TIC OCEAN
VEDEN
FINLAND
RUSSIA
ESTONIA
LATVIA
LITHUANIA
BELARUS
POLAND
KAZAKHSTAN
CZ.
UKRAINE
UZBEKISTAN
SLK.
AUS.
HUNG.
MOLDOVA
SLN.
CR.
ROMANIA
MONGOLIA
KYRGYZSTAN
TAJIKISTAN
B. H.
SE.
GEORGIA
BULGARIA
MO.
ALBANIA
MAC.
N. KOREA
GREECE
TURKEY
ARMENIA
TURKMENISTAN
CYPRUS
AZERBAIJAN
S. KOREA
JAPAN
MALTA
SYRIA
LEBANON
ISRAEL
IRAQ
IRAN
AFGHANISTAN
PEOPLE'S REPUBLIC OF CHINA
JORDAN
PACIFIC OCEAN
BAHRAIN
BHUTAN
LIBYA
EGYPT
KUWAIT
QATAR
PAKISTAN
NEPAL
SAUDI ARABIA
BANGLADESH
MYANMAR (BURMA)
UNITED ARAB EMIRATES
OMAN
INDIA
Taiwan
Wake I. (U.S.)
LAOS
Mariana Islands (U.S.)
CHAD
ERITREA
YEMEN
VIETNAM
SUDAN
THAILAND
PHILIPPINES
MARSHALL ISLANDS
DJIBOUTI
CAMBODIA (KAMPUCHEA)
Guam (U.S.)
ETHIOPIA
SRI LANKA
CENTRAL AFRICAN REP.
BRUNEI DARUSSALAM
PALAU
MALDIVES
SOMALIA
UGANDA
MALAYSIA
FEDERATED STATES OF MICRONESIA
KENYA
KIRIBATI
SINGAPORE
RWANDA
DEM. REP. OF CONGO
NAURU
INDIAN OCEAN
PAPUA NEW GUINEA
SEYCHELLES
BURUNDI
TANZANIA
INDONESIA
SOLOMON IS.
TIMOR LESTE
TUVALU
COMOROS
ABBREVIATIONS
NGOLA
ZAMBIA
MALAWI
VANUATU
FIJI
AUS. AUSTRIA
BEL. BELGIUM
NAMIBIA
ZIMBABWE
MADAGASCAR
B. H. BOSNIA AND HERZEGOVINA
MAURITIUS
CR. CROATIA
BOTSWANA
New Caledonia (France)
CZ. CZECH REPUBLIC
MOZAMBIQUE
AUSTRALIA
SWAZILAND
DEN. DENMARK
SOUTH AFRICA
LESOTHO
HUNG. HUNGARY
K. KOSOVO
LUX. LUXEMBOURG
MAC. MACEDONIA
MO. MONTENEGRO
NETH. NETHERLANDS
NEW ZEALAND
SE. SERBIA
SLK. SLOVAKIA
SLN. SLOVENIA
Mercator Projection
SWITZ. SWITZERLAND
20°E
40°E
60°E
80°E
100°E
120°E
140°E
160°E

Geography Overview

Maps are among the most powerful of human inventions, showing us where we are, where we have been, and where we might go in the future. They are essential tools in nearly every aspect of social life, enabling politicians to govern their people, soldiers to defend against invasions, and merchants to conduct trade and commerce. As noted in the *Introducing World History* essay, maps also create mental images of the world and, hence, help shape the way people look at the world and their place in it.

Maps are especially useful for the historian or student of history. Historical maps show us where different peoples lived and interacted, at one point in time or over long periods. Typically, they use lines, symbols, shading, and text to present a combination of physical and political information. The physical part pertains to the natural world—the shape of landmasses and bodies of water—and serves as a kind of background or screen onto which political information is projected. Categories of political information commonly featured on historical maps include the location and names of important cities and states, the changing borders of nations and empires, and the routes people traveled as they explored, migrated, traded, or fought with one another. In order to read a historical map, one must first understand its legend. The legend provides a key for interpreting the map's graphical symbols.

The first map in this overview, Map 1.3: The Indo-European Migrations and Eurasian Pastoralism, uses colored shading to show that around 4000 B.C.E. a people called the Indo-Europeans lived by the Caucasus Mountains in western Asia, and blue arrows to show that over the next three thousand years various Indo-European tribes migrated into western and northern Europe, Central and southwestern Asia, and northern India. Black capital letters are used to name important regions of human settlement, such as Anatolia and Mesopotamia, and black italic capitals for topographical features, such as mountains and desert. Red italic capitals indicate how people in different parts of Eurasia and Africa sustained themselves at this time—whether by raising livestock, farming, hunting and gathering, or some combination of these.

Every map is designed to convey only selected categories of information and, therefore, may leave certain questions about the geographical area and its inhabitants at either the same or different points in history unanswered. Thus, Map 1.3 tells us very little about the other human populations that lived in Eurasia between 4000 and 1000 B.C.E. The names *Sumer* and *Akkad* appear, but their status as regions where the world's first urban societies arose is something the student will only discover by reading the beginning of Chapter 2 and looking at Map 2.1 Ancient Mesopotamia. Arrows show the probable routes taken by different Indo-European tribes as they migrated from their homeland, but these tribes are not named, and the student must read the rest of Chapter 2 and all of Chapter 3 before learning that they included the Greeks in Europe and the Aryans in northern India.

To introduce you to the maps in this text, and the world history they help to illuminate, seven maps have been reproduced in this section, each provided with an analytical introduction and set of questions. Every part of the world is covered, and every historical period is represented by one map—except for the Early Modern Era, which is represented by two maps. The introductions help explain the content of each map by placing it in its broader historical context. That context includes the other maps in this text, and these are referenced whenever possible. For almost any subject about which the student would like to learn more, there are several maps that should be consulted. A list of all the maps in this text follows the table of contents.

The Indo-European Migrations and Eurasian Pastoralism

After the first human communities learned to domesticate native plants and animals, between 11,500 and 7,000 years ago, two types of cultures arose: farming societies in fertile river basins and pastoral societies in areas dominated by grassland, mountainous terrain, or desert (see Map 1.2). Important early farming societies include the city-states of Sumer and Akkad in Mesopotamia (see Map 2.1), the Harappan cities of the Indus Valley in India (see Map 2.2), the Egyptian and Nubian states along the Nile River in Africa (see Map 3.1), and the Shang state by the Yellow River in China (see Map 4.1). Bordering these peoples were pastoral societies who raised livestock as their main source of food and raw material and lived in smaller, dispersed groups over large areas of Eurasia, Africa, and Arabia. One such society, or collection of tribes, were the Indo-Europeans, who lived near the Caucasus Mountains around 4000 B.C.E. Over the next three thousand years, various Indo-European peoples migrated from their homeland: the Greeks settled in the eastern Mediterranean, the Hittites in central Anatolia, and the Aryans in northern India. Most European languages and many languages of southwestern Asia, Central Asia, and India are direct descendants of the prehistoric language spoken by the Indo-Europeans.

Maps referenced

Visit the website and eBook for additional study material and interactive tools: www.cengage.com/history/lockard/globalsocnet2e

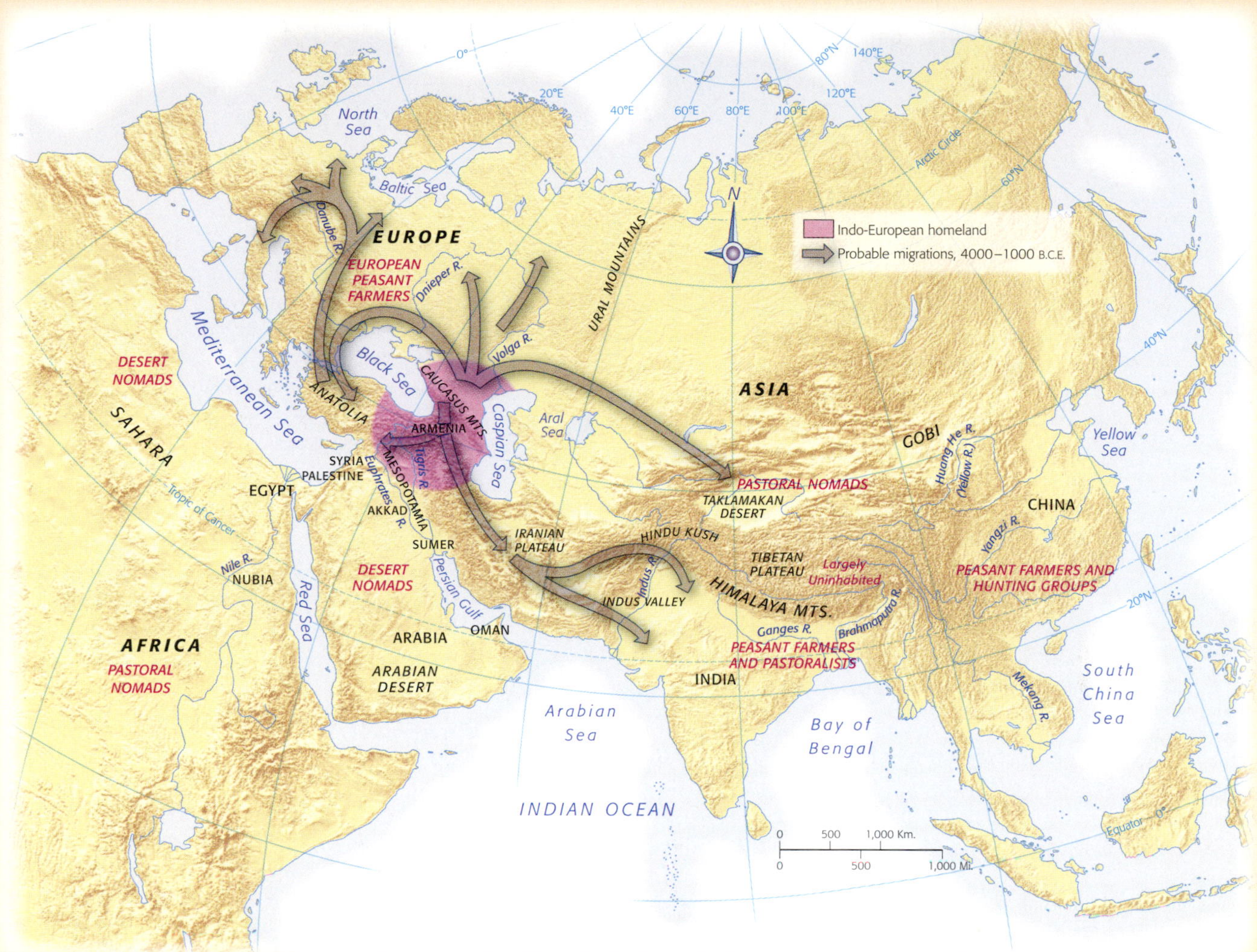

MAP 1.3
The Indo-European Migrations and Eurasian Pastoralism
Some societies, especially in parts of Africa and Asia, adapted to environmental contexts by developing a pastoral, or animal herding, economy. One large pastoral group, the Indo-Europeans, eventually expanded from their home area into Europe, southwestern Asia, Central Asia, and India.

Questions

1. The Indo-Europeans were pastoral nomads, most of whom later became farmers. Which regions on this map are suited to pastoralism and which to farming economies?

2. The blue arrows on this map show the probable migration routes taken by various Indo-European tribes from 4000 to 1000 B.C.E. Identify the main geographical features (rivers, seas, mountain ranges, etc.) of the Indo-European homeland and the regions settled by Indo-Europeans during their migrations.

THE ROMAN EMPIRE, CA. 120 C.E.

Rome was founded in the eighth century B.C.E. by the Latin people, a tribe of Indo-European pastoralists. In 509 B.C.E., influenced by the cultures of the neighboring Greek and Etruscan city-states (see Map 8.1), the Romans established a republic—a form of government in which political power is exercised by elected representatives of the people. The Roman Republic became a great military power, defeating the trading empire of the Carthaginians, and, by 58 B.C.E., under Julius Caesar, the Celtic tribes in Gaul (modern France). With the rise to power of Octavian, who defeated Mark Antony and Queen Cleopatra of Egypt at the naval Battle of Actium in Greece in 31 B.C.E., the Republic became a military dictatorship. At the time of Emperor Hadrian's death in 138 C.E., the Roman Empire dominated the whole of the Mediterranean basin, bounded in the west by the Atlantic Ocean, in the south by the Sahara Desert, to the north by Germanic and Celtic tribes, and to the east by the Parthian empire and the Arabian Desert. The Roman Empire was unified by a network of over 150,000 miles of roads and linked to the peoples of Africa and Asia by numerous land and sea trade routes (see map on page 233, "Great Empires and Trade Routes").

Maps referenced

Visit the website and eBook for additional study material and interactive tools: www.cengage.com/history/lockard/globalsocnet2e

MAP 8.2
The Roman Empire, ca. 120 C.E.

The Romans gradually expanded until, by 120 C.E., they controlled a huge empire stretching from Britain and Spain in the west through southern and central Europe and North Africa to Egypt, Anatolia, and the lands along the eastern Mediterranean coast.

Questions

1. Which three rivers helped define the borders of the Roman Empire by the death of Augustus (Octavian) in 14 C.E.?

2. Which Roman emperor had a 73-mile wall built to secure the province of Britain from Celtic tribes to the north?

DAR AL-ISLAM AND TRADE ROUTES, CA. 1500 C.E.

The rise and spread of Islam in the Intermediate Era is paralleled by that of Christianity in Europe and Buddhism in Asia (see the map on page 378, "World Religions and Trade Routes, 600–1500"). By 750 C.E. the Umayyad Caliphate had conquered Spain and North Africa in the west (see Map 10.1), and a year later Arab armies defended their conquest of Central Asia by defeating Chinese forces from the Tang Empire at the Battle of Talas (see Map 11.1). From its capital in Baghdad, the Abbasid Caliphate ruled an empire stretching from Egypt to the Indus River (see Map 10.2). Like Latin culture in Europe, Arabic literature and science flourished during this period; new long-distance trade routes enriched Arab merchants and rulers and stimulated interest in the wider world. The confidence and curiosity of Islamic culture at this time are shown by the life and writings of the fourteenth-century Moroccan jurist and explorer Ibn Battuta. Logging more than 60,000 miles in thirty years, Ibn Battuta traveled to the far reaches of the Islamic world, from Timbuktu in the West African empire of Mali (see Map 12.1) to the Delhi Sultanate in India (see Map 13.1) and the cities of Pasai and Melaka in Southeast Asia (see Map 13.3).

Maps referenced

Visit the website and eBook for additional study material and interactive tools: www.cengage.com/history/lockard/globalsocnet2e

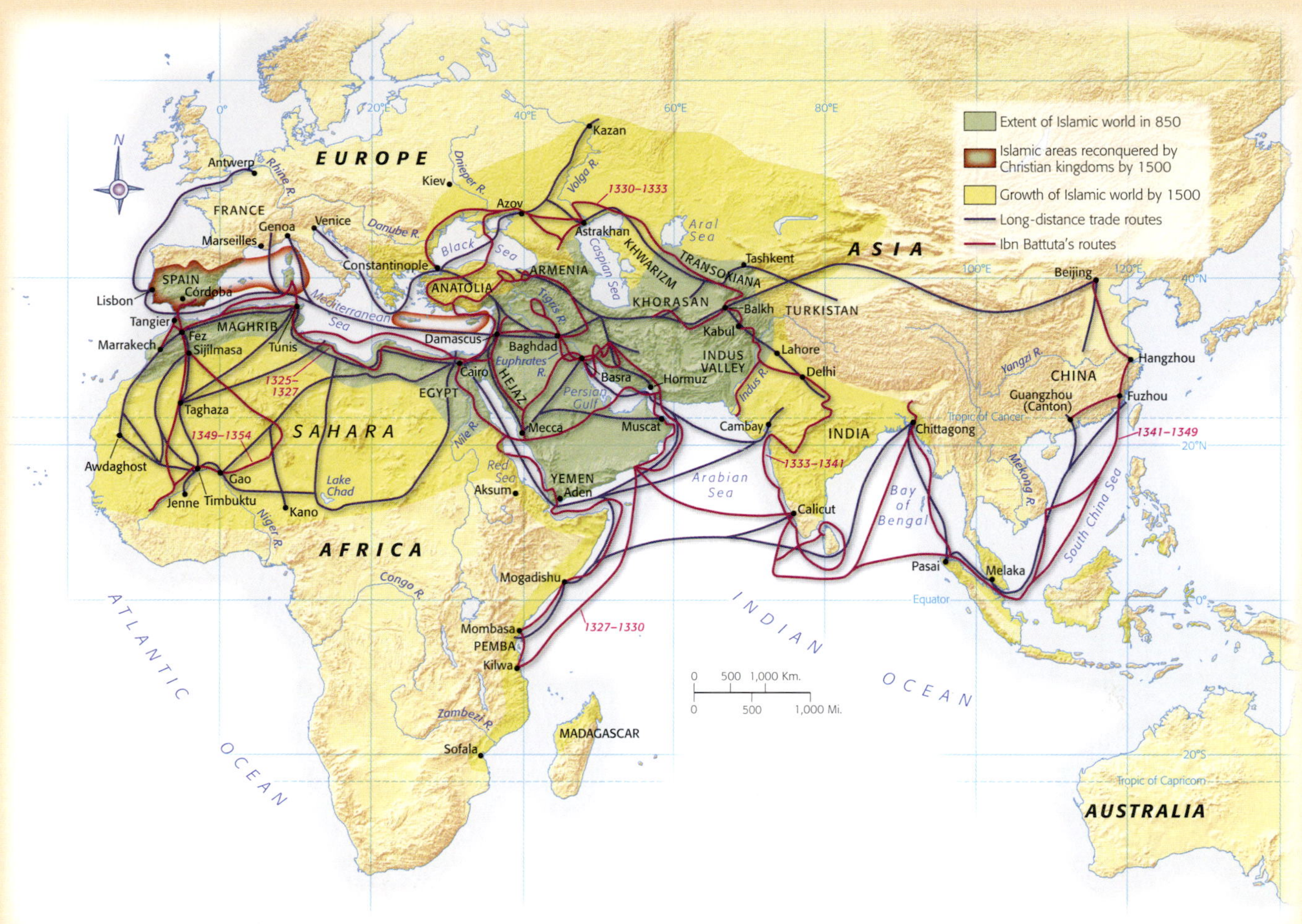

MAP 10.3
Dar al-Islam and Trade Routes, ca. 1500 C.E.
By 1500 the Islamic world stretched into West Africa, East Africa, and Southeast Asia. Trade routes connected the Islamic lands and allowed Muslim traders to extend their networks to China, Russia, and Europe.

Questions

1. Which European cities conducted maritime trade with Islamic societies in the Intermediate Era?

2. Islam spread to which western European land during the early Intermediate Era? (See also Map 10.1.)

THE ATLANTIC ECONOMY

The rise of European political and economic power in the Early Modern Era was made possible by maritime exploration (see Map 15.1) and missions of conquest in the Americas (see Map 17.1). In four voyages between 1492 and 1504, Christopher Columbus crossed the Atlantic Ocean and surveyed much of the Caribbean Basin, claiming it for Spain. Hernán Cortés sailed from Cuba to eastern Mexico and conquered the Aztec Empire in 1521, and in 1535 the Inca Empire in South America was conquered by Francisco Pizarro. By 1700, Portugal controlled Brazil, while England, France, and Spain claimed most of North America (see Map 17.2). European colonization was devastating to indigenous peoples. The introduction of infectious diseases like smallpox, to which Native Americans had no immunity, reduced their population by 90 percent from 1500 to 1700. Millions of West Africans were enslaved and transported to the Americas, where they mined gold and silver and produced sugarcane and tobacco on plantations (see Map 16.2). European states prospered from the development of capitalist economies, and the revenue from colonial slave labor and increased global trade put them in a position to dominate the world.

Maps referenced

Visit the website and eBook for additional study material and interactive tools: www.cengage.com/history/lockard/globalsocnet2e

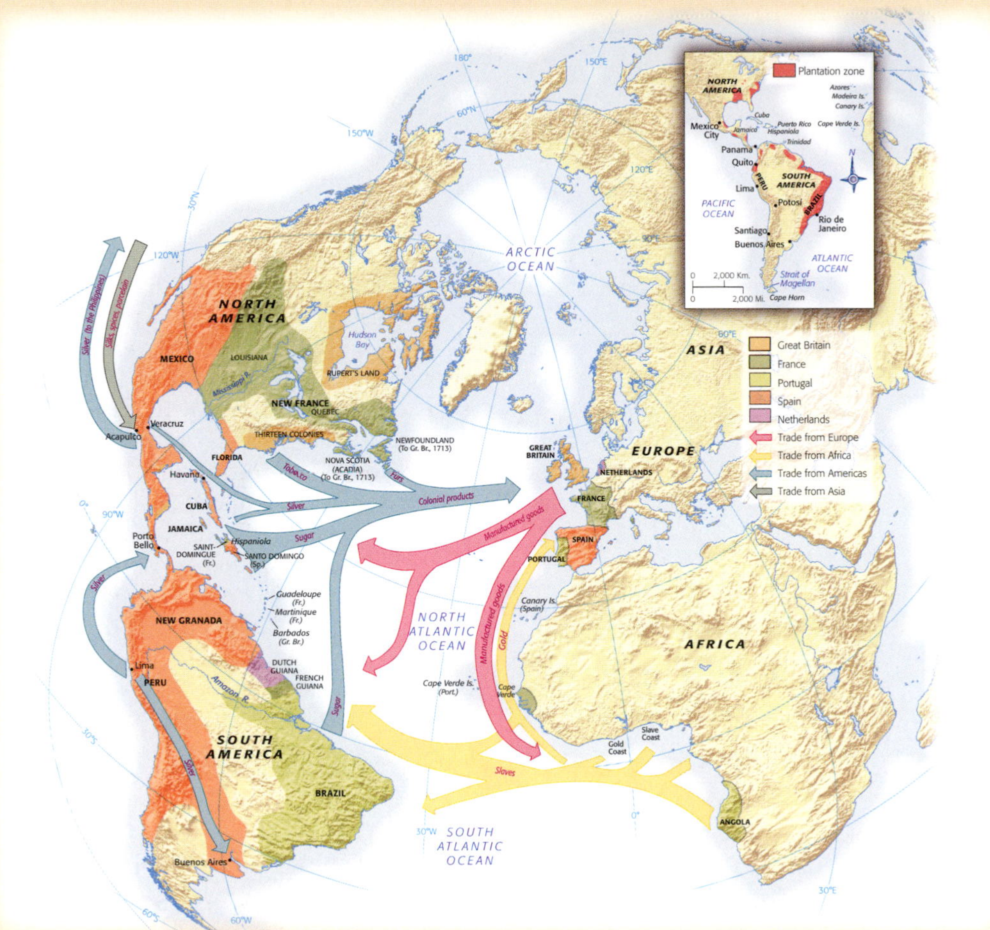

MAP 17.3
The Atlantic Economy

The Atlantic economy was based on a triangular trade in which African slaves were shipped to the Americas to produce raw materials that were chiefly exported to Europe, where they were turned into manufactured goods and exported to Africa and the Americas.

Questions

1. Which Caribbean islands were colonized by Spain, France, and Great Britain?

2. Which Spanish American port imported silks, spices, and porcelain from Asia?

3. Settlers from which American colony exported furs to Europe?

U.S. Expansion Through 1867

The successful revolution in 1776 of Great Britain's thirteen North American colonies inaugurated a series of revolutions throughout the Western Hemisphere. Apart from Cuba and Puerto Rico, all of Spain's Latin American colonies achieved independence by 1840 (see Map 19.2). In 1783 the United States extended as far west as the Mississippi River; in 1803 its territory was doubled by the Louisiana Purchase; by 1848, after a war with Mexico, the territories of Texas, New Mexico, and California were annexed. Beginning in England in the 1770s, the Industrial Revolution had—and continues to have—far-reaching effects on the social and political history of the world. Europe's population soared, and industrial capitalism enriched nations and wealthy investors, but also impoverished and dislocated millions of people. From 1821 to 1920 more than 30 million Europeans emigrated to the United States (see Map 20.1). In 1865, after a bloody Civil War, slavery was abolished in the southern states. Only four years later, a large and diverse workforce, including African Americans and Chinese immigrants, completed the first transcontinental railroad. Immigrants from Britain also settled Oceania during the Modern Era (see Map 20.3), seizing the lands of Aborigines in Australia and Maori in New Zealand, just as European colonists had seized the lands of Native Americans two centuries before.

Maps referenced

Visit the website and eBook for additional study material and interactive tools: www.cengage.com/history/lockard/globalsocnet2e

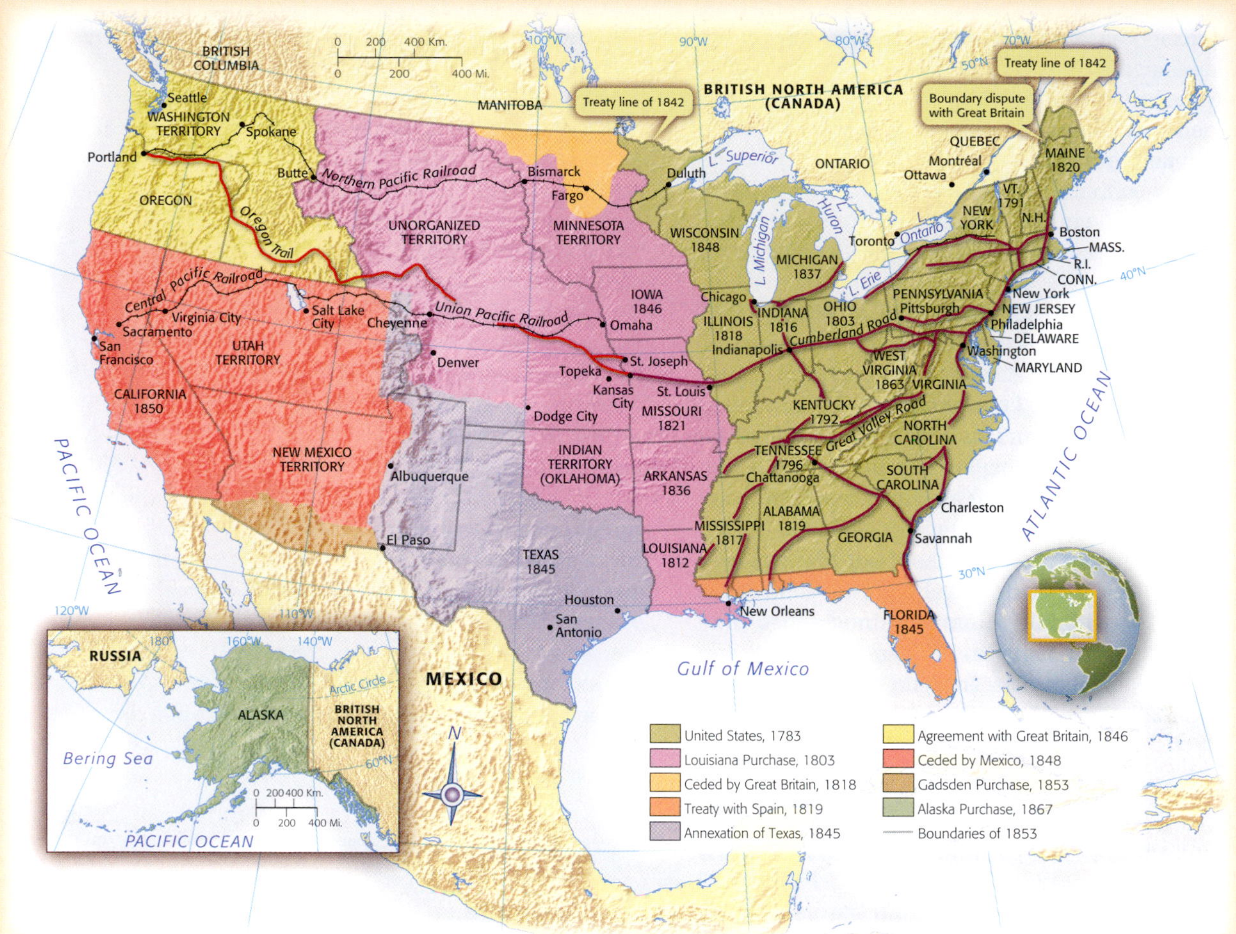

MAP 20.2
U.S. Expansion Through 1867
The United States expanded in stages after independence, gaining land from Spain, France, Britain, and Mexico until the nation stretched from the Atlantic to the Gulf and Pacific coasts by 1867. During the same period Canadians expanded westward from Quebec to British Columbia.

Questions

1. First mapped in 1811, the Oregon Trail became the primary overland route for settlers migrating to the Pacific Northwest. Which future states did it pass through?

2. Which cities in the western United States benefited from the California Gold Rush of 1849?

3. The first transcontinental railroad was a joint effort of the Union Pacific and Central Pacific Railroads. What two cities did it join by 1869?

Africa in 1914

After losing their American colonies, European nations projected their power to the south and east, and by 1914 they had colonized most of Africa, India, and Southeast Asia (see Map 19.4). Numerous Africans resisted European colonization, such as the Mandinka king Samory Toure, who fought the French in West Africa, and the confederation of Shona and Ndebele peoples, who fought the British in Southern Rhodesia. Ultimately, however, a combination of deceitful diplomacy and superior firearms made the Europeans unstoppable. Belgium seized the Congo River Basin, France took control of most of West Africa, and Great Britain conquered lands in a north-south band stretching from Cairo to Cape Town. The remaining African territories, with the exception of independent Ethiopia and Liberia, were colonized by Germany, Italy, and Portugal. The spread of Muslim culture beyond the Middle East and Central Asia, begun in the Intermediate Era, was unaffected by European colonialists and Christian missionaries: today Islam is the majority religion in northern Africa and Southeast Asia (see Map 26.3 and Map 30.2).

Maps referenced

MAP 19.4 **The Great Powers and Their Colonial Possessions in 1913** (p. 541)

MAP 26.3 **World Religions** (p. 759)

MAP 30.2 **The Islamic World** (p. 877)

Visit the website and eBook for additional study material and interactive tools: www.cengage.com/history/lockard/globalsocnet2e

MAP 21.1
Africa in 1914

Before 1878 the European powers held only a few coastal territories in Africa, but in that year they turned to expanding their power through colonization. By 1914 the British, French, Belgians, Germans, Italians, Portuguese, and Spanish controlled all of the continent except for Ethiopia and Liberia.

Questions

1. Which European state had a single African colony?

2. What world religions are predominant in northern and southern Africa, respectively (see also Map 26.3)?

3. Around which two African river basins did the British and French base their colonies?

World Population Growth

World population increased more rapidly in the contemporary era than at any time in history: from 2.5 billion to more than 6.5 billion. This map shows the relative size of nations as measured by their populations in 2002. It also shows their projected average annual growth rates between 2002 and 2015. Currently, population growth is moderate in the world's five largest nations, and higher in developing nations like Pakistan, Nigeria, and Mexico. For a number of reasons, including women's desire to work outside the home and to prevent pregnancy by using birth control, Japan and many European nations have declining birthrates and aging populations. Since 1900 there has been a massive increase in global industrial output, consumption of resources, and all forms of pollution. Although the developing nations of Asia have the largest populations, most of the world's wealth is concentrated in North America, western Europe, and Japan (see the map on page 938, "Global Distribution of Wealth"). In 2000, over 1 billion people were desperately poor. People living in wealthier nations consume a much greater share of the earth's raw materials and cause more damage to the environment than those in developing nations. The average American consumes some twenty times the resources of the average Pakistani.

Map referenced

SNT 6 Global Distribution of Wealth (p. 938)

Visit the website and eBook for additional study material and interactive tools: www.cengage.com/history/lockard/globalsocnet2e

MAP 26.2
World Population Growth

This map shows dramatically which nations have the largest populations: China, India, the United States, Indonesia, and Brazil. It also shows which regions experience the most rapid population growth: Africa, South Asia, and Central America.

Questions

1. In 2002, the population of India was how many times greater than that of the United States? How many times greater was the population of China?

2. What challenges confront developing nations with large and growing populations?

3. What are some things developing nations can do to meet these challenges?

Societies, Networks, and Transitions

A Global History

Second Edition

Craig A. Lockard
University of Wisconsin—Green Bay

Australia • Brazil • Japan • Korea • Mexico • Singapore • Spain • United Kingdom • United States

Societies, Networks, and Transitions, 2e
Craig A. Lockard

Senior Publisher: Suzanne Jeans

Senior Acquisitions Editor: Nancy Blaine

Development Manager: Jeff Greene

Senior Development Editor: Tonya Lobato

Assistant Editor: Lauren Floyd

Editorial Assistant: Emma Goehring

Senior Media Editor: Lisa Ciccolo

Senior Marketing Manager: Katherine Bates

Marketing Coordinator: Lorreen Pelletier

Marketing Communications Manager: Christine Dobberpuhl

Senior Content Project Manager: Carol Newman

Senior Art Director: Cate Rickard Barr

Print Buyer: Becky Cross

Senior Rights Acquisition Account Manager: Katie Huha

Text Permissions Editor: Tracy Metivier

Senior Photo Editor: Jennifer Meyer Dare

Photo Researcher: Carole Frohlich

Production Service: Lachina Publishing Services

Text Designer: Henry Rachlin

Cover Designer: Dutton & Sherman Design

Cover Image: Jerusalem: Odel Baililty/AP Images

Compositor: Lachina Publishing Services

Library of Congress Control Number: 2009935606

Student Edition:

ISBN-13: 978-1-4390-8520-2

ISBN-10: 1-4390-8520-X

Wadsworth
20 Channel Center Street
Boston, MA 02210
USA

Printed in the United States of America
1 2 3 4 5 6 7 13 12 11 10 09

Brief Contents

Contents

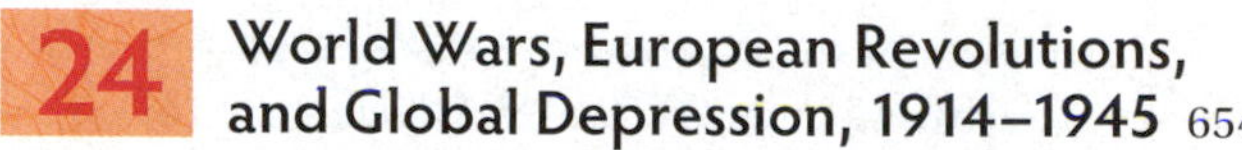

Maps

Features

PROFILE

WITNESS TO THE PAST

HISTORICAL CONTROVERSY

SOCIETIES • NETWORKS • TRANSITIONS

PREFACE

Awareness of the need for a universal view of history—for a history which transcends national and regional boundaries and comprehends the entire globe—is one of the marks of the present. Our past [is] the past of the world, our history is the first to be world history.[1]

—GEOFFREY BARRACLOUGH

British historian Geoffrey Barraclough wrote these words over two decades ago, yet historians are still grappling with what it means to write world history, and why it is crucial to do so, especially to better inform today's students about their changing world and how it came to be. The intended audience for this text is students taking introductory world history courses and the faculty who teach them. Most of these students will be taking world history in colleges, universities, and community colleges, often with the goal of satisfying general education requirements or building a foundation for majoring in history or a related field. Like the contemporary world, the marketplace for texts is also changing. Both students, many of whom have outside jobs, and instructors, often facing expanded workloads, have increasing demands on their time. New technologies are promoting new pedagogies and a multiplicity of classroom approaches. Hence, any textbook must provide a sound knowledge base while also enhancing teaching and learning whatever the pedagogy employed.

To make this second edition even more accessible than the first edition, we have changed from a two-column to a more reader-friendly one-column format, streamlined and shortened the narrative, and added a brand-new map program. We believe that these changes will make the text more visually dynamic, easier to follow, and even more user friendly. Furthermore, students and many faculty are more interested in technology than ever before, and this second edition places more emphasis on the many website resources that are available through icons that tell students where to find online primary sources and interactive maps related to the text, as well as through a suggested list of online resources at the end of each chapter. I believe that these changes and additions enhance the book's presentation and clarity and enable it to convey the richness and importance of world history for today's students and tomorrow's leaders while also making the teaching of the material easier for both high school and college instructors using this text.

Twenty-first-century students, more than any generation before them, live in multicultural countries and an interconnected world. The world's interdependence calls for teaching a wider vision, which is the goal of this text. My intention is to create a meaningful, coherent, and stimulating presentation that conveys to students the incredible diversity of societies from earliest times to the present, as well as the ways they have been increasingly connected to other societies and shaped by these relationships. History may happen "as one darn thing after another," but the job of historians is to make it something more than facts, names, and dates. A text should provide a readable narrative, supplying a content base while also posing larger questions. The writing is as clear and thorough in its explanation of events and concepts as I can make it. No text can or should teach the course, but I hope that this text provides enough of a baseline of regional and global coverage to allow each instructor to bring her or his own talents, understandings, and particular interests to the process.

I became involved in teaching, debating, and writing world history as a result of my personal and academic experiences. My interest in other cultures was first awakened in the multicultural southern California city where I grew up. Many of my classmates or their parents had come from Asia, Latin America, or the Middle East. There was also a substantial African American community. A curious person did not have to search far to hear music, sample foods, or encounter ideas from many different cultures. I remember being enchanted by the Chinese landscape paintings at a local museum devoted to Asian art, and vowing to one day see some of those misty mountains for myself. Today many young people may be as interested as I was in learning about the world, since, thanks to immigration, many cities and towns all over North America have taken on a cosmopolitan flavor similar to my hometown.

While experiences growing up sparked my interest in other cultures, it was my schooling that pointed the way to a career in teaching world history. When I entered college, all undergraduate students were required to take a two-semester course in Western Civilization as part of the general education requirement. Many colleges and universities in North America had similar classes that introduced students to Egyptian pyramids, Greek philosophy, medieval pageantry, Renaissance art, and the French Revolution, enriching our lives. Fortunately, my university expanded student horizons further by adding course components (albeit brief) on China, Japan, India, and Islam while also developing a study abroad program. I participated in both the study abroad in Salzburg, Austria, and the student exchange with a university in Hong Kong, which meant living with, rather than just sampling, different customs, outlooks, and histories.

Some teachers and academic historians had begun to realize that the emphasis in U.S. education on the histories of the United States and western Europe, to the near exclusion of the rest of the world, was not sufficient for understanding the realities of the mid-twentieth century. Young Americans were being sent thousands of miles away to fight wars in countries, such as Vietnam, that few Americans had ever heard of. Newspapers and television reported developments in places such as Japan and Indonesia, Egypt and Congo, Cuba and Brazil, which had increasing relevance for Americans. Graduate programs and scholarship directed toward Asian, African, Middle Eastern, Latin American, and eastern European and Russian history also grew out of the awareness of a widening world, broadening conceptions of history. I attended one of the new programs in Asian Studies for my MA degree, and then the first PhD program in world history. Thanks to that program, I encountered the stimulating work of pioneering world historians from North America such as Philip Curtin, Marshall Hodgson, William McNeill, and Leften S. Stavrianos. My own approach, developed as I taught undergraduate world history courses beginning in 1969, owes much to the global vision they offered.

To bring some coherence to the emerging world history field as well as to promote a global approach at all levels of education, several dozen of us teaching at the university, college, community college, and secondary school levels in the United States and Canada came together in the early 1980s to form the World History Association (WHA), for which I served as founding secretary and, more recently, as a member of the Executive Council. The organization grew rapidly, encouraging the teaching, studying, and writing of world history not only in the United States but all over the world. The approaches to world history found among active WHA members vary widely, and my engagement in the ongoing discussions at conferences and in essays, often about the merits of varied textbooks, provided an excellent background for writing this text.

The Aims and Approach of the Text

Societies, Networks, and Transitions: A Global History provides an accessible, thought-provoking guide to students in their exploration of the landscape of the past, helping them to think about it in all its social diversity and interconnectedness and to see their lives with fresh understanding. It does this by combining clear writing, special learning features, current scholarship, and a comprehensive, global approach that does not omit the role and richness of particular regions.

There is a method behind these aims. For forty years I have written about and taught Asian, African, and world history at universities in the United States and Malaysia. A cumulative seven years of study, research, or teaching in Southeast Asia, East Asia, East Africa, and Europe gave me insights into a wide variety of cultures and historical perspectives. Finally, the WHA, its publications and conferences, and the more recent electronic listserv, H-WORLD, have provided active forums for vigorously discussing how best to think about and teach world history.

The most effective approach to presenting world history in a text for undergraduate and advanced high school students, I have concluded, is one that combines the themes of connections and cultures. World history is very much about connections that transcend countries, cultures, and regions, and a text should discuss, for example, major long-distance trade networks such as the Silk Road, the spread of religions, maritime exploration, world wars, and transregional empires such as the Persian, Mongol, and British Empires. These connections are part of the broader global picture. Students need to understand that cultures, however unique, did not emerge and operate in a vacuum but faced similar challenges, shared many common experiences, and influenced each other.

The broader picture is drawn by means of several features in the text. To strengthen the presentation of the global overview, the text uses an innovative essay feature entitled "Societies, Networks, and Transitions." Appearing at the end of each of the six chronological parts, this feature analyzes and synthesizes the wider trends of the era, such as the role of long-distance trade, the spread of technologies and religions, and global climate change. The objective is to amplify the wider transregional messages already developed in the part chapters and help students to think further about the global context in which societies are enmeshed. Each "Societies, Networks, and Transitions" essay also makes comparisons, for example, between the Han Chinese, Mauryan Indian, and Roman Empires, and between Chinese, Indian, and European emigration in the nineteenth century. These comparisons help to throw further light on diverse cultures and the differences and similarities between them during the era covered. Finally, each essay is meant to show how the transitions that characterize the era lead up to the era discussed in the following part. In addition, the prologues that introduce each of the six eras treated in the text also set out the broader context, including some of the major themes and patterns of wide influence as well as those for each region. Furthermore, several chapters concentrate on global rather than regional developments.

However, while a broad global overview is a strongly developed feature of this text, most chapters, while acknowledging and explaining relevant linkages, focus on a particular region or several regions. Most students learn easiest by focusing on one region or culture at a time. Students also benefit from recognizing the cultural richness and intellectual creativity of specific societies. From this text students learn, for instance, about Chinese poetry, Indonesian music, Arab science, Greek philosophy, West African arts, Indian cinema, Latin American economies, and Anglo-American political thought. As a component of this cultural richness, this text also devotes considerable attention to the enduring religious traditions, such as Buddhism, Christianity, and Islam, and to issues of gender. The cultural richness of a region and its distinctive social patterns can get lost in an approach that minimizes regional coverage. Today most people are still mostly concerned with events in their own countries, even as their lives are reshaped by transnational economies and global cultural movements.

Also a strong part of the presentation of world history in this text is its attempt to be comprehensive and inclusive. To enhance comprehensiveness, the text balances social, economic, political, and cultural and religious history, and it also devotes some attention to geographical and environmental contexts as well as to the history of ideas and technologies. At the same time, the text highlights features within societies, such as economic production, technological innovations, and portable ideas that had widespread or enduring influence. To ensure inclusiveness, the text recognizes the contributions of many societies, including some often neglected, such as sub-Saharan Africa, pre-Columbian America, Southeast Asia, and Oceania. In particular, this text offers strong coverage of the diverse Asian societies. Throughout history, as today, the great majority of the world's population has lived in Asia.

Organizing the Text

All textbook authors struggle with how to organize the material. To keep the number of chapters corresponding to the twenty-eight or thirty weeks of most academic calendars in North America, and roughly equal in length, I have often had to combine several regions into a single chapter to be comprehensive, sometimes making decisions for conveniences sake. For example, unlike texts that may have only one chapter on sub-Saharan Africa covering the centuries from ancient times to 1500 C.E., this text discusses sub-Saharan Africa in each of the six chronological eras, devoting three chapters to the centuries prior to 1500 C.E. and three to the years since 1450 C.E. But this sometimes necessitated grouping Africa, depending on the era, with Europe, the Middle East, or the Americas. Unlike texts that may, for example, have material on Tang dynasty China scattered through several chapters, making it harder for students to gain a cohesive view of that society, I want to convey a comprehensive perspective of major societies such as Tang China. The material is divided into parts defined as distinct eras (such as the Classical and the Early Modern) so that students can understand how all regions were part of world history from earliest times. I believe that a chronological structure aids students in grasping the changes over time while helping to organize the material.

For the second edition I have reorganized Part II. The chapter on southern and Central Asia now leads off this part as Chapter 5, introducing the development and beliefs of Buddhism as well as examining Central Asian societies such as the Sogdians and Huns. This makes the discussion of Buddhism and of the Silk Road in Chapter 6 on East Asia more understandable. The coverage of the Greeks and Persians in the Eastern Mediterranean (Chapter 7) is now followed immediately by the chapter on the Western Mediterranean and Roman Empire (Chapter 8).

Distinguishing Features

Several features of *Societies, Networks, Transitions: A Global History* will help students better understand, assimilate, and appreciate the material they are about to encounter. Those unique to this text include the following.

Introducing World History World History may be the first and possibly the only history course many undergraduates will take in college. The text opens with a short essay that introduces students to the nature of history, the special challenges posed by studying world history, and why we need to study it.

Balancing Themes Three broad themes—uniqueness, interdependence, and change—have shaped the text. They are discussed throughout in terms of three related concepts—societies, networks, and transitions. These concepts, discussed in more detail in "Introducing World History," can be summarized as follows:

- **Societies** Influenced by environmental and geographical factors, people have formed and maintained societies defined by distinctive but often changing cultures, beliefs, social forms, institutions, and material traits.
- **Networks** Over the centuries societies have generally been connected to other societies by growing networks forged by phenomena such as migration, long-distance trade, exploration, military expansion, colonization, the spread of ideas and technologies, and webs of communication. These growing networks modified individual societies, created regional systems, and eventually led to a global system.
- **Transitions** Each major historical era has been marked by one or more great transitions sparked by events or innovations, such as settled agriculture, Mongol imperialism, industrial revolution, or world war, that have had profound and enduring influences on many societies, gradually reshaping the world. At the same time, societies and regions have experienced transitions of regional rather than global scope that have generated new ways of thinking or doing things, such as the expansion of Islam into India or the European colonization of East Africa and Mexico.

Through exposure to these three ideas integrated throughout the text, students learn of the rich cultural mosaic of the world. They are also introduced to its patterns of connections and unity as well as of continuity and change.

"Societies, Networks, and Transitions" Minichapters A short feature at the end of each part assists the student in backing up from the stories of societies and regions to see the larger historical patterns of change and the wider links among distant peoples. This comparative analysis allows students to identify experiences and transitions common to several regions or the entire world and to reflect further on the text themes. These features can also help students review key developments from the preceding chapters.

Historical Controversies Since one of the common misconceptions about history is that it is about the "dead" past, included with each "Societies, Networks, and Transitions" feature is a brief account of a debate among historians over how an issue in the past should be interpreted and what it means to us today. For example, why are the major societies dominated by males, and has this always been true? Why and when did Europe begin its "great divergence" from China and other Asian societies? How do historians evaluate contemporary globalization? Reappraisal is at the heart of history, and many historical questions are never completely answered. Yet most textbooks ignore this dimension of historical study; this text is innovative in including it. The Historical Controversy essays will help show students that historical facts are anything but dead; they live and change their meaning as new questions are asked by each new generation.

Profiles It is impossible to recount the human story without using broad generalizations, but it is also difficult to understand that story without seeing historical events reflected in the lives of men and women, prominent but also ordinary people. Each chapter contains a Profile that focuses on the experiences or accomplishments of a woman or man, to convey the flavor of life of the period, to embellish the chapter narrative with interesting personalities, and to integrate gender into the historical account. The Profiles try to show how gender affected the individual, shaping her or his opportunities and involvement in society. Several focus questions ask the student to reflect on the Profile. For instance, students will examine a historian in early China, look at the spread of Christianity as seen through the life of a pagan female philosopher in Egypt, relive the experience of a female slave in colonial Brazil, and envision modern Indian life through a sketch of a film star.

Special Coverage This text also treats often-neglected areas and subjects. For example:

- It focuses on several regions with considerable historical importance but often marginalized or even omitted in many texts, including sub-Saharan Africa, Southeast Asia, Korea, Central Asia, pre-Columbian North America, ancient South America, the Caribbean, Polynesia, Australia, Canada, and the United States.
- It includes discussions of significant groups that transcend regional boundaries, such as the caravan travelers and traders of the Silk Road, Mongol empire builders, the Indian Ocean maritime traders, and contemporary humanitarian organizations such as Amnesty International and Doctors Without Borders.
- It features extensive coverage of the roots, rise, reshaping, and enduring influence of the great religious and philosophical traditions.
- It blends coverage of gender, particularly the experiences of women, and of social history generally, into the larger narrative.
- It devotes the first chapter of the text to the roots of human history. After a brief introduction to the shaping of our planet, human evolution, and the spread of people around the world, the chapter examines the birth of agriculture, cities, and states, which set the stage for everything to come.
- It includes strong coverage of the world since 1945, a focus of great interest to many students.

Witness to the Past Many texts incorporate excerpts from primary sources, but this text also keeps student needs in mind by using up-to-date translations and addressing a wide range of topics. Included are excerpts from important Buddhist, Hindu, Confucian, Zoroastrian, and Islamic works that helped shape great traditions. Readings such as a collection of Roman graffiti, a thirteenth-century tourist description of a Chinese city, a report on an Aztec market, and a manifesto for modern Egyptian women reveal something of people's lives and concerns. Also offered are materials that shed light on the politics of the time, such as an African king's plea to end the slave trade, Karl Marx's *Communist Manifesto,* and the recent *Arab Human Development Report*. The wide selection of document excerpts is also designed to illustrate how historians work with original documents. Unlike most texts, chapters are also enlivened by brief but numerous excerpts of statements, writings, or songs from people of the era that are effectively interspersed in the chapter narrative so that students can better see the vantage points and opinions of the people of that era.

Learning Aids

The carefully designed learning aids are meant to help faculty teach world history and students actively learn and appreciate it. A number of aids have been created, including some that distinguish this text from others in use.

Geography Overview Located at the front of the textbook, the Geography Overview pairs key maps found in the text with critical-thinking questions that help students interpret the variety of geographic and historical information that a map can convey.

Part Prologue and Map Each part opens with a prologue that previews the major themes and topics—global and regional—covered in the part chapters. An accompanying world map shows some of the key societies discussed in the part.

Chapter Outline, Primary Source Quotation, and Vignette A chapter outline shows the chapter contents at a glance. Chapter text then opens with a quotation from a primary source pertinent to chapter topics. An interest-grabbing vignette or sketch then funnels students' attention toward the chapter themes they are about to explore.

Focus Questions To prepare students for thinking about the main themes and topics of the chapter, a short list of thoughtfully prepared questions begins each chapter narrative. These questions are then repeated before each major section. The points they deal with are revisited in the Chapter Summary.

Special Boxed Features Each chapter contains a Witness to the Past drawn from a primary source, and a Profile highlighting a man or woman from that era. The Historical Controversy boxes, which focus on issues of interpretation, appear at the end of each part and before each "Societies, Networks, and Transitions" essay. Questions are also placed at the end of the primary source readings, historical controversies, and profiles to help students comprehend the material.

Maps and Other Visuals Maps, photos, chronologies, and tables are amply interspersed throughout the chapters, illustrating and unifying coverage and themes.

Section Summaries At the end of each major section within a chapter, a bulleted summary helps students to review the key topics.

Chapter Summary At the end of each chapter, a concise summary invites students to sum up the chapter content and review its major points.

Annotated Suggested Readings and Endnotes Short lists of annotated suggested readings, mostly recent, and websites providing additional information are also found at the end of each chapter. These lists acknowledge some of the more important works used in writing as well as sources of particular value for undergraduate students. Direct quotes in the text are attributed to their sources in endnotes, which are located at the end of the book.

Key Terms and Pronunciation Guides Important terms likely to be new to the student are boldfaced in the text and immediately defined. These key terms are also listed at the end of the chapter and then listed with their definitions at the end of the text. The pronunciation of foreign and other difficult terms is shown parenthetically where the terms are introduced to help students with the terminology.

New to this Edition

In developing this new edition, I have also benefited from the responses to the first edition, including correspondence and conversations with instructors and students who used the text. Incorporating many of their suggestions, this second edition is somewhat shorter than the first. The chapter structure is now streamlined by combining some materials and hence eliminating superfluous heads. Yet the new one-column format also allows for short call-outs of paragraph topics to be placed in the margins, along with key terms and definitions, helping students to organize the material and study for exams. New "eBook and Website Resources" sections at the end of every chapter indicate important corresponding online assets, including Primary Sources and Interactive Maps. I have also eliminated redundancies, corrected factual errors, and revised the suggested readings lists.

In addition to all these changes, I have updated the narrative to incorporate new scholarly knowledge and historical developments since the first edition was completed in 2006. Hence, many chapters include new information. Paleontology, archaeology, and ancient history are lively fields of study that constantly produce new knowledge, and the chapters in Part I include updates on subjects such as human evolution, the spread of modern humans, the rise of agriculture, the emergence of states, and early human settlement in the Americas. Later chapters incorporate new material on such subjects as politics in Muslim Spain, the invention of the Cherokee alphabet, and the contributions of the abolitionist Frederick Douglass. As most readers know, many important developments have occurred in the last few years, and hence the chapters in Part VI have required the most revision. As a result, Chapter 26 on the Global System includes, among other topics, new material on the 2008–2009 global recession, increasing global warming, the spread of Christianity (especially Pentacostalism), political protests and instant messaging (especially in China and Iran), and the world response to the death of Michael Jackson. Chapter 27 on East Asia examines economic challenges, human rights protests in China, violence in Tibet and Xinjiang, Japanese politics, and North Korean developments and regional tensions. The discussion of Europe and Russia in Chapter 28 ponders recent economic challenges, immigration issues, Russian-Georgian tensions, Vladimir Putin's government, and changing attitudes toward the European Union. In Chapter 29 on the Americas, I have added material on such topics as the Reagan and Bush legacies, the 2008–2009 economic meltdown, the election of Barack Obama, the wars in Iraq and Afghanistan, politics in various Latin American nations, the drug wars in Mexico and Colombia, and Chinese investment. New material in Chapter 30 on the Middle East and Africa includes Turkish politics, continuing Israel-Arab conflicts, the 2009 Iran elections, Iraq and Afghanistan updates, conflicts in Somalia, politics in varied African nations, the spread of Christianity, and the growing Chinese economic presence. Finally, Chapter 31 addresses the 2009 Indian elections, India's challenges, Pakistani politics, the Sri Lankan defeat of Tamil rebels, the Southeast Asian economic crisis, and politics and violence in various Southeast Asian nations. These chapters should give students a good introduction to the world in which they live.

Ancillaries

A wide array of supplements accompany this text to help students better master the material and to help instructors teach from the book.

Instructor Resources

PowerLecture CD-ROM with ExamView® and JoinIn® This dual-platform, all-in-one multimedia resource includes the Instructor's Resource Manual; a Test Bank (developed by Candace Gregory-Abbott of California State University, Sacramento; includes key term identification and multiple-choice, short answer/essay, and map questions); Microsoft® PowerPoint® slides of lecture outlines and of images and maps from the text, which can be used as offered or customized by importing personal lecture slides or other material; and JoinIn® PowerPoint® slides with clicker content. Also included is ExamView®, an easy-to-use assessment and tutorial system that allows instructors to create, deliver, and customize tests in minutes. Instructors can build tests with as many as 250 questions using up to 12 question types; using ExamView®'s complete word-processing capabilities, they can enter an unlimited number of new questions or edit existing ones.

HistoryFinder This searchable online database allows instructors to quickly and easily download thousands of assets, including art, photographs, maps, primary sources, and audio/video clips. Each asset downloads directly into a Microsoft® PowerPoint® slide, allowing instructors to easily create exciting PowerPoint presentations for their classrooms.

eInstructor's Resource Manual Prepared by Rick Gianni of Purdue University Calumet, this manual has many features, including instructional objectives, annotated chapter outlines, chapter summaries, lecture suggestions, suggested debate and discussion topics, and writing and research assignments. It is available on the instructor's companion website.

WebTutor™ on Blackboard®, WebTutor™ on WebCT®, and WebTutor™ on Angel® With WebTutor™'s text-specific, preformatted content and total flexibility, instructors can easily create and manage their own custom course website. Its course management tool gives instructors the ability to provide virtual office hours, post syllabi, set up threaded discussions, track student progress with the quizzing material, and much more. For students, WebTutor™ offers real-time access to a full array of study tools, including animations and videos that bring the book's topics to life, plus chapter outlines, summaries, learning objectives, glossary flashcards (with audio), practice quizzes, and weblinks.

Student Resources

Book Companion Site This website features a wide assortment of resources to help students master the subject matter. Prepared by Jason Ripper of Everett Community College, it includes a glossary, flashcards, crossword puzzles, learning objectives, preclass quizzes, tutorial quizzes, critical thinking exercises, and matching exercises. Throughout the text, icons direct students to relevant exercises and self-testing material located on the student companion website, which can be accessed at: *www.cengage.com/history/lockard/globalsocnet2e.*

CL eBook This interactive multimedia ebook links out to rich media assets such as Internet field trips and MP3 chapter summaries. Through this ebook, students can also access self-test quizzes, chapter outlines, focus questions, fill-in-the-blank exercises, chronology puzzles, essay questions (for which the answers can be emailed to their instructors), primary source documents with critical thinking questions, and interactive (zoomable) maps. Available on iChapters.

iChapters The website *www.iChapters.com* saves students time and money by giving them a choice in formats and savings and a better chance to succeed in class. iChapters.com, Cengage Learning's online store, is a single destination for more than 10,000 new textbooks, eTextbooks, eChapters, study tools, and audio supplements. Students have the freedom to purchase a-la-carte exactly what they need when they need it. They can save 50 percent on the electronic textbook and can pay as little as $1.99 for an individual eChapter.

Wadsworth World History Resource Center Wadsworth's World History Resource Center gives students access to a "virtual reader" with hundreds of primary sources, including speeches, letters, legal documents and transcripts, poems, maps, simulations, timelines, and additional images that bring history to life, along with interactive assignable exercises. A map feature including Google Earth™ coordinates and exercises will aid in student comprehension of geography and use of maps. Students can compare the traditional textbook map with an aerial view of the location today. It's an ideal resource for study, review, and research. In addition to this map feature, the resource center also provides blank maps for student review and testing.

Writing for College History, 1e Prepared by Robert M. Frakes, Clarion University, this brief handbook for survey courses in American history, Western Civilization/European history, and world civilization guides students through the various types of writing assignments they encounter in a history class. Providing examples of student writing and candid assessments of student work, this text focuses on the rules and conventions of writing for the college history course.

The History Handbook, 1e Prepared by Carol Berkin of Baruch College, City University of New York, and Betty Anderson of Boston University, this book teaches students both basic and history-specific study skills, such as how to read primary sources, research historical topics, and correctly cite sources. Substantially less expensive than comparable skill-building texts, *The History Handbook* also offers tips for Internet research and evaluating online sources.

Doing History: Research and Writing in the Digital Age, 1e This text was prepared by Michael J. Galgano, J. Chris Arndt, and Raymond M. Hyser of James Madison University. Whether they are starting down the path as a history major or simply looking for a straightforward and systematic guide to writing a successful paper, students will find it an indispensable handbook to historical research. This text's "soup to nuts" approach to researching and writing about history addresses every step of the process, from locating sources and gathering information to writing clearly and making proper use of various citation styles to avoid plagiarism. It enables students to learn how to make the most of every tool available—especially the technology that helps them conduct the process efficiently and effectively.

The Modern Researcher, 6e Prepared by Jacques Barzun and Henry F. Graff of Columbia University, this classic introduction to the techniques of research and the art of expression is used widely in history courses but is also appropriate for writing and research methods courses in other departments. Barzun and Graff thoroughly cover every aspect of research, from the selection of a topic through the gathering, analysis, writing, revision, and publication of findings. The research process is presented not as a set of rules but through actual cases that put the subtleties of research in a useful context. Part One covers the principles and methods of research; Part Two covers writing, speaking, and getting one's work published.

Reader Program Cengage Learning publishes a number of readers, some containing exclusively primary sources, others a combination of primary and secondary sources, and some designed to guide students through the process of historical inquiry. A complete list of readers can be found at *www.cengage.com.*

Custom Options

Cengage Learning offers custom solutions for this course that can tailor-fit students' learning needs—whether it's making a small modification to *Societies, Networks, and Transitions* to match the syllabus or combining multiple sources to create something truly unique. Instructors can pick and choose chapters, include their own material, and add additional map exercises along with the *Rand McNally Historical Atlas of the World* to create a text that fits the way they teach. They can ensure that students get the most out of their textbook dollar by giving them exactly what they need. A Cengage Learning representative can help instructors explore custom solutions.

Rand McNally Historical Atlas of the World, 2e This valuable resource features over seventy maps that portray the rich panoply of the world's history from preliterate times to the present, illustrating how cultures and civilizations were linked and interacted. The maps make it clear that history is not static; rather, it is about change and movement across time, a process of expansion, cooperation, and conflict. This atlas includes maps that display the world from the beginning of civilization; the political development of all major areas of the world; Africa, Latin America, and the Middle East in increased detail; the current Islamic World; and the world population change in 1900 and 2000.

Document Exercise Workbook Prepared by Donna Van Raaphorst, Cuyahoga Community College, this is a two-volume collection of exercises based around primary sources.

Formats

The text is available in a one-volume hardcover edition, a two-volume paperback edition, a three-volume paperback edition, and as an interactive ebook. *Volume I: To 1500* includes Chapters 1–14; *Volume II: Since 1450* includes Chapters 15–31; *Volume A: To 600* includes Chapters 1–9; *Volume B: From 600 to 1750* includes Chapters 10–18; and *Volume C: Since 1750* includes Chapters 19–31.

Acknowledgments

The author would like to thank the following community of instructors who, by sharing their teaching experiences and insightful feedback, helped shape the final textbook and ancillary program:

Susan Autry, Central Piedmont Community College
Brett Berliner, Morgan State University
Edward Bond, Alabama A & M University
Gayle K. Brunelle, California State University, Fullerton
Clea Bunch, University of Arkansas at Little Rock
Steve Corso, Elwood-John Glenn High School
Gregory Crider, Winthrop University
Jodi Eastberg, Alverno College
Eve Fisher, South Dakota State University
Rick Gianni, Purdue University Calumet
Candace Gregory-Abbott, California State University, Sacramento
Gregory M. Havrilcsak, University of Michigan–Flint
Linda Wilke Heil, Central Community College
Mark Hoffman, Wayne County Community College District
Bram Hubbell, Friends Seminary
Frances Kelleher, Grand Valley State University
Kim Klein, Shippensburg University
Rachel Layman, Lawrence North High School
Christine Lovasz-Kaiser, University of Southern Indiana
John Lyons, Joliet Junior College
Mary Ann Mahony, Central Connecticut State University
Laurence Marvin, Berry College
Patrick McDevitt, University at Buffalo SUNY
David K. McQuilkin, Bridgewater College
Bill Mihalopoulos, Northern Michigan University
W. Jack Miller, Pennsylvania State University-Abington
Edwin Moise, Clemson University
Aarti Nakra, Salt Lake Community College
Peter Ngwafu, Albany State University
Melvin Page, East Tennessee State University
Craig Patton, Alabama A & M University
William Pelz, Elgin Community College
Paul Philp, John Paul II HS/Eastfield Community College
Jason Ripper, Everett Community College
Rose Mary Sheldon, Virginia Military Institute
Anthony Steinhoff, University of Tennessee–Chattanooga
Bill Strickland, East Grand Rapids High School
Kurt Waters, Centreville High School

The author would also like to acknowledge the following instructors who lent their insight and guidance to the previous edition: Siamak Adhami, Saddleback Community College; Sanjam Ahluwalia, Northern Arizona University; David G. Atwill, Pennsylvania State University; Ewa K. Bacon, Lewis University; Bradford C. Brown, Bradley University; Gayle K. Brunelle, California State University–Fullerton; Rainer Buschmann, California State University, Channel Islands; Jorge Canizares-Esguerra, State University of New York–Buffalo; Bruce A. Castleman, San Diego State University; Harold B. Cline, Jr., Middle Georgia College; Simon Cordery, Monmouth College; Dale Crandall-Bear, Solano Community College; Cole Dawson, Warner Pacific College; Hilde De Weerdt, University of Tennessee, Knoxville; Anna Dronzek, University of Minnesota, Morris; James R. Evans, Southeastern Community College; Robert Fish, Japan Society of New York; Robert J. Flynn, Portland Community College; Gladys Frantz-Murphy, Regis University; Timothy Furnish, Georgia Perimeter College; James E. Genova, The Ohio State University; Deborah Gerish, Emporia State University; Kurt A. Gingrich, Radford University; Candace Gregory-Abbott, California State University, Sacramento; Paul L. Hanson, California Lutheran University; A. Katie Harris, Georgia State University; Gregory M. Havrilcsak, University of Michigan–Flint; Timothy Hawkins, Indiana State University; Don Holsinger, Seattle Pacific University; Mary N. Hovanec, Cuyahoga Community College; Jonathan Judaken, University of Memphis; Thomas E. Kaiser, University of Arkansas at Little Rock; Carol Keller, San Antonio College; Patricia A. Kennedy, Leeward Community College–University of Hawaii; Jonathan Lee, San Antonio College; Thomas Lide, San Diego State University; Derek S. Linton, Hobart and William Smith Colleges; David L. Longfellow, Baylor University; Erik C. Maiershofer, Point Loma Nazarene University; Afshin Marashi, California State University, Sacramento; Robert B. McCormick, University of South Carolina Upstate; Doug T. McGetchin, Florida Atlantic University; Kerry Muhlestein, Brigham Young University–Hawaii; Peter Ngwafu, Albany State University; Monique O'Connell, Wake Forest University; Annette Palmer, Morgan State University; Nicholas C. J. Pappas, Sam Houston State University; Patricia M. Pelley, Texas Tech University; John

Pesda, Camden County College; Pamela Roseman, Georgia Perimeter College; Paul Salstrom, St. Mary-of-the-Woods; Sharlene Sayegh, California State University, Long Beach; Michael Seth, James Madison University; David Simonelli, Youngstown State University; Peter Von Sivers, University of Utah; Anthony J. Steinhoff, University of Tennessee-Chattanooga; Nancy L. Stockdale, University of Central Florida; Robert Shannon Sumner, University of West Georgia; Kate Transchel, California State University, Chico; Sally N. Vaughn, University of Houston; Thomas G. Velek, Mississippi University for Women; and Kenneth Wilburn, East Carolina University.

The author has incurred many intellectual debts in developing his expertise in world history, as well as in preparing this text. To begin with, I cannot find words to express my gratitude to the wonderful editors and staff at Wadsworth, Cengage Learning—Nancy Blaine, Tonya Lobato, Carol Newman, and Jean Woy—who had enough faith in this project to tolerate my missed deadlines and sometimes grumpy responses to editorial decisions or some other crisis. I also owe an incalculable debt to my development editor on the first edition, Phil Herbst, who prodded and pampered and helped me write for a student, rather than scholarly, audience. Tonya Lobato adroitly supervised the second edition. Carole Frohlich ably handled photos; Charlotte Miller, maps; Susan Zorn, copyediting; Jake Kawatski, indexing; and Katherine Wetzel, general project management. Katherine Bates provided great help with marketing. I also owe a great debt to Pam Gordon, whose interest and encouragement got this project started. Ken Wolf of Murray State University prepared the initial drafts of several of the early chapters and in other ways gave me useful criticism and advice. I am grateful to Edwin Moise, Michelle Pinto, Rick Gianni, and Ibrahim Shafie for pointing out factual errors in the first edition. I would also like to acknowledge the inspiring mentors who helped me at various stages of my academic preparation: Bill Goldmann, who introduced me to world history at Pasadena High School in California; Charles Hobart and David Poston, University of Redlands professors who sparked my interest in Asia; George Wong, Bart Stoodley, and especially Andrew and Margaret Roy, my mentors at Chung Chi College in Hong Kong; Walter Vella, Robert Van Niel, and Daniel Kwok, who taught me Asian studies at Hawaii; and John Smail and Philip Curtin, under whom I studied comparative world history in the immensely exciting PhD program at Wisconsin. My various sojourns in East Asia, Southeast Asia, and East Africa allowed me to meet and learn from many inspiring and knowledgeable scholars. I have also been greatly stimulated and influenced in my approach by the writings of many fine global historians, but I would single out Philip Curtin, Marshall Hodgson, L. S. Stavrianos, William McNeill, Fernand Braudel, Eric Hobsbawm, Immanuel Wallerstein, and Peter Stearns. Curtin, Hobsbawm, and McNeill also gave me personal encouragement concerning my writing in the field, for which I am very grateful.

Colleagues at the various universities where I taught have been supportive of my explorations in world and comparative history. Most especially I acknowledge the friendship, support, and intellectual collaboration over three and a half decades of my colleagues in the interdisciplinary Social Change and Development Department at the University of Wisconsin-Green Bay (UWGB), especially Harvey Kaye, Lynn Walter, Larry Smith, Andy Kersten, Kim Nielsen, Andrew Austin, and the late Tony Galt, as well as members of the History faculty. I have also benefited immeasurably as a world historian from the visiting lecture series sponsored by UWGB's Center for History and Social Change, directed by Harvey Kaye, which over the years has brought in dozens of outstanding scholars. My students at UWGB and elsewhere have also taught me much.

I also thank my colleagues in the World History Association (WHA), who have generously shared their knowledge, encouraged my work, and otherwise provided an exceptional opportunity for learning and an exchange of ideas. I am proud to have helped establish this organization, which incorporates world history teachers at all levels of education and in many nations. Among many others, I want to express a special thank-you to longtime friends and colleagues in the WHA from whom I have learned so much and with whom I have shared many wonderful meals and conversations.

Finally, I need to acknowledge the loving support of my wife Kathy and our two sons, Chris and Colin, who patiently, although not always without complaint, for the many years of the project put up with my hectic work schedule and the ever-growing piles of research materials, books, and chapter drafts scattered around our cluttered den and sometimes colonizing other space around the house. Kathy also spent many hours selflessly helping me to complete chapter revisions to meet deadlines for the second edition.

About the Author

Craig A. Lockard is Ben and Joyce Rosenberg Professor of History in the Social Change and Development Department at the University of Wisconsin–Green Bay, where since 1975 he has taught courses on Asian, African, comparative, and world history. He has also taught at SUNY-Buffalo, SUNY-Stony Brook, and the University of Bridgeport, and twice served as a Fulbright-Hays professor at the University of Malaya in Malaysia. After undergraduate studies at the University of Redlands, during which he was able to spend a semester in Austria and a year as an exchange student at a college in Hong Kong, the author earned an MA in Asian Studies at the University of Hawaii and a PhD in Comparative World and Southeast Asian History at the University of Wisconsin–Madison. His published books, articles, essays, and reviews range over a wide spectrum of topics: world history; Southeast Asian history, politics, and society; Malaysian studies; Asian emigration and diasporas; the Vietnam War; and folk, popular, rock, and world music. Among his major books are *Southeast Asia in World History* (2009); *WORLD* (2009); *Dance of Life: Popular Music and Politics in Modern Southeast Asia* (1998); and *From Kampung to City: A Social History of Kuching, Malaysia, 1820–1970* (1987). He was also part of the task force that prepared revisions to the U.S. National Standards in World History (1996). Professor Lockard has served on various editorial advisory boards, including the *Journal of World History* and *The History Teacher,* and as book review editor for the *Journal of Asian Studies* and the *World History Bulletin*. He was one of the founders of the World History Association, served as the organization's first secretary, and is currently a member of the Executive Council. He has lived and traveled widely in Asia, Africa, and Europe.

Note on Spelling and Usage

Transforming foreign words and names, especially those from non-European languages, into spellings usable for English-speaking readers presents a challenge. Sometimes, as with Chinese, Thai, and Malay/Indonesian, several romanized spelling systems have developed. Generally I have chosen user-friendly spellings that are widely used in other Western writings (such as *Aksum* for the classical Ethiopian state and *Ashoka* for the classical Indian king). For Chinese, I generally use the *pinyin* system developed in the People's Republic over the past few decades (such as *Qin* and *Qing* rather than the older *Chin* and *Ching* for these dynasties, and *Beijing* instead of *Peking*), but for a few terms and names (such as the twentieth-century political leaders *Sun Yat-sen* and *Chiang Kai-shek*) I have retained an older spelling more familiar to Western readers and easier to pronounce. The same strategy is used for some other terms or names from Afro-Asian societies, such as *Cairo* instead of *al-Cahira* (the Arabic name) for the Egyptian city, *Bombay* instead of *Mumbai* (the current Indian usage) for India's largest city, and *Burma* instead of *Myanmar.* In some cases I have favored a newer spelling widely used in a region and modern scholarship but not perhaps well known in the West. For example, in discussing Southeast Asia I follow contemporary scholarship and use *Melaka* instead of *Malacca* for the Malayan city and *Maluku* rather than *Moluccas* for the Indonesian islands. Similarly, like Africa specialists I have opted to use some newer spellings, such as *Gikuyu* rather than *Kikuyu* for the Kenyan ethnic group. To simplify things for the reader I have tried to avoid using diacritical marks within words. Sometimes their use is unavoidable, such as for the premodern Chinese city of *Chang'an;* the two syllables here are pronounced separately. I also follow the East Asian custom of rendering Chinese, Japanese, and Korean names with the surname (family name) first (e.g., *Mao Zedong, Tokugawa Ieyasu*). The reader is also referred to the opening essay, "Introducing World History," for explanations of the dating system used (such as the Common Era and the Intermediate Era) and geographical concepts (such as Eurasia for Europe and Asia, and Oceania for Australia, New Zealand, and the Pacific islands).

Introducing World History

A journey of a thousand miles begins with the first step.

—Chinese Proverb

This introduction helps you take the important "first step" toward understanding the scope and challenge of studying world history. By presenting the main concepts and themes of world history, it serves as your guide in exploring the story of the world presented in the rest of the book while providing a foretaste of the lively debates among historians as they try to make sense of the past, especially how societies change and how their contacts with one another have created the interconnected world we know today. By examining world history, you can better understand not only how this connection happened, but also why.

What Do Historians Do?

History is the study of the past that looks at all of human life, thought, and behavior and includes both a record and an interpretation of events, people, and the societies they developed. Therefore, the job of the historian is to both describe *and* interpret the past. Although beginning students generally see history as the story of "what happened," most professional historians want to make sense of historical events. Two general concepts help historians in these efforts. When they look at humans in all their historical complexity, historians see both changes and continuity. The legal system in the United States, for example, is unlike any other in the world, and yet it has been shaped in part by both English and ancient Roman legal practices.

Historians face their greatest challenges in their role as interpreters of the past. Although historians agree on the need for extensive evidence to support their generalizations, they often disagree on how an event should be interpreted. Often the disagreements reflect political differences. In 1992 a widely publicized disagreement took place on the occasion of the 500-year anniversary of the first cross-Atlantic voyage of Christopher Columbus to the Western Hemisphere in 1492. Some historians pictured Columbus as a farsighted pioneer who made possible communication between the hemispheres, while others saw him as an immoral villain who mistreated the local peoples, beginning a pattern of exploitation by Europeans. Similar debates have raged about whether it was necessary for the United States to drop atomic bombs on Japan in 1945, killing thousands of Japanese civilians but also ending World War II.

While the events of the past do not change, our understanding of them does, as historians both acquire new information and use the old information to answer new questions. Only within the past fifty years, for example, have historians studied the diaries and journals that reveal the important role of women on the home front during the American Civil War. Recently historians have used long-neglected sources to conclude that, a millennium ago, China had the world's most dynamic economy and sophisticated technology. Similarly, historians have recently discovered, in the West African city of Timbuktu, thousands of old books written in African languages, forcing a rethinking of literacy and scholarship in West African societies hundreds of years ago.

What history "tells us" is constantly evolving. New evidence, changing interests, and the asking of new questions all add up to seeing things in a new light. As you read the text, remember that no text contains the whole or final truth. Historical revision, or changing understanding of the past, is at the heart of historical scholarship. This revision and the difficulties of interpretation also make history controversial. In recent years heated debates about what schools should teach about history have erupted in many countries, including Japan, India, France, and the United States.

Historians bridge the gap between the humanities and the social sciences. As humanists, historians study the philosophies, religions, literatures, and arts that people have generated over the ages. As social scientists, historians examine political, social, and economic patterns, though frequently asking questions different from those asked by anthropologists, economists, political scientists, and sociologists, who are generally more concerned with the present and in theoretical questions. Historians also study people in their many roles and stations in life—the accomplishments of the rich and famous as well as the struggles and dreams of common women and men—and must be familiar with the findings of other relevant academic disciplines.

Why Study World History?

World or global history is the broadest field of history. It studies the human record as a whole and the experiences of people in all the world's inhabited regions—Africa, the Americas, Asia, Europe, and the Pacific Basin—and also helps us better understand individual societies by making it easier to look at them comparatively. Studying history on a global scale also brings out patterns of life, cultural traditions, and connections between societies that go beyond a particular region, such as the spread of Buddhism, which followed the trade routes throughout southern and eastern Asia nearly two thousand years ago. World history takes us through the forest of history in which the individual societies represent the individual trees. World history helps us comprehend both the trees and the forest, allowing us to situate ourselves in a broader context.

This helps us understand our increasingly connected world. Decisions made in Washington, D.C., Paris, or Tokyo influence citizens in Argentina, Senegal, and Malaysia, just as events elsewhere often affect the lives of people in Europe and North America. World historians use the widest angle of vision to comprehend how diverse local traditions and international trends intermingle. International trends spread from many directions. Western phenomena such as McDonald's, Hard Rock Cafes, French wines, Hollywood films, churches, the Internet, cell phones, and text messaging have spread around the world but so have non-Western products and ideas, among them Mexican soap operas, Chinese food, Japanese cars, Indonesian arts, African rhythms, and the Islamic religion. When we study individual nations, we must remember that, for all their idiosyncrasies, each nation develops in a wider world.

Along with the growing interconnectedness of the world, a global perspective highlights the past achievements of all peoples. The history of science, for example, shows that key inventions—printing, sternpost rudders, the compass, the wheelbarrow, gunpowder—originated in China and that the modern system of numbering came from India, reaching Europe from the Middle East as "Arabic" numerals. Indeed, various peoples—Mesopotamians, Egyptians, Greeks, Chinese, Indians, Arabs—built the early foundation for modern science and technology, and their discoveries moved along the trade routes. The importers of technology and ideas often modified or improved on them. For example, Europeans made good use of Chinese, Indian, and Arab technologies, as well as their own inventions, in their quest to explore the world in the fifteenth and sixteenth centuries. The interdependence among and exchanges between peoples is a historical as well as a present reality.

The World History Challenge

When we study world history, we see other countries and peoples, past and present. We do not, however, always see them accurately. Nevertheless, by studying the unfamiliar, world history helps us to recognize how some of the attitudes we absorb from the particular society and era we live in shape, and may distort, our understanding of the world and of history. Coming to terms with this mental baggage means examining such things as maps and geographical concepts and acquiring intellectual tools for comprehending other cultures.

Broadening the Scope of Our Histories

During much of the twentieth century, high school and college students in North America were often taught some version of a course, usually called Western Civilization, that emphasized the rise of western Europe and the European contributions to modern North American societies. This course recognized the undeniably influential role of Western nations, technologies, and ideas in the modern world, but also reflected historians' extensive acquisition of data on Europe and North America compared with the rest of the world. This approach often exaggerated the role that Europe played in world history before modern times, pushing Asian, African, and Native American peoples and their accomplishments into the background while underplaying the contributions these peoples made to Europe. Students usually learned little about China, India, or Islam, and even less about Africa, Southeast Asia, or Latin America.

In the 1960s the teaching of history began to change in North America. The political independence of most Asian, African, and Caribbean nations from Western nations fostered a more sophisticated understanding of African, Asian, Latin American, Native American, and Pacific island history in North America and Europe. The increased knowledge has made it easier to write a history of the entire globe. As a result, world history courses, rare before the 1960s, became increasingly common in U.S. universities, colleges, and high schools by the late twentieth century and have been proliferating in several other countries, such as Australia, Canada, South Africa, China, and the Netherlands.

Revising Maps and Geography

Maps not only tell us where places are; they also create a mental image of the world, revealing how peoples perceive themselves and others. For example, Chinese maps once portrayed China as the "Middle Kingdom," the center of the world surrounded by "barbarians." This image reflected and deepened the Chinese sense of superiority over neighboring peoples. Similarly, 2,500 years ago, Greek maps showed Greece at the center of the inhabited world known to them.

Even modern maps can be misleading. For example, the Mercator projection (or spatial presentation) still used in many school maps in North America and elsewhere and standard in most atlases, is based on a sixteenth-century European model that distorts the relative size of landmasses, greatly exaggerating Europe, North America, and Greenland while diminishing the lands nearer the equator and in the Southern Hemisphere. Hence, Africa, India, Southeast Asia, China, and South America look much smaller than they actually are. In the United States, maps using a Mercator projection have often tellingly placed the Americas in the middle of the map, cutting Asia in half, suggesting that the United States, appearing larger than it actually is, plays the central role in the world. Some alternative maps give a more accurate view of relative size. For example, the oval-shaped Eckert projection uses an ellipse that shows a better balance of size and shape while minimizing distortion of continental areas. A comparison between the Mercator and Eckert world maps is shown on the following spread.

The same shaping of mental images of geography found in maps is also seen in concepts of geographical features and divisions, such as continents, the large landmasses on which most people live. The classical Greeks were probably the first to use the terms *Europe, Africa,* and *Asia* in defining their world 2,500 years ago, and later Europeans transformed these terms into the names for continents. For centuries Western peoples have taken for granted that Europe is a continent although Europe is not a separate landmass, and the physical barriers between it and Asia are not that significant. If mountains and other geographical barriers define a continent, one can make a better case for India (blocked off by truly formidable mountains) or Southeast Asia than for Europe. At the same time, seeing Asia as a single continent is also a problem, given its spectacular size and geographical diversity. Today world geographers and historians usually consider Europe and Asia to constitute one huge continent, Eurasia, containing several subcontinental regions, such as Europe, South Asia, and East Asia.

Popular terms such as *Near East, Middle East,* or *Far East* are also misleading. They were originally formulated by Europeans to describe regions in relationship to Europe. Much

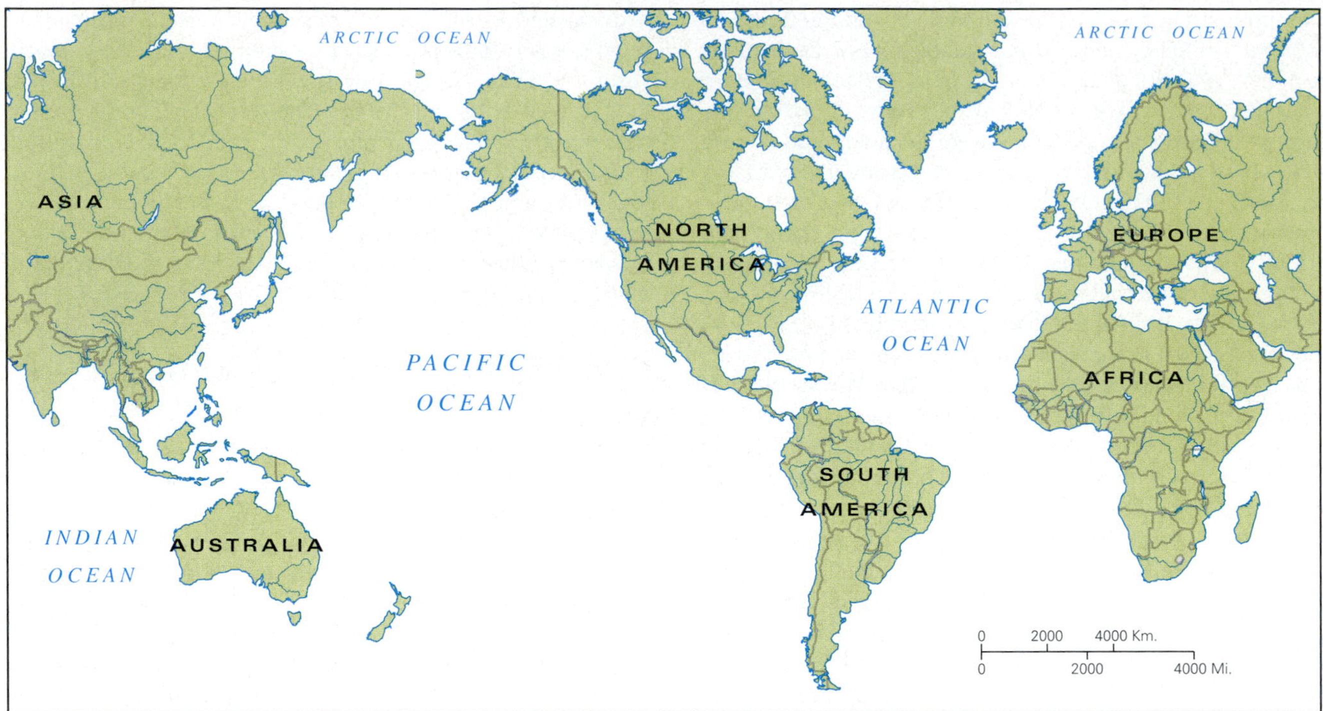

Mercator Projection

depends on the viewer's position; Australians, for example, often label nearby Southeast and East Asia as the "Near North." Few Western scholars of China or Japan today refer to the "Far East," preferring the more neutral term *East Asia.* This text considers the term *Near East,* long used for western Asia, as outdated, but it refers to Southwest Asia and North Africa, closely linked historically (especially after the rise of Islam 1,400 years ago), as the Middle East, since that term is more convenient than the alternatives. The text also uses the term *Oceania* to refer to Australia, New Zealand, and the Pacific islands.

Rethinking the Dating System

A critical feature of historical study is the dating of events. World history challenges us by making us aware that all dating systems are based on the assumptions of a particular culture. Many Asian peoples saw history as moving in great cycles of birth, maturation, and decay (sometimes involving millions of years), while Westerners saw history as moving in a straight line from past to future (as can be seen in the chronologies within each chapter). Calendars were often tied to myths about the world's creation or about a people's or country's origins. Hence, the classical Roman calendar was based on the founding of the city of Rome around 2,700 years ago, reflecting the Romans' claim to the territory in which they had recently settled.

The dating system used throughout the Western world today is based on the Gregorian Christian calendar, created by a sixteenth-century Roman Catholic pope, Gregory XIII. It uses the birth of Christianity's founder, Jesus of Nazareth, around 2,000 years ago as the turning point. Dates for events prior to the Christian era were identified as B.C. (before Christ); years in the Christian era were labeled A.D. (for the Latin *anno domini,* "in the year of the Lord"). Many history books published in Europe and North America still employ this system, which has spread around the world in recent centuries.

The notion of Christian and pre-Christian eras has no longer been satisfactory for studies of world history because it is rooted in the viewpoint of only one religious tradition, whereas there are many in the world, usually with different calendars. Hence, the Christian calendar has little relevance for the non-Christian majority of the world's people. Muslims, for example, who consider the revelations of the prophet Muhammad to be the central event in history, begin their dating system with Muhammad's journey, within Arabia, from the city of Mecca to Medina in 622 A.D. Many Buddhists use a calendar beginning with the death of Buddha around 2,500 years ago. The Chinese chronological system divides history into cycles stretching over 24 million years. The Chinese are now in the fifth millennium of the current cycle, and their system corresponds more accurately than does the Gregorian calendar to the beginning of the world's oldest cities and states, between 5,000 and 6,000 years ago. Many other alternative dating systems exist. Selecting one over the others constitutes favoritism for a particular society or cultural tradition.

Therefore, most world historians and many specialists in Asian, African, and European history have moved toward a more secular, or nonreligious, concept, the Common Era. This system still accepts as familiar, at least to Western readers, the dates used in the Western calendar, but it calls the period after the transition, identified by Christians with the birth of Jesus, a "common" era, since many influential, dynamic societies existed two millennia ago throughout the world, not only in the Judeo-Christian Holy Land. Two millennia ago, the beginning of the Common Era, the Roman Empire was at its height, Chinese and Indian empires ruled large chunks of Asia, and many peoples in the Eastern Hemisphere were linked by trade and religion to a greater extent than ever before. Several African societies also flourished, and states and cities had long before

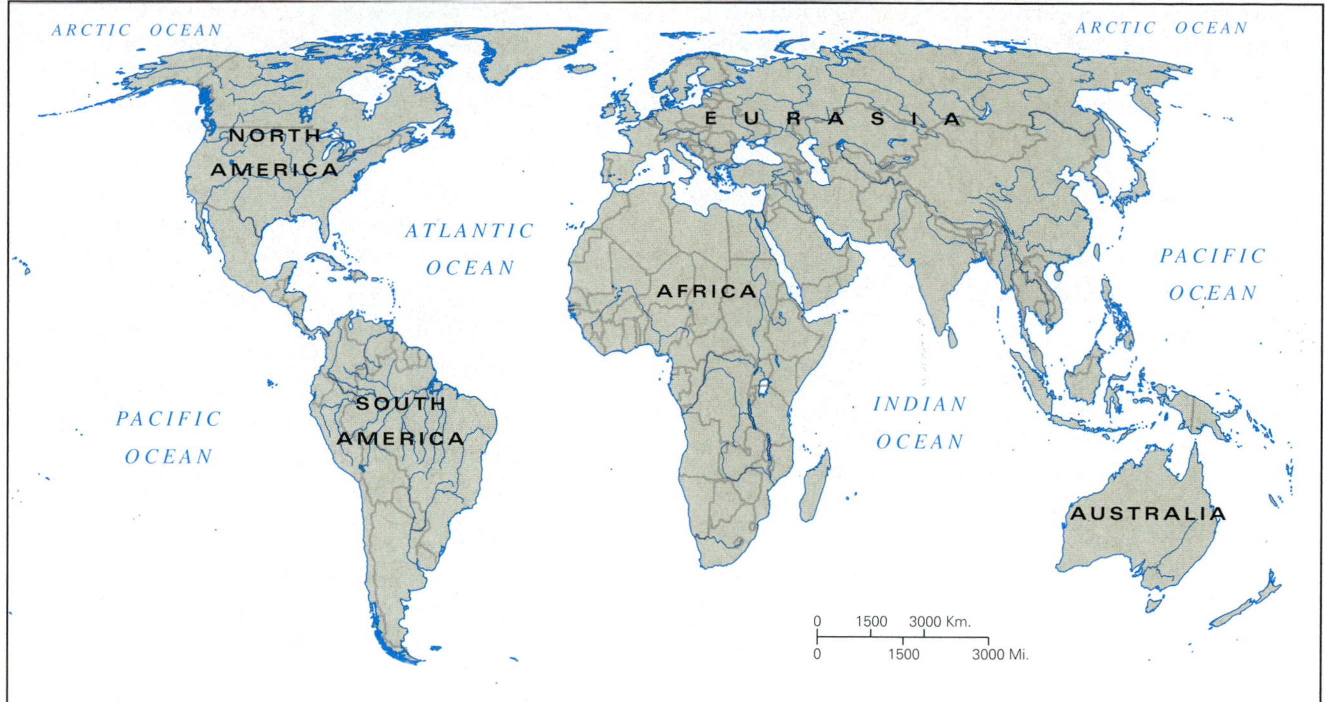

Eckert Projection

developed in the Americas. Hence this period makes a useful and familiar benchmark. In the new system, events are dated as B.C.E. (before the Common Era) and as C.E. (Common Era, which begins in year 1 of the Gregorian Christian calendar). This change is an attempt at including all the world's people and avoiding preference for any particular religious tradition.

Rethinking the Division of History into Periods

To make world history more comprehensible, historians divide long periods of time into smaller segments, such as "the ancient world" or "modern history," each marked by certain key events or turning points, a process known as **periodization**. For example, scholars of European, Islamic, Chinese, Indonesian, or United States history generally agree among themselves on the major eras and turning points for the region they study, but world historians need a system that can encompass all parts of the world, no easy task since most historic events did not affect all regions of the world. For instance, developments that were key to eastern Eurasia, such as the spread of Buddhism, or to western Eurasia and North Africa, such as the spread of Christianity, did not always affect southern Africa, and both the the Americas and some Pacific peoples remained isolated from the Eastern Hemisphere for centuries.

Given the need for an inclusive chronological pattern, this book divides history into periods, each of which is notable for significant changes around the world:

1. **Ancient (100,000–600 B.C.E.)** The Ancient Era, during which the foundations for world history were built, can be divided into two distinct periods. During the long centuries known as Prehistory (ca. 100,000–4000 B.C.E.), Stone Age peoples, living in small groups, survived by hunting and gathering food. Eventually some of them began simple farming and living in villages, launching the second period, the era of agrarian societies. Between 4000 and 600 B.C.E., agriculture became more productive, the first cities and states were established in both hemispheres, and some societies invented writing, allowing historians to study their experiences and ideas.
2. **Classical (600 B.C.E.–600 C.E.)** The Classical Era is marked by the creation of more states and complex agrarian societies, the birth of major religions and philosophies, the formation of the first large empires, and the expansion of long-distance trade, which linked distant peoples.
3. **Intermediate (600–1500 C.E.)** The Intermediate Era comprises a long middle period or "middle ages" of expanding horizons that modified or displaced the classical societies. It was marked by increasing trade connections between distant peoples within the same hemisphere, the growth and spread of several older religions and of a new faith, Islam, and oceanic exploration by Asians and Europeans.
4. **Early Modern (1450–1750 C.E.)** During the Early Modern Era, the whole globe became intertwined as European exploration and conquests in the Americas, Africa, and southern Asia fostered the rise of a global economy, capitalism, and a trans-Atlantic slave trade while undermining American and African societies.
5. **Modern (1750–1945 C.E.)** The Modern Era was characterized by rapid technological and economic change in Europe and North America, Western colonization of many Asian and African societies, political revolutions and ideologies, world wars, and a widening gap between rich and poor societies.

6. **Contemporary (1945–present)** The Contemporary Era has been marked by a more closely interlinked world, including the global spread of commercial markets, cultures, and communications, the collapse of Western colonial empires, international organizations, new technologies, struggles by poor nations to develop economically, environmental destruction, and conflict between powerful nations.

Understanding Cultural and Historical Differences

The study of world history challenges us to understand peoples and ideas very different from our own. The past is, as one writer has put it, "a foreign country; they do things differently there."[1] As human behavior changes with the times, sometimes dramatically, so do people's beliefs, including moral and ethical standards. For example, in Asia centuries ago, Assyrians and Mongols sometimes killed everyone in cities that resisted their conquest. Some European Christians seven hundred years ago burned suspected heretics and witches at the stake and enjoyed watching blind beggars fight. Across the Atlantic, American peoples such as the Aztecs and Incas engaged in human sacrifice. None of these behaviors would be morally acceptable today in most societies.

Differences in customs complicate efforts to understand people of earlier centuries. We need not approve of empire builders, plunderers, human sacrifice, and witch burning, but we should be careful about applying our current standards of behavior and thought to people who lived in different times and places. We should avoid **ethnocentrism**, viewing others narrowly through the lens of one's own society and its values. Historians are careful in using value-loaded words such as *primitive, barbarian, civilized,* or *progress* that carry negative or positive meanings and are often matters of judgment rather than fact. For instance, soldiers facing each other on the battlefield may consider themselves civilized and their opponents barbarians. And progress, such as industrialization, often brings negative developments, such as pollution, along with the positive.

Today anthropologists use the term **cultural relativism** to remind us that, while all people have much in common, societies are diverse and unique, embodying different standards of proper behavior and thought. For instance, cultures may have very different ideas about children's obligations to their parents, what happens to people's souls when they die, or what constitutes music pleasing to the ear. Cultural relativism still allows us to say that the Mongol empire builders in Eurasia some eight hundred years ago were brutal, or that the mid-twentieth-century Nazi German dictator, Adolph Hitler, was a murderous tyrant, or that laws in some societies today that blame and penalize women who are raped are wrong and should be protested. But cultural relativism discourages us from criticizing other cultures or ancient peoples just because they are or were different from us. Studying world history can make us more aware of our ethnocentric biases.

The Major Themes

Determining major themes is yet another challenge in presenting world history. This text uses certain themes to take maximum advantage of world history's power to illuminate both change and continuity as we move from the past to the present. Specifically, in preparing the text, the author asked himself: What do educated students today need to know about world history to understand the globalizing era in which they live?

Three broad themes help you comprehend how today's world emerged. These themes are shaped around three concepts: societies, networks, and transitions.

1. **Societies** are broad groups of people that have common traditions, institutions, and organized patterns of relationships with each other. The societies that people have organized and maintained, influenced by environmental factors, were defined by distinctive but often changing cultures, beliefs, social forms, governments, economies, and ways of life.
2. **Networks** are arrangements or collections of links between different societies, such as the routes over which traders, goods, diplomats, armies, ideas, and information travel. Over the centuries societies were increasingly connected to other societies by growing networks forged by phenomena such as population movement, long-distance trade, exploration, military expansion, colonization, the diffusion of ideas and technologies, and communication links. These growing networks modified individual societies, connected societies within the same and nearby regions, and eventually led to a global system in which distant peoples came into frequent contact.
3. **Transitions** are passages, changes, events, or movements that reshape societies and regions. Each major historical era was marked by one or more great transitions that were sparked by events or innovations that had profound, enduring influences on many societies and that fostered a gradual reshaping of the world.

The first theme, based on societies, recognizes the importance in world history of the distinctiveness of societies. Cultural traditions and social patterns differed greatly. For example, societies in Eurasia fostered several influential philosophical and religious traditions, from Confucianism in eastern Asia to Christianity, born in the Middle East and later nourished both there and in Europe. Historians often identify unique traditions in a society that go back hundreds or even thousands of years.

The second theme, based on networks, acknowledges the way societies have contacted and engaged with each other to create the interdependent world we know today. The spread of technologies and ideas, exploration and colonization, and the growth of global trade across Eurasia and Africa and then into the Western Hemisphere are largely responsible for spurring this interlinking process. Today networks such as the World Wide Web, airline routes, multinational corporations, and terrorist organizations operate on a global scale. As this list shows, many networks are welcome, but some are dangerous.

The third theme, transitions, helps to emphasize major developments that shaped world history. The most important include, roughly in chronological order, the beginning of agriculture, the rise of cities and states, the birth and spread of philosophical and religious traditions, the forming of great empires, the linking of Eurasia by the Mongols, the European seafaring explorations and conquests, the Industrial Revolution, the forging and dismantling of Western colonial empires, world wars, and the invention of electronic technologies that allow for instantaneous communication around the world.

With these themes in mind, the text constructs the rich story of world history. The intellectual experience of studying world history is exciting and will give you a clearer understanding of how the world as you know it came to be.

KEY TERMS

history
periodization
ethnocentrism
cultural relativism
societies
networks
transitions

SUGGESTED READING

After each chapter and essay, you will find a short list of valuable books and useful websites to help you explore history beyond the text. The books listed below will be of particular help to beginning students of world history because they examine the field of world history, offer an overview of history, or place key themes in a broad context for the general reader. The websites listed are megasites containing links to many essays, primary readings, and other sources.

Books

Bender, Thomas. *A Nation Among Nations: America's Place in World History.* New York: Hill and Wang, 2006. Looks at the history of the United States as part of modern world history.

Bentley, Jerry H. *Shapes of World History in 20th Century Scholarship.* Washington, DC: American Historical Association, 1996. A brief presentation of the scholarly study of world history.

Buschmann, Rainer F. *Oceans in World History.* Boston: McGraw-Hill, 2008. An innovative overview of how oceans connected distant societies.

Chanda, Nayan. *Bound Together: How Traders, Preachers, Adventurers, and Warriors Shaped Globalization.* New Haven: Yale University Press, 2007. A lively examination by an Indian journalist.

Christian, David. *Maps of Time: An Introduction to Big History.* Berkeley: University of California Press, 2004. A detailed but pathbreaking study by an Australian scholar that mixes scientific understandings into the study of world history.

Crossley, Pamela Kyle. *What Is Global History?* Malden, MA: Polity Press, 2008. Briefly examines approaches to understanding world history.

Dunn, Ross, ed. *The New World History: A Teacher's Companion.* Boston: Bedford/St. Martin's, 2000. A valuable collection of essays on various aspects of world history and how it can be studied. Useful for students as well as teachers.

Fernandez-Armesto, Felipe. *Pathfinders: A Global History.* New York: W.W. Norton, 2006. Readable survey of exploration.

Headrick, Daniel R. *Technology in World History.* New York: Oxford University Press, 2009. Good summary of this important topic.

Hodgson, Marshall G. S. *Rethinking World History: Essays on Europe, Islam, and World History.* Edmund Burke III, ed. New York: Cambridge University Press, 1993. Written by one of the most influential world historians for teachers and scholars but also offering many insights for students.

Manning, Patrick. *Migration in World History.* New York: Routledge, 2005. Explores population movements from prehistory to today.

McNeill, J. R., and William H. McNeill. *The Human Web: A Bird's-Eye View of World History.* New York: W.W. Norton, 2003. A stimulating overview of world history using the concept of human webs to examine interactions between peoples.

McNeill, William H., et al., eds. *Berkshire Encyclopedia of World History,* 5 vols. Great Barrington, MA: Berkshire, 2005. One of the best of several fine encyclopedias, with many essays on varied aspects of world history.

Nieberg, Michael S. *Warfare in World History.* New York: Routledge, 2001. Focuses on wars as agents of long-term change.

Ponting, Clive. *A New Green History of the World: The Environment and the Collapse of Great Civilizations.* New York: Penguin, 2007. Provocative study by a British scholar for a general audience.

Stavrianos, Leften S. *Lifelines from Our Past: A New World History.* rev. ed. Armonk, NY: M. E. Sharpe, 1997. A brief but stimulating reflection on world history by a leading scholar.

Stearns, Peter N. *Western Civilization in World History.* New York: Routledge, 2003. A brief examination of how Western civilization fits into the study of world history.

Wiesner-Hanks, Merry E. *Gender in World History.* Malden, MA: Blackwell, 2001. A pioneering thematic survey of a long-neglected subject.

WEBSITES

Bridging World History (***http://www.learner.org/courses/world history/***). Rich site with essays and multimedia presentations.

The Encyclopedia of World History (***http://www.bartleby.com/67/***). A valuable collection of thousands of entries spanning the centuries from prehistory to 2000.

Internet Global History Sourcebook (***http://www.fordham.edu/halsall/global/globalsbook.html***). An excellent set of links on world history from ancient to modern times.

Internet History Sourcebooks Project (***http://www.fordham.edu/halsall/***). Huge invaluable collection of public domain historical readings on many topics and regions.

Women in World History (***http://chnm.gmu.edu/wwh/***). Invaluable collection of links covering many societies and all eras.

World Civilizations (***http://www.wsu.edu/~dee***). An Internet anthology maintained at Washington State University.

World History Connected (***http://worldhistoryconnected.press/illinois.edu)/***). This e-journal contains essays of use to both students and teachers.

World History for Us All (***http://worldhistoryforusall.sdsu.edu***). A growing site with useful essays and other materials, sponsored by San Diego State University.

World History Sources (***http://worldhistorymatters.org***). Valuable annotated links on different subjects, based at George Mason University.

PART I

Foundations: Ancient Societies, to 600 B.C.E.

Most of us carry pictures in our minds of the world's ancient peoples and their ways of life: prehistoric cave dwellers huddling around a fire, wandering desert tribes, towering pyramids, and spectacular ruins of cities and temples. In fact, the centuries between 100,000 and 600 B.C.E. saw the evolution of these and many other social and cultural phenomena, more complex and often more significant to us today than these mental pictures convey. These centuries also saw humans take the first steps in establishing regular contacts and exchanges, often those of trade, with one another, creating the networks that linked many societies over wide areas.

Human societies have emerged only recently in earth's long history. Simple life began on earth over 3 billion years ago. Several million years ago in Africa the earliest near ancestors of humans began to walk upright and use simple tools. Gradually they evolved into modern humans who commanded language, controlled fire, and eventually populated the entire world. For thousands of years, small bands of people, carrying their stone and wood tools as they moved from campsite to campsite, lived by hunting and gathering. With the first great transition in human history, the introduction of agriculture some 10,000 years ago, people began to deliberately cultivate plants and raise draft animals. Although some societies remained hunters and gatherers or herders, most people around the world shifted eventually to farming. Congregating in villages and towns and farming the neighboring fields with their simple hoes and plows, they experienced profound changes in their ways of life. For some societies, the production of an agricultural surplus—more food than was needed by the farmers—and growing commercial activity provided the economic and labor support that enabled the development of formal governments and religious institutions. Farming, town life, trade, and more advanced technology set the stage for the second great transition, the building of cities and the forming of states.

The world's first societies emerged in various parts of the world, and each society gradually created its own distinctive traditions. The first cities and states arose between 5,500 and 4,000 years ago in the lands stretching from southern Europe and northern Africa eastward through western and southern Asia to China. For most of history the vast majority of the world's people lived in these regions of Africa and Eurasia. Between 5,000 and 3,000 years ago cities and states also developed in the Americas. The most densely populated ancient societies emerged where agriculture, aided by irrigation, flourished: in large river valleys, particularly the floodplains of the Nile in Egypt, the Tigris-Euphrates in Mesopotamia, the Indus in India, and the Yellow in China. The ancient world also benefited from great advances in metalworking, especially of copper, bronze, and iron, which spread widely. Growing networks of trade and transportation

Courtesy of the Trustees of the British Museum

Cuneiform Tablet This letter, impressed on a clay tablet in Mesopotamia around 1900 B.C.E., records a merchant's complaint that a shipment of copper that he had paid for contained too little metal. Mesopotamian letters, written chiefly by merchants and officials, were enclosed in envelopes made of clay and marked with the sender's private seal.

increasingly connected many societies to each other by land and sea. Although societies exchanged ideas, products, and technologies with others, each ancient society created unique religions, cultural values, social structures, and systems for recording information. These traditions sometimes continued over several thousand years, even though modified with time. A few traditions, such as the ancient Hebrew and Indian religions, have survived into the present.

Contacts between peoples in different regions had already begun to increase greatly with the appearance of farming. Societies traded agricultural and hunting tools, as well as minerals, wood, clothing, and food. Between 2500 and 600 B.C.E. the Eastern Hemisphere experienced much more active trading networks. Improved transportation, including seaworthy sailing vessels, horse-drawn chariots, and camel caravans, fostered trade by shrinking distances. Long-distance trade served to spread ideas and expand horizons. Some peoples migrated far from their ancestral homes, with major movements into the Pacific islands (Oceania) and the southern half of Africa. Like trade, other encounters between societies, friendly or hostile, often became major forces for change.

Most ancient societies, such as Egypt and Mesopotamia, have long since disappeared, leaving only crumbling ruins or long-buried artifacts to remind us of their achievements. In their ancient forms, these societies never survived through the centuries, although their religions and values often influenced the societies that displaced them, and many of their descendants still live in the region. On the other hand, the Chinese and Indian societies persisted in some recognizable form and are familiar to us today. The Ancient Era built the framework for much that came later.

EUROPE
Ancient cities and states formed on the Mediterranean island of Crete and in Greece. Minoans, the residents of Crete, were successful maritime traders. After their collapse, the Mycenaeans of mainland Greece traded widely and exercised regional power until they declined. Migrants into Greece mixed with the Mycenaeans to form the foundation for later Greek society. These southern European societies worked bronze and participated in trade networks linking them to North Africa, eastern Europe, and western Asia.

WESTERN ASIA
The world's first farmers probably lived in western Asia, east of the Mediterranean Sea, where the oldest known cities and states also arose. The diverse societies that formed in the Tigris-Euphrates River Valley in Mesopotamia developed bronzeworking, writing, science, and mathematics, and they also traded with India and Egypt. Western Asians perfected iron technology, which eventually spread around Eurasia. The Phoenicians were the greatest traders of the Mediterranean region and also invented an alphabet later adopted by the Greeks. Another notable people, the Hebrews, introduced a monotheistic religion, Judaism.

EASTERN ASIA
Farming developed very early in the Yellow and Yangzi River Basins in China, fostering the region's first cities and states. Chinese culture then expanded into southern China. The Chinese invented a writing system and worked bronze and iron. Mixing Chinese influences with their own traditions, Koreans took up farming and metalworking. Some Koreans migrated into Japan, where they and the local peoples mixed their traditions to produce the Japanese culture.

AFRICA
Farming appeared very early in North, West, and East Africa. Africa's earliest cities and states formed along the Nile River Valley in Egypt. The Egyptians invented a writing system and flourished from productive agriculture and trade with other African societies and Eurasia. Cities and states also arose in Nubia, just south of Egypt. Africans south of the Sahara Desert developed ironworking technology very early, and iron tools and weapons helped the Bantu-speaking peoples gradually expand from West Africa into Central and East Africa.

SOUTHERN ASIA AND OCEANIA
Farming and metalworking developed early in South and Southeast Asia. The people of the Harappan cities in the Indus River Basin grew cotton, made textiles, and traded with western and Central Asia. After the Harappan society collapsed, Aryan peoples from western Asia moved into India, and the mixing of Aryan and local traditions formed the basis for the Hindu religion. Meanwhile, Austronesian peoples migrated from Taiwan into the Southeast Asian and Pacific islands. Southeast Asians pioneered in maritime trade and formed their first states. Hunters and gatherers flourished in Australia.

CHAPTER

1

The Origins of Human Societies, to ca. 2000 b.c.e.

Chapter Outline

- Prehistory: The Cosmos, Earth, and the Roots of Humanity
- The Odyssey of Early Human Societies
- The Agricultural Transformation, 10,000–4000 b.c.e.
- The Emergence of Cities and States

PROFILE
The !Kung Hunters and Gatherers

WITNESS TO THE PAST
Food and Farming in Ancient Cultural Traditions

Kazuyoshi Nomachi/Pacific Press Photo

Tassili Archers
Thousands of ancient paintings on rock surfaces and cave walls record the activities of African hunters, gatherers, and pastoralists. This painting of archers on a hunt was made in a rock shelter on the Tassili plateau of what is today Algeria, probably long before the Sahara region had dried up and become a harsh desert.

We are long past the time when we could deal with the human story apart from the life story, or the earth story, or the universe story.

—Cosmologist Brian Swimme and Historian Thomas Berry[1]

FOCUS QUESTIONS

1. According to most scientists, what were the various stages of human evolution?
2. How did hunting and gathering shape life during the long Stone Age?
3. What environmental factors explain the transition to agriculture?
4. How did farming and metallurgy establish the foundations for the rise of cities, states, and trade networks?

The human story was already old and the life story far older when, at Abu Hureyra (AH-boo hoo-RAY-rah) in the Euphrates (you-FRAY-teez) River Valley of what is now Syria, a group of villagers became some of the first farmers, thus taking a large step in shaping world history. People who hunted game and gathered vegetables and nuts occupied Abu Hureyra 13,000 years ago, when the area was wetter and blessed with many edible wild plants and herds of Persian gazelles. But a long cold spell brought a drought, challenging their good life; to survive, the Abu Hureyra villagers began to cultivate the most easily grown grains and later also raised domesticated sheep and goats. By 7600 B.C.E. they had shifted completely to farming and animal herding.

The Abu Hureyra farmers pursued a life familiar to rural folk for millennia afterwards. Several hundred people crowded into a village of narrow lanes and courtyards. Families dwelled in one-story, multiroom mud houses with polished plaster floors, some decorated with red designs. At night family members studied the sky and pondered the mysteries of the universe. Men did much of the farm work while women carried heavy loads on their heads, prepared meals, and ground grain in a kneeling position, an activity that was hard on arms, knees, and toes. Work for both women and men involved repetitive tasks and called for muscle power. Many villagers suffered from arthritis and lower back injuries. Abu Hureyra was abandoned in 5000 B.C.E.

Prehistory includes a vast span of time, from the earliest humans to the beginnings of agriculture and the emergence of complex societies with cities and states. Much of what we know about these millennia comes from archaeologists, who study the material remains of past cultures, and anthropologists, who study human biology and culture in relation to the physical and social environment. During the long saga of our planet, all living creatures appeared and developed, including eventually humans. Over many millennia humans evolved physically, mentally, and culturally, learning to make simple tools and then spreading throughout the world. Later most societies, like the Abu Hureyra villagers, made the first great historical transition from hunting and gathering to farming and animal herding. This transition profoundly changed the relationship between people and the environment and prompted the working of metals for better tools. The rise of agriculture all over the world made possible another important transition, the emergence of larger societies with cities and states. In turn this stimulated long-distance trade and the rise of social, cultural, and economic networks linking distant societies.

e Visit the website and eBook for additional study materials and interactive tools: www.cengage.com/history/lockard/globalsocnet2e

PREHISTORY: THE COSMOS, EARTH, AND THE ROOTS OF HUMANITY

According to most scientists, what were the various stages of human evolution?

Some scholars have promoted a "big history" that places the development of human societies and networks in a much longer and more comprehensive framework, the "universe story." They argue that we cannot comprehend the rise of complex societies without a knowledge of prefarming peoples, the ancestors of humans, and, before that, the beginning of life on earth and the formation of our planet within the larger cosmic order. Recurring patterns of balance and imbalance and of order and disorder in the natural world, such as global warming and cooling, have always played a role in human history. Inspired by such large forces around them, people have speculated about the origins of the cosmos, earth, life, and humanity for countless generations. Over the years their views have been integrated into religions.

Perceptions of Cosmic Mysteries

Human development on earth constitutes only a tiny fraction of the long history of the universe, which most astronomers think began in a cosmic Big Bang explosion some 14 billion years ago. As the universe expanded, matter coalesced into stars, and stars formed into billions of galaxies spread over vast distances. Our solar system emerged about 4.5 billion years ago out of clouds of gas. On our planet, earth, the developing atmosphere kept the surface warm enough for organic compounds to coalesce into life forms. This is the story presented by modern science.

Over the centuries most human societies, to explain their existence, have crafted creation stories and cosmologies, systematic expressions of their views on the natural and supernatural worlds. These explanations have varied greatly, but usually they have involved myths or legends of some divine creator or creators. The earliest known creation story, from Mesopotamia, claimed that heaven and earth were formed as one in a primeval sea and then were separated by the gods, humanlike beings unperceivable to mortals and far more powerful. Mesopotamian beliefs influenced the seven-day creation story in the Hebrew book of Genesis.

e **Primary Source: The *Rig Veda*** Read how Indra, "the thunder-wielder," slew Vritra, "firstborn of dragons," and how Purusha created the universe through an act of ritual sacrifice.

Many cosmological traditions, however, were very different. Ancient Hindu holy books, for example, describe the creation of a universe out of nothingness: "There was neither non-existence or existence then; there was neither the realm of space nor the sky which is beyond. Darkness was hidden by darkness in the beginning, emptiness."[2] Then a great heat formed the cosmos and generated life. The ancient Chinese believed that the universe was created out of chaos and darkness and that the creator Pan Ku fashioned the sun, moon, and stars to put everything in proper order. The result was a unifying force in the universe, known as the "way," or *dao* **(DOW)**. A related Chinese theory, *feng shui* **(fung-SHWAY)**, suggests that the earth itself contains natural forces that people must comprehend in order to properly situate buildings and graves. Some ideas from the feng shui tradition have recently gained a following in Western countries.

Early Life and Evolutionary Change

Life on Earth

"Life," meaning organisms that are able to consume food, grow, and reproduce with a genetic code, has a long history. Simple, single-celled life emerged by perhaps 3.5 to 3.8 billion years ago and remained dominant until about a half billion years ago, when life forms became increasingly complex and proliferated in incredible variety. Animal life colonized the land between 400 and 500 million years ago and evolved into many species. Throughout its long history, life has been influenced by natural forces such as geology and climate. Volcanic and earthquake activity caused by plate movements has influenced human history, and sometimes intense volcanic eruptions have dramatically altered regional climates. As we will see, warmer or cooler climates helped shape human societies and also sometimes undermined them.

Most natural scientists agree that living things change over many generations through evolution, the process by which they modify their genetic composition to adapt to their environment. In the nineteenth century the British biologist Charles Darwin explained the process with his theory of natural selection. He believed individuals developed variations that helped them to compete for food and domination within their own species and to triumph over rival species. Scientists still debate evolution's precise mechanisms, but modern biology has mostly confirmed Darwin's

CHRONOLOGY

	Cosmos	Human Evolution	Prehistory Transitions
14 billion years ago	**14 billion years ago** Big Bang **4.5 billion years ago** Solar system and earth	**5–6 million years ago** Earliest proto-humans	
400,000 B.C.E.		**400,000–200,000 B.C.E.** *Homo sapiens* **135,000–100,000 B.C.E.** Modern humans in Africa	
100,000 B.C.E.		**100,000 B.C.E.** Modern humans in Eurasia	**100,000–9500 B.C.E.** Old and Middle Stone Ages **9500–8000 B.C.E.** New Stone Age; beginning of agriculture **3500–3200 B.C.E.** First cities in western Asia **3000 B.C.E.** Introduction of bronze **1500 B.C.E.** Introduction of iron

basic insights that species, including humans, are shaped by their changing biological and physical environment.

Species Extinctions

A half dozen massive species extinctions have occurred in the past 400 million years. For example, 250 million years ago gigantic volcanic eruptions produced enough climate-changing gases to almost wipe out all life. The best-known extinction involved the dinosaurs, which flourished for 150 million years before dying out about 65 million years ago, probably from environmental changes: the cooling of the planet from increasing volcanic activity, the cataclysmic impact of one or several large asteroids or comets smashing into the earth, or both. The resulting toxic acid rain and long winter destroyed food sources, thus killing off about 70 percent of all species. The demise of the dinosaurs opened the door for mammals to rise and flourish. One group of these mammals eventually evolved into humans. So far humans have been lucky. Scientists estimate that 99 percent of all species eventually became extinct when conditions changed dramatically, as they did for the dinosaurs. In our own time, species have been dying rapidly over the past two hundred years, most likely because of environmental changes such as pollution, habitat removal, and global warming generated by human activity.

Human Ancestors

Eventually, after several billion years, evolutionary changes among one branch of mammals led to the immediate ancestors of humans. Humans are part of the primate order, the mammal category that includes the apes. Our closeness to the apes is shown by the fact that over 98 percent of human DNA is the same as that of chimpanzees. Human–chimp lines diverged sometime before 5 or 6 million years ago.

Humans ultimately became dominant among large animal species by using their superior brain to gain an evolutionary edge. One key to their success was the ability to form *complex* social organizations that emphasized cooperation for mutual benefit. Humans also developed tools, mastered fire, and learned how to use speech, all of which gave them great advantages. Ultimately they began using a more complex technology that enabled them to manipulate the physical environment in many ways to meet their needs.

Hominids (HOM-uh-nids), a family including humans and their immediate ancestors, first evolved 5 to 6 million years ago from more primitive primates. The first chapters of the human story began in Africa, where the span of human prehistory is much longer than anywhere else. The most extensive fossil evidence comes from the southern African plateau and the Great Rift Valley of East Africa, a wide, deep chasm stretching from Ethiopia south to Tanzania. There are heated disagreements among scientists over fossil and artifact remains and whether teeth, skulls, and bones belong to ancestors of humans or of apes. Fossil discoveries point to several stages and branches in early human evolution (see Chronology: Hominid Evolution). A common ancestral, apelike group lived in the woodlands and savannahs of East Africa. One division (the ancestors of most apes) began

hominids A family including humans and their immediate ancestors.

CHRONOLOGY

Hominid Evolution

20 Million B.C.E. Common ancestor to humans and apes (Africa)

5–6 Million B.C.E. Earliest proto-humans

4–5 Million B.C.E. Australopithecines

2.5 Million B.C.E. *Homo habilis*

2.2–1.8 Million B.C.E. *Homo erectus*

400,000–200,000 B.C.E. *Homo sapiens* (archaic humans)

135,000–100,000 B.C.E. *Homo sapiens sapiens* (modern humans)

specializing in forest dwelling and climbing with all four limbs. Another division developed occasional and then permanent bipedalism, walking upright on two feet. This made more activity possible because it left the hands free for holding food or babies, manipulating objects, and carrying food back to camp. Bipeds, being higher off the ground, could also scan the horizon for predators or prey.

Several hominid groups apparently coexisted at the same time, but only one led to modern humans. Several branches of early hominids known as **australopithecines** (aw-strah-lo-PITH-uh-seens) lived in eastern and southern Africa 4 or 5 million years ago. The brains of these proto-humans were about one-third the size of our brains. One example was found in Ethiopia, where archaeologists unearthed the bones of a small female, named Lucy by anthropologists, who lived some 20 years and probably walked mostly on her feet. Scholars disagree as to whether these hominids might be the ancestors to modern humans.

Some 2.5 million years ago one branch of australopithecines evolved into our direct ancestor, a transition probably due to environmental change. The earth cooled, fostering the first of a series of Ice Ages, which covered large areas of northern Eurasia and North America with deep ice sheets and glaciers. This cooling pattern also affected Africa and its hominid inhabitants, bringing a drier climate and more open habitats. Increased intelligence was needed to deal with the challenges posed by this climate change. ***Homo habilis*** (HOH-moh HAB-uh-luhs) ("handy human") was so named because of this species' larger brain size and its ability to make and use simple stone tools for hunting and gathering. Stone choppers and later hand axes made possible a more varied diet, more successful hunting, and larger groups that could cooperate to share food. The other branches of australopithecines died out, losing the competition to *Homo habilis.*

australopithecines Early hominids living in eastern and southern Africa 4 to 5 million years ago.

Homo habilis ("handy human") A direct ancestor of humans, so named because of its increased brain size and ability to make and use simple stone tools for hunting and gathering.

As hominid societies developed, males increasingly became the hunters or scavengers for meat and females the gatherers of nuts and vegetables. The receding of the forests and their food sources may have made meat a more crucial protein source. Nonetheless, gathering still probably brought more food than hunting or scavenging. Indeed, these early humans were probably mainly vegetarians, like many primates today. In any case, cooperation between the sexes and group members was the key to survival and probably involved communication through gestures and vocal cries.

Homo Erectus and Migrations Out of Africa

Probably between 1.8 and 2.2 million years ago, some more advanced hominids evolved from *Homo habilis* in East Africa. Most scholars have termed these hominids ***Homo erectus*** ("erect human"). Their achievements were remarkable. They had a brain about two-thirds the size of ours and eventually developed a more complex and widespread tool culture that included hand axes, cleavers, and scrapers. They spread to other parts of Africa, preferring the open savannah.

Homo erectus ("erect human") A hominid that emerged in East Africa probably between 1.8 and 2.2 million years ago.

Pioneers in Eurasia

Between 1 and 2 million years ago, as southern Eurasia developed a warmer climate, some *Homo erectus* bands began migrating out of Africa, carrying with them refined tools, more effective hunting skills, and an ability to adapt to new environments. Perhaps the first migrants were following game herds. This was the first great migration in human history, and it corresponded to the ebb and flow of the Ice Ages as well as the periodic drying out of the Sahara region. Over thousands of years these hominids came to occupy northern Africa, the Middle East, South and Southeast Asia, China, Europe, and perhaps Australia. Some of the earliest non-African sites, perhaps 1.8 million years old, have been found in the Caucasus (KAW-kuh-suhs) Mountains of western Asia. Farther east, bones and tools discovered in Chinese caves and skulls from the island of Java in Indonesia, then connected to mainland Asia, have been dated at 1.6 to 1.9 million years ago. These finds suggest that *Homo erectus* may have been widespread in East and Southeast Asia by 1.5 million years ago. Fossils from eastern Siberia date back 300,000 years, indicating how adaptable and resourceful the species had become if it could survive in that brutal climate. Europe has proved a bigger puzzle. These hominids lived in Spain by 800,000 B.C.E. However, their tool cultures differed somewhat from those of Chinese *Homo erectus*, indicating cultural diversity and perhaps, some scholars believe, major variation from the Asian species.

By 500,000 years ago *Homo erectus* in China lived in closely knit groups, engaged in cooperative hunting, and probably used both wood and bamboo for containers and weapons. Most lived in caves, but some built simple wooden huts for shelter. Their hand axes were the Swiss army knives of their time, with a tip for piercing, thin edges for cutting, and thick edges for scraping and chipping. Scientists debate whether *Homo erectus* could use speech.

One of the key discoveries, how to start and control fire, was perhaps the most significant human invention ever. But we do not yet know precisely where or when people first used fire or how many millennia it took for knowledge of fire to spread widely. Fire opened up many possibilities, providing warmth and light after sunset, frightening away predators, and making possible a more varied diet of cooked food, which tasted better and fostered group living and cooperation as people gathered together around campfires and hearths. Fire also enabled ancestral humans to spread to cooler regions, such as Europe and eastern Asia.

John Reader/Photo Researchers, Inc.

The Laetoli Footprints Some 4 million years ago in Tanzania, three australopithecines walked across a muddy field covered in ash from a nearby volcanic eruption. When the mud dried, their tracks were permanently preserved, providing evidence of some of the earliest upright hominids.

The Evolution and Diversity of *Homo Sapiens*

The transition from *Homo erectus* to archaic forms of ***Homo sapiens*** ("thinking human"), a species that was physically close to modern humans, began around 400,000 years ago in Africa. By 200,000 years ago a more complex tool culture was widespread, evidence for *Homo sapiens* occupation. With this development humanity became a single species, despite some superficial differences. Eventually members of *Homo sapiens* were the only surviving hominids.

Members of *Homo sapiens* had many advantages over *Homo erectus*. With a larger brain, they were more adaptive and intelligent, able to think conceptually. Archaic *Homo sapiens* may have used language, lived in fairly large organized groups, built temporary shelters, created crude lunar calendars, and killed whole herds of animals. They also raised more children to adulthood. Possession of symbolic language gave *Homo sapiens* an advantage over earlier hominids and all other creatures, allowing them to share information over the generations. Language enabled people to adjust to their environment and overcome challenges not just individually but also collectively.

Homo sapiens ("thinking human") A hominid who evolved around 400,000 years ago and from whom anatomically modern humans (*Homo sapiens sapiens*) evolved around 100,000 years ago.

Scientists debate precisely how and where *Homo erectus* evolved into *Homo sapiens,* and several competing theories explain the transition. Some scholars argue that the evolution into *Homo sapiens* occurred in different parts of the Afro-Eurasian zone. The most widely supported scenario, known as the African Origins theory, suggests that *Homo sapiens* evolved only in East Africa and then spread throughout Afro-Eurasia, displacing and ultimately dooming the remaining *Homo erectus* groups. The evidence for this theory includes the fact that (so far, anyway) the earliest *Homo sapiens* remains have been found in East Africa. One of the most useful tools in tracing human evolution is the study of genetic codes, which mostly support the African Origins theory.

Debating Race

Whether the evolution into *Homo sapiens* occurred only in Africa or on several continents, all humans came to constitute one species that could interbreed and communicate with each other. There were a few differences in physical features, such as skin and hair color and eye and face shape, but it remains unclear whether these developed earlier or later in *Homo sapiens* evolution. The diverse groupings that evolved from *Homo sapiens* were once labeled "races," meaning large groups that shared distinctive genetic traits and physical characteristics. But the race concept is for good reasons often dismissed by experts for its inability to classify human populations. Observable physical attributes such as skin color and eye shape reflect a tiny portion of one's genetic makeup

CHRONOLOGY
The Spread of Modern Humans

135,000–100,000 B.C.E. Eastern and southern Africa

100,000 B.C.E. Palestine

60,000–45,000 B.C.E. Australia

50,000–40,000 B.C.E. India, Southeast Asia

50,000–35,000 B.C.E. China

45,000–35,000 B.C.E. Europe

40,000 B.C.E. Japan, Americas (disputed)

35,000–30,000 B.C.E. New Guinea

20,000 B.C.E. Siberia

15,000–12,000 B.C.E. Americas (traditional view)

2000 B.C.E. Western Pacific islands

1500 B.C.E. Samoa

200 B.C.E. Marquesas Islands

400–500 C.E. Hawaii

1000 C.E. New Zealand

and thus cannot always predict whether two groups are genetically similar or different. There has been much genetic intermixing between human populations, and many people are difficult to classify. Humans are much more similar than different.

Sometime between 150,000 and 100,000 years ago in Africa, anatomically modern humans with slightly larger brains, known as *Homo sapiens sapiens*, developed out of *Homo sapiens*. With this biological change, language and culture expanded in new directions and developed many variations. Scholars debate whether creativity, intelligence, and even language abilities were innate to *Homo ssapiens sapiens*, as suggested by engraved pigments in South African caves from 75,000 to 100,00 years ago, or arose only some 50,000 years ago, possibly as a result of a genetic mutation. With this great transition humanity reached its present level of intellectual and physical development, and humans established the foundation for the constant expansion of information networks to a global level.

Modern humans eventually developed their languages in ways that made possible complex cultures with shared learning. Spoken language was the main method of communication for much of history. Perhaps there was one original language used by all humans. But eventually, some 5,000 or 6,000 languages emerged around the globe. Some languages, such as English and German, have a clear common ancestry, but scholars debate the relationships and origins of most of the world's languages. Human intellectual development also included abstract, symbolic thought, which was revealed early in decoration and art. Ocher (O-ker), for example, a natural red iron oxide, was mined in various African locations and probably used for body decoration. The gorgeous cave and rock art of southwestern Europe, Africa, western Asia, and Australia has been traced back at least 30,000 to 40,000 years. These creations probably had magical, religious, or ritual purposes, such as the celebration of spirits or valued animals.

The Globalization of Human Settlement

Between 50,000 and 12,000 years ago much of the world was settled by restless modern humans. As people spread, genetic differences grew and *Homo sapiens sapiens* proved able to adapt to many environments all over the world. By 100,000 years ago some had already left Africa to settle in Palestine. *Homo sapiens sapiens* settlement might not have expanded much beyond Africa and southwestern Asia until 50,000 years ago. But rising sea levels at the end of the last Ice Age may also have covered evidence that might allow us to trace migration routes along the southern Asian coasts. Eventually modern humans reached central and eastern Eurasia, from where some moved on to Australia, the Americas, and Europe (see Chronology: The Spread of Modern Humans).

Modern humans crossed to the eastern fringe of Asia before they populated Europe (see Map 1.1). They arrived in India and Southeast Asia between 40,000 and 50,000 years ago, in China between 35,000 and 50,000 years ago, and in Europe between 35,000 and 45,000 years ago. To reach Australia from Southeast Asia across a very shallow sea required rafts or boats, but modern humans may have settled there between 60,000 and 45,000 B.C.E. While New Guinea had human settlers between 50,000 to 60,000 years ago, the peopling of the Pacific islands to the east began much later, around 2000 B.C.E.

Neanderthals Hominids who were probably descended from *Homo erectus* populations in Europe and who later spread into western and Central Asia.

Cro-Magnons The first modern, tool-using humans in Europe.

Beginning around 200,000 years ago, a vibrant new tool culture developed in Europe that has been identified with the **Neanderthals** (nee-AN-der-thals), hominids who were probably related to *Homo erectus* populations. The Neanderthals gradually spread to inhabit a wide region stretching from Spain and Germany to western and Central Asia; fossils have also been found in North Africa. Skillful hunters, the Neanderthals maintained social values, buried their dead, and cared for the sick. Their cranial capacity equaled or even exceeded that of *Homo sapiens*, and they had larger bodies. Although they probably lacked spoken language, they were capable of communication. They also used tools, made bone flutes, and wore jewelry. The relationship of the Neanderthals to *Homo sapiens sapiens* is debated. By 70,000 years ago both Neanderthals and modern humans lived in Palestine. When the modern, tool-using humans known as **Cro-Magnons** (krow-MAG-nuns) arrived in Europe from Asia, they also coexisted with Neanderthals for several millennia. DNA studies suggest that Neanderthals were a rather different species from Cro-Magnons. There is little convincing evidence of significant interbreeding. Around 28,000 years ago, the last Neanderthals died out. Whether they were ultimately annihilated, outnumbered, outcom-

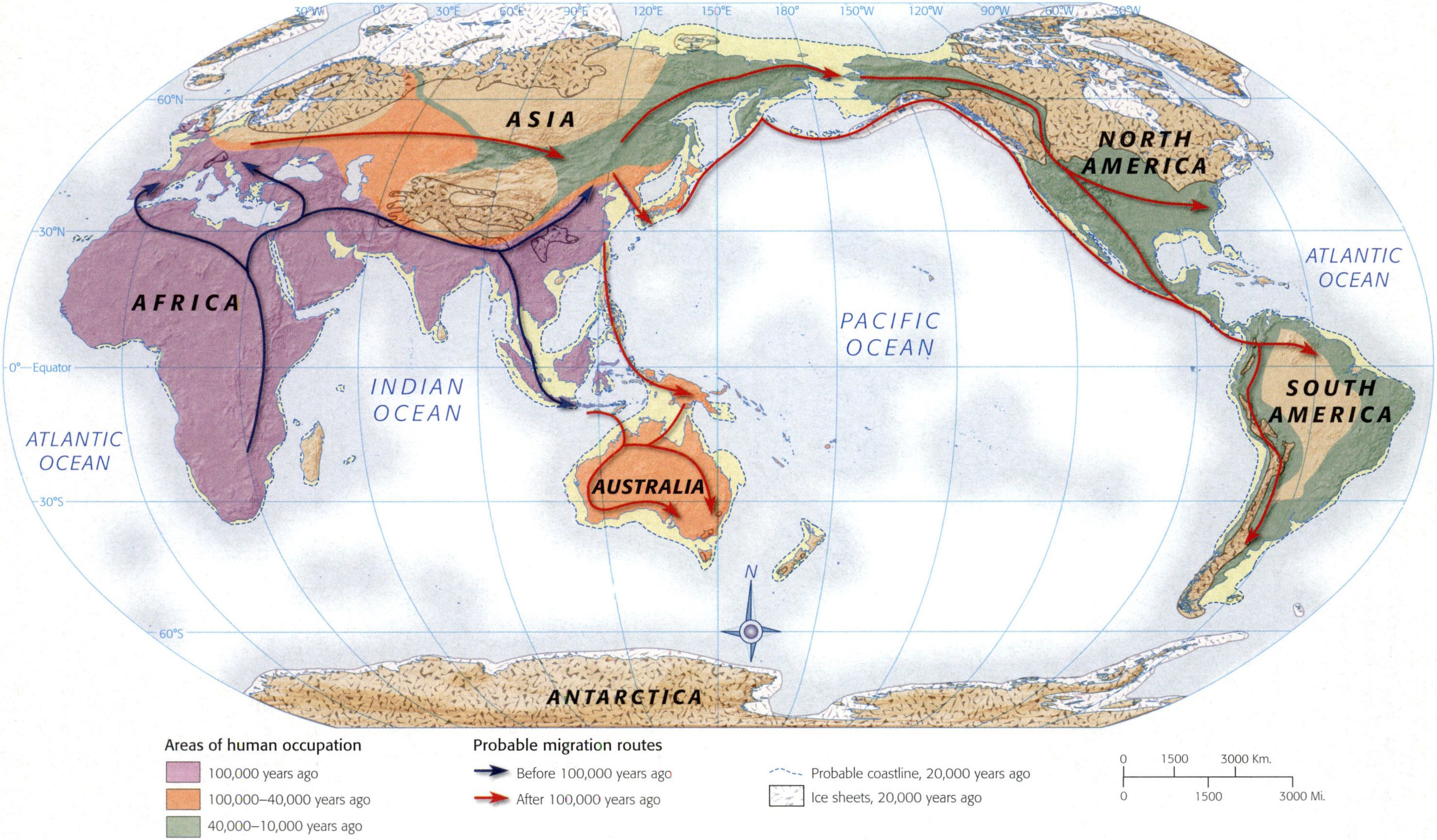

Map 1.1
Spread of Modern Humans Around the Globe

Most scholars believe that modern humans originated in Africa and that some of them began leaving Africa around 100,000 years ago. Gradually they spread out through Eurasia. From Eastern Asia some crossed to the Americas.

Interactive Map

peted, or assimilated by the more resourceful and adaptable *Homo sapiens sapiens,* who had better technology and warmer clothing, remains unknown.

Peopling the Americas

Archaeologists long thought that the peopling of the Americas came very late and that the earliest migration into North America occurred only 12,000 to 15,000 years ago. But recent discoveries have led some scholars to speculate that the pioneer arrivals may have crossed from Northeast Asia, probably in very small numbers, as early as 20,000 or possibly even 30,000 or 40,000 years ago (see Chapter 4). At various times a wide Ice Age land bridge connected Alaska and Siberia across today's Bering Strait, and the evidence for a migration chiefly from Asia over thousands of years is strong. The first settlers moved by land or by boat along the coast. Gradually people of Asian ancestry settled throughout the Western Hemisphere, becoming the ancestors of today's Native Americans.

SECTION SUMMARY

- To fully understand human history, it is helpful to first examine the origins of our planet, the beginning of life on earth, and our prehuman ancestors.
- Throughout the millennia, various peoples have developed stories of creation and universal order.
- In order to survive, species must adapt to their changing environments.
- Humans are closely related to chimpanzees and other great apes; they eventually became dominant because of their use of intelligence.
- Early hominids first evolved in Africa (most likely East Africa) 4 to 6 million years ago.
- Of the early hominids, our direct ancestor, *Homo habilis,* was most successful because it used simple stone tools.
- *Homo erectus* developed more refined tools and migrated to Eurasia and throughout Africa.
- *Homo sapiens* had larger brains and evolved into modern humans, who developed language and spread throughout the world.
- Though humans from different parts of the world may have different appearances, their genetic differences are insignificant.

THE ODYSSEY OF EARLY HUMAN SOCIETIES

How did hunting and gathering shape life during the long Stone Age?

Paleolithic The Old Stone Age, which began 100,000 years ago with the first modern humans and lasted for many millennia.

Mesolithic The Middle Stone Age, which began around 15,000 years ago as the glaciers from the final Ice Age began to recede.

Neolithic The New Stone Age, which began between 10,000 and 11,500 years ago with the transition to simple farming.

For thousands of years humans lived at a very basic level during what is often called the Stone Age, although they also used other materials, such as wood and bone, to help them sustain life. The Stone Age included three distinct periods. The long **Paleolithic** (pay-lee-oh-LITH-ik) period (or Old Stone Age) began about 100,000 years ago. The **Mesolithic** (mez-oh-LITH-ik) period (Middle Stone Age) began around 15,000 years ago, when the glaciers from the final Ice Age receded. Major meat sources in Eurasia and North America that were adapted to Ice Age climates, such as the vast herds of woolly mammoths and mastodons, died out from warming climates, catastrophic disease, or zealous hunting by humans. During the Paleolithic and Mesolithic eras peoples organized themselves into small, usually mobile, family-based societies. The **Neolithic** (nee-oh-LITH-ik) period (New Stone Age) began between 9500 and 8000 B.C.E. in Eurasia, with the transition from hunting and gathering to simple farming.

Hunting, Gathering, and Cooperation

Small groups of twenty to sixty members were the earliest and simplest forms of society. Their subsistence life depended on fishing, hunting live animals, scavenging for dead or dying animals, and gathering edible plants, a way of life that depended on naturally occurring resources. Members cooperated in gathering or hunting to obtain food. Improved tools made possible both more food options and better weapons against predators or rivals. Hunting became more important when the bow and arrow were invented in Africa, Europe, and southwestern Asia at least 15,000 years ago. Now hunters could kill large animals at a safer distance. Although men gained prestige from being the main hunters, meat was usually a small part of the diet.

Survival Strategies

The gathering by women of edible vegetation such as fruits and nuts was probably more essential for group survival than obtaining meat, and it gave women status and influence. Ethnographic studies indicate that this is still true among many of the remaining hunting and gathering peoples today. Furthermore, women probably helped develop new technologies such as grinding stones, bone needles, nets (possibly used to catch small animals like rabbits and foxes), baskets, and primitive cloth. The oldest known woven cloth clothing was made in eastern Europe some 28,000 years ago. Pottery was made at least 12,500 years ago in Japan.

The hunting and gathering way of life may not have been as impoverished and unfulfilling as we sometimes imagine it was, with people continually searching for food in harsh environments. Many societies were creative, inventing fishhooks, harpoons, fuel lamps, dugout boats, and canoes. Studies over the past fifty years of groups who still hunt and gather, such as the Mbuti (em-BOO-tee) of the Congo rain forest and the !Kung of the Kalahari Desert, have found that they enjoy varied, healthy diets, surprisingly long life expectancies, considerable economic security, and a rich communal life. Many spend only ten to twenty hours a week in collecting food and establishing camps. Generally these people have plenty of time for activities such as music, dance, and socializing. On the other hand, hunters and gatherers have always faced serious challenges. Early humans had to make their own weapons and clothing and construct temporary huts. For some groups, life remained precarious and many died young, since not all enjoyed access to adequate food resources.

Hunting and gathering generally encouraged cooperation, which led to closely knit communities based on kinship. Members were able to communicate with one another, and they also passed information from one generation to another, conveying a sense of the past and traditions. Gradually humans increased in numbers, and societies became more complex. In societies founded on family ties, personal relationships were paramount, while little value was given to obtaining material wealth. The mostly nomadic way of life made individual accumulation of material possessions impractical. These small groups shared food resources among the immediate family and friends, thus helping to ensure survival. Cooperative work and food sharing also promoted an intense social life.

Cooperation and Conflict

But living close to others did not always result in harmony and mutual affection. Those who violated group customs could be killed or banished, temporarily or permanently, and sometimes groups split apart because of conflicts. Most hunters and gatherers lived in small bands that had no system of government or leader; everyone played a needed role, and social responsibilities linked people together. In these egalitarian social structures, all members in good standing often had equal access to resources. At the same time, groups often tended to reward the most resourceful members.

Women and men probably enjoyed a comparable status, as they do in many hunting and gathering societies today. As key providers of food, women may have participated alongside men in group decision making. They also likely held a special place in religious practice as bearers of life. Midwives were highly respected. **Matrilineal** (mat-ruh-LIN-ee-uhl) **kinship** patterns, which trace descent and inheritance through the female line, were probably common, as they are today in these societies. But these societies mostly maintain a clear sexual division of labor and give men some advantages over women. Although childbearing influenced women's roles, women were not constantly pregnant. Since it was necessary to limit group size to avoid depleting resources from the environment, most hunting and gathering societies practiced birth control and abortion. In addition, the practice of breastfeeding an infant for several years suppressed ovulation and created longer intervals between pregnancies. Paleolithic populations grew slowly, perhaps by only 10 percent a century.

matrilineal kinship A pattern of kinship that traces descent and inheritance through the female line.

Cultural Life and Violence

Some aspects of culture that we might recognize today were taking shape, such as religious belief. As people sought to understand dreams, death, and natural phenomena, they developed a perspective known as **animism** (ANN-uh-miz-um), the belief that all creatures, as well as inanimate objects and natural phenomena, have souls and can influence human well-being. Many early peoples also practiced **polytheism** (PAUL-e-thee-ism), the belief in many spirits or deities. Since spirits were thought capable of helping or harming a person, **shamans** (SHAW-mans), specialists in communicating with or manipulating the supernatural realm, became important members of the group. Many shamans were women.

Some activities with a social function that we might consider essential for enjoyment developed early, including music, dance, making and drinking beer or wine, and painting on rocks and cave walls. Primitive flutes can be traced back 45,000 years. Dancing and singing may have promoted feelings of togetherness and lessened personal rivalries.

animism The belief that all creatures as well as inanimate objects and natural phenomena have souls and can influence human well-being.

polytheism A belief in many spirits or deities.

shamans Specialists in communicating with or manipulating the supernatural realm.

Egalitarian, self-sufficient societies enriched by spirituality and leisure activities may sound appealing to many modern people, but this was not the complete story. Violence between and within different societies has been a part of human culture throughout history, and the seeds were planted in the Paleolithic period. People were hunters, but they were also hunted by predators such as bears, wolves, and lions. This reality may have instilled in early societies not only a terror of dangerous animals, apparent in myths and folklore, but also a tendency to justify violence. Men were often expected to prove their bravery to attract females.

Anthropologists disagree about whether humans are inherently aggressive and warlike or peaceful and cooperative. The experiences of societies still based on hunting and gathering or simple agriculture suggest that both patterns are common. Some peoples, such as the Hopi and Zuni Indians of the American Southwest, the Penan of Borneo, and many Australian Aborigines, have generally avoided armed conflict. But most societies have engaged in at least occasional violence, such as when their survival or food supply was threatened. Some societies have admired military prowess and male bravado. For example, the Dani of New Guinea, who engaged in frequent conflict with their neighbors, lost a third of their men to war-related death.

War and Peace

Humans may not be genetically programmed for either violence or cooperation. They have a capacity but not a compulsion for aggressive behavior. On the other hand, humans may naturally seek self-preservation; social and cultural patterns that have promoted certain behaviors, such as violence against neighboring groups, have often arisen in response to environmental conditions that have threatened existence.

The Heritage of Hunting and Gathering

Hunting and gathering never completely disappeared. Throughout history some peoples have found this way of life the most realistic strategy for survival. Although not environmentalists in the modern sense, most recent hunting and gathering societies have made only a marginal impact on the surrounding environment because of their small numbers and limited technology. Since they have learned to live within environmental constraints, these peoples could be seen as highly successful adapters. Although it has generated little material wealth, hunting and gathering has remained viable for many societies, such as Australian Aborigines, until

Cave Paintings in Europe This Ice Age painting of bison is from a cave at Altamira, Spain. Many paintings on cave walls have been found in France and Iberia. Paleolithic peoples all over the world painted pictures of the animals they hunted or feared as well as of each other, suggesting an increasing self-awareness.

Jean Clottes

modern times. Indeed, Australia was the only inhabitable continent where agriculture never developed before modern times, largely because populations remained small, much of the continent was harsh desert, and the Aborigines were such skillful hunters and gatherers. But trade routes spanned the continent, and many Aborigines developed detailed notions of land management as well as rich mythologies about their origins and their relationship to the fragile environment.

Although we must be cautious in comparing modern hunters and gatherers to peoples who lived several millennia ago, today's few remaining hunting and gathering peoples, to the extent that they have not yet been significantly changed by the outside world, can probably reveal much about ancient societies (see Profile: The !Kung Hunters and Gatherers). But this way of life, which has survived for many millennia, may disappear during the twenty-first century. In recent decades many hunters and gatherers have seen their lives disrupted or destroyed by logging, commercial fishing, plantation development, dam building, tourism, and other activities that exploit their environments. For example, in the Amazon Basin, the burning of rain forests and opening of new land for farming or mining overwhelms many Native American groups. In the end these peoples, defenseless against modern technology, may have to make the same transition to new survival strategies as other peoples did millennia ago.

SECTION SUMMARY

- During the Paleolithic and Mesolithic eras, people lived in small groups of hunters and gatherers.
- In general, women gathered fruits and nuts, which provided the majority of the food, while men hunted game.
- Hunting and gathering groups were usually close-knit and egalitarian, though violence was not unknown.
- Anthropologists are undecided as to whether humans have a natural tendency toward violence or peace.
- Some hunting and gathering groups still exist, but they are threatened by modernity.

The Agricultural Transformation, 10,000–4000 B.C.E.

What environmental factors explain the transition to agriculture?

Between 10,000 and 11,500 years ago, people who had survived largely by hunting and gathering during the Mesolithic period began to develop simple agriculture. This momentous change marked the beginning of the Neolithic period, a time when humans began to master the environment and change natural biological relationships in unprecedented ways. People now deliberately altered the ecological system by cultivating the soil, selecting seeds, and breeding animals that could help them survive. The often-used term *Agricultural Revolution* is misleading, because the development did not involve rapid, electrifying discoveries but occurred over hundreds of years. Nonetheless, the shift from hunting and gathering to farming was one of the greatest transitions in history, and it changed human life all over the world. The production of a food surplus set the stage for everything that came later, including cities, states, social classes, and long-distance trade.

Environmental Change and the Roots of Agriculture

Probably the first farmers did not even see themselves as pioneers forging a new way of life. Even before farming began, some people were preparing themselves for permanent village life. Some, like the villagers at Abu Hureyra in Syria, were settling alongside lakes or in valleys rich in wild grains that were easy to collect. Around the world, archaeologists have discovered clay-walled houses from the Neolithic period, as well as baskets, pottery, pits for storing grain, and equipment for hunting, fishing, and grain preparation. However, documenting the steps taken in the transition to agriculture and settled life is not easy. For the earliest periods we have no written sources, since writing appeared only around 3500 B.C.E. Many material artifacts still lie buried, while others have long since turned to dust or were covered by rising sea levels.

Climate Change and Population Growth

Climate change was probably one key factor in triggering the shift to agriculture. After the last great Ice Age, the earth entered a long period of unusual warmth, which still persists. The melting glaciers caused rising sea levels, covering about a fifth of previously available land. Some scholars contend that the spread of the Persian Gulf, the Black Sea, and the Mediterranean onto once occupied lowlands may have led to legends in the Middle East of a great flood and human expulsion from a "garden of Eden." Rising sea levels also covered over many land links, including those connecting the British Isles to continental Europe and Japan to Asia. Another factor was probably population growth. Around 10,000 B.C.E., the world population had grown to perhaps 5 or 10 million, and in

THE !KUNG HUNTERS AND GATHERERS

Although we need to remember that all societies change over time, often in response to environmental conditions, the remaining hunting and gathering peoples today may give us a glimpse of how some prehistoric peoples lived. The !Kung, a subgroup of the San people (once known as Bushmen), live in the inhospitable Kalahari Desert in southwestern Africa, chiefly in what is today Botswana and Namibia. Several thousand years ago they were widespread in the southern half of Africa, and some probably adapted to desert life a long time ago.

The !Kung became skilled hunters and gatherers. Women obtain between 60 and 80 percent of the food, collecting nuts, berries, bulbs, beans, leafy greens, roots, and bird eggs, as well as catching tortoises, small mammals, snakes, insects, termites, and caterpillars. While the women gather, the men hunt animals, snare birds, and extract honey from beehives. These hunters are skilled trackers who can follow animal tracks and other clues for many miles without rest. The !Kung utilize some fifty species of plants and animals for food, medicine, cosmetics, and poisons. Although Western peoples may disregard many of the food sources because of cultural biases, these sources are in fact highly nutritious. Termites, for example, are about half protein.

The !Kung have adapted well to a harsh environment. Even during periodic drought conditions that devastate the more vulnerable farmers, the diversity of !Kung food sources ensures a steady supply. Furthermore, their diet is low in salt, carbohydrates, and saturated fats, and high in vitamins and roughage. Their diet, combined with a relatively unstressful life, helps them avoid modern health problems like high blood pressure, ulcers, obesity, and heart disease. But because they live far from clinics, they die more easily from accidents and malaria, and some scholars doubt that their diet is nutritionally sound. Nonetheless, !Kung life expectancy is similar to that in many industrialized countries.

Since they spend only about fifteen to twenty hours a week in maintaining their livelihood, the !Kung have ample free time for resting, conversing, visiting friends, and playing games. Children have few responsibilities because their labor is not needed for the !Kungs' survival. The !Kung value interdependence between the genders and are willing to do the work normally associated with the opposite sex. For example, fathers take an active role in child rearing. The intense social life is symbolized by a large communal space in the midst of the camp surrounded by family sleeping huts; they prefer companionship to privacy. The !Kung strongly discourage aggressiveness. Their folk stories praise the animal tricksters who evade the use of force.

Throughout history farming peoples have affected hunters and collectors. The !Kung have faced many challenges in recent decades that have altered the lives of many bands. Most are no longer completely self-sufficient. They trade desert products to nearby farming villages for tools and food. Others have been drafted into the military, have taken up wage labor, or have been displaced because their territory has been claimed by governments or business interests. Today, forced or induced to abandon their traditional ways of life, some disoriented !Kung have moved to dilapidated, impoverished villages on the edges of towns. The future for their ancestral lifestyle is unpromising.

THINKING ABOUT THE PROFILE

1. What role does the gathering by women play in the !Kung economy?
2. How does the traditional !Kung way of life promote leisure activity?
3. What problems do the !Kung face today?

M. Shostak/Anthro-Photo

!Kung Women Returning to Camp These !Kung women in the Kalahari Desert of southwestern Africa are returning to camp after gathering wild berries and vegetables, sometimes by using digging sticks. Many Stone Age societies were sustained by such activity.

some regions hunting and gathering could no longer meet the basic needs of everyone, especially as good land was submerged. Soon food gatherers gravitated to areas rich in wild grains and grazing animals, some of them abandoning their nomadic ways to live permanently near these rich food sources.

The Great Transition to Settled Agriculture

Crop Domestication

The environment continued to change, posing new challenges. The earth cooled again briefly about 9000 B.C.E., reducing food supplies, and a drought in the Middle East presented a crisis for some food-gathering societies because they had no real concept of saving or storing for the future. Responding to the challenges, hunters and gatherers began to store food and learn how to cultivate their own fields. Some people experimented with new foods, especially cereal grains collected in a wild state. Former hunters and gatherers began to pioneer **horticulture** (HORE-tee-kuhl-chur), the growing of crops with simple methods and tools, such as the hoe or digging stick. These efforts eventually resulted in a profound reorganization of human society. Women may well have taken the lead in domesticating plants and some animals and in molding clay for storage and cooking pots. As the chief gatherers, women knew how plants grew in certain types of soil and sprouted from seeds, and they also knew the amount of water and sunshine needed to sustain plants. Women are generally the main food producers in horticultural societies today.

horticulture The growing of crops with simple methods and tools.

One major food-producing strategy was shifting cultivation, a method still practiced today by millions of people, especially in Southeast Asia, Africa, and Latin America. Shifting cultivation was especially adaptable in wooded areas, where people could clear trees and underbrush by chopping and burning (hence the common term *slash and burn*). Once the area was cleared, people loosened the soil with digging sticks and finally scattered seeds around the area. Natural moisture such as rain helped the crops mature. But since the soil became eroded after a few years, shifting cultivators moved periodically to fresh land, returning to the original area only after the soil had recovered its fertility.

Farming promoted many radical changes in the way people lived and connected with their environments. Whether agriculture made life more secure, predictable, and healthy than hunting and gathering remains subject to debate. But the domestication of plants and animals increased the production of food in a given amount of land. Agriculture could produce a much higher yield per acre and thus could support much denser populations in the same area. Permanent settlements also made possible the storage of food for future use, since the pots and buildings did not have to be moved periodically. Most people apparently believed farming was necessary for survival.

However, since farmers depended on fewer plant foods than food gatherers, they were in some ways more vulnerable to disaster from drought or other natural catastrophes. Food shortages may have become more rather than less common. The earliest farmers could probably grow enough to feed themselves and their families with three or four hours of work a day. But as they required more food to feed growing populations, they were forced to exploit local resources more intensively and to work harder in their fields. Some people complained. The Hebrew writer who recorded the biblical garden of Eden story blamed women for the hard work of farming: "Cursed is the ground for your sake; in toil you shall eat of it all the days of your life. In the sweat of your face you shall eat bread til you return to the ground."[3] Agriculture eventually depended on peasants, mostly poor farmers who worked small plots of land that were often owned by others. Hard-working peasants were the backbone of most societies before the Industrial Revolution.

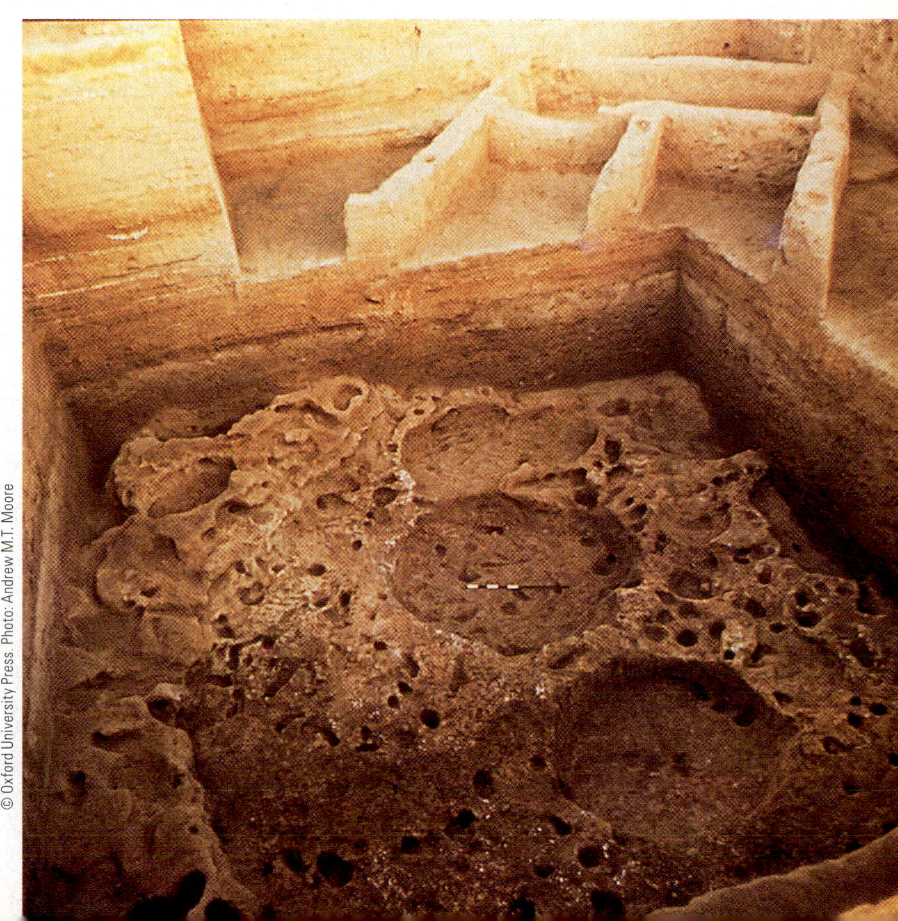

Ruins of Abu Hureyra The site of this ancient village overlooks the floodplain of the Euphrates River in northeastern Syria. The earliest settlement included intersecting pits that were turned into huts by roofs of reeds, branches, and poles.

The Globalization and Diversity of Agriculture

The agricultural transformation eventually reached across the globe. Agriculture came first to Eurasia, where geography favored the movement of people to the east or west along the same general latitude, without abrupt climatic changes. By contrast, the Americas are constructed along a north-south axis, and northern and southern temperate regions are linked only through a huge tropical zone stretching from southern Mexico to northern and eastern South America. Some peoples, such as those in Australia and the Arctic, did not or could not make the transition from food gathering because of environmental and geographical constraints. Nonetheless, the different regions all contributed significantly to the discovery and production of the food resources we use today.

CHRONOLOGY
The Transition to Agriculture, 10,000–500 B.C.E.

9500–8000 B.C.E. Southwestern Asia (Fertile Crescent)

7000 B.C.E. Nubia (date disputed), China, Mexico, New Guinea

6500 B.C.E. Greece

6000 B.C.E. Northwestern India, Egypt, Andes, West Africa (disputed)

5000 B.C.E. Thailand

4900 B.C.E. Panama

4500 B.C.E. Ethiopia

4000 B.C.E. Britain, Scandinavia

3000 B.C.E. Island Southeast Asia, tropical West Africa

1500 B.C.E. Amazon Basin

1000 B.C.E. Colorado

500 B.C.E. Southeast North America

Where did agriculture begin? Most archaeologists believe the earliest transition to farming occurred in the area of southwestern Asia known as the "Fertile Crescent." This includes what is today Iraq, Syria, central and eastern Turkey, and the Jordan River Valley. This region had many fast-growing plants with high nutritional value, such as wheat, barley, chickpeas, and peas. The breakthrough came between 9500 and 8000 B.C.E. Food growing also began independently in several other parts of the world, although we still do not know precisely when (see Map 1.2). Hot, humid climates such as those in Southeast Asia, tropical Africa, and Central America are poor for preserving plant, animal, and human remains. But clearly several Asian peoples were among the earliest farmers. Crop cultivation began around 7000 B.C.E. in China and New Guinea, 7000 or 6000 B.C.E. in India, 5000 or 4000 B.C.E. in Thailand, and 3000 B.C.E. in Island Southeast Asia.

The dates for the beginning of agriculture vary considerably (see Chronology: The Transition to Agriculture, 10,000–500 B.C.E.). In the Mediterranean region, farming began in the Nile Valley by at least 6000 B.C.E., if not earlier, and in Greece by 6500 B.C.E. Agriculture reached northward to Britain and Scandinavia between 4000 and 3000 B.C.E. Farming may have spread into Europe with migrants from western Asia who intermarried with local people. While some historians suspect that farming in the southeast Sahara dates to between 8000 and 6000 B.C.E., others doubt it began that early. People in Ethiopia were farming by 4500 B.C.E. In the Americas cultivation apparently began in central Mexico between 7000 and 5500 B.C.E. and in the Andes **(ANN-deez)** highlands by 6000 B.C.E., if not earlier. Farming reached the Amazon Basin by 1500 B.C.E., Colorado by 1000 B.C.E., and the southeastern part of North America by 500 B.C.E.

The earliest crops that were grown varied according to local environments and needs. Millet dominated in cold North China, rice in tropical Southeast Asia, wheat and barley in the dry Middle East, yams and sorghum in West Africa, corn in upland Mesoamerica, and potatoes in the high Andes. Some crops such as flax were grown for fiber to make clothing. Other plants had medicinal properties. Southwest Asians began making wine from grapes and beer from barley between 6000 and 3000 B.C.E. Over time farming became deeply ingrained in the psychology, social life, and traditions of many societies (see Witness to the Past: Food and Farming in Ancient Cultural Traditions). Farming technology gradually improved. People living in highlands where slopes are steep, such as in Peru, Indonesia, China, or Greece, made their fields on terraces, which were laborious to construct and maintain. Then, as more people moved from highlands into valleys, they used water from nearby marshes or wells or built large-scale water projects such as irrigation canals.

Animal Domestication

Humans and Animals

The domestication of animals for human use developed in close association with crop raising. As they were bred in captivity, animals were gradually modified from their wild ancestors. Men may have tamed and looked after the larger animals such as oxen and cattle, while women may have taken charge of smaller species such as sheep and pigs. Wild boars were domesticated into pigs in several different regions. Animals were raised to supply meat and leather, to aid in farming, to produce fertilizer, or to supply transportation. For example, horses and camels made long-distance travel and communication easier. Plows became more efficient tools when pulled by oxen or cattle. One disadvantage was that domesticated animals passed on diseases to humans, although this eventually led to immunities among peoples in Eurasia.

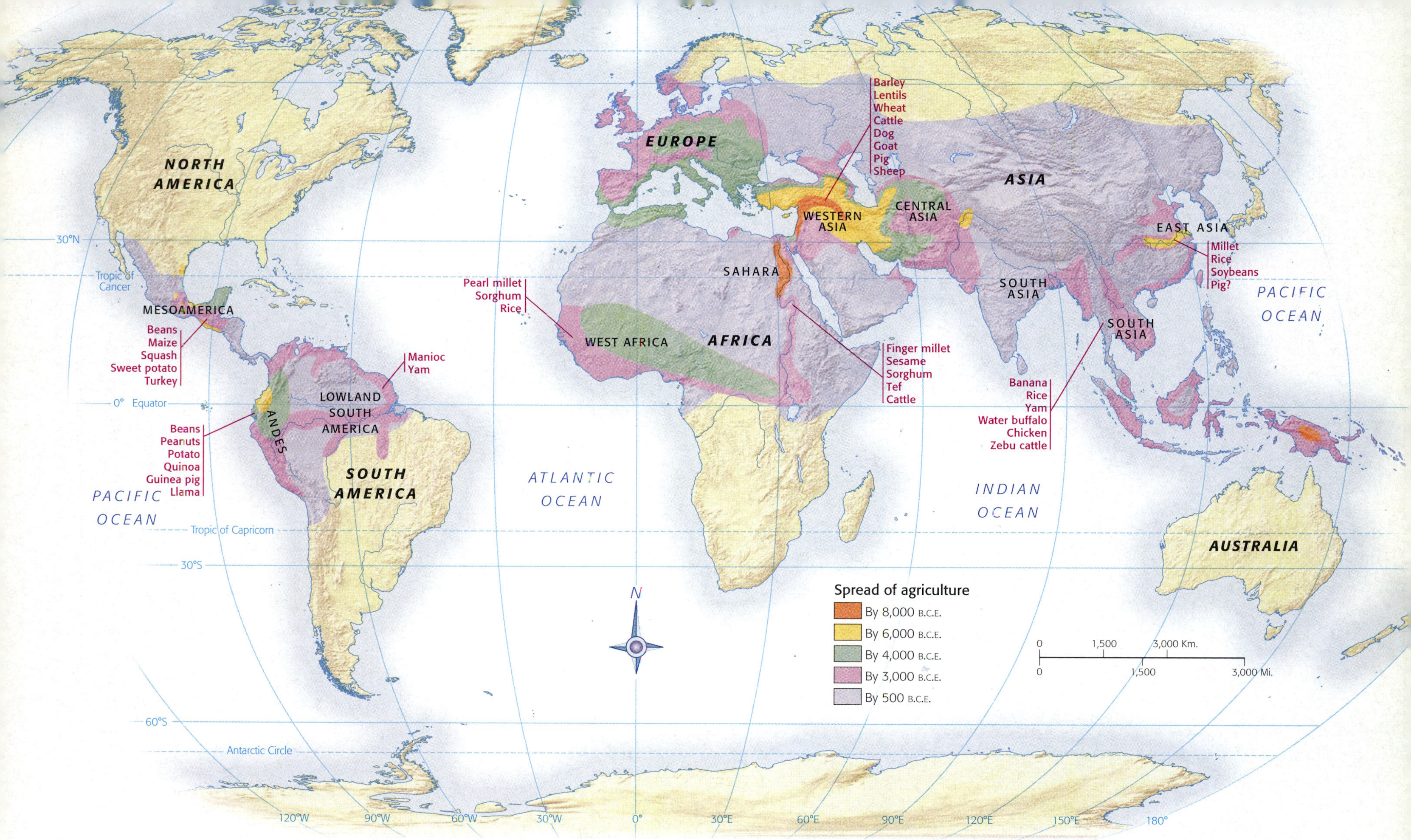

NORTH AMERICA
MESOAMERICA
Beans
Maize
Squash
Sweet potato
Turkey
LOWLAND SOUTH AMERICA
Manioc
Yam
ANDES
Beans
Peanuts
Potato
Quinoa
Guinea pig
Llama
SOUTH AMERICA
PACIFIC OCEAN
ATLANTIC OCEAN
EUROPE
Barley
Lentils
Wheat
Cattle
Dog
Goat
Pig
Sheep
WESTERN ASIA
CENTRAL ASIA
ASIA
EAST ASIA
Millet
Rice
Soybeans
Pig?
PACIFIC OCEAN
SAHARA
Pearl millet
Sorghum
Rice
WEST AFRICA
AFRICA
Finger millet
Sesame
Sorghum
Tef
Cattle
SOUTH ASIA
SOUTH ASIA
Banana
Rice
Yam
Water buffalo
Chicken
Zebu cattle
INDIAN OCEAN
AUSTRALIA
30°N
Tropic of Cancer
0° Equator
Tropic of Capricorn
30°S
60°S
Antarctic Circle
120°W 90°W 60°W 30°W 0° 30°E 60°E 90°E 120°E 150°E 180°
N

Spread of agriculture
By 8,000 B.C.E.
By 6,000 B.C.E.
By 4,000 B.C.E.
By 3,000 B.C.E.
By 500 B.C.E.

0 1,500 3,000 Km.
0 1,500 3,000 Mi.

Map 1.2
The Origins of Agriculture

Between 11,500 and 7,000 years ago, people in western Asia, North and sub-Saharan Africa, southern Asia, East Asia, New Guinea, Mesoamerica, and South America developed agriculture independently and domesticated available animals. Later most of these crops and some of the animals spread into other regions.

Interactive Map

Food and Farming in Ancient Cultural Traditions

As agriculture became an essential foundation for survival, it became increasingly important in the traditions and mindsets of societies around the world. The following excerpts show three examples of how food and farming were reflected in the cultural traditions of ancient societies. The first, an Andean ritual chant many centuries old, is a prayer for successful harvests addressed to an ancient deity. The second is from a farmer's almanac from eighteenth-century B.C.E. Mesopotamia that offers guidance on cultivating a successful grain crop; this excerpt deals with preparing the field and seeding. The third reading, a song collected in China around 3,000 years ago, celebrates a successful harvest and explains how some of the bounty will be used.

Andean Chant

Oh Viracocha, ancient Viracocha, skilled creator, who makes and establishes
"on the earth below may they eat, may they drink" you say; for those you have established, those you have made
may food be plentiful.
"Potatoes, maize, all kinds of food may there be"

Excerpt from Farmer's Almanac

Keep a sharp eye on the openings of the dikes, ditches and mounds [so that] when you flood the field the water will not rise too high in it. . . . Let shod oxen trample it for you; after having its weeds ripped out [by them and] the field made level ground, dress it evenly with narrow axes weighing [no more than] two thirds of a pound each. . . . Keep your eye on the man who puts in the barley seed. Let him drop the grain uniformly two fingers deep. . . . If the barley seed does not sink in properly, change your share. . . . Harvest it at the moment [of its full strength].

Chinese Harvest Song

Abundant is the year, with much millet, much rice;
But we have tall granaries,
To hold . . . many myriads and millions of grain.
We make wine, make sweet liquor,
We offer it to ancestor, to ancestress,
We use it to fulfill all the [religious] rites,
To bring down blessings upon each and all.

THINKING ABOUT THE READING

1. Who did the Andeans believe determined the success of their harvest?
2. How did Mesopotamian farming depend on draft animals and cooperation?
3. How did ancient Chinese farmers use surplus grain and rice to fulfill obligations?

Sources: Brian M. Fagan, *Kingdoms of Gold, Kingdoms of Jade* (London: Thames and Hudson, 1991), p. 88; *The Book of Songs*, translated by Arthur Waley (London: George Allen and Unwin, 1954), ©1954 by permission of The Arthur Waley Estate.

Much remains unclear about the chronology and location of animal domestication. For example, dogs may have been domesticated from gray wolves by at least 12,000 or perhaps 15,000 years ago in East Asia or the Middle East. Dogs were welcome for companionship, guarding, assistance in hunting, and sometimes food. Migrants took Asian dogs to the Americas. Sheep, goats, pigs, chickens, and cattle were all domesticated in the Middle East and South Asia between 9000 and 7000 B.C.E. Some contested evidence also suggests early cattle domestication in East Africa and in the Sahara region . The first domesticated horses and donkeys, which date back to around 4000 B.C.E., enabled the improved transportation that stimulated long-distance trade networks.

Zoological Differences

Zoological differences among the continents were crucial to the evolution of advanced agriculture. Eurasia contained many species of large, plant-eating, herding mammals whose habits and mild dispositions made their domestication into draft animals possible. But outside Eurasia, the lack of draft animals hindered the development of agriculture. Africa (except for cattle) and Australia lacked such animals, and most of the candidates in the Americas, such as the horse and camel, were extinct by 10,000 B.C.E. The only American possibilities were the gentle llamas and alpacas of the South American highlands. Though Andean people used them as pack animals by 3500 B.C.E., they were not well suited for farming.

Agriculture and Its Environmental Consequences

At the same time that the environment influenced farming, the resulting population growth also contributed to environmental changes, some with negative consequences such as cutting trees.

Human activities have had an impact on environments since the time of *Homo habilis*. Indeed, Stone Age hunters in both hemispheres may have contributed to the extinction of many animal species. But intensive agriculture more radically altered the ecology, especially as technology improved. Technological innovation solved some problems for a while, but it did not always prove advantageous in the long run. For example, the invention of the plowshare made it easier to loosen dirt and eliminate weeds so that seeds could be planted deeper in nutrient-rich soil. But it also exposed topsoils to water and wind erosion. Similarly, vast irrigation networks provided the economic foundations for flourishing agriculture and denser settlement. But irrigation requires more labor than dry farming, and it also tends to foster centralized governments that can allocate the water resources among the people, with the result that more controls are placed on people's behavior. In addition, adding water to poor soils can produce waterlogged land and also produce a thick salt surface that ruins farming. In Mesopotamia and the Americas, where irrigation ultimately created deserts, it helped account for the rise and fall of entire societies.

Seated Goddess from Western Asia This baked-clay figure from one of the oldest towns in western Asia, Çatal Hüyük in Anatolia, shows an enthroned female, probably a goddess giving birth, guarded on both sides by catlike animals—perhaps leopards.

Environmental Destruction

Various activities contributed to environmental destruction. Farming and animal raising placed new demands on the land. Goats, for example, caused considerable damage as they browsed on shrubs, tree branches, and seedlings, thus preventing forest regeneration. Cattle required much pasture. People exploited nearby forests for lumber to build wagons, tools, houses, furniture, and boats. Contemporary observers were aware of the deforestation. For example, twenty-four centuries ago the philosopher Plato bemoaned the deforestation of the Greek mountains, which he called "a mere relic of the original country. What remains is like the skeleton of a body emaciated by disease. All the rich soil has melted away, leaving a country of skin and bone."[4] Overgrazing and deforestation in the mountains feeding the main rivers produced silt that contained harmful salt and gypsum, which moved downstream to the sea, clogging canals and dams.

The changing relationship of humans to their environment with farming generated new religious ideas. Early sacred and philosophical texts often justified human domination over nature. For example, the authors of the Hebrew book of Genesis believed God told humans to "be fruitful and multiply; fill the earth and subdue it; have dominion over the fish of the sea, over the birds of the air, and over every living thing that moves upon the earth."[5] Many ancient thinkers saw an ordered world in which every part had a role and purpose in a divine plan, with humans the ultimate beneficiaries.

SECTION SUMMARY

- The shift from hunting and gathering to farming had tremendous consequences, but it occurred gradually, over hundreds of years.
- The end of the last great Ice Age and increased population density led people to shift from hunting and gathering to farming.
- Settled farming could support much denser populations and allowed for food storage, but it also led to some new health problems.
- Farming probably began in the area of southwestern Asia known as the "Fertile Crescent."
- Irrigation and other technological advances led to larger crops but also caused great environmental damage.

The Emergence of Cities and States

How did farming and metallurgy establish the foundations for the rise of cities, states, and trade networks?

Farming generated more complex societies. Given the prospects for ample food, some western Asian people moved to fertile areas to farm. They unloaded their stone tools, clay pots, and plant seeds and built flimsy huts of mud and reeds. Families formed small villages, which had more children to help in the fields. They built houses with a sleeping platform, bread oven, grain silo, and a corral for their domesticated animals. Older women served as religious specialists, acting as midwives, reciting myths, and composing verses. Over time people began to see themselves as part of larger communities. To honor a special deity the villagers built a temple. Eventually these villages with their temples grew into the first cities. In turn, cities established a foundation for the rise of states, trade networks, and writing.

The Rise of New Technologies

Agriculture also fostered new technologies. Many times in history people came up against a serious resource problem, such as lack of food and water, and had to overcome the problem or perish. Often their solution was to develop some new technology, and many of these inventions had long-lasting value. One innovation, metalworking, made possible a new level of human control over resources supplied by the environment. The first metalworking was done with copper, used in Europe for making weapons and tools as early as 7000 B.C.E. and in the Middle East by 4500 B.C.E. In fact, copper mining may have been the first real industry of the ancient world. Traded over considerable distances, copper also became perhaps the first major commodity to enjoy a world market. Gold was also used and valued very early. These two soft metals could be fairly easily cut and shaped with stones.

Metallurgy

Soon specialist craftsmen emerged to mine and work metals. By 3000 B.C.E. some of these specialists in western Asia had developed heating processes by which they could blend copper together with either tin or arsenic to create bronze. The bronze trade became a major spur to commerce in early Mesopotamia. By 1500 B.C.E. the technology for making usable iron had also been invented, although it took many centuries for people to perfect the new alloy for practical use. Bronze and iron made better, more helpful, and more durable tools (such as plows), but they also made more deadly weapons, and their use shaped many societies of the ancient and classical worlds (see "Societies, Networks, Transitions," page 96).

Urbanization and the First Cities

Agriculture also fostered population growth. By using cow's milk and grain meal for infant's food, women could now breastfeed for a shorter period and consequently bear children more frequently. In the Middle East the population is believed to have grown from less than 100,000 in 8000 B.C.E. to over 3 million by 4000 B.C.E. Some farming villages grew into substantial, often prosperous towns. In one of the oldest towns, Çatal Hüyük **(cha-TAHL hoo-YOOK)** in central Turkey, roughly 10,000 residents lived in cramped mud-brick buildings. The residents decorated the white plaster walls of their houses with paintings. Çatal Hüyük and similar towns became centers of long-distance trade. By around 3700 B.C.E. Tell Hamoukar **(Tell HAM-oo-kar)** in northeastern Syria had grown from a village into a town enclosed by a defensive wall. It contained both a bakery and a brewery, evidence of some residents organizing people and resources, and seems to have had a growing bureaucracy, perhaps even a king. By 3500 B.C.E. Tell Hamoukar had grown into a city that later traded with the cities of southern Mesopotamia. Road networks linked the various cities of the Tigris-Euphrates Basin.

Urban Life

As people grouped together, they pioneered new ways of living. Permanent settlements became larger, dominating nearby villages and farms. A city is a permanent settlement with a greater size,

James Mellaart/Catalhoyuk Research Projects

Çatal Hüyük A view of rooms and walls in one of the first known towns, Çatal Hüyük in eastern Turkey. The ruins contained many art objects, murals, wall sculpture, and woven cloth.

population, and importance than a town, and it usually contains many shops, public markets, government buildings, and religious centers. Cities emerged where farmers produced more food than they needed for themselves and so could be taxed or coerced to share their excess crops. This surplus was critical to sustain people with no time or land for farming, and priests, scribes, carpenters, and merchants increasingly congregated in the growing settlements.

Urban Revolution

What some call the urban revolution constituted a major achievement in different parts of the world, perhaps as significant as the agricultural transformation. In Southwest Asia the first small cities were formed between 3500 and 3200 B.C.E.; they were administered by governments and dominated by new social hierarchies. Soon cities appeared elsewhere, many surrounded by walls (see Chronology: The Rise of Cities). City people enjoyed new amenities. Many streets were lined by small shops and crowded with makeshift stalls selling foodstuffs, household items, or folk medicines. Hawkers peddled their wares from door to door. Craftsmen in workshops fashioned the items used in daily life, such as pottery, tools, and jewelry. Some of the goods made, mined, or grown locally were traded by land or sea to distant cities. Thus the rise of cities reshaped societies and fostered networks of communication and exchange.

The Rise of States, Economies, and Recordkeeping

Food production and urbanization eventually led to the formation of states: formal political organizations or governments that controlled a recognized territory and exercised power over both people and things. The people within them, often from diverse ethnic and cultural backgrounds, did not necessarily share all the same values or allegiances. Furthermore, they exchanged influences with neighboring peoples. Complex urban societies organized into states developed at least 3,000 years ago on all the inhabited continents except Australia.

CHRONOLOGY
The Rise of Cities

3500–3200 B.C.E. Western Asia

3500–3000 B.C.E. Northwestern India

3100–3000 B.C.E. Egypt

3100–2500 B.C.E. Peru

2000 B.C.E. Northern China

1800 B.C.E. Nubia

1600 B.C.E. Crete

1200 B.C.E. Mesoamerica (Mexico)

100 C.E. West Africa

These urban societies relied on diversified economies that generated enough wealth to support a division of labor and social, cultural, and religious hierarchies. Farmers, laborers, craftsmen, merchants, priests, soldiers, bureaucrats, and scholars served specialized functions. The priests served the religious institutions that emerged as societies organized and standardized their beliefs. Some states constructed monumental architecture, such as large temples, palaces, and city walls. While men dominated most of the hierarchies and heavy labor, women also played key economic roles. Women made the cloth: preparing the raw materials, spinning the yarn, weaving the yarn into fabrics, and fashioning and sewing the clothing, blankets, and other useful items, while passing along their knowledge from mother to daughter. Most urban societies were connected to elaborate trade networks extending well beyond the immediate region. By 4000 B.C.E. a network of merchant contacts linked India and Mesopotamia, 1,250 miles apart. Clay counting tokens used for trade had appeared by 3100 B.C.E., if not earlier. By 5000 B.C.E. the first seafaring vessels had been built around the Persian Gulf

The early urban societies also introduced cultural innovations such as recordkeeping and literature. A system of recordkeeping could involve a written language, such as those developed by the Egyptians, Greeks, Chinese, and Maya, among others. Or records could be kept by a class of memory experts, such as the professional "rememberers" among many African and South American peoples. In most literate societies writing was usually reserved for the privileged few until recent centuries, so knowledge of literature was not widespread unless it was passed on orally. Most societies created rich oral traditions of stories, legends, historical accounts, and poems that could be shared with all the people.

Some historians apply the term *civilization* to larger, more complex societies such as ancient Egypt and China, but this is a controversial concept with a long history of abuse. Since ancient times some peoples have seen themselves as "civilized" and criticized their neighbors, or any people unfamiliar to them, as "barbarians." Modern historians may focus too much on societies, such as Egypt, that left more of an archaeological and written record, giving lesser attention to those societies that did not. The term *civilization* could also refer to a large grouping of people with a common history and traditions, such as the Chinese, Maya, Arabs, or western Europeans. Or it could be restricted to those large, complex urban societies that developed or borrowed certain useful patterns such as bureaucratic governments, monumental architecture, and writing. Thus the term is too subjective to have much value in understanding world history. It is not used in this text.

The Rise of Pastoral Nomadism

pastoral nomadism An economy based on breeding, rearing, and harvesting livestock.

Some societies adopted an alternative to agriculture and cities known as **pastoral nomadism**, an economy based on breeding, rearing, and harvesting livestock. The interaction between pastoral nomads and settled farmers was a major theme in history for many centuries. On the marginal land unsuitable for farming, some people began specializing in herding, moving their camps and animals seasonally in search of pasture. They traded meat, hides, or livestock to nearby farmers for grain. Both trade and conflict between the two contrasting groups, farmers and herders, became common. Pastoral nomadism involved dispersed rather than concentrated populations. Yet some pastoral nomads exercised a strong influence on societies with much greater populations.

Pastoral nomads mostly concentrated in grasslands and deserts, which could sustain only small populations. Grasslands covered much of central and western Asia from Mongolia to southern Russia, as well as large parts of eastern and southern Africa. An even more inhospitable area was the Sahara region of northern Africa, which by 2000 B.C.E. was part of a great arid zone stretching from the western tip of Africa eastward through Arabia into western Asia and then to the frontiers of China.

Pastoral Life

Living along or beyond the frontiers of settled farming, the pastoralists lived very differently than farmers, but they were not culturally unsophisticated. For example, they domesticated horses in Central Asia around 4300 B.C.E. and camels in Arabia around 3000 or 2500 B.C.E. Although they had few material possessions, like other societies, pastoralists often had humane values and a rich cultural life. The nomadic pastoral life had many similarities regardless of the region. Since a large area was needed to support each animal, herds had to be kept small to prevent overgrazing. As a result, the herders lived in small, dispersed groups, generally organized by extended families that were often part of **tribes**, associations of clans that traced descent from a common ancestor.

tribes Associations of clans that traced descent from a common ancestor.

There were also many differences among pastoralists. While some societies maintained egalitarian social structures, others were headed by chiefs. In some of the pastoral societies of Central Asia, women seem to have held a high status and to even have served as warriors. Burial mounds in Turkestan contain the remains of what may be female warriors from 2,500 years ago. These women, unusually tall, were buried with daggers, swords, and bronze-tipped arrows. Some pastoralists became tough, martial peoples who were greatly feared by the farmers. Central Asian pastoralists like the Huns and Mongols played a central role in world history before modern times.

Indo-European Expansion

Among the pastoral nomads who had a great historical influence were the various tribes known collectively as the **Indo-Europeans**. Historians derive this term from the original common tongue that spawned the many related languages spoken today by these peoples' descendants. Scholars have long debated where the original Indo-European homeland was located, but it was probably in the Caucasus Mountains, the adjacent southern Russian plains to the north, or in eastern Anatolia (modern Turkey). Eventually, because of the spread of these seminomadic and strongly patriarchal tribes and their languages, most people in Europe, Iran, and northern India came to speak Indo-European languages.

Indo-Europeans Various tribes who all spoke related languages deriving from some original common tongue and who eventually settled Europe, Iran, and northern India.

Indo-European expansion apparently occurred in several waves. Some Indo-Europeans may have moved into Europe and Central Asia as early as 6500 or 7000 B.C.E., perhaps carrying with them not only their language but also farming technology. The culturally mixed people who resulted may have been the ancestors of the Celts and Greeks. Sometime between 3000 and 2000 B.C.E. many of the Indo-European pastoralists were driven from their western Asian homeland by some disaster. The various tribes dispersed in every direction, splitting up into smaller units and driving their herds of cattle, sheep, goats, and horses with them. As they encountered farming peoples, they turned to conquest in order to occupy the land (see Map 1.3).

This dispersal set the stage for profound changes across Eurasia. The Hittites gained dominance in Anatolia and then, around 2000 B.C.E., expanded their empire into Mesopotamia. Other tribes pushed on between 2500 and 1500 B.C.E., some to the west into Greece, some east as far as the western fringe of China, some south into Persia (Iran). From Persia some tribes moved southeast through the mountain passes into northwestern India. Everywhere they went the Indo-Europeans spread their languages and imposed their military power, eventually absorbing or subduing the peoples they encountered. Most eventually abandoned pastoral nomadism for farming, but their spread opened a new chapter in the history of Europe, the Middle East, and India.

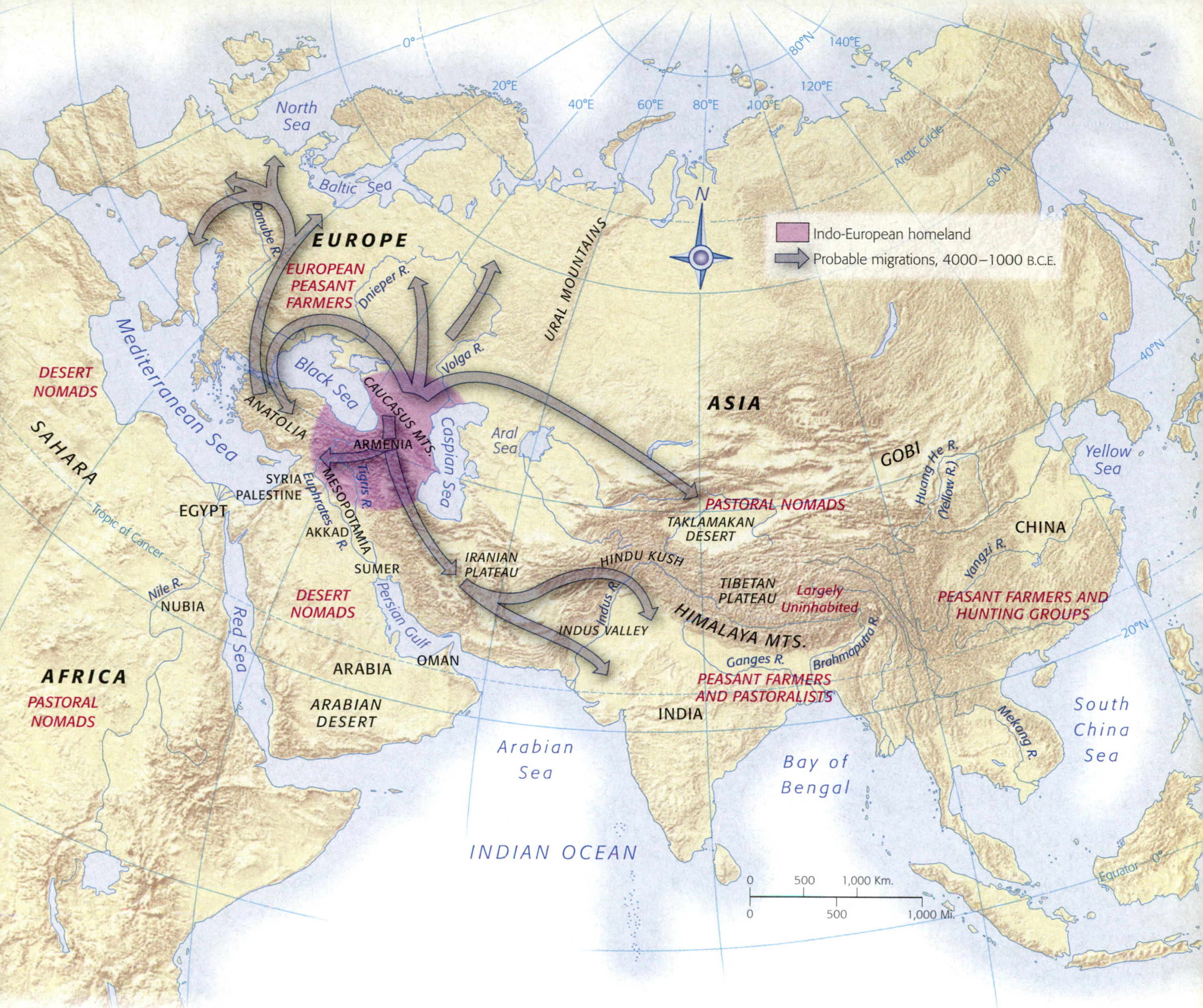

Map 1.3
The Indo-European Migrations and Eurasian Pastoralism

Some societies, especially in parts of Africa and Asia, adapted to environmental contexts by developing a pastoral, or animal herding, economy. One large pastoral group, the Indo-Europeans, eventually expanded from their home area into Europe, southwestern Asia, Central Asia, and India.

e **Interactive Map**

SECTION SUMMARY

- Metals such as bronze and iron helped improve farming tools and weaponry.
- Highly productive farming allowed for the formation of the first cities, which became centers of trade.
- People in cities developed forms of recordkeeping and writing.
- Pastoral nomads, or herders, kept their animals in areas that were unsuitable for farming.
- Herders played an important role in spreading culture across Eurasia, though most eventually took up farming.

CHAPTER SUMMARY

The story of humans and their societies constitutes only a tiny part of the broader 4.5-billion-year history of the earth. Some 4 million years ago our hominid ancestors emerged in Africa, learning to walk upright, to make and use tools, and to control fire. Eventually, evolution produced modern humans, who developed language and more complex social structures. During the long Paleolithic age, all humans, using simple technologies and living in small groups, hunted wild animals and gathered wild plants, surviving by maintaining a balance with their environment. While many such societies survived over the millennia, eventually environmental changes and other factors encouraged most peoples to adopt farming.

Beginning between 10,000 and 11,500 years ago, the climate warmed and populations increased. Some people began to grow their own food. The great transition from hunting and gathering to a farming-based economy also involved the domestication of wild animals. Farming probably emerged first in southwestern Asia. By 2000 B.C.E. various peoples in Eurasia, Africa, and the Americas were farming. Agriculture led to larger populations and changed people's relationship to the environment. It also set the stage for another transition, the emergence of the first societies with cities, states, social classes, and recordkeeping. In the Afro-Eurasian zone, where many peoples were in contact with others, these societies first developed between 3000 and 3500 B.C.E. The first cities and states formed in sub-Saharan Africa and the Americas between 3000 and 1000 B.C.E. Some people living in the grasslands and deserts became nomadic pastoralists and interacted with settled farmers. The formation of distinctive societies and increased contact between peoples inaugurated a new era of human history.

KEY TERMS

hominids
australopithecines
Homo habilis
Homo erectus
Homo sapiens
Neanderthals
Cro-Magnons
Paleolithic
Mesolithic
Neolithic
matrilineal kinship
animism
polytheism
shamans
horticulture
pastoral nomadism
tribes
Indo-Europeans

EBOOK AND WEBSITE RESOURCES

PRIMARY SOURCE

The *Rig Veda*

INTERACTIVE MAPS

Map 1.1 Spread of Modern Humans Around the Globe
Map 1.2 The Origins of Agriculture
Map 1.3 The Indo-European Migrations and Eurasian Pastoralism

LINKS

About Archaeology (http://archaeology.about.com/science/archaeology). Contains much material on archaeology and ancient societies.

ArchNet Home Page (http://archnet.asu.edu/). This Arizona State University site contains links to information on human origins, prehistory, and archaeology.

Becoming Human (http://www.becominghuman.org/). Material on hominds compiled at Arizona State University.

Evolution of Modern Humans (http://anthro.palomar.edu/homo2/default.htm). Valuable site maintained by Palomar College.

Human Origins Program (http://anthropology.si.edu/humanorigins/). Smithsonian Institution site covers a range of topics.

Internet Ancient History Sourcebook (http://www.fordham.edu/halsall/ancient/asbook.html). Good collection of essays and links on prehistory.

The Internet Public Library: Archaeology (http://www.ipl.org/div/subject/browse/soc06.00.00/). Extensive collection of links on the ancient world and prehistory.

World Civilizations (http://www.wsu.edu/~dee/). A useful collection of materials on prehistory and ancient history, operated by Washington State University.

Plus flashcards, practice quizzes, and more. Go to: www.cengage.com/history/lockard/globalsocnet2e.

SUGGESTED READING

Barfield, Thomas J. *The Nomadic Alternative.* Englewood Cliffs: Prentice Hall, 1993. Examines current and past nomadic societies in Asia ad Africa.

Bellwood, Peter. *First Farmers: The Origins of Agricultural Societies.* Malden, MA: Blackwell, 2005. A detailed scholarly account summarizing recent knowledge.

Bogucki, Peter. *The Origins of Human Society.* Malden, MA: Blackwell, 1999. A detailed and up-to-date scholarly study of human prehistory.

Christian, David. *Maps of Time: An Introduction to "Big History."* Berkeley: University of California Press, 2004. The most extensive presentation of the "big history" approach.

Clark, Robert B. *The Global Imperative: An Interpretive History of the Spread of Humankind.* Boulder, CO: Westview, 1997. A well-written, brief overview of human expansion and the development of agriculture.

Diamond, Jared. *Guns, Germs and Steel: The Fates of Human Societies.* New York: W.W. Norton, 1997. A fascinating interpretation of early human societies, with emphasis on environmental influences.

Fagan, Brian. *The Long Summer: How Climate Changed Civilization.* New York: Basic Books, 2004. An up-to-date assessment of the connection between history and climate over the past 5,000 years.

Fagan, Brian. *People of the Earth: An Introduction to World Prehistory*, 12th ed. Upper Saddle River, NJ: Prentice-Hall, 2006. A standard overview of human evolution and prehistory, from early hominids through the Neolithic.

Goudsbloom, Johan. *Fire and Civilization.* London: Penguin, 1992. Examines the impact of fire use on prehistorical and early farming peoples.

Lee, Richard B. and Richard Daly. *The Cambridge Encyclopedia of Hunters and Gatherers.* New York: Cambridge University Press, 2004. A major source on these societies today.

Manning, Patrick. *Migration in World History.* New York: Routledge, 2005. A provocative study of human migrations, with much on prehistory and ancient history.

Megarry, Tim. *Society in Prehistory: The Origins of Human Culture.* New York: New York University Press, 1995. A sociological study of human evolution and Stone Age societies.

Mithen, Steven. *After the Ice: A Global Human History, 20,000–5000 BC.* Cambridge: Harvard University Press, 2004. An unorthodox but fascinating portrayal, based on the latest research, of 15,000 years of prehistory.

Panter-Brick, Catherine. *Hunter-Gatherers: An Interdisciplinary Perspective.* New York: Cambridge University Press, 2001. Scholarly study of past and present peoples.

Ristvet, Lauren. *In the Beginning: World History from Human Evolution to the First States.* New York: McGraw-Hill, 2007. Readable overview of prehistoric patterns.

Tattersall, Ian. *The World from Beginnings to 4000 BCE.* New York: Oxford University Press, 2008. A brief, up-to-date survey of human prehistory and the Neolithic period.

CHAPTER 2

Ancient Societies in Mesopotamia, India, and Central Asia, 5000–600 B.C.E.

CHAPTER OUTLINE

- Early Mesopotamian Urbanized Societies, to 2000 B.C.E.
- Later Mesopotamian Societies and Their Legacies, 2000–600 B.C.E.
- The Earliest Indian and Central Asian Societies, 6000–1500 B.C.E.
- The Aryans and a New Indian Society, 1500–600 B.C.E.

PROFILE
Hammurabi the Lawgiver

WITNESS TO THE PAST
Hindu Values in the *Bhagavad Gita*

Michael Holford

Bull's Head from Sumerian Lyre
This bull's head is part of the soundbox of a wooden harp. The harp, made in Sumeria around 2600 B.C.E., is covered with gold and lapis lazuli and reflects the popularity of music in Mesopotamian society.

Inanna filled Agade [a Mesopotamian city], her home, with gold. She filled the storerooms with barley, bronze, and lumps of lapis lazuli [a stone used in jewelry]. The ships at the wharves were an awesome sight. All the lands around rested in security.

—Poem praising the goddess of love and generosity, written in 2250 B.C.E.[1]

FOCUS QUESTIONS

1. Why did farming, cities, and states develop first in the Fertile Crescent?
2. What were some of the main features of Mesopotamian societies?
3. What were some of the distinctive features of the Harappan cities?
4. How did Indian society and the Hindu religion emerge from the mixing of Aryan and local cultures?

Some 5,000 years ago in the Mesopotamian (MESS-uh-puh-TAIM-ee-an) city of Uruk (OO-rook), an unknown artist carved a beautiful narrative relief on a large stone-pedestaled vase, the first such sculpture known in history, and donated it to the city's temple for the goddess of love, Inanna (ih-NON-a), the first known goddess in recorded history. The scenes of domestic and religious life celebrate a festival honoring the goddess. The artist divided the vase into three bands, each illustrating different aspects of Uruk life and traditions. The lowest band presents an agricultural scene, with sheep, barley, and water, the staples of the area's economy. The central band portrays a procession of men carrying foodstuffs that they will present as gifts of gratitude to Inanna. Finally, the uppermost band features a female figure wearing a tall horned headdress, perhaps Inanna or her priestess. The vase reflects artistic skill and also pictures for us the social order and rituals of one of the world's earliest cities.

Sometime after the people in southwest Asia and India had become comfortable with the farming technology necessary for successful living, they began to make the next great transition by founding the first cities like Uruk and states. Various urban societies eventually formed in the Indus Valley in northwestern India and all along the **Fertile Crescent**, a large semicircle of fertile land that included the valleys of the Tigris (TIE-gris) and Euphrates (you-FRAY-teez) Rivers stretching northwest from the Persian Gulf to the eastern shores of the Mediterranean Sea. The Mesopotamians divided their specialized workers into full-time farmers, professional soldiers, government officials, artisans, traders, and priests. Ancient Indians also established social classes and the foundations for several religions of enduring appeal.

Fertile Crescent A large semicircular fertile region that included the valleys of the Tigris and Euphrates Rivers stretching northwest from the Persian Gulf to the eastern shores of the Mediterranean Sea.

The Mesopotamians and Indians were among various Afro-Eurasian peoples who built the foundations to sustain large populations. For at least three millennia a large majority of the world's population has lived in an arc stretching from Egypt and Mesopotamia eastward through India to China and Japan. The people of western Asia created the first systematic use of writing for both business transactions and literature, the first working of bronze, the first large states, and the first institutionalized religions to worship deities like Inanna. These societies also constructed networks to exchange products and information over long distances by land and sea. The city Agade (uh-GAH-duh) was visited by traders from near and far. Over time southwest Asia became a crossroads or bridge between Europe, Africa, and southern Asia and a great hub for trade and communication networks extending to distant lands.

e Visit the website and eBook for additional study materials and interactive tools: www.cengage.com/history/lockard/globalsocnet2e

EARLY MESOPOTAMIAN URBANIZED SOCIETIES, TO 2000 B.C.E.

Why did farming, cities, and states develop first in the Fertile Crescent?

Small city-states emerged in Mesopotamia around 5,000 years ago, especially in the southern part of the Tigris-Euphrates Valley. Geography played a key role in this region's transition to farming, urbanization, and state building. The connections between diverse peoples helped cultures change and grow. Over the centuries various peoples moved into the area, each adopting and building on the achievements of their predecessors. Their cities were dominated by religious temples and had elaborate social class structures. As conquerors combined various city-states into a series of ever larger states, empires were formed, and Mesopotamian societies were soon linked by trade to the Mediterranean and North Africa.

Western Asian Environments

Geographical Foundations

Life in these early societies owed much to the geographic features that brought people together. Most early urban societies began first in wide river valleys such as the Tigris-Euphrates, Indus, and Nile Valleys because such places provided life-giving irrigation for the crops that supported larger populations. In Mesopotamia (the Greek word for the "land between the rivers"), the flooding of the Tigris and Euphrates Rivers made possible a flourishing society. The Tigris-Euphrates Basin stretches from the western edge of the Persian Gulf through today's Iraq into Syria and southeastern Turkey. The long river valley promoted interaction, both friendly and hostile, between peoples. For example, it invited frequent invasions through mountain passes by people living to the north and east. To the northwest is the mountainous Anatolia (ANN-uh-TOE-lee-uh) Peninsula (modern Turkey). East of Mesopotamia lay Iran (known through most of history as Persia), a land of mountains and deserts and the pathway to India and Central Asia. To the south the Arabian peninsula, largely desert, was characterized by oasis agriculture and nomadic pastoralism.

Although water was plentiful, other characteristics of this region and its climate were not so generous. Ancient Mesopotamia had a climate similar to southern California today. Most rain fell in the winter, and summer temperatures in some places reached 120 degrees Fahrenheit. During the long, scorching summer, the land baked stone-hard and searing winds blew up a choking dust. Vegetation withered. In the winter, winds, clouds, and the occasional rains made for stormy days. In spring the rains and melting snows in the nearby mountains swelled the rivers to flood level, sometimes submerging the plains. Still, the annual but unpredictable floods created natural levees that could be drained and planted, and the nearby swamps contained abundant fish and wildlife.

Diverse peoples and languages contributed to the history of western Asia. Many different peoples settled the region, some of them speaking Semitic languages, including Arabic and Hebrew, which are related to some African tongues. Speakers of Turkic and of Indo-European languages such as Persian, Armenian, and Kurdish arrived later. Europeans later referred to southwestern Asia as the Orient, Asia Minor, or the Near East (since it was part of the "East" nearest to them), and to the region along the eastern Mediterranean coast as the Levant (luh-VANT) ("rising of the sun"). Geographers today use the label "southwest Asia" and often lump the region together with Islamic North Africa under the broader concept of the "Middle East," since Europeans saw it as midway between East Asia (the "Far East") and themselves ("the West").

The Tigris and Euphrates Rivers, which flow southeast from eastern Anatolia, fostered several Mesopotamian societies. The modern city of Baghdad is midway up the Tigris, and the ancient city of Babylon was only a few miles away on the Euphrates. Such cities arose when the population of farmers and herders in the fertile hills on either side of these rivers increased and needed more food. Possibly pushed by a cooler climate, they left the hill country and created the first towns in the marshy areas near the head of the Persian Gulf. After moving

CHRONOLOGY
Mesopotamia, 5500–330 B.C.E.

5500 B.C.E. First Sumerian settlements

3200 B.C.E. First cuneiform writing

3000–2300 B.C.E. Sumerian city-states

2750 B.C.E. Model for legendary Gilgamesh rules Uruk

ca. 2500–2100 B.C.E. Jiroft

ca. 2350–2160 B.C.E. Akkadian Empire unifies Mesopotamia

ca. 2100–2000 B.C.E. Neo-Sumerian Empire led by city of Ur

ca. 2000 B.C.E. *Epic of Gilgamesh* written in cuneiform

ca. 1800–1595 B.C.E. Old Babylonian Empire

ca. 1790–1780 B.C.E. Hammurabi's Law Code

ca. 1600–1200 B.C.E. Hittite Empire

ca. 1115–612 B.C.E. Assyrian Empire

745–626 B.C.E. Height of Assyrian Empire

ca. 626–539 B.C.E. Chaldean (Neo-Babylonian) Empire

ca. 539–330 B.C.E. Persian Empire

CHRONOLOGY

	Mesopotamia	India and Central Asia
3000 B.C.E.	**3000–2300 B.C.E.** Sumerian city-states	
2500 B.C.E.	**2350–2160 B.C.E.** Akkadian Empire	**2600–1750 B.C.E.** Harappan city-states **2200–1800 B.C.E.** Oxus cities
2000 B.C.E.	**1800–1595 B.C.E.** Old Babylonian Empire	**1600–1400 B.C.E.** Aryan migrations **1500–1000 B.C.E.** Aryan age
1000 B.C.E.	**1115–605 B.C.E.** Assyrian Empire	

to the river valleys, they worked together to build elaborate irrigation canals so they could grow food after the annual floods. This irrigation had significant consequences, for it necessitated the cooperation that laid the foundations for organized societies and then cities. Yet irrigation also slowly degraded the soil, the salts it added eventually creating infertile desert.

The Pioneering Sumerians and Their Neighbors

People built the first Mesopotamian cities and states in Sumer **(soo-MUHR)**, the lower part of the Tigris-Euphrates Valley in southern Iraq (see Map 2.1). The Sumerians originally came from the north or the east and settled in southern Mesopotamia about 5500 B.C.E. By 3500 B.C.E. Uruk had grown into a city, eventually reaching a population of 50,000. Some scholars suspect that other Mesopotamian peoples, such as those in the north at Tell Hamoukar (see Chapter 1), may have been as important as the Sumerians in forging the first states. But our knowledge of the Sumerians is much more extensive.

By 3000 B.C.E. Sumerians had created a network of city-states, urban centers surrounded by agricultural land controlled by the city and used to support its citizens (see Chronology: Mesopotamia, 5500–330 B.C.E.). These earliest territorial political units allowed Sumerian societies to grow to several million people by 2500 B.C.E. Uruk was surrounded by 5 miles of fortified walls and had extended its influence through trade as far north as modern Turkey by 3500 B.C.E. An attack by Uruk on Tell Hamoukar is the world's oldest known example of large-scale organized warfare.

Sumerians were clearly proud of their cities. A Sumerian myth begins with the lines "Behold the bond of Heaven and Earth, the city. Behold the kindly wall . . . its pure river, its quay where the boats stand. Behold its well of good water. Behold its pure canal."[2] The Sumerians felt that city life made them superior to others. The city-dwellers lived in mud-baked brick houses constructed around courtyards. The largest building in any Sumerian city was the temple, or **ziggurat (ZIG-uh-rat)**, a stepped, pyramidal-shaped building (almost an artificial mountain) that was seen as the home of that city's chief god. One of these temples may have inspired the later Hebrew story of the tower of Babel **(BAY-buhl/BAH-buhl)**.

ziggurat A stepped, pyramidal-shaped temple building in Sumerian cities, seen as the home of the chief god of the city.

Sumerian Society and Economy

In Sumerian society some people had higher ranks than others. At first decision-making assemblies of leading citizens governed the cities. Scholars have long debated whether these assemblies, which included elders and other free citizens, amounted to a kind of democratic government. The assemblies seem to have appointed a city leader, sometimes a woman, with both secular and religious authority. However, with the waging of wars, rulers, priests, and nobles came to dominate large numbers of lower-class people, workers, and slaves. Women lost the right to be elected leader and serve in the assemblies. War leaders became kings, or hereditary monarchs, and weakened the power of the assemblies and priests. The nobility and priests controlled most of the land in and around the city, which was tilled by tenant farmers or slaves. Thus many common people became dependent on the nobles or priests for their survival. A Sumerian proverb claimed that "the poor man is better dead than alive; if he has bread, he has no salt; if he has salt, he has no bread."[3] The many slaves, who included captives taken in battles and criminals, were treated as personal property but allowed to marry. Eventually royal officials, nobility, and priests controlled most of the economic life of the cities.

Map 2.1
Ancient Mesopotamia

The people of Mesopotamia and the adjacent regions of the Fertile Crescent pioneered farming. The Mesopotamians also built the first cities and formed the first states. The Sumerian cities dominated southern Mesopotamia for over a millennium, only to lose power to societies from northern Mesopotamia.

e **Interactive Map**

patriarchy A system in which men largely control women and children and shape ideas about appropriate gender behavior.

As the first of many male-governed societies, Sumeria introduced **patriarchy**, a system in which men largely control women and children and also shape ideas about appropriate gender behavior. Sumerian women were generally subservient to men and excluded from government, but they could inherit property, run their own businesses, and serve as witnesses in court. A queen enjoyed much respect as the wife of the king. Sumerian religion also allowed a woman to be the high priestess if the city divinity was female. Sumerians treasured the family; a proverb suggested the importance of women in the family but also the stereotypes they faced: "The wife is a man's future; the son is a man's refuge; the daughter is a man's salvation; the daughter-in-law is a man's devil."[4]

Trade and Trade Networks

The trade networks involving Sumeria may have been some of the first in world history with significant consequences. Because of their location and lack of natural resources, the Sumerian cities engaged in extensive trade, which helped form networks with neighboring societies. Sumerians imported copper from Armenia in the Caucasus Mountains and then discovered how to mix it with tin to make bronze. This alloy made for stronger weapons, which they often used against each other. Thus the Bronze Age originated in western Asia, and later the use of bronze helped shape other societies in Eurasia and North Africa. The Sumerians also imported gold, ivory, obsidian, and other necessities from Anatolia, the Nile Valley, Ethiopia, India, the Caspian Sea, and the eastern shore of the Mediterranean.

The Persian Gulf became a major waterway, with many trading ports. Bahrain **(bah-RAIN)** Island served as a transshipment point for goods flowing in from all directions and as a hub where various traders and travelers met. Mesopotamian merchants traveled to this port carrying textiles, leather objects, wool, and olive oil and returned with copper bars, ivory, precious objects, and rare woods from various western Asian societies and India. Mesopotamian traders traveled widely. Trade helped people learn and profit from each other's skills and surplus goods.

The Sumerians also seem to have had some trade and other connections with another urban-based farming society, Jiroft **(JEER-oft)** in southeastern Iran. Jiroft emerged sometime between 3000 and 2500 B.C.E., which had an economy based on cultivating date palms. Jiroft, which had emerged by 2500 B.C.E., had an economy based on gaily decorated capital city had lofty red brick towers, and the rulers supplied craftsmen to Uruk. The ruins of Jiroft city include a two-story citadel, a Sumerian-like ziggurat, the world's oldest known board games, and staggering numbers of decorated vases, goblets, cups, and boxes. The people adorned their products with precious stones from India and Afghanistan.

Jiroft

Sumerian Writing and Technology

Writing

The Sumerians were innovators in many areas. Although a few scholars think the Egyptians, Indians, or Chinese might have developed a simple writing system at least as early, most still credit the Sumerians with producing the first written records. Trade and the need to keep accurate records of agricultural production and public and private business dealings led around 3200 B.C.E. to the **cuneiform** **(kyoo-NEE-uh-form)** (Latin for "wedge-shaped") writing system, by which temple recordkeepers, or scribes, began to keep records of financial transactions by making rough pictures (say, of an animal or fish) on soft clay with a stylus that made wedges in the clay. They then baked the bricks on which these pictograms were scratched. Sumerian scribes soon let a stylized version of the pictogram stand for an idea, and later they converted an even more abstract version into a phonetic sign describing a speech sound.

cuneiform ("wedge-shaped") Latin term used to describe the writing system invented by the Sumerians.

Writing provided a way of communicating with people over long distances and allowed rulers to administer larger states. Those who controlled the written word, like those who master electronic communication in our day, had power, prestige, and a monopoly over a society's official history. Writing also gave temple scribes and other religious leaders the power to determine how written texts attributed to the gods or political authorities should be interpreted. Since writing required mastery of at least three hundred symbols, few people learned to write, and those who did largely came from the upper class. In part to produce scribes, the Sumerians created the world's first schools, where strict instructors beat students for misbehavior or sloppy work. A clay tablet from the eighteenth century B.C.E. describes the life of a pupil who spent twenty-four days a month in school and was frequently beaten: "My teacher said: 'Your hand [writing] is unsatisfactory.' [He] caned me. I [begin to hate] the scribal art."[5] However, because cuneiform eventually transformed pictures into phonetic sounds, it made the written word more accessible, even for people whose only goal was a good recipe for a meal of red broth and meat.

Writing became crucial in history for a number of reasons. First, written language made it easier to express abstract ideas and create an intellectual life based on a body of literature. The

Hirmer Verlag Munchen

Overview of Early City of Uruk This photo shows the ruins of one of the earliest Mesopotamian cities, a rich source of art objects and fine architecture. The best-known king of Uruk was the legendary Gilgamesh.

oldest known signed poetry was composed by Enheduanna **(en-who-DWAHN-ah)**, a Sumerian priestess and princess living around 2300 B.C.E. Royal women were often authors. In addition, a written language based on clearly understood symbols allowed communication among people who spoke different languages but understood the same written symbols. For example, the number 5 is understood today the same way by Spanish speakers, who pronounce it "cinco," and German speakers, who say "funf." Finally, writing was one key to the interaction among societies. It not only gave a strong sense of identity to all who shared the language but also eventually encouraged the spread of trade and culture, including religion, to those outside a particular homeland.

Sumerian Inventions

Sumerians were innovative in many areas. They pioneered the first use of the wheel, glass, and fertilizer, inventions that we still live with today. Sumerians also created some of the earliest calendars, which were based on their observations of the movements of various celestial bodies, and one of the first mathematical systems, based on the number 60. Remnants of this system can be seen today in our 60-minute hours and 60-second minutes. Many other peoples eventually adopted all of these inventions. Humanity also owes to the Sumerians the decision to divide night and day into twelve hours each. Like us, the Sumerians enjoyed alcoholic beverages. Although they were not the first to convert barley into beer, they designated a special goddess to supervise its production, called Ninkasi or "the lady who fills the mouth." The many taverns fostered early drinking songs: "I will summon brewers and cupbearers to serve us floods of beer and keep it passing round! Our hearts enchanted and our souls radiant."[6]

The Akkadian Empire and Its Rivals

Sargon's Empire

Eventually the political structure of the region changed. For centuries each city had its own king who ruled the people in the name of the city's god. This independence ended about 2350 B.C.E. when Sargon **(SAHR-gone)**, the ruler of Akkad **(AH-kahd)**, a region just north of Sumer whose capital was Agade, conquered Uruk as a prelude to uniting the other Sumerian cities under the rule of his family. Sargon formed the world's first known empire, a large state controlling other societies through conquest or domination. The Akkadians enslaved many other people in addition to the Sumerians; in fact, slaves constituted perhaps a third of the empire's population. Under Sargon trade between Mesopotamia and India reached a peak. Indeed, Akkad became the major center for regional trade, and merchant ships from as far as Oman **(O-mahn)** in eastern Arabia and, even further away, India, docked at the wharves, carrying copper and various exotic products.

Sargon's empire soon came into conflict with one created by another imperial city, Ebla **(EBB-luh)**, in northern Mesopotamia. Ebla had created a large empire based on trade that stretched from eastern Turkey to the ancient city of Mari **(MAH-ree)**, several hundred miles north of Akkad. The Akkadian Empire was destroyed by the twenty-first century B.C.E., probably from a combination of internal conflicts, external attacks, and less rainfall. A disastrous drought between 2200 and 1900 B.C.E. affected much of Eurasia. Mesopotamian societies such as Sumer and Akkad were powerless against abrupt climate change. Sumerian legends expressed dread of the periodic droughts: "The famine was severe, nothing was produced. The fields are not watered. In all the lands there was no vegetation [and] only weeds grew."[7] Irrigation canals silted up and settlements became ghost towns as people migrated.

As the Akkadian Empire collapsed, a new Sumerian dynasty led by Ur took over much of the lower valley between 2100 and 2000 B.C.E., forming the Neo-Sumerian Empire. Some Ur kings boasted of their commitment to art and intellectual life, one ordering that the places of learning

The Royal Standard of Ur This mosaic from around 2500 B.C.E., made of inlaid shells and limestone, was found in a royal tomb. It depicts various aspects of life in the Mesopotamian city-state of Ur. The bottom panel shows a four-wheeled battle wagon drawn by a horselike animal. The middle panel features soldiers wearing armor and helmets. The top panel shows war prisoners being brought before the king.

British Museum/Michael Holford

should never be closed. But Ur was devastated by a coalition of enemies and sacked and burned along with other Sumerian cities. Its temples were destroyed, its populations killed or enslaved, and its treasures plundered. A surviving lamentation describes the destruction of Ur: "Ur is destroyed, bitter is its lament. The country's blood now fills its holes like hot bronze in a mould. Our temple is destroyed, the gods have abandoned us, like migrating birds. Smoke lies on our city like a shroud."[8]

The Akkadians, Eblaites, and the later Sumerians established the first empires in history, even though their creations were short-lived and were not the large bureaucratic organizations we see in later empires. They were largely collections of city-states that acknowledged one city as overlord. It soon became clear that whoever had the best army would dominate Mesopotamia.

SECTION SUMMARY

- The first urban societies of Mesopotamia developed in the Tigris-Euphrates Basin.
- Sumerian society was hierarchical and patriarchal.
- The earliest writing system was probably the cuneiform system, developed by the Sumerians.
- The world's first empire, the Akkadian Empire, was founded by Sargon in an area just north of the Sumerians.

Later Mesopotamian Societies and Their Legacies, 2000–600 B.C.E.

What were some of the main features of Mesopotamian societies?

The Sumerians and Akkadians established a pattern of city living, state building, and imperial expansion. From 2000 B.C.E. and continuing for the next 1,500 years, a series of peoples coming mainly from the north—the Babylonians, Hittites, and Assyrians—successively dominated Mesopotamia and created new empires. Each made important contributions to the politics, laws, culture, and thought of the region. This pattern changed only when the entire area was incorporated into the Persian Empire in 539 B.C.E.

The Babylonians and Hittites

The Babylonians

Several states dominated Mesopotamia during the second millennium B.C.E., beginning with Babylon. In 1800 B.C.E. the Amorites **(AM-uh-rites)**, a Semitic people, conquered Babylon, a city about 300 miles north of the Persian Gulf, and gradually extended their control in the region. Babylon's most famous king, Hammurabi **(HAM-uh-rah-bee)**, who ruled from 1792 to 1750 B.C.E., reunified Mesopotamia. Hammurabi had nearly three hundred laws collected and posted on a black basalt pillar. These laws were designed, he said, "to make justice appear in the land, to destroy the evil and the wicked [so] that the strong might not oppress the weak."[9] It remains famous today because some of its principles appeared later in the laws of the Hebrews and also because of its most noted principle, the law of retaliation: an eye for an eye and a tooth for a tooth.

The Hittites

By 1595 B.C.E. the Babylonian Empire had disintegrated in the face of attacks by the Hittites **(HIT-ites)**, an Indo-European people who moved into Mesopotamia from their base in central Anatolia. The Hittites were most famous for their later use of iron weapons, which were superior to those made of bronze, but these had not yet been invented when the Hittites invaded Mesopotamia. The Hittites expanded their power until they met the equally strong Egyptians in Syria and Palestine. The Hittites may also have used the first known biological weapons, since one of their tactics was to send plague victims into enemy lands. The Hittite Empire dominated various parts of western Asia from 1600 to 1200 B.C.E. but treated their subjects less harshly than the Babylonians. They followed a tolerant attitude toward other religions and adopted many Mesopotamian gods, establishing a tradition of tolerance in the region.

The Assyrian Empire and Regional Supremacy

In 1115 B.C.E. the Assyrians **(uh-SEER-e-uhns)** began conquering an empire in western Asia that was eventually larger than any before, the first that was more than a collection of city-states. They did this by creating a large, well-organized military; systematically using terror against enemies; and devising methods of bureaucratic organization that later empires imitated. One of the greatest kings, Tiglath-pileser **(TIG-lath-pih-LEE-zuhr)** III (745–727 B.C.E.), conquered the entire eastern shore of the Mediterranean. Later Assyrian rulers added Egypt to the empire. One

Assyrian king described himself with some accuracy as "obedient to his gods and receiving the tribute of the four corners of the world."[10] Using iron weapons while their enemies still relied on softer bronze ones, the Assyrians launched armies of over 50,000 men that were carefully divided into a core of infantrymen aided by cavalry and horse-drawn chariots. They conducted sieges in which they used battering rams and tunnels against the city walls of their enemies. They also employed guerrilla, or irregular hit-and-run, tactics when fighting in the forests or mountains.

Assyrian Government

Assyrian kings created a systematic bureaucracy to rule over several million people in the Tigris-Euphrates heartland alone. To improve their administrative control, the rulers used horsemen to create an early version of the "pony express," which allowed them to send messages hundreds of miles within a week. Some kings were both brutal and learned. Ashurbanipal **(ah-shur-BAH-nugh-pahl)** (680–627 B.C.E.) founded a great library to collect tablets from all over the country. He boasted of his learning, noting that, in school, he learned to solve complex mathematical problems and discovered the "hidden treasure" of writing.

Violence and the Fall of the Assyrians

The Assyrians were most remembered, and deplored, for their brutality, which ultimately contributed to their downfall. King Ashurbanipal bragged about mutilating and burning prisoners. After destroying the state of Elam in Iran, he boasted that "like the onset of a terrible hurricane I overwhelmed Elam. I cut off the head of . . . their braggart king. In countless numbers I killed his warriors." As to the capital city, "I destroyed it, I devastated it, I burned it with fire."[11] Soldiers routinely looted cities, destroyed crops, and both flailed and impaled their enemies. To prevent revolts, the Assyrians often simply moved people to another part of the vast empire. For example, according to legends, inhabitants of one of the two Hebrew kingdoms were sent to Mesopotamia, where they disappeared from history (see Chapter 3). Yet the Assyrians also tolerated other religions, a policy that allowed the Hebrew faith to survive the conquest of their state.

The terror tactics undermined Assyrian popularity. In 612 B.C.E., a coalition including the Chaldeans **(kal-DEE-uhns)** (also known as neo-Babylonians) captured the Assyrian capital at Nineveh **(NIN-uh-vuh)**. The Chaldeans, who formed the last Mesopotamian empire, adopted the Assyrian administrative system and flourished from 626 B.C.E. until they were conquered by the much larger Persian Empire in 539 B.C.E. Their most memorable ruler, Nebuchadnezzar **(NAB-oo-kuhd-nez-uhr)** II (r. 605–562 B.C.E.), a brutal strongman, rebuilt Babylon and adorned it with magnificent palaces and the elaborate terraced "hanging gardens," which were built to please one of his wives and which became famous throughout the ancient world. Nebuchadnezzar led the conquest of the remaining Hebrew kingdom in 586 B.C.E.

Mesopotamian Law

Hammurabi's Code

Several very different documents tell us much about Mesopotamian life and beliefs. The eighteenth-century B.C.E. Law Code of Hammurabi gives us a good look at the social structures of this early urban society (see Profile: Hammurabi the Lawgiver). Hammurabi's Code makes clear both what people valued and how people themselves were valued; it is also one of the earliest systematic records we have of how ancient peoples viewed laws, government, and social norms. The Code probably reflected a high crime rate in the cities, no doubt because of the tremendous gap between rich and poor. Families were responsible for the crimes of any of their members. To keep lines of inheritance clear, Hammurabi prescribed harsh punishments for sexual infidelity and incest, as did many societies. Women who violated social norms generally suffered harsher punishments than men, just as the eyes and teeth of poor men or slaves were worth less than the same body parts among the upper classes. Each slave was branded with the owner's symbol, and some endured harsh lives of forced labor. Yet, while it may seem contradictory to their status as property, some slaves also owned their own assets, carried on business, and even acquired their own slaves.

The Code also addressed economic issues. In this class-conscious society, a surgeon could lose his hand if his patient was a free man who failed to survive the operation, certainly a disincentive to take up medicine. If the patient was a slave, however, the surgeon had only to replace him with another. If a builder's house collapsed and killed its inhabitants, the builder could be executed. The existence of a thriving commercial class is confirmed by the existence of high interest rates on loans. In general, the punishments in Hammurabi's Law Code tell us how precarious life must have been in this society, where even a single small break in an irrigation canal wall could spell disaster.

Hammurabi the Lawgiver

No person personifies Mesopotamian society better than Hammurabi, a Babylonian king (r. 1792–1750 B.C.E.) who was also at times a diplomat, warrior, builder of temples, digger of canals, and, most famously, lawgiver. Many surviving tablets, inscriptions, and letters, some from Hammurabi himself, made the king and his era the best documented in Mesopotamian history. He seems to have been a good administrator and able general who governed fairly and efficiently. Like other Mesopotamian kings, Hammurabi probably had a chief queen and various concubines, as well as several sons and daughters.

When Hammurabi became king, Babylon (which meant "gateway of the gods" in Akkadian) was an insignificant city-state. To expand its power, Hammurabi shrewdly allied with the powerful king of Ashur, probably by becoming a vassal, and allowed him to conquer some nearby cities. For some years Hammurabi's small domain remained one of many rival states, as noted by one of his officials: "There is no king who by himself is strongest. Ten or fifteen kings follow Hammurabi." Like other kings, Hammurabi had intelligence agents in other cities keeping him abreast of important developments such as pending alliances and troop movements. A spy for another king became close to him, writing that "whenever Hammurabi is perturbed by some matter, he always sends for me. He tells me whatever is troubling him, and all of the important information I continually report to my lord." After his army repulsed an invasion by a coalition of rivals, a confident Hammurabi engaged in a long series of wars that added all of southern Mesopotamia and then much of the north to his kingdom. Finally he conquered the strongest power, his former ally Ashur.

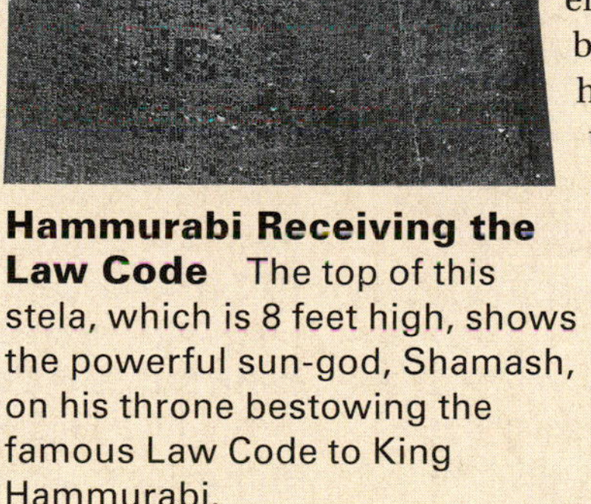
Hirmer Verlag Munchen

Hammurabi Receiving the Law Code The top of this stela, which is 8 feet high, shows the powerful sun-god, Shamash, on his throne bestowing the famous Law Code to King Hammurabi.

Kingship brought responsibilities. Hammurabi's letters reveal him sitting in an office at his palace, dictating to a secretary who recorded his orders or thoughts with a reed stylus on a clay tablet. Most letters conveyed commands to governors. Messengers brought letters from officials, which the secretary read aloud. In his replies, Hammurabi tried to resolve problems, for example, suggesting ways to clear a flooded shipping channel, warning delinquent tax collectors of their obligations, punishing corrupt officials, improving agricultural productivity, or protecting frontiers. He also held daily audiences for petitioners seeking justice. Many decisions concerned temple property and administration, indicating the link between church and state.

Hammurabi realized the need to have uniform laws in his diverse country. He compiled older laws, recent legal decisions, and social customs, arranged them systematically, and placed them on an 8-foot block of basalt stone in the temple of Babylon's patron god, Marduk. At the top, an artist pictured Hammurabi receiving the symbols of kingship from Shamash, the sun-god and lawgiver. The Code of 282 laws informed citizens of their rights and demonstrated to both gods and people that the king was doing his job to uphold justice in a moral universe.

For close to four millennia, the principles of this ancient Mesopotamian law code have intrigued us. The Code reflected the harsh views of the era. It mandated two kinds of punishments, a monetary penalty and a retribution in kind, and the harshness of the punishment depended on the class of the people involved. The Code recognized three social classes: nobles and landowners, commoners, and slaves. Many of Hammurabi's laws discouraged burglary by prescribing instant death for those caught. This emphasis may have reflected the fact that mud-brick homes were not very secure. On the other hand, prostitution was legal. Some laws protected women and children from abuse and arbitrary treatment. For example, a husband who divorced his wife because she bore no sons had to return the dowry she brought into the marriage and forfeit the money he had given her parents for a bridal price. Since the Hebrews borrowed some of these laws, often in modified form, and passed them into Christian and Islamic traditions, Hammurabi's legacy remains influential today.

THINKING ABOUT THE PROFILE

1. How did Hammurabi increase the power of Babylon?
2. What were the purposes of his great Law Code?

Note: Quotations from William H. Stiebing, Jr., *Ancient Near Eastern History and Culture* (New York: Longman, 2003), 88–89.

Mesopotamian Religion and Literature

Gods and Godesses

Like most early people, the Mesopotamians believed in a host of gods and goddesses, such as Inanna, later called Ishtar **(ISH-tar)**, the beautiful goddess of love who created desire. But this polytheistic religion imposed no moral demands. These divinities came with human weaknesses, yet they were powerful enough to punish humans, who were created to serve them. People saw themselves as subject to the gods' whims. The gods were housed in massive and opulent temples, where ritual ceremonies were held. The Babylonians and later the Assyrians changed the names of some of the earlier Sumerian gods but maintained the basic Sumerian view of the universe.

Epic of Gilgamesh

The *Epic of Gilgamesh* **(GILL-guh-mesh)**, first written down about 2000 B.C.E. but revised and retold by Mesopotamians for 1,500 years, reveals some of their religious values and attitudes. Perhaps humanity's first epic adventure story, *Gilgamesh* echoes Hammurabi's view of the world as a dangerous place in which happiness is hard to find. Although only one part of a very rich legacy of literature and mythology, *Gilgamesh* had the most enduring and widespread influence, enriching the traditions of varied Eurasian societies.

Primary Source: The *Epic of Gilgamesh* Find out how Gilgamesh's friend Enkidu propels him on a quest for immortality, and whether or not that quest is successful.

In one version of the Gilgamesh story, the hero, modeled after a real king in Uruk about 2750 B.C.E. and created to be two-thirds god and one-third man, engages in a series of adventures involving both the gods and men. With his friend Enkidu, Gilgamesh challenges and defeats the evil but divine giant who guards a mysterious cedar forest. Following this adventure, Gilgamesh rejects a proposal from Ishtar, the goddess of love, telling her that she is fickle and recounting the disagreeable things she has done to her previous lovers, such as turning one of them into a wolf. In revenge at being snubbed, Ishtar causes the death of Enkidu. Reflecting on the death of his friend, Gilgamesh decides to search for the key to eternal life, an ultimately futile quest involving many setbacks that reflects the general pessimism of Mesopotamian culture. A Uruk master scribe lamented around 1300 B.C.E.: "Gilgamesh, what you seek you will never find. For when the Gods created Man they let death be his lot, eternal life they withheld. Let your every day be full of joy, love the child that holds your hand, let your wife delight in your embrace, for these alone are concerns of humanity."[12]

Legacy of *Gilgamesh*

Scholars have noted the similarities between this story and stories found in the later Hebrew book of Genesis. In both there is a paradise: the garden of Eden for the Hebrews, Dilmun for the Mesopotamians. In both a great flood destroys humankind. In both a man challenges the god(s). And in both a serpent comes between a man and immortality. However, although the writer or writers of Genesis may been influenced by *Gilgamesh,* there are some differences in tone and attitude between the Babylonian and Hebrew versions. In the Hebrew story, God sends a flood to punish humans for evil living. In more urban Mesopotamia, where floods were frequent and destructive, the gods "decide to exterminate mankind" because "the uproar of mankind is intolerable and sleep is no longer possible by reason of the babel."[13] But a dissenting god causes his favorite mortal to survive by building a boat and loading it with his family and "the seed of all living creatures, the game of the field, and all the craftsmen."

The parallels between the Gilgamesh legend and Genesis remind us that the Gilgamesh story became widely known far beyond Mesopotamia. Some motifs can be found in the literature of the Greeks, such as the Homeric epics. They also reappear in the much later Islamic period, such as the stories of Aladdin and Sinbad, and they are still found in the folk cultures of some villages. The Gilgamesh epic became one of the many unique traditions that shaped the societies of southwestern Asia and made them different from other early societies such as India and Egypt.

SECTION SUMMARY

- The Babylonians, Hittites, Assyrians, and Chaldeans created empires in Mesopotamia.
- The Babylonian king Hammurabi created a legal framework that included harsh punishments and reflected strict class divisions.
- The Assyrian Empire, known for its brutality, dominated a large region but was finally defeated by a coalition of enemies.
- The *Epic of Gilgamesh,* which shows parallels with the book of Genesis, reflects Mesopotamian values and perspectives, including a pessimistic view of life.

THE EARLIEST INDIAN AND CENTRAL ASIAN SOCIETIES, 6000–1500 B.C.E.

What were some of the distinctive features of the Harappan cities?

India developed a society with cultural features vastly different from those of the Middle East, Europe, or China. Aided by environmental factors, some Indians made the transition to farming very early, and the first cities and states east of Mesopotamia were founded around 2600

B.C.E. (see Chronology: Ancient India and Central Asia, 7000–600 B.C.E.). Most scholars trace the foundations of Indian urban society to the city-states and the widespread Bronze Age culture they shared, often called **Harappan** (huh-RAP-un), that were centered in the Indus (IN-duhs) River Valley and nearby rivers in what is now Pakistan and northwest India. Harappan culture eventually covered some 300,000 square miles, the largest in geographical extent of the ancient societies. Although the Harappans built no pyramids like the Egyptians or ziggurats like the Sumerians, they developed a remarkable society. To the north, an urban society also developed in Central Asia.

Harappan Name given to the city-states and the widespread Bronze Age culture they shared that were centered in the Indus River Valley and nearby rivers in northwest India.

South Asian Environments and the Rise of Farming

Geographical Foundations

River valley environments strongly shaped the early societies of India, just as they did Mesopotamia, Egypt, and China. The Indian subcontinent, about half the size of Europe, is rimmed by the Indian Ocean and the Himalayan Mountains, which boast the half dozen highest peaks in the world, including Mt. Everest at nearly 30,000 feet. The Himalayas, which stretch some 1,500 miles from east to west, inhibited regular communication between China and India. Just north of the Himalayas, the Tibetan Plateau is the source of great rivers, including the Indus and Ganges in India, the Yellow and Yangzi in China, and the Irrawaddy and Mekong in Southeast Asia, which eventually reach great plains and deltas. The land proved highly fertile in these river basins, allowing for productive farming and dense settlement. Rice and wheat became the staple crops for most peoples in both South and East Asia, and scavenging animals like chickens and pigs were more important food sources than beef cattle, which requires extensive pasture.

South Asian Regions

As with all societies, India's distinctive features resulted in part from its physical environment and climate. The fertile north Indian plains, watered by the Indus and Ganges Rivers, are relatively flat and so encouraged cultural unity and the formation of cities and kingdoms. By contrast, mountainous south India developed more cultural diversity. The southern peoples and languages differ greatly from those of north India. Other regions with highly distinctive local cultures include Bengal, framed by the delta of the Ganges River, and the fertile island of Sri Lanka (once known as Ceylon), just a few miles off India's southern tip.

The tropical climate affected Indian life. Some areas enjoy high rainfall, especially in the south and northeast, but much of the northwest is today desert. Although the annual rains sustain life, seasonal flooding can be a chronic problem. Water has been an especially sacred commodity in Indian life and thought, and a frequent subject of literature. Because they had many domesticated cattle, most Indians learned to consume dairy products, including yogurt, a local invention. Thanks to surpluses of wheat and barley, by 3000 B.C.E. the population of the Indus Valley may have reached 1 million, and regional trading networks emerged, setting the stage for the emergence of cities.

Harappan Cities

Around 2600 B.C.E., the first Indian urban society emerged from regional cultures in the Indus River Valley, a semiarid region similar ecologically to the Nile and Tigris-Euphrates Valleys (see Map 2.2). Along the banks of the Indus, which later inspired the English term *India,* and nearby rivers such as the Saraswati, a vibrant urban-based culture thrived for hundreds of years and planted some seeds for the rich Indian culture that endures to the present. Silt spread by regular river floods served as a natural fertilizer, while nearby forests provided enough wood for baking the bricks used in building cities. Like the Nile in Egypt, the flat, easily navigable Indus and its tributary rivers gave Harappan society considerable uniformity. Most of the Harappan cities were in the Punjab (PUHN-jab) and Sind provinces of modern Pakistan, a crossroads of major trading routes, but some were hundreds of miles to the west or east. Indeed, the Indus culture covered an area far larger than the Mesopotamian and Egyptian cultures combined. The two major Indus cities, called by archaeologists Harappa and Mohenjo-Daro (moe-hen-joe-DAHR-oh), stood 400 miles apart. The 1,500 Harappan cities and towns contained a total population of perhaps 5 million people at their zenith.

CHRONOLOGY
Ancient India and Central Asia, 7000–600 B.C.E.

7000–6000 B.C.E. Agriculture begins in Indus River Basin

2600–2500 B.C.E. Harappan cities established

2300–1900 B.C.E. Harappan cities at height

2200–1800 B.C.E. Oxus cities in Central Asia

1900–1750 B.C.E. Harappan society collapses in Indus Basin

1600–1400 B.C.E. Beginning of Aryan migrations into India

1500–1000 B.C.E. Aryan age of conquest and settlement

1000–700 B.C.E. Compilation of *Brahmanas*

1000–450 B.C.E. Height of Indo-Aryan synthesis

800–600 B.C.E. Compilation of *Upanishads*

Map 2.2
Harappan Culture and Aryan Migrations

The Harappan culture emerged in the city-states of the Indus River Basin. They had collapsed by around 1500 B.C.E., when the Aryan peoples from Iran began migrating into India and setting up states.

e Interactive Map

City Life

All the cities had many common features, in construction as well as in society, government, religion, and culture. The uniformity among Harappan cities reveals a society that valued order, organization, and cleanliness. Administrators used the same pattern, carefully laying out the cities using a north-south grid pattern with wide streets and large rectangular city blocks. They built most buildings of sturdy baked brick molded to a standardized size. Residential and commercial districts were separated from a smaller area for public affairs. Shops probably lined the main streets. The largest city, Harappa, some 3 $^{1}/_{3}$ miles in circumference, contained perhaps 80,000 people at its height. Massive brick ramparts 40 feet thick at their base partially protected it from the river waters and any potential human attackers. Large granaries provide evidence of wealth and stored voluminous supplies, perhaps of wheat for the local population, or export goods. The Harappan people had exceptional housing for ancient times. More affluent residents lived in spacious homes constructed on strong brick foundations with interior courtyards that provided considerable privacy. But even the common people enjoyed well-built accommodations.

The urban Harappans enjoyed the most advanced sanitation system in the ancient world. Most houses had a bathroom and drains to carry away the wastewater. The covered drains along the city streets were a technological masterpiece and more sanitary than those found in many modern cities. Indeed, not until modern times did urban sanitation anywhere duplicate and then exceed Harappan models. The close attention to providing and carrying away water and the huge public baths suggest an emphasis on washing and personal cleanliness for ritual purity, which later became important in Indian religion.

Dravidian A language family whose speakers are the great majority of the population in southern India.

Scholars debate the identity of the Harappan people. Most believe that they spoke a **Dravidian (druh-VID-ee-uhn)** language, although speakers of other languages may also have lived there. The term *Dravidian* refers to a specific language family and the people who speak these languages. Most modern Dravidian speakers live in southern India, where they are the great majority of the population.

Josephine Powell, photographer. Courtesy of Special Collections, Fine Arts Library, Harvard College

Ruins of Mohenjo-Daro The photo shows the great bath at Mohenjo-Daro. Like modern Indians, the Harappans valued bathing for hygienic and possibly religious reasons.

Harappan Society and Its Beliefs

The Harappan governments, social system, and religious beliefs remain a puzzle. The available evidence for an organized monarchy is thin, and there were no elaborate palaces, temples, or monuments glorifying leaders. Each city was probably independent, perhaps governed by some powerful guild of merchants or a council of commercial, landowning, and religious leaders. The ruins contain few weapons, suggesting that, in contrast to Mesopotamia, war was uncommon. But some people owned beautiful objects of personal adornment, such as necklaces and beads, while others apparently lacked such valuable possessions. The ruins also contain many toys made from clay or wood, indicating a prosperous society that valued leisure for children.

Government and Gender Relations

Harappan society had unusual gender relations for that era, different from the rigid patriarchies that characterized Mesopotamia or China as governments grew more powerful. Apparently Harappan husbands moved into their wives' households after marriage, a practice that suggests a matrilineal system. Yet some customs harmed women. At least some Harappans may have practiced *sati* (suh-TEE), the custom of a widow killing herself by jumping onto the funeral pyre as her dead husband is being cremated.

Arts and Writing

Harappan city-dwellers developed an artistic appreciation, mixing art with religion and even commerce. They made small, square, clay seals, possibly used by merchants for branding their wares. Some of the seals contain brilliant portraits of indigenous animals, including bulls and water buffaloes as well as the tigers, elephants, and rhinoceros that inhabited the nearby forests. Small bronze statues of dancers suggest the Harappans enjoyed dance. Most scholars argue that the Harappans created a written language by at least 2600 B.C.E., although other historians question whether the Harappans had a true writing system comparable to the Mesopotamians and Chinese. By Harappan times the seals, pottery, and various clay tablets contained some four hundred different signs that were completely unrelated to the scripts of Mesopotamia and Egypt. Unfortunately, modern scholars have not been able to decipher the Indus language. Most likely many of the signs represent the names of merchants, businesses, or the commodities being sold.

Harappan Religion

Shiva The Hindu god of destruction and of fertility and the harvest.

Some Harappan religious notions contributed to Hinduism, a religion that developed after Harappan times. For example, one of the seals features a human figure sitting in a yogalike position, surrounded by various animals. The figure appears to have multiple faces, a regular feature of later Hindu icons, and may depict what later became the great Hindu god **Shiva** (SHEEV-uh) in one of his major roles as "Lord of the Beasts." Harappans apparently already worshiped Shiva in his dual role as god of destruction and of fertility and the harvest. Possibly the later Hindu notions of reincarnation and the endless wheel of life derived from Harappan beliefs. Mother-goddess worship seems also to have been prominent in Harappan religious life, as it was in the Fertile Crescent and ancient Europe. Many small clay figurines featuring exaggerated breasts and hips may have represented the mother goddess. Such artistic representations of voluptuous female deities remain common today in India. The goddesses symbolized earth and the life-bearing nature of women. Whereas a female orientation largely disappeared in the religions of many other societies, it remained prominent in Hinduism.

The Harappan Economy and the Wider World

Agriculture

The Harappan cities were hubs tied to surrounding regions, especially southwestern and Central Asia, through trade and transportation networks that fostered extensive contact. This foreign trade grew out of a diverse local economy based on cultivating barley and wheat and producing cotton and metal products. These innovations helped Harappan society to remain stable and prosperous for hundreds of years. A highly sophisticated irrigation system and animal husbandry aided farming. Harappans or their ancestors domesticated the camel, zebu (oxen), elephant, chicken, and water buffalo. The raising of fowl enriched the diet, and water buffalo and zebu greatly aided farming as draft animals. Possibly the Harappans worshiped these two animals, becoming the basis for the later respect accorded cows in Hinduism.

Harappans also made other long-lasting contributions. They invented cotton cloth and made cotton textiles for clothing, one of ancient India's major gifts to the world. For many centuries, cotton spinning and weaving remained the most significant Indian industry, producing materials for eager markets both at home and abroad. Cotton was a chief item in the interregional trading system, shipped in bulk to Mesopotamia. Since there were few metals in the Indus Basin, the Harappans obtained metals in exchange for cotton and other products.

Harappan Seal The seal from Mohenjo-Daro features a humped bull. The writing at the top has yet to be deciphered.

J. M. Kenoyer/Courtesy, Department of Archaeology and Museums, Government of Pakistan

The desirable Harappan agricultural and manufactured products led to extensive foreign trade that linked India with the wider world of western and Central Asia. A huge dock, massive granaries, and specialized factories at the coastal port of Lothal reflected a high-volume maritime trade. Many Harappan seals found at the Mesopotamian city of Ur suggest a steady trade between 2300 and 2000 B.C.E. Bahrain Island in the Persian Gulf functioned as a major crossroads for the Harappan-Sumerian trade. The Harappans exported surplus food, cotton, timber products, copper, and gold, as well as luxury items such as pearls, precious stone products, ivory combs, beads, spices, peacock feathers, and inlay goods made from shell or bone. The Harappans imported precious stones from southern India and silver, turquoise, and tin from Persia and Afghanistan.

The Decline and Collapse of Harappan Society

Eventually, Harappan society declined, for reasons not altogether clear. Sometime between 1900 and 1750 B.C.E. a combination of factors disrupted the urban environment of this once wealthy and highly efficient society. By 1700 B.C.E. most of the Harappan cities had been destroyed or abandoned, although a considerable rural population remained. The decay is obvious in the archaeological excavations. Seals and writing began to disappear. The careful grid pattern for city streets was abandoned, the drainage systems deteriorated, and even home sizes were reduced. Some evidence points to plundering and banditry.

Collapse

Harappan decline may have resulted from several factors. Perhaps the Harappans exhausted the land. Some evidence points to ecological catastrophes resulting from climate change, deforestation, increased flooding, excessive irrigation of marginal lands, and soil deterioration. Apparently rainfall decreased significantly, one major river, the Sarawati, drying up entirely. These catastrophes probably led to economic breakdown. The crop surpluses that had long sustained the cities disappeared, and people abandoned farms. Perhaps disease epidemics weakened the population.

The end of some of the Indus Valley cities may have been sudden, the result perhaps of a disastrous flood. A mud slide after an earthquake may have temporarily dammed the Indus River or one of its tributaries, unleashing an awesome flood that quickly overwhelmed low-lying cities. The hoards of jewelry, skeletons buried in debris, and cooking pots found strewn across kitchens indicate hastily abandoned homes. The rising floodwaters may have been accompanied by more earthquakes. The chaos of the last days spread rapidly along the river. Harappa, located on higher ground, and some other cities survived a while longer, although with much reduced populations.

The fate of the Harappan people and their cultures is unclear. Some cities east of the Indus Valley remained populated for several more centuries, practicing modified forms of Harappan culture until around 1300 B.C.E. Many Harappans may have migrated into central and southern India, mixing with local Dravidian populations. They carried with them a culture, technology, and agriculture that contributed to the Indian society to come. The calamities left the remaining Indus peoples weak and unable to resist later migrations of peoples from outside.

Central Asian Environments and Oxus Cities

Central Asia is the vast area of plains (**steppes**), deserts, and mountains that stretches from the Ural Mountains and Caspian Sea eastward to Tibet, western China, and Mongolia. Before modern times Central Asians played a role in history far greater than their relatively small populations would suggest, not only as invaders and sometimes conquerors but also as middlemen in the long-distance trade that developed on the land routes between China, India, the Middle East, and Europe.

steppes The plains of Central Asia.

Much of Central Asia offered a harsh living environment suitable mainly for pastoralists. It was inhabited largely by people speaking Ural-Altaic languages, including various Turkik and Mongol tongues. Many different peoples lived in the region known today as Turkestan, from east of the Caspian Sea to Xinjiang **(SIN-john)** on China's western frontier. Large-scale population movements and frequent warfare between competing tribal confederations became common. Most of the steppe societies had skilled horsemen and were led by warrior chieftains. Some Central Asian peoples attacked and occasionally conquered northern China, and over the centuries various Central Asian peoples also migrated through the mountain ranges into northwest India.

Central Asian Societies

Although much of Central Asia was steppe lands, some areas supported city life. Archaeologists regularly find previously unknown sites, such as Jiroft in southern Iran, to expand our knowledge. In recent years these discoveries have revealed an early urban society in Central Asia, which some call the Oxus **(OX-uhs)**, after the river that runs through the area. The Oxus society apparently thrived between 2200 and 1800 B.C.E., when the Harappan culture was also at its height, building walled cities with mud-brick buildings around desert oases in what is now Uzbekistan and Turkmenistan. Enjoying a wetter climate than now, the people grew wheat and barley. They also forged bronze axes, carved figurines of women from stone and ivory, and decorated pottery. A tiny stamp seal with letter-like symbols dated to 2300 B.C.E. is evidence for writing, and so far the writing has not been linked to any other society. The Oxus cities, perhaps independent city-states, were situated along the "Silk Road" trade routes between India and China, suggesting that this trade may be older than is often thought. They were closely linked to the Harappans and probably traded with China, Jiroft, and Mesopotamia. Eventually the cities were abandoned and, over the centuries, buried by sand.

SECTION SUMMARY

- The earliest Indian urban society, the Harappan, emerged in the Indus River Valley around 2600 B.C.E.
- The peaceful Harappans had well-planned cities with advanced sanitation, a culture that gave women high status, and a written language.
- The Harappans invented cotton cloth, and Harappan cities enjoyed extensive foreign trade with western and Central Asia.
- Harappan cities declined for unknown reasons, possibly due to environmental catastrophe.
- The steppes of Central Asia were home to mostly horsemen, but evidence of an urban society has been discovered on the Oxus River.

THE ARYANS AND A NEW INDIAN SOCIETY, 1500–600 B.C.E.

How did Indian society and the Hindu religion emerge from the mixing of Aryan and local cultures?

Aryans Indo-European-speaking nomadic pastoralists who migrated from Iran into northwest India.

Indo-Aryan synthesis The fusion of Aryan and Dravidian cultures in India over many centuries.

Throughout India's long history, many people migrated from elsewhere into the subcontinent, some of them conquering parts of India, and the assimilation of these various newcomers resulted in an increasingly diverse Indian society. One such group of invaders were the **Aryans** (AIR-ee-unzs), Indo-European-speaking nomadic pastoralists who migrated into northwest India, expanded across northern India, and introduced new traditions to the area. The Aryan expansion between 1500 and 1000 B.C.E. built the foundation for a new society that mixed Aryan culture with the traditions of the indigenous peoples, including the Dravidians. Over many centuries a fusion of Aryan and Dravidian cultures occurred that historians label the **Indo-Aryan synthesis**, forging a new social system and Hinduism, a religion of diverse beliefs. But the Aryans had a greater impact in the north than in the mostly Dravidian south, which retained its own languages and writing systems. Despite regular contact with western, Central, and Southeast Asia, the patterns that developed were so distinctive and enduring that India even today is unlike any other society.

The Aryan Peoples and the Vedas

Aryan Migrations

Most scholars agree that the Aryans began migrating by horse-drawn chariot from Iran (the Persian word for "Aryan") or Turkestan into northwestern India between 1600 and 1400 B.C.E., after the collapse of the Harappan cities. The migration to India came when rainfall in the Indus region was increasing again, improving economic conditions. Some historians and Indian nationalists argue that Aryan settlement in India was far older and that the Harappans may have been Aryans. However, in the mainstream view, the Aryans arrived in small groups over several centuries, bringing with them a rich oral literature and unusual ideas about government, society, and religion. For the next 500 years, the Aryans expanded throughout northern India as more arrived. But archaeologists have found little material evidence, such as pots or weapons, that might tell us more about Aryan migration and settlement. Furthermore, unlike the Chinese and Greeks, ancient Indians never developed a tradition of historiography, the study and writing of history, perhaps because their conceptions of time emphasized the temporary nature of existence.

Vedas The Aryans' "books of knowledge," the principal source of religious belief for Hindus: a vast collection of sacred hymns to the gods and thoughts about religion, philosophy, and magic.

Much of what we know about the ancient Aryans comes from their literature, the **Vedas** (VAY-duhs) ("books of knowledge"). A vast collection of sacred hymns to the gods and thoughts about religion, philosophy, and magic, the Vedas were based on oral accounts carefully preserved by bards, the memory experts of each Indo-European tribe, through a vibrant oral tradition. The Vedas reflected the world-view of the priestly class and were already old when written down. They are the principal early source of Hindu religious belief. From the Vedas we can infer that the Aryans were organized into tribes that frequently moved their settlements. Their class system consisted of warriors, priests, and commoners. They were a cattle-raising people, as is reflected in one of the hymns: "A bard am I, my father a leech, And my mother a grinder of corn. Diverse in means, but all wishing wealth, Alike for cattle we strive."[14]

Conflict and Conquest

They were also a militaristic people who harnessed horses to chariots and skillfully wielded bows and arrows and bronze axes. They had fought their way through blistering deserts and snowy mountains to reach India. Some Vedas celebrate Aryan victories against fortified settlements inhabited by peoples, probably including Dravidians, who had darker skins than the Aryans: "For fear of thee fled the dark-hued races, scattered abroad, deserting their possessions."[15] The various Aryan tribes could unite against a common enemy, but most of the time they fought against each other.

Sanskrit The classical language of north India, originally both written and spoken but now reserved for religious and literary writing.

In India the Aryans mixed their language with those of local people, creating **Sanskrit** (SAN-skrit), the classical written and spoken language of north India, through which the Vedas were preserved. By the fourth century B.C.E., however, vernacular (everyday) Indo-European spoken languages like Hindi and Bengali had become dominant in north India, and Sanskrit gradually became mostly a written language for religious and literary works. Since few Indians today learn to write or speak Sanskrit, some fear the language may eventually become extinct.

Early Aryan Government, Society, and Religion

The early Aryan political and social structure was tribal and marked by persistent military conflict. Each tribe was governed by an autocratic male, known as a *raja*, who sought as much power for himself and his group as possible. The most powerful tribe seems to have been the Bharata (BAA-ray-tuh). Later the ***Mahabharata*** (MA-huh-BAA-ray-tuh) ("Great Bharata"), an Aryan epic and the world's longest poem, spun a complex and entertaining tale of many cousins and their titanic battles for supremacy. Reflecting life around 1000 B.C.E., the *Mahabharata* is, like Homer's *Iliad*, drenched in the blood of endless struggles over succession and supremacy. The *Ramayana* (ruh-MA-yawn-uh) ("The Story of Rama"), another Aryan epic written down sometime after 500 B.C.E., may be based on the extension of Aryan power into southern India.

Mahabharata ("Great Bharata") An Aryan epic and the world's longest poem.

Aryan Families

Aryan family structure was patriarchal, with the father dominating his wives and children. In the centuries to follow, both male supremacy and a hierarchy based on age became the standard Indian family pattern. The Aryans developed a living pattern known as the joint family, also common in China, in which the wives of all the sons moved into the larger patriarchal household, which included members from three or even four generations. The status of Aryan women changed with time. The early Aryans educated both daughters and sons in the Vedas. One Vedic hymn encouraged women to speak publicly, and women may have composed some of the hymns. Later women became more restricted and daughters less valued. They needed to obtain dowries (gifts for the prospective in-laws) in order to marry, could not participate in the sacrifices to gods, and did not inherit property.

The Vedas also reveal something of Aryan recreational interests. The leading sports seem to have been horse-drawn chariot racing and gambling. Both dice and chess were invented in India. Gambling features prominently in the *Mahabharata;* one raja loses his kingdom through his fondness for games of chance. The Aryans were fond of wine and music, using such instruments as lutes, flutes, and drums. Song and dance remain an integral component of Indian religious worship and ritual.

Aryan Religion

As sacred texts, the Vedas contained considerable information about Aryan religion, the significance of various gods, and the role of priests. Each Aryan tribe boasted its own bards, poets who were also priests. Because they alone had memorized the Vedic hymns, these bards presided over sacrifices and rituals. The oldest and most important Veda, the *Rig Veda* ("Verses of Knowledge"), probably composed between 1500 and 1000 B.C.E., contains over 1,000 poems written in Sanskrit, most of them soliciting the favor of Aryan gods.

The Aryans worshiped a pantheon of nature gods, to whom they offered sacrifices. The *Rig Veda* describes some thirty-three deities, several of which are prominent. They are led by the thunderbolt-wielding war-god Indra (INN-druh), who is ever youthful, heroic, and victorious. Many poems celebrate the awesome power of the deities, as in the following tribute to the storm-gods: "You are terrible and powerful, O storm gods. You bring everlasting rain in the desert. Dark rain clouds shroud the sky, Turning day into night, drenching the earth."[16] Aryan religion also included speculations on the deepest mysteries of existence. One poem, the "Hymn of Creation," is one of the most ancient expressions of questions about the creation of the universe: "Who really knows? Who will here proclaim it? Whence was this creation? The gods came afterwards, with the creation of the universe. Who then really knows whence it has arisen?"[17] This hymn also suggests a time before time when there was no space or sky, night or day, life or death. Then, in a kind of Big Bang, the cosmos was created by the power of heat (see Chapter 1).

Aryan Expansion and State Building in North India

Many Aryans eventually moved eastward into the Ganges (GAN-geez) Valley between 1000 and 450 B.C.E., building kingdoms and mixing with local peoples. During this time they changed through conflict, cooperation, and assimilation with the peoples they encountered. They eventually adopted Dravidian systems of farming, village structure, and some religious concepts, but they also contributed their language, social system, and many religious beliefs to the mix.

Political Development

Throughout north India, city development and economic growth encouraged political consolidation into kingdoms. By the sixth century B.C.E. sixteen major Aryan kingdoms stretched from Bengal westward to the fringes of Afghanistan, most of them in the central Ganges region. However, kings did not have unlimited power; they were still advised by councils of warriors. Thus no kingdom was yet strong enough to conquer all the others and create a unified government for all north India until the establishment of the Mauryan Empire in 321 B.C.E. (see Chapter 7).

The Roots of the Caste System

The Indo-Aryan synthesis modified the social structure, which became increasingly complex as the expanding Aryans integrated diverse people. Perhaps incorporating some Harappan traditions, a four-tiered class division emerged that comprised the **brahmans** (BRAH-munz),

brahmans The priests, the highest-ranking caste in Hindu society.

[17]Burton Stein, *A History of India*. Copyright ©1988 by Wiley-Blackwell Publishing Ltd. Reprinted with permission.

Aryan Warfare Vedic stories remain popular in modern India. This scene from an old temple wall of Aryan warfare depicts embattled gods and demons from the *Mahabharata*.

Eliot Elisofon/Getty Images

kshatriyas Warriors and landowners headed by the rajas in the Hindu caste system.

vaisyas The merchants and artisans in the Hindu caste system.

sudras The poorer farmers, farm workers, and menial laborers in the Hindu caste system.

or priests; the **kshatriyas** (kuh-SHOT-ree-uhs), the warriors and landowners; the **vaisyas** (VIGH-shuhs), or merchants and artisans; and the **sudras** (SOO-druhs), mostly poorer farmers, farm workers, and menial laborers. The Aryans allocated the three highest categories to themselves. The priests enjoyed many special privileges as guardians and interpreters of sacred knowledge. Over time the sudras, mostly of non-Aryan origins, were locked into a permanent low status and were prohibited from studying the magically potent Vedic hymns.

The Sanskrit term for a class division, or ritual status, was *varna* (VARN-uh), which meant "[skin] color." The term suggests that the lighter-skinned Aryans wanted to maintain their domination over, and purity from "pollution" by, the darker-skinned indigenous people. Many centuries later, Portuguese visitors referred to the system as *castas* ("pure"); hence the origin of the Western term *caste*. Aryans used religion to justify this class system. One of the hymns in the *Rig Veda* attributed the classes to the Lord of Beings, the originator of the universe: "When they divided the Man, into how many parts did they divide him? What was his mouth, what were his arms, what were his thighs and his feet called? The brahman was his mouth, of his arms was made the kshatriya. His thighs became the vaisya, of his feet were born the sudra."[18]

The Caste System

caste system The four-tiered Hindu social system comprising hereditary social classes that restrict the occupation of members and their relations with members of other castes.

pariahs The large group of outcasts or untouchables below the official Hindu castes.

Gradually, over many centuries, this four-tiered class hierarchy evolved into the immensely complex **caste system**. Each hereditary social class was restricted to certain occupations, and its members were restricted in their relations with members of other castes. For example, only members of closely allied groups could intermarry. Below the caste system were a large group of outcasts (**pariahs**) or untouchables, labeled such because the higher castes considered their touch defiling. The pariahs performed tasks considered "unclean," such as tanning animal hides and removing manure. This system, firmly in place by 500 B.C.E., differed in many respects from the modern caste system. Although the system was never rigid and changed over time, it provided the basic structure of Hindu society for several millennia.

Indo-Aryan Society and Economy

Bhagavad Gita

Bhagavad Gita ("Lord's Song") A poem in the *Mahabharata* that is the most treasured piece of ancient Hindu literature.

The Vedas reveal some of the expectations and attitudes of ancient Indian society. For example, contained within the *Mahabharata* is a philosophical poem called the ***Bhagavad Gita*** (BAA-guh-vad GEE-tuh) ("Lord's Song"), the most treasured piece of ancient Hindu literature (see Witness to the Past: Hindu Values in the *Bhagavad Gita*). It encourages people to do their duty to their superiors and kinsmen resolutely and unselfishly. It also explains that death is not a time of grief because the soul is indestructible. The other great ancient epic, the *Ramayana,* resembles the *Odyssey* of the Greek Homer in that it tells of endless court intrigues and a hero's wanderings while his wife remains chaste and loyal.

We know something of Indo-Aryan gender relations. The *Ramayana* illustrates the early Hindu notion of perfect manhood and womanhood through the main characters: Rama, the husband, and Sita (SEE-tuh), his wife, who demonstrate mutual loyalty, devotion, and self-sacrifice. But Sita

Hindu Values in the *Bhagavad Gita*

The *Bhagavad Gita*, a philosophical poem in the *Mahabharata*, helped shape the ethical traditions of India while providing Hindus with a practical guide to everyday life. The following excerpt is part of a dialogue between the god Krishna (Vishnu) and the poem's conflicted hero, the warrior Arjuna (are-JUNE-ah), on the eve of a great battle in which Arjuna will slaughter his uncles, cousins, teachers, and friends. The reading summarizes some of Krishna's advice in justifying the battle. Krishna suggests that Arjuna must follow his destiny, for while the physical body is impermanent, the soul is eternal. The slain will be reborn. Furthermore, humans are responsible for their own destiny through their behavior and mental discipline. They also, like Arjuna, need to fulfill their obligations to society.

The wise grieve neither for the living nor for the dead. There has never been a time when you and I and the kings gathered here have not existed, nor will there ever be a time when we will cease to exist. As the same person inhabits the body through childhood, youth, and old age, so too at the time of death he attains another body. The wise are not deluded by these changes.

When the senses contact sense objects, a person experiences cold or heat, pleasure or pain. These experiences are fleeting; they come and go. Bear them patiently. . . . Those who are not affected by these changes, who are the same in pleasure and pain, are truly wise and fit for immortality. Assert your strength and realize this!

The impermanent has no reality; reality lies in the eternal. Those who have seen the boundary between these two have attained the end of all knowledge. Realize that which pervades the universe and is indestructible; no power can affect this unchanging, imperishable reality. The body is mortal but he who dwells in the body is immortal and immeasurable. . . . As a man abandons worn-out clothes and acquires new ones, so when the body is worn out a new one is acquired by the Self, who lives within. . . . Death is inevitable for the living; birth is inevitable for the dead. Since these are unavoidable, you should not sorrow. . . .

Now listen to the principles of yoga [mental and physical discipline to free the soul]. By practicing these you can break through the bonds of karma. On this path effort never goes to waste, and there is no failure. . . . When you keep thinking about sense objects, attachment comes. Attachment breeds desire, the lust of possession that burns to anger. . . .

They are forever free who renounce all selfish desires and break free from the ego-cage of "I," "me," and "mine" to be united with the Lord. This is the supreme state. Attain to this, and pass from death to immortality. . . . Strive constantly to serve the welfare of the world; by devotion to selfless work one attains the supreme goal of life. Do your work with the welfare of others always in mind.

THINKING ABOUT THE READING

1. What key aspects of Hindu thought are revealed in the poem?
2. How do the attitudes toward life, death, and desire influence the behavior of individuals?
3. What are some of the viewpoints in this ancient poem that might be considered universal in their appeal?

Source: From *The Bhagavad Gita,* trans. by Eknath Easwaran, founder of the Blue Mountain Center of Meditation, copyright 1985. Reprinted by permission of the Nilgiri Press, P.O. Box 256, Tomales, CA 94971, www.easwaran.org.

is also patient and faithful in supporting her husband and family. The Sita ideal strongly influenced cultural expectations of womanhood, especially in north India. Women enjoyed a higher status in south India, where both matriarchal and matrilineal traditions persisted for centuries, and goddesses remained especially central to religious life. But even in the north some women mastered the Vedas and mixed freely with men.

Indo-Aryan technology derived from both foreign and local developments. The Aryans used iron, especially once they reached iron-rich districts in the Ganges region around 1000 B.C.E. Soon after they arrived in India they made the transition from a pastoral economy to a combination of pastoral and agricultural pursuits that emphasized grains like barley and wheat. One Veda prays: "Successfully let the good ploughshares' thrust part the earth, successfully let the ploughman follow the beasts of draft."[19] The use of plows and the expansion of irrigated agriculture greatly increased the available food supply and thus fostered population growth. India's population in 500 B.C.E. has been estimated at 25 million, including 15 million in the Ganges Valley.

Hinduism: A New Religion of Diverse Roots

Although Indian religion has changed much since the Harappans, it has remained unique. Nothing in the Middle East or Europe remotely resembles basic bedrock Indian beliefs such as reincarnation. What modern Indians would clearly recognize as Hinduism had probably not fully formed until the beginning of the Common Era. The term Hinduism was not applied to these traditions until recent centuries. But the foundations were clearly established in ancient times. Hinduism can be seen historically as a synthesis of Aryan beliefs with Harappan and other Dravidian traditions that developed over many centuries. As the religion became more complex, it probed ever more deeply into cosmic mysteries, resulting in ferment and questioning.

Hindu Beliefs

The Hindu religious system became one of the richest and most complex in the world, with gods, devotions, and celebrations drawn from various regional cultures. The Aryans gradually turned from their old tribal gods to deities of Harappan origin such as Shiva. Hence the rise of the great gods of Hinduism: *Brahma* (BRA-ma) (the Creator of life); *Vishnu* (VISH-noo) (the Preserver of life); and *Shiva* (among other functions, the Destroyer of life). Vishnu is a benevolent deity who works continually for the welfare of the world. Shiva personifies the life force and embodies both constructive and destructive power. Hinduism never developed a rigid core of beliefs uniting all followers; instead, it loosely linked together diverse practices and cults that shared a reverence for the Vedas. The Vedic thinkers were influenced by pre-Aryan meditation techniques and mystical practices of possible Harappan origin, such as those that were later known as *yoga*. In the eternal quest for divine favor, the Hindus came to believe that everyone must behave properly so that the universe can function in an orderly manner. They came to see human existence as temporary and fleeting and only the realm of the gods as eternal.

Religious Development

Brahmanas Commentaries on the Vedas that emphasize the role of priests (brahmans).

Upanishads Ancient Indian philosophical writings that speculated on the ultimate truth about the creation of life.

The Vedas underwent three major stages of development to become accepted as revealed literature. The earliest stage included the poems and hymns in the *Rig Veda* and several other collections. From around 1000 to 700 B.C.E. a series of prose commentaries on the earlier Vedas appeared, elaborating on the meaning of the Vedic literature and also prescribing proper procedures for worshiping the gods. These commentaries are called the ***Brahmanas*** (BRA-ma-nus), since they emphasize the central role of the priests, or brahmans. At this time, the prevailing religion can be termed Brahmanism. Later still, between 800 and 600 B.C.E., a third group of more philosophical writings appeared, mostly in the form of 108 poetic dialogues known as the ***Upanishads*** (oo-PAHN-ih-shahds) ("sitting around a teacher"). These writings, which speculated on the ultimate truth about the creation of life, offered a striking contrast to the emphasis on ritual, devotion, and ethics in the older works because they came from an atmosphere of questioning and rebellion against priestly power. They also gave women more importance; for example, the dialogues include the story of an exceptionally learned female. The religious atmosphere of ancient India was dynamic, with growing tensions between competing ideas about the nature of existence and appropriate human behavior. For example, the *Ramayana* contrasts the luxury-filled decadence of the royal courts with the austere existence of hermit-sages dwelling in the forest and practicing forms of meditation and mysticism. The movements that developed out of this ferment in the first millennium B.C.E. transformed the framework of Indian religion, fostering both Buddhism and the modified form of Brahmanism known today as Hinduism, as we shall see in Chapter 5 .

SECTION SUMMARY

- The Indo-European Aryans, a cattle-raising tribal people, migrated into north India 3,500 years ago.
- The Vedas, written in Sanskrit, are religious writings that reveal information on the Aryan religion and their patriarchal culture.
- Aryan priests supervised the worship of the religion's many nature gods.
- Eventually Aryans built kingdoms in the Ganges River Basin.
- Aryan and local cultures mixed together over the centuries and eventually produced a unique four-tiered caste system.
- The *Bhagavad Gita,* which emphasizes one's earthly duty and the soul's immortality, became the most treasured piece of Indian literature.
- Hinduism developed over many centuries but never became a rigid belief structure.
- The philosophical *Upanishads* represented a departure from the emphasis on priestly ritual.

CHAPTER SUMMARY

Mesopotamian society and early Indian society were two of humankind's first experiments with farming, cities, and states, both using technologies that were unheard of in Neolithic times. These ancient societies also developed different religious notions, social systems, and political structures. They were shaped by the challenges and opportunities of flood-prone river valleys: Mesopotamian society arose between the Tigris and Euphrates Rivers, and Harappan society arose in the Indus River Valley. Mesopotamians introduced the first cities and states, the cuneiform system of writing, bronze metalworking, mathematics, and science. Their many kingdoms were united under several different empires. Mesopotamia was also part of the early trade networks linking the Mediterranean Basin with India. Such connections among societies were a crucial and continuing part of history.

In northwest India the Harappans built peaceful, bustling, and well-planned cities. They produced cotton products and developed sophisticated sanitation systems. The Harappans also participated in a trading network that reached into the Fertile Crescent and Central Asia. After the Harappan collapse, Aryan migrants established political control. The mixing of Harappan and Aryan cultures shaped a new Indian society, establishing the foundation for a caste system and the religion of Hinduism.

KEY TERMS

Fertile Crescent
ziggurat
patriarchy
cuneiform
Harappan
Dravidian
Shiva
steppes
Aryans
Indo-Aryan synthesis
Vedas
Sanskrit
Mahabharata
brahmans
kshatriyas
vaisyas
sudras
caste system
pariahs
Bhagavad Gita
Brahmanas
Upanishads

EBOOK AND WEBSITE RESOURCES

PRIMARY SOURCE
The *Epic of Gilgamesh*

e **INTERACTIVE MAPS**
Map 2.1 Ancient Mesopotamia
Map 2.2 Harappan Culture and Aryan Migrations

LINKS

Exploring Ancient World Cultures (http://eawc.evansville.edu/). Excellent site run by Evansville University, with essays and links on the ancient Near East and Europe.

Harappa: The Ancient Indus Valley and the British Raj in India and Pakistan (www.harappa.com). Essays and photos on the Indus societies and excavations.

Indus Valley Civilization (http://ancienthistory.about.com/od/indusvalleyciv/Indian_Subcontinent.htm). Gives access to many sites and links on ancient India, run by About.com.

Internet Ancient History Sourcebook (http://www.fordham.edu/halsall/ancient/asbook.html). Exceptionally rich collection of links and primary source readings.

Internet Indian History Sourcebook (http://www.fordham.edu/halsall/india/indiasbook.html). An invaluable collection of sources and links on ancient India.

Plus flashcards, practice quizzes, and more. Go to: www.cengage.com/history/lockard/globalsocnet2e.

SUGGESTED READING

Allchin, F. R. *The Archaeology of Early Historic South Asia: The Emergence of Cities and States.* Cambridge: Cambridge University Press, 1995. A scholarly overview.

Avari, Burjor. *India: The Ancient Past. A History of the Indian Sub-Continent from 7000 BC to AD 1200.* New York: Routledge, 2007. A balanced, up-to-date overview.

Basham, A. L. *The Wonder That Was India,* 3rd ed. London: Macmillan, 1968 (reprinted 1999 by Rupa and Company, New Delhi). An older study but still the best survey of premodern India.

Bottero, Jean. *Everyday Life in Ancient Mesopotamia.* Baltimore: Johns Hopkins University Press, 2001. Summarizes recent discoveries about Mesopotamian social and cultural life.

Crawfurd, Harriet. *Sumer and the Sumerians,* 2nd ed. Cambridge: Cambridge University Press, 2004. An up-to-date and interdisciplinary summary of the achievements of the Sumerians.

Dunstan, William E. *The Ancient Near East.* New York: Harcourt Brace, 1998. Designed for the general reader, this work makes sense of the confusing array of states and empires in western Asia.

Kenoyer, Jonathan Mark. *Ancient Cities of the Indus Valley Civilization.* New York: Oxford University Press, 1998. A valuable, well-illustrated summary of the most recent discoveries.

McIntosh, Jane. *A Peaceful Realm: The Rise and Fall of the Indus River Civilization.* Boulder, CO: Westview, 2001. A comprehensive, well-illustrated survey of the Harappans, based on recent archaeological research.

Noble, D. Brendan. *The Ancient World: A Social and Cultural History,* 7th ed. Upper Saddle Back, N.J.: Prentice Hall, 2009. Survey text with much on Mesopotamia.

Sandars, N. K., trans. *The Epic of Gilgamesh.* New York: Penguin Books, 1972. An easy introduction to the ancient Mesopotamian world-view.

Stiebing, William H. *Ancient Near Eastern History and Culture.* New York: Longman, 2003. An up-to-date survey of ancient western Asia, Egypt, and the eastern Mediterranean.

Thapar, Romila. *Early India from the Origins to AD 1300.* Berkeley: University of California Press, 2002. A valuable revision of the standard history of early India, detailed and comprehensive.

Wolpert, Stanley. *A New History of India,* 8th ed. New York: Oxford University Press, 2009. One of the most readable survey texts.

CHAPTER

3

Ancient Societies in Africa and the Mediterranean, 5000–600 B.C.E.

CHAPTER OUTLINE

- The Rise of Egyptian Society
- Egyptian Society, Economy, and Culture
- Ancient Sub-Saharan African Societies
- Early Societies and Networks of the Eastern Mediterranean

PROFILE
Hekanakhte, an Egyptian Priest

WITNESS TO THE PAST
The World-view of an African Society

George Holton/Photo Researchers, Inc.

Abu Simbel
The great temple with its colossal statues at Abu Simbel overlooking the Nile River in Egypt was built as a monument to honor the powerful thirteenth-century B.C.E. pharaoh Rameses the Great, who presided over empire building and economic prosperity.

Behold, the heart of his majesty was satisfied with making a very great monument; never has happened the like since the beginning. He made it as an everlasting fortress. It is wrought with gold and many costly stones.

—Temple inscription at Thebes, Egypt, fourteenth century B.C.E.[1]

Around 1460 B.C.E. Queen Hatshepsut (hat-SHEP-soot), the powerful ruler of Egypt, issued a decree to build a temple on the banks of the Nile River for the glory of the highest god, Amon-Re (AH-muhn-RAY). The temple would have terraced gardens planted with fragrant myrrh. To obtain the myrrh, the queen ordered an expedition to be sent down the Red Sea to Punt (poont) on the coast of northeast Africa, probably modern Somalia (so-MAH-lee-uh). Egyptian ships had previously visited Punt at various times. Now Hatshepsut, for reasons of commerce, religion, and personal ambition, ordered that contact with Punt to be renewed. The new expedition was extremely successful, returning with myrrh trees, jewels, incense, and other treasures. Like other rulers before and after her, Queen Hatshepsut commemorated her achievements with inscriptions and pictures, in this case by summarizing the results of the trading expedition on the walls of her magnificent new temple: "The loading of the cargo-boats with great marvels of Punt, with all the good woods, ebony, pure ivory, gold, monkeys, [and] skins of leopard. Never were brought such things to any king, since the world was."[2] To obtain such luxury products, Egyptians became shipbuilders and sailors, becoming connected to a much wider world. Foreign trade made Egypt the ancient world's wealthiest society.

FOCUS QUESTIONS

1. How did the environment shape ancient Egypt?
2. What were some unique features of Egyptian society?
3. What were some achievements of the ancient Nubian, Sudanic, and Bantu peoples?
4. What were the contributions of the Hebrews, Minoans, Mycenaeans, Phoenicians, and Dorian Greeks to later societies in the region?

Among the Egyptians and some other African and eastern Mediterranean societies—including the Hebrews, Minoans (mih-NO-uhns), Mycenaeans (my-suh-NEE-uhns), Phoenicians (fo-NEE-shuhns), and early Greeks—we see the same kind of dramatic changes resulting from contact among different peoples that fostered urban life in Mesopotamia and India. Egypt greatly influenced neighboring peoples and was also influenced by them. This interaction among neighbors promoted cultural development in the Nile Valley and the Mediterranean. Like the Tigris-Euphrates and Indus Valleys, the Nile Valley made possible population growth, social organization, large state structures, and elaborate religious systems.

Ancient peoples also created unique and complex societies elsewhere in Africa and the eastern Mediterranean. Diverse sub-Saharan African societies developed or borrowed farming and metal technologies, and some built cities. However, unlike Egypt's spectacular pyramids, over the centuries many of the sub-Saharan people's monuments and buildings were covered by rain forest, blowing sand, or wayward rivers. Meanwhile, on the islands and shores of the eastern Mediterranean, various peoples traded widely, built cities whose ruins still interest visitors, and developed religious concepts that endure to this day.

Visit the website and eBook for additional study materials and interactive tools: www.cengage.com/history/lockard/globalsocnet2e

The Rise of Egyptian Society

How did the environment shape ancient Egypt?

The formation of Egyptian society involved interactions among many different peoples, producing a mixed society so successful that it survived in more or less its basic form for nearly 2,000 years. The classical Greek historian Herodotus **(heh-ROD-uh-tuhs)** called Egypt the "gift of the Nile" because it owed its existence to the Nile River. The river valley's African location allowed the Egyptians to develop many traditions and ideas completely different from those in nearby Mesopotamia, Palestine, and Crete.

North African Environments

North Africa, a region stretching from Morocco to the Red Sea, has been shaped by several environmental features. In ancient times maritime routes in the Mediterranean Sea linked societies along its shores and islands and enabled the spread of products, ideas, technologies, and peoples. The Red Sea connected Egypt to northeast Africa, Arabia, and India. Agriculture, then and now, is mainly possible only in a narrow fertile valley in Egypt nourished by the Nile River. To the west of the Nile lies the vast Sahara Desert, which stretches all the way to the western coast of Africa. In northwestern Africa (today's Tunisia, Algeria, and Morocco) mountain ranges separate the desert from the Mediterranean and Atlantic coastal plains, where farming is also possible.

The Nile River is the key to understanding the formation of Egyptian society (see Map 3.1). The settlers in the northern Nile Valley enjoyed many centuries of uninterrupted development thanks to the inhospitable deserts on both sides of the valley. This environment allowed Egypt to thrive for a thousand years without significant outside challenge. Since the Nile was navigable and slow moving, boats drifted northward with the current and used southerly winds to move south; thus the river was a great highway that promoted political stability and uniformity. By the fourth millennium B.C.E. the grasslands and forests of earlier times had turned to desert and the valley was fertile only because of the silt deposited by the fall flooding of the Nile.

Foundations of Egyptian Society

The same process that transformed farming societies into urban societies in Mesopotamia took place a few centuries later, around 3100 or 3000 B.C.E., in the Nile Valley. Here too, with little rainfall, irrigation works were necessary to take advantage of the rich silt. But unlike the 100-mile-wide Tigris-Euphrates Valley, the river valley here was only 10 miles wide, with the result that the population was more protected from the outside and more concentrated.

The Nile Valley continued to be shaped by the arrival of new peoples. Many of the earliest settlers were migrants from a Sahara region that had been fertile but began drying out some 6,000 to 7,000 years ago. This environmental change forced the peoples to move to the grasslands of western Africa, the northern coast, or into the Nile Valley. Other early migrants came from western Asia and from the Horn of Africa, southeast of Egypt. The Egyptian population eventually included peoples of Semitic, Berber **(BUHR-bur)**, Ethiopian, Somali, black African, and, later, Greek origins. Egypt also enjoyed close relationships with the Nubians, black African peoples living along the Nile in what is today southern Egypt and northern Sudan. The ancient Egyptian language belonged to the Afro-Asiatic family, which included Semitic and Berber languages and many African tongues. Most of the people in northwest Africa were Berbers.

Unlike the floods in Mesopotamia, the Nile floods came on an exact schedule. Egyptians formed a central government to organize large numbers of people to prepare the cropland to take best advantage of the flooding, such as by building dikes to contain the floodwater used in irrigation. The backbreaking work required to maintain the irrigation canals reminds us that, for peasants at least, a complex society was a mixed blessing. If the floodwaters were not carefully channeled, little would grow. In periods of political disorder, when weak central governments left the dikes untended, the desert spread and famine struck the land. When order prevailed and the dikes were maintained, the valley could support a high population. By 1000 B.C.E., the population had reached 3 or 4 million. Given their general good fortune, it is not surprising that Egyptians saw themselves as the center of the world. As far as they knew for many centuries, they were.

In earliest times, the 100-mile-long area from the modern city of Cairo down the Nile to the sea was considered Lower Egypt or the northern kingdom, at the end of which was the fertile Nile

CHRONOLOGY

	Egypt	Sub-Saharan Africa	Eastern Mediterrnean
3000 B.C.E.	**2686–2181** B.C.E. Old Kingdom		
2000 B.C.E.	**2040–1786** B.C.E. Middle Kingdom **1550–1064** B.C.E. New Kingdom	**2000** B.C.E.–**1000** C.E. Bantu migrations **1800–1500** B.C.E. Nubian kingdom of Kerma	**2000–1400** B.C.E. Minoan Crete **1600–1200** B.C.E. Mycenaea **1500–650** B.C.E. Phoenicia
1000 B.C.E.		**900** B.C.E. Rise of Kush	**1000–722** B.C.E. Hebrew kingdoms

Delta (see Map 3.1). The area from Cairo to Aswan **(AS-wahn)**, some 650 miles south, was Upper Egypt or the southern kingdom. These two states were united by the legendary Upper Egyptian King Menes **(MEH-neez)** in about 3000 B.C.E. The rest of Egyptian history is usually divided into three successive eras: the Old Kingdom (2686–2181 B.C.E.), the Middle Kingdom (2040–1786 B.C.E.), and the New Kingdom (1550–1064 B.C.E.). During each period various dynasties ruled Egypt, and the intermediate periods were marked by disorder or foreign conquest. After 1075 B.C.E. Egypt increasingly fell victim to the empire building of western Asian, Mediterranean, and other African peoples.

pharaohs Rulers of ancient Egypt.

The Old Kingdom: Egypt's Golden Age

When we think of ancient Egypt, most of us picture the Old Kingdom because of the pyramids built in this splendid era. The pyramids, which have awed visitors for thousands of years, illustrate the Egyptian self-confidence of this period. Perhaps the greatest and most enduring of the ancient world's construction projects, they reflected a powerful government, unsurpassed organizing talent, a prosperous society, and unique values and beliefs (see Chronology: Ancient Egypt, 3100–525 B.C.E.). The largest pyramid, that of the twenty-fifth-century pharaoh Cheops at Giza, is nearly 500 feet high, covers an area of nearly 200 square yards, and remained the tallest building in the world until the twentieth century. All the nearly 6 million tons of limestone used in the building was moved into place on ramps and wooden rollers by tens of thousands of workers without the benefit of winches, pulleys, or scaffolds. Most of the workers were not slaves, and many were highly skilled artisans. Workers and their families lived in villages where the government supplied them with ample food and good housing. This did not prevent complaints, however. One disgruntled draftsman wrote to his superior: "If there is some beer, you do not look for me, but if there is work, you do look for me. I am a man who has no beer in his house."[3]

The rulers of Egypt, known as **pharaohs (FAIR-os)** (from *per-o* or "great house"), had immense power to order such projects because their subjects believed them to be the divine

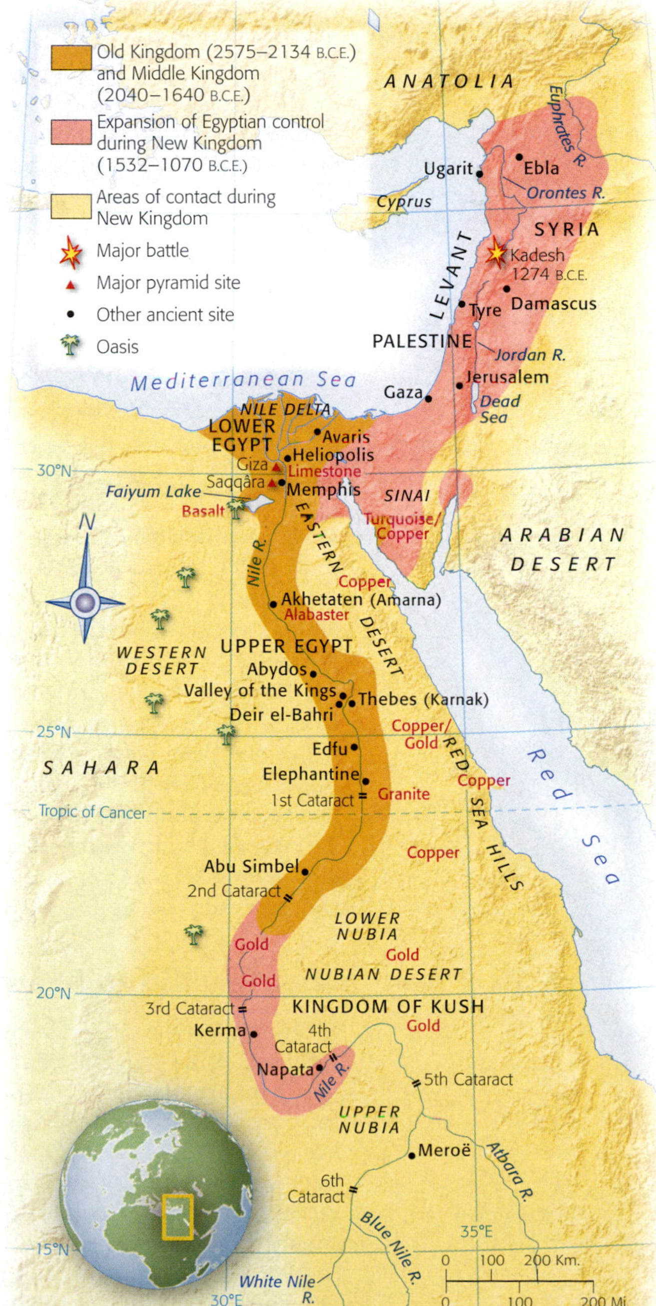

Map 3.1
Ancient Egypt and Nubia

The Egyptian and Nubian societies developed along the Nile River. Egypt traded with, and sometimes controlled, the peoples of the Levant on the eastern Mediterranean coast.

e Interactive Map

CHRONOLOGY

Ancient Egypt, 3100–525 B.C.E.

3100–3000 B.C.E. Upper and Lower Egypt unified

2686–2181 B.C.E. Old Kingdom and age of pyramids

2181–2041 B.C.E. First Intermediate Period

2040–1786 B.C.E. Middle Kingdom

1786–1550 B.C.E. Second Intermediate Period

1550–1064 B.C.E. New Kingdom

1064–525 B.C.E. Third Intermediate Period

offspring of the sun-god Re, the creator of heaven, earth, and humans. Pharaohs also had soldiers as well as the authority of priests and religion to support their rule. Writing, invented by 3000 B.C.E., enabled the administration to function smoothly. The Egyptian writing system of **hieroglyphics** **(hi-ruh-GLIF-iks)**, like Sumerian cuneiform, evolved from pictograms into stylized pictures expressing ideas. The pharaohs, who were considered the owners of all the land and people in Egypt, governed a highly centralized state from the city of Memphis, strategically located where the Nile Valley met the delta. A chief minister supervised the administrative structure and ensured that taxes were collected, grain properly stored in government warehouses, and salaries paid to government officials. Most ministers came from noble families, but occasionally pharaohs recruited for talent. One advised his son: "Do not distinguish the son of a noble man from a poor man, but take to thyself a man because of the work of his hands."[4]

The royal government also expanded trade through regional networks. The pharaohs dispatched expeditions east to Arabia, south to Nubia **(NOO-bee-ah)**, and northeast to Lebanon, Syria, and Anatolia. Although the Egyptians may not have invented international maritime trade, the records from the Pharaoh Snefru **(SNEF-roo)** around 2600 B.C.E. provide the first known written accounts of this activity. They describe the arrival of forty ships filled with cedar logs, probably from today's Lebanon, to make the cedar wood doors of the royal palace.

hieroglyphics The Egyptian writing system, which evolved from pictograms into stylized pictures expressing ideas.

Some historians believe that the expense of the great royal tombs eventually impoverished the country during the final decades of the twenty-second century B.C.E. The royal governors became more independent of the ruler at Memphis, whose authority was thereby weakened. Egyptian beliefs led people to accept this development. Many peasants reasoned that if the power of the ruler was weakened, it must mean that the gods were displeased. But environmental change may also have undermined the government. A dramatic and sudden drop in rainfall led to many years of poor harvests and starvation in Upper Egypt. The demise of the Old Kingdom led to a century of social disorder during which thieves ransacked some royal tombs. One scribe lamented the consequences of this upheaval: "The son of the high-born is no longer to be recognized. Men do not sail to Byblos **(BIB-loss)** [Phoenicia] today. Gold is diminished. To what purpose is a treasure without its revenues? Laughter hath perished. It is grief that walketh through the land."[5]

The Middle Kingdom and Foreign Conquest

The pharaohs of a new dynasty restored strong government, moving the capital to Thebes in the south and establishing stronger control over the governors. This Middle Kingdom lasted for 400 years and saw Egyptian influence extend to Palestine and, briefly, to Nubia. Amon-Re, a fusion of two great gods, now became Egypt's chief god and was proclaimed the ancestor of the divine pharaoh.

However, foreign conquest and domestic disorder brought an end to the Middle Kingdom. The Hyksos **(HICK-soes)**, an iron-using Semitic people from Syria and Palestine, conquered a portion of the Nile Delta region. Hyksos rule led to further divisions: an Egyptian dynasty began to rule Upper Egypt from Thebes, and the Nubians established yet a third state. The Hyksos adopted Egyptian customs and brought several improvements to Egypt that would later pay dividends, including increased trade with the peoples of the eastern Mediterranean and Mesopotamia, and military innovations, such as iron and the practice of using smaller shields, body armor, powerful bows, and, especially, horse-drawn chariots.

The New Kingdom and Egyptian Expansion

Empire Building

In the mid-1500s B.C.E. a dynamic new set of rulers reestablished Egypt's regional power and fostered social and religious changes. Using the new military technology, the pharaohs began the most expansionist period of ancient Egyptian history. During the New Kingdom, Egypt became more active in the western Asian and Mediterranean worlds. By 1500 B.C.E. its rulers were leading armies on repeated campaigns into Palestine, Syria, and the Euphrates River, as well as south into Nubia. Foreigners from Libya in the west and from as far away as Babylon in the east came to serve in the Egyptian court. Egypt's power derived partly from its position as the major regional supplier of gold, which it obtained mostly from Nubia and Punt.

For a few years Egypt was ruled by the female pharaoh introduced at the beginning of this chapter. Hatshepsut (r. ca. 1479–1458), the daughter and wife of pharaohs, ruled in her own name

Michael Holford

Great Pyramid at Giza Three Egyptian pharaohs from the twenty-sixth century B.C.E. were buried in these magnificent pyramids, which symbolized the power of Old Kingdom Egypt. The rearmost pyramid, built for Pharaoh Cheops, remains the largest all-stone building ever constructed anywhere.

between 1473 and 1458. The Egyptians had no word for a female ruler and described a queen only as the "king's wife." To ensure that she looked like a proper pharaoh, Hatshepsut apparently wore male clothing and the headdress and false beard that were symbols of royalty. Hatshepsut supervised military campaigns in both the north and south and also sponsored the marine expedition to Punt to collect luxury goods.

Another New Kingdom pharaoh, Amenophis (AH-men-o-fis) IV (r. 1353–1333), rebelled against the priests of Amon-Re and promoted the worship of a new sun-god, Aten, who he claimed was the only god (other than the pharaoh himself). Amenophis changed his name to Akhenaten (AH-ke-NAH-tin) ("servant of Aten") and wrote a famous hymn to Aten: "Beginner of Life. How manifold are thy works? They are hidden from the sight of men, O Sole God. Thou didst fashion the earth according to thy desire."[6] His experiment with **monotheism**, the belief in a single, all-powerful god, has long intrigued historians because it occurred at roughly the same time that the Hebrews were developing their belief in a single god. Some scholars see cross-cultural influences at work, since Hebrews were within the Egyptian sphere of influence, and some may have lived in Egypt. Some Hebrew psalms and proverbs are clearly derived from Egyptian writings, including Akhenaten's hymn to Aten. At Akhenaten's death, however, the priests successfully pressured his successor to return to Amon-Re worship.

Religious Diversity

monotheism The belief in a single, all-powerful god.

The New Kingdom continued its military successes for a while before faltering. The high point of Egyptian empire building was reached when Rameses (ram-ih-SEEZ) II (r. 1290–1224) signed a treaty with the Hittites dividing Syria and Palestine between them. In 1208 B.C.E. Libyan tribes invaded the Nile Delta. Although they were pushed out, Egypt began its long decline as a power in the eastern Mediterranean. From about 750 to 650 B.C.E., a dynasty of pharaohs from the kingdom of Kush in Nubia ruled Egypt. They adopted Egyptian customs and wrote their language in hieroglyphics. Finally, Egypt was conquered by the Assyrians in the seventh century and by the Persians in the late sixth century B.C.E.

SECTION SUMMARY

- The regular flooding of the Nile River provided the ancient Egyptians with a highly fertile valley and a dependable growing season.
- A strong central government allowed the Egyptians to make the most of their agricultural system.
- The pyramids were built by the Egyptian pharaohs of the Old Kingdom, thought to be descendants of the sun-god.
- During the Middle Kingdom, the Egyptian capital moved from Memphis to Thebes.
- The New Kingdom was a time of Egyptian expansion into western Asia and the Mediterranean, but it ended with the decline of Egyptian dominance.

Egyptian Society, Economy, and Culture

What were some unique features of Egyptian society?

Like other ancient societies, the Egyptians had many distinctive customs, technologies, and beliefs. Egypt was a generally tolerable place to live. Perhaps because of the Nile inundation each fall, Egyptians of all social classes, blessed with many centuries of good crops, seemed to view themselves as favored. One writer celebrated the Nile Delta as "full of everything good—its ponds with fish and its lakes with birds. Its meadows are verdant, its melons abundant. Its granaries are so full of barley that they come near to the sky."[7] Although many peasants and workers worked hard and had fewer comforts than the upper classes, they at least had a life that was secure and a routine that was predictable. Women enjoyed considerable freedom. Finally, Egyptian cities could grow rich by trading with many distant suppliers and markets.

Society

Social Classes

Like other urban societies, Egypt was divided into social classes with different responsibilities and roles. The pharaoh theoretically owned everything in the kingdom and had particular estates reserved for him. The priests and nobles owned 80 to 90 percent of all the usable land (see Profile: Hekanakhte, an Egyptian Priest). The scribe, or "writing man," held an honored upper-class occupation. "Be a scribe," a young man was advised in one source. "Your limbs will be sleek. Your hands will grow soft. You will go forth in white clothes with courtiers saluting you."[8] Not all enjoyed such amenities. Peasants maintained the irrigation works and paid high taxes. At the bottom of society were slaves, perhaps 10 or 15 percent of the population. They were mostly prisoners of war and foreigners, including Nubians and people from Palestine, among them some Hebrews. Most worked in the homes of the wealthy, in the palaces, or on temple estates. Some helped build pyramids and monuments.

Egyptians valued security and regularity more than social equality. Since it was relatively easy to plant in the soft soil left after the floods, they did not need heavy plows. Despite occasional grueling labor on construction projects, peasants showed little discontent except during the troubled intermediate periods. Although the rich ate meat and the poor had beer, bread, and beans ("beer and bread" was an ancient Egyptian greeting, much like "have a good day"), most people thought themselves lucky. Their massive tombs and mummies may seem gloomy to us today, but their temples were once bright with paint and gold. Egyptians told bawdy stories (often about their gods), played musical instruments such as flutes, pipes, and harps, and got drunk. Both men and women used cosmetics to enhance their physical attractions, including scented oils and colorful eyeliners. In seeking beauty aids, Egyptians became the world's first chemists. Young people wrote sentimental poems to sweethearts. One love poem by a girl reported on a swim with her lover:

> Diving and swimming with you here,
> Gives me the chance I've been waiting for,
> To show my looks,
> Before an appreciative eye.
> My bathing suit of the best material.
> Nothing can keep me from my love,
> Standing on the other shore.[9]

Gender Relations

Gender roles were flexible, and women had more independence and rights, especially in law, than women in any other ancient society. Hatshepsut was the most famous of at least four women pharaohs. The status of New Kingdom Egyptian women was higher than that of women in Mesopotamia or later in classical Greek and Roman society, and legal distinctions seemed to be based more on class than on gender. A woman could inherit, bequeath, and administer property, conclude legal settlements, take cases to court, initiate divorce, and testify. Some women could probably read and write, and many were involved in well-paying economic activities. Women weavers produced some of the finest cloth in world history. Wives also enjoyed rough equality with husbands and assumed the public and family responsibilities of their deceased spouses. Women served as doctors and priestesses, and a few women even held administrative positions. Despite all these exceptions, public duties were normally reserved for men. An Old Kingdom sage advised men to "love your wife at home, as is proper. Fill her belly and clothe her back. Make her heart glad as long as you live. You should not judge her, or let her gain control."[10]

Cities, Trade, and Technology

Mesopotamian cities had been trading centers almost from their beginnings. Egyptian cities, by contrast, were largely administrative centers to house tax collectors, artisans in government workshops, shopkeepers, and the priests who cared for the local temple. Most trade involved the

HEKANAKHTE, AN EGYPTIAN PRIEST

Hekanakhte **(heh-KHAN-akt)** who lived about 2000 B.C.E., was the *ka*-priest of a chief government minister who had died a generation earlier. As a *ka*-priest, it was his duty to tend the tomb of his patron, near the city of Thebes, in order to protect the deceased individual's guardian spirit or soul (*ka*). Wealthy individuals, like the great minister Ipi whom Hekanakhte served, left money or other resources to support a priest who would perform these duties. If the *ka* were not honored with these ceremonial offerings, Egyptians feared that it would die a "second death" or be annihilated.

In this case, the minister Ipi had left a large estate to support Hekanakhte and his family. Hekanakhte also supervised other properties left to his care, and he had to be gone visiting them much of the year. We know much about him because during his absences he wrote many letters to his eldest son, Mersu. Mersu read and eventually discarded them in a local tomb, where they were forgotten but where the dry desert climate preserved them until they were discovered by an archaeologist in 1922. These letters give us an interesting picture of family life in the Middle Kingdom. We discover that Hekanakhte had a large family that included five sons, two of them married, and all of them living at home. He also supported his mother, a poor female relative, and a widowed daughter.

Perhaps because he had such a large household, Hekanakhte's letters to Mersu give advice on cultivating and tending the grain crops. Some of the letters were written during a bad year, when harvests were slim because of inadequate Nile flooding. The priest tells his son that he is sending some food, but he carefully lists what each family member is to receive. He tells Mersu to remind family members not to complain, since "half life is better than dying together." Hekanakhte orders that only those who work should get food and urges Mersu to "make the most of my land, strive to the uttermost, dig the ground deep with your noses." He also tells his son exactly what seeds to plant and where to plant them. And he warns his son not to overpay the help, saying that if he does, his own personal funds will be reduced. Trust between father and son seems to have been in short supply.

Family disputes in Hekanakhte's household were a frequent topic in these letters. Apparently Hekanakhte had spoiled Mersu's younger brother, Snerfu, because he constantly reminds Mersu to give this youngest son things he wants. In addition, Hekanakhte apparently decided late in life, after his wife died, to take a young concubine, Iutenhab **(YOU-ten-hob)**, who disrupted the household with her many requests. In one letter, the priest tells his son to fire a maid who had offended Iutenhab. Given the nagging tone of many of Hekanakhte's letters to his long-suffering son, it may not surprise us that one of the letters found in the debris of the tomb had been left unopened.

THINKING ABOUT THE PROFILE

1. What were the duties of a *ka*-priest?
2. What do these letters tell us about family relationships in this social class?

Note: Quotations from Barbara Mertz, *Red Land, Black Land: Daily Life in Ancient Egypt* (New York: Dodd, Mead, 1978), 127.

Measuring and Recording the Egyptian Harvest This wall painting from a tomb in the city of Thebes shows officials and peasants figuring the size of the annual harvest.

Michael Holford

import of luxury goods by the wealthy. Also, Egyptian city-dwellers, unlike their Mesopotamian counterparts, did not think of themselves as attached to the city. They were, like all Egyptians, subjects of the pharaoh. Most Egyptians lived in villages, and market towns were scattered up and down the river. The Egyptians' long-distance trade systems were more wide-ranging than those of the Mesopotamians. Egyptians traded with sub-Saharan Africans as far south as the Congo River Basin, with the Berber peoples of Libya and Algeria to the west, with the societies along the Red Sea to the east, with Palestine, Phoenicia, and Mesopotamia to the northeast, and with southeastern Europe. Gold, semiprecious stones, and such exotic things as frankincense, myrrh, ivory, ostrich feathers, and monkeys came from sub-Saharan Africa through Nubia or via the Red Sea and were exchanged for furniture, silver, tools, paper, and linen. Egyptians mined copper in the nearby Sinai (SIGH-nigh) Peninsula and along the Red Sea coast, and the Nile Delta provided papyrus and waterfowl.

Economic Life

The Egyptians understood enough mathematics and physics to make the pyramids perfectly level and to match the corners of each pyramid with the four points of the compass. The Egyptians also used a solar calendar that divided the year into 365 days and twelve months, more accurate than the Sumerian lunar calendar. Egyptian arithmetic, however, was less sophisticated. The Egyptians understood fractions, but they had no concept of zero. In medicine, Egyptians used both surgery and herbal remedies to treat illnesses. They recognized that the heart was a pump, were able to cure some eye diseases, and did some dental work. Modern observers still admire Egyptian technical skill in treating the dead, reflected in the mummies held in museums worldwide. Using a form of salt found abundantly in Egypt, and taking advantage of the extremely dry climate, Egyptian morticians were able to preserve human tissue well enough that the distinct features of individuals can be seen 4,000 years later.

Mathematics and Science

Religion

Gods and Myths

Egyptian religious and moral beliefs included many myths, unique views of death, and some 2,000 gods and goddesses, most of them benevolent. Like their Mesopotamian counterparts, the Egyptian gods were created to explain nature, but they were also made in the image of humans and shared human weaknesses. The emphasis on preserving bodies indicates a chief feature of Egyptian religion, the belief that a person's soul could be united with his or her body after death, but only if the body was properly preserved. In the Old Kingdom, only pharaohs could expect this afterlife, which mirrored life on earth. By the Middle Kingdom, however, all who could afford some form of mummification and whose souls passed a final moral judgment after death were candidates for immortality. As a result, people devoted vast resources to this quest.

e **Primary Source: Egyptian *Book of the Dead*** Read the number of potential sins that would likely tarnish a journeying spirit and prevent entrance into the realm of the blessed.

The most dramatic and long-lived of the Egyptian myths is the story of Osiris (oh-SIGH-ris), a god-king, and his wife Isis (EYE-sis). Murdered by his brother, Osiris descended to the underworld, where he established justice there as he had done on earth. A famous Egyptian drawing from the *Book of the Dead,* which depicts the afterlife, shows Osiris weighing the heart of a dead princess against the symbol of justice and truth. The *Book of the Dead* describes a confession that the dead person is to repeat as part of this judgment by Osiris. This confession includes statements by the deceased indicating that he or she has not murdered or cheated anyone.

Because of the *Book of the Dead,* the durability of the pyramids, other Egyptian tombs, and mummified remains, some scholars have viewed the ancient Egyptians as people preoccupied with death and the afterlife. However, the tombs are the only artifacts that remain because they were made of stone. The Egyptians were probably not as preoccupied with death as the physical remains suggest. They no doubt enjoyed life as much or more than other people. Many wall paintings suggest that even the lower classes accepted their lot as part of the natural order of things and found ways to cope. They show farmers and herders telling jokes, women bringing them their lunches, children squabbling, and shepherds asleep under a tree, a dog or flask of beer beside them. They could find solace in religion and awe of the pharaoh who sat, as the gods ordained, at the apex of the social pyramid.

SECTION SUMMARY

- Though Egyptian society was divided into classes, with the rich enjoying lavish lifestyles, even the poor were relatively comfortable.
- Women had greater independence and rights in Egypt than in any other ancient society, but their roles were still quite limited.
- Ancient Egyptians had great technical skill in architecture, medicine, and preserving the dead.
- Ancient Egyptians believed they could obtain immortality if their bodies were mummified and if they passed a moral judgment after death.
- Ancient Egyptians traded widely with societies in sub-Saharan Africa and western Asia.

Ancient Sub-Saharan African Societies

What were some achievements of the ancient Nubian, Sudanic, and Bantu peoples?

Africa is the original homeland for all of humanity, and Egypt was only the best-known of the early farming societies and states that emerged on the continent. Africans fostered varied societies that became linked to each other and the wider world by growing networks. Just as the annual Nile floods fostered Egypt's distinctive development, so the environment also influenced sub-Saharan Africans and helped or hindered their early development of farming and technology. While historians tend to emphasize state building and monarchs, many Africans rejected political centralization, choosing public participation rather than kings and bureaucracies. However, strong states emerged in Nubia and the Sudan. Meanwhile, migrating **Bantu** (BAN-too) spread farming, iron metallurgy, and their languages widely in the southern half of the continent.

Bantu Sub-Saharan peoples who developed a cultural tradition based on farming and iron metallurgy, which they spread widely through great migrations.

Sub-Saharan African Environments

Geographical Foundations

Both geography and climate have shaped African history. Africa, with one-fifth of the earth's landmass, is the second largest continent after Eurasia and occupies more space than the United States, Europe (excluding Russia), China, and India combined. The equator bisects Africa, giving most of the continent a tropical climate. Lush rain forests have flourished along West Africa's Guinea coast and in the vast Congo River Basin in the heart of the continent. These equatorial regions are home to many insects, parasites, and bacteria that cause debilitating diseases like malaria, yellow fever, and sleeping sickness. Since the last is deadly to cattle and horses, it was impractical to use a plow or wheel. Most of the continent, however, is parched desert or savannah grasslands. African weather can be erratic, with fluctuating and often unpredictable rains. Rain quickly diminishes north and south of the equator, producing a huge dry zone that receives less than 10 inches of rain a year. The deserts have largely been occupied by pastoral societies and herds of large wild animals. In some regions the poor-quality soil has been easily eroded by overuse, fostering low agricultural productivity. Nonetheless, early farmers cultivated the grassland-covered region known as the **Sudan** (soo-DAN), which stretches along the southern fringe of the Sahara Desert from the western tip of Africa to the Nile Basin.

Sudan A grassland region stretching along the southern fringe of the Sahara Desert from the western tip of Africa to the Nile Valley.

Geography has often hindered communication. The eastern third of Africa includes extensive plateau and mountain regions, where in some plateau districts great lakes and volcanic soils have permitted denser populations. The eastern highlands also produced great river systems, including the Nile, the Congo, and, in the south, the Zambezi (zam-BEE-zee), but all these rivers have numerous rapids and waterfalls that have limited boat travel. Only the Niger (NIGH-jer) River, which flows through the West African plains, is navigable over large distances. Prevailing winds also made it difficult to sail along the West African coast, and much of the African coast has sandbars that create great swells, making it difficult to land a boat. Furthermore, there are few bays, gulfs, inland seas, or natural harbors to serve as maritime hubs. Only along the eastern, Red Sea, and Mediterranean coasts did a few protected bays and prevailing winds favor seagoing trade.

The Expanding Sahara

The catastrophic climatic change that created and expanded the Sahara Desert strongly shaped early African societies. In 3500 B.C.E. the Sahara region was relatively wet, a rich grazing land with lakes and rivers and occupied by societies that flourished from hunting, gathering, fishing, and some farming. Ancient rock art portrays people dancing, worshiping, riding chariots, and tending horses and cattle. The paintings endow women with dignity as they raise children, gather plants, and make baskets, pottery, and jewelry. Then, as rain patterns shifted southward, **desertification**, the process by which productive land is transformed into mostly useless desert, began. By 2000 B.C.E. the Sahara region was harsh desert. People contributed to this process by overgrazing marginal lands and burning forests to create grasslands. The same desertification processes continue today on the Sahara's southern fringe. The Sahara was left largely to nomadic herders of cattle, goats, and camels, and most other inhabitants migrated to the north and south or into the lower Nile Valley. Eventually the Sahara marked a general boundary between the Berber and Semitic peoples along the southern Mediterranean coast and the darker-skinned peoples in the rest of Africa. But the desert barrier did not prevent considerable social, cultural, and genetic intermixing and exchange.

desertification The process by which productive land is transformed into mostly useless desert.

The Origins of African Agriculture

Africa's geographical disadvantages did not prevent agriculture from developing early as the result of both local and imported discoveries. Some 12,000 or 13,000 years ago, people in the eastern Sahara were perhaps the first in the world to make pottery, probably for storing food and water, two centuries earlier than Middle Eastern people. Between 8000 and 5000 B.C.E., people in Nubia and the Sahara region had become farmers, followed by Ethiopians (see Chronology: Ancient Sub-Saharan Africa, 8000 B.C.E.–350 C.E.). By 2500 B.C.E. farming was widespread in West, Central, and East Africa. In West Africa almost all food crops developed from local wild African plants like sorghum, millet, yams, and African rice. Rice gradually spread south to become a major crop in the rain forest zone. People in the eastern Sahara domesticated cotton and worked it into fabrics using spindles of baked clay, perhaps by 5000 B.C.E. Other crops came later from outside Africa, including wheat, barley, and chickpeas from the Middle East and bananas from Southeast Asia. But the movement went in both directions. Crops domesticated in West Africa such as sorghum and sesame reached India and China well before 2000 B.C.E.

CHRONOLOGY
Ancient Sub-Saharan Africa, 8000 B.C.E.–350 C.E.

8000–5000 B.C.E. Earliest agriculture in the Sahara and Nubia

5000–4000 B.C.E. Earliest agriculture in Ethiopia

3100–2800 B.C.E. First Nubian kingdom (disputed)

2500 B.C.E. Widespread agriculture in West, Central, and East Africa

2000 B.C.E. Beginning of Bantu migrations

1800–1500 B.C.E. Kerma kingdom in Nubia

1200 B.C.E. Early urbanization in western Sudan

1000–500 B.C.E. Bantu settlement of Great Lakes region

1000–500 B.C.E. Beginning of trans-Saharan trade

1000–500 B.C.E. Early ironworking technology

900–800 Mande towns

900 B.C.E.–350 C.E. Early Kush

Animal domestication presented a great challenge to sub-Saharan Africans. Cattle were probably domesticated very early from local sources in the southern Sahara and East Africa. But no other African animals were suitable for domestication, and some were dangerous predators. Rock art reveals possible failed attempts to domesticate giraffes, antelopes, and elephants. Most draft animals had to come from North Africa and Eurasia. Goats and sheep were brought in from the Middle East.

African peoples overcame geographical challenges in many ways. The major response to difficult climate and soils was to create a subsistence economy, rather than the high-productivity agriculture possible in Egypt, China, India, Southeast Asia, or southern Europe. One such subsistence strategy, pastoral nomadism, became the specialty of some groups in dry regions. Others chose farming by shifting cultivation, a creative adaptation to prevailing conditions. Shifting cultivators moved their fields around every few years, letting recently used land lie fallow for a while to regain its nutrients. If not abused, this system worked well for centuries. Only in a few fertile areas was intensive sedentary agriculture possible.

Ancient African Metallurgy

Most sub-Saharan peoples learned to make metal tools and weapons. Copper may have been mined in the Sahara by 1500 B.C.E. There was no pronounced bronze age, and generally the use of bronze came around the same time as or later than iron. Sub-Saharan Africans were among the world's earliest ironworkers, probably making iron by at least 1000 B.C.E. on the northern fringe of the Congo Basin. Iron smelters were built around 900 B.C.E. in the Great Lakes region, slightly earlier than the first Egyptian works. Between 600 and 300 B.C.E., iron was being mined, smelted, and forged widely in West and East Africa, with West Africans possibly being influenced by iron and bronze metallurgy established on the North African coast after 700 B.C.E. Since major iron ore deposits were rare, ore and iron artifacts had to be transported over long distances. Mining and working iron were both difficult operations, and those who did them probably occupied a special position in the community. Among the Haya (HI-uh) people in Tanzania (TAN-zeh-NEE-uh), when a new king was installed on the throne, he made a ritual visit to the blacksmith's hut, symbolizing the special relationship between the king and the ironworkers.

Iron Technology

Iron technology gradually improved and the number of products increased. In many places miners had to dig open pits or even put down vertical shafts to reach ore deposits deep underground. Furnaces for smelting ranged from simple open holes in the ground to elaborate clay structures 6 or 8 feet high with blower systems. The craftsmen made spear blades and arrowheads for warriors and hunters; hoes, axes, machetes, and knives for farmers and traders; bangles and rings for jewelry; gongs to produce music; hammers, hinges, and nails for household use; and iron bells for ceremonies and rituals.

Agriculture and metallurgy came to various African regions at different times, depending on circumstances, and they spread to the southern half of the continent last. Originally much of this region was inhabited by expert hunters and gatherers such as the !Kung (see Chapter 1), successful adapters to their environment who had little incentive to develop agriculture or ironworking. Gradually most of these groups were pushed farther south by iron-using farmers.

Early Urban Societies in Nubia

The first known urban African state after Egypt emerged in the region known in ancient times as Nubia (see Map 3.1), occupying what is today the northern half of the country of Sudan and far southern Egypt. Like Egyptians, Nubians turned to the Nile for survival. The region is mostly desert, but a thin area along the Nile was fertile, and copper and gold could be mined nearby. The first Nubian kingdom may have formed as early as 3100 B.C.E. Egypt dominated the region for many centuries, occasionally through military occupations. Egypt and Nubia also established a two-way trade, with Egypt exporting materials such as pottery and copper items to Nubia and importing ivory, ebony, ostrich feathers, and slaves from the Nubians. An independent Nubian kingdom, Kerma **(CARE-ma)**, appeared between 1800 and 1600 B.C.E. Extensive ruins of stone and mud-brick buildings, massive cemeteries, and large towers testify to a prosperous and well-organized society. Kerma was also distinguished for painted pottery and copper vessels and weapons. Around 1500 B.C.E. Egyptian forces once again occupied Nubia and destroyed the Kerma state.

Nubia and the Nile

When Egyptian power declined around 900 B.C.E., after the end of the New Kingdom, a larger Nubian state known as Kush **(koosh)** emerged, laying the foundations for a golden age of trade, culture, and metallurgy. The Kushites conquered Egypt in the eighth century B.C.E. but were pushed out by the Assyrians after nearly a century of occupation. Kush became a major regional trading hub. Overland caravan routes linked Kush with the Niger Basin, the Congo Basin, and the Ethiopian highlands. This enterprising society provided goods from central and southern Africa to the Mediterranean and Red Sea regions, as well as to markets as distant as India and China. From these places Kush imported Roman goblets and Chinese copper vessels.

Kush clearly benefited from its contacts with other societies, adding imported ideas to Nubian traditions. For example, irrigation technology imported from Egypt and western Asia made farming possible in this barren area. In religion, Kushites worshiped both Egyptian and local gods and buried their kings in Egyptian-style pyramids. A sixth-century B.C.E. inscription tells us that King Aspelta **(as-PELL-ta)**, as the son of the Egyptian sun-god, Ra, built for his son a pyramid of white stone. However, while Kushite art reflected Egyptian and even sometimes Greek influence, the overall effect remained distinctively Nubian. The unique Kushite society may have also been matrilineal, and some women held key political positions, including that of queen. Kings sometimes traced their descent back through female ancestors.

Eventually Kush linked the peoples of Africa and the Mediterranean. By 600 B.C.E. Kush had become the major African producer of iron, a position that gave it an even more crucial economic influence on the ancient world. The ancient Greek poet Homer described Kushites as "the most just of men; the favorites of the gods. The lofty inhabitants of Olympus **(oh-LIM-pus)** (home of Greek gods) journey to them, and take part in their feasts."[11]

Coronation Stela of Kushite King Aspelta (ca. 600 B.C.E.) The stela and inscription celebrate the coronation of King Aspelta. Related to the royal line through his mother, he was chosen from among many candidates by high priests acting in the name of the gods.

The Sudanic Societies and Trade Networks

In ancient times peoples in the Sudan grasslands of West Africa also developed towns and long-distance trade routes, and perhaps a few small kingdoms. Trade extended to Nubia and Egypt. By 1200 B.C.E. farmers in Mauritania **(MORE-ee-TAIN-ee-uh)** had built over two hundred stone villages and towns in what is now mostly uninhabited desert. They may have been the ancestors of the Mande **(MAN-da)** peoples, who now occupy a large area of the western Sudan. By 900 or 800 B.C.E. population increase had changed walled villages into large, well-constructed towns. Eventually this flourishing society was swallowed by the expanding Sahara and the people probably moved south.

Werner Forman/Art Resource, NY

Nok Terracotta Sculpture of Head Elaborate, life-size, technically complex sculptures reveal something of Nok material life in ancient Nigeria. Some figures sit on stools, carry an axe, or wear beads.

Long-distance trade, especially the caravan routes crossing the Sahara Desert, greatly aided the growth of Sudanic societies by forging enduring communication networks. The earliest caravan activity dates back to 1000 or 500 B.C.E. Gradually some groups took up commerce as their primary activity. The trans-Saharan trade depended on pack animals introduced by Berbers from North Africa, initially mules and horses and later camels. First domesticated in parched Arabia, camels stimulated trans-Saharan trade because they could endure many days of caravan travel without water. Eventually a large trade system linked the Sudanic towns with the southern Mediterranean coast and the forest zone to the south.

African societies gradually shaped their beliefs into complex artistic and religious traditions. On the southern fringe of the Sudan, in what is now central Nigeria, the Nok people, mostly farmers and herders, were working iron by 500 B.C.E., and they created enduring artistic traditions. Nok artists fashioned exquisite terracotta pottery and sculpture, including life-size and realistic human heads. The later art of several Nigerian societies shows Nok influence. While each society developed some distinctive notions of the cosmic order and their place within it, there were common patterns (see Witness to the Past: The World-view of an African Society). Many peoples, like the Mande and the Igbo **(EE-boh)**, believed in one divine force or supreme being, either male or female, who created the cosmos, earth, and life and then remained remote from human affairs. Africans needing immediate spiritual help appealed to secondary gods and spirits. Thus sub-Saharan African religion became a mix of monotheism, polytheism, and animism.

The Bantu-Speaking Peoples and Their Migrations

Bantu Migrations

Today people who speak closely related Bantu languages occupy most of Africa south of a line stretching from today's Kenya in the east to Cameroon in West-Central Africa. All of these societies can trace their distant ancestry back to the same location in West-Central Africa originally occupied by the Bantu (see Map 3.2). In their migrations, the Bantu incorporated many of the peoples they encountered and modified their own cultures to suit local conditions. The Bantu occupation of central, eastern, and southern Africa is the result of one of the great population movements in world history, a saga similar to that of the sea voyages that resulted in the settlement of the Pacific islands and the Indo-European migration into western and southern Eurasia. As the Bantu spread out over a wider area, they gradually divided into over four hundred different ethnic groups.

The Bantu originated along the Benue **(BAIN-way)** River in eastern Nigeria and western Cameroon **(KAM-uh-roon)**. But agricultural progress fostered overcrowding by 2000 B.C.E., spurring some to migrate eastward into the lands just north of the Congo River Basin. Bantu settled the Great Lakes region of East Africa between 1000 B.C.E. and 500 B.C.E. Some land-short Bantu from the Benue also began moving south into the Congo River Basin. Bantu mixed with the local peoples, exchanging technologies and cultural patterns.

Bantu Technologies

The Bantu benefited from metallurgy and agricultural technologies. They had learned to smelt iron, a knowledge that they spread along the Bantu communication network. Metallurgy allowed the Bantu to use iron tools and weapons to open new land and subdue the small existing populations. Although skilled farmers, some also adopted cattle and goat raising. By 2,000 years ago some Bantu living in northeast Africa had also learned to grow domesticated bananas and plantains (large bananas) imported from Southeast Asia, as well as sorghum **(SOAR-gum)** from the Nile Valley. These high-yielding crops replaced yams as their primary staple food and provided a spur to population growth, encouraging new migration into southern Africa.

The World-view of an African Society

Few primary sources survive for the ancient period in sub-Saharan Africa. Although it is difficult to extrapolate the distant past from contemporary oral traditions, we can get some insight into ancient understandings of the natural and spiritual realms from such accounts. This excerpt on the world-view of the Igbo people in southeastern Nigeria was compiled by an Igbo anthropologist, who summarized Igbo thought. Many Igbo perspectives may well derive from the Nok and Bantu cultures, whose ancestral homelands are near the region where the Igbo live today.

There is the world of man peopled by all created beings and things, both animate and inanimate. The spirit world is the abode of the creator, the deities, the disembodied and malignant spirits, and the ancestral spirits. It is the future abode of the living after their death. . . . Existence for the Igbo is a dual but interrelated phenomenon involving the interaction between the material and the spiritual, the visible and the invisible, the good and the bad, the living and the dead. . . . The world of the "dead" is a world full of activities. . . . The principle of seniority makes the ancestors [in the world of the "dead"] the head of the [extended kinship system in the world of man]. . . .

The world as a natural order which inexorably goes on its ordained way according to a "master plan" is foreign to Igbo conceptions. Rather, their world is a dynamic one—a world of moving equilibrium. It is an equilibrium that is constantly threatened, and sometimes actually disturbed by natural and social calamities. . . . But the Igbo believe that these social calamities and cosmic forces which disturb their world are controllable and should be "manipulated" by them for their own purpose. The maintenance of social and cosmological balance in the world becomes . . . a dominant and pervasive theme in Igbo life. They achieve this balance . . . through divination, sacrifice, and appeal to the countervailing forces of their ancestors . . . against the powers of the malignant spirits. . . . The Igbo world is not only a world in which people strive for equality; it is one in which change is constantly expected. . . . Life on earth is a link in the chain of status hierarchy which culminates in the achievement of ancestral honor in the world of the dead. . . .

The idea of a creator of all things is focal to Igbo theology. They believe in a supreme god, a high god, who is all good. . . . The Igbo high god is a withdrawn god. He is a god who has finished all active works of creation and keeps watch over his creatures from a distance. . . . Although the Igbo feel psychologically separated from their high god, he is not too far away, he can be reached, but not as quickly as can other deities who must render their services to man to justify their demand for sacrifices. . . . Minor gods [can] be controlled, manipulated, and used to further human interests. . . . Given effective protection, the Igbo are very faithful to their gods.

THINKING ABOUT THE READING

1. How do the Igbo understand the relationship between the human and spiritual worlds?
2. What is the role of the supreme god in their polytheistic theology?
3. How might their beliefs about the relationship of the human and spiritual realms shape Igbo society?

Source: From Uchendu, THE IGBO OF SOUTHEAST NIGERIA, 1E

SECTION SUMMARY

- African geography is extremely varied, ranging from jungles with abundant rainfall to deserts with practically no rainfall.
- The area now covered by the Sahara Desert was once lush and fertile, but it gradually dried out as rain patterns shifted southward.
- Small-scale agriculture flourished in Africa, though widespread disease made it difficult to domesticate animals.
- Sub-Saharan Africans worked with iron at the same time or before they worked with bronze.
- Early sub-Saharan societies were linked by trade.
- Nubia had a close relationship with Egypt, which eventually destroyed the Nubian kingdom of Kerma.
- The Nubian kingdom of Kush increased in power as Egypt declined and became a major trading hub linking the peoples of Africa to the Mediterranean.
- Caravan routes through the Sahara allowed for trade and for links among widely separated African peoples.
- The Bantu spread widely throughout Africa, mixing their culture and traditions with those of local peoples.

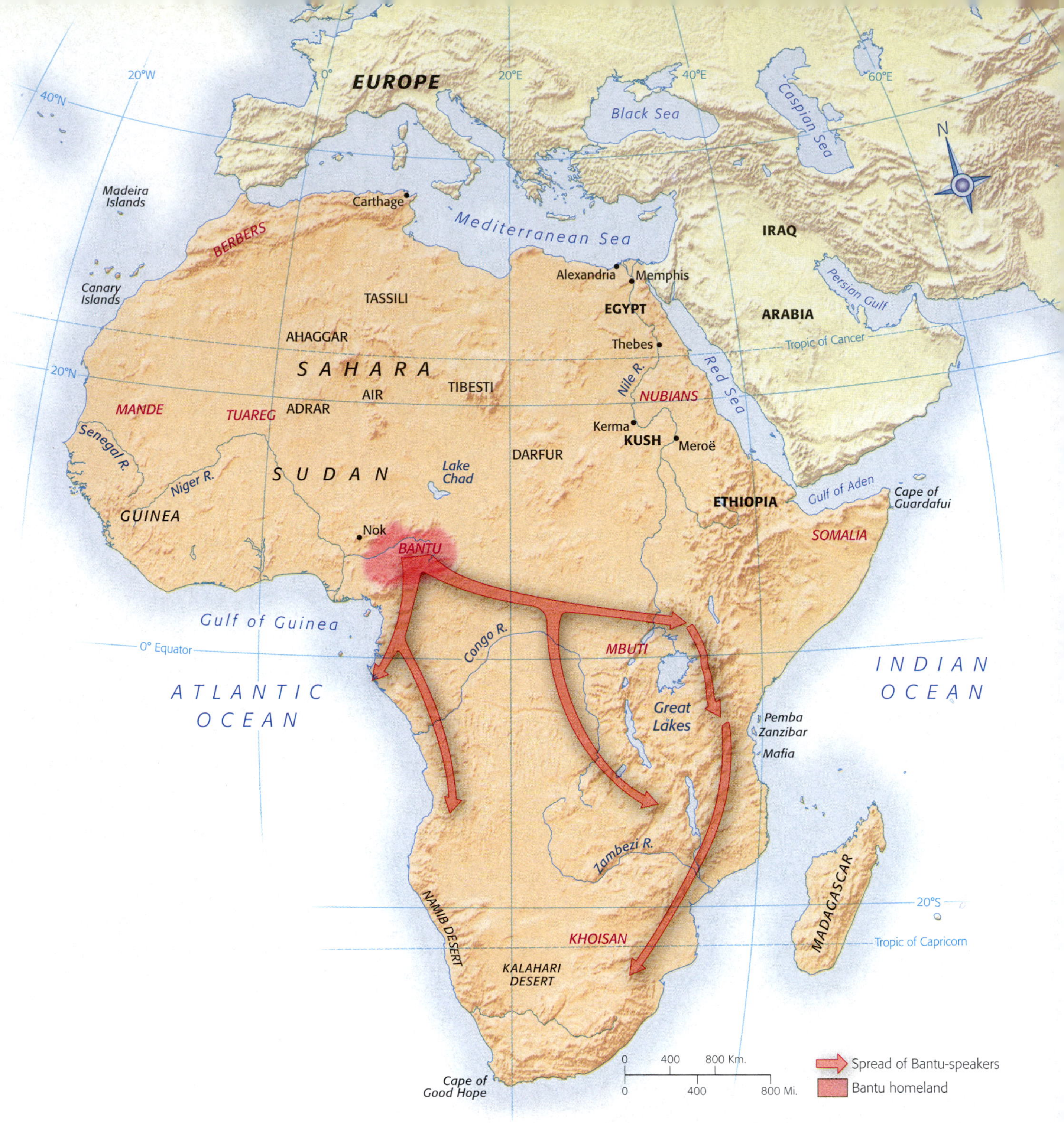

Map 3.2
Bantu Migrations and Early Africa

The Bantu-speaking peoples spread over several millennia throughout the southern half of Africa. Various societies, cities, and states emerged in West and North Africa.

e **Interactive Map**

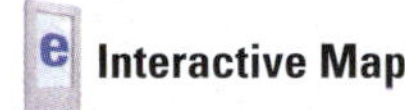

Early Societies and Networks of the Eastern Mediterranean

What were the contributions of the Hebrews, Minoans, Mycenaeans, Phoenicians, and Dorian Greeks to later societies in the region?

During the second millennium B.C.E., when the Egyptian and Mesopotamian societies were rising and falling, smaller bronze- and then iron-using societies in the eastern half of the

Mediterranean Basin were developing influential ideas or establishing cities and states. Among these, the Hebrews created the foundation for three major religions. The Minoans became a flourishing economic bridge between western Asia and southeastern Europe, and the warlike Mycenaeans built the first cities in Greece. The Phoenicians created an important new alphabet, established colonies in the western Mediterranean, and forged trade links with people as far away as England, fostering networks connecting many ancient societies. Greek migrants also began building an influential society.

Eastern Mediterranean Environments

Geographical Foundations

The history and diet of peoples living around the eastern Mediterranean were influenced by the regional climate, with its cool, rainy winters and hot, dry summers, and by the Mediterranean Sea. On the plains of the northern shores, people grew grain and made bread. The many hills also encouraged the planting of olive trees and grape vines, and both olive oil and wine became export crops. Pastoralism was common in the drier lands of Lebanon and Palestine. Finally, the eastern Mediterranean Sea, a mostly placid body of water, fostered boat building, maritime trade, and other contacts between diverse societies (see Map 3.3).

One of the densest populations emerged in Greece, located across the Aegean **(ah-JEE-uhn)** Sea from Anatolia. The Greeks were destined to live in relatively small, independent city-states and to be a seafaring, trading people. Unlike Mesopotamia and Egypt, where river valleys invited the creation of large political units, Greece consists of small valleys separated by numerous mountains. Physical separation encouraged political fragmentation and intellectual diversity. Greece also has an extensive coastline with many good harbors. Greeks could travel by sea east to Ionia (today western Turkey), south to Crete, or west to southern Italy more easily than they could establish connections with nearby inland towns. Thus the Mediterranean linked the societies of the Greek peninsula to other peoples such as the Minoans, Egyptians, and Phoenicians.

The Hebrews and Religious Innovation

The Hebrews, a Semitic people, were one of many groups of pastoral nomads led by powerful men known as patriarchs (from the Greek word for "rule by the father"). Their population was small, their economic and technological developments unimpressive, and their political achievements short-lived. The united Hebrew monarchy lasted less than a century. Yet the Hebrew contribution to religious history, especially to Christian and Islamic traditions, exceeds that of either the Mesopotamians or Egyptians.

The various books of the Hebrew Bible contain their basic laws and are the main source for their early history. The Hebrews trace their ancestry back to Abraham, a patriarch who supposedly lived in Mesopotamia sometime between 2000 and 1500 B.C.E. (see Chronology: The Eastern Mediterranean, 2000–539 B.C.E.). Whether Abraham was a real person or mythical may never be resolved by archaeological research. The patriarch and his two sons, Isaac and Ishmael, are considered the spiritual ancestors of three monotheistic religions—Judaism, Christianity, and Islam—which are often called the Abrahamic faiths and collectively have some 3 billion followers today. Historians and archaeologists have heatedly debated the historical reliability and antiquity of the Hebrew Bible, which was probably based in part on oral traditions. Little of it can be confirmed by archaeology. Some scholars think the biblical books are quite old, while others argue that most or all of the books were composed after 700 B.C.E. to support the claims of Hebrew political and religious factions. Some Bible stories seem based on Mesopotamian and Egyptian traditions, such as the great flood in the *Epic of Gilgamesh,* suggesting the spread of ideas. For example, some of the advice in the Hebrew Book of Proverbs, such as helping neighbors rather than acquiring wealth, closely echoes ideas in more ancient Egyptian writings. These ongoing controversies in biblical scholarship underline the importance of Hebrew religion to later history.

In the biblical account, Abraham led a few followers on a migration from southern Mesopotamia to Palestine, on the Mediterranean coast. Although born into a polytheistic world, Abraham recognized one supreme god. Peoples from Palestine had migrated, either voluntarily or as slaves, to Egypt since at least 2000

CHRONOLOGY
The Eastern Mediterranean, 2000–539 B.C.E.

2000–1500 B.C.E. Possible time frame for Abraham (biblical account)

2000–1400 B.C.E. Minoan society

1630 B.C.E. Volcanic eruption destroys Thera (Santorini)

1600–1200 B.C.E. Mycenaean society

1500–650 B.C.E. Phoenician society

1300–1200 B.C.E. Hebrew Exodus from Egypt led by Moses (biblical account)

1200–800 B.C.E. Greek "Dark Age"

1250 B.C.E. Destruction of Troy, possibly by Mycenaeans

1000 B.C.E. First Hebrew kingdom (biblical account)

922–722 B.C.E. Hebrew kingdoms of Israel and Judah

750 B.C.E. Carthage colony established by Phoenicians

722 B.C.E. Assyrian conquest of Israel

586 B.C.E. Neo-Babylonian (Chaldean) conquest of Judah

539 B.C.E. End of Babylonian captivity

Map 3.3
The Ancient Eastern Mediterranean

The Hebrew, Minoan, Mycenaean, Phoenician, and Greek societies developed along the eastern shores of the Mediterranean Sea. They exchanged goods and ideas with each other and with other western Asians and the Egyptians.

e Interactive Map

B.C.E. A group of Hebrews who had gone to Egypt to escape drought and been enslaved were freed and left Egypt, probably in the thirteenth century. This "Exodus" from Egypt and eventual return to Palestine was led by Moses, whom the later Hebrews believed to be the founder of their religion. Moses gave his name to a code of laws, including the Ten Commandments.

Hebrew Political History

Around 1000 B.C.E. the Hebrews had enough unity to establish a monarchy centered in the small city of Jerusalem. But Hebrew unity proved short-lived. After the death of King Solomon in 922 B.C.E., the monarchy split into a northern kingdom of Israel and a southern kingdom of Judah. In 722 the Assyrians conquered Israel and resettled its inhabitants elsewhere in their empire. When Assyria fell, the Hebrew prophet Nahum **(NAY-hum)** expressed the joy of many: "Nineveh [the Assyrian capital] is laid waste; who will bemoan her? All who hear the news of you will clap their hands over you."[12] In 586 the Chaldeans conquered Judah and moved its leaders to Babylon. The bitterness of the "Babylonian Captivity" was reflected in a Hebrew psalm: "By the rivers of Babylon, there we sat down, yea, we wept when we remembered Zion."[13] This exile ended in 539 when the Persians conquered the Chaldeans and allowed the Hebrews to return to Palestine. Later Palestine became part of the Roman Empire. The Jews were again dispersed after a revolt against Roman rule in 70 C.E., and from that time until the establishment of modern Israel in 1948 C.E., there was no Jewish state.

Religious Concepts

Despite their lack of political power, the religious history of the Hebrews, especially their ethical code, makes them memorable in world history. Over their long history the Hebrews developed four religious concepts that made them stand out among ancient peoples and that later influenced the Western and Islamic traditions: monotheism, morality, messianism, and meaning in history. Many Hebrews worshiped a single god, *Yahweh* **(YA-way)**. They believed Yahweh had made an agreement, or covenant, with their earliest patriarchs and reinforced it when Moses received the Ten Commandments. If they would obey him, he would protect them. Some neighboring peoples may also have adopted monotheistic views around the same time. Gradually the Hebrews reshaped monotheism, asserting that there is only one God, Yahweh, for all peoples, as the prophet Isaiah proclaimed: "There is no other God besides Me, a just God. Look to Me, and be saved, all you ends of the earth!"[14]

Hebrew holy men known as prophets refined two other Hebrew religious concepts, morality and messianism. These men emphasized that it was not enough to obey the Bible's social and ritual commandments. Following Yahweh also meant leading a moral life, refraining from lying, stealing, adultery, and persecution of the poor and oppressed. One of the differences between the code of Hammurabi and the law of Moses was that the latter also emphasized compassion for the poor. Also, unlike the Mesopotamian law, Hebrew law required that only the wrongdoer be punished, and not members of his or her family. Hebrew ethics emphasized mercy as well as justice. Another major concept, **messianism**, was the belief that God had given the Hebrew people a special mission in the world. As the Hebrews faced their time of troubles after the division of Solomon's kingdom, and especially after the fall of Judah to the Chaldeans, messianism acquired a broad spiritual meaning of bringing proper ethical behavior to all peoples. The book of Isaiah refers to Israelites as models from whom other people can learn moral truth: "I will give you as a covenant to the people, as a light to the [nations]. To open blind eyes, to bring out prisoners from the prison, those who sit in darkness."[15] This idea later inspired Christian missionary work.

messianism The Hebrew belief that their God, Yahweh, had given them a special mission in the world.

The final contribution is the idea that history itself has meaning and that it moves forward in a progressive, linear fashion and not in great repetitive cycles. Sanctifying a linear view of time meant that this earthly world was where human beings worked out their salvation by choosing good over evil. This belief also helped give birth later to the idea of progress, the notion that the future will be better than the past. It stood in contrast to ideas enshrined in the Indian religions of Hinduism and Buddhism that the material world is illusory and that time is cyclical.

Minoan Crete and Regional Trade

Minoan Cities

An influential urban society and network hub, now called Minoan (mi-NO-an), thrived on the island of Crete (kreet) between about 2000 and 1400 B.C.E. Crete lies just south of the Aegean Sea and the Greek peninsula, a strategic location that made it a logical center for sea trade between Egypt, western Asia, and southeastern Europe. Historians have remained intrigued by the achievements of Minoan society. Some of the cities had indoor plumbing and streets with drains and sewers, like the cities in ancient India. Paintings and sculptures show some Mesopotamian and Egyptian influences, but they are also different in style. Minoans apparently worshiped a large number of female deities, including an important mother goddess. The Minoans built no fortresses or defensive walls, apparently relying on their fleet to protect them. Around 1630 B.C.E. many cities on the island were destroyed, perhaps from earthquakes that followed a massive volcanic explosion that blew apart the nearby island of Thera (THER-uh) (today's Santorini). The

The Captivity of Israeli Women at Nineveh This relief comes from the palace of the Chaldean king Sennacherib in Nineveh. It was probably carved at the beginning of the seventh century B.C.E.

Erich Lessing/Art Resource, NY

Julie M. Fair

Wall Painting from Thera, Crete The paintings in palaces and homes show slices of Minoan life. This portrays female boxers, hinting that women played many roles in Minoan society.

sinking of most of Thera and the dispersal of the survivors may have given rise to the legend of the lost continent of Atlantis.

The first great Mediterranean sea power, the Minoans were innovators and played a key role in regional trade. They pioneered a mixed agriculture that was well suited to the region's sunny, dry climate. Minoans traded extensively with Sicily, Greece, and the Aegean islands and sent wine, olives, and wool to Egypt and southwest Asia. Ancient Crete also served as a hub or meeting place connecting, through trade, western Asians and North Africans with various European societies. The Cretan ports were counterparts to the Persian Gulf ports that linked western and southern Asia. Though the Minoans' writing has not been deciphered, tablets found in the palace appear to be written in two scripts, one perhaps of Mesopotamian origin and the other related to early forms of Greek.

The Mycenaeans and Regional Power

The Mycenaeans, Indo-Europeans named after the city of Mycenae **(my-SEE-nee)** in southern Greece, also became an important power between 1600 and 1200 B.C.E. after migrating into the Greek peninsula. A warrior society, their graves contain bronze swords and armor. Their state-controlled economy was tightly organized by the king and his scribes. Eventually the Mycenaeans conquered Crete (whose Minoan society had already collapsed), all of southern Greece, and the Aegean islands, forming an empire from which they collected taxes and tribute. They continued the Minoan trading networks, dispatching ships to Sicily, Italy, and Spain and into the Black Sea, and also engaged in war with rivals, operating out of strong fortresses. According to legends, around 1250 the Mycenaeans conquered Troy, a prosperous Hittite trading port along the northwestern coast of Anatolia. This event inspired Homer's epic story, the *Iliad,* some 500 years later. Scholars differ as to whether an actual Trojan War ever took place, and some suspect that the Homeric stories combine oral accounts of various conflicts. Whatever their accuracy, they strongly influenced the later Greeks and Romans.

Conquest and Trade

By 1200, however, the Mycenaeans themselves faced collapse, although the reasons remain unclear. A prolonged drought resulting from climate change or a possible series of earthquakes may have been factors. Many historians blame civil wars and attacks by warlike Indo-Europeans known as the Dorian Greeks, who were migrating into the peninsula. In the several centuries after 1200 various groups known as "Sea Peoples" pillaged and disrupted trade throughout the Aegean and eastern Mediterranean. But eventually a creative society emerged in Greece that incorporated many influences from the Dorian Greeks, Mycenaeans, Phoenicians, and Egyptians.

Collapse

The Phoenicians and Their Networks

The Phoenicians linked Mediterranean and southwest Asian peoples by trade networks and by their invention of a phonetic alphabet. Between 1500 and 1000 B.C.E. this Semitic people, known to the Hebrews as the Canaanites (KAY-nan-ites), established themselves along the narrow coastal strip west of the Lebanon mountains, where they built the great trading cities of Tyre (tire), Sidon (SIDE-en), and Byblos (BIB-los). Tyre was a major hub, the place where luxury goods from many societies were collected and the finest artists and craftsmen worked. The Hebrew prophet Ezekial denounced the rich, vibrant city and the extraordinary network of mercantile connections: "Your borders are in the midst of the seas. All the ships of the sea were in you to market your merchandise."[16] Although sometimes dominated by Egypt, these cities were fiercely competitive and independent states headed by kings. While the Phoenicians spoke a common language and worshiped the same gods, they never united. The Phoenicians' relatively rich land was the home of the now long-gone "cedars of Lebanon" prized by the tree-starved Sumerians, Egyptians, and Hebrews. The most famous cultural achievement of the Phoenicians, their simplification of Mesopotamian cuneiform writing into an alphabet of twenty-two characters, became the basis of later European alphabets.

Trading Cities

Only a few tablets containing information on Phoenician government, society, and religion survive. Most of what we know comes from Egyptian, Greek, and Hebrew sources; these peoples generally admired the Phoenicians' skills as scribes, seafarers, engineers, and artisans but also denounced them as immoral profiteers and cheaters. The Phoenician image as schemers, deserved or not, survives into modern times. Our term for a shameless woman, Jezebel, is derived from a princess of Tyre. Yet the Phoenician creation of an alphabet helped spread Phoenician influence in the Mediterranean.

Between 1000 and 800 B.C.E., the seafaring Phoenicians began to replace the declining Mycenaeans as the leaders in Mediterranean trade with western Asia. In addition, the Phoenicians became experts in new methods of dyeing cloth, and they may have traveled as far as England to get supplies of tin. They established colonies or trading posts beyond the Strait of Gibraltar on the southern coast of Spain and in Morocco, Sicily, and southern Italy. Some historians think the Phoenicians may have reached the Canary Islands and Madeira, off the coast of Morocco. Thus the Phoenicians became the greatest mariners of the ancient Mediterranean.

Trade and Colonization

Between 1000 and 500 B.C.E., the Mediterranean Sea became a major source of goods and wealth, partly because of Phoenician efforts. Solid bars of precious metals served as currency. Using their colonies as ports for resupply and repair, the Phoenicians traveled long distances to secure iron, silver, timber, copper, gold, and tin, all valuable commodities in western Asia and Egypt during the second and first millennia B.C.E. Legends suggest that around 600 B.C.E., under the sponsorship of the Egyptian king, a Phoenician fleet may even have sailed around Africa in an expedition lasting three years, but these journeys cannot be substantiated. In 650 B.C.E. the Assyrians conquered the Phoenician home cities and brought an end to their dynamic power, but some Phoenician colonies lived on. The most famous colony was Carthage in North Africa near what is today Tunis. Carthage became the capital of a major trading empire and the chief competitor to the Romans in the western Mediterranean by the third century B.C.E. As great sailors the Carthaginians later explored far down the coast of West Africa.

The Eclectic Roots of Greek Society

The fall of the Phoenicians and the Mycenaeans set the stage for another seafaring people, the Greeks, to found an influential urban society. During the centuries from the destruction of Mycenae around 1200 B.C.E. down to around 800 B.C.E., called the Greek "Dark Age," organized states and writing disappeared, the economic and social environment changed considerably, and there was great population movement. Dorian Greeks settled much of the Greek peninsula, and many Mycenaeans dispersed, some settling the offshore islands and others crossing the Aegean Sea to Ionia, where they established cities. The Greek world, scattered, as the philosopher Plato later put it, like frogs around a pond, became a mix of Mycenaean and Dorian peoples and traditions. Various tribes struggled for power.

Although the Greeks were famous as maritime traders, they were also warriors. Their respect for military strength is reflected in the works of Homer, oral epics written down between the eleventh and the eighth centuries B.C.E. that became an integral part of the Greek tradition. Historians disagree as to whether Homer was an actual person or the collective name for several authors who compiled these epic poems, perhaps a composite of various stories, into a narrative. Many themes in the epics may reflect influences from Mesopotamian literature such as the *Epic of Gilgamesh*, indicating the spread of ideas around the eastern Mediterranean world.

Homeric Epics

The first Homeric epic, the *Iliad*, is set during an attack by some Greek cities, led by their king Agamemnon (ag-uh-MEM-non), on Troy. The poem emphasizes the value of valor in war but also warns its readers against excessive pride. Arrogance leads the Greeks to make some nearly fatal mistakes. For example, the Greek hero Achilles **(uh-KIL-eez)** refuses to fight after a quarrel with Agamemnon. When Achilles' friend Patroclus **(puh-TROW-klus)** takes Achilles' place in the battle and is killed by Hector, the Trojan leader, a remorseful Achilles then kills Hector, warning that there can be no truce until one of them has fallen. The poem ends when Hector's father, Priam, comes to ask Achilles for his son's body. Achilles is moved by Priam's courage, and both men share their grief. This poem and Homer's second epic, the *Odyssey*, a story of the adventures of Odysseus **(oh-DIS-ee-us)**, or Ulysses, who is returning home after the Trojan War, portrayed the Greek gods as superheroes who intervened frequently to help their human friends and hinder their enemies. The Homeric world measured virtue by success in combat rather than justice or mercy. Yet these great epics continue to be read, not only because of their dramatic and often brutal war scenes, but also because they tell us something about the tragedy of human life. This emphasis on both human power and suffering remained a part of Greek literature throughout the following centuries.

The Homeric epics and belief in the gods that they introduced greatly influenced the emerging Greek society. The Greeks also borrowed ideas from neighboring peoples, including the Egyptians and western Asians, although the degree of outside influence on early Greek culture is debated (see the Historical Controversy feature in "Societies, Networks, Transitions," page 94). Certainly the Mediterranean was a zone of interaction for peoples living around its rim. Phoenician ships, which had avoided a turbulent Greece for several hundred years, began to show up again, restoring Greek contact with the eastern Mediterranean and its regional trade networks. Soon the Greeks adopted and modified the Phoenician alphabet. These centuries built a foundation for a dynamic Greek society in the Classical Era.

SECTION SUMMARY

- Mountainous Greece favored the development of many small, independent communities, rather than one homogenous community.
- The Hebrews were politically fragmented, but their religious writings, with their emphasis on monotheism, morality, messianism, and meaning in history, have had a tremendous impact on religious history.
- Minoan Crete was the first great Mediterranean sea power and had a well-developed urban infrastructure.
- Around 1250 B.C.E., the Mycenaeans possibly conquered Troy; this event later inspired Homer's epic, the *Iliad*.
- The Phoenicians, the region's greatest maritime traders, simplified the Mesopotamian cuneiform writing into an alphabet, which served as the basis for later European alphabets.
- The Homeric epics, the *Iliad* and the *Odyessy*, greatly influenced the emerging Greek society, which was a synthesis of Mycenaean and Dorian Greek peoples.

CHAPTER SUMMARY

Egypt is often called "the gift of the Nile" because it arose in the flood-prone Nile River Valley. The Egyptian system lasted for several thousand years in its basic form. The Egyptians developed a state led by kings and invented the hieroglyphics writing system. In their stable and predictable environment, they developed a more optimistic world-view and culture than the Mesopotamians. Egyptians also participated in trade networks linking western Asia and the Mediterranean Basin with sub-Saharan Africa and India.

Many sub-Saharan African peoples also invented or adopted agriculture and metallurgy, both of which built the framework for cities and states. An environment of grasslands, forests, and the expanding Sahara Desert shaped their history, and the gradual drying out of the Sahara region forced many people to migrate. Cities arose early in Nubia (along the central Nile), probably stimulated by long-distance trade and contacts with Egypt. The Sudan fostered distinctive cultures. The Bantu peoples, in one of the greatest migrations in history, spread their farming and iron-based culture and languages widely in the southern half of Africa.

The Mediterranean societies also benefited from regional connections. The trade routes of the seafaring Minoans, Mycenaeans, and Phoenicians enriched the peoples of western Asia and the Mediterranean Basin by bringing them material goods, markets, cultural contacts, and a practical new alphabet. The Hebrews' evolving understanding of their mission, and of Yahweh, was influenced by their contact with Egyptians and Mesopotamians. Some of these contributions, such as the Phoenician alphabet and Hebrew religious and ethical concepts, have influenced many peoples down to the present day. Greece arose from interaction among several Mediterranean societies in a turbulent period during which Homer wrote his great epics.

KEY TERMS

pharaohs
hieroglyphics
monotheism
Bantu
Sudan
desertification
messianism

EBOOK AND WEBSITE RESOURCES

PRIMARY SOURCE

Egyptian *Book of the Dead*

INTERACTIVE MAPS

Map 3.1 Ancient Egypt and Nubia
Map 3.2 Bantu Migrations and Early Africa
Map 3.3 The Ancient Eastern Mediterranean

LINKS

African Timelines (http://web.cocc.edu/cagatucci/classes/hum211/timelines/htimelinetoc.htm). Offers many links to essays and other sources on Africa; maintained by Central Oregon Community College.

Ancient Jewish History (http://www.us-israel.org/jsources/Judaism/jewhist.html). Offers much useful information.

Exploring Ancient World Cultures (http://eawc.evansville.edu/). Excellent site run by Evansville University, with essays and links on the ancient Near East and Europe.

Internet African History Sourcebook (http://www.fordham.edu/halsall/africa/africasbook.html). This site contains much useful information and documentary material on ancient Africa.

Internet Ancient History Sourcebook (http://www.fordham.edu/halsall/ancient/asbook.html). Exceptionally rich collection of links and primary source readings.

Plus flashcards, practice quizzes, and more. Go to: www.cengage.com/history/lockard/globalsocnet2e.

SUGGESTED READING

Armstrong, Karen. *The Great Transformation: The Beginning of Our Religious Traditions*. New York: Alfred Knopf, 2006. Good discussion of ancient religions.

Castledon, Rodney. *Minoans: Life in Bronze Age Crete*. New York: Routledge, 1993. A valuable recent survey.

Connah, Graham. *African Civilization: An Archaeological Perspective*, 2nd ed. Cambridge: Cambridge University Press, 2004. A good overview of early African societies; emphasizes the rise of cities and states.

Dunstan, William E. *The Ancient Near East*. New York: Harcourt Brace, 1998. Designed for the general reader, this work makes sense of the confusing array of states and empires in western Asia and Egypt.

Ehret, Christopher. *The Civilizations of Africa: A History to 1800*. Charlottesville: University of Virginia Press, 2002. A pathbreaking introduction to African history, with nearly half devoted to the ancient period.

Grimal, Nicolas. *A History of Ancient Egypt*. Oxford: Blackwell, 1992. A clear account of this society for beginning students.

Harris, Nathaniel. *History of Ancient Egypt: The Culture and Lifestyle of the Ancient Egyptians*. New York: Barnes and Noble, 1997. A richly illustrated overview of Egyptian life.

Markoe, Glenn E. *The Phoenicians*. Berkeley: University of California Press, 2000. A fine account of the history, cities, economy, and literature of this maritime society.

McNutt, Paula M. *Restructuring the Society of Ancient Israel*. Louisville: Westminster John Knox Press, 1998. Survey of knowledge and scholarly debates.

Mertz, Barbara. *Red Land, Black Land: Daily Life in Ancient Egypt*, rev. ed. New York: Peter Bedrick, 1990. A lively and readable recreation of the lives and values of ancient Egyptians.

Newman, James L. *The Peopling of Africa: A Geographic Interpretation*. New Haven: Yale University Press, 1995. An excellent summary of what we know about the early history and migrations of Africa's people.

Niditch, Susan. *Ancient Israelite Religion*. New York: Oxford University Press, 1997. An account of the Hebrew religion that shows its debt to the Canaanites as well as those features that made it unique.

Shaw, Ian, ed. *The Oxford History of Ancient Egypt*. New York: Oxford University Press, 2004. A well-rounded, up-to-date survey.

Stiebing, William H. *Ancient Near Eastern History and Culture*, 2nd ed. New York: Longman, 2008. An up-to-date survey of ancient western Asia, Egypt, and the eastern Mediterranean.

Tyldesley, Joyce. *Hatshepsut: The Female Pharaoh*. New York: Viking, 1996. A readable biography of this remarkable leader.

Welsby, Derek A. *The Kingdom of Kush: Napatan and Meroitic Empires*. Princeton: Markus Wiener, 1996. A well-illustrated and up-to-date survey of Kushite society.

CHAPTER

4

Around the Pacific Rim: Eastern Eurasia and the Americas, 5000–600 B.C.E.

CHAPTER OUTLINE

Shang Axe Head
The Shang Chinese made some of the ancient world's finest bronze tools. This axe head, decorated with a human face, may have been used to behead rivals of the Shang rulers.

He encouraged the people and settled them. He called his superintendent of works [and] minister of instruction, and charged them with the building of the houses. Crowds brought the earth in baskets. The roll of the great drum did not overpower [the noise of the builders].

—Chinese poem from the second millennium B.C.E.[1]

FOCUS QUESTIONS

1. How did an expanding Chinese society arise from diverse local traditions?
2. What were some key differences between the Shang and Zhou periods in China?
3. How did the traditions developing in Southeast and Northeast Asia differ from those in India and China?
4. How do scholars explain the settlement and rise of agriculture in the Americas?

According to Chinese tradition, around 1400 B.C.E. a ruler named Pan Keng supervised the building of a new capital city, Anyang **(ahn-yahng)**, on a flat plain alongside the Huan River. The king and his officials supervised the citizens in the hard construction labor, which was done to the beat of a drum. The king had high expectations for his new capital. Thanks to the rich soil, productive farms would stretch out into the distance. The river could supply water and aid in defense. People could find timber, hunt, or seek relief from the summer heat in mountains a short chariot ride away. Anyang was likely China's first planned city. Surrounded by four walls facing the points of the compass, it reflected the ancient adage that without harmony nothing lasts. Three and a half millennia later archaeologists digging at Anyang found exquisite ritual bronzes and "dragon bones," animal bones carved with some of the earliest Chinese writing. For hundreds of years, local chemists, not knowing their priceless historical value, had been grinding up these bones to make folk medicine. But they showed that ancient China, like Mesopotamia and Egypt, had both cities and a writing system. Although Anyang's buildings crumbled with time and ruling families came and went, the legacy of early China did live on for centuries.

Cities, states, agriculture, and trade networks developed in various societies on both sides of the Pacific Ocean. People in China and Korea were among the earliest people in the world to develop farming and metalworking, and Southeast Asians pioneered in maritime technology. The ancient Chinese established a foundation for a society that has retained many of its original ideas and customs down to the present day. Despite formidable geographical barriers, China and Southeast Asia also became connected very early to other parts of Eurasia by trade networks. On the American side of the Pacific, too, many peoples underwent the great transitions to farming, cities, and complex social structures. Although mountains, deserts, and forest barriers tended to isolate North, Central, and South American societies from each other, regional networks of exchange still formed during the ancient period.

Visit the website and eBook for additional study materials and interactive tools: www.cengage.com/history/lockard/globalsocnet2e

The Formation of Chinese Society, 6000–1750 B.C.E.

How did an expanding Chinese society arise from diverse local traditions?

China was one of the first societies with cities and states, joining Harappa, Mesopotamia, Egypt, and Minoan Crete in pioneering new ways of life. Societies change in part through contact with each other, but forbidding desert and mountain barriers, including the high Tibetan **(tuh-BET-en)** Plateau on China's western borders, complicated contact with China, although they did not prevent some influences from crossing borders. But productive farming, creative cultures, and the rise of states laid the framework for a distinctive society, now at least 4,000 years old.

China and Its Regional Environments

The Chinese faced many challenges in communicating both with each other and with distant peoples. China's vast size, combined with a difficult topography, made transportation difficult and also encouraged regional cultural and political loyalties. The early Chinese were sometimes divided into competing states, and governments struggled to enforce centralizing policies. The Himalayas **(him-uh-LAY-uhs)**, the Tibetan Plateau, and great deserts inhibited contact with South and West Asia. However, the Chinese did have regular exchanges, including both trade and conflict, with the peoples in Central Asia, North Asia, Southeast Asia, and Tibet, whose cultures, languages, and ways of life were very different from the Chinese. The Chinese sometimes extended political control over these peoples and sometimes were invaded and even conquered by them.

Geographical Foundations

China's large land area was one major factor that fostered regionalism. Modern China covers as much land as western and eastern Europe combined. But most people lived in the eastern third of the modern country. Most Chinese also lived in inland river valleys rather than along the coast. As a result, maritime commerce was not very significant until 1000 C.E. China's three major river systems helped shape Chinese regionalism. The Yellow, or Huang He **(hwang ho)**, River; the Yangzi **(yahng-zeh)**, or Yangtze, River; and the West, or Xijiang **(SHEE JYAHNG)**, River all flow from west to east and hence do not link the northern, central, and southern parts of China. The Yellow River, sometimes termed "China's sorrow" because of its many destructive floods, flows some 3,000 miles through north China to the Yellow Sea, but it is easily navigable only in some sections. The more navigable but also flood-prone Yangzi, the world's fourth-longest river, flows through central China, a region of moderate climate that has long had the densest population. The shorter West River system helps define mountainous and subtropical south China.

China's neighboring regions had diverse environments and distinctive cultures. The deserts and grasslands of Central Asia, with their blazing hot summers and long, bitterly cold winters, were mostly unpromising for intensive agriculture. The rugged, pastoralist Central Asian societies that lived there traded with, warred against, and sometimes conquered the settled farmers of China, Korea, and India. The Central Asians who most affected Chinese history included diverse Turkik-speaking peoples, some of whom lived in the dry Xinjiang **(SHIN-jee-yahng)** region of far western China. The Tibetans were subsistence farmers and herders. The ancient Chinese also forged occasional relations with people in mainland Southeast Asia, Manchuria, and Korea.

CHRONOLOGY
Ancient China, 7000–600 B.C.E.

7000 Agriculture begins in Yellow River Basin

5000 Agriculture begins in Yangzi River Basin

5000–3000 Yangshao culture in northern China

3000–2200 Longshan culture in northern China

2600 Copper mining

2183–1752 Xia dynasty in northern China (disputed)

1752–1122 Shang dynasty in northern China

1400 Beginning of bronze-casting industry

1122–221 Zhou dynasty

Early Chinese Agriculture

Agriculture in China began around 7000 B.C.E., perhaps 1,000 years later than in Mesopotamia (see Chronology: Ancient China, 7000–600 B.C.E.). The remains of Neolithic settlements have been discovered all over China, suggesting the diverse roots of Chinese society. The Yellow and Wei River Valleys in north China were major centers of early farming. The modest annual rainfall and frequent flooding made the region somewhat similar to the Nile, Tigris-Euphrates, and Indus Basins. In addition, winds blowing in from the Gobi Desert of Mongolia to the northwest deposited massive amounts of dust, which enriched the soils of north China. The people planted the wheatlike, highly drought-resistant millet. Later, wheat, likely imported from India or

CHRONOLOGY

	China	Japan and Southeast Asia	The Americas
10,000 B.C.E.		**10,000–300** B.C.E. Jomon culture	
5000 B.C.E.	**5000–3000** B.C.E. Yangshao culture	**4000–2000** B.C.E. Austronesian migrations	
3000 B.C.E.	**3000–2200** B.C.E. Longshan culture		**3000–1600** B.C.E. Peruvian cities
2000 B.C.E.	**1752–1122** B.C.E. Shang dynasty **1122–221** B.C.E. Zhou dynasty		**1200–300** B.C.E. Olmec **1200–200** B.C.E. Chavín
1000 B.C.E.		**1000–800** B.C.E. First Southeast Asian states	

Mesopotamia, became northern China's main cereal grain. Ancient songs tell us something about the farming routine:

> They clear away the grass, the trees; Their ploughs open up the ground. In a thousand pairs they tug at weeds and roots, Along the low grounds, along the ridges. They sow the many sorts of grain, The seeds that hold moist life. How that blade shoots up, How sleek, the grown plant.[2]

Farther south, the Chinese in the Yangzi River Basin began cultivating rice by 5000 B.C.E. Thus very early two distinct agricultural traditions emerged. In the cooler, drier north drought-tolerant crops like wheat, millet, pears, and apricots were mainstays. In the wetter, warmer southern half of China, irrigated rice predominated. But rice became so important that for several thousand years Chinese have greeted each other by asking, Have you eaten rice yet?, and have described losing a job as breaking one's rice bowl.

Highly productive agriculture was always a key to China's success. Making wise use of the land, the Chinese sustained reasonably adequate diets over many millennia. Despite sporadic famine, the Chinese people were basically well fed and well housed throughout much of history, beginning in ancient times. Productive farming also promoted population growth: China contained between 2 and 4 million people by 3000 B.C.E. The Chinese ate well enough that they came to perceive food as more than simple fuel. Cooking became an art form and an essential component of social life, and a God of the Kitchen became an important deity of folk religion. Many regional cooking variations developed, as any traveler will see by exploring the Cantonese, Hunanese **(hoon-ahn-eez)**, Mandarin, and Sichuanese **(SUH-chwahn-eez)** restaurants in large cities around the world. The use of chopsticks for eating meals probably goes back 4,000 years.

Neolithic China included several societies with distinctive regional traditions that established a foundation for Chinese cultural development. The Yangshao **(YANG-shao)** ("painted pottery") culture, which began in the middle Yellow River region around 5000 B.C.E., covered an area of north China larger than Mesopotamia or Egypt. Yangshao people made fine painted pottery, used kilns, bred pigs and dogs, weaved thread, and buried their dead in cemeteries, suggesting belief in an afterlife. They also raised silkworms and fashioned the silk into clothes. In the centuries to follow, silk making become a unique Chinese activity, and Chinese silk was exported all over Eurasia. Music was popular; a 7,000-year-old seven-holed flute is the oldest still playable musical instrument ever found anywhere in the world. Evidence for jade carving, for which the Chinese later became famous, has been found in several regions. Finally, since floods and earthquakes were common, the early Chinese sought various ways to avert disaster. This search led to religious speculation and experimentation with techniques to predict the future.

The Growth and Spread of Chinese Culture

About 3000 B.C.E., when the Sumerians were building their cities, the exchange of ideas and technologies over the developing trade networks began to produce an expansive Chinese culture out

[2] *The Book of Songs*, translated by Arthur Waley (London: George Allen and Unwin, 1954), © copyright by permission of The Arthur Waley Estate.

Peasant Life in Zhou China The decorations on bronze vessels from Zhou China offer information on peasant life. This decoration, from the Warring States Period, shows people in varied activities: fighting, hunting, making music, performing rituals, and preparing food.

E. Consten, Das alte China

of various regional traditions. As late as 2000 B.C.E. many societies with different cultures and languages remained in China, but gradually the societies in northern and central China merged their traditions into a common social and cultural zone. The Yellow River Basin remained a major core of creativity. The Longshan **(LUNG-shahn)** ("black pottery") culture flourished between 3000 and 2200 B.C.E. Occupations were now more specialized, fostering a division of labor and social classes. The Longshan people built strong houses, lived in walled villages and towns, and had weapons. They also made pottery almost as hard as metal, carved high-quality jade, and created a simple pictographic writing system. Millennia before any other society, the Chinese of this era also used industrial diamonds to polish ceremonial ruby and sapphire axes, giving them a fine sheen. Chinese in other regions also made contributions. For example, the people in the Yangzi Basin produced distinctive traditions of agriculture, animal domestication, town building, and bronze metallurgy that were at least as old, if not older, than those of north China.

During the first millennium B.C.E., Chinese identity and customs gradually expanded from the Yellow and Yangzi Basins into south China. The Chinese displaced or absorbed most of the indigenous **(in-DIJ-uh-nuhs)** peoples (the original inhabitants) in the south, although many ethnic minorities still live there. This mixing of different peoples produced a Chinese culture that encompassed many regional traditions and, at times, different states, all held together by many common customs as well as a standardized written language. Political unity helped but was not essential to this sense of a shared cultural identity.

Population growth and shared culture made possible the first state. Chinese historians labeled this state the Xia **(shya)** (Hsia) dynasty (2183–1752 B.C.E.), but its existence is still debated. A possible Xia capital city, one square mile in size, was built around 2000 B.C.E. near the Yellow River. The Xia may have presided over an occupationally diverse society including scribes, metallurgists, artisans, and bureaucrats. Some influences also filtered in from Central Asia, including the horse and chariot, ironworking, and certain philosophies, but in general, the Chinese themselves developed the ideas and institutions that gave their society the ability to expand, grow, adapt, and coordinate large populations. Many of the ancient traditions remain influential even today.

SECTION SUMMARY

- Early Chinese society was concentrated inland from the sea and was frequently fragmented into various states.
- In the cold, dry Chinese north, crops such as wheat and millet were grown, while in the wetter, warmer south, rice was dominant.
- Members of the Yangshao ("painted pottery") society were skilled craftspeople who excelled at carving, weaving, and village design.
- As time passed, the widely diverse Chinese peoples began to knit themselves together in one broad society with traditions that persist to this day.
- The first Chinese state may have appeared late in the third century B.C.E.

The Reshaping of Ancient Chinese Society, 1750–600 B.C.E.

What were some key differences between the Shang and Zhou periods in China?

China had clearly made the great transition to cities and states when the Shang **(shahng)** dynasty established a powerful state and an expanding culture based on bronze technology. The Shang were followed by a more decentralized, iron-using Zhou **(joe)** dynasty, when the Chinese improved writing and developed literature. Some religious notions of enduring influence in China also appeared in these centuries. Isolation from other Eurasian states fostered a feeling of cultural superiority. The Chinese perceived themselves surrounded by less developed neighbors who either adopted Chinese customs or invaded China to enjoy its riches. Strong governments, technological developments, and writing helped make China the most influential East Asian society.

The Shang Dynasty Reshapes Northern China

Shang Conquests and Government

The Shang (1752–1122 B.C.E.), the first Chinese dynasty that can be well documented, began around the same time that Hammurabi ruled in Babylon and the Harappan society was collapsing in India. A people from the western fringe of China, the Shang, like the Aryan migrants into India, had adopted horse-drawn chariots for warfare and owed their success partly to contacts with Central Asian pastoralists. They conquered the eastern Yellow River Basin, imposing a hierarchy dominated by landowning aristocrats (see Map 4.1), presiding over a growing economy and the building of more cities. However, many Chinese outside Shang control maintained their own states and unique customs.

The Shang established an authoritarian state, perhaps in part to coordinate irrigation and dam building. Shang kingship was passed on to a monarch's brother or son. Kings presented themselves as father figures who headed the country as a father did a family, claiming both political and spiritual leadership. Like the Aryans who were then moving into India, they devoted much of their energy to military matters, using a lethal combination of archers, spearmen, and charioteers. One of their concerns was defending their northern borders, a recurring theme in Chinese history. The relative prosperity of China in comparison to the marginal existence possible in the grasslands and deserts beyond the frontiers often prompted pastoral nomads to invade the Yellow River Valley.

Shang Cities, Technology, and Society

Economically and technologically the Shang was a flourishing period. Many cities were built as administrative and commercial centers. Anyang, the ruler Pan Keng's new capital city discussed in the chapter opening, was surrounded by a wall 30 feet high and 60 feet wide that enclosed 4 square miles; altogether, the city and its suburbs spread out over some 10 square miles. It apparently took some 10,000 workers eighteen years to build Anyang, reflecting considerable political and social organization. Technology improved, especially with the introduction of bronze in 1400 B.C.E. and the earliest porcelain. This was the great age of bronze, and the Shang are often considered the most skilled bronze casters in the Afro-Eurasian world. They produced flawless bronze arrows, spears, sculpture, pots, and especially ritual vessels for drinking wine. The Shang also produced glazed pottery that was the forerunner of the porcelain ("china") for which the Chinese would later become so famous.

The Shang social hierarchy was dominated by landowning aristocrats, many of them government officials. They enjoyed luxurious surroundings, and their residences were built on cement-like foundations. Aristocratic women also enjoyed a high status. For example, Fuhao **(foo-HOW)**, a wife of a Shang king, led military campaigns and owned large estates. Shang leaders and their families were buried in elaborate royal tombs with great quantities of valuable objects.

Shang Bronze Pots These bronze ritual vessels, some featuring animal designs, were made during the Shang or early Zhou period. They were used for ceremonies.

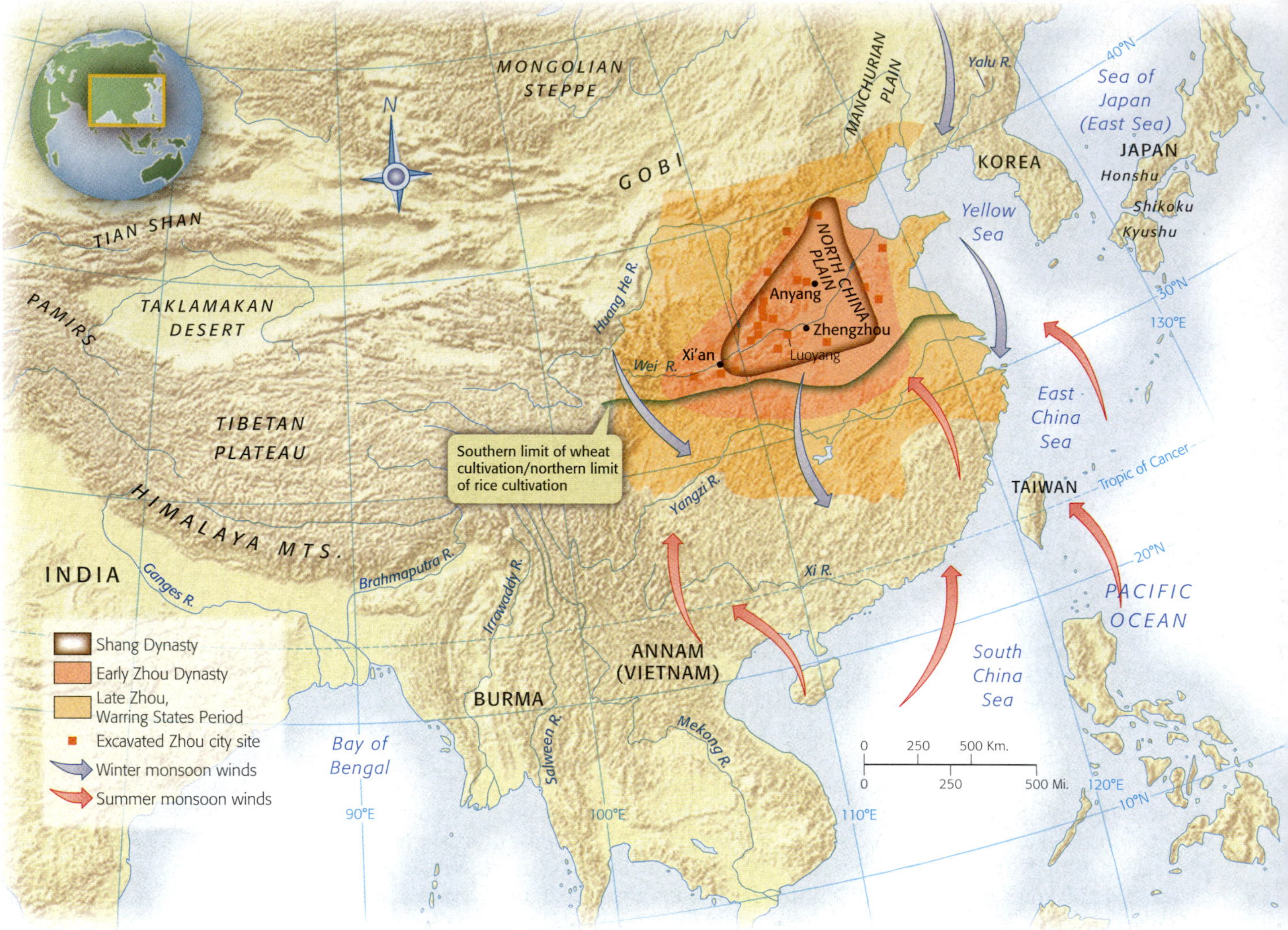

Map 4.1
Shang and Zhou China

The earliest Chinese states arose in north China along the Yellow River and its tributaries. The bronze-using Shang dynasty presided over the first documented state and were succeeded by the iron-using Zhou, who governed much of north and central China.

 **Interactive Map**

However, many people were commoners, included skilled artisans, scribes, and merchants. The scribes may have formulated the world's earliest simple decimal system. Farmers and laborers, including many slaves, occupied the bottom of the social hierarchy, and they were often mobilized by the powerful state for major building projects. The Shang were harsh masters. They practiced human and animal sacrifice as part of their religious observances, often using slaves as victims.

Shang Writing

The Shang's momentous contribution was an elaborate writing system. In an attempt to predict the future, influential people wrote questions addressed to the gods on bones of animals and tortoise shells. The variety of subjects included the abundance of the next harvest, the outcome of a battle, the weather, or the birth of an heir. For example, one inquired whether "if the king hunted, whether the chase would be without mishap."[3] Some prestigious officials were experts in interpreting the future with these bones. The writing found on oracle bones was clearly the forerunner of today's Chinese writing.

The Early Zhou and Their Government

Political Change

As Shang power faded, the Zhou, a state on the western fringe of China, invaded and overthrew the Shang, forming a new dynasty, the Zhou (1122–221 B.C.E.), and a new type of government. The Duke of Zhou supposedly urged that "we must go on, abjuring all idleness, until our reign is universal and there shall not be one who is disobedient to our rule."[4] But the decentralized Zhou system differed considerably from the Shang approach. A relatively weak central government ruled over small states that had considerable autonomy but owed service obligations to the king.

This decentralization reflected the Zhou realization that, despite their impressive military technology, Chinese culture had spread too far for them to administer the entire society effectively. The royal family directly ruled the area around their capital but parceled out the rest to followers and relatives. The regional leaders became local lords with much local power. Hence the Zhou kings presided, however symbolically, over a much larger land area than that of the Shang, from southern Manchuria to the Yangzi Basin (see Map 4.1).

To solidify their position, the Zhou justified their triumph over the Shang with a new concept: the **Mandate of Heaven**. According to this belief, rulers had the support of the gods ("heaven") so long as conditions were good. However, when there was war, famine, or other hardships, heaven withdrew its sanction and rebellion was permissible. The decadent and cruel Shang, the Duke of Zhou argued, lost their right to rule because their last kings mocked the gods by their behavior. But over time this radical new concept was used against the Zhou and all later dynasties. Monarchs lost their legitimacy if their misrule led to a crisis. Ever since the Chinese have invoked the Mandate of Heaven to justify the demise of a discredited government.

Mandate of Heaven A Chinese belief that rulers had the support of the supernatural realm as long as conditions were good, but rebellion was justified when they were not.

Furthermore, Chinese scholars began to view their political history in terms of the **dynastic cycle**. Instead of seeing a straight line of progress in history, as the Hebrews did, the Chinese focused on dynasties of ruling families, all of which more or less followed the same pattern as their predecessors. The cycle always began with a new dynasty, which brought peace and prosperity for a few decades. Then overexpansion and corruption led to increasingly costly government, bankruptcy, social decay, and rebellions, eventually resulting in a new dynasty. This concept shaped Chinese thinking for the next 2,500 years.

dynastic cycle The Chinese view of their political history, which focuses on dynasties of ruling families.

The Zhou system was unstable, plagued by chronic warfare between the various substates, with larger substates conquering smaller ones. As a result, the 1,700 substates of the early Zhou years were reduced to 7 by 400 B.C.E. These larger substates now had considerable power in counteracting the weakening Zhou kings. Furthermore, Central Asians were obtaining faster ponies, forcing the Chinese to erect better defenses against their relentless pressure.

Early Zhou Society and Economy

Social Patterns

Zhou government not only brought political fragmentation and a figurehead monarchy, but it also fostered a rigid society clearly divided into aristocrats, commoners, and slaves. The nobility, who owed allegiance to the king as vassals but governed their own realms as they liked, owned large estates defended by private armies and worked by slaves. As influential commoners, the merchants had more freedom of action and often became rich. The majority of slaves were soldiers from rival ministates captured in the frequent wars. Criminals and sometimes their relatives were enslaved for their misdeeds. Peasants were mostly bound to the soil on aristocracy-owned land (see the Witness to the Past: The Poetry of Peasant Life in Zhou China), assigned work and punished if it was not done. Their songs reflected resignation: "We rise at sunrise, We rest at sunset. Dig wells and drink, Till our field and eat—What is the strength of the emperor to us?"[5] Yet, there were some checks on landowner power. The more repressive and exploitive lords lost many of their workers and slaves, who migrated or absconded, depopulating the land and ruining the landlord.

Gender roles were rigid in this patriarchal society. All marriages were arranged by parents. A song from the times states: "How does one take a wife? Without a matchmaker she cannot be got." Before or after marriage most women worked hard, and their assigned place was in the home, preparing food, doing housekeeping, and making clothes. Women at all levels were expected to be submissive, and they enjoyed no official role in public affairs. While many elite women were literate, few peasant women or men enjoyed opportunities to learn to read and write. Both genders valued friendship and kinship, as another song illustrates: "Of men that are now, None equals a brother. When death and mourning affright us, Brothers are very dear."[6]

Iron and Agricultural Technology

Zhou China nurtured many significant technological and economic developments. Ironworking reached China from Central Asia by around 700 B.C.E. Iron made much better plows and tools than bronze but also improved weaponry for the increasing warfare. Newly introduced soybeans provided a rich protein source and also enriched the soil. Chinese agriculture became so productive, and surpluses so common, that the population by 600 B.C.E. was around 20 million. Trade grew, merchants became more prominent, and China developed a cash economy with copper coins.

Zhou social life often revolved around food. The Chief Cook of the ruler was a high state official, and lavish feasts cemented social ties. Indeed, the banquet was a chief tool of diplomacy at

The Poetry of Peasant Life in Zhou China

We can learn something of the lives of ancient Chinese common folk, especially the peasants who worked the land, from *The Book of Songs*, a collection of 305 poems, hymns, and folk songs compiled between 1000 and 600 B.C.E.

Some songs address ordinary people at their labor. Men weed the fields, plant, plow, and harvest. Women and girls gather mulberry leaves for silkworms, carry hampers of food to the men in the fields for lunch, and make thread:

> *The girls take their deep baskets, And follow the path under the wall, to gather the soft mulberry-leaves.*

Some of the songs deal with courtship and love, sometimes revealing strong emotion, as in this song by a girl about a prospective sweetheart:

> *That the mere glimpse of a plain cap, Could harry me with such longing, Cause me pain so dire. . . . Enough! Take me with you to your house. . . . Let us two be one.*

Within the family, the father had nearly absolute authority over his wife and children. When the family patriarch died, his wife became the family head. Children were expected to obey their parents, but some songs reveal that mutual affection and gratitude were common:

> *My father begot me. My mother fed me, Led me, bred me, Brought me up, reared me, Kept her eye on me, tended me, At every turn aided me. Their good deeds I would requite.*

Peasant lives were filled with toil and hardship, but they could find some relief from drudgery in friendship and kinship. Entertaining relatives and friends was a major leisure activity:

> *And shall a man not seek to have his friends? He shall have harmony and peace. I have strained off my liquor in abundance, the dishes stand in rows, and none of my brethren are absent. Whenever we have leisure, let us drink the sparkling liquor.*

Peasants faced many demands on their time and labor. Songs complain and even protest about an uncaring government and its rapacious tax collectors:

> *Big rat, big rat, Do not gobble our millet! Three years we have slaved for you. Yet you took no notice of us. At last we are going to leave you, And go to the happy land . . . where no sad songs are sung.*

Some songs record abject poverty and misery:

> *Deep is my grief. I am utterly poverty-stricken and destitute. Yet no one heeds my misfortunes. Well, all is over now. No doubt it was Heaven's [the supernatural realm's] doing. So what's the good of talking about it!*

Zhou peasants needed all the help they could get, and some songs seem to be prayers to Heaven to bless their lives:

> *Good people, gentle folk—Their ways are righteous. . . . Their thoughts constrained. . . . Good people, gentle folk—Shape the people of this land. . . . And may they do so for ten thousand years!*

THINKING ABOUT THE READING

1. What do the songs tell us about the importance of families and friends to the Zhou Chinese?
2. What did peasants think about those who ruled them? Can you say why?

Source: The Book of Songs, translated by Arthur Waley (London: George Allen and Unwin, 1954) © copyright by permission of The Arthur Waley Estate.

all levels of society, often lubricated by wine: "When we have got wine, we strain it; When we have got none, we buy it!"[7] However, the costly and complicated ceremonies enjoyed by the rich did not extend down to peasants, who had little money for anything more than basic hospitality.

The Evolution of Chinese Writing and Religion

A distinctive Chinese writing system arose to solve the special problems posed by the many, often mutually unintelligible spoken languages. Some six hundred dialects of Chinese are still spoken today, a heritage of many local cultures. Most of the Chinese north of the Yangzi River speak closely related Northern Mandarin dialects, but other Chinese, especially in the southern half of China, have vastly different dialects. Chinese from Guangzhou **(GWAHN-cho)** and Beijing **(bay-JING)** would not understand each other if they only spoke their local dialects. Another difficulty is that the monosyllabic Chinese languages are tonal: that is, the stress placed on a sound changes its meaning. For example, depending on the tone employed by the speaker, in

Mandarin the sound *ma* can mean "mother," "hemp," "horse," or the verb "to curse." It can also indicate a question. To overcome these problems, the Chinese gradually developed one written language based not on sound but on characters. The pictographs of early Shang times resemble crude pictures of an object, such as a man or bird. Later they evolved into complex ideographs, in which characters stand for ideas and concepts. Some 50,000 new characters have been created since the Shang (see Figure 4.1). The practicality of this system became apparent in modern times when Chinese linguists faced great difficulty converting tonal words into a Western-type alphabet.

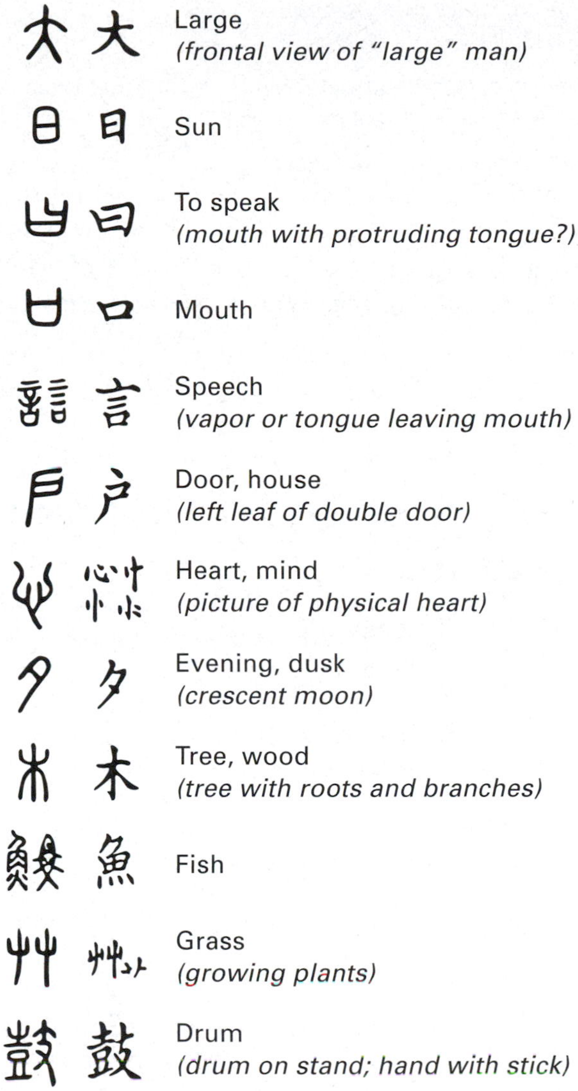

大	Large *(frontal view of "large" man)*
日	Sun
曰	To speak *(mouth with protruding tongue?)*
口	Mouth
言	Speech *(vapor or tongue leaving mouth)*
户	Door, house *(left leaf of double door)*
心 忄 ⺗	Heart, mind *(picture of physical heart)*
夕	Evening, dusk *(crescent moon)*
木	Tree, wood *(tree with roots and branches)*
魚	Fish
艸	Grass *(growing plants)*
鼓	Drum *(drum on stand; hand with stick)*

Figure 4.1 Evolution of Chinese Writing This chart shows early and modern forms of Chinese characters, revealing how pictographs, often recognizable, matured into increasingly abstract ideographs.

As in Mesopotamia and Egypt, writing had vast social and cultural implications, promoting political and cultural unity by making possible communication between people speaking different dialects. Otherwise the Chinese might have split into many small countries, as occurred in India and Europe for much of history. Thus writing helped to create the largest society on earth, unifying rather than dividing peoples of diverse ancestries, regions, and languages. The written language also gave prestige to those who mastered it. As the writing brush became the main writing instrument, writing became an art form, and every literate Chinese became something of an artist. Yet the demands of memorizing thousands of characters mostly limited literacy to the upper classes with the time and money to study writing. Education, scholarship, and literature became valued commodities.

Chinese ideas on the mysteries of life and the cosmic order also developed in ancient times. Shang religion emphasized ancestor worship, magic, mythology, agricultural deities, and local spirits. These ideas evolved by later Zhou times into distinctive ideas, including the notion of a generalized supernatural force the Chinese called *tian* (tee-an), which was believed to govern the universe. The ***Yijing*** (yee-CHING) (Book of Changes), a collection of sixty-four mystic hexagrams and commentaries that was used to predict future events, later became influential throughout East Asia. The *Yijing*'s main theme was that heaven and earth are in a state of continual change.

***Yijing* (Book of Changes)** An ancient Chinese collection of sixty-four mystic hexagrams and commentaries upon them that was used to predict future events.

The *Yijing* was closely related to Chinese cosmological thinking as expressed in the theory of *yin* and *yang*, which had appeared in simple form as early as the Shang period. To the Chinese, yin and yang are the two primary cosmic forces that power the universe through their interaction. Neither one permanently triumphs; rather they are balanced, in conflict and yet complementary in a kind of cosmic symphony. Many things were correlated with these principles:

Yang: bright, hot, dry, hard, active, masculine, heaven, sun

Yin: dark, cold, wet, soft, quiescent, feminine, earth, moon

Given the Chinese preference for hierarchy, yang was superior to yin, and male superior to female. Thus the philosophy justified inequalities in society. The yin-yang dualism remains important throughout East Asia. The Chinese strongly influenced their neighbors in Korea, Vietnam, and Japan, and over the centuries many Chinese ideas and institutions diffused to the peoples on their fringe.

SECTION SUMMARY

- The western Shang established an authoritarian state, with the king playing the role of father to the entire country.
- Under the Shang, society became increasingly stratified, divided up into a dominant aristocracy, a middle class, farmers and laborers, and slaves.
- After a slave rebellion overthrew the Shang, the Zhou established a more widespread, less centralized empire.
- The Zhou introduced the concepts of rule by the "Mandate of Heaven" and of the dynastic cycle, which have endured to this day.
- A common written language provided a unifying link for the Chinese, who spoke hundreds of different dialects (many of which are still spoken today).
- One of the first Chinese books was the *Yijing*, which was related to the idea of the universal opposing forces, *yin* and *yang*.

ANCIENT SOUTHEAST AND NORTHEAST ASIANS

How did the traditions developing in Southeast and Northeast Asia differ from those in India and China?

China's neighbors in Southeast and Northeast Asia also made important early contributions in farming and technology in an environment somewhat different from China and India. These cultures, although influenced by China or India, demonstrated many unique characteristics. Chinese influence was especially strong in Korean and Japan, beginning in the Shang period. But the Koreans and Japanese had already established the foundations for complex societies. Over the following centuries they integrated Chinese influences with their own ideas and customs, maintaining separate ethnic identities.

CHRONOLOGY

Northeast and Southeast Asia, 10,000–600 B.C.E.

10,000–300 B.C.E. Jomon culture in Japan

8000–6000 B.C.E. Agriculture begins in Southeast Asia

7000–4000 B.C.E. Agriculture begins in New Guinea

5000–2000 B.C.E. Agriculture begins in Korea

4000–2000 B.C.E. Austronesian migrations into Southeast Asia islands

2000–1500 B.C.E. Bronze Age begins in Southeast Asia

1600–1000 B.C.E. Melanesian and Austronesian migrations into South Pacific

1000–800 B.C.E. First Southeast Asian states

1000 B.C.E. Austronesian settlement of Fiji and Samoa

Southeast Asian Environments and Early Agriculture

While historically linked to both China and India, Southeast Asian peoples developed in distinctive ways that were shaped in part by geography and climate. Southeast Asia, which stretches from modern Burma (or Myanmar) eastward to Vietnam and the Philippines and southward through the Indonesian archipelago, is separated from the Eurasian landmass by mountain and water barriers. The region has a tropical climate, with long rainy seasons. Rain forests once covered much of the land. But the great rivers that flow through mainland Southeast Asia, such as the Mekong **(MAY-kawng)**, Red, and Irrawaddy **(ir-uh-WAHD-ee)** Rivers, also carved out broad, fertile plains and deltas that could support dense human settlement.

The topography both helped and hindered communication. Southeast Asians say that the water unites and the land divides. The shallow seas fostered maritime trade, seafaring, and fishing and linked the large islands such as Sumatra **(soo-MAH-truh)**, Java **(JA-veh)**, and Borneo (Kalimantan) to their neighbors. In contrast, the heavily forested highlands inhibited overland travel and encouraged diverse religions, languages, and states. An Indonesian proverb well describes the mosaic of cultures that resulted: different fields, different grasshoppers; different pools, different fish.

Agriculture and technology arose early. Some scholars think that, as in the Fertile Crescent, the transition to food growing began in Thailand and Vietnam by 8000 or 9000 B.C.E., but most doubt that it began earlier than 6000 B.C.E. (see Chronology: Northeast and Southeast Asia, 10,000–600 B.C.E.). Horticulture may have began in the island of New Guinea even earlier. Rice was probably first domesticated in south or central China first and then spread into Southeast Asia, where it became a major crop. Southeast Asians may have been the first to cultivate bananas, yams, and taro and domesticated chickens, pigs, and perhaps even cattle. Southeast

Asians also developed or improved technologies originally from India, Mesopotamia, and China. By 1500 B.C.E. fine bronze was being produced in northeast Thailand in villages like Ban Chiang **(ban chang)**, whose people lived in houses perched on poles above the ground, still a common pattern in Southeast Asia. Ban Chiang women made beautiful hand-painted and durable pottery. Village artists fashioned jewelry and many household items of bronze and ivory. Elsewhere in Eurasia the Bronze Age was synonymous with cities, kings, armies, huge temples, and defensive walls, but in Southeast Asia bronze metallurgy derived from peaceful villages. Evidence for trade networks can be found in Dong Son village, Vietnam, where people made huge bronze drums that have been found all over Southeast Asia. Tin mined in Southeast Asia may have been traded to the Indus cities. Southeast Asians worked iron by 500 B.C.E., several centuries later than northern China.

Erich Lessing/Art Resource, NY

Dong Son Bronze Drum These huge Dong Son bronze drums, named for a village site in Vietnam, were produced widely in ancient Southeast Asia and confirm the extensive long-distance trade networks.

Migration and New Societies in Southeast Asia and the Pacific

Gradually new societies formed from local and migrant roots. The early Southeast Asians probably included the Vietnamese, Papuans **(PAH-poo-enz)**, Melanesians **(mel-uh-NEE-zhuhns)**, and Negritos **(ne-GREE-tos)**. Migrants came into Southeast Asia from China sometime before the Common Era, assimilating local peoples or prompting them to migrate eastward through the islands. Today Papuans and Melanesians are found mostly in New Guinea and the western Pacific islands, while the few thousand remaining small-statured, dark-skinned Negritos mostly live in remote mountains and islands. The newcomers probably mixed their cultures and languages with those of the remaining indigenous inhabitants, producing new peoples such as the Khmers **(kuh-MARE)** (Cambodians), who later established states in the Mekong River Basin.

Over the course of several millennia peoples speaking Austronesian **(AW-stroh-NEE-zhuhn)** languages and possessing advanced agriculture entered island Southeast Asia from the large island of Taiwan, just east of China. Beginning around 4000 B.C.E., Austronesians began moving south into the Philippine Islands, and by 2000 B.C.E. some moved into the Indonesian archipelago (see Map 4.2), settling Java, Borneo, and Sumatra. Austronesian languages became dominant in the Philippines, Indonesia, the Malay Peninsula, and the central Vietnam coast. Indonesian islanders were the major seafaring traders of eastern Eurasia before the Common Era.

Pacific Cultures

The Austronesian migrations affected other regions as well. Melanesians had migrated eastward into the western Pacific islands beginning around 1500 or 1600 B.C.E., carrying Southeast Asian crops, animals, and house styles as far east as Fiji. Traveling in outrigger canoes and, later, in large double-hulled canoes, some Austronesians also sailed east into the Pacific, mixing their cultures, languages, and genes with those of the Melanesians. By around 1000 B.C.E. Austronesian settlers had reached Samoa and Tonga. These voyages were intentional efforts at discovery and colonization by fearless mariners who developed remarkable navigation skills, reading the stars with their eyes and the swells with their backs as they lay down in their canoes.

The ancient western Pacific culture known as **Lapita**, stretching some 2,500 miles from just northeast of New Guinea to Samoa, was marked by distinctive pottery and a trading network over vast distances. In Samoa and Tonga, Polynesian culture emerged from Austronesian roots. Some Polynesians eventually reached as far east as Tahiti and Hawaii, both 2,500 miles from Tonga.

Lapita The ancient western Pacific culture that stretched some 2,500 miles from just northeast of New Guinea to Samoa.

The Austronesians, Khmer, Vietnamese, and others established societies based on intensive agriculture, fishing, and interregional commerce. By 1000 B.C.E. Austronesian trade networks stretched over 5,000 miles, from western Indonesia to the central Pacific. Austronesians built advanced boats and carried out maritime trade with India by 500 B.C.E. Indonesian cinnamon even reached Egypt. The Vietnamese created the first known Southeast Asian states between 1000 and 800 B.C.E. and believed in a god that "creates the elephants [and] the grass, is omnipresent, and has [all-seeing] eyes."[8]

The Foundations of Korea and Japan

Geographical Foundations

Korea and Japan are neighbors, but they were shaped by different environments (see Map 4.1). The 110 miles of stormy seas that separate them at their closest point did not prevent contact between the two societies but did make it sporadic. Korea occupies a mountainous peninsula some 600 miles long and 150 miles in width. Japan is a group of 3,400 islands stretching across

Map 4.2
The Austronesian Diaspora

Austronesians migrated from Taiwan into Southeast Asia, settling the islands. Later some of these skilled mariners moved east into the western Pacific, settling Melanesia. Eventually some of their ancestors settled Polynesia and Micronesia.

Interactive Map

several climatic zones. Over 90 percent of the land is on three islands: densely populated Honshu **(hahn-shoo)**, frigid Hokkaido **(haw-KAI-dow)** in the north, and subtropical Kyushu **(KYOO-shoo)** in the south. Because mountains occupy much of Japan, only a sixth of the land is suitable for intensive agriculture. The archipelago is also weak in all metals except silver.

Koreans

Koreans began farming between 5000 and 2000 B.C.E.. Later they creatively adapted rice growing, which originated in warm southern lands, to their cool climate. As Korean agriculture became more productive, the population grew rapidly, generating a persistent migration of Koreans across the straits to Japan. Growing occupational specialization led to small states based on clans. In a pattern still common today, female shamans led the animistic religion. Despite centuries of contact, the Koreans were never assimilated by the neighboring Chinese, in part because the nontonal Korean and tonal Chinese spoken languages were very different. Korean belongs to the Ural-Altaic language family and is related (although not closely) to Mongol, Turkish, and the Eastern Siberian tongues.

The ancient Koreans imported some useful ideas, adopting bronze and then ironworking, probably from China and Central Asia. Shang refugees brought more Chinese culture and technology, but Koreans also created their own useful products and technology, including some of the era's finest pottery. To contend with the frigid winters, the early Koreans invented an ingenious method of radiant floor heating, still widely used today, that circulates heat through chambers in a stone floor. Much later both the Chinese and Romans devised similar schemes.

The ancient Japanese were more isolated than the Koreans from China and no less creative. Human settlement began perhaps 40,000 years ago, before rising sea levels isolated Japan from the mainland. Pottery, for example, was produced earlier than in China and is among the world's oldest. The identity of these early settlers is unknown, but they were probably the ancestors of the Ainu **(I-noo)**, who are genetically close to other East Asians despite their unusually light skin and extensive body hair. The ancestral Ainu built seaworthy boats, for they settled the Kurile **(KOO-reel)** Islands north of Japan and traded with eastern Siberia. Ainu relics have also been found in the Aleutian **(ah-LOO-shan)** Islands off Alaska, suggesting some connection there in ancient times. Ancestral Ainu also were perhaps among the northeast Asians who settled the Americas. Today the remaining few thousand Ainu, who mostly live on Hokkaido and Sakhalin Island, face cultural extinction.

Little is known about when the non-Ainu ancestors of today's Japanese arrived in the islands. Some may have come from Korea beginning 3,000 or 4,000 years ago. Ainu and newcomers mixed over the millennia. Genetic studies link modern Japanese to the Ainu, Siberians, and especially Koreans.

Dogu Figurine Jomon fired-clay figures, like this one, typically portray women and may have been used in fertility rites. Many have a heart-shaped face and elaborate hairstyle.

Tokyo National Museum/The Art Archive

Jomon Society

The best documented Japanese early society is called **Jomon** (JOE-mon) ("rope pattern"), because of the ropelike designs on their pottery. The Jomon period began around 10,000 B.C.E. and endured until 300 B.C.E. The Jomon were probably an Ainu culture that was divided by various languages and regional customs, a diversity that may have reflected the arrival of migrants from Korea. However, the major migrations that brought waves of iron-using settlers from Korea came later, between 500 and 700 B.C.E. The Jomon traded with Korea and Siberia.

Jomon The earliest documented culture in Japan, known for the ropelike design on its pottery.

The Jomon lived primarily from hunting, gathering, and fishing, but by 5000 B.C.E. they lived in permanent wooden houses containing elaborate hearths, probably the centers for family gatherings. A wide range of foods made up their well-balanced, highly nutritious diet, including shellfish, fish, seals, deer, wild boar, and yams. The Jomon may have been better fed than the Chinese and Korean farmers. There is no evidence for complex agriculture until around 500 B.C.E.

A very different spoken language helped preserve cultural distinctiveness despite much Chinese cultural influence over the centuries. Whether the Japanese language was spoken by the Jomon or brought by later immigrants remains uncertain. Japanese is distantly related to modern Korean and not at all to the surviving Ainu languages. Probably between 500 B.C.E. and 500 C.E., most of the Ainu languages were overwhelmed by a Japanese language possibly based on a now lost Korean dialect. The environment also helped shape the language. Perhaps in response to increasingly crowded conditions, the language promoted tact and vagueness, and the Japanese became adept at nonverbal understanding. These tendencies, which are useful in discouraging social conflict, remain part of Japan's unique heritage.

SECTION SUMMARY

- The peoples of Southeast Asia established early maritime trading networks, while inland geographical boundaries led to the development of extremely diverse cultures.
- Extensive migration occurred among China, Southeast Asia, and the Pacific islands.
- Korea and Japan, while being strongly influenced by the Chinese, were shaped by different environments and created unique cultures and societies.
- Partly because of its distinct language, Korea was never assimilated into China and developed special technologies, such as radiant floor heating, to meet its needs.
- The ancestors of modern Japanese probably included, among others, the Ainu, the Jomon, and later the Koreans.
- Japan's language promoted tact and vagueness, probably to prevent social conflict in an increasingly populated area.

ANCIENT AMERICANS

How do scholars explain the settlement and rise of agriculture in the Americas?

After the migrations of humans from Eurasia to the Americas thousands of years ago, American societies developed in isolation from those in the Eastern Hemisphere. Early Americans created diverse cultures that often flourished from hunting and gathering, and later Americans, in some regions, pioneered agriculture and, in Mexico and the Andes, created urban societies and states. Population movement and adaptations to differing environments shaped these varied people's most ancient history, but Americans also shared some common ideas.

Diverse American Environments

Most of the land area of the Western Hemisphere is found on two continents, North and South America, which are linked by the long, thin strand of Central America. A string of fertile islands, both large and small, also rings the Caribbean Sea from Florida to Venezuela. Unlike the east-west axis of Eurasia, the Americas lie on a north-south axis, with a large forest-covered tropical zone separating more temperate regions. This meant that migrating peoples or long-distance travelers encountered very different environmental and climatic zones.

Geographical Foundations

Although the total land area is smaller, the Western Hemisphere contains as much diversity of landforms and climate as the Eastern. Extensive tropical rain forests originally covered much of Central America, the Caribbean islands, and the vast Amazon and Orinoco **(or-uh-NO-ko)** River Basins of South America, making intensive farming difficult, although some people developed simple farming. Rain-drenched forests also once covered the northern Pacific coast and southern Chile, while the southeastern part of North America had more temperate woodlands. The long winters in much of North America made hunting and gathering the most practical subsistence option. Great mountain ranges discouraged communication. Like the Himalayas in Asia, the high Andes, which stretch nearly 5,000 miles down the western side of South America, limited travel. In North America, the Rocky Mountains also provided an east-west barrier. Mountains also run along the Pacific coast of North America, trapping rain clouds and creating huge deserts in western North and South America, as well as extensive grasslands in the interior of the continents. Some of the great river systems, such as the Mississippi, fostered long-distance trade.

The Antiquity and Migration of Native Americans

Debates on Origins

The ancestry and antiquity of Native Americans generate scholarly debate. Most anthropologists agree that modern Native Americans are descended from stone tool–using Asians who crossed the Bering Strait from Siberia to Alaska, probably when Ice Age conditions lowered ocean levels and created a wide land bridge. Some may have crossed by boat even when no land bridge existed. Seeking game like bison, caribou, and mammoths, migrants could have moved south through ice-free corridors or by boat along the Pacific coast and gradually dispersed throughout the hemisphere. Waves of migrants, probably in small numbers, from different cultural backgrounds in East and North Asia might account for the over two thousand languages among Native Americans. The last wave some 5,000 years ago brought the Inuit **(IN-oo-it)** and Aleuts **(AH-loots)**.

American Origins

The traditions of many Native American peoples place their origins in the areas where they lived 500 years ago, but some may have lived in these places for many centuries before that. While their origin stories, rich in spiritual meaning, deserve respect, much evidence supports the notion of ancient migration from Asia. No remains of any hominids earlier than modern humans have been found in the Americas. Furthermore, the common ancestry of modern Native Americans is clear from the remarkable uniformity of DNA, blood, virus, and teeth types, which all connect them to peoples in northeast Asia. Some evidence hints that the ancestors of the Ainu, skilled boatbuilders in Japan, might have been early migrants. A few recent tool and skeletal finds in North America and Brazil resemble those in Southeast Asia. Several scholars have also suggested that some tool cultures in eastern North America are similar to those of Stone Age peoples who lived in Spain and France several millennia earlier. But the evidence for possible European or Southeast Asian ancestry is sparse. If such migrants did once settle in the Americas, they likely died out or were absorbed by the peoples of Northeast Asian ancestry.

Clovis A Native American culture dating back some 11,500 to 13,500 years.

The question of when the first migrants arrived in the Americas perplexes archaeologists. Most trace the migration back to the **Clovis** culture some 11,500 to 13,500 years ago, named after spear points discovered at Clovis, New Mexico, but widespread in North and Central America (see Chronology: The Ancient Americas, 40,000–600 B.C.E.). However, skeletons and artifacts have lately been discovered in North and South America that are much older. Monte Verde **(MAWN-tee VAIR-dee)**, a campsite in southern Chile that is over 10,000 miles from the Bering Strait, may be at least 12,500 years old. Some think it is much more ancient. Monte Verde people lived in rectangular houses with log foundations and exploited a wide variety of vegetable and animal foods. Various other sites in North America, Mexico, and Brazil challenge the Clovis-first theory, but none offers conclusive evidence that convinces skeptics. Various sites in Pennsylvania, South Carolina, and

Virginia may place people in eastern North America between 17,000 and 19,000 years ago. These scattered discoveries hint at but do not yet prove an ancient migration somewhere between 20,000 and 40,000 years ago. The debate will rage for years to come as more sites are excavated.

The earliest Americans, known to scholars as Paleo-Indians, survived by hunting, fishing, and gathering while adapting to varied environments. Being skilled hunters and armed with spears, they may have helped bring about the extinction of large herbivore animals such as horses, mammoths, and camels, which disappeared from the Western Hemisphere between 9000 and 7000 B.C.E. A similar die-off of animals also occurred in Eurasia at the end of the Ice Age, suggesting that climate change was a factor. Most likely, the extinctions of the animals in both hemispheres was caused by some combination of overhunting, environmental change, and perhaps an apocalyptic disease that affected the large mammals. Hunters mostly shifted to smaller game. But on the North American Great Plains, many peoples hunted bison, without benefit of horses. Only in the nineteenth century C.E. did this hunting way of life become impossible, as newly arrived white Americans slaughtered the bison herds on which these Native Americans depended.

Some people in favored locations flourished from hunting, fishing, and gathering for many millennia. In the Pacific Northwest, coastal peoples built oceangoing boats and sturdy wood houses. Along the Peruvian coast deep-sea fishermen exploited the rich marine environment. The Monte Verde villagers used more than fifty food plants and twenty medicinal plants. In southern California the Chumash **(CHOO-mash)** society, like the Jomon culture of Japan, lived well from a varied vegetation and meat diet that included large marine mammals such as seals. The Chumash built large, permanent villages headed by powerful chiefs. Yet Pacific coast peoples such as the Chumash were also subject to climate change, which periodically brought drought by altering plant and animal environments.

The eastern third of what is now the United States also provided an abundant environment for hunting and gathering, augmented by trade. By 4000 B.C.E. extensive long-distance trade networks linked people over several thousand miles from the Atlantic coast to the Great Plains. Dugout canoes moved copper and red ocher from Lake Superior, jasper (quartz) from Pennsylvania, obsidian from the Rocky Mountains, and seashells from both the Gulf and East Coasts. Great Lakes copper was traded as far away as Mexico, New England, and Florida.

CHRONOLOGY
The Ancient Americas, 40,000–600 B.C.E.

40,000–20,000 B.C.E. Possible earliest migrations to Americas (disputed)

11,500–9,500 B.C.E. Beginning of Clovis culture

8000 B.C.E. Beginning of agriculture in Mesoamerica and Andes

6000 B.C.E. Potato farming in Andes

4000 B.C.E. Early trade routes in North America

2500 B.C.E. Earliest mound-building cultures

3000–2500 B.C.E. Farming along Peruvian coast

3100–1600 B.C.E. Peruvian city of Caral

2500 B.C.E. Agriculture in lower Mississippi Valley

2000 B.C.E. Earliest agriculture in southwestern North America

1500 B.C.E. Agriculture in Amazon Basin

1200–300 B.C.E. Olmec

1200–200 B.C.E. Chavín

1000–500 B.C.E. Poverty Point culture

650 B.C.E. Olmec writing

Early Societies and Their Cultures

Over many millennia Americans organized larger societies and developed some distinctive social and cultural patterns that emphasized cooperation within families, animistic religion, and, for some, building huge mounds. Most people lived in egalitarian bands linked by kinship and marriage. Hunting was often a communal activity. Americans shared a belief in supernatural forces, spirits, or gods. For example, men often sought a personal guardian spirit through a visionary experience induced by fasting, enduring physical pain, or taking hallucinogenic drugs. Shamans claiming command over spirits or animal souls were vehicles to connect the human and spirit worlds. The ceremonies for such events as initiations into adult life and courtship probably included ritual dancing. Since the land furnished food, most Americans revered the earth as sacred. Some of them also adopted creation stories that were widely shared with other peoples.

Some Americans organized communities around **mound building**, the construction of huge earthen mounds, often with temples on top. The oldest mound so far discovered, in Louisiana, dates to 2500 B.C.E. Beginning around 1600 B.C.E., some peoples in North America's eastern woodlands and Gulf Coast also developed distinctive mound-building cultures. One major site, Poverty Point in northeastern Louisiana, was occupied between 1000 and 500 B.C.E. (see Profile: The Poverty Point Mound Builders). Occupying about 3 square miles and home to perhaps 5,000 people at its height, Poverty Point had the most massive earthworks in all the Americas at that time. The largest mound, an effigy of a bird that can only be seen from the air, was 70 feet high, comparable to an eight-story apartment building, and 700 feet long. Poverty Point served as the hub of a trading system, importing goods from as far away as the Ohio and upper Mississippi River Valleys and exporting stone and clay products such as pendants and bowls to Florida, Missouri, Oklahoma, and Tennessee.

mound building The construction of huge earthen mounds, often with temples on top, by some ancient peoples in the Americas.

THE POVERTY POINT MOUND BUILDERS

While the spectacular mounds at Poverty Point are the site's most striking legacy, the archaeological research has also revealed a remarkable community. The inhabitants did not need farming because their location, in a fertile valley nourished by annual Mississippi River floods, offered a benign hunting and gathering environment and a gentle climate. The people enjoyed a rich and varied diet that many modern people might envy. Men used simple weapons—for example, spears, spear throwers, darts, and knives—to hunt. The woods provided turkey, duck, deer, and rabbit, while the rivers offered bass, catfish, alligator, and clams. Women collected acorns, hickory nuts, walnuts, wild grapes, persimmons, sunflower seeds, squash, and gourds.

Life seems to have been agreeable. The people lived in wood houses around a central plaza and six mounds, probably governed by chiefs. In their houses men and women crafted many tools and art objects, some of which they traded hundreds of miles away. Small decorated baked-clay balls, found by the thousands in the ruins, were heated for use in cooking or boiling water. Since cooking was women's work, women probably made these clay balls, perhaps helped by their children. Each woman had her own preference for design and shape. Stoneworkers also ground and polished hard stones into ornaments and useful artifacts, and they chipped various stones into points, blades, and cutting tools. Those with an artistic bent made solid-clay female figurines, sometimes pregnant, possibly as fertility symbols. Using red jasper, they fashioned beautiful bead necklaces, bird-head pendants, and human effigies.

Located at the intersection of important waterways, Poverty Point was the central hub for a large region and was linked to trade networks that supplied the townsmen with Appalachian metal for bowls and platters, stone from the Ozarks and Oklahoma, and flint from as far away as Illinois and Ohio. The finely crafted red jasper items, often shaped like animals such as owls, have been found in distant settlements. Some of the Poverty Point men may have ventured out on trading expeditions or to bring home valuable stones from as far away as Missouri. Men and perhaps women undoubtedly arrived regularly in canoes full of trade goods to exchange.

At times the people were mobilized to build new mounds or rebuild old ones that were eroding with time. The complete earthworks contain an immense 1 million cubic yards of soil; to make them, the people probably had to transport 35 to 40 million 50-pound basket loads to the site. Several thousand people may have participated in the construction, and the project had to be carefully planned and directed so that it followed a geometric design. The mounds perhaps aided astronomical observations as a solar calendar, or perhaps served as a regional ceremonial center for social, political, or religious purposes. Some priestly or ruling class may have lived atop the mounds, as was common in some mound-building societies around the hemisphere. At least 150 smaller satellite sites, scattered along the Mississippi for several hundred miles, all contain similar artifacts, suggesting that Poverty Point was the center of both an economic and a political network.

The culture disappeared by 500 B.C.E., the people having dispersed to smaller settlements. There are no signs of war or major environmental change. Perhaps some political or religious crisis disrupted society. Whatever the case, the Poverty Point people and their culture were lost to history, leaving only the badly eroded but still impressive ruins of today.

THINKING ABOUT THE PROFILE

1. What sort of life did the Poverty Point people experience?
2. What role did Poverty Point play in the region?

Gilcrease Museum, Tulsa, Oklahoma

Poverty Point Jasper Bead Trade goods, such as this red jasper bead shaped like a locust, were produced at Poverty Point in Louisiana and traded over many hundreds of miles in eastern and central North America.

The Rise of American Agriculture

Americans were some of the earliest farmers, but they developed very different crops than the peoples of Afro-Eurasia. Population growth, long-distance trade, and the ebb and flow of weather conditions helped spark this great transition. Hunting and gathering peoples were vulnerable to devastating droughts in years when the periodic weather change known today as *El Niño* (EL

NEE-nyo) warmed the Pacific Ocean, shifting both rainfall patterns and the marine environment, perhaps prompting them to experiment with growing food sources. Some of the chief crops, such as maize (corn), were much more difficult to master than the big-seeded grains of the Fertile Crescent. Furthermore, since there were no potential draft animals, farmers needed to be creative in growing and transporting food.

Early Farming

Some Americans made the transition not long after Southwest Asians had. In Mesoamerica (the region from central Mexico through northern Central America), bottle gourds and pumpkins may have been raised by 8500 or 8000 B.C.E. and maize, sweet potatoes, and beans by 3500 B.C.E. Andes people cultivated chili peppers and kidney beans by about 8000 B.C.E. Later potatoes and maize flourished there. Some Andeans, like early farmers in Eurasia, built elaborate irrigation canals that created artificial garden plots. By 3000 or 2500 B.C.E. societies along the Peruvian coast raised cotton, squash, and maize. By 1500 B.C.E. farming had spread to the Amazon Basin. Farming later spread to North American societies, probably influenced by a wetter climate. The southwestern peoples were particularly ingenious in adapting farming to their poor soils and desert conditions, growing maize, squash, beans, and corn. By 2500 B.C.E. people in the lower Mississippi Valley grew sunflowers and gourds. Eventually maize, beans, and squash became mainstays from the Southwest to the northeastern woodlands, providing a nutritionally balanced diet.

Three basic farming patterns eventually shaped American societies. People in the highland and valley regions of Mesoamerica relied on maize, beans, and squash. Another pattern emphasizing potatoes and other frost-resistant tubers was developed in the high altitudes of the Andes. Tropical forest societies in South America grew manioc, sweet potatoes, and root crops. The differing farming patterns proved significant for later world history because the great diversity later enriched modern food supplies. Americans domesticated more different plants than had all the Eastern Hemisphere peoples combined, including three thousand varieties of potatoes, as well as chocolate, quinine, and tobacco.

The Americans practiced less intensive agriculture than people in the Eastern Hemisphere because of the lack of draft animals. The only large herd animals available for domestication, the llama and alpaca of the Andes, were tamed by 3500 B.C.E., mostly for use as pack animals and wool sources. Americans domesticated turkeys and guinea pigs for eating. But there were no surviving counterparts to horses, cattle, and oxen. With no animals to aid in pulling, people could not use a plow or wheel. In any case, wheeled vehicles were useless in the steep Andes and the tropical rain forests. People made other innovations, including various ingenious irrigation schemes such as terracing of hillsides and the floating gardens in Central Mexico, which turned swamps into productive fields. But the intensive farming that supported huge populations in China or India was not possible in the Americas.

Health

The lack of draft animals also meant that Americans were exposed to fewer infectious diseases and epidemics. In the Eastern Hemisphere, domesticated animals passed diseases such as measles and smallpox to humans through germs and parasites, precipitating outbreaks that could kill many people. Historians disagree over whether Americans may have been healthier than people across the oceans. Many of them enjoyed long lives, but many people also suffered from various ailments. Furthermore, isolation from the Eastern Hemisphere left Native Americans vulnerable to the diseases brought by Europeans and Africans beginning in 1492 C.E., for which they had no immunity. These diseases eventually killed the great majority of Native Americans.

Farming Societies, Cities, and States

Ancient Religions

Archaeologists are learning more about the social and cultural patterns that led to cities and states among early farming peoples. Communal activity was essential in early villages as people cooperated for survival. In the northern Andes, people fashioned the oldest known ceramics in the hemisphere between 3000 and 2500 B.C.E. Institutionalized religions took shape, led by a priestly caste. Some Mesoamericans practiced human sacrifice by 7000 B.C.E., and human sacrifice became common in both Mesoamerica and the Andes to honor the gods and keep the cosmos in balance. Far earlier than the more famous Egyptian mummies, some South American and North American societies developed processes for mummifying the bodies of the deceased through drying, perhaps because of religious beliefs about death and the afterlife. Like the North American mound builders, some Andean and Mesoamerican societies also began building permanent structures for religious, governmental, or recreational purposes. Pacific coast and Andean cultures in South America constructed some of the oldest monumental architecture, including stepped pyramids, by the third millennium B.C.E., about the same time as Egypt, India, and China. A site in southern Mexico from 5000 B.C.E. contained a dance ground or ball

Architecture

court, and ceremonial ballgames involving small teams of players attempting to knock a rubber ball through a high stone hoop became a fixture of Mesoamerican life for millennia.

The First Cities

Agriculture, monumental construction, population growth, and long-distance trade provided a foundation for the first cities and states in the Andes and Mesoamerica between 3000 and 1000 B.C.E. (see Map 4.3). People worked metals like copper, gold, and silver to create tools, weapons, and jewelry. Growing towns with public buildings became centers of political, economic, and religious activities. Massive ceremonial centers hundreds of feet long were constructed along the Peruvian coast, and elsewhere huge mounds laid the foundation for great pyramids. Between 4000 and 1 B.C.E. the population of the Americas grew from 1 or 2 million to around 15 million; over two-thirds of this number were concentrated in Mesoamerica and western South America. Long-distance trade routes also became more common, moving commodities such as obsidian, mirrors, seashells, and ceramics.

South American Societies: Caral and Chavín

Chavín The first major urban civilization in South America (900–250 B.C.E.).

Olmec The earliest urban society in Mesoamerica.

The first large settlements built around massive stone structures emerged around 3100 B.C.E. in the Norte Chico region between the Andes and the Pacific coast in north-central Peru. The largest of these settlements and America's first known city, Caral, was built perhaps as early as 2500 or 3000 B.C.E., about the same time as the Harappan cities and the Egyptian pyramids. Caral had some 3,000 residents and was a 150-acre complex of plazas, pyramids, and residential buildings that probably required many thousands of laborers to build. The major pyramid, 60 feet tall and covering the equivalent of four football fields, contained an amphitheater capable of seating hundreds of spectators for civic or religious events. The local economy was clearly able to support an elite group of priests and planners who lived in large, well-kept rooms atop the pyramids. Eventually some twenty pyramid complexes occupied land for many miles around.

We know only a little of Norte Chico life. The economy was based on marine resources such as fish and growing squash, sweet potatoes, fruits, beans, and cotton. The Norte Chico people do not seem to have made ceramics or enjoyed many arts and crafts. However, Caral was a major hub for trade routes extending from the Pacific coast through the Andes to the Amazonian rain forest. There is evidence for human sacrifice. The people evidently enjoyed music, and many animal bone flutes have been found. But Caral collapsed for unknown reasons around 1600 B.C.E., several hundred years before the rise of the better-known American societies of Chavín and the Olmec.

Olmec Head This massive head from San Lorenzo is nearly 10 feet high. The significance of such heads (and the helmets they wear) remains unclear, but they might represent chiefs, warriors, or gods.

Chavín (cha-VEEN), situated 10,000 feet above sea level in northwestern Peru, emerged the same time as the Olmec, around 1200 or 1000 B.C.E., and collapsed by 200 B.C.E. The Chavín people created flamboyant sculpture and monumental architecture. They also developed a highly original art focusing on real or mythical animals, and they worked gold and silver. Chavín exercised considerable influence in surrounding regions. At its height, the main city probably had some 3,000 inhabitants. Elaborate burial sites reveal class divisions. Chavín became a major regional power, trading widely with the coast and spreading its religious cult to distant peoples. The people worshiped two main deities, and their ceremonial center became a site of pilgrimage for the faithful from a wide area. Chavín perpetuated some of the architectural and religious patterns that became common in the Andes. Its capital, Chavín de Huántar, was located high in the Andes Mountains of Peru. Chavín became politically and economically dominant in a densely populated region that included two distinct ecological zones, the Peruvian coastal plain and the Andean foothills.

Mesoamerican Societies: The Olmec

The **Olmec** (OHL-meck), a people who lived along the Gulf coast of Mexico, formed the earliest known urban society in Mesoamerica by 1200 or 1000 B.C.E., flourishing until 300 B.C.E. (see Map 4.3). Each Olmec city was probably ruled by a powerful chieftain. Olmec cities reflected engineering genius. The earliest city, known today as San Lorenzo, was built on an artificial dirt platform three-quarters of a mile long, half a mile wide,

Map 4.3 Olmec and Chavín Societies

The earliest known American states arose in Mesoamerica and the Andes. The Olmec and Chavín both endured for a millennium.

and 150 feet high. Home to some 2,500 people, San Lorenzo was situated above fertile but frequently flooded plains. Another Olmec city, La Venta, included huge earth mounds that required massive labor to build. The stones for Olmec sculptures and temples had to be brought from 60 miles away, and some of the blocks weigh more than 40 tons. The Olmec studied astronomy to correctly orient their cities and monuments with the stars.

Olmec Arts and Writing

The Olmec created remarkable architecture, art, and a writing system. The purpose of the huge sculptured stone heads they erected is unknown, but they might represent rulers. The Olmec built temples and pyramids in ceremonial centers and palace complexes. Their artists carved human and animal figures as well as supernatural beings in sculpture and relief. By around 650 B.C.E. the Olmec had also developed perhaps the first simple hieroglyphic writing in the Americas, which influenced other Mesoamerican peoples, especially the Maya. Mesoamerican writing kept records of kings, rituals, and the calendar, much as writing did in Egypt.

Olmec Economy

Commerce and the networks it created were a key to Olmec influence. The Olmec traded with Mexico's west coast and Central America, importing basalt, obsidian, and iron ore. One of the major trade goods was jade, which the Olmec fashioned into ceremonial objects, masks, and jewelry. The Olmec may also have exploited cocoa trees for chocolate. Extensive communication between the Olmec and neighboring peoples contributed to some cultural homogeneity in Mesoamerica, especially in religion. Olmec religious symbols and myths emphasized fearsome half-human, half-animal supernatural beings, the prototypes of later Mesoamerican deities. Religious ceremonies required precise measurement of calendar years and time cycles, which fostered mathematics and writing. Although Olmec society eventually disappeared, the Olmec established enduring patterns of life, thought, and kingship in Mesoamerica that influenced later peoples like the Maya (see Chapter 9).

SECTION SUMMARY

- The lands of the Western Hemisphere are smaller in area than those of the Eastern and are constructed on a north-south axis rather than an east-west one, but they are just as varied in terms of landforms and climate.
- Scientific evidence suggests that Native American peoples migrated from Eurasia to North America at least 12,000 years ago, and possibly between 20,000 and 40,000 years ago.
- Early American peoples survived by hunting, gathering, and fishing, as well as trading over large distances, but some societies clustered around huge mounds that served religious purposes.
- Mutual cooperation, earth worship, personal connections with guardian spirits, and shamanism were prominent features in early American cultural and spiritual life.
- In response to the challenges posed by different climates, American peoples domesticated more different plants than all the peoples of the Eastern Hemisphere.
- Lacking draft animals, Americans came up with ingenious approaches to farming, but they could not grow the amount of food necessary to support the population levels of India or China.
- The absence of draft animals also meant that Native Americans were not exposed to many diseases before the arrival of Europeans and Africans after 1492 C.E.
- Various technological breakthroughs led to the development of urban societies in Mesoamerica and the Andes, including Caral, America's first known city.
- Chavín of South America and the Olmec in Mesoamerica were early urban societies that served as patterns for later American urban societies.

CHAPTER SUMMARY

Chinese society emerged in river valleys, where the Chinese made the transition to agriculture, cities, and states. The Himalayan Mountains, the Tibetan Plateau, and vast deserts allowed only sporadic contact between China and most other societies. Gradually an expanding Chinese society incorporated many local traditions. The Shang built a powerful state while developing bronze technology and a unique writing system. The Zhou replaced the Shang and presided over a more decentralized system that saw further technological and cultural development, including more advanced writing and literature. China's neighbors in Southeast Asia, Korea, and Japan were also creative in farming and technology, forming unique cultural identities and traditions. Austronesians migrating into Southeast Asia were skilled mariners, and some of them settled the western Pacific islands.

Scholars still debate the origin and antiquity of settlement in the Americas, but most conclude that migrants moved from eastern Eurasia by land or boat many millennia ago. For centuries, hunting, fishing, and gathering supported a viable way of life. The Americans did not have the rich farmland and draft animals common in Eurasia. Nonetheless, farming appeared nearly as early as in the Eastern Hemisphere, a result of population growth, climate change, and technological development. Americans domesticated a wide variety of crops and also forged long-distance trade networks, religious institutions, cities, and states.

KEY TERMS

Mandate of Heaven
dynastic cycle
Yijing
Lapita
Jomon
Clovis
mound building
Chavín
Olmec

EBOOK AND WEBSITE RESOURCES

e **INTERACTIVE MAPS**

Map 4.1 Shang and Zhou China
Map 4.2 The Austronesian Diaspora
Map 4.3 Olmec and Chavín Societies

LINKS

Ancient and Lost Civilizations (http://www.crystalinks.com/ancient.html). Offers some useful essays on various world regions and ancient cultures.

Ancient Mesoamerican Civilizations (http://angelfire.com/ca/humanorigins/index.html). Links and information about the Olmec and other premodern societies.

Internet East Asian History Sourcebook (http://www.fordham.edu/halsall/eastasia/eastasiasbook.html). An invaluable collection of sources and links.

Internet Guide for China Studies (http://www.sino.uni-heidelberg.de/igcs/). A good collection of links on premodern and modern China.

The Ancient East Asia Website (http://www.ancienteastasia.org/). Offers useful essays and other materials on China, Japan, and Korea.

Plus flashcards, practice quizzes, and more. Go to: www.cengage.com/history/lockard/globalsocnet2e.

SUGGESTED READING

Barnes, Gina L. *China, Korea and Japan*, rev. ed. New York: Thames and Hudson, 2000. A well-illustrated summary of the archaeology.

Chang, Kwang-Chih. *The Archeology of Ancient China*, 4th ed. New Haven: Yale University Press, 1986. The major study of ancient China and lavishly illustrated.

Coe, Michael D. *Mexico: From the Olmecs to the Aztecs*, 7th ed. London: Thames and Hudson, 2005. A readable overview of pre-Columbian Mexico, with much on the Olmec.

Creel, Herlee G. *The Birth of China: A Survey of the Formative Period of Chinese Civilization.* New York: Frederick Ungar, 1961. This study remains one of the best introductions to the society of early China.

Ebrey, Patricia, et al. *East Asia: A Cultural, Social, and Political History*, 2nd ed. Boston: Houghton Mifflin, 2009. An excellent survey text on the region.

Ebrey, Patricia Buckley. *The Cambridge Illustrated History of China.* New York: Cambridge University Press, 1999. A readable survey incorporating recent findings.

Fagan, Brian M. *Kingdoms of Gold, Kingdoms of Jade: The Americas Before Columbus.* London and New York: Thames and Hudson, 1991. A nicely illustrated and readable introduction.

Fairbank, John K., Edwin O. Reischauer, and Albert M. Craig. *East Asia: Tradition and Transformation*, rev. ed. Boston: Houghton Mifflin, 1989. A major text with good coverage of ancient China, Korea, and Japan.

Fiedel, Stuart J. *Prehistory of the Americas*, 2nd ed. Cambridge: Cambridge University Press, 2008. A readable introduction.

Habu, Junko. *Ancient Jomon of Japan.* New York: Cambridge University Press, 2004. Excellent study of Jomon society.

Higham, Charles. *The Archaeology of Mainland Southeast Asia.* Cambridge: Cambridge University Press, 1989. A useful and scholarly study of early Southeast Asia.

Higham, Charles. *The Bronze Age of Southeast Asia.* New York: Cambridge University Press, 1996. Scholarly study of ancient Southeast Asia and China.

Imamura, Keiji. *An Introduction to Prehistoric Japan: New Perspectives on Insular East Asia.* Honolulu: University of Hawaii Press, 1996. An up-to-date introduction to what is known about early Japan.

Keightly, David N., ed. *The Origins of Chinese Civilization.* Berkeley: University of California Press, 1983. Scholarly essays on various aspects of ancient China.

Kirch, Patrick V. *The Lapita Peoples: Ancestors of the Oceanic World.* London: Blackwell, 1997. A recent overview of the ancient Pacific peoples.

Totman, Conrad. *A History of Japan.* Malden, MA: Blackwell, 2000. A recent survey with much on this era.

Patriarchy and Matriarchy in the Ancient World

Today, as in the past, men generally hold political, economic, and religious power in most societies. This dominance is due to patriarchy, a system whereby men largely control women and children, shape ideas about appropriate gender behavior, and generally dominate society. Many people assume that patriarchal social organization springs from some innate characteristic of the human species, symbolized by the common expression that this is a "man's world." But the situation is more complex historically.

THE PROBLEM

The prevalence of patriarchy raises three important questions. First, was there ever a time when women held equal power and status to men? Second, was matriarchy, in which women enjoy social and political dominance, ever common? And third, assuming women once enjoyed a higher status in society, can we identify a particular period when patriarchy triumphed? These questions spark heated scholarly debates.

THE DEBATE

The first question is the easiest to answer. Historians are reasonably sure that, among many peoples, women had greater equality with men during the Stone Age. The small, closely knit societies, like the !Kung of southern Africa, were often egalitarian, had weak leaders, and had little private property to fight over. But, despite a rough equality due to women's ability, essential for a society's survival, to gather food and medicinal herbs, there is little evidence that many prefarming societies allowed women more publicly recognized authority than men. Some peoples who practiced simple farming, such as the Iroquois, Cherokee, Hopi, and Zuni in North America, gave women considerable influence within a matrilineal culture, even if men usually had ultimate decision-making power.

In response to the second question, some scholars have argued that a "golden age of matriarchy" existed before the rise of urban societies and states in Europe and the Middle East, and perhaps also in India, Japan, Southeast Asia, and the Americas. Supporters of the ancient matriarchy thesis point to the many figurines of females, many perhaps of goddesses, unearthed at archaeological sites worldwide. They believe that goddess worship correlated with high female status and that women were cherished for giving birth and nurturing the young, which gave them a connection to the earth and spirits. Patricia Monaghan identifies more than 1,500 different goddesses worldwide, representing everything from mother to warrior.

Perhaps the most debated recent studies are by Lithuanian archaeologist Marija Gimbutas, whose writings, based on discoveries at sites such as Çatal Hüyük in Turkey, the Minoan palace at Knossos, and Stonehenge, portray ancient people in Europe and Anatolia as egalitarian and peaceful farmers led by influential women. These female-oriented societies, she says, were destroyed around 3500 B.C.E. by more violent Indo-European nomads from Central Asia, who brought patriarchy with them. From then on, patriarchy spread across Europe. Similarly, Riane Eisler and Judith Lorber describe ancient, goddess-worshiping farming cultures in eastern and southern Europe, where men and women ruled equally, with no war or inequalities of wealth. And like Gimbutas, they contend that Indo-European newcomers imposed male governments on these earlier societies.

Most scholars dispute the views of Gimbutas, Eisler, and Lorber about ancient matriarchies and equal status for each gender. For example, Lotte Motz, Lucy Godison, and Christine Morris argue that goddess worship theories are unproven. Motz claims that female images are no more common in early Europe than those of men and animals. Furthermore, the figurines may have been used in fertility rites rather than revered as spiritual forces. Motz and Cynthia Eller also suggest that mother goddess theories reflect not ancient realities but modern political and cultural attitudes, including a feminism that challenges patriarchy and biases about women's roles. Nor can we assume, such critics say, that worshiping female deities, if it happened, actually gave real power to women. After all, the patriarchal ancient Mesopotamians and Greeks worshiped various female deities, including a goddess of love, and many modern patriarchal cultures, including the Chinese, Japanese, Hindu Indian, and Yoruba, have female deities in their pantheons. Many Europeans have revered the Virgin Mary over the past two millennia, but men have still dominated European society.

If the notion of ancient matriarchies transformed by force into patriarchies cannot be proven, we are still left with the third question, how and when did patriarchy emerge? Anthropologist Sherry Ortner argues for a slow but inevitable transition from the egalitarianism of food collecting to male domination in the early cities and states. To Ortner, patriarchy was a product of technological and social upheavals rather than a will to power by aggressive men. Childbearing played a role because, while women stayed home having and raising children, men could travel and engage in more paid work and governmental, leisure, and religious activities, as well as warfare. That led to the gender stereotypes of women in unpaid work at home and men at paid work elsewhere. Also arguing for a gradual change, anthropologist Elizabeth Barber contends that farming people needed products, such as metal ores, that had to be gained through long-distance trade. This gave power to the more mobile and physically stronger men, who could travel to distant places and transport the heavy cargoes home. To be sure, knowledge of cloth making and the fiber arts gave women importance in ancient societies, since men also used products such as clothing and blankets; nevertheless, patriarchy emerged gradually as society slowly changed and began to reward strength and mobility.

There is considerable evidence that men increased their power over women in many early urban societies. Historian Gerda Lerner analyzed male power in the Mesopotamian city-states, where kings or male assemblies ruled. Law codes

Erich Lessing/Art Resource, NY

Goddess Figure This female figure, probably a mother-goddess, found in France was probably used in fertility rights. Such figures have been found in many ancient societies studied by archaeologists.

such as Hammurabi's favored men, and only women could be divorced or sold into slavery for adultery. Laws also restricted women's freedom of movement and treated them as private property. By this time, Lerner argues, gods had become more important than goddesses, and male power was legally recognized and sanctioned by religion.

EVALUATING THE DEBATE

What, then, was the status of women in ancient societies? The weight of scholarship favors those who doubt that full-blown matriarchal societies were once widespread. But few societies have ever been entirely controlled by the activities or wishes of men. Until recently historians and archaeologists have neglected the role of women. When we study ancient societies, we may unknowingly be influenced by modern patriarchal attitudes, since these are prominent in today's culture. We are more likely to study kings and wars than the beginnings of herbal medicine, cloth production, and the role of women as negotiators in community disputes. We have not heard the last word from scholars on the question of ancient matriarchies and patriarchies, but their disputes have made us more aware of the role of women in history.

THINKING ABOUT THE CONTROVERSY

1. Why can worship of a mother-goddess be understood in different ways?
2. Why do we need to understand patriarchy to comprehend world history?

EXPLORING THE CONTROVERSY

Some major works supporting the ancient goddess and matriarchy thesis include Marija Gimbutas, *Goddesses and Gods in Old Europe, 6500–500 B.C.: Myths and Cult Images* (Berkeley: University of California Press, 1982); Gimbutas, *The Language of the Goddess: Unearthing the Hidden Symbols of Western Civilization* (New York: Harper and Row, 1989); Gimbutas, *The Living Goddesses* (Berkeley: University of California Press, 1999); and Riane Eisler, *The Chalice and the Blade: Our History, Our Future* (San Francisco: Harper and Row, 1995). Judith Lorber challenges basic assumptions about gender in *Paradoxes of Gender* (New Haven: Yale University Press, 1994). Patricia Monaghan, *The New Book of Goddesses and Heroines* (New York: Llewellyn Publications, 1997), provides a useful reference on mythological and legendary female deities from many lands and eras.

Strong criticism of the ancient matriarchy thesis can be found in Lucy Godison and Christine Morris, eds., *Ancient Goddesses: The Myths and the Evidence* (Madison: University of Wisconsin Press, 1999); Lotte Motz, *The Faces of the Goddess* (New York: Oxford University Press, 1997); and Cynthia Eller, *The Myth of Matriarchal Prehistory: Why an Invented Past Won't Give Women a Future* (Boston: Beacon Press, 2001). Among major books on the making of patriarchy and gender roles are Elizabeth Barber, *Woman's Work: The First 20,000 Years: Women, Cloth, and Society in Early Times* (New York: W.W. Norton, 1994); Gerda Lerner, *The Creation of Patriarchy* (New York: Oxford University Press, 1986); and Sherry Ortner, *Making Gender: The Politics and Erotics of Culture* (Boston: Beacon Press, 1997).

Ancient Foundations of World History, 4000–600 B.C.E.

People today live in the shadow of the ancient peoples who began farming and later founded the Bronze Age cities in western Asia, Africa, South Asia, East Asia, and southern Europe. These ancient centuries, and the transitions that marked them, constructed the foundations for much that came later, including organized societies and the growing networks that connected them.

After thousands of years of prehistory, some peoples congregated in villages and began to practice agriculture. This was perhaps one of the two greatest transitions in human history, the other being the Industrial Revolution of the eighteenth and nineteenth centuries C.E. We can thank early farmers for giving us, between 10,000 and 5000 B.C.E., valuable inventions such as pottery, cloth, and the plow. Agriculture was the essential building block that stimulated other major developments, in particular the founding of cities and states and the invention of metalworking. New developments then fostered other changes. For example, better means of transportation allowed people, goods, ideas, and even diseases to travel longer distances in a shorter time. This transportation also became the basis for networks of trade and cultural exchange linking distant societies. In turn, this wider sharing of ideas helped bring about further transformations in social and cultural patterns. Today, like the ancients, we still get our food mostly from intensive agriculture and livestock raising, work metals into useful products like tools, ride in wheeled vehicles and boats that allow us to travel over long distances, worship in religious buildings, and often live in cities, where people representing several classes and many occupations work and trade. These cities are located in powerful states that are administered by bureaucratic governments and protected by military forces.

Ancient transitions happened as the result of many influences, among them environmental factors such as disease, climate change, the availability of fertile land, and the annual flooding of rivers. Local conditions helped shape such distinctive societies as Sumeria, Egypt, Nubia, Minoan Crete, Phoenicia, the Harappan cities, Shang China, and the Olmec. At the same time, there was much contact and communication among Eurasian and northern African societies as well as long-distance migrations by peoples like the Austronesians, Bantu, and Indo-Europeans. Such movement ensured that even largely distinctive societies shared certain common features.

Technological Foundations

We can thank the ancient peoples for inventing useful technologies such as metallurgy and for vastly improving transportation. Today we take these technologies for granted; indeed, they are basic to modern industrial life. In ancient times, however, people developed these technologies to help them solve particular problems. Once developed, they had many consequences. For example, metallurgy became a key to economic growth. Bronze and, a few centuries later, iron aided agriculture, transportation, and communication. Improvements in land and sea transportation helped move people and products over long distances, fostering trade networks. Expanded trade encouraged cities, and metal weapons and improved transportation allowed city rulers to build or expand states.

The Copper and Bronze Ages

The first metal to be worked was copper. Stoneworkers discovered that heating copper reduced it to liquid form and allowed it to be shaped in a mold. As it cooled, it could be given a good cutting edge. Many peoples in both hemispheres made copper tools and weapons, and they traded copper widely. Excavations of sunken trading ships from this era in the Mediterranean often discover large cargoes of copper. The Sumerian city-states were the first great metal-using society, followed soon after by the Egyptians, who used copper instruments to build the great pyramids. But metallurgy also led to deforestation, as forests were cut to make charcoal to fire the kilns. For example, it took 140 pounds of wood to produce 1 pound of copper.

Beginning around 3000 B.C.E. in western Asia, metalworkers figured out how to mix copper with tin or arsenic to create bronze. This discovery launched the Bronze Age in Afro-Eurasia. The Sumerians were the first society known to use bronze in commerce. Between 2600 and 2000 B.C.E. bronze technology was adopted or invented in Egypt, eastern Europe, Nubia, India, China, and Southeast Asia. The Chinese were the greatest users and mass producers of bronze. In South America, some peoples made use of another copper-arsenic alloy, as well as silver and gold.

Bronze technology affected life. Easier to make and more durable than copper, bronze was well suited for tools, drinking vessels, and weapons. In Hebrew tradition, the formidable biblical Philistine warrior Goliath had a bronze helmet, bronze armor on his legs, and a bronze javelin. Bronze making probably spurred both trade networks and warfare. Since tin deposits are less common than copper, tin was traded over great distances, and industries arose to obtain copper and tin and to manufacture bronze products. Armies were formed in part to protect mines, markets, and trade routes. Metalsmiths were so valuable that invading armies often carried them home in captivity. Finally, copper and bronze, as well as gold and silver, were used for the first coins, which gradually became the major medium of exchange.

The Iron Age

The making of iron provided the next technological breakthrough (see map). Western Asia had little tin but large quantities of iron ore. Iron was much harder to work than copper: artisans needed to produce higher temperatures, and heating produced a spongy mass rather than a liquid. Eventually inventive workers, possibly in the Hittite kingdom along the Black Sea or in Palestine, discovered a completely new but laborious technology that involved repeatedly heating and hammering the iron and plunging the result into cold water.

Metals and Great States ca. 1000 B.C.E.

The earliest states arose in river valleys—the Nile, Tigris-Euphrates, Indus, and Yellow—and these early states also worked metals, first bronze and then iron, to produce tools and weapons.

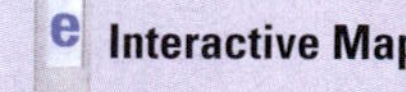
Interactive Map

The Iron Age began in western Asia and Egypt by around 1600 B.C.E. Between 900 and 500 B.C.E. iron technology was also adopted or invented in Greece, India, western and central Europe, Central Asia, China, Southeast Asia, and West and East Africa. Some peoples acquired iron through trade, and others through contact with ironworking peoples like the Bantu. Since ironworking never developed in the Americas or Australia, these societies had no iron weapons or tools. Eurasians and Africans may have benefited from having societies close enough to each other to regularly exchange ideas. In contrast, many thousands of miles, much of it rain forest or desert, separated the societies of Mesoamerica from those in the Andes region, limiting contact.

Ironworking brought many advantages. The metal was both more adaptable and cheaper to make than bronze. With it people could produce better axes for cutting wood, plows for farming, wagon wheels for transport, and swords for warfare. For example, in Hebrew tradition, the Israelites could not drive the Canaanites out of the Palestinian lowland because they had iron chariots. Centuries later metalworkers learned how to add carbon to iron to make steel. But like many technologies, iron proved a mixed blessing. While it improved farming, it also made for deadlier weapons. Armies equipped with iron-tipped weapons enjoyed a strategic advantage over their neighbors. Although iron shields afforded some protection, more men may have died as warfare became more frequent.

Transportation Breakthroughs and Human Mobility

Metalworking was only one of several valuable technologies invented in ancient times. Land transport was dramatically transformed by the anonymous inventor of the wheel, to whom we owe much. Wheels were first used in pottery making, an activity that involved both men and women. But sometime between 3500 and 3200 B.C.E., probably in Mesopotamia, artisans found that fitting an axle to a cart allowed two wheels (often made of iron) to turn freely, and the wheeled cart was invented. Wagons followed rapidly, and then horse-drawn chariots. These wheeled vehicles made possible longer journeys and enabled people to carry more cargo, increasing long-distance trade. This increased travel inspired the first maps, drawn in Mesopotamia around 2300 B.C.E.

These maps, drawn onto small tablets and then baked, recognized distant relationships in portraying agricultural land, town plans, and the world as known to Babylonians. Such a map from the sixth or seventh century B.C.E. reveals how trade and communication had expanded their horizons. The map shows the Babylonian world, including rivers, canals, cities, and neighboring states, in the center of a flat earth, with the remote lands on the fringe inhabited by legendary beasts. The mapmaker noted that his sketch showed the "four corners" of the earth.

The inventors of the first boats are unknown. The ancestors of Australian Aborigines and some of the first migrants to the Americas may have used boats, perhaps canoes or rafts, to reach their destinations many thousands of years ago. Archaeologists have discovered the remnants of 10,000-year-old boats in northwest Europe. By 5000 B.C.E. people living in Mesopotamia and along the Nile had invented square sails, and wind could then be harnessed to drive boats through the water. The use of sails spread quickly. Reed and tar boats began sailing between Kuwait, on the Persian Gulf, and India. The Greek writer Homer reported how the Mycenaeans prepared ships for voyages: "they dragged the vessel into deeper water, put the mast and sails on board, fixed the oars in leather hoops, all ship-shape, and hauled up the white sail."[1] Austronesians were probably the first to construct boats capable of sailing the deep oceans. As with land transport, better ships made it easier for distant peoples to come into contact with one another and share their ways of life. Maritime trade networks, such as those linking Pacific islands with Southeast Asia and the eastern Mediterranean with northwest Europe, stretched over vast distances.

The invention and spread of wheeled vehicles and boats also made it easier for people to migrate over longer distances. The ancient era saw several great migrations involving large numbers of people. Using seagoing boats, especially large outrigger canoes, Austronesians sailed to and settled most of the widely scattered Pacific islands. Using carts and chariots, Indo-European peoples occupied large areas of Eurasia. Traveling by foot or in canoes, and also possessing iron technology, Bantu-speaking peoples settled the forests and grasslands of the southern half of Africa.

Urban and Economic Foundations

The first cities, some of them with populations over 100,000, became the cultural focal points and organizing centers for surrounding regions. The first states formed around cities, which also fostered the first writing. The urban revolution also encouraged expanded economic activities, so that merchants became prominent members of society. In turn, merchants established the first long-distance trade networks that connected people over long distances and helped spread the influence of urban societies.

The Functions and Social Organization of Cities

From the very beginning, ancient cities served a variety of functions. Some, like several Mesopotamian cities and South American cities such as Caral and Chavín, developed as centers for religious ceremonies. An Akkadian text boasted that, in Uruk, "people are resplendent in festive attire, where each day is made a holiday."[2] Cities in Egypt and China, by contrast, seem to have been founded chiefly as administrative centers to govern the surrounding territories. Many others, including the Harappan, Nubian, and Olmec cities, formed around marketplaces. Perhaps the first large city, Tell Hamoukar in Mesopotamia, sat alongside a major trade route. Many cities served all these functions.

Cities produced more organized societies by fostering more elaborate class structures than could be found in the countryside. Political elites staffed the government bureaucracies such as the law courts, while religious leaders directed the

Terracotta Figures from Harappan Cities These terracotta figures found in the ruins of Harappa show the diverse hairstyles and ornaments popular in the city. Archaeologists believe that these indicate the diversity of social classes and ethnic groups that inhabited Harappa.

temples. In Mesopotamian, Egyptian, Chinese, Harappan, and American cities, these upper-class groups generally lived in the center, around the temples and public buildings. Just outside this central zone, the middle-class merchants and skilled craftsmen lived with their families above their workshops and stores. This was true in both Sumerian Ur and Chinese Anyang. In Mesopotamia, craftsmen accounted for 20 percent of the city population. Different neighborhoods were often defined by occupation. For example, at Anyang potters apparently concentrated in one district, metalworkers in another. On the city outskirts lived the laborers, including household servants, small farmers, and slaves. Cities also attracted people from neighboring societies, and ethnically diverse populations were common. Some merchants migrated from elsewhere but probably maintained ties to their hometowns through the extensive commercial networks.

Most urban women led busy lives. As households began to stir each morning, women prepared a quick meal for husbands and sons heading out to their work, perhaps as artisans, peddlers, soldiers, or laborers. Many used pots and pans made of copper or bronze to cook and serve the food. After cleaning up the meal, many women walked through dusty streets to market stalls to buy food grown on nearby farms. As they returned home, they may have passed children playing in the narrow alleys, perhaps watched by grandparents. In some societies, the wealthier women were increasingly restricted inside walled courtyards. The poorest women and men begged, searched through trash, or offered their services to those who were better off.

Cities, Trade, and Networks of Exchange

Because trade was a major city activity, merchants became prominent members of urban society. In their shops and market stalls, they made available products from near and far. One of the most popular products was salt, which was used to preserve and add taste to food. Another was obsidian, a volcanic glass that made sharp tools and was found naturally only where volcanic activity had occurred. Diverse peoples, among them Greeks, Pacific islanders, and Mesoamericans, actively sought obsidian. By 1500 B.C.E. long-distance traders supplied various Mediterranean and Middle Eastern societies with opium and other drugs, which were mostly used to ease the pain of disease, surgery, and childbirth. As it does today, trade could also foster disagreements. An Ur merchant, complaining about the poor quality of copper shipped from Bahrain, wrote to the sender: "Who am I that you treat me in this manner and offend me?"[3]

Growing trade required the creation of currencies, without which our modern economic life would be impossible. Simple forms of money, mostly varied weights of precious metals like silver, were invented between 3000 and 2500 B.C.E. in Mesopotamian cities. Legal codes were then written that specified fines, interest rates, and even the ideal price of some common goods. By 600 B.C.E. the first gold coins were being struck in Anatolia. Money made exchange easier, especially in cities, and it may have stimulated the development of mathematics as a tool for calculating wealth. Various ancient societies in both hemispheres developed some system of mathematics.

Trade networks moving objects of value, from raw materials to luxury goods, linked major cities and even distant societies. Between 4000 and 3000 B.C.E. traders began shipping minerals, precious stones, and other valued commodities over long distances, and Mesopotamia became a commercial hub linking southern Asia with Egypt. Beginning around 1200 B.C.E., heavily urbanized Phoenicia, which established many trading ports around the Mediterranean, became the first known society to flourish mostly through interregional commerce rather than farming. Gradually trade routes expanded over long distances, increasing contacts between societies with different cultures and institutions. Goods traveled initially by riverboat and by donkey or horse caravans. By 2000 B.C.E., however, sea trading in the Mediterranean Sea, Persian Gulf, and Indian Ocean had become more important.

Some areas became trade centers. Mesopotamia was the center of a vast trade network, with links eastward to India and Central Asia and westward to Egypt and Italy. Its location as the hub of this network allowed it to draw ideas, produce, and people from a huge hinterland. Similarly, Egypt connected Africa and Eurasia. By 2000 B.C.E. cities like Dilmun on Bahrain Island in the Persian Gulf flourished as trade hubs located between major societies. The Persian Gulf itself has served as a contact zone for over five millennia.

Trade fostered other transitions. The need to guide ships or caravans to distant destinations, as well as the belief that the changing skies could influence human activity (astrology), sparked the study of the stars. Babylonian astrological beliefs and the zodiac may have been spread by trade to western Asia and southern Europe, where they became popular.

Victor Boswell/NGS

Fragments of Egyptian-Hittite Treaty This carved stone fragment contains a treaty, signed around 1250 B.C.E., between Egypt and the Hittite kingdom in Anatolia that ended a war between the two states. The treaty is inscribed in the widely used cuneiform script of the Akkadian language. It eloquently demonstrates the reality of ancient warfare but also expresses the age-old quest for peace.

Political Foundations

Closely related to urbanization was the emergence of the first states, with their bureaucratic structures and powerful ruling elites. States marked a transition to more complex and organized societies. The first known states formed in Mesopotamia around 3500 B.C.E. and in Egypt by 3000 B.C.E. Between 3000 and 1000 B.C.E. states were also established in India, China, Vietnam, Nubia, and southeastern Europe, as well as in Mesoamerica and South America. Today we take for granted the notion of large political units to whom people owe allegiance, but in the ancient world they were major innovations. Among the consequences of states was the rise of conflict between them as well as with nearby pastoral peoples, which resulted in increased warfare. Although warfare long predates state building, now it was waged on a larger scale, becoming a common pattern in world history.

Kings and Political Hierarchies

States were hierarchically organized political structures. The rulers—mostly kings and emperors, but sometimes queens, such as the Egyptian Hatshepsut—ruled over many rural peasants and city-dwellers living within the territories they controlled. These people paid taxes, in money or in agricultural products, in acknowledgment of the king's ability to keep order, promote justice, and protect his subjects from harm. The great Law Code associated with the Babylonian ruler Hammurabi is one illustration of this basis of ancient governments. Many kings sought the kind of support accorded the Aryan kings in the Hindu sacred writings: "Him do ye proclaim, O men as kings and father of kings, the lordly power, the suzerain of all creation, the eater of the folk, the slayer of foes, the guardian of the law."[4] Bureaucracies were formed to administer the states, including the first empires. As royal power increased, the institutions that allowed merchants and other leading citizens to participate in government, such as the assemblies in Sumerian cities, lost their importance.

The rulers of large states had to possess legal and military power to reward their supporters and punish their enemies. This required sufficient income from either taxes or the spoils of war. Some of this money was also used to build great monumental architecture, such as the Egyptian pyramids and Olmec mounds whose ruins still astonish tourists. Rulers also had to convince their subjects that they ruled, either as gods themselves (such as the pharaoh of Egypt) or with the permission of divine forces (such as the Zhou dynasty rulers in China, who claimed to rule by the "Mandate of Heaven"). We often imagine ancient pharaohs and emperors as all-powerful despots, and in many respects they were. But kingship was not always an easy job. Officials might ignore their policies, rivals could challenge them, and disenchanted groups might rebel.

After states came empires, which were generally formed by conquest. The Akkadian Sargon in Mesopotamia established the earliest known imperial state around 2350 B.C.E. Sargon's use of a standing army (with over five thousand soldiers) set the pattern that prevailed in the Fertile Crescent for the next several millennia as various states gained influence or control over their neighbors, often to secure scarce resources like silver, copper, or timber. Various ancient societies established empires, among them Assyrians, Egyptians, Mycenaeans, and Hittites. This expansion prompted states to set up forts on their frontiers to control the local population and the flow of traffic. An Egyptian inscription ordered a garrison along the Nile "to prevent any Nubian from passing northward, whether on foot or by boat," except for traders or messengers.[5]

States and Warfare

With the rise of competing states and improved military technology, warfare became more common. One of the chief tasks of the ruler was to protect and perhaps expand his state, and often rulers waged war to acquire land and capture people. More land and population meant more resources and tax revenues. As part of the rise of warfare as an institution, rulers were expected to be or honor heroic warriors. Even today people remember the legends of great ancient warriors (real or mythical) like Hercules at Troy or Arjuna in the *Bhagavad Gita*. Ancient soldiers were armed with "shock" weapons such as clubs or swords and "missiles" such as arrows or spears. Warfare by settled peoples required a powerful state. To wage war, kings had to marshal resources such as food and metals as well as recruit soldiers. They also had to discourage dissent and instill among the population a sense that warfare was worthwhile. Opposition to the ruler and his policies was viewed as treason and could mean death or imprisonment.

In Afro-Eurasia many wars matched states against pastoral nomads, who were attracted by the wealth of the farming societies and their cities. These mobile nomads, often viewed by the farming peoples as "barbarians," pioneered the development of chariot and cavalry warfare and possessed many horses or camels. Between 2000 and 1000 B.C.E. nomadic peoples occasionally conquered cities and states. Eventually many of these pastoralists, such as the Hittites in western Asia and the Aryans in India, adopted some of the ways of the conquered farmers, while the urban peoples acquired the pastoralists' military technologies. Incursions into farming societies by nomadic pastoralists remained an important pattern in world history until the seventeenth century C.E.

Ancient armies, like modern ones, depended on their weapons and on soldiers who were not always enthusiastic about their job. One Egyptian text said of a soldier: "He is awakened when an hour has passed and he is driven like an ass. He works till the sun sets. He is hungry, his body is exhausted, he is dead while still alive. His body is broken with dysentery."[6] Some conscripts in Zhou China shared the disenchantment: "What plant is not wilting? What man is not taken from his wife? Alas for us soldiers!"[7] Then as now, soldiering was a dangerous activity that required bravery and self-discipline.

Warfare became increasingly lethal as weaponry and strategy improved. When the Assyrians swept through Mesopotamia in the ninth century B.C.E., their advanced cavalry and siege weaponry enabled them to level and burn the great city of Babylon. Later the Assyrians themselves experienced defeat, as their capital, Ninevah, fell to "the noise of the whip and of rattling wheels, galloping horses, clattering chariots!"[8] Even though many ancient cities were surrounded by defensive walls, they were still vulnerable to well-armed foes. But the costs of war, in treasure and people, also prompted rulers to make peace treaties with rival powers and prompted prophets to call for beating "their swords into ploughshares, their spears into pruning hooks; nation shall not lift up sword against nation."[9] The quest for peace was as old as the urge to wage war.

Social and Cultural Foundations

Beginning around 3500 B.C.E. the social forms common to hunters and gatherers began to change as more and more people settled down to farming and developed more organized societies. Metallurgy, cities, and states fostered new structures, systems, and attitudes, along with social inequality and more varied activities. Perhaps the two most significant cultural innovations were writing, which allowed for record-keeping and improved communication, and institutionalized religion, which shaped the values and behavior of societies. The social and cultural patterns that emerged in antiquity endured because they fulfilled basic human needs for group survival and personal satisfaction.

Inequality, Conflict, and Leisure

The shift from the relatively egalitarian ethos of hunting and gathering to a more hierarchical social organization changed people's lives. Increasingly people were divided into social classes, with the wealthier groups controlling the distribution and consumption of economic resources. Ancient graves reveal the differences in social status. Some graves were elaborate, filled with offerings of material goods such as jewelry, and others were very simple. Legal codes, such as that of Hammurabi, usually favored the wealthy.

At the same time, with productive agriculture, populations grew. Between 8000 and 500 B.C.E. the world's population jumped from 5 or 10 million up to an estimated 100 million. The great majority of these people lived in Mesopotamia (the most densely populated area), Egypt, India, China, and southeastern Europe. People were also living longer than during the Stone Age, when a third died before age twenty and only a tenth lived past forty. Bronze Age peoples lived into their early forties, and probably 5 to 10 percent lived past sixty.

With less equality but more people, the potential for social conflict increased. Most communities included haves and have-nots, landlords and landless, free citizens and slaves. The gap between rich and poor made crime a serious problem that was addressed through harsh codes like that of Hammurabi. Theft was common in major Mesopotamian and Egyptian cities. Large enslaved populations, which included debtors and prisoners of war, might revolt. Slavery was more pervasive in Mesopotamia than in China, Egypt, and India, but slaveholding was common in all ancient agricultural societies.

Patriarchy was another source of inequality and remains a feature of life today (see Historical Controversy: Patriarchy and Matriarchy in the Ancient World). Men increasingly believed that women were unsuited to run governments, and few of them were allowed to do so. Social changes that required heavy physical labor in farming, warfare, and long-distance trade influenced gender and family relations. Women now became known as the "weaker sex" and were often assigned chiefly domestic tasks. An ancient Chinese saying asserted that "men plow and women weave."[10] Although women continued to produce some of the pottery and most of the cloth, they were no longer equal contributors to food needs because they now spent more time at home. In farming families, women were also encouraged to bear a larger number of children to help in the fields. In many places, men, especially rulers and the rich, had multiple wives or took concubines. In some societies, among them Sumeria, Egypt, and Shang China, the remnants of older matrilineal family systems were only fading memories, but middle-class urban women fought hard to retain their property and other rights. Sexual options became more limited for women because men wanted to ensure that their personal wealth would be passed on to their children of known paternity. Increasingly dependent on men for support, women became more preoccupied with physical appearance, hoping to attract male favor. Women used eye makeup and perfume, both invented in ancient Egypt and still popular today.

Despite the social inequality and long hours of toil, leisure activities developed that are familiar to us today. For example, the Sumerian city-dwellers enjoyed dancing and music and invented beautiful, elaborate harps and lyres for their pleasure. Zhou Chinese music lovers preferred flutes and drums, and Egyptians preferred metal horns. Music was used for worship, festivals, and work, but the oldest known love songs had also appeared by 2300 B.C.E. in Egypt. Wrestling became a popular sport in many cultures. Alcoholic drinks like beer and wine were also common, often consumed in public taverns. Drinking became an integral part of leisure and social relationships in many societies. Homer summed up the pleasures favored in early Greece: "The things in which we take a perennial delight are the feast, the lyre [a musical instrument], the dance, clean linen in plenty, a hot bath and our beds."[11] These are pleasures that most modern people share, indicating that some things have not changed much in 3,000 years.

Writing and Its Consequences

Imagine how different our modern worlds of education and work would be without reading and writing. Although limited to a relatively small group of people for much of history, writing was a critical invention of several early societies. A Sumerian legend recalled a key discovery: "The High Priest of Kulaba formed some clay and wrote words on it as if on a tablet; with the sun's rising [to dry the clay], so it was!"[12] Writing fostered increasing occupational specialization, including the emergence of clerks, scribes, bureaucrats, and eventually teachers, scholars, and historians.

Initially developed chiefly to keep commercial accounts, codify legends and rituals, or record political proclamations, writing later gave birth to literature, historiography, sacred texts, and other forms of learning and culture that could now be transmitted and expanded. For example, writing helped spread the Sumerian epic of Gilgamesh so widely that it influenced the Hebrew book of Genesis and the *Iliad* and the *Odyssey* of the Greek Homer many centuries later. Similarly, Indian stories such as the *Ramayana* became popular in Southeast Asia. Writing also allowed rulers to communicate over long distances with district governors and foreign leaders, and it allowed merchants to make arrangements with merchants in other cities, enhancing the role of communication networks.

Writing, however, had contradictory consequences. On the one hand, it clearly stimulated creativity and intellectual growth while allowing for a spread of knowledge. But writing also often became a tool for preserving the social and politi-

Bell of Marquies Music had a key function in the court life of Zhou China. This sixty-four-piece bell set was found in the tomb of a regional ruler, which also contained many flutes, drums, zithers, pan pipes, and chimes. Five men using mallets and poles were needed to play this set of bells.

cal order, especially when literacy was restricted to a privileged elite such as bureaucrats, lawyers, or priests. For example, a soldier in Zhou China complained that he and his colleagues wanted to return home, but they "were in awe of the [official] orders in the tablets."[13] Sacred literature was also frequently closed to debate, since it supposedly came from the gods.

Institutionalized Religions

The rise of agriculture and then cities gradually transformed the belief that nature was alive with spiritual forces (animism) to more systematic theologies and organized religious observances. These beliefs and practices gave order and meaning to people's lives and may have promoted cooperation and a sense of community. Ideas about the fate of individual humans after death as well as notions of right and wrong differed widely as societies developed unique traditions and beliefs. While most ancient peoples were polytheists or animists, believing in many gods or spirits, a few, such as the Hebrews and some African societies, were monotheists, believing in one high god who presided over the universe.

Full-time religious specialists also evolved, often replacing the shamans, the part-time spiritual leaders associated with earlier times. With the rise of agriculture and larger communities, a priestly class arose who were seen as able to communicate with the gods and interpret their will. Because they provided essential services such as writing or calculating the time of the annual floods, priests were the first social group to be freed from direct subsistence labor. They also staffed the temples, which in some cities were massive monumental buildings serving thousands of believers.

The supernatural and natural worlds were usually explained through myths, stories about the past or about the interaction of gods with the human world. Mythology explained the birth of the universe, the progression of seasons, the uncertainties of agriculture, the flooding of rivers, and human dramas such as battlefield losses and victories. Myths and legends were included in sacred books. Several thousand years later some of these ancient books, such as the Hindu Vedas and the Hebrew Bible, are still revered by many millions of people.

Institutionalized religions influenced societies. Because religious ceremonies and ideas provided supernatural sanction for the social and political order, they became a powerful force for social control. Challenging the political or social system, which was seen as divinely inspired, now constituted blasphemy and condemned one to eternal punishment after death. Many of the ancient religions, led by men and worshiping chiefly male gods, supported patriarchal attitudes. Religious views also spread from one society to another. For example, Egyptian ideas of the afterlife and a final Day of Judgment were influential around the larger Mediterranean basin. Hebrews may have acquired their notions of a weekly Sabbath and a Garden of Eden from Mesopotamians. Many centuries later all these ideas were reflected in Christianity and Islam.

Suggested Reading

Books

Adas, Michael, ed. *Agricultural and Pastoral Societies in Ancient and Classical History*. Philadelphia: Temple University Press, 2001. A useful collection of essays on various aspects of premodern world history.

Armstrong, Karen. *The Great Transformation: The Beginning of Our Religious Traditions.* New York: Knopf, 2006. Good discussion of ancient religions and beliefs.

Bogucki, Peter. *The Origins of Human Society*. Malden, MA: Blackwell, 1999. A detailed and up-to-date scholarly study of prehistory and the rise of ancient societies.

Casson, Lionel. *The Ancient Mariners: Seafarers and Sea Fighters of the Mediterranean in Ancient Times*, 2nd ed. Princeton, NJ: Princeton University Press, 1991. A fascinating study of ancient maritime trade and connections.

Christian, David. *Maps of Time: An Introduction to "Big History."* Berkeley: University of California Press, 2004. The most extensive presentation of the "big history" approach, with much on the ancient era.

Curtin, Philip D. *Cross-Cultural Trade in World History.* Cambridge: Cambridge University Press, 1984. A pioneering comparative study.

Diamond, Jared. *Guns, Germs and Steel: The Fates of Human Societies*. New York: W.W. Norton, 1997. A fascinating interpretation of prehistoric and ancient human societies, with emphasis on environmental influences.

Fagan, Brian. *The Long Summer: How Climate Changed Civilization*. New York: Basic Books, 2004. An up-to-date assessment of the connection between history and climate over the past 5,000 years.

Fagan, Brian M. *People of the Earth: An Introduction to World Prehistory*, 12th ed. New York: Longman, 2003. Contains much up-to-date material on the ancient societies and prehistory.

Headrick, Daniel R. *Technology: A World History.* New York: Oxford University Press, 2009. Valuable discussion of ancient agriculture and metallurgy.

Manning, Patrick. *Migration in World History.* New York: Routledge, 2005. A provocative study, with much on prehistory and ancient history.

Matossian, Mary Kilbourne. *Shaping World History: Breakthroughs in Ecology, Technology, Science, and Politics.* Armonk, NY: M.E. Sharpe, 1997. A general examination of science, technology, and ecology, with much material on early farmers and the ancient societies.

Ristvet, Lauren. *In the Beginning: World History from Evolution to the First States.* New York: McGraw-Hill, 2007. Good overview of topics on ancient global history.

Snooks, Graeme D. *The Dynamic Society: Exploring the Sources of Global Change.* London: Routledge, 1996. A challenging view of world history by an economist, with much on the ancient world.

Trigger, Bruce D. *Understanding Early Civilizations.* New York: Cambridge University Press, 2003. A detailed scholarly examination of ancient societies, including Egypt, Mesopotamia, and Shang China.

Wood, Michael. *Legacy: The Search for Ancient Cultures.* New York: Sterling, 1994. A well-written survey of ancient societies for the general reader.

WEBSITES

Ancient and Lost Civilizations (*http://www.crystalinks.com/ancient.html*). Offers some useful essays on various world regions and ancient cultures.

Exploring Ancient World Cultures (*http://eawc.evansville.edu/*). Excellent site run by Evansville University, with essays and links on the ancient Near East, Egypt, India, China, and Europe.

Geology Project (*http://www.unr.edu/sb204/geology*). Provides brief but useful information on the history of copper, bronze, and iron technology.

Internet Ancient History Sourcebook (*http://www.fordham.edu/halsall/ancient/asbook.html*). An exceptionally rich collection of links and primary source readings.

Internet Global History Sourcebook (*http://www.fordham.edu/halsall/global/globalsbook.html*). An excellent set of links on world history from ancient to modern times.

World Civilizations (*http://www.wsu.edu/~dee/TITLE.HTM*). A useful collection of materials on prehistory and ancient history, operated by Washington State University.

PART II

Blossoming: The Classical Societies and Their Legacies, ca. 600 B.C.E.–ca. 600 C.E.

The Classical Era, roughly the centuries between 600 B.C.E. and 600 C.E., was a formative period that saw a flourishing of societies and networks in nearly every inhabited part of the globe. The foundations for this era had been laid with the agricultural transition and the rise of the first cities and states in both the Eastern and Western Hemispheres. The classical societies typically became more complex and often larger than their ancient predecessors, and their art, literature, politics, and religion have had a lasting significance. Today's popular images of the Classical Era—Greek philosophers debating the meaning of existence, Roman gladiators battling in the Colosseum, and the Buddha meditating under a leafy tree—while limited, testify to the ongoing prominence this era has held in our thought.

These centuries saw innovations in thought, government, writing, and metalworking and an increase in long-distance trade aided by new transportation technologies. Improved communications between societies spread ideas and products, helping foster change. Trading zones expanded, and societies as distant from each other as Persia and China established diplomatic communication. People began to envision a larger world than their own village or kingdom, and that larger world changed them. In the increasingly cosmopolitan milieu of the Eastern Hemisphere, for example, Chinese influence began to reshape Korea and Japan, Indian religions and political ideas sparked state building in Southeast Asia, and Greek culture reached into Europe, Asia, and Africa. In the ferment sparked in the Eastern Hemisphere by local growth and contact with other societies, many of the laws, political traditions, literatures, philosophies, and religions associated with the major cultures emerged. Similarly, in both sub-Saharan Africa and the Americas, societies exchanged religious ideas, trade goods, and notions of government. Population movement into the Pacific islands (Oceania) and southern Africa continued.

The early classical centuries in Greece, Israel, Persia, India, and China were marked by philosophical speculation. This creative evolution in human thought between 600 and 250 B.C.E., often called the Axial Age, laid the groundwork for the core beliefs of some classical societies. Many of the greatest thinkers in history, such as Buddha, Confucius, and Socrates, lived at the same time or were near-contemporaries. Several billion people in Asia continue to revere the teachings of Confucius and the Buddha, Hebrew thinkers influenced later religions, and schools in North America and western Europe still introduce students to the ideas of the classical Greek philosophers.

Between 350 B.C.E. and 250 C.E. large parts of the Afro-Eurasian zone were transformed by large regional empires.

Persian Rhyton This gilded silver drinking cup, made in Persia in the fourth or fifth century B.C.E., has the figure of the ibex, a local animal, at the base. The cup is an example of the artistic treasures produced by classical peoples.

During the imperial age great states dominated the Mediterranean Basin, western Asia, India, and China. Diverse peoples, including Persians, Hellenistic Greeks, Romans, Mauryan Indians, and Han Chinese, presided over regional empires greater in scale than any that had come before. Some of the empire builders, such as the Macedonian Alexander the Great and the Roman Julius Caesar, are still famous today. Eventually, however, the empires overextended themselves territorially and collapsed. In contrast, most American and sub-Saharan African states were small and often decentralized.

The great Afro-Eurasian empires were in regular contact with each other by way of extensive trade networks. Distances narrowed. The best-known network was the overland Silk Road, named after the main commodity shipped, which linked China across Central Asia with India, the Middle East, and Europe. Caravans also linked North and West Africa across the harsh Sahara Desert, while trade routes around the Indian Ocean connected Southeast Asia and India with East Africa and Western Asia. Thanks to conquest or trade, Greek and Roman ideas and institutions permeated the Mediterranean region, and Indian cultural influences spread into Central, East, and Southeast Asia. Deadly diseases, such as plague, also moved along the trade routes, killing millions. Thus societies all over the world were increasingly altered, at times dramatically, by contact with others through various kinds of networks of trade, migration, disease, and conquest. Nonetheless, despite this contact, major societies largely remained distinct from each other.

As the Afro-Eurasian empires declined, divided, or collapsed, three religions rose in influence and enjoyed a wide appeal: Buddhism, Hinduism, and a new faith, Christianity. As these religions crossed cultural boundaries, attracting people of diverse backgrounds, they became universal religions, promoting social stability while also fostering cultural exchange. Since the Classical Era, regions have often been identified with their dominant religion, such as Hindu India or Christian Europe. These religious heritages were formed in the Classical Era.

EUROPE
Greek city-states, notably Athens, experimented with democracy and fostered philosophy and science. By conquering a large empire, Alexander the Great spread Greek culture into western Asia and Egypt. The Romans built an empire that encompassed the Mediterranean Basin and much of Europe, spreading Roman influence. By late Roman times Christianity was becoming the dominant religion in the Mediterranean, and Germanic tribes migrated into southern Europe, contributing to the collapse of Roman power. To the east, Byzantium conquered a large empire while mixing Roman, Greek, and Christian traditions.

WESTERN ASIA
The Persians established a large empire over much of western Asia and Egypt, promoting Persian thought. After their collapse the Hellenistic Greeks dominated the region and spread Greek culture. The Hellenistic Greeks were then displaced by the Romans. In Roman-ruled Palestine the teachings of a Hebrew, Jesus, sparked a new religion, Christianity, which during the later Classical Era spread around the Mediterranean Basin. With Roman decline the Persians regained power over much of western Asia.

EASTERN ASIA
Chinese philosophies emerged during a time of rapid change, and Confucianism, Daoism, and Legalism became enduring influences. The Qin dynasty reunified China, and then the Han dynasty established a huge empire and overland trade with western Asia and Rome. When the Han collapsed, Buddhism filtered in from India. Chinese science and technology during this era were innovative. Koreans and Japanese formed states and imported Confucianism, Buddhism, and political models from China.

AFRICA
Egypt fell successively under Persian, Hellenistic Greek, and finally Roman rule. Carthage was another major North African power and trade center until the Romans conquered the region. In northeast Africa, Kush was a trade center and major iron producer, and another trading state, Aksum, adopted Christianity. Trading cities and then empires, notably Ghana, emerged in the Sudan region. Elsewhere the Bantu peoples continued their expansion, settling much of central, eastern, and southern Africa. Long-distance trade networks connected West Africans with North Africa and East Africans with India and western Asia.

SOUTHERN ASIA AND OCEANIA
Buddhism arose in India, where it was later adopted by the kings of the region's first empire, the Mauryas. However, Hinduism remained India's majority faith, and Buddhism later split into rival schools. Indians traded with western Asia, Africa, Rome, and Southeast Asia. Various groups migrated into India from Central Asia. The Gupta kingdom made India a world leader in science, and Indian influence, including Buddhism and Hinduism, spread into Southeast Asia, helping foster states. Maritime trade linked Southeast Asia with China, India, western Asia, and East Africa. During this same time Austronesians continued settling the Pacific islands and traded with each other over vast distances.

CHAPTER

5

Classical Societies in Southern and Central Asia, 600 B.C.E.–600 C.E.

CHAPTER OUTLINE

- The Transformation of Indian Society, Religion, and Politics
- South and Central Asia After the Mauryas
- The Gupta Age in India
- The Development of Southeast Asian Societies

PROFILE
The Trung Sisters, Vietnamese Rebels

WITNESS TO THE PAST
Basic Doctrines in the Buddha's First Sermon

C.M. Dixon/Ancient Art & Architecture Collection

Gold Coin
This gold coin, showing a horseman, was made in India during the reign of King Chandragupta II, who presided over a great and prosperous Indian empire, with a dynamic economy, between 380 and 415 C.E.

The merchants used to move about in the rivers as they wished, in the forests as if in gardens and on mountains as if in their own houses. As [the King] used to protect the earth so it too gave him gems out of mines, corns from the fields, and elephants from forests.

—INDIAN WRITER KALIDASA (KAHL-I-DAHSS-UH), FIFTH CENTURY C.E.[1]

FOCUS QUESTIONS

1. How did Buddhism and the Mauryas shape Indian society?
2. What were some of the ways in which classical India connected with and influenced the world beyond South Asia?
3. What were the main achievements of the Gupta era?
4. How did Southeast Asians blend indigenous and foreign influences to create unique societies?

Sometime around 80 C.E. an unknown Greek boarded a trading ship that left the Egyptian port of Berenike **(BER-eh-nick-y)** headed for India. The ship sailed down the Red Sea and then along the coast of Arabia, braving the dangers from pirates. At the Indus River the merchants exchanged clothing, silverware, and glassware for semiprecious stones from Afghanistan, Chinese silks, and Indian textiles. Proceeding down India's west coast, they stopped near present-day Bombay, trading silverware and Italian wine for pepper. The travelers then reached the great port of Muziris **(MOO-zir-us)** in southwest India, where the sailors probably haunted the waterfront dives. A second-century Indian poet recorded the arrival of such ships at Muziris: "The beautiful vessels stir white foam on the river, arriving with gold and departing with pepper."[2] The ship then sailed around the southern tip of India and up the east coast, stopping to collect pearls, textiles, spices, and gems. Finally the ship returned to Egypt, the merchants aboard hoping to make a fortune from their cargo.

From Egypt, western Asia, and East Africa ships arrived annually at Indian seaports to trade, collecting fabulous trade goods, such as pepper, cinnamon, cotton, and gems, for sale in distant markets. India also attracted sojourners and permanent settlers arriving by sea or overland. For those who arrived over the mountains from windswept Central Asia, the Indian sun was a blazing fury and the drenching summer rains a shock. To all the newcomers, the Indian culture and religion were more unusual than the climate. But Indian society was adaptable and accommodating. Most immigrants found themselves gradually enfolded into Indian religions, which allowed for many paths to understanding. Hinduism was resilient, bending to meet the varying needs of dissimilar people. This adaptability also helped Indian culture to spread into Southeast Asia.

The Classical Era was a time of flowering in South and Southeast Asia, particularly in state building, the development of new trade networks, and religious thought. Many of the patterns forged in this era endured into modern times. Several great empires brought unusual political unity to South Asia and made India a leading world power. India also remained closely connected to land and sea networks of exchange that helped reshape the society. Hinduism developed new schools of thought, while Buddhism **(BOO-diz-uhm)** arose to become a major faith in many parts of Asia. Meanwhile, various Central and Southeast Asian societies established states and social systems that differed greatly from those in India and China while becoming major participants in international maritime trade.

Visit the website and eBook for additional study materials and interactive tools: www.cengage.com/history/lockard/globalsocnet2e

The Transformation of Indian Society, Religion, and Politics

How did Buddhism and the Mauryas shape Indian society?

The forging of a new society from the synthesis of Aryan and local traditions continued for centuries, affecting many aspects of life and thought. The distinctive caste system became a key foundation of Indian society, and Hinduism grew even more diverse and complex. In addition, Jainism and Buddhism were born out of the religious ferment of the Axial Age, that great philosophical awakening across Eurasia during the early Classical Age that spawned many new ways of thinking from Greece to China. India's first large centralized state, the Mauryan **(MORE-yuhn)** Empire, emerged in part as a response to contact with peoples to the west. Like the Hellenistic Greeks and Romans, the Mauryans were linked to trade and communication networks.

Caste and Indian Society

The social configuration we know today as the caste system began to take shape early in the Classical Era. Members of a caste generally practiced a common occupation: some were priests, others warriors, merchants, artisans, or farmers, while still others performed the more menial tasks. Caste membership was also supported by Hindu values, including beliefs in reincarnation. Although the social and religious characteristics became similar throughout India over the centuries, the caste system was never uniform and unchanging. Still, it produced a social stability that allowed it to persist for several thousand years.

Over time the caste system became more fully developed. A political and legal document with advice for a Hindu king, usually known as the Code of Manu **(MAN-oo)**, formalized many rules regarding caste relations. Gradually, during the first millennium of the Common Era, the four main castes (*varna*) subdivided into thousands of subcastes known as *jati* ("birth groups"), each with its own rules and, frequently, occupational specialization. Eventually the caste system became hereditary. Each person was born into a certain caste that maintained a moral code stipulating such duties as family maintenance and specifying which jatis could supply marriage partners. Strong food regulations prescribed the types of food that could be consumed by each caste, who could cook and serve the food, and who could accompany the diner. Gradually vegetarianism became more common among the higher castes, and cows were protected against being killed. Beef eating was probably common in ancient times, but by 500 C.E. pious Hindus avoided eating beef because the cow had come to be considered sacred, the symbol of life and motherhood. Cows wandered at will, eating whatever grain they found. Foreign observers have often argued that the cows spread disease and consume scarce food resources. However, some anthropologists argue that cow tolerance makes economic sense, ensuring an ample supply of cow dung for fuel and fertilizer as well as milk.

Village Scene, Second Century C.E. In classical times most Indians lived in villages. This drawing of a village scene is based on a relief made at Amaravati, a Buddhist temple complex built in the second century C.E. It shows members of different caste groups carrying out various village activities.

From A. L. Balsham, *The Wonder That Was India* [London: Sidgwick and Jackson, 1954]

Hindu ideas sanctioned the caste system. The doctrine of *karma* held that one's status in the present life was determined by deeds in past lives. Every action had repercussions, and the sum of one's karma in past lives determined one's fate in this life. The three top caste groupings were considered further along the path of reincarnation. Low-caste Indians were held responsible for their status because of their presumed past sins. Their only hope lay in dutifully performing their present duties

CHRONOLOGY

	India	Southeast Asia
600 B.C.E.	**563–483** B.C.E. Life of the Buddha	
400 B.C.E.	**322–185** B.C.E. Mauryan Empire	
200 B.C.E.		**111** B.C.E.–**939** C.E. Chinese colonization of Vietnam
1 C.E.	**50–250** C.E. Kushan era	ca. **75–550** C.E. Funan ca. **192–1471** C.E. Champa
200 C.E.	**320–550** C.E. Gupta era	

and obligations. Below the formal caste system were the untouchables, or *pariahs* **(puh-RYE-uhz)**. Some 10 percent of the population, untouchables were generally condemned to trades and crafts regarded as undesirable (such as carrying water to village houses) or unclean because their function involved being polluted by filth or the taking of animal life. They worked as sweepers of village streets, fishermen, butchers, gravediggers, tanners, leatherworkers, and scavengers, and they lived largely in their own neighborhoods.

Caste in Indian Life

The caste system has functioned in some form for the past 2,500 years, providing stability and security. It promoted mutual aid within each caste and regulated village life, as subcastes exchanged goods or services with other subcastes in the village. Regional variations also developed: no single hierarchy or ranking was recognized throughout India. In south India, Bengal, and northwestern India, the caste system remained less complex. This system contributed greatly to the long-term continuity of Indian society, providing meaning and direction to the lives of Indians. Caste, along with village and family, became the pillar of Indian society, contributing to a group orientation and an acceptance of authority. It still remains strong in many villages. However, today the system has been rapidly breaking down in the larger cities. It is difficult to avoid close contact with members of other castes while eating in a restaurant, being confined in a hospital, or working in an office or factory.

The Shaping of Hinduism

New Spiritual Movements

The religion known today as Hinduism faced increasing dissent during the Classical Era, fostering new thinking. Power had been concentrated in the priestly class, the *brahmans*. They alone had mastered the scriptures and hymns for worship and presided over rituals. Enriched by gifts from the devout, many priests became wealthy landowners. Eventually, however, some Indians resented priestly wealth and corruption, and new movements emphasized new approaches to worship and spirituality, especially meditation, over ritual. The critics proposed other paths to spiritual fulfillment. Some of their writings were collected in the *Upanishads*, the final portion of the vast Hindu scriptures.

Brahman The Universal Soul, or Absolute Reality, that Hindus believe fills all space and time.

As a result of this new spirituality, Hinduism's highest ideal came to be the escape from sensual pleasures and the material world (seen as an "illusion") and the joining of one's individual soul with **Brahman**, the Universal Soul, or Absolute Reality, that fills all space and time. To achieve this goal, some seekers rejected society and sought mystical unity with the divine. *Yoga* **(YOH-guh)** ("yoke" or "union") was a system of physical and mental exercises that emphasized control of breathing to promote mental concentration, calmness, and a trancelike state that produced a mystical awareness of a universal soul. Holy men who abandoned worldly pleasures through such practices as yoga were greatly admired. Union with the universal soul meant ending the cycle of reincarnation through devotion to God, selfless action, and knowledge achieved through intense meditation. Only by escaping from one's ego could a person end the round of reincarnation and finally achieve the ultimate bliss of merging with Brahman, described in the *Upanishads* as a deep, dreamless sleep. But achieving this state necessitated abandoning the desires and actions that prevent release from earthly lives. "In thinking 'This is I' and 'That is mine,'" warns the *Upanishads*, "one binds himself to himself, as does a bird with a snare!"[3]

Spiritual Practices

Vedanta ("Completion of the Vedas") A school of classical Indian thought that offered Hindus mystical experience and a belief in the underlying unity of all reality.

New forms of worship stressed devotion or prayer focused on specific gods such as Vishnu or Shiva. Every home had a shrine to worship such deities. Frequent religious festivals had mass appeal, and great throngs made annual pilgrimages to sacred places such as the Ganges River. Eventually the spiritual quest led to new schools of Hindu thought such as **Vedanta** (vay-DAHNT-uh), meaning the "completion" of the Vedas. Vedanta offered mystical experience, a belief in the underlying unity of all reality, and sophisticated interpretations of the countless gods found in popular Hinduism, a diversity often summed up by the phrase "33,000 gods." Vedanta thinkers rejected polytheism and viewed these gods and spirits as only manifestations of the single Absolute Reality that pervades everything. The *Upanishads* states that Brahman is

> *God, all gods, the five elements—earth, air, fire, water, ether; all beings, great or small, born of eggs, born from the womb, born from heat, born from soil; horses, cows, men, elephants, birds; everything that breathes, the beings that walk and the beings that walk not.*[4]

Hindu Tolerance

Hinduism developed a broad and tolerant approach to religious differences. Many invaders swept into India, but most of them found a place in Hinduism, which incorporated a wide variety of beliefs, even integrating some non-Hindu figures into devotional cults. Indians worshiped God in many forms. As an old Indian folk song puts it: "Into the bosom of the great sea, flow streams that come from hills on every side. Their names are various as their springs. And thus in every land do men bow down, To one great God, though known by many names."[5] Hinduism developed not as a cohesive, rigidly defined theology with a centralized church but as a broad collection of loosely connected sects with many variations of belief and practice. Toleration and accommodation allowed Hinduism to retain its popularity among both the better educated and the villagers, despite the clearly inequitable divisions of caste and the burdens of karma.

Jainism and Buddhism

Mahavira and Jainism

Jainism An Indian religion that believes that life in all forms must be protected because everything, including animals, insects, plants, sticks, and stones, has a separate soul and is alive.

Two dissident ascetics eventually gave up on reforming Hinduism and founded new movements that became separate religions, Jainism (JINE-iz-uhm) and Buddhism. Jain ideas were organized by a famed teacher, Mahavira (MA-ha-VEER-a) ("Great Hero"), the pampered son of a tribal chief who abandoned his affluent life to wander naked as an ascetic around 500 B.C.E. Mahavira practiced self-torture as the route to salvation, eventually starving himself to death. The basic tenet of **Jainism** is that life in all forms must be protected because everything, including animals, insects, plants, and even sticks and stones, has a separate soul and is alive. While walking, a devout Jain sweeps the ground to avoid stepping on insects and wears a cloth over the nose to prevent inhaling insects. In Mahavira's words, "All things living, all beings whatever, should not be slain, or treated with violence."[6] Jains are vegetarians, but the most devout will not even eat vegetables such as carrots or potatoes because uprooting them damages the microorganisms living in the soil. Most Jains became merchants and bankers and are prominent today in India's economic elite. Given the emphasis on austere behavior and a spartan diet, the Jain sect never became very large; there are perhaps 1 million Jains in the world today. But Jainism had a major intellectual influence on Hindu ideas of nonviolence. Twenty-five centuries after Mahavira, Mohandas Gandhi, a devout Hindu, utilized Jain ideas in developing his philosophy of nonviolence and passive resistance to generate political change.

Buddhism A major world religion based on the teachings of the Buddha that emphasized putting an end to desire and being compassionate to all creatures.

More important in the long run than Jainism was **Buddhism**, based on the teachings of a major Axial Age thinker, which eventually spread out of India to become a major faith in Central, East, and Southeast Asia and Sri Lanka. The religion's founder, Siddartha Gautama (si-DAHR-tuh GAUT-uh-muh) (563–483 B.C.E.), was a prince of a small kingdom in what is now southern Nepal and a contemporary of Confucius, Mahavira, and several other Axial Age thinkers. As with Jesus of Nazareth and Confucius, his life and thought are known largely through the accounts written by his followers. Siddartha led a privileged, carefree, and self-indulgent life, and then was shocked when he ventured from the palace and encountered the miseries experienced by common people. He abandoned his royal life, wife, and family to search for truth as a wandering holy man, living in the forest, practicing yoga, meditating, begging for his food, and nearly dying from fasting. He met skeptics who argued that there is no afterlife or god. Eventually, Siddartha believed he understood cosmic truths and began traveling to teach his new religion, attracting many disciples, who called him the Buddha ("The Enlightened One"). He also rejected the Hindu caste system as immoral.

The Four Noble Truths

Buddha emphasized the Four Noble Truths (see Witness to the Past: Basic Doctrines in the Buddha's First Sermon): that this life is one of suffering and ignorance; that suffering stems from desiring what one does not have and clinging to what one already has for fear of losing it; that one must stop all desire; and that one does this by following the Noble Eightfold Path of correct

Jean-Louis Nou/akg-images

Worship of Buddhist Relics In the first century C.E. Buddhists erected a pillar containing this frieze of a stupa housing relics of the Buddha. The stupa is surrounded by throngs of worshipers and pilgrims making music and bringing offerings to honor the Buddha.

views, intent, speech, actions, trade (or profession), effort, mindfulness, and concentration. Following this path means leading a good life that does no harm to others. To Buddhists, the world is in a constant state of flux; when mortals try in vain to stop the flow of events, they suffer. Buddhism is neither monotheistic nor polytheistic, and the Buddha was ambivalent as to whether a god or gods existed. Buddhists were encouraged to live morally, nonviolently, and moderately and consider the needs of others. For example, men were urged to treat their wives with respect. Asked to summarize his beliefs, the Buddha replied: "Avoid doing evil deeds, cultivate doing good deeds, and purify the mind."[7] The Buddha did not oppose acquiring wealth but believed that wealth alone did not bring happiness. He also condemned the irresponsible use of wealth, such as wasting it on drinking, gambling, and laziness rather than saving some for emergencies and donating some to worthy causes.

Other Buddhist Beliefs

Although rejecting priestly power and the caste system, Buddha adopted many Hindu ideas and modified them. To be released from the chronic cycle of birth and rebirth, Buddhists were urged, as were Hindus, to abandon all sense of self. But the goal was not unity with Brahman but rather **nirvana** (neer-VAHN-uh) (literally, "the blowing out"), a kind of everlasting peace or end of suffering achieved through perfection of wisdom and compassion. Buddha also urged his followers to avoid taking animal life if possible. As a result, many Buddhists became vegetarians. Buddha also seems to have been the world's first religious leader to introduce the idea of **monasticism** (muh-NAS-tuh-siz-uhm), the pursuit of a life of penance, prayer, and meditation in a community of other seekers. He advocated that monks adopt chastity, poverty, and nonviolence and suspend family ties. Monks and nuns followed the rules of proper conduct and also used such techniques as yoga for concentration, meditation, and self-discipline. They begged for their food, thus affirming their humility and allowing believers to gain merit by giving them food and other necessities. Eventually Buddhism became a major influence on the first great Indian imperial state, the Mauryan Empire.

nirvana ("the blowing out") For Buddhists a kind of everlasting peace or end of suffering achieved through perfection of wisdom and compassion.

monasticism The pursuit of a life of penance, prayer, and meditation, either alone or in a community of other seekers.

Foreign Encounters and the Rise of the Mauryas

Persian and Greek Invaders

For several centuries in this era, northwest India remained in close communication with Persia and then Hellenistic Greece. Under their great king, Darius, the Persians conquered much of the Indus River Valley in 518 B.C.E., bringing India to the attention of the Greek historian Herodotus, whose fabulous tales may have stimulated the imagination of the young Alexander the Great (see Chapter 7). By 326 B.C.E. Alexander's forces had reached the Indus River and soon subdued several small Aryan kingdoms east of the Indus (see Chronology: Classical India). Impressed with wealthy India, the Macedonian conqueror discussed religion and philosophy with Indian scholars and apparently dispatched his notes back to his own teacher, Aristotle, making some

Basic Doctrines in the Buddha's First Sermon

Buddhist tradition holds that, after achieving enlightenment, the Buddha preached his first sermon in a deer park in the outskirts of the Ganges city of Varanasi (Benares) around 527 B.C.E. The sermon became one of the most important sources of belief for all Buddhists. It laid out the framework of Buddha's moral message, including the Middle Way between asceticism and worldly life, the Noble Eightfold Path, and the Four Noble Truths. These are the most important concepts in all branches of Buddhism.

There are two ends not to be served by a wanderer. What are these two? The pursuit of desires and of pleasure which springs from desire, which is base, common, leading to rebirth, ignoble and unprofitable; and the pursuit of pain and hardship [asceticism], which is grievous, ignoble, and unprofitable. The Middle Way of the [Buddha] avoids both of these ends. It is enlightened, it brings clear vision, it makes for wisdom, and leads to peace, insight, enlightenment, and Nirvana. What is the Middle Way? It is the Noble Eightfold path—Right Views, Right Resolve, Right Speech, Right Conduct, Right Livelihood, Right Effort, Right Mindfulness, and Right Concentration. . . .

And this is the Noble Truth of Sorrow. Birth is sorrow, age is sorrow, disease is sorrow, death is sorrow; contact with the unpleasant is sorrow, separation from the pleasant is sorrow, every wish unfulfilled is sorrow—in short, all of the five components of individuality are sorrow.

And this is the Noble Truth of the Arising of Sorrow. It arises from craving, which leads to rebirth, which brings delight and passion, and seeks pleasure from here, now there—the craving for sensual pleasure, the craving for continued life, the craving for power.

And this is the Noble Truth of the Stopping of Sorrow. It is the complete stopping of the craving, so that no passion remains, leaving it, being emancipated from it, being released from it, giving no place to it.

And this is the Noble Truth of the Way which Leads to the Stopping of Sorrow. It is the Noble Eightfold Path. . . .

THINKING ABOUT THE READING

1. What does the Buddha mean by the Middle Way?
2. What causes suffering, and how can people stop it?
3. What conduct do these ideas promote?

Source: From *Sources of Indian Tradition, Vol. 1* by William Theodore de Bary et al., eds.

CHRONOLOGY
Classical India

563–483 B.C.E. Life of the Buddha

326 B.C.E. Alexander the Great's army reaches western India

322–185 B.C.E. Mauryan Empire

269–232 B.C.E. Reign of Ashoka

200 B.C.E.–150 C.E. Division of Buddhism into Theravada and Mahayana schools

ca. 50–250 C.E. Kushan Empire in northwest India

ca. 320–550 C.E. Gupta era

Greek thinkers aware of Buddhist and Hindu ideas. Faced with a rebellion by his soldiers, Alexander turned back before entering the Ganges Valley and returned to Persia. His legacy endured, however; Hellenistic cultural influence persisted in northwest India, and Greek artistic styles helped to shape Buddhist art. As an outpost of their Persian venture, the Greek imperialists set up a state in northern Afghanistan known as Bactria **(BAK-tree-uh)**, which flourished as a regional power. Some Greeks also remained behind in northwest India, intermarrying with local women.

Alexander's invasion into western India created a political vacuum that was filled by the military forces of Chandragupta **(CHUHN-druh-GOOP-tuh)** Maurya, who established the first imperial Indian state, the Mauryan Empire (322–185 B.C.E.). Perhaps inspired by Alexander, Chandragupta transformed himself from the ruler of a Ganges state, Magadha **(MAH-guh-duh)**, into the monarch of half the subcontinent (see Map 5.1). At its height the Mauryan Empire included parts of Afghanistan, most of north and central India, and large parts of south India. The Mauryas maintained diplomatic relations with many societies, including Greece, Syria, and Egypt. Chandragupta, skilled in manipulating power, was influenced by his chief adviser, Kautilya **(cow-TILL-ya)**, who favored political centralization and compiled the initial draft of a manual for rulers on obtaining and holding power.

Forming a Mauryan Empire

The empire was ruled by the most efficient government in the classical world. A large army and secret police maintained order, and spies kept government officials under constant surveillance. An ambassador from Greece particularly admired the conscientious justice system, in which the king presided personally over court sessions and settled disputes. To maintain the expensive government, the state heavily taxed agriculture, trade, mining, herding, and other economic activities. Village councils composed of older men from leading families enjoyed considerable local autonomy, a pattern that became entrenched over the centuries. The Mauryan monarch lived in great splendor, often in seclusion and surrounded by an entourage of women who cooked his food, served his wine, and in the evening carried him to his apartment, where they lulled him to sleep with music. To discourage opposition, since Vedic times Indian rulers had claimed to be blessed by the gods and endowed with supernatural and magical powers. Yet,

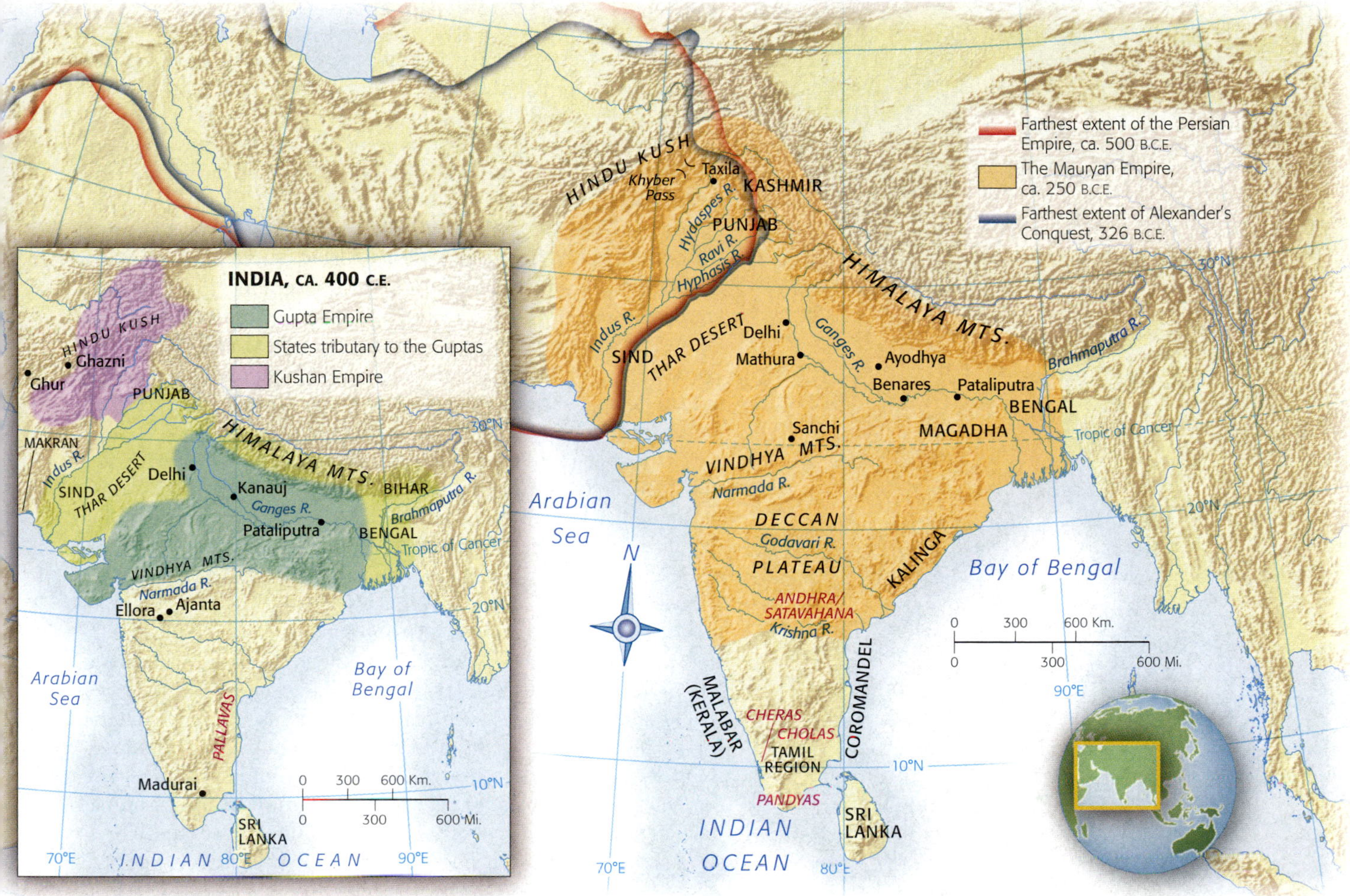

Map 5.1
The Mauryan Empire, 322–185 B.C.E.

During the Classical Era major states arose in north India, most notably the Mauryan, Kushan, and Gupta Empires. The brief encounter with the Greek forces led by Alexander the Great, which reached the Indus River Valley in 326 B.C.E., may have stimulated the Mauryas to build India's first empire.

e **Interactive Map**

the realization that excessive taxes and forced labor might drive the people into rebellion provided checks on autocratic power.

Mauryan Life, Institutions, and Networks

Many of the 50 to 100 million people in densely populated Mauryan India lived in cities, the centers for a prosperous economy. The Mauryan capital city, Patna **(PUHT-nuh)** (then called Pataliputra) on the Ganges River, was widely celebrated for its parks, public buildings, libraries, and a great university that attracted many foreign students. The accounts of Greek ambassadors suggest that Patna, with some 500,000 residents, was very likely the world's largest city. The fortified timber wall around the city, which had 570 towers, was roughly 21 miles long, suggesting that Patna was about twice as large as Rome several centuries later.

City Life

Mauryan prosperity depended on the world's most advanced trading system and craft industries. Many skilled woodworkers, ivory carvers, and stonecutters populated the cities, which also produced fine cotton fabrics. Products and merchants moved along the major east-west highway, which stretched from a seaport near present-day Calcutta **(kal-KUHT-uh)** through the Ganges and Indus Valleys to the borders of Afghanistan. Many foreign merchants resided in the empire, and an active exchange took place with China, Arabia, and the Middle East over trade networks. Artisan and merchant guilds, ruled by councils, supervised the private sector, while the government owned mines and forests and engaged in shipbuilding, arms manufacture, and textile production. Public granaries stored surplus food.

Mauryan Economy

Borromeo/Art Resource, NY

Ashoka Column This 32-foot-tall sandstone column, erected in northeast India around 240 B.C.E., weighs 50 tons. The inscriptions on the pillar outline Ashoka's achievements and offer advice on how citizens of the empire should behave.

Ashoka and Buddhist Monarchy

The Mauryas reached their height under Chandragupta's grandson, the enlightened king Ashoka **(uh-SHOH-kuh)** (whose name means "Sorrowless"), one of the major political and religious figures in world history. The ambitious Ashoka became a general and rose to power through a bloody campaign of eliminating rivals and expanding into frontier lands. We know much about Ashoka (r. 269–232 B.C.E.) from the many edicts he had carved in rocks and sandstone pillars. His early edicts boast of many enemies slain and captured. At some point, however, he experienced a spiritual conversion and became a devout Buddhist, proclaiming his remorse at past atrocities and his commitment to nonviolence. One edict noted that Ashoka "began to follow righteousness, to love righteousness. The greatest of all victories is the victory of righteousness."[8]

Ashoka spent his remaining years in power promoting the Buddha's pacifist teachings. He pledged to bear wrong without violent retribution, to look kindly on all his subjects, and to ensure the safety, happiness, and peace of mind of all living beings. To fulfill his pledge, he designed laws to encourage compassion, mutual tolerance, vegetarianism, and respect for all forms of life. He also sponsored many public works, including hospitals and medical care paid for by the state. Ashoka dispatched Buddhist missions to spread the religion into Sri Lanka, Southeast Asia, and Afghanistan. Despite his own strong beliefs, however, he neither made Buddhism the state religion nor persecuted other faiths. While Ashoka financed the building of Buddhist temples and *stupas* **(STOOP-uhz)** (domed shrines), government aid was distributed to all religious groups. The king argued that "all sects deserve reverence. By thus acting a man exalts his own sect and at the same time does service to the sects of other people."[9] Ashoka styled himself "Beloved of the Gods," which meant he was considered at least a semideity. For both Hindus and Buddhists, the Mauryas created a political legacy of the universal emperor, a divinely sanctioned leader with a special role in the cosmic scheme of things.

Ashoka ruled with popular acclaim, but his successors were less able. Within a half century after his death, the Mauryan Empire had collapsed. Difficult communications in a large empire fostered local autonomy, and the mounting costs of a centralized bureaucracy drained the treasury. The end of the Mauryan Empire set a political pattern different from that of China, where long periods of unity were interspersed with short intervals of political fragmentation. In India, periods of unity were relatively brief, followed by prolonged fragmentation. But while Indians did not always possess political unity, they did possess a strong sense of cultural unity and loyalty to the social order, including the family and caste, rather than to the state.

SECTION SUMMARY

- The Indian caste system, which began to take form in the Classical Era, was based on the idea of karma and placed limits on one's occupation, diet, religious practice, and social interactions.
- New spiritual movements within Hinduism, such as yoga and Vedanta, challenged priestly control and emphasized the goal of escaping the ego.
- Jainism and Buddhism split off from Hinduism, but only Buddhism, which offered guidelines for achieving nirvana, gained wide appeal.
- Through the conquests by Darius and Alexander the Great, northwest India experienced significant influence from the West.
- After Alexander's retreat, Chandragupta established the first imperial Indian state, the centralized, autocratic Mauryan Empire, which included the Indus and Ganges Basins.
- The Mauryan capital city, Patna, was among the largest in the world, and the empire excelled in crafts and trade.
- King Ashoka, Chandragupta's grandson, became a pacifist convert to Buddhism, which he helped to spread to Sri Lanka, Southeast Asia, and Afghanistan.
- Unlike those of China, India's periods of unity were relatively brief; and, several decades after Ashoka died, the Mauryan Empire broke down.

South and Central Asia After the Mauryas

What were some of the ways in which classical India connected with and influenced the world beyond South Asia?

Although the end of the Mauryas in the early second century B.C.E. was followed by 500 years of political fragmentation before the rise of the next empire, that of the Guptas, these centuries saw increasing contact between India and the outside world. Indian cultural influence, especially Buddhism, spread into Central Asia. Various Central and West Asian peoples swept into northwestern India, conquering the Indus Valley and mixing with local peoples, who eventually absorbed the invaders and their ways. Substantial foreign trade and Buddhist missions to neighboring societies also occurred.

Indians and Central Asians

During this time India had constant relations with Central Asia, the area stretching from Russia eastward to the borders of China. The Turkestan region north of India, where many people spoke Turkik languages, was a key contact zone for networks stretching east to China, south to India, and west to Persia and Russia. As trade between China and western Asia developed, cities developed along the overland route (known as the "Silk Road") through Turkestan. The Sogdians (SAHG-dee-uhns), mostly Persian-speaking Zoroastrians or Buddhists who had a written language and literature, developed a flourishing mercantile society and dominated Turkestan's commerce. Over the centuries various pastoral Central Asian groups, unable to penetrate China's defenses or under pressure from Chinese expansion, moved westward, including the Huns, who developed the most effective weapon of the day, a reflex bow. Pressure from the horseback-riding Hun soldiers had long pushed various peoples into Europe. Some Huns followed into southern Russia and Hungary. In the fourth and fifth centuries C.E. Huns invaded the weakened Roman Empire (see Chapter 8).

The Silk Road and the Sogdians

Diverse peoples migrated through the mountain ranges into northwest India from Central Asia and western Asia, introducing new cultural influences. The Hellenistic kingdom of Bactria in Afghanistan was a crossroads between east and west where Greek, Persian, and Indian cultures met and mixed, and invaders from this city reintroduced Greek influence to the Indus Basin. Bactrian Greeks inspired a Greek- and Roman-influenced form of Buddhist painting and sculpture, but eventually they became absorbed into the broad fold of Indian society.

Migrations into India

In 50 C.E. the **Kushans** (KOO-shans) from Central Asia conquered much of northwest India while constructing an empire that also encompassed Afghanistan and many Silk Road cities. The Kushans promoted extensive trade between India and China, the Middle East, and the eastern Mediterranean. Some Kushan leaders embraced Buddhism and were instrumental in spreading the religion into Central Asia, from which it then diffused to China. The Kushans also encouraged the mix of Indian and Greco-Roman culture over a wide area. The much respected Kushan king Kanishka (ka-NISH-ka) (r. 78–144 C.E.) patronized artists, writers, poets, and musicians and tolerated all religions. Like invaders before them, the Kushans intermarried with local people, enhancing the hybrid character of the culture in northwestern India. When Kushan rule ended in 250, northern Indians replaced it with a patchwork of competing states.

Kushans An Indo-European people from Central Asia who conquered much of northwest India and western parts of the Ganges Basin, constructing an empire that also encompassed Afghanistan and parts of Central Asia.

South India and Sri Lanka

The political instability in northwestern India was duplicated elsewhere in the subcontinent, where there was frequent warfare between competing states. Some southern states had long flourished from maritime trade networks stretching from China to the Persian Gulf, and south India was renowned as far west as Greece and Rome for products such as gold. During this time both south India and the large island of Sri Lanka saw considerable political and cultural development. North Indian culture, partly rooted in Aryan traditions, spread southward, including Aryan myths, values, rituals, and ideas such as divine kingship, which appealed to south Indian rulers. South Indians also adopted the caste system, although in a less rigid form than in north India.

North Indian Influences

Southern Regional Traditions

Despite their influence, however, Aryan ideas did not destroy regional traditions in south India. For example, the Tamils, who speak a Dravidian language and inhabit India's southeastern corner, developed a vigorous cultural tradition with poetry as the most esteemed art. The temple-filled mountain city of Madurai **(made-uh-RYE)** had several colleges and became a major center of Hinduism, literature, and education. A Tamil poem from the second century C.E. describes Madurai's function as a religious center filled with devout people:

> *The great and famous city of Madurai, Is like the lotus flower of God Vishnu. Its streets are the petals of the flower. God Shiva's temple is the center. The citizens are the plentiful pollen; The poor, the crowding beetles. And in Madurai, we wake to the chanting of the four Vedas, Sacred sculptures from the tongue of Brahma, born of the lotus flower.*[10]

Sri Lankan Society

Just south of India, on Sri Lanka (Ceylon), a very different south Asian society developed. Over the centuries, migrants from India intermarried with the local people, formed kingdoms, and eventually produced the Sinhalese **(sin-huh-LEEZ)** society. Sri Lanka became a trading hub between Southeast Asia and the Middle East. In the first century B.C.E. the Sinhalese, to improve their rice growing, began constructing one of the most intricate irrigation systems in world history, building canals dozens of miles long and artificial lakes covering thousands of acres, an engineering requiring complex hydraulic technology. Sri Lankan water control was comparable to that of ancient China and Mesopotamia. During Ashoka's reign Buddhist missionaries converted most Sri Lankans to Buddhism, and the Sinhalese came to view themselves as the protectors of Buddhism. Tamil-speaking Hindus also crossed the narrow straits and settled in the northern part of the island. For the next two millennia, Sinhalese Buddhist and Tamil Hindu societies coexisted, sometimes uneasily, in Sri Lanka.

Indian Encounters with the Afro-Eurasian World

Maritime Trade

The post-Maurya era stands out as a time of unprecedented Indian communication with other cultures and connection to networks of exchange. Even merchants from the Mediterranean visited India. India dispatched spices, cloth, silks, ivory, and works of art to the Roman Empire in exchange for gold coins, copper, tin, lead, and wine. Around 80 C.E. a Greek handbook for merchants interested in trade with India described sailing routes and India's products and culture. The author recommended a south Indian port offering a large quantity of cinnamon and pepper as well as multicolored textiles, tin, copper, gems, diamonds, sapphires, fine-quality pearls, ivory, and Chinese silk. Various Indian words were incorporated into the Greek language, especially words for spices, such as *ginger,* and for foods, like *rice.*

Indian Trade

Trade with China continued along the Silk Road, while many Indian traders traveled to Southeast Asia. Expanding foreign and domestic trade brought much wealth to the Indian commercial and artisan castes, fostering considerable economic growth. Gold coins led to the creation of banking and financial houses. But this commercial dynamism mostly occurred in the cities. Foreign products did not often reach the villages, where the bartering of services between farmers, craftsmen, and servants continued to define social and economic relations.

Exporting Religious Traditions

Indian philosophy and religious ideas also gained a foreign audience. Some Indian philosophers seem to have visited western Asia, and their ideas may have influenced some of the religious movements percolating in the region. The Buddhist idea of monasticism also expanded from India to western Asia and may have influenced the rise of Christian monasticism. Buddhism and Buddhist art continued to spread into Central Asia, especially into the Silk Road cities. Indian cultural influence thus flowed out to the world, in a manner similar to the spread of Hellenistic Greek culture throughout the eastern Mediterranean and western Asia.

Religious Changes in South Asia

Buddhist Divisions

The post-Mauryan centuries saw considerable religious change, including the decline of Buddhism in India, the resurgence of Hinduism, and the arrival of both Christianity and Judaism. The division of Buddhism into two major schools with competing visions occurred in the two centuries just before the Common Era. Some followers criticized the religion as being remote from the real world, atheistic in its rejection of a god, excessively individualistic, requiring too much self-discipline, and denying any afterlife. In response, in the second century C.E., during the Kushan domination of northern India, the division into two schools, the mainstream Theravada **(THERE-eh-VAH-duh)** and the reformist Mahayana **(MAH-HAH-YAH-nah)**, became complete.

Theravada, which means "Teachings of the Elders," remained closer to Buddha's original vision and clearly descended from Ashoka's Buddhism. To its followers the Buddha was not a god but rather a human teacher. Since the ever-changing universe had no supreme being or gods, people could only take refuge in the wise and compassionate Buddha, his teachings, and the community of monks who maintained them. Each believer was responsible for acquiring merit through devotion, meditation, and good works, such as feeding monks or supporting a temple. The only sure way to end rebirth and reach nirvana was to become a monk and abide by strict monastic rules, and many men did so for at least a few years.

The other school, **Mahayana** ("the Greater Vehicle" to salvation), was a more popularized and less demanding form of belief and practice. Mahayana developed many sects, most of which considered the Buddha a god. Mahayana followers found comfort in devotion to a loving deity (Buddha) and stressed charity and good works as paths toward salvation. A central concept is the **bodhisattva** (boe-dih-SUT-vuh) ("one who has the essence of Buddhahood"), a loving and compassionate "saint" who has died but postponed his or her own attainment of nirvana to help others find salvation. In China, Mahayanists converted nirvana into an appealing heaven, while the wicked were assigned to a terrifying hell. Some historians wonder whether Mahayana ideas about achieving salvation with the help of a saint contributed to Hebrew concepts of a messiah or the reverse. Perhaps the link, if any, was Persian Zoroastrianism, which may have influenced both Mahayana Buddhism and Christianity as it had earlier provided ideas to the Hebrews.

Although several Buddhist monastic orders and some believers remained, Indian Buddhism was gradually absorbed into Hinduism. Perhaps Buddhism was too pessimistic a faith, portraying life as suffering in contrast to the many life-affirming Hindu gods. But Buddhism flourished abroad by providing spiritual support in times of rapid political change or instability. It spread along the trade routes, accommodating itself to local traditions and faiths. The Mahayana school eventually became dominant in Central Asia, including Tibet and Mongolia, from where it filtered into China, Korea, Vietnam, and Japan. The Theravada school became entrenched in Sri Lanka and eventually expanded into mainland Southeast Asia, in the process replacing Mahayana Buddhism (see Map 5.2).

New religions also arrived in India. According to local legends, around 52 C.E. the Christian apostle St. Thomas established Christian churches and attracted followers along the Malabar (MAL-uh-bahr) coast of southwestern India. Such a trip along active maritime trade routes was certainly possible. Large Christian communities still flourish in the Malabar state of Kerala (KER-uh-luh), especially in the ancient coastal ports. Jewish settlers also came to India's west coast, where they established permanent communities in Kerala and to the north at Bombay. In the later twentieth century C.E., many Indian Jews emigrated to the new Jewish state of Israel.

Theravada ("Teachings of the Elders") One of the two main branches of Buddhism, the other being Mahayana, that arose just before the Common Era. Theravada remained closer to the Buddha's original vision.

Mahayana ("the Greater Vehicle" to salvation) One of the two main branches of Buddhism; a more popularized form of Buddhist belief and practice than Theravada. Mahayana Buddhism tended to make Buddha into a god and also developed the notion of the bodhisattva.

bodhisattva ("one who has the essence of Buddhahood") A loving and ever compassionate "saint" who has postponed his or her own attainment of nirvana to help others find salvation through liberation from birth and rebirth.

SECTION SUMMARY

- Various peoples, among them the Kushans from Central Asia, invaded northwest India and ended up adopting various aspects of Indian culture.
- Aspects of northern Indian culture spread to the south, and Buddhism was adopted in Sri Lanka.
- During the post-Mauryan era, there was great demand for Indian goods among traders from western Asia and the Mediterranean.
- Buddhism split into Theravada, a more traditional form, and Mahayana, a more accessible form.
- Buddhism declined in popularity in India as Hinduism adopted many of its ideas, but it spread to Central Asia, China, and Southeast Asia, where it flourished.

The Gupta Age in India

What were the main achievements of the Gupta era?

In the fourth century C.E. the great Gupta (GOOP-tuh) Empire brought political unity to India once again. The Gupta era (320–550 C.E.) was a brilliant period that saw the assimilation of both immigrants and the foreign cultural influences that reshaped an ancient society. Today Indians consider the Gupta their golden age, with prosperity, tolerant government, and major contributions in science, medicine, mathematics, and literature. In comparison with the declining Roman Empire and turbulent post-Han China, Gupta India was perhaps the world's most dynamic society, visited by travelers and pilgrims from all over Asia.

Government and Economy

The Gupta family and their allies conquered most of north India. The Gupta Empire was somewhat like the Mauryan Empire in that the Gupta Empire was decentralized, with local rulers

Gupta Empire

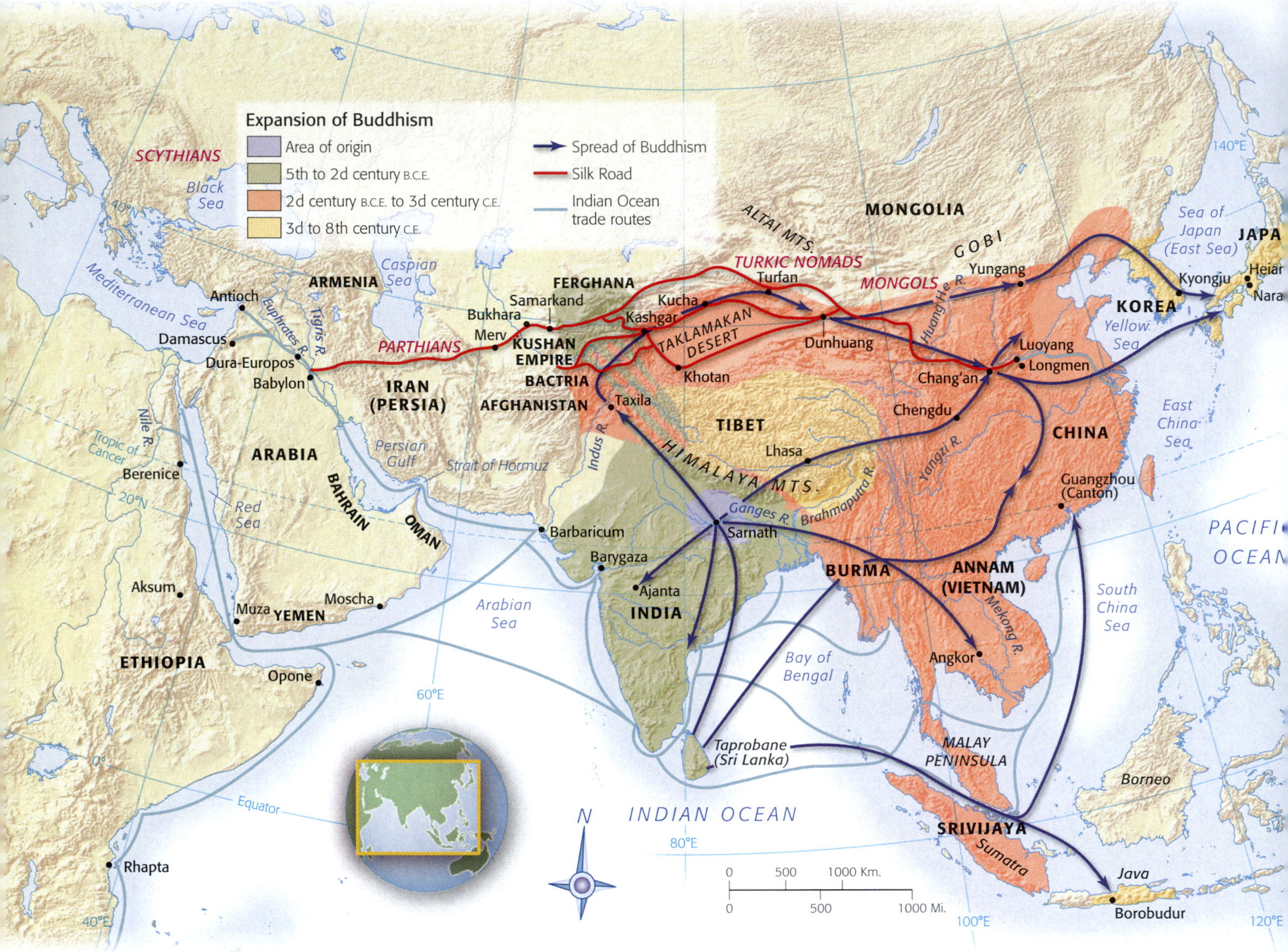

Map 5.2
The Spread of Buddhism in Asia, 100–800 C.E.

Buddhism originated in what is today Nepal and became a major religion in India during the Classical Era. From India it spread into Central Asia, China, Korea, Japan, and Southeast Asia as far east as Java.

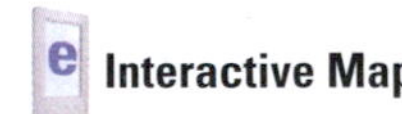

acknowledging Gupta overlordship. The Gupta zenith came under King Chandra Gupta II (r. 375–414), one of the most revered figures in Indian history, praised as enlightened, bold, and resourceful.

Gupta Economy

Gupta India enjoyed a prosperity fostered by internal and external trade, the widespread use of gold and silver coins, and highly productive agriculture. India increasingly became the world's textile center, producing fabrics like linen, wool, and cotton; it also produced pepper and spices for export to the Middle East, Europe, China, and Indonesia. Although the Gupta government favored merchants and farmers, it continued the practice of using enforced labor for one day a month to assist in public projects. The Gupta rulers, like the Mauryas, operated all metal and salt mines as well as various industrial enterprises such as arms factories and textile mills.

Gupta Tolerance

Gupta Indians generally enjoyed domestic peace, personal freedom, and tolerance for minority views. One fifth-century Chinese Buddhist pilgrim, Faxian **(fah-shee-en)** (Fa-hsien), was impressed by the prosperity, state services, and humane justice system: "The people are very well off. The king governs without corporal punishment. Criminals are fined according to circumstances, lightly or heavily. Even in cases of repeated rebellion, they only cut off the right hand. The people kill no living thing."[11] While the rulers were Hindu, there was no official discrimination against Buddhists or Jains. The Guptas even helped build a great Buddhist monastery and university at Nalanda **(na-LAN-da)**, where students from all over Asia explored not only Buddhist subjects but also logic, medicine, and Hindu philosophy. However, as before the Gupta age, tolerance did not extend to the untouchables, who still occupied a degraded status.

The Gupta capital city, Patna, reflected prosperity, with hospitals that provided free care to the poor and handicapped. A great university attracted 10,000 students, many from other Asian societies. One observer reported that he saw in Patna "the workshops thriving along the royal road, the river furrowed by boats, and maidens flirting with youths in the parks on the outskirts of town."[12]

Gupta Society

Patriarchy and Gender Relations

Primary Source: The Code of Manu See how the principle of dharma justifies the traditional roles of men and women and of priests, warriors, merchants, and servants in Hindu society.

Indian social patterns were never stagnant, and patriarchy became more dominant over time. As male authority grew, women's status gradually declined throughout northern India. By Mauryan times women enjoyed fewer opportunities to pursue intellectual or religious leadership. The *Mahabharata* warned men not to put "confidence in a woman or a coward, a lazybones, a violent man, a self-promoter, a thief, much less an atheist."[13] However, patriarchy remained weaker in south India. Some southern peoples were matrilineal, a kinship system still common in Kerala, and southern women often enjoyed more freedom and options than northern women. In contrast to the mostly male deities in the north, Hinduism in south India placed more emphasis on goddess worship, which may have given women higher status in society. An exception to the idea of the submissive female was also found in the *Kama Sutra*, a detailed sexual handbook written in the third century C.E. that offered ideas about gender that seem almost modern, including a liberal approach to sexual freedom and a somewhat understanding approach to homosexuality.

The Gupta age was not a golden age for women. Brahmans attempted to impose their rigid views on gender relations. The Code of Manu, devised by brahmans, tied women to the patriarchal family, urging that "in childhood a female must be subject to her father, in youth to her husband, and when her lord is dead, to her sons; a woman must never be independent."[14] The code restricted women's property rights and recommended early marriage to preserve chastity. It became common for girls to be married well before puberty, after negotiations were made between the senior men of the two families involved. In addition, widows could no longer remarry. The ancient custom of *sati* **(suh-TEE)**, in which wives joined their late husbands on the funeral pyre, became more widespread. Many Indian writers denounced it, since families often forced an unwilling wife to agree.

Gupta Science, Mathematics, and Culture

Science and Aryabhata

In the Gupta era intellectual and cultural pursuits flourished, and India became the world's leading producer of scientific knowledge, planting some of the roots of modern science. One of the world's major astronomers, mathematicians, and physicists, Aryabhata **(AR-ya-BAH-ta)** (ca. 476–550), taught that the earth was round, rotated on its own axis, and revolved around the sun as one of a family of planets. He also correctly analyzed lunar eclipses, accurately calculated the moon's diameter and the circumference of the earth, and precisely determined the length of a solar year at 365.36 days. In verse, Aryabhata discussed physics, including the earth's rotation and the nature of gravity. Many of these insights did not spread outside India until many centuries later.

Decimals and Numerals

In mathematics the Gupta Indians surpassed all other classical peoples. Aryabhata analyzed quadratic equations and the value of *pi*. The greatest Gupta achievement was the concept of zero and the consequent evolution of the decimal system. The base could have been any number; Indians probably chose 10 because it corresponded to the number of fingers. With this system, individual numbers were needed only for 0 through 9. By contrast, for the ancient Greeks each 8 in 888 was different. And for the Romans, 888 was written as DCCCLXXXVIII, rendering multiplication and division difficult. The simple and logical Indian numbering system eventually reached the Middle East and later was carried to Europe by Arabs, becoming known as Arabic numerals. Only in the fifteenth century, a thousand years after Gupta times, did European scientists and mathematicians adopt "Arabic" numerals, opening the door to modern science and mathematics. The Indian formulation of the zero and decimal system compares to the invention in western Asia of the wheel and alphabet: all pathbreaking and revolutionary in their consequences.

Chemistry and Medicine

The Guptas were also remarkably creative in industrial chemistry and medicine. They made soap and cement, produced the world's finest tempered steel, and transformed sugar-cane juice into granulated crystals for easy storing or shipping. India's fine dyes and fabrics were later adopted

Benoy K. Behl

Ajanta Cave Paintings This painting, made on a cave wall in central India during or just after the Gupta era, depicts one of the Buddha's earlier lives as a king listening to his queen. This and other wall paintings made at Ajanta were part of a complex of Buddhist shrines.

by Europe; *cotton*, *calico*, and *cashmere* are all Indian words. The Guptas also built on a long tradition of medicine. Yoga practitioners required body control to promote mental and spiritual discipline, studying posture, breath control, and regulation of the pulse. Indian physicians also discovered the function of the spinal cord and sketched out the structure of the nervous system. The new knowledge of physiology and herbal medicines contributed to a better understanding of health. Gupta India had the world's best medical system, drugs, and therapeutic methods. Doctors sterilized wounds, did Caesarian deliveries, developed plastic surgery, and vaccinated patients against smallpox. By 1000 C.E. vaccination had traveled the trade routes to China, and by the 1700s to Europe.

The Gupta era was also a great period for literature and performing arts. Writing mostly in Sanskrit, Gupta writers produced religious works, poetry, and prose. The most popular writer, Kalidasa (kahl-i-DACE-uh) (ca. 400–455), rendered ancient legends and popular tales into drama and lyrics. Kalidasa's famous poem, "The Cloud Messengers," uses a passing cloud surveying the panoramic landscape to capture the heartache of lovers separated by a vast distance: "I see your body in the sinuous creeper, your gaze in the startled eyes of deer, your cheek in the moon, your hair in the plumage of peacocks, and in the tiny ripples of the river I see your sidelong glances."[15] Theater, music, and dance flourished, establishing the basis for the Indian performing arts of today. Instruments such as the lute, or *vina* (VEE-nuh), and zither, or *sitar* (si-TAHR), were adopted after being imported from western Asia. Improvisational instrumental pieces known as *ragas* (RAHG-uhz) were designed for religious and philosophical contemplation. Gupta artists also produced many religious sculptures and paintings, especially on cave or temple walls.

Decline of the Guptas

Hun Invasion

The arrival of Central Asian peoples brought an end to the Guptas. In the last half of the fifth century C.E. Huns conquered part of northwestern India. Although they were blocked by Gupta power, the cost of holding them off badly depleted the treasury. Soon the empire disintegrated, and other Central Asian invaders followed the Huns into north India. After the Gupta collapse, the varied Hindu states could not unite. India entered a period of fragmentation, political instability, and frequent warfare that persisted for several centuries and left Indians open to conquest by Muslim peoples.

Nevertheless, the many rival states that now constituted India remained part of the wider world. Seafarers from the southeastern coast made piratical raids deep into Southeast Asia, while the maritime trade linking southern India with Southeast Asia and China intensified dramatically. Cargo-laden Indian fleets sailed with the monsoon winds far to the east.

SECTION SUMMARY

- Under the decentralized Gupta Empire, based in northern India, the government attained prosperity while pursuing religious tolerance.
- Over time, the status of Indian women declined, particularly in the north.
- During the Gupta era, science, mathematics, literature, and the arts all thrived.
- The Guptas formulated the concept of zero, which made the decimal system possible and made mathematical computation infinitely more powerful.
- The Gupta Empire was greatly weakened by Hun invasion, and soon thereafter it collapsed and other Central Asian groups invaded India.

The Development of Southeast Asian Societies

How did Southeast Asians blend indigenous and foreign influences to create unique societies?

In the tropical lands east of India and south of China, many societies borrowed political, religious, and cultural ideas from the two neighboring regions, although the impact of these ideas varied greatly. Southeast Asian states were products of indigenous as well as outside forces. Most of the early Southeast Asian societies were centered on coastal plains and in river valleys, where they flourished from both productive agriculture and extensive foreign trade and established enduring patterns in government, religion, and economics.

Austronesian Seafaring, Trade, and Migrations

Maritime Trade

Seafaring and maritime trade were major forces in the development of some Southeast Asian societies. One group of Austronesians (AW-stroh-NEE-zhuhns), the Malays (muh-LAYZ), enjoyed a strategic position for maritime commerce and intercultural exchange. The Straits of Melaka (muh-LAK-uh), between Sumatra (soo-MAH-tra) and Malaya (muh-LAY-a), had long been a crossroads through which peoples, cultures, and trade passed, some taking root in the area. The lands bordering the straits had also enjoyed fame as a source of gold, tin, spices, and forest products, some of which were traded as far west as Rome, and they became one of the world's most important contact zones. The prevailing climatic patterns in the South China Sea and Indian Ocean allowed ships sailing southwest and southeast to meet in the straits, where their goods could be exchanged.

Ancient Art & Architecture Collection

Relief of Indonesian Ship The Indonesians were skilled mariners. This rock carving, from a Buddhist temple in central Java, depicts a sailing vessel of the type commonly used by Indonesian traders in the Indian Ocean and South China Sea in this era. These ships also carried Indonesian colonists to East Africa and Madagascar.

Malay States and Seafarers

Early in the Common Era small Malay trading states emerged in the Malay Peninsula and Sumatra, prospering from maritime commerce. Like the Phoenicians and Greeks, Malays specialized in maritime trade to distant shores, and they and other Melanesians became prominent in the expanding networks of exchange. In the third century B.C.E., Malay ships visited China using a sail that may have been the model for the revolutionary four-sided lateen **(luh-TEEN)** sail used later by Arabs and Polynesians, which allowed ships to sail directly into the wind. Malays opened the maritime trade between China and India by obtaining cinnamon grown on the China coast and carrying it across the Indian Ocean to India and Sri Lanka. Some Austronesian sailors returned from India with Indian ideas about government and religion. Other Austronesians from central Indonesia introduced Southeast Asian foods (especially bananas and rice), outrigger canoes, and musical instruments (including the xylophone) to East Africa.

Indian Ocean Connections

Between the fourth and sixth centuries C.E., instability in Central Asia disrupted the Silk Road, making the Indian Ocean connection more crucial. Some Southeast Asians benefited from the growing seagoing trade between China, India, and the Middle East. But the voyages held many dangers. For example, the Chinese Buddhist pilgrim Faxian, sailing from Sri Lanka to Sumatra in 414 C.E., reported that he "set sail on a large merchant ship which carried about two hundred passengers. A small boat trailed behind, for use in case the large vessel should be wrecked, as sailing on this sea was most hazardous. [We] were caught up in a typhoon [which] lasted for thirteen days. That sea is [also] infested with pirates."[16]

Austronesian Migrations

Austronesian seafaring also led to migration. Between 100 and 700 C.E. some Austronesians from southern Borneo **(BOR-nee-oh)** and Sulawesi **(soo-luh-WAY-see)** migrated across the Indian Ocean to the East African coast. Later most of them settled on the large island of Madagascar **(mad-uh-GAS-kuhr)**, off the southeast coast of Africa. Today their descendants account for the majority of the island's population and speak Austronesian languages. Beginning in ancient times, other Austronesians moved from Southeast Asia into the western Pacific. Eventually their descendants, known today as the Polynesians **(pahl-uh-NEE-zhuhns)** and Micronesians **(my-kruh-NEE-zhuhns)**, settled nearly all of the islands of the central and eastern Pacific (see Chapter 9). As a result of these movements, Austronesian-speaking societies stretched thousands of miles from Madagascar eastward through Indonesia and the Philippines to Hawaii and Easter Island in eastern Polynesia.

Indianization and Early Mainland States

First Cities and States

Various states developed on the Southeast Asian mainland by early in the Common Era, but their foundations had been established a few centuries earlier. The most populous societies emerged along the fertile coastal plains or in the valleys of great rivers like the Mekong and Red, where irrigated rice cultivation was possible, providing a highly productive and labor-intensive economic mainstay that could be sustained for many generations. Because it promoted social cooperation, this kind of economy led to centralized kingdoms. By 500 B.C.E. a few small states had emerged that used bronze and iron. The kings of Van Lang in northern Vietnam ruled through a landed aristocracy who controlled vast rice-growing estates worked by peasants. During the third century B.C.E. the earliest cities with monumental architecture appeared. At Co Loa, near modern Hanoi, King An Duong built a huge citadel surrounded by a wall 5 miles long and 10 yards wide. Urban societies also emerged among peoples such as the Khmers **(kuh-MEERZ)** (Cambodians).

Indianization The process by which Indian ideas spread into and influenced many Southeast Asian societies; a mixing of Indian with indigenous ideas.

Outside influences from China and India also generated change. In the second century B.C.E., Han China conquered northern Vietnam, imposing a colonial rule that endured for a millennium (111 B.C.E.–939 C.E.) and spreading many Chinese cultural patterns into Vietnam (see Chronology: Classical Southeast Asia). Chinese traders regularly visited many Southeast Asian states over the centuries. Elsewhere Indian influence was paramount in fostering a very different form of society. Around the beginning of the Common Era, Indian traders and brahman priests began regularly traveling the oceanic trade routes and settling in some of the states, where they married into or became advisors to influential families. They brought with them Indian concepts of religion, government, and the arts. Thus Gupta India provided a political model for Southeast Asians.

The process by which Indian ideas spread into and influenced many Southeast Asian societies is often termed **Indianization**, a mixing of Indian with indigenous ideas. This occurred about the same time as classical Greco-Roman culture was spreading around the Mediterranean. For a millennium, Southeast

CHRONOLOGY
Classical Southeast Asia

111 B.C.E.–939 C.E. Chinese colonization of Vietnam

39–41 C.E. Trung Sisters' rebellion in Vietnam

ca. 75–550 C.E. Funan

ca. 100–1200 C.E. Era of Indianization

ca. 192–1471 C.E. Champa

ca. 450–750 C.E. Zhenla states

Asian peoples such as the Khmers in the Mekong Basin, the Chams along the central coast of Vietnam, and the Javanese **(JAH-vuh-NEEZ)** on the fertile island of Java were closely connected to India, adapting Indian writing systems to local spoken languages. Mahayana Buddhism and Hinduism became popular in Southeast Asia, especially among the upper classes, fusing with indigenous animisms that focused on communicating with spiritual forces. Many Southeast Asians blended outside and local religions rather than following one exclusively. In politics, Southeast Asian rulers adopted the Indian concept of powerful kings who possessed supernatural powers and religious sanction, which made their positions difficult to challenge.

However, although centuries of borrowing helped shape Southeast Asians, they rarely became carbon copies of their mentors. Like the Japanese and western Europeans, they took ideas that they wanted from outsiders and adapted them to their own use, creating a distinctive synthesis. For example, the Hindu and Buddhist architecture and temples of Burma, Cambodia, or Java differed substantially from the South Asian models as well as from each other.

Map 5.3
Funan and Its Neighbors
The first large mainland Southeast Asian states emerged during the Classical Era. The major states included Vietnam, which became a Chinese colony in the second century B.C.E., Funan, Zhenla, and Champa.

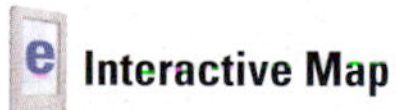
Interactive Map

Funan, Zhenla, and Champa

Productive agriculture, maritime commerce, and Indianization fostered stronger mainland states. Between 75 and 550 C.E. Funan **(FOO-nan)** flourished in the fertile Mekong Delta of southern Vietnam. While the Khmer people made up most of the population, Austronesians did most of the maritime trade. Indianized Funan traded with China, valued literacy, and built complex irrigation systems to turn swamps into productive agricultural land. Funan apparently had some authority over Cambodia and southern Thailand (see Map 5.3). Trade goods from as far away as Rome, Arabia, Central Asia, and perhaps East Africa have been found in its ruins, and merchants from various countries (including India and China) lived in the major port city. Another Khmer state, Zhenla, in the middle Mekong basin, became prominent in the fifth century when Funan declined.

Meanwhile, the coastal, Austronesian-speaking Cham people of central Vietnam formed an Indianized state, or possibly several states, known as Champa **(CHAM-pa)**, which tried to control the coastal commerce between China and Southeast Asia. The Chams, a strongly Hindu people, became renowned as sailors and merchants and sometimes resorted to piracy. They frequently fought the Vietnamese, who continually pushed southward. Champa existed from 192 to 1471 C.E., when the Vietnamese finally conquered Champa.

Vietnam and Chinese Colonization

Chinese Rule

During Chinese colonial times, Vietnamese society was largely confined to what is today the northern third of Vietnam. China's final conquest and annexation of Vietnam in 111 B.C.E. ended the independence of a densely populated kingdom. The Chinese policy to assimilate the Vietnamese and implant Chinese values, customs, and institutions fostered some revolutionary changes. Chinese philosophies and religions like Confucianism, Daoism, and Mahayana Buddhism were adopted by most Vietnamese but also mixed with earlier ancestor and spirit worship. China's patriarchal family system, written language, and political ideas also sank deep roots.

Vietnamese Resistance

Yet, while the Vietnamese adopted many Chinese patterns, they also sustained a hatred of Chinese rule and resisted cultural assimilation. The survival of the Vietnamese identity, language, and many customs during a millennium of colonialism constituted a display of national determination unparalleled in world history. Perhaps the Vietnamese were able to avoid cultural and national extinction because they already had several centuries of state building and cultural identity behind them when the Chinese colonized. A long history of resistance to the Chinese, a sense of nationhood, and a desire for independence also helped them resist assimilation. Chinese and later foreign conquerors such as the French in the modern era found that they had to conquer each village, one by one.

Anti-Chinese Revolts

Many revolts punctuated the Chinese colonial period, all of them well remembered today as symbols of patriotism. The rebellions were sometimes led by women, including the Trung Sisters (see Profile: The Trung Sisters, Vietnamese Rebels). Chinese officials recommended harsh retaliation to rebellion: "At every stream, cave, marketplace, everywhere there is stubbornness. Repression is necessary."[17] This history of resistance to foreign invaders meant frequent warfare. A Vietnamese Buddhist poet described the results: "War, no end to it, people scattered in all directions. How can a man keep his mind off it? The winds dark, the rains violent year after year, laying waste the land, over and over."[18] The Vietnamese eventually regained independence from China in the tenth century.

Economies, Societies, and Cultures

Regional Patterns

Despite the great differences between societies like Champa, Funan, and Vietnam, there were many commonalities throughout the region. Most of the larger Southeast Asian states were multiethnic in their population, including foreign merchants in temporary or permanent residence. Many Southeast Asians also lived well. Chinese envoys who visited Funan around 250 C.E. described walled cities, palaces, and houses occupied by people who ate with silver utensils and paid their taxes with gold, silver, perfumes, and pearls. The Chinese envoys were also impressed with the many books available and the well-kept archives, indicating that an Indian writing system was already in use. Commerce was prevalent in most places, but most Southeast Asians were farmers and fishermen living in self-sufficient villages held together by ties of kinship and a communal spirit of cooperation for mutual survival.

Family Systems and Gender Relations

Many Southeast Asian family systems contrasted with those in China or India. While the Vietnamese followed a patriarchal pattern like China, others developed flexible systems incorporating both paternal and maternal kin. The Chams were matrilineal, and their women enjoyed considerable political influence. Both Cham men and women could have more than one spouse. In Southeast Asia women generally enjoyed a higher status and played a more active public role than they did in China, India, the Middle East, and Europe; for example, they took charge of most village markets. The Southeast Asian pattern of inclusion and blending of religions and cultures, along with extensive trade, made Southeast Asian societies distinctive.

SECTION SUMMARY

- The lands bordering the Straits of Melaka were rich in natural resources, and their peoples engaged in wide-ranging maritime trade.
- Austronesians settled over a wide area, from Madagascar, off the coast of Africa, to the Pacific islands of Polynesia.
- Southeast Asians were influenced by both Chinese and Indian culture, but they retained distinct aspects of their native cultures.
- Some principal states in this era were Funan, Zhenla, and Champa on the Southeast Asian mainland.
- Vietnam showed great resistance in its long struggle against Chinese colonization.
- Though different from each other, Southeast Asian societies tended to be multiethnic and able to blend diverse elements into cultural unity.

CHAPTER SUMMARY

The Classical Era saw dramatic changes in India and Southeast Asia, some generated by outside influences such as migration and long-distance trade. India developed unique social systems and religious ideas. The caste system divided the population into categories based on descent and occupation. Hinduism flowered into various schools of speculative thought. Buddhism challenged Hinduism and the caste system in the first millennium B.C.E. Hinduism and Buddhism shared many beliefs, such as reincarnation and karma, but differed in their conception of gods and the path to ending reincarnation.

India's political, economic, and intellectual life also changed. The Mauryan Empire united India, and under Ashoka the empire reflected humane and peaceful Buddhist values. The Classical Era also saw the forging of deeper cultural and trade connections between India and other regions, and many peoples migrated into the country from Central Asia. Buddhism spread into

THE TRUNG SISTERS, VIETNAMESE REBELS

Some of the major anti-Chinese rebellions in Vietnamese history were led by women such as the Trung Sisters in 39 C.E. Even after 2,000 years, the Vietnamese honor the two sisters and their martyrdom with annual ceremonies at cult shrines dedicated to their memory. Our knowledge of the two sisters and their experiences is limited. Some historians consider them semimythical rather than flesh and blood. Their revolt was caused by Chinese attempts to raise taxes and consolidate their control over the indigenous landed aristocracy. The Trung Sisters became enshrined in images of brave but beautiful, sword-bearing women mounted on elephants, leading their troops against the Chinese.

The sisters are believed to have been daughters of a prominent family of landed aristocrats from near Hanoi. The older sister, Trung Trac, had married a member of another landed family. When her husband protested an increase in taxes by Chinese colonial authorities, he was apparently executed. The spirited sisters then sparked a rebellion that rapidly spread throughout the entire country and involved both the elite and the peasantry. With local Chinese officials in retreat, her followers declared Trung Trac queen of a newly independent country. Some sources suggest the sisters served as joint queens, ruling for two years. They abolished taxes, but, as traditionalists, they also sought to restore the pre-Chinese order dominated by landed aristocrats and protect local autonomy. Despite the sisters' aristocratic agenda, the common people joined the revolt because of their hostility to the authoritarian rule of the Chinese governors.

Han dynasty rulers, not about to allow this valuable part of their empire to secede, dispatched their most able general and his army to destroy the rebellion. As the fighting and repression intensified, most of the sisters' upper-class supporters abandoned their cause. Eventually their remaining forces were defeated in 41 C.E., and the sisters either committed suicide or were captured and executed. China now intensified its direct control of the colony and launched a more deliberate cultural assimilation policy to integrate Vietnam politically into China proper.

Although the revolt failed to dislodge the Chinese, the Trung Sisters established a model for later rebels, some of them also women. Another famous anticolonial leader, the nineteen-year-old Lady Trieu in the third century C.E., demonstrated a similar commitment. When advised to marry rather than fight, she replied: "I want to ride the storm, tread the dangerous waves, win back the fatherland and destroy the yoke of slavery. I don't want to bow down my head working as a simple housewife." The Lady Trieu seems an almost modern figure in her patriotic and social defiance.

Even in the nineteenth and twentieth centuries, Vietnamese women inspired by the Trung Sisters and Lady Trieu took up arms alongside men to fight oppressive governments and invading forces. Although men led the movements, women were prominent in the struggle against French colonialism and in the revolution by Communist forces to overthrow the U.S.-backed government in South Vietnam in the mid-twentieth century.

THINKING ABOUT THE PROFILE

1. What sparked the rebellion led by the Trung Sisters?
2. What does the experience of the Trung Sisters tell us about Vietnamese society under Chinese rule and the role of women in that society?

Note: Quotation is from Thomas Hodgkin, *Vietnam: The Revolutionary Path* (New York: St. Martin's, 1981), 22.

The Trung Sisters This painting by a Vietnamese artist shows the Trung Sisters riding into battle on war elephants against the Chinese.

both Central and Southeast Asia, becoming a major world religion. During the Gupta golden age, Indians achieved new knowledge in science and mathematics that later influenced the Middle East and Europe.

The states that emerged in Southeast Asia were based on maritime trade, rice agriculture, and the blending of local and foreign influences. The Austronesian sailors fostered trade networks over vast distances, and kingdoms arose in Cambodia and Vietnam. Indian religious, political, and cultural ideas had a great impact in many parts of the region, and China's conquest of Vietnam spread Chinese influence.

KEY TERMS

Brahman
Vedanta
Jainism
Buddhism
nirvana
monasticism
Kushans
Theravada
Mahayana
bodhisattva
Indianization

EBOOK AND WEBSITE RESOURCES

PRIMARY SOURCE
The Code of Manu

INTERACTIVE MAPS
Map 5.1 The Mauryan Empire, 322–185 B.C.E.
Map 5.2 The Spread of Buddhism in Asia, 100–800 C.E.
Map 5.3 Funan and Its Neighbors

LINKS

Austronesian and Other Indo-Pacific Topics (http://w3.rz-berlin.mpg.de/~wm/wm3.html). A useful collection to sources on Austronesian languages and cultures, operated by Germany-based scholars.

Internet Indian History Sourcebook (http://www.fordham.edu/halsall/india/indiasbook.html). An invaluable collection of sources and links on India from ancient to modern times.

Silk Road Narratives (http://depts.washington.edu/uwch/silkroad/texts/texts.html). Explores cultural interaction in Eurasia through excerpts from Silk Road travelers.

Virtual Religion Index (http://virtualreligion.net/vri/). An outstanding site with many links on the history of Buddhism and Hinduism.

Plus flashcards, practice quizzes, and more. Go to: www.cengage.com/history/lockard/globalsocnet2e

SUGGESTED READING

Armstrong, Karen. *Buddha.* New York: Viking Penguin, 2001. A brief and readable introduction to the Buddha's life and thought.

Auboyer, Jeannine. *Daily Life in Ancient India: From 200 BC to 700 AD.* Translated by Simon Watson Taylor. London: Phoenix, 2002. A fascinating and readable examination of classical Indian society.

Avari, Burjor. *India: The Ancient Past. A History of the Indian Subcontinent from c. 7000 BC to AD 1200.* New York: Routledge, 2007. Good overview by an Indian scholar.

Basham, A. L. *The Wonder That Was India*, 3rd ed. London: Macmillan, 1968 (reprinted 1999 by Rupa and Company, New Delhi). Although dated, this is still the best general study of pre-Islamic India.

Foltz, Richard C. *Religions of the Silk Road: Overland Trade and Cultural Exchange from Antiquity to the Fifteenth Century.* New York: St. Martin's, 1999. An introduction to trade and the spread of religions, especially Buddhism, in Central Asia.

Frye, Richard N. *The Heritage of Central Asia: From Antiquity to the Turkish Expansion.* Princeton: Markus Wiener, 1996. One of the best surveys of Central Asia in this era.

Hall, Kenneth. *Maritime Trade and State Development in Early Southeast Asia.* Honolulu: University of Hawai'i Press, 1985. Useful study of trade, politics, and international connections.

Higham, Charles. *Early Cultures of Mainland Southeast Asia.* Chicago: Art Media Resources, 2002. Scholarly study with good coverage of this era.

Kulke, Hermann, and Dietmar Rothermund. *A History of India*, 2nd ed. London and New York: Routledge, 2010. A concise but stimulating general history that incorporates recent scholarship on the Classical Era.

Mabbett, Ian, and David Chandler. *The Khmers.* London: Blackwell, 1995. An authoritative study of early Cambodian history.

O'Reilly, Dougald J.W. *Early Civilizations of Southeast Asia.* Lanham, MD.: AltaMira Press, 2007. Excellent survey of classical Southeast Asia.

Oxtoby, Willard G. *World Religions: Eastern Traditions.* New York: Oxford University Press, 1996. Contains valuable essays on the Buddhist, Hindu, and Jain traditions.

Ray, Himanshu Prabha. *The Archaeology of Seafaring in Ancient South Asia.* New York: Cambridge University Press, 2003. A scholarly study of India's maritime trade and contacts in this era.

Shaffer, Lynda Norene. *Maritime Southeast Asia to 1500.* Armonk, NY: M.E. Sharpe, 1996. A very readable brief introduction to premodern Southeast Asia, including Funan and the Austronesian maritime trade.

Stein, Burton. *A History of India.* Malden, MA: Blackwell, 1998. A survey text especially strong on social and religious history.

Taylor, Keith Weller. *The Birth of Vietnam.* Berkeley: University of California Press, 1983. The major study on Vietnam before and during Chinese colonization.

Thapar, Romila. *A'soka and the Decline of the Mauryas.* Delhi: Oxford University Press, 1997. An update of an earlier study, with much information on the Mauryas.

Thapar, Romila. *Early India from the Origins to AD 1300.* Berkeley: University of California Press, 2002. A valuable revision of the standard history of early India, detailed and comprehensive.

CHAPTER

6

Eurasian Connections and New Traditions in East Asia, 600 B.C.E.–600 C.E.

CHAPTER OUTLINE

- Changing China and Axial Age Thought, 600–221 B.C.E.
- Chinese Imperial Systems and the World
- China After the Han Empire: Continuity and Change
- Korea, Japan, and East Asian Networks

PROFILE
Sima Qian, Chinese Historian

WITNESS TO THE PAST
The Analects and Correct Confucian Behavior

Courtesy, Dunhuang Academy/ Lois Conner, photographer

Fresco from Mogao Caves
The Mogao Caves, situated along the Silk Road in western China, contain many frescoes reflecting Silk Road life and the spread of Buddhism into the region. This fresco, painted in the third century C.E., shows a caravan resting at an oasis.

After the Han had sent its envoys to open up communications with the state of Da Xia [in today's Afghanistan], all the barbarians of the distant west craned their necks to the east and longed to catch a glimpse of China.

—CHINESE DIPLOMAT ZHANG QIAN, REPORTED BY HISTORIAN SIMA QIAN, CA. 100 B.C.E.[1]

FOCUS QUESTIONS

1. What were the distinctive features of the Chinese philosophies that emerged during the late Zhou period?
2. What developments during the Han dynasty linked China to the rest of Eurasia?
3. What outside influences helped shape China after the fall of the Han?
4. How did the Koreans and Japanese assimilate Chinese influences into their own distinctive societies?

In 138 B.C.E. the Chinese emperor, Wu Di **(woo tee)**, sought to make contact with a Central Asian group, the Yuezhi **(yueh-chih)**, in order to forge an alliance against their mutual enemy, another Central Asian group, the Xiongnu **(SHE-OONG-noo)**, who were threatening China. An attendant at the imperial court, Zhang Qian **(jahng chee-YEN)**, volunteered to undertake the dangerous diplomatic mission. A strong man known for his generosity who inspired trust and easily made friends with non-Chinese, Zhang set off on the overland journey west with only a small escort. After being captured by the Xiongnu and held prisoner for ten years, Zhang finally escaped. Hoping to complete his mission, he and his party made their way west, following a route that soon became known as one of the classical world's great networks of exchange: the Silk Road. They crossed the Pamir **(pah-MEER)** Mountains and visited lands in what is today Afghanistan and Turkestan, whose people already knew of China because they avidly imported Chinese silk (hence the name *Silk Road*). Although his diplomatic mission failed, after twelve years away Zhang brought back useful products, including the grape, and informed Wu Di about the lands to the west and their resources.

For over a millennium after Zhang's journey, China connected with the lands much farther west by way of overland trade and travel through Central Asia. Every year merchants gathered just outside the walls of the Chinese capital, Chang'an **(CHAHNG-ahn)** (today's Xian **[SEE-ahn]**), to form a caravan. The merchants loaded bundles of metals, ceramics, spices, scrolls of paintings, seeds, and above all piles of silk on their horses and donkeys. The veteran caravaners, Chinese and Central Asian, understood the dangers ahead, which could include blinding sandstorms and ruthless bandits, but also the fabulous profits that would be made from their venture. They traveled west for weeks, skirting the Great Wall of China. At the last outpost of Chinese society, marked by the Jade Gate, the horses and donkeys were exchanged for camels, better suited to the upcoming journey through harsh deserts. After weeks of travel across waterless wastes, the caravan crossed the snow-covered Pamir Mountains. Finally, several thousand miles from Chang'an, the travelers would arrive at the cities of Turkestan, where their precious commodities were traded or sold. Much of this cargo was then on its way to India, western Asia, and even southern Europe. In spite of great distances and immense geographical barriers, this vast network of trails tied China to the world beyond and made peoples as far west as Rome aware of China.

China and its neighbors, Korea and Japan, built their societies far away from the influence of the Middle East, India, and Europe, fostering unique technologies, governments, religions, and philosophies. But East Asians were also influenced by peoples, ideas, and commercial goods that traveled the trade networks from faraway places such as Central Asia and India. These were the centuries of the classical blossoming of East Asian cultures, which established frameworks for the development of these societies in the centuries to follow.

e Visit the website and eBook for additional study materials and interactive tools: www.cengage.com/history/lockard/globalsocnet2e

Changing China and Axial Age Thought, 600–221 B.C.E.

What were the distinctive features of the Chinese philosophies that emerged during the late Zhou period?

Chinese technology, science, and philosophy developed largely independently from outside influences. Yet Chinese originality also responded to many of the same challenges faced by other societies. The Chinese needed ideas to explain the workings of the universe and to bring order to their lives. Such ideas appeared during the late Zhou period, when changes in society and politics produced unsettled conditions. Chinese philosophers seeking to restore order spawned several schools of thought that endured for several millennia.

Late Zhou Conflicts

Warring States

The Zhou dynasty endured for nearly 900 years (1122–221 B.C.E.), but after 500 B.C.E. it experienced rapid social and economic change as well as chronic warfare, worsened through advances in iron weapons (see Map 6.1). This era of particularly intense fighting is known as the "Warring States Period." Local lords did not challenge the Zhou king directly but increasingly ignored him, fighting instead among themselves for supremacy. This prolonged crisis fostered changes in many areas of Chinese life, not all of them detrimental. For example, despite the fighting, by 250 B.C.E. China had become the most populous society on earth, with 20 to 40 million people. Improving technol-

Map 6.1
China in the Sixth Century B.C.E.

During the late Zhou era China was divided into competing, often warring, states, only loosely ruled by the Zhou kings. Some, such as Ch'u and Wu, were large. In the third century B.C.E. the westernmost state, Qin, conquered the others and formed a unified empire.

e Interactive Map

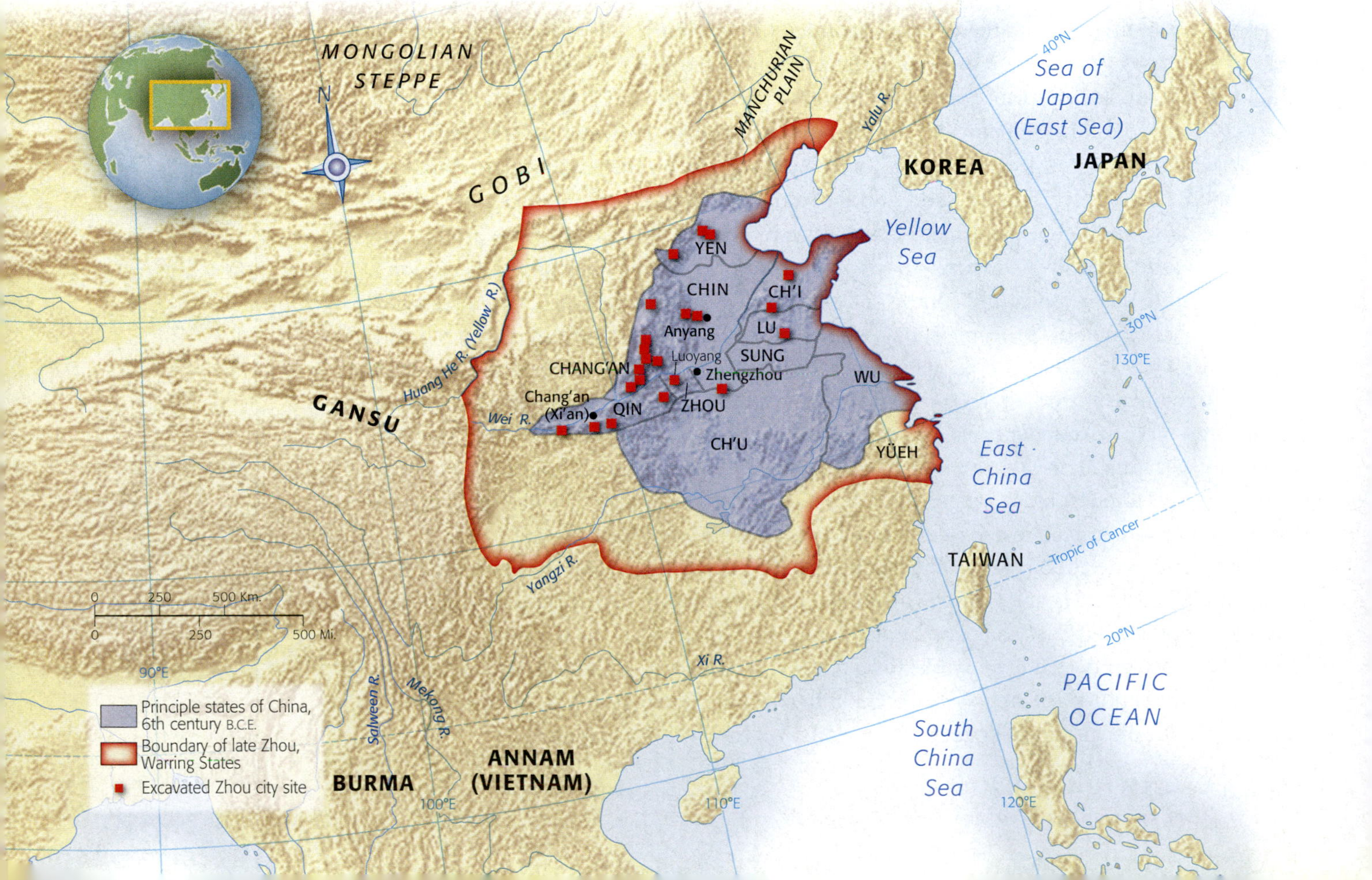

CHRONOLOGY

	China	Korea	Japan
1200 B.C.E.	**1122–221** B.C.E. Zhou dynasty		
300 B.C.E.	**221–206** B.C.E. Qin dynasty **206** B.C.E.–**220** C.E. Han dynasty	**108** B.C.E.–**313** C.E. Chinese colonization	**300** B.C.E.–**552** C.E. Yayoi culture
300 C.E.	**222–581** C.E. Three Kingdoms and Six Dynasties	**350–668** C.E. Koguryo Empire	
500 C.E.	**581–618** C.E. Sui dynasty		**552–710** C.E. Yamato state

ogy and communications also fostered commerce and cities. Political and economic power gradually shifted to the eastern part of the Yellow River Basin, while Chinese culture expanded south of the Yangzi River Basin, which became the major agricultural region because of its greater fertility and favorable climate. Social mobility also increased. Many peasants and slaves abandoned their homes and moved to open land or to the fast-growing cities. The growing merchant class also gained influence. A Chinese historian recorded the situation: "The law honors farmers, yet farmers have become poorer; the law degrades merchants, yet merchants have become richer."[2]

Late Zhou Technology and Science

Iron Technology

China joined the Iron Age in the sixth century B.C.E., thus achieving equal technological footing with western Asia. Knowledge of ironworking, which probably filtered into China from Central Asia over trade networks, led to the use of iron-tipped ox-drawn plows, which improved agricultural productivity. The Zhou Chinese also became the first people to make the breakthrough to cast iron, which is much easier to shape into products; with this discovery they could make superior axes, hoes, ploughshares, picks, swords, and chariots. Indeed, Chinese iron plows were the world's most efficient farm tools before the second millennium C.E. The Chinese also made major advances in water control and conservation. In 250 B.C.E., for example, a vast complex of dikes, canals, and dams was constructed to control the fickle upper Yangzi River, a huge system that worked so well that it is still used today. Other advances included the growing of soybeans, which provided a rich protein source and enriched the soil. The late Zhou Chinese also invented the first compasses and became pioneers in mathematics, amending the Shang decimal system by adding a place for the zero in equations. While the Chinese had long produced silk from strands made by a caterpillar of a moth that fed on mulberry trees, in Zhou times they developed better methods of weaving the silk.

One Hundred Philosophical Schools

The later Zhou was the most creative period in traditional Chinese thought, producing so many competing philosophies that it was called the era of the "hundred schools of thought." These diverse approaches were part of the widespread intellectual creativity in Eurasia during the Axial Age, so named because it fostered ways of thought that endured through the centuries. New philosophies and widening intellectual horizons also emerged in the Mediterranean world, western Asia, and India between 600 and 250 B.C.E. (see Chapters 5 and 7 and "Societies, Networks, Transitions," for Part II; see also Chronology: Classical China). To help explain the fighting and restore peace and harmony, philosophers across Eurasia emphasized ethical principles, criticized political conditions, and proposed new ideas about government and society. At the end of this period, powerful empires

CHRONOLOGY
Classical China

1122–221 B.C.E. Zhou dynasty

550–350 B.C.E. Height of Axial Age in China

481 B.C.E. Beginning of Warring States Period

551–479 B.C.E. Life of Confucius

221–206 B.C.E. Qin dynasty

206 B.C.E.–**220** C.E. Han dynasty

141–87 B.C.E. Reign of Wu Di

105 C.E. Invention of paper

222–581 C.E. Three Kingdoms and Six Dynasties Era

581–618 C.E. Sui dynasty

British Museum/Visual Connection Archive

Confucius Stone rubbing of a portrait of Confucius from an ancient temple. For 2,500 years Confucius was the most honored and influential Chinese thinker, remembered in countless paintings, woodblock cuts, and carvings on walls.

emerged in China, India, and the Mediterranean that reflected a new order of technological and organizational planning. In China, the hundred schools resulted in part from the constant conflict during the Warring States Period and the increased knowledge of the outside world resulting from contact with Turkik pastoralists, who brought horses to China in exchange for grain, wine, and silks.

Chinese thought differed dramatically from that developed in other societies. From the late Zhou period onward, Chinese philosophy, unlike that in, for example, India, viewed people as social and political creatures within communities and placed less emphasis on an afterlife and powerful gods. While Chinese thinkers did not ignore the supernatural, and some practiced magic or mystical techniques, their main emphases were humanistic. This practical approach reflected the philosophers' position in society. Although literate and thoughtful, they were also pragmatic men who often served in government. Some wandered from one Zhou state to another offering their services, thus becoming teachers. Their disciples collected their sayings or thoughts into the classic texts venerated by later generations. The leading masters created with their followers the philosophies of Confucianism, Daoism, and Legalism, all of which ultimately stood the test of time and influenced China for the next two millennia. The divisions between and within the various schools were never rigid, but each had certain core ideas.

Confucius and His Legacy

The most influential new philosophy, **Confucianism** (kun-FYOO-shu-NIZ-um), was based on the ideas of Confucius and emphasized the relations among people. Kong Fuzi (kong foo-dzu) ("Master Kung"), better known in the West as Confucius, probably lived from 551 to 479 B.C.E. (see Chronology: Classical China). As with the Buddha in India or Jesus of Nazareth, we know of his life and ideas through the writings of followers. Confucius left no direct writings, but his sayings were collected by his disciples and published a century or two after his death in a book called ***The Analects*** (see Witness to the Past: *The Analects* and Correct Confucian Behavior). Born into a modest but aristocratic family, he attempted unsuccessfully to gain a government position in various states and then spent years as a teacher of dazzling ability. Over his career he taught some three thousand students from all social classes. The sage claimed that he had "never refused to teach anyone, even though he came to me on foot, with nothing more to offer as tuition than a package of dried meat."[3] Maintaining that education was the key to promoting morality, Confucius stressed the study of history, philosophy, literature, poetry, and music. Considering himself not a creator of new ideas but rather a transmitter of ancient wisdom, he revived traditional ideas and reorganized them into a coherent system of thought. Hence, he extolled the past as an example for the future.

Confucianism is not primarily a religion concerned with otherworldly issues, but a philosophy of social relations, a moral and ethical code designed to promote social stability. The Chinese never considered Confucius a god, but rather a wise sage to be honored by offerings. Confucius could best be described as an agnostic, arguing that, since people know little about life, they cannot know about death and the supernatural world. Like the Ionian Greeks a world away, Confucius was developing a rationalist view opposed to superstition. He asserted that wisdom was working to improve society and keeping one's distance from the gods and spirits while showing them reverence. The answer to the world's problems, Confucius argued, was virtue, ethics, and, above all, benevolence and moderation in behavior. Confucius also advised people to think about the future, contending that if they do not think about problems that are still distant, they will have to worry about them when they arrive.

Confucius advocated an autocratic but paternalistic form of government in which the ruler was responsible for the people's welfare. The family constituted the model for the state. Just as children should respect and obey their parents, a custom known as **filial piety** (FILL-eal PIE-uh-ty), so citizens should obey a fair government and play their assigned roles in a society defined by order and hierarchy: "Let the ruler be ruler, and the minister minister; let the father be father, and the son son."[4] Confucius talked about duty and obedience of inferiors to superiors: of wife to husband, son to father, younger to older, and citizen to king. But authority, he emphasized, must be wielded justly and wisely. Government was fundamentally a matter of ethics: if power was abused, it became illegitimate. When asked what thought should guide the conduct of both leaders and citizens throughout life, he replied: "Do not do to others what you yourself do not desire."[5]

Confucianism A Chinese philosophy based on the ideas of Confucius emphasizing the relations among people.

The Analects The book of the sayings of Confucius collected by his disciples and published a century or two after his death.

filial piety The Confucian rule that children should respect and obey their parents.

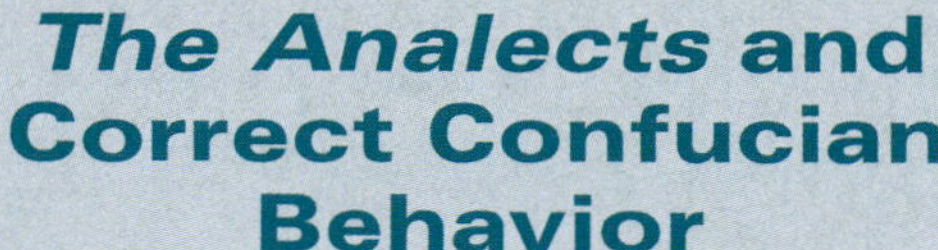

The Analects and Correct Confucian Behavior

The Analects is the main record of Confucius and his thought that survived the Warring States Period and the book burnings of the next dynasty. Compiled by his disciples many years after his death, it is presented largely in the form of questions from his followers and answers, short aphorisms, or long discourses by the sage. Divided into twenty chapters, the book covers many topics, mostly peoples' conduct and aspirations. It became the most important book in China from the Han dynasty down to modern times. These fragments present a few of Confucius's thoughts about the correct behavior of gentlemen (the rulers and other leaders), sons and daughters, and people in general.

[About the gentleman], Confucius said, "The gentleman concerns himself with the Way [the natural order that is also a moral order]; he does not worry about his salary. Hunger may be found in plowing; wealth may be found in studying. The gentleman worries about the Way, not about poverty. . . . The gentleman reveres three things. He reveres the mandate of Heaven; he reveres great people; and he reveres the words of the sages. Petty people do not know the mandate of Heaven and so do not revere it. They are disrespectful of great people and they ridicule the words of the sage. The gentleman aspires to things lofty; the petty person aspires to things base. The gentleman looks to himself; the petty person looks to other people. The gentleman feels bad when his capabilities fall short of some task. He does not feel bad if people fail to recognize him. . . ."

[About filial piety or respect for parents], Confucius said, "Nowadays, filial piety is considered to be the ability to nourish one's parents. But this obligation to nourish even extends down to the dogs and horses. Unless we have reverence for our parents, what makes us any different? Do not offend your parents. . . . When your parents are alive, serve them according to the rules of ritual and decorum. When they are deceased, give them a funeral and offer sacrifices to them according to the rules of ritual and decorum. . . . It is unacceptable not to be aware of your parents' ages. Their advancing years are a cause for joy and at the same time a cause for sorrow. . . ."

[About humanity], Confucius said, "If an individual can practice five things anywhere in the world, he is a man of humanity. . . . [These are] Reverence, generosity, truthfulness, diligence, and kindness. If a person acts with reverence, he will not be insulted. If he is generous, he will win over the people. If he is truthful, he will be trusted by the people. If he is diligent, he will have great achievements. If he is kind, he will be able to influence others. . . . When you go out, treat everyone as if you were welcoming a great guest. Employ people as if you were conducting a great sacrifice."

THINKING ABOUT THE READING

1. What are some of the main qualities expected of a gentleman?
2. How might Confucian views on respect for parents have influenced the family system?
3. How did the advice reflect Confucius's humanistic emphasis?

Source: Reprinted with the permission of The Free Press, a Division of Simon & Schuster Inc. from CHINESE CIVILIZATION AND SOCIETY, A Sourcebook, Second Revised & Expanded Edition by Patricia Buckley Ebrey.

Impact of Confucianism

Confucian teachings have had a more enduring influence on East Asia than those of any other thinker, becoming in some form or another the official doctrine in China, Korea, Vietnam, and Japan and helping set the common East Asian pattern of compromise. As a Chinese proverb advised, people should "bend like bamboo" to avoid conflict with other people. To promote harmony, Confucianism stressed adherence to rules of courtesy. For example, a book of etiquette from late Zhou times advised men on rules for visiting another man of equal status: if the host should "yawn, stretch himself, ask the time of day, order his dinner, or change his position, then [the guest] must ask permission to [leave]."[6] Confucian societies used ritual and etiquette to maintain stability and discipline. Confucian ideas were designed to promote social order and continuity across generations, and, in the centuries to follow, they generally did. China became one of the most stable societies in history.

Later Confucian Thinkers

The ideas of Confucius were revised to some extent by his followers and became increasingly rigid in application over the centuries, leading in some cases to a conservatism and inflexibility that Confucius might have condemned. Two of the main followers of Confucius represented opposing schools of interpretation. Both lived one and a half centuries later than their master. Mengzi **(MUNG-dze)** (Mencius) (372–289 B.C.E.) advocated a liberal, even permissive government in which the ruler embraced benevolence and righteousness as his main goals. Mengzi believed human nature was essentially good, and hence he was extremely optimistic about the prospects for society. Xunzi **(SHOON-dze)** (Hsun Tzu) (310–220 B.C.E.) disagreed; viewing human nature as essentially bad, he maintained that the state must enforce goodness and morality. Xunzi also contributed to the authoritarian tendencies of Confucianism by claiming that Confucian writings were the source of all wisdom.

Daoism and Chinese Mysticism

Daoism A Chinese philosophy that emphasized adaptation to nature.

The second major philosophy, **Daoism** (DOW-iz-um), taught that people should adapt to nature. Daoism's main ideas are attributed to Laozi (lou-zoe) (Lao Tzu or "Old Master"). According to legends, Laozi was an older contemporary of Confucius and a disillusioned bureaucrat who became a wandering teacher. If such a man ever lived, he probably did not write the two main Daoist texts, which were most likely composed during the third century B.C.E.

Daoist Beliefs

Daoism was a philosophy of withdrawal for people appalled by the warfare of the age. Daoist thinkers held that the goal of life was to follow the "way of the universe," or *dao*, described by Daoist teachers as "unfathomable, the ancestral progenitor of all things, everlasting. All pervading, dao lies hidden and cannot be named. It produces all things. He who acts in accordance with dao becomes one with dao."[7] Convinced that people could never dominate their environment, Daoists urged them to ally with it, becoming simple, without desire and striving, and content with what is. A Daoist text expressed disgust with everyday life: "To labor away one's whole lifetime but never see the result, and to be utterly worn out with toil but have no idea where it is leading, is this not lamentable?"[8] Daoists advised Chinese to conform to the great pattern of the natural world rather than, as was the emphasis of Confucians, to social expectations and governments. One of the main texts argued that the wise person prefers fishing on a remote stream to serving as emperor. To the Daoists, societies were obstacles and all governments corrupt and oppressive. Daoism was mystical and romantic, fostering an awareness of nature and its beauties. This attitude became pronounced in Chinese poetry and landscape painting, which often recorded towering mountains, roaring waterfalls, and placid lakes.

Diverse Traditions

Daoism later fragmented into several traditions. Popular Daoism became a religion of countless deities and magic. Some followers sought to find the elixir of immortality, often by experimenting with a wide variety of foods. By contrast, philosophical Daoism, which appealed to the better educated, suggested that the individual should turn inward and experience oneness with the universe. Daoist writers found it difficult to express their basic ideas in words, one claiming that "those who know do not speak; those who speak do not know."[9]

Some of the early Daoist writings contained stories such as this one, which is filled with mysticism, a sense of unity with nature, and a humbling relativism:

> *One time, Chuang-tzu dreamed he was a butterfly, flitting around, enjoying what butterflies enjoy. The butterfly did not know that it was Chuang-tzu. Then Chuang-tzu started, and woke up, and he was Chuang-tzu again. And he began to wonder whether he was Chuang-tzu who had dreamed he was a butterfly dreaming that he was Chuang-tzu.*[10]

Balancing Confucianism, Daoism tapped a different strand of Chinese experience, adding enjoyment, reflection, and a sense of freedom. Daoists advised Confucianists to flow with the heart rather than struggle with the intellect. The man in power was a Confucianist, but out of power he became a Daoist. The active bureaucrat of the morning became the dreamy poet or nature lover of the evening. Daoism complemented Confucianism by enabling the Chinese to balance the conflicting needs for social order and personal autonomy.

Legalism and the Chinese State

Legalism A Chinese philosophy that advocated harsh control of people by the state.

Among the dozens of other competing philosophies, **Legalism**, which advocated that the state maintain harsh control of people, also had an enduring influence. Borrowing ideas from the Confucian Xunzi, the Legalists emphasized that an authoritarian government must secure prosperity, order, and stability by controlling all economic resources and making people well disciplined through compulsory military duty and harsh laws. Taken to extremes, Legalism led to unrestrained state power. The ruler needed to be strong and to have no regard for the rights or will of the people. Legalists wrote that people can be controlled by means of punishments and rewards, commands and prohibitions, and they ridiculed Confucian humanism.

Although Legalism exercised a long-term influence on Chinese politics, the Chinese always balanced it with the more humane ideas of Confucius and Mengzi, who stressed moral persuasion rather than coercion. Hence, many Chinese did not follow one philosophy to the exclusion of others. Laws were sometimes severe, but local officials had flexibility in implementing them and took into account the social context.

SECTION SUMMARY

- Despite being marred by chronic civil warfare, China became the most populous society on earth, and its economy evolved rapidly.
- The belated development of iron technologies and other breakthroughs made China competitive with western Asia.
- Instability resulting from military conflict led intellectuals to question basic tenets of society and government, thus creating the era of the "hundred schools of thought."
- Three enduring Chinese philosophies from this period—Confucianism, Daoism, and Legalism—have influenced Chinese state and culture through two millennia.
- Chinese philosophies emphasized humanism rather than the supernatural or gods.

CHINESE IMPERIAL SYSTEMS AND THE WORLD

What developments during the Han dynasty linked China to the rest of Eurasia?

Chinese society, more than Indian, Middle Eastern, or European societies, was characterized by cohesion and continuity, as well as by blending of diverse influences. For example, although China was often attacked and even occasionally conquered by Central Asians, the invaders maintained continuity with China's past by adopting Chinese culture, a process known as **Sinicization** **(SIN-uh-sigh-ZAY-tion)**. But one major transition quickly changed the face of premodern China: the replacement of the multistate Zhou system by a centralized empire. Because of this development, China after 221 B.C.E. was different from the China before it and set the pattern for the centuries to follow. The new imperial China was forged by the harsh rulers of Qin **(chin)** and by the Han dynasty, which conquered a large empire, fostered foreign trade, and established enduring political patterns. During this time the Chinese family matured into its basic form, and the economy grew dramatically, affecting peasant life. Chinese examined their own history, looking for lessons from the past. The Han were also highly creative in technology and science, making advances in mathematics and health.

Sinicization The process by which Central Asian invaders maintained continuity with China's past by adopting Chinese culture.

The Qin Dynasty

Qin Legalism

Late Zhou political turmoil ended when the Qin dynasty (221–206 B.C.E.) conquered the other states and implemented repressive Legalist ideas, transforming the China of many states into an empire with a powerful authoritarian central government. Advised by Legalist thinkers, the state of Qin had gradually become the strongest state within the Zhou system, controlling the economy and establishing government monopolies over many trade goods. Like Sparta in Greece, the population was militarized, the men serving as citizen-warriors. Slowly Qin began conquering other Zhou states. The brutal prime minister, Li Si **(lee SHE)** (Li Ssu), a Legalist thinker and the chief deputy to the man who would eventually become the first emperor of all of China, argued that those who used the past to oppose the present, meaning the Confucians, had to be exterminated.

The First Emperor and His Empire

In 221 B.C.E. the Qin, after finally defeating and absorbing all the remaining Zhou states, established a new government that ruled most of the Chinese people. The first Qin ruler assumed the new and imposing title of Shi Huangdi **(SHE hwang-dee)** ("first emperor"). This extraordinary autocrat surrounded himself with mystery and pomp to enhance his prestige, but in so doing he also concealed himself from the consequences of his decrees. Shi Huangdi lived in carefully guarded privacy, moving secretly from one apartment to another in his vast palaces. To reveal his movements was a crime that was instantly punished with death. The new dynasty implemented dramatic policies. The Qin sent armies to incorporate much of southern China and, for a while, Vietnam into the empire. Many in the south were eventually assimilated into Chinese society. Mandating a total reordering of China along Legalist lines, the emperor constructed a monolithic and united state that sought to control all aspects of Chinese life. Given this unification, the name *Qin* is fittingly the origin of the Western name for China.

Qin Repression

Later Chinese historians viewed the Qin Empire as one of the most terrible periods in the country's long history. The common people hated the forced labor, strict laws, spies, general surveillance, and thought control that were paramount in the Qin police state. Intellectuals despised the Qin for launching attacks on non-Legalist thought, including Confucianism, as subversive doctrines. The Qin burned thousands of books and executed many scholars, often by burying them alive. In so doing they ended the intellectual creativity of the hundred schools.

Qin Achievements

Despite the repression, Shi Huangdi's policies led to many achievements, fostering public works projects, economic growth, and social change. The Qin standardized weights and measures, unified agricultural practices, and codified laws. To aid communication, they built roads, bridges, dams, and canals and ordered that all wheel axles be the same length so that wagons could use the ruts made by other wagons in the dusty roads. The Qin standardized the written language so that all literate Chinese anywhere in the empire could communicate easily. To foster economic growth, the Qin established state monopolies over essential commodities like salt, and ever since the Chinese have accepted a strong government role in economic matters. Taxes were high and involved forced labor on government projects. The harsh Qin laws also ended crime, as a later Chinese scholar conceded: "Nothing lost on the road was picked up and pocketed, the hills were free of bandits, men avoided quarrels at home."[11] Finally, Qin land reform undermined the power of the old aristocracy, a mighty blow to the Zhou social structure.

The Great Wall

The most famous public works project of the Qin era was the construction of an early and limited version of a Great Wall along China's northern borders as a barrier against the encroachment of Central Asian warriors. The Chinese traded with their Central Asian neighbors but also fought with and feared them. A few partial earthen walls had already been built in Zhou times, but the Qin consolidated these into a more formidable structure, later known as the Great Wall. As part of their tax obligation, vast numbers of laborers were drafted for building the Great Wall, one of the greatest architectural feats of the ancient world. Later dynasties periodically rebuilt and added to the wall. The present brick and stone wall that so astounds tourists derives mostly from reconstruction and expansion work six centuries ago, after which the wall stretched over 1,400 miles across north China. Properly manned, it could be an effective defense, but only the most affluent emperors could afford that expense. The wall was seldom successful in curbing invaders but was a symbolic affirmation of empire and territorial limits.

Qin Defeat

But the Qin dynasty itself was short-lived. Many hated Shi Huangdi, and his expansionist policies provoked conflict with neighboring peoples. His inner circle kept the first emperor's death in 210 B.C.E. secret for fear of general revolt. He was buried in a huge underground mausoleum together with seven thousand astonishingly realistic life-size terracotta horses and warriors brandishing real bronze weapons. When news finally spread of Shi Huangdi's death, peasant revolts broke out. In 206 B.C.E. the Qin forces were defeated by a rebel alliance. As the various rebel groups then vied for power, a former peasant led his forces to victory, establishing a new dynasty, the Han (HAHN).

The Great Wall This panorama from the region just north of Beijing shows a portion of the wall reconstructed in the fifteenth century C.E. The wall was an attempt to mark the northern boundary of China and keep out nomadic invaders.

Georg Gerster/Photo Researchers, Inc.

The Han Empire

The Han is the most respected Chinese dynasty because during these four centuries (206 B.C.E.–220 C.E.) China became a major force in Eurasian trade, diplomacy, and imperialism. The Han built a huge empire stretching far into Central Asia (see Map 6.2), and trade across this area allowed greater contact with people to the west. Like the Qin, the Han built a strong state, but they also modified the Qin's harsh Legalist structure. The brilliance of Han rule and the expansion of Chinese society southward set the pattern for later dynasties and led the Chinese to call themselves the Sons of Han.

Age of Empires

The middle Classical Era was the age of empires, when large segments of Eurasia and North Africa were dominated by large imperial structures like the Han. All the empires built on the ideas of the Axial Age sages, resolving the crises that had sparked their rise. But the classical empires eventually declined as their structures and finances weakened, the conquered populations revolted, and nomadic peoples invaded the imperial heartlands. The Han and Roman Empires reached their zenith around the same time and resembled each other in population, although Rome's empire was larger in territorial size. In 2 C.E. the Han Empire contained at least 60 million people, most of them in China proper, and the Roman Empire ruled some 55 million, most of them outside Italy.

Map 6.2
The Han Empire

The Han Empire fluctuated in size but at its height controlled most of today's China, Korea, northern Vietnam, and a long corridor through Central Asia to Turkestan.

Emperor Wu Di

The pinnacle of Han imperial power came under the emperor mentioned in the chapter opening: Wu Di, who ruled for over half a century (141–87 B.C.E.). After he established firm control at home, Wu Di, a firm believer, like many Chinese emperors, that the best defense is a good offense, used bloody campaigns to counteract the encroaching pastoral nomads to the north and west. Some groups, such as the Huns, were deflected to the west, where they then disrupted the Roman Empire. The branch of Huns the Chinese called Xiongnu, a large tribal confederation, had constantly threatened China.

Han Expansion

Empire building and diplomacy soon linked China to western Eurasia as well as to Northeast and Southeast Asia. The Han sent ambassadors such as Zhang Qian to distant Central Asians seeking allies against common enemies. Wu Di also dispatched great armies, some numbering as many as 150,000 men, to conquer southwestern China, northern Korea, Vietnam, the Xinjiang **(shin-jee-yahng)** region on China's western borders, Mongolia, and parts of Turkestan. Wu Di wrote a poem about a successful military campaign that brought many horses as tribute: "The heavenly horses are coming from the Far West. They crossed the Flowing Sands, for the barbarians are conquered."[12] The Chinese ruled Korea for four centuries and Vietnam for 1,000 years. Soon Chinese power extended even further, as states in today's Afghanistan acknowledged themselves vassals of China, sending tribute to Han emperors. But not all soldiers celebrated these achievements. One Han soldier wrote a protest song: "In the wilderness we dead lie unburied, fodder for crows. Tell the crows for us, 'We've always been brave men.'"[13] In later Han times a Chinese army of 90,000 men reached as far as the Caspian Sea in southeastern Russia, and a small force led by a General Gan Ying apparently traveled through Parthia to the Persian Gulf in 97 C.E., the first Chinese known to reach there. On his return General Gan reported on the customs and topography of these western states, as well as on the vast Roman Empire.

The Silk Road and Eurasian Trade

Silk Road A lively caravan route through Central Asia that linked China with India, the Middle East, and southern Europe.

The Han security presence in Central Asia fostered overland trade networks between China and western Asia. A lively caravan route, known as the **Silk Road** for its most valuable cargo, linked China with India, the Middle East, and southern Europe. Central Asian cities such as Kashgar **(kahsh-gar)** and Samarkand **(SAM-mar-kahnd)** grew up along the Silk Road to service the trade and the merchants. Indeed, the string of cities along the road was an important contact zone between East and West. Chinese silk, porcelain, and bamboo were carried west across the deserts and mountains to Baghdad and the eastern Mediterranean ports. Eventually some Chinese goods, especially silk, reached Rome. Since silk was lightweight and easily packed, large quantities were carried west by each caravan. Caravans then returned with horses and luxury goods such as Egyptian glass beads, Red Sea pearls, and Baltic amber.

The Silk Road trade networks greatly influenced the peoples who participated in the trade. To pay for Chinese luxuries, the Romans dispatched silver to China, causing a serious trade imbalance that contributed to the decline of the Western Roman Empire. Thus the Han Empire ultimately had a political and economic impact on distant Europe. Relations with Central and West Asians also brought new products to China, such as stringed musical instruments and new foods. Imperial power and foreign trade generated an economic boom and the rapid growth of commerce. The Silk Road network also fostered a Central Asian melting pot as peoples moved, met, and mixed.

Han Government and Politics

Han Politics

The Han government structure survived in its basic form until the early twentieth century. Whereas the Qin had sought to transform China in one brutal stroke, the Han were more pragmatic and cautious, relying on elements of Qin authoritarianism but using less repression. The Han softened Legalism with Confucian humanism, demonstrating that Confucian philosophy could maintain stability in the wake of momentous change. This Han pattern of mixing Legalism with Confucianism, power with ethics, characterized the Chinese political system for the next 2,000 years. During Han times the civil service developed to include some 130,000 officials, or 1 for every 400 to 500 people, a small number in relationship to the total population. The central government had a restricted role, mainly ensuring law, order, and border defense. Its bureaucrats collected taxes, administered the legal system, and officered military forces. Yet the many rebellions during Han times suggest that high taxes and demands that peasants provide military or labor service, such as rebuilding river dikes or repairing washed-out roads, generated occasional unrest.

The Han bureaucracy was staffed by educated men later called **mandarins**. Chinese proverbs claimed that the country might be won by the sword but could be ruled only by the writing brush—in other words, by an educated elite. The Han Chinese invented the civil service examination system to select officials based on merit. These exams tested knowledge of the Confucian writings, an indication that Confucianism was becoming the official state ideology, legitimizing the regime and promoting faithful service. The prestige of the scholars staffing the bureaucracy also moderated the tendency toward despotism, since they served as intermediaries between the emperor and the people. The development of the Han bureaucracy marked the rise of the **scholar-gentry**, a social class based on learning and officeholding but also on landowning, since many of the mandarins came from wealthy landowning families. Still, the social system was somewhat fluid. Scholars could not guarantee that their sons would be competent, and some poor men did rise by passing the civil service exams.

mandarins Educated men who staffed the Chinese bureaucracy.

scholar-gentry A Chinese social class of learned office-holders and landowners that arose in the Han dynasty.

Han Ideology

During the Han the concept of the Mandate of Heaven and of history in terms of the dynastic cycle became ingrained in Chinese thinking (see Chapter 4). Most premodern Chinese scholars believed that emperors ruled as deputies of the cosmic forces, but only so long as they possessed justice, benevolence, and sincerity. In each dynasty, able early rulers were succeeded by debauched weaklings, who indulged their pleasures, keeping harems of wives, concubines, and sometimes boys. When an emperor misruled, rebellion was justified. The rise and fall of dynasties also correlated with economic trends. A strong new dynasty initially generated security and prosperity, luring ambitious emperors into overextending imperial power and squandering human and financial resources, not only on expansion but also on court luxury. Such luxury included some extraordinary art produced for the Han elite; for example, the tomb of one princess contained a 2,000-piece jade suit that was sown with gold wire.

Han Decline

Wasteful expenditures created financial difficulties and military stagnation. Governments could no longer fund the large military commitment to protect the country, and some bureaucrats became corrupt. To meet the growing deficits the government raised taxes, forcing many poorer peasants to sell their land to large landlords, who could then evade taxes through their wealth and influence. This pattern was illustrated by Han emperor Wu Di. His glorious empire came at a huge cost, straining the imperial treasury. Some Han scholars opposed military expansion as a senseless waste of lives and tax revenues, and in 81 B.C.E. Wu Di's successor invited some of them to make their case before him. They did so, arguing that,

> *at present, morality is discarded and reliance is placed on military force. Troops are raised for campaigns and garrisons are stationed for defense. It is the long-drawn-out campaigns and the ceaseless transportation of provisions that burden our people at home and cause our frontier soldiers to suffer from hunger and cold.*[14]

But higher government officials responded that the spending was necessary to protect the country from the Xiongnu.

The Han dynasty finally collapsed in 220 C.E., not unlike the fall of Rome several centuries later. Critical factors for both empires included inadequate revenues, peasant revolts, powerful landed families contending for power, and raids by pastoralists from the borderlands. Across Eurasia the unusually warm conditions between 200 B.C.E. and 200 C.E. came to an end, and the colder weather affected agriculture. Both empires were also ravaged by epidemics in the second century C.E., which killed millions and thus reduced tax revenues.

Han Society and Economy

Family System

Han social life revolved around the family system, which endured for over 2,000 years because it offered many strengths. In part because of Confucian ideas, the family became the central focus of allegiance. Each person belonged to a large, continuing family that went backward and forward in time. The Chinese were expected to honor their ancestors while also considering the welfare of future generations. The family provided great psychological and economic security. The Chinese ideal was the joint family, that is, three or four generations living together under one roof. But only wealthy families could support the large houses and private courtyards that made the joint family way of life possible. The family was also an autocratic institution led by a patriarch, or senior male, who commanded respect. Chinese traced descent exclusively through the male line. Children were expected to respect both parents and to venerate their elders, and family interests always took precedence over individual ones. Laws held the family accountable for the actions of its members, discouraging disgraceful behavior by individuals.

Gender Relations and Women

This family system increasingly put most women at a disadvantage. Women were expected to be devoted to their parents, then to their husband and sons; care of the family and children was their central preoccupation. Parents arranged marriages with the goal of linking families, and a young wife joined her husband's family and was subject to the authority of his parents. Although many marriages seem to have been happy, the sorrows of unhappy women became a common literary theme. Many Chinese novels and plays concerned unrequited love or lovers forced to marry others. In one small part of central China, some women developed among themselves a special and secret form of writing, known as **nuxu** (nu-shu), to share their life experiences. Its origins remain obscure.

nuxu A secret form of writing developed by some Chinese women to share their experiences, possibly beginning in the Han period.

We know much about the experiences of Han women. Ban Zhao (ban chao), an accomplished historian, astronomer, and mathematician, wrote an influential book on women's place in society. Her advice to women stressed the Confucian obligations of selfless behavior, devotion, and obedience. Although gender roles became more rigid than they had been a few centuries earlier, many women engaged in some small-scale trade or worked long hours in the fields in addition to doing housework and caring for children. They also formed groups to spin or weave together. Women's experiences were never standardized, and the independence and influence they enjoyed depended on their age, social class, and local practices. There were always women like Ban Zhao who achieved wide acclaim. Some elite women received an education, and some were celebrated for their poetry writing. The mother of the Confucian thinker Mengzi was widely esteemed as a model of astuteness and assertiveness, yet she was reported by a male Han era biographer to have said that a "woman's duties are to cook the five grains, heat the wine, look after her parents-in-law, make clothes, and that is all!"[15] In contrast, some peasant women, who worked in the fields alongside their men, were strong-willed and exercised influence in their families and villages.

During the Han period and for over 2,000 years thereafter, China's economy was dominated by intensive farming, especially the growing of cereal crops by peasants. Landowning became the major goal of economic endeavor and investment, and peasants had to produce a food surplus for the 20 percent of the people living in towns and cities. Working fertile land, peasants achieved high yields, becoming some of the world's most efficient farmers through hard physical labor, especially in growing rice. Fields had to be flooded with irrigation water and drained, and the rice had to be sown, transplanted, and harvested, all by hand. Peasants did not lead easy lives. Most rarely went farther than the local market town to which they brought their produce. Family land and movable property were divided equally among sons. A Han scholar complained that poor peasants were left with too little land to live on and thus reduced to eating the food of pigs and dogs. As a result, many peasants were forced into tenancy to landlords. However, slavery, an important feature of Shang and Zhou society, became less common during the Han.

Han Farmer Stone relief of Han farmer using an ox-drawn plow. These plows fostered the expansion of cultivated land during the Han.

From Patricia Buckley Ebrey, *The Cambridge Illustrated History of China*, 1996

Population pressure and land shortage posed problems to peasants and also created political stability. By the second century B.C.E., practically all the good agricultural land in north and north-central China was being used. The labor-intensive nature of the economy was also apparent outside agriculture. Transportation meant porters with carrying poles, men pushing wheelbarrows, and men bearing the sedan chairs of the elite. Men also walked along narrow paths pulling boats upriver through the narrow gorges of the Yangzi River. While the famous sericulture (silk-making) industry produced silks and brocades of the finest weave, producing 150 pounds of silk required feeding and keeping clean the trays of 700,000 worms.

Chinese Historiography

The Chinese developed one of the greatest traditions of studying and writing about history, known as historiography. The recording of history was probably inevitable among a people who looked to the past for guidance in the present. History writing in China goes back at least as far as the Zhou dynasty. Beginning with the Han, most dynasties employed a group of professional historians, such as the Han era's Sima Qian **(SI-mu tshen)** (see Profile: Sima Qian, Chinese Historian). Later Chinese historians were influenced by Sima Qian's belief that past events, if not forgotten, also taught about the future. The Chinese historians tended to ignore social and economic history in favor of political history, concentrating on personalities, stories, wars, and the doings of emperors while neglecting long-term trends.

The greatest Chinese historians wrote monumental works and had much in common with each other. They aimed for objectivity, carefully separating their editorial comments from the narrative text. Like all historians, they still had to decide what to include and omit, focusing more on information about human beings and their foibles than on supernatural intervention. Historical literature also served as a manual for government, since it discussed the success and failure of past policies with the goal of achieving wisdom and promoting morality.

SECTION SUMMARY

- Through military conquest, the Qin dynasty unified the warring states into a new centralized, imperial China.
- Legalism, with its strict authoritarianism and negative view of human nature, was the dominant philosophy of the Qin rulers.
- Both the Han dynasty and the Roman Empire reached their peaks at about the same time, with roughly similar population sizes.
- The diplomatic and military expansion under the Han rulers set the stage for expanded trade, including the development of the Silk Road linking China to western Asia and Europe.
- The structure of government established during the Han, characterized by a blending of central and local authority and a softening of Legalism with Confucian humanism, endured until the early twentieth century.
- The family structure became the central social institution; its patriarchal hierarchy, codified in law, put the needs of the group above the needs of the individual.
- Despite subservience to all males in the family, some women of this period made many artistic and intellectual contributions.
- Peasant labor, as well as backbreaking labor in general, continued to be the foundation of the economy and characterized most people's existence.

China After the Han Empire: Continuity and Change

What outside influences helped shape China after the fall of the Han?

After the collapse of the Han in 221 C.E., China experienced three and a half centuries of disorder and political fragmentation known as the Three Kingdoms and Six Dynasties. China was divided into several states, once as many as sixteen, some ruled by Chinese and others by invaders. Just as the incursion of new peoples shaped Europe and India in the ashes of the Roman and Mauryan Empires, so this era in China was marked by frequent incursions by pastoral nomads. In the seventh century, the Chinese restored centralized government and reaffirmed the classical tradition.

Disunity, Invasion, and Cultural Mixing

Nomadic Invasions

The post-Han period was a troubled one as pastoral nomads crossed the Great Wall and attacked north China. They included the Huns, Mongols, and Turks, all of whom spoke Ural-Altaic languages. Although chiefly livestock herders, most used bronze and iron. Brutal winters and keen competition for good grazing land made them martial peoples scornful of but also attracted to the richer life available to the agricultural Chinese. Sometimes they succeeded in breaching the Great Wall thanks to their skills in horseback warfare, especially when they united in confederations under strong chiefs. These invasions produced what historians term the "Great Wall Complex": a natural Chinese paranoia about the security of borders and the perpetual fear of outsiders seeking to conquer. The Chinese believed that all non-Chinese were barbarians hoping to share in China's cultural glory and material wealth. This fear prompted them to rally to fight invaders. A much loved fifth-century ballad, perhaps based on an actual person, recalls the

SIMA QIAN, CHINESE HISTORIAN

Perhaps the greatest Han dynasty historian was Sima Qian (ca. 145–90 B.C.E.). His father, a high court official who also wrote about Chinese history, begged his son on his deathbed to continue compiling a history of China and its neighbors from earliest times. "I have failed to set forth a record of all the enlightened rulers and wise lords, the faithful ministers and gentlemen who were ready to die for duty," he conceded. His dutiful son replied, "I shall not dare to be remiss," and made the project his life's work. At the age of twenty, Sima Qian, who had grown up in the ancestral home in northwest China, began a grand tour of the empire. During the tour, he devoted time to examining historical sites, such as the tomb and family home of Confucius.

After receiving an official appointment in the Han government, the young scholar was sent on a mission to newly conquered territories in the southwest. Later he visited far northwestern outposts, including Mongolia, and also traveled extensively with the emperor Wu Di. Like his father, Sima Qian was appointed Grand Astrologer, a post dealing with time and the heavens, and helped to reform the calendar. But, being an honest man who spoke his mind, he alienated the emperor by defending a respected general whose brave attack against the Huns had failed for lack of support. As punishment Sima Qian was castrated.

Using his immense learning, combined with access to the vast imperial library containing the public records, Sima Qian produced his major book, *Records of the Grand Historian*. An invaluable source, *Records* covered some 2,000 years of history in 130 chapters, roughly 10,000 pages of text. Attempting to be universal, this monumental history ranges across a variety of topics, including astronomy, astrology, science, music, religious sacrifices, and economic patterns. It offers sketches of famous men from many walks of life, including political and military leaders, merchants, philosophers, scholars, comedians, assassins, rebels, bandits, and poets. *Records* also describes all foreign peoples and lands well known to the Chinese, from Korea to Afghanistan. Because it also covers rivers and canals, we know much of Wu Di's ambitious conservation and irrigation schemes. In addition, Sima Qian was the first historian to offer a comparative appraisal of China's various philosophical traditions, in which he showed particular sympathy to Daoism.

The book is strongest on the history of his times. Because Sima Qian's castration had embittered him toward Wu Di, some chapters are filled with covert satires on the emperor and warnings about his increasing power. His most original writing came in the chapters on people and contemporary affairs. Consider this criticism of those abusing their power:

> *We see that men whose deeds are immoral and who constantly violate the laws end their lives in luxury and wealth and their blessings pass down to their heirs without end. And there are others who expend anger on what is not upright and just, and yet, in numbers too great to be reckoned, they meet with misfortune and disaster. I find myself in much perplexity.*

Sima Qian Painting of Sima Qian. This modern painting, by an unknown artist, imagines what Han China's great historian, Sima Qian, might have looked like.

Sima Qian's vital narrative and lively prose made his book popular reading among Chinese scholars for many centuries. Above all, the historian was concerned with both his literary and his moral legacy. As Sima Qian concluded, in words that still stir historians everywhere: "I have assembled and arranged the ancient traditions, and if they may be handed down and communicated surely I would have no regrets," and, "those who do not forget the past are masters of the future." Sima Qian set the standard to be followed by later historians in China.

THINKING ABOUT THE PROFILE

1. How did Sima Qian become a historian?
2. What does his life tell us about the pleasures and hazards of being a high official in Han China?
3. What made his historical writing so valuable to later readers?

Note: Quotations from Ben-Ami Scharfstein, *The Mind of China: The Culture, Customs, and Beliefs of Traditional China* (New York: Dell, 1974), 89–91; and Sima Qian, *Historical Records*, translated by Raymond Dawson (Oxford: Oxford University Press, 1994), 177.

deeds of a young woman warrior, Mulan, who disguises herself as a man in order to fight invading Central Asians. Only after she distinguishes herself in battle do her comrades discover her gender. The ballad makes a case for gender equality: "For the male hare has a lilting, lolloping gait, and the female hare has a wild and roving eye; But set them both scampering side by side, And who so wise could tell you 'This is he?'"[16] These invasions also prompted many Chinese to move south, solidifying the Chinese character of the Yangzi Basin.

Assimilation

The Chinese learned to endure both division and invasion by outsiders. In dealing with invaders, the Chinese developed a remarkable defense mechanism: assimilation. Most of the barbarian conquerors eventually ruled in a Chinese way, using the Confucian bureaucracy while also adapting many elements of Chinese culture. The Chinese believed that rule by foreigners could be tolerated as long as Chinese culture was respected and protected. Chinese culture, social institutions, and economic patterns thus proved able to survive the shock of conquest. But the Chinese also learned from the invaders. This merging of cultures provided a foundation for the later rejuvenation of a China that would be greater than the empires of Qin and Han.

China and the World

After the Han era, China became even more connected to the world outside, fostering a vital, cosmopolitan culture. One fifth-century emperor loved everything foreign: dress, art works, food, beds, chairs, harps, dances. Ideas and products traveled both directions along the Silk Road and by land and sea between China and Southeast Asia. Chinese objects from this era often showed Indian, Persian, Mesopotamian, Greek, or Roman influences. The graves of wealthy Chinese frequently contained Roman glass, Persian silver vessels, images of Greek gods, and cups made from Indonesian shells. China's openness to ideas from outside also led many Chinese to embrace an Indian religion, Buddhism.

Buddhism and China's Eclectic Religious Tradition

Spread of Universal Religions

During the later Classical Era, universal religions—faiths that appealed to people from many cultures—became much more prominent in Eurasia and North Africa, marking another great transition. The decline and collapse of the great Afro-Eurasian empires, from China to Rome, produced political instability and social strife challenging established ways. In response, universal religions diffused along the trade networks: Christianity from western Asia to Europe, where it soon became the dominant religion; Hinduism throughout India and into Southeast Asia; and Mahayana (mah-HAH-YAH-nah) Buddhism into Central and East Asia. These universal religions incorporated existing local beliefs, creating hybrid artistic forms and value systems. The most pronounced synthesis took place in East Asia as Buddhism encountered earlier belief systems such as Confucianism.

Werner Forman/Art Resource, NY

Buddha Statue at Yungang This huge statue of the Buddha, created around 290 C.E., is 45 feet tall. It is one of thousands found along cliffs in western China and elsewhere along the Silk Road.

The Buddhist Age

The arrival of Buddhism was a momentous transition for East Asia, fostering the Buddhist Age in both Chinese and, more generally, Asian history between the fourth through the ninth centuries C.E. Buddhism in some form became dominant in much of East, Central, and Southeast Asia as well as in portions of South Asia (see Chapter 5). The basic Buddhist beliefs about overcoming suffering through good deeds and thoughts derived from the sixth-century B.C.E. teachings of the Indian sage known as the Buddha ("the Enlightened One"), but the religion later split into several rival schools. One of these, Mahayana Buddhism, was carried by merchants and missionaries along the Silk Road into Central Asia. From there it spread into western China during later Han times, serving to tie China to distant India. Later the religion spread from China to Korea, Vietnam, and Japan. Buddhism, a religion of compassion and gentleness, offered meaning and hope to people experiencing hardship, warfare, and instability. It also offered the Chinese a spiritual outlook largely missing in Confucianism, which appealed to reason and practical ethics but said little about gods or life after death, and it offered more than Daoist mysticism, which could not explain the fate of the individual in the cosmic order. Mahayana Buddhism thus promised salvation in an afterlife. But Buddhism also adapted to Chinese traditions. For example, the Buddhist notion of reincarnation clashed with Chinese beliefs in ancestor worship, so most Chinese never accepted this idea.

Buddhism in China

Because it had traveled from India through Central Asia, Chinese Buddhism acquired a cosmopolitan outlook. Buddhism's peaceful spread was accompanied by Indian artistic, literary, and cultural influences, such as the huge sculptures of the Buddha found along the Silk Road and in northwestern China. Many Buddhist missionaries entered China, and several hundred Chinese pilgrims went to India, either overland or along the sea route through Southeast Asia. For example, the monk Faxian **(fah-shee-en)** spent fifteen years in India and also visited Buddhist centers in Southeast Asia in the fifth century C.E. On their return to China the pilgrims spread knowledge of the societies they encountered.

The Three Ways

As a result of this mixing, by the middle of the first millennium C.E. an eclectic Chinese religious tradition embraced three very different viewpoints—Buddhism, Confucianism, and Daoism—known as "the three ways." The three schools interacted with each other, creating a rich synthesis, and many Chinese could no longer clearly differentiate between them. An old but still popular Chinese story has Confucius, Laozi, and Buddha walking and talking together, debating the merits of their respective positions; as they cross a bridge, they are obscured in mist. When spotted again only one somewhat larger figure can be seen in the distance. Yet some distinctions were maintained. Only Buddhism developed a fully organized church, with monks and nuns. Confucianism, a philosophy of social relations rather than a true religion, had no priests. Many Chinese, believing that people's needs could not be satisfied by any one set of doctrines and hence not identifying themselves exclusively with any of the three belief systems, saw the three traditions as different roads to the same destination, personal happiness.

Secular Worldviews and Popular Religion

Gradually a gap between the relatively secular worldview of the educated elite and the popular religion of the common people widened. The intellectuals favored Confucian humanism and Daoist naturalism, with moral perfection of humankind as the ultimate goal. Since Confucius and his followers had revealed a doctrine centered on humanity rather than on gods, many intellectuals viewed popular religion, with its gods, spirits, ghosts, and magic, as superstition. One Han scholar wrote that "the number of persons who have died since the world began must run into thousands of millions. If everyone of them has become a spirit, there must be at least one to every yard as we walk along the road."[17] Meanwhile, although more Chinese may have been indifferent to religion than was common elsewhere, many peasants, artisans, and merchants believed in thousands of gods and goddesses of Buddhist, Daoist, or animist origin, using shamans to communicate with the spirit realm. They also accepted notions of heaven and hell introduced by Mahayana Buddhism, and of **geomancy** **(JEE-u-MAN-see)**, known in Chinese as *feng shui* **(fung shway)** ("wind and water"), a popular Daoist-influenced system for determining the auspicious settings of buildings and graves. Geomancy is still widely employed today in East Asia, and some architects even use it to assess the auspiciousness of modern houses and skyscrapers in North American and European cities.

geomancy Known in Chinese as *feng shui* ("wind and water"), a system for determining the auspicious settings of human dwellings and graves.

Science and Technology in the Classical Era

Han Technology

During this era China developed one of the world's oldest scientific and technological traditions, establishing along with the Indians, Mesopotamians, Egyptians, and Greeks the foundation for modern science. The Zhou and Han are credited with many important breakthroughs, including porcelain ("china"), rag paper, the water-powered mill, the shoulder harness for horses, the foot stirrup (possibly adapted from Central Asian models), the magnetic compass, the seismograph, the wheelbarrow, the stern-post rudder for boats, the spinning wheel, and linen. Most of these inventions did not reach western Eurasia over the trade routes until a few centuries—in some cases a millennium—later. Paper may have been the most significant innovation. Before paper Chinese scribes wrote with a pointed stylus on strips of wood, bamboo, or woven cloth. Eventually an ingenious first-century C.E. artisan tried beating the cloth into fiber and forming thin sheets. In seeking ways to mass-produce Buddhist texts and images for believers and Confucian classics for students preparing for the examinations, Han craftsmen made ink rubbings on paper from stone carvings, often of entire Buddhist books. Elementary block printing was in limited use in China by the sixth century C.E. By the ninth century woodblock printing had become a major activity in East Asia.

Han Mathematics and Science

The Han also made great strides in mathematics and science. Besides making the most accurate calculation of *pi* at the time, the Chinese were many centuries ahead of the rest of the world in the use of fractions, a simple decimal system, the concept of negative numbers, and in certain aspects of algebra and geometry. Around 190 C.E. they invented the *abacus,* a primitive computer still used widely in Asia today that proved an unparalleled tool for calculations. The abacus was constructed by fastening balls on wires attached to a board carved with divisions. Han astronomers compiled catalogues of stars, speculated on sunspots, and explained the causes of lunar eclipses. Astronomy was essential for an agricultural society, which needed accurate calendars to regulate planting and harvesting.

Chinese Medicine

Chinese science, especially medicine, owed much to the cosmological thinking exemplified in yin-yang dualism and also to Daoism, which inspired an interest in nature. To the Daoists the body was a microcosm of the universe. An enduring medical discovery, *acupuncture,* developed from the belief that good health was the result of proper yin-yang balance in the body. In this procedure, thin needles are inserted at predetermined points to alleviate pain or correct some condition. Chinese experts learned the parts of the body and how to read a pulse. Acupuncture is still practiced today and has spread around the world. The Chinese also stressed good hygiene and preventive medicine, including a well-balanced diet and regular exercise. In their quest for the elixir of immortality, Daoist alchemists discovered many edible foods, herbs, and potions that improved health, and they developed the greatest list of pharmaceuticals in the premodern world. By the Han period doctors could diagnose gout and cirrhosis of the liver. Many ancient Chinese folk remedies remain popular to this day in China.

Maritime Technologies

The Chinese also continued to develop innovative technologies. Although never a great seafaring people like the Austronesians and Greeks, the Chinese became some of the world leaders in shipbuilding, some taking up maritime trade. Even in Han times, Chinese ships carried trade goods back and forth to Korea, Japan, and Southeast Asia. By at least the fifth century C.E. the Chinese had constructed large oceangoing vessels with stern-post rudders for maneuvering, which permitted longer and farther journeys. Chinese ships and navigational skills were probably adequate to even cross the vast Pacific, although there is no compelling evidence that any did so.

The Sui Reunification of China

Chinese Unity

To an observer in the fourth century it might have seemed that the Roman Empire, although visibly weakening, could endure, while the Chinese empire was overrun by "barbarian" invaders, broken apart, and turning to foreign, otherworldly religions. Yet China was eventually reunified under a powerful, centralized government, whereas Rome, facing the same kinds of challenges, fragmented and collapsed. Several factors contributed to China's reassembly. First, reestablishment of a centralized state was made easier by the large population of the Chinese core area, which was 50 million by 400 C.E., probably double the population of Europe. In addition, the Chinese shared more cultural unity than the varied peoples of western Asia, India, and Europe. The nomadic invaders, small in numbers, may have been easily absorbed in China. Culture and politics probably also played a role. Confucian ethical humanism, the merit-based civil service exams, and the Chinese writing encouraged cultural unity. In contrast, India contained many very different spoken languages but also diverse writing systems, and in Europe, the speakers of Romance languages based on phonetic alphabets splintered into many competing countries, never to be reunited.

Sui Government and Society

The ruthless Sui (sway) dynasty (581–618 C.E.) played the same role in history as the Qin, reuniting China after several centuries of turmoil and division. The Sui emperors were tyrants but also patrons of arts and letters, and they created the largest library at that time in the world. Like the Qin, the Sui were builders, mobilizing 6 million forced workers to construct the Grand Canal linking the Yangzi and Yellow Rivers. At 1,200 miles long, the longest human-made channel ever constructed, the canal ensured the prosperity of later dynasties, since each year huge quantities

Sui Decline

of grain could be shipped north. Tree-shaded parks and inns lined the route. However, like earlier dynasties, the Sui overreached and collapsed. Exhausting campaigns of conquest temporarily extended imperial frontiers into Korea and Central Asia, but the Sui drove the Chinese people too hard, resulting in overwork and food shortages. Soon rebellions broke out. The victor in the ensuing struggles established the Tang **(tahng)** dynasty (618–907 C.E.), which launched China into its great golden age, extending over many centuries, and linked it more closely to Korea and Japan, whose societies we turn to now.

SECTION SUMMARY

- Spurred by invasions of nomadic peoples from the north, the population shifted south, but the invaders were assimilated by existing Chinese government structures.
- Buddhism took root in China during this tumultuous period, spreading along the trade routes from India and melding with existing Confucian thought.
- The Chinese attitude toward religion was characterized by an easy interchange of beliefs, in which individuals drew from a variety of religious or philosophical perspectives depending on their need.
- Developments in science and medicine were influenced by Daoism, which promoted the idea of a yin-yang balance in the natural world.
- Fractured by invasions, Chinese reunification was nevertheless made easier by the population's shared written language, culture, and history.
- Like the Qin before them, the Sui rulers also reunited China using harsh measures but made lasting contributions, such as the Grand Canal.

KOREA, JAPAN, AND EAST ASIAN NETWORKS

How did the Koreans and Japanese assimilate Chinese influences into their own distinctive societies?

Large, densely populated China dominated East Asia for much of history. Consequently, eastern Asia did not develop the political diversity, with many rival states, that prevailed in India, western Asia, or Europe after classical times. Korea and Japan adopted intensive farming and thus became receptive to Chinese cultural influence. Although more developed than Japan for many centuries, Korea was often in the shadow of China. Separated by water, Japan was able to remain more independent. Yet both Korea and Japan creatively forged distinctive societies.

Korea and China

As a close neighbor, Korea experienced regular and extensive interaction with China, which brought many advantages but also political pressures. During the first millennium B.C.E. Chinese cultural and technological influences began permeating the Korean peninsula. Koreans adopted iron technology from the Chinese, including advanced weapons, which later fostered the rise of agriculture-based Korean states. However, these were soon overwhelmed by Chinese influence. In 108 B.C.E. Wu Di's Han armies, reportedly 60,000 troops strong, conquered northern Korea against fierce resistance. China ruled the territory as a colony for the next four centuries, providing models to the Koreans in government structure, architecture, and city planning (see Chronology: Classical Japan and Korea).

The end of Chinese colonization in 313 C.E. allowed Korean society to flower, and three native kingdoms emerged that dominated Korea between the fourth and seventh centuries, occasionally warring against each other. However, Chinese cultural influences, including the writing system and Confucianism, also spread more widely. Mahayana Buddhism, introduced from China in 372 C.E., strongly influenced Korean painting, sculpture, and architecture. But the Koreans never became carbon copies of the Chinese. For example, unlike in China, where family status rose or fell with dynastic change and civil service examination results, an aristocracy of inherited position thrived for most of Korean history. And although most Koreans adopted Buddhism, the animism that had long flourished never disappeared.

CHRONOLOGY
Classical Japan and Korea

300 B.C.E.–552 C.E. Yayoi culture in Japan

18 B.C.E. Rise of Koguryo in northern Korea

108 B.C.E.–313 C.E. Han Chinese colonization of Korea

250 C.E. Beginning of Yayoi tomb culture

350–668 C.E. Koguryo Empire

676–935 C.E. United Silla state

538 C.E. Introduction of Buddhism to Japan

552–710 C.E. Yamato state in Japan

604 C.E. First Japanese constitution

Eventually one Korean kingdom, Koguryo **(ko-GUR-yo)**, became the most influential (see Map 6.3). In the fifth century, with China divided, Koguryo expanded far to the north, annexing much of Manchuria and southeastern Siberia and becoming one of the largest states in Eurasia between 350 and 668 C.E. At the same time, several smaller Korean states controlled the southern part of the peninsula. Koguryo's army repulsed seven major Chinese invasions by the Sui and Tang dynasties between 598 and 655 C.E., when a resurgent China was the most powerful state in eastern Eurasia. In 612 C.E. they routed an invading Sui army that, according to legend, numbered at least 1 million soldiers but was probably closer to a still formidable 300,000. The huge cost of the Chinese campaigns in Korea contributed to the collapse of the Sui dynasty. Finally, in 668 C.E., Chinese armies, allied with the southern Korean state of Silla **(SILL-ah or SHILL-ah)**, overran Koguryo. Soon Silla drove out the Chinese armies and reunified much of Korea under the Silla state in 676.

Map 6.3
Korea and Japan in the Fifth Century C.E.
During the Classical Era Korea was often divided into several states. Koguryo in the north was the largest state, ruling part of Siberia. By the sixth century the Yamato state governed much of the main Japanese island, Honshu.

Yayoi and Yamato Japan

Like Korea across the straits, Japan experienced dramatic change in this era. The pottery-making Jomon culture (see Chapter 4) persisted until around 300 B.C.E., when a new culture, Yayoi **(ya-YOI)**, emerged, based on exceptionally productive wet rice farming and establishment of close links with Korea. During the Yayoi era (300 B.C.E.–552 C.E.), Korea remained a source of learning and population for Japan, with a continuous flow of Korean immigrants, including skilled craftsmen, scribes, and artists, as well as both Korean and Chinese ideas and technology from the mainland into the islands. Korean migrants brought horses, and the armored warrior on horseback later became a vivid feature of Japanese life. Immigration from Korea continued until the ninth century. By 600 C.E. the Japanese people as we know them today had come together from the genetic and cultural mixing over many centuries of Korean immigrants with earlier settlers and the indigenous Ainu people.

The Yayoi also traded sporadically with China. A Chinese visitor in 297 C.E. left us much information about Yayoi society, reporting the preoccupation with taboos, class distinctions, and especially ritual cleanliness. Like modern Japanese, the Yayoi were fond of dancing, singing, drinking rice wine, and eating raw vegetables; experienced no theft and little other crime; and revered nature. The Yayoi used the potter's wheel, were expert weavers, and had mastered both bronze and iron technology, later fashioning iron into highly effective swords and armor. The Yayoi formed no centralized governments but were organized into many clans, each ruled by a hereditary priest-chieftain. During the second century C.E., when Japan was engulfed in conflict, a woman, Pimiko **(pih-MEE-ko)**, became a powerful queen-priestess and brought peace by imposing strict laws. However, most clan elites were men who governed farmers, artisans, and a few slaves and who mobilized people to build hundreds of large earthen tombs, often surrounded by moats, all over south-central Honshu Island. The tombs housed the remains of prominent leaders, who were buried with jewels, swords, and clay figurines.

Rise of Yamato

Japan entered the light of written history in the sixth century C.E. with the Yamato **(YA-ma-toe)** (552–710 C.E.), the first state ruling a majority of the Japanese people. The Yamato was centered in south-central Honshu, where the cities of Kyoto and Osaka now stand. Yamato was not a centralized state like Han China or Koguryo but rather a national government ruling over smaller groups based on territorial clans, each headed by a hereditary chief. Eventually Yamato extended its influence into southern Japan while expanding the northern frontier deep into Ainu territory.

Yamato Government

Yamato was headed by emperors and occasionally empresses—all ancestors of the same imperial family that rules Japan today, fifteen centuries later. Political continuity under the same royal family gave the Japanese a strong sense of identity and cultural unity. The Japanese viewed their earlier history in mythological terms, believing the imperial family descended from the Sun Goddess. This beautiful spirit, *Amaterasu* **(AH-mah-teh-RAH-soo)**, and her male consort experienced violent mood swings and periodic conflict that may have been modeled on the frequent storms,

Prince Shotoku This painting from the eighth century C.E. shows Prince Shotoku, one of the major Yamato leaders, and his sons in the Japanese clothing style of the times. Prince Shotoku launched a period of intensive borrowing from China.

Imperial Household Agency

volcanic eruptions, and earthquakes that rock the islands. Despite her tantrums, a female creator deity may also have reflected a high status for women in early Japan. Before the eighth century C.E. around half of the imperial sovereigns were women. However, patriarchy became the common pattern by 1000 C.E.

Japanese Isolation and Cultural Unity

The Japanese forged a particularly distinctive society through a mixing of the local and the foreign. The islands were over a hundred miles from the Eurasian mainland. Since communication with other societies was sporadic, mainly restricted to Korea and China, the Japanese had to become very creative. At the same time, the space and resources available to the steadily growing population on the mountainous islands were restricted, resulting in a tightly woven society with intense social pressures. Since personal privacy became rare in this crowded land, people learned how to erect psychological walls that allowed them to "tune out" the surrounding noise and activity.

Cultural Borrowing

Isolation also made the Japanese expert at borrowing selectively from the outside during periods of intensive contact. Japanese history featured an interplay between the indigenous (native) and the foreign, borrowing from Korea, China, and, much later, the West. While conscious of borrowing, the Japanese have always selected foreign ideas that suit their own needs, seldom leaving a borrowed idea in its original form. For example, they adopted the Chinese idea of an exalted emperor but not the concept of the Mandate of Heaven, which allowed for incompetent or tyrannical dynasties to be overthrown. The Japanese also created much of their own culture. Leading technological innovators for millennia, they developed the best tempered steel of the classical world. They also created artistic forms and styles of universal appeal, such as carefully planned gardens and *bonsai* **(bon-sigh)** (miniature) trees, as well as ingenious solutions to chronic problems such as urban crowding and limited resources. Thus the Japanese house itself, containing thick straw floor mats, sliding paper panels rather than interior walls, a hot tub for communal bathing, and charcoal-burning braziers, conserved building materials and minimized fuel needs for heating and cooking.

Japanese Encounters with China

Shinto ("way of the gods") The ancient animistic Japanese cult that emphasized closeness to nature and enjoyed a rich mythology that included many deities.

Japan was greatly influenced by the Chinese several times in history. The importation of Chinese ideas began on a large scale in the middle of the sixth century C.E. Mahayana Buddhism was introduced around 538 and became a major medium for cultural change, bringing, for example, new forms of art. Chinese teachers, artisans, and Buddhist monks crossed over to Japan, and Japanese journeyed to Korea and China, coming back as converts to Buddhism. Just as the Chinese maintained three distinct traditions of thought, in Japan Buddhism coexisted with the ancient animistic cult later known as **Shinto** **(SHIN-toe)** ("way of the gods"), which emphasized closeness to nature and enjoyed a rich mythology that included many deities.

A growing realization among Japanese leaders that China and Korea were much stronger than Japan in the political, economic, and cultural spheres led the Japanese to launch an era of deliberate borrowing from China to reshape Japanese society. The Yamato expanded relations with Sui China and began to reorganize government structures, integrating Chinese writing and Confucian notions of social organization and morality. The adoption of Chinese ideas accelerated under the auspices of Prince Shotoku **(show-TOW-koo)** (573–621 C.E.), an ardent Buddhist who sponsored the building of temples and also promoted Confucian values. His ideas also foreshadowed later Japanese values emphasizing group interests: "Harmony is to be cherished, and opposition for opposition's sake must be avoided as a matter of principle,"[18] he wrote into the first Japanese constitution, issued in 604. Shotoku became one of the most revered figures in Japanese history. His support for Buddhism has led some historians to compare Shotoku to the Indian king Ashoka, who also embraced Buddhism, and the Roman emperor Constantine, who promoted Christianity. Over the next two and a half centuries many official embassies were exchanged between China and Japan, further promoting the exchange of ideas.

SECTION SUMMARY

- Like most of China, Korea and Japan were agricultural societies, a similarity that facilitated the easy transmission of Chinese culture.
- Korea's proximity to China led to the adoption of Chinese writing and other technologies in Korea.
- Both Buddhism and Confucianism from China permeated Korean culture and were blended with the native belief system of animism, keeping Korean culture distinctive.
- The flow of ideas and people from Korea and China to Japan introduced Buddhism, writing, and other influences into Japan, but the Japanese culture, arts, and religion remained distinctive.
- From the beginning, Japan's small land area prompted the Japanese to deal creatively with lack of space and the social problems of overcrowding.
- The Yamato were Japan's first centralized state and began actively importing cultural and political ideas from China in the sixth century.

Chapter Summary

The classical societies that flowered in eastern Asia were distinctive in many ways. China was large, densely populated, and an innovator in government, culture, religion, science, and technology. During the warfare and political instability of the late Zhou period, Confucius promoted ethical values and suggested how people could live in harmony with each other through a well-defined and hierarchical social structure. In contrast, the Daoists advocated a life in accordance with the rhythms of the natural world. The Legalists argued that a powerful government must harshly regulate society to preserve order. These classical ideas persisted in Chinese thought into modern times. The Legalist leaders of the Qin dynasty used brutal policies to transform China into a centralized imperial state. Following the short-lived Qin, the great Han dynasty established a large Asian empire and traded with western Asia and Europe across the

Silk Road, becoming a major force in eastern Eurasia. The social structure became more patriarchal, and women were expected to be dutiful to their men.

After the Han collapsed, Central Asians frequently invaded and divided China politically. In this turbulent period, Mahayana Buddhism became popular in China, where it mixed with Confucianism, Daoism, and animism. Eventually the Sui dynasty reunified China, an achievement that contrasted with the Roman Empire in the West, which disintegrated into various fragments. China also became a model for neighboring societies. First the Koreans and then the Japanese adopted many Chinese ideas, including some technologies, writing, Confucianism, and Buddhism. But they also creatively blended them with their own unique traditions, resulting in a distinctive mix of the imported with the local.

KEY TERMS

Confucianism	**Legalism**	**scholar-gentry**
The Analects	**Sinicization**	**nuxu**
filial piety	**Silk Road**	**geomancy**
Daoism	**mandarins**	**Shinto**

EBOOK AND WEBSITE RESOURCES

INTERACTIVE MAPS

Map 6.1 China in the Sixth Century B.C.E.
Map 6.2 The Han Empire
Map 6.3 Korea and Japan in the Fifth Century C.E.

LINKS

History of China (http://www.chaos.umd.edu/history). Collection of essays and timelines on Chinese history maintained by the University of Maryland.

Internet East Asian History Sourcebook (http://www.fordham.edu/halsall/eastasia/eastasiasbook.html). An invaluable collection of sources and links on China, Japan, and Korea from ancient to modern times.

Internet Guide for China Studies (http://www.sino.uni-heidelberg.de/igcs/). Good collection of links on premodern and modern China, maintained at Heidelberg University.

Monks and Merchants (http://www.asiasociety.org/arts/monksandmerchants/index.html). Interesting essays, timelines, maps, and images for an Asia Society exhibition on the Silk Road as a zone of communication.

A Visual Sourcebook of Chinese Civilization (http://depts.washington.edu/chinaciv/). A wonderful collection of essays, illustrations, and other useful material on Chinese history.

Plus flashcards, practice quizzes, and more. Go to: www.cengage.com/history/lockard/globalsocnet2e

SUGGESTED READING

Adshead, S. A. M. *China in World History*, 3rd ed. New York: St. Martin's, 2000. A good introduction to Han China's interaction with Central Asia, western Asia, and Europe.

Clements, Jonathan. *Confucius: A Biography*. New York: Sutton, 2005. A brief study written for a popular audience.

Cotterell, Arthur. *The First Emperor of China*. New York: Penguin, 1981. A readable and fascinating study of the first emperor and his times.

Di Cosmo, Nicole. *Ancient China and Its Enemies: The Rise of Nomadic Power in East Asian History*. Cambridge: Cambridge University Press, 2002. An important study of China and the northern peoples from the Zhou through the Han dynasties.

Ebrey, Patricia Buckley. *The Cambridge Illustrated History of China*. New York: Cambridge University Press, 1996. A very readable survey with much on the classical period.

Ebrey, Patricia Buckley, et al. *Pre-Modern East Asia: to 1800: A Cultural, Social, and Political History*, 2nd. ed. Boston: Houghton Mifflin, 2009. An excellent survey of China, Japan, and Korea.

Hane, Mikiso. *Premodern Japan*, 2nd ed. Boulder, CO: Westview, 1991. A readable survey.

Hinsch, Bret. *Women in Early Imperial China*. Lanham, MD: Rowman and Littlefield, 2002. A stimulating study of the factors shaping women's experiences in Qin and Han China.

Holcombe, Charles. *The Genesis of East Asia, 221 B.C.–A.D. 907*. Honolulu: University of Hawai'i Press, 2001. A provocative examination of this era.

Hudson, Mark J. *Ruins of Identity: Ethnogenesis in the Japanese Islands*. Honolulu: University of Hawai'i Press, 1999. Scholarly study of forming Japanese identity and people.

Imamura, Kenji. *Prehistoric Japan: New Perspectives on Insular Japan.* Honolulu: University of Hawai'i Press, 1996. A scholarly study of the Yayoi and Yamato periods.

Lewis, Mark E. *The Early Chinese Empires: Qin and Han.* Cambridge: Belknap Press, 2007. Good study of these two dynasties.

Loewe, Michael. *Everyday Life in Early Imperial China: During the Han Period 202 B.C.–A.D. 220.* Indianapolis: Hackett, 2005. Reprint of a classic work on Han life and society.

Mote, Frederick W. *Intellectual Foundations of China,* 2nd ed. New York: Knopf, 1989. A brief, readable introduction to classical Chinese philosophy.

Seth, Michael J. *A Concise History of Korea from the Neolithic Period through the Nineteenth Century.* Latham, MD.: Rowman and Littlefield, 2006. One of the best general surveys of premodern Korea.

Shaughnessy, Edward L., ed. *China: Empire and Civilization.* New York: Oxford University Press, 2005. Contains many short essays on premodern Chinese society and culture.

Sima Qian. *Historical Records,* translated by Raymond Dawson. New York: Oxford University Press, 1994. A brief introduction to the writings of the Han era historian.

Wright, Arthur. *The Sui Dynasty: The Unification of China,* A.D. *581–617.* New York: Alfred A. Knopf, 1978. A valuable study of government and society.

CHAPTER 7

Western Asia, the Eastern Mediterranean, and Regional Systems, 600–200 B.C.E.

CHAPTER OUTLINE

Persepolis
During the height of their empire, Persian kings built a lavish capital at Persepolis, in today's Iran. This photo shows the audience hall, the part of the grand palace where the kings greeted their ministers and foreign diplomats.

Wonders are many on earth, and the greatest of these, is man, who rides the ocean. He is master of the ageless earth. The use of language, the wind-swift motion of brain he learned; found out the laws of living together in cities. There is nothing beyond his power.

—CHORUS IN *ANTIGONE*, BY THE FIFTH-CENTURY GREEK PLAYWRIGHT SOPHOCLES (SAHF-UH-KLEEZ)[1]

FOCUS QUESTIONS

1. How did the Persians acquire and maintain their empire?
2. What were some features of Greek government, philosophy, and science?
3. In what ways did Persians and Greeks encounter and influence each other?
4. What impact did Alexander the Great and his conquests have on world history?

Thales (THAY-leez) and Anaximander (uh-NAK-suh-MAN-der), pioneering Greek philosophers and scientists, had the great fortune to grow up in prosperous Miletus (my-LEET-uhs), a commercial city on the southwestern coast of Anatolia (modern Turkey). Miletus had long served as a crossroads for the entire region, mingling Greek and foreign cultures. Young men like Thales and Anaximander haunted the bustling docks and seaside bars, listening to the reports of sailors returning from distant shores and of travelers from foreign lands. Milesian merchants sent ships to the far corners of the Mediterranean carrying the treasured wool developed by Miletus sheep breeders and the fine furniture produced by its cabinetmakers. Along the shores of the Black Sea, Milesian settlements supplied fish and wheat that enriched the city's traders. Some sailors brought scraps of learning from older societies such as Egypt and Mesopotamia. This intermingling led to new thinking about geography and cartography. Thales worked out a geometrical system to calculate the position of a ship at sea. Thales' student, Anaximander, made the first map of the Mediterranean world and the first Greek chart of the heavens. Later Hecataeus (HEK-a-TAU-us) of Miletus published a map of the world known to the Greeks, from India to Spain. Miletus matured into a great intellectual center and a meeting place for the Greek and Persian worlds.

The Greeks developed not only a penchant for maritime trade and an understanding of regional geography but also a unique society on the rocky shores of the Aegean Sea. In cities such as Miletus and Athens, they introduced many ideas and institutions that endured through the centuries. The view of humanity's greatness offered by Sophocles in the opening quotation reflects an obsession with individuality and freedom that made the Greeks role models for modern democracies. But the Greek achievements are only part of the story. Connected to a wider world through cities like Miletus, the Greeks flourished by participating in regional trade, colonizing other territories, and borrowing ideas from neighboring societies. Another creative society and even greater regional power, the Persian Empire, dominated the eastern Mediterranean and western Asia and also introduced many innovations that affected the lives of many peoples. Ultimately, the rival Greek and Persian societies were temporarily brought together in a political union that mixed Greek and Persian culture.

The Persians and Their Empire

How did the Persians acquire and maintain their empire?

Although its period of greatest political influence lasted only two centuries, the Persian Empire played an important role in world history. The Persians established a larger, more multicultural empire than any people before them, encompassing Anatolian Greeks, Phoenicians, Hebrews, Egyptians, Mesopotamians, and Indians. Domination of the east-west trade routes made the empire the meeting ground of the early classical world. The Persians' wars with Greece and their empire building in western Asia paved the way for the later rule of the Greek Alexander the Great and his successors.

Building the Persian Empire

The Persian homeland was located on a plateau just north of the Persian Gulf (see Map 7.1). Overland routes connected Mesopotamia and Anatolia to India and Central Asia through Persia's mountains and deserts. The Caucasus Mountains between the Black and Caspian Seas were also linked to Persia historically. Two pastoral societies on the Persian plateau, the Indo-European Medes (MEEDZ) and the Persians, competed for power. By 600 B.C.E. the Persians were subjects of the Medes, who had joined with the Babylonians to overthrow the Assyrians (see Chronology: Persia, 1000–334 B.C.E.). But the Medes were soon displaced by the Persians.

Achaemenid The ruling family of the classical Persian Empire.

The Persian Empire, usually known as **Achaemenid** (a-KEY-muh-nid) Persia after the ruling family, was an extraordinary achievement. At its peak, it extended from the Indus Valley in the east to Libya in the west and from the Black, Caspian, and Aral (AR-uhl) Seas in the north to the Nile Valley in the south (see Map 7.1). This empire was created by a series of four kings. Cyrus II, better known as Cyrus the Great, began the expansion. Cyrus and his successors, Cambyses (kam-BY-seez) II, Darius (duh-RY-uhs) I, and Xerxes (ZUHRK-seez) I, conquered vast territories. Their autocratic but tolerant government established a model for later Middle Eastern empires and challenged the Greeks in the west.

Cyrus the Great (r. 550–530 B.C.E.) overthrew the Median king to become the "king of the Medes and Persians." By 539 he had conquered Mesopotamia, Syria, Palestine, Lydia (a kingdom in the western part of Anatolia), and all the prosperous Greek cities in Anatolia. As much diplomat as soldier, Cyrus followed moderate policies in the conquered territories, making only modest demands for tribute. After conquering Babylonia, Cyrus issued a proclamation on a cylinder, which some consider the world's first charter of human rights: "Protect this land from rancor, from foes, from falsehood, and from drought." Cyrus claimed that the main Babylonian god, Marduk (MAHR-dook), ordered him to help the Babylonians by becoming their ruler and bringing them "justice and righteousness."[2] Under his rule, the Jews taken to Babylon by the Assyrians were allowed to return to Palestine and rebuild their temple. When Cyrus was killed while campaigning against nomads east of the Aral Sea, he was replaced by his son Cambyses II (r. 530–522 B.C.E.), who subjugated Egypt and wisely presented himself as a new Egyptian ruler who would bring stability, good fortune, health, and gladness.

CHRONOLOGY
Persia, 1000–334 B.C.E.

600 B.C.E. Persians become vassals of Medes

640 B.C.E. Kingship of Cyrus the Great

547–546 B.C.E. Conquest of Lydia

530–522 B.C.E. Kingship of Cambyses II

525–523 B.C.E. Conquest of Egypt

521–486 B.C.E. Kingship of Darius I

518 B.C.E. Persian conquest of Indus Valley

499 B.C.E. Rebellion by Ionian Greeks against Persian rule

499–479 B.C.E. Greco-Persian Wars

486–465 Kingship of Xerxes

404 B.C.E. Egyptian independence from Persia

330 B.C.E. Conquest of Persian Empire by Alexander the Great

Cambyses' successor and distant cousin, Darius I (r. 521–486 B.C.E.), was a usurper who had seized power. Not a modest man, he boasted that "over and above my thinking power and understanding, I am a good warrior, horseman, bowman, spear-man."[3] Darius crushed a revolt in Egypt and spread Persian power east and west, even annexing Afghanistan and parts of the Indus River valley in northwestern India. Today many peoples in Afghanistan and Central Asia speak languages closely related to Persian. Darius claimed that within his territories he cherished good people, rooted out the bad, and prevented people from killing each other. To promote justice and ensure his posterity as a great lawgiver, he fashioned a law code for Babylonia that basically reaffirmed Hammurabi's laws made almost 1,500 years earlier.

The Persians were among the classical world's greatest engineers and builders. For example, to forge closer links with Egypt, Darius completed the first Suez Canal, 125 miles long and 150 feet wide, that briefly connected the

CHRONOLOGY

	Greece	Persia	Hellenistic World
600 B.C.E.	**ca. 594 B.C.E.** Solon's reforms in Athens	**550–530 B.C.E.** Kingship of Cyrus the Great **525–523 B.C.E.** Conquest of Egypt **521–486 B.C.E.** Kingship of Darius I	
500 B.C.E.	**499–479 B.C.E.** Greco-Persian Wars **460–429 B.C.E.** Periclean era in Athens **431–404 B.C.E.** Peloponnesian War		
400 B.C.E.			**338 B.C.E.** Macedonian conquest of Greece **336–323 B.C.E.** Reign of Alexander the Great **330 B.C.E.** Occupation of Persia

Mediterranean and the Red Seas. Darius also began the building of a new capital at Persepolis (puhr-SEP-uh-luhs). The architecture of this spectacular city, centered on a massive stone terrace on which stood monumental royal buildings, was drawn from Egyptian, Mesopotamian, and Greek traditions, and its craftsmen and workers included Egyptians, Greeks, Hittites, and Mesopotamians.

Imperial Policies and Networks

Persian Government

Unlike their Assyrian and Babylonian predecessors, the Persian empire builders used laws, generous economic policies, and tolerance toward the conquered to rule successfully. Leading citizens came from many backgrounds. Generals might be Medes, Armenians, Greeks, Egyptians, or Kurds, a people living in the mountains just north of Persia and Mesopotamia. Some of the Persian techniques were imitated by their successors, including the Greeks and Romans, when they created even larger imperial structures several centuries later.

Although their power was in theory absolute, Persian kings were expected to consult with important nobles and judges. Each of the Persian provinces was governed by a **satrap** (SAY-trap) ("protector of the kingdom"), an official who ruled according to established laws and paid a fixed amount of taxes to the king each year. The Persians had several grand capitals, including Babylon and Susa (SOO-zuh) in Mesopotamia, before Persepolis was completed. Communications were aided by the "royal road" stretching 1,700 miles from east to west. A messenger of the

satrap ("protector of the kingdom") A Persian official who ruled according to established laws and procedures and paid a fixed amount of taxes to the emperor each year.

Oriental Institute, University of Chicago, Photo #P57121

Bas Relief of Darius and Xerxes Holding Court This relief was carved in one of the palaces at the Persian capital of Persepolis.

Map 7.1
The Persian Empire, ca. 500 B.C.E.

At its height around 500 B.C.E., the Persians controlled a huge empire that included northern Greece, Egypt, and most of western Asia from the Mediterranean coast to the Indus River in India.

Interactive Map

king could travel the road by horse in nineteen days. The Persians became famous for building roads and then protecting those who traveled them. The Greek historian Herodotus marveled at the communication network, writing that "neither snow, nor rain, nor heat, nor darkness of night prevents these couriers from completing their designated stages with utmost speed."[4]

Persian Economy

The highways promoted economic growth and exchange, a second Achaemenid practice that strengthened their empire. The use of standard weights and measures, along with minted coins of recognized value, fostered trade throughout the empire. In addition, the Persian rulers did not steal the wealth of the conquered lands but allowed conquered peoples to continue to benefit from the same economic activities as before. Phoenicians, for example, continued their Mediterranean trade. To open new networks for exchanging goods and technologies, Darius sent an expedition to India that returned by sailing around Arabia to Suez. This expedition laid the foundation for the conquest of the Indus River Valley and also more maritime trade.

Cultural Mixing

Perhaps most crucial to their imperial success, the Persians generally treated the people they conquered with respect, allowing them to maintain their own social and religious institutions. In Egypt, for instance, Cambyses was a pharaoh, not a Persian ruler. The Persians prided themselves on their ability to unify vastly different peoples under the "king of kings," a title that respected other rulers with limited rights in their own territories. For this reason, many Greeks fought for Persia in the Greco-Persian Wars.

The Persians also utilized various official languages. Eventually, Aramaic **(ar-uh-MAY-ik)**, spoken by many peoples of western Asia, became the official language. After a time Greek also was widely used. Herodotus reported of the Persians that "there is no nation which so readily adopts foreign customs. As soon as they hear of any luxury, they instantly make it their own."[5]

Persian Religion and Society

The Persians made another distinct contribution to later world history in their promotion of **Zoroastrianism** (zo-ro-ASS-tree-uh-niz-uhm), a religion founded by Zoroaster (whose name means "With Golden Camels") that later became the state religion of Persia. Some of the key ideas in Judaism, Christianity, and Islam are foreshadowed by, and perhaps even derived from, Zoroastrianism. Zoroaster was one of the first non-Hebrew religious leaders to challenge the prevailing polytheism. Scholars debate whether he lived between 630 and 550 B.C.E., as earlier studies concluded, or centuries earlier, perhaps around 1000 or 1200 B.C.E., as some recent studies suggest. He may have been a priest in the early Persian religion, which was closely related to the religion of the Aryans who migrated to India.

Zoroastrianism A monotheistic religion founded by the Persian Zoroaster, and later the state religion of Persia. Its notion of one god opposed by the devil may have influenced Judaism and later Christianity.

Zoroaster had a monotheistic vision of one supreme god, **Ahura Mazda** (ah-HOOR-uh MAZZ-duh) (the "Wise Lord"), who was opposed by an evil spirit, a Satan-like figure who was the source of lies, cowardice, and evil (see Witness to the Past: Good, Evil, and Monotheism in Zoroastrian Thought). Ahura Mazda allowed humans to freely choose between himself and evil, between heaven and hell. By serving Ahura Mazda, men and women were promoting ultimate goodness and truth. At the end of time, Zoroaster believed, Ahura Mazda would win a final victory over the spirit of evil and even hell would come to an end. Zoraster also banned use of intoxicants and animal sacrifice. However, some Persians worshipped other gods and several religions coexisted in Persia.

Ahura Mazda (the "Wise Lord") The one god of Zoroastrianism.

The Zoroastrian Legacy

The Jews may have adopted some of their religious ideas about good and evil, God and the devil, heaven and hell, and a last judgment from Zoroastrians while the Jews were held captive in Babylon (586–539 B.C.E.). Such ideas were later incorporated into Christianity, and the Zoroastrian watchwords of "good thoughts, good words, good deeds" also became key ideas of other religions. Darius I did much to spread Zoroastrianism, publicly attributing his victories to Ahura Mazda and honoring him for creating earth, sky, and humankind. While Zoroastrianism was displaced in western Asia by Christianity and, later, Islam, the faith lives on today among small groups in Iran as well as in the wealthy Parsee (PAR-see) minority in India, descendants of Persian Zoroastrians.

Persian Class System

The Persians did not develop as politically diversified a society as did the Greeks. At the top of the system were the nobles, many of them warriors who had been granted large estates by the king, followed by priests, merchants, and bankers. In Babylonian cities ruled by Persia these citizens met in formal assemblies to make important judicial decisions. Zoroastrian priests schooled the princes of the noble families to prepare for government careers. The middle class included brewers, butchers, bakers, carpenters, potters, and coppersmiths. Peasants and slaves constituted the bottom of the social structure. Many peasant farmers were impoverished, becoming poor renters or sharecroppers bound to the land. Slaves, mainly debtors, criminals, and prisoners of war, filled various functions. Some were apprenticed in trades while others operated small businesses.

Families and Gender Relations

Persian society was patriarchal and polygamous. Persian men believed that the greatest proof of masculinity was to father many sons, and many, especially at upper levels, had several wives. Persian women were usually kept secluded in harems and probably veiled themselves, an ancient practice in western Asia. But some queens and other noble women exercised strong influences on their husbands, and many even controlled large estates. A few women became independently wealthy. For instance, one entrepreneur of commoner origins, Irdabama, was a major landowner who not only controlled a large labor force of several hundred but also operated her own grain and wine business.

Warfare and Persian Decline

First Greco-Persian War

Darius and his successors eventually encountered some major problems. Darius campaigned unsuccessfully against the Scythians (SITH-ee-uhnz), warlike Indo-European pastoral nomads whose territory stretched from Ukraine to Mongolia. Skilled horsemen and master workers of gold and bronze, the Scythians had both fought and traded with the Greek cities. A more serious defeat came with the first Greco-Persian War, in which the tiny disunited Greek states turned back the world's most powerful empire. Persians and Greeks were rivals for regional power, but many Greeks lived in Persian territories. Inspired by Scythian resistance to Darius, some Greek cities on the Ionian (eye-OH-nee-uhn) coast of Anatolia rebelled against Persian control (see Map 7.1). In response Darius decided to attack the cities on the Greek peninsula that supported the Ionian Greek rebels. While the Persians failed to occupy most of Greece, they reclaimed the Ionian Greek cities, brutally punishing the most rebellious. Darius then turned to favoring democratic forces in Ionian cities, a tactical move he unrealistically hoped would inspire democrats in the peninsula to cooperate with Persian aims.

Second Greco-Persian War

Xerxes (r. 486–465 B.C.E.), the son of Darius, tried again to conquer the Greeks in 480 B.C.E., attacking with a huge army and naval force; the result was a fierce two-year struggle. Perhaps

Good, Evil, and Monotheism in Zoroastrian Thought

The Persian thinker Zarathustra, better known today as Zoroaster, the name given him by the Greeks, offered an ethical vision that, he believed, came from God. The early Persians apparently believed in three great gods and many lesser ones, but Zoroaster preached that only one of these, *Ahura Mazda* (the "Wise Lord"), was the supreme deity in the universe, responsible for creation and the source of all goodness. A rival entity, Angra Mainyu ("Hostile Spirit"), embodied evil and was the source of all misery and sin. Zoroaster asked people to join the cosmic battle for good and worship Ahura Mazda while opposing evil and Angra Mainyu, referred to as the Liar. This excerpt outlining Zoroaster's beliefs comes from one of the devotional hymns, the Gathas, contained within the Zoroastrian holy scriptures. It was written down in final form centuries after Zoroaster's life but was probably based on earlier writings by the prophet or his disciples.

Then shall I recognize you as strong and holy, Mazda, when by the hand in which you yourself hold the destinies that you will assign to the Liar [Angra Mainyu] and the Righteous [Ahura Mazda] . . . the might of Good Thought shall come to me.

As the holy one I recognized you, [Ahura Mazda], when I saw you in the beginning at the birth of Life, when you made actions and words to have their reward—evil for the evil, a good Destiny for the good—through your wisdom when creation shall reach its goal. At which goal you will come with your holy Spirit, O Mazda, with Dominion, at the same with Good Thought, by whose action the settlements [human societies] will prosper through Right. . . .

"I am Zarathustra, a true foe to the Liar, to the utmost of my power, but a powerful support would I be to the Righteous, that I may attain the future things of the infinite Dominion, so I praise and proclaim you, Mazda. . . ."

As the holy one I recognized you, [Ahura Mazda], when Good Thought [a good spirit created by Ahura Mazda] came to me, when the still mind taught me to declare what is best: "Let not a man seek again and again to please the Liars, for they make all the righteous enemies."

And thus Zarathustra himself . . . chooses the spirit of thine that is holiest, Mazda. May Right be embodied, full of life and strength! May Piety abide in the Dominion where the sun shines! May Good Thought give destiny to men according to their works [good actions]!

This I ask you, tell me truly, Ahura. . . . Who determined the path of sun and stars? Who is it by whom the moon waxes and wanes again? . . . Who upheld the Earth beneath and the firmament from falling? Who the water and the plants? Who yoked swiftness to winds and clouds? . . .

This I ask you, tell me truly, Ahura—whether we shall drive the Lie away from us to those who being full of disobedience will not strive after fellowship with Right, nor trouble themselves with counsel of Good Thought. . . .

I will speak of that which [Ahura Mazda], the all-knowing, revealed to me first in this earthly life. Those of you that put not into practice this word as I think and utter it, to them shall be woe at the end of life. I will speak of that which the Holiest declared to me as the word that is best for mortals to obey: he, [Ahura Mazda] said, "They who at my bidding render [Zarathustra] obedience, shall all attain Welfare and Immortality by the actions of the Good Spirit." In immortality shall the soul of the righteous be joyful, in perpetuity shall be the torments of the Liars [the followers of evil]. All this does [Ahura Mazda] appoint by his Dominion.

THINKING ABOUT THE READING

1. What supreme powers did Zoroaster attribute to Ahura Mazda?
2. How did Zoroaster expect individuals to work for good and combat evil?
3. What fate awaited those who chose the path of evil?

Source: Yasnas 43–45, in James Hope Moulton, *Early Zoroastrianism* (London: Williams and Norgate, 1913), 364–370.

Xerxes' most effective ally was the Ionian Greek Queen Artemisia **(AHRT-uh-MIZH-ee-uh)**, who was praised for her bravery and the wise counsel she gave the Persian king. But the Persian thrust failed. Although Xerxes still held a large chunk of the Greek world and regained control of Egypt, defeat in this second Greco-Persian War was a turning point in Persian history.

Persian Collapse

The Persian Empire was not finally conquered until the army of Alexander the Great defeated Persian forces in 330 B.C.E., but the seeds of decline were planted when Xerxes imposed heavy taxation on the satrapies, weakening support for Persian rule. By 424 B.C.E. the Persian Empire was suffering from civil unrest caused by fights within the Achaemenid family, currency inflation, and difficulty collecting taxes. Under Xerxes and his successors, the wise policies of Cyrus and Darius were gradually reversed. Many merchants and landlords were ruined by having to borrow money at very high interest rates, and fewer attempts were made to include other ethnic groups in governing. Some regions rebelled. For example, Egypt ended Persian control in 404 B.C.E. and restored pharaonic rule. Thus support for the increasingly remote kings weakened long before Alexander's superior armies ended Achaemenid Persia and its once-great empire.

SECTION SUMMARY

- The Persian Empire, centered on a trade crossroads, was larger than any empire that preceded it.
- The Persians often won the support of peoples they had conquered through their respect for native cultures and their institution of the rule of law.
- The monotheistic Persian religion, Zoroastrianism, may have contributed some key ideas to Judaism, Christianity, and Islam.
- The Persian Empire suffered several setbacks, including an unsuccessful campaign against the Scythians and repeated failure to completely conquer Greece.
- Though the Persian Empire was conquered by Alexander the Great in 330 B.C.E., it had begun to decline over a century earlier.

THE RISE AND FLOWERING OF THE GREEKS

What were some features of Greek government, philosophy, and science?

When people today think of the classical Greeks, they envision the "golden age" of Athenian democracy, with philosophers debating the meaning of life and thinkers pondering the mysteries of science, but these were only part of a complex, often conflicted society. The Greeks had to struggle to forge democracy. How much of their culture the Greeks created and how much they adopted from others remains subject to debate. The Mediterranean was a zone of interaction for peoples living around its rim, and by 700 B.C.E. the Greeks became active participants in maritime trade. Soon this activity led to prosperity and new forms of government. Like people today, they debated how populations should be ruled, how leaders should be chosen, and how youngsters should be educated. But the Greek society modern people admire was also far from egalitarian and had many unattractive features.

polis A Greek city-state that embraced nearby rural areas, whose agricultural surplus then helped support the urban population.

oligarchy Rule by a small group of wealthy leaders.

The Greek City-States

The Greek world was shaped by varied influences. Mountainous terrain, coastal plains, and scattered islands encouraged the development of many city-states rather than one centralized state, as well as the maritime trade that fostered growth and prosperity between 800 and 500 B.C.E. (see Chronology: The Greeks, 750–338 B.C.E.). A growing population, a shortage of good farmland at home, and commercial interests led many Greeks to leave their home cities to establish new settlements along the Ionian coast, around the Black Sea, in Italy, and even the Mediterranean coasts of France and Spain (see Map 7.2). Trade and migration opened the Greeks to new ideas. Greeks even visited and lived in Egypt.

Prosperity led to a new conception of the city and the citizen's role in it. The result was the **polis** (POE-lis), a city-state that became the major institution of classical Greek life and gave citizens a sense of community, loyalty, personal identity, and meaning. All business, from building a new temple to making war, was decided by the free male citizens meeting in an open assembly. The worst punishment a Greek could suffer was being asked to leave the polis. Some Greeks committed suicide rather than face ostracism. City-states competed fiercely with each other, including in sports events. The Olympic Games, begun in the eighth century B.C.E., were associated with a religious festival to honor the god Zeus. Each polis sent athletes who competed naked in track and field events or personal contests of strength, such as wrestling. The idea was to win, even if it meant cheating.

Not all inhabitants of the polis were equal. Many cities developed **oligarchy** (AHL-uh-gar-kee), rule by a small group of wealthy leaders. As much as 80 percent of the population, including women, slaves, children, and resident foreigners, were not citizens and thus had no right to vote or hold office. Even among the citizens, members of old, aristocratic families were treated with greater respect than others. By the seventh century, however, aristocratic power weakened. Although aristocrats generally scorned trade in favor of the wealth to be gained from owning land, the growing trade created wealth for other citizens, allowing them to compete with the upper class. Furthermore, a new battle formation was developed that relied

CHRONOLOGY
The Greeks, 750–338 B.C.E.

ca. 750–550 B.C.E. Greek colonization in Mediterranean, Black Sea

ca. 594 B.C.E. Solon's reforms in Athens

561–527 B.C.E. Peisistratus tyrant in Athens

507 B.C.E. Athenian democracy under Cleisthenes

499–479 B.C.E. Greco-Persian Wars

477 B.C.E. Founding of Delian League

469–399 B.C.E. Life of Socrates

ca. 460–429 B.C.E. Era of Pericles in Athens

431–404 B.C.E. Peloponnesian War

428–347 B.C.E. Life of Plato

384–322 B.C.E. Life of Aristotle

338 B.C.E. Philip of Macedonia's conquest of Greece

Map 7.2
Classical Greece, ca. 450 B.C.E.

Greek settlements, divided into rival city-states, occupied not only the Greek peninsula but also Crete and western Anatolia. Two alliances headed by Athens and Sparta fought each other in the Peloponnesian War (431–404 B.C.E.).

on infantry more than the aristocracy-dominated cavalry. The city of Sparta perfected an infantry formation, the phalanx **(FAY-langks)**, that other cities quickly adopted. The phalanx consisted of a square of soldiers that moved in unison, each man protected with heavy armor and carrying a sword or spear. Greek armies became citizen-armies, not paid professional forces. As men other than aristocrats risked their lives for their polis, they wanted a greater role in governing it.

Roots of Democracy

The new military system, combined with population expansion and increased wealth from trade with the Greek cities in Ionia, contributed to the rise of democracy. Some Greeks tried to combine the contradictory ideas that people are politically free and that they also owe their loyalty to the community. Some Greeks also discovered how people could live with each other without being controlled by gods or kings, and many cities developed notions of political freedom and equality for adult male citizens. These were radical ideas for that era, or even for ours.

Athenian Political Change

Reform, Tyranny, and Democracy in Athens

The most dramatic political changes occurred in Athens, a polis on the eastern Greek peninsula of Attica. Athens became progressively more democratic, partly as a result of a crisis. The soil was wearing out, and farmers borrowed money and went deeply into debt. As the bad wheat harvests continued, farmers sold themselves and their families into slavery. The poor demanded reform. Around 594 B.C.E. the Athenians elected Solon **(SOH-luhn)**, a general, poet, and merchant, to lead the city and rewrite the old constitution. To avoid civil war, he canceled the debts of the poor, forbade enslavement for default of debts, made wealth rather than birth the criterion for membership on the council that controlled the city, and established a Council of 400 to review issues before they came before an Assembly of Citizens, which now served as a court of appeals where people, rich or poor, could bring a case to court. However, he also reduced the freedom of women by, for example, allowing fathers to sell into slavery daughters who lost their virginity before marriage.

Stages of Democracy

The Athenian path to a more democratic system came in several stages, from reform to tyranny to democracy. Solon's reforms failed to please either side in this social and economic struggle. The poor wanted him to give them land from the rich, while the aristocrats resented their loss of power. Tensions returned, allowing Peisistratus **(pie-SIS-truht-uhs)** (r. 561–527 B.C.E.) to seize power as a **tyrant**, not necessarily a brutal ruler but someone who ruled outside the law. Peisistratus gave the poor land he had confiscated from aristocratic estates and launched a building program, including an aqueduct to bring water directly to the city center.

tyrant Someone who ruled a Greek polis outside the law, not necessarily a brutal ruler.

Another aristocrat, Cleisthenes **(KLICE-thuh-neez)**, established genuine democracy in Athens in 507 B.C.E. Instead of emphasizing noble birth or wealth as a criterion of citizenship, Cleisthenes created geographical units that chose people by lot to serve in a new Council of 500. The council submitted legislation to the Assembly, which consisted of 40,000 citizens who also selected by lot the city officials. In the mid-fifth century the power of the aristocrats was further reduced, and lower-income citizens were allowed to serve as officials. Euripides **(you-RIP-uh-deez)** described the system in his play, *The Suppliant Woman*: "The city is free, and ruled by no one man. The people reign, in annual succession. They do not yield power to the rich; the poor man has an equal share in it."[6] The Athenians believed that ordinary citizens could serve in any government positions except as military officers, and they chose representatives by lot rather than by more divisive elections. However, only a small aristocracy of adult males enjoyed these rights. Moreover, many Greeks did not think that democracy of any type was a good thing.

The Spartan System

Military Power

In the Peloponnese **(PELL-eh-puh-NEESE)** peninsula in southern Greece, the landlocked city-state of Sparta followed a course much different from that of Athens (see Map 7.2). Spartans saw military power as essential to their prestige and influence. When the Spartans found themselves short of land, they conquered their neighbors rather than establish overseas colonies, then made the conquered peoples agricultural slaves with no political or human rights; slaves could be killed by a Spartan almost at will. Since slaves outnumbered Spartans ten to one, Sparta developed a rigid military state, led by two kings and a Council of Elders who were elected for life by an Assembly of all citizens over thirty. The Assembly could vote only yes or no to measures prepared for it by the Council of Elders and the king. Thus the Spartans discouraged independence of thought or behavior. Spartan boys who seemed physically unfit were generally taken to a remote rural area and allowed to die. The other boys were given a rigid military training and taught that self-discipline and courage were the highest virtues. One legend tells of a young boy who found a small fox and concealed it under his shirt while engaged in military drill. While standing quietly at attention, the boy suddenly fell over dead. The fox had eaten into his vital organs, but self-discipline had kept him from crying out in pain. From ages twenty to thirty, Spartan males served in the army, and they were allowed to live at home with their wives only after this time.

Scala/Art Resource, NY

Narrative Drawing on Pottery The Francois vase, made around 570 B.C.E., is considered a masterpiece of narrative drawing on pottery, with fine detail and vivid coloring. It shows scenes of battle.

Although enjoying no political rights, Spartan women acquired a higher status than other Greek women, and their husbands' frequent absences from home allowed some of them to acquire wealth and land. Athenian men criticized Spartan women for their independence, portraying them as greedy, licentious, and needing male control. The playwright Euripides scolded the "Spartan maidens, allowed out of doors with the young men, running and wrestling in their company, with naked thighs."[7]

Religion, Rationalism, and Science

The Greeks may have been practical people, but they were also concerned with the supernatural realm. The multitude of gods and legends introduced by the Homeric epics profoundly shaped

Greek thinking and values, although Greek religion also owed something to the Egyptians and Phoenicians. Chief gods and goddesses represented various natural and human activities. Zeus, a sky-god who guaranteed the natural and social order, was the leader. His wife, Hera (HEER-uh), represented marriage and the family. Poseidon (puh-SIDE-uhn), the brother of Zeus, was the lord of the sea. Athena, Zeus's favorite daughter, was the goddess of wisdom. Other notable deities were Apollo, patron of music, philosophy, and other finer things in life; Dionysus (DIE-uh-NYE-suhs), the god of wine; and Aphrodite (af-ruh-DITE-ee), goddess of sex and fertility. Although these gods and goddesses had human virtues and vices, they were also seen as immortal and more powerful than humans. To defy the gods was to invite disaster. Proper sacrifices to the gods, usually incorporated into festivals and official ceremonies, guaranteed harmony between humans and the heavens.

Rational Thought

Interest in the deeper meaning of life also led the Greeks to develop a rational approach to the search for truth. They produced some of history's greatest thinkers, joining the Mesopotamians, Egyptians, Indians, and Chinese in laying the foundation for modern science. Some Greek thinkers questioned supernatural explanations of natural events. The Ionian philosopher Xenophanes (zi-NAHF-uh-neez) was skeptical of the gods:

> *Mortals deem that the gods are begotten as they [humans] are, and have clothes like theirs and voice and form. . . . The Ethiopians make their gods black. The Thracians* (THRAY-shuhns) *say theirs have blue eyes and red hair.*[8]

Scientific Thought

Creative thought erupted throughout the Greek world. Thales of Miletus (ca. 636–546) was the first person we know of to perceive the universe as orderly and to seek a natural explanation of phenomena rather than attributing them to gods. Anaximander of Miletus (611–547) said the first creatures lived in water and came close to the idea, developed several millennia later, that human beings evolved from lower forms of life. Democritus (di-MAHK-ruht-uhs) announced his belief that all matter was composed of tiny seeds known as atoms and that these moved, creating different objects. Heracleitus (HER-uh-KLITE-uhs) of Ephasus (EF-uh-suhs) in Ionia declared that the universe is in a constant state of flux and that only change was permanent. The Ionian Pythagoras (puh-THAG-uh-ruhs) helped establish the foundations of modern mathematics by emphasizing the number 10 and developing the multiplication tables as well as major mathematical theorems.

These early thinkers laid the foundations of natural science and philosophy by emphasizing the explanatory power of human reason and evaluating evidence by human rather than divine standards. However, some Greek thinkers also opened the door to the more troubling idea that human standards are relative rather than absolute. The **Sophists** (SAHF-uhsts) emphasized skepticism and the belief that there is no ultimate truth. People have struggled with this twin legacy of Greek thinkers ever since.

Sophists Thinkers in classical Greece who emphasized skepticism and the belief that there is no ultimate truth.

Axial Age Philosophy and Thinkers

Axial Age Thinkers

Views of the Greek contribution to world thought often focus on the specific ideas of three major fifth- and fourth-century Athenian thinkers. The first two, Socrates and Plato, studied the nature of truth; the third, Aristotle (AR-uh-staht-uhl), examined the truth to be found in nature. These men were part of an outpouring of philosophical and religious genius across Eurasia between 600 and 200 B.C.E. that historians often term the Axial Age. The ideas of Buddha in India, Confucius in China, Hebrew prophets, Zoroaster, and various Greeks shaped classical societies and remained influential for many centuries.

Socrates

The earliest Greek philosophical giant, the Athenian Socrates (469–399 B.C.E.), believed that "the unexamined life" was not worth living. Shabbily dressed, eccentric, passionate, and indifferent to money and pleasure, he spent much time asking people leading questions that helped them examine the truth of their ideas, an approach called the **Socratic Method**. Unlike the Sophists, Socrates believed in absolute truths that would make people virtuous. But he also was suspicious of democracy, favoring government by the chosen few who had acquired superior knowledge. Although often credited as the founder of Western moral philosophy, some of his elitist views might be unpopular even today. For undermining the polis by asking so many, often embarrassing, questions and "corrupting the youth," Socrates was condemned to death for treason by the citizens of Athens in 399 B.C.E. The prosecutor said of him: "Socrates is an evil doer and a curious person, searching into things under the earth and above the heavens, and making the worse appear the better, and teaching all this to others."[9] Although he could have secured a lighter sentence or gone into exile, Socrates chose death, making him, in modern eyes at least, a

Socratic Method The method, introduced by Socrates, of asking people leading questions to help them examine the truth of their ideas.

martyr for truth and free expression, although most of his contemporaries may not have viewed him in this way.

Socrates' leading pupil, Plato (428–347 B.C.E.), became disillusioned with city politics after his mentor's execution. After a sojourn in Egypt, Plato founded a school in Athens that he called the Academy (the source of our word *academic*). Plato elaborated Socrates' belief in ultimate truth, beauty, and goodness, but he believed most people are ruled by emotions and cannot see reality. Only a special class, the Guardians, trained to use reason to control the emotions and will, can understand ultimate truth and goodness and therefore should govern. Later in his life, Plato retreated from this elitist conception and suggested that strong laws could control democratic excesses. Some charge that Plato's thinking sanctioned dictatorships in which a small group of men claimed special wisdom and virtue.

Aristotle (384–322 B.C.E.) was the Athenian philosopher whose ideas seem most similar to ours today. The son of a Greek physician working for the king of Macedonia, Aristotle came to Athens to study philosophy with Plato and eventually founded a school of his own. Like Socrates, he was charged with impiety, but he chose to go into exile. Aristotle offered many enduring insights. Although he distrusted democracy, he encouraged people to pursue their personal desires. Aristotle was pragmatic, emphasizing how human nature and physical nature worked rather than exploring the ultimate truths that lay behind our actions. His writings spanned the social sciences, humanities, and natural sciences. He was also one of the first psychologists, describing human emotions like affection, anger, bravery, fear, hate, joy, and pity. Aristotle was particularly interested in classifying and analyzing nature and dissecting animals, and he was the first to classify animals zoologically. His work was a key foundation for both Western and Islamic science. He also wrote works on logic and ethics and studied political systems. In philosophy, he speculated on **metaphysics**, the broad field that studies the most general concepts and categories underlying people and the world around them (such as "time" and "causation").

HIP/Art Resource, NY

Socrates This statue, made several centuries after his death, celebrates the Athenian philosopher Socrates, who had a strong influence on the thinking of Greek philosophers who came after him, including his student, Plato.

Literature

Greek cultural creativity, especially in Athens, reflected dynamism and freedom. Athens attracted many great writers and artists because prosperity generated spending money for entertainment. Perhaps the Athenians' most enduring contribution, drama, arose from annual religious festivals and was based on historical or mythological themes. Plays, which were mostly tragedies, were usually performed in outdoor amphitheaters and accompanied by music. The dramatists had different styles. Aeschylus **(ESS-kuh-luhs)** (525–456 B.C.E.) emphasized traditional values, the gods, and justice issues while portraying the disasters brought on by too much pride. Sophocles **(SAUF-uh-klees)** (ca. 497–406 B.C.E.) was a humanist, treating emotional issues with restraint. Aristophanes **(AR-uh-STAHF-uh-neez)** (448–380 B.C.E.) wrote comedies that ridiculed Athenians and their pretensions. For example, in *The Knights*, a general tries to convince an ignorant sausage seller to unseat the Athenian leader: "To be a leader of the people isn't for learned men, or honest men, but for the ignorant and vile."[10] Some of his criticism reflected Athenian losses during a terrible war. Some playwrights also offered vivid images of women who refused to be silenced or abused. In *Agamemnon* **(ag-uh-MEM-non)**, a great tragic drama by Aeschylus, the wife of Agamemnon, the hero of the Trojan War, kills him upon his return for sacrificing their daughter to the gods to get a favorable wind to sail to Troy.

Greek lyric poets, especially in the Ionian cities, reflected an individualistic and openly intellectual way of thinking. For example, in contrast to Spartan heroism, Archilochus **(ahr-KIL-uh-kuhs)** mocked the Spartan order to their soldiers to "return with your shield—or on it," writing: "Some lucky Thracian has my shield, For, being somewhat flurried, I dropped it by a wayside bush, As from the field I hurried. To blazes with the shield. I'll get another just as good, When next I take the field."[11] Perhaps the most intensely personal poet was Sappho **(SAFF-oh)**, from the Ionian island of Lesbos. A director of a girl's school, Sappho wrote passionate love lyrics to her students: "A host of horsemen, some say, is the loveliest sight upon the earth; some say a display of soldiery; some a fleet of ships, but I say it's whomever one loves."[12] Sappho was considered the equal of Homer as a poet, and her poems were read in the Mediterranean world long after her death.

metaphysics The broad field that studies the most general concepts and categories underlying people and the world around them (such as "time" and "causation").

Aristotle on Politics Discover the strengths and weaknesses, as Aristotle saw it, of kingdoms, aristocracies, and democracies.

Greek Society

Social Classes

The differences between social classes and genders were pronounced. Freedom was reserved primarily for males. Greek society consisted, from top to bottom, of free men (only some of whom were citizens), many resident foreigners, free women, and slaves. Most free men, if not wealthy landowners or small farmers, worked as laborers, artisans, or shopkeepers. Resident foreigners, including Phoenicians, Lydians, and Syrians, were primarily merchants, bankers, and artisans. Many became wealthy, and they were required to serve in the military. Free women could not vote, hold office, or serve on juries. Socrates supposedly asked a colleague: "Is there anyone of your acquaintance with whom you have less conversation than your wife?" The reply: "Hardly anyone, I think."[13] Women from elite families generally stayed inside the home, in contrast to many less affluent women.

Slavery

About one-third of the population were slaves, mostly captives taken in battle or debtors. Slaves were often household servants or paid artisans, but many served as teachers, instructing generations of young people how to write and play music. Slaves also built some of the great buildings and worked on agricultural plantations or in mines owned by aristocrats. Life for many was harsh; slaves could be tortured and executed for mere suspicion of a crime.

Women Fetching Water The painting on this vase portrays everyday life in a Greek city. Women have congregated at a public fountain to fill jugs with water to be carried back home, where it will be used for drinking, cooking, and cleaning. The women's hair coverings and long robes reflect the fashion of the day.

Like the nuclear family system of the modern West but unlike the extended family pattern of many African and Asian societies, most Greek families consisted of a husband, a wife, and children. The principal tasks of women were to feed and clothe their families and to bear and raise children. While a woman did not have the same sexual freedom as men, she could own property and divorce her husband. Women's participation was also essential in religious festivals. For example, the oracle at the temple of Delphi **(DELL-fye)**, which many leaders consulted to determine the will of Apollo, spoke through a woman's voice.

But women also experienced strong prejudice in a patriarchal society. Aristotle articulated the misogynist, or antiwoman, views of many men when he described women as deformed males. A popular saying expressed male views: "Respectable women should stay at home; the street is for worthless hussies." Some women expressed their discontent, as reflected in a tragic play by Euripides: "[Men] say we lead a safe life at home. What imbeciles! I'd rather stand to arms three times than bear one child."[14] In contrast to their role in politics, in Greek literature women are often powerful and capable of great anger, humor, faithfulness, and intelligence. The last two are the chief qualities of Penelope, the wife of Ulysses in Homer's *Odyssey* who waits patiently for her husband, ruling the state wisely until his return while escaping the clutches of many men who want to marry her. In the bawdy comedy *Lysistrata* **(lis-uh-STRAH-tuh)** by Aristophanes, a group of women organize to end war by refusing to have sex with their husbands until the men stop fighting. Lysistrata tells her husband: "We women got together and decided we were going to save Greece. Listen to us and keep quiet, as we've had to do up to now, and we'll clear up the mess you've made."[15]

Scala/Art Resource, NY

Some social customs might be considered controversial today. While their wives stayed at home, men attended parties, sometimes enlivened by the presence of courtesans celebrated for their wit and charm. Some courtesans had high status as free people and probably a good education, such as Aspasia **(ass-PAY-zhee-uh)**, a vivacious, literate Milesian who operated a meetinghouse in Athens where educated men came for sex and conversation with intellectual women. An advocate of gender equality, Aspasia became the mistress of the Athenian leader Pericles **(PER-eh-kleez)**, whose enemies accused her of writing his speeches, violating the tradition that politics was for men only. But most prostitutes were slaves whose lives were far different from Aspasia's.

Homosexuality has existed in all societies from earliest times, but Greek men were particularly open about their same-sex relationships. Artists fashioned many naturalistic statues of naked men and women. Diverse homosexual practices and relationships were tolerated. For example, homosexual behavior between older and younger upper-class men was accepted as part of a training or mentoring relationship for career preparation, and many famous Greeks had such relationships. In Sparta some top military units comprised homosexual couples. Boys and girls were often brought up separately, reducing heterosexual contact. But we must not assume that the concepts of same-sex or even opposite-sex relationships 2,500 years ago were precisely the same as those today.

In general, men of superior status took for granted that, with or without consent, they could have intimate relations with anyone of inferior status, including servants, slaves, and foreigners. In contrast, nonelite Greeks often condemned homosexual relations between two adults.

SECTION SUMMARY

- The mountainous, maritime geography of Greece fostered the development of multiple city-states rather than one centralized state.
- The polis system of governance allowed extensive political rights for some but no political rights for many.
- Increased trade and the rise of the infantry reduced the power of Greek aristocrats.
- After a period of reform and tyranny, Athens emerged as a democracy for the minority who were citizens.
- Sparta had the strongest army in Greece and often attacked its neighbors and enslaved them.
- Though Greeks had a well-developed religion, they were also notable for their commitment to using reason to understand the world.
- Three of the greatest Greek philosophers were Socrates, who believed in absolute truths; Plato, who described an ideal society in the *Republic;* and Aristotle, who explored human nature and the workings of the physical world.
- Greek drama tended to focus on tragedy, as in the works of Euripides, Aeschylus, and Sophocles; writers like Aristophanes wrote comedies.
- Greek women were generally expected to stay at home and out of politics, but they were often featured as powerful characters in plays.
- Homosexual relations among men were considered acceptable and were common among the upper classes.

Greeks, Persians, and the Regional System

In what ways did Persians and Greeks encounter and influence each other?

The Greeks and Persians fought and connected with each other as well as with other societies. During the early fifth century B.C.E. Greek cities successfully fought a series of wars with the greatest power of western Asia, the Persian Empire. But the rival Greek states also fought ruinous wars with each other. Both Greeks and Persians borrowed many ideas from neighboring peoples, including the Egyptians and western Asians. The legacy of classical Greece and Persia for Europe and the Middle East is subject to debate.

The Greco-Persian Wars

First Greek Victory

The Greco-Persian conflict began in 499 B.C.E., when some Greek cities in Persian-held Anatolia, supported by Athens, rebelled against their Persian overlords; they were defeated in 494. To punish the peninsular Greeks, the Persian king Darius I dispatched a fleet to Greece in 492, but storms destroyed his ships. He then sent a larger Persian force into Greece, which was defeated at the Battle of Marathon in northern Greece in 490 B.C.E. Herodotus reported that the Greeks carried out a slaughter and the Persians fell in heaps, many of them drowning in the sea.

Second Greek Victory

The Persians made another attempt to conquer the Greeks in 480 B.C.E., sparking the second war. Persia's King Xerxes sent a huge army, supported by the entire Persian navy, to engage an alliance led by Athens and Sparta. A Spartan force of three hundred fought to the death holding a strategic pass, but they were betrayed by some Greeks who showed the Persians a path around them. The Persians swept down into Athens and burned the city. Expecting final victory, they attacked the Athenian fleet trapped in the Bay of Salamis (SAL-uh-muhs). Surprisingly, the Greeks won the battle. The large Persian force was difficult to supply and control effectively, and the Athenians had also developed the world's most advanced fighting ship, the well-armored *trireme* (TRY-reem), which had three banks of oarsmen and deadly bronze rams. The following year (479) the Greeks defeated the remaining Persian infantry force at the battle of Plataea (pluh-TEE-uh). Some historians argue that the Greek victory over the Persians also led to a growing divide between "Europe" and "Asia," as the Greeks increasingly viewed themselves as different from, and superior to, the people to the east.

Empire and Conflict in the Greek World

Intra-Greek Warfare

Delian League A defensive league organized by Greek cities in the fifth century B.C.E. to defeat the Persians.

With the Persian threat ended, the old rivalries of the Greek cities reemerged. The period following the Greek victories was marked not only by great philosophers and playwrights but also by nearly constant warfare among Greek cities. To defeat the Persians the Greek cities had organized a defensive alliance, called the **Delian** (DEE-lee-uhn) **League**, led by the richest state and largest naval power, Athens, while other cities contributed funds or ships to the alliance. But in 467 the island of Naxos (NAK-suhs) tried to withdraw from the league and Athens refused, taking military action to stop Naxos. Some Athenians protested, worrying that a democracy, which allows varied opinions, could not manage an empire. But the Delian League had changed from a defensive alliance to an Athenian empire. In midcentury, Athens moved the league treasury to Athens and began to spend some of the money on Athenian civic improvements.

Periclean Athens

Peloponnesian War A long war between Athens and Sparta and their respective allies in 431–404 B.C.E. that resulted in the defeat of Athens.

Athens reached its golden age under Pericles (ca. 495–429 B.C.E.), a visionary leader and spellbinding orator whose reforms brought more democracy to the legal system. Athenians had many reasons to be proud of their city, especially of the magnificent public buildings, such as the Parthenon (PAHR-thuh-nahn), a temple dedicated to the city's patron goddess, Athena, on the hilltop known as the Acropolis (uh-KRAHP-uh-luhs). But while Athenians embraced self-fulfillment and individualism, not all of them believed in unrestrained freedom, fearing that too much pride or self-expression spelled trouble. Playwrights, poets, and historians all taught how pride or arrogance could lead to punishment by the gods and personal disaster. Despite the warnings, the Athenians' arrogance and pride in their city eventually brought disaster, as increasing resentment of Athenian power by rival cities generated the long **Peloponnesian War** (431–404 B.C.E.) between Athens and Sparta and their respective allies. In a famous "funeral oration" delivered in memory of dead Athenian soldiers, the city's nationalistic leader, Pericles (r. 460–429 B.C.E.), reportedly contrasted Athenian democratic institutions and equality before the law with Spartan discipline and lack of freedom:

> *. . . We are called a democracy, for the administration is in the hands of the many and not of the few. . . . I have dwelt upon the greatness of Athens because I want to show you we are contending for a higher prize than those who enjoy none of these privileges. For in magnifying the city I have magnified the men whose virtues made her glorious.*[16]

The Acropolis The Acropolis dominated the surrounding city of Athens. The marble Parthenon at the center, dedicated to Athena, was built during the time of Pericles.

Michael Freeman Photography

In this speech Pericles introduced the novel ideas that war was not just to defend hearth and home but to spread better ideas and systems, and also that citizens who enjoyed freedom had a responsibility to their community. The assumption that because they had such high ideals Athenians were superior to their neighbors was one of the reasons other Greek cities despised Athens.

Athenian Defeat

The war proved a disaster for Athens and a boon for Sparta. The Athenians' strategy was to use their navy to combat the superior land army of Sparta and its allies. But Athens was hit by a deadly plague in which a third of the population, including Pericles, died. The Athenians also blundered in an unwise attempt to capture Syracuse, a city founded by Greek settlers on Sicily. Later the Spartans, with Persian advice, destroyed the Athenian fleet. The victorious Spartans disbanded the Athenian navy, destroyed the city walls, and killed or exiled thousands of Athenians.

Although the war made Sparta the most powerful Greek state, decades of instability followed. The frequent conflicts between the Greek cities proved too destructive. Less than a century after the Peloponnesian War ended, Greece was conquered and became the base for a much greater empire led by the northern state of Macedonia.

Historiography: Universal and Critical

Concepts of History

The Greeks developed concepts of history that are still used today, but they did so in the context of their connections to other societies. Of course, peoples before them had some sense of history. The legends passed down through oral traditions, such as the stories in the Hebrew Bible and the Homeric epics, were narratives of history, although we cannot prove their accuracy. The Chinese also wrote historical accounts. But the Greeks were the first to pursue critical, analytical, and universal history. The two most famous Greek historians were Herodotus and Thucydides (thyou-SID-uh-deez).

Herodotus

Herodotus (ca. 484–425 B.C.E.) wrote history on a scale never attempted before, providing most of what we know of the Greco-Persian Wars. Integrating information on geography and cultural traditions, Herodotus wrote vividly about neighboring societies such as Persia and Egypt. Born in a Persian-ruled Ionian city, he traveled around the Persian Empire and sojourned in Egypt, concluding that some Greek gods could be equated with Egyptian divinities. He visited Tyre, where he learned that Phoenicians had invented the alphabet. A sophisticated man with an inquiring mind, Herodotus lived for a time in Athens and portrayed the Athenians favorably, attributing the Greek victory over the Persians to the Greeks' free society, which gave them more incentive than the armies of the absolute Persian monarch. Because his interests and travels went well beyond the Greek world, Herodotus might be considered the first world historian. Although he too often reported unverified hearsay and failed to subject all of his material to critical scrutiny, he did not adopt Greek prejudices against other cultures, offering sympathetic views of the Persians and criticisms of the Greeks.

Thucydides

Much of what we know about Greek politics and wars during the fifth century B.C.E. comes from a single book, *The Peloponnesian War*, written by Thucydides (ca. 460–ca. 400 B.C.E.), an Athenian general who was exiled from Athens for losing an important battle. Despite his exile, Thucydides objectively evaluated the strengths and weaknesses of his home city, setting an example of careful observation. Unlike earlier writers, he added critical judgments to his narrative, for example, criticizing the Athenians for ignoring Pericles' warnings to attempt no new conquests. He also evaluated the strengths and weaknesses of democracy and asked fundamental questions about the nature of power. Thucydides looked for patterns and moral lessons in the past. Whenever historians seek to interpret the past, they are acknowledging a debt to Thucydides, a historian who was not just a teller of tales but also a teacher of wisdom.

Interregional Trade and Cultural Mixing

Trade Networks

Throughout this time period the Mediterranean Basin remained a vast zone of exchange in which Greeks played the leading commercial role once dominated by Phoenicians, trading wine and olive oil through the eastern Mediterranean. They also established colonies and spread Greek culture. Like the Greeks, the Persians also welcomed foreign traders. Port cities like Persian-ruled Miletus in Ionia prospered as hubs of regional trade, and Persian gold coins were widely used in the Mediterranean Basin. Persian leaders patronized Greek traders living in their domains, and in 510 B.C.E. one of them, Scylax of Caryanda (SKY-lax of KAR-ee-AN-da), headed a Persian trade mission to India. Tribute flowed to the Persian capital, including camels from Arabia and Bactria, gold from India, horses from the Scythians, bulls from Egypt, leather goods from Anatolia, and silver from Ionia.

Long-distance trade was crucial to the Mediterranean world in many ways. Merchants traveling elsewhere to trade eventually evolved into what historians call a **trade diaspora**, living

trade diaspora Merchants from the same city or country who live permanently in foreign cities or countries.

permanently in foreign cities or countries. Most of the shipowners, traders, and moneylenders of Athens came from western Asia or from the Greek diaspora colonies such as Massalia (today's Marseilles) and the Crimea, and communities of expatriate Greek merchants were established in Egypt, western Asia, and around the Black Sea. Trade also contributed to the growth of a strong Athenian navy that helped the Greeks defeat the Persians. Athens became the leading Greek commercial and financial hub, controlling rich silver mines worked by over 20,000 slaves and importing huge amounts of wheat from Egypt, Sicily, and southern Russia. It developed a reputation as the most profitable and safest city to do business in, a place where even those of humble origins could achieve wealth.

Athens as a Hub

The Mediterranean Basin also provided a context for the intermingling of southern European, western Asian, and North African cultures. Though themselves highly creative, Persians and Greeks also learned much from other peoples. For example, Persians blended Ionian Greek, Mesopotamian, and Scythian art styles and motifs with their own traditions. Greeks were especially open to influences from the Phoenicians, Lydians, Egyptians, and Mesopotamians. Phoenician traders brought art forms and styles that inspired the Greeks to modify their columns, pottery, statues, and ceramic styles, and Greek music used many instruments and melodies from western Asia. The Greeks also adopted the Phoenician alphabet and several Phoenician, Egyptian, and Anatolian gods. In addition, many Greek colonists absorbed local influences. For example, Greeks in Massalia (modern Marseilles), on the southern coast of France, had to understand the local Celtic customs and language.

Cultural Exchange

Greeks visited, worked in, or settled in other societies, learning about other cultures. Many Ionian merchants lived in Egypt. The Athenian lawgiver Solon visited Egypt as a merchant, studied with priests, and wrote poems about living along the Nile. Some Egyptian medical ideas are found in his influential writings of the Athenian physician Hippocrates **(hip-AHK-ruh-teez)**. Some Greeks even fought as mercenaries for Egyptian kings and worshiped Egyptian gods. Other Greeks served in Mesopotamian and Persian armies. The scientist Democritus visited Babylonia and Persia, and both Plato and Aristotle knew something about Zoroastrianism. Cosmopolitan Ionia, where Greek and Asian cultures mixed, produced pathbreaking thinking in philosophy and science, often under Persian patronage. In fact, rational thinking appeared there earlier than in Athens. Thales, a Lydian subject, studied in Egypt, where he learned geometry; he was the first Greek to inscribe a right-angled triangle and to determine the sun's course from solstice to solstice, something the Babylonians had long known how to do. The Ionian-born mathematician Pythagoras (ca. 580–ca. 500 B.C.E.) may have visited Egypt and Babylon.

Greek Diaspora

The Persian and Greek Legacies

Persian Contributions

Both the Persians and Greeks influenced the peoples around them while leaving a rich legacy for later societies. Persians built the world's first large empire and multinational state, bringing together diverse societies under one flexible and tolerant canopy and fusing traditions from many cultures while spreading learning, such as Babylonian astronomy, to peoples such as the Greeks. Two thousand years later Persians still looked back to Cyrus the Great for inspiration. The Persians also made contributions to other cultures. Zoroastrian ideas influenced several religions, including Judaism, Christianity, and Islam, and many Persian words entered other languages. For example, the Persian word for "garden" became the English word *paradise*. Persian culture and language also strongly influenced Afghanistan and Central Asia. Under Persian rule, science and mathematics continued to develop in Ionia and Mesopotamia.

Many historians credit the Greeks with creating the Western tradition. They have admired the Greeks as the direct cultural, intellectual, and political ancestors of modern Europeans and North Americans, and they have perceived Greek society as culturally richer than any other before modern times. The Athenian era of Pericles, Plato, and Aeschylus is viewed as the "golden age" that launched Western literature, history, philosophy, science, and the democratic ideal. However, the view of Greece as the fountainhead of Western culture has problems. Some historians argue that the Romans founded the Western tradition. Perhaps, they suggest, the Greeks were an extension of the western Asian and North African societies that influenced them. From a modern perspective, the Greeks seem both very strange and quite familiar. Many Greek customs and social inequalities, especially their sometimes cruel

SECTION SUMMARY

- The Persians attacked the Greeks several times, but the Greeks, against great odds, fended them off.
- Following the Greek victory over the Persians, Athens's growing arrogance eventually led to the Peloponnesian War between Athens and Sparta, which ended with Spartan victory.
- Herodotus, who wrote of the Greco-Persian Wars, and Thucydides, who wrote of the Peloponnesian War, were the first historians to write critical and analytical history.
- The eastern Mediterranean and western Asia were zones of intense trade and cultural mixing.
- The long-held idea that the Greeks created the Western tradition is controversial, as are the merits of some Greek customs and ideas.

treatment of women and slaves, appall people today. To critics, Greek thinkers were not very liberal or secular, their democracy was elitist and flawed, and what ideas western Europe derived from the Greeks came in modified form through the Romans. Later, Europe rediscovered much of Greek thought through the Arabs. Moreover, modern science is based not only on Greek but also on Chinese, Indian, and Middle Eastern discoveries.

The debate suggests how fascinating the Greeks have been to various societies over the centuries, beginning with the Romans. Middle Eastern societies also treasured Greek thinkers and science, and Greek philosophy influenced some Islamic scholars. The debate also indicates that the Greeks, however imperfect their society, fostered ideas and institutions that were unusual for their time and that have endured for over two millennia.

The Hellenistic Age and Its Afro-Eurasian Legacies

What impact did Alexander the Great and his conquests have on world history?

Between 334 and 323 B.C.E., Alexander of Macedonia **(MASS-uh-DUHN-ia)**, a student of classical Greek ideas, created a huge empire, spreading Greek culture over a wide area. Alexander's achievements established new networks of communication, and his legacy lived on for centuries in **Hellenism**, a widespread culture that combined western Asian (mainly Persian) and Greek (Hellenic) characteristics. During the Hellenistic Age, Greeks ruled over large parts of western Asia and North Africa, a domination that ended only with the rise of the Roman Empire and new Persia-based empires that continued to influence Middle Eastern history.

Hellenism A widespread culture flourishing between 359 and 100 B.C.E. that combined western Asian (mainly Persian) and Greek (Hellenic) characteristics.

Alexander the Great, World Empire, and Hellenism

Macedonian Conquest

The Greek disunity spawned by the Peloponnesian War opened the door to the armies of Macedonia to conquer a vast empire. The war had so weakened all the Greek cities that no one city could unite the peninsula. That task was left to the state of Macedonia, on the northern fringe of Greece. Led by King Philip II (382–336 B.C.E.), who developed a paid professional army and devised a more effective infantry phalanx, the Macedonian army conquered the Greek cities in 338 B.C.E. (see Chronology: Hellenistic Age, 359–100 B.C.E.). Two years later, on the eve of an expedition to Asia, Philip was assassinated. The hard-living, hard-drinking Philip had many enemies among Greeks, Persians, and Macedonian nobles.

Rise of Alexander

Philip's twenty-year-old son, Alexander (r. 336–323 B.C.E.), a former student of Aristotle, became king. A fearless and resolute megalomaniac, his ambitions for conquest were evident as a child. Alexander reportedly lamented that, with such a multitude of other countries, it was a shame that he had not yet conquered even one of them. Later, he wrote to the Persian king that he was seeking vengeance on Persia for its invasions of Greece a century and half earlier. During his thirteen-year reign from 336 to his death in 323 B.C.E., Alexander, a brilliant military strategist and leader of men, used Macedonian, Greek, and mercenary troops to conquer the world from Greece east to western India, and from the Nile valley in the south to the Caucasus Mountains and the Black and Caspian Seas in the north. He employed ruthless tactics against enemies, sometimes destroying entire cities and slaughtering their inhabitants. The powerful Persian Empire was dismantled in three major battles between 334 and 331. The last Persian emperor, Darius III, was murdered by his own troops after Alexander had burned Persepolis and taken his place as Persian ruler. Alexander's forces then moved through Afghanistan, fighting difficult battles with the tough peoples of that mountainous region. The inhabitants destroyed their homes and farms rather than surrender. Many of Alexander's horses died and his grain ran out. Finally reaching the Indus Valley, the Macedonian wanted to move into the heart of India, but his exhausted and homesick troops refused to go farther. Alexander and his remaining troops made a difficult desert journey back to western Asia.

Extraordinary for the times, Alexander saw himself as a new world ruler, a governor to all peoples. His empire incorporated most of the major ancient Afro-Eurasian societies, including Egypt, Crete, Mycenae, Phoenicia, Mesopotamia, and

CHRONOLOGY

Hellenistic Age, 359–100 B.C.E.

359–336 B.C.E. Reign of King Philip of Macedonia

338 B.C.E. Philip's conquest of Greek states

336–323 B.C.E. Reign of Alexander the Great

332 B.C.E. Invasion of Egypt

330 B.C.E. Occupation of Persia

327–325 B.C.E. Invasion of India

306–30 B.C.E. Ptolemaic Egypt

238 B.C.E. Parthian state in Persia

141 B.C.E. Parthians' conquest of Seleucids

Alexander Defeating Persians at Battle of Issus In this Roman copy of an earlier Greek painting, Alexander the Great is shown on his horse in the battle that brought defeat to Persian king Darius III in 333 B.C.E.

Scala/Art Resource, NY

the Indus Valley. The burning of Persepolis symbolized the end of one era of cultural exchange and the beginning of another.

Alexander initially organized his empire like the Persians. Although he was probably bisexual or homosexual and continued to have an intimate relationship with a male adviser, Alexander married a princess from Bactria (northern Afghanistan) and encouraged his soldiers to take Asian wives. He adopted the dress of a Persian ruler, wearing a purple and white cloak and a head ribbon previously worn by Persian royalty. After Alexander died in Babylon at age thirty-three, probably from a fever acquired after a night of heavy drinking, the conquered territories would retain a mixed Greek and Persian cultural flavor for centuries under the influence of Hellenism.

The Hellenistic Age and the Greek Heritage

The Hellenistic Age in the eastern Mediterranean and western Asia lasted several centuries. During this time, the Greek legacy was passed on in a form that fifth-century Greeks might have found hard to understand. Hellenistic culture placed less emphasis on individual freedom and the use of reason and more emphasis on the emotions. Some of Alexander's soldiers settled in Afghanistan and western India, and Greek ideas had an enduring influence on the local art. For centuries afterward people as far away as Ethiopia, Nubia, and western India studied the Greek language and borrowed Greek artistic styles.

Imperial Divisions

Alexander's empire soon fragmented. When asked to whom he left his empire, Alexander was alleged to have said: "to the strongest." Within twenty years, by the end of the fourth century B.C.E., Alexander's empire had been divided by his former generals, all Macedonians. A dynasty begun by Ptolemy **(TAHL-uh-mee)** controlled Egypt and the eastern Mediterranean coast; the family of Seleucus **(suh-LOO-kuhs)** controlled Persia, Mesopotamia, and Syria; and followers of Antigonus **(an-TIG-uh-nuhs)** controlled the Macedonian kingdom and northern Greece (see Map 7.3).

Parthian Empire

The dominance of the Hellenistic Seleucid kings, who governed Persia and Mesopotamia, was short-lived. They were challenged by the Parthians **(PAHR-thee-uhnz)**, Indo-European pastoral nomads who migrated from Central Asia into eastern Persia in the third century B.C.E. In the second century B.C.E. the Parthians conquered large parts of Persia, Afghanistan, and Mesopotamia and seized the Seleucid capital on the Tigris River. Over the next few decades they expanded their empire into the Caucasus and then crushed an invading Roman army in 53 B.C.E. The Parthians adopted many Hellenistic traditions, making Greek the official state language. Gradually Persian influences grew stronger, and the Parthians became Zoroastrians. But frequent wars with the Romans, who replaced the other Hellenistic kingdoms, sapped their strength. In 224 C.E. the last Parthian ruler was defeated by a new Persian power, the Sassanians **(suh-SAY-nee-uhnz)**, who ruled much of western Asia for the next four centuries, coming into frequent conflict with the Romans.

Hellenistic Cities and Economic Networks

City Life

Hellenistic cities differed from the polis in Golden Age Greece. Alexander had founded many cities named after him, the most famous of which was the still-surviving city of Alexandria on the Mediterranean coast of Egypt (see Map 7.3). Hellenistic cities were not politically independent

Map 7.3
The Hellenistic Kingdoms

The empire conquered by Alexander the Great was divided into rival Hellenistic kingdoms on his death in 323 B.C.E. By 140 B.C.E. the Parthians had conquered some of the eastern territories.

Interactive Map

city-states but rather part of kingdoms, and their citizens did not enjoy much political participation. Wealthy aristocrats, professional soldiers, and bureaucrats ran the cities' governments. Although centers of Greek culture, the cities also existed in a predominantly non-Greek environment and so were influenced by local traditions. For example, the Ptolemaic dynasty in Egypt ruled with the pomp of the pharaohs. Hellenistic monarchs relied on Greeks, Persians, and others to govern, but they were vastly outnumbered by their Asian and African subjects.

The cities were no longer vibrant democratic communities, and the urban culture glorified hedonism. The upper classes enjoyed high living, and poets celebrated activities like horse racing, lovemaking, and drinking. A satirical Egyptian poem mocked a drunken and gluttonous harpist who showed up at weddings and festivals: "He disputes with the party-goers, shouting: 'I can't sing when I'm hungry, I can't hold my harp without my fill of wine!' And he drinks wine like two people and eats the meat of three."[17] Hellenistic cities were also more cosmopolitan and ethnically diverse than their earlier Greek counterparts. Alexandria, Egypt, for example, had large Egyptian, Greek, and Jewish populations and was a melting pot where many religions met and new ones sprouted up. It was here that the Zoroastrian holy books and the Hebrew Bible were translated into Greek. Many poets and scholars also moved to Alexandria. The Syrian Greek poet Meleager expressed the Hellenistic attitude: "Stranger, we live in the same motherland, the world."[18]

Trade Networks

Alexander's conquests also linked the Mediterranean and western Asia in a vast trading network. Alexander used part of the great wealth he found in the Persian capital to build and repair roads and harbors. Greek colonists introduced or expanded money-based economies. Long-distance trade expanded rapidly as silk from China and sugar from India were traded for onions from Egypt, wood products from Macedonia, and olive oil from Athens. As caravans of vegetables and wine moved eastward, they crossed caravans of spices and other goods moving westward out of India, Arabia, and northeast Africa. This trans-Eurasian trading network remained strong long after the Hellenistic states had disappeared.

Science, Religion, and Philosophy

Scientific Thought

Hellenistic thinkers maintained the classical Greek interest in scientific, religious, and philosophical questions. Scientists and mathematicians were rigorous in collecting and evaluating data, then offering hypotheses to explain mathematics problems, natural phenomena, and the workings of the universe. Alexandria in Egypt, with the largest library in the ancient world (700,000 papyrus scrolls), was the research center of the Hellenistic world, and Alexandrian thinkers and inventors anticipated the scientific, mathematical, and technological developments of the modern world. Here Euclid wrote his text on plane geometry, a book used for 2,000 years. Herophilus **(hair-OFF-uh-lus)** improved understanding of the brain and the nervous system. Aristarchus **(AR-uh-STAHR-kuhs)** proposed that the sun rather than the earth was the center of the universe, an idea most Europeans rejected for the next 1,000 years. The geographer Eratosthenes **(ER-uh-TAHS-thuh-neez)** calculated the circumference of the earth within about 200 miles. The inventor Hero devised a steam turbine, although it was treated only as an amazing toy. Other other major thinkers, such as the engineer and mathematician Archimedes, spent time in Alexandria (see Profile: Archimedes, a Hellenistic Mathematician and Engineer).

Cynicism A Hellenistic philosophy, made famous by the philosopher Diogenes, that emphasized living a simple life, shunning material things and all pretense.

Greek philosophical and religious thought went in new directions. Some thinkers put less emphasis on reason to solve problems and more on resigning oneself to life in ways that often seemed fatalistic, taking life as it comes. The school of thought known as **Cynicism**, made famous by Ionia-born Diogenes **(die-AHJ-uh-neez)** (ca. 412–ca. 323 B.C.E.), emphasized living a simple life, shunning material things and all pretense. A famous legend of the meeting of Diogenes and a young Alexander conveys the flavor of Cynic philosophy. Diogenes asked Alexander about his greatest desire, and the Macedonian replied, "to subjugate Greece." Next he would subjugate Southwest Asia and then the world. And after that, Alexander said, "I will relax and enjoy myself," prompting Diogenes to reply: "Why not save yourself all the trouble by relaxing and enjoying yourself now?[19]

Stoicism A Hellenistic philosophy that emphasized the importance of cooperating with and accepting nature, as well as the unity and equality of all people.

Another Hellenistic philosophy, **Stoicism** **(STOH-uh-siz-uhm)**, emphasized cooperating with and accepting nature, as well as the unity and equality of all people. Founded by Zeno **(ZEE-noh)** (ca. 334–ca. 265 B.C.E.) in Athens, Stoicism was a cosmopolitan and optimistic philosophy that accepted cultural diversity. Stoics also taught that the law of nature governing human affairs was common to all people and transcended the limited human laws created by kings. The Stoic emphasis on basic human equality survived over the centuries to influence modern lawmakers.

Mithraism A Hellenistic cult that worshiped Mithra, a Persian deity associated with the sun; had some influence on Christianity.

Hellenistic religion, like its major philosophies, offered people individual happiness and eternal life. The religion of Isis, originally an Egyptian fertility goddess, promised personal salvation. **Mithraism** **(MITH-ruh-iz-uhm)**, a very popular cult that worshiped Mithra, a Persian deity associated with the sun, promised salvation, providing people were properly initiated into the community of the faith. Some historians believe that these Hellenistic religions, which shared features with Christianity, help explain the appeal of the teachings and life of Jesus several centuries later. Christianity borrowed from Mithraism the concept of purgatory as well as the winter solstice and birthday of Mithra (December 25). Hellenistic ideas also influenced the Romans (see Chapter 8) and remained important in western Asia and the eastern Mediterranean for many centuries.

SECTION SUMMARY

- After the Peloponnesian War, no Greek city was strong enough to unite the rest of the Greek peninsula.
- King Philip II of Macedonia conquered several Greek cities, and, after he died, his ambitious son Alexander the Great established an empire that ranged from Egypt to India.
- Alexander's legacy included a vast trading network that linked the Mediterranean, western Asia, and India, as well as the spread of Hellenism, a mix of Greek and Persian culture.
- Hellenism was marked by rigorous scientific inquiry, philosophies such as Cynicism and Stoicism that urged people to take life as it came, and mystical religions that had some influence on Christianity.

ARCHIMEDES, A HELLENISTIC MATHEMATICIAN AND ENGINEER

Archimedes was an outstanding mathematician, the greatest engineer of the Hellenistic world, and perhaps the most wide-ranging mind of his time. Some historians consider Archimedes and Aristotle the two greatest thinkers of Greek society. Archimedes was born around 287 B.C.E. to an influential family—his father was apparently an astronomer—in Syracuse, a Greek city on the island of Sicily. He studied in the intellectual capital of the Hellenistic world, Alexandria in Egypt, where inquisitive souls of financial means or, like Archimedes, political connections traveled widely and learned from varied cultures. In cosmopolitan Alexandria Archimedes became acquainted with famous scientists, including the astronomer Aristarchos. Eventually Archimedes returned to Syracuse, where he spent the rest of his days. We know little of his personal life and do not know whether he ever married.

In mathematics Archimedes introduced many new ideas, some of which added to Euclid's geometry. He offered a new system of numerals to handle large numbers; calculated the value of *pi*, the ratio of the circumference to the diameter of a circle, more accurately than anyone before him; and discovered the laws for finding the centers of gravity of plane figures. A book he wrote, lost for centuries but recently rediscovered, hints that 1,800 years before anyone else he was exploring calculus, the basis for much twenty-first-century technology. Archimedes also studied astronomy and built an instrument for measuring the movements of the sun, moon, and planets. This early clock may have inspired later timekeeping inventions.

Archimedes is equally well known for his engineering innovations. His later biographer, the Greek writer Plutarch, claimed that, like Plato, Archimedes disdained practical applications. Certainly he wrote much less about his applied than his theoretical studies. Nonetheless, his contributions were immense. He discovered "Archimedes' law," still tested in high school classrooms, which states that a body wholly or partly immersed in a fluid loses weight equal to the weight of the fluid displaced. This insight apparently came to him while in the public baths, as he watched water flow over the side as he entered the pool. According to Plutarch, he leaped from the pool and ran home naked, crying aloud: "Eureka!" ("I have found it!"). (The public nudity would not have astonished Greeks, who were used to seeing people in public without their clothes.) With such discoveries, Archimedes founded the science of hydrostatics, which involves balance and weights.

Archimedes also made other practical contributions. For instance, he supervised construction of the world's first three-masted ship, a huge combination of warship, yacht, and cargo ship that had horse stalls, fish tanks, cargo holds for wheat, and luxurious cabins. He also worked out the law of the lever and the theory of mechanical advantage, using his knowledge to launch his ship with the use of compound pulleys. He also solved a major problem of the time in irrigation and mining by discovering how to move great volumes of water up a steep incline by using a large pipe with a tightly fitted screw.

With Roman power on the rise, Archimedes was put in charge of Syracuse defenses. For a while Roman attackers were repulsed by his ingenious weapons, including missiles dropped from cranes that swung out over the fortified walls, and darts and balls delivered by catapults. Some legends, which many historians doubt, credit him with experimenting with mirrors to direct the sun's rays at enemy ships to set them on fire.

In 212 the Romans captured Syracuse and killed the aged Archimedes—according to one legend, as the famously absent-minded scientist was working on geometrical diagrams. This Roman triumph helped end the Hellenistic Age and begin the Roman Age in the central Mediterranean. The engineering and mathematical discoveries of Archimedes now became part of Roman and later world traditions.

THINKING ABOUT THE PROFILE

1. How did Archimedes' career reflect the Hellenistic Age?
2. Why was Archimedes considered one of the major classical engineers and mathematicians?

The Archimedes Palimpsest In 1889 scholars discovered a crumbling, long-lost parchment containing a copy of a major work by Archimedes, the treatise called "On Floating Bodies." This work, on buoyancy, suggests that he was centuries ahead of the rest of the world in his thinking on mathematics and physics, even suggesting ideas that did not reappear until the past several centuries.

Chapter Summary

The Greeks and Persians dominated the Mediterranean and western Asia during the early Classical Era, influencing many other peoples in the region. The Persians built a huge multiethnic empire. Their emphasis on governing through mutual tolerance, a skillful bureaucracy, and good roads influenced the Macedonian Alexander the Great and his successors, as well as the Roman and the Muslim rulers of West Asia after them. Persian religious ideas, including Zoroastrianism, also spread to neighboring peoples such as the Hebrews. The Greeks reached their golden age during the fifth century. The Athenians practiced democracy, however imperfectly, in a society where there were many slaves and where women had few legal rights. Democracy developed as citizens demanded a voice in the decisions that ordered them to war. The classical Greeks were also pioneers in philosophy and science. Influenced by the increasing emphasis on reason, Greek thinkers like Socrates, Plato, and especially Aristotle established a foundation for critical thinking and natural science. Their legacy influenced people in both the Middle East and Europe.

The Greeks and Persians were also fierce rivals for regional power, fighting a series of destructive wars but also exchanging trade goods and ideas. The eastern Mediterranean zone fostered cultural mixing, maritime commerce, and the sharing of knowledge and products. Alexander the Great's conquests made Greek language and culture part of the eastern Mediterranean world for several centuries after his death. The Hellenistic world mixed Greek arts and philosophy with many Persian or western Asian ideas of government. The later Roman, Christian, and then Muslim rulers in these areas retained some of this Greco-Persian heritage.

KEY TERMS

Achaemenid
satrap
Zoroastrianism
Ahura Mazda
polis
oligarchy
tyrant
Sophists
Socratic Method
metaphysics
Delian League
Peloponnesian War
trade diaspora
Hellenism
Cynicism
Stoicism
Mithraism

EBOOK AND WEBSITE RESOURCES

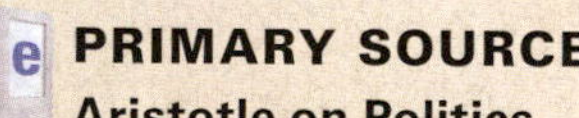

PRIMARY SOURCE
Aristotle on Politics

INTERACTIVE MAPS
Map 7.1 The Persian Empire, ca. 500 B.C.E.
Map 7.2 Classical Greece, ca. 450 B.C.E.
Map 7.3 The Hellenistic Kingdoms

LINKS

Ancient/Classical History (http://ancienthistory.about.com/library). Essays and timelines for many ancient civilizations and societies.

Diotima: Women and Gender in the Ancient World (http://www.stoa.org/diotima/). Contains excellent materials on gender and women in the early Mediterranean world.

Exploring Ancient World Cultures (http://eawc.evansville.edu/). Excellent site run by Evansville University, with essays and links on the ancient Near East and Europe.

Internet Ancient History Sourcebook (http://www.fordham .edu/halsall/ancient/asbook.html). Exceptionally rich collection of links and primary source readings.

Livius: Articles on Ancient History (http://www.livius.org). Very useful site with many short essays on the Greeks, Persians, Parthians, Romans, and other ancient and classical societies.

Plus flashcards, practice quizzes, and more. Go to: www.cengage.com/history/lockard/globalsocnet2e

SUGGESTED READING

Allen, Lindsay. *The Persian Empire.* Chicago: University of Chicago Press, 2005. A wonderfully illustrated recent survey of the classical Persians.

Armstrong, Karen. *The Great Transformation: The Beginning of Our Religious Traditions.* New York: Knopf, 2006. Good coverage of Greek and Persian religious development.

Briant, Pierre. *From Cyrus to Alexander: A History of the Persian Empire.* New York: Eisenbraun, 2001. An excellent and up-to-date survey.

Bridenthal, Renate, et al. *Becoming Visible: Women in European History,* 3rd ed. Boston: Houghton Mifflin, 1998. Contains excellent chapters on ancient and classical societies.

Brosius, Maria. *Women in Ancient Persia, 559–331 B.C.* New York: Oxford University Press, 1996. Examines women and their roles, providing a detailed picture of their lives.

Casson, Lionel. *The Ancient Mariners: Seafarers and Sea Fighters of the Mediterranean in Ancient Times,* 2nd ed. Princeton: Princeton University Press, 1991. A pathbreaking study of maritime trade, migration, and warfare.

Cook, J. M. *Persian Empire.* New York: Schocken, 1987. A useful scholarly survey, especially strong on political history.

Faceliere, Robert. *Daily Life in Greece at the Time of Pericles.* London: Phoenix, 2002. A detailed examination of various aspects of life in classical Athens.

Fox, Robin Lane. *Alexander the Great.* New York: Penguin, 2004. Updated edition of a readable introduction.

Levi, Peter. *The Greek World.* Oxford: Stonehenge, 1992. A comprehensive, well-illustrated, and readable survey.

Lloyd, G. E. R. *The Ambitions of Curiosity: Understanding the World in Ancient Greece and China.* New York: Cambridge University Press, 2002. An interesting scholarly study of the achievements and limitations of scientific inquiry in these two societies.

Martin, Thomas R. *Ancient Greece from Prehistoric to Hellenistic Times.* New Haven, CT: Yale University Press, 1996. A clear survey of Greek history, written for the general reader.

Pomeroy, Sarah B., et al. *Ancient Greece: A Political, Social, and Cultural History,* 2nd ed. New York: Oxford University Press, 2007. An excellent and readable overview.

Pomeroy, Sarah B. *Goddesses, Whores, Wives and Slaves: Women in Classical Antiquity.* New York: Schocken, 1995. An excellent study of women's lives in classical Greece and Rome.

Samons, Loren J., ed. *Athenian Democracy and Imperialism.* Boston: Houghton Mifflin, 1988. A valuable collection of writings on an important theme.

Vernant, Jean-Pierre, ed. *The Greeks,* translated by Charles Lambert and Teresa Lavender Fagan. Chicago: University of Chicago Press, 1995. A collection of essays interpreting Greek political, economic, social, and religious life.

Wood, Michael. *In the Footprints of Alexander the Great: A Journey from Greece to Asia.* Berkeley: University of California Press, 1997. A fascinating recreation of Alexander the Great's route to, and experiences reaching, India.

CHAPTER

8

Empires, Networks, and the Remaking of Europe, North Africa, and Western Asia, 500 B.C.E.–600 C.E.

CHAPTER OUTLINE

- Etruscans, Carthage, Egypt, and the Roman Republic
- The Rise and Decline of Imperial Rome
- Christianity: From Western Asian Sect to Transregional Religion
- Revival in the East: Byzantines, Persians, and Arabs

PROFILE
Hypatia of Alexandria, a Pagan Philosopher

WITNESS TO THE PAST
The Voices of Common Romans

Erich Lessing/Art Resource, NY

Santa Sophia
The magnificent Santa Sophia Church in Constantinople, rebuilt during the reign of the emperor Justinian in the sixth century C.E., had interior walls covered in gold mosaics that glowed from reflected sunlight. This mosaic from the Zoe panel shows Jesus holding a Bible.

Remember, Roman, that it is for you to rule the nations. This shall be your task: to impose the ways of peace, to spare the vanquished and to tame the proud by war.

—Roman poet Virgil[1]

FOCUS QUESTIONS

1. What were the main political and social features of the Roman Republic?
2. How did the Romans maintain their large empire?
3. How did Christianity develop and expand?
4. How did the Byzantine and Sassanian Empires reinvigorate the eastern Mediterranean world?

Around 320 B.C.E. Pytheas **(PITH-ee-us)**, a scientist from the Greek colony of Massalia **(ma-SAL-ya)**, today's city of Marseilles **(mahr-SAY)** on the Mediterranean coast of France, wrote a book about his remarkable travels in Europe. According to his account, the brave and curious Pytheas reached the western coast of France, from where he arranged to sail on a boat owned by local Celtic **(KELL-tik)** people to southwest England. He continued north through the Irish Sea and then ventured down the east coast of Britain before exploring the North Sea coast as far as Denmark. Some of his contemporaries called him a liar. Today many scholars credit Pytheas for providing Mediterranean societies with their first eyewitness account of the remote northern coast and its mysterious peoples, whom they considered dangerous barbarians.

The western Mediterranean where Pytheas lived was crisscrossed by trade networks: Greeks, Etruscans **(ee-TRUHS-kuhns)**, Carthaginians **(kar-thuh-JIN-ee-uhns)**, and the upstart Romans competed for economic resources and political power. These societies were all part of an interdependent world incorporating southern Europe, North Africa, and western Asia, where commodities flowed and ideas were exchanged. Three hundred years after Pytheas's voyage, Europe was much more closely linked, thanks largely to a people who in Pytheas's time were an ambitious but still minor power, the Romans.

The Roman success in creating a large empire and rich society, celebrated in the opening quote by the Roman poet Virgil, had a considerable impact on world history. Roman expansion reshaped much of Europe, marginalizing or incorporating the northern peoples while also transforming North African and western Asian politics. When the Roman Empire finally ended after half a millennium, it left several legacies for later European, western Asian, and North African societies. The Romans passed on to later Europeans legal and governmental concepts, some of which derived from the Greeks. Also during Roman times, Christianity emerged, forming the cultural underpinning of a post-Roman European society while also spreading in Asia and Africa.

A version of the Roman Empire in the eastern Mediterranean, Greek-speaking Byzantium **(buh-ZANT-ee-uhm)**, served as a transcontinental trade center and a buffer between western Europe and West Asian states, including a revived Persian Empire. Byzantine-Persian struggles set the stage for the rise of another society, the Arabs.

Visit the website and eBook for additional study materials and interactive tools: www.cengage.com/history/lockard/globalsocnet2e

ETRUSCANS, CARTHAGE, EGYPT, AND THE ROMAN REPUBLIC

What were the main political and social features of the Roman Republic?

By 300 B.C.E. the Mediterranean world was politically and culturally diverse, divided between Etruscans, Carthage, Greek city-states, various Hellenistic kingdoms including Egypt, and the rising Romans, who eventually dominated the entire region. The Romans learned much from the older Etruscan society that they eventually absorbed, and they were influenced by Greek ideas in building their republic. Eventually Rome conquered peoples in southern Europe and then beyond, establishing the framework of a huge empire.

European Geography, the Etruscans, and Early Rome

Geographical Foundations

Geography and climate were influential in shaping western Mediterranean society. The geological spine of Italy is the Apennine mountain range running down the eastern side of the narrow peninsula, to the west and north of which spread rich agricultural plains. This fertile land and mild climate fostered intensive agriculture. The Romans exported wine and olive oil while importing grain from the nearby islands of Sicily and Sardinia (sahr-DIN-ee-uh) and from northern Africa. In contrast to Greece, agricultural success and the ease of contact in the peninsula encouraged large states. Italy's inhabitants also were pressed to defend themselves against northern peoples attracted to the warmer lands of the south. These Indo-European Celtic and Germanic peoples living in the forested hills and plains of western and northern Europe made frequent invasions of Italy using passes through the Alps, a formidable complex of mountains.

As the Romans expanded beyond Italy, they drew upon the natural resources of the larger Mediterranean world (see Map 8.1) and beyond. Spain offered rich supplies of silver, copper, and tin. Egypt provided wheat. Beginning about 200 B.C.E., overland trade routes connected the Mediterranean with China along the famous Silk Road, named after the most important product acquired from East Asia, which was bartered in return for gold, silver, precious stones, and some textile products from the west.

The Etruscans

The Romans were greatly influenced by the Etruscans, who founded a dozen or so city-states in central and northern Italy by the eighth century B.C.E. The Etruscans were chariot warriors and also sailors who traded with the western Mediterranean islands and Spain. Eventually they dominated more of Italy and the nearby island of Corsica. They also had considerable contact and sometimes conflict with nearby Greek settlements. They adopted the Greek alphabet and myths, and Greek craftsmen worked in some Etruscan cities.

The Etruscan language is only partially understood, and none of their major literature survives. Their huge cemeteries with well-decorated tombs show that they were skilled artists and artisans, and their cities were well planned and linked together by a good road system. Each city apparently had its own king. The Etruscans were also known for working iron ore into excellent iron axes, sickles, and tools. Their rigid social system included slavery, although Etruscan women apparently had a high social status, conversing with men in public, driving their own chariots, owning real estate, and sometimes running businesses like pottery workshops.

Initially the relationship between the Romans and the Etruscans was peaceful. A small city-state in central Italy just south of Etruscan territory, Rome was established in the eighth century B.C.E. by Indo-European pastoralists known as the Latins (see Chronology: The Roman Republic, 753–58 B.C.E.). Built on seven hills along the Tiber River, Rome was originally founded as a base for trade with the Etruscans. However, the Etruscans soon dominated Rome. The Romans adopted the twenty-six-character alphabet that the Etruscans had themselves borrowed from the Greeks, as well as the Greek-inspired Etruscan phalanx infantry formation. Skilled Etruscan engineers taught the Romans to make the weight-bearing semicircular arch, which Romans used to construct city walls, aqueducts to carry water, and doorways. Although Etruscan kings won support by building new public buildings, at the end of the sixth century B.C.E. the last Etruscan king was driven out for his brutality, and Rome became independent. Later the Romans conquered and assimilated the Etruscans.

CHRONOLOGY The Roman Republic, 753–58 B.C.E.

753 B.C.E. Founding of Rome (traditional date)

ca. 616–509 B.C.E. Etruscan kings rule over Rome

509 B.C.E. Beginning of Roman Republic

265 B.C.E. Roman control of southern Italy

264–241 B.C.E. First Punic (Roman-Carthaginian) War

218–201 B.C.E. Second Punic War

149–146 B.C.E. Third Punic War

113–105 B.C.E. First German-Roman conflicts

60–58 B.C.E. Julius Caesar completes conquest from Rhine to Atlantic

CHRONOLOGY

	Roman Republic	Roman Empire	Byzantium and Western Asia
500 B.C.E.	**509** B.C.E. Roman Republic		
300 B.C.E.	**264–146** B.C.E. Punic Wars		
100 B.C.E.		**31** B.C.E.–**180** C.E. *Pax Romana* **7–6** B.C.E.–**30** C.E. Life of Jesus	
1 C.E.			**240–272** C.E. Founding of Sassanian Empire
300 C.E.		**395** C.E. Division of eastern and western empires	**330** C.E. Founding of Constantinople
500 C.E.		**476** C.E. Official end of western Roman Empire	**527–565** C.E. Reign of Justinian

The Roman Republic and Expansion

Using political ideas borrowed from the Greeks, the Romans built a system of self-government for their city-state. In 509 B.C.E. they established a republic, a state in which supreme power is held by the people or their elected representatives. Over the next three centuries, the Romans developed a system of representative government that introduced enduring political ideas. Many modern English words taken from Latin—such as *senate, citizenship, suffrage* (the right to vote), *dictator* (a man given full power), *plebiscite* (PLEB-i-site) (a special vote by citizens on a political issue), and even *republic*—suggest the influence of the Romans on modern political life.

Initially, power rested entirely with the aristocratic upper class, or **patricians** (puh-TRISH-uhnz). Patricians controlled the Senate, a body that had previously advised the kings and later dominated foreign affairs, the army, and the legislative body made up of soldiers, the **Centuriate Assembly**. The Senate, composed of three hundred former government officials, claimed the right to ratify resolutions of the Centuriate Assembly before they became law. As the Republic developed, the Centuriate Assembly elected two men each year to serve as **consuls**, who had executive power.

patricians The aristocratic upper class who controlled the Roman Senate.

Centuriate Assembly A Roman legislative body made up of soldiers.

consuls Two patrician men, elected by the Centuriate Assembly each year, who had executive power in the Roman Republic.

The patricians were heavily outnumbered by the commoners, or **plebeians** (pli-BEE-uhnz). As wealth flowed into Rome as a result of military expansion in the peninsula and then beyond, the plebeian soldiers wanted to share in this wealth. Long years of army service had taken them away from their farms and left them in debt, and they demanded a greater political voice and economic equality. A Roman historian reported the bitterness of a plebeian leader toward those who opposed reform: "[You] realize vividly the depth of the contempt in which you are held by the aristocracy. They would rob you of the very light you see by; they grudge you the air you breathe, the words you speak."[2] Political power, the plebeians believed, would allow them to pass laws that distributed the state's wealth more fairly.

plebeians The commoner class in Rome.

Gradually social and political rights expanded. In 494 B.C.E. the plebeians selected two of their number, called **tribunes**, to represent their interests in the Centuriate Assembly, much as the consuls represented patrician interests. By 471 a separate Plebeian Assembly was established to elect tribunes and to conduct votes of the plebeian class, called plebiscites. Plebeians later gained the right to share with the patricians lands that the Roman state had won in war. Full equality for plebeians was won by 267 B.C.E., when their assembly became the principal lawmaking body of the state.

tribunes Roman men elected to represent plebeian interests in the Centuriate Assembly.

In the fourth century, the Roman Republic turned to imperialism, the control or domination by one state over another, as a way of resolving some of its problems. A major defeat at the hands of the Gauls (gawlz), a Celtic people who plundered Rome in 390 B.C.E., shocked Roman leaders, who decided to expand their territory to keep their frontiers safely distant from the city of Rome. Thus motivated, the Romans successfully fought wars with other Italian city-states. At the end of each conflict, they often granted either full or limited Roman citizenship to the inhabitants of the defeated cities. Being a Roman citizen thus became a great honor entitling a person to special legal treatment, an honor that fathers were proud to pass on to their sons. By wisely treating former enemies fairly, the Romans spread their power without encouraging revolts and ensured that more men would join their army.

Imperialism

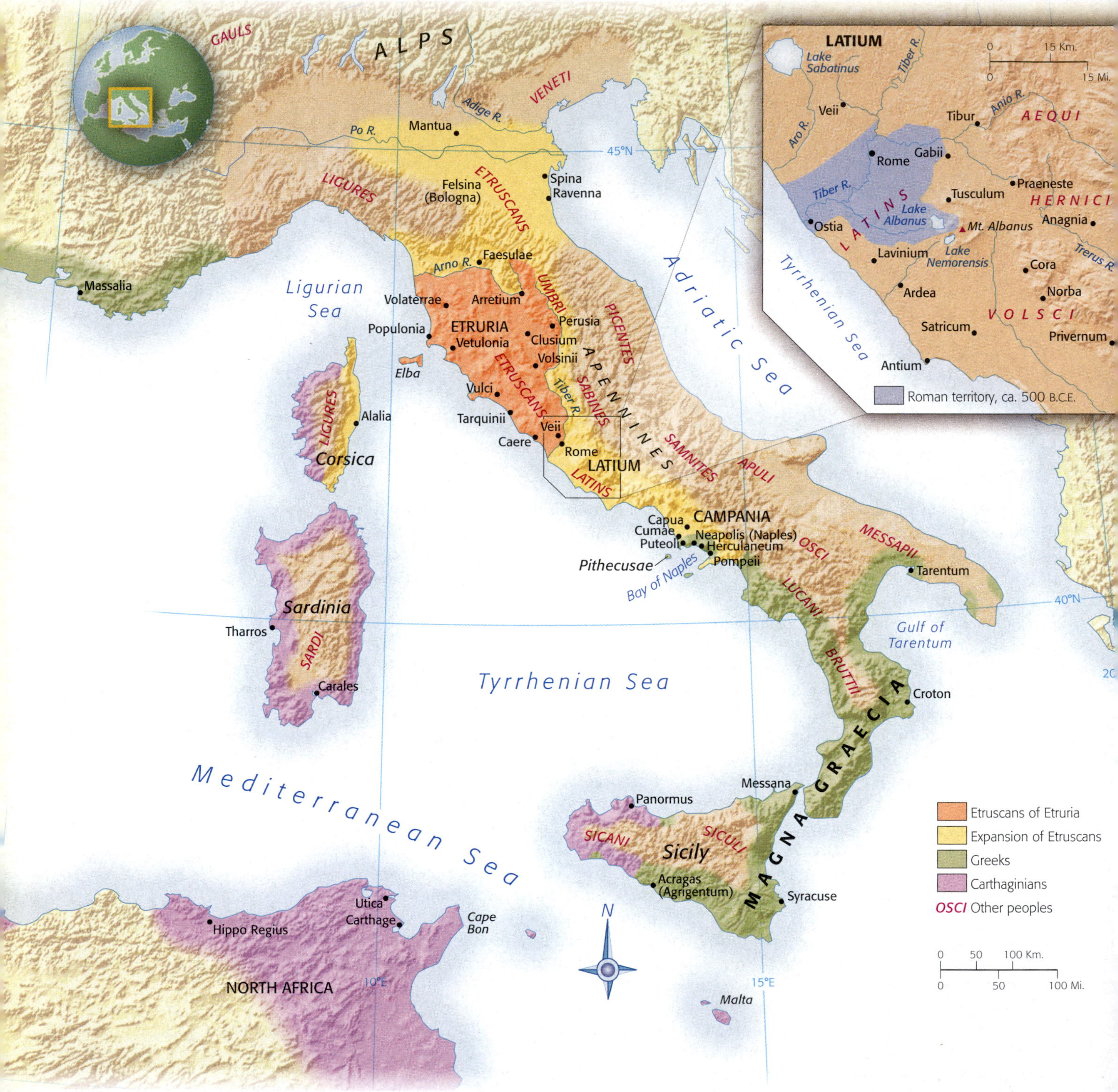

Map 8.1
Italy and the Western Mediterranean, 600–200 B.C.E.

During the early Classical Era the Etruscan cities in the north and the Greek city-states in the south held political power in Italy. Carthage held a similar status in northeast Africa. Eventually the Latins, from their base in Rome, became the dominant political force in the entire region.

Carthage, Egypt, and Regional Trade

The Carthaginians

After first conquering the Etruscan cities, weakened by conflicts with the Gauls, the Romans were then able to conquer the Greek cities in southern Italy and Sicily in 265 B.C.E. Across the sea from Sicily, however, the Romans encountered their greatest enemy, the Carthaginians. Both

John Elk III/www.bciusa.com

The Roman Forum The Forum, located amidst various religious and governmental buildings, was the center of Roman political life.

Carthage and Egypt played key roles in Mediterranean trade. The city-state of Carthage **(KAHR-thij)** was originally a Phoenician colony founded in 814 B.C.E. on the North African coast near where the city of Tunis is today. The other great power on the southern shores of the Mediterranean was Egypt, where the Hellenistic Greek Ptolemaic **(taw-luh-MAY-ik)** dynasty had fostered great prosperity for over a century.

With a fine harbor and a strategic position, Carthage grew into the wealthiest Phoenician outpost, described by a Greek from Sicily as having "gardens and orchards of all kinds, no end of country houses built luxuriously, land cultivated partly as vineyards and partly as olive groves, fruit trees, herds of cattle and flocks of sheep."[3] However, the autocratic city government experienced political instability as rival leaders vied for power, and differences between the prosperous Phoenician settlers and the native Berbers created tensions. The Carthaginians also fought frequent wars with their commercial rivals, the Greeks.

The Carthaginians used their maritime skills to develop trade networks. Around 425 B.C.E. an admiral, Hanno, led a naval expedition through the Strait of Gibraltar and down the coast of West Africa, seeking markets. He founded trading posts along Morocco's coast and sailed at least as far as the Senegal River. Other Carthaginian expeditions apparently reached the British Isles and perhaps several of the Atlantic islands off the northwest African coast. By the third century B.C.E. the Carthaginians had created an empire along the southern and western shores of the Mediterranean Sea, controlling a large part of Spain, much of the North African coast, and the islands of Corsica and Sardinia. In 264 B.C.E. they moved troops to Sicily to aid several Greek cities allied with them against Rome.

Ptolemaic Egypt

In Egypt, Ptolemaic power was becoming more tenuous by the second century B.C.E. The Ptolemies had increased agricultural and crafts production, in part by demanding more work from Egyptians. As in earlier times, Egypt remained a major supplier of wheat to other Mediterranean societies. It also exported papyrus, the preferred medium for scientific, philosophical, and literary texts throughout the region; textiles; pottery; and metal objects. Greeks and Phoenicians owned some of the ships that carried these goods to foreign ports. Despite the economic growth, many Egyptians tired of foreign occupation, hardship, and high taxes, and several rebellions threatened the government. In 180 B.C.E. Cleopatra I became sole ruler, the first in a long chain of assertive queens. During this time Egyptian rulers sought alliances with rising Rome to maintain their own independence. In 47 B.C.E., an ambitious eighteen-year-old became ruler as Queen Cleopatra VII, just as years of poor harvests and official corruption fostered more unrest. Her skills enabled the unstable country to maintain domestic peace and deflect Rome for nearly two decades.

The Punic Wars and Afro-Eurasian Empire

Carthage-Rome Conflict

The result of Roman expansion southward was three Punic **(PYOO-nik)** Wars, which pitted the two major powers and bitter rivals, Rome and Carthage, against each other. The first Punic War

(264–241 B.C.E.) resulted in several Roman naval expeditions against Carthage and finally ended with Roman occupation of Sicily, Corsica, and Sardinia. In the second conflict (218–201), the brilliant Carthaginian general Hannibal (247–182 B.C.E.) led his troops through Spain and France to invade Italy across the Alps, defeating every Roman army sent against them. Modern people may have images in their mind, probably accurate, of war elephants used by Hannibal's army lumbering through the rugged mountains. The Carthaginians had carefully trained these elephants to charge and possibly terrify the enemy on the battlefield. But the elephants and Hannibal's troops were not used to the snow and ice of the mountains, and they perished by the thousands.

Forming the Roman Empire

The arrival and early military success of Hannibal's force alarmed the Romans. With his supply lines overstretched, however, Hannibal could not conquer the Italian cities. Eventually the Romans drove him out and defeated Carthage, which had to surrender all its overseas possessions, including Spain. In the final Punic War (149–146), Romans laid siege to Carthage city and destroyed it, spreading salt on the fields around the city to make it difficult to plant crops there in the future. Northwest Africa became a Roman province, a source of copper, grain, and West African gold.

Roman victory encouraged additional Roman imperial expansion, aimed either at punishing Carthage's allies or at restoring stability. Rome ended Macedonian control of the Greek cities in 197 B.C.E. and in 146 B.C.E. made Greece and Macedonia into a Roman province. Few could resist the Roman infantrymen, armed with swords and rectangular shields, or the armor-clad Roman archers, who rode in carts carrying large crossbows, among the era's most feared weapons. By the middle of the first century B.C.E. the Romans had built an empire that commanded the entire Mediterranean and its vast resources, binding together Europe, western Asia, and North Africa. The empire included most of Anatolia, Syria, and Palestine, as well as much territory in northern and western Europe. The Ptolemies still controlled Egypt, but they were careful to not offend the Romans. The Romans absorbed much of the Hellenistic east, with its rich web of international commerce centered on several hubs, including Alexandria in Egypt, which distributed goods from as far away as India and East Africa.

CHRONOLOGY
The Roman Empire and Its Successors, 60 B.C.E.–526 C.E.

60–44 B.C.E. Julius Caesar rises to dominance in Roman politics

31 B.C.E.–14 C.E. Reign of Octavian (Caesar Augustus)

31 B.C.E.–180 C.E. *Pax Romana*

7–6 B.C.E.–30 C.E. Jesus's life and preaching in Palestine

64 C.E. Death of Peter (first bishop of Rome) and of Paul of Tarsus

66–73 C.E. Jewish revolt against Rome

251 C.E. Germans defeat Roman armies and sack Balkans

306–337 C.E. Reign of Constantine

313 C.E. Legalization of Christianity

325 C.E. Council of Nicaea

354–430 C.E. St. Augustine of Hippo

391 C.E. Paganism banned by Emperor Theodosius I

395 C.E. Final division of eastern and western empires

410 C.E. Ostrogoths sack Rome

410 C.E. Huns invade western Europe

452 C.E. Huns plunder northern Italy

455 C.E. Vandals sack Rome

476 C.E. Official end of western Roman Empire

481–511 C.E. Clovis and Franks conquer Gaul

493–526 C.E. Ostrogoths rule Italy

The Decline of the Republic

But imperial success also led to major changes in Roman society. The Roman historian Tacitus (TASS-uh-tuhs) observed how the growth of empire increased the love of power: "It was easy to maintain equality when Rome was weak. World-wide conquest and the destruction of all rival[s] opened the way to the secure enjoyment of wealth and an overriding appetite for it."[4] Imperial expansion provoked various crises that reshaped Roman politics and undermined the Republic, turning the representative institutions into window-dressing. Warfare gave excessive power to military leaders, weakening the influence of the Senate, and growing Roman wealth increased the gap between the very rich and desperately poor. As the empire expanded, upper-class families bought farmland from peasants who had become impoverished by long service in the army. Many farmers then moved to the city of Rome, where the government supported hundreds of thousands of displaced people to maintain their loyalty. With fewer farmers willing to serve in the army, the tribune Tiberius Graccus (tie-BIR-ee-uhs GRAK-uhs) proposed turning over public land to farmers who agreed to serve in the Roman legions when needed. When the poor gathered in Rome to support this measure, some wealthy Romans panicked and spurred a mob to club Tiberius and many of his followers to death, demonstrating both the determination of the wealthy not to give up power and the mobilization of many poor people to support one leader or another. The Senate was unable to control the military leaders.

The changing nature of military power also undermined democracy. In 107 B.C.E., the victorious general Gaius Marius (GAY-uhs MER-ee-uhs) was elected consul for five straight years, violating a law that prohibited a person from holding the office more than one year. Marius brought his military veterans to pressure the senators to vote for a law that gave the veterans public land. Skillful military leaders thereafter used their armies to enhance their political power and outmaneuver civilian leaders and the Senate, resulting in civil and foreign wars. Between 78 and 31 B.C.E., ambitious military leaders expanded Roman territory in Europe and Asia, including Syria and Palestine, while finally destroying republican institutions within Rome itself.

Military Power and Politics

The young Julius Caesar proved the most ambitious. He completed the conquest of Europe from the Rhine River west to the Atlantic and sent the first Roman forces into Britain, after which he won a civil war against former allies. Caesar also weakened the Senate by enlarging it to nine hundred men, thus making it too large to be an effective governing body. Finally, in 44 B.C.E. he had himself declared "perpetual dictator" (see Chronology: The Roman Empire and Its Successors, 60 B.C.E.–526 C.E.). This act led to his assassination, made famous centuries later in the play *Julius Caesar* by the English author William Shakespeare.

Civil War

Caesar's death led to civil war, the end of any pretence of democracy, and the conquest of Egypt. Caesar's adopted son, Octavian **(ok-TAY-vee-uhn)**, fought Mark Antony, a general who had fallen in love with the Egyptian ruler Cleopatra. A remarkable personality who had borne a son by Julius Caesar, Cleopatra was described by a Greek historian as someone whose "presence was irresistible; the attraction of her person, the charm of her conversation, was something bewitching. She could pass from one language to another."[5] The turmoil and the Republic itself ended when Octavian defeated Antony and Cleopatra at the naval Battle of Actium **(AK-tee-uhm)**, in Greece, in 31 B.C.E. Antony and Cleopatra committed suicide and their armies surrendered to Octavian, giving Rome control of Egypt. The Romans then placed Egypt under a tighter grip than most of their colonies, imposing heavy taxes and encouraging more wheat production to feed the city of Rome.

SECTION SUMMARY

- The agricultural plenty of Italy allowed for the development of larger states than had been possible in Greece, and the Mediterranean Sea allowed for Roman expansion.
- The Etruscans, a non-Indo-European people most likely from western Asia, formed the first urban society in Italy; they influenced and were eventually conquered by the Romans.
- Rome formed a republic, in which citizens rule the state; initially upper-class patricians dominated, but over time the plebeians attained increasing amounts of power.
- After a major defeat by the Gauls, the Romans decided that the key to safety was to expand their territory so their frontiers would be safely distant from Rome.
- Rome defeated Carthage, its primary rival, in the Punic Wars and then conquered an empire.
- With the shift from Roman Republic to empire, military leaders gained power, farmers grew impoverished, and the people had less voice in government.

The Rise and Decline of Imperial Rome

How did the Romans maintain their large empire?

Athenians had pondered whether empire and democracy were compatible, and eventually they proved incompatible. Likewise, in Rome the rise of empire, with its clash of personal ambitions and greed created by the wealth gained through conquest, had important consequences. The expanding empire led to the replacement of the Republic with a more autocratic and arrogant imperial system. This period of imperial rule saw the full development of Roman culture and of those elements of the Roman heritage, such as law, that formed a significant legacy to European society. The Roman Empire lasted in the west for about five hundred years. Its decline began when a long period of internal and external disorder challenged the *Pax Romana*. Some of this decline resulted from various population movements that put pressure on the frontiers of the empire, leading to imperial division and then collapse.

Augustus and the *Pax Romana*

Imperial Government

Rome and its empire were now ruled by emperors (*caesarsi*) who controlled the military and much of the government bureaucracy. This trend was begun by Octavian (63 B.C.E.–14 C.E.), who called himself Augustus, a Latin term meaning "majestic, inspiring awe." His long reign (r. 31 B.C.E.–14 C.E.) gave Augustus time to establish and consolidate a system in which the Senate appointed governors to the peaceful provinces while he governed provinces where troops were stationed. Augustus enacted or vetoed legislation and called the Senate into session. The writer Juvenal **(JOO-vuhn-uhl)** deplored the consequences of the lost popular voice and its replacement by entertainments to divert public attention: "The people that once bestowed commands now meddles no more and longs eagerly for just two things: bread and circuses."[6]

Pax Romana The period of peace and prosperity in Roman history from the reign of Augustus through that of Emperor Marcus Aurelius in 180 C.E.

The period in Roman history from Augustus through the reign of Emperor Marcus Aurelius **(aw-REE-lee-uhs)** in 180 C.E. is known as the ***Pax Romana*** ("Roman Peace"). For the first and last time, the entire Mediterranean world was controlled by one power and remained at peace for two centuries (see Map 8.2). Some historians refer to the Mediterranean Sea in those centuries as a "Roman lake." During this time Rome experienced few challenges from the Germanic peoples, who mostly remained east of the Rhine and north of the Danube Rivers. In western Asia the Romans faced only a weak Parthian kingdom in Persia and Mesopotamia. Whether in London or Paris, Vienna or Barcelona—all cities founded by the Romans—people lived under the same laws.

Peace and prosperity encouraged trade and population growth. Great fleets of ships moved mountains of goods around the Mediterranean Sea. Trade also flourished along the Silk Road between China and Rome through Central and western Asia. Rome governed a huge population, estimated at 54 million in the first century C.E., including 6 million in Italy. Rome may have been the world's largest city, with a half million to 1 million inhabitants. In this diverse empire the Roman ideal, like that of the Hellenistic Greeks, was cosmopolitan. Hence, Emperor Marcus Aurelius (r. 161–180 C.E.) wrote: "Rome is my city and country, but as a man, I am a citizen of the world."[7] Non-Romans were incorporated into the ruling class, and half of the Roman Senate were non-Italians. Men of wealth and military skill, whatever their ethnic background, could rise to the highest levels in the army and government. Many people migrated to Rome, bringing with them cultural forms such as musical instruments and dances. Thus the empire slowly changed into a multinational state that fostered diversity within unity. It was no accident that the phrase chosen as the slogan of the new United States in the eighteenth century C.E., *e pluribus unum* **(EE PLUR-uh-buhs OO-nuhm)**, "one from many," is written in Latin.

Civic Virtue and Law

Roman society owed much to the Greeks' political, ethical, and philosophical ideas. But the Romans also made something distinctive from this Greek legacy, developing a practical way of looking at the world. In particular, the Romans extended the meaning of some of the classic Greek ideas, such as citizenship, and developed a concept of civic virtue, an idea close to what people today call public duty. Codified laws underpinned the Roman system and encouraged public responsibility. Several principles of Roman law have survived the centuries to become an accepted part of the laws of most modern nations and modern international law. For example, the Romans believed that all people, regardless of wealth or position, were equal before the law. They promoted individual responsibility; a family could not be held responsible for one member's misdeeds. Roman jurists also said that the burden of proof in a trial should rest with the person making the charge, not with the defendant.

The Roman concept of law was influenced by the Greek Stoic belief in eternal truths that transcended particular cultures. Leading Roman Stoics included the philosopher Seneca (4 B.C.E.–65 C.E.), the great Roman lawyer and essayist Cicero (106–43 B.C.E.), and the second-century emperor Marcus Aurelius **(uh-REAL-yus)**, famous for his humanity and justice. These thinkers believed that all people were alike in their use of reason to determine that certain things were right and others wrong. Stoics promoted tolerance, moderation, and acceptance of life's travails. Because of such beliefs, the Romans generally allowed conquered peoples to govern themselves and keep their own customs and leaders so long as they paid their taxes and did not revolt.

Religion and Society

Gods and Godesses

Roman religion and society, like government, changed over the centuries. Religion comprised a pantheon of gods and goddesses who were worshiped for practical reasons, such as to ensure good fortune. The Romans honored each god or goddess and expected favorable results. For example, specific gods or goddesses were associated with agricultural tasks, and there was even a goddess for thieves and one for door hinges. Roman religion was an integral part of civic life, there being no "separation of church and state" in Roman society. Priests were state officials who performed public sacrifices to please the gods and ceremonies promoting the welfare of the state. Reflecting these practical goals, Caesar Augustus commissioned the building in Rome of the *Ara Pacis,* or Altar of Peace, a sacrificial marble altar to celebrate the end of the wars of conquest in Gaul and Spain and, hopefully, launch a long era of peace. Not wishing to offend any divinity who might help them, the Romans also adopted the gods and goddesses of other

Roman Empire by death of Augustus, 14 C.E.
Territory added by death of Hadrian, 138 C.E.
Territory gained and lost, with dates held
Parthian Empire, ca. 200 C.E.
Major battle

Map 8.2
The Roman Empire, ca. 120 C.E.

The Romans gradually expanded until, by 120 C.E., they controlled a huge empire stretching from Britain and Spain in the west through southern and central Europe and North Africa to Egypt, Anatolia, and the lands along the eastern Mediterranean coast.

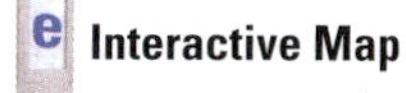
Interactive Map

Ara Pacis The Altar of Peace, built in 9 B.C.E., resided in a large enclosure, whose walls contain relief sculptures. This scene depicts Mother Earth and her children, with the cow and sheep at her feet representing the prosperity resulting from peace.

Scala/Art Resource, NY

peoples. This was especially true of the Greek deities, which the Romans equated with their own gods. For example, the Greek leader of the gods, Zeus, became the Roman Jupiter, Zeus's wife Hera became the Roman Juno (JOO-noh), and the Greek god of wine, Dionysus, became the Roman Bacchus (BAK-uhs).

Although there was some mobility, Roman society remained stratified into sharply defined upper and lower classes, as well as sharply divided by wealth. Below the upper classes were middle-class merchants and artisans, who ranked above the urban workers. Many peasants became seriously impoverished. We know something of a wide range of the concerns and values of the middle and lower classes from the graffiti and tombstone memorials that they left (see Witness to the Past: The Voices of Common Romans).

Social Classes

As in Greece, slaves, one-third of the Italian population, occupied the bottom of the social ladder. Most slaves were war captives, but some people were enslaved as payment for debt or as the result of a crime. Some slaves lived very hard lives, working in mines, on vast plantations growing cash crops such as olives and grapes, or as oarsmen of Roman ships. A Roman historian described the lives of slaves working in a silver mine in Spain: "The slaves secure for their masters riches which are almost beyond belief. They, however, are physically destroyed, their bodies worn down. Many die because of the excessive mistreatment they suffer. They are given no break from their toil."[8] Most of the gladiators who fought in the arenas to entertain the public were highly skilled slaves who had studied at gladiator schools. In these deadly contests, few participants lived to old age. Slave rebellions were not uncommon and brutally crushed. The Romans were generous in freeing slaves after years of good service, but ex-slaves were still stigmatized socially.

Patriarchy and Gender Relations

Like most classical societies, the Romans were patriarchal. Only men had a political voice, and they enjoyed extensive power over women, children, and slaves. The oldest male in a family had the power of life and death over other family members and was even free to kill his children without fear of legal problems. Wives were advised to accept the extramarital sexual exploits of their husbands: "Let the matron be subject to her husband." Yet, some women stepped outside expected bounds. Seneca criticized those daring women who copied "male indulgences, they keep just as late hours, and drink as much liquor; they challenge men in carousing."[9]

Adult women also enjoyed some legal rights, including possession of their own property, even if married. Some women enjoyed considerable wealth, using it for such community ends as financing public monuments. Moreover, a wife could escape her husband's legal control by spending three days and nights away from his house, and she could sue her husband if he abandoned her. For example, a woman whose husband had moved to Alexandria and married another woman asked the court to make her husband return the dowry she brought to the marriage. Roman women also had more freedom to leave their homes and travel through the city than did their Greek sisters. Finally, abortion and contraception were common until they were outlawed around 200 C.E.

In the later years of the Republic, Romans became free to choose their own spouse. By 17 B.C.E., adultery and avoidance of marriage by both genders had become serious social problems. To attempt to halt a population decline among native Italians, a law was passed requiring men to marry or pay higher taxes. Views on human sexuality were diverse. For example, Romans were generally tolerant of homosexual activity and did not view it as immoral. Acknowledged homosexuals participated openly in Roman life.

Economy and Trade Networks

Roman society flourished from expanding trade and industry. Roman industries, such as mining and pottery making, depended mostly on slave labor. Those who acquired wealth beyond that needed for public display invested it in land rather than in business or industry. The Romans built over 150,000 miles of roads, most of them 4 feet thick. The phrase "all roads lead to Rome" reflects these accomplishments, as well as the fact that Rome became a communications center for a large area of Afro-Eurasia.

Trade Routes

Maritime trade routes linked the Romans to peoples in Asia and Africa. The Egyptian port of Berenike **(BER-eh-nick-y)**, on the Red Sea, was a transfer point for fabrics, spices, gems, and other exotic goods from India and Southeast Asia, frankincense and myrrh from Arabia, and ivory, drugs, tortoise shells, and slaves from Somalia and Ethiopia. During the *Pax Romana* over a hundred ships a year set off from Berenike and nearby ports for India. Merchant ships, the largest able to carry 1,200 tons of grain, plied the Mediterranean between Egypt and Rome. Roman coins have been found in India, China, and Vietnam.

The Romans also traded widely over land. Roman-ruled North Africa obtained gold from West African societies across the Sahara Desert. The Silk Road across Central and western Asia allowed Chinese products to reach Rome. Romans shipped much gold and silver east in return for spices, jewelry, cut gems, glassware, and silk. Eventually, however, the Roman economy was harmed by the expanding Roman appetite for Chinese goods. The historian Pliny **(PLIN-ee)** the Elder bemoaned the wealth shipped east and blamed it on Roman women's fondness for silks, pearls, and perfumes: "India and China and [Arabia] together drain our empire. That is the price that our luxuries and our womankind cost us."[10] However, the criticism was misplaced, since both men and women coveted imported Asian goods.

Literature, Architecture, and Technology

Poetry and History

As in the realm of public works and trade, the achievements of Roman literary culture during the late Republic and early empire were considerable, although they mostly reflected the views of the aristocratic elite. Virgil (70–19 B.C.E.) was Rome's greatest epic poet. To promote Roman greatness, his *Aeneid* **(i-NEE-id)** described the journey of the legendary Trojan hero Aeneas **(i-NEE-uhs)**, who, according to the poem, left Troy and eventually founded the city of Rome. The love poems of Ovid (43 B.C.E.–17 C.E.) were irreverent and erotic, with his treatise on the art of love advising men to indulge their sexual cravings. In disgust, the moralistic emperor Augustus eventually sent Ovid into bitter exile along the Black Sea.

Historians also made substantial contributions to Roman literature. Tacitus (56–117 C.E.) wrote a history of the early emperors in which he lamented the end of the Republic, which had a more open political atmosphere and sense of equality. He also authored a description of the Germanic tribes north of the Rhine and Danube, in which he contrasted the sexual purity and other virtues of the Germans with the vices of his fellow Romans. Of the corrupt emperor Domitian, Tacitus wrote that he "fancied that the voice of the Roman people [was] obliterated; he banished teachers of philosophy and exiled every noble pursuit, so that nothing honorable might anywhere be encountered."[11]

Architecture and Engineering

The Romans' quest to provide public services fostered notable architecture and engineering. The great dome of the Pantheon **(PAN-thee-ahn)**, or temple to all the gods in Rome, has no interior-supporting pillars and forms a perfect sphere, as high as it is wide. The famous Colosseum in Rome was the world's largest outdoor arena until the twentieth century. Aqueducts carried water hundreds of miles from the mountains of Italy and Spain into the Roman cities. This abundance of water encouraged the development of public baths, which were social centers containing gardens, exercise and game rooms, and libraries. A Roman writer observed that baths, sex, and wine ruin bodies but make life worth living. The Romans are also remembered for some creature comforts. Some of the homes of the wealthier citizens were heated from furnaces under the floor that spread heat to the house through ductwork. The Koreans at the other end of Eurasia also developed similar heating systems. In addition, Romans invented glass windowpanes, scales with weights, chemical

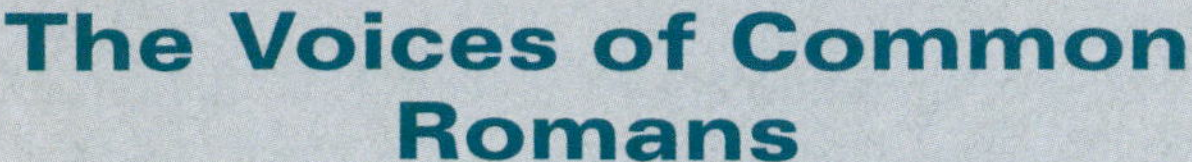

WITNESS TO THE PAS

The Voices of Common Romans

As with most premodern societies, we know much more from the surviving records and literature about the prominent and wealthy Romans than about the common people who constituted most of the population. But we can learn something about the middle and lower classes from the graffiti preserved in the ruins of ancient cities like Pompeii and the epitaphs on tombstones. Romans used graffiti and epitaphs to voice frank opinions on many matters and to summarize their lives. Like modern graffiti, some of the remarks address sexual activities and bodily functions or insult rivals with profanity. The following are some examples of less profane but often humorous graffiti and epitaphs from various Roman cities.

Graffiti

I'm amazed, O wall, that you've not collapsed under the weight of so much written filth.

A bronze urn has disappeared from my tavern. Whoever returns it will get 65 sesterces reward. Whoever informs on the thief will get 20 sesterces, if we recover it.

Perarius, you're a thief.

No loiterers—scram!

Livia, to Alexander: "If you're well, I don't much care; if you're dead, I'm delighted."

Samius Cornelius, go hang yourself!

Stronnius is an ignoramus.

Crescens is a public whore.

Whoever doesn't invite me to dinner is a barbarian.

Whoever is in love, may he prosper. Whoever loves not, may he die. Whoever forbids love, may he die twice over!

Marcus loves Spendusa.

If you haven't seen the Venus that Apelles painted, take a look at my girl—she's just as beautiful.

Thraex makes the girls sigh.

All the goldsmiths support Gaius Cuspious Pansa for public works commissioner.

The mule-drivers support Gaius Julius Polybius for mayor. Genialis supports Bruttius Balbus for mayor. He'll balance the budget.

I ask you to support Marcus Cerrinus Vatia for public works commissioner. All the late-night drunks back him.

Epitaphs

If you wish to add your sorrow to ours, come here and shed your tears. A sad parent has laid to rest his only daughter, whom he treasured with sweet love as long as the Fates permitted. Now her dear face and form are mere shadow and her bones mere ash.

For my dearest wife, with whom I lived two years, six months, three days, and ten hours. On the day she died, I gave thanks before gods and men.

I was once famous, preeminent among thousands of strong Bavarian men. I swam across the Danube in full armor. I once shot an arrow in the air and split it with a second in midair. No Roman or barbarian ever beat me with a spear, no Parthian with the bow. This tombstone preserves the story of my deeds. But I am still unique, the first to do such things as these.

THINKING ABOUT THE READING

1. What do these graffiti tell us about political life?
2. What do the graffiti and epitaphs reveal about what common people valued?
3. In what ways do the sentiments seem familiar to modern readers?

Source: From *Lives and Times: A World History Reader, Volume I* 1st edition by HOLOKA/UPSHUR. © 1985 Wadsworth, a part of Cengage Learning, Inc. Reproduced with permission. www.cengage.com/permissions.

fertilizer, the theater curtain, the door key, the heavy plow, and a primitive dental drill. Finally, a calendar introduced by Julius Caesar created a year of 365 days and a few minutes. His calendar had to be reformed, but not until the sixteenth century.

The Decline of the Western Roman Empire

Political and Economic Problems

Political and economic problems eventually undermined the imperial system. Roman leaders had never found a good way to pass power on to a successor. The reliance on the army to decide who ruled resulted in twelve soldier-emperors between 235 and 260 C.E., none of whom died peacefully in old age. To control their possessions, the Romans spent more of their wealth to support a growing bureaucracy and the military, pushing the state toward bankruptcy. Paying the taxes was a particular problem in the western half of the empire, where serious inflation substantially decreased real wealth. The Roman economy was stronger in the east, where the older, larger cities provided a stronger tax base. Thus a serious "balance of payment" problem developed between the west and the east. The frontier lands west of Italy consumed more than they produced, and to pay for goods and food they had to constantly find more precious metals (such as gold and silver) or more wealth in the form of slaves, which they could sell or trade to the east for manufactured products.

No matter how advanced, with its aquaducts, central heating, and bureaucracy, the empire gradually decayed from within. Leaders became consumed by rivalries while corruption, ineptitude, and civil wars eroded government, making the state vulnerable to invaders. The early third century was a turning point. Roman rulers were forced by increasing costs and the difficulties of controlling a growing empire to end further conquests and merely defend the existing frontiers, cutting themselves off from the income that conquest provided and further impoverishing the government. Some gold and silver mines in the western lands became exhausted, as did some of the fertile soil in Italy, making goods more expensive. Alongside these troubles were a steadily widening gap between rich and poor, a serious trade deficit with China, declining levels of literacy, and growing corruption, apathy, and loss of public spirit. A cooler climate may have diminished crop yields. Because of contacts with distant lands, Rome was also increasingly vulnerable to the spread of diseases and epidemics that killed many thousands. A plague in the empire from 251 to 266 C.E., which reached Europe from North Africa, caused dramatic population decline and weakened Roman military forces. At the height of the epidemic, 5,000 people were said to have died each day just in the city of Rome.

Celtic and Germanic Societies and the Romans

Celtic Societies

The decline of Rome also corresponded with the rise of two northern European societies, Celts and Germans, both of Indo-European origin. The Celtic peoples, whose culture had developed by the twelfth century B.C.E. in the Danube River Basin north of the Alps, posed a challenge to the expanding Romans. Powerful chiefs ruled small Celtic states, and priests, known as *druids*, organized the worship of their many gods. Many Celts lived in large fortified towns, and some had coins and writing. Aided by bronze and then iron technologies, the Celts had occupied large sections of central and western Europe, from Germany and France to the British Isles and Spain. Fierce warriors and fine horsemen, by 400 B.C.E. Celtic tribes had raided into Italy, sacked Rome, and weakened the Etruscan states. A Roman writer describing the Celtic armies in Gaul said that the many trumpeters and horn blowers, as well as their war cries, terrified their opponents.

However, the well-drilled, disciplined Roman legions overwhelmed the Celtic fighters, which were divided by tribal rivalries. Most of the Celts were eventually colonized by the Romans or dislodged by the Germans. In 225 B.C.E. the Romans overran the Celts in northern Italy, and first the Carthaginians and then the Romans crushed Celtic power in Spain. Julius Caesar conquered the Celts of Gaul. In 60–61 C.E., however, the Romans faced a temporary setback when Celts led by a warrior-queen, Boudica **(boo-DIK-uh)** (d. 61 C.E.), destroyed several Roman settlements in England. Boudica had good reason to despise the Romans, who had pillaged her territory, flogged Boudica, and raped her daughters. A Roman historian lamented the defeat brought by a woman, which caused the Romans great shame. In retaliation, the Romans sent in a larger force, killing 80,000 of Boudica's subjects. The queen committed suicide rather than surrender to the Romans.

Celtic societies and culture remained strong mostly in Ireland and the rugged hills of Wales and Scotland, where the challenge of overcoming long lines of communication kept the Romans from extending their rule. Indeed, the Roman emperor Hadrian **(HAY-dree-uhn)** had a remarkable 73-mile-long rock wall built across northern England to keep Celtic tribes out of Roman territory. Celtic culture was eventually modified by Christianity, which reached Ireland in the fifth century. Today the Irish, Scottish, and Welsh people still honor their Celtic heritage, but few are fluent in their original Celtic languages. In most of mainland Europe and England, Celtic culture was gradually Latinized and Germanized, although even today pockets of Celtic identity can be found in Brittany **(BRIT-uhn-ee)** (western France) and in northwest Spain.

Roman Army Camp This carving shows a camp being built by Roman legionnaires during a military campaign. Soldiers' helmets, shields, and pikes are propped up at the right side. Some men build walls and dig ditches.

Alinari/Art Resource, NY

Gilles Mermet/Art Resource, NY

Life on a Late Roman Empire Estate The painting, of a fortified manor house and its surroundings, shows typical farming activity for each season.

The Germanic peoples put pressure on the empire's northern borders and eventually began migrating into the empire. German societies seem to have been organized in Scandinavia and the northern plains of Germany. No known German cities or states existed. The Roman historian Tacitus praised the Germans for their hospitality, noting that they considered it a crime to turn any visitor away from their door. Expanding to the south and west, the Germans inflicted several defeats on Roman legions in Gaul in 113 B.C.E. Although the Romans reorganized their legions and crushed the Germans, fear of Germanic invasions was a major reason the Romans expanded northward. As a result, some Germans were brought into the Roman fold, and some served in the Roman army. However, most Romans viewed the Germans as dangerous "barbarians."

For the next several centuries Romans and Germans watched each other warily on the fringes of the empire. German tribes joined to form confederations, whose combined strength made them a greater threat. Pushed by their own enemies such as the westward-moving Huns from Central Asia, some Germans began looking to the Roman lands for new homes, and German-Roman conflict intensified as Germanic peoples began moving into the empire. In 251 C.E. the Germans defeated a Roman army and plundered the Balkans. The declining Roman Empire was unable to field enough high-quality soldiers to defeat the invaders because its shrinking population meant that men needed to farm could not be spared for the army. In 381 the Romans began drafting men into service, but many draftees mutilated themselves to avoid service.

German expansion had a major impact on Roman society. High taxes needed to support the Roman armies alienated all classes, but they fell primarily on poor peasants, many of whom lost their land and became workers on large landed estates. Sometimes whole villages placed themselves under the protection of a wealthy landlord. This system, in which men and women worked the land of their patrons, eventually reshaped the peasant class as they gave up their freedom in exchange for protection. Meanwhile, the upper classes increasingly escaped the cities, which they had earlier supported with their money and public service, for their country estates. Thus Roman cities slowly but steadily shrank in size as fewer children were born and the upper classes moved away.

The Division of the Roman Empire

Imperial Division and Roman Defeat

The mounting problems led to the division of the empire. Emperor Diocletian **(DIE-uh-KLEE-shuhn)** (r. 285–305) recognized the weakness of the western empire and divided the empire in half, making the Adriatic Sea an east-west dividing line. He ruled the east from Nicomedia **(NIK-uh-MEED-ee-uh)** in Anatolia and appointed another man, Maximian, as emperor in the west. A later emperor, Constantine (r. 306–337), temporarily reunited the empire under one ruler. He also established a new eastern capital on the Straits of Bosporus **(BAHS-puhr-uhs)**, first named New Rome and then Constantinople **(cahn-stan-tih-NO-pul)**—today's Istanbul **(IS-tahn-BUL)**. In 395 Constantinople became the capital of the eastern, or Byzantine Empire, which survived the western Roman Empire by nearly a thousand years.

The worst military defeats suffered by Roman armies occurred in the fourth and fifth centuries C.E., forcing emperors to abandon claims to many territories, including Britain. In 410 the Germanic Ostrogoths **(AH-truh-GAHTHS)** (eastern Goths) plundered the city of Rome. Also around 410, a branch of the Huns, fierce horse-riding Central Asian pastoralists, conquered Hungary and later pushed various Germans west into Gaul, Italy, and Spain. Led by the able warrior Attila **(uh-TIL-uh)** (406–453), the Huns ravaged the Balkans and Greece before plundering northern Italy in 452. Hun power soon collapsed, but Rome was again sacked by another German group, the Vandals, in 455 C.E. The official end of the western empire came in 476, when Germans deposed the last Roman emperor.

The western Mediterranean world was now ruled by various Germanic kingdoms, including the Vandals in Northwest Africa, the Visigoths (VIZ-uh-gahths) in Spain, and the Ostrogoths in Italy. Another German group, the Franks, under their leader Clovis (KLO-vuhs), conquered what is now France and western Germany. Meanwhile, Germanic Angles and Saxons migrated into England. These Germanic peoples retained a considerable amount of Roman culture; moreover, some adopted local versions of Latin, which formed the basis for **Romance languages** such as French, Italian, and Spanish.

Romance languages Languages that derive from Latin, such as French, Italian, and Spanish.

SECTION SUMMARY

- The *Pax Romana,* which began with Augustus, was a time of peace, prosperity, and cosmopolitan living, but also of imperial rule and a passive populace.
- The Romans set long-lasting legal standards and offered allegiance to a wide variety of gods, many of them borrowed from other peoples.
- Roman society was highly stratified; slaves performed much of the manual labor, and women, although accorded some significant legal rights, were generally subjugated.
- Rome served as a nexus for trade and communication, and it excelled in architecture and engineering.
- Beset by a range of problems, including uneasy succession, economic imbalance, overexpansion, climate change, and disease, the Roman Empire began to decline.
- The Celts, fierce warriors, posed a threat to the Romans, but they were eventually conquered and Latinized except for some in rugged areas of the British Isles.
- The Germans, whom the Romans considered barbarians, exerted a tremendous amount of pressure on the Roman Empire.
- The Roman Empire had trouble fielding enough soldiers or gathering enough money to fend off the German threat, since many of its poor had traded their rights for protection by the rich, and many of the rich had left the cities to live on their estates.
- The Roman Empire fell in 476 C.E., but an offshoot, the Byzantine Empire, lasted for another thousand years.

Christianity: From Western Asian Sect to Transregional Religion

How did Christianity develop and expand?

The one institution that was a vigorous part of the life of the Roman cities even in the final decades of the western empire was the Christian church. Christianity arose in Palestine (in western Asia) in the first century C.E. as a Jewish sect (see Map 8.3). The religious and social institutions of Christianity accompanied Greco-Roman culture into the new Germanic kingdoms, and together they defined the culture of the new societies that dominated Europe in the centuries following the Classical Age. To understand the history of the Western societies, we need to analyze the rise and values of Christianity.

Roman Palestine and Jesus of Nazareth

Palestine and Hebrew Traditions

Christianity was founded on the teachings of Jesus of Nazareth, a Jewish teacher in first-century C.E. Roman-ruled Palestine. Palestine and the surrounding region contained a mix of several traditions. For example, most people, including the Jews, spoke Aramaic (ar-uh-MAY-ik), the official language in the later Persian Empire, and most literate people wrote in Greek, a legacy of Hellenism. Various ideas from Egyptian, Mesopotamian, Phoenician, Persian, and Greek traditions undoubtedly influenced the Jewish and then Christian faiths. Palestine was one of the most restless Roman provinces and had a history of rebellion against Rome. Over the centuries the Hebrew prophets, such as Isaiah in the eighth century B.C.E. and Jeremiah, Ezekiel, and the "Second" Isaiah during the early Axial Age, explored the relations of the Hebrews to their God and other peoples. Jewish society was characterized by diverse beliefs and practices. Various mystical Jewish sects rejected both Hellenistic cosmopolitanism and the formal Jewish leadership. Jesus inherited these prophetic traditions and spoke of himself as the fulfillment of Jewish law.

Jesus and the Gospels

Much uncertainty surrounds the life of Jesus. Roman records confirm religious conflicts and instability in Palestine but make no mention of Jesus. According to Christian tradition, Jesus was a

Jewish carpenter, teacher, and healer who probably lived from around 7 or 6 B.C.E. to 30 C.E. As with Buddha and Confucius, our knowledge of Jesus and his career comes from the writings of followers, primarily through the four gospel (literally "good news") accounts of the Christian New Testament. The earliest of these narratives, the Gospel of Mark, was written around 70 C.E., some forty years after the death of Jesus. Like the other three gospels in the official canon compiled in the middle of the second century C.E., Mark was written not as a historical account but as a faith statement, a "witness" to the power of God in the lives of the early followers of Jesus. As a result, modern theologians and historians vigorously debate the historical accuracy of gospel accounts. Several dozen other gospels or fragments of gospels were not included in the Christian Bible, and some of them differ considerably from the official gospels. Thus it is unclear whether the gospel accounts were based largely on eyewitness testimonies, oral traditions, or earlier writings that have since been lost.

The gospels describe Jesus as, among other things, a moral reformer who confronted the Jewish leaders, especially the *Pharisees* **(FAR-uh-seez)**, a group that emphasized ritual purity, obeyed strict ceremonial laws, and awaited the coming of a messiah who would free them from the Romans. Jesus favored a simple life that included love of others, forgiveness of enemies, acceptance of the poor and other despised groups, and opposition to excessive legalism and ceremony. According to the Gospel of Matthew, Jesus summed up his teachings in two commandments: "Love God with all your heart, soul, and mind; and love your neighbor as yourself."[12] Matthew also reported that Jesus angered influential Jews and Romans by advising the wealthy to give their money to the poor since rich people were unwelcome in God's kingdom. Some modern theologians argue that Jesus made no claims to be divine or a "son of God," but described himself only as a healer and wisdom teacher. Other scholars emphasize that Jesus was seen as much more than a wisdom teacher by his followers.

Jesus's enemies, especially the Roman governor and a few Jewish religious leaders, accused him of treason against Rome, and Jesus was tried, convicted, and executed by crucifixion. Followers of Jesus claimed that he was revived or resurrected from death and that he "appeared to" his disciples. This belief in the continuing divine presence of Jesus probably motivated his followers to preach his message to others and honor his teachings by gathering for worship as a special sect within the first-century C.E. Jewish community.

Paul and the Shaping of Christianity

The evolution of the religion of Jesus into Christianity was greatly affected by the activities and writings of Paul of Tarsus **(TAHR-suhs)**, a port city in southeast Anatolia. Paul was a first-century Romanized Jew from a Pharisee family who said that he was miraculously converted to belief in Jesus as a young man. He then spent the rest of his life spreading this faith to non-Jews, traveling extensively to western Asian and Greek cities before his death in a prison in Rome about 64 C.E. Paul's teaching emphasized that Jesus was a divine being, the "son of God" who earned forgiveness for the sins of humankind by his death on the cross. By accepting Jesus as the Christ (*Christus* meant "anointed one"), Paul taught, a person could be saved from damnation to an eternity in Hell. Paul also preached that a non-Jew who did not follow Jewish laws and ritual could become a follower of Jesus. By arguing that there was neither Jew nor Greek, slave nor free person but instead a spiritual equality, he was challenging fundamental Roman assumptions such as those behind slavery. These kinds of beliefs prompted many otherwise broad-minded Roman citizens to regard Christians as a threat. Paul's patriarchal views also strongly influenced Christian thinking. Paul valued celibacy above marriage and urged wives to be subject to their husbands and remain silent in church.

Paul and His Mission

Paul disagreed strongly with those in Jerusalem who believed that Christians had to follow Jewish laws. Paul's decision to exempt converts from undergoing the circumcision required by Jewish law was crucial for the success of Christianity, for, in those days before antibiotics and anesthesia, such operations would have discouraged many. Peter, the chief disciple of Jesus, agreed that God made no distinction between Jews and others, and in Roman Catholic tradition Peter became the first bishop of Rome (and hence the first pope). Peter was probably killed in Rome during the persecution of Christians in 64. Eventually, most Christians believed they were saved by faith in Jesus, not by following any Jewish tradition.

Jewish Revolt and Dispersal

The victory of Paul in convincing Peter to include non-Jews was crucial in establishing Christianity as a world religion (see Map 8.3). A Jewish revolt from 66 to 73 C.E. resulted in the Roman destruction of the Jewish temple in Jerusalem and the dispersion of many Jews to other lands. During the revolt the *Zealots*, a group of Jewish rebels, held out in a hilltop fort known as Masada **(muh-SAHD-uh)** overlooking the Dead Sea. Although the Romans eventually took the fort, Masada stood through history as a symbol of Jewish resistance to oppression. After the Roman victory, any Jew became discredited in Roman eyes, so it was fortunate for the early Christians that they had broken

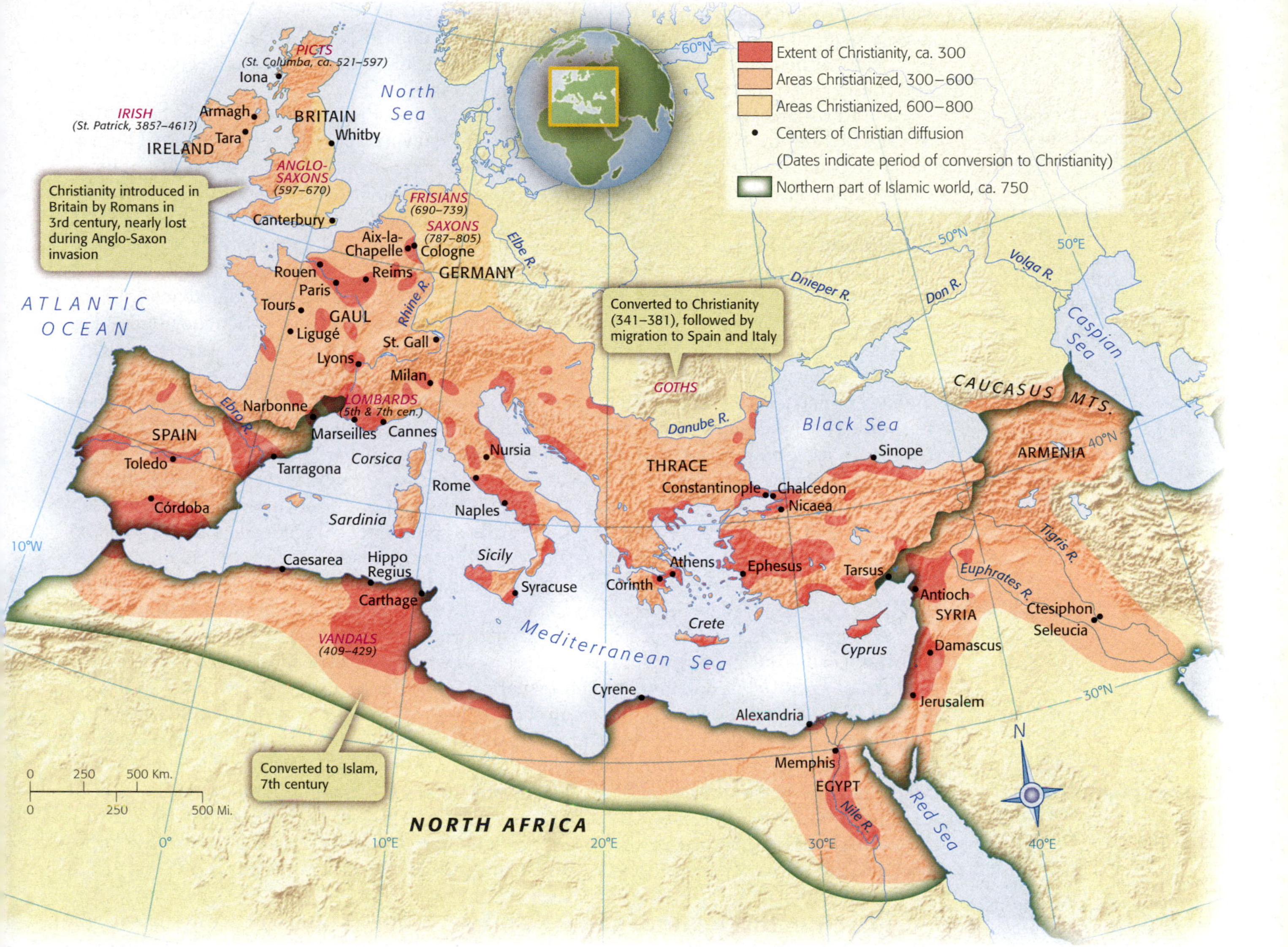

Map 8.3
Spread of Christianity

Christianity arose in Palestine in the first century C.E. and gradually gained footholds in parts of western Asia, North Africa, and southern Europe by 300 C.E. Over the next five centuries Christianity became the dominant religion in much of western and central Europe and expanded its influence in western Asia and North Africa.

with Judaism. Meanwhile, while Jews scattered across Eurasia and North Africa, the number of non-Jewish Christians continued to grow throughout the empire as the religion spread along the networks of trade and occupation throughout western Asia, North Africa, and southern Europe.

Christianity in the Mediterranean Zone

Christianity and Eastern Religions

The Roman context shaped Christian growth and institutions. Christianity had similarities to "mystery religions," many from western Asia, that were becoming popular in the Roman world at the same time. Some had their roots in Persian and Hellenistic traditions. Like the followers of Mithra **(MITH-ruh)** or Isis **(ICE-uhs)**, Christians believed in a life after death and had practices, such as a special initiation rite (baptism), that fostered a sense of religious community. But Christianity offered a greater emotional appeal than its competitors because of a belief in the spiritual equality of all people and a concern for the poor. Christians used the terms *heathen* and *pagan*, which had negative connotations, to describe those who followed polytheistic or animistic religions or were irreligious. These advantages helped Christianity gain greater acceptance. In 313 C.E. it became a legal religion by an edict of the Roman emperor Constantine, who believed he had won a battle because of the help of the Christian God. After this the organized church, loosely headed by the bishop of Rome, became more significant. By 400 C.E. non-Christian faiths had been banned and Christianity had become the official Roman religion, thus uniting state and church in a troubled marriage for over a millennium.

Arianism A Christian sect that taught that Jesus was not divine but rather an exceptional human being.

Nicene Creed A set of beliefs, prepared by the council at Nicaea in 325 C.E., that became the official doctrine of the early Christian church.

But Christians also had to contend with theological divisions. For example, the sect of **Arianism** (AR-ee-uh-niz-uhm) taught that Jesus was not divine but rather an exceptional human being. To combat what most Christians saw as heresies and to establish core beliefs, the emperor Constantine called a church council at Nicaea (nye-SEE-uh), in Anatolia, in 325 C.E., where he ordered the bishops to resolve their doctrinal differences and determine which beliefs to follow. The **Nicene** (NYE-seen) **Creed** they produced became the official doctrine of the early church and is still recited in many denominations.

The early Christians borrowed much Greco-Roman culture. Their main difference with the state was to refuse to acknowledge the emperor's official divine status, for which they sometimes were persecuted. Nevertheless, as the Christian religion spread, most Christians were left alone to worship as they wished, and they, in turn, acquired a Roman education and even celebrated traditional Roman festivals along with the new Christian ones, such as the Christians' celebration of the birthday of Jesus on the date of the old Roman and Mithraist festival of the winter solstice. Early Christians also generally adopted the Greco-Roman tolerance toward homosexuality. There were also tensions between Christians and non-Christians, such as those that led to the murder of the philosopher Hypatia (hye-PAY-shuh) by Christian mobs in Alexandria around 416 C.E. (see Profile: Hypatia of Alexandria, a Pagan Philosopher). And some early church leaders already blamed the Jews for the death of Jesus. In general, however, Christians adapted successfully to Roman life.

By the early fifth century, the political and social leaders in most Roman cities were Christian, but some Christian leaders began to be troubled by their social and political success. Followers of Jesus were supposed to focus on spiritual instead of worldly success, on Heaven instead of earth. One result of this questioning was monasticism, the pursuit of a life of penance, prayer, and meditation, either alone or in a community of other seekers. For instance, Benedict of Nursia (ca. 480–ca. 543) became so disillusioned by the hedonistic life in Rome that he moved into a cave and later founded western Europe's first monastic order, the Benedictines (ben-uh-DIK-teenz). Benedict formulated monastic rules that explained how to live a spiritually fulfilling life. Many monks and nuns practiced **asceticism**, austere religious practices, such as intense prayer, that were used to strengthen spiritual life and seek a deeper understanding of God. As part of this increasing tendency to withdraw from society, some church leaders began to reemphasize the superiority of a life of virginity over that of marriage, a value earlier stressed in the writings of Paul.

asceticism Austere religious practices, such as intense prayer, that were used to strengthen spiritual life and seek a deeper understanding of God; began to be used in the Christian church in the fifth and sixth centuries C.E.

Augustine and Roman Christianity

e Primary Source: Saint Augustine Denounces Paganism and Urges Romans to Enter the City of God In *City of God,* Augustine uses sarcasm to condemn the rituals of Rome's pre-Christian religion.

As Christianity expanded, it developed church institutions and produced thinkers who shaped the theology. In the declining decades of the empire, the North African bishop Augustine of Hippo (354–430 C.E.) redefined Christianity's relation to the Roman world and described Christian morality and history in a form that dominated western European culture for a thousand years. Augustine had tried several faiths before becoming a convinced Christian and eventually a priest, and then, in 395, bishop of Hippo, a city near Carthage. Like many Roman cities, Hippo had followers of many faiths, including various pagan and Persian traditions, all seen as heretical by the established church. After the sack of Rome by the Ostrogoths in 410, Augustine became troubled by the pagan accusation that it was the refusal of Christians to fight (many early Christians were pacifists) and the abandonment of the Roman gods that caused Roman society to wither. In his book, *City of God*, completed in 427, Augustine defended Christianity against its critics. He argued that the "city of God" comprised all who followed God's laws (i.e., Christians), while the "city of man" consisted of non-Christians, who ignored God's teachings and would be damned in a final judgment at the end of time. Augustine contended that all of history was in God's hands. He promoted a view of history as a straight line of progress from past to future, in which, at the end of history, Jesus would return to judge all humanity, living and dead.

In developing a moral thinking he viewed as superior to that of the tolerant Roman culture, Augustine also urged Christian men and women to remain celibate, viewing marriage as only for those with low self-control. He criticized sex outside of marriage, sanctioned sex within marriage only for procreation, and proclaimed men superior to women. Augustine's writings and theology strongly influenced the Roman Catholic tradition, as Christians increasingly separated themselves from hedonistic Roman traditions. For example, in 498 Christian leaders introduced an annual feast day in honor of St. Valentine to replace a holiday honoring Juno, the Roman goddess of love and marriage, and a popular, somewhat raunchy, Roman fertility festival.

HYPATIA OF ALEXANDRIA, A PAGAN PHILOSOPHER

Hypatia was a female philosopher and mathematician in the old Hellenistic city of Alexandria in Egypt, then part of the Roman Empire. At a time when Christianity was becoming more influential, she followed a non-Christian polytheistic religion and thus in Christian eyes was a "pagan." Perhaps nothing better shows the complex relationship between Christians and pagans in the late Roman Empire, and the tension within the Christian community itself, than her murder at the hands of a Christian mob in 415 C.E. To critics of religious intolerance such as the eighteenth-century English historian Edward Gibbon, Hypatia was a beautiful woman torn to pieces by a fanatic mob because she believed in the Greek spirit of reason instead of, in his view, the irrational beliefs of Christianity. But it was not that simple.

Hypatia was born around 355 C.E., the daughter of a well-educated mathematician and astronomer. As a youth she studied the works of the mathematician Euclid and other great thinkers of the Hellenistic era and became known for making geometry intelligible to students. She was also attracted to the study of philosophy, but not of the purely rational sort Gibbon imagined. She became a neo-Platonist, a person who saw philosophy as almost a religion, a way to discover the hidden spirit of the divine within each person. She also stressed the feminine aspects of culture and argued that women benefited from honoring goddesses. Hypatia wrote commentaries on mathematical and astronomical subjects and lived quietly as a teacher, did not publicly participate in pagan worship, and, like many Christian women of her day, practiced celibacy, although she was married to another philosopher. Women philosophers were uncommon in those days, but Hypatia's wisdom and learning were celebrated. Admirers claimed she had "the spirit of Plato and the body of Aphrodite [the Greek goddess of love]." Her students were both pagan and Christian. One of them became a Christian bishop in Anatolia but remained Hypatia's lifelong friend.

Conditions in Alexandria began to change after 391 C.E., when the Roman emperor Theodosius forbade pagan worship in the empire. During the next twenty years, more and more Christians felt called to eradicate all non-Christian religions, and violent attacks on Jews and pagans became more frequent. By then Christians were a majority of the city population, though they were divided into feuding factions. Tensions grew worse in the city after the fanatic Cyril, who was generally intolerant of non-Christians, won election as bishop in 412. Since Hypatia was a close friend and supporter of Orestes, the city's Christian governor, his bitter rival Cyril spread the rumor that the widely respected Hypatia was a witch and practiced black magic. He also encouraged attacks on Jews.

In 415 a semimilitary gang of young Christians allied with Cyril dragged Hypatia from her carriage, stripped off her clothes, murdered her, and burned her body. Cyril had not ordered this, but he had created a social climate that made such a crime possible. After this event, Alexandria became a more thoroughly Christian city. The Jews, who had been a substantial community in Alexandria for over 600 years, were expelled, and Orestes returned to Rome. Cyril was never punished for his part in Hypatia's death.

Later critics were probably wrong to view Hypatia mostly as a martyr to her non-Christian beliefs. She was also, at least partly, a victim of a jealous bishop. However, Gibbon and others were correct to see her as one of the last representatives of a tolerant paganism rooted in the cosmopolitan ethos of Hellenistic and Roman culture, which was replaced by an intolerant form of Christianity. Her death also represented the displacement of philosophers from the public forum by religious men who claimed that the ideas they preached were superior because they came from God rather than from book learning.

THINKING ABOUT THE PROFILE

1. What does Hypatia's career tell us about Alexandrian society?
2. What does her experience reveal about conflicts between Christians and non-Christians in the late Roman Empire?

Note: Quotation from Maria Dzidzka, *Hypatia of Alexandria* (Cambridge: Harvard University Press, 1995), 5.

Statue of Hypatia This statue honors the great pagan philosopher and mathematician of fifth-century Alexandria who was murdered by Christian rivals.

Ancient Art & Architecture Collection

Christian Society

Christianity filled the vacuum in the western Mediterranean as Roman government collapsed and many people left the cities in the fifth century. The population of the city of Rome fell from 800,000 in 300 to 60,000 in 530. The Christian clergy often provided the only semblance of order for those who remained. Church officials also achieved a huge boost when the Franks, a Germanic people, were converted to Latin Christianity under their ruler Clovis. Then, in the late sixth century, Europe was hit by many disasters, which were enumerated in 599 by an alarmed

Pope Gregory: "as the end of the world approaches, many things menace us which never existed before: inversions of the climate, horrors from the heavens and storms contrary to the season, wars, famine, plagues, earthquakes."[13] But the widespread mood of doom proved premature. A new age was dawning in western Europe. It was largely German and Christian in tone, with a Greco-Roman overlay of language and culture.

SECTION SUMMARY

- Christianity was born in Palestine, an area with a tradition of rebellion against Rome, and grew out of the Jewish prophetic tradition.
- Jesus opposed excessive legalism and ceremony, but scholars debate whether he saw himself as divine, or the "son of God."
- Paul was instrumental in spreading and shaping Christianity after Jesus's death, as well as in arguing that one did not have to be Jewish to become a Christian.
- Aided by the popularity of mystery religions similar to it and by the decline in quality of life, Christianity took hold and became the official Roman religion.
- In defending Christianity against its critics, Augustine distinguished between Christians, who would be saved, and non-Christians, who would be damned, and he also argued for strict standards of sexual morality that favored celibacy.

Revival in the East: Byzantines, Persians, and Arabs

How did the Byzantine and Sassanian Empires reinvigorate the eastern Mediterranean world?

A century after Roman emperor Constantine dedicated his new capital city, later known as Constantinople, in 330 C.E., the western part of the empire fell to various German groups while the eastern empire fostered a new and distinctive society, Byzantium. Byzantium saw itself as a continuation of the Roman Empire but developed a different political structure as well as a culture and church that was more Greek than Latin. By taking the brunt of attacks by resurgent western Asian peoples such as the Sassanian Persians, Byzantium gave the struggling new states in western Europe time to develop into a separate Latin Christian culture. The Persian-Byzantine conflict also helped shape the rising Arab society.

Early Byzantium and the Era of Justinian

Byzantium's Empire

Byzantium emerged as the most powerful state in the eastern Mediterranean region, a status it maintained for many centuries. Its capital, Constantinople, straddled the narrow waterway linking the Aegean and Black Seas and separating Europe from western Asia, symbolically linking diverse peoples and traditions. The large eastern Roman Empire initially encompassed the Balkans, Greece, Anatolia, Syria, Palestine, and Egypt. Few emperors in Rome enjoyed the power that the Byzantine government had over its people, economy, and religious institutions.

The most important early ruler of the Byzantine Empire was the Emperor Justinian **(juh-STIN-ee-uhn)** (r. 527–565 C.E.) (see Chronology: Byzantium and Western Asia, 224–616 C.E.). Spurred on and advised by his powerful and ambitious wife, Theodora **(THEE-uh-DOR-uh)**, Justinian was determined to defeat the German states in the west and reunite the old Roman Empire. His armies reconquered a large part of the western territories. They defeated the Ostrogothic kingdom in Italy in 563 after long years of fighting, but repeated battles for control of Rome left the city devastated, with only a few thousand impoverished, disease-ridden inhabitants. Moreover, Justinian's victories were accomplished only at the cost of high taxes, and he was barely able to defend his own domains from Huns, Persians, and various peoples migrating into Europe. During the first half of the seventh century, Justinian's successors had to fight the Sassanian Persians, and the western lands were once again lost (see Map 8.4).

Justinian's Government

Justinian also established a political pattern of despotism in which the Byzantine emperors were treated as near-gods by their subjects and thus gained absolute power over nearly every area of national life. They presided over a centralized and complex bureaucracy (hence our term *byzantine* for complicated and puzzling systems). Spies monitored the population. Justinian had many critics, among them the great Byzantine historian Procopius, who described the emperor as "at once villainous and amenable; as people say colloquially, a moron. He was never truthful with anyone. His nature was an unnatural mix of folly and wickedness."[14] But Justinian also collected all existing Roman laws into one legal code, preserving Roman legal principles for later generations.

In 540 the Byzantines encountered one of the most terrible epidemics in world history, often known as the plague of Justinian. The sickness, probably bubonic plague, began in Egypt and spread along the trade routes into western Asia before reaching Europe. At its height some 10,000 people a day perished. Ships were loaded with corpses, rowed out to sea, and abandoned. Agriculture largely halted and many communities were abandoned. A Christian bishop in Palestine wrote that "all the inhabitants, like beautiful grapes, were trampled and squeezed dry without mercy."[15] The plague returned several times until 590. When Justinian died at age eighty-three, his empire was much poorer, weaker, and less populated than it had been when he took power.

Byzantine Society, Economy, and Religion

Cities and Economic Life

Despite its many political misfortunes, the Byzantine Empire survived for centuries because of its social and economic strengths. The empire remained much more urban than western Europe. Constantinople grew to perhaps a million people and was described by a visitor as "a splendid city, how stately, how fair. It would be wearisome to tell of the abundance of all good things."[16] The rich in the cities lived in splendor, with luxury goods like silk clothes, carpets, and elegant tapestries provided by local industry. A huge gap separated rich and poor, but the Byzantine peasants faced unique restrictions. Laws required peasants who had lived many years in one place to remain there. They became bound to the soil, under the control of powerful landlords. Although Byzantine society was patriarchal, upper-class women in the large cities enjoyed influence, and some queens exercised considerable power. Women had the legal right to control their own property and to have their dowry returned if their husbands divorced them. However, men enjoyed greater legal safeguards, and wife-beating was common. In an era when maternal and infant mortality rates were high, pregnancy remained hazardous and childbirth dangerous.

CHRONOLOGY
Byzantium and Western Asia, 224–616 C.E.

224–226 B.C.E. Sassanians overthrow Parthians, begin building empire

306–337 B.C.E. Reign of Constantine

330 B.C.E. Founding of Constantinople

395 B.C.E. Final division of eastern and western empires

527–565 B.C.E. Reign of Justinian

540–590 B.C.E. Plague of Justinian

607–616 B.C.E. Sassanians conquer Syria, Palestine, and Egypt

The Byzantine economy flourished. Merchants and bankers were prominent members of the urban aristocracy and benefited from Constantinople's position astride the principal trade routes between Europe and Asia. Ships and caravans brought many products and resources to Constantinople: spices, cotton, and copper from India and Southeast Asia; jewels, silk, gold, and silver from China and Central Asia; gold, ivory, and slaves from Africa; cotton and grain from Egypt; grains, wool, and tin from northwestern Europe; olive oil and silver from Spain and Italy; timber, fur, copper, hides, and slaves from Russia and Scandinavia. The government placed a 10 percent tax on all goods that passed through the capital. Byzantine currency was internationally recognized, and Byzantine coins have been found as far away as China. But most trade with China and India had to go through Persian-controlled lands, and the Persian-Byzantine relationship alternated between uneasy peace and armed conflict.

Culture and Religion

The Byzantine society and culture, fundamentally Hellenistic Greek, inevitably diverged from the western Roman tradition in many ways, but especially in religion and culture. The Byzantines preserved and later passed on to the Latin west (often through the Muslims) the works of Plato, Aristotle, Homer, Sophocles, and other Greeks. The Christian church in the east also became separated from its Latin counterpart, over time evolving into the Greek Orthodox Church, which developed many customs and viewpoints quite foreign to the Roman church. Religion permeated all aspects of Byzantine life. The church, especially monasteries, gained control of considerable land and hence wealth. From the ruler, who controlled both temporal and religious affairs, to the ordinary citizen, religious questions were avidly discussed. Emperors proposed church reforms and called church councils to deal with what mainstream Christians considered heresies, including that of the **Monophysites** (muh-NAHF-uh-sites), who argued that Jesus had a single divine nature rather than both a divine and human form; and the **Nestorians**, who believed that the divine and human natures of Jesus were independent of each other. Christianity also affected gender relations. A goddess figure who represented urban prosperity was replaced by the much beloved Christian image of the Holy Virgin Mary, which gave women moral stature. But the church also viewed women as weak and inferior, both physically and morally, and easily tempted by sin.

Monophysites A heretical sect that argued that Jesus had a single divine nature rather than both a divine and a human form.

Nestorians A heretical Christian sect that believed that the divine and human natures of Jesus were independent of each other.

Werner Forman/Art Resource, NY

Interior of Santa Sophia Cathedral The great cathedral of Santa Sophia in Constantinople, rebuilt for Byzantine emperor Justinian, was famous for its spectacular interior.

Over time theological disputes between the eastern and western churches grew. In general, Greek Christians came to emphasize ritual and also refused to accept the notion that the bishop of Rome (later known as the pope) was superior in authority to the other bishops. Conflicts over authority and doctrine contributed to the final split between the Latin and Greek churches in the eleventh century. Meanwhile, the Monophysites formed the Armenian, Coptic, and Syrian Orthodox Churches. The Nestorians migrated to Persia, becoming the basis of the modern Chaldean and Assyrian Churches. From Persia they spread their faith along the Silk Road into India and China.

Byzantine art and architecture reflected the cultural diversity of this huge empire and was strongly influenced by western Asian traditions. The fusion of some Persian and Greco-Roman influences can be seen, for example, in the great dome in the Church of Santa Sophia (Holy Wisdom) in Constantinople, built under Justinian. The church was designed to symbolize inner Christian spirituality in contrast to human pride. Hence, the external appearance was modest but the interior was richly decorated with mosaics, marble columns, tinted glass, and gold leaf.

Sassanian Persians and Their Networks

Both the Roman Empire and the Byzantines had to deal with a revived Persia under the Sassanian dynasty, which generated frequent conflict during their four centuries of rule. Considering themselves the successors to the Achaemenids a half millennium earlier, the Sassanian court, based in modern Iraq, provided a focus for a brilliant culture mixing Hellenistic and Persian influences. Between 240 and 277 the Sassanians pursued empire. In the east they fought with the Kushans (KOO-shans), whose Afghanistan-based empire controlled parts of western India and Central Asia. The Sassanians overthrew the Parthians in 224 and spent the rest of the third century building their own empire. Eventually the Sassanians occupied much of Afghanistan and some of the Silk Road cities of Central Asia, but they lost these territories to the Huns in the fourth century C.E. To the west the Sassanians expanded into the Caucasus and Mesopotamia, creating chronic conflict with Rome in and around Syria. They also occupied parts of Arabia, including Yemen (YEM-uhn) in the south. In the sixth and early seventh centuries the Sassanians occupied the eastern Byzantine Empire, including Syria, Palestine, and Egypt (see Map 8.4). But years of war with Byzantium weakened both societies. In 651 the last Sassanian king was murdered and Arab Muslim armies gained control of all Sassanian territories.

Controlling much of the Persian Gulf, Sassanian Persia became a contact zone for international trade. Sassanian trade links stretched east as far as India, Central Asia, and China, and south into Africa. Byzantine and Sassanian coins were used as currency in the Silk Road cities. Persians produced some of the world's finest pottery, silver plates, pearls, brocades, carpets, and glassware, exchanging these for gems, incense, perfume, and ivory.

Sassanian Religion and Culture

In contrast to the religiously tolerant Achaemenids, the Sassanians mandated a state religion, Zoroastrianism. The government imposed orthodoxy, supporting the priesthood and sometimes persecuting other religions. However, state religions tend to decay, and Zoroastrianism was no exception. The Zoroastrian establishment became corrupt and rigid, and by the fifth century the faith was losing influence and followers. Yet Zoroastrianism spawned various religions that combined this faith with others. One of these new religions, Mithraism, became popular in the Roman Empire and spread as far west as England. Another new religion, **Manicheanism** (man-uh-KEE-uh-niz-uhm), founded by the Persian Mani (MAH-nee) (216–277 C.E.), was a blend of Zoroastrianism, Buddhism, and Christianity that emphasized a continuing struggle between the equally powerful forces of light and dark. Although Mani was executed for heresy, his faith suppressed by both the Sassanians and Christians, his religious dualism was later incorporated into Islam and some Christian sects.

Manicheanism A blend of Zoroastrianism, Buddhism, and Christianity, founded by Mani, that emphasized a continuing struggle between the equal forces of light and dark.

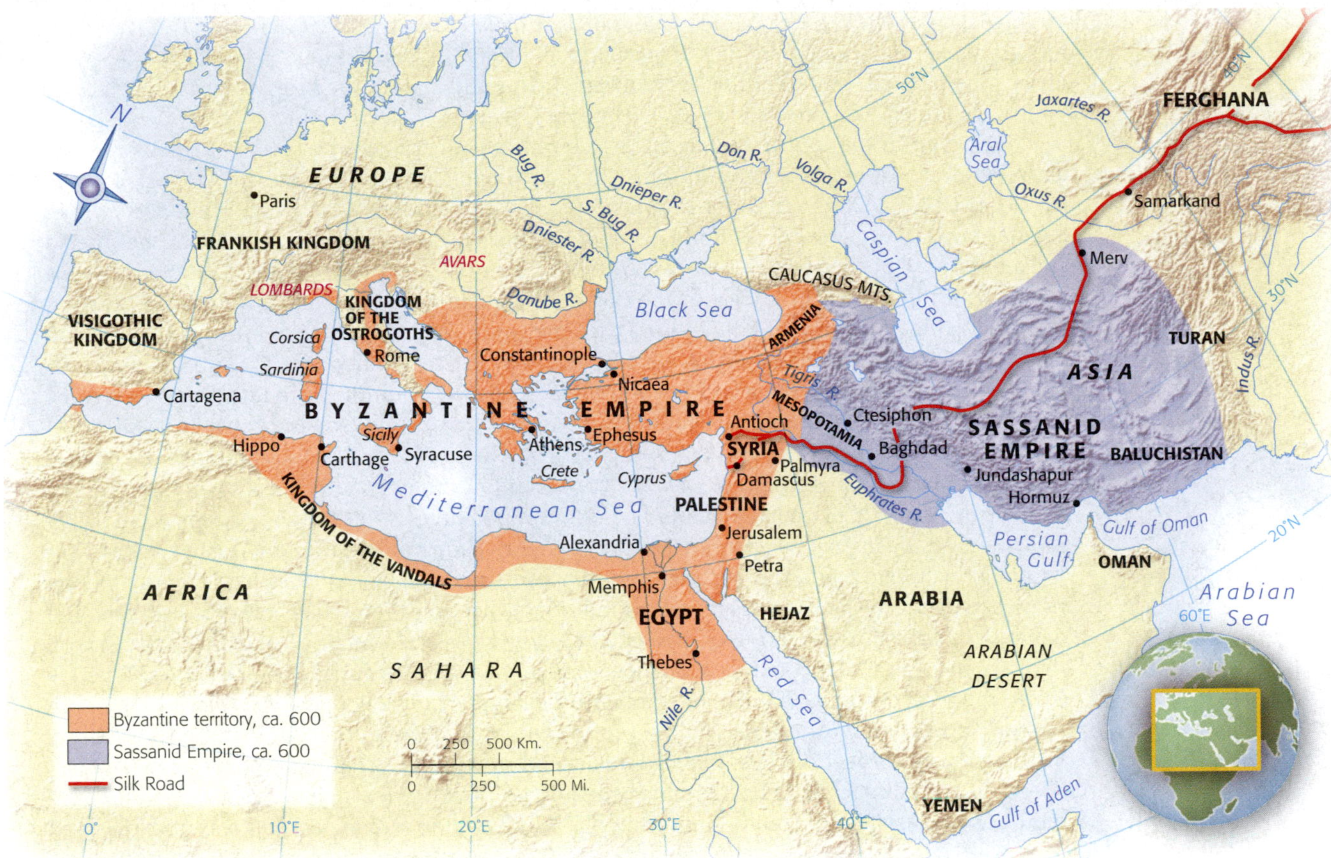

Map 8.4
The Byzantine and Sassanian Empires

By 600 C.E. the Byzantine Empire controlled much of southern Europe and the eastern end of the Mediterranean Basin, and the Sassanian Empire dominated most of the rest of western Asia, part of Turkestan, and Egypt. Various Germanic kingdoms held political sway in far western Europe, northern Europe, and northeast Africa.

Interactive Map

As Zoroastrianism gradually lost influence, the state became more tolerant of diversity and turned the capital city, Jundashapur, into a cosmopolitan intellectual center. Christian minorities such as the Armenians of the Caucasus region were allowed freedom of religion, and the Sassanians also welcomed Nestorian Christians fleeing Byzantine repression. Foreign scholars migrated to the newly tolerant state, as did Jews and others who feared persecution in Christian Europe. The Sassanians also collected scientific and literary books from many neighboring peoples, translated Greek writings, and established a renowned hospital and medical school. Sassanian Persia's multiculturalism provided a framework that enabled later Islamic governments to rule diverse peoples and faiths. But Zoroastrianism, too closely connected to Sassanian domination, became only a minor faith after Islam swept through the region.

Interregional Trade, Cities, and the Arabs

Geographical Foundations

The ebb and flow of long-distance trade in western Asia, often influenced by the activities of the Hellenistic Greeks, Romans, Byzantines, and Sassanians, helped foster Arab culture. Diverse Semitic societies lived in the Arabian peninsula, a dusty region of mountains, dry plains, and harsh deserts stretching from the Jordan River and Sinai southeast to the Indian Ocean. Most of the Arabian peoples were pastoral nomads divided into tribes. Roman sources described these mobile people: "All alike are warriors of equal rank, ranging widely with the help of swift horses and slender camels."[17] Others lived from trade or farming. Eventually all of these groups coalesced into the Arab society.

The Nabataeans

One of the peoples out of which Arab society arose were the Nabataeans **(NAB-uh-TEE-uhnz)**, who traded all over the Middle East and into Europe by land and sea. The Nabataean writing system became the inspiration for the Arabic script. They also established a kingdom and built a major trading city, Petra **(PE-truh)**, in today's Jordan, astride the overland caravan routes. Built in a narrow gorge, Petra had a population of 30,000 at its peak. The Petra residents developed an ingenious system for collecting and storing rainwater in this arid region. The ruins of Petra's spectacular tombs, with their elaborate facades carved into rock, still astonish visitors.

Beginning in the fourth century B.C.E., Petra flourished as a crossroads for goods moving between India, Arabia, Greece, and Egypt. But in 106 B.C.E. the Romans occupied Petra, and the city began a long decline as its trade shifted north to Palmyra **(pal-MY-ruh)**, on the Euphrates River in today's Syria. Palmyra thrived until 273 C.E., when the Romans crushed a revolt led by the shrewd and ambitious Queen Septimia Zenobia **(zuh-NO-bee-uh)**. After their conquest of the prosperous and ancient trading city in 114 B.C.E., the Romans had cultivated Palmyra to protect their eastern frontier. Taking advantage of Roman wars with the Goths, Zenobia sent her army into Egypt and then occupied much of Roman Asia. As ruler she invited Greek thinkers to Palmyra and encouraged religious tolerance. However, by controlling Egypt she controlled the Roman grain supply. After fierce battles the Romans reoccupied Palmyra and took Zenobia to Rome, where she died.

Yemenite Societies

The farming-based kingdoms that rose and fell in Yemen in southern Arabia since the days of the fabled Queen of Sheba around 1000 B.C.E. constituted another source for Arab culture. Yemen included an area of high, cool mountains and well-watered valleys. The Yemenite people were highly skilled, especially in civil engineering and architecture. They produced an abundant harvest with the aid of elaborate dams and terraces, and they constructed splendid cities in valleys and along mountainsides. City-states emerged, among them Saba, possibly the Sheba of the Hebrew Bible. The Yemenites traded by sea with India and East Africa, as well as across Arabia by land with the eastern Mediterranean and Mesopotamia. Frankincense from the region was prized as far away as Rome.

In the sixth century C.E. Arabian conditions began to change. Political disarray, an Ethiopian invasion, and commercial depression began to undermine Yemenite society and power. To the north, renewed conflict between the Sassanians and Byzantines led both of them to actively seek allies in central Arabia. As a result, Arabia became a political pawn caught between Orthodox Byzantium, Zoroastrian Persia, and Coptic Ethiopia. This situation also increased the traffic over land trade routes and fostered the settlement of many Christian and Jewish merchants in desert towns like Mecca **(MEK-uh)**. Some Arabs adopted these religions. In the seventh century all these trends fostered the emergence of a new Arab faith, Islam, out of classical roots. Eventually Islamic armies overran most of the Byzantine Asian territories and the Sassanian Empire.

SECTION SUMMARY

- Justinian ruled the Byzantine Empire absolutely and tried to retake the Roman Empire, with mixed results.
- More urban and wealthy than western Europe, the Byzantine Empire served as a trading hub for goods from across Europe and Asia.
- Byzantine culture became more Greek and less Roman, and the Byzantine church denied the authority of the pope and came to emphasize ritual and doctrine to a greater degree than did the Roman church.
- The Sassanians revived the strength of Persia and adopted Zoroastrianism as a state religion.
- Arab culture began to rise out of tribes of pastoral nomads, the trading cities of Petra and Palmyra, and the farming-based kingdoms of Yemen.

CHAPTER SUMMARY

The middle and late Classical Era in the Mediterranean world and western Asia was shaped largely by the activities and cultures of the Romans, Germans, Greeks, and Persians. The Romans adopted and spread some of the values of the classical Greeks, while also making major contributions in government, law, and architecture. For several centuries they had a republic in which some of the people had a voice in government and elected Rome's leaders. To acquire more resources and preempt challengers, the Romans gradually expanded their territory until it encompassed much of Europe, North Africa, and western Asia. In the process they defeated and conquered rivals, including the Etruscans, Carthage, Egypt, and the Celts. Eventually the Republic was replaced by a more autocratic system led by powerful emperors. Controlling the far-flung territories was expensive, however, and the Roman forces became overextended. Soon the Romans were also defending their territories against the incursions of the Germanic peoples.

New forces also developed in the eastern end of the Mediterranean basin. Christianity arose out of Jewish society in Palestine and spread throughout the Mediterranean world, western Asia, and North Africa. The power of the Christian church rose as Roman political power declined. In the east Byzantium emerged out of the eastern Roman Empire, developing into a distinct society that incorporated Hellenistic Greek political and cultural traditions. It also fostered the Greek Orthodox Church. Meanwhile, the Sassanians reinvigorated Persian society and built a large empire, eventually putting pressure on Byzantium. These conflicts increased travel over the trade routes and generated new currents in Arab society.

KEY TERMS

patricians
Centuriate Assembly
consuls
plebeians
tribunes
Pax Romana
Romance languages
Arianism
Nicene Creed
asceticism
Monophysites
Nestorians
Manicheanism

EBOOK AND WEBSITE RESOURCES

PRIMARY SOURCE

Saint Augustine Denounces Paganism and Urges Romans to Enter the City of God

LINKS

Diotima: Materials for the Study of Women and Gender in the Ancient World (http://www.stoa.org/diotima/). Contains excellent materials.

Exploring Ancient World Cultures (http://eawc.evansville.edu/). An excellent site with essays and links on the ancient Near East and Europe.

From Jesus to Christ: The First Christians (http://www.pbs.org/wgbh/pages/frontline/shows/religion). Valuable essays linked to a documentary series on U.S. Public Broadcasting.

Internet Ancient History Sourcebook (http://www.fordham.edu/halsall/ancient/asbook.html). An exceptionally rich collection of links and primary source readings.

e

INTERACTIVE MAPS

Map 8.1 Italy and the Western Mediterranean, 600–200 B.C.E.
Map 8.2 The Roman Empire, ca. 120 C.E.
Map 8.3 Spread of Christianity
Map 8.4 The Byzantine and Sassanian Empires

Livius: Articles on Ancient History (http://www.livius.org). Very useful site with many short essays on the Romans.

The Roman Empire (http://www.roman-empire.net/). Offers extensive materials and essays on the Romans.

Plus flashcards, practice quizzes, and more. Go to: www.cengage.com/history/lockard/globalsocnet2e

SUGGESTED READING

Aldrete, Gregory S. *Daily Life in the Roman City: Rome, Pompeii, and Ostia.* Norman: University of Oklahoma Press, 2009. Readable and accessible.

Boren, Henry C. *Roman Society*, 2nd ed. Lexington, MA: D.C. Heath, 1992. An overview of how Roman society developed.

Chauveau, Michael. *Egypt in the Age of Cleopatra.* Ithaca: Cornell University Press, 2000. A wide-ranging, readable study by a French scholar.

Cunliffe, Barry. *Europe Between the Oceans: 9000 BC–AD 1000.* New Haven: Yale University, 2008. Innovative interdisciplinary study of European development.

Cunliffe, Barry. *The Ancient Celts.* New York: Penguin, 1997. A detailed but fascinating overview of Celtic history and culture.

Dupont, Florence. *Daily Life in Ancient Rome.* Oxford: Blackwell, 1992. Discusses material culture and social values.

Fox, Robin Lane. *Pagans and Christians.* New York: Alfred A. Knopf, 1987. Explores the early rise of Christianity.

Grant, Michael. *The Fall of the Roman Empire.* New York: Macmillan, 1990. A brief and readable account.

Lynch, Joseph H. *Early Christianity: A Brief History.* New York: Oxford University Press, 2009. Covers the foundations and first half millennium.

Pomeroy, Sarah B. *Goddesses, Whores, Wives and Slaves: Women in Classical Antiquity.* New York: Schocken, 1975. An excellent study of women's lives in classical Greece and Rome.

Taylor, Jane. *Petra and the Lost Kingdom of the Nebateans.* New York: I.B. Taurus, 2001. An overview of this pre-Arab society.

Treadgold, Warren. *A Concise History of Byzantium.* New York: Palgrave, 2001. A comprehensive recent survey.

Wiesehofer, Josef. *Ancient Persia.* London: I.B. Taurus, 2001. Scholarly essays on pre-Islamic Persia and the Sassanians.

Young, Gary K. *Rome's Eastern Trade: International Commerce and Imperial Policy, 31 BC–AD 305.* London: Routledge, 2001. A recent scholarly investigation of the Roman trading system.

CHAPTER 9

Classical Societies and Regional Networks in Africa, the Americas, and Oceania, 600 B.C.E.–600 C.E.

CHAPTER OUTLINE

- Classical States and Connections in Northeast Africa
- The Blossoming of West and Bantu Africa
- Classical Societies and Networks in the Americas
- Populating the Pacific: Australian and Island Societies

PROFILE
A Moche Lord

WITNESS TO THE PAST
A Shopper's Guide to Aksum

Werner Forman/Art Resource, NY

Aksum Stele
Early in the Common Era the kings of the African state of Aksum, in what is today Ethiopia, decorated their capital city with tall, flat-sided pillars known as steles, some nearly 70 feet high, possibly as monuments to the royal family.

When the day dawns the trader betakes himself to his trade; the spinner takes her spindle; the warrior takes his shield; the farmer awakes, he and his hoe handle; the hunter awakes with his quiver and bow.

—Ancient Yoruba proverb about daybreak in a West African town[1]

FOCUS QUESTIONS

1. What were some of the similarities and differences between Kush and Aksum?
2. How did the spread of the Bantus reshape sub-Saharan Africa?
3. How did the Mesoamerican, Andean, and North American societies compare with each other?
4. How were some of the notable features of Australian and Pacific societies shaped by their environments?

In the classical world, few settlements were as specialized as those serving the caravans that crossed the trackless sands of the vast Sahara Desert of Africa, a barren landscape where scorching sun and arid soil made it nearly impossible to plant crops or trees. The journeys were interrupted by rest stops at caravan way stations, isolated oasis towns with gardens, date palms, and flocks of sheep where weary travelers could find fresh water and restock before resuming their journeys. The round trip of many weeks between the cities of the North African coastal zone and those on the southern fringe of the desert held many dangers besides thirst and discomfort, including fierce raiders on horseback. Camels, the major beast of burden in the caravan trade, were not always cooperative animals and often waged battles of wills with their handlers, but they could travel many days without water. Thanks to these caravans and the brave men who led them, sub-Saharan African products reached a wider world, and goods and ideas from North Africa and Eurasia found their way along the trade networks to peoples living south of the Sahara.

The diverse societies that arose in sub-Saharan Africa, the Americas, and Oceania (the Pacific Basin) were all shaped by their environment, whether that was a desert like the Sahara, a highland, a flood-prone river valley, or a rain forest, savannah, seacoast, or small island. Societies were also influenced by their contacts—friendly, hostile, or both—with other societies. Various Africans established connections with the wider world through long-distance trade, such as that carried on by the camel caravans across the bleak Sahara or by boat around the Indian Ocean. These connections ensured that few societies were completely isolated. During the Classical Era diverse societies developed in sub-Saharan Africa, the Americas, and Australia, and intrepid mariners settled most of the Pacific islands. These various communities worshiped their own deities, created their own artistic styles, valued some products more than others, and evolved their own social and political structures, including some states. At the same time, they had much in common.

Visit the website and eBook for additional study materials and interactive tools: www.cengage.com/history/lockard/globalsocnet2e

CLASSICAL STATES AND CONNECTIONS IN NORTHEAST AFRICA

What were some of the similarities and differences between Kush and Aksum?

In classical times tropical Africa and Eurasia were connected largely through intermediaries, including the North Africans linked to the trans-Saharan caravan trade and the maritime traders of the Indian Ocean. Two African societies, Kush **(koosh)** in Nubia and Aksum **(AHK-soom)** in Ethiopia, became trading hubs and powerful states. Both enjoyed particularly close ties with Egypt and western Asia.

CHRONOLOGY
Classical Africa

2000 B.C.E.–1000 C.E. Bantu migrations into Central, East, and South Africa

800 B.C.E.–350 C.E. Meroë Kingdom of Kush

500 B.C.E.–600 C.E. Garamante confederation dominates trans-Saharan trade

400 B.C.E.–800 C.E. Aksum kingdom in Ethiopia

200 B.C.E. Founding of Jenne-Jenno

300 C.E. Introduction of Christianity to Kush and Aksum

ca. 500 C.E. Founding of kingdom of Ghana

Iron, Cities, and Society in Kush

The kingdom of Kush, along the Nile south of Egypt, existed from about 800 B.C.E. to 350 C.E. (see Chronology: Classical Africa), flourishing as the major African producer of iron and an important crossroads for trade between sub-Saharan Africa and the Mediterranean (see Map 9.1). Its capital city, Meroë **(MER-uh-wee)**, became an industrial powerhouse of the classical world. Kush had many sources of iron ore, and heaps of iron slag litter the ruins of Meroë today. The Nubians in Kush imported pottery, fine ceramics, wine, olive oil, and honey from Egypt and western Asia, and they exported both iron and cotton cloth. Both the Greeks and Romans admired the Nubians. Some Nubians seem to have visited Greece, and others were members of the Persian armies that attacked Greece. Africans, possibly Nubians, went to Rome to trade or work as musicians, actors, gladiators, athletes, and day laborers in the city. At its height Meroë was a grand city of perhaps 25,000 inhabitants, containing massive temples, large brick-lined pools that may have been used for public baths, and rows of pyramids, similar to those in Egypt, where kings and queens were buried in splendor. The highly skilled builders used masonry, stonework, fired brick, and mud brick. As in the Indus cities, washing and sanitation facilities, with many latrines, serviced Meroë's population.

Kushite Society and Politics

Although influenced by Egypt, Kushite society and culture were distinctive. At the top of the social hierarchy were absolute monarchs, including some queens, who both governed the state and served as guardians of the state religion and the temples. Besides worshiping some Egyptian gods, Kushites considered their monarchs, like those in Egypt, to be divine. Inscriptions testify to the piety of rulers, and Roman sources report that kings were guided by laws and traditions:

> *It is their custom that none of the subjects shall be executed, even if the person condemned to death appears to deserve punishment. Instead the king sends one of his servants bearing a symbol of death to the criminal. He upon seeing [it], immediately goes to his own house and kills himself.*[2]

Queen mothers seem to have played an influential role in politics. Below the ruler were the military and bureaucratic elite. Kush's military officers led an army feared for both its weapons and the appearance of its soldiers. The Greek historian Herodotus described the soldiers of Kush:

> *[They] were clothed in panthers' and lions' skins, and carried long bows made from branches of palm trees, and on them they laced short arrows made of cane tipped with stone. Besides this they had javelins, and at the tip was an antelope horn, made sharp like a lance; they also had knotted clubs. When they were going into battle they smeared one half of their body with chalk, and the other half with red ocher.*[3]

Below the bureaucratic and military elite were free peasants and slaves. Women played a variety of economic roles, working in gold mines and engaging in farming and craft production. They also served as priestesses, perhaps specializing in the honoring of female deities.

Kushite Culture

Kushites enjoyed a rich culture. Some Greek-speaking teachers apparently lived at Meroë, and at least one Kushite king studied Greek philosophy. Meroë also had artists who produced highly polished, finely carved granite statues of their monarchs. Music played on trumpets, drums, harps, and flutes was a part of ceremonial and religious life, and some of the instruments may have been

CHRONOLOGY

	Africa	The Americas	Oceania
800 B.C.E.	**800 B.C.E.–350 C.E.** Kush		
400 B.C.E.	**400 B.C.E.–800 C.E.** Aksum		**300 B.C.E.–1200 C.E.** Polynesian settlement of Pacific
200 B.C.E.	**200 B.C.E.** Founding of Jenne-Jenno	**200 B.C.E.–600 C.E.** Hopewell mound builders **200 B.C.E.–700 C.E.** Moche **200 B.C.E.–750 C.E.** Teotihuacan **150 B.C.E.–800 C.E.** Flourishing of Maya society	
500 C.E.	**ca. 500 C.E.** Founding of Ghana		

imported from Egypt and Greece. People of all classes and both genders wore jewelry, and the ruins of at least one tavern have been found littered with thousands of goblet fragments, suggesting that wine was a popular drink. Finally, the presence of writing on numerous tombstones as well as graffiti suggests that literacy was widespread among all classes. Along with other distinctive achievements, Kushites developed their own alphabet, **Meroitic** (mer-uh-WIT-ik), a cursive script that can only be partly read today. Meroitic gradually replaced Egyptian hieroglyphics in monumental inscriptions. Indeed, over time Egyptian influence apparently faded while indigenous culture flourished.

Meroitic A cursive script developed in the Classical Era by the Kushites in Nubia that can only be partly read today.

The Legacy of Kush

After a millennium of power and prosperity, by 200 C.E. Kush was in decline, in part from environmental deterioration. Centuries of deforestation and overgrazing had helped produce a drier climate. Climate change was widespread in the world at that time, and it may have also hastened the decline of the Han Chinese and Roman Empires. Chronic warfare with the Ethiopian state of Aksum also contributed to Meroë's problems. In 350 C.E. an invasion by the Aksum army destroyed what remained of the Kush kingdom.

Spread of Kushite Traditions

However, the culture of Kush was kept alive in some neighboring societies. Some of its people, including the rulers, may have migrated elsewhere in Africa, spreading their iron technology and culture. Some West African societies developed political traditions not unlike those in Kush, and some peoples now living a few hundred miles to the southwest of Meroë still show many signs of Kushite influence, including recreational activities (such as wrestling), fashion, body art, and material life.

Several new kingdoms arose from the ashes of Kush, and contacts with the outside world eventually brought a new religion, Christianity, that became dominant in Nubia between the fourth and sixth centuries C.E. During this time many churches were built. Nubian Christianity was a branch of the **Coptic** (KAHP-tik) **Church**, which followed Monophysite thought (see Chapter 8) and had become influential in Egypt. Many Copts still live in Egypt. But the Christian kingdoms of Nubia, isolated from other Christians to the north by the Islamic conquest of Egypt in the seventh century C.E., gradually faded. Around 1400 C.E. Muslims conquered the last Christian Nubian state, and most people converted to Islam. Today only the ruins of Christian churches and monasteries of Nubia remain, along with the Meroite pyramids, the material legacy of Kush.

Coptic Church A branch of Christianity, based on Monophysite ideas, that had become influential in Egypt and became dominant in Nubia between the fourth and sixth centuries C.E.

The Aksum Empire and Society

Another literate urban African state, **Aksum**, emerged in the rocky but fertile Ethiopian highlands beginning around 400 B.C.E. Despite difficult geographical terrain and an unpredictable climate, its peoples traded with Egypt and also benefited from proximity to the Red Sea, the major maritime route between the Mediterranean Sea and the Indian Ocean. At the Red Sea's narrow-

Aksum A literate, urban state that appeared in northern Ethiopia before the Common Era and grew into an empire and a crossroads for trade.

Map 9.1 Classical Africa, 1500 B.C.E.–600 C.E.
During this era, Kush, Aksum, and Jenne were major African centers of trade and government. Trade routes crossed the vast Sahara Desert, and the Bantu-speaking peoples expanded into central, southern, and eastern Africa.

Interactive Map

est point, only 20 miles of water separates the southern tip of Arabia from Northeast Africa. Many Semitic people from Arabia crossed into Ethiopia and settled. Although many deep gorges inhibited communication across the plateau, accessibility to Arabia greatly benefited the northern Ethiopians and may have allowed them to establish links to the Hebrews. Ethiopian legends claim that the Queen of Sheba (Saba), who, according to biblical accounts, met the Hebrew King Solomon, was in fact an early Ethiopian monarch, Queen Makeda **(ma-KAY-da)**, who went to Israel in search of knowledge. In the tale Makeda supposedly told her people:

> *Let my voice be heard by all of you, my people. I am going in quest of Wisdom and Learning. My spirit impels me to go and find them out where they are to be had, for I am smitten with the love of Wisdom and I feel myself drawn as tho by a leash toward Learning. Learning is better than treasures of gold, better than all that has been created upon earth.*[4]

Semitic immigrants from Yemen, the probable location of the ancient Sheba kingdom, may have brought the story with them to Ethiopia and adapted it for local needs. The son of Solomon and Makeda, Menelik **(MEN-uh-lik)**, supposedly founded a new kingdom, called Aksum.

Located on the northern edge of the Ethiopian plateau near the Red Sea, Aksum was a center of agriculture and both bronze- and ironworking inhabited by the ancestors of the Amharic **(am-HAR-ik)** people who today dominate central Ethiopia. Between 400 B.C.E. and 100 C.E. Aksumites built their first temples and palaces of masonry, as well as a city, dams, and reservoirs. Irrigation and terracing supported productive farming. The Aksumites also developed an alphabet and enjoyed close economic and cultural exchange with both southwestern Asia and eastern Africa. In about 50 C.E. they built an empire that dominated a large section of Northeast Africa and flourished chiefly from trade. Soon Aksum had eclipsed Meroë and gained control of the trade between the Red Sea and the central Nile. It became so well known that the Persian prophet Mani included it with Persia, Rome, and China among the world's four great kingdoms.

From Graham Connah, *African Civilizations*, p. 44. Reproduced by permission of Cambridge University Press

Queen Amanitere Queen Amanitere ruled Meroë along with her husband, King Natakamani, around 2,000 years ago. In this relief on the Lion Temple at Naqa, Kush, she holds vanquished foes by the hair while brandishing swords, thus demonstrating the power of the royal couple and the Kushite state.

The Aksumites traded all over the Middle East, eastern Mediterranean, and East Africa. The trade network also reached to Sri Lanka and India, and many Indian coins have been found at Aksum (see Witness to the Past: A Shopper's Guide to Aksum). The Aksumites exported ivory, gold, obsidian, emeralds, perfumes, and animals and imported metals, glass, fabrics, wine, and spices. They used the Greek language in foreign commerce and were the first sub-Saharan Africans to mint their own coins. Byzantium sent envoys to the court, seeking alliances against common enemies in Arabia. The Aksumites' extensive ties with the Semitic peoples of Yemen led to considerable genetic and cultural intermixing between these two peoples. The classical Amharic language, **Geez (gee-EZ)**, is a mixture of African and Semitic influences. There was also much Hebrew influence on Ethiopian literature and religion. Indeed, the modern Amharic royal family, descendants of Aksumite kings, claimed ancestry from King Solomon and Queen Makeda. The Jewish communities known as *Falasha* **(fuh-LAHSH-uh)** have lived in northern Ethiopia for many centuries.

Geez The classical Amharic language of Ethiopia, a mixture of African and Semitic influences.

Aksum's social structure was dominated by kings who had a paternalistic attitude toward their people. A fourth-century C.E. king left an inscription in which he claimed: "I will rule the people with righteousness and justice, and will not oppress them."[5] Judging from their spectacular palaces, kings also enjoyed great wealth and power. A sixth-century Byzantine ambassador reported on the royal family's pomp and ceremony, writing that the king wore *a golden collar. He stood on a four-wheeled chariot drawn by four elephants; the body of the chariot was high and covered with gold plates. The king stood on top carrying a small gilded shield and holding in his hands two small gilded spears.*[6]

Below the royal family was an aristocracy that supplied the top government officials, a substantial middle class including many merchants, and peasants and slaves, who could be conscripted for massive building projects.

The capital city of Aksum was a wealthy and cosmopolitan trading center widely known for its monumental architecture, including magnificent pillars, thin stylized representations of multistoried buildings (some over 100 feet high), many stone platforms, and huge palaces. The making and transporting of the huge monoliths and stone slabs required remarkable engineering skills.

The Aksum Legacy

Christianity in Aksum

Christianity became influential just as Aksum reached its height of economic and military power in the fourth century C.E. Christian missionaries traveled the trade routes from western Asia, with whom the Aksumites had long exchanged goods and ideas. The king adopted the faith, making Christianity the official religion of the kingdom. According to a Roman source, he "began to search out Roman merchants [at Aksum] who were Christian and to give them great influence and to urge them to establish [churches], supplying sites for buildings, and in every way promoting the growth of Christianity."[7] The king had political reasons for conversion, since he wanted to establish closer relations with Rome, Byzantium, and Egypt. But the Amharic population only slowly adopted the new faith. Ethiopian Christianity resembled the Coptic churches of Egypt and Nubia but also incorporated some of the long-entrenched spirit worship and various Hebrew practices, including the Jewish sabbath and kosher food.

Aksum eventually collapsed as a result of several forces. By 400 C.E., reduced rainfall and the resulting pressure on the land had produced an ecological crisis. Political problems added to imperial decline. In addition, the conquest of southern Arabia by Aksum's enemy, Sassanian Persia, in 575 diverted the Indian Ocean commerce from the port of Adulis. Then the rapid Islamic conquests of western Asia and North Africa beginning in the middle of the seventh century cut Aksum off from the Christian world. Aksum's trade withered, and it fell into economic stagnation, cultural decline, and political instability. By 800 C.E. the capital city was abandoned. Unlike Kush, Ethiopian society persisted in recognizable form. Over the centuries Christianity became a deeply ingrained local religion in the Ethiopian highlands, producing the unique Ethiopian Christianity of today. The Ethiopian church, closely connected to the monarchy, owned many landed estates. Ethiopians remained relatively isolated in their mountain fastness for the next ten centuries.

SECTION SUMMARY

- The kingdom of Kush in Nubia, with its capital city of Meroë, was a major African iron producer and crossroads of trade between sub-Saharan Africa and the Mediterranean.
- Kush was influenced by Egypt but was also remarkable for its rich culture and its fearsome warriors and absolute monarchs.
- Aksum, in the Ethiopian highlands, had contact with Egypt and Arabia, may have forged links with the Hebrews, and after a time eclipsed Meroë as the region's primary trade center.
- Aksum's king converted to Christianity as a means of establishing closer relationships with Rome, Byzantium, and Egypt.
- Like Kush, Aksum may have declined in part because of climate change, but it was also hurt by the Islamic conquest of its neighbors; unlike Kush, however, the society endured into modern times.

THE BLOSSOMING OF WEST AND BANTU AFRICA

How did the spread of the Bantus reshape sub-Saharan Africa?

Complex urban societies also arose in West Africa, especially in the Sudanic region, on the Sahara's southern fringe, among peoples like the Mande **(MAHN-day)**. These societies were linked to North Africa and beyond by trade networks. Meanwhile, Bantu-speaking Africans continued to spread their languages, cultures, and technologies widely, occupying the southern half of the continent. Some became connected to trade networks linked to east coast port cities.

WITNESS TO THE PAST

A Shopper's Guide to Aksum

The following account of the trade of Aksum comes from the *Periplus of the Erythrean Sea,* written by an unknown Greek sometime in the second half of the first century C.E. The Periplus was a guide prepared for merchants and sailors that outlines the commercial prospects to be found in Arabia, the Indian Ocean, and the Persian Gulf. It also describes many of the bustling ports of this region. Hence, the *Periplus* is an excellent source for understanding Classical Era networks of exchange. In this excerpt, we learn about the port city of Adulis (A-doo-lis) on the Red Sea. Adulis, now called Massawa (muh-SAH-wuh), was the chief Aksumite trade distribution center, where goods from the Ethiopian interior and from faraway places such as India, Egypt, and the Mediterranean were brought for sale or transshipment.

Adulis [is] a port . . . lying at the inner end of a bay. . . . Before the harbor lies the so-called Mountain Isla, . . . with the shores of the mainland close to it on both sides. Ships bound for this port now anchor here because of attacks from the land [by bandits]. . . . Opposite Mountain Island, on the mainland, . . . lies Adulis, a fair-sized village, from which there is a three day's journey to Coloe, an inland town and the first market for ivory. From that place to the [capital] city of the people called Aksumites there is a five day's journey more; to that place all the ivory is brought from the country beyond the Nile. . . .

There are imported into these places [Adulis], undressed cloth made in Egypt for the Berbers; robes from . . . [modern Suez]; cloaks of poor quality dyed in colors; double-fringed linen mantles; many articles of flint glass, and others of . . . [agate] made in . . . [Thebes, Egypt]; and brass, which is used for ornament and in cut pieces instead of coin; sheets of soft copper, used for cooking utensils and cut up for bracelets and anklets for the women; iron, which is made into spears used against the elephants and other wild beasts, and in their wars. Besides these, small axes are imported, and adzes and swords; copper drinking cups, round and large; a little coin for those coming to the market; wine of Laodicea [on the Syrian coast] and Italy . . . ; olive oil . . . ; for the King, gold and silver plate made after the fashion of the country, and for clothing, military cloaks, and thin coats of skin. . . . Likewise from the district of Ariaca [on the northwest coast of India] across this sea, there are imported Indian cloth [fine-quality cotton]. . . . There are exported from these places ivory, and tortoise-shell and rhinoceros-horn. The most [cargo] from Egypt is brought to this market [Adulis] from the month of January to September.

THINKING ABOUT THE READING

1. What were some of the societies that were linked to the trade at Adulis?
2. What does this reading tell us about the networks of exchange that connected Aksum to a wider world?

Source: W. H. Schoff, trans. and ed., *The Periplus of the Erythraen Sea: Travel and Trade in the Indian Ocean by a Merchant of the First Century* (London, Bombay & Calcutta, 1912).

Sudanic Farming, Cities, and the Trans-Saharan Networks

Geographical Foundations

In the vast but dry grassland region known as the Sudan (soo-DAN), lying in West and Central Africa between the Sahara and the tropical forests, societies adapted their economic life to the prevailing ecology. Most Sudanese became farmers living in small, largely self-sufficient villages, growing vegetables and cereal crops, especially millet and sorghum, that needed little water. West Africans also grew cotton and developed richly colored cotton clothing. The food grown in a large fertile delta region along one stretch of the Niger (NYE-juhr) River helped to feed the people of the trading cities.

Some Sudanese along the Niger River congregated in large towns and cities that reached 30,000 or 40,000 in population. The major hub, Jenne-Jenno, located in what is now the nation of Mali, developed as early as 200 B.C.E. The residents built circular houses made of straw and coated with mud and also worked copper, gold, and iron, which they obtained from mines several hundred miles away. Gold dust and small copper ingots (ING-guhts) apparently served as currency throughout the Sudan. By 400 C.E. Jenne-Jenno had become a crucial transshipment point where goods arriving by camel or donkey caravan were exchanged for goods moved by boat along the Niger River. Jenne-Jenno continued to flourish as a commercial center for many centuries, closely tied, like other Sudanic cities, to hemispheric trade by the caravans across the Sahara. Eventually a wall over a mile in circumference surrounded the city to protect the residents. Built upon a

Ghana The first known major Sudanic state, formed by the Soninke people of the middle Niger Valley.

Mande Diverse Sudanic peoples who spoke closely related languages, shared many customs, and dominated the western Niger River Basin and adjacent areas of West Africa.

griots A respected class of oral historians and musicians in West Africa who memorized and recited the history of the group, emphasizing the deeds of leaders.

productive agriculture, Jenne-Jenno exported grain, fish, and animal products in exchange for metals. Historians suspect that Jenne-Jenno and other commercial centers in the Niger Valley were probably independent city-states for most of the first millennium C.E.

Large cities and states were less common in sub-Saharan Africa than in Eurasia and North Africa, in part because of smaller population densities. The African agricultural system, mostly based on shifting cultivation, suited the soils but could not generally support large settled populations. At the beginning of the Common Era the African continent may have contained between 15 and 25 million people, much less than half that of China. About half lived in Egypt, Kush, and along the Mediterranean coast. Small population densities meant that societies were held together by social and economic ties and did not require a powerful state to maintain order. The establishment of various caravan routes crossing the Sahara's barren sands, which greatly aided the growth of Sudanic societies by fostering interregional trade, began well before the Common Era. Eventually a large trade system spanned the Sahara, linking the Sudanic towns with the southern Mediterranean coastal societies such as Carthage. The gold used in coins minted in Carthage may have come from western Africa. Salt moving south to the Sudan and gold moving north to the Mediterranean drove the complex Saharan trade. Sudanic cities also shipped north cotton cloth, leather goods, pepper, and slaves, which the merchants in North Africa then sold to Europe.

Although Sudanic societies were largely self-sufficient, they needed salt mined in the central Sahara and along the West African coast. The salt trade was mostly controlled by the *Garamante* tribal confederation, which inhabited a large desert region north of the Sudan. These Berber (BUHR-buhr) people dominated the caravan trade routes as intermediaries from around 500 B.C.E. to 600 C.E., managing a vast commercial network. The Garamantes used camels as pack animals and horses to pull light chariots. To the Greeks and Romans, they were warlike barbarians, but in fact, these Saharans made the parched desert livable by combining pastoral stock raising with irrigated farming. They constructed several thousand miles of underground canals to cultivate their farms, lived in walled cities and villages, built stone citadels as military outposts, and were apparently governed by royal families. Their state collapsed around the same time as the Roman Empire, and the remnants were later overrun by Muslims.

West African States and Peoples

As in Kush and Aksum, commerce stimulated the growth of states in the Sudan and West Africa. Kingdoms apparently grew out of markets and taxed the trade in gold and other commodities. The Soninke (soh-NIN-kay) people of the middle Niger Valley formed the first known major Sudanic state, **Ghana** (GAH-nuh). Although Ghana existed by at least 700 C.E., it was probably formed several centuries earlier. Excavations of the probable capital city show a stone town that was built sometime between 500 and 600 C.E. Ghana reached its height as a trade-based empire in the ninth century and flourished until the thirteenth.

Diverse **Mande** (MON-day) peoples may have been typical of classical Sudanic societies. The Mande spoke closely related languages, shared many customs, and dominated the western Niger River Basin and adjacent areas. Mande speakers included such ethnic groups as the Soninke (who established Ghana), Mandinka (man-DING-goh), Malinke (muh-LING-kee), and Bambara (bam-BAHR-uh) peoples. By 900 or 800 B.C.E. Mande farmers lived in large walled villages, and they may have built Jenne-Jenno. Later, Mande speakers dominated much of the western Sudan.

The Mande groups shared many common social, political, and religious traditions. Their societies included aristocratic, warrior, and commoner classes and a special group of ritual and religious specialists. The Mande eventually developed theocracies in which chiefs and village heads combined religious and secular duties. A respected class of oral historians and musicians known widely as **griots** (GREE-oh) memorized and recited the history of the community, emphasizing the deeds of leaders. Many Mande of all classes enjoyed considerable prosperity, often from making their elaborate and

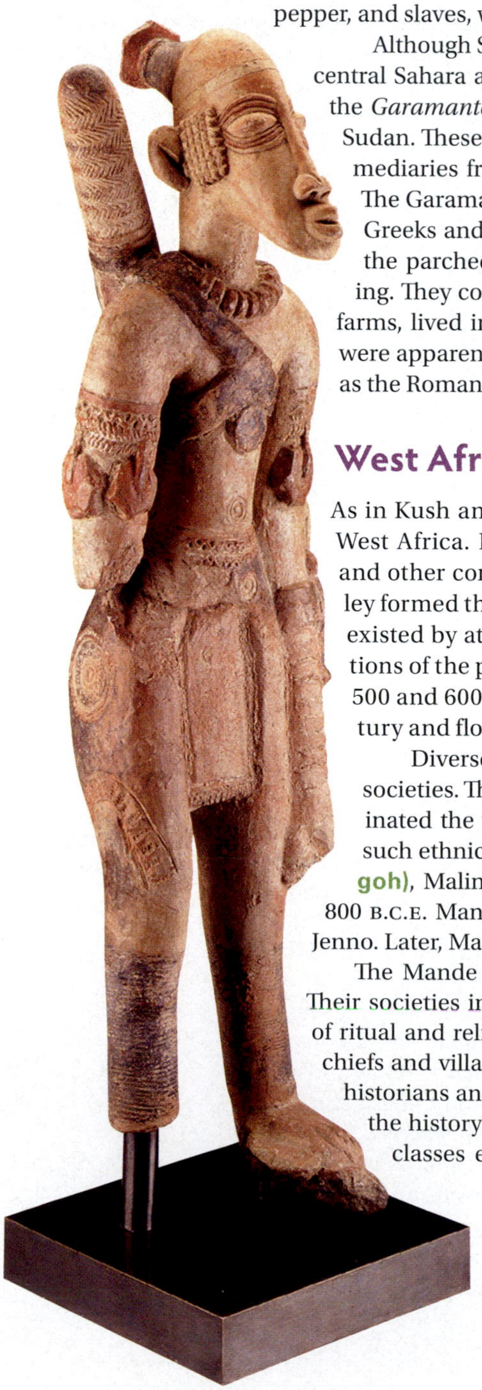

A Jenne Warrior This statuette, about 2 feet tall and made of a baked clay known as terracotta, likely portrays a warrior in Jenne, probably of high status, although some experts believe it portrays a founding ancestor.

beautiful cotton clothing, which was traded widely. The Mande and other Sudanic peoples also developed some common ideas about religion, including animism. Although they believed in a distant creator god, spirits of nature and ancestors loomed large in daily life. The Mande drew no neat line between the living and the dead, and they also wanted to keep the favor of good spirits and avoid the hostility of bad ones.

Guinea Coast

Over time various peoples, including some from the Sudan, migrated into the Guinea **(GIN-ee)** coast, a migration made possible by new tools and agricultural techniques. The Guinea coast, which stretches some 2,000 miles from modern Senegal **(sen-i-GAWL)** to southeastern Nigeria **(nie-JEER-ee-uh)**, was mainly covered by forest and swamp and had few edible plants or game animals. The mixing of Sudanic and other traditions in this area produced unique new societies. To survive their challenging environment, the people lived mostly in small, self-sufficient villages with rich social networks. They practiced subsistence agriculture, with yams and bananas as the staple crops, often working the land communally. The Guinea peoples also traded with the Sudanic societies, over land or by boat up the rivers such as the Niger and Volta **(VAHL-tuh)**, and thus became linked to wider networks of economic and cultural exchange. Many of the coastal societies came to practice some common customs, including Sudanese traditions such as theocratic political systems and pronounced social class divisions.

The Bantu-Speaking Peoples and Their Migrations

Settling Eastern and Southern Africa

Over several thousand years, many iron-using speakers of Bantu languages had migrated from their original homeland in eastern Nigeria into Central and East Africa (see Chapter 3). During the Classical Era, Bantu peoples accelerated their expansion to the south and east. Some Bantu-speaking peoples moved into the southern Congo region now known as Katanga **(kuh-TAHNG-guh)**, an area of savannah grasslands but prone to drought and disease. Much of the region south of the Congo Basin rain forest is relatively arid because of irregular rainfall. Fortunately, the Bantu successfully adapted sorghum and millet from the Sudanic region and Ethiopia to this dry southern climate. From Katanga many Bantu began moving to the west, south, and east. By 200 B.C.E. Bantu culture had reached the Zambezi **(zam-BEE-zee)** River Basin, and by the third century C.E. the first Bantu settlers entered what is now the nation of South Africa. Networks of trade and migration spanning vast distances eventually connected the southern third of Africa to the Sudan and the East African coast.

Cultural Mixing

Bantu-speaking migrants encountered local peoples and incorporated new influences. Because they worked iron, the Bantu possessed military and agricultural technologies more effective than those of many non-Bantu, some of whom were pushed into marginal economic areas suitable only for hunting and gathering. For example, the Mbuti Pygmies of the Congo region moved into thick rain forests, while many of the Khoisan **(KOY-sahn)** peoples in southern Africa, such as the Kung! hunters and gatherers discussed in Chapter 1, became desert dwellers. But many Bantu intermingled with, and probably culturally assimilated, those they met. Sudanese cultural forms carried by the Bantu, such as drums and percussive music, woodcarving, and ancestor-focused religions, became widespread. The contacts also influenced the Bantu cultures. For example, the Xhosa **(KOH-sah)** and Zulu peoples, who settled along the southeastern coast of today's South Africa, mixed their languages and cultures with the local Khoisan cattle herders, incorporating cattle herding into their economic life.

The migrating Bantu also gradually absorbed various societies in East Africa, including pastoralists and farmers. Various ironworking pastoralists from the eastern Sudan, known as **Nilotes** **(nie-LAHT-eez)** because they speak Nilotic **(nie-LAHT-ik)** languages very different from the Bantu tongues, were also settling in East Africa. Their relationships with the Bantu were not always peaceful. Some Bantu adopted pastoralism (herding cattle and goats) while others mastered new crops, including Southeast Asian foods like bananas, coconuts, sugar cane, and Asian yams available on the East African coast. These foods, as well as domesticated chickens and possibly pigs, were brought to East Africa by Indonesian mariners and migrants early in the Common Era (see Chapter 5) and eventually spread throughout Africa. Some of the Indonesian mariners settled along the coast, establishing trading posts and marrying local people. Between 100 and 700 C.E. Indonesians settled the large and previously uninhabited island of Madagascar, implanting there a mixed Indonesian-Bantu culture and language that still survive.

Nilotes Ironworking pastoralists from the eastern Sudan who settled in East Africa and there had frequent interactions with the Bantu.

Maritime Trade and the East African Coast

The East African coast developed a cosmopolitan society based on maritime trade. The winds and currents in the Indian Ocean reverse direction every six months, allowing boats from

SECTION SUMMARY

- The Sudan region included trading hubs such as Jenne-Jenno, but the population in the Classical Era was not dense enough to require a powerful state; Ghana was the first state to arise, probably around 500 C.E.
- The Garamante peoples controlled the extensive caravan routes through the Sahara Desert to bring salt from the African Mediterranean coast to Sudan, which exported gold in return.
- The Bantu peoples, equipped with iron tools, continued to migrate south and east, mixing with and sometimes pushing out other peoples, as they made their way to South Africa by the third century C.E.
- Indonesian mariners settled on the East African coast and, to a greater extent, in Madagascar, where a mixed Indonesian-Bantu culture survives to this day.
- Winds that switched direction every six months made it easy to travel back and forth between East Africa and southwestern Asia, India, and Southeast Asia.

southwestern and southern Asia to sail to East Africa and back each year. The trading ports to which merchants from southern Arabia sailed were located along the coast from Somalia to present-day Tanzania. The main port city, Rhapta **(RAHP-ta)** in Tanzania, had a large Arab merchant community.

The east coast trade grew slowly during the Classical Era. A first-century C.E. Greek reported that ships left Egypt's Red Sea ports and then visited Adulis and various Somalian ports before sailing to East African ports such as Rhapta. They then headed to India rather than venturing farther down the coast, avoiding what they considered the mysterious ocean stretching southward. Growing numbers of traders came to the coastal towns. East Africa exported ivory, rhinoceros horn, and tortoise shell to Egypt, India, and western Asia and imported iron goods, pottery, and glass beads. Egyptian, Roman, and West Asian coins found in the region indicate trade with the Mediterranean area, and Persian pottery was distributed widely along the coast and inland. Eventually, the coast developed many port cities and a culture that mixed Bantu ideas with those of southwestern Asia. But it was many centuries before any ships established contact with the Western Hemisphere, to which we now turn.

CLASSICAL SOCIETIES AND NETWORKS IN THE AMERICAS

How did the Mesoamerican, Andean, and North American societies compare with each other?

As in Eurasia and Africa, the first cities and states in the Americas developed during ancient times, including the Olmec in Mesoamerica and the Chavín in the Andes (see Chapter 4). Population increase helped to stimulate the growth of more American urban societies during the Classical Era. By around 1 C.E. there may have been around 15 million people in the Americas, over two-thirds of them concentrated in Mesoamerica and western South America, where several cities became the centers of prosperous states. Most of these American societies thrived from highly productive agriculture and developed diverse cultures, governments, and ways of life.

The Emergence of the Early Maya

Maya The most long-lasting and widespread of the classical Mesoamerican societies, who occupied the Yucatán Peninsula and northern Central America for almost 2,000 years.

To the east of the pioneering Olmec, in the lowland rain forests of Central America and the Yucatán **(YOO-kuh-TAN)** Peninsula in southeast Mexico, the **Maya** **(MIE-uh)** became the most long-lasting and widespread Mesoamerican society, forging a literate culture that excelled in some sciences and mathematics (see Map 9.2). Building on early regional traditions, Maya farming by shifting cultivation and ceramic making date back to at least 1100 B.C.E. The Maya introduced intensive cultivation of maize (corn) and other foods into the tropical forests. According to Maya legends, the gods had fashioned people out of corn. Maya farmers built artificial platforms and terraces on which they could grow enough crops to generate surpluses that supported a ruling elite, as well as large underground reservoirs to store groundwater where rainfall was scarce. As more productive agriculture led to more population, the Maya spread southward into the mountains and coastal zones of what is today Chiapas **(chee-AHP-uhs)** (Mexico), Guatemala **(GWAHT-uh-MAHL-uh)**, Honduras, El Salvador, and Belize **(buh-LEEZ)**.

Mayan Building Projects

As their power increased, the Maya elite organized ambitious building projects, constructing the first Maya pyramids and elaborate stone buildings by 600 B.C.E. Unlike Egyptian pyramids, which served as burial tombs for top leaders, Maya pyramids had temples on top to house the gods and were built for religious worship and ceremonies. According to Maya folklore:

There had been five generations of people since the origin of light, of life and of humankind. And they built houses for the gods, putting these in the center of the highest part of the citadel. After that their domains grew larger and more crowded.[8]

As notions of divine kingship became widespread, the Maya began making stone statues and carvings of their rulers and painting sophisticated murals illustrating Maya myths.

At the height of their culture, 150 B.C.E.–800 C.E., the Maya built many cities, each boasting masonry buildings, large temples, spacious plazas and pyramid complexes, and elaborate carvings (see Chronology: Classical Americas). Suburbs containing residences, markets, and workshops stretched for several miles out from the city centers. The major early city was El Mirador, where some of the earliest examples of Maya writing were inscribed on pot fragments and sculpture. Influenced by Olmec models, the Maya developed the most comprehensive writing system in the Americas, a hieroglyphic script used for calendars, religious regulations, and many sacred books, as well as to record dynastic histories, genealogies, and military successes. A later Spanish observer admired "those who carried with them the black and red ink, the manuscripts and painted book, the wisdom, the annals, the books of song."[9]

Map 9.2
Classical Societies in the Americas
The major American centers of complex agriculture, cities, and states emerged in Mesoamerica, where the Maya were the largest and longest-lasting society, and the Andes regions, where Chavín, Moche, and Tiwanaku were important societies.

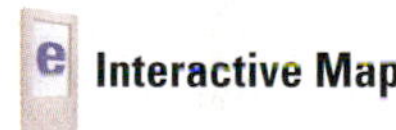
Interactive Map

Tikal **(ti-KAHL)**, in what is today eastern Guatemala, was one of the major Maya cities between 200 and 900 C.E., with a population of 50,000 at its height. Tikal contained three hundred large ceremonial buildings dominated by temple pyramids 200 feet high that were decorated with carvings made of stucco plaster. The first ruler used the jaguar as the symbol of kingship, military bravery, and religious authority. His descendants, King Great Jaguar Paw and General Smoking Frog, led Tikal to a great victory over the rival city Uaxactun in 378 C.E., ensuring Tikal's regional supremacy for the next two hundred years.

Maya Politics and Trade

Maya identity was more cultural than political. There was much cultural uniformity among the competing cities, probably because of the region's dense population and the close proximity of the trading cities with one another. Perhaps 10 million people lived in the Maya lowlands by 600 C.E. By around 500 C.E. the system shifted from one in which many small city-states competed to one in which a few cities, such as Tikal, dominated the others in their particular region. But no united Maya state or empire ever existed. Warfare between competing city-states over resources was frequent and brutal, and prisoners of war were usually enslaved or sacrificed. As in various Eastern Hemisphere and American societies, human sacrifice was common. Captured leaders from other cities faced especially agonizing deaths. Maya ruling families were interconnected, often marrying sons or daughters into ruling families of rival cities to cement alliances or discourage attack. Cities were ruled by kings and sometimes queens, who combined political, military, and religious leadership. The kings consolidated their position by linking themselves to gods and ancestors and erecting stone monuments containing inscriptions glorifying their deeds and ancestry. Because the scribes who wrote these inscriptions were a respected and influential group, when a city-state was defeated in battle the scribes of the losing king might also be killed.

Warfare and Leadership

Maya cities were linked in networks of interregional trade that were forged by hacking paths through the often dense rain forests. While rulers taxed and may have distributed goods, some recent findings suggest that many cities had marketplaces for traders. The Maya traded widely with non-Maya societies, some of them hundreds of miles away in central Mexico and deep into Central America. Dugout canoes carried Mayan and Central American goods to eastern Caribbean islands at least 1500 years ago. Merchants from the great non-Maya city of Teotihuacan **(teh-o-tee-WAH-kahn)**, located near what is today Mexico City, lived in Maya cities, and Maya merchants and craftsmen settled in Teotihuacan. Mayan trading rafts probably sailed up and down the Central American coast and to some Caribbean islands. Unlike the societies of the Eastern Hemisphere,

Regional Networks

CHRONOLOGY
Classical Americas

1100–150 B.C.E. Early Maya society

600 B.C.E.–1100 C.E. Tiwanaku Empire in the Andes

400 B.C.E.–1000 C.E. Monte Alban in Mexico

300 B.C.E.–1400 C.E. Hohokam society in southwest North America

200 B.C.E.–600 C.E. Hopewell mound-building culture in eastern North America

200 B.C.E.–700 C.E. Moche in Peru

200 B.C.E.–750 C.E. Teotihuacan in Mexico

150 B.C.E.–800 C.E. Flowering of Maya city-states

100–900 C.E. Anasazi society in southwest North America

the Maya did not work bronze or iron, but they did use copper and imported gold from Panama. One of the most prized materials obtained through long-distance trade was jade, a very hard stone. Skilled Maya artists carved in jade, as well as in stone and wood, and their jade products were traded widely.

Maya Society, Religion, and Science

The Maya maintained a hierarchical social structure. The upper class included nobles, who staffed the bureaucracy, architects, priests, and scribes. Below them were many artisans, including sculptors, potters, painters, and stoneworkers. The laborers and farmers, who supplied manual work and food, occupied a lower rung still. Slaves, most of them criminals, war prisoners, orphans, or children sold by debtors, did the manual work of wealthy households. The strict legal code forced convicted robbers to restore stolen goods, pay for them, or work for the victim as a slave until the debt was paid.

The Maya had an extended, multigenerational family structure. Although descent was patrilineal, each person had two names, one from the father's family and one from the mother's. Parents arranged marriages for their children at an early age. Maya society accorded men more rights, prestige, and privileges than women. Boys and young men often lived apart from their families in special communal houses, learning the arts of war. Mothers kept their daughters close at hand, giving them a strict upbringing; girls, but not boys, were severely punished for compromising their chastity. Yet, some royal women wielded considerable power behind the kings, and a few served as rulers.

City people had some time for leisure activities. Regular festive local markets featured dancing to the drum and flute as well as ball games. Ball courts were built in all settlements. In the middle of each court was a stone ring, often 20 or 30 feet high, and players used a ball 6 inches in diameter, which they could only hit with their buttocks, fists, and elbows. Since the main goal, directing the ball through the ring, was difficult, teams were probably also rewarded for keeping the ball in play as long as possible. The rapid action was exhausting. In an important match involving war captives, losers were sometimes sacrificed. The game, over 2,000 years old, is still played in some Mexico villages but without dire consequences for losing. Each city was fed by thousands of peasants growing maize and *cacao* **(kuh-COW)**, from which chocolate is made. Cacao cultivation might go back to the Olmec. Although each farm family had its own plot, clearing and cultivating were done communally with neighbors. The Maya and other Americans had no draft animals to assist in farming, so they could not practice the intensive agriculture as people did in the Eastern Hemisphere. Instead the peasants had small plots, which they worked for perhaps fifty days a year. They were also subject to labor on public works or military duty.

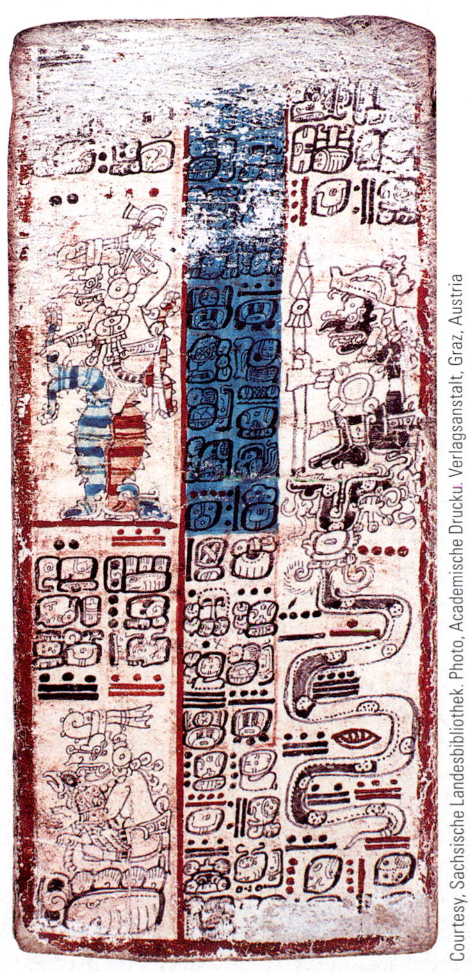

Maya Codex Only three Maya books (or codices) are known to have survived the Spanish conquest. This beautiful illustrated folding-screen book, the Dresden Codex, compiled around 1200 C.E., records astronomical calculations, tables of eclipses, and ritual detail. It is written on a long strip of bark paper coated with stucco.

Courtesy, Sachsische Landesbibliothek. Photo, Academische Drucku. Verlagsanstalt, Graz, Austria

Maya religion, science, and mathematics were linked together. The Maya worshiped a creator god and many other deities. The only surviving book of Maya religion, the *Popul Vuh* ("Book of Council"), claimed that the earth was sacred and that humankind was "given memory to count the days, [to be] bearers of respect for its divinity; to keep the rituals which connect humanity, nature and the heavens."[10] The Maya were obsessed with placating the gods through ritual practices, including human sacrifice. The gods needed victims, and so did the kings, to maintain their reputations for power. The Maya also emphasized purification of the body. There were many sweat baths, buildings fashioned to contain heat and steam generated by hot rocks. Sweat baths also may have been the scene of religious ceremonies.

Calendars and Astronomy

The Maya's concern for using the correct times and seasons for religious celebrations motivated them to make calendars and to study astronomy. Cosmic phenomena determined which days were best for war, marriage, trade, rituals, and other activities. The Maya conceived of time as cyclical, and priests marked this time by observing the movement of planets and stars. The Maya secular calendar, based on a solar year at 365 days, was the world's most accurate before the sixteenth century. Their religious calendar, however, was based on 260 days. Every fifty-two years the two calendars coincided, at which time great festivals and religious observances were held.

The Maya were wise to study the sun, stars, and planets because cyclical variations in the sun's energy brought on debilitating droughts roughly every two hundred years. This climate change may have undermined the legitimacy of leaders linked to the gods and may also have provoked wars over scarce resources. Eventually increasing droughts probably contributed to the collapse of the Maya cities. The interest in time also contributed to a mathematics system simpler and much easier to use than the Roman numerals of Europe. Like the mathematicians of India, the Maya also introduced the concept of zero. Unfortunately, most of the Maya books (known as codices) were destroyed by the Spanish invaders in the 1500s C.E. Being zealous Christians, many Spanish considered the writing pagan, one arguing that the "books contained nothing [but] superstition and lies of the devil, [so] we burned them all which caused [the Maya] much affliction."[11] This terrible loss has made it much more difficult for historians to understand Maya history and culture.

Monte Alban and Teotihuacan

Mexican Cities

The Maya were not the only Mesoamerican peoples to develop cities and states in this era. By 400 B.C.E. small states were emerging among the Zapotec (ZAHP-uh-TEK) people in southern Mexico, especially around Monte Alban (MON-teh ahl-BAHN), a hilltop city and large ceremonial center with several huge pyramid platforms. Monte Alban was ruled by a hereditary elite of kings and priests. Many large carved stones may have been portraits of slain war captives, indicating military activity. Thanks to population growth and migration to the prosperous state, the capital city may have had a population of 25,000 to 30,000 people at its peak between 300 and 750 C.E. The Zapotec developed a complex alphabet and calendar that were similar to, and may have been derived from, those of the Olmec. Around 750 C.E. Monte Alban city began a long decline and was later mostly abandoned.

The large Valley of Mexico (the site of present-day Mexico City) also became an important site for urban societies. The valley had long been a center for mining *obsidian* (uhb-SID-ee-uhn), a glassy, volcanic rock prized for its razor-sharp edges. By 200 B.C.E. **Teotihuacan** ("the City of the Gods") became the largest city in the Americas and the capital of an empire in central Mexico, allowing the city to extend its influence over much of Mesoamerica. By 600 C.E. Teotihuacan was home to between 120,000 and 200,000 inhabitants, probably one of the half dozen largest cities in the world. It was laid out on a north-south axis that was bisected by wide avenues. The city boasted plazas, markets, apartment buildings, palaces, and hundreds of temples. Like the Harappan cities of ancient India, a complex drainage system aided removal of unwanted water. A huge Pyramid of the Sun rose over 200 feet high in the ceremonial center of the city, built from some 3 million tons of volcanic rock that was dug up and then transported to the city without benefit of iron tools or beasts of burden to pull wheeled vehicles. These American pyramids, smaller in size and built differently than the great Egyptian and Nubian pyramids, nonetheless demonstrate that the human mind can create the same symbols, however widely separated by geography and time. Teotihuacan also contained ball courts for games played with rubber balls.

Teotihuacan ("the City of the Gods") The largest city in the Americas and the capital of an empire in central Mexico during classical times.

Teotihuacan Government and Economy

Teotihuacan was a political, religious, and economic center. The kings seem to have been viewed as divine and left administration to bureaucrats and aristocrats. The people had writing and an ingenious numbering system, which no doubt assisted trade and administration. Priests and artisans, perhaps a quarter of the city's population, resided in houses built around small courtyards, where some fashioned obsidian tools or manufactured ceremonial pottery. Teotihuacan may also have functioned as the hub for the many trade networks spanning Mesoamerica and extending far to the north and south. Some neighborhoods were set aside for merchants and for sojourners or settlers, many of them traders and artisans, from the Maya cities and other regions, and Teotihuacan merchants also traveled widely. Maya-carved jade statues have been found in the city's ruins, and some archaeologists think there may have been close links between Teotihuacan and Maya royal families.

Eventually Teotihuacan society collapsed. The rulers seem to have become increasingly militaristic and human sacrifice became more common, earning Teotihuacan many enemies and

Georg Gerster/Photo Researchers, Inc.

Teotihuacan This overview shows the two largest pyramids at Teotihuacan, the Pyramid of the Moon (bottom center) and the Pyramid of the Sun. There were six hundred smaller pyramids in the city.

harming trade. In 750 C.E. invaders burned the city down, and the population scattered. The causes of the collapse may have been environmental (such as a prolonged drought) or the result of internal revolt or invasion by a rival state. But even in ruins the city's splendor lived on. A millennium later the Aztecs who had settled the area told the Spanish conquerors of their reverence for the sacred spirit of the pyramids: "And this they call Teotihuacan, because it is where they bury the lords."[12]

Andean Societies

Moche A prosperous, powerful state that formed along the northern Peruvian coast from 200 B.C.E. to 700 C.E.

The Maya and other Mesoamerican states were not the only societies that emerged and often flourished in the Americas during the Classical Era. The great Andes state of Chavín collapsed by 200 B.C.E., but some of the architectural and religious patterns it pioneered spread through the Andes and into adjacent lands, including **Moche** (MO-che), a prosperous and powerful state that formed around 200 B.C.E. in the desert region along the northern Peruvian coast. In this dry region farming required maintaining irrigation canals to channel the runoff from the Andes to grow corn, beans, peppers, squash, and cotton, which the Moche skillfully wove into textiles. They also exploited the abundant, protein-rich maritime resources just offshore, including fish and mollusks.

Coastal Societies

The Moche were part of a distinctive culture that emerged on the north coast of Peru in the second century B.C.E. These societies built monumental architecture, with platforms and courtyards, and fashioned beautiful jewelry, mirrors, and pottery. Coastal peoples traded some of their agricultural and maritime bounty to Andes societies for potatoes and other highland crops. Eventually trade networks linked distant societies over much of western South America. Some took up seagoing trade. Between 500 B.C.E. and the 1600s C.E., the Manteno people from the coast of Ecuador used balsa wood rafts equipped with sails and loaded with textiles, ceramics, precious metals, and prized shells to forge a coastal trade network stretching from Mexico to Chile. Because of such long-distance trade networks, coastal and interior peoples came to depend on each other, encouraging the formation of states in both places.

Moche Cities

The Moche capital city centered around two massive brick pyramids dedicated to the sun and the moon. The well-planned city was home to perhaps 10,000 people. Separate and perhaps hostile city-based Moche kingdoms were spread over hundreds of miles, all with similar customs, buildings, and pyramids. Burial chambers and a huge assortment of clay pottery painted with highly realistic scenes of social activity provide much knowledge of Moche society, such as the sometimes elegant, sometimes brutal life of the elite (see Profile: A Moche Lord). Enormous amounts of gold and silver artifacts were buried with Moche dignitaries.

The painted pots also reveal a colorful slice of everyday life. They show midwives attending birthing mothers and women carrying babies on their backs in shawls. Nearly everyone wears headgear in these scenes, from the feathered headdresses of the elite to the decorated cotton turbans of the common folk. Men often tattooed their faces. Like most Andes peoples, the Moche consumed maize beer. The paintings also show erotic scenes of lovemaking between men and women and between gods and humans, as well as scenes showing war leaders drinking the blood of their unfortunate captives. While many of their customs shock us and may not have made them popular neighbors, the Moche should be remembered for more than bloodshed. They were excellent gold workers and also made products from a copper and gold alloy as well as silver. They created one of the world's finest ceramic traditions and apparently also developed a mathematical system based on 10.

Eventually the Moche faced challenges they could not overcome, including a series of natural disasters, among them severe *El Ñinos* **(el NEEN-yoz)**, the periodic warm water currents in the Pacific that bring higher temperatures and torrential rain to the region, as well as prolonged drought and massive earthquakes. Moche leaders may have responded to the resulting food shortages with increasing warfare to obtain resources and human sacrifice to appease the gods. The ecological and political crises that these disasters generated brought the Moche to an end by 650 or 700 C.E.

Tiwanaku

At about the same time that the Moche dominated the northern Peruvian coast, various states continued to rise and fall in the Andes and along the southern Peruvian coast. In the Lake Titicaca **(tit-i-KAHK-uh)** region (in modern Bolivia and southern Peru) of the Andes highlands between 600 and 100 B.C.E., the ancestors of the Aymara **(AYE-muh-RAH)** people built a state and constructed impressive stone sculpture. Even in ruins, their plazas, palaces, and brightly colored temples decorated with gold-covered reliefs could impress the Spanish 1,500 years later; one wrote: "There is a hill made by the hands of men, on great foundations of stone. What causes most astonishment are some great doorways of stone, some made out of a single stone."[13] The capital city, Tiwanaku **(tee-wah-NA-coo)**, emerged by 100 C.E. and reached its height in 600 C.E., when it had a population of perhaps 40,000 and controlled much of the southern Andes. Tiwanaku was over 10,000 feet above sea level. A statue of the sun-god atop a platform greeted visitors, and in the city center was a huge, sacred platform, 650 feet long and 50 feet high. The rulers staged elaborate festivals with much drug and alcohol consumption to recruit labor for public works projects. Little is known of gender relations at Tiwanaku, but in the neighboring and rival state of Wari, just to the north, women of elite status operated a mountaintop brewery that made hundreds of gallons of corn beer every week.

Tiwanaku influenced a large region of western South America. The local art and the religion, which probably involved human sacrifice, seem to have spread into neighboring societies. The lands around the capital, rich in llama herds and a center of copper mining, flourished from a system of raised field agriculture—seeds planted on long artificial ridges separated by ditches—which improved drainage, replaced nutrients in the poor soil, and protected crops such as potatoes from frost. Tiwanaku agriculture was some 400 percent more productive than the farming in the region today. The Aymara, like other Andean peoples, were also skilled at using fibers. For example, they made boats to sail on the lake by weaving together reeds. But by 1100 C.E. the capital and surrounding fields were abandoned, perhaps because of climate change that generated a drought so severe that rivers dried up.

Another peoples, the Nazca **(NAHZ-kuh)**, a decentralized agrarian society that flourished in the harsh desert in southern Peru from 200 B.C.E. to 600 C.E., became notable for the beautiful multicolored pottery and textiles it manufactured and the ceremonial centers it constructed. But the Nazca are most famous for creating geometric lines along their windswept plateau by clearing away surface stones to reveal the underlying rock and then laying the stones along the edges of the lines. Constructed on a huge scale, the lines depict either geometric shapes or animals such as monkeys and birds. These enigmatic markings have puzzled modern observers; scholars think they were created to mark the seasons, to communicate with gods believed to dwell in the nearby mountains, or to mark water sources. Or they may have just been artistic expressions of shapes and animals.

North American Societies

Southwestern Peoples

Sophisticated societies also emerged in North America before the Common Era. Several cultural traditions and permanent towns emerged among the desert farmers of the American Southwest, including the Hohokam **(huh-HOH-kuhm)**, Anasazi **(ah-nah-SAH-zee)**, and Mogollon

A MOCHE LORD

Outside of Mesoamerica, no American society left written records to help us understand individual lives. Nearly all we know of the Moche comes from recent archaeological investigations. As in Egypt, an arid climate preserved many objects and remains, allowing scholars to examine jewelry, weapons, clothing, ceramics, and skeletons. Many paintings on pots portray slices of Moche life. In addition, excavations at royal tombs in several cities have told us much about how the leaders of Moche society lived and died, even if we have no idea of their names, personalities, family ties, or precise governmental functions. These findings allow us to trace some of the experiences of one leader, probably a warrior-priest, who is known to archaeologists as one of the lords of Sipan, a Moche city. He was in his mid-thirties when he was buried around 390 C.E.

Archaeologists know what Moche men and women looked like. Moche men were stocky and averaged about 5 feet 3 inches in height, but this lord was 3 inches taller. He cut his hair in bangs over his forehead, wore it long in back, pierced his ears and nose, painted his face, and tattooed his arms and legs. The Moche women, such as those in the lord's family, stood about 4 feet 7 inches tall and wore their hair long, often braided with colorful woolen strands. At ceremonies women's dress consisted of a multicolored woven smock heavily laden with long strands of beads. Women lived much longer than men, but men had far richer costumes.

Bildarchiv Preussisc her Kulturbesitz/Art Resource, NY

A Moche Lord This Moche lord, memorialized for posterity in ceramic, wears the headgear and ear ornaments common to the Moche nobility. The potter skillfully captured the lord's facial features, giving the portrait a lifelike quality.

The lord of Sipan was buried in all the finery he probably wore in his official and ceremonial life. Like other warrior-priests, he dressed ostentatiously to demonstrate his wealth and power. He wore a long tunic completely covered with platelets of gilded copper, and he had copper sandals on his feet. On his wrists he sported large beaded bracelets of turquoise, gold, and shell. A beaded chest-plate and a spectacular necklace of gold and silver beads covered his chest and shoulders, and probably gleamed like the sun. Around his waist he wore a belt that supported crescent-shaped bells. A crescent-shaped gold nose ornament completely covered his mouth and lower face. Large ear ornaments were inlaid with gold and turquoise. On his head, the Sipan lord wore a large, crescent-shaped headdress ornament made of gold. In one hand he held a gold and silver scepter, an insignia of high rank. Moche art frequently depicted high-status men dressed like the Sipan lord.

The lord led a privileged life, but it was also one with many dangers. Moche society had a great concentration of wealth, and a few people, like the lord, lived in extreme opulence. Every valley may have had one or more royal courts that were connected to one another through marriage alliances and trade, like the kings of the Maya cities. Moche art frequently depicts warriors parading in front of royalty, perhaps preparing for war against rival courts. Like Maya royalty, the lord of Sipan may have gone into battle to personally fight rival lords.

Battle was a grueling and fateful experience for the combatants. Warriors used clubs to beat the heads of enemies, or they hurled stones and arrows with a sling. Like Roman gladiators, Moche warriors participated in hand-to-hand combat, with the ultimate goal of capturing the enemy for torture and sacrifice. A complex set of rules may have governed the conduct of warriors on and off the field. Battles ended when one warrior caught hold of another's hair and dragged him down. The loser, stripped of his clothes and weapon, was then paraded before the royalty of the winners. Painted bottles show the victorious lord presiding over a horrific sacrificial ceremony, drinking a goblet of blood drawn from the slit throats of captive enemy warriors. The lord of Sipan never suffered that fate. He was buried along with several young women, perhaps wives, concubines, or attendants; two burly men armed with shields and war clubs, possibly to protect him in the afterlife; and a dog, probably the lord's pet hound.

THINKING ABOUT THE PROFILE

1. How do burials and paintings on pots help us understand Moche life?
2. What do the lord's clothing and symbols of royalty tell us about Moche society?
3. What role did warfare play in the life of a Moche lord?

(MOH-guh-YOHN). By around 300 B.C.E. the Hohokam of what is now southern Arizona and northwest Mexico were trading extensively with other southwestern peoples and the southern California coast. Hohokam farmers used advanced irrigation, dams, terraces, and other strategies to grow maize, beans, squash, and cotton. The Hohokam survived for some 1,500 years, building large towns. The total Hohokam population in the vicinity of present-day Phoenix may have reached 40,000. The presence in Hohokam settlements of ball courts and rubber balls, as well as Mesoamerican-style platform mounds, indicates Mesoamerican influence over long-distance trade networks. But there is no evidence for human sacrifice or warfare. Eventually overpopulation, deforestation, and drier climates increased conflict and put more stress on the society, and by the fifteenth century the Hohokam settlements had been abandoned. Their modern descendants include the Pima and Papago Indians of Arizona.

The Anasazi and the closely related Mogollon culture were the direct ancestors of the Pueblo Indians in what is today Arizona and New Mexico. The Anasazi were once much more widespread and had towns in Arizona, Utah, and Colorado. The culture, which arose around the first century C.E., reached its high point between 750 and 900 C.E. The Mogollon peoples emerged around 200 B.C.E. and covered a territory stretching from central Arizona and New Mexico into northern Mexico. They flourished from a combination of corn growing and skillful gathering until the fifteenth century C.E.

Eastern Moundbuilders

Another great era of mound building characterized the eastern woodlands between around 500 B.C.E. and 400 C.E. Mound building had begun in North America around 2500 B.C.E. (see Chapter 4). But this new mound-building culture became even more widespread, encompassing the Mississippi, Ohio, Tennessee, and lower Missouri River Basins and their tributaries as well as the South Atlantic coast, a total area larger than India. The most prominent mound-builder tradition, known today as Hopewell, was centered in the Ohio River region. Hopewell artistic styles, maize cultivation, religious beliefs, ceremonial traditions, and burial customs spread throughout the eastern woodlands, but there is no evidence for any large state. The Hopewell peoples created extraordinary earthworks and other engineering projects. Elaborate geometric designs such as hexagons and circles mark their mounds. The Great Serpent Mound, built on a hilltop in Ohio around 2,000 years ago, was one of the most spectacular. Shaped like a snake, it ran 800 feet long from head to tail and was 4 feet tall and 20 feet wide. Some of the mounds were burial chambers for members of the elite. The Ortuna, a Hopewell culture in northern Florida, built a maze of 20-foot-wide canals that allowed them to reach both the Atlantic and Gulf coasts by dugout canoe, thus connecting them to a trading network stretching north to Ohio.

The Hopewell and other mound-building cultures were supported by two major economic changes. First, agriculture became more intensive, especially after the spread of maize. Second, long-distance trade expanded into a network spanning a large section of North America. Along the river trade routes moved obsidian from the Rocky Mountains, copper from the Great Lakes and later southern Appalachia, ceramic figurines and vessels from the lower Great Lakes, ore from Kansas, silver from Ontario, shells from the Gulf of Mexico and Florida, freshwater pearls from the Mississippi, and marine products from the Gulf coast such as sharks' teeth and turtle shells. Thanks to this trade network, sharks' teeth have been found in Illinois, over a thousand miles from the Caribbean.

The Hopewell culture began to decline around 300 C.E. and collapsed by 600 C.E. Overpopulation and the resulting competition for land might have put too much stress on the environment and economic system, and trade networks may have been disrupted. The maize crop diminished, possibly in part because of a cooling climate. In addition, around 300 C.E. someone invented or imported the bow and arrow into the region, altering the balance of power and stimulating warfare.

Changing States and the Spread of Cultures

While the traditions of the earliest urban societies, the Olmec and Chavín, remained influential in Mesoamerica and the Andes region, much change occurred over the centuries, although often on a different timeline from the Eastern Hemisphere. For example, around 200 or 300 C.E., various societies experienced a major transition. Small states such as Monte Alban, Teotihuacan, Tikal, and Tiwanaku grew into larger states, often regional empires. Long-distance trade increased, merchants became more influential, and ideas (such as writing and ball games in Mesoamerica) spread more widely. Many American peoples revered the land, seeing it as the source of both physical and spiritual life. The land also deserved reverence because of its close relationship to the supreme spirits or gods. As a result, people such as the Maya and some North American societies held maize as sacred, a gift from the gods.

SECTION SUMMARY

- The Maya society on the Yucatan Peninsula lived largely on corn, developed a comprehensive writing system and a numbering system that included zero, and built impressive buildings and large pyramids that served as religious centers.
- A few cities, such as Tikal, came to dominate Maya society, but there was no overarching Maya state.
- The Maya tried to please their gods through human sacrifice, which became more common with time, and self-purification, for which they used sweat baths; religion also motivated them to study astonomy and devise very accurate calendars.
- The Zapotecs built the city and state of Monte Alban.
- Teotihuacan, near present-day Mexico City, grew into one of the largest and best-designed cities in the world and had an extremely advanced infrastructure, including a complex drainage system.
- In the Andes, Chavín was succeeded by Moche, whose pottery depicts a violent culture of war and sacrifice but also of advanced metalwork and architecture.
- In the desert Southwest of North America, the Hohokam people developed extensive irrigation systems, and their cultural artifacts show some Mesoamerican influence.
- Supported by corn and expanded trade networks, mound-building cultures spread across eastern North America.

Except for the exceptionally enduring Maya and Tiwanaku, South American and Mesoamerican states exhibited a pattern of rise and fall after a few centuries, perhaps due in part to environmental and climate changes, which affected agriculture and fishing. Chronic warfare may also have played a role. Although the classical states established frameworks for later empires such as the Aztec and Inca, they did not survive in their original form, as the classical Chinese and Ethiopian states did.

The widespread presence of pyramids in Mesoamerica and South America has caused some observers to speculate about possible contacts across the Atlantic to North Africa and the Mediterranean long before the arrival of Norse Vikings around 1000 C.E. and, five centuries later, Spanish ships. But there is no firm archaeological evidence for any ties to the Eastern Hemisphere, and most specialists are skeptical that such contacts were ever made. Pyramids are based on practical principles of monument construction that were probably available to builders in any culture. Some American peoples were building mounds nearly as early as the first Egyptian pyramids.

Along the American west coast, from California to Peru, are scattered hints of trans-Pacific contacts in pottery design, artwork, and plants, leading to occasional speculation about possible Chinese, Japanese, or Polynesian voyages to the Americas. Some studies claim to find Japanese pottery in Ecuador, Olmec hieroglyphics that resemble Shang Chinese characters, Polynesian musical instruments and loan words in western South America, or Polynesian words and boat designs along the California coast. The world's most skilled mariners, Polynesians were capable of trips over several thousand miles of uncharted ocean, and they could have occasionally visited the American coast and then returned home. This might explain the presence of the South American sweet potato in Polynesia. However, no conclusive proof exists for any trans-Pacific contacts, and if any voyages did occur, they left no obvious long-lasting influence.

POPULATING THE PACIFIC: AUSTRALIAN AND ISLAND SOCIETIES

How were some of the notable features of Australian and Pacific societies shaped by their environments?

Although the original settlers of Australia and the Pacific islands migrated from or through Southeast Asia, the societies they developed remained largely isolated from the historical currents of Eurasia for many centuries. Australian Aborigines mastered a hostile environment and flourished from hunting and gathering. In extraordinary voyages, Austronesians migrated over thousands of miles of open ocean to inhabit most of the Pacific islands, adapting to new environments, creating diverse cultures, and developing long-distance trade networks.

Australian Geography and Aboriginal Societies

Geographical Foundations

Australia was settled at least 50,000 years ago. By 1000 B.C.E. Aboriginal tribes spoke some two hundred distinct languages. The environments that shaped the varied societies included the tropical, heavily forested coasts of the north and northeast, the temperate river basins and coasts of the southeast and southwest, and the deserts that dominate much of the interior. Aboriginal life was based largely on hunting and gathering, exploiting many food sources such as sea life along the coast and wild plants and insects in the harsh desert interior. Women gathered plants and small animals, prepared meals for the family, looked after the children, made the clothing, and built the huts. Men fished, hunted large animals, and manufactured implements. Aborigines developed an intimate understanding of weather patterns and their relationships to plants, animals, and land, knowledge still used by meteorologists today. In terms of nourishment, most Aborigines ate at least as well as peoples in Afro-Eurasia, and malnutrition and starvation were largely unknown. Agriculture never developed because most of the land was infertile, the rains erratic, and there were no native plants or animals capable of domestication. Even today large-scale irrigation is needed to sustain farming, and, as in ancient Mesopotamia, this irrigation has increased the salt content in groundwater, endangering fresh water supplies. Instead, Aboriginal societies developed land management and usage that enabled them to conserve their resources over thousands of years. They evolved a close relationship to the earth that remained at the center of their customs and beliefs over centuries. They also studied the night sky to survive the challenging landscape, using stories to explain the tides, eclipses, the rising and setting of the sun and moon, and the changing positions of the stars and planets throughout the year. The sky served as a calendar that indicated the change of seasons and when certain foods were available.

Many Aboriginal practices operated in tandem with the environment. For example, fire could be used to clear land to encourage regrowth of edible plants and rejuvenate the natural ecosystem. Whether deliberate or a result of natural processes, fires have always been a regular occurrence in Australia, but they have complicated modern life for the now urbanized regions. At least one Aboriginal society, the Gunditjmara in southern Australia, built an ingenious artificial lake where they operated eel farms beginning around 6000 B.C.E. The abundant eels raised there were traded around southern Australia. The Gunditjmara may also have lived in a permanent town with stone houses.

Customs and Beliefs

Aboriginal societies had many similar customs and beliefs. Since they had to move by foot with the seasons, most communities owned few possessions and prided themselves on not loading themselves down. Aboriginal men carried spear throwers and spears while women carried digging sticks and baskets to hold foodstuffs. Their seasonal moves, designed to maximize food availability, involved relocating to the same camps every year over regular trails. Aboriginal societies were divided into tribes organized either through the patrilineal or the matrilineal line, and nuclear families operated with considerable independence. Although few tribes had chiefs, older males exerted considerable influence in religious and social life. Women made critical decisions about the campsite and controlled their own ceremonial life. Relations between the genders were apparently flexible. Periodic disputes between neighboring tribes sometimes led to fighting, but they were usually settled by diplomacy involving the tribal elders.

Since most people had to spend only about three days a week in search of food, they had considerable time for rituals, ceremonial expression, and religious matters, including a widely shared belief in the mythology of the **dreamtime**, the distant past when the spiritual ancestors gave order and form to the universe at the world's creation. The dreamtime myths were remarkably consistent around the continent, passed down through countless generations by a rich oral literature. Aborigines also recognized an animistic world inhabited by many spirits and ghosts. Their art had a religious base and included body decoration, bark paintings, and especially rock carvings and paintings.

dreamtime In Aboriginal Australian mythology, the distant past when the spiritual ancestors gave order and form to the universe at the world's creation.

A complex trade system spanned the continent. Pearls and shells from the northern coast reached southern Australia, and quartz, flint, and other stones to make tools, as well as animal skins, wood products, and ornaments, were exchanged over wide areas. By classical times Indonesian trading ships probably visited the northwest coast to obtain pearls. Later, Chinese ships may have also engaged in such exchanges. But these outside contacts had little influence on most Australian societies. Today, after two centuries of change brought by European conquest and settlement, the life that sustained Australia's Aborigines for thousands of years has largely passed. Where once songs were sung about the history of the lands and the peoples, today, largely settled on rural land reserves or living in poor urban neighborhoods, the Aborigines lament the loss of their traditions. Their stories still recollect tribal pasts and beliefs, but the storytellers inhabit a very different reality from their ancestors.

Austronesian Expansion

Austronesian Migrations

Today some 1,200 different Austronesian languages are spoken from Madagascar eastward through Indonesia, Malaysia, the Philippines, and most of the Pacific islands. This book has elsewhere discussed the migrations of Indo-Europeans from southern Russia into Europe, western Asia, and India, as well as the long movement of Bantu-speaking peoples into the southern half of Africa. But no premodern peoples migrated over as wide an area in so short a time as did the Austronesians. Before the Classical Era some Austronesian-speaking peoples moved from Southeast Asia into the western Pacific islands just northeast of Australia (see Chapter 4). There they

CHRONOLOGY
The Pacific Islands, 1500 B.C.E.–1000 C.E.

1500–1000 B.C.E.	Micronesian settlement of Marianas
ca. 500 B.C.E.	Emergence of Polynesian culture in Fiji, Samoa, and Tonga
300–200 B.C.E.	Polynesian settlement of Marquesas and Tahiti
400–600 C.E.	Polynesian settlement of Hawaii
800–1000 C.E.	Polynesian settlement of New Zealand

encountered Melanesians (mel-uh-NEE-zhuhnz) who had earlier migrated from Southeast Asia. Over time the two traditions mixed, and Melanesians adopted Austronesian languages. Eventually some Austronesian-speaking peoples from the western Pacific sailed farther east and north to colonize other islands, in the process fostering new groups later known as Polynesians (PAHL-uh-NEE-zhunz) and Micronesians (MIE-kruh-NEE-zhunz).

Using only the stars, moon, sun, winds, and waves to guide them, the migrants endured the hardships of long open-sea voyages to discover new lands. Navigation and boat-building were a science; voyagers spent many days selecting the right tree for their canoes since worm-ridden wood might prove disastrous at sea. An ancient Tahitian prayer reveals the voyagers' fears: "O gods! Lead us safely to land. Leave us not in the ocean. Give us a breeze. Let the weather be fine and the sky clear."[14] These intentional migrations were spurred by overpopulation on islands with limited resources, fresh water, or fertile land. Some Pacific islands were mountainous and often covered by dense rain forests, while others were flat atolls only a few feet above sea level, which left the inhabitants vulnerable to high waves due to fierce storms. Islanders either learned to limit population growth or suffered the effects of deforestation and natural resource depletion, which generated conflict or migration. Excellent naval technology made the migrations possible: each double-hulled outrigger canoe, up to 100 feet long and consisting of two hulls with a platform lashed between them for living, cooking, work space, and storage, was capable of carrying up to eighty people, along with foods, plants, and animals.

Micronesians

The Micronesians, who settled many central and north Pacific islands, made ingenious navigation charts from cowrie shells tied together. The Austronesian-speaking ancestors of some Micronesians eventually colonized many small islands in the central Pacific, including the Carolines. The Marianas (MAR-ee-AN-uhz), including the islands of Guam and Saipan, may have been settled directly by Austronesians sailing east from the Philippines and possibly Taiwan between 1500 and 1000 B.C.E. (see Chronology: The Pacific Islands, 1500 B.C.E.–1000 C.E.). The Chamorro (cha-MOR-roe) people of the Marianas were the only Pacific society to grow Asian rice, suggesting they had continuing connections with the Philippines.

Polynesian Migrations and Societies

Polynesian Dispersal

Polynesian culture seems to have flowered first in the neighboring Fiji, Tonga, and Samoa (suh-MO-uh) island groups around 500 B.C.E. (see Map 9.3). Within a few centuries some were on the move again. By around 300 or 200 B.C.E. Polynesian mariners from Tonga may have reached the Marquesas (mar-KAY-suhs) Islands and soon thereafter Tahiti (tuh-HEE-tee), 1,500 miles east of Tonga. Polynesians sailed from Samoa 1,500 miles north to the Kiribati (kear-uh-BAH-tee) Islands, and then on to the Marshall Islands. Later, between 400 and 600 C.E., mariners from the

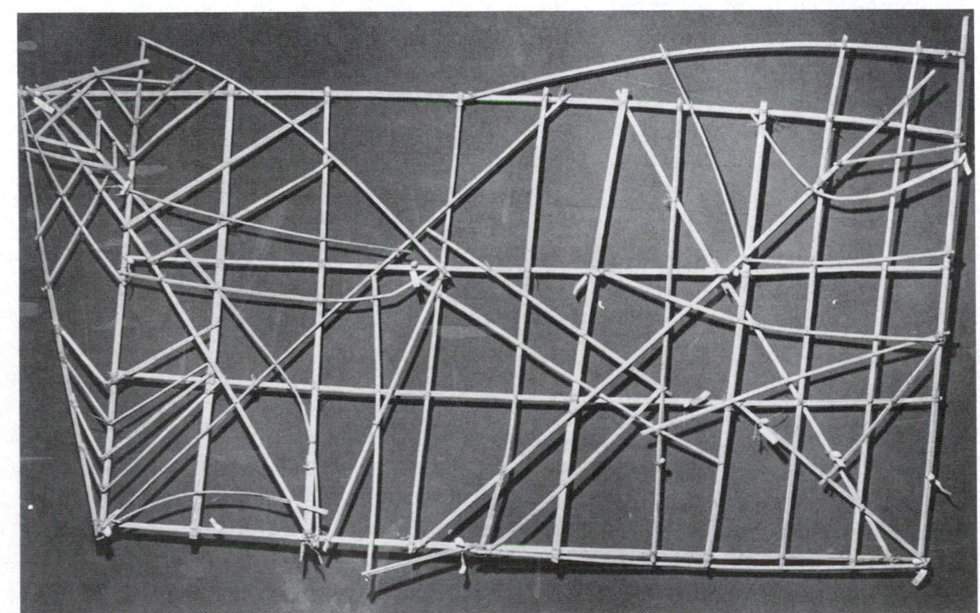

Polynesian Palm-Frond Navigational Map This nautical map, made in the Marshall Islands from palm fronds, shows distances between islands as measured by time traveled. The map may have originally had bits of shell or coral to mark islands. Polynesians and Micronesians often made such maps for their ocean voyages.

Bishop Museum

Map 9.3
Pacific Migrations in the Classical Era
During this era, Austronesian peoples scattered across the vast Pacific Basin, using ingenious canoes and navigation techniques to settle nearly all the inhabitable islands. From bases in Tonga and Samoa in the west, the Polynesians settled a large expanse of the basin ranging from Hawaii in the north to Easter Island in the east and New Zealand in the south.

Interactive Map

Marquesas settled Hawaii after crossing over 2,000 miles of ocean, followed around 1100 or 1200 C.E. by a migration from Tahiti 2,500 miles east to Easter Island. Finally, between 800 and 1000 C.E., some Tahitians moved west another 2,500 miles to Aotearoa **(ow-TEH-a-ROW-uh)** (which a Dutch explorer much later named New Zealand), the largest landmass settled by Polynesians. These settlers, the ancestors of the Maori **(MAO-ree)** people, faced a very different climate and topography from that of the tropical Pacific islands, as well as a new mix of plants and animals. Polynesian sailors may even have visited the Peruvian coast. Such contact might explain the presence of sweet potatoes, a South American crop, in eastern Polynesia and New Zealand for at least 1,000 years.

Polynesian Agriculture and Cultures

Polynesian agriculture was based on Southeast Asian crops such as yams, taro, bananas, coconuts, and breadfruit and animals such as pigs, chickens, and dogs. But survival required some modifications, including elaborate terracing, artificial ponds, and irrigation. Polynesians also exploited local food sources such as coconuts and the abundant marine life of the lagoons, coral reefs, and deep sea. Cloth made out of bark furnished clothing. But fragile island ecologies were easily unbalanced. Imported animals like pigs, dogs, and (unintentionally) rats consumed local birds. Overhunting eliminated some species, and deforestation was also a problem. As an extreme example, Easter Island, which was heavily forested when Polynesians arrived, was completely denuded over the centuries, and the people were reduced to poverty and chronic conflict over ever scarcer resources.

Early Polynesians lived in clans that were generally dominated by hereditary chiefs who controlled the lands. Conflict between rival clans over status and land led to tensions and sometimes war. Eventually the most elaborate social hierarchies emerged in Tonga, Tahiti, and Hawaii, where paramount chiefs ruled many thousands of followers and controlled much of the economy. While men held most political power, women often enjoyed a high status, and most Micronesian and some Polynesian societies were matrilineal. Polynesian women often ranked higher than their brothers in spiritual and ritual authority and, by marrying into other clans or ruling families, could help

SECTION SUMMARY

- Aboriginal Australians developed great understanding of natural phenomena and were very successful hunters and gatherers for thousands of years.
- Aborigines across Australia believed in the dreamtime of the mythic past and felt that spirits and ghosts inhabited much of the physical world.
- Austronesian peoples from Southeast Asia took to the sea and settled on various Pacific islands.
- Polynesian culture probably began in Fiji, Tonga, and Samoa, but it spread out over a remarkable expanse of the Pacific Ocean.
- An extensive trading network developed among the Pacific islands, and, despite their isolation from each other, the islands' cultures remained quite homogenous.

political relations. The far-flung Polynesian societies also shared many other cultural traits, including elaborate facial and body tattooing (the word *tattoo* is of Polynesian origin), myths, reverence for ancestors, and art forms such as woodcarving. Many of these customs were also common in Melanesia and Micronesia.

The huge triangle of Polynesia, anchored at the ends by Hawaii, New Zealand, and Easter Island, is one of the largest expanses of territory in the world. One of the first outsiders to explore the area, British captain James Cook, wrote in 1774: "It is extraordinary that the same [people] should have spread themselves over all the isles in this vast Ocean, almost a fourth part of the circumference of the Globe."[15] Migration over such vast distances did not necessarily mean isolation. Thanks to a large maritime network, obsidian mined on the island of New Britain, northeast of New Guinea, was traded as far west as Borneo and as far east as Fiji, some 4,000 miles apart. Nearby island groups traded with each other and maintained social links. For example, the Tongan and Fijian chiefly families frequently intermarried. But the sailing required remarkable observation and could be dangerous, as Captain Cook reported from Tonga in 1777: "In these Navigations the Sun is their guide by day and the Stars by night; when these are obscured they have recourse to the points from whence the Wind and waves come upon the vessel. If [these] shift, they are bewildered."[16] Even today Polynesian traditions honor great navigators of the past such as Moikeha and Pa'ao, who sailed back and forth between the Marquesas and Hawaii over a millennium ago.

CHAPTER SUMMARY

During the Classical Era some sub-Saharan Africans became more closely linked by trade with North Africa and Eurasia. Kush became a center for iron production, and Aksum, in the Ethiopian highlands, flourished as a trading hub. Cities and small states that emerged in the Sudanic region of West Africa participated in the growing trans-Saharan caravan trade network linking them with the Mediterranean world. Cities also appeared along the East African coast, tied by trade networks to the Mediterranean, western Asia, and India. Bantu-speaking peoples settled the southern half of Africa, carrying with them iron technology and many Sudanic influences.

Various urban societies dominated Mesoamerica and the Andes, including the Maya, Moche, Tiwanaku, Teotihuacan, and Monte Alban. The Maya forged a particularly enduring society based on competing city-states, developed a writing system, and understood much about astronomy and mathematics. The Moche on the Peruvian coast and Tiwanaku in the highlands formed empires. In Mesoamerica, Teotihuacan became the greatest city in the Americas and a major trading hub. In North America many peoples adopted farming, built permanent towns, and took up mound building. In the Pacific, Australian Aborigines adapted well to their harsh environment, flourishing for millennia from hunting and gathering. And various Austronesian peoples, particularly the Polynesians, made spectacular migrations into the vast Pacific Ocean by using remarkable seagoing technologies and adapting to diverse island environments.

KEY TERMS

Meroitic
Coptic Church
Aksum
Geez
Ghana
Mande
griots
Nilotes
Maya
Teotihuacan
Moche
dreamtime

EBOOK AND WEBSITE RESOURCES

INTERACTIVE MAPS

Map 9.1 Classical Africa, 1500 B.C.E.–600 C.E.
Map 9.2 Classical Societies in the Americas
Map 9.3 Pacific Migrations in the Classical Era

LINKS

About Archaeology (http://archaeology.about.com/library). About.com offers many essays and links relevant to early Africa and the Americas.

Africa South of the Sahara: Selected Internet Sources (http://www-sul.stanford.edu/depts/ssrg/africa/guide.html). Useful collection of links from Stanford University.

African Timelines (http://www.cocc.edu/cagatucci/classes/hum211/timelines/htimeline.htm). Has many links to specific periods and cultures as well as essays on controversial topics.

Ancient Mesoamerican Civilizations (www.angelfire.com/ca/humanorigins). Links and information about the premodern societies.

History and Cultures of Africa (http://www.columbia.edu/cu/lweb/indiv/africa/cuvl/cult.html). Extensive links provided by Columbia University.

Internet African History Sourcebook (http://www.fordham.edu/halsall/africa/africasbook.html). This site, maintained at Fordham University, contains much useful information and documentary material on African societies.

Plus flashcards, practice quizzes, and more. Go to: www.cengage.com/history/lockard/globalsocnet2e

SUGGESTED READING

Adams, Richard E. W. *Ancient Civilizations of the New World.* Boulder: Westview, 1997. Brief survey of Mesoamerican and South American societies before 1500 C.E.

Burstein, Stanley M. *Ancient African Civilizations: Kush and Axum.* Princeton: Markus Wiener, 1998. Good brief introduction and collection of primary sources.

Coe, Michael. *The Maya,* 7th ed. London and New York: Thames and Hudson, 2005. The standard overview of Maya history.

Connah, Graham. *African Civilization: An Archaeological Perspective,* 2nd ed. Cambridge: Cambridge University Press, 2001. An overview of early African societies, emphasizing the rise of cities and states.

Ehret, Christopher. *An African Classical Age: Eastern and Southern Africa in World History, 1000 B.C. to A.D. 400.* Charlottesville: University Press of Virginia, 1998. A pathbreaking study rethinking the role of classical Africa in world history.

Fagan, Brian M. *Kingdoms of Gold, Kingdoms of Jade: The Americas Before Columbus.* London and New York: Thames and Hudson, 1991. A nicely illustrated and readable introduction to the premodern American societies.

Fischer, Steven Roger. *A History of the Pacific Islands.* New York: Palgrave, 2002. A readable introduction to Pacific societies and history.

Kehoe, Alice Beck. *America Before the European Invasions.* New York: Longman, 2002. A recent overview of the North American peoples and history before 1600 C.E.

Kirch, Patrick. *On the Road of the Winds: An Archaeological History of the Pacific Islands.* Berkeley: University of California Press, 2000. A comprehensive study of the Austronesians in the Pacific.

Knight, Alan. *Mexico: From the Beginning to the Spanish Conquest.* New York: Cambridge University Press, 2002. An introduction to Mesoamerican societies.

Mann, Charles C. *1491: New Revelations of the Americans Before Columbus.* New York: Alfred A. Knopf, 2005. A readable summary of recent scholarship on the American societies.

Newman, James L. *The Peopling of Africa: A Geographic Interpretation.* New Haven, CT: Yale University Press, 1995. An excellent summary of what we know about the early history and migrations of Africa's people.

Nile, Richard, and Christian Clark. *Cultural Atlas of Australia, New Zealand and the South Pacific.* New York: Facts on File, 1996. A well-written overview with much on early histories and cultures.

Phillipson, David W. *African Archaeology,* 3rd ed. Cambridge: Cambridge University Press, 2005. A general study of the archaeology of premodern Africa, from prehistory into the second millennium of the Common Era.

Phillipson, David W. *Ancient Ethiopia: Aksum, Its Antecedents and Successors.* London: British Museum Press, 2005. A general study of the archaeology of premodern Africa, from prehistory into the second millennium of the Common Era.

Shillington, Kevin. *History of Africa,* revised 2nd ed. New York: Palgrave Macmillan, 2005. A recent survey text.

Welsby, Derek A. *The Kingdom of Kush: The Napatan and Meroitic Empires.* Princeton: Markus Wiener, 1996. A well-illustrated and up-to-date survey of Kushite society.

Whitlock, Ralph. *Everyday Life of the Maya.* Reprint of 1976 edition. New York: Dorset Press, 1987. Although somewhat dated, this remains an excellent introduction to Maya life.

The Afrocentric Challenge to Historians of Antiquity

For many years the writings by Western scholars about world history emphasized Europe, a biased perspective known as Eurocentrism. In the conventional story line, history began in Egypt, Mesopotamia, and Palestine before moving to Greece and Rome and then on to northwestern Europe and finally to North America. The rest of the world, except perhaps for India and China, constituted an exotic aside to the European mainstream. The academic fields of classics (the study of the Greco-Roman world) and Egyptology specialized in the ancient Mediterranean world, excluding the rest of Africa and Asia. Before the 1970s most Western historians either ignored Africa or argued that Africa was unimportant throughout world history.

THE PROBLEM

Today a historical perspective that incorporates Africa has become common, but for much of the twentieth century many scholars openly agreed with an eminent British historian, who wrote in 1928 that Africa had no history and that most Africans had stayed stagnant and sunk in barbarism for many centuries. In reacting to racial discrimination and lingering contempt for Africa's historical legacy, many historians have made a convincing case for the importance of Africa and its critical role in world history. But questions remain. Was Africa a central part of the larger ancient and classical world? Was Egypt essentially an African or a Mediterranean society? Finally, did Egypt strongly influence classical Greece?

THE DEBATE

In dramatic contrast to Eurocentrism, an alternative approach known as Afrocentrism emphasizes Africa's, rather than Europe's, centrality in history. The more radical Afrocentrists provide a mirror image to the old Eurocentric model, dismissing the older history as a lie designed to glorify European culture and perpetuate the power of white people. They assert that Africa was the fountainhead of Mediterranean culture and that a new way of understanding world history must be developed. Afrocentrists like the Senegalese Cheikh Anta Diop and the American Molefe Asante argue that black Africans, including Egyptians, originated and developed many of the arts, philosophies, and technologies of the ancient and classical Mediterranean societies.

Critics accuse the radical Afrocentrists, like the rigid Eurocentrists, of exaggeration and selectivity in their use of historical evidence, charging that they rely on largely outdated and discredited sources. Some Afrocentrists, for example, promote the dubious notions that Egyptian queen Cleopatra (a Hellenistic Greek) and Athenian philosopher Socrates were black, or that African mariners established the Olmec society of Mexico. Such unsubstantiated theories convince few scholars, regardless of their ethnic background. The British scholar Stephen Howe even asserts that Afrocentric writings replace outmoded Eurocentric scholarship with a misleading version that offers a fictional history.

One prong of the debate is whether ancient Egypt should be seen as essentially Mediterranean or as an African society rooted in African traditions. There is some truth to both propositions. Most scholars now acknowledge extensive Egyptian connections to Africa, western Asia, and southeastern Europe. African ties were certainly extensive. For example, the ancient Egyptian language was closely related to many African tongues. In addition, historians of Africa now believe that many ideas that Egyptians shared with African peoples diffused to Egypt from the south, including the notion and rituals of divine kingship that underpinned Egyptian royalty, various myths and gods, and much material culture. But Egypt's connections were diverse. Populated by migrants from all directions, Egypt produced people of many skin colors and physical features. As a trade crossroads, it maintained trade relations with Africans, Asians, and Europeans. People moved around and intermarried. Thus the Nile Valley was a zone of contact between many groups, where there was not only considerable mingling of people but also, with that, creative cultural borrowing and invention, making it difficult for historians to precisely identify the foreign influences on Egyptian culture.

Another controversy concerns whether Egypt spread African ideas and influences to the Greek culture emerging across the Mediterranean. In his three-volume study, *Black Athena*, the British-born, U.S.-based scholar Martin Bernal contends that, until the early nineteenth century, Western historians stressed the Afro-Asiatic origins of Greek culture, acknowledging Egypt and Phoenicia as core influences. Then, in a sharp turn from that position, he argues, because of increasing racism toward black people and rising European imperialism and nationalism, Western scholars began to stress the Greeks as being a creative source of culture rather than derivative—the pure and original source of European society. African and Middle East influences, such as those from Egypt and Phoenicia, were removed from the scenario.

To argue his point, Bernal uses the myths and historical writings of the Greeks themselves, including, for example, the claims by the Greek historian Herodotus that the Egyptians invented mathematics and that the names of Greek gods originated in Egypt. Herodotus spent time in Egypt around 450 B.C.E. and admired the Egyptian heritage. Influenced by his views, Bernal agrees with Diop that a significant proportion of Greek religion, political philosophy, architecture, science, and even language was imported from Phoenicia and Egypt. For example, Bernal suggests that Athena, the Greek goddess of wisdom and patron goddess of Athens, was a transplanted version of Neith, a goddess from the Nile Delta.

Bernal's work has provoked a storm of controversy. Critics accuse Bernal of misreading Greek myths and historical accounts. They suggest that the Greeks credited Egypt with these accomplishments because they wanted to legitimize their own position by connecting with the older and much respected Egyptian culture, a plausible argument. Furthermore, as most historians are aware, Herodotus often exaggerated or relied on unreliable hearsay, and so is not always a convincing source. Reliance on Herodotus, critics charge, led Bernal to unsubstan-

Athena, Greek Goddess of Wisdom Some scholars suspect that some Greek deities, such as Athena, portrayed here in a Greek sculpture, were based on Egyptian deities.

tiated links, such as one tracing the origins of Greek philosophy to Egyptian literature on wisdom, despite many differences. In one of the more articulate critiques of Bernal, Mary Lefkowitz links Bernal to radical Afrocentrism (an approach he criticizes), deploring his scholarship for disputing that the Greeks invented democracy, philosophy, and science.

In this debate, few classicists disagree that the Greeks admired the Egyptians and traded with them extensively. Some leading Greek thinkers, including Herodotus, Solon, Plato, Thales, and Euclid, visited or studied in Egypt. But, like Lefkowitz, many classicists believe Bernal greatly overstates Afro-Asian influence and underestimates Greek genius. At the same time, however, many other scholars defend Bernal, while some, including the Africanist Basil Davidson and the classicist Jacques Berlinblau, take a more balanced middle view. And the controversy has also inspired more studies placing Egypt and Africa in a larger regional or world context, such as those by Schofield and Davies and by Gilbert and Reynolds.

EVALUATING THE DEBATE

Both sides of the debate have been accused of having a political agenda: to influence how the histories of Europe and Africa are taught in North American and European schools. Hence, the controversy illustrates the danger of what historians call "present mindedness," the tendency to interpret the past largely in light of present social and political concerns. While we can never entirely escape this tendency, we can try to see the people of the past as they saw themselves. This means not using their experiences as ammunition in current social and political debates, as both Eurocentric and Afrocentric historians have often done. While many particular points made by Afrocentrists have found little favor among most historians, we can credit Bernal and others for their useful critique of Eurocentric scholarship. In any case, the sources for Greek thinking may be less important than the creative uses they made of them. Since the issues of how much Egypt contributed to Greece and how much it reflected or stimulated sub-Saharan African cultures are legitimate subjects for historical investigation, the debates will continue. But both Afrocentrism and Eurocentrism are inadequate in providing a global framework that looks at the contributions of all societies.

THINKING ABOUT THE CONTROVERSY

1. What is the argument labeled by critics as Eurocentrism?
2. What is the Afrocentric criticism of Eurocentrism?
3. What are the insights and problems of Bernal's *Black Athena*?

EXPLORING THE CONTROVERSY

Afrocentric history was pioneered by Cheikh Anta Diop in *Civilization or Barbarism: An Authentic Anthropology* (Brooklyn: Lawrence Hill, 1991) and *The African Origin of Civilization: Myth or Reality* (New York: Lawrence Hill, 1974). A more radical approach can be found in Molefe Asante's *Afrocentricity* (Trenton: Africa World Press, 1988) and *The Afrocentric Idea* (Philadelphia: Temple University Press, 1987). The most significant scholarly challenge to the views of mainstream classicists can be found in Martin Bernal, *Black Athena: The Afroasiatic Roots of Classical Civilization*, 3 vols. (New Brunswick, NJ: Rutgers University Press, 1987, 1991, 2001). Bernal responds to his critics in *Black Athena Writes Back* (Durham, NC: Duke University Press, 2001). The major rebuttals to Bernal and Afrocentrism include Stephen Howe, *Afrocentrism: Mystical Pasts and Imagined Homes* (London: Verso, 1998); Mary Lefkowitz, *Not Out of Africa: How Afrocentrism Became an Excuse to Teach Myth as History* (New York: Basic Books, 1996); and Mary Lefkowitz and Guy MacLean, eds., *Black Athena Revisited* (Chapel Hill: University of North Carolina Press, 1996).

For thoughtful discussions of the Afrocentrist controversy, see Basil Davidson, *The Search for Africa: History, Culture, Politics* (New York: Times Books, 1994); and Jacques Berlinblau, *Heresy in the University: The "Black Athena" Controversy and the Responsibility of American Intellectuals* (New Brunswick, NJ: Rutgers University Press, 1999). Useful studies of Egypt and Africa in world history include Louise Schofield and W. Vivian Davies, eds., *Egypt, the Aegean and the Levant: Interconnections in the Second Millennium* (London: Trustees of the British Museum, 1995); and Erik Gilbert and Jonathan T. Reynolds, *Africa in World History: From Prehistory to the Present* (Upper Saddle River, NJ: Prentice-Hall, 2004).

Classical Blossomings in World History, 600 B.C.E.–600 C.E.

In the second century B.C.E. a Greek historian, Polybius, recognized the expanding horizons of his time and concluded that "the world's history has been a series of unrelated episodes, but from now on history becomes an organic whole. The affairs of Europe and Africa are connected with those of Asia and all events bear a relationship and contribute to a single end."[1] In his perception of increasing connections across cultures, Polybius identified a crucial transition. During the Classical Era a vast exchange of ideas, cultures, and products grew in the Afro-Eurasian zone. For example, the Chinese sent missions into western Asia, where they met Persians and Greeks. Alexander the Great, born on the northern fringes of Greece, conquered Egypt and later looked out on the Indus River in India, dreaming of moving on to the Ganges and even farther.

The commercial exchanges that were carried out along the trade routes represented the first glimmerings of a world economy centered on Asia. Greek merchants traveled as far as south India, and one, based in the Egyptian city of Alexandria, wrote a manual describing the ports and listing the products traded in East Africa and South Asia. Warehouses in the south Indian port of Pondicherry were filled with casks of Roman wine. Goods from Persia and Rome reached Funan in Southeast Asia, while the statue of an Indian goddess was carried to the Italian city of Pompeii. Romans craved Chinese silk, Arabian incense, and Indian spices. Merchants near Kabul, in today's Afghanistan, dealt in Greek glass, Egyptian pots, Chinese lacquer ware, and Hindu carvings.

Thanks in part to greater interregional communication over widening networks of exchange, the Classical Era was a period of blossomings of many kinds. Creative philosophies established new value systems or reinforced existing ones in the Mediterranean world and Asia. Between 350 B.C.E. and 200 C.E. the Afro-Eurasian world was also transformed by large regional empires. In the wake of these empires, universal religions such as Buddhism and Christianity crossed cultural boundaries, becoming permanent fixtures of world history. Classical peoples also refined their economic and social patterns. In this process, each society, while having its own dynamics, was also altered by contact with others.

The Axial Age of Philosophical Speculation

Between around 600 and 400 B.C.E., several societies of Eurasia faced a remarkably similar set of crises. People in China, India, Persia, Israel, and Greece were all beset by chronic warfare, population movement, political disruption, and the breakdown of traditional values. Improved ironworking technology produced better tools but also more effective weapons. Political instability was common, as rival states competed with each other for power in China, India, the Middle East, and Greece. These troubled conditions led to a climate of spiritual and intellectual restlessness, provoking a questioning of the old order. Because of the many influential and creative thinkers of this age, some scholars have called this an "axial period" or turning point, a crucial transition in history. This idea understates some crucial religious developments that occurred after 350 B.C.E., such as the reshaping of Hinduism, the division of Buddhism, and the rise of Christianity and Islam. The Axial Age also produced enduring philosophical, religious, and scientific ideas that became the intellectual underpinning of many cultural traditions and fostered new ways of thinking.

Axial Age Thinkers

Many of the greatest thinkers in history were near-contemporaries; that is, they lived at roughly the same time, between 600 and 350 B.C.E. Laozi (credited by tradition as the inspiration for Daoism) and Confucius in China lived and taught in the sixth century around the same time as Buddha and Mahavira (the founder of the Jain faith) in India and the Greek thinkers Thales and Heracleitus. Other major Axial Age thinkers included the Hebrew prophets Jeremiah, Ezekiel, and the second Isaiah, as well as Socrates, Plato, and Aristotle in Greece. Although he may have lived much earlier, the teachings of the Persian Zoroaster also became prominent in this era. Many people today are still influenced by these thinkers: Laozi's advice to live in accordance with nature, the Confucian dream of an ordered society based on proper ethical conduct, the Buddha's rules for ending human suffering, Mahavira's belief in absolute nonviolence, the prophetic Hebrew vision of universal justice and monotheism, the Greek emphasis on rational analysis, and the Zoroastrian notion of opposing forces of darkness and light still have meaning.

Some of these men were not only thinkers but also teachers. To pass along their ideas, leading intellectuals such as Confucius and Plato took on students. Confucius reflected the passion for education: "I am not someone who was born wise. I am someone who tries to learn [from the ancients]."[2] It was a time of exciting exchanges, as mystics and teachers traveled through India, dozens of philosophers spread their ideas in China, and students of Socrates competed with followers of the Stoics in the schools of Athens.

Causes and Characteristics of Axial Age Thought

In trying to identify the causes of the Axial Age, historians point to social and political instability, the effects of commercial exchanges along far-flung trade networks, economies productive enough to support a class of thinkers, and the first glimmerings of the belief that individuals have intrinsic worth apart from their role in society. Other possible causes include the increase in cultural exchanges among Afro-Asian peoples with the spread of writing, iron tools and vehicles, and

Confucius and Laozi in Conversation This picture engraved on a stone tablet in an old Confucian temple shows Confucius visiting Laozi in the city of Loyang and amiably discussing with him views on ritual and music.

improved boats. These inventions helped widen intellectual horizons and stimulated human intellect and imagination. Exactly where many of the great Axial Age ideas began, however, has led to controversy (see Historical Controversy: The Afrocentric Challenge to Historians of Antiquity).

Whatever the causes, several themes became common to Axial Age thinkers. First, especially in China and Greece, thinkers questioned the accepted myths and gods and promoted a humanistic view of life, one more concerned with the social and natural order than the supernatural order. Second, most thinkers stressed moral conduct and values, a vision that often rejected the violent, selfish pursuit of material power they saw around them. Some, like the Buddha, Mahavira, and Laozi, were pacifists who denounced all violence, the Jains going to the extreme of preventing harm even to insects. Third, Confucius, the Hebrew prophets, and several Greeks were also among the first people to think about history and its lessons for societies. Fourth, while few of these thinkers favored social equality, many argued that rulers should govern with a sense of obligation to the powerless and less fortunate. Finally, all the Axial Age thinkers believed that the world could be improved, either by the actions of ethical individuals or by the creation of an ideal social order, or both. For example, Plato devised a model government led not by kings but by a special class of wise men.

But the Axial Age thinkers disagreed as to whether truth was absolute. Socrates and Plato, for example, argued for universal concepts, Plato writing that "those who see the absolute and eternal have real knowledge and not mere opinions." Yet, some Greeks and Chinese also explored the notion that truth was relative and dependent on circumstances. As one Chinese thinker wrote: "Monkeys prefer trees: so what habitat can be said to be absolutely right? Fish flee at the sight of women whom men deem lovely. Whose is the right taste absolutely?"[3] Philosophers still struggle with the question of universal or relative truth.

The Axial Age had not only philosophical and religious but also scientific and political consequences. Across Eurasia people raised fundamental questions about many phenomena and answered them by systematic investigation. Greek thinkers such as Aristotle, who pondered and classified everything from political systems to animals, influenced European and Middle Eastern science, and their ideas inspired new discoveries by Hellenistic, Roman and, later, Islamic scientists. At the other end of Eurasia, Chinese influenced by Confucianism and Daoism also created another rich scientific tradition. Indians became some of the classical world's greatest mathematicians and astronomers. Together, the classical Greeks, Chinese, Indians, and the ancient Mesopotamians and Egyptians built the foundations for modern science. Axial Age ideas also became the basis for new political ideologies. For example, in China, Confucianism mixed with Legalism provided the ideas for building stronger states, while Romans rose to power using modified Greek ideas of democracy. As a result of strengthening state institutions and leaders, in China, India, Persia, and Greece the Axial Age ended in mighty empires that reflected a new order of technological and organizational planning.

The Age of Regional Empires

The empires that arose in much of Eurasia during or at the end of the Axial Age were greater in size and impact than those that had flourished in ancient times. The Persian Empire set the stage, thriving for nearly three centuries. More regional empires appeared between 350 B.C.E. and 250 C.E., from China in the East to Rome in the West, that were much grander in scale than such earlier empires as the Assyrian and the Shang Chinese. In the Mediterranean Basin Rome built on the heritage of Alexander the Great. The Parthians and then the Sassanian Persians governed some of western and Central Asia, the Chinese Han Empire dominated much of East and Central Asia, and in India the Mauryan state controlled much of the subcontinent for over a century. Most of the empires built upon the ideas of classical sages and religious leaders, such as Confucius, Zoroaster, and Plato, in organizing society. In so doing they helped resolve the crises, such as political instability, that had sparked the rise of the Axial Age reformers. Empires also appeared in sub-Saharan Africa and the Americas, including Aksum, Teotihuacan, and Tiwanaku, but on a smaller scale than in Eurasia.

The Rise of Empires

The first great regional empires in the Eastern Hemisphere developed during the Axial Age. The Achaemenid Empire of Persia (550–334 B.C.E.) dwarfed its Middle Eastern predecessors and was the first large empire that ruled many diverse societies. At its height it reached from Egypt and northern Greece across western Asia to Central Asia and the Indus Basin. Persian kings had reason to brag, as did Xerxes, that they were kings of lands containing many people, of the great earth far and wide. Like many leaders, the Persian kings claimed to improve society. Darius I boasted that he had "changed many bad things that had been done to good things. . . . so that people did not kill each other any more."[4] The Hellenistic Empire created by Alexander and the Macedonian Greeks built directly on the experiences of Persian imperial rule. The dynasties that succeeded Alexander dominated much of western Asia, Egypt, and southeastern Europe for the next two centuries.

By the end of the Axial Age, in the third and fourth centuries, new empires arose in Eurasia in part as a result of increased warfare, such as fighting between warring states in India, China, and the western Mediterranean. In each region one state eventually subdued its rivals; the Mauryan, Han, and Roman Empires were the results of these conflicts. Changing social and economic conditions also helped spur the rise of these empires. Rapid economic growth due to expanding long-distance trade networks made merchants more important in all of these societies, and merchants then sought more political influence and social equality. The upper classes, such as the priestly brahman caste of India and the wealthy senatorial class in Rome, protected their own privileges while increasingly exploiting the peasants. The gap between rich and poor widened, causing increased tensions. Rulers surrounded themselves with the trappings of wealth and power, enjoying lavish ceremonies and giving themselves exalted titles. But the move toward empire alleviated some social conflicts by providing large, stable environments in which resources could be acquired and distributed. During this period, the growing states required extensive administrative machinery, larger armies, standardized laws, and governing philosophies. Administrators were needed to collect taxes, organize social services, and serve as judges. From China to Rome, provinces paid taxes and supplied soldiers to the large armies needed to sustain and expand the empires. For example, during the early Roman Empire the armed forces received 58 percent of all government revenue. At the same time the Han emperor stationed 300,000 troops along the Great Wall. Since everything was bigger and the stakes were higher, wars against competing states could be terribly destructive: after three wars with Carthage spanning more than a century, Rome razed that great city to the ground and laced salt into the soil to render it unfit for farming.

Philosophical and religious beliefs maintained community standards but were also used by rulers of these large states to sustain and legitimize their power. For example, Stoic philosophy encouraged Romans to accept their lot in life. In China Confucian ideas urged people to respect leaders, and Legalist thinkers told leaders to exercise power ruthlessly. Thus, the Confucian scholar Dong Zhongshu (ca. 179–104 B.C.E.) elevated the role of the Chinese emperor, arguing that "heaven, earth, and man are the source of all creatures. Heaven gives birth to them, earth nourishes them, and human beings complete them. Who else but a king could connect them all?"[5] In Mauryan India, Ashoka enhanced his position by using Buddhist moral injunctions emphasizing peace, tolerance, and welfare to win popular support. Ashoka recorded his goals on pillars: "All men are my children, and just as I desire for my children that they should obtain welfare and happiness, so do I desire [the same] for all men."[6]

Increasing Cultural Unity and Contact

These new regional empires imposed peace and uniformity within their boundaries. Bureaucratic structures standardized practices throughout an empire so that the weights, measures, currencies, calendars, tax codes, and official languages used throughout the far-flung provinces of an empire were the same. For example, Greek spread widely in the Hellenistic kingdoms of Asia. Latin became the common language in the Roman Empire, in the process fostering the western European "romance" languages, such as Spanish and French. Latin influences also found their way into Germanic languages such as English and German. But in Roman Asia few outside the political elite spoke or read Latin. Similarly, the northern Chinese dialect of Mandarin became China's official spoken language even though, outside of the educated class, few in the southern half of China spoke Mandarin.

By stimulating commerce and communication, the empires fostered the spread of ideas and technologies into neighboring societies and increased contact among distant peoples (see map). For example, Hellenistic Greeks and Mauryan Indians encountered each other in Afghanistan, a crossroads where Eurasian peoples both fought with each other and exchanged ideas. Spurred by imperial expansion, Roman culture and then Christianity permeated the Mediterranean Basin, Hellenistic Greek culture spread in western Asia and North Africa, and China influenced Japan, Korea, Vietnam, and Central Asia.

In Eurasia trade routes grew out of transportation systems constructed to channel resources to imperial capitals. China built canals unprecedented in scale, Achaemenid

Great Empires and Trade Routes

During the Classical Era, great empires often dominated East Asia, India, western Asia, North Africa, and southern Europe. Extensive land and maritime trade routes linked East Asia with western Eurasia, West Africa with the Mediterranean, and East Africa with southern Asia.

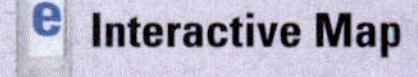
Interactive Map

Persia and Mauryan India constructed east-west highways, and the Romans developed 150,000 miles of paved roads. These roads and canals, along with seaports, became linked to long-distance trade networks, which brought many societies, such as the Celts and Germans in northern Europe, the Sogdians in Central Asia, the Sudanic peoples of West Africa, the East African coastal dwellers, and the Japanese and Koreans, into closer contact with major empires.

Decline of Empires

Throughout history states rise and fall, and the classical empires did as well. While each of the great regional empires declined for different reasons, the Roman and Han Chinese Empires suffered from some of the same problems. Each empire expanded beyond its ability to support itself, weakening administrative structures and finances. Some conquered territories brought wealth to the empire, but others did not. The British Isles, for example, were a net drain on the imperial Roman treasury, and it was costly to maintain Chinese control in Central Asia. Both of these empires also suffered from civil wars and growing domestic unrest. Eventually both empires, unable to acquire new wealth through further expansion, made economic cutbacks and raised taxes to sustain the imperial structure, which caused widespread resentment. Contemporary observers recorded the decline. The third-century C.E. Roman writer Cyprian argued that "the World itself testifies to its own decline by giving manifold concrete evidence of the process of decay. This loss of strength and stature must end, at least, in annihilation."[7]

Both the Han and Roman Empires were also plagued by environmental problems. Because the empires formed as the global climate was warming, they could benefit from increased food supplies, and both flourished during the peak of warmth between 200 B.C.E. and 200 C.E. With the return of colder weather after 200 C.E., however, agricultural production declined and the great empires collapsed or weakened. Soil exhaustion in Italy was also a factor in Rome's declining food supply. In addition, diseases traveled along the land and sea routes, undermining Rome and China in the second century C.E. Some outbreaks, like the terrible plague identified with Justinian's Byzantium, killed millions and made life miserable over wide areas. Probably originating in Africa, the plague killed nearly half the population of Constantinople in the 540s. By the time the pandemic reached its end in the 590s, some 25 million West Asians, North Africans, and Europeans had perished.

When pastoral nomads began to put more pressure on the Roman and Chinese Empires, these states had been weakened so much by economic and environmental problems that they could no longer effectively resist. For instance, Chinese emperors could no longer afford to maintain the garrisons along the series of walls built across north China. The Germanic tribes proved a long-term threat to Rome, and various Central Asians, among them Huns, Scythians, and Turkish peoples, continuously intruded along the fringes of Persia, India, and China. By 200 C.E. population growth and climate change pushed some of them to more aggressively seek wealth in the declining Roman and Han Empires. In the end, the imperial orders were undermined in part by forces beyond their control.

Various peoples eventually conquered or displaced the great empires, although they also usually adopted Roman, Indian, Persian, or Chinese culture. But the imperial idea never died. It proved particularly strong in Persia, where the Achaeminid, Hellenistic Seleucid, Parthian, and finally Sassanian Empires succeeded each other over a millennium. Even in India, where fragmented states were the norm, the Gupta rulers claimed kinship with the Mauryas five centuries earlier. The belief in the need for large regional empires also endured for centuries in China and served as a model for later dynasties that conquered vast territories. Hence, the China of the eighteenth century C.E., which incorporated many non-Chinese societies, clearly descended in recognizable form from the Han of 150 B.C.E. Similarly, the Byzantine Empire controlled vast European and western Asian territories once part of the old Roman Empire. After the fall of the western Roman Empire, however, western Europeans never succeeded in reviving that empire, even though some Christian German kings centuries later claimed the title of "Holy Roman Emperor." In contrast to China, where the Sui dynasty revived much of the early Han system, western European societies were never able to restore the Roman heritage.

World Religions and Their Influences

During the later centuries of the Classical Era, universal religions became more prominent in Afro-Eurasia, marking another great transition that reshaped societies. Instead of the gods of the ancient world, which were local and identified with particular cities or cultures, these new religions were portable and appealed across cultural boundaries. They could be carried along trade routes, attracting believers far from their lands of birth. The Eurasian faiths with the most followers—Christianity, Buddhism, Hinduism, and Zoroastrianism—filled a vacuum created by political instability and cultural decline.

The Spread of Universal Religions

Religions spread along land and sea trade routes. Missionaries accompanied or were themselves traders, as a fourth-century C.E. Christian hymn in Syria acknowledged: "Travel like merchants, That we may gain the world. Fill creation with teaching."[8] About six centuries after its founding in India, Buddhism reached China via the Silk Road and Southeast Asia over the maritime trade routes. Christianity, with roots in the eastern Mediterranean, spread to Rome, where it became prominent by the fourth century C.E.; it permeated northern Europe beginning around 500 C.E. Christianity also established roots in western Asia, Egypt, Nubia, and Ethiopia. Other faiths also established a presence. Manicheanism, a mix of Christian and Zoroastrian influences, attracted believers from North Africa to China. Judaism also gained some converts in Arabia, the Caucasus, and Ethiopia. By 500 or 600 C.E. small Christian and Jewish communities had even been established in Central Asia, western India, and northern China. Networks of exchange helped shape religious traditions as well as spread them. For example, Zoroastrian ideas probably influenced Ionian Greek, Mahayana Buddhist, and Judeo-Christian beliefs and art forms.

The universal religions gave people hope in the face of the political and social crises that marked the decline of the great regional empires from the second through the fifth centuries C.E. Sometimes these new religions merged with or incorporated existing beliefs. In East Asia, for example, Buddhism gradually blended with or accommodated Confucianism, Daoism, and Shinto, and, in northern Europe, Christianity acquired a Germanic or Celtic flavor over the centuries. Not all the religious changes were accommodating, however. Religion could also divide families. In one case, a Roman writer told of conflict between a Christian wife and her husband, who practiced his traditional faith: "She is engaged in a fast; her husband has arranged a banquet. She celebrates the Easter Vigil throughout the entire night; her husband expects her in his bed."[9]

In sub-Saharan Africa and the Americas, some religious beliefs reached across many societies, becoming the counterparts to the organized Eurasian religions. The polytheistic beliefs of the Mande and other Sudanic peoples, for instance, gradually spread to the Guinea coast and Central Africa, and from there to eastern and southern Africa. In the Americas the Olmec introduced gods and views of the universe that contributed to the later religious beliefs of the Maya, and some Maya ideas may have spread to other Mesoamericans. Chavín religious traditions, including gods and shamanistic practices, probably influenced the views of other Andean peoples such as the Moche and Tiwanaku. Some of the American peoples practiced human sacrifice as part of their religious devotions, as offerings to the gods. Human sacrifice was also found in some Afro-Eurasian societies, among them the Celts, Minoan Crete, ancient Egypt, and Shang China.

Religion, Culture, and Society

The universal religions became a major force in shaping the societies and regions in which they became dominant, eventually creating, for example, a largely Hindu India, a Buddhist Sri Lanka, and a Christian Europe. To be sure, religion was only a part of life, and religions changed over time, dividing into varied sects such as the Mahayana and Theravada Buddhists. But after the regional empires collapsed into many rival states in the Mediterranean, India, and China, religious institutions transcended political divisions, fostering cultural unity across borders. Hindus, Buddhists, and Christians often saw themselves as part of larger communities. As a result, Chinese Buddhist pilgrims such as Faxian made the long and arduous journey to India to study with Indian Buddhists. And

Bibliothèque nationale de France

King David For centuries artists in the Christian Ethiopian kingdom, in the highlands of Northeast Africa, painted biblical figures on the pages of religious manuscripts. The artists often used Ethiopian motifs, and this painting of the Hebrew king David, adorned in rich robes and crown and playing a harp-type instrument, resembles that of an Ethiopian king.

many Christians looked to the bishops in faraway cities such as Rome for guidance. Spirituality permeated the lives of people all over the world. Religion also offered the poor the hope that they might end their suffering and low status, if not in this life then through reincarnation or in some form of heaven.

All the universal religions, as well as the religions of urban American societies such as the Maya, had certain features, practices, and beliefs in common. They had sacred writings or scriptures, such as the Hindu Vedas and Christian Bible, strict moral codes, organized priesthoods, theologies laying out core beliefs, and some concept of existence after death. Most faiths also encouraged followers to treat others as they wanted to be treated themselves, although in practice many people ignored this advice. The devout shared a belief in the universal truth of their faith. All the religions were patriarchal to one degree or another, adding religious sanction to the growing suppression of women. Christian and Buddhist leaders also dispatched missionaries into neighboring societies, although Buddhism later lost most of its missionary zeal.

For all the spiritual comfort and insight they provided believers, these new religions, like their predecessors, were also important as forces of social control. For example, Hindu ideas of reincarnation and karma underpinned the Indian caste system, encouraging people to accept their status. Christians focused on attaining heaven and were warned that questioning religious authority and beliefs might prevent salvation. Some of the religious establishments grew intolerant of dissent. For this reason, Christian bishops established a consensus on doctrine, excluding ideas considered to be heresy. Those who disagreed with Christian or Zoroastrian orthodoxy might be banned or punished, and they were expected to face retribution after death in Hell, the abode of evil, an underworld for wicked people and disbelievers.

Monasticism and Its Diffusion

Some of the universal religions spawned a new social and spiritual movement, monasticism. It may have first developed as a movement within both Buddhism and Jainism. Buddha himself supposedly ordained the first monks as well as nuns, including his mother. In Theravada Buddhist societies most men spent some period as monks, bound by their rigid code of celibacy and poverty. But the concept then perhaps spread over the trade networks into western Asia. Whether or not inspired by Buddhist models, monasticism became a growing component of organized Christianity by the third century C.E.

Whether Christian or Buddhist, monasteries provided educational and charitable services while providing a focus for community religious life. In societies as far removed as England, Nubia, and China, a substantial number of men (and some women) joined monastic orders, abandoning the humdrum existence of everyday life for a focus on prayer and meditation. Most monks and nuns practiced austere religious practices to strengthen spiritual life. This could involve sexual abstinence, fasting, and solitary contemplation. In the Hindu tradition wandering holy men who abandoned the comforts of settled life and families provided a counterpart to organized monastic life.

Changing Economic and Social Patterns

Increased migration and communication fostered major social and economic changes. Population growth encouraged migration, which led to the intermixing of peoples and the exchange of ideas. Deadly disease epidemics moving along migration networks testified to this widespread contact between distant peoples. The long-distance trade routes also spread both diseases and new ideas. The result was that certain social attitudes became more common over a wide area, including attitudes toward women and slaves that lasted for centuries. The social and economic systems of the Classical Era, some alien and some familiar to modern people, suggest both how much and how little the world has changed since the Classical Era.

The Growth and Decline of World Population

Successful agricultural systems in the great empires allowed for substantial population growth from Europe to China. In 4000 B.C.E., at the dawn of the ancient world, the world population was well under 100 million. At the beginning of the Common Era there were probably between 200 and 250 million people, over 70 percent living in Asia and about 20 million each in Africa and the Americas. China was the largest society, with some 60 million people. In addition, more people now lived in cities. In 450 B.C.E. the world's largest city was probably Babylon, with 200,000 people. By 200 B.C.E. Patna in Mauryan India had 400,000, and by 100 C.E. Rome was the largest metropolis, with at least 500,000 people and perhaps a million.

But diseases began to limit population growth in the later Classical Era. Networks of communication were often networks of contagion, port cities being the major hubs of transmission. Epidemics of smallpox and plague resulted from travelers unknowingly spreading new diseases into areas where people had not yet built up immunities to them. Epidemic diseases may have killed as much as 25 percent of the population of China and the Roman Empire during the second and third centuries C.E. Indeed, plague outbreaks contributed considerably to the decline of the classical empires; for example, they undermined the Roman state and, by producing widespread misery and disillusionment, aided the spread of Christianity among demoralized or desperate Roman subjects. As a result of the various disease outbreaks, by 600 B.C.E. the world population remained between 200 and 240 million, similar to what it had been six centuries earlier.

Population growth led to increased movement, as people sought open lands and better opportunities. Responding to population pressures, Chinese migrants moved into central and southern China; Germanic and Turkish peoples spread into central Europe and western Asia, respectively; Bantu-speaking peoples occupied the southern half of Africa; and Austronesians settled remote Pacific islands. As groups migrated, they assimilated local peoples and cultures and adapted their lives to new surroundings.

Trade and Cultural Contact

The networks of trade, like those of imperial expansion and missionary activity, linked distant peoples while spreading the influence of cultures more widely. The Greeks picked up scientific and mathematical knowledge as well as some religious notions from the Egyptians and Phoenicians. Indian cultural influences, including Buddhism, spread over the trade routes into central, east, and southeast Asia, reaching as far as Korea, Japan, and Indonesia. Aksum was linked by commerce with the Mediterranean world and India, a link that brought Christianity to the Ethiopian highlands. Precious spices from southern Arabia, textiles from India, and gold from Malaya and West Africa found their way to the Mediterranean societies. The Roman writer Pliny was surprised at Roman demand for Indian pepper, which "has nothing in it that can plead as a recommendation [other than] a certain pungency; and yet it is for this that we import it all the way from India!"[10] Trade also connected Mesoamerica with neighboring regions and fostered networks of exchange in both eastern North America and western South America. For example, copper from the North American Great Lakes reached the Gulf Coast, and Mesoamerican ball games spread far and wide. Crops also traveled American trade routes; maize from Mexico became a major crop in both North and South America, and tomatoes from the Andes carried into Central America and Mexico.

Crossing the Pamir Mountains The Pamir Mountains, separating the deserts of what is now western China from the deserts and grasslands of Turkestan and Afghanistan, were one of the more formidable barriers faced by camel caravans traveling the Silk Road. To avoid the blistering summer heat of the desert, the caravans often traveled in winter and thus had to maneuver through mountain snows.
Michael Fairchild/Peter Arnold, Inc.

The Silk Road endured as a major overland long-distance network of exchange—in effect the first transcontinental highway—and allowed people, goods, and ideas to travel thousands of miles. As a Han dynasty historian put it: "Messengers come and go every season and month, foreign traders and merchants knock on the gates of the Great Wall every day."[11] In Eurasia the introduction of coinage encouraged trade by offering widely recognized tokens of value. Coins from Sassanian Persia and Byzantium as well as Chinese silk served as the network currency. Indeed, the huge amounts of gold and silver exported by Rome to pay for Chinese silk and Indian spices did some damage to the Roman economy. Overland trade expanded with the growing use of camels. After the invention of an efficient saddle allowed this pack animal to be used for longer journeys across the deserts and plains of Asia and Africa, camels became the trucks of the premodern Afro-Eurasian zone. And the merchants who used the camels carried not only bullion and products but also religions, especially Buddhism and Manicheanism, which spread along the Silk Road into Central Asia and China.

Cities grew up along the Silk Road across Central Asia to serve as suppliers and middlemen to the merchants. These cities, such as Kashgar in Xinjiang and Samarkand in Turkestan, became part of a contact zone linking many societies. Hubs at the eastern end of the Mediterranean, such as Petra, Palmyra, Alexandria, and Constantinople, served as transshipment points for goods traveling between China and Rome. This trade aided some societies. For example, Nabataean Arabs constructed a trade network linking Egypt, western Asia, and southern Europe, while the Sogdians dominated Central Asian trading cities and even had communities in western China. Chinese sources described the Sogdians as trained for trade: "At birth honey was put in their mouths and gum on their hands. They learned the trade from the age of five. On reaching twelve they were sent to do business in a neighboring state."[12]

Maritime trade also flourished during this period, enriching various ports. Hence, both trade goods and cultural influences were carried by sea between eastern and western Asia. Sailing networks connected the entire Mediterranean Basin. For several centuries one key network hub was the tiny Greek island of Delos (DEH-los) in the Aegean Sea, of which it was said, "Merchant, sail in and unload! Everything is as good as sold."[13] Merchants from all over, including Greeks from around the Mediterranean, Romans, Syrians, Jews, Phoenicians, Nabataean Arabs, and Yemenite Arabs, flocked to Delos to trade. Maritime counterparts to the overland trade diaspora of the Sogdians developed. For example, a Jewish trading community sunk roots in southwest India, Indian merchants settled in Funan (Cambodia), Indonesians and Arabs sailed to East Africa to trade or settle, and Greeks established communities all over the Mediterranean and Black Sea Basins.

Eventually a vast maritime route linked China, Vietnam, and Cambodia in the East through Malaya and the Indonesian archipelago to India and Sri Lanka, and then stretched westward to Persia, Arabia, and the East African coast. Europe and North Africa were connected to this system through the Arabs, Aksumites, and Persians. The Greek geographer Strabo wrote that since merchants from Roman-ruled Alexandria had sent trading fleets to India, "these regions have become better known to us today."[14] Some cities flourished as hubs for this maritime trade. For instance, between 100 and 500 C.E. the Egyptian port of Berenike on the Red Sea was regularly visited by ships from India. Products from as far away as Java and Cambodia reached the markets of Berenike, and eleven different written languages, including Greek and Sanskrit, were used there. Berenike was also linked through Alexandria to the Mediterranean societies.

Maritime commerce faced serious limitations, however. Because of formidable currents, only the strongest oars would allow a boat to pass through the Strait of Gibraltar separating Spain from North Africa. This problem inhibited trade between Mediterranean and Atlantic societies for many centuries. Similarly, the vast distances of the Pacific Ocean, crossed in that day only by outrigger canoes, limited the volume and type of goods carried along the trading networks there. Some people, using balsa rafts, traded along the Pacific Coast of South and Central America, while others used canoes to travel between Caribbean islands, but the volume and frequency of such maritime trade remain unclear.

Social Systems and Attitudes

The social systems and attitudes of the Classical Era set the patterns for centuries to come. In many places gender roles hardened. For example, in Greece and China, customs and laws allowed men far greater social freedom than women. Because the great empires were made through military conquest, they were very masculine in nature. In addition, patriarchal attitudes were encouraged by some of the new philosophies and religions. For example, Confucianism gave power to older men, and influential Christian leaders urged women to stay in the background. In addition, the faiths that replaced Greek and Roman religions removed goddesses as objects of worship in the Mediterranean world, although in southern Asia many Hindus continued to revere female deities.

Homosexuality existed in all classical societies and was generally tolerated in some, especially in Greece and Rome. Chinese historians reported that many emperors of the era, including the empire-builder Wu Di of the Han dynasty, had male lovers in addition to their wives and concubines. The Han era historian Sima Qian wrote numerous biographies of those men "who served the ruler and succeeded in delighting his ears and eyes, [winning] his favor and intimacy."[15] Chinese also tolerated lesbian relationships among women in polygamous households. But in many places official attitudes concerning gender roles and sexual behaviors became more rigid over time, pushing homosexuals to the margins of society.

Changing social and religious attitudes affected women. Although women had some legal protections in Greece and Rome, many also lived generally domestic and often secluded lives. For instance, when Roman women in 195 B.C.E. took to the streets to protest a law, passed during a costly war, that limited the amount of gold and finery a woman could wear, many men complained that women should stay home and out of politics. A Roman politician noted that "women cannot partake of [local office], priesthoods, [military] triumphs, badges of office, or spoils of war; elegance, finery and beautiful clothes are women's badges; in these they find joy and take pride."[16] Women faced increasing restrictions in China and northern India, where they were expected to be obedient to men. Patriarchy was also common in Africa, the Americas, and the Pacific islands. While there were notable exceptions, the leaders in Aksum and in the Maya city-states were mostly men.

But wherever they lived, women had varied experiences. Some were treated as property, assigned by their fathers to husbands, and many faced permanent dependency on fathers, husbands, and sons. But those who were well loved by male relatives could perhaps gain substantial personal advantages. Only a small minority of women anywhere were educated, Hypatia of Alexandria and Ban Zhao in China being notable examples. However, a few, such as Queen Zenobia in Palmyra, Cleopatra VII in Egypt, Queen Theodora in Byzantium, and several Kushite queens, attained great power. Some women asserted their own interests, a behavior reflected in some Greek plays. Thus, in *Antigone* **(an-TIG-on-ee)** by Sophocles, the main female character defies King Creon, who refuses to allow her to give her dead brother a proper burial.

Like patriarchy, slavery was practiced in many classical societies around the world. Most people saw slavery as a part of the natural order of things and essential to economic life. Slaves everywhere were bought and sold at the whim of the owner, and their lives and labor were controlled. Most slaves were poor, but not all lived in misery. Some Greek and Roman slaves held high positions in society or were attached to prosperous families. In societies such as Han China, Mauryan India, Aksum, and the Maya society, slaves were only one segment of the lower class, whereas in Greece and Rome slaves constituted a large part of the population and were used in every area of the economy, from mining and construction to prostitution and domestic work. For example, in Rome it was chiefly slaves who built the Colisseum, the Forum, and the great aqueducts that so impress modern tourists. Slavery mostly died out in China and India during the first millennium C.E. and became less important in Europe after the collapse of the Roman Empire, showing that societies do change, often dramatically, over time.

Suggested Reading

Books

Adas, Michael, ed. *Agricultural and Pastoral Societies in Ancient and Classical History*. Philadelphia: Temple University Press, 2001. A useful collection of essays on various topics.

Armstrong, Karen. *The Great Transformation: The Beginning of Our Religious Traditions.* New York: Knopf, 2006. Excellent introduction to the Axial Age and its thinkers.

Bentley, Jerry H. *Old World Encounters: Cross-Cultural Contacts and Exchanges in Pre-Modern Times.* New York: Oxford University Press, 1993. An up-to-date survey of trade routes and the spread of universal religions.

Bulliet, Richard W. *The Camel and the Wheel.* Cambridge: Harvard University Press, 1975. A classic study of the caravan trade in Asia and Africa.

Curtin, Philip D. *Cross-Cultural Trade in World History*. Cambridge: Cambridge University Press, 1984. Contains much material on long-distance trade in the Classical Era.

Fernandez-Armesto, Felipe. *Civilizations: Culture, Ambition, and the Transformation of Nature*. New York: Touchstone, 2001. A fascinating and wide-ranging survey across eras and regions that emphasizes adaptations to varied environments.

Foltz, Richard C. *Religions of the Silk Road: Overland Trade and Cultural Exchange from Antiquity to the Fifteenth Century*. New York: St. Martin's, 1999. Analyzes the spread of religions.

Headrick, Daniel. *Technology: A World History.* New York: Oxford University Press, 2009. Good summary of metallurgy and long distance trade in this era.

Lloyd, Geoffrey, and Nathan Sivin. *The Way and the Word: Science and Medicine in Early China and Greece.* New Haven, CT: Yale University Press, 2003. Compares these two great traditions of learning, arguing that modern science derives from both as well as from Indian, Islamic, and other cultures.

McClellan, James, and Harold Dorn. *Science and Technology in World History: An Introduction*. Baltimore: Johns Hopkins University Press, 1999. A survey of science and technology traditions.

Pearson, Michael. *The Indian Ocean.* New York: Routledge, 2003. A history of the maritime connections.

Prazniak, Roxann. *Dialogues Across Civilizations: Sketches in World History from the Chinese and European Experiences*. Boulder: Westview, 1996. Contains interesting comparative essays.

Smart, Ninian. *The Long Search.* Boston: Little, Brown and Co., 1977. A very readable introduction to the various universal religious traditions of Eurasia and their modern offshoots.

Super, John C., and Brian K. Turley. *Religion in World History.* New York: Routledge, 2006. A brief study of religious diffusion and change.

Wood, Frances. *The Silk Road.* Berkeley: University of California Press, 2002. Surveys 2,000 years of history.

WEBSITES

Ancient and Lost Civilizations (*http://www.crystalinks.com/ancient.html*). Contains essays and other materials on ancient and classical societies.

Exploring Ancient World Cultures (*http://eawc.evansville.edu/*). A very helpful collection of essays and other useful material.

Internet Ancient History Sourcebook (*http://www.fordham.edu/halsall/ancient/asbook.html*). An exceptionally rich collection of links and primary source readings.

Monks and Merchants (*http://www.asiasociety.org/arts/monksandmerchants/index.html*). Interesting essays, timelines, maps, and images for an Asia Society exhibition on the Silk Road as a zone of communication.

Silk Road Narratives (*http://depts.washington.edu/uwch/silkroad/texts/texts.html*). Explores cultural interaction in Eurasia through excerpts from Silk Road travelers.

PART

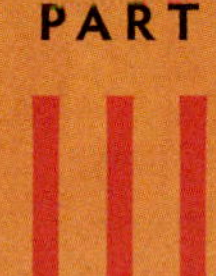

Expanding Horizons: Encounters and Transformations in the Intermediate Era, ca. 600–1500

By 600 C.E. most of the great classical Eastern Hemisphere empires and states, such as Rome, Han China, Gupta India, and Kush, were only memories. The classical American societies, such as the Maya, were to flourish a few centuries longer, only to collapse. Yet vigorous new societies were emerging. Even while some classical patterns hung on or were modified to suit new needs, the Afro-Eurasian zone was in transition. During this era many societies developed a more cosmopolitan outlook. New trade networks emerged and old ones were revitalized. Though characterized by long periods of conflict, this era also saw worldwide innovations.

Historians disagree as to what this era should be called. Borrowing from European history, scholars often refer to the medieval period, a "middle ages" stretching from around 600 to 1500. The term *medieval* suggests societies with relatively weak governments, rigid social orders, and one dominating religion, a description that best fits Europe in this era and perhaps Japan and parts of India. However, the term has little relevance for China, the Islamic states, and most of Africa, Southeast Asia, and the Americas. *Intermediate Era* is a more neutral term to describe this creative transitional period, which linked the Classical Era, when contacts between distant societies were still limited, with the rise of global connections that marked the centuries after 1500.

The Intermediate Era experienced dramatic transformations of societies. The explosive rise of Islam from a local faith in Arabia in the early 600s to a hemisphere-wide religion by 1400 was one of the main transitions. The resurgence of China as a political, economic, and cultural force was another. Also during this time, Buddhism became a major influence in the eastern half of Eurasia, while Christianity became Europe's dominant faith. Mighty empires arose in Africa, Southeast Asia, and the Americas.

These nine centuries also differed from the preceding Classical Era by virtue of the increasing contacts between peoples. Contacts became more frequent and substantial beginning around 600. New interregional communications took place across Afro-Eurasia, including trade, cultural exchange, and religious links. As a result, a maritime trading network connected China and Southeast Asia through India and the Persian Gulf to East Africa

Courtesy, Museo Prehistorico et Etnografico, Rome

Sape Ivory Saltholder Africans had traded and carved ivory since ancient times. This magnificent ivory carving, made, probably in the fifteenth century, by an artist of the Sape people, who lived in what is today Sierra Leone in West Africa, was used to store salt. The carving reflected artistic influence brought to the region by the earliest Portuguese explorers and traders.

and the Mediterranean. A growing caravan trade across the Sahara Desert brought West Africa and the Mediterranean closer together. The spread of religions also reshaped societies. For example, Arab culture expanded with Islam. The cosmopolitan Islamic world, stretching from Morocco to Indonesia, enjoyed much cultural diversity but also shared many beliefs and practices. In the Western Hemisphere, Mesoamerican cultural and agricultural influences spread deep into North and Central America.

The era was also marked by conflicts that changed societies. Spurring the rise of interregional encounters was the expansion of several Central Asian peoples. Turkish migrations and conquests in western Asia occured throughout the period. In the thirteenth century the Mongols conquered the largest land empire in world history, stretching from Korea and China westward to Russia and eastern Europe, a momentous achievement with major consequences. For example, as a result, East Asian technology flowed along the trade routes to Europe. However, the Mongol period also witnessed the spread along these same trade routes of a catastrophic plague, known as the Black Death, that devastated societies all across Eurasia and North Africa, killing countless millions of Chinese, Persians, Arabs, and Europeans.

The Intermediate years also saw major innovations such as economic growth, technological change, the rise of new states, and maritime exploration. China became the world's most commercialized and industrialized society, often exercising influence far from its borders. In the early 1400s Chinese maritime expeditions reached East Africa and the Persian Gulf. Islamic states were also dynamic, and Muslim scholars and artisans made numerous contributions to the world. West African kingdoms, East African coastal cities, and Southeast Asian states were closely tied to world trade. In the Americas, the Aztec and Inca Empires had arisen on the foundations of earlier societies. Europeans made key intellectual and technological discoveries, and they also benefited when the expansion of Islam and the Mongols introduced to Europe Asian-derived ideas, plants, and tools. In the 1400s, making good use of naval technology and weaponry from all over Eurasia and energized by economic growth and religious fervor, Europeans began voyages of discovery that set the stage for connecting the entire world after 1500.

EUROPE

In western Europe a rigid society, dominated by a powerful Christian church, slowly emerged, reaching its zenith around 1000 C.E. Dozens of small rival states fought each other. Urban and commercial growth, technological innovation, and the Black Death eventually undermined feudalism and church power, and political, intellectual, artistic, and religious change began reshaping western Europe in the 1400s. At the same time, imported Chinese and Arab naval and military technology helped spur maritime explorations. Meanwhile, Byzantium struggled to hold its eastern Mediterranean empire but also spread its culture to the Russians.

WESTERN ASIA

The rise of Islam in Arabia in the 600s transformed the region. Arab Muslim armies conquered much of Western Asia, and most of the region's peoples eventually embraced Islam. Islam also spread west through North Africa and into Spain, as well as east to India, Central Asia, and Indonesia, linking Western Asians with a vast Islamic community. Islam divided into rival Sunni and Shi'a schools. Muslim scholars fostered science and literature, and major Islamic states, especially the Abbasid Empire, dominated the region. Eventually the Ottoman Turks formed the most powerful Western Asian state, conquering Byzantium.

EASTERN ASIA

China stood out for its influence and creativity. During the Tang and Song dynasties, China's economy grew rapidly and science flourished, attracting merchants and scholars from many countries. At the same time, Chinese cultural influences spread to neighboring Korea, Japan, and Vietnam. Under Mongol rule, China remained open to the world, but it later turned inward. Meanwhile, Japanese and Koreans combined Chinese influences, such as Buddhism, with their own traditions.

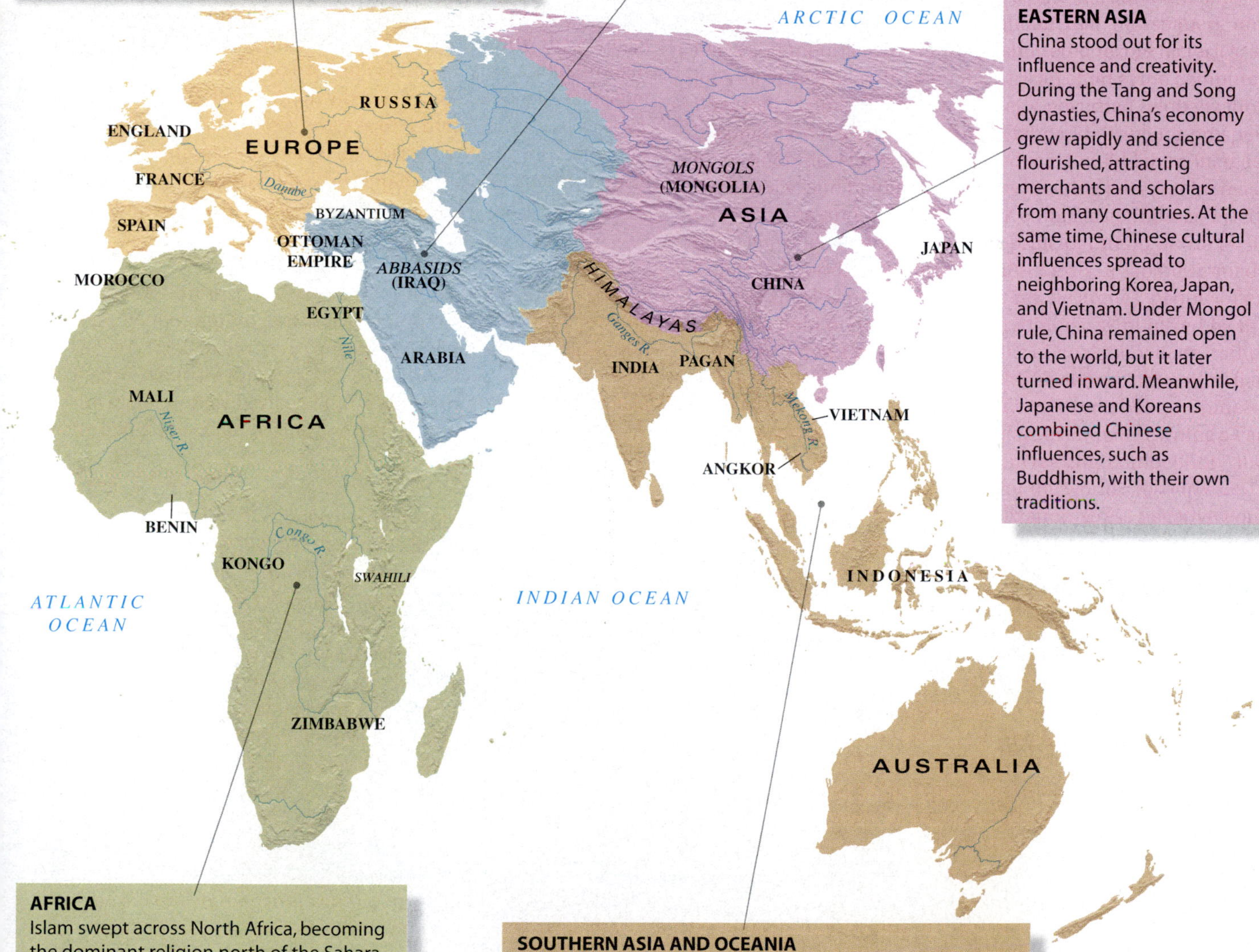

AFRICA

Islam swept across North Africa, becoming the dominant religion north of the Sahara. It also reshaped societies as it spread into West Africa and East Africa. Sub-Saharan African peoples formed large empires, such as Mali, and flourishing states, such as Benin, Kongo, and Zimbabwe. West African kingdoms and East African coastal cities were closely tied to world trade. In the 1400s the Portuguese explored the West African coast and disrupted African states.

SOUTHERN ASIA AND OCEANIA

Although politically fragmented into diverse rival states, India remained a major commercial and manufacturing center. Muslims from West and Central Asia conquered parts of north India, spreading Islam there. In response, Hinduism became reinvigorated. Southeast Asians flourished from farming and maritime trade, and major kingdoms, notably Angkor and Pagan, emerged. Southeast Asians imported ideas from India, China, and the Middle East, and many people adopted Theravada Buddhism or Islam. Maritime trade, especially the export of spices, and the spread of Islam and Buddhism linked Southeast Asia to the wider Afro-Eurasian world. Meanwhile, Polynesians settled the last uninhabited Pacific islands, including Hawaii and New Zealand.

CHAPTER

10

The Rise, Power, and Connections of the Islamic World, 600–1500

CHAPTER OUTLINE

- Early Islam: The Origins and Spread of a Continuous Tradition
- Early Islamic States and Empires
- Cultural Hallmarks of Islam: Theology, Society, and Learning
- Globalized Islam and Middle Eastern Political Change

PROFILE
Ibn Battuta, a Muslim Traveler

WITNESS TO THE PAST
The Holy Book, God, and the Prophet in the Quran

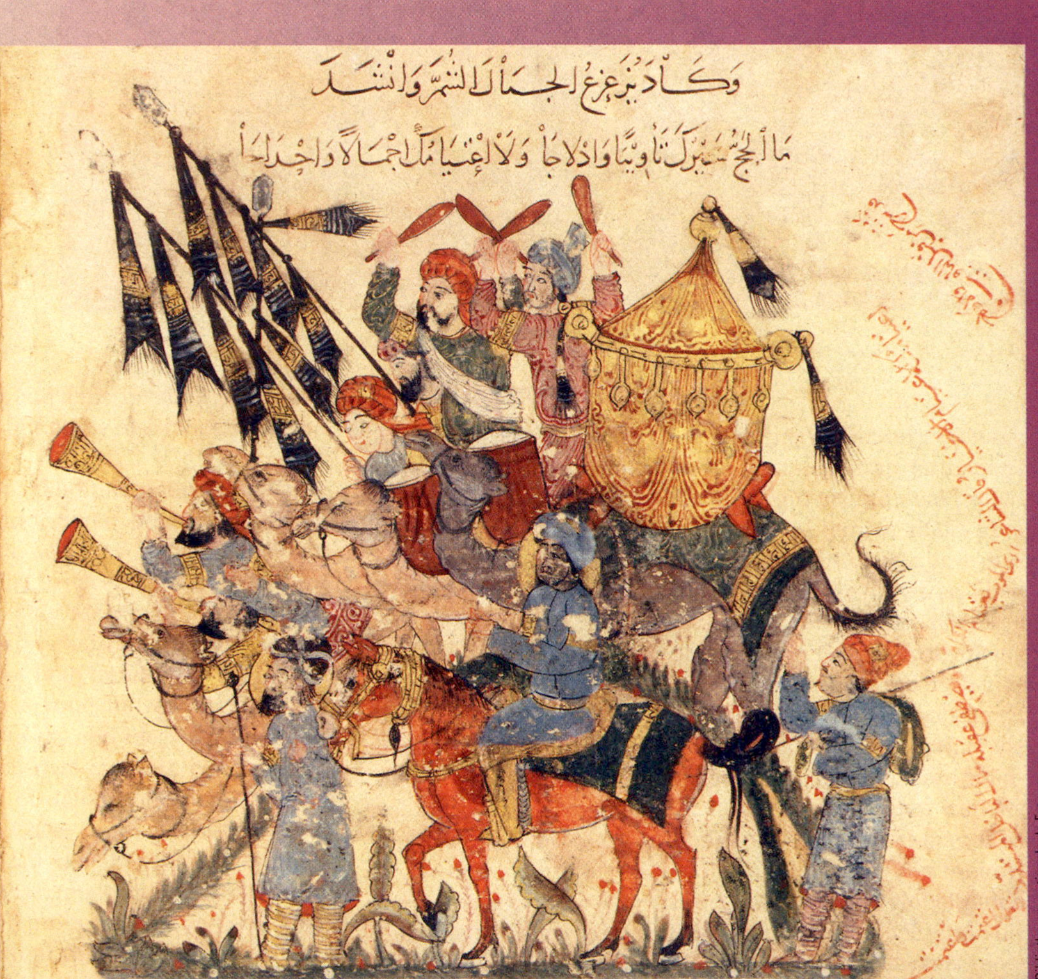

Bibliotheque nationale de France

Pilgrimage Caravan
Every year caravans of Muslim pilgrims converged on Islam's holiest city, Mecca, in Arabia. This painting shows such a caravan led by a band. Pilgrims came from as far away as Morocco and Spain in the west and Indonesia and China in the east.

Then came Islam. All institutions underwent change. It distinguished [believers] from other nations and ennobled them. Islam became firmly established and securely rooted. Far-off nations accepted Islam.

—Ibn Khaldun, fourteenth-century Arab historian [1]

FOCUS QUESTIONS

1. How did Islam arise and spread?
2. What were the major achievements of the Islamic states and empires?
3. What were the major concerns of Muslim thinkers and writers?
4. Why do historians speak of Islam as a hemispheric culture?

In 1382 the author of these words on history, the fifty-year-old Arab scholar Abd al-Rahman Ibn Khaldun **(AHB-d al-ruh-MAHN ib-uhn kal-DOON)**, left his longtime home in Tunis in North Africa and moved east to Egypt. He was already a well-traveled man and renowned as a thinker, and his work, like his life, reflected the expansive cosmopolitan nature of Islamic society, which crossed many geographical and cultural borders. He had recently completed his greatest work, a monumental history of the world known to educated Muslims. The book was the first attempt by a historian anywhere to discover and explain the changes in societies over time. Rational, analytical, and encyclopedic in coverage, it also offered a philosophy of history rooted in the scientific method.

Ibn Khaldun came from a family with roots in Arabia that had later settled in Spain and several generations later in Tunis. Ibn Khaldun visited and worked in various cities of North Africa and Spain, serving diverse rulers as a jurist, adviser, or diplomat. Now he was finally settling in Cairo, Egypt, a city he praised as the "metropolis of the world, garden of the universe, meeting-place of nations, ant hill of peoples, high place of Islam, seat of power."[2] Cairo remained his home as he served as a judge and a teacher, wrote voluminously, and traveled with high Egyptian officials to Palestine, Syria, and Arabia. Six centuries after his family left Arabia for the western Mediterranean, he could feel at home in their ancestral homeland. The Islamic world he chronicled enjoyed an extraordinary unity of time and space.

The rise of Islam that produced Ibn Khaldun was a major historical turning point that led to widespread social, cultural, and political changes over the centuries. The Islamic religion originated in seventh-century Arabia and eventually spread across several continents. Today Islam is, after Christianity, the largest religion in the world, embraced by about one-fifth of the world's population. A dynamic faith, Islam adapted to new cultures while remaining close to its founding ideals. It also had extensive dialogue with, and often tolerance toward, other traditions. For nearly a thousand years Islamic peoples greatly influenced or dominated much of the Eastern Hemisphere. Muslim thinkers salvaged or developed major portions of the science and mathematics that formed the basis for later industrial society, and Muslim sailors and merchants opened or extended networks that spread goods, technologies, and ideas throughout Afro-Eurasia.

e Visit the website and eBook for additional study materials and interactive tools: www.cengage.com/history/lockard/globalsocnet2e

EARLY ISLAM: THE ORIGINS AND SPREAD OF A CONTINUOUS TRADITION

How did Islam arise and spread?

The Islamic religion was founded in the Arabian peninsula, a parched land inhabited mainly by nomads who lived on the fringes of more powerful societies. A fervently monotheistic faith influenced by Jewish and Christian thought, Islam was inspired by the visions of a single influential man, Muhammad (moo-HAM-mad), considered by his followers to be the last of God's prophets. Islam quickly developed explosive energies that propelled it from a small Arab sect into the dominant faith of many millions of people from one end of the Eastern Hemisphere to the other. Within 130 years of Islam's birth, Arab armies and navies had conquered much of the territory from Spain to Persia and in the years to follow penetrated India, Central Asia, and China, in the process implanting Islam far from its homeland. These conquests and the accompanying spread of the new religion dramatically reshaped many societies across the Afro-Eurasian zone. Arab language and culture spread with Islam, providing a new identity for the once diverse Middle Eastern societies.

The Middle Eastern Sources of Islam

In Muhammad's day the Middle East, which includes western Asia and North Africa, was a region of great cultural diversity, a major factor in the rise of Islam. The Byzantine Empire had filled the vacuum left by the collapse of Roman control in western Asia and North Africa. Between 611 and 619 Sassanian Persia conquered Syria, Palestine, and Egypt. The Persians, Byzantines, and Ethiopians all interfered in Arabian politics. Many Middle Eastern people were Christians, including sects such as the Monophysites (among them the Copts of Egypt) and Nestorians, which were considered heretical by Roman Christians. These diverse traditions eventually influenced Islam.

Arab Society and Culture

Islam was also the product of a distinctive Arab society and culture. The Arabs, a Semitic people, occupied a desolate environment where life was sustained by scattered oases and a few areas of fertile highlands. Survival in a sparsely populated environment depended on cooperation within families, clans, and tribes. Each tribe was governed by a council of senior males, who selected a supreme elder respected for his generosity and bravery. Some Arabs, like the Nabataeans, became traders who ranged widely in the Middle East, and Arab trading cities and farmers flourished in Yemen in the south. But many Arab tribes were tent-dwelling nomadic pastoralists, known as **Bedouins** (BED-uh-wuhnz), who wandered in search of oases and grazing lands. Some resorted at times to raiding trade caravans. Poetry among the Arabs was so popular that, one month a year, raids and battles were halted so that poets could gather and compete. The Arab romantic poetry tradition may have been taken to Europe centuries later by Christian crusaders, probably influencing the chivalric love songs of medieval European performers known as troubadours.

Bedouins Tent-dwelling nomadic Arab pastoralists who wandered in search of oases, grazing lands, or trade caravans to raid.

Arabia was saturated with diverse religious traditions, including Judaism, Christianity, and Zoroastrianism. Like their Hebrew neighbors, the Arabs believed that they were descended from Abraham. While some Arabs had adopted Judaism or Christianity, most were polytheistic, believing in many gods, goddesses, and spirits. Some tribes believed that the chief god was housed in a huge sacred cube-shaped structure made out of stone, known as the **Ka'ba** (KAH-buh), in Mecca, a bustling trading city in central Arabia near the Red Sea to which people made annual pilgrimages. Meccan merchants obtained hides, leather goods, spices, and perfumes in Yemen and exchanged them in Syria for textiles, olive oil, and weapons.

Ka'ba A huge sacred cube-shaped stone in the city of Mecca to which people made annual pilgrimages.

The Prophet Muhammad and His Revelations

The founder of Islam was Muhammad Ibn Abdullah (ca. 570–632). Historians debate the origins of all the major religions, and Islam is no exception. Just as historians disagree about the accuracy of the historical accounts contained in the Hebrew Bible and the Christian gospels, and lack adequate sources to trace fully the lives of the Buddha and Confucius, there is controversy, especially among non-Muslim scholars, concerning Muhammad's life, how much Islamic thought arose out of older ideas, and the factors that shaped the expansion of the Arabs and Islam. The sources available for understanding early Judaism, Christianity, and Islam were com-

CHRONOLOGY

	Middle East	Europe	Central Asia
600	**622** Hijra of Muhammad to Medina **634–651** Arab conquests in Middle East **632–661** Rashidun Caliphate **661–750** Umayyad Caliphate		
700	**750–1258** Abbasid Caliphate	**711–1492** Muslim states in Spain	**705–715** Islamic conquests
1000		**1096–1272** Christian Crusades in Middle East	
1200			**1218–1360** Mongol conquests in Central and western Asia
1300		**1300–1923** Ottoman Empire	**1369–1405** Reign of Tamerlane

piled decades, sometimes centuries, after the events described and can be interpreted by historians in different ways.

According to the traditional accounts, Muhammad was a member of the Hashimite (HASH-uh-mite) clan of the prosperous mercantile Quraysh (KUR-aysh) tribe of Mecca (see Chronology: The Islamic World, 570–1220). Raised by an uncle after his parents died, he became a merchant, shipping goods for a wealthy twice-widowed older woman, Khadija (kah-DEE-juh), who had capitalized on the opportunities that city life sometimes gave ambitious women. They soon married. Although Muhammad's trade caravans flourished, he believed that Meccan merchants had become greedy and materialistic, contrary to Arab traditions of generosity.

Primary Source: The Quran: Call for Jihad Discover what the Quran says about the duty of Muslims to defend themselves from their enemies, and how this duty is qualified.

Muhammad's Revelations

In seeking answers to his concerns, Muhammad often meditated in the barren mountains around Mecca. In 610 he had a series of visions in which he believed God revealed the secrets of existence. He reported that he was visited by an angel, who brought God's command to "recite in the name of your lord who created the human."[3] Alarmed, he consulted one of his wife's cousins, a monotheist who encouraged him to accept the visions he received as revelations from God. Fearing that he was possessed by demons, Muhammad often agonized about the visions. The spiritual experiences continued over the next twenty-three years. However, Muhammad eventually came to accept the authenticity of the messages, largely because of the support given by his wife Khadija: "She believed in me when no one else did. She considered me to be truthful when the people called me a liar. She helped me with her fortune when the people had left me nothing."[4] Muhammad began preaching the new faith of *Islam* ("submission to God's will") to a few followers. The early believers, or *Muslims* (MUZ-limz) ("those who had submitted to God's will"), were mostly drawn from among his middle-class friends and relatives and a few other Meccans, some from lower-class backgrounds. Gradually some rich members of the Quraysh tribe also joined.

In the 650s, several decades after Muhammad's death, his followers compiled his revelations into an official version, the **Quran** (kuh-RAHN), meaning "Recitation." The Quran, beloved by Muslims for its beautiful poetic verses, became Islam's holy book, to believers the inspired word of God. A second book revered by many Muslims as a source of religious guidance and law, the **Hadith** (hah-DEETH), meaning "narrative," compiled by Muslim scholars into an official version during the ninth and tenth centuries, collected the remembered words and deeds of Muhammad himself.

Quran ("Recitation") Islam's holiest book; contains the official version of Muhammad's revelations, and to believers is the inspired word of God.

Hadith ("Narrative") The remembered words and deeds of Muhammad, revered by many Muslims as a source of religious guidance and law.

Muhammad insisted that he was human, not divine, and his followers accepted him as a prophet whose visions were the last of several occasions in history during which God spoke to prophets. The earlier prophets were Adam, Abraham, Moses, and Jesus, and Muhammad was considered the final voice superseding the others (see Witness to the Past: The Holy Book, God, and the Prophet in the Quran). Muhammad's faith mixed older traditions with new understandings, and many of the principal ideas of Islam clearly resembled some beliefs of the Christians and Jews living in Mecca. Like these traditions, Muhammad's views were strictly monotheistic. All other gods were put aside, and believers were assured of an afterlife. In contrast to the dominant Arab social customs, Islam guaranteed women certain rights formerly denied them and promoted the equality

CHRONOLOGY

The Islamic World, 570–1220

ca. 570 Birth of Muhammad in Mecca

622 Hijra of Muhammad and followers to Medina

632 Death of Muhammad; Abu Bakr becomes first caliph

634 Muslim conquests begin

632–661 Rashidun Caliphate

636–637 Arab military victories over Byzantine and Sassanian forces

642 Arab conquest of Egypt

651 Completion of Arab conquest of Persia

661 Murder of Ali and establishment of Umayyad dynasty in Damascus

705–715 Arab conquests of Afghanistan and Central Asia

711–720 Arab conquest of Spain

732 European defeat of Arabs at Battle of Tours

750 Abbasid defeat of Umayyads and new caliphate

756–1030 Umayyad dynasty in Spain

825–900 Arab conquest of Sicily

969–1171 Fatimid dynasty in Egypt and neighboring areas

1061–1091 Norman conquest of Sicily from Arabs

1071 Beginning of Seljuk Turk conquest of Anatolia

1085 Spanish Christian seizure of Umayyad capital

1095–1272 Christian Crusades in western Asia and North Africa

1171–1193 Reign of Saladin in Egypt

1218 Beginning of Mongol conquests in Muslim Central Asia

of all believers. Muhammad also advocated principles of equality and justice, sharing all wealth, living simply, and creating a spirit of unity.

Emigration and Triumph

Muhammad soon faced challenges that led him to leave Mecca. His ideas divided his Quraysh tribe, and the Mecca leaders rejected Muhammad's views and following as a threat to their position. Some enemies harassed Muslims and even plotted Muhammad's murder. In 619 Khadija died, followed by the uncle who raised him, leaving Muhammad in despair. Meanwhile, the nearby city of Medina became engulfed in strife. To find a solution, the contending factions invited Muhammad, respected for his fairness and honesty, to come to Medina and arbitrate their disputes. In 622 Muhammad led seventy Muslims and their families from Mecca to Medina, an event known as the **hijra** (HIJ-ruh), or "emigration." Hence, to believers, 622, which begins the Muslim calendar, represents humanity's response to God's message. In Medina the Muslims formed a new community of believers, or **umma**. Many Medinans came to accept Muhammad as the Prophet, and he built his first mosque for worship and prayers. Muhammad was aided by his forceful personality and leadership. He also used a wise strategy of tolerating differences. For example, he accommodated Jews by respecting the stories of their past prophets.

Some historians argue that the boundaries between Muslims and Jews were not clearly defined at this time. Muhammad also said that the original Jewish and Christian teachings had been distorted by these religions' followers. In Medina Muhammad also took new wives. Because frequent warfare and raiding killed off many men, Arab men often had several wives so they could protect vulnerable women and procreate more children. Concerned for the welfare of women without husbands, Muhammad urged his men to marry widows. He also required that all wives be treated equally and fairly.

Muhammad's growing popularity earned him more enemies. Some Medina Jews mocked his beliefs. Muhammad urged his followers to respect sympathetic Christians and Jews, saying, "Dispute not with the People of the Book. We believe in what has been sent down to us, and what has been sent down to you; our God and your God is One."[5] But, believing he needed strong methods to preserve his umma, he expelled two Jewish tribes and had all the men of another killed because he suspected them of aiding his opponents. Muhammad's followers also fought and won various military skirmishes, usually against much larger armies. The Muslims, mostly city-dwellers, quickly learned desert warfare. In general Muhammad was a flexible, pragmatic leader, usually willing to negotiate and compromise rather than shed blood, but his brilliant military victories and shrewd diplomacy made him the most powerful man in Arabia. Muhammad pardoned most of his foes and assumed power in Mecca, sharing the taxes from trade with those who became Muslim. His triumph marked a shift of power and expanded the umma in central Arabia.

hijra The emigration of Muslims from Mecca to Medina in 622.

umma The community of Muslim believers united around God's message.

Muhammad's message of monotheism, community, equality, and justice proved a powerful attraction because it dissolved social barriers between tribes and encouraged a larger spiritual community. In his last sermon, Muhammad told his audience to deal justly with each other, treat women kindly, and consider all Muslims as brothers.[6] His message emphasized the one and only, all-powerful God, **Allah** (AH-luh): "He knows what is hidden and what is evident. He is the merciful lord of mercy. There is no God but him. He is the king, the holy, the peace, the faith keeper, the preserver, the strong, the all-disposing."[7]

Allah To Muslims the one and only, all-powerful God.

Muhammad began delivering his message amidst social and economic changes in western Arabia. Meccan merchants had become more deeply involved in long-distance trade. Some Mec-

WITNESS TO THE PAST

The Holy Book, God, and the Prophet in the Quran

The Quran is organized according to the length of individual chapters, so that early and later revelations are mixed together; it does not follow a rigid organization of thoughts. In addition, the beauty of the powerful, poetic writing style is not always apparent in English translation, where most of the nuances of the Arabic language are lost. In Arabic the Quran clearly comes across as both a scripture and an elegant literature that has inspired millions. The following brief excerpts present some basic ideas about the holy book itself, the unity and power of the monotheistic God, and the recognition of Muhammad as a human prophet or apostle to God.

In the name of the Merciful and Compassionate God. That is the Book! There is no doubt therein; a guide to the pious, who believe in the unseen, and are steadfast in prayer, and of what we have given them expend in alms; who believe in what is revealed to thee, and what was revealed before thee, and of the hereafter they are sure. These are in guidance from their Lord, and these are the prosperous. . . .

God, there is no god but He, the living, the self-subsistent. Slumber takes Him not, nor sleep. His is what is in the heavens and what is in the earth. Who is it that intercedes with Him save by His permission? He knows what is before them and what behind them, and they comprehend not aught of His knowledge but of what He pleases. His throne extends over the heavens and the earth, and it tires him not to guard them both, for He is high and grand. . . . On Him is the call of truth, and those who call on others than Him shall not be answered at all, save as one who stretches out his hand to the water that it may reach his mouth, but it reaches it not! The call of the misbelievers is always in error. . . . In the name of the Merciful and Compassionate God, Say "He is God alone!"

Muhammad is but an apostle; apostles have passed away before his time; what if he die or is killed, will ye retreat upon your heels? He who retreats upon his heels does no harm to God at all; but God will recompense the thankful. . . . Muhammad is not the father of any of your men, but the Apostle of God, and the Seal of the Prophets; for God all things doth know!

THINKING ABOUT THE READING

1. What is the purpose of the Quran?
2. What are the powers of God?
3. What is the relationship between Muhammad and God?

Source: Excerpts taken from Chapters 2, 3, 13, and 33 of the Quran, as reprinted in L. S. Stavrianos, ed., *The Epic of Man to 1500* (Englewood Cliffs, NJ: Prentice-Hall, 1970), 210–211.

cans had become richer and others poorer, fostering social instability. But Muhammad, like Jesus of Nazareth six hundred years earlier, emphasized social justice, thus winning support among the poor.

When Muhammad died at age sixty-two, the umma faced a challenge. Muhammad had left little guidance on future leadership, and the issue provoked disagreements. The four men closest to him formed a **caliphate** (KAL-uhf-uht), an imperial state headed by an Islamic ruler, or *caliph* (KAL-uhf), considered the successor of the Prophet in civil affairs. The umma was ruled from Medina by the Arab merchant aristocracy through Muhammad's four consecutive successors, known later as the Rashidun ("rightly guided") caliphs, between 632 and 661, but disagreements about succession continued.

caliphate An imperial state headed by an Islamic ruler, the caliph, considered the designated successor of the Prophet in civil affairs.

Islamic Beliefs and Society

Like Christians, Muslims considered their faith the last revealed religion, and they possessed a strong missionary impulse to share their faith with all people. The basic tenets of the religion provided a framework for a new world-view that changed history and for a sense of community in the wider brotherhood of believers. Believers have clear duties, known as the five pillars. These include, first, the profession of faith. Theologically the religion is blunt: "There is no God but Allah and Muhammad is his messenger."[7] Muhammad is not considered divine but a teacher chosen by God to spread the truth of a monotheistic God said to be eternal, all powerful, all knowing, and all merciful. Second is the formal worship, to be performed with words and action five times daily. The third pillar requires giving assistance to the poor and disadvantaged, for which Muslims are expected to donate a tenth of their wealth, which also benefits the giver. The fourth pillar, the annual fast or **Ramadan** (RAHM-uh-dahn), lasts one month, during which time Muslims have to abstain from eating, drinking, and having sex during daylight hours, to sacrifice for their faith and understand the hunger of the poor. They are supported

The Five Pillars of Faith

Ramadan The thirty days of annual fasting when Muslims abstain from eating, drinking, and sex during daylight hours, to demonstrate sacrifice for their faith and understand the hunger of the poor.

Muhammad Enters a City in Triumph Although Islamic custom discourages painting images of the Prophet, Muslim artists, especially Persians and Turks, have done so over the centuries, emphasizing his spiritual qualities and destiny. This painting from an Islamic collection shows Muhammad leading his followers into Mecca for the first time after his exile while an angel on the gate cries, "Thou art the prophet of God."

by lively gatherings of families and friends just before sunrise and then again following sunset. Finally, if possible, at least once in their lives Muslims make a pilgrimage, or **haj** (HAJ), to the holy city of Mecca, where they worship with other believers from around the world. Among other spiritual activities, pilgrims circle the great Ka'ba shrine, as Arabs had done before Islam.

haj The Muslim pilgrimage to the holy city of Mecca to worship with multitudes of other believers from around the world.

jihad Effort to live as God intended; a spiritual, moral, and intellectual struggle to enhance personal faith and follow the Quran.

Islam places other demands on believers. A puritanical moral code prohibits adultery, gambling, usury, or the use of intoxicating liquors. Heavy drinking was common among Arabs. Like Judaism, Islam also has strict dietary laws, including a ban on pork. An important concept is the necessity to pursue effort, or **jihad** (ji-HAHD), to live as God intended. Most perceive this as a spiritual, moral, and intellectual struggle to enhance personal faith and follow the Quran. However, a minority has interpreted jihad as involving military conflict or violent struggle with nonbelievers or enemies, somewhat like the Christian crusading tradition. Many Islamic beliefs are similar to Judeo-Christian beliefs. Muslims believe in angels, heavenly servants who serve as God's helpers, and a Devil who flouts God's command, and they also anticipate a last judgment, when each individual will be accountable for his or her own actions. The good will attain Heaven, a garden paradise, while the wicked will suffer an eternity in Hell.

Muslims applied the idea of unity to society, seeking to build a moral and divinely guided community by regulating how people lived together. People were asked to pursue justice, avoid excesses, and practice mercy. Islamic laws also protected the freedom of religious minorities to worship as they pleased, promoting toleration of Christians and Jews as "protected peoples." The Quran stated: "Lo! those who believe [in Islam], and those who are Jews and Christians, whoever believeth in Allah on the last day and doeth right—surely their reward is with their Lord, and no fear shall come upon them, neither shall they grieve."[8] Some Christian groups, angry with the corruption of the Byzantine Empire, aided the Muslim expansion and viewed the Arabs as liberators.

Islam and Women

Islamic ideas influenced gender relations, improving the position of women in Arab culture. Before Islam, Arab women had few rights, and many were kept in seclusion. Men took as many wives as they could afford, and women were considered prized booty in raids. Under Islam, men could have up to four wives as long as they could support them and treated them equally, and men had more rights under the divorce and inheritance rules than women. However, women had some legal protection, could own property and engage in business, and were considered partners before God alongside men. Scholars debate how Muhummad viewed women's roles in society. Muhammad enjoyed the company of women, helped out with household chores, listened with interest when his wives asserted their own opinions, and emphasized that men should treat women kindly. He had taken more wives after Khadija's death, and his favorite wife, A'isha, played a prominent political role, especially after his death. Muhammad also encouraged female modesty in dress, suggesting that women draw their cloaks about them when they went out. Whether this meant full veiling of the face remains a matter of dispute. Veiling was common in many earlier Middle Eastern societies, going back to ancient Mesopotamia. Several generations after Muhammad, veiling became expected of devout women. While this enforced modesty has restricted women, many Muslim men and women have believed the custom protects women's dignity and virtue. This practice has also separated the sexes, preventing what most Muslims considered inappropriate romantic entanglements.

Arab Conquests and the Making of an Islamic World

Arab Expansion

The Arabs rapidly expanded from their base in central Arabia. Between 634, shortly after the Prophet's death, and 651 Muslim armies conquered Iraq, Syria, Palestine, Egypt, and Persia.

Map 10.1 Expansion of Islam, to 750 C.E.
The Arabs rapidly conquered much of western Asia, North Africa, and Spain, in the process expanding Islam into the conquered territories. By 750 their empire stretched from Morocco and Spain in the west to western India and Central Asia.

e Interactive Map

Arab ships sailed into the Mediterranean, taking Cyprus (649), Carthage (698), Tunis **(TOO-nuhs)** (700), and then Spain (711–720). In 732 Islamic expansion in Europe was finally stopped in southern France, at the Battle of Tours **(toor)**, by a combined Christian force led by the Frankish general Charles Martel. Had Arab forces won that conflict, the history of Europe might have been different. Following the armies, Islam, within two centuries, had become the dominant religion in the Middle East and North Africa at the expense of Christianity and Zoroastrianism. In the centuries to follow, Islam spread across the Sahara to West Africa, down the East African coast, and north into Anatolia and then the Balkans. Arab expansion spread Arab identity and the Arabic language to many peoples in western Asia and North Africa. Adoption of the Arabic language and Islam united diverse peoples by transforming them into Arabs.

Arabs also expanded eastward, carrying Islam with them. After completing the conquest of Sassanian Persia, Arabs conquered Afghanistan, Sind **(sind)** in the lower Indus Basin, and Central Asia between 705 and 715 (see Map 10.1). By 751 Arab armies had reached the western fringes of the Chinese Empire, where they won a fierce engagement at the Talas River, blocking Chinese westward expansion and turning Central Asian Turks away from China and toward the Islamic world. Muslims now controlled most Silk Road cities, such as Samarkand and Bukhara. Muslim Arabs were already carrying out seaborne trade with China, and some Arab merchants settled in coastal cities there. In the eleventh century, Muslims began ruling large parts of India. Later, in the fifteenth and sixteenth centuries, Islam spread through the islands of Southeast Asia.

Factors in Expansion

Historians have struggled to explain the energies involved in the rapid Arab expansion. Factors in Arabia, including long-term drought, poverty, and overpopulation, may have provided a spur to seek new lands. Arab leaders may have needed to capture lucrative trade routes and productive lands to obtain more resources to support their followers. In addition, the Byzantine and Sassanian Empires, exhausted from warfare and infighting, made an easy target for conquest. Furthermore, the Arab fighters were often motivated by religious faith. Yet most historians agree that Muslims made no systematic attempt to impose their religion on the conquered, and some suggest that Islam was still not clearly differentiated from Judaism and Christianity.

SECTION SUMMARY

- Islam was born in Arabia, a harsh land where many people lived in cooperative tribes or clans.
- Islam's holiest book, the Quran, is believed to be a record of the divine revelations of the prophet Muhammad, who is considered the last prophet after Adam, Abraham, Moses, and Jesus.
- Facing some opposition in Mecca and drawn to resolve a dispute in Medina, Muhammad and his followers moved there and won many new converts.
- Muhammad's teachings were monotheistic (like Christianity and Judaism) and emphasized equality and mutual respect among peoples from different tribes.
- Islam is based on the five pillars: profession of faith; formal worship; charity; annual fasting, or Ramadan; and the pilgrimage, or haj, to Mecca.
- Islam spread extremely rapidly via Arab conquest of the Middle East, North Africa, Central Asia, and parts of India and Europe.
- Arab identity and language gradually spread to many of the conquered peoples.
- Explanations for the rapid Arab expansion include the need for resources, the weakness of other empires, and the need for a common cause to hold the Arabs together.

The dynamics within the fragile Islamic community itself provided a motive for expansion. Muhammad's death confronted his followers with a crisis, since they had lost their charismatic spiritual leader. By providing a common cause, conquest discouraged members from leaving the community. Warfare also capitalized on a long tradition of tribal fighting. Arab armies were cohesive, mobile, and well led. To prevent the rise of rival factions, Muhammad's first successor, his best friend Abu Bakr **(ab-boo BAK-uhr)**, forbade people from leaving the umma and declared Muhammad God's final prophet. Abu Bakr allied with other tribes, among them often feuding nomadic Bedouins whose fighting spirit could be turned against non-Arab foes. Arab fighters divided up the spoils of conquest, spreading wealth within the community, maintaining unity, and keeping the allegiance of the many Muslims who believed strongly in a radical egalitarianism that challenged those with wealth and power.

By the eleventh century Islam had become the dominant religion over a wide area of Afro-Eurasia, joining older universal religions such as Buddhism and Christianity. Late-seventh-century Muslims thought of themselves as carriers of a global movement and new religion encompassing many peoples rather than an Arab cult. They ruled over self-governing religious communities of Greek Orthodox Christians, Nestorians, Copts, Zoroastrians, Manicheans, and Jews. Rather than remaining minority rulers over non-Muslim majorities, the Arab Muslims began encouraging conversion and cultural synthesis. Contrary to Western myth, conversion by force was the exception rather than the rule. Many found the religion and the increasingly cosmopolitan community of believers an attractive alternative to their old traditions.

EARLY ISLAMIC STATES AND EMPIRES

What were the major achievements of the Islamic states and empires?

Islamic expansion established a framework by which powerful states could rule millions of Muslims and non-Muslims, aided by unique concepts of government and law. For over half a millennium Arabic-speaking Muslims ruled a large segment of the Eastern Hemisphere. Great states and empires dominated the Middle East, and Islamic states on the fringe of Christian Europe served as conduits of knowledge. Peoples and ideas spread widely, fostering a dynamic society mixing Arab, Persian, Indian, and Greek cultures. But Islam also divided into rival sects, a split that created enduring tensions and that influenced Middle Eastern politics for many centuries.

Islamic Government and Law

sultan A Muslim ruler of only one country.

Shari'a The Islamic legal code for the regulation of social and economic as well as religious life.

Many Muslims viewed government and religion as the same, and Islamic states tended to punish those Muslims who violated religious prohibitions. Islamic political and religious power were often combined in a theocracy headed by a caliph or more commonly a **sultan**, a Muslim ruler of only one country. Although such far-reaching power could be easily abused, the moral authority of respected religious scholars could sometimes check abuses of political power. Muslim leaders established a legal code, or **Shari'a** **(shah-REE-ah)**, for the regulation of social and economic as well as religious life. The Shari'a provided a comprehensive guide to life, covering areas such as divorce, inheritance, debts, and morality. Based chiefly on the Quran and the Hadith, it was also rooted in Arab cultural traditions and customs, supplemented by Persian and Byzantine concepts. But conflicts over the interpretation and application of the Quran led to the rise of several competing interpretative traditions that differed slightly in their emphasis on such tools as reasoning and scriptural authority.

Religious scholars such as judges, preachers, and prayer leaders played a major role in elaborating the Shari'a and in sustaining Islamic culture. Their legal decisions and writings provided cohesion and stability over the centuries, independent of the rise and fall of rulers. Muslims valued education based on studying with renowned religious and legal scholars, whose students then became teachers. By the tenth century religious boarding schools, known as **madrasas** (muh-DRAH-suhz), headed by a religious scholar, began appearing. Today thousands of these schools can be found all over the Muslim world.

madrasas Religious boarding schools found all over the Muslim world.

Early Imperial Caliphates: Unity and Strife

The imperial caliphates, beginning with the Rashidun, attempted to maintain unity but also faced challenges. After 661, the end of the Rashidun era, political power shifted outside of Arabia with two successive imperial dynasties, the Umayyad (oo-MY-ad) and the Abbasid (ah-BASS-id). Both dynasties were installed by members of Muhammad's Quraysh tribe. Arabia was the fountainhead, but power shifted elsewhere. While Mecca and Medina remained spiritual hubs, reinforced by annual pilgrimages, new cities emerged as more important political and economic centers for the Islamic world.

The sense of social and religious unity within a growing umma did not prevent political conflict. The early conquests greatly enriched Medina and Mecca merchant clans, and some Muslims grew critical of the new materialism. A full revolt against the Rashidun leadership erupted, and dissidents murdered the unpopular third caliph, Uthman (ooth-MAHN), installing Ali (ah-LEE) (ca. 600–661), Muhammad's son-in-law, as the fourth caliph. Although well qualified, pious, and generous, Ali proved weak. He moved the capital from Medina to Kufah (KOO-fa) in what is today Iraq, but others challenged Ali for leadership. Muhammad's widow, A'isha, helped rally the opposition to Ali, resulting in a civil war. Ali was finally killed by Uthman's relatives, who blamed him for their leader's murder. With Ali's death, the Rashidun era ended, but the divisions generated a permanent split in the Islamic world. Centuries later, many Muslims viewed the Rashidun period as a golden age with a simple government and a righteous cause, and some called for reinstating the caliphate to rule the Muslim world.

Sunni ("The Trodden Path") The main branch of Islam, comprising those who accept the practices of the Prophet and the historical succession of caliphs.

The caliphate moved to Damascus (duh-MAS-kuhs), in what is today Syria, under the leadership of the Umayyad dynasty (661–750). The Islamic empire was now led by men with no direct connection to, or descent from, the Prophet. With the move to Damascus, Arab politics came to be defined by large bureaucratic states with remote leaders who passed on their rule to their sons. Military expansion continued, and the Umayyad caliphs extended the Islamic empire deep into Byzantine territory. But the Umayyad system soon experienced unrest. Although the rulers encouraged Islam and called themselves deputies of God, they did not practice Islamic morality. Devout Muslims opposed to the Umayyads emphasized Muhammad's role as God's prophet, clearly setting Islam apart from rival monotheistic religions, and the Umayyads' legendary drinking, womanizing, and laxness in religious devotion generated civil war and division. Among the challengers was the Prophet's only remaining male heir, his grandson Husayn (hoo-SANE), who attracted support from those who believed the caliph must be a direct descendant of Muhammad. Husayn's rebellion in 680 failed, however, and he was killed in the Battle of Karbala (KAHR-buh-LAH), a city in Iraq. In death he and his father Ali, the murdered caliph, became martyrs against the Umayyads.

The Great Umayyad Mosque in Damascus This mosque, built between 709 and 715, is the oldest surviving monumental mosque.

Jane Taylor/Sonia Halliday Photographs

The Sunni-Shi'a Split

After the death of Ali, Islam began to split into two main branches due to disagreements over the nature of the umma and the full meaning of Muhammad's revelations. The main branch, **Sunni** (SOO-nee) ("The Trodden Path"), accepted the practices of the

Prophet and the historical succession of caliphs. Today about 85 percent of all Muslims, including most of those in North Africa, Turkey, the Balkans, South and Southeast Asia, and China, as well as the majority of Arabs, are Sunni. Sunni, which embraces a wide variety of opinions and practices and was probably not named until the ninth or tenth century, adheres to one of four main schools of Islamic law and a broad view of who qualifies for political power.

Shi'a ("Partisans" of Ali) The branch of Islam emphasizing the religious leaders descended from Muhammad through his son-in-law, Ali, who they believe was the rightful successor to the Prophet.

The other main branch began in a dispute over the leadership of the faithful. The **Shi'a** **(SHEE-uh)** ("Partisans" of Ali) emphasized only the religious leaders descended from Muhammad through his son-in-law, Ali, who they believed was the rightful successor to the Prophet. Karbala and nearby Najaf **(NAH-jaf)**, where respectively Husayn and Ali are buried, became holy Shi'ite pilgrimage centers. Over time Shi'ites provided an alternative religious vision to Sunni Islam. Shi'ism itself divided into three rival schools, based on which leader after Ali should be followed. The main concentrations of Shi'ites are found today in Iran, where most Persians adopted the school after 1500, and also in Iraq, Lebanon, and the Persian Gulf states. Smaller minorities are scattered across Central Asia, western India, and Pakistan.

Although they shared many commonalities, the differences between these two branches were deep. In general, Shi'ites followed strong religious leaders, a tradition not unknown to some Christians, ultra-Orthodox Jews, and Hindu sects. There was often much antagonism between the two groups, as there would later be, for example, between Catholics and Protestants in some Western countries. Sunni majorities sometimes persecuted Shi'ite minorities, producing a Shi'ite martyrdom complex and a tradition of dissent against Sunni rulers. Over the centuries Shi'ite movements established various states, often ruling uneasily over Sunni majorities.

Arabian Nights: The Abbasid Caliphate

The Abbasid Caliphate (750–1258), the next dynasty after the Umayyad, enjoyed great power and fostered a dynamic society for several centuries, surviving for half a millennium. The Abbasid caliphs embodied the unity of the Islamic umma and established a style for later Muslim rulers. The Abbasids, a Sunni branch of the Quraysh tribe descended from Muhammad's uncle, Abbas, had attracted support from both Sunnis and Shi'ites to defeat the Umayyad army. The lone Umayyad survivor fled to Spain, where he established a separate state that flourished for three centuries. The Abbasids expanded the empire to the east and maintained pressure against Byzantium in the west. By 800 the Abbasid Empire ruled some 30 million people (see Map 10.2).

Abbasid Baghdad

The Abbasids moved their capital to Baghdad, located where the Tigris and Euphrates Rivers come closest together in today's Iraq. This move placed the capital strategically along major trade routes and in the middle of a farming district made fertile through irrigation. Baghdad became one of the world's greatest hubs, its bazaars filled with goods from as far away as China, Scandinavia, and East Africa, and the city boasted joint-stock companies and banks. In a public show of piety and generosity, the Abbasid government employed thousands of people in public works projects, building palaces, schools, hospitals, and mosques. Some Baghdad citizens, however, openly flouted Islamic prohibitions against hedonistic behavior, and in general Baghdad reflected the cosmopolitan flavor of Islamic society. In the 1160s a rabbi from Muslim-ruled Spain, Benjamin of Tudela, visited Baghdad and wrote of the ethnically diverse city and, in particular, its large Jewish community:

> *This great Abbasid [caliph] is extremely friendly towards the Jews, many of his officers being of that nation. Baghdad contains about one thousand Jews, who enjoy peace, comfort, and much honor. Many of the Jews are good scholars and very rich. The city contains 28 Jewish synagogues.*[9]

Indeed, Islam became a far-reaching influence because of its ability to receive and absorb culture from all parts of the Eastern Hemisphere. For example, although the Abbasids were Arabs, Persian influence on their system was strong, and many Persians occupied high government positions. The Abbasids also acquired knowledge from faraway lands. Muslims first learned papermaking technology from Chinese captured in the Battle of Talas of 751, and by 800 Baghdad had its first paper mill. By the twelfth century paper was also manufactured in Morocco and Spain. Papermaking allowed for a wider distribution of the Quran, helping to spread Islam.

City Life

The height of Abbasid Baghdad conjures up the images of affluence and romance reported in *The Arabian Nights*, a cycle of stories that later also influenced European writers, artists, and composers. For example, the famous *Scheherazade* symphony by the nineteenth-century Russian composer Nikolai Rimsky-Korsakov **(RIM-skee KAWR-suh-kawf)** attempted to evoke the atmosphere

Map 10.2 The Abbasid Empire, ca. 800 C.E.
The Abbasids, a dynasty based in what is today Iraq, established the largest Muslim empire in the early Intermediate Era, ruling lands from Central Asia to Egypt before losing most of their territories. Among other major Islamic states, the Umayyads ruled Spain and Northwest Africa and the Fatimids ruled Egypt and neighboring lands.

e Interactive Map

of Abbasid Baghdad. Some images of old Baghdad come from fanciful children's books and films based loosely on the great literary work, where we read of flying carpets and genies in magic lamps. Under the most famous Abbasid caliph, Harun al-Rashid **(hah-ROON al-rah-SHEED)** (786–809), there were no flying carpets, but many people enjoyed a comfortable life. Harun had a large harem of wives, concubines, and slave girls, perhaps 2,000 in all. The royal harems had an image, perhaps partly true, as a secluded world of luxury, idleness, and endless plotting for royal favor. Like some other Abbasid rulers, Harun also had a reputation for heavy drinking and pursuing the temptations of the flesh.

As they adopted the ways of the conquered, Arabs were gradually transformed from desert herders and traders into imperial rulers. The Abbasids often ruled through traditional leaders, such as the Coptic Church patriarchs of Egypt. In Iraq they resolved disputes among Nestorian Christians just as the Sassanian governors had done. Like the Sassanians, the caliphs patronized a state religion, now shifted from Zoroastrianism to Islam, and lavishly supported arts and crafts. They also appointed Muslim judges and built mosques.

The growth of cities followed Islamic conquests. New cities like Cairo began as Muslim garrisons. The caliphates needed administrative centers, however, and these drew in surrounding people seeking work. Hence Baghdad rapidly swelled to perhaps a million people by 900, becoming the world's largest city. The caliphs adopted the Sassanian system of dividing cities into wards marked by ethnic and occupational groups and of governing these groups through their own leaders.

Abbasid Decline and the End of the Arab Empire

Like all empires, the Abbasids eventually faced mounting problems and gradually lost their grip on power by the tenth century. Turkish soldiers, assigned to guard the caliphs, became more powerful in the government. Disaffected Shi'ites fomented bloody revolts as the caliphate became a mere figurehead, and parts of the empire broke away. Anti-Abbasid Shi'ites who claimed descent from Fatima, the daughter of Muhammad, established the Fatimid **(FAT-uh-mid)** Caliphate in Egypt and North Africa based in Cairo, which eventually became a rival to

CHRONOLOGY
The Islamic World, 1095–1492

1095–1272 Christian Crusades in western Asia and North Africa

1250–1517 Mamluk rule in Egypt and Syria

1258 Mongol seizure of Baghdad and end of Abbasid Caliphate

1260 Mamluk defeat of Mongols in Battle of Ayn Jalut

1260–1360 Mongol Il-Khanid dynasty in Persia and Iraq

1300–1923 Ottoman Empire

1369–1405 Reign of Tamerlane in Central and Southwest Asia

1371 Ottoman conquest of Bulgaria and Macedonia

1396 Ottoman defeat of European forces at Battle of Nicopolis

1453 Ottoman capture of Constantinople and end of Byzantine state

1492 Christian seizure of Granada; expulsion of Muslims and Jews from Spain

Baghdad as an intellectual and economic center. The university founded in Cairo by the Fatimids in 970, Al-Azhar, became the most influential in the Islamic world and remains the unrivaled center of Islamic higher learning. Shi'ites also ruled various smaller states, where most of the population remained Sunni or non-Muslim yet generally enjoyed religious freedom. The Mongols, Central Asian nomads who built a great regional empire stretching from East Asia to eastern Europe in the thirteenth century (see Chapter 11 and the essay concluding Part III), were attracted by the wealth of the Abbasid realm. In 1258 Mongol armies sacked and destroyed Baghdad and executed the last Abbasid caliph (see Chronology: The Islamic World, 1095–1492), shattering the symbolic unity of the Muslim world. Throughout the Middle East, Arab dominance was challenged by Persians, Berbers, Kurds, and Turks as well as by Mongols.

Despite these setbacks, political weakness and loss of cultural dynamism did not become evident in the Islamic world until the sixteenth and seventeenth centuries, and even then there were important exceptions. Although few later Muslim rulers could match the power of the early Abbasids, Islamic society flourished and Islam accelerated its diffusion to new peoples. Between 1258 and 1550 the territorial size of the Islamic world doubled. Scholars, saints, and mystics assumed leadership throughout this world, establishing legal structures, dogmas, social forms, standards of piety, aesthetic sensibilities, styles of scholarship, and schools of philosophy that helped define the vital core of Islamic culture.

Cultural Mixing in Muslim Sicily and Spain

Islamic culture also flourished in Sicily and Spain, fostering a cosmopolitan mixed culture that brought prosperity and the sharing of scientific knowledge. Between 825 and 900 Muslim forces conquered Sicily, the largest Mediterranean island. Under Muslim rule, Sicily benefited from close ties to the Arab-dominated maritime trade system. Muslim rulers repaired long-decayed Roman irrigation works and vastly increased agricultural production. Many Arabs, Berbers, Africans, Greeks, Jews, Persians, and Slavs gravitated to the island, mixing with the local peoples and creating a cosmopolitan society. The Muslim capital, Palermo, was larger than any other city in Europe except Constantinople. But political divisions among Muslims left the island open to a gradual Christian reconquest. Between 1061 and 1091 the Normans, descendants of Vikings who had settled in France, replaced a Muslim government with their own. By 1200 Christian German rulers had established a Sicilian state and were persecuting Muslims and Jews, gradually bringing to an end an era when the islanders blended Islamic and Christian traditions into a dynamic fusion.

A more enduring Muslim society emerged in Spain, much of which was first conquered by Umayyad forces between 711 and 720. Their capital, Cordoba **(KAWR-duh-buh)**, became Europe's largest city by 1000, home to half a million people. Under Umayyad rule, Spain was for several centuries a famed center of culture and learning, drawing scholars and thinkers from all over Europe and the Islamic world. Cordoba's library held 400,000 volumes, when libraries in Christian Europe owned only several hundred.

The Splendor of Cordoba

The mood of tolerance generated a productive relationship between diverse peoples and traditions, with Christian, Muslim, and Jewish thinkers working together to share and advance knowledge. To one Arab poet, Cordoba was the garden of the fruits of ideas. Intellectuals discussed ancient Greek thought and the latest astronomical discoveries and translated books from and into Arabic. From this cosmopolitan intellectual milieu, much of the classical Greco-Roman heritage, Islamic and Indian science and mathematics, and some Chinese technology, such as papermaking, were passed on to Europe. Europe also benefited from Arab vocal and instrumental music, which were important in Islamic Arab culture for ceremonies, pleasure, and worship. Arab folk songs and musical instruments, such as the guitar and lute, diffused northward, influencing the courtly love songs of European troubadours and, later, Western popular music.

Decline and Conquest

By 1000 decline, marked by civil wars and factionalism, had begun to set in and the Umayyad government fragmented into smaller, often warring states. Intolerant Muslim invaders from Morocco took power in some regions and persecuted anyone not sharing their rigid interpretation of Islam. Many Spaniards had remained loyal to Catholicism, providing a base of support for efforts at reconquest, and much of northern Spain gradually came under Christian control. In 1085

Evers/Visual Connection Archive

Alhambra, Court of Lions The Alhambra, or Palace of Lions, built in Granada in southern Spain in the fourteenth century, is one of the finest architectural treasures from Muslim Spain. It features a courtyard with a fountain.

Christian knights conquered Cordoba, the center of Islamic power. Constant Christian military pressure gradually pushed Muslim rule into southern Spain, and by 1252 Christian princes controlled much of Spain and Portugal. Finally, in 1492, Christians took the last Muslim stronghold at Granada **(gruh-NAHD-uh)**. The new Christian rulers, militant and intolerant, forced Muslims and Jews to either convert to Christianity or face expulsion. Many converted but thousands fled, usually to Muslim countries in North Africa or to Anatolia.

SECTION SUMMARY

- Muslim leaders imposed Shari'a, a legal code that regulated social, economic, and religious life.
- In the period of the early Rashidun Caliphate, dissidents murdered the third caliph and installed Muhammad's son-in-law Ali as the fourth caliph, and after Ali's murder Islam began to split into two branches: the Sunni majority branch and the Shi'a dissident branch who believed Ali was the only successor to the Prophet.
- Throughout history, Sunni persecution of Shi'ite minorities has created a Shi'ite martyrdom complex and a tradition of dissent against Sunni rulers.
- The Umayyad dynasty, which succeeded the Rashidun Caliphate, was led by men with no connection to Muhammad who extended the empire into Byzantine lands.
- Under the Abbasid Caliphate, during which *The Arabian Nights* was set, Baghdad became a cosmopolitan hub of trading and culture.
- As they expanded, Arabs adopted the imperial ruling structures of the peoples they conquered and were targeted by numerous invaders, including the Mongols.
- Spain and Sicily were ruled by Muslims for several centuries, though Christians gradually reclaimed them and failed to maintain the tolerance of the early Muslim rulers.

CULTURAL HALLMARKS OF ISLAM: THEOLOGY, SOCIETY, AND LEARNING

What were the major concerns of Muslim thinkers and writers?

Islamic expansion launched a thousand-year era, from the seventh to the seventeenth century, that brought many Afro-Eurasian peoples into closer contact with one another and allowed for a mixing of cultures within an Islamic framework. Muslims synthesized elements from varied traditions, including the Arab, Greek, Persian, and Indian, to produce a new hybrid culture, vital and durable, that was rooted in theology, social patterns, literature and art, science, and learning. Islamic theology continued to develop, fostering several distinct strands of thought and behavior, and Islamic societies fashioned a distinctive social system and a renowned cultural heritage. In addition, Islamic scholars contributed major scientific achievements and historical studies to the world.

Theology, Sufism, and Religious Practice

Theological Debates

From the very beginning, Muslims' debates over theological questions led to divergent interpretations of the Quran. As in all religions, a variety of views about the great questions of life and death developed, reflecting the mixing of intellectual traditions. Some Muslim thinkers emphasized reason and free will, while others believed that Allah preordained everything. Throughout the Islamic world, influential thinkers mastered several fields of knowledge. Abu Yusuf al-Kindi (a-BOO YOU-suhf al-KIN-dee) (ca. 800–ca. 870), an Arab who lived in Iraq, praised the search for truth and popularized Greek ideas. Although he emphasized logic and mathematics, he also published work on science, music, medicine, and psychology. Abu Ali al-Husain Ibn Sina (a-BOO AH-lee al-who-SANE IB-unh SEE-nah) (980–1037), known in the West as Avicenna (av-uh-SEN-uh), was both a philosopher and a medical scholar. A native of Bukhara (boo-CAR-ruh), a Silk Road city in Central Asia, he spent most of his career in Persia. Ibn Sina believed everyone could exercise free will but that the highest goal was communion with God. Afghanistan-born Abu Hamid al-Ghazali (AH-boo HAM-id al-guh-ZAL-ee) (1058–1111), a teacher in Baghdad, used Aristotelian logic to justify Islamic beliefs. This rationalistic approach remained influential in Shi'a thinking but lost support in Sunni circles from the fourteenth century onward.

Sufism A mystical approach and practice within Islam that emphasized personal spiritual experience.

Among both Sunnis and Shi'ites a mystical approach and practice developed and gained many followers. **Sufism** (SOO-fiz-uhm) emphasized personal spiritual experience rather than nit-picking theology. Sufis stressed the superiority of the heart over the mind and sought communion with God. Such mysticism was suggested in the Quran: "Wherever ye turn there is the face of God."[10] A famous Sufi poet in Persia, Baba Kuhi, saw God in everything: "In the market, in the cloister—only God I saw; In the valley and on the mountain—only God I saw. Him I have seen beside me oft in tribulation; in favor and in fortune—only God I saw."[11] Many Sufis exchanged information with Christian, Hindu, and Jewish mystics, were willing to synthesize Islam with other ideas as long as the central spirit was maintained, and considered their practices useful even for non-Muslims. But Sufism constituted a supplement rather than a challenge to conventional Islam.

Diverse Practices

Sufis congregated in orders led by masters who taught prescribed techniques and attracted devoted followers. The whirling *dervishes* (DUHR-vish-iz) of Turkey are one of the most famous Sufi orders. Dervishes practiced special exercises and methods, including the trance dancing from which they get their name, to achieve a state of divine ecstasy. Several Sufi orders were renowned as peace-loving and tolerant of different views and customs. Followers credit some Sufi masters with magical powers and make their tombs pilgrimage destinations. However, Sufism remained a controversial movement. While the tendency to tolerate religious flexibility won Sufis converts, many non-Sufis condemned the way some Sufis suspended ordinary Islamic biases against wine, drugs, and music in worship. Sufis produced most Islamic poetry, and millions of Sufis revere the Persian Sufi poet Hafez (hah-FEZ) (1326–1389), who loved God and the grape with equal devotion: "Here we are with our wine and the ascetics with their piety. Let us see which one the beloved [God] will take."[12]

As Islam spread into diverse cultures, it developed several distinct patterns of practice. The adaptationists showed a willingness to make adjustments to changing conditions. These Muslims have provided the base for reform and for secular and modernizing movements. Conservatives, on the other hand, strove to preserve established beliefs and customs, such as the rigid division of the sexes, and mistrusted innovation. The most dogmatic conservatives argued that the divine revelations channeled through Muhammad set a permanent standard to use in judging existing conditions, an unchangeable authority of universal validity. Finally, some stressed the personal aspects of the faith. These diverse patterns all have large followings among both Sunnis and Shi'ites, providing the basis for political and social conflict in Muslim societies.

Social Life and Gender Relations

As Islamic culture expanded and matured, the social structure became more complex and marked by clear ethnic, tribal, class, occupational, religious, and gender divisions, especially in the Middle East. Arabs generally had a higher social status than Turkish, Berber, African, and other converts. Those who can claim descent from the Prophet and members of the Hashimite clan to which he belonged have held an especially honored status in Islamic societies around the world. Many Arabs were also members of tribes, such as Muhammad's Quraysh tribe. In addition, because the first Muslims were merchants, the religion had a special appeal for people in the commercial sector, providing spiritual sanction of their quest for wealth, which could finance pilgrimages to Mecca and also help the poor through almsgiving. There was, however, discrimination against Christian and Jewish minorities, who did not always have the same rights as Muslims. They paid higher taxes and were prohibited from owning weapons, and so were exempt from military duty. However, they did enjoy some protection under the law. On the whole these communities were allowed to follow their own laws, customs, and beliefs and to maintain their own religious institutions.

Slavery was common. Slaves served as bureaucrats and soldiers, workers in businesses and factories, household servants and concubines, musicians, and plantation laborers. One Abbasid caliph kept 11,000 slaves in his palace. Islamic law encouraged owners to treat slaves with consideration, and many were eventually freed. Many slaves were war captives and children purchased from poor families or from Christian European states like Byzantium and Venice. In addition, for over a dozen centuries, but especially after 1200, perhaps 10 to 15 million African slaves were brought to the Middle East across the Sahara or up the East African coast by an Arab-dominated slave trade. African slave soldiers were common in Egypt, Persia, Iraq, Oman **(oh-MAHN)** in eastern Arabia, and Yemen.

Families were at the heart of the social system. Marriages were arranged, with the goal of cementing social or perhaps business ties between two families. Although Shari'a law allowed men to have up to four wives at a time, this privilege remained largely restricted to the rich and powerful. Many poor men never married at all because they could not afford the large bridal gifts expected. While divorce was theoretically easy for men, marriage contracts sometimes discouraged divorce by specifying that men pay a large gift to the wife upon divorce. Within the family, parents expected children to obey and respect them, even after they became adults. Family gatherings were usually segregated by gender and often involved poetry recitations, musical performances, or Quran readings. Although Islamic law harshly punished homosexuality, homosexual relationships were not uncommon, and same-sex love was often reflected in poetry and literature, most notably in Muslim Spain. European visitors were often shocked at the tolerant attitudes of Arabs, Persians, and Turks toward homosexual romantic relationships.

The status of women in Islamic society has been subject to debate by both Western and Islamic observers for centuries. For example, the philosopher Ibn Rushd **(IB-uhn RUSHED)** (1126–1198), known in the West as Averroes **(uh-VER-uh-WEEZ)**, attacked restrictions on women as an economic burden, arguing that "the ability of women is not known, because they are merely used for procreation [and] child-rearing."[13] Although the Quran recognized certain rights of women, prohibited female infanticide, and limited the number of wives men could have, it also accorded women only half the inheritance of men and gave women less standing in courts

Persian Women at a Picnic This miniature from sixteenth-century Persia shows women preparing a picnic. The ability of women to venture away from home varied widely depending on social class and regional traditions.

Bodleian Library, Oxford University, MS Elliot 189

of law. While some Muslims criticized the many restrictions on women as institutionalizing their social inferiority, other Muslim men and women have contended that these restrictions liberate women from insecurity and male harassment. Scholars have also disagreed over whether restrictions such as veiling and seclusion were based on Quranic mandates or on patriarchal pre-Islamic Arab, Middle Eastern, and Byzantine customs. Some Muslim communities in the Middle East, and many outside the region, never adopted these practices.

Gender Relations

Women played diverse roles. Some of the wives of Abbasid caliphs played political roles, albeit mostly behind the scenes. For instance, Khayzuran, noted for her compassion and generosity, rose from a simple Yemenite slave girl to become the great love and wife of the Caliph Mahdi, dominating his harem and investing in land reclamation and charitable works. On his death, she helped smooth the transition to the rulership of her son, Harun al-Rashid. During Abbasid times some elite women, while excluded from public life, enjoyed considerable power behind the scenes, and some exceptional women circumvented restrictions. For example, Umm Hani (also known as Mariam) in fifteenth-century Cairo studied law and religion with many famous teachers, wrote poetry, owned a large textile workshop, and became a renowned teacher and scholar of the Hadith. She also had seven children by two husbands and made thirteen pilgrimages to Mecca. While formal education for girls in the Middle East was generally limited, women monopolized certain occupations such as spinning and weaving, and they also worked in the fields or in some domestic industries beside men. And in some Muslim societies, particularly in sub-Saharan Africa and Southeast Asia, women often maintained their relative independence and were free to dress as they liked, socialize outside the home, and earn money. Turks and Mongols also seem to have been more liberal on gender issues than Arabs and Persians. In short, patterns of gender relations varied considerably.

Pen and Brush: Writing and the Visual Arts

Although Islamic societies became identified with literacy and literature, writing derived from pre-Islamic roots. The Arabic alphabet originated in southern Arabia long before Muhammad's time, and Islam enhanced the script further by emphasizing literacy. The Quran stated: "Read, and thy Lord is most generous, Who taught with the pen, Taught man what he knew not."[14] Muslims adopted the Arab poetic tradition but modified romantic ideas into praise not for a lover but for the Prophet and Allah.

Literature and Poetry

One of the greatest writers of Abbasid times, also an astronomer and mathematician, was the Persian Omar Khayyam **(OH-MAHR key-YAHM)**. In his famous poem *Rubaiyat* **(ROO-bee-AHT)**, he noted the fleeting nature of life: "One thing is certain, that Life flies; and the rest is Lies; the flower that once has blown forever dies." This fact led him to regret never knowing the purpose of existence:

> *Ah, make the most of what ye yet may spend, Before we too into the Dust descend; Dust unto Dust, and under Dust to lie, [without] Wine, Song, Singer, and End! Into this Universe, and Why not knowing, Nor Whence, like Water willy-nilly flowing; And out of it, as Wind along the Waste, I know not Whither, wily-nilly blowing.*[15]

The most famous Sufi poet was the thirteenth-century Persian Jalal al-Din Rumi **(ja-LAL al-DIN ROO-mee)**. Born in Afghanistan, as a youth he lived in Central Asia and Anatolia, a fact reflecting Islam's wide reach. Rumi blended liberal spirituality with humor in writings about love, desire, and the human condition, and he often danced while reciting his poems to disciples. He was optimistic, joyful, and ecumenical, stating: "I am neither Christian, nor Jew, nor Zoroastrian, nor Muslim."[16] At the beginning of the twenty-first century, over seven hundred years after his death, Rumi became the best-selling poet in the United States after his poems were translated into English.

History and Social Sciences

The modern study of history and of social sciences, especially geography, owes much to Muslim research and writing. With the expansion of Islam and Arab trading communities to the far corners of the Eastern Hemisphere, some Muslims traveled to distant lands. Educated Muslims enjoyed reading these travelers' accounts of other countries and peoples, and modern historians are indebted to travelers such as the Moroccan jurist Ibn Battuta **(IB-uhn ba-TOO-tuh)** for much of what we know today about sub-Saharan Africa and Southeast Asia from the ninth to the fifteenth centuries (see Profile: Ibn Battuta, a Muslim Traveler). Geographers and cartographers such as Al-Idrisi **(al-AH-dree-see)** from Muslim Spain also produced atlases, globes, and maps.

Ibn Khaldun (1332–1406), the well-traveled North African introduced at the beginning of the chapter, was the first known scholar anywhere to look for patterns and structure in history. His monumental work connected the rise of states among tribal communities with a growing feeling of solidarity between leaders and their followers. His recognition of the role in history of "group feeling" (what today we call ethnic identity) and of religion was pathbreaking. In studying other cultures, he advocated "critical examination":

> *Know the rules of statecraft, the nature of existing things, and the difference between nations, regions and tribes in regard to way of life, qualities of character, customs, sects, schools of thought, and so on. [The historian] must distinguish the similarities and differences between the present and the past.*[17]

Ibn Khaldun put the Arab expansion into the broader flow of regional history.

Some Muslims emphasized the visual arts. For example, since Arabic is written in a flowing style, the artful writing of words, or **calligraphy** (kuh-LIG-ruh-fee), became a much admired art form. An elegant script offered not just a message but also decoration. Islamic Persia, India, and Central Asia also fostered a tradition of painting, especially landscapes. In addition, Muslims produced world-class architecture that included lavishly decorated buildings such as the Taj Mahal in India. Some architecture, such as mosques with domes and towers, reflected Byzantine church influence. Then as now, Muslims were famed for weaving carpets and fabrics that were valued in many non-Muslim societies.

calligraphy The artful writing of words.

Science, Technology, and Learning

Integrating Traditions

During the Islamic golden age many creative thinkers emerged. Muslims also borrowed, assimilated, and diffused Greek and Indian knowledge and were familiar with some Chinese technologies. Thanks to this knowledge, certain classical and Hellenistic Greek traditions of philosophy and science that had been nearly forgotten in Europe survived in the Middle East. Many advances in science and medicine were also made in the Islamic world as experts synthesized the learning of other societies with their own insights. Some of this knowledge was carried into the Middle East by Nestorian Christians, who taught Greek sciences under Abbasid sponsorship. The Abbasid caliphs opened the House of Wisdom in Baghdad, a research institute staffed by scholars charged with translating Greek, Syrian, Sanskrit, and Persian books on philosophy, medicine, astronomy, and mathematics into Arabic. Aristotle's writings were particularly influential. The institute also included schools, observatories, and a huge library. Other scientific centers arose, from Spain and Morocco to Samarkand in Central Asia. For example, in the tenth and eleventh centuries the Shi'ite Fatimids built the House of Knowledge in Cairo with a massive library holding 2 million books, many on scientific subjects.

Arab and Persian scholars were not just translating but also actively assimilating the imported knowledge. As the influential eleventh-century Persian philosopher Al-Biruni (al-bih-ROO-nee) wrote: "The sciences were transmitted into the Arabic language from different parts of the world; by it [the sciences] were embellished and penetrated the hearts of men, while the beauties of [Arabic] flowed in their veins and arteries."[18] The dialogue resulting from a diversity of ideas produced an open-minded search for truth that is apparent in the work of Ibn Khaldun, Ibn Sina, al-Kindi, and Ibn Rushd. For instance, the philosopher al-Kindi wrote that Muslims should acknowledge truth from whatever source it came because nothing was more important than truth itself. Ibn Rushd (Averroes), who lived in Cordoba, influenced Christian thinkers with his assertion of the role of reason. In the eleventh century, Christian Europe became aware of the Muslim synthesis of Greek, Indian, and Persian knowledge from libraries in Spain.

Medicine and Chemistry

Muslims also turned their attention to medicine. Although much influenced by Greek ideas, Muslim medical specialists did not accept ancient wisdom uncritically. Instead, they developed an empirical tradition. Baghdad hospitals were the world's most advanced. Muslim surgeons learned how to use opium for anesthesia, extract teeth and replace them with false teeth made from animal bones, remove kidney stones, and do a colostomy by creating an artificial anus. After many Islamic medical books were translated into Latin in the twelfth century, they became the major medical texts in Europe for the next five centuries. Two medical scientists, Abu Bakr al-Razi (a-boo BAH-car al-RAH-zee) (ca. 865–ca. 932) and Ibn Sina (Avicenna), compared Greek ideas with their own research. Al-Razi, a Persian, directed several hospitals and wrote more than fifty clinical studies as well as general medical works. The latter included the *Comprehensive Book,* the longest medical encyclopedia in Arabic (eighteen volumes), which was used in Europe into the 1400s. Al-Razi also studied what we would today call sociological and psychological aspects of medicine, and a century later Ibn Sina stressed psychosomatic medicine and treated depression. He also pioneered the study of vision and

IBN BATTUTA, A MUSLIM TRAVELER

Among the Islamic travelers who journeyed to, and often sojourned in, distant lands, the most famous was Abdallah Muhammad Ibn Battuta, a gregarious and pious fourteenth-century Moroccan who spent thirty years touring the length and breadth of the Islamic world, as far east as Southeast Asia and, he claimed, the coastal ports of China. His travels demonstrated the reach of the Islamic community. He was a pilgrim, judge, scholar, Sufi, ambassador, and connoisseur of fine foods and elegant architecture. Ibn Battuta's writings about his remarkable journeys, the autobiographical *Rihla* (Book of Travels), provide detailed, often unique eyewitness accounts of many societies. A collaborator compiled the *Rihla* in a literary form near the end of the adventurer's life.

Born in Tangier, Morocco, in North Africa, to a Berber family of scholars and trained in Islamic law, Ibn Battuta left home in 1325 at the age of twenty-one to seek adventure and learning. His apparent wanderlust proved difficult to quench. Such extensive travel would have been impossible for any woman, Muslim or otherwise, in that era, since women were expected to stay close to home and family. Traveling by camel, horse, wagon, or ship, Ibn Battuta covered between 60,000 and 75,000 miles and visited dozens of countries. He never had a conventional family life and married several times for short periods, leaving children all over the hemisphere. The politically ambitious jurist often sojourned in a society for months or years; his largest career stint was seven years' service in the Delhi Sultanate of northern India. But wherever he went, Ibn Battuta made observations on a wide variety of subjects, from cuisine and botany to political practice and Sufi mystics. For example, he reported on the "continuous series of bazaars [along the Nile] from Alexandria to Cairo. Cities and villages succeed one another without interruption." And, coming from a more patriarchal North African society, he marveled at the "respect shown to women by the [Central Asian] Turks, for they hold a more dignified position than the men. Turkish women do not veil themselves."

Although a repeated visitor to Mecca and the Islamic heartland, his experiences in the frontier regions of Islam, such as India and the Maldive Islands, Southeast Asia, the East African coast, the western Sudan, Turkish Central Asia, Anatolia, and Mongol-ruled southern Russia, provide the most useful information for the historian. They reveal a vivid picture of an expanding, vigorous Islamic realm encountering diverse structures, peoples, and practices. For example, from him we learn about the sexual customs of the Maldive Islands, where he married the widow of a sultan, and the Arab religious scholars, Persian merchants, and Chinese painters who gathered at Delhi "like moths around a candle."

Whereas the Christian Marco Polo a century earlier was always a stranger in his travels in Asia, in most places Ibn Battuta went he encountered people who shared his world-view and social values. From Morocco to Central Asia and around the Indian Ocean Rim, people worshiped in mosques and recognized the Shari'a as a legal framework. Far and wide, Ibn Battuta enjoyed the company of merchants, scholars, Sufis, and princes, with most of whom he could converse in Arabic on many topics, including developments in faraway lands. His knowledge of Islamic law and Arabic allowed him to work as a judge and legal scholar from Morocco to India. But, while cosmopolitan and open-minded by the standards of the day, he was clearly uncomfortable in non-Islamic societies such as China and in those frontier Islamic cultures where Islamic orthodoxy was greatly modified by local custom, such as Mali in West Africa. The traveler finally returned home to Tangier, where he died around 1368.

THINKING ABOUT THE PROFILE

1. Why was Ibn Battuta one of the great travelers of the Intermediate Era?
2. What do his travels tell us about the values and reach of Islamic religion and culture?

Notes: Quotations from Ross Dunn, *The Adventures of Ibn Battuta: A Muslim Traveller of the 14th Century* (Berkeley: University of California Press, 1986), 45, 183; Nikki R. Keddie, "Women in the Middle East Since the Rise of Islam," in *Women's History in Global Perspective*, ed. Bonnie G. Smith, vol. 3 (Urbana: University of Illinois Press, 2005), 81.

Bibliotheque nationale de France

The Journey to Mali No known paintings of Ibn Battuta exist. However, this map of Africa and the Mediterranean world, made by a Jewish cartographer in Spain in 1375, features a drawing of a camel-riding Muslim traveler that some historians think represents the journey of the Moroccan to Mali.

eye disease and performed complicated operations on the eye. His medical encyclopedia provided about half of the medical curriculum in medieval European universities. Muslims also pioneered many of the apparatus, techniques, and language of chemistry later adopted in the West.

Mathematics and Astronomy

The scientific revolution that later occurred in Europe would have been impossible without Arab and Indian mathematics. In Baghdad the Persian Zoroastrian al-Khuwarizmi **(al-KWAHR-uhz-mee)** (ca. 780–ca. 850) developed the mathematical procedures he called algebra, building on Greek and Indian foundations. Omar Khayyam, the beloved Persian poet who worked at Baghdad's House of Wisdom, helped formulate trigonometry. From Indian math books Muslims adopted a revolutionary system of numbers. Today we know them as Arabic numerals because Europe acquired them from Muslim Spain. The most revolutionary innovation of Arabic numerals was not just their greater convenience but also the use of a dot to indicate an empty column. This dot eventually became the zero. All these innovations had practical uses. Thus, advances in mathematics and physics made possible improvements in water clocks, water wheels, and other irrigation apparatuses that spread well beyond the Islamic world.

Muslim astronomers combined Greek, Persian, and Indian knowledge of the stars and planets with their own observations to improve astronomical observations. Applying their knowledge of mathematics to optics, they constructed a primitive version of the telescope. One astronomer reportedly built an elaborate planetarium that reproduced the movement of the stars, and a remarkable observatory built at Samarkand in Central Asia in 1420 produced charts for hundreds of stars. Some astronomers noted the eccentric behavior of the planet Venus, which challenged the widespread notion of an earth-centered universe. Indeed, many Muslim astronomers accepted that the world was round.

Between the eighth and thirteenth centuries Islamic societies also made innovations in agriculture, demonstrating an expansion of production that amounted to what we today might call a "green revolution." As a result, improved diets and health spurred dramatic population growth. The agricultural improvement resulted partly from Islamic expansion. When the Arab conquests opened the door to India, Arabs could bring to the Middle East South Asian crops such as cotton, hard wheat, rice, and sugar cane; fruits such as the coconut palm, banana, sour orange, lemon, lime, mango, and watermelon; and vegetables such as spinach, artichokes, and eggplant. These imports from wetter lands encouraged better irrigation, including the use of enormous water wheels to supply water. Indeed, the spread of agricultural products was one of the Islamic peoples' major contributions to world history. Most of these crops filtered westward to Spain, where they thrived, and cotton became a major crop in West Africa. Many crops reached Christian Europe from Spain and Sicily, but they were adopted only slowly, since Europe at that time had a lower population density and limited irrigation technology.

SECTION SUMMARY

- Sufism, a mystical approach to Islam that emphasized flexibility and a personal connection with God, drew both Sunni and Shi'ite followers.
- Although the Quran and most Muslim societies restricted women, some Muslim societies did not, and both Muslims and non-Muslims have debated the origins and benefits of such practices as wearing a veil.
- Literature, especially poetry, was very important in Islamic culture, as was calligraphy, the artful writing of words.
- Islamic science and medicine were very advanced and pioneered such practices as anesthesia and the replacement of false teeth.
- The Scientific Revolution would not have occurred without the help of Islamic mathematicians who passed on to Europe Indian mathematics.
- Islamic peoples helped to spread a great variety of agricultural products across Eurasia.

Globalized Islam and Middle Eastern Political Change

Why do historians speak of Islam as a hemispheric culture?

The major theme of early Islam was the transformation of a parochial Arab culture into the first truly hemisphere-wide culture connected by many religious and commercial networks. Between the eighth and seventeenth centuries Islam expanded out of its Arabian heartland to become the dominant religion across a broad expanse of Africa and Eurasia, and Muslim minorities emerged in places as far afield as China and the Balkans. From this expansion was created **Dar al-Islam** (the "Abode of Islam"), the Islamic world stretching from Morocco to Indonesia and joined by both a common faith and trade. Networks fostered by Islam reached from the Atlantic eastward to the Pacific, spreading Arab words, names, social attitudes, cultural values, and the Arabic script to diverse peoples. Eventually several powerful military states

Dar al-Islam ("Abode of Islam") The Islamic world stretching from Morocco to Indonesia and joined by both a common faith and trade.

rose to power and ruled over large populations of Muslims and non-Muslims. The Islamic world also faced severe challenges—expanding Turks, Christian crusaders, Mongol conquerors, and horrific pandemics—that set the stage for the rise of new political forces in the fifteenth and sixteenth centuries. Yet, the Islamic tradition was resistant and overcame factionalism and political decay to remain creative well past the 1400s.

The Global Shape of Dar al-Islam

More than half of the world's 1.5 billion Muslims today live outside the Middle East, and Arabs are significantly outnumbered by non-Arab believers. The majority of all Muslims live in South and Southeast Asia. After the destruction of the Abbasid Caliphate, Arab political power diminished, but Islam grew rapidly in both Africa and South Asia (see Chapters 12–13). Dozens of prosperous Muslim trading cities, from Tangier in northwest Africa to Samarkand in Central Asia to Melaka in Malaya, offered goods from distant countries. Beginning in the thirteenth century, Muslims constructed a hemisphere-spanning system based not just on economic exchange but also on a shared understanding of the world and the cosmos, linked by informal networks of Islamic scholars and saints. The Quran and its message of a righteous social order provided a framework for Dar al-Islam.

Trade Networks

The spread of Islam corresponded with the growth of Muslim-dominated long-distance trade, especially the maritime trade around the Indian Ocean Basin. Except for the Chinese, Arabs enjoyed the world's most advanced shipbuilding and navigation between 1000 and 1450. The lateen sails that Arabs devised, or perhaps adapted from Southeast Asians, later allowed European ships to undertake long-distance voyages in the 1400s. An increasingly integrated Muslim-dominated maritime trading system gradually emerged that linked the eastern Mediterranean, Middle East, East African coast, Persia, and India with the societies of East and Southeast Asia (see Map 10.3). One Arab merchant expressed his commercial ambitions: "I want to send Persian saffron to China, where I hear that it fetches a high price, and then ship Chinese porcelain to Greece, Greek brocade to India, Indian iron to Aleppo [a Syrian port], Aleppo glass to the Yemen and Yemeni material to Persia."[19]

The Straits of Melaka in Southeast Asia and Hormuz **(HAWR-muhz)** at the Persian Gulf entrance stood at the heart of the key mercantile system of the Intermediate world. Over these sea routes the spices of Indonesia and East Africa, the gold and tin of Malaya, the textiles of India, the gold of southern Africa, and the silks, porcelain, and tea of China traveled to distant markets. The maritime network achieved its height in the fifteenth and sixteenth centuries, when Muslim economic and cultural power remained strong. Arab and Persian merchant communities could be found as far east as the ports of Korea and south China. By intermarrying with local women and practicing their faith, Muslim merchants in these trade diasporas converted others to Islam.

Turks and Crusaders

Rise of the Turks

Between the eleventh and fifteenth centuries the Middle East faced a series of interventions by Turks and Crusaders that reshaped the region politically. The rise of the Turks is a major theme in this period of world history. The Turks were originally pastoral nomads from Central Asia who were divided by tribe and dialect. For centuries these skilled horsemen had intruded into Chinese, Indian, and western Asian societies, and some Turks adopted such religions as Nestorian Christianity, Judaism, and Buddhism. Gradually they drew closer to Middle Eastern cultural patterns, and most eventually embraced Islam. Some Turkish groups sent boys to the Abbasids, where they trained to serve the Abbasids as soldiers or administrators.

Late in the tenth century a group of Muslim Turks, the Seljuks **(SEL-jooks)**, achieved regional power. Expanding from Central Asia and recruiting other Turkish tribes into their confederation, they swept westward through Afghanistan and Iran into Iraq. Allied with the declining Abbasids, Seljuk forces conquered many Muslim and Christian societies in the Caucasus region, eventually creating a large empire stretching from Palestine to Samarkand. The weakening of the Byzantine state allowed the Seljuks in 1071 to seize much of Anatolia, which had for many centuries been populated largely by Greek-speaking Orthodox Christians. Even when the Seljuks' power soon diminished elsewhere and their empire crumbled, they continued to govern Anatolia.

The First Crusade

By the eleventh century some Islamic states faced increasing challenges from European Christians. Between 1095 and 1272 Christians from various European societies launched a long series of Crusades to win back what they saw as the Judeo-Christian Holy Land from Muslim occupation (see Chapter 14). The First Crusade capitalized on Muslim weakness, since the various feuding

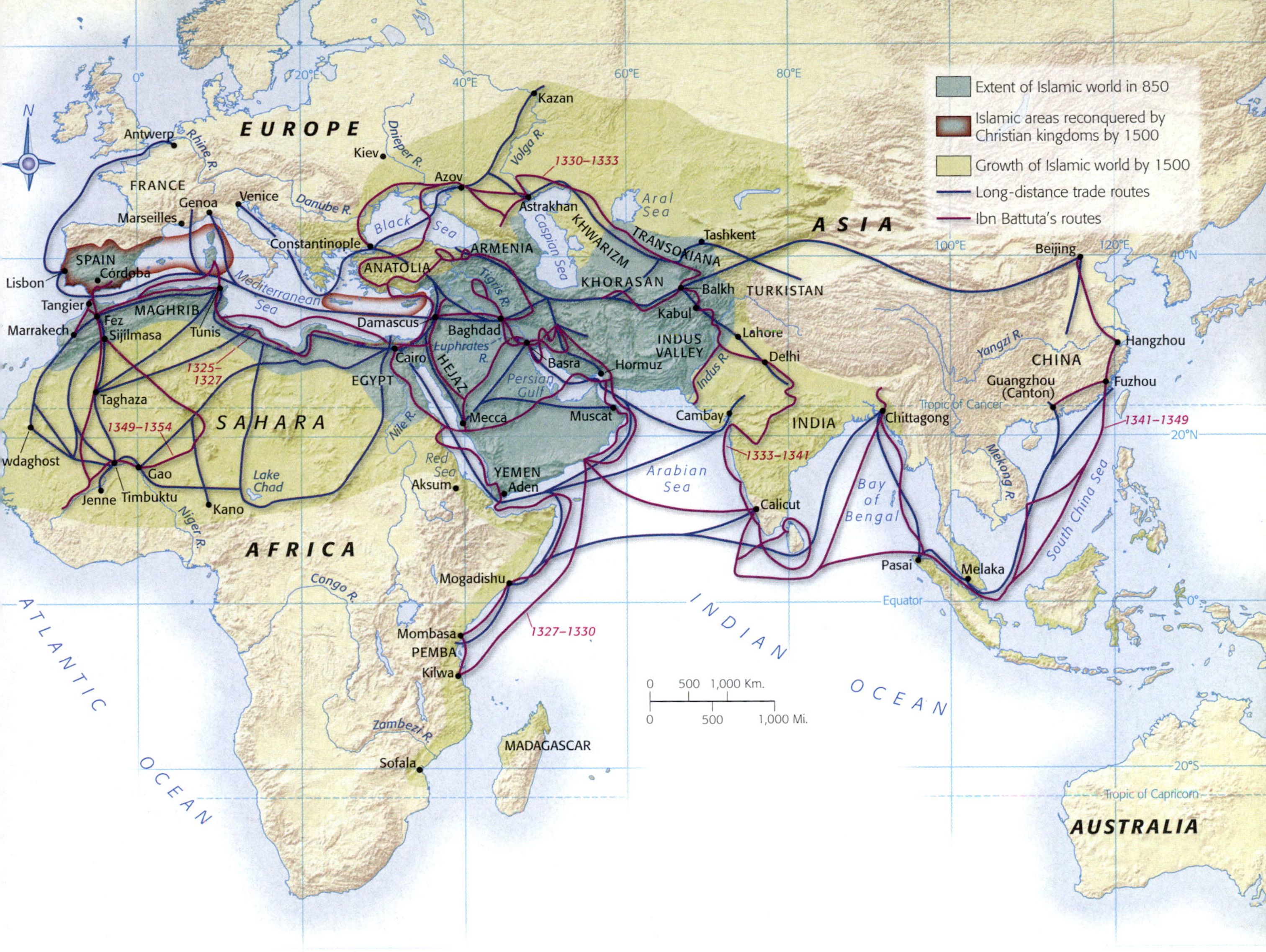

Map 10.3 Dar al-Islam and Trade Routes, ca. 1500 C.E.
By 1500 the Islamic world stretched into West Africa, East Africa, and Southeast Asia. Trade routes connected the Islamic lands and allowed Muslim traders to extend their networks to China, Russia, and Europe.

Interactive Map

Muslim states could not cooperate. Some states, such as Fatimid Egypt, even maintained lucrative trade ties with Europe, and parts of the Middle East still had substantial Christian and Jewish populations as well as many dissident Muslims. In the end, however, the Crusades failed to achieve their goal.

The First Crusade (1095–1099) was triggered by the encroachment of Seljuk Turks on Byzantine territory and a division of the Christian church into rival branches in 1054. Roman popes, worried about Seljuk expansion and anxious to assert their primacy over the leaders of the breakaway Greek Orthodox Church based in Constantinople, promoted the idea of positive violence to defend the faith. Using untrue stories of Arab and Seljuk atrocities against Christians in Palestine, Pope Urban II called on Christians to reclaim the Holy Land and protect the churches and relics of Jerusalem. His plea attracted some 100,000 European volunteers, some pious, others just hungry for booty. The crusaders fought their way along the coast and reached Jerusalem in 1099, when they took the city and killed thousands of Muslims, Jews, and even local Christians. Some crusaders stayed on to guard the sites but also to colonize the surrounding territory, and four small crusader states were established in what is today Israel and Lebanon. As Muslim forces regrouped, another pope dispatched the Second Crusade (1147–1149), in which the crusaders mostly slaughtered Jews in Europe and pillaged the Byzantine Empire.

Muslim-Christian Conflicts

However, crusaders often fought each other, undermining their own power. In the mid-twelfth century Muslims effectively counterattacked, pushing back Christian forces and prompting the Third Crusade (1189–1192). The Muslim armies were led by General Salah al-Din, or Saladin **(SAL-uh-din)** (1138–1193), an Iraqi-born Kurd who once served the Fatimid rulers of Egypt, then deposed them and became sultan, replacing Shi'ite with Sunni rule. Saladin's forces stopped a crusader invasion of Egypt and then, between 1187 and 1192, captured Jerusalem from the crusaders and extended his power into Syria. A tolerant leader, Saladin spared the Christians who surrendered in Jerusalem and employed the great Cordoba-born Jewish sage and legal authority Moses Maimonides **(my-MAHN-uh-deez)** (1135–1204) as his physician. His military exploits made Saladin a hero in Muslim eyes, and he is still revered today. The final six crusades failed to wrest control of North Africa, Jerusalem, and Anatolia from Muslim hands.

The Crusader's Legacy

Historians still debate the heritage of the Crusades. Many crusaders were undoubtedly inspired by a sincere religious zeal to preserve access to Christian holy sites, but many also looted captured cities and sacked the Orthodox Christian capital, Constantinople. Likewise, Muslim armies often showed little mercy on their enemies. Some believe that the militant Christian challenge to Islam represented by the Crusades ultimately made both religions less tolerant and more zealous, complicating relations between the two groups. For centuries afterward some Muslim rulers viewed their Christian subjects as untrustworthy, while Christians persecuted the remaining Muslim populations in southern Europe. Even today, hundreds of years later, Islamic militants still capitalize on lingering resentment against Western "crusaders."

Mongol Conquests and the Black Death

Another people from outside the region, the Mongols **(MAHN-guhlz)**, also swept into western Asia, destroying various states, creating instability, and unwittingly laying the foundation for a hemisphere-wide disease that caused much devastation and death in the Middle East. The Mongols, Central Asian pastoral nomads, constituted a much greater short-term threat to Islam than the Christian crusaders. Led by Genghis Khan **(GENG-iz KAHN)** (ca. 1162–1227), the Mongols, prompted perhaps by environmental stress and overpopulation, began their expansion out of their Mongolian homeland in the late twelfth century. Between 1218 and 1221 they fought their way through the lands inhabited mostly by Turkish-speaking Muslims just north of Afghanistan, destroying several great Silk Road cities.

Mongol atrocities were legendary. For example, they killed 700,000 mostly unarmed residents in the Persian city of Merv. Their goal was to paralyze the Muslim societies with enough fear to prevent opposition. It usually worked. An Arab chronicler wrote of the Mongol invaders that "in the countries that have not yet been overrun by them, everyone spends the night afraid that they may appear there too."[20] After Genghis Khan's death in 1227, the Mongols turned to conquering China, Russia, and eastern Europe but also put pressure on the Caucasus and Anatolia. In 1243 they defeated the remnants of the Seljuk Turks.

Hulegu's Empire

In 1256 a grandson of Genghis Khan, Hulegu **(hoo-LAY-goo)** (1217–1275), led new attacks on the Middle East that had more lasting consequences for the region. Crossing the mountains into Iraq, Hulegu's army, faced with fierce resistance, responded with brutal force. In 1258 the Mongols pillaged Baghdad, burning schools, libraries, mosques, and palaces, killing perhaps a million people, and executing all the Abbasids. Some historians see Hulegu's destruction of Baghdad as a fateful turning point for Arab society that ended the prosperity and intellectual glory once represented by the now-gutted city. Hulegu's forces pushed on west, occupying Damascus and destroying the key eastern Mediterranean port of Aleppo **(uh-LEP-oh)**. The pastoralist Mongols also badly disrupted agriculture, returning some farms to pasture and dispersing the peasants. In some places farming never recovered. But the Islamic tradition proved resilient. In 1260 Hulegu's armies tried to invade Egypt but were defeated by the Mamluks **(MAM-looks)**, ex-slave soldiers of Turkish origin who had taken power in Egypt. Hulegu's Mongols stayed in Iraq and Persia, calling themselves the Il-Khanid **(il-KHAN-id)** dynasty, assimilating Persian culture, and eventually adopting Islam. Many descendants of Mongol invaders in Russia, known today as Tartars, also eventually became Muslim. The Il-Khanids practiced religious toleration and encouraged monumental architecture, learning, and a literary renaissance, during which scholars wrote pathbreaking histories of the world that tell us much about the Mongol empire.

The Great Pandemic

By building a large empire across Eurasia, the Mongols fostered overland trade and travel, but in so doing they also provided a path over which deadly diseases could spread. Like Europe and China, much of the Islamic world was deeply affected by the terrible fourteenth-century pandemic known in the West as the Black Death, a catastrophic disease, probably bubonic plague, that killed quickly and spread rapidly over the networks of exchange. Initially carried into the Black Sea region from eastern Asia by fleas infesting rats that stowed away on caravans along the Mongol-controlled Silk Road or on board trading ships, the pandemic hit the Middle East repeatedly over the course of a century, reducing the population of Egypt and Syria by two-thirds. Ibn Khaldun wrote that "cities and towns were laid waste, roads and way signs were obliterated, settlements and mansions became empty. The entire inhabited world changed."[21] Ibn Khaldun felt he might be living at the end of history, but by the 1400s the Middle East had stabilized and regained some of its lost economic and cultural dynamism.

The Rise of Muslim Military States

In the thirteenth and fourteenth centuries, several powerful Muslim military states arose, including those of the Mamluks in Egypt, the Timurids in Central Asia, and the Ottoman Turks in Anatolia. Gunpowder, a Chinese invention that filtered westward along the Silk Road during Mongol times, forever changed the nature of warfare and also had an impact on politics. After 1350 possession of firearms gave some states and groups an advantage over rivals and led to the rise of stronger, more bureaucratic states.

The Mamluks, who had thwarted Mongol expansion, ruled Egypt and Syria from 1250 to 1517, making Egypt the richest Middle Eastern state. After extending their power into Arabia and capturing Mecca and Medina, they were able to control and tax the flow of Muslim pilgrims. The Mamluks also enjoyed an active trade with the two major Italian trading cities, Genoa and Venice, that supplied valuable Asian goods to Europe. Merchants from Venice established trading posts around the Mamluk lands, where they exchanged timber, metals, and gold for spices, dyes, and Indian textiles. Eventually, however, Mamluk corruption and demands for increased taxes prompted seafaring European merchants to seek a maritime route to the East to avoid Mamluk territory. In 1516–1517 another Turkish group, the Ottomans, defeated the Mamluks and absorbed their lands into the growing Ottoman Empire (see Map 10.4).

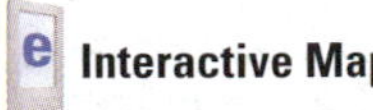

Map 10.4 The Ottoman Empire, 1566
Between 1300 and the mid-1500s the Ottoman Turks expanded out of western Anatolia to conquer a large empire in western Asia, Egypt and North Africa, and eastern Europe, making the Ottomans one of the world's largest states.

Venetian Ambassadors Visiting Mamluk Damascus Venetians and Genoese merchants, fierce rivals, regularly visited the Middle East to acquire silks, spices, and other valuable products. This painting from the 1400s shows Venetians being received by the Mamluk governor of Damascus, who wears a horned hat and sits on a low platform, in today's Syria.

Tamerlane

In Central Asia, the Timurid state became the dominant regional power for over a century. The state's ruthless founder, Tamerlane **(TAM-uhr-lane)** (1336–1405), a Muslim prince of Turkish and Mongol ancestry, had been crippled by an arrow wound as a young man but hoped to emulate Genghis Khan. From his capital at Samarkand, Tamerlane's army rampaged through the Caucasus, southern Russia, Persia, Iraq, and Syria, killing thousands of people and destroying cities and farms. He then turned against India, wreaking havoc in the north (see Chapter 13). Only Tamerlane's death in 1405 halted his forces from invading China and Ottoman Turkey. Although Tamerlane protected merchants and Sufi mystics, his heritage was largely one of smoking ruins and pyramids of human heads. However, his successors built mosques and patronized scholars, and later his grandson established a great empire in India in the early 1500s.

The Ottomans

The most powerful and enduring military state was established by the Ottoman **(AHT-uh-muhn)** Turks. The Ottomans originated as a small Anatolian state led by a chief, Osman **(ohs-MAHN)** (*Ottoman* means "followers of Osman"), who came under the influence of Sufis dedicated to the destruction of Byzantium, which was reeling from temporary occupation of Constantinople by crusaders and weakening influence in Anatolia. The Ottomans capitalized on this vacuum and, by 1300, began raiding and then annexing the remaining Byzantine strongholds in Anatolia. Ultimately they used gunpowder weapons to conquer much of the Byzantine Empire, creating one of the most dynamic states in western Eurasia and a link between Middle Eastern Islam and European Christianity. The once great Byzantium was increasingly a shell of a state surrounding Constantinople.

Soon the Ottomans moved into the Balkans, where they defeated the strongest Christian power in southeastern Europe, Serbia. The Ottomans favored Muslims in taxes, and over the next several centuries many Albanian and Serb-speaking Christians adopted Islam, perhaps partly for economic reasons, creating a division in the Balkans between Catholic, Orthodox, and Muslim peoples that complicated politics for centuries to come. At the Battle of Nicopolis **(nuh-KAHP-uh-luhs)** in 1396, the Ottomans defeated a Hungarian-led force drawn from throughout Europe to oppose further Ottoman expansion. Then in 1453 Sultan Mehmed **(MEH-met)** the Conqueror (1432–1481) finally took Constantinople and converted the city into the Ottoman capital, eventually renamed Istanbul.

Ottoman Empire

The Ottoman Empire was now the major regional power, an empire of many peoples. Istanbul attracted a multiethnic and multireligious population and remained a major trade hub. Mehmed the Conqueror, who patronized the arts, even invited some of Italy's most famous artists and architects to work in his cosmopolitan capital, which by 1500 was Europe's largest city. Ottoman sultans used the administrative and military skills of the subject peoples and promoted men of merit regardless of their backgrounds. Through the **millet** ("nationality") system, the leaders of religious and ethnic minorities administered their own communities. For instance, the Greek patriarch had authority over all Orthodox Christians in Ottoman territory. Christians and Jews also practiced their religions freely for the most part. Thus the millet system allowed the Turks to divide and hence rule diverse peoples and faiths.

millet The nationality system through which the Ottomans allowed the leaders of religious and ethnic minorities to administer their own communities.

Under a dynamic and militarily powerful state, the Ottomans continued to expand. By 1500 they had solidified control over Greece and the Balkans (see Map 10.4). In the 1500s, the so-called Ottoman golden age, Ottoman rule was extended over much of western Asia as far east as Persia and also through North Africa from Egypt to Algeria. However, the Ottomans were defeated when they attempted to take Hungary in 1699. This event marked the end of Ottoman, and Islamic, expansion in western Eurasia and symbolized the decline of Islamic power, but the Ottoman Empire continued until 1923.

Islamic Contributions to World History

By linking peoples of varied cultures, ideas, religions, and languages, the Arab conquests fostered intellectual and artistic creativity. The Islamic faith and culture they spread profoundly influenced the development of Southern Asian, African, and European societies, and to the east the gradual Islamic conquest of India posed an alternative to Hinduism. As Islamic influence and Arab merchants traveled south across the Sahara and along the East African coast, various African societies also adopted the Islamic faith as well as some Muslim customs and technologies. From the ninth through the eleventh centuries, the Arabs in Sicily and Spain passed on some of the fruits of the advanced science, mathematics, and technology of the Middle East, India, and even China to Europe. In many respects the Muslims served as the critical link between the classical Greeks and Indians and the late medieval Europeans. Greco-Roman and Islamic learning was now studied in medieval universities. Western Europeans profited from this exchange of knowledge, and eventually it helped spark not only a scientific and technological revolution in Europe but also a questioning of the entrenched Christian church that ultimately led to more diverse ideas within Western societies. But the exchange was not one way, and Muslims also benefited from European knowledge of medicine, science, and art.

Cultural Mixing and Diversity

The mixing of Arab, Persian, Turkish, Byzantine, Christian, Jewish, African, and Indian influences created a hemispheric-wide Islamic world that connected culturally and politically diverse societies sharing a common faith and, often, values. While most people in what is today Iraq, Syria, Egypt, and North Africa adopted the Arabic language and called themselves Arabs, the Persians and Turks continued to speak their own languages, which they now wrote using the Arabic script. Indeed, for many centuries Persian remained a language of government and the elite, from the Seljuk Turkish empire in Anatolia to various Muslim states in India and Central Asia.

Non-Muslims played key roles in the Islamic world, especially in commerce. From the eighth through eleventh centuries Jews were the key trade middlemen between Christian Europe and the Muslim world. Hence, Jews from Narbonne in southern France traded in Spain, North Africa, and the eastern Mediterranean, becoming fluent in Arabic. After the eleventh century the Jews lost ground as intermediaries to the Italians in the west and the Armenian Christians in the east.

Muslim scholars were proud of the expanse of their horizons. For example, the Egyptian scholar Jalal al-Din al-Suyuti **(juh-LALL al-din al-sue-YOU-tee)** (1445–1505) boasted that he and his books had traveled as far as West Africa and India. Yet, after the defeat of the last Muslim kingdom in Spain in 1492, he also saw the Muslim world in need of intellectual and social renewal. Although the Ottoman Turks were on the rise, al-Suyuti could not know that after 1500 Muslim states would also have a resurgence in Persia and India, nor that various Europeans, benefiting from the encounter with Islam, would become serious rivals to Muslim power and a challenge to the interconnected Islamic world.

Several powerful Islamic states, including the Ottoman Empire, continued to exercise political and economic influence in the sixteenth and seventeenth centuries. But, with the occasional exception of Ottoman Turkey, technological innovation, scientific inquiry, and the questioning of accepted religious and cultural ideas fell off in the Middle East after 1500. The madrasas, while training Muslim clerics and providing spiritual guidance, tended to have narrow, theology-based curriculums that deemphasized

SECTION SUMMARY

- Trade routes spread Islam throughout the hemisphere, eventually creating Dar al-Islam, an Islamic world stretching from Indonesia to Morocco, in which Arabs constituted a minority of Muslims.
- The series of Christian Crusades to win back the Judeo-Christian Holy Land from Muslims led to long-lasting resentment on the part of Muslims.
- The Mongols, led by Genghis Khan and Hulegu, one of his grandsons, ruthlessly attacked Muslims in Central Asia and sacked Baghdad, but the Islamic tradition continued throughout Mongol rule.
- The arrival of gunpowder from China allowed Muslim military states, such as the Mamluks and the Timurids, to gain power.
- The Ottoman Turks established an extremely successful empire in the territory of the former Byzantine Empire by allowing subject minorities to administer their own affairs.
- By conducting and preserving a great deal of scientific and philosophical learning, the Muslims contributed much to European culture.

secular learning. Some historians believe this trend undermined the humanist, tolerant tradition of Islamic scholarship, such as the open-minded approach of Baghdad's House of Wisdom and the schools in Muslim Spain. Over the next three centuries, most of the Middle Eastern peoples who had boasted innovative and cosmopolitan traditions for a millennium gradually lost military and economic power while Europeans surged.

CHAPTER SUMMARY

The rise of Islam in Arabia during the seventh century changed world history. Islam forged a community of believers around a set of monotheistic ideas, and Muhammad's message proved so popular that, within a few decades, Muslim Arabs had conquered a large empire and spread Islam to many Arab and non-Arab peoples. Islam offered a distinctive set of religious, political, and social ideas, such as pilgrimage, annual fasting, a legal code, and an emphasis on social justice, but it also was influenced by Christian, Jewish, Persian, and other traditions. Islamic societies flourished under powerful theocratic governments, such as the Umayyad and Abbasid Caliphates, while Islamic writers and scientists assimilated and developed knowledge from many societies. Muslim thinkers preserved classical Greek learning while pioneering new ideas in astronomy, mathematics, the physical sciences, and agriculture. Arab links also contributed knowledge to medieval Europe, spurring the scientific and technological rise of the West.

The Islamic world became a cosmopolitan network of peoples, linked by trade and religious scholars. While the end of the Abbasids brought some political fragmentation, Islam still expanded, overcoming several challenges in the millennium after Muhammad. By 1500 the Ottoman Turks controlled a vast empire. Stretching from western Africa and southwestern Europe eastward to Southeast Asia and western China, Islam became a hemispheric culture, even extending its influences into non-Islamic regions. After 1500, however, the Islamic Middle East began to fade as a political power and a center for intellectual inquiry.

KEY TERMS

Bedouins	**umma**	**jihad**	**Shi'a**
Ka'ba	**Allah**	**sultan**	**Sufism**
Quran	**caliphate**	**Shari'a**	**calligraphy**
Hadith	**Ramadan**	**madrasas**	**Dar al-Islam**
hijra	**haj**	**Sunni**	**millet**

EBOOK AND WEBSITE RESOURCES

PRIMARY SOURCE
The Quran: Call for Jihad

INTERACTIVE MAPS
Map 10.1 Expansion of Islam, to 750 C.E.
Map 10.2 The Abbasid Empire, ca. 800 C.E.
Map 10.3 Dar al-Islam and Trade Routes, ca. 1500 C.E.
Map 10.4 The Ottoman Empire, 1566

LINKS

History of the Middle East Database (http://www.nmhschool.org/tthornton/mehistorydatabase/mideastindex.php). A fine set of essays and links on the early and modern Middle East and Islam.

Ibn Battuta's Rihla (http://www.sfusd.k12.ca.us/schwww/sch618/Ibn_Battuta/Ibn_Battuta_Rihla.html). A useful site on Ibn Battuta and his wide travels.

Internet Islamic History Sourcebook (http://www.fordham.edu/halsall/islam/islamsbook.html). A comprehensive examination of the Islamic tradition and its long history, with many useful links and source materials.

Islam and Islamic History in Arabia and the Middle East (http://www.islamicity.com/education). A comprehensive site sponsored by a moderate Muslim organization.

Islamic Studies, Islam, Arabic, and Religion (http://www.arches.uga.edu/~godlas). A comprehensive collection of links and resources maintained at the University of Georgia.

Virtual Religion Index (http://virtualreligion.net/vri/). Has many links on all major religions, including Islam.

Plus flashcards, practice quizzes, and more. Go to: www.cengage.com/history/lockard/globalsocnet2e

SUGGESTED READING

Armstrong, Karen. *Muhammad: A Biography of the Prophet.* San Francisco: Harper, 1992. A readable and sympathetic survey of Muhammad and his life.

Aslan, Reza. *No God but God: The Origins, Evolution, and Future of Islam.* New York: Random House, 2005. An account of Islamic religion and history by a liberal, Iranian-born, U.S.-based Muslim scholar.

Berkey, Jonathan P. *The Formation of Islam: Religion and Society in the Near East, 600–1800.* New York: Cambridge University Press, 2003. A fine scholarly study of the rise of Islam to 1500.

Bloom, Jonathan, and Sheila Blair. *Islam: A Thousand Years of Faith and Power.* New Haven, CT: Yale University Press, 2002. A well-written overview of Islamic history and society from 600 to 1700.

Dunn, Ross. *The Adventures of Ibn Battuta: A Muslim Traveller of the 14th Century.* Berkeley: University of California Press, 1986. A fascinating look at Dar al-Islam through the writings of the famed Arab traveler.

Eaton, Richard M. *Islamic History as Global History.* Washington, D.C.: American Historical Association, 1993. A valuable short pamphlet showing the significance of Islamic societies to world history.

Egger, Vernon O. *A History of the Muslim World to 1405: The Making of a Civilization.* Upper Saddle River, NJ: Prentice-Hall, 2004. A recent and comprehensive survey.

Esposito, John L. *Islam: The Straight Path*, revised 3rd ed. New York: Oxford University Press, 2005. Balanced and accessible introduction to Islamic faith and history.

Inalcik, Halil. *The Ottoman Empire: The Classical Age, 1300–1600.* London: Phoenix Press, 2000. A reprint of one of the best introductions to the early Ottoman Empire and society, first published in 1973.

Kennedy, Hugh. *The Great Arab Conquests: How the Spread of Islam Changed the World We Live In.* New York: Da Capo Press, 2007. Well-written overview of Islamic expansion.

Kennedy, Hugh. *When Baghdad Ruled the World: The Rise and Fall of Islam's Greatest Dynasty.* Cambridge, MA: Da Capo Press, 2005. A readable study of the Abbasid dynasty and era.

Lewis, David Levering. *God's Crucible: Islam and the Making of Europe, 570–1215.* New York: W.W. Norton, 2009. Recent study of Muslim-European exchanges.

Menocal, Maria Rosa. *The Ornament of the World: How Muslims, Jews, and Christians Created a Culture of Tolerance in Medieval Spain.* Boston: Little, Brown and Co., 2002. Uses profiles of historical figures to explore the cultural flowering of Muslim Spain.

Morgan, Michael H.. *Lost History: The Enduring Legacy of Muslim Scientists, Thinkers, and Artists.* Washington, D.C.: Smithsonian Institution, 2008. Profiles Islamic thinkers and their influence on Europe.

Nasr, Seyyed Hossein. *Islam: Religion, History, and Civilization.* San Francisco: HarperSanFrancisco, 2003. An insightful overview of the Islamic tradition by an Iranian-born scholar.

Risso, Patrica. *Merchants of Faith: Muslim Commerce and Culture in the Indian Ocean.* Boulder: Westview, 1995. A readable survey of Muslim trade networks.

Robinson, Francis, ed. *The Cambridge Illustrated History of the Islamic World.* Cambridge: Cambridge University Press, 1996. An authoritative, richly illustrated survey of Islamic society and history.

Walther, Wiebke. *Women in Islam from Medieval to Modern Times.* Princeton: Markus Wiener, 1999. One of the most valuable and readable studies of gender issues, by a German scholar.

CHAPTER 11

East Asian Traditions, Transformations, and Eurasian Encounters, 600–1500

CHAPTER OUTLINE

- Tang China: The Hub of the East
- Song China and Commercial Growth
- Mongol Conquest, Chinese Resurgence, and Eurasian Connections
- Cultural Adaptation in Korea and Japan

PROFILE
Lady Murasaki, Heian Novelist

WITNESS TO THE PAST
Life in the Chinese Capital City

Rafael Macia/Photo Researchers, Inc.

Giant Japanese Buddha at Kamakura
During this era, most Japanese adopted Buddhism, some expressing their faith in art. This gigantic statue, erected in the city of Kamakura in 1252, shows the Buddha in meditation.

China is a sea that salts all rivers that flow into it.

—Italian traveler Marco Polo (1275 c.e.)[1]

FOCUS QUESTIONS

1. What role did Tang China play in the Eurasian world?
2. Why might historians consider the Song dynasty the high point of China's golden age?
3. How did China change during the Yuan and Ming dynasties?
4. How did the Koreans and Japanese develop their own distinctive societies?

Early in the twelfth century the Chinese artist Zhang Zeduan, noted for his realistic drawings, painted a massive scroll of people at work and leisure throughout the city of Kaifeng (KIE-FENG), then China's capital and home to perhaps 1 million people. Set during the annual spring festival, the scroll, the surviving portions of which are 17 feet long, portrays a bustling city, from its riverside suburbs to the high protective walls and the towering city gates to the downtown business district, during one of premodern China's most creative and prosperous eras. Kaifeng's streets are crowded with people (mostly men) going about their daily activities, including foreign merchants, streetside hawkers touting their goods, fortune tellers, scholars, and monks. The scroll also shows people working in warehouses, iron smelters, arsenals, and shipyards. Zhang's record of Kaifeng's commercial life is particularly vivid, showing building material suppliers, textile firms, and drug and chemical shops, as well as hotels, food stalls, teahouses, and restaurants. Cargo and pleasure barges cruise the river, while camels heavily laden with goods enter the city.

Much of the prosperous city life Zhang portrayed was familiar to Chinese of earlier and later generations, for Chinese society showed considerable continuity over time. The Han's eventual succession by the Sui and then by the Tang (tahng) and Song (soong) dynasties ensured that Chinese society continued along traditional lines, in contrast to the dramatic changes that took place in Japan, the Middle East, India, Southeast Asia, and Europe during the Intermediate Era. Once the Tang adopted a modified version of the Han system, the ensuing millennium proved to be a golden age, broken only occasionally by invasion or disorder. Some scholars call the Intermediate Era in world history the "Chinese Centuries." China became perhaps the world's richest and most populous society, enjoying a well-organized government and economy, a flourishing artistic and literary culture, and creativity in technology and science. Many commercial and cultural networks connected China to the rest of Eurasia. Furthermore, China's neighbors in Korea and Japan adopted many aspects of Chinese culture, though they also forged their own highly distinctive societies during this period. China did indeed, as Marco Polo recognized, influence or awe all those with whom it came into contact.

e Visit the website and eBook for additional study materials and interactive tools:
www.cengage.com/history/lockard/globalsocnet2e

TANG CHINA: THE HUB OF THE EAST

What role did Tang China play in the Eurasian world?

The harsh Sui dynasty that united China after the disintegration of the Han ruled for only a short time (581–618 C.E.) before rebellions brought it to an end. The victor in the struggles between rival rebel forces established the Tang dynasty (618–907). The three centuries of Tang rule set a high watermark in many facets of Chinese life and provided a cultural and political model for neighboring Asian societies. The only comparable power in Eurasia at that time was the expanding Muslim Abbasid empire; India and Europe were divided into many small states and often threatened by invaders. Tang models shaped China until the early twentieth century.

The Tang Empire and Eurasian Exchange

In the seventh and eighth centuries Tang China—an empire of some 50 or 60 million people—was the largest and most populous society on earth, with immense influence in the eastern third of Eurasia (see Map 11.1). Like the Han before them, the Tang launched ambitious campaigns that brought Central Asia (as far west as the Caspian Sea), Tibet, Mongolia, Manchuria, and parts of Siberia under Chinese rule. Vietnam had long been a colony. The Koreans became a vassal state, and the Japanese established close ties. Chinese garrisons protected the Silk Road, fostering the flow of goods and people across Eurasia.

Silk Roads

The Tang were the most outward-looking of all Chinese dynasties, and during these years China became an open forum, a world market of ideas, people, and things arriving over the networks of exchange. The overland Silk Road across Central Asia remained a transcontinental high-

Map 11.1 The Tang Empire, ca. 750 C.E.

The Tang dynasty forged a large empire across Central Asia into Turkestan before their expansion was halted by Muslim armies at the Battle of Talas River in 751. Control of Central Asia allowed the Tang to protect the Silk Road trade route. The Tang also controlled Vietnam and dominated Korea.

CHRONOLOGY

	China	Korea	Japan
600	**618–907** Tang dynasty	**676–918** Silla	**710–784** Nara period **794–1184** Heian period
900	**960–1279** Song dynasty	**935–1392** Koryo	
1100	**1279–1368** Yuan dynasty		**1180–1333** Kamakura Shogunate
1300	**1368–1644** Ming dynasty **1405–1433** Voyages of Admiral Zheng He	**1392–1910** Yi dynasty (Choson)	**1338–1568** Ashikaga Shogunate

way for traders, adventurers, diplomats, missionaries, and pilgrims traveling east or west, carrying goods and ideas. Nestorian Christian, Manichean, Buddhist, and Muslim missionaries arrived, and merchants from around Asia formed communities in several Chinese cities, many arriving by sea. Indeed, a lively sea trade, a kind of maritime Silk Road, linked China with Southeast Asia, India, and the Middle East. Perhaps two-thirds of the 200,000 inhabitants of the southern port of Guangzhou **(gwahng-jo)**, also known as Canton, were immigrants, including Arabs, Persians, Indians, Cambodians, and Malays, and the city boasted both Sunni and Shi'ite mosques. Indian astronomers and mathematicians joined the Tang government as scientific officials. Meanwhile, several hundred Chinese scholars visited or sojourned in India, most of them seeking Buddhist literature.

China and the World

Tang wealth and power stimulated commerce throughout Eurasia. By land or sea, many Chinese inventions reached into western Eurasia. In 753 C.E. a Chinese craftsman reported that, in Baghdad: "As for the weavers who make light silks, the goldsmiths who work gold and silver there, and the painters; the arts which they practice were started by Chinese technicians."[2] Chinese products such as silk and porcelain were much prized in Europe and the Middle East, and Chinese culture also spread to Korea and Japan. This multicultural exchange benefited China as well. Diverse societies in places such as Burma, Java, and Nepal regularly sent embassies to the Tang court bearing gifts, and renewed contacts with India and the Middle East fostered China's creativity. New products also appeared, most notably tea from Southeast Asia. After the Chinese began drinking tea, originally a medicinal substance, as a beverage, teahouses opened in every marketplace. Another new arrival was the chair from the Middle East, replacing seating pads; the Chinese became the only chair users in East Asia. However, some Chinese scholars criticized the cosmopolitan attitude and complained about too much foreign culture.

Chang'an

The Eurasian exchange fostered dynamic and culturally rich cities. Tang China boasted many cities larger than any cities in Europe or India, and the capital, Chang'an **(CHAHNG-ahn)**, present-day Xi'an **(SHEE-AHN)**, had 2 million inhabitants. The world's largest city, Chang'an was a model of urban planning, with its streets carefully laid out in a grid pattern and the city divided into quadrants. The broad thoroughfares were crowded with visitors and sojourners from many lands, among them Arabs, Persians, Syrians, Jews, Turks, Koreans, Japanese, Vietnamese, Indians, and Tibetans. Many foreign artists, artisans, and merchants worked in the capital, as well as entertainers such as Indian jugglers and Afghan actors. The city contained four Zoroastrian temples, two Nestorian Christian churches, and several mosques. The only contemporary cities that could come close to matching Chang'an's size and amenities were Baghdad, the center of the powerful Abbasid Caliphate, and Byzantine-ruled Constantinople.

Imperial Government and Economic Growth

The centralized imperial government reached a high level of efficiency and maintained one of the world's most productive economies. Despite bloody rebellions, invasions, assassinations, palace coups, and dynastic upheavals, the hallmark of China's political system for many centuries was stability. Later dynasties followed the basic Tang model. According to Confucian theory, the family was the model for the state, so the emperor at the top of the system was the symbolic father of the people, governing by moral example, not physical force. The Chinese considered the emperor the Son of Heaven—not a divine figure but the intermediary between the terrestrial and supernatural realms—and the first scholar of the land. He held daily audiences during which

© Cultural Relics Press

Musicians on the Silk Road This glazed pottery figurine, one of many similar pieces from the Tang era, shows musicians playing Persian musical instruments while riding a camel on their travels along the Silk Road to China, demonstrating China's ties to the Middle East.

diplomats from distant lands sometimes presented gifts as a symbol of their submission to his authority. In return the emperor bestowed on them a title, state robes, and gifts, a ceremony followed later by a banquet.

While women sometimes had power behind the throne, only one woman, the Empress Wu Zhao **(woo chow)** (625–705), ever officially led the government. She had become an imperial concubine at age thirteen and used her political skills and ruthless ambition to eventually displace the sickly emperor, maintaining her power for over fifty years. While Empress Wu generally ruled ably, Chinese scholars viewed her as an evil usurper and warned future generations that women should not rule the country.

In theory the emperor held absolute power, but his actual power was circumscribed in various ways. He had to consider the Censorate, an agency unique to China that monitored the workings of the government, rooted out corruption, proposed changes in state policies, and criticized the government for failings. Only the strongest emperors could punish the Censorate for criticism. Furthermore, the doctrine of the Mandate of Heaven, that people have a right to overthrow an evil, corrupt, or ineffective government, meant that emperors had to consider the consequences of their policies and behavior.

Because administering such a large and diverse empire required a competent bureaucracy, the Tang revived the competitive civil service exams from Han times. The Chinese believed that government officials, known as mandarins, should be the wisest and ablest men in the land. The merit-based exams were intended to seek out talented individuals, regardless of birth, for government service. To help train potential officials, the government also operated a national university and hundreds of local-level academies. During the Tang and the succeeding Song dynasties, perhaps 15 percent of the mandarins did not come from upper-class backgrounds, indicating that the examinations led to some social mobility.

The system consisted of a series of examinations at local, provincial, and national levels. Usually less than 5 percent of candidates passed and moved on to the next level. By passing the highest level a man received the equivalent of a PhD degree, a prerequisite to hold office. The exams largely tested knowledge of literary composition and the contents of the Confucian classics. This competitive merit exam system was the most important institution contributing to the long duration of the political system, giving the ruling elite a shared Confucian ideology emphasizing ethics and loyalty. The Tang bureaucracy numbered around fifteen thousand officials, an extraordinarily small number for a country as huge as China. Clearly they ruled with the cooperation of the local people. From now on whoever ruled China had to rule through the bureaucracy of scholars.

Tang officials pursued policies that maintained economic growth, especially agricultural production. The 80 percent of Chinese who tilled the soil were generally able—though often just barely—to produce a food surplus for the other 20 percent in towns and cities. The Chinese worked to achieve better yields and became one of the world's most efficient farming peoples. The Tang also attempted to circumvent the power of powerful landowning families by experimenting with land reform. In the "equal field system," officials assigned each peasant family a plot of around 19 acres, in the hope that this would provide enough for the family's needs. For a time the reforms brought the peasantry some prosperity. When the Tang declined after some 120 years, the equal field system also disintegrated. Still, throughout history some emperors and officials sought a more equitable land system.

Religion, Science, and Technology

Buddhism in China

The early Intermediate Era was the golden age for Buddhism in Central, Southeast, and East Asia. Under the Tang, Buddhism grew to be a dominant faith, while Confucianism and Daoism remained influential. As Buddhist monks, pilgrims, and artists traveled between India and China, they drew the two societies into closer contact. However, competing Buddhist sects presented the government with some problems. Furthermore, the Buddhist monasteries came to control vast amounts of tax-exempt land and wealth, becoming an alternative power center. In the mid-ninth century the government cracked down on Buddhist institutions. Emperor Wuzong **(woo-chong)** (840–846), in desperate need of more revenues, seized 4,600 monasteries and defrocked all monks under the age of fifty. Although Wuzong's successors restored the monasteries, his actions reduced the political and economic power of the Buddhist orders enough to ensure that they never again exercised significant secular power.

Some new religions also moved east along the Silk Road. Nestorian Christianity, a sect considered heretical in Byzantium, gained a small following, and Islam became strong in northwest China and in pockets of southwest and southern China. Jewish merchants also settled in several northern China cities, founding Jewish communities that endured for centuries. Except for Wuzong, the Tang court generally took a tolerant, ecumenical view of religion. As one Tang emperor proclaimed: "The Way [truth] has more than one name. There is more than one sage. Doctrines vary in distant lands, their benefits reach all mankind."[3]

Tang scholars and craftsmen made significant scientific and technological achievements. Tang astronomers established the solar year at 365 days and studied sunspots, and some argued that the earth was round and revolved around the sun. They were also the first to analyze, record, and then predict solar eclipses. Chinese engineers built the first load-bearing segmental arch bridge. Another important development was the perfection of gunpowder, an elaboration of the firecracker. By using a mix of sulphur, saltpeter, and charcoal, Chinese military forces could now use primitive cannon and flaming rockets to protect their borders or resist rebels. Tang scholars made great strides by inventing woodblock printing. For centuries Chinese had carved texts into stone and then taken ink rubbings for mass distribution as demand for copies of religious and Confucian texts outpaced supply. Finally, some creative men began carving texts into wooden blocks, which could be used to reproduce text on paper with ink, satisfying the need to produce texts for the civil service exams and spread Buddhist writings. The first known book printed on paper with this method was a Buddhist text from 868 (see Chronology: China During the Intermediate Era). The Chinese had an insatiable desire to classify the wisdom of the past for use by future generations, and they could now compile encyclopedias to record their accumulated knowledge. Woodblock printing also gave rise to a written popular culture.

CHRONOLOGY
China During the Intermediate Era

581–618 Sui dynasty

618–907 Tang dynasty

751 Battle of Talas River

868 First books from woodblocks on paper

907–960 Five Dynasties

960–1279 Song dynasty

1167–1227 Life of Genghis Khan

1279–1368 Yuan dynasty (Mongols)

1368–1644 Ming dynasty

1405–1433 Voyages of Admiral Zheng He

The Arts and Literature

Landscape Painting

Some of China's greatest painters and sculptors lived in Tang times. Painting, an activity avidly pursued by scholars and government officials, was closely associated with calligraphy, the beautiful rendering of Chinese characters used to render a meaningful poem, quote, or passage in a refined, balanced form. Both calligraphers and painters used brush and ink on silk or paper. Chinese paintings were generally restrained, understated, and philosophical in presentation. Influenced by Daoism, many painters specialized in landscapes. An eleventh-century writer explained why: "Why does a virtuous man take delight in landscapes? That in a rustic retreat he may nourish his nature; amid the carefree play of streams and rocks, he may take delight. Haze, mist, and the haunting spirits of the mountains are what human nature seeks, and yet can rarely find."[4] But Confucian ideas were also expressed in the people who were usually a small part of the picture. Like Confucian philosophy, Chinese arts stressed order, morality, and tradition. But there were exceptions. Some artists were free spirits and experimented wildly; one eccentric flipped ink-soaked hair at silk, and another splashed while dancing. Artists also reflected their times. Wind-tossed bamboo and choppy water, for example, might indicate turbulent politics. The traveler to Tang China also experienced art when sipping tea from nearly transparent porcelain cups, the most sanitary utensils in the world at that time. China became famous for splendid lacquer ware, furniture made with mother of pearl, gold and silver inlay, and luxurious brocades.

Tang Poetry

Many of China's greatest poets lived in this era, and annual literary festivals were held in Chang'an to select prizewinners. Many poems depicted the hardships of life—poverty, war, the ups and downs of romantic love, the passing of time, the imminence of death—but many lyrical poems explored life and its wonders, as well as the parting of friends. Chinese poems usually blended emotion with restraint, reflecting their Daoist and Buddhist influences. For example, Wang Wei **(wahng way)** expressed a Daoist appreciation of nature: "Walking at leisure we watch laurel flowers fall. In the silence of this night the spring mountain is empty. The moon rises, the birds are startled, As they sing occasionally near the spring fountains." The poem describes a changing landscape of falling laurel leaves, a quiet spring mountain, a rising moon, and birds singing, all of which create Daoist feelings of peace, detachment, and purity.

The two giant figures of Tang poetry were Li Po **(lee po)** and Du Fu **(too foo)**, close friends but very different in their personalities and styles. The eccentric Li (701–762) was romantic, disrespectful

The Nelson-Atkins Museum of Art, Kansas City, Missouri. Purchase: William Rockhill Nelson Trust, 47-71. Photograph by John Lamberton.

Song Landscape This painting, completed around 1000, shows a Buddhist temple dwarfed by towering mountain peaks.

of authority, and humorous but often melancholy: a true free spirit. Influenced by Daoism, Li said that a good person must be carefree, maintaining the heart and mind of a child. Li is believed to have drowned on a boat trip when he reached out in a drunken ecstasy for the reflection of the moon in the water. In "The Joys of Wine" he wrote: "Since Heaven and Earth love wine, I can love wine without shaming Heaven. With three cups I penetrate the Great Dao. Take a whole jugful and I and the world are one. Such things as I have dreamed in wine, Shall never be told to the sober."[5] Li also occasionally wrote about public issues. In a piece about the Tang military campaigns in Central Asia, he outlined the hardships of conscripted soldiers and wondered who would cultivate their fields.

The opposite of Li Po, Du Fu (712–770) was a Confucian humanist, the preeminent poet of social consciousness and deeply concerned with the human condition. Du's poems held up a mirror to his times. His antiwar poems remain powerful even a millennium later: "When will men be satisfied with building a wall against the barbarians? When will the soldiers return to their native land?" His sympathies were with the soldiers and their families rather than with imperial aims:

The war-chariots rattle, The war-horses whinny. Each man of you has a bow and quiver in his belt. Father, mother, son, wife, stare at you going. At the border where the blood of men spills like the sea. And still the heart of Emperor Wu is beating for war. Do you know that, east of China's mountains, in two hundred districts, And in thousands of villages, nothing grows but weeds? And though strong women have bent to the ploughing, East and west the furrows are all broken down.

Du was also capable of great tenderness and celebrated the pleasures of everyday life: "Clear waters wind, Around our village. With long summer days, Full of loveliness. My wife draws out, A chessboard on paper, While our little boys, Bend needles into fish hooks. What more could I wish for?"[6]

Changes in the Late Tang Dynasty

Significant changes took place in China between the eighth and tenth centuries. The overwhelming majority of Chinese now lived in central and south China, where the fertile Yangzi Basin was the most productive economic region. New crop strains were introduced from Southeast Asia that eventually made it possible to harvest two crops of rice a year. This increased productivity, combined with better transportation, led to more trade and substantial increases in the urban population. Crafts and merchant guilds and the world's first paper money appeared, and Chinese traders visited Southeast Asia to obtain luxury goods.

Like the Han, the Tang ultimately found its empire too expensive to maintain and too difficult to defend. After a bitter defeat by Arab forces at the Battle of Talas River (near Samarkand) in 751, the Tang declined as a military power in Central Asia. Muslim forces filled the vacuum, and Islam became the dominant religion in Turkestan and in the Xinjiang **(shin-jee-yahng)** region just west of China proper. Finally the Tang lost control of China itself. The country broke apart, and in 907 Chinese rebel bands, spurred by famine and drought, sacked Chang'an. The Tang demise allowed Vietnam to finally free itself from the long yoke of Chinese rule.

During the next five decades after the Tang collapse, China was divided into several competing states known as the Five Dynasties. But Chinese society was now too massive and deeply rooted to experience the centuries of anarchy that occurred between the Han and Sui, and from the Tang onward the interludes of disorder between great dynasties proved brief. Perhaps the Chinese might have remained more innovative if imperial unity had been replaced by smaller competing states, as

[5]Poem by Wang Wei "Bird-singing Stream" as seen in *The White Pony: An Anthology of Chinese Poetry* by Robert Payne (NY: Mentor, 1960). Poem by Li Po "Joys of Wine" as seen in *The White Pony: An Anthology of Chinese Poetry* by Robert Payne (NY: Mentor, 1960).

happened in western Europe. But the Chinese came to deplore disunity. A proverb stated: "Just as there cannot be two suns in the sky, there cannot be two rulers in China." The centralized imperial system remained in place for nearly a millennium after the Tang.

SECTION SUMMARY

- The Tang Empire was marked by ambitious expansion, inclusion of visitors from around the world, and the spread of Chinese goods across Eurasia.
- Under the Tang, stability was maintained by keeping the emperor's authority somewhat in check and by rewarding high achievers through the civil service exam system.
- Buddhism reached its peak influence during the Tang, but it was greatly weakened when Emperor Wuzong seized Buddhist monasteries.
- During the Tang, the first book was printed using woodblocks.
- Poetry and other arts were very popular during the Tang; while usually stressing Daoist harmony, they sometimes expressed criticism of the government.

Song China and Commercial Growth

Why might historians consider the Song dynasty the high point of China's golden age?

The next great dynasty, the Song (Sung) (960–1279), presided over a sophisticated period of achievement. Although lacking the Tang's empire building and world leadership, the Song was in many respects more refined in the arts of living and in technological development and material richness. Described by some historians as premodern China's most exciting period, the Song was characterized by unprecedented innovation, economic dynamism, urban sophistication, and cultural flowering. Late Song China contained perhaps 120 million people, between a quarter and a third of the world's total population, living in an area that stretched a thousand miles east to west and north to south.

Cities, Economies, and Technologies

Song China boasted the world's largest cities, at least five cities having populations over a million, and nearly fifty other cities each containing over 100,000 people. Meanwhile, once-great cities in western Eurasia had fallen in population: Rome to 35,000 and Baghdad to 125,000. Chinese urban residents enjoyed a high quality of life. A modern scholar described the vibrant activity in one of the cities:

> *The day started with the booming of temple bells. Peddlers began to make their way up and down the streets, calling out the foods they had for sale. Carts laden with meats and vegetables moved in toward the markets. Businesses of all kinds opened. Many of these, such as the tailors, hairdressers, dealers in paper and brushes, and caterers, served the city's taste for*

Scroll of Kaifeng This segment from the scroll "Spring Festival on the River," discussed in the chapter opening, shows people thronging the Rainbow Bridge while boatmen lower their masts to pass under the cantilevered structure. Along the streets and bridge stalls sell their goods.

Werner Forman/Art Resource, NY

luxury. As night fell, lanterns lit up taverns and restaurants, the largest of which had staffs of hundreds. In the theater district dozens of houses offered varied bills, including the latest songs, puppet shows, acrobats, wrestlers, storytellers, and comedians.[7]

In the later Song era, when the government had been pushed south of the Yangzi River by nomadic invaders, the capital was Hangzhou **(hahng-jo)**, a city of several million on the southern end of the Grand Canal (see Witness to the Past: Life in the Chinese Capital City). A later and well-traveled Italian visitor, Marco Polo, called it unquestionably the greatest city in the world. Hangzhou would be followed by Nanjing in the fifteenth century, and then Beijing from the sixteenth into the nineteenth centuries, as the world's largest cities.

Song Economy

The Song also marked the high point for Chinese commerce and foreign trade. The merchant class grew substantially, and tax revenues were three times higher than for the Tang. The Grand Canal, which linked the Yellow and Yangzi River Basins, provided an economic cornerstone, allowing the mass movement of goods between north and south. China also developed the world's first fully monetized economy, putting paper money and silver coins into wide use. In addition, Song China had the world's most advanced farming, with expanding productivity meeting the needs for agricultural products. Farmers doubled the rice crop and vastly increased the growing and marketing of sugar, once a minor crop. While foreign trade continued to flourish, now it was based more on maritime networks that connected China to the rest of Afro-Eurasia. Chinese merchants regularly visited Southeast Asia and traded around the Indian Ocean, and Chinese industrial and food products found markets as far away as Persia, East Africa, and Egypt. The cosmopolitan southern seaports of Guangzhou (Canton) and Quanzhou (Zayton) were home to thousands of foreigners, including many Arab, Indian, Persian, and even East African merchants. To accommodate these varied peoples, the cities contained numerous mosques and Hindu temples.

Primary Source: The Craft of Farming Look inside a twelfth-century Chinese treatise on farming, with advice on when to plow, which crops to plant, and how to use compost as fertilizer.

Song China's industry was the world's most advanced. China's world leadership was reflected in its export of manufactured goods (silks, porcelain, books) and import of raw materials (spices, minerals, horses). Chinese porcelain was traded all over Asia, the Middle East, and parts of Africa, and the name *china* became synonymous with the very finest porcelain products. China's iron industry was the world's largest before the eighteenth century, producing the finest steel for tools, weapons, stoves, ploughshares, cooking equipment, nails, building materials, and bridges. Mass production and metal-casting techniques supplied standardized iron products to the world's largest internal market, and the Song mined coal for fuel and produced salt on an industrial scale. Spurred by domestic and foreign trade, Song China also developed a significant shipbuilding industry. Its huge compartmentalized ships had four decks and four to six masts and were capable of carrying five hundred sailors and extensive cargo. Thousands of cargo ships plied the rivers and canals. This maritime technology was the world's best at that time.

Technology and Science

The Song also maintained the Chinese technological and scientific tradition. Between the first and fifteenth centuries C.E., the Chinese produced a majority of the world's major inventions. For example, they built the world's longest bridge (2.5 kilometers) and expanded the use of water-powered clocks and mills. Major Chinese inventions of the era that later spread throughout Eurasia included the magnetic compass (for naval navigation), the sternpost rudder, and the spinning wheel. Song craftsmen also made movable type, first from fired clay and then from tin or copper, an invention that greatly facilitated the printing of books. In weaponry, Song technicians developed the fire lance, a bamboo tube filled with gunpowder that was the precursor of the metal-barrel gun. Song ships were fitted with missile launchers, flamethrowers, cannons, and bombs, all used to keep the coast free of pirates. Song engineers also invented a mechanized spinning process for the reeling of silk and later hemp thread. Developed over half a millennium before the Industrial Revolution began in western Europe, this was the world's first industrial machine. The Song also had notable achievements in astronomy and medicine. Today astronomers still use data the Song collected from observation of the skies, such as on the supernova that created the Crab Nebula. A Song calendar precisely measured the solar year (365.2425 days). In medicine, Chinese doctors inoculated against smallpox, a disease that ravaged much of Afro-Eurasia. Some Chinese medical ideas reached the Middle East and Europe by the thirteenth century.

Society and Religion

Men, Women, and Families

The Song also saw the development of an urbane elite culture. Printed books fostered the spread of education, exposing a wider audience to the values of the social and political elite, and the Song government established schools in every district. Although only a small percentage of these students ever became mandarins, a degree or some educated background became a certificate of status, even if it never led to a government post. The cultivated gentleman, whether or not in government service, was expected to be proficient in music (especially lute playing), chess,

WITNESS TO THE PAST

Life in the Chinese Capital City

The following excerpts are from a description of Hangzhou, the capital city of China during the southern Song dynasty, written by a Chinese observer in 1235. It reveals the life of urban people in China during one of its most creative eras. The writer describes the city's many amenities, including shops, restaurants, and taverns, and also its cultural and social activities. The many specialized enterprises and diverse clubs indicate a highly complex society.

During the morning hours, markets extend from . . . the palace all the way to . . . the New Boulevard. Here we find pearl, jade, talismans, exotic plants and fruits, seasonal catches from the sea, wild game—all the rarities of the world. . . . In the evening . . . the markets are as busy as during the day. . . . In the wine shops and inns business also thrives. . . . In general the capital attracts the greatest variety of goods and has the best craftsmen. For instance, the flower company at Superior Lane does a truly excellent job of flower arrangement, and its caps, hairpins, and collars are unsurpassed in craftsmanship. Some . . . famous fabric stores sell exquisite brocade and fine silk which are unsurpassed anywhere in the country.

Among the various kinds of wine shops, the tea-and-food shops sell not only wine, but also various foods to go with it. However, to get seasonal delicacies . . . one should go to the inns, for they also have a menu from which one can make selections. The pastry-and-wine shops sell pastries with duckling and goose fillings. . . . In the large teahouses there are usually paintings and calligraphies by famous artists on display. . . . Most restaurants here are operated by people from the old capital [Kaifeng], like the lamb rice shops which also serve wine. . . . There are special food shops such as meat-pie shops and vegetable-noodle shops. . . . The vegetarian restaurants cater to [Buddhist] religious banquets and vegetarian dinners. . . . There are also shops specializing in snacks. Depending on the season, they sell a variety of delicacies. . . . In the evening, food vendors of all sorts parade the streets and alleys . . . chanting their trade songs. . . .

The entertainment centers . . . are places where people gather. . . . In these centers there are schools for musicians offering thirteen different courses, among which the most significant is opera. . . . In each scene of an operatic performance there are four or five performers who first act out a short, well known piece. . . . Then they give a performance of the opera itself. . . . The opera is usually based on history and teaches a moral lesson, which may also be a political criticism in disguise. . . . There are always various acting troupes performing, and this usually attracts a large crowd.

For men of letters, there is a unique West Lake Poetry Society. Its members include both scholars residing in the capital and visiting poets from other parts of the country; over the years, many famous poets have been associated with this society. . . . Other groups include the Physical Fitness Club, Angler's Club, Occult Club, Young Girl's Chorus, Exotic Foods Club, Plants and Fruits Club, Antique Collector's Club, Horse-Lover's Club, and Refined Music Society. . . .

There are civil and military schools inside . . . the capital. Besides lineage schools, capital schools, and country schools, there are at least one or two village schools, family schools, private studios, or learning centers in every neighborhood.

THINKING ABOUT THE READING

1. What do the main goods sold in the markets say about economic prosperity?
2. What does the reading tell us about popular pleasures and entertainments in Hangzhou?
3. What do the main recreational and educational activities available suggest about leisure time and societal values?

Source: Reprinted with permission of The Free Press, a Division of Simon & Schuster Inc., from CHINESE CIVILIZATION AND SOCIETY, A Sourcebook, Second Revised & Expanded Edition by Patricia Buckley Ebrey.

calligraphy, poetry, and painting. Although Song commercial growth allowed women to operate restaurants and sell fish and vegetables in markets, women experienced more restrictions than they had known earlier. Tang paintings and statues had shown aristocratic women in swept-up hair riding horses or standing dignified, wearing loose-fitting gowns. Now, however, women's status began to decline. Fearing that the new economic opportunities for women might undermine patriarchy, conservatives sought to limit women's roles. Men more often took concubines (official mistresses) in addition to their official wives, and families increasingly frowned upon remarriage for widows. Peasant wives had the most equitable position because they worked in the fields alongside men and were therefore crucial to family economic livelihood. Still, children belonged to the father's family, and the wife was ruled by her husband's mother. Divorce was possible but uncommon because it was a disgrace for the woman. In addition, old age was especially difficult for poor women, as a male Song writer sympathetically described:

> *For women who live a long life, old age is especially hard to bear, because most women must rely on others for their existence. Some wives with stupid husbands are able to manage the family's finances. But the most remarkable are the women who manage a household after their husbands have died leaving them with young children.*[8]

Still another source of suffering for women was footbinding, which was introduced during the Song period among the elite and some of the common folk. Mothers tightly bound the feet of five- or six-year-old daughters to prevent normal growth, crippling a girl's feet and giving her a dainty walk, which enhanced what Chinese men viewed as her beauty and eroticism. But many peasants rejected the practice as too physically debilitating, since women's labor was necessary for family survival. Footbinding was not widespread until later dynasties.

neo-Confucianism A form of Confucianism arising in China during the Song period (960–1279) that incorporated many Buddhist and Daoist metaphysical ideas.

qi In Chinese thought, the energizing force pervading the universe.

The Song also saw the rise of **neo-Confucianism**, a form of Confucianism that incorporated many Buddhist and Daoist metaphysical ideas. Neo-Confucianism was associated particularly with Zhu Xi (JOO shee) (1130–1200), a child prodigy and one of the most influential thinkers in Chinese history, who resigned from government service in disgust at corruption. Zhu Xi believed that the original ideas of Confucius had become rigid and altered over the centuries, and he advocated rediscovering the essence of the sage's ideas. The influence of Daoism can be seen in Zhu Xi's rational and humane approach, which recognized a dualism between the material world and the energy thought by Chinese to pervade the universe, or **qi** (ch'i). Harnessing this qi for personal centering became the goal of *tai qi* (tai ch'i), exercises to build mind and body. In the spirit of Confucius, Zhu identified reason or principle as the unchanging law, and morality as the measure of all human affairs: "For every person the most important thing is the cultivation of himself as an ethical being."[9] However, because Zhu was indifferent to natural science, his ideas did not help sustain scientific inquiry. Over time neo-Confucianism became the dominant mindset of China's educated elite and a force for stability but not innovation.

The Song in World History

Barriers to Chinese Transformation

Although in many ways the Song could have been a turning point in Chinese and world history, they did not foster a major transition. The profound economic, technological, and urban developments remind some historians of eighteenth-century Europe at the dawn of rapid industrialization. But unlike that revolution's transforming impact in the West, the commercial and agricultural dynamism never revolutionized Chinese society. Instead, these developments were contained and absorbed. For example, the Chinese had the technology to sail the seas and colonize other lands, but they lacked the incentive because China was largely self-sufficient. Since the highly bureaucratic empire easily adjusted to economic change, it could keep the merchants from disrupting China's social order. With an agriculture productive enough to feed a huge population, convenient transportation by water through canals, and many natural resources, the Chinese had no great need to develop additional mechanized technologies. The Mongol conquest of the Song, as well as a cooler climate by the thirteenth century and the Black Death pandemic in the fourteenth, also undermined economic dynamism. Finally, population pressure became a growing burden as land available for farming filled up.

Confucian disdain of merchants also led to stagnation. In its domination of the merchants, the imperial government played a central role in containing economic growth. Song commercial growth resulted partly from the influence of unusually large number of mandarins from wealthy merchant families in this period. Yet, many essential commodities remained government monopolies, such as iron, grain, cloth, and salt, while public granaries to check famine were financed by taxes on the wealthy. This socialist policy reflected the low esteem accorded merchants in Confucian ideology. Monopolies over essential products enriched the state and protected the population from price and supply problems, but they restricted merchants to handling nonessential products.

The Song government, more interested in economic than political growth and empire, was generally disinterested in military expansion. Prosperity, trade, and urban living made peace more attractive than conquest. Although maintaining the world's largest army, the Song, unlike the Han and Tang, reduced the power of military leaders so they could not threaten civilian authority, a chronic problem in the Tang. As a result, the Song adopted a passive attitude toward controlling the pastoral nomads across the border, attempting not to conquer but to appease them with generous payments. Ultimately the policy failed. In the twelfth century a nomadic people, the Jin (Chin), conquered northern China, forcing the Song court to move south across the Yangzi, where it continued to rule central and southern China from Hangzhou until the invasion by the Mongols.

SECTION SUMMARY

- The Song dynasty was notable for its bustling urban life, its maritime trade, and its advanced economy.
- Song China made great advances in the manufacture of porcelain, ships, and bridges and in the prevention of disease.
- During the Song, the pursuit of education and cultivation became widespread among the elite.
- However, the status of women declined, and footbinding began to be practiced by the elite and some commoners.
- The Song's achievements did not lead to a major historical transition because China at this time felt self-sufficient, was not interested in conquest, and kept merchants out of important industries; it also tried to deal with neighboring pastoral nomads peacefully, a strategy that ultimately failed.

Mongol Conquest, Chinese Resurgence, and Eurasian Connections

How did China change during the Yuan and Ming dynasties?

From the thirteenth through the nineteenth centuries the Chinese way of life showed great stability. Three ruling houses held power between the downfall of the Song and the end of the imperial system in the twentieth century, an almost unprecedented record of political stability, perhaps matched only by that of the ancient Egyptian kingdoms. Two of the three dynasties were conquest dynasties imposed by non-Chinese nomadic peoples riding in on horseback. The two dynasties that held power between the thirteenth and seventeenth centuries were the Yuan **(yu-wenn)**, established by invading Mongols, and the Ming, which marked a return to Chinese rule.

The Mongol Empire and the Conquest of China

Central Asian Pastoralists

For several millennia the Chinese had feared what they considered the "barbarian" scourge, fast-riding horsemen who came out of the Central Asian grasslands and deserts killing, looting, and taking captives. The strongest rulers could control these nomadic tribal peoples by conquest or effective divide-and-rule diplomacy. The ever-present Central Asian influence on China's political life was based on the close proximity of the arid grasslands north and west of China, which, compared to the lush farmlands of China, were suitable only for mobile herding. These contrasting environments had produced very different societies. In the grasslands a pastoral economy and few resources necessitated seasonal migration and chronic poverty for the tough, self-reliant herding people. When China was weak, the Great Wall proved no major barrier to peoples anxious to taste China's affluence. In the thirteenth century the Chinese realized their worst nightmare when a new confederation of warlike peoples, the Mongols, conquered all of China.

Mongol Expansion

Before invading China the Mongols conquered much of Eurasia, including eastern Europe and western Asia. Traditionally divided into often feuding tribes, the Mongols became united under Temuchin (ca. 1167–1227), a ruthless but brilliant man of humble origins who defeated or co-opted his rivals and then changed his name to Genghis Khan **(GENG-iz KAHN)** ("Universal Emperor"). He had simple motives: "A man's greatest pleasure is to defeat his enemies, to drive them before him, to take from them that which they possessed, to see those whom they cherished in tears, to ride their horses, to hold their wives and daughters in his arms."[10] Skilled horse soldiers, more agile than their foes, the Mongols were formidable opponents. Their well-organized fighting units possessed powerful bows that could kill at 600 feet, disc-shaped stirrups that gave the rider maneuverability, and the world's most advanced siege weaponry, including catapults. Because of China's strength, it was one of the last countries to fall to Mongol control. Genghis Khan had conquered parts of northern China in 1215. The Mongol conquest of the rest of China, which came fifty years after the death of Genghis, was accomplished by his grandson, Khubilai Khan **(koo-bluh KAHN)** (r. 1260–1294), who created a new dynasty, the Yuan (1279–1368). China became, for the first and only time, part of a great world empire, one that stretched from eastern Europe to Korea and from the Black Sea to the Pacific Ocean (see Map 11.2 and the essay at the end of Part III).

The Yuan Dynasty

The Mongols imposed a distinctive government system and fostered new cultural forms in China. By Mongol standards Khubilai Khan was a rather enlightened ruler, far less cruel and more pragmatic than most of the Mongol leaders elsewhere in Eurasia. He patronized Buddhism, built granaries for food storage, operated an efficient postal system, and improved the transportation network. But Chinese historians have condemned Khubilai Khan for the sins committed by the Mongols generally, such as maintaining Mongol cultural identity and actively resisting assimilation into Chinese society. Later Chinese viewed the Yuan as China's darkest hour, an intolerable rule by aliens who would not be absorbed. Khubilai Khan moved the capital to Beijing ("Northern Capital"), before this a provincial city close to the Great Wall but situated alongside the major highways leading north and west. Except for brief periods since, Beijing has remained the capital of China, politically eclipsing more ancient cities like Chang'an and Hangzhou.

The Mongols mistrusted and did not patronize intellectuals, but they were tolerant in religious matters. They invited missionaries from all over Eurasia to come to the court for religious debates, among them Christians of various sects (including Catholics); Khubilai Khan's mother was a Nestorian Christian. Khubilai Khan ruled over a religiously diverse society and wanted to avoid conflict. Indeed, China was far more accepting of religious diversity than Christian Europe. However, the Mongols had more rigid gender expectations and marriage practices than the Chinese, stressing

Map 11.2 China in the Mongol Empire
After the Mongols conquered much of Central Asia, western Asia, and eastern Europe, they added China and Korea to their huge empire, the largest contiguous land empire in world history. During the Mongol era many Asians and some Europeans, including the Italian Marco Polo, visited or worked in China.

e Interactive Map

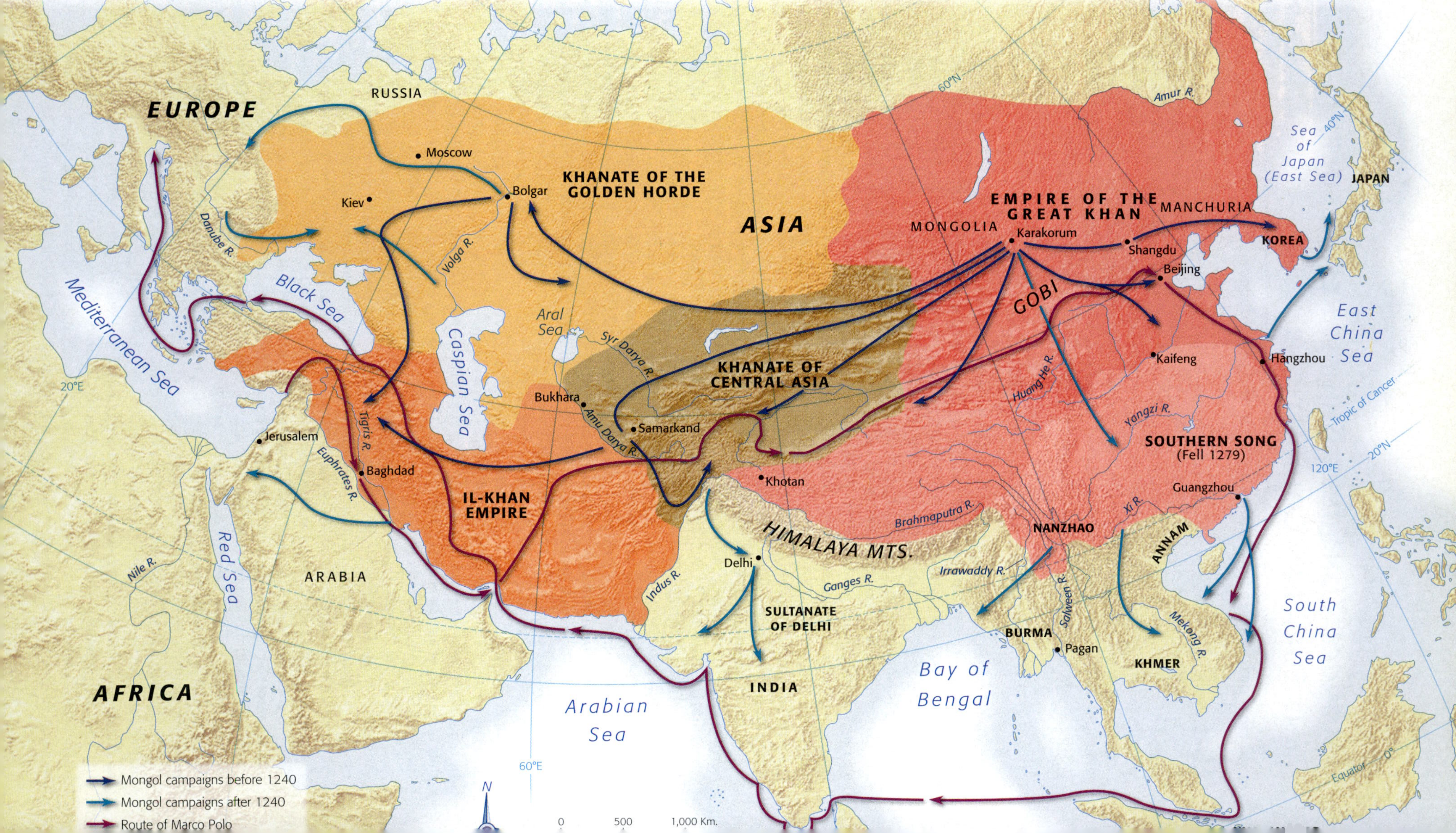

National Palace Museum, Taipei, Taiwan

Khubilai Khan and His Entourage Hunting This painting by a Chinese artist of the time shows Khubilai Khan, dressed in ermine, and Mongol colleagues, including a woman, hunting on horseback, a popular activity among Mongols.

the need for widows to remain chaste and dutifully serve their aging parents-in-law. Chinese men now also expected women to remain at home and emphasize feminine behavior, including the growing fashion of tightly bound feet to set them apart from non-Chinese women.

Mongol China and Eurasian Networks

The Mongols paved the way for enhanced global communication, opening China's doors to the world. By protecting the Silk Road, the Mongols revived networks for the exchange of goods, ideas, and technologies between East and West. Chinese inventions like gunpowder, printing, the blast furnace for cast iron, silk-making machinery, paper money, and playing cards moved westward. Bubonic plague, which killed millions of Chinese during Mongol rule, also traveled the overland trade routes, fostering the Black Death that ravaged the Middle East and Europe in the fourteenth century (see Chapters 10 and 14). Many foreigners came to Mongol China by land and sea. Although Khubilai Khan attempted to win Chinese support by modeling his government along Chinese lines and dutifully performing Confucian rites, the Mongols failed to get the cooperation of most scholars and bureaucrats. To rule the vast country, they were forced to rely administratively on foreigners who came to China to serve in what was effectively an international civil service. These included many Muslims from Central Asia, western Asia, and North Africa, as well as a few Europeans who found their way to "fabled Cathay," as they called China.

Marco Polo in China

One of the European visitors was the Italian merchant Marco Polo (ca. 1254–1324), who, with his father and uncle, initially went to China seeking trade goods but spent seventeen years there, mostly in government service. Eventually Polo returned to Italy and told of the wonders he had encountered (or heard about from other travelers). Europeans, few of whom knew much about the world east of Palestine, were unbelieving. Most dismissed Polo's book as full of lies, but the general accuracy of his account has been confirmed by historians. He was a keen observer and recorded the resentment of the Chinese people toward the Mongols, who once slaughtered a city's entire population for the killing of one drunk Mongol soldier. Polo wrote of China's great cities, such as Beijing and Hangzhou. Standing along the shores of beautiful West Lake, Hangzhou could not help but charm the Italian. Polo wrote in the thirteenth century that "the city is beyond dispute the finest and noblest in the world in point of grandeur and beauty as well as in its abundant delights. The natives of this city are of peaceful character, thoroughly honest and truthful and accustomed to dainty living."[11] The city boasted parks, a fire department, garbage collection, a pollution-control agency, and paved streets—all things nonexistent in Polo's much smaller Venice, then one of the major European cities. Indeed, China in this era was far more developed in many fields than the rest of Eurasia and probably had the world's highest standard of living. Polo noted, for example, that the Chinese had for a thousand years burned black stones (coal) for heat and that they took regular baths, astonishing information to medieval Europeans, who seldom if ever bathed.

Mongol Decline

While the Mongol conquests had enormous consequences for Central Asia, the Middle East, and Europe, Mongol rule in China lasted only a century and did not leave a deep imprint. Although the Mongols long dominated regions such as Russia and Turkestan, they failed to hold China. For one thing, they were always hated, and their leadership deteriorated after the death of Khubilai Khan. Furthermore, the Mongols in China lost their fighting toughness and came to desire luxury more than sacrifice. As Mongols in Central Asia and Persia adopted the cultures and religions of the conquered, Mongol unity fragmented and power struggles grew rampant. Then too, a terrible plague outbreak raged and the Yellow River flooded severely, bringing famine. Soon rebellions broke out all over China, and eventually a Chinese commoner established a new dynasty. Mongol military forces returned to Central Asia. Today Mongols venerate Genghis Khan as their greatest leader, building gawdy memorials and even a theme park to honor the conqueror.

Ming Government and Culture

The new Ming dynasty (1368–1644) fostered orderly government, social stability, and a rich culture. The founder, Zhu Yuanzhang **(JOO yu-wen-JAHNG)** (1328–1398), was a former Buddhist monk and the son of an itinerant farm worker who, like the founder of the Han, rose from abject poverty through sheer ability and ruthless behavior in a time of opportunity. Ming China's people lived for nearly three centuries in comparative peace and prosperity, with living standards among the highest and mortality rates among the lowest of anywhere in the world. During this time China more than doubled in population, from around 80 million to between 160 and 180 million.

South China University of Technology Library, Canton (Guangzhou)

A Ming Imperial Workshop Printers' shops, such as the one shown here, used movable type to publish encyclopedias with information on engineering, medicine, agriculture, and other practical topics.

The Ming installed a government similar to that of the Han and Tang but somewhat more despotic. Perhaps because of the bitter experience of Mongol rule, the Ming emperors exercised more power than earlier emperors and placed the bureaucracy under closer scrutiny, eliminating the office of prime minister, who had kept his hand on the pulse of the country. The Censorate also became more timid, reducing the checks on royal abuses. Hence, the Ming emperors became more isolated from the real world. As in previous dynasties, some Ming emperors had male lovers as well as many wives and concubines, a practice that reflected a tolerance of same-sex relationships among many Chinese court officials and commoners.

A sense of order infused the arts. Although culturally the Mongol period had proved relatively sterile, musical drama (Chinese opera) became a popular form of entertainment, appealing mostly to the Chinese common folk rather than the elite. In the Ming era, however, theater reached its highest level, with Chinese operas including extended arias and spoken dialogue. Each performance of a play aimed at harmonizing song, speech, costume, makeup, movement, and musical accompaniment. Much Chinese music was composed for operas or for ritual and ceremonial purposes. String, wind, and percussion instruments were popular, especially the flute, lute, and zither.

The Chinese began writing novels in Yuan times, an elaboration of age-old storytelling. The first novelists were intellectuals who refused to work for the Mongols but sought alternative sources of income by writing books for a popular audience. Although most Ming scholars considered fiction worthless, it had a large audience. Most novels had a Confucian moral emphasizing correct behavior, but some offered social criticisms or satires. Perhaps the greatest Ming novel, *The Water Margin* (also known as *All Men Are Brothers*), presented heroes who were also bandits, Robin Hoods driven into crime by corrupt officials. Ming authors also wrote some of the world's first detective stories. Rulers encouraged intellectual pursuits, expanding the *Hanlin* ("Forest of Culture") Academy established in the Tang. The brightest scholars were assigned there and paid to read and write whatever they liked. Ming scholars also compiled a 11,000-volume encyclopedia (with 20,000 chapters) and a 52-volume study of Chinese pharmacology.

Ming China and the Afro-Eurasian World

The early Ming rulers pursued territorial expansion, including a failed attempt to recolonize Vietnam. But China was now oriented more to the sea. Rather than send armies far into Central Asia, the emperor dispatched a series of grand maritime expeditions to southern Asia and beyond to reaffirm China's preeminence in the eastern half of Asia. Admiral Zheng He **(jung huh)** (Cheng Ho) (ca. 1371–1435), a huge man and a trusted court eunuch of Muslim faith, commanded seven voyages between 1405 and 1433. The world had never before seen such a large-scale feat of seamanship: the largest fleet comprised sixty-two vessels carrying 28,000 men, and the largest "treasure ships," as they were known, weighed 1,500 tons, were 450 feet long, boasted nine masts nearly 500 feet high, and carried a crew of five hundred. Observers must have been astounded as these ships approached their harbors. A few decades later Christopher Columbus sailed from Spain in three tiny vessels carrying a total of only about a hundred men.

Exploring the Indian Ocean World

Zheng He's extraordinary voyages carried the Chinese flag through Southeast Asia to India, the Persian Gulf, the Red Sea, and the East African coast (see Map 11.3). Had they continued, the Chinese ships could have sailed around Africa to Europe or the Americas, but they had no incentive to do so. During these voyages the Chinese undertook only a few military actions, but some thirty-six countries in southern and western Asia officially acknowledged Chinese preeminence. The ruler of the East African city of Malindi sent ambassadors bearing tribute, including a giraffe.

Historians still debate the reasons for Zheng He's great voyages. Some point to the desire to have so many foreign countries reaffirm the emperor's position as the Son of Heaven. Zheng He may also have sought to locate a deposed boy emperor who had disappeared, possibly fleeing into exile. Others suspect that the ambitious emperor wanted to demonstrate China's military capabilities. Some historians see commercial motives as primary, since these voyages occurred at a time of increased activity by Chinese merchants in Southeast Asia. During the early Ming many thousands of Chinese visited or had settled in the Philippines, Indonesia, Siam, and Vietnam, creating a closer commercial link to China, and Yuan and Ming porcelain was sold as far west as South-Central Africa.

Tribute System

Zheng He's voyages may also have revitalized the traditional tribute system, which during Han and Tang times shaped China's relations with its neighbors. China considered friendly East,

Map 11.3 The Voyages of Zheng He

After replacing the Mongols, the Ming reestablished a strong Chinese state, attempted to recolonize Vietnam, and rebuilt the Great Wall. Ming emperors also dispatched a series of grand maritime expeditions in the early 1400s that reached the Middle East and East Africa.

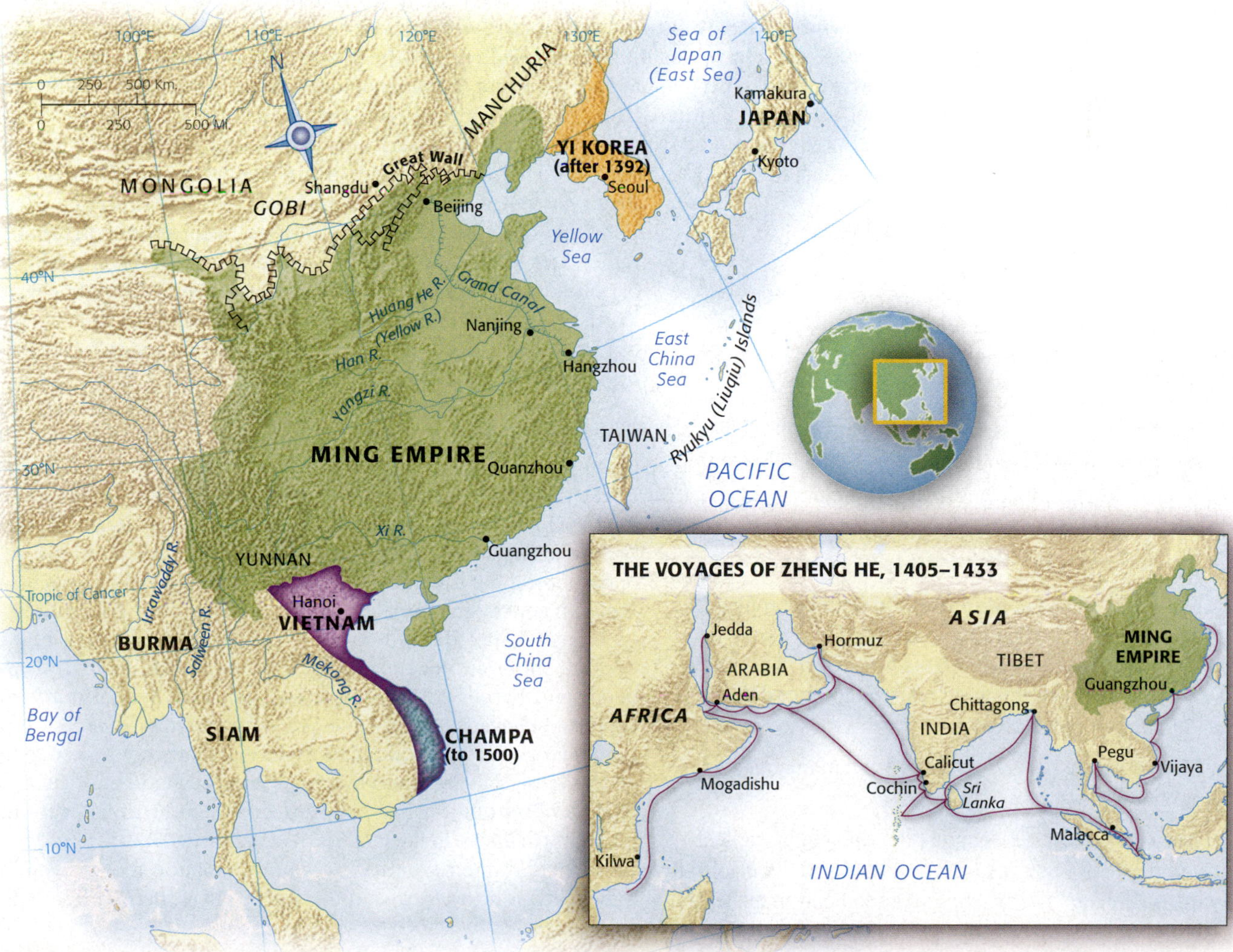

Southeast, and Central Asian states as vassals and granted them trade relations but rarely intervened to support their allies. In return the tributary states sent periodic envoys bearing gifts to the emperor, confirming his superiority in ritual form and playing along because they desired China's goodwill and trade goods. In Ming times tribute came regularly from states in Korea, Vietnam, Cambodia, Borneo, Indonesia, South Asia, and Central Asia.

Inevitably the Chinese saw themselves as the Middle Kingdom surrounded by barbarian societies. The Chinese never recognized any other society as an equal; they felt that they were superior not just materially but also culturally and that barbarians could not resist their appeal, a view reinforced when other East Asian societies borrowed from China. For the Chinese, to be civilized was to embrace Chinese culture, and a virtuous ruler, they believed, irresistibly attracted barbarians. When a tribute mission arrived in the capital, part of the rite was the **kotow**, the tribute-bearers' act of prostrating themselves before the emperor, a practice from which we get the modern English word *kowtow* ("to pander to authority"). This practice, above all others, left little doubt as to who was superior and who was inferior, reflecting a Confucian sense of hierarchy.

kotow The tribute-bearers' act of prostrating themselves before the Chinese emperor.

Ming China Turns Inward

Ending the Grand Voyages

In the early Ming, China remained perhaps the world's wealthiest and most developed country. Hindu India faced Muslim conquests, Middle Eastern societies struggled to overcome various setbacks, and western Europeans were just beginning to enjoy political and economic dynamism. Commercially vibrant and outward-thrusting, Ming China had the capability to open maritime communication between the continents and become the dominant world power. Instead China turned inward. The grand voyages and the commercial thrust to distant lands came to a sudden halt when the Ming emperor ordered them ended and outlawed Chinese emigration altogether. But some Chinese continued to illegally travel abroad for trade, and foreign merchant ships still came to China. The tribute system provided cover for extensive trade and smuggling.

The causes of the stunning reversal of official Chinese engagement with the world that, in the perspective of later history, seemed so counterproductive remain subject to debate. Perhaps Zheng He's voyages were too costly even for the wealthy Ming government. The voyages were not cost-effective, since the ships mostly returned with exotic goods rather than mineral resources and other valuable items. Unlike Christian and Muslim societies, the Chinese lacked any missionary zeal, having little interest in spreading Chinese religion and culture except to near neighbors such as Vietnam. Furthermore, despite their flourishing guilds and frequent wealth, the merchants held a low status in the Confucian social system. Ming leaders were convinced that profit was evil, and mercantile interests inevitably conflicted with political ones. Confucian officials often despised the merchants, and a later Ming scholar wrote that "one in a hundred [Chinese] is rich, while nine out of ten are impoverished. The poor cannot stand up to the rich. The lord of silver rules heaven and the god of copper cash reigns over the earth."[12] Hence many mandarins opposed foreign trade.

Military factors also influenced the turn inward. With the Mongols regrouping in Central Asia, the Ming court shifted its resources to defense of the northern borders and the pirate-infested Pacific coast, spending millions rebuilding and extending the Great Wall. What tourists see today of the Great Wall near Beijing is mostly work done by the Ming. In addition, military operations along the northern border and an ill-fated invasion of Vietnam generated a fiscal crisis that weakened the government.

Finally, after the bitterness of the Mongol era, the Chinese became more ethnocentric and antiforeign. China had always been land-based, self-centered, and self-sufficient. Later Ming Chinese believed that they needed nothing from outside. China remained powerful, productive, and mostly prosperous, enjoying generally high living standards, well into the eighteenth century, when profits from overseas colonies and the Industrial Revolution tipped the balance in favor of northwest Europe. By the later Ming, China had entered a period of relative isolation that was ended only by the forceful intrusion of a newly developed Europe in the early 1800s.

SECTION SUMMARY

- The ancient Chinese fear of Central Asian nomads was realized when the Mongols, under Genghis and Khubilai Khan, conquered China and established the Yuan dynasty.
- Khubilai Khan made a number of improvements in China's transportation system and moved the capital to Beijing.
- Because of lack of cooperation from Chinese scholars and bureaucrats, the Mongols established an international civil service, in which Marco Polo served.
- After the decline of the Mongols, the Chinese enjoyed three centuries of prosperity under the Ming dynasty, and their sense of well-being was displayed in Zheng He's grand sailing expeditions, which enhanced China's position among its neighbors.
- The Ming dynasty received tribute from many peoples throughout Asia.
- For reasons that are still debated, the Ming emperor suddenly ordered all overseas activity halted and China turned inward, beginning an isolation that ended only in the 1800s.

Cultural Adaptation in Korea and Japan

How did the Koreans and Japanese develop their own distinctive societies?

As the cultural heartland of East Asia, China strongly influenced its three large neighbors of Vietnam (see Chapter 13), Korea, and Japan. All derived considerable culture from China, including writing systems, philosophies, and political institutions. At the same time, they adapted these Chinese influences to their indigenous customs, retaining their cultural identity. During the second half of the Intermediate Era, the Japanese developed a very different way of life and outlook than they had enjoyed a few centuries earlier.

Korea and China

Silla Society

Several strong states emerged on the Korean peninsula. In the mid-seventh century the southern Korean state of Silla **(SILL-ah)** defeated its main rival, Koguryo, and eventually united most Koreans, but at the price of becoming a vassal of China. Political unity allowed Korean culture to become homogenized. Like earlier states, Silla also borrowed Chinese culture and institutions. Buddhism triumphed, and the Tang system became the model in government, with Confucianism used as a political ideology; many Korean monks also traveled to China. But Koreans were selective in their borrowing. The Korean social structure continued to place more emphasis than the Chinese did on inherited status instead of merit, and the gap between rich and poor was much wider than in China. Moreover, among Silla's rulers were three queens, suggesting less gender bias than in China. For example, Queen Sondok (r. 632–647) fostered science and promoted a tolerant mixing of Buddhism and shamanism. Silla women generally shared in the social status of their menfolk and enjoyed many legal rights.

During the period when Silla dominated much of the peninsula (676–935), Koreans adapted Chinese writing to their own very different spoken language, creating a distinctive literary tradition in history, religion, and poetry. To mass-produce these works, Silla craftsmen developed woodblock printing as early as China. The oldest still extant example of woodblock printing in the world, a Korean Buddhist writing, dates from 751. Koreans also studied astronomy. A great observatory built in this era is the oldest still standing in East Asia. Korea also formed connections with the rest of the world. Buddhist pilgrims came from as far away as India, and many Arabs traded or settled down there. One Arab wrote that "seldom has a stranger who has come there from Iraq or another country left it afterwards. So healthy is the air there, so pure the water, so fertile the soil and so plentiful of all good things."[13]

Koryo Society

Gradually Silla declined, damaged by elite rivalries, corruption, and peasant uprisings, and it was replaced by a new state, Koryo **(KAW-ree-oh)**, which lasted for over four centuries (935–1392). Chinese influence continued in politics and philosophy: Koreans set up an examination system, and neo-Confucianism became popular. But Koreans retained a distinctive political and social system. Korean kings, never as strong as Chinese emperors, were greatly influenced by the court, military, and aristocratic landowning families; unlike in China, Korean farming relied on large estates. The status of women also changed. In contrast to Silla, Koryo court women mainly exercised influence behind the scenes. For example, Lady Yu successfully urged her reluctant husband, Wang Kon, the founder of the Koryo dynasty, to seize power from a despotic ruler, arguing, "It is an ancient tradition to raise a banner of revolt against a tyrant. How can you, a great military leader, hesitate?"[14] While most Koryo women played a lesser role in public affairs, they took full responsibility for family affairs and farmed.

Buddhism in Korea, which assimilated many elements from animism, gradually became a powerful economic and political force. But the involvement of monks in political life fostered religious corruption and a worldly orientation that alienated some believers. As a result, although for the past 1,500 years Korea has been a nominally Buddhist society, the religion gradually lost influence. A more secular interest fostered such developments as a publishing industry; by 1234 Koreans had invented the world's first metal movable-type printing.

Choson and the Yi Dynasty

After the Mongols conquered the peninsula, Koryo became a colony in their vast empire. When Koreans resisted, the Mongols devastated the land, carrying off hundreds of thousands of captives and imposing heavy taxes on peasants. Yet, thanks to closer links to trade networks, more Chinese and western Asian learning and technology reached Korea during the Mongol era. In 1392

Map 11.4 Korea and Japan, ca. 1300
Japanese society developed in an archipelago, the major early cities rising in central Honshu. In 1274 and 1281 the Japanese repulsed Mongol invasions by sea. Throwing off the Mongols, Korea was unified under the Yi dynasty in 1392.

e Interactive Map

a new Korean dynasty took over from the Mongols, the Yi **(yee)**, whose state was known as Choson **(cho-suhn)** (see Map 11.4). They lasted until 1910, an incredible longevity of 518 years.

Yi rulers maintained a tribute relationship with China, and Koreans learned to better use Chinese social and political models. Mastery of Confucian scholarship became the road to government careers, as Confucianism provided a philosophical justification for government by a benevolent bureaucracy under a virtuous ruler. Education expanded to prepare students for the civil service exams. Confucian influence also remade Korean social institutions such as the family. Believing that Korean women had too much freedom and hence behaved immorally, the Yi encouraged women's seclusion at home and imposed arranged marriages, veiling of the face when out in public, female chastity, and strict obedience to husbands and fathers. However, commoner women, who needed to work in the fields, usually had more freedom of movement. Today Confucianism is arguably a stronger force than Buddhism, especially in rural Korea.

Yi Korea continued to develop literature, technology, and science. King Sejong **(say-jong)** (r. 1418–1450) was a particularly strong supporter of scientific progress. Respected by his people for improving the Korean economy, helping poor peasants, and prohibiting cruel punishments, Sejong wrote books on agriculture and formed a scholarly think tank, the Hall of Worthies, where Yi scholars invented a phonetic system for indicating Korean pronunciation of Chinese characters and for writing the Korean language. But Chinese was still used for serious scholarship. These years also saw a renaissance of intellectual activity and technology. Koreans created the world's first rain gauges, which were installed throughout the country to keep accurate rainfall records. Choson remained among the more creative of the late Intermediate Afro-Eurasian societies.

Japan in the Nara Era

Although adopting many Chinese and Korean influences, Japan, like Korea, produced a highly distinctive society. In the mid-sixth century the Japanese embarked on three centuries of deliberate cultural borrowing from China, creating a robust, expansive, and sophisticated society. The changes began with the *Taika* **(TIE-kah)** ("Great Change") reform of 646 C.E., which the rulers hoped would transform Japan into a centralized empire on the Tang model, establishing a governmental system made to resemble, on the surface at least, the Chinese centralized bureaucracy. The Japanese now used the Chinese writing system. The adoption of Buddhism from China also brought with it a rich constellation of art and architecture.

Nara and the Tang

The high point of conscious borrowing from China (710–784) takes its name from Nara **(NAH-rah)**, Japan's first capital city, which was built on the model of the Tang capital, Chang'an (see Chronology: Korea and Japan During the Intermediate Era). Nara had a population of some twenty thousand, while the total Japanese population was probably 5 or 6 million. During the Nara period land was nationalized in the name of the emperor and, using Tang models, reallocated on an equal basis to the peasants. In return, the peasants paid a land and labor tax. This system was abandoned as unworkable after a few decades, but it illustrated that in agrarian societies land control is the key to political power, a fact demonstrated vividly throughout Japanese history.

dyarchy A form of dual government that began in Japan during the Nara period (710–784), whereby one powerful family ruled the country while the emperor held mostly symbolic power.

Although these changes were designed to strengthen imperial authority, the Japanese emperor never became an unchallenged and activist Chinese-style ruler. Powerful aristocrats maintained control of the bureaucracy and also retained large tax-exempt landholdings. In practice Japan became a **dyarchy**, a form of dual government whereby one powerful family filled the highest government posts and dominated the emperors, whose power was mostly symbolic.

Courtesy, Yushin Yoo

King Sejong This modern painting portrays the Yi dynasty King Sejong, revered by Koreans for his political, economic, and scientific achievements, observing stars, supervising book printing, and contemplating a musical instrument he commissioned. Sejong patronized learning, supported agricultural innovations that increased crop yields, introduced humane laws, and fostered economic growth.

The emperors passed their lives in luxurious seclusion, guaranteeing an unbroken succession through having sons. This dyarchical system remained the pattern in Japan into the nineteenth century.

Nara leaders promoted aspects of Chinese culture but blended them with Japanese traditions. The rituals and ceremonies of the imperial court, largely based on Tang Chinese models, included stately dances and orchestral music using Japanese versions of Chinese musical instruments such as the flute, lute, and zither. They are still maintained at the Japanese court. More significantly, the Chinese written language gained great prestige, and Chinese ideographs were adapted to Japan's very different nontonal spoken language, in what must have been a difficult conversion process. Chinese literary forms, including poetry and calligraphy, became popular.

Religion and Culture

The Japanese also adopted and reshaped Chinese philosophical and religious doctrines that they found appealing. They modified Confucianism's ethical and political doctrines to suit their own social structure. They also borrowed Mahayana Buddhism, whose world-view that all things are impermanent greatly influenced their art and literature. Many artists and poets focused on the passage of time and the changing of the seasons. But the Japanese also retained their original animist religion known today as Shinto, a kind of nature worship. Shinto and Buddhism addressed different needs and easily blended into a synthesis. The deities of Shinto were not gods but beautiful natural phenomena such as Mt. Fuji **(FOO-jee)**, waterfalls, thunder, or stately trees. Shinto also stressed ritual purity, encouraging bathing and personal cleanliness. It offered no coherent theology or moral doctrine, no concept of death or an afterlife.

Economic unrest characterized the late Nara period. Peasants resented forced labor and military conscription, which often resulted in economic ruin. Many abandoned their fields, becoming wandering *ronin* **(ROH-neen)** ("wave people"), some of whom were hired by large landowners as workers. To stop people from becoming ronin, the government abolished compulsory service and gave the responsibility for police and defense to local officials. Eventually the ronin these officials hired as troops were transformed into the provincial warrior class, whose activities reshaped Japanese life.

Heian Cultural Renaissance

The imitation and direct cultural borrowing from China came to an end during the Heian **(HAY-en)** period (794–1184). After the capital moved from Nara to Heian, or Kyoto, 28 miles north, Japan gradually returned to relative isolation. The leaders discontinued foreign contacts in the ninth century and set about consciously absorbing and adapting the Chinese cultural patterns imported during the Nara era under the slogan "Chinese learning, Japanese spirit." Buddhism gradually harmonized with Shinto beliefs while generating new sects, art, and temple building. A rich and unique court society arose that fostered a distinctly Japanese writing system, literary styles, arts, and world-view. The

CHRONOLOGY
Korea and Japan During the Intermediate Era

646 Taika reforms in Japan

668 Destruction of Koguryo

676–935 Domination of Korea by Silla

710–784 Nara period in Japan

794–1184 Heian period in Japan

935–1392 Unification of Korea by Koryo

1180–1333 Kamakura Shogunate in Japan

1274, 1281 Mongol invasions of Japan

1338–1568 Ashikaga Shogunate in Japan

1392–1910 Yi dynasty in Korea

kana A Japanese phonetic script developed in the Heian period (794–1184) that consisted of some forty-seven syllabic signs derived from Chinese characters.

modification of Chinese influence was exemplified in the development of **kana** **(KAH-nah)**, a phonetic script consisting of forty-seven syllabic signs derived from Chinese characters. Now Japanese could write their language phonetically, allowing more freedom of expression, especially when the kana letters were combined with Chinese characters. The Japanese written language of today combines the two systems.

Heian elite culture, a world enormously remote from us today in time, attitudes, and behavior, reached its high point around 1000 C.E. It flourished among a very small group of privileged families in Kyoto, which then had a population of around 100,000. Many elite residents derived their incomes from bureaucratic jobs and land ownership. The Kyoto aristocracy, extraordinarily withdrawn from the outside world, created a culture governed by standards of form and beauty in which the distinction between art and life was not clearly made. Passionately concerned with their social rank, they created some of Japan's greatest literature and art, admiring nothing so much as the ability to write in an artistic hand, compose a graceful poem, and create an elegant costume. The finest energies went into creating beauty, such as putting together harmonious syllables and lines of ink on the page or perfumes on the body. The Heian period was probably unique in world history for the careful attention spent in choosing an undergarment, or the time writing a love note, with perhaps a tastefully faded chrysanthemum to emphasize the melancholy nature of the contents. The superficial Heian aristocrats were not interested in pure intellect or social morality but were obsessed by mood, especially the sense of the transience of beauty.

Women's Roles

Women from affluent families had their highest position in Japanese history during the Heian era. Romantic affairs and sexual promiscuity were acceptable for both men and women. Aristocratic women spent their days playing games, writing diaries, listening to romantic stories, or practicing art. Some women, such as the novelist Lady Murasaki **(MUR-uh-SAH-kee)**, gained a formal education and wrote because, without demanding jobs, they had abundant free time and could focus on their feelings (see Profile: Lady Murasaki, Heian Novelist). A poet might deftly turn a scene of nature into one of emotion: "The flowers withered, their color faded away, while meaninglessly, I spent my days in the world, and the long rains were falling."[15]

The Heian aristocracy saw love as an art to be cultivated. People wrote poems before meeting their lover and then the next morning following their meeting. Here are two morning-after poems from the diary of a prominent woman writer, Izumi Shikibu:

> *Woman: "painful though it were, to see you leave before dawn [to avoid discovery], better by far than when the dawn's grey light, so cruelly tears you from my side." Prince: "to leave you while the leaves are moist with dew, is bitterer by far, than if I were to say farewell at night, without a single chance to show my love."*[16]

Heian women wore their hair long to the ground, applied white skin powder and lipstick, plucked their eyebrows, and blackened their teeth with dye. In one novel, a lady refuses to do these things, and her attendants are disgusted: "Those eyebrows of hers, like hairy caterpillars, aren't they; and her teeth—like peeled caterpillars."[17] Men also used cosmetics and were equally concerned with their personal dress and appearance.

Heian Decline

Heian culture was perhaps too removed from real life to survive. Only a tiny fraction of Japan's population could afford to enjoy this hedonistic way of life. The common people outside Kyoto lived vastly different lives, usually working at bare subsistence levels as farmers and craftsmen. They were mostly illiterate and saddled by unremitting work, and most knew nothing of Heian court life or Chinese literature. Heian aristocrats called the provinces "uncivilized, barbarous, wretched" places.[18] The late Heian literature shows a growing pessimism as the Kyoto elite became aware that their world of aesthetic perfection might soon vanish. Such indeed was the case. Social and economic changes were clearing the path for a more decentralized system as powerful regional families gained considerable wealth and began building up their own warrior bands, based on kinship and vassal ties to their lord, to keep the peace. By the twelfth century the Heian era had ended and Japan had moved into a new phase of its history with a much different social system.

The Warrior Class and a New Japanese Society

The Heian aristocracy served as a transmitter of the now fully assimilated residue of Chinese culture to another vigorous group, the provincial warrior class, in whose hands the future of Japan was to lie. This warrior class gradually became the dominant force in Japanese politics

LADY MURASAKI, HEIAN NOVELIST

Women produced much of the best Heian literature. The greatest of the books was *The Tale of Genji*, the world's first psychological novel, written by a lady-in-waiting, Lady Murasaki (Murasaki Shibiku), beginning around 1008. Murasaki worked as the maid to Empress Akiko, who was a consort of the emperor and the daughter of a political leader. We know only a little of Murasaki's life, much of it from a diary she kept. She was born around 978 into a leading aristocratic family steeped in literature. Her grandfather was a famed poet and her father a provincial governor. Her father apparently lamented that she had not been a boy and allowed her to study. Murasaki's writing showed that she was familiar with Chinese history, literature, and poetry and had a considerable education. Indeed, she criticized young people who expected good jobs without undergoing the appropriate training.

Perhaps because she avidly pursued learning, she was married late, at age twenty, but her much older husband died only a few years later from illness. She had at least two children, including a daughter who later became a well-known writer. Murasaki is believed to have died sometime between 1025 and 1031, perhaps after several years as a Buddhist nun. Her self-description in her diary suggests an introverted woman:

> *Pretty yet shy, unsociable, fond of old tales, conceited, so wrapped up in poetry that other people hardly exist, spitefully looking down on the whole world—such is the unpleasant opinion that people have of me. Yet when they come to know me they say that I am strangely gentle, quite unlike what they had been led to believe.*

Murasaki's novel, *The Tale of Genji*, is much more sophisticated in language and thoughtful in sensibility than the literature that came before in Japan. In *Genji* she made contemporary language rather than the formal Chinese writing style a medium for art. Even today words and phrases from *Genji* are common in Japanese language. She also had other goals, claiming that the novel should always have "a definite and serious purpose." In focusing on the emotional and psychological interplay of her characters, her writing betrays a strongly feminine perspective. *Genji* also constitutes a treasure trove on social history, revealing much about the times.

The engaging *Genji* story chronicles the life and amorous adventures of Prince Genji, the son of an emperor and a model for all the qualities of taste and refinement admired by the Kyoto aristocracy. Genji is an accomplished poet, painter, dancer, musician, and athlete. But his supreme gift is the art most prized: "pillowing" (lovemaking). Genji and his friends devote little time to their government jobs. They spend their days largely in the search for pleasure, attend countless ceremonial functions, recite poetry endlessly, and move from one romantic affair to another. The mood of the novel is subdued melancholy and nostalgia for the passing of lovely things. Both men and women freely express their emotions. Hence, Genji shows a keen sensitivity to nature: "I hope that I shall have a little time left for things which I really enjoy—flowers, autumn leaves, the sky, all those day-to-day changes and wonders that a single year brings forth; that is what I look forward to." The novel ends with Genji making plans to give up his posts and retire to a mountain village, perhaps to continue with his poetry, music, and painting while focusing more on religious knowledge.

Lady Murasaki This eighteenth-century painting of Lady Murasaki writing while observing the moon reflected the styles of the artist's times but also suggests the continuing significance of the beloved Heian era writer.

THINKING ABOUT THE PROFILE

1. What sort of background did Murasaki come from?
2. Why is *Genji* such an important work of literature?

Notes: Quotations from Ivan Morris, *The World of the Shining Prince* (New York: Kodansha, 1994), 251; Ryusaku Tsunoda et al., eds., *Sources of Japanese Tradition*, vol. 2 (New York: Columbia University Press, 1958), 178–179; and Mikiso Hane, *Japan: A Historical Survey* (New York: Charles Scribner's, 1972), 56.

and society, helping to produce a very different Japanese government and culture. Rural society was changing. Powerful, land-hungry families and Buddhist communities were often able to seize land by force. By gaining tax exemptions, they increased the tax load on peasants, some of whom fled to the north or joined roving bands of unattached ronin. Other peasants signed over themselves and their lands to lords of manors, at the cost of becoming bound to the land and supplying food in exchange for protection. Thus the Heian era estates were replaced by a system in which a lord ruled over the villages on his parcel of land. By the end of the twelfth century, tax-paying land amounted to 10 percent or less of the total cultivated area, and local power had been taken over by the new rural aristocracy. Soldiers and ronin signed on as military retainers to aristocratic families headed by mounted warriors. Since conscription had ended earlier, imperial forces were weak, and political and military power dispersed to rural areas. Periodic fighting resulted in part from overpopulation: too many people competing for control of too little good land.

Rural Society

This warrior class led Japan into a type of social and political organization more like that of Zhou China or medieval Europe than the centralized Tang state. Historians disagree as to when between the twelfth and fourteenth centuries the transition to a new Age of Warriors was completed, but it continued in some form to the nineteenth. During this time, military, political, and economic power all became defined in terms of rights to land and relations between lords and vassals. Despite many similarities between post-Heian Japan and medieval Europe, the Japanese rulers were at times stronger than most European kings.

Warrior Society

samurai ("one who serves") A member of the Japanese warrior class, which gained power between the twelfth and fourteenth centuries and continued until the nineteenth.

Bushido ("Way of the Warrior") An idealized ethic for the Japanese samurai.

The warrior class, or **samurai** (SAH-moo-rie) ("one who serves"), who gradually assumed military supremacy over the emperor and the court, resulted from a relationship formed between the rural lords and their military retainers, based on an idealized feudal ethic later known as **Bushido** (boo-SHEE-doh) ("way of the warrior"), which was not completely developed until the seventeenth century. The samurai had two great ideals: loyalty to leaders, and absolute indifference to all physical hardship. They enjoyed special legal and ceremonial rights and in return were expected to give unquestioning service to their lords. Although only a few women of the samurai class engaged in combat, most received some martial arts training. Their main job was to run and defend the family estates.

Although the samurai occupied the highest level of the social system, they were a small percentage of the population. If a samurai failed to do his duty or achieve his purpose, suicide was a purposeful and honorable act that served as conclusive evidence that here was a man who could be respected by friend and enemy alike for his physical courage, determination, and sincerity. Homosexuality was also common among the samurai, as among several other warrior castes in history, such as the Spartans in classical Greece, perhaps because of male bonding and an ethic extolling male values. However, Japanese society generally tolerated same-sex relationships. Such unique cultural patterns as Zen Buddhism and the tea ceremony also rose to prominence among the samurai class.

The Shogunates and Economic Change

Kamakura Shogunate

shogun ("barbarian-subduing generalissimo") A Japanese military dictator controlling the country in the name of the emperor.

By the twelfth century Japan was controlled by competing bands of feudal lords, and a civil war broke out between two powerful families and their respective allies. One lord, Minamoto-no-Yoritomo (MIN-a-MO-to-no-YOR-ee-TO-mo), emerged victorious and set up a military government in Kamakura (kah-mah-KOO-rah), near Tokyo (TOE-kee-oh), which lasted from 1180 to 1333. The emperor commissioned him **shogun** (SHOW-guhn) ("barbarian-subduing generalissimo"), in effect a military dictator controlling the country in the name of the emperor, who remained in seclusion in Kyoto. The shogun was responsible for internal and external defense of the realm, and he also had the right to nominate his own successor. No shogun seriously attempted to abolish the imperial house, which had become politically impotent but symbolized the people and the land. The Kamakura shoguns, nominally subordinate to the emperors, had real power, but before 1600 the system was not very centralized.

During the Kamakura Shogunate the Mongols failed twice, in 1274 and 1281, to invade Japan. The 1281 Mongol attempt involved up to 150,000 men transported by over 4,000 conscripted Chinese ships, some armed with ceramic projectile bombs, the world's first known seagoing exploding projectiles. On both occasions, the Mongol armies landed, met fierce resistance, and were destroyed when great storms scattered and shipwrecked their fleets. These divine winds, or *kamikaze* **(KAHM-i-KAHZ-ee)**, convinced the Japanese of special protection by the gods, and any inferiority complex toward China ended. Japan was not successfully invaded and defeated until 1945.

In 1333 the Kamakura Shogunate dissolved through intrigues and civil wars and was replaced by a government headed by the Kyoto-based Ashikaga **(ah-shee-KAH-gah)** family (1338–1568). But the Ashikaga shoguns never had much real power beyond the capital. Political power became increasingly decentralized as local lords struggled to obtain more land, leading to the rise of several hundred landowning territorial magnates called **daimyo (DIE-MYO)** ("great name"). Each daimyo monopolized local power, had his supporting samurai, and derived income from the peasants working on his land.

Ashikaga Shogunate

daimyo ("great name") Large landowning territorial magnates who monopolized local power in Japan beginning during the Ashikaga period (1338–1568).

Between 1200 and 1500 Japan experienced rapid change in both economic and political spheres. Agriculture became more productive, and an increasingly active merchant class lived in the fast-growing towns. The Japanese developed a new interest in foreign trade, and Japanese sailors and merchants traveled to China and Southeast Asia. The rigid political and social system strained to accommodate these new energies. In the next century civil war and the arrival of European merchants and Christian missionaries aggravated these problems and resulted in a dramatic modification of the political system.

Japanese Society, Religion, and Culture

The new Japanese society and culture, shaped by the warrior class, reflected an even more rigid structure than before. Inequality started in the family, headed by a patriarchal male: children owed obedience to their parents, and the young honored the old. Women now commonly moved into their husband's household and were expected to be dutiful, obedient, and loyal to their menfolk. Marriages were arranged for the interest of the family, not from romantic love. While women lost some freedom, marriage became more durable and divorce more difficult, giving married women more security. Aristocratic women dominated the imperial court staff and ran the emperor's household. As in China, the interest of the group always took precedence over that of the individual.

Many Buddhist sects emerged, but three became the most significant. The largest, the *Pure Land,* emphasized prayer and faith for salvation, stressed the equality of all believers, and was very popular among the lower classes. It also rejected the notion of reincarnation, maintaining that believers went straight to nirvana. The *Nicheren* **(NEE-chee-ren)** sect has sometimes been compared to Christianity and Islam because of its militant proselytizing and concern for the afterlife. Whereas most Japanese Buddhist sects were peaceful and tolerant, Nicheren was angry, seeing rival views as heresy. The third major Buddhist sect, **Zen**, which originated in China under Daoist influence, emphasized meditation, individual practice and discipline, self-control, self-understanding, and intuition. Knowledge came from seeking deep into the mind, rather than from outside assistance. One Zen pioneer wrote, "Great is mind. Heaven's height is immeasurable but Mind goes beyond heaven; the earth's depth is unfathomable, but Mind reaches below the earth. Mind travels outside the macrocosm."[19] Zen practitioners expected enlightenment to come in a flash of understanding. The Zen culture was devised over the centuries to bring people in touch with their nonverbal, nonrational side. It stressed simplicity and restraint, contending that "great mastery is as if unskillful."[20]

Japanese Buddhism

Zen A form of Japanese Buddhism called the meditation sect because it emphasizes individual practice and discipline, self-control, self-understanding, and intuition.

Religious perspectives affected the arts. Zen values permeate Japanese rock gardens, landscape gardening, and flower arrangements. Gardens, ponds, and buildings, such as the beautiful Golden Pavilion of Kyoto, built in the thirteenth century, were all constructed in harmony with their natural surroundings. The tea ceremony emphasized patience, restraint, serenity, and the beauty of simple action involving the commonplace, that is, preparing and drinking tea. The highly formalized ceremony could last two hours, suggesting withdrawal from the real world. Japanese ceramics and pottery later became famous throughout the world for their subtlety and understated beauty. Potters made cups, bowls, and vases using rough textures and irregular lines to suggest weathering and the effects of time, a Japanese preoccupation. Japanese painting was also an old art and emphasized not creativity or self-expression but skill and technique through self-discipline. The **Noh** drama, plays that presented stylized gestures and spectacular masks, also appeared in this era.

Japanese Arts

Noh Japanese plays that use stylized gestures and spectacular masks; began in the fourteenth century.

SECTION SUMMARY

- The Korean state of Silla was subordinate to China and borrowed a great deal from China's culture, adapting it to Korean traditions.
- The Koryo state was dominated by the aristocracy and saw the decline of Buddhist influence.
- The Yi, who ruled Korea after the Mongols, sought good relations with China and instituted the Chinese educational and civil service exam system.
- In the Nara period, Japan borrowed heavily from Chinese culture, but its government was a dyarchy in which one powerful family dominated the emperor, and imports such as Buddhism were melded with native cultural features such as Shinto.
- In the Heian period, borrowing from China ended, foreign contacts were stopped, and a small elite group, concerned almost exclusively with the pursuit of aesthetic beauty, created some of Japan's best art and literature.
- Affluent women in the Heian period had great sexual freedom and the time to learn to write.
- In Japan, the warrior class, or samurai, gradually attained supremacy over the emperor and the court, and an organization like that of medieval Europe, based on lords and vassals, became dominant.
- The Kamakura Shogunate began after the winner of a Japanese civil war was given the title of shogun, or military dictator, who ruled while the emperor retreated behind the scenes.
- The Ashikaga Shogunate, which followed the Kamakura, had little power over the provinces, which became ruled by landowning lords called daimyo.
- Three enduring Buddhist sects developed in Japan: Pure Land, which stressed equality; Nicheren, which was militant; and Zen, which stressed meditation, discipline, and simplicity, qualities that are shown in such Japanese arts as gardening, flower arranging, and the tea ceremony.

CHAPTER SUMMARY

The Intermediate Era was in many respects a golden age for much of East Asia. The Tang and Song dynasties represented perhaps the high point of Chinese history and culture. While the Tang enjoyed great external power, the Song featured dramatic commercial growth. The Chinese continued to develop distinctive forms of literature, visual arts, philosophy, and government, as well as new technologies and scientific understandings. The Mongol conquest and brief period of rule weakened China's dynamism but extended overland trade routes that linked China even more closely to the outside world and promoted the spread of Chinese science and technology to western Eurasia. During the Ming, China briefly reasserted its transregional power and maintained an advanced technology. But, in part because of the experience of Mongol rule, Ming China also increasingly turned inward, becoming less involved in world affairs.

The Koreans and Japanese synthesized Chinese learning, writing, Confucianism, and Buddhism with their own native traditions to produce highly distinctive societies. Significant change occurred in Japan as it moved from the aristocratic court culture of Heian to a warrior-dominated culture based on large landowning families and their military retainers, or samurai. By the end of the 1400s the East Asian societies remained strong but faced new challenges when Europeans began to expand their power in the world.

KEY TERMS

neo-Confucianism
qi
kotow
dyarchy
kana
samurai
Bushido
shogun
daimyo
Zen
Noh

EBOOK AND WEBSITE RESOURCES

PRIMARY SOURCE
The Craft of Farming

INTERACTIVE MAPS
Map 11.1 The Tang Empire, ca. 700 E
Map 11.2 China in the Mongol Empire
Map 11.3 The Voyages of Zheng He
Map 11.4 Korea and Japan, ca. 1300

LINKS

Ancient Japan (http://www.wsu.edu/~dee/ANCJAPAN/ANCJAPAN-HTM). A useful site from Washington State University offering many essays and links on premodern Japan.

A Visual Sourcebook of Chinese Civilization (http://depts.washington.edu/chinaciv/). A wonderful collection of essays, illustrations, and other useful material on Chinese history.

East and Southeast Asia: An Annotated Directory of Internet Resources (http://newton.uor.edu/Departments&Programs/AsianStudiesDept/index.html). Varied collection of links, maintained at University of Redlands.

Internet East Asian History Sourcebook (http://www.fordham.edu/halsall/eastasia/eastasiasbook.html). An invaluable collection of sources and links on China, Japan, and Korea from ancient to modern times.

Internet Guide for China Studies (http://www.sino.uni-heidelberg.de/igcs/). A good collection of links on premodern and modern China, maintained at Germany's Heidelberg University.

Silk Road Narratives (http://depts.washington.edu/uwch/silkroad/texts/texts.html). Explores cultural interaction in Eurasia through excerpts from Silk Road travelers.

Plus flashcards, practice quizzes, and more. Go to: www.cengage.com/history/lockard/globalsocnet2e

SUGGESTED READING

Adshead, S. A. M. *China in World History*, 3rd ed. New York: St. Martin's, 2000. A study of China's relations with the world during this era.

Adshead, S. A. M. *T'ang China: The Rise of the East in World History.* New York: Palgrave Macmillan, 2004. A provocative examination of the rise and decline of China.

Benn, Charles. *China's Golden Age: Everyday Life in the Tang Dynasty.* New York: Oxford University Press, 2002. A comprehensive look at the society, economy, and culture of Tang China.

Cohen, Warren. *East Asia at the Center: Four Thousand Years of Engagement with the World.* New York: Columbia University Press, 2000. A good summary of China, Korea, and Japan in Eurasian history.

Ebrey, Patricia Buckley, Anne Walthall, and James B. Palais. *East Asia: A Cultural, Social, and Political History* 2nd ed. Boston: Houghton Mifflin, 2009. A readable, comprehensive survey, especially strong on the Intermediate Era.

Ebrey, Patricia Buckley. *The Inner Quarters: Marriage and the Lives of Chinese Women in the Sung Period.* Berkeley: University of California Press, 1993. A fascinating study of this neglected topic.

Gernet, Jacques. *Daily Life in China on the Eve of the Mongol Invasion 1250–1276.* Stanford: Stanford University Press, 1962. Dated but still a fascinating study of Song life.

Kuhn, Dieter. *The Age of Confucian Rule: The Song Transformation of China.* Cambridge: Harvard University Press, 2009. In-depth study of the Song era and society.

Lane, George. *Genghis Khan and Mongol Rule.* Indianapolis: Hackett, 2004. Good introduction with much on China.

Levathes, Louise. *When China Ruled the Seas: The Treasure Fleet of the Dragon Throne, 1405–33.* New York: Simon and Schuster, 1994. A recent study of the Ming voyages for the general reader.

Merson, John. *The Genius That Was China: East and West in the Making of the Modern World.* Woodstock, NY: Overlook Press, 1990. Lavishly illustrated with good coverage of Song and Ming China.

Morris, Ivan. *The World of the Shining Prince: Court Life in Ancient Japan.* New York: Kodansha International, 1994. A reprint of the classic 1964 study of Heian society and culture.

Rossabi, Morris. *Kublai Khan: His Life and Times.* Berkeley: University of California Press, 1987. A study of China under Mongol rule.

Seth, Michael J. *A Concise History of Korea from the Neolithic Times to the Nineteenth Century.* Lanham, MD: Rowman and Littlefield, 2006. Knowledgeable study of Korea and the larger East Asian context.

Shaughnessy, Edward, ed. *China: Empire and Civilization.* New York: Oxford University Press, 2005. Contains essays on many aspects of Chinese society in this era.

Souyri, Pierre F. *The World Turned Upside Down: Medieval Japanese Society*, translated by Kathe Roth. New York: Columbia University Press, 2001. A major scholarly study of later Intermediate Japan and warrior society.

Turnbull, Stephen. *Samurai: The World of the Warrior.* New York: Osprey, 2003. Well-written examination of samurai life.

Varley, Paul. *Japanese Culture,* 2nd ed. updated and expanded. Honolulu: University of Hawai'i Press, 2000. A good overview.

CHAPTER

12

Expanding Horizons in Africa and the Americas, 600–1500

Chapter Outline

- Diverse African States and Peoples
- African Societies, Thought, and Economies
- American Societies in Transition
- The American Empires and Their Challenges

PROFILE
Sundiata, Imperial Founder

WITNESS TO THE PAST
An Aztec Market

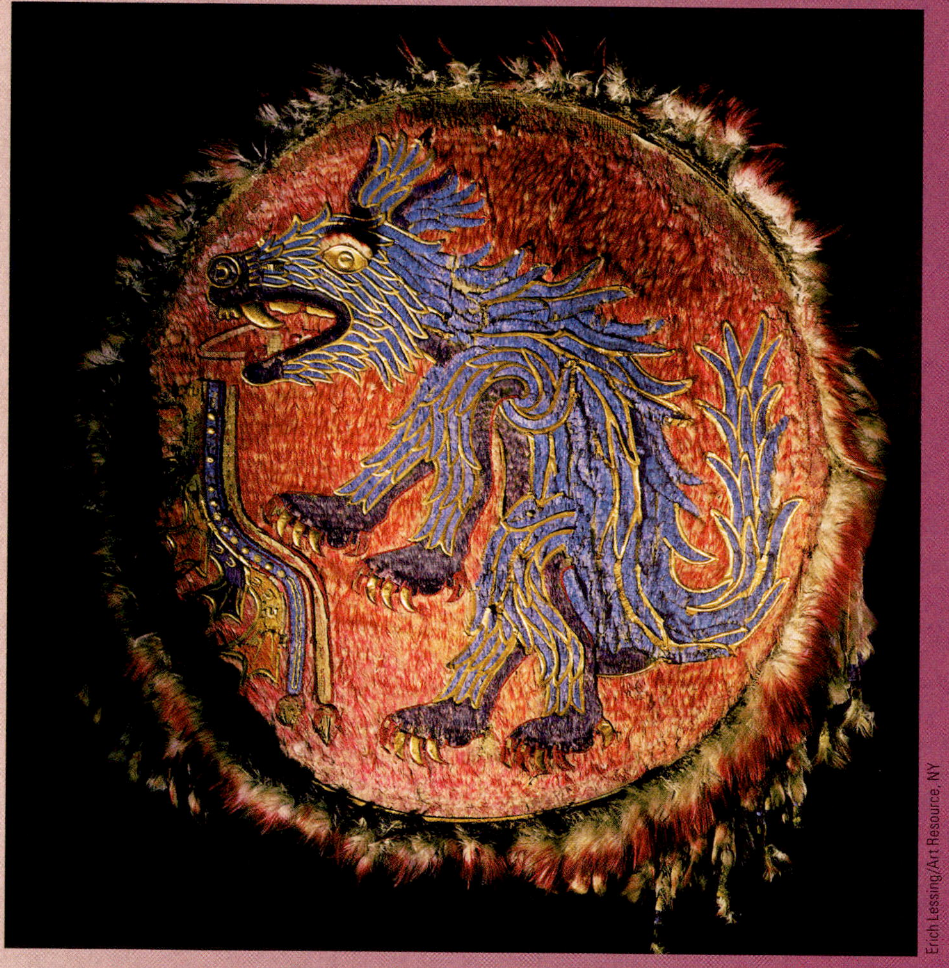

Erich Lessing/Art Resource, NY

Feathered Shield
This brightly colored feathered mosaic shield, used for ceremonial purposes by an Aztec warrior in the fifteenth century, has an image of the Aztec water god, a monster that resembled a coyote, outlined in gold.

A long time ago, when the Arabs arrived in Lamu [a port in today's Kenya, East Africa], they found local people there. The Arabs were received with friendliness and they wanted to stay on. The local people offered to trade land for cloths. Before the trading was finished, the Arabs had the land, and the [local people] had the cloth.

—A Lamu oral tradition[1]

FOCUS QUESTIONS

1. How did contact with Islamic peoples help shape the societies of West and East Africa?
2. What were some distinctive patterns of government, society, thought, and economy in Intermediate Africa?
3. What factors explain the collapse of the early Intermediate Era American societies?
4. How were the Aztec and Inca Empires different, and how were they similar?

Around 912 the Baghdad-born Arab geographer Abdul Hassan Ibn Ali al-Mas'udi sailed to East Africa with mariners from Oman, in eastern Arabia, on their regular trading expedition to what Arabs described as *Zanj* ("the land of black people"). The journey up and down the East African coast could be perilous, with reefs and strong winds that generated high waves. Al-Mas'udi spent three years visiting ports as far south as Sofala **(so-FALL-a)**, a city in Mozambique **(moe-zam-BEEK)**. After further travels to Persia, India, and China, al-Mas'udi finally settled in Cairo, where he wrote several scholarly books. The most influential, titled *Meadows of Gold and Mines of Gems,* described East African society in a key period of state formation while also recording the many links between these coastal towns, the Arabs, and other Eurasian societies. Al-Mas'udi praised the energetic traders and skilled workers of the coast, reported that the Sofala region produced abundant gold for export, and described how Arabs carried ivory from Zanj to Oman, from where they shipped it to India and China. He wrote that "in China the Kings and military and civil officers use ivory [to decorate furniture]. In India ivory is much sought after. It is used for the handles of daggers. But the chief use of ivory is making chessmen and backgammon pieces."[2]

During the Intermediate Era many societies in East Asia, Southeast Asia, South Asia, West Asia, North Africa, and Europe benefited from extensive links by which they exchanged technologies, products, religions, and ideas. As al-Mas'udi's description confirms, some sub-Saharan Africans also became connected to this vast network as trade expanded. African peoples like the gold producers near Sofala became integral parts of hemispheric commerce. But many sub-Saharan Africans had only indirect links, and the American societies across the Atlantic Ocean had no known links at all, to these busy Afro-Eurasian networks of exchange; thus they had to independently address the challenges they faced. Despite lack of contact with each other, Africans and Americans also shared some patterns of social and political development, some thriving in forbidding desert, forest, or highland environments. States rose and fell, among them a few regional empires. However, in contrast to the more densely populated areas of Eurasia, many Africans and Americans lived in self-governing villages rather than large, centralized governments. In the Western Hemisphere, trade routes existed over wide areas, but geography inhibited the growth of long-distance networks such as those linking East Africa to China. Only after 1492 did maritime exploration permanently connect African, American, and Eurasian peoples.

e Visit the website and eBook for additional study materials and interactive tools: www.cengage.com/history/lockard/globalsocnet2e

Diverse African States and Peoples

How did contact with Islamic peoples help shape the societies of West and East Africa?

After 600, several important kingdoms arose in the Sudanic region and along the Guinea coast. As in Eurasia, empires sprouted, flourished, and decayed. Scholars studied and disputed in centers of learning, and what Chinese artists accomplished with ink and Europeans with paint, African artists achieved with bronze and wood. The rise of great Sudanic kingdoms coincided with the expansion of Islam and a global commerce that linked West Africa with North Africa, the Mediterranean Basin, and western Asia. Meanwhile, the expansion of Bantu-speakers continued as the Bantus settled the vast expanses of central, eastern, and southern Africa, some building great kingdoms. The East African coast became a flourishing mercantile region closely linked to Eurasia, allowing Islam to spread into the area. Like the Sudanic kingdoms and most Eurasian societies, some Bantu peoples built cities, kept records, engaged in extensive trade, and boasted diverse social classes.

Trade, State Building, and the Expansion of Islam in the Sudan

For hundreds of years camel caravans had plied the trackless Sahara sands, where dry conditions, towering sand dunes, and searing sun conspired against crops, grasses, and trees. The caravans transported gold, salt, ivory, slaves, and ceramics between West and North Africa. The people benefiting the most lived in the Sudan, the largely grasslands region just south of the Sahara. Because its generally flat geography and the long but sluggish Niger River allowed for easy communication, the Sudan became a meeting place of people and ideas.

Islam in the Sudan

Beginning in the 800s Islam filtered down the Saharan trade routes, carried peacefully by merchants, teachers, and mystics in much the same way it arrived in the islands of Southeast Asia (see Chapter 13). As Muslim merchants settled in Sudanic towns, they helped form stable governments to protect the trade. Many political and economic leaders, and eventually most Sudanic peoples, embraced Islam. Islamic influence produced changes in customs, names, dress, diet, architecture, and festivals, and Islamic schools spread literacy in the Arabic language. The Sudanic religious atmosphere promoted tolerance, by Muslims toward animists and vice versa. Still, Islamic practice was often superficial, and it took several centuries for the religion to permeate into the villages.

A few kingdoms already existed by the time that Islam reached the Sudan. The kings in these animist societies were considered divine, remaining aloof from the common people and ruled through bureaucracies. But many kings had to consult a council of elders, who frequently had to approve a decision to go to war, and some kings were elected by elders or chiefs. The women of the royal families also had great power, and, in a few societies, they could rule as queens. Some kingdoms became empires. States had no fixed territorial boundaries, only fluctuating spheres of influence, and they often included diverse ethnic groups, making them inherently unstable.

The earliest known Sudanic kingdom was Ghana, centered on the northwestern Niger River (see Map 12.1). Founded by Mande speakers of the Soninke **(soh-NIN-kay)** ethnic group, Ghana was probably established around 500 C.E. (see Chapter 9) but reached its golden age in the ninth and tenth centuries (see Chronology: Africa in the Intermediate Era), prospering from its control of the trans-Saharan gold trade. Of Ghana and its profitable commerce, the Spanish Muslim traveler Abu Hamid al-Andalusi wrote: "In the sands of that country is gold, treasure immeasurable. Merchants trade salt for it, taking the salt on camels from the salt mines. They travel on the desert as if it were a sea, having guides to pilot them by the stars or rocks."[3] Many of the 20,000 inhabitants of Ghana's capital, Koumbi, were immigrants, including Arab and Berber merchants. Ghana's rulers converted to Islam, increasing the wealth and splendor of the royal court. An Arab visitor wrote that the king's attendants had gold-plaited hair and carried gold-mounted swords, and that even the guard dogs wore collars of gold and silver. But a civil war erupted, and Berbers from North Africa attacked and destroyed the kingdom in 1203.

CHRONOLOGY
Africa in the Intermediate Era

ca. 500–1203 Kingdom of Ghana

1000–1200 Rise of Hausa city-states

ca. 1200–1450 Zimbabwe kingdom

1200–1500 Golden age of East African coastal cities

1220–1897 Kingdom of Benin

1234–1550 Mali Empire

ca. 1275 Rise of Yoruba kingdom of Oyo

1324–1325 Mansa Musa's pilgrimage to Mecca

ca. 1375 Rise of Kongo kingdom

1464–1591 Songhai Empire

1487 Bartolomeu Dias rounds Cape of Good Hope

CHRONOLOGY		
	Africa	The Americas
700	**ca. 500–1203** Ghana	**700–1400** Anasazi **800–1475** Chimu Empire **900–1168** Toltec Empire
1000	**ca. 1000–1450** Zimbabwe	
1200	**1220–1897** Benin **1234–1550** Mali Empire	
1400	**1464–1591** Songhai Empire	**1428–1521** Aztec Empire **1440–1532** Inca Empire

Mali and Songhai: Islam and Regional Power

Islam in Mali

The greatest Sudanic empire, Mali **(MAHL-ee)**, was formed in 1234 by another Mande-speaking group, the Malinke **(muh-LING-kay)**, led by the Keita **(KAY-ee-tah)** clan, whose leader, Sundiata **(soon-JAH-tuh)**, became the **mansa (MAHN-suh)**, or king, of Mali (see Profile: Sundiata, Imperial Founder). Farmers and traders, the Malinke conquered much of the western Sudan, including the territory once controlled by Ghana. The empire's total area stretched some 1,500 miles from east to west and incorporated dozens of ethnic groups. The Malinke mansa was both a secular and religious leader who surrounded himself with displays of wealth and ceremonial regalia and expected his subjects to approach him on their knees, instilling respect and obedience in his people. Sundiata apparently converted to Islam, perhaps to secure better relations with North Africa, but he never seriously practiced the religion and also made use of Malinke animism and magic.

mansa ("king") Mande term used by the Malinke people to refer to the ruler of the Mali Empire.

Islamic influence gradually grew stronger, expanding communication and travel. Some later Mali emperors made glittering pilgrimages to Mecca. When Sundiata's descendant, Mansa Musa **(MAN-sa MOO-sa)** (r. 1312–1337), went to Mecca in 1324 riding a white Arab horse, he took fifty slaves bearing golden staffs, one thousand followers, and one hundred camels, each loaded with 300 pounds of gold. According to an Arab official writing of Mansa Musa's visit to Egypt en route to Arabia, he "spread upon Cairo the flood of his generosity; there was no person or holder of any office who did not receive a sum of gold from him. The people of Cairo earned incalculable sums from him, whether by selling or gifts."[4] An Arab observer credited Mansa Musa with building grand mosques in Mali and importing Islamic jurists. But the majority of Mali's people remained animist, and even the elite were lax in their Islamic practice.

Malian Society

Most Malians lived in small villages and cultivated rice, sorghum, or millet, supplemented by herding or fishing. Mali also supplied most of Europe's gold reserves and about two-thirds of the world's gold supply in this era. Local Africans mined the gold in open pits or in underground passages while women extracted the gold dust from the dirt dug out by the men. Gold traders then met salt merchants from the north and silently matched piles of gold and salt until a fair exchange was agreed upon. Imports came to Mali from as far away as China and India, and the Mali trading city of Timbuktu **(tim-buk-TOO)** emerged as the major southern terminus of the trans-Saharan caravan trade. The international links provided by Islam and the trans-Saharan commerce enticed many visitors and sojourners to Mali, including poets, architects, teachers, and traders from places such as Spain and Egypt, and at least one Italian merchant reached Timbuktu. The fourteenth-century Moroccan traveler Ibn Battuta spent months in Mali, whose many "admirable qualities" he admired, commenting that "they are seldom unjust, and have a greater abhorrence of injustice than any other people." He also found that "neither traveler nor inhabitant in it has anything to fear from robbers or men of violence."[5] But the pious Muslim frowned on what he considered the immodest dress and independent behavior of women and the custom of eating dogs.

Rise of Songhai

Mali rapidly declined in the 1400s because of internal factionalism and raids by other peoples. Soon the fringes broke away, and by 1550 the Mali of former days was gone, replaced as the dominant Sudanic empire by Songhai **(song-GAH-ee)**, a kingdom formed by several ethnic groups. By 1464 Songhai's empire was as large as the former Mali Empire. Some of the Songhai rulers were

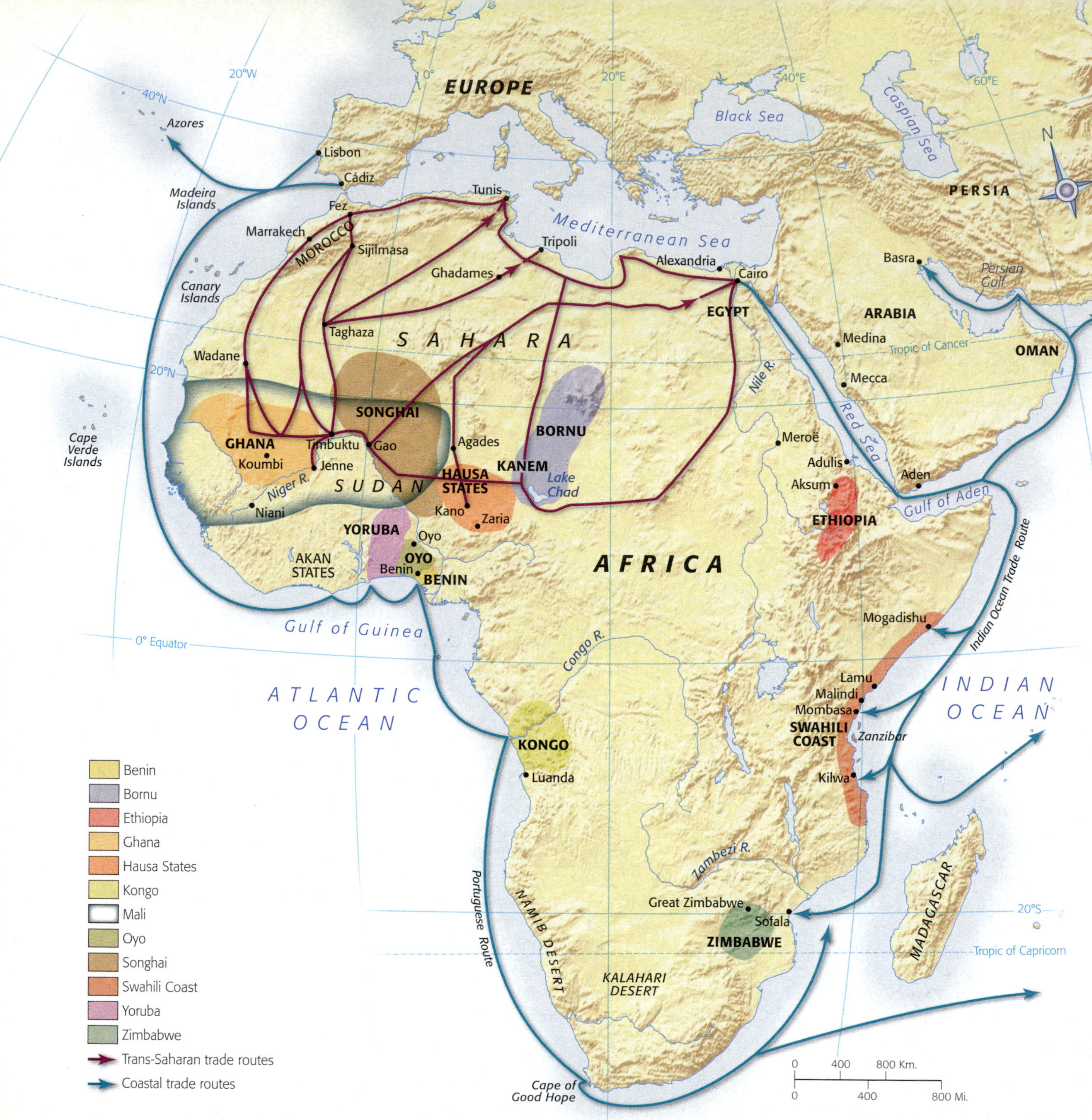

Map 12.1 Major Sub-Saharan African Kingdoms and States, 1200–1600 C.E. Many large kingdoms and states emerged in Intermediate Africa. Large empires dominated the Sudan in West Africa, while prosperous trading cities sharing a Swahili culture dotted the east coast.

e Interactive Map

nominal Muslims, and others were devout. The most revered leader was Aksia **(ACK-see-a)** the Great (1483–1528), a humane, pious, and tolerant man who was devoted to learning. The imperial capital at Gao **(ghow)** on the Niger River was a substantial city containing perhaps 100,000 people. As demand for gold and slaves increased in both North Africa and Europe, Songhai flourished from the trans-Saharan caravan trade. Slaves were obtained from nearby peoples and sold in the Gao slave market, and many were taken on the arduous journey across the Sahara to the Mediterranean societies. In exchange for gold and slaves, Songhai received glass, copperware, cloth, perfumes, and horses.

Under Songhai rule, Timbuktu flourished, becoming a major intellectual center with a famous Islamic university that specialized in teaching astronomy, astrology, medicine, history, geography,

Arabic, and Quranic studies. The thousands of scholars and students in the city patronized bookstores and libraries containing thousands of books, many in African languages using Arabic script. In recent years over 30,000 lost books, hundreds of years old, on many subjects have been found underneath Timbuktu's mud houses and in nearby desert caves. One North African, on visiting Timbuktu, noted many shops and abundant food and described the people as "of a gentle and cheerful disposition, and spend a great part of the night in singing and dancing through all the streets of the city."[6] Songhai flourished until 1591, when Moroccans destroyed its military power.

The Central Sudan and Guinea Coast

Hausa States

After 1000 another dynamic Sudanic society developed farther east, in northern Nigeria, eastern Niger, and southern Chad, where the Hausa **(HOUSE-uh)** people erected fiercely competitive city-states, ruled by kings, that came to dominate some of the trans-Saharan trade. The prosperity of these city-states attracted many non-Hausa immigrants, including Arabs and Berbers, and Hausa society became increasingly Islamic. Hausa cities such as Kano **(KAHN-oh)** were centers for manufacturing cotton cloth and leatherwork, some of which was sold as far away as Europe. The Hausa were also farmers, famed craftspeople, and skilled traders, whose pursuit of wealth ranged all over West Africa. Today the Hausa language, which mixed Arab, Berber, and West African influences, remains the major trading language of the central Sudan and the most widely spoken sub-Saharan African language.

Like many Sudanic peoples, the Hausa possessed a strong class system, headed by royal families and the aristocracy. Islamic intellectuals, such as teachers, and wealthy merchants were influential. Hausa women enjoyed a high status compared with women in many African societies. In the fifteenth century a queen, Amina, ruled one of the major Hausa states, Zaria **(zah-REE-uh)**. An oral poem praised her as "like the moon at its full, like the morning star. She is a lion as precious as gold among all women."[7]

Hausa Houses in Kano Hausa towns and cities feature houses with large courtyards behind high walls. Structural beams made from local palm trees protrude from the walls.

Werner Forman/Art Resource, NY

SUNDIATA, IMPERIAL FOUNDER

According to tradition, the founder of the great Mali Empire was Sundiata Keita, the "Lion Prince" of the Malinke people. It is difficult to separate myth from fact about his life, but most historians believe there was a real Sundiata. Arab historians such as Ibn Khaldun mention him in their accounts. Nonetheless, any account must use oral epics, which tend to glorify his heroism and reflect a Malinke view of a glorious past.

At the time Sundiata was born in the early thirteenth century, Ghana was collapsing and various other groups were contending to fill the power vacuum. Sundiata was one of twelve sons of a Malinke king, Nare Fa Maghan, and Sogolon Conde, a hunchback. As a child Sundiata was sickly and had stiff legs that made walking difficult. Hence he was spared when a rival state, Kaniaga, under their brutal king, Sumaguru, conquered Sundiata's town, Niane, and executed all his brothers as potential threats. According to the oral epic:

> *He had a slow and difficult childhood. At the age of three he still crawled along on all-fours. He had nothing of the great beauty of his father. He had a head so big that he seemed unable to support it. He was taciturn and used to spend the whole day just sitting in the middle of the house. Malicious tongues began to blab. All Niane talked of nothing but the stiff-legged son.*

However, soothsayers predicted greatness for him, and eventually he overcame his physical problems so that "at the age of eighteen he had the stateliness of the lion and the strength of the buffalo."

As a young man he went into exile, and then he returned to rally his people against the tyrannical Sumaguru: "The sun will arise, the sun of Sundiata." Determined and diplomatic, he skillfully used traditional clan and kinship groups as well as a reputation for possessing knowledge of magic to build and solidify his power. Persuading other Malinke chiefs to surrender their titles to him, he became his peoples' sole king, enhancing his position in preparation for war. Sundiata put together a military force and triumphed over Sumaguru in the battle of Kirina about 1235, and then he conquered much of the old Ghana territories.

As king, Sundiata acquired the power to reshape Malinke government and society. According to the epics, "He left his mark on Mali for all time and his [rules] still guide men in their conduct [today]." As ruler for over two decades, Sundiata transformed his small state into the core of an imperial system based in his hometown of Niane, alongside the Niger River and near valuable gold fields. His rule brought peace, happiness, prosperity, and justice: "He protected the weak against the strong. The upright man was rewarded and the wicked one punished." The epic account is undoubtedly an idealized version of truth, but it also recorded that Sundiata punished his enemies. Malinke custom allowed high-status men to have many wives, and Sundiata, like his father, followed this practice, leaving many descendants.

Sundiata died about 1260, but his legend lived on. As the epics retold even today put it:

> *Sundiata was unique. In his time no one equaled him and after him no one had the ambition to surpass him. Men of today, how small you are beside your ancestors. Sundiata rests but his spirit lives on and today the Keitas still come and bow before the stone under which lies the father of Mali.*

THINKING ABOUT THE PROFILE

1. What does Sundiata's career tell us about the personal qualities admired by the Malinke people and helpful in forging a Sudanic empire?
2. How do the epic stories told over the centuries remember Sundiata and his deeds?

Note: Quotations from D. T. Niane, *Sundiata: An Epic of Old Mali* (London: Longman, 1965), 15, 40, 47, 81, 83–85.

From Ada Konare Ba, *Sunjata: Le Fondateur L'Empire du Mali* (Dakar: Nouvelles Editions Africaines, 1983)

Sundiata This modern depiction of Sundiata Keita memorializes the legendary founder of the Mali Empire. Even today, nearly a millennium after his death, Sundiata remains a hero to Africans for his political and military skills.

Along the Guinea coast, a region of rain forest and grasslands just south of the Sudan, Sudanic influence and trade fostered the growth of states among societies like the Yoruba **(YORE-uh-buh)**. By about 1000 the Yoruba in western Nigeria had developed several states, each based on a large city ruled by a king or prince. The kings were powerful and considered sacred, but they were influenced by elders and aristocrats. However, no united Yoruba kingdom existed: Yoruba identity was more cultural than political, based on a common language and culture, including complex animistic traditions that are still influential today. One Yoruba kingdom, Oyo **(OY-oh)**, rose rapidly after 1275 to become the most powerful state in the area, flourishing until the late eighteenth century. Many towns dotted Yoruba country, serving as both commercial and political centers and ruled by elaborate bureaucracies. Merchants were respected and closely connected to the north-south trade networks. Since Yoruba women were not expected to work in the fields, many developed wealth and influence as traders. The Yoruba were also famed as artists. For example, the Yoruba at Ife **(EE-fay)** cast beautiful bronze portraits of their rulers. Since the Yoruba prized submissiveness to superiors and their culture discouraged conflict, crime was rare.

The Nelson-Atkins Museum of Art, Kansas City, Missouri. Purchase: William Rockhill Nelson Trust, 58–3. Photograph by Jamison Miller.

Benin King and Musicians This bronze plaque shows the king, preparing for war, wearing beads and flanked by royal musicians on both sides. Such plaques were hung on palace walls and pillars to glorify the ruler.

Another great Guinea kingdom, Benin **(buh-NEEN)**, situated just east of Yoruba territory, was the state of the Bini **(bean-ee)** people, who shared some cultural traditions with the Yoruba. Benin emerged around 1220, and under King Ewuare **(ee-WAHR-ee)** the Great it established a sizable empire in the mid-1400s. Early kings like Ewuare were warriors, but later they became more spiritual leaders, leading secluded lives but subject to influence by powerful local chiefs. Benin artists cast beautiful bronzes and carved ivory to glorify the accomplishments of the king and state. Since Benin was located near the Atlantic coast, it was one of the first African kingdoms to be visited by Europeans in the 1400s, who wrote of the prosperous society they admired.

Benin city was protected by high walls and included an elaborate royal palace, neat houses with verandas (porches), and neighborhoods linked by broad avenues. An elite commercial class traded with the Hausa, Yoruba, and Songhai. Bini merchants dealt in woodcarvings, foodstuffs, ironwork, farm tools, weapons, and later cloth. Because they produced most of the cloth, Bini women also benefited from this trade. The upper classes dressed and dined well, consuming beef, mutton, chicken, and yams, while the poor ate yams, dried fish, beans, and bananas. However, the poor were protected from becoming beggars because an innovative welfare system supported those unable to work. Benin began to decline in 1550 but only collapsed in 1897.

The Bantu Diaspora

Bantu migrations persisted during the Intermediate Era. In eastern Africa the migrating Bantu came into contact with the Nilotic-speakers, who themselves had migrated from North-Central Africa. Bantu and Nilotes **(NAI-lots)** competed over good grazing land and salt, but they also traded, coexisted, and sometimes mixed together. For example, the Bantu Gikuyu **(kee-KOO-yoo)**, who settled in Kenya, intermarried, traded, and sometimes fought with the Nilotic Masai **(mah-SIE)** people, who were mainly cattle herders.

Over time the Bantu peoples scattered over forest, savannah, and highlands in the southern half of Africa, developing diverse cultures, languages, political systems, and economic patterns but also maintaining many common traditions. Most Bantu-speakers remained farmers, practicing shifting cultivation where necessary but using more complex methods where possible. Bananas became the staple crop of East Africa. Some Bantu lived in towns, and centralized kingdoms on the Sudanic model appeared, especially in the Great Lakes region. But most kings had religious and ceremonial rather than real political power, and the village usually remained supreme.

East African Commerce and Swahili Culture

Indian Ocean Networks

The expansion of both Islam and global commerce integrated the East African coastal peoples, including many Bantu, into Dar al-Islam and the wider world. The 1,200 miles of coast stretching from Somalia down to Mozambique was a cultural melting pot, where a growing trade network linking East Africa with the societies around the rim of the Indian Ocean brought in diverse cultures, languages, and religions, fostering a unique hybrid society. Because the prevailing monsoon wind patterns made it relatively easy to sail up and down the coast, the East African coastal peoples had long been in regular contact with seafaring folk from Arabia, Persia, India, and Southeast Asia. Indonesians visited East Africa for centuries, bringing with them bananas, coconuts, and yams, which spread throughout tropical Africa. Some Indonesians also settled on the island of Madagascar. Eventually seafaring Arabs from the Persian Gulf, Oman, and Yemen dominated the coastal trade, seeking ivory, tortoise shell, leopard skin, and later gold and copper.

City States

As trade increased, many city-states developed along the coast, among them Mogadishu (mo-ga-DEE-shoo), Lamu (LAH-moo), Malindi (ma-LIN-dee), Mombasa (mahm-BAHS-uh), Zanzibar (ZAN-zuh-bahr), Kilwa (KILL-wa), and Sofala. Leaders of these states were chiefly interested in trade, not military expansion, and governed only a small hinterland. Settlers came from Arabia, Persia, and India. Each independent city-state was dominated by a royal court, often claiming Persian or Arab ancestry, and powerful trading families. Trade networks into the interior expanded with the discovery of gold in the highlands of Zimbabwe (zim-BOB-way). Because of its access to these gold fields, Sofala at the mouth of the Zambezi (zam-BEE-zee) River became a wealthy city.

The golden age of the coast reached its peak from the twelfth through the fifteenth centuries as Islam became entrenched. Ships from Arabia, Persia, and India regularly visited. One passenger, the Moroccan jurist Ibn Battuta, traveled as far south as Kilwa, a prosperous city on an island off Tanzania, and described it as "one of the most beautiful and well-constructed towns in the world, elegantly built [with] good buildings of stone and mortar, entirely surrounded by a wall and towers."[8] Kilwa, which had perhaps 20,000 people, was a collection hub for goods coming in from north and south. The upper classes built three-story stone houses with indoor plumbing and lavished themselves with large quantities of gold and silver jewelry as well as Chinese silk and porcelain. Ibn Battuta described the Kilwa Muslims as devout, chaste, and virtuous and its rulers, a family claiming Yemenite descent, as humble and pious. Still, he disliked some local customs, such as their preference for a rich diet. He approved of the chicken, meat, fish, vegetables, and mangoes but not the rice cooked with butter and yogurt chutney, which probably had South Asian origins. His reports show that East Africans had become closely linked to the Islamic world by trade and religion but also maintained various local customs.

The East African city-states became an integral part of the greatest maritime trading network of the Intermediate world, a system of ports and trade routes that linked economies around the rim of the Indian Ocean stretching from Indonesia to East Africa. Foreign traders brought pottery, Chinese porcelain, glass beads, and Indian cotton to East Africa and traded them for iron, ivory, tortoise shell, leopard skins, gold, and slaves. The beautiful homes of the coastal cities, some with tropical gardens, fountains, and pools, attested to the wealth that was available to the upper and middle classes.

Swahili Name for a distinctive people, culture, and language, a mix of Bantu, Arab, and Islamic influences, that developed during the Intermediate Era on the East African coast.

Over time, intermarriage and the blending of Bantu, Arab, and Islamic influences in the coastal cities produced a distinctive new African culture and language, **Swahili** (Arab for "people of the coast"). The mixing of the Bantu and Arabic tongues created the new Swahili language, and Arabic script was used to produced poetry, historical legend, and religious speculation, in addition to commercial accounts. Eventually Swahili became the major trading language of the entire coastal region, its influence reaching as far inland as the eastern Congo River Basin. Today Swahili is second only to Hausa as a first or second language in sub-Saharan Africa.

The Swahili favored Arab architectural styles, ideas of inheritance, and dress, including long gowns for men and modest attire for women. Whereas the interior Bantu peoples practiced either patrilineal or matrilineal descent, the Swahili were, like Arabs, firmly patrilineal. However, it took many centuries for Islam to penetrate the hinterland. Islam spread in part because it was a flexible religion, willing to tolerate the incorporation of Bantu beliefs in spirits and ancestor worship. Today Muslims are numerous in all the East African countries, but five hundred years ago Islam was found mostly in the coastal towns.

Zimbabwe and the Kongo

Shona States

The East African trading cities were only a part of the wider Bantu diaspora, which also included various kingdoms in central and southern Africa. On the fertile plateau of south-central Africa one of the greatest kingdoms, Zimbabwe, which means "houses built of stone," emerged and flourished from trade with the coast. Today little remains of the kingdom's monumental buildings except for dozens of impressive stone ruins that dot the landscape for hundreds of miles. The Shona (SHO-nah) people constructed these buildings and a great state between the thirteenth

Visual Connection Archive

The Great Zimbabwe Complex Great stone enclosures, most probably used as royal residences or religious sanctuaries, were built around the Zimbabwe kingdom. This one, surrounded by high walls, was at the center of the kingdom's capital city.

and fifteenth centuries, eventually controlling much of the plateau. The granite buildings had various functions. Some were walls enclosing towns, and others seem to have been courts. In the heart of the capital city, which probably contained 10,000 to 20,000 people, the largest enclosure is an oval space surrounded by a wall 1,800 feet long, 32 feet high, and 17 feet thick that may have housed the royal family or perhaps served as a sanctuary in which the royal family worshiped their patron deity.

Zimbabwe's Mineral Wealth

Mining was the key to Zimbabwe's prosperity. The Shona had migrated from the southern Congo River Basin, an area of many copper mines. Discovering gold, copper, and iron ore on the plateau, they extracted it from open-pit and occasionally underground mines and traded these minerals down the Zambezi River to the coast. By 1500 some 10,000 Arab and Swahili traders lived along the river, buying and then exporting the gold to the Middle East and India through Sofala and Kilwa. Shona exports corresponded to a rapid growth in the world demand for gold. In exchange Zimbabwe received Indian textiles and Chinese ceramics. Shona artists produced copper, bronze, and gold ornaments. In the 1400s the empire broke up into two rival states, and the capital city was largely abandoned by 1450. Perhaps Zimbabwe was a casualty of overpopulation, soil exhaustion, and overgrazing by cattle. As Zimbabwe declined, the trade routes and then the government may have shifted north to the upper Zambezi River Valley, but the Shona continued to export gold to the coast.

Kongolese Society

Another great Bantu kingdom, Kongo, was established by the Bakongo **(bah-KOHNG-goh)** people in the 1300s near the Atlantic coast of northern Angola and western Congo. Eventually its population reached 2.5 million. The king's compound, nearly a mile around, was located in the capital city of Mbanga **(um-BAHN-ga)**. Royal musicians bearing drums and ivory trumpets announced visitors and ceremonies. High-status people wore finely woven cloth fabrics, beautifully dyed, which European visitors compared to velvet, silk, and brocade. Although in theory absolute and divine, the king faced some restrictions: he was elected by elders and governors and had to seek advice from a council formed by the heads of the leading clans.

Kongo village chiefs settled disputes but referred serious quarrels or crimes to district judges. Villagers lived in houses with walls of palm matting and thatch roofs. Every day women ground millet into a white flour and stirred it in boiling water to make a stiff porridge, which was eaten with peas or beans and spicy sauces made of palm oil. Meat such as chicken, fish, or game, as well as bananas, yams, and pumpkins, provided some variety. Trade flourished, and people used a seashell-based currency to buy salt, colored cloth from India, palm cloth, palm belts, and animal skins.

SECTION SUMMARY

- The area south of the Sahara, known as the Sudan, benefited most from the Sahara caravan trade and gradually embraced Islam.
- In the kingdom of Ghana, which prospered from the trans-Saharan gold trade, councils of elders held the power of kings in check.
- The kingdom of Mali also grew fabulously wealthy because of the caravan trade, but like Ghana, it ultimately declined because of infighting and external threats.
- The Songhai, who split off from Mali, amassed great wealth from the demand for gold and slaves, and Timbuktu became a major center of Islamic learning.
- The Hausa city-states also participated in trade, and their women enjoyed high status.
- South of the Sudan, on the Guinea coast, the Yoruba developed a balance of power between kings and aristocrats and were generally peace-loving traders and artists, and the prosperous kingdom of Benin developed an innovative welfare system.
- The Bantu continued to expand across eastern and southern Africa and established numerous coastal city-states that were greatly influenced by trade with Arabs.
- The East African coast became largely Muslim, though it retained a great deal of its native African culture along with influences from such cultures as Arabia and South Asia.
- The fusion of Bantu, Arab, and Islamic culture yielded a new language, Swahili, and led to the adoption of many Arab practices by East Africans.
- Zimbabwe rose to prosperity as a result of mining and built large granite buildings whose precise use is still debated by historians.

AFRICAN SOCIETIES, THOUGHT, AND ECONOMIES

What were some distinctive patterns of government, society, thought, and economy in Intermediate Africa?

Societies across Africa shared many common patterns of social organization, religion, culture, and economy. Nonetheless, African societies also varied considerably, depending partly on how closely they were connected to the Islamic world and on whether they had centralized or village-based governments. While intensive agriculture did not develop to the same extent as in Eurasia, trade with the wider world attracted European explorers to the region.

Political and Social Patterns

Stateless Societies

Although the powerful kingdoms such as Mali, Benin, and Zimbabwe governed many Africans, there were also many people who lived in stateless societies, decentralized, village-based political systems featuring self-governing villages where government involved family relationships. A council of elders normally assisted the chief and applied customary law to regulate conduct. Some of these stateless societies were small and some large, but each was unique. The Tiv **(tihv)** of eastern Nigeria developed an egalitarian society in which legal and economic rights were based on kinship. Their politics can be described as local democracy. Village elders and family heads allocated land, administered justice, and organized community activities, and custom influenced the authority of leaders and the behavior of citizens. Women controlled their own fields and did much of the farm work, but they were aided by men in harvesting and planting. The Gikuyu **(kee-KOO-you)**, Bantu farmers in the temperate, green highlands around Mount Kenya in East Africa, had no local chiefs and mostly lived in individual family homesteads. Each extended family was headed by the senior male, who represented the family to the broader Gikuyu society. Younger Gikuyu men formed a special council that handled military affairs, and village councils elected representatives to district councils of elders. This democratic Gikuyu system relied heavily on group discussion and the power of public opinion.

Social Networks

Whether living in kingdoms or stateless societies, individuals were connected to others through varied social networks. The family formed an economic unit that cooperated in most matters and frequently included all the members of living generations and their spouses and children. Some societies practiced matrilineal kinship, tracing descent and inheritance through the female line. In kingdoms with kings, the queen sister or queen mother was usually a highly respected figure. For example, the Bini people still revere Idia, an early-sixteenth-century queen mother who raised an army and used her magical powers to aid her son in overcoming his enemies. Queen mothers often controlled access to rulers, managed treasuries, presided over court systems, and helped enthrone or depose rulers. Some queens ruled in their own right. However, women's status varied widely. Men dominated most families and often had multiple wives. Since the chief goal of marriage was children, a woman's status depended on her childbearing ability. To win the highest regard meant bearing many children, and women looked to their children rather than their husbands for support in old age.

A web of associations defined socially acceptable behavior. The family was part of a clan or lineage that traced descent to a particular ancestor. People related to other villagers through work or music groups, secret societies, religious cults, and age grades that promoted cooperation between people of the same generation. Most groups prized collective effort and responsibility instead of individual initiative. The *ethnic group,* often mistakenly called the "tribe" by modern observers, included people, not necessarily related by kinship ties, who spoke the same language, practiced similar customs, and lived in the same general territory. Some ethnic groups were quite large. Both the Yoruba and Hausa numbered in the millions and were divided into various states. Distinct cultures, languages, and religions marked off groups such as the Yoruba, Hausa, Shona, and Gikuyu.

African Slavery

Like many societies around the world, some sub-Saharan peoples condoned slavery and engaged in slave trading. Slaves were often war captives or debtors. Ibn Battuta wrote that, in many Sudanic cities, the wealthy "vie with one another in regard to the number of their slaves and serving-women. They never sell the educated female slaves, or but rarely and at a high price."[9] Slaves filled diverse social and economic roles. The Wolof (WOH-lohf) of Senegal assigned slaves to household work; Kongolese slaves were soldiers or plantation workers; the Akan (ah-KAHN) on the Guinea coast employed slave labor for gold mining; and some Hausa slaves were palace advisers and hence enjoyed a high social status. Some slaves were considered members of households, and many could marry and have their children freed. While slave life was often hard, among many African peoples slaves had more rights and could expect better treatment than slaves in most European, Islamic, Asian, and American societies.

Religious and Artistic Traditions

Religious Diversity

African religion was diverse, including not only Muslim and Christian believers but also many millions who practiced monotheism, a rich polytheism with many gods and spirits, animism (spirit worship), or a mix of the three. Africans often recognized a supernatural world of sorcery, magic, spirits, ancestors, and multiple gods that was mediated by shamans, male or female specialists who were skilled in curing disease and had knowledge about the spiritual realm. They were often successful as healers because they understood that many illnesses had spiritual and psychological as well as physical dimensions. Some male elders, considered sages, collected wisdom and challenged individuals to become better and more knowledgeable. Scholars compare these sages, who were constantly probing for truth, to classical Greek, Indian, and Chinese philosophers. Reverence toward cosmic forces blended into worship and spirituality, and many Africans believed in a life force that was part of all living and material entities. Deceased family members and ancestors, believed to be present in spirit, were also revered. Since most societies envisioned an unapproachable high god who held himself aloof from daily affairs, people prayed to ancestors and spirits.

The Dogon people, who live on an arid plateau in today's nation of Mali, may represent what African society and religion were like before the formation of states and the coming of outside religions. Their society is ruled by priest-chiefs. People work the fields collectively and center their lives on community religious festivals and arts. The Dogon order the cosmos and their society through myths that perceive the cosmos as dualistic, mixing male and female, order and change.

Africans also developed oral and written literatures. Most societies relied on **oral traditions**, verbal testimonies concerning the past passed down through the generations by professional rememberers, known as *griots* in West Africa, who served as local historians and recordkeepers and sometimes became councilors to kings and tutors to princes. Griots could recount past events while also updating the story with contemporary happenings, becoming walking libraries who transmitted knowledge to their successors. As a modern griot explained: "We are vessels of speech, the repositories which harbor secrets many centuries old. We are the memory of mankind."[10] Some griots concentrated on genealogy, remembering lists of kings or queen mothers. many top West African writers and popular musicians today come from griot families.

oral traditions Verbal testimonies concerning the past; the major form of oral literature in cultures without writing.

Some African peoples also had written languages and produced poetry and philosophical speculation. The most widespread written languages included Arabic, Hausa, Amharic, and Swahili. However, writing spread slowly because most Africans relied on well-defined customs to maintain order and so did not need written laws; because they had communal ownership, they also did not need to track land use and inheritance. Merchants in the Sudanic and East African cities recorded the buying and selling of large quantities of goods in Arabic or Swahili, but elsewhere writing was difficult, since paper deteriorates quickly in the tropical climate.

Art and Music

Africans produced a rich artistic heritage, including sculpture, dance, and music. Paleolithic Africans were among the first people anywhere to paint on rocks and cave walls. When farming developed, painting declined and sculpture in wood, clay, ivory, bronze, or gold became the major visual art form. Many Africans made wooden masks for religious festivals, as well as carvings of animal, human, and spiritual figures, and African sculpture has influenced modern artists around the world. Music and dance were both closely integrated into work, leisure, and religion and usually involved everyone's participation. Musical groups often accompanied people working in the fields, and at the end of the day the farmers and musicians returned to the village for an impromptu party. While African musicians emphasized percussion and used many types of drums, they also played various wind and string instruments. African musical traditions filtered into the Middle East along the trade routes, influencing Islamic music. Then, beginning in the 1500s, African slaves carried their musical traditions to the Americas, where they blended with European and Native American styles to foster many of the popular music styles of the twentieth century, such as blues, jazz, rock, calypso, salsa, and samba.

Agriculture and Trade

Sub-Saharan Africans successfully exploited the resources of their tropical environment to foster farming and trade. Whereas Eurasian societies had horses and oxen to pull plows and large wheeled carts, in much of tropical Africa these animals could not be bred or survive because of various tropical diseases or insect pests; they could only be used in the northeast highland regions and in the dry Sudan and Sahara. Because economic production and transportation therefore had to rely on human muscles, most Africans were small farmers who produced food primarily for their own use. With often poor soils, irregular rainfall, and no manure from draft animals for fertilizer, Africans could not match the highly productive agriculture found in China, India, and Europe. Instead many practiced shifting cultivation, a practical adaptation to local conditions. This system worked well as long as population densities remained small; by 1500 there were probably some 40 million people in sub-Saharan Africa, compared to over 100 million in China. More sophisticated techniques such as irrigation or terracing were used where possible.

Commercial Life

Trading networks interlaced tropical Africa. Great markets emerged at Sudanic cities such as Gao and Timbuktu, where traders bought and sold ivory, ebony, and honey from the Guinea coast and books, wheat, horses, dates, cloth, and salt from the north. Most market traders were women, and most traveling merchants were men. Some peoples were renowned as long-distance traders. Hausa merchants traveled to the Guinea coast to buy kola nuts, a rain forest tree crop that can be made into one of the few stimulants allowed Muslims. Various items, including gold, ivory, and kola nuts, were exported from tropical Africa to North Africa, Asia, and Europe. Both gold and cowry **(KOW-ree)** shells, collected on the Indian Ocean coast, were used as local currency.

However, local trade was often more essential than international commerce. People bought and sold things needed for everyday life, such as cloth, salt, ironware, and copper, and women made cloth from cotton and bark. Because sources of abundant salt were rare, it commanded a high price, and traders sometimes had to obtain it from hundreds of miles away. Iron ore was more common. Copper was valued from ancient times for making bangles and bracelets, but there were few good sources. The most extensive copper mining took place in the copper-belt region south of the Congo Basin and in South Africa.

Africans, Arab Slave Traders, and the Portuguese

Slave Trades

Africa was connected to Eurasia primarily by trade across the Sahara Desert or along the East African coast. As international trade expanded, Arab, Berber, and African traders shipped more African slaves north, where they were sold in North Africa, Iberia, Arabia, Persia, India, and Christian Europe. Between 650 and 1500 the trans-Saharan caravans transported perhaps 2 to 4 million slaves from West Africa to the Mediterranean societies, while up to 2 million were shipped from East Africa. These were significant numbers but considerably smaller in scale than the trans-

Atlantic slave trade carried out by Western nations between 1500 and 1850. African slaves in the Middle East became domestic servants, laborers, soldiers, and even administrators. Perhaps 250,000 descendants of African slaves, traders, and sailors live in India and Pakistan today.

Portuguese Explorations

The trans-Saharan slave trade inspired western Europeans to eventually seek slaves directly in West Africa. Portuguese exploration began a new era in African history. In search of Asian spices and African gold as well as slaves, the well-armed Portuguese began sailing south along the West African coastline in the early 1400s (see Chapter 14). They became involved in African affairs, colonizing the Cape Verde **(VUHRD)** Islands in the Atlantic and the nearby coastal region of Guinea-Bissau **(GIN-ee bis-OW)** and establishing various trading forts to obtain gold, ivory, and slaves. Some West Africans picked up artistic and religious ideas from the Portuguese merchants and Christian missionaries.

In 1487 a Portuguese expedition led by Bartolomeu Dias rounded the Cape of Good Hope at the tip of Africa and sailed into the Indian Ocean, thus opening up a whole new chapter in Western exploration and intensifying Portuguese interest both in Africa and the world to the east. Even after Christopher Columbus, sailing for Spain, announced his "discovery" of what he thought was India in 1492, the Portuguese concentrated on the sea route around Africa. In 1497 Portuguese ships commanded by Vasco da Gama sailed up the East African coast to the trading city of Malindi and, engaging an Indian or Arab pilot, sailed on to southern India. Da Gama had discovered the fastest oceanic path from Europe to the Indian Ocean maritime trading network.

In the 1480s the Portuguese began a long relationship with the Kongo kingdom, sending Catholic missionaries and skilled craftsmen. The resulting blend of Christian and Kongolese traditions reshaped the region. In 1491, after two court officials claimed that the Virgin Mary appeared to them in dreams, the Kongolese king, Nzinga a Nkuwu **(en-ZING-a ah en-KOO-WOO)**, and some of the aristocracy adopted Christianity and sent their children to Portugal for study. The king wanted Portuguese teachers, craftsmen, and weapons to use against a rival kingdom. By the early 1500s, however, after the Portuguese realized the economic possibilities of the Americas, they became far more interested in obtaining slaves than in helping the Kongolese economy or treating the Kongolese as equals. In 1514 they began exporting Kongolese slaves to nearby islands, and eventually many Kongolese were shipped to the Americas. This began a new era for Africa and a direct relationship with the peoples of Europe and the Americas, the region to which we now turn.

SECTION SUMMARY

- Many Africans lived in "stateless societies" in which family relationships, rather than rulers or governments, organized people's lives.
- Africans were part of a variety of social networks, including the family, the village, and the ethnic group, often mistakenly called the "tribe."
- In addition to Muslims and Christians, many Africans were polytheistic, believers in multiple gods and spirits.
- In Africa the oral tradition was much stronger than the written one, and writing spread slowly because African custom did not depend on recordkeeping and important knowledge was passed down orally by griots.
- African agriculture faced a number of challenges, including the difficulty of obtaining and using draft animals, poor soil, and irregular rainfall.
- Several million African slaves were shipped to the Middle East, and the Portuguese laid the groundwork for the much larger European slave trade to the Americas.

American Societies in Transition

What factors explain the collapse of the early Intermediate Era American societies?

Like Africans, most Americans creatively exploited their environments, whether they lived in urban societies or in smaller agricultural or nomadic communities. Whereas many Africans had direct or indirect contact with Eastern Hemisphere networks, Americans remained a world apart from that interconnecting zone and the influences that flowed through it. Furthermore, these American societies were often separated from each other by great distances and by more geographical barriers—high mountains, harsh deserts, and thick forests—than was true for their counterparts in Eurasia. Yet cultures, technologies, and trade goods spread over a wide area. Powerful states with dense populations in Mesoamerica and the Andes, such as the Maya, declined or collapsed, while less centralized governments formed elsewhere, including in North America.

The Collapse of the Classical States

Unlike their Afro-Eurasian counterparts such as Rome, Gupta India, and Han China, most of the major American states of the Classical Era survived into the early Intermediate Era. Great cities such as Teotihuacan, Tikal in the Maya lands, and Tiwanaku in the southern Andes had

CHRONOLOGY
The Americas in the Intermediate Era

200 B.C.E.–700 C.E. Moche

300–1450 Mogollon culture

600 B.C.E.–1100 C.E. Tiwanaku

300–1400 Hohokum culture

600–800 High point of Maya

700–1400 Anasazi culture

700–1700 Mississippian culture

800–900 Abandonment of southern Maya cities

800–1475 Chimu Empire

900–1168 Toltec Empire

ca. 1000 Norse settlement in Newfoundland

1050–1250 High point of Cahokia

1200 High point of Chimu Empire

1428–1521 Aztec Empire

1440–1532 Inca Empire

1492 Columbus reaches Caribbean

flourished for centuries. Their success was based on productive and innovative farming, trade, and metalworking, combined, in some cases, with warfare with their neighbors. Americans were creative plant breeders. Combining maize, a very nutritious crop, with beans, squash, and fish or game provided many people with a well-balanced, healthy diet. Americans also discovered many plant drugs still used today to cure disease or alleviate pain, including quinine and coca.

However, during the early Intermediate Era older centers of religious, economic, or political power were replaced by newer ones. In eighth-century Mesoamerica, Monte Alban, the capital of the Zapotec state, declined while Teotihuacan collapsed, removing a unifying commercial and political hub for central Mexico. Although the Maya had flourished for centuries, by 900 they had abandoned many of their cities. In South America, Moche collapsed around 700, but Tiwanaku only fell apart around 1000 (see Chronology: The Americas in the Intermediate Era). The reasons for these rapid changes of political and economic fortunes remain somewhat unclear, but climate change probably played a role. In Mesoamerica and the Pacific coast of South America, a warming climate baked the land as rains failed and brought drought. Grassy hillsides turned brown, streams dried up, and crops withered.

The Zenith and Decline of the Maya

The Maya of Yucatán and northern Central America declined rapidly and then suddenly collapsed, opening the way for new powers to rise. Maya society reached its peak between 600 and 800, with growing populations and massive monument building. Population densities reached a staggering 600 people per square mile, similar to China today, testifying to the Maya success in mastering a marginal environment for farming. Tikal may have contained 50,000 people. Complex irrigation systems supported a Mayan population of 3 to 5 million people between 600 and 900.

Warfare between states was frequent, but victories were short-lived and resulted in no large empires. The battles were mostly for royal glory and economic predominance, not conquest. The Maya were in close commercial contact with central Mexico; in Teotihuacan, for example, a whole neighborhood was reserved for Maya merchants. Maya also sometimes ventured by boat to Caribbean islands, trading jade, salt, feathers, and chocolate. They were excellent sculpturers, builders, astronomers, and mathematicians and had a well-developed writing system that could express any thought or concept. Thousands of folding-screen books called codices, made of bark paper, were produced, although only a handful survived after the Spanish arrival in the early 1500s. The early Maya evidently practiced forest conservation, considering certain groves of trees sacred, but as they built larger temples they increasingly cut down forests for timber.

Southern Mayan Collapse

Eventually this society faced the same transition as the other classical states. Between 800 and 900 most of the Maya cities in the southern lowlands were deserted, and the whole region lost perhaps two-thirds of its population. Climate change seems to have caused a drought lasting over a century, emptying the complex system of canals and reservoirs that collected rainwater for farming and drinking. Overpopulation may have prompted frantic attempts to increase agricultural productivity on marginally fertile land. The resulting soil degradation and deforestation may have fostered crop failures, reduced rainfall, famine, malnutrition, starvation, epidemics, and increased warfare. Governments may have become more unstable, prompting revolts. As people abandoned the southern Maya cities, some moved to fortified villages in remote areas. The political and religious hierarchy of kings, aristocrats, and priests may have disappeared, and merchants, scribes, and craftsmen ceased their work.

Northern Mayan Cities

However, these dramatic developments seem not to have affected the northern Maya cities such as Uxmal **(oosh-MAHL)**, which flourished until around 1000. Only the northern Yucatán coast enjoyed continuity after 900. But more frequent warfare also engulfed this region, and human sacrifice increased. The city of Chichen Itza **(chuh-chen uht-SAH)**, founded around 800, dominated the Yucatán Peninsula between 1000 and 1250, when it was succeeded by the state of Mayapan **(MY-uh-PAHN)**, itself destroyed by a rebellion in 1441. By the 1500s the Yucatán Maya were fragmented into small states in chronic conflict with each other. The remnants of the Maya people still existed over a wide area of Mesoamerica, but their once-brilliant history was fading from memory.

The Toltecs and Chimu

Rise of the Toltecs

As the older Mesoamerican and Andean states declined or collapsed, other peoples established powerful states not unlike the kingdoms that flourished in West Africa. The Toltecs (TOLL-teks) moved into Mexico's central valley from the desert north and created an empire that lasted from 900 to 1168, systematically recording their history in writing. Their empire seems to have been a loose military alliance involving newcomers from the north mixing with the local people, whose roots lay in Teotihuacan. The Toltecs adopted the cult of **Quetzalcoatl** (kate-zahl-CO-ah-tal), the feathered serpent, which goes back deep in Mesoamerican history. In Toltec tradition, Quetzalcoatl was a human leader who was banished to sea by the war-gods, a story probably based on Topiltzin (to-PILLT-sen) (b. ca. 947), a cult high priest who succeeded his father as Toltec king but whose opposition to human sacrifice and promotion of peace angered more warlike leaders. Forced into exile, the man gradually blended into the god in myth. But the legend also said that the banished man-god, bearded and of fair complexion, would return to seek revenge, and this prophecy haunted later Mesoamericans.

Quetzalcoatl The feathered serpent, a symbol that goes back deep in Mesoamerican history.

The Toltecs achieved influence throughout the region, even over some of the northern Maya cities. Their capital city, Tula, was filled with ceremonial architecture and reached a population of 30,000 to 60,000. Tula was a center for obsidian mining, with Tula craftsmen producing obsidian and copper tools. The Toltecs may have even established some contact with societies in the Andes, and some Toltec trade goods have been found as far north as New Mexico and Arizona. But in the twelfth century the Toltec state, weakened by long-term drought, famine, and war, collapsed, disrupting the trade routes.

Rise of Chimu

Along South America's Pacific coast, the Chimu (chee-MOO) Empire, whose ruling class may have descended from Moche nobles, rose to prominence around 800. By 1200 the Chimu controlled a sizable empire stretching some 600 miles north to south. Their capital, Chan Chan (CHAHN CHAHN), was a substantial city, filled with many adobe-walled compounds and a population of 25,000 to 50,000. The Chimu lords, who lived in seclusion in magnificent walled palaces up to three stories high, had elaborate funerals in which several hundred men and women were sacrificed to serve as attendants in the afterlife. Workers drafted into the army labored on vast construction and irrigation projects, including 25-foot-wide roads. To irrigate the fields of maize, beans, cotton, gourds, squash, peanuts, and fruits, they constructed hundreds of miles of terraces and large storage reservoirs that controlled the flow of water down the mountainsides. These activities allowed the Chimu to avoid all but the most severe droughts and to achieve two or three crops a year.

Pyramid at Tula Each figure on this pyramid at the Toltec capital is made of fitted stone sections and represents a warrior carrying a throwing stick in one hand and a bag of incense in the other.

Robert Harding World Imagery

Map 12.2 Major North American Societies, 600–1500 C.E.
Farming societies were common in North America. The Pueblo peoples such as the Anasazi in the southwestern desert and the Mound Builders in the eastern half of the continent lived in towns. The city of Cahokia was the center of the widespread Mississippian culture and a vast trade network.

Interactive Map

Eventually, however, the Chimu faced challenges they could not overcome. Even with their productive farming, El Niño climate changes could disrupt irrigation. By the fourteenth century the Chimu were in decline, perhaps because of overpopulation and increased salinization of the soil. Around 1475 they were conquered by the Incas and incorporated into a vast Andean empire.

Pueblo Societies

Southwestern Peoples

While only a few American societies formed kingdoms or built large cities, many peoples creatively farmed in challenging environments and supported towns and long-distance trade. Some of the most successful societies developed in the southwestern desert of North America, whose modern descendants are known as the Pueblo Indians because of their permanent towns, called *pueblos* in Spanish. By learning to farm this dry region, the Pueblo peoples survived and sometimes flourished, becoming experts at selecting just the right soils for maize. Southwestern peoples also grew cotton and wove cotton cloth. Towns were often built around human-made dams, terraces, irrigation canals, and reservoirs. The Pueblo peoples also traded with central Mexico and the Pacific coast, mining and exchanging turquoise with Teotihuacan and the Toltecs for craft goods. Some Mesoamerican religious beliefs and customs, such as the tradition of the feathered serpent and ball courts and games, filtered north into some Pueblo communities.

By 700 the Hohokum and Mogollon societies dominated parts of southern Arizona, New Mexico, and northern Mexico (see Map 12.2). Among their large buildings, Casa Grande in northern Mexico, three stories high, was constructed around 1325 of thick adobe atop a platform mound. The surrounding town housed some 2,200 people. By 1000 the neighboring Mogollon people had developed masonry technology for house building. But climate change caused drought in the 1300s, and both the Hohokum and Mogollon settlements were eventually abandoned.

The Anasazi **(ah-nah-SAH-zee)**, meaning "ancient ones" in the Navaho **(NAH-vuh-ho)** language, flourished between 700 and 1400, reaching their height of prosperity between 900 and 1250. Using huge sandstone blocks to build masonry houses, they constructed towns over large sections of Arizona, Colorado, New Mexico, and Utah, including major centers at Mesa Verde and Chaco **(CHAHK-oh)** Canyon. Mesa Verde, ingeniously built into steep cliff walls, probably housed 2,500 people, while another 30,000 lived in the surrounding area. In Chaco Canyon, eight adobe towns sat in or on the rim of the canyon, in which multistoried houses, some six stories high, were built around central plazas. The Anasazi constructed these pueblos with wood beams, stone, and clay carried from distant forests. Wide roads connected the Chaco pueblos with Anasazi towns a hundred miles away. The total Anasazi population probably numbered 100,000.

Anasazi Society

The Anasazi, like many Pueblo Indians, lived in egalitarian communities that practiced matrilineal kinship and matrilocal residence, with men moving into their wife's household. Women owned the houses, crops, and fields, but men dominated the council of elders who administered each town.

Environmental challenges eventually precipitated collapse. By 1200 Anasazi agriculture had declined from severe drought. Deforestation, soil erosion, disease epidemics, and invasions by outsiders may also have been factors. Hard times resulted in increased warfare between pueblos, and some pueblos, their social order undermined, may have resorted to human sacrifice or cannibalism. By 1300 many Anasazi had moved to the Rio Grande River Valley, where they mixed with other newcomers, producing the Pueblo peoples of central and northern New Mexico. By 1400 the older Anasazi culture had collapsed and the pueblos of Chaco and Mesa Verde had long been abandoned. Those Anasazi who survived were probably the ancestors of southwestern tribes like the Hopi **(HOH-pee)** and Zuni.

Anasazi Collapse

The Mississippian and Eastern Woodlands Societies

In the vast Mississippi and Ohio River Basins of eastern North America, where the land was more fertile than in the southwest, mound-building cultures flourished, based on trade and shifting cultivation of maize. The Mississippian culture, the most widespread between 700 and 1700, featured several cities, monumental architecture, social hierarchies, and religious art. The main Mississippian center, Cahokia **(kuh-HOH-kee-uh)**, was strategically located near the juncture of the Mississippi and Missouri Rivers, a few miles from today's St. Louis. At their peak between 1050 and 1250, the city and suburbs probably had a population of 30,000 to 60,000. Cahokia was the North American counterpart to cities such as Teotihuacan and Tula, and Mesoamerican influences are clear in Mississippian communities, which had central plazas that included platform mounds topped by temples and elite houses, probably surrounded by markets. The largest Cahokia pyramid, 1,000 feet long, 700 feet wide, and 100 feet tall, was much larger than the Egyptian pyramids. Circles of standing timbers tracked the seasons by marking the sun's position. As in Mesoamerican cities, Cahokia's priest-rulers probably presided over lavish rituals atop the pyramids, and the chief religious cult worshiped the sun and had a religious symbolism of mythical creatures.

Cahokia

The matrilineal Cahokia society was divided into distinct classes. At the death of a ruler some commoners were sacrificed to accompany him on the voyage to the hereafter. According to oral traditions, a lord showed his status by riding in a flotilla of large canoes decorated with gold objects. Warfare over territory may have been common. Cahokia artisans made baskets, pottery, shell beads, leather clothes, copper ornaments, wooden utensils, and stone tools, and they carved artistic images into their buildings. Cahokia was the major hub of a vast trade network that stretched from the Great Lakes to the Rockies to the Gulf Coast along the Mississippi, Missouri, and Ohio Rivers. Cahokians imported Great Lakes copper to make jewelry, as well as marine shells and shark and barracuda jaws from the Gulf Coast. Cultural influences from Cahokia also spread through the eastern woodlands, including new strains of maize better adapted to cooler climates.

By 1550, the Mississippian culture had collapsed and the Mississippi River Basin population had dwindled, due probably to overpopulation, soil depletion, epidemics, and a cooling climate

SECTION SUMMARY

- American classical states survived longer than their counterparts in Eurasia, though they ultimately declined, perhaps because of climate change.
- The Maya supported an extremely dense population, but by 900 C.E. the southern Maya had collapsed, while the northern Maya continued on fitfully before collapsing by 1500.
- The Toltecs, a loose military empire based in central Mexico, adopted the cult of Quetzalcoatl, the feathered serpent.
- The Pueblo peoples of the American Southwest thrived on maize, grew and wove cotton, and were largely egalitarian and matrilineal.
- In the Mississippi and Ohio River Basins, mound-building cultures thrived on the fertile land and built some of the largest structures in the world.

that damaged agriculture. Growing tensions between the elites and the common folk also may have undermined the political system. By the early 1700s the surviving Mississippian peoples were devastated by diseases such as malaria and smallpox brought by European invaders. The last remnants of the Mound Builders, the sun-worshiping Natchez people in the lower Mississippi valley, were wiped out by French colonizers in a battle in 1731.

In the eastern woodlands of North America, few states had developed, and most farming communities resembled the African stateless societies such as the Tiv and Gikuyu. Although villages had chiefs, often elected by elders, they lacked much authority. Every family participated in decision making. Eastern woodland farming produced abundance. An English observer visiting Massachusetts in 1614 noted that the land was "so planted with gardens and corn fields, and so well inhabited with a goodly, strong people [that] I would rather live here than any where."[11] The men cleared the fields but were often gone for long periods, hunting or fighting. While warfare using bows and arrows was common, it generally led to few casualties. Since the women, working in groups, produced most of the food and many societies were matrilineal, their social and political status was high. Women elders often had the power to approve or prohibit warfare, and often a senior clan mother known for her wisdom nominated a new chief, who would then be elected or rejected by the rest of the tribe. The relative freedom of women resulted in a stronger emphasis on romantic courtship.

The American Empires and Their Challenges

How were the Aztec and Inca Empires different, and how were they similar?

The collapse of the Maya and the decline of the Toltecs and Chimu resulted in the rapid rise of the Aztec **(AZ-tek)** and Inca **(IN-kuh)** societies, who built the largest empires and most sophisticated states ever seen in the Americas before 1500 (see Map 12.3). Thanks to strong armies and well-organized governments, both empires dominated large regions, but both also rapidly collapsed when confronted in the 1500s with the power of Spanish military forces and the epidemic diseases they brought from the Eastern Hemisphere.

The Aztec Empire, Religion, and Warfare

Foundations of Empire

The Aztec society that developed out of the competition for power in Mesoamerica was created by the warlike Mexica, immigrants from the north known for their military skills who spoke Nahuatal **(NAH-what-uhl)**. An early leader told them that "we shall conquer all peoples of the universe. I shall make you lords and kings of all that is in the world."[12] The Mexica took pride in their reputation as warriors and wrote much about their history, identifying themselves as the successor to the Toltecs and adopting many Toltec gods, rituals, and cultural forms. By 1325 they had established a strong state that soon controlled much of the Valley of Mexico, the lake-filled basin where Teotihuacan had once flourished and where they built their capital, Tenochtitlan **(teh-noch-TIT-lan)**. In 1428 they expanded into neighboring regions. Their greatest ruler, Moctezuma **(mock-teh-ZOO-ma)** I (1440–1468), declared that war was the main Aztec preoccupation and its purpose was to gain new territories while acquiring prisoners for sacrifice to the gods. By 1519 the empire controlled much of central and southern Mexico, and it even collected tribute from people as far south as Guatemala and El Salvador. The tribute from the conquered became an important revenue source.

Aztec Religion

Religion supported the warfare. The Aztecs believed the sun to be a warrior-god who daily battled his way across the skies to prevent the destruction of the universe by the forces of darkness. To help the sun-god remain fit for this struggle, the Aztecs had to feed the deity with blood from non-Aztec warriors captured in their frequent fighting, who were regularly sacrificed in gruesome

Map 12.3 South America and Mesoamerica, 900–1500 C.E.
The Maya and Aztecs in Mesoamerica and the Incas in the Andes forged the most densely populated societies, the most productive farming, and the best-organized governments. The Incas built one of the world's largest empires. Other urban societies also flourished in Mexico and South America.

rituals. In Aztec myths, their god Huitzilopochtli **(wheat-zeel-oh-POSHT-lee)** ("The Hummingbird Wizard") commanded them to feed him with human hearts torn from the recently sacrificed. The Aztec practiced human sacrifice on a greater scale than any other major society ever did, sacrificing several thousand captured warriors a year throughout the empire. Other central Mexican people practiced blood sacrifice as well.

Aztec Challenges

By 1500 the Aztecs faced growing economic, political, and military problems. The need for a regular supply of captives fostered a permanent state of war and terror, making for an unstable imperial system and fierce resistance. The conquered peoples paid tribute, but rebellions were frequent, providing an excuse to fight and obtain more captives. As a result of their brutal policies, the Aztecs had many enemies, some of whom were willing to cooperate with the newly arrived Spanish to invade Tenochtitlan. Even before this, Aztec leaders seem to have had a deepening sense of insecurity and to have been haunted by bad portents. These worries increased in 1518, when word reached Tenochtitlan of winged towers (Spanish ships) bearing white men with beards who were landing on Mexico's east coast. Because the Spanish arrival coincided with the prophesied return of Quetzalcoatl, historians debate whether Emperor Moctezuma II identified the Spanish with the god and thus lost the will to resist. However, the crucial fact was that Aztec tools and weapons were still based on sharp minerals, such as obsidian, which were no match for Spanish guns and steel swords. Although the Spanish encountered a vigorous Aztec society, Spanish conquest and occupation in 1521 ended the Aztec era.

Aztec Warrior These drawings, made by a sixteenth-century Aztec artist, show Aztec warriors, wearing costumes that reflect their status, who have defeated their opponents and forced them to kneel in submission. Many such captives would later be sacrificed.

Bodleian Library, Oxford University, Ms. Selden A.1, fol. 64r

Aztec Economy and Society

Trade and Agriculture

The Aztecs developed a prosperous economy and a dynamic social system. Tenochtitlan (the site of today's Mexico City), on a swampy island in the middle of a large lake, was one of the world's great cities: large palaces, temples, forty pyramids, and diverse markets served some 150,000 to 300,000 residents. The Spanish marveled at the markets, where each kind of merchandise was sold in its respective street (see Witness to the Past: An Aztec Market). Thousands of canoes carrying passengers or produce traversed the six major canals daily. The first Spaniards to reach the city in 1519 were awed by the sight:

> *And when we saw all those towns and villages built in the water, and other great towns on dry land, and that straight and narrow causeway leading to Mexico [Tenochtitlan], we were astounded. These great towns and buildings rising from the water, all made of stone, seemed like an enchanted vision. Indeed, some of our soldiers asked whether it was not all a dream.*[13]

chinampas Artificial islands built along lakeshores of the central valley of Mexico for growing food.

Highly productive farming and trade underpinned the Aztec economy. The Aztecs grew their food on artificial islands, called **chinampas**, built on the lakes of the central valley, a technology that dated back hundreds of years. Tenochtitlan served as the core of a trade system that stretched into North America and Central America. Whole villages produced copper items or textiles. Merchants enjoyed a privileged position but were careful to maintain the state's goodwill, some probably serving as spies in outlying areas.

Social Classes

The Aztecs had a hierarchical social structure headed by emperors, true despots who were considered semigods and selected by a group of high officials, priests, and warriors. Then came the warrior-noble caste, whose men were divided into war lodges such as the eagle knights and jaguar knights. If captured by the enemy, they were expected to die with honor. According to an Aztec poem: "There is nothing like death in war. Far off I see it; my heart yearns for it!"[14] The priesthood, mostly celibate, played a key role in Aztec life, preparing the calendars and most of the books. An Aztec remembered the priests as "sages wise in words. They watch over, they read, they lay out the books. They lead us, they tell us the way."[15]

The elite classes held the commoners in contempt. Some commoners were entertainers and some were artisans, who created beautiful representations of the human figure for the elite. Indeed, Aztec sculpture, painted codex books, and murals were traded all over Mesoamerica. Many com-

WITNESS TO THE PAST

An Aztec Market

The Spanish conquistadors who made their first visit to the Aztec capital of Tenochtitlan in 1519, two years before their conquest, were impressed with the wealth of foods and other trade goods available in the markets in and around the city. This account by Bernal Diaz del Castillo (DEE-as del kah-STEE-yoh), a Catholic priest who observed the Spanish conquest, describes the great market of Tlatelolco, near Tenochtitlan. Every day the market was thronged with as many as 25,000 people, and special market days might have attracted twice that number.

We were astounded at the number of people and the quantity of merchandise that [the market] contained, and at the good order and control that was maintained, for we had never seen such a thing before. . . . Each kind of merchandise was kept by itself and had its fixed place marked out. Let us begin with dealers of gold, silver, and precious stones, feathers, mantles, and embroidered goods. Then there were other wares consisting of Indian slaves, both men and women. . . . Next there were other traders who sold great pieces of cloth and cotton, and articles of twisted thread. . . . There were those who shod cloths of hennequen [a tough fiber] and ropes and the sandals with which they are shod. . . .

Let us go and speak of those who sold beans and sage and other vegetables and herbs, . . . and to those who sold fowls, cocks, . . . rabbits, hares, deer, mallards, young dogs and other things of that sort in their part of the market, and let us also notice the fruiterers, and the women who sold cooked food, dough and tripe; . . . then every sort of pottery made in a thousand different forms from great water jars to little jugs; . . . then those who sold . . . lumber, boards, cradles, beams, blocks and benches. . . . Paper . . . and reeds scented with liquid [amber], and . . . tobacco, and yellow ointments. . . .

I am forgetting those who sell salt, and those who make the stone knives, . . . and the fisherwomen and others who sell some small cakes . . . [and] a bread having a flavor something like cheese. There are for sale axes of brass and copper and tin, and gourds and gaily painted jars made of wood. I could wish that I had finished telling of all the things which are sold there, but they are so numerous and of such different quality and the great market place with its surrounding arcades was so crowded with people, that one would not have been able to see and inquire about it all in two days.

THINKING ABOUT THE READING

1. What does the reading tell us about Aztec society and its material culture?
2. In what ways does the Aztec market remind you of a modern supermarket or department store?

Source: Bernard Diaz del Castillo, "The Discovery and Conquest of Mexico," trans. by A. P. Maudslay (NY: Farrar, Straus and Cudahy, 1956).

moners worked as tenant farmers on land owned by nobles. While the upper classes regularly ate sumptuous meals of meat, tortillas, and tamales, followed by a chocolate drink, commoners lived on ground maize meal, beans, and vegetables, cooked with chili, and rarely ate meat. At the bottom of society were many slaves, often debtors or criminals.

Gender Relations

Men and women led very different lives. While their menfolk served the state, elite women enjoyed wealth but had two main roles: childbearer and weaver. Noble fathers advised their daughters "to learn very well the task of being a woman, which is to spin and weave. It is not proper for you to learn about herbs or to sell wood, peppers, [or] salt on the streets"[16] like the commoner women. Elite girls were kept at home until their arranged marriage, when they moved into their husband's family. In contrast, commoner women were freer to leave the house and pursue careers such as street vendors and midwives. While many young boys went to school to learn religion, history, rhetoric, and the arts of war, girls were taught domestic skills and religion as they prepared for marriage at around age sixteen.

The Inca Imperial System

Rise of the Incas

The Incas conquered an empire in the Andes much larger than the Aztec Empire. The Inca society, led by warrior chiefs, came together in central Peru around 1200. In the early 1400s a new leader, Viracocha (VEE-ruh-KOH-chuh) Inca, who claimed to be a living god, launched a new era of conquest with an army led by professional officers. By 1440 Viracocha's son, the pragmatic and visionary Pachacuti (PA-cha-koo-tee) ("World Remaker") (r. 1438–1471), became the major empire builder, eventually conquering the Lake Titicaca Basin and the Chimu Empire. By 1525, after uniting the highlands and the coastal zone for the first time, the Incas dominated nearly the whole region from southern Colombia to central Chile, ruling from their capital city, Cuzco (KOO-skoh), which contained between 60,000 and 100,000 people. Their empire stretched for nearly 3,000 miles, much of it above 8,000 feet in altitude, and became the most politically

Alison Wright/Photo Researchers, Inc.

Machu Picchu This dramatic mountaintop settlement in the high Andes was probably built as a spiritual retreat for Inca royalty, who enjoyed its well-constructed drains, baths, fountains, and administrative buildings.

integrated in all of the Americas. The Incas also treated conquered peoples much more generously than did the Aztecs, incorporating them into their armies, rewarding their service, and tolerating their religions and cultures.

Empire building derived in part from the Inca religion and ideas of royalty, which considered kings to be divine, offspring of the sun and responsible for defending the order of the universe. The kings enjoyed great wealth and pomp. In describing a royal procession, a Spanish observer said that the king wore a collar of huge emeralds and was borne on a sedan throne made of massive gold, lined with the feathers of tropical birds and studded with gold and silver plates. On their death the kings' bodies were mummified and became the center of a cult. Since deceased kings were still considered the owners of their property and land, their successors had an incentive to seek new conquests so as to acquire their own property and land.

Inca Imperial Policies

The Incas conquered or frightened into submission nearly all the farming societies, but their culture and power did not permeate far into the rain forests and deserts. The Incas deliberately resettled peoples to prevent rebellion or to develop new districts. In contrast to the brutal Aztecs, however, the Incas faced relatively few rebellions, in part because many non-Inca appreciated the peace imposed after several centuries of warfare. To win support, the Incas encouraged sons of non-Inca leaders to attend school with the sons of Inca nobles in Cuzco, where they studied history, geometry, military tactics, and oratory. Vast quantities of maize beer were consumed at festivals and celebrations to create goodwill and cooperation among the conquered. The Incas also practiced human sacrifice but on a smaller scale than the Aztecs, mostly on ceremonial occasions. For example, several children from noble families of conquered peoples might be killed on top of a mountain as honored gifts to the mountain gods, and their bodies were then mummified by the cold.

Like most empires, the Inca system was hierarchical and rigid. The royal family kept their bloodline undiluted by having siblings marry each other. Each ruler had a large harem of concubines but also a chief queen, his sister, who had her own magnificent palace and often considerable power behind the scenes. She headed a cult of the moon, led ceremonies for the major goddesses, and also gave birth to the male royal heirs. After some time rebellions became more frequent, and rivalry for the throne sometimes led to civil war. When the Spanish arrived in 1532, such a conflict had just ended, weakening the Inca resistance and allowing the Spanish to triumph militarily and replace the Inca political system with Spanish rule.

Inca Political Economy, Society, and Technology

The Inca Empire was supported by the most productive agriculture and creative technology in the Americas. Food collected by imperial storehouses was distributed as needed to others. In contrast to the Aztecs, the Inca state operated the imperial economy, taking the place of merchants in collecting and distributing goods. The state also required subjects to serve in the army, work state-owned farms, or serve on public works projects. Officials regularly visited villages to monitor work productivity or to check on sanitation.

Inca society was patriarchal, and most Inca commoners were part of large extended families. Both men and women made pottery and worked in the fields, the men plowing and the women sowing the seeds. Peasant women also spent considerable time each day weaving and collecting firewood or llama dung for cooking. The ancient Andean creator-god and chief Inca deity, Viracocha, had both male and female characteristics, and the Incas worshiped several female deities, including the Earth Mother.

Whereas the Aztecs mainly pursued sacrificial victims, the Incas wanted control of labor and land, building administrative centers throughout their territories. Some of these centers were retreats for the elite, such as Machu Picchu (MAH-choo PEE-choo), a spectacular collection of buildings built high atop a narrow mountain ridge above a remote river valley. Because communications were a priority in ruling conquered lands, the Incas linked this vast empire with 14,000 miles of roads radiating out from Cuzco. The roads were graded and paved and had gutters for drainage. Inca engineers even tunneled through rocks and built suspension bridges across gorges and pontoon bridges of reeds across rivers. The road system awed the Spanish, one of whom wrote, "I believe there is no account of a road as great as this, running through deep valleys, high mountains, banks of snow, torrents of water, living rock, and wild rivers."[17] Along these roads relay runners, averaging some 150 miles per day, conveyed administrative messages, and llama pack trains carried supplies.

e **Primary Source: The Chronicles of Cieza** Learn how the Incas used mysterious knotted ropes called quipus as recordkeeping devices that helped them govern a vast empire.

Unlike the Mesoamericans, the Incas had no formal writing system, but they did have an efficient form of recordkeeping that involved differently colored knotted strings, called **quipus**, to record commercial dealings, property ownership, and census data. The Incas also created an oral literature with narrative power, including tales, prayers, and plaintive love songs, all passed down through the generations.

quipus Differently colored knotted strings used by the Incas to record commercial dealings, property ownerships, and census data.

The Incas were particularly skilled in technology and science, and their vast agricultural engineering projects, such as terraces and irrigation canals, generated a widespread prosperity. An extensive irrigation system surpassed most of those in the Eastern Hemisphere, and Inca agriculture was far more productive than Peruvians can manage today. The main crops were potatoes, maize, peanuts, and cotton. Since the Incas practiced soil conservation, they rarely experienced famine. They also developed sophisticated medicine and surgical techniques, including simple anesthesia procedures. Using copper, bronze, and silver, they fashioned beautiful metal objects and were also among the world's greatest cloth maker s, weaving luxurious woolen fabrics from the fleece of the alpaca and making bridges from cords and roofs from fibers. Engineers built fortresses and temples with great blocks of stone so perfectly joined that even a knife could not be inserted between them.

American Societies and Their Connections

Regional Exchanges

The various American societies exchanged ideas and goods with each other over extended networks. As a result of trade and conquest, many people in western South America worshiped the same gods, shared mythologies, practiced human sacrifice, and made similar textiles, artworks, and metal products. Mesoamerican religious ideas, such as the cult of Quetzalcoatl, influenced the Anasazi and even reached into the Mississippi Valley. Mesoamericans traded with the Pueblo peoples for turquoise and with Central Americans for jade. But the Andean and Mesoamerican societies were separated by thousands of miles of forests and mountains, which limited direct contact. The only known direct communication between the two regions was undertaken by traders known as the Manteno, from coastal Ecuador, who for centuries had sailed large balsa rafts carrying cargo up and down the Pacific coast from Chile to Mexico.

However, geographical barriers did not prevent the Andean and Mesoamerican societies from developing some common social and political features. Gender relations, for instance, were very similar in the two regions. Unlike North America, where matrilineal patterns were common, these were patriarchal societies in which men dominated central governments and village life, and older males led the extended family households. Women took care of food, wove cloth, and ran households. Unlike the kings and nobles, who might have several wives, most commoners practiced monogamy. In both regions, warfare was common but ritualized, and conflict involved much protocol, including declarations of war. Armies in close formation fought hand to hand, with the goal of capturing rather than killing opponents. Since most battles occurred far from cities, civilians and settlements were largely left alone.

Demography and Disease

The Americas had far fewer people than the Eastern Hemisphere. Historians debate the size of the Western Hemisphere population in the late 1400s, but recent studies estimate 60 to 75 million. Mesoamerica had the most people, perhaps 20 to 30 million, while the Andes region was home to 12 to 15 million. Perhaps 7 million lived in North America, two-thirds of them in the eastern woodlands and southwestern regions. Compared to the Eastern Hemisphere, Americans faced fewer deadly diseases, and some peoples were quite healthy. Yet, farmers and urbanites, especially Mayans,

SECTION SUMMARY

- The Aztecs lived in a state of constant war and conquest, sacrificing thousands of enemy warriors a year, but their enemies helped the Spanish to conquer them.
- The Aztecs were productive farmers and active traders, and they had a hierarchical social structure in which priests played a central role.
- The Incas conquered a wide area in the Andes and had a hierarchical social structure, but they were far more inclusive and tolerant than the Aztecs.
- Trade in the Inca Empire was tightly controlled by the state, and an extensive irrigation system and soil conservation program yielded a consistent and abundant food supply.
- Despite extremely limited contact between Andean societies and Mesoamerican ones, they were similar in terms of gender relations and warfare protocols.

experienced more health risks than hunters and gatherers and general health seems to have been deteriorating for some centuries prior to the Columbian voyages. Famine caused by sporadic climate change was a bigger problem.

Eventually, however, the American societies faced a challenge coming from the Eastern Hemisphere. The only known European visits to the Americas before 1492 took place in eastern Canada. Around 1000 C.E. a small group of Greenland-based Norse (Norwegian) Vikings led by Leif Ericson visited the area and established a base camp in Newfoundland (see Chapter 14). The Vikings alienated the local people and abandoned their settlement after a few years, but occasional Norse trading visits to the area may have continued for decades, even centuries. The isolated Norse did not publicize their discoveries to Europe, although Portuguese fishermen who visited Iceland may have picked up some information.

Five centuries later a more enduring connection between the hemispheres was forged. In search of Asia, a Spanish expedition led by an Italian mariner, Christopher Columbus, ventured out in three small ships, eventually reaching the Bahamas. In later voyages Columbus visited more parts of the Caribbean and the coast of South America. Even before 1492 some Americans had premonitions of a coming disaster. A chronicle compiled a few years earlier by the Tarascan **(tuh-RAH-skuhn)** people of western Mexico, rivals of the Aztecs, forecast a time when

> *there will be no more temples or fireplaces, everything shall become a desert because other men are coming to the earth. They will spare no end of the earth, and everywhere all the way to the edge of the sea and beyond.*[18]

Despite creating technologies and ways of life that met their needs, thousands of years of isolation had left the Americans vulnerable to the devastating diseases and more effective steel weapons brought from more densely populated Afro-Eurasia. The new oceanic link altered American history forever, as epidemics wiped out millions of people, great empires fell, and Europeans colonized the hemisphere.

CHAPTER SUMMARY

African and American societies were separated by a vast ocean but shared certain patterns. They both formed some great centralized kingdoms and empires as well as many village-based stateless societies, and their contacts with Eurasian states and networks ranged from modest to none. Most Africans were settled ironworking farmers. The Sudanic kingdoms of Ghana, Mali, and Songhai had a complex political, cultural, and intellectual life, as well as trade connections to the Mediterranean. The increase in long-distance trade and the widespread acceptance of Islam helped integrate West Africa into hemispheric networks. Similar trends reshaped the East African coast, where city-states emerged and became linked to the Middle East and the great Indian Ocean maritime trade networks. Some coastal Bantu blended Islam and Arab culture with their own traditions, creating a Swahili culture. Other Bantu formed great kingdoms such as Zimbabwe, which flourished from gold exports. Throughout Africa, however, many people lived in small stateless societies. African religion included both polytheistic and monotheistic traditions, and many people believed in diverse spirits.

Across the Atlantic in the Americas, the classical states, including the long-enduring Maya and its cities, eventually collapsed from climate change and chronic warfare. These societies were replaced by vigorous new peoples, such as the Toltecs and Chimu. The Aztecs and Incas built the largest empires that ever existed in the Americas. The Americans also showed a pattern of continuity with the past. Both the Aztecs and Incas made use of long-established religious traditions and highly efficient agricultural techniques. The Aztecs practiced human sacrifice and commerce on a much greater scale than the Incas, while the Incas were outstanding engineers and road builders. Both empires had productive agriculture and well-organized states, but neither was prepared for the diseases and iron weapons that were brought by the Spanish.

KEY TERMS

mansa
Swahili
oral traditions
Quetzalcoatl
chinampas
quipus

EBOOK AND WEBSITE RESOURCES

PRIMARY SOURCE
The Chronicles of Cieza

INTERACTIVE MAPS
Map 12.1 Major Sub-Saharan African Kingdoms and States, 1200–1600 C.E.
Map 12.2 Major North American Societies, 600–1500 C.E.
Map 12.3 South America and Mesoamerica, 900–1500 C.E.

LINKS

Africa South of the Sahara (http://www-sul.stanford.edu/depts/ssrg/africa/guide.html). Useful collection of links from Stanford University.

Ancient Mexico.com (http://www.ancientweb.org/mexico/). Contains useful features on art, culture, and history.

Ancient Mesoamerican Civilizations (http://www.angelfire.com/ca/humanorigins/). Links and information about the premodern American societies.

Civilizations in Africa (http://www.wsu.edu/~dee/CIVAFRCA/CIVAFRCA.HTM). Contains useful essays on premodern Africa.

History and Cultures of Africa (http://www.columbia.edu/cu/lweb/indiv/africa/index.html). Provides valuable links to relevant websites on African history.

Internet African History Sourcebook (http://www.fordham.edu/halsall/africa/africasbook.html). This site contains much useful information and documentary material on ancient Africa.

The Aztecs/Mexicas (http://www.indians.org/welker/aztec.htm). Essays and information on the Aztecs.

Plus flashcards, practice quizzes, and more. Go to: www.cengage.com/history/lockard/globalsocnet2e

SUGGESTED READING

Connah, Graham. *African Civilization: An Archaeological Perspective*, 2nd ed. Cambridge: Cambridge University Press, 2001. An overview of early African societies, emphasizing the rise of cities and states.

D'altroy, Terence N. *The Incas.* Malden, MA: Blackwell, 2003. An excellent, up-to-date introduction to the Andes societies in this era.

Davidson, Basil. *The Lost Cities of Africa*, rev. ed. Boston: Atlantic-Little, Brown, 1987. A revision of a classic and a very readable study of early African societies from the Sudan to Zimbabwe.

Ehret, Christopher. *The Civilizations of Africa: A History to 1800.* Charlottesville: University of Virginia Press, 2002. A survey text with detailed coverage.

Fagan, Brian M. *Kingdoms of Gold, Kingdoms of Jade: The Americas Before Columbus.* London and New York: Thames and Hudson, 1991. A nicely illustrated, readable introduction to the American societies.

July, Robert W. *A History of the African People*, 5th ed. Prospect Heights, IL: Waveland Press, 1998. A very readable survey of African history.

Kehoe, Alice Beck. *America Before the European Invasions.* New York: Longman, 2002. A recent overview of the North American peoples and history before 1600 C.E.

Knight, Alan. *Mexico: From the Beginning to the Spanish Conquest.* New York: Cambridge University Press, 2002. An introduction to Mesoamerican societies through the Aztecs.

Longhena, Maria and Walter Alva. *The Incas and Other Ancient Andean Civilizations.* New York: Barnes and Noble, 2007. Lavishly illustrated study of pre-Inca and Inca cultures.

Mann, Charles C. *1491: New Revelations of the Americas Before Columbus.* New York: Alfred A. Knopf, 2005. A readable summary of recent scholarship on the American societies.

Nurse, Derek, and Thomas Spear. *The Swahili: Reconstructing the History and Language of an African Society, 800–1500.* Philadelphia: University of Pennsylvania Press, 1985. An excellent summary of what we know about the Swahili and their early history.

Pearson, Michael. *The Indian Ocean.* New York: Routledge, 2003. Integrates East Africa into the hemispheric trading system.

Shaffer, Lynda Norene. *Native Americans Before 1492: The Mound-building Centers of the Eastern Woodlands.* Armonk, NY: M. E. Sharpe, 1992. A brief overview, for the general reader, of some early North American societies.

Smith, Michael E. *The Aztecs*, 2nd ed. Malden, MA: Blackwell, 2003. A recent scholarly study.

Thobhani, Akbarali. *Mansa Musa: The Golden King of Ancient Mali.* Dubuque, IA: Kendall-Hunt, 1998. A readable introduction to Mali and its rulers.

Townsend, Richard F. *The Aztecs*, rev. ed. New York: Thames and Hudson, 2000. A readable, well-illustrated survey of Aztec history and society.

CHAPTER

13

South Asia, Central Asia, Southeast Asia, and Afro-Eurasian Connections, 600–1500

CHAPTER OUTLINE

- Hinduism, Buddhism, and South Asian Society
- The Coming of Islam to India and Central Asia
- Cultural Adaptation and Kingdoms in Southeast Asia
- Buddhist, Confucian, and Islamic Southeast Asian Societies

PROFILE
Pwa Saw, a Burmese Queen

WITNESS TO THE PAST
The Songs of Kabir

Fujita Art Museum

Xuan Zang Arriving in China
A seventh-century Buddhist Chinese pilgrim, Xuan Zang, spent many years traveling in India, collecting Buddhist wisdom and observing Indian life. This Chinese painting shows him and his caravan returning to China with pack loads of Buddhist manuscripts.

India's shape is like the half-moon. The administration of the government is founded on benign principles. The taxes on the people are light. Each one keeps his own worldly goods in peace. The merchants come and go in carrying out their transactions. Those whose duty it is sow and reap, plough and [weed], and plant; and after their labor they rest awhile.

—XUAN ZANG, SEVENTH-CENTURY CHINESE VISITOR TO INDIA[1]

FOCUS QUESTIONS

1. How did Hinduism and Buddhism change in this era?
2. How did Islam alter the ancient Indian pattern of diversity in unity?
3. What political and religious forms shaped Southeast Asian societies in the Early Intermediate Era?
4. What was the influence of Theravada Buddhism, Confucianism, and Islam on Southeast Asia?

In 630 C.E. a determined Chinese Buddhist monk, Xuan Zang **(swan tsang)** (ca. 600–664), traveled the Silk Road to India on an extended pilgrimage to collect holy books and ended up spending fifteen years visiting every corner of the subcontinent. He was very observant and politically astute, but he also chafed at the perception of many Indian Buddhists that China was too remote to truly claim Buddhism. In a debate at the great Nalanda **(nuh-LAN-duh)** Monastery, Xuan Zang told the monks that

> *Buddha established his doctrine so that it might be diffused to all lands. Who would wish to enjoy it alone? Besides, in my country the emperor is virtuous and the subjects loyal, parents are loving and sons obedient, humanity and justice are highly esteemed.*[2]

Xuan Zang found much to admire in India, including the Indian tolerance for diverse viewpoints. Even though Hinduism was dominant, Buddhism enjoyed protection and royal patronage. Xuan Zang's writings described an Indian society that had a rigid social structure but was also creative and open to foreign influences, including regular contact with China, Europe, the Middle East, and Indonesia. Xuan Zang was also much impressed with India's high standard of living, efficient governments, and generally peaceful conditions. But some customs troubled him. Despite the bias in Indian religions against eating animals, many Indians consumed fish, venison, and mutton. He also criticized the caste restrictions, such as confining untouchables to their own shabby neighborhoods. After covering some 40,000 total miles in his many years of travel, Xuan Zang returned to China in 643, taking with him hundreds of Buddhist books to be translated into Chinese. He also became a confidant of the Tang emperor and fostered closer relations between India and China.

India's cultural diversity and openness to foreign influence were due in part to the repeated invasions of Central Asian peoples, who brought with them varied beliefs and customs. Hindu religion and society absorbed these newcomers and their ideas. Groups with differing customs generally lived peacefully side by side, and Indian ideals spread to neighboring peoples. But Hindu political domination and the assimilation of newcomers faced a particularly severe challenge with the arrival of Muslims, who gained control over large parts of the subcontinent. Having their own strong religious ideas, Muslims were not easily absorbed into the complex world of Hindu culture. The coming of Islam constituted a great turning point in the region's development, a transition comparable to that initiated by the Aryan migrations into India several millennia earlier.

e Visit the website and eBook for additional study materials and interactive tools: www.cengage.com/history/lockard/globalsocnet2e

Southeast Asians also adopted new political systems and religions. Powerful kingdoms emerged, some of them strongly influenced by Indian culture. By the fifteenth century new faiths from outside, Theravada Buddhism and Islam, had reshaped the political map and created diverse cultures that remained a hallmark of Southeast Asian societies.

Hinduism, Buddhism, and South Asian Society

How did Hinduism and Buddhism change in this era?

No Hindu leaders recreated an empire like the Maurya or Gupta Empire. Instead India encompassed many states, cultures, and languages. Despite a broad Hindu tradition and the common heritage it created, India became a collage of microcultures in which many images coexisted on the same canvas, shaping each other while retaining their own distinctive character, thus demonstrating one of the great themes in Indian history: diversity in unity. Although dividing into competing schools of thought and practice, Hinduism experienced a Renaissance and grew in popularity. While Hinduism increasingly shaped Indian life, Buddhism faded in India but found new influence in neighboring societies. Hindu culture flourished in India for half a millennium before facing the concerted challenge from Islamic peoples.

Unity and Disunity in Hindu India

The political disunity following the fall of the Gupta state in the fifth century proved to be a long-term pattern. King Harsha Vardhana (600–647) briefly united parts of north India (see Chronology: South Asia, 600–1500). A man of enormous energy, he amassed a formidable army of 100,000 cavalry and 60,000 elephants and skillfully held together his small empire while cultivating close relations with Tang China. Harsha had a fondness for philosophy and was renowned as a poet. While enjoying the pomp of kingship, he also listened patiently to the complaints of his humbler subjects. A strong Buddhist like Ashoka, he tolerated all faiths but also prevented his beloved sister, a Hindu, from committing sati at her husband's cremation. Harsha ruled for forty-one years, but his empire collapsed on his death.

Harsha

Despite Harsha's brilliant reign, dozens of states proliferated in the subcontinent. Many Hindu states were absolute monarchies in which rulers owned many economic resources, such as forests, mines, and weaving operations, and tried to control outlying regions through appointed governors. Holding a precarious position of power, they buttressed their rule by claiming a divine mission and employed Brahmans (Hindu priests) as court advisers to give them legitimacy.

Rajputs ("King's Sons") A Hindu Indian warrior caste formed by earlier Central Asian invaders.

North and south India developed somewhat different political patterns. **Rajputs** ("King's Sons"), members of a Hindu warrior caste formed by earlier Central Asian invaders, controlled some north Indian states. Rajputs were raised in traditions of chivalry, honor, and courage not unlike those of Japanese samurai or medieval European knights, their code emphasizing mercy toward enemies and precise rules of conduct in warfare. However, the Rajput-led kingdoms often fought wars against each other for regional power. In contrast, many south Indian states were oriented to the sea and hence specialized in piracy and foreign trade. South Indian merchants had more political influence than north Indian merchants and continued their lucrative maritime trade with Southeast Asia, China, and the Middle East. Indeed, many visited or settled in Southeast Asia, bringing with them lasting south Indian ideas on art, politics, and religion.

Village Life

Whatever the fragmentation of politics and regions, the continuity of Indian culture was reflected in the countless villages that remained the basic unit of Indian life. Even today, about 80 percent of Indians still live in villages. Farmers had to feed an Indian population that reached around 100 million by 1500. Land was regarded as the property of the ruler, who was entitled to either a tax or a share of the produce. The land tax remained the main source of state revenue and the main burden on the villagers. As long as they regularly met their tax obligations, peasants had the hereditary right to use the land they farmed. Village governments included a council elected annually from among village elders and caste leaders that dispensed local justice and collected taxes.

The typical village remained largely self-sufficient and organized through the caste system, which promoted stability. Members of different castes lived separately in their own neighborhoods, but all contributed to the livelihood of the larger community. Each village had a potter, carpenter,

CHRONOLOGY

	South Asia	Southeast Asia
600	**600–647** Empire of Harsha	**600–1290** Srivijaya Empire
800	**846–1216** Chola dynasty	**802–1432** Angkor Empire
1000	**1192–1526** Delhi Sultanate	**1044–1287** Pagan kingdom
1200	**1336–1565** Vijayanagara state	**1238–1419** Sukhotai state
1400		**1403–1511** Melaka state

blacksmith, clerk, herdsman, teacher, astrologer, and priest as well as many farmers who served each other on a barter basis in what was essentially a symbiotic community. Some modern writers romanticize traditional village life, portraying people living peacefully together, and village life did offer psychological and economic security. Each villager had a recognized status, rights, and duties, a supportive caste community, and many personal relationships. When the rulers maintained peace, repressed banditry, and kept the tax burden reasonable, most people were probably contented.

Many Indians also lived in towns and cities. Merchants helped administer the towns, but, as in China, they were heavily taxed and not allowed to become too independent of government. During the eighth century, to escape the Islamic conquest of Persia, some Zoroastrians fled to western India, where they formed the distinctive *Parsee* (Persian) community and became known as businessmen and manufacturers. Indeed, India was one of the world's leading manufacturing centers. Urban workshops produced cloth, textiles, pottery, leather goods, and jewelry for local use or export to markets as distant as China, Africa, and eastern Europe. India and China provided most of the world's industrial goods until the eighteenth century, and the average per capita incomes for Indians remained high by world standards.

CHRONOLOGY
South Asia, 600–1500

600–647 Empire of Harsha in north India

620–649 First Tibetan kingdom and introduction of Buddhism

711 First Muslim invasion of northwest India

846–1216 Chola kingdom in south India

1192–1526 Delhi Sultanate

1336–1565 Kingdom of Vijayanagara in south India

1398–1399 Devastation of Delhi by Tamerlane

The Hindu Social System and Scientific Traditions

Family System

The Hindu social system demonstrated great continuity over the centuries and, as in China, subordinated the individual to the group. Indians owed their most basic obligations to their extended family, a relationship described in an old saying as "joint in food, worship, and property." The family, which included people of several generations, lived together in the same household, enforced caste regulations among their members, and also collectively owned their economic assets, such as farmland. Because families shared their wealth, they constituted an effective source of social security. Most families, especially in north India, were patriarchal, headed by a senior male, although older women enjoyed considerable influence. Children lived in close contact with cousins, aunts, uncles, and grandparents. Child rearing became a group obligation.

Marriage customs reflected regional differences. In north India, parents arranged marriages. Girls were married off young, sometimes by the age of seven or eight, usually to a boy in a neighboring village. Because the bride's family paid for the wedding and was expected to give lavish presents, families preferred sons. In South India girls were more likely to marry boys whom they already knew, often a cousin. In Kerala (CARE-a-la) in southwestern India, one large group practiced **polyandry**, marriage of a woman to several husbands. Most Indian families viewed divorce as a humiliation.

polyandry Marriage of a woman to several husbands.

Gender Relations

The Indian social system favored men, who enjoyed many privileges, and male leaders became obsessed with preserving social stability and controlling female sexuality. From puberty females of all castes were taught to keep a distance from all men except their closest relatives. High-caste women were expected to spend their time at home, only occasionally visiting friends or family. Low-caste and untouchable women enjoyed more mobility because they had to earn the incomes needed for family survival. Most women led lives marked by obedience, sacrifice, and service, submitting to parents, husband, and children. The young bride, usually much younger than her

Benoy K. Behl

Sculpture of Two Lovers from Konarak Temple This sculpture of two embracing lovers comes from the Konarak temple in the north Indian state of Orissa. The Hindu temple, dedicated to the sun-god, was built in the thirteenth century and featured many erotic sculptures.

husband, moved into her husband's household and obeyed her new mother-in-law. Yet, husbands often treated their brides indulgently. Indians also revered motherhood. After she bore children (especially sons), the wife's status improved considerably, and she enjoyed more freedom and respect. As a woman grew older and became a mother-in-law herself, she gained even more influence.

Of course, not all wives were silent and subservient. Women also enjoyed some legal rights, and ill-treatment of women was condemned, although it was undoubtedly common. But widowhood could prove catastrophic if a woman had no son. Since Hindu custom frowned on remarriage, to be a young and childless widow was to face a difficult situation. To avoid surviving their deceased husband, some women, especially in north India, chose or were forced to die on their husband's funeral pyre. An ancient Indian expression captures the challenge for women: "As a girl she is under the tutelage of her parents; as an adult her husband; as a widow her sons."

Indians held diverse views about sex. Many books commended celibacy and advised married men to exercise their sexual prerogatives sparingly if they wanted health and virtue. Yet, the worldly views of many are reflected in many Indian texts such as the *Kama Sutra*, a manual of lovemaking and related matters. Even the Hindu gods and goddesses were portrayed in art and writings as highly sexual beings, a view very unlike that of the virginal Madonna and celibate Jesus of Christian tradition, the image of a spiritually and morally pure Buddha, and the puritanical restrictions of Islam. During this era Indians made many contributions in mathematics and science. One of the greatest Indian mathematicians and astronomers, Bhaskara (bas-CAR-a), living in the twelfth century, proved that zero was infinity. He also designed a perpetual motion machine by filling a wheel rim with quicksilver. Bhaskara's book on the subject, translated into Arabic, later reached Europe and inspired drawings of quicksilver wheels that influenced modern scientific thought. The first weight-driven clocks, built in Europe after 1300, may have been based in part on Bhaskara's ideas.

Some Indian astronomers and mathematicians found employment in Tang China, fostering a fruitful exchange of knowledge between the two societies. However, while Indians developed a rational system of mathematics and the basis for scientific reasoning, the indifference of the higher castes to applied or practical inquiry hindered the development of science. As the brahmans became more powerful, those with technical expertise lost status. Some visitors reported a growing disdain among Hindu thinkers for foreign ideas. An astute Muslim observer wrote that "the Hindus believe that there is no country, king, religion, [or] science like theirs."[3]

Hindu Diversity and Renaissance

Diverse Beliefs

Hinduism provided the spiritual framework for the great majority of South Asians until the coming of Islam. Its strength lay in its diversity, which could accommodate all classes, personalities, and intellects. It gave the scholars and mystics abstract and speculative thought and the more worldly individuals a wealth of ritual, art, and gods for every occasion. The values of Hinduism permeated the diverse Indian society. Recognizing that individuals varied in their spiritual and intellectual capacities, Hindus tolerated many different practices and beliefs and relied on no fixed and exclusive theology. As the earliest Hindu holy book, the *Rig Veda*, put it: "Reality is one; sages speak of it in different ways."[4] Concepts of spiritual power ranged from an indescribable but all-pervading, omnipotent God, to personal gods with human attributes, to demons and spirits. Hinduism remained undogmatic, a philosophy and way of life with no central institution or church to monitor the faith or to codify beliefs. Muslims introduced the collective term *Hindu*, from the Persian term for "Indians," to describe the varied Indian sects, and in the nineteenth century Europeans began referring to the diverse collection of Indian beliefs as "Hinduism."

The tradition of tolerance suggested that all approaches to God were valid, although mystics and intellectuals tended to consider their approaches more worthy. For example, mother-goddess worship was common among the lower castes, especially in south India, but was less popular among the higher castes. People worshiped the many gods and goddesses in various ways. Many men and women believed that the wives and consorts (companions) of the main male gods were more responsive to their needs than the male gods. Thus many cults worshiped Shiva's wife, Shakti **(SHAHK-tee)**, who was kind and beautiful but also cruel and fearsome. Most Hindus perceived the universe as a collection of temporary living quarters inhabited by individual souls going through a succession of lives. The most devout had the ultimate goal of being liberated from human consciousness and freed from the endless cycle of birth and rebirth, but only a small minority seriously sought to escape from the earthly world with all its pain and pleasures. While wandering holy men were respected for their withdrawal from worldly activities, most Hindus met their social obligations to family, caste, and village while practicing moderation and temperance.

Hindu Tolerance

Hinduism helped establish a common culture throughout India. Brahmans served as advisers to kings, standardizing political ideas and rituals. But while they monopolized reading the Sanskrit scriptures, the Hindu classics were available to all through storytellers. The collections of ancient prayers and hymns, the Vedas, were also translated from Sanskrit into regional languages.

Many thinkers who embellished or revitalized Hindu traditions lived during these centuries, creating the Hindu Renaissance. Through his itinerant preaching, debates with rivals, and written commentaries on the *Upanishads*, Shankara **(shan-kar-uh)** (788–820), a south Indian brahman, revitalized the mystical *Vedanta* tradition, with its belief in the underlying unity of all reality. To Shankara, all the Hindu gods were manifestations of the impersonal, timeless, changeless, and unitary Absolute Reality, *Brahman*, and the individual soul only a tiny part of the whole unity of the universe. While accepting the Hindu scriptures as divine revelation, he wanted to prove them through logical reasoning and debate, yet he also argued that all knowledge was relative because humankind's grasp of reality is warped by ignorance. The truth of existence could only be understood through ascetic meditation. Shankara's views remain very popular among modern Indian intellectuals.

The Hindu Renaissance

Other philosophers offered different visions of Hinduism. Ramanuja **(RAH-muh-NOO-ja)** emphasized **bhakti**, devotional worship of a personal god, arguing that the gods should be accessible without priestly help. A few centuries later some Christian reformers in Europe would develop a similar notion of establishing a personal relationship with God without priestly aid. The bhakti tradition emphasized pilgrimage to holy places such as the city of Benares **(buh-NAHR-uhs)** (Varanasi), alongside the Ganges; Hindus who died in Benares had their sins washed away. Many early bhakti thinkers, most of them non-brahmans, also opposed or downplayed the caste system. The bhakti tradition appealed particularly to women. An early female poet, Antal, urged women devotees to revere Lord Krishna (an incarnation of Vishnu).

bhakti Devotional worship of a personal Hindu god.

The Hindu Renaissance included the building of flamboyant temples, whose sculptural art illustrated the intricate mythology of the faith. One of the best examples was a temple constructed in Khajuraho **(kah-ju-RA-ho)** that was dedicated to Vishnu. Sculptures carved into the temple walls suggested the delights enjoyed by the gods, including lovemaking. The erotic, sexually explicit paintings or carvings in many Hindu temples reflected a rather open view about portraying sexuality.

Transitions in Indian and Tibetan Buddhism

While Hinduism was enjoying its resurgence, the influence of Indian Buddhism gradually declined except in northeast India, where governments patronized the religion and its institutions, such as the college at the Nalanda Monastery, which attracted religious students from around Asia. Pilgrims from distant lands, such as Xuan Zang, showed how much Buddhism was becoming a major influence in the eastern half of Eurasia as the faith spread in Central Asia, Tibet, China, Korea, Japan, and Southeast Asia, adapting to different cultures. The intellectual environment of northeast India also promoted a dialogue between Hinduism and Mahayana Buddhism, fostering new schools of Buddhist and Hindu thought. One new Buddhist school, the **Vajrayana** ("Thunderbolt"), featured female saviors and magical powers. It spread during the eighth century into Nepal and Tibet.

Vajrayana ("Thunderbolt") A form of Buddhism that featured female saviors and the human attainment of magical powers.

In Bengal the contact between Mahayana Buddhists and Hindu followers of Shiva who revered his consort, the goddess Shakti, led to **Tantrism (TAN-triz-uhm)**, which worshiped the female essence of the universe. Both the Tantric and Vajrayana schools exalted female power as earth mother and divine strength. Tantric sects developed within both Hinduism and Buddhism, and some were mystical sects that presented male-female sexual union as a symbolic unity between

Tantrism An approach within both Buddhism and Hinduism that worshiped the female essence of the universe.

the earthly and cosmic worlds. Other sects promised release from life's pain in a single lifetime to those who cultivated hedonism, pleasure, and ecstasy. Tantric Hindus were often hostile to the caste system. Most Hindus and Buddhists denounced Tantrism as an excuse for debauchery and sexual desire, and Tantrism gradually became a minor strand in the two religions.

While Buddhism declined in India, the remote high plateau of Tibet became a refuge for the religion. The first known pre-Buddhist Tibetan state emerged when Songsten-gampo **(SONG-sten-GOM-po)** (r. 620–649 C.E.) unified several tribes. Interested in connecting to an Asian world where Buddhism was expanding, he established close relations with Tang China and married a Chinese princess. Although not a Buddhist, he allowed the religion to spread in his kingdom. Tibetans also made the Sanskrit script from India their written language. By the eighth century Buddhism had become the dominant Tibetan faith, and its monasteries enjoyed many legal protections and financial support from the government. But many Tibetans also continued to follow the ancient folk religion, *bon*. The two faiths competed for popular support and political influence, and violent religious conflicts destroyed the unified state.

Rise of Tibetan Buddhism

However, both Tibetan Buddhism and state building were later reinvigorated in the thirteenth century when many Buddhist monks fled to Tibet to escape Islamic persecution in India. Political relations with the predominantly Buddhist Mongols, who had conquered China and established some control in Tibet, also boosted Tibetan Buddhism. A unified Tibetan government was reestablished in 1247 under the leadership of one Buddhist sect and then by aristocratic families, which persisted into the seventeenth century.

Lamaism The Tibetan form of Buddhism, characterized by the centrality of monks (*lamas*) and huge monasteries.

Tibetans developed a distinctive religious tradition in their harsh highlands environment. Their Buddhism is often termed **Lamaism** **(LAH-muh-iz-uhm)** because of the centrality of monks, or *lamas* **(LAH-muhz)**, and huge monasteries. Perhaps a quarter to a third of male Tibetans became career monks, and Buddhism came to permeate every aspect of Tibetan life. Believers practiced magic, made pilgrimages to shrines, and provided generous support to monasteries and Buddhist teachers. Tibetans also blended Buddhism with strong beliefs in the supernatural, including evil spirits. For example, people spun hand-held or roadside prayer wheels and carved prayers into stones, seeking the help of the Buddha.

SECTION SUMMARY

- In the Intermediate Era, India was fragmented into many small states; the north was influenced by earlier Central Asian invaders and the south by maritime trade with Southeast Asia.
- The village, which was based on cooperation and caste, remained the basic unit of Indian life and provided people with a sense of security.
- Indian merchants in the cities were heavily taxed, but India and China produced most of the world's manufactured goods in this era.
- In the Hindu social system, the individual was subordinate to the group and people tended to live in extended families that supported their members.
- Indian men had much more power than women, who were forced to marry early and earned respect through bearing children, particularly boys.
- The mathematician Bhaskara discovered perpetual motion, which influenced science in the West.
- Hinduism adapted itself to the needs of a wide variety of people, from the worldly to the scholarly, and helped to establish a common culture throughout India.
- Shankara, a major thinker of the Hindu Renaissance, emphasized the importance of reason and of ascetic meditation, while Ramanuja emphasized the worship of a personal god.
- Indian Buddhism declined generally, but it remained important in the northeast, where Vajrayana and Tantrism grew out of the interplay between it and Hinduism.
- Buddhism became the dominant religion in Tibet, where it became Lamaism, and many Indian Buddhist monks took refuge there to escape Islamic persecution.

THE COMING OF ISLAM TO INDIA AND CENTRAL ASIA

How did Islam alter the ancient Indian pattern of diversity in unity?

The spread of Islamic religion and government in India was a major transition in Indian history, as important as the coming of the Aryans several millennia earlier. Since Muslims and Hindus were almost exact opposites in their beliefs, Islam created a great divide in South Asian society. As Al-Biruni, an eleventh-century Muslim scholar, put it: "Hindus entirely differ from us in every respect. In all manners and usages they differ from us to such a degree as to frighten their children with us."[5] For centuries Hinduism had absorbed invaders and their faiths, but Islam, a self-confident, missionary religion, could not be assimilated. The tension between the two faiths sometimes resulted in conflict. However, Islam enriched Indian culture, establishing new connections with western Asia while also promoting the spread of Indian ideas, especially in mathematics and science, to the Middle East and Europe. Many Indians embraced the new faith, and Muslims also gained political dominance over large parts of India.

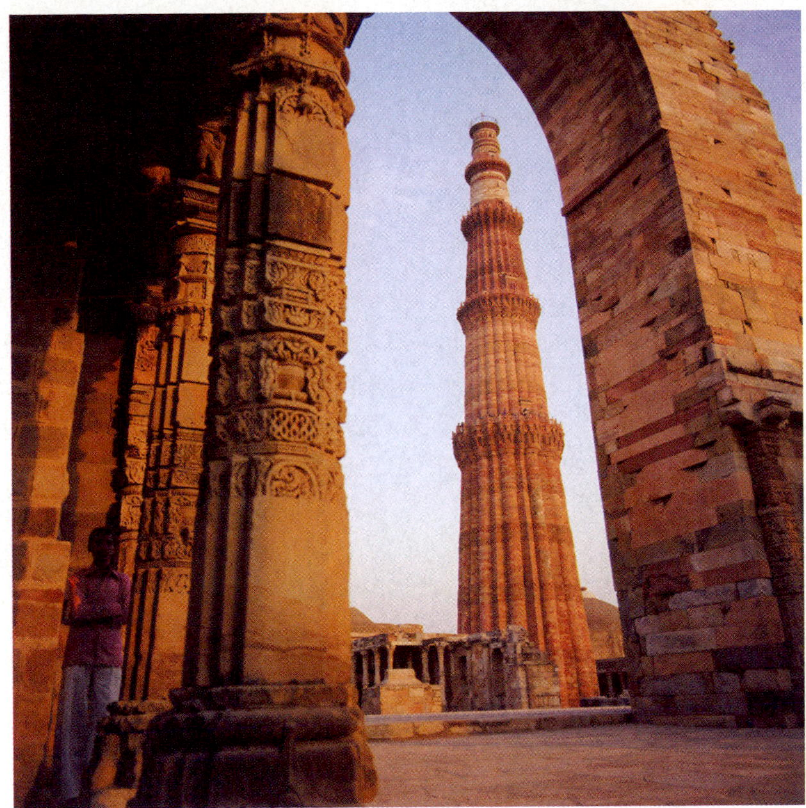

Robert Harding World Imagery

The Kutb Minar Tower in Delhi The 240-foot-high Kutb Minar temple in Delhi was built between the twelfth and fourteenth centuries to celebrate Muslim victory in north India.

Early Islamic Encounters

Islamic forces reached Central Asia and India within a few decades of the religion's founding. Western Asians had long been linked to Central Asia through Silk Road trade, and they were well aware of India's riches. Arab sailors had been active in South Asia for centuries before the rise of Islam, linking India by trade to western Asia and East Africa. Islamic rulers hoped to dominate these valuable regions, and military conflict increased.

During the seventh century Arab forces expanded into Afghanistan. By 673 Arab armies were moving into Silk Road cities such as Bukhara and Samarkand, dominated by the Sogdian **(SOG-dee-uhn)** merchants, mostly Buddhists and Zoroastrians. The rival Central Asian city-states could not come together against the dynamic Arabs, and although many Sogdians resisted, by the early eighth century Arabs had conquered most of the cities. The Arab defeat of Chinese forces at the Battle of Talas River in 751 marked the end of serious resistance to Muslim dominance in Central Asia, and eventually most Central Asians adopted Islam. In India, conflict between Hindus and Muslims began slowly. In 711 Indian pirates plundered an Arab ship near the mouth of the Indus River, and Arab armies responded by briefly conquering the western Indus Basin. But not all encounters were violent. Arab traders from Yemen settled in the ports of southwestern India, bringing Islam to some of the people there.

Afghan Sultanates

The expansion of Islam through western and Central Asia presented a challenge to India. By the eleventh century various Turkish peoples had formed Islamic sultanates in Afghanistan, of which Ghazni **(GAHZ-nee)** was the most powerful. Sultan Mahmud **(MACH-mood)** of Ghazni (r. 997–1030) led his soldiers on campaigns into India, as much for plunder as for conquest. Seeing the multitude of Hindu idols as an abomination to Islamic monotheism, the invaders destroyed Hindu temples while they looted cities. The vast wealth they took from northwestern India to Ghazni helped that city become a great center of Islamic learning and arts that attracted famed scholars such as the Persian Al-Biruni.

Muslim Conquests

The Rajputs led the major Indian opposition to Muslim invaders, maintaining a spirited Hindu resistance for many decades. But Rajput military tactics were outdated, and the military forces were divided in their political loyalties. In addition, Indian wars had been fought largely between rulers and their respective warrior castes rather than by conscripted civilians. The caste system allowed only warriors such as the Rajputs to be trained in arms, so they could not effectively mobilize other Indians to help in the fight. Eventually the Rajput armies were defeated by the more mobile, horse-riding Muslims.

The pillaging and destruction by the early Muslim invaders fostered long-term Hindu antipathy toward Muslims. Many Hindus were killed, enslaved, or robbed. For example, even Al-Biruni concluded that Mahmud "utterly ruined [India's] prosperity. To Mahmud the Hindus were infidels, to be dispatched to hell as soon as they refused to be plundered."[6] The Muslim newcomers zealously persecuted Buddhists as well, destroying their monasteries and schools, including the

Map 13.1 India and the Delhi Sultanate, ca. 1300 C.E.

At its height, the Delhi Sultanate controlled much of northern India. South India was divided into many major states, with the Cholas and Pandyas the largest. Indian ports were connected by a vigorous maritime trade to the Middle East, East Africa, and Southeast Asia.

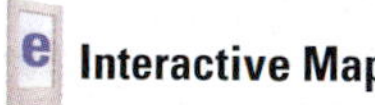
Interactive Map

complex at Nalanda. Thousands of monks either were killed or fled to sanctuary in the Himalayas or Tibet. This repression helped eradicate Buddhism from the land of its birth.

The Rise and Fall of the Delhi Sultanate

A new chapter in Muslim expansion began in 1191 when a Turkish prince, driven by religious fervor and lust for the region's riches, conquered most of northern India and founded the Delhi Sultanate (see Map 13.1). The sultanate (1192–1526) reached its height in the 1200s and 1300s and brought political unity to north India for the first time in centuries. Under the Delhi regime Islamic authority and religion spread throughout north India. But the Delhi system was unstable and experienced frequent bloodshed and treachery as leaders competed for power.

Delhi Sultans

The Delhi sultans had diverse ruling styles. Some were patrons of the arts, supporters of science, experts in Greek philosophy, and builders of architecturally splendid structures. Many others, however, were tyrannical and cruel, routinely killing rivals and their families. Some ruined the country with reckless spending. All the sultans employed Persian-style royal pomp, but they also styled themselves after Hindu monarchs, demanding prostration and toe-kissing from subordinates. This blending of ruling styles suggests that Muslim and Hindu cultures were mixing among the elite. Some sultans expanded Delhi's power into central India and, briefly, south India, creating an empire larger than the Gupta realm.

Two of the most able Delhi sultans were Iltutmish **(il-TOOT-mish)** (1211–1236), who made the Delhi Sultanate the most powerful state in north India, and his remarkable daughter, Raziya (r. 1236–1240). Iltutmish kept out the Mongol armies of Genghis Khan by skillful diplomacy, gradually followed more tolerant policies toward Hindus, and welcomed Muslim refugees, among them scholars and artists, fleeing the Mongols. Their large numbers helped to abort any possibility of Hinduism gradually absorbing Islam. Iltutmish's chosen successor, Raziya, became the only female Muslim ruler in Indian history, praised by scholars of her time for fostering trade, building roads, planting trees, supporting poets and artists, and opening schools. A male Muslim observer described her as "a great monarch, wise, just and generous. She was endowed with all the qualities befitting a king, but she was not born of the right sex, and so in the estimation of men all these virtues were worthless."[7] Raziya was resented as a female leader in a patriarchal society. She further offended Muslim conservatives by abandoning the veil, dressing in male garb, and having a close, perhaps romantic, relationship with a male personal attendant. She died defending her position from male rivals.

By the mid-fourteenth century north India was humbled by severe drought and famine caused in part by climate change. The Delhi Sultanate went into a rapid decline, devastated by rebellion and civil war. Meanwhile, a new Muslim threat appeared in the northwest, the Mongol and Turkish forces of Tamerlane (1336–1405). The ruthless warrior had already conquered Central Asia and Persia, creating the Timurid Empire based at Samarkand (see Chapter 10). In 1398 Tamerlane's forces invaded India, looting Delhi and killing perhaps 100,000 inhabitants in the city, mostly Hindus. Thousands more were dragged away as slaves. Tamerlane defended his actions, arguing that "although I was desirous of sparing them it was the will of God that this calamity should befall the city."[8] Tamerlane and his army returned to Central Asia, leaving Delhi's few surviving inhabitants to perish by plague or starvation. His invasion had a great impact on India, destroying the grand city of Delhi and with it political unity in north India. The Delhi Sultanate survived for several centuries, but in a shrunken form. By the fifteenth century India was fragmented into dozens of Muslim and Hindu states.

Hindu Politics and Culture

The Nelson-Atkins Museum of Art, Kansas City, Missouri. Purchase: William Rockhill Nelson Trust, 34-7. Photography by Jamison Miller

Shiva as Lord of the Dance This famous bronze statue of Shiva as Lord of the Dance was made by Chola artists in southeast India. Displaying himself as a god of many qualities, Shiva grasps the flame of destruction in one hand and the drum of creation in another. The small figure under his foot represents the illusions that Shiva undermines.

While the Delhi Sultanate governed part of India, various Hindu monarchies survived elsewhere, especially in south and east India. Like post-Heian Japan and medieval Europe, these states featured economic self-sufficiency and political decentralization, with warriors receiving land from the monarch in exchange for military service. Commerce flourished, especially in south India. Merchants on the southwest coast, including Jews and Arabs, maintained close ties to western Asia and North Africa and enjoyed wealth. Ports such as Cochin **(KOH-chin)** and Calicut **(KAL-ih-cut)** in Kerala and Cambay **(kam-BAY)** in Gujarat **(GOO-jur-ot)** played major roles in Indian Ocean trade.

The Tamil **(TAA-mill)** people of southeast India, controlled by a Hindu dynasty known as the Cholas **(CHO-luhs)** (846–1216), profited from both piracy and foreign trade. The powerful Chola navy controlled the eastern Indian Ocean and conquered both Kerala and Sri Lanka (Ceylon). Chola merchant castes organized a dynamic maritime trade that brought great wealth to the society and revenue to the kings, and sometimes Chola seafaring led to plunder and conquest as far away as Southeast Asia. Some Chola rulers also established close diplomatic and trade ties to Burma, Cambodia, and China.

The Tamils developed an outstanding artistic tradition, including many fabulous Hindu temples featuring magnificent bronzes. Perhaps the greatest creation was made by some unknown tenth-century genius, a bronze figure of Shiva portrayed as "Lord of the Dance," ready to commence the cosmic dance of life and restore vitality to the world. For centuries artists and historians praised this work, one writing that

> *rarely has an artist achieved such perfect balance and harmony in any medium as in this metal statue, whose symbolism embraces all of Hindu civilization in its mythic power. . . . The workmanship of the artists was flawless in its beauty, magically transmuting metal to flesh-like texture, imparting the breath of life to their subjects.*[9]

Vijayanagara

The Cholas declined, and the power vacuum was eventually filled by another Hindu kingdom, Vijayanagara **(vij-uh-yuh-NUHG-uhr-uh)** ("City of Victory"), established in 1336. This militarily powerful state, which eventually dominated much of south and central India, built a magnificent temple-filled capital city but was destroyed by rivals in 1565. The persistence of Hindu rule in southern India preserved Hindu customs and institutions, disappearing in some northern areas.

Muslim Rule and the Reshaping of Indian Life

Hindu-Muslim Conflict

The growing number of Muslims and Islamic political power changed Indian history. Muslims and Hindus experienced chronic conflict, the natural result of tensions created by their very different values. To Muslims, Hinduism, with its many deities, elaborate rituals, powerful priests, fondness for images, and preference for eating pork but not beef, constituted the opposite of all Islam held sacred. At the same time, Hindus despised the intolerance of some Muslim rulers and desperately resisted Muslim control. Since Muslim governments could not afford to permanently alienate their Hindu subjects, who constituted a huge majority of the population, some compromises between rulers and ruled were made. Although Muslim rulers often confiscated the wealth of rich Hindu nobles, life in the villages went on largely undisturbed. Eventually many Muslim scholars and leaders came to respect Hindus and the small Zoroastrian community as peoples of the book, counterparts to Christians and Jews in western Asia. But non-Muslims still faced second-class status and special tax payments.

Growth of Islam

Over the centuries many Indians converted from Hinduism to Islam, especially in the Indus River Valley in the northwest and in Bengal in the northeast. A much smaller proportion of southerners embraced Islam. Converts included rich Hindus who wanted to safeguard their positions and secure government offices in Muslim-ruled states, as well as many poor Hindus who converted to escape low or untouchable status and to avoid the heavier taxes on non-Muslims. Over 90 percent of today's Muslims in South Asia are descendants of converts from Hinduism or Buddhism rather than Muslim immigrants. Today Muslims constitute one-fourth of the South Asian population. Sufi mystics, who sought personal union with god, were the key to many Hindus' conversion. Bengali folk tradition celebrates a Sufi who moved to a village and built a mosque: "For the whole day [he] sat under a fig tree. His fame soon spread far and wide. Everybody talked of the occult [healing and psychic] powers he possessed."[10] People respected the intensity of the Sufis' spiritual discipline and the depth of their religious understanding. Perhaps the Sufi message also became popular because it closely resembled bhakti Hinduism, which also emphasized emotional commitment. Today many South Asian Muslims and some Hindus still venerate Sufi mystics of earlier centuries as saints.

purdah The Indian Muslim custom of secluding women.

Religious and cultural mixing occurred. Some Hindu and Muslim mystics came together to form a group emphasizing a love of god. Some poets, honored later as saints, promoted a mixture of Sufi and bhakti ideals, among them Kabir (kah-BEER) (1440–1518), a member of a low-status caste of weavers from Benares (see Witness to the Past: The Songs of Kabir). Although blind and illiterate, Kabir wrote poetry that is still revered today by both Hindus and Muslims. The cultural mixing also fostered a new language, Urdu (ER-doo), a combination of Persian, Turkish, Arabic, and Indian words superimposed on a Hindi grammar and written with the Arabic script, that was used by many Muslims in north and northwest India. Muslim influences, including Persian words and Persian food, were also incorporated into Hindu social life. Many Hindu males adopted Muslim clothing styles, and in north India some Hindus began practicing the local Muslim custom of **purdah**, seclusion of women. Some intermarriage also occurred, and, at the village level, Muslims fit themselves into the caste system to some extent. Thus the Muslim society that developed in India, like the Hindu society, was not egalitarian but rather was led by an upper class who descended from immigrants.

However, despite some mixing, from the thirteenth century onward, the life of India became two distinct currents flowing side by side. Under the challenge of the missionary Islam, Hinduism became more conservative, emphasizing tradition and priestly leadership, while most Muslims refused to be assimilated into the social and religious fold of Hinduism and remained disdainful of Hindus and of the caste system. But, unlike Buddhism, which was centered in vulnerable monasteries, Hinduism's decentralized structure proved stable. Thus Hindus and Muslims mingled to some extent along the lines of contact but never formed a single stream. This persistent division greatly affected twentieth-century India, when the British colony of India (most of the subconti-

SECTION SUMMARY

- Hindu warriors fended off Muslim invaders for a time, but they were outmatched and eventually defeated by their aggressive opponents.
- The destruction inflicted by Muslim invaders caused long-term Hindu resentment and also contributed to the decline of Buddhism in India.
- The Islamic Delhi Sultanate brought unity to north India for the first time in centuries, but its rulers ranged from the enlightened to the tyrannical.
- Various Hindu monarchies, including the Cholas, maintained power in southern and eastern India, while Hindu traditions died out in the north.
- The Delhi Sultanate declined because of climate change and civil war, and north Indian unity was shattered by the invasion of Tamerlane.
- Muslim and Hindu beliefs were radically opposed, but over time Muslim rulers came to tolerate Hindu subjects, many of whom eventually converted to Islam.
- While there was some cultural interchange between Hindus and Muslims in India, for the most part, the traditions remained separate.

WITNESS TO THE PAST

The Songs of Kabir

Coming from a Hindu family that had recently converted to Islam, Kabir was well acquainted with both religious traditions. His mystical poems of passionate love for a monotheistic god rejected religious prejudice, rigid dogmatism, and the caste system. Modern Indian intellectuals seeking to bridge the gap between the two faiths particularly admired his attempt to see beyond the limitations of the two religions and his absolute opposition to violence. The following poem argues that individuals must experience God for themselves.

O servant, where dost thou seek Me? Lo! I am beside thee.

I am neither in temple nor in mosque; I am neither in Kaaba [Muslim shrine] nor in Kailash [abode of Shiva].

Neither am I in rites and ceremonies, nor in Yoga and renunciation.

If thou art a true seeker, thou shalt at once see Me: . . .

It is needless to ask of a saint the caste to which he belongs; For the priest, the warrior, the tradesman, and all the thirty-six castes, alike are seeking for God.

It is but folly to ask what the caste of a saint may be; The barber has sought God, the washerwoman, and the carpenter . . .

Hindus and Muslims alike have achieved the End, where remains no mark of distinction. . . .

O brother! when I was forgetful, my true Guru [Hindu teacher] showed me the Way.

Then I left off all rites and ceremonies, I bathed no more in the holy water: . . .

From that time forth I knew no more how to roll in the dust in obeisance:

I do not ring the temple bell; I do not set the idol on its throne; I do not worship the image with flowers.

It is not the austerities that mortify the flesh which are pleasing to the Lord,

When you leave off your clothes and kill your senses, you do not please the Lord,

The man who is kind and who practices righteousness, who remains passive amidst the affairs of the world, who considers all creatures on earth as his own self,

He attains the Immortal Being, the true God is ever with him.

Kabir says: "He attains the true Name whose words are pure, and who is free from pride and conceit."

If God be within the mosque, then to whom does this world belong?

If Ram [God] be within the image which you find upon your pilgrimage, then who is there to know what happens without?

Hari [Lord Vishnu] is in the East; Allah is in the West. Look within your heart, . . .

All the men and women of the world are His Living Forms. Kabir is the child of Allah and of Ram [God]: He is my *Guru*, He is my *Pir* [Sufi saint].

THINKING ABOUT THE READING

1. Why would someone of mixed religious background be open to questioning rigid doctrines?
2. What does Kabir think about the traditions of organized religions?
3. Where does Kabir believe that God is to be found?

Source: William Theodore De Bary, ed., *Sources of Indian Tradition*, Vol. 1

nent) was eventually divided into separate nations, the Hindu-dominated India and the Muslim-dominated Pakistan. A third religion also maintained a South Asian base, since the island of Sri Lanka remained a bastion of Theravada Buddhism.

Cultural Adaptation and Kingdoms in Southeast Asia

What political and religious forms shaped Southeast Asian societies in the Early Intermediate Era?

Owing partly to the stimulus from India and, to a lesser extent, China, several great Southeast Asian kingdoms developed near the end of the first millennium C.E., establishing their main centers in what is today Cambodia, Burma, the Indonesian islands of Java and Sumatra, and Vietnam (see Map 13.2). These Southeast Asian states mixed outside influences with their own traditions to foster new societies (see Chronology: Southeast Asia, 600–1500).

Map 13.2 Major Southeast Asian Kingdoms, ca. 1200 C.E.

By 1200 the Khmer Empire (Angkor), which once covered much of mainland Southeast Asia, had declined. Sukhothai, Pagan, Srivijaya, Champa, and Vietnam were other major states.

Interactive Map

Indianized Kingdoms and Societies

From early in the Common Era until around the fourteenth century, many Southeast Asian societies made selective use of Indian models in shaping their political patterns, a process known as Indianization. For example, the rulers declared themselves god-kings, not just China-style intermediaries between the human realm and the cosmos but rather a reincarnated Buddha or Shiva worthy of cult worship. By maintaining order in the world, they ensured cosmic harmony. Kings enjoyed enormous prestige but also faced continuous threats from rivals, who often succeeded in acquiring the throne, and neighboring states.

The economic foundations of the Indianized kingdoms differed. Some were based largely on agriculture, while others, including the states alongside the Straits of Melaka, depended heavily on maritime trade. These contrasting patterns represented skillful adaptations to the environment. In the agriculture-based economies, rice-growing technology became productive enough to sustain large centralized states, but in places with large areas of swampland people compensated for their lack of good farmland by maximizing their access to the open frontier of the sea.

The migration and mixing of peoples and their cultures were significant themes in Southeast Asia, as they had been in India, Europe, and Africa. Peoples such as the Burmans **(BUHR-muhnz)** in the ninth century and the Tai **(tie)** peoples in the seventh to thirteenth centuries moved from Tibet and China into mainland Southeast Asia. The Burmans established the dynamic state of Pagan **(puh-GONE)** in central Burma (1044–1287).

Religion played a central role in the new states. Though the peasantry remained chiefly animist, Southeast Asian elites adopted Mahayana Buddhism and Hinduism. At its height in the twelfth century, the city of Pagan was one of the architectural wonders of the world, filled with magnificent temples and shrines for the glory of Buddhism and Hinduism. At Pagan and elsewhere religion infused government and the arts, and Hindu priests became advisers on court rituals. Hindu Indian epics such as the *Ramayana* and *Mahabharata* became deeply imbedded in the cultures, and the Hindu kings, gods, and demons animated the arts.

Southeast Asian societies shared many common features. Extensive trade networks, both land and maritime, had linked the region from earliest times, and many people specialized in local or foreign commerce. Most of the larger states were multiethnic in their population, including many foreign merchants, a diversity that fostered a cosmopolitan attitude. Still, most Southeast Asians were farmers and fishermen and lived in villages characterized by a spirit of cooperation for mutual survival. Unlike in India, however, Southeast Asian family patterns ranged from flexible structures to a few patriarchies and matriarchies. In contrast to India and China, women held a relatively high status in most Southeast Asian societies, and some, like the Burmese queen Pwa Saw **(pwah saw)**, exercised political influence behind the scenes (see Profile: Pwa Saw, a Burmese Queen). An enduring gap in world-views separated the social and cultural traditions of the courts, including the royal families, administrations, and capital cities, from the villages. For example, Indian scripts became the basis for many Southeast Asian written languages, such as Khmer, Burman, and Thai, and fostered poetry, religious speculations, and historical chronicles, important components of Southeast Asia's elite culture.

The Angkor Empire and Society

The Khmer people created the greatest Indianized state, the kingdom of Angkor **(ANG-kor)** in Cambodia. A visionary king, Jayavarman **(JAI-a-VAR-man)** I (r. 802–834), who identified himself with the Hindu god Shiva, established the state in 802, and his successors extended the kingdom, which persisted until 1432. The magnificent temples still standing today testify to the prosperity and organization of Angkor society. By the twelfth century the bustling capital city, Angkor Thom

(ANG-kor tom), contained perhaps a million people, making it much larger than medieval European cities and comparable to all but the largest Chinese and Arab cities. Trade with China and other countries flourished, and many Chinese merchants lived in the kingdom.

At its height in the twelfth and thirteenth centuries, Angkor had an empire controlling much of what is now Cambodia, Laos, Thailand, and southern Vietnam. The Khmers acquired and maintained their empire by warfare, diplomacy, and pragmatism, usually giving regional governors considerable autonomy. Many kings were art patrons and builders of roads and temples. Zhou Daguan (joe ta-kwan), a Chinese ambassador in Angkor in 1296, left vivid descriptions of Angkor, including the system of justice presided over by the king: "Disputes of the people, however insignificant, always go to the king. Each day the king holds two audiences for affairs of state. Those of the functionaries or the people who wish to see the king, sit on the ground to wait for him."[11] The well-financed state held much power over the population and supported substantial public services, including hospitals, schools, and libraries. Conscripted workers constructed an extensive canal and reservoir network for efficient water distribution and storage, exhibiting some of the most advanced civil engineering in the premodern world. The Khmers also may have had the most productive agriculture in world history, producing three to four crops of rice a year.

CHRONOLOGY
Southeast Asia, 600–1500

192–1471 Kingdom of Champa

600–1290 Srivijaya Empire

802–1432 Angkor Empire

939 End of Chinese colonization in Vietnam

1044–1287 Pagan kingdom in Burma

1292–1527 Madjapahit kingdom on Java

1238–1419 Sukhotai kingdom in Siam

1350–1767 Ayutthaya kingdom in Siam

1403–1511 Melaka kingdom and Sultanate

1428–1788 Le dynasty in Vietnam (founded by Le Loi)

Religion played an important political and cultural role. The Angkor government resembled a theocracy: it presided over a cult for the popular worship of the god-kings, and priestly families held a privileged position. The numerous temples and Hindu priests controlled massive wealth. Hindu values were also reflected in theater, art, dance, and the many magnificent stone temples, some of them as huge as small mountains. Designed to represent the Hindu conception of the cosmos centered on the abode of the gods, the temples provided vivid symbols of a monarch's earthly power, since the construction involved amazing engineering skills and massive conscripted labor. The largest religious complex in the premodern world, Angkor Wat (ANG-kor waht), was built by some 70,000 workers in the twelfth century. The reliefs carved into stone at Angkor Wat and other temples provide glimpses of daily life, showing fishing boats, midwives attending a childbirth, merchant stalls, festival jugglers and dancers, peasants bringing goods to market, the crowd at a cockfight, and men playing chess.

In exchange for material security, Khmer commoners tolerated a highly inequitable distribution of wealth and power as well as substantial labor demands. Angkor had numerous slaves and people in temporary servitude. Although no India-style caste system existed despite the strong Hindu influence, the social structure was rigid. Each class had its appointed role: below the king were the priests, and below them were the trade guilds. The vast majority of the population were of the farmer-builder-soldier class. Khmer women played a much more important role in society and politics than women did in most other places in the world. According to Zhou Daguan, women operated most of the retail stalls: "In this country it is the women who are concerned with commerce."[12] Some royal women were noted for intellectual or service activities. Jayarajadevi (JAI-ya-RAJ-adeh-vee), the first wife of King Jayavarman VII, took in hundreds of abandoned girls and trained and settled them. After her death the king married Indradevi (IN-dra-deh-vee), a renowned scholar who lectured at a Buddhist monastery. Women dominated the palace staff, and some were even gladiators and warriors. Chinese visitors were shocked at the liberated behavior of Khmer women, who went out in public as they liked. Women were also active in the arts, especially as poets.

Angkor Wat Temple Complex This photograph shows the inner buildings of the Angkor Wat temple complex in northern Cambodia. The towers represented the Hindu view of the cosmos. Mount Meru, the home of the gods, rises 726 feet in the middle.

Robert Harding World Imagery

Indianized Urban Societies in Java and Sumatra

Several Indianized states developed in the Indonesian archipelago on the large islands of Java and Sumatra. The encounters between Indian influence and local traditions produced in Java a distinctive

PWA SAW, A BURMESE QUEEN

Women in royal families played important political roles in many Southeast Asian states, mostly behind the scenes, but few had the influence of thirteenth-century Queen Pwa Saw of Pagan. Much of what we know about her life comes from a chronicle of the country's history compiled by Burmese scholars in the nineteenth century, and modern historians are divided on whether it represents more myth than fact. Whatever the accuracy, in their traditions the Burman people remember Queen Pwa Saw as witty, wise, and beautiful and as exercising political influence for forty years during one of their most difficult periods.

The girl who would become queen was born to a prosperous peasant family in a remote village around 1237. According to the legends, a deadly king cobra approached her when she was asleep but failed to attack, considered a favorable omen for a bright future, and a jasmine bush she tended astonished her neighbors by blooming in three colors. This unusual event drew the attention of the young King Uzana (r. 1249–1256), a playboy fond of hunting and drinking who was visiting the district with a large entourage of attendants. The unexpected visit of a king and his party riding on elephants spurred the villagers into frenzied preparations for a proper reception to demonstrate their respect. Infatuated with the bright, pretty, graceful, and talkative sixteen-year-old girl, Uzana took her back to Pagan as one of his many wives and appointed her a deputy queen. A short time later, Uzana died in an accident while hunting wild elephants.

With her husband's death, Pwa Saw was thrown into the schemes and rivalries of the royal court as various factions maneuvered for power. Placed in a precarious position as a young bride resented by rival queens, she quickly forged an alliance with the able and wily Chief Minister Yazathingyan **(YAH-za-THING-yan)**, who feared the accession of the king's oldest son, the unpopular Prince Thitathu **(thee-TAH-thoo)**, with whom he had long quarreled. Together they convinced officials to support another son, Narathihapade **(NAR-a-THITH-a-PAH-dee)** (r. 1256–1287), as king and make Pwa Saw chief queen. But the young king proved arrogant, quick-tempered, and ruthless, alienating many at court and earning the nickname "King Dog's Dung." While the economy declined, the king boasted that he was "the commander of 36 million soldiers, the swallower of 300 dishes of curry daily," and had 3,000 concubines. His zeal to build an expensive Buddhist pagoda fostered the proverb that "the pagoda is finished and the great country ruined." Pwa Saw remained loyal but lost respect for the king.

After her ally Yazathingyan died leading royal forces to suppress a rebellion in the south, Pwa Saw skillfully survived the king's paranoid suspicions and the constant intrigues of the court nobles, attendants, and other queens. Because the king trusted the widely revered queen, she could often overrule his destructive tendencies and talk him into making wiser state decisions. She also convinced the erratic king to appoint capable officials. But she had to maintain her wits. Increasingly paranoid, Narathihapade executed any perceived enemies and burned another queen to death. In the 1270s, anxious to prove himself a great leader, he rejected Pwa Saw's advice to meet Mongol demands for tribute and avoid conflict and instead escalated tensions, thus bringing on war, disaster, and the temporary Mongol occupation of Pagan.

Even as the Pagan state declined, Pwa Saw asserted a benevolent influence. For instance, in 1271 she donated some of her lands and properties to a Buddhist temple, expressing hope that in future existences she would "have long life, be free from illness, have a good appearance, melodic of voice, be loved and respected by all men and gods, [and] be fully equipped with faith, wisdom, nobility." In 1287 the mad king was murdered by one of his sons. In 1289 Queen Saw and surviving ministers selected a new king, Kyawswar **(kee-YAH-swar)** (1287–1298). With that last effort to help her country, she retired in style to her home village.

THINKING ABOUT THE PROFILE

1. What skills did Pwa Saw use to influence the court?
2. What does this profile tell us about the relations between queens and kings at Pagan?

Notes: Quotations from D. G. E. Hall, *A History of South-East Asia*, 4th ed. (New York: St. Martin's Press, 1981), 169; and Michael Aung-Thwin, *Pagan: The Origins of Modern Burma* (Honolulu: University of Hawaii Press, 1985), 41.

Robert Harding World Imagery

Court Life of Pwa Saw No known paintings of Pwa Saw exist. This fresco, from the Ananda Buddhist temple at Pagan, shows rich court ladies, much like Pwa Saw herself, relaxing in an upstairs room of a magnificent Buddhist temple while, downstairs, stallholders hawk their wares to visitors.

religious and political blend known as Hindu-Javanese, which was based on an agricultural economy. According to Hindu-Javanese thinking, because the earthly order mirrored and embodied the cosmic order, people must avoid disharmony and change to preserve the cosmic order. The god-king's duty was to prevent social deterioration and maintain order in a turbulent human world. The greatest Javanese kingdom, Madjapahit (MAH-ja-PA-hit) (1292–1527), reached its peak in the fourteenth century under the fabled Prime Minister Gajah Mada, when it loosely controlled a large empire embracing much of present-day Indonesia. As in Angkor, the capitals and palaces of Javanese kingdoms like Madjapahit were built to imitate the cosmic order. Hindu-Buddhist ideas can be seen vividly in temple complexes such as the temple mountain of Borobodur (BOR-uh-buh-door) in central Java, as well as in the shadow puppet plays, or **wayang kulit** (WHY-ang KOO-leet), which were based on the Hindu epics like the *Ramayana* but had much local content as well.

Hindu-Javanese Society

wayang kulit Javanese shadow puppet play based on Hindu epics like the *Ramayana* and local Javanese content.

Social inequality permeated Hindu-Javanese society, and a complex etiquette regulated the relations between those of varied status. The aristocracy, who administered the realm, expected deference from commoners, most of whom lived in villages whose cultures differed substantially from those of the royal capitals. Much village work was planned and carried out on a communal basis, following a tradition of mutual aid. Peasants identified more with their village community than with distant kings in their palaces.

Trading States

Coastal states on Sumatra were shaped more heavily by international trade than were the agricultural kingdoms of Java and Cambodia. The Straits of Melaka separating Sumatra from the Malay Peninsula was a major passageway through which a complex maritime trading system gradually emerged that linked the eastern Mediterranean, Middle East, East African coast, Persia, and India with East and Southeast Asia. Between 600 and 1290 many of the small trading states in the Straits region came under the loose control of Srivijaya (SREE-vih-JAI-ya), an empire based in southeastern Sumatra that exercised considerable power over the region's international commerce and maintained a close trade relationship with powerful China. Srivijaya's naval force both fought and engaged in piracy. Srivijaya was also a major international center of Buddhist study, attracting thousands of Buddhist monks and students from many countries.

International Influences and the Decline of the Indianized States

The great Indianized states of Southeast Asia came to an end between the thirteenth and fifteenth centuries, but the changes were mostly gradual. Some causes of decline were internal. Angkor experienced a combination of military expansion that overstretched resources; increased temple building that resulted in higher tax levies and forced labor that antagonized much of the population; and growing breakdown of the irrigation system, which took more and more labor to maintain. Increasingly unpredictable rains due to climate change overstretched the hydraulic system. But international influences also played a role in the disintegration of Angkor and neighboring states.

Migrations and Invasions

Over several centuries various groups from mountainous southwestern China speaking Tai languages migrated into Southeast Asia, some of them setting up their own states in the Mekong Basin and northern Thailand. These were the ancestors of the closely related Siamese (SYE-uh-meez), today known as the Thai, and the Lao (laow) peoples. As they moved south, the Tai conquered or absorbed the local peoples while also adopting some of their cultural traditions. Eventually they came into conflict with Angkor, repeatedly sacking the capital and seizing much of the empire's territory. The Khmer Empire soon disintegrated, and the Angkor capital was abandoned. As the monuments to their glorious past were overtaken by jungle, the Khmers became pawns perched uneasily between the expanding Vietnamese and Siamese states.

Meanwhile, the Mongols encountered Angkor's neighbors. After conquering China, in 1288 they attacked Pagan because the Burmans refused to recognize Mongol overlordship. When the Mongols soon withdrew, they left instability in Burma as rival groups competed for power. Elsewhere in Southeast Asia the Mongols found mostly frustration. Although a land-and-sea invasion of Vietnam and Champa inflicted terrible damage, it was ultimately repelled by a temporary Vietnamese-Cham military alliance. A Mongol naval expedition to Java also proved a costly failure. Southeast Asians were among the few peoples to successfully resist Mongol conquest and power.

Theravada Buddhism and Islam

A third force for change was religion. By early in the second millennium of the Common Era, Theravada Buddhism and Islam began filtering peacefully into the region from outside. Theravada Buddhism had been a strong influence in Burma, but a revitalized form came from Sri Lanka and provided a challenge to the Indianized regimes. The Buddhist message of egalitarianism, pacifism, and individual worth proved attractive to peasants weary of war, public labor projects, and tyrannical kings. Theravada Buddhism was a tolerant religion able to exist alongside the rich animism of the peasants, who could honor the Buddha while worshiping local spirits. By the fourteenth century most of the Burman, Khmer, Siamese, and Lao peasants had adopted Theravada Buddhism, while the elite mixed the faith with the older Hindu–Mahayana Buddhist traditions.

From the thirteenth through sixteenth centuries, Sunni Islam filtered in from the Middle East via India and spread widely. Like Buddhism, Islam offered an egalitarian message and a complex theology that appealed to peasants and merchants in the Malay Peninsula, Sumatra, Java, and some of the other islands. Some adopted Sunni Islam in a largely orthodox form, while others mixed it with animism or Hinduism-Buddhism. Sufism also blended well with the existing mysticism. Only a few scattered peoples maintained Indianized societies. Among the Balinese **(BAH-luh-NEEZ)** on the Indonesian island of Bali, Hinduism and other classical patterns remained vigorous, emphasizing arts like dancing, music, shadow plays, and woodcarving. Thus the many visitors to Bali today can glimpse patterns that were once widespread in the region.

SECTION SUMMARY

- Southeast Asian kingdoms were heavily influenced by India, and, as in India, their rulers considered themselves god-kings, although their power was limited in the provinces.
- Most Southeast Asian states were multiethnic and were influenced by immigrants and the migration of Mahayana Buddhism and Hinduism from India.
- The Indianized kingdom of Angkor controlled a large swath of Southeast Asia and completed advanced civil engineering projects, such as an extensive canal system and the huge temple complex of Angkor Wat.
- Hindu priests played a very important role in Angkor, and the social structure was extremely rigid, though an Indian-style caste system did not take hold and women were more important in society and politics than in most places in the world.
- On Java, a highly stratified Indianized society that championed harmony developed, while on Sumatra, Srivajaya became a powerful commercial empire.
- Southeast Asians fended off the Mongols, but new peoples such as the Tai invaded and destroyed Angkor, and the gradual introduction of Theravada Buddhism and Sunni Islam challenged the hierarchical order and displaced Indian influence in many states.

Buddhist, Confucian, and Islamic Southeast Asian Societies

What was the influence of Theravada Buddhism, Confucianism, and Islam on Southeast Asia?

By the fifteenth century Southeast Asia had experienced a major transition. The Indianized kingdoms had gradually been replaced by less despotic states, and networks of trade and religion linked the region even more closely to Afro-Eurasia. The major Southeast Asian societies diverged from the earlier Indian and Chinese-influenced patterns, and Theravada Buddhism, Confucianism, and Islam permeated further into the countryside. By the fifteenth century three broad but very distinctive social and cultural patterns had developed: the Theravada Buddhist, the Confucian-Buddhist Vietnamese, and the Malayo-Muslim or Indonesian.

Theravada Buddhist Society in Siam

Rise of Siamese States

The Siamese established several states in northern and central Thailand. Sukhotai **(SOO-ko-TAI)** (1238–1419), founded by former Angkor vassals, controlled much of the central plains of Thailand. According to Siamese tradition, Sukhotai's glory was established by Rama Kamkheng **(RA-ma KHAM-keng)** ("Rama the Brave"), a shrewd diplomat who established a close tributary relationship with China. Sukhothai adopted the Khmer script and incorporated Khmer influences in literature, art, and government. Siamese chronicles portray Rama as a wise and popular ruler. A temple inscription tells us that

> *the Lord of the country levies no tolls on his subjects. If he sees someone else's wealth he does not interfere. If he captures some enemy soldiers he neither kills them nor beats them. In the [palace] doorway a bell is suspended; if an inhabitant of the kingdom has any complaint or any matter irritates his stomach and torments his mind, and he desires to expose it to the king ring the bell.*[13]

This may have exaggerated his merits, but Rama did make Theravada Buddhism the state religion and adopted humane laws. By 1350, however, Sukhotai was eclipsed by another Siamese state with its capital at Ayutthaya (ah-YUT-uh-yuh), which developed a regional empire whose influence extended into Cambodia and the small Lao states along the Mekong River. Its rivalry with the Burmans and Vietnamese for regional dominance occasionally led to war.

Class System and Gender Relations

In most Theravada Buddhist states, people viewed kings as semidivine reincarnated Buddhas. Kings lived in splendor, advised by Brahman priests in ceremonial and magical practices. They had many wives and therefore many sons, all of whom could be rivals for the throne, and unclear political succession rules meant chronic instability. Despite a bureaucratic government, royal power lessened as distance to the capital increased.

The Siamese society had many similarities to those of the Theravada Buddhist Khmer, Burmans, and especially the Lao. The Siamese social order was divided into a small aristocracy, many commoners, and some slaves (many of them prisoners of war). Deference to higher authority and recognition of status differences were expected. In contrast to the extended families of China or India, small nuclear families were the norm. While Theravada peoples encouraged cooperation within the family and village, they also valued individualism. Although women did not enjoy absolute equality and were expected to show their respect for men, free women enjoyed many rights. They inherited equally with men, could initiate marriage or divorce, and operated most of the stalls in village or town markets. Visitors from China, India, Europe, and the Middle East were shocked at the relative freedom of Siamese women. A Muslim Persian diplomat in Ayutthaya wrote that "it is common for women to engage in buying and selling in the markets and even to undertake physical labor, and they do not cover themselves with modesty. Thus you can see the women paddling to the surrounding villages where they successfully earn their daily bread with no assistance from the men."[14]

Theravada Buddhist Values

Siamese society reflected Theravada Buddhist values, such as gentleness, meditation, and reincarnation, as well as the concept of *karma*, the idea that one's actions in this life or past lives determined one's destiny. To escape from the endless round of life, death, and rebirth, believers were expected to attain merit by performing generous deeds, with the ultimate goal of reaching *nirvana*, or release from suffering. Many men became Buddhist monks who played key roles in local affairs and operated many village schools, with the result that Theravada societies had some of the highest literacy rates (especially for males) in the premodern world. Women could not gain merit as monks, although some became nuns. Most Siamese were tolerant of those who were less devout, believing that an individual's spiritual state was his or her own responsibility. Peasants moved easily between supporting their local Buddhist temple and placating the animist spirits of the fields.

Confucianism, Buddhism, and Vietnamese Society

Vietnam, another important Southeast Asian state, had been a Chinese colony for over a thousand years, but a Vietnamese rebellion finally succeeded in pushing the Chinese out in 939 and establishing independence. Vietnam continued to borrow ideas from China and even became a vassal state, sending tribute missions to the Chinese emperor. By the fourteenth century it offered a striking contrast to Theravada Buddhist societies.

Vietnam and China

Despite Vietnam's formal subservience, Chinese forces occasionally attempted a reconquest, inspiring the Vietnamese to become masters at resisting foreign invasions. In 1407 the new Ming dynasty invaded and conquered Vietnam. In response to the harsh Chinese repression, Le Loi (lay lo-ee) (1385–1433) organized a Vietnamese resistance movement that struggled tenaciously for the next two decades. After finally expelling the Chinese in 1428, Le Loi founded a new Vietnamese dynasty, the Le (1428–1788). His social and economic reforms and victory over Chinese domination made him one of the heroes of Vietnam's long struggle for independence. As Le Loi told his people: "Over the centuries, we have been sometimes strong, sometimes weak; but never yet have we been lacking in heroes. In that let our history be the proof."[15] Thus over the centuries, a sense of common identity and national feeling greatly aided Vietnamese survival on the fringes of powerful China. When the country was at peace, literature, poetry, and theater flourished.

Vietnam's imperial system was modeled on China's, headed by an emperor considered a "son of heaven," an intermediary between the terrestrial and supernatural realms ruling through the Mandate of Heaven. As in China, emperors governed through a bureaucracy staffed by scholar-administrators (*mandarins*) chosen by civil service examinations designed to recruit men of talent. The official ideology of Confucianism stressed ethical conduct, social harmony, and hierarchy. Vietnam also sought to influence or control the peoples of the highlands as well as the neighboring Cham, Khmer, and Lao states.

Le Dynasty Ruler This Vietnamese drawing shows the Le emperor being carried in state, accompanied by his mandarins, parasol- and fan-bearers, and a royal elephant. The drawing was printed in an eighteenth-century British book, with an English description of the procession.

From Churchill, *A Collection of Voyages and Travels*, 1732

Peasant society differed considerably from the imperial court and political elite. In the villages religious life mixed Mahayana Buddhism, Confucianism, and Daoism, all adopted from China, with spirit and ancestor worship. Villages were self-governing, their autonomy summarized in the expression that "the authority of the emperor ends at the village gate." Communal land in the village was set aside to be farmed by landless peasants. Although the Vietnamese social system was patriarchal, women dominated the town and village markets, doing most of the buying and selling of food and crafts, and they saw their influence increase with age.

Vietnamese Expansion

Beginning in the tenth century, some Vietnamese left the overcrowded Red River Valley and Tonkin Gulf to migrate southward. These Vietnamese settlers, supported by imperial forces, overran the Cham people in central Vietnam and by 1471 the kingdom of Champa had ended. By the sixteenth century the Vietnamese were pushing toward the Khmer-dominated Mekong River Basin in southern Vietnam. As a result of this migration, the Vietnamese became more involved with Southeast Asia, and the central and southern dialects and cultures gradually came to differ from those in the northern part of Vietnam.

Islam, Maritime Networks, and the Malay World

Maritime Trade

Southeast Asians had long excelled as seafaring traders, traveling as far away as East Africa. During the Intermediate Era Southeast Asian port cities became essential intermediaries in the trade between China, India, and the Middle East. This trade brought Southeast Asians into contact with the Muslim Islamic merchants from Arabia, Persia, and India, who spread Islam along the Indian Ocean trading routes. Commercial people were attracted to a religion that sanctioned the accumulation of wealth and preached cooperation among believers, and some Hindu-Buddhist rulers of coastal states in the Malay Peninsula and Indonesian islands grew eager to attract Muslim traders. Impressed by the cosmopolitan universality of Islam, they adopted the new faith, converting themselves into sultans. The increased trade spurred the growth of cities and new maritime trading states and gave merchants more influence in local politics. This transformation in the international maritime economy created an unprecedented commercial prosperity and cosmopolitan culture in Southeast Asia. At the same time, more intensive agricultural growth, including new crops and varieties of rice, spurred population increase, migration, and more bureaucratic states.

Rise of Melaka

The spread of Islam in the region coincided with, and was spurred by, the rise of the great port of Melaka **(muh-LACK-uh)** on the southwest coast of Malaya facing the Straits of Melaka. In 1403 the Hindu ruler of the city, Parameswara, adopted Islam and transformed himself into a sultan. The Melakans blended Islamic faith and culture with the older Hindu-Buddhist and animist beliefs, creating an eclectic cultural pattern. Because Islam in the region was closely identified with the Malay people of Melaka, historians often refer to the Muslim Southeast Asian societies as Malayo-Muslim. Malay identity spread to many societies in Malaya, Sumatra, and Borneo who practiced Islam and spoke the Malay language.

Melaka replaced Srivijaya as the region's economic power and became the crossroads of Asian maritime commerce. Its rulers sent tributary missions to China and made their port a waystation for the series of grand Chinese voyages to the western Indian Ocean led by Admiral Zheng He (see Chapter 11). In exchange for Melaka's service, the Ming supported the young state in regional disputes. Soon merchants from around Asia began coming to the new emporium, rapidly transforming the port into the archipelago's major trading hub, as well as the southeastern terminus for the Indian Ocean maritime trading network. One of the major commercial centers in the world, Melaka rivaled other great trading ports such as Calicut, Cambay, Guangzhou (Canton), Hormuz, Alexandria, Genoa, and Venice. In 1468 Melaka's sultan Mansur wrote to the king of the Ryukyu Islands, "We have learned that to master the blue oceans people must engage in commerce. All the lands within the seas are united in one body. Life has never been so affluent in preceding generations as it is today."[16] Gradually, Melaka became the center of a highly decentralized empire that dominated much of coastal Malaya and eastern Sumatra.

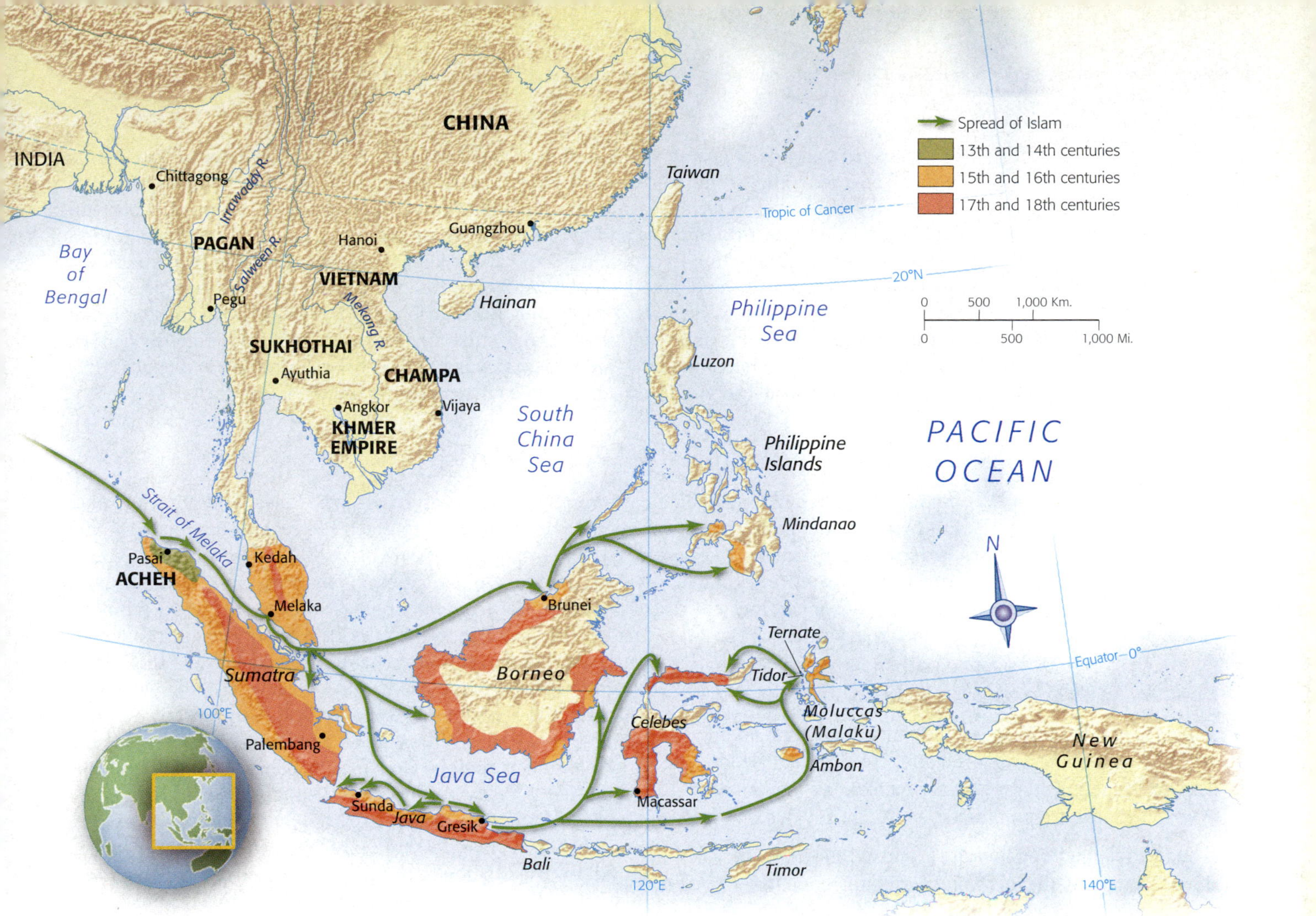

Map 13.3 The Spread of Islam in Island Southeast Asia

Carried by merchants and missionaries, Islam spread from Arabia and India to island Southeast Asia, eventually becoming the major faith on many islands and in the Malay Peninsula.

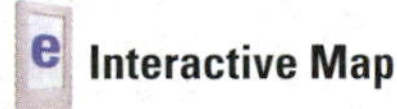
Interactive Map

Melaka flourished until 1511 as a vital link in world trade. An early-sixteenth-century Portuguese visitor wrote that it had "no equal in the world" and extolled the importance of Melaka to peoples and trade patterns as far away as western Europe: "Melaka is a city that was made for merchandise, fitter than any other in the world. Commerce between different nations for a thousand leagues on every hand must come to Melaka."[17] Melaka had a special connection to the Indian port of Cambay, nearly 3,000 miles away. Every year trading ships from around the Middle East and South Asia gathered at Cambay and Calicut to make the long voyage to Melaka, carrying with them grain, woolens, arms, copperware, textiles, and opium. Goods from as far north as Korea also reached Melaka.

The flourishing trading port attracted merchants from many lands. By the late 1400s Melaka's 100,000 to 200,000 people included 15,000 foreign merchants, whose diversity reflected Melaka's global importance. The foreigners included Arabs, Egyptians, Persians, Armenians, Jews, Ethiopians, Swahilis, Burmese, and Indians from the west, and Vietnamese, Javanese, Filipinos, Japanese, and Chinese from the east and north. Some eighty-four languages were spoken on the city's streets. Visitors claimed that more ships crowded the Melaka harbor than in any other port in the world, attracted by a stable government and a free trade policy. City shops offered textiles from India, books from the Middle East, cloves and nutmeg from Maluku, batiks and carpets from Java, silk and porcelain from China, and sugar from the Philippines. Gold brought from various places was so plentiful that children played with it.

Spread of Islam

Melaka also became the main center for the spread of Islam in the Malay Peninsula and western Indonesian archipelago (see Map 13.3), spurring political change and economic growth as rulers embraced the new faith for religious, political, and commercial reasons. Some Islamic states, such as Acheh **(AH-chay)** in northern Sumatra, became regional powers. The sultanates of Ternate **(tuhr-NAH-tay)** and Tidor **(TEE-door)** in the Maluku **(muh-LUKE-uh)** (Moluccan) Islands of northeastern Indonesia prospered from the spices they produced (especially cloves and nutmeg) that were prized in Europe and the Middle East. Gradually many people followed the example of their rulers and adopted Islam, joining Southeast Asia to the wider Islamic world. But there also remained many village-based societies, some of them still practicing animism, in more isolated or fringe areas such as the Philippine Islands, with no political authority higher than local chiefs.

Islamic Diversity

Various patterns of Islamic belief and practice, more diverse than elsewhere in the Islamic world, emerged in the scattered island societies. In most cases Islam did not completely displace older customs. For example, on Java Indianized kings and courts combined Islamic beliefs with older Hindu-Buddhist ceremonies and mystical traditions. Yet, many peasants maintained their mystical animist beliefs and practices under an Islamic veneer, tolerating diverse religious views, while others (especially merchants) adopted a more orthodox Islamic faith, following prescribed Islamic practices and looking toward the Middle East for models. The complex Javanese religion mirrored a hierarchical social system. The sultans in their palaces remained aloof from the people, while the aristocracy remained obsessed with practicing refined behavior rooted in mystical Hinduism. Javanese of all classes placed a great value on avoiding interpersonal conflict.

Southeast Asia and the Wider World

Southeast Asia had long been a cosmopolitan region where peoples, ideas, and products met, and visitors and sojourners from many lands continued to reach the region. For example, the intrepid Italian traveler Marco Polo passed through in 1292 on his way home from a long sojourn in China. His writings praised the wealth and sophistication of Champa, Java, and Sumatra, arousing European interest in seeking direct trade connections with these seemingly fabulous lands. Polo wrote that "Java is of unsurpassing wealth, producing all kinds of spices, frequented by a vast amount of shipping. Indeed, the treasure of this island is so great as to be past telling."[18]

Indeed, the Southeast Asia Marco Polo and other travelers such as the Moroccan Ibn Battuta encountered was one of the world's more prosperous and urbanized regions. Major cities like Ayutthaya, Melaka, and Hanoi (Vietnam) were as large as the major European urban centers like Naples and Paris. By the 1400s, though having perhaps 15 to 20 million people, Southeast Asia was still dwarfed by the dense populations of nearby China and India. Still, blessed with fertile land and extensive trade, Southeast Asians often enjoyed better health, more varied diets, and adequate material resources than most peoples.

Southeast Asia's connections to the wider world, as well as its famed wealth, eventually attracted arrivals who were not welcome. By the beginning of the sixteenth century a few Portuguese explorers and adventurers, with deadly weapons, state-of-the-art ships, Christian missionary zeal, and desire for wealth, reached first India and then Southeast Asia seeking "Christians and spices." The Portuguese standard of living was probably inferior to that of Siam, Vietnam, Melaka, or Java, but the Portuguese were the forerunners of what became a powerful, destabilizing European presence that gradually altered the region after 1500.

SECTION SUMMARY

- Siamese states such as Sukhotai and Ayutthaya were Theravada Buddhist monarchies that valued individualism and peacefulness, offered women a fair amount of freedom, and were permeated by Buddhist values.
- Despite gaining freedom from Chinese rule, Vietnam retained a great deal of Chinese cultural influence.
- Inhabitants of the Malay and Indonesian archipelagoes embraced Islam, which arrived via increasing maritime trade, and grafted it onto Hinduism and Buddhism to create many different patterns of Islamic belief, while native animist traditions survived to some extent in the villages.
- Melaka displaced Srivajaya as the center of Southeast Asian trading power and became an international crossroads.
- Southeast Asia would eventually attract less friendly visitors, such as the Portuguese.

CHAPTER SUMMARY

Although many earlier patterns of life and thought persisted in India and Southeast Asia during the Intermediate Era, these regions also experienced tremendous changes. A constant stream of West Asian and Central Asian peoples into India brought more diversity to Indian social patterns and beliefs. Although India remained politically fragmented, Hinduism enjoyed a kind of renaissance. Most people owed allegiance to their family, caste, and village. Hinduism spawned diverse ideas and cults and gradually brought some cultural unity, while Buddhism gradually lost influence in much of India. Hindu society faced its greatest challenge from Muslim conquerors, who became politically dominant in north India. Muslims would not be assimilated, although there was some mixing of Hindu and Muslim traditions. Islam added a major new strand to India's heritage, influencing the political, religious, and cultural realms but increasing diversity at the expense of unity.

Hindu and Buddhist ideas along with various other Indian traditions diffused to Southeast Asia, where they helped foster the rise of great kingdoms. The Angkor Empire dominated much of mainland Southeast Asia by mixing Indian and local patterns. New religions and new peoples, especially the Tais, eventually reshaped Southeast Asia. Theravada Buddhism became a major influence in several societies, including Siam, while Islam became strong in peninsula and island societies such as Melaka and Java. International trade fostered economic dynamism, and Melaka served as a major international port in which many cultural traditions flourished.

KEY TERMS

Rajputs
polyandry
bhakti
Vajrayana
Tantrism
Lamaism
purdah
wayang kulit

EBOOK AND WEBSITE RESOURCES

INTERACTIVE MAPS

Map 13.1 India and the Delhi Sultanate, ca. 1300 C.E.
Map 13.2 Major Southeast Asian Kingdoms, ca. 1200 C.E.
Map 13.3 The Spread of Islam in Island Southeast Asia

LINKS

Internet Indian History Sourcebook (http://www.fordham.edu/halsall/india/indiasbook.html). An invaluable collection of sources and links on India.

WWW Southeast Asia Guide (http://www.library.wisc.edu/guides/SEAsia/). An impressive, easy-to-use site from the University of Wisconsin-Madison.

WWW Virtual Library: South Asia (http://www.columbia.edu/cu/web/indiv/southasia/cuvl/). This Columbia University site offers many useful resources.

WWW Virtual Library: Southeast Asia (http://www.library.leiden.edu/collections/special/intro_se_asia.jsp). A Dutch site offering portals to all the countries of the region.

Plus flashcards, practice quizzes, and more. Go to: www.cengage.com/history/lockard/globalsocnet2e

SUGGESTED READING

Andaya, Barbara Watson, and Leonard Andaya. *A History of Malaysia*, 2nd ed. Honolulu: University of Hawaii Press, 2000. Contains an overview of Melaka and the spread of Islam in Southeast Asia.

Asher, Catherine B. and Cynthia Talbot. *India Before Europe*. New York: Cambridge University Press, 2006. Contains a good summary of this era.

Aung-Thwin, Michael. *Pagan: The Origins of Modern Burma*. Honolulu: University of Hawaii Press, 1985. The most comprehensive study of the Pagan society in Burma.

Avari, Burjar. *India: The Ancient Past: A History of the Indian Sub-Continent from c.7000 BC to AD 1200*. London: Routledge, 2007. Useful survey by an Indian scholar.

Basham, A. L. *The Wonder That Was India*, 3rd rev. ed. New Delhi: Rupa and Company, 1967 (reprinted 1999). Although dated, this is still a valuable general study of pre-Islamic India.

Chaudhuri, K. N. *Trade and Civilization in the Indian Ocean: An Economic History from the Rise of Islam to 1750*. Cambridge: Cambridge University Press, 1985. A scholarly study of trade and Islam, with much on India and Southeast Asia.

Hall, Kenneth R. *Maritime Trade and State Development in Early Southeast Asia*. Honolulu: University of Hawaii Press, 1985. One of the few studies of trade and politics in Southeast Asia before 1500 C.E.

Higham, Charles. *The Civilization of Angkor*. Berkeley: University of California Press, 2001. A scholarly but readable summary of Cambodia's early history.

Kulke, Hermann, and Dietmar Rothermund. *History of India*, 4th ed. London and New York: Routledge, 2004. A concise but stimulating general history, incorporating recent scholarship on India in this era.

Mabbett, Ian, and David Chandler. *The Khmers*. London: Blackwell, 1995. An authoritative study of Cambodian history, with much on Angkor.

Risso, Patricia. *Merchants and Faith: Muslim Commerce and Culture in the Indian Ocean*. Boulder: Westview, 1995. Connects Islam and Indian Ocean commerce, with much of southern Asia.

Rizvi, S. A. A. *The Wonder That Was India*, Part 2. New Delhi: Rupa and Company, 1987 (reprinted 2000). A comprehensive discussion of India under the impact of Islam from 1200 to 1700.

Taylor, Jean G. *Indonesia: People and Histories*. New Haven: Yale University Press, 2003. Well-written examination with much on this era.

Thapar, Romila. *Early India: From the Origins to A.D. 1300*. Berkeley: University of California Press, 2003. A recent revision of the standard work by an Indian historian.

CHAPTER

14

Christian Societies in Medieval Europe, Byzantium, and Russia, 600–1500

CHAPTER OUTLINE

- Forming Christian Societies in Western Europe
- Medieval Societies, Thought, and Politics
- Eastern Europe: Byzantines, Slavs, and Mongols
- Late Medieval Europe and the Roots of Expansion

PROFILE
Heloise, a French Scholar and Nun

WITNESS TO THE PAST
A Literary View of Late Medieval People

Robert Harding World Imagery

Wells Cathedral The importance of Christianity in European life was symbolized by magnificent cathedrals. This cathedral, built in the town of Wells in England in the thirteenth century C.E., was designed to reflect the glory of God.

The most Christian man beloved by God, the glorious king of the Franks, while he was building this [Christian] monastery, wished that [its] consecration and the battles which he [waged] should not be consigned completely to oblivion.

MONASTERY DEDICATION ATTRIBUTED TO CHARLEMAGNE, NINTH-CENTURY FRANKISH EMPEROR[1]

FOCUS QUESTIONS

1. How did Europeans create new societies between 500 and 1000?
2. What institutions and ideas shaped medieval European life?
3. How did Byzantine society differ from that of western Europe?
4. What developments between 1300 and 1500 gave Europeans the incentive and means to begin reshaping the world after 1500?

It was Christmas, 800 C.E., and the city of Rome, filled with magnificent buildings and monuments, still possessed majesty and was the center of western Christendom. Along one of the many roads that connected the fabled metropolis to a wider Europe had come the most powerful ruler in Europe, Charlemagne **(SHAHR-leh-mane)**, the king of the Germanic people called the Franks, arriving from his capital of Aachen **(AH-kuhn)**, some 700 miles away in northwest Germany, to celebrate Christmas mass with Pope Leo III, the head of Christendom. A towering man, 6 feet 4 inches tall, and wearing a Roman toga and Greek cloak, Charlemagne entered the spectacular St. Peter's cathedral. When the Christmas service ended, the pope placed upon Charlemagne's head a golden crown encrusted with sparkling jewels while the crowd chanted, "Crowned by god, great and peace-loving Emperor of the Romans, life and victory."[2] For the first time the pope had crowned an emperor of a new, church-blessed Roman Empire. For the next few centuries popes tried to influence secular affairs and shape monarchies, while kings worked to control the church and, like Charlemagne, used religion—even the building of monasteries—for their own purposes. The complex relations between the Roman church and diverse European states helped shape the tapestry of European life in this era.

In the 1400s Italian historians first coined the term ***medieval*** to describe the centuries, in their view a superstitious and ignorant "Dark Age," between the classical Romans and their own time. But the reality of what later scholars often called the "Middle Ages" in Europe was more complex. Linked by faith and culture, western Europeans combined Christianity with practices inherited from both the Romans and Germanic groups like the Franks. Although the mixing of religion and politics went back to ancient times, in both western Europe and Byzantium to the east, the strong influence of the Christian churches in all aspects of society, including politics, was an innovation, and medieval people tended to think of themselves as part of Christendom rather than Europe. Christian culture spread into northeastern Europe and Russia; at the same time, however, Europeans borrowed much from other cultures, especially from Muslims. Finally, the many tensions of European life, including conflicts between Christian leaders and kings for power, struggles between kings and nobles, debates over how to reconcile faith and reason, and the differing priorities of the rural-based aristocracy and urban merchants, fostered a competitive spirit that helped spur overseas exploration in the fifteenth century.

medieval A term first used in the 1400s by Italian historians to describe the centuries between the classical Romans and their own time.

e Visit the website and eBook for additional study materials and interactive tools: www.cengage.com/history/lockard/globalsocnet2e

FORMING CHRISTIAN SOCIETIES IN WESTERN EUROPE

How did Europeans create new societies between 500 and 1000?

The disintegration of the western Roman Empire in the fifth century led to political and social instability, clearing the ground for the rise of new societies between 500 and 1000. These were centuries of creativity, spurred by the mixing of Roman and Germanic traditions as well as by relations with non-European peoples. While western European societies varied, they also developed many common features, including a dominant Christian church and similar social, political, and economic systems. Economic change and technological development also set a foundation for a new Europe.

Environment and Expanding Christianity

Climate and Geography

Climate change and disease shaped post-Roman Europe. A cooling climate brought shorter growing seasons between 500 and 900, after which warmer trends returned. The terrible plague that devastated Europe during Justinian's time reappeared occasionally. Given these challenges, it was not surprising that people turned to religion for support. Between 200 and 800 western Europe also suffered repeated incursions by migrating peoples. Various Germanic groups occupied much of the region, destroying forever the western Roman Empire and culture and preventing any imperial restoration like that in China, where classical society reemerged during the Tang dynasty. Today few people study the Latin that was once the dominant language of the Mediterranean world.

Yet, Europe's favorable geography enabled similar religious, social, economic, and political patterns to spread. Much of western and central Europe was blessed by fertile, well-watered plains rich in minerals, while a long coastline offered many fine harbors along the Mediterranean and Baltic Seas and the Atlantic Ocean. Long navigable rivers such as the Danube **(DAN-yoob)** and Rhine and accessible mountain passes through the Alps made communication within the region much easier than for Asia, Africa, and South America. Hence, land and sea networks linked diverse societies, fostering the movement of ideas, products, peoples, technologies, and diseases.

Rise of the Roman church

As Roman power melted away, the church became the major source of authority, and local bishops and monasteries were often the only government in rural areas. Over time the bishops of Rome gained authority, eventually claiming the title of pope (Holy Father) and heading the vast church apparatus. Increasingly the papacy meant an independent church that was not controlled by any one government and that could assert its influence over kings. The popes continued their efforts to spread the faith to those Germanic peoples who still followed their ancient gods. Around 600 Pope Gregory I sanctioned turning pagan worship sites into churches rather than destroying them. As a result of missionary efforts, the Anglo-Saxon kingdom of Kent in England converted, and from its capital, Canterbury, missionaries were sent to German lands. The most famous, Boniface **(BON-uh-face)** (ca. 675–754), a member of the Benedictine order, won many converts in Germany.

Christians helped spread the faith by blending German values and practices into their religion. For instance, the pagan use of special amulets or charms to ward off evil was changed to the Christian practice of wearing medals around the neck honoring Jesus or his mother. Once they had acquired key positions in governments, Christians often persecuted non-Christians by destroying their houses of worship or denying them government positions. Since many church bishops came from upper-class German families, Christian leaders began valuing warriors and fighting, which was not a prominent feature of early Christianity. Even local church leaders often were more concerned with protecting their territory and family than they were with promoting Christian values.

Religious Orders

The church also included religious orders. From Christianity's earliest centuries, some men and women had tried to escape what they felt were the corruptions of cities by moving to isolated places to pray and prepare for Heaven. Many monks joined monasteries, communities for men who had taken holy orders. Monasteries grew their own food, and monks cleared forests for crops. Some of the large monasteries provided social services such as shelter for travelers, emergency food, and clothing for the poor. Some women also joined convents for lives of service or prayer. While monks and nuns tried to escape the concerns of society, they actually helped create a new culture. With the slogan "to work is to pray," monks filled their lives with activity to avoid idleness; one form of

CHRONOLOGY

	Early Medieval Western Europe	Later Medieval Western Europe	Byzantium and Russia
600	**750–1200** Viking attacks in Europe **768–814** Reign of Charlemagne		
800	**843** Treaty of Verdun		**988** Russian conversion to Christianity
1000		**1066** Norman conquest of England **1095–1272** Crusades	**1054** Schism between Roman and Byzantine churches
1200		**1337–1453** Hundred Years War **1348–1350** Peak of Black Death	**1237–1241** Mongol invasions
1400		**1420** Beginning of Portuguese exploration of Africa	**1453** Fall of Constantinople to Turks

work, copying manuscripts, eventually created the bound book. The willingness of monks to serve God and their neighbors with their hands as well as their hearts gave manual labor a respect that it never had in the classical Mediterranean world.

The Frankish and Holy Roman Empires

Rise of the Franks

Between 500 and 1000 the political map of Europe changed. Muslim armies conquered North Africa, the eastern shore of the Mediterranean, and most of Spain during the seventh and eighth centuries (see Chapter 10), and Muslim bands raided Italy and France. The victory of the Frankish ruler Charles Martel at the Battle of Tours in 732 finally stopped these raids (see Chronology: The Early Middle Ages, 500–1000). Following this victory, the Franks created a large state in western Europe. In 753 Pope Stephen sought the aid of the Franks against the Germanic Lombard kingdom in northern Italy, which was threatening papal control of central Italy. He then anointed the Frankish king Pepin **(PEP-in)** the Short as the special protector of Italy, indicating the sacred nature of kingship in Christian thought and the pope's belief that he had the right to designate political rulers. In return for the pope's blessing, Pepin defeated the Lombards and donated land in central Italy to the pope, the basis of a collection of small Papal States surrounding Rome that remained under papal control for over 1,000 years. From this time on the attention of western Europe's chief religious leaders became divided between their spiritual and earthly concerns.

The Carolingians

The special relationship between the popes and the Franks grew during a new dynasty known as the Carolingians **(kah-roe-LIN-gee-uhnz)** after their greatest ruler, Charlemagne (r. 768–814), who, as dramatized in the chapter opener, was crowned by the pope in Rome. Charlemagne spread Frankish power from France and northern Italy deep into the lands of another Germanic people, the Saxons, in north and central Germany, temporarily uniting the heart of western Europe (see Map 14.1). Charlemagne took great interest in the religious lives of his people. He promoted both education and Christianity, using the church to strengthen his empire as he appointed bishops and priests, influenced ceremonies and doctrines, ordered execution for those who violated religious obligations, and controlled the monasteries. To enhance his power, he also sent diplomatic missions to Byzantium and various Islamic states. Charlemagne told Pope Leo III that he would defend the church from its enemies and that the pope's job was only "to assist the success of our arms with your hands raised in prayer to God."[3] In return for this protection and promotion of Christianity, the Carolingians expected church leaders, from priests and bishops to abbots of monasteries, to be loyal to the king.

When the pope crowned Charlemagne "Emperor of the Romans," he revived the Roman Empire in the west symbolically. However, papal relations with the Carolingian rulers also set the stage for later church-state conflict. Popes argued that lay control over church matters should only be exercised with papal approval, while later German rulers wanted some political control in Italy.

Map 14.1 Europe During the Carolingian Empire

At the height of their power under Charlemagne, the Carolingian rulers of the Franks controlled much of northwestern Europe, including what is today France, the Low Countries, western and southern Germany, and northern Italy.

Interactive Map

Rise of Holy Roman Empire

Charlemagne's empire did not long outlive him. In the Treaty of Verdun **(vuhr-DUN)** in 843, it was divided among his three grandsons, and eventually other Germanic peoples challenged the Franks for influence. The Saxon ruler Otto I, known as Otto the Great (r. 936–973), built a new German empire by establishing his control over rebellious princes in Germany and leading an army into northern Italy, and in 962 the pope declared Otto "Roman Emperor." From this point until 1806, rulers in Germany retained this title, eventually proclaiming their lands to be the "Holy Roman Empire." But this empire had little in common with the classical Roman Empire. Much of its territory had never been under Roman control, and most Germans, Italians, Slavs, Czechs, and Hungarians within its domains had little sense of common citizenship or even much awareness of the political connections beyond the local level. Like the Carolingians, Otto and his successors continued to both defend and dominate the church, even appointing bishops in their lands.

CHRONOLOGY
The Early Middle Ages, 500–1000

529 First Benedictine monastery

732 Battle of Tours

750–1200 Viking attacks in Europe

756–1492 Muslim states in Spain

768–814 Reign of Charlemagne over Franks

800 Papal crowning of Charlemagne

843 Division of Carolingian Empire in Treaty of Verdun

874 Viking settlement of Iceland

955 Defeat of Magyars

962 Revival of Holy Roman Empire by Otto the Great

986 First Norse settlements in Greenland

Vikings and Other Invaders

The European heartland continued to attract other peoples seeking wealth. The biggest threat came from the Vikings, or Northmen, who faced population pressures that led them to launch raids out of Scandinavia, a region with limited productive farmland. Viking warriors burned and looted towns and monasteries in England, France, Holland, and Ireland. While rumors may have exaggerated Viking atrocities, it was a scary time, and people prayed: "From the violence of the men from the north, O Lord, deliver us."[4] The Vikings were also skilled craftsmen who built ingenious shallow-draft boats capable of both oceanic and riverine voyages.

Between 750 and 1200 various Vikings raided, traded, and settled around Europe. After some time the Scandinavians adopted Christianity and established the kingdoms of Denmark, Norway, and Sweden. Some Swedish Vikings moved east into the heartland of Russia, establishing several states and also sailing downriver to the Black Sea to trade with Byzantium and the Middle East. Danish and Norse Vikings established permanent settlements in coastal England, Ireland, and the islands north of Scotland. Other Vikings settled down in western France, in Normandy (named after Normans or Northmen). Normans who descended from these Vikings conquered England in 1066.

Eventually the Vikings gave up raiding for trade and farming. Those who settled outside Scandinavia adopted the cultures of the local Celtic, Latin, Germanic, or Slavic peoples. But their heritage remains in the many place names and words in the local languages. The Vikings left other legacies as well. Among the world's greatest maritime explorers, Norse Vikings began settling Iceland in 874 and founded several settlements on Greenland around 986. Then around 1000 a small group of Greenland Vikings established an outpost along the coast of eastern Canada, and Vikings made occasional trading visits to the area for the next several centuries. These Viking explorers also fostered a democratic ideal. Icelanders created an elected assembly in 930 to make and administer laws.

Bulgars and Magyars

Two other warlike peoples, the Bulgars **(BUL-gahrz)** and Magyars **(MAG-yahrz)**, migrated from Russia into central Europe. The Slavic Bulgars created a large state but were contained by

Viking Longship This longship from the ninth century, excavated from a burial mound in Norway in 1904, boasted intricate decorations and carvings. Probably used for ceremonial purposes, it became the burial chamber of a royal Viking woman.

"Tilling the Fields" Most medieval Europeans were peasants growing food. This French painting from the 1400s shows peasants working land on a manor.

The Bridgeman Art Library International

Byzantine armies, and eventually they converted to Eastern Orthodox Christianity and settled in the eastern Balkan region known as Bulgaria. The Magyars, excellent horsemen who spoke a Ural-Altaic language related to Turkish, moved into the Hungarian plain and threatened Germany and Italy. However, German forces under Otto the Great crushed a large Magyar army in 955, and the Magyars then settled permanently in Hungary and adopted Roman Christianity.

Early Medieval Trade, Muslim Spain, and Technology

Merchants

Trade also shaped the new Europe. While most Europeans were peasants, growing food or raising livestock, some were merchants who traded wool hides, salt, fish, wine, and grain over long distances, often by sea or riverboat. Trade continued briskly in the eastern Mediterranean, where it was tightly controlled by the Byzantine rulers. As time passed, the east-west trade grew dynamic. The Italian city of Venice was an active trading center throughout the Middle Ages, and Venice and Genoa competed to dominate trade with the Middle East and Byzantium. Other Italian cities remained connected to the Byzantine economy. Even the most remote northern towns received occasional visits from merchants, and aristocrats purchased luxury goods such as silk produced in the East. By 800, multiple networks of exchange were reconnecting western Europeans to each other and to eastern Europe and the increasingly Islamic Middle East.

Islamic Influences

Europeans benefited from the growing connections with, and borrowings from, the Muslim world. Islamic expansion stimulated a wider movement of people, goods, and information, such as Asian science and classical Greek thought, that gradually influenced many Afro-Eurasian societies. The exchange of products and ideas between Christian Europe and cosmopolitan Islamic Spain and Sicily, where various cultures met, proved especially fruitful for European intellectual life. Scholars and merchants from all over the Mediterranean world and the Frankish kingdom gravitated to Spanish cities such as Cordoba (see Chapter 10). The meeting of Christian, Jewish, and Muslim traditions in Muslim-ruled Spain and Sicily allowed the philosophical, scientific, and technological writings of many Classical Greek and Indian as well as Persian and Arab thinkers to spread among educated Europeans. In the 1140s, an Italian translator of Arabic texts wrote that "it befits us to imitate the Arabs especially, for they are our teachers and the pioneers."[5]

Technological Innovation

Various technological improvements, some originating in Asia, came into common use in western Europe during these early centuries, laying the basis for European expansion after 1000. Some of the major technological innovations improved agriculture, spurring the higher grain yields that sparked population growth in Europe. The rugged *moldboard plow* included a blade that dug the earth and an attached moldboard that turned over the furrow, enabling farmers to turn and drain the heavy, wet soil of northern Europe, where difficult farming conditions had kept the populations sparse. The horseshoe, which Europeans adopted from Central Asians in the ninth century, allowed farmers to make greater use of horses to plow fields, especially when they were combined with the horse collar. Invented in China, the horse collar distributed the weight of the burden across the animal's shoulders so that the horse could pull more weight and work longer hours. The most crucial agricultural improvement was the three-field system, which replaced the Roman two-field system. Europeans divided their fields into three parts and let only one-third lie fallow each year, increasing their yield by planting winter and summer wheat in the other two fields. Increased grain consumption produced a better-balanced diet.

Other innovations fostered the growth of industry. First invented in Roman times, watermills were built along rivers and streams to generate power, freeing up human and animal labor for other tasks. By 1056 over 5,600 watermills in England provided power for such activities as sawing logs and grinding wheat into flour. Waterpower thus allowed some industries to be mechanized. By the 1100s Europeans also used windmills, invented in Persia around 650, to generate power for such industries as grinding grain. By then the wheelbarrow had also reached Europe from China.

SECTION SUMMARY

- With the decline of the Roman Empire, the Christian church became a power in its own right with influence over kings, and monasteries created a new culture that respected manual labor.
- Under Germanic influence, Christians more aggressively spread their faith, assimilating pagan practices and transforming them into Christian ones and sometimes persecuting non-Christians, as well as beginning to value warfare and fighting.
- During this time the Papal States were created, Charlemagne's Carolingian empire temporarily united much of Europe, and Otto the Great began the tradition of calling Germany the "Holy Roman Empire."
- The Vikings of Scandinavia, who raided European lands for over four centuries, were also good traders and eventually settled in Iceland, Greenland, and various European territories; they also made forays to eastern Canada and experimented with democracy.
- As merchants engaged in growing networks of exchange, trade with the expanding Muslim world and contact with Muslim Spain introduced Europeans to Classical Greek, Indian, Arab, and Persian ideas.
- Technological advances such as the moldboard plow, the horseshoe, and the horse collar improved agriculture, as did the three-field system, and the watermill helped to improve European industry.

Medieval Societies, Thought, and Politics

What institutions and ideas shaped medieval European life?

Medieval Europe was dominated by three institutions between 800 and 1300. The papacy was significant in religion and church state relations, feudalism in the realm of politics and social structure, and manorialism in the economic realm. Both feudalism and manorialism developed from roots in the late Roman Empire and varied greatly across western Europe. The pluralism of religious, social, political, and economic institutions forged in early medieval Europe, combined with an unusually warm climate, spurred changes in many areas of life between 1000 and 1300, centuries historians term the "High Middle Ages." The power of the Roman church and its popes grew, fostering conflict with rulers and intellectuals. European societies were beset by tensions not only between religious and lay rulers but also between Roman and Byzantine Christian leaders and between Christians and Muslims. These varied conflicts, along with the growing divergence between cities, with their merchant classes, and the traditional feudal aristocrats ruling in the countryside, helped reshape European society.

The Emergence of Feudalism

Although some historians consider the concept to be misleading and overgeneralized, most have characterized the complex and decentralized social, political, and economic system of these centuries as **feudalism**, a political arrangement characterized by a weak central monarchy ruling over smaller states and aristocratic families that were largely autonomous but owed military and labor service obligations as vassals to the monarch. In turn, these nobles ruled as lords over the warriors and farmers on their estates, who, as subordinates, owed them service as **vassals**. Church leaders supported this arrangement, arguing that "it is the will of the Creator

feudalism A political arrangement characterized by a weak central monarchy ruling over smaller states or influential families that were largely autonomous but owed service obligations to the monarch.

vassals In medieval Europe, a subordinate person owing service to a lord.

CHRONOLOGY
The High Middle Ages, 1000–1300

987–1328 Capetian kings in France

1066 Norman conquest of England

1095–1272 Christian Crusades to reclaim Holy Land

1198–1216 High point of medieval papacy under Innocent III

1215 Signing of Magna Carta

1231 Beginning of Inquisition

1265 First English Parliament

that the higher shall always rule over the lower. Each individual and each class should stay in its place [and] perform its tasks."[6] This feudalistic political and social formation was strongest in France, England, and parts of Italy. Although many monarchs had little power beyond the region around their capital, some small states were part of a larger unit, such as the Holy Roman Empire, their princes owing allegiance to the king but also exercising power in the states they ruled.

Despite the Christian church's role in creating a common culture and the accomplishments of strong rulers such as Charlemagne and Otto the Great, certain forces worked toward the decentralization that characterized feudalism. The old Roman roads had fallen into disrepair, disrupting transportation and trade, and Europe remained sparsely populated with few cities. By 1000 the most densely populated region, France, boasted a population of only 8 or 9 million people, England had only a million and a half, and Europe as a whole only around 40 million, less than half of Song China's 100 million. Since both money and talent were scarce and land was the source of wealth, Charlemagne rewarded his best soldiers and officials by giving them control over land. Vassals who held such grants of land from a lord, called **benefices**, took an oath of personal loyalty to the king and promised him military service. In return they had a free hand to govern their territory, collect taxes from the inhabitants, and administer justice.

benefices In medieval Europe, grants of land from lord to vassal.

fief In medieval Europe, the thing granted in a feudal contract, usually land.

knights In medieval Europe, armored military retainers on horseback who swore allegiance to their lord.

chivalry The rigid code of behavior, including a sense of duty and honor, of medieval European knights.

Feudalism also refers to legal relations between lords and vassals, including the ***fief***, the thing granted in a feudal contract, usually land but sometimes something such as the right to collect tolls on a bridge. If a fief of land were large enough, the vassal could subdivide it and have vassals of his own. Thus feudalism allowed a king to rule a large country without personally administering it. This rule through subordinates was most common in England, especially after William, Duke of Normandy, conquered that island in 1066 and set up a feudal monarchy (see Chronology: The High Middle Ages, 1000–1300).

Feudal society included **knights**, armored military retainers who swore allegiance to their lord and who fought mostly on horseback. Since warhorses and elaborate armor were expensive, lords imposed this expense on their vassals. Knights had a rigid code of behavior, including a sense of duty and honor known as **chivalry**. A thirteenth-century French writer explained the chivalric ideal: "A knight must be hardy, courteous, generous, loyal and of fair speech; ferocious to his foe, frank and debonair to his friend. [He] has proved himself in arms and thereby won the praise of men."[7] Despite romantic images of knights wielding lances in jousts or defending maidens from fire-breathing dragons, the reality was usually more mundane. Knights wore 60 pounds of chain-mail armor and were often felled by heat exhaustion. The steel suits of armor seen in museums did not come into general use until the 1400s. Since states and rival lords fought each other regularly, knights were kept busy. But despite the dangers, the rewards could be great, including acquiring wealth and marrying into an aristocratic family. The mounted cavalry was the chief fighting force, made possible by the stirrup, brought by Central Asians who probably adopted it from the Chinese. The stirrup enabled the knight to stand when delivering a blow, making him much more powerful than if he delivered a blow while seated.

Manors, Cities, and Trade

manorialism The medieval European system of autonomous, nearly self-sufficient agricultural estates.

serfs In medieval Europe, peasants legally bound to their lord and tied to the land through generations.

The rural economy was based on **manorialism**, a system of autonomous, nearly self-sufficient agricultural estates. As the Roman cities became expensive places to live, wealthy Romans retreated to their large country estates and hired low-wage agricultural workers. Eventually these Roman estates and villages became the manors. With money and trade goods in short supply, each manor supplied its own needs, from mills to grind the grain to blacksmiths to shoe the horses. The manors, often organized around a castle, were owned by nobles who had the right to the produce grown by the large class of hereditary **serfs**, peasants who were legally bound to their lord and tied to the land through the generations. Serfs tilled the lord's fields as well as their own and were given the use of the manor's resources, such as farming tools or crafts, and protection in the manor house or castle in case the settlement was attacked. Serfs were not allowed to change their status or leave without permission, but they could not be dispossessed unless they failed to live up to their obligations. Warned to work hard to receive their eventual reward in Heaven, they paid for their security with a lifetime of drudgery. Occasional peasant revolts indicated some dissatisfaction.

Although serfdom became far more pervasive, slavery did not disappear altogether in Europe. Mostly farmers or domestic servants, slaves constituted perhaps 10 percent of the English population until the eleventh century, were common in Italy and Spain, and also worked papal estates and the farms of French monasteries. Leading Christian thinkers like St. Thomas Aquinas argued that slavery was morally justified and an economic necessity. An active Mediterranean slave trade based in Byzantium acquired slaves, mostly Slavs, Greeks, and Turks, from the Black Sea region and shipped them to southern Europe and North Africa. The Carolingians and Venetians also sold European slaves to the Arabs, and Vikings sold English and French slaves to Byzantium and Islamic Spain. By the 1400s Arabs and Portuguese were selling enslaved West Africans in southern Europe.

Urban Growth

During the High Middle Ages, populations, towns, and cities grew. Compared to Byzantium, China, and the Islamic world, early medieval western Europe was economically underdeveloped and its cities small: by 1000 Rome had only 35,000 people, Paris 20,000, and London 10,000. By contrast, Constantinople had 300,000, Kaifeng in China had 400,000, Cordoba in Muslim Spain nearly 500,000, and the world's largest city, Baghdad, a million people. However, between 1000 and 1300 the increased food resulting from the new methods of growing crops spurred a doubling of Europe's population to about 75 million. Western European cities increased in population and became centers of trade and industry. Milan and Paris grew to almost 100,000 during these three centuries. London had 30,000 people and a problem with air pollution due to the burning of coal.

As in our own day, some medieval people thought cities were degenerate places. An eleventh-century English monk detested London:

> *I do not like that city. All sorts of men crowd together there from every country. Each race brings its own vices. No one lives in it without falling into some sort of crime. Actors, jesters, smooth-skinned lads, flatterers, effeminates, pederasts, singing and dancing girls, quacks, belly-dancers, sorceresses, extortioners, magicians, mimes, beggars, buffoons: all this tribe fill all the houses. Therefore, if you do not want to dwell with evildoers, do not live in London.*[8]

Indeed, urban life and the money to be made attracted many people to cities. A German expression, "city air makes one free," referred to the fact that a serf who left the manor and was able to spend "a year and a day" in a city without being caught was considered legally free. Thus cities increasingly operated outside the feudal social and political structure. City craftsmen and merchants organized themselves into **guilds**, fraternal organizations designed to protect the economic interests of members and to win exemptions from feudal obligations. Eventually city charters, secured from the local lord or the king, allowed the cities to have their own courts and other privileges of self-government. Rulers granted such privileges because of the wealth that city commerce and payments brought them.

guilds In medieval Europe, collective fraternal organizations of craftsmen and merchants designed to protect the economic interests of their members.

Rise of Merchants and Bankers

The expansion of cities and commerce opened new possibilities for merchants, but they had to overcome social prejudices. In feudal society, people belonged to one of three categories, in order of importance: "those who prayed" (churchmen, priests, and monks), "those who fought" (aristocratic warriors, knights), and "those who worked" (peasants). Merchants and bankers had no place in this hierarchy unless they could marry the daughter of an impoverished aristocrat and hence acquire land. But most merchants also shared society's values and Christian faith. The English merchant Godric of Pinchale (ca. 1069–1170) left home as a teenager to peddle goods in nearby villages, then traded goods by sea between England, Scotland, Denmark, and Holland. Eventually he owned a small fleet of vessels and became quite wealthy, even making pilgrimages to Jerusalem. He never married and later in life gave away all his wealth to the poor and became a hermit, writing religious poetry and gaining fame for his piety.

People resented merchants because they sold goods for more than they paid for them and consorted with foreigners. Greed was considered a serious sin, and the practice of loaning money at interest was regarded as **usury**, a sin because the lender was making a profit without doing any labor. But moneylending was necessary to commerce, and even popes borrowed money at interest. While Italians became renowned as bankers, moneylending was often left largely to Jews, thus allowing Christians to benefit from borrowing money without committing usury. Gradually using and lending money became more acceptable

usury The practice of loaning money at interest; considered a sin in medieval Europe, although necessary to commerce.

Long Distance Trade

Long-distance trade reached its peak between 1100 and 1350 as western Europeans shipped woolen textiles, flax, hemp, wines, olive oil, fruit, and timber to the East in return for luxury goods from Byzantium and Asia such as spices, silk, perfumes, and precious gems. Trade and commerce around Europe also grew and prejudice against merchants declined. Cities such as Constantinople, Venice, Genoa, Bruges (broozh) and Amsterdam in the Low Countries, and Strassburg in the Rhineland became major commercial hubs. Italian merchants acquired goods from the Middle East and Byzantium and shipped them over the Alps to Belgium and Holland in exchange for woolen

A Medieval Town
This painting shows a variety of town enterprises, including a tailor's shop, barbershop, and an apothecary.

Bibliotheque nationale de France

textiles. One feudal French ruler, the Count of Champagne (shahm-PAHN-yuh), established the "fairs of Champagne" where goods were displayed at town fairs lasting seven weeks, with the count providing various services for the merchants. The wealth created by such activities fostered a commercial revolution and made merchants and bankers more influential.

Eventually commerce became more central to the European economy than agriculture, although the broad repercussions of the commercial revolution—the rise of capitalism; the incorporation of merchants as a vital social class; stronger monarchies; and the weakening of both feudalism and the Christian church—became clear only centuries later. In the short term, both the popes and the political leaders of Europe seemed stronger than ever, but the merchant class gradually gained political and economic power to challenge feudal nobles and eventually the monarchies.

Social Life and Groups

Families and Gender Relations

Medieval society was patriarchal, though family life and gender relations varied with social status and local customs. Generally, men supported the family and women ran the household and raised children. Sons were considered more important than daughters because they passed on the family line, property, and name. Parents arranged most marriages. Men were allowed to have sex outside marriage, while women were valued for their virginity and faithfulness. From the church's perspective, marriage was a necessary evil, and it legitimized sex only for procreation, not pleasure. A leading theologian, St. Thomas Aquinas, contended that "woman was created to help man, but only in the act of procreation, because in all other tasks he can find far better support elsewhere." One priest even warned married people to avoid sex on the Sabbath because "monsters, cripples, and all sickly children [are] conceived on Saturday nights."[9] However, rulers often flouted custom. Charlemagne enforced rigid Christian morality on his people while also marrying four times, having five mistresses, and siring eighteen children.

Today's Western middle-class model of a husband, wife, and their unmarried children living in one independent household, separate from the larger family, was the exception rather than the rule. Many medieval women tended to marry late, and large numbers of both men and women remained unmarried. Children often left their birth families at an early age to become apprentices in a trade, servants, or novices in religious orders. Laws favoring men spurred many young women to join Christian convents, all-female religious communities where they could find physical and social protection and possibilities for leadership.

Medieval society had an almost contradictory view of women. On the one hand, gender stereotypes in the Bible led people to believe that women had to be subordinate to men and were depraved, leading men into sin, as Eve did Adam. Women were also considered intellectually inferior to men. On the other hand, Mary, the Virgin Mother of Jesus, became one of the most popular objects of devotion. Many cathedrals were named after Notre Dame **(NO-truh DAHM)** ("Our Lady"). Furthermore, women could inherit property, and they worked in many occupations, including farming, ale making, small-scale trade, glassmaking, and the textile industry.

By the 1100s **courtly love**, a new concept of passionate but pure relationships between knights and ladies and celebrated in song by wandering troubadours, brought romance to male-female relations and, combined with the cult of the Virgin Mary, elevated the status of aristocratic women. Courtly love probably originated in Muslim Spain, where women poets flourished. But whether courtly or not, romantic love existed mostly outside of marriage. In medieval tales, knights often sought the favors of fair maidens (usually the wife of another, perhaps their lord) who were unattainable. Since adultery was considered a high crime, the knight's love was usually unrequited.

courtly love A standard of polite relationships between knights and ladies that arose in the 1100s in medieval Europe. Courtly love was celebrated in song by wandering troubadours.

Outsiders

The early Christian tolerance of homosexuality survived through the Early Middle Ages. Although various church leaders and rulers condemned what they called "sodomites," after the immoral inhabitants of the biblical city of Sodom, public attitudes toward same-sex relationships were often more accepting. Indeed, considerable homosexual fiction and poetry was published in the eleventh and twelfth centuries, and several prominent bishops and English kings were thought to be homosexuals. Beginning in the thirteenth century, however, public attitudes shifted. As states became stronger, they promoted uniformity in social relations and religious views and fostered suspicion of those perceived as outside the social and religious mainstream. The church launched a violent campaign against heresy and unconventional behavior that often targeted people suspected of homosexuality. Whereas in 1250 homosexual behavior was legal in most of Europe, by 1300 it had become a capital offense in many societies.

Medieval society was tightly ordered but also rife with tensions. Daily life was precarious for rich and poor alike, and violent crime remained common. Many tensions arose because of a major distinction between Christians and "outsiders"—nonbelievers, Muslims, Jews, and heretics. Christians used the term *pagan* to describe Muslims, who reciprocated by calling Christians *infidels* (unbelievers). The drive to destroy all beliefs outside of the Christian mainstream eventually led to a long series of crusades against Islam and persecution of Jews.

Christians and Jews

Many European towns had Jewish communities. Jews worked in many occupations but were best known as merchants and bankers because Christians were forbidden to loan money at interest. Resentment of their commercial success and moneylending made them scapegoats for misfortunes, such as epidemics, that were hard to explain. Although Christians mostly tolerated the Jews before 1150, anti-Semitism **(AN-tee-SEM-uh-tiz-uhm)** increased dramatically as more Christians took up banking and as Christians became more militant in asserting their faith. In 1182 the Jews were ordered to leave France, and this expulsion was imitated in other countries during the next three centuries. Governments also placed restrictions on Jewish businesses and residences. Our modern term *ghetto* originally described the part of medieval cities where the Jews were compelled to live. Many expelled Jews migrated to Poland and Byzantium, which developed large Jewish populations.

Disdain was also directed at people considered to be heretics. Christians struggled to differentiate correct belief from heresy. Some devout Christians criticized church corruption, including ill-educated priests and arrogant bishops, but church leaders viewed reformers challenging their power as heretics. As a result, they organized military attacks on the Albigensians **(AL-buh-JEN-shunz)**, a group in southern France who criticized the church's material wealth, urged clerical poverty, and wanted the Bible to be translated from Latin into the vernacular languages such as French and German so that ordinary people could read it for themselves. The church destroyed the Albigensians by killing their followers and confiscating their property.

The Church as a Social and Political Force

Europeans experienced both exuberance and turmoil during the High Middle Ages. Massive cathedrals with lofty spires inspired deep emotions, and the church claimed to help its members reach Heaven and avoid Hell. But the church of the High Middle Ages was also a powerful social and political force. The basis of clerical power was the sacrament, a rite believed to be a spiritual milestone. Medieval Christians measured the stages of their lives by sacraments such as baptism and matrimony, which had to be administered by a priest. In the village church, people did not just receive spiritual nourishment but also registered births and marriages and paid taxes. Because they had the power to deny someone the sacraments, which were considered

Church Sacraments

excommunicate To expel a person from the Roman Catholic Church and its sacraments.

necessary for salvation, medieval priests had enormous power. They could also **excommunicate**, or expel a person from the church and its sacraments, an act that was psychologically devastating.

Not all priests and bishops lived up to their responsibilities or growing expectations for celibacy. Many priests had so little education that they could barely recite the Latin liturgy, and some were corrupt and took bribes. Many priests and monks were also married, a practice that reformist church leaders attempted to end because they felt priests should not be distracted by families and did not want priests to pass on their parishes to their children. Nonetheless, even after the final ban many priests were married, kept mistresses, or were either homosexual or assumed to be so. Many people had ambivalent attitudes toward the clergy, fearing priests because of their power and ridiculing them because of their shortcomings.

Reformers

In the eleventh century, reformers attempted to change the church and end abuses by priests, monks, and high officials. New religious orders tried to restore monastic life to its original purity, insisting that all monks remain celibate, and several German rulers revived the papacy by appointing reform-minded popes who tried to end **simony** (SIGH-muh-nee), a common practice whereby wealthy families paid to have their sons appointed bishops. Such an appointment was desirable because bishops collected significant revenues in their territories. In an attempt to keep European rulers from interfering in papal elections, the church also established the College of Cardinals in 1059 to elect the pope. Churchmen made Roman law the basis of church law because it referred all matters to the person at the top, in this case the pope.

simony In medieval Europe, a practice whereby wealthy families paid to have their sons appointed bishops.

The Papacy

The papacy's growing political power was made clear when a major church-state conflict erupted over the appointment of bishops. For centuries rulers had appointed their leading nobles to key church offices. But in 1075 Pope Gregory VII (ca. 1020–1085) excommunicated the German emperor for appointing the archbishop of Milan (mi-LAHN). Gregory had a low opinion of kings, who, he said, "derive their origin from men ignorant of God who raised themselves above their fellows by pride, plunder, treachery, murder, at the instigation of the Devil."[10] In 1122 both men compromised and agreed that both emperor and pope would invest the new bishops. This dispute strengthened papal authority and weakened the German emperors. As German rulers began intervening in Italian politics to regain control over the church, they lost influence over their own princes at home, leading eventually to decentralized government and political warfare in the German-speaking lands. Another pope, Innocent III (r. 1198–1216), dramatically extended papal authority over secular rulers, using his control over the sacraments to force King John of England to accept the pope's candidate for archbishop of Canterbury and requiring the king of France to take back a wife he had divorced. In 1215 he required Jews to wear distinctive clothing and also aggressively punished "heretical depravity."

Holy Inquisition A church court created in 1231 in medieval Europe to investigate and eliminate heresy; inquisitions continued into the 1600s.

The papal drive to investigate and eliminate heresy led to the **Holy Inquisition**, a church court created in 1231. Churchmen tried thousands of people with views outside the mainstream, and popes sanctioned torture and starvation to induce confessions. Those found guilty faced punishments, including penances, banishment, prison, mutilation, and death. Over the next two centuries several thousand people were executed. The most notorious inquisition began, under state rather than church control, in Spain in 1478 and perpetrated brutal persecution of Jews and Muslims, burning at least 2,000 people at the stake. The inquisitions continued into the 1600s and also included bans on books viewed as dangerous to the faith.

Beliefs on History and Nature

Christians had adopted from the ancient Jewish tradition ideas about nature and history still apparent in the West today, including the concept of progress. Early Christian thinkers supported the notion of human society improving with time, an idea then foreign to most of the world. This linear rather than cyclical concept viewed history as leading from one point to another in a line of progressive movement. The basis for the view was found in the seven-day creation story in Genesis. To many Christian thinkers, God planned the world, including the natural environment, for human benefit, which necessitated exploiting nature. Hence, no item had any purpose but to serve humans, and it was God's will that people improved land by clearing forests and wetlands, which some monasteries did with great enthusiasm. The crass medieval attitude toward nature gave ideological justification for the great technological and economic development to later emerge in the West but also caused environmental problems.

Some Christian and Jewish thinkers dissented from these views and affirmed that nature was also God's creation and required care and stewardship. One was St. Francis of Assisi (1182–1226), who renounced wealth to found a new religious order, the Franciscans (fran-SIS-kuhnz), dedicated to lives of poverty, humility, and serving the urban poor. St. Francis saw all creatures as part of God's plan. And the twelfth-century Jewish philosopher Moses Maimonides wrote that "it should not be believed that all beings exist for the sake of the existence of man."[11] In addition, kings and lords often protected the forests where they enjoyed hunting.

New European States

English Monarchs

Threatened by the increase in papal power, and with less need for feudal vassals as economies grew, rulers sought to gain more control over their lands (see Map 14.2). The English kings were most successful at this centralization of power. After leading the Norman conquest of England in 1066, William of Normandy (1027–1087) had divided the land among his chief vassals. But by the 1100s, William's successors were taking authority away from the local nobility, appointing justices and tax collectors. King Henry II (r. 1154–1189) expanded the power of the royal courts over feudal and church courts. He also invaded Ireland in 1171 and established English control of the island's eastern region.

However, some of Henry II's successors unintentionally laid the foundations for a later representative government in England. John (the Prince John of the Robin Hood legend) weakened royal power in 1215 by signing the **Magna Carta** (MAG-nuh KAHR-tuh) or "Great Charter," an agreement that limited the feudal and taxation rights of the king and his officials while protecting the rights of the church, lords, and merchants. The Magna Carta was later used to support the notion that rulers had to have the consent of their subjects, one of the foundations of modern English constitutional monarchy. Henry III (r. 1216–1272) also contributed to representative government. His incessant demand for taxes to fight foreign wars made him unpopular, and, in 1265, rebellious barons called together a parliament (literally, a "speaking place") that included middle-class townspeople and knights to air their grievances and demand that the king consider their views. This parliament became the model for later meetings called by kings to secure approval of their policies.

Magna Carta ("Great Charter") An agreement signed by King John of England in 1215 that limited the feudal rights of the English king and his officials while protecting the rights of the church, lords, and merchants.

French and German Monarchs

The Capetians (kuh-PEE-shuhnz), who succeeded the Carolingians as kings in France (987–1328), also tried to increase their power and expand their territory. King Philip II (r. 1180–1223) gained control over Normandy, replacing noblemen with paid officials who would be more loyal to the crown. Louis IX, or St. Louis (r. 1226–1270), a pious man, curbed the power of the nobility while persecuting heretics and Jews. Philip the Fair (r. 1285–1314) may have had the most impact on France and Europe. To raise money for his wars, he arrested all the Jews and seized their property before expelling them from the kingdom in 1306. He also had the leaders of a militant religious order, the Knights Templar (TEM-plahr), burned at the stake as heretics so that he could default on a loan they had given him. When Pope Boniface VIII (r. 1294–1303) challenged Philip's growing power, Philip accused the pope of sexual perversion and murder and sent a force to Italy to arrest him. Townspeople rescued the pope by driving French troops away. For the next seventy years (1305–1377), the College of Cardinals, bowing to French pressure, elected popes, most of them French, who chose to live in the papal territory of Avignon (ah-vee-NYON) in southern France. Philip's ruthless action showed that the days of papal control over European rulers were ending and that France was emerging as the strongest kingdom in western Europe.

e **Primary Source: Magna Carta: The Great Charter of Liberties** Learn what rights and liberties the English nobility, on behalf of all free Englishmen, forced King John to grant them in 1215.

German rulers of the Hohenstaufen (HO-uhn-SHTOU-fuhn) dynasty (1152 and 1254) had the least success in centralizing their lands, largely because they spent too much time trying to control Italy while the feudal nobility in Germany remained powerful. Frederick I (r. 1154–1190) reasserted his authority as Holy Roman Emperor over the wealthy cities in northern Italy, but this involved war with the pope, who organized an Italian coalition that defeated Frederick's forces. Frederick I's successors gradually lost power to German princes. It would be seven hundred years before Italy, divided up into small papal-ruled and nonpapal states, and Germany finally achieved the territorial unity enjoyed by France and England.

The Crusades and Intellectual Life

Christian-Muslim Conflict

The religious and political tensions helped foster the Crusades, a series of military expeditions or holy wars between 1095 and 1272 to reclaim the "Holy Land," Palestine, from Muslim control (see Chapter 10). European Christians had long made pilgrimages to Jerusalem and considered the city part of their world. The crusading began after the Byzantine emperor sought help to dislodge the Muslim Seljuk Turks, who now dominated much of western Asia. Medieval Christians had a militant zeal to spread their faith and destroy Islam, through the use of force if necessary, and early Christian thinkers like Augustine of Hippo had sanctioned war to defend the faith. Except for Islam, no other world religion maintained such a strong missionary impulse to convert the world to what its believers considered the only true faith. Although many crusaders were motivated by religious beliefs and idealism, these often became mixed with lust for wealth and land. Political rivalries between European leaders also played a role.

In 1095 Pope Urban II urged Christian rulers to unite to protect the Christian holy sites, prompting the first of nine crusades by land and sea. Fabricating or exaggerating stories of Muslim

Map 14.2 Medieval Europe, 900–1300

During the High Middle Ages, the Holy Roman Empire, comprising dozens of smaller states, covered much of what is today Germany, Austria, eastern France, and northern Italy. France, England, Hungary, and Poland were also major states.

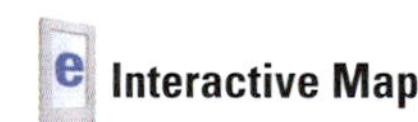

atrocities against Christians, he proclaimed that the Turks "have completely destroyed some of God's churches. They ruin the altars with filth and defilement. They are pleased to kill others. And what shall I say about the shocking rape of the women."[12] Various kings, nobles, and bishops joined the cause. Some crusaders temporarily occupied parts of the Holy Land, such as Jerusalem, even establishing crusader-led states, but eventually they were forced out. Other crusaders were diverted to ransacking Constantinople or Egypt.

Looting and pillaging cities, the crusaders often slaughtered thousands of Muslims, Jews, and Byzantine Christians, burning mosques and synagogues with people inside. The Muslim defenders often responded by killing local Christians. The streets of Jerusalem, it was said, ran ankle-deep in blood. Crusaders even slaughtered 12,000 Jews in Germany in 1096. Non-Christians viewed crusaders as terrorists. In the thirteenth century, however, the crusading energies dissipated. The long conflicts left a bitter heritage between Christians and Muslims that still complicates political and cross-cultural relations in the modern world.

Rise of Universities

Some medieval tensions also derived from robust intellectual debates, often in universities, involving theologians and philosophers. By the twelfth century, guilds of scholars formed centers of higher learning. While universities had existed earlier in India and the Islamic world, they mostly specialized in religious studies. European universities taught not only religion but also secular knowledge, such as the ideas of Aristotle, raising eyebrows among church leaders (see Profile: Heloise, a French Scholar and Nun). The most famous European universities were at Paris, Oxford

HELOISE, A FRENCH SCHOLAR AND NUN

A scandalous love affair between two brilliant people, Abelard and Heloise, reveals much about the life and values of medieval times, including church politics and attitudes toward sexuality. Over the centuries the romance and its sad repercussions inspired countless works of poetry and prose. Often portrayed as a forbidden affair between a smitten schoolgirl and her unprincipled teacher, a famed but controversial theologian, the relationship between the two figures was in reality far more complex.

Heloise (1101–1164) was the niece of a high church official in Paris. Coming from a wealthy, influential family, she had more educational opportunities than most women of her time and was educated at a well-financed convent, where she showed a keen intelligence. In 1117 her uncle Fulbert, a high-ranking cleric, arranged for the seventeen-year-old to study with Peter Abelard (1079–1142), the most famous teacher and a nonclergyman, at the school of the Notre Dame Cathedral. Born into an aristocratic family in Brittany, Abelard had studied with renowned teachers and had taught at several schools. He was notorious for both his arrogance and his intellect and made enemies in the church by championing reason, logic, and progressive thinking on religious doctrine.

Despite a twenty-year age difference, Abelard and Heloise fell passionately in love. Abelard wrote of how they went from reading books to kissing. They composed love songs and letters to each other, but their affair also reflected a friendship and intellectual respect, and her letters reveal a good knowledge of Roman and Christian writers. The two lovers tried to keep their affair quiet and were secretly married after she became pregnant. Their romance came at a time when the church was not just encouraging but mandating that clergy as well as secular teachers, such as Abelard, and students in church schools remain celibate. Abelard realized that his marriage would end his current position and his future church career. Heloise gave birth to a son, who was raised by Abelard's sister and eventually became a church official. However, when Heloise's family learned of the affair, they sought revenge, and Fulbert hired two men to beat and then castrate Abelard. Now disgraced, Abelard joined a Benedictine monastery, and, at his encouragement, Heloise entered a convent. Eventually she became the community's director.

Although separated, Heloise and Abelard continued to write letters to each other. Expressing her affection, Heloise wrote him that "I seek to please thee rather than [God]. Thy command brought me, not the love of God, to the [nunnery]." Strongly influenced by the thought of Aristotle, Abelard restored his scholarly reputation by writing books and essays about the possibilities of mixing philosophy and religion, for which he was for a time condemned as a heretic. Later, as an abbot (head) of a large monastery, he helped Heloise and her nuns establish a new convent, although he maintained a personal distance from her. Her ability to gain support and funding helped her convent to flourish. She remained ambivalent about her career, however, writing Abelard that "I am judged religious at a time when there is little in religion that is not hypocrisy." Heloise became known for her learning, and one top male cleric praised her knowledge of the liberal arts, saying, "You have surpassed all women and have gone further than almost every man." However, Heloise resented Abelard's desire to remain aloof from her, and she wrote, "Of all the wretched women I am the most wretched, for the higher the ascent, the heavier the fall."

Although they died twenty years apart, the pair were buried alongside each other at the convent, a fitting conclusion to a relationship and an era. Heloise was one of the last educated churchwomen to maintain close contact with male scholars and church officials. Obsessed with celibacy, the church increasingly separated the men and women engaged in religious life.

THINKING ABOUT THE PROFILE

1. What does the love affair and its consequences tell us about life at this time?
2. How did the different ways in which Abelard and Heloise rebuilt their lives reflect the values of medieval people?

Notes: Quotations from Barbara A. Hanawalt, *The Middle Ages: An Illustrated History* (New York: Oxford University Press, 1998), 88; Jane Slaughter and Melissa K. Bokovoy, *Sharing the Stage: Biography and Gender in Western Civilization*, vol. 1 (Boston: Houghton Mifflin, 2003), 255, 261–262; and James Burge, *Heloise and Abelard: A New Biography* (San Francisco: HarperSanFrancisco, 2003), 271.

Heloise and Abelard This painting, from a fourteenth-century French manuscript, shows Heloise (in nun's habit) and Abelard in conversation, years after their torrid love affair had shocked church authorities.

in England, and Salerno and Bologna **(boe-LOAN-yuh)** in Italy. Students learned the "seven liberal arts"—astronomy, geometry, arithmetic, music, grammar, rhetoric, and logic—and then specialized in medicine, law, or philosophy. As today, students did not spend all of their time studying. When one student wrote home for money because "the city is expensive and makes many demands," his father replied: "I have recently learned that you live dissolutely, preferring play to work, and strumming your guitar while others are at their studies."[13]

Debating Faith and Reason

Heated debates over the relative importance of faith and reason, often against church opposition, contributed much to later Western thought. Thomas Aquinas **(uh-KWINE-uhs)** (1225–1274), an Italian monk of the Dominican order and professor at the University of Paris, argued that much could be determined by reason, even the existence of God, but that at some point a believer had to accept on faith many mysteries. He also believed that human domination over nature was part of a divine plan and that women were passive and incapable of moral perfection. Some thinkers influenced by Aristotle argued that real knowledge came only from direct observation, a position that supported scientific inquiry.

Literature

Literature was diverse and contradictory. The *Song of Roland*, from twelfth-century France, described the great deeds of a loyal knight who died fighting in Charlemagne's army. But the warlike tone of this epic contrasted with many French lyric poems and stories that exalted personal happiness and romantic love as an ideal in a society that generally arranged marriages. Writers all over Europe took up the Celtic legend of the British King Arthur and his court. In some versions Arthur's wife, Guinevere **(GWIN-uh-veer)**, and his best friend, Lancelot, followed their hearts and became doomed lovers. In a lighter vein, we have this parody of the Christian Apostles' Creed written by a student more delighted by spirits than by the Spirit: "I believe in the tavern of my host, More than in the Holy Ghost. The tavern will my sweetheart be, and the Holy Church is not for me."[14]

SECTION SUMMARY

- Feudalism was a medieval political arrangement in which a king gave nobles the right to rule over sections of his territory in exchange for their allegiance.
- The owners of rural manors had a right to the crops of their serfs, peasants who were bound to the land, and they were protected by their knights, armored warriors on horseback.
- Agricultural advances helped to fuel growing populations in European cities, though they remained smaller than cities in the Muslim world and China.
- As trade in luxury goods flourished, European merchants gradually gained influence, but they suffered from people's image of them as greedy and usurious.
- Medieval society was patriarchal and considered women to be inferior to men; children usually left home early; and most marriages were arranged by parents.
- In the Early Middle Ages homosexuality was widely tolerated, but by the Late Middle Ages it had become unacceptable.
- Many of the tensions in medieval society were caused by the intolerance for "outsiders": non-Christians and heretics, Muslims, and Jews, all of whom were disdained and treated harshly, killed (as in the Crusades), or expelled.
- The church and its priests had a great deal of power over people's lives, but many priests were unqualified or incompetent.
- In some instances, popes became more powerful than kings, and they also orchestrated the Holy Inquisition, which killed thousands of "nonbelievers."
- Christians adopted the Jewish belief in progress over time and the belief that everything in the world was for the use of humans, a view that laid the ground for later industrialization in the West.
- While English rulers eventually consolidated their power and Philip the Fair of France ruthlessly seized power and property and even attacked the pope, German rulers had trouble centralizing their lands because they were too interested in struggling with the pope in Italy.
- Spurred on by a mix of religious idealism and greed, Christians mounted a series of Crusades to wrest the "Holy Land" from Muslim control, thereby creating a resentment among Muslims that has lasted to today.

EASTERN EUROPE: BYZANTINES, SLAVS, AND MONGOLS

How did Byzantine society differ from that of western Europe?

Byzantium, and the eastern European societies it influenced, remained very distinct from western Europe. Despite Christianity and long-standing trade connections, deep political, economic, and religious differences separated them and still do. Demonstrating a remarkable longevity, the Byzantine Empire fought for its life but, from the eleventh century, experienced steady political decline until its final defeat by the Ottoman Turks in 1453 (see Chronology: Byzantium, Russia, and Eastern Europe, 600–1500). In the process, it served as a buffer zone protecting central and western Europe against Muslim, Slavic, and Mongol invaders. Most of the Slavic societies in eastern Europe adopted Eastern Orthodox Christianity, and one of these, the Russians, eventually created a powerful state.

CHRONOLOGY
Byzantium, Russia, and Eastern Europe, 600–1500

632 First Arab expansion into the Byzantine Empire

825 First Swedish Viking bases in Russia

863 Cyrillic alphabet created

988 Conversion of Vladimir of Kiev to Christianity

1054 Schism between Roman and Byzantine churches

1091 Battle of Manzikert

1237–1241 Mongol invasions of Russia and eastern Europe

1453 Ottoman Turk conquest of Constantinople

1459 Ottoman Turk defeat of Serbs

Byzantium and Its Rivals

Byzantium faced nearly continuous pressure from neighboring peoples. In the sixth and seventh centuries the Sassanian Persians and Byzantines fought wars that weakened both empires and made Arab conquest of their lands easier. The Arabs attacked Constantinople in 673 and 717, but the Byzantines survived. For the next three and a half centuries, they were challenged by various Slavic peoples who had begun moving into eastern Europe in late Roman times, becoming the dominant population in a vast region of mountains, forests, and grasslands stretching north from Greece to the eastern Baltic and eastward through Russia. The major Slavic threats came from the Bulgars and Serbs. The Byzantine ruler known as "Basil the Bulgar-Slayer" defeated a Bulgar army in 1014 and blinded 15,000 Bulgarian prisoners of war before releasing them to return home. The defeat of the Bulgars opened the door to the Serbs, who set up several small states in the Balkans, bringing them into conflict with Byzantium. After a series of wars, the Ottoman Turks conquered the Serbs in 1459.

Byzantine-Turk Conflicts

Byzantine political fortunes declined. In 1071, Byzantine forces were driven from southern Italy by Norman knights, and in 1091, at the Battle of Manzikert (MANZ-ih-kuhrt), they were defeated by Seljuk Turks in eastern Anatolia. The shrunken Byzantine territories now faced regular attacks from both east and west. Turks soon completed the conquest of Anatolia and left Constantinople a beleaguered fortress. The desperate Byzantines requested the help of western knights to defend them against the Turks, but instead crusader armies occupied Palestine and Syria between 1096 and 1200. The Byzantines also did not expect the crusaders in 1204, bribed by the Venetians, Byzantine trading rivals, to use a disputed imperial succession in the empire as an excuse to conquer Constantinople itself and govern it until forced out in 1261. Capitalizing on these disasters, the expanding Ottoman Turks finally conquered Constantinople and the surrounding territory in 1453, ending the Byzantine state and transforming the capital city, which the Turks eventually renamed Istanbul.

Despite its many misfortunes, the Byzantine Empire survived as long as it did because of its economic and religious strengths. Because Constantinople lay astride the principal trade routes between Europe and Asia, the merchant class remained vital. Slave traders shipped eastern European slaves, many of them Slavs from the Black Sea region, to be sold in the Mediterranean. Our English word for "slave" comes from the word *Slav.* Taxes from these goods and people as well as silk production enriched the treasury, and Byzantine coins were used around Eurasia.

Church and State

Byzantine church and state were intertwined, with Christianity and its rituals influencing all aspects of society and filling it with lengthy religious ceremonies and an intense prayer life. Unlike in western Europe, however, governments dominated the church, and rulers regularly interfered in church affairs. Byzantines also engaged in hair-splitting theological disputes. For example, they bitterly disagreed on the use of icons, painted images of holy figures, and over whether the Holy Spirit proceeded from God or from both God and Jesus. Byzantine Christians refused to recognize the supreme position of the bishop of Rome over other bishops. These conflicts over theology and authority spurred the final split between the Roman Catholic and Greek Orthodox Churches, which came when the pope and the patriarch of Constantinople angrily excommunicated each other in 1054.

Although the Byzantine church supported male power, a few women achieved political or intellectual influence. Empress Irene, an orphan who married an emperor, ruled Byzantium for two decades (780–802). Although her detractors considered her cruel and ruthless, Irene fostered prosperity, made peace with Muslim states, and temporarily resolved the dispute over icons. Byzantium's best-known historian, the princess Anna Comnena (1083–1148), studied literature, astronomy, medicine, and Greek philosophy.

Byzantium, Russians, and Mongols

Spread of Byzantine Culture

The Byzantines held off foes long enough so that Byzantine culture spread north and east, allowing Byzantine religion and culture to survive the defeat of the empire. The differences between eastern and western versions of Christianity gave some of the eastern European peoples a choice of which to adopt. In the ninth century, two Byzantine brothers, known later as Saints Cyril and Methodius **(mi-THO-dee-uhs)**, converted many Slavs to eastern Christianity. The brothers devised an alphabet, known as Cyrillic **(suh-RILL-ik)**, for the Slavs, and Cyril began translating the Bible and other church writings from Greek. The Bulgars, Serbs, Russians, and many Ukrainians eventually adopted Byzantine culture, including Orthodox Christianity. The Russians and other societies they influenced, including the Georgians in the Caucasus, learned their Christian culture and their politics from a society with an autocratic emperor and close connections between church and state, in contrast to western Europe, where church-state conflicts remained common. Other Slavs, among them Croats **(KRO-ATS)**, Czechs **(checks)**, Lithuanians **(lith-oo-ANE-ee-uhnz)**, Poles, Slovaks **(SLO-vaks)**, Slovenes **(SLO-veenz)**, and many Ukrainians, adopted Roman Catholicism. Eastern and western European cultures remain distinct even today, partly because of the differences between the Greek and Roman churches of 1,000 years ago.

Rise of Russia

Russian identity descended from the Rus **(roos)**, whose capital was at Kiev **(KEE-yev)**, in today's Ukraine **(you-CRANE)**. Swedish Vikings, who founded trading cities in the Slavic regions, had become the Rus ruling class, both trading with and raiding the Byzantines. Viking trade networks crisscrossed the Russian and Ukrainian plains, and the Vikings were eventually assimilated by the Slavs. From the tenth to the twelfth centuries, the Russians expanded, forming settlements as far north as Novgorod **(NOHV-goh-rod)**, from which timber was shipped south to the Black Sea. The Rus ruler Vladimir **(VLAD-ih-mir)** I (ca. 956–1015) in Kiev opened the doors to Byzantine influence. Vladimir had several wives and eight hundred concubines but, hoping for political advantage, sought marriage to a Byzantine princess. After she refused to marry a pagan polygamist, he agreed to accept Orthodox Christianity in 988 and make her his only wife. When Vladimir ordered his soldiers to be baptized, he guaranteed that a large part of eastern Europe would become Eastern Orthodox.

By the time western Europeans heard rumors about the brutal Mongols, the Russians had already encountered them. Mongol armies conquered Central Asia and parts of China and the Middle East (see Chapters 10 and 11 and the essay at the end of Part III) and repeatedly sacked Russian cities beginning in 1237. A papal envoy who visited Kiev after an attack reported, "We found lying in the fields countless heads and bones. [The city] has been reduced to nothing: barely 200 houses [still] stand there."[15] Until the fifteenth century most Russians remained subject to the Golden Horde, a Mongol state on the lower Volga River. Muscovy **(MUSS-koe-vee)**, a Russian state centered on Moscow, benefited, since the Golden Horde treated its ruler as the senior Russian leader.

An Orthodox Church in Novgorod, Russia The distinctive architecture of this church represents the fusion of Slavic, Byzantine, and Viking influences.

Novosti

Western Europe was fortunate to escape Mongol conquest. In 1241, Mongol armies moved far into Europe, crushing Polish and Hungarian forces sent against them. Soon they stood at the Danube contemplating an invasion into German lands. But the Germans and Europeans farther west were spared because Mongol generals returned to Mongolia when they heard of the death of the Mongol leader, Ogodei. Had the Mongol conquests continued westward, European history might have been very different. But Europe was much less tempting than the far richer societies of China and Islamic western Asia.

Eventually Muscovy became the dominant Russian state as Mongol political power declined and the head of the Russian Orthodox Church, appointed by the patriarch of Constantinople, moved from Kiev to Moscow. During the reign of Ivan III (1440–1505), Muscovy escaped Mongol control and established domination over other Russian states. Ivan began to call himself *czar* (meaning "caesar") to indicate his superiority over lesser rulers, and he married the niece of the last Byzantine emperor. The Russian Orthodox Church broke with the patriarch of Constantinople, and Russian clergy began referring to Moscow as the Third Rome, successor to Constantinople. The Russians also expanded into the territories of the Catholic Lithuanians, adding religious antagonisms to the political tensions between Orthodox and Catholic peoples in eastern Europe.

SECTION SUMMARY

- The Byzantines were under almost constant attack by Sassanian Persians, Bulgars, Slavs, and western European Christians, but Byzantium survived until it was conquered by the Turks in 1453.
- Byzantium's culture and Orthodox Christianity survived because they were spread to many eastern European peoples, including the Russians, the Bulgars, the Serbs, and many Ukrainians.
- The Russians, who had adopted Orthodox Christianity, were attacked by the Mongols but emerged as one of the strongest societies in eastern Europe.

LATE MEDIEVAL EUROPE AND THE ROOTS OF EXPANSION

What developments between 1300 and 1500 gave Europeans the incentive and means to begin reshaping the world after 1500?

The Late Middle Ages (1300–1500) were a period of transition. For a century the population shrunk dramatically as a result of famine, plague, and warfare, contributing to the gradual end of feudalism. Royal power increased many places at the expense of the feudal nobility, while the Roman church also lost influence as questioning of church practices and beliefs increased. Yet, the ferment fostered intellectual and cultural creativity, trade increased, and brave mariners began exploring the world beyond Europe, fostering the resurgence of the West.

The Black Death and Social Change

Late medieval Europe was an unhappy place, ravaged by famine, disease, and war. Europe's climate turned colder about 1300, fostering "the Little Ice Age." As a result, the Norse farming settlements in Greenland collapsed from deforestation, expanding glaciers, and conflict with the local Inuit. The same cooler temperatures shortened the European growing season, causing serious food shortages.

Hemispheric Pandemic

Europe also repeatedly suffered from the Black Death, a terrible *pandemic,* or massive epidemic that crossed many regions, named for the black bruises that appeared under the skin. In 1347 a trading ship coming from the Black Sea limped into a Sicilian harbor with all of the crew either dead or dying from a deadly infection spread by fleas that lived on rats who had scampered aboard ship—probably bubonic plague, perhaps mixed with pneumonic **(noo-MON-ik)** plague. The pandemic caused unprecedented death and suffering as it spread along and disrupted the networks of exchange all over Eurasia and North Africa (see Chronology: The Late Middle Ages, 1300–1500). During its peak years from 1348 to 1350, the pandemic killed a third of all Europeans. Over 65 percent of the population in some congested cities died, greatly reducing commerce, and Europe's population in the fourteenth century dropped from around 70 or 75 million to some 45 or 50 million people, most killed by either a fast-acting respiratory infection or by swelling and internal bleeding. Pope Clement VI wrote that "the living were barely sufficient to bury the dead, or so horrified as to avoid the task. So great a terror seized nearly everyone."[16] The horrors endured in nursery rhymes: "Ring around the rosies, a pocketful of posies, ashes, ashes, we all fall down." Those who survived developed some immunities: although the Black Death reoccurred for decades, it killed fewer people each time.

Impacts on Society

The troubles reshaped European social patterns, especially for the upper classes. With far fewer peasants alive to till the fields, those remaining asked for more privileges and money, and peasant revolts demanding an end to serfdom increased, most notably in France in 1358 and in England in 1381. Meanwhile, some people challenged social norms. In addition to writing works of history, ethics, and poetry, the French author Christine of Pasan (1364–ca. 1430) proclaimed that women were equals of men, systematically disproved all the negative stereotypes men held of women's character, and shrewdly critiqued the patriarchal social structure. She wrote that "those who blame women out of jealousy are those wicked men who have seen many women of greater intelligence and nobler conduct than they themselves possess."[17] Some literature, such as the fiction of the fourteenth-century English writer Geoffrey Chaucer **(CHAW-suhr)** (see Witness to the Past: A Literary View of Late Medieval People), reflected the changing social customs and relations.

The death and despair influenced emotional and social life. Many people assumed the pandemic was divine punishment. Feelings of utter hopelessness overwhelmed people who vainly tried to dig graves for their family members before they too succumbed to death, which usually came in a matter of days. While famine and disease raged, aristocrats regaled themselves with magnificent banquets and pageants and wore ostentatious clothing. The poor sought escape through prayer, meditation, and self-flagellation, imitating the torture of Jesus by beating themselves with whips until their blood flowed. Some places people, looking for scapegoats, blamed outsiders, especially Jews, for the troubles. In the mid-1300s thousands of Jews were burned alive or driven out of cities, especially in the German states.

The pandemic's impact on western and eastern Europe proved quite different. Because eastern Europe had fewer cities and more villages, fewer peasants died. Since the eastern monarchs were also weaker, the aristocracy imposed serfdom on many of their peasants, creating large agricultural estates. The nobility were strengthened socially, while their western European counterparts were weakened by labor shortages and higher costs. Hence, eastern Europe remained primarily an agricultural area, while western European rulers continued to strengthen their central governments.

CHRONOLOGY
The Late Middle Ages, 1300–1500

1309–1377 Avignon papacy

1337–1453 Hundred Years War between France and England

1348–1350 Peak of Black Death

1378–1417 Great Schism in papacy

1455–1485 War of the Roses in England

1455 Printing of Gutenberg Bible

1478 Beginning of Spanish Inquisition

1487 Dias arrival at Indian Ocean

1492 First voyage by Columbus to America; Spanish Christian defeat of last Muslim state

Warfare and Political Centralization

The Hundred Years War

Warfare in late medieval western Europe, which was common, strengthened kings and states (see Map 14.3). For example, the intermittent fighting between English and French troops known as the Hundred Years War (1337–1453) enhanced royal power in France and also, eventually, in England. This war, caused by the English kings' desire to hold on to their feudal lands in France, eventually resulted in a French victory. At first the English gained victories by using trained commoners and a new weapon, the longbow, that launched powerful arrows and thus diminished the knights as an effective fighting force. However, aided by Jeanne d'Arc **(zhahn DAHRK)** (ca. 1412–1431), a sixteen-year-old peasant who believed that voices from saints told her to lead troops into battle, the French broke the English siege of the city of Orleans **(or-lay-AHN)** and slowly recovered most of the English-held territory in France. Jeanne, meanwhile, was captured and burned at the stake, becoming the most famous martyr to French nationhood.

During the conflict's final stages, the French monarchs introduced new direct taxes that lessened their dependence on the feudal nobility. Kings also reorganized the royal armies to depend more on mercenary troops hired with tax revenues. In England, military defeat fostered a long conflict between two rival royal houses, the War of the Roses (1455–1485), that ended with Henry VII founding a new Tudor dynasty. Henry VII sent in armies to reclaim Ireland, which were followed by English settlers who repressed the Celtic Irish. The Tudors established England as a world power during the 1500s.

Royal power also increased during the late 1400s in Spain. In 1085 Christians began the long reconquest of the peninsula

Praying for Relief This image of survivors carrying away plague victims in Rome was commissioned by a French duke for an illuminated book in the early 1400s. It illustrates the despair and devastating loss of life caused by the Black Death, especially in cities.

WITNESS TO THE PAST

A Literary View of Late Medieval People

The English writer Geoffrey Chaucer (ca. 1340–1400) wrote one of the best-known books of the Late Middle Ages, *The Canterbury Tales*, set in the time of the Black Death. Born in London, Chaucer was a cosmopolitan poet, soldier, and diplomat who served in the English Parliament and was familiar with French and Italian intellectual and cultural trends. His writings reflected these trends while also strongly influencing spoken and written English. *The Canterbury Tales* also offered a witty and sophisticated picture of English society. This excerpt presents stereotypical and satirical views of various pilgrims on their way to visit Canterbury, the seat of church power in England.

The knight there was, and he was a worthy man, Who, from the moment that he first began To ride about the world, loved chivalry, Truth, honor, freedom, and all courtesy. . . . Of mortal battles he had fought fifteen . . . And always won he sovereign fame for prize . . . He never yet had any vileness said [about him] in all his life . . . He was a truly perfect, gentle knight. . . .

There was also a nun, a prioress, Who, in her smiling, modest was and coy . . . At table she had been well taught withal, And never from her lips let morels fall, Nor dipped her fingers deep in sauce, but ate With so much care the food upon her plate That never driblet fell upon her breast. In courtesy she had delight and zest. . . .

A monk there was, one made for mastery [and loved hunting] . . . A manly man, to be an abbot able. Full many a blooded horse had he in stable: And when he rode men might his bridle hear A-jingling in the whistling wind as clear, Aye, and as loud as does the chapel bell Where this brave monk was of the cell. . . . This said monk let such lowly old things [strict old monastic rules] slowly pace And followed new world manners in their place. What? Should he study as a madman would Upon a book in cloister cell? Or yet, go labor with his hands and . . . sweat [as St. Augustine commanded]? . . .

There was a merchant with forked beard, and girt . . . Upon his head a Flemish beaver hat; His boots were fastened rather elegantly. He spoke [his opinions] pompously, Stressing the times when he had won, not lost [his profits] . . . At money changing he could make a crown. This worthy man kept all his wits well set; There was no one could say he was in debt, So well he governed all his trade affairs. . . .

There was a good man of religion, too, A country parson, poor . . . but rich he was in holy thought and work. He was also a learned man also [a scholar] . . . who Christ's own Gospel truly sought to preach. Devoutly his parisoner's would he teach . . . Benign he was and wondrous diligent, Patient in adverse times and well content . . . But rather would he give . . . unto those poor parishioners about, Part of his income, even of his goods . . . That first he wrought and after words he taught [first he practiced, then he preached]. . . .

THINKING ABOUT THE READING

1. What are the various clerical stereotypes presented?
2. How is the merchant portrayed?

Source: General Prologue to Geoffrey Chaucer's *Canterbury Tales*, electronic edition prepared by Edwin Duncan (*http:www.towson .edu/~duncan/chaucer/titlepage.htm*)

from Muslims. By 1249 they had reclaimed Portugal, and by the 1300s Spanish Christians had displaced all of the Muslim states except for Granada **(gruh-NAH-duh)** in the far south. In 1469 the two largest kingdoms were united when King Ferdinand of Aragon **(AR-uh-gon)** married his cousin, Isabella of Castile **(kas-TEEL)**. These monarchs finally crushed Granada in 1492 and then, obsessed with religious uniformity, demanded that the Spanish Jews and Muslims either convert or be expelled. Hoping to increase royal wealth, they also sponsored the first trans-Atlantic voyage by the Italian mariner, Christopher Columbus, in 1492.

Holy Roman Empire

The nobility remained strong in the Holy Roman Empire, which included many of the German-speaking lands and parts of Italy. The Habsburg **(HABZ-berg)** family, who took power in 1273, were unable to create a strong centralized state. In 1356 they reduced the pope's influence over the election of Holy Roman Emperors but also confirmed the power of the princes. During the coming centuries imperial Habsburg rulers concentrated on increasing the personal territorial holdings of their family. In the later 1400s, by royal marriage alliances, they gained control of the Netherlands and much of southern Italy.

Hemispheric Connections, New Intellectual Horizons, and Technology

Long Distance Trade

The Late Middle Ages fostered new intellectual horizons and technologies, some of them derived from contacts with Asia and Africa. The Mongols did not conquer western Europe but reenergized

Spread of Roman Christendom

- In 1000 C.E.
- Added 1000–1200
- Lost 1000–1200 (Regained 1200–1500)
- Added 1200–1500
- Lost 1200–1500
- English holdings, 1360
- Boundary of the Holy Roman Empire

Map 14.3
Europe, 1400–1500
During this period France became western Europe's strongest kingdom, but Spanish kings gradually reunified much of the Iberian peninsula. The Holy Roman empire remained decentralized. Meanwhile, Lithuania, Hungary, and Poland controlled much of eastern Europe.

Interactive Map

Eurasian trade, allowing inventions and ideas to flow to Europe from China and western Asia. Some of these inventions, such as printing, gunpowder, and the compass, eventually revolutionized European technology. Europeans, especially Italians, imported spices, carpets, silks, porcelain, glassware, and even painting supplies from Muslim Spain, Ottoman Turkey, Mamluk Egypt, and Persia. The cosmopolitan Ottoman ruler Mehmed the Conqueror (1430–1481) read and published Greek and Latin books on history and philosophy and invited Italian merchants, craftsmen, artists, and architects to work in Istanbul (formerly Constantinople). Some Italians, especially Venetians, were influenced by the magnificent palaces and mosques they saw in Islamic cities. By the later 1400s the Portuguese brought back artworks and fabrics from West Africa and the Kongo that also influenced European artists.

Papal Decline

At the same time, moral and political corruption contributed to the decline of papal political power and the Roman church. Some historians argue that all power tends to corrupt. In the case of the church, dissidents complained about the buying of church offices, favoritism to relatives, and the absenteeism of bishops who served more than one diocese; to collect the extra revenue, such bishops were necessarily absent from one or other of their jobs. His detractors claimed that Cardinal Wolsey, archbishop of both Canterbury and York in England, entered the cathedral at York only once, for his funeral. Skeptics also viewed practices such as venerating holy relics and making pilgrimages as superstition that encouraged fraud, while defenders argued that relics and pilgrimages gave people something tangible to cling to when seeking God's help.

Papal prestige declined after the popes moved to Avignon in southern France (1309–1377). The Avignon popes required that candidates for bishop pay a large sum to the papal treasury, a form of extortion that reserved high church offices for the wealthy. When the papacy finally returned to Rome, two men claimed to be the rightful pope, and Europeans picked sides in this "Great Schism" (1378–1417). Although the split ended, much damage had been done to the papacy's prestige. After a council of bishops unsuccessfully tried to replace papal monarchy with a church government by such councils, popes refused to call any further councils on church reform.

The Renaissance

Renaissance ("Rebirth") A dramatic flowering in arts and learning that began in the Italian city-states around 1350 and spread through Europe through the 1500s.

humanism The name for the European Renaissance philosophy, which emphasized humanity, worldly concerns, and reason rather than religious ideals.

Imported ideas and products along with dissent in the church contributed to the dramatic flowering of arts and learning later known as the **Renaissance**, or "rebirth," that began in the Italian city-states around 1350 and intensified through the 1400s and 1500s, spreading to other societies. In Florence, artists and thinkers rediscovered the ideas of the Classical Greeks and Romans. Renaissance philosophy, called **humanism**, emphasized humanity, worldly concerns, and reason rather than religious ideals. The books of Dante Alighieri (DAHN-tay ah-lee-GYEH-ree) (1265–1321), especially *The Divine Comedy*, attacked the pope and promoted vernacular language, in this case Italian, rather than Latin, while painters in Italy, such as Sandro Botticelli (SAHN-dro BOT-i-CHEL-ee) (1445–1510), and in the Netherlands depicted space and the human figure realistically. Scholars debate whether the Renaissance undermined medieval world-views by fostering individualism, secularism, and scientific inquiry or was mainly a cultural movement among a small privileged elite that had little impact on the larger society. Nonetheless, Renaissance artists and writers emphasized tolerance of diverse views and new ideals of beauty, weakening church influence. The Renaissance eventually spread into northern Europe in the 1500s.

New Technologies

Extraordinary technological development, greatly aided by imports from other regions, also characterized late medieval Europe. European scholars translated Arab and Greek scientific writings in Muslim Spain, while Asian and Muslim technologies reached Europe, including the Chinese spinning wheel and loom, which spurred improved textile manufacturing. During the fourteenth and fifteenth centuries western Europeans developed better ships, in part by improving Chinese inventions such as the compass and sternpost rudder and by adapting the Arab lateen sails. By the 1490s, thanks to these advances in navigation, sailing, and weaponry, Europeans were masters of the oceans. They also devised time-measuring devices, including mechanical clocks, that allowed people to control and standardize units of time.

Perhaps the most crucial invention was printing by movable type, allowing information to be produced and spread in unlimited quantities. The Chinese invented woodblock printing and movable type made of clay and metal centuries earlier (see Chapter 11), and knowledge of Chinese techniques may have traveled the trade routes to Europe. By the 1400s Europeans used block printing for books and playing cards, and in 1455 the German goldsmith Johann Gutenberg (yoh-HAHN GOO-ten-burg) (1400–1468) introduced the first known metal movable type outside of East Asia, using it to print a Bible. From then on the printed word became an essential medium of mass communication and no longer the monopoly of the few who could afford the expensive hand-copied volumes. This development undermined both feudalism and the church.

Imported technology, especially gunpowder from China, made for more lethal warfare. By the 1200s, the Chinese had developed primitive guns capable of ejecting flame and projectiles 40 yards, a major reason it took the Mongols so long to conquer China. This and other weapons reached

Europe during the Mongol era and were then improved, making warfare far deadlier than it had been before. But gunpowder weapons, while killing many knights and nobles in wars, also gave Europeans a huge military advantage over societies that did not have them, among them those in sub-Saharan Africa and the Americas.

Population and Economic Growth

Technological advance was matched by population and economic growth. Increased agricultural development spurred a European population increase of 40 to 50 percent between the tenth and fourteenth centuries, the highest rate in the world. After the Black Death, Europe's population again increased rapidly, grain production doubled, and many peasants moved into eastern Europe to open lands.

Expanding Commerce

Commerce also expanded. When feudalism and manorialism were dominant, merchants mostly dealt in luxury goods for the aristocracy. Indeed, the feudal ethic was somewhat hostile to the accumulation of wealth, and it devalued merchants. By the 1300s, however, this feudal ethic began to break down. As foreign trade became more economically important, commerce became a part of everyday life. Valuable spices from India and Southeast Asia were distributed by Venetian merchants who had trading posts all over the Middle East and around the Black Sea, as well as from Genoa. Observers were awed by the vast quantity of merchandise, much of it from the East, in fifteenth-century Venice:

> *It seems as if the whole world flocks here. Who could count the many shops so well furnished that they seem almost warehouses, with so many cloths of every make—tapestry, brocades, carpets of every sort, silks of every kind; and so many warehouses full of spices, groceries and rugs. These things stupefy the beholder.*[18]

Gold from West Africa, used in coins, treasuries, and jewelry, also stimulated the European economy. European merchants borrowed and used Arab trading practices and mathematics. In the early 1200s Fibonacci **(fee-bo-NACH-ee)**, a merchant from Pisa in Italy, wrote of the Arab and Indian numerals and calculations he had studied in Algeria, Egypt, and Syria. Soon the mathematical and commercial innovations he learned were adopted in Venice, Genoa, and Florence.

Unique Cities

Western European cities were unique in their growing political power and autonomy. Unlike in centralized China or the Ottoman Empire, these cities existed in a politically fragmented region and thus could bargain with kings for advantages and autonomy. In 1241 various north German cities expanded a trade alliance, the Hanseatic **(han-see-AT-ik)** League, that eventually had over 165 member cities, including some in Holland and Poland, and its own army and navy, making it almost an independent political power. These developments gave European merchants a status and power unique in the world. In China, for instance, merchants, while often prosperous, had a low ranking in the Confucian social system, were heavily taxed, and faced many restrictions. In western Europe merchants steadily gained influence, becoming city political leaders. Governments now supported merchants and their interests, fostering a social and institutional structure that encouraged profits. Not everyone approved, however. The Dutch philosopher Erasmus complained about greed, asking, "When did avarice reign more largely and less punished?"[19] Nonetheless, late medieval Europeans laid the foundation for an economic revolution that began to fundamentally alter western European life in the 1500s and later spread its influences around the world.

The Portuguese and Maritime Exploration

Portuguese Motives

In the 1400s a few Europeans, pushed by the growth of commerce, and taking advantage of the new maritime and military technologies, began to explore the world beyond Europe by sea. The Portuguese, who had recently been unified in a kingdom and whose standard of living was probably lower than that of many Africans and Asians, began sailing south in search of slaves, gold, and other trade goods. Although shocked at the wealth of some of the societies they encountered, they enjoyed the advantage of guns, better ships, and a maritime tradition, and they were motivated by a missionary desire to outflank Islam and spread Christianity, as well as a compelling appetite for plunder and conquest. The Portuguese also had a larger strategic purpose: to find a way around Africa and sail directly to the fabled lands of Southeast Asia, the source of the spices so valued in Europe. They also sought the sources of African gold. Finally, European legends spoke of a great Christian emperor in Africa, "Prester John," perhaps derived from the king of Ethiopia, who they believed could be a possible ally against Muslims.

Hence, in search of, in their words, "Christians and spices," the Portuguese began systematically exploring the West African coast in 1420 under the sponsorship of Prince Henry the Navigator (1394–1460), an innovator in shipbuilding design and cartography. Soon Henry's caravels, small ships that could sail both on the ocean and into shallow coastal waters and rivers, discovered Madeira **(muh-DEER-uh)** Island and the Azores **(A-zorz)** and Canary Islands in the Atlantic off North Africa. By the 1480s the Portuguese had visited much of the African coast as far south as Angola (see Chapter 12). In 1487 Portuguese ships led by Bartolomeu Dias **(DEE-uhsh)** reached the Indian Ocean, intensifying Portuguese interest both in Africa and the world to the east. One of the sailors who had manned Portuguese ships was a Genoese immigrant to Portugal, Christopher Columbus, who later developed an alternative strategy for reaching the East. In 1492 Columbus, under Spanish sponsorship, sailed west across the Atlantic to the Americas, changing world history forever.

Portuguese Discoveries

SECTION SUMMARY

- The Black Death killed a third of Europe's people and reduced the power of western European nobles while increasing the power of eastern European nobles.
- French rulers increased their power in the Hundred Years War, England's Tudor dynasty later made England a world power, and Spanish Christians gradually drove out the Muslims, while in Germany and Italy the nobility remained strong.
- The church entered a decline in power and prestige as it came to be seen as corrupt, and the papacy was weakened by the Great Schism.
- During the Renaissance, artists and writers rediscovered classical influences and championed worldly concerns, individualism, and realism rather than spirituality.
- Major technological developments, influenced in part by ideas imported from China and the Muslim world, included the printing press, which further undermined the church, and guns, which killed many in European wars and were especially deadly against Africans and Americans.
- Despite the Black Death, Europe's population soared and its merchants grew increasingly successful and powerful.
- The Portuguese were the first to begin exploring the West Coast of Africa for slaves, gold, and other trade goods, and their adventures eventually led to Columbus's voyage to the Americas.

CHAPTER SUMMARY

European societies changed dramatically between 600 and 1500. By mixing Greco-Roman, Christian, and Germanic legacies between 500 and 1000, western Europeans constructed new societies based on new values and practices. These societies also acquired knowledge from and traded with the Islamic world, especially Muslim Spain. Feudalism, manorialism, and the papacy became the major medieval institutions, but they generated conflict between popes and kings, kings and nobles, nobles and merchants, cities and countryside, and Christians and outsiders. The church played a crucial social and political role in European societies. Priests dominated village life, while popes fought heresy and spurred crusades against Muslims.

The social, political, economic, and religious systems of Byzantium were different from those in western Europe. The Byzantine emperors were more powerful and had more control over the church. Eventually the Byzantine church broke completely with the Roman church, becoming the Greek Orthodox Church. Byzantium also passed on many traditions to various eastern European societies such as the Russians. Russia later became a strong state with a rival Orthodox Church.

Western Europeans were linked by trade networks to other societies of Eurasia and North Africa. These networks, including those formed by the Mongol expansion, allowed the movement from east to west not only of valuable goods, technologies, and ideas but also of diseases such as the Black Death. Between 1300 and 1500 western European states grew larger and, in some cases, more centralized, the church faced decline as a political force, and warfare became more deadly. Sparked in part by Afro-Asian influences, the Renaissance fostered new humanistic ideas and artistic currents, while economic growth and social change enhanced the influence of merchants. In the fifteenth century, aided by Asian and Islamic seafaring technologies, western Europeans began exploring the world.

KEY TERMS

medieval
feudalism
vassals
benefices
fief
knights
chivalry
manorialism
serfs
guilds
usury
courtly love
excommunicate
simony
Holy Inquisition
Magna Carta
Renaissance
humanism

EBOOK AND WEBSITE RESOURCES

PRIMARY SOURCE
Magna Carta: The Great Charter of Liberties

INTERACTIVE MAPS
Map 14.1 Europe During the Carolingian Empire
Map 14.2 Medieval Europe, 900–1300
Map 14.3 Europe, 1400–1500

LINKS

Byzantium: Byzantine Studies on the Internet (http://www.fordham.edu/halsall/byzantium). Contains useful texts, images, essays, and bibliography.

The Internet Medieval Sourcebook (http://www.fordham.edu/halsall/sbook.html). This is one of the best, most extensive sources for texts and essays.

Lectures in Medieval History (http://www.ku/kansas/medieval/108/lectures/index.html). Many useful essays for the general reader by a leading expert.

Medieval and Renaissance Europe: Primary Historical Documents (http://eudocs.lib.byu.edu/index.php/Main_Page). Many links to primary sources.

The WWW Virtual Library: Medieval Europe (https://www.msu.edu/~georgem1/history/medieval.htm). Contains many links to many topical sites.

The World of the Vikings (http://www.worldofthevikings.com). Contains many links to texts, images, and essays.

Plus flashcards, practice quizzes, and more. Go to: www.cengage.com/history/lockard/globalsocnet2e.

SUGGESTED READING

Bridenthal, Renate, et al., eds. *Becoming Visible: Women in European History,* 3rd ed. Boston: Houghton Mifflin, 1998. Valuable essays.

Brotton, Jerry. *The Renaissance Bazaar: From the Silk Road to Michelangelo.* Oxford: Oxford University Press, 2002. An important revisionist interpretation by a British scholar that places European developments in a hemispheric context.

Cruz, Jo Ann, H. Moran, and Richard Gerberding. *Medieval Worlds: An Introduction to European History, 300–1492.* Boston: Houghton Mifflin, 2004. A readable and comprehensive recent text.

Cunliffe, Barry. *Facing the Ocean: The Atlantic and Its Peoples, 8000 BC–AD 1500.* New York: Oxford University Press, 2001. Examines the societies on Eurasia's western rim.

Davies, Norman. *Europe: A History.* New York: Harper Perennial, 1998. A fascinating examination with much on this era.

Gies, Frances, and Joseph Gies. *Marriage and the Family in the Middle Ages.* New York: Harper and Row, 1987. A thorough account of marriage and family life, written for the general reader.

Hanawalt, Barbara A. *The Middle Ages: An Illustrated History.* New York: Oxford University Press, 1998. A well-written overview aimed at the general reader.

Kelly, John. *The Great Mortality: An Intimate History of the Black Death, the Most Devastating Plague of All Time.* New York: HarperCollins, 2005. A readable account of the calamity and its effects on people.

Logan, F. Donald. *The Vikings in History,* 3rd ed. London: Routledge, 2005. A wide-ranging survey that stresses the importance of the Vikings in European history.

Lowney, Chris. *A Vanished World: Medieval Spain's Golden Age of Enlightenment.* New York: Free Press, 2005. Examines Islamic Spain's connections to Europe.

Madden, Thomas F. *A New History of the Crusades.* Lanham, MD: Rowman and Littlefield, 2005. A recent and well-written overview.

McCormick, Michael. *Origins of the European Economy: Communication and Commerce, A.D. 300–900.* New York: Cambridge University Press, 2001. Pathbreaking work.

Ostrowski, Donald. *Muscovy and the Mongols: Cross-Cultural Influences on the Steppe Frontier, 1304–1589.* Cambridge: Cambridge University Press, 1990. A scholarly study of Byzantine and Mongol influences on the Russians.

Treadgold, Warren. *A Concise History of Byzantium.* New York: Palgrave, 2001. A comprehensive recent survey.

Wells, Colin. *Sailing from Byzantium: How a Lost Empire Shaped the World.* New York: Delta, 2006. Readable study of Byzantium and its legacy.

Eastern Predominance in the Intermediate World

For over a century now the prosperous and powerful nations of North America and western Europe—often known today as the West—have dominated the world economically and politically. But before 1500 the world looked very different, and various societies in Asia and North Africa were much stronger and more influential than they are today. Some Eastern societies enjoyed power and status far beyond their borders, helping to shape much of the Eastern Hemisphere in these centuries. However, historians debate to what degree we can consider this to have been an era of Eastern predominance in Afro-Eurasia.

THE PROBLEM

Some historians believe that the rise to influence and prosperity of the East, especially China, India, and various Islamic societies, was a major theme of the Intermediate Era. In their view, for most of these centuries, these Eastern peoples developed and sustained more dynamic governments, productive economies, and creative technologies than any other societies. Others disagree, contending that after 1000 the advantage shifted to western Europeans, who laid the foundations for rapid growth and eventual world dominance. These arguments are part of a vigorous scholarly debate.

THE DEBATE

Many historians identify Eastern predominance in this era, but they disagree on which society made the greatest contributions to the world. The largest number point to China as the Eurasian leader in the Intermediate Era, and they offer a variety of factors to explain China's status. S. A. M. Adshead, for example, sees Tang China as taking center-stage in the world economy and becoming the world's best-ordered state between 600 and 900. William McNeill refers to an era of Chinese predominance especially from 1000 to 1500, with China as the engine of the Eurasian economy. Various historians of Asia, among them Rhoads Murphey, describe an especially dynamic and creative Song China that had many of the conditions that would, in the later eighteenth century, foster industrialization in northwest Europe: urbanization, commercialization, widening local and overseas markets, rising demand, and mechanical invention. A few scholars such as Mary Matossian label the entire Intermediate Era the "Chinese Millennium," when China was more populous, productive, and wealthy than any other society, enjoying an orderly society and advanced technology.

There is a growing consensus among world historians that Chinese innovations and commercial expansion energized Eurasian trade and that Chinese inventions contributed much to the Intermediate world. The British scholar Robert Temple goes even further, crediting the Chinese with inventing modern agriculture, shipping, astronomical observatories, oil industries, paper money, decimal mathematics, wheelbarrows, fishing reels, multistage rockets, guns, umbrellas, hot-air balloons, chess, whiskey, and even the essential design of the steam engine. Without Chinese naval technology, he and others argue, Columbus would never have sailed to America. China and India were the two great centers of world manufacturing before 1500, and their exports fueled Afro-Eurasian trade.

But China was not the only Asian powerhouse and great source of knowledge. Indians fostered two universal religions, Buddhism and Hinduism, while inventing and exporting scientific, technological, and agricultural techniques to China, the Islamic world, and later Europe in a process the historian Lynda Shaffer terms "southernization." Such innovations as Indian granulated sugar crystals, the decimal system, "Arabic" numerals, and cotton plants had revolutionary implications for Eurasia. Then there are historians of the Middle East, such as Marshall Hodgson and Richard Eaton, who argue for the centrality of the Islamic societies. They contend that, before 1600, the Islamic culture and economy were the world's most expansive, influential, and integrating force. Islam provided a widespread, sophisticated culture as many peoples joined the Muslim-dominated hemispheric economy. Islam was cosmopolitan, egalitarian, and flexible, allowing Muslims to rebound from the Mongol conquests and Black Death and reestablish powerful states such as Ottoman Turkey.

Still other historians think China, India, and Islam all played key roles as powerhouses in an Eastern-dominated Intermediate world. For instance, Robert Marks argues that the Eastern Hemisphere in the 1300s and 1400s had three centers, with dynamic but linked regional systems based on China, India, and Islam. In the 1400s, from Ottoman Turkey eastward to Japan, agricultural efficiency, consumer goods, social welfare, and civilian and military technology were generally the equal of, and often superior to, European counterparts. British scholar John Hobson makes a strong case that the rise of the East made possible the later rise of the West. He argues that the globalization of the era allowed the advanced Eastern inventions, the products of more dynamic societies, to flow westward, where they were gradually assimilated by Europe. Many historians contend that Europe in this era was economically weak, with small, insignificant states, and did not show renewed vigor until 1400. Nor did Europe have, as some historians suggest, any unique cultural advantages. Jack Goody concludes that there were few decisive cultural differences between East and West in rationality, economic tools, family patterns, and political pluralism.

Other scholars doubt that any Eastern societies had a great advantage in this era, and they contend that medieval Europe was not backward compared to China, India, or Islam. David Landes, for example, while conceding that Europe was well behind China and Islam in many areas of life in 1000, suggests that things had changed considerably 500 years later. With what he considers many cultural and geographical advantages, Europeans, argues Landes, caught up to the East with the growth of manufacturing and trade. Landes and others describe an inventive Europe with impressive technological progress using increased nonhuman power, especially in agriculture. Toby Huff has favorably contrasted European science with its Chinese counterpart, especially after 1200. Restless human energy, influential merchants, and competing states made late medieval Europe dynamic. Rodney Stark credits the medieval Catholic Church's emphasis on reason and belief in progress for fostering economic growth, asserting that these ideas were lacking in other religions, a view many scholars have challenged. Landes and Huff also challenge the notion of Eastern leadership. They see China by 1450 as overpopulated, intellectually dormant, indifferent to technology, negating commercial success, and resistant to change. Some historians of China, such as Adshead, concur that the balance of power was shifting toward Europe in the later Intermediate Era.

If several Eastern societies, and especially China, did have some advantages and great power during much of the Intermediate Era, they lost their predominance between 1450 and 1800, raising the question of when and how the East declined. As for when, some historians believe the decline of the East preceded and made possible the rise of the West. Janet Abu-Lughod describes a well-integrated hemispheric system linking Afro-Eurasia by trade for several centuries, with no single country dominant. This network declined after 1350, reducing Europe's commercial competition. Other historians blame Eastern decline on the Mongols and their heirs, who devastated western Asia and North India and ended the creative Song dynasty.

Others credit what the historian L. S. Stavrianos termed the "Law of the Retarding Lead"—that nothing fails like success—for undermining China and helping underdeveloped Europe. This concept holds that the best-adapted, most successful societies have the most difficulty in changing and retaining their lead in a period of transition. They lose their dynamic thrust. Conversely, the less successful societies are more likely to eventually adapt and forge ahead. In the 1400s China still had an edge over other societies, with an advanced technology, efficient government, great regional power, and the world's largest commercial economy. As a result, the Chinese had a stake in preserving rather than dramatically altering their system, which seemed to work so well. Indeed, some argue that the leading Eastern societies, especially China, remained successful until overtaken by a rising West between 1600 and 1800.

EVALUATING THE DEBATE

A plausible case can be made for Eastern predominance, and most global historians now agree that, while other societies played key roles, China and the Islamic world were the two major poles of global trade and technological innovation for much of this era, at least before the 1400s. But the Eastern advantage was eventually lost. We are left with tantalizing questions. What if the Mongols or Ottomans had conquered some of western Europe, or Ming admiral Zheng He had continued his voyages and headed all the way to West Africa, Europe, or the Americas? Had they occurred, these Mongol, Ottoman, or Chinese achievements might have created a world unrecognizable to us today. Perhaps China, with many prerequisites already in place and enriched by greater trade with West Africa and Europe, might have sparked an industrial revolution. It did not happen, however. Humanity stood at a crossroads in the middle of the millennium, posed between several very different futures. During the next several centuries Europe gradually forged ahead—what some historians call "the rise of the West"—partly by assimilating Eastern technologies and science, while

Courtesy of South China University of Technology Library, Canton (Guangzhon)

Chinese Foundries By the second century B.C.E. Chinese iron masters had developed highly sophisticated techniques for producing iron and steel, including a basic blast furnace similar to those invented in Europe in the nineteenth century.

the Islamic societies, India, and finally China struggled, making the world after 1500 very different from the world before it.

THINKING ABOUT THE CONTROVERSY

1. Why do some historians emphasize China as the predominant power in this era?
2. What role did India and the Islamic societies play in the Intermediate world?
3. What points support the argument that Europe began its rise to world power in this era?

EXPLORING THE CONTROVERSY

Among books making the case for Eastern predominance and leadership are John M. Hobson, *The Eastern Origins of Western Civilisation* (New York: Cambridge University Press, 2004); Robert B. Marks, *The Origins of the Modern World: A Global and Ecological Narrative* (Lanham, MD: Rowman and Littlefield, 2002); and Jack Goody, *The East in the West* (Cambridge: Cambridge University Press, 1996). On China as the major power, see S. A. M. Adshead, *Tang China: The Rise of the East in World History* (New York: Palgrave, 2004); William H. McNeill, *The Pursuit of Power: Technology, Armed Force, and Society Since A.D. 1000* (Chicago: University of Chicago Press, 1982); Rhoads Murphey, *East Asia: A New History*, 3rd ed. (New York: Longman, 2004); Mary Kilbourne Matossian, *Shaping World History: Breakthroughs in Ecology, Technology, Science, and Politics* (Armonk, NY: M.E. Sharpe, 1997); and Robert Temple, *The Genius of China: 3,000 Years of Science, Discovery and Invention* (London: Prion Books, 1986). For Indian and Islamic influence, see Lynda Shaffer, "Southernization," *Journal of World History* 5, no.1 (Spring 1994): 1–22; Marshall Hodgson, *Rethinking World History* (Cambridge: Cambridge University Press, 1993); and Richard Eaton, *Islamic History as Global History* (Washington, DC: American Historical Association, 1993). Among books that argue for European superiority are Toby E. Huff, *The Rise of Early Modern Science: Islam, China, and the West* (Cambridge: Cambridge University Press, 1993); David S. Landes, *The Wealth and Power of Nations: Why Some Are So Rich and Some Are So Poor* (New York: Norton, 1998); and Rodney Stark, *The Victory of Reason: How Christianity Led to Freedom, Capitalism, and Western Success* (New York: Random House, 2005). For a broader study of the rise and demise of the East, see Janet L. Abu-Lughod, *Before European Hegemony: The World System A.D. 1250–1350* (New York: Oxford University Press, 1989).

SOCIETIES • NETWORKS • TRANSITIONS

Expanding Horizons in the Intermediate Era, 600 B.C.E.–600 C.E.

Societies change largely in interaction with one another rather than in isolation, and world historians emphasize these interactions. In world history, the formation of broad connections among peoples is more crucial than the rise and fall of individual states and even great empires. World history differs from regional history primarily because the world historian stresses contacts, collisions, and networks of exchange, as well as the spread from one society to another of products, technologies, ideas, and people. From earliest times parts of Eurasia and North Africa formed an interconnecting zone, and the links continually expanded to incorporate more of Eurasia and Africa and then, after 1500, the Americas and Oceania.

These patterns can be clearly seen in the Intermediate Era, or Middle Ages between 600 and 1500 C.E., when the world changed profoundly. During this time, the Chinese, Indian, and Islamic societies stood out for their power and creativity, but by the 1400s western Europe was also emerging as a dynamic center. In the Eastern Hemisphere vigorous societies also flourished in Northeast Asia, Southeast Asia, Central Asia, and sub-Saharan Africa. Many far-flung cultures became linked as people, armies, goods, and religions moved more easily and frequently, expanding horizons. These movements and exchanges connected peoples from one end of Afro-Eurasia to the other and generated several transitions, such as the reshaping of many societies by the spread of universal religions. Connections were also growing within the Americas. Large empires such as those of the Aztecs, Incas, and their predecessors enjoyed widespread influence, and trade networks bound societies over great distances. Thanks to European voyages of discovery, by 1500 the long divided Eastern and Western Hemispheres came into regular communication, furthering global contacts.

Today the term *globalization* refers to the increasing interconnectedness of nations and peoples around the world through international trade, investment, ideas, popular culture, and travel. Globalization is sometimes viewed as a twentieth-century phenomenon. But extensive exchanges between widespread peoples and travel over vast distances came many centuries earlier, especially in Afro-Eurasia. An English observer, William Fitzsteven, described the results of such connections in the 1170s when he noted how the markets of London carried products that reflected the cosmopolitan tastes of the city's people:

> *Gold from Arabia, from Sabaea [Yemen] spice*
> *And incense; from the Scythians [Central Asians] arms of steel*
> *Well-tempered; oil from the rich groves of palm*
> *That spring from the fat lands of Babylon;*
> *Fine gems from Nile, from China crimson silks;*
> *French wines; and sable . . .*
> *From the far lands where Rus and Northmen [Vikings] dwell.*[1]

This essay examines some of these early forms of globalization during the Intermediate Era, such as long-distance trade, the spread of world religions and the social changes they fostered, the connections sparked by the Mongol expansion, and the acceleration of maritime exploration in the Late Intermediate Era.

Increasing Economic Exchange

Interregional trade was a major theme in world history, especially because it fostered other forms of exchange, including the spread of religions, cultures, and technologies over trade routes. Merchants carried with them their own traditions and learned of other traditions in their travels. During the Intermediate Era, several trade zones developed in the Americas, while in the Eastern Hemisphere overland trade routes reached across Eurasia and Africa. Maritime trade also flourished around the rim of the Indian Ocean. Though it was dominated by Islamic merchants, who spread their faith far and wide, many peoples of various faiths engaged in long-distance commerce by land and sea, serving as links between diverse societies.

Trade and Interregional Contact

The roots of the growing commerce between societies go far back in history. Long-distance trade routes had long existed to move cargo and people by boat, camel, or horseback. The contacts between societies that occurred through trade and military expansion spread various cultural and religious ideas (see map). For instance, Indian influences, including Buddhism, were carried over the trading routes into Central Asia, Tibet, China, Japan, and Southeast Asia between 200 B.C.E. and 1500 C.E. Similarly, between 700 and 1500, Islam expanded by land and sea into West and East Africa, southern Europe, India, and Southeast Asia. Muslim-dominated trade routes ultimately reached from the Sahara to the South China Sea. Once established, these trade routes became a stimulus for travel. Indeed, the annual pilgrimage of devout Muslims proved a boon for merchants as pilgrims from all over brought their local products to Mecca, transforming it into one of the world's great fairs. In 1184 one observer marveled that "no merchandise in the world is absent from this meeting."[2]

Beginning around 200 B.C.E., the Silk Road, a 4,000-mile-long route linking China through Central Asia to India, western Asia, and the Mediterranean, provided the most outstanding example of overland trade and a symbol of east-west contacts. Cities such as Samarkand and Bukhara grew up along the overland Silk Road routes across Central Asia to service trade and merchants. The people in these cities prospered as middlemen between merchants and suppliers of caravans. Chinese silk, porcelain, and bamboo were carried west to Baghdad and the eastern Mediterranean ports, from which they were shipped by sea to Constantinople and Rome. Silk clothes were coveted by European bishops and aristocrats as well as by Mahayana Buddhist monks. The lively caravan trade that developed along

Bildarchiv Preussischer Kulturbesitz/Art Resource, NY

Silk Road Travelers The Silk Road remained a key trade route during this era. This painting, from a fourteenth-century atlas made in Spain, shows one of the horse and camel caravans that traveled between China and Central Asia.

the Silk Road had other consequences too. Over the centuries many Chinese inventions, such as gunpowder, wheelbarrows, and the compass, were transported westward over the Silk Road and profoundly changed Western society. The trade even influenced food preferences. Chinese noodles, for example, spread widely in Asia, and Arabs may have brought Chinese-derived pasta to Italy. But the exchange was not entirely one way. Arabs marveled at a Chinese scholar who sojourned in Baghdad around 900, learned Arabic, and made copies of important medical texts to take back to China.

The Silk Road was not the only major land trade network. Other major overland trade routes linked West Africa and the Mediterranean across the Sahara Desert, allowing the movement of commodities such as salt and gold. Land and riverine routes also tied northern and eastern Europe into the broader Eurasian trade system. For example, between 800 and 1000 Swedish Vikings established a major trading network stretching from Scandinavia through Russia to Byzantium. Persia, Mali in West Africa, Byzantium, the northern Italian city-states, and Muslim Spain also prospered from their strategic locations along major trade routes. An Arab source reported that, thanks to their extensive travels, Jewish merchants who came to Cordoba in Spain "speak Arabic, Persian, [Italian], and the language of the Franks and Slavs."[3] At about the same time that these routes were expanding in Eurasia and Africa, in the Americas overland trade also carried Mesoamerican influences deep into North America while spreading Andean technologies, crops, and religious cults widely around South America. Although oceanic exchange in the Americas was limited, people in North and South America moved products by canoe along rivers, a lively canoe and raft trade linked the Caribbean islands, and some traders sailed along the Pacific coast on rafts.

The Rise of Maritime Trade

By 1000 an increasingly lucrative maritime trade, perhaps spurred by improving naval technology, grew in the Eastern Hemisphere, despite the dangers from pirates and storms. At one end of the Afro-Eurasian zone, much trade crisscrossed the Mediterranean, around which Venice, Genoa, Constantinople, Aleppo in Syria, Alexandria, and Algiers served as the major ports. Sailing networks along Europe's Atlantic coast later linked the Baltic and North Seas to Mediterranean ports and helped foster the Hanseatic League of Baltic ports.

Farther east, the Indian Ocean routes became the heart of the most extensive maritime trade network in the Intermediate world. The Abbasid caliph al-Mansur, writing from Baghdad, boasted that "there is no obstacle to us and China; everything on the sea can come to us on it."[4] The Indian Ocean system linked China, Japan, Vietnam, and Cambodia in the east through Malaya and the Indonesian archipelago to India and Sri Lanka, and then westward to Persia, Arabia, Russia, the eastern and central Mediterranean, and the East African coast as far south as Mozambique. Over these routes the spices of Indonesia, the gold and tin of Malaya, the textiles, sugar, and cotton of India, the cinnamon of Sri Lanka, the gold and ivory of East Africa, the coffee of Arabia, the carpets of Persia, and the silks, porcelain, and tea of China moved to distant markets. Many of these products reached Europe, sparking interest there in reaching the sources of the riches of the East.

The spices, aromatic and pungent derivatives of vegetables grown in tropical lands, were among the main products moving from east to west. Black pepper was cultivated chiefly in India, Siam, and Indonesia, while cloves, nutmeg, and mace came from the Maluku (Moluccan) Islands of eastern Indonesia. Cinnamon was grown in Indonesia and Sri Lanka. All of them found a market in the Middle East and Europe. Asia was not the only source for spices, since red or cayenne pepper from West Africa was traded to the Middle East and reached Europe in the 1300s. While they became ingredients in cosmetics and perfumes, spices were more commonly used as medicine or as condiments to flavor food. Intermediate Era people treated a range of illnesses and aided digestion with spices, and many

World Religions and Trade Routes, 600–1500

Much of the Eastern Hemisphere was linked by land and maritime trade routes. Along with goods and travelers, Buddhism, Christianity, and Islam spread along these trade routes, attracting believers from many societies.

Interactive Map

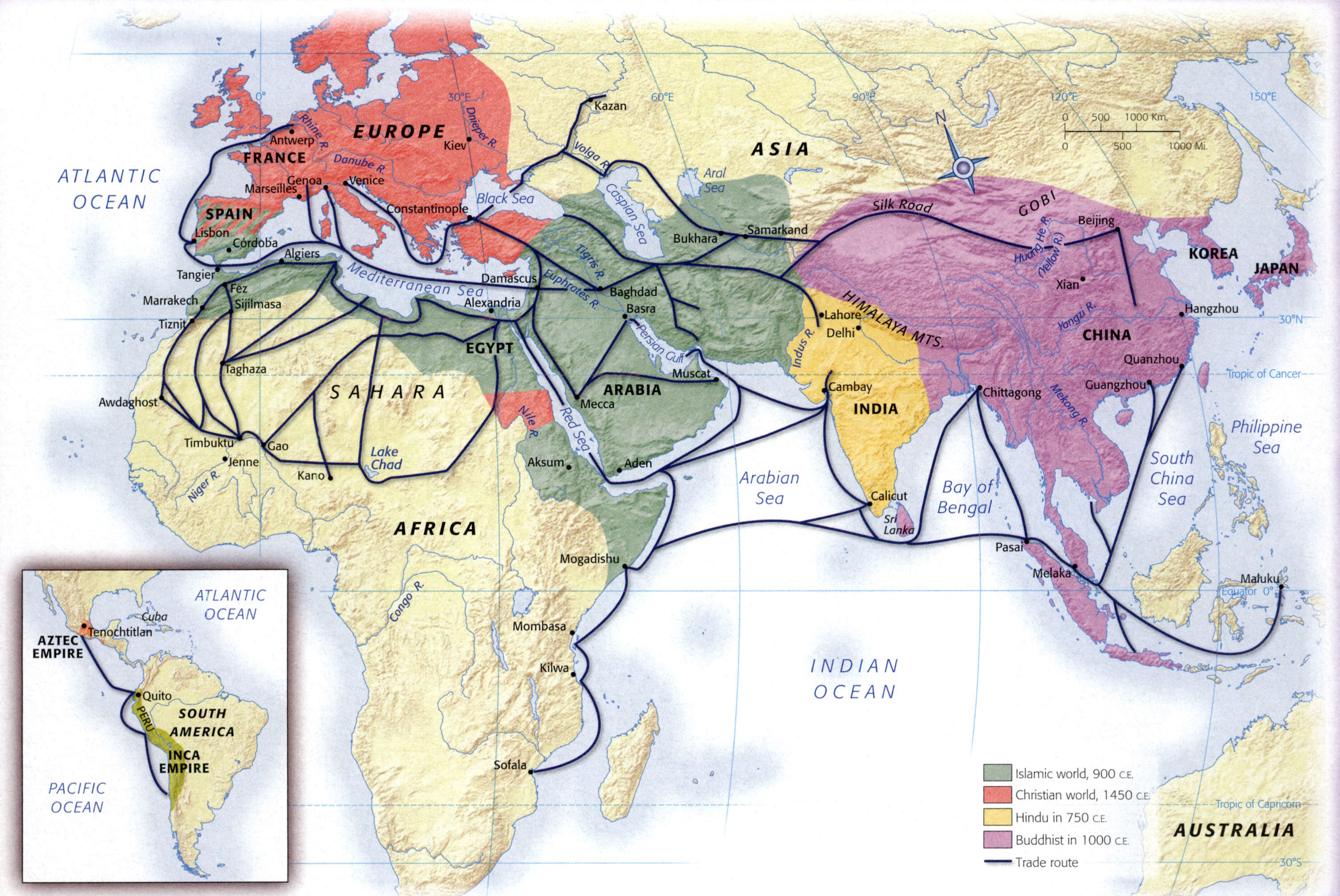

cultures used copious quantities of spices in cooking. Asian spices such as almonds, ginger, saffron, cinnamon, sugar, nutmeg, and cloves improved late medieval European diets. An English book from the early 1400s reported the popularity of pepper, which helped disguise the bad taste of heavily salted preserved meat during the long European winter: "Pepper is black and has a good smack, And every man doth it buy."[5]

Various states around the Persian Gulf, Indian Ocean, and South China Sea were closely linked to maritime trade. However, no particular political power dominated the Indian Ocean trading routes. The trade dynamism depended on cosmopolitan port cities, especially hubs such as Hormuz in Persia, Kilwa in Tanzania, Cambay in northwest India, Calicut on India's southwest coast, Melaka in Malaya, and Quanzhou **(chwan-cho)** in southern China. These trading ports became vibrant centers of international commerce and culture, drawing populations from various societies. The thirteenth-century traveler Marco Polo was fascinated by the coming and going of ships at Quanzhou: "Here is a harbor whither all ships of India come, with much costly merchandise. It is also the port whither go the [Chinese] merchants [heading overseas]. There is such traffic of merchandise that it is a truly wonderful sight."[6]

A hemispheric trade system developed in which some people came to produce for a world market. This system was fueled by China and India, the great centers of world manufacturing in this era (see Historical Controversy: Eastern Predominance in the Intermediate World). Together China and India probably produced over three-quarters of all world industrial products before 1500. China exported iron, steel, silk, refined sugar, and ceramics, while India was the great producer of textiles. Their industrial products might be transported thousands of miles. Hence, the work of a cotton weaver in India might be sold in China or East Africa, and Chinese ceramics might reach Zimbabwe and Mali. The Muslim soldiers who resisted the Christian crusaders used steel swords smelted in India from East African iron. Merchants from all over Afro-Eurasia—Arabs, Armenians, Chinese, Indians, Indonesians, Jews, Venetians, Genoese—traveled great distances in search of profits, often forming permanent trade diasporas. For instance, it was said of the Genoese, whose merchant networks stretched from Portugal to the Middle East and Russia, that they were so spread "throughout the world that wherever one goes and stays he makes another Genoa there."[7] One Cairo-based Jewish family firm had branches in India, Iran, and Tunisia. Most of the goods traded over vast distances were luxury items meant for the upper classes, but some goods, such as pepper and sugar, also reached consumers of more modest means.

Universal Religions and Social Change

The power and reach of universal, or world, religions such as Buddhism, Christianity, and Islam increased during the Intermediate Era. Religion and its mandates dominated the lives of millions around the world. These religions were early agents of globalization, propagating ideas and fostering trade across regional boundaries. By 1500 the religious map of the Eastern Hemisphere looked very different than it had in 600. Millions of people had embraced ideas, beliefs, and ways of life vastly different from those of their ancestors. The religions promoted moral and ethical values that helped preserve harmony in societies that were increasingly cosmopolitan. The Christian injunction to "love thy neighbor as thyself," the Buddhist emphasis on good thoughts and actions, and the Muslim ideals of social justice and the equality of believers fostered goodwill and cooperation. Religious beliefs also spurred the emergence of new values and social forms.

The Triumph of Universal Religions

During the Intermediate Era, most people in Eurasia and many in Africa eventually embraced one or another universal religion. Islam became the most widespread, rapidly expanding through the Middle East and eventually claiming Central Asia and parts of Europe while gaining a large following in West Africa, the East African coast, South Asia, China, and Southeast Asia. Islam fostered religious, social, and economic networks that linked peoples from Morocco and Spain to Indonesia and the Philippines with a common faith, values, and trade connections. Some Muslim scholars and jurists, such as the Moroccan Ibn Battuta, traveled, sojourned, and even settled thousands of miles from their homelands.

Older faiths also spread in this era, changing societies in varied ways. Theravada Buddhism was established in Sri Lanka and then expanded into mainland Southeast Asia, where it gradually displaced earlier faiths and reshaped cultures by teaching moderation, pacifism, unselfish acts, and individualism. To the north, Mahayana Buddhism first reached Central Asia and then China early in the Common Era, and during the Intermediate Era it became entrenched in Japan, Korea, Vietnam, Mongolia, and Tibet. In most places Buddhism existed alongside rather than replacing earlier religious traditions, such as animism in Siam and Tibet, Shinto in Japan, and Confucianism in China. By 1000 a Buddhist world incorporating diverse societies and several sects stretched from India eastward to Vietnam and Japan, but the temples, pagodas, and statues constructed to honor the Buddha reflected local styles and taste. Whereas many kinds of people, including merchants and jurists, moved along Islamic networks, Buddhist networks tended to facilitate the movement of pilgrims, such as the seventh-century Chinese monk Xuan Zang **(swan tsang)**, who sojourned in India.

Christianity expanded to encompass nearly all of Europe in its fold by 1200, filtering north into the Germanic and Celtic lands and east among the Slavs. But the original Christian church divided. The Roman church dominated the west while the Orthodox church claimed Russia and much of eastern Europe. Although Christianity was pushed back by Islam in western Asia and North Africa, sizable Christian communities grew and sometimes flourished in these regions, aided by the tolerance Muslims usually accorded Christian practice. Nonetheless, chronic tensions arose between Christian Europe and the Islamic world, derived from political and economic conflicts as well as a clash between the strong missionary impulses of both religions. Christians and Muslims often viewed each other as barbarians. A tenth-century Arab geographer argued after visiting Europe that the manners of Christian Europeans "are harsh, their understanding dull and their tongues heavy. Those of them who are furthest to the north are the most subject to stupidity, grossness and brutishness."[8] Tensions between the two rival faiths generated the European Crusades to regain the Holy Land, which left a legacy of bitterness on both sides.

All universal religions nurtured a respect for learning. An admiring Arab described a great library, the House of Knowledge, opened by the Shi'ite Fatimid caliph in Egypt in 1005: "People could visit it, and whoever wanted to copy something that interested him could do so. Lectures were held there by the Quran readers, astronomers, grammarians, philologists, and physicians."[9] The House of Wisdom in Abbasid-ruled Baghdad attracted scholars from all over the Islamic world and beyond, and scholars from Arabia and Spain even made the long journey across the Sahara to West Africa to teach or study in the university at Timbuktu. Some Buddhist centers of higher education, such as the university at Nalanda in India and the monasteries in Srivijaya, in Sumatra, attracted students from all over Asia. In Europe, various Christian orders and thinkers encouraged the preservation of knowledge, laying the foundation for universities, such as Paris and Oxford, and spurring philosophical speculation. Eventually the European universities broadened their studies, mixing theology with secular subjects such as science and logic. Confucians also revered knowledge, and Chinese rulers patronized centers of scholarship such as the Hanlin Academy. Jewish communities honored theologians and produced philosophers such as Spanish-born Moses Maimonides (971–1030), an expert on Aristotle who became a court physician in Egypt.

Gender Roles and Family Patterns

The expansion of universal religions during the Intermediate Era, combined with increasing trade, also influenced many aspects of social life, thought, and attitudes. All of the religions had patriarchal institutional structures that were led by men who promoted notions of female inferiority. For instance, even humanist Christian thinkers believed that women belonged in the home. A fifteenth-century Italian warned that "it would hardly win us [men] respect if our wife busied herself among the men in the marketplace. It also seems somewhat demeaning to me to remain shut up in the house among women when I have manly things to do among men."[10] Islam incorporated many Arab and Persian customs that constrained women, including those that prescribed female seclusion and modesty, but seclusion and veiling of women became the main pattern primarily in Muslim societies that already had a strong patriarchal tradition, such as Arabia, Egypt, north India, and the former Byzantine territories. Where pre-Islamic cultures had less rigid gender roles, as in Spain, Southeast Asia, and West Africa, Islamic patriarchy was considerably modified. The pious Arab traveler Ibn Battuta, for example, was astonished that, in his view, the Mali women wore much too revealing clothing and seemed to have a higher status than the men.

The status of women varied around the world. As Confucianism dug deeper roots in East Asia, patriarchy became a stronger force there than it had been in classical times. By Ming times it was more common to seclude upper-class Chinese women, and even bind their feet. Japanese society also became more patriarchal, as the warrior culture replaced the Heian culture in which elite women had flourished. But some Mahayana Buddhists favored gender equity, at least in principle. The Japanese Zen master Dogen (DOE-joan) argued that there was nothing special about masculinity: "The elements that make up the human body are the same for a man as for a woman. You should not waste your time in futile discussion of the superiority of one sex over another."[11] In mainland Southeast Asia, Theravada Buddhism proved a generally moderating force in gender relations, although men had more opportunity than women to acquire the merit needed to reach nirvana because only men could become monks. In societies as different as Byzantium, Carolingian France, West Africa, Southeast Asia, and the Inca Empire, individual women, such as the Burmese queen Pwa Saw, could still gain power as queens or as powers behind the throne. But in most societies religious hierarchies and military organizations remained mostly male, with priesthoods and warfare giving men more access to prestige and resources. In addition, in most places education was largely restricted to boys.

Religious values influenced family patterns and sexual attitudes. Islam allowed men to have four wives, but polygamy for some men meant that women were unavailable to others, who then could not marry. Christian teachings favored monogamy and marriage, but many men and women joined clerical orders or for other reasons never married. And European kings often flouted church teachings by having concubines and mistresses. Only a minority of western Europeans, mostly in the middle class, lived in nuclear families like those common today in the West. In many societies around the world, men of elite status, and especially in royal families, had multiple wives and concubines. Only a few societies allowed women to have more than one husband.

Attitudes toward homosexuality and gender identity varied widely. Followers of Christianity, Judaism, Islam, and Confucianism all shared an aversion to homosexual relations, in part because they did not produce children. But this sexual behavior had long been practiced and even tolerated in all these traditions. Christian tolerance turned to fierce repression only in the thirteenth century, and such repression was not a global pattern. Perhaps because there were many unmarried Muslim men, and also owing to the rigid segregation of the sexes, some Islamic societies ignored homosexual activity. Homosexual literature was common in western Asian cities under the Abbasid Caliphate. The Japanese, Chinese, and some Southeast Asian and Native American societies also tended to accept homosexuality as part of life. Gender categories could be flexible. Some Asian and American tribal peoples identified more than two genders, including homosexual or heterosexual men who lived as women and served the village as shamans.

Slavery and Feudalism

Most societies were hierarchical, and many people lived in slavery or faced severe restrictions on their freedom. Sanctioned by various religions or simply by custom or economic necessity, slavery had long been common throughout the world and remained so in the Intermediate Era, except for East Asia, where it largely died out by 1000. Islam permitted slavery but encouraged owners to treat slaves well. In Arab, Persian, and Turkish societies, the availability of slaves to do the physical work made the seclusion of elite women possible. Many Muslim African societies, and some that were non-Muslim, had slaves, including the West African kingdoms and East African city-states, although their status varied widely. Africans had been shipped north for centuries to work in the Islamic world, and some African slaves in the Persian Gulf region revolted. Slaves were also common in Southeast Asian societies such as Angkor and Siam. A Persian observer wrote that, in Indonesia, the people "reckon high rank and wealth by the quantity of slaves a person owns."[12] Various American peoples, among them the Mayas and Aztecs, enslaved prisoners of war, debtors, and criminals.

In Europe, slavery's decline after the end of the Roman Empire, and gradual replacement by serfdom, a less restrictive form of bondage, did not end the slave market there. Some slaves still labored in parts of western Europe, sometimes even on lands of Christian monasteries. An active Mediterranean slave trade shipped Slavs, Greeks, and Turks from the Black Sea region to southern Europe and North Africa. Some northwestern Europeans were also sold as slaves to Mediterranean societies. By the fifteenth century Africans appeared in southern European slave markets.

Although some scholars question the usefulness and scope of the concept of feudalism, others identify it as a major new social and political pattern in the world in the Intermediate Era. In feudal societies, relations between people of different status, especially between lords and vassals, were prescribed by agreements or law, and governments were weak or decentralized. The feudal model, which included lords and knights, independent manors, serfdom, small states, and chronic warfare, was best represented by some medieval European societies between 800 and 1300. Some historians also apply feudalism to post-Heian Japan under the warrior class and shogunates, and others to parts of India and Southeast Asia, where many small states competed for power. Feudal societies such as Norman England, the Carolingian realm, and perhaps Ashikaga Japan differed in many ways from the large centralized states such as Song China, Abbasid Iraq, Mali, or the Inca Empire, where emperors or kings exercised great power through bureaucracies.

In most hierarchical societies, whether feudal or centralized, political, military, and religious elites lived off wealth from the primary producers, such as peasants, herders, and artisans. Workers were more or less controlled by, and owed obligations to, those in power, such as Inca kings and Chinese emperors, who ruled despotically. For example, in medieval Europe the dominant Christian church encouraged people who wanted to reap rewards in Heaven to accept the social order, and some governments standardized work requirements. Hence, in 800 the Frankish king Charlemagne proclaimed that the peasant living on church and royal estates "must plow his lord's land a whole day [but not also be asked] to do handiwork service during the same week. The dependent shall not withdraw from these services and the lords shall not ask more from them."[13] In both western Europe and Japan, feudalism established a basis for future change by building up intense pressures that eventually erupted.

The Mongol Empire and Hemispheric Connections

The Mongol expansion, which united a large chunk of the Eurasian population and indirectly affected millions of other people, was one of the most crucial developments in world history. Between 1250 and 1350 the Mongols established the largest land empire in world history, stretching from lands on the western shores of the Black Sea east to the Pacific coast of China and Korea. The building of the Mongol Empire was a ruthless but amazing feat. Within the span of a century the Mongol armies, supported by a Mongol population of less than 2 million, swept out of their arid Central Asian grasslands to put over 200 million people under their control. By reopening Central Asian trade routes closed by political turmoil and by connecting with many different peoples and countries, the Mongols fostered communication networks and the transfer of technology between once remote parts of the Eastern Hemisphere. In doing so, they were major catalysts of change, laying a foundation for the gradual transition from the Intermediate to the Early Modern Era.

The Mongol Empire

The forces prompting the Mongols to build their empire are not altogether clear. Warfare was common among the Mongols, who were tough steppe herders of horses and camels. Historically, various other Central Asian pastoralists, including Turks, Huns, and Tibetans, had forged large but short-lived empires

Edinburgh University Library, Orms. 20, fol. 124v

Catapults The Mongols used advanced military technology, including catapults, to conquer cities. This battle scene, painted by a Persian artist, shows the Mongols attacking a city around 1300.

or confederations. Various factors in Central Asia, including ecological instability, climate change, and population growth, may have prompted the Mongol expansion by fostering competition for limited resources. Another factor was the religions, such as Mahayana Buddhism and Nestorian Christianity, that reached remote Mongolia, which heightened awareness of the riches to be found in the world beyond the steppes. These forces led to the emergence of Genghis Khan (ca. 1162–1227), a visionary leader who effectively united the Mongol tribes. His warriors, mounted and well armed, and aided by siege weaponry and innovative military strategies of rapid attack, made a formidable fighting force.

Within a few decades Mongol armies conquered Central Asia, Tibet, Korea, Russia, part of eastern Europe, Afghanistan, and a large part of western Asia, including Persia and Anatolia. The Mongols were at the Danube, preparing to sweep through Hungary into western Europe, when Genghis Khan's successor, his son Ogodei (1185–1241), died, aborting that thrust. Thus western Europe did not suffer the ravages experienced by other peoples. In the mid-1200s the Mongols expanded their domination in western Asia, overpowering the Arab Abbasid Caliphate. The widespread destruction they caused in the Middle East and Central Asia ended the Islamic golden age and reshaped politics and agriculture in these regions. Later, China, the most formidable foe and tempting prize, and Korea were also eventually added to the Mongol-ruled realm.

Coming from a harsh environment with few resources, the Mongols, with an army of perhaps 130,000 men, sometimes used brutal methods, as had conquerors of earlier eras such as the Assyrians and Alexander the Great. Contemporary accounts credit the Mongols with massacring hundreds of thousands, perhaps millions, of people and burning many cities. A Persian historian concluded that "it is unlikely that mankind will [ever again] see the like of this calamity."[14] The death toll, however, was probably exaggerated by both Mongols and their foes. Some historians doubt that many civilians were killed en masse, since they were needed for production and transportation.

However, the Mongol Empire proved short-lived. One reason was that the Mongols never connected with maritime commerce. They were also victims of their success. Before he died, Genghis Khan worried that his successors would forsake the rigorous life for the comforts of wealthy conquered peoples such as Arabs and Chinese, predicting that "after us, [our] people will wear garments of gold; they will eat sweet, greasy food, ride splendid coursers, and hold in their arms the loveliest women, and they will forget that they owe these things to us."[15] This warning proved prophetic. The Mongols succumbed to wealth and power, their harsh and increasingly corrupt rule provoking rebellions that would end their domination.

The Heritage of the Mongols and Their Networks

In 2000 some world historians named Genghis Khan the most crucial figure of the second millennium C.E. because, despite his brutality, the Mongol conquests he led established an early form of globalized communication characterized by technology and product transfer moving chiefly from east to west along the Silk Road. During the Mongol era, for example, Chinese inventions such as the spinning wheel, medical discoveries, and domesticated fruits and plants such as the orange and lemon reached Europe and the Middle East. People moved by way of these routes, too. A Chinese Nestorian Christian monk of Turkish ancestry, Rabban Sauma, even visited Rome, France, and England in 1287 as a diplomat for the Mongol ruler of Persia, the first known visitor to western Europe from East Asia and an early example of politics on a hemispheric scale.

Because of the Mongols, travel from one end of Eurasia to the other became easier than ever before. During Mongol times many men of talent moved from west to east. In China the Mongols relied administratively on a large number of foreigners who came to serve in the civil service. These included many Muslims from West and Central Asia and a few Europeans such as Marco Polo who found their way to the fabled land the Europeans called Cathay. Polo's reports on his travels increased European interest in Asia and inspired later explorers, such as Christopher Columbus, to seek a sea route to East Asia.

Some historians consider the Mongols the great equalizers of history by having made possible technology transfer from East Asia to western Europe and the Middle East. The Mongols unwittingly set in motion changes that allowed Europeans to acquire and improve Chinese technologies such as printing, gunpowder, and the magnetic compass while developing new inventions of their own. These Chinese inventions had a major impact in Europe. In the seventeenth century the English philosopher Francis Bacon noted that Chinese printing, gunpowder, and the magnet "changed the whole face and state of things" in European literature, warfare, and navigation.[16] Europeans improved Chinese weapons such as flamethrowers and primitive guns, making late medieval warfare far deadlier. Gunpowder and Chinese military technology, coming by way of routes opened by the Mongols, also helped reshape Middle Eastern politics and fostered the rise of the Ottoman Empire.

Disaster and Dynamism in the Late Intermediate Era

A combination of natural disasters, including a terrible pandemic and abrupt climate change, also helped reshape Eurasian societies. Increased trade by land and sea and the migration of peoples such as the Turks, Germans, and Mongols fostered the spread of diseases across the Eastern Hemisphere. Many regions also experienced much cooler climates beginning around 1300, which caused agricultural failures and with them, widespread famine. But these disasters also sparked dynamic new energies that revived trade, which in turn spurred maritime exploration.

The Spread of Diseases

Diseases have long played a major role in human life. Sometimes they have come in terrible pandemics, deadly disease outbreaks affecting millions of people in many societies. Among the most dangerous diseases was bubonic plague, carried by fleas that infested rats. The fleas jumped from rats to humans, causing enlarged lymphatic glands in the victim's groin, armpit, or neck and a high fever, usually followed by death. The disease was sporadic, often not returning for many years. Pandemics had political consequences. A major plague epidemic from the sixth through eighth centuries, for example, weakened both Byzantium and Sassanian Persia, making it more difficult for these empires to repulse Islamic forces.

The worst pandemic in world history, known in the West as the Black Death, may have resulted from the Mongol conquests, in particular the greater contact they brought between Eurasian societies. Climate change may also have been a factor. Eurasia was unusually wet during the 1300s, perhaps increasing the number of fleas and rats. The Black Death, which most scholars think was chiefly caused by bubonic plague, apparently originated in China or Central Asia, where it killed millions. By the mid-1300s it had been carried by merchants and soldiers along the Silk Road to southern Russia. Ships leaving the Genoese trading colony at Calfa, on the Crimean peninsula at the north end of the Black Sea, carried it unwittingly to the Middle East and Europe, where it raged through cities and towns. In the affected societies, from China to Egypt to England and even to fishing villages in remote Greenland, perhaps a third of the total population died in the first outbreak, the higher mortality being in congested cities. Surveying the damage, the Italian writer Petrarch wrote that future generations would be "incredulous, unable to imagine the empty houses, abandoned towns, the squalid countryside, the fields littered with dead, the dreadful silent solitude which seemed to hang over the whole world. Physicians were useless, philosophers could only shrug their shoulders and look wise."[17] Millions more died as the pandemic reappeared in intervals in western Eurasia over the next century.

Ultimately the Black Death disrupted the complex system of interregional trade and communication that had flourished around Eurasia in the thirteenth and fourteenth centuries. Agricultural and industrial production declined and financial crises and labor shortages wrecked economies from China to France. The pandemic also helped undermine Mongol rule in East Asia and the Middle East. Some of the problems resulted from the huge population losses. When the Black Death came to an end, a spurt of growth saw population levels soar from East Asia to Europe. By 1500 the world population had reached between 400 million and 600 million people, about twice the population of 1000. China accounted for a fourth of the total, and India for at least a fifth. Europe, including Russia, grew rapidly to 70–95 million. The Black Death did not affect sub-Saharan Africa or the Americas, each of which probably had 60 to 80 million people by 1500.

Climate Change and Societies

Climate change has helped shape, and sometimes destroyed, societies since the dawn of humankind. It spurred the transition to farming in western Asia 10,000 years ago, undermined the Mesopotamian and Indus societies 4,000 years ago, and hastened the decline of the Chinese Han and Roman Empires around 200 C.E. Eurasian weather became more erratic during the 1200s, and the fluctuations may have helped prompt the Mongol expansion. In the Americas climate change during the Intermediate Era probably contributed to the collapse of various societies, including Tiwanaku, Moche, Teotihuacan, the southern Maya, and the Anasazi.

Around 1300 an unusually warm period gave way to much cooler weather that lasted until 1850, sparking what scientists call the "Little Ice Age," with serious results for societies. Whatever the causes, which are still debated, longer and more frigid winters periodically affected Europe, North America, Central Asia, and China. Bitter cold drove the Norse Vikings out of Greenland, and Icelandic farming floundered. Severe storms and flooding in Europe were followed by drought and crop failures, causing widespread famine. Rivers and canals froze, inhibiting boat traffic. Between 1315 and 1317 perhaps 15 percent of Europe's population starved to death. Hunger apparently made northern Europeans and Chinese less resistant to the Black Death. In addition, rainfall declined in India and Africa, drying up many lakes.

In North America great droughts in the late 1200s may have contributed to Cahokia's decline and caused the dispersal of the Anasazi. Pueblo peoples responded to hard times by migrating, as they said in their songs and poems: "Survival, I know this way. It rains. Mountains and canyons and plants grow. We traveled this way."[18] The Hohokum and Mogollon societies collapsed from drought, and their people moved elsewhere in the southwest. The North Atlantic climate became even colder from the mid-1600s to mid-1700s, and such discomfort may have inspired some adventurous Europeans to seek greener pastures abroad, in the Americas.

The Roots of Oceanic Exploration

The Mongol conquests had connected distant peoples and fostered trade. With the Mongol Empire's demise, however, and the security of Silk Road travel reduced, maritime trade became more crucial and naval technology improved considerably. As a result, late in the Intermediate Era there was a trend toward oceanic exploration over vast distances. The fame of Melaka, Calicut, Hormuz, and other Asian ports as commercial hubs for valuable goods had reached Europe, and by the late fourteenth century some European merchants were beginning to dream of a sea route to the East that would enable them to trade directly with China and the Indies.

By the early 1400s the Chinese had the most advanced ships and navigational techniques and the most outward-looking attitude. The Chinese took the initiative of exploration, dispatching unprecedented voyages of discovery led by Zheng He that sailed as far as the Middle East and East Africa. Zheng's ships followed long-established maritime networks, reflecting the crucial role played in world history by Afro-Eurasian maritime commerce. This Chinese thrust did not have lasting effects on the world, however. Although they had the naval capability, the Chinese, unlike the Europeans, lacked the economic incentive and religious zeal, and hence never sailed around Africa in search of Europe. However, some historians think a few Arabs and Indians may have. A navigation manual written by the Arab navigator Shihab al-Din Ahmad Ibn Majid **(SHE-hob al-DIN AH-mad ibn MA-jeed)** in the later 1400s, and probably based on earlier voyages, gives quite detailed, and mostly accurate, instructions for sailing down the East African coast, around the Cape of Good Hope, up the West African coast, and then into the Mediterranean.

The Portuguese and then the Spanish, both peoples with long maritime traditions and coastal locations, used Chinese, Arab, and European naval technology to construct ships and equip crews for successful long-distance voyages. In search of gold, spices, slaves, and other resources, Portuguese ships sailed to West and Central Africa, where they established outposts and eventually colonies. By the end of the fifteenth century the Portuguese had rounded the Cape of Good Hope to reach the Indian Ocean, the East African trading ports, and finally India. The Portuguese were not the only Europeans dazzled by Asian wealth. A historian in the early 1500s reported on another mariner and his ambitions:

> *Christopher Columbus, a Genoese, proposed to the Catholic King and Queen [of Spain] to discover the islands which touch the Indies. He asked for ships, promising not only to propagate the Christian religion, but also certainly to bring back pearls, spices and gold beyond anything imagined.*[19]

The Spanish expedition led by Columbus landed in the Americas in the 1490s. With these new networks of communication between distant societies, the history of the world was profoundly altered. An even more connected world and the Early Modern Era were at hand.

Suggested Reading

Books

Bentley, Jerry H. *Old World Encounters: Cross-Cultural Contacts and Exchanges in Pre-Modern Times.* New York: Oxford University Press, 1993. An up-to-date survey of trade routes and the spread of universal religions.

Curtin, Philip D. *Cross-Cultural Trade in World History.* Cambridge: Cambridge University Press, 1984. A sweeping examination of world trade and cross-cultural exchange.

Fernandez-Armesto, Felipe. *Millennium: A History of the Last Thousand Years*. New York: Scribner, 1995. An idiosyncratic but interesting overview of the world over the past millennium, for the general reader.

Gilbert, Erik, and Jonathan Reynolds. *Trading Tastes: Commodity and Cultural Exchange to 1750.* Upper Saddle River, NJ: Prentice Hall, 2006. A readable survey of the salt, silk, spice, and sugar trades and their impacts.

Gordon, Stewart. *When Asia Was the World: Traveling Merchants, Scholars, Warriors, and Monks who Created the "Riches of the East."* Philadelphia: Da Capo, 2008. Profiles eight great travelers and their experiences in Eurasia.

Headrick, Daniel R. *Technology: A World History*. New York: Oxford University Press, 2009. Good survey of maritime, military, and productive technologies.

Hobson, John M. *The Eastern Origins of Western Civilisation.* New York: Cambridge University Press, 2004. A fascinating, well-researched study offering an Asia-centric history of the era.

Keay, John. *The Spice Route: A History*. Berkeley: University of California Press, 2006. Readable description of Afro-Eurasian trade.

Lane, George. *Daily Life in the Mongol Empire*. Indianapolis: Hackett, 2006. Readable account of societies and cultures.

Larner, John. *Marco Polo and the Discovery of the World.* New Haven, CT: Yale University Press, 1999. A readable study of the impact of Marco Polo's writings on European exploration.

McNeill, William H. *Plagues and Peoples*, rev. ed. Garden City, NJ: Anchor, 1998. One of the best studies of the history and role of diseases, including the Black Death.

Morgan, David. *The Mongols.* New York: Basil Blackwell, 1986. A fine study of the Mongols and their empire.

Pacey, Arnold. *Technology in World Civilization.* Cambridge: MIT Press, 1990. Discussion of Asian and European technologies in this era.

Pearson, Michael. *The Indian Ocean.* New York: Routledge, 2000. A comprehensive look at the role this ocean played in world history.

Ringrose, David R. *Expansion and Global Interaction, 1200–1700*. New York: Longman, 2001. Explores the relationship between expansion and global interaction that began with the Mongols.

Risso, Patricia. *Merchants and Faith: Muslim Commerce and Culture in the Indian Ocean.* Boulder: Westview, 1995. A readable survey of Islam-centered commerce from the beginning through the nineteenth century.

Stearns, Peter. *Gender in World History.* New York: Routledge, 2000. A brief but general study with good material on this era.

Super, John C., and Briane K. Turley. *Religion in World History.* New York: Routledge, 2006. A brief overview of religious traditions and change.

Weatherford, Jack. *Genghis Khan and the Making of the Modern World.* New York: Crown, 2004. A readable and provocative examination of the Mongol role in world history.

Whitfield, Susan. *Life Along the Silk Road.* Berkeley: University of California Press, 1999. A readable portrait of Silk Road life through the experiences of travelers and residents.

WEBSITES

Internet Global History Sourcebook (*http://www.fordham.edu/halsall/global/globalsbook.html*). An excellent set of links on world history from ancient to modern times.

Silk Road Narratives (*http://depts.washington.edu/uwch/silkroad/texts/texts.html*). Explores cultural interaction in Eurasia through excerpts from Silk Road travelers.

Virtual Religion Index (*http://virtualreligion.net/vri/*). An outstanding site with many links on all major religions from ancient times until today.

PART IV

Connecting the Globe: Forging New Networks in the Early Modern World, 1450–1750

A major theme of history is global integration, as networks were built that increasingly connected distant societies. The roots of global integration go back deep into history, to the trade routes of the Classical Era, such as the Silk Road, that spread products and ideas, expanding horizons. However, global connections increased dramatically in the Early Modern Era, between 1450 and 1750.

Europeans played a major role in building the new connections. After many centuries in which various Asian and Islamic societies had led the world in economic development, science, and effective government, western Europeans revitalized their societies, improved their military and naval technology, and honed their economies, often through their increasing contacts with the wider world. The Portuguese began maritime exploration around Africa to locate the sources of the valuable commodities, especially spices, coming into Europe from Asia. The Spanish joined the search for Asian wealth in 1492, and the expedition led by Christopher Columbus forged the first permanent link across the Atlantic to the Americas. The Dutch, English, and French soon began their own explorations. What was originally an active system of exchange and communication within an Afro-Eurasian zone became genuinely global, making it possible to speak of a world history linking all peoples. The Early Modern Era established the basic framework for the connected world we live in today.

European exploration, often followed by military conquest and colonization of other societies, affected millions of people around the world, but especially in the Americas and parts of Africa. In the Americas the Europeans encountered often prosperous societies, including the Aztec Empire of Mesoamerica and the Inca Empire of South America. Technologically stronger, Europeans established colonial governments in the Americas and built new economies based on mining, ranching, and plantations and on slave labor brought from Africa. The European and African encounters with Native Americans led in turn to the spread of diseases from Eurasia that ravaged the American population. The European quest to acquire enslaved Africans for their American colonies also transformed the political and economic life of West and Central Africa. European activities eventually stretched into the Islamic Middle East and southern Asia, where Europeans colonized several ports and islands by 1750. The connections established between Europeans and other societies fostered the rise of a truly world economy, fueled by the new capitalist economy of Europe.

Chinese Porcelain Chinese products attracted merchants from all over Eurasia. This Chinese-made porcelain bowl from the 1700s, made for export, is decorated with a view of the major southern Chinese port city and commercial center, Guangzhou (also known as Canton).

However, while historians often speak of the rise of the West in this period, it is misleading to assume that the spread of Western influences constituted the whole story. Europe's impact on large, still-powerful Asian societies, such as China, India, Persia, and the Ottoman Empire, was modest at best. Despite growing European power,

China and India remained key centers of the Eurasian economy, and several other Asian and some African societies enlarged their territories and remained dynamic. Some of the same political, economic, and intellectual trends that were then reshaping Europe also sprouted independently in a few Asian societies. Indeed, many Asian, African, and even American peoples were scarcely aware that European merchants, adventurers, and missionaries were seeking out wealth, power, and converts around the world. From the perspective of a Chinese mandarin official, Japanese samurai warrior, Siamese Buddhist monk, Indian peasant, Turkish architect, Arab governor, Persian artist, Ethiopian noble, or Hausa merchant, the West was chiefly a curiosity rather than a threat. By 1750 Western influence and power around the world were growing but still very incomplete.

Historians consider this period the *Early* Modern Era because, while much of the globe was now more closely linked, life was still vastly different from what it is today. Before Europeans and North Americans saw their lives transformed by industrialization in the nineteenth century, they lived more like their ancestors of 1,500 years ago than like their descendants in the twenty-first century. Much of their work, technologies, and household goods would not have astonished earlier generations. As the chapters in Part V will show, the changes since 1750, a date commonly used to mark the end of the Early Modern period, have been much more far-reaching. However, by 1750, closer contacts than ever before between the world's many societies—contacts that often widened the gap in power and wealth between Europeans and the peoples they came to dominate politically and economically—had set the stage for the modern world.

EUROPE
Several European societies emerged as major world powers. The Portuguese and Spanish in the 1500s, followed by the Dutch, English, and French in the 1600s and 1700s, established footholds and colonies in Africa, the Americas, and Asia. The resources obtained abroad, especially the minerals and plantation crops of the Americas and Southeast Asia, brought wealth to Europe. Exposure to a wider world fostered capitalism, science, technology, and a questioning of long-standing religious doctrine, resulting in the Protestant Reformation and the Enlightenment.

WESTERN ASIA
The Ottoman Empire became the world's major Islamic power, controlling not only much of Western Asia but also much of North Africa and southeastern Europe. Rivals of the major European powers, especially the Russians, the Ottoman Turks prospered by fostering learning, accommodating ethnic minorities, and importing military and technical expertise. To their east, the Persians under the Safavid dynasty dominated parts of Central Asia and flourished for several centuries.

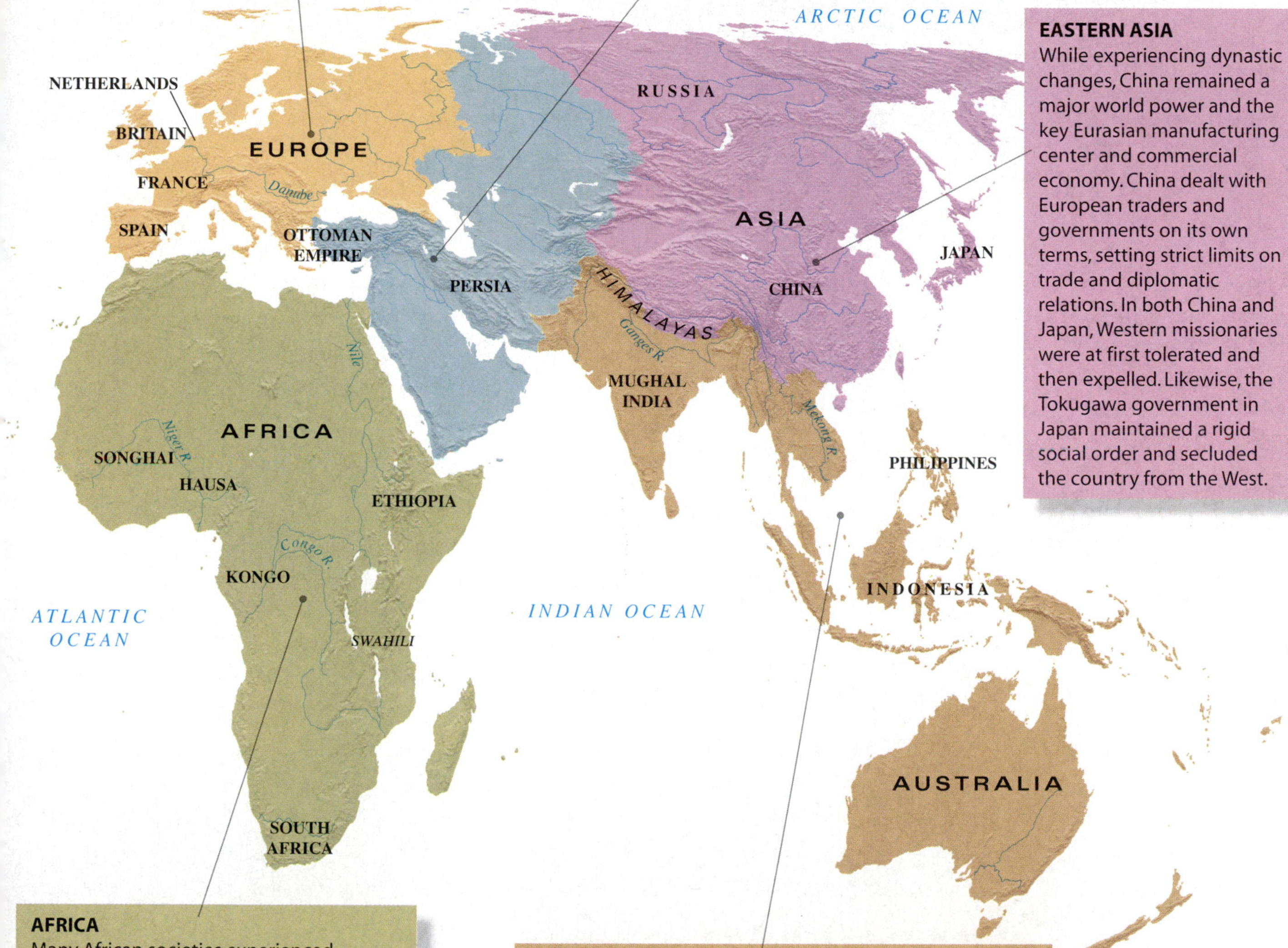

EASTERN ASIA
While experiencing dynastic changes, China remained a major world power and the key Eurasian manufacturing center and commercial economy. China dealt with European traders and governments on its own terms, setting strict limits on trade and diplomatic relations. In both China and Japan, Western missionaries were at first tolerated and then expelled. Likewise, the Tokugawa government in Japan maintained a rigid social order and secluded the country from the West.

AFRICA
Many African societies experienced dramatic change. The need by European powers for cheap labor in their American colonies fostered the trans-Atlantic slave trade, which disrupted much of the West and Central African coast as millions of Africans were enslaved and shipped to the Americas. Although some African states, such as Ashante and Benin, flourished from the slave trade and other commerce, warfare between states became more common. The Portuguese conquered the states of Angola and Kongo and destabilized the East African coastal cities, while the Dutch established a foothold in South Africa.

SOUTHERN ASIA AND OCEANIA
India, ruled by the Islamic Mughal dynasty, was one of the world's major powers, with a flourishing economy that attracted merchants from many societies. After obtaining footholds in India, Europeans then sought wealth in nearby Southeast Asia. First the Portuguese and then other European powers gained a modest presence in Southeast Asia, the Spanish colonizing the Philippines and the Dutch parts of Indonesia. While Europeans began exploring the Pacific Basin, their impact on Oceania was slight. Nonetheless, the Spanish trade across the Pacific between the Philippines and Mexico laid a foundation for the global economy.

CHAPTER

15

GLOBAL CONNECTIONS AND THE REMAKING OF EUROPE, 1450–1750

CHAPTER OUTLINE

- TRANSITIONS: OVERSEAS EXPANSION AND CAPITALISM
- THE RENAISSANCE AND REFORMATION
- CHANGING STATES AND POLITICS
- THE TRANSFORMATION OF CULTURES AND SOCIETIES

PROFILE
Rembrandt van Rijn, Dutch Artist

WITNESS TO THE PAST
Queen Elizabeth I Rallies Her People

Amsterdams Historisch Museum

Amsterdam Stock Exchange During the seventeenth century, the Dutch port city of Amsterdam was the center of European commerce and played a key role in the world economy. The Amsterdam stock market, shown here in a painting by Dutch artist Job Adriaenz, attracted merchants and financiers from all over Europe.

"O, wonder! How many goodly creatures are there here! How beauteous mankind is! O brave new world That hath such people in't!"

—Miranda, in *The Tempest* by William Shakespeare, 1611[1]

FOCUS QUESTIONS

1. How did exploration, colonization, and capitalism increase Western power and wealth?
2. How did the Renaissance and Reformation mark a crucial cultural and intellectual transition?
3. What types of governments emerged in Europe in this era?
4. How did major intellectual, scientific, and social changes help to reshape the West?

The European and world economies changed rapidly in the sixteenth century, and few places exemplified change more than the Flemish port city of Antwerp (AN-twuhrp), with its fabulous Bourse (boors), a huge building that served as a combination of marketplace and stock exchange. The posted motto above its entrance read: "For the service of merchants of all nations and all languages." An economic boom enriched Antwerp's merchants and bankers, as well as the businesspeople from many lands who came to the Bourse to buy and sell. As many as 2,500 ships from different lands anchored at one time in the harbor, many laden with gold and silver from the Americas. Every day goods were put on sale in the Bourse, and bustling crowds of merchants, foreign visitors, and affluent local consumers thronged the rooms to buy spices from Southeast Asia and India, American sugar, tin from England, Venetian glass, Spanish lace, German copper, paintings by great Flemish artists, and even the service of assassins or professional soldiers. Thus one great city linked the economies of Europe and the wider world. The Antwerp Bourse represented a postmedieval Europe shaped by overseas exploration, conquest, and expanding commerce, contributing the changes in life and thought that the English playwright Shakespeare referred to as a "brave new world."

In 1500, western Europeans were still medieval in many respects: they were dominated by the Roman church, had little national identity, were skeptical of science, were minor participants in hemispheric commerce, and were barely aware of distant lands. By the mid-1700s, however, Europe had undergone a profound economic, intellectual, and political transition. Europeans were conquering and settling the Americas, as well as establishing colonies or trading networks in Asia and Africa. Wealth flowed into Europe, fostering investment in science and technology, while new knowledge of, and influences from, non-European cultures reshaped European thinking. The Catholic Church also faced severe challenges as some European thinkers became influenced by secular ideas, including science. Such changes often produced long and bloody wars. By 1750 many Europeans had left their medieval institutions and beliefs behind and were on the verge of introducing even more profound changes to the world.

e Visit the website and eBook for additional study materials and interactive tools: www.cengage.com/history/lockard/globalsocnet2e

Transitions: Overseas Expansion and Capitalism

How did exploration, colonization, and capitalism increase Western power and wealth?

capitalism An economic system in which property, exchange, and the means of production are privately owned.

The foundations for the dramatic changes in many Early Modern European societies were established in the 1400s and early 1500s. The European encounter with America and its riches, the growth of a trans-Atlantic slave trade, and the opening of direct trade with Asia all increased European wealth and fostered **capitalism**, an economic system in which property, exchange, and the means of production, such as factories, are privately owned. Capitalism gradually expanded its operations to a global level, so that by the 1600s valuable Asian spices and precious American metals and plantation crops were pouring into Europe. The economic revolution also fostered stronger European states and reshaped the daily lives of most Europeans.

Roots of Change

Some of the changes continued trends already apparent in western Europe. During the 1400s, when merchants flourished, cities grew larger, the feudal social systems and values broke down, and commerce became a part of everyday life. By 1500 cities such as Paris and London had grown to over 200,000; though still small by Asian standards, they were unique for their growing political power and autonomy. Unlike Chinese or Ottoman cities, European cities existed in a politically fragmented region rather than a centralized empire. Thus city leaders could bargain with kings for advantages and autonomy. As the middle classes bought more luxury goods, especially fine clothes, industries like textile manufacturing grew.

Cities and Farms

However, most Europeans were still peasants who worked the soil, their lives organized around the male-dominated household: men tilled the fields while women had responsibility for the house, barn, and gardens. Although many peasants were now free or tenant farmers rather than serfs, they were still burdened with taxes and service obligations to lords and to the church. Yet, population growth and climate change fostered economic change. The European population (excluding Russia) increased from 70 to 100 million between 1500 and 1600, and then to 125 million by 1750, making for larger commercial markets. The global cooling that began around 1300 reached its height in the late 1600s and finally ended in the mid-1800s. This "Little Ice Age" brought winter freezing to canals and rivers, caused poor harvests, and helped motivate overseas explorers to seek better conditions and food sources elsewhere. Imported foods from the Americas, such as maize and potatoes, helped avert mass famine.

Commerce and Politics

Merchants benefited from more favorable attitudes toward commerce, which gave them a status and power unusual in the world. Many western European societies offered an opportunity for making profit and also had institutions, such as banks, that favored economic growth. Blessed with these advantages, late medieval Europeans laid the foundation for an economic transition that began to fundamentally alter western European life and later spread its influences around the world. Some western European societies developed capitalism, a dynamic system highly oriented to economic growth. In the 1400s cities such as Venice and Genoa in Italy, and Bruges **(broozh)** and Antwerp in Belgium, became centers of capitalistic enterprise. Venetians and Genoese, fierce competitors, traded all over Europe, western Asia, and North Africa. However, early capitalism was limited by the Catholic Church's condemnation of usury, and not until after 1500 did capitalism change dramatically, allowing the Antwerp merchants to build a Bourse that became a marketplace for world products.

Western European politics also began to shift in the 1500s. Medieval Europe had remained politically fragmented, and in 1500 it contained some five hundred states or ministates. Unlike in China, Ottoman Turkey, or Mughal India, no single bureaucratic imperial state could dominate the economy and enforce conformity. But in the 1500s some of the small states were gradually transformed into integrated monarchies, enriched by resources obtained in Africa, the Americas, and Asia. Both merchants and monarchs resented the independence of the landed aristocracy and cooperated to destroy their influence in a series of bloody wars. For the first time since the Carolingians, large but competitive centralized states developed in Europe, particularly in England and France, making the political system dynamic and unstable.

Intellectual Currents

During this time new intellectual currents fostered broader horizons, especially improvements in mapmaking. In 1375 Abraham Cresques **(kres-kay)**, a Jewish cartographer on the Span-

CHRONOLOGY

	Cultural and Intellectual Changes	Political Changes
1300	**1350–1615** Renaissance	
1400		
1500	**1517–1615** Protestant Reformation	**1588** Defeat of Spanish armada
1600	**1600–1750** Scientific Revolution **1675–1800** Enlightenment	**1618–1648** Thirty Years War **1641–1645** English Civil War **1688–1689** English Glorious Revolution

ish island of Majorca **(muh-JOR-kuh)**, used Christian, Muslim, and Jewish traditions and travelers' accounts to produce a map that placed Jerusalem rather than Europe at the center of the world. Innovative Portuguese maps from the 1400s influenced Flemish mapmakers of the 1500s such as Gerardus Mercator **(muhr-KAY-tuhr)**. But these maps, unlike Cresques' effort, did not decenter Europe. Mercator's 1569 world map vastly exaggerated the size of Europe and North America while diminishing the size of Africa, India, China, and South America. In spite of these distortions, Mercator's approach, which pictures the earth as an uncurved rectangle intersected by straight lines for latitude and longitude, is still widely used.

New Technologies

Developments in technology and mathematics, often inspired by earlier Arab, Chinese, and Indian innovations, also fostered change. Between 1450 and 1550 Europe's technology surpassed that of the Arabs and was catching up to China, with major improvements in shipbuilding, navigation, weaponry, and printing. European ships took advantage of Arab lateen sails and Chinese sternpost rudders, and they also used the Chinese magnetic compass to navigate. Facing much rougher, stormier waters than the placid Mediterranean, the people along Europe's Atlantic coast also built sturdier ships that gave them a naval advantage. Gunpowder weapons and printing processes, both invented in China, were improved, and the printing press fostered the dissemination of knowledge to an increasingly literate audience. Europeans also blended the Indian numerical system and Arab algebra with their own insights to improve quantification.

"Gold, God, and Glory": Explorations and Conquests

European Motives

The rise of Europe as a world power resulted from overseas expansion and conquest (see Chapters 16–18). The phrase "Gold, God, and Glory" describes European motives. "Gold" was the search for material gain by acquiring and selling Asian spices, African slaves, American metals, and other resources. A desire to directly connect with Asian trade led to the first voyages of discovery in the 1400s. "God" refers to the crusading tradition of Christianity, the rivalry with Islam, disdain of non-Christian religions, and the desire to convert the world to Christianity. Reflecting this view, a Catholic missionary in Spanish America argued that "it is a great thing that so many souls should have been saved and that so many evils, idolatries, and great offenses against God [by Native Americans] should have been halted."[2] "Glory" describes the goals of the competing monarchies, who sought to establish their claims to newly contacted territories so as to strengthen their position in European politics. Motivated by these three aims, various western European peoples expanded overseas, gaining control over widening segments of the globe. By the late nineteenth century Europeans dominated much of the world politically and economically.

Iberian Voyagers

During the 1400s the seafaring Spanish and Portuguese ventured out from the Iberian peninsula into the Atlantic and discovered the Azores, Madeira, and Canary island chains off northwest Africa (see Map 15.1). These Iberians enjoyed a favorable geographic location facing the Atlantic Ocean and North Africa, a tradition of deep-sea fishing, a history of aggressive crusading, and possession of Europe's best ships and navigation techniques. They also had economic motives. For centuries West African gold had passed through North Africa to southern Europe, where it was used for coins, treasuries, and jewelry. Furthermore, the Portuguese sought a way to break the Venetian monopoly over the valuable trade from southern Asia through Persia and Egypt.

Maritime exploration required new technologies. The Portuguese invented the caravel, an easily maneuverable ship designed to travel long distances. Later the Iberians built larger galleons,

Antwerp Marketplace The marketplace at the center of Antwerp, in what is today Belgium, was the main hub for European trade in the 1500s, the place where goods from all over Europe and from Africa, the Americas, and Asia were bought and sold.

which provided much more cargo space and room for larger crews. To chart the position of the sun and stars, Iberian sailors used the Arab astrolabe **(AS-truh-labe)**. Learning how to mount weapons on ships enabled Europeans to overwhelm coastal defenses and defeat lightly armed ships. The Spanish in the Americas and the Portuguese in Africa and Asia, using artillery, naval cannon, and muskets, could control large territories if the inhabitants lacked guns. By the late 1500s, the English were building the most maneuverable ships and the best iron cannon, and by the 1700s European land and sea weapons greatly outclassed those of once militarily powerful China, India, Persia, and Ottoman Turkey. Europeans now posed a threat to the great Asian states.

The intense competition between major European powers led to increased exploration and a scramble for colonies, subject territories where Europeans could directly control primary production. In the 1400s the Portuguese began direct encounters with western Africa, and by 1497 they had reached East Africa and then sailed across the Indian Ocean to India. Soon they seized key Asian ports such as Hormuz on the Persian Gulf, Goa in India, and Melaka in Malaya. Meanwhile, the Spanish discovered that a huge landmass to the west, soon to be named America, lay between Europe and Eastern Asia. The Spanish explored the Americas and conquered many of its peoples, including the great Inca and Aztec Empires, making them the most powerful European state in the 1500s. Portugal, England, France, and Holland also colonized in the Americas and sent emigrants to what they called "the New World." European states also established colonies or footholds in coastal Africa and carried enslaved Africans to the Western Hemisphere to work on plantations growing cash crops, such as sugar, cotton, and coffee, for European consumption. The Portuguese, Dutch, and Spanish colonized various Southeast Asian islands, including the Philippines, Java, and the Spice Islands of Indonesia. American minerals, especially silver, supported a great expansion of the European economy and allowed Europeans to buy into the rich Asian trade. These developments enabled the transfer of vast quantities of resources to Europe, especially silver, gold, sugar, coffee, and spices, and the fortunes of European trading ports such as Venice, Genoa, Lisbon, Seville, Antwerp, and Amsterdam rose or fell depending on overseas trade.

Conquest and Colonization

During the Early Modern Era Europeans laid the foundations for Western dominance in the world after 1750. The Portuguese and Spanish prospered in the 1500s, while in the 1600s the overseas trade of the Dutch, English, and French enabled them to become the most powerful European countries. But European influence was still limited in many regions. Asian and African societies such as China, Siam, Japan, and Morocco remained powerful and successfully resisted or ignored

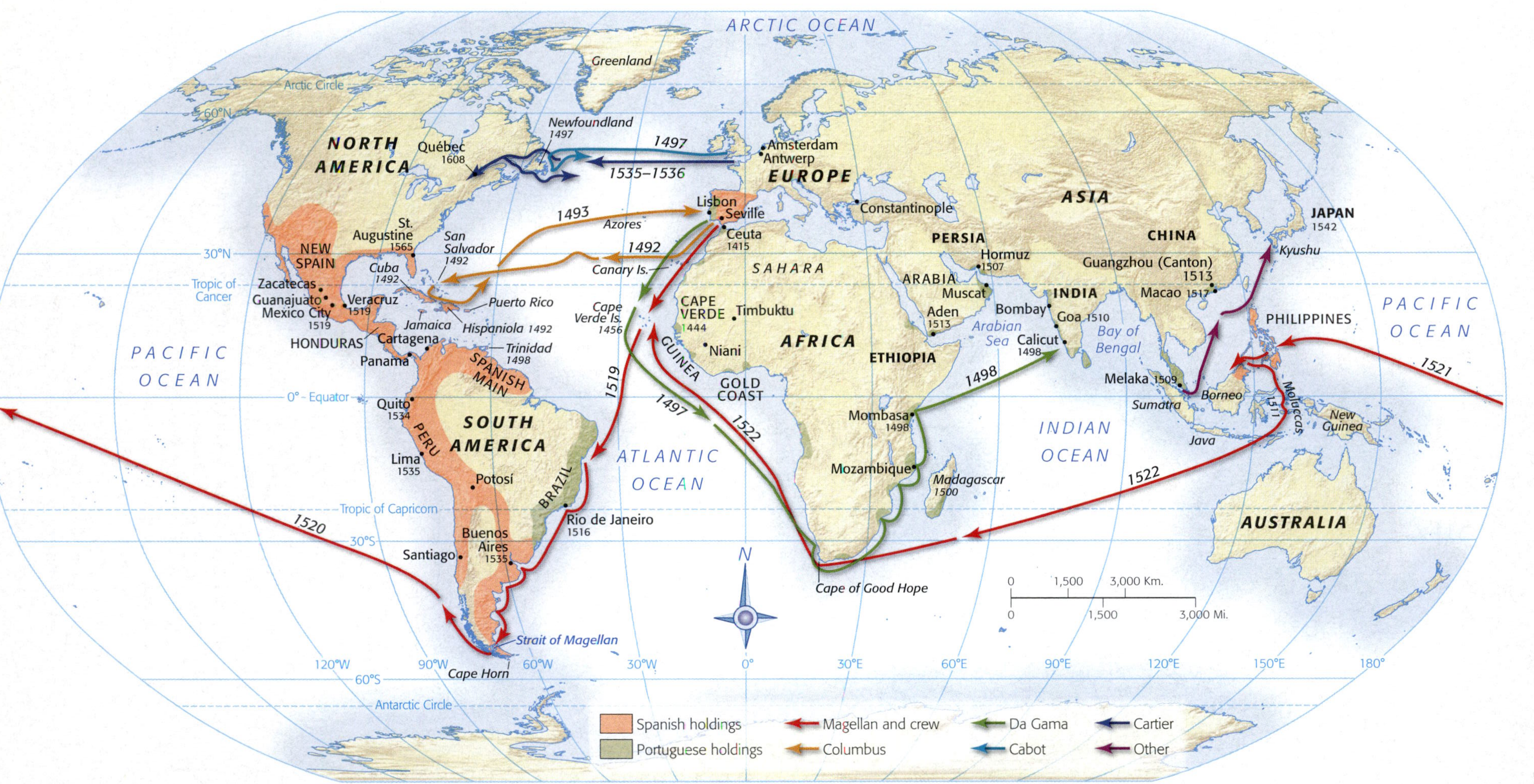

Map 15.1
European Exploration, 1450–1600

Between the early 1400s and mid-1600s explorers sponsored by Portugal, Spain, France, Holland, and England discovered the sea route around Africa to South and Southeast Asia and crossed the Atlantic to the Americas, permanently connecting the two hemispheres. They also sailed across the Pacific Ocean from the Americas to Asia.

Interactive Map

European demands. Nonetheless, overseas trade and exploitation provided some European societies with valuable human labor and natural resources, contributing to the growth of capitalism.

The Rise of Capitalism

Features of Capitalism

Capitalism has taken many forms and fostered new values around the world. Under capitalism, the drive for profit from privately owned and privately invested capital has largely determined what goods are produced and how they are distributed. Capitalism was revolutionary because, on a greater scale than before, money in the form of investment capital was used to make profits. The various forms of capitalism had certain common features—the need for constant accumulation of additional capital, economic self-interest, the profit motive, a market economy of some sort, and competition—that shaped relations between people. For example, carpenters who once shared their services with the community on a barter basis and their profits with their guild began to charge fees instead, competing for customers with other carpenters. Later capitalism included private ownership of the means of production, such as factories, businesses, and farms. However, the profit motive, wealth accumulation, and competition were incompatible with some cultural values. Many traditional cultures had a bias against people accumulating more wealth than their neighbors or working hard only to maximize income. Even today, some Asian, African, American Indian, and Latin American cultures value cooperation, religious piety, or generosity more than acquiring great wealth. In precapitalist societies governments siphoned off surplus wealth, and the elite spent their resources on conspicuous consumption of luxuries, such as the building of the magnificent cathedrals, palaces, and pyramids that now impress tourists. Medieval Europe's merchant and craft guilds accepted a strict regulation of economic activity for the greater good. By contrast, to make more money capitalists invested some profits in further exchange or production, fostering an economic expansion and transforming small-scale trade into global capitalism.

While western Europe became increasingly capitalist, eastern European nobles discouraged capitalism. Allied with the landowning aristocracy, who faced a labor shortage on their estates, kings in Poland, Lithuania, Prussia, and Russia mandated serfdom on the peasantries and imposed laws forbidding people to leave the land. By providing little support to merchants, they thwarted capitalist expansion. Foreign merchants, including Dutch, Germans, Jews, and Armenians, became the major middlemen and gradually dominated eastern Europe's commerce. As the economies became chiefly agrarian, many once-vibrant cities declined into sleepy provincial towns, inhabited by many foreign-born merchants or their descendants. For example, many Polish and Lithuanian cities had large populations of Jewish merchants and artisans.

During the 1500s capitalism took hold in northwest Europe. The English, Flemish, and Dutch developed the most dynamic capitalism and soon eclipsed Italy, shifting the economic balance of power from the Mediterranean to the English Channel and North Sea. Enriched by distributing American silver and controlling Baltic grain, Antwerp became Europe's main financial capital. By the 1620s Amsterdam emerged as Europe's capitalist powerhouse, dominating much European and Asian trade. This clean, orderly, and prosperous Dutch city boasted amenities rare elsewhere, such as street lamps. In 1728 the English writer Daniel Defoe concluded that "the Dutch are the Middle Persons of Trade, the Factors and Brokers of Europe. They buy to sell again, and the greatest part of their vast commerce consists in being supply'd from all parts of the world that they may supply the world again."[3] Old concepts of investing wealth in land gradually gave way to investing capital in business and industry to increase production of ships, arms, and textiles, creating more capital. Many western Europeans were affected by the new materialism, purchasing consumer goods from tea, coffee, and sugar to clocks, china, and glassware.

People needed more money because the import of American metals caused a rapid rise in prices. Increasing capital changed business methods, especially the use of credit, which fostered banking. As a result, many Europeans shifted their attitudes toward charging interest for loans and seeking profit. The medieval church had denounced charging interest as usury, a mortal sin, and had also opposed commercial profit. A good Christian could not become a merchant or

CHRONOLOGY
Political, Economic, and Intellectual Developments, 1500–1750

1500–1770 Era of commercial capitalism

1533–1586 Reign of Ivan the Terrible in Muscovy

ca. 1600–1750 Scientific Revolution

ca. 1600–1750 Baroque era

1609 Dutch independence

1618–1648 Thirty Years War

1641–1645 English Civil War

1648 Congress of Westphalia

1661–1715 Reign of Louis XIV in France

1675–1800 Enlightenment

1682–1725 Reign of Peter the Great in Russia

1688 Bill of Rights

1688–1689 Glorious Revolution and Declaration of Rights in England

1700–1709 Great Northern War

1701–1714 War of the Spanish Succession

1707 United Kingdom of England, Scotland, and Wales

banker, leaving much commerce and banking to the Jewish minority. By the late 1500s, however, many rejected these church teachings and heeded the cynical saying that "he who takes usury goes to hell; he who doesn't goes to the poorhouse." Acceptance of interest by Christians reflected a gradual shift to an entirely different type of society in western Europe.

Capitalism also produced a new social group, the **bourgeoisie** (BUR-swah-zee), an urban-based, mostly commercial, middle class ranging from small-scale merchants to financiers. Jacob Fugger (FOOG-uhr) (1459–1525) of Augsburg, a southern German city, was proof that an ambitious commoner could prosper from the capitalist trends. The grandson of a weaver and son of a successful merchant, Fugger built a financial empire of banks, factories, silver mines, and farmlands, becoming Europe's richest man, loaning money to royal houses, and acquiring a castle and the title of count. He praised himself as "behind no one in attainment of extraordinary wealth, in generosity, purity of morals and greatness of soul."[4] His sons also published the first newsletter for merchants and bankers, which tracked political and economic developments in Europe.

bourgeoisie The urban-based, mostly commercial, middle class that arose with capitalism in the Early Modern Era.

Capitalism continually changed in character and expanded in scope. Under **commercial capitalism**, dominant in western Europe between 1500 and 1770, most capital was invested in commercial enterprises such as trading companies, including the world's first joint-stock companies (see Chronology: Political, Economic, and Intellectual Developments, 1500–1750). These precursors of today's giant multinational corporations pooled their resources by selling shares, or stocks, to merchants and bankers. Under directors chosen for their experience, joint-stock companies encouraged investment and mobilized great capital. A typical company employed many cashiers, bookkeepers, couriers, and middlemen skilled in languages, and it invested in diversified economic activities such as real estate, mining, and industry. Few Asian or African merchants could compete with this collective power.

commercial capitalism The economic system in which most capital was invested in commercial enterprises such as trading companies, including the world's first joint-stock companies.

Commercial capitalism was strongly shaped by the state and big business enterprises working together for their mutual benefit. In particular, England, Holland, France, and Spain practiced **mercantilism**, an economic approach based on building a nation's wealth by expanding its reserves of precious metals such as gold and silver bullion. Trading was controlled by semimilitary, government-backed companies that were protected from competition. To attract bullion held by other nations, these governments tried to limit imports and increase exports. Some joint-stock companies obtained royal charters granting them monopolies and the right to colonize other lands in the name of the state. In England such companies financed overseas exploration and supported piracy against Spanish and French shipping. Spurred by mercantilism, commercial capitalism expanded out of western Europe and into Africa, Asia, and the Americas.

mercantilism An economic approach that emerged in Early Modern Europe based on a government policy of building a nation's wealth by expanding its reserves of precious metals.

SECTION SUMMARY

- Europe's political decentralization allowed for the growth of cities and the development of capitalism.
- Europeans made great strides in mapmaking and improved technologies such as shipbuilding, navigation, weaponry, and printing by borrowing and building on the work of Arabs, Chinese, and Indians.
- Motivated by "Gold, God, and Glory," Europeans, led by the Spanish and the Portuguese, acquired colonies in the Americas, Africa, and Asia.
- Despite entrenched value systems that opposed an emphasis on accumulating wealth, capitalism took hold in western Europe, while eastern European leaders resisted it and instead mandated serfdom.
- Amsterdam established itself as the center of capitalist Europe in the 1600s.
- Commercial capitalists, assisted by the mercantilist policies of their countries, increased their market power by pooling resources in such organizations as joint-stock companies.

The Renaissance and Reformation

How did the Renaissance and Reformation mark a crucial cultural and intellectual transition?

Two major movements, the Renaissance and the Reformation, reshaped European thought and culture in the 1500s. During the Renaissance, a dramatic flowering in arts and learning that began in Italy around 1350 (see Chapter 14), new philosophical, scientific, artistic, and literary currents paved the way for more creative, secular societies. The movement reached its peak in the 1500s as the gold and silver imported from the Americas provided more people with money to purchase art and books (see Chronology: The Renaissance and Reformation, 1350–1615). Many historians believe that the Renaissance, sparked in part by trade with Asia and North Africa, provided a bridge between medieval and modern western Europe. **The Reformation**, the movement to reform Christianity, spawned new Christian churches that provided alternatives to the Roman Catholic Church. Both movements helped to undermine the pillars of medieval society and changed western European cultural and religious life.

The Reformation The movement to reform Christianity that was begun by Martin Luther in the sixteenth century.

Renaissance Thought, Art, and Literature

Primary Source: The Prince: Power Politics During the Italian Renaissance Learn from the man himself what it means to be "Machiavellian."

During the Renaissance spurt in knowledge, thinkers and artists rediscovered the ideas of the Classical Greeks and Romans while consuming products and ideas from the Islamic world and China. The Renaissance promoted individualism, secularism, tolerance, beauty, creativity, and a philosophy, known as humanism, that emphasized humanity and its creations rather than God and a troubled church. A crisis of confidence in the Roman Catholic Church, including abuses by leadership and clergy, grew after 1400. Some Renaissance thinkers favored church reform and less rigid ideas. The Dutch philosopher Erasmus (uh-RAZ-muhs) (1466–1536) called for a more personal religion and tolerance of diverse beliefs, arguing that Jesus commanded people nothing except to love one another. He also advocated the use of living languages rather than Latin. The French humanist writer François Rabelais (RAB-uh-lay) (ca. 1494–1553) was even more critical, calling monks "a rabble of counterfeit saints, hypocrites, pretended zealots, who deceive the world."[5] By spurring freedom of thought and offering critical insights, humanists undermined medieval attitudes that had crippled scientific investigation. But popes rejected any changes in doctrine or institutions.

Political Thought

In humanist political thought, Niccolò Machiavelli (MAK-ee-uh-VEL-ee) (1469–1527), the Florentine author of a political manual, *The Prince*, studied power as separate from moral doctrine. Machiavelli claimed to draw on the lessons of history, but he also used his experience as a diplomat. *The Prince* argued that the ruler must always keep the end in mind and apply ruthless policies, such as deception and violence, in pursuing vital national interests. But since rulers must avoid being hated, they ignore popular moral values at their peril; a leader need not have piety, faith, integrity, and humanity, but must seem to have them. Machiavelli's writings became very influential guides for European leaders.

Some thinkers developed more interest in science, employing direct experimental methods and observation. The Florentine Leonardo da Vinci (lay-own-AHR-doh dah VIN-chee) (1452–1519), a painter, sculptor, architect, scientist, mathematician, and engineer, exemplified the versatile Renaissance personality and openness to varied influences. Knowledgeable about Muslim science and architecture, he negotiated unsuccessfully with the Ottoman sultan to build a bridge in Istanbul. Polish astronomer Nicolaus Copernicus (koh-PUR-nuh-kuhs) (1473–1543) studied the skies and Islamic scholarship on astronomy that suggested the earth might not be the center of the universe. Copernicus transformed astronomy and physics when he devised his revolutionary "heliocentric," or sun-centered, theory of the solar system in 1507, refuting the traditional idea that earth was the center of the universe and arguing that earth and the planets revolved around the sun. He did not dare publish his findings until after his death, fearing persecution by the church.

The Renaissance spread Italian artistic influence that deepened knowledge of humanity by more accurately representing real life in sculpture, painting, architecture, and literature. Some of the inspiration came from contacts with Islamic, Asian, and African peoples and their artistic traditions. Italians such as the Venetian painter Giovanni Bellini (ca. 1430–1516) worked in or visited Muslim cities, spreading Italian influences but also returning with new perspectives. Rome replaced Florence as the hub of Italian art, attracting the eccentric Florentine Michelangelo Buonarroti (mi-kuhl-AN-juh-loh bwawn-uh-RAW-tee) (1475–1564), who became famous for his realistic sculptures, paintings, and frescoes. The attitudes and gestures of each figure he painted on the ceiling of the Vatican's Sistine Chapel are carefully rendered. Later Venice became the main Italian art center, where rich merchants and aristocrats offered artists generous financial support to produce landscapes and portraits rather than the religious artworks that had once been common. One Venetian, Titian (TISH-uhn),

CHRONOLOGY
The Renaissance and Reformation, 1350–1615

ca. 1350–1615 Era of Renaissance

ca. 1517–1615 Protestant Reformation

1532 Formation of Church of England (Anglicans)

1534 Founding of Society of Jesus (Jesuits)

1536 Move of John Calvin to Geneva

1545–1563 Council of Trent

1558–1603 Elizabethan era in England

1562–1589 Wars of religion in France

1571 Defeat of Turks at Lepanto by "Holy League"

1588 English defeat of Spanish armada

1598 Edict of Nantes

Musée de la Ville de Paris, Musée Carnavalet/The Bridgeman Art Library International

Bruegel's *Peasant Wedding* Painted around 1567, Pieter Bruegel's *The Peasant Wedding* celebrates the rituals of peasant life, in this case a wedding dinner for a village. The Flemish artist may also have intended the painting of the feasting villagers as a satire on self-indulgence. The bride, composed and radiant, presides over the feast under a canopy.

(ca. 1488–1576), broke with Christian tradition by painting nudes and pre-Christian fables. Some women artists also gained a following. Artemisia Gentileschi (1593–ca. 1652), who survived a rape by her art teacher and torture to test her allegations, painted heroic women from Greek mythology and the Bible. Beyond Italy, in the Low Countries, Pieter Bruegel **(BRU-guhl)** the Elder (ca. 1525–1569) painted realistic landscapes and sympathetic scenes of peasant and town life. El Greco **(ell GREK-oh)** (1541–1614), a native of Crete who studied in Italy before settling in Spain, blended Venetian, Byzantine, and Spanish traditions.

Literature

The growing secularism and humanism also had literary consequences. In England during the brilliant reign of Queen Elizabeth I (r. 1558–1603), writers replaced concern for the hereafter with stories of human passions. The plays of William Shakespeare (1564–1616) reflected the Elizabethans' celebration of the individual person and their nation. The son of a prosperous businessman, Shakespeare acted in the theater and began writing histories, comedies, and tragedies that many literary scholars have believed transcend time and place. Yet, his work was shaped by his milieu, and some of his plays, such as *Henry V* and *Julius Caesar*, addressed English or ancient history. Other plays, such as *Othello*, *Hamlet*, and *The Merchant of Venice*, commented on the world beyond England. One of his best-known characters, Hamlet, voiced Renaissance exuberance: "What [a] piece of work is a man, how noble in reason, how infinite in faculties."[6] In Spain in 1615, Miguel de Cervantes **(suhr-VAN-teez)** Saavedra (1547–1616) published one of the era's great novels, *Don Quixote* **(kee-HO-tee)**. Cervantes had worked as a steward and soldier, was enslaved in Algiers, and then became a purchasing agent eventually imprisoned for debt. His book portrayed Spain at the end of it's golden age. The main character, Don Quixote, sets out to battle dragons and evil men, right injustice, and defend the oppressed, but he mainly makes a grand nuisance of himself. Cervantes dignified the human spirit but also, like some classical Greek playwrights, made fun of its plight.

Growing knowledge about other cultures forced some Europeans to reconsider their assumptions about the world and also stimulated debate about the nature of Native American society. In *Utopia*, published in 1516, the English author Thomas More (1478–1535) portrays Native Americans as living in a paradise and views European society as filled with poverty, injustice, hatred, and war. The French writer Michel Eyquem de Montaigne **(mon-TANE)** (1533–1592) idealized Native American societies, popularizing the notion of a "Noble Savage" uncorrupted by "civilization." In his 1611 play *The Tempest*, Shakespeare mocked the Noble Savage idea, contrasting the civilized Prospero and the savage Caliban **(KAL-uh-ban)** (an anagram for *cannibal*), who is fierce and brutal. The play may reflect the often hostile encounters between English settlers and Native Americans in Virginia.

The Reformation and Religious Change

A questioning of the old order also spawned the Reformation (1517–1615), a movement that transformed the religious makeup of Europe and profoundly reshaped Western thought (see Map

15.2). For centuries the Roman church had dominated Europe. But to critics, it had become corrupt, often led by incompetent popes who intervened rashly in political affairs and by church leaders and clergy who sometimes blatantly violated requirements for celibacy and poverty. The spread of literacy inspired some to examine Christian writings for themselves, and throughout the 1500s various groups sought church reform. Some, later called **Protestants**, broke completely with the Roman Catholic Church. By 1600 almost 40 percent of non-Orthodox Europeans, mostly in the north, had renounced the Catholic faith and adopted some form of Protestantism. Protestant faiths were then carried across the Atlantic by English and Dutch settlers into North America. Eventually dozens of differing Protestant churches competed with each other and with Catholics for influence.

Protestants Groups that broke completely with the Roman Catholic Church as the result of the Reformation.

Luther

Martin Luther (1483–1546), a German, launched the movement that ended the unity of Western Christianity. The Holy Roman Emperor's power was weakening as conflicts with princes and cities produced widespread discontent, and many Germans also resented the pope and the bishops for leading luxurious lives. Luther, an Augustinian monk who later taught at the University of Wittenberg **(WIT-n-burg)**, concluded that nothing in scripture justified papal power and church rituals. Tormented, he came to believe that only faith, not good works, could wipe away a person's sin and ensure salvation. Luther's break with the church was prompted by the lucrative church practice of selling indulgences, clerical statements that canceled punishment due for sins in exchange for cash contributions to the church. In 1517 Luther distributed a paper attacking indulgences. His arguments became the talk of the country. After Pope Leo X excommunicated Luther in 1520 for refusing to retract his views, Luther translated the Bible into German and developed his religious doctrines, condemning Rome as "the greatest thief and robber that has ever appeared on earth or ever will. Poor Germans, we have been deceived."[7] Lutherans formed a church rooted in the Augsburg Confession, a doctrinal statement issued in 1530 that argued for the Bible as the only source of faith, stated that every believer had the freedom to interpret scripture, and attacked the cults of the Virgin Mary and the saints, priestly celibacy, and the monastic orders.

Lutheranism spread widely in northern Germany, Scandinavia, and the eastern Baltic coast. Many German city officials, princes, priests, professors, and common people threw their support to the reform cause. But in 1524 a major conflict split the reform movement when peasants revolted against the lords and church leaders who owned the land. Luther unsuccessfully mediated between the sides and then supported the nobles, who crushed the uprisings, causing over 100,000 deaths. The Lutheran Church became closely linked to governments, and many German princes became Lutheran, while the Holy Roman Emperor remained staunchly Catholic.

Calvinism

Inspired by Luther's example, non-Germans founded Protestant movements. Calvinism was more radical than Lutheranism in rejecting Catholic doctrine. Its founder, John Calvin (1509–1564), was forced to leave France and settled in Geneva **(juh-NEE-vuh)**, Switzerland. Unlike Luther, Calvin believed not in human free will but in predestination, the doctrine that an individual's salvation or damnation was already determined at birth by God. Since good behavior and faith could not guarantee reaching Heaven, governments must enforce morality. Calvin demanded strict morality and attacked worldly pleasures such as dancing and playing cards. Under Calvin, Geneva became a theocratic society, ruled by church leaders with growing intolerance of other views who burned some dissenters at the stake. Calvinism spread rapidly in Switzerland, England, and Holland, and in 1561 the Calvinist John Knox founded the Presbyterian Church in Scotland, where it became the dominant church.

English Protestantism

In England, the initiative for religious change came from the king, Henry VIII (r. 1509–1547). When Henry had no male heir with his wife, Catherine of Aragon, a Spanish princess, he asked the pope to annul his marriage so that he could marry Anne Boleyn (1501–1536), the much-courted daughter of English aristocrats. When Rome refused, Henry broke with the church in 1532, rejecting papal supremacy. He announced his divorce, married Anne Boleyn, and arranged to be made head of the newly formed Church of England, later known as the Anglican Church, which retained much Catholic dogma and ritual. Quickly moving to suppress both Calvinism and the Catholic Church, Henry closed the English monasteries and distributed their lands to his aristocratic and business allies. However, he grew disenchanted with Anne Boleyn, who also bore him no sons, and had her beheaded in 1536. Henry married four more times. Henry's moves generated religious strife in England. His only male heir died at sixteen of tuberculosis and was succeeded by Henry's daughter by Catherine of Aragon, Queen Mary Tudor **(TOO-duhr)** (r. 1553–1558), a Catholic who suppressed the Anglican Church. But she was replaced by Elizabeth I (1533–1603), the daughter of Henry VIII and Anne Boleyn, who restored the Anglican Church. English Calvinists (known as Puritans) were persecuted by Elizabeth's successors, and some emigrated to Holland. From there one Puritan group, the Pilgrims, moved to North America in 1620 to seek more religious freedom, helping plant Puritan influence in the New England colonies.

Map 15.2
Reformation Europe

The Protestant Reformation reshaped Europe's religious landscape in the 1500s and early 1600s. By the mid-1550s some form of Protestantism had become dominant in much of northern Europe, England, and Scotland. Catholicism remained predominant in the southern half of western Europe and parts of eastern Europe.

Interactive Map

Protestantism, Capitalism, and Catholic Reaction

The emergence of Protestantism had many consequences. Modern historians avidly debate whether the rise of capitalism and Protestantism were connected and how much Protestant doctrines supplied religious underpinnings for capitalist values. Calvinists believed that citizens demonstrated their fitness for salvation by being law-abiding, industrious, thrifty, and sober, all values that supported the capitalist order. Like Protestants, capitalists favored productive labor, frugality, and accumulation of wealth as good in themselves. Both Protestantism and capitalism also encouraged individualism. Although capitalism also emerged in some Catholic societies, it flourished especially in the Protestant societies of Holland, England, and northern Germany. The strongest capitalist societies were also the most intellectually diverse and produced some secularized free thinkers. Although Luther and Calvin were intolerant of other religious views, they opened the doors to democracy: once people had freely voiced their opinions on religion, they moved on to seeking a voice in government. Similarly, when women became literate so that they could read the scriptures, they also gained some new options.

Counter Reformation A movement to confront Protestantism and crush dissidents within the Catholic Church.

The Protestant challenge generated the **Counter Reformation**, a movement to confront Protestantism and crush dissidents within the Catholic Church using varied strategies, including the Holy Inquisition, the church court formed in medieval times to combat heretical ideas (see Chapter 14). Several thousand people believed to hold dissident ideas were burned at the stake in Spain. The pope formed the Congregation of the Index to censor books and to decide which ones were to be forbidden altogether. To outflank Protestantism, the Spanish Basque former soldier, Ignatius Loyola (1491–1556), founded a new, highly disciplined missionary order, the Society of Jesus, in 1534. One Jesuit, the Spanish Basque St. Francis Xavier (ZAY-vee-uhr) (1506–1552), became a pioneering missionary in India, Southeast Asia, and Japan.

Council of Trent

For all their harsh punitive measures, the Inquisition and Index did not suppress dissidence, prompting the pope to sponsor the Council of Trent (a city in northern Italy) to reconsider church doctrines. However, the council (1545–1563) reaffirmed most Catholic dogma, supporting the value of both tradition and scripture, endorsing the church hierarchy and papal authority, and maintaining priestly celibacy. But the council did impose more papal supervision on priests and bishops, and it mandated that all clergy be trained in seminaries. The Trent reforms enabled Catholicism to check its loss of believers to Protestantism, to recover some lost ground, and to survive and flourish in a modified form.

But religious passions fostered intolerance. Religious minorities, such as Jews, French Protestants, and English Catholics, faced discrimination and sometimes violence. Several popes pursued anti-Jewish policies, while Luther advocated burning synagogues, arresting rabbis, and confiscating Jewish property. Many Jews faced expulsion from their countries or segregation in city ghettoes. To escape this persecution, many Jews and minority Catholics and Protestants emigrated to other European countries or to the Americas.

Religious Wars and Conflicts

Protestant-Catholic Tensions

Religious divisions contributed to European wars and conflicts from the late sixteenth through early eighteenth centuries. Habsburg-ruled Spain, which controlled a vast empire in the Americas and Southeast Asia, was particularly troubled by religious tensions. The Spanish Habsburgs also ruled Portugal, the Low Countries, and parts of Italy. King Philip II of Spain (r. 1556–1598), known as "the most Catholic of kings," put imperial resources toward defending the Catholic cause in Europe while spreading the faith abroad.

In the Low Countries, Philip's suppression of Calvinism antagonized businessmen and the nobility, who demanded autonomy and freedom of worship. Inflamed Protestants attacked Catholic churches, and Spain's execution of dissident leaders spurred a general revolt in 1566, with both Catholics and Protestants rallying behind the Calvinist leader, the Dutchman William of Nassau (NAS-aw), Prince of Orange. Philip dispatched an occupation army that executed over 1,100 Protestants and, in 1576, sacked Antwerp. In 1579, Philip promised political liberty to the ten largely Catholic Flemish-and French-speaking southern provinces of the Low Countries, forging the foundations of modern Belgium and Luxembourg. Because of English assistance to the Low Country rebels and English attacks on Spanish shipping in the Americas, Philip II tried to invade England by sea in 1588 but faced a determined foe in Queen Elizabeth I (see Witness to the Past: Queen Elizabeth I Rallies Her People). The English ships outmaneuvered Spain's armada of 130 ships and then triumphed when a fierce storm in the English Channel devastated the once-invincible Span-

Queen Elizabeth I Rallies Her People

Few women have ever enjoyed the power and respect of England's Renaissance queen, Elizabeth I. Her forty-five years of rule (1558–1603) marked a brilliant period for English culture, especially in literature and theater. On her death, the admiring playwright Ben Jonson wrote her epitaph: "For wit, features, and true passion, Earth, thou hast not such another." The queen may have been, as her detractors claimed, deceptive, devious, and autocratic, but her intelligence and formidable political skills helped her maneuver successfully through the snake pit of both English and European politics. But English-Spanish relations deteriorated, prompting war. In 1588, as the powerful Spanish armada sailed toward the English coast, Elizabeth launched the English ships with a speech to her subjects that ironically played off her gender to reinforce her link with the English people. With the help of foul weather, the English defeated the Spanish, changing the fortunes of both countries.

My loving people. We have been persuaded by some that are careful for our safety, to take heed how we commit ourselves to armed multitudes, for fear of treachery, but I assure you, I do not desire to live to distrust my faithful and loving people. Let tyrants fear; I have always so behaved myself, that, under God, I have placed my chiefest strength and safeguard in the loyal hearts and good will of my subjects, and therefore I am come amongst you, as you see, at this time, not for my recreation and disport, but being resolved in the midst and heat of the battle, to live or die amongst you all, to lay down for my God, and for my kingdoms, and for my people, my honor and my blood, even in the dust.

I know I have the body of a weak and feeble woman; but I have the heart and stomach of a king, and of a king of England too; and I think foul scorn that . . . Spain, or any prince of Europe should dare to invade the borders of my realm; to which rather than any dishonor shall grow by me, I myself will take up arms, I myself will be your general, judge, and rewarder of every one of your virtues in the field.

I know already for your forwardness you have deserved rewards and crowns; and we do assure you in the word of a prince, they shall be duly paid you. In the meantime my lieutenant general shall be in my stead, than whom never prince commanded a more noble or worthy subject; no doubting but by your obedience to my general, by your concord in the camp, and your valor in the field, we shall shortly have a famous victory over those enemies of my God, of my kingdoms, and of my people.

THINKING ABOUT THE READING

1. How did Elizabeth justify the forthcoming battle with Spain?
2. What personal qualities did this Renaissance monarch suggest she could offer to her people in their time of peril?

Source: Charles W. Colby, ed., *Selections from the Sources of English History* (Harlow: Longmans, Green, 1899), pp. 158–159. Quotation in introduction from A. L. Rowse, *The Elizabethan Renaissance: The Life of the Society* (New York: Charles Scribner's, 1971), p. 59.

ish fleet. The mostly Protestant, Dutch-speaking northern provinces broke away from Spain in 1588 and became fully independent in 1609, forming the Netherlands, popularly known as Holland.

Religious conflicts also raged across France. The French Calvinists, known as Huguenots **(HYOO-guh-nauts)**, were led by the powerful Bourbon family. In 1572, after the assassination of Calvinist leaders sparked Huguenot rioting in Paris, Catholic forces massacred 30,000 Huguenots. In 1593 Henry of Bourbon (1553–1610), remarking that "Paris is well worth a mass," renounced Calvinism for Catholicism in order to become King Henry IV. In 1598 he signed the Edict of Nantes **(nahnt)**, which recognized Roman Catholicism as the state church but gave Huguenots the right to freely practice their religion.

Christian-Muslim Conflicts

While Protestant-Catholic tensions in Europe were intense, Christian-Muslim conflicts also simmered and often translated into political and military conflict. The Muslim Ottoman Turks sought to expand their empire, which already included Greece, much of the Balkans, and Bulgaria (see Chapter 16). When some Balkan people abandoned Christianity for Islam, the Holy Roman Emperor Charles V marshaled allies to defeat the Turks at Vienna in 1529. In 1571 the so-called Holy League of Spain, Rome, and Venice used advanced naval gunnery to destroy the Turkish fleet at the Battle of Lepanto **(li-PAN-toh)**, off Greece, temporarily ending Turkish ambitions. Then in 1683 the Turks besieged Vienna, but Polish intervention saved Austria. The Austrians pushed the Turks out of Hungary, ending Ottoman expansion in Europe and with it the Christian fear of more losses to Islam.

SECTION SUMMARY

- Renaissance humanists questioned the authority of the Catholic Church, while thinkers such as Machiavelli, Leonardo da Vinci, and Copernicus challenged accepted truths of morality, science, and astronomy.
- Renaissance artists such as Michelangelo aimed to represent humanity more realistically, and writers such as Shakespeare and Cervantes examined the concerns of individuals and the broad sweep of society.
- Martin Luther, who criticized the corruption of the Catholic Church, set the Reformation in motion; it was propelled by figures such as John Calvin, whose ideas were taken up by the Puritans, and King Henry VIII of England, who made England Protestant.
- While not all capitalists were Protestant, many historians see a link between the individualism and thrift of Protestants and their success in business.
- In the Counter Reformation, the Catholic Church attempted to reassert its dominance, but ultimately it focused its energy on converting non-Europeans rather than combating Protestants.
- Religion sparked several wars: Spain's attempts to keep the Low Countries Catholic led to costly conflict with England and the eventual fragmentation of the area; Catholics massacred Huguenots in France; and several battles finally ended Ottoman expansion in Europe.

CHANGING STATES AND POLITICS

What types of governments emerged in Europe in this era?

Capitalism, Renaissance humanism, the Protestant Reformation, and the encounters with the wider world fostered new institutions, beliefs, and politics. The transition unleashed forces that consumed Europe in bloody wars: kingdoms were torn asunder and reconfigured, old states declined, and new states gained influence. These states were not nations in the modern sense but multiethnic entities ruled by royal families who married across national lines. Patriotic feelings were mostly restricted to the elites. While in some states royal absolutism flourished, a few others developed representative governments with elements of democracy.

Regional Wars and National Conflicts

Various wars raged, some prompted by religious divisions, others spawned by tensions between rival states and within large multinational empires such as the Habsburg-ruled Spain and the Holy Roman Empire. Even after religious tensions subsided, warfare remained a constant reality. The major conflict that continued the religious wars and national rivalries of the 1500s was the Thirty Years War (1618–1648), a long series of bloody hostilities that claimed millions of lives and involved many countries. This complex struggle started in the Holy Roman Empire, as Czech Protestants revolted against Habsburg Catholic rulers who were trying to limit religious freedom. Eventually the fighting drew in German princes and mostly Lutheran Denmark and Sweden. Finally France, although mostly Catholic, went to war against its Habsburg rivals who ruled Austria and Spain. In 1648 the conflict ended after a four-year-long congress produced the Treaty of Westphalia (west-FALE-yuh), which reaffirmed religious freedom but failed to end Protestant-Catholic conflict. France enjoyed unrivaled prestige after 1659, while Spain and the Holy

Thirty Years War

Courtesy of the Trustees of the British Museum

Soldiers' Return In the early 1600s the French artist Jacques Callot made a series of moving etchings about the Thirty Years War called "Miseries of War." This etching shows a group of discharged soldiers, so impoverished and brutalized by war that they either beg for food or die alongside the road.

Roman Empire were militarily exhausted. The conference also recognized Swiss independence from Habsburg rule, and the Dutch benefited because the long struggle had weakened their former ruler, Spain. After Westphalia, Europe fought wars with well-drilled professional soldiers, large warships, and more deadly cannon and rifles.

War of Spanish Succession

The most widespread conflict, the War of the Spanish Succession (1701–1714), brought together England, Holland, Austria, Denmark, Portugal, and some German states to battle France and Spain over who would inherit the Spanish throne from the last Habsburg king, and how the Spanish Empire might be partitioned as a result. The human costs of war increased. For example, in one battle 40,000 French soldiers were killed or wounded. The Treaty of Utrecht **(YOO-trekt)**, which ended the war, forced Spain to transfer its territory in Belgium and Italy to Austria. The once-prosperous Dutch had overextended themselves, damaging their economy. England received most of the war's spoils, including the strategic Gibraltar peninsula at Spain's southern tip, which commanded the entrance to the Mediterranean Sea, as well as some French territory in eastern Canada. Utrecht fostered a new European system dedicated to maintaining a balance of power between rival states.

Absolutist and Despotic Monarchies

The conflicts and new mindsets fostered diverse political patterns by the seventeenth century, among them **absolutism**, a system of strong monarchial authority in which all power was placed under one supreme authority, a king or queen. Supporters saw absolutism as the best way to avoid chaos. Spain and Habsburg-ruled Austria, the Papal States of central Italy, governed by the Vatican, and the Turk-dominated Ottoman Empire all exercised absolutist power. But the French kings and the Russian czars best represented this increasing concentration of power.

absolutism A system of strong monarchial authority in which all power is placed in a supreme authority, a king or queen.

French Absolutism

For a time the French absolute monarchy of King Louis XIV (r. 1661–1715), envied by other rulers, dazzled Europe. French became the language of European diplomacy, while French art and architecture were imitated as far away as imperial Russia. By the mid-1600s France, with 18 million people, was western Europe's largest country, was self-sufficient in agriculture, and had thriving industries. Louis XIV believed that he was the state and that his power derived from God; thus he was a monarch by divine right. Known as "the Sun King" for the brilliant extravagance of his court, Louis demanded obedience from all at the expense of the nobility. His dominant passion was love of glory. Few French kings valued marital fidelity, and Louis had many mistresses and children, legitimate and illegitimate.

The king imposed mercantilism, fostering industries and companies subject to royal domination; he also revoked the Edict of Nantes, forbade Protestant pastors to preach, and closed Protestant schools and churches, leading 200,000 Huguenots to emigrate to England, Holland, and North America. Some 5,000 servants and courtiers lived on the grounds of the Sun King's spectacular palace at Versailles **(vuhr-SIGH)**, a Paris suburb. Versailles became the center of French cultural life, regularly visited by French nobles and foreign leaders, all spied upon by the king. Louis' brilliant finance minister, Jean Baptiste Colbert **(kohl-BEAR)**, complained that "every day is one long round of dances, comedies, music of all kinds, promenades, hunts and other entertainments."[8] The king patronized the arts and literature by giving annual allowances to a court composer and financing playwrights and ballet dancers.

Louis XIV's search for power caused four major wars aimed at preventing Habsburg dominance. French power reached its height around 1680, but the wars proved financially ruinous and fell short of their objectives. The War of the Spanish Succession sapped the French treasury and military, enabling Austria, England, and Holland to counterbalance French power. Although France remained a major state, it had lost some of its glory. The absolutist French monarchy collapsed in revolution in the late 1700s.

Russian Absolutism

Russia also developed a tyrannical government led by czars. After the Russians had freed themselves from Mongol domination, Ivan **(ee-VON)** IV (r. 1533–1584), known as Ivan the Terrible because of his paranoia and brutality, built a centralized state while fighting wars with neighboring Poland and Sweden and conquering the Tartar states founded by Mongols and Turks. Ivan also ordered the death or torture of Russians whom he considered enemies. To gain support from the landed nobility, Muscovite czars after Ivan imposed tight control over the Russian Orthodox Church and a serfdom-based rural economy. Lords could sell their serfs, making them little better than slaves. The czars also began extending their sovereignty toward the Black and Baltic Seas, where the Russians came into conflict with the Poles and Lithuanians.

Peter I the Great (r. 1682–1725), an enlightened but despotic czar nearly 7 feet tall, attempted to transform his backward realm into a modern state by copying Western technology and

St. Petersburg This painting, made around 1760, shows the Winter Palace, inhabited by the Russian royal family, occupying the left side of the Neva River in St. Petersburg, a major port that attracted many trading ships. Other government buildings occupy the right bank.

Michael Holford

administrative techniques. He secretly toured Europe for eighteen months, visiting factories, museums, government offices, hospitals, and universities, and even worked as a carpenter in a Dutch shipyard to view firsthand the most advanced industrial and military technology. Returning to Russia, the czar launched ambitious political, economic, military, and educational reforms and hired foreign specialists to advise him. Peter's Westernizing policies had mixed consequences. Some were superficial and unpopular, such as banning beards, no longer fashionable in western Europe. Peter also increased royal power at the expense of the church and nobility, often in a harsh manner. With such great power, Peter expanded Russia's frontiers, established industries, strengthened serfdom, formed a navy to protect his Baltic flank, and developed a more efficient government. Since he hated gloomy, medieval Moscow, he began building a new capital on the Baltic, modeled on Amsterdam and Venice, and named it St. Petersburg.

Russian Expansion

Peter had many foreign achievements. Wanting a stronger presence on the Baltic Sea, mostly dominated by Sweden, he forged a secret alliance with Denmark and Poland. During the Great Northern War (1700–1709), Russia and its allies battled the formidable Swedes, finally forcing them to abandon the eastern Baltic to Russia. Anxious to forge permanent access to the Mediterranean Sea, which was open to shipping year-round, Russian forces pushed south toward the Black Sea and the Straits of Bosporus (see Map 15.3). They also began acquiring territory in Siberia and Muslim Central Asia (see Chapter 16). By eventually creating a huge empire and exploiting its resources, Russia developed a largely self-sufficient economy but had limited trade with western Europe, since most czars after Peter were wary of Western influence. Today Russia remains the last great land empire, ruling over various non-Russian peoples.

The Rise of Representative Governments

Some European countries moved toward greater political freedom. Iceland had an elected assembly, while Switzerland was a multilingual, decentralized, and constitutional confederation of Catholic and Protestant districts. A fading power, Venice was a self-governing republic, although noble and merchant families dominated political life. The Netherlands and England developed the most open and accountable governments because, enriched by sea trade, the commercial classes and many nobles amassed huge fortunes and hence played political roles, eventually demanding more influence.

Dutch Golden Age

The Netherlands enjoyed a golden age during much of the 1600s, building a colonial empire with holdings in the Americas, South Africa, Sri Lanka, and Southeast Asia and dominating the Atlantic, Baltic, and Indian Ocean trade. Large Dutch joint-stock companies controlled the overseas market. The Dutch East India Company, formed in 1602, monopolized the spice trade from Southern Asia, making huge profits from cinnamon and pepper, and imported Chinese silks and porcelain, Japanese art, Indian cotton textiles, and precious metals. Some of the capital amassed was invested in Dutch industry. The Netherlands became Europe's most prosperous society, with Amsterdam serving as a major hub of world trade, and the flow of wealth also fostered an innovative republican political system. Holland's long-standing climate of freedom and tolerance

Map 15.3
Russian Expansion, 1300–1750

Beginning in the 1300s the Russians expanded from a small remote northern state, based in Moscow, into an empire. By the mid-1700s the Russians had spread over a wide area and gained political domination over western Siberia, the northern Caucasus, and part of what is today the eastern Baltic region and the Ukraine.

e Interactive Map

attracted people fleeing from persecution, such as Portuguese Jews, or seeking a more open intellectual atmosphere. After breaking away from Spain, the predominantly Protestant Netherlands became a republic linked by assemblies of delegates. But the powerful Nassau family held the top post, Stadhouder General, and controlled the army and navy. The Nassaus' desire for more authority put them chronically at odds with the merchant elite, who favored provincial autonomy, resulting in continued tensions.

English Politics and Civil War

The English also forged a colonial empire. England sent Protestant settlers to some districts in their mostly Catholic colony of Ireland, and the English East India Company, founded in 1601, pursued commerce and conquest in Asia while England established colonies in North America and the Caribbean. By 1700 it overtook its rivals as major international traders. Empire and growing profits fostered profound political changes, with two upheavals in the 1600s securing first a republic and then a constitutional monarchy. The English had long struggled to define the rights of kings and parliaments. The Stuarts, the Scottish royal family who became the monarchs after Elizabeth I died without an heir, had absolutist ambitions and made Anglicanism the only recognized faith, antagonizing the Puritans and Presbyterians. In 1641, Parliament condemned despotic Stuart policies, prompting the English Civil War. Oliver Cromwell (1599–1658), a zealous Puritan convinced he was doing God's will, led parliamentary troops who defeated the royalist forces in 1645 and beheaded Stuart king Charles I.

Parliament abolished the monarchy and proclaimed a republican Commonwealth (1649–1660) dominated by Cromwell. The defeat of the royalists was a turning point as Puritans favoring capitalism and property rights ended the last vestiges of English feudalism. But the Puritan majority in Parliament were fanatics determined to root out "godlessness" and establish laws based solely on the biblical edicts of Moses. They had no patience with constitutional government and expelled the Presbyterians from Parliament. Eventually, Cromwell became dictator and imposed Puritan morality, banning newspapers, executing dissidents, and crushing a Catholic rebellion in Ireland by burning crops and massacring many thousands of Irish resistors. On Cromwell's death Parliament restored the Stuarts to the throne after they agreed to guarantee individual freedom of religion. However, the Protestant-Catholic conflicts resumed and eventually led to a stronger Parliament, now dominated by Anglicans, which offered the kingship to Dutch Stadhouder William of Orange (r. 1689–1702), a champion of the Protestant cause. Riots in London forced pro-Catholic James II (r. 1685–1688) to abdicate and flee to France. In the Glorious Revolution (1688–1689), Parliament decreed William and his wife, Mary, sovereigns after they accepted a Bill of Rights recognizing the right of petition and requiring parliamentary approval of taxes. The Toleration Act, establishing freedom of religion, followed.

England's Glorious Revolution

After the Glorious Revolution, royal power was modified but the government represented only the landed nobility, wealthy merchants, and property owners, who had political influence and wealth. Only the aristocrat-dominated Parliament could vote the money for the king and his army. In 1707 England, Scotland, and Wales officially combined as the United Kingdom, often known as Great Britain. But English supremacy came at the expense of ethnic minorities. To better control them, the feisty Scottish highlanders were cleared from their lands, and their Celtic language, Gaelic **(GAY-lik)**, was banned. In colonized Ireland, Protestant English and Scottish settlers acquired land and Catholics became second-class citizens. Laws denied the majority Irish Catholics the right to education, property, and political office.

Rising New States, Declining Old States

German States

The forces unleashed by capitalism, religious change, warfare, and shifting political fortunes fostered several powerful new states and harmed several longtime powers (see Map 15.4). German-speaking, Catholic Austria under the Habsburg monarchs became a major empire after the Thirty Years War, governing Czechs, Croats, Slovenians, Hungarians, and some Italians, Romanians, and Serbs. Sweden became independent of once mighty Denmark in 1520, forging a hereditary but not absolutist monarchy with an efficient administration, a national assembly, and Lutheranism as the state religion. Soon Sweden dominated Baltic trade but eventually lost its economic position to the Dutch. Under King Gustavus Adolphus (r. 1611–1632), an earthy but brilliant military strategist, Sweden conquered parts of Poland and Prussia and most of the eastern Baltic societies. By 1721, however, the Swedes had lost all their possessions in the eastern Baltic, except Finland, to Russia or Prussia.

Prussia, a small, mostly German-speaking state along the eastern Baltic coast, became independent from Poland in 1660. In the mid-1700s Prussia built a formidable standing army under an authoritarian but constitutional monarchy. Under King Frederick the Great (r. 1740–1786) Prussia rapidly expanded at the expense of Poland, Austria, and the Holy Roman Empire. A brilliant leader and strategist, Frederick was warlike and ruthless but also a fine musician who enjoyed conversations with philosophers.

Holy Roman Empire

Several older states declined. The Holy Roman Empire had little coherence. The emperors, elected by leading princes, were figureheads presiding symbolically over some three hundred states representing assorted Germans, eastern Europeans, and Italians. The French writer Voltaire **(vawl-TARE)** mocked the entity as neither holy nor Roman nor an empire. The empire was effectively swept away in 1740, when Austria and Prussia began a 130-year struggle for dominance in the region. Italians remained divided into small states ruled by the pope, the Habsburgs, or the Holy Roman Empire. Predominantly Catholic Poland and Lithuania had been major states and in 1569 combined to form a republican commonwealth under elected kings and noble-dominated national and local assemblies, launching a golden age of economic prosperity and religious tolerance. Their large Jewish communities enjoyed many legal rights. But by the mid-1600s the commonwealth struggled amid rebellion and invasion, losing territory to the Russians, who slaughtered Jews. Catholics turned on Protestants, and after 1717 Poland became an appendage to the Russian Empire, Lithuania became a Russian province, and Catholicism became crucial to Polish and Lithuanian identity.

Map 15.4
Europe in 1740

By the mid-1700s France and Great Britain were the most powerful western European states. While once powerful Spain and Portugal had lost influence and the Germans and Italians remained divided, Prussia, Sweden, Russia, and Habsburg-ruled Austria were gaining strength.

Interactive Map

SECTION SUMMARY

- Europeans fought a series of wars, some religiously motivated and some not; in the Thirty Years War, which involved many countries, Catholic France triumphed over the Catholic Habsburgs.
- Louis XIV of France, the archetypal absolutist monarch, lived in astounding luxury and wielded great power.
- Russian czars from Ivan the Terrible on exercised tight control while expanding Russia's territory, traditions that Peter the Great continued while pushing to modernize and Westernize his country.
- The Dutch were successful colonial merchants and instituted a decentralized republican system of government that was strained by the military power held by the Nassau family.
- Through a series of struggles between Parliament and monarchs, English political power became more equally shared, though it was still held largely by wealthy aristocrats and merchants.
- Amid the ongoing political turmoil in Europe, Austria and Prussia became major powers, Sweden saw its fortunes rise and fall, and Poland and Lithuania came under Russian power.

THE TRANSFORMATION OF CULTURES AND SOCIETIES

How did major intellectual, scientific, and social changes help to reshape the West?

Europeans' voyages of discovery and colonization altered their view of the world, broadened their horizons, and contributed to intellectual change. In England, Scotland, Switzerland, Poland-Lithuania, and especially the Netherlands some religious tolerance and diversity undermined barriers to free thought so that science, philosophy, and technology could proceed with fewer obstacles than elsewhere, while the Islamic world, China, and India produced less creative thought than before. Nevertheless, European thinkers borrowed Islamic and Asian ideas. Capitalism spurred by overseas expansion reshaped social patterns and fostered an increasingly urban society.

Arts and Philosophy

baroque An extravagant and, to many, shocking European artistic movement of the 1600s that encouraged release from restraints of thought and expression.

The expanding horizons of the Renaissance and Reformation led to an extravagant artistic movement in the 1600s, the **baroque** ("contorted" or "grotesque"), that shocked people by encouraging release from restraints on expression and questioning accepted ideas. In Italy baroque art, such as the marble statues and fountains of the Roman sculptor Gianlorenzo Bernini **(buhr-NEE-nee)** (1598–1680), was expressive and sensuous, emphasizing freedom. Many Dutch painters concentrated on landscapes, still lifes, and domestic scenes, a sharp break from medieval preoccupation with religious themes. The paintings of Rembrandt van Rijn (see Profile: Rembrandt van Rijn, Dutch Artist) and Jan Vermeer (1632–1675) conveyed emotion, immediacy, personality, and the thoughts and feelings of individuals. Some of the paintings of artists like Vermeer also showed some of the imported foreign products, such as Chinese bowls, Turkish carpets, Southeast Asian spices, and American tobacco, that reflected a growing world economy. In contrast to Renaissance artists, Dutch artists saw their work as a capitalist enterprise and often produced for the wider market rather than for individual patrons.

Not all creative people worked in the baroque spirit. The German Lutheran composers George Frederick Handel (1685–1750) and Johann Sebastian Bach **(BAHCH)** (1685–1759) produced work of enduring popularity that appealed to a wide audience. Handel settled in London, where he wrote his famous choral work, *The Messiah*. Bach wrote pieces for both Protestant and Catholic churches as well as a cantata about a young woman so madly in love with coffee that her father feared she would never find a husband. The growing fad for coffee that Bach memorialized suggested the significance of products obtained from abroad.

European Thought

Baroque art corresponded to the greatest era of philosophical and scientific speculation in Europe since the classical Greeks. The Englishman Francis Bacon (1561–1626), once a politician, sought to eliminate intellectual restraints on science by separating philosophy from theology and advocating the use of reason. He developed a famous maxim: "Knowledge is power." Bacon's scientific method involved developing an idea, testing it experimentally, and then drawing conclusions. These ideas, considered unsettling at the time, made him a major influence on later thinkers.

The founding father of modern philosophy, René Descartes **(DAY-cart)** (1596–1650), promoted a rationalist view of the world. Born in France, Descartes traveled widely and at various times served in both the Dutch and Bavarian armies. Human rationality, he believed, was founded on a distinction between mind and body. He wanted to sweep away traditional learning, much of which he doubted, and establish a new system of knowledge. The only thing he could not doubt was his own existence, writing: "While I wanted to think everything false, it was absolutely necessary that I, who was thinking thus, must be something. I think, therefore I am."[9] Besides being a philosopher, he also studied mathematics, optics, physics, and physiology.

The English political thinker Thomas Hobbes (1588–1679) believed that society was not perfectible, even using reason or Christian teachings. Hobbes, a pessimist, held that with no government to control humanity's anarchic, power-seeking instincts, life was "solitary, poor, nasty, brutish, and short."[10] His disturbing book, *The Leviathan* **(la-VIA-thin)**, provided a new view of the state and its relationship to the individual, arguing that people needed despotic power to control them. Truth, reason, or justice were just artificial attributes created by social convention and language. Many of Hobbes's contemporaries condemned his views, including his royalist slant and apparent atheism. But his idea of a social contract between citizens and rulers influenced later thinkers.

Science and Technology

The Scientific Revolution (ca. 1600–1750), an era of rapid advance in knowledge, particularly in mathematics and astronomy, built on the work of Bacon and Descartes to gain a new understanding of the natural and physical world. European scientists demolished the medieval view of the earth's position in the cosmos, stimulated European intellectual life, and laid the groundwork for later intellectual and industrial transitions. Although offering new ideas could be dangerous in a continent full of religious conflicts and despotic monarchs, advances occurred in many areas.

The Scientific Revolution An era of rapid European advance in knowledge, particularly in mathematics and astronomy, that occurred between 1600 and 1750.

The Scientific Revolution derived in part from imported Asian and Islamic ideas and technologies. European scientists were familiar with the writings of earlier Muslim thinkers. The Jesuits who sojourned in China sent back reports that praised Chinese scientific traditions and inventions. Prompted by scientists, French King Louis XIV sent a mission to China to acquire scientific and technical knowledge. As Europeans assimilated and improved imported models while creating new ones, the leadership in science and technology gradually shifted from China and the Middle East to Europe.

Astronomy

Astronomers made some of the most significant discoveries. The German mystic Johannes Kepler (1571–1630) used mathematics to amplify Copernicus's discovery that all the planets revolved around the sun. The Italian Galileo Galilei **(gal-uh-LAY-oh gal-uh-LAY-ee)** (1564–1642) proved experimentally that Copernicus's theories were correct. By adapting spectacles, invented by the Dutch, Galileo built the first telescope in 1609. With this telescope Galileo discovered that the moon had mountains, Jupiter had four large moons, and our solar system was but a small part of a Milky Way galaxy containing countless stars that could not be seen with the naked eye. These findings were dangerous, especially given Galileo's talent for insulting critics, mocking conventional wisdom, and arguing that the biblical view of astronomy was ignorant. In 1615 the Catholic Church summoned the scientist to Rome to be tried as a heretic, and he was forced to publicly recant his views in order to leave prison. When he continued to publish, Inquisition officials placed him under house arrest for life.

Newton

Scientific activity reached its height with Sir Isaac Newton (1642–1727), a mathematics professor at Cambridge University who discovered some fundamental laws of physics. Newton's work was a synthesis of Bacon's methodologies, Descartes' mathematics, Galileo's discoveries, and other scientific findings. His importance was proclaimed in a famous epitaph by the poet Alexander Pope: "Nature and Nature's laws lay hidden in night; God said, 'Let Newton be!' and all was light."[11] In 1687 Newton published *Mathematical Principles of Natural Philosophy*, which accounted for all the motions of the planets, the comets, the moon, and the sea. He had found the connection, especially the law of universal gravitation, that tied together varied parts of the physical world into an ordered whole. Newton's ideas dominated Western scientific thinking for the next two hundred years.

New Technologies

In the wake of scientific discoveries, technology improved. Such useful items as the watch, lead pencil, thermometer, and concrete became available. An English mathematician developed the first slide rule, and a German mathematician invented the first mechanical calculator to perform multiplication, division, and much more. The Dutch scientist Christian Huygens **(HYE-guhnz)** introduced a more accurate clock. In the early 1700s, an English farmer, Jethro Tull, using a two-millennia-old Chinese model, developed a drill to sow seeds, the first step toward rural

REMBRANDT VAN RIJN, DUTCH ARTIST

The bounty from Dutch commerce in the 1600s helped foster a brilliant period of painting in the Netherlands. For the first time, artists made their livelihood in a free market, and they could be found in every town. Wealthy Dutch merchants commissioned works of art to decorate their houses, town halls, and guild halls. The painters catered to this taste, offering realistic pictures of everyday life, group portraits, landscapes, and the interiors of well-appointed houses. Most art celebrated personal success, the material world, and the Protestant faith. Nearly every Dutch family of means owned at least one original piece of art.

No artist had more success meeting this demand than Rembrandt van Rijn, born in 1606 in Leiden, a city on the Rhine River where his father's mill stood. As a youth, Rembrandt enjoyed watching ships and walking in the countryside. He studied for a while at Leiden University but left to apprentice with a local artist. In 1631 he moved to Amsterdam and soon made a good living painting portraits of churchmen, poets, rich merchants, and fashionable ladies. His income enabled him to decorate his art studio and home with fabulous silks, velvets, and swords from all over the world, as well as paintings from Italian Renaissance artists. At twenty-seven the artist married Saskia van Uylenburgh, the daughter of a prominent city official, and showered her with fine jewelry. He also often painted her portrait. They had several children, but only one lived to adulthood.

Rembrandt's work took art beyond the traditions of the Renaissance and even of the baroque. The prolific artist produced many etchings (300 survive), some 2,000 drawings, and 650 paintings. For Rembrandt, influenced by baroque interest in emotions and light, the subject was usually humankind, its pain, power, and pride. He found that by manipulating the direction, distance, and intensity of light and shadow, he could reveal nuances of mood and character. He mastered light, which washes over all forms in his paintings with a special glow.

In his portraits, including sixty remarkable self-portraits, Rembrandt penetrates deeply into souls and inner feelings. In one of his most famous group portraits, the *Syndics of the Cloth Guild* (often called "The Cloth Makers"), a splendid oriental rug covers a table around which black-coated drapers discuss the guild's affairs. Perhaps Rembrandt's finest work is *The Night Watch,* painted in 1642, where he discards the conventional portrait format to portray a military company scurrying about organizing themselves for a march. The public was confounded when *Night Watch* transformed a typical group scene into a luminous baroque drama of movement and lighting filled with many mysteries. According to legend, the soldiers in shadow refused to pay their share of the commission. Rembrandt was the first major European artist to paint for himself rather than a patron, to pursue his own impulses and interpretations.

After Saskia's death from tuberculosis, Rembrandt painted little for a while and had to sell his house and furnishings to pay his debts to merchants and bankers. He proved a poor businessman and gradually became removed from his clients. When he resumed painting, he concentrated on depicting Bible stories and celebrating the humility of Jesus. His religious paintings reveal a personal piety. This final stage in Rembrandt's career, in which he sought inner truth, was the least understood. While some admirers supported his work, this more introspective art did not attract a mass audience, and he died bankrupt in 1669. Modern critics revere Rembrandt as an artist of great versatility and a unique interpreter of Protestant conceptions of biblical scripture.

THINKING ABOUT THE PROFILE

1. What does Rembrandt's life tell us about Dutch society in the 1600s?
2. Why do you think Rembrandt is considered one of the greatest artists in European history?
3. How did his work reflect the baroque tradition?

Rijksmuseum, Amsterdam/The Bridgeman Art Library

Rembrandt's *Night Watch* Rembrandt's most famous painting, *Night Watch,* completed in 1642, depicts a militia group that policed Amsterdam's streets. The masterful use of light and the portrayal of the men in action rather than just posing were artistic innovations.

mechanization. Perhaps also inspired by old Chinese models, the Englishman Thomas Newcomen invented the first crude steam engine for use in pumping water from mines. By the 1730s the English textile industry became more efficient with spinning machines, similar to those introduced in China in the 1200s, for making cotton products.

The Enlightenment

The Enlightenment, which began in 1675 and continued until 1800, was a philosophical movement based on science and reason that rejected many traditional ideas. This Age of Reason, as it was sometimes called, was perhaps the most fertile period in Western philosophy. The movement owed something to Bacon, Descartes, and Newton as well as to growing European knowledge of Native American societies and of secular Chinese thought. In 1687 a French observer wrote that the Confucian "moral system is infinitely sublime, simple, sensible. Never has Reason appeared so well developed with so much power."[12] Some historians call Confucius the Enlightenment's patron saint. An intellectual attitude more than a set of opinions, the Enlightenment replaced unquestioning religious faith with observed fact and suggested that objective truth could be established through reason, taking human destiny away from God and placing it in human free will. Many Enlightenment thinkers admired Christianity's moral authority but opposed the dogmatic attitudes of organized churches. Some adopted **deism**, the belief in a benevolent God who designed the universe but does not intercede in its affairs.

The Enlightenment A philosophical movement based on science and reason that began in Europe in the late seventeenth century and continued through the eighteenth century.

deism Belief in a benevolent God who designed the universe but does not intercede in its affairs.

In England, France, and Scotland, new notions of tolerance, individual rights, and the relationship between citizens and the state emerged. The Enlightenment spread a humanistic secularism, promoted critical approaches to knowledge, and addressed gender issues such as women's education and equality in marriage. In France Louise d'Epinay (1726–1783) condemned gender discrimination and negative female stereotypes, arguing that both women and men "struggle against pain, difficulties, obstacles [and] have the same nature."[13] Some male thinkers also favored women's education and equality in marriage. Yet, gender issues were often marginalized, and many Enlightenment thinkers accepted the prejudices of the era.

The Englishman John Locke (1632–1704), a physician who lived for a decade in France and Holland, made experimental studies of science that led him to proclaim the value of **empiricism**, an approach stressing experience and testing of propositions rather than reason alone to acquire knowledge. Empirical approaches later became common in the social and natural sciences. Locke's influential political theories also provided a foundation for the modern democratic state and notions of human freedom. Unlike Hobbes, he condemned absolute monarchy and advocated defending freedom by cooperating for common goals and allowing the state only limited powers over the individual. If the state transgressed freedom and self-government, people had the right to oppose it. Locke favored individual rights, such as the separation of church and state, while proposing some limits, such as restricting political participation to people with property. Many of his ideas became influential not only in England but also among the founders of the United States, and

empiricism An approach that stresses experience and the testing of propositions rather than reason alone in acquiring knowledge.

Painting of Madame Geoffrin's Salon This mid-eighteenth century painting by French artist Lemoinnier shows a gathering of Enlightenment thinkers and artists at the elegant Paris salon operated by Madame Geoffrin, seated toward the right. These salons offered dinners and stimulating conversation that allowed for a free exchange of ideas.

his view that people were entitled to life, liberty, and estate became enshrined in the United States Declaration of Independence in 1776, drafted by Thomas Jefferson.

philosophes The intellectuals who fostered the French Enlightenment.

The French Enlightenment was fostered by intellectuals known as **philosophes** (fill-uh-SOHF) (philosophers). In Paris, educated women such as Madame Maria-Therese Geoffrin (JOFF-rin) (1699–1777) operated salons (sa-LAW): elegant rooms where thinkers and artists gathered for conversation. Baron de Montesquieu (maw-tuh-SKYOO) (1689–1755) attacked arbitrary, absolutist power and proposed a republican government with checks and balances, including the separation of powers between the executive, legislature, and judiciary. He also criticized religious dogma. His ideas, like Locke's, were widely discussed in the North American colonies. The best-known philosophe, Voltaire (1694–1778), a poet, dramatist, and historian, believed that science, empiricism, and rational behavior fostered happier lives. Occasionally imprisoned in France, he spent many years in England, Switzerland, and Prussia. Voltaire viewed China as an admirable political model of a despotic but secular and benevolent state, in contrast to absolutist France. A deist, he supported tolerance toward other views but fiercely attacked established religion and also disliked the Jews for their separation, often involuntary, from mainstream society.

Capitalism and Rural Society

Displaced Peasants

Capitalism gradually reshaped rural society and turned many peasants into a displaced labor force. In sixteenth-century England King Henry VIII seized the lands of the Catholic Church and distributed some to wealthy businessmen, who began buying land as an investment, turning agriculture from subsistence living to a commercial venture. The new hard-hearted landowners increased demands on peasants or shifted from agriculture to more profitable sheep raising, ejecting peasants from the land. The English peasantry, now landless, became tenant farmers and poor farm workers working for big landlords. Some former peasants found jobs in towns, some became rural craftsmen, and many became rural vagabonds, drifting around the countryside and resorting to any measures, including crime, to stay alive. Their plight and the negative, "blame the victim" attitudes they encountered are evident in nursery rhymes: "Hark hark the dogs do bark, the beggars are coming to town. Some give them white bread, and some give them brown, and some give them a good horsewhip and send them out of town." Whereas under feudalism people saw individual well-being as a product of the inequitable manor system, under capitalism people were considered responsible for their own condition. Some communities imprisoned debtors and flogged the homeless.

The peasants' loss of their land ruined many lives but also created a labor pool for fledgling industries, thus giving the English an advantage over the French, who were reluctant to abandon feudal laws protecting peasants, and the labor-short Dutch. Businessmen gave crafts production to displaced peasants and paid them for each item they made, undermining guilds and destroying medieval concepts of economic justice. Eventually these trends reached other western European societies. Nothing comparable to the forced poverty of the peasantry happened elsewhere in the world. The imperial power of the Chinese or Ottoman state could curb the greed of landowners and merchants, preventing peasant ejection from the land. Western European peasants, many of whom heavily consumed alcohol as an escape, were far worse off than peasants in Islamic societies.

Uprisings and Movements

The great contrast between the few rich and the many poor, amplified by famine and the devastations of war, brought on uprisings, such as the bloody peasant revolt in Germany in 1524. In England, the suffering of the Civil War fostered widespread discontent and radical movements such as the Levellers. Led by lower-class soldiers, the Levellers advocated equality, democracy, and complete religious freedom: in their 1648 manifesto, they pleaded, "May the pressing needs of our stomachs reach Parliament and the City [London]; may the tears of our starving babies be preserved; may the cries of their tender mothers begging for bread to feed them be graven in metal."[14] Life was increasingly dangerous and unhealthy. Bandits prowled the roads and mercenary soldiers roamed the countryside attacking merchant convoys and plundering villages. Many rural folk fled to the overcrowded cities, filled with beggars, drunks, trash-filled streets, polluted water, the stench of human waste, and disease. In the 1600s one-third of London's children died before the age of one. In France people said that nine-tenths of the people die of hunger, one-tenth of indigestion.

Families and Gender Relations

Family life and gender relations also changed. For the growing middle classes of northern Europe, the nuclear family of parents and their natural-born children, rare in medieval times, became more common, in contrast to the large extended families of southern and eastern Europe. Societies increasingly recognized childhood as a distinct phase of life, inventing toys and games and opening more schools, mostly for boys. However, half or more of children left their families by their early teens, many to become apprentices or servants with other families.

The economic roles and status of women shifted. With the growing availability of consumer goods, women no longer always had to produce but could now purchase such items as cotton clothing. Men now made much higher wages than women. These trends lowered women's social status. In contrast to medieval times, when many women never married and also worked in diverse occupations, women were now encouraged to look chiefly to marriage, motherhood, and the home. While women in northwest Europe married in their twenties, many women elsewhere married by their early teens. Still, between 10 and 20 percent of people never married at all, and the Roman Catholic Church encouraged church vocations over marriage. At the Council of Trent church leaders rejected the Protestant pattern of married clergy, denouncing the notion that "it is better and happier to be united in matrimony than to remain in virginity and celibacy."[15]

Gender Relations

The experiences of women varied across Europe. Many Dutch women enjoyed liberated lives, some becoming merchants. Elsewhere, some women also engaged in trade. The German Jewish merchant Glukel of Hameln **(HAH-muhln)** (1646–1724), the mother of eight, traveled widely to trade fairs. But few women controlled enough financial resources to become traders. A few educated French women achieved influence in the intellectual and cultural realms. Voltaire's friend and then lover, Emilie Du Chatelet **(EM-ih-lee de SHA-the-lay)** (1706–1749), wrote works on mathematics and natural philosophy and analyzed the ideas of scientists such as Newton.

At the opposite extreme, many Russian women were, according to a German visitor, "most miserable; for men consider no woman virtuous unless they live at home, and be so closely guarded that she go out nowhere."[16] Lower-class women faced exploitation, mostly finding paid work as servants in affluent households. Some women faced worse problems. Because millions of people believed in magic, astrology, prophecy, ghosts, and witches, thought to destroy crops and cause personal misfortunes, official persecution of alleged witches provided a diversion from wars and religious conflicts. Thousands of women suspected of being witches were executed or banished from the community, often after horrific ordeals. In a Polish trial, a suspected witch was stripped naked, bound hand and foot, and suspended from the ceiling before she confessed.

More restrictive views of sexuality led to punishment of women and men who defied convention. Often prompted by churches, governments regulated sexual and moral behavior to encourage family life, prosecuting adultery and premarital sex. Despite this, premarital pregnancy rates ranged from 10 to 30 percent. Catholic and Protestant churches condemned homosexuality, and such behavior faced severe sanctions, including execution. Yet, laws were enforced erratically, especially in tolerant England and Scandinavia, and male homosexuals congregated in large cities. Moreover, antisodomy laws in Catholic countries often ignored the nobility and clergy, some of whom openly advocated same-sex relationships. Some very influential men were possible or probable homosexuals, among them Leonardo da Vinci, Michelangelo, Francis Bacon, and several popes and kings such as Prussian king Frederick the Great, and many European kings had same-sex bedmates. Fewer lesbians were public about their love life, but the Swedish queen Christina (1626–1689) was a notable exception. The cosmopolitan, flamboyant Christina, an outspoken supporter of the French Enlightenment and science who spoke some ten languages, had a long affair with one of her ladies-in-waiting and, after abdicating her crown, maintained an active sexual life in

SECTION SUMMARY

- The extravagant baroque style that followed the Renaissance emphasized artistic freedom, while Dutch painters eschewed religious themes for natural ones.
- Bacon and Descartes emphasized the role of reason in science and philosophy, respectively, while Thomas Hobbes developed a pessimistic political philosophy.
- Advances in astronomy, particularly those made by Galileo, greatly antagonized Catholic officials, while Isaac Newton discovered fundamental laws of physics.
- Locke, Montesquieu, and Voltaire were among the prominent thinkers of the Enlightenment, a movement that favored reason over unquestioning faith.
- First in England and then elsewhere in western Europe, rural peasants were impoverished by landowners' greed and served as a ready source of labor for industry.
- As imported goods became more available, the economic role of women declined, as, in many cases, did their social standing.

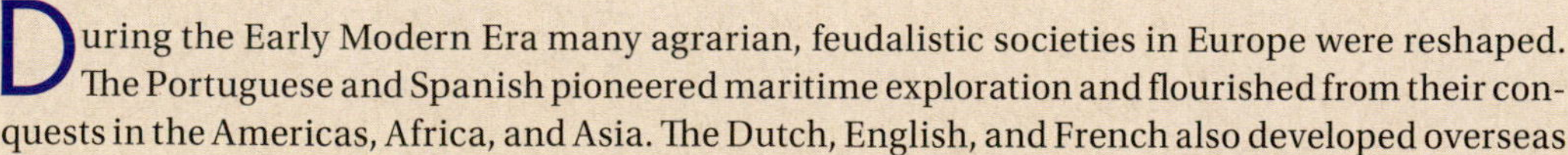

Chapter Summary

During the Early Modern Era many agrarian, feudalistic societies in Europe were reshaped. The Portuguese and Spanish pioneered maritime exploration and flourished from their conquests in the Americas, Africa, and Asia. The Dutch, English, and French also developed overseas empires that brought them considerable wealth. The growth of trade, capitalism, and mercantilism fostered a new commercial orientation while shifting economic and political power to the countries of the Atlantic seaboard. The Renaissance, which spread humanist and secular values, and then the Reformation changed Europe's philosophical and religious terrain, challenging the Roman church. Protestants organized churches, and by the mid-1500s much of northern Europe had become Protestant. These challenges generated a Counter Reformation within the Catholic Church.

Wars raged during much of the era and contributed to political changes. France and Russia developed absolutist monarchies, whereas England and Holland enjoyed greater political freedom. Powerful new states such as Austria and Prussia emerged while older states such as the Holy Roman Empire declined. The discovery of new lands as well as the changing political, religious, and economic forces renewed interest in scientific discovery and a stress on individual rights, leading to the Enlightenment. The Scientific Revolution produced such revolutionary thinkers as Newton and allowed Europe to surpass China and the Middle East technologically. Capitalism made many rural peasants homeless, and family life, including the status of women, also changed.

KEY TERMS

capitalism
bourgeoisie
commercial capitalism
mercantilism
The Reformation
Protestants
Counter Reformation
absolutism
baroque
The Scientific Revolution
The Enlightenment
deism
empiricism
philosophes

EBOOK AND WEBSITE RESOURCES

PRIMARY SOURCE

The Prince: Power Politics During the Italian Renaissance

INTERACTIVE MAPS

Map 15.1 European Exploration, 1450–1600
Map 15.2 Reformation Europe
Map 15.3 Russian Expansion, 1300–1750
Map 15.4 Europe in 1740

LINKS

British History (http://www.british-history.com/). Contains links to short essays on various periods of British history.

Medieval, Renaissance, Reformation: Western Civilization, Act II (http://www.omnibusol.com/medieval.html). A treasure trove of links on many aspects of society in these centuries.

Modern History Sourcebook (http://www.fordham.edu/halsall/mod/modsbook.html). A very extensive online collection of historical documents and secondary materials.

Russian History Index: The World Wide Web Virtual Library (http://vlib.iue.it/hist-russia/Index.html). Contains useful essays and links on Russian history, society, and politics.

Plus flashcards, practice quizzes, and more. Go to: www.cengage.com/history/lockard/globalsocnet2e.

SUGGESTED READING

Ames, Glenn J. *The Globe Encompassed: The Age of European Discovery, 1500–1700.* Upper Saddle River, N.J.: Pearson Prentice Hall, 2008. Good brief summary of European explorations.

Brook, Timothy. *Vermeer's Hat: The Seventeenth Century and the Dawn of the Global World.* New York: Bloomsbury, 2008. Fascinating examination of global trends through Dutch paintings.

Cameron, Euan, ed. *Early Modern Europe: An Oxford History.* New York: Oxford University Press, 1999. Includes excellent essays on various aspects of the era.

Davies, Norman. *Europe: A History.* New York: Oxford University Press, 1996. An interesting and valuable survey.

Goldstone, Jack. *Why Europe? The Rise of the West in World History, 1500–1850.* New York: McGraw-Hill, 2009. Places the rise of Europe in a comparative global context.

Hughes, Lindsey. *Russia in the Age of Peter the Great.* New Haven, CT: Yale University Press, 1998. A readable, detailed study.

Jacob, Margaret. *The Cultural Meaning of the Scientific Revolution.* Philadelphia: Temple University Press, 1988. Places scientific discoveries in a larger social and cultural context.

Jensen, De Lamar. *Reformation Europe: Age of Reform and Revolution*, 2nd ed. Lexington, MA: D.C. Heath, 1992. Places the movements in a broader social, political, and economic context.

Kamen, Henry. *Empire: How Spain Became a World Power, 1492–1763.* New York: Perennial, 2003. A provocative chronicle.

MacCulloch, Diarmaid. *The Reformation: A History.* New York: Penguin, 2005. A fascinating, readable study of the era.

Porter, Roy. *The Enlightenment*, 2nd ed. New York: Palgrave Macmillan, 2000. An up-to-date synthesis.

Schama, Simon. *Embarrassment of Riches. An Interpretation of Dutch Culture in the Seventeenth Century.* New York: Knopf, 1987. A popular study of the Netherlands during the golden age.

Weir, Alison. *The Life of Elizabeth I.* New York: Ballantine, 1999. One of the best and most readable biographies of the English ruler.

Wiesner-Hanks, Merry. *Early Modern Europe, 1450–1789.* New York: Cambridge University Press, 2006. Excellent survey emphasizing social history.

Wiesner-Hanks, Merry. *Women and Gender in Early Modern Europe.* New York: Cambridge University Press, 2008. A readable and comprehensive study.

CHAPTER

16

New Challenges for Africa and the Islamic World, 1450–1750

CHAPTER OUTLINE

- Sub-Saharan African Societies
- Early European Imperialism and the Trans-Atlantic Slave Trade
- The Ottomans and Islamic Imperial Revival
- Persia, Morocco, and Central Asia

PROFILE
Pasha Sinan, Ottoman Architect

WITNESS TO THE PAST
A Kongolese King Protests the Slave Trade

Topkapi Palace Museum

Glassblowers' Procession The Ottoman rulers periodically had the members of several hundred occupational guilds in Istanbul parade before them, including storytellers, taxidermists, potters, and even executioners. This painting, from an illuminated manuscript finished around 1582, shows the glassblowers, some of them on a wheeled cart demonstrating their skills.

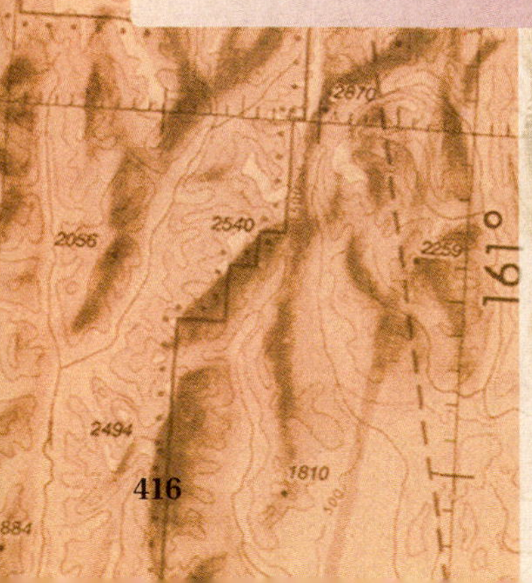

Warriors will fight scribes for the control of your institutions; wild bush will conquer your roads; your soil will crack from the drought; your sons will wander in the wilds. Yes, things will fall apart.

—IGBO ANCESTRAL CURSE[1]

FOCUS QUESTIONS

1. How did the larger sub-Saharan African societies and states differ from each other in the sixteenth century?
2. What were the consequences of African-European encounters and the trans-Atlantic slave trade?
3. What factors made the Ottoman Empire such a powerful force in the region?
4. How did the Persian and Central Asian experience differ from that of the Ottomans?

Things fell apart for many Africans in the Early Modern Era, including Ayuba Suleiman Diallo (ah-YOO-bah SOO-lay-mahn JAH-loh). In 1731 the thirty-year-old educated prince from the West African kingdom of Bondu visited Senegambia, at the western tip of Africa, on a trading mission. Captured by enemies and sold to the British as a slave, he was eventually shipped to a plantation growing tobacco in Maryland. After he attempted escape, Thomas Bluett, an English entrepreneur, recognized both his talents and his connections to West African commercial life. Diallo's Islamic faith and ability to read and write Arabic reflected the influence of Islam in parts of West Africa. Bluett emancipated Diallo, took him to London, and presented him at the royal court. The British hoped he might help their commercial activity in Senegambia. After agreeing to act as middleman in obtaining more slaves, Diallo returned to Bondu and resumed his life. Until his death, Diallo profited as a trading partner of British merchants. He had been both victim and beneficiary of the new challenges of his times.

Some aspects of Ayuba Suleiman Diallo's story represent the changing Atlantic world as Europe, Africa, and the Americas became increasingly linked in unprecedented ways. Diallo's West African trading world now included English, Portuguese, Dutch, and French companies seeking gold, gum, hides, ivory, and especially slaves. Goree (go-ray) Island, near the present-day city of Dakar (duh-KAHR), became a major slave collection center. Diallo's story is unique because he gained freedom quickly and eventually returned home. But the ancient Igbo curse proved prophetic for the many Africans who were shipped off as slaves. At the same time, many Africans remained untouched by the various slave trades and other disruptive European activities and continued to pursue their ways of life as they always had, expanding and flourishing or declining and decaying from local conditions unrelated to what Europeans might be doing along the coasts.

The growing European power was also gradually felt in the Islamic Middle East (western Asia and North Africa) and Central Asia. By the 1500s Islam, the monotheistic religion that had arisen in Arabia a millennium earlier, dominated a huge chunk of Afro-Eurasia, from the westernmost fringe of Africa to central Indonesia and the southern Philippines. Islamic political ideas, trade networks, and literary traditions linked many millions of people. The powerful Ottoman Empire, which included much of western Asia, North Africa, and southeastern Europe, and a new Persian state, the Safavid Empire, had increasing connections of trade and conflict with non-Islamic societies. But while these Islamic societies experienced changes, they also maintained long-standing traditions and remained largely in control of their own destinies.

e Visit the website and eBook for additional study materials and interactive tools: www.cengage.com/history/lockard/globalsocnet2e

Sub-Saharan African Societies

How did the larger sub-Saharan African societies and states differ from each other in the sixteenth century?

Many African societies flourished in the 1500s. Like Asians and Europeans, some Africans formed great states and engaged in extensive long-distance trade (see Chapter 12). Many had adopted Islam, while others mixed monotheism, polytheism, and animism. Many African societies possessed valuable human and natural resources that attracted Europeans, posing new challenges and changing Africa's relationship to the world. In the 1400s the Portuguese commenced exploratory voyages down the West African coast that foreshadowed dramatic changes to come.

The West African States

Songhai and Timbuktu

The last of the great Sudanic empires, Songhai **(song-GAH-ee)**, remained strong through much of the 1500s (see Map 16.1). Based at Gao on the Niger River, Songhai's empire stretched 1,500 miles from east to west. Songhai's people blended Islam with local customs. In contrast to Arab society, however, Sudanic women enjoyed a high social position and considerable personal liberty, much to the shock of Arab visitors. Women dominated village markets and in some cities were free to have lovers as they desired.

The city of Timbuktu became a major terminus for the trans-Saharan trade that shipped to North Africa gold, ivory, and slaves for Arab and European markets. Timbuktu was also a major center of Islamic scholarship, boasting schools, libraries, well-stocked bookstores, and universities teaching theology, law, and literature. An early-sixteenth-century Arab visitor, Leo Africanus, reported that Timbuktu had "numerous judges, doctors of letters, and learned Muslims. The king greatly honors scholarship. Here too, they sell many hand-written books. More profit is had from their sale than from any other merchandise."[2] The Islamic University of Sankore at Timbuktu employed several well-known Arab scholars on its faculty, and its student body was drawn from throughout the Islamic realm. Thousands of crumbling books, written in Arabic and several African languages, have recently been found in forgotten Timbuktu storage rooms. However, Songhai's leadership deteriorated and succession struggles emerged. In 1591, a Moroccan invasion ended the kingdom and the era of large imperial states in the western Sudan (see Chronology: Africa and the Atlantic World, 1482–1750).

Several other West African societies exercised regional influence and profited from trade. The Sudanic kingdoms formed by the Mandinka, Bambara **(bahm-BAH-rah)**, and Mossi peoples in the upper Niger Basin had effective, cavalry-based armies. The Dyula **(JOO-lah)**, a Mandinka Muslim mercantile clan, expanded operations throughout West Africa, moving goods such as gold and salt with caravans of porters, canoe fleets, and donkey trains. Thus the first Europeans to visit West Africa could tap into well-established trade networks and weekly markets that had been held in various towns and villages for many centuries. Many societies were matrilineal, and some West Africans had women chiefs or queens. Queen mothers of kings enjoyed great power, and Africans often venerated women elders for their wisdom and closeness to the ancestors.

Several strong trade-based Islamic kingdoms arose in the central and eastern Sudan. Kanem-Bornu **(KAH-nuhm-BOR-noo)**, centered on Lake Chad, prospered from trading slaves to North African Arabs for horses. The kingdom reached its height in the late 1500s and early 1600s under King Idrus Aloma **(IH-dris ah-LOW-ma)**, a devout Muslim who extended his territories deep into the Sahara and imported guns from the Ottoman Empire. The most purely Islamic state in sub-Saharan Africa, Kanem-Bornu declined only in the later 1700s. Other states included the fiercely competitive city-states of the Hausa people, of what is now northern Nigeria, eastern Niger, and southern Chad. These states were centers for manufacturing cotton cloth and leatherwork, some of which was sold as far away as Europe, and Hausa merchants traded around West Africa. Although Islam gradually became the dominant faith throughout the Hausa lands, in contrast to the Middle East, Hausa women, like those in other savannah states such as Songhai and Kanem-Bornu, continued to play vital political and social roles. For instance,

CHRONOLOGY
Africa and the Atlantic World, 1482–1750

- **1482** First Portuguese-Kongo encounter
- **1487** Portuguese discovery of Cape of Good Hope
- **1497** Vasco da Gama's first voyage to East African coast
- **1505** Portuguese pillage of Kilwa
- **1514** First African slaves to Americas
- **1507–1543** Rule of Alfonso I in Kongo
- **1526–1870** Trans-Atlantic slave trade
- **1575** End of Portuguese technical assistance to Kongo
- **1591** Destruction of Songhai
- **1652** Dutch settlement of Cape Town

CHRONOLOGY

	Sub-Saharan Africa	Middle East
1300		**1300–1923** Ottoman Empire
1400	**1497** Portuguese encounters with East Africa	
1500	**1526–1870** Trans-Atlantic slave trade	**1501–1736** Safavid Persia **1520–1566** Suleiman the Magnificent
1600	**1591** Destruction of Songhai **1652** Dutch settlement of Cape Town	**1554–1659** Sa'dian Morocco

Queen Amina of Zaria **(ZAH-ree-uh)** extended her city's power while building effective walled defenses against rival states and raiders.

Guinea Coast

Important non-Muslim states occupied the Guinea Coast from today's Ghana to eastern Nigeria. The Akan **(AH-kahn)** peoples of the Volta **(VAWL-tuh)** River Basin built small states that prospered from mining and trading gold to the north. In western Nigeria, the Yoruba states were each based on a large city ruled by a king or prince. Yoruba women exercised political influence by electing a woman representative to the council of chiefs. Oyo, the most powerful Yoruba kingdom, had a feared cavalry force equipped with bows, javelins, and swords and flourished until the late 1700s under able kings. Another great Guinea kingdom, Benin **(buh-NEEN)**, in south-central Nigeria, shared many cultural and political traditions with the Yoruba. European visitors admired this prosperous society, including the capital city of wide streets and large wooden houses with verandas. A Dutch merchant marveled at the palace of the Benin king, which had galleries "as big as those on the Exchange at Amsterdam [supported by] wooden pillars encased with copper where their victories are depicted."[3]

Bantu Trading Cities and Kingdoms

Swahili Cities

By the sixteenth century peoples speaking closely related Bantu languages had settled much of eastern, Central, and southern Africa. The closest ties to hemispheric networks were forged by city-states along the East African coast, thriving centers of trade where Bantu settlers and Arab immigrants had created a Swahili culture that mixed African and Islamic traditions. Indonesians, Indians, Persians, and Arabs had regular contact with East Africa, bringing ideas, products, technologies, and immigrants. Some cities boasted large stone and mortar buildings with terraces, towers, and luxuriant trees and gardens. Prosperous East African

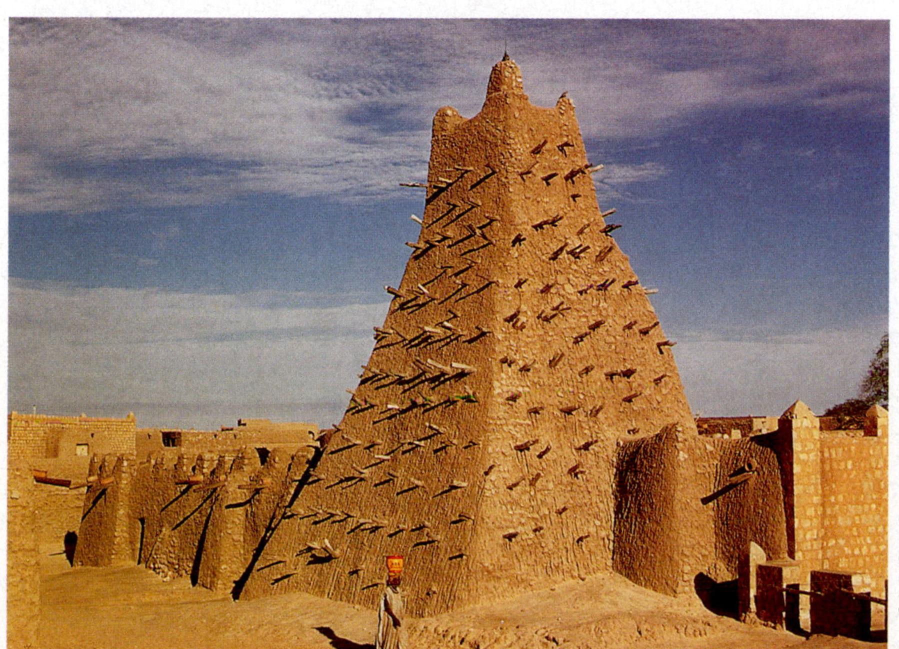

Aldona Sabalis/Photo Researchers, Inc.

Sankore Mosque Built in the fourteenth century, the Sankore Mosque in the Sudanic city of Timbuktu, a center of commerce and scholarship in the Songhai Empire, symbolized the spread of Islam in the region but also the adaptation of the faith to West African traditions, reflected in the mosque's unique architecture.

Map 16.1
African States and Trade, 1500–1700

Some African states, such as Songhai, Kanem-Bornu, Benin, Lunda, Buganda, and Ethiopia, remained powerful in this era. West African coastal societies were increasingly drawn into world trade, while the East African coastal cities remained significant in Indian Ocean trade.

Interactive Map

city-states such as Kilwa and Malindi, with their royal courts, mosques, and luxury goods, were part of the great trading network around the Indian Ocean dominated by seafaring Arabs and Indian Muslims, and ships from Arabia, Persia, and India regularly visited the coast from the twelfth through the fifteenth centuries. These Swahili ports collected goods from the African interior, such as iron, ivory, tortoise shell, leopard skins, gold, and slaves, to be exchanged for Chinese porcelain, glass beads, and Indian cotton. Portuguese visitors to Malindi reported that the "king wore a robe of damask trimmed with green satin, and a rich turban. He was seated on two cushioned chairs of bronze, beneath a round sunshade of crimson satin attached to a pole. Two trumpets of ivory made sweet harmony."[4]

Other major Bantu states emerged inland. On the southeastern plateau bordering the great Zambezi **(zam-BEE-zee)** River the Shona people flourished from exporting gold and ivory to the Middle East and India through the coastal city of Sofala. By 1500 the once-great Shona kingdom of Zimbabwe had collapsed, replaced by competing kingdoms. In the fertile rolling hills just west of Lake Victoria in southeastern Uganda, Buganda **(boo-GON-da)** emerged in the 1500s, and by the 1700s it had a well-developed bureaucracy, a powerful military, and extensive trade with the coastal cities. As the kingdom grew in wealth and influence, art, poetry, dance, and philosophy flourished. The large Kongo kingdom arose in the 1300s along the Congo River in northern Angola and western Congo, ruling some 2.5 million people by 1500. It boasted many large towns and a royal capital containing some 30,000 residents. To the east, the Luba **(LOO-buh)** and Lunda kingdoms built substantial empires in the southern Congo. Their location far inland and their access to trade networks running through Central Africa allowed them to resist European power into the nineteenth century.

Most of the Bantu societies in southern Africa formed small states led by chiefs and combined farming with cattle herding. The largest, the Xhosa **(KHO-sa)** and Zulu, mostly lived along the Indian Ocean coast. Around 50,000 Khoikhoi **(KOI-KOI)**, non-Bantu pastoralists also called Hottentots **(HOT-n-TOTS)**, lived around the Cape of Good Hope at Africa's southern tip.

Three Traders This bronze plaque, from the sixteenth century, shows three Benin merchants, possibly appointed by the king to negotiate with the Europeans who were then arriving in the region. The merchant in the center holds a staff signifying his royal appointment and royal authority over commerce with non-Benin people.

Africa in the Hemispheric System

Africans had long played key roles in the Eastern Hemisphere economic system, but the rapid rise of European power between 1450 and 1600 presented them with serious challenges, reshaping their role in the world. Sub-Saharan Africans were vulnerable to European and Arab power because they did not enjoy the same environmental advantages and interregional connections that had benefited parts of Eurasia and North Africa. By 1500 Eurasian and North African societies had invented or borrowed cutting-edge technologies such as printing and gunpowder weapons and had also developed more productive economies than those of sub-Saharan Africa. Most Africans never encountered the Chinese technology and Indian mathematics that spurred Middle Eastern and European development. In addition, much of sub-Saharan Africa had marginally fertile soils, scarce exploitable minerals, and few good harbors.

West and East Africans had been major suppliers of gold, ivory, and other commodities to the Middle East and Europe for centuries. Although this trade increased European interest in Africa, only a few Europeans and Africans had made direct contact with each other. By the 1300s the few remaining Christian Nubian kingdoms in the central Nile Valley had been conquered by Muslims, and Christianity died out in Nubia. Only in remote Ethiopia, where the Amharic **(ahm-HAHR-ik)** people had adopted a form of Christianity related to Eastern Orthodoxy, did the religion flourish. Ethiopia's state had survived 1,500 years in the highlands of Northeast Africa, building splendid churches, often on steep mountainsides. But the expansion of Islam cut off the Ethiopians from Europe.

Europe-Africa Connections

Direct contacts between Europe and sub-Saharan Africa only began in the early 1400s, when the Portuguese began exploring down the West African coast in search of gold, Christian allies against Islam (possibly a murky recollection of Ethiopian and Nubian Christians), and a hoped-for sea route to China and Southeast Asia, the sources of the silk and spices so valued in Europe. The Europeans' ignorance of black Africa helped create the myth of **Darkest Africa**, those areas of Africa least known to Europeans but, in European eyes, awaiting to be "opened" to the "light of Western civilization." At the same time, Europeans also perplexed Africans. In southern Nigeria, the first appearance of white men along the coast shocked a local fisherman, who reportedly "raced home [in a panic] and told his people what he had seen; whereupon he and the rest of the town set out to purify themselves, [to] rid themselves of the influence of the strange thing that had intruded into their world."[5]

Darkest Africa Those areas of Africa least known to Europeans but, in European eyes, awaiting to be "opened" to the "light of Western civilization."

After they began establishing control in the Americas, Europeans became interested in acquiring large numbers of enslaved Africans. Slavery existed in many African societies, just as it had in

Slave Trades

other areas of the world, and slaves were for centuries exported from Africa. Muslim merchants, usually Arabs or Berbers, acquired slaves in the Sudan and transported them by caravan across the Sahara to North Africa, where they were sold to Arab or, sometimes, European owners. A similar Arab-run slave trade from East Africa shipped slaves northward to Arabia, the Persian Gulf, Persia, and India. Over twelve centuries perhaps 10 to 15 million enslaved Africans were taken north by Muslim slave traders. Europeans also tolerated slavery. Slaves from eastern Europe, particularly Russians and Greeks, had for centuries been dispatched, first by the Byzantines and then by the Ottomans, from the Black Sea region and Balkans to Spain, Portugal, Italy, France, Central Asia, and the Middle East. Thus slavery had no particular "racial" identity yet. But the forging of plantation economies in the Americas focused more attention on Africa as a source of slaves. Europeans did not invent the African slave trade, but they soon transformed it.

The Portuguese and Early African Encounters

Early Portuguese Explorations

The Portuguese were the first Europeans to have direct encounters with sub-Saharan African societies. Having the world's most advanced ships and well armed with gunpowder weapons, the Portuguese, spurred by Prince Henry the Navigator, began exploring the West African coastline in the early 1400s (see Chapters 12 and 14). They soon discovered and settled the uninhabited Azores and Madeira Islands. By 1471 they had reached as far as the modern nation of Ghana, where they tapped into the gold trade from the Akan states, calling the region the Gold Coast. Shifting from exploration to exploitation, they colonized the Cape Verde Islands, the nearby coastal region of Guinea-Bissau, and the small islands of Sao Tome **(tuh-MAY)** and Principe near Nigeria, while establishing trading forts to obtain gold, ivory, and slaves. In the 1480s the Portuguese began a long relationship with the prosperous Kongo kingdom, near the Atlantic coast of south-central Africa. They sent Catholic missionaries and skilled craftsmen to the Kongo, and the Kongolese king and some of the people adopted Christianity, blending it with their own religious concepts. The Portuguese and Kongolese enjoyed similar standards of living and had similar views of government, both favoring strong monarchy.

The Sea Route to Asia

In 1487 Bartolomeu Dias (ca. 1450–1500) led a Portuguese expedition that sailed round the southern tip of Africa into the Indian Ocean, intensifying Portuguese interest in both Africa and Asia. Dias believed that he had discovered the best route to Asia and its fabulous goods, leading the Portuguese king to rebuff Christopher Columbus when the Italian sailor sought sponsorship to sail west. Even when Columbus, leading a Spanish expedition in 1492, returned from his first voyage to the Americas and announced, incorrectly, that he had found a sea route to India, the skeptical Portuguese pursued the route around Africa. Their encounter with the Khoikhoi herdsmen at the Cape of Good Hope foreshadowed the conflict to come between Europeans and Africans. After being at sea for months, Dias and his thirsty sailors helped themselves at a watering hole without asking permission. The Khoikhoi threw stones, and Dias killed a herdsman with a crossbow.

More Portuguese exploration followed, eventually reshaping the hemispheric trade system. In 1497 four ships commanded by Vasco da Gama **(VAS-ko dah GAH-ma)** (ca. 1469–1525) left Portugal. Surviving hurricanes and mutinies, da Gama's ships sailed around the Cape and then up the East African coast, visiting the Swahili trading cities of Mozambique, Mombasa, and Malindi. There he discovered that the merchants had no interest in his meager trade goods, such as hats and cloaks of much poorer quality than Asian and Arab products. Refocusing his attention on India, da Gama then turned to local expertise, engaged a skillful pilot, and sailed from Malindi to southwestern India. Even though the Indians told him his merchandise was unworthy of even the poorest local merchant and could not compete with the more valuable and better-made products from India, China, Indonesia, and Persia, da Gama had located the sea route to the East. He acquired a small cargo of spices and precious stones and returned home in triumph. In the following years, often using force, the Portuguese set up trading bases around the Indian Ocean, while their warships attempted to limit the maritime commerce of their Arab, Ottoman, Persian, and Indian rivals.

SECTION SUMMARY

- Songhai, the last great Sudanic kingdom with its trading city Timbuktu, produced many scholars of Islam, but its society was much more open to contributions from women than was Arab society.
- West African states were extremely varied and included the strict Islamic kingdom of Kanem-Bornu, the Hausa traders, the Yoruba in western Nigeria, and the prosperous kingdom of Benin.
- In Bantu-speaking East Africa, coastal city-states such as Kilwa and Malindi grew wealthy from the sale of goods from across Africa to Arabia, Persia, and India; the Shona exported gold and ivory; and Buganda traded extensively with East African coastal cities.
- Enslavement of many peoples—for example, Africans by Africans, Africans by Arabs, eastern Europeans by western Europeans—was widespread when western Europeans began to obtain African slaves.
- Early Portuguese relations with Africa included cooperation with the Kongo kingdom, conflict with the Khoikhoi, and failed attempts to trade with East African coastal city-states.

Early European Imperialism and the Trans-Atlantic Slave Trade

What were the consequences of African-European encounters and the trans-Atlantic slave trade?

As Portuguese ships began making ever-longer journeys along the West African coast, their encounters fostered trade but also conflict and destruction. The Portuguese made contact with the Kongo, which they eventually colonized, and then became active in East Africa, undermining the coastal trading cities. Meanwhile, the Dutch gained a foothold in South Africa. These activities led to the trans-Atlantic slave trade, which affected the millions of Africans who were captured, transported, and sold in the Americas, the African states where slaves were obtained, the American societies that imported slave labor, and the European and North American merchants, shippers, and planters who profited from the trade. These European activities contributed to a new global system of trade and empire that harmed some African societies. By the 1700s the gulf in wealth, power, and development, once narrow, between Africa and Eurasia had grown very wide, greatly influencing the relationship between European and African peoples.

Kongo, Angola, and the Portuguese

Portugal and Kongo

The Portuguese had their major impact in the Kongo and the surrounding region. An enlightened king and a dedicated Kongolese Christian, Alfonso I (r. 1507–1543), ruled the Kongolese, who were open to foreign influence. A Portuguese merchant noted that "the grandees of the court began to dress like Portuguese, wearing mantles, capes, cloaks of scarlet silk, hats, and velvet and leather sandals."[6] Alfonso used Portuguese weapons to expand his empire, and he clearly wanted to modernize the kingdom along Western lines with Portuguese help. He might have succeeded had the Portuguese not become less concerned with political alliance and more interested in acquiring enslaved Kongolese, which they began to do in 1514. Although opposed in principle, Alfonso was willing to sell slaves to the Portuguese in exchange for goods and services he regarded as essential to his kingdom's progress. In his tradition, moreover, Kongolese owners had a responsibility to treat slaves well. However, demands for slaves multiplied as the Portuguese developed plantations to grow sugar on Sao Tome, northwest of Kongo. In their new colony in Brazil, across the Atlantic from Kongo, the Portuguese set up many more plantations to grow sugar and other tropical crops, multiplying the need for enslaved labor. Since Alfonso and his successors permitted only a modest trade in slaves, the Portuguese resorted to armed raids to procure slaves. Alfonso repeatedly asked the Portuguese to halt their coercive activities, which were damaging and depopulating his country (see Witness to the Past: A Kongolese King Protests the Slave Trade), but his pleas were unsuccessful. Alfonso grew disillusioned with the rapacious Portuguese, who halted their cooperation with the Kongo government in 1575.

Conquests in Angola

Eventually the Portuguese turned to conquest. After setting up a base at Luanda (loo-AHN-duh) in 1580, they began a war against a vassal state of Kongo, Ndongo (uhn-DONG-go), whose ruler was called the Ngola, hence the Portuguese name for the region, Angola (ahng-GO-luh). Like the Kongolese, the Ndongo warriors were skilled but armed only with arrows and lances against Portuguese guns, cannon, and steel swords. The Portuguese encountered a formidable adversary in Queen Nzinga (en-ZING-a) of Ndongo (1624–1663), born a slave in the royal court. A brilliant diplomat, eloquent debater, and skilled warrior who dressed as a man and had a harem of men, she led her own troops into battle. She also shrewdly negotiated with the Portuguese to preserve her kingdom, demanding to be treated as an equal with Europeans. Her charismatic personality rallied her people. After years of diplomacy alternating with war, the pragmatic Nzinga made peace, a victim of Portugal's superior arms and ruthless quest for gold and slaves, and after her death Ndongo became the foundation for the Portuguese colony of Angola, under a government run by Portugal.

Kongolese Wars

In the early seventeenth century the Portuguese and displaced Africans they had hired began raiding Kongo. The Christian monarchy sent a series of moving appeals to the papacy for help. The popes pursued some of these appeals with the Portuguese government, but most were ignored. Kongo became engulfed in civil wars, generating more captives to be sold as slaves. An unusually charismatic Kongolese woman, Dona Beatriz Kimpa Vita, led a spiritual movement combining Catholic and traditional elements and aiming to reform Kongolese political life, but in 1706 Catholic missionaries had her burned at the stake.

A Kongolese King Protests the Slave Trade

In the early sixteenth century the Kongolese king Alfonso I, who had embraced Catholicism and welcomed the Portuguese to his kingdom, wrote over twenty letters in Portuguese to the king of Portugal, creating the earliest known African commentary on European activities in Africa. Some letters complained of aggressive Portuguese activities and asked that the king halt the slavers from obtaining Kongolese citizens. They also requested educational, medical, and religious assistance from Portugal. The letters, usually polite in tone, revealed gradually diminished hopes as friendly early encounters turned into Portuguese plunder and exploitation. These are excerpts from several letters written in 1526.

Sir, Your Highness should know how our Kingdom is being lost in so many ways that it is convenient to provide the necessary remedy, since this is caused by the excessive freedom given by your factors and officials to the men and merchants who are allowed to come to the Kingdom to set up shop with goods and many things which have been prohibited by us. . . .

And we cannot reckon how great the damage is, since the mentioned merchants are taking every day our natives, sons of the land and the sons of our noblemen and vassals and our relatives, because the thieves and men of bad conscience grab them wishing to have the things and wares of this Kingdom which they are ambitious of; they grab them and get them to be sold; and so great, Sir, is the corruption and licentiousness that our country is being completely depopulated, and Your Highness should not agree with this nor accept it as in your service. And to avoid it we need from . . . [your] Kingdoms no more than some priests and a few people to teach in schools. . . . It is our will that in these Kingdoms there should not be any trade of slaves nor outlet for them. . . . And as soon as they are taken by the white men they are immediately ironed and branded with fire. . . .

It happens that we have continuously many and different diseases which put us very often in such a weakness that we reach almost the last extreme; and the same [thing] happens to our children, relatives and natives owing to the lack in this country of physicians and surgeons who might know how to cure properly such diseases. And as we have got neither dispensaries nor drugs which might help us in this forlornness, many of those who had already been confirmed and instructed in the holy faith of Our Lord Jesus Christ perish and die; and the rest of the people in their majority cure themselves with herbs and breads and other ancient methods, so that they put all their faith in the mentioned herbs and ceremonies if they live. . . . And this is not much in the service of God. . . . We beg of you to be agreeable and kind enough to send us two physicians and two apothecaries and one surgeon, so that they may come with their drug-stores and all the necessary things to stay in our kingdoms, because we are in extreme need of them all.

THINKING ABOUT THE READING

1. What do these examples of letters tell us about Portuguese slaving activities and growing power in the Kongo?
2. What did Alfonso believe his kingdom needed from the Portuguese?
3. Why were the Portuguese unlikely to grant Alfonso's requests?

Source: Basil Davidson, ed., *African Civilization Revisited: Chronicles from Antiquity to Modern Times* (Trenton, N.J.: Africa World Press, 1991), pp. 223–226. This excerpt has been reprinted with the permission of Africa World Press in Trenton, NJ.

Eventually most of the Kongolese were incorporated into Portuguese Angola and lost faith in Christianity. Angola and Kongo became deeply enmeshed in the trans-Atlantic slave trade, which, by the later 1600s, had grown much larger than the Arab and Black Sea slave trades. Angola and Kongo were the major suppliers of slaves to Brazil—indeed, the largest single source of enslaved men and women to the Americas, accounting for some 35 to 40 percent of the total.

Eastern Africa and the Portuguese

Portugal and the Trading Cities

Portuguese activity extended into the eastern side of Africa. In 1502 Vasco da Gama led a squadron of twenty ships to occupy the trading ports of Mozambique and Sofala. To establish commercial control, Portuguese forces attacked and occupied other Swahili trading cities, plundering them and burning some to the ground. In Mombasa, according to a Portuguese eyewitness, "everyone started to search the houses, forcing open the doors with axes and iron bars. A large quantity of cotton cloth, rich silk and gold embroidered clothes was seized."[7] Kilwa was pillaged in 1505, and much of the population fled. Today all that remain of Kilwa are stone ruins. Their conquests gave the Portuguese bases from which, using ruthless methods, such as attacking and

Courtesy, Dr. Michael Araldi

Queen Nzinga This drawing by an Italian priest, Father Cavazzi, shows the formidable Queen Nzinga of Ndongo, in Angola, sitting on her throne, wearing a crown topped by a Christian cross and bracelets befitting her royal dignity while giving an order to attendants.

sinking Arab, Persian, and Indian ships, they gradually gained control of the Indian Ocean maritime trading network and the valuable goods it moved from southern and eastern Asia to the Middle East and Europe. The Portuguese established control of key trading ports in the Persian Gulf, India, Malaya, Indonesia, and China and seized the Spice Islands of eastern Indonesia, the main source for the priceless clove and nutmeg supplies.

Although the Portuguese also controlled key East African ports, they never prospered because the city-states declined into poverty as many traders fled elsewhere. The fanatically Christian Portuguese suppressed the Islamic Swahili culture, burning books that contained epic poems, religious writings, and historical chronicles. While they dominated coastal commerce for a century, their power over Indian Ocean maritime trade gradually diminished, and their influence waned all over the coast except in Mozambique. The power vacuum was filled by Arabs from Oman, on the northeast Arabian coast, who overran the Portuguese settlements in the late 1600s and established a sultanate on Zanzibar, an island off Tanzania. The Omani Arabs now supervised the lucrative slave and ivory trade to the Middle East and India, maintaining their political and commercial position into the late 1800s.

Portugal and the Shona States

Eventually the Portuguese became interested in acquiring gold on the plateau occupied by the Shona people. Portuguese adventurers began moving up the Zambezi River to the largest Shona kingdom, Monomotapa **(MO-no-mo-TOP-a)**, and gradually took control of the lower Zambezi Valley, the foundation for a Portuguese-governed colony later called Mozambique. Because the Portuguese died in large numbers from tropical diseases such as malaria, the Shona were able to hold out for many years. By 1628, however, a decaying Monomotapa had become a virtual Portuguese puppet state.

But in trying to control the gold trade the Portuguese destroyed it. Monomotapa was eventually overrun by neighboring African states, forcing the Portuguese out of the plateau, and the gold fields became less productive. The Portuguese then began concentrating their efforts on coastal Mozambique. Those Portuguese who settled there, especially in the Zambezi Valley, tended to marry African women and adopt many aspects of local culture and customs. Mozambique became a supplier of slaves to the Indian Ocean islands and to the Americas, but on a small scale relative to West and Central Africa. Only in the nineteenth century did Portugal gain firm control over the settlers and solidify their Mozambique colony.

Portugal and Ethiopia

The Portuguese also intervened briefly in Ethiopia, where a Christian culture maintained traditions forged many centuries earlier. In the 1520s the Portuguese sent a small force to help Ethiopians successfully repulse an invasion by Muslim neighbors backed by the rising Ottoman Turkish Empire. Then in the early 1600s the Portuguese sent Jesuit missionaries in an effort to convert the king from the state church to Catholicism. He adopted the new faith and, at Portuguese urging, began to reform Ethiopian society and the Ethiopian Church. When both the church and the Amharic population resisted, civil war erupted, the pro-Portuguese king abdicated, the missionaries and other Portuguese were expelled, and Ethiopia went back to its old ways and faith. This episode and the Portuguese activities in Kongo were the first of various later attempts by zealous Westerners to change African society, attempts which, like these, often harmed local people.

South Africa and Dutch Colonization

Colonizing the Cape

European activity also affected the peoples living at the southern tip of Africa. The social, political, and economic evolution of the present country of South Africa differed greatly from that of most sub-Saharan Africans. In 1652 the Dutch established a settlement, Cape Town, on the Cape of Good Hope, to provision the Dutch ships sailing between Europe and Indonesia, where the Dutch were trading and establishing bases. Dutch settlers arrived and took up farming. At first they traded with the local Khoikhoi people, but, since they had guns, they soon began seizing what they wanted. In 1659 the Khoikhoi rose against the Dutch. After crushing the poorly armed resistance, the Dutch claimed the Khoikhoi land and eventually enslaved or killed all the Khoikhoi and began imposing white supremacy rule over Africans in the lands they controlled. To obtain a labor supply for their farms and households, the Dutch imported slaves from Madagascar, Mozambique, and Indonesia. Masters and slaves lived close together, producing the roots of the mixed-race (known as "Colored") population of today. But whites always held a politically, legally, and economically superior status.

Boers Dutch farming settlers in South Africa in the eighteenth century.

trekking The migrations of Boer settlers in cattle-drawn wagons into the interior of South Africa whenever they wanted to flee government restraints.

Continued Dutch immigration led to rapid population growth, and some Dutch, chafing at governmental rules, began looking eastward for new land to settle. The Dutch settlers, later called **Boers** ("farmers"), began a movement not unlike the Bantu migrations centuries earlier, many adopting the sheep- and cattle-herding economy of the Bantu. As some Boers expanded east in search of farmland in the 1700s, they encountered the Xhosa and later the Zulu peoples, generating a series of bitter conflicts over land that lasted for nearly half a century. Thousands of Africans and some Boers died in the fighting. Nonetheless, these migrations of Boer settlers in cattle-drawn wagons, known as **trekking**, became a tradition, occurring whenever a Boer group wanted to flee government restraints. But eventually the Dutch government extended its influence into the lands settled by Boer trekkers.

The Trans-Atlantic Slave Trade

Roots of the Slave Trade

Modern relations between people of different groups that are commonly but misleadingly called races have their origins in the expansion of Europe and the trade in African slaves, which forged a global distribution of power and privilege along the lines of skin color. The most prominent factor in these relations, the trans-Atlantic slave trade—usually dated from 1526, when the first large shipments to the Americas began, to 1870, when it was completely abolished—fostered both commerce and cultural change in the lands bordering the Atlantic Ocean (see Map 16.2). The economic value of the plantations and mines in Europe's new American colonies created a labor market that could not be filled by free men and women, European slaves and criminals, or coerced Native Americans, especially since the Native American population declined massively during the first hundred years of European conquest and colonization. African slaves provided the lowest available cost option and thereby created the racial basis of trans-Atlantic slavery. Europeans easily rationalized the ruthless exploitation of Africans because of their different culture and appearance.

In the early 1600s the English, Spanish, French, Dutch, Danish, and English colonists in North America began following the Portuguese example by obtaining enslaved West Africans and shipping them across the Atlantic to meet the limitless demands of the American plantation economies, especially after the introduction of sugar planting (see Chapter 17). The West African coastal region was fragmented into many small states, making resistance to European slavers difficult and enabling Europeans to manipulate rivalries between states. Furthermore, the region's sedentary

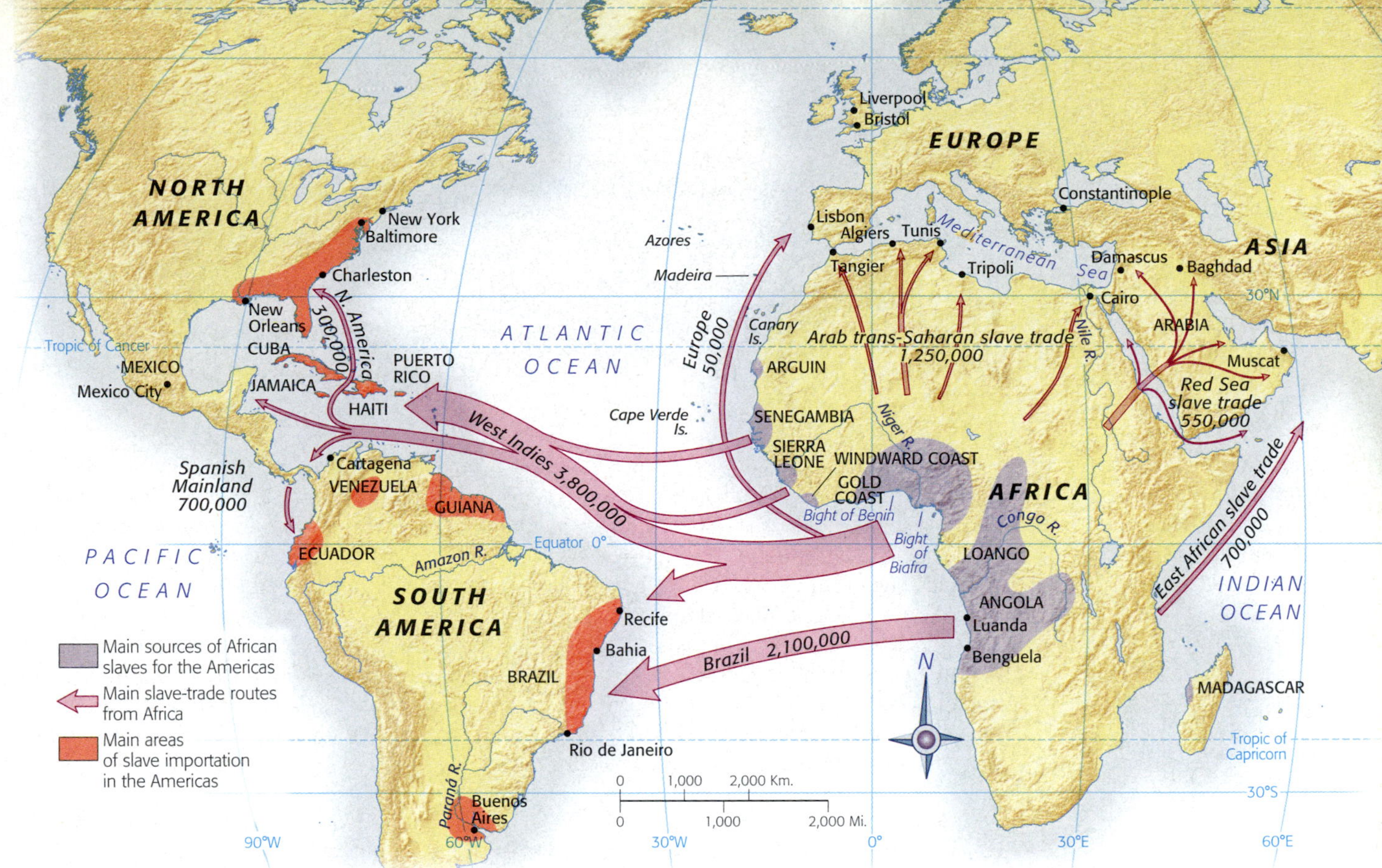

Map 16.2
Trans-Atlantic Slave Trade, 1526–1870
While the Arab-run slave trade from West and East Africa to North Africa and western Asia continued, the trans-Atlantic slave trade was far larger in scope. Millions of Africans were transported across the Atlantic, the greatest number ending up in Brazil and the West Indies. The majority of slaves came from what is today Angola, Congo, and Nigeria.

e **Interactive Map**

population was familiar with tropical agriculture and mining. Slave trade profits soared along with the volume of transported Africans. European forts to obtain, store, and ship slaves soon dotted the West African coast from Senegal down to Angola. Several holding centers, such as Calabar in Nigeria and Goree in Senegambia, processed many slaves for sale to slave ships. Europeans traded cotton goods, guns, iron, rum, and tobacco for slaves, often with the cooperation of local African chiefs, but sometimes they acquired Africans directly by force, as in Kongo and Angola.

Transporting Slaves

How many Africans were originally enslaved for the trade is uncertain, but probably some 25 to 30 million people. Between 9 and 12 million Africans were landed in the Americas over four centuries, perhaps a third women, to be sold at auction. Millions of slaves died in holding cells in West Africa or on the notorious **Middle Passage**, the slave's journey by ship from Africa to the Americas. Those who survived the Middle Passage faced a bleak future, sold without regard to personal ties, mostly to sugar, cotton, or coffee plantations. The trans-Atlantic slave trade reached its peak between 1700 and 1800, with perhaps 100,000 Africans a year being shipped to the Americas. Both the Middle Passage and the fate of the Africans who survived the trip were horrific. The trip from Africa to the Americas took one or two months, and conditions on the notoriously overcrowded, disease-ridden slave ships were terrible, as this description by an American observer attested:

Middle Passage The slave's journey by ship from Africa to the Americas.

> *The [naked] men were shackled two by two, the right wrist and ankle of one to the left wrist and ankle of another. The women—usually regarded as fair prey for the sailors—spent the night between decks, in a space partitioned off from that of the men. All the slaves were forced to sleep without covering on bare wooden floor. In a stormy passage the skin over their elbows might be worn away to the bare bones. Every man was allowed a space six feet long by sixteen inches wide (and usually about two feet seven inches high).*[8]

Olaudah Equiano (oh-LAU-duh ay-kwee-AHN-oh), an Igbo seized in Nigeria in the 1750s, described the intolerable stench of the hold and the floggings on the deck for misconduct that sometimes resulted in death.

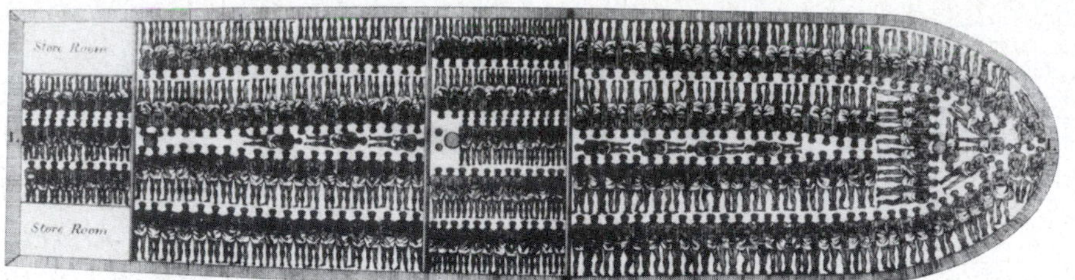

From a Parliamentary Report

The Middle Passage This painting from the era vividly shows the overcrowded conditions on the ships that carried African slaves, packed like sardines, on the "Middle Passage" across the Atlantic to the Americas. Such brutal conditions resulted in the deaths of many slaves and eventually prompted reformers to demand the end of the slave trade.

The mortality rates on the voyages probably averaged around 10 to 20 percent. Slavers hotly debated whether cramming as many slaves as possible into the ships (known as "tight pack") or carrying slightly fewer slaves ("loose pack") would land the greater number of slaves for eventual sale. Many slaves committed suicide before reaching the Americas. Equiano recounted a case when two other Igbos, in despair, jumped overboard while chained together, and many crews installed nets along the sides of slave ships to catch jumpers. There were also many mutinies. For instance, in 1839 slaves took control of a small Spanish ship, the *Amistad*, bound from Sierra Leone to Cuba. Led by Joseph Cinque, the son of a Mande chief, the ringleaders picked the locks on their chains and then killed the captain and some of the crew. After months at sea, and not knowing how to sail the ship home, they somehow found their way to New York. Cinque and his comrades were tried for mutiny in the United States, but the courts eventually ruled that they were kidnapped and freed them.

racism A set of beliefs, practices, and institutions based on devaluing groups that are supposedly biologically different.

Europeans quickly developed feelings of superiority to Africans that resulted in **racism**, a set of beliefs, practices, and institutions based on devaluing groups that are supposedly biologically different. To rationalize the trade, they invented the cruel fiction that Africans were subhuman savages unworthy of civilized treatment. For instance, in 1589 the English adventurer Richard Hakluyt described Africans as "a people of beastly living, without a God, law, religion, or common wealth."[9] Western scholars argued that Africans were naturally inferior to Europeans in intelligence. And slave traders and owners felt little guilt, seeing the inequality of peoples as ordained by God. Some even thought slavery helped Africans by exposing them to Western values and Christianity.

The Slave Trade and African Societies

Legacies for Africa

The harm done by the trans-Atlantic slave trade varied from region to region. Some coastal peoples of West and Central Africa succumbed to chronic raiding, kidnapping, and warfare, in an "enslave your neighbor or be enslaved" syndrome. European guns traded for slaves resulted in plundered villages and broken families. Some peoples, among them Kongolese, Angolans, Yorubas, Igbos, and Akans, were disproportionately transported to the Americas, leaving their societies badly disrupted. Over three-quarters of the Africans in the Americas came from these groups. In Angola, European settlers later took over the land in depopulated districts. By linking Atlantic Africa closely to Europe and the Americas, the slave trade created an **Atlantic System**, a large network that spanned western and Central Africa, the east and gulf coasts of North America, the Caribbean Basin, and the Atlantic coast of South America.

Atlantic System A large network that arose with the trans-Atlantic slave trade; the network spanned western and Central Africa, the east and gulf coasts of North America, the Caribbean Basin, and the Atlantic coast of South America.

The slave trade fostered economic change in Africa. While their major target was slaves, Europeans also coveted gold and cloth, and Western merchants soon monopolized the coastal trade. But some Africans and people of mixed African and European ancestry also flourished as merchants and slave traders. Other Africans refused to cooperate in slave trading and dealt with Europeans on their own terms. Hence, the kings of Benin prohibited the sale of male slaves and instead obtained the firearms needed to protect the state by trading cotton textiles, mostly made by women, as well as pepper, ivory, and beads. Some states such as Dahomey (duh-HO-mee), whose powerful army included women soldiers, prospered by cooperating with the slave traders at the expense of their neighbors.

Changing African States

Along the Gold Coast, the Ashante (a-SHAN-tee) had formed a state in the seventeenth century under their great king Osei Tutu (OH-say TOO-too), who introduced a constitution that made other chiefs members of an advisory council to the king. With access to gold fields, a powerful military force, and firearms acquired from Europeans, by the mid-1700s the Ashante dominated a large area while trading gold to North Africa and slaves to the Europeans.

The most far-reaching changes occurred along the coast from Senegambia to Angola, sometimes reaching several hundred miles inland. Some states, such as Kongo, declined, while others, such as Ashante, rose in power. Most West and Central African societies far from the coast, such as Kanem-Bornu, had little direct contact with the European slavers or the coastal states. However, the

Arab slave trade badly disrupted some East African regions, even reaching into the eastern Congo River Basin. The Sudan region remained a source of slaves for North Africa. The trans-Atlantic slave trade hence created economic imbalances that hindered local industries and integrated Africa into the world economy as a supplier of human and later natural resources. For example, the European presence fostered the diffusion of American food crops, such as maize and peanuts, to Africa. Some African artists incorporated Western ideas and Christian symbols into their work, while some African traditions influenced Western artists. But Portuguese and Dutch colonization in southern Africa foreshadowed the division of sub-Saharan Africa by several European nations in the 1800s.

One of the main results of the European intrusion was **imperialism**, the control or domination, direct or indirect, of one state or people over another. Often imperialism led to **colonialism**, government by one society over another society. The Cape Verde Islands, Angola, and parts of Senegambia, Mozambique, and South Africa became Western colonies in the era of the slave trade. But the full-blown Western colonial scramble for Africa only began with rapid industrialization in Europe, which accelerated the need for natural resources such as peanuts, palm oil, gold, timber, and cotton that could be processed into industrial or commercial products, as well as for new markets to consume these goods.

imperialism The control or domination, direct or indirect, of one state or people over another.

colonialism Government by one society over another society.

European Views on Africans

Racism made Africans and their descendants in the Americas a permanent underclass, treated with contempt by people of European ancestry. The first Europeans to encounter great African states like Benin, Kongo, and Kilwa in the late 1400s and early 1500s were awed by their prosperity and marveled at how even the poorest were treated with dignity. By the 1700s Europeans and North Americans viewed Africa as in desperate need of Western tutelage, setting the stage for, and justifying, colonization. Meanwhile, the Islamic Middle East also encountered rising Western power but, for most societies, with less dramatic consequences.

SECTION SUMMARY

- Under Christian King Alfonso I, Kongo attempted to emulate Portugal, but relations soured as the Portuguese began to enslave large numbers of Kongolese to work on sugar plantations in Africa and Brazil, and eventually the Portuguese conquered both Angola and Kongo, which then became the major source of slaves for the trans-Atlantic slave trade.
- In their ultimately unsuccessful attempt to dominate Indian Ocean trade, the Portuguese established control over the East African coast but eventually lost influence as the city-states declined.
- Dutch settlers in southern Africa, later called Boers, imposed white supremacy over the lands they seized but lived in close contact with their imported African and Asian slaves, producing the mixed-race "Colored" population of today; as Dutch population grew, some Boers trekked to other areas, creating continual conflict with local Africans.
- Millions of West African slaves were shipped to North America because they were the cheapest form of labor available to work the farms and mines and because the Native American population had been decimated.
- The conditions of the Middle Passage, from West Africa to America, were horrific, and many slaves died, committed suicide, or mutinied en route.
- The slave trade led to racist views, as many Europeans justified it by claiming that Africans were inherently inferior or arguing that it benefited slaves by exposing them to Western culture and religion.
- The slave trade destabilized and harmed many African societies, but some peoples and states armed themselves to resist the slave trade, while others prospered by selling neighboring peoples into slavery.
- As a result of the slave trade, European nations established imperial and colonial control over much of Africa and their impression of Africa shifted from respect to condescension.

THE OTTOMANS AND ISLAMIC IMPERIAL REVIVAL

What factors made the Ottoman Empire such a powerful force in the region?

The Islamic societies of the Middle East did not experience the jarring transitions felt by many Africans. While European nations established supremacy of the seas, Islamic states remained major land powers. The greatest, the Turkish Ottoman Empire, eventually ruled much of southeastern Europe, the western fringe of Asia, and much of North Africa and nearly conquered much of eastern and central Europe. By the 1700s, however, the Ottomans and other Middle Eastern states suffered from chronic warfare, poor leadership, a growing rigidity, and

CHRONOLOGY
The Middle East, 1500–1750

1501–1736 Safavid dynasty in Persia

1514–1517 Ottoman conquest of Syria, Egypt, and Arabia

1520–1566 Reign of Ottoman sultan Suleiman the Magnificent

1529 First Ottoman siege of Vienna

1554–1659 Sa'dian dynasty in Morocco

1682–1699 Ottoman wars with Habsburg Austria

1715 Beginning of Russian conquest of Turkestan

1722 Afghan invasion of Safavid Persia

1736–1747 Rule of Nadir Shah in Persia

a superiority complex toward the upstart Europeans. These Islamic societies soon became targets of European imperialism.

The Ottoman Empire, Government, and Economy

From their base in central Anatolia, the Ottoman Turks gained power over much of the once-great Byzantine Empire in the 1300s. The Ottoman conquest of the Byzantine capital, Constantinople, in 1453 demonstrated conclusively the power of Islamic society, as the center of Orthodox Christianity was transformed into Muslim-ruled Istanbul. By 1512 the Ottomans controlled Anatolia, Bulgaria, Greece, Albania, Serbia, and Romania. They had also unsuccessfully invaded southern Italy. Had they conquered Italy, the history of Europe might have been very different. During the sixteenth century the Ottomans defeated Persian forces, added Syria, Lebanon, Palestine, and Egypt to their domains, and controlled much of the Mediterranean.

The Ottoman golden age came under Sultan Suleiman **(SOO-lay-man)** the Magnificent (r. 1520–1566), famed as a just lawgiver but also a merciless conqueror who presided over military expansion and the pushing back of Christian power (see Chronology: The Middle East, 1500–1750). Suleiman's forces pushed into the eastern Balkans and north of the Danube River, defeating the Hungarians and besieging Vienna, and also gained control of Egypt and then the North African coast. After defeating the Persians and incorporating Iraq, Suleiman's empire stretched from Algeria to the Persian Gulf and from Hungary to Armenia (see Map 16.3). But the Ottomans never controlled much of the Arabian Peninsula, enabling Oman to extend its power to the East African cities. Suleiman's reign revived the Islamic glory that had faded with the downfall of the Iraq-based Abbasid Empire in the 1200s. Ottoman sultans claimed to have restored the caliphate, the blending of political and religious power of early Islamic times that was thought to be ordained by God. In 1538 the Ottoman ruler could boast proudly of his wide-ranging power: "I am God's slave and sultan of this world. I am head of Muhammad's community . . . who sends his fleets to the seas of Europe, the Maghrib [northwest Africa] and India."[10]

Suleiman's strategic position often involved him in conflicts. At various times, the Ottomans allied with France or with northern European Protestants against the Habsburgs, who ruled Austria and a large area of eastern Europe. Suleiman also controlled the overland trade routes between Europe and the Indian Ocean, selling spices and other products from India, Southeast Asia, and China to Venetian and other European merchants. Ottoman success owed much to military power. Gunpowder weapons, especially cannon, often built and operated by Hungarian Christians in Ottoman service, equaled the best of European gunnery, and the effective navy had ships that were often designed and crewed by Christian mercenaries.

Ottoman Government and Economy

For decades the Ottoman government was led by able sultans who governed through an imperial council headed by a prime minister and chose officials based on merit, allowing Arabs and other non-Turks to serve as officials and military officers. A Habsburg envoy wrote, "No distinction is attached to birth among the Turks. Honors, high posts, and judgeships are the rewards of great ability and good services."[11] The ruling elite resided in beautiful palaces with large harems of wives and concubines, as well as their children and many servants.

The Ottomans especially recruited administrators and soldiers from Christian peoples. The sultan's agents selected Christian youth for training and essentially made them slaves, who were required to embrace Islam. The most talented were sent to the palace school and prepared for administration, learning to read and write Arabic, Persian, and Turkish. Prime ministers usually came from this group. The other conscripts joined the well-armed, well-paid, highly disciplined elite military corps of infantrymen known as **janissaries** ("new troops"), who lived in barracks and were not allowed to marry.

janissaries ("new troops") Well-armed, highly disciplined, and generally effective elite military corps of infantrymen in the Ottoman Empire.

The Ottoman commercial economy flourished. Istanbul and other major cities served as centers for transregional trade, where merchants from different lands bought or sold European woolens, Persian silk, Chinese porcelain, Indian spices and textiles, Arab sugar, and Anatolian iron. Artisan and merchant guilds controlled many economic activities. But the dynamic international trade mostly involved luxuries, and the empire was largely self-sufficient in necessities such as food.

Map 16.3
The Ottoman and Safavid Empires, 1500–1750
By the later 1500s the Ottoman Empire included large parts of western Asia, southeastern Europe, southern Russia, and North Africa. Their major rivals, the Safavids, controlled Persia and parts of Iraq, the Caucasus, Afghanistan, and Central Asia.

Interactive Map

Ottoman Society, Culture, and Thought

Multiethnic Population and City Life

The diverse Ottoman society and culture thrived. The empire's multiethnic population, about evenly divided between Christians and Muslims, contained some 50 million people at its peak, dwarfing the largest European country, France, which had perhaps 15 million. The sultans governed the sizable Jewish, Greek Orthodox, and Armenian Christian communities through their own religious leaders, laws, and courts. Although they faced some legal disabilities, religious minorities enjoyed a toleration rare in the world at that time. The vibrant social life in Ottoman cities revolved around coffeehouses, public baths, and taverns. An Ottoman observer of one coffeehouse wrote: "Some read books and fine writings, some were busy with backgammon and chess, some brought new poems and talked of literature. Pious hypocrites said: 'People have become addicts of the coffee-house; nobody comes to the mosques.'"[12]

Many immigrants, including Jews and Muslims fleeing persecution in Spain, settled in Ottoman territory, bringing with them valuable expertise and international connections. The Ottomans also attracted European merchants and technicians by exempting them from taxes and laws, privileges that gave them a commercial advantage over their local-born competitors. Many Christian peasants from southern and eastern Europe migrated into Ottoman territory or welcomed Ottoman conquest, which generally brought them a better life. Balkan peasants said that the turban of the Turk was better than the tiara of the pope.

Gender Relations

Despite patriarchy, women had a higher status in Turkish society than in Arab tradition. Royal women exercised considerable political clout. Princes were brought up in royal harems, whose women influenced their thinking while financing buildings and social service activities. Upper-class women often owned land, managed businesses, and controlled wealth. Women took their grievances to Islamic courts, which protected their rights to inheritance and property. Having sons provided women even more security. Since men tended to die younger, women often became heads of households. Yet, women could also be abused by men and more easily divorced, and sometimes families punished or killed women suspected of illicit sexual activity.

Literature and Art

The Ottomans also stimulated literary and artistic creativity. Istanbul attracted artists and artisans from all over Europe and the Middle East. For example, Suleiman the Magnificent welcomed humanist thinkers from Italy, while Sultan Mehmed II (1432–1481) arranged to have the most famous Venetian artist, Giovanni Bellini, decorate his palace with paintings. Ottoman architects, such as the innovative Pasha Sinan, designed beautiful domed mosques and other public buildings that combined form with function (see Profile: Pasha Sinan, Ottoman Architect). In this creative environment, Ottoman and European architects and artists influenced each other. One sultan who admired Italian art even tried to woo two of the greatest talents, Michelangelo and Leonardo da Vinci, to work in Istanbul. Ottoman medicine remained vibrant, and scholars published many volumes on astronomy, mathematics, and geography and produced world maps more sophisticated than those of Europe. However, by the 1700s Ottoman science fell behind that of western Europe, as Ottoman intellectuals remained largely disinterested in and uninformed about scientific and technological developments elsewhere. The emphasis on law and theology rather than science in higher education inhibited technological innovation.

Islam and Sufism

In Ottoman religious life, various mystical Sufi sects, seeking a personal experience of God, had large followings. Seyh Bedreddin (SAY beh-DREAD-en), who founded an order of practitioners known as dervishes, wrote about his discoveries: "Ecstasy came to me, and I remained in wonderment at God's presence. The mystic who has perceived God spreads to the whole universe; he is one with the mountains and streams. There is no here or hereafter; everything is a single moment."[13] To achieve a trancelike state, dervishes danced feverishly, whirling around faster and faster while their long skirts billowed out, creating a hypnotic effect. Although some Sufi sects operated with official support, others, including the dervishes, were suspected of political disloyalty and of modifying too many Islamic principles.

Perhaps because the Ottomans drew the religious establishment close to the state, Islam became more rigid during these centuries in the Ottoman realms and the Middle East. Most religious leaders emphasized memorization rather than analysis of the sacred texts, punished deviation from orthodoxy, and were increasingly hostile to technological innovation. Meanwhile, Christian minorities flocked to schools set up by Christian missionaries from Europe and North America, some of which taught commercial and technical subjects, thus exposing them to knowledge from the wider world.

Ottoman Decline and the West

Military and Political Problems

Eventually the Ottomans faced new challenges that undermined the state and reduced the empire. Ottoman armies continued to effectively battle against European and Persian rivals into the 1670s, when they annexed part of the Ukraine. However, in 1683 Austria and its allies repulsed the last Ottoman attack of Vienna. Soon the Ottomans were pushed south of the Danube River, lost the Ukraine and southern Greece, and ceded Hungary to the rival Habsburgs. As their military practices and technology fell behind, Ottoman power was no longer feared, and European diplomats began calling the empire "the sick man of Europe." Janissary military discipline weakened while the officers spent winters in Istanbul, thus limiting military campaigns to warm weather months. Eventually the sultans eliminated the whole training system for young men and led campaigns personally, exhausting their energy. The Ottomans' technology also fell behind. The Ottoman navy had once enjoyed the most advanced technology, but by the 1600s European ships were now better armed and more maneuverable. Ottoman weaponry, especially artillery, stagnated just as European military technology was rapidly improving.

Compared to China or the emerging European states, the Ottoman state also was not very centralized, making imperial control difficult to maintain. Government through the religious communities or provincial leaders focused peoples' loyalty on their ethnic group or region rather than on the Ottoman state. The Kurds, a Sunni Muslim ethnic group occupying a large region in today's eastern Turkey, northern Iraq and Syria, and northwest Iran, increasingly resented Turkish control. Many Arabs and Balkan Christians who once welcomed Ottoman rule began to think of their own peoples as nations repressed by the empire. Ottoman citizens also disliked higher taxes, growing

PASHA SINAN, OTTOMAN ARCHITECT

One of the most innovative architects in world history, Pasha Sinan (1491–1588), served as the royal architect to Ottoman sultans for fifty years and perfected the Ottoman style. Sinan's work reflected the meeting and mixing of Christian and Muslim cultures in Istanbul, the former Byzantine city of Constantinople that became the Ottoman capital. Spectacular architecture symbolized the grandiose Ottoman spirit, thanks in part to Sinan, who eventually occupied a key state office. In his long career Sinan designed over three hundred works, ranging from grand government buildings and mosques taking years to build to fountains, tombs, bridges, and baths.

Sinan was born into a Christian Greek family in central Anatolia. Selected for the Ottoman military in 1512, he was converted to Islam and then trained as a janissary warrior and fought in various military campaigns. During his military service Sinan developed a reputation for his engineering skills. For example, he figured ways to float artillery across lakes and engineered the quick building of a bridge across the Danube River. In 1538 he was appointed royal architect, based in Istanbul, by the great sultan Suleiman the Magnificent, a patron of art and architecture. In this highly visible post, Sinan developed, procured funding for, and supervised the construction of projects that would be seen by millions. To succeed, he needed the skills of a visionary, planner, administrator, and manager.

Istanbul was filled with inspiring architecture from Byzantine times, including the beautiful cathedral of Hagia Sophia, with its huge dome. Sinan was fascinated by these domed structures and concentrated on incorporating them into his own architecture. The Santa Sophia church design, with its ascending hierarchy of sanctity ending at the altar, had reflected the Byzantine world-view and the values of the Greek Orthodox Church. Sinan sought to outdo the architects who built Hagia Sophia for the Byzantine emperor Justinian a thousand years earlier. He also wanted to adapt the dome structure to the needs of an Islamic house of worship, providing open spaces where all could face Mecca from an equal position. Sinan experimented constantly in pursuit of his vision.

During his career Sinan designed several great mosques in Istanbul in which he tried to incorporate the best features of Hagia Sophia into an Islamic setting. The Suleimaniye **(SOO-lay-man-iya)** mosque, for instance, finished in 1557, sits atop a high hill, dominating the city and proclaiming the triumph of Islam. A sixteenth-century English traveler, John Sanderson, exclaimed that the mosque passed "in greatness, workmanship, marble pillars, and riches all the churches of [Christian] emperors [and merited] to be matched with the 7 Wonders of the [ancient] World." The main dome is surrounded by over four hundred lesser domes. Within this huge complex were several of Istanbul's most elite schools.

Sinan's last great mosque, the Edirne **(eh-DURN-a)**, completed in 1575, had a dome that surpassed that of Hagia Sophia. Sinan considered it his masterpiece and boasted that "architects among Christians say that no Muslim architect would be able to build such a large dome. With the help of God I erected a dome higher and wider than Hagia Sophia." In designing this mosque, Sinan tried to assert what he considered the superiority of Islam over Christianity and brought Ottoman architecture to its highest point. The mosque expressed the imperial Ottoman achievement and the splendor of Islam.

Various rich Ottomans, to show their piety and provide themselves with a burial place, endowed mosques. The women of the imperial family and the wives of wealthy Ottoman officials also financed mosques, among other good works. Sinan designed some of these mosques and also built great tombs to commemorate the powerful men and women of his day. He also designed parts of the sultan's great palace, the Topkapi Sarai **(sah-RYE)** (Abode of Felicity). This huge complex boasted beautiful interiors and contained a series of pavilions, gardens, courts, treasuries, reception halls, baths, kitchens, and other buildings. Begun by Sinan, it was constructed over several centuries with no particular master plan. The palace and the grand mosques remain as testimonies to Sinan's talents and the cultural vibrancy of the Ottoman Empire in the 1500s.

THINKING ABOUT THE PROFILE

1. What does Sinan's career tell us about the Ottoman system?
2. How did Sinan's architecture reflect a mixing of Islamic and Christian traditions?

Notes: Quotations from Andrew Wheatcroft, *The Ottomans* (New York: Viking, 1993), 143; and Aptullah Kuran, *Sinan: The Grand Old Master of Ottoman Architecture* (Washington, DC: Institute of Turkish Studies, 1987), 168–169.

Robert Frerck/Woodfin Camp and Associates

Suleimaniye Mosque Between 1548 and 1557 Sinan designed and supervised the building of one of Istanbul's most magnificent mosques, the Suleimaniye, honoring God and Sinan's patron, Sultan Suleiman the Magnificent, who was buried in the mosque. Overlooking the Straits of Bosporus, the mosque complex contains schools, shops, and a hospital.

corruption, a bloated bureaucracy, and increasing peasant poverty. Finally, the ruling elite exercised more power over weak or incompetent sultans, some of whom were mentally unstable or despots. "Ibrahim the Mad" proved particularly tyrannical when he took power, once ordering the drowning of 280 concubines who angered him. Nobody grieved when he was deposed and executed. With weaker male leaders, senior palace women gained more influence, supporting one or another of the factions that contended for favor.

Ottoman sultans had difficulty controlling restless provinces in North Africa and western Asia, brutally crushing occasional rebellions during the 1600s. Although formally remaining vassals of Istanbul, leaders of Ottoman descent in Algeria and Tunisia became increasingly independent. In Mesopotamia and Egypt, the Ottomans ruled through local Arab leaders who sought more autonomy. By the mid-1700s Ottoman influence was deteriorating in large parts of the empire, and the Russians pressured Ottoman territory north of the Black Sea.

The Ottomans also faced increasing economic and military challenges from the rising western Europeans, the Habsburgs, and Russia. The growing European role in Asian trade weakened Anatolia's historic position as a middleman just as western Europe was becoming wealthier. Because the Portuguese and Dutch preferred to ship Asian resources around Africa to Europe's Atlantic ports, the Asian-Europe trade that flowed through Ottoman ports was gradually reduced. Moreover, because Ottoman rulers gave little support to the empire's merchant class, most of them Greeks, Armenians, and Jews, the once self-sufficient empire became increasingly dependent on imports from Europe. Hence Western merchants gradually gained control over large sectors of the Ottoman economy. Large Western trading firms, armed with both great capital and better business methods and backed by their own governments, became influential, ultimately reducing the Ottomans, once a hub of international commerce, to a secondary power in the emerging global trade system.

The rise of European power led to fierce debates. Reformers interested in European products and customs favored the importing of some European technology, but these reformist forces struggled against conservatives, who preferred the status quo and also found it difficult to overcome a Muslim superiority complex regarding the once-upstart Europeans. Many reformers looked backward to the era of Suleiman the Magnificent for inspiration. In this fashion the creaking Ottoman state limped into the twentieth century.

SECTION SUMMARY

- Under Suleiman the Magnificent, the Ottoman Empire stretched across vast areas of the Middle East, North Africa, and southeastern Europe, and it controlled the overland trade routes between Europe and the Indian Ocean.
- Leaders of the Ottoman Empire were chosen on the basis of merit, not birth, and even Christians served as administrators and soldiers.
- The Ottoman Empire was culturally and religiously diverse; religious minorities were allowed a measure of self-governance, and many immigrants were attracted by the empire's tolerance.
- The Ottoman Empire attracted and encouraged a range of artists and thinkers from across Eurasia, though state support for Islam may have caused it to become more rigid and close-minded.
- Though the Ottoman Empire remained strong through much of the seventeenth century, its military discipline, weaponry, and political stability soon began a gradual decline.
- As Europeans began to trade directly with Asia, the Ottomans lost their traditional role as middlemen and became increasingly dependent on European imports.

PERSIA, MOROCCO, AND CENTRAL ASIA

How did the Persian and Central Asian experience differ from that of the Ottomans?

Like the Ottomans, Islamic societies from Morocco to Central Asia also underwent significant changes. In Persia, a Shi'ite dynasty, the Safavids, revived Persian culture and became an internationally recognized power. Persian leaders, thinkers, and officials had long played a key role in the Islamic world, and Persian, widely spoken by Muslim elites from Istanbul to India, was the closest thing to a hemispheric language. In northwest Africa, Morocco became notable for its military prowess. Various Islamic societies in Central Asia struggled to maintain the Silk Road trade networks while facing pressure from the expanding Russian Empire.

The Safavid Empire

Rise of Safavids and Shi'ism

The Safavid dynasty came to power in Persia at the beginning of the sixteenth century, founded by a Turkish group from Azerbaijan (AZ-uhr-bye-ZHAHN) in the Caucasus Mountains who belonged to a militant Shi'ite Sufi order. In 1501, the Safavids, led by a charismatic thirteen-year-old boy, Isma'il (1487–1524), invaded and began conquering Persia, then a center of Sunni practice. Isma'il claimed descent from Muhammad and Sassanian princes. A Venetian diplomat described the youth as "of noble presence and a truly royal bearing, as in his eyes and brows there was something so great and commanding, which plainly showed that he would some day become a great ruler."[14] Isma'il, who thought of himself as an agent of God, mandated the conversion of the Persians to Shi'ism. Tensions between the majority Sunni and minority Shi'a had simmered since the Islamic community divided centuries earlier, and the Safavids used force when necessary on reluctant Sunni Persians, confiscating property and executing religious leaders. The shift to Shi'ism took some years, with many Sunni families emigrating to India, Central Asia, or Ottoman territories. Many Persians, however, enjoyed the rich Shi'ite ceremonies and wanted to differentiate themselves from the hated Sunni Ottomans. Eventually Persians came to view Shi'ism as central to Persian identity. Today the large majority of Iranians are Shi'ites of Persian or Azeri Turkish background.

Political and Military Power

The Safavids established a strong political system but never acquired the gunpowder-based military power of their Sunni Ottoman rivals. Safavid armies rode on horseback and viewed guns as both awkward and unmanly, leaving them vulnerable to the gunpowder weapons possessed by their Portuguese and Ottoman enemies. The Portuguese seized and held the strategic port of Hormuz **(hawr-MOOZ)**, on Persia's southeast coast, for decades, and in 1514 the Ottomans occupied Safavid lands in Armenia and Anatolia. The battle losses to the hated Ottomans demoralized Safavid military leaders, and Isma'il, unable to cope with defeat, became an alcoholic recluse in the palace. Although the Safavids soon regained their confidence, they did not attempt to expand their empire. They also adopted many of the governmental practices that had long been common in the region. Like the Ottomans, they acquired slave boys, primarily from Christian peoples such as the Armenians and Georgians, to be trained for administrative or military purposes, and over time they adapted to local Persian customs.

Safavid rule reached its peak under Shah (king) Abbas **(ah-BAHS)** I (r. 1587–1629), who consolidated his power by manipulating or executing his enemies, including Sufi leaders. His capital, Isfahan **(is-fah-HAHN)**, became a beautiful, tree-shaded city of some 1 million people, filled with mosques, public baths, parks, and a great bazaar that one visitor described as "the surprisingest piece of Greatness in Honor of Commerce that the world can boast of."[15] The shah reserved a few days each year, with men kept away, for the normally secluded women to visit the bazaars and promenade in the evening on Isfahan's spectacular main boulevard lined with gardens, pavilions, and a water channel. Shah Abbas enjoyed visiting the city's teahouses, where he listened to poets and storytellers and chatted with citizens. Many peasants worked on land owned by the king and received a share of the crop for their labors. Abbas was also tolerant in religion and admitted Christian missionaries. Abbas maintained good relations with European powers and imported English advisers to train his military forces and manufacture modern cannon and muskets. With these new weapons, he waged successful wars against the invading Ottomans and Uzbeks and recaptured Hormuz from the Portuguese. For their part, Europeans sought Persia as an ally against their mutual Ottoman enemy.

Decline and Collapse

By the eighteenth century the Safavid sultans had become weaker, the Shi'ite religious officials had become stronger, and the empire's economy had declined. Unable to control the clergy or trust their sons plotting for the throne, later Safavid rulers often turned to alcohol and concubines for comfort, while corruption grew rampant. In 1722 Afghans seized Isfahan and then repulsed Ottoman forces invading from the west. Isfahan, once one of the world's most beautiful cities, was nearly destroyed. In 1736 a new Persian leader, Nadir Shah (1688–1747), led a force that drove out the Afghan invaders and launched a vigorous new state. His armies marched into Ottoman lands and north India, plundering the major city, Delhi. But Nadir Shah proved ruthless against suspected foes, antagonizing many, and economic collapse exposed millions to famine. After ill-advised efforts to reconvert the Persians from Shi'a to Sunni Islam, Nadir Shah was assassinated in 1747, and his empire soon collapsed. In the decades to follow Persia was again divided into smaller states while Western pressure intensified.

Persian Economy, Society, Culture, and Thought

Commerce and the Armenians

Safavid Persia flourished for several centuries, remaining a major exporter of silk, a trade dominated by Armenian settlers who also operated the lucrative gold and silver crafts industries. Long-distance trade by land and sea continued, and Persian merchants remained active in the Indian Ocean trade and operated as far away as China, Southeast Asia, and East Africa. Foreign merchants flocked to Isfahan's great bazaar, where artisans produced fine carpets, textiles, metalwork, and ceramics. Armenians based in Persia also competed fiercely with Dutch, English,

Portuguese, and Indian merchants in parts of Eurasia. The Armenian network radiated outward from New Julfa **(JOOL-fa)**, an Armenian city near Isfahan run by a central council of merchants. Sharing a common culture and the Christian religion, Armenian merchants played a key role in the overland trade from India to Central Asia and the Middle East. The New Julfa network eventually stretched eastward to India, Burma, Java, and China; westward to Venice, Marseilles, Amsterdam, and London; and northward through Russia to northern Europe. English, Dutch, and French merchants visited Persian ports, and English and Russian merchants were also active in northern Persia, whetting the European appetite for more extensive trade. By cooperating with these traders, the Persians counteracted the Ottoman control of overland routes.

Gender Relations and Culture

Persian society was patriarchal, with women largely restricted to the home and expected to veil themselves when they went out of the household. Yet, Persian women often had more influence than was the case among Arabs. Royal women in harems raised royal sons and also tried to shape government policies. Some women became wealthy and owned land and businesses. Even in seclusion, women could use agents to help run their enterprises and manage property or money. Poor women had no such opportunities.

The Safavids patronized art and literature. Like some Muslim rulers in India, princes in Renaissance Europe, and Chinese emperors, the Safavid shahs were often themselves artists and poets. The major cities, especially Isfahan, became centers for writers, craftsmen, and artists who became famous for miniature paintings, a style that spread to the Ottoman and Mughal Empires. In 1525 the Safavid sultan commissioned an ambitious, decade-long project to produce an illustrated version of an old epic poem recounting Persian history. The completed version contained 258 paintings by many artists. Poetry also thrived, and well-known Persian poets were recruited by Muslim Indian courts, some of which used Persian as an official language. Finally, this was a golden age for crafting carpets, textiles, and ceramics. Carpet weaving became both an art form and a national industry, with government-run factories producing silks, brocades, velvets, and other fabrics.

Persian Shi'ism

Persian Shi'ism underwent some changes. The Safavids encouraged passion plays and annual religious processions commemorating the tragic death of the prophet Muhammad's grandson,

Persian Tiles As Isfahan flourished under Shah Abbas I, wealthy Persians decorated their homes and mosques with tiles featuring scenes, often gardens, painted by local artists. This tile painting shows a woman at leisure in her garden, holding a vase while her servant offers her fruit.

Husayn, in the Battle of Karbala in 680, the event that split the Islamic community. Hundreds of men fulfilled vows of faith by beating their bodies with chains while chanting religious dirges. Sufi influence gradually declined, while religious teachers emphasized their own authority over that of the Quran. The result was that Islamic leaders enjoyed greater power and wealth than was common elsewhere in the Islamic world. Even the shahs claimed to represent divine power, giving the state a theocratic cast. But tensions over religious power between the shahs and Shi'ite leaders continued to simmer.

Moroccan Resurgence and Expansion

While the Ottomans and Safavids dominated much of the Islamic world, the Moroccans on the far northwestern fringe of Africa forged one of the stronger Islamic states and conquered an empire. Moroccan society comprised Berbers, Arabs, and an influential Jewish community. The gradual displacement of Islamic rule in Iberia resulted in many Muslims and Jews migrating across the Strait of Gibraltar to Morocco, and the Jews invigorated commercial life. Morocco traded widely with North Africa, West Africa, and Europe, with ships from Venice and Genoa regularly visiting Moroccan ports to exchange metals, textiles, spices, hardware, and wine for leather, carpets, wool, grain, sugar, and African slaves.

The Sa'dians

Encounters with the Portuguese brought the Sa'dians to power. Portugal's cultivation of sugar on the Atlantic islands began undermining Moroccan sugar production, and the establishment of Portuguese forts along the coast threatened the Moroccan government. In response, Sufi movements organized tribal coalitions to resist the Portuguese. In 1554 the Sa'dians, a Moroccan family who claimed descent from the prophet Muhammad, conquered much of Morocco with the support of Sufi and tribal leaders, ruling Morocco until 1659. The greatest Sa'dian leader, Sultan al-Mansur (man-SOOR) (r. 1578–1603), recruited mercenary European and Turkish soldiers who knew how to use firearms and modern artillery. The Netherlands and England, both rivals of the Portuguese, sold Morocco ships, cannon, and gunpowder, allowing the Moroccans to capture the Portuguese ports along the Atlantic coast. In 1591 Moroccan forces seized the trading city of Timbuktu in Songhai, undermining that Sudanic state, and gained control of the trans-Saharan trade linking West and North Africa.

After the Sa'dian system fragmented, a new Moroccan dynasty, the Alawis (uh-LAH-wees), who also claimed descent from the prophet Muhammad, came to power in 1672. This dynasty still rules Morocco today. Sufi influence continued to expand, but powerful Sufi movements sometimes clashed with the royal governments. Alawi-ruled Morocco traded even more heavily with Europe, North Africa, and the Sudan.

Central Asia and Russian Expansion

Silk Road Cities

The most direct and long-lasting confrontations between Muslims and Europeans resulted from Russian imperial expansion into Central Asia and Ottoman territories. The Russians had long coveted the dry lands of Central Asia, where long-distance trade flourished. Central Asia contained large Muslim communities where Sufi masters often gained political power. In many of the cities, including Silk Road hubs such as Bukhara (boo-CAR-ruh) and Samarkand (SAM-ar-kand), social, political, and religious patterns closely resembled those of Persians and Arabs. As the remnants of the Mongol Empire broke up, Russia capitalized by extending its own power first into Siberia and then into the Black Sea region and Central Asia. Seeking resources and land for possible settlement by Russians, it acquired a great land-based territorial empire. The Russian eastward and southward expansion over huge distances was a saga comparable to the later westward expansion of the United States and Canada across North America, with a key role played by the **Cossacks** (KOS-aks), tough, hard-drinking adventurers and fierce soldiers from southern Russia who descended from Russians, Poles, and Lithuanians fleeing serfdom, slavery, or jail.

Russian Conquests

Cossacks Tough adventurers and soldiers from southern Russia who were descendants of Russians, Poles, and Lithuanians fleeing serfdom, slavery, or jail.

The expansion east across sparsely populated Siberia to the Pacific coast began in the 1500s and accelerated into the eighteenth century. In 1689 conflict with China forced the Russians to temporarily abandon the Amur (AH-moor) River Basin north of China (see Chapter 18), but they continued to add other Siberian territory, often after overcoming fierce local resistance. Siberia yielded the Russians furs, metals, and forest products. Seeking direct access to maritime trade routes, Russian leaders also coveted the Black Sea and the Straits of Bosporus, through which Russian ships could reach the warm Mediterranean. The southward thrust meant confronting the Tartars (TAHR-tuhrz), Muslim descendants of Mongols. In the 1400s and 1500s Tartars, Russians, Ottoman Turks, Poles, and Lithuanians fought for control of southern Russia. The Russians seized the Tartar state of

Kazan **(kuh-ZAN)**, slaughtering many residents in the capital and making possible domination of the northern Caspian Sea and direct trade between the Baltic lands and Persia through Russia.

Soon the Russians turned toward Muslim Central Asia, settled largely by Turkish peoples and often known as Turkestan. By the early 1700s the Russians had gained territory occupied by the Kazakhs **(kah-ZAHKS)**, a pastoral people, and by 1864 they controlled all the Kazakh lands to the eastern border with China. They then targeted the Silk Road cities but faced formidable opponents in the Uzbeks **(OOZ-beks)**, a people of mixed Turkish, Persian, and Mongol ancestry. Uzbek sultans promoted Sunni Islam, which made them enemies of the Shi'ite Safavids. When Safavid hostility closed Persia to Uzbek trade, the prosperity of the Silk Road cities declined. The Uzbeks and their neighbors earned smaller revenues while the sultans lost power to tribal chiefs. In the early 1700s the Persians gained control of some Uzbek territory and much of Afghanistan, and by the later 1800s an expanding Russia was able to conquer all of southern Turkestan.

SECTION SUMMARY

- Under the leadership of a charismatic boy named Isma'il, the Safavids, originally from Azerbaijan, conquered Persia and made the Persians convert from Sunni to Shi'a Islam.
- Under the Safavids, Persia was a major exporter of silk and remained a major conduit of trade, and its beautiful capital, built by Shah Abbas I, attracted merchants from many countries.
- The Safavid Empire patronized art and literature, and Safavid artists became famous for their miniature painting and their carpet weaving.
- Safavid religious leaders, increasingly relying on their own authority rather than that of the Quran, eventually became more influential as the power of Safavid rulers declined and then collapsed.
- Morocco, the far western outpost of Islam, absorbed many fleeing Iberian Muslims and grew into a powerful state that, under the Sa'dians, eventually defeated the Portuguese.
- With the aid of the Cossacks, Russia engaged in a large territorial expansion to create a land-based empire, an expansion that brought it into conflict with Siberian and Islamic Central Asian peoples, including the Uzbeks in Turkestan.

CHAPTER SUMMARY

The overseas expansion of Europe affected different regions in different ways but was only one of the forces at work in most societies. Various African societies, among them Songhai, Kanem-Bornu, the Hausa states, Benin, and Buganda, remained strong in the 1500s. Eventually, however, the Europeans' arrival set in motion forces that reshaped parts of Africa, especially societies along the western and eastern coasts, and many Africans became linked more closely to Europe and the Americas. The Portuguese undermined Kongo, Angola, and the East African city-states and established the first European colonies in sub-Saharan Africa, Angola, and Mozambique. With the trans-Atlantic slave trade, which arose in the sixteenth century, various Europeans procured slaves in West and Central Africa and shipped them across the Atlantic to meet the limitless demands of the American plantations. This trade benefited a few African societies but devastated others and created chronic conflict along the West African coast.

Several Islamic societies remained powerful, including the empires of the Ottomans, Safavids, and Morocco. The Ottomans, Sunni Turks, built an empire over much of western Asia, North Africa, and southeastern Europe, reuniting a large part of the Islamic world. At their zenith they had a powerful military, flourishing economy, and vibrant cultural life. The Safavids fostered a lively culture and economy in Persia and converted the Persians from Sunni to Shi'a Islam, increasing the rivalry with the Ottomans. Sa'dian Morocco repulsed the Portuguese and built a regional empire. But by the early 1700s these great Islamic states as well as Muslim societies in Central Asia experienced new challenges, some posed by Russian expansion into Muslim lands.

KEY TERMS

Darkest Africa
Boers
trekking
Middle Passage
racism
Atlantic System
imperialism
colonialism
janissaries
Cossacks

EBOOK AND WEBSITE RESOURCES

INTERACTIVE MAPS

Map 16.1 African States and Trade, 1500–1700
Map 16.2 Trans-Atlantic Slave Trade, 1526–1870
Map 16.3 The Ottoman and Safavid Empires, 1500–1750

LINKS

History and Cultures of Africa (http://www.columbia.edu/cu/lweb/indiv/africa/cuvl/cult.html). Provides valuable links to relevant websites on African history.

Internet African History Sourcebook (http://www.fordham.edu/halsall/africa/africasbook.html). This site contains useful information and documentary material.

Internet Islamic History Sourcebook (http://www.fordham.edu/halsall/islam/islamsbook.html). Useful links and source materials.

Middle East Studies Internet Resources (http://www.columbia.edu/cu/lweb/indiv/mideast/cuvlm/ancient/html). A useful collection of links.

The Trans-Atlantic Slave Trade (www.whc.neu.edu/afrintro.htm). A demographic simulation created at Northeastern University.

Plus flashcards, practice quizzes, and more. Go to: www.cengage.com/history/lockard/globalsocnet2e.

SUGGESTED READING

Balandier, Georges. *Daily Life in the Kingdom of the Kongo: From the Sixteenth to the Eighteenth Century.* New York: Meridian Books, 1968. A classic study of an important African kingdom.

Barendse, R. J. *The Arabian Seas: The Indian Ocean World of the Seventeenth Century.* Armonk, NY: M. E. Sharpe, 2002. A lengthy but wide-ranging scholarly study of the political economy connecting Europe, Africa, India, and the Middle East.

Barkey, Karen. *Empire of Difference: The Ottomans in Comparative Perspective.* New York: Cambridge University Press, 2008. Situates the Ottomans in world history.

Findley, Carter Vaughn. *The Turks in World History.* New York: Oxford University Press, 2005. A survey over many centuries.

Goldschmidt, Arthur, Jr., and Lawrence Davidson. *A Concise History of the Middle East*, 9th ed., revised and updated. Boulder, CO: Westview Press, 2009. A good introduction, especially to the Ottoman and Safavid Empires.

Khodarkovsky, Michael, *Russia's Steppe Frontier: The Making of a Colonial Empire, 1500–1800.* Bloomington: Indiana University Press, 2002. A scholarly study.

Klein, Herbert S. *The Atlantic Slave Trade.* New York: Cambridge University Press, 1999. An overview that incorporates social, economic, political, and cultural history.

Lindsay, Lisa A. *Captives as Commodities: The Transatlantic Slave Trade.* Upper Saddle River, N.J.: Pearson Prentice Hall, 2008. Concise overview with much on African context.

Northrup, David. *Africa's Discovery of Europe, 1450-1850.* New York: Oxford University Press, 2002. A sweeping survey of Africa's engagement with Europe and the varied responses.

Pearson, Michael N. *Port Cities and Intruders: The Swahili Coast, India, and Portugal in the Early Modern Era.* Baltimore: Johns Hopkins University Press, 1998. A scholarly study of the coast.

Robinson, Francis. *The Cultural Atlas of the Islamic World Since 1500.* Oxford: Stonehenge, 1992. A useful compilation of materials.

Savory, Roger. *Iran Under the Safavids.* Cambridge: Cambridge University Press, 1980. The standard survey.

Shillington, Kevin. *History of Africa,* rev. 2nd ed. New York: Palgrave Macmillan, 2005. A readable survey with much on this era.

Thornton, John. *Africa and Africans in the Formation of the Atlantic World, 1400–1800,* 2nd ed. Cambridge: Cambridge University Press, 1998. An excellent examination of Africa and the diaspora.

Wheatcroft, Andrew. *The Ottomans.* New York: Viking, 1993. A readable, lively discussion with particular attention to the elites.

CHAPTER

17

Americans, Europeans, Africans, and New Societies in the Americas, 1450–1750

CHAPTER OUTLINE

- Early American-European-Pacific Encounters
- The European Conquest of the Americas
- The Consequences of American Colonization
- New Economies, Slavery, and the Atlantic System

PROFILE
Caetana, Slave Rebel Against Patriarchy

WITNESS TO THE PAST
Spanish Men and Inca Women

Scala/Art Resource, NY

A Mestizo Family
The intermarriage of Europeans and Indians was common in Latin America, especially in Mexico. This Mexican painting, by the eighteenth-century artist Las Castas, shows a Spanish man, his Indian wife, and their mixed-descent, or *mestizo*, daughter.

Truly do we live on earth? Not forever on earth; only a little while here. Although it be jade, it will be broken. Although it is gold, it is crushed.

—AZTEC POEM ON THE MEANING OF LIFE, CA. 1500[1]

FOCUS QUESTIONS

1. How did encounters between Europe and the Americas increase in the 1500s?
2. How did Europeans conquer and begin settling the American societies?
3. What were the major consequences of European colonization of the Americas?
4. How were the new American economies and the trans-Atlantic slave trade connected?

In the sixteenth century Spanish colonists in Mexico trained an Aztec historian, Chimalpahin Cuahtlehuanitzin (chee-MAL-pin QUAT-al-WANT-zen), how to read and write in the Western alphabet. Using this alphabet but writing in his native Nahuatl (NAH-waht-l) language, he gave us a record of the Mexican world at the threshold of the changes instigated by European arrival. He wrote of Aztec victories over neighboring people and of how Aztec kings improved their great capital, Tenochtitlan (teh-noch-TIT-lan), by constructing an aqueduct to convey fresh water and rebuilding temples. But Cuahtlehuanitzin also told of ominous developments. He recorded that reports reached Tenochtitlan in 1519 of pale-skinned men in huge boats arriving on the eastern coast from the sea, where gods might come from. Aztec legends claimed that, centuries earlier, a Toltec king driven into exile had become a god, Quetzalcoatl (kate-zahl-CO-ah-tal) ("the plumed serpent"), who promised to return some day and seek revenge. These strange men seemed suspiciously godlike: they dressed in metal, had unfamiliar but lethal metal weapons, and rode on large animals as tall as the roof of a house—perhaps some kind of deer. The god's reappearance would threaten the Aztec social order. Cuahtlehuanitzin wrote that 1492 in the Gregorian calendar had been an unusually bad year, bringing an eclipse of the sun, volcanic eruptions, and widespread famine. The Aztec philosophy of life understood such occasional setbacks. But the Aztecs were not prepared for the Europeans who arrived in the Aztec lands or for a terrible and unknown disease that began killing off the people. And within two years, these men from afar, with horses, metal armor, and gunpowder weapons, had conquered the heart of the Aztec Empire, giving new meaning to the broken jade and crushed gold in the Aztec poem.

The first Europeans to arrive in the Americas claimed to have discovered a "new world," but it was actually an old one, long populated by a mosaic of peoples. The exploratory voyages of Christopher Columbus and the conquests of European adventurers destroyed or reshaped many long-existing societies, in reality *creating* a "new world." During the 1500s the Spanish and Portuguese conquered and colonized large areas of Latin America that contained millions of people. The English, French, and Dutch followed in North America and the Caribbean. As a result of these incursions, few regions experienced more changes than the Americas, and the two hemispheres became closely linked. European exploration also led to the first encounters between Europeans and the Pacific island societies. The resulting transitions affected both sides of the Atlantic and forged a complex global exchange of crops and animals, peoples and cultures. Soon European ships regularly crisscrossed the Atlantic, moving people, plants, animals, natural resources, and manufactured goods, while Eastern Hemisphere diseases set off a demographic disaster for Native Americans.

The societies that emerged from colonization reflected diverse influences from all over the Atlantic world. Europeans, Africans, and Native Americans in Latin America and the Caribbean formed mixed cultures that differed from those in English- and French-ruled North America. In some regions a plantation economy engaged enslaved Africans and their

Visit the website and eBook for additional study materials and interactive tools: www.cengage.com/history/lockard/globalsocnet2e

descendants as a work force. Millions of Africans transported across the Atlantic against their will now lived in conditions that were often unendurable, requiring them to develop strategies for survival.

EARLY AMERICAN-EUROPEAN-PACIFIC ENCOUNTERS

How did encounters between Europe and the Americas increase in the 1500s?

American peoples developed diverse ways of life long before the European voyages of exploration permanently connected the two hemispheres and posed a great challenge . Christopher Columbus began the historic change in 1492. In his wake various European nations first explored and then gradually conquered and settled the entire Western Hemisphere, drawing the Americas closer to Europe. The exploration of the Americas also spilled over into the Pacific Ocean.

American Societies in 1500

Aztecs and Incas

Before the arrival of Europeans, American peoples had developed distinctive institutions, customs, and survival strategies as they adapted to different environments. Those who lived by hunting, gathering, and fishing mostly inhabited the North American Great Plains, the Pacific Northwest coast, Alaska, northern Canada, and some tropical forest regions of Central and South America. Small-scale farmers concentrated in eastern North America, parts of the North American desert and Amazon Basin, and southeastern Brazil. The most complex societies flourished from intensive farming in Mesoamerica (Mexico and northern Central America) and the Andes region of western South America (see Chapter 12). By 1500 the Aztecs of central Mexico were the most powerful Mesoamerican society and the Incas **(IN-kuhz)**, centered in central Peru, controlled most of the Andes region. Like their predecessors, the Aztecs and Incas lived in cities, farmed, and worked metals and fibers for tools, decoration, and weapons.

The Aztecs, through military conquest and a well-organized government, completed their empire building in 1428 (see Chronology: American Societies and European Discoveries, 1400–1524). Aztec warfare relied on disciplined battle formations, shrewd tactics, and deadly weapons such as bows and arrows, stone-bladed broadswords, spears, and spear-throwers. But the Aztecs only loosely controlled their empire, and they faced military confrontations with rival societies, especially the Tlaxcalans **(tlax-CALL-uns)** on their eastern fringe. Cruel Aztec imperialism and extensive human sacrifice had created enemies, some of whom later cooperated with the Spanish to overthrow Aztec power.

The Incas completed the conquest of their empire in 1440. Even more impressive than the Aztecs in material accomplishments, they formed an empire larger than the Roman or Han Chinese Empires of the Classical Era, stretching nearly 2,500 miles north to south, much of it above 8,000 feet in altitude. The Inca state was the most dynamic and integrated in all the Americas, geared for conquest and paternalistic regimentation. In the later 1500s the writer Garcilaso de la Vega **(GAHR-suh-LAH-so duh luh VAY-guh)**, the son of a Spanish captain and an Inca princess, acknowledged the misery of people colonized by the Incas but also praised the highly productive farming system and generosity of Inca society, which "had attained perfection. No thoughtful man can fail to admire so noble a government."[2]

In part due to climate change, some societies had long passed their peak by 1500. The last Maya cities of southern Mexico and northern Central America had collapsed, but some 5 to 6 million Mayan-speaking people lived in villages, remnants of a once-vibrant society that was over 2,000 years old. In North America, Cahokia **(kuh-HOE-key-uh)**, the main city of the mound-building, trade-oriented Mississippian culture, had been deserted by 1250. By the 1400s the Anasazi **(ah-nah-SAH-zee)** and other societies of the southwestern desert had already abandoned their major settlements. However, flourishing societies besides the Aztecs and Incas remained, such as the Taino **(TIE-no)** in the Caribbean islands and the farming peoples along the Atlantic coasts of North America and Brazil.

CHRONOLOGY
American Societies and European Discoveries, 1400–1524

1428–1521 Aztec Empire

1440–1532 Inca Empire

1492 Landing in Bahamas by Columbus

1494 Treaty of Tordesillas

1497 John Cabot's landing in North America

1500 Portuguese claim of Brazil

1513 Balboa's sighting of Pacific Ocean

1519–1521 Ferdinand Magellan's circumnavigation of globe

1524 French claim of Canada

CHRONOLOGY

	Exploration	Latin America	North America
1400	**1492** First Columbian voyage		
1500	**1519–1521** Magellan's circumnavigation of the globe	**1521** Spanish conquest of Aztecs **1535** Spanish conquest of Incas	
1600			**1604** French settlement in Canada **1607** English settlement in Virginia **1627** Colony of New France
1700			**1759** English defeat of French in Quebec

Population

While the first European settlers wrongly considered the Americas to be largely empty land, some regions were densely populated. By 1492 the population of the Western Hemisphere probably numbered between 60 and 75 million people, and perhaps even over 100 million, the majority in Mesoamerica and the Andes region. But the coming of the Europeans was to change that. Because of many millennia of isolation from the Eastern Hemisphere, American peoples had no immunity to the diseases brought by Europeans and later African slaves. Hence, the coming of the West brought a terrible mortality. Native Americans also had no metal swords or firearms to resist Europeans.

Bridging the Atlantic and the Columbian Voyages

The stormy Atlantic Ocean was the major barrier between the hemispheres, but a few Europeans steadily overcame the challenge. The first known contact between Americans and Europeans did

Courtesy of John Carter Brown Library at Brown University

Arawak Women This woodcut, made in the sixteenth century, shows Arawak women on a Caribbean island preparing a meal of cornmeal tortillas and stew.

not have a long-lasting impact. In the tenth century some Norse Vikings sailed west from Iceland and established small farming settlements in several coastal valleys in southern Greenland. By around 1000 a few of these hardy Norse sighted eastern Canada and explored the coast. They built a small village on Newfoundland, a large island, where they harvested fish and cut timber. Largely as a result of conflicts with Native Americans, the Norse abandoned the Newfoundland settlement after only a few years, but the Greenland Norse apparently sent occasional trading and lumbering expeditions to eastern Canada. A few Norse artifacts have been found scattered across eastern Canada and the Arctic islands. The Greenland settlements also collapsed by 1450, possibly from factional disputes, conflicts with the native Inuit **(IN-yoo-it)** people, deforestation, and colder climates, which made farming impossible. Portuguese ships occasionally visited Iceland, where people knew of the Canada settlement, and this knowledge probably circulated in Europe.

The Norse

The Norse may not have been the only people to spot the North American coast before 1492. As cold weather brought poor harvests and reduced fish catches along Europe's Atlantic coast, some desperate fishermen ventured farther from home. Portuguese, Basque, Danish, English, Breton, and Moroccan fishermen worked the North Atlantic waters in search of cod, whales, and sardines. Some of them probably found the fish-rich Grand Banks off Newfoundland. A few scattered non-Norse European artifacts reported by early explorers in eastern North America suggest that some coastal people may have encountered Europeans, but any landings apparently went unreported in Europe. It was the quest for riches, national glory, and Christian converts that encouraged other Europeans to explore the Atlantic (see Chapter 15). While Portuguese expeditions concentrated on the African route to the East (see Chapters 16 and 18), others, led by Christopher Columbus, hoped to sail westward from Europe to Asia. Contrary to myth, many educated Europeans accepted that the earth was round and hence could be circumnavigated.

Columbus

The first explorer to brave the Atlantic in order to reach Asia, Christopher Columbus (see Chapter 15), came under the Spanish flag. Columbus (1451–1506), born in Genoa, had lived for many years in Lisbon, which had a large Genoese merchant community. His connections helped him marry Donha Felipa Moniz, the aristocratic daughter of the governor of Portuguese-settled Madeira. Columbus worked in Madeira and visited the Canary and Azores Islands farther out in the Atlantic. He also likely sailed to Iceland and down the West African coast on Portuguese ships, and he was probably familiar with both the Norse discoveries and the tales of Portuguese fishermen.

Soon Columbus, described by a contemporary as a man of great spirit and lofty thoughts, formed grander plans of exploration. Inspired by the writings of the thirteenth-century Italian adventurer Marco Polo, who traveled in Asia and sojourned in China, Columbus hoped to find the sea route to the silk- and spice-rich lands of China and Southeast Asia. A devout Christian, he claimed that he wanted to introduce Christianity to China. But his inaccurate maps vastly underestimated the size of the earth and the distance to Asia. Rebuffed in Portugal, Columbus eventually convinced the Spanish monarchs, King Ferdinand and Queen Isabella, to finance his exploration in hopes of establishing direct ties to Asia. Commanding ships far smaller than the great junks of the Chinese explorer Zheng He in the early 1400s, Columbus surveyed much of the Caribbean and some of the South American coast in four voyages over the next decade and believed that he had discovered outlying regions of Asia. When Ferdinand and Isabella realized he was wrong, they were at first disappointed.

Columbus and the Taino

On his first voyage in 1492, Columbus reached the Bahamas and encountered the Taino, an Arawak **(AR-uh-wahk)**-speaking people who lived on Caribbean islands (see Map 17.1). The Taino proved friendly, but they wore few clothes in the tropical heat, shocking the straight-laced Spanish. The Taino themselves may have desired to cultivate a potential ally. They had often resisted incursions by the Caribs **(KAR-ibs)**, a more warlike group that had originated in South America. The Taino smoked cigars, slept in hammocks, and possessed a little gold, and some lived in sizable towns built around Mesoamerican-style plazas. Combining fishing with cultivation of corn (maize) and manioc, they carried on interisland trade in large canoes that were capable of holding up to 150 people. Taino women did the farming and often served as community leaders, confounding the patriarchal Spanish. Columbus developed favorable views of the hospitable, patient, and peaceable Taino, seeing them as innocent children of nature: "They are uncovetous people [who] love their neighbors as themselves."[3] Later, when Columbus encountered Taino noncooperation or armed resistance to Spanish demands, he changed his views.

Columbus then moved on to the island he called Hispaniola **(HIS-puhn-YO-luh)**, today the home of Haiti and the Dominican Republic. Leaving a small colony of Spaniards there, Columbus began his return voyage to Europe by way of Cuba, which Columbus believed might be China.

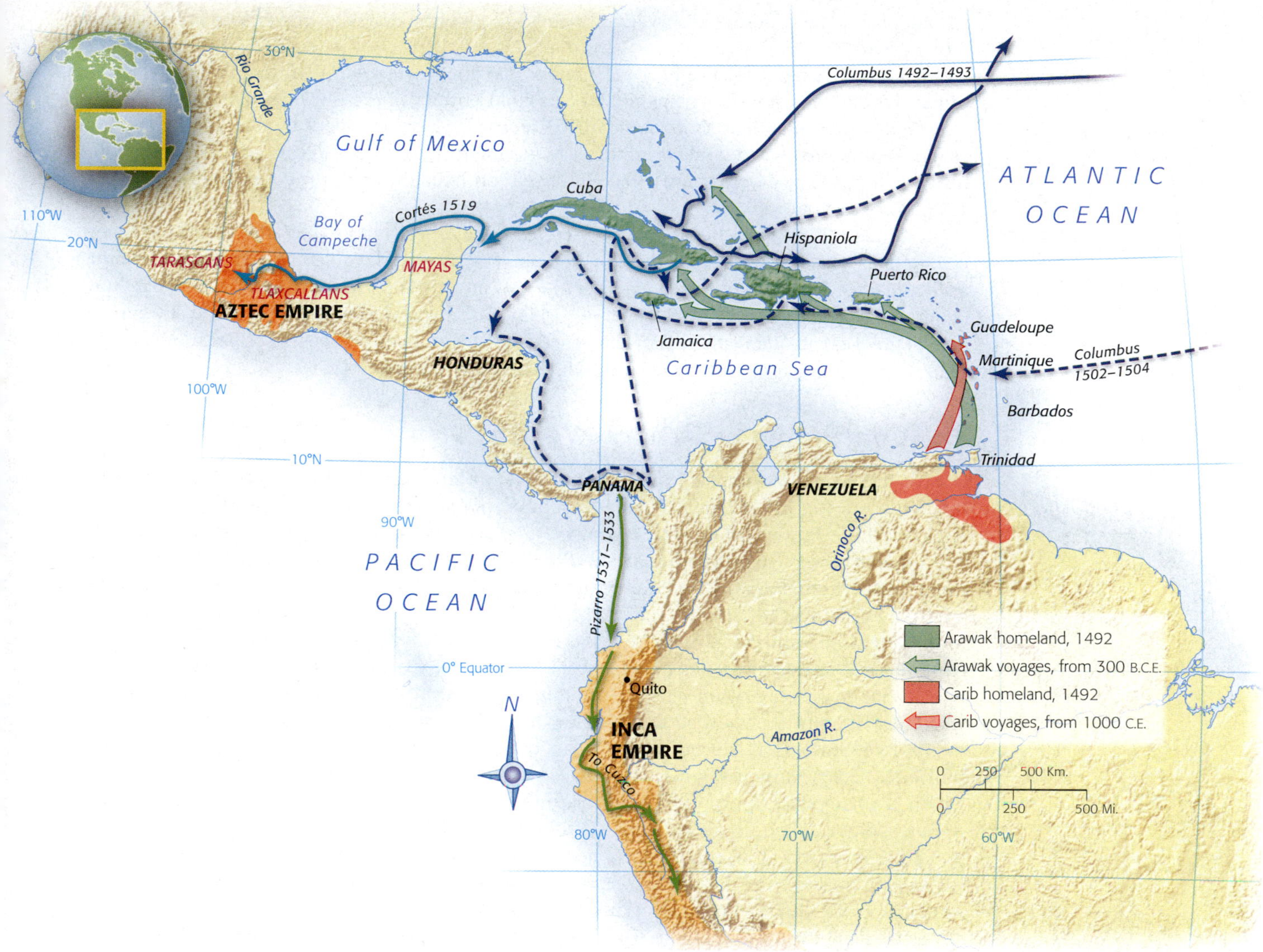

Map 17.1
The Americas and Early European Exploration
The several voyages across the Atlantic led by Columbus explored the Caribbean Basin and set the stage for Spanish conquest of many American societies, most notably of the Aztec and Inca Empires.

Interactive Map

There he dispatched a small party to search the interior for the Chinese ruler. They returned only with mysterious dried leaves called *tobacos*, which local people smoked. Later other Europeans would take tobacco back to Europe and start a smoking fad. Columbus and his crew sailed back to Spain with six Taino Indians to present at court so that he could seek funding for a second voyage, and he was feted as a hero and promoted to admiral.

Later Columbian Voyages

Although Columbus did not find China, he launched a new era of exploration. Spanish authorities quickly planned a second voyage and, to counteract a possible Portuguese challenge, persuaded the pope to issue the Treaty of Tordesillas **(tor-duh-SEE-yuhs)** in 1494 giving Spain the rights to most of the Americas while the Portuguese received Africa and Brazil. Both Iberian countries promised the pope that they would evangelize and colonize the "heathen" peoples they encountered. During his four voyages, Columbus explored much of the Caribbean region. He brought Spanish colonists with him in 1493 and established the first permanent European settlement in the Americas on Hispaniola. The colony's success depended on exploiting the local Taino through forced labor and then slavery. As Columbus wrote, "The Indians of this island are its riches, for it is they who dig and produce the bread and other food for the [Spanish] Christians and get the gold from the mines, and perform all the services and labor of men and of draft animals."[4] Columbus also explored the coasts of Cuba and Jamaica and sighted Puerto Rico. On his third voyage, in 1498, he found Trinidad and the Venezuelan coast. But his mismanagement as governor of

Hispaniola and his failure to discover vast riches brought him disgrace, and he was ordered home under arrest.

However, Queen Isabella allowed Columbus one final voyage to find a strait that might lead to India. This expedition in 1502 explored the coast of Central America. Though Columbus encountered a Maya trading raft he thought might be Chinese, he began to speak of the Caribbean islands as the "West Indies" as separate from the eagerly sought "East Indies" (India and Southeast Asia). After he and his crew were shipwrecked for a year on Jamaica, he returned to Spain and died in 1506, a broken man.

Eventually Europeans began referring to the Native Americans as "Indians," confusing American peoples with those of India. The label remains controversial, and some activists prefer terms such as *Native American* or *First Nations* to *Indian.* The term *America* derives from an Italian merchant, Amerigo Vespucci **(ves-POO-chee)** (1454–1512), who claimed to have made several voyages to the Western Hemisphere. His letters to powerful European princes described a "new world" that was soon known as "Amerigo's land," which became *America.*

The Continuing Search for Wealth

Other Expeditions

Others followed Columbus's example, and exploration soon became a multinational effort involving the English, French, Portuguese, and Spanish. By 1525 European expeditions had explored the Atlantic and Caribbean coasts from eastern Canada to South America's southern tip. Some explorers sought to enrich themselves and the European monarchs who sponsored them. Others hoped to gain God's favor through Christian missionary activity. These expeditions stimulated still further voyages and claims. Following an expedition led by another Genoese, John Cabot, the English claimed the Atlantic coast of North America in 1497, setting off a fruitless search for a northwest sea passage from the Atlantic Ocean through North America to the Pacific, but no practical route existed. In 1500 Portugal established its claim to Brazil, which fell within the longitudes awarded to it by the pope in the Treaty of Tordesillas, and began settlements. By 1511 the Spanish controlled Cuba, Puerto Rico, and Jamaica. In 1513 a Spanish expedition led by Vasco Nunez de Balboa **(bal-BOH-uh)** crossed Panama and sighted the Pacific Ocean, which he claimed for Spain. The French claimed eastern Canada in 1524 with a voyage led by an Italian captain, Giovanni da Verrazano **(VER-uh-ZAH-no)**.

Magellan and the Pacific Crossing

The only practical sea route to Asia via the Americas was finally discovered in 1520, in a Spanish expedition led by a Portuguese captain, Ferdinand Magellan **(muh-JELL-un)** (1480–1521). After falling out with the Portuguese king, he gained support from the Spanish monarch to explore a possible Pacific route to the Spice Islands via the Americas. His ships sailed down the Atlantic and rounded the southern tip of South America; they then survived a torturous trip through the stormy strait that today bears his name: the Strait of Magellan. Magellan continued on across the Pacific, a long, difficult journey during which no inhabited islands were spotted before Guam **(gwahm)**, with the crewmen living off rat meat and boiled leather for months. Eventually the expedition landed in the Philippine Islands, where Magellan was killed in a clash with local people. Magellan's ship and surviving crew continued on westward around Africa to Spain. Europeans now had a better idea of world geography and turned to the conquest and settlement of the Americas.

Some explorers, greedy for quick wealth, engaged in piracy and looting. The Spanish conqueror of Aztec Mexico, Hernán Cortés, admitted that the Spanish "suffer an affliction of the heart which can only be cured by gold."[5] As governor of Hispaniola, Columbus supported the killing of the Taino who refused to supply gold. The harsh exploitation generated Taino resistance attacks on the Spanish, prompting Columbus to order that Taino rebels and their families be enslaved and shipped to Spain in chains. Later the Spanish also raided other islands for slaves. Within thirty years all the Taino on Hispaniola, and many elsewhere, had been enslaved or killed, had died of disease or overwork, or had committed suicide because of their suffering. A Spanish priest lamented that many Caribbean islands were ruined "by men who wished to depopulate them and to kill the Indians who lived there. They were laid to waste."[6]

New Horizons and Exploration in the Pacific

Polynesian Societies

The continued search for a sea route to Asia led to European exploration of the Pacific Basin. The Pacific islanders, scattered across many island chains, developed diverse cultural and political traditions. Many Polynesians living on mountainous islands had varied food sources from farming and fishing that supported states led by kings or powerful chiefs. For instance, the eight inhabited Hawaiian Islands, divided into four rival chiefdoms, had a population of perhaps 200,000. Some 100,000 to 150,000 Maori **(MOW-ree)**, also organized into chiefdoms, lived on the two main New Zealand islands. By contrast, people living on small atolls only a few feet above sea level relied chiefly on resources from the sea.

Many island societies traded over vast distances. Warfare between rival islands was common, and some islanders also faced destruction of their fragile environments. The Polynesians who settled on remote Easter Island in the eastern Pacific deforested the small island over the centuries, leaving no wood for building new boats. Long isolated from other Polynesians, and with offshore fishing now impossible, they engaged in chronic civil war for control of scarce resources. Most Pacific islanders, like indigenous Americans, had not been in direct touch with Asia for millennia, making them vulnerable to Eurasian diseases later brought by Europeans.

Spain and Guam

Although Spanish ships annually sailed across the Pacific Ocean between the Philippines and Mexico beginning in 1565 (see Chapter 18), Europeans made little effort to colonize the vast Pacific region in this era. They did not locate some island chains, including Hawaii, until the later 1700s, when English settlement in Australia also began. Magellan's ships chanced on Guam, where they clashed with the local Chamorro **(chuh-MOR-oh)** people, the first of many unhappy encounters between Pacific islanders and European visitors. In the 1500s and 1600s Spanish, Portuguese, English, and Dutch expeditions discovered many islands, as well as Australia, but the islands, with few easily exploitable resources, looked unpromising compared to Asia and the Americas. Spain colonized Guam in 1663, founding a Catholic mission. But 90 percent of the Chamorros died over the next two decades, mostly from disease. In 1671 a demoralized Chamorro chief complained to a missionary that "the Spanish would have done better to remain in their own country. We have no need of their help to live happily. They treat us as gross barbarians."[7]

SECTION SUMMARY

- In 1500, many American peoples lived by hunting, gathering, and fishing, while others lived in the large, often repressive empires created by the Incas and the Aztecs.
- From 1000 on, Norse from Greenland intermittently settled in Newfoundland, and other Europeans may have crossed the Atlantic in search of fish long before Columbus discovered America.
- Beginning in 1492, Christopher Columbus explored the Caribbean and the South American coast under the impression that they were outlying areas of Asia, opening up exploration of the Americas.
- Columbus focused on the island of Hispaniola, where he enslaved the native Taino, and gradually gave up on the idea that he had discovered an Atlantic route to Asia, which was later discovered by Magellan.
- European nations divided up the Western Hemisphere according to the Treaty of Tordesillas, and as Europeans explored the Americas, some seeking riches and others converts, their diseases and their habit of enslaving or killing the local people decimated native populations.
- Pacific Island societies, which ranged from the highly stratified Hawaiians and the Maori of New Zealand to subsistence atoll inhabitants, were generally of less interest to Europeans, and most were not colonized until later.

THE EUROPEAN CONQUEST OF THE AMERICAS

How did Europeans conquer and begin settling the American societies?

European explorations and the search for riches led to colonization in the Americas. Native Americans lacked the guns to resist and were also divided into often-hostile societies. Thousands of Spanish adventurers roamed the Americas in the 1500s, many of them soldiers engaged in armed conquest, known as **conquistadors** **(kon-KEY-stuh-dorz)**. The major Spanish conquests came in Mexico and the Andes, while the Portuguese annexed Brazil. Later, the English, French, and Dutch obtained footholds in North America, the Caribbean, and the northeast coast of South America. By 1750 many American societies were under firm colonial control by various European powers.

conquistadors The leaders of Spanish soldiers engaged in armed conquest in the Americas.

The Fall of the Aztec and Inca Empires

Cortes and the Aztecs

Seeking to conquer the rich Aztec Empire, in 1519 Hernán Cortés **(kor-TEZ)** (1485–1547) and 550 soldiers from Spanish-controlled Cuba landed on Mexico's east coast, where they founded the settlement of Veracruz **(VER-uh-KROOZ)**. The Aztecs' understanding of war, which was to secure captives for sacrifice, not to kill opponents, along with their less-deadly weapons, put them at a disadvantage to the Spanish. First Cortés defeated and then forged an alliance with the Tlaxcalans, who had long resisted the Aztecs. Impressed by Spanish power, the Tlaxcalan nobles adopted Christianity, and their soldiers joined Cortés. After defeating several other peoples on the empire's perimeter, Cortés and his growing force marched west through the mountains into the Valley of Mexico, the heart of an Aztec Empire of 25 million. With its gleaming temples and canal network, the Aztec capital city, Tenochtitlan, astonished the Spanish. Cortés called it the world's most beautiful city. The Aztec leader, Moctezuma II **(mock-teh-ZOO-ma)**, warmly greeted them. Moctezuma (r. 1502–1520) may initially have identified Cortés with Quetzalcoatl and believed the Spaniards to be gods. Taking advantage of the confusion, the Spanish arrested Moctezuma. With sixty Spanish soldiers supplied with horses and guns, and many Indian allies, Cortés temporarily controlled the capital.

CHRONOLOGY
European Conquest and Settlement of the Americas, 1521–1650

1521 Spanish conquest of Aztec Empire

1532 First permanent Portuguese settlement in Brazil

1535 Spanish conquest of Inca Empire

1587 First English colony at Roanoke

1604 First French settlement in Acadia

1607 First permanent English settlement in Virginia

1608 French settlement at Quebec City

1624 Dutch settlement at New York

1627 Colony of New France

But soon violence erupted. Seizing gold and behaving arrogantly created hostility, and Aztec mobs killed or captured some Spaniards. Moctezuma, no longer a credible leader, was killed, either by enraged Aztecs or his Spanish captors. The Spanish had to fight their way out of the city, at great cost in life. Some fleeing Spaniards, loaded down with stolen Aztec gold, fell into the canals and drowned. Forced to return to the coast, Cortés made alliances with more Aztec enemies and recruited more Spanish soldiers from Cuba. His enlarged army, numbering around 1,000 Spaniards and 10,000 Indian allies, laid siege to Tenochtitlan, where Aztecs resisted fiercely while a smallpox epidemic, inadvertently spread by the Spanish, ravaged their population. In 1521 the Spanish occupied the city and captured the last emperor while revengeful Tlaxcalans massacred thousands of city residents (see Chronology: European Conquest and Settlement of the Americas, 1521–1650). The Spanish military force had horses and was armed with deadly muskets, cannon, steel swords, and crossbows. Aztec poets, who had written about their violent culture in melancholy verses, now turned to bemoaning their destruction, one lamenting that "broken spears lie in the roads; we have torn our hair in our grief. The houses are roofless now, and their walls are red with blood."[8]

Spanish Conquests

The Spanish now ruled the Aztec Empire, using the efficient Aztec administration to collect tribute from the former Aztec subjects. The conquest revealed the possibilities for wealth in the Americas. From their Mexico base, Spanish conquerors pushed south to seize Central America, Panama, and, a few years later, the northern part of South America. Others moved north as far as

Codex of Aztec Resistance Illustrations in a book published around 1580 revealed a local perspective on the Spanish conquest of the Aztec Empire. This illustration shows Aztec warriors besieging a Spanish force in Tenochtitlan and the difference in weapons technology.

New Mexico and northern California. By 1750 the Spanish empire included a third of the territory of what later would become the United States, stretching from San Francisco through Santa Fe and San Antonio all the way to St. Augustine in Florida.

Spain and the Incas

The Spanish also conquered the huge Inca Empire. The conquistador Francisco Pizarro (ca. 1476–1541) explored down the west coast of South America, and in 1531 his forces marched into the Andes Mountains to conquer the Incas. As in Mexico, smallpox had already wiped out millions of Incas, including much of the leadership. Hence, the empire was divided by civil war between two rivals for the throne. With only 160 Spaniards but artillery and horses, Pizarro captured Atahualpa **(AH-tuh-WAHL-puh)**, one of two rival claimants. The Spanish killed thousands of Incas, many unarmed. Holding the king for ransom, Pizarro demanded and received gold and silver, then executed Atahualpa. Ignoring pleas from Catholic priests to treat the Incas with more leniency, Pizarro retorted that he had not come to spread Christianity but to take the Incas' gold. The conquistadors seized the Inca capital, Cuzco **(KOOZ-ko)**, converting it into a Spanish settlement, and founded the city of Lima along the Pacific coast. Over the next few years they gained control over much of Peru, Ecuador, Bolivia, and Chile and brutally crushed Indian uprisings. Pizarro and his men placed themselves at the top of the efficient Inca administrative system. Pizarro was later murdered by supporters of a rival Spanish leader.

Colonization of Brazil and the Caribbean

Portugal and Brazil

The Portuguese established small trading posts along the Brazilian coast, an area blessed by regular rainfall, striking natural beauty, and a benign climate. Vespucci had called Brazil a paradise for possible settlement. The Portuguese began obtaining and shipping brazilwood, which made an excellent dye for European textiles. For some years, however, they remained more focused on exploiting the wealth of Africa and Asia than on exploiting the Americas. In 1532 the Portuguese founded a permanent colony along the southern Brazilian coast and began awarding land grants to private entrepreneurs. Facing not large settled societies but seminomadic food collectors and small farmers, they considered the Indians potential slaves who had to be compelled to work. Portuguese from the settlement at São Paulo **(sow PAU-low)**, and hence known as **Paulistas**, pushed deep into the interior raiding for slaves. The colonial government began to combat these activities, and expand its control in the interior, only in 1680.

Paulistas Portuguese slavers from the southern Brazilian settlement at São Paulo.

The Dutch also coveted Brazil as a location for tropical plantations. In the seventeenth century they gained control over much of northeastern Brazil, setting up plantations that grew huge quantities of sugar for the European market. But the Portuguese eventually expelled their rivals and soon took over the profitable northeast, building a city, Salvador da Bahia, at Bahia **(ba-HEE-a)**.

Although the Spanish colonized Cuba, Puerto Rico, and much of the Caribbean coast of Central and South America, they had to contend with the Dutch, English, and French, all of whom founded settlements in the Caribbean. Expelled from Brazil, the Dutch moved to several small Caribbean islands and established a colony, Dutch Guiana **(ghee-AHN-a)** (now Suriname), in northeastern South America. The French seized Haiti **(HAY-tee)**, the western half of Hispaniola, which became a center for plantations and a major source of wealth, as well as French Guiana and the islands of Guadeloupe **(GWAD-e-loop)** and Martinique **(mahr-ten-EEK)**. Meanwhile, the English made Jamaica, Barbados **(bahr-BAY-doz)**, British Guiana (now Guyana), and later Trinidad their colonial linchpins.

Piracy

In the Caribbean, piracy by Europeans became a major economic activity, much of it directed at Spanish settlements or at the Spanish galleons hauling rich cargoes of silver, sugar, or imported Asian goods to Europe. In 1670 the English pirate Sir Henry Morgan undertook a particularly brazen attack, leading a force of 1,400 men to sack Panama City, where warehouses stored wealth from Asia and Latin America. The Spanish burned the city rather than allow it to fall to the buccaneers. Some pirates, such as Morgan, John Hawkins, and Sir Francis Drake, became respected figures in England, celebrated for the wealth they captured from rival countries. In 1577 Drake (ca. 1540–1596) set sail from England on a secret mission for Queen Elizabeth I. This journey, which eventually took him around the entire world, was part of a strategy to outflank and plunder the Spanish empire. Drake's fleet sailed through the Strait of Magellan and up the Pacific coast to Mexico and San Francisco Bay, and perhaps as far north as the Columbia River, looting unsuspecting Spanish settlements and treasure-laden ships along the way. Drake then sailed across the Pacific to the Spice Islands and then around Africa to England. He was also instrumental in the English defeat of the Spanish armada sent against England in 1588, a battle that decisively shifted European political power. Drake's swashbuckling career illustrated how the world had changed after 1492.

The English, French, and Indians in North America

The English and French focused their colonizing efforts on North America's eastern seaboard at the expense of Native American farming societies, often matrilineal and sometimes matriarchal. Europeans described the people as healthy, enjoying a nutritious diet. However, the Indians soon disdained the Europeans as unintelligent, physically weak, and smelly. While Indians valued personal cleanliness, the British and French seldom bathed. Nonetheless, at first the Indians usually offered hospitality, traded with, and sought allies among the newcomers. Soon the newcomers had established settlements, wearing out their welcome.

English Settlements

Coveting the land and wanting to outflank rival countries, the English planted settlements up and down the Atlantic coast. The first English settlement, at Roanoke in Virginia in 1587, failed, but a successful English colony was established in 1607 at Jamestown in Virginia. To bolster their settlements, which struggled to survive in the unfamiliar land, families were brought from England to farm. In many cases only the generosity of Native Americans sharing their knowledge or supplying food enabled the colonists to survive. The Dutch settlement at New York, founded in 1624, also came under English control because the Dutch could not recruit enough settlers from Holland to offset English immigration.

French Canada

The French established their first settlement in Acadia (the Canadian province of Nova Scotia) in 1604, followed by outposts along the St. Lawrence River at Quebec **(ke-BEK)** City in 1608 and Montreal. These settlements became the basis for New France, a colony established in 1627 and covering much of eastern Canada. French Jesuit missionaries (known as "Black Robes") traveled widely, as far west as today's Illinois, in their campaign to convert Native Americans to Catholicism. Using

Map 17.2
The English and French in North America, ca. 1700
While the English colonized much of the Atlantic coast of North America, the French concentrated on what is today eastern Canada and the interior of North America, including the Great Lakes and the Mississippi and Ohio River Basins.

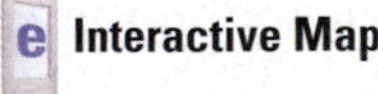 Interactive Map

canoes, French explorers and trappers, known as **voyageurs** **(voi-uh-ZHUR)**, mapped and established trading outposts throughout the Great Lakes and Mississippi River Basin. To counter English and Spanish expansion, in 1699 the French founded New Orleans, the base for French activities and territorial claims in Louisiana and the Mississippi Valley (see Map 17.2).

voyageurs French explorers and trappers in North America.

The English colonies north of Maryland developed largely as agricultural economies of free white settlers. Many English and French settlers also came to North America to exploit two valuable commodities, fish and fur. The seas off New England and eastern Canada teamed with cod, which became a major part of the European diet. As cod stocks off Europe greatly diminished, fishermen established bases along the North American coast. Later some English and French settlers moved inland in search of beavers, whose fur was popular in Europe for women's and men's coats and hats. Fur remained the major Canadian export until the rise of wheat farming in the nineteenth century.

Europeans and Indians

Both French and English settlement disrupted the Indian tribes (now known as "First Nations" in Canada). The French generally maintained better relations with local peoples than did the English, forging alliances with tribal leaders. Nonetheless, most Native Americans died from either disease or armed conflict, were pushed north and west, or eventually were forced onto reservations. In the early 1700s various tribes, among them the Tuscarora **(tus-kuh-ROR-uh)** and Delaware, were forced by English colonists to move west of the Appalachian Mountains, relocations foreshadowing worse treatment to come. Yet, some Indians proved formidable opponents. The Iroquois **(EAR-uh-coy)** Confederation, a coalition with a complex political structure, formed in the 1500s to unite five once-warring tribes living between Lake Erie and the Hudson River in upstate New York. These longhouse-dwelling tribes felt a shared ethnicity and a common enemy in the Huron of southern Ontario, who established a rival confederation. In the 1690s, it became a pantribal government with a council of chiefs and an oral constitution. Unanimity was needed for any decision. Some scholars credit Iroquois political ideas, such as a representative congress and freedom of speech, as an influence on the later constitution of the United States. The Iroquois were an effective military alliance, generally defeating rival tribes while holding off or outmaneuvering European arrivals for many years. Later the Iroquois supported the English in conflicts against the French, who were allied with their traditional rivals, the Huron and Algonquins **(al-GAHN-kwinz)**. But eventually the Iroquois, Huron, and Algonquins, like other Native Americans, were colonized.

SECTION SUMMARY

- The Spanish under Cortés were able to conquer the Aztecs because of their superior weaponry, their alliances with other American peoples, and a smallpox epidemic that ravaged the Aztecs.
- From their base in Mexico, the Spanish pushed north and south, and Pizarro conquered the Incas, the Spanish proceeding to rule much of South America with great cruelty, using the Inca administrative system.
- The Portuguese colonized Brazil and enslaved many of its Indians.
- The Spanish, Portuguese, Dutch, French, and English all struggled for colonial control of the Americas, with pirates from each country preying on other countries' ships.
- The English established colonies in what is now the eastern United States, while the French did so in eastern Canada, New Orleans, and the Mississippi River Basin.
- Many North American colonies thrived on fish and fur, while others practiced agriculture, and all eventually pushed native peoples off their lands.

The Consequences of American Colonization

What were the major consequences of European colonization of the Americas?

By the late sixteenth century the Spanish had explored and claimed an empire stretching from northern California and the Rocky Mountains to southern Chile and Argentina, forming local governments and founding cities. The English, French, and Dutch gained territory in the Caribbean basin and North America. Despite many similarities, the American colonies differed from each other. However, in all cases colonization came at the expense of Native Americans, who suffered especially from the colonists' diseases, faced Christian missionary activity, and experienced violent repression of their resistance and culture.

The Columbian Exchange

Columbian Exchange The transportation of diseases, animals, and plants between the hemispheres that resulted from European exploration and conquest.

The **Columbian Exchange** refers to the transfer of diseases, animals, and plants between hemispheres. Virulent microbes brought from the Eastern Hemisphere caused massive depopulation and suffering in the Americas. Although often healthier than Eastern Hemisphere peoples, the Native Americans had suffered from polio, hepatitis, some varieties of tuberculosis, many intestinal parasites, and syphilis. Yet, only syphilis, a sexually transmitted disease, made any serious impact when carried to Europe. It was more an unpleasant nuisance than a mass killer. The Native Americans had no immunity to diseases brought from the Eastern Hemisphere like measles, typhus, influenza, and especially smallpox, which reduced the Native American population by around 90 percent. Smallpox was widespread in Europe, and most ships from Europe carried the virus. No group remained untouched as the diseases spread havoc. A Maya writer reported that "great was the stench of the dead. The dogs and vultures devoured the bodies. We were born to die!"[9] Men died at higher rates than women, leaving widows to support households and young girls to grow up without the protection of fathers and male relatives.

Disease and Demography

American population numbers began recovering as the most resistant individuals survived and as immigrants from Europe and Africa, who had some immunity, married Native Americans, producing less-susceptible children. Eventually Native American populations grew. Today the descendants of the Maya, Incas, and other peoples are numerous in the highlands and forests of Central and South America.

Atlantic Connection

The Columbian Exchange affected both sides of the Atlantic. European immigrants imported their political systems, social institutions, religious beliefs, and urban forms to the Americas as well as Eurasian plants, such as wheat, orange trees, and grape vines, and domesticated animals such as horses, pigs, chickens, goats, and sheep. Native Americans found some imports useful. Horses brought by the Spanish enabled some tribes in the North American Great Plains to hunt buffalo more effectively. Many American products also moved eastward across the Atlantic, including drugs such as quinine and coca and crops such as tobacco, rubber, American cotton, potatoes, tomatoes, and maize (corn), increasing the abundance of food in Europe. South American chilies became a mainstay of South and Southeast Asian cooking, making the spicy foods even hotter. Finally, gold and silver from American mines had a major impact on the Eurasian economy.

The Spanish Empire and New Latin American Societies

The conquered Americans paid the costs of the conquest. In Spanish America and Portuguese Brazil, some Europeans made great fortunes by exploiting the people, land, minerals, animals, and plants. American gold and silver financed the Spanish empire. The Spanish and Portuguese seized all the riches they could locate, forced or persuaded the Indians to adopt Christianity, destroyed their religious centers, murdered Indian leaders who refused to cooperate, and discouraged or suppressed local languages in favor of Spanish or Portuguese. While many peoples resisted as best they could, these efforts were usually futile. The European settlers learned from the native people how to survive in these lands, and they also intermarried or had sexual relations with local women, producing people of mixed descent.

Colonial Governments and Societies

The Spanish appropriated American political structures but also introduced their own institutions and ways. Some Spanish settlements became large cities, such as Havana, Buenos Aires, Lima, and Mexico City, the last built on the site of Tenochtitlan. Spain divided its vast empire into two smaller divisions (viceroyalties): New Spain (governed from Mexico City) and Peru (governed from Lima), each headed by a viceroy who was always Spanish-born and held great power. In 1739 Colombia, Ecuador, Venezuela, and Panama became part of the Viceroyalty of New Granada, administered from Bogotá. Each large viceroyalty had to be subdivided into smaller political units, **audiencias**, judicial tribunals with administrative functions. The Spanish held all key political offices, from governors down to local mayors.

audiencias Judicial tribunals with administrative functions that served as subdivisions of viceroyalties in Spanish America.

The Spanish sometimes faced resistance. Maya Yucatán fell only in 1545 after a long, bitter military struggle. Sporadic Indian resistance in Peru continued for two centuries, and the last major rebellion, in 1780–1781, involved over 10,000 Inca descendants led by Tupac Amaru II **(TOO-pack ah-MAR-oo)**, named after an Inca emperor executed by the Spanish. In New Mexico resentment by some Pueblo peoples against the Spanish and the Catholic Church, which held little tolerance

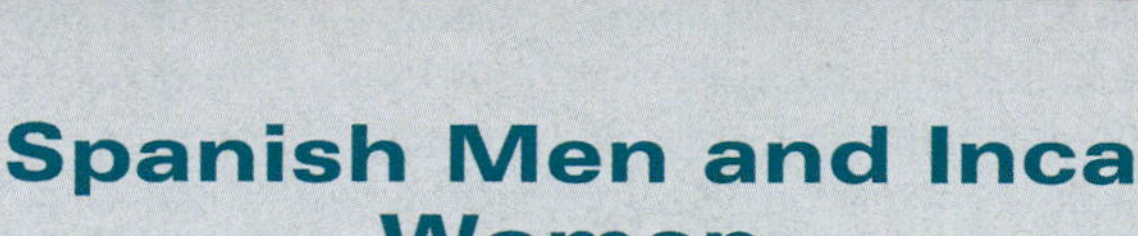

Spanish Men and Inca Women

In many parts of Latin America, Spaniards married or cohabitated with Native American women, fostering a mixed, or mestizo, population. In Peru some Spaniards deliberately sought to marry Inca princesses, perhaps to establish local connections in a factionalized colonial society. In this account from the early seventeenth century by the Peruvian historian Garcilaso de la Vega, himself the product of such a match, we learn of an Inca princess who was less than enthusiastic about her Spanish suitor, a captain from a modest background. Her ambivalent response has been viewed by some historians as representing a mixed attitude common in Latin America toward the imposition of European culture: contempt for many European customs and the brutal conquest but also admiration of some European values and Europeans' military power.

. . . a daughter of [Inca leader] Huaina Cápac and herself . . . the owner of the Indians [workers], was married to a very good soldier called Diego Hernández, a very worthy man, who was said in his youth to have been a tailor. . . . [Before the marriage] the princess learned this and refused the match, saying that it was unjust to wed the daughter of Huaina Cápac with a . . . tailor. Although the Bishop of Cuzco as well as . . . other personages who went to attend the ceremony of betrothal, begged and pleaded with her, it was all to no purpose. They then sent to fetch her brother. . . . When he came, he took his sister into a corner of the room and told her privately that it was impolitic for her to refuse the match, for by doing so she would render the whole of the [Inca] royal line odious in the eyes of the Spaniards, who would consider them mortal enemies and never accept their friendship again. She agreed, though reluctantly, to her brother's demands, and so appeared before the bishop, who wished to honor the betrothed by officiating at the ceremony.

When the bride was asked through an Indian interpreter if she consented to become the bride and spouse of the aforesaid, the interpreter said "did she want to be the man's wife?" for the Indian language had no verb for consent or for spouse, and he could therefore not have asked anything else.

The bride replied in her own tongue: . . . "Maybe I will, maybe I won't." Whereupon the ceremony continued. . . . They were still alive and living as man and wife when I left Cuzco.

Other marriages of this kind took place throughout the empire, and were arranged so as to give allocations of Indians to [Spanish] claimants and reward them with other people's properties. Many, however, were dissatisfied, some because their income was small and others because their wives were ugly; there is no perfect satisfaction in this world.

THINKING ABOUT THE READING

1. What does the reading tell us about social attitudes among Incas and Spaniards in colonial Peru?
2. What do we learn about the treatment of women?
3. How might the princess's attitude be seen as a form of resistance?

Source: Garcilaso de la Vega, *Royal Commentaries of the Incas and General History of Peru,* Part Two. Translated by Harold V. Livermore (Austin: University of Texas Press, 1966), pp. 1229–1230.

for Native American customs, led to several revolts. In 1680, a respected shaman led a force that pushed the Spanish out of the area. Although the Spanish returned and brutally crushed the Pueblo rebels, they now adopted a more cooperative policy.

Distinctive societies gradually emerged in Spanish America and Brazil, now called Latin America. The **creoles (KREE-awl)**, people of Iberian ancestry who were born in Latin America, were the key group. The mixing of peoples fostered **mestizos**, who blended of white and Indian ancestry, and **mulattos**, a mix of African with white or Indian ancestry or both (see Witness to the Past: Spanish Men and Inca Women). While most creoles enjoyed high status, the mixed groups held a social status between Europeans at the top and Indians and Africans at the bottom. The mixed groups eventually represented a sizable portion of the population in many colonies. Mexico and Peru developed large mestizo groups, while mulattos were especially prominent in Brazil and Cuba. People born in Europe (**peninsulares**), who monopolized wealth and power, viewed the creoles, mestizos, and mulattos with either condescension or contempt, considering them rustics. A Mexico-born scholar with Spanish parents complained that Europeans "think that not only the original Indian inhabitants but also those of us who were, by chance, born in [the Americas] either walk on two legs by divine dispensation or that they are hardly able to discover anything rational in us."[10]

creoles People of Iberian ancestry who were born in Latin America.

mestizos Groups in Latin America that blended white and Indian ancestry.

mulattos Groups in Latin America that blended African ancestry with white or Indian ancestry or both.

peninsulares Europe-born residents in Latin America who monopolized wealth and power.

Of the many writers and artists born and educated in Spanish America, perhaps the greatest was the creole Mexican nun Sor (Sister) Juana Inez de la Cruz (1651–1695), a renowned poet, playwright, philosopher, and scientist influenced by European Enlightenment thinkers. As a young woman she mastered Latin and Aztec while studying logic, history, mathematics, and literature. To pursue her intellectual interests, the well-born Sor Juana chose life in a convent over marriage, eventually collecting the largest private library in Mexico. Sor Juana struggled against patriarchal customs, arguing that "like men, do women not have a rational soul? Shall they not enjoy the privilege of the enlightenment of letters? Why is she not as able to receive as much learning and science?"[11]

Spanish American Cultures

Despite creative, broad-minded figures such as Sor Juana, Latin American culture remained more closely connected to the Catholic Church than to a western Europe reshaped by the Renaissance, Enlightenment, and Reformation. To screen out what they considered dangerous ideas, the church had to approve all printed matter entering the colonies. The church-controlled universities, set up to train creole men for careers as colonial officials and priests, taught largely in Latin and employed clerics as instructors. To root out heresy in the colonies, Spanish officials also brought the ruthless Holy Inquisition, which tried suspected secret Jewish or Protestant sympathizers. *Conversos*, Jews forced to convert to Christianity in Spain, were subject to investigation, imprisonment, and sometimes gruesome executions.

Latin Americans exhibited dramatic contradictions: while the elite looked toward Europe for inspiration, the majority wanted to preserve the languages, beliefs, and ways of life from pre-Columbian times. Latin American writers examined the conflicted relationship between Spain and Latin America, describing a mix of good and evil or sun and shadow, as in the bullfight ring. Women faced the greatest dilemmas, often both accepting and repudiating patriarchal Spanish rule. They now enjoyed new food sources, such as chickens and pigs, but they clung to their native dress and pride and had to be flexible and adaptive to survive. Since men had higher mortality rates, women were often heads of households. Some Indian and mestizo women engaged in commerce, worked in domestic service, tended animals, or made clothing, including carding, spinning, and weaving wool from sheep.

Christian Missions, the Black Legend, and Native Americans

Spreading Catholicism

Both the Spanish and Portuguese pledged to spread Catholicism. Although they enjoyed only mixed success, missionaries gave Indians a superficial Christianity, changing local gods into Christian saints. They were frequently militant in their faith and often had a profound influence, sometimes altering people's settlement and even economic patterns. The Spanish Franciscan missionary Fray Junipero Serra (1713–1784), known as the "walking friar" because he traveled by foot, established mission stations along the coast of California from San Diego to San Francisco. He converted many Indians while also encouraging and sometimes requiring seminomadic hunters and gatherers, like the Chumash **(CHOO-mash)** of the Santa Barbara area, to live in towns and cultivate European crops.

To extend their control, the Spanish built forts near mission stations. The missionaries often faced resistance. In the Inca territories, many women openly rejected Catholicism. According to a Spanish observer: "They do not confess, attend catechism classes, or go to mass. Returning to their ancient customs and idolatry, they do not want to serve God or the [Spanish] crown."[12] Native Americans could also put their stamp on Christianity. Although some historians believe the story was introduced decades later to promote conversions, an Aztec peasant in 1531 supposedly saw a vision of the Virgin Mary at a shrine to the Aztec mother goddess. Officials built a church there to honor "Our Lady of Guadalupe," and the image of the virgin as an Indian woman became a symbol of Mexican nationalism.

Repression and Exploitation

Missionary activity sometimes proved disastrous. In Yucatán, a few missionaries gained control over many Maya people. Although sometimes admiring Maya culture, they were intolerant of non-Christian beliefs and destroyed Maya books and religious symbols. In 1562 priests who suspected that converts still secretly worshiped Maya gods launched a terrible inquisition, torturing 4,500 Indians, 158 of whom died. One witness reported that "the friars ordered great stones attached to their feet, and so they were left to hang, and if they did not admit to [worshiping] idols, they were flogged as they hung there and had burning wax splashed on their bodies."[13] The church punished the priest in charge but later made him a bishop. The Spanish also zealously persecuted homosexuality, which was tolerated by many Native American peoples, including the Maya and Caribs. The

Courtesy of John Carter Brown Library at Brown University

Indian Slavery Spain's enemies publicized cases of Spanish brutality toward Native Americans. This sixteenth-century engraving, by the Dutch observer Theodore de Bry, portrays the misery of Native Americans subjected to slavery and forced labor.

Spanish brought homosexuals before the Inquisition or sometimes executed them without trial, and they used the charge of widespread homosexuality to treat Native Americans like animals.

Spanish actions led to the **Black Legend**, the Spanish reputation for brutality toward Native Americans, including the repression of native religions, execution of rebels, and forced labor. Although the Black Legend exaggerated Spanish atrocities, Spain's enemies in Europe eagerly passed along such stories. Actually, disease killed far more Indians than murder and brutality. Furthermore, other Europeans could be just as intolerant and forceful in their dealings with local peoples. While many Spaniards saw the Native Americans as savages needing to be Christianized and ruled, some Catholic clerics advocated humane policies and sought to protect them. The Dominican friar Bartolomé de Las Casas (lahs KAH-suhs) (1474–1566), although an ardent missionary, proclaimed that Indians were humans like the Spanish and bemoaned the destruction they experienced. The Spanish lawyer Francisco de Vitoria questioned the whole project of Western colonization, suggesting that policies should always promote Indian welfare and interests and not only Spanish profits. In 1637 the Jesuits in Uruguay (YOOR-uh-gwye) even armed the Indians to help protect them against slave raiders.

Black Legend The Spanish reputation for brutality toward Native Americans, including the repression of native religions, execution of rebels, and forced labor.

Primary Source: A Dominican Voice in the Wilderness: Preaching Against Tyranny in Hispaniola A Dominican friar, and former landholder, expresses his outrage at the injustices committed against the native people of "New Spain."

But the battle over how to treat Indians was won by intolerant people reflecting a Europe engulfed in Catholic-Protestant conflict (see Chapter 15). Most Spaniards considered the Indians justly conquered and favored exploitation of people they considered born for servitude. A Spanish scholar expressed a common contempt for Indians as "naturally lazy and vicious, in general a lying, shiftless people [whose] chief desire is to eat, drink, worship heathen idols, and commit bestial obscenities."[14] These harsh attitudes affected women even more than men. In 1625, an Indian writer in Peru charged that white men exploited both women's labor and their bodies: "In the mines, Indian women are made into concubines, daughters of Indian men are kidnapped. In the villages, [Spanish men convert] single women, married women, all women into prostitutes. Parish priests have concubines. There is no one who takes these women's side."[15] This contempt, along with economic needs, led to the drafting of Indians to work in mines or farms. Although eventually the church treated Indians indulgently and paternalistically, as children needing guidance, the Indian quality of life—health, morale, leisure, and joy—mostly declined, generating alcoholism and despair. Today many Latin American Indians remain dominated politically, socially, and economically by creoles and mestizos.

English and French Colonies in North America

Immigration and Diversity

The English and French expanded and competed in North America (see Map 17.2). By the mid-1700s the territory from New England to Georgia was divided into thirteen English colonies, each administered by an appointed English governor. European immigration increased, especially from England but also from Scotland, Ireland, Germany, and the Netherlands. Some from poor or criminal backgrounds arrived as indentured laborers to work on farms or in businesses, workshops, or households to repay their passage. By 1730 the thirteen colonies contained around 500,000 whites. African slaves or their descendants, some 20 percent of the colonial population, were concentrated in the South but were also found in northern colonies.

Intellectual and religious diversity characterized English colonial life. Educated colonists influenced by English and French Enlightenment thinkers espoused democratic ideals and reason, and many English immigrants were Protestant dissenters seeking freedom of religion. The Puritans influenced the colonial culture, implanting Calvinist attitudes about the value of work and commerce. In 1695 Cotton Mather, a famed Puritan preacher, stated the Puritan case vigorously: "How can you ordinarily enjoy any rest at Night, if you have not been well at work in the Day? Let your Business ingross the most of your time."[16] Puritans also maintained patriarchal attitudes. One, John Winthrop, the first governor of the Massachusetts colony, argued that women lost their reason if they gave themselves wholly to reading and writing instead of attending to household affairs. Yet, colonial life also fostered change in gender roles. Although deference to men remained deeply ingrained, and a husband had the legal right to his wife's property and wages and the couple's children, given the labor shortage, many women worked in the fields alongside men, and a few even managed farms or plantations.

English-French Conflict

The English and French clashed for decades over control of Acadia (Nova Scotia) and New France in eastern Canada. This conflict resulted in part from a larger, globe-spanning English-French competition for influence in Europe, the Caribbean, and southern Asia and in part over access to sources of fish and fur. Eventually England triumphed over France in North America. In

Johnson Hall This grand house, built in the mid-eighteenth century by American fur trader William Johnson in what is now upstate New York, became a meeting place for Native American tribes, such as the Iroquois, allied with the British against the French.

1713 the English took control of Acadia, and in 1755 they deported much of the Acadian French population to the French colony of Louisiana, forming the basis for the French-speaking Cajun **(KAY-juhn)** community there (see Chronology: The Americas, 1650–1760). In 1759 English forces defeated the French near Quebec City and then captured Montreal, acquiring New France. French cultural influence was eventually confined chiefly to the area now known as Quebec. In 1774 the English, recognizing the tenacity of French culture, allowed the French in Quebec to hold public office, speak their language, and freely practice their religion.

The French Canadians became a growing presence in Quebec. French immigration to Canada largely ended, but the French Canadian population increased dramatically, today totaling more than 7 million, one-fourth of Canada's population. Until the mid-1900s the influential Catholic Church in Quebec encouraged early marriage and large families. The French Canadians always felt threatened by the dominant English, perhaps fostering cultural conservatism. Both the French and the English Canadians settled down to farming.

CHRONOLOGY
The Americas, 1650–1760

ca. 1605–1694 Palmares maroon state

1713 English control of Acadia

1739 Stono Rebellion in South Carolina

1755 Deportation of French Acadians to Louisiana

1759 English defeat of French in Quebec

Europeans and Indians

The relations between European settlers and Indian societies reflected both conflict and alliance. Indians resented and often fought the foreigners' occupation of their land, and the English and French had to deal carefully with the better organized tribes. But some Indians were inevitably drawn into the often-violent English-French competition for global influence. The Huron allied with the French; the Iroquois allied with the English; and some tribes opposed both. Because European traders acquired fur from Indians, white-Indian alliances largely reflected trading partnerships. As French fur traders ventured into the interior and set up trading posts, they tended to intermarry with Indians, producing the **Metis (may-TEES)**, people of mixed French and Indian descent. Today Metis communities are scattered around Canada. In contrast, English colonists tended to immigrate as families, reducing the rates of intermarriage with Indians.

Metis People in Canada of mixed French and Indian descent.

The encounter with Europeans reshaped Indian life and made living much more difficult. An English observer, Robert Beverley, noted that "they have on several accounts to lament the arrival of the English [who] have taken away great part of their country, and consequently made everything less plenty among them."[17] Indians mistrusted Europeans, who often broke treaties, and were often repelled by European culture, but they also desired European goods, especially metalwork and guns. A few tribes, like the Cherokee in the Carolinas and Georgia, actively adopted European influences, such as new farming methods, although this change often disadvantaged women, who once did the farming and hence enjoyed high status. Some Indians responded creatively. The Cherokee still honor Sequoyah, who created a writing system for his peoples' language in the early 1800s. Christian missionaries had less success in North America than in Latin America. Most success came among settled farmers. Among matrilineal societies like the Huron and Cherokee, missionaries undermined women's power and freedom because patriarchal Christian marriage practices emphasized the obedience of wives to husbands. Spousal abuse often increased as men unable to support their families turned on their wives.

SECTION SUMMARY

- As a result of American colonization, huge numbers of Native Americans died from smallpox, and many animal and plant species were exchanged between Europe and the Americas in the Columbian Exchange.
- The Spanish exploited the resources of their American colonies and ruled them harshly, inspiring several rebellions and fostering the "Black Legend."
- In the Spanish American colonies, a recognizable culture developed, more rigidly Catholic than in Europe and featuring American-born Spanish (creoles) and mixed-race peoples (mestizos and mulattos).
- In their attempts to convert Native Americans to Catholicism, the Spanish and Portuguese often trampled on Native American customs and beliefs, and they crushed perceived resistance harshly. As English colonists solidified their control of the East Coast and eventually took over all of French Canada, Indian tribes were often caught between the warring powers.

New Economies, Slavery, and the Atlantic System

How were the new American economies and the trans-Atlantic slave trade connected?

Different economic and social systems emerged in Latin America and northern English America. In much of Latin America, the Caribbean, and the southern colonies of North America, European rule produced an inequitable economic relationship between the colonies and their colonizing countries as these colonies all produced natural resources for the growing world economy. The plantations and mines depended chiefly on slave labor imported from Africa (see Chapter 16). In contrast, the northern English colonies in North America emphasized commerce and family farming and gradually moved toward economic independence. The trans-Atlantic slave trade and the emergence of the American plantation zone forcibly linked West Africa, the Americas, and Europe into a larger Atlantic System, a triangular trade that moved enslaved Africans to the Americas, where they became largely plantation labor growing sugar, cotton, and tobacco for shipment to Europe. European merchants then used the lucrative proceeds from slave labor to purchase guns, rum, textiles, and other commodities for shipment to Africa to obtain more enslaved labor. The profits from the slave trade and the enterprises it served also influenced the development of European economies.

Economic Change in Latin America

Mining and Ranching

The Latin American colonies were largely geared to export natural resources (see Map 17.3). In the Andes and Mexico the Spanish developed rich gold and silver mines. The silver mines in Bolivia became some of the richest. Coerced Indian miners in the main Andean mining center, Potosi (po-tuh-SEE), found life difficult, "working twelve hours a day, going down to where night is perpetual, the air thick and ill smelling. When they arrive at the top out of breath, [they] find a mineowner who scolds them because they did not bring enough load."[18] By the late 1600s Mexican mines produced over half of the hemisphere's mineral wealth, and gold mines in Brazil, mostly worked by African slaves, supplied over half of the world's gold. While benefiting very few Native Americans, mining enriched merchants, filled royal treasuries, and linked the colonies to the world economy. Much of the exported gold ultimately passed through Spain and Portugal to northern Europe as payment for manufactured goods, enriching Flanders, Holland, and England. American silver also bought Europeans access to Asian markets. A large portion of American silver was shipped to China to purchase desirable Chinese products such as silk and tea.

Cattle and horses brought from Europe enabled ranching to become a major economic activity, especially in the vast grasslands of Argentina, Brazil, and Venezuela. As Indians perished, good land passed into European hands. Vast cattle ranches, known in Spanish America as **haciendas**, were often over 1 million acres in size. Ranching remained a key economic activity in several countries, providing great incomes for monarchs, merchants, and investors.

haciendas Vast ranches in Spanish America.

To ensure Indian labor, the Spanish imposed the **encomienda** ("entrustment"), the Crown's grant to a colonial Spaniard of a certain number of Indians from whom he extracted tribute. In exchange for providing labor for mines or ranches, the Indians were instructed in Christianity by clergy. While in theory protecting Indians, this system fostered many abuses. A Spanish Franciscan condemned the cruel mine owners who pursued profit at the expense of encomienda workers: "The Indian slaves who up to the present have died in these [gold] mines cannot be counted. Gold, in this land, was adored as a god."[19] Because of the abuses, Spanish monarchs sometimes abandoned the encomienda but relented in the face of revolt by Spanish colonists. By the mid-1500s the institution had been reformed, but it still allowed temporary conscription of Indian labor until the later 1600s.

encomienda ("entrustment") The Crown's grant to a colonial Spaniard in Latin America of a certain number of Indians from whom he extracted tribute.

Economic Stagnation

Despite early Spanish and Portuguese successes, by the 1800s an increasingly stagnant Latin America eventually fell behind a vibrant North America in economic development. Initially, Latin America had many advantages British North America lacked: rich mines, abundant fertile land, and a much larger population. By the 1700s Latin Americans, unlike North Americans, had built a half dozen large cities and several fine universities, and they produced great wealth, although it was inequitably distributed. But the rise of single-product, slave-based plantations, which, like mining or ranching, fostered specialized economic production for a world market, thwarted development in Latin America and the Caribbean as well as the southern English colonies. The plantations were a **monoculture**, an economy dependent on the production and export of one chief commodity.

monoculture An economy dependent on the production and export of one chief commodity.

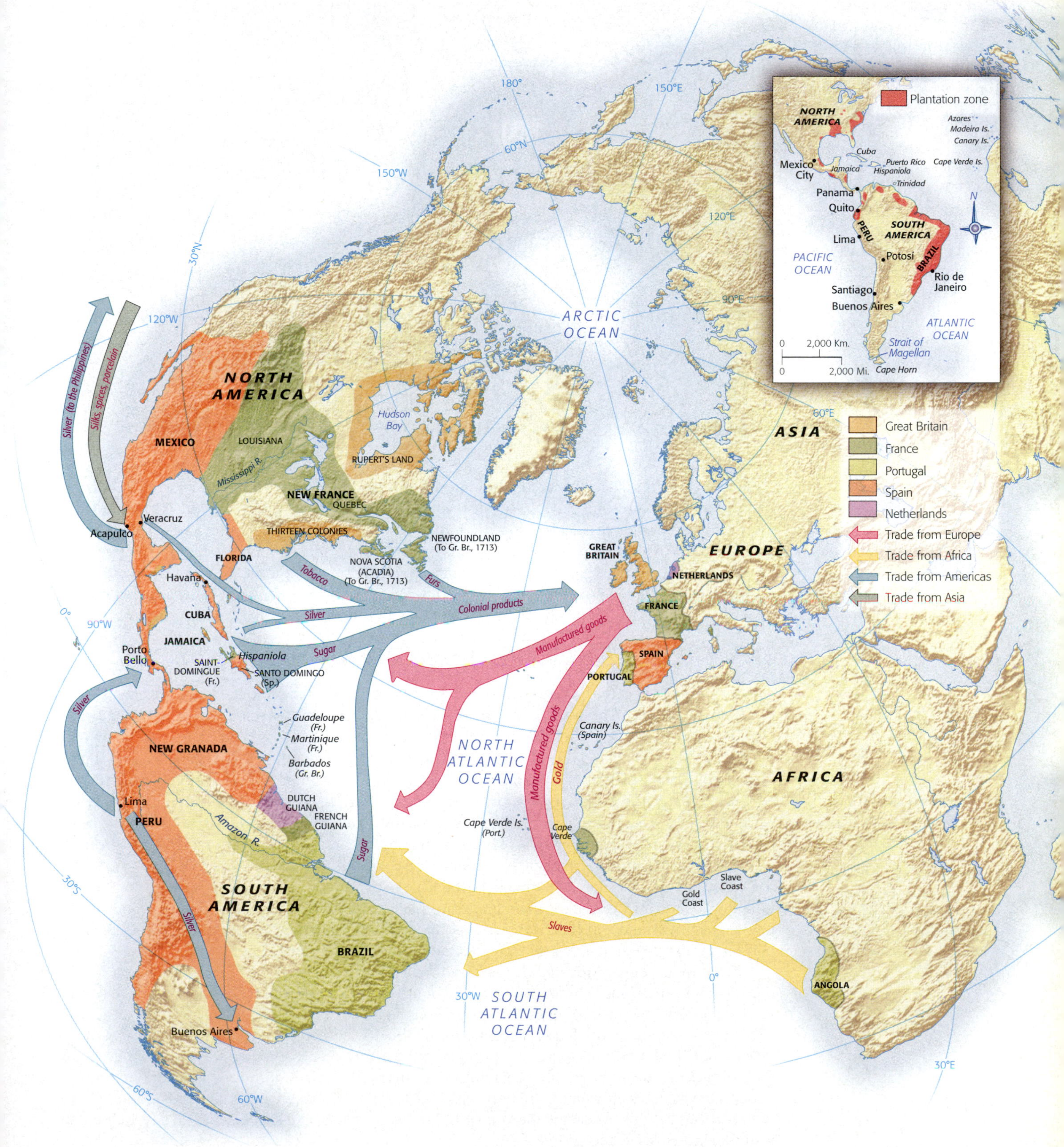

Map 17.3
The Atlantic Economy

The Atlantic economy was based on a triangular trade in which African slaves were shipped to the Americas to produce raw materials that were chiefly exported to Europe, where they were turned into manufactured goods and exported to Africa and the Americas.

Caribbean Sugar Mill On a West Indian plantation this windmill crushed sugar cane into juice, which was boiled down in the smoking building on the right to produce sugar granules. Such plantations were the dominant economic activity on the Caribbean islands and in parts of South America, Central America, and southeastern North America.

From William Clark, *Ten Views in the Islands of Antigua*, 1823. British Library

Usually based on slave or coerced labor, monocultures depended completely on the colonizing country to buy the resource, such as sugar, silver, or beef, they produced in return for supplying food and other necessities. Plantation, mining, or ranching-based economies cannot generate overall **development**, growth in a variety of economic areas that benefits the majority of people. Monoculture economies generally benefit only a minority, and they prosper or decline depending on world prices for their export commodity. With few alternative forms of employment or ways to generate wealth, plantation and mining societies created significant poverty.

development Growth in a variety of economic areas that benefits the majority of people; the opposite of monoculture.

The Plantation Zone and African Slavery

Plantation Economies and Sugar

Plantations soon became the key economic institution in much of the tropical and subtropical areas of the South American mainland, the Caribbean islands, and southeastern North America. By the later 1600s, when most of the richest silver mines in the Andes and Mexico had been exhausted, plantations flourished in many regions, growing sugar, coffee, cotton, bananas, and sisal (a tough fiber used to make rope) for shipment to North America and Europe. The transition to a plantation economy created the **plantation zone**, a group of societies with economies relying on enslaved African labor and stretching from Virginia and Kentucky southward through the West Indies and Central America to central Brazil and Peru. In the Caribbean islands, sugar planting transformed whole economies. Initially European settlers set up self-sufficient farms that grew diverse crops in Caribbean islands such as Jamaica, Barbados, Hispaniola, Cuba, and Puerto Rico. But in the mid-1600s the growing of sugar, much more profitable than the other crops, expanded. Since sugar needed plentiful land and cheap labor, slaves replaced white farmers. Some white farmers became planters, some migrated to North America, and the more desperate became pirates.

plantation zone A group of societies with economies that relied on enslaved African labor; the plantation zone stretched from Virginia and Kentucky southward through the West Indies and the east coast of Central America to central Brazil and the Pacific coast of Colombia.

The growing sugar industry also fostered transitions in Europe. Europeans, especially Venetians, had imported sugar from the Arabs and Southeast Asia, but supplies were limited. To satisfy increasing demand, the Portuguese began growing sugar on small Atlantic islands such as Madeira. The desire to acquire more land for sugar boosted the drive for empire. With more American plantations and cheaper supplies, sugar was transformed from a rare luxury to a staple of the European diet, sweetening bland foods and providing more calories for the undernourished working classes. Foods such as jam sandwiches and beverages like tea that contained sugar allowed people to take their lunches to work, replacing the large midday family meals, and stay at work all day, helping to foster an industrial economy in Britain.

Sugar and Slavery

The plantations of the Caribbean islands and some coastal districts in Brazil, the Guianas, Venezuela, Colombia, and Mexico were essentially sugar "factories," relying on mass production of raw sugar by enslaved workers. A seventeenth-century saying noted that "without sugar, no Brazil; without slaves, no sugar; without Angola, no slaves."[20] The southern English colonies of North America differed only in that the crops were more varied, including cotton, rice, and tobacco as well as sugar. The populations of all the plantation-based societies were composed chiefly of enslaved people of African ancestry. Slavery dominated southeastern North America, the Caribbean basin, and coastal South America.

Trans-Atlantic Slave Trade

The high mortality rates of enslaved labor required the constant importation of new slaves from Africa. Between 1500 and 1850 some 9 to 12 million Africans were brought into the Americas, especially to the plantation zone, as slaves. Most went to the Caribbean islands and to Brazil, which today has the largest population of African descent in the Americas. However, African slaves were also used outside the plantation zone, in northern English colonies such as New York, New Jersey, and Massachusetts and as far south as Argentina, though on a much smaller scale. By 1850 Brazil received some 40 percent of all enslaved Africans, followed by the British Caribbean (21 percent), French Caribbean (15 percent), Spanish America (15 percent), and British North America (5 percent). About one-third of all people of African descent live in the Western Hemisphere today. Given their status as enslaved workers, Africans occupied the bottom of the social ladder, where life was extremely harsh. On some sugar plantations, as many as half the slaves died within two or three years of arrival. Today the descendants of enslaved Africans constitute the large majority of people in Jamaica, Haiti, Barbados, the Bahamas, and most other Caribbean islands; half the population of Trinidad, Belize, Suriname, and Guyana; and substantial minorities in Brazil, Cuba, Puerto Rico, the Dominican Republic, Panama, Venezuela, Colombia, and the United States.

Slave Life and African American Cultures

Chains of Slavery

The imperatives of the marketplace and not humane considerations governed the lives of African slaves and their unfree descendants. In contrast to many African societies, colonial Americans gave enslaved people few if any legal or customary rights, treating them simply as cost items in the production process, to be bought and sold at their owner's whim. Since the markets for plantation crops constantly expanded, slave owners sought maximum profit regardless of the human consequences. Enslaved Africans experienced a high mortality rate, dying from mistreatment, disease, infant mortality, and disrupted family life. Slave women faced rape or sexual harassment by male owners and slaves. In Brazil, while slaves labored in many economic activities, including gold mining and cattle ranching, most worked on sugar, coffee, and tobacco estates. The average Brazilian sugar plantation owned between eighty and one hundred slaves. Some worked as mule drivers, sugar makers, household servants, or even low-level managers, but most were field hands expected to produce three-quarters of a ton of sugar a year each. The slave owner recovered the cost of purchasing and maintaining slaves after about three years but had little incentive to maintain the health of slaves no longer able to work hard. Encouraged by the Catholic Church to marry, many Brazilian slaves formed families, even though they could be broken up by sale.

Slave Resistance

Africans and their descendants often resisted the slave system. Some, like the Brazilian woman Caetana, risked severe punishment by defending their interests (see Profile: Caetana, Slave Rebel Against Patriarchy). Some slaves, known as **maroons** in the English Caribbean, escaped from plantations and set up African-type societies in the interior of Brazil, Colombia, Jamaica, Haiti, Dutch Guiana, and some of the southern colonies in North America, often recreating African cultures by mixing influences from various African ethnic groups. Women led at least two of the ten major maroon societies in Brazil. Since the colonial governments sent in military forces to recapture or control maroons, some of the communities were only temporarily independent. The largest maroon community formed in northeast Brazil, where rebellious slaves established a state around 1605, Palmares (paul-MARYS), with a government led by an African-style king and chiefs. With a population of perhaps 30,000, Palmares resisted nearly annual Portuguese assaults before being crushed by the Portuguese in 1694. Slave revolts also erupted in Haiti, Mexico, the North American colonies, and elsewhere, but they were brutally repressed and the leaders executed. For example, the 1739 Stono Rebellion in South Carolina, the deadliest of the North American uprisings, largely involved recently imported Kongolese. The captured rebels were beheaded.

maroons Slaves who escaped from plantations and set up African-type societies in the interior of several American colonies.

Some slaves were eventually freed, a process known as *manumission,* which was rare in the English colonies and more common in Latin America, especially Brazil, where women, mulattos, and local-born children were most likely to be freed. In both English and Latin America, a few slaves earned enough to buy their own freedom, and some slave owners gave favored slaves an inheritance.

CAETANA, SLAVE REBEL AGAINST PATRIARCHY

Thanks to a fascinating court case from Brazil in the 1830s, we learn about a remarkable female slave, Caetana, who challenged patriarchy. Caetana was born around 1818 on a large Rio Clara plantation owned by Captain Luis Mariano de Tolosa, in the Paraiba (par-uh-EE-buh) River Valley in southeastern Brazil. The plantation life Caetana experienced had not changed dramatically since the 1700s. At Rio Clara about half of the slaves had been born in Africa while the other half, like Caetana, were born in Brazil. By 1835 coffee had become a major cash crop. Most of the 134 Rio Clara slaves, both men and women, planted, maintained, and harvested the 30,000 coffee bushes, often with children in tow. Some slaves raised other crops, tended cattle, or worked as artisans such as carpenters, blacksmiths, and stonemasons. The house slaves worked in Tolosa's mansion, experiencing less strenuous indoor work such as cooking, cleaning, laundering and ironing clothes, carrying water, emptying kitchen slop and human waste, delivering messages, nursing infants, or taking care of the older Tolosa children. In exchange for better food and medical care than was given the field hands, they were expected to be obedient and loyal.

Caetana lived in a close-knit relationship to kin, including her mother, Pulicena, and her sister, married to the free-born mulatto, Joao Ribeira da Silva, who was probably a supervisor of field hands. Caetana was also close to her aunt, the freed slave Luisa Jacinta, whose husband, Alexandre, served as Caetana's godfather and male authority figure. Caetana grew up speaking Portuguese with no direct knowledge of African ways or the terrible Middle Passage across the Atlantic. From a young age she served in the Tolosa house as a personal maid to the Tolosa women, including two daughters, and was trusted and allowed into their private quarters.

In 1835 Tolosa, without consulting her, ordered Caetana, then around seventeen, to marry Custodio, a slave in his mid-twenties, in a wedding blessed by the Catholic Church. Custodio was a master tailor who may have cut and sewn the rough cotton clothes worn by slaves and probably also made clothes for the Tolosa family. Like many slave owners, Tolosa may have believed that slave marriages fostered social stability and diminished the threat of rebellion. Perhaps he also feared that an unmarried house slave, representing unyoked female sexuality, might be a bad influence on his two daughters, twelve and two years old, and temptation for his three adolescent sons. Most adult slave women at Rio Clara were married. Caetana, however, refused Tolosa's order, saying, according to court records, that she felt "a great repugnance for the state of matrimony" and found Custodio especially distasteful. In the end she obeyed, succumbing to the pleas of her family and fearing Tolosa's threats to punish her by assigning her to field work or selling her to another plantation. But after priests performed the ceremony and the couple moved into her aunt and uncle's house, she refused to sleep with Custodio, humiliating and enraging him.

After her uncle and godfather, Alexandre, threatened to beat her if she did not submit to her husband, and with few options, Caetana fled to Tolosa's mansion and pleaded to have the marriage ended. Her rebellion was apparently not against plantation slavery as such but against male authority over her. Caetana's action against the entire system of male power—slave owner, uncle, husband, church—threw Rio Clara into turmoil. After his threats to sell Caetana or reassign her to onerous field work failed, Tolosa relented, giving her protection from her husband and asking a church court to issue an annulment. In court, Caetana complained that she was "reduced to the hard necessity of obeying solely from fear of grave punishment and lasting harm." The legal case took five years, including appeals, with the church ultimately refusing the annulment request.

We do not know why, against such long odds, she rebelled, why she despised marriage, or what ultimately happened to Caetana. Perhaps she envied unmarried free women, who were often respected, or the chaste nuns in the convents. The records do not indicate whether she continued to evade the marriage, but it seems unlikely she complied. She might have been sold to another plantation, before or after Tolosa died in 1853. What we do know is that Caetana bravely refused a demand to do something against her will.

THINKING ABOUT THE PROFILE

1. What does Caetana's experience tell us about life on a Brazilian plantation?
2. What does her rebellion tell us about the Brazilian system of patriarchy?

Note: Quotations from Sandra Lauderdale Graham, *Caetana Says No: Women's Stories from a Brazilian Slave Society* (New York: Cambridge University Press, 2002), 2, 57.

Courtesy, Fundacao Biblioteca Nacional, Rio de Janeiro

Women Slaves in Brazil This 1861 painting shows a personal maid, much like Caetana, instructing slave girls in making lace on a Brazilian plantation. Such slave girls often wore colorful skirts and, like the instructor, earrings.

As a result, free blacks filled niches in Latin American life. The enslaved and freed people of color constituted some two-thirds of the population in parts of Brazil and Cuba. While racism remained influential throughout the Americas, Latin Americans tended to rank people according to their occupation and status as well as skin color, fostering a flexible social order. In contrast, the English colonies rigidly divided people largely by skin color and whether they had any African ancestry.

Mixed Cultures

The harsh conditions of slave life notwithstanding, unique African American cultures emerged. Africans and their descendants frequently mixed Western and African customs, and some created hybrid religions based on both African and Christian beliefs. The ceremonies of Haitian voodoo, Cuban *santaria* **(san-tuh-REE-uh)**, and Brazilian *candomblé* **(can-dum-BLAY)** involved West African practices such as animal sacrifice and worship of African spirits and gods. Yet, many followers of these faiths also believed in the Christian God and saints. Combining African rhythms with local European and sometimes Native American musical traditions, African Americans also laid the foundations for musical forms that would gain wide appeal in the twentieth century, including North American jazz and blues; Caribbean salsa, reggae, and calypso; and Brazilian samba. A few even developed new languages, such as the Gullah **(GULL-uh)** dialect of the Georgia Sea Islands, which mixes English and African words.

African American cultures also influenced other ethnic groups in the Americas. African words enriched the English, French, Spanish, and Portuguese spoken locally. Brazilian Portuguese, for instance, contains many words of Kongolese and Yoruba origin. Many non-Africans enjoyed folktales and traditions of African origin, such as the Brer Rabbit stories of the southern United States, and the Angolan-based *capoiera* martial arts of Brazil, which involved music as well as physical movements. Africans introduced several African crops, including watermelons, black-eyed peas, okra, and rice, and contributed their knowledge of blacksmithing and ironworking to colonial life. The survival of African cultural forms and values was probably strongest in Brazil, Haiti, and Caribbean islands such as Cuba, Jamaica, and Trinidad. In Brazil, the Portuguese eventually learned to accept African influences, brought by the thousands of Africans arriving every year for over three centuries. Thus Brazilian culture developed as a mix of African and European influences. In contrast, Spanish American and North American authorities often tried to repress African music and religion, with some success.

Economic Growth in English North America

Some English North American colonies had a different economic, and eventually political, fate than monoculture colonies. Some historians contrast the English culture, energized by capitalism and religious diversity, with the semimedieval Catholic culture of Spain and Portugal. In this view, an unwillingness to fight authority, acceptance of poverty as God's will, and disinterest toward new ideas inhibited Latin Americans. Other historians believe that colonial policies were responsible for the differences between English and Latin America: the northern English colonies enjoyed more autonomy than the Spanish colonies. Historians also contend that, while both the cultural and colonial patterns were influential, the colonial economies and the social diversity they fostered also played a role. The northern English colonies fostered economies that were strikingly different from the monocultures. The northern colonies lacked mines to fill galleons with gold and silver, a large Native American labor force to exploit, the soil or climate for profitable tropical crops, or open grasslands for ranching. Slaves in the north mostly worked for farms, businesses, or households. The immigrant European population was largely composed of farmers, artisans, and merchants, making them less dependent on slave plantations and the severe social inequality they fostered.

The economic conditions contributed to differing administrative policies. The British allowed their colonies from New Jersey north through New England considerable freedom to build diversified economies for the local market. More concerned with their more valuable Caribbean islands such as Jamaica, the world's largest sugar producer in the 1700s, as well as plantation-dominated colonies such as South Carolina and Virginia, the British imposed fewer restrictions on New York or Massachusetts. Merchants from Boston, Providence, and New York competed with the English in the Caribbean to obtain sugar and molasses, which was converted to rum and shipped to Africa for slaves. Hence, some North Americans amassed huge profits from the slave trade to invest in their own broad-based economies. At the same time, the northern English colonies moved toward development, while the southern English colonies, Latin America, and the Caribbean maintained largely undiversified, monoculture economies. Those Latin American and Caribbean colonies with the most abundant natural and human resources to exploit had the greater short-term economic growth but less eventual development than the northern English colonies with fewer resources. As a result, some of the most profitable American colonies of the past, such as Haiti, Jamaica, Peru,

Bolivia, and Guatemala, are now among the world's poorest countries, and northeast Brazil is one of Brazil's poorest regions, while the less-profitable northern English colonies eventually became among the most developed regions in the world.

The Americas, the Atlantic System, and European Wealth

Atlantic System

Trans-Atlantic migration, voluntary and forced, and increasingly close economic ties created an Atlantic System, a large network that spanned western and Central Africa, the east and gulf coasts of North America, the Caribbean Basin, and the coastal zones of South America, and that was defined by trans-Atlantic shipping, plantations, slavery, and the prominence of Africans and their descendants in the Americas. Ultimately, this system spurred the rise of European capitalism and wealth. The slave trade and plantation economies provided enormous capital to Europeans and North Americans. The prosperity of eighteenth-century cities such as Bristol and Liverpool in England, as well as Boston, Providence, Charleston, Savannah, and New Orleans in North America, depended heavily on the slave trade. Since the slavers, the cooperating African chiefs and merchants, the plantation owners, the shipbuilders, and the other groups linked directly or indirectly to the trade were all reluctant to abandon a lucrative activity, the trade endured for four hundred years, finally coming to an end only in the 1870s.

The Atlantic System also contributed to European industrialization and colonialism. Some of the profits were invested in enterprises and technology in England, the Netherlands, France, and North America, helping to bring economic development to these societies and later spurring rapid industrialization in England. Some of the investment capital for inventing industrial technologies came from individuals and companies linked to the slave trade and plantations. For example, Glasgow merchants known as the "tobacco lords" because of their ties to North American tobacco plantations set up printing companies, tanneries, and ironworks and also invested in cotton textile plants and coal mines in Britain. However, the vast profits earned from overseas commerce did not always result in substantial economic development in European countries. While Spain and Portugal largely squandered opportunities, becoming poor countries within Europe, the Dutch and English pursued wiser investment policies.

Spanish and Portuguese Decline

Spain, the most powerful European country for most of the 1500s, had reaped vast riches from American silver mines and the galleons that brought Chinese goods and tropical products from the Philippines to Mexico. But it did not ultimately use this wealth in ways that promoted its own economic improvement. In fact, much of the exploitation of the Americas hurt Spain. The flood of American bullion into Spain caused severe inflation, resulting in importing lower-priced products from other European countries. Moreover, the Spaniards who went to the Americas and Asia created a labor shortage at home. By heavily taxing peasants and merchants in Spain for large investments in the colonies, Spanish investment did not spur capitalism, and most Spanish merchants used their profits to buy land rather than investing in trade or industry. By 1600 Spain was bankrupt, and a Spanish official charged that the country had wasted its wealth on frivolous spending rather than manufacturing: "the cause of [our] ruin is that riches ride on the wind, instead of [producing] goods that bear fruit. Spain is poor because she is rich [in gold and silver]."[21] Much of the silver ended up elsewhere in Europe or in China. The wealth also tempted the monarchy to pursue expensive and ultimately futile wars in Europe.

The Portuguese were second only to the English in slave trading, and Brazil was the world's largest exporter of gold, diamonds, and sugar and a major producer of coffee and cotton. But the Portuguese squandered their colonial wealth through nonproductive investments, such as building magnificent churches and monasteries rather than financing local industry. As a small country with a small population, Portugal had a tiny domestic market and hence little incentive to build its local industries. Investment in Brazil was more profitable.

Rise of Holland and England

The Dutch and English did much better investing their profits than the Spanish and Portuguese. The Netherlands became a major banking center and also boasted the world's largest commercial fleet. During the 1600s, the Dutch earned vast profits from selling Indonesian coffee and spices to other Europeans, and they invested much of these profits in their domestic economy. A large share of Portuguese and Spanish wealth ended up in the Netherlands. England, which had replaced the Netherlands as the dominant European power by the end of the 1600s, enjoyed the most long-term success, benefiting from profits earned in the Americas and India. England held the most powerful position in the Atlantic System, with wealth flowing into Liverpool, Glasgow, and Bristol from the slave, tobacco, and sugar trades, enriching businessmen and bankers who could now easily mobilize capital for investment in trade, technology, and manufacturing. These factors gave England unique advantages that it fully exploited in the 1700s and 1800s.

Global Consequences

The Americas were transformed and linked to the rest of the globe, reshaping world history. The conquest of Native Americans and the acquisition of American resources gave some Europeans a decided economic advantage over China, India, and the Ottoman Empire. The profits from American metals, often mined by Native Americans, and American crops, chiefly grown by African slaves, shifted world economic power and added to European political and military strength. By the late 1700s Britain had surpassed China in wealth, living standards, and power.

SECTION SUMMARY

- Using Indian labor imposed through the encomienda system, Spanish colonists became wealthy at first through ranching and mining gold and silver, but their economies eventually suffered from lack of diversification.
- Plantations run with African slave labor and focused on producing a single product—sugar in Latin America and the Caribbean, cotton in southeastern North America—also eventually created impoverished societies.
- As a result of the plantation system, sugar went from being a rarity to being a fundamental part of the European diet, and its use helped make the English Industrial Revolution possible.
- African slaves in the Americas were treated as commodities, and resistance to slavery was rarely successful, though freed slaves had somewhat more success in Latin America than they did in North America.
- Elements of African religion, music, language, and agriculture all found their way into American culture, though they were accepted more readily by the Portuguese than by other European colonists.
- Areas of the Americas with the greatest natural resources ended up being the poorest, while those with the least natural resources, such as the northern English colonies, were forced to develop more broad-based economies and became wealthy and well developed.
- The slave trade and plantation economies helped spur European capitalism and were extremely profitable to Europeans and North American colonists.
- Spain and Portugal wasted the wealth they derived from their colonies, but the Dutch and the English invested it wisely and, as a result, gained an advantage over other world powers.

CHAPTER SUMMARY

The Columbian voyages unleashed powerful forces around the Atlantic Ocean that generated a great historical transition. European explorers seeking a route to Asia and then conquerors seeking wealth brought the Americas and their peoples into a permanent relationship with the Eastern Hemisphere. The Spanish, Portuguese, English, and French built vast colonial empires in the Americas, using their superior military power to subjugate American peoples. The majority of Native American people perished from disease and other causes; American societies, including the great Aztec and Inca Empires, were destroyed and placed under European colonial control; and the survivors saw their lives changed enormously. The Native American and mixed-descent peoples had to adjust to colonial rule, Africans to the trauma of servitude, and the European colonizers and settlers to cultural resistance.

The economic evolution of the Americas, especially mining and plantation agriculture, created a tremendous market for labor. Mine owners conscripted Native American workers, and planters exploited enslaved Africans and their descendants. The slave trade linked the Americas closely to the larger world, and the emerging Atlantic System closely connected Europe, West Africa, and the Americas, mostly to the benefit of Europe and European colonists. Some colonists in English North America built more diversified economies, in contrast to the monocultures of the Caribbean and Latin America. The Spanish and Portuguese initially prospered from their conquests but later squandered the resources they obtained, while the English and Dutch capitalized on their activities to achieve greater wealth and power. American history was thus not only a dynamic saga of indigenous development but also the story of increasing integration into larger global processes.

KEY TERMS

conquistadors
Paulistas
voyageurs
Columbian Exchange
audiencias
creoles
mestizos
mulattos
peninsulares
Black Legend
Metis
haciendas
encomienda
monoculture
development
plantation zone
maroons

EBOOK AND WEBSITE RESOURCES

PRIMARY SOURCE

A Dominican Voice in the Wilderness: Preaching Against Tyranny in Hispaniola

INTERACTIVE MAPS

Map 17.1 The Americas and Early European Exploration
Map 17.2 The English and French in North America, ca. 1700
Map 17.3 The Atlantic Economy

LINKS

Africans in America: America's Journey Through Slavery (http://www.pbs.org/wgbh/aia/home.html). A useful website offering materials relevant to a documentary series broadcast on Public Television.

Native Americans and the Land (http://nationalhumanitiescenter.org/tserve/nattrans/ntecoindian/ecolinksce.htm). A useful set of essays compiled by Alfred Crosby.

Early America (http://earlyamerica.com/earlyamerica/index.html). Offers primary sources on the thirteen North American colonies in the eighteenth century.

Internet Resources for Latin America (http://lib.nmsu.edu/subject/bord/laguia/). An outstanding site with links to many resources.

1492: An Ongoing Voyage (http://metalab.unc.edu/expo/1492.exhibit/Intro.html). An electronic exhibit from the Library of Congress on pre-and post-Columbian Europe, Africa, and the Americas.

Pictorial Images of the Transatlantic Slave Trade: A Media Database (http://hitchcock.itc.virginia.edu/Slavery/index.php). A searchable collection of three hundred images on the experiences of enslaved Africans.

Plus flashcards, practice quizzes, and more. Go to: www.cengage.com/history/lockard/globalsocnet2e.

SUGGESTED READING

Altman, Ida, et al. *The Early History of Greater Mexico*. Upper Saddle River, NJ: Prentice-Hall, 2003. An excellent survey of Mexico in this era.

Ames, Glenn J. *The Globe Encompassed: The Age of European Discovery, 1500–1700*. Upper Saddle River: Pearson Prentice Hall, 2008. Good brief review with much on the Americas.

Brown, Jonathan C. *Latin America: A Social History of the Colonial Period*, 2nd ed. Belmont, CA: Wadsworth, 2004. A detailed survey on Europeans, Indians, and Africans.

Captive Passage: The Transatlantic Slave Trade and the Making of the Americas. Washington, DC: Smithsonian Institution Press, 2002. Excellent collection of essays for the general reader.

Conniff, Michael L., and Thomas J. Davis. *Africans in the Americas: A History of the Black Diaspora*. New York: Blackburn Press, 2002. An introduction to the slave trade and the African heritage in the Americas.

Cook, Noble David. *Born to Die: Disease and New World Conquest, 1492–1650*. New York: Cambridge University Press, 1998. One of the best scholarly introductions to the topic.

Crosby, Alfred W. *The Columbian Exchange: Biological and Cultural Consequences of 1492*, 30th anniversary ed. New York: Praeger, 2002. A pioneering study of the exchange of plants, animals, diseases, and foods.

Curtin, Philip D. *The Rise and Fall of the Plantation Complex: Essays in Atlantic History*. Cambridge: Cambridge University Press, 1990. One of the best studies of the plantation zone in the Americas.

Eakin, Marshall C. *The History of Latin America: Collision of Cultures*. New York: Palgrave Macmillan, 2007. Recent interpretative study.

Egerton, Douglas R., et al. *The Atlantic World*. Wheeling, Il.: Harlan Davidson, 2007. Stresses trans-Atlanic connections.

Fischer, Steven R. *A History of the Pacific Islands*. New York: Palgrave, 2002. Provides coverage of these centuries.

Fuentes, Carlos. *The Buried Mirror: Reflections on Spain and the New World*. Boston: Mariner Books, 1999. A readable overview by a Mexican scholar of the interaction of peoples and cultures.

Guarneri, Carl. *America in the World: U.S. History in Global Context*. New York: McGraw-Hill, 2007. Useful brief survey.

Hoffer, Peter C. *The Brave New World: A History of Early America*, 2nd ed. Baltimore: Johns Hopkins University Press, 2006. A lively, comprehensive portrait of North America in this era.

Kicza, John E. *Resilient Cultures: America's Native Peoples Confront European Colonization, 1500–1800*. Upper Saddle

River, NJ: Prentice-Hall, 2003. A brief survey of the encounters throughout the Americas.

Lindsay, Lisa A. *Captives as Commodities: The Transatlantic Slave Trade.* Upper Saddle River: Pearson Prentice Hall, 2008. Concise and readable study.

Martin, Cheryl E., and Mark Wasserman. *Latin America and Its People,* 2nd ed. New York: Longman, 2007. A readable survey text.

Mattoso, Katia M. de Queiros. *To Be a Slave in Brazil, 1550–1888.* Translated by Arthur Goldhammer. New Brunswick: Rutgers University Press, 1986. An in-depth look at the context of Brazilian slavery and the slave experience.

Mintz, Sidney W. *Sweetness and Power: The Place of Sugar in Modern History,* reprint ed. New York: Penguin, 1995. The best introduction to the role of sugar and sugar planting in this era.

Thornton, John. *Africa and Africans in the Making of the Atlantic World, 1400–1800,* 2nd ed. Cambridge: Cambridge University Press, 1998. A provocative examination of Africa and the African diaspora in the Atlantic world.

Viola, Herman J., and Carolyn Margolis, eds. *Seeds of Change: Five Hundred Years Since Columbus.* Washington, DC: Smithsonian Institution Press, 1991. Excellent collection of readable essays on the changes fostered by European exploration and conquest.

CHAPTER

18

South Asia, Southeast Asia, and East Asia: Triumphs and Challenges, 1450–1750

CHAPTER OUTLINE

Michael Holford

"Southern Barbarians"
This painting on a sixteenth-century Japanese screen, decorated with gold leaf, depicts a Portuguese sea captain, shaded by a parasol carried by his black servant, being greeted by black-robed Jesuit missionaries in the port of Nagasaki. His porters carry gifts for the Japanese merchants.

The Portuguese saw that Melaka was magnificent, and its port exceedingly crowded. The people gathered around to see what the Portuguese looked like, and they were all surprised by their appearance. [But] these [Portuguese] know nothing of manners.

—Malay Chronicles[1]

FOCUS QUESTIONS

1. What were the major achievements and failures of the Mughal Empire?
2. How did Southeast Asia become more fully integrated into the world economy?
3. What factors enabled China to remain one of the world's strongest and most dynamic societies?
4. How did Korea and Japan change during this era?

Sultan Mahmud Shah (MA-mood shah) (r. 1488–1511), the Malay ruler of Melaka, the great trading state on the southwest coast of the Malay Peninsula, had a problem. In 1509 five well-armed Portuguese ships, each with a banner bearing a cross and full of menacing pale-skinned men, lowered anchor off his port city, in an exploratory visit prompted by Melaka's fame as a treasure-trove of Asian luxury goods, such as the Indonesian spices that fetched huge profits in Europe. Portuguese intentions were unclear. They did not act like the peaceful Asian merchants who arrived regularly in trading ships, nor did they bring the customary valuable gifts for the sultan and his officials. Initially, curious Melakans gathered around a Portuguese envoy, twisting his beard, taking off his hat, and grasping his hand. However, the encounter quickly became strained. The Portuguese violated local customs, antagonized Melaka officials, and alarmed influential local Indian traders, who feared competition, while the Portuguese considered Sultan Mahmud Shah arrogant and treacherous. Fighting between Portuguese sailors and Malay visitors to their ship broke out. After the Melakans arrested some Portuguese sailors shopping in town, the remaining force, unprepared for an assault on the heavily defended city, sailed away, vowing revenge.

Two years later a Portuguese fleet of some forty ships, mounted with cannon and carrying hundreds of soldiers armed with deadly muskets, sailed back to Melaka to capture the city. The sultan led the defense mounted on his elephant. As the Portuguese gained the upper hand after a bloody month-long assault, their commander, Admiral Affonso de Albuquerque (al-ba-KER-kee), told his soldiers to cast the "Moors" (Muslims) out of the country, and his men slaughtered much of the population and looted the city. This episode was a preview of both the conflicts and the connections forged between Europeans and Asians that followed over the next four centuries.

Many eastern and southern Asians had better success than the Melakans in deflecting the Europeans, who competed with each other and Asians for markets and resources. The Portuguese in the 1500s, the Dutch in the 1600s, and the English in the 1700s established some control over the Indian Ocean maritime network and colonized a few areas, such as Melaka. But, for all their deadly gunpowder weapons, the Europeans did not yet have a clear military and economic advantage over the stronger Asian states; their influence in these regions was modest. Various Asian leaders manipulated the rival Europeans and sometimes forced them to leave. Asian countries were also protected by distance, since they could be reached only by long and dangerous voyages from Europe.

Visit the website and eBook for additional study materials and interactive tools: www.cengage.com/history/lockard/globalsocnet2e

Most Asian societies did not undergo the transitions that were reshaping the Americas and parts of Africa in this era. A Muslim kingdom dominated much of India, many Southeast Asian states flourished from trade, China was still a major power, able to deal with Europeans on Chinese terms, and Japan fiercely defended its own interests. As late as 1750 China and India together still accounted for over half of world manufacturing. Trade between Asia and Europe largely involved luxuries such as Chinese tea and silk, Indonesian spices, Indian textiles, and European silver and gold. Yet, in spite of spirited resistance to European incursions, by the mid-1700s most of the great Asian states were under stress or collapsing from internal problems and destabilizing Western activities.

Mughal India, South Asia, and New Encounters

What were the major achievements and failures of the Mughal Empire?

During its history India had developed a culture shaped by Hinduism and Muslim conquerors. The Mughals **(MOO-guhlz)**, Muslim Central Asians of mixed Mongol-Turkish descent, ruled much of India, reaching their height in the later 1500s and early 1600s. The Mughals fostered artistic and religious innovations while fashioning a prosperous economy, and many Indians also participated in international trade. In the early 1700s the Mughals rapidly declined, just as pressures from European states were mounting.

The Rise and Decline of the Mughal Empire

In 1526 Babur **(BAH-bur)** (1483–1530), a Muslim descendant of Genghis Khan and Tamerlane, led 12,000 troops from Afghanistan and conquered much of north India, forming a new ruling dynasty, the Mughal (see Map 18.1). A learned man and gifted poet in the Persian language, the ambitious Babur fashioned one of world's most magnificent societies. A French visitor to the imperial court wondered whether any other monarch possessed more gold, silver, and jewels; the English used the term *mogul* to mean someone of extreme wealth. Mughal India had few rivals in military strength, government efficiency, economic power, and royal patronage of the arts.

Like earlier Indian governments, the Mughals also had to manage a highly diverse society. Buddhism had nearly died out in India but thrived in Tibet and on Sri Lanka (Ceylon). Most Indians practiced Hinduism, a religion of varied beliefs and customs. However, since the ninth century a succession of Muslim states had ruled parts of the subcontinent,

Map 18.1 The Mughal Empire, 1526–1761
By the mid-1600s the Mughals, a Muslim dynasty based in north India, controlled much of the Indian subcontinent. However, some ports fell under European rule. The Portuguese had a colony at Goa, and, by the early 1700s, the British had established outposts at Bombay, Calcutta, and Madras, while the French occupied Pondicherry.

Interactive Map

CHRONOLOGY

	India	Southeast Asia	China	Japan and Korea
1300		**1350–1767** Ayuthia	**1368–1644** Ming dynasty	**1392–1573** Ashikaga Shogunate **1392–1910** Yi dynasty in Korea
1400				
1500	**1526–1761** Mughal Empire **1556–1605** Reign of Akbar	**1511** Portuguese conquest of Melaka **1565** Spanish conquest of Philippines		
1600			**1644–1912** Qing dynasty **1689** Treaty of Nerchinsk	**1603** Tokugawa Shogunate founded

and perhaps a quarter of the Indian population embraced Islam. Polytheistic Hinduism and monotheistic Islam offered starkly different visions of the cosmic and social order. But while Hindus and Muslims often disagreed, at the village level they often lived side by side, sharing many customs. Indian society was also fragmented by caste divisions and hundreds of different regional languages, such as Bengali in the northeast and Tamil in the southeast. The adaptable Mughals used **Urdu**, a mix of Hindi, Arabic, and Persian written in the Persian script, as their language of administration.

Urdu A language developed in Mughal India that mixed Hindi, Arabic, and Persian and was written in the Persian script.

Akbar's India

Akbar **(AK-bahr)** (r. 1556–1605), a grandson of Babur, became the most outstanding Mughal ruler (see Profile: Akbar, Mughal Ruler). Akbar, whose name means "Very Great," expanded Babur's empire over all of north India and deep into south India. After winning the support of various Hindu groups, including some of the Hindu warrior caste, the Rajputs **(RAHJ-putz)**, Akbar gave Hindus high positions in the government, removed the extra taxes earlier Muslim rulers in India had imposed on non-Muslims, and promoted religious toleration and compromise between communities. Akbar also reformed the government, strictly checking bribery and corruption while seeing that the law was justly administered. He tried to abolish what he considered the most pernicious social customs, such as *sati* (burning the wife on the husband's funeral pyre), child marriage, and trial by ordeal, and ended the enslavement of prisoners of war. Akbar's India also enjoyed an enlightened criminal code, with all citizens having the right of appeal to the ruler if they believed themselves wrongly convicted of a crime or mistreated in the courts. Peace and prosperity prevailed during Akbar's reign.

Akbar presided over a golden age, but his successors had less tolerance and wisdom. The Mughals never worked out a stable pattern of succession, and Muslim rulers had many wives and concubines, producing numerous ambitious male heirs to the throne. Akbar was poisoned by a rebellious son, who then occupied the throne as Jahangir **(ja-HAN-gear)** ("World Seizer"). Royal Mughal women had considerable power at court, and Jahangir was strongly influenced by his Persian wife, Nur Jahan **(nur ja-HAN)**. Jahangir wrote that he had handed government business over to Nur Jahan and that he only needed wine and meat to be happy. While Jahangir generally pursued Akbar's wise policies, his son, Shah Jahan (r. 1628–1658), promoted Islam, destroyed several Hindu temples, and assembled a harem of 5,000 concubines. Sitting on his splendid jewel-encrusted Peacock Throne in Delhi, Shah Jahan doubled the tax bills, but his extensive building projects and unsuccessful military campaigns in Afghanistan and Central Asia virtually bankrupted the state. Eventually Shah Jahan was imprisoned by his even more intolerant son, Aurangzeb **(ow-rang-ZEB)** (r. 1658–1707), who greatly expanded the empire in the south but also undermined the Mughal state and its revenues.

Mughal Decline

Eventually the Mughals' endless wars and extravagant royal spending drained state coffers and power. Their military strength had once been sufficient to keep Europeans and other enemies at bay. The Mughal army, numbering some 1 million soldiers, was equipped with gunpowder weapons such as muskets and field artillery that rivaled European arms, and it had thousands of elephants to ride into battle. By the early 1700s, however, the Mughals lacked the money to match European military capabilities. Increasing tax demands on both merchants and peasants sparked increasing opposition to Mughal rule, and Aurangzeb's ruthless, intolerant, and corrupt policies alienated both Muslims and non-Muslims. A dogmatic Muslim, Aurangzeb placed higher taxes on non-Muslims and persecuted—sometimes even executed—Hindu and Sikh leaders. One pious

Muslim wrote that "bribery is everywhere; mean people have become governors, May God damn the tyrant! In this world he is an infidel; in the next he is in hell."[2]

Revolt eventually led to the dismantling of the Mughal state. To expand his empire Aurangzeb had significantly increased the size of his already huge army, creating logistical problems in supplying the troops just as anti-Mughal forces were becoming bolder. The Marathas **(muh-RAH-tuhz)**, a Hindu group from western India, began raiding the faltering empire in the later 1600s, using guns given by some disenchanted Hindu merchants. When Safavid Iran conquered Mughal-controlled Afghanistan, Mughal leaders were too busy plotting against each other to respond. The Mughal rulers were finally defeated in 1761 by Hindu and Sikh insurgents but continued to rule a small territory from Delhi until 1857.

The decline and near demise of the Mughal state left India open to penetration and eventually conquest by Europeans. The anti-Mughal forces could not unite, leaving India fragmented and vulnerable. The growing division between Muslims and Hindus also played a critical role in the gradual establishment of European domination. After they began annexing parts of India in the 1700s, the English encouraged the Hindu-Muslim division to fragment opposition, but they also had trouble subduing the Sikhs. The religious divide greatly affected twentieth-century South Asia, which became divided into rival Hindu and Muslim nations.

Indian Economy, Society, Religion, and the Arts

Manufacturing and Trade

Thanks to manufacturing, especially of textiles, India had long been one of the world's most industrialized societies. During this period demand continued for Indian textiles all over Eurasia, and India's iron industry produced high-quality steel and cannon. By 1750 India still accounted for one-quarter of the world's industrial output, and it remained the largest producer of textiles. In agriculture, efficient farming, which benefited from investments in reservoirs and irrigation, produced large yields of wheat and rice, as well as cash crops that found a ready market at home or abroad, such as cotton, indigo, pepper, sugar, and opium. This productive Indian economy supported a doubling of the population between 1500 and 1750. At the same time, the bullion brought by foreign trade benefited the Mughal treasury. India had, for much of recorded history, been a major core of the Afro-Eurasian trading networks, trading fine fabrics such as cashmere and gingham to Europe and the Middle East for gold and silver. In the 1600s an influx of American silver, used by European merchants to obtain other Indian products, tripled the money supply.

Indian merchants and bankers expanded commercial networks over vast distances. The Indian maritime trade diaspora stretched from Arabia, Persia, northeast Africa, and the Red Sea to Malaya, Sumatra, Siam, and China. Hindu and Muslim merchants from Gujerat **(goo-juh-RAHT)** in northwest India had a strong position in trade and finance around the Indian Ocean, including Melaka. Thousands of Indians also traded across Central Asia, Afghanistan, Tibet, Persia, the Caucasus states, and Russia. In fact, Indians were the dominant commercial group at the Russian trading port of Astrakhan **(AS-truh-kan)** on the Caspian Sea.

Indian merchant networks enjoyed vast amounts of capital, sophisticated credit and financing arrangements, and reputations for shrewdness. Heavily capitalized firms competed successfully against European and Asian rivals. Some merchants in Surat **(SOO-raht)**, the main Gujerat port, were among the world's richest entrepreneurs. A Dutch diplomat wrote that the merchants of Bengal were "exceptionally quick and experienced. They are always sober, modest, thrifty, and cunning in identifying the source for their profit."[3]

Social System

Indian society was divided by caste and gender divisions. Most of the Hindu merchants belonged to various subcastes (*jati*) of the larger *vaisya* caste grouping, who ranked below the priests (*brahmans*) and warriors in a caste system that had been evolving for over two thousand years. Subcastes moved up or down in the system. Women's influence depended on their caste and family situation. In north India both Muslim and Hindu women were often kept in seclusion, expected to be chaste and obedient to fathers and husbands in a patriarchal, patrilineal society. Yet, some women in the Mughal court exercised influence. Khanzada Begum (1478–1545), Babur's oldest sister, successfully interceded with rebellious brothers to end a family split and keep Babur's son, Humayun, on the throne, avoiding bloodshed. Mughal women had financial resources, which they often devoted to endow mosques and support religious scholars.

Religion

The coming of Islam had dramatically changed India's religious and cultural environment. Unlike earlier invaders into India, Muslims resisted assimilation into the tolerant Hindu fold and remained disdainful of Hindus and of the caste system. The two groups never united to form a single people. The early Mughals, especially Akbar, mostly left the Hindus free to practice their own faith and customs. However, in later years, less-tolerant policies deepened the religious divide, and mysticism became increasingly popular among both Muslims and Hindus. Muslim rulers welcomed Indian, Arab, and

AKBAR, MUGHAL RULER

During the early Mughal period in the sixteenth century, Akbar, one of the most respected political leaders of history, ruled India, coming to power at the age of thirteen after his father died. A contemporary of Queen Elizabeth I of England and Shah Abbas of Persia, he was also a possible epileptic (like Julius Caesar and Napoleon) and subject to bouts of depression. His military conquests, in which he could be ruthless against his enemies, were not the source of his reputation for greatness. Rather, his greatness lay in his skills as an administrator and his ability to respect and blend the diverse traditions of India. Always seeing himself as an Indian rather than a foreign ruler, he worked hard to blend all the strands of Indian culture and religion into a unified country. Although raised a Muslim, he married a Christian and two Hindu princesses, winning non-Muslim support. The marriages symbolized acceptance of India's religious diversity.

Foreign visitors were charmed by Akbar. A Jesuit missionary who visited India in the early 1580s wrote that he was

> *of a stature and type of countenance well suited to his royal dignity, so that one could easily recognize even at first glance that he is the king. He creates an opportunity almost every day for any of the common people or of the nobles to see him and converse with him. It is remarkable how great an effect this courtesy and affability has in attaching to him the minds of his subjects.*

Visionary, energetic, and versatile, Akbar lived to the fullest, becoming a skilled metalworker, draftsman, polo player, and musician. Although himself illiterate, he had an insatiable love of learning and had books of all kinds read to him. His personal library included 24,000 volumes. He also patronized poets, musicians, painters, and architects, even honoring his architects and artisans by having them build a new capital at Fatepuhr Sikri near Agra, where he then lived. Akbar took a particular interest in the lovely gardens constructed around Mughal buildings in the capital and elsewhere, which featured shade trees, fountains, and pools. To show his respect to Hindus, he encouraged Hindi literature and even appointed a Hindi court poet. In response to orthodox Muslims who criticized his support of Hindu court painters, some of whose subject matter violated Islamic prejudices against human images, he argued that God loved all beauty.

Although the Mughals were officially Muslims, Akbar espoused complete freedom of religion. This was not just a political expediency but rather a reflection of an enlightened man with a restless, inquiring mind. Investigation of the mysteries of creation, he claimed, should be done according to the light of reason. He believed that all faiths had something truthful to offer and that all religions were untrue when they denied other religions' sincerity of purpose. Once a week, representatives of all religions held debates in the palace at his invitation; when Jesuit missionaries arrived from the West, they stayed with Akbar for several years and joined in the spirited debates. Indeed, Akbar had the Christian gospels translated into Persian and even attended the occasional mass out of curiosity.

Akbar never completely bought into any religion totally, believing that no one faith had a monopoly on truth. He remained skeptical and found some beliefs in all of them that he thought contradicted reason. Later in life he adopted the Hindu custom of vegetarianism and gave up his favorite sport of hunting. Influenced by the inclusive spirit of Sufi mysticism, in the end he created his own religion, incorporating what he saw as the best features of all religions. But, since he would not impose his views on others, Akbar's religion found few takers and died with him.

THINKING ABOUT THE PROFILE

1. How did Akbar foster Indian cultural life?
2. How could Akbar afford to show so much tolerance of other religions?

Note: Quotation from Rhoads Murphey, *A History of Asia*, 4th ed. (New York: HarperCollins, 2003), 178.

Akbar The great Mughal emperor, Akbar, enjoyed pomp and circumstance. This miniature painting shows him entertaining guests at a reception in his palace.

Persian Sufi masters to their courts to compose songs, poems, and sermons to lead their followers to communion with God. Akbar and Jahangir were particularly sympathetic to Sufism, horrifying Muslim dogmatists, who regarded the mystics as heretics. Sufis argued that a personal bond existed between each believer and God, and some Sufi movements, such as the Chishtiya (CHIS-tee-ya), avoided association with secular powers. The Indian Chishti saint Nizam al-Din Awliya (KNEE-zam al-DIN aw-LEE-ya) wrote that "my room has two doors. If the sultan comes through one door, I will leave through the other."[4]

Many Hindus, particularly from lower castes, had gravitated toward the mystical bhakti (BUK-tee) devotional movement. Some bhakti groups opposed the caste system, ignoring the high-caste brahmans and sympathizing with the poor. Bhakti worship often focused on commitment to a particular Hindu god, such as Shiva or Vishnu. Mysticism forged a gradual accommodation between some Muslims and Hindus who venerated both Sufi and bhakti saints. Many women were bhakti poets. The most famous, Mirabai (MEERA-buy) (ca. 1498–ca. 1546), a Rajput who was widowed at a young age, refused to commit sati and spent the rest of her life writing praises to Vishnu. Bhakti women like Mirabai could defy social conventions and even become saints, and Muslim women were more likely than men to honor and visit the graves of Sufi sheiks.

Sikhism

Sikhs Members of an Indian religion founded in the Early Modern Era that adopted elements from both Hinduism and Islam, including mysticism.

Other Indians tried to blend or transcend Hinduism and Islam by forming new religions. The largest of these sects, the **Sikhs** ("Disciples"), adopted elements, including mysticism, from both Hinduism and Islam. Eventually the Sikhs numbered several million people, mostly living in northwest India's Punjab region. The founder, Guru Nanak (GOO-roo NAN-ak) (1469–1539), born a Hindu, had been influenced by bhakti movements but argued that devotion was not enough; people were saved by their deeds alone: "God will not ask a man his tribe or sect, but what he has done. There is no Hindu and no Muslim. All are children of God." Nanak was followed by nine spiritual leaders who refined the faith during Mughal times. Arjan (1563–1606) established the holy scripture, which announced: "I do not keep the Hindu fast, nor the Muslim Ramadan. I have broken with the Hindu and Muslim. I shall put my heart at the feet of one Supreme Being."[5] Akbar granted Sikhs land for a great temple in Amritsar (uhm-RIT-suhr) in the Punjab.

Like Muslims, Sikhs worshiped one universal and loving God, rejected the caste system and priests, promoted egalitarianism, forbade alcohol and tobacco, and stressed discipline, hard work, and charity for the needy. Sikhs also developed distinctive customs. Observant Sikh men sported a beard, wore a steel bracelet, and carried a dagger or sword at all times. Prohibited from cutting their hair, many men wore a turban on their head. Sikh women enjoyed great freedom compared to Hindus and Muslims. Persistent persecution by Mughal leaders after Akbar led Sikhs, once pacifists, to become militaristic and excellent soldiers, well represented in modern India's military and police forces. The Sikhs also became skilled and practical farmers.

Arts

The arts flourished. Based on Persian models, the distinctive Mughal school of miniature painting represented a synthesis between Islamic and Hindu cultures. The Mughals were also great builders of tombs, mosques, forts, and palaces. Their Indian-Persian architectural style, known as Indo-Islamic, made lavish use of mosaics, domes, and gateways. The Mughal elite lived in large houses with courtyards, trees, gardens, water basins, and handsome subterranean apartments furnished with large fans where people escaped the heat of the day. In the audience hall of his spectacular Delhi palace, Shah Jahan had inscribed: "If on earth be an Eden of bliss, it is this, it is this, it is this!"[6] East of Delhi, at Agra (AH-gruh), Shah Jahan left another legacy, the Taj Mahal (tahzh muh-HAHL). Often considered the world's most beautiful building, the Taj—a marble mausoleum with pools, archways, domes, and minarets—took 22,000 workers twenty-two years to complete. It was the final resting place for Shah Jahan's favorite wife and close political adviser, Mumtaz Mahal (MOOM-taz muh-HAHL).

South Asia and European Challengers

Portuguese Exploration

The Mughals were the last great precolonial Indian rulers, and with their collapse Europeans filled the power vacuum. Europeans' interest in southern Asia as a source of spices and textiles spurred the Portuguese to seek a sea route around Africa and the Spanish to sponsor the Columbian voyages across the Atlantic in search of "the Indies." The Portuguese adventurers came from a country with superior naval technology, missionary zeal, and a compelling appetite for wealth but a standard of living little if any higher than that enjoyed by many Indians, Southeast Asians, and Chinese. The Portuguese were the first Europeans to arrive in India directly by sea around Africa. Following the Indian Ocean maritime trade route from East Africa, Vasco da Gama (ca. 1469–1525) reached the southwestern Indian port of Calicut in 1498 with the help of a pilot hired in East Africa (see Chronology: South Asia, 1450–1750). At Calicut he encountered merchants from as far away as northwest Africa and quickly realized both the economic potential of Asia and the small value of the European goods he carried. Da Gama had one military advantage over the Indians—mounted cannon on his ships—but he was able without force to obtain a cargo of spices, which he sold in Europe at 3,000 percent profit. In 1500 a second Portuguese fleet returned to Calicut, and, after fighting broke out ashore between the Portuguese and some Arabs and local people, the Portuguese used their cannon to bombard Calicut to rubble and destroy the less-maneuverable Indian and Arab ships that were defending the city.

Like all the European powers that followed them to Asia, the Portuguese resorted to violence to enforce their power and acquire wealth. Seeking to control the trade from Asia to the West, they established fortified settlements at strategic locations around the Indian Ocean, including Hormuz **(hor-MOOZ)** at the entrance to the Persian Gulf, Mombasa in East Africa, Diu **(dee-YOU)** in northwest India, Goa on India's southwestern coast, and Melaka in Malaya. In 1515 they occupied Colombo **(kuh-LUM-bow)** in Sri Lanka, a source of cinnamon. Soon the Portuguese used their warships and sometimes terrorism, extorting payments from Ottoman, Arab, Indian, and Indonesian merchant ships in the Indian Ocean. In 1502 Vasco da Gama attacked, plundered, and burned an Arab passenger ship bound for Calicut carrying over three hundred people, including several of Calicut's richest merchants and many women and children, killing all the people aboard.

CHRONOLOGY
South Asia, 1450–1750

1498 Arrival of Vasco da Gama in India

1510 Portuguese conquest of Goa

1515 Portuguese occupation of western Ceylon

1526–1761 Mughal Empire

1556–1605 Reign of Akbar

1600 Founding of British East India Company

1640s Dutch conquests in Ceylon

1717 British settlement in Calcutta and Bombay

Portugal and Indian Ocean Trade

But, despite devoting some eight hundred ships and controlling several key ports, the ambitious Portuguese never completely dominated the Indian Ocean commerce. Asian merchants often found ways to outmaneuver or evade Portuguese ships, and Asian states resisted Portuguese demands. The Portuguese mostly purchased or seized trade goods but still had to compete with wily Asian merchants. But the Portuguese made a lasting contribution to South and Southeast Asian cooking by introducing chilies from the Americas, making the spicy food even hotter. Before chilies, the heat in Indian dishes came from black or red peppers. In Goa the Portuguese and local Indians created a fiery hot dish, *vindaloo*, that combined European vinegar, American potatoes, chilies, and local ingredients and became a fixture of South Asian cuisine.

Although they later lost all their other South and West Asian footholds, the Portuguese retained Goa as a colony until 1961, when India assumed control. The Portuguese were also zealous Christians. Da Gama had told Calicut leaders that the Portuguese sought "Christians and spices," a useful shorthand for understanding their motives. Hostility to Islam, a cornerstone of Portuguese policy, sometimes led to persecution of Islamic institutions and believers in Portuguese-held territories. Portuguese men settled in Goa and Colombo, marrying local women and fostering permanent mixed-descent, Portuguese-speaking Catholic communities.

Dutch and French Activities

By 1750 European influence and Indian-European trade remained modest. But the Portuguese activity foreshadowed an increasingly active European presence, as the Dutch, French, and English all attempted to impose their influence on parts of South Asia. The overextended Portuguese were hard-pressed to sustain their power against these European rivals, who had larger populations and were developing better ships and gunpowder weapons.

In the early 1600s the Dutch destroyed Portuguese power in South and Southeast Asia and gained partial control over the Indian Ocean commerce. Amsterdam merchants formed the well-financed private Dutch East India Company in 1602, with government backing and its own armed

A Goa Market A Dutch traveler, Jan Huygen Van Linschoten, made this plate while living in the Portuguese-ruled port city of Goa in the 1580s. It shows a street scene, including market stalls and, on the far right, a Portuguese woman walking with two Indian maids. Some Indians, wearing crosses, have become Christians.

fleet that operated in conjunction with other Dutch activities. Then in the 1640s the Dutch gained control of some of the coastal regions of Sri Lanka from the Portuguese. They remained in Sri Lanka, often intermarrying with local people, until the British ousted them in the early 1800s and colonized Sri Lanka.

The French joined the competition, establishing a trading presence at Surat and Calcutta and building a military and commercial base at the southeast coast town of Pondicherry **(pon-dir-CHEH-ree)** in the later 1600s and early 1700s. Long-standing English-French political and commercial rivalries spilled over into conflict during the Seven Years War (1756–1763), during which the two nations fought in Europe, North America, the Caribbean, and Asia. As part of this conflict the English and French engaged in fierce battles for dominance in southeast India that destabilized the region's politics.

England and India

The English, with a rapidly growing commercial economy, became the main threat to the Mughals, Dutch, and French. In 1600 British investors formed the British East India Company, and Company traders visited various ports. The English built a fort at Madras **(muh-DRAS)** (today known as Chennai) on the southeast Indian coast and established a trading base at Surat in northwest India, where they forged a commercial alliance with the Parsis **(PAHR-seez)**, the Zoroastrian descendants of Persian refugees. In 1717 the English established bases at Bombay (today called Mumbai) and Calcutta, both then sparsely populated backwaters, for collecting and exporting textiles, indigo, and saltpeter (an ingredient for gunpowder). Many Parsis left Surat for better prospects in Bombay, again working closely with the English for their mutual benefit.

Elsewhere in India English officials still had to negotiate with the Mughals or local princes for trading privileges. When banditry grew rapidly as Mughal authority collapsed, the law and order in the three English-run towns attracted Indian settlers, and merchants prospered. Competition from Indian textile imports spurred English textile manufacturers to cut costs, helping stimulate English industrialization. By the mid-eighteenth century the English were strong enough to treat local rulers with less deference and expand their control into the surrounding regions, often resorting to military force against Indian resistance. From their Calcutta base in Bengal, they began their long period of military conquest in South Asia, continually weakening what little remained of Mughal authority and eventually controlling nearly all of South Asia except for a few small enclaves, such as Portuguese Goa and French Pondicherry. South Asians had often been conquered by outsiders of different cultural and religious backgrounds, such as the Mughals. But now India faced a major new challenge.

SECTION SUMMARY

- The Muslim Mughal Empire attained great riches and, especially under Akbar, maintained an enlightened rule over religiously diverse India, but it began to decline after the fall of Akbar.
- The Indian economy, already strong, expanded greatly as extensive foreign trade brought an influx of silver and enriched entrepreneurs.
- Tensions existed between Indian Muslims and Hindus, though some were able to bridge the gap through mysticism and others joined sects such as the Sikhs that blended or transcended the dominant religions.
- The Mughal decline hastened under Aurangzeb, a harsh and corrupt ruler who was particularly resented by non-Muslims, whom he persecuted and taxed at high rates.
- As a result of their military prowess, Portuguese traders gained a share of trade with India and some control of Indian Ocean commerce.
- The Dutch, French, and English all competed with each other and with the Portuguese for dominance of trade with India, with the English growing increasingly strong by the mid-eighteenth century.

SOUTHEAST ASIA AND GLOBAL CONNECTIONS

How did Southeast Asia become more fully integrated into the world economy?

Southeast Asia, the region south of China and east of India, had long been a cosmopolitan center where peoples, religions, ideas, and products met. Southeast Asians participated in the wider hemispheric trade, and most adopted Theravada Buddhism, Confucianism, or Islam. The Portuguese arrival at Melaka inaugurated a new era during which European adventurers, traders, missionaries, and soldiers actively reshaped Malaya, the Philippine Islands, and parts of Indonesia. However, in most parts of Southeast Asia Western influence remained weak until the nineteenth century.

Southeast Asian Transitions and Societies

Economic and Political Growth

Southeast Asians experienced commercial growth, political change, increasingly productive agriculture, and expansion of Islam and Buddhism in this era. Increasing connections with European, Chinese, Arab, and Indian merchants spurred commerce between the 1400s and

1700s, with Southeast Asia remaining an essential hub in the maritime trade network linking East Asia with India and the Middle East. Sailing ships still stopped in the region's ports to exchange goods or wait for the monsoon winds to shift. Merchants came from as far as the Middle East, Central Asia, Africa, and India.

Larger, more centralized states such as Burma, Siam, and Vietnam absorbed neighboring smaller states. Economic dynamism enhanced the value of regional ports such as Melaka, Ayuthia **(ah-YUT-uh-yuh)** in Siam, Hoian **(hoy-AHN)** in Vietnam, Pegu **(peh-GOO)** in Burma's Irrawaddy Delta, and Banten **(BAN-ten)** in West Java. Thanks to the increased amounts of trade and the wealth this created, urban merchants gained political influence. However, agriculture remained a major activity, and new crops and varieties of rice spurred population growth. Theravada Buddhism dug deeper roots on the mainland, and Islam continued to spread throughout the Malay Peninsula and the islands of Indonesia and the southern Philippines. Increased trade and exposure to new religions opened cultures to the outside world.

CHRONOLOGY
Southeast Asia, 1450–1750

1350–1767 Ayuthia kingdom in Siam

1511 Portuguese conquest of Melaka

1565 Spanish conquest of Philippines

1619 Dutch base at Batavia

1641 Dutch seizure of Melaka from Portuguese

1668 Siamese expulsion of French

Ayuthia

Various Southeast Asian societies remained vigorous (see Map 18.2). The kings of Ayuthia, a mostly Theravada Buddhist state, governed much of Siam from 1350 to 1767), participating in maritime trade while extending their influence into Cambodia and some of the small Lao **(laow)** states along the Mekong River (see Chronology: Southeast Asia, 1450–1750). Ayuthia's competition with the Burmese, Vietnamese, and the largest Lao state, Lan Xang **(lan chang)**, for regional dominance occasionally led to war. In the 1560s a Burmese army ravaged Siam and sacked Ayuthia, carrying back to Burma thousands of Siamese prisoners who reflected diverse occupational skills: actor, actress, architect, artist, blacksmith, carpenter, coiffeur, cook, coppersmith, goldsmith, lacquerware maker, painter, perfume maker, silversmith, stone carver, wood carver, and veterinarian.

Siam eventually recovered from Burma's conquest and flourished. King Narai **(na-RY)** (r. 1656–1688) fostered a cultural renaissance by promoting literature and art, often with a Buddhist emphasis. Since Buddhist monks sponsored many village schools, Siam had one of the highest literacy rates in the premodern world, providing an audience for writers. For example, a long poem by Sri Mahosot **(shree ma-HO-sut)** describes the courtship rituals of young people along the Ayuthia riverside during the evening hours: "O beautiful night! Excited voices on the riverbank. Couples closely embraced, they stare at each other. There is smiling, touching, singing in chorus, looking eye to eye. There is excitement, craving and longing forever."[7]

Siamese society was hierarchical but tolerant by world standards. The royal family and aristocracy remained aloof from the commoners and a large class of slaves. Women operated village and town markets. In 1636 a Dutch trader contrasted the tolerance of Siamese Buddhists with the zealous proselytizing of Christians and Muslims in that era. He observed that the Siamese did not condemn any "opinions, but believe that all, though of differing tenets, living virtuously, may be saved, all services which are performed with zeal being acceptable to the great God. And the Christians [and Muslims] are both permitted the free exercise of their religions."[8] Ayuthia's openness to merchants and creative people from all over Eurasia made it a vibrant crossroads of goods and ideas.

However, Ayuthia had to contend with increasing activity by English, French, and Dutch traders. King Narai sent three diplomatic missions to the French court of Louis XIV to obtain Western maps and scientific knowledge. He also employed several foreigners as officials, including a Persian Muslim as prime minister and a Greek merchant, Constantine Phaulkon **(FALL-kin)**, as superintendent of foreign trade. When the Siamese learned that the opportunistic Phaulkon and French officials had plotted to convert Narai to Christianity and station French troops near the capital, they expelled the French diplomats, missionaries, and merchants from Siam in 1688 and executed Phaulkon. The Siamese, who once welcomed foreign traders, now mistrusted Europeans.

Islamic Expansion and Societies

Trade networks fostered the expansion of Islam. Southeast Asian Muslims often made the long pilgrimage to Mecca and some sent their sons to the Middle East for study, reinforcing links between the regions. Various societies adapted Islam to their own cultural traditions. For example, many Javanese superimposed Islam, often with a Sufi flavor, on the existing foundation of Hinduism and mystical animism (spirit worship), producing an eclectic and tolerant mix of faiths. Some other peoples, including most Malays, embraced a more orthodox version of Islam. Muslim merchants, who preferred calling at ports with Muslim rulers, enriched these states. The mixing of Islam and maritime trade encouraged connections to the wider world. For example, Hamzah Fansuri **(HOM-sah fan-SIR-ee)**, a Sufi poet from Sumatra famed for his mystical and romantic writings, lived for a time in Ayuthia and then Baghdad. Fansuri was a follower of an earlier Spain-born mystic, Ibn al-Arabi (1165–1240), who taught, like Vedanta Hinduism, that all reality is one and everything that exists is part of the divine.

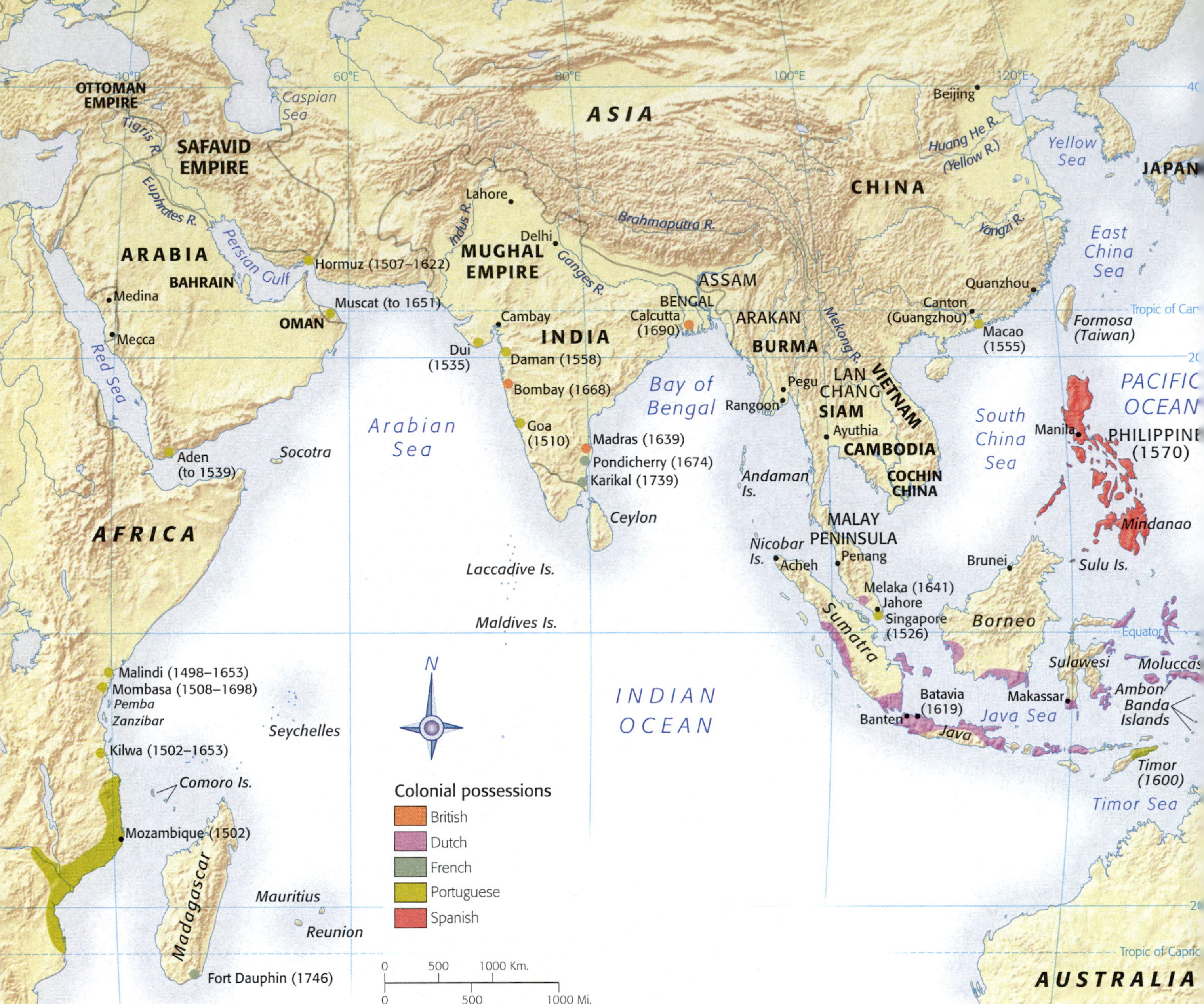

Map 18.2 Southeast Asia in the Early Modern Era

Much of Southeast Asia remained independent, able to deflect European ambitions, but the Portuguese had captured the port of Melaka, Timor, and the Moluccas (Maluku), and the Spanish had colonized the Philippines. In the 1600s the Dutch displaced the Portuguese from Melaka and the Moluccas, and ruled part of Java from Batavia.

Interactive Map

Rooted in patriarchal Arab traditions, Islam diminished women's rights and traditional independence in some Indonesian societies. In Acheh **(AH-cheh)** in northern Sumatra, where four successive women had ruled in the 1600s, women were now prohibited from holding royal power. Yet, Muslim royal courts on Java and other islands were filled with hundreds, sometimes thousands, of women, some wives and concubines but most attendants, guards, or textile workers making *batik*, the beautiful cloth produced in Java by a wax and dying process. Batik arts later spread throughout the world.

Portugal in Southeast Asia

Southeast Asia's wealth and resources, especially spices such as cloves, nutmeg, and pepper, attracted European merchants and conquerors to the region. The Portuguese who occupied Melaka were the forerunners of a powerful and destabilizing European presence that transformed Southeast Asia between 1500 and 1914. The Portuguese now had an advantage against their rivals and had reshaped world trade, as the victorious admiral Albuquerque boasted: "Melaka is the source of all the spices and drugs which the [Muslims] carry every year to [the Middle East]. Cairo and Mecca will be entirely ruined, and Venice will receive no spices unless her merchants go and buy them in Portugal."[9] A few years later the Portuguese brutally conquered the Spice Islands, known as Maluku **(muh-LOO-ku)** (Moluccas), in northeast Indonesia, thus gaining nearly total control of the valuable spice trade to Europe.

But, as in India, Portuguese power in Southeast Asia proved short-lived. Like the East African ports they occupied earlier, Melaka languished because few Muslim merchants chose to endure the higher taxes and Portuguese intolerance of Islam. The Portuguese employed brutal force against their rivals and challengers. The Jesuit missionary St. Francis Xavier, a Spaniard, described Portuguese behavior in the Spice Islands as little more than discovering new ways of conjugating the verb *to steal*. Although the Dutch replaced the Portuguese in Melaka in 1641, a small Catholic, Portuguese-speaking community still lives there. Furthermore, for several centuries Portuguese became a language of trade and commerce in some coastal regions of Asia, from Basra in Iraq to ports in Vietnam.

Other Europeans

Portuguese activities spurred the Spanish, Dutch, English, and French to compete for markets, resources, Christian converts, and power in Southeast Asia. The Spanish conquered the Philippines, the Dutch gained some control of the Indian Ocean maritime trade and conquered Java and the Spice Islands, while the English mainly sought trade relations. Beginning in 1615, the French sought trade with Vietnam but also dispatched Catholic missionaries, who recruited a small following of Vietnamese. The Vietnamese used the Chinese writing system, and to undercut Confucian influence on Vietnamese culture, French missionaries created a romanized Vietnamese alphabet, which in the twentieth century became the official Vietnamese writing system. Southeast Asian states such as Siam, Vietnam, Burma, and Acheh were strong enough to resist over three hundred years of persistent effort by Westerners to gain complete political, social, and economic domination, which they achieved only by 1914.

The Philippines Under Spanish Colonization

Magellan in the Philippines

The greatest Western impact in Southeast Asia before 1800 came in the Philippine Islands. The first Spanish ships to reach the islands in 1521, commanded by Ferdinand Magellan, were part of the first successful effort to circumnavigate the world. Magellan pressured the Filipinos he encountered to adopt Christianity, ordering a local chief to burn all his peoples' religious figures and replace them with a cross. Magellan's arrogant demands resulted in his death during a skirmish with hostile Filipinos. Today, on the beach on Cebu Island where Magellan died, a memorial honors Lapulapu (LAH-pu-LAH-pu), the chief who led the attack, as the first Filipino to repel European aggression. When, after visiting the Spice Islands, Magellan's ships returned to Spain, they had proved that Columbus was correct that Asia could be reached by sailing west from Europe (see Chapter 17).

Magellan had chanced upon an archipelago inhabited by diverse people speaking over a hundred Malay languages and scattered across 7,000 islands, although the majority lived on the two largest islands, Luzon (loo-ZON) and Mindanao (min-duh-NOW). Muslims occupied the southernmost islands, but most Filipinos mixed belief in one supreme being with animism, for which the Spanish labeled them immoral devil worshipers. The remote islands had historically received relatively little cultural influence from India or China. Yet, a few hundred Chinese traders lived in the major towns, and some Filipinos traveled as far as Melaka and Burma as maritime traders. Many Filipinos used a simple writing system, and the largest Filipino political units were villages led by chiefs.

Colonizing the Philippines

When the Spaniards returned to conquer and evangelize, they renamed the islands the Philippines after their monarch, Philip II, known as "the most Catholic of kings." The militarily superior Spanish had little trouble conquering the islands and co-opting local chiefs. But the Muslims in the south, called **Moros** by the Spanish, were never completely pacified. Today some southern Muslims seek independence from the Christian-dominated country. The Spanish set up their colonial government in Manila, located in Luzon along a fine natural harbor, which they hoped to use as a base for trade with China.

Moros The Spanish term for the Muslim peoples of the southern Philippines.

For over nearly three centuries of its colonial rule, beginning in 1565, Spain imposed the Catholic religion and many aspects of Spanish culture on the people with a policy known as **Hispanization**. The Catholic Church governed various regions and acquired great wealth as priests collected taxes and sold the crops, such as sugar. Several Catholic religious orders competed to gain the most converts, their efforts financed by the Spanish crown. To better control and evangelize the Filipinos, missionaries required people to move into towns. What little formal education existed was in church hands and emphasized religious doctrine. As in Latin America, the Spanish destroyed nearly all of the pre-Spanish writings, which they considered pagan. Eventually around 85 percent of the Filipinos adopted Roman Catholicism.

Hispanization The process by which, over nearly three centuries of Spanish colonial rule beginning in 1565, the Catholic religion and Spanish culture were imposed on the Philippine people.

However, Filipinos accepted Christianity on their own terms, disgusting the Spanish by incorporating their own animist traditions, such as by transforming the friendly spirits into Christian saints and magic into miracles attributed to Jesus or the Virgin Mary. Some Filipinos used religious

From Edgar Wickberg, *The Chinese in Philippine Life 1850–1898* (New Haven and London: Yale University Press, 1965)

Chinese Mestizo Couple This painting by a French artist shows two wealthy, well-dressed Chinese mestizos riding in Manila. Chinese mestizos, products of marriages between Chinese immigrants and Filipino or Spanish women, played a key role in colonial life.

festivals to subtly express opposition to Spanish rule, rewriting Spanish passion plays on the life and death of Jesus into plays expressing their anticolonial sentiments, such as by presenting Jesus as a social activist of humble background tormented by a corrupt ruling class. Since the Spanish conquerors had contempt for the common people, few Filipinos were able to rise in the church hierarchy or in government.

Colonial Economy and Society

Inequality also permeated the colonial economy, which was based on plantation agriculture and tenant farming, implanting a permanent gap between the extraordinarily rich landowners and the impoverished peasants. The Spanish emphasized lucrative cash crops, such as sugar and hemp, for sale on the world market, and Spanish officials, corporations, and clerics owned most of the farmland. Peasant revolts became common. Priests and landowners told Filipinos that their religious duty was to labor hard for others and receive their just rewards later in heaven.

Although the Spanish created a country and expanded the economy, they did not construct a cohesive society. Regional and ethnic loyalties remained dominant. The Spaniards occupied the top spots, mostly living in Manila, often in luxury, and few outside the church learned to speak local languages. As in Latin America, many Spaniards returned to Spain after acquiring wealth. Below them were mixed-descent mestizos, who resulted from unions between Spanish men with Filipinas, and a few Filipino families who descended from chiefs. Chinese immigrants worked as merchants and craftsmen, some becoming rich but most remaining middle class. The Chinese often became Catholic, and Chinese men frequently married Filipinas, forming the basis for a Chinese mestizo community. Many leaders of the Philippines today are of Chinese or Spanish mestizo ancestry. But while the Spanish needed the Chinese as middlemen, they also despised, feared, persecuted, and sometimes expelled them. On occasion Spanish forces slaughtered the residents of Manila's large Chinatown.

Indios The Filipinos at the bottom of the Spanish colonial social structure, who faced many legal restrictions.

The vast majority of Filipinos, whom the Spanish called **Indios** (Indies people), occupied the lowest social status and faced many legal restrictions; for example, they were prohibited from dressing like Spaniards. While the Filipinos retained their close family ties, Filipinas lost the high position they had enjoyed in pre-Spanish society because the Spanish culture and church devalued women. The female priestesses integral to Filipino animism were pushed to the margins of society by Catholic priests, one of whom described the priestesses as "loathsome creatures, foul, obscene, truly damnable. My task [is] to reduce them to order."[10] Despite male prejudice and a narrowing of gender roles, Filipinas continued to control family finances and engage in small-scale trade.

Indonesia and the Dutch

Dutch Conquests

In the seventeenth century the Dutch arrived, displacing the Portuguese from most of their bases and becoming the dominant European power in Southeast Asia. The Dutch became Europe's most prosperous society during the 1600s, in large part because of their trade and conquests in Asia, especially Indonesia. In 1595 a Dutch fleet visited the Spice Islands of Maluku and brought back spices to Holland. Over the next several decades the Dutch, after bloody battles, dislodged the Portuguese from most of their scattered outposts, including Maluku. Finally, they captured the Portuguese-controlled port of Melaka in 1641, but the city never recovered its earlier glory. The Dutch sought wealth but, unlike the Portuguese and Spanish, cared little about spreading their culture and religion.

Over three hundred years the Dutch gradually gained control of the Indonesian islands, except for Portuguese-ruled Timor. They ruthlessly eliminated all competition, often by military force, including a 1623 massacre of the English residents of a base on Ambon **(am-BOHN)** Island. As Dutch forces attacked and occupied the prosperous trading city of Makassar **(muh-KAS-uhr)**, in southeast Sulawesi **(SOO-la-WAY-see)**, in 1659, the city's sultan asked: "Do you believe that God has preserved for your trade alone islands which lie so distant from your homeland?"[11] Both sides sparked conflict, but the militarily superior Dutch often slaughtered their Indonesian opponents by the thousands. The Dutch were also well-organized, resourceful, and shrewd diplomats, allying themselves with one state against a rival state, but this sometimes drew them into civil wars or sparked stiff resistance. For example, Shaikh Yusuf (ca. 1624–1699), a Sulawesi-born, Arabia-educated spiritual adviser to the sultan of Banten in western Java, led 2,000 followers into a holy war against the Dutch in 1683. It failed and Yusuf was exiled to Dutch-ruled South Africa.

For several centuries the Dutch left administration of their Indonesian bases to the Dutch East India Company, which had great capital and large resources for pursuing profit. Since Holland was ten months away by boat, there was little guidance and few restraints on the company's power as it pursued a trade monopoly in Southeast Asia . If Spice Islanders grew restless, Dutch forces might exterminate them or carry them off as slaves to Java, Ceylon, or South Africa. To increase demand and reduce supply, the Dutch sometimes chopped down spice-growing trees and bushes, leaving the population with no income.

The Dutch in Java

Eventually the Dutch concentrated on the rich island of Java, which had a flourishing mercantile economy, living standards comparable to those in most of western Europe, several competing sultanates, and several large cities with cosmopolitan populations drawn from throughout Asia. Javanese artisans were noted for fine craftsmanship, and the island's smiths made perhaps the finest steel swords in the world. Javanese commercial prowess was renowned in the region. Javanese women were prominent in business alongside the men, as an English observer noted: "It is usual for a husband to entrust his pecuniary affairs entirely to his wife. The women alone attend the markets, and conduct all the buying and selling."[12]

Capitalizing on Java's political divisions, the Dutch slowly extended their power after establishing a base at a village they renamed Batavia, on the northwestern coast, in 1619. Batavia later grew into a city, today known as Jakarta. Most of Java came under direct or indirect Dutch control by the end of the eighteenth century. Chinese traders had operated in Java for centuries, and the Dutch invited more to come. Over time, Dutch and Chinese entrepreneurs slowly displaced the Javanese merchant class, once major players in the world economy.

Colonial Economy and Society

Soon the Dutch concentrated on making Java a source of wealth by exploiting the rice-growing peasantry. They forced the peasants in the highlands of west Java and Sumatra to grow coffee through a system of annual quotas. Coffee, domesticated in Ethiopia and grown in southern Arabia, had become a popular beverage in both the Middle East and Europe. The Dutch earned huge sums from monopolizing the world coffee trade, enough to finance much of Holland's later industrialization. Thus coffee came to be called "java" in the West.

The Dutch gradually transformed Javan society and life, with inequality characterizing colonial society. Europeans occupied the top rung, followed by mixed-descent Eurasians and the co-opted aristocracy, who encouraged the peasants to treat the aristocratic officials with great awe.

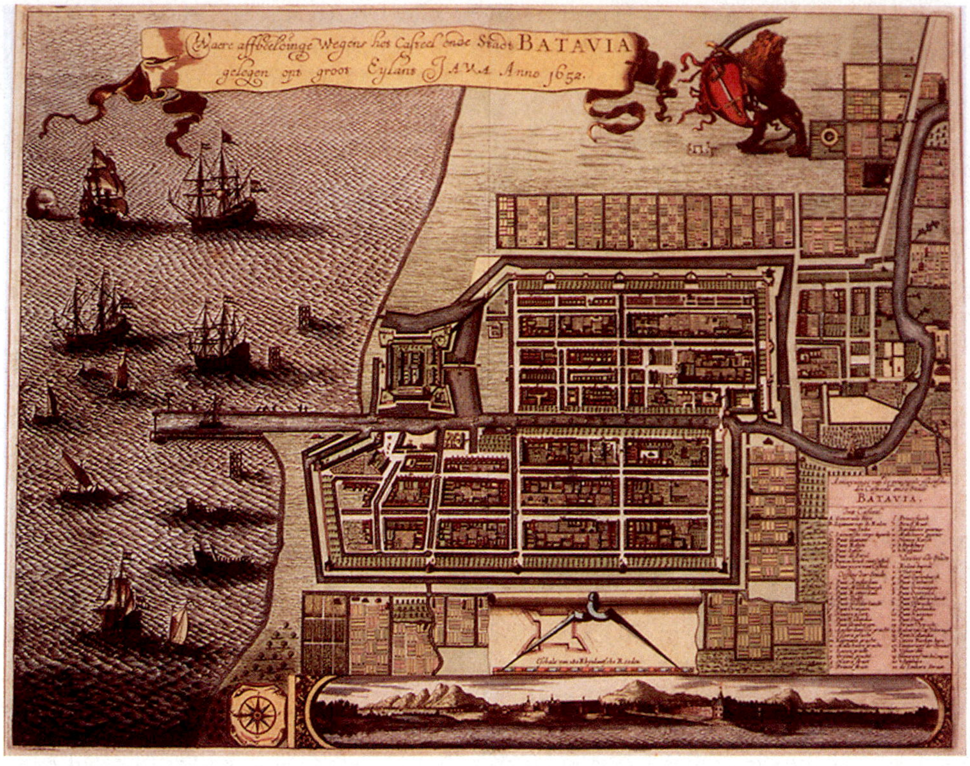

Batavia The Dutch built a port they called Batavia on the northwest coast of Java. Batavia, shown on this map from 1652, grew rapidly as the political and commercial center of the Dutch empire in Southeast Asia.

The middle class was mostly Chinese. Like the Spanish, the Dutch came to fear the growing Chinese community, sometimes massacring Chinese in Batavia. Denied real power, the Javanese royal courts turned inward, creating more fluid, graceful, and stylized royal dances and intricate batik fabrics.

Many Dutch found Javanese culture seductive and took local wives, owned slaves, dressed in Javanese clothes, and indulged in the delicious spicy curries, now enriched by American chilies. Most Dutch lived in Batavia, built to resemble a city in the Netherlands. Its close-packed, stuffy houses and stagnant canals were poorly suited to the tropics, and the puritanical Dutch wore heavy woolen clothes in the tropical heat but bathed only once a week. Like many Southeast Asian cities, Batavia had a multiethnic society.

SECTION SUMMARY

- Increased trade in Southeast Asia led to greater political centralization and increased the influence of major world religions such as Islam and Buddhism.
- Theravada Buddhism thrived in Siam while Islam flourished on the Malay Peninsula and in the Indonesian archipelago, where it blended with local traditions.
- Europeans, beginning with the violent Portuguese and later including the Spanish, Dutch, English, and French, were attracted by Southeast Asia's riches and resources.
- The Spanish conquered the Philippine Islands and eventually succeeded in converting local people to Christianity, though the Filipinos shaped Christianity to their own ends.
- The militaristic Dutch came to dominate Indonesia, particularly Java, which they turned into a highly profitable coffee exporter.
- As a result of European colonization, Southeast Asia entered the world economy, though European speculators often focused on making quick money rather than strengthening the region's economy for the long term.

Southeast Asians and the World Economy

The major changes experienced by Southeast Asians reshaped global commerce. With the Portuguese, Dutch, and Spanish exporting luxury items and natural resources from their colonies, the region became an even more crucial part of the developing world economy. The founding of Manila in 1571, which became the first hub linking Asia and the Americas across the Pacific, fostered a truly global economy. Asian products, including Chinese silk and porcelain, were brought to Manila for export to Mexico, and from there on to Europe. These Spanish galleons symbolized the new global reality. The galleons returned to Manila with European goods, mail, personnel, and vast amounts of silver to pay for Asian goods, draining Spanish imperial coffers and enriching Asian treasuries. Over half the silver mined in the Americas ended up in China. The American silver gave the Asian economy a great push, encouraging increased production of Philippine sugar, Chinese tea, and Indian textiles.

The Manila galleon trade was highly speculative, since Spanish businessmen bet their fortunes that the galleons would arrive in Mexico safely. Pirates, storms, and other obstacles made the voyages dangerous, and some galleons never completed their voyages. The unpredictable galleon trade fostered a "get rich quick" mentality rather than a long-term strategy to bring prosperity to the Philippines.

In spite of all the economic changes, Southeast Asians retained considerable continuity with the past. The West was not yet dominant in either political or economic spheres, except in a few widely scattered outposts such as Melaka, the Spice Islands, and the Philippines. The Europeans had to compete with Chinese, Arab, Indian, and Southeast Asian merchants. The Vietnamese, continuing their long expansion down the Vietnamese coast, annexed the Mekong Delta in the 1600s, while the Siamese forced the French to leave. Only by the eighteenth century did the Southeast Asian societies begin to collapse under the weight of accelerating Western military and economic activity, combined with internal strife and increasingly expensive government structures.

Early Modern China and New Challenges

What factors enabled China to remain one of the world's strongest and most dynamic societies?

Two dynasties, the Ming followed by the Qing **(ching)**, ruled China between the overthrow of the Mongols in the 1300s and the advent of a republic in 1912, making one of the great eras of orderly government and social stability in history (see Map 18.3). In this era China remained one of the most industrialized societies, boasting a vibrant culture and economy. Although encoun-

Map 18.3 Qing China and East Asia in the Early Modern Era
Qing China remained the colossus of eastern Eurasia, controlling a huge empire that included Tibet, Xinjiang, and Mongolia. Korea and Vietnam remained tributary states of China, but the Russians expanded into eastern Siberia. The Japanese partly secluded themselves from the outside world.

Interactive Map

The Qing Empire
Qing homeland
Dominant by 1644
Dominant by 1659
Acquired from Russia, 1689
Dominant by 1783
Principal tributary states
Great Wall

ters with Europeans indicated the challenges ahead just as China experienced political and technological decay, no other country could match the size, wealth, and power of Early Modern China.

The Later Ming Dynasty

China under the Ming (1368–1644) remained dynamic (see Chronology: China, 1450–1750). Highly productive agriculture and the world's largest, most diversified commercial economy supported the imperial political system administered by the mandarins. Although heavily regulated, commerce provided numerous products and services, and the rebuilding of the Grand Canal made it easier to ship goods and stimulated manufacturing. Along with silk and tea, cotton textiles were produced and exported to Japan and Southeast Asia for silver and spices. For centuries China had also been a world leader in science and technology. Late Ming and early Qing Chinese developed color woodblock printing, while better cotton gins, spinning wheels, and other technologies for textile and silk production fostered growth .

CHRONOLOGY
China 1450–1750

1368–1644 Ming dynasty

1557 Portuguese base at Macao

1610 Death of Matteo Ricci in Beijing

1644–1912 Qing dynasty

1689 Treaty of Nerchinsk

At the same time, Ming China turned somewhat inward, concentrating on home affairs and the defense of the northern borders. Always self-sufficient and self-centered, China became increasingly ethnocentric; the great maritime voyages of the early 1400s had ended, and the Ming court viewed foreign states mainly as tribute providers. Although some foreign merchants still came to China and Chinese merchants went to Southeast Asia, the later Ming encouraged isolation, in contrast to the cosmopolitanism of the earlier Tang, Song, and Yuan periods. The Chinese were not patrolling the seas when the first Portuguese ships arrived.

Misrule and other mounting problems led to dynastic change. Crop failures and a terrible plague killed millions in north China, and in the 1590s the Ming dispatched military forces to defend their Korean vassal from the Japanese, at a huge cost to the treasury. Japanese and Chinese pirates ravaged the southern coast and peasant revolts broke out. These problems opened the doors to the Manchus **(MAN-chooz)**, a seminomadic pastoral people from Manchuria just northeast of China who found Chinese collaborators tired of the Ming failures. Manchu forces swept into China on horseback, routing the Ming. However, it took several decades to occupy and pacify the country, and Ming loyalists held out in the south and on the large offshore island of Taiwan for several decades.

Qing Empire, Society, Thought, and Culture

Qing Government and Empire

The new Manchu-installed Qing dynasty ruled from 1644 to 1912. The first Qing rulers, exceptionally able, governed, like their Chinese predecessors, through the Chinese bureaucracy and patronized Confucianism. Although forbidding intermarriage with Chinese, the Manchus knew that to succeed they needed to adopt Chinese institutions and culture to win Chinese support. Like most earlier foreign rulers, therefore, the Manchus assimilated Chinese ways and relied on the mandarins, scholars educated in the Confucian classics, for administration.

Some Qing emperors were outstanding managers, aware of their awesome responsibility. The most admired Qing ruler, the reflective Kangzi **(kang-shee)** (r. 1661–1722), wrote that "giving life to the people and killing people—these are the powers that an emperor has. He knows that administrative errors in government bureaus can be rectified, but that a criminal who is executed cannot be brought back to life any more than a chopped string can be joined together again."[13] Kangzi toured the provinces inspecting public works and joining hunting expeditions. He was also a writer and painter, exemplifying the Confucian ideal of the virtuous ruler. His son and successor, Yongzheng **(young-cheng)** (r. 1723–1735), improved social conditions, ordering that anyone held in hereditary servile status anywhere in the empire be freed.

The Manchus created the greatest Eurasian land empire since the Mongols. Qing armies reasserted Chinese control of the western and northern frontier, annexing Xinjiang **(shin-chang)** ("New Dominions"), a desert region largely inhabited by Turkish-speaking Muslims, and Mongolia. Long a tributary state to China, Tibet was brought into the Manchu fold. While Tibetans shared with Manchus and Mongols the same mystical version of Buddhism known as Lamaism **(LAH-muh-iz-uhm)**, they were culturally different from Chinese. The Qing also incorporated Taiwan, a large island whose original inhabitants were Malay peoples. Chinese began immigrating there in the 1600s.

Laurie Platt Winfrey, Inc

Emperor Kangxi The Qing emperor Kangxi had one of the longest reigns in Chinese history, and his birthdays were given lavish public celebrations. In this print of Beijing, a crowd gathers around the royal dais while women observe the festivities from courtyards (foreground) and shopkeepers look on from their businesses.

Gentry and Society

Ming and Qing China owed their political and social stability in part to the gentry, who combined office and land ownership in an agrarian-based bureaucratic empire. As landlords and moneylenders, the gentry dominated rural economic life. Because they could afford tutors, gentry men also received a formal education and held scholarly degrees. The mid-Qing novel, *The Story of the Stone*, revealed the expectations for gentry sons: "A boy's proper business is to read books in order to gain an understanding of things, so that when he grows up he can play his part in governing the country."[14]

A close relationship developed between the local gentry and the imperial bureaucracy. Together the Chinese gentry and the Manchu rulers sought to preserve the status quo. However, some of the gentry could not negotiate the dynastic change. For example, the celebrated essayist, poet, historian, and degree-holder Zhang Dai **(chang die)** (1597–1680) lived a comfortable life during the late Ming, his privileged status and wealth allowing him to support a wife and several consorts, by whom he had eight or ten children. As a rich man Zhang spent his ample leisure time at a lakeside villa in Hangzhou **(hahng choh)**, visiting tourist sites, collecting handcrafted lanterns, playing the lute, and getting together with a crab-eating club. However, in the 1640s the Zhangs ran afoul of changing political winds during the dangerous transition between the Ming and Qing dynasties, and they were reduced to poverty.

Gender Relations

Women had a complex status in patriarchal Qing society. The elite debated, and some intellectuals encouraged, the education of women. Some women from gentry and merchant families were educated informally, reading and even writing literature. However, elite women also had limited physical mobility because of footbinding, a custom introduced half a millennium earlier but that only became widespread during the Ming. Peasant women were usually illiterate but nonetheless played a key economic role; for example, women improved and promoted spinning and weaving tools. The men planted but the women picked the cotton, processed it into yarn, and wove the finished product for sale. An eighteenth-century government report observed that "whole peasant families assemble, young and old; the mother-in-law leads her son's wives, the mother supervises her daughters; when the wicker lantern is lit and the starlight and moonlight come slanting down, still the click-clack of the spindle-wheels comes from the house."[15] But in many districts peasant women were gradually marginalized as their menfolk or large commercial farmers took over their livelihood in search of greater profits.

Chinese attitudes toward homosexuality fluctuated. Visiting Europeans were shocked at the Chinese tolerance toward homosexuality, which was fiercely punished in Europe. However, some Chinese scholars blamed the Ming downfall on lax morality and convinced the Qing to penalize homosexuality. Yet, by Europeans' standards, the Qing punishments were mild, and the repression gradually ebbed. At least half of the Qing emperors are thought to have had same-sex bedmates. These relationships did not preclude marriage and family, and one Qing emperor with a male lover also fathered twenty-seven children with his wives and concubines.

Chinese Thought

Philosophy also contributed to the stability of the Ming and Qing period. Most Chinese remained comfortable with the eclectic mix of Confucianism, Buddhism, and Daoism that had evolved in the Classical Era. Nonetheless, a renaissance of Confucian thought flourished during the Ming and early Qing. Some scholars developed an interpretation of Confucianism, known as neo-Confucianism, that incorporated elements of Buddhism and Daoism, stressed rational thinking, and reemphasized the natural goodness of people.

Like European Renaissance and Enlightenment thinkers, Ming and Qing philosophers sought knowledge, whether or not it conformed to religious doctrine. Like Sir Francis Bacon and Rene Descartes, the neo-Confucian Wang Yang-Ming (1472–1529) pondered the unity of knowledge and conduct and wondered how people know the external world, concluding that "whatever we see, feel, hear, or in any wise conceive or understand is as real as ever."[16] Like Bacon and John Locke, scholars contended that the mind is reason. Others turned to the critical study of the past. Like Enlightenment thinkers, a few Chinese scholars studied knowledge from other societies. The philosopher and poet Tai Chen made comparative studies of Chinese and Western mathematics. However, neo-Confucianism became the new orthodoxy, limiting Chinese interest in alternative ideas. Some Qing scholars argued that no more writing was needed because the truth had been made clear by ancient thinkers: all that was left was to practice their teachings. By the 1700s, few Chinese intellectuals showed interest in practical inquiry or technological development. Thus, although neo-Confucianism contributed to the unparalleled continuity of Chinese society, it fostered intellectual conformity hostile to originality or ideas from outside.

Art and Literature

China's art and literature, in contrast, remained creative. As they had for centuries, artists painted landscapes featuring misty distances, soaring mountains, and angular pine trees. However, many innovative painters drew on Daoist mysticism to create fanciful, untraditional scenes. The eccentric Zhu Da (ca. 1626–1705) painted bizarre conceptions of nature: huge lotuses in ponds, birds with wise-looking eyes, and surging landscapes. Qing authors wrote some of China's greatest fiction. Some scholars who had failed the civil service examinations became writers. *The Scholars,* by Wu Jingzi **(woo ching-see)**, satirized the examination system and revealed the foibles of the pompous and ignorant. The 1,300-page *The Story of the Stone,* by Cao Xueqin **(tsao swee-chin)**, used a large, declining gentry family to discuss, and sometimes satirize, Qing life. Qing scholars also compiled the world's greatest encyclopedia, 5,000 volumes long.

China and the World Economy

Commercial and Industrial Growth

China had flourishing industrial production, extensive foreign trade, and the world's largest and best-integrated commercial economy (see Witness to the Past: A Mandarin's Critique of Chinese Merchants). Government taxation policies encouraged both agriculture and industry. Gradually the fertile lower Yangzi **(yahng-zeh)** Basin, linked by the Yangzi River and Grand Canal to west and north China, became China's industrial heartland, commercial hub, and most prosperous

Chinese Porcelain Like other peoples around Eurasia, people in southwestern Asia prized Chinese porcelain. This Turkish miniature painting shows several valued pieces of Chinese porcelain, probably part of a bride's dowry, being carried in a decorated cart for display during a wedding procession.

Topkapi Palace Museum

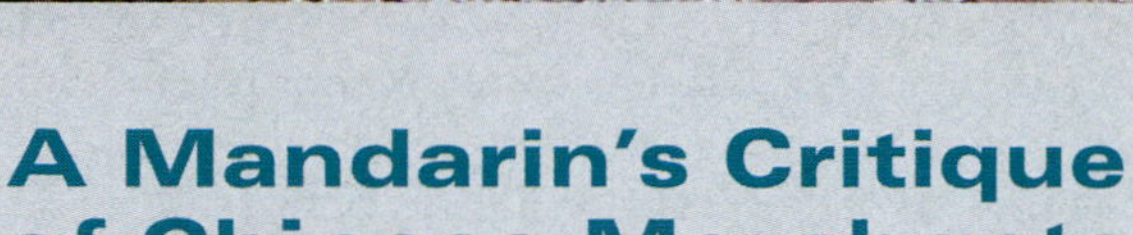

A Mandarin's Critique of Chinese Merchants

In the late sixteenth century, a Ming official, Zhang Han (Chang Han) (1511–1593), wrote an essay criticizing merchants. Himself from a wealthy merchant family, Zhang had the ambivalent attitude toward merchants that was typical of the Confucian elite of the day. He asserted that merchants were greedy, self-serving, arrogant, and pampered. However, he also admired the products provided by commerce and the efficiency with which they were distributed throughout the empire. And he suggested that China could benefit from lower taxes on mercantile activity.

Money and profit are of great importance to men. They seek profit, then suffer by it, yet they cannot forget it. They exhaust their bodies and spirits, run day and night, yet they still regard what they have gained as insufficient. Those who become merchants eat fine food and wear elegant clothes. . . . Opportunistic persons attracted by their wealth offer to serve them. Pretty girls in beautiful long-sleeved dresses and delicate slippers play stringed and wind instruments for them and compete to please them. Merchants boast that their wisdom and ability are such as to give them a free hand in affairs. They believe that they know all the possible transformations in the universe and therefore can calculate all the changes in the human world, and that the rise and fall of prices are under their command. They are confident that they will not make one mistake in a hundred in their calculations. These merchants do not know how insignificant their wisdom and ability really are. As [the *Chuang Tzu,* an ancient Daoist text] says: "Great understanding is broad and unhurried; little understanding is cramped and busy."

Because I have traveled to many places during my career as an official, I am familiar with commercial activities and business conditions in various places. . . . Those who engage in commerce, including the foot peddler, the cart peddler, and the shopkeeper, display not only clothing and fresh foods from the fields but also numerous luxury items such as priceless jade from [K'un-lun], pearls from the [southern] island of Hainan, gold from Yunnan (in southwest China), and corals from Vietnam. These precious items, coming from the mountains or the sea, are not found in central China. But people in remote areas and in other countries, unafraid of the dangers and difficulties of travel, transport these items step by step to the capital, making it the most prosperous place in the empire. . . . The profits from the tea and salt trades are especially great, but only large-scale merchants can undertake these businesses. Furthermore, there are government regulations on their distribution. . . .

Turning to the taxes levied on Chinese merchants, though these taxes are needed to fill the national treasury, excessive exploitation should be prohibited. . . . But today's merchants are often stopped on the road [at checkpoints] for additional payments and also suffer extortions from the [marketplace] clerks. Such exploitation is hard and bitter enough but, in addition, the merchants are taxed twice. How can they avoid becoming more and more impoverished? . . . Levying taxes on merchants is a bad policy. We should tax people according to their degree of wealth or poverty.

THINKING ABOUT THE READING

1. What criticisms does Zhang make of merchants?
2. In Zhang's view, what benefits does China gain from merchant activity?
3. How does Zhang believe merchant activity could be stimulated?

Source: Reprinted with the permission of The Free Press, a Division of Simon & Schuster Inc., from *Chinese Civilization and Society, A Sourcebook,* Second Revised and Expanded Edition by Patricia Buckley Ebrey.

region. The people of the Yangzi Basin enjoyed living standards comparable to those of England and the Netherlands, both enriched by overseas colonization. A French visitor in the early 1700s, amazed that China's internal trade vastly exceeded the commerce of all Europe, wrote that the Chinese put "merit ceaselessly in competition with merit, diligence with diligence, and work with work. The whole country is like a perpetual fair."[17]

A major force in an international economy, China exported porcelain, cotton textiles, silk, tea, quicksilver, and zinc, and as a market for and source of valuable products influenced economic decisions made in Southeast Asia, the Middle East, Europe, and the Americas. Europeans shipped silver to China to pay for Chinese products. Moreover, Chinese population growth resulted in part from the Spanish introduction of American crops such as corn, sweet potatoes, and peanuts, as well as Chinese development of a new fast-growing rice. China's population numbered some 100 million in 1500 and reached 250 or 300 million by 1750, a quarter of the world total. Several major cities had over a million residents, including Nanjing **(nahn-JING)**, Beijing, and Guangzhou **(gwong-joe)** (known in the West as Canton).

Limits to Growth

However, despite China's economic dynamism, full-scale capitalism and industrialization did not develop. The commercial revolution and technological advances of the Tang, Song, and Ming failed to foster the revolutionary changes that transformed western European feudalism into capitalism. Unlike the English and Dutch, the Chinese lacked an overseas empire that could be exploited to acquire capital for investment. Another basic difference from Europe was the continuity of Chinese traditions. The essential Han pattern was continued by successive dynasties until 1912. The bureaucracy-gentry, often contemptuous of merchants and their values, kept merchants politically weak, whereas in Europe economic growth undermined the old system. With a fast-growing population, China also had no labor shortage and hence no great spur for technological innovation. Its economy met its basic needs well.

The imperial government restricted and taxed the merchant class, a major difference from early modern Europe, where business enterprises had a growing influence in politics. Although a wealthy Chinese merchant class existed and the laws encouraged markets, the government feared that if merchants became too powerful they might threaten the regime, and hence circumscribed their activities. Chinese industrialists and merchants organized themselves into guilds certified by the government and responsible for their members' behavior. During the Song commercial revolution, many mandarins came from merchant backgrounds and protected business generally. By the Qing this was no longer true. The government also maintained monopolies over the production and distribution of essential commodities, including arms, textiles, pottery, salt, iron, and wine.

Government policies reflected a centralized, agriculture-based empire. Hence, the Ming emperor stopped Zheng He's overseas voyages and ordered Chinese merchants to return home. That edict did not stop wily Chinese merchants from going abroad. Those from Fujian **(fu-JEN)** province, on the southeast coast, remained prominent in Asian trade, especially in Southeast Asia. Mountainous Fujian offered poor conditions for farming, and a Chinese official commented that Fujian men, of necessity, made fields from the sea. But, unlike their European rivals, they received no official support and often had to pay bribes to local officials. Thus Chinese energies focused inward at a fateful turning point in world history, leaving the world's oceans open to Western enterprise.

China's Encounters with the West

Portugal and Christian Missions

Primary Source: Journals: Matteo Ricci This story about Jesuit missionaries in China provides an interesting look at the nexus of religion and politics in the early seventeenth century.

However, China did not cut itself off completely from the outside world. In the 1500s and 1600s European ships seeking silk, tea, porcelain, lacquerware, and other products reached Chinese shores. The Portuguese landed on the China coast in 1514 and began a troubled relationship with China, soon earning reputations as pirates and religious fanatics. With their naval forces spread thinly around Asia and Africa, the Portuguese were no match for Chinese armed junks. In 1557, to stop the piracy, the emperor allowed the Portuguese to establish a trading base at a small unpopulated peninsula, Macao **(muh-cow)**, near Guangzhou on the southeast coast. When the Qing declined in the 1800s, the Portuguese transformed Macao from a trading base into the first Western colony on Chinese soil.

Christian missionaries, especially Jesuits, also became active in the late Ming and early Qing. The most influential Jesuit, the Italian Matteo Ricci **(ma-TAY-o REE-chee)** (1552–1610), was a brilliant scholar and linguist trained in law, mathematics, and geography. In 1583 he entered China to study the Confucian classics and foster an interest in Christianity among Confucian scholars. Ricci impressed Chinese officials with his great learning and began training young scholars for the civil service exams. Eventually the emperor allowed Ricci and his Jesuit colleagues to settle in the capital, Beijing. Ricci became a scientific adviser to the imperial court, helping improve clocks, calendars, and astronomical observations. On Ricci's death the Chinese buried him with honors in Beijing. Yet, Ricci attracted only a few converts to his faith.

China-European Connections

Thanks to the Jesuits, some Chinese leaders became interested in Western scientific knowledge. The emperor Kangzi wrote:

> *I often worked several hours a day with [the Jesuits]. I examined each stage of the forging of a cannon. I worked on clocks and mechanics. [Father] Pereira taught me to play a tune on the harpsichord. . . . I also learned to calculate the weight and volume of spheres, cubes, and cones, and to measure distance and the angles of riverbanks.*[18]

A few Chinese even visited Europe. The Christian convert Michael Alphonsus Shen demonstrated chopstick techniques for French king Louis XIV and catalogued Chinese books in the Oxford University library. For their part, the well-educated Italian Jesuits were much impressed with a China that had more wealth and a more advanced technology than did Europe. Jesuit letters home describing Chinese ideas and inventions circulated widely in Europe. The Jesuits lived like mandarins and wore Chinese clothing, and their admiration of Chinese traditions led them to harmonize Christianity with Chinese philosophy to attract support from Chinese scholars.

The efforts of Ricci and his colleagues introduced Roman Christianity to China, and by 1700 some 100,000 Chinese had become Catholics, a tiny percentage of the vast population. The less-tolerant missionaries who followed the early Jesuits made even less progress. After the pope prohibited mixing Christianity and Confucianism, the faith had less appeal. Many Chinese considered Christianity intellectually false and resented the missionary enterprise for its arrogance. The emperor Yongzheng asked the missionaries: "What would you say if I sent a troop of Buddhist monks into your country to preach their doctrines? You want all Chinese to become Christians. Shall we become subjects of your king? You will listen to no other voices but yours."[19] In the early 1700s the Qing banned Christianity for undermining such Chinese traditions as ancestor worship, persecuted converts, and expelled missionaries.

Holland, Russia, and China

Other challenges from the Western countries faced China. Before 1800 Europeans could be rebuffed because China was militarily and economically strong. But relations with the Dutch and Russians suggested changes to come. The Dutch had established a base on Taiwan in 1624 but were expelled in 1662 by the militarily stronger Ming resistance forces that had moved to the island. In 1683 the Qing took control of Taiwan, but the Dutch remained active in the China trade. Meanwhile, Russian expeditions crossed Siberia, seeking trade with China as well as sable fur, over time consolidating control of the sparsely populated Siberian regions. They coveted the Amur River Valley, in eastern Siberia north of the Manchu homeland and under loose Qing suzerainty, as a gateway to the Pacific. The Chinese defeated Russian forces in several battles in Siberia but then granted Russians commercial privileges in the Treaty of Nerchinsk of 1689, the first treaty between China and a European power and a symbol of things to come. Russia maintained its ambitions in eastern Siberia, occasionally testing Qing power.

Needing little from outside, China still retained control of its relations with European powers before the 1800s. The Qing restricted foreign trade to a few border outposts and southern ports, especially Guangzhou (Canton), and firmly refused diplomatic relations with the Western nations. The Chinese were willing to absorb useful technologies to improve mapmaking and astronomy, but they were less interested in foreign ideas like Christianity. By the mid-Qing, China was also increasingly self-centered and complacent, underestimating the Western challenge.

China's internal problems mounted just as Western economic, industrial, and military power increased, and foreign pressures on China intensified in the later 1700s. An overconfident China was eclipsed within a few decades by the West. Having lived under foreign rulers such as the Manchus, the Chinese understood political subjugation but could not comprehend that foreign forces might force them to rethink their cultural traditions, which they wanted to preserve at all costs. During the later 1800s the 2,000-year-old imperial system declined rapidly.

SECTION SUMMARY

- During the Ming dynasty, China maintained its economic power, but it turned increasingly inward and antiforeign and was ultimately undermined by plague, famine, and pressures from Japan.
- The Qing dynasty was established by foreign Manchus, who assimilated to many Chinese ways, amassed the greatest Eurasian land empire since the Mongols, and added Taiwan to China's holdings.
- Chinese neo-Confucians incorporated elements of Buddhism and Daoism in their thinking and, like their European contemporaries, emphasized reason, but over time neo-Confucianism hardened into a new orthodoxy and discouraged the growth of new ideas.
- China's economy remained extremely strong but never developed full-scale capitalism or industrialization, perhaps because it lacked an exploitable overseas empire, and perhaps because the government failed to encourage entrepreneurship.
- China had fitful encounters with Europeans, including Portuguese traders who irked Chinese authorities and established a colony at Macao, and missionaries who had little success and were ultimately banned for undermining Chinese traditions.
- Over time, China faced increasing pressure from the Russians, who fought for commercial privileges in the area north of China.

CONTINUITY AND CHANGE IN KOREA AND JAPAN

How did Korea and Japan change during this era?

Koreans, Japanese, and Chinese were neighbors but developed very different societies. Korea faced little Western pressure, local issues and conflicts with Japan being far more important. For a brief period Japan encountered a significant European presence, but when the experience proved destabilizing, the Japanese became aloof from the West.

Choson Korea, Ashikaga Japan, and European Encounters

Yi Korea

Korea and Japan remained more isolated than China from the wider world. The Koreans mixed Chinese influences with local traditions, adapting and modifying Chinese political models, Confucian social patterns, and Mahayana Buddhism. The Yi (YEE) dynasty, which called its state Choson, ruled from 1392 until 1910, a longevity of over five centuries (see Chronology: Korea and Japan, 1450–1750). Strongly Confucian, the Yi borrowed Chinese models and maintained close relations with China. The early Yi era enjoyed progress in science and technology as well as in writing and literature. However, Choson was damaged by factional disputes and a disastrous Japanese invasion.

CHRONOLOGY
Korean and Japan, 1450–1750

1338–1568 Ashikaga Shogunate

1392–1910 Yi (Choson) dynasty in Korea

1549 Beginning of Christian missions in Japan

1592–1598 Japanese invasions of Korea

1603 Founding of Tokugawa Shogunate

1637 Christian rebellion against Tokugawa

1639–1841 Japanese seclusion policy

In 1592 a Japanese army of 160,000 attempted to conquer some of the peninsula, capturing the capital, Seoul (soul). The Koreans, aided by China, eventually prevailed because of their invention of the world's first ironclad naval vessels, which they used to cut Japanese supply lines, forcing the Japanese to withdraw. But the invasion destroyed countless buildings, weakened the central government, and generated severe economic problems.

While the Yi maintained their power, Koreans abandoned or modified some customs borrowed from China. The rigid social class system was modified, with class lines becoming more open. Agriculture became more productive, and population grew, reaching 7 million by 1750. Commerce and the merchant class also expanded. Yet, growing dissension fostered movements for change that grew during the 1700s.

Japanese society was marked by its samurai (SAH-moo-rie) warrior class, its distinctive mix of Buddhism, Confucianism, and Shinto, and its long history of adapting foreign influences. But by 1500, Japan under the Ashikaga (ah-shee-KAH-gah) Shogunate (1338–1568), like Yi Korea, experienced rapid economic change, population growth, and then civil war that strained the political and social system. The Ashikaga shoguns, military leaders who dominated the imperial family in Kyoto and the central government, never had much power beyond the capital.

Japanese Growth

As technological advances improved agriculture, production per acre tripled, and Japan's population doubled from 16 million in 1500 to 30 million in 1750. The increased productivity stimulated trade and the growth of cities, and by 1600 Kyoto contained some 800,000 people. Urban merchants and craftsmen organized themselves into guilds that obtained monopoly rights to sell or make a product, thus earning higher status and more freedom than most Japanese enjoyed. Active merchants spurred foreign and domestic trade. Whereas only a few Japanese diplomats and Buddhist monks had ever ventured to Korea and China, now Japanese traders and pirates visited Korea, China, and Southeast Asia. Japanese settled in Vietnam, Cambodia, Siam, and the Philippines, and one even became a governor in Siam. Japan also became a major supplier of silver, copper, swords, lacquerware, rice wine, rice, and other goods to Asia. If the economic and military expansion had continued, the Japanese might have challenged the Europeans for influence in Southeast Asia and might even have developed capitalism. But growing instability turned Japan in a different direction.

Civil War

Political turmoil and civil war were a factor. Political power became increasingly decentralized, as several hundred daimyo, great territorial landowning magnates, each with a supporting samurai force, increasingly dominated rural Japan. The rise of the daimyo precipitated a century-long civil war from the mid-1400s into the late 1500s. Military engagements mostly involved hand-to-hand conflict between samurai wielding long, slightly curved, two-handed swords with great efficiency, supported by commoner spearmen. A famous poet visited a historic battleground and offered a retrospective on the fleeting nature of the fighters' causes: "The summer grasses! All that is left of the warrior's dream!"[20]

Three men who successively became shogun gradually restored order. All were brutal warlords and also devotees of the refined tea ceremony. The first, Oda Nobunaga **(OH-da no-boo-NAG-ga)** (1534–1582), was so wild as a youth that a family servant committed suicide hoping this desperate act might settle the young man down. Of daimyo background, Oda proved a brilliant military strategist who once defeated an army of 25,000 with his own small force of 2,000 men. He usually performed a folk dance and then sang a delicate verse about life's transience before leading his samurai into bloody battles. Hideyoshi Toyotomi (1536–1598), of peasant origins, had ambitions abroad, demanding unsuccessfully that the Spanish governor of the Philippines send him tribute; he also dreamed of conquering China. When the Koreans refused his request to use Korea as a staging base for the China invasion, he instead invaded Korea in 1592 but was repulsed by the fierce Korean resistance. The last of the three, Tokugawa Ieyasu **(ee-yeh-YAH-soo)** (1542–1616), one of Hideyoshi's chief generals, ended the warfare and became shogun in 1603.

Europeans in Japan

During the civil war European traders and missionaries arrived in Japan, and their encounter with the Japanese sparked cultural exchange but also conflict. In 1542 the Portuguese reached Japan, causing a sensation, as we learn from a Japanese observer:

> *There came on a [merchant ship] a creature one couldn't put a name to, that [appeared to have] human form at first [glance], but might as well be a long-nosed goblin. Careful inquiry [revealed] that the creature was called a "Padre." The first thing one noticed was how long the nose was! It was like a wartless conch-shell.*[21]

The Europeans were equally astonished at what they found. An Italian Jesuit in the 1500s struggled with the cultural differences:

> *Japan is a world the reverse of Europe. Hardly in anything do their ways conform to ours. They eat and dress differently. Their methods of doing business, their manner of sitting down, their buildings, their domestic arrangements are so unlike ours as to be beyond description or understanding.*[22]

But for all the mutual astonishment, the Europeans had an economic, religious, and military impact. The Portuguese traded Chinese silk for Japanese gold, and soon Spanish and Dutch merchants arrived. Francis Xavier (1506–1552), a Spanish Jesuit missionary, began to preach Christianity in 1549. As a result of energetic Spanish and Portuguese missionary efforts, by 1600 perhaps 300,000 of the 18 million Japanese were Christians, including some daimyo on the southern island of Kyushu **(KYOO-shoo)**, who converted to gain a closer relationship to European traders and acquire advanced military technology. But many Japanese grew suspicious of the missionaries, resented their intolerance of Japanese faiths and customs, and could not comprehend the fierce competition between Portuguese and Spanish priests and between rival Catholic orders. Japanese leaders viewed the Christian communities, often armed by the missionaries, as posing a threat to their power.

Borrowing from Europe

Thanks to the warfare, the Japanese were now more open to borrowing from outside than they had been since the Heian **(HAY-an)** era. But the Japanese adopted what was useful to them: Western technologies. They acquired, then quickly improved, muskets from the Portuguese and Spanish. European guns sharpened warfare and, since even nonsamurai could obtain them, contributed to the breakdown of social class lines. The increasingly common and deadly violence resulting from guns often prompted peasants to seek solace in religion, and some adopted Christianity. Japanese leaders became alarmed by the superiority of Western military and naval technology, as well as the surprising effectiveness of Western Christian missionaries.

The Tokugawa Shogunate: Stability, Seclusion, and Society

Rise of the Tokugawa

The civil war, intensified by gunpowder weapons, ended with the Tokugawa Shogunate, which ruled Japan from 1603 to 1868. Tokugawa Ieyasu was a great warrior and able administrator, but also cruel and treacherous. He subdued his rivals and established a shogunate at Tokyo, then known as Edo, presiding over the most centralized state in premodern Japanese history. The Tokugawa leaders imposed a government mixing authoritarian centralization with a hierarchical social system led by the samurai, resembling medieval European feudalism in some respects. The imperial family in Kyoto remained powerless. To discourage rebellion, some members of each daimyo family were required to live in Edo as hostages. A samurai scholar instrumental in developing the code of chivalry (*bushido*) claimed that farmers, merchants, and artisans were too busy to master the warrior ways, while the samurai, "is one who does not cultivate, manufacture, engage in trade. The business of the samurai consists in reflecting on his own station in life, in discharging loyal service to his master, in devoting himself to duty above all."[23]

Japanese Seclusion

To stop the conflict between the various Europeans and Catholic orders, Tokugawa eventually declared a seclusion policy, closing off Japan from Western pressure and ordering home Japanese traders in Southeast Asia. He ejected the Catholic missionaries and merchants and broke the power of the Christian communities. When Japanese Christians rebelled in 1637, Tokugawa responded by massacring 37,000 of them. The shogun warned the Portuguese and Spanish that they should justly be killed, but he generously spared their lives if they left Japan and never returned. But while Japan was closing itself to the West, trade with China, Korea, and Southeast Asia continued, with Japan paying for silk with its main mineral resource, silver. Several thousand Chinese merchants lived in Japanese ports, especially Nagasaki.

After 1639 a few Dutch traders were allowed to set up a base on a small island, Deshima (DEH-shi-ma), in Nagasaki (nah-gah-SAH-kee) Bay. The Dutch were not interested in converting the Japanese to Christianity, only in commerce, and for the next two centuries the Dutch base served as Japan's only link to the European world. The Deshima station chief for the Dutch East Indies Company reported in 1650 that the restrictions and humiliations they endured were worth the gains, since Japan was the most profitable of all the company's operations.

Tokugawa Society

Tokugawa leaders believed that society could be frozen, but under the surface new social forces and tensions simmered. Even when the rulers restricted travel between cities or regions, merchants evaded the rules and moved their wares. The rapidly growing population strained the country's resources, and peasant protests, riots, and uprisings were common. Led by Tokyo and Osaka, each with over a million inhabitants by 1800, cities became prosperous centers of commercial networks, and merchants and their values became more influential.

The Tokugawa tried to restrict Japanese women. European visitors in the 1500s were surprised that elite women had more independence than their European contemporaries. In contrast to some Asian societies, Japanese women were never secluded and participated in community life. Some were literate, and a few became noted writers. Nonetheless, Tokugawa women had few legal or property rights, faced arranged marriages, and were encouraged to be dependent on men. Severe laws against adultery only punished women. The Tokugawa advised peasants that "however good looking a wife may be, if she neglects her household duties by drinking tea or sight-seeing or rambling along the hillside, she must be divorced."[24]

Cultural Life

ukiyo-e Colorful Japanese woodblock prints that celebrated the life of the "floating world," the urban entertainment districts.

bunraku The puppet theater of Tokugawa Japan.

kabuki The all-male and racy drama that became the favored entertainment of the urban population in Tokugawa Japan.

haiku The seventeen-syllable poem that proved an excellent vehicle for discussing the passage of time and the change of seasons in Early Modern Japan.

Distinctive new cultural forms also emerged. In the major cities entertainment districts known as the "floating world" were filled with restaurants, theaters, geisha houses, and brothels. A playwright described a lively district in Osaka: "Through the thronged streets young rakes were strolling, singing folk-songs as they went, reciting fragments of puppet dramas, or imitating famous actors at their dialogues. From the upper rooms of many a teahouse floated the gay plucking of a *samisen* [lute]."[25] The master artist Moronobu (more-oh-NOH-boo) introduced the colorful woodblock prints known as **ukiyo-e** (oo-kee-YO-ee), which celebrated the floating world. These prints achieved wide distribution, making famous the actors, geishas, and courtesans who were portrayed. Later, landscapes, such as views of Mt. Fuji, became popular themes for woodcuts. By the 1800s many European artists collected and were influenced by these prints.

New theater forms also appeared, such as the **bunraku** puppet theater and the racy **kabuki** drama, the favored entertainment of the urban merchant class. Kabuki featured gorgeous costumes, beautiful scenery, and scripts filled with violent passion. Men played all the roles. Professional female impersonators were highly honored and spent years mastering the voice, gestures, and other aspects of femininity. The seventeen-syllable **haiku** poem also became popular. Haiku proved an excellent vehicle for discussing the passage of time or briefly summarizing some action or scene through a series of images, such as the presentation by the samurai turned wanderer and greatest haiku poet, Matsuo Basho (BAH-show) (1644–1694), of a sudden event on a quiet pond:

Werner Forman/Art Resource, NY

Kabuki Theater The urban middle classes, especially the merchants and samurais, enjoyed kabuki drama. This eighteenth-century print by one of the most acclaimed artists, Moronobu, shows the audience enjoying a play about a vendetta involving two brothers.

"An old pond. Frog jumps in. Sound of water." Another Basho poem commented on the change of seasons and human emotions: "No blossoms and no moon, and he is drinking *sake* [rice wine], all alone."[26] Japanese did not need to be lonely on a dark winter's night to appreciate Basho's delicate word art.

Tokugawa Stagnation

Tokugawa Japan largely enjoyed security, stability, and peace for 250 years. But it came at a price. Although commerce thrived, Japan, like China, experienced no political transformation or social rejuvenation. The lack of dynamism left Japan vulnerable to a later return of Western power. The Tokugawa had merely papered over the cracks. When the West intruded in the mid-nineteenth century, the latent tensions boiled over and the Tokugawa lost their grip on power, but Japan, unlike China, was able to respond creatively. Whereas Chinese feared cultural change more than political conquest, the Japanese were more afraid of conquest, and their history of borrowing from abroad made them uniquely prepared to assimilate Western techniques and customs to Japanese traditions, as they had done with Chinese, Korean, and Western imports in earlier eras. China and Japan eventually met the challenge from the West in very different ways.

SECTION SUMMARY

- The Chinese helped Korea to rebuff a 1592 Japanese invasion, but as a result Korean culture began to liberalize and shed some customs borrowed from China.
- Ashikaga Japan saw tremendous economic and population growth, but it was undermined by a lengthy civil war, during which European merchants made incursions and introduced guns and Christianity, upsetting Japan's social order.
- The Tokugawa Shogunate ended Japan's civil war, restored strict order, and expelled European missionaries and traders, with the exception of a small group of Dutch traders who were uninterested in missionary work.
- Despite the Tokugawa leaders' attempt to halt change, the Japanese economy grew rapidly, tensions in Japanese society increased, and Japan's culture flourished in the urban "floating world" and in new theatrical and literary forms.
- Tokugawa Japan was quite stable, but its rigidity hampered its growth and made it vulnerable to overthrow when Western powers returned in the mid-nineteenth century.

CHAPTER SUMMARY

European expansion had much less impact in most of southern and eastern Asia than it had in the Americas and Africa. Many Asian societies remained strong and militarily powerful, able to manipulate or deflect the Europeans who came in search of valuable trade resources and products. Mughal India, especially under the tolerant Akbar, developed creative art and architecture and a prosperous export economy. By the 1700s, however, the Mughals weakened from overspending and religious intolerance as new challenges mounted. While various Southeast Asian states remained strong, the Portuguese and then the Dutch successively captured Melaka and the Spice Islands, and the Dutch gradually conquered Java. The Spanish carved out a colony in the Philippines and began exporting Asian goods from Manila to the Americas, helping build a world economy. Increasing commerce more closely tied Southeast Asia to the growing world economy.

China during the late Ming and early Qing remained among the world's most powerful and prosperous countries, with outstanding leaders, extensive industry, and the world's largest commercial economy. However, while it remained creative in arts and philosophy, overpopulation and declining support for merchants eventually hindered China just as European pressures increased. Both Japan and Korea imposed policies of partial seclusion. After welcoming Western traders and missionaries, Japan restricted their access. The Tokugawa Shogunate maintained a rigid social and political system but also fostered a creative culture. Hence, European activity was only one of many factors influencing Asian societies.

KEY TERMS

Urdu
Sikhs
Moros
Hispanization
Indios
ukiyo-e
bunraku
kabuki
haiku

EBOOK AND WEBSITE RESOURCES

PRIMARY SOURCE
Journals: Matteo Ricci

INTERACTIVE MAPS
Map 18.1 The Mughal Empire, 1526–1761
Map 18.2 Southeast Asia in the Early Modern Era
Map 18.3 Qing China and East Asia in the Early Modern Era

LINKS

Internet East Asian History Sourcebook (http://www.fordham.edu/halsall/eastasia/eastasiasbook.html). An invaluable collection of sources and links on China, Japan, and Korea from ancient to modern times.

Internet Guide for China Studies (http://www.sino.uni-heidelberg.de/igcs/). A good collection of links maintained at Germany's Heidelberg University.

Internet Indian History Sourcebook (http://www.fordham.edu/halsall/india/indiasbook.html). An invaluable collection of sources and links on India from ancient to modern times.

East and Southeast Asia: An Annotated Directory of Internet Resources (http://newton.uor.edu/Departments&Programs/AsianStudiesDept/general.html). This site, prepared at the University of Redlands, offers many links on history, culture, and politics, with much on this era.

Nakasendo Highway: A Journey to the Heart of Japan (http://www.nakasendoway.com). This website, hosted at Hong Kong University, uses a famous highway to introduce Tokugawa Japan.

A Visual Sourcebook of Chinese Civilization (http://depts.washington.edu/chinaciv/). A wonderful collection of essays, illustrations, and other useful material on Chinese history.

WWW Southeast Asia Guide (http://www.library.wisc.edu/guides/SEAsia/). An impressive, easy-to-use site from the University of Wisconsin-Madison.

WWW Virtual Library: South Asia (http://www.columbia.edu/cu/libraries/indiv/area/sarai/). This Columbia University site offers many useful resources.

Plus flashcards, practice quizzes, and more. Go to: www.cengage.com/history/lockard/globalsocnet2e.

SUGGESTED READING

Andaya, Barbara Watson. *The Flaming Womb: Repositioning Women in Early Modern Southeast Asia.* Honolulu: University of Hawai'i Press, 2006. Fascinating scholarly study of gender relations.

Brook, Timothy. *The Confusions of Pleasure: Commerce and Culture in Ming China.* Berkeley: University of California Press, 1998. A readable exploration of Ming China, including the lives of China's people.

Chaudhuri, K. N. *Trade and Civilization in the Indian Ocean: An Economic History from the Rise of Islam to 1750.* Cambridge: Cambridge University Press, 1985. A scholarly study of trade and Islam, focusing on India and Southeast Asia.

Cohen, Warren. *East Asia at the Center: Four Thousand Years of Engagement with the World.* New York: Columbia University Press, 2000. A good summary of China, Korea, Japan, and Southeast Asia in Eurasian history.

Crossley, Pamela Kyle. *The Manchus.* Cambridge, MA: Blackwell, 1997. An excellent study of Manchu history and culture.

Ebrey, Patricia Buckley, Anne Walthall, and James D. Palais. *East Asia: A Cultural, Social, and Political History*, 2nd ed. Boston: Houghton Mifflin, 2009. A readable, comprehensive survey.

Lal, Ruby. *Domesticity and Power in the Early Mughal World.* New York: Cambridge University Press, 2005. Examines women's complex roles in the Mughal court.

Matsunosuke, Nishiyama. *Edo Culture: Daily Life and Diversions in Urban Japan, 1600–1868.* Honolulu: University of Hawaii Press, 1997. A detailed look at popular culture and ways of life during the Tokugawa era.

Mungello, D. E. *The Great Encounter of China and the West, 1500–1800*, 3rd ed. Lanham, MD: Rowman and Littlefield, 2009. A readable account of the meeting of Chinese and European societies in the Early Modern Era.

Phelan, John L. *The Hispanization of the Philippines: Spanish Aims and Filipino Responses, 1565–1700.* Madison: University of Wisconsin Press, 1959. Dated but still the best general study of the topic.

Prakash, Om. *European Commercial Enterprise in Pre-Colonial India.* New York: Cambridge University Press, 1998. A valuable scholarly study.

Reid, Anthony. *Southeast Asia in the Age of Commerce, 1450–1680.* 2 vols. New Haven: Yale University Press, 1988 and 1993. A major scholarly source on the Southeast Asian societies and their interaction with the wider world.

Richards, John F. *The Mughal Empire.* Cambridge: Cambridge University Press, 1993. The major scholarly study of Mughal India.

Schimmel, Annemarie. *The Empire of the Great Mughals: History, Art and Culture.* New York: Oxford University Press, 2005. A well-illustrated survey emphasizing social and cultural history.

Seth, Michael J. A *Concise History of Korea: From the Neolithic Period through the Nineteenth Century.* Lanham, MD.: Rowman and Littlefield, 2006. A recent overview.

Spence, Jonathan D. *Emperor of China: Self-Portrait of Kang-Hsi.* New York: Vintage, 1974. A fascinating study of an important Qing emperor.

Statler, Oliver. *Japanese Inn.* Honolulu: University of Hawaii Press, 1981. A reprint of one of the best portrayals of life in Early Modern Japan.

Subrahmanyan, Sanjay. *The Portuguese Empire in Asia, 1500–1700: A Political and Economic History.* New York: Longman, 1993. An overview of the Portuguese and their impacts.

Taylor, Jean Gelman. *Indonesia: Peoples and Histories.* New Haven: Yale University Press, 2003. A highly readable survey with much on this era.

Historical Controversy

The Great Divergence Between Europe and Asia

In recent years historians have debated the roots of Europe's rise to world leadership, power, and wealth while other societies, especially in Asia, lost the political and economic leadership they once enjoyed—what some call "the great divergence." To many historians the surprising rise of Europe during the Early Modern Era needs explaining. It was not inevitable; history could have turned out very differently.

THE PROBLEM

How, why, and when Europe rather than a major Asian society like China came to dominate the world remain some of the principal questions of modern world history. If several Asian societies had an edge in power and wealth over other societies during most of the Intermediate Era, then why was the world so very different by 1800? Some western European societies, especially Britain, moved toward an unprecedented level of industrialization while once-influential Asian societies, including China, increasingly faced challenges from the West. And when did western Europe begin to diverge from other dynamic, commercialized economies, especially China's? The debate divides into several schools of thought.

THE DEBATE

Many historians argue that the great divergence began in the Intermediate Era, when western Europe developed unique advantages that intensified after 1500. They contend that social, cultural, and political factors gave Europeans an advantage. David Landes believes Europe enjoyed a superior social heritage because its values and institutions promoted economic growth. In his view, European countries prospered because they were vital and open, valuing both hard work and knowledge, and these values led to increased economic productivity and positive attitudes toward change. Rodney Stark emphasizes what he considers a tradition unique to Christianity of stressing reason and progress. Offering another explanation, scholars such as E. L. Jones and Nathan Rosenberg stress the political pluralism represented by fiercely competing states. The chronic warfare between states stimulated a quest for increased revenues and more effective weapons. Furthermore, the flexibility of Western institutions, including the shift toward more representative government in England and Holland, made it easier to take advantage of overseas discoveries. In contrast to dynamic Europe, Landes and Jones argue, the rest of the world was static. China, in their view, had by 1700 reached an economic, political, and intellectual dead end, possessing wealth and power but introducing few inventions leading to any breakthroughs.

Other historians reject the notion of European social and cultural superiority. James Blaut and Andre Gunder Frank contend that the key to Europe's rise was not a unique culture but European countries' acquisition of wealth, especially in precious metals, from their conquests in the Americas. Between 1500 and 1800 the colonized Americas supplied 85 percent of the world's silver and 70 percent of the gold, a huge windfall to European merchants and governments, who were selling much of it to China in exchange for tea, silk, porcelain, and other valuable Chinese exports. The rise of the slavery-based plantation economy in the Americas in the 1600s produced additional profits for the Western colonizers. The sale of profitable American minerals and cash crops such as sugar not only stimulated European capitalism but also gave Europeans new advantages as they tapped into the lucrative Asian market. Blaut also believes that Europe benefited from being much closer than was Asia to the Americas.

Many who dispute the claim that Western social and cultural traditions or the pluralistic state system were an advantage agree that Europeans capitalized on events, such as the American conquests and the acquisition of Asian and Middle Eastern technology, to foster economic growth. Scholars such as John Hobson, Alan Smith, L. S. Stavrianos, and Eric Wolf have shown that western European economies were rapidly commercializing from late medieval times and produced a full-blown commercial capitalism between 1450 and 1800 that helped generate a more widespread and powerful world economy. Nonetheless, while Europeans developed better weaponry and business organization, some historians conclude that Europe had no real advantage over China until the late eighteenth or early nineteenth centuries, when industrialization gave the British and later some other western Europeans a vastly superior technology.

Many historians disagree that China was at a dead end and in economic decline. They argue that China's commercial economy dwarfed all others, making China a major player in world trade. In 1800 China still produced a third of all the world's manufactured goods. China also imported over half of all the silver mined in the Americas. Chinese in the commercialized core regions may have enjoyed as high, if not higher, standards of living, per capita incomes, and long life spans as northwest Europeans before 1800. Chinese merchants and craftsmen were intensely competitive, hardly constrained by the Ming and Qing state. Indeed, China's commercial economy grew rapidly from the early Ming to the mid-1700s, producing abundant export products that were eagerly sought by merchants from all over Afro-Eurasia.

Scholars also question whether other Asian societies, including India, were in decline, even though their states were clearly weakening. By 1800 India could not match China's economy but still produced around a quarter of the world's industry, about the same as Europe. With their many exports and imports, China and India remained the engines for the Eastern Hemisphere trading system well into the 1700s. In the early Mughal era India enjoyed a far larger, more productive economy than England. Although the Mughal state was collapsing by the early 1700s, Indian manufactured goods still attracted a vigorous international trade. R. Bin Wong,

Kenneth Pomeranz, Jack Goldstone, and Andre Gunder Frank suggest that eighteenth-century China, India, western Europe, and perhaps Japan had comparable levels of economic development. The Indian scholar Amiya Kumar Bagchi agrees, stressing that western Europeans enjoyed no decisive advantage over China and India in economic production, consumption, and growth before Britain's Industrial Revolution, and that China only fell behind in the 1850s. Furthermore, he argues, most Europeans saw little improvement in their lives until the late nineteenth century.

In asking why sustained economic growth began first in northwestern Europe rather than in eastern Asia, Pomeranz argues that the densely populated Yangzi River Delta of China, Japan's Tokyo region, and possibly even India's Gujerat region were similar in many respects to the northwest European core regions, England and the Netherlands, in the seventeenth and eighteenth centuries, and that all these regions were facing similar ecological and demographic stress, such as overpopulation. The great divergence came in the 1800s, he suggests, when one country, England, developed fossil fuels, especially its coal industry, for power while increasingly reaping the benefits of cheap, often slavery-produced resources from the Americas. China had used coal many centuries before Europe, but its remaining coal reserves were remote from the major population centers. The availability of slave-produced American wealth and easily tapped coal reserves, Pomeranz suggests, put first England and then northwestern Europe on a completely new development path unavailable to China, Japan, and India, changing world history.

EVALUATING THE DEBATE

This debate will likely thrive for years, making thoughtful arguments on all sides. Some scholars see the rise of the West as inevitable, a result of certain advantageous trends building for centuries, while others argue that things could have turned out differently had Western nations not been able to exploit American resources and China had sustained its dynamism. The Industrial Revolution in Europe, beginning in the late 1700s, which gave Europeans the technology and wealth to achieve global dominance, may have been the product of long-standing and unique European attitudes, or it may have resulted from a late shift in global economic power, fueled by American resources, that favored Europe and undermined China and India. Whether or not Europe was exceptionally enterprising or simply lucky in finding useful resources, the new, expanded world economy that emerged between 1500 and 1800 benefited primarily western Europe and later North America, but it eventually touched everyone, bringing about changes in many aspects of life around the world.

THINKING ABOUT THE CONTROVERSY

1. Why do some historians believe the great divergence between Asia and the West did not come until after 1750?
2. How did Western expansion into the Americas give some European countries an advantage over Asian countries in the global economy?

EXPLORING THE CONTROVERSY

Historians emphasizing Europe's social, cultural, and political advantages include David S. Landes, *The Wealth and Power of Nations: Why Some Are So Rich and Some Are So Poor* (New York: Norton, 1998); Rodney Stark, *The Victory of Reason: How Christianity Led to Freedom, Capitalism, and Western Success* (New York: Random House, 2005); E. L. Jones, *The European Miracle: Environments, Economies and Geopolitics in the History of Europe and Asia*, 3rd ed. (Cambridge: Cambridge University Press, 2003); and Nathan Rosenberg and L. E. Birdzell, Jr., *How the West Grew Rich* (New York: Basic Books, 1986). On the rise of the European-dominated world economy, see Alan K. Smith, *Creating a World Economy: Merchant Capital,*

Tea-Packing Factory in China This painting from the 1700s shows a tea-packing factory in China's major trading port, Guangzhou (Canton) in southern China. A European merchant negotiates with a Chinese manager while Chinese workers prepare tea for export.

Colonialism, and World Trade, 1400–1825 (Boulder, CO: Westview Press, 1991); L. S. Stavrianos, *Global Rift: The Third World Comes of Age* (New York: William Morrow, 1981); and Eric Wolf, *Europe and the Peoples Without History* (Berkeley: University of California Press, 1983). Scholars dubious of innate European advantages include Andre Gunder Frank, *ReORIENT: Global Economy in the Asian Age* (Berkeley: University of California Press, 1998); James Blaut, *The Colonizer's Model of the World: Geographical Diffusionism and Eurocentric History* (New York: Guilford Press, 1993); Amiya Kumar Bagchi, *Perilous Passage: Mankind and the Global Ascendancy of Capital* (Lanham, MD: Rowman and Littlefield, 2005); and John M. Hobson, *The Eastern Origins of Western Civilization* (New York: Cambridge University Press, 2004). On China's continuing strength, see Kenneth Pomeranz, *The Great Divergence: China, Europe, and the Making of the Modern World Economy* (Princeton: Princeton University Press, 2000); and R. Bin Wong, *China Transformed: Historical Change and the Limits of European Experience* (Ithaca, NY: Cornell University Press, 1997). For an excellent discussion of the great divergence debate and related issues, see David D. Buck, "Was It Pluck or Luck That Made the West Grow Rich?" *Journal of World History*, 10, no. 2 (Fall 1999): 413-430; and Jack Goldstone; *Why Europe? The Rise of the West in World History, 1500–1850.* New York: McGraw-Hill, 2009.

Connecting the Early Modern World, 1450–1750

In 1552 a Spanish historian called the landing in the Americas by a naval expedition led by Christopher Columbus "the greatest event since the creation of the world."[1] It was a claim that ignored many previous achievements, yet the permanent connecting of the hemispheres that followed Columbus in fact reshaped the world, helping to make the Early Modern Era vastly different from the Intermediate Era that preceded it. History was now painted on a larger canvas, and peoples' horizons around the world rapidly expanded. In this new global age, greatly increased communication and mobility resulted in encounters, some friendly others hostile, between societies once remote from each other. Travel and exploration revealed the resources of the inhabited world. As a result of this discovery, the exchange among societies of people, diseases, ideas, technologies, capital, resources, and products occurred on a greater scale than ever before. Europeans forged a new world economy, while disrupting, changing, and sometimes destroying the societies they encountered, especially in the Americas and parts of Africa and Southeast Asia. Because of the growing contacts spanning the two hemispheres, for the first time in history an interconnected world became a reality.

But the encounters between Europeans and peoples they could reach only after long sea voyages were only part of the story. The world had many political and economic centers between 1450 and 1750. In the Afro-Eurasian zone, Morocco, the Ottoman Empire, several western European societies, Safavid Persia, Mughal India, China, and a few Southeast Asian societies such as Siam were wealthy, populous, and linked to each other by trade networks and diplomatic ties. They all enjoyed military prowess, had effective states, and fostered creative thinkers. Some African kingdoms, such as Ashante and Buganda, also enjoyed influence and connections to hemispheric trade. No single country or region dominated world politics or the world economy. Yet, the links forged during the Early Modern Era laid a foundation for the building, often by force, of an even more integrated global system, encompassing even the most remote peoples, in the Modern Era.

New Empires and Military Power

From the dawn of recorded history some peoples have used military power to impose their will on others and create empires. As a result, people often think of history in terms of great empires such as Assyria, Rome, Tang China, the Inca, and, the largest of all, the Mongol. Increasing wealth and power, as well as more deadly weapons, led some Early Modern Era societies to build large empires. Some, such as Safavid Persia, Mughal India, Qing China, and Russia, ruled land empires. In contrast to these empires, which annexed nearby and often sparsely populated territories, the Ottoman Turks controlled large areas of southeastern Europe, western Asia, and North Africa, and the Omani Arabs established footholds in East Africa. The Portuguese, Spanish, Dutch, English, and French empires were even more ambitious, incorporating distant peoples in Africa, Asia, and the Americas. These conquests created empires on a geographical scale never imagined before, even by the Mongols. But empire also had limits, and many peoples were able to resist the imperial designs of the major powers.

Gunpowder Empires

Historians characterize most Early Modern empires as "gunpowder empires" because they depended on bigger and better gunpowder weapons, including cannon mounted on ships, field artillery, and guns used by individual soldiers. Gunpowder empires dominated Eurasia and the Americas. Various Asian and European societies sought to acquire resources and markets in neighboring societies by building empires rather than relying chiefly on trade. Only a few European countries, however, had the means, including sea power, to envision dominating very distant societies, and those countries sought resources and then territory in Africa, the Americas, Asia, and the Pacific. Only those few European countries also had the incentive: the quest for "gold, god, and glory." The worldwide exploration, trade, missionary activity, and conquest that took place during this era resulted from the transformation of various European societies by various forces—the rise of capitalism, powerful merchants, and competitive, centralizing states, as well as by rivalry between Christian churches actively seeking converts—while improved military and maritime technology provided the means for all this activity.

Europeans took advantage of their economic growth and military expansion to improve their position in the world and to compete more effectively for resources in the East, where Islamic societies, India, and China had long enjoyed the most political, economic, and cultural power. Advanced naval and military technology, including gunpowder weapons unknown in the Americas and in much of Africa and Southeast Asia, allowed the Portuguese to seize various African and Asian trading ports, and the Spanish to construct a huge empire in the Americas. The Dutch, English, and French soon followed, establishing footholds in North America, the Caribbean, coastal Africa, and southern Asia. The European powers used some of their weapons against each other. For example, the Dutch and Portuguese were bitter rivals for influence and territory in Southeast Asia, Sri Lanka, and Brazil. Europeans controlled Atlantic shipping and also gained considerable power over Indian Ocean trade, which brought them great wealth. As the English adventurer Sir Walter Raleigh recognized in 1608,

From Olfert Dapper, *Beschreibung von Africa*, Amsterdam, 1670

Dutch Diplomats In this print, a Dutch delegation, eager to make an alliance with the Kongolese against the Portuguese, prostrate themselves before the Kongolese king, sitting on his throne under an imported chandelier, in 1642.

"Who so commands the sea commands the trade of the world; who so commands the trade of the world commands the riches of the world."[2]

A Polycentric World

Despite the growth of empires, the Early Modern world had varied centers of political and economic power, a situation known as polycentrism. No one country could dominate all other rivals. Despite their weaponry, Europeans did not become dominant all over the world during this era. European power was limited in Asia, the Middle East, and parts of Africa and South America, and much of North America and the Pacific remained untouched by European exploration. For much of the era, the Ottomans, Mughals, and Chinese were more politically, economically, and culturally influential in Eurasia than European societies. For example, many Muslims admired Mughal India, which became a destination for merchants, writers, and religious scholars. A Persian poet proclaimed: "Great is India, the Mecca of all in need. A journey to India is of essence to any man made worthy by knowledge and skill."[3] The major Asian states also collected far larger tax revenues than did any European government. Societies in Eurasia, from China to England, and in Africa, from Buganda to Songhai, extended their power into nearby territories, centralized their governments, fostered commerce, and worked to integrate ethnic minorities into the broader society.

The era was dynamic for many peoples. Across Eurasia varied societies experienced economic innovation, free markets, industrialization, and rising living standards. For example, cities such as Amsterdam in Holland, Isfahan **(is-fah-HAHN)** in Persia, and Ayuthia **(uh-YUT-uh-yuh)** in Siam were bustling trade crossroads, attracting merchants from all over Eurasia. A Jesuit who visited Surat in northwest India in 1663 found countless foreign ships and thousands of foreign merchants, among them traders from over a dozen European societies, including Swedes and Hungarians, as well as many Asians, from Turks to Chinese. Foreign merchants, such as the Dutch and Persians at Ayuthia or at Surat, had to adapt to local customs to succeed. Sometimes, as in Siam, Tokugawa Japan, and Morocco, Europeans who disregarded local customs or threatened local governments were expelled.

The encounters between peoples fostered compromises and information exchange. Many Asians and Africans adapted ideas from other cultures to meet their own needs. Among other leaders, the Chinese emperor Kangzi **(KANG-see)**, the Siamese king Narai **(na-RY)**, the Mughal sultan Akbar **(AK-bahr)**, and the Kongo king Alfonso I showed a keen interest in Western ideas and technologies. Kangzi, for instance, studied Western science with Italian Jesuits, and Alfonso asked the Portuguese for technical assistance. But Europe was not the only source of knowledge. For example, Narai also borrowed architectural styles and medical knowledge from the Persians and Chinese.

The main European advantage had been in acquiring the resources of the Americas for exploitation, often using enslaved African labor. But the large-scale trans-Atlantic slave trade became possible because the kings or chiefs of some African states, such as Ashante **(ah-SHAN-tee)** and Dahomey **(da-ho-MAY)**, profited by collaborating with it. Similarly, Spanish rule in the Americas survived only because the conquerors ultimately made compromises with Indian societies. For example, in Peru, well-placed Spaniards intermarried with the Inca elite and Spanish officials adopted some Inca administrative traditions. In the Spanish empire, as well as in other empires of the era such as the Ottoman and Mughal, laws recognized local customs, and different groups often maintained their own legal codes.

Innovative thought reflected the vigor of many societies. Science and technology remained creative all over Eurasia. The Chinese and British, for example, published important scientific books and invented new technologies, especially for the textile industry. New astronomical observatories were built in China, India, and the Middle East, although Europeans had by now developed a much keener interest than Asians in clocks and mathematics. Japan's fostering of schools gave it the world's highest literacy rate and an audience for a publishing industry. Siam and Burma also enjoyed high rates of literacy, though it was chiefly restricted to males. Leaders of the European Renaissance, Reformation, and Enlightenment, Sufi mystics in the Ottoman and Mughal Empires, the Hindu bhakti **(BUK-tee)** movement in India, and some Chinese thinkers challenged accepted wisdom. Various European and Chinese philosophers emphasized reason, as did some Latin Americans such as the Mexican nun and scientist Sor Juana Ines de la Cruz. Indeed, some participants in the European Enlightenment were inspired by their growing knowledge of secular China, which was ruled by emperors who dabbled in philosophy. A French ambassador in 1688 praised Qing China for promoting "virtue, wisdom, prudence, good faith, sincerity, charity, gentleness, honesty [and] civility."[4]

European achievement of global power was not inevitable. In this era China as well as several western European societies had sizable empires and the potential for great economic and political success (see Historical Controversy: The Great Divergence Between Europe and Asia). Early Modern China, boasting the world's largest commercialized economy, remained the engine of the Eurasian economy. Not only Europe but also China experienced commercial growth, increases in cash cropping, growing industrial production, and widening marketing networks.

The maritime expansion of Europe, however, contrasted sharply with that of the Chinese. Just as western Europeans turned outward and developed a naval technology to match that of the Chinese, the Chinese pulled back from their grand maritime expeditions of the early 1400s and turned inward, although some Chinese merchants continued to venture out to trade. China enjoyed huge budget surpluses until the late 1700s and did not need colonies or foreign trade to prosper. Unlike western European states, the Chinese government did not depend on rich merchants for economic and political support. Chinese rulers feared that if merchants gained more wealth and influence, they could threaten the state and undermine Confucian values. In contrast, western European merchants had the support of their mercantilist governments, especially in England, the Netherlands, Spain, and France. The resulting political competition between European states fostered exploration and colonization.

Gunpowder and Warfare

Gunpowder weapons were not new. The Chinese invented gunpowder and then made the first true guns in the tenth century C.E., primarily for defensive purposes. The Mongols improved these Chinese weapons into a more effective offensive force, to blow open city gates. By 1241 these weapons had reached Europe. Early Modern Europeans, Turks, Mughals, and Chinese owed their strength in part to improvements in gunpowder weaponry. Combined with better military organization and seagoing capability, advanced weaponry inevitably affected political and social systems.

As they spread around Eurasia and North Africa, gunpowder weapons changed warfare. Europeans learned how to make particularly deadly weapons, improving the technology in part because they had easier access to metals. In Europe—full of competitive, often hostile states—no ruler had a monopoly on weapons, such as siege cannon. Hence rulers had an incentive to constantly improve their armaments, such as handheld muskets, to maintain the balance of power. As a result, the wars in Europe became far more deadly. Indeed, even in Asia and the Americas, Europeans often used the weapons more against each other than against the local people. The French writer Voltaire wrote that after 1500 all the pepper from Calicut came dyed red with blood, and a Portuguese poet lamented that the spices of the Indies were bought with Portuguese blood. The Portuguese, Dutch, and English slaughtered each other in Southeast Asia, and the English and French fought long wars in North America that spilled over into South Asia.

A similar increase in battlefield casualties came in Japan in the civil war era of the 1500s, when Japanese sword-smiths learned how to replicate Portuguese and Spanish guns and cannon. Japanese small arms soon proved superior to European rifles. In contrast, the Ottomans did not create a class of Turkish and Arab craftsmen and instead relied heavily on hiring European craftsmen to manufacture their military and naval technology. Ashante and Dahomey achieved military success in West Africa because they had large armies equipped with muskets acquired from European slave traders.

But Asians took the development of their gunpowder arsenals only so far. With gunpowder weapons, the Qing greatly expanded China's land frontier deep into Central Asia and Tibet, thereby stabilizing their border regions. After that, secure in their power, the Manchu emperors had little need to increase their offensive capability, while the land-oriented Mughals saw little gain in developing naval armaments. The Chinese, Japanese, and Koreans all had some naval power but no interest in challenging the Europeans in the Indian Ocean. When Chinese came into contact with foreign firearms in 1500s, they found them superior to their own. A Chinese military manual published in 1644 concluded that "nothing has more range than the Ottoman musket. The next best is the European one."[5] Nonetheless, Chinese firearms were adequate for ejecting the Dutch from Taiwan and the Russians from the Amur Valley in the 1600s. But two centuries later, European military technology far surpassed that of Asian powers, dramatically changing the hemispheric balance of power.

The Emerging World Economy

With the opening of the Atlantic and Pacific Oceans to regular sea travel, connections spanning not just hemispheres but the entire world were forged during the Early Modern Era. Western Europeans gradually created a global network of economic and political relationships that increasingly shaped the destinies of people around the world. Rather than the luxuries of earlier times, such as silks and spices, long-distance trade increasingly moved bulk items: essential natural resources, such as sugar and silver from the Americas, and manufactured goods, such as textiles from Europe and Asia. Traders moved commodities and capital faster and more cheaply over greater distances than ever before. These trends wove together different societies in a world economy. European merchants were actually only a small part of global commerce; some Asian and African merchant groups also flourished, and some Asian states, particularly China and Siam, benefited from the increasing trade. Nonetheless, western Europeans usually benefited more, and it was Europeans who laid the foundations for a new global system to emerge after 1750.

The New Trading System

Europeans became the main beneficiaries of the increased communication and travel that shaped a gradual globalization of trade. The capitalist market economy that gradually developed was increasingly centered on northwestern Europe, especially England and the Netherlands, but a half dozen other European countries were also enriched by trade (see map). For example, the Portuguese as well as the Dutch established regular maritime trade routes between Europe and Asia around Africa that allowed Europeans to avoid the overland routes through the Middle East while harming their Muslim rivals by diminishing Persian and Ottoman commerce. The Spanish conquest of the Americas provided huge quantities of silver from Peru, Bolivia, and Mexico, which financed expansion of the European economy and, since Asian governments valued silver, enabled Europeans to gain access to Asian markets. The Spanish establishment of a base at Manila in 1571 provided an essential economic link between eastern Eurasia and the Americas, forging a major foundation for a truly world economy. European exploration and settlement in the Americas brought access to resources such as timber, marine mammals, fish, and wildlife (particularly fur-bearing beavers) only lightly exploited before by local peoples.

Growing commercial activity stimulated production for the market, in mining and manufacturing but especially in tropical agriculture. The highly profitable plantations that sprung up around the Caribbean Basin, along the Atlantic coast of North and South America, and on the Atlantic and Indian Ocean islands and the Philippines reflected the expansion of production. A growing trans-Atlantic slave trade provided cheap labor to the American plantations, enabling them to produce inexpensive calories for Europe in the form of sugar and, after 1700, abundant cotton for English mills. Thousands of slaves obtained in eastern Europe, East Africa, Sri Lanka, and Indonesia also labored for European and Muslim enterprises in the Middle East, South Africa, and Southeast Asia.

As a result of the growing commercial activity, including the slave trades, by 1750 millions of people worked thousands of miles from their place of birth or otherwise experienced lives very different from those of their ancestors. For example, Chinese merchants lived on Java, Persians served in the Siamese government, Turkish soldiers fought for the sultans of Acheh **(AH-cheh)** in Sumatra, Portuguese settled in Mozambique, Kongolese labored in Brazil, and French traders explored the Mississippi Basin. Some merchants flourished by having operations in many lands. One of the most successful was the German commercial agent Ferdinand Cron in the late sixteenth and early seventeenth century. Born in Augsburg and then based in Portuguese-ruled Goa on India's west coast, Cron supervised a network of couriers who collected information on markets and prices from Europe in the West to Melaka and Macao in the East and then used that information to make lucrative investments.

Asia and Europe in the New World Economy

The transition to a European-dominated trading system took place over several centuries in Asia. Before the 1800s, when the transition was completed, Asia boasted the bulk of world

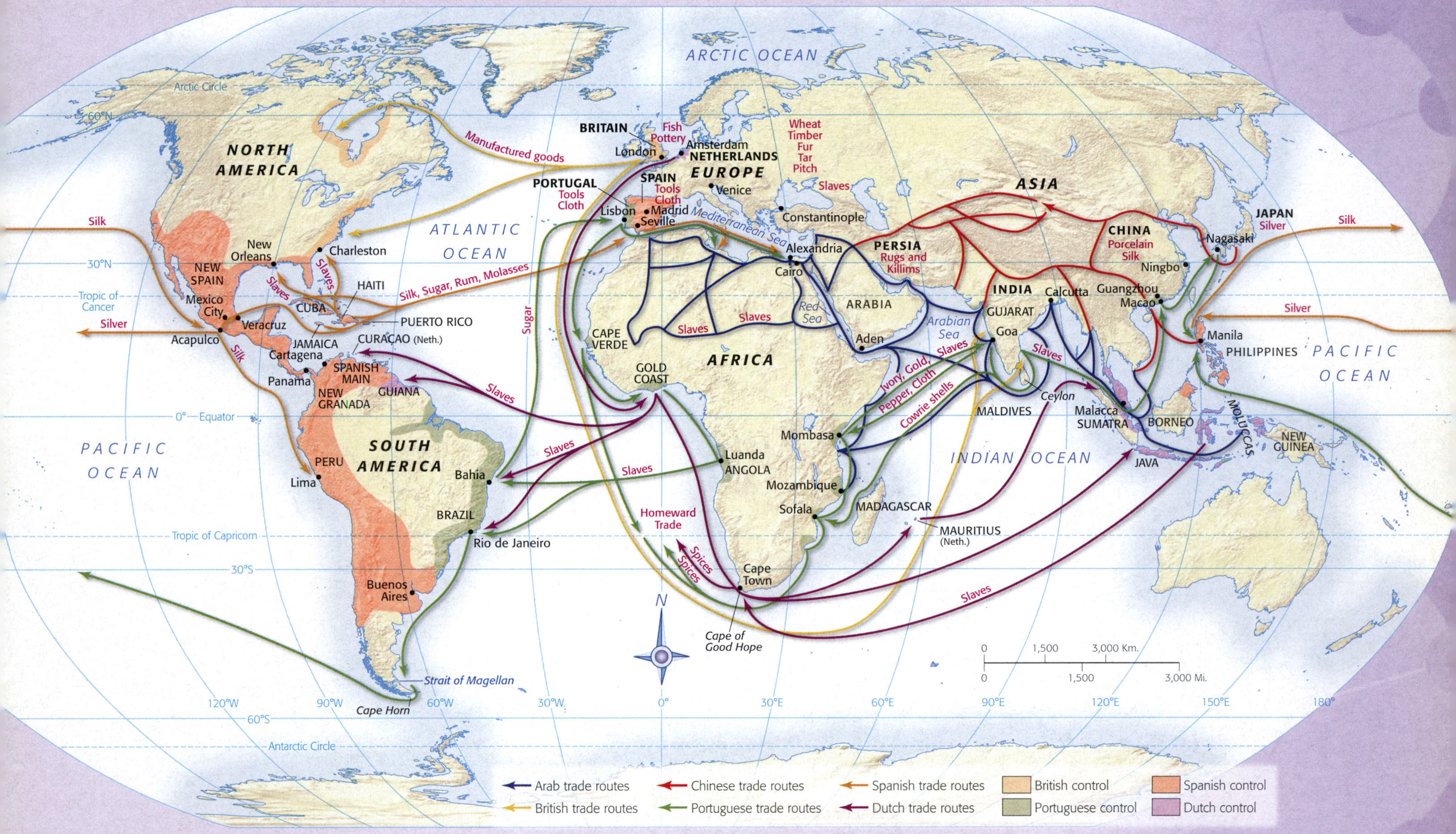

Early Modern Trade Routes

Between 1500 and 1700 the world economy developed and new trade routes proliferated. Major maritime routes linked Asia and the Americas across the Pacific; Europe, Asia, and the Americas across the Atlantic; and eastern and southern Asia with Africa and Europe across the Indian Ocean.

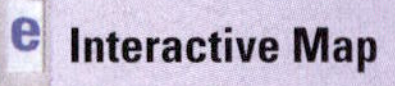

Interactive Map

economic activity. Asians produced some 80 percent of goods as late as 1775, and this production had probably increased since 1500. The industries of China and India remained the twin pillars of Asian commerce well into the 1700s. Indian textiles such as cashmere and cotton cloth were so popular in Asia, Africa, and Europe that they almost constituted a form of currency. Handicraft industries also flourished in the Ottoman Empire, Persia, Sri Lanka, Burma, Siam, and Java during the sixteenth and seventeenth centuries. These societies imported raw materials from India (including raw cotton), China (especially silk), and Japan (copper) for production into exportable consumer goods. For example, Javanese women used beeswax and dying to transform Indian cloth into beautiful batik clothing. The economies of India and China dwarfed those of any other country. The most economically developed regions within China, Japan, India, and northwestern Europe may have enjoyed roughly comparable standards of living, including health and income levels.

Asian merchants, enjoying lower overhead and shrewd business skills, could often outcompete those from Europe. After 1670 Indian merchants even took the Indonesian textile market away from the Dutch. Like Europeans, Asians also traded over long distances. In the 1600s, for example, Arab and Persian traders remained influential at the main Mughal port, Surat, while north Indian merchants were found all over the Persian Gulf. Many wealthy Asian trading magnates had huge capital resources. The trader Virji Vohra **(VEER-gee VOOR-ah)** in Surat was as rich as Europe's wealthiest merchant family, the Fuggers in Germany. A European visitor to Goa in 1510 was amazed at the competition provided by fabulously rich Arab and Indian merchants: "We [Europeans] believe ourselves to be the most astute men that one can encounter, and the people here surpass us in everything. And they can do better calculations by memory than we can do with the pen."[6] European merchants competed best when they were, like the Dutch East Indies Company traders, supported by military force.

European-Asian trade relations often favored Asians. Since Asians had little interest in European manufactured goods such as clothing, which they considered inferior in quality to their own goods, Europeans bought Asian goods and resources with American silver and gold. For example, since Europeans traded with China for products such as tea, vast amounts of American silver ended up in China, where it served as the basis of the monetary system and promoted economic growth. The Ottoman, Safavid, and Mughal Empires also needed an expanding money supply to meet the investment needs of their expanding economies and were, like the Chinese, ready to trade goods for silver.

Asian goods found a ready market around the world. Europeans shipped bullion to Persia for silk, and Persia shipped bullion to India for cotton textiles. Chinese goods transported from the Philippines were so much cheaper than Spanish ones in Peru that the Spanish viceroy complained it was "impossible to choke off the trade since a man can clothe his wife in Chinese silks for 25 pesos, whereas he could not provide her with clothing of Spanish silks with 200 pesos."[7] While European ships carried a growing amount of seaborne trade, European merchants accounted for only a small proportion of trade from India and China. Mughal India traded far more with Central Asians and Ottomans than with the Dutch or English. Asian exports to Europe grew slowly; intra-Asian trade was far larger.

Expanding Trade Networks

The growth of long-distance trade corresponded to the expansion of trade networks operated by different commercial communities. The rise of European power allowed Dutch, English, and French merchants to establish themselves in India, Southeast Asia, West Africa, eastern Europe, Russia, and the Caribbean Basin. At the same time, Sephardic Jews, originally from Iberia, spread their trading networks throughout western Europe, flourishing particularly in Antwerp, Amsterdam, Seville, and Geneva. Eventually, Jews also became active as merchants in parts of South America, the Caribbean, and the Indian Ocean. Some entered the Asian spice trade, developing ties as far east as Melaka. The Mendes family, for instance, expelled from Spain in 1492 and eventually based in Istanbul, had business connections in several European cities and, with their banks, helped finance the gem and spice trades across Asia, Europe, and Africa.

Groups specializing in trade were prominent in many lands. Chinese remained active all over Southeast Asia, establishing permanent settlements in many cities and towns. For example, the Spanish in the Philippines depended on the Chinese merchant class to supply many consumer goods. A Spanish friar observed in the mid-1600s that although Manila "is small, and the Spaniards are few, nevertheless, they require the services of thousands of Chinese."[8] When the Chinese and Japanese governments banned direct trade with each other, Chinese trading ships carried shipments from China and Japan to Southeast Asian ports such as Hoian in Vietnam and Ayuthia, where the goods were exchanged. Traders of French or mixed French and Indian descent traveled deep into the North American continent contacting local peoples. In East Africa, it was the Omani Arabs who had a leading role. In West Africa, Hausa merchants increasingly dominated the trade networks of the Sudan by the 1600s. This trade domination brought prosperity to walled cities like Kano **(KAH-no)**, famous for its cloth manufacturers, and Katsina. Hausa merchants became influential in the Niger Basin as far west as the Ashante kingdom and supplied resources such as kola nuts to the far-reaching trans-Saharan trade, which still flourished despite growing European trade along the west coast. In far western Africa the Dyula **(JOO-lah)**, Mandinka Muslims, held the leading commercial position.

Similarly, some Asian merchants, especially Indians and Armenians, maintained and even expanded commercial networks over vast distances. The Indian maritime trade network stretched from Arabia, Persia, Northeast Africa, and the Red Sea to Melaka, Sumatra, Siam, and China. Although the Portuguese cut into the Indians' power in the Indian Ocean, Indians remained active in the 1700s. Meanwhile, Indian overland trade networks extended across Central Asia, Afghanistan, Tibet, Persia, the Caucasus states, and much of Russia. Armenian merchants based in Safavid Persia flourished in the overland trade from India to Central Asia and the Middle East, and from Persia to Russia, England, and the Baltic. Some Armenians traveled widely. Hovannes Ter-Davtian (tur-DAHV-ti-an) left Isfahan in 1692, traded on the western and eastern coasts of India, and then spent seven years in Tibet before arriving in Calcutta in 1693 with a cargo of Chinese porcelain, gold, and musk that earned him a handsome profit. Growing Eurasian trade clearly involved, and often benefited, varied groups.

Environmental Changes

Human activity reshaped the natural world and was influenced by it in turn. As they had for millennia, people tapped the earth for underground resources, such as coal and iron ore, but large-scale manufacturing, which often pollutes the environment, was found in only a few widely scattered countries, mostly in Eurasia. For farming and light industries, Early Modern economies relied chiefly on traditional power sources, such as people, animals, water, and wind. For example, windmills were common in the Middle East and Europe, and spinning wheels, often operated by women, were widespread in Eurasia and North Africa. Nonetheless, natural systems came under more stress as the global population nearly doubled, putting severe pressure on land and resources. Expanding settlements and farming in frontier regions displaced woodlands, grasslands, and wetlands and reduced the variety of plant and animal life. More spectacularly, the exchange of diseases, plants, and animals across the Atlantic altered entire environments and resulted in huge population losses in the Americas.

Climate Change and Population Growth

Between 1300 and 1850 much of the world experienced a fluctuating "Little Ice Age," probably caused by a dimming sun and increased volcanic activity, that had significant consequences for many societies. In North America and Eurasia, this period brought cool temperatures, shorter growing seasons, and famine. The coldest years came between 1570 and 1730, and then through the early 1800s. For example, in the 1600s China often received either too much rain, which caused widespread flooding, or too little rain and late springs, which produced drought and reduced the growing season to allow for only one crop of rice rather than two. The lands bordering the North Atlantic saw much colder and wetter conditions, which diminished agricultural production and resulted in widespread starvation in much of Europe. Indeed, harsh weather conditions, combined with occasional outbreaks of bubonic plague, may have been one of the factors that spurred Europeans to seek new lands abroad. Climate change also affected tropical regions. For example, West Africa had abundant rain until 1700, when rainfall began diminishing, allowing desert to claim much of the Sahel and pushing savannah farming southward by several hundred miles.

Nonetheless, despite the poor weather, the distribution of new food sources and other resources was widening. For instance, western European societies obtained more food, particularly grain, from eastern Europe, and thus became more linked to that region. Seaborne trade, especially from the Americas, also provided valuable resources, especially to coastal maritime states such as the Netherlands and Britain. The increased diffusion of resources fostered population growth. Indeed, American crops such as the potato helped Europe stave off even worse climate-related famines. To the east, the Mughals cleared the forests and wetlands of Bengal to create a large area for rice growing, which allowed them to feed more people. Around the world the expansion of farming to sustain more people came at the expense of shifting cultivators, pastoralists, and food collectors. Some peoples, such as the pastoral Khoikhoi (KOI-KOI) in South Africa, died off or were enslaved or killed.

Partly because of the spread of food crops, especially from the Americas to Afro-Eurasia, world population increased significantly. In 1500 the earth contained between 400 and 500 million people. Perhaps 60 percent lived in Asia, with China and India each accounting for nearly a quarter of the world total. By 1750 the world population had grown to between 700 and 750 million, probably 80 percent of them peasants living on the land. China and India together, totaling perhaps 400 million, still accounted for over half, while Europe held perhaps 20 percent and Africa 10 percent of the world total.

The Exchange of Diseases, Animals, and Crops

In this era people, chiefly Europeans and Africans, moved voluntarily or involuntarily to distant lands, deliberately or accidentally carrying with them species of animals, insects, bacteria, and plants that reshaped local ecosystems. These biological invasions, what historians have termed the Columbian Exchange, particularly accompanied the encounter between Eurasia and the Americas. The European settlers in the Americas brought with them horses and food animals: pigs, chickens, sheep, and cattle. To raise beef cattle, Europeans introduced ranching. Ships returning to Europe carried with them American turkeys, which enriched Eurasian diets.

The exchange of diseases between the Eastern and Western Hemispheres was not one-way, but it had a greater impact on the Americas than on Eurasia and Africa. Native Americans had never experienced, and hence had developed no immunities to, Afro-Eurasian diseases such as smallpox, diphtheria, measles, chicken pox, whooping cough, malaria, bubonic plague, yellow fever, cholera, typhoid fever, and influenza.

These diseases devastated the Americas. Smallpox brought the greatest known demographic catastrophe in world history, killing off around 90 percent of the peoples of the Americas. This was a much greater percentage of population than that destroyed by the terrible Black Death, which ravaged much of Eurasia and North Africa in the 1300s. The demographic disaster for the Americas emptied productive land and hence paved the way for Europeans to settle the Americas and to import captive Africans to labor in mining and agriculture. Only in the highlands, such as the Andes Mountains in South America, where European diseases had a smaller impact, did substantial concentrations of Native Americans survive. In contrast, only a few American diseases, especially syphilis, brought suffering to people in Europe and Africa.

Crop exchanges also proved momentous. Eurasian and African crops transformed some American regions and required the introduction of new agricultural practices. Most Native Americans had grown crops such as corn (maize) and potatoes on small plots, but settlers found that Afro-Eurasian crops such as wheat, rice, coffee, barley, and sugar were most successfully grown on large farms or estates. Among these imported crops, sugar had the most impact on the Americas, and vast acreage was devoted to its growth, mostly on plantations worked by African slaves and their descendants. Much of the sugar was exported to Europe for use to sweeten foods such as jam and breads, and beverages such as tea and coffee.

American crops spread widely in the Eastern Hemisphere, where people adopted them to enhance their lives or resolve some of their own food problems. Tobacco, for instance, gained popularity in China and Europe, generating both avid devotees (some of whom considered it medicinal) and opponents who considered it unhealthy or immoral. Many imports,

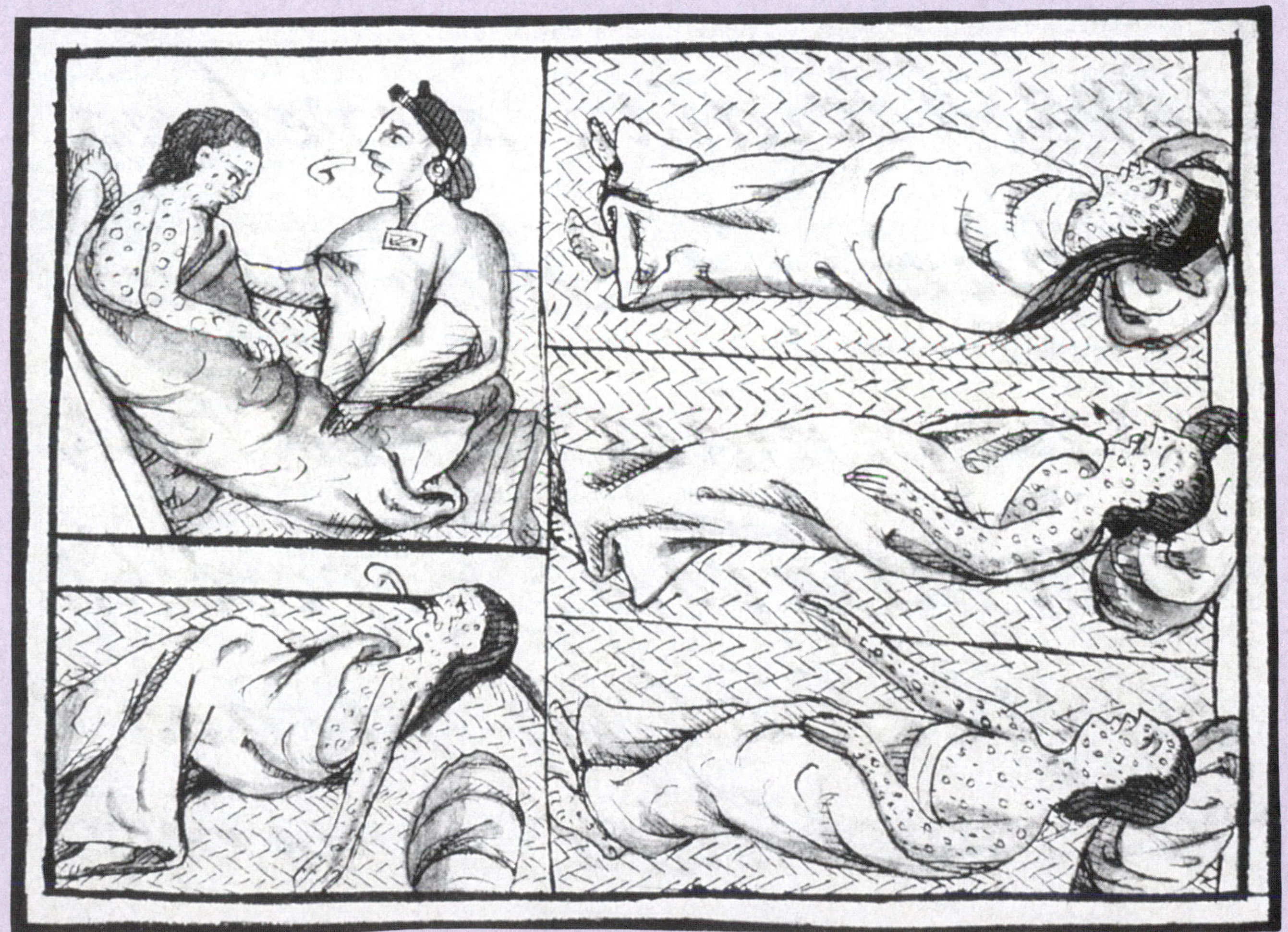

Biblioteca Medicea Laurenziana

Smallpox Victims in the Americas Eurasian diseases accompanied the Europeans to the Americas, causing a catastrophic loss of life for the Native Americans, who had no immunity. As shown in this print from the 1500s, millions of people sickened and died from smallpox.

such as tomatoes, made the once-bland European meals more varied. Potatoes became a mainstay of the European diet and the major crop grown in several societies, including Ireland and Scotland. Maize (corn) could be grown on marginal land and proved a boon in Africa, Southwest Asia, and China, where it was planted on unused hillsides. Corn also fed livestock, and the stalks could be used to make huts and sheds. American chilies, hotter than Asian black peppers, proved hugely popular in South and Southeast Asian cooking, adding a sharp bite to curries and other foods. Peanuts became a key crop in West Africa. The new foods offered not only a more varied diet but also a healthier one. By 1750 a diner in many cities in the world could enjoy a fruit salad mixing pieces of Southeast Asian bananas and mangos, Chinese peaches, Southwest Asian pears, African watermelons, Mesoamerican papayas, South American pineapples, and Mediterranean grapes.

European expansion and colonization owed much to the spread of the Eurasian biota, a distinct package of plants, animals, and germs that overwhelmed the rest of the world, especially the Americas and, later, Oceania. Eurasian plants, such as wheat and apple trees, and animals, such as cattle, often replaced indigenous ones in the temperate zones of the Americas and, after 1800, Australia and New Zealand. These changes occurred in part because Europeans viewed animals, plants, and land largely as commodities, to be exploited for their own benefit. The English scientist Sir Francis Bacon expressed these attitudes well: "The world is made for man, not man for the world."[9]

Social and Cultural Change

During the Early Modern Era, the growing networks of trade, information, and technology fostered changes in societies all over the world. Some changes resulted from the increasing migration of peoples, voluntarily or by force. Intermarriage or sexual contact between people from different ethnic groups produced new peoples with mixed cultural backgrounds. Other contributing factors were changing economic systems, the growth of international trade, and the exchange of ideas. Encounters with other ways of living and thinking stimulated curiosity and fostered rethinking. Several religions expanded their boundaries and sought converts, challenging the ancient faiths of the Americas and parts of Asia.

Migration and Hybrid Groups

Improved maritime technology made it possible for people to cross vast oceans and to do so in larger numbers than ever before. The resulting contacts between peoples reshaped societies. A new system of global migration brought people with very different customs and values together, not always happily. The largest population movement involved Europeans settling in the Americas and bringing with them enslaved Africans but few European women. Women comprised perhaps only a fifth of the Spanish and Portuguese who went to the Americas; men thus frequently sought partners among Native American and African women.

Intermarriage and sexual relations across social boundaries led to the creation of American societies that contained many mixed-descent people. By 1750 in Latin America and in French colonies such as Haiti and Louisiana a large part of the population blended European and Native American backgrounds, creating mestizos, or European and African ancestries, fostering mulattos. For example, many people in Mexico City were mestizo, while in New Orleans blacks and mulattos predominated. In turn, these groups' cultures often mixed the varying social influences, as in northeast Brazil, where people blended African religions and Catholic traditions. Unlike English North America, where any African ancestry usually meant classification as black, in much of Latin America a complex hierarchy of social categories developed based on gradations of skin color.

Migration and intermarriage also occurred in the Eastern Hemisphere. Dutch and Portuguese adventurers and merchants, most of them men, settled in southern Africa and the port cities of South and Southeast Asia, often taking wives from the local population. Some of the Russians who moved into Siberia and the Black Sea region mixed with local peoples. As had been true for centuries, Arab and Indian traders relocated to distant lands in Africa and Eurasia, often settling permanently and sometimes taking local wives. Many Chinese also migrated, usually with their families, and moved into nearby territories such as Taiwan, and male merchants settled in Southeast Asia, where they often intermarried. For example, several thousand Chinese lived in the major Siamese city, Ayuthia; one of them wrote in the early 1600s that "Siam is really friendly to the Chinese."[10] Many of the Chinese married Ayuthia women and stayed permanently, their descendants mixing Chinese and Siamese culture. More Chinese also arrived, and by 1735 some 20,000 lived in the kingdom.

Groups of mixed European and Asian ancestry appeared in European colonies in Asia. For instance, the Portuguese men who settled in Goa, Colombo, and Melaka married local women and raised their children as Portuguese-speaking Catholics. But their descendants adopted many local customs. Hence, in Melaka today, while Catholic churches, schools, and festivals remain at the heart of Portuguese community life, the local Portuguese language contains many Malay words, the cuisine has borrowed extensively from Malay and Chinese cooking, and, unlike their merchant, sailor, and soldier ancestors, most men work as fishermen. Throughout the era Portuguese was the lingua franca of maritime Asia, spoken in many ports, and some of its words were incorporated into local languages such as Malay.

In Africa too—South Africa, Mozambique, Angola, and along the West African coast—the mixing of Europeans and Africans led to hybrid social groups. The offspring of relations between Dutch men and African or Asian women were so common in South Africa that they became a distinct racial group, known as the Coloreds. Prominent slave-trading and merchant families of West Africa often descended from Portuguese men who married women from local chiefly or royal families. Like Brazilian mulattos and many Asian mestizos, African mulattos often spoke a version of Portuguese, the first language with a global reach.

Changing Gender Relations

Although men, voluntarily or involuntarily, were much more likely than women to join overseas ventures or cross oceans, women were also affected by the changes of the era. In the Americas many European men sought Indian women, often by force. One-third of enslaved Africans taken to the Americas were women, some of whom were brought into close contact with slave-owning men, mostly white, who exercised control over their lives. The result was forced sexual activity and mixed-descent children. Since slave couples were often separated by sale, women held together many slave households, a social pattern that continued among many African Americans after the abolition of slavery. Christian missionaries working among North American Indians often pursued policies that marginalized women in once-egalitarian cultures such as the Algonquians of eastern Canada and the Iroquois of New York.

Gender patterns were modified around the world, including in Africa. For instance, in the parts of Africa most affected by slave trading, the absence of men in their productive years encouraged the remaining men to take multiple wives, a practice that may or may not have made life easier for women. The traditional role of West African women in local commerce, however, also meant that, along the coast, some became active as slave traders. A few of these, such as Senhora Philippa, who in the 1630s controlled the trading center of Rufisque **(ROO-feesk)** in today's Senegal, became immensely wealthy and owned trading ships and magnificent houses. Women also played powerful roles in some of the newer kingdoms fostered by the trans-Atlantic slave trade, where they controlled access to the kings. For example, in Dahomey queen-mothers wielded extraordinary power in a palace occupied by a few men and thousands of women, many of them wives and concubines of the king. Dahomey women also served as soldiers and bodyguards. A Portuguese missionary to one Senegambia kingdom described a powerful woman, the king's aunt, who was "so respected and obeyed that nothing of importance took place in the kingdom without her knowledge."[11] Of course, most African women, whether slave or free, enjoyed much less wealth and power in their communities than these merchants and royal women.

In much of Eurasia women experienced increasing subordination by men. Hence, women generally became more restricted in Mughal India, China, and Japan as patriarchal attitudes strengthened, largely as a result of internal factors. For example, Qing leaders turned more socially conservative, imposing harsher laws against behavior considered deviant, such as homosexuality, and stressing the purity of women, which meant less freedom for women to leave home. Adopting the idea of the "chaste widow," more Chinese widows than ever before, forever faithful to their late husbands, frequently refused to remarry. In addition, Western missionaries and officials often sought to impose their own patriarchal prejudices on Asians. Hence, in Southeast Asia, the Spanish and Portuguese were often appalled at the relative freedom of women. Spanish officials criticized Filipinos for tolerating adultery and premarital sex, and they punished those who engaged in these activities.

But there were exceptions to the growing restrictions on women. The Mughal emperor Akbar ordered that no woman could be forced by family or community pressures to immolate herself on her husband's funeral pyre, arguing that "it is a strange commentary on the magnanimity of men that they seek their own salvation by means of the self-sacrifice of their wives."[12] Many Qing women from elite families published essays and poetry that were widely read and admired. One Chinese poet recalled how her father nurtured her talent: "Understanding that I was quite intelligent, He taught his daughters as he taught his sons, [advising us to] Develop together, support, and do not impede each other."[13]

Missionaries and Religious Change

The encounters between widely differing cultures around the world also had a religious dimension, forcing people to confront different belief systems while widening or sparking divisions in established faiths. Some of the major conflicts came in Europe. Tensions simmering for several centuries finally fragmented Western Christianity into Catholic and diverse Protestant churches in the 1500s, spurring religious wars, militancy, and hostility toward non-Christians. Dissenters were punished by those in the majority. Scientists such as the Italian astronomer Galileo Galilei and the Flemish biologist Andreas Vesalius **(an-DRAY-us ve-SAL-yus)**, who produced the first reference manual on human anatomy, were tried by the Holy Inquisition, a Catholic Church institution organized to root out heresy.

Meanwhile, other religious traditions also dealt with tensions and divisions. Mystical Sufi orders became more influential in Islamic societies from Indonesia to West Africa. For example, the early Mughal emperors Babur and Akbar were fervent Sufis. Babur wrote in a poem that "I am their follower in heart and soul. I am a king, but yet a slave [follower] of the Dervishes [mystics]."[14] But the Sufis' popularity distressed dogmatists, fostering debate on Sufism's role and value among Ottoman, Mughal, and Central Asian Muslims. Islamic division hardened in Persia, too. Ordered by their Safavid rulers, Persians shifted from the Sunni to the Shi'a branch of Islam, causing many Sunnis to emigrate. But tensions sometimes led to secular approaches rather than to religious zeal. One such movement, neo-Confucianism, became a strong influence in China, helping secular values to triumph there while Buddhism lost influence among the elites. To comprehend a world charged with diverse and changing ideas, Chinese thinkers, European Enlightenment philosophers, and several Mughal emperors questioned religious dogmas and sought to broaden intellectual horizons.

In contrast to those who explored new ideas, many were religious militants and engaged in missionary activity. Christians actively sought converts in the Americas, Africa, and Asia. Christian missionaries were often intolerant of local traditions and scornful toward the people they were trying to reach. One prominent Spanish clergyman strongly supported conquest and evangelization as a way of "civilizing" Native Americans, whom he described as "these pitiful men, in whom you will scarcely find any vestiges of humanness. They were born for servitude. How are we to doubt that these people, so uncultivated, so barbarous, and so contaminated with such impiety and lewdness, have not been so justly conquered."[15] Catholicism eventually triumphed in Latin America, Kongo, and the Philippines, and it found a few thousand converts in East Asia. Protestant missionaries mostly concentrated on Catholic Europe, Southeast Asia, and North America, where they particularly targeted Native Americans and slaves.

At the same time, the Christian missionary enterprise faced challenges, including stiff resistance. To gain acceptance, missionaries often had to blend Christianity with local traditions, often against the opposition of church leaders. The intolerance of many Christian missionaries toward other faiths led to their expulsion from Japan and China. East Asians assimilated some useful Western technical and scientific knowledge from the missionaries, such as clock-making and mapmaking, but most rejected Christianity. Christian missionary efforts had little success among Muslims, Theravada Buddhists, and Hindus. Indeed, missionary activity sometimes prompted non-Christians to solidify support for traditional ways, as was the case in China and Japan.

Christianity was not the only missionary religion: millions of Europeans, Africans, and Asians embraced Islam. Islam spread into the Balkan societies under Ottoman control, and many Serbs, Albanians, and Bulgarians adopted the faith, forging a permanent divide between Christians and Muslims in the region. Islam continued to gain strength in sub-Saharan Africa, Mughal India, and Island Southeast Asia. Unlike Christianity, Islam was not identified with unpopular Western conquest, and it continued to link distant societies. For instance, in the 1600s Nuruddin al-Raniri **(new-ROOD-in al-RAN-eer-ee)**, from Gujerat in India, studied in Mecca and then traveled widely, finally settling in Acheh, Sumatra, and becoming an adviser to the king. Under Nuruddin's influence, the sultan promoted the more vigorous practice of Islamic customs, such as fasting, strict dietary laws, and alms-giving.

Some trends promoted accommodation between divergent faiths. For example, in India the Mughal emperor Akbar preached tolerance and cultural diversity. Indeed, in some respects Akbar and his ancient Indian predecessor, the Mauryan emperor Asoka, were global pioneers in promoting respect for different traditions. Akbar's more zealously Islamic successors, however, repressed Hinduism, reviving a long conflict between the two faiths. Theravada Buddhists generally respected all religions. Hence, when the French king, Louis XIV, sent a mission to King Narai of Ayuthia requesting that he and his people adopt Roman Catholicism, the Siamese monarch sent a letter back, arguing that God rejoiced not in religious uniformity but in theological diversities, preferring to be honored by different worships and ceremonies. Meanwhile, Muslims and animists lived side by side without conflict in parts of Africa. Similarly, in some European societies, notably the Netherlands and Poland, Protestants and Catholics learned to live in peace. And growing European knowledge of Chinese society, including Confucianism, led some leaders of the European Enlightenment, such as Voltaire, to view China as an admirable, secular alternative model to the religious divisions and orthodoxies of Europe. In this way Asian ideas influenced some Europeans just as European ideas spread to some non-European peoples, a testament to an increasingly connected world.

Suggested Reading

Books

Adas, Michael, ed. *Islamic and European Expansion: The Forging of a Global Order*. Philadelphia: Temple University Press, 1993. Contains excellent essays by William McNeill, Alfred Crosby, and Philip Curtin on major developments in this era.

Black, Jeremy. *War in the World: Military Power and the Fate of Continents, 1450–2000.* New Haven: Yale University Press, 1998. A global history of land and sea warfare and its contexts.

Brandon, William. *New Worlds for Old: Reports from the New World and Their Effect on the Development of Social Thought in Europe, 1500–1800.* Athens: Ohio University Press, 1986. Examines the impact on Europe of the American discoveries and cultures.

Brook, Timothy. *Vermeer's Hat: The Seventeenth Century and the Dawn of the Global World.* New York: Bloomsbury Press, 2008. Fascinating examination of how global commerce influenced European consumer culture.

Canizares-Esquerra, Jorge and Erik R. Seeman, eds. *The Atlantic in Global History, 1500–2000.* Upper Saddle River: Pearson Prentice Hall, 2007. Interesting essays on varied topics.

Crosby, Alfred W. *Ecological Imperialism: The Biological Expansion of Europe, 900–1900.* Cambridge: Cambridge University Press, 1993. A pioneering exploration of the environmental changes in the past millennium.

Curtin, Philip D. *The World and the West: The European Challenge and the Overseas Response in the Age of Empire.* Cambridge: Cambridge University Press, 2000. Explores relevant themes in world history since 1500.

Darwin, John. *After Tamerlane: The Rise and Fall of Global Empires, 1400–2000.* New York: Penguin, 2008. Informative overview of interactions and empires.

Eltis, David. *The Rise of African Slavery in the Americas.* New York: Cambridge University Press, 2000. Overview of slavery and the Atlantic system.

Goldstone, Jack. *Why Europe? The Rise of the West in World History, 1500–1850.* New York: McGraw-Hill, 2009. Provocative interpretation that decenters the West.

Gunn, Geoffrey C. *First Globalization: The Eurasian Exchange.* Lanham, MD: Rowman and Littlefield, 2003. An idiosyncratic but absorbing study of East-West encounters.

Hobhouse, Henry. *Seeds of Change: Five Plants That Transformed Mankind*. New York: Harper and Row, 1985. A fascinating study of how quinine, sugar, tea, cotton, and the potato changed the world.

Marks, Robert B. *The Origins of the Modern World: A Global and Ecological Narrative*, 2nd ed. Lanham, MD: Rowman and Littlefield, 2007. A stimulating, readable, and concise account of how the modern world emerged.

McVay, Pamela. *Envisioning Women in World History, 1500–Present.* New York: McGraw-Hill, 2009. A good comparative overview.

Pacey, Arnold. *Technology in World Civilization.* Cambridge: MIT Press, 1990. Provides a global overview of technological change in this era.

Pilcher, Jeffrey M. *Food in World History.* New York: Routledge, 2006. Examines changing food cultures around the world.

Pomeranz, Kenneth, and Steven Topic. *The World That Trade Created: Society, Culture, and the World Economy, 1400 to the Present,* 2nd ed. Armonk, NY: M.E. Sharpe, 2006. Contains dozens of brief essays written for the general public.

Richards, John F. *The Unending Frontier: An Environmental History of the Early Modern World*. Berkeley: University of California Press, 2003. A detailed but stimulating study of environmental change, with many case studies.

Smith, Alan K. *Creating a World Economy: Merchant Capital, Colonialism, and World Trade, 1400–1825*. Boulder, CO: Westview Press, 1991. A valuable survey of the world economy in this era.

Wiesner-Hanks, Merry E. *Christianity and Sexuality in the Early Modern World: Regulating Desire, Reforming Practice*. New York: Routledge, 2000. A wide-ranging study of the impact of spreading Christianity on sexual practices.

Wills, John E. *1688: A Global History*. New York: W.W. Norton, 2001. A very readable and informative exploration of various peoples and societies around the world in the late seventeenth century.

WEBSITES

Native Americans and the Land (*http://www.nhc.rtp.nc.us:8080/tserve/nattrans/ntecoindian/essays/columbian.htm*). Contains varied materials on the Columbian Exchange.

Columbus and the Age of Discovery (*www.millersville.edu/~columbus/*). This site, maintained by Millersville University, offers many sources related to the linking of the hemispheres during this era.

Early Modern Resources (*http://www.earlymodernweb.org.uk/emr/*). A useful British site offering many links to essays and sources.

Internet Global History Sourcebook (*http://www.fordham.edu/halsall/global/globalsbook.html*). An excellent set of links on world history from ancient to modern times.

Internet Modern History Sourcebook (*http://www.fordham.edu/halsall/*). An extensive online collection of historical documents and secondary materials.

PART V

Global Imbalances: Industry, Empire, and the Making of the Modern World, 1750–1945

The Early Modern Era from the mid-1400s to the mid-1700s, discussed in Part IV, constituted a key stage in the building of today's world. During that era European overseas expansion established permanent communication between the Eastern and Western Hemispheres, building ever closer political and economic ties between Europe, the Americas, the West and East African coasts, and some Asian societies. These ties in turn fostered a global economy while dramatically altering the lives, for better or worse, of many people.

The next key stage in creating the world we live in today came during the Modern Era, between around 1750 and 1945, which was marked by revolutions in political, intellectual, economic, and social life around the world. In countries such as France, Britain, the United States, and Japan, political revolutions or major reforms replaced old governments with more democratic or progressive governments, inspiring other peoples to seek similar changes. Latin Americans became independent from Spanish and Portuguese colonialism. In many countries political change went hand in hand with new ideas about the relationship between citizens and governments, new visions of a better life, and more skeptical attitudes toward organized religions. At the same time, Western nations transformed world politics by asserting their power in Asia, Africa, and Latin America, a few of them establishing huge colonial empires. The peoples they colonized, however, often resisted Western rule. Meanwhile, in the economic realm, the Industrial Revolution, which produced unprecedented goods and fostered technological advances, reshaped Western economic life. In some societies assertive workers', peasants', and women's movements challenged old aristocratic social orders. Overall, great progress was made toward improving social and economic conditions, especially in providing material goods. But the progress was purchased at a high cost in the dislocation of human lives, the suppression of colonized peoples, the ravaging of the natural environment, growing antagonism toward the powerful Western nations, and the deadliest wars in history.

The increasing military, political, and economic domination of the rest of the world by several European nations, soon joined by the United States, was a major trend in the nineteenth and early twentieth centuries. While Western peoples controlled some

The Robert Opie Collection

Colonial Advertisement As imperialism became a part of European life, advertisers capitalized on the interest in the colonial realm. This nineteenth-century advertisement for a British biscuit company shows a scene of the British in India.

35 percent of the world's land surface in 1800, they controlled over 84 percent by 1914. This domination encouraged European emigration and helped to spread capitalism, Western languages, and Western ideas such as Christianity and Marxism. It also contributed to huge changes in the world economy. Strongly shaped by Western activity, the world economy reshuffled natural resources, so that rubber, for example, a plant native to Brazil, became a major cash crop in Southeast Asia, often grown by Indian or Chinese immigrants. Around the world men and women now often worked for wages to produce goods primarily for sale in distant markets rather than the local community.

But Western expansion and domination also created imbalances. The major imbalance was a growing gap by the early 1900s between rich nations and poor societies. Rich nations enjoyed industrialization and, in some cases, imperial expansion. The poor societies, by contrast, were usually colonies of Western nations, economically subordinate to the West, or, like China and Latin America, subject to informal Western power. Most Asian societies powerful in the Early Modern Era, including China and India, declined. The West, including North America, increasingly exported industrial and consumer goods while people elsewhere largely exported raw materials. Six hundred years ago many Chinese and Southeast Asians and some Native Americans lived longer and healthier lives than did most Europeans. By the early twentieth century, however, the balance had changed and most societies in western Europe and North America were far richer and healthier, and had far more influence on the world, than other peoples.

By the first decade of the twentieth century Western imperialism had generated global integration, the increasing connections between societies. Sparked partly by these connections, major changes came to the world during the first half of the twentieth century, some of them creating widespread misery. The hopes for a more democratic, equitable world were undermined by two ruinous world wars, the decade-long collapse of the world economy, and some of history's most brutal, despotic governments. Meanwhile, people in Asia, Africa, and Latin America increasingly challenged Western power and unpopular local governments. These developments set the stage for a new world order to emerge after 1945.

EUROPE
The Industrial Revolution, which began in Britain in the later 1700s, sparked dramatic economic, social, and political change. The French Revolution and the rise of parliamentary democracy in nations such as Britain benefited the middle classes and fostered new national loyalties. Russia conquered Siberia and Central Asia. Britain, France, and Germany renewed imperialism in the later 1800s, forging large empires in Asia and Africa. After 1914 Europe was reshaped by World War I, communist revolution in Russia, economic collapse, the rise of fascism, and World War II.

WESTERN ASIA
Although gradually losing its grip on southeastern Europe and North Africa, the Ottoman Empire maintained control of much of western Asia until after World War I, when Britain and France acquired the Arab territories and the Ottomans collapsed, replaced by a modernizing Turkish state. Persia attempted reforms but still fell under Western domination. Arab nationalism challenged Western power, while secular reformers and pro- and antimodern Muslims struggled for influence throughout the region.

EASTERN ASIA
China remained strong until the early 1800s, when, unable to reform and thwart Western ambitions, it lost several wars to the West and experienced rebellions. After a revolution ended the imperial system in the early 1900s, China lapsed into warlordism and then civil war, opening the door for Japanese invasion. Fearing Western power, the Japanese had rapidly industrialized and modernized their society in the later 1800s but, ravaged by economic depression, came under military rule in the 1930s, which eventually led to their defeat in World War II.

AFRICA
Although some African states, such as Ashante, Buganda, and Egypt, remained strong into the 1800s and instituted reforms, they could not halt increasing Western power. The ending of the trans-Atlantic slave trade by the mid-1800s opened the door to Western colonization of the entire continent. The British and French built large empires in both sub-Saharan Africa and North Africa. Western imperialism created artificial countries, undermined traditional societies, and drained Africa of resources. After World War I African and Arab nationalist movements struggled against Western domination.

SOUTHERN ASIA AND OCEANIA
Overcoming local resistance, the British gradually conquered India, and their rule exploited India's resources, reshaped Indian life, and generated opposition from Indian nationalists seeking independence. Dynamic Southeast Asian states repulsed the West until the mid-1800s, when the British, French, and Dutch colonized all of these resource-rich societies, except Thailand, often against fierce resistance, and the United States replaced Spanish rule in the Philippines, crushing a local independence movement. To the east, Western powers colonized the Pacific islands and Europeans settled in Australia and New Zealand.

CHAPTER 19

Modern Transitions: Revolutions, Industries, Ideologies, Empires, 1750–1914

CHAPTER OUTLINE

- The Age of Revolution
- The Industrial Revolution and Economic Growth
- Nationalism, Liberalism, and Socialism
- The Resurgence of Western Imperialism

PROFILE
Tommy Armstrong, Bard of the English Coal Mines

WITNESS TO THE PAST
The Communist View of Past, Present, and Future

British Museum/Laurie Platt Winfrey, Inc.

Crystal Palace Exposition of 1851
Attracting more than 6 million visitors, the Great Exhibition, held at the Crystal Palace in London in 1851, showcased industrial products and the companies that produced them from all over the world but especially from Europe.

From this foul drain the greatest stream of human industry flows out to fertilize the whole world. From this filthy sewer pure gold flows. Here humanity attains its most complete development and its most brutish.

—French writer Alexis de Tocqueville on Manchester, England, 1835[1]

FOCUS QUESTIONS

1. How did the Caribbean and Latin American revolutions compare with those in North America and Europe?
2. How did industrialization reshape economic and social life?
3. How did nationalism, liberalism, and socialism differ from each other?
4. What factors spurred the Western imperialism of the later 1800s?

On a spring day in 1851 Londoners celebrated their era's technological achievements. People of all social classes, from bankers and nobles to sailors, day laborers, and barmaids, headed for the spectacular new Crystal Palace in Hyde Park to see the official opening, led by Queen Victoria herself, of the Great Exhibition. The less affluent walked while the wealthy rode in horse-drawn carriages or steam-powered buses. Some came by railroad from other British cities or by steamships from France and Belgium to honor "The Works of Industry of All Nations," with Progress as the organizing theme. The first "world's fair" was dazzling. Some 14,000 firms had displays showcasing British industrial leadership and the mineral basis for British industry such as coal and iron ore. The hall of machinery contained inventions that had revolutionized British life: power textile looms, hydraulic presses, printing presses, marine engines, and locomotives that had attained the unimaginable speed of 60 miles per hour. Another hall featured industrial products that British merchants sold all over the world, including fine textiles made from wool, cotton, linen, and silk. Many of these products were made in Manchester, the city condemned as a "foul drain" but praised for fostering development. Nearly half of the exhibitors represented other countries of Europe and North America, illustrating the spread of industrialization.

The Great Exhibition celebrated the industrialization that had begun three-quarters of a century earlier and was already transforming the social and physical landscapes in parts of Europe. The British, enamored with the idea of progress, saw in modern industry, a growing economy, and creative science humanity's triumph over the natural world. Industrialization gave Britain and other European and North American countries the economic and military power to increase their influence around the world. Political revolutions and new ideologies also redefined Europe and the Americas between 1750 and 1914. Historians refer to an "age of revolutions," violent conflicts that spurred the rise of modern European, North American, and Latin American nations. In turn, the economic and political changes resulting from industrialization and revolutions fostered new political ideas. Great Britain, France, Germany, and Russia emerged as the main powers in Europe while the United States became the strongest American country. But the trends yielded mixed blessings. The British writer Charles Dickens, commenting on the French Revolution, summed up the era: "It was the best of times, it was the worst of times. It was the age of wisdom, it was the age of foolishness, it was the season of light, it was the season of darkness, it was the spring of hope, it was the winter of despair."[2] These trends had also sparked a renewal of the imperialism that resulted in various European nations acquiring or expanding empires in Asia and Africa.

Visit the website and eBook for additional study materials and interactive tools: www.cengage.com/history/lockard/globalsocnet2e

The Age of Revolution

How did the Caribbean and Latin American revolutions compare with those in North America and Europe?

Age of Revolution The period from the 1770s through the 1840s when revolutions rocked North America, Europe, the Caribbean, and Latin America.

The **Age of Revolution** refers to the period from the 1770s through the 1840s, when violent upheavals rocked North America, Europe, the Caribbean, and Latin America as revolutionaries employed armed violence to seize power (see Chronology: The North American and European Revolutions, 1770–1815). While political revolutions changed the personnel and structure of government, social revolutions transformed both the political and social order. The Age of Revolution began when the American Revolution ended British colonial rule and led to a new democratic form of government. The French Revolution, the major social revolution, overthrew a discredited old order of royalty and aristocratic privilege and also inspired other peoples to seek radical change. As in British North America, dissatisfaction with colonialism was common in the Caribbean and Spanish America and led to revolutions and wars of independence in these regions. For the next two centuries revolutions transformed states, ideologies, and class structures in Europe, Latin America, and Asia.

These revolutions were brutal but momentous events in modern world history and had much in common. Though often well educated and from middle-class or upper-class backgrounds, revolutionary leaders mobilized followers from among disenchanted peasants and urban workers. Many revolutions, including the French, moved from moderate to more extreme actions such as purging dissidents, rivals, or opponents. Although they replaced repressive and inequitable systems, few revolutionaries satisfied the demands of their people.

British Colonialism and the American Revolution

Resentments had festered for decades between American colonists and the imperial British government. Then in the late 1700s Europeans and Latin Americans watched fascinated as the disaffected citizens in the thirteen British colonies in North America ended British rule and established the United States. The American revolutionary leaders proclaimed Enlightenment political theories, such as democracy and personal freedom, while forming their new representative government.

Colonial Governments

In the mid-1700s the British hold on these colonies seemed strong. Each colony from New Hampshire to Georgia had unique institutions and economies. The southern colonies depended largely on plantation slavery, while the northern colonies combined commerce and manufacturing with farming, a more balanced economy. Only 2 million persons lived in the colonies in the 1760s, and the largest town, Boston, had only 20,000 residents. A fifth of the colonial population was African American, mostly slaves concentrated in the southern plantation zone. The white American colonists were generally prosperous, enjoyed considerable self-government and religious toleration, could vote for local assemblies and mayors if they were adult white males who owned sufficient property, and faced much lighter taxes than did people in Britain. Most colonists eagerly consumed British culture.

But tensions increased between the governing British and many colonists who, claiming for themselves the label of Americans, felt divorced from Britain and increasingly resented British policies, such as taxation without representation in the British Parliament. The British also placed more restrictions than before on local American manufacturing. Clumsy British attempts to raise taxes, enforce long-ignored laws, and reserve the coveted land west of the Appalachians for Indians angered many colonists, who mounted boycotts of British goods. In 1773, protesters of a higher tax on tea, dressed as Indians, raided three British ships in Boston harbor and dumped their cargo of tea overboard, an event known as the Boston Tea Party.

Patriots and Loyalists

Colonists favoring independence, known as Patriots, and those opposed, called Loyalists, increasingly clashed. Most of the Patriot and Loyalist leaders were wealthy lawyers, physicians, journalists, merchants, and landowners. Patriot leaders admired European Enlightenment thinkers such as John Locke in England and Baron de Montesquieu in France and favored democracy and a republic. The Patriots were also stirred by the writings of the antiroyalist Englishman Tom Paine (1737–1809), a sailor and teacher turned journalist who settled in Philadelphia and promoted independence, separation of church and state, social equality, women's rights, abolition of slavery, and other ideas then considered radical. Paine's passionate pamphlet *Common Sense*, which urged Americans to oppose tyranny and free themselves by force in order to "begin the world over again," helped galvanize public opinion against colonialism.

CHRONOLOGY

	Europe	The Americas
1750	**1770s–1870s** First Industrial Revolution **1789–1815** French Revolution	**1776–1783** American Revolution **1791–1804** Haitian Revolution
1800	**1815** Congress of Vienna	**1810–1826** Spanish-American wars of independence
1850	**1859–1870** Unification of Italy **1862–1871** Unification of Germany **1870s–1914** Second Industrial Revolution	

The colonies' many competing churches and schools of thought fostered intellectual diversity. Some of the Patriots were devout Protestants or Catholics; others were free thinkers. Some, including Paine, Thomas Jefferson, James Madison, Benjamin Franklin, and George Washington, were deists, believing in an impersonal creator who left humanity alone, and were often suspicious of organized churches. Patriot leaders also reflected their times: some owned slaves, smuggled, took mistresses, had illegitimate children, and, like many other male colonists, drank heavily.

Struggle for Independence

After preliminary American-British skirmishes, delegates met and declared that the thirteen colonies ought to be free and independent states, with no allegiance to the British crown. On July 4, 1776, the delegates approved the Declaration of Independence, written largely by Thomas Jefferson (1743–1826), a Virginia planter, which stated, "We hold these truths to be self-evident, that all men are created equal, that they are endowed by their Creator with certain inalienable Rights, that among these are Life, Liberty and the pursuit of Happiness."[3] Perhaps a third of the colonists remained Loyalists, and many others, especially less-affluent white colonists, were neutral or apathetic. A revolutionary army organized and commanded by George Washington (1732–1799), a wealthy Virginia farmer and decorated veteran of earlier wars against France and its Indian allies, then fought the British and their allies for six bitter years, famously described by Tom Paine as "the times that try men's souls."

Women aided the Patriot cause by raising funds for the army, serving as cooks and nurses in army camps, and engaging in sabotage and spying. A few women disguised themselves as men to join the combat. Britain's rivals, France and Spain, aided the Patriot cause. The British enjoyed support from many Indians, who resented the colonists for aggressively occupying Indian lands, and from some black slaves, who were promised their freedom by a British general. Some Loyalists and British officials accused the Patriots of hypocrisy, wanting freedom for themselves while maintaining slavery for nonwhites. The American defeat of British forces at Yorktown, Virginia, in 1781 proved decisive, and Britain recognized American independence in 1783. Despite their democratic values, the Patriots treated the Loyalists harshly, confiscating their land and jailing them. Ultimately 100,000 Loyalists were expelled or fled to Canada, and many others left for England.

The thirteen former colonies formed an independent federation, the United States of America. The new country's founders debated the relative powers of the states and of a national government that could unite them. The first weak confederation proved unworkable. Seeking a stronger central government, in 1787 delegates met in Philadelphia and approved a constitution, mostly written by James Madison (1751–1836), a well-educated Virginian, that established an elected president and congress presiding over a federal system that granted the states many powers. The delegates then elected the war hero Washington (g. 1789–1797), admired for his integrity and managerial skills, as the republic's first president. The first elected congress approved ten constitutional amendments, known as the Bill of Rights, which enshrined Enlightenment values such as freedom of speech, assembly, press, and religion.

However, the founders of the new republic made no effort to transform the American social order. Despite their rhetoric, they did not challenge slavery, recognize Native American claims to land, or expand voting rights even to all white men, much less to persons other than white men. Although some Patriots, including

CHRONOLOGY
The North American and European Revolutions, 1770–1815

1770s–1840s Age of Revolution

1773 Boston Tea Party

1776 American Declaration of Independence

1783 Britain's recognition of United States independence

1787 United States constitutional convention; Northwest Ordinance for forming new states

1789–1815 French Revolution

1791–1792 Constitutional state in Poland-Lithuania

1804 Crowning of Napoleon as emperor of France

1810–1811 Height of Napoleon's empire

1815 Defeat of Napoleon at Battle of Waterloo; Congress of Vienna

Washington, freed their slaves, and most northern states gradually abolished slavery, blacks who fought for Britain were often executed or reenslaved, and some left with other Loyalists for Canada. Indians could only watch bitterly as the government claimed and promoted settlement of most of the Indian land east of the Mississippi River and as the U.S. Congress approved the Northwest Ordinance, allowing frontier settlements to join the United States. Women did not gain equal rights with men, even though they too had sacrificed to win independence and had managed their absent husbands' shops, businesses, and farms during the war. However, new laws made it somewhat easier for women to obtain a divorce, a right long enjoyed by men.

American "Exceptionalism"

Americans also believed they had formed a society unique to history, an idea known as American "exceptionalism." They viewed themselves as the most democratic, individualistic, enterprising, prosperous, technological, and self-determining society on earth, unhindered by the burdens of history that held down other peoples. Yet, Americans also argued that their ideas and institutions were relevant for the whole world, agreeing with the Puritan Massachusetts governor, John Winthrop, who claimed in 1630 that his new society constituted a "City upon a Hill, [with] the eyes of all people upon us."[4] A century and a half later, Jefferson declared that America was a standing monument and example for the world. These attitudes have remained powerful in American thought.

The French Revolution

The French Revolution electrified Europe by replacing the monarchy with a republic and spreading values of liberty and social equality, but it also generated terrible violence, the rise of despotic leaders, and long years of war. The shock waves it generated strongly shaped nineteenth-century Europe. The Revolution was traumatic but also inspiring: it preached "liberty, equality, and fraternity" and a fairer distribution of wealth, and the middle classes took over the government in the name of the common people. But the Revolution also plunged Europe into a prolonged crisis and a series of wars between France and its European rivals, who feared the spread of radical ideas and sought to restore royal government to France.

Causes

The Revolution had many causes. France's participation in the American War of Independence, aiding the Patriot's anti-British cause, worsened long-standing financial problems rooted in an unjust economic system that badly needed reform. The Roman Catholic clergy and the privileged nobility were exempt from most direct taxes, putting the entire burden on artisans and peasants. While several bad harvests increased hunger and misery, high prices, food shortages, and high unemployment spurred resentment. The difficulty the poor had in buying bread led Marie-Antoinette, the king's wife, to contemptuously remark: "Let them eat cake."

To calm rising passions, King Louis XVI (1754–1793) called the Estates General, a long-dormant consultative body that included representatives of the clergy, the nobility, and finally a Third Estate comprising the middle classes and peasants. Every town debated political issues and then elected delegates to the Estates General. The leaders of the Third Estate, who represented over 90 percent of the population, demanded influence reflecting their numbers. Many middle-class men and women had read the works of Enlightenment thinkers and had found the American Revolution inspirational. Stalemated in the Estates General, the Third Estate delegates formed a rival national assembly and began writing a new French constitution. In response, the king called in the army to restore order, provoking anger and violence.

Eruption of Conflict

The Revolution erupted in Paris in 1789 after armed crowds stormed the Bastille, the royal prison and a hated symbol of tyranny, to release the prisoners and seize gunpowder and cannon. The bloody Bastille attack proved so inspirational that the date (July 14) later became France's national holiday. Both men and women took up arms to oppose royal power, and the terrified nobility fled. Members of the Third Estate formed a new Constituent Assembly, which voted to destroy the social order and then adopted the Declaration of the Rights of Man and of the Citizen, a document strongly influenced by the English Bill of Rights of 1689 and the new United States constitution. The Declaration announced that all people everywhere had a natural right to liberty, property, equality, security, religious toleration, and freedom of expression, press, and association. A new constitution made the king bound by laws and subject to an elected assembly, outlawed slavery, and reorganized and weakened the church, confiscating the vast wealth of the higher clergy. The French example inspired other Europeans to adopt political reform. In 1791 reformers in Poland-Lithuania reshaped the state and expanded voting rights. But Russia, supported by the Polish nobility, invaded and crushed the reformist government.

Continental War

With several European states demanding a restoration of royal power in France, French leaders who thought that war might unify the nation behind the revolution declared war in 1792. The

Kunsthistorisches Museum Vienna/The Bridgeman Art Library International

Storming the Bastille This painting celebrates the taking of the Bastille, a castle prison in Paris that symbolized hated royal rule, by armed citizens and soldiers. The governor and his officials are led out and will soon be executed.

army recruited volunteers, identifying the defense of France with revolutionary ideals and proclaiming that "young men shall go forth in battle, married men shall forge weapons, women shall make tents and clothing, and shall serve in hospitals."[5] A national convention, elected by universal male suffrage, made France a republic, ending the monarchy. In the name of all the world's people, the French began a crusade to end absolute monarchies and social inequality in Europe. With patriotic enthusiasm the French public rallied behind the revolutionary government, singing a song, the *Marseillaise* (mar-sye-EZ), that was written as a call to oppose tyranny and is now France's national anthem. In 1793 the revolutionaries executed King Louis XVI for treason.

Revolutionary Divisions and Terror

Military conflict intensified internal dissent and worsening economic problems in France. Some leaders emphasized preserving the Revolution's libertarian principles, such as freedom of speech and assembly. However, a more radical faction known as **Jacobins** (JAK-uh-binz), who believed these rights had to be set aside in the crisis, took control of the state and imposed a dictatorship to promote internal security. The Jacobins' Committee of Public Safety used terror against real or imagined opponents, often cutting off their victims' heads in public using the gruesome guillotine. Perhaps 40,000 French citizens, mostly rebellious peasants and provincial leaders, were executed, and tens of thousands more were arrested, often on flimsy evidence, to restore internal order. The Jacobins' leader, Maximilien Robespierre (1758–1794), a lawyer and dedicated republican, started as an idealistic humanist but became the most zealous promoter of the terror against alleged counterrevolutionaries, some of them his former allies. As the violence and radicalism intensified, sowing dissension, some Jacobin leaders themselves, including Robespierre, were executed in factional disputes. The terror abated when the Jacobins lost power in 1795, but several constructive Jacobin policies endured, including guaranteeing the right to public education for all children.

Jacobins A radical faction in the French Revolution that believed civil rights had to be set aside in a crisis and that executed thousands of French citizens.

Legacies

Although not all its accomplishments proved long-lasting, the French Revolution showed that a new order could be created, inspiring generations of revolutionaries to come. Ultimately the Revolution constructed a middle class–dominated state much more powerful than that of the Bourbon kings. During these years much of the vocabulary of modern politics emerged, including terms such as *conservative* and *right-wing*, referring to those who favored retaining the status quo or restoring the past, and *liberal* and *left-wing*, meaning progressives wanting faster change. Revolutionary France also transformed warfare by introducing conscription and promotion through the ranks. The countries occupied or conquered by France, such as Belgium, were turned into "sister republics," where new revolutionary governments promoted human rights.

But the Jacobins' terrible violence undermined personal liberty and dampened the Revolution's appeal. The French trauma turned North Americans against revolutions, which they now feared too often degenerated into anarchy and then despotism. Observers also debated whether the "Rights of Man" included women. Olympe de Gouges (1748–1793), a French butcher's daughter, published a manifesto complaining that women were excluded from decision making and tried to organize a female militia to fight for France, arguing that needles and spindles were not the only weapons women knew how to handle. For her efforts she was executed by the Jacobins. A British campaigner for women's rights, Mary Wollstonecraft (1759–1797), moved to Paris and wrote the *Vindication of the Rights of Women* in 1792, calling for equal opportunities for women in education and society. But despite the efforts of reformers such as de Gouges and Wollstonecraft, women remained excluded from active citizenship in France and nearly everywhere else.

The Napoleonic Era and a New European Politics

Rise of Bonaparte

Although the republican system had inspired many, the terror and the shifting fortunes of war led to a resurgence of pro-monarchy feelings and prompted antiroyalists to turn to the ambitious General Napoleon Bonaparte **(BOW-nuh-pahrt)** (1769–1821), a lawyer's son and a brilliant military strategist from the French-ruled island of Corsica, whose rise to power was astounding. A lowly artillery officer once imprisoned for alleged Jacobin ties, through political connections and his forceful personality he rapidly rose through the ranks to command major military victories in France, Italy, Austria, and Egypt. In 1799 Bonaparte gained the most powerful political office in revolutionary France, that of First Consul. In 1804, responding to a widespread belief that only a dictator could provide stability, Bonaparte crowned himself emperor in a regal coronation, attended by the pope, that harked back a millennium to the crowning of Charlemagne. Quickly promoting reconciliation and economic prosperity within France, he standardized revolutionary laws, including the equality of all citizens before the law, thus making permanent the Revolution's core values. However, Bonaparte's dictatorial tendencies betrayed French liberty, and he developed a taste for the trappings of royal power. Wanting an heir, he divorced his childless wife, the popular Empress Josephine, and married an eighteen-year-old Austrian princess, Marie-Louise.

Napoleonic Wars

The wars soon began again. In 1805 Britain, the world's dominant sea power, forged a coalition with Austria, Prussia, and Russia to defeat France. France won most of the land battles, enabling it to occupy much of western Europe. Bonaparte's family now ruled Spain, Naples, and some German states. But armed resistance in Spain and the German states, a costly invasion of Russia resulting in humiliating retreat, and an invasion of France by rival powers all sapped Bonaparte's military strength. In 1814 allied armies entered Paris. Bonaparte abdicated and was imprisoned on an Italian island. He escaped and regrouped his forces, but was finally overcome by British and Prussian armies at Waterloo, a Belgian village, in 1815. While the Bourbon family reclaimed the French throne, Bonaparte spent his remaining years in exile on St. Helena, a remote, British-ruled South Atlantic island.

The demise of revolutionary France and Napoleon's empire allowed for a partial return to the European status quo. The victorious allies met in 1815 at the Congress of Vienna to remold the European state system (see Map 19.1). Europeans who preferred monarchy and church-state alliance rejoiced at French defeat. The men who overthrew French control in Naples sang, "Naples won't stay a republic. Here's an end to equality. Here's an end to liberty. Long live God and his Majesty."[6] Dominated by Austria, Britain, Russia, and the revived royalist government of France, the Congress reaffirmed pre-Napoleonic borders and restored most of the former rulers displaced by revolutionaries and reformers. However, thirty-nine German states began moving toward national unity by forming the German Confederation. Russia invaded Poland-Lithuania, destroying the constitutional government and partitioning the nation between Russia and Prussia.

Later Upheavals

Once the revolutionary genie was out of the bottle, however, all the best efforts of the established order could not put it back again. Revolutionary ideas combined with popular discontent and frequent wars continued to unsettle Europe as various revolutions broke out in 1830–1831 because of discontent with despotic political systems. The French overthrew the despotic Bourbon king, Charles X, and installed his more progressive cousin, Louis-Philippe (1773–1850), as a constitutional monarch who recognized some liberties. Uprisings in several German and Italian states and in Poland sought voting rights, and a peasant rebellion caused by poverty and unemployment rocked Britain.

Even more turbulent European revolts erupted in 1848, a result of poor harvests, rising unemployment, massive poverty, and a desire for representative government. These upheavals began

Map 19.1 Europe in 1815

With the Napoleonic wars ended, the Congress of Vienna redrew the map of Europe. France, Austria, Spain, Britain, and a growing Prussia were the dominant states, but the Ottoman Turks still ruled a large area of southeastern Europe.

e Interactive Map

in France, forcing the increasingly unpopular King Louis-Philippe to abdicate, and soon spread to Austria, Hungary, and many German and Italian states. In German cities students met in city marketplaces to demand elected parliaments and civil liberties such as free speech and a free press. But conservative regimes violently crushed the uncoordinated dissident movements within a few months. A French observer said that "nothing was lacking" in the repression in Paris, "not grapeshot, nor bullets, nor demolished houses, nor martial law, nor the ferocity of the soldiery, nor the insults to the dead."[7] Still, the uprisings helped further spread democratic ideas, and parliamentary power increased in countries such as Denmark and the Netherlands. To prevent revolutionary outbursts, many European governments also began to consider social and economic reforms, such as higher wages, to improve people's lives.

Caribbean Societies and the Haitian Revolution

In the Caribbean, the first successful movement to overthrow colonialism came in Haiti, where slaves of African ancestry fought their way to power. Most of the small Caribbean islands and the

Guianas in northeast South America were colonies of Britain, France, or the Netherlands, inhabited chiefly by African slaves working on plantations. The Afro-Caribbean peoples mixed European cultural forms and languages with African traditions. In British-colonized islands such as Jamaica, Barbados, and Antigua, for example, most slaves adopted Christianity and Anglo-Saxon names.

Haitian Conflicts

Slave revolts were common throughout the colonial era, but only the Haitian Revolution overthrew a regime. In 1791 some 100,000 Afro-Haitian slaves, inspired by the French Revolution and its slogans of liberty and equality, rose up against the oppressive society presided over by French planters (see Chronology: The Caribbean and Latin American Revolutions, 1750–1840). Toussaint L'Ouverture **(too-SAN loo-ver-CHORE)** (1746–1803), a freed slave with a vision of a republic of free people, became the insurgent leader. Raised a Catholic, Toussaint learned French and Latin from an older slave.

The Haitian revolution went from triumph to tragedy. For a decade the Afro-Haitians fought the French military and anti-French British and Spanish forces hoping to capitalize on the turmoil, and by 1801 Toussaint's forces controlled Haiti and freed the slaves. But Napoleon Bonaparte sent in a larger French force and French soldiers captured Toussaint, who died in a French prison. In 1804 Afro-Haitians defeated Napoleon's army and established the second independent nation in the Western Hemisphere after the United States. Around the Americas the Haitian Revolution cheered slaves and abolitionists but alarmed planters, who became more determined to preserve slavery, and the United States, still a slave-owning nation, withheld diplomatic recognition of the black Haitian republic. In Haiti, French planters were either killed or fled, and the ex-slaves took over sugar production. The promise of a better life for Haiti's people proved short-lived, however. Toussaint's successor as revolutionary leader, the Africa-born Jean Jacques Dessalines **(de-sah-LEEN)** (1758–1806), ruled despotically, beginning two centuries of tyranny.

Latin America's Independence Wars

Spanish and Portuguese Empires

The Spanish and Portuguese ruled much larger and more populous American empires than did the British. By 1810 some 18 million people lived under Spanish rule from California to South America's southern tip, including 4 million Europeans, 8 million Indians, 1 million blacks, and 5 million people of mixed descent. Corruption ran deep, and the planters, ranchers, mine owners, bureaucrats, and church officials who benefited from Spanish rule opposed any major change, preferring a system that sent raw materials, such as silver and beef, to Spain rather than developing domestic institutions or markets.

The Spanish ruled their colonies differently than did the British in North America, allowing little self-government, maintaining economic monocultures, and imposing one dominant religion: Roman Catholicism. Latin American social conditions did not promote unity or equality. The creoles, whites born in the Americas, resented the influential newcomers from Spain, but they also feared that resistance against Spain might get out of control and threaten their position. The huge underclass of Indians, enslaved Africans, and mixed-descent people faced growing unemployment and perhaps the world's most inequitable distribution of wealth. In contrast to British America, a rigid Catholic Church wary of dissent discouraged intellectual diversity. The Inquisition denounced as seditious any literature espousing equality and liberty and punished "heretics." Local critics accused the government and church of "[keeping] thought in chains."[8]

Given the political and social inequalities, revolts punctuated Spanish colonial rule. For instance, in Mexico the Maya revolted against high taxes and church repression of Maya customs in 1761, leading to Spanish reprisals. A mass uprising led by Tupac Amaru II (1740–1781), the wealthy, well-educated mestizo who claimed to be a descendant of an Inca king, spread over large areas of Peru in the 1780s. Tupac and Michaela Bastidas, his wife and a brilliant strategist, organized a broad-based coalition that quickly overran much of the colony. They hoped to establish an independent state, with Tupac as king, where Indians, mestizos, and creoles would live in harmony. Many of Tupac's peasant followers revived the Inca religion and attacked Catholic churches and clergy. However, the better-armed Spanish defeated the rebel bands and executed Tupac and his family.

Eventually, dissatisfaction in Spanish America exploded into wars of national independence. Creole merchants and ranchers criticized Spain for its commercial monopoly, increasing taxes, and the colonial government's favoritism toward those

CHRONOLOGY
The Caribbean and Latin American Revolutions, 1750–1840

1791–1804 Haitian Revolution

1808 Move of Portuguese royal family to Brazil

1810–1826 Wars of independence in Spanish America

1810–1811 First Mexican revolution

1816 Argentine independence

1821 Founding of Gran Colombian republic by Bolivar

1822 Mexican independence; Dom Pedro emperor of Brazil

1830 Independence of Colombia, Venezuela, and Ecuador

1839 Division of Central American states

born in Spain. They also wanted a role in government. Creoles also often felt more loyalty to their American region than to distant Spain, and some were influenced by the Enlightenment and the American and French Revolutions. The British, who were pressuring the Spanish and Portuguese to open Latin American markets to British goods, also secretly aided anticolonial groups. At the same time, Spain experienced political problems at home, including French occupation during the Napoleonic wars.

Since Spain refused to make serious political concessions, middle-class creole revolutionaries waged wars of independence between 1810 and 1826. Two separate independence movements began in Venezuela and Argentina, led respectively by Simon Bolivar **(bow-LEE-vahr)** and Jose de San Martin. Born into a wealthy Caracas family that owned slaves, land, and mines, Bolivar (1783–1830) had studied law in Spain, was a free thinker who admired rationalist Enlightenment thought, and had a magnetic personality that inspired loyalty. He offered an inclusive view of his Latin American people: "We are a microcosm of the human race, a world apart, neither Indian nor Europeans, but a part of each."[9] Bolivar also spent time in Haiti and Jamaica, where he gained sympathy for blacks. He formed an army in 1816 to liberate northern South America, offering freedom to slaves who aided his cause. After many setbacks, Bolivar's forces triumphed and created the republic of Gran Colombia in 1821, uniting Colombia, Ecuador, and Venezuela. San Martin (1778–1850), a former colonel in the Spanish army, helped Argentina gain independence in 1816 and Chile in 1818. In 1824 San Martin and Bolivar cooperated to liberate Peru, where royalist sympathies were strongest.

akg-images

Simon Bolivar The main leader of the anti-Spanish war of independence in northern South America, Bolivar came to be known as "the Liberator," a symbol of Latin American nationalism and the struggle for political freedom.

But the wars damaged economies and caused people to flee the fighting. The creoles who now governed these countries often forgot the promises made to the Indians, mestizos, mulattos, and blacks who had provided the bulk of the revolutionary armies. And although some slaves were freed, slavery was not abolished. Some women enthusiastically served the revolution as soldiers and nurses. For example, Policarpa Salavarrieta helped Bolivar as a spy until she was captured by the Spanish. Before she was executed in Bogota's main plaza, she exclaimed: "Although I am a woman and young, I have more than enough courage to suffer this death and a thousand more."[10] But women still lived in patriarchal societies that offered them few new legal or political rights. Finally, unlike the founders of the United States, Latin America's new leaders were largely unable to form democratic governments. Bolivar could not hold his own country together, and in 1830 Gran Colombia broke into Colombia, Ecuador, and Venezuela. Meanwhile, Uruguay and Paraguay split off from Argentina, and Bolivia separated from Peru. Disillusioned, Bolivar concluded that Latin America was ungovernable.

Political change also came to Mexico and Brazil but less violently (see Map 19.2). In 1810 two progressive Mexican Catholic priests, the creole Manuel Hidalgo and the mestizo Jose Maria Morelos **(moh-RAY-los)**, mobilized peasants and miners and launched a revolt promoting independence, the abolition of slavery, and social reform. Creole conservatives and royalists suppressed that revolt, but a compromise between various factions brought Mexico independence in 1822 under a creole general, Agustin de Iturbide **(ah-goos-TEEN deh ee-tur-BEE-deh)** (1783–1824), who proclaimed himself emperor. However, the anti-Spanish alliance of creoles, mestizos, and Indians unraveled and a republican revolt ousted Iturbide. The Central American peoples split off from Mexico and by 1839 had splintered into five states.

e **Primary Source: The Jamaican Letter** Simon Bolivar shares his thoughts in 1815 on the present and future of the Latin American independence movement.

Brazilian Political Change

Portuguese Brazil also experienced dissension. By the late 1700s Brazil was the wealthiest part of the Portuguese colonial realm, but only the white plantation and gold mine owners benefited from the prosperity. Since Brazil was the major importer of slaves, accounting for a quarter to a

OREGON COUNTRY (Joint U.S.-British occupation)
BRITISH NORTH AMERICA (CANADA) (Gr. Br.)
UNITED STATES
MEXICO 1821
New York
Philadelphia
Washington, D.C.
Charleston
San Antonio
New Orleans
Mississippi R.
Colorado R.
Rio Grande
Gulf of Mexico
ATLANTIC OCEAN
BAHAMA IS. (Gr. Br.)
Havana
CUBA (Spain)
HAITI 1804
PUERTO RICO (Spain)
Mexico City
Veracruz
BRITISH HONDURAS (Gr. Br.)
JAMAICA (Gr. Br.)
GUATEMALA
Guatemala City
Caribbean Sea
UNITED PROVINCES OF CENTRAL AMERICA 1823–1839
Panama
TRINIDAD (Gr. Br.)
Caracas
VENEZUELA
BR. GUIANA (Gr. Br.)
DUTCH GUIANA (Neth.)
FRENCH GUIANA (France)
Magdalena R.
Orinoco R.
Socorro
Bogotá
GRAN COLOMBIA 1819–1830
Quito
ECUADOR
Galápagos Islands
Equator 0°
Amazon R.
EMPIRE OF BRAZIL 1822
PACIFIC OCEAN
Lima
PERU 1824
BOLIVIA 1825
La Paz
Sucre
Salvador
Paraná R.
PARAGUAY 1811
São Paulo
Rio de Janeiro
CHILE 1817
UNITED PROVINCES OF THE RIO DE LA PLATA 1816
URUGUAY 1828
Montevideo
Valparaíso
Santiago
ARGENTINA
Buenos Aires
Bahía Blanca
PATAGONIA (Disputed between Argentina and Chile)
Islas Malvinas (Falkland Islands)
40°W
40°N
20°N
20°S
80°W
60°W
0 500 1000 Km.
0 500 1000 Mi.
1811 Year independence gained
Colony

Map 19.2 Latin American Independence, 1840
By 1840 all of Latin America except for Cuba and Puerto Rico, still Spanish colonies, had become independent, with Brazil and Mexico the largest countries. Later the Central American provinces and Gran Colombia would fragment into smaller nations, and Argentina would annex Patagonia.

third of all Africans arriving in the Americas, blacks vastly outnumbered Native Americans. Disgruntled Afro-Brazilians demanded a better life, but they faced many setbacks, including the defeat of a 1799 revolt in the northeastern state of Bahia **(buh-HEE-uh)**. Yet, Brazil enjoyed a nearly bloodless transition to independence. In 1808 the Portuguese royal family and government sought refuge in Brazil to escape the Napoleonic wars, and Brazilians increasingly viewed themselves as separate from Portugal. A member of the royal family still in Brazil, Dom Pedro (1798–1834), severed ties with Portugal completely in 1822 and became emperor of Brazil as Pedro I. However, although an elected parliament was set up, most Brazilians had no vote and Pedro I governed autocratically. Politics involved a small group of merchants, landowners, and the royal family.

SECTION SUMMARY

- Many people in the North American colonies chafed against British rule and, inspired by Enlightenment thinkers, pushed for independence, while others, including many Indians and black slaves, sided with the British.
- After a first failed attempt at confederation, the thirteen American colonies agreed upon a system that balanced federal and state powers, but the American Revolution did little to change the social order and did not extend equal rights to blacks, women, and Indians.
- The French Revolution, which aimed to wrest control from the nobility and the clergy, achieved some of its progressive goals and was an inspiration to some societies, but it led to a period of war and widespread terror, and its excesses turned others away from revolution.
- In the tumultuous aftermath of the French Revolution, Napoleon Bonaparte seized power, implemented some of the Revolution's egalitarian ideals in law, and waged a series of overly ambitious wars that eventually led to his defeat and the Congress of Vienna, at which many pre-Revolution boundaries were restored. Throughout the first half of the nineteenth century, other revolutions against despotic regimes rose up and were usually crushed, but nevertheless democratic ideals made gradual progress.
- After over a decade of revolutionary struggle, the Afro-Haitian slaves won their freedom from the French, but they soon fell under the control of an African-born despot.
- Spain controlled its American colonies extremely tightly, leaving little room for intellectual freedom or economic mobility, and put down many revolts through the end of the eighteenth century.
- Rising dissatisfaction among South Americans, particularly creoles, led to successful independence movements throughout the continent, though the newly free nations had trouble forming representative and democratic governments.
- After Mexico obtained its independence, the coalition that had opposed the Spanish fell apart, while members of the Portuguese royal family who fled to Brazil helped it to obtain its independence peacefully.

The Industrial Revolution and Economic Growth

How did industrialization reshape economic and social life?

The **Industrial Revolution**, a dramatic transformation in the production and transportation of goods, was a major force reshaping the economic, political, and social patterns of Europe and later of North America and Japan. For the first time in history, the shackles were taken off the productive power of societies. Henceforth, people became capable of the rapid, constant, and seemingly limitless increase of goods and services. This revolution was perhaps the greatest transformation in society since settled farming, urbanization, and the first states arose thousands of years ago. In the late 1700s breakthroughs in productivity were made in Britain and then spread across the English Channel to western Europe and the Atlantic to North America, eventually transforming the limited European power of 1750 into Western domination over much of the world by 1914.

Industrial Revolution A dramatic transformation in the production and transportation of goods.

The Age of Machines

The Industrial Revolution and the changes it generated had deep roots. The Renaissance, Reformation, Scientific Revolution, and Enlightenment had generated new ways of thought and understandings of the natural and physical world, and the discovery of new lands, animals, plants, peoples, and cultures stimulated curiosity about the world. Commercial capitalism and conquest overseas formed political and economic links between the Americas, the African coast, some Asian societies, and western Europe, allowing Europeans to acquire natural resources and great wealth overseas for investment in new technologies and incentives for producing more commodities for the world market.

Rise of British Industries

Great Britain became the world's leading trading nation. By the early 1700s British inventors experimented with steam power and spinning machines, and accelerating world demand spurred Britain to replace India as the main supplier of cotton textiles. Britain had many advantages over rival countries, including a diverse intellectual atmosphere, a reasonably democratic political system, favorable terrain on which to build transportation networks, abundant raw materials like coal and iron, and many water sources to run machines. As a result, between the 1780s and 1830s Britain dominated European industrialization. Profits from the British-controlled Caribbean islands and North American colonies and from British trading posts in India were particularly crucial in funding the Industrial Revolution. Some British companies made vast fortunes from the trans-Atlantic slave trade, and companies owning sugar, cotton, and tobacco plantations in the Americas often invested their excess capital in new British industries. The English Midlands region east of Liverpool, a slave trade port, and northern Wales, near rich coal and iron ore fields, became the center of British industry (see Map 19.3).

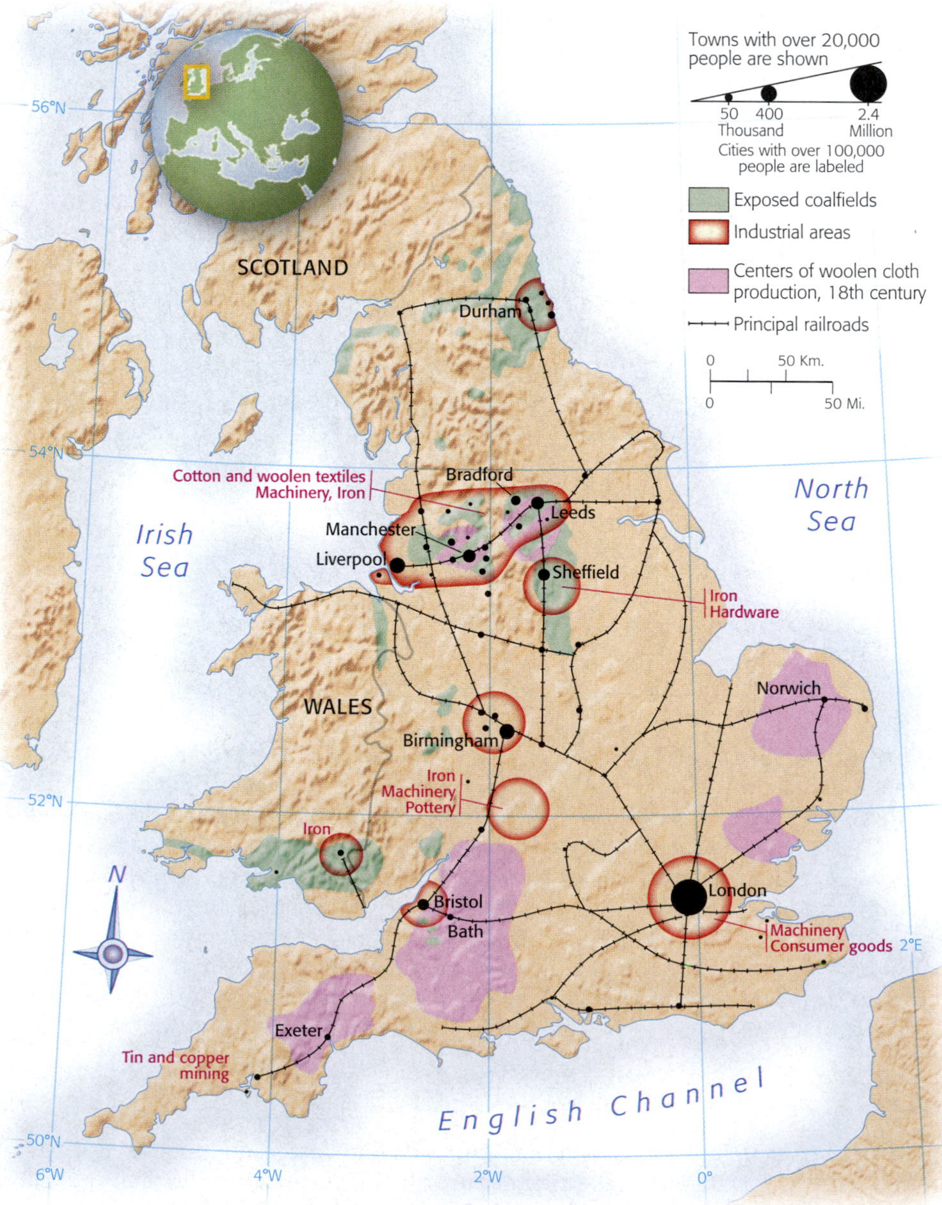

Map 19.3 Industrial Transformation in England

British industrialization mostly occurred near coalfields and iron ore deposits, spurring the rise of cities such as Birmingham, Leeds, Liverpool, and Manchester.

e **Interactive Map**

The Industrial Revolution introduced an era in which machines produced goods and increasingly performed more human tasks, reshaping peoples' lives. Instead of making things by hand with the aid of simple tools, workers now used increasingly complicated chemical processes and machines moved by energy derived from steam and other inanimate sources rather than people or animals. By tapping the resources of the earth's crust and turning them into commodities, the Industrial Revolution created great material richness and great misery. Between the 1770s and 1914 a Europe of peasant holdings, country estates, and domestic workshops became a Europe of sprawling and polluted industrial cities such as Manchester, with a wide gap between the few rich and the many poor (see Chronology: European Politics and Economy, 1750–1914). In the past 250 years the material culture of Europe changed more than it had in the previous 750 years. Today citizens of industrialized nations use transportation, wear fabrics, and employ building materials inconceivable in 1750. As one measure of how the world changed, one need only consider some of the words that first appeared in the English language between 1780 and 1850: *industry, factory, middle class, working class, engineer, crisis, statistics, strike,* and *pauper.*

CHRONOLOGY
European Politics and Economy, 1750–1914

1770s Beginning of Industrial Revolution in England

1774 James Watt's first rotary steam engine

1776 Adam Smith's *The Wealth of Nations*

1800 British Act of Union

1821–1830 Greek war of independence

1830–1831 Wave of revolutions across Europe

1831 Formation of Young Italy movement by Mazzini

1845–1846 Irish potato famine

1848 Wave of revolts across Europe; *The Communist Manifesto* by Marx and Engels

1851 Great Exhibition in London

1859–1870 Unification of Italy

1862–1871 Unification of Germany

1870s–1914 Second Industrial Revolution

The Industrial Revolution triggered continual technological innovations and a corresponding increase in economic activity. Inventions in one industry stimulated inventions in others. New cotton machines created a demand for more plentiful and reliable power than could be provided by traditional water wheels and horses. The steam pump invented in England in 1712 was inefficient, but in 1774 James Watt (1736–1819), a Scottish inventor who gained financial support from a wealthy merchant, produced the first successful rotary steam engine. Useful in many types of industrial activities, steam engines provided power for the textile mills, iron furnaces, flour mills, and mines. When used in railroads and steamships, steam power conquered time and space, bringing the world much closer together. Watt's backer, Matthew Boulton, argued that he had to sell steam engines to all the world to make money.

The new machines and engines required increased supplies of iron, steel, and coal, spurring improved mining and metalworking and then transportation facilities to move the coal and ore. After a while technological and economic growth came to be accepted as normal. The British novelist William Thackeray celebrated the changes in 1860: "It is only yesterday, but what a gulf between now and then! *Then* was the old world. Stagecoaches, riding horses, pack-horses, knights in armor, Norman invaders, Roman legions. But your railroad starts a new era."[11] Mechanization also provoked fear. Between 1815 and 1830 anti-industrialization activists in Britain known as **Luddites**, mostly skilled textile workers, invaded factories and destroyed machines in a mass protest against the effects of mechanization. Ultimately the Luddite cause proved futile. The British government sent in troops to stop the destruction and made the wrecking of machines a crime punishable by death.

Luddites Anti-industrialization activists in Britain who destroyed machines in a mass protest against the effects of mechanization.

For decades Britain was the world's richest, most competitive nation, with a reputation as the workshop of the world. The new factories mass-produced goods of better quality and lower price than traditional handicrafts, giving British merchants marketable goods and a powerful need to sell them to the world to recoup their heavy investments in machinery and materials. By the mid-1800s Britain produced two-thirds of the world's coal, half the iron, and half the cotton cloth and other manufactured goods. A British poet boasted that "England's a perfect World, hath Indies, too, Correct your Maps, Newcastle [a center of the coal industry] is [silver rich] Peru."[12] No other state could substantially threaten Britain's economic and political position.

Spreading the Industrial Revolution

However, the British also invested some of their huge profits in western Europe, spreading the Industrial Revolution across the English Channel between the 1830s and 1870s. Industrial operations became concentrated in regions rich in coal and iron ore. Capitalizing on its mineral reserves, prosperous trading cities, and a strategic location, Belgium industrialized in the early 1800s, building an ambitious railroad system to transport coal, iron, and manufactured goods. By the 1830s France, where the government helped fund industrial activity, also begun constructing a national railroad network. In the German states, political fragmentation before 1870 discouraged industrialization, except in several coal-rich regions, and some countries, including Portugal, Spain, and Austria-Hungary, remained largely agricultural. By 1914, however, industrialization was widespread around Europe and had also taken root in North America and Japan, and large numbers of people lived in cities and worked in factories.

Industrial Sheffield
This painting of one of the key British industrial cities, Sheffield, in 1858 shows the factories, many specializing in producing steel and metal goods, that dominated the landscape.

Courtesy, Sheffield Archives and Local Studies Library

Industrial Capitalism and Society

Industrialization and the vast increase in manufactured goods transformed commercial capitalism, dominated by large trading companies, into industrial capitalism centered around manufacturing. European industrial firms made and exported manufactured goods and imported raw materials, such as iron ore, to make more goods. Since economic success depended on a large and steady turnover of goods, advertising developed to create demand, and banking and financial institutions expanded their operations. Governments supported the industrialists, bankers, and financiers by fostering policies to maximize private wealth.

Economic Philosophers

laissez faire Restriction of government interference in the marketplace, such as laws regulating business and profits.

Economic philosophers emerged to praise and justify British-style capitalism. The Scottish professor and Enlightenment supporter Adam Smith (1723–1790) helped formulate modern economics theory, known as neoclassical economics, in his book *The Wealth of Nations* (1776), which advocated the principle of **laissez faire**. Rather than allowing government to interfere in the marketplace through laws regulating business and profits, Smith believed in self-interest, arguing that the "invisible hand" of the marketplace would turn the entrepreneur's individual greed into a rising standard of living for all. He also introduced the new idea of a permanently growing economy, reinforcing the long-standing Western view of progress. History was going somewhere.

Smith's free trade philosophy refuted medieval Christian attitudes that condemned mercantile activity and also helped end the mercantilism of the Early Modern Era. The free traders believed that Britain should serve as the world's industrial center, into which flowed raw materials and out of which flowed manufactured goods. But Smith saw the potential for both good and evil in capitalism, acknowledging that free enterprise did not necessarily generate prosperity for all, since the interests of the manufacturers were not necessarily those of society. Hence, he encouraged businesses to pay their employees high wages, writing that "no society can surely be flourishing and happy of which the far greater part of its members are poor and miserable. [They should be] well fed, clothed and lodged."[13]

Second Industrial Revolution

Around 1870, the Second Industrial Revolution, characterized by technological change, mass production, and specialization, commenced, led by the United States and Germany. The increasing application of science to industry spurred improvement in the electrical, chemical, optical, and automotive industries and brought new inventions such as electricity grids, radio, the internal combustion engine, gasoline, and the flush toilet. By 1900 Germany was Europe's main producer of electrical goods and chemicals. Factory production was now often done on an assembly line of separate specialized tasks; for example, a worker in an automobile assembly line might only install wheels. The Second Industrial Revolution promoted a shift from many competitive enterprises to giant monopolies, led by tycoons with unprecedented wealth.

The concentration of capital in "big business" gave a few businessmen and bankers, such as the Krupp family in Germany and the Rockefellers in the United States, vast economic power and control over many industries. For instance, Alfred Krupp (1812–1887) became Europe's leading manufacturer of arms and also owned steel mills and mines. The monopolies emerged because the factories, including new industries producing such useful innovations as aluminum and electrical power, required a heavy capital investment to start, eliminating many small businesses. A long depression in the late 1800s also undermined competition, encouraging businesses to merge or cooperate and to moderate slumps by fixing prices. These economic changes reshaped government policies and generated a drive to colonize more of the world to ensure access to resources and markets.

Social Consequences

The Industrial Revolution also affected both men and women and all social and economic classes (see Chapter 20). In 1800 Europe remained mainly agricultural. A century later there was a greater division of labor, growing social problems, most people living in cities, and the replacement of human workers by machines. The factory system compelled the migration of millions of people from the countryside into cities, which were overcrowded and unhealthy, with high rates of alcoholism, prostitution, and crime. City people crowded into festering slums, worked long hours for low wages, and learned new lifestyles. French writer Alexis de Tocqueville **(TOKE-vill)** described the atmosphere of Manchester in 1835:

> *The footsteps of a busy crowd, the crunching wheels of machinery, the shriek of steam from boilers, the regular beat of the looms, the heavy rumble of carts, these are the noises from which you can never escape in the somber half-light of these streets. Crowds are ever hurrying this way and that, but their footsteps are brisk, their looks preoccupied, and their appearance somber and harsh.*[14]

Industrial Workers

Factories, mines, and cities reshaped European life. Many factory workers labored fourteen- or even eighteen-hour days in a system of rigid discipline, with no insurance for accidents, ill health, or old age. Many children worked seven days a week in mines or factories. In the mid-nineteenth-century English cotton mills, about one-quarter of workers were adult men, over half were women and girls, and the rest were boys younger than eighteen. Workers such as the English coal miner Tommy Armstrong sometimes used songs to express their solidarity with each other and resentment of those they worked for (see Profile: Tommy Armstrong, Bard of the English Coal Mines). Gradually many people began to think of themselves as members in a social and economic class that had interests of its own in opposition to other classes. The working classes, such as the coal miners and factory workers, were the largest group. The middle classes included businesspeople, professionals, and prosperous farmers. A salaried labor force, today known as "white-collar" workers, emerged to handle sales and paperwork. For example, some 90,000 women worked as secretaries in Britain by 1901. The middle class prided itself on a keen work ethic and attributed poverty to poor work habits and lack of initiative. Meanwhile, in many countries the beleaguered aristocrats struggled to maintain their dominance over the governments and churches. Crime increased as the gap between the haves and the have-nots became more apparent.

SECTION SUMMARY

- The Industrial Revolution began in England, which had great stores of capital derived from overseas trade, an openness to new ideas, and abundant natural resources, and the revolution gradually spread throughout western Europe and North America.
- As technology played an increasingly important role in the economy and in people's lives, with machines constantly evolving and being put to new uses, some people marveled at the technological change while others, such as the Luddites, resisted it.
- Commercial capitalism was changed into industrial capitalism centered on manufacturing, and economic philosophers such as Adam Smith advocated laissez faire, the idea that the market, if left alone, would improve everyone's standard of living and create ever-increasing wealth and progress.
- The Second Industrial Revolution ushered in an age of specialization and mass production, and it favored monopolistic corporations that could afford enormous investments in new technology.
- The Industrial Revolution brought many people from the countryside to cities, where they encountered crowding, noise, new social problems, and hard labor conditions.
- As a result of the revolution, new classes arose—the working class; the middle classes, including a new secretarial force; and the aristocrats—and the gap between the haves and the have-nots widened.

TOMMY ARMSTRONG, BARD OF THE ENGLISH COAL MINES

Tommy Armstrong (1849–1919) was one of the most famous song-makers who came out of the new industrial working class of Britain. From a poor family and with little formal schooling, Armstrong began working in the mine pits around Durham in the Northumbrian region of north England at age nine. Since the youngster was born with crooked legs, his older brother William carried him to work on his back. Tommy worked first as a trapper-boy, opening the ventilation doors for coal and miners to pass through. Later he went on to more demanding jobs in the pits.

In the later nineteenth century many miners in Durham and elsewhere composed rhymes and songs. Armstrong was already writing song lyrics at age twelve. Eventually he married, but miners' wages barely covered expenses for his large family—his overworked wife and fourteen children—prompting Armstrong to seek additional money by writing songs and having them printed. Single sheets, known as broadsides, containing lyrics were then sold in pubs to raise money for his family but also to buy beer for himself. The balladeer of Tyneside, as he was known, referring to the nearby Tyne River, developed a legendary thirst. His son claimed, "Me dad's Muse was a mug of beer." Armstrong engaged in song duels with rival songwriters and even made up verses about the people in the houses he passed on his way home from work or pub. His songs usually had a strong sense of social class and social criticism. One of them encouraged educating the young, in part to avoid trouble with the law: "Send your bairns [children] to school, Learn them all you can. Make scholarship your faithful friend, and you'll never see the school-board man [truant officer]." He set his songs to folk and music-hall tunes as well as to Irish melodies brought by the thousands of Irish immigrants to the mines.

Armstrong became renowned for writing songs reflecting the miner's increasingly radical views and ballads to memorialize mining disasters, usually to raise money for union funds or the relief of orphans and widows. For example, in 1882, after an explosion killed seventy-four miners, Armstrong produced a song commemorating the lost men: "Oh, let's not think of tomorrow lest we disappointed be. Our joys may turn to sorrow as we all may daily see. God protect the lonely widow and raise each dropping head; Be a father to the orphans, never let them cry for bread." Conscious of his responsibility, he claimed that "when you're the Pitman's [coalminer's] Poet and looked up for it, if a disaster or a strike goes by without a song from you, they say: What's with Tommy Armstrong? Has someone let out all the inspiration?"

Armstrong was especially productive in the last two decades of the 1800s when strikes were common and the Miners' Union grew rapidly from 36,000 to over 200,000 members. As the struggles between miners and mine owners became more bitter, the union grew more assertive and organized. Armstrong wrote strike songs to give information and courage to miners, but also to collect money for hungry families of strikers. Some of the worst conflicts erupted in 1892, when the Durham miners were asked to take a large pay cut. When the union refused, the workers were locked out of their workplaces, prompting one of Armstrong's most famous songs: "In our Durham County I am sorry for to say, That hunger and starvation is increasing every day. For want of food and coals, we know not what to do, But with your kind assistance, we will stand the battle through. Our work is taken from us now, they care not if we die, For they [the mine owners] can eat the best of food, and drink the best when dry." After months of labor strife, the union pragmatically agreed to a lower pay reduction. The songs of Tommy Armstrong and other industrial balladeers provide a chronicle of the Industrial Revolution and the ways it shaped the lives of millions of people.

THINKING ABOUT THE PROFILE

1. How did Armstrong's life reflect the working conditions and often hardships imposed on workers by the Industrial Revolution?
2. What did the songs of industrial balladeers like Armstrong tell us about how working-class people confronted the realities of industrial society?

Tommy Armstrong Known as the "Pitman's (coalminer's) Poet," Armstrong worked in the coalfields around Durham, in England, and wrote many songs celebrating the miners' struggles for a better life.

Nationalism, Liberalism, and Socialism

How did nationalism, liberalism, and socialism differ from each other?

Modern Europe also produced three new ideologies—nationalism, liberalism, and socialism—that influenced societies and that continue to shape our world. An **ideology** is a coherent, widely shared system of ideas about the nature of the social, political, and economic realm. Nationalism fostered unified countries, liberalism encouraged democratic governments, and socialism sparked movements to counteract the power of industrial capitalism and the social dislocations generated by industrialization.

ideology A coherent, widely shared system of ideas about the nature of the social, political, and economic realm.

Nations and Nationalism

Nationalism, a primary loyalty to, and identity with, a nation bound by a common culture, government, and shared territory, greatly influenced Europe and the Americas in this era. Nationalists insisted that support for country transcended loyalty to family, village, church, region, social class, monarch, or ethnic group. Many peoples had a growing sense of belonging to a nation, such as France or Italy, that shared a common identity separate from, and often better than, those of other nations. For example, a Swiss newspaper proclaimed in 1848 that the "nation [Switzerland] stands before us as an undeniable reality. The Swiss of different cantons [small self-governing states] will henceforth be perceived and act as members of a single nation."[15] Some historians conceive of the nation as an "imagined community" that grew in the minds of people living in the same society.

nationalism A primary loyalty to, and identity with, a nation bound by a common culture, government, and shared territory.

Nationalist Visions

Nationalism provided a cement that bonded all citizens to the state but also fostered wars with rival nations. With its vision of uniting people who shared many traditions and a sense of common destiny, nationalism became a popular, explosive force, appealing particularly to the rising middle classes and intellectuals struggling to gain more political power while claiming that the nation included all the people, regardless of social status. This perception of collective identity and the nation's special nature was captured by the India-born English poet Rudyard Kipling: "If England was what England seems, An' not the England of our dreams, But only putty, brass an' paint, 'Ow quick we'd drop 'er! But she ain't!"[16]

Most historians credit the birth of modern nationalism to France and Great Britain in the late eighteenth and early nineteenth centuries. The French revolutionaries proclaimed that all sovereignty emanated from the nation, rather than from individuals or groups, and the British began to conceive of themselves as one nation composed of several peoples. England and Wales had united in 1536 under English monarchs, joined by Scotland in 1707, but there was not yet a Britain; the peoples who shared the island identified themselves as English, Scottish, or Welsh. But the spread of English power led to the suffocation of the Scottish and Welsh cultures and languages. Although some Welsh and Scots remained wary of England, eventually most accepted being part of Great Britain, a linking formalized in the British Act of Union in 1800.

Changing Political Landscape

Nationalism also transformed Europe's political landscape. In 1750 large parts of Europe were dominated by multinational states with ethnically diverse populations. One royal family, the Vienna-based Habsburgs, ruled Austria, Hungary, the Czech lands, Belgium, and parts of Italy. In contrast, nationalism fostered **nation-states**, politically centralized countries with defined territorial boundaries, such as Italy, Belgium, and Norway. By 1914 only the Russian and Habsburg-ruled Austro-Hungarian empires remained major multinational states in Europe.

nation-states Politically centralized countries with defined territorial boundaries.

Making Greece and Italy

Greeks, Italians, and Germans made some of the most dramatic efforts to create unified nations. The Greeks, long a part of the Turkish-dominated Ottoman Empire, claimed nationhood through violence. While Greeks served in the Ottoman government and Greek merchants dominated commerce in Ottoman-ruled western Asia, some Greeks sent their sons to western Europe to study. Returning home with nationalist ideas, they organized an uprising for independence in 1821, killing many Turks. The Ottomans responded by massacring Greek villages, pillaging churches, and hanging the leader of the Greek Orthodox Church in Istanbul, inflaming western European opinion. Aided by the intervention of Britain, France, and Russia, Greece became independent in 1830, inspiring other restless Ottoman subjects. In 1862 Romania also became independent.

Unlike the Greeks, Italians long cultivated a dream of unity. The Italian speakers were divided into many small states ruled by the Habsburgs, the Holy Roman Empire, or the pope. In 1831 the fiery Giuseppe Mazzini (jew-SEP-pay mots-EE-nee) (1805–1872), an exiled Genoese political philosopher, founded the Young Italy movement, which advocated one Italian nation. He also promoted a republican government and women's rights, radical ideas in Italy. Mazzini's example inspired nationalists and democrats elsewhere in Europe, who formed imitative organizations such as Young Poland. In 1859 Italian nationalists began an armed struggle for Italian unity. Forces under Giuseppi Garibaldi **(gar-uh-BOWL-dee)** (1807–1882), who had nurtured his passion for Italy during years of exile in South America, created the kingdom of Italy in 1861. In 1870 Italian troops entered the last Papal State, Rome, reuniting Italy for the first time since the Roman Empire. The job of creating Italians who shared a common national vision would take longer.

German Unification

German unification also came in stages. In 1862 the Prussian prime minister, Otto von Bismarck (1815–1898), brought together many northern German states under Prussian domination. Bismarck came from the landed nobility and had spent his youth gambling and womanizing before beginning a rapid political ascent. Hostile to business and democratic political rights, he united the Germans through warfare, a policy he characterized as "blood and iron." War with Denmark added to Prussian territory, and the defeat of Austria in 1866 drove the Habsburgs out of all their German holdings west of Austria. A war with France added southern Germany and the Alsace-Lorraine border region. In 1871 King William I of Prussia was declared *kaiser* (emperor) of a united Germany, by now one of Europe's major powers.

Frustrated Nationalisms

Zionism A movement that sought a Jewish homeland.

Some peoples could not satisfy their nationalist aspirations. The Poles frequently but unsuccessfully rebelled against their Russian and German rulers. Jewish minorities, scattered around Europe and often having little in common, faced daunting barriers. Many east European and Russian Jews had been restricted to all-Jewish villages and urban neighborhoods known as ghettoes, where they often maintained conservative cultural and religious traditions. Yet, many Jews, especially in Germany, France, and Britain, adopted a secular approach, moving toward assimilation with the dominant culture. Reacting against widespread anti-Semitism, other Jews gravitated to revolutionary groups or to **Zionism**, a movement founded by Hungarian-born journalist Theodor Herzl **(HERT-suhl)** (1860–1904) that sought a Jewish homeland. In 1948 the Zionists formed the state of Israel in Palestine.

Ireland had been a colony of England for centuries, and Irish opposition to harsh English rule simmered, sometimes erupting in violence. The English attempted to destroy the language, religion, poetry, literature, dress, and music of the Irish people. As an Irish folk song from 1798 protested, "She's the most distressful country that ever yet was seen. [The English] are hanging men and women for the wearing of the green [Ireland's unofficial national color]."[17] Much of Ireland's farming land belonged to rich English landlords, and after 1800 the English mounted even more laws restricting Irish rights, deporting thousands who resisted to Australia. Many Irish men, with few job prospects, were recruited into the British army, to fight in England's colonial wars abroad. Irish ballads are filled with men going out to fight, of mothers or wives greeting their wounded men when they returned, or of families grieving for those who would never return. Then during the 1840s the potato crop failed for several successive years because of a fungus blight. One and a half million

Battle of Langhada The Greek war for independence from the Ottoman Turks gained strong support from liberals and nationalists all over Europe. This painting, by the Greek artist Panagiotis Zographos, uses Byzantine art traditions to show Greek soldiers riding to fight the Turks in the Battle of Langhada.

Irish died from starvation while English landlords ejected Irish peasants from the land so that they could replace subsistence food growing with more profitable sheep raising. As a result, millions of Irish sought escape from poverty and repression by emigrating to the Americas and Australia.

But the Irish still rebelled against British rule. The Fenians (FEE-nians), a secret society dedicated to Irish independence, were transformed by 1905 into Sinn Fein (shin FANE) (Gaelic for "Ourselves Alone"), which turned to violence against English targets. Sinn Fein extremists formed the Irish Republican Army, which organized a rebellion on Easter Monday, 1916, in which some 1,500 volunteers seized key buildings in Dublin and proclaimed a republic in Ireland. The English quickly crushed the rising, executed the ringleaders, and jailed 2,000 of the participants, but Sinn Fein, the IRA, and terrorism continued to bedevil the English colonizers.

Liberalism and Parliamentary Democracy

Democracy and Freedom

While nationalism reshaped states, another ideology offered a vision of democracy and individual freedom. Influenced by Enlightenment thinkers such as John Locke and Baron de Montesquieu, **liberalism** favored emancipating the individual from all governmental, economic, or religious restraints. Liberals, mainly of middle-class background, favored representative government, the right to vote, and basic civil liberties such as freedom of speech, religion, assembly, and the press. The Scottish philosopher John Stuart Mill (1806–1873) offered the most eloquent defense of free expression, writing that no one should restrict what arguments a legislature or executive should be allowed to hear. Liberal politicians fought against slavery, advocated religious toleration, and worked for more popular participation in government.

liberalism An ideology that favored emancipating the individual from all restraints, whether governmental, economic, or religious.

Democratic decision making is an old and widespread idea. Village democracies that allowed many residents to voice their opinions and shape decisions had long existed in various tribal and stateless societies of Asia, Africa, and the Americas. The classical Greeks and Romans had also introduced democratic institutions, but political rights were restricted to a small minority of male citizens. Representative institutions later appeared in England, the Netherlands, Switzerland, Iceland, and Poland. By the nineteenth century liberal democracy came to mean choice and competition, usually between contending political parties and policies, within a constitutional framework that allows free choice for the electorate. Eventually some nations such as Britain adopted **parliamentary democracy**, government by representatives elected by the people. Liberalism proved particularly popular in Britain and the United States, providing the bedrock for the United States' democratic Constitution and Bill of Rights. To protect against tyranny, the nation's founders mandated a separation of executive, legislative, and judicial powers.

parliamentary democracy Government by representatives elected by the people.

British Democracy

Democracy had gradually grown in Britain as royal power declined over several centuries. The popular Queen Victoria (r. 1837–1901) reigned over Britain for sixty-four years after becoming queen at eighteen, and, with her German-born husband, Prince Albert, provided a model of morality and stability. But the British monarch, even one as respected as Queen Victoria, was no longer very powerful, exercising influence mostly behind the scenes. Prime ministers, elected by the majority of Parliament members, now made national and foreign policy. The base of democracy gradually widened as the elected House of Commons exercised more power than the appointed and hereditary House of Lords. Both houses featured lively debate between political parties.

But democratic access remained somewhat limited in Britain, and British reformers wanted average people to have more voice in the electoral system. While the Reform Act of 1832 increased the number of voters, all voters were upper- and middle-class males. The major working-class protest movement, Chartism, called for universal adult male suffrage, a secret ballot, and paying members of Parliament so that people without wealth could run for office. Some Chartists, led by Elizabeth Neesom, advocated the right of women to participate in government. Chartists used demonstrations, strikes, boycotts, and riots to support their demands; however, because the wealthy feared that radical ideas such as wealth redistribution might be proposed, these measures had little success.

Socialism, Marxism, and Social Reform

Socialist Visions

While liberals favored preservation of wealth and property rights and feared radical popular movements, a third ideology encouraged protest. In contrast to liberalism's promotion of individual liberty, **socialism** offered a vision of social equality and the common, or public, ownership of economic institutions such as factories. Socialism grew out of the painful social disruption that accompanied the Industrial Revolution. Utopian socialists in Britain, France, and North America, many influenced by Christian ideals, offered visions of perfect, cooperative

socialism An ideology offering a vision of social equality and the common, or public, ownership of economic institutions such as factories.

societies shaped by the common good. A few even founded communal villages based on service to the community and renunciation of personal wealth. The British industrialist Robert Owen (1771–1858) set up a model factory town around his cotton mill and later founded a model socialist community, New Harmony, in Indiana. Some proponents of women's rights, such as Emma Martin (1812–1851) in Britain and Flora Tristan (1801–1844) in France, promoted socialism as the solution to end female oppression, stirring controversy. Clergymen opposed to feminism and socialism urged their congregations to disrupt Martin's speeches, and outraged mobs chased and stoned her.

Karl Marx

Karl Marx (1818–1883) had the most long-lasting influence on socialist thought, and his ideas, known as Marxism, became one of the major intellectual and political influences around the world. Marx, a German Jew with a passion for social justice, studied philosophy at the University of Berlin and then worked as a journalist before settling in London. He worked closely with his German friend, Friedrich Engels (1820–1895), who managed his father's cotton factory in England. Engels, who collaborated in writing and editing some of Marx's books, introduced Marx to the degraded condition of English industrial workers. In *The Communist Manifesto* (1848), Marx developed a scenario in which the downtrodden could redress the wrongs inflicted upon them by rising up in a violent socialist revolution, seizing power from the capitalists, and creating a new society (see Witness to the Past: The Communist View of Past, Present, and Future). Marx argued that, through violent revolution, peoples can change the inequitable political, social, and economic patterns inherited from the past. He also opposed nationalism, writing that working people had common interests and needed to cooperate across borders. In 1864 Marx helped form the International Workingmen's Association to work toward those goals.

Marx was a product of his scientific age and considered his ideas as laws of history. In his most influential work, the three-volume *Capital*, he argued that historical change resulted from struggle between antagonistic social classes. All social and economic systems, he suggested, contain contradictions that doom them to conflict, which generates a higher stage of development. For example, feudalism was undermined by the confrontation between nobles, merchants, and serfs, leading to capitalism. Eventually, Marx predicted, this process would replace capitalism with socialism, where all would share in owning the means of production and the state would serve the interests of the masses rather than the privileged classes. Finally would come communism, where the state would wither away and all would share the wealth, free to realize their human potential without exploitation by capitalists or governments. Such a vision of redistributing wealth and power proved attractive to many disgruntled people in Europe and later around the world.

Marxian Ideas

Marx offered ideas that economists and historians have debated ever since. He believed that the nature of the economic system and technology determined all aspects of society, including religious values, social relations, government, and laws. In each system, such as feudalism or capitalism, the ways in which land and labor were allocated to production, work was organized (such as on medieval manors or in capitalist factories), and products were distributed, as well as the tools used, determined such patterns as family relationships and the gods people worshiped. Marx also argued that religion was the "opiate of the people," encouraging people not to protest but to fatalistically accept their lot in life in hopes of earning a better afterlife. He criticized capitalism for fostering extremes of wealth and poverty and for separating workers from ownership and management of the means of production—the farms, mines, factories, and businesses where they labored—to furnish wealth to the owners as well as to the urban-based, mostly commercial, middle class that Marx called the bourgeoisie. Marx observed that the industrial working class, the **proletariat**, grew more miserable as wealth became concentrated in giant monopolies in the later 1800s.

proletariat The industrial working class.

Spread of Marxism

Marxist ideas attracted a wide following, first in Europe and later in various American, Asian, and African countries. In Europe they stimulated unrest. In 1871, in the aftermath of a disastrous war with Germany and the election of a conservative government, a people's government comprising Marxists, republicans, and other groups briefly gained control of Paris. The Paris Commune, as this government was called, experimented with some socialist programs such as better wages and working conditions. The French government attacked Paris with ruthless force, and in response the Commune supporters (Communards) burned public buildings and killed the Catholic archbishop. The brutality of the French government troops prompted a horrified British reporter to conclude that "Paris the beautiful is Paris the ghastly, the battered, the burning, the blood-splattered."[18] When the dust had cleared, 38,000 Communards had been arrested, 20,000 executed, and 7,500 deported to the South Pacific. Later rebels across Europe would hoist the Marxist banner for radical redistribution of power and privilege.

With its promise of a more equitable society, Marxism became a major world force. Socialist parties were formed all over Europe in the late 1800s and early 1900s, and more radical socialists

WITNESS TO THE PAST

The Communist View of Past, Present, and Future

In 1848 Karl Marx and Friedrich Engels published *The Communist Manifesto* as a statement of beliefs and goals for the Communist League, an organization they had founded. In this excerpt Marx and Engels outlined their view of history as founded on class struggle, stressed the formation of the new world economy, and offered communism as the alternative to an oppressive capitalist system. They ended their summary of the problems of contemporary society by inviting the working class to take its future into its own hands through unity and revolution.

A specter is haunting Europe—the specter of communism. All the powers of old Europe have entered into a holy alliance to excise this specter. . . . Where is the party in opposition that has not been decried as communistic by its opponents in power? . . . The history of all hitherto existing society is the history of class struggles. . . . Oppressor and oppressed stood in constant opposition to one another, carried on in an uninterrupted, now hidden, now open fight, a fight that each time ended, either in a revolutionary reconstitution of society at large, or in the common ruin of the contending classes.

In the earlier epochs of history, we find almost everywhere a complicated arrangement of society into various orders, a manifold gradation of social rank. In ancient Rome we have patricians, knights, plebeians, slaves; in the Middle Ages, feudal lords, vassals, guild-masters, journeymen, apprentices, serfs; in almost all these classes, again, subordinate gradations. The modern bourgeois [middle class] society that has sprouted from the ruins of feudal society has not done away with class antagonisms. It has but established new classes, new conditions of oppression, new forms of struggle in place of the old ones.

Our epoch, the epoch of the bourgeoisie, possesses, however, this distinctive feature: it has simplified the class antagonisms. Society as a whole is more and more splitting up into two great hostile camps, into two great classes directly facing each other: bourgeoisie and proletariat (working class). . . . The discovery of America, the rounding of the Cape [of Good Hope], opened up fresh ground for the rising bourgeoisie. The East Indian and Chinese markets, the colonization of America, trade with the colonies, the increase in the means of exchange and in commodities generally, gave to commerce, to navigation, to industry, an impulse never before known, and, thereby, a rapid development to the revolutionary element in the tottering feudal society. . . . Meantime the markets kept ever growing, the demand ever rising. Even manufacture no longer sufficed. Thereupon, steam and machinery revolutionized industrial production. The place of manufacture was taken by the giant, modern industry, the place of the industrial middle class, by industrial millionaires. . . .

Modern industry has established the world market, for which the discovery of America paved the way. . . . The bourgeoisie, by the rapid improvement of all instruments of production, by the immensely facilitated means of communication, draws all, even the most barbarian, nations into civilization. The cheap prices of its commodities are the heavy artillery with which it batters down all Chinese walls. . . . It compels all nations, on pain of extinction, to adopt the bourgeois mode of production. . . . It creates a world after its own image. . . .

[The Communists] have no interests separate from those of the proletariat as a whole. . . . The immediate aim of the Communists is . . . the formation of the proletariat into a class; the overthrow of the bourgeois supremacy; and the conquest of political power by the proletariat. . . . The Communists disdain to conceal their views and aims. They openly declare that their ends can be attained only by the forcible overthrow of all existing social conditions. Let the ruling classes tremble at a Communistic revolution. The proletarians have nothing to lose but their chains. They have a world to win. WORKING MEN OF ALL COUNTRIES, UNITE!

THINKING ABOUT THE READING

1. What did Marx and Engels identify as the opposing classes in European history?
2. What developments aided the rise of the bourgeoisie to power?
3. What is the goal of the communists?

Source: From *The Communist Manifesto,* trans. 1880. *http://www.anu.edu.au/polisci/marx/classics/manifesto.html.*

soon split off to establish parties that called themselves communist. But while many poor people or industrial workers envied the rich and thought life unfair, they were also inhibited by family, religion, and social connections from joining radical movements or risking their lives in a rebellion that might fail. An English pub toast reflected the desires of people for more immediate pleasures: "If life was a thing that money could buy, the rich would live and the poor might die. Here's oceans of wine, rivers of beer, a nice little wife and ten thousand a year."[19] North Americans had a weaker sense of social class, and Marxism never became as influential in the United States as in parts of Europe. Furthermore, Marx mistakenly believed that socialist revolution would first occur in leading capitalist nations such as Britain and Germany. Instead the first successful socialist revolution came, over three decades after Marx had died, in Russia.

SECTION SUMMARY

- With the rise of nationalism, the inhabitants of a given country came to identify with each other as distinct from, and often better than, the inhabitants of other countries.
- Greece attained nationhood through revolution, Italy through a unification movement, and Germany through war against others, while the Poles, the Irish, and the Jews struggled unsuccessfully to form nations.
- Liberalism, which favored maximizing individual liberty, was particularly influential in Britain and the United States of America.
- Socialism aimed to achieve economic equality through common ownership of industry, and its major proponent, Karl Marx, argued that history is driven by class struggle and that capitalism would inevitably give way to a communist society.
- Marx's ideas exerted a strong influence on the Paris Communards and the founders of labor unions.
- Social Democrats, who rejected Marx's revolutionary ideas and instead favored working to better the lot of workers within a capitalist democracy, managed to

In contrast to the call for revolution, some Marxists favored a more gradual, evolutionary approach of working within constitutional governments and establishing social democracy, a system mixing capitalism and socialism within a parliamentary framework. The first Social Democratic Party was formed in Germany in 1875. Criticizing Marxist revolutionaries, a German Social Democratic leader, Eduard Bernstein (1850–1932), argued that socialists should work less for the better future and more for the better present. Socialists often felt a kinship with people of shared views and class backgrounds in other countries, leading in 1889 to the founding of the Second International Workingmen's Association by nonrevolutionary socialist parties, with the goal of working for world peace, justice, and social reform.

Social Democrats and Marxists actively supported labor unions and strikes to promote worker demands. Although most employers were opposed, unions gradually gained legal recognition as representatives of the work force in many nations. In Britain, France, Germany, the Netherlands, and Sweden, trade unions and labor parties acquired enough political influence to force governments to legislate better working conditions. In the later 1800s governments implemented social reforms to address the ills of the Industrial Revolution, laying the foundation for state-run welfare systems. Many European nations legislated the length of the working day, working conditions, and safety rules. To tackle poverty, Germany and Britain introduced health and unemployment insurance and created old-age pensions. Thus, contrary to Marx's expectations, life for many European workers improved considerably by the early 1900s. But many people still worked in dangerous and unhealthy conditions or faced a ten-hour working day, and child labor continued.

THE RESURGENCE OF WESTERN IMPERIALISM

What factors spurred the Western imperialism of the later 1800s?

The Industrial Revolution provided economic incentives, and nationalism provided political incentives, for European merchants and states to exploit the resources of other lands to enrich their own nations and thwart the ambitions of rival nations. Initially the British were most successful in dominating the growing world economy. But economic, political, and ideological factors eventually fostered a resurgence of imperialism, leading European nations to colonize and dominate much of Asia and Africa, reshaping the global system. With the entire world connected by economic and political networks, history now transcended regions and became truly global.

British Trade, Industrialization, and Empire

British Economic Power

The quest for colonies diminished somewhat in the first phase of the Industrial Revolution, even for Great Britain, who feared no competitor in world trade because it had none. The British free traders, wanting neither economic nor political barriers to their operations, viewed the acquisition of more colonies as too expensive. Britain already controlled or had gained access to valuable territories in the Americas, Africa, Asia, and the Pacific. Although it lost its thirteen North American colonies, it took control of French Canada and Australia. Furthermore, Britain's Spanish and Portuguese rivals suffered even graver losses; most of their Latin American colonies became independent, opening doors for British commercial activity.

British merchants also benefited from new technologies that enabled them to compete all over the world. Steam power meant that sailors were no longer dependent on trade winds, allowing British ships to reach distant shores faster. The first exclusively steam-powered ships, in 1813, took 113 days to travel from England around Africa to India, in contrast to eight or nine months by sailing ships. The completion of the Suez Canal linking the Mediterranean Sea and the Red Sea in 1869 dramatically cut the travel time, and Britain, the canal's major shareholder, extended its influence to East Africa and Southeast Asia. By 1900 the England-India trip took less than twenty-five days, making for more efficient transport of resources, goods, and people.

Despite a pragmatic preference for peaceful commerce, Britain did obtain some colonies between 1750 and 1870, taking over territories or fighting wars when local governments refused to trade or could not protect British commerce. For example, as states in India grew weaker and banditry increased, the British began expanding the territory under their influence and gradually gained direct control or indirect power over most of India. They also established footholds in Malaya, Burma, China, and South Africa. But the British preferred to undercut the economic power of their rivals, as they did in Argentina, Brazil, and Chile. They could flood a society with cheap manufactured goods, as shown when they greatly diminished India's crafts and industries for their own benefit. British industrialists and merchants also opposed any attempts to foster rival enterprises, such as textile mills, in Asian and African states.

Challenges to Britain

However, the British advantage in world markets gradually diminished as world economic leadership changed during the later 1800s. The British invested many of the profits that they earned from India and their Caribbean colonies in other nations, especially in the United States, Canada, and Australia, all countries settled largely by British immigrants. This investment helped the United States become a serious competitor. British investment also benefited some European nations, and increasingly the United States and Germany were able to gain on Britain. Because British investors found it more profitable to invest abroad rather than at home, British industrial plants became increasingly obsolete. In 1860 Britain had been the leading economic power, with France a distant second followed by the United States and Germany. By 1900, however, the hierarchy had changed: the United States was now at the top, followed by Germany and then a fading Britain and France.

Revival of Imperialism

As industrializing Germany, France, and the United States became more competitive with Britain, their growing economic and political competition renewed the quest for colonies abroad. The shift to domestic economies dominated by large monopolies stimulated empire building by piling up huge profits and hence excess capital that needed investment outlets abroad to keep growing. Furthermore, by the 1880s some of the wealth generated by the industrial economy began to filter down to the European working classes, stimulating new consumer interests in tropical products such as chocolate, tea, soap, and rubber for bicycle tires. Businessmen in Britain, Germany, Italy, France, Belgium, and the United States looked for new opportunities to exploit environments in Africa, Asia, and the Pacific and then pressured their governments to pursue colonization to assist their efforts.

National rivalries also motivated imperialism. Nations often seized colonies to prevent competing nations from gaining opportunities. While expanding British control in southern Africa, the British imperialist Cecil Rhodes (1853–1902) was moved by the words of his Oxford University professor, the philosopher and art critic John Ruskin: "This is what England must either do, or perish: found colonies as fast and as far as [it] is able, seizing every piece of waste ground [it] can get [its] foot on."[20] The national rivalries and the intense competition for colonies also planted the roots of conflict in Europe. By the early 1900s Germany and Austria-Hungary had forged an alliance, prompting Britain, France, and Russia to do likewise and setting the stage for future wars.

The conflicts between European powers led to a resurgence of Western imperialism between 1870 and 1914, often resulting in colonialism or, less commonly, neocolonialism. Seizure of colonies not only brought profits for business interests but also strengthened a nation's power in competition with rival nations. The result was the greatest land grab in world history: a handful of European powers dividing up the globe between themselves.

The Scramble for Empire and Imperial Ideologies

New Conquests and Resistance

With the resurgent Western imperialism, millions of Africans, Asians, and Pacific islanders were conquered or impacted by Western nations and thus brought into the Western-dominated world economic system. Many peoples fiercely resisted conquest. The Vietnamese, Burmese, and various Indonesian and African societies held off militarily superior European armies for decades, and even after conquest guerrilla forces often continued to attack European colonizers. For fifteen years after the French annexed Vietnam, anticolonial fighters refused to surrender, preferring to fight to the death. Countless revolts punctuated colonial rule, from West Africa to the Philippines, and Western ambitions were sometimes frustrated. Ethiopians defeated an Italian invasion force bent on conquest, while the slaughter of British occupiers by Afghans discouraged direct colonization. The Japanese prevented Western political domination by modernizing their own government and economy, and the Siamese (Thai) used skillful diplomacy and selective modernization to deflect Western power.

Lipton Tea European imperial expansion brought many new products to European consumers. Tea, grown in British-ruled India, Sri Lanka (Ceylon), and Malaya, became a popular drink, advertised here in a London weekly magazine.

The Illustrated London News Library

Despite these efforts, by 1914 Western colonial powers controlled 90 percent of Africa, 99 percent of Polynesia, and 57 percent of Asia (see Map 19.4). The British Empire, the world's largest, included fifty-five colonies containing 400 million people, ten times Britain's population, inspiring the boast that "the sun never sets on the British Empire." France acquired the next largest empire of twenty-nine colonies. Germany, Spain, Belgium, and Italy joined in the grab for African colonies. Between 1898 and 1902 the United States took over Hawaii, Samoa, Puerto Rico, and the Philippines. Russia also continued its expansion in Eurasia that had begun in the Early Modern Era (see Chapter 23).

New Technologies

New technologies permitted and stimulated imperial expansion. The Industrial Revolution gave Europeans better weapons to enforce their will, including the repeating rifle and the machine gun, such as the lightweight, quick-firing Maxim Gun. A British writer boasted: "Whatever happens we have got the Maxim Gun, and they have not."[21] These weapons gave Europeans a huge advantage against Asians and Africans, and the discovery of quinine to treat malaria enabled European colonists and officials to survive in tropical Africa and Southeast Asia. Later, better communication and transportation networks, such as steamship lines, colonial railroads, and undersea telegraph cables, helped consolidate Western control and more closely connected the world. In 1866 a speaker at a banquet honoring Cyrus Field, the American most responsible for building the trans-Atlantic cable linking Europe and North America, noted that on the statue of Christopher Columbus in Genoa, Italy, was the inscription: "There was one world; let there be two." Now, with the cable, the speaker boasted, "There were two worlds and [now] they [are] one."[22]

Imperial Networks

Western imperialism forged networks of interlinked social, economic, and political relationships spanning the globe. Hence, decisions made by a government or business in London or Paris affected people in faraway Malaya or Madagascar, and silk spun in China was turned into dresses worn by fashionable women in Chicago and Munich. Westerners also enjoyed advantageous trade relations with, or strong influence over countries such as China, Siam, Persia, and Argentina, a condition known as neocolonialism. The scope of this imperialism changed world power arrangements. In 1750 China and the Ottoman Empire remained among the world's strongest countries, but by 1914 they could not match Western military and economic power. In 1500 the wealth gap between the more economically developed and the less developed Eurasian and African societies was small, and China and India dominated world trade and manufacturing. By 1914 the gap in total wealth and personal income between industrialized societies, whether in Europe or North America, and most other societies, including China and India, had grown very wide.

Social Darwinism

Supporters of imperialism embraced a new ideology, Social Darwinism, based on the ideas about the natural world developed by the British scientist Charles Darwin, who described a struggle for existence among species (see Chapter 20). Social Darwinists concluded that this struggle led to

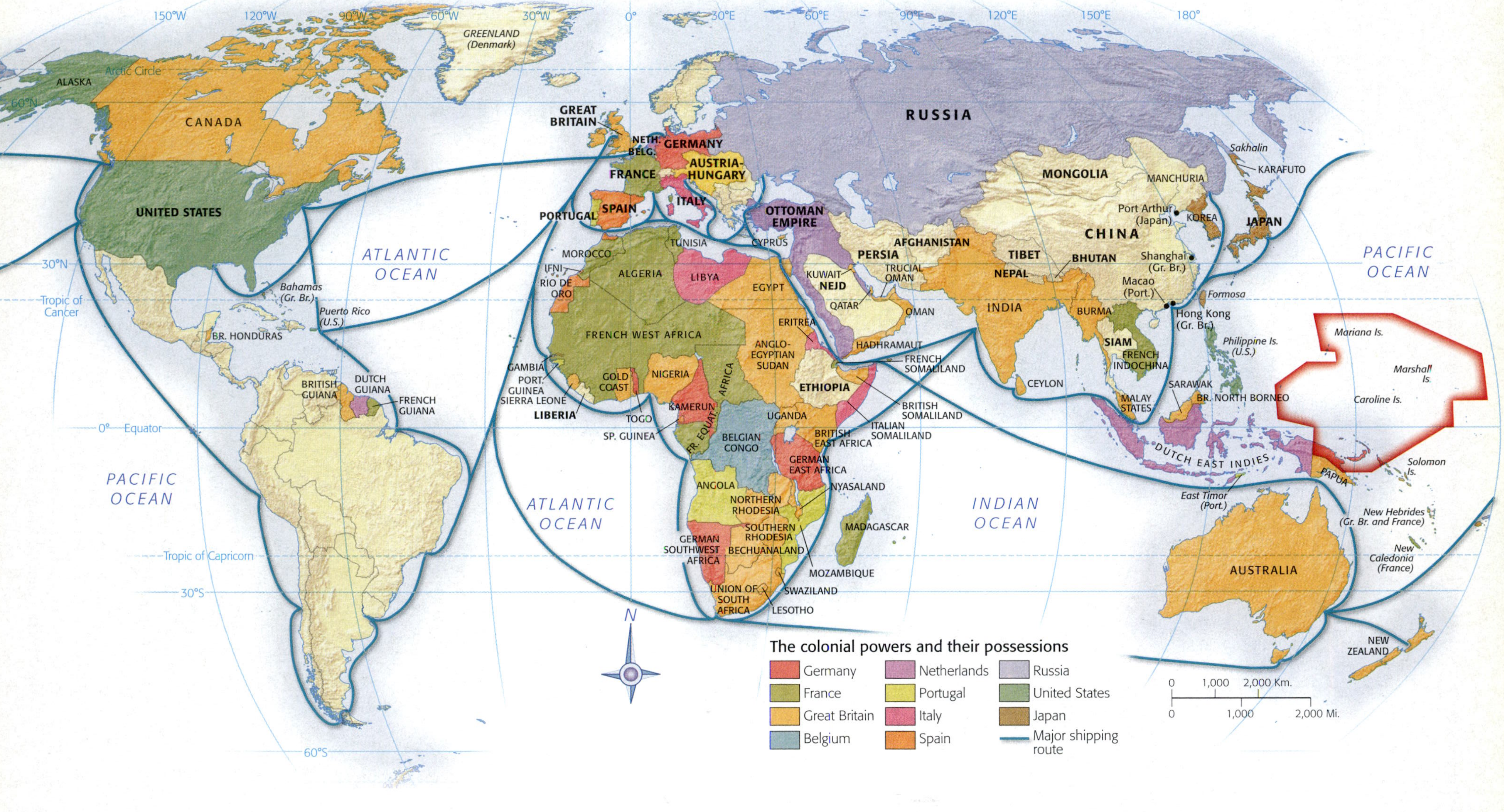

Map 19.4 The Great Powers and Their Colonial Possessions in 1913

By 1913 the British and French controlled huge empires, with colonies in Africa, southern Asia, the Caribbean zone, and the Pacific Basin. Russia ruled much of northern Eurasia, while the United States, Japan, and a half dozen European nations controlled smaller empires.

Interactive Map

the survival of the fittest and applied this notion to the human world of social classes and nations. The industrialized peoples considered themselves the most fit and saw the poor or exploited as less fit. A German naval officer wrote in 1898 that "the struggle for life exists among individuals, provinces, parties and states. The latter wage it either by the use of arms or in the economic field. Those who don't want to, will perish."[23] Social Darwinists stereotyped the Asian and African societies as "backward" and held their own nations up as "superior" peoples who had the right to rule. As most Westerners took the innate inequality of peoples for granted, Western racism and arrogance toward other peoples increased. For example, whereas many Western observers had once admired the Chinese and Enlightenment thinkers had seen China as a model of secular and efficient government, by the 1800s Europeans and North Americans had developed scorn for "John Chinaman" and the "heathen Chinee." These stereotypes were popularized by intellectual and political leaders. Cecil Rhodes boasted, "I contend that we British are the finest race in the world, and that the more of the world we inhabit the better it is for the human race."[24]

This self-proclaimed superiority legitimized the effort to "improve" other people by bringing them Western culture and religion. The French proclaimed their "civilizing mission" in Africa and Indochina, the British in India claimed that they were "taking up the white man's burden," and the Americans colonized the Philippines claiming condescendingly to "uplift" their "little brown brothers." Western defenders argued that colonialism, despite much that was shameful, gave "stagnating" non-Western societies better government and drew them out of isolation into the world market. A British newspaper in 1896 claimed that "the advance of the Union Jack means protection for weaker races, justice for the oppressed, liberty for the down-trodden."[25] However, most people in Asia, Africa, and the Pacific opposed colonialism, seeing it only for the terrible toll it took on their lives. The Indian nationalist leader Mohandas Gandhi, educated in Britain, reflected the resentment. When asked what he thought about "Western civilization," he replied that civilizing the West would be a good idea.

SECTION SUMMARY

- Even after losing thirteen of its North American colonies, Britain continued to dominate the world economy through its other holdings and its technological advantages, but it gradually lost ground, especially to the United States.
- As Germany, France, and the United States became more competitive with Britain, the powers competed for colonies that could provide natural resources for their industries and power over their rivals.
- In the renewed scramble for colonial domination, many African, Asian, and Pacific peoples resisted Western imperialism, but the technological advantage of Western nations often proved insurmountable.
- Westerners rationalized imperialism and colonization as good for the colonized, who were offered the fruits of Western culture in exchange for their independence.

CHAPTER SUMMARY

The years between 1750 and 1914 were an age of revolutions that reshaped economies, governments, and social systems in Europe and the Americas. Colonists in North America overthrew British rule and established a republic that included democratic institutions. The French Revolution ended the French monarchy and brought the middle classes to power. Although the Revolution was consumed in violence and then modified by Napoleon Bonaparte's dictatorship, the shock waves reverberated around Europe, carrying with them new ideas about liberty and equality. The American and French Revolutions also inspired peoples in the Caribbean and Latin America. Haitians ended slavery and forced out the French colonial regime and planters, and in South America creoles waged successful wars of independence against Spanish rule.

The Industrial Revolution, which began in Britain in the late 1700s, transformed societies profoundly, reorienting life to cities and factories and producing goods in unparalleled abundance. Until the 1850s Britain enjoyed unchallenged economic power. With the spread of industrialization, positions of world economic leadership began to change. New ideologies contributed to the creation of new states and government structures. Nationalism introduced new ideas of the nation and provided a glue to bind people within the same nation. Liberalism promoted increasing freedom and democracy. Socialism addressed the dislocations industrialization created and sought to improve life for the new working classes by forging a system of collective ownership of economic property. Capitalism, industrialization, and interstate rivalries in the West also generated a worldwide scramble for colonies and neocolonies in the later 1800s, allowing Western businesses to seek resources and markets abroad. This imperialism brought many more societies into a global system largely dominated by the West.

KEY TERMS

Age of Revolution
Jacobins
Industrial Revolution
Luddites
laissez faire
ideology
nationalism
nation-states
Zionism
liberalism
parliamentary democracy
socialism
proletariat

EBOOK AND WEBSITE RESOURCES

PRIMARY SOURCE

The Jamaica Letter

INTERACTIVE MAPS

Map 19.1 Europe in 1815
Map 19.2 Latin American Independence, 1840
Map 19.3 Industrial Transformation in England
Map 19.4 The Great Powers and Their Colonial Possessions in 1913

LINKS

The American Revolution (http://revolution.hnet.msu.edu/intro.html). An excellent collection of links, essays, and other resources.

BBC Outline: History (http://www.bbc.co.uk/history/). Offers valuable information by topic and time.

British History (http://www.british-history.com/). Contains links to short essays on various periods of British history.

Internet Resources for Latin America (http://lib.nmsu.edu/subject/bord/laguia/). An outstanding site with links to many resources.

Modern History Sourcebook (http://www.fordham.edu/halsall/). An extensive online collection of historical documents and secondary materials.

Plus flashcards, practice quizzes, and more. Go to: www.cengage.com/history/lockard/globalsocnet2e.

SUGGESTED READING

Abernethy, David B. *The Dynamics of Global Dominance: European Overseas Empires, 1415–1980.* New Haven, CT.: Yale University Press, 2002. Classic study of Western imperialism.

Anderson, Benedict. *Imagined Communities: Reflections on the Origin and Spread of Nationalism,* rev. ed. London: Verso, 1991. An influential scholarly examination of the rise of nationalism.

Anderson, M. S. *The Ascendancy of Europe, 1815–1914,* 3rd ed. Harlow, UK: Pearson, 2003. A good overview of the era by a British historian.

Baumgart, Winfried. *Imperialism: The Idea and Reality of British and French Colonial Expansion, 1880–1914.* New York: Oxford University Press, 1986. A readable analysis of the imperial quest.

Connelly, Owen, and Fred Hembree. *The French Revolution and Napoleonic Era,* 3rd ed. New York: Harcourt, 1999. A thoughtful survey emphasizing the Revolution's long-term consequences.

Countryman, Edward. *The American Revolution,* rev. ed. New York: Hill and Wang, 2003. An excellent treatment of the conflict and its context.

Grosby, Steven. *Nationalism: A Very Short Introduction.* New York: Oxford University Press, 2005. Highlights social, historical, and philosophical perspectives.

Headrick, Daniel R. *The Tools of Empire: Technology and European Imperialism in the Nineteenth Century.* New York: Oxford University Press, 1981. A pathbreaking study of the role of technology in European expansion.

Heilbroner, Robert L. *The Worldly Philosophers: The Lives, Times and Ideas of the Great Economic Thinkers,* 7th ed. New York: Simon and Schuster, 1999. A classic and readable introduction to these thinkers.

Hobsbawm, Eric. *The Age of Revolution, 1789–1848; The Age of Capital, 1848–1875; The Age of Empire, 1875–1914.* New York: Vintage, 1996. This outstanding trilogy by an esteemed British historian remains the standard survey of the period.

Martin, Cheryl E., and Mark Wasserman. *Latin America and Its People,* 2nd ed. New York: Longman, 2007. An introductory survey, especially strong on this era.

Samson, Jane. *Race and Empire.* New York: Longman, 2005. Examines the relationship of racism and imperialism.

Sperber, Jonathan. *Revolutionary Europe, 1780–1850.* Harlow, UK: Pearson, 2000. A good overview of these turbulent decades.

Stearns, Peter N. *The Industrial Revolution in World History,* 3rd ed. Boulder, CO: Westview Press, 2007. An overview from a global perspective.

Wesseling, H. L. *The European Colonial Empires, 1815–1919.* Harlow, UK: Pearson, 2004. A useful overview of the entire colonial enterprise by a Dutch scholar.

CHAPTER

20

Changing Societies in Europe, the Americas, and Oceania, 1750–1914

CHAPTER OUTLINE

- The Reshaping of European Societies
- The Rise of the United States
- Latin America and the Caribbean in the Global System
- New Societies in Canada and the Pacific Basin

PROFILE
Euclides da Cunha, Brazilian Writer

WITNESS TO THE PAST
Protesting Sexism and Slavery

The Art Archive

Australian Gold Rush
The discovery of gold in southeastern Australia set off a gold rush in the 1850s. Hoping to strike it rich, miners, often from other countries, among them Chinese, flocked to the gold fields, and immigration to Australia boomed.

Of course, some day we [Americans] shall step in. We are bound to. We shall be giving the word for everything: industry, trade, law, journalism, art, politics, and religion. We shall run the world's business whether the world likes it or not. The world can't help it, and neither can we, I guess.

—American millionaire in Joseph Conrad's Novel *Nostromo* (1904)[1]

FOCUS QUESTIONS

1. How and why did European social, cultural, and intellectual patterns change during this era?
2. What impact did westward expansion, immigration, and industrialization have on American society?
3. What political, economic, and social patterns shaped Latin America after independence?
4. Why did the foundations for nationhood differ in Canada and Oceania?

In 1871 a thirty-three-year-old Japanese samurai and Confucian scholar, Kume Kunitake (1839–1931), boarded an American steamship at Yokohama and began a three-week voyage to San Francisco as a member of an official information-gathering delegation sent from Japan to the United States and then Europe. Kume's delegation traveled around the country, visiting factories, museums, schools, churches, public parks, and scenic mountains. Kume faithfully recorded his perceptive impressions of Western life but also filtered them through the Japanese cultural lens, concluding that "the customs and characteristics of East and West are invariably different." Kume admired U.S. democracy but also saw its potential for disorder, since Americans were "careless about official authority, each person insisting on his own rights." Kume recorded the Americans' friendliness but also their brashness, ambition, and sense of destiny, attitudes satirized four decades later by the Polish-born British novelist Joseph Conrad through the words of his fictional American millionaire quoted above. Kume's delegation then traveled around Europe, where he noted how Europeans treasured and even imitated Japanese art. He loved the cafes, theaters, and art museums of Paris. But, as an ardent Confucian rationalist, he viewed Christianity as irrational and the Christian Bible as full of "absurd tales." Kume contrasted the splendor of the churches with the poverty of the people. But he preferred Europe's constitutional monarchies to the untidy U.S. republic and saw rapidly industrializing Germany as Japan's natural model. Returning by ship to Japan, Kume's delegation passed through Western colonies such as Ceylon, Singapore, and Hong Kong. Kume wrote that "Europeans treated the natives with arrogance and cruelty."[2] He later became a distinguished professor of history at Tokyo University.

Spurred by revolutions, industrialization, nation building, and overseas imperialism, Europeans reshaped their social, cultural, and intellectual patterns. By 1914 the United States, Canada, and Mexico occupied all of North America, while Latin America was divided into many countries large and small. Some Caribbean societies were independent, but many remained colonies of European nations. The Europeans also settled the Pacific region known today as Oceania, which comprises Australia and the two large islands of New Zealand, while colonizing the smaller Pacific islands. Although Europe, the Americas, and Oceania were separated from each other by vast distances and had unique characteristics, their societies were shaped by similar patterns of capitalism, migration, and nation building.

The United States, Canada, Australia, and New Zealand, but also Latin American countries such as Argentina, Uruguay, Brazil, and Chile, were settled chiefly by European immigrants who planted European institutions and ideas after the indigenous populations were largely displaced. These European traditions and institutions, while remaining influential, were modified by time, circumstances, and the cultures of ethnic minorities, either indigenous peoples, such as Native Americans and New Zealand Maori, or imported societies, such as Afro-Brazilians and Afro-Cubans. At the same time, the United States and Canada gradually diverged from the Latin American and Caribbean societies. By expanding its frontiers and rapidly industrializing in the 1800s, the United States became a world power, often extending its political and economic influence into Latin America and the Caribbean.

The Reshaping of European Societies

How and why did European social, cultural, and intellectual patterns change during this era?

Thanks to destabilizing revolutions in political and economic life (see Chapter 19), modern Europeans lived in a world of cities, new forms of work, and rising populations, prompting millions of people to emigrate to the Americas, southern Africa, and Oceania in search of work and a better life. Industrialization transformed social structures and family systems. Thought, the arts, and science reflected and also shaped the new Europe, with the resulting innovations influencing peoples around the world.

Population Growth, Emigration, and Urbanization

Expanding economies, better public health, and new crops such as potatoes from the Americas lowered Europe's mortality rate and fostered population growth. People married earlier, increasing the birthrate, and more people married than in Early Modern times. Europe's population (including Russia) grew from 100 million in 1650 to 190 million in 1800 and to 420 million in 1900, creating new problems. Thomas Malthus, an English clergyman and economist, argued in 1798 that poverty, disease, war, and famine checked population growth, but if these problems were eliminated, population would outgrow its means of subsistence. Overpopulation did indeed bring bleak poverty and underemployment to many areas of Europe, problems accelerated by the replacement of small family farms by large farms that needed fewer workers. But the growth of cities and industries also provided new employment opportunities.

Population Movement

Population growth and poverty led to migration within Europe and emigration overseas. Many Poles, for example, moved to the mines of northern France and western Germany, and Irish immigrants built railroads, canals, and roads in England. Emigration cut Ireland's population by half between 1841 and 1911. As an identifiable, non-Christian minority, the Jews in eastern Europe and Russia became public scapegoats for unresolved problems and were sometimes subjected to violent, usually coordinated mob attacks known as *pogroms* (from the Russian word meaning "roundup"), prompting them to seek better lives in western Europe and the Americas. In total, some 45 million Europeans emigrated to the Americas, Australia, New Zealand, Algeria, and South Africa to escape their difficulties (see Map 20.1).

Growing Cities

Rural Europeans also moved to industrial cities. The population of Manchester, the British center of the cotton industry, grew tenfold between 1800 and 1900. By 1900 Britain had the world's most urban society, with 90 percent of its people living in towns and cities. Between 1800 and 1900 London increased from 900,000 to 4.7 million, Paris from 600,000 to 3.6 million, and Berlin from 170,000 to 2.7 million. Urbanization increased social problems. Rapidly expanding cities lacked social services such as sanitation, street cleaning, and water distribution. Huge numbers of people lived in poverty, crammed into overcrowded housing in crime-ridden slums with high disease rates, overflowing privies, and littered streets. As the English poet William Blake wrote: "Every night and every morn, some to misery are born." The standard of living did not rise much for most Europeans until the 1880s, when incomes began to improve and several countries, including Britain and Germany, began building a social safety net for their citizens. By 1900 British and French workers were earning nearly twice the wages of workers in 1850.

While cities grew dramatically, western European rural life also changed. Agricultural technology and practices developed rapidly, resulting in better yields, more mechanization, and improved animal breeding. Market agriculture largely displaced the subsistence production of earlier times. But peasants often earned low wages, and many small farmers frequently lost their land to more highly capitalized and mechanized operations. Occasional famines also occurred, notably in

CHRONOLOGY

	United States	Latin America	Canada and Oceania
1800	**1803** Louisiana Purchase **1846–1848** U.S.-Mexican War islands	**1823–1889** Abolition of slavery	**1840s–1890** Colonization of Pacific islands
1850	**1861–1865** Civil War **1898–1902** Spanish-American War	**1889** Brazilian republic	**1850** Treaty of Waitangi **1867** Canadian Confederation
1900		**1910–1920** Mexican Revolution **1914** Panama Canal	**1901** Australian Commonwealth

Ireland and Russia. In contrast to rural life in western Europe, some feudal traditions remained influential in eastern Europe, especially in Russia and Poland, where the landed gentry retained authority over peasant lives.

Social Life, Families, and Gender Relations

Europeans enjoyed wider social horizons than their ancestors. After 1870 the rise of mass-distribution newspapers, organized football (soccer) leagues, more widespread vacation travel, and other activities connected peoples within and between nations. The world's first cinema opened in Paris in 1896, launching a film industry that would produce one of the most popular entertainments in Europe and then the world. People enjoyed a growing range of options in areas of life once fixed by tradition, such as where to live, work, or worship and whom to marry. Choice brought more personal freedom but also more social instability. Some observers viewed these changes as liberation, while others concluded that they fostered anxious uncertainty.

Changing Sexual Attitudes

Industrialization also reshaped sexual attitudes, particularly in Britain. The middle class, who considered unbridled passion a sign of bad character, increasingly discouraged sexual activity before marriage and limited sexual intercourse within marriage. In contrast, the working classes experienced higher rates of illegitimacy and more frequent sexual relations than ever before. Marital infidelity became common in the urban slums, fostering negative middle-class stereotypes of the poor. Thus, a British factory girl in 1909 complained, "I wanted no one to know that I was a factory girl because I was ashamed at my position. I was always hearing people say that factory girls were loose-living and corrupt."[3] Thanks to improved diets, children of all classes reached sexual maturity at a younger age, making it more difficult to maintain boys' choirs as male voices changed earlier.

Family Life

Home life and families underwent changes. During the Early Modern Era people in England and the Low Countries began to marry later and live in nuclear families, which usually included just parents and their children. During the 1800s the nuclear pattern became common in most of northern Europe, especially among the middle classes, while large extended families remained the norm in southern and eastern Europe. Families now included fewer nonrelated members, such as servants and apprentices, than had been usual in earlier centuries. In the 1700s western Europeans began to adopt the notion that people should have the freedom to choose their partner and marry for love rather than to meet family demands or economic need, but critics argued that love matches would lead to marital instability and divorce when romance faded. Married men and women often spent more time with their same-sex friends than their spouses, and sometimes the line between these friendships and homosexual relationships was murky.

People also began to redefine family life. By the later 1800s some men and women criticized marriage as stifling and old-fashioned, living out of wedlock with lovers. Prominent people in the artistic and political worlds, such as the popular French actress Sarah Bernhardt, openly had affairs or, like the fiery German socialist Rosa Luxemburg, lived openly with same-sex partners. Homosexuals occupied all levels of society, but they often faced discrimination and persecution. The Irish poet, novelist, and playwright Oscar Wilde (1854–1900), the married father of two, was tried and imprisoned in 1895 for engaging in homosexual relationships, known as sodomy. The increasing attention to homosexuality and the first scientific studies of it sparked heated and ongoing debates as to whether the behavior was rooted in nature or perversion.

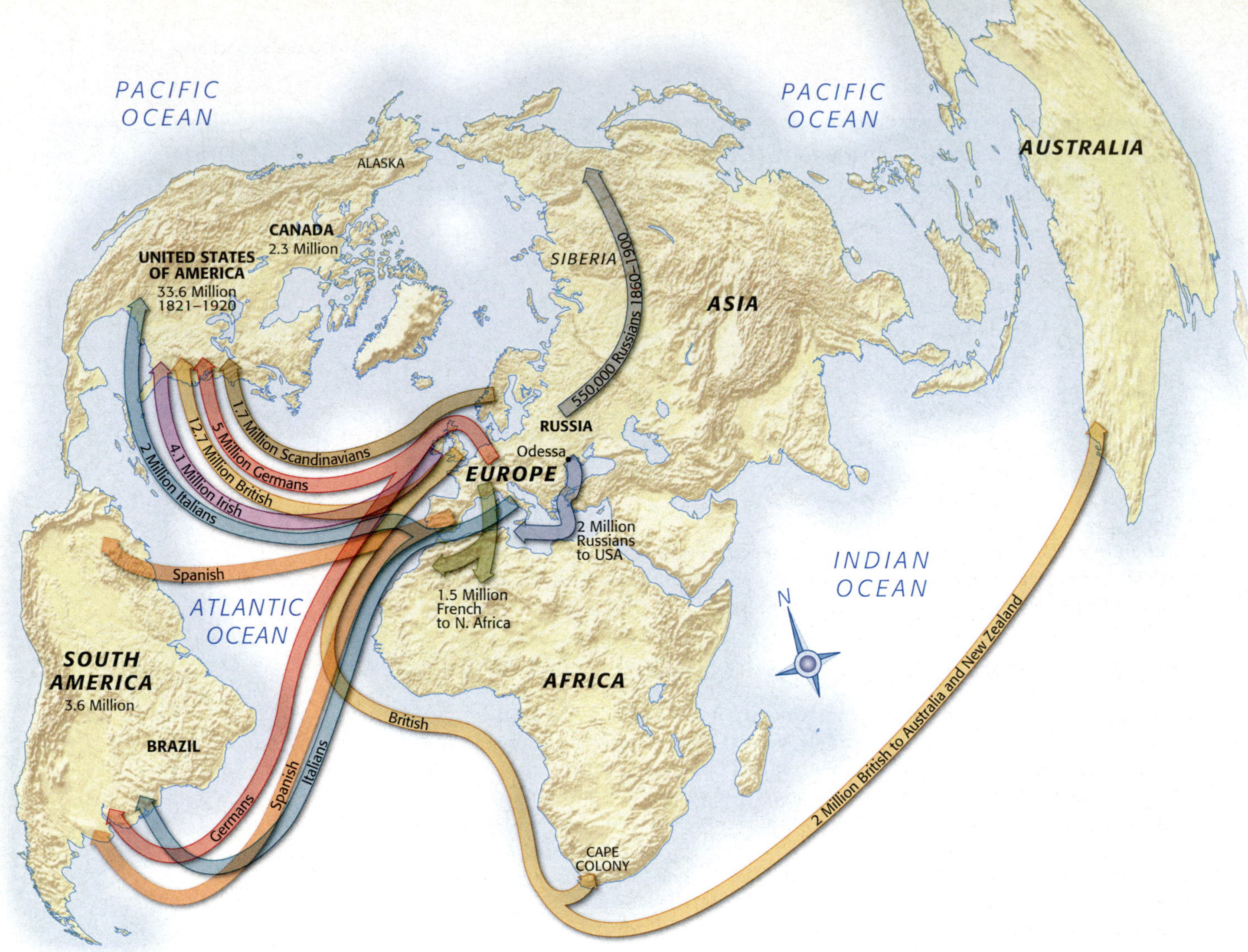

Map 20.1 European Emigration, 1820–1910

Pushed by rapid population growth and poverty, millions of Europeans left their homes to settle in the Americas (especially the United States), North and South Africa, Siberia, Australia, and New Zealand. The British and Irish accounted for the largest numbers of emigrants, nearly 17 million combined.

Interactive Map

Reprinted by permission of HarperCollins Publishers, Ltd. © *Times Atlas of World History*, 3rd. ed. Some data from Eric Hobsbawm, *The Age of Empire, 1875–1914* (New York: Pantheon, 1987)

Gender Relations

The industrial economy was hard on families, particularly on women and children. Seldom viewed as breadwinners, women typically earned only 25 percent of men's wages. Single mothers found it especially difficult to earn a living, and some were forced to turn to prostitution for survival. Women and children often did hard manual labor in cotton mills and mines. In 1838 a liberal member of the British Parliament reported: "I saw a cotton mill, a sight that froze my blood, full of women, young, all of them, some large with child, and obliged to stand twelve hours each day. The heat was excessive in some of the rooms, the stink pestiferous. I nearly fainted."[4] By the early 1900s, when machines did more of the factory work, fewer women and far fewer children worked full-time in the industrial sector.

The Industrial Revolution reshaped life for both genders, putting men and women into separate work worlds and lowering women's status by increasing their dependence on men. Moving the workplace from the home to the factory increased men's power over their wives. No longer needed in economic production, middle-class women lost their roles as direct producers, becoming instead home managers ("housewives") charged with keeping the house clean. Middle-class men assumed that women belonged at home as submissive helpmates and encouraged them to cultivate their beauty and social graces to please their menfolk. Men remained dominant in the political, social, economic, and religious spheres, and women's roles were increasingly restricted to marriage, motherhood, and child rearing. Moreover, often women had no legal standing and could not divorce their husbands. Upper- and middle-class women practiced artificial birth control and had fewer children than in earlier eras. By 1900, however, women enjoyed longer life expectancies and devoted fewer years to childbearing and rearing.

In the later 1800s European women gained more legal rights and economic opportunities. Some European women took new jobs as secretaries, telephone operators, or department store sales clerks, and occasionally doors opened to professional jobs. The Netherlands had Europe's first woman physician in 1870, and France the first woman lawyer in 1903. Leading professional women such as the Italian educator Maria Montessori (mon-ti-SAWR-ee) (1870–1952), who devised innovative schools allowing children to develop at their own pace; the Polish-born French scientist Marie Curie (1867–1934), who won a Nobel Prize in physics in 1903; the influential German composer and pianist Clara Schumann (1819–1896); and the British nurse Florence Nightingale (1820–1910), who revolutionized nursing practices, provided role models. In 1867 the University of Zurich in Switzerland became the first university to admit women, and it was soon followed by universities in France, Sweden, and Finland.

In quest of more rights, some women espoused views later known as **feminism**, a philosophy promoting political, social, and economic equality for women with men. Inspired by pioneers such as Mary Wollstonecraft in the late 1700s, the first feminist movements emerged in Britain and Scandinavia, with some activists, later known as **suffragettes**, pressing for the same voting rights as men. In 1896 Finland became the first European nation to accept female suffrage (see Chronology: European Society and Culture, 1750–1914). In Britain suffragettes led by Emily Pankhurst (1858–1928) campaigned for the right to vote by giving speeches, canvassing door-to-door, and demonstrating. In southern and eastern Europe feminists had only a small following.

CHRONOLOGY
European Society and Culture, 1750–1914

1859 Publication of Charles Darwin's *On the Origin of Species*

1860s Beginning of impressionist artistic movement in France

1896 Women's suffrage in Finland

1905 Publication of Albert Einstein's special theory of relativity

feminism A philosophy promoting political, social, and economic equality for women with men.

suffragettes Women who press for the same voting rights as men.

Thought, Religion, and Culture

The industrial and political revolutions, and the social changes they sparked, fostered new directions in European thought and culture. Philosophers such as the Germans Immanuel Kant (1724–1804) and Friedrich Nietzsche (NEE-chuh) (1844–1890) debated the values of the Enlightenment. An Enlightenment thinker, Kant believed that experience alone was inadequate for understanding because the perceptions it fosters are ultimately shaped by the mind, which imposes a structure on the sensations we see. Kant doubted that a perfect society could ever be achieved, arguing that "man wishes concord, but nature, knowing better what is good for his species, wishes discord."[5] Nietzsche rejected the Enlightenment notions of progress, perceiving a growing decadence in European culture that he blamed on Christian values and democratic ideas. To Nietzsche, there was no fundamental moral and scientific truth, as the Enlightenment philosophers had thought, but rather misconceptions developed by each culture as its members tried to understand the world. With no absolute truth, absolute good and evil cannot exist. In the twentieth century extreme nationalists and racists distorted Nietzsche's ideas to persecute ethnic minorities, while many European and North American intellectuals used Nietzsche's notion that truth is relative to argue that all knowledge was culturally constructed.

"Convicts and Lunatics" The movement for women's right to vote, or suffrage, was particularly strong in Britain. This poster, "Convicts and Lunatics," designed by the artist Emily Harding Andrews for the Artist's Suffrage League around 1908, shows a woman graduate, deprived of basic political rights, treated similarly to a convict and a mentally disturbed woman.

Library of Congress

Religion

Religion also changed with the times. Gradually Protestants and Catholics learned to tolerate each other. In the later 1700s and early 1800s a religious revival inspired many European Protestants to move to the United States. Evangelicals stressed personal relations with God, favored missionary activity, and condemned behavior they considered sinful, such as social dancing and drinking. Soon new churches appeared. The charismatic British Anglican preacher John Wesley (1703–1791), seeking a more emotional faith, founded the Methodist movement, which later formed its own church. The Society of Friends, better known as Quakers, who believed in nonviolence, human dignity, and individual conscience, fought against slavery and for social and political freedom and humanitarian causes.

Many middle-class Protestants sought a liberalized faith stressing social tolerance rather than the hellfire and damnation preached by some evangelicals. As the relevance of religion declined, by 1851 only half of the English population attended church. The divide between the more liberal and the more devout resulted in public debates across Europe about the role of religion in society. In Britain evangelicals sought to impose their values on the increasingly secular society by trying to ban alcohol and gambling and by requiring all businesses to close on Sunday, moves fiercely opposed by many Protestants and Catholics.

The Roman Catholic and Greek Orthodox Churches also faced challenges. Spurred by the French Revolution, the Catholic clergy in France and Belgium lost the privileged status they had enjoyed for centuries. France opened a public school system in the 1890s and mandated state neutrality toward religion in 1905. At the same time, the Catholic Church generally strengthened church dogma and organization, and popes reasserted their theological infallibility and announced new doctrines such as the Immaculate Conception of the Virgin Mary. The church also remained a major spiritual force and landowner in Austria, southern Germany, Poland, Spain, Portugal, and Italy. Meanwhile, the Greek Orthodox world fragmented into national churches in Greece, Serbia, Romania, and Bulgaria.

Literature and the Arts

The growth of a literate public eager and able to consume cultural products liberated writers, composers, and artists from dependence on wealthy patrons. Imbibing various movements, European classical music enjoyed a golden age, and the compositions of this era are still enjoyed by audiences around the world. The Austrian Wolfgang Amadeus Mozart **(MOTE-sahrt)** (1756–1791) wrote thirty-five symphonies, eight operas, and many concertos. Inspired by the Age of Revolution, some thinkers and artists adopted **romanticism**, a philosophical, literary, artistic, and musical movement that questioned the Enlightenment's rationalist values and instead glorified emotions, individual imagination, and heroism. Some romantics celebrated great figures such as Napoleon Bonaparte. The German writer Friedrich Schiller (1759–1805) offered intense romantic images with a nationalist tinge, such as a poem that turned the story of William Tell, a legendary hero of Swiss resistance against foreign invasion, into a manifesto for German political freedom. Romanticism also inspired the German composer Ludvig von Beethoven (1770–1827), whose much-admired Ninth Symphony set Schiller's poem, "Ode to Joy," to music.

romanticism A philosophical, literary, artistic, and musical movement that questioned the Enlightenment's rationalist values and instead glorified emotions, individual imagination, and heroism.

In contrast, writers and artists embracing another movement, realism, portrayed a grimy industrial world filled with uncertainty and conflict. For example, the liberal Spanish painter Francisco de Goya's (1746–1828) moving series on the Napoleonic invasion of Spain portrayed not warfare's heroism but its horrors: orphans, pain, rape, blood, and despair. The British realist novelist and former factory worker Charles Dickens (1812–1870) revealed the hardships of industrial life, the injustices of capitalism, and the miseries of the poor.

Several significant movements shaped the visual arts in the later 1800s and reflected influences from Asian, African, and Pacific art. **Modernism** embraced progress and welcomed the future. Realistic landscape paintings, the appearance of photography, and the introduction of Japanese prints contributed to the rise in France of **impressionism**, an artistic movement that expressed the immediate impression aroused in momentary scenes, bathed in changing light and color. Impressionists painters such as Claude Monet **(moe-NAY)** (1840–1926) and Pierre Renoir **(ren-WAH)** (1841–1919) achieved worldwide fame. Some French artists rebelled against impressionism, returning to familiar shapes and compositions. The most influential included Paul Cezanne **(say-ZAN)** (1839–1906), famous for his landscapes, still lifes, and portraits; the prolific Dutch-born Vincent Van Gogh **(van GO)** (1853–1890), who introduced intense primary colors and thick brushstrokes; and Paul Gauguin **(go-GAN)** (1848–1903), a former stockbroker whose richly colored paintings often featured idyllic scenes of Polynesian life based on his long residence there, stimulating European interest in the wider world. Pablo Picasso (1881–1973), a young Spaniard who settled in Paris, revolutionized Western art by integrating ideas from African sculpture and masks. The new European art bore little resemblance to medieval European art.

modernism A cultural trend that embraced progress and welcomed the future.

impressionism An artistic movement that sought to express the immediate impression aroused by momentary scenes that were bathed in light and color.

Science and Technology

The Modern Era saw spectacular achievements in science and technology. The British naturalist Charles Darwin (1809–1882), after years spent traveling around the world studying plants, animals, and fossils in many lands, formulated the theory of evolution emphasizing the natural selection of species. In his book, *On the Origin of Species*, Darwin argued that all existing species of plants and animals, including humans, had evolved into their present forms over millions of years. Species either adapted to their environment or died out. Eventually evolution became the foundation for the modern biological sciences, confirmed by many studies and accepted by most scientists, but it generated opposition from many churches, whose leaders saw Darwin's evolutionary ideas as a degradation of humans and a negation of religious faith.

Darwin

The German-born Jewish physicist Albert Einstein (1879–1955) ranks with Galileo, Newton, and Darwin as a pathbreaking European scientist. His papers on the theory of relativity, published in the early 1900s, provided the basis for modern physics, our understanding of the universe, and the atomic age. Einstein offered a new view of space and time, showing that distances and durations are not, as Newton thought, absolute but are affected by one's motion. He also proved that matter can be converted into energy and that everything is composed of atoms, insights that provided the basis for atomic energy. Einstein's papers electrified the scientific world. He taught in Swiss, Czech, and German universities before immigrating to the United States in 1934.

Einstein

New and rapid health and technological discoveries all over Europe also characterized the age, improving people's lives. Physicians introduced the first effective vaccines against deadly diseases such as smallpox that had ravaged the world for centuries, and drugs and medical technologies improved. In 1895 the German physicist Wilhelm Rontgen **(RUNT-guhn)** (1845–1923) discovered x-rays, spurring progress in diagnosis and surgery. Medical advances and improved sanitation also led to better public health. Thanks to cleaner water, cholera was eradicated from Europe's industrial cities. Electric batteries, motors, and generators emerged as new sources of power. The Italian Guglielmo Marconi (1874–1937) introduced wireless telegraphy, and in 1901 he used his invention to communicate between England and Canada, opening another network connecting the world. Two Germans, Gottlieb Daimler and Karl Benz, became the "fathers of the automobile," producing the first petroleum-powered vehicle in the 1880s.

Meanwhile, some scientists worried about the effects of industrial pollution on the environment. The observation that carbon dioxide emissions from coal-burning factories heated the atmosphere led the Swedish scientist Svante Arrhenius to speak of a "greenhouse effect" that potentially threatened modern societies. Scientific studies over the next century confirmed his fears. The world still struggles with the promise but also the perils of the technologies and industrial processes developed in this era.

SECTION SUMMARY

- In Europe, better crops and health care produced larger populations, which led to increasing urbanization, impoverishment, and emigration.
- As Europe became more industrialized and interconnected, the nuclear family and love marriages became increasingly common, and some began to question the institution of marriage itself.
- Industrialization made men more powerful and relegated women to the home, but in the late nineteenth century women began to gain legal rights and economic opportunities.
- While some Protestants attempted to stamp out behavior they considered sinful, Europeans as a whole became more secular and the Catholic Church's influence declined.
- Artists, writers, and composers became dependent on the public marketplace rather than wealthy patrons, and artistic trends such as romanticism, realism, modernism, and impressionism became dominant.
- Advances in science and technology led to the theory of evolution, greater understanding of the physical world, improved medical care, new sources of energy, and new concerns about pollution and its effects.

The Rise of the United States

What impact did westward expansion, immigration, and industrialization have on American society?

After the American Revolution, the former colonists turned to building their new nation. During the early republic Americans established new forms of government, reshaped economic patterns, fostered a new culture, and began the movement westward, conquering Native Americans, acquiring Mexican territory, and becoming involved in the wider world. Then between 1860 and 1914 the United States changed dramatically. The Civil War maintained the territorial unity of the nation, ended slavery, and led to the increased centralization of the federal government, which, combined with economic protectionism, allowed the United States to duplicate the economic and political growth that was spurred by mercantilism in Early Modern western Europe. Industrialization created more wealth, supported U.S. power, and reshaped American society. By 1900 the United States had a larger population than all but one European nation, boasted the world's most productive economy, owned half a continent, enjoyed a powerful, stable, democratic government, and exercised its power abroad, all sustained by an abundance of natural resources.

The Early Republic and American Society

The new American republic, weak and surrounded by hostile neighbors in British Canada and the Spanish American Empire, found nation building a challenge. Unity was fragile, and Americans faced the daunting task of establishing principles to unite the diverse states. Ultimately they forged a new distinctive form of representative democracy and constructed an economic framework to preserve independence and encourage free enterprise capitalism. The Constitution and Bill of Rights established a relatively powerful central government, elected by voters in each state, within a federal system that recognized the lawmaking powers of each member state (see Chronology: The United States and the World, 1750–1914). By the mid-1800s all white adult males enjoyed the right to vote, but the government maintained slavery and excluded Native Americans and women from political activity.

protectionism Use of trade barriers to shield local industries from foreign competition.

Professing a love for freedom, Americans have had to constantly redefine the balance between the rights of the state and the individual, and of the majority and the minority. The U.S. political system reflected a mix of liberalism, which underpinned the Bill of Rights, and fear of disorder. The founders made tyranny difficult through the separation of powers into executive and legislative branches and an independent judiciary. But, wary of radicalism and shocked by the French Revolution's excesses, American leaders also discouraged attacks on the upper classes by limiting voting rights, such as through property and literacy qualifications for voting and the indirect election for the presidency through the Electoral College, in which each state chose electors to cast their votes, producing results that did not always reflect the popular vote.

CHRONOLOGY
The United States and the World, 1750–1914

1787 U.S. Constitution

1803 Louisiana Purchase

1812–1814 U.S.-British War of 1812

1823 Monroe Doctrine

1825 Completion of Erie Canal

1846–1848 U.S.-Mexican War

1848 U.S. acquisition of Texas, California, and New Mexico

1849 California gold rush

1861–1865 Civil War

1862 Lincoln's Emancipation Proclamation

1867 U.S. purchase of Alaska from Russia

1869 Completion of transcontinental railroad

1898 U.S. incorporation of Hawaii

1898–1902 Spanish-American War

1902 U.S. colonization of Philippines

1903 First powered flight by Wright Brothers

American leaders also had to establish a sound economic foundation for the new nation. The southern plantation interests favored free trade to market their crops abroad without obstacles. But many founders insisted that economic independence was necessary to safeguard political independence and thus preferred self-reliance and **protectionism**, the use of trade barriers to shield local industries from foreign competition. The first treasury secretary, the West Indian-born Alexander Hamilton (1757–1804), established a national bank, favored tariffs to exclude competitive foreign goods, and provided government support for manufacturing. Continued conflicts with Britain brought about a U.S. decision in 1807 to temporarily embargo all foreign trade, which stimulated domestic manufacturing to offset the lost imports.

Trade and border conflicts between Britain and the United States led to the War of 1812 (1812–1814), during which the British captured Washington, burned down the White House, and repulsed a U.S. invasion of Canada. After some U.S. victories, however, the two sides negotiated peace. Industrialization proceeded in the U.S. northeast, and the first large textile mills to convert raw cotton into finished cloth opened in New England. The northern industrialists who favored protectionist policies soon prevailed over the southern planters who wanted free trade. Meanwhile, to move resources and products, Americans also built over 3,300 miles of canals, including the Erie Canal across New York State, linking the markets and resources of the Midwest to New York City.

Gradually Americans forged a society distinct from Britain's. The French writer Alexis de Tocqueville (1805–1859), who visited the United States in the early 1830s, noted the American commitment to democracy and individualism and Americans' "unbounded desire for riches."[6] But he also condemned slavery and feared that too much individualism and greed undermined community. De Tocqueville was fascinated by America's gender relations, admiring the independence of single American women, the tendency to view marriage as a voluntary contract between loving equals, and the resulting influence of married women in the family. Nonetheless, unmarried women and many wives were still under the strong control of men who believed that women's place was centered on the home.

African Americans

Enslaved African Americans, mostly plantation workers, were the majority in many southern districts, constantly replenished by new arrivals from Africa. They created music, including spirituals, that was based in part on African rhythms and song styles and that used Christian images to indirectly express a longing for freedom. In "Go Down Moses," for example, the refrain emphasized "let my people go," a clear call for emancipation, just as the Hebrews in Egypt were led to freedom by Moses. Many white Americans also wanted to eliminate slavery and other social ills. The abolitionists Sojourner Truth (ca. 1797–1883) and Frederick Douglas (1818–1895), both former slaves, also eloquently advocated gender equality and women's suffrage. Sarah Grimke (1792–1873), a Quaker from a South Carolina slaveholding family, became an active abolitionist and one of the first American feminists, rejecting the notion of different male and female natures (see Witness to the Past: Protesting Sexism and Slavery). Discovering that their deceased brother had fathered two sons with one of his slaves, Sarah and her sister Angelina flouted custom and laws by raising and educating their nephews.

Religion

This period also saw the development of distinctively American religious and cultural beliefs that often ignored rigid doctrines and dogmatic church leaders. Many Americans embraced secular values, showing tolerance for diverse ideas and indifference to organized religion. Others actively sought a personal and intense religious experience. Religious dissenters, such as Quakers and Methodists, had long flocked to North America, and Protestant denominations there multiplied, reinforced by the religious revivals that periodically swept the country. Yet, Puritan and Calvinist values remained influential, promoting a dedication to hard work and criticism of music, dancing, and reading for pleasure.

Manifest Destiny and Expansion

The nation gradually expanded westward, acquiring abundant fertile land and rich mineral deposits, thus providing a counterpart to European imperialism in Asia and Africa (see Chapter 19). As pioneers began moving across the Appalachian Mountains in search of new economic opportunities, they developed the potent notion of their **Manifest Destiny**, the conviction that their country's unmatched institutions and culture gave them a God-given right to take over the land. Manifest Destiny offered a religious sanction for U.S. nationalism and the thrust outward. In 1823 Secretary of State John Quincy Adams set a goal of transforming the United States into "a nation, coextensive with the North American continent, destined by God and nature to be the most populous and powerful people ever combined under one social compact."[7]

Manifest Destiny Americans' conviction that their country's unmatched institutions and culture gave them a God-given right to take over the land.

Library of Congress

American Progress This 1893 painting by the American artist John Gast extols progress and shows Americans, guided by divine providence, expanding across, and bringing civilization to, the forests and prairies of the Midwest and West. The painting reflects views held by many Americans of their destiny and special role in the world.

Map 20.2 U.S. Expansion Through 1867

The United States expanded in stages after independence, gaining land from Spain, France, Britain, and Mexico until the nation stretched from the Atlantic to the Gulf and Pacific coasts by 1867. During the same period Canadians expanded westward from Quebec to British Columbia.

Interactive Map

Territorial Expansion

After acquiring the Ohio territory, in 1787 the new nation extended from the Atlantic to the Mississippi River. In 1803 President Thomas Jefferson (g. 1800–1809) astutely bought from France, in the Louisiana Purchase, a huge section of the Midwest and South that doubled the size of the country. Then the United States acquired Florida and the Pacific Northwest. While many Americans moved into the Midwest, others continued on to Oregon by wagon train, crossing vast prairies, deserts, and mountains. In 1848, as a result of the U.S.-Mexican War, the United States obtained Texas, California, and New Mexico from Mexico. Then the discovery of gold near Sacramento in 1849 prompted over 100,000 Americans, known as "49ers," to board sailing ships or covered wagons and head for California from the distant east, hoping to strike it rich. In California the "49ers" sometimes clashed with the long-settled Mexicans and immigrant Chinese. The 1867 purchase of Alaska from Russia eliminated all European rivals from North America (see Map 20.2). By 1913 the United States had grown to forty-eight states.

Frontier Life

The vast North American frontier offered conditions where settlers could develop new ways of life and ideas. The rise of cattle ranching on the Great Plains fostered a new occupation, that of

Protesting Sexism and Slavery

Sarah Grimke and her younger sister, Angelina, were the daughters of a wealthy slaveholding family in Charleston, South Carolina. Adopting the Quaker faith, which emphasized human dignity, and rejecting their positions as members of the state's elite, they dedicated their lives to advocating women's rights and the abolition of slavery. In 1837 they moved north and began giving lectures before large audiences. Because they spoke out so publicly, they were often criticized by churches for violating gender expectations. Sarah Grimke responded in 1838 by writing letters to her critics that often used Christian arguments to defend women's right and obligation to voice their views. When the letters were published together in one volume, they became the first American feminist treatise on women's rights. The following excerpts convey some of Grimke's arguments.

Here then I plant myself. God created us equal; he created us free agents; he is our Lawgiver, our King and our Judge, and to him alone is woman bound to be in subjection, and to him alone is she accountable for the use of those talents with which her Heavenly Father has entrusted her. . . . As I am unable to learn from sacred writ when woman was deprived by God of her equality with man, I shall touch upon a few points in the Scriptures, which demonstrate that no supremacy was granted to man. . . . [In the Bible] we find the commands of God invariably the same to man and woman; and not the slightest intimation is given in a single passage, that God designed woman to point to man as her instructor. . . .

I hope that the principles I have asserted will claim the attention of some of my sex, who may be able to bring into view, more thoroughly than I have done, the situation and degradation of women. . . . During the early part of my life, my lot was cast among the butterflies of the *fashionable* world; and of this class of women, I am constrained to say, both from experience and observation, that their education is miserably deficient; that they are taught to regard marriage as the one thing needful, the only notice of distinction; hence to attract the notice and win the attentions of men, by their external charms, is the chief business of fashionable girls. They seldom think that men will be allured by intellectual acquirements, because they find, that where any mental superiority exists, a woman is generally shunned and regarded as stepping out of her "appropriate sphere," which, in their view, is to dress, to dance, to set out to the best possible advantage her person. . . . To be married is too often held up to the view of girls as [necessary for] human happiness and human existence. For this purpose . . . the majority of girls are trained. . . . [In education] the improvement of their intellectual capacities is only a secondary consideration. . . . Our education consists almost exclusively of culinary and other manual operations. . . .

There is another class of women in this country, to whom I cannot refer, without feelings of the deepest shame and sorrow. I allude to our female slaves. . . . The virtue of female slaves is wholly at the mercy of irresponsible tyrants, and women are bought and sold in our slave markets, to gratify the brutal lust of those who bear the name of Christians. . . . If she dares resist her seducer, her life by the laws of some of the slave States may be . . . sacrificed to the fury of disappointed passion. . . . The female slaves suffer every species of degradation and cruelty, which the most wanton barbarity can inflict; they are indecently divested of their clothing, sometimes tied up and severely whipped. . . . Can any American woman look at these scenes of shocking . . . cruelty, and fold her hands in apathy, and say, "I have nothing to do with slavery"? *She cannot and be guiltless.*

THINKING ABOUT THE READING

1. What do the letters tell us about the social expectations and education for white women from affluent families?
2. In what way do Grimke's letters address the issue of slavery?

Source: Sarah M. Grimke, *Letters on the Equality of the Sexes, and the Condition of Woman* (Boston: Issac Knapp, 1838).

cowboys on horseback, who were needed to guide herds of several thousand cattle on long, lonely drives to railroad towns for shipment east. These cowboys—whites, Mexicans, African Americans, and men of mixed descent—often learned survival skills and knowledge of horses from Native Americans. Individualists sought adventure, social equality, and a better life in the West. Life on the frontier was often hard, especially on women. An Illinois farm wife, Sara Price, lamented her hardship in poetry, writing that "life is a toil and love is a trouble. Beauty will fade and riches will flee. Pleasures will dwindle and prices they double, And nothing is as I would wish it to be."[8]

Westward Expansion and Native Americans

Westward expansion came at the expense of the Mexicans, Spaniards, and Native Americans already there. Indians saw whites as invaders and often resisted violently. To whites, Indians represented an alien culture and needed to be restricted to reservations. The U.S. Supreme Court ruled in 1831 that the Indians' "relation to the United States resembles that of a ward to his guardian."[9] Over time many Indians, even tribes who lived in peace with whites, were removed from their native lands. The Cherokee, farmers of Georgia and the Carolinas who had developed an alphabet, published a newspaper, written a constitution, and had long cultivated good relations with their white neighbors, were forced into concentration camps and then in 1838 sent on a forced march of 1,200 miles, the "Trail of Tears," to Oklahoma. Four thousand Cherokee died from starvation or exposure on the journey. Other tribes were broken up in coerced relocations. Some tribes also resisted removal. The Seminole **(SEM-uh-nole)** in Florida, led by Chief Osceola **(os-ee-OH-luh)** (ca. 1804–1838), fought two wars with the U.S. army, attacking with guerrilla tactics and then retreating into the Everglades swamps. Finally Osceola was captured, after which the Seminole resistance faded and many of the tribe were exiled to Oklahoma.

United States and Latin America

The Americans' quest for resources and markets led ultimately to territorial expansion into Latin America and the formation of a new kind of empire. In 1823 President James Monroe (1758–1831) authored one of the major principles of U.S. foreign policy. The Monroe Doctrine was a unilateral statement warning European nations against interfering in the Western Hemisphere and affirming U.S. commitment to shape the Latin American political future after the overthrow of Spanish colonialism. The doctrine effectively marked off Latin America as an American **sphere of interest**, an area in which one great power assumes responsibility for maintaining peace and monopolizes the resources of that area. The Monroe Doctrine forged complex links between the United States and the rest of the Americas, often provoking hostility in Latin America, and set the stage for the rise of the United States as a world power.

sphere of interest An area in which one great power assumes responsibility for maintaining peace and monopolizes the area's resources.

As a result of the U.S.-Mexican War of 1846–1848, the United States greatly expanded its national territory. Some 35,000 Americans and their slaves had settled in the Mexican province of Texas. Chafing at Mexican rule and its antislavery policies, in 1836 the Americans rebelled and pushed the Mexican forces out, declaring themselves an independent republic. Soon the Texans sought annexation to the United States, a move favored by the proslavery southern states and opposed by the antislavery northern states. After Texans talked of alliance with Britain, the U.S. president and Congress moved to admit Texas to statehood in 1844, provoking the pride of Mexicans, who had never recognized Texan independence and now reasserted their claims. The war that followed stirred divisive and passionate debate in the United States, where many people opposed the conflict. After President James Polk (1795–1849) ordered military action, a Massachusetts legislative resolution proclaimed "that such a war of conquest, so hateful, unjust and unconstitutional in its origin and character, must be regarded as a war against freedom, against humanity, against justice, against the Union."[10] The war ended when 14,000 U.S. troops invaded Mexico and captured Mexico City. This victory allowed the United States to permanently annex Mexican territories from Texas to California. However, the conflict had killed 13,000 Americans and 50,000 Mexicans, and it had also fostered an enduring Mexican distrust of the United States.

United States and Asia

Many Americans supported the extension of Manifest Destiny to Latin America and Asia. Polk wanted to seize California and its harbors to increase the profitable commerce with China. In 1853 Senator William Seward placed expansion in global perspective, advising Americans: "You are already the great continental power. But does that content you? I trust that it does not. You want the commerce of the world. The nation that draws the most from the earth and fabricates most, and sells the most to foreign nations, must be and will be the great power of the earth."[11] American traders participated in the lucrative China trade, including opium smuggling, while the United States Navy opened up reclusive Japan. Hence, after the American revolution, merchants from New England ports such as Salem (Massachusetts) established, and grew rich from, operations in Asian ports such as Macao and Madras. U.S. traders, missionaries, adventurers, diplomats, and soldiers flocked to Asia (see Chapters 22–23).

During the nineteenth century the United States began to build, not a territorial empire like the British and Spanish, but chiefly an "informal" empire based on extending U.S. power through financial controls, trade, and military operations. American naval forces intervened in Southeast Asia almost annually from the 1830s through the 1860s. For example, in 1832 a U.S. naval expedition bombarded a port on the Indonesian island of Sumatra, whose officials had seized a private U.S. ship for illegal activities; U.S. officials boasted that the demolition of the port had "struck terror" into the Sumatrans, forcing them to release the ship. Some American leaders advocated military action to gain trade agreements, an aggressive attitude that increasingly influenced U.S. policies during the century. Presidents also sought to obtain nearby Cuba from Spain, even financing Cuban revolts.

The Civil War, Abolition, and Industrialization

North-South Conflict

The Civil War (1861–1865) reshaped U.S. society by ending slavery. Like Sarah Grimke, many Americans had believed that slavery mocked liberal democracy. By the early 1800s it had largely disappeared from northern states, and in 1810 the U.S. government outlawed the slave trade.

Thousands of free blacks occupied a precarious position in the southern states. The Civil War was a last gasp for the slavery-based southern plantation society, which desperately tried to break free from the urbanization, industrialization, and social change percolating in the northern states. By 1860, the North was the home of industry, banks, and great ports such as New York, Boston, and Philadelphia. By contrast, the South was largely a monocultural plantation economy, inhabited by 350,000 white families and 3 million black slaves, which depended on exports to survive.

In 1860–1861 eleven southern states seceded from the union, forming the proslavery Confederate States of America. President Abraham Lincoln (1809–1865), a lawyer from Illinois who wanted to end slavery and preserve the union, mobilized the military forces of the remaining states to resist the secession. In 1862 he issued the Emancipation Proclamation, freeing all slaves in the Confederacy. After four years of war the North defeated the South, mainly because the North's dynamic economy better mobilized resources for war and the North also had a population advantage of nearly 4 to 1.

The northern victory ultimately displaced the southern plantation system, crushed the southern struggle for self-determination, destroyed the South's economic link to Britain, firmly established protectionism as economic policy, and fostered a much stronger federal government. The war resulted in more American deaths than all other wars fought by Americans combined, killing 360,000 Union and 258,000 Confederate troops. The South began to enjoy balanced economic development only with the growth of industry in the mid-twentieth century, largely paid for by northern investors.

African Americans

Although the Civil War emancipated African Americans, it did not eliminate the disadvantages faced by them and other ethnic minorities. Many former slaves taught themselves to read, and some opened schools to expand opportunities for young blacks. Many African Americans left the plantations, but their job prospects were chiefly limited to sharecropping or physical labor. Long after slavery ended, African Americans also faced laws restricting their rights and barriers to voting. The southern states and some northern states had rigid laws against intermarriage and, unlike Latin America, little separate recognition for people of mixed ancestry, who were lumped with African Americans and treated as such. Any trace of African ancestry meant automatic relegation to inferior status. Skin color became the major determinant of social class, and racial segregation of schools, housing, and public facilities remained the norm in the South until the 1960s. Those who violated these laws and customs faced jail, beatings, or even executions by white vigilantes. The journalist Ida B. Wells (1862–1931), born into slavery, sparked a long movement to end mob violence, including hangings (known as "lynchings").

Resurgent Expansion

As peace brought a resumption of expansion into central and western North America, more Native Americans lost control of their destinies. Whites subdued the Great Plains with new technology, including the six-shooter, the steel plough, and the barbed-wire fence. Settlers, railroad builders, and fur traders massacred 15 million bison, the chief source of subsistence for Great Plains tribes, while farmers and ranchers reshaped the environment of the prairies and northern woodlands. Indians resisted but eventually faced defeat. In 1890, the United States Army's massacre of three hundred Lakota Sioux followers of the Ghost Dance, an Indian spiritual revival movement, at Wounded Knee in South Dakota marked the triumph of U.S. colonization of the west. Defeated and impoverished, Indians were put on government-controlled reservations. Their children, prohibited from speaking their native languages or practicing tribal traditions in boarding and public schools, were stripped of their cultural heritage.

Industrial Growth

The northern victory in the Civil War and protectionism spurred the improved material life and great industrial growth in the later 1800s, with the rise of the food processing, textile, iron, and steel industries and growing coal, mineral, and oil production. In 1860 the United States ranked fourth among industrial nations, but by 1894 it ranked first; American exports had tripled, and the nation was second only to Britain as a world trader. Technological innovations changed economic life. Electricity as a power source, combined with improved production methods, turned out goods faster, more cheaply, and in greater quantities than ever before, increasing U.S. competitiveness. New inventions by Americans such as the typewriter, cash register, adding machine, telegraph, and telephone increased business productivity, while American and European inventions such as water-tube boilers, steam-powered forging hammers, portable steam engines, and the internal combustion engine revolutionized industry. Thomas Edison (1847–1931) benefited the public and industry by perfecting the light bulb.

Improved transportation and communication networks reshaped American life and population patterns. The transcontinental railroad, completed in 1869, opened western lands for settlement. Many of the workers who drove the spikes and blasted the passages through rocks and mountains for the railroad tracks were African Americans, Chinese, or Irish. Henry Ford (1863–1947) started a motor company in 1903, turning out the first affordable cars and refining the

Corbis

Women Textile Workers In both Europe and North America women became the largest part of the work force in the textile industry. These women, working in a New England spinning mill around 1850, endured harsh work conditions and the boring, often dangerous, job of tending machines.

mass-production assembly line. Orville and Wilber Wright became the first men to achieve powered flight in 1903, launching the age of aviation.

Capitalists and Workers

But industrialization also led to a monopolistic concentration of industrial and financial resources similar to Europe's that worsened the inequitable distribution of wealth. A few fabulously wealthy tycoons such as John D. Rockefeller and J. P. Morgan, known to their critics as the Robber Barons, influenced politicians, controlled much of the economy, and expected workers to labor at subsistence wages. The Social Darwinist Rockefeller claimed that "the growth of large business is merely survival of the fittest and a law of God."[12] The wealthy flaunted their success, and many less-affluent Americans also valued and hoped to acquire wealth, believing that the United States was a land of opportunity where anyone could succeed with hard work regardless of social background.

Industrialization fostered industrial workers, who often experienced a hard life. In the coal mines of the southern Appalachians and Ohio River Valley, the work was dangerous, the hours long, and the wages low. Children worked alongside their parents, and miners often died young from breathing coal dust. Before the Civil War the textile industry, centered in New England, was based on exploitation of women and children. Companies recruited teenage girls from poor rural families to work in dark, hot mill rooms filled with cotton dust. They labored fourteen hours a day, six days a week, and were housed in company dormitories, six to eight girls per room. By the 1880s the textile industry had moved south to Virginia and the Carolinas, where wages were lower and people even more desperate for jobs.

Social Change, Thought, and Culture

Immigration

This era was also marked by social change. Some 25 million Europeans immigrated to the United States between 1870 and 1916. At first they came largely from northwestern Europe, especially

English, Irish, Germans, and Scandinavians. Later many arrived from southern and eastern Europe, including Italians, Greeks, Serbs, and Poles. Many Jews fleeing persecution in Europe saw the United States as the Promised Land, and by 1927 the Jewish population totaled 4 million. Meanwhile, thousands of Chinese, Japanese, and Filipino immigrants landed on the Pacific Coast. Most of these European and Asian newcomers faced discrimination. Some businesses posted signs saying, "No Irish need apply." Chinese and Japanese immigrants, mostly living in the western states, faced harsher restrictions and sometimes violence.

In less than a century the United States went from a mostly rural nation along the Atlantic coast to a transcontinental powerhouse. The federal government encouraged migration westward by giving free land to settlers in the Midwest for farming. The United States also became urbanized, with half of the people living in cities, including metropolises such as New York and Chicago.

Economic and Social Movements

These decades also saw movements seeking economic and social change. Since factories poured out more goods than Americans could consume, by the 1890s economic depression, panics, and bloody labor conflicts fostered working-class radicalism. Farmers and workers resented the wealth of the Robber Barons and the power of large corporations and railroads. Even while the United States became the world's leading agricultural producer, many farmers went bankrupt, losing their land to banks, and popular movements, some led by women, fought those with power and privilege. Labor unions had first appeared in the 1820s, and by midcentury mill girls were campaigning for better conditions and a shorter workday in New England textile mills. Eugene Debs (1855–1926), the socialist leader of the railway union, explained in 1893 that "the capitalists refer to you as mill hands, farm hands, factory hands. The trouble is he owns your head and your hands."[13] By the early 1900s the radical, Marxist-influenced International Workers of the World (better known as the Wobblies) gained influence among industrial workers, miners, and longshoremen. Union militants such as Mary Harris ("Mother") Jones (1830–1930), an Irish immigrant who called herself a hellraiser and organized coal miners and railroad workers, fought the power of big business. Employers and their political allies disparaged union members as communists and fought their demands.

Struggle for Women's Rights

Women also struggled for their civil rights. During the 1800s, although large numbers of women worked in factories, shops, and offices while also managing their homes, religious leaders urged women to be more pious, self-sacrificing, and obedient to men. They wore stiff, uncomfortable whalebone corsets that constrained movement and accentuated their figure, a symbol of their submission to male expectations. Many women wanted more options; the banners carried by striking factory workers in 1912 read, "We want bread and roses too." But women gained basic privileges on a par with men only after a long, nonviolent suffrage movement for the vote that declared that "all men and women are created equal." Suffragettes opposed a system in which women had no rights to property or even to their own children in case of divorce. After seven decades of marching, publicizing their cause, and lobbying male politicians, they convinced Congress to give women the right to vote in 1920.

Literature and Culture

Some Americans increasingly created their own distinctive literary and intellectual traditions. Walt Whitman (1819–1892), a journalist influenced by European romanticism, celebrated democracy, the working class, and both heterosexual and homosexual affection while addressing the transformations of the Industrial Revolution. Whitman described his ethnically diverse and dynamic nation as "a newer garden of creation, dense, joyous, modern, populous millions, cities and farms. By all the world contributed."[14] Mark Twain (1835–1910), a former printer and riverboat pilot from Missouri turned journalist, was inspired by European realism and sought material all over the country and the world. Twain emphasized the underside of American life and character, was skeptical about technology's value, and opposed the increasing U.S. imperial thrust in the world.

American philosophy and religion also went in new directions. The leading American philosophers, such as William James and John Dewey, broke with the European tradition by claiming that ideas had little value unless they enlarged people's concrete knowledge of reality, an approach known as pragmatism. While many Americans embraced secular and humanist views, many others sought inspiration in religion. The Protestant missionary impulse fostered religious and moral fervor, and Americans became active as Christian missionaries around the world. The nation itself became more religiously diverse. In 1776 most Americans were Protestant, often Calvinist, but by 1914 the United States contained followers of many faiths, including some Buddhist and Muslim immigrants from Asia.

Americans also produced unique music, largely the result of mixing black and white traditions. In the South, blues and jazz music developed in the early 1900s out of African American culture. The blues grew out of the plantation economy, the songs detailing personal woes in a world of harsh reality and racism. Bluesmen sang of lost love, the brutality of police, jail, joblessness, and oppression. Some songs celebrated black heroes such as the legendary hand driller John Henry, who allegedly died competing against a steam drill to build a railroad tunnel in the later 1800s. The blending of black blues with white folk music and popular music provided a foundation for several forms of American popular music in the twentieth century, including rock, rhythm and blues, and soul, which spread around the world.

American Capitalism and Empire

Imperialism

As in Europe, industrial capitalism fostered imperialism and warfare. A series of economic depressions from the 1870s through the 1890s spurred public demand for foreign markets, as many American businessmen, farmers, and workers favored acquiring territories overseas to improve national economic prospects. Others hoped to spread American conceptions of freedom and a capitalist marketplace economy. Many argued that since domestic problems, such as the wide rich-poor gap, were not easily resolved, only acquiring resources and markets by directly or indirectly controlling other societies could generate enough wealth to avoid domestic turmoil. These pressures led to military interventions. The United States sent military forces to at least twenty-seven countries and territories between 1833 and 1898 to protect American economic interests or to suppress the piracy that threatened U.S. shipping. Troops were dispatched to many Latin American nations, China, Indonesia, Korea, and North Africa, and for decades U.S. gunships patrolled several of China's rivers to protect American businessmen and missionaries from Chinese who resented Western imperialism.

Colonization of Hawaii

U.S. forces also brought the Hawaiian Islands, a Polynesian kingdom where Americans had long settled as traders, whalers, planters, and missionaries, into the U.S. empire. The growing American population resented the Hawaiian monarchy. In 1891 Liliuokalani **(luh-lee-uh-oh-kuh-LAH-nee)** (1838–1917), a Hawaiian nationalist who wanted to restrict settler political influence, became queen. Although strong and resolute and beloved by her people as a songwriter, she faced economic disaster when the U.S. Congress abandoned preferential treatment for Hawaiian sugar imports. In 1893 American settlers, aided by 150 U.S. troops, overthrew the monarchy, formed a provisional government, and announced that they would seek affiliation with the United States. A heated debate in the United States on the advantages and disadvantages of direct colonization delayed annexation of the islands until 1898. The end of the monarchy also transformed the islands socially, as thousands of Japanese, Chinese, Korean, and Filipino immigrants become the main labor force, mostly working on plantations owned by American settlers and companies. By the 1930s, Asians constituted the large majority of Hawaii's population.

Spanish-American War

The major conflict involving the United States was the Spanish-American War (1898–1902), which pitted American against Spanish forces in several Spanish colonies. The war helped make the United States a major world power and empire and was motivated by President William McKinley's (1843–1901) desire to obtain foreign markets for America's surplus production. To that end, the United States fought with Spain over that country's remaining, restless colonies: Cuba, Puerto Rico, Guam, and the Philippines. The war unleashed American nationalist fervor, one observer describing patriotism as oozing out of every boy old enough to feed the pigs. While the United States quickly triumphed against the hopelessly outmatched Spanish, 5,500 Americans died in Cuba, mostly of disease; a surgeon who labored among the survivors wrote of pale faces, sunken eyes, staggering gaits, and emaciated forms.

The war also changed Americans' outlook on the world. A future president, Woodrow Wilson, boasted about America's emergence as a major power: "No war ever transformed us quite as the war with Spain. No previous years ever ran with so swift a change as the years since 1898. We have witnessed a new revolution, the transformation of America completed."[15] However, to colonize the Philippines, the United States had to brutally suppress a fierce nationalist resistance by Filipinos opposed to U.S. occupation, resulting in the deaths of thousands of Filipinos and Americans and indicating the costs of exercising power in the world. Many Americans protested the bloody U.S. invasion of the distant islands (see Chapter 22). The colonization of the Philippines, Puerto Rico, and Guam, as well as economic and political domination over nominally independent Cuba, also transformed the United States from an informal into a territorial empire much like the Netherlands and Portugal.

SECTION SUMMARY

- Americans were more individualistic and offered more independence to women than Europeans, and a struggle raged between supporters and opponents of slavery.
- Americans gradually pushed toward the West Coast, taking advantage of abundant natural resources and inflicting great suffering on Native Americans.
- The Monroe Doctrine announced that the United States saw Latin America as its own sphere of interest, off-limits to European powers.
- The bloody and divisive U.S.-Mexican War brought a large chunk of Mexican territory under American control.
- The Civil War killed hundreds of thousands, did tremendous damage to the South's economy, and freed the slaves, though discrimination and segregation continued for at least another century.
- American industry advanced rapidly, producing immense wealth for a small number of tycoons, helping others to prosper, and creating difficult, hazardous work for many.
- Millions of immigrants poured into the United States, seeking opportunity and often finding discrimination, while social movements seeking better treatment for workers and greater rights for women came into being.
- A distinctive American culture developed that celebrated democracy and practicality and that reflected the diverse origins of the American people.
- In the interests of promoting and protecting American business interests, the U.S. military intervened in the affairs of many foreign countries and territories, most notably in the Spanish-American War, which brought the United States its first formal colonies.

LATIN AMERICA AND THE CARIBBEAN IN THE GLOBAL SYSTEM

What political, economic, and social patterns shaped Latin America after independence?

Brazil and most of Spain's Latin American colonies won their independence in the early 1800s, although the Caribbean islands mostly remained colonies (see Chapter 19). But the new states did not forge the enduring democracy of their northern neighbors or foster significant economic change; instead most Latin Americans experienced political instability and regional conflicts. By the 1870s conditions stabilized as expanding European markets created a greater demand for Latin American exports, though free-trade policies also deepened the economic monocultures. Black slaves gained their freedom, waves of European immigrants changed the social landscape, and the United States increasingly exercised power in the region.

New Latin American Nations

Political Instability

Latin Americans faced new political and economic challenges. Some countries, such as Argentina, Brazil, and Mexico, were large and unwieldy, while others, such as El Salvador and the Dominican Republic, were small and had limited resources. Creating stable republics and political unity proved to be a struggle because the new governments did not always win the allegiance of all the people, and civil wars often pitted those favoring federalism and regionalism against partisans of a strong centralized government. In addition, various frontier disputes fostered occasional wars. Chile fought Peru and Bolivia in 1837 and again in 1879–1884, acquiring territory from those two countries as a result (see Chronology: Latin America and the Caribbean, 1750–1914).

Political instability often led to military dictatorships, since Spain and Portugal had never fostered democratic conditions in their colonies. Thus although most of the Latin American countries adopted elections and U.S.-style constitutions, authoritarian governments often ignored their provisions. Tensions between central governments and remote regions also became chronic. For example, the Argentine government did not impose its authority on the southernmost provinces until the 1870s.

Economic and Political Power

Despite political independence, most leaders did not favor dramatic social and economic change. The wealthy upper class, mostly creoles, owned large businesses, plantations, and haciendas; mestizos and mulattos dominated the small middle class of shopkeepers, teachers, and skilled artisans; and over half of the population, including most Indians and blacks, were lower class. Economies based chiefly on plantation agriculture or mining had similar, highly unequal social structures and offered limited educational opportunities. Planters, ranchers, mine owners, merchants, and military officers dominated politics and often restricted the political participation of the poor nonwhite majority. To contain or prevent unrest, military strongmen, known as **caudillos**, who acquired and maintained power through force, governed many Latin American countries. Some of these, such as the dictator Juan Manuel de Rosas (huan man-WELL deh ROH-sas) (1793–1877) in Argentina, were tyrants. Rosas's police and thugs beat up, tortured, or murdered opponents, often poor peasants. For their armies, caudillos and regional leaders sometimes recruited local cowboys, known as **gauchos** in Argentina and Uruguay, who worked on large ranches and were skilled horsemen and fighters.

caudillos Latin American military strongmen who acquired and maintained power through force.

gauchos Cowboys in Argentina and Uruguay who worked on large ranches and were skilled horsemen and fighters.

Despite these problems, most Latin American nations established some stability by the 1850s. Many countries sought both "progress and order," which usually meant caudillo rule, but a few fostered multiparty systems in which competing parties sought access to national power. Liberals generally favored federalism, free trade, and the separation of church and state; often irreligious, they opposed the institutional power of the Catholic Church as contrary to individual liberty. Conservatives sought centralization, trade protectionism, and maintenance of church power. Conflicts between these groups were sometimes violent.

Political Changes

Brazil was the only Latin American nation governed by a monarchy, which seemed unwilling to consider popular aspirations toward abolishing slavery and forming a republic. As tensions simmered, the army seized power in 1889, exiled Emperor Dom Pedro II, and replaced the monarchy with a republic. However, although a federal system emerged, suffrage was highly restricted, the majority of Brazilians gained neither property nor civil rights, and many remained desperately poor. In the end Brazil maintained an authoritarian tradition, but rebellions and regionalism constantly challenged the government.

Social and economic inequalities in Latin American countries often led to reforms and sometimes to revolutions. The birth of the Mexican republic in 1824 did not bring stability to the vast country, which stretched from northern deserts to southern rain forests. Between 1833 and 1855 a caudillo, General Antonio Lopez de Santa Anna (1797–1876), led a series of dictatorships punctuated by civil war. Santa Anna also lost half of Mexico's territory, including Texas and California, in the disastrous U.S.-Mexican War (1846–1848), a humiliation that is still felt by Mexicans today. Growing social problems and Santa Anna's misadventures sparked upheaval. In 1861 Mexican liberals led by Benito Juarez (WAHR-ez) (1806–1872), a pragmatic lawyer and Zapotec Indian, defeated the conservatives and suspended repayment of the foreign debt, provoking a short-lived occupation by France that made a member of the Habsburg family, Maximilian of Austria (1832–1867), emperor of Mexico. However, France withdrew its troops and Maximilian's regime collapsed in 1867. Juarez again served as president until his death in 1872, seeking social justice, fighting corruption, subordinating the church to the secular state, and assigning church and communal lands to individual families to create free peasants. His reformist policies and his Indian ancestry made Juarez Mexico's most honored leader and a symbol of the nation.

In 1876 Mexico came under the dictatorship of Porfirio Diaz (DEE-ahs) (1830–1915), a mestizo caudillo. Diaz brought stability and economic progress but also allowed foreign business interests and investors to take over much of Mexico's economy, doing little to help the poor majority. Under his free enterprise policies many Indians sold their land to large haciendas and land companies to pay off debts. The Diaz regime ended in civil war and the Mexican Revolution (1910–1920). One of several revolutionary factions was led by the liberal creole Francisco Madero (1873–1913), a landowner's son educated in France and the United States. Another rebel leader, Pancho Villa (VEE-uh) (1877–1923), a former cowboy, attracted support chiefly from ranchers in northern Mexico. In the south, the charismatic mestizo former peasant Emiliano Zapata (zeh-PAH-teh) (1879–1919) organized a peasant army that seized haciendas and fought the federal army.

CHRONOLOGY

Latin America and the Caribbean, 1750–1914

1861–1872 Benito Juarez president of Mexico

1876–1911 Diaz dictatorship in Mexico

1842 End of trans-Atlantic slave trade by most nations

1862–1867 French occupation of Mexico

1886 Abolition of slavery in Cuba

1889 Abolition of slavery in Brazil

1889 Brazilian republic

1879–1884 War between Chile and Peru-Bolivia

1895–1898 Cuban revolt against Spain

1898–1902 Spanish-American War

1901 Platt Amendment to Cuban constitution

1910–1920 Mexican Revolution

1912 U.S. intervention in Nicaragua

1914 Completion of Panama Canal

With the defeat of Diaz, largely by Zapata's forces, the idealistic Madero was elected president but, unable to hold the revolutionary movement together, was murdered by a rival, generating a free-for-all between the armies of Madero, Villa, Zapata, and other leaders. Mexico was engulfed in sporadic violence, all factions used ruthless tactics, and alliances formed and collapsed. A novel recorded the confusion: "thinkers prepare the Revolution; bandits carry it out. At the moment no one can say with any assurance: 'So-and-so is a revolutionary and What's his-name is a bandit.' Tomorrow, perhaps, it will be clearer."[16] Zapata was assassinated by a rival in 1919, but his reputation lived on after death, making him the most celebrated revolutionary hero.

The fighting had raised expectations for social change and fostered a yearning for peace. Women played a critical revolutionary role. They cooked and commanded troops, served as spies and couriers, shot carbines and pistols, and fought disguised as men. Some of their hopes for more rights seemed realized in a constitution introduced in 1917, which set forth progressive goals such as an eight-hour work day and paid maternity leave. In 1920 the conflict wound down after claiming 1 million lives. While most Mexicans remained impoverished, a new party led by former revolutionaries formed a government and brought political stability while also opening some space for women to enter the business world and state governments.

Archivo General de la Nación, Mexico, courtesy of Martha Davidson

Women Revolutionaries in Mexico Women joined men in fighting, and sometimes dying, for one or another faction during the Mexican Revolution. Many women hoped that the revolution would bring social change and a greater emphasis on improving women's political and economic rights.

Spanish-ruled Cuba also experienced revolt. By the later 1800s an independence movement had developed led by the journalist Jose Marti (1853–1895), who had traveled and lived in Europe, the United States, and various Latin American nations. Marti's writings promoting freedom, equality, and social justice helped inspire a Cuban revolt in 1895. Marti welcomed Afro-Cubans and women, who became the backbone of the struggle. However, Marti was killed in the fighting, and eventually the revolution was sidetracked by U.S. intervention during the Spanish-American War. Americans soon dominated the economy and strongly influenced the Cuban government.

Latin American Economic and Social Change

Like North Americans, Latin Americans debated free trade and heavy involvement in the world economy as opposed to protectionism and self-sufficiency. But, as exports and investments declined, Latin American leaders, unlike U.S. leaders, decided to maintain the monoculture based on plantations, mines, and ranches, concentrating on the export, mainly to the United States and Europe, of raw materials such as Ecuadorian cocoa, Brazilian coffee, Argentine beef, Cuban sugar, and Bolivian and Chilean ores. The decision left Latin American societies economically vulnerable because earnings from minerals and cash crops ebbed and flowed with the fall or rise of world commodity prices. By the twentieth century economic conditions in Latin America were closely tied to fluctuating, "boom or bust" world prices for those countries' exports. Hence, the politically unstable Central American countries, whose economies depended on tropical agriculture, were derisively called "banana republics."

Growth Without Development

Because Latin American economic policies fostered growth but not development, the majority of people saw few benefits and the gap between the rich and the poor widened. The impoverished state of most Indians and blacks gave them little purchasing power to support any local industries that might be developed. Efforts to industrialize in Brazil, Colombia, and Mexico in the 1830s and 1840s failed because of competition from European imports. Independence also opened Latin America to North American, French, and especially British merchants and financiers, who used their economic power to dominate banking and the import trade for industrial goods while also investing in mines and plantations. By the mid-1800s British businessmen and bankers controlled the imports and exports of both Brazil and Argentina. Argentina was sometimes called an informal member of the British Empire, and an Argentine nationalist complained that "English capital has done what English armies could not do. Today our country is tributary to England."[17] After 1890 the United States also became a powerful economic influence in Latin America.

Foreign economic domination had several consequences. First, foreign corporations increasingly owned the plantations and mines. For example, the U.S.-based United Fruit Company dominated Central American banana growing. Latin America became a major contributor to world commodity markets, producing some 62 percent of the world's coffee, 38 percent of the sugar, and 25 percent of the rubber by World War I. Although growing U.S. demand for markets and raw materials fostered economic expansion, inequalities grew. In some rural areas of Brazil, for example, powerful landed families maintained the peasantry in what was essentially bondage through private armies and gunmen. Throughout Latin America powerful families or foreign corporations increasingly owned the usable land, fostering social and economic imbalances that produced political unrest in the twentieth century.

Abolition of Slavery

Yet, the abolition of slavery opened the door to social change. Some of the leaders who overthrew Spanish rule freed slaves who fought in the wars of independence. Between 1823 and 1854 slavery was legally abolished in most of Latin America and the Caribbean, and most European and American countries outlawed the trans-Atlantic slave trade. The Spanish rulers finally granted Cuban slaves their freedom in 1886, and abolitionists became more outspoken in Brazil. Increasing resistance by slaves, growing opposition by educated Brazilians, and the desire to promote European immigration led finally to abolition in 1889. However, as in the United States, emancipation did not dramatically improve economic conditions. Many Latin American and Caribbean blacks shifted from being slaves to low-status sharecroppers, tenant farmers, and laborers. As a popular Brazilian verse lamented: "Everything in this world changes; Only the life of the Negro [black] remains the same. He works to die of hunger."[18]

Immigration and Class System

While life for most blacks changed little, the immigration of millions of Europeans and Asians reshaped many Latin American societies. Latin America's population doubled between 1850 and 1900 to over 60 million. Italians, Spaniards, Germans, Russians, and Irish sought better economic prospects, especially in Argentina, Brazil, Chile, Uruguay, and Venezuela. The majority of people in Buenos Aires, Argentina, trace their roots to Italy. The continued immigration generated a long-term market for European products and fashions.

People from overcrowded lands in Asia and the Middle East also immigrated to the Americas. In Trinidad, British Guiana, and Dutch Guiana, the abolition of slavery prompted labor-short planters to import workers from India, with the result that Indians eventually accounted for around half of the population in these colonies. Japanese settled in Brazil, Peru, and Paraguay as farmers and traders, Arab immigrants from Lebanon and Syria developed trade diasporas throughout Latin America, and Indonesians moved to Dutch Guiana as plantation workers. Chinese flocked to Peru and Cuba and, in smaller numbers, to Jamaica, Trinidad, and the Guianas. Much cultural mixing occurred as a result. For example, an Afro-Trinidadian might have a Spanish surname, belong to the Presbyterian Church, possess a Hindu love charm, enjoy English literature, and favor Chinese food. People of Asian or Middle Eastern ancestry have sometimes headed Latin American or Caribbean governments.

Despite the newcomers, Latin American society remained more conservative than North America. The creole elite dominated most countries, while European and Asian immigrants and mixed-descent people constituted the middle class. Many mulattos and most blacks and Indians remained in the lower class. Indians often withdrew into their village communities and limited contact with the national society. In 1865 a Mexican described the wide gap between whites and Indians: "The white is the proprietor; the Indian the worker. The white is rich; the Indian poor and miserable."[19] In Brazil, large populations of European, African, and mixed-descent people fostered a unique, multiracial society. Unlike in the United States, economic class and skin color did not always coincide, and intermarriage and cultural mixing were common. Millions of Brazilians of all backgrounds blended African religions with Catholicism, creating new sects. Yet blacks were also more likely than whites to experience prejudice and to be poor, a fact reflected in Rio de Janeiro's largely black hillside shantytowns.

Latin American and Caribbean Cultures

Literature

Latin Americans struggled to reconcile indigenous with imported European and African cultural traditions. Rejecting European models, novelists focused on social themes. Euclides da Cunha **(KOO-nyuh)** (1866–1909) helped create a realistic Brazilian literature that described the life of the country's poor (see Profile: Euclides da Cunha, Brazilian Writer). The radical Chilean essayist Francisco Bilbao praised freedom and rationalism while denouncing slavery, Catholicism, and U.S. expansionism. In contrast, the well-traveled Nicaraguan poet Ruben Dario (1867–1916) favored escapist and fantastic images while stressing beauty as an end in itself.

Musics

Especially creative cultural innovations came in music and dance. The sensuous dance called the tango emerged in the working-class bars and clubs of Buenos Aires, becoming the most popular music in Argentina and Uruguay. The tango mixed African and European traditions, since its rhythms were derived from African drumming and the music featured the accordion-like *bandoneon,* carried to Argentina by Italian immigrants. The tango became a symbol of lower-class identity, and by the early 1900s it had also become popular in the ballrooms and nightclubs of Europe. Brazil's unique music also blended European melody and African rhythms. The migration of Afro-Brazilians from the poor northeast to Rio de Janeiro fostered **samba**, a popular music and dance developed by Bahian women who settled in Rio's hillside shantytowns. Popular with all classes, samba became integral to Carnival, the three-day celebration before the long Christian period of fasting and penitence known as Lent.

samba A Brazilian popular music and dance.

Caribbean peoples also mixed African and European influences to produce distinctive cultures. On Trinidad, the British officials, who feared the black majority, prohibited African-based musical forms. Two traditions emerged to reflect Afro-Trinidadian identity and defiance of British rule. The first, **calypso**, a song style featuring lyrics addressing daily life and topical subjects, eventually became the major popular music in the English-speaking eastern Caribbean islands. The second tradition, the pre-Lent Carnival already mentioned, became a major festival. Calypso songs performed during Carnival often questioned colonial policies. A song in the 1880s protested colonial restrictions on music during Carnival: "Can't beat my drum, In my own native land. Can't have Carnival, In my native land."[20] Informal calypso presentations in makeshift theaters evolved by the 1920s into elaborate, heavily rehearsed shows.

calypso A song style in Trinidad that featured lyrics addressing daily life and topical subjects.

The United States in Latin America

Latin Americans both envied and feared the increasingly powerful United States, whose military forces occasionally intervened in Central America and the Caribbean. In 1856 William Walker, an American adventurer financed by influential U.S. businessmen, invaded Nicaragua with a well-armed American mercenary force and proclaimed himself president. Despite opposition by Central American leaders, the United States granted his government diplomatic recognition. Walker introduced slavery before being forced out in 1857, becoming a hated symbol in Central America of what Latin Americans often called Yankee imperialism.

United States and Cuba

Cuba was another example of U.S. interference. The Spanish-American War turned Cuba into a U.S.-dominated neocolony, and the Platt Amendment to the Cuban constitution, imposed by the United States in 1901, integrated the Cuban and U.S. economies and required that the U.S. Congress approve any treaties negotiated by Cuban leaders. The American military governor summarized the situation: "There is little or no real independence left to Cuba. She is absolutely in our hands, a practical dependency of the United States."[21] U.S. businessmen soon owned much of Cuba's economy, including railroads, banks, and mills, and the United States acquired a naval base at Guantanamo Bay. Later Cuban nationalists blamed Cuba's squalid condition not on the often despotic Cuban governments but on the United States. The Platt Amendment was finally repealed in 1934.

United States and Central America

The United States became deeply involved in some parts of Central America and the Caribbean. To build a canal across Central America linking the Pacific and Atlantic Oceans, the United States helped Panama secede from Colombia in 1903. Now essentially a U.S. protectorate, Panama then leased a 10-mile-wide zone across the isthmus in perpetuity to the United States for the canal. Several thousand workers from Panama and various Caribbean islands died in the ten arduous years of construction. In 1914 the Panama Canal, 51 miles long, was completed, one of the great engineering feats of history. U.S. and other ships could now sail between the Atlantic and Pacific Oceans safely and conveniently. In 1912 Americans also overthrew the president of Nicaragua, whom they suspected of inviting the British to build a rival canal across his country. But unrest followed, prompting the United States to send in a military force, which remained until 1933. U.S. soldiers also occupied Haiti (1915–1933) and the Dominican Republic (1916–1924) to quell unrest or maintain friendly governments. These interventions set the stage for a more active U.S. imperial policy in Latin America and the Caribbean.

EUCLIDES DA CUNHA, BRAZILIAN WRITER

Euclides da Cunha (1866–1909) was one of Latin America's greatest writers, respected for his prose style, and the spokesman for a rising Brazilian nationalism. Born near Rio de Janeiro to a family originally from Bahia in the northeast, Cunha grew up at a time of great social change and political turmoil, when Brazilians abolished slavery and the Brazilian empire became a republic. He attended a military college to study engineering but rebelled against the rigid discipline. After angrily hurling down his sword in front of the Minister of War, he left the college before graduating to work as a journalist. Cunha was also a scientist interested in geography and a sociologist interested in people. A man of many skills, later in life he worked as a sanitary engineer and surveyor as well as a professor of logic. He lived most of his life in Rio de Janeiro and São Paulo.

Cunha's generation of urban Brazilian intellectuals, influenced by European writers, sought political democracy, national unity, and an end to violence and racial prejudice. A voracious reader, Cunha came to passionately share these progressive views. He also wanted Brazilians to free themselves from slavish imitation of European philosophical and intellectual trends and make Brazil rather than Europe their spiritual home. Perhaps because of his unhappy military school experience, he became antimilitarist, writing that war is "a monstrous thing, utterly illogical." Nonetheless, Cunha rejoined the army for a while to defend the new republican government that had replaced the conservative imperial state. But the republic's inability to maintain democracy proved demoralizing, and he left the army to work as a civil engineer before returning to writing.

Cunha's greatest literary contribution was his book *Rebellion in the Backlands*, published in 1902, which is often called the bible of Brazilian nationality and a major work of world literature. Cunha's book challenged the nation's conscience and stimulated other authors to question accepted political wisdom. The book examined a rebellion, the Canudos War of 1896–1897, in an impoverished and parched rural region of Bahia State in the northeast, where most people worked on cattle ranches. Cunha's somber book recounted the powerful story of a rural mystic, Antonio Conselheiro, who, preaching a primitive Christianity that rejected private property, gathered a fanatic group, numbering in the thousands, to oppose Brazil's republican government. Federal officials responded with force, brutally crushing the uprising and killing most of the rebels. The book was a sociological analysis that reads like fiction.

Cunha called his searing account of the struggle a "cry of protest" against an "act of madness" by the government, an attack on the barbarity of the "civilized" against the weak. He portrayed sympathetically the mestizo backwoods people, detailing their customs, occupations, joys, diversions, and sorrows. For example, he described their "multitude of extravagant" beliefs, a mix of Christian and African traditions, and their ceremonies to revere the dead: "It is a charming sight to see a backwoods family at nightfall kneeling before their rude altar, by the dim light of oil lamps, praying for the souls of their loved ones who have died or seeking courage against the storms of this life."

Few urbanites knew anything about the northeast backlands people, who were alien to urban Brazilians. "It was not an ocean which separates us from them," Cunha wrote, "but three whole centuries." Cunha portrayed the confrontation between two cultures, the coast and interior, a theme that became popular in Latin American literature. The deeply religious backlanders could not comprehend the antireligious, rationalist ideas popular in the major cities, while the urbanites could not understand why rural people did not want the modern vision of political and social progress offered them. Cunha admired the rural men who had thrown off European culture and desired to be left alone, finding in the northeastern cowboy "the very core of our nationality." He believed that mestizos, blacks, and Indians were all part of the nation but that bringing the urban and rural people together in one nation would take many years.

Cunha's writing laid the groundwork for artists, writers, and scholars in Brazil and the rest of Latin America to explore new topics. Sadly, Cunha himself would not live to see his influence spread. In 1909 he was a victim of the violence he deplored. Discovering that his wife was having an affair with an army officer, Cunha rashly confronted the rival and was mortally wounded in the ensuing exchange of gunfire.

THINKING ABOUT THE PROFILE

1. How did Cunha's ideas reflect the Brazil of his era?
2. How did he view the backlanders and their role in the Brazilian nation?

Note: Quotations from Euclides da Cunha, *Rebellion in the Backlands*, translated by Samuel Putnam (Chicago: University of Chicago Press, 1957), xiii, v, iii, 112, 161, xvi.

Courtesy, Fundacao Biblioteca Nacional, Rio de Janeiro

Euclides da Cunha Euclides da Cunha was one of the major writers and social critics of late-nineteenth-century Brazil.

SECTION SUMMARY

- After gaining independence from Spain, Latin American nations were plagued by instability, undemocratic governments, and socioeconomic inequality along racial lines.
- After a disastrous period as a republic, a brief occupation by the French, and a probusiness dictatorship, a long, violent revolution finally led to political stability in Mexico.
- Latin American economies tended to focus on the export of one or two natural resources, which created instability and made them susceptible to foreign domination.
- The abolition of slavery in Latin America did not greatly improve the economic conditions of former slaves, and millions of immigrants from Europe, India, Japan, and elsewhere flowed into Latin American countries.
- The tango developed in lower-class Buenos Aires, and samba was a result of cultural mixing in Rio de Janiero, while Caribbean calypso was a legacy of resistance to British efforts to stamp out African-based music on Trinidad.
- The United States repeatedly intervened in Latin American affairs, most directly in Cuba, whose diplomatic affairs it dominated for three decades, and Panama, through which it built the Panama Canal.

New Societies in Canada and the Pacific Basin

Why did the foundations for nationhood differ in Canada and Oceania?

The United States became the most powerful and prosperous of the societies founded in the Americas and Oceania by European settlers, but it was not the only one to build a democratic nation and foster growing economies. Canada also expanded across North America to the Pacific. Western nations also colonized the island societies scattered around the Pacific Basin. In Australia and New Zealand, Britain established settler colonies, the British immigrants bringing with them their traditions and transforming these South Pacific territories.

Making a Canadian Nation

English and French Canadians

By 1763 the British had defeated the French and gained control of eastern Canada, including the main French colony, Quebec (see Chronology: Canada and the Pacific Basin, 1750–1914). The victorious British had to forge a stable relationship with French Canadians, who maintained their language, culture, and identity, and by 1774 the British pragmatically recognized the influential role of the Catholic Church and French civil law in Quebec. Meanwhile, British colonists settled chiefly in the Maritimes along the Atlantic coast, as well as west of Quebec in Ontario. Although the British governed Quebec and the English-speaking regions separately until 1841, relations between British and French Canadians remained uneasy, causing a British official in the 1830s to conclude that Canada was "two nations warring in the bosom of a single state."[22] The influence of France in North America ended in 1803, when the United States acquired the vast Louisiana territory, including the Mississippi River Basin long coveted by Americans.

Canada and the United States

Canada's peoples had to deal with the ambitions of the United States, whose leaders hoped that Canada might eventually join the Union. In a U.S.-British treaty in 1783, the United States recognized British control north of the Great Lakes and the Saint Lawrence River. After the American Revolution, many pro-British Loyalists moved to Canada, increasing the English-speaking population, especially in Ontario. Loyalists promoted democratic reforms and representative assemblies in Canada. The relations between the United States and Canada remained tense for years. Americans feared that their northern neighbors were aiding the Native Americans who resisted U.S. expansion in the Ohio region, such as the powerful and charismatic Shawnee chief Tecumseh (1768–1813), who gathered a large alliance of tribes to drive the white settlers out of Ohio and reinvigorate Indian ways. During the War of 1812 Americans repeatedly invaded Canada but were repulsed. The war ended U.S. attempts to expand north and also laid the seeds for a Canadian identity separate from the United States and Britain. In 1846 another treaty fixed the U.S.-Canada boundary in the west.

CHRONOLOGY

Canada and the Pacific Basin, 1750–1914

1763 British defeat of French forces in Canada

1774 British recognition of French culture and laws in Quebec

1770s Cook expeditions to Polynesia, New Zealand, and Australia

1788 First British penal colony in Australia

1792 First British settlers in New Zealand

1812–1814 U.S.-British War of 1812

1840s–1900s Western colonization of Pacific islands

1850 Treaty of Waitangi

1851 Discovery of gold in Australia

1867 Canadian Confederation

1885 Canadian transcontinental railroad

1901 Formation of Australian Commonwealth

1907 New Zealand self-government

Canadians could now turn to building a democratic nation in peace while working to modify British control. Between 1815 and 1850 Canada welcomed 800,000 British immigrants, and gradually the British approved reforms that fostered a unified Canada, an elected national parliament, and waning British influence over the Canadian government. But Canadians rejected complete independence in favor of self-rule within the British Empire as a strategy to resist U.S. power. In 1867 leaders from Ontario, Quebec, and New Brunswick and Nova Scotia in the Maritimes negotiated a Canadian Confederation that guaranteed strong provincial rights and preservation of the French language wherever it was spoken. Canada then became a **dominion**, a country having autonomy but owing allegiance to the British crown.

dominion A country having autonomy but owing allegiance to the British crown.

However, expansion of white settlement and political power to the west fired resentment among Indians and people of mixed French-Indian descent, the French-speaking Metis (may-TEES). The combative Metis leader, Louis Riel (ree-EL) (1844–1885), who had once studied to be a Catholic priest, led two rebellions before being executed for treason. Eventually, however, Manitoba and British Columbia joined the confederation and the federal government promised to build a transcontinental railroad, which Canada's first prime minister, Scottish-born John MacDonald (g. 1867–1873, 1878–1891), hoped would transform the 4 million Canadians into a unified nation. Crossing over 2,000 miles of forests, prairies, and high mountains, the railroad was completed in 1885. The government also negotiated treaties with Native Americans, allocating reservations to many of them as white settlers moved to the western provinces. By 1905 Canada included all the present provinces except Newfoundland.

The Canadian economy and ethnic structure were transformed between the 1860s and 1914. Beaver fur and fish had been the major exports since the 1600s, but now wheat grown in the Great Plains became the major export. Gold strikes in the Yukon and the offering of free land in western Canada attracted several million immigrants from many lands, including many from eastern and southern Europe as well as China and Japan, enriching the ethnic mosaic. By 1911 Canadians took control of their own foreign affairs and diplomacy. Over the next several decades Canada fostered increased industrialization and established warmer relations with the United States while maintaining the British monarch as symbolic head of state.

Exploration and Colonization of the Pacific Islands

The peoples who lived on the small mountainous islands and flat atolls scattered across thousands of miles in the vast Pacific Ocean Basin were the last to experience European expansion, but when it came, the impact was significant. The Spanish colonized Guam, in the Marianas, in 1663, but otherwise there had been little European contact with Pacific islanders. By the mid-

Library and Archives Canada, #PA 38667

Along the Canadian Pacific Railroad During the late nineteenth century both native-born Canadians and immigrants from many lands—British, Dutch, Germans, Poles, Russians, Scandinavians—followed the Canadian Pacific Railroad to settle the newly opened lands of the midwestern prairies and western mountains. Some people set up temporary tent villages by railroad stops before taking up farming, mining, logging, trade, or fishing.

1700s, however, the British and French had begun a race to explore what they considered the last frontier, eventually colonizing, along with Spain, Germany, Russia, and the United States, all the inhabited islands. The English captain James Cook (1728–1779), the son of an agricultural laborer, led some of the most extensive explorations. Cook reached the eastern Polynesian island of Tahiti in 1769, where he recruited a Polynesian high priest, Tupaia (ca. 1725–1771), whose skills as a navigator and speaker of several Polynesian languages greatly aided the expedition. Tupaia drew up the charts that helped Cook map Polynesia, including New Zealand, and the coast of Australia. Cook made two more expeditions to the Pacific in the 1770s, locating the Hawaiian Islands in 1778. His early reports created an image of the South Sea islands as a "Garden of Eden" with amiable people, an image that still survives in popular culture, but Cook himself was killed in Hawaii after antagonizing local leaders.

Exploring and Colonizing the Pacific

European explorations eventually led to economic exploitation and Christian missionary activity. In the late 1700s the Russians established a foothold in Alaska and the Aleutian Islands as a base for hunting seals and sea otters for their fur. Both animals were hunted to near extinction, and thousands of Aleuts died from exposure to European diseases. Deep-sea whaling lasted longer, attracting Western sailors. Western traders also visited the Pacific islands, seeking resources such as sandalwood, greatly valued in Asia for building furniture. Soon all of Fiji's sandalwood was gone. Meanwhile, Protestant and Catholic missionaries went to the islands, with varied results. The Samoans welcomed the missionaries, often adopting Christianity, and the Fijians initially rejected missionaries but later tolerated them, often pragmatically mixing Christianity with their own traditions. One chief, Ratu Tui Levuka, reportedly said that his right hand was Methodist, his left hand Catholic, and his body heathen. Some peoples were hostile to outside influences. For instance, the New Hebrides people killed the first missionaries who reached the islands.

Traders and missionaries opened the way for colonization, and between the 1840s and 1900 Western powers colonized all of the Pacific societies. The French gained domination over many island chains, such as the Society Islands, which included Tahiti, while the British colonized various others, among them Fiji. The Germans and Americans divided up Samoa. The Germans also acquired most of Micronesia, and Britain and France controlled much of Melanesia. By 1875 the smallpox, measles, and venereal diseases introduced by Western visitors and settlers to Hawaii had reduced the population from 150,000 to 50,000. Hawaii remained a Polynesian kingdom until 1893, when American settlers seized control.

The Rise of Australia and New Zealand

Britain and Australia

The British colonized the continent they named Australia and the two large islands they called New Zealand (see Map 20.3 and Chapter 9). European settlement in Australia began when the British began transporting convicts, often Irish, from overcrowded British jails to a penal colony they founded on the southeast coast in 1788. As more penal colonies were founded, settlements formed around the fine harbor at Sydney, and former convicts and discharged soldiers began settling the land. Agriculture, ranching, and mining became the basis for the modern economy. The British divided the continent into six colonies, with New South Wales and Victoria in the southeast having the largest populations.

British colonization came at the expense of the Aborigines, peoples completely different from the Pacific islanders in language, culture, and ways of life whose ancestors had lived on the continent for thousands of years. Divided into hundreds of scattered tribes, Aborigines lived chiefly by fishing and nomadic hunting and gathering, and the European settlers considered them to be an inferior people with a primitive way of life. Many Aborigines resisted encroachments on their land by raiding British settlements. While early British settlers killed as many as 20,000 Aborigines, diseases brought by Europeans such as smallpox and influenza were responsible for killing the majority of the Aboriginal population. By 1875 only 150,000 Aborigines remained, and whites forcibly settled their land. Eventually many Aborigines had little choice but to move to cities or to work on European cattle and sheep ranches. However, large numbers remained on tribal reservations, where they maintained many of their traditions and beliefs.

Building an Australian Nation

Creating a common Australian identity and nationhood took over a century. Throughout the 1800s Europeans clung to the coastal regions suitable for farming and ranching and avoided the inhospitable desert interior. The discovery of gold in southeastern Australia in 1851 attracted settlers from Europe and also prompted Chinese and other Asians to seek their fortunes in Australia, creating resentments among the Europeans. Violence between Europeans and Asians, especially in the mining camps, led to laws restricting Asian immigration. Meanwhile, white women struggled for influence in the male-dominated Australian society. By the 1880s women's movements were

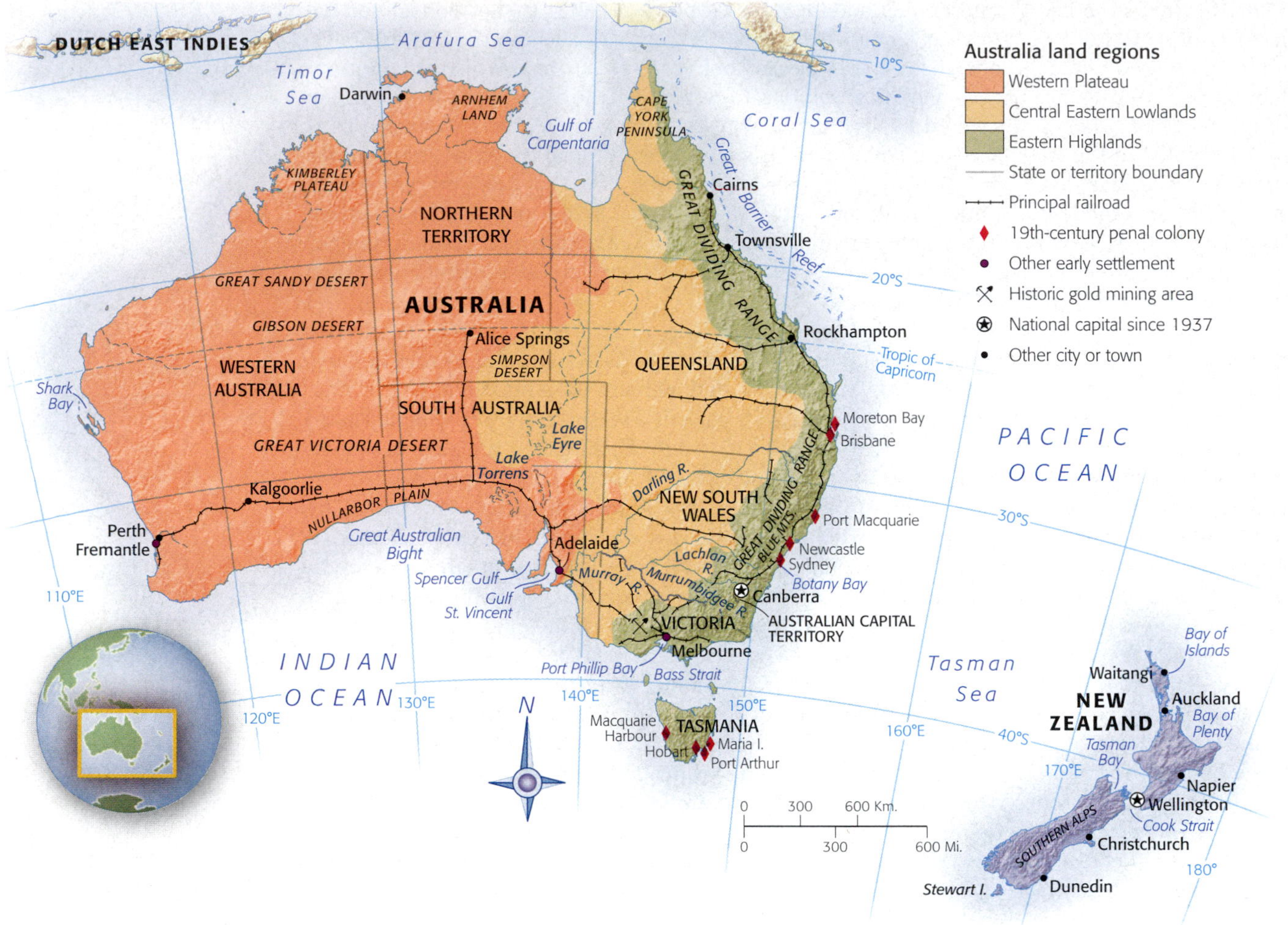

Map 20.3 Australia and New Zealand
The British colonized and gradually settled Australia and New Zealand between the late 1700s and 1914. In 1901 the six Australian colonies became a federation, with a capital eventually built in Canberra.

pressing for moral reform and suffrage, and white women gained the right to vote in 1902. However, Aborigines only gained the right to vote in 1962.

Gradually Australia became a nation. By 1890 Britain had turned all six of its Australian colonies into self-governing states, which formed the Commonwealth of Australia in 1901 (see Map 20.3). Like Canada, Australia became a self-governing, democratic dominion and maintained close political links with Britain, but it gradually formed its own identity. A transcontinental railroad system, completed in 1917, connected the vast country. Yet the majority of white Australians lived in or near five coastal cities. Distance from European supplies fostered some local manufacturing, including steel production.

Colonizing New Zealand

The British also colonized the two large mountainous islands of New Zealand, 1,200 miles east of Australia, at the expense of the Polynesian Maori people. The Maori had lived on the islands, which they called Aotearoa, for a millennium, gradually dividing into sometimes warring tribes headed by chiefs. In 1792, when the first British settlers arrived, the Maori numbered around 100,000. Some Maori took advantage of the British newcomers for their own purposes. One chief, Hongi Hika (ca. 1772–1828), befriended a Protestant missionary, who took him to England. Returning with guns, Hongi and his warriors raided rival tribes. Maori intertribal warfare became more deadly and made it harder for the rival tribes to cooperate against the British.

As more British settlers came, territorial disputes with the Maori increased. The Treaty of Waitangi in 1850 between the British and five hundred Maori chiefs seemingly confirmed the Maori's right to their land while acknowledging British sovereignty. But the English-language and Maori-language versions differed. While Maori chiefs thought they still had authority over their lands and people, the British asserted that the treaty gave them political and legal power. Disagreement over the treaty provisions and occupation of more Maori land by British settlers led to deadly wars that ended only in the 1870s. The British skillfully exploited Maori tribal rivalries and had the military advantage of heavy artillery and armored steamships. Eventually Maori resistance subsided, leading to an 1881 peace agreement that accorded Maori control over some districts.

Gradually British identity in New Zealand grew stronger. The discovery of gold in 1861 stimulated British immigration, so that by 1881 the Maori accounted for only 10 percent of the half-million population. Immigrants were attracted by high living standards, a colonial economy based on farming and sheep raising, and a growing government welfare system. New Zealand prospered after 1882, when steamships acquired refrigerated holds to carry lamb and dairy products from the islands to Europe. A parliamentary government including Maori representatives was formed in 1852, and by 1893 both men and women of all communities enjoyed universal suffrage. New Zealand gained self-government as a British dominion in 1907, but it continued a close alliance with Britain as a guarantee of security and proudly remained an outpost of the British Empire well into the twentieth century.

SECTION SUMMARY

- Canada had to contend with the challenge of forming a unified country that included French and English speakers, as well as with the threat of the neighboring United States.
- Over time, Canada became increasingly independent of Britain and stretched across the continent, and wheat eventually surpassed beaver fur as the country's top export.
- Western nations, starting with Britain and France but later including Russia, the United States, and Germany, colonized the Pacific islands and exploited their natural resources.
- Starting as penal colonies, British settlements in Australia expanded and pushed the native Aborigines off their land and then clashed with Asians who came to mine gold.
- British colonizers of New Zealand clashed repeatedly with the native Maori, ultimately deceiving them into signing away the rights to their land in the Treaty of Waitangi, which led to a series of wars that ended only in the late nineteenth century.

CHAPTER SUMMARY

During the Modern Era European populations grew and millions of people emigrated to the Americas and Oceania. More people lived in cities, where social problems and poverty increased. The industrial system influenced the relations between men and women, as family life changed and European women lost status, fostering feminist movements. Reacting to political and social turbulence, some European thinkers abandoned Enlightenment ideas. The pace of scientific and technological innovation also increased.

Across the Atlantic, the new democratic republic in the United States gradually became a regional and then world power with a diversified economy and distinctive culture. The United States expanded westward, eventually incorporating large sections of North America, some of it acquired after war with Mexico. As Americans settled the frontier, they subdued Native Americans and fostered new social patterns. The Civil War temporarily divided the nation and ended slavery. In the aftermath, economic growth and industrialization spurred massive immigration from Europe and social movements to improve the lives of workers and women. Industrial capitalism also motivated Americans to increase their influence in the wider world, eventually leading to the Spanish-American War. The U.S. victory in that conflict made the United States a world power.

Other new nations arose in the Americas and Oceania during the Modern Era. After Latin Americas gained independence from Spain and Portugal, the new governments remained authoritarian and fostered little economic or social change. Latin American and Caribbean economies remained monocultures geared to the export of raw materials and under foreign domination. While millions of European immigrants arrived, most blacks and Indians remained poor. Social inequalities produced tensions and, in Mexico, a revolution. Latin American and Caribbean societies created unique cultures that reflected the mix of peoples from around the world. The United States also played an increasing role in the region, fostering resentments that have lingered into the present.

Despite a division between French and English speakers, Canada expanded to the Pacific and became a nation with a self-governing democracy. Meanwhile European powers colonized the Pacific islands. Europeans settled in Australia and New Zealand and, like Canadians, elected to remain tied to Britain even while developing their own democratic nations.

KEY TERMS

feminism
suffragettes
romanticism
modernism
impressionism
protectionism
Manifest Destiny
sphere of interest
caudillos
gauchos
samba
calypso
dominion

EBOOK AND WEBSITE RESOURCES

INTERACTIVE MAPS

Map 20.1 European Emigration, 1820–1910
Map 20.2 U.S. Expansion Through 1867
Map 20.3 Australia and New Zealand

LINKS

WWW-VL: History: United States (http://vlib.iue.it/history/USA/). A virtual library that contains links to hundreds of sites.

Internet Resources for Latin America (http://lib.nmsu.edu/subject/bord/laguia/). An outstanding site with links to many resources.

Latin American Resources (http://www.oberlin.edu/faculty/svolk/latinam/htm). An excellent collection of resources and links on history, politics, and culture.

Modern History Sourcebook (http://www.fordham.edu/halsall/mod/modsbook.html). A very extensive online collection of historical documents and secondary materials.

The World of 1898: The Spanish-American War (http://www.loc.gov/rr/hispanic/1898). A Library of Congress site that provides excellent documents and resources.

Plus flashcards, practice quizzes, and more. Go to: www.cengage.com/history/lockard/globalsocnet2e.

SUGGESTED READING

Christensen, Carol and Thomas. *The U.S.-Mexican War*. San Francisco: Bay Books, 1998. A well-illustrated survey for the general public.

Clayton, Lawrence A. and Michael L. Conniff, *A History of Modern Latin America*, 2nd ed. Boston: Wadsworth, 2005. Good discussion of this era.

Costa, Emilia Viotti da. *The Brazilian Empire: Myths and Histories*. Chicago: The Dorsey Press, 1985. A study of the nineteenth century by a Brazilian historian.

Davies, Edward . *The United States in World History*. New York: Routledge, 2006. Access review of U.S. history and world connections.

Dubofsky, Melvyn. *Industrialization and the American Worker, 1865–1920*, 3rd ed. Wheeling, IL: Harlan Davidson, 1996. A good summary of the Industrial Revolution and its impact.

Fischer, Steven R. *A History of the Pacific Islands*. New York: Palgrave, 2002. A recent overview including New Zealand.

Foner, Eric. *The Story of American Freedom*. New York: W.W. Norton, 1998. A provocative examination of how Americans have pursued the dream of a free society.

Gonzalez, Michael J. *The Mexican Revolution, 1910–1940*. Albuquerque: University of New Mexico Press, 2002. Scholarly study of the conflict.

Keen, Benjamin, and Keith Haynes. *A History of Latin America*, 8th ed. Boston: Houghton Mifflin, 2009. A good general survey.

Knight, Alan. *The Mexican Revolution*. Cambridge: Cambridge University Press, 1986. A readable synthesis of this major uprising.

Kraut, Alan M. *The Huddled Masses: The Immigrant in American Society, 1840–1921*, 2nd ed. Wheeling, IL: Harlan Davidson, 2001. A brief survey.

Longley, Lester D. *The Americas in the Modern Age*. New Haven: Yale University Press, 2004. Relates recent relationships to developments around the hemisphere since the mid-1800s.

Nile, Richard, and Christian Clerk. *Cultural Atlas of Australia, New Zealand, and the South Pacific*. New York: Facts on File, 1996. A comprehensive and readable overview of history and cultures.

Paterson, Thomas G., et al. *American Foreign Relations: A History*, 6th ed. Boston: Wadsworth, 2005. A fine survey.

Riendeau, Roger E. *A Brief History of Canada*. Toronto: Fitzhenry and Whiteside, 2000. A short work covering 400 years of Canadian development.

Smith, Bonnie G. *Changing Lives: Women in European History Since 1700*. Lexington, MA: D.C. Heath, 1989. A comprehensive study of women's lives and their roles in public life.

Stearns, Peter N., and Herrick Chapman. *European Society in Upheaval: Social History Since 1750*, 3rd ed. New York: St. Martin's, 1991. A readable survey with lively material.

Stephanson, Anders. *Manifest Destiny: American Expansion and the Empire of Right*. New York: Hill and Wang, 1995. A readable brief analysis of this important American doctrine and its consequences.

Tyrrell, Ian. *Transnational Nation: United States History in Global Perspective Since 1789*. London: Palgrave, 2007. Study by an Australian scholar places U.S. history in a global context.

CHAPTER

21

AFRICA, THE MIDDLE EAST, AND IMPERIALISM, 1750–1914

CHAPTER OUTLINE

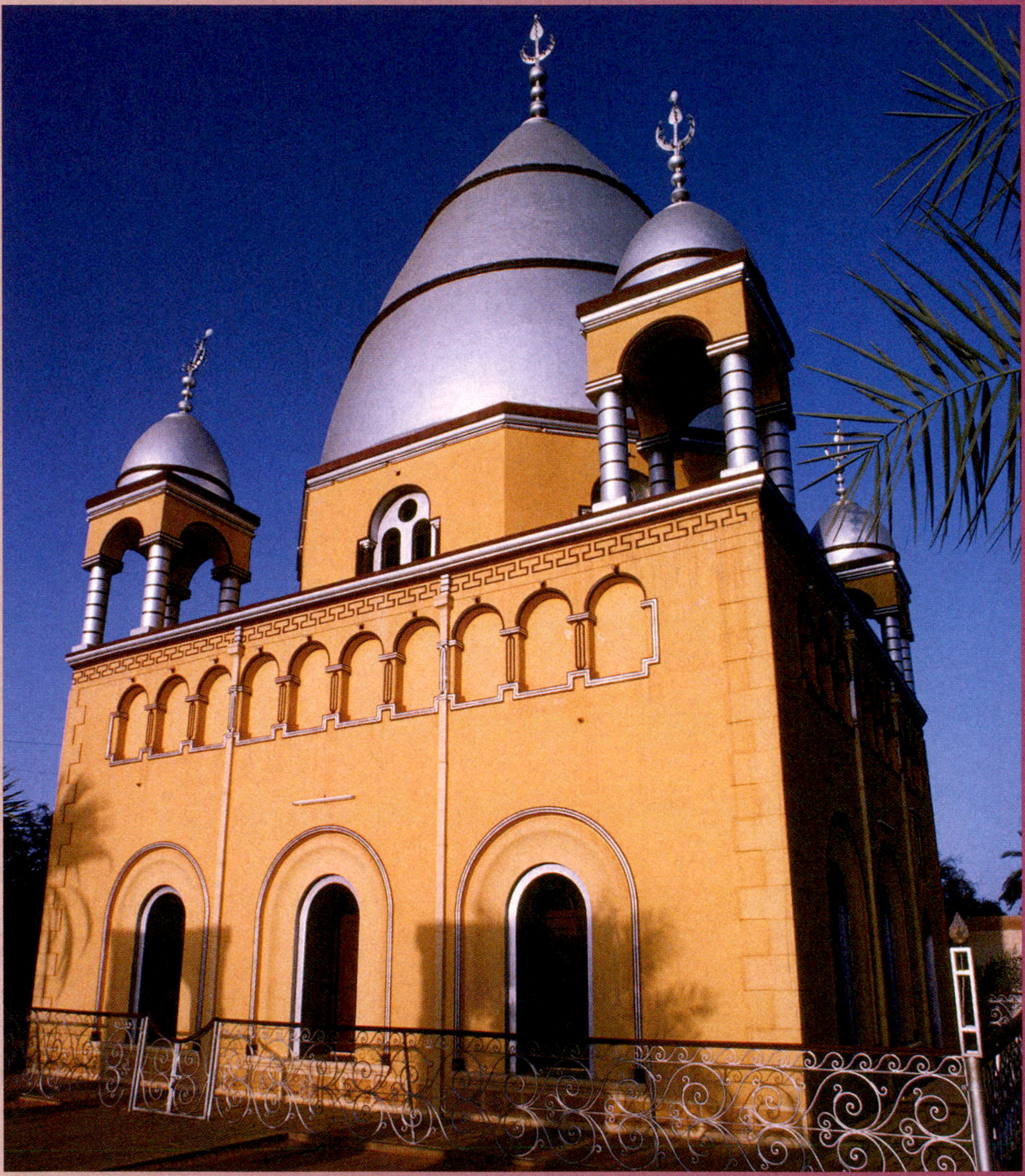

Tim Beddow/Eye Ubiquitous

Tomb of Muhammad Ahmad in Khartoum
Muhammad Ahmad ibn 'Abd Allah, known to history as the Mahdi ("Divinely Guided One"), used Islamic appeals to recruit a large army and lead opposition to the joint British and Egyptian rule in Sudan. He died soon after routing the British forces in 1885, but his tomb remains a popular place of pilgrimage and a symbol of Muslim resistance to Western power.

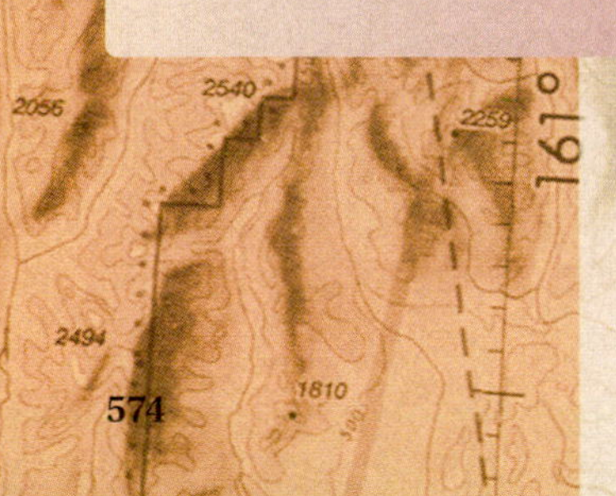

The power of these Europeans has advanced to a shocking degree and has manifested itself in an unparalleled manner. Indeed, we are on the brink of a time of [complete] corruption. As for knowing what tomorrow holds, I am blind.

—Moroccan historian Ahmad Ibn Khalid al-Nasri, 1860[1]

FOCUS QUESTIONS

1. How did various Western nations obtain colonies in sub-Saharan Africa?
2. What were some of the major consequences of colonialism in Africa?
3. What political and economic impact did Europe have on the Middle East?
4. How did Middle Eastern thought and culture respond to the Western challenge?

Fresh from his victories in Italy and Austria, in 1798 the French general Napoleon Bonaparte vowed to join the illustrious European conquerors who had achieved glory before him in the Middle East. Alexander the Great had conquered Egypt and Persia, Roman and Byzantine emperors had controlled the eastern Mediterranean, and medieval Christian crusaders had established temporary footholds in western Asia. Bonaparte admired the earlier military commanders and coveted the rich lands they had gained. In his mind, Europe was hardly a match for his talents when the rich Muslim world beckoned. He planned to invade Egypt and then reduce the Ottoman Turks and Persians to French vassals. With four hundred ships carrying 50,000 soldiers, Bonaparte quickly established control over northern Egypt. He also brought some five hundred French scholars to gather valuable information on Egyptian history, society, language, and environment. In the Nile River Delta they discovered the multilanguage Rosetta stone, a tablet made in 196 B.C.E. that allowed scholars for the first time to translate ancient Egyptian hieroglyphics. In a bid for popular support, the French general confidently announced: "People of Egypt, I come to restore your rights; I respect God, His Prophet and the Quran. We are friends of all true Muslims. Happiness to the People!"[2] He also claimed to have liberated the people from Egypt's repressive Mamluk rulers. But Bonaparte's policies soon alienated Egyptians, who came to see the French as even worse. The French army, small and ill-equipped, withered in the desert heat. An attempt to conquer Syria having failed, Bonaparte left for Paris in 1799, becoming just another example of westerners unsuccessfully attempting to control and change Muslim societies.

The unsuccessful French invasion of Egypt provided a harbinger of more conflicts, as the Moroccan historian Ahmad ibn Khalid al-Nasri had feared. Bonaparte's expedition was the cutting edge of a European imperial thrust in sub-Saharan Africa and the Middle East. Industrializing Europe's accelerating need for natural resources and new markets, combined with European political rivalries and a powerful military technology, launched ruthless colonization. European colonialism generally lasted for only a century or less, and sub-Saharan and North Africans often resisted Western power. Yet the power of Western governments, technologies, and ideas reshaped African societies and their economies, cultures, and political systems while linking them more closely to a European-dominated world economy. While western Asian societies experienced less disruption, the Ottomans lost their North African and European territories, and the Ottoman and Persian states struggled to meet the challenges posed by increased European power.

Visit the website and eBook for additional study materials and interactive tools: www.cengage.com/history/lockard/globalsocnet2e

THE COLONIZATION OF SUB-SAHARAN AFRICA

How did various Western nations obtain colonies in sub-Saharan Africa?

Between the later 1700s and later 1800s the diminishing importance of the trans-Atlantic slave trade gradually changed the relationship between Africans and Europeans. The Western impact on Africa had been uneven during the slave trade, which had integrated Africa into the world economy chiefly as a supplier of human beings while impeding most other trade between Europeans and Africans. But, as the demand for slaves waned, Europeans became more interested in acquiring African agricultural and mineral resources and more territories. Thus the full-blown quest for colonies, what a British newspaper called the "scramble for Africa," began only with the end of the trans-Atlantic slave trade and the spread of the Industrial Revolution in Europe in the mid-1800s. The European powers divided up the African continent among themselves, often against fierce resistance, and accelerated economic penetration of the continent. By 1914 the colonization process was complete.

The End of the Slave Trade and African Societies

For over three centuries the trans-Atlantic slave trade (1520–1870) dominated relations between Africa, Europe, and the Americas, but humanitarian opposition and economic concerns spurred an abolitionist movement. British abolitionists hoped to open Africa to both Christian missionaries and trade in commodities other than slaves. Many abolitionists were Christians prompted largely by moral outrage at slavery, while others were influenced by the Enlightenment vision of human equality. One sympathizer wrote that people "are not objects. Everyone has his rights, property, dignity. Africa will have its day."[3]

Africans and African Americans also struggled against slavery. Olaudah Equiano (1745–1797), an Igbo taken from Nigeria to Barbados and then Virginia, eventually purchased his freedom and then actively campaigned in Europe for abolition. Equiano published a best-selling book chronicling his own horrific experiences and pointing out the contradiction in self-proclaimed devout Christians mistreating their slaves. Slave revolts in the Americas, including the successful revolution in Haiti (see Chapter 19), indicated the willingness of many slaves to risk their lives for freedom. American and European opposition to slavery was also fueled by the widely read poetry and Christian writings of Phyllis Wheatley (ca. 1753–1785), a Senegal-born slave in Boston who learned Latin and Greek and eventually won her freedom. Her published writings undermined the widespread notion that Africans were incapable of sophisticated thought.

The Industrial Revolution made slavery uneconomical as overseas markets for factory-made goods became more desirable than cheap labor for plantations. So many colonies produced sugar that the market was flooded, making the plantations less profitable while African states charged more to provide slaves. Investing in manufacturing proved more profitable. As a result of these moral and economic factors, the slave trade and slavery came to an end in the Atlantic world in the nineteenth century. Denmark outlawed the slave trade in 1804, followed by Britain in 1807, and then all British-controlled territories, including their plantation-rich Caribbean colonies, in 1833 (see Chronology: Sub-Saharan Africa, 1750–1914). The British government declared war on the slave traders, intercepting slave ships in the Atlantic and returning the slaves to Africa. By 1842 most European and American countries had made it illegal to transport slaves across the Atlantic. The Civil War ended slavery in the United States in 1865, and in the later 1880s Brazil and Cuba also finally outlawed slavery.

The East African trade that sent slaves to the Middle East and the Indian Ocean islands, run chiefly by Arabs from Oman, continued longer. In 1835 the Omani leader, Sayyid Sa'id **(SIGH-id SIGH-eed)** (r. 1806–1856), moved his capital to Zanzibar, an island just off the coast of Tanzania, and built a commercial empire shipping ivory to India, China, and Europe and slaves to India, the Persian Gulf, and South Arabia. The Omanis also profited from growing Indonesian cloves on slave plantations on Zanzibar. To obtain slaves and ivory, Omani and Swahili merchants expanded over-

CHRONOLOGY
Sub-Saharan Africa, 1750–1914

1804 Launching of Fulani jihads by Uthman dan Fodio

1804 Abolition of slave trade by Denmark

1806 British seizure of Cape region from Dutch

1807–1833 Abolition of slave trade in Britain and its territories

1816 Beginning of Shaka's Zulu Empire

1838 Great Trek by South African Boers

1842 Ending of trans-Atlantic slave trade by most European nations

1847 First American freed slave settlement in Liberia

1874–1901 British-Ashante wars

1878 Belgian colonization in Congo

1884–1885 Berlin Conference

1884–1885 Discovery of gold in South Africa

1898 French defeat of Samory Toure

1899–1902 Boer (South African) War

1905 Maji Maji Rebellion in Tanganyika

1912 Founding of African National Congress in South Africa

CHRONOLOGY

	Sub-Saharan Africa	The Middle East
1800		**1805–1848** Rule of Muhammad Ali in Egypt **1830** French colonization of Algeria
1850	**1870** Ending of trans-Atlantic slave trade **1874–1901** British-Ashante wars **1884–1885** Berlin Conference on colonialism **1899–1902** Boer War	**1859–1869** Building of Suez Canal **1882** British colonization of Egypt

land trade routes through Tanzania into the eastern Congo River Basin. In 1873 the British convinced the Zanzibar sultan to close the island's slave market, and as compensation imported vast amounts of ivory. But slavers still raided African villages to acquire the labor needed to carry the huge ivory tusks to the coast for export. Although the British gained control of Zanzibar in 1890, some slave trading continued on a modest scale in parts of East and Central Africa until the early 1900s.

New States

Even before abolition, freed slaves who chose, or were pressured, to return to Africa from the Americas had established several West African states and port cities. The black founders and white financers of these states wanted to give the freed slaves opportunities to run their own lives while also setting up new centers of Western trade. The two largest settlements of freed slaves emerged in Sierra Leone and Liberia. In 1787 the British settled four hundred former slaves around the fort at Freetown, which became the core of their colony of Sierra Leone. The British also shipped more former slaves to Freetown from their West Indian colonies and from British-ruled Canada, where they had fled for supporting the Loyalist cause during the American Revolution. Freed slaves from the United States were first shipped to Liberia in 1847 and then were joined by others after the Civil War. One of the first African nationalists, West Indian–born Edward Blyden (1832–1912), emigrated to Liberia after being denied admission to universities in the United States because he was black. Blyden believed that, given the racism in the Americas and Europe, people of African ancestry could realize their potential only in Africa.

However, some problems remained. Although Liberia remained an independent state governed by the descendants of former slaves, its economy was dominated by U.S.-owned rubber plantations. In addition, in both Sierra Leone and Liberia, the local Africans often resented the freed slave settlers, mostly English-speaking Christians, because they occupied valuable land, dominated commerce, and held political power. In recent decades conflicts between the two groups have torn apart both countries.

Western Explorers

The decline of the trans-Atlantic slave trade also made Africa more accessible to Western explorers who wanted to discover whether the great African rivers were navigable for commercial purposes. The Scottish explorer Mungo Park (1771–1806), a doctor for an English trading company in West Africa who traveled along the Niger, hoped to open to British industry new sources of wealth. Adventurers were obsessed with finding the source of Africa's greatest river, the Nile, and they finally located Lake Victoria in 1860. David Livingstone (1813–1873), a Scottish cotton mill worker turned medical missionary, spent over two decades traveling in eastern Africa, where he collected information and opened the region to Christian missionary activity and trade with the West. The European adventurers claimed to have "discovered" inland African societies and geographical features, but they discovered little that Africans and Arabs did not already know and usually followed long-established trading routes using local guides. The ethnocentric stereotype of intrepid white explorers struggling in hardship through virgin territories is a myth, but it shaped Western views. Explorers spread the notion of "Darkest Africa" awaiting salvation by Christian missionaries and Western traders.

European Traders

In the 1800s European traders began to obtain various raw materials needed by the West, such as peanuts, palm oil, gold, timber, and cotton. They had to contend with dynamic West African merchants who, with the end of the slave trade, had set up cash crop plantations, many producing palm oil, the main lubricant for industrial machinery in Europe before the development of petroleum. To avoid the African middlemen on the coast, British traders traveled up Nigeria's rivers to buy palm oil directly from the Igbo **(EE-boh)** producers. With superior financial resources and support from their governments, European companies eventually undermined African merchants and states that were reluctant to grant trade concessions, and by 1890 in the trading port of Lagos only one African merchant was still able to compete with British merchants.

From John H. Hanson, *Migration, Jihad, and Muslim Authority in West Africa* (Bloomington and Indianapolis: Indiana University Press)

African Muslim Warrior While Western pressure on coastal societies increased, several Muslim peoples expanded their influence in the West African interior. Some military forces, having acquired Western arms in exchange for slaves and gold, conquered regional empires that flourished for a century or more.

Some major developments derived largely from forces within African societies rather than from relations with the West. For example, tensions within the Islamic societies of the Sudan fostered militancy and political expansion, and conflicts between those who wanted to purge Islamic practice of pre-Islamic customs and those who mixed Muslim and African traditions broke out sporadically in West Africa. By the 1790s these conflicts had spread to the Fulani, a pastoral and trading people scattered across the Sudan from Senegal east to Chad. Some Fulani were devout Muslims, some nominal Muslims, and some animists.

One Fulani, Uthman dan Fodio **(AHTH-mun dahn FOH-dee-oh)** (1754–1817), a respected Muslim scholar and ardent follower of Sufi mysticism who lived in the prosperous Hausa states of northern Nigeria, began criticizing the religious tolerance of Hausa rulers, called for the conversion of non-Muslim Fulani, and advocated making Islam central to Sudanic life. His magnetic personality and Islamic zeal soon attracted a Fulani and Hausa following. Uthman's attacks on high taxes and social injustice and his promise to build an Islamic government alarmed Hausa rulers, who feared the unrest he was causing. After an attempt on his life, Uthman launched a jihad (holy war) in 1804. He conquered the Hausa states and created a caliphate based in the city of Sokoto **(SOH-kuh-toh)**, ruling much of northern Nigeria. Uthman divided his empire into small, Fulani-led states led by governors, known as *emirs*.

Uthman's jihad and his vision of a purified Islam sparked others to take up his cause, and several other jihadist states, often led by Fulani religious scholars, formed in the Sudan. The Islamic revival, which continued into the 1880s, allowed a more orthodox Islam to spread widely just as Western influence was increasing in Africa. But by the later 1800s, the Fulani states declined and Sokoto's power waned. The Fulani resisted French and British expansion but eventually were unable to stop it; however, Islam remained a vital force in the Sudanic zone.

European Conquest and Partition

Britain, France, Germany, Spain, Belgium, and Italy all acquired African colonies in the late 1800s, often by intimidating African leaders through warfare or the threat of force (see Map 21.1). Several factors made this possible. Western companies sought their government's help to pressure states to admit Western merchants; advances in tropical medicine, especially the use of quinine for malaria, freed Europeans from high tropical mortality rates; and the invention of more powerful weapons gave Europeans a huge military advantage over African forces armed only with rifles or spears. When possible, Europeans achieved conquest peacefully by using deceptive treaties, offering bribes, dividing up states, and convincing African leaders that resistance was futile. When faced with resistance, however, Europeans used ruthless force.

King Leopold of Belgium took the lead in colonization. In 1878 he hired Henry Stanley (1841–1904), a Welsh-born American and former Confederate soldier and journalist who had earlier searched successfully in East Africa to find David Livingstone. Stanley then explored the Congo River Basin, which King Leopold now commissioned him to acquire for Belgium. Soon other European powers joined the scramble to obtain colonies, and in 1884–1885 the colonizing nations held a conference in Berlin to set the ground rules for colonization. For a claim to be recognized, the colonizer had to first give notice of its intent and then occupy the territory with a military presence. Agents of European governments such as Stanley asked African chiefs, who knew no Western languages, to sign treaties of friendship or protection that actually gave the land to European countries. African chiefs usually had no right to sign over land, since it was owned by their people. If chiefs refused to sign, they were threatened with war. Fearing a slaughter or war with their neighbors, many chiefs signed. The king of Buganda reflected the Africans' distress when he concluded that the Europeans were coming to eat his country.

European Advantages

Europeans achieved domination for several other reasons. The colonial scramble came at a time of famine when rains failed and while epidemics of smallpox and cholera were killing mil-

Map 21.1 Africa in 1914

Before 1878 the European powers held only a few coastal territories in Africa, but in that year they turned to expanding their power through colonization. By 1914 the British, French, Belgians, Germans, Italians, Portuguese, and Spanish controlled all of the continent except for Ethiopia and Liberia.

Interactive Map

lions. One French missionary reflected the despair: "wars, drought, famine, pestilence, locusts, cattle-plague! Why so many calamities in succession? Why?"[4] For most Africans these were bitter years indeed. In addition, the military disparity in weapons and tactics, already mentioned, played a major role. The British had the hand-cranked Gatling gun, which could fire hundreds of rounds per minute, and then the Maxim gun, a totally automatic machine gun invented in 1884. Europeans willingly slaughtered thousands. In Southwest Africa (today's Namibia), the Germans killed all but 15,000 of the 80,000 Herero **(hair-AIR-oh)** people after a rebellion in 1904. In Kenya, British military expeditions attacked villages for chasing away tax collectors or ambushing Western military patrols sent to intimidate potential resisters. A British officer in Kenya in 1902 boasted of giving orders that every living thing in a Gikuyu village, except children, should be killed without mercy because an

Englishman had been killed nearby. The British then burned all the huts and destroyed the banana farms. They called their policy of establishing law and order, often by force, the "Pax Britannica," or British peace.

After centuries of rivalries and slave wars, Africans could not unite for common defense, and Europeans took advantage of this weakness by pitting state against state and ethnic group against ethnic group. The region that became Nigeria had been the home of various independent kingdoms and village-based stateless societies. Thanks to the slave trade, some of these societies were already unstable, and the Yoruba had engaged in a bitter civil war for much of the 1800s. Between 1887 and 1903 the British conquered or annexed these diverse societies, creating the colony they called Nigeria because it occupied both sides of the lower Niger River.

Partitioning the Continent

By 1914 European powers, by drawing boundaries and staking claims, had divided up the entire continent except for Ethiopia and Liberia. The French empire was concentrated in North, West, and Central Africa, extending across the Sahara from Senegal to Lake Chad. The British had four colonies in West Africa, including Nigeria, but built most of their empire in eastern and southern Africa. The four German colonies were scattered, while Italy concentrated on the Horn region of Northeast Africa, including Somalia and Eritrea, and on Libya in North Africa.

European nations competed fiercely for territories, sometimes coming to the brink of war over rival claims. Britain wanted to control the whole eastern region from Cairo in the north to the Cape of Good Hope, while the Germans dreamed of an empire in Central Africa. German colonization of Tanganyika spurred Britain to move into Kenya, Uganda, and Zanzibar. In South Africa, the brash British imperialist Cecil Rhodes (1853–1902), a clergyman's son who had made millions in the South African diamond mining industry, was largely responsible for extending British influence into the territory he arrogantly named Northern and Southern Rhodesia to outflank Germany and Portugal. British settlers migrated to Southern Rhodesia (today's Zimbabwe) and Kenya, solidifying the British hold on the region.

African Resistance

Although outgunned, many Africans offered spirited resistance to European conquest. The Mandinka leader Samory Toure, in the western Sudan, resisted for decades (see Profile: Samory Toure, Mandinka King and Resistance Leader). In 1903 many people in Fulani-ruled Sokoto chose to die in battle against the British rather than surrender. In Muslim West Africa, the mystical Sufi brotherhoods sometimes rallied opposition to the French or British. In Senegal, when the French tried to rule the Wolof people through their kings and chiefs, Wolof resisters turned to Muslim clerics, especially Amadu Bamba Mbacke **(AH-mah-doo BOM-ba um-BACK-ee)** (ca. 1853–1927), who had founded a peaceful Sufi order, the *Murids* ("learners seeking God"). The French exiled him for many years but eventually realized that they could only rule Senegal with the cooperation of the Murids. Amadu Bamba acknowledged French administration but was free to expand the Murids. The only decisive African military triumph over Western forces, however, came in Ethiopia. In 1896, under the reforming Emperor Menelik **(MEN-uh-lik)** II (1844–1914), Ethiopia, fortified in high mountains difficult to penetrate, defeated an invasion force of 10,000 Italian troops with his French-trained army of 80,000 men.

In the Gold Coast (today's Ghana), the Ashante kingdom offered particularly strong political and military resistance. The British, seeking to protect their coastal forts, repeatedly clashed with the prosperous, powerful, expanding Ashante. In 1874 the British dispatched a large force against Ashante and secured the coast, but effective Ashante resistance prevented them from pushing into the interior. The British then deliberately fomented a civil war in the Ashante territories, but the Ashante king refused British ultimatums to surrender. In 1896 three thousand well-armed British troops finally occupied the Ashante capital, Kumasi, and exiled the king. However, resistance continued, often spurred by royal women such as the queen-mother Yaa Asantewa, who offered to lead Ashante forces if the men would not. Not until 1901 did the British manage to incorporate the Ashante into their Gold Coast colony.

SECTION SUMMARY

- Opposed by many Europeans on humanitarian and religious grounds, African slavery became less profitable than manufacturing as the Industrial Revolution gained momentum, and it was phased out by the end of the nineteenth century.
- With the end of the slave trade, Europeans began to explore Africa's interior and to take advantage of its vast store of natural resources.
- At the same time, tensions increased between purist and moderate West African Muslims, and Uthman dan Fodio, who led the Fulani jihads, established the Sokoto Caliphate, under which Islam became a strong presence in the Sudan.
- European nations rapidly colonized Africa by engaging in deceptive negotiations, by threatening and often carrying out acts of violence, and by exploiting existing rivalries among groups of Africans.
- By 1914, all but a small portion of Africa had been divided up among the European powers, which sometimes feuded over control of various territories and sometimes met fierce resistance from Africans such as the Ashante.

SAMORY TOURE, MANDINKA KING AND RESISTANCE LEADER

Samory Toure (1830–1900) was an effective resistance leader in West Africa and a powerful empire builder. He grew up an animist in a Mandinka village in what is today Guinea. Samory's mother was an animist Mandinka, and his father was a farmer descended from the Dyula, a Muslim merchant caste with branches throughout West Africa. His father's family had earlier abandoned Islam, but their connections to the Dyula trading world gave Samory links to a broader community and an understanding of both merchant and farmer concerns. The growing Atlantic trade brought prosperity to the Dyula and firearms to the interior, at a time when regional Islamic movements were energizing Muslims and fomenting conflict between varied Muslim and animist groups.

Samory began his career as a foot soldier and eventually became an inspirational military commander. By 1870 he had recruited a large, well-armed, well-trained, and intensely loyal force from many Mandinka groups. Skillfully exploiting divisions among his opponents while maintaining connections to both Muslims and animists, Samory built a large state, Kankan, in the Guinea highlands and western Niger River Basin. He personally adopted Islam, perhaps chiefly for political reasons, and earned Dyula support by keeping open the trade routes. Islamic revivalism in West Africa influenced Samory to view Islam as a unifying force that could hold his ethnically diverse empire together, and in 1884 he transformed the kingdom into an Islamic state. However, the required conversion of animists led to rebellion. In a pragmatic move that showed his willingness to ignore Islamic scruples to further his political goals and personal ambitions, Samory abolished the theocracy and replaced it with a state based not on Islam but on personal loyalty and national unity.

A political rather than a religious figure, Samory was aware of the traditions of Mandinka empires going back to the great Mali Empire founded by Sundiata in the thirteenth century, and he became the architect of a revived Mandinka Empire modeled on Mali. His later admirers viewed him as an early nationalist trying to maintain a Mandinka state. Samory recruited friends and relatives to form an advisory council, and its members became ministers responsible for specialized tasks such as supervising the treasury, the system of justice, religious affairs, and relations with Europeans. At the same time, Samory also respected the authority of local chiefs. In addition, he gained merchant support by seeking a stable and crime-free order where, as he said, "a woman alone should be able to travel as far as Freetown" in Sierra Leone without facing assaults or robberies.

Samory spent his last ten years defending his state against the French. He had long avoided conflict with Europeans, but his state posed a barrier to French expansion into the interior, and in the 1880s French forces began to move into the gold-rich area. After being defeated by Samory's army, they sent a larger force but again faced stiff resistance and were forced to negotiate a truce. During the 1890s the two sides fought a war for seven years. To oppose the French effort, the British in Sierra Leone gave Samory firearms in exchange for slaves and gold, and Samory built workshops to maintain and make muskets and rifles. His army of 30,000 men included mostly foot soldiers and an elite core of cavalry. A clever military strategist who made good use of guerrilla tactics, Samory also developed an effective system of intelligence throughout the villages to detect French movements. Asked how he repeatedly discovered French movements without giving away his own, he replied, "It is because I eat alone" (thus keeping his secrets).

But the French had more and better weapons, including heavy artillery and machine guns. Samory was also disadvantaged by not being able to unite with rival African states after years of conflict. The French gradually pushed Samory eastward, where he forged a new empire in today's northern Ivory Coast and Ghana. As they retreated into the interior, Samory's forces carried out a scorched earth policy that devastated the inhabitants and cost him popular support. In 1898 the French finally defeated Samory's brave but exhausted and hungry army, captured the ruler, and exiled him to the new French colony of Gabon in South-Central Africa, where he died.

THINKING ABOUT THE PROFILE

1. What does Samory's career tell us about Sudanic politics in this era?
2. How was Samory able to resist the French for decades?

Note: Quotations from *The Horizon History of Africa* (New York: American Heritage, 1971), 431; and Robert W. July, *A History of the African People,* 5th ed. (Prospect Heights, IL: Waveland, 1998), 207.

Samory Toure Samory Toure, the ruler of a Mandinka state, led a military force that resisted French incursion into their West African region in the late nineteenth century, but he was eventually captured by the French. This photo shows him (front, left) in custody.

The Colonial Reshaping of Sub-Saharan Africa

What were some of the major consequences of colonialism in Africa?

The experience of living under Western colonial domination from the 1880s to the 1960s reshaped sub-Saharan Africans' politics, society, culture, and economy. The trans-Atlantic and East African slave trades had devastated parts of Africa for four centuries, but the colonial conquests undermined the autonomy of all African societies. Colonialism created artificial states and transformed Africans into subject peoples who enjoyed few political rights. Europeans also took over large tracts of land as settlers. The largest settler colony, South Africa, experienced an unusual history: over three centuries of white supremacy introduced by the Dutch colonizers and perpetuated by the British. South Africa's political, social, and economic system reshaped life for both Europeans and Africans. European immigrants also settled in British East Africa, the Rhodesias, and the Portuguese colonies. Asian migrants joined them, often as traders. Colonialism also allowed Western business interests to penetrate the continent and integrate Africa into the global system as a supplier of valuable raw materials.

Colonial States and African Societies

Colonial Governments

The colonial policies devised in London, Paris, Berlin, Lisbon, and Brussels introduced new kinds of governments in Africa, as each colonizing power sought the best way to achieve maximum control at minimum expense. The French grouped their colonies into large federations such as French West Africa that were headed by one governor, while the British preferred to handle each colony, such as the Gold Coast and Nigeria, separately. Despite little understanding of or interest in African cultures, Europeans always held ultimate political authority and usually supervised administration, and Africans had to abide by decisions made by European bureaucrats. Under **direct rule** the administration was largely European, even down to the local level, and chiefs or kings were reduced to symbolic roles. Under **indirect rule** the Europeans gave the traditional kings or chiefs considerable local power but kept them subject to colonial officials. Indirect rule, which left much of the original society intact, caused less disruption than direct rule, but African leaders were required to consult with the local European adviser on many matters. Since Europeans lacked enough officials to administer a large colony such as Nigeria , indirect rule was inspired by pragmatism. In order to work with local leaders, Europeans sometimes strengthened chiefs or appointed chiefs where none previously existed, undermining village democracy.

direct rule A method of ruling colonies whereby a largely European colonial administration supervised all activity, even down to the local level, and native chiefs or kings were reduced to symbolic roles.

indirect rule A method of ruling colonies whereby districts were administered by traditional (native) leaders, who had considerable local power but were subject to European officials.

Nigeria, a huge unwieldy colony that contained some 250 distinct African ethnic groups, provided an example of both kinds of administration. As the British struggled to keep the largely Muslim north pacified, they needed the collaboration of the Hausa and Fulani emirs. Lord Lugard, the British governor, proclaimed that every emir "will rule over the people as of old time but will obey the laws of the [British] Governor."[5] The British also left the traditional Hausa-Fulani courts and social structure largely undisturbed. By contrast, they governed southern Nigeria chiefly through direct rule, with the result that greater change occurred in the south, including the introduction of Christian missions and cash crop farming. Peoples such as the Igbo and Yoruba adapted to these changes. The Igbo, particularly receptive to Christianity, became prominent in Nigeria's educated middle class. The Yoruba blended their rich artistic tradition and polytheism with imported English literary forms and Christianity, maintaining tolerance for divergent views. Rejecting fate and helplessness, the Yoruba described their culture as a river that is never at rest, caught up within swift-moving currents that can either run deep and quietly or be turbulent and overpowering.

However, many policies politically handicapped the Africans. Supporters of Western colonialism claimed it provided "a school for democracy," but by 1945 only a few Africans enjoyed political rights or access to democratic institutions. A few thousand urban merchants and professionals in British Nigeria and the Gold Coast could vote for and serve on city councils, while males in French Senegal elected members of the colonial council and a representative to the French parliament. Meanwhile, the traditional African chiefs and kings, to keep their positions, implemented colonial policies, such as by supervising cash crop agriculture and recruiting people for labor and war. Africans often viewed these privileged and wealthy leaders as little better than paid agents of colonialism.

Fostering "Tribalism"

Misunderstanding African ethnic complexities, to simplify administration colonizers identified people of similar culture and language as "tribes," such as the Yoruba of Nigeria and Gikuyu of

Kenya, even though these peoples were actually collections of subgroups without much historical unity. In reality, African peoples such as the Yoruba, Gikuyu, Igbo, Xhosa, and Mandinka were ethnic groups, not unlike the politically divided Italians, Irish, and Poles of early-nineteenth-century Europe. Thus the boundaries drawn up to partition Africa into colonies created artificial countries that often ignored traditional ethnic relationships. Countries such as Nigeria, Ghana (the former Gold Coast), Congo, and Mozambique were colonial creations, not nations built on shared culture and identity. Colonizers ignored the interests of local people, sometimes dividing ethnic groups between two or more colonial systems. The Kongolese, once masters of a great kingdom, were split between Portuguese Angola and the Belgian and French Congos. Rival societies were also sometimes joined, creating a basis for later political instability. In Nigeria the tensions between the Igbo, Yoruba, Hausa-Fulani, and other groups have fostered chronic conflict since the end of British rule. Other countries have also experienced ethnic conflicts that have sometimes led to violence.

European and Asian Immigrants

Several colonies restricted African civil and economic rights, particularly South Africa, Portuguese-ruled Angola, and British-ruled Kenya and Southern Rhodesia. They reserved for immigrant white farmers not only the best land, such as the fertile Kenyan highlands once dominated by the Gikuyu people, but also the most lucrative crops, such as coffee. African farmers also faced barriers in obtaining bank loans. The whites participated in government and perpetuated white supremacy, and the settler colonies erected rigid color bars to limit contact between whites and Africans except as employers and hired workers.

To Europeans, African culture was irrational and static, having no history of achievement. An ethnocentric British scholar argued in 1920 that "the chief distinction between the backward and forward peoples is that the former are of colored skin."[6] This prejudice translated into the demeaning idea that Africans were unfit to rule themselves and badly in need of Western leadership. Racist ideology spawned the French and Belgian idea of the "civilizing mission," which viewed Africans as children who could attain adulthood only by adopting French language, religion, and culture. Europeans also imposed a color bar that kept Africans out of clubs, schools, and jobs reserved for Europeans.

Asian minorities also became part of colonial societies. Beginning in the 1890s Indians arrived to build railroads, work on sugar plantations, or become middle-level retail traders. Indians became the commercial middle class of East Africa and occupied a key economic niche in South Africa, the Rhodesias, Mozambique, and Madagascar. Cities such as Nairobi in Kenya, Kampala in Uganda, and Durban in South Africa had substantial Indian populations, their downtowns dominated by Indian stores and Hindu temples. In West and Central Africa, Lebanese became shopkeepers in cities and towns. The Asians' growing influence and wealth, resented by black Africans, led after independence to many governments restricting Asian economic power. However, Europeans recognized Asians' value in perpetuating divide-and-rule tactics, since Africans often focused their resentment on the Asian traders they dealt with rather than European officials.

Europeans and Africans in South Africa

White Supremacy and Conflict

South Africa was shaped by conflicts between European settlers and the Bantu-speaking African peoples. The first Dutch settlement, Cape Town, was established at the Cape of Good Hope in 1652. As they expanded, the Dutch settlers, known as Boers (Dutch for "farmers"), established a system based on white rule over nonwhites that enforced physical separation of the groups in all areas of life. The system of white supremacy became even more rigid in the late 1700s and early 1800s among Boers who boarded wagon trains and migrated east along the coast and into the interior, a journey they called trekking, to find good farming land and to escape government restrictions on their freedom of action.

Trekking led to chronic conflict between the Boers and the Xhosa (KHO-sa) farmers and pastoralists who lived in the eastern Cape region. The two groups fought for nearly half a century, and many Xhosa died. When fearing attack, trekkers pulled their wagons into a circle, known as a **laager**, a tradition that symbolized Boer resistance to new ideas and their desire for separation from other peoples. In 1806 the British annexed the Cape Colony, giving Boers even more reason to migrate into the interior. Boers viewed white supremacy as sanctioned by their strict, puritanical Calvinist Christian beliefs, and the system also ensured them a cheap labor supply for their farms and ranches. By ending South African slavery, the British harmed the Boer economy, which depended on thousands of slaves of African and Asian origin. The Boers were also outraged when later the British granted the right to vote to Africans and mixed-descent people, known as coloreds.

laager A defensive arrangement of wagons in a circle. Used by the Boers in South Africa in the eighteenth and nineteenth centuries to guard against attacks by native Africans.

Zulu Expansion

The migrating Boers had to contend with the largest Bantu people, the Zulus. In the early 1800s some Zulus began a military expansion under an ambitious military genius, Shaka (ca. 1787–1828), who overcame the disadvantage of being born out of wedlock to gain fame as a courageous warrior and become a powerful chief. Shaka united various Zulu clans in Natal **(nuh-TALL)**, the region along South Africa's Indian Ocean coast, into a powerful nation. Soil exhaustion, severe drought, population growth, and fears of potential Boer migration may all have been factors provoking Zulu expansion. Shaka organized a disciplined army of some 40,000 warriors and invented effective new military tactics, such as dividing his troops into regiments armed with short, stabbing spears. In 1816 he began invading other groups' territories, and the resulting wars killed thousands of Zulus and non-Zulus while wreaking widespread disruption. After conquering much of the interior plateau, Shaka grew more despotic and was assassinated by his brother, and eventually the Zulu empire fell to the Boers. Ironically, by depopulating large areas of the mineral-rich interior plateau, the wars made it easier for the Boers to later move in.

The Sotho Kingdom

Some Bantu leaders avoided conquest by the Zulus and Boers. For example, Moshoeshoe **(MOE-shoo-shoo)** (b. ca. 1786) created a kingdom for his branch of the Sotho **(SOO-too)** people. With the region in turmoil because of the Zulu and Boer expansion, Moshoeshoe moved his people to an easily defended flat-top mountain in 1824, taking in African refugees regardless of their ethnic origin. The king preferred peaceful negotiation to warfare; he offered tribute, such as cattle, to his African rivals and cultivated friendship with the British as a counterweight to the Boers. He also invited Christian missionaries to his state and used them to acquire guns and horses. British support for Moshoeshoe allowed his Sotho kingdom to remain independent until 1871, when it was absorbed into the British-ruled Cape Colony.

The Great Trek
Many Boers migrated into the South African interior in wagon trains. These migrants, known as trekkers, endured hardships but also eventually subjugated the local African peoples, taking their land for farming, pasturing, and mining.

Conflict between the Boers and the expanding British intensified. In 1838 a large minority of Boers began what they called the Great Trek, heading in well-armed wagon caravans of several hundred families with their sheep and cattle into the interior. After many hardships and fighting with Zulus, they moved into the high plateau and formed two independent Boer republics, Transvaal **(TRANS-vahl)** and the Orange Free State. After conquering the Africans, the Boers seized their cattle and forced them to work on Boer farms. As they consolidated control over Africans, their ideas of keeping themselves separate, preserving their culture, and upholding what one Boer leader called the proper relations between white "master" and African "servant" grew stronger. Boers despised the British and considered black Africans an "inferior race" hostile to European values.

Mansell/Time & Life Pictures/Getty Images

However, the discovery in the Boer republics of diamonds and gold spurred the British to seek control over the Boer republics, leading to the South African War (1899–1902), often called the Boer War. The war culminated in British victory but also intensified Boer resentment of the British. To eradicate local support for the Boer fighters, the British burned farms, destroyed towns, and interned thousands of Boers, including women and children, in concentration camps, where 26,000 died of disease and starvation. Moreover, the British relied on African troops, thousands of whom died fighting in hopes that the British would be less oppressive.

But Africans found they had merely exchanged one set of white masters for another. British and Boer leaders worked out a compromise in which the South African government, now a collaboration between the two groups, extended discriminatory Boer laws, restricting African civil and political rights and putting many Africans on reserves, rural lands with few resources from which workers desperate for jobs could be recruited. Africans were valued chiefly as cheap unskilled labor for the white-owned economy, and laws limited their movement and reserved the more desirable neighborhoods and jobs only for whites. Continued African resistance led the government to build a police state to enforce their racial policies. Furthermore, British-Boer tensions simmered as thousands of British settlers arrived, eventually becoming a third of the white population. The Boers began to call themselves Afrikaners (people of Africa) and their Dutch-derived language Afrikaans.

Christian Missions and African Culture

Mission Schools

Supported by colonial governments, Christian missionaries, whose primary goal was to reshape African culture and religious life, established most of Africa's modern hospitals and schools. Mission doctors practiced Western medicine and denounced African folk medicine, and mission schools taught new agricultural methods, mathematics, reading, writing, and Western languages, giving a small group of Africans valuable skills in the colonial economy and administration. Critics complained that the mission schools not only taught Western values and European history but also ignored African history and derided African beliefs as superstition. Some African nationalists, themselves products of mission schools, charged that these schools, as an Igbo writer put it, "miseducated" and "de-Africanized" them, perpetuating their status as "hewers of wood and haulers of water."[7] The Africans who attended mission schools and adopted individualistic Western ways often became divorced from their village traditions, loosening the social glue of African communities. Yet, before 1945 only 5 percent of children attended any government or mission school. The first modern African college was established in Sierra Leone in 1827, but before 1940 the few Africans who could attend a university had to do so usually in Europe or the United States.

Spreading Christianity

Millions of Africans adopted Christianity. Some Africans became devout Catholics or Protestants, while others only accepted those beliefs they liked while rejecting others. Africans often emphasized Bible passages that called for justice and equality. Some African churches combined Christian doctrines with African practices and beliefs, such as condoning men having more than one wife. Yorubas often just added the Christian and Muslim gods to their polytheistic pantheon. Christianity also marginalized the female deities and shamans who had been influential, reducing women's religious roles. Moreover, when Christian leaders sometimes asked men to give up multiple wives, these women were left without support or their children. Yet, women often welcomed monogamy and favored Christian social values such as promoting education for girls.

Africans in the World Economy

Colonial Economies

The transformation of African economic life was at least as significant as the political reorganization. Extracting wealth from a colony required tying its economy closely to that of the colonizer. European businessmen now controlled the top level of the economies, including the banks, import-export companies, mines, and plantations. Colonial policies transformed Africans into producers for the world market, replacing the subsistence agriculture, which could not produce enough revenues for the government or investors. Requiring taxes to be paid in cash promoted a shift from growing food to growing cash crops such as cotton, cocoa, rubber, and palm oil or mining copper, gold, oil, chrome, cobalt, and diamonds. If taxation did not spur the changes, authorities resorted to forced labor, most notoriously in the Belgian Congo, where much of the population was required to grow rubber for Belgian planters. An American missionary reported in 1895 that the Belgian policies "reduced the people to a state of utter despair. Each town is forced to bring a certain quality [of rubber]. The soldiers drive the people into the bush. If they will not go they are shot down, and their left hands cut off. The soldiers often shoot poor helpless women and harmless children."[8] Over half of the Congo's population died from overwork or brutality over a twenty-year period.

Colonial Africa became linked to the West and the world economy, often leaving Africans vulnerable as their livelihoods became subject to the fluctuations in the world price for the commodities they produced, a price determined by the whims of Western consumers and corporations. Colonies also became markets for Western industrial products, which displaced village handicrafts. Africans became exporters of cash crops they did not consume, such as cocoa and rubber, and importers of goods they did not produce. Many of the cash crops that dominated African lives had been

Punch Cartoon Library & Archive

Rubber Coils in Belgian Congo The Belgians colonized the Congo hoping to exploit its resources. This critical cartoon, published in the British satirical magazine *Punch* in 1906, shows a Congolese ensnared in the rubber coils of the Belgian king Leopold in the guise of a serpent. Rubber was the major cash crop, introduced by the Belgians to generate profits.

introduced from outside. Peanuts and rubber were brought from South America, and cocoa from Mexico. With the growth of an automobile culture in the West, an oil-drilling industry also emerged along the West African coast, making these societies dependent on oil exports. Colonies often became economic monocultures. Hence Northern Rhodesia (now Zambia) mostly exported copper, Senegal peanuts, and the Gold Coast cocoa. The dependence of Ghanaians on growing and selling cocoa was well described in a local popular song from the 1960s: "If you want to send your children to school, build your house, marry, buy cloth [or] a truck, it is cocoa. Whatever you want to do in this world, it is with cocoa money that you do it."[9]

The opportunities and demands of the colonial economy profoundly affected the lives of both men and women. As men were recruited or forced to migrate to other districts or colonies for mining or industrial labor, a permanent pattern of labor migration became established. Hence, the white-owned farms and mines of South Africa recruited thousands of workers from Mozambique and British Central Africa on renewable one-year contracts, and men from the Sahel migrated to the cocoa estates of the Ivory Coast and Gold Coast. This migration disrupted family and village life. The male migrants lived in crowded dormitories or huts that offered little privacy, enjoyed few amenities other than drinking beer in makeshift bars, and were able to visit their families back home for only a few days a year.

Africans were heavily recruited into the white-owned South African economy. Many thousands moved to cities, especially the Transvaal mining center of Johannesburg, thus becoming temporarily or permanently removed from their farming villages. They experienced dreadful work conditions on white-owned factories and farms, and even worse in the mines, where safety regulations were few and hundreds of miners died each year. The Zulu poet B. W. Vilakezi described the miner's life in the early 1900s: "Roar, without rest, machines of the mines, Roar from dawn till darkness falls. To black men groaning as they labor, Tortured by their aching muscles, Gasping in the fetid air, Reeking from the dirt and sweat. The earth will swallow us who burrow. And, if I die there, underground, What does it matter? All round me, every day, I see men stumble, fall and die."[10]

In many African societies women had long played a major role as traders and farmers. As men migrated for work or took up cash crop farming, women became responsible for the less lucrative food production, increasing their workload. The agricultural workweek for women in the German-ruled Cameroons went from forty-five to seventy hours. The Baule women of the Ivory Coast, who had long profited from growing cotton and spinning it into thread, lost their position to Baule men when cotton became a cash crop and textiles an export item. Women traders who had dominated town markets now faced competition from Indians or Lebanese. Some women responded with self-help organizations. Ashante market women in Kumasi organized themselves under elected leaders later known as market queens to promote cooperation and settle disputes among themselves. Thanks to education, self-help, and ambition, some African women also gained skills to support themselves as teachers, nurses, and traders. But many poor women were overwhelmed by the challenges of trying to preserve their families while fulfilling their new responsibilities.

African Responses and the Colonial Legacy

Cultural Resistance

Africans responded to colonialism in various ways. In South Africa the small educated middle class of professionals and traders found ways to oppose white supremacy. One of these, the

[9]Song lyrics by Fred Sarpong as seen in Dennis Austen, *Politics in Ghana* (London: Oxford University Press, 1964).

Johannesburg lawyer Pixley ka Isaka Seme **(PIX-ley ka I-sa-ka-SE-me)**, a graduate of Columbia University in New York, helped found the African National Congress in 1912 to promote African rights and cultural regeneration. In Nigeria many educated Igbos became cash crop farmers, merchants, professionals, or clerks. Other Africans dealt with change by enriching traditional ways. The imaginative Yoruba artist Olowe of Ise **(oh-LO-way of ee-SAY)** (ca. 1875–1938) emphasized Yoruba themes and ideals in the woodcarvings and elaborately carved doors he sculpted for Yoruba kings but creatively added richly textured surfaces and the illusion of movement. Some Africans mixed Western and African ideas. The Black Zion movement in South Africa had Christian overtones, claiming that Jesus was African, but also promoted African traditions such as faith healing.

Africans also used their traditional cultural forms to express their sentiments. Igbo women used a combination of dance and theater to influence their individualistic but patriarchal society, dancing and singing their grievances in a strategy known as "sitting on a man." The dance performances sometimes encouraged noncooperation with colonial demands, such as increased taxes, or with excessive male Igbo chauvinism. When local leaders ignored the dance messages of dissatisfaction, the women took stronger action, including rioting. In South Africa Zulu workers reworked dance tunes and turned them into songs to protest white domination. The Sotho people transformed their poetry praising influential people and ancestors into songs expressing the experiences of male migrants working in the mines and the women left behind in the villages. Some South African composers mixed Christian hymns with traditional Xhosa or Zulu choral music. The African National Congress adopted one such hymn, "God Bless Africa," as their official anthem. Later the song, with its uplifting message of hope, became the anthem of black empowerment:

> *Bless the youth, that they may carry the land with patience. Bless the wives and young girls. Bless agriculture and stock raising. Banish all famine and diseases. Fill the land with good health. Bless our effort, of union and self uplift, of education and mutual understanding.*[11]

Noncooperation

Many Africans chose noncooperation. Tax evasion and passive protest were rampant, especially in rural areas. Others chose a more activist strategy and formed labor unions, usually illegal in colonial systems that protected Western-owned businesses. Strikes were common, especially among mine workers, but governments arrested strike leaders and added them to the political prisoners rotting away in colonial prisons. Rebellions sparked by unpopular policies, such as new taxes or forced labor, also punctuated colonial rule. The Maji Maji Rebellion, which broke out in German-ruled Tanganyika in 1905, began as a peasant protest against a new cotton-growing scheme that forced people to work in the cotton fields for only 35 cents a month. Africans' preference to grow their own food rather than be commercial farmers led to a new religious cult known as Maji Maji ("water medicine"), which used magic water in hopes of better crops. In their uprising, the rebels occupied towns and sprinkled their bodies with magic water in hopes it would make them immune from bullets. The Germans, using machine guns, soon regained the towns and in 1907 defeated the Maji Maji at the cost of 26,000 African lives. However, the resistance caused the Germans to end forced labor.

Colonial Legacies

Some historians contend that colonialism increased the productive capacity of the land, built cities and transportation networks, brought advances in technology, and stimulated Africans to produce more wealth than they ever had before. Other historians argue that colonial rulers stole land, exploited labor, gained profitable access to raw materials, shifted profits back to Europe, limited Africa's economic growth, and created artificial, unstable countries. While profits from Africa supported European industrialization and enriched European businesses, colonial Africa enjoyed little balanced economic growth that benefited the majority of the people. One observer in the early 1900s noted that in Portuguese-ruled Mozambique a man "works . . . all his life under horrible conditions to buy scanty clothing for his wife and daughters. The men and boys can rarely afford proper clothing."[12] Moreover, many former colonies are economically vulnerable monocultures today. As for progress, seventy-five years of Belgian colonialism in the Congo failed to build any paved road system linking the major cities or to establish more than a handful of schools and medical clinics for the millions of Congolese. As a result sub-Saharan Africa was the most impoverished region of the world at the end of the colonial era, a legacy difficult to overcome.

SECTION SUMMARY

- African colonial governments served the interests of the colonizers, though the colonizers' involvement in local affairs varied between direct and indirect rule.
- Colonizers divided Africa into countries with artificial boundaries, sometimes splitting an ethnic group into more than one country and sometimes throwing rival groups into a single country, thus creating lasting tensions.
- Dutch settlers of South Africa, called Boers, pursued a policy of white supremacy in spite of more liberal British policies.
- South Africa was also shaped by the conquests of Shaka, a Zulu leader.
- The Boers fled inland to escape British control, but when diamonds and gold were discovered in the Boer republics, the British won the South African War, after which they agreed to enforce white supremacist policies to gain Boer cooperation.
- In several colonies whites reserved the best resources and all political power for themselves, while Indians and Lebanese came to form the middle class in many African societies.
- Christian missionary schools provided a small minority of Africans with skills they could use in the colonial world but largely ignored and often damaged the native African culture.
- As African economies came to depend on a single commodity desired by Europeans, colonized Africans lost their subsistence skills and were often forced to work far from home.
- Blacks suffered greatly in white-dominated South Africa, but many resisted through poetry, music, dance, and political organizations such as the African National Congress.
- Some Africans took advantage of opportunities offered by colonization, others enriched their traditional ways, and a few, such as the Maji Maji, openly rebelled, though never successfully.
- While some historians think that colonization brought beneficial development to Africans, economic growth benefited mainly the colonizers, did little to materially improve African lives, and prevented Africans from building diversified and strong economies.

IMPERIALISM, REFORM, AND THE MIDDLE EASTERN SOCIETIES

What political and economic impact did Europe have on the Middle East?

Between 1750 and 1914 most Muslim societies suffered repeated challenges from western Europe and Russia. The Ottoman Empire remained the only significant Muslim power and, despite a remarkable ability to rejuvenate itself, fell behind the industrializing West. Expanding European empires ate at the fringes of Persia and the shrinking Ottoman domain, and European economic penetration and cultural influences forced responses that differed from society to society.

Challenges to the Ottoman Empire

Russian Expansion

During the Early Modern Era the Ottoman Turks forged a huge empire in southeastern Europe and western Asia, as well as gaining a strong influence across North Africa. Many Muslims viewed the Ottoman sultan as the caliph, the successor to the Prophet and leader of the Islamic community, giving Ottoman leaders enormous prestige. But by 1750, as a result of both Western pressure and internal problems, the Ottoman power had diminished. In the nineteenth century rising pressure from European nations, especially Russia, undermined the Ottoman Empire and its more than 60 million people (see Map 21.2). Since the 1500s the Russians had expanded south toward the Black Sea, and in 1768 they defeated Ottoman forces and gained control over part of the northern Black Sea coast. They extended this control to include the Crimean peninsula, and in 1829 they took over the largely Christian Caucasus state of Georgia (see Chronology: The Middle East, 1750–1914). In 1853 Czar Nicholas I characterized the weakening Ottoman Empire as "the sick man of Europe," a reputation that would stick.

Revolts

The European powers schemed to outflank each other while building up their influence in the weakening empire. With European support, the Greeks, Serbs, Romanians, and Bulgarians threw off Ottoman rule in the 1800s, revealing Ottoman weaknesses (see Chapter 19). An Anglo-French fleet and the Russian army intervened to aid the Greeks, shifting the military balance. The 1830 treaty ending the war recognized Greek independence and gave autonomy to Serbia and Moldavia.

Map 21.2 The Ottoman Empire and Persia, 1914
The Ottoman Empire once included much of southeastern Europe, western Asia, and North Africa. By 1914, after losing most of its European, Caucasian, and North African territories, it was restricted largely to parts of western Asia.

e Interactive Map

Ethnic Minorities

Weakened by military losses, the central government had difficulty satisfying the empire's multiethnic population. Because the Turks had long benefited from tapping the empire's varied peoples to enrich their state, non-Muslim minorities played major roles in commerce, the professions, and government. The Ottomans had generally been tolerant of minorities such as Kurds (mostly Sunni Muslims), Jews, and Arab Christians, allowing each group to basically rule itself through its own religious establishment, such as the Greek Orthodox Church. Christians and Jews felt particularly secure in the major Ottoman cities, and Jews generally enjoyed more rights and prosperity than they did in Europe. Multiethnic Istanbul was described in 1873 as "a city not of one nation but of many. Eight or nine languages are constantly spoken in the streets and five or six appear on the shop fronts."[13] Various religious sects also settled in the Lebanon mountains, maintaining their traditions.

But some ethnic minorities became restless, especially in eastern Turkey and the Caucasus, where Turkish relations with the Christian Armenians deteriorated. Armenians had generally remained loyal Ottoman subjects, and some held high government positions, but the nationalist and socialist ideas percolating in Europe influenced some to want their own state. Armenians founded their own schools, colleges, libraries, hospitals, presses, and charitable organizations and looked to Europe and North America for financial and moral support. In the 1890s and early 1900s the Ottoman government responded to increasing Armenian assertiveness, including terrorist attacks, by seizing Armenian property, killing over 100,000 Armenians, and exiling thousands more. Many moved to North America to escape the persecution. Then in 1915, during World War I, the government charged Armenians with supporting Russia and began removing Armenians from eastern Anatolia, where in response Armenian nationalists declared a republic. During the turmoil the Ottoman army, aided by local Turks and Kurds, killed around a million Armenians. Many

CHRONOLOGY

The Middle East, 1750–1914

1768–1829 Russians gain control of northern Black Sea lands and Georgia

1794–1925 Qajar dynasty in Persia

1798–1799 French occupation of Egypt

1805–1848 Rule of Muhammad Ali in Egypt

1830 Greek independence from Ottoman Empire

1830 French colonization of Algeria

1859–1869 Building of Suez Canal

1882 British colonization of Egypt

1890s–1915 Turkish genocide against Armenians

1897 First Zionist conference

1899 British protectorate over Kuwait

1905–1911 Constitutional revolution in Persia

1907–1921 Russian and British spheres of influence in Persia

1908 Young Turk government in Ottoman Turkey

1908 Discovery of oil in Persia

1911–1912 Colonization of Libya and Morocco

historians consider the violent assault a genocide, the singling out of one group for mass killing, but Turkish nationalists view it as an incidental side effect of war. The mass killings still complicate Armenian-Turkish relations. The surviving Armenians formed a small republic in the Caucasus, Armenia, that was absorbed by Russia in 1920.

To survive and match Western power, Ottoman sultans tried hard to reform and modernize, building a more secular and centralized government. However, this was no easy task because the Islamic religious leaders, the privileged Janissary military force, and governors of distant Arab provinces, who were virtually independent, benefited from weak central authority. Gradually Ottoman leaders and thinkers recognized the need to obtain knowledge and aid from the West. The reformist sultan Mahmud II **(MACH-mood)** (r. 1808–1839) tried to reestablish central authority by eliminating the Janissaries, once an effective fighting force but now resisting change and a costly burden. Mahmud recruited a new military force that crushed the Janissaries and then slowly built a modern army trained by Prussian officers. His successors set up new schools that taught European learning and languages, and by 1900 the University of Istanbul had become the Muslim world's first modern institution of higher education. The Ottomans also replaced many older Islamic laws with laws based on French revolutionary codes. Increasingly the rulers marginalized Islam and treated Islamic knowledge as irrelevant, demoralizing conservatives.

The growth of a more centralized government and a modern, secular Ottoman nationality continued through the 1800s. To foster a national identity, the Ottoman sultans declared all citizens equal before the law, announcing that "the differences of religion and sect among the subjects is something not affecting their rights of citizenship. It is wrong to make discriminations among us."[14] But attempts to involve the people in government largely failed, and the reforms proved inadequate. In the 1880s a modernizing group known as the **Young Turks** emerged in the military and the universities. With a goal to make Turkey a modern nation with a liberal constitution, in 1908 the Young Turks, espousing Turkish nationalism, led a military coup that deposed the old sultan. Under the facade of parliamentary government, they ruled as autocrats and military modernizers. During World War I, as an ally of Germany and Austria-Hungary, the Young Turks embraced a Turkish ethnic identity, secularization, and closer ties to the Western world. After their defeat in World War I, the Ottoman Empire was dissolved and the Arab peoples once ruled by the Ottomans fell under British or French rule. By 1920 the Turks were struggling to hold on to their Anatolian heartland.

Egypt: Modernization and Occupation

Young Turks A modernizing group in Ottoman Turkey that promoted a national identity and that gained power in the early twentieth century.

The most extensive effort to deflect Western pressure through modernization came in Egypt, but only after Ottoman influence was minimized. The Ottomans had governed the province through the Mamluks, a Muslim caste of Turkish origin whose corruption and repression gave French general Napoleon Bonaparte an excuse to invade the country. When Bonaparte abandoned his Egyptian adventure, Egypt came under the rule of Muhammad Ali (r. 1805–1848), a Turkish-speaking Albanian who had led the Ottoman forces that helped eject the French. After being appointed viceroy by the Ottoman sultan, Muhammad Ali made Egypt effectively independent but was forced by the European powers to remain loosely bound to the weakening Ottoman state. The charming sultan impressed Europeans with his talents: "If ever a man had an eye that denoted genius, [he] was the person. Never dead nor quiescent, it was fascinating like that of a gazelle; or, in the hour of storm, fierce as an eagle's."[15]

Muhammad Ali's Reforms

Muhammad Ali introduced ambitious reforms to transform Egypt into a European-style industrial nation. He used government revenues from increased agricultural exports to establish foundries, shipyards, and textile, sugar, and glass factories, as well as a conscript army trained by Western instructors, a navy, and an arms industry. He also replaced Islamic with French legal codes, sent Egyptians to study technical subjects in Europe, fostered the first Arab newspapers, and laid the foundation for a state educational system to train people for the military and bureaucracy. However, Muhammad Ali's programs did not ultimately protect Egyptian independence and foster development, a failure that invited British interference. Unlike European nations, Egypt lacked iron and coal, and the work force was not used to industrial regimentation. As Muhammad Ali and his successors welcomed Western investment, they became more shackled to European finance, and an influx of cheap British commodities also stifled Egypt's textile and handicraft manufacturing. Europeans were more interested in procuring Egyptian raw cotton for processing in their own mills than they were in buying finished textiles.

Following the European model, Muhammad Ali turned to seeking resources and markets through conquest. Egyptian armies moved south into the Sudanic lands along the Nile River, which they made into an Egyptian colony, and also into Ottoman-ruled Arabia, Palestine, Syria, and Greece. But this aggression alarmed the European powers, who intervened to push the Egyptians back. The British sought to undermine Egypt in order to have more influence in the region and to gain control of the Suez Canal, built as a French-Egyptian collaboration between 1859 and 1869. The 100-mile-long canal, a magnificent technological achievement whose construction had cost the lives of thousands of Egyptian workers, linked the Mediterranean and Red Seas, greatly decreasing the shipping time between Europe and Asia. British merchant and naval ships became the canal's major users, and Britain then gained control of the canal by capitalizing on Muhammad Ali's failure to transform Egypt. In 1875 Muhammad Ali's grandson was forced by skyrocketing national debt to sell Egypt's share of canal ownership to the British government.

British Occupation

To preempt the ambitions of other European powers, the British decided to seize Egypt using military force. Egypt was bankrupt and deeply in debt to European financiers and governments, while the country's political and commercial elite, including many Coptic Christians, were committed to modernization. But most Egyptians, influenced by conservative Islamic ideas and leaders, opposed the growing Western influence. In 1882 local unrest and threats to European residents provided an excuse for the British to invade the country. Egypt became part of Britain's growing worldwide empire.

Soon the British had to deal with a challenge coming from the Sudanic region to Egypt's south (today the nation of Sudan). In 1881 a militant Arab Muslim in the Sudan, Muhammad Ahmad (1846–1885), declared that he was the Mahdi (MAH-dee) ("the Guided One") sent to restore Islam's purity and destroy the corrupt Egyptian-imposed government. He recruited an army that defeated the Egyptian forces and their British officers, then formed an Islamic state. However, the Mahdist government wasted money in wars, and in 1898 British and Egyptian forces defeated it and formed a new state known as the Anglo-Egyptian Sudan, which was effectively a British colony.

Persia: Challenges and Reforms

Qajar Rule

Persia, increasingly known as Iran, faced many problems. After the Safavid collapse in 1736 and the following decades of turmoil, in 1794 one Persian tribe, the Qajars (KAH-jars), established control from their base in Tehran and ruled uneasily until 1925. The early Qajar rulers were unable to resolve most of Persia's problems and became noted instead for greed, corruption, and

Mary Evans Picture Library

Muhammad Ali Meets European Representatives Muhammad Ali, the Egyptian sultan who tried to modernize his state, cultivated ties with Western nations. This painting shows the sultan in 1839 meeting with representatives from several European governments.

lavish living. One particularly extravagant shah married 158 wives, fathering nearly 100 children, and was survived by some 600 grandchildren. Qajar Persia was more a diverse collection of tribes, ethnic groups, and religious sects than a nation, fostering conflict. The majority of Persia's people, including the Turkish-speaking Azeri minority in the northwest, were Shi'ites, but Christian Armenians, Jews, Zoroastrians, and Sunni Kurds all sought increased autonomy. Shi'ite clerics controlled education, law, and welfare and enjoyed vast wealth from landholdings and tithes, and the top Shi'ite clerics engaged in power struggles with the Qajar shahs. Shi'ites also persecuted as heretical the **Bahai** (buh-HI) religion. Founded in 1867 by the Persian Bahaullah (bah-hah-oo-LAH) (1817–1892) as an offshoot of Shi'ism, Bahai called for universal peace, the unity of all religions, and service to others. Shi'ites killed many Bahais and forced their leaders into exile.

Bahai An offshoot of Persian Shi'ism that was founded in 1867; Bahai preached universal peace, the unity of all religions, and service to others.

Foreign Pressures

Persia also faced continuous pressure from Russia and Britain. By the 1870s Russia had gained territory on both sides of the Caspian Sea, including the Caucasus, and between 1907 and 1921 it asserted a sphere of influence in northern Persia. British power also steadily grew in the Persian Gulf and along Arabia's Indian Ocean coast. The British, who wanted to keep the Russians away from the Persian Gulf and India, asserted a sphere of influence in southeastern Persia, which gave them a foothold at the entrance to the Persian Gulf. British entrepreneurs gained a monopoly on Persian railroad construction and banking, and the Anglo-Persian Oil Company (later British Petroleum), which struck oil in 1908, became Persia's dominant economic enterprise, with profits going chiefly to Britain. Persians considered the powerful British economic role a humiliation. A weak government combined with foreign pressure led to reforms, as some Qajar shahs attempted to restore central government power, rebuilt an army, set up a Western-style college, introduced a telegraph system, and allowed Christian missionaries to establish schools and hospitals. While some celebrated the reforms, they threatened the conservative Shi'ite clergy, who hoped to thwart modernization.

Constitutional Revolution

From 1905 to 1911 Persia enjoyed a constitutional revolution and a brief period of democracy, unique in the Middle East. The more liberal Shi'ite clergy, allied with Tehran merchants, Armenians, and Western-educated radicals, imposed a democratic constitution that curbed royal power by setting up an elected parliament and granting freedom of the press. When a conservative, pro-Russian shah took power and attempted to weaken the parliament, liberal newspapers, writers, and musicians lampooned him and his allies, with troubadours singing songs about the love of country, democracy, freedom, justice, and equality. However, Britain and Russia pressured Persia to grant them more influence, straining the progressive leadership. The constitutionalist forces soon split into pro-Western nationalists seeking separation of religious and civil power, land reform, and universal education, and Shi'ite clerics who, alarmed at the secular direction, favored slower change. As violence increased in 1911, the royal government closed down the parliament and ended the democratic experiment. Aref Qazvini, a popular prorevolution songwriter, lamented the setback: "O let not Iran thus be lost, if ye be men of truth."[16] By then, Britain and Russia, stationing troops in Persia, had reduced Persia's political and economic independence.

Western Asia, Northwest Africa, and Europe

Syria and Lebanon

Declining Ottoman power and growing Western activity eventually reshaped the Arab provinces of the eastern Ottoman Empire, especially Syria and Lebanon, which the Ottomans governed as one province. Despite their diverse ethnic and religious mosaic, including Arab and Armenian Christians, Sunni and Shi'ite Arabs, and Sunni Kurds, the peoples had mostly lived in peace. By recognizing each community's autonomy, the Ottoman government promoted religious tolerance. A British writer reported that under Lebanon's generally stable conditions, "every man lives in a perfect security of life and property. The peasant is not richer than in other countries, but he is free."[17] However, in the 1850s poverty and a stagnant economy fostered occasional conflicts, and the densely populated region around Mount Lebanon came under the influence of several Western powers. The French developed a special relationship with the Maronites (MAR-uh-nite), Arab Christians who sought a closer connection with the Roman Catholic Church, and American Protestant missionaries established a college in the main Lebanese city, Beirut, that spread modern ideas. The weak economy also encouraged emigration, especially of Lebanese Christians to the United States. Other Lebanese Christians and Muslims moved to West Africa, Latin America, or the Caribbean. By 1914 perhaps 350,000 Syrians and Lebanese had emigrated to the Americas.

Iraq

Under Ottoman rule, Iraq, the heart of ancient Mesopotamia, lacked political unity and had not prospered. The Ottomans divided Iraq into three provinces: a largely Sunni Arab and Kurdish north, a chiefly Sunni Arab center, and a Shi'ite Arab–dominated south. Iraqis suffered from major floods and repeated plague and cholera epidemics. A British official described Iraq as "a country of extremes, either dying of thirst or of being drowned."[18] Iraq also lacked order, foreign capital, and a transportation system such as railroads or steamships. Pirates attacked Persian Gulf shipping, and Bedouin tribes raided land caravans. The literacy rate remained extremely low. Yet, Western interest in this Ottoman backwater's economic potential and strategic location grew. In 1899 the British established a protectorate over the small neighboring kingdom of Kuwait **(koo-WAIT)** at the west end of the Persian Gulf, which allowed them to station troops and agents. But both the British and Germans came to believe that Iraq might have considerable oil, and in the early 1900s the Ottomans and foreign investors poured money into Iraq.

France and Algeria

The Arabic-speaking societies along Africa's Mediterranean coast from Libya to Algeria had never been under firm Ottoman control, and their proximity to Europe made them natural targets for colonization. In 1830 the French embarked on full-scale colonization of Algeria. Abd al-Qadir **(AB dul-KA-deer)**, a Muslim cleric, used Islamic appeals to unite Arab and Berber opposition to the French. His resourceful followers quickly learned how to make guns. Facing years of determined resistance, the French attempted to demoralize the Algerians by driving peasants off the best land and selling it to European settlers while also relocating and breaking up tribes. Yet anti-French revolts, often spurred by appeals to Islam, erupted until the 1880s. The ruthless French conquest cost tens of thousands of French and hundreds of thousands of Algerian lives.

The French intended to impose French culture, settlers, and economic priorities on the Algerians. General Bugeaud, the conqueror of Algeria, conceded in 1849 that "the Arabs with great insight understand very well the cruel revolution we have brought them; it is as radical for them as socialism would be for us."[19] Between the 1840s and 1914 over a million immigrants from France, Italy, and Spain poured into Algeria, erecting a racist society similar to South Africa. The European settlers eventually elected representatives to the French parliament as Algeria was incorporated into the French state. Vineyard cultivation and wine production displaced food crops and pasture, an economic change that mocked Islamic values prohibiting alcoholic beverages.

Colonizing North Africa

Gradually European power in Northwest Africa increased. In Morocco, Sultan Mawlay Hassan (r. 1873–1895) skillfully worked to preserve the country's independence by playing the rival European powers off against each other. However, the French and Spanish, attracted by Morocco's economic potential and strategic position, had divided the country between them by 1912. Tunisia, just east of Algeria, had long enjoyed considerable autonomy under Ottoman rule, and the port city of Tunis prospered as a center of trade and piracy. Coveting this trade, in 1881 France sent in troops to occupy Tunisia. Libya, a sparsely populated, mostly desert land between Tunisia and Egypt, was conquered by the Italians in 1911 and 1912. The country's Islamic orders led repeated resistance efforts, and the resulting conflicts killed one-third of Libya's people. European colonialism now dominated the whole of North Africa.

SECTION SUMMARY

- After 1750, the Ottoman Empire's power began to wane under pressure from Russia and western Europe and also from the Armenians, who exerted pressure from within the empire for greater autonomy.
- The Ottomans modernized their army, adopted French-style laws, and became increasingly secular, but their decline continued until the empire was broken apart after World War I.
- After Napoleon left Egypt, an Ottoman-appointed governor, Muhammad Ali, attempted an ambitious and somewhat successful program of modernization; ultimately, however, Britain gained control of the Suez Canal and made Egypt a colony.
- Persia, fragmented under the rule of the Qajars, came to be dominated economically by Britain, and interference by both Britain and Russia helped to end a brief period of progressive rule.
- Westerners became increasingly influential in Syria and Lebanon, as well as in Iraq, which was backward and undeveloped but attracted Western attention because of its economic potential.
- Europeans colonized Northwest Africa: first Algeria, where settlers established a racist society; then Morocco, which was shared by France and Spain; and finally Tunisia and Libya.

Middle Eastern Thought and Culture

How did Middle Eastern thought and culture respond to the Western challenge?

West Asians and North Africans responded to the challenges facing them in three ways. Some formed vibrant Islamic revivalist movements that promoted a purer version of Islamic practice rooted in early Muslim tradition. Others mounted reform movements that combined Islam with modernization and secularization. The early stirrings of Arab nationalism constituted a third response. While governments stagnated or struggled, revivalist, reform, and nationalist movements pumped fresh vitality into Islamic culture and religious life, influencing social and cultural patterns. But none of these movements offered an effective resistance to Western economic and military power.

Islamic Revivalism

Islamic revivalism Arab movements that sought to purify Islamic practices by reviving what they considered to be a purer vision of Islamic society.

Influential movements of **Islamic revivalism** sought to purify Islamic practices by reviving what they considered a purer vision of Islamic society rooted in the earliest form of Islam, embracing what they regarded as God's word in the Quran and the sayings of the Prophet Muhammad. They also reaffirmed the ideal of the theocratic state of the early caliphs in Mecca, which blended religion and government. The revivalists criticized as corrupt the scholarly and mystical additions that had resulted from encounters with Persian, Hindu, Indonesian, African, and European cultures over the centuries. In many African and Southeast Asian societies, Muslims still consulted shamans skilled in magic and healing, revered Sufi saints, and permitted women to engage in trade and reject veiling. Muslim revivalists despised Sufism and its mystical practices, such as music and dance, and in response several Sufi brotherhoods eventually moved away from mystical beliefs toward an emphasis on the original teachings of the Prophet Muhammad.

Religious Leaders

While political leaders lost prestige and authority, religious leaders allied to merchant and tribal groups seized the initiative to spread revivalist thought. Revivalists such as Othman dan Fodio in West Africa and the Mahdist Army in Sudan interpreted the early Muslim idea of jihad, or struggle for the faith, as a call to wage holy war against other Muslims who disagreed with them. Carried by scholars, merchants, and missionaries, revivalist Islam spread from the Middle East to every other part of the Islamic world. Many sub-Saharan African, Indian, and Southeast Asian Muslims visited, studied, or sojourned in the Middle East, often embracing the revivalist ideas. Revivalist movements stiffened resistance against French colonization in Algeria and West Africa and Dutch colonization in Indonesia.

Wahhabism A militant Islamic revivalist movement founded in Arabia in the eighteenth century.

Revivalism had its greatest impact in Arabia, spurring a militant movement in the 1700s known as **Wahhabism** (wah-HAH-bi-zuhm). The movement's founder, Muhammad Abd al-Wahhab (al-wah-HAHB) (1703–1792), led a long campaign to purify Arabian Islam. Al-Wahhab studied Islamic theology in Medina and Iraq, adopting a strict interpretation of Islamic law and promoting intolerance toward all alternative views, such as Sufism and Shi'ism, and those lax in their faith. In 1744 his campaign gained a key ally, Muhammad Ibn Saud (sah-OOD), a tribal chief, and together they put together a fighting force to expand their influence. During the later 1700s the Wahhabis used military force to take over parts of Arabia and then advanced into Syria and Iraq, occupying the city of Karbala, the major Shi'ite holy site, which they destroyed. By 1805 the Wahhabis controlled Mecca and Medina, Islam's two holiest cities, where they horrified non-Wahhabis by massacring the residents and trying to destroy all sacred tombs to prevent saint worship. Muhammad Ali, the governor of Egypt, used his European-style army and modern weapons to push the Wahhabis back from the holy cities. However, Wahhabi ideas, puritanism, and zeal spread widely during the 1800s as Western power undermined Middle Eastern governments. Yet many Muslims condemned Wahhabi intolerance, extremism, and such practices as the forced veiling of women.

Forming Saudi Arabia

In 1902 the descendants of al-Wahhab and Ibn Saud launched a second great expansion. The head of the Saud family, Abdul Aziz Ibn Saud (1880–1953), sent Wahhabi clergy among the Bedouins to convince them to abandon their nomadic ways and join self-sufficient farming communities that adopted extreme asceticism and a literal interpretation of the Islamic legal code, the Shari'a. Wahhabi clergy beat men for arriving late for prayers, and Wahhabi men pledged to die fighting for their beliefs. In 1925 the Saud family established Saudi Arabia, a state based on the Shari'a, and discovery of oil in 1938 gave the Saud family and their Wahhabi allies the wealth to maintain their control.

e **Primary Source: The History and Doctrines of Wahhabis** Read Abdullah Wahhab's response to critics about the beliefs of the Wahhabis.

Modernist Islamic Thought

Some reformist Muslim thinkers, rejecting a rigid, backward-looking vision of Islam such as Wahhabism, promoted modernization as a strategy for transforming Islamic society and meeting the Western challenges. Intellectuals argued that Muslims should reject blind faith and welcome fresh ideas, social change, and religious moderation. Modernists detested many conservative traditions. Qasim Amin **(KA-sim AH-mean)**, a French-educated Egyptian lawyer, argued that the liberation of women was essential to the liberation of Egypt, that acquiring their "share of intellectual and moral development, happiness, and authority would prove to be the most significant development in Egyptian history." Women reformers such as Bahithat al-Badiya **(buh-TEE-that al-buh-DEE-ya)** echoed these sentiments (see Witness to the Past: Egyptian Women and Their Rights). The radical male Iraqi poet Jamil Sidqi az-Zahawi **(ja-MILL SID-key az-za-HA-wi)** identified the veil as the symbol of female exclusion, imploring women to "unveil yourself for life needs transformation. Tear it away, burn it, do not hesitate. It has only given you false protection!"[20]

Modernist Visions

Muslim modernists believed that introducing change would be a straightforward process, that by buying weapons and machines they could strengthen their armies and industries to deflect Western pressure, enrich their countries, and avoid domestic unrest. But their dreams proved impractical because the visionaries were ahead of their largely conservative populations. The challenges increased as Western technical and economic capabilities grew. Like European Enlightenment thinkers, some Muslim modernists struggled with how to reconcile faith and reason. They worried that modernization required adopting Western philosophical and scientific theories, which were often contrary to Islamic beliefs about society, God, and nature. Belief in equality contradicted the low status of Muslim women, and the Western notions of popular sovereignty and the nation troubled those who believed that only God could make laws or establish standards, which the state must then administer. Some reformers also doubted whether Islam, with its universalistic idea of a multiethnic community guided by God, was compatible with nationalism, which emphasized the unity of one group of people defined by a common state. The Moroccan historian Ahmad ibn Khalid al-Nasri, writing of military cadets being trained in Western weapons and tactics, worried that "they want to learn to fight to protect the faith, but they lose the faith in the process of learning how."[21] What role, the modernizers wondered, could clerics and the Shari'a have in a world of machines and nations?

Egyptian Thinkers

Egypt-based thinkers especially argued the compatibility of Islam with modernization. The Persia-born teacher Jamal al-Din al-Afghani (1838–1895) favored modern knowledge and believed that reason and science were not contrary to Islam, arguing that rigid interpretations of Islam and the weight of local traditions contributed to Arab backwardness. He lamented that, intolerant of new ideas, "the Arab world still remains buried in profound darkness,"[22] while rational interpretations of Islam would free Muslims for positive change. But his strong criticisms of British activity in Egypt and Persia as well as of Arab leaders he viewed as puppets led to his exile to Paris, where he

Hulton/Getty Images

Cairo Opera House Hoping to demonstrate modernization, Egyptian leaders built an opera house in Cairo in the 1860s. One of the first pieces staged was an opera by Italian composer Giuseppe Verdi to celebrate the opening of the Suez Canal in 1869.

Egyptian Women and Their Rights

One of the leading women writers and thinkers in early-twentieth-century Egypt, Bahithat al-Badiya (buh-TEE-that al-buh-DEE-ya) (1886–1918), advocated greater economic and educational rights for women in a rapidly changing society. She wrote at a time when Egyptian nationalists were demanding independence from Britain and a modern state and intellectuals were debating the merits of modernity as opposed to tradition. In 1909, in a lecture to an Egyptian women's club associated with a nationalist organization, Bahithat offered a program for improving women's lives. Struggling against male and Islamic opposition to women's rights, she sought a middle ground between Islamic conservatism and European secular liberalization.

Ladies, I greet you as a sister who feels what you feel, suffers what you suffer, and rejoices in what you rejoice. . . . Complaints about both men and women are rife. . . . This mutual blame which has deepened the antagonism between the sexes is something to be regretted and feared. God did not create man and women to hate each other but to love each other and to live together so the world would be populated. . . . Men say when we become educated we shall push them out of work and abandon the role for which God has created us. But isn't it rather men who have pushed women out of work? Before, women used to spin and to weave cloth for clothes, . . . but men invented machines for spinning and weaving. . . . In the past, women sewed clothes . . . but men invented the sewing machine. . . . Women . . . [made bread] with their own hands. Then men invented bakeries employing men. . . . I do not mean to denigrate these useful inventions which do a lot of our work. . . . Since male inventors and workers have taken away our work should we waste our time in idleness or seek other work to occupy us? Of course, we should do the latter. . . .

Men say to us categorically, "You women have been created for the house and we have been created to be breadwinners." Is this a God-given dictate? . . . No holy book has spelled it out. . . . Women in villages . . . help their men till the land and plant crops. Some women do the fertilizing, haul crops, lead animals, draw water for irrigation, and other chores. . . . Specialized work for each sex is a matter of convention, . . . not mandatory. . . . Women may not have to their credit great inventions but women have excelled in learning and the arts and politics. . . . Nothing irritates me more than when men claim they do not wish us to work because they wish to spare us the burden. We do not want condescension, we want respect. . . .

If we had been raised from childhood to go unveiled and if our men were ready for it I would approve of unveiling those who want it. But the nation is not ready for it now. . . . The imprisonment in the home of the Egyptian woman of the past is detrimental while the current freedom of the European is excessive. I cannot find a better model [than] today's Turkish woman. She falls between the two extremes and does not violate what Islam prescribes. She is a good example of decorum and modesty. . . . We should get a sound education, not merely acquire the trappings of a foreign language and rudiments of music. Our education should also include home management, health care, and childcare. . . . We shall advance when we give up idleness.

THINKING ABOUT THE READING

1. How does Bahithat evaluate women's roles and gender relations in Egypt?
2. What does her moderate advice to Egyptian women suggest about Egyptian society and the power of patriarchy?

Source: Bahithat al-Badiya, "A Lecture in the Club of the Umma Party, 1909," trans. by Ali Badran and Margot Badran, in *Opening the Gate: A Century of Arab Feminist Writing,* ed. by Margot Badran and Miriam Cooke, (Bloomington: Indiana University Press, 1990), pp. 228–238.

published a weekly newspaper that promoted his views. Another major and well-traveled thinker, Muhammad Abduh (AHB-doo) (1849–1905), wanted to reform his native Egypt and rejuvenate Islam. Although opposed to wholesale Westernization, Abduh admired major European thinkers and contended that no knowledge, whatever its origin, was incompatible with Islam. Occupying a top Islamic legal position, he promoted modernist Islam at Al-Azhar University, the most influential institution of higher education in the Middle East.

The Roots of Arab Nationalism and the Zionist Quest

Challenges to Nationhood

During the 1800s an Arab national consciousness developed in response to domination by the Ottoman Turks and then by the British and French. Some proposed a pan-Arab movement uniting Arabs from Morocco to Iraq in a common struggle for political and cultural independence. But Arabs were divided by different religious and group affiliations. Most were Sunni Muslims, while others, particularly in the Persian Gulf and southern Iraq, were Shi'ites. Some in Egypt, Lebanon, and Syria were Christians. Arabs were also divided into feuding patriarchal tribes that sometimes disliked rival tribes as much as they disliked Ottoman or European overlords. Many Arabs remained loyal to Ottoman rule, and in 1876, hoping to defuse ethnic nationalism, the Ottomans gave the Arabs seats in the national legislature based on their large population in the empire.

Syrian Roots

Yet, some thoughtful Arabs envisioned self-governing Arab nations. Arab nationalism emerged from a Syrian literary and cultural movement in the later 1800s that included Lebanese Christians, one of whom published a poem calling on Arabs to "arise and awake." Modernist Muslim writings were also influential. The witty books of Abd-al-Rahman al-Kawabiki **(AB-dul RAH-man al-KA-wa-BIK-ee)** (1849–1903), a Syrian who had studied in Egypt and Mecca and hated intolerance and injustice, criticized Ottoman despotism as contrary to Islam and promoted Arab politics. Arab nationalist groups formed all over the Ottoman Empire, but before World War I they were small and had little public influence.

Zionism and Jewish Immigration

While Islamic societies struggled to respond to Western power, the Zionist movement (see Chapter 19) introduced another challenge. In the Jewish ghettoes of eastern Europe, especially Poland and Russia, some thinkers began a quest for a state for their long persecuted and widely scattered people. Prayers in Jewish synagogues for worshiping "next year in Jerusalem," the ancient Hebrew capital in Palestine, had endured for centuries. Few European Jews spoke Hebrew, and many rejected Zionism, identifying with the country where they lived. But for others, Zionism functioned like nationalism. The first Zionist conference, held in Basel, Switzerland, in 1897, identified Palestine, then under Ottoman rule, as the potential Jewish homeland. Jews had long visited or settled in Palestine, and perhaps 20,000 lived there in 1870, but the Ottomans refused Zionist leaders permission to organize a massive settlement of Jews, prompting the Zionist leader, the Hungarian-born journalist Theodor Herzl (1860–1904), to propose accepting a British offer for a temporary home in East Africa.

Soon militant Zionists promoted Jewish migration to Palestine without Ottoman permission or support from European governments. By 1914 some 85,000 Jews, many of them newcomers from Russia and Poland, lived in Palestine alongside some 700,000 Arabs. Committed to creating a socialist society, the immigrants established Jewish collective farms, each known as a **kibbutz**, whose members shared their wealth and promoted Hebrew rather than the German-based Yiddish widely spoken by central and east European Jews. Settlement in Palestine was funded by international Zionist organizations, who bought land from absentee Arab and Turkish landowners. The Zionists had a flag, an anthem, and an active Jewish press. However, since Jewish institutions had no legal recognition in Palestine, the stage was set for future conflict with Palestinian Arabs, who resented the newcomers and their plans to acquire more land for a Jewish state

kibbutz A Jewish collective farm in Palestine that stressed the sharing of wealth.

SECTION SUMMARY

- One response to European pressure was Islamic revivalism, which advocated a pure form of Islam, favored a theocratic state, and sometimes used violence.
- Revivalism was most influential in Arabia, where militant followers of al-Wahhab and Ibn Saud took over a number of cities and eventually formed Saudi Arabia.
- Some intellectuals tried to modernize their religion, but modern European ideas such as equality continued to clash with Islamic practices such as the subjugation of women, and Western nationalism was at odds with the idea of a universal brotherhood under God.
- Some tried to inspire Arab nationalism, but religious divisions and rivalries made this a difficult task.
- Muslims were also challenged by European Zionists, who moved to Palestine in spite of Ottoman objections and also in spite of the Palestinian Arabs, setting the stage for future conflict.

CHAPTER SUMMARY

Sub-Saharan Africa underwent extensive changes between 1750 and 1914. The ending of the trans-Atlantic slave trade opened Africa to exploration and trade by Europeans, and industrial Europe's need for resources and markets fostered a "scramble for Africa" as various Western nations colonized African societies, sometimes by military force against protracted resistance. The French colonized a vast area of West and Central Africa; Britain forged a large empire in West, Central, and East Africa; and the Germans, Belgians, and Italians also acquired African colonies. European settlers flocked to colonies in southern and eastern Africa, most notably South Africa, where they established white supremacist societies. Colonialism created artificial, multiethnic countries. It replaced subsistence agriculture with cash crop farming, plantations, and mineral exploitation while enmeshing Africa in the world economy as a supplier of natural resources. Africans mounted strikes and rebellions against colonialism, but all such efforts were eventually defeated.

The Middle East also experienced European imperialism. The Ottoman Empire attempted to stall its decline with Western-style reforms, but it still lost territory and influence. Egypt attempted an ambitious modernization program, but it proved inadequate to prevent British colonization. In Persia, Western economic and political influence sparked reforms that were later rejected by Persian conservatives. France and Italy colonized North Africa, and French settlers displaced Algerians from valuable land. In response, some Muslims, most notably the Wahhabis, pursued a revivalist strategy to purify the religion and reject Western influence, while modernist reformers sought to adapt secular Western ideas to Islam in order to energize Muslim societies. Arab nationalist movements also arose but remained weak before World War I. Finally, Jewish Zionists posed a threat to Palestinian Arabs by beginning to settle in Palestine, where they hoped to build a Jewish state.

KEY TERMS

direct rule
indirect rule
laager
Young Turks
Bahai
Islamic revivalism
Wahhabism
kibbutz

EBOOK AND WEBSITE RESOURCES

PRIMARY SOURCE
The History and Doctrines of Wahhabis

INTERACTIVE MAPS
Map 21.1 Africa in 1914
Map 21.2 The Ottoman Empire and Persia, 1914

LINKS

Africa South of the Sahara (http://www-sul.stanford.edu/depts/ssrg/africa/). A valuable site that contains links relevant to African history.

History and Cultures of Africa (http://www.columbia.edu/cu/lweb/indiv/africa/cuvl/cult/html). Provides valuable links to relevant websites on African history.

Internet African History Sourcebook (http://www.fordham.edu/halsall/africa/africasbook.html). Contains useful information and documentary material on Africa.

Internet Islamic History Sourcebook (http://www.fordham.edu/halsall/islam/islamsbook.html). A comprehensive examination of Islamic history and culture.

Middle East Studies Internet Resources (http://www.columbia.edu/cu/lweb/indiv/mideast/cuvlm/index.html). A useful collection of links.

Plus flashcards, practice quizzes, and more. Go to: www.cengage.com/history/lockard/globalsocnet2e.

SUGGESTED READING

Cleveland, William L. *A History of the Modern Middle East*, 4th ed. Boulder: Westview, 2008. One of the best surveys of the era.

Esposito, John L. *Islam: The Straight Path*. Revised 3rd ed. New York: Oxford University Press, 2005. Good discussion of Islamic thought in this era.

Goldschmidt, Arthur and Lawrence Davidson. *A Concise History of the Middle East*. 9th ed. Boulder: Westview, 2008. Well-written, up-to-date survey.

Hochschild, Adam. *King Leopold's Ghost: A Story of Greed, Terror, and Heroism in Colonial Africa*. Boston: Houghton Mifflin, 1998. A study of the Belgian Congo.

MacKinnon, Aran S. *The Making of South Africa: Culture and Politics*. Upper Saddle River, NJ: Prentice-Hall, 2003. A comprehensive, readable survey.

Marsot, Afaf Lufti al-Sayyid. *Egypt in the Reign of Muhammad Ali*. New York: Cambridge University Press, 1984. An excellent study.

Northrup, David. *Africa's Discovery of Europe, 1450–1850*. New York: Oxford University Press, 2002. A sweeping survey.

Palmer, Alan. *The Decline and Fall of the Ottoman Empire*. New York: Barnes and Noble, 1992. A readable narrative.

Quataert, Donald. *The Ottoman Empire, 1700–1922*, 2nd ed. New York: Cambridge University Press, 2005. Fine survey of major trends.

Robinson, Francis. *The Cultural Atlas of the Islamic World Since 1500*. Oxford: Stonehenge, 1992. A useful compilation of materials.

Rodney, Walter. *How Europe Underdeveloped Africa*. Washington, DC: Howard University Press, 1982. An influential and controversial critique of the West in Africa by a Guyanese scholar.

Shillington, Kevin. *History of Africa,* rev. 2nd ed. New York: Palgrave Macmillan, 2005. A standard text with good coverage of this era.

Wheatcroft, Andrew. *The Ottomans*. New York: Viking, 1993. A lively discussion with particular attention to the governing elites.

CHAPTER

22

South Asia, Southeast Asia, and Colonization, 1750–1914

CHAPTER OUTLINE

- Forming British India
- The Reshaping of Indian Society
- Southeast Asia and Colonization
- The Reshaping of Southeast Asia

PROFILE
Kartini, Indonesian Feminist and Teacher

WITNESS TO THE PAST
Challenging British Imperialism with Spiritual Virtues

Universiteits-Bibliotheek, Leiden. Snouk Hurgronje Collection, Codex Orientales 7398

Dipenegara
This painting shows Prince Dipenegara, a Javanese aristocrat who led a revolt against the Dutch colonizers in the 1820s, reading, with several attendants at hand.

Rice fields are littered with our battle-killed; blood flows or lies in pools, stains hills and streams. [French] Troops . . . grab our land, our towns, roaring and stirring dust to dim the skies. A scholar with no talent and no power, could I redress a world turned upside down?

—Protest by Vietnamese poet Nguyen Dinh Chieu against French Conquest, late nineteenth century[1]

FOCUS QUESTIONS

1. How and why did Britain extend its control throughout India?
2. How did colonialism transform the Indian economy and foster new ideas in India?
3. How did the Western nations expand their control of Southeast Asia?
4. What were the major political, economic, and social consequences of colonialism in Southeast Asia?

Frustrated by the Vietnamese emperor's refusal to liberalize trade relations with Western nations and protect Christian missionaries, the French, seeking to expand their empire, attacked Vietnam with military force in 1858 and over the next three decades conquered the country against determined resistance. A blind poet, Nguyen Dinh Chieu **(NEW-yin dinh chew)** (1822–1888), symbolized the Vietnamese resistance when he wrote an oration honoring the fallen Vietnamese soldiers after a heroic defense in a battle in 1862: "You preferred to die fighting the enemy, and return to our ancestors in glory rather than survive in submission to the [Westerners] and share your miserable life with barbarians." The French retaliated by seizing Chieu's land and property. The poet, unbowed, refused to use Western products and forbade his children to learn the romanized Vietnamese alphabet developed by French Catholic missionaries. In verse spread by word of mouth and painstakingly copied manuscripts distributed throughout the land, Chieu heaped scorn on his countrymen who collaborated with the French occupiers and promoted the struggle: "I had rather face unending darkness, Than see the country tortured. Everyone will rejoice in seeing the West wind [colonialism],Vanish from [Vietnam's] mountains and rivers."[2] The son of a mandarin in southern Vietnam, Chieu overcame blindness to become a physician, scholar, teacher, and writer famous for his epic poems sung in the streets extolling the love of country, friendship, marital fidelity, family loyalty, scholarship, and the military arts. He rejected the French offer of a financial subsidy and the return of his family land if he would rally to their cause. The Vietnamese continue to revere his stirring poems.

With enhanced military, economic, and technological power provided by the Industrial Revolution (see Chapters 19–20), Britain, France, the Netherlands, and the United States colonized all of South and Southeast Asia except Thailand. Western domination destroyed traditional political systems, reoriented economies, and posed challenges for societies and their world-views, including the Vietnamese whom Nguyen Dinh Chieu attempted to rally. Since Western domination occurred while western Europeans were at the high point of their military and industrial development and cultural arrogance, colonialism proved a transforming experience. It linked these regions more closely than ever to a European-dominated world economy and transmitted to the colonies the ideas and technologies of Western life. In turn, Asian workers produced resources that spurred Western economic growth. But the exchange of ideas was not all one way: Asian religions and arts attracted interest in the West and even developed a small following there. The unyielding resistance to imperialism exemplified by Nguyen Dinh Chieu also gave hope to colonized people in Africa and the Middle East. Resentment against colonialism simmered for decades, and eventually the Indians and Filipinos, among others, asserted the rights of their peoples for self-determination.

Visit the website and eBook for additional study materials and interactive tools: www.cengage.com/history/lockard/globalsocnet2e

Forming British India

How and why did Britain extend its control throughout India?

Marathas A loosely knit confederacy led by Hindu warriors from west-central India; one of several groups that challenged British domination after the decline of the Mughals.

Black Hole of Calcutta A crowded jail in India where over a hundred British prisoners of a hostile Bengali ruler died from suffocation and dehydration in 1757. This event precipitated the beginning of British use of force in India.

By the early 1700s the Muslim Mughals who ruled much of India (see Chapter 18) were in steep decline, challenged by both Indians and Europeans. The splendor of the Mughal court and India's valuable exports had earlier attracted the Portuguese, Dutch, and British. As the Mughals lost power, the British took advantage of a fragmented India and began their conquest of the subcontinent in the mid-1700s. By the mid-1800s Britain controlled both India and the island of Sri Lanka. India had often been conquered by outsiders from Western and Central Asia, but unlike those invaders, who often became assimilated into Indian society, the British maintained their own separate traditions.

Mughal Decline and the British

Europeans had long coveted South Asia for its spices and textiles. Even today, small, single-masted sailing barges ply the coastline between western India, the Persian Gulf, and East Africa, continuing the ancient exchange of merchandise with the coming and going of monsoon winds. Between 1500 and 1750 European powers controlled some of the Indian Ocean maritime trade but conquered only a few scattered outposts in South Asia. The Dutch, who destroyed Portuguese power in South and Southeast Asia, concentrated on Sri Lanka and Indonesia. By 1696 the British possessed three fortified trading stations in India: Calcutta (now Kolkata) in Bengal, Madras (today known as Chennai) on the southeastern coast, and Bombay (today called Mumbai) on the west coast.

By 1750 the Mughals were corrupt and weak, since many Indians had already broken away from Mughal control. Emperors might sit on the spectacular Peacock Throne in Delhi's spectacular Red Fort, but they had little actual power much beyond Delhi, often consoling themselves with the large royal harem or smoking opium. Mughal factions quarreled while the countryside became increasingly disorderly. Without a powerful imperial state to unite it, Indian society, with its diverse cultures, castes, languages, regions, and religions, was unable to effectively resist European encroachments. Mughal governors whose allegiance to the emperor was nominal formed new Muslim states. The **Marathas** (muh-RAH-tuhs), a loosely knit confederacy led by Hindu warriors from west-central India, and the Sikhs, a religious minority in northwest India, built powerful new states. By 1800 the Marathas ruled much of western India, and the Sikhs, under the dynamic Ranjit Singh (RUN-ji SING) (1780–1839), had conquered the Punjab and Kashmir in the northwest. Mounted on sturdy ponies, the Marathas became feared for their plundering raids deep into central India against helpless Mughal armies. In southern India, the Mughal collapse left a power vacuum that both Britain and France attempted to fill by supporting their respective Indian allies in the struggle for regional advantage. Ultimately, none of the rising Indian states gained enough power or acquired enough weapons to repulse the West.

The British posed the gravest challenge. Bengal, India's richest and most populous region, was ruled by Muslim governors who mostly ignored the Mughal government. The Bengali ruler, Aliverdi Khan (r. 1740–1756), had left British trade unmolested. But his successor, Siraja Dowlah (see-RAH-ja DOW-luh) (ca. 1732–1757), considered the British bothersome leeches on his land's riches. Dowlah alienated Western merchants and in 1757 rashly attacked British trading stations. After capturing Calcutta, Dowlah's forces placed 146 captured British men, women, and children in a crowded jail known as the **Black Hole of Calcutta**. The next day only 23 staggered out, the rest having died from suffocation and dehydration. The enraged British blamed Siraja Dowlah for the atrocity and dispatched a force under Robert Clive (1725–1774) to regain Britain's holdings. A former clerk turned into a daring war strategist, the ambitious Clive and his 3,200 soldiers defeated 50,000 Bengali troops at the Battle of Plassey in 1757 and recaptured Calcutta (see Chronology: South Asia, 1750–1914). Clive allied with Hindu bankers and Muslim nobles unhappy with Siraja Dowlah, who was executed, and by 1764 he controlled Bengal.

CHRONOLOGY
South Asia, 1750–1914

1744–1761 Anglo-French struggle for Coromandel coast

1757 Battle of Plassey

1764 British acquisition of Bengal

1774–1784 Warren Hastings governor of Bengal

1793 New land policy in Bengal

1799 British defeat of Mysore

1796–1815 British colonization of Sri Lanka

1816 British protectorate over Nepal

1819 British occupation of all Maratha lands

1820s Beginning of British Westernization policy

1839–1842 First Anglo-Afghan War

1849 British defeat of Sikhs in Punjab

1850 Completion of British India

1857–1858 Indian rebellion

1858 Introduction of colonial system in India

1877 Founding of Muslim college at Aligarh

1878–1880 Second Anglo-Afghan War

1885 Formation of Indian National Congress

1903 British invasion of Tibet

1906 Formation of All-India Muslim League

CHRONOLOGY

	South Asia	Southeast Asia
1750	**1757** Battle of Plassey	**1788–1802** Tayson rule in Vietnam
1796–1815	**1802** British colonization of Sri Lanka	**1819** British colony in Singapore **1824–1886** Anglo-Burman Wars
1850	**1850** Completion of British India **1857–1858** Indian Rebellion	**1858–1884** French conquest of Vietnam **1898–1902** United States conquest of Philippines
1900	**1885** Indian National Congress	

The British government, following a policy of mercantilism to acquire wealth for the state, allowed the British East India Company (often known as "the Company") to govern Indian districts as they were acquired and to exploit the inhabitants while sharing the profits with the British government. As they acquired more Indian territory, the British, much like the former Mughal rulers, expected the Indians to serve them. They also showed a lust for riches equal to that of the Spanish conquistadors in the 1500s. As governor of Bengal (1758–1760, 1764–1767), Clive launched an era of organized plunder, allowing British merchants and officials to drain Bengal of its wealth while Company officials, including Clive, lived like kings. Praised by British leaders and celebrated in the press and schoolboy stories, Clive became the idol of every young Englishman who dreamed of marching to glory and wealth via India's battlefields and bazaars. The cry of "Go East," inspired by Clive's rags-to-riches story, fueled British imperialist ambitions. Eventually accused and later cleared of corruption and fraud charges, a depressed Clive committed suicide at the age of forty-nine.

British Ambitions

To undo the economic chaos left by Clive and consolidate the British position, the Company appointed Warren Hastings to serve as governor-general (1774–1784) of Bengal. Hastings redesigned the revenue system, made treaty alliances, and annexed nearby districts to safeguard the British bases. A scholarly man influenced by Enlightenment thought, Hastings respected the people he governed, in contrast to other British officials, and, he claimed, hoped to never see the whole of India colonized. Like the English, he argued, many Indians had intellect and integrity and should enjoy the same equal rights as the English colonizers. His successors, however, often disregarded his advice. Hastings himself was accused of corruption and forced out of office, living the rest of his life in disgrace.

Expanding British India

Company Rule

Success in Bengal fueled further British expansion in the subcontinent. The British government gave the Company authority to administer all British-controlled Indian territories while also seeking profit, but it forbade further annexation. Despite the ban, governor-generals after Hastings authorized the occupation of more areas, often against opposition, to prevent trade disruption or to counteract rival European nations. Some imperialists talked about Britain's sacred trust to reshape the world, viewing the extension of British authority, culture, religion, and free trade policies a great blessing for Asians. The reality, however, was often different. In expanding its territory, the British mixed military force, extortion, bribery, and manipulation of India's diversity. British agents and merchants could play one region off against another and Hindu against Muslim, aided by Indian collaborators, especially businessmen eager to increase their connections to the world market. Employing superior weapons and disciplined military forces, the British overcame spirited resistance. They recruited mercenary soldiers, known as **sepoys**, under the command of British officers, and by 1857 the Company forces comprised nearly 200,000 sepoy troops and 10,000 British officers and soldiers.

sepoys Mercenary soldiers recruited among the warrior and peasant castes by the British in India.

The French provided a serious roadblock to British expansion, and European wars involving the British and French were extended into a contest for India's southeastern Coromandel coast. Victory there over the French in 1761 soon led the British into actions against other Indian states, including formidable Mysore in south-central India led by Haidar Ali Khan (r. 1761–1782), a devout Muslim who modeled his army on Western lines. A brilliant military strategist, Haidar warned the British, "I will march your troops until their legs swell to the size of their bodies. You shall not have a blade of grass, nor a drop of water."[3] Only in 1799, after twenty years of bloody wars, was Mysore defeated.

Clive Meets Indian Leaders In this painting, Robert Clive meets the new Bengali official, Mir Jafir, after the British victory in the 1757 Battle of Plassey. Clive supported Mir Jafir's seizure of power from the anti-British leader, Siraja Dowlah.

National Portrait Gallery, London

Gradually the British imposed their control over western, central, and northern India. The Maratha confederacy was divided by rivalries, and in 1805 the British occupied the Marathas' northern territories and entered Delhi, where they deposed the aged Mughal emperor. After taking the remaining Maratha lands in 1819, they turned their attention to northwest India, dominated by Rajputs, a declining Hindu warrior caste, and Sikhs. The Rajputs, aware of their weakness, now signed treaties giving Britain claims on their lands. The death of the Sikh leader, Ranjit Singh, in 1839 shattered the Sikhs' unity and undermined their powerful military state. In 1849, after a series of bloody British-Sikh wars, Britain finally triumphed. Britain then stationed troops in the many small independent principalities scattered around India. By 1850, the British ruled all Indians directly or through princes who collaborated with them (see Map 22.1).

Britain and Sri Lanka

British expansion in India eventually led to interventions in neighboring societies, including Sri Lanka (Ceylon), the large, fertile island just south of India. Fearing that the French might establish a base there, in 1796 the British acquired the territory the Dutch had held since the 1630s, and by 1815, after conquering the last remaining Sri Lankan kingdom, Kandy, they controlled the entire island. The British seized rice-growing land from peasants to set up coffee, tea, and rubber plantations and recruited Tamil-speaking workers from southeast India as laborers. By 1911 the poorly paid Tamil laborers and their families made up 11 percent of the Sri Lankan population, maintaining their own customs, language, and Hindu religion and having little contact with Sri Lanka's majority population, the Buddhist Sinhalese. Since many Sinhalese considered both the British and the Tamils unwanted aliens, Sinhalese-Tamil tensions simmered and, after independence, led to a long civil war in Sri Lanka.

Nepal and Afghanistan

Fearing that the Russians, who were conquering Muslim Central Asia, intended to expand into South Asia, the British also attempted to secure India's land borders. First they invaded Nepal, a kingdom in the Himalayan Mountains, defeated Nepal's Hindu ruling caste and fierce fighters, the Gurkhas **(GORE-kuhz)**, in 1814–1816, and turned Nepal into a British protectorate. Soldiers later recruited from Nepal, also known as gurkhas, were employed on battlefields around the world in support of British objectives. Mountainous Afghanistan, an ethnically diverse but Muslim region that had enjoyed only short periods of political unity, seemed the most vulnerable to Russian expansion. However, the Pashtun tribes in the south possessed the fighting skills to oppose Europeans bent on conquest. The British twice invaded Afghanistan and occupied the major eastern city, Kabul, but faltered against fierce Pashtun resistance. In the first Afghan War (1839–1842), Pashtuns massacred most of the 12,000 retreating British and sepoy troops and the British civilians, including women and children, who had accompanied them. Undeterred, the British fought the second Afghan War (1878–1880). Concluding that Afghanistan could not be annexed by military force, they

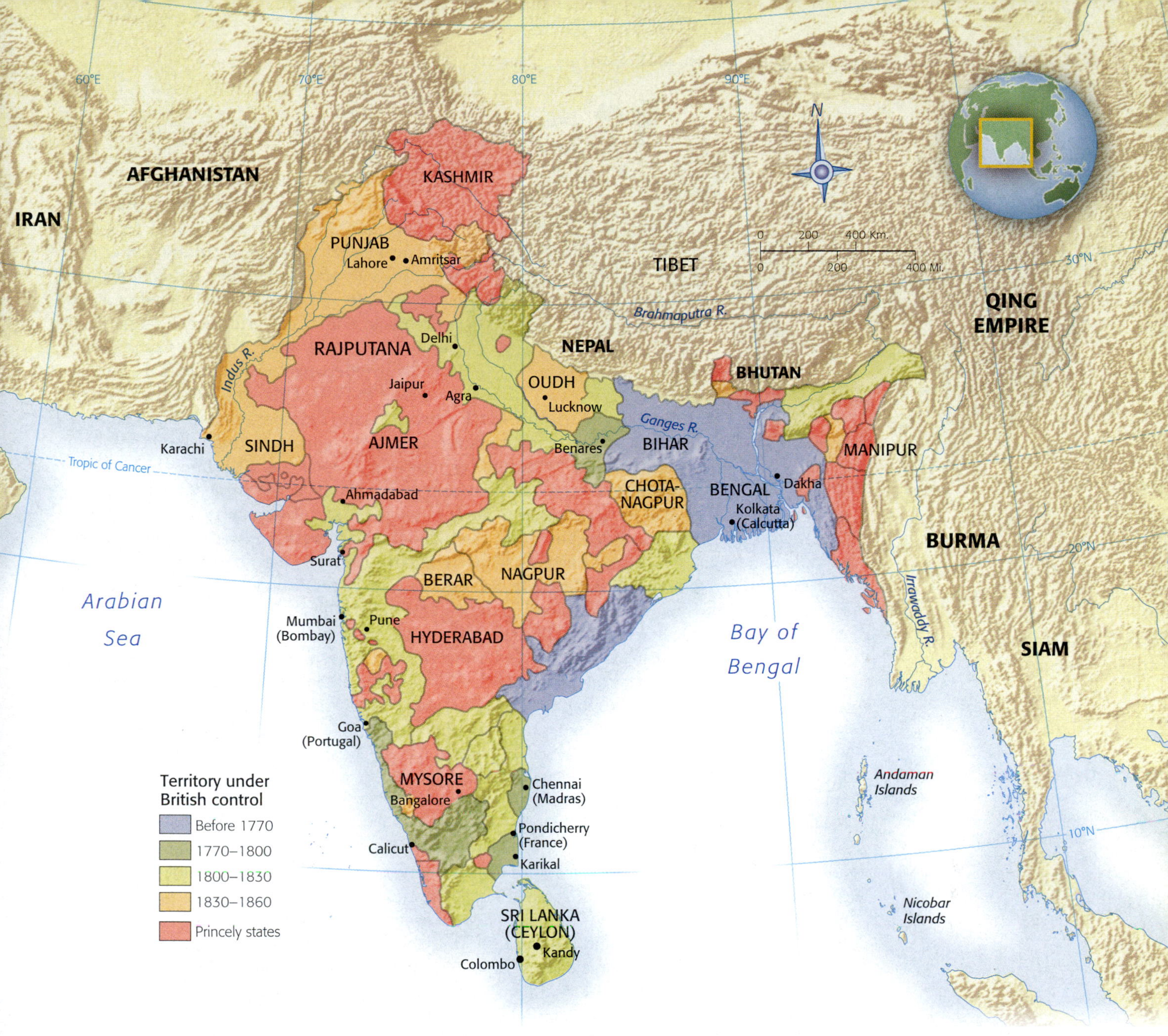

Map 22.1 The Growth of British India, 1750–1860
Gradually expanding control from their bases at Calcutta, Madras, and Bombay, the British completed their military conquest of the final holdout states by the 1850s.

e Interactive Map

replaced a Pashtun leader who favored the Russians with one who was pro-British and who gave Britain control of Afghanistan's foreign affairs.

India Under the East India Company

Reforming India

The British East India Company gradually tightened its control of India and shifted from sharing government with local rulers to administering India through British officials. In arrogant colonial language, Sir Thomas Munro, governor of Madras from 1820 to 1827, explained the imperial mission, claiming that the British must maintain their rule until the Indians, sometime in the distant future, abandoned their "superstitions" and became "enlightened" enough to govern themselves. In the 1820s, the Company began promoting a policy of **Westernization**, a deliberate attempt to spread Western culture and ideas. Protestant evangelism, then strong in Britain, influenced the reform ideas. One devout Company director argued that Britain must diffuse Christian teachings among Indians, whom he described as sunk in darkness and misery. British officials, often disregarding Indian traditions, encouraged Christian missions and tried to ban customs they disliked. Many Indians rejoiced when they banned *sati*, the custom of widows

Westernization A deliberate attempt to spread Western culture and ideas.

Courtesy of the Trustees of the Victoria & Albert Museum

British East India Company Court This painted wood model shows an Indian court presided over by an official of the British East India Company.

throwing themselves on their husband's funeral pyre, but there was less enthusiasm for British attempts to tinker with Muslim and Hindu law codes.

The British also established schools that taught in English. Lord Macaulay (1800–1859), a reformer and firm believer in Western cultural superiority, considered it pointless to teach Indian languages, declaring in 1832 that "a single shelf of a good European library is worth the whole native literature of India and Arabia." Consequently, Macaulay, reflecting Western racist views, proposed creating "a class of persons Indian in blood and color but English in taste, opinions, morals and intellect."[4] While many Indians considered English-medium schools a threat to both Hindu and Muslim customs, some welcomed the schools because they opened Indian students to a wider world. Indians themselves formed the first English-medium institution of higher education, the Hindu College in Calcutta, in 1818.

Orientalism A scholarly interest among British officials in India and its history that prompted some to rediscover the Hindu classical age.

Yet, some British, reflecting what came to be called **Orientalism**, showed a scholarly interest in India and its history. Warren Hastings, who encouraged the study of Indian culture, languages, and literature, preferred reading the European and Asian languages he had mastered—Greek, Latin, Persian, and Urdu—to pursuing his official duties. One of his officials, William Jones (1746–1794), who mastered Arabic, Persian, and Sanskrit, became the most influential Orientalist scholar, but his views often reflected an attempt to fit India into Western concepts of history and religion. Just as Christians and Jews believed the Bible reflected historical truth, Jones treated ancient Vedic texts as accurate historical records rather than religious teachings and claimed that the classical Greeks, such as the mathematician Pythagoras and the philosopher Plato, derived their theories from the same ancient source as the classical Indian sages. Jones's ideas shaped scholarly understanding of Indian history. Several religious movements based on Hindu concepts, such as reincarnation, also gained a small following in the West. Yet by the later 1800s Orientalist respect for India had largely been replaced by British nationalism and intolerance.

The encounter between India and the West also fostered a Hindu social reform movement and philosophical renaissance led by the brilliant Bengali scholar Ram Mohan Roy (1772–1833). After seeing his sister burn to death on a funeral pyre, and concerned that customs such as *sati* and caste divisions were harmful, Roy hoped to adopt certain Western ways to reform and strengthen Hinduism. To better understand the world by studying non-Hindu religions, Roy mastered their source languages—Hebrew, Greek, Arabic, and Persian—and thus became the world's first modern scholar of comparative religion. Roy and his followers attempted to create a synthesis of the best in Hinduism and Christianity; he also founded secondary schools, newspapers, and a Hindu reform organization. Viewing the British as promoters of knowledge and liberty, Roy wanted Britain to promote modernization while also seeking Indian advice.

Economic Policies

In order to make India more profitable, the British East India Company built roads, railroads, and irrigation systems; most significantly for rural Indians, it revised the land revenue collection, the principal source of public finance. The British viewed Indian rural society as stagnant, unable to provide the tax revenues needed to support British administration. In precolonial times, most Indians, living in self-sufficient villages that were governed by the family and caste, had enjoyed a measure of social stability and had the hereditary right to use the land. One British observer wrote that "the village communities [have] everything they want within themselves. They seem to last when nothing else lasts. Dynasty after dynasty tumbles down; but the village communities remain the same."[5]

zamindars Mughal revenue collectors that the British turned into landlords who were given the rights to buy and sell land.

Yet, Company officials, seeking higher revenues, began collecting taxes from farmers in money rather than, as had long been common, a portion of the crop. In 1793 British officials in Bengal converted the Mughal revenue collectors, or **zamindars**, into landlords, who, in addition to collecting taxes, were given the rights to buy and sell land if they paid additional high taxes whenever they did so. Under this system, peasant farmers became tenants to landlords, losing their hereditary rights to land. Many landlords sold their land rights to businessmen who became absentee landlords growing rich from the crops grown by the peasants. In Madras, however, the governor, Munro, mistakenly believed that the peasants were or could be converted into profit-seeking individualists like English farmers. In his system the peasant farmer dealt directly with the government but had to pay tax in cash and could be evicted for nonpayment. Under both systems a barter economy, in which villagers agreed to exchange their services or products with each other, was changed to a money economy. Since some villagers earned more money, the cash-based system undermined the stability and security peasants had once enjoyed and benefited a moneylender caste that came to control much of the land. The Company also encouraged a switch from food crops to cash crops such as opium, coffee, rubber, tea, and cotton, often grown on plantations rather than peasant farms.

Resistance: The 1857 Revolt

Roots of Revolt

In spite of Indian reform movements such as Roy's, most Indians resented the Company's Westernization and economic policies. Many once-prosperous families lost land or become indebted, and the courts enforced laws based on British traditions, fueling hostility. As a result of such grievances, local revolts were common. Furthermore, sepoys increasingly resented the aggressive attempts of British officers to convert them to Christianity. Those stationed in Bengal were particularly outraged by new army rifle cartridges, which had to be bitten off with the teeth before being rammed down the gun barrel. A rumor, probably true, spread that the cartridges were greased with beef and pork fat, violating the religious dietary prohibitions of both cow-revering Hindus and pork-avoiding Muslims.

British-Indian Conflict

In 1857 one revolt, which the British called the Indian Mutiny and Indian nationalists later termed the first War of Independence, spread rapidly and offered a serious challenge to British authority. The revolt began among sepoys and was soon supported by peasant and Muslim uprisings. A few members of princely families also joined the rebel cause, including the widow of the Maratha ruler of Jhansi, who led her troops into battle dressed as a man. The revolt was confined largely to north and northeast India. Because no rebel leaders envisioned a unified Indian nation, British observers argued that the rebels had limited and selfish goals, but many Indians perceived their customs and religions threatened by British policies. Some rebel leaders attempted to unite Hindus and Muslims against their common British enemy. A few wanted to restore the Mughal order.

The rebels captured Delhi and besieged several cities. Both sides used ruthless tactics and committed massacres. Rebels murdered a thousand British residents when they occupied the city of Kanpur, and, when British troops recaptured Delhi, they engaged in widespread raping, pillaging, and killing. The Muslim poet Ghalib mourned: "Here is a vast ocean of blood before me. Thousands of my friends are dead. Perhaps none is left even to shed tears upon my death."[6] The anti-British sentiment was not widespread enough, however, to overcome the rebels' problems: inadequate arms, weak communications, and lack of a unified command structure or strategy. In addition, the rebels received no support from people in other parts of India. Linguistic, religious, cultural, and regional fragmentation made a united Indian opposition impossible. When the British captured the last rebel fort, held by the rani (queen) of Jhansi, in 1858, she was killed and the rebellion collapsed, although a few small rebel groups fought skirmishes with the British until 1860.

Indian Railroad Train The railroads built during British rule carried both resources and passengers. This lithograph shows a Sikh signalman at the station and a train conveying Indian women and a European.

SECTION SUMMARY

- Fragmented after the decline of the Mughals, India was unable to resist encroachment by the Portuguese, Dutch, British, and French.
- In reaction to the Black Hole of Calcutta, the British under Robert Clive took over Bengal and proceeded to plunder its riches; though his successor, Warren Hastings, was more respectful, many governor-generals disregarded Indians' rights.
- Though initially opposed by the French, the British East India Company gradually expanded its control over India by employing local collaborators and playing groups off against each other, and by 1850 Britain controlled all of India.
- The British expanded into Sri Lanka, where they imported Tamils to work on the tea plantations; into Nepal, where they recruited effective soldiers; and into Afghanistan, where they met fierce resistance but ultimately installed a friendly ruler.
- Many British tried to make Indians more Western by abolishing customs they considered backward, while others became interested in studying traditional Indian teachings.
- By having peasants pay their taxes in cash rather than in crops, the British began to shift India from a barter economy to a money economy, a change that undermined centuries of rural stability.
- Though some Indians supported Westernization, periodic revolts occurred, and in 1857 the sepoys began a large rebellion that led to much bloodshed and eventually Indian defeat.

THE RESHAPING OF INDIAN SOCIETY

How did colonialism transform the Indian economy and foster new ideas in India?

The 1857 revolt prompted the British to replace the British East India Company government with direct colonial rule. The British felt betrayed by the rebels, but some officials viewed the troubles as symptoms of deeper discontents that needed to be addressed. To move in that direction, the 1858 Government of India Act transferred sovereignty to the British monarch. In 1876 Queen Victoria was proclaimed Empress of India, head of the government known as the British *Raj*, named for the ancient title of Hindu kings. India became the brightest "jewel in the imperial crown," a source of fabulous wealth. The policies pursued by the British Raj reshaped economic, intellectual, and social patterns and eventually inspired movements reflecting a new sense of the Indian nation.

Colonial Government and Education

Colonial Rule

The British Raj bore many similarities to the Mughal system. The top British officials, the viceroys, lived, like Mughal emperors, in splendor in Delhi, enjoying pomp and circumstance, including Mughal-style ceremonies, and building a new capital at New Delhi next to the old Mughal capital of Delhi, with gigantic architecture. The British built palatial mansions, museums, schools, universities, and city halls but also faced health problems from the tropical heat and diseases such as malaria. They also connected India with a network of roads, bridges, and railways, so that by 1900 India had over 25,000 miles of track, the world's fourth largest rail system.

Although British officials mistrusted Indians after 1857, they allowed the traditional princes to keep their privileges and palaces in exchange for promoting acceptance of British policies. The British also deliberately pitted the Hindu majority against the Muslim minority by favoring one or the other group in law, language, and custom. For example, Hindus protested that the main Muslim language, Urdu, was used in many north Indian courts, exacerbating hatreds that remain today. To promote security, local revenue supported a huge army of 200,000 men, mostly Indian volunteers, who were needed to keep the peace in India and fight British battles abroad. As part of what Kipling called the "Great Game" of strategic rivalry with Russia, Britain invaded Tibet in 1903, prompting Tibetan leaders to agree not to concede territory to Russia or any other foreign power.

The British typically believed that Western colonialism improved Asian and African societies. Rudyard Kipling (1865–1936), a Bombay-born, Britain-educated English poet and novelist, reflected this view in his writings: "Take up the White Man's burden—Send forth the best ye breed—Go, bind your sons in exile. To serve your captives' need."[7] Some policies reflected racism. Much like colonized Africans, Indians were excluded from European-only clubs and parks as well as high positions in the bureaucracy, enjoying no real power or influence. The Raj continued the Westernization policy, promoting British and often Christian values through an expanded English-medium education system. English became the common language for educated Indians; however, only a privileged minority, mostly drawn from higher-caste Hindus, could afford to send their children, mostly boys, to the English schools. By 1911 only 11 percent of men and 1 percent of women were literate in any language. Although only a tiny minority of Indians converted to Christianity, an English-educated middle class emerged, with a taste for European products and ideas. They sent their sons and a few daughters to British universities, where they learned about notions like "freedom" and "self-determination of peoples" that stood in sharp contrast to nondemocratic conditions in India. This growing British-educated professional class organized social, professional, and political bodies concerned with improving Indian life and acquiring more influence in government.

Westernization

Economic Transformation

The British also transformed the Indian economy. Long an economic powerhouse and the world leader in producing cotton textiles, India still produced a quarter of all world manufactured goods in 1750. However, two centuries later, conditions had changed. Many historians believe that British policies, designed to drain India of its wealth to benefit Britain, harmed the Indian economy. British land policies commercialized agriculture, while tax and tariff policies diminished the existing manufacturing. The Company's land tax system exploited the peasantry, planting the roots of one of contemporary India's greatest dilemmas, inequitable land ownership. Many fell hopelessly into debt, and as peasants had to grow cash crops such as cotton, jute, pepper, or opium rather than food, famine became more common, killing millions as food supplies and distribution became more uncertain.

Rural Policies

Other changes also affected rural life. The introduction of steamships freed shipping from the vagaries of monsoon winds, and the opening of the Suez Canal in 1869 made it easier and much faster to ship raw materials from India to Europe. The return ships brought to India cheap machine goods, which undermined the role of village craftsmen such as weavers and tinkers. In addition, the quest for revenues, which included felling forests and ploughing grassland to grow more cash crops, placed massive pressure on the physical environment.

Many historians argue that British rule fostered the decline of Indian manufacturing. Hoping to find new markets abroad for its own industrial products, the British denied India tariff protection for its more expensive handmade products, excluded Indian manufactured goods from Britain, and prohibited the import of industrial machinery by Indians. Meanwhile British products flooded India, destroying the livelihood of many skilled craftsmen. Textile imports increased sixfold between 1854 and 1913, ruining millions of Indian weavers, who, along with metalworkers and glass blowers, often became farm laborers. Yet, industrial activity did not disappear completely from India, and a few Indians found ways to prosper. Some Indians continued to compete with British imports by manufacturing cotton textiles and initiated a modern iron and steel sector. For example, the Gujerati industrialist Jamsetji N. Tata **(JAM-set-gee TA-ta)** (1839–1904) built cotton mills, while his son, Sir Dorabji Tata **(DOR-ab-ji TA-ta)** (1859–1932), founded the Indian steel industry in 1907. Unable to get British funding, they raised money among Indian investors and used their wealth to promote scientific education and found technical colleges.

Industrial Decline

By the late 1800s the limits on India's industries became a subject of heated controversy. Indian critics alleged that tariffs protected British industries while strangling Indian competition. The gap between British and Indian wealth grew. By 1895 the per capita income in Britain was fifteen times higher than India's, a much greater gap than existed two hundred years earlier. Britain's defenders contended that British rule brought investment, imported goods, railroads, and law and order. But critics questioned whether these innovations benefited most Indians as it enriched the British merchants, industrialists, and collaborating Indian businessmen and landlords. Indian scholars attacked what one called "The Drain" of wealth and argued that British policies gave India "peace but not prosperity; the manufacturers lost their industries; the cultivators were ground down by a heavy and variable taxation; the revenues were to a large extent diverted to England."[8] By 1948, after two centuries of British influence, most Indians remained poor.

Population Growth and Indian Emigration

Population growth worsened the plight of the peasantry. As a result of peace and improved sanitation and health, the Indian population rose from perhaps 100 million in 1700 to 300 million by 1920. While encouraging agricultural productivity, the British also provided economic incentives to have more children to help in the fields. Although a similar population increase occurred in Europe at the same time, the growing numbers could be absorbed by industrialization or emigration to the Americas and Australia. India enjoyed neither an industrial revolution nor an increase in food growing. Moreover, Indian landlords had a stake in the cash crop system and discouraged innovation. As a result, population numbers far outstripped the amount of available food and land, creating dire poverty and widespread hunger.

Leaving India

As these problems mounted, millions of desperately poor Indians were recruited to emigrate to other lands. After the abolition of slavery in the Americas, African American workers often left the plantations. The need to replace them created a market for Indian labor in Trinidad, British Guiana (today's Guyana), and Dutch Guiana (now Suriname). Plantations in Sri Lanka, Malaya, Fiji, the Indian Ocean island of Mauritius, and South Africa also wanted Indian labor. But travel was hazardous. For example, in 1884 a family of low-caste landless laborers facing starvation in Bihar state boarded a sailing ship at Calcutta bound for the distant Fiji Islands in the South Pacific. The family was led by Somerea, a fifty-year-old widow, and included her two sons, a daughter-in-law, and four grandchildren. After three months the ship arrived in the islands, but, thanks to cholera, dysentery, typhoid, and a shipwreck, 56 of the 497 passengers had died during the trip. Somerea's family apparently survived the journey.

Indian Diaspora

Most Indian emigrants, including Somerea's family, were destined for plantations and were indentured, meaning they had signed contracts that obligated them to work for a period of years (usually three to five) to repay their passage. Somerea's family probably worked on a sugar plantation. The indenture contracts also stipulated the number of days per week (six) and hours per day (usually nine to ten) that must be worked. Many Indian merchants, moneylenders, and laborers also emigrated, flocking to British Burma, Singapore, Malaya, and East Africa. Between 1880 and 1930 around a quarter million people a year left India. Few returned. The mortality rates were so high and the indenture terms so unfavorable that critics considered the system another form of slavery. Moreover, the pay was so low that many Indians could never pay off their contracts.

Indians now had key economic roles in many countries. Cities such as Nairobi in Kenya, Rangoon in Burma, and Port of Spain in Trinidad had large Indian neighborhoods, and Indian trade networks reached around the Indian Ocean and Pacific Rim. The future leader of the Indian nationalist movement, Mohandas Gandhi (GAHN-dee), experimented with his ideas of nonviolent resistance to illegitimate power while working among Indians in South Africa. Today people of Indian ancestry make up half or more of the populations of Mauritius, Trinidad, Guyana, Suriname, and Fiji and are substantial minorities in Sri Lanka, Malaysia, Singapore, Burma, Kenya, and South Africa. However, although many Indian emigrants succeeded in business or the professions, the majority still labor on plantations growing cocoa, rubber, tea, or sugar.

Indian Thought, Literature, and Society

Hindu Reform and Revival

Indian intellectuals responded to British rule and ideas in several ways. A small group of well-educated Indians, like Ram Mohan Roy mentioned earlier, wanted to combine the best of East and West while reforming customs, such as the ban on widow remarriage, that they saw as corruptions of Hinduism. But their influence waned after 1900. Another group, hostile to Western ways, sought to revive Hindu culture, emphasizing the glories of the past and arguing that India needed nothing from the West. Swami Vivekananda (SWAH-me VIH-vee-keh-NAHN-da) (1863–1902) was an influential proponent of ending British cultural and political domination: "O India, this is your terrible danger. The spell of imitating the West is getting such a strong hold upon you. Be proud that thou art an Indian, and proudly proclaim: 'I am an Indian, every Indian is my brother.'"[9]

Theosophy A nineteenth-century North American and European movement that blended Hindu thought with Western spiritualist and scientific ideas.

Swami Vivekananda was also a reformer, condemning the oppression of untouchables and the conditions of the poor. His writings and lectures gave Indians great pride in their own culture and also helped spread Hindu thought to the West. In 1893, on a visit to New York, he formed the Vedanta Society, which promoted a philosophical view of Hinduism based on the ancient *Upanishads*. Vedanta thought portrayed the Hindu holy books, the Vedas, compiled over 2,500 years ago, as the supreme source of religious knowledge, although not necessarily authored by either God or humans. Vedanta ideas had contributed to another movement, **Theosophy**, that attracted some

Western followers by blending Hindu notions with Western spiritualist and scientific ideas. Theosophy promoted the idea that India was more spiritual than other societies.

Muslim Revival and Reform

Like Hindus, Muslims were forced to rethink their values and prospects. Although the British left many Muslim institutions untouched, Muslims resented the Christian missionary activity supported by British officials openly critical of Islam. To them, India seemed increasingly dominated by European and Hindu values. In response, some Muslims traveled to the Middle East to pursue Islamic knowledge and came home with Islamic revivalist ideas, some opening schools. In the northwest frontier and Bengal, dogmatic Wahhabism (see Chapter 21) gained a following. Opposed to modernization, the revivalists clashed with other Muslims, Christians, Sikhs, and Hindus.

In contrast, Muslim modernists, led by the cosmopolitan Sayyid Ahmad Khan (1817–1898), wanted Muslims to gain strength, suggesting that "the more worldly progress we make, the more glory Islam gains." Khan believed that Islam was compatible with modern science, and in 1877 he founded a college at Aligarh **(AL-ee-GAHR)** that offered Western learning within a Muslim context. Trained for jobs in government service, Aligarh students, often not devout, studied many subjects in English, and typically learned how to play the British game of cricket. Many went on to study at top British universities. A satirist observed the secular atmosphere at Aligarh, whose leaders "neither believe in God, nor yet in prayer. They say they do, but it is plain to see, What they believe in is the powers that be."[10] Aligarh graduates dominated Muslim political activity in India until independence.

Literature

Indian literature took on a more nationalist flavor. The Tagore family, Hindus from Calcutta, pioneered the movement to awaken national pride and expand literary expression. The hugely influential Rabindranath Tagore **(RAH-bin-drah-NATH ta-GORE)** (1861–1941) was a poet, educator, patriot, and internationalist whose writings won him the Nobel Prize for literature in 1913 (see Witness to the Past: Challenging British Imperialism with Spiritual Virtues). His wealthy family, he wrote, adopted foreign customs but also nurtured a pride in the Indian nation. Tagore sought a new and freer India, "where the mind is without fear and the head is held high; Where knowledge is free; where the clear stream of reason has not lost its way into the dreary desert sand of dead habit; Into that heaven of freedom, let my country awake."[11]

Caste and Gender Relations

British policies also affected society, including the caste system. Historians debate whether the elaborate caste system of modern times had existed for centuries as an active, continually changing part of Indian life, or whether the modern system was shaped by the views of colonial era officials seeking to classify Indians for administrative and census purposes. Before the colonial era, Hindus in Bengal, Punjab, and south India generally saw the formal differences among varied castes as of only moderate importance. But British policies sharpened caste identities by classifying people largely through their caste affiliations, thus making the system more rigid and favoring the higher castes. Furthermore, as different Indians increasingly came into contact with one another, some Indians sought firmer social boundaries by further dividing castes from each other. In the nineteenth century, much of India became more caste conscious than ever before, with upper castes stressing their uniqueness and lower castes wanting to emulate the upper castes to improve their social status. Envying the highest caste, brahmans (priests), other castes adopted brahman rituals and ideas, such as vegetarianism. For example, some untouchable leather workers joined a movement that opposed the caste system but, like brahmans, avoided eating meat. For their part, higher castes tried to preserve their privileged positions by demanding that members of lower castes be excluded from government jobs. Hindu thinkers were divided about the caste system. Some reformers called for abolishing caste, while defenders praised the system's ideals of conduct and morality.

Gender relations also changed. Traditionally women and men had performed separate but interdependent roles within a patriarchal household. Ploughing was men's work; transplanting and weeding were shared duties; and women tended the house and garden. But both men and women lost work as absentee landlords emphasized growing cash crops rather than food. Lower-caste men emulated the upper castes, often forcing women into seclusion. But new opportunities also arose for women. More girls attended school, becoming teachers, nurses, midwives, and even doctors, and by the 1870s women published biographies of their experiences and struggles. For centuries girls had been married early with little choice of husband. Now a small minority of "new women" in Indian cities led more independent lives and married later, in their twenties or thirties, or sometimes not at all.

Indian and British reformers also sought to improve the lives of Indian women and foster greater gender equality. For example, a controversial new marriage act in 1872 provided for both civil marriage and marriage across caste lines. The British tried incremental reforms, such as allowing widow remarriage and raising the age of female consent from ten to twelve. But although

Challenging British Imperialism with Spiritual Virtues

On the last day of the nineteenth century Rabindranath Tagore wrote a poem in Bengali protesting the brutal imperialism of the war Britain was waging against the Boers in South Africa, driven, Tagore believed, by British nationalism. The poem suggested that the patient cultivation of the "spiritual virtues" of India and the East would become a force in the world after the reckless power of Western imperialism, sparked by nationalism, had lost its control over humankind. In this, he echoed the views of many Hindu nationalists and reformers that Hinduism and India had a special devotion to peace and spiritual insights that could benefit the Western world. For this poem and other influential writings, Tagore won the Noble Prize for literature in 1913.

The last sun of the century sets amidst the blood-red clouds of the West and the whirlwind of hatred.
The naked passion of self-love of Nations, in its drunken delirium of greed, is dancing to the clash of steel and the howling verses of vengeance.
The hungry self of the Nation shall burst in a violence of fury from its own shameless feeding, for it has made the world its food.
And licking it, crunching it, and swallowing it in big morsels, It swells and swells,
Till in the midst of its unholy feast descends the sudden shaft of heaven piercing its heart of grossness.
The crimson glow of light on the horizon is not the light of thy dawn of peace, my Motherland.
It is the glimmer of the funeral pyre burning to ashes the vast flesh—the self-love of the Nation—dead under its own excess.
The morning waits behind the patient dark of the East, Meek and silent.
Keep watch, India.
Bring your offerings of worship for that sacred sunrise.
Let the first hymn of its welcome sound in your voice and sing
"Come, Peace, thou daughter of God's own great suffering.
Come with thy treasure of contentment, the sword of fortitude,
And meekness crowning thy forehead."
Be not ashamed, my brothers, to stand before the proud and the powerful, With your white robe of simpleness.
Let your crown be of humility, your freedom the freedom of the soul.
Build God's throne daily upon the ample barrenness of your poverty.
And know that what is huge is not great and pride is not everlasting.

THINKING ABOUT THE READING

1. How does Tagore perceive nationalism?
2. How does he believe India should respond to Western power?

Source: From *Sources of Indian Tradition, Vol. 2,* William Theodore de Bary, ed.

reformers often supported the idea of marriage based on love, they also encouraged wives to show their husbands and children self-sacrificing devotion. This was not enough progress for some women. Pandita Ramabai (1858–1922) urged women to take control of their lives. Her father, a noted reformer, declined to marry her off as a child, and her knowledge of Sanskrit won her the reputation of *Saraswati*, after the Hindu goddess of wisdom. She married a lawyer of low-caste background, a shocking move for a brahman woman, and then traveled to England, where she became a Christian. Upon returning, Ramabai opened a school for girls, especially child widows, and later a refuge for female famine victims.

The Rise of Nationalism

National Feeling

British rule inevitably produced a nationalist reaction. The Western idea of the "nation," defined by a feeling of inclusiveness among people living within the same state (see Chapter 19), was new for Indians, who thought of themselves as joined by a common Hindu or Muslim culture rather than a centralized state. By establishing political unity in India, educating Indians in European ideas but then largely excluding Indians from administration, Britain fostered national feelings but also bitterness toward the colonizers. Furthermore, by 1900, Indians were publishing six hundred newspapers, which reported on world events such as the Irish struggle for independence from England, the Japanese defeat of Russia in war, and the U.S. conquest of the Philippines, all of which inspired Indians to oppose British rule. In 1885 nationalists formed the Indian National Congress, which worked for peaceful progress toward self-government. But the Congress mostly attracted well-educated professionals and merchants, especially Bengalis, of brahman backgrounds. British officials heaped scorn on the Congress, and constitutional reforms in 1909 brought a measure of representative government but no true legislative and financial power.

Rise of the Congress

By 1907 a radical nationalist group led by a former journalist, Bal Gangadhar Tilak **(BAL GAGN-ga-DAR TEA-lak)** (1856–1920), transformed the Congress from a gentleman's pressure group into the spearhead of an active independence movement. Tilak fiercely defended Hindu orthodoxy and custom; however, many Indians disliked Tilak and remained wary of the Congress, while Muslims perceived the Hindu-dominated Congress, particularly radical leaders like Tilak, as anti-Muslim. As Hindu-Muslim tensions increased, the All-India Muslim League was founded in 1906 with the goal of uniting Muslims scattered all over the country. Hindus constituted 80 percent of India's population; Muslims were a majority only in eastern Bengal, Sind, north Punjab, and the mountain districts west of the Indus Valley. The influential Muslim reformer and educator Sayyid Ahmad Khan opposed potential Hindu majority rule, arguing that "it would be like a game of dice, in which one man has four dice and the other only one."[12] The Muslim League's first great victory came in 1909, when British reforms guaranteed some seats in representative councils to Muslims. The Congress was enraged, charging divide and rule. Hindu-Muslim rivalries continued to complicate the nationalist movement throughout the twentieth century, eventually leading to separate Hindu and Muslim-majority nations, India and Pakistan, in 1949.

SECTION SUMMARY

- After 1857, the British monarchy ruled India through the British Raj, which built palatial buildings, a large railroad system, and an expanded English-language school system, thereby educating Indians about Western ideals such as nationalism and sowing the seeds for an Indian revolution against Britain.
- Britain stifled Indian industry by using India as a market for British industrial products, and it turned Indian peasants into tenants who had to grow cash crops for Britain rather than their own food, thus destroying the centuries-old village economy and exacerbating famine and poverty.
- As the Indian population increased, many poor Indians were driven to work abroad in indentured servitude, while other Indians emigrated to work as laborers, merchants, and moneylenders.
- While some Hindus wanted to combine the best in British and Indian culture, others, such as Vivekananda and Tagore, sought to revive more traditional Hindu traditions, while a Muslim college at Aligarh trained Muslims in English government and science.
- The caste system became more rigid under British rule, with lower castes imitating upper castes, upper castes trying to strengthen their privileges, and women facing greater restrictions in some cases and expanded opportunity in others.
- As Indian nationalists began to unite in their opposition to the British, members of the Hindu majority formed the Indian National Congress in 1885, but it was opposed by many Muslims, who formed the All-India Muslim League in 1906.

Southeast Asia and Colonization

How did the Western nations expand their control of Southeast Asia?

Like Indians, Southeast Asians also had colonization imposed on them by Western military force. During the 1800s the Western challenges became more threatening, and by 1914 all the major Southeast Asian societies except the Siamese had come under Western colonial control. The major changes came in Indonesia, Vietnam, and Burma, where the Dutch, French, and British, respectively, increased their power, and in the Philippines, which by 1902 was controlled by the United States. Thus Southeast Asian societies became tied, more than ever before, to the larger world but lost their political and economic independence.

Colonialism in Indonesia and Malaya

Dutch Expansion

cultivation system An agricultural policy imposed by the Dutch in Java that forced Javanese farmers to grow sugar on rice land.

The Dutch expanded their power in the Indonesian archipelago. The Dutch East India Company already controlled the Spice Islands (Maluku) and Java, territories that supplied them with great wealth. In 1799 the Dutch government abolished the Company because of debts and corruption and replaced it with a formal colonial government that concentrated its economic exploitation in Java and Sumatra (see Chronology: Southeast Asia, 1750–1914). In 1830 the Dutch introduced the **cultivation system**, an agricultural policy that forced farmers on Java to grow sugar on

CHRONOLOGY

Southeast Asia, 1750–1914

1786 British base at Penang Island

1799 Abolition of Dutch East India Company

1788–1802 Tayson rule in Vietnam

1802 Nguyen dynasty in Vietnam

1819 British base at Singapore

1824–1826 First Anglo-Burman War

1830–1870 Cultivation system in Java

1851–1852 Second Anglo-Burman War

1858–1884 French conquest of Vietnam

1868–1910 Kingship of Chulalongkorn in Siam

1869 Opening of Suez Canal

1885–1886 Completion of British conquest of Burma

1887 Formation of Federation of Indochina

1898–1902 U.S. conquest of Philippines

1908 Dutch defeat of last Balinese kingdom

their rice land and allowed the government to set a low fixed price to pay peasants for sugar, even when world prices were high, enriching the Dutch but ultimately impoverishing many peasants. A Dutch critic described the results: "If anyone should ask whether the man who grows the products receives a reward proportionate to the yields, the answer must be in the negative. The Government compels him to grow on *his* land what pleases *it;* it punishes him when he sells the crop to anyone else but *it*."[13] Dutch-owned plantations growing sugar and other cash crops replaced the cultivation system in the 1870s.

In the later 1800s the Dutch turned their attention to gaining control, and exploiting the resources, of the other Indonesian islands, such as Borneo and Sulawesi (see Map 22.2). In some areas they used violence to impose their rule and suppress resistance. For example, between 1906 and 1908 they crushed the small kingdoms on Bali, an island just east of Java. After the valiant Balinese resistance failed, the royal family of the largest kingdom committed collective suicide, walking into the guns of the Dutch forces rather than surrendering, shaming the Dutch and depriving them of any sense of victory. The Dutch also united the thousands of scattered societies and dozens of states of the vast Indonesian archipelago into the Dutch East Indies. But the diverse colony, governed from Batavia (now Jakarta) on Java, promoted little common national feeling, making it difficult later to build an Indonesian nation with a shared identity.

Meanwhile the British became more active in Malaya and eventually subjugated the varied Malay states. Seeking a naval base, the British East India Company purchased Penang **(puh-NANG)** Island, off Malaya's northwest coast, from a cash-strapped sultan in 1786. Then in 1819 a visionary British East India Company agent, Jamaica-born Thomas Stamford Raffles (1781–1826), capitalized on local political unrest to acquire sparsely populated Singapore Island, at the tip of the Malay Peninsula. A fine harbor and strategic location on the Straits of Melaka, the midpoint for shipping between China and India, made Singapore a valuable base and a great source of profit to both British businessmen and government treasuries. As the British welcomed Chinese immigrants, Singapore became the major hub for both British and Chinese economic activity and networks in Southeast Asia. By the 1860s Singapore, with a mostly Chinese population, had become the key crossroads of Southeast Asian commerce. Finally, after obtaining Melaka from the Dutch in 1824, Britain governed the three Malayan ports as one colony, the Straits Settlements.

British Expansion

Pressured by British merchants in the Straits Settlements, the British soon extended their influence into the Malay states. For some time Chinese had been immigrating to western Malaya, where they contracted with local Malay rulers to mine tin and gold. Growing demand for metals in industrializing Europe spurred British merchants, competitors of the Chinese, to seek control of the mining. By the 1870s the British used order and security as their rationale for threatening or forcing the Malay sultans to accept British advisers and then British domination. Britain soon achieved formal or informal control over nine sultanates, which, together with the Straits Settlements, became British Malaya. The British also colonized the northern third of Borneo, creating the states of Sabah (British North Borneo) and Sarawak and imposing a protectorate over the old sultanate of Brunei.

British rule changed Malaya, encouraging the planting of pepper, tobacco, oil palm, and especially rubber on the west coast while attracting many more Chinese and Indian immigrants. Malayan tin was shipped to Europe and North America for making household utensils, tin cans, and barrels for storage of food and oil. Malay villagers, pressured by British taxes to take up rubber planting, lost their self-sufficiency, while the British maintained the Malay sultans and aristocracy as symbolic and privileged leaders of the Malay states. Thus a **plural society** developed, a medley of peoples—Malays, Chinese, and Indians—that mixed but did not blend. The different groups generally maintained their own cultures, religions, languages, and customs, confirming a Malay proverb : "raven with raven, sparrow with sparrow."

plural society A medley of peoples who mix but do not blend, maintaining their own cultures, religions, languages, and customs.

Vietnam and Burma: Colonization and Resistance

The Taysons

Vietnam fell to French colonialism after a bitter struggle. In 1771 three brothers from Tayson, a village in southern Vietnam, launched the Tayson Rebellion. Social revolutionaries committed to a unified Vietnamese nation and fed up with corruption and misrule, the Taysons fought against the Vietnamese emperors and their French allies, using the slogan "seize the property

Map 22.2 The Colonization of Southeast Asia
Between 1800 and 1914 the European powers gradually conquered or gained control over the Southeast Asian societies that had not been colonized in the Early Modern Era. Only Siam remained independent.

e Interactive Map

of the rich and redistribute it to the poor."[14] In 1788 the Taysons defeated their foes and reestablished national unity, after which they sponsored economic expansion and rallied the people against a Chinese invasion.

Nguyen Dynasty

In 1802, Nguyen Anh **(NEW-yin ahn)** (1761–1820), the leader of a princely family based in Hue, defeated the Taysons with French assistance and established a new imperial dynasty. But the Nguyen dynasty proved unpopular and unable to address the inequalities that had inspired the Tayson Rebellion. *The Tale of Kieu*, a 3,300-line poem cherished by the Vietnamese even today, sympathetically portrays an intelligent and beautiful young woman, Kieu, forced by poverty to become a concubine and then a prostitute but who keeps her sense of honor. Kieu symbolized the Vietnamese people mistreated by the upper-class Vietnamese and their French allies. Another critic of the imperial court and of patriarchal Confucianism, the outspoken woman poet Ho Xuan Huong **(ho swan wan)**, had been a concubine to several high officials. Using wit and sarcasm, she wrote freely about sex, championed women's rights, and attacked polygamy: "One wife gets quilts, the other wife must freeze. To share a husband . . . what a fate! I labor as a wageless maid."[15]

French Conquest

In 1858 the militarily powerful French, hoping to control the Mekong and Red River trade routes to China, began what they arrogantly called a "civilizing mission" to spread French culture and Christianity, launching a bloody campaign of conquest against a determined but badly outgunned Vietnamese resistance. The French first conquered the south and then moved north, facing Vietnamese opposition the whole way. By 1884 the French were victorious but still faced prolonged

can vuong ("aid-the-king") Rebel groups who waged guerrilla warfare for fifteen years against the French occupation of Vietnam.

resistance for another fifteen years against the heroic efforts of thousands of poorly armed rebels known as the **can vuong** (kan voo-AHN) ("aid-the-king"), who waged guerrilla warfare throughout the country, just as their ancestors had resisted the Chinese and Mongol invaders, often against hopeless odds. One of the rebel leaders rejected any compromise with the French: "Please do not mention the word *surrender* any more. You cannot give any good counsel to a man who is determined to die." As a French witness admitted, the Vietnamese resisted fiercely: "We have had enormous difficulties in imposing our authority. Rebel bands disturb the country everywhere, appear from nowhere, arrive in large numbers, destroy everything, and then disappear into nowhere."[16] The rebels received food and shelter from the local population. In suppressing the can vuong struggle, the French massacred thousands and executed surrendered or captured rebels. The can vuong rebels became powerful symbols of resistance for later generations of Vietnamese fighting colonialism and foreign invasion.

Federation of Indochina

In 1887 the French created the Federation of Indochina, an artificial unit linking Vietnam, which the French broke into three separate colonies, with newly acquired Cambodia and Laos, all of which had very different social, cultural, political, and historical legacies. The French maintained their rule by force while allowing French commercial interests and settlers to exploit natural resources and markets. The colonial regime also destroyed the traditional autonomy of the Vietnamese villages by appointing leaders and by greatly increasing the tax burden to finance colonial administrative costs. Many peasants lost their land or access to communal lands to private landowners, investors, and rubber planters, mostly French. Powerful French enterprises prospered even if Indochina proved a financial drain for the French government.

Britain and Burma

As with the French in Vietnam, it took decades for the British to colonize Burma and overcome resistance. As they expanded their power in India, the British coveted Burma's rich lands and worried about Burmese claims to border regions. In three wars—between 1824–1826, 1851–1852, and 1885–1886—the British conquered Burma (today Myanmar), with both sides suffering huge casualties. Vastly differing cultures and clashing strategic interests produced violent British-Burmese conflict, and the gradual loss of independence proved devastating to the Burmans, the country's majority ethnic group. As they lost territory, they felt an impending doom, expressed in a frenzied cultural activity, including drama, love poetry, and music. The court, fearing that the Burmese heritage might disappear if the British triumphed, also compiled *The Glass Palace Chronicle*, a history of Burma from earliest times.

Between 1853 and 1878 a new Burmese king, the idealistic Mindon, tried to salvage his country's prospects by pursuing modernization and seeking good relations with the British. However, worried that he might succeed, the British tried to humiliate Mindon, and in 1886, after completing their conquest, they exiled the royal family. When some Burmese resisted British rule, the British, calling it "pacification," destroyed whole villages and executed rebel leaders. The Burman aristocracy and royal system were abolished as Burma became a province of British India, a humiliating fate. For the next fifty years the British undermined Burmese Buddhism and cultural values, established Christian mission schools, and recruited non-Burman hill peoples into the government and army.

Bastille Day Parade in Vietnam This painting, by an unknown Vietnamese scholar, subtly criticizes the unpopular French colonization by satirizing the annual French holiday. A French man is shown with his arm around a Vietnamese woman while unarmed Vietnamese lantern-bearers are being commanded by a French official.

Courtesy of l'Ecole d'Extreme Orient, Paris

Siamese Modernization

Burma's traditional enemies, the Siamese (Thai), were the only Southeast Asians who retained their independence. In the early 1800s Siam was a strong state under the vigorous new Bangkok-based Chakri dynasty. Seeing Burma's dilemma, able Chakri kings mounted a successful strategy to resist Western pressures. With Britain and France, which both coveted Siam, preoccupied with controlling Malaya, Burma, and Indochina, Siamese leaders had time to strengthen government institutions, improve their economic infrastructure, cultivate a long-standing alliance with China, and broaden their popular support. The farsighted Siamese kings understood the changes in Southeast Asian politics and the rise of Western power, and they promoted a modernization policy, yielding to the West when necessary and consolidating what remained. Siamese leaders agreed to commercial agreements that opened the country to Western businesses. Recognizing Siamese determination and pressed to maintain their control of restless Burma and Indochina, Britain and France decided that conquering Siam would be too costly and left Siam as a buffer between British Burma and French Indochina.

Modernizing Kings

Two kings and their advisers were most responsible for Siam's success. The first, the scholarly, peace-loving Mongkut **(MAHN-kut)** (r. 1851–1868), had served as a Buddhist monk and teacher for several decades, studying science and learning to read Latin. Rather than inviting invasion, he signed treaties with various Western powers, often with terms unfavorable for Siam, invited Western aid to modernize his kingdom, and hired the wives of Christian missionaries to teach English to his wives and sons. Mongkut's widely traveled son and successor, Chulalongkorn **(CHOO-lah-LONG-corn)** (r. 1868–1910), emphasized diplomacy and modernization. His reforms abolished slavery, centralized government services, strengthened the bureaucracy, and established a Western-style government education system. He also stimulated economic growth by encouraging Chinese immigration and opening new land for rice production, making Siam one of the world's leading rice exporters. As a result, Siam's economic development generally kept pace with that of its colonized neighbors but under Siamese rather than colonial direction. When Chulalongkorn died in 1910, Siam (today Thailand) was still independent, and the Western appetite for new colonies had waned.

The Philippines, Spain, and the United States

Revolt Against Spain

As in Latin America (see Chapter 19), hostility toward the corrupt, repressive, and economically stagnant rule of Spain had simmered for decades in the Philippines. Many educated Filipinos of Spanish, indigenous, and mixed (mestizo) background resented colonial power, the privileged immigrants from Spain, and the Catholic Church's domination. Writers such as the poet and novelist Jose Rizal **(ri-ZAHL)** (1861–1896), who had lived for a time in Spain and Germany, encouraged anti-Spanish feeling. Rizal's novels satirized the government and the church, earning him official condemnation as a subversive heretic, and he was publicly executed for alleged treason against the colonial government in 1896. Rizal's death united varied opposition groups and turned nationalists toward revolution. One nationalist leader, Emilio Aguinaldo **(AH-gee-NAHL-doe)** (1870–1964), called on the Filipinos to rebel: "Filipinos! Open your eyes! Lovers of their native land, rise up in arms, to proclaim their liberty and independence."[17] Women played active roles in the movement, serving as soldiers, couriers, spies, and nurses. Despite the revolutionary's heroic efforts, however, the Spanish had contained the revolution by 1897, though they failed to crush scattered resistance.

U.S. Intervention

The situation changed dramatically in 1898 when a U.S. fleet sailed into Manila Bay and destroyed the Spanish navy. Americans had engaged in occasional naval skirmishes in Southeast Asia throughout the 1800s, and they now sought control of resources and markets. The United States intervened in the Philippines as an episode of the Spanish-American War (see Chapter 20), the first of four ground wars that it would fight in East and Southeast Asia over the next eight decades. The U.S. attack on Manila rejuvenated the revolutionaries, who received American support and soon controlled much of the country. The revolutionaries declared independence and established a semidemocratic republican government. But the factionalized leaders disagreed in their objectives, and U.S. leaders had other plans for the country.

The decision by the United States to remain in the Philippines as a colonizer led to its suppression of the nationalist revolution. U.S. president William McKinley answered Rudyard Kipling's call to assume "the white man's burden" and reflected the American idea of Manifest Destiny, the notion that God supported U.S. expansion. Ignoring centuries of Filipino history and deep desire for independence, McKinley proclaimed: "It is our duty to uplift and civilize and Christianize and by God's Will do our very best by [the Filipinos]."[18]

Philippine-U.S. War

But McKinley underestimated the Filipino opposition to the U.S. occupation. Some 125,000 American troops fought during the four-year Philippine-American War, with over 5,000 Americans and some 16,000 Filipinos dying in battle. Another 200,000 Filipinos perished either in guarded compounds the Americans set up to keep villagers from helping the revolutionaries or from famine and disease generated by the conflict. Since Filipino soldiers often enjoyed the active support of the local population, Americans had to fight for every town. The elusive revolutionaries' guerrilla warfare demoralized the American soldiers, who had expected a quick victory. While Americans controlled the towns, the revolutionaries controlled the countryside. Both sides committed atrocities, including torture. Americans destroyed whole villages and looted Catholic churches, while Filipinos killed captured Americans. Angered by American deaths, U.S. general Jacob Smith ordered his men to turn Samar Island into a "howling wilderness," to "kill and burn. The more you kill and burn the better you will please me."[19]

The war also divided Americans. Strong supporters coveted Philippine resources and markets, and U.S. newspapers urged the slaughter of all Filipinos who resisted. But an organized protest movement opposed the war. The writer Mark Twain satirized American economic motives in his 1900 rewriting of "The Battle Hymn of the Republic": "Mine eyes have seen the orgy of the launching of the Sword; He is searching out the hoardings where the strangers' wealth is stored; He hath loosed his fateful lightnings, and with woe and death has scored; His lust is marching on." American critics also rejected the imperialism: "We've taken up the white man's burden, of ebony and brown; Now will you tell us, Rudyard [Kipling], how we may put it down."[20]

U.S. Colonialism

By 1902, with the revolutionaries defeated and many wealthy Filipinos, to protect their interests, supporting U.S. rule, the Philippines became an American colony. Americans reshaped the society of those they paternalistically called "our little brown brothers," establishing an elected legislature filled mostly by Filipinos. The colonial government fostered modern health care and education, and the schools produced many Filipinos fluent in English. But American rule ignored peasant needs while perpetuating the power of the Filipino landowners, who controlled the lives of millions of impoverished peasant tenants, and reinforcing the cash crop economy now linked to American economic needs.

SECTION SUMMARY

- As the Dutch expanded their control over the Indonesian archipelago, they joined together vastly disparate cultures and disrupted the traditional economy, such as by forcing Javanese farmers to grow sugar on rice land and to sell it at unfairly low prices.
- The British expanded control over the Malay Peninsula, which they used to supply raw materials such as tin and rubber, and Singapore, which became a key crossroads of Southeast Asian and India-China trade.
- After conquering Vietnam, the French faced fierce resistance from can vuong rebels, but they ultimately conquered the rebels and opened the country to exploitation by French commercial interests.
- As the British gradually conquered Burma, native Burmans attempted to preserve their culture, but after the British victory in 1886 the Burmese traditions were largely undermined.
- Unlike the rest of Southeast Asia, Siam (now Thailand) avoided colonization because of its fortunate geographical location and its farseeing leaders, who gave in to some Western demands and consolidated popular support.
- After defeating the Spanish in the Philippines and supporting local rebels, the U.S. government turned against the Filipinos and, after a bloody struggle, established a colony geared toward American economic needs.

THE RESHAPING OF SOUTHEAST ASIA

What were the major political, economic, and social consequences of colonialism in Southeast Asia?

Colonialism in Southeast Asia had many parallels to that in India and Africa. Although some Southeast Asians benefited, many others experienced worsening living conditions. A chant popular among Vietnamese peasants lamented the seizure of Vietnamese resources by the French: "Ill fortune, indeed, for power has been seized by the French invaders. It's criminal to set out the food tray and find that one has nothing but roots and greens to eat."[21] From a global perspective, colonialism linked Southeast Asia more firmly to a Western-dominated world economy. But colonial policies also affected local political, social, intellectual, and cultural life. Like Indians, Southeast Asians responded to the challenges of colonialism in creative ways.

Colonial Governments and Economies

Colonialism proved a shattering experience. The only colony with much self-government, the U.S.-ruled Philippines, had an elected legislature, but its decisions had to be approved by U.S. officials. The British allowed some influential Malayans participation in local government and, in 1935, formed a legislature in Burma that included both elected and appointed members. But France and the Netherlands allowed little democracy, and colonialism often meant government by stodgy, autocratic European bureaucrats.

Colonial Governments

Colonial governments varied widely. As in sub-Saharan Africa (see Chapter 21), direct rule, which removed traditional leaders, such as the Burmese kings, or made them symbolic only, as with the Vietnamese emperors, was used in Burma, the Philippines, and parts of Vietnam and Indonesia. Europeans mostly applied indirect rule in Malaya, Cambodia, Laos, and some parts of Indonesia, governing a district through the traditional leaders, such as Malay sultans or Javanese aristocrats. The traditional leaders frequently supported colonial rule and enjoyed considerable local power. Colonial authorities also played one ethnic group or one region off against another, creating problems that persisted after independence and made national unity difficult. Also as in Africa, colonial boundaries sometimes ignored traditional ethnic relationships and rivalries, laying a basis for political instability. Countries such as Burma, Indonesia, and Laos were artificial creations of European colonialism rather than organic unities with culturally similar populations.

Economic Change

As in India, colonialism transformed economic life. Since subsistence food farming could not produce enough revenues for colonial governments or investors, it was replaced by cash crop farming, plantations, and mines, tying the colony's economy more closely to that of the colonizer. Western businessmen mostly controlled the banks, import-export companies, mines, wells, and plantations. As a result, Southeast Asia became one of the world's most valuable economic areas. Colonial taxation policies encouraged people to grow rubber, pepper, sugar, coffee, tea, opium, and palm oil; cut timber; mine gold and tin; and drill oil. Some key cash crops, such as rubber from

British Library

Java Coffee Plantation This painting from the nineteenth century shows a European manager supervising barefoot laborers who are raking and drying coffee beans, a major Javanese cash crop.

Brazil and coffee from the Middle East, originated elsewhere. Many colonies became specialized monocultures emphasizing one or two major commodities, such as rubber and tin from Malaya, or rubber and rice from Vietnam, but the world price for these exports fluctuated with unstable global demand. Moreover, these economic activities often harmed the natural environment, as forests were cleared for plantations or logged for timber to be shipped out of the region.

Many Southeast Asians now depended on rubber growing for their livelihood. The invention of bicycles and then automobiles opened up markets for rubber tires. To meet this need, the British introduced rubber to Malaya, from where it spread to Sumatra, Borneo, southern Thailand, Vietnam, and Cambodia, grown mostly on European-owned plantations. Malaya supplied over half of the world's natural rubber by 1920. Plantation workers endured long hours, strict discipline, monotonous routine, and poor food, generally arising before dawn to tend the rubber trees and replace the buckets that collected the sap, trying to finish their labor before the blazing tropical sun made hard physical work unhealthy. A Vietnamese writer described rubber estate workers: "every day one was worn down a bit more, cheeks sunken, eyes hollow. Everyone appeared almost dead."[22]

Economic growth did not benefit all equally. The European colonizers and the local officials and merchants who cooperated with them gained wealth, and the peasants on Java who grew sugar and coffee for the Dutch initially earned new income. But costs also rose faster than the compensation earned, forcing the peasants to grow more and work longer hours to earn the same profit as before. The peasants now depended on sugar or coffee profits for survival but often became impoverished because of the rising costs. They also faced disaster when world prices for sugar and coffee declined and then, in the 1930s, collapsed altogether.

Social Change

Population Growth and Immigration

As in India, colonial policies also sparked rapid population growth. In 1800 perhaps 30 to 35 million people lived in Southeast Asia, but by the late 1930s it was around 140 or 150 million. The greatest increases came on Java, where the population in 1800 was some 10 million but increased to 30 million by 1900 and 48 million by 1940, creating a burden for contemporary Indonesia. As Dutch policies fostered better health care, people lived longer, while economic incentives encouraged larger families to provide more labor for the fields. However, women faced not only more hours working in the fields but also increased expectations for bearing more children. Fast-growing populations, especially in Java, Vietnam, and the Philippines, resulted in smaller farm plots and more landless people.

Between 1800 and 1941 millions of Chinese and Indians immigrated to Southeast Asia to work as laborers, miners, planters, and merchants. The Chinese chiefly came from poor, overcrowded coastal provinces in southeast China. Although some established businesses or joined relatives, the majority immigrated under the indenture system, which obligated them to work for years in mines, plantations, or enterprises. Chinese immigrants, mostly males, hoped to make enough money to return to their native village wealthy and respected, but some remained poor, spending their lives as laborers, miners, or plantation workers. Many other Chinese prospered as merchants, planters, and mine owners, and often decided to remain in Southeast Asia. Dominating retail trade, they become the commercial middle class, operating general stores, specialty shops, and restaurants in every town. As a result, some cities, such as Kuala Lumpur **(KWAW-luh loom-POOR)** in Malaya and Singapore, became largely Chinese in population. Many Chinese married local women or brought families from China, their descendants often adopting aspects of local culture and language. By adjusting to local conditions, the Chinese became a permanent presence in Southeast Asian life.

British Malaya also attracted Indian settlers. Indian immigrants had long come to Malaya as traders, craftsmen, and workers. Beginning in the 1880s, the British imported Tamil-speaking people from southeast India to work on rubber plantations, and the Chinese and Indians together eventually outnumbered the Malays. The British governed the various communities through their own leaders: Malay chiefs, Chinese merchants, and urban Indian traders. But this strategy separated and discouraged cooperation between the three groups.

Gender Relations

The changes during the colonial era particularly affected women, who had traditionally played a major economic role as farmers, traders, and weavers. Now, as men took up cash crop farming, the responsibility for growing the family's food was often left to women, increasing their workload.

As Chinese, Indian, and sometimes Arab men increasingly took over small-scale trade in towns, many women also lost their role in the local marketplace and thus their status as income earners for the family. The expansion of textile imports also affected women's status. Women had previously dominated weaving, spinning, and dyeing. Although weaving was hard work, even drudgery, women could do it at home with friends and relatives while caring for children. But after 1850, as inexpensive factory-made textiles came from Europe, people stopped buying local handwoven cloth, slowly forcing women out of the textile business. A Javanese noblewoman wrote in a 1909 essay that "little by little [women] feel that their life is no longer of such value, considered by men only as ornaments as they are no longer contributing to the household coffers."[23] Women had to find other income sources, which often took them away from the home and children.

Some women joined movements to assert their rights, as European feminist movements had some influence in Southeast Asia in the late nineteenth and early twentieth centuries. For example, Siamese feminists opposed polygamy and supported girls' education. Today many Indonesians honor an inspirational Javanese woman, Raden Adjeng Kartini, as a heroine whose writings and life influenced the rise of Indonesian feminism and nationalism (see Profile: Kartini, Indonesian Feminist and Teacher). Although she died young, the schools for girls she founded in 1900 multiplied. Like Kartini, other women struggled to cope with the changing world.

Urbanization

Southeast Asia already had large cities, but Western rule encouraged more rapid urbanization. Cities such as Manila, Jakarta, Rangoon (today known as Yangon), Singapore, Kuala Lumpur, and Saigon (today Ho Chi Minh City) grew as colonial capitals. Cities attracted immigrants, such as the Chinese, and migrants from nearby districts. Most colonial towns and cities offered a diverse assortment of food stalls and restaurants, schools that catered to different ethnic groups, as well as Muslim mosques, Buddhist, Hindu, and Chinese temples, and Christian churches. While most people remained attached to their own culture, some descendants of Chinese and Indian immigrants assimilated into the surrounding culture; friendships and even marriages crossed ethnic lines. For example, much of Thailand's political and economic leadership has some mix of Chinese and Siamese ancestry.

Cultural Change

Religion and Education

Colonial governments differed in educating people and fostering indigenous cultures. Most colonies left education to the Christian missions. Some Vietnamese, Indonesians, and Chinese became Christian, and hill peoples frequently did so, but few Theravada Buddhists or Muslims abandoned their faiths. A few colonies set up government schools. The U.S.-ruled Philippines had the best record, enrolling 75 percent of children in elementary schools. Independent Siam also opened public schools that made education widely available for both boys and girls. At the other extreme, French Indochina spent little public money on schools. Some communities developed alternatives to Western education. Buddhist and Muslim groups expanded their schools and taught from a non-Western perspective, while other schools mixed Eastern and Western ideas. Schools opened by a mystical Javanese religious organization provided an alternative to both Islamic and Christian instruction, emphasizing Indonesian arts such as music and dance but also Western ideas such as expressing one's own ideas and social equality.

New Cultural Forms

Southeast Asians also developed new cultural forms. On Java, musicians mixed European string instruments with the rhythms of the largely percussion Javanese gamelan orchestra to create a romantic new popular music, *kronchong*. In the 1800s the sentimental songs were particularly favored by Indonesian sailors and soldiers, as well as by disreputable young men, known as kronchong crocodiles, who dressed flamboyantly, gambled, and drank heavily. By the early 1900s kronchong became respectable, and it was eventually embraced by Indonesian nationalists as an artistic weapon against the Dutch, offering songs on topical and nationalist themes.

The cultural exchange was not one-way. Western composers who observed performances by Javanese and Balinese gamelan orchestras incorporated gamelan influences into their music. In most colonies, a modern literature also developed that reflected alienation from colonialism and an awareness of rapid change. But since criticism of the colonial regime was suppressed, authors made their points indirectly to avoid censorship or arrest. Vietnamese writers used historical themes or critiques of Vietnamese society to discuss contemporary conditions, and Indonesian writers explored characters experiencing despair and disorientation because of the colonial system.

KARTINI, INDONESIAN FEMINIST AND TEACHER

The inspirational social activist and teacher Raden Adjeng Kartini **(RAH-den AH-jeng KAR-teen-ee)** (1879–1905), usually known to Indonesians simply as Kartini, represented a feminist consciousness new to Indonesia. In her life, she shared the problems and faced the prejudices Indonesian women encountered in the colonial system and their own societies. The daughter of a Javanese aristocrat, she chafed against the confined lives of her social class, which expected young women to obey men, especially their fathers, without question, stay home, and train for marriage. However, Kartini's parents were unusually liberal, subscribing to Dutch-language newspapers and hiring Dutch tutors for their sons and daughters. Kartini's progressive father sent her and her siblings to a Dutch-language primary school. Her brothers later moved on to a Dutch-language high school, and one even attended a university in Holland. A good student, Kartini also keenly wanted to complete high school and then study in Holland, but attending high school or a Dutch university would have required her to leave home. Since Javanese customs discouraged aristocratic women from traveling without their families, her father would not permit it. In conformity with aristocratic custom, at puberty Kartini was restricted to the family's house and ordered to prepare herself for an arranged marriage by learning domestic skills.

But Kartini had larger ambitions. From her experience in Dutch-language school and friendships with Dutch women, she drew a model of personal freedom contrary to that of her Javanese society, including a commitment to educate Javanese

Courtesy, Photo Gallery, Indonesian Embassy, London

Raden Adjeng Kartini This painting, completed decades after Kartini's death, honors the young Javanese woman who founded girls' schools.

SECTION SUMMARY

- Colonized Southeast Asian peoples were allowed very little autonomy and were frequently combined into countries with little ethnic or cultural unity.
- Economic life in colonies was reshaped to serve Western nations' needs for raw materials, especially rubber, and for markets for their goods, and in many cases it led to destruction of the natural environment and the impoverishment of local people.
- Millions of Chinese immigrated to Southeast Asia, where many prospered as merchants and retailers, while Indians came to work in Malayan rubber plantations.
- Economic changes due to colonization forced women to grow food for their families and eliminated the market for their handmade textiles, thus taking away their traditional ability to earn an income.
- Education in colonies included both Western-style and more traditional schools, and cultural and artistic interchange between Westerners and colonized peoples produced new cultural forms, such as kronchong music.

women in order to give them more options in life. Eventually Kartini bowed to her parents' demands and entered an arranged marriage with a man she scarcely knew who already had two other wives, but who agreed to support her plan to open a school for girls. Kartini sent a memorandum to the colonial government entitled "Educate the Javanese," and then, at twenty, she opened Indonesia's first girls' school, which combined Javanese and Western values.

Kartini wrote a series of fascinating letters to Dutch friends in Java and Holland that reveal much about her thinking. Her correspondents were often nonconformist career women with socialist leanings, known in Holland as "modern girls," who encouraged Kartini's educational plans and thirst for knowledge. In 1899 she told a pen-friend, the radical feminist Stella Zeehandelaar: "I have been longing to make the acquaintance of a 'modern girl,' that proud independent girl who has all my sympathy." Mixing her Dutch friends' ideas with her own, Kartini's letters asserted women's right to education and freedom from polygamy and child marriage.

Like European feminists, in her letters Kartini criticized the constraints of marriage, family, and society. She had serious doubts about the advantages of marriage in her own society: "But we must marry, must, must. Not to marry is the greatest sin which the Muslim women can commit. And marriage among us? Miserable is too feeble an expression for it. How can it be otherwise, when the laws have made everything for the man and nothing for the woman. When law and convention both are for the man; when everything is allowed to him." She thought women repressed: "The ideal Javanese girl is silent and expressionless as a wooden doll, speaking only when it is necessary." She also condemned religious prejudice, whether by Muslims or Christians: "We feel that the kernel of all religion is right living, and that all religion is good and beautiful. But, o ye peoples, what have you made of it?" But she had hope for change: "I glow with enthusiasm toward the new time which has come. My thoughts and sympathies are with my sisters who are struggling forward in the distant West."

Kartini died in childbirth at age twenty-five. Her Dutch friends, such as Zeehandelaar, later published Kartini's letters, ensuring her fame. Thanks partly to the royalties from her published letters, the schools Kartini founded multiplied after her death, educating thousands of Indonesian girls in the twentieth century. But Kartini left a controversial legacy for Indonesians. Her schools filled a great need, for which many Indonesians are grateful, and although Kartini had criticized Javanese culture and admired Western ideals, in 1964 the Indonesian president named her a national heroine and honored her as the nation's *ibu*, or "mother." But conservatives accused her of abandoning Islam and Javanese culture. Because of her close ties to Dutch friends, her detractors labeled Kartini an apologist for colonialism, and some contrasted her unfavorably to Rahma El-Yunusiah, a devout Muslim woman from Sumatra who taught Arabic and the Quran and who refused any contact with the Dutch. Nonetheless, today Kartini is honored as a proponent of Indonesian women's rights and a precursor of Indonesian nationalist sentiment.

THINKING ABOUT THE PROFILE

1. What does Kartini's life tell us about the challenges that faced Javanese women of her day?
2. How do Kartini's thoughts reflect the meeting of East and West?

Note: Quotations from Raden Adjeng Kartini, *Letters of a Javanese Princess*, edited with an introduction by Hildred Geertz (New York: W. W. Norton, 1964), 31, 34, 42, 45, 73.

CHAPTER SUMMARY

Change was more obvious than continuity in South and Southeast Asia. Gradually Britain extended its control over the Indian subcontinent, using military force but also outmaneuvering rivals, forging alliances, and intimidating small states into accepting British domination. By 1850 the British East India Company controlled all of India directly or indirectly. The Company introduced policies to reshape India's economy and culture, including a Westernizing education system. The rebellion of 1857, suppressed with great difficulty, shocked the British into replacing the Company with colonial government rule. The new British Raj allowed little Indian participation in government. British policies transformed the Indian economy by favoring landlords at the expense of peasants and by suffocating traditional industries to benefit British manufactures. Population growth and poverty fostered emigration. The encounter with the West also prompted Indian thinkers to reassess their cultural traditions. Some Indians adopted Western influences, some rejected them, and others tried to mix East and West. Finally, unpopular British policies generated a nationalist movement that challenged British rule.

The European powers finished colonizing Southeast Asia. Using military force or threats, the Dutch became dominant throughout the Indonesian archipelago, reaping its wealth in part by compelling Javanese to grow cash crops. Britain gained control of Burma through warfare but needed less force in Malaya, which proved profitable as a source of minerals and cash crops. Against strong resistance the French occupied Vietnam, exploiting and reshaping rural Vietnamese society.

The Americans displaced the Spanish as the colonial power in the Philippines after suppressing a nationalist revolution. While they maintained the cash crop economic system, they also fostered some political participation. Only Siam, led by perceptive kings, avoided colonization. Colonialism reshaped social patterns, undermining the economic activities of women, fostering urbanization, and promoting the immigration of Chinese, who later became the commercial class. Southeast Asians responded by forming creative schools and unique cultural activities.

KEY TERMS

Marathas
Black Hole of Calcutta
sepoys
Westernization
Orientalism
zamindars
Theosophy
cultivation system
plural society
can vuong

EBOOK AND WEBSITE RESOURCES

INTERACTIVE MAPS

Map 22.1 The Growth of British India, 1750–1860
Map 22.2 The Colonization of Southeast Asia

LINKS

Asian Studies (http://coombs.anu.edu.au/WWWVLAsianStudies.html). A vast Australian metasite.

East and Southeast Asia: An Annotated Directory of Internet Resources (http://newton.uor.edu/Departments&Programs/AsianStudies-Dept/general.html). This site offers many links.

Internet Indian History Sourcebook (http://www.fordham.edu/halsall/india/indiasbook.html). An invaluable collection.

Virtual Library: South Asia (http://www.columbia.edu/cu/libraries/indiv/area/sarai/). A major site on India.

WWW Southeast Asia Guide (http://www.library.wisc.edu/guides/SEAsia/). An easy-to-use site.

Plus flashcards, practice quizzes, and more. Go to: www.cengage.com/history/lockard/globalsocnet2e.

SUGGESTED READING

Bayly, C. A. *Indian Society and the Making of the British Empire.* New York: Cambridge University Press, 1988. A masterly scholarly synthesis of research on the Company era.

Bayly, Susan. *Caste, Society and Politics in India from the Eighteenth Century to the Modern Age.* New York: Cambridge University Press, 1999. A major scholarly study.

Bose, Sugata. *A Hundred Horizons: The Indian Ocean in the Age of Global Empire.* Cambridge: Harvard University Press, 2006. Examines British India's connections to the wider world.

Bose, Sugata, and Ayesha Jalal. *Modern South Asia: History, Culture, Political Economy,* 2nd ed. New York: Routledge, 2004. A recent brief survey text.

Brown, Ian. *Economic History in South-East Asia, c. 1830–1980.* Kuala Lumpur: Oxford University Press, 1997. A detailed but readable scholarly assessment.

Brown, Judith M. *Modern India: The Origins of an Asian Democracy,* 2nd ed. New York: Oxford University Press, 1994. A detailed study of India since 1750, especially strong on politics.

Crossette, Barbara. *The Great Hill Stations of Asia.* New York: Basic Books, 1999. Entertaining study of Western colonialism through hill towns.

Forbes, Geraldine. *Women in Modern India,* rev. ed. New York: Cambridge University Press, 1999. A scholarly study since 1750.

Karnow, Stanley. *In Our Image: America's Empire in the Philippines*. New York: Ballantine, 1989. A readable survey.

Larkin, John. *Sugar and the Origins of Modern Philippine Society*. Berkeley: University of California Press, 1993. Study of the sugar industry's impact on the colonial Philippines.

Marr, David G. *Vietnamese Anticolonialism, 1885–1925*. Berkeley: University of California Press, 1971. A scholarly examination of the resistance to French colonization.

Metcalf, Thomas R. *Imperial Connections: India in the Indian Ocean Arena, 1860–1920.* Berkeley: University of California Press, 2007. Studies the crucial role of Indians in the British Empire.

Owen, Norman G., et al. *The Emergence of Modern Southeast Asia: A New History*. Honolulu: University of Hawaii Press, 2005. The best survey, comprehensive and readable.

Tandon, Prakash. *Punjabi Century, 1857–1947*. Berkeley: University of California Press, 1968. A personal view of a century of change.

Tarling, Nicholas, ed. *The Cambridge History of Southeast Asia*, vol. 2. New York: Cambridge University Press, 1992. Contains interpretive essays on varied topics by major scholars.

Wyatt, David K. *Thailand: A Short History*, 2nd ed. New Haven: Yale University Press, 2003. The best general survey.

CHAPTER

23

East Asia and the Russian Empire Face New Challenges, 1750–1914

CHAPTER OUTLINE

- The Zenith and Decline of Qing China
- From Imperial to Republican China
- The Remaking of Japan and Korea
- Russia's Eurasian Empire

PROFILE
Ando Hiroshige, Japanese Artist

WITNESS TO THE PAST
Planning a Revolutionary New China

Visual Connection Archive

Treaty Between Japan and China
After an industrializing Japan defeated a declining China in a war over Japanese encroachments in Korea (1894–1895), diplomats from both nations met to negotiate a peace treaty. This painting shows the Chinese and Japanese representatives, easily identified by their different clothing styles, discussing the terms.

The sacred traditions of our ancestors have fallen into oblivion. Those who watch attentively the march of events feel a dark and wonderful presentiment. We are on the eve of an immense revolution. But will the impulse come from within or without?

—A Chinese official, 1846[1]

FOCUS QUESTIONS

1. What were the causes and consequences of the Opium War?
2. Why did Chinese efforts at modernization fail?
3. How did the Meiji government transform Japan and Korea?
4. What factors explain the expansion of the Russian Empire?

In 1820 Li Ruzhen (LEE ju-chen) (1763–1830) published a satiric novel that boldly attacked Chinese social conditions. Set in the Tang dynasty, *Flowers in the Mirror* explored, among other themes, a sensitive topic only superficially discussed by earlier male Chinese writers: the relationship between the sexes. Li described a trip by three men to a country in which all the gender roles followed in China for centuries have been reversed, where men suffered the pain of ear piercing and footbinding and endured hours every day putting on makeup, all to please the women who run the country. One of the men, Merchant Lin, is conscripted as a court "lady" by the female "king":

> *His [bound] feet lost much of their original shape. Blood and flesh were squeezed into a pulp and little remained of feet but dry bones and skin, shrunk to a dainty size. Responding to daily anointing [with oil], his hair became shiny and smooth. With blood-red lipstick, and powder adorning his face, and jade and pearl adorning his coiffure and ears, Merchant Lin assumed a not unappealing appearance.*[2]

Li seemed an unlikely man to address so sympathetically the daily challenges faced by women. A conventionally educated Confucian scholar who had failed the civil service examinations, Li became a writer on language, political philosophy, mathematics, and astrology. But growing Western pressure to open China's borders to foreign trade, unchecked population growth, domestic unrest, political corruption, and growing opium addiction spurred Chinese scholars such as Li to reassess the relevance of Chinese traditions, such as outmoded civil service examinations and women's footbinding. Li addressed the social inequities that kept women from actively participating in China's regeneration. The growing dissatisfaction with China's practices that Li's provocative book represented, combined with Western intervention in China, set the stage for the immense revolution that would eventually transform this ancient society.

China was still powerful in the late 1700s, but in the 1800s it experienced three military defeats, a devastating rebellion, and increasing poverty for millions of Chinese. In response, the imperial government supported some reforms, but these did not foster the modernization that China needed to control foreign influence, and eventually revolutionary movements overthrew the imperial system. Like the Chinese, the Japanese also faced challenges, even before Western ships forced the nation open in the 1850s. Soon the old system fell, and Japan's new leaders began an all-out program of modernization to prevent Western domination. By 1900 the Japanese had heavy industry, a modern military, and a comprehensive educational system; they also sought their own resources and markets abroad and were soon colonizing their neighbor, Korea. Although historically linked more closely to Europe than to Asia, Russia, perched on the borders of Europe, East Asia, and the Islamic Middle

e Visit the website and eBook for additional study materials and interactive tools: www.cengage.com/history/lockard/globalsocnet2e

East and Central Asia, also became a factor in Asian politics by expanding across Siberia to the Pacific. After it became dominant in parts of eastern Europe, pushed its borders southward into Ottoman territories, and conquered the Central Asian states, Russia was the largest territorial power in Eurasia.

THE ZENITH AND DECLINE OF QING CHINA

What were the causes and consequences of the Opium War?

Established by the Manchus, the Qing **(ching)** (1644–1912) was the last dynasty in China's 2,000-year-old imperial history (see Chronology: China, 1750–1915). After reaching its zenith in the eighteenth century, Qing China experienced decay in the nineteenth as several catastrophic wars resulted in unequal treaties that increased Western penetration and fostered major rebellions. Meanwhile, China's economy underwent changes, and increasing poverty prompted millions of Chinese to seek their fortunes abroad. Qing decline had as much to do with Europe's rise as with China's failures.

Qing China in an Imperial World

Manchu Rule and Economy

Eighteenth-century China was still one of the world's most powerful, prosperous, and technologically sophisticated societies, self-sufficient and self-centered. But although the Manchus had followed the political example of earlier Chinese dynasties, they were more despotic and forbade intermarriage with the Chinese. While the Chinese accepted Manchu rule, as they had tolerated alien rule in the past, they resented the ethnic discrimination. The Qing had built a great empire by occupying predominantly Muslim Xinjiang **(shin-jee-yahng)**, a mostly desert region just west of China; conquering the Mongols; annexing Tibet; and adding the fertile island of Taiwan, known in the West as Formosa, to which many Chinese migrated. This expansion stretched Qing military power and proved economically costly.

Yet the Qing generally maintained prosperity for nearly two centuries. New crops from the Americas, such as corn, sweet potatoes, and peanuts, provided additional food sources. Cash cropping of cotton, tea, and American tobacco expanded but also led to a growing concentration of land ownership. In 1830 China, with growing domestic trade, new textile factories, and increased copper mining, remained the world's largest commercial economy and still accounted for a third of world manufacturing. Some historians suggest that the mid-Qing commercialized economy resembled the patterns that sparked economic change in Early Modern western Europe. For example, China's population nearly tripled from 150 million in 1700 to 432 million by 1850. Peasants responded to population pressure by farming marginal land and expanding their use of irrigation and fertilizer.

Society and Culture

But population growth still outstripped the growth of the food supply, straining resources and fostering corruption and Chinese resentment of the Qing government. Although in the 1700s living standards in the more developed regions of China were probably comparable to those of the more affluent parts of western Europe, they deteriorated in the 1800s. Chinese culture and society also became more conservative, as the Qing government prohibited books and plays that it considered treasonable or subversive to traditional Chinese values. Some scholars, arguing that moral laxness caused the fall of dynasties, applauded the crackdown. The Qing also introduced harsher laws against homosexuality, which Chinese governments had generally tolerated, and increased social pressures on women to conform to such gender expectations as refusing to remarry after they became widows. Imperial edicts read in monthly public meetings emphasized Confucian notions of moral virtue, heaping honor on filial sons, loyal officials, and faithful wives. The government also published instructional books containing historical writings on female obligations such as not laughing aloud, talking loudly, or swaying their skirts. Yet, women also read popular literature, such as the satirical novel *Flowers in a Mirror.* And, in a few districts in central China, peasant women wrote their communications in a secret script, *nuxu* **(noo-shoe)**, that was perhaps developed by and for women centuries earlier.

China and Europe

China's problems resulted from both internal decay and foreign pressure. Greedy officials took bribes to allow the smuggling and sale of narcotic drugs, and local rebellions against the Qing were suppressed, but at great cost. As conditions deteriorated at home, European nations demanded more privileges, including freedom to travel inside China. The Portuguese had established a base at Macao on the southern coast and gradually turned it into a colony, and in the 1700s Dutch and

CHRONOLOGY

	China	Japan and Korea	Russia and Central Asia
1800	**1839–1842** Opium War		
1850	**1850–1864** Taiping Rebellion	**1853** Opening of Japan by Perry **1867–1868** Meiji Restoration	**1800–1870s** Russian conquest of Turkestan and Caucasus
1900	**1911** Chinese Revolution	**1910** Japanese colonization of Korea and Taiwan	**1905** First Russian Revolution

English traders were granted permission to trade at the southern port of Guangzhou (gwahng-jo) (known to the British as Canton).

Chinese merchants in coastal cities, who had long traded with Southeast Asia, often supported contact with the West because they could make fortunes by trading with the Europeans. For example, some merchants specialized in **Chinoiserie** (chin-WAH-zur-ee), a Western vogue for Chinese ceramics, painting, lacquerware, and decorative furniture whose quality Europeans could not duplicate. Western merchants and diplomats also commissioned Chinese artists to paint Chinese people, costumes, and city scenes using Western artistic techniques. In the early 1800s a merchant's guild, the **Co-hong**, had a monopoly on Guangzhou's trade with the West, and its head, Howqua (how-kwah) (1769–1843), became one of the world's richest men. Howqua was famous in China for his spectacular pleasure garden and lavish mansion, which employed five hundred servants.

Nevertheless, largely self-sufficient in food and resources, China did not need foreign trade, and Qing emperors were unwilling to make concessions to the more open trade system desired by the Europeans. They restricted trade to a few ports such as Guangzhou and refused diplomatic relations on an equal basis with the West. The Chinese knew little of the Western world and were confused by the diverse European nationalities. Moreover, Chinese leaders viewed European merchants as barbarians bearing tribute, and they required visiting diplomats to perform the humiliating custom of prostrating themselves before the emperor. But the British righteously saw themselves as benefiting China by opening the country to free trade. China's attitude toward foreign trade and the outside world was well exemplified in a letter written by the Qing emperor Qianlong (chee-YEN-loong) (r. 1736–1795) to King George III of Britain following a British trade mission in 1793 requesting more access. The emperor denied Britain permission to establish an embassy but commended the king for his respectful spirit of submission and humility in sending tribute: "Our dynasty's majestic virtue has penetrated into every country under heaven. Our celestial empire possesses all things in prolific abundance. It behooves you, O king, to display ever greater devotion and loyalty in the future, so that by perpetual submission to our throne, you may secure peace and prosperity for your country hereafter."[3]

CHRONOLOGY
China, 1750–1915

1644–1912 Qing dynasty

1839–1842 Opium War

1842 Treaty of Nanjing

1856–1860 Arrow War

1850–1864 Taiping Rebellion

1894–1895 Sino-Japanese War

1898 100 Days of Reform

1900 Boxer Rebellion

1911 Chinese Revolution

1912 Formation of Chinese Republic

1915 Japan's 21 Demands on China

Chinoiserie An eighteenth- and nineteenth-century Western vogue for Chinese painting, ceramics, lacquerware, and decorative furniture.

Co-hong A nineteenth-century Chinese merchant's guild that had a monopoly on Guangzhou's trade with the West.

The Opium Trade and War

Half a century after Emperor Qianlong blithely dismissed the British request, the tables were turned. Two wars in the mid-1800s, in which Qing China suffered humiliating defeats, forcibly jarred the Chinese from their complacency and made clear that the world was changing. The British badly wanted more Chinese silk and tea, which had become valued revenue sources for British merchants. But China, desiring little from the West, accepted only precious gold and silver bullion as payment. Between the 1760s and 1780s the import of silver into China increased over 500 percent, presenting a serious balance of payments problem for Western economies. Seeking a marketable product that would solve this unfavorable trade disparity, the British found it in opium, an addictive drug that was grown in India and the Middle East.

The Chinese had used opium as a painkiller since the 1600s and then discovered that they could smoke opium for pleasure by mixing it in a pipe with tobacco. By the later 1700s opium dens, where people could buy and use opium, began to appear. The drug gave users a dreamy, relaxed experience that temporarily relieved boredom, stress, physical pain, and depression. Opium

Photograph Courtesy Peabody Essex Museum, E79708 View of Guangzhou ca. 1800

Guangzhou During the eighteenth century, the Western traders in China were restricted to one riverside district in Guangzhou (Canton), where they built their warehouses, businesses, and homes in European style.

Primary Source: Letter to Queen Victoria, 1839 On behalf of the emperor, Lin Zexu implores Queen Victoria to halt the British opium trade in China.

appealed to bored officials, wealthy women cooped up at home, busy clerks, anxious merchants, nervous soldiers, and overworked peasants. Highly addictive, it also produced severe withdrawal symptoms such as cramps and nausea.

The British, who began to grow opium as a cash crop in Bengal, soon found foreign markets around Asia. In fact, the sale of opium, chiefly obtained from the British, became an important revenue source for all the European colonial governments in Southeast Asia. As British and American traders began smuggling opium into China, reaping huge profits, they were indifferent to the terrible moral and social consequences of their enterprise. Between 1800 and 1838 opium imports to China increased sixfold, and 5 to 10 million Chinese became addicts. As the opium trade undermined Chinese society and impoverished families, one Chinese official concluded that "opium is nothing else but a flowing poison [which] utterly ruins the minds and morals of the people, a dreadful calamity."[4] Another argued that opium smokers should be strangled and the pushers and producers beheaded.

Repressing the Opium Trade

After the Qing emperor issued decrees forbidding the marketing, smuggling, and consumption of opium, British, American, and other Western traders were forced officially to trade through the Co-hong merchant's guild in Guangzhou. But the British found that officials could be bribed to overlook opium smuggling. The British doubled opium imports during the 1830s while also pressing for reform of the trading system. Chinese leaders responded by further isolating the Western traders and attacking the opium trade. The emperor appointed the mandarin Lin Zexu **(lin tsay-shoe)** (1785–1850) to go to Guangzhou and end the opium trade. Lin, an incorruptible Confucian moralist, wrote to Britain's Queen Victoria: "Suppose there were people from another country who carried opium for sale to England and seduced your people into buying and smoking it. Certainly you would be bitterly aroused."[5] Lin ordered his officials to raid the Western settlement, where they seized and destroyed 20,000 chests of opium worth millions of dollars.

Opium War

Lin's seizure of opium outraged Western traders, and Britain declared war. In the Opium War (1839–1842), as the British called it, the British fleet raided up and down the Chinese coast, blockading and bombarding ports, including Guangzhou. The Chinese fought back, often resisting against hopeless odds, but they lacked the weapons to triumph. Although China had formidable military forces in 1600, Europeans had now greatly surpassed China in naval and military technology. A few alarmed officials were concerned with the inadequacy of Chinese military technology. Lin Zezu wrote to a friend that China badly needed ships and guns like the British had, but most officials rejected such ideas, detesting the British and remaining scornful of all things Western. Average Chinese reacted with rage. One placard in Canton in 1841 was addressed to "rebellious barbarian dogs. If we do not completely exterminate you we will not be manly Chinese able to support the sky over our heads. We are definitely going to kill you, cut your heads off, and burn your bodies in the trash."[6]

Treaty of Nanjing

When the British prepared to blow down the walls of the major city of Nanjing, the Qing were forced to negotiate for peace, and in 1842 they signed the Treaty of Nanjing, the first of a series of humiliatingly unequal treaties that nibbled away at Chinese sovereignty. The treaty gave Britain permanent possession of Hong Kong, a sparsely populated coastal island downriver from Guangzhou; opened five ports to British trade; abolished the Co-hong and its trade monopoly; set fixed tariffs so that China no longer controlled its economic policy; and gave the British **extraterrito-**

extraterritoriality Freedom from local laws for foreign subjects.

riality, or freedom from local laws. The Chinese were also forced to pay Britain the war costs. Soon other Western countries signed treaties with China that gave them the same rights as the British. Each successive treaty expanded foreign privileges. The Opium War became to the Chinese a permanent symbol of Western imperialism.

The Treaty System and Rebellion

Unequal Treaties

The debacle of the Opium War soon led to other wars, a treaty system that opened China to the West, and rebellions. The British remained dissatisfied with the amount of trade, and the Chinese sought to evade their obligations, ensuring that another conflict would develop. China had imprisoned some Chinese sailors for suspected piracy aboard a Chinese ship, *The Arrow*, registered in Hong Kong, giving Britain a pretext to attack China and generating the Arrow War (1856–1860). France also entered the war. China was again defeated and forced to sign a new unequal treaty that opened more coastal and interior ports to Western traders, established foreign embassies in Beijing, and permitted Christian missionaries to enter the Chinese interior. Again forced to pay the war costs, China fell deeper into debt. It was also forced to give up its claim to Vietnam, a longtime vassal state being colonized by France, and to acquiesce in the Russian takeover of eastern Siberia.

By restricting control of China's economy and power to make rules for Western residents, the treaty system deprived China of some of its autonomy. It also led to **international settlements**, zones in major Chinese port cities, such as Guangzhou and Shanghai, that were set aside for foreigners and in which most Chinese were not allowed. For example, a small island on the riverfront adjacent to downtown Guangzhou, and accessible only by a footbridge, became the home of Western merchants, officials, and missionaries. It boasted mansions, warehouses, clubs, and churches built by and serving the largely British, American, and French population. Chinese were clearly unwelcome except as servants and businessmen.

international settlements Special zones in major Chinese cities set aside for foreigners, where most Chinese were not allowed; arose as a result of China's defeat in the Opium and Arrow Wars.

China's Challenges

The Opium and Arrow Wars and the treaty system forced the Chinese to debate how best to respond to the new dangers. Some Chinese officials understood the need for China to learn from the West, to examine Western books, build modern ships and guns, and study science, mathematics, and foreign languages. These views influenced the provincial official and reformer Zeng Guofan (zung gwoh-FAN) (1811–1872), who recommended making modern weapons and steamships. But, failing to see the magnitude of the challenges, few mandarins showed interest, one conservative rejecting Western knowledge as based largely on earlier Chinese discoveries.

While scholars debated, China's problems multiplied, especially in the coastal provinces. To pay for the wars, the government had to raise taxes, causing many peasants to lose their land, and some turned to begging or banditry. Natural disasters also demoralized the country. Between 1800 and 1850 the Yellow River flooded twenty times and then changed course, wiping out hundreds of towns and villages. Western cultural influence increased, as Christian missionaries from the United States and Britain opened most of China's Western-type schools and hospitals, providing educational and health benefits to those Chinese who had access to them. By the 1920s there were 2,500 American missionaries in China and thirteen American-operated colleges. However, Christian missionaries, who often lived well and were protected by Western military power, challenged Chinese religions and provoked negative opinions. Western residents, often ethnocentric and seeing themselves as representing a superior Western civilization, tended to view the Chinese as depraved heathens and mocked their culture. Chinese generally distrusted the several hundred thousand Chinese who became Christian.

Taiping Rebellion

Deteriorating conditions eventually generated the Taiping Rebellion (1850–1864), the most critical of several midcentury upheavals against the Qing (see Map 23.1). Guangdong (GWAHNG-dong) province, on the southeast coast, experienced particularly severe social and economic dislocations that increased popular unrest. Many peasant families had no food surplus and were reduced to eating the chaff of the wheat. The rebellion was fueled by economic insecurity, famine, loss of faith in government, and a desire for social change. The leader, Hong Xiuquan (hoong shee-OH-chew-an) (1813–1864), who had failed to pass the civil service examinations and had also studied with Christian missionaries, believed that God had appointed him the new Son of Heaven to exterminate evil. Impressed by Western military power but also proudly Chinese, Hong preached a doctrine blending Christianity and Chinese thought, a mixing of local and Western ideas that was typical in Asia and Africa as a response to Western disruption.

Hong promoted a new form of government, equal distribution of goods, communal property, and equality between men and women. The puritanical Hong also prohibited opium use, polygamy, footbinding, prostitution, concubinage, and arranged marriages. He established a sect, the

Taipings (Heavenly Kingdom of Great Peace), that rejected Confucian traditions and envisioned a God-oriented utopia where all people would be equal. Many of the Taiping men and women were, like Hong himself, Hakkas, a dialect group in south China whose assertive women never bound their feet. Hong organized an army and in 1850 launched a rebellion, invoking Chinese nationalism: "We raise the army of righteousness to liberate the masses for the sake of China."[7] Soon he had attracted millions of supporters from among the poor and disaffected.

Taiping Defeat

Taiping armies conquered large parts of central and southern China, but the Taipings suffered from leadership conflicts, and their hostility to traditional Chinese culture cost them popular support. Conservative Confucians disliked the Taipings' espousal of women's rights, which threatened the patriarchal family system, and intellectuals accused them of opening China to Westernization. Thus most of the educated elite rallied to the Qing and organized provincial armies to oppose the Taipings. Westerners often sympathized with the progressive Taiping social message but knew that a weak Manchu government meant more Western ability to continue exploiting China. Hence, various Western nations aided the Qing with money, arms, mercenary soldiers, and military advisers. The Taipings were defeated, and the process of dynastic renewal was aborted. The conflict left

Map 23.1 Conflicts in Qing China, 1839–1870

During the mid-1800s Qing China experienced repeated unrest, including several major rebellions. The largest and most destructive, the Taiping Rebellion, engulfed a large part of southern and central China between 1850 and 1864.

Interactive Map

China in shambles, with provinces devastated and 20 million Chinese killed. An American missionary described the destruction: "Ruined cities, desolated towns and heaps of rubble still mark their path. The hum of busy populations had ceased and weeds and jungle cover the land."[8] The Qing were now deeper in debt to the West and compelled to adopt even more conciliatory attitudes.

Economic Change and Emigration

Western Economic Influence

China's encounters with the West generated several economic changes. The extension of Western businesses into the interior stimulated the growth of the Chinese merchant class and small-scale Chinese-owned industries, such as match factories and flour mills, but the merchants disliked Western economic domination and the weak Qing government. Gradually a new working class formed that labored in mines, factories, railways, and docks. The gulf between peasants in the interior and the merchants and workers in the coastal cities was vast. The unequal treaties enabled Western economic penetration into China, and China's economy became increasingly geared to Western needs. Westerners often ran Qing government agencies, banks, railroads, factories, and mines and guarded them with Western police. By 1920 foreign companies controlled most of China's iron ore, coal, railroads, and steamships, and Western businessmen became inspired by the notion of the vast China market. One U.S. firm launched an advertising campaign to put a cigarette in the mouth of every Chinese man, woman, and child. Finally, women were harmed by imported British textiles, which frequently displaced Chinese women from textile production. Although women continued to weave, they earned lower incomes than before.

Some scholars view Western economic imperialism as a spur to the growth of China's domestic economy. Others argue that Western competition ruined Chinese industries such as cotton spinning and iron and steel production, hurting China's ability to compete with the West. Western businesses succeeded because they had greater capital and the support of Western governments and military power. China's traditional exports also declined because of competition with other Asian countries. By 1900 India and Sri Lanka had become the world's largest producers of tea and Japan the largest producer of silk. The Qing, already deeply in debt, had little money left for building China's economic institutions.

Chinese Emigration

From the 1840s through the 1920s, deteriorating economic, social, and political conditions in hard-hit coastal provinces, combined with natural disasters, prompted millions of Chinese to

Courtesy, Daniel Wolf Collection, NY

Rattan Factory in Guangzhou This photo, taken around 1875, shows Chinese men and women workers, mostly of peasant background, in a factory making rattan, along with the factory's European owners.

emigrate, usually to places where Western colonialism and capitalism were opening new economic opportunities. Several hundred thousand people a year left from southern ports, usually headed for Southeast Asia but, in many cases, bound for Pacific islands such as Hawaii and Tahiti or for Australia, Peru, Cuba, North America, and South Africa (see Chapters 20 and 22). The Chinese emigrants who joined or opened businesses in these new countries formed the basis for local middle-class Chinese communities. But many left China as part of the notorious "coolie trade." Under this labor system, desperate Chinese were recruited or coerced to become indentured workers in faraway places, signing contracts that required them to labor for years in harsh conditions on plantations or in mines or to build railroads.

Chinese Diaspora

As a result of this emigration, the societies where Chinese settled, especially in Southeast Asia, became more closely connected to China through economic and social networks than ever before. Chinese businesses overseas often had branches in China, and families in China maintained ties to family members abroad. While Chinese emigrants often returned to their native villages with wealth earned abroad, others never earned enough money to return to China, and many settled permanently abroad. The emigrants and their descendants, while often sustaining Chinese culture and language, often mixed Chinese and local customs. Today some 30 million people of Chinese ancestry live outside of China, the large majority in Southeast Asia. Some finance businesses, industries, and educational institutions in China.

SECTION SUMMARY

- In the eighteenth century, Qing China was still thriving on the strength of its agriculture, trade, and manufacturing, but its rapidly growing population began to intensify internal problems such as poverty and corruption.
- In the nineteenth century, China faced increasing problems as well as pressure from Westerners for greater trade opportunities, but the Qing refused to allow an open trading system, thus creating a severe trade imbalance between the West and the East.
- To solve this imbalance, the British began smuggling opium into China, and when China resisted the British defeated China in the Opium War and forced the Chinese to agree to highly unfavorable terms that allowed the British to trade in China.
- After another war, China was forced to set aside special areas exclusively for Westerners, called international settlements, and to also allow Christian missionaries into the country.
- Economic insecurity, famine, and Western interference eventually led to the Taiping Rebellion, a widespread and devastating revolt that was ultimately put down by the Qing with help from Western powers.
- China's economy was increasingly penetrated and transformed by Western powers, and millions of Chinese emigrated throughout the world, some to be indentured workers and others to go into business.

FROM IMPERIAL TO REPUBLICAN CHINA

Why did Chinese efforts at modernization fail?

The rebellions, government stagnation, poverty, and growing Western demands brought about a crisis for the Qing. Some Chinese still concluded that China should reaffirm its traditional ways and reject the West. But just as for centuries China had absorbed invaders to survive, a growing number of reformers wanted to adapt useful Western technologies to Chinese ways. As challenges and setbacks mounted, some gave up on reform and organized revolutionary movements. Eventually revolutionaries overthrew the imperial system, but these developments did not solve China's problems.

Chinese Debates and New Challenges

Conservatives and Liberals

China's elite divided over how much China should modernize its society. The conservatives, who dominated the bureaucracy, advised that China hold fast to Confucian traditions. Believing China could learn nothing from Westerners, they opposed railroads, underground mines, and other innovations because these disrupted the harmony between humanity and nature and put boatmen and cart drivers out of work. One conservative wrote that it was "better to see the nation die than its way of life change."[9] Conservatives believed that new technologies inevitably undermined social, economic, and even political values. Liberals, believing China had to adopt certain Western ideas to survive, sponsored impressive government innovations. They streamlined central and regional governments, set up a foreign ministry, formed a college to train diplomats, and sent some students to schools in the West, especially to the United States. A few argued that Confucius favored democracy and gender equality. Few liberals, however, wanted radical transformation, preferring to simply graft on some technological innovations. To most reformers, Western ideas such as political democracy and nationalism were too foreign to easily adapt to China's family-centered society. As one noted, "China should acquire the West's superiority in arms and machinery, but retain China's superiority in Confucian virtue."[10]

Self-Strengtheners

Meanwhile, reformers in the provinces, calling themselves "self strengtheners," aimed to strengthen China by building arsenals and shipyards. By 1894 China had a better-trained army and sixty-five warships. But this was still insufficient against a fully industrialized enemy. The reforms also failed to save the Qing because the technological innovations generated new problems. The new warships required coal to make steam to power them, which meant improving coal-mining technology. Railroads had to be built to move the coal, and they in turn required telegraphs to communicate train movements. Training workers for these new enterprises required technical schools. In addition, the new working class did not fit into Confucian social categories, which divided society into scholars, peasants, artisans, and merchants. China also employed Western advisers to help set up and run the new industries and government departments. But the new enterprises were often poorly run. The innovations were also expensive, further complicating the economic problems of a Chinese government financing a growing debt to Western nations and banks.

Empress Dowager

China's problems grew less manageable. China was too large, overpopulated, and saddled with a poorly led, bureaucratic, and overly conservative government. From 1861 to 1908 the Empress Dowager Ci Xi **(zoo shee)** (1835–1908), a concubine of the old emperor who had become the regent of the new child emperor, dominated the imperial government. Forceful and intelligent, she was also covetous and irresponsible. She diverted money intended to build a modern navy to construct the magnificent Summer Palace, just outside Beijing, for her imperial retreat. China's inability to deflect the growing challenges fostered escapism among many thoughtful Chinese, expressed by a poet official: "I'll drink myself merry, Thrash out a wild song from my lute, And let the storms rage at will."[11]

Peter Newark's Military Pictures

Chinese Study Maxim Gun After the Taiping Rebellion, the Qing emperor sent two Chinese mandarins to England to examine and purchase new weapons. In this photo, they examine a Maxim gun, one of the first machine guns that gave Western nations a great military advantage.

China and the West

In addition to these problems, foreign economic and political pressures placed constraints on what China could accomplish, putting Chinese leaders into a siege mentality. By the late 1800s Western gunboats patrolled China's rivers, international settlements existed in the major cities, Christian missionaries challenged Chinese values, and Westerners influenced the imperial government and the economy. Some foreign powers dominated particular regions as spheres of influence, such as Britain in Guangdong and the Germans in Shandong, acquiring resources, establishing enterprises, and manipulating local governments.

gunboat diplomacy The Western countries' use of superior firepower to impose their will on local populations and governments in the nineteenth century.

The United States, Britain, France, and Germany exercised power over China through **gunboat diplomacy**, the use of superior firepower to impose a country's will on local populations and governments. Western gunboats patrolled some of China's rivers and seacoasts in the late 1800s and early 1900s, interceding to protect Western businessmen, missionaries, and diplomats whose activities generated Chinese hostility. A notorious U.S. naval force, the Yangzi Patrol, comprising shallow-draft gunboats, destroyers, and cruisers, patrolled the hundreds of miles of the Yangzi River in order "to make every American feel perfectly safe in coming to live or to transact business, until such time as the Chinese themselves are able to afford these guarantees."[12] Sovereign Chinese rights and the people's outrage at foreign intrusion counted for little. Americans also promoted free trade, generously funded Christian missionaries, and donated to humanitarian causes such as flood relief and orphanages. Yet China never became a full Western colony such as India or Vietnam, perhaps because too many foreign powers were involved. The United States discouraged full colonization by promoting an "Open Door" policy that allowed equal access by all the foreign powers to China's vast markets and resources. The Open Door enabled the industrialized nations to avoid conflict and acquire wealth without the high political and military costs of conquering and governing China.

Wars, Reforms, and Nationalism

New Conflicts

The growing foreign challenge soon included rapidly industrializing Japan. In search of resources and markets, in the 1890s Japan began intervening in Korea, long a vassal state of China. The Koreans pleaded for help from China, and the resulting Sino-Japanese War (1894–1895) ended in a humiliating Chinese defeat. China was forced to pay an indemnity to Japan and to recognize Korean independence, and in 1910 Korea became a Japanese colony. The Qing were also forced to cede the large island of Taiwan, populated largely by Chinese, to Japan. The Manchus had already lost influence over other tributary states, such as Vietnam (to France) and Burma (to Britain). The defeat by Japan proved a blow to Chinese pride and to the credibility of the Qing rulers.

These crises brought a group of progressive reformers to the attention of the young Manchu emperor, Guangxu, and in 1898 he called for dramatic changes, later known as the 100 Days of Reform, including a crash program of economic modernization. But the Empress Dowager Xi Ci and her conservative allies blocked the proposals, arrested the reformers, placed the emperor under house arrest, promoted an antiforeign atmosphere, and encouraged the Chinese to organize antiforeign militias. The ensuing tensions led to the Boxer Rebellion, a popular movement in 1900 that aimed to drive the foreigners out of China but resulted in an even stronger Western presence. The Qing strongly backed the Boxers ("Righteous Harmony Fists"), an anti-Western, anti-Christian secret society comprising mostly poor peasants. While the Boxers attacked foreigners in north China, occupied Beijing, and besieged the foreign embassies, the Qing declared war on the foreign powers. In response, the British, Americans, and French organized an international force that routed the Boxers, occupied Beijing, and forced the Qing to pay another huge indemnity and to permit foreign military forces to stay in China. The Europeans talked openly of dismantling China, and the Russians used the rebellion as an excuse to occupy Manchuria.

Reformist Efforts

The string of defeats generated final frantic efforts at reform and modernization, setting the stage for more dramatic transitions. Fearing China might soon be divided into colonies, the chastened Manchus now looked to Japan for models. They abolished the 2,000-year-old Confucian examination system, set up modern, Western-style schools, and sent 10,000 students to Japan. But the 57,000 state schools enrolled only a fraction of China's school-age children. The Qing also allocated more money to the military and strengthened provincial governments.

Reformist ideas also sparked movements among women. Some women studying in Japan formed the Encompassing Love Society, with the goal of making Chinese women full participants in society. Other women worked to raise female literacy and expand economic opportunities. The feminist Qin Jin **(chin jin)** (1877–1907) left her arranged marriage for study in Japan and then started a women's magazine and pursued political activity. Later she was executed as a revolutionary. She wrote in a poem, "Our women's world is sunk so deep, who can help us? Unbinding my feet I clear out a thousand years of poison."[13] She expressed the hope that one day China would see free women "blooming like fields of flowers."

Liberals who had criticized the Qing reformers for going too slowly now became more influential. Many reformers had read and even translated European literature and scholarship and were deeply impressed by Japan's modernization. The leading liberal reformer, Liang Qichao **(Li-ANG chi-CHAO)** (1871–1929), a scholar and journalist, promoted a modernization that blended Confucian values and Western learning. He also believed China should industrialize, form a constitutional government, and focus on the idea of nation instead of culture. Liang's colleague, Kang Youwei **(KANG yoo-WAY)** (1858–1928), envisioned a world government, the end of nationalist strife and gender discrimination, and a welfare state. He also began a movement against footbinding, the long-time Chinese practice that severely hampered women; as a song passed among illiterate women put it, "Your body is so heavy a burden for your feet that you fear you may stumble in the wind."[14]

Sun Yat-Sen and Nationalism

For some Chinese inspired by nationalism, most importantly Sun Zhong Shan, better known as Sun Yat-Sen **(soon yot-SEN)**, the fiasco of the Boxer Rebellion showed the futility of trying to change China by reform from above and prompted them to organize a revolution from below. Sun (1866–1925) mixed tradition and modernity. Unlike the liberal reformers such as Liang and Kang, Sun did not come from an upper-class mandarin background and had no commitment to the traditional system. He identified with the poor and downtrodden. Born near Guangzhou to a peasant family that had supported the Taipings, Sun moved to Hawaii at age thirteen to join an elder brother. There he studied in an Anglican high school and became a semi-Christian. He then received a medical degree in British-ruled Hong Kong. He began dressing in Western clothes and visited England, where he learned that Westerners often criticized their own systems.

Convinced that the Qing system was hopeless, Sun decided to devote his life to politics and became the chief architect of the Chinese Revolution. In 1895 he founded a secret society dedicated to replacing the imperial system with a Western-style republic, setting up branches in China, Japan, and Hawaii (see Witness to the Past: Planning a Revolutionary New China). Facing arrest in China for treason, Sun traveled extensively, recruiting support among Chinese merchants in Southeast Asia, North America, and the treaty ports; Chinese students in Japan; and sympathetic military officers. Sun and his followers thought of themselves as nationalists, more interested in China as a nation than as a culture.

Sun's Program

Sun also began to develop his program, which he termed the "Three Principles of the People." The first principle, nationalism, involved overthrowing the Manchus, restoring ethnic Chinese to power, and reclaiming China's historical greatness. His second principle, republicanism, proposed a constitutional democracy with an elected representative government rather than the constitutional monarchy sought by the liberal reformers. The third principle, people's livelihood, envisioned an equitable economic status for all. Sun was vague on the details but favored partial state control of the economy and the reshaping of China into a modern, wealthy, powerful nation. Sun did not necessarily want to imitate Europe and the United States, but eventually the day would come, he hoped, when the Chinese could look over their shoulder and find the West lagging far behind.

Chinese Revolution and Republic

Outbreak of Revolution

Sun was traveling in the United States raising money for his cause when, on October 10, 1911, some of his followers began the uprising. Soldiers in the Yangzi River city of Wuhan **(WOO-HAHN)** mutinied and were soon joined by sympathizers in other cities. Within two months the revolutionary soldiers controlled provinces in central and southern China. As Qing authority quickly crumbled outside the north, Sun returned to China for the first time in sixteen years. The revolution had wide popular support, and Sun's nationalist message spread rapidly, especially among students, military officers, and Chinese in the treaty ports. Sun now reorganized his anti-Manchu secret society into a political party, the Guomindang **(gwo-min-dong)** (Chinese Nationalist Party), which gathered together varied nationalists and liberal reformers. However, Sun was not a forceful leader, and the revolutionaries could agree only on opposing the Manchus. Meanwhile, from Beijing, the Manchus asked an ambitious general, Yuan Shikai **(yoo-AHN shee-KAI)** (1859–1916), to deal with the revolutionaries. In control of a large army, Yuan decided to replace the dynasty with his own rule by playing the Manchus off against the revolutionaries.

Two centers of power now existed. While General Yuan held the dominant position in the north and influence over the Qing leaders, the revolutionaries, who controlled the Yangzi Valley and parts of south China, made plans to establish a provisional government. Sun sought a compromise to save China from civil war, offering to make Yuan president if Yuan arranged for the abdication of

Planning a Revolutionary New China

In 1905 various radical Chinese groups met in Japan and merged into one revolutionary organization, the *Tongmen Hui* (Chinese Alliance Association), led by Sun Yat-Sen, then based in Tokyo. Most of the members were drawn from among the 10,000 Chinese students enrolled in Japanese universities. Unhappy with the Qing government and impressed by modernizing Japan, they sought to change China through revolution. In their founding proclamation, which was influenced by Western thought, they set out their agenda, visionary but vague, for a three-stage passage from military to constitutional government and a more equitable society.

Since the beginning of China as a nation, we Chinese have governed our own country despite occasional interruptions. When China was occasionally occupied by a foreign race, our ancestors could always . . . drive these foreigners out . . . and preserve China for future generations. . . . There is a difference, however, between our revolution and the revolutions of our ancestors. The purpose of past revolutions . . . was to restore China to the Chinese, and nothing else. We, on the other hand, strive not only to expel the ruling aliens [Manchus] . . . but also to change basically the political and economic structure of our country. . . . The revolutions of yesterday were revolutions by and for the heroes; our revolution, on the other hand, is a revolution by and for the people. . . . everyone who believes in the principles of liberty, equality, and fraternity has an obligation to participate in it. . . .

At this juncture we wish to express candidly and fully how to make our revolution today and how to govern the country tomorrow.

1. Expulsion of the Manchus from China. . . . We shall quickly overthrow the Manchu government so as to restore the sovereignty of China to the Chinese.
2. Restoration of China to the Chinese. China belongs to the Chinese who have the right to govern themselves. . . .
3. Establishment of a Republic. Since one of the principles of our revolution is equality, we intend to establish a republic. . . . all citizens will have the right to participate in the government, the president of the republic will be elected by the people, and the parliament will have deputies elected by and responsible to their respective constituencies. . . .
4. Equalization of land ownership. The social and economic structure of China must be so reconstructed that the fruits of labor will be shared by all Chinese on an equal basis. . . .

To attain the four goals . . . , we propose a procedure of three stages. The first . . . is that of military rule . . . [in which] the Military Government, in cooperation with the people, will eradicate all the abuses of the past; with the arrival of the second stage the Military Government will hand over local administration to the people while reserving for itself the right of jurisdiction over all matters that concern the nation as a whole; during the . . . final stage the Military Government will cease to exist and all governmental power will be invested in organs as prescribed in a national constitution. This orderly procedure is necessary because our people need time to acquaint themselves with the idea of liberty and equality . . . , the basis on which the republic of China rests. . . . On . . . restoring China to her own people, we urge everyone to step forward and to do the best he can. . . . Whatever our station in society is, rich or poor, we are all equal in our determination to safeguard the security of China as a nation and to preserve the Chinese people.

THINKING ABOUT THE READING

1. How does the proclamation use Western revolutionary and nationalist ideas?
2. How will revolution build a new China?

Source: Pei-Kai Cheng and Michael Lestz with Jonathan D. Spence, eds., *The Search for Modern China: A Documentary Collection* (New York: W.W. Norton, 1999), 202–206.

Republican Government

the five-year-old Qing emperor. In February 1912 the Qing dynasty, and with it the 2,000-year-old imperial system, was ended, and a republic was established in Nanjing. Symbolizing a change of direction, the new government adopted the Western calendar. But Sun had underestimated Yuan's ambitions. Hoping to restore an autocratic system with himself at the top, Yuan moved the capital back to Beijing.

During the first year, the republic's leaders established liberal institutions, including a constitution written by Sun that provided for a two-chamber parliament and a president, and in 1913, in the first general election in China's long history, a restricted electorate chose a national assembly and provincial assemblies. A new women's suffrage movement, influenced by its counterparts in Europe, also pressed for equal rights for women. But although Sun's Guomindang won a majority of seats in the election, it lacked a consensus about the directions of change, and the republican system failed to bring stability and liberty, dashing Sun's hopes. Convinced that China needed a strong leader, Yuan had Guomindang leaders assassinated, bought off, or, in Sun's case, forced into exile. Supported by much of the army, the imperial bureaucracy, and the foreign powers, who preferred a strongman to the democratic uncertainties of Sun, Yuan soon outlawed the Guomindang, suspended parliament, and banned the women's suffrage movement. Sun and his closest followers moved to Japan, embittered and demoralized, and Yuan became increasingly autocratic and announced plans to found a new dynasty.

New Challenges

Yuan's plans, however, were put on hold by financial problems, constant pressure from foreign powers, and the secession of regions occupied largely by non-Chinese. Although growing nationalism made concessions to foreign powers unpopular, China was bankrupt, and Yuan was forced to borrow heavily from foreign governments to keep the country afloat. In 1911 much of Mongolia declared independence and later became allied with Russia. Tibet also expelled the Chinese administration. Although China remained neutral during World War I, Japan, allied with Britain, occupied the German sphere of influence in the Shandong peninsula. Then in 1915 Japan presented Yuan with 21 Demands, including control of Shandong, more rights in Manchuria, and the appointment of Japanese advisers to the Chinese government. The 21 Demands set off huge Chinese protests and boycotts against Japan and Yuan's inability to protect China's interests. His imperial restoration plans aborted, a humiliated Yuan died in 1916. Yuan's years in power had wrecked the republican institutions, and his submission to Japan's 21 Demands suggested that China was even weaker than before. After Yuan's death, China fell into the abyss of prolonged civil war.

SECTION SUMMARY

- In the debate over what China should do next, conservatives thought China should stick to its traditions, while liberals tried to modernize China, but their reforms failed to bring it to the technological and military level of the West.
- By the late 1800s, China's autonomy had been all but eliminated by gunboat diplomacy, under which Western powers ensured the safety of Westerners in China through the use of force.
- After China lost its influence over Korea in the Sino-Japanese War and the Boxer Rebellion failed to rid China of foreigners, liberals moved to modernize and Westernize Chinese education and culture.
- Sun Yat-Sen, born to Chinese peasants but educated in Western schools, formed a secret society devoted to replacing imperial rule with a Western-style republic and set out three principles: nationalism, republicanism, and economic equality.
- A revolution inspired by Sun Yat-Sen succeeded in toppling the Qing dynasty with the assistance of General Yuan Shikai.
- Yuan seized power after Sun Yat-Sen's party won the republic's first election, but he was weakened by Japanese encroachment and the loss of influence over areas such as Mongolia and Tibet, and after his death China entered a period of civil war.

The Remaking of Japan and Korea

How did the Meiji government transform Japan and Korea?

In the later nineteenth century Japan met the Western challenge more successfully than China, rapidly transforming itself into a powerful industrialized nation. Despite serious internal problems, Japan possessed significant strengths that fostered success. The shoguns, military dictators from the Tokugawa family, had governed Japan since 1600 and tightly controlled Japanese society (see Chronology: Japan and Korea, 1750–1914). When the first Western ships arrived demanding to open Japan, the Japanese, largely shut off from the outside world, were just as far behind the West in military and industrial technology as other Asian societies. Yet, the ultimate Japanese response to Western intrusion was radically different from China's, allowing Japan to avoid the shackles of colonialism and become the only non-Western nation to successfully industrialize before World War II. This transition owed much to a revolution that ended Tokugawa rule and created a new government that fostered dramatic reforms that helped Japan resist the West. Across the straits, Korea had also chosen a seclusion policy, and it, too, faced severe challenges, eventually becoming a Japanese colony.

Late Tokugawa Japan

Japanese-Chinese Contrasts

Like China, Japan faced foreign pressures that led to change, but Japan successfully met the challenge of the Western intrusion while China, failing to rally, gradually lost some of its autonomy. The differences between these two ancient neighbors help explain the different outcomes. Japan,

CHRONOLOGY
Japan and Korea, 1750–1914

1392–1910 Yi dynasty in Korea

1600–1867 Tokugawa Shogunate

1853 Opening of Japan by Perry

1854 Treaty of Kanagawa

1867–1868 Meiji Restoration

1894–1895 Sino-Japanese War

1904–1905 Russo-Japanese War

1910 Japanese colonization of Korea and Taiwan

being geographically compact and linguistically homogeneous, had a strong loyalty to the emperor as a national symbol, whereas China's vastness created difficulties, and Chinese loyalties were restricted largely to the family. While new ideas, such as Buddhism, reached China over the centuries, their assimilation was a slow process, whereas Japan had a long tradition of readily borrowing from outside. Hence, Japanese leaders could more easily decide to import and adopt new ideas, technologies, and institutions.

The two neighbors also differed in economic, political, and military systems. The Japanese merchant class was assertive and rapidly expanding its scope and power, whereas in China the government restricted commercial energies. In contrast to China's centralized empire, the Tokugawa shoguns, based in Edo (today's Tokyo), had to balance the interests of the influential leaders (daimyo) of regional landowning families while keeping the Kyoto-based emperor powerless. Although the samurai had lost their fighting edge under the long-enforced Tokugawa peace, they still held a respected position and power in society. Never having been successfully invaded, the Japanese also felt vulnerable when they encountered the well-armed Westerners. Unlike the Chinese, they prized political independence far more than cultural purity. Thus Japanese leaders, learning of Western intentions and capabilities through the Dutch traders at the southern port of Nagasaki, were far more sensitive to the Western threat than the Chinese elite.

Japanese Borrowing

Japan also benefited from an openness to new ideas. Its many schools fostered high literacy rates, and Western knowledge acquired from Dutch traders included sciences such as medicine, physics, and chemistry. One reformer argued that "Dutch [Western] learning is not perfect, but if we choose the good points, what harm could come? What is more ridiculous than to refuse to discuss its merits?"[15] Even some women, who generally suffered a low status, gained an education. For example, the poet and painter Ema Saiko (1787–1861) compared her reading with her father's: "My father deciphers Dutch books; His daughter reads Chinese poetry. Divided by a single lamp, We each follow our own course."[16] The Japanese also valued hard work, thrift, saving, and cooperation—attributes that lent themselves to modernization. Cities such as Edo and Osaka, already among the world's largest, offered a flourishing commerce and diverse entertainments. A description of a carnival in Edo in 1865 recorded the following amusements, services, and vendors: kabuki theater, archery booths, fortunetellers, wandering balladeers, massage healers, barbershops, and peddlers of chilled water, sushi (raw fish), confectionery, stuffed fritters, dumplings, fried eel livers, toys, and lanterns.

Tokugawa Arts

Vigorous Tokugawa arts produced creations that achieved renown worldwide and were prized in the West, such as ceramics, jewelry, and furniture, enriching the Dutch traders at Nagasaki. This was also a great age for painting and woodblock prints, with the two greatest artists blending Japanese and imported art styles. Katsushika Hokusai **(HO-koo-sie)** (1760–1849) produced thousands of paintings, but he was most famous for landscape prints such as the *Thirty-six Views of Mount Fuji.* He strove to improve his craft, predicting that "by ninety I will surely have penetrated the mystery of life. At one hundred, I will have attained a magnificent level and at one hundred and ten, each dot of my work will vibrate with life."[17] Ando Hiroshige **(AN-do hir-o-SHEE-gee)** (1797–1858) concentrated on Tokyo scenes and landscapes emphasizing nature (see Profile: Ando Hiroshige, Japanese Artist). The treatment of atmosphere and light in Japanese color prints influenced the French impressionist painters of the later 1800s (see Chapter 20), especially the influential Dutch artist Vincent van Gogh. Both Japanese prints and French impressionism asked the viewer to look at an everyday scene in a new way.

Growing Problems and the Opening of Japan

Tokugawa Decline

By the early 1800s many Japanese blamed the Tokugawa for growing problems: inflation, increasing taxes, social disorder, and the gradual impoverishment of the samurai. As daimyo families, burdened with heavy expenses, had to cut samurai salaries, the samurai borrowed money from merchants to support their families. In the 1830s Japan also experienced widespread famine. The growing social tensions fostered urban riots, peasant revolts, and various plots to depose the Tokugawa shogun. Japanese officials were even more concerned about the growing Western presence in the region. They knew that Russians had been active in Siberia and the North Pacific and that British ships had sailed along Japan's coast. The shogun ordered samurai to fire on foreign ships approaching the coast, and after China's defeat in the Opium War, Japan's shocked leaders encouraged the samurai to develop more effective weapons. The Japanese considered the Westerners money-grasping barbarians who did not understand the proper rules of social

ANDO HIROSHIGE, JAPANESE ARTIST

The nineteenth-century Japanese artist Ando Hiroshige (1797–1858) gained a worldwide reputation for work that reflected a distinctly Japanese vision of landscape and urban life. His work, along with that of his four-decades-older contemporary, Katsushika Hokusai, portrayed old Japan on the eve of dramatic change, a Japan of rice fields, small shops, traveling peddlers, sedan chairs, samurai warriors, and dirt roads rather than the later Japan of factories, conglomerates, railroads, and steamships. By portraying scenery and diverse urban scenes, Hiroshige and Hokusai carried printmaking far beyond the early Tokugawa tradition, which emphasized life in the restaurants, teahouses, theaters, and bordellos of the "Floating World" entertainment districts.

Hiroshige was born into a samurai family in Edo (Tokyo) in 1797. His father was a member of the fire brigade, and the family lived at the fire station. As a child, Hiroshige learned to read, write, and master martial arts, and he also developed a talent for poetry. Like other young samurai, he probably visited the Floating World to enjoy kabuki theater and to patronize courtesans. In 1809 the twelve-year-old youngster succeeded to his father's position as a fireman. Underpaid and enjoying art more than firefighting, he began studying with several famous artists. From this time on he used the name Utagawa Hiroshige, a tribute to the Utagawa school of art in which he had been trained. Dutch traders at Nagasaki had introduced Western art to Japan, and Hiroshige probably assimilated ideas from imported Dutch etchings. Inspired by mountains, rivers, rocks, and trees, the young artist gained a working knowledge of different modes and the techniques to use in depicting them. Influenced by Hokusai's pioneering work, Hiroshige began favoring rural landscapes and Edo scenes. At the age of twenty-seven he passed on his fire brigade post to his son and pursued art full time.

Street Stalls and Tradesmen in Joruricho This print by Hiroshige portraying the street life in Edo reveals the artist's sympathy for common people, such as the peddlers, barbers, and food-sellers shown at work and their customers.

Although having much in common, Hokusai and Hiroshige had different outlooks. Hokusai's landscapes divided attention between the setting and the people in it, usually workers such as weavers, carpenters, and spinners. By contrast, Hiroshige subordinated everything to the setting, especially to the mood established by weather, season, time of day, and angle of view. Influenced by Chinese art, Hiroshige portrayed the insignificance of humans against the vastness of nature. His rain and snow scenes are marvels of mood, showing mastery of light and subtle harmony, mixing fact with imagination.

Hiroshige's art often reflected his personal experiences. In 1832, while accompanying an embassy of the Tokugawa shogun to the imperial court in Kyoto, Hiroshige gathered material for his famous work, *The 53 Stations of the Tokaido,* which depicts scenes of villages, inns, and lakes along the Tokaido (Eastern Sea Route) highway connecting Tokyo and Kyoto. Hiroshige immortalized the highway, which skirted the Pacific coast of Honshu Island, where mountains sweep down to the sea, and then traversed inland through majestic snowcapped mountains and past beautiful Lake Biwa. A continued stream of people—daimyo and their processions, couriers, monks, pilgrims, merchants, adventurers, entertainers—traveled the well-maintained Tokaido to and from the shogun's court. Stations with inns, restaurants, brothels, and bathhouses flourished as rest stops for the bustling traffic.

Since many Japanese had money to indulge in art, Hiroshige's later collections of prints sold thousands of copies, and he remained a very popular artist. Townspeople loved this art reflecting daily life or the worldly dreams of the merchant class. Hiroshige produced some 5,500 different prints, sold individually or in collections such as the *53 Stations of the Tokaido* and *One Hundred Views of Famous Places in Edo.* However, his personal life was often troubled. Hiroshige never prospered financially and was often pressed to finance his beloved nightly cup of rice wine. He married several times and sired several children. His eldest daughter's husband, known as Hiroshige II (1826–1869), continued Hiroshige's artistic tradition. At the age of sixty Hiroshige became a Buddhist monk, not an unusual step for aging Japanese men. He died at age sixty-two in 1858 of cholera during a great epidemic. On his deathbed, he discouraged his family from holding a lavish funeral by reciting an old verse: "When I die, Cremate me not nor bury me. Just lay me in the fields, to fill the belly of some starving dog."

Hiroshige was the last of the major Japanese print masters. Shortly after he died, Westerners opened up Japan, ending the secluded world that had nourished the woodblock prints and the artists who produced them. But Hiroshige prints continued to be traded around the world, giving foreigners their most vivid impressions of Japan. When Europeans imported the pictures in the late 1800s, they proved a revelation to artists looking for new ways to portray landscapes. Hence woodblock prints, born of isolation, became one of the first major cultural links between Japan and the outside world.

THINKING ABOUT THE PROFILE

1. How did Hokusai and Hiroshige's prints differ from earlier Japanese prints?
2. What do Hiroshige's life and art tell us about late Tokugawa Japan?

Note: Quotation from Julian Bicknell, *Hiroshige in Tokyo: The Floating World of Edo* (San Francisco: Pomegranate Artbooks, 1994), 50.

behavior. Samurai, vowing to fight to the death to resist Western invasion, put pressure on the shogun to deal firmly with the threat.

The Tokugawa responded with reforms at the national level, such as establishing a bureau to translate Western books and reducing the number of government officials to save money, but they failed to energize the system. Some provincial governments in the southwest attempted more daring changes, recruiting talented men to their administrations, emphasizing "Dutch studies," and even sponsoring industrial experiments, including an electric steam engine. Some samurai also learned how to cast better guns and iron suitable for making modern cannon.

Opening Japan

The need for change was made urgent by external threats that arose in the 1850s. The most dramatic attempt to break down Japanese seclusion came from the Americans. American ships had occasionally visited the Dutch base at Nagasaki to trade, and U.S. leaders also wanted Japan to protect shipwrecked sailors and provide fresh water and coal to ships making the long trip between California and China. In 1853 a fleet of eleven U.S. warships commanded by Commodore Matthew Perry sailed into Tokyo Bay and delivered a letter from the U.S. president, Millard Fillmore, to the shogun, demanding that the Japanese sign a treaty opening the country or face war when Perry returned the following year. The three U.S. steamships with the expedition shocked the Japanese with their ability to move against the wind and tide.

The shogun, more realistic than his critics, granted Perry's demands in the Treaty of Kanagawa (1854) and then accepted the blame for the nation's humiliation. The treaty opened two ports to U.S. trade and allowed for the stationing of a U.S. consul. Soon, American diplomats demanded a stronger treaty, the opening of more ports, extraterritoriality, and the admission of Christian missionaries. The shogun reluctantly agreed and soon signed similar treaties with the Dutch, British, French, and Russians. Although the changes still limited the Westerners' movement, most Japanese leaders saw Japan as the loser. As they had done earlier in China and India, Western merchants flooded the nation with cheap industrial goods to create a market and destroy the native industries. International settlements restricted to foreigners arose in major port cities, and Westerners enjoyed ever-increasing economic and legal privileges.

Government Crisis

Western encroachment provoked a government crisis and a national debate about how Japan should respond. Some Japanese believed accommodation was preferable to war and favored opening to the West. One prominent Westernizer, Fukuzawa Yukichi **(FOO-koo-ZAH-wa you-KEE-chee)** (1835–1901), traveled in the West and became a strong proponent of liberalism, rationalism, and political freedom. Another group advocated complete defiance and the use of force to expel the intruders, arguing that the Americans had dishonored and might enslave Japan. Turning against the ineffective Tokugawa shoguns but not the powerless emperor who symbolized the nation, one faction proclaimed, "Revere the Emperor, Expel the Barbarians."

Shaken, the Tokugawa government launched efforts at modernization. It established a shipbuilding industry, promoted manufacturing, hired two hundred Western teachers, sent a few Japanese students abroad, established an institute of Western studies, and expanded the study of foreign languages. The Japanese who had already become interested in Western science and technology, however, saw these innovations as too little and too late. Despite the reforms, the shogun was now widely perceived as weak. Aware of Japan's military disadvantage, the shogun always chose negotiation, even when the Westerners badly misused their power and retaliated for any attacks on Western residents. The shogun's strategy of avoiding confrontation led a respected poet to complain angrily: "You, whose ancestors in the mighty days, Roared at the skies and swept the earth, Stand now helpless to drive off wrangling foreigners—How empty your title, 'Queller of the Barbarians.'"[18] By the 1860s the Japanese seemed to be repeating the experience of China, gradually losing control of their political and economic future.

Tokugawa Defeat and the Meiji Restoration

Meiji Restoration A revolution against the Tokugawa Shogunate in Japan in 1867–1868, carried out in the name of the Meiji emperor; led to the successful modernization of Japan.

The deteriorating situation in Japan led to a revolution against the Tokugawa Shogunate, known as the **Meiji Restoration** (1867–1868) because it was carried out in the name of the emperor, whose reign name was Meiji **(MAY-gee)**. The revolution resulted from a conspiracy by progressive daimyo and younger samurai from southwestern Japan, united by their hatred of the status quo, but with varied goals. Generally pragmatic, some were avid Westernizers, others extreme nationalists. Although from privileged families, they allied with commoners, especially merchants.

As an alternative to the discredited shogun, Japanese dissidents turned to the relatively powerless Meiji emperor who lived in seclusion in Kyoto. In 1868 anti-Tokugawa leaders, backed by military force, seized the imperial palace and convinced the emperor to decree the restoration of his own rule. The decree ousted the Tokugawa family from their land and positions, opened the government to men of talent, appointed the rebels as imperial advisers, and announced that "the evil customs of the past shall be broken off. Knowledge shall be sought throughout the world."[19] The Tokugawa fought back, sparking a bloody one-year civil war. The rebel forces crushed all armed resistance.

Crash Modernization

The Meiji regime's crash modernization program lasted for thirty years. Under the new regime, Japan joined the world community and agreed to honor all treaties. As a symbolic attack on tradition, the imperial residence was moved from Kyoto to Tokyo (formerly Edo), a much larger and more dynamic city. Perceiving change as a necessary evil, the Meiji leaders pragmatically sought ways to achieve national unity, wealth, defense, and equality with the West. Although influenced by Western political and economic models, Meiji reformers also incorporated Japanese traditions in building a distinctive form of industrial society, defusing the Western threat. Despite its flaws, the Meiji system proved productive for Japan and, in recent decades, an attractive model for the rapidly industrializing nations in East and Southeast Asia.

To establish an effective governmental structure and secure popular loyalty, the Meiji leaders formed a State Council to advise and control the emperor. To defuse potential opposition, they recruited both samurais and commoners into the new bureaucracy while convincing the daimyos to give up control of their land, in exchange for generous financial settlements and often for appointment as regional governors. Many newly freed peasants moved to cities in search of manufacturing or service work. The government also employed thousands of Western advisers, teachers, and workers, who were required to train Japanese assistants to replace them when their contracts expired. By financing these programs through tax revenues, Meiji Japan did not need foreign loans, hence avoiding the debt trap that ensnared most Latin American and Middle Eastern societies as well as China.

Political Change

The new political system had some democratic trappings, but the Japanese, with no tradition of political freedom, had to invent a new word for the concept. A small group of men made most of the key decisions. Nonetheless, responding to a growing movement for more popular participation in decision making, in 1889 the Meiji leaders wrote the first constitution in Japanese history, forming a constitutional monarchy symbolically headed by the emperor. The constitution introduced an independent judiciary and a two-house parliament, elected by the 450,000 men who were taxpaying property holders, that chose members for the policy-making cabinet. Former samurai formed the first political parties, but they remained factionalized and weak as a political force.

Using the slogan "rich country, strong army," the government stressed industrial development and built railroads and telegraphs. Anxious about Western imperialism, the Japanese also built up the armed forces, including a modern navy, by drafting commoners as soldiers, once a profession

Laurie Platt Winfrey, Inc.

First Commercial Bank in Edo During the Meiji era the banking industry grew. This bank, built in Western style in Edo, was owned by the Mitsui family, which also owned large stores, breweries, factories, coal mines, and other enterprises. Mitsui was one of the major business conglomerates in Japan, with branches all over Asia.

limited to samurai. By breaking down the distinction between samurai, merchant, and peasant, the military draft promoted social leveling. Military service also fostered literacy and nationalism. Since pressure from the West gradually diminished, the Meiji leaders enjoyed more freedom of action compared with China to strengthen the nation. Japan was also a much less inviting target for the West, since it had few natural resources that could be profitably exploited. Although Westerners viewed Japan as a market for their goods, China had many more potential consumers. The various Western powers, largely preoccupied elsewhere, saw Japan mainly as a potential ally against each other.

Meiji Economy and Society

state capitalism An economic system in which the state takes a leading role in supporting business and industrial enterprises; introduced by the Meiji government in Japan.

zaibatsu The most powerful Japanese corporations that dominated the national economy beginning during the Meiji regime and that maintained an especially close relationship to the government.

In building a modern economic foundation, the Meiji created **state capitalism**, an economic system in which the state takes a leading role in supporting business and industrial enterprises and then regulates and closely monitors the economy once it is privatized. The state subsidized or purchased stock in light industries such as textiles and in heavy industries such as mines and steel mills. Sometimes it also formed new corporations that were sold to a few companies with political connections, such as Mitsui (MIT-soo-ee), a family-owned business from Tokugawa times. The most powerful corporations, the **zaibatsu**, maintained especially close ties to the government.

State capitalism and industrial growth often favored city people over the rural peasantry, and capital for industrialization was obtained by squeezing the peasants through the land tax. In exchange, the government spurred agricultural productivity by providing new seeds, improving land use, and supplying better irrigation. However, public investment favored the cities, prompting one liberal scholar to complain that "steel bridges glisten in the capital, and horse-drawn carriages run on the streets, but in the country the wooden bridges are so rotten one cannot cross them."[20]

Industrialization

The new economic structure perpetuated the traditional group orientation and social controls of Japanese society. Most Japanese identified closely with the company that employed them, and the economy flourished by exploiting Japanese workers. The government kept wages low so that scarce capital could be devoted to building factories, shipyards, and railroads, ultimately creating new jobs and fostering national wealth, but life in the Meiji era was not easy. As in the United States and Europe, the textile mills mainly employed women, half of them below the age of twenty and 15 percent younger than fourteen, chiefly recruited from rural villages. The young factory women, paid half the salary of male workers, lived in crowded, often locked dormitories and worked twelve-hour shifts, interrupted only by one half-hour meal break. Mill workers experienced high death rates from overwork, physical abuse from supervisors, and diseases such as tuberculosis caused by crowded working conditions.

Social Reforms

Meiji reforms also attacked the rigid Tokugawa class system. New laws allowed people to change occupations and travel or move freely. Losing their monopoly on military occupations, some samurai became lawyers, teachers, or journalists, while disgruntled samurai joined opposition political movements. To involve all Japanese in modernization, the regime emphasized mass education and constructed a universal school system paid for by both taxes and tuition, adopting the examination-based educational system of European nations such as Germany. It also opened technical schools and universities and dispatched students to Europe and the United States. By 1900 Japan was training its own scientists, engineers, and technicians.

Meiji policies stimulated debate about Japanese society. Some reformers blamed the patriarchal family for discouraging personal independence, while conservatives worried that the individual was replacing the family. To preserve gender roles and female obedience to men, Meiji policies promoted the idea of "Good Wife, Wise Mother" to strengthen families by having mothers stay at home with their children. Thus married women, with little income, had a low social status. Some women struggled to improve their position and change society. For example, Fukuda Hideko founded a magazine in 1907 to promote feminist and socialist thought, writing that "virtually everything [for women] is coercive and oppressive, making it imperative that we women rise up and develop our own social movement."[21]

Burakumin ("Hamlet people") A despised Japanese subgroup who traditionally performed jobs considered unclean and undignified.

But it proved difficult to completely eradicate old social prejudices. For instance, the **Burakumin** (boo-ROCK-uh-min), or "hamlet people," a poor, despised subgroup who performed jobs considered unclean and undignified, such as meat processing and leatherworking, remained subject to discrimination. Despite Meiji laws giving the Burakumin legal equality, Japanese still discouraged intermarriage with Burakumin and banned them from temples and shrines.

Westernization, Expansion, and the Meiji Legacy

Synthesizing East and West

The Japanese became acquainted with Western philosophy, social theory, economic thought, literature, and fashions, all of which influenced Japanese society. During the peak of Westernization in the 1870s, the Japanese adopted the Western calendar, added European words to the Japanese language, became familiar with chairs and couches, began eating more meat, wore leather shoes, attended fancy dress balls, carried umbrellas, sported watches, wore trousers, shook hands rather than bowed, and often married in the Western style. The Meiji also ended the prohibition on Christianity, though missionaries never converted more than a few thousand Japanese. Writers found that Western literary styles such as realism and romanticism allowed them freer expression. For example, Futabatei Shimei **(FOO-ta-BA-tay shi-MAI)** (1864–1909) wrote the first modern Japanese novels, in colloquial language rather than the highly formal language of tradition.

Many Westerners were amazed at Japan's dramatic transformation. A German doctor wrote that he felt lucky to be an eyewitness to the interesting experiment as Japan tried to make, in one great leap, the changes toward industrial society that took Europeans five centuries to complete. But in 1911 a Japanese novelist worried about a "nervous collapse" that would devastate the society as a result of cultural confusion. Japan seemed neither traditional nor Western.

By the later 1880s the mania for Western fads had abated. Hoping to keep Westernization from overwhelming Japan, the Meiji leaders carefully fostered a synthesis of old and new, reemphasizing traditional values, including ancient myths and the divinity of the emperor. Although the Japanese were never slavish imitators of the West, the dramatic changes created tensions between Japan and other nations that ultimately fostered a more imperialistic foreign policy, and some samurai advocated an invasion of Korea as a way for them to serve their nation in glory. But the Meiji leaders, fearful of antagonizing the Western powers, followed a cautious foreign policy. Nonetheless, they sponsored a vast colonization of the large northern island of Hokkaido **(ho-KIE-do)** to protect the country from potential Russian aggression.

Wars with China and Russia

Eventually Meiji Japan fought two wars (see Map 23.2). In the first one, the Sino-Japanese War (1894–1895), China and Japan battled each other over their competing influence in Korea, which Japan had long coveted for its fertile land but now also viewed as a market for Japanese products. After a smashing military victory, Japan dominated Korea as well as the Chinese island of Taiwan, and in 1910 it transformed both into colonies. Impressed, Britain forged an alliance with Japan that endured through the Meiji era. Britain's rival, Russia, had ambitions in Korea and had acquired a foothold in China's resource-rich Manchuria region, which Japan wanted to exploit. The rising tensions led to the Russo-Japanese War (1904–1905). During the conflict the Japanese seized a Russian-held Manchurian port and then destroyed the Russian fleet sent out from Europe. The Japanese victory electrified the world. A non-Western nation had defeated a major European power, giving hope to societies under Western domination and spurring Asian nationalisms. The triumph in the war further enhanced the pride of the Japanese people in their nation and confirmed that Japan had, in three decades, become a world power. Among the fruits of victory was the transfer to Japan of some Russian holdings in Manchuria and control of the southern half of Sakhalin island, off the Siberian coast.

The Meiji era, which came to an official end with the death of the Meiji emperor in 1912, had achieved stunning successes, giving Japan national security and a position as a powerful regional power. Although Japan's wealth and influence were still less than that of the major industrial powers—the United States, Britain, France, and Germany—Japan was now an industrial nation with 50 million people, on a par with countries such as Russia and Italy.

The Meiji Legacy

The Meiji changes have provoked debate. Some historians view the Meiji policies as a political and social revolution, not unlike the French Revolution in uprooting the old society. Others emphasize the longtime Japanese willingness to modify culture to strengthen the country. Some Japanese found the changes shattering, while others took them in stride. One supporter proclaimed Japan's "marvelous fortune. I feel as though in a dream and can only weep tears of joy." Another enthusiast wrote that "we are no longer ashamed to stand before the world as Japanese, known by the world."[22] But concerned that the growing military power would corrupt his country, one writer called on his people to open their eyes to the dangers ahead. His fears were realized three decades later in World War II, when Japan's conquest of an Asian and Pacific empire provoked U.S. retaliation, ultimately leading to Japanese military defeat and occupation by U.S. forces.

Map 23.2 Japanese Modernization and Expansion, 1868–1913
Japan undertook a crash modernization in the later 1800s. By 1910 its military power had increased, and it had won a war with Russia and colonized Korea, Taiwan, and Sakhalin (then known as Karafutu).

Interactive Map

Korean Transitions

Late Yi Dynasty

The last of the Korean dynasties, the Yi **(YEE)** (1392–1910), who ruled the state they called Choson **(choh-SAN)** for over five centuries, had chosen seclusion from the outside world, earning Korea the label of "the Hermit Kingdom." However, Korea still had relations with China. Korean scholars who visited China, where some met Westerners, later criticized Korea's overly rigid and inequitable social system. Yet, several strong kings in the 1700s fostered learning, printing encyclopedias and historical records. Aristocratic women wrote memoirs, diaries, and stories of court life, and even some commoners wrote stories and novels.

However, by the early 1800s Choson, like Qing China and Tokugawa Japan, began to succumb to stress. The rigid social structure crumbled as the economy and population grew, increasing pressure on the land. With Buddhism losing influence, some Koreans turned to Christianity, and although officially prohibited, a few French and Chinese Christian missionaries had illegally entered Korea. Korea also experienced recurrent famines and peasant uprisings, for which the Choson government blamed and hence persecuted Christians and Western missionaries. Korean intellectuals debated the value of Western learning, and some pushed for reforms of the traditional system. With the Yi refusing direct commercial negotiations with the West, Korean military forces drove away French and American ships seeking to open Korea to Western trade. The Yi also worried about Russian expansion in eastern Siberia. By the later 1800s Korea seemed in need of rejuvenation.

Opening Korea

In 1876, Meiji Japan, adopting the model used by the United States to open Japan, sent a naval expedition to Korea that forced the Yi government to open five ports and sign unequal treaties that gave Japan a strong role in Korea's economy, sparking changes within Korea. Impressed by Meiji modernization, the Yi government introduced reforms, such as toleration of Christianity, and signed trade agreements with Western nations. In 1886 Christians opened Korea's first modern girls' school, whose graduates later promoted women's rights. Many Korean peasants joined the Tonghak ("Eastern Learning"), a protest movement not unlike the Taipings in China that mixed Confucianism, Buddhism, Christianity, and hatred of Japan and the West. Spurred by famine, the movement grew into the nationwide Tonghak Rebellion against the Yi government in 1894. When Korea's longtime ally, China, sent in troops to help repress the rebellion, Japan responded by sending in a force and capturing the Korean capital, Seoul, holding the Yi royal family hostage. This led to the Sino-Japanese War, which resulted in a humiliating Chinese withdrawal, a stronger Japanese presence, and an end to the decrepit Yi dynasty. Some 18,000 Koreans died in fighting the Japanese.

Japanese Colonization

In 1910 Japan forcibly transformed Korea into a Japanese colony and Korea remained a heavily exploited, harshly ruled Japanese colony until 1945, enduring brutal suppression of Korean nationalism and culture, although the Japanese also increased educational opportunities and built a modern economy. The Japanese seized Korean land for Japanese companies and restricted civil liberties, and in 1919 the Japanese police brutally crushed peaceful demonstrations calling for independence, killing or injuring some 24,000 demonstrators and arresting 47,000. Resentment simmered as repressive measures, such as forcing students to speak only Japanese, increased. Some Koreans found solace in Christianity, and perhaps a fifth became Catholics or Protestants. Others turned toward Marxism and joined an underground Communist Party founded by Korean workers in China and Russia. Many Koreans, however, rejected Western ideas, believing the best strategy was to strengthen Confucianism. Japanese relations with Koreans became even more exploitative during World War II. Korean men were conscripted as soldiers and workers, and young Korean women, termed by the Japanese "comfort women," were forced to serve as sex slaves for Japanese soldiers. Even today many Koreans have a deep antipathy for Japan as a result of colonial repression and exploitation.

SECTION SUMMARY

- Japan was better able than China to deal with foreign pressures because of its compactness and homogeneity, its openness to outside ideas, its balance of power between groups of elites, its strong merchant class, and its sensitivity to the threat posed by foreigners.
- Late Tokugawa Japanese culture was vigorous, open to Western learning, and marked by thriving urban centers and ambitious artists.
- Internal decay in Japan led to riots and revolts, but officials, more concerned with external threats, embarked on reforms designed to strengthen the country and enable it to withstand pressure from Westerners. However, when faced with a choice between war and opening Japan to American trade, the Japanese shogun chose trade, which led to trade agreements with other Western nations, a flood of cheap manufactured goods, and special privileges for Westerners in Japan.
- After the Meiji Restoration, which overthrew the Tokugawa Shogunate, Japanese samurai and others frustrated with the Tokugawa Shogunate established a regime that was dedicated to making Japan open to and competitive with the rest of the world.
- The Meiji regime modernized Japan by breaking down social distinctions, pursuing industrial and military strength, and establishing a constitutional monarchy.
- The Meiji state supported and closely regulated industry, gave workers new rights to change occupation and travel freely but kept wages deliberately low, stripped samurai of their traditional privileges, and attempted to preserve traditional gender roles.
- In the late 1800s, Meiji leaders worked to balance traditional practices with newly adopted Western ones and, while there was debate over how to conduct foreign policy, Japan fought successful wars against both China and Russia.
- Historians debate whether the Meiji era was a fundamental transformation or a continuation of Japan's ability to change with the times.
- The Yi dynasty had closed Korea off from the rest of the world, earning for itself the label "the Hermit Kingdom," and when Korea experienced famine and instability in the 1800s, its leaders blamed the influence of Christian missionaries.
- Meiji Japan forced Korea to accept unequal trade agreements and, after defeating China in the Sino-Japanese War, turned Korea into a colony and ruled it extremely harshly, brutally suppressing dissent and exploiting its men and women during World War II.

Russia's Eurasian Empire

What factors explain the expansion of the Russian Empire?

Between 1750 and 1914 Russia built a vast Eurasian empire stretching 3,200 miles from the Baltic Sea to the Bering Straits, creating more intensive ties to Asian societies. Russians continued to push their frontiers across Siberia and into Central Asia and south toward the Black Sea, making Russia a hemispheric power bordering Europe, Central Asia, and the Middle East. Shaped by autocratic governments, a rural system with some resemblance to medieval feudalism, and chronic discontent, Russia played an increasing role in both Asian and European politics.

Europeanization, Despotism, and Expansionism

Russian Government

Russians had long debated whether they belonged to the European tradition or had a unique heritage; Russian politics reflected these debates. Western European influence was particularly strong during the long reign of Catherine the Great (r. 1762–1796), who carried on Peter the Great's Europeanization campaign (see Chronology: Russia and Central Asia, 1750–1914). Influenced by the Enlightenment, Catherine denounced slavery, hailed liberty, and presided over a golden age of opulence for the nobility. Wearing sumptuous gowns, the czarina gave elegant private parties and masked balls and, like many European kings, had a series of lovers, some twenty-one in all. The Russian elite copied royal France and learned French, increasing the huge gulf between them and the peasants bound to estates as serfs. Despite her liberal views, Catherine could not encourage freedom among the disgruntled common people because she needed support from the landed aristocracy. To gain their favor, she extended serfdom to Ukraine and denounced the French Revolution as irreligious and immoral. Continuing Russian expansionism, Catherine's energetic foreign policy added Poland and Finland and extended the empire south to the Black Sea, annexing the Crimean peninsula in 1783.

CHRONOLOGY
Russia and Central Asia, 1750–1914

1762–1796 Reign of Catherine the Great

1861 Emancipation of Russian serfs

1800–1870s Russian conquest of Caucasus and Turkestan

1891–1915 Building of Trans-Siberian Railroad

1904–1905 Russo-Japanese War

1905 First Russian Revolution

To maintain order and their own power, the czars who followed Catherine often relied on the brutal despotism common in Russian history. Alarmed by the social changes in western Europe, the aristocracy opposed industrialization, which they worried might upset serfdom. Czar Nicholas I (r. 1825–1855) feared alienating the aristocracy and instead suppressed the restless Poles and formed a secret police force with wide powers to harass, imprison, or eliminate opponents. Nicholas also invaded Hungary and sought dominance over the Ottomans to secure Russia's grain exports through the Black Sea to the Mediterranean. His attempts to absorb the Ottoman-held Balkans by encouraging rebellion and occupying several Ottoman provinces provoked Britain and France, leading to the bloody Crimean War of 1854, which pitted Russia against a British-French-Ottoman alliance. Armies of conscripted Russian serfs were no match for modern British and French forces, and Russia had to withdraw from Ottoman territory. Nicholas's successor, Czar Alexander II (r. 1855–1881), was more oriented to western Europe and followed a reformist domestic policy, emancipating the serfs in 1861 and decentralizing government. But many serfs were unable to pay the landowners for the lands they wanted to use, and discontent grew.

Expansion in Asia

The Russians became more engaged with Asia, expanding their power in Siberia, the Caucasus, and Central Asia to form the largest contiguous land empire in the world (see Map 23.3). In search of imperial glory, markets, and resources such as sable fur, Russia had expanded across Siberia and reached the Pacific coast in the 1600s before losing to the Chinese forces and pulling back from the fertile Amur River Basin. By the early 1800s the Russians occupied the Amur Basin and in 1860 gained official Chinese recognition of their claims in exchange for helping negotiate the end of the Arrow War. They also acquired a coastal zone on Siberia's Pacific shore, building the port city of Vladivostok ("Ruler of the East") as a base for commercial and military activity in the Pacific Basin.

For several centuries the Russians had expanded around the Black Sea, seeking an outlet to the Mediterranean Sea. Between 1800 and the 1870s they expanded their control south through the mountainous Caucasus, absorbing Armenia and Georgia, both largely Christian, as well as Muslim Azerbaijan **(az-uhr-bye-JAHN)**. Sometimes facing fierce resistance, they needed four decades to conquer the strongly Islamic Chechens **(CHECH-uhnz)**. The Russians triumphed in 1859 by ravaging Chechen lands, herds, and crops and beheading their captives, fostering a Chechen hatred of Russian rule.

Russian expansion in Europe and Asia

- Russian territory, 1533
- Territory added by 1598
- Territory added by 1689
- Territory added by 1914
- Boundaries as of 1914
- 1965 territory of U.S.S.R.

Map 23.3 Expansion of the Russian Empire
Between the 1500s and 1914 Russia gradually gained control of Siberia, Turkestan, the Caucasus, Ukraine, Poland, the Baltic states, and Finland, becoming the world's largest contiguous territorial empire.

Interactive Map

Catherine the Great Resplendent in her royal robes, Catherine the Great triumphantly enters one of the ports of the Crimean peninsula recently captured from the Turks. Catherine presided over an expansion of the Russian Empire and efforts at modernization.

Colonizing Muslim Central Asia

The Russians also colonized Muslim Central Asia, the first step in gaining direct access to the Indian Ocean trade and countering British influence in the region. By 1864 the Russians controlled all the Kazakh (KAH-zahk) lands east of the Caspian Sea and looked south to Turkestan's old and declining Silk Road cities. Although the cities remained vigorous centers of Islamic learning and Sufism, only Bukhara, a strong Uzbek (OOZ-bek)–dominated state, maintained a thriving trade. By the 1870s Russia dominated Turkestan. Russia now coveted Afghanistan, but the forbidding terrain and formidable reputation of Afghan warriors discouraged occupation. Eventually Afghanistan became a buffer between British India and Russian Central Asia.

Russification A czarist policy in the nineteenth century that promoted Russian language and culture for non-Russian peoples; created resentment among many Muslims.

Czarist policy in Central Asia and the Caucasus promoted changes that chiefly benefited Russians, as some Central Asian land suitable for growing cotton was given to several hundred thousand Russian farmers. The czars also gradually introduced a policy of **Russification**, the promotion of Russian language and culture for the non-Russian peoples, sparking resentment and spiritual revival among many Muslims. But Russian expansion brought problems along with the gains. The mighty empire's sheer size hindered governance, fostered corruption, and prevented the ready exploitation of the vast resources. Moreover, colonization of non-Russian lands made Russian leaders permanently fear rebellion and build a huge army to maintain security. The world's longest railroad, the Trans-Siberian, built between 1891 and 1915 and linking St. Petersburg with Vladivostok, fostered Russian settlement of eastern Siberia and helped Russian traders penetrate Manchuria and Korea. But expansion brought conflict with Japan, generating the Russo-Japanese War (1904–1905), in which Russia's humiliating defeat undermined its last czar, Nicholas II (r. 1894–1917).

Russian Economy, Society, and Revolution

Economic Growth

Territorial expansion and political developments created changes in many areas of Russian life. Spurred by acquiring Caucasus and Central Asian markets, the Russian economy grew. Russia enjoyed increased industrialization, financed largely by western European capital and by local bankers and businessmen of German or Jewish origin, and by 1914 Russia ranked fifth in the world as an industrial power. The factory workers, who increased in number fivefold between 1860 and 1914, resented the exploitation they faced when housed in crowded dormitories and expected to work thirteen hours a day. However, most Russians still lived in villages, dominated by the local nobility.

Gender Relations

Some Russian women sought to improve their status. While noblewomen frequently enjoyed some public influence, most commoner women had little power. Some were beaten and abused by husbands, since the laws gave men the right to control their wives and children. Peasants often spent their entire lives in the village where they were born. Even when some elite women became scholars and writers, they still had fewer rights than men. By the mid-nineteenth century, however, a women's movement had emerged that emphasized access to higher education. Thanks to these efforts, more women earned degrees and worked as doctors, midwives, and teachers.

Russian Thought and Culture

Russian thinkers tormented themselves over their national identity and goals. Many were Westernizers who admired the efforts of rulers such as Catherine the Great to promote modernization, and some wanted to abolish serfdom and the nobility. The work of some Russian writers, such as Russia's beloved poet Alexander Pushkin **(POOSH-kin)** (1799–1837), reflected familiarity with western European literature and thought. In contrast, the **Slavophiles** rejected Western models and defended Russian culture, such as respect for the Russian Orthodox Church, which remained a dominant force. Slavophiles often advocated that Russians unite with other Slavs in eastern Europe and the Balkans to confront the West.

Slavophiles Nineteenth-century Russians who emphasized Russia's unique culture and rejected Western models.

Whether Westernizers or Slavophiles, Russians were proud of their rich literary and artistic tradition. The novels of Fyodor Dostoyevsky **(dos-tuh-YEF-skee)** (1821–1881), reflecting his experiences as an exile in Siberia for revolutionary activities and his travels in Europe, were shaped by his awareness of poverty and the troubled human soul. Leo Tolstoy **(tuhl-STOI)** (1828–1910), master of the psychological novel, fought in the Crimean War. His epic work, *War and Peace* (1869), which profiled two noble families during war, portrayed people as mere victims of chance. One of Russia's most honored composers, Pyotr Tchaikovsky **(chi-KOF-skee)** (1840–1893), traveled widely in Europe and was criticized by Russian nationalists for his cosmopolitan approach to music and by conservatives for his homosexuality. He wrote operas as well as ballets of enduring popularity around the world, especially *Swan Lake* and *The Nutcracker*.

Dissent and Rebellion

Increasing discontent with the autocratic system and the rising costs of empire building resulted in violent resistance. To crush opposition, the czars sent thousands of dissidents to remote Siberian prison camps, where many died of illness, starvation, overwork, or the harsh climate. Some dissidents joined the illegal Socialist Revolutionary Party, founded in 1898, that used terror to strike against the regime. After assassinating a minister of state, the party proclaimed that "the crack of the bullet is the only possible means to talk with our ministers, until they listen to the voice of the country."[23]

In 1905 the sacrifices imposed on common people by the Russo-Japanese War sparked a major socialist-led revolutionary movement involving both men and women and widespread violence. The unrest began when 100,000 factory workers in the capital, St. Petersburg, who were required to work longer hours to produce war supplies, went on strike and marched demanding equality before the law, freedom of speech, an eight-hour workday, social insurance, and other progressive goals. Russian troops opened fire on the peaceful marchers, killing some 200 and wounding hundreds more. The violence shattered public support for the czar and fueled outrage, which soon spread to the armed forces. The revolutionaries were split in their goals, enabling the government to crush the uprising, execute thousands of rebels, and burn pro-rebel villages. But the czar bowed to public demands and allowed an elected national assembly with limited powers. The socialist movement fractured into hostile factions; however, conflicts simmered, and in 1917 they produced the greatest upheaval in Russia's history, which ended the czarist system (see Chapter 24).

SECTION SUMMARY

- The Russian leader Catherine the Great paid lip service to Enlightenment values, but she presided over an era of royal opulence, territorial expansion, and expanded serfdom, and she was followed by the despotic Nicholas I, who led the nation to defeat in the Crimean War.
- Russian expansion brought it control of eastern Siberia, Muslim Central Asia, and the Caucasus states, although some peoples, such as the Chechens, fiercely resisted.
- Russia's economy expanded along with its territory, creating a discontented proletariat; while many Russian thinkers embraced Western ideals, the Slavophiles argued for the superiority of traditional Russian culture.
- Russians increasingly discontented with the demands of empire building and autocratic rulers joined terrorist groups and supported a revolution in 1905, which, while put down, led to reforms.

CHAPTER SUMMARY

China faced daunting challenges from the Western powers. Qing China had long been able to rebuff Western demands for more trade, but the government and economy were declining by the early 1800s. China's attempts to halt British opium smuggling led to the Opium War, and its defeat in that war resulted in an unequal treaty system that gave Western nations greater access to China and its resources. Increasing poverty and rebellions further undermined Qing power. Attempts at modernization failed because of China's vast size, conservative opposition, and fears of radical culture change. In 1911 revolution ended the imperial system, but the new republic soon collapsed in civil war.

While the Western challenges progressively undermined China, they prompted Japan to transform its society. The arrival of American ships demanding that Japan open itself to the West forced the issue and undermined the shogunate, which then lost power in the 1868 Meiji Restoration. Capitalizing on dynamic merchants, high literacy rates, a tradition of cultural borrowing, and national loyalties, the Meiji government launched a crash program to modernize Japan's government, military, economy, and social patterns, importing Western ideas and institutions. By 1900 the Meiji had industrialized Japan, deflected Western ambitions, and turned Japan into a world power, able to defeat China and Russia in two wars and to colonize Korea.

Despotic Russian leaders pushed Russian control across Siberia and into eastern Europe and colonized Central Asia and the Caucasus. By the later 1800s Russia dominated large parts of Eurasia, forming the world's largest contiguous land empire. But maintaining an empire against restless colonized societies strained Russian capabilities. Russia also industrialized and promoted social change, but repression of the Russian peasants ultimately brought dissent and revolutionary movements.

KEY TERMS

Chinoiserie
Co-hong
extraterritoriality
international settlements
gunboat diplomacy
Meiji Restoration
state capitalism
zaibatsu
Burakumin
Russification
Slavophiles

EBOOK AND WEBSITE RESOURCES

PRIMARY SOURCE

Letter to Queen Victoria, 1839

INTERACTIVE MAPS

Map 23.1 Conflicts in Qing China, 1839–1870
Map 23.2 Japanese Modernization and Expansion, 1868–1913
Map 23.3 Expansion of the Russian Empire

LINKS

East and Southeast Asia: An Annotated Directory of Internet Resources (http://newton.uor.edu/Departments&Programs/AsianStudies-Dept/general.html). Links on history, culture, and politics.

The Floating World of Ukiyo-e: Shadow, Dreams, and Substance (http://www.loc.gov/exhibits/ukiyo-e/). Introduces the Japanese prints at the Library of Congress.

Internet Guide to Chinese Studies (http://www.sino.uni-heidelberg.de/igcs/). An excellent collection of links, maintained by a German university.

Internet East Asian History Sourcebook (http://www.fordham.edu/halsall/eastasia/eastasiasbook.html). Sources and links on China, Japan, and Korea.

Russian History Index: The World Wide Web Virtual Library (http://vlib.iue.it/hist-russia/Index.html). Useful links.

Plus flashcards, practice quizzes, and more. Go to: www.cengage.com/history/lockard/globalsocnet2e.

SUGGESTED READING

Allworth, Edward, ed. *Central Asia: 130 Years of Russian Rule*, 2nd ed. Durham, NC: Duke University Press, 1994. A collection of essays.

Benson, John and Takao Matsumura. *Japan, 1868–1945: From Isolation to Occupation*. New York: Longman, 2001. Revisionist interpretation of political, economic, and social changes.

Chang, Hsin-Pao. *Commissioner Lin and the Opium War*. New York: W.W. Norton, 1964. The classic account.

Cumings, Bruce. *Korea's Place in the Sun: A Modern History*, 2nd ed. New York: W.W. Norton, 2005. Good coverage of this era.

Ebrey, Patricia Buckley, Anne Walthall, and James B. Palais. *East Asia: A Cultural, Social, and Political History*, 2nd ed. Boston: Houghton Mifflin, 2009. A recent, balanced survey.

Evtuhov, Catherine, et al. *A History of Russia: Peoples, Legends, Events, Forces*. Boston: Houghton Mifflin, 2004. A detailed survey.

Fahr-Becker, Gabriele, ed. *Japanese Prints*. New York: Barnes and Noble, 2003. A well-illustrated introduction to this wonderful art.

Madariaga, Isabel de. *Russia in the Age of Catherine the Great*. London: Phoenix Press, 1981. Reprint of a well-balanced and panoramic examination of Catherine and her era.

Matsunosuke, Nishiyama. *Edo Culture: Daily Life and Diversions in Urban Japan, 1600–1868*. Honolulu: University of Hawaii Press, 1997. A fascinating look at popular culture during the Tokugawa era.

McClain, James L. *Japan: A Modern History*. New York: W.W. Norton, 2002. An excellent survey of events since 1600.

Schirokauer, Conrad, and Donald N. Clark. *Modern East Asia: A Brief History*, 2nd ed. Belmont, CA: Wadsworth, 2007. A survey of China, Japan, and Korea in this era.

Schoppa, R. Keith. *Revolution and its Past: Identities and Change in Modern Chinese History*, 2nd ed. Upper Saddle River, NJ: Prentice-Hall, 2006. Well-written survey of continuity and change.

Smith, Richard J. *China's Cultural Heritage: The Ch'ing Dynasty, 1644–1913*, 2nd ed. Boulder, CO: Westview Press, 1994. A readable and comprehensive study.

Spence, Jonathan D. *The Search for Modern China*, 2nd ed. New York: W.W. Norton, 1999. A provocative examination.

CHAPTER 24

World Wars, European Revolutions, and Global Depression, 1914–1945

CHAPTER OUTLINE

- The Roots and Course of World War I
- The Revolutionary Path to Soviet Communism
- The Interwar Years and the Great Depression
- The Rise of Fascism and the Renewal of Conflict
- World War II: A Global Transition

PROFILE
Yoshiya Nobuko, Japanese Writer and Gender Rebel

WITNESS TO THE PAST
The Doctrine of Fascism

Global Communism
The communist leaders of the Soviet Union hoped that their revolution in Russia in 1917 would inspire similar revolutions around the world, ending capitalism and imperialism. This poster reflects the dream of a triumphant communism.

My beautiful, pitiful era. With an insane smile you look back, cruel and weak, like an animal past its prime, at the prints of your own paws.

—Osip Mandelstam, Russian poet[1]

FOCUS QUESTIONS

1. What was the impact of World War I on the Western world?
2. How did communism prevail in Russia and transform that country?
3. How did the Great Depression reshape world politics and economies?
4. What were the main ideas and impacts of fascism?
5. What were the costs and consequences of World War II?

By April 1917 the French army had been fighting the Germans for over two and a half years during World War I. With growing casualty lists and tremendous hardship on soldiers, the French officers were divided over mounting a more aggressive strategy, likely to result in many more deaths, or a more defensive approach. Finally a new French commander, General Philippe Pétain **(peh-TANH)** (1856–1951), advocated a strategy to minimize French casualties. A peasant's son with an aristocratic demeanor, a sweeping white moustache, and many love affairs with other men's wives, Pétain regarded his soldiers as more than cannon fodder, endearing him to the fighting men. But Pétain was overruled, and the French launched another frontal assault on the well-fortified German lines, resulting in a military disaster that caused 120,000 deaths and broke the troops' fighting spirit. Mutinies broke out in the units, with the mutineers protesting the futile military strategy of suicidal assaults. Some soldiers proposed a protest march on Paris, and 20,000 deserted. In response, the army executed about 50 mutineers but also granted the frontline troops better food and more generous rations of wine. Mutinies and an overwhelming war-weariness occurred among all the combatant nations. Pétain emerged from World War I as a hero but later lost his stature when he served as the nominal head of the French government under hated Nazi occupation in World War II. He died in prison, a broken man looking back on three tumultuous decades that had brought so much distress and destruction to the world.

Those decades included not only two great military struggles but also a mighty revolution in Russia, a terrible worldwide economic depression, and the rise of new ideologies. The Russian Jewish poet Osip Mandelstam described an era full of achievements and atrocities, heroism and hardship, as "beautiful [and] pitiful." Before World War I some Europeans believed that Western democracy might spread throughout the world and the horrors of war could be ended forever. Liberals even hoped World War I would be the war to end all wars. But the hopes of the idealists were dashed by two world wars, fought partly in Europe, that challenged the liberalism and rationalism spawned by the Enlightenment. Dictatorship in Russia, economic collapse, and organized slaughter shattered faith in progress. The disarray in Europe helped undermine Western political influence in the world, except for the rising Western power, the United States.

[1]Quoted in Anne Applebaum, *Gula: A History* (NY: Doubleday, 2003), p. 3.

Visit the website and eBook for additional study materials and interactive tools: www.cengage.com/history/lockard/globalsocnet2e

The Roots and Course of World War I

What was the impact of World War I on the Western world?

In August 1914, as war broke out between the major powers of Europe, the British foreign secretary remarked, "The lights are going out all over Europe. We shall not see them again in our lifetime."[2] The conflict pitted two alliances. Britain, France, and Russia formed the Triple Entente, which later included Serbia, Japan, Italy, Portugal, Romania, Greece, and eventually the United States. These nations, also known as the Allies, faced the Central Powers: Germany, Austria-Hungary, the Ottoman Empire, and Bulgaria. Although most of the military action took place in and around Europe, the leaders of the countries involved saw the conflict as nothing short of a struggle to control the global system, with its industrial economies and colonial empires. The Great War, as many Europeans called it, was history's first total war, an armed conflict between industrialized powers that lasted four terrible years. The war brought down empires and dynasties, made the United States a world power, and weakened western Europe's hold over the colonial world. And the end of the conflict made a second major war almost inevitable.

Preludes to War

Early 20th Century Europe

In the early 1900s, Europeans enjoyed affluence, social stability, and growing democracy. The European economies benefited from their links to each other and their access to the world's resources and markets. Some thinkers believed nations tied by economic interdependence would never wage war against each other. European nations cooperated in many things. Treaties bound their nations to protect the right of workers to pensions and health insurance while restricting child labor. Whatever their nationality, educated Europeans loved the music of the Austrian composer Wolfgang Amadeus Mozart and the novels of the Russian writer Leo Tolstoy. Europeans frequently spoke two or three languages and traveled in other countries, and royal families intermarried across borders. In 1899 European nations agreed to limit armaments and create the International Court to settle disputes between nations. Although the court was seldom invoked, Europeans hoped it would discourage a sudden outburst of war. They looked to the future with confidence and felt superior to the rest of the world. Thanks to imperial expansion, rising populations, and expanded markets, Europeans consumed new products such as chocolate and rubber tires, while European emigration to the Americas and Australia increased markets there for European goods, and automobiles and large ships made it easier to move people, natural resources, and manufactured products over long distances. European capital financed South African gold and diamond mines, Malayan rubber plantations, Australian sheep stations, Russian railways, Canadian wheat fields, and every sector of the growing U.S. economy.

National Rivalries

However, the prosperity, interdependence, and idealism had their limits, and other conditions led to tensions and resentments. The quest for imperial glory increased competition between the European powers for economic and political influence outside of Europe, and each nation felt threatened in some way by competitors. Britain, France, and Germany were the wealthiest, most powerful nations and fierce rivals with large empires in Africa, Asia, the Pacific, and the Caribbean. Because they began empire building later than Britain and France, the Germans resented those nations' political control of much of the world. Britain, which generally commanded the seas, became concerned when Germany began building a naval fleet. As Germany challenged Britain for dominance in overseas markets, the two nations bolstered their military strength, stepping up the manufacture of heavier weapons and drafting more young men into the military. Still considering wars necessary struggles rather than terrible evils, by 1911 leaders began to plan for war. The chief of the German General Staff told the German chancellor, "I hold war to be inevitable, and the sooner the better. Everyone is preparing for the great war, which they all expect."[3]

As economic and military rivalries grew, alliances formed. Britain, France, and Russia were all wary of an aggressive Germany, which felt encircled by these three hostile powers, while Austria-Hungary and the Ottoman Empire shared German dislike of Russia. The growing nationalist agitation for self-determination by the many ethnic minorities within the multinational German, Russian, Austro-Hungarian, and Ottoman Empires added to the combustible mix. Austria-Hungary faced a particularly difficult challenge in governing the restless Czech, Slovak, and Balkan peoples within its empire. The Balkans, populated by feuding ethnic groups, was coveted by the Ottomans, Russia, and Austria-Hungary. In 1908 Austria-Hungary annexed Bosnia-Herzegovina **(boz-nee-uh-HERT-suh-go-vee-nuh)**, a territory containing Croats, Serbs, and Muslims that neighboring

CHRONOLOGY

	World War I and Aftermath	Era of Great Depression	World War II
1910	**1914–1918** World War I **1917** Russian Revolution		
1920	**1926** Fascist state in Italy	**1929–1941** Great Depression	**1939–1945** World War II
1930		**1933** Nazi triumph in Germany **1937** Japanese invasion of China	
1940			**1941** Japanese attack on Pearl Harbor **1944** Bretton Woods Conference

Serbia also wanted (see Chronology: World War I, 1914–1919). If their ally Germany could restrain Russia, Austria-Hungary's leaders thought war with Serbia might salvage their decaying empire, which once ruled large parts of Europe.

Historians often blame World War I on failures of diplomacy, breakdowns in communication among nations, and the personal ambitions of leaders. Although a grandson of Britain's Queen Victoria, the German monarch, Kaiser Wilhelm II (r. 1888–1918), who saw himself as a king answerable only to God, grew to envy British power. Political and military leaders also underestimated the human costs and long-term consequences of conflict. Although overstating the case, a key British leader later conceded that "the nations slithered over the brink into the boiling cauldron of war without a trace of apprehension or dismay."[4] Other issues also paved the road to war. Some governments hoped war might divert public attention from festering domestic problems, such as Irish resistance to English policies and growing German social ills. And while the general public did not pressure its governments for war, it did not try to restrain them. Feminists and socialists opposed war on principle, but, when war came, they often closed ranks. In the Austrian capital, Vienna, vast crowds paraded through the streets singing patriotic songs through the night, even though a local observer wrote that his people expected a nightmare. Meanwhile leaders, although believing war was preferable to maintaining a fragile peace, also feared their people would tire of it.

CHRONOLOGY
World War I, 1914–1919

1908 Austria-Hungarian annexation of Bosnia-Herzegovina

1914 Outbreak of conflict

1916 Battle of Verdun

June 1917 U.S. intervention

March 1917 Fall of czarist government in Russia

October 1917 Bolshevik revolution in Russia

March 1918 Brest-Litovsk Treaty

November 1918 End of conflict

1919 Paris Peace Conference

The Course of the European War

Renewed Conflict

The pretext for war was the assassination of the Austrian archduke Franz Ferdinand (1863–1914), the heir to the Habsburg throne, and his wife, Sophie, while they rode through the crowded streets of Sarajevo (sar-uh-YAY-vo), Bosnia-Herzegovina's capital city, during an official visit. Although conciliatory toward the empire's Slavic minorities, to Serb nationalists in Bosnia the archduke symbolized continuing Austro-Hungarian domination. The Serb group behind the assassination, the Black Hand, wanted to merge Bosnia with Serbia. Austria-Hungary responded to the assassination by declaring war on Serbia, whose leaders they suspected of aiding the assassination. Germany supported Austria-Hungary, while Britain, France, and Russia entered the conflict against Germany. Soon Ottoman Turkey joined the Central Powers, closing off British and French access to the Black Sea. Germany planned a quick knockout blow against France, hoping that this would allow most troops to then be sent east to face Russia. These plans were thwarted.

European leaders expected a short war; instead they got a long, brutal conflict, the first war to be fought in three dimensions: air, sea, and land. It became a war of attrition and the first fully industrialized conflict as combatants employed more efficient and indiscriminate ways of killing, including long-range artillery, poison gas, flamethrowers, and aerial bombing. A generation of men was cut down by shrapnel that tore flesh to pieces, high explosives that pulverized bone, and gas that seared the lungs. The German soldier turned writer Erich Maria Remarque remembered the "great brotherhood [caused by] the desperate loyalty to one another of men condemned to die," while the British poet Wilfred Owen wrote: "By his dead [comrade's] smile I knew we stood in hell."[5] Many surviving soldiers were maimed mentally or physically, often suffering from shellshock, a

e **Primary Source: Mud and Khaki: Memoirs of an Incomplete Soldier** Read from the memoirs of a British soldier, and imagine the horrors of trench warfare and poison gas in World War I.

Imperial War Museum/The Bridgeman Art Library International

John Nash, *Over the Top* This painting, by the British artist John Nash, shows the trench warfare common on the western front during World War I. Here Allied soldiers leave their trenches to attack across "No Man's Land" on a snowy day.

horrific nervous condition that made normal life difficult or impossible. The war also generated disease and starvation among civilians.

Battlefronts

The war on the western front in Belgium and northern France largely involved soldiers huddling in muddy trenches, gas masks at hand, and using artillery and machine guns to pound the enemy troops in their trenches, combined with attacks across the barbed wire–filled ground, known as "No Man's Land," between the opposing trenches. This resulted in countless casualties. But for all the sacrifices, the front lines moved little in four years. The cataclysmic Battle of Verdun in northeastern France in 1916, during which the French stopped a surprise German assault, killed a million men, symbolizing the senseless slaughter. More soldiers may have been killed per square yard at Verdun than in any other battle in history. But despite the carnage, Verdun had little impact on the war itself. However, by 1917 the British had invented the first armored tank, "Big Willie," which was equipped with large guns and belted treads. Able to cross over No Man's Land and German trenches, it put more pressure on German lines.

The war had several fronts (see Map 24.1). In the east, Germany and its allies quickly overran Serbia and Romania and pushed deep into western Russia against poorly organized Russian armies. By 1917 the war had killed or wounded over 7 million Russians and caused Russian peasants to flee eastward, only to face hunger, disease, and homelessness. Originally a German ally, Italy switched sides in 1915 but lost heavily in unsuccessful battles. In the Middle East the Ottomans initially inflicted a heavy toll on the Allied troops that were sent to invade Turkey, including many soldiers from Australia and New Zealand. But an Arab uprising begun in 1916 and a British invasion of Ottoman-controlled Iraq forced the Ottoman forces eventually to retreat from that area. Some fighting also broke out in East Africa, as the British and South Africans invaded the German colony of Tanganyika. On the other side of the world, Japan, a British ally, occupied German-held territory in China and colonies in the Pacific islands.

Although the Germans won more battles than they lost, eventually the tide turned against them. Over time the Allies' superior wealth, better weapons, larger forces, and sea power proved decisive. Britain and Germany, possessing the world's two most powerful navies, with gigantic battleships known as dreadnoughts, engaged each other in the North Sea and the eastern Mediterranean. Eventually the Germans used their submarines to break Allied supply lines. Their attacks on British and U.S. shipping carrying supplies to Britain, however, enraged Americans and brought a reluctant United States into the war.

Turning Points

Two fateful developments in 1917—two Russian Revolutions and the intervention of the United States—altered the conflict. The first Russian Revolution overthrew the czarist government and the second, led by communists, took Russia out of the war. Freed from the eastern front, German armies made breakthroughs against the British and French forces in the west. But the U.S.

Map 24.1
World War I

World War I pitted the Triple Entente of Britain, France, and Russia, and its allies, against the Central Powers: Germany, Austria-Hungary, and the Ottoman Empire. The worst fighting occurred along the western front and in eastern Europe and Russia. The intervention of the United States in 1917 against the Central Powers proved decisive.

Interactive Map

intervention on the Allied side, the first major U.S. interference in European affairs, eventually offset German success. The United States had remained neutral, but, as a German victory seemed more likely, U.S. military leaders, munitions makers, politicians, and businessmen all pressed for intervention. U.S. companies and banks worried that an Allied defeat might prevent payment on orders for American products and investments in the British and French economies. Eventually President Woodrow Wilson committed the United States to war, linking the military commitment to idealistic American values when he told Congress that "the world must be made safe for democracy. We are the champions of the rights of mankind."[6]

Allied Victory

The U.S. intervention secured an Allied victory. Beginning in June 1917, American troops—ultimately over a million—arrived in Europe. Many of the young men, often from rural backgrounds, struggled to comprehend European ways; others developed a taste for European culture and a fondness for cities such as London and Paris. The United States helped the Allies blockade German ports, creating severe economic problems, and pushed the German forces back. Soon Germany's allies began surrendering. Demoralized, its overextended army in disarray, and suffering food and fuel shortages at home, Germany was forced to agree to peace in November 1918. Kaiser Wilhelm II and the Austro-Hungarian emperor both abdicated, ending two long-standing European monarchies. The Allies dictated the peace terms, which changed the old global order and began a new one.

Consequences of World War I

Reshaping Europe

World War I undermined German power and shifted more influence to Britain, France, and the United States. The Paris Peace Conference of 1919, held in the opulent former royal palace in the Paris suburb of Versailles (vuhr-SIGH), reshaped Europe and resulted in the Treaty of Versailles. The U.S. president, Woodrow Wilson, hoped to use his prestige and his nation's growing power to sell an agenda, known as the Fourteen Points, to skeptical British and French leaders. Favoring political freedom and stability, Wilson proposed conciliatory treatment of Germany because he worried that a humiliated, crippled Germany would become chaotic. However, the hardline French wanted to divide Germany. The final treaty, a compromise, required Germany to partly dismantle its military; abandon its Asian, African, and Pacific colonies; and shift land to its European neighbors, leaving 3 million ethnic Germans in countries such as Czechoslovakia and Poland. The treaty also forced Germany to pay huge annual payments, known as reparations, to the Allies to compensate for their war costs. Ultimately the treaty failed to create a lasting settlement, left Germany virtually disarmed and bankrupt, and planted the roots for future problems, as Wilson had feared. The new German leader, Fridrich Ebert, saw a troubled future: "The armistice will not produce a just peace. The sacrifices imposed on us must lead to our people's doom."[7]

The war had taken an appalling human toll on both sides. Altogether 9 to 10 million soldiers died, including 2 million Russians, 2 million Germans, 1.5 million French, and 75,000 Americans. Since some 10 million civilians died, the total killed was around 20 million. The brutality and waste radicalized many workers and peasants, especially in eastern Europe, and leftist political parties—Socialists and Communists—gained strength. In 1914 Europeans had gone to war with patriotic enthusiasm, but by 1918 some philosophers and writers feared that the war meant the rejection of Enlightenment rationality; they also concluded that the slaughter had destroyed the Western claim to moral leadership in the world. Pacifist, antiwar sentiments grew. The French writer Henri Barbusse, a soldier himself, reflected these sentiments: "Shame on military glory, shame on armies, shame on the soldier's calling that changes men by turns into stupid victims and ignoble brutes."[8]

Imperial Consequences

The war destroyed several old states and created new ones. Four long-standing empires—the Russian, Ottoman, Austro-Hungarian, and German—collapsed, while Communists gained power in Russia, launching a new political and economic system. Elsewhere, Wilson, believing that ethnically homogeneous nation-states could prevent nationalist rivalries, promoted the self-determination of peoples in Europe. As a result, the Paris Peace Conference redrew national boundaries to give ethnic minorities their own states. Poland, Czechoslovakia, Yugoslavia, and Finland were carved out of the ruins of the German, Austro-Hungarian, and Russian Empires, but they later became pawns in the struggle between Germany and Russia that helped launch World War II. Many of the new states also placed various ethnic groups within arbitrary boundaries. For example, Yugoslavia included Orthodox Serbs, Catholic Croats and Slovenes, and Muslim Slavs and Albanians; these peoples had fought each other for centuries and did not share a common national identity.

The sacrifices of war, and the appeal of national independence, also led to changes within the British Empire. Britain faced uprisings and civil war in its longtime colony, Ireland, and in 1921 it was forced to grant most of the island special status within the British Empire as the self-governing

Irish Free State. In 1937 Ireland became completely independent of the British crown, finally realizing the centuries-old dream of Irish nationalists.

The victorious powers ignored the principle of self-determination for their colonies. In seeking to strengthen the main U.S. allies, Britain and France, Woodrow Wilson supported the preservation of their colonies in Asia, Africa, the Pacific, and the Caribbean. The peace settlement transferred Germany's African colonies to Britain, France, Belgium, and South Africa and its Asian and Pacific territories to Britain, France, Australia, New Zealand, and Japan. Britain and France also gained control of the Middle Eastern societies formerly ruled by Ottoman Turkey. The peace settlements, by ignoring the political struggles of colonized peoples, thus spurred opposition to the West. The death of thousands of Asian and African colonial subjects conscripted or recruited to fight for Britain, France, or Germany in World War I sparked even deeper resentments. Thus World War I was one of the key factors in the rise of nationalism, the desire to form politically independent nations, in the colonies between 1918 and 1941 (see Chapter 25).

A New Global System

Although the global system shaped by colonial empires and Western economic power survived after the war, European prestige and influence were weakened. The war undermined European economies, allowing the United States to leap ahead of Europe. Like British leaders in the nineteenth century, Wilson, heading the world's largest, most productive economy, wanted free trade and an open world in which American industry could assert its supremacy. Since European nations had borrowed from the United States to finance the war, they now owed the United States money, allowing the United States, long a debtor nation, to become a creditor nation. By 1919 it was producing 42 percent of all the world's industrial output, more than all of Europe combined, and had replaced Britain as the banker and workshop of the world. Wilson also helped form a League of Nations, the first organization of independent nations to work for peace and humanitarian concerns. But Wilson could not persuade the U.S. Congress, controlled by the largely isolationist Republican opposition, to approve U.S. membership in the league. Hence, the only nation with the power and stature to make the league work stayed outside, leaving Britain and France alone to deal with European and global issues.

SECTION SUMMARY

- The early 1900s in Europe were marked by great affluence and stability, expanding markets, and shared notions of culture, justice, and human rights.
- Many factors contributed to the start of World War I, including Germany's resentment of British and French colonial holdings, which led to a military buildup on both sides; competing claims on Bosnia-Herzegovina; and a few governments' desire to divert attention from domestic problems.
- Sparked by the assassination of Austrian archduke Franz Ferdinand in Sarajevo, the war soon involved Austro-Hungary, Germany, Britain, France, and Turkey, all of which employed unprecedented military technology that caused millions of deaths.
- In 1917 Germany seemed on the verge of victory when the United States entered the fighting, in part because of pressure by business interests that provided goods to France and Britain and in part because of outrage over German submarine attacks on U.S. ships.
- The United States helped the French and British win the war, but U.S. president Woodrow Wilson could not prevent the French from dictating harsh settlement terms that required Germany to partially dismantle its military, abandon its colonies, give up some of its territory, and pay heavy reparations.
- The horrors of World War I led to the radicalization of many Europeans; a growth of antiwar sentiment; the breakup of the Ottoman and German Empires, much of which were colonized by Britain and France; the breakup of much of the Russian and Austro-Hungarian Empires, which were carved into new countries; and the world dominance of the United States.

The Revolutionary Path to Soviet Communism

How did communism prevail in Russia and transform that country?

The Russian Revolution, a major consequence of World War I, was a formative event of the twentieth century, shaping European and world history, politics, and beliefs. In the wake of the revolution, Russia provided a testing ground for a radical new ideology, communism, which fostered a powerful state that reshaped Russian society and provided an alternative to the capitalist democracy dominant in North America and western Europe.

The Roots of Revolution

The Russian Revolution had deep roots in Russian society and its history under the despotic czars (see Chapter 23). Controlling a huge Eurasian empire, Russia had enjoyed some industrialization, but the powerful landed aristocracy opposed further development. Socially and economically, Russia was still a somewhat feudalistic country, with peasants often remaining subject to the landowners and enjoying little social mobility or wealth. Growing discontent among intellectuals, the floundering middle class, underpaid industrial workers, and peasants, who hated the autocratic czarist system, fomented radical movements.

Bolsheviks The most radical of Russia's antigovernment groups at the turn of the twentieth century, who embraced a dogmatic form of Marxism.

In 1905 a revolution broke out, only to be brutally crushed by the government, but it left a revolutionary heritage for the **Bolsheviks**, the most radical of Russia's antigovernment groups, who transformed the revolutionary socialist views promoted by Karl Marx into a dogmatic communist ideology. The Bolshevik founder and leader, Vladimir Lenin **(LEN-in)** (1870–1924), a lawyer from a middle-class family, was humorless and uncompromising but a clever political strategist who recruited supporters with his passionate beliefs and persuasive speeches. Influenced by the works of Karl Marx, he was further radicalized when the government executed his older brother for having joined an assassination plot against the czar. Most of the Bolshevik leaders, including Lenin, had spent time as political prisoners in harsh Siberian labor camps. To avoid another arrest Lenin had lived in exile elsewhere in Europe since 1907, organizing his movement.

The Bolsheviks espoused a goal of helping the downtrodden workers and peasants redress the wrongs inflicted upon them by the rich and privileged, claiming that revolutionary violence could bring about a new, classless communist society with a more equitable distribution of wealth and power. Lenin advocated a small, disciplined revolutionary organization that would work for workers' interests and whose leaders were full-time revolutionaries. All members had to abide by the decisions made by the leaders, a system known as the party line. When World War I broke out, the Russian people and even most opposition political parties rallied around the unpopular government, seeing it as a patriotic war of defense against the hated Germans. Only the Bolsheviks opposed the war, which they saw as an imperialistic struggle over markets and colonies. But the war soon lost its allure as Russian military forces collapsed in the face of stronger German armies.

Lenin The Bolshevik leader Vladimir Lenin stirred crowds with his fiery revolutionary rhetoric, helping to spread the communist message among Russians fed up with ineffective government, war, and poverty.

Sovfoto

By 1917 the demoralized Russian people were seeking change, sparking two revolutions. The first, in March, toppled the czar, imprisoned the imperial family, and set up a provisional government (see Chronology: Russia, 1917–1938). This unplanned revolution erupted while riots and strikes paralyzed the cities. Working women had begun the protests by swarming the streets of the capital, St. Petersburg, demanding relief and food, and they soon gained support from the soldiers sent to control them. The new provisional government leaders, such as the lawyer Aleksandr Kerensky (1881–1970), were well-meaning urban liberals who wanted reform and Western-style democracy, but they had no roots among the population. They failed because they refused to provide the two things most Russians wanted: peace and land. Because of their commitments to the Allies, they vowed to continue fighting the war, declining to redistribute land from the aristocracy to the peasantry until the war ended and elections could be held to form a new, more representative, government.

While the increasingly discredited provisional government asked for time, radicals organized **soviets**, local action councils that enlisted workers and soldiers to fight the factory owners and military officers. This grassroots movement for change undermined government authority. As the soviets and the government jockeyed for control of St. Petersburg, the Germans, hoping to weaken the Russian government, helped Lenin, in exile in Switzerland, to secretly return to Russia hidden in a railroad box car. Using the slogans of "peace, bread, and land" and "all power to the soviets," Lenin rapidly built up Bolshevik influence in the soviets. The provisional government tried to prevent the peasants from seizing land, and soldiers from deserting their units, but government control was weak.

CHRONOLOGY

Russia, 1917–1938

1917 March revolution

1917 October revolution

March 1918 Brest-Litovsk Treaty

1918–1921 Russian Civil War

1922 Formation of Soviet Union

1924 Death of Lenin

1928 Beginning of Five-Year Plans

1929–1953 Stalin's dictatorship

1936–1938 Stalin's Great Purge

The Bolshevik Seizure of Power and Civil War

In October 1917, the Bolsheviks and their 240,000 party members staged an uprising and grabbed power from Kerensky's crumbling provisional government. Aided by the soviets, they seized key government buildings in St. Petersburg. With a fragile hold on power, the Bolsheviks had to allow diverse parties to contest elections for an assembly, which met in January 1918. After the assembly refused to support a Bolshevik bid for leadership, however, the Bolsheviks used troops to take over the national and city governments, pushing other parties aside and terrorizing or executing opponents, including the moderate, prodemocracy socialists. Claiming that his goal was to transfer power to the working class, Lenin defended the violence, asserting that chefs cannot make an omelet without breaking eggs. The Bolsheviks then renamed themselves the Communist Party and gained popular support by pulling Russia out of the war. In the Treaty of Brest-Litovsk, negotiated with Germany in March 1918, Russia gave up some of its empire in the west to Germany, abandoning the Ukraine, eastern Poland, the Baltic states, and Finland. The Bolsheviks also moved the capital from St. Petersburg, which they renamed Leningrad, to Moscow.

soviets Local action councils formed by Russian radicals before the 1917 Russian Revolution that enlisted workers and soldiers to fight the factory owners and military officers.

Once in power, the communists had to develop a strategy for dealing with the wider world. In 1919, Lenin, hoping to protect Russia's revolution by promoting world revolution, organized the Communist International, often known as the Comintern, a collection of communist parties from around the world. However, the prospect of world revolution soon faded because of U.S. aid to Europe after the war.

Russian Civil War

The Russian Revolution sparked the Russian Civil War (1918–1921) (see Map 24.2). The leaders of the conservative, anticommunist forces, who called themselves White Russians in contrast to the communists' military force, the Red Army, included czarist aristocrats and generals who were angry at losing their dominance and a few pro-Western liberals favoring democracy. Heavily funded and armed by Western nations alarmed by the Revolution, the White Russians fought the communist forces for three years. However, the communists, with a cohesive party and brilliant military leadership, capitalized on the disunity among White Russian leaders and their Western backers. Most crucially, they received growing support from the working class and the peasants, who feared the return of the hated landowners with a White Russian victory. Although the communists initially looked vulnerable, they eventually gained the advantage, defeating the White Russians and even reclaiming some of the territory lost in the Brest-Litovsk Treaty, including the Ukraine.

Foreign Interventions

Outside intervention by Japan, Britain, France, and the United States added an international flavor to the Russian Civil War. Japan, which concentrated on eastern Siberia, and Britain sent 60,000 and 40,000 troops, respectively, into Russia. The liberal idealist Wilson sent two separate American military forces to Russia to roll back the communist regime and, he claimed, spread democratic values. Five thousand American troops went to northern Russia to battle the Red Army for control of two port cities, but brutal winter weather, poor provisions, and high casualties drove the U.S. troops to near mutiny. Another contingent of 10,000 Americans entered eastern Siberia. Soon recognizing the intervention as a quagmire, Wilson lamented that it was harder to get out than it was to go in, and U.S. and other Western troops were finally removed in 1920. The Western intervention only helped solidify the communist government, widely seen by Russians as fighting a nationalist war against foreign powers seeking to restore the old discredited czarist order.

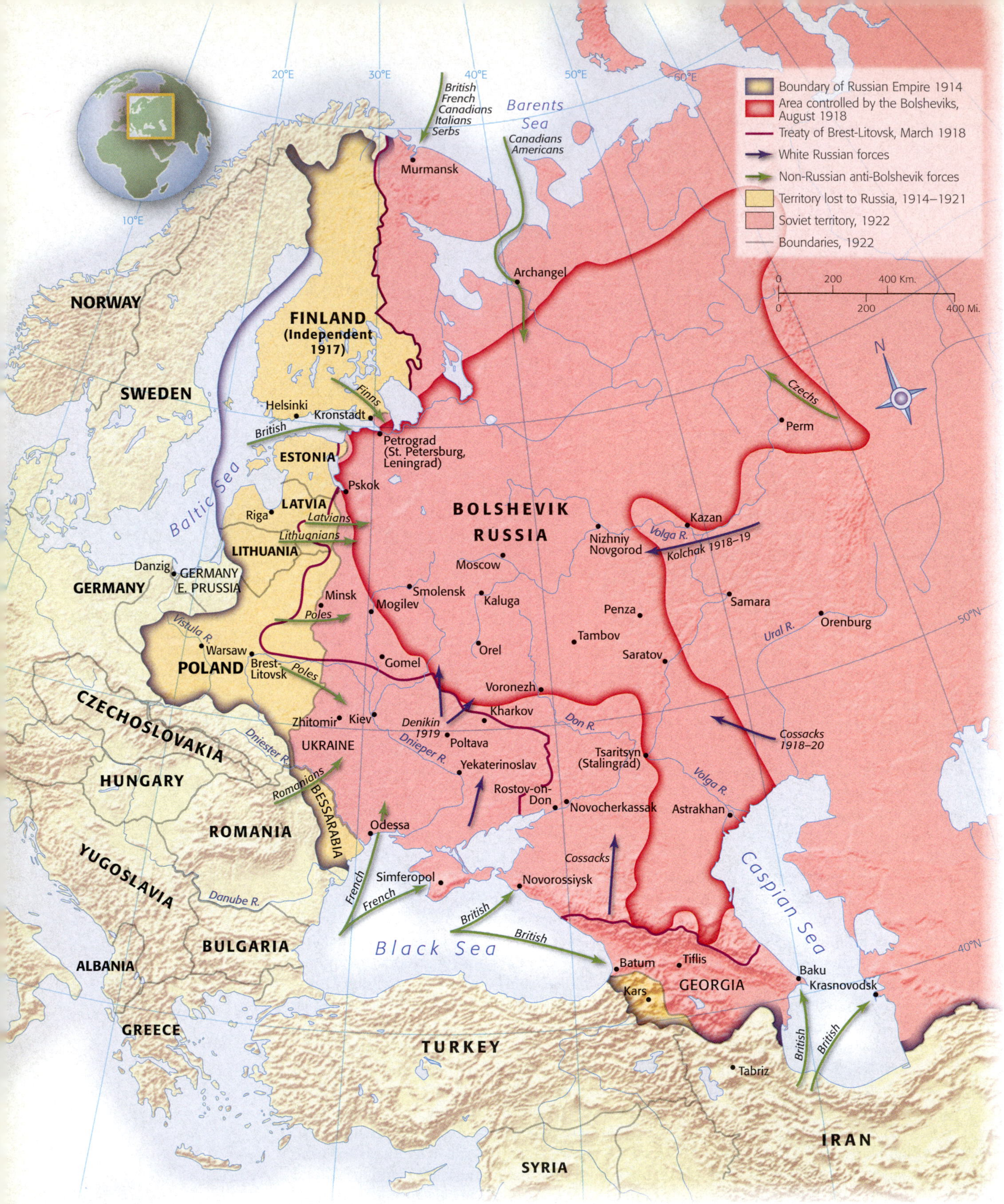

Map 24.2 Civil War in Revolutionary Russia (1918–1921)
The communist seizure of power in Russia in 1917 sparked a counteroffensive, backed by varied Western nations and Japan, to reverse the Russian Revolution. The communists successfully defended the Russian heartland while pushing back the conservative offensive.

e Interactive Map

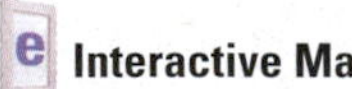

Lenin, Stalin, and Dictatorship

By 1922 the Communist Party controlled much of the old Russian Empire, but the country was devastated and its people starving, and the civil war had made good relations with the capitalist democracies impossible, as well as reinforcing the paranoid, authoritarian, and militaristic attitudes of the communists. The party was forging the world's first state based on communist ideas, inspiring the growth of communist groups in other countries. Russia's leaders proclaimed their nation the Union of Soviet Socialist Republics (USSR), in theory a federation of all the empire's diverse peoples—such as Kazakhs, Uzbeks, Armenians, and Ukrainians—but largely controlled by Russians, and hence a continuation of the Russian Empire. Soon the USSR turned from world revolution to building "socialism in one country"—using coercion against reluctant citizens if necessary.

Building the Soviet Union

Since Soviet leaders had no model of a communist state, they experimented while using their secret police to eliminate opponents, among them liberals and moderate socialists. The basis for Soviet communism was **Marxism-Leninism**, a mix of socialism (collective ownership of the economy) and **Leninism**, a political system in which one party holds a monopoly on power. Lenin initially favored centralization of all economic activity, but he was forced by peasant opposition to adopt the **New Economic Policy** (NEP), a pragmatic approach that mixed capitalism and socialism, allowing peasants to sell their produce on the open market. The NEP brought economic recovery. However, with few consumer goods available, the peasants had no incentive to sell their produce for profit because there was little to buy with the money they earned.

Marxism-Leninism The basis for Soviet communism, a mix of socialism (collective ownership of the economy) and Leninism.

Leninism A political system in which one party holds a monopoly on power, excluding other parties from participation.

New Economic Policy Lenin's pragmatic approach to economic development, which mixed capitalism and socialism.

Lenin became dissatisfied with the results of the revolution, which he called socialist in appearance but not substance: "czarism slightly anointed with Soviet oil,"[9] and he criticized the bloated bureaucracy. Decades later, Lenin's assessment of his government's failures remained accurate, since the USSR never became the egalitarian communist society envisioned by Karl Marx. Lenin himself, who combined ruthless authoritarianism with concern for the exploited, deserves some of the blame. While Lenin constructed myths about mass support for the "dictatorship of the proletariat," led by the Communist Party, the ties between the political leaders and the Soviet people remained weak. The instability and divisions caused by World War I and the Russian Civil War made the communist leaders even less willing to trust the people or allow dissent, which they feared would provoke unrest.

The long czarist tradition of authoritarian, bureaucratic government and an obedient population fostered communist dictatorship. The communists were a small party, and most leaders were, like Lenin, intellectuals from urban middle-class backgrounds. To regenerate the economy, they eventually adopted not popular control of farms and enterprises by workers and peasants but a top-down managerial system staffed by officials chiefly of middle-class origin. The middle class was now largely composed of state employees, managers, and bureaucrats with salaries and privileges that were denied the masses and dedicated not to fostering social change but to maintaining their own power. Lenin hoped to reform the party but died in 1924.

Stalin's Dictatorship

Lenin's successor was a master bureaucrat, Joseph Stalin (STAH-lin) (1879–1953), who reshaped Soviet communism. Born in the Caucasus province of Georgia, he studied to be a Russian Orthodox priest before being expelled from the seminary. After joining the Bolsheviks, he adopted the name Stalin ("Man of Steel"). In control of the Communist Party apparatus, Stalin outmaneuvered his party rivals to succeed Lenin, coming to power as the peasants, no longer fearing landlords, increasingly turned away from the Communist Party. Stalin urged a hard line against those who resisted state policies, eliminated all his competition in the party, and became a dictator. The system he imposed, **Stalinism**, included state ownership of all property, such as lands and businesses, a planned economy, and one-man rule.

Stalinism Joseph Stalin's system of government, which included state ownership of all property, such as lands and businesses, a planned economy, and one-man rule.

In 1928 Stalin ended Lenin's NEP and introduced an annual series of Five-Year Plans for future production, formulated by state bureaucrats. These plans produced basic industrial goods, such as steel and coal, but few consumer products. Stalin also launched a massive crash industrialization program and withdrew the country from the global system, mobilizing Russian resources and refusing foreign investment. In order to introduce tractors and harvesters to increase farm production, Stalin strengthened the party's grip and collectivized the land, turning private farms into commonly owned enterprises and destroying the wealthier small farmers, the *kulaks*, by exiling to Siberia those who refused to join the collective farms.

The 1930s and 1940s were hard, terror-filled years for the Soviet people. Stalin ordered purges to eliminate actual or potential opponents; forced-labor camps for suspected dissidents; and the widespread use of the secret police (the KGB), which spied on and intimidated the people. When the collectivization of farming provoked a widespread famine, the growing dissent led to the Great

gulags Harsh forced-labor camps in Siberia.

Purge of 1936–1938, marked by well-publicized trials of some party leaders as traitors. Stalin also deported millions to the harsh forced labor camps in Siberia known as **gulags** (Russian shorthand for State Camp Administration). Some 4 to 5 million people were arrested and half a million executed for alleged subversion, and from 1929 until 1953 some 18 million people passed through the massive gulag system, 4.5 million of these never returning home. Gulag inmates toiled, starved, and died building railroads, cutting timber, or digging canals. Not even beloved artists were spared the repression, especially if they were Jewish. One of Russia's most revered poets, Osip Mandelstam (MAHN-duhl-stuhm) (1891–1938), died in the gulag in 1938. The total dead and jailed from Stalin's repression numbered around 40 million people. The Russian poet Anna Akhmatova (uhk-MAH-tuh-vuh) (1889–1966), in her requiem for a lost generation, summarized the horror: "Madness has already covered, Half my soul with its wing. And gives to drink of a fiery wine, And beckons into the dark valley."[10]

Economic Costs

The repression also came at a high economic cost. Peasants often destroyed their equipment and livestock as a protest, and agriculture suffered from these losses for decades. Peasants also adopted passive resistance, doing just the minimum to survive. As a result, Russia's annual food production between 1928 and 1980 was less than in 1924. Since the government could not use agricultural surplus to finance industrialization, it squeezed the urban workers, forced to labor long hours for low wages and few consumer goods. Workers in turn became alienated and passively resisted, voicing their feelings in the common expression: "The government pretends they are paying us so we pretend we are working." The economic system was hurt by a lack of initiative and creativity, as well as by high rates of alcoholism and theft.

Reshaping Russian Society

At the same time, the communists introduced modern ideas. The crash industrialization raised the gross national product (GNP), the annual total of all economic activities, to second in the world by 1932, and the Five-Year Plans mobilized the population for industrialization; as with Meiji Japan, the state, rather than private capital, was the main agent for change. The industrial work force nearly tripled between 1928 and 1937. In addition, mass education raised the literacy rate from 28 percent in 1900 to over 90 percent by the 1980s, and better medical care raised life expectancy from thirty-two in 1914 to seventy in 1960.

Communism also reshaped social patterns. Lenin wanted to promote social equality by breaking up traditional institutions, including the patriarchal family. In 1918 the Soviet official and feminist Alexandra Kollontai (1872–1952), arguing that the state should fund child care and domestic work, envisioned public kitchens, laundries, and nurseries so that women could work outside the home. Lenin also made divorce easier, legalized homosexuality, sanctioned free love and abortion, and forbade Muslim women from wearing the veil and men from having multiple wives. Stalin, however, reversed Lenin's policies, restoring the family, making divorce more difficult, banning abortion, and persecuting homosexuals. Kollontai, whose outspokenness on women's freedom antagonized party leaders, later became the Soviet ambassador to Sweden, the world's first female ambassador.

Unlike the atheistic Lenin, who considered religion a form of spiritual oppression by promoting a belief in a better life after death, Stalin moderated official atheism and pragmatically reached some accommodation with the Russian Orthodox Church, while keeping it subject to state control. While many Soviet citizens professed atheism, at least half identified themselves as religious in the 1936 census. Stalin also ordered literary and artistic works to depict Soviet life from a revolutionary perspective, a style known as **socialist realism**.

socialist realism Literary and artistic works that depicted life from a revolutionary perspective, a style first introduced in Stalin's Russia.

The USSR was the first society to leave the capitalist world order, industrialize rapidly under direct state control, and establish a socialist society. Although aimed at catching up to the West in a short time, it came at a high cost in human rights and lives, and its pervasive system of political repression and state control limited its appeal to other societies. Historians debate how much of the Soviet system was due to communism and how much to an autocratic Russian tradition that despised merchants and promoted deference to state power. The USSR combined Marxist ideology, czarist despotism, and the missionary impulse, derived from Christianity, to spread the "true faith" to the world.

SECTION SUMMARY

- The Bolsheviks, a group of Marxist revolutionaries led by Vladimir Lenin, were energized by the unsuccessful 1905 Russian revolution and organized a core of professional activists devoted to violent revolution and more equitable distribution of wealth and power.
- In March 1917, a spontaneous revolution overthrew the czar, but its urban liberal leaders could not satisfy the people's demand for reform and an end to the war, so radical soviets, allied with the Bolsheviks, organized, and in October they seized power and then removed Russia from the war.
- In the interest of spreading the revolution, Lenin founded the Communist International, but he was soon fighting the Russian Civil War against the White Russians, who included defenders of the aristocracy and were funded and armed by Western nations disturbed by the Bolshevik revolution.
- After winning the civil war, the Bolsheviks focused on establishing Marxism-Leninism in the USSR, a brand of socialism achieved through one-party rule that treated opponents ruthlessly and failed to achieve a true connection between the masses and the government.
- Lenin's successor, Joseph Stalin, sent millions to forced-labor camps called gulags and imposed state ownership of all property and a planned economy, which led to decreased harvests and widespread misery.
- Rapid industrialization made the USSR the second largest world economy by 1932, and other advances greatly increased the literacy rate and life expectancy, but at the cost of many lives and limitations of human rights even more severe than under the czars.

The Interwar Years and the Great Depression

How did the Great Depression reshape world politics and economies?

Peace in Europe had brought a great questioning of the old order. By the early 1920s, however, western Europe had stabilized and most countries had democratically elected governments, while the United States enjoyed widespread prosperity. But Western affluence was dramatically undermined by the **Great Depression**, a collapse of the world economy that lasted in varying degrees of severity through the 1930s. The Depression's global reach illustrated the economic interdependence of societies. As the distress affected both industrialized nations and those countries and colonies supplying raw materials, it also fostered radical political movements.

Great Depression A collapse of the world economy that lasted in varying degrees of severity through the 1930s.

Postwar Europe and Japan

Political and Economic Changes

The 1920s was a decade of political, economic, and social change throughout western Europe and Japan. Europe's very slow and painful recovery fostered political opposition movements, placing conservatives on the defensive. Many European governments were weakened by political infighting, and conservative-dominated regimes usually rebuffed the demands of workers for better conditions or unions, causing socialist and social democratic parties, such as the British Labor Party, to grow stronger and try to extend workers' rights through legislation. Some countries remained politically and economically unstable. Under a new democratic government, the Weimar (VIE-mahr) Republic, Germany struggled with high unemployment and a devastated economy, and in 1923 France occupied the industrialized Ruhr district of western Germany to enforce reparations payments. The costly reparations caused hyperinflation in Germany, which in turn fostered extremist groups. Since German prosperity was essential for the European economy, the Allies reduced reparations and the United States extended loans, but the Weimar regime continued to face challenges. Multiethnic countries such as Poland, with its large German, Russian, and Ukrainian minorities, and a Czechoslovakia that mixed Czechs and Slovaks with Germans, Poles, Hungarians, and Ukrainians, also experienced tensions.

However, some countries enjoyed an economic recovery that curbed inflation and unemployment. After Europeans borrowed U.S. mass production processes, including the assembly lines pioneered at Ford Motor Company in Detroit, the growing middle classes could afford cars, radios, refrigerators, vacuum cleaners, and central heating. Although the urban white-collar class tended to oppose working-class socialism, labor unions also gained strength, helping some workers achieve an eight-hour day. Yet Europe's economies were more and more bound up with the world economy, losing ground to the United States and Japan.

Various forces fostered European unity to safeguard peace. To promote peace and unity among European nations, some leaders emphasized their common roots in classical Greece, Rome, and Christianity. The visionary French foreign minister, Aristide Briand **(bree-AHND)** (1862–1932), led efforts to renounce war among European nations, proposing a federal union and common market. His vision only came to fruition two decades later, with the formation of the European Common Market.

Cities and Gender Relations

Social change in the cities included new patterns of leisure and consumption. Affluent people found entertainment at nightclubs, cabarets, and dancehalls and shopped at large department stores, and U.S. culture, especially jazz, became widely popular. Religious observance declined because some Europeans felt abandoned by God on the battlefields or rejected Christianity as a patriarchal faith out of tune with their lives. Women's fashions emphasized short hair and a boyish figure, while the "new woman" sought financial independence through paid work. As the war had left fewer young men to marry or hire, women moved into office jobs, the female secretary replacing the male clerk. More women also became lawyers, physicians, and even members of parliaments. Finally, in many countries, women fought for and often achieved suffrage. Before the war only Norway and Finland had women's suffrage. Denmark gave women the vote in 1915 and Germany in 1919, while Britain extended it to women over thirty in 1918 and to all women over eighteen in 1928. But many countries, including France and Italy, ignored these demands.

As gender standards changed, once-shocking attitudes became common, including an openness about sexuality and a rejection of traditional marriage. Women now wore clothes that showed off their figure, and beauty contests featured women in revealing swimsuits that would have once been considered scandalous. Yet, official attitudes toward homosexuality shifted toward repression. In the nineteenth century, despite antisodomy laws on the books, courts had usually dismissed charges of homosexual relations, and Europeans understood that some men and women had same-sex relations or emotional ties. By the early 1900s, however, the media identified homosexuals as different in attitudes from heterosexuals. While gay men and lesbians lived openly in cities such as Paris and Berlin, they were often watched and suffered police raids on their clubs. Although Soviet Russia and Weimar Germany legalized homosexuality, these tolerant policies were later reversed. In 1934 Stalin defined homosexuality as a crime against the state, and in 1935 Nazi Germany prosecuted 50,000 men for homosexual activity. Many European nations also banned abortion and birth control.

Changing Japan

As in Europe, industrialization, democratic politics, and liberalization reshaped Japan during the 1920s, generating prosperity and new possibilities for the growing urban middle class. Japan's population tripled between 1860 and 1940 to 60 million, but lack of land forced many rural people to move to cities or emigrate to the Americas to find work. Cheap labor helped to gain foreign markets for Japanese consumer goods, especially textiles. Powerful business interests dominated the democratic system, and corrupt and volatile politics disillusioned many Japanese of all social classes.

Japan played a visible role in the world. Even before World War I, it had already colonized Taiwan and Korea and gained footholds in northern China, and during the war it acquired the German colonies in the Pacific and the German sphere of influence in eastern China. This assertive role created enemies. Tensions with the United States increased, fostered in part by the American racist laws restricting the rights of Japanese immigrants and in part by U.S. hostility to Japanese ambitions in Asia and the Pacific.

As in the 1870s, a wave of Western influence permeated Japan's cities. American popular culture influenced urban middle-class Japanese, and baseball became a popular sport. In Tokyo, young men and women, known as the "modern boy" and "modern girl," wore the latest imported styles while enjoying jazz, beer halls, and Western films. Young women avidly read mass women's magazines, many questioned the tradition of the submissive female and dominant male, and many young people sought freedom to choose their own marriage partners. Feminism also grew. For conservatives, nontraditional Japanese such as the openly lesbian writer Yoshiya Nobuko **(yo-SHE-ya no-BOO-ko)**, whose work had a large following among youth (see Profile: Yoshiya Nobuko: Japanese Writer and Gender Rebel), were leading Japan in the wrong direction. The feminist poet Yosano

Akiko celebrated the emerging women's movement: "All the sleeping women, Are now awake and moving."[11] Another leading feminist, Kato Shidzue (KAH-to shid-ZOO-ee) (1897–2001), sojourned in the United States and then advocated family planning and equal political rights for women. Japanese thinkers and artists also pondered the divide between traditional and modern values and cultural identity. The writer Akutagawa Ryunosuke (1892–1927), who combined Western and Japanese traditions, wrote an influential short story, *Rashoman*, that tells of a rape and murder from several eyewitness perceptions. However, the working classes and rural population were alienated from the Westernized middle class culture of the cities, seeing little benefit in either the liberalization of customs or individualistic Western thought. Nor did they share in the economic prosperity.

CHRONOLOGY
Europe, North America, and Japan, 1919–1940

1919–1920 First Red Scare in United States

1921 Irish Free State

1921 Formation of Italian fascist movement

1926 Formation of fascist state in Italy

1929–1941 Great Depression

1931 Japanese occupation of Manchuria

1933–1945 Presidency of Franklin D. Roosevelt

1932 Nazi electoral victory in Germany

1933–1938 Anti-Jewish legislation in Germany

1935–1936 Italian conquest of Ethiopia

1936 Start of fascist government in Japan

October 1936 Hitler-Mussolini alliance

1936–1939 Spanish Civil War

1937 Japanese invasion of China

March 1938 Austrian merger with Germany

1938 German annexation of western Czechoslovakia

August 1939 Nazi-Soviet pact

September 1939 German invasion of Poland

1940 Tripartite Pact between Germany, Italy, and Japan

U.S. Society and Politics

In the United States, anticommunism prompted by the Russian Revolution and growing middle-class prosperity bolstered conservative forces. Americans were hostile to socialism of any kind and especially communist ideology, and hatred of Russians and communism replaced hatred of Germans. In 1919–1920 widespread public fear of communism, known as the "Red Scare," generated the first in a series of government crackdowns on dissidents that suppressed strikes, harassed labor unions, arrested political radicals, and deported foreigners (see Chronology: Europe, North America, and Japan, 1919–1940). The Red Scare froze attitudes toward communist movements for generations, as the United States pursued a policy of isolating the USSR. A U.S. senator and critic of this policy concluded in 1925, "So long as you have a hundred and fifty million people [in the U.S.S.R.] outlawed, it necessarily follows that you cannot have peace."[12] Not until 1933 would the United States soften its policy and extend diplomatic recognition.

Various forms of domestic unrest also existed. Desperate workers struck for better wages, while left-wing unions fought against the power of "big business." In response, alarmed federal, state, and local governments helped employers fight labor unions in the Appalachian coal fields, Detroit auto plants, and South Atlantic textile mills, sending police to break up strikes and arrest union organizers. There was also widespread resentment of the U.S. Congress for passing Prohibition, which outlawed alcohol production and made it harder to obtain liquor. In addition, World War I veterans protested when the government was slow in providing their back pay and they had trouble finding jobs. Federal government policies often made life worse for the less affluent, and political leaders ignored terrorism, including lynchings by white racists of African Americans in the South. To escape mistreatment and limited economic prospects, several million African Americans moved from southern states to the north and west in the 1920s, doubling the black populations of cities such as Chicago, Detroit, and New York. Dominating the federal government, the Republicans, oriented toward big business, neglected the country's natural and human resources, contributing to eroded croplands and fouled rivers.

The Roarin' 20s

For the top half of the U.S. population, however, including a growing middle class, these were the "Roarin' 20s," the hedonistic era when high society had few inhibitions. Affluent whites evaded Prohibition by buying illegally produced liquor. Gatsby, a character in a novel by the popular writer and playboy F. Scott Fitzgerald (1896–1940), exemplified the optimistic American values of the time: "Gatsby believed in the green light, the future that year by year recedes before us. It eluded us then, but that's no matter—tomorrow we will run faster, stretch out our arms farther, and one fine morning . . ."[13] Other changes affected all Americans. Jazz music, rooted in southern black culture, provided employment for black musicians and became so popular that the era was often known as "the Jazz Age." Women finally won the vote in 1920, allowing more of them to enjoy a larger public role. And all Americans celebrated the first nonstop flight between North America and Europe, made by Charles Lindbergh (1902–1974) in 1927, a feat demonstrating both heroism and advances in technology.

Isolationism

In contrast to Woodrow Wilson's idealistic globalism, American leaders proclaimed an isolationist foreign policy; in reality, however, they often practiced interventionism. Restless American citizens sought new Christian converts, commercial markets, and business investments, reflecting

YOSHIYA NOBUKO, JAPANESE WRITER AND GENDER REBEL

Yoshiya Nobuko (1896–1973) was a popular, gender-bending writer who lived through major transitions as Japan moved from a parochial society through imperial power and world war to become an industrial powerhouse. She was born in the northern Honshu city of Niigata just after the Japanese victory over China in the Sino-Japanese War (1894–1895). Her middle-class, culturally conservative parents trained her for the "good wife, wise mother" role expected of women in Meiji Japan. Yoshiya observed that her mother encouraged her to adopt traditional roles of female domesticity and obedience to men while she herself remained in a loveless arranged marriage to Yoshiya's father.

Yoshiya, who began writing as a child, published her first short stories at age twelve. In 1915 she moved to Tokyo, where she began to diverge from Japanese society's career and gender expectations. Rising Japanese literacy was opening doors to literature aimed at a popular audience, allowing writers such as Yoshiya to make a living from their work. Between 1916 and 1924 Yoshiya's short stories were serialized in a popular magazine, *Girl's Illustrated*, aimed at young, chiefly female readers. The stories she published inspired a generation of women writers and made Yoshiya famous. They appealed to schoolgirls and to the growing group of women not yet committed to marriage and children. According to tradition, women were supposed to be married by age twenty-four, but many young women now worked in the public sector as clerks, cafe hostesses, ticket sellers, schoolteachers, typists, and telephone operators. Yoshiya's core audience came from this group, especially the so-called modern girl, a Westernized urban woman who avoided or postponed marriage. Critics accused these women of being un-Japanese and manly.

Kyoto News Photos

Yoshiya Nobuko A prominent Japanese writer for popular audiences, especially for girls and young women, Yoshiya Nobuko represented the modern girl. She wore her hair short and usually dressed in a mannish style that defied gender expectations.

In her writing and life, the very modern Yoshiya took advantage of the new public sphere opened to women for redefining relations between them. She challenged the conventions of family life, openly avowing her lesbianism. Japanese had traditionally tolerated homosexuality, including public displays of affection by people of the same gender. Now more openly passionate friendships between females were becoming common among students, educators, civil servants, and actresses. Japanese society viewed female homosexuality as spiritual, in contrast to the popular image of the carnal male version, and gradually lesbianism developed from a phase of life among girls to an adult subculture. Despite laws requiring women to have long hair, Yoshiya was one of the first Japanese women to emulate Western fashion in the 1920s by cutting her hair short, symbolizing her maverick persona. In 1923 Yoshiya met her life partner, Monma Chiyo, a mathematics teacher at a Tokyo girls' school. They remained inseparable and openly lived together as a couple, writing steamy, often erotic, love letters to each other even when together. In 1957 Yoshiya adopted Monma, the only legal way for homosexual couples to share property and make medical decisions for each other. Yoshiya also flouted gender expectations in other ways. She designed her own house, was one of the first Japanese to own a car, and was the first Japanese woman to own a racehorse.

Yoshiya became one of Japan's most successful and highest-paid writers. A literary critic wrote in 1935 that "there isn't a [Japanese] woman alive who hasn't heard of Yoshiya." Her Japanese readership included many middle-class men and women, gay and straight, single and married. She published girls' fiction, social commentary, and autobiographical essays. Some literary critics criticized Yoshiya for seeking a mass audience, but her defenders argued that Yoshiya's writing broadened minds. She and Monma spent 1929 traveling in Russia, Europe, and the United States, where she was impressed by what she considered America's liberated women. After the trip, she vowed to no longer write about women "who cried a lot and simply endured their miserable lot in life."

While an ardent feminist, Yoshiya mistrusted political parties and never became active in the organized Japanese feminist movement. She also disliked the militaristic turn of the 1930s, which brought more censorship. To avoid political harassment or imprisonment, she joined a government writers' group that toured Southeast Asia and China during World War II and wrote stories and reports praising Japanese imperial ambitions. After the war she continued to publish fiction and nonfiction, winning numerous awards. She began to write historical novels to redress female stereotypes in male fiction, such as the dutiful wife, and to restore the voice of women to Japanese history. She died at home at age seventy-seven, holding Monma's hand. Yoshiya's writings remain popular in Japan today.

THINKING ABOUT THE PROFILE

1. How did Yoshiya's life reflect the social changes of the era in Japan?
2. Why might her writing have attracted a large audience?

Note: Quotations from Jennifer Robertson, "Yoshiya Nobuko: Out and Outspoken in Practice and Prose," in Anne Walthall , ed., *The Human Tradition in Modern Japan* (Wilmington, DE: SR Books, 2002), 156, 167.

the optimistic, unsettled character of American society, which emphasized free enterprise and the belief in America's political and economic model. In 1904 President Theodore Roosevelt had proclaimed that America should intervene as an international police power whenever a country, in his estimation, committed chronic wrongdoing. This view, adopted by later U.S. presidents, justified military interventions to punish opponents and reward allies in Latin America. U.S. Marines remained in Nicaragua for decades (1909–1933), and El Salvador, Haiti, Mexico, and the Dominican Republic all experienced major U.S. military incursions between 1914 and 1940.

The Great Depression

Roots of Disaster

The major spur to change, the Great Depression, began in the United States in the fall of 1929, when prices on the New York Stock Exchange fell dramatically, ruining many investors. This crash ultimately precipitated a worldwide economic disaster unprecedented in intensity, longevity, and spread that lasted until 1941 and affected industrial and agricultural economies alike. The flow of wealth into the United States had intensified existing imbalances in world trade and investment. Generally self-sufficient, the U.S was less dependent on world trade than Britain had been when it was the world's leading economic power. While the British had invested profits abroad, Americans mostly invested and spent at home to satisfy a self-indulgent society. Meanwhile, stiff U.S. government tariff barriers against manufactured goods hurt European economies, and the nation refused to shift to an aggressive free trade position until well into the 1930s. Furthermore, the world banking and credit structure was very unstable, partly because the United States did not use its unmatched economic power to make the world economy work efficiently. Instead U.S. banks, too anxious for profits, became overextended in loans to Britain, France, and Germany. Conditions within the United States also generated the Great Depression. A "get-rich-quick" philosophy led to reckless financial practices, such as risky loans and investments. Income inequality was stark: by 1929 the top 20 percent of American families earned 54 percent of the income while the bottom 40 percent earned 12.5 percent. As more people fell into poverty, purchasing power declined, while more consumer products became available, causing a glut. As a result, many manufacturers could not sell enough products to stay in business or avoid layoffs.

Economic Collapse

These problems led to the stock market crash, followed later by bank failures. As U.S. banks faced ruin, they called in their debts from western European banks, triggering a chain reaction of bank failures. In the United States the GNP and industrial output fell by one-half in four years, and unemployment rose to 25 percent of the labor force by 1932. All areas of the U.S. economy were hurt, and the misery was widespread. President Herbert Hoover (g. 1929–1933), who opposed government intervention in the economy, failed to stem the collapse or the pain. Things were even

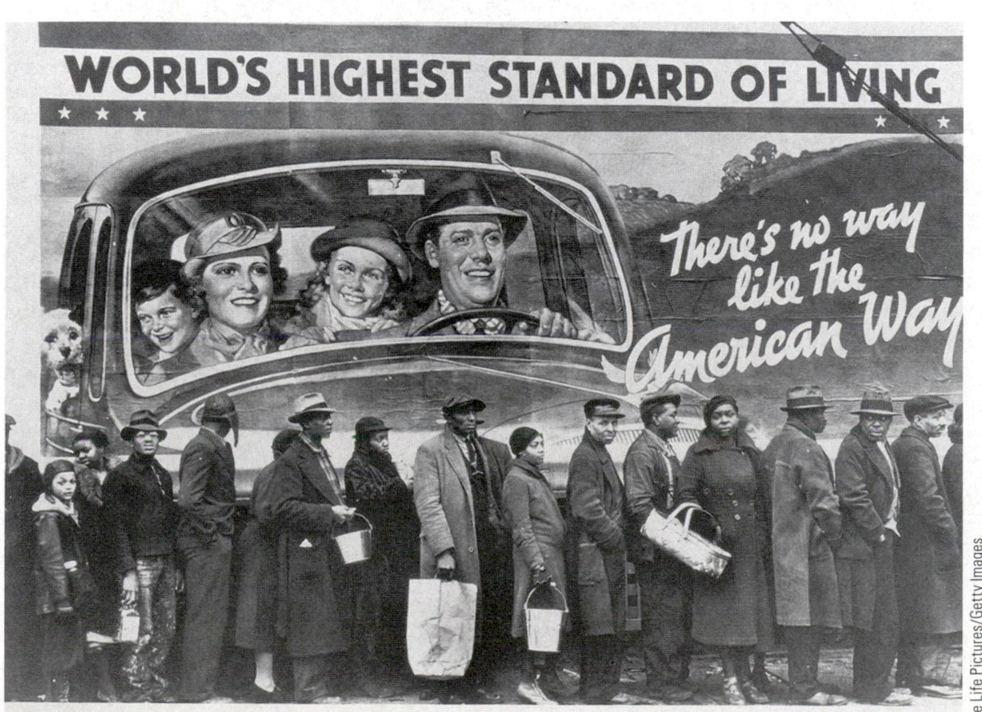

Time Life Pictures/Getty Images

Depression Breadline During the Depression, breadlines, such as this one in New York City, were common in the United States as millions of unemployed and desperate people sought food from social service providers, including religious groups.

worse in European nations. Some 30 percent of Germans were out of work by 1932, and German industrial output declined by half. A French politician summed up the disaster in his nation: "The oceans were deserted, the ships laid up in the silent ports, the factory smokestacks dead, long lines of workless in the towns, poverty throughout the countryside. Nations were economically cut off from one another, but they shared the common lot of poverty."[14] Many societies in Asia, Africa, Latin America, and the Caribbean were also devastated as demand for, and hence the price of, raw materials such as rubber, tin, and sugar plummeted. Only the USSR avoided major pain, since it was largely outside the world economy and hence somewhat insulated from the dislocations.

U.S. Distress

The Great Depression brought severe economic distress to the United States. Homeowners and farmers saw banks foreclose on their property, migrant workers moved around in a futile search for jobs, hungry Americans flocked to breadlines and soup kitchens for food and milk supplied by charitable organizations, and sidewalk vendors hoped to make a few pennies selling apples. Shantytowns known as "Hoovervilles" sprang up on the edges of cities to house the unemployed and dispossessed, and parts of the Midwest and Southwest became a **Dust Bowl**, as terrible drought and disappearing topsoil, caused by erosion and government neglect, put agriculture badly out of balance. Farm income dropped 50 percent, causing 3 to 4 million people, mostly farmers, to head to the West Coast after selling or losing their land. A witness in 1932 told a congressional committee: "The roads of the West and Southwest teem with hungry hitchhikers. The campfires of the homeless are seen along every railroad track."[15] The experiences of these impoverished migrants were chronicled in the novels of John Steinbeck (1902–1968), such as *The Grapes of Wrath*, and by the leftwing Oklahoma-born folksinger, Woody Guthrie (1912–1967), in songs such as "Pastures of Plenty": "I've worked in your orchards of peaches and prunes, Slept on the ground in the light of the moon, On the edge of your city you've seen us and then, We come with the dust and we go with the wind."[16]

Dust Bowl Parts of the U.S. Midwest and Southwest during the 1930s where disappearing topsoil and severe drought threw agriculture badly out of balance.

Panic, despair, and disillusionment seized the country. Unlike some western Europeans, Americans had no social security, unemployment insurance, or welfare system to turn to. In 1932, when ragged World War I veterans marched in Washington, D.C., demanding payment of the bonuses once promised them, President Hoover ordered federal troops to disperse them at gunpoint. As a result, the union movement and leftwing political parties such as the communists grew rapidly, and labor militancy and strikes led to confrontations between workers and the police. Women had to stay with their children in tent cities while their husbands looked for work. Jobless men lost status and often turned to drink. The Depression also intensified the poverty of African Americans, whose unemployment rate approached 70 percent.

Roosevelt's Presidency

The Depression caused a change of leadership and turnaround in U.S. government policy. Discontent against inaction drove the Republicans from office in 1933 and brought in a new president, Democrat Franklin Delano Roosevelt (1882–1945). Roosevelt expressed optimism, telling the nation that they had nothing to fear but fear itself. He introduced the **New Deal**, a new government policy of liberal reform within a democratic framework to alleviate the suffering. Roosevelt proposed what he called the "four freedoms"—freedom of speech and worship and freedom from want and fear. His reforms included regulations on banks and stock exchanges to prevent future depressions, public welfare programs, and social security, which guaranteed retirement income for workers. For the first time, the federal government took responsibility for providing pensions and other supportive help to citizens. Roosevelt also supported union organizing. Although it did not end the Depression, the New Deal made government popular and modified the pain. By defusing the appeal of socialism and communism, it also saved U.S. capitalism. In the later 1930s, when the recovery faltered, Roosevelt used the ideas of the British economist John Maynard Keynes (1883–1946), who advocated deficit spending by governments to spur economic growth. Keynes argued that free markets were not self-correcting and needed government regulation. The mobilization of military forces and manufacturing during World War II finally ended the Depression.

New Deal A new U.S. government program of liberal reform within a democratic framework introduced by President Franklin Roosevelt to alleviate suffering caused by the Great Depression.

European Distress

By devastating the economies of Europe and Japan, the Depression challenged the weaker democratic systems. A quarter to a third of Europeans became jobless. Germans often faced malnutrition, and hunger marches became common in Britain. A French observer described Paris as an "abyss of misery, suffering, and disorder, the theaters nearly empty, factories shut, businesses bankrupt; grey faces and bad news everywhere."[17] Countries developed public works programs to create jobs and also discouraged imports, further reducing international trade. However, some nations lacked the resources for a New Deal type of reform. To pay the World War I reparations, Germany had borrowed heavily, especially from the United States, and had no way to repay the loans.

A few nations gradually relieved the distress. Newer British industries such as motor and aircraft production and electronics showed rapid growth, and increased consumer demand gradually turned around the British economy. The Scandinavian nations of Denmark, Norway, and Sweden had the most success by pursuing "the Middle Way," a combination of undogmatic socialist economics with long-established democratic traditions based on community action. Social democratic parties, favoring a mix of free markets, a welfare state, and democratic politics, had come to power in Scandinavia in the 1920s. By increasing government intervention in the economy, the social democrats ensured full employment and protected people from hardship.

Japan in Crisis

The Depression hit Japan even harder than Europe and the United States, making clear its nearly total dependence on foreign trade. As the world economy collapsed, many foreign markets closed, unemployment skyrocketed, and Japan's foreign trade was cut in half in two years, forcing Japan's 100 million people to dramatically reduce consumption of necessities such as food and fuel. Because Japan had no access to the resource-rich Western colonies in Southeast Asia, Japanese leaders, becoming more authoritarian, turned to radical solutions, including expansion abroad and building a heavy arms industry.

Western Cultures, Thought, and Science

Rise of Mass Culture

Tempered by the trauma of war and then the Depression, Western culture went in new directions, including the rise of mass culture, popular entertainments appealing to a wide segment of the population and disseminated by radio and motion pictures. Radio stations appeared and the recording industry grew. By 1930, 40 percent of U.S. families owned a radio; by 1940, 86 percent did. In North America and Europe the urban middle class found solace especially in popular music. American jazz musicians such as Louis Armstrong, Duke Ellington, and Billie Holiday had an international following, and songs written by New York City–based writers, known collectively as Tin Pan Alley, reached millions around the world through radios, records, movies, and musical theater. The sophisticated and romantic songs written by Americans like Richard Rodgers and Lorenz Hart, George and Ira Gershwin, Irving Berlin, Jerome Kern, and Cole Porter buoyed peoples' spirits. Porter's song, "Anything Goes" (1934), chronicled changing fashions: "In olden days a bit of [women's] stocking, was looked on as something shocking. Now, heaven knows, anything goes." By contrast, some popular songs of the 1930s, such as "The Boulevard of Broken Dreams" and "Brother, Can You Spare a Dime?," addressed harsh reality.

Arts and Science

Cultural vistas expanded. Painters, poets, and novelists settled in a few run-down Paris neighborhoods and produced work that vigorously broke from older traditions. The innovative and versatile painter Pablo Picasso (1881–1973), a Spaniard who settled in Paris, helped invent **cubism**, a form of painting that rejected visual reality and emphasized instead geometric shapes and forms that often suggested movement. Soon Picasso, who later joined the Communist Party, abandoned representational art entirely and sought visual experience as transformed by the artist in his mind. Literature explored the inner world of thought and feelings. The Irishman James Joyce (1882–1941), who had enjoyed no formal education, broke traditional rules of grammar, and his books were often banned for using obscenity. In England Virginia Woolf (1882–1941) converted the novel from a narrative story into a succession of images, thoughts, and emotions known as stream of consciousness. Her 1929 novel, *A Room of One's Own*, championed women's growing economic independence.

cubism A form of painting that rejected visual reality and emphasized instead geometric shapes and forms that often suggested movement.

The social and natural sciences also brought a greater understanding of human behavior and the physical world. Sigmund Freud **(FROID)** (1856–1939), an Austrian Jewish physician, developed psychoanalysis, a combination of medical science and psychology, and shocked the world by arguing that sex was of great subconscious importance in shaping people's behavior. In physics, Albert Einstein (1879–1955) radically modified the Newtonian vision of physical nature and rejected the absolutes of space and time, arguing that time depended on the relative motion of the measurer and the thing measured. Einstein fled the anti-Jewish atmosphere of Nazi Germany for the United States, where he helped convince President Roosevelt to sponsor research on atomic weapons. He spent the rest of his life seeking a unifying theory to explain every physical process in the universe.

SECTION SUMMARY

- After the war Germany experienced rapid inflation because of its postwar debt, Europe lost economic ground to the United States and Japan, and women entered the work force and the political sphere.
- Many Japanese benefited from postwar economic growth, though some rural Japanese had to move to cities or emigrate, while Japan played a larger role in world affairs and clashed with the United States over its treatment of Japanese immigrants and Japanese ambitions in Asia.
- American fear of communism led to the "Red Scare," a harsh crackdown on dissidents and union organizers, while the split widened between the poor, who suffered under government policies, and the affluent, who enjoyed the "Roarin' 20s."
- Among the factors contributing to the Great Depression were America hoarding its profits, American tariffs against European imports, risky investment practices (which helped cause the stock market crash of 1929), and uneven distribution of income.
- With millions of Americans jobless, homeless, and hungry, radical movements grew in power and President Franklin Delano Roosevelt instituted the New Deal, a sweeping series of programs that put people to work, provided pensions, and protected against future depressions.
- The Great Depression hit Europe and Japan even harder than the United States, rendering Germany unable to pay its heavy debts and causing Japan to become more authoritarian and expansionist, while Scandinavian nations emerged in better condition by combining socialism, free markets, and democracy.
- The United States took the lead in developing the new mass media of radio and motion pictures, painters such as Picasso broke radically with earlier forms, and Freud and Einstein did pioneering work in psychoanalysis and physics.

The Rise of Fascism and the Renewal of Conflict

What were the main ideas and impacts of fascism?

fascism An ideology that typically involved extreme nationalism, hatred of ethnic minorities, ruthless repression of opposition groups, violent anticommunism, glorification of the state, and authoritarian government.

By devastating the economies of Germany and Japan, the Great Depression helped spread a new ideology in these countries. This ideology, **fascism**, typically involved extreme nationalism, hatred of ethnic minorities, ruthless repression of opposition groups, violent anticommunism, glorification of the state, and authoritarian government. Fascist movements often included a party with a large membership, such as the German Nazis (National Socialist German Workers), that was headed by a charismatic leader and supported military expansion. Fascism, which assaulted liberal values and rational thinking, was embraced by Italy, Germany, and Japan and also influenced China and several eastern European and Latin American nations.

The March to Fascism

Fascism in Italy

First emerging in Italy in 1921, fascism was a response to political corruption, an economic slump, and the instability of democratic politics. Domestic unrest increased as peasants and workers demanded a fairer share of wealth, and fascism arose from a pragmatic alliance of upper-class conservatives in the military, bureaucracy, and industry with discouraged members of the middle class who faced economic hardships. Both groups feared communism. Benito Mussolini (1883–1945), a one-time teacher and journalist and former socialist and World War I veteran, founded the Italian fascist movement, which advocated national unity and strong government. A spellbinding orator, Mussolini aroused mass enthusiasm by promising a vigorous and disciplined Italy. He especially attracted war veterans with his nationalistic rhetoric, using an ancient Roman symbol, the *fasces*, a bundle of sticks wrapped around an ax handle and blade, to symbolize the unity he wanted to bring Italy. Landowners and industrialists funded his movement because it battered labor and peasant organizations, and the upper classes viewed Mussolini as a bulwark against the radical workers.

Mussolini also won the support of the Italian king, the Catholic Church, and the lower middle class, from which he organized a uniform-wearing paramilitary group, the Blackshirts, who violently attacked, intimidated, and sometimes murdered opponents. In 1922 the king asked Mus-

The Doctrine of Fascism

Benito Mussolini gradually developed an ideology for his movement that appealed to the Italian people's nationalistic emotions. The following excerpt comes from an essay under Mussolini's name that was published in an Italian encyclopedia in 1932. In fact, the true author was a Mussolini confidant, the philosopher Giovanni Gentile. The essay reflected Mussolini's vision of fascism as the wave of the future, in which the individual would subordinate her or his desires to the needs of the state.

Fascism, the more it considers and observes the future and the development of humanity quite apart from political considerations of the moment, believes neither in the possibility nor the utility of perpetual peace. It thus repudiates the doctrine of Pacifism—born of the renunciation of the struggle and an act of cowardice in the face of sacrifice. War alone brings up to its highest tension all human energy and puts the stamp of nobility upon the peoples who have the courage to meet it. . . . Fascism [is] the complete opposite of . . . Marxian Socialism, the materialist conception of history. . . . Above all Fascism denies that class-war can be the preponderant force in the transformation of society. . . .

After Socialism, Fascism combats the whole complex system of democratic ideology, and repudiates it, whether in its theoretical premises or in its practical application. Fascism denies that the majority, by the simple fact that it is a majority, can direct human society; it denies that numbers alone can govern by means of periodic consultation. . . . The democratic regime . . . [gives] the illusion of sovereignty, while the real effective sovereignty lies in the hands of other concealed and irresponsible forces. . . .

But the Fascist negation of Socialism, Democracy, and Liberalism must not be taken to mean that Fascism desires to lead the world back to the state of affairs before 1789 [the French Revolution]. . . . Given that the nineteenth century was the century of Socialism, of Liberalism, and of Democracy, it does not . . . follow that the twentieth century must also be the century of Socialism, Liberalism, and Democracy: political doctrines pass, but humanity remains. . . .

The foundation of Fascism is the conception of the State, its character, its duty, and its aim. Fascism conceives of the State as an absolute, in comparison with which all individuals or groups are relative, only to be conceived of in their relation to the State. . . . The Fascist state is itself conscious, and has itself a will and a personality. . . . The Fascist state is an embodied will to power and government, the Roman tradition is here an ideal of force in action. . . . Government is not so much a thing to be expressed in territorial or military terms as in terms of morality and the spirit. It must be thought of as an Empire—. . . a nation which directly or indirectly rules other nations. . . . For Fascism the growth of Empire, . . . the expansion of the nation, is an essential manifestation of vitality, and its opposite a sign of decadence. . . . But Empire demands discipline, the co-ordination of all forces and a deeply felt sense of duty and sacrifice; this fact explains many aspects of the practical working of the regime, the character of many forces in the State, and the necessarily severe measures which must be taken against those who would oppose this spontaneous and inevitable movement of Italy in the twentieth century, and would oppose it by recalling the outworn ideology of the nineteenth century.

THINKING ABOUT THE READING

1. Why does fascism reject pacifism, socialism, and liberal democracy?
2. What role does the state play under fascism?

Source: B. Mussolini, "The Political and Social Doctrine of Fascism," *Political Quarterly*, IV (July–September, 1933), pp. 341–356.

solini to form a government, and by 1926 Mussolini had killed, arrested, or cowed his opponents, turned Italy into a one-party state with restricted civil liberties, and created a cult of personality around himself (see Witness to the Past: The Doctrine of Fascism). Many Italians believed Mussolini was restoring social order, and they appreciated that the government was efficient; the trains ran on time, a rare experience under democratic Italian regimes.

German Fascism

Fascism also became dominant in Germany after the Depression undermined the moderate, democratic Weimar Republic. Germany had no colonies to tap for resources and markets that might aid recovery from World War I, and Weimar leaders could not solve the severe problems. The German people, who had an authoritarian political tradition and an economy in shambles, resented the reparation payments imposed after World War I, which drained the treasury. Thus many Germans, preferring security to freedom, were willing to listen to a charismatic leader who offered simplistic answers to complex problems. The upper and middle classes also feared working-class socialism.

The Nazi (National Socialist) Party, led by Adolph Hitler (1889–1945), offered a strategy for regaining political and economic strength and for keeping workers under control. Hitler, an Austrian-born social misfit, had made a precarious living painting signs and doing odd jobs before joining the German army in World War I, at which time he already nurtured a hatred of Jews and labor unions. In 1920 Hitler helped form the Nazi Party, which promised to halt

Hitler's Motorcade
In this photo from 1938, Adolph Hitler, standing stiffly in his car, salutes members of a paramilitary Nazi group, the Brownshirts, who parade before him at a Nazi rally in Nuremburg.

Time Life Pictures/Getty Images

the unpopular reparations payments and capitalized on the Great Depression to increase their strength. With economic collapse, the industrial workers moved left toward the communists while the middle classes moved right toward the Nazi movement, financed by big industrialists. Thus Germany became a polarized society. Many Germans were willing to believe that Germany's problems could be blamed on unpopular minorities and foreign powers, and Hitler, understanding propaganda and how to use a few basic ideas, made up "facts" to gain support. In his book *Mein Kampf* (My Struggle), written in 1924, he argued that "all effective propaganda has to limit itself to a very few points and to use them like slogans. A political leader must not fear to speak a lie if this might be effective."[18] Hitler developed a catchy slogan: "one people, one government, one leader."

Nazi Policies

The Nazis won the largest number of seats in the 1932 elections, and Hitler became chancellor (the equivalent of prime minister) in 1933. Even though the Nazis won only 44 percent of the vote, Hitler tightened his grip on power and moved immediately to impose dramatic changes, including a thorough purging of the schools, theater, cinema, literature, and press so that he could manipulate them. The Nazis outlawed leftist parties, suspended civil liberties, imposed heavy censorship, mobilized youth, told women to stay at home and take care of their husbands and children, and expanded the army. They also regeared the economy toward rearmament, thus solving the terrible unemployment problem. By 1939 Germany's GNP was 50 percent higher than it had been in 1929, mainly because of the manufacture of heavy machinery and armaments. The Nazi myth about maintaining a pure German people—what Hitler termed the Aryan race, after the ancient Indo-Europeans who settled Europe, Persia, and India—also led to anti-Semitic laws between 1933 and 1938. Hitler banned marriage and sexual relations between Jews and so-called Aryan Germans, and he excluded the Jews, many of them assimilated into German culture, from many occupations and citizenship, pushing them into ghettos in German cities, where they could be watched. The Nazis also enacted harsh laws against homosexuals and the Romany, or Gypsies, another unpopular minority.

Japanese Fascism

During the 1930s Japan and Germany came to resemble each other fairly closely, even if their forms of fascism were very different. Although Japan never developed a mass-based Fascist Party, Japanese leaders blamed foreign nations, especially the United States and the USSR, for Japan's problems, and big business supported military expansion to gain resources and markets. To this end, military officers assassinated liberal politicians and fomented violence in the Chinese province of Manchuria, which was rich in natural resources and had open land on which to settle Japanese. In 1931 Japan invaded and occupied Manchuria, but the League of Nations imposed no stiff penalties on Japan, a failure that helped to discredit that organization. By 1936 the military, in alliance with big business and bureaucratic interests, controlled Japan and imposed a fascist government that promoted labor control, censorship, the glorification of war, police repression, and hatred of foreign powers. The schools and media indoctrinated the population in obedience, patriarchy, and the sacred origins of the Japanese people while attacking Western individualism and democracy. Then in 1937 a military skirmish outside Beijing provided an excuse for Japan to launch a full-scale invasion of China, and by 1938 Japan controlled most of eastern China. When Japan signed a pact with Germany and Italy in 1940, the United States and Britain introduced strong economic sanctions, including an oil embargo. Japan now faced economic collapse or war.

CHRONOLOGY
World War II, 1939–1945

1939 Beginning of war in Europe

June 1941 German invasion of Soviet Union

December 1941 Japanese bombing of Pearl Harbor; invasion of Southeast Asia

1942 Battle of Midway

1944 Allied landing at Normandy

July 1944 Bretton Woods Conference

February 1945 Yalta Conference

April 1945 Allied invasion of Germany

August 1945 U.S. bombing of Hiroshima and Nagasaki

The Road to War

During the later 1930s the European nations moved toward war, forming various alliances. The United States, Britain, and France, known as the Allies, led democracies that wanted to preserve the European state structure, the global economy, and the colonial system in Asia and Africa. The fascist countries, led by Germany, Italy, and Japan, known as the Axis Powers, sought to change the political map of Europe and Asia and gain world economic dominance. The prelude to another world war was also marked by diplomatic problems caused in part by a massive arms buildup and the imperialism of the Axis nations. Hitler pursued an aggressive policy to dominate eastern Europe, arguing that Germany needed living space and colonies, and to unite the several million ethnic Germans living in eastern Europe. In 1936 Hitler's troops occupied the German territory west of the Rhine River that was demilitarized after World War I, and in 1935 Italy invaded and brutally conquered the last independent African kingdom, Ethiopia. The League of Nations voted ineffective sanctions against Italy. While Hitler and Mussolini forged a close alliance, the later Tripartite Pact of 1940, linking Germany and Italy with Japan, was a marriage of necessity, strained and wary. The Japanese pursued the pact partly to warn the United States that opposing Japanese expansion also meant facing the Germans and Italians.

Spanish Civil War

Civil war in Spain heightened European tensions by drawing in foreign intervention. Liberals and conservatives had long struggled to shape Spanish politics, and Spain was polarized between left and right. During the 1936 elections, Spain's Republicans, a leftwing coalition of liberals, socialists, and communists promising reforms, edged out the National Front of conservatives, monarchists, and staunch Catholics. The right rallied around the fascist military forces led by General Francisco Franco (1892–1975), launching the Spanish Civil War (1936–1939). The Loyalist government, aided by the USSR, ultimately lost to Franco's fascists at a huge cost in lives. Germany and Italy helped the Spanish fascists with weapons and advice, and several thousand volunteers from North America and European nations fought for the Loyalist cause. But the Western Allies refused to support the Loyalists, viewing them as too radical. The German bombing of Guernica (GWAR-ni-kuh), a village in northern Spain, caused an international outcry and prompted Pablo Picasso to paint a celebrated testament to the atrocity. Spain endured Franco's fascist dictatorship until 1975.

German Aggression

In the late 1930s the Allies followed a policy of appeasement toward fascist aggression. They were not yet prepared for war, and the catastrophe of World War I led many to see another war as too terrible to contemplate, even the end of civilization. Historians debate whether the appeasement policy, generally supported by public opinion, was realistic, the best of the available options, or a shameful betrayal that only whetted fascist appetites and postponed the inevitable conflict. War did become inevitable. In 1938 Hitler succeeded through threats to merge German-speaking Austria, with many pro-Nazi citizens, into Germany, and then stimulated riots by German minorities in western Czechoslovakia, launching a claim to the territory. Czechoslovakia was handed over and occupied by German troops. Hitler declared: "We shall not capitulate—no never! We may be destroyed, but if we are, we shall drag a world with us—a world in flames."[19] In August 1939 Hitler and Stalin signed the Nazi-Soviet Pact, a nonaggression agreement, and in September, with the Soviet threat temporarily removed, Germany invaded Poland, forcing France and Britain to declare war against Germany (see Chronology: World War II, 1939–1945).

SECTION SUMMARY

- The Italian fascists, led by Benito Mussolini, appealed to those upset by instability, corruption, and economic problems and viciously fought communists and any others who opposed them.
- A new ideology, fascism, that developed out of economic collapse, stressed extreme nationalism, an authoritarian state, and hatred of minorities and leftists.
- Suffering from the Depression, resentful of post–World War I reparations, and fearful of socialism, many Germans supported Adolph Hitler's Nazi Party, which blamed problems on minorities such as the Jews and revived the economy through a military buildup.
- Japan became increasingly nationalistic and imperialistic, blamed its problems on foreigners, took over most of eastern China, and signed a pact with Germany and Italy.
- Tensions rose as Italy invaded Ethiopia, fascists took over Spain, and Germany took over Austria and Czechoslovakia; France and Britain declared war after Germany signed a nonaggression pact with the Soviet Union and invaded Poland.

WORLD WAR II: A GLOBAL TRANSITION

What were the costs and consequences of World War II?

Historians have sometimes viewed World War II as a continuation and amplification of World War I. Both wars shared some of the same causes, including nationalist rivalries, threats to the European balance of power, and a struggle to control the global economic system. But there were differences, too. World War II involved an ideological contest between democracy, fascism, and communism, and the trench warfare of World War I was superseded by the widespread aerial bombing and mobile armies used in World War II, with civilians now fair game. For the first two years, major battles were confined largely to Europe, the North Atlantic, and North Africa. Then the war spilled over to East and Southeast Asia and the western Pacific. The conflict, the most costly war in world history, brought staggering misery, 50 million deaths, one of history's worst genocides, and the use of the deadliest weapons ever known. It marked a major transition that reshaped world politics and international relations.

Cataclysmic War and Holocaust

Outbreak of War

In September 1939, Europe plunged into armed struggle. Germany and its allies overran nearly all of Europe except for valiant Britain and neutral Switzerland and Sweden (see Map 24.3). Germany then imposed puppet regimes in the conquered territories, including the Vichy **(VISH-ee)** government in France headed by World War I hero, General Philippe Pétain. The occupied countries had to send raw materials and food to Germany, and millions of civilians were enslaved to work on German farms and in factories. But Germany failed to achieve all of its strategic objectives. In a heroic resistance, Britain withstood a blitz of aerial bombing in 1940, prompting Prime Minister Winston Churchill (1874–1965) to boast that it was Britain's finest hour. Moreover, German submarines failed to sever Britain's maritime link with North America. Italian efforts to carve out a Mediterranean empire also faltered, as Greeks pushed the Italians back and the British seized parts of Italian North Africa and destroyed Italy's navy, compelling the Germans to divert military resources to confront British power in North Africa and Greece. Finally, underground movements emerged all over Europe to fight the Nazis. One of the major resistance heroes, the Swedish diplomat Raoul Wallenberg (1912–ca. 1947), stationed in occupied Hungary, risked death to save some 100,000 Jews by giving them Swedish passports and smuggling many out to safety.

German Invasion of Russia

In June 1941 Germany broke its nonaggression pact and invaded Russia. Top German officers opposed the invasion, but Hitler wanted the rich resources, especially Caucasus oil, and open lands for German colonization. Believing himself to be a military genius, he took control of all military operations and made many strategic blunders. Hitler also had an obsessive fear of communism. This invasion relieved pressure on Britain, since two-thirds of the German army was now committed to the eastern front. After misjudging German intentions and reeling from the invasion, the Soviet leader, Joseph Stalin, joined the anti-Axis alliance and received aid from the United States and Britain that helped the USSR resist, even though Western leaders, who mistrusted Stalin and still despised the Soviet system, expected Russia to remain a long-term threat to their interests. German forces reached the outskirts of Moscow and another major city, Stalingrad. But although German military forces were superior, they failed to capture the major Russian cities because the Red Army began an effective counterattack. Soon the German high command realized the folly of the invasion. The turning point came in February 1943, as the Soviet Red Army stopped the Germans at Stalingrad. By the summer, German forces, like the French army of Napoleon Bonaparte, began a long, humiliating retreat from Russia.

Map 24.3 World War II in Europe and North Africa
The Axis Powers, led by Germany and Italy, initially occupied much of Europe, and in 1941 they invaded the Soviet Union, but they were unable to hold their gains against the counteroffensive of the United States, Britain, the Soviet Union, and the Free French forces.

e Interactive Map

Nazi Genocide

Holocaust The Nazis' deliberate murder of Jews and Romany (Gypsies), one of the worst genocides in world history.

German racist nationalism led to horrific campaigns of extermination against unpopular minorities and conquered peoples. Hitler ordered the "final solution" of the "Jewish Question," and the resulting **Holocaust**, the Nazis' deliberate murder of Jews and Romany (Gypsies), was one of the worst genocides in history, killing some three-quarters of Europe's Jews. During 1942 the Germans erected death camps, such as Bergen-Belsen **(BUR-guhn-BEL-suhn)** in Germany and Auschwitz **(OUSH-vits)** in Poland, targeting especially the large Jewish communities of Germany, Poland, and Ukraine. But Jews everywhere in Nazi-occupied Europe—Vichy France, the Netherlands, Hungary, Russia—were rounded up and put in death camps, to be killed in gas chambers, starved, or worked to death. In addition to the 6 million Jews and half a million Romany (Gypsies) murdered in the Holocaust, the Nazis were responsible for the deaths of 11 million Slavs (including over 3 million Poles) and many German communists, socialists, anti-Nazi Christians, homosexuals, children deemed physically or mentally unfit to serve the German nation, and prisoners of war.

Historians differ on how complicit the German people were in the Nazis' genocide. Some blame the grip of a terrorist dictatorship that suppressed information. Nazi police chief Heinrich Himmler told the murderous special force, the SS, that "among ourselves, we can speak openly about it [the Holocaust], though we can never speak of it in public. That is a page of glory in our history that never can be written."[20] Other historians also assign responsibility to the German people, many of them anti-Semitic. Only a few brave Germans dared to resist Nazi policies. Those who did, such as the Lutheran theologian Dietrich Bonhoeffer **(BON-ho-fuhr)** (1906–1945), a strong critic of anti-Semitism who supported the underground resistance, were executed.

Globalization of the War

U.S.-Japan Conflict

Conflict between Japan and the United States eventually globalized the war (see Map 24.4). Japanese leaders had a plan for a new economic order in the East led by Japan, and they knew that they had to eliminate both the Western colonial powers and the threat from the United States. On December 7, 1941, what President Franklin D. Roosevelt called "a date which will live in infamy," Japanese planes attacked the U.S. naval base at Pearl Harbor, Hawaii, destroying much of the U.S. Pacific fleet, killing 2,400 Americans, and ending U.S. neutrality. At the same time, Japanese military forces invaded Southeast Asia. Within several months they controlled most of the region, having forced the Americans out of the Philippines and jailed the British and Dutch residents of their respective colonies. However, already bogged down and unable to expand their occupation of China, Japan badly needed Southeast Asian resources, especially oil and rubber from the Dutch East Indies (Indonesia). Preoccupied with war in Europe, and with only modest military forces left in Asia, the Western powers were unable to resist the Japanese advance.

Japanese leaders disagreed about challenging U.S. power. Some top military officers argued against the Pearl Harbor attack, knowing that the superior U.S. military and economic power could defeat Japan if Americans geared up to do so. But other leaders, impressed by Hitler's quick victories in Europe, thought they could duplicate that success in the Pacific, immobilizing the U.S. fleet and gaining time to consolidate control of Asia and the Pacific. If Germany kept the United States focused on Europe, they thought Roosevelt might avoid a costly war in Asia. They also assumed that Americans, addicted to creature comforts, lacked the will to mobilize. But the surprise Pearl Harbor attack proved a strategic blunder, uniting Americans in support for war. Admiral Isoruku Yamamoto **(EE-so-ROO-koo YAH-muh-MO-toe)**, the former university student in the United States who planned the attack, somberly told colleagues: "I fear all we have done is to awaken a sleeping giant and fill him with a terrible resolve."[21]

Roosevelt had been looking for ways to turn U.S. public opinion toward war and end his nation's isolationism, and Pearl Harbor served that purpose well. Historians remain divided about how much U.S. officials, including Roosevelt, knew about the forthcoming attack and whether they let it happen to shock the U.S. public into supporting the war. U.S. officials anticipated a military conflict with Japan but apparently expected an assault on the Philippines, an American colony, rather than on Hawaii, where Japanese Americans constituted over half of the population. The United States quickly mobilized and regeared the economy for war. A patriotic wave swept the country as America entered the war on both fronts.

Pacific War and U.S. Society

The war affected American society. Six million women joined the work force, replacing the men going off to fight. Although many men objected to the trend, by 1943 the government encouraged women as their "patriotic duty" to take up jobs once considered unladylike, such as on factory assembly lines. A popular song celebrated "Rosie the Riveter" who was "making history working for victory." The song could have described Sybil Lewis, an African American from Oklahoma, who

Map 24.4 World War II in Asia and the Pacific
After invading China in 1937, Japan disabled the U.S. fleet at Pearl Harbor in 1941 and in 1941–1942 occupied most of Southeast Asia and the western Pacific. The United States and its allies pushed back the Japanese forces from their bases in the Pacific and bombed Japan from those bases, but Japan did not surrender until 1945, when the United States dropped atomic bombs on Hiroshima and Nagasaki.

Interactive Map

moved to Los Angeles to work as a waitress, became a riveter making airplane gas tanks for Lockheed Aircraft, and then worked as a shipyard welder. Anxious for workers, companies often hired African Americans, posing a challenge to prevailing racial attitudes, and millions of southern blacks found jobs in northern and western cities. When the war ended, over 19 million American women had full-time paid jobs, and the black population of many American cities had doubled. After defeating fascism, more white Americans were also sympathetic to black demands for democracy in the United States, especially in the segregated South.

But racism aimed at 110,000 Japanese Americans, many U.S.-born or naturalized citizens living in western states, fueled one of the greatest invasions of civil liberties in U.S. history. Many Japanese Americans joined U.S. military units to fight in Europe. Nevertheless, suspecting but offering little proof that some Japanese Americans might be spies or support the Japanese war effort, the U.S. government seized their property and sent them to sparse, remote internment camps, such as Manzanar in the harsh California desert, for the duration of the conflict. Their property was never returned. With a few exceptions, German and Italian Americans faced no similar treatment.

The End of the War

German Defeat

The U.S. entry changed the shape of the conflict. The Axis forces had been triumphant through 1942, as Germany dominated much of Europe and North Africa, and Japan controlled most of Asia east of India and large areas of the western Pacific. In 1943, however, the tide began to turn. The Germans were defeated in North Africa, and Allied landings in Italy knocked that country out of the war. In June 1944, British and American forces landed on five beaches at Normandy, on France's Atlantic coast. Although German defenses did not collapse, resulting in huge Allied casualties, the Allies, including the Free French forces under General Charles DeGaulle (1890–1970), finally began pushing the Germans back in France.

Germany was defeated only by massive Allied ground offensives and an aerial bombardment that demoralized the civilian German population. The British firebombed several German cities; in Hamburg, 30,000 civilians were killed in a firestorm. While the Soviet Red Army pushed the Germans back in the east, U.S. and British forces retook Italy, France, and other Nazi-occupied countries. By December 1944, Allied forces had reached Germany, and the Allies gained command of the skies. The German war economy collapsed. As the losses mounted, Hitler lost touch with reality, giving orders to nonexistent army divisions. In spring 1945, as British and U.S. armies moved into Germany from the west and the Soviet Red Army from the east, Hitler and his mistress, Eva Braun, went through a marriage ceremony and then committed suicide in their underground bunker in Berlin. Germany surrendered. Soon the liberation of the concentration camps revealed the full extent of Nazi atrocities to a shocked world.

A major reason for the Nazi defeat was Hitler's racist and imperialistic policies. Hitler believed that Germans were racially superior to all other peoples, including the conquered Slavs, and brutally exploited the occupied areas to supply Germany. Had the Germans patronized the east Europeans and Russians, they might have won their support. Some Ukrainians, Russians, Lithuanians, and Latvians worked with the Nazis because they hated the communists more, but they were hated as collaborators with the German occupiers and often pursued and punished after the war.

Japanese Defeat

The Japanese defeat was more dramatic. In 1942, the United States stopped the Japanese advance at the battle of Midway Island, west of Hawaii, and began to isolate the Japanese bases in the Pacific. By mid-1944 they pushed the Japanese out of most of the western Pacific islands and began launching bombing raids on Japan. By early 1945, U.S., Australian, and British forces started to retake Southeast Asia and China. The invasion of Okinawa, in the Ryukyus Islands just south of Japan's main islands, cost the lives of 10,000 American troops and 80,000 Japanese civilians, warning what an invasion of the main Japanese islands might entail. U.S. and Japanese leaders could not agree on negotiations for peace, as Japan resisted American demands for total surrender.

In August 1945, the United States forever changed warfare by dropping an atomic bomb on the Japanese city of Hiroshima, demolishing most of the city and killing 80,000 people; thousands more were maimed or died later from injuries or radiation. The Japanese cabinet, divided on surrender, debated whether the United States had more than one bomb. Three days later, a second bomb hit Nagasaki, killing 60,000 Japanese civilians. Japanese emperor Hirohito (1901–1989) opted for surrender, asking his people to "suffer the insufferable, endure the unendurable," and cooperate with the U.S. occupation. For the first time in its long history, Japan had been defeated and successfully invaded. Disgraced, more than five hundred military officers committed suicide. But a long-imprisoned Japanese leftist celebrated the defeat: "Ah, such happiness, At somehow living long enough, To see this rare day, When the fighting has ceased."[22] World War II had come to an end.

Historians debate whether it was necessary militarily to drop the atomic bombs on Japan, causing so many civilian deaths. Many contend that the Japanese would have fiercely resisted an invasion and hence the bombs saved many American and Japanese lives. Others argue that Japan was near surrender but U.S. leaders misread its intentions. Still others say that the United States rushed to defeat Japan because the Soviet Union was going to join the struggle against Japan and would demand territory or a role in the occupation. Soviet forces had already moved into Manchuria as Japanese resistance collapsed. The bomb warned the Soviet Union about U.S. capabilities to dissuade Stalin from expansionism.

Japan lost the war primarily because it overstretched its forces and failed to convert Southeast Asian resources into military and industrial products fast enough to defeat the larger, wealthier United States. Japan also imposed increasingly authoritarian, brutal policies on its subject peoples. Hence, Japanese troops, upon capturing China's capital in 1937, killed thousands of Chinese in an orgy of destruction that became known as "the Rape of Nanjing." In most cases Japan's military alienated the Chinese and Southeast Asians, and eventually most Southeast Asians looked on the Japanese as perhaps even worse than the Western colonizers.

The Costs and Consequences of Global War

War Deaths and Economic Destruction

World War II took a terrible toll in lives: approximately 15 million military and 35 million civilian deaths. Soviet Russia, which lost over 20 million people, or 10 percent of its population, now had one more bitter memory in a long history of threats and invasions by countries to the west. Poland and Yugoslavia both lost over 10 percent of their people. Britain lost 375,000 people and France 600,000, while strategic bombing blasted every major German city to rubble. Over 2 million Japanese military personnel and probably a million Japanese civilians died, and 7 million Chinese were killed or wounded. Fighting on both fronts, some 300,000 American military personnel died.

The European and Asian countries involved were also economically devastated, clearing the way for new global economic arrangements. In 1944 U.S. president Roosevelt summoned representatives of forty-four countries to a conference held in Bretton Woods, New Hampshire, to establish the postwar world economic order, including international monetary cooperation to prevent the financial crises that caused the Great Depression. The Bretton Woods Conference set up the U.S.-dominated World Bank and International Monetary Fund to provide credit to states requiring financial investment. Bretton Woods also fixed currency exchange rates and encouraged trade liberalization, benefiting the United States.

New World Politics

World War II also transformed world politics, first by removing the twin threats of German Nazism and Japanese militarism. Unlike in World War I, the victorious Allies were more generous toward the vanquished. Germany, Italy, and Japan lost their colonies and were required to adopt democratic governments. In addition, U.S. forces occupied Japan for several years, while Germany was temporarily divided into sectors controlled by Russia, Britain, France, and the United States. But the Allies gave the defeated nations massive aid and guidance to speed recovery. Meanwhile, Chinese, Korean, and Vietnamese communists took advantage of Japanese occupation to gain support for their movements. In fact, Japanese occupation undermined Western colonial rule throughout Southeast Asia, while in India, nationalists who had been jailed for opposing the use of Indian troops in the war were even more embittered against British rule (see Chapter 25).

In February 1945, Roosevelt, Churchill, and Stalin met at a conference at Yalta **(YAWL-tuh)**, in Russia's Crimean peninsula, to determine the postwar political order. They proposed goals, an institutional structure, and a voting system for the new world organization, the United Nations. The Yalta Conference also divided Europe into anticommunist and communist spheres of interest. Western leaders, drained by war and seeking postwar stability, reluctantly agreed that the Soviet Union could dominate eastern Europe by stationing troops and influencing governments.

A new rivalry between the two emerging superpowers, the United States and the USSR, complicated the new global political order. The United States, which had not fought on its own soil, emerged from the war much less devastated than other major combatants and politically and economically stronger. Now the dominant world power, it took the lead in protecting a global system in which it held the strongest cards. But the USSR emerged from the war as a military power with imperialist ambitions, and U.S. leaders realized that thwarting Soviet ambitions required reconstructing Europe and Japan to restore political stability.

U.S. Air Force/AP Images

Bombing of Nagasaki This photo shows the awesome power of the atomic bomb dropped by the United States on the Japanese city of Nagasaki in August 1945, three days after the atomic bombing of Hiroshima. Some 60,000 Japanese died in the Nagasaki bombing.

U.S.-Soviet Conflict

The political history of the world between 1945 and 1989 revolved around the conflict between these two competing superpowers with very different governments and economies. The USSR replaced Germany as the dominant power in eastern Europe and installed communist governments, including one in the eastern part of Germany. World War II also increased the appeal of communism worldwide and led to communist regimes in Yugoslavia and North Korea and later in China and North Vietnam. Both Soviet and U.S. leaders tended to look at the world through the lens of their World War II experience. For the USSR that meant paranoia about any threat from the West, while Americans perceived a repeat of Hitler's aggression anywhere in the world where they experienced a political threat, such as a nationalist or communist-inspired revolution. The U.S.-Soviet rivalry created a world very different from that existing before World War II.

SECTION SUMMARY

- Germany rapidly took over most of Europe and used it as a source of raw materials, but the British withstood extended bombing and Germany wasted valuable resources on an ultimately unsuccessful invasion of the Soviet Union.
- Nazi Germany deliberately killed 6 million Jews and a half million Gypsies in death camps, along with millions of others; historians are divided on how much the German people knew about the death camps and how responsible they were for them.
- After Japan attacked Pearl Harbor, the United States entered the war in both Asia and Europe, and many women and blacks found work in professions that had until then been closed to them, while Japanese Americans were put in internment camps.
- After the United States entered the war, the Allies slowly began to win the war in Europe, and in the spring of 1945, with U.S. forces advancing from the west and the Soviets from the east, Hitler committed suicide and Germany surrendered.
- After Japan refused to agree to a total surrender despite serious setbacks, the United States dropped atomic bombs on Hiroshima and Nagasaki, killing, injuring, and sickening scores of thousands; historians still debate whether these bombs were necessary.
- World War II killed 50 million military personnel and civilians, but in its aftermath, Germany, Italy, and Japan were aided rather than punished, and the United States and the Soviet Union emerged as the world's dominant powers.

CHAPTER SUMMARY

War and its aftermath dominated the years between 1914 and 1929 in the industrialized Western nations. Growing tensions between European powers led to World War I, in which new weapons killed millions of civilians and soldiers alike. The terrible losses fostered widespread disillusionment and brought major political changes to Europe and the wider world. New nations were carved out of the German, Russian, Austro-Hungarian, and Russian Empires, while the United States emerged as a major world power. The communist Bolsheviks seized power in Russia and created the Soviet Union. Lenin forged a one-party state, and his successor, Stalin, imposed a brutal dictatorship under which he collectivized the economy, used Five-Year Plans to encourage industrialization, and modernized the society.

During the 1920s much of Europe, the United States, and Japan experienced liberal democracy and middle-class prosperity. However, in the 1930s, the Great Depression brought economic collapse, a sharp decline in world trade, and millions of unemployed workers. A few wealthy nations, especially the United States, pursued recovery through liberal reform and government spending, sustaining democracy despite the economic hardship. But for Germany, Italy, and Japan, economic disaster fostered fascism, an ideology that favored an authoritarian state, extreme nationalism, and repression of minorities. The increasing aggression of the fascist nations, in search of lands to exploit for their resources and markets, led to World War II. During the war, Nazi brutality perpetrated genocide against the Jews and other minorities. Germany initially occupied eastern Europe and much of western Europe, while Japan invaded China and Southeast Asia. With the entry of the United States into the war, the Allies eventually won. The war cost 50 million lives and devastated Europe and much of Asia. The United States emerged as the world's major superpower, with the Soviet Union as its major rival.

KEY TERMS

Bolsheviks
soviets
Marxism-Leninism
Leninism
New Economic Policy
Stalinism
gulags
socialist realism
Great Depression
Dust Bowl
New Deal
cubism
fascism
Holocaust

EBOOK AND WEBSITE RESOURCES

PRIMARY SOURCE

Mud and Khaki: Memoirs of an Incomplete Soldier

LINKS

The Great War (http://www.pitt.edu/~pugachev/greatwar/ww1.html). A useful site on World War I with many essays and links.

WWW-VL: History: United States (http://vlib.iue.it/history/USA/). A virtual library, maintained at the University of Kansas, that contains links to hundreds of sites.

Russian History Index: The World Wide Web Virtual Library (http://vlib.iue.it/hist-russia/Index.html). Contains useful essays and links on Russian history, society, and politics.

INTERACTIVE MAPS

Map 24.1 World War I
Map 24.2 Civil War in Revolutionary Russia (1918–1921)
Map 24.3 World War II in Europe and North Africa
Map 24.4 World War II in Asia and the Pacific

Modern History Sourcebook (http://www.fordham.edu/halsall/mod/modsbook.html). A very extensive online collection of historical documents and secondary materials.

Plus flashcards, practice quizzes, and more. Go to: www.cengage.com/history/lockard/globalsocnet2e.

SUGGESTED READING

Boyle, John Hunter. *Modern Japan: The American Nexus.* Fort Worth: Harcourt Brace Jovanovich, 1993. Good study of U.S.-Japanese relations.

Brendon, Piers. *The Dark Valley: A Panorama of the 1930s.* New York: Alfred A. Knopf, 2000. A readable account of this decade in both Europe and North America.

Doughty, Robert A., et al. *World War II: Total Warfare Around the Globe.* Lexington, MA: D.C. Heath, 1996. A brief account emphasizing military history.

Dower, John. *War Without Mercy: Race and Power in the Pacific War.* New York: Pantheon, 1986. A provocative look at the U.S.-Japan conflict.

Fitzpatrick, Sheila. *The Russian Revolution,* 3rd ed. New York: Oxford University Press, 2008. A provocative, concise, and readable account of developments from 1917 through the 1930s.

James, Harold. *Europe Reborn: A History, 1914–2000.* New York: Longman, 2003. An excellent survey of the period.

Kitchen, Martin. *A World in Flames: A Short History of the Second World War in Europe and Asia, 1939–1945.* New York: Longman, 1990. A readable narrative.

Kitchen, Martin. *Between the Wars,* 2nd ed. New York: Longman, 2006. Examines Europe's economic and international history.

Lee, Stephen J. *European Dictatorships, 1918–1945,* 2nd ed. New York: Routledge, 2000. An interesting study of the major dictatorships and their leaders.

Lewin, Moshe. *The Soviet Century.* New York: Verso, 2005. A provocative and critical overview of the Soviet Union and Soviet Communism.

Lyons, Michael J. *World War I: A Short History,* 2nd ed. Upper Saddle River, NJ: Prentice-Hall, 2000. A readable and comprehensive overview.

Mann, Michael. *Fascists.* New York: Cambridge University Press, 2004. A detailed but readable study of European fascism in this era.

Martin, Russell. *Picasso's War: The Destruction of Guernica and the Masterpiece That Changed the World.* New York: Plume, 2002. Examines the era through the artist and his most famous painting.

Mazower, Mark. *Hitler's Empire: How the Nazis Ruled Europe.* New York: Penguin, 2008. Explores life under German domination.

McClain, James L. *Japan: A Modern History.* New York: W.W. Norton, 2002. A very readable recent account with good coverage of these decades.

Moss, George Donelson. *America Since 1900,* 6th ed. Upper Saddle River, NJ: Prentice-Hall, 2007. A readable survey of the United States in this period.

Neiberg, Michael S. *Fighting the Great War: A Global History.* Cambridge: Harvard University Press, 2005. A scholarly analysis of the conflict.

Parrish, Michael E. *Anxious Decades: America in Prosperity and Depression, 1920–1941.* New York: W.W. Norton, 1994. An examination of this era in the United States.

Sato, Barbara. *The New Japanese Women: Modernity, Media, and Women in Interwar Japan.* Durham: Duke University Press, 2003. A fascinating scholarly study.

Wilkenson, James, and H. Stuart Hughes. *Contemporary Europe: A History,* 10th ed. Upper Saddle River, NJ: Prentice-Hall, 2004. A comprehensive general survey.

CHAPTER 25

Imperialism and Nationalism in Asia, Africa, and Latin America, 1914–1945

CHAPTER OUTLINE

- Western Imperialism and Its Challengers
- Nationalism and Communism in China
- British Colonialism and the Indian Response
- Nationalist Stirrings in Southeast Asia and Sub-Saharan Africa
- Remaking the Middle East and Latin America

PROFILE
Mohandas Gandhi, Indian Nationalist

WITNESS TO THE PAST
Sukarno Indicts Dutch Colonialism

Photo12/The Image Works

Mao Zedong Organizing Communists in China
This later artist's rendition shows the young Mao Zedong, the future Chinese communist leader, organizing a communist group in his native province, Hunan, around 1921. A portrait of Karl Marx decorates the wall.

What unhappiness strikes the poor, Who wear a single worn-out, torn cloth. Oh heaven, why are you not just? Some have abundance while others are in want.

—Peasant folk song protesting colonialism in Vietnam[1]

FOCUS QUESTIONS

1. What circumstances fostered nationalism in Asia, Africa, and Latin America?
2. How and why did the communist movement grow in China?
3. What were the main contributions of Mohandas Gandhi to the Indian struggle?
4. How did nationalism differ in Southeast Asia and sub-Saharan Africa?
5. What factors promoted change in the Middle East and Latin America?

In 1911 Nguyen Tat Thanh **(NEW-win tat-tan)**, a young man from an impoverished village in French-ruled Vietnam, signed on as a merchant seaman on a French ship; he would not return to his homeland for another thirty years. Nguyen hated colonialism. The seaman visited North African and American ports, and he developed both a distaste for America's white racism and an admiration for its freedom. After working as a cook in London, Nguyen moved to Paris, where he worked chiefly as a photo retoucher while seeking to develop an anticolonial movement among the Vietnamese exiles in France. Adopting a new alias, Nguyen Ai Quoc **(NEW-win eye-kwok)** ("Nguyen the Patriot"), he spent his free time reading books on politics and working with Asian nationalists and French socialists to oppose colonialism.

At the Paris Peace Conference after World War I, Nguyen Ai Quoc became famous among Vietnamese exiles for his efforts to address the delegates about the self-determination of colonized peoples. He attempted to enter the meetings and present a moderate eight-point plan for changes in France's treatment of its Southeast Asian colonies, including basic freedoms, representation in government, and release of political prisoners. But the Western powers refused to permit his entry. Disillusioned with Western democracy, the Vietnamese exile helped found the French Communist Party, which promised to abolish the French colonial system. He then moved to the Soviet Union and later, under a new name, Ho Chi Minh **(ho chee-min)** ("He Who Enlightens"), led the communist forces in Vietnam in their long struggle against French colonialism and then against the Americans. Concluding that communism was the most effective strategy for promoting nationalism, Ho became a worldwide symbol of opposition to Western imperialism and sympathy for peasants suffering under colonial policies in Vietnam and elsewhere.

Between 1914 and 1945 nationalistic Asians and Africans challenged the imperialism of the European powers, now weakened by World War I, that had reshaped Asian and African politics and economies. From Indonesia to Egypt to Senegal, but especially in India and Vietnam, rapid, often destabilizing change sparked nationalism aimed at escaping Western domination. Similar trends also influenced independent countries such as Siam (now Thailand), Persia (now Iran), and particularly China. The Great Depression and World War II unsettled the world even more, sometimes sending discontented people to join those seeking to overturn the status quo, such as Ho Chi Minh. Despite frequent uprisings and protests, the Western powers maintained their empires until after World War II. During and after that war, however, nationalist movements became even stronger, making a return to the world of the 1930s impossible.

Visit the website and eBook for additional study materials and interactive tools: www.cengage.com/history/lockard/globalsocnet2e

Western Imperialism and Its Challengers

What circumstances fostered nationalism in Asia, Africa, and Latin America?

The events that rocked the industrialized nations—two world wars, the Russian Revolution, and the Great Depression—also affected the nonindustrialized societies of Asia, Africa, and Latin America. These societies, which enjoyed little power in the global system, also suffered from destabilizing social and economic changes resulting from colonialism. Many disenchanted Asians and Africans adopted nationalism and Marxism to struggle for power.

The Impact of Colonialism

World War I and the Colonies

Western colonialism had a major impact on Asians, Africans, and West Indians. The slaughter of millions of people during World War I undermined Western credibility and whatever moral authority Western peoples claimed to possess. Resentment also grew from the deaths of thousands of Asians and Africans conscripted as soldiers and workers to support the colonial powers in the war effort. Both France and Germany drafted men, often through harsh methods similar to forced labor, from their African colonies, while Britain sent Africans and Indians. Some 46,000 Kenyans died fighting for Britain, and at least 25,000 West Africans perished helping France on the front lines. Although British and French officials promised democratic reforms and special treatment for war veterans, these promises were not carried out, and few families of dead African soldiers ever received any compensation for their loss.

Colonial Systems

Colonialism also reshaped societies. As discussed in Chapters 21 and 22, colonization formed artificial states that often ignored social, economic, and historical realities in the region. Colonies such as Dutch-ruled Indonesia, British Nigeria, and the Belgian Congo incorporated diverse and often rival ethnic groups who had little sense of national unity. In addition, to cover the costs of managing the colonies, the colonial governments used a variety of methods, including higher taxes and forced labor, that increased resentment. In Portuguese-ruled Mozambique, men and women who had no cash to pay the required taxes were assigned to work on plantations or in mines in a system not unlike slavery. After months of labor they often received little more than a receipt saying they had met their tax obligation for the year. Among the worst abuses were the opium and alcohol monopolies that provided revenues for colonial governments in Southeast Asia. In French-ruled Vietnam all villages were required to purchase designated amounts of these products, so that by 1918 opium sales accounted for one-third of all colonial revenues in Vietnam, and some Vietnam-

Exporting Resources from Indonesia Small boats brought cash crops grown in eastern Java, part of the Dutch East Indies, to the port of Surabaya, from where they were shipped to Europe.

Royal Commonwealth Society Collection, Cambridge University Library Y30333/A9

CHRONOLOGY

	Asia	The Middle East and Africa	Latin America
1910	**1916–1927** Warlord Era in China		
1920	**1928–1937** Republic of China	**1920–1922** Nationalist unrest in Kenya **1922** Formation of Turkish republic **1925–1979** Pahlavi dynasty in Iran	
1930	**1930** Indochinese Communist Party **1935–1936** Chinese Communist Long March		**1930–1945** Estado Novo in Brazil **1934–1940** Cardenas presidency in Mexico
1940	**1941–1945** Japanese occupation of Southeast Asia **1942** Gandhi's Quit India campaign		

ese became addicted to opium. Moreover, villages that bought too little alcohol or were discovered making their own illicit alcoholic beverages were fined.

Among other problems, rising birth rates and declining death rates, abetted by colonial economic policies and, in some cases, improved health and sanitation, fostered rapid population growth in colonies such as India, Indonesia, the Philippines, and Vietnam. This population growth outstripped economic resources, exacerbating poverty and stimulating emigration. Furthermore, the production and export of one or two primary commodities, such as rice and rubber from Vietnam, sugar from Barbados and Fiji, copper from Northern Rhodesia, and oil from Trinidad and Iraq, put a brake on later economic diversification. Colonized peoples also disliked the arrogance of the Western colonizers. Assuming that their societies were superior, Europeans and North Americans had enshrined their racist attitude in the Covenant for the new League of Nations formed after World War I, which considered the colonized peoples not yet able to govern themselves in the modern world. Finally, Western officials, businessmen, and planters in the colonies lived in luxury—with mansions, servants, and private clubs—while many local people lived in dire poverty, often underfed and underemployed.

Colonial Economies

At the same time, colonial governments built a modern communications and economic infrastructure that often spurred economic growth. British India, Dutch Indonesia, and British East Africa built railroads that facilitated the movement of goods and people. Colonialism also fostered the growth of cities. For example, in 1890, to service their new East African Railroad from the Kenyan coast to Uganda, the British opened a settlement with a hotel and bar at Nairobi, a Gikuyu village in the Kenyan highlands. Nairobi, with its cool climate, later became the colonial capital. Port cities founded by Western colonizers, such as Hong Kong on the China coast, Jakarta in Indonesia, Singapore at the tip of Malaya, Bombay (today's Mumbai) in India, and Cape Town in South Africa, became key hubs of world trade. However, critics questioned how much these developments benefited Asians and Africans.

The capitalism introduced by the West also spurred resentment. Some non-European merchants, such as the Chinese in Southeast Asia and the Lebanese in West Africa, profited from the growing economic opportunities. But colonial policies that promoted the spread of the capitalist market, expanded communications, and eroded traditional political authority also destabilized rural villages, laying the groundwork for the rise of revolutionary responses in countries like Vietnam. The commercialization of agriculture transformed traditional, often communal, landowning arrangements into money-based private property systems with competitive values and policies that converted land into a commodity to be exploited on the free market. In many colonies, among them British India, French Vietnam, and Portuguese Angola, a powerful landlord class now flourished at the expense of once-self-sufficient peasant farmers. The remaining peasant farmers had no control over the constantly fluctuating prices paid for their crops. Lacking money or connections to influential people, many peasants fell into dire poverty. A Vietnamese peasant later recalled the bitter years of hardship under French colonization: "My father was very poor. He and my mother, and all of my brothers and sisters, had to pull the plow. In the old days, people did the work of water buffalo."[2]

The Great Depression of the 1930s brought economic catastrophe to many nonindustrialized societies as demand for their resources in the industrialized nations plummeted. In Southeast Asia and Africa, prices for rubber, sugar, and coffee fell, in Argentina livestock and wheat prices collapsed, and Brazilians threw their nearly worthless sacks of coffee beans into the sea. To protect Western investors during this time, international agreements restricted rubber growing to large plantations, causing distress to small farmers, rubber workers, and the shopkeepers who serviced them in Malaya, Sri Lanka, and the Belgian Congo. As these exports declined, colonial revenues fell. Because rubber and tin provided the bulk of tax revenues in British Malaya, price collapse necessitated huge budget cuts, undermining such activities as education and road building.

The Great Depression

Unequal landowning, growing mass poverty, few economic opportunities for displaced peasants, and foreign control of the economy produced political unrest. For example, on the Caribbean island of Trinidad, a British colony, the depression led to strikes and labor unrest. The calypso singer Growling Tiger implored the colonial government not to ignore human suffering: "The authorities should deal much more leniently with the many unemployed in the colony; work is nowhere to be found but there is rent to pay while the money circulation decreases by the day."[3] But most colonial regimes harassed and jailed protest leaders.

Nationalism, Marxism, and Imperial Expansion

Nationalism and Radical Movements

As a result of these hardships, ideologies of resistance, including nationalism and Marxism, became influential in the colonized world, fostering movements for independence. Since colonial governments jailed or exiled dissenters, nationalists had to organize underground. Nationalism appealed especially to the educated middle class—lawyers, teachers, merchants, and military officers—who faced white racism. The few existing universities in the colonies offered a venue for nationalist-government conflicts and campus protests. In British Burma (today's Myanmar) during the 1920s and 1930s, students, both men and women, at the University of Rangoon repeatedly went on strike to protest British policies. After a major strike in 1936, student leaders were expelled, but the administration also met some student demands such as introducing scholarships for poor students.

Nationalism promoted a sense of belonging to a nation, such as Indonesia or Nigeria, that transcended parochial differences such as social class and religion. Whereas colonialism had uprooted people from their villages, families, customs, and traditions, nationalists sought to foster stability and help the poor, often linking capitalism with foreign control. But the "nation" sometimes existed only in people's imagination: in the multiethnic colonies of Africa, Southeast Asia, and the Caribbean, ethnic rivalries hindered a feeling of nationhood.

Some Asians, Africans, and Latin Americans who sought radical change, such as Ho Chi Minh, mixed nationalism with Marxism, which provided an alternative vision to colonialism, capitalism, and discredited local traditions and leaders. Young Asians, Africans, and West Indians studying in Europe and North America often adopted Marxism after facing racism in the West and bleak employment prospects and political repression back at home. Some of them gravitated to the communism imposed on and practiced in the Soviet Union (see Chapter 24), which addressed social inequality and political powerlessness under the leadership of a centralized revolutionary party. Many found persuasive the theories of the Russian communist leader, Vladimir Lenin, who blamed the poverty of the colonial and neocolonial societies on the industrialized nations that had imposed a capitalist system on subject peoples. Lenin saw the world as divided between imperial countries (the exploiters) and dominated countries (the exploited). An Indian nationalist observed in the 1930s that younger Indian men and women who used to admire Western democracies now found inspiration in Soviet Russia. Although the Soviet Union also proved capable of blatantly imperialistic policies, many viewed Lenin's theory of capitalism-based imperialism as valid.

Asserting Western Power

At the same time that anti-imperialist feelings were rising, powerful nations expanded their imperial reach and intervened in less-powerful countries. Britain and France took control of the former Ottoman colonies in western Asia and the German colonies in Africa, some of which had valuable resources, while Australia and Japan occupied the German-ruled Pacific islands. Supported by colonial governments, Europeans continued to settle in Algeria, Angola, Kenya, South Africa, and Southern Rhodesia, dispossessing local people from their land. Moreover, Western military conquests in Africa had not ended. In 1935–1936 Italy invaded and brutally conquered the last independent African state, Ethiopia, killing some 200,000 Ethiopians. Despite their spirited defense, they succumbed to superior Italian aerial bombing and firepower.

Meanwhile, the United States exercised influence in the Americas. During the Mexican Revolution, President Woodrow Wilson sent thousands of U.S. troops into Mexico to restore order. Americans also owned a large share of the Mexican economy, including most of the oil industry. The longest U.S. intervention came in Nicaragua, where U.S. Marines overthrew a government hostile to the United States and then remained there from 1909 to 1933, often fighting a peasant resistance led by Augusto César Sandino **(san-DEE-no)** (1895–1934), who became a hero to nationalist Central Americans. In its desire to protect U.S. investments in Central America, the United States often supported governments led by landowners and generals, such as the notoriously corrupt Nicaraguan dictator, Anastasio Somoza (1896–1956). President Franklin D. Roosevelt defended this policy by maintaining that "they may be SOBs, but they're our SOBs."[4] These repeated U.S. interventions in the region left an aftertaste of local resentment against what Central Americans called "Yankee imperialism."

SECTION SUMMARY

- World War I affected colonies in Asia, Africa, and the Caribbean as thousands of colonial subjects were forced to fight and die for France, Germany, and Britain, and promises of democratic reforms and special treatment for war veterans were not carried out.
- Colonial governments imposed heavy taxes and hard labor on the colonial peoples, who often lived in poverty while their Western counterparts lived in luxury, a state of affairs that was defended by the Western idea that the colonial peoples could not yet govern themselves.
- Western capitalism disrupted traditional rural life in many colonies, placing formerly self-sufficient farmers at the mercy of landowners and the world economy, which led to misery, political unrest, and activism during the Great Depression.
- Nationalism appealed to many frustrated colonial subjects, though many multiethnic colonies struggled to develop a sense of nationhood, and Marxism appealed to many, such as Vietnam's Ho Chi Minh, as an alternative to exploitative capitalism.
- Despite local opposition, Western nations expanded their colonial reach between 1900 and 1945: Italy brutally conquered Ethiopia, France and Britain took over former Ottoman colonies, and the United States continued to meddle in Central America.

Nationalism and Communism in China

How and why did the communist movement grow in China?

The Chinese Revolution of 1911–1912, which ended the 2,000-year-old imperial system (see Chapter 23), had led to a republic that Chinese hoped would foster renewed strength in the world, but these hopes were soon dashed (see Chronology: China, 1911–1945). China lapsed into warlordism and civil war, nominally independent but subject to pressure from the West and Japan. Alarm at China's domestic failures and continuing Western imperialism sparked a resurgent nationalism more influential than in most nonindustrialized countries, as well as the formation of a communist party and China's eventual reunification.

Warlords, New Cultures, and Nationalism

During the demoralizing Warlord Era (1916–1927), China was divided into territories controlled by rival **warlords**, local political leaders who had their own armies, taxing and terrorizing the population. Some warlords called themselves reformers interested in promoting education and industry. Still others took bribes to carry out policies favoring merchants or foreign governments. High taxes, inflation, famine, accelerating social tensions, and banditry made life difficult for most Chinese, increasing frustration.

warlords Local political leaders with their own armies.

Radical Currents

One result was that cities became enclaves of new intellectual, social, cultural, and economic thought. New schools and universities opened, and by 1919 4.5 million girls were in school, although vastly more boys enjoyed access to formal education. By the 1920s many women worked as nurses, teachers, and civil servants, but few rural women became literate or enjoyed these new opportunities. Exposure to Western ideas in universities, especially those run by Christian groups, led some Chinese students to question their own cultural traditions. Women activists and sympathetic men

CHRONOLOGY
China, 1911–1945

1911–1912 Chinese Revolution

1915 Beginning of New Culture Movement

1916–1927 Warlord Era

1919 May Fourth Movement

1926–1928 Northern Expedition to reunify China

1927 Guomindang suppression of communists

1927–1934 Mao Zedong's Jiangxi Soviet

1928–1937 Republic of China in Nanjing

1931 Japanese occupation of Manchuria

1935–1936 Long March by Chinese communists

1937–1945 Japanese invasion of China

campaigned against footbinding, which largely disappeared except in remote rural areas by 1930. Chambers of commerce and labor unions also appeared.

Many Chinese intellectuals supported the **New Culture Movement**, which sought to wash away the discredited past and sprout a literary revival. The movement originated in 1915 at Beijing University, China's intellectual mecca that hired radical professors and that encouraged a mixing of Chinese and Western thought. University professors published the literary magazine *New Youth,* which became the chief vehicle for attacking China's traditions, including Confucianism, which they believed kept China backward by promoting conformity and discouraging critical thinking. The magazine's editor, Chen Duxiu **(chen too-shoe)** (1879–1942), promoted republican government and science. Contributors to the magazine, while detesting Western imperialism, admired the liberal, open intellectual atmosphere in Western nations and viewed modern science as liberation from superstition. Essays derided the traditional Chinese family system as contrary to individual rights and advised women to seek equality with men.

Chinese rage against Western and Japanese imperialism increased in the aftermath of World War I. China had remained neutral until 1917, but Japan had occupied the German sphere of influence in the Shandong peninsula of eastern China, and in 1915 it presented China with 21 Demands, including control of Shandong, increased rights in Manchuria, and appointment of Japanese advisers to the Chinese government. The decision by the Western allies to allow Japan to take over Shandong provoked a radical nationalist resurgence in 1919, known as the **May Fourth Movement**, that opposed imperialism and the ineffective, warlord-controlled Chinese government. Decrying social injustice and government inaction, students and workers, many of them women, mounted mass demonstrations, strikes, and boycotts of Japanese goods. Merchants closed their businesses in sympathy. Capitulating to the protests, the Chinese government refused to sign the Versailles treaty. The new Soviet Union sided with China and renounced the special privileges that had been obtained by the czars, winning admiration among the Chinese.

New Culture Movement A movement of Chinese intellectuals started in 1915 that sought to wash away the discredited past and sprout a literary revival.

May Fourth Movement A radical nationalist resurgence in China in 1919 that opposed imperialism and the ineffective, warlord-controlled Chinese government.

In 1921 professors and students at Beijing University, many of them active in the New Culture and May Fourth Movements, organized the Chinese Communist Party (CCP). Some of the party founders, such as the *New Youth* editor, Chen Duxiu, were Europe- or Japan-educated reformers who admired Western science and culture. Others were nationalists who despised Western models and believed the Chinese people could liberate China if they were mobilized for revolution. Soviet advisers, while encouraging the party to organize among the urban working class, considered the Chinese communists unlikely to become influential. But the communists formed peasant associations, labor unions, women's groups, and youth clubs, and by 1927 the party had some 60,000 members.

The Communist Party was only one strand of a resurgent nationalism. Sun Zhongshan, better known as Sun Yat-sen (1866–1925), whose revolutionary ideas helped overthrow the Qing dynasty (see Chapter 23), began to rebuild his Guomindang, or Nationalist Party. Receiving no help from the Western nations, who benefited from China's disarray, Sun accepted advisers and military aid from the Soviet Union. In the mid-1920s Sun's Guomindang and the Chinese communists worked together, in an alliance known as the United Front, to defeat warlordism. However, Sun's ideology grew more authoritarian, as he concluded that China's 400 million people—in his view just "loose sand"—were not ready for democracy. Sun died in 1925, and the new Guomindang leader, Sun's brother-in-law, Jiang Jieshi (better known in the West as Chiang Kai-shek **(CHANG kai-shek)**) (1887–1975), was more conservative. Chiang, who came from a wealthy landowning family, was a pro-business soldier and a patriot, but indifferent to social change. He began building a modern military force.

The Republic of China

Between 1926 and 1928 the Guomindang forces and their communist allies reunified China with a military drive, the Northern Expedition, that defeated or co-opted the warlords. The foreign powers recognized Chiang's new Republic of China. However, during the drive, tensions had grown between leftwing and rightwing factions. Whereas communists and leftist Guomindang leaders sought social change and mobilization of workers, the right wing, led by Chiang, was allied with the antiprogressive Shanghai business community. In 1927 Chiang expelled the communists from the United Front and began a reign of terror, killing thousands of leftists; those who survived went into hiding or fled into the rural interior or abroad.

Northern Expedition

From 1928 to 1937 Chiang's Republic of China, based at Nanjing (nahn-JING) along the Yangzi River, launched a modernization program. The Republic's leaders, many of them Western-educated Christians, built railroads, factories, a banking system, and a modern army, streamlined the government, fostered public health and education, and adopted new legal codes. New laws promoted monogamy and equal inheritance rights for women, though Chiang's government had little power to carry them out. The regime also negotiated an end to most of the unequal international treaties imposed by the Western nations and Japan in the 1800s. The U.S. government, closely allied with Chiang's regime, and private Americans provided generous political and financial support for Chiang's modernization efforts. Feeling a paternalistic responsibility for China, Americans funded schools, hospitals, orphanages, and Christian missions. In 1940 a prominent U.S. senator, reflecting the notion that Americans could enrich and Westernize China, proclaimed: "We will lift Shanghai up, ever up, until it is just like Kansas City."[5]

Chiang's Government

Yet the Republic faced daunting challenges. While the urban elite in big coastal cities prospered, Chiang was unable or unwilling to deal with the growing poverty of the peasantry. Commercialization of agriculture shifted more land to landlords, and half of China's peasants lacked enough land to support their families. Chiang also tolerated government corruption and rewarded his financial backers in the merchant and banking sector. As antigovernment sentiment grew, Chiang, influenced by European fascism, built an authoritarian police state that brutally repressed dissent. China also faced problems with Japan. In 1931 Japanese forces seized Manchuria, the large northeastern region rich in mineral resources and fertile farmland, and set up a puppet government under the last Manchu emperor, Henry Pu Yi (1906–1967) (see Map 25.1). As Japan gradually extended its military and political influence southward, Chiang, unable to match Japanese military power, followed a policy of appeasement. His attempts to strengthen the Chinese military diverted scarce resources from economic development, and his reluctance to fight Japan left him open to charges that he was unpatriotic.

China's challenges were reflected in cultural life. Disillusioned by China's weakness in the world and continued despotism, many intellectuals lost faith in both Chiang's regime and Chinese traditions. The writer Lu Xun (LOO shun) (1881–1936), who had studied in Japan and became proficient in several foreign languages, published satires on Chinese failures to meet the challenges of the modern world. Lu Xun later formed a leftist writers' group and supported the communists. In criticizing both imperialism and greedy Chinese leaders, he argued, "Our vaunted Chinese civilization is only a feast of human flesh prepared for the rich and mighty, and China is only a kitchen where these feasts are prepared."[6] Ding Ling (1904–1985), one of China's first feminist writers, had fled her native village to avoid an arranged marriage, participated in the May Fourth Movement, and lived a liberated city life. Her early novels and short stories focused on women's issues and featured independent women unable to find emotional or sexual satisfaction. After the Guomindang killed her politically activist husband, she dedicated her writing to the revolutionary cause but was later persecuted by the communists for her feminism and reluctance to follow the party line.

Cultural Life

The Rise of Chinese Communism

As the communists who survived Chiang's terror worked to rebuild their movement, one of the younger party leaders, Mao Zedong (maow dzuh-dong) (1893–1976), pursued his own strategy to mount the revolution to reshape China. From a peasant family dominated by a father who abused Mao's mother, Mao had run away from home to attend high school. Moving to Beijing, he found work in the Beijing University Library, where he embraced communism. He then edited a radical magazine, became an elementary school principal, and organized workers and peasants. In 1927, as Chiang eliminated communists, Mao fled to the rugged mountains of Jiangxi (kee-ON-see) province in south-central China, where he set up a revolutionary base, known as the **Jiangxi Soviet**, and organized a guerrilla army out of peasants, bandits, and former Guomindang soldiers to fight the Guomindang. Rejecting the advice of Soviet advisers to depend on support from the urban working class, Mao opted instead to rely on China's huge peasantry.

Mao and Communist Leadership

Jiangxi Soviet A revolutionary base, established in 1927 in south-central China, where Mao Zedong organized a guerrilla force to fight the Guomindang.

Mao believed that violence was necessary to oppose Chiang, writing that "a revolution is not a dinner party, or writing an essay, or painting a picture, or doing embroidery; it cannot be so refined, so leisurely and gentle. A revolution is an act of violence by which one class overthrows another."[7] Between 1928 and 1934 Mao expanded the Jiangxi Soviet, redistributing land from the rich to the poor. As Chiang's repression intensified, top Chinese Communist Party leaders, who had once scorned Mao, moved to the Jiangxi Soviet.

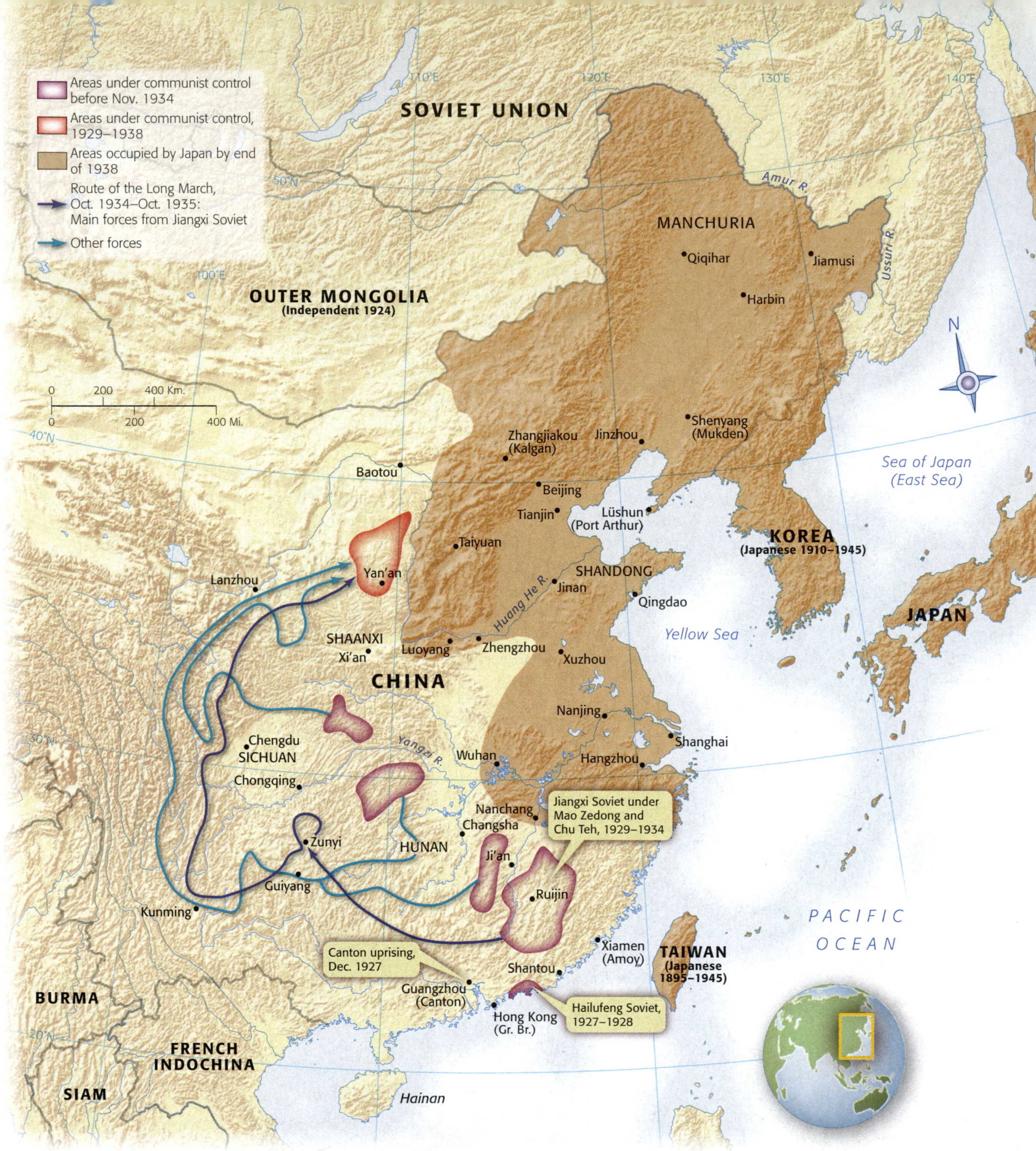

Map 25.1 Chinese Communist Movement and Chinese-Japanese War
Japan occupied much of northern and eastern China by 1939. In 1935–1936 the Chinese communists made the famous 6,000-mile Long March from their base in Jiangxi in southern China to Yan'an in northwest China.

e **Interactive Map**

Long March An epic journey, full of hardship, in which Mao Zedong's Red Army fought their way 6,000 miles on foot and horseback through eleven Chinese provinces to establish a safe base.

Increasingly alarmed by Mao's growing base, Chiang had his army blockade the Jiangxi Soviet to keep out essential supplies, forcing Mao to reluctantly abandon his base. In 1935 Mao and 100,000 soldiers and followers broke through the blockade and, in search of a safer base, began the **Long March**, an epic journey, full of hardship, in which Mao's Red Army fought their way 6,000 miles on foot and horseback through eleven provinces. The communists crossed eighteen mountain ranges, forded twenty-four rivers, and slogged through swamps, losing 90 percent of their people to death or desertion. Finally in late 1936 the ragtag survivors arrived in a poor northwestern prov-

The Long March This painting glorifies the crossing, over an old iron chain bridge, of the Dadu River in western Sichuan province by the communist Red Army during the Long March. This successful crossing, against fierce attacks by Guomindang forces, was a key event in the communists' successful journey to northwest China.

ince, where they moved into cavelike homes carved into the hills around the dusty city of Yan'an (YEH-nan). The Long March saved the communists from elimination by Chiang, making Mao the unchallenged party leader. Mao celebrated the achievement: "The Long March is the first of its kind in the annals of history [and has] proclaimed that the Red Army is an army of heroes."[8] But the communists were still vulnerable to Chiang's larger, better-equipped forces and would be saved only by the Japanese invasion of China in 1937, which forced Chiang to shift his military priorities to fighting the Japanese. These developments allowed the communists to regroup and spread their message of change in wartime China.

Japanese Invasion and Communist Revolution

The Japanese invasion and the disastrous Chinese-Japanese war that followed altered China's politics as Chiang had to divert money from modernization to the military. Mao captured the patriotic mood of the country by proposing a united front against Japan, and Chiang had little choice but to agree. The Japanese soon occupied the major cities of north China and the coast, and by the end of 1938 Japanese forces controlled most of eastern China, including the best farmland and the major industrial cities, but became bogged down and unable to expand their control. War and occupation undermined Chiang's government and enabled the communists to recruit support, thus setting the stage for major changes in Chinese politics in the later 1940s.

Nationalist Retreat

Chiang's government relocated inland to Chongqing (CHUNG-king), a city protected by high mountains on the Yangzi River. This move was followed by a mass migration of Chinese fleeing the Japanese. Unlike the cosmopolitan coastal cities, Chongqing offered no bright lights or French restaurants and had a depressing climate of fog and humidity. Fatigue, cynicism, and inflation discouraged the Guomindang's followers. Virtually broke, Chiang's government squeezed the peasants in the areas they still controlled for tax revenues to support an army of 4 to 5 million men. But it gradually lost support. Militarily ineffective, politically repressive, and economically corrupt, it offered limited resistance to the Japanese, killed and imprisoned opponents, and put the personal gain of its leaders above the economic well-being of China's people. Although the United States supported Chiang as an ally against imperial Japan, it was able to supply the Guomindang-held areas only by difficult, mountainous routes from Burma and India. Moreover, Chiang often ignored U.S. advice in military and political matters. As the war wore on, he lost much of his popular support.

Communist Resurgence

Meanwhile, the communists at Yan'an were able to improve their prospects. Used to poverty, they had a more disciplined army with a higher morale. While Chiang's much larger forces had the main responsibility to fight the Japanese, the communists mobilized the people by forging a close relationship with the peasantry in north China and by mounting guerrilla bands to harass the Japanese. Their unconventional struggle, which Mao called "**people's war**," combined military action and political recruitment. In Mao's military strategy, "the enemy advances, we retreat; the enemy halts, we harass; the enemy retreats, we pursue."[9] In the political strategy, communist activists set up village governments and peasant associations and encouraged women's rights, punishing abusive husbands. The communist message of social revolution and nationalism offered hope to the downtrodden. Thousands of Chinese, students, intellectuals, and writers such as Ding Ling flocked to Yan'an to join the communist cause. By 1945 the party had 1.2 million members.

people's war An unconventional struggle combining military action and political recruitment, formulated by Mao Zedong in China.

Maoism An ideology promoted by Mao Zedong that mixed ideas from Chinese tradition with Marxist-Leninist ideas from the Soviet Union.

The communist experiences at Yan'an fostered what later came to be known as **Maoism**, an ideology promoted by Mao that mixed ideas from Chinese tradition with Marxist-Leninism from the Soviet Union. Mao emphasized the subordination of the individual to the needs of the group (a traditional Chinese notion), the superiority of political values over technical and artistic ones, and belief in the human will as a social force. To combat elitism, Mao introduced mass campaigns in which everyone engaged in physical labor, such as building dams and roads. The communists sent intellectuals into villages to teach literacy and learn from the peasants. Mao expressed faith that the Chinese people, armed with political understanding, had the collective power to triumph over nature, poverty, and exploitation to build a new society.

During the Japanese occupation the communists gained domination over much of rural north China, where Mao's ideas on social change and economic justice had gained support. Hence, when the war ended in 1945, the communists had improved their prospects while Chiang's Guomindang, although still a superior military force, was beset with problems resulting from its inability to defeat the Japanese and maintain popular support. In 1949 the communists won a bitter civil war and established a government.

SECTION SUMMARY

- After the end of the imperial system, rival warlords controlled China during a period of civil war, and intellectuals formed the New Culture Movement, which called for a modernized China that fostered individualism and equality rather than traditions such as Confucianism.
- Japan's aggressive demands after World War I enraged the Chinese, and some were attracted to communism, but Sun Yat-sen's successor, the probusiness Chiang Kai-shek, allied the nationalist movement with the United States.
- Chiang Kai-shek's Republic of China launched a modernization program, but it was hampered by a split with the communists, persistent rural poverty, and the Japanese seizure of Manchuria.
- Mao Zedong organized peasants into a communist revolutionary army and then led them on the punishing Long March in search of safety from Chiang Kai-shek's far-stronger army, which might have triumphed had it not been diverted by a 1937 Japanese invasion.
- The Chinese people lost faith in Chiang's government as it squeezed them for taxes to support a failing war against Japan, while Mao's communists instilled hope through guerrilla attacks on the Japanese and a promise of equality and progress through shared sacrifice.

British Colonialism and the Indian Response

What were the main contributions of Mohandas Gandhi to the Indian struggle?

In India, resentment of British colonialism and an inequitable social order sparked a powerful nationalist movement. Those Indians who hoped that World War I would bring them self-determination could see that the British rhetoric about democracy did not apply to India. Growing opposition to British rule, spurred by the Indian National Congress, led to unrest that forced the British to modify some of their policies. Nationalism also set the stage for the turmoil that eventually created separate Hindu and Muslim nations after World War II.

The Nationalist Upsurge and Gandhi

The severe dislocations caused by World War I spurred nationalist opposition to the British Raj. To pay for the war, the British raised taxes and customs duties on Indians, sparking several armed uprisings. Over 1 million Indians fought for Britain in France and the Middle East, and 60,000 were killed. Many Indians expected a better future because of their sacrifices in a war they did not start—perhaps a self-government similar to that of Australia and Canada, both former colonies. But the British dashed these hopes by declaring that they would maintain India as an integral part of their empire. However, the losses in World War I showed that British power was no longer unchallengeable.

Indian Discontent

A severe economic slump heightened Indian discontent, causing the alarmed British to clamp down on dissent and maintain the harsh wartime laws. In 1919, in the Punjab city of Amritsar, British officers, fearing a mass uprising, ordered their Indian soldiers to open fire on an unarmed crowd at an unauthorized rally held in a walled field where escape was difficult (see Chronology: South Asia, 1914–1945). The attack killed 400 protesters and wounded 1,000, including women and children. Throughout India, the Amritsar massacre was greeted with outrage. The anger intensified when the British hailed the officer in command, General Dyer, as a national hero. Prominent Indians, many once pro-British, were appalled at the cruelty. The Nobel Prize–winning writer Rabindranath Tagore **(tuh-GAWR)** (1861–1941) wrote, "The enormity of the measures taken up for quelling some local disturbances had, with a rude shock, revealed to our minds the helplessness of our position as British subjects in India."[10]

CHRONOLOGY
South Asia, 1914–1945

1919 Amritsar massacre

1930 Gandhi's Great Salt March

1931 London Conference

1935 Government of India Act

1937 Provincial elections

1942 Gandhi's Quit India campaign

The unrest brought to the fore new Indian nationalist leaders, the most outstanding of whom was Mohandas K. Gandhi **(GAHN-dee)** (1869–1948) (see Profile: Mohandas Gandhi, Indian Nationalist). After getting his law degree in Britain, Gandhi lived for twenty-two years in South Africa, where the British colonial regime practiced racial segregation and white supremacy (see Chapter 21). To assert the rights of the Indian immigrants in South Africa, Gandhi developed tactics of **nonviolent resistance**, noncooperation with unjust laws and peaceful confrontation with illegitimate authority. Influenced by his pacifist wife, Kasturbai, Gandhi adopted ideas against taking life that had been introduced 2,500 years earlier by the Jains and Buddhists and also promoted by the Quakers, a pacifist Christian movement Gandhi had encountered in England. Nonviolence—Gandhi often called it passive resistance—was, he wrote, "a method of securing rights by personal suffering; it is the reverse of resistance by arms."[11] Gandhi believed that violence was never justified. The enemy was to be met with reason, and if he responded with violence, this had to be endured in good spirit.

nonviolent resistance Noncooperation with unjust laws and peaceful confrontation with illegitimate authority, pursued by Mohandas Gandhi in India.

Gandhi and His Strategies

After returning to India, in 1920 Gandhi became the president of the Indian National Congress. His message of resisting nonviolently led him to mount mass campaigns against British political and economic institutions. Inspired by his example, huge numbers of ordinary people—factory workers, peasants, estate laborers—joined his movement, shaking the foundations of British colonial rule. Gandhi made mass civil disobedience, involving marches, sit-ins, hunger strikes, peaceful violation of law, refusal to pay taxes, and boycotts of government and businesses, the most effective expression of nonviolence. Gandhi's Congress colleague, Jawaharlal Nehru **(JAH-wa-HAR-lahl NAY-roo)**, placed Gandhi's strategy in perspective: "Gandhi was like a powerful current of fresh air that made us stretch ourselves and take deep breaths, like a Whirlwind that upset many things but most of all the working of people's minds."[12]

Yet, some of Gandhi's ideas were outside the mainstream of nationalist thought, confounding allies. Gandhi opposed the global economic system because it involved competitive capitalism and trade between societies with unequal power and wealth. He believed that India should reject Western models and return to the self-sufficient, village-based precolonial economy, where everyone could spin their own cloth. He called industrialization "a machinery which has impoverished India. India's salvation consists in unlearning what she has learned during the past fifty years. The railways, telegraphs, hospitals, [and] lawyers have all to go."[13] Critics considered Gandhi's ideal of self-sufficient villages living in simplicity a utopian fantasy that was impractical and out of touch with the modern world, unable to improve people's lives. Gandhi also insisted that Indian society's lowest social group, the untouchables, be included in political actions, much to the distress of high-caste Hindus. He coined the term *harijans* (children of God) as a more dignified label to replace *pariahs,* the centuries-old name for untouchables. Gandhi did not entirely reject the caste system, but he wanted all people to enjoy the same dignity. In his conception, harijan toilet cleaners would have the same status as members of the priestly caste but would go on cleaning toilets. Even untouchable leaders often considered Gandhi's views unrealistic and patronizing.

Rising Congress Influence

Thanks to Gandhi's efforts, during the 1920s the Congress developed a mass base that was supported by people from all of India's cultures, religions, regions, and social backgrounds. His tactics bewildered the British, who, while claiming to uphold law, order, and Christian values, clubbed hunger strikers, used horses to trample nonviolent protesters, and arrested Gandhi and other leaders. One Indian observer told British officials in 1930 that the Congress "has undoubtedly acquired a great hold on the popular imagination. On roadside stations where until a few months ago I could hardly have suspected that people had any politics, I have seen demonstrations and heard Congress slogans."[14] Each campaign led to British concessions and a growing realization that Britain could not hold India forever.

The Great Depression lowered the standard of living for most Indians, collapsing prices for India's cash crops and rural credit, causing distress and suffering, and sparking a new Gandhi-led campaign in 1930, the Great Salt March. Gandhi and several dozen followers marched to the west coast, where they produced salt from the Indian Ocean seawater. In doing so they broke British laws,

MOHANDAS GANDHI, INDIAN NATIONALIST

Few individuals have had as much impact on history as Mohandas Gandhi (1869–1948), who became the leading figure of Indian nationalism in the 1920s by formulating ideas of nonviolent opposition to repressive colonial rule that influenced millions both inside and outside India. Gandhi was born into a well-to-do family of the vaisya caste in the western state of Gujerat; although vaisyas were commonly involved in commerce, his father was a government official. His parents maintained traditional attitudes, and his mother was a devout Hindu. Like many Hindu families, they arranged for him to marry young. The thirteen-year-old Mohandas married Kasturbai Kapada (KAST-er-by ka-PO-da) (1869–1948), the daughter of a rich merchant. Kasturbai proved a courageous helpmate in his later political activities.

Gandhi wanted to study law in London, but his family feared he would be corrupted there because his young wife, now with a son, had to stay in India. To gain their approval, he vowed to live a celibate life in England and never to touch meat or wine. In England he expanded his knowledge by reading Indian works such as the *Bhagavad Gita* and Western books such as the Christian Bible. His three years in London also gave him contact with Western nationalism and democracy, as well as a law degree.

At first unable to find a suitable position back in India, in 1893 Gandhi was hired by a large Indian law firm to work in South Africa, where the racist government and white minority mistreated not only Africans but also the thousands of Indians who had been recruited as laborers and plantation workers. With his wife's encouragement, he turned to helping the local Indians assert their rights, for which he was jailed, beaten by mobs, and almost killed by angry opponents, both white and Indian. The British who ruled South Africa raised taxes on Indians, shut down Indian gatherings, and refused official recognition of Hindu marriages. In response, and influenced by Kasturbai's advocacy of justice and nonviolence, Gandhi began developing his strategy of nonviolent resistance against oppressive rule, ideas that later inspired admirers throughout the world and that were used by Dr. Martin Luther King, Jr., in the U.S. civil rights movement of the 1950s and 1960s.

Bettman/Corbis

Gandhi Addressing Calcutta Meeting Mohandas Gandhi addressed some of his followers—many women as well as men—on a lawn following a meeting with British officials in Calcutta in 1931.

since salt production was a lucrative government monopoly. Gandhi's action and arrest caught the popular imagination, setting off a wave of demonstrations, strikes, and boycotts. In quelling the unrest, the British killed 103, injured 420, and imprisoned 60,000 resisters. They released Gandhi a few months later, and he agreed to halt civil disobedience campaigns if the British would promote Indian-made goods and hold a conference to discuss India's political future.

Social Change: Caste and Gender Relations

Caste System

These events took place against a backdrop of nationalist politics, economic dislocations, and rapid population growth that affected India's social structure. India's population grew from 255 million in 1871 to 390 million in 1940. The trends reshaping the caste system in the 1800s continued, including the adoption by lower castes of high-caste practices such as vegetarianism and more awareness of caste identities. Although Gandhi urged fair treatment for all groups, increasing attention to caste identities led to more discrimination against untouchables, the most disadvantaged group and perhaps a fifth of India's population. As a result, untouchables mounted movements promoting their rights. Dr. Bhimrao Ramji Ambedkar (BIM-rao RAM-jee am-BED-car) (1893–1956), who rose from one of the lowest groups, the sweepers who cleaned village streets, to earn a Ph.D. and a law degree from major U.S. and British universities, started schools, newspapers, and political parties. He rejected Gandhi's policies as inadequate for real change and successfully lobbied the government to offer untouchables government jobs and scholarships for higher education. Later in life, believing untouchables could never flourish within Hinduism, Ambedkar led thousands of followers to adopt Buddhism, which by then had only a small following in India.

Between 1906 and 1914 Gandhi carried on his fight for justice for Indians in South Africa, spreading ideas of nonviolence. He led hunger strikes, public demonstrations, and mass marches, in which thousands of Indians resisted oppression by willingly risking beating or arrest for their cause. In 1914 the colonial regime bowed to the constant pressure and lifted the worst legal injustices against the Indians. Gandhi was forty-five years old when the triumph in South Africa earned him fame and the respected title of *Mahatma* (Great Soul) among Indians in South Africa and at home.

With the outbreak of World War I in Europe, Gandhi, Kasturbai, and their four children left South Africa to return to India. In 1915 he established a spiritual center near the Gujerat capital, Ahmedebad, where he trained followers in his ideas of nonviolence. Though Gandhi was deeply religious, he also believed that everyone had to reach truth in his or her own way, writing that "there are innumerable definitions of God, because His manifestations are innumerable. But I worship God as Truth only. I have not yet found Him, but I am seeking after Him." Moved by the poverty and suffering of the Indian masses, he also took up their cause. To identify with their plight, the high-caste Gandhi adopted the dress of the simple peasant and always traveled third class.

The British massacre of Indian protesters at Amritsar in 1919 shook Gandhi's faith in British justice. In 1920 he became the leader of India's major nationalist organization, the Indian National Congress, and over the next three decades he was at times a religious figure and at other times the consummate politician, crafty and practical. Needing mass support to build a policy of massive noncooperation, he launched three great campaigns of civil disobedience, in 1920, 1930, and 1942. Each time the British jailed him for long periods. His self-discipline was reflected in his practice of fasting to protest oppression, which added to his saintly image.

In his personal life, Gandhi was also troubled. His wife, Kasturbai, aided in his campaigns, but Gandhi was gone for long periods, neglecting her and their four children. One embittered son rejected his father entirely. When Gandhi took a lifelong vow of chastity in 1906, Kasturbai did also. Both kept their vows. Although both were born into affluent families, the Gandhis agreed to live simply. Critics accused Gandhi of sometimes humiliating his wife by, for example, asking her to do menial tasks such as cleaning toilets. Arrested during Gandhi's "Quit India" campaign, Kasturbai, in failing health, died in her husband's lap in prison in 1944. Before she passed away, she noted that they had shared many joys and sorrows and asked that she be cremated in a sari (dress) made from yarn he had spun.

Gandhi helped lead India to independence from Britain. Shortly thereafter, when trying to end accelerating Hindu-Muslim violence in 1948, he was assassinated by a Hindu fanatic who opposed Gandhi's tolerant approach (see Chapter 31). India's first prime minister, Jawaharlal Nehru, called Gandhi's death the loss of India's soul: "The light has gone out of our lives and there is darkness everywhere."

THINKING ABOUT THE PROFILE

1. How did Gandhi's South African experiences shape his political strategies?
2. How did Gandhi's ideas and activities have a great influence in the world?

Note: Quotations from Judith M. Brown, *Modern India: The Origins of an Asian Democracy*, 2nd ed. (New York: Oxford University Press, 1994), 211; and Rhoads Murphey, *A History of Asia*, 4th ed. (New York: Longman, 2003), 437.

Gender Relations

Attitudes toward women were also changing. Hindus increasingly favored widow remarriage, once forbidden, to help offset the higher Muslim birthrate. But greater emphasis on what traditionalists considered proper female conduct largely favored male authority. Yet, while the feminist movement remained weak, many women joined the Congress, and some demanded a vote equal to men for representative institutions. With British assent, all the provincial legislatures granted women the franchise between 1923 and 1930. Educated women published magazines. Rokeya Hossain (1880–1932), a Bengali Muslim raised in seclusion who had opened girls' schools and campaigned for equal rights, published a utopian short story, "Sultana's Dream," that portrayed men confined to seclusion because of their uncontrolled sexual desires while women governed. Gandhi's views on women were mixed. He advocated gender equality, encouraged women's participation in public life, and also urged women to abandon seclusion and join a nationalist women's corps. But women were usually offered the more menial tasks such as picketing and cooking. Gandhi promoted women's traditional roles as wives, mothers, and supporters of men and believed women were especially suited to passive resistance. Some women with a more militant vision joined men in terrorist organizations. Pritilata Waddedar (1911–1932), a brilliant Bengali university graduate, led and died in an armed raid on a British club that reportedly boasted a sign: "Dogs and Indians not allowed."

Hindu-Muslim Division

Congress and the Muslims

A growing Hindu-Muslim division posed a problem for Indian nationalism. Although some Muslims supported the Congress, its largely Hindu membership sparked concerns among Muslims about their role in India. While Gandhi respected all religions and welcomed Muslim support,

Muslim leaders, fearing that independence would mean Hindu domination, mounted their own nationalist organizations to work for a potential Muslim country of their own. In 1930 student activists in Britain called their proposed Muslim nation Pakistan, meaning "Land of the Pure" in the Urdu language spoken by many Indian Muslims. Accounting for some 20 percent of British India's population and largely concentrated in the northwest and Bengal, Muslims occupied all niches of society but were divided by social status, ancestry, language, and sect. The great majority were Sunni, but some were Shi'a.

While Muslim leaders often focused on the need for a state that enshrined their religious values, Congress leaders were chiefly Western-oriented Hindu intellectuals. Jawaharlal Nehru (1889–1964), who succeeded Gandhi as Congress leader in 1929, wanted a secular state that was neutral toward religion and, in contrast with Gandhi, a modern India. Born into a wealthy brahman family and endowed with unusual charisma and rare public speaking skills, Nehru was a Marxist-influenced product of an elite Western education with a passion for the welfare of the common people. But while Gandhi wanted to reshape colonial society, Nehru and other Congress leaders focused more on political independence. Few of the Indian nationalists shared the Chinese communist goal of radical social transformation.

The Muslim League

By the 1930s the main rival to the Congress was the Muslim League, led by the Western-educated Bombay lawyer Muhammed Ali Jinnah **(jee-NAH)** (1876–1948), a dapper figure in his tailored suits who always spoke English and never learned Urdu. Jinnah argued that Islam and Hinduism were different social orders and that it was a naive dream that the two groups could ever forge a common nationality. Jinnah developed the Muslim League into a mass political movement in competition with the Congress. His claim to speak for all Muslims outraged the Congress, which had over a hundred thousand Muslim members and saw itself as a national party representing all religions and castes. But Jinnah cultivated good relations with the British and convinced regional Muslim leaders to support the Muslim League. The Congress tried to marginalize the Muslim League and refused to form a coalition with it, which proved a mistake in the long run.

Competing Visions

The competing visions of the Congress and the Muslim League complicated British efforts to introduce representative government institutions. The two rival organizations clashed in 1931, when Indian leaders and British officials met in London to discuss expanded elections. Representatives of various minorities, including Muslims, Sikhs, and untouchables, demanded separate electorates to ensure that their groups gained representation. Seeing this as a tactic that would allow the British to divide and rule, Congress objected, but the minorities won electoral rights in India's many provinces. The electoral agreement also did not end anticolonial unrest and counterviolence by the British. However, in the Government of India Act of 1935 the British introduced a new constitution that allowed some 35 million Indians who owned property to vote for newly formed provincial legislatures. In the first provincial elections, in 1937, the Congress won 70 percent of the popular vote and the majority of seats, defeating the Muslim League even for seats reserved for Muslims. More Indians also rose to leadership positions in the army, police, and civil service. However, British officials argued that the communal divisions necessitated the continuation of British rule to maintain order, and Jinnah redoubled his efforts to unite Muslims against the Congress.

World War II and India

World War II reshaped the nationalist dialogue by increasing the Hindu-Muslim divide. The British committed Indian troops without consulting Congress leaders, and in 1942 Gandhi, fearing that the British had no intention of ending their colonial rule, mounted a campaign calling on the British to "Quit India." The British arrested the entire Congress leadership and 60,000 party activists, jailing many of them for the duration of the war. During World War II, the rural poor and urban workers suffered as prices for essential goods soared, and famine in Bengal killed 3 to 4 million people. In response to these hardships, Nehru's main rival for Congress leadership, the militant Bengali Marxist Subhas Chandra Bose (1895–1945), allied with imperial Japan. With Japanese backing, Bose organized an Indian National Army, recruited largely from the British Indian army and Indian emigrants in Southeast Asia, that invaded India from Japan-held Burma. The invasion failed, but many Indians saw Bose as a national hero.

Meanwhile, the arrest of Congress leaders left a vacuum that allowed Jinnah to strengthen his Muslim League. The British cultivated Jinnah, who joined the government and demanded the creation of a separate Muslim state based on the provinces where Muslims were the majority. Rejecting Muslim separatism, the jailed Gandhi unsuccessfully urged Muslims to resist what he termed the suicide of partition. After World War II, the struggle between Indian nationalists and the British, and between Hindus and Muslims, resumed, leading to the end of British rule and the creation of two separate independent nations, predominantly Hindu India and a chiefly Muslim Pakistan.

SECTION SUMMARY

- In the aftermath of World War I Indians were angry that Britain denied them greater autonomy and imposed higher taxes to pay for the war, and resentment peaked with the massacre of hundreds of peaceful protesters at Amritsar.
- Mohandas Gandhi, the foremost Indian nationalist leader, promoted nonviolent resistance to British rule, including strikes, boycotts, and refusal to pay taxes, and won a massive popular following for the Indian National Congress.
- While even his Indian supporters considered some of Gandhi's ideas naive and utopian, campaigns such as the Great Salt March were highly effective in winning concessions from the British.
- Leaders of the untouchables, the lowest Hindu caste, pushed for and obtained greater opportunities, and women were allowed somewhat more freedom, though many Indian men, including Gandhi, did not see them as entirely equal to men.
- Feeling threatened by the predominantly Hindu National Congress, the Muslim League, led by Jinnah, argued that Indian Muslims should have a country of their own, which they called Pakistan.
- The British jailed tens of thousands of Indian National Congress activists after Gandhi objected to Indian troops being forced to fight in World War II, a Bengali Marxist led a failed invasion of India, the Muslim League grew increasingly independent, and eventually, after the end of World War II, both Pakistan and India gained independence from Britain.

Nationalist Stirrings in Southeast Asia and Sub-Saharan Africa

How did nationalism differ in Southeast Asia and sub-Saharan Africa?

The challenges posed by European colonialism were also addressed by nationalist movements and protests in Southeast Asia and sub-Saharan Africa, though none were as influential as the Indian National Congress. In 1930 the Indonesian Nationalist Party, struggling against Dutch colonialism, urged Indonesians to be zealous in the cause of national freedom. The plea symbolized nationalist assertions in Southeast Asian colonies, especially French-ruled Vietnam. In sub-Saharan Africa nationalist movements, often based on ethnicity, were weaker.

Nationalism in Southeast Asia

The first stirrings of Southeast Asian nationalism came in the Philippines in the late 1800s, but the revolution was thwarted by the American occupation. The U.S. promise of eventual independence and its co-optation of nationalist leaders into the colonial administration reduced radical sentiments. By 1941 nationalists had a large following in Vietnam, British Burma, and Indonesia, all of which experienced oppressive colonial rule. In French-ruled Cambodia and Laos and in British Malaya and Borneo, all colonies that had experienced less social, economic, and political disruption, nationalism was weaker.

Burma and Siam

In Burma (today's Myanmar), despite limited self-government by the 1930s, the colony's majority ethnic group, the Burmans, hated British rule and resented British favoritism toward Christian ethnic minorities and the large, often wealthy Indian community, who dominated the economy. The colony's schools encouraged their students to adopt Western ways, including Western clothing styles, and devalued Buddhist traditions. The nationalist leaders, mostly graduates of these schools, used Theravada Buddhism as a rallying cry to press for reform, and some favored women's rights. When the Japanese invaded Burma in 1941, many Burmans welcomed them as liberators.

Although Siam (today's Thailand) was not a colony, nationalism emerged from tensions between the aristocratic elite and the rising middle class of civil servants, military officers, and professionals, who resented political domination by the royal family and aristocracy. Middle-class discontent was further fueled by the Great Depression, which forced salary and budget cuts. In 1932 military officers who called themselves nationalists took power in a coup against the royal government (see Chronology: Southeast Asia and Africa, 1912–1945), and the Siamese king agreed under pressure to become a constitutional, mostly symbolic monarch. Military leaders then ran the government through the 1930s, pursuing nationalist policies, renaming the country Thailand

CHRONOLOGY

Southeast Asia and Africa, 1912–1945

1912 Formation of African National Congress in South Africa

1912 Formation of Islamic Union in Indonesia

1920 Formation of Indonesian Communist Party

1920–1922 Nationalist unrest in Kenya

1926–1927 Communist uprising in Indonesia

1927 Formation of Indonesian Nationalist Party

1928–1931 Peasant rebellions in the Congo region

1930 Founding of Indochinese Communist Party

1932 Nationalist coup in Thailand

1935–1936 Conquest of Ethiopia by Italy

1941 Formation of Viet Minh in Vietnam by Ho Chi Minh

1941–1945 Japanese occupation of Southeast Asia

("Land of Free People"), and urging the Thais to live modern lives, including dressing in a modern Western fashion, with hats and shoes. Thailand forged an alliance with imperial Japan and introduced fascist policies, militarizing the schools and suppressing dissent.

The most powerful nationalist movement in Southeast Asia emerged in Vietnam, which was destabilized by French rule. The earliest leader was the passionately revolutionary Phan Boi Chau **(FAN boy chow)** (1867–1940), born into a mandarin family and educated in Confucian learning. By the time of his death in a French prison, Phan had inspired Vietnamese patriotism and resistance. As he wrote in his prison diaries, "It has been but a yearning to purchase my freedom even at the cost of spilling my blood, to exchange my fate of slavery for the right of self-determination."[15] But the older Confucian scholars gradually lost influence to the younger, urban, French-educated intellectuals of the Vietnamese Nationalist Party, which had few options other than terrorism: they assassinated colonial officials and bombed French buildings. A premature uprising in 1930 sparked greater French repression that destroyed the major nationalist groups except for the communists, thus becoming a turning point in Vietnamese history.

The rise of Vietnamese communism owed much to Ho Chi Minh, a mandarin's son and former sailor turned political activist who had spent many years organizing the communist movement among Vietnamese exiles in Thailand and China. Ho believed that revolution was the answer to economic exploitation and political repression in Vietnam, and he favored equality for women and improving the lives of the peasants and plantation workers. In 1930 Ho established the Indochinese Communist Party, which united anticolonial radicals from Vietnam, Cambodia, and Laos. Vietnamese Marxists linked themselves to the patriotic traditions of the Vietnamese rebels who for 2,000 years resisted Chinese, Mongol, and French conquerors. As one Vietnamese Marxist said: "Behind us we have the immense history of our people. There [are] still spiritual cords attaching us."[16] Vietnamese communism took on a strongly nationalist flavor. In 1941 Ho established the **Viet Minh**, or Vietnamese Independence League, a coalition of anti-French groups that waged war against both the French colonizers and the Japanese, who occupied Vietnam during World War II.

Viet Minh The Vietnamese Independence League, a coalition of anti-French groups established by Ho Chi Minh in 1941 that waged war against both the French and the Japanese.

lingua franca A language widely used as a common tongue among diverse groups with different languages.

Nationalist activity also emerged in the Dutch East Indies in the early twentieth century. Diverse organizations sought freedom from Dutch control while seeking ways to unite the colony's hundreds of ethnic groups. One strategy was to adopt a unifying language. Malay was the mother tongue for many peoples in the western Indonesian islands, and elsewhere it served as a trading language. Malay was thus a **lingua franca**, a language widely used as a common tongue among diverse groups that also had their own languages. Nationalist intellectuals began using Malay and called it Indonesian, which gradually became the language of magazines, newspapers, books, and education. Indonesian religious traditions were also reshaped. Some Muslims, impressed with but also resenting Western power, sought to reform and purify their faith by purging it of practices based on older pre-Islamic influences, such as mysticism, which they believed held Indonesians back. *Muhammadiyah* ("Way of Muhammad") and its allied women's organization, *Aisyah,* criticized local customs, promoted the goal of an Islamic state, stressed the five pillars of Islam, and favored the segregation of men and women in public, a custom long ignored by most Indonesians.

In 1912 Javanese batik merchants who mixed reformist religious ideas with nationalism established the colony's first true political movement, the Islamic Union, which by 1919 had recruited 2 million members. As Marxism became influential in Indonesia after the Russian Revolution, the colonial government responded by arresting Marxists. The more radical Marxists established the Indonesian Communist Party in 1920, which grew rapidly by attracting support from nondevout Muslim peasants and labor union members in Java. Overestimating their strength, the communists sparked a poorly planned uprising in 1926. The Dutch crushed the uprising and executed the communist leaders.

Sukarno and Indonesian Nationalism

The destruction of the communists left an opening for other nationalists. The Indonesian Nationalist Party, led mostly by Javanese aristocrats who rejected Islamic reform ideas, was established in 1927 and promoted a new national identity. Sukarno **(soo-KAHR-no)** (1902–1970), the key founder, was born into a wealthy aristocratic Javanese family. After studying engineering, he dedicated his life to politics and a free Indonesia. Sukarno loved the shadow puppet stories that had been popular on Java for centuries. Like the characters in those stories, Sukarno (who had no first name) brought together contradictory ideas, such as Islamic faith and atheistic Marxism. The mass popularizer of Indonesian nationalism, he created a slogan: "one nation—Indonesia, one people—Indonesian, one language—Indonesian." He even designed a flag and wrote a national anthem. The

Sukarno Indicts Dutch Colonialism

Sukarno, the fiery Indonesian nationalist, was skilled at articulating his criticisms of colonialism. A splendid orator, he attracted a large following through his use of Indonesian, especially Javanese, religious and cultural symbols and frequent historical references in his speeches. Arrested by the Dutch in 1930, Sukarno delivered a passionate defense speech, known as "Indonesia Accuses," at his trial that became one of the most inspiring documents of Indonesian nationalism. Sukarno stressed the greatness of Indonesia's past as a building block for the future.

The word "imperialism" . . designates a . . . tendency . . . to dominate or influence the affairs of another nation, . . . a system . . . of economic control. . . . As long as a nation does not wield political power in its own country, part of its potential, economic, social or political, will be used for interests which are not its interests, but contrary to them. . . . A colonial nation is a nation that cannot be itself, a nation that in almost all its branches, in all of its life, bears the mark of imperialism. There is no community of interests between the subject and the object of imperialism. Between the two there is only a contrast of interests and a conflict of needs. All interests of imperialism, social, economic, political, or cultural, are opposed to the interests of the Indonesian people. The imperialists desire the continuation of imperialism, the Indonesians desire its abolition. . . .

What are the roads to promote Indonesian nationalism? . . . First: we point out to the people that they have had a great past. Second: we reinforce the consciousness of the people that the present is dark. Third: we show the people the pure and brightly shining light of the future and the roads which lead to this future so full of promises. . . . The P.N.I. [Indonesian Nationalist Party] awakens and reinforces the people's consciousness of its "grandiose past," its "dark present" and the promises of a shining, beckoning future.

Our grandiose past? Oh, what Indonesian does not feel his heart shrink with sorrow when he hears the stories about the beautiful past, does not regret the disappearance of that departed glory! What Indonesian does not feel his national heart beat with joy when he hears about the greatness of the [Intermediate Era] empires of Melayu and Srivijaya, about the greatness of the empire of Mataram and Madjapahit. . . . A nation with such a grandiose past must surely have sufficient natural aptitude to have a beautiful future. . . . Among the people . . . again conscious of their great past, national feeling is revived, and the fire of hope blazes in their hearts.

THINKING ABOUT THE READING

1. What is Sukarno's evaluation of imperialism?
2. How does he think Indonesians should capitalize on their past?

Source: Harry J. Benda and John A. Larkin, eds., *The World of Southeast Asia: Selected Historical Readings* (New York: Harper and Row, 1967), pp. 190–193.

Dutch authorities arrested Sukarno in 1929 and exiled him to a remote island prison for the next decade, making him a nationalist symbol (see Witness to the Past: Sukarno Indicts Dutch Colonialism). With Sukarno in jail, the Indonesian Nationalist Party and the nationalist vision grew slowly throughout the 1930s.

The Japanese Occupation and Its Consequences

The occupation of Southeast Asia by Japanese forces from 1941 to 1945 boosted nationalism and weakened colonialism. Before 1941 colonial authority had remained strong, with only Vietnamese nationalism posing a serious threat. Then everything changed. Japan had already bullied Thailand and the Vichy-controlled French colonial regime in Vietnam to allow the stationing of Japanese troops. Then the bombing of Pearl Harbor in 1941 was quickly followed by a rapid Japanese invasion of Southeast Asia. The Japanese easily overwhelmed the colonial forces, and within four months they controlled major cities and heavily populated regions, shattering the mystique of Western invincibility. As an Indonesian writer later remembered, the Japanese occupation "destroyed a whole set of illusions and left man as naked as when he was created."[17] European and American officials, businessmen, planters, and missionaries were either in retreat or confined in prison camps. The Japanese talked of "Asia for the Asians," and some Japanese officers with anticolonial sentiments sympathized with Southeast Asian nationalists. But this rhetoric also masked the Japanese desire for resources, especially the rubber, oil, and timber of Indonesia, British Borneo, and Malaya.

Japanese Invasion

Japanese domination was brief, less than four years, yet it led to significant changes. Conflicts between ethnic groups often increased because of selective repression. In Malaya, Japanese policy allowed Malay government officials to keep their jobs while the Chinese minority often faced

Japanese Rule

property seizures and arrest, creating antagonisms that persisted long after the war. By destroying the link to the world economy, the occupation also caused hardship. Western companies closed, while Japanese forces seized natural resources and food. By 1944 living standards, crippled by severe shortages of food and clothing, were in steep decline. Southeast Asians also suffered from harassment by the Japanese police, who treated even minor violators of occupation regulations with brutality. The Japanese forcibly conscripted thousands of Southeast Asians: Javanese men became slave laborers, and Filipinas, called "comfort women" by the Japanese, served the sexual needs of Japanese soldiers. As their war effort faltered, the desperate Japanese resorted to even more repressive policies.

Japan and Southeast Asian Nationalism

Japanese rule also offered some political benefits for Southeast Asians. Since they needed experienced local help, the Japanese promoted Southeast Asians into government positions once reserved for Westerners. To purge the area of Western cultural influences, they closed Christian mission schools, encouraged Islamic or Buddhist leaders, and fostered a renaissance of indigenous culture and local literature. This policy also promoted Southeast Asian nationalism, at least indirectly. Whereas under colonialism most nationalists had been in jail or exile and hence powerless, the Japanese freed nationalist leaders such as Sukarno and gave them official positions, if little actual power. The nationalists now enjoyed a new role in public life and used radio and newspapers to foster their beliefs. The Japanese also recruited young people into armed paramilitary forces, which became the basis for later nationalist armies in Indonesia and Burma that resisted the return of Western colonialism.

Opposing Japan

Some Southeast Asians actively opposed Japanese rule, especially in Vietnam. Vietnamese communism might never have achieved power so quickly had it not been for the Japanese occupation, which discredited the French administration and imposed great hardship on most of the population. The Viet Minh, led by Ho Chi Minh, were now armed and trained by American advisers, who had been sent to help anti-Japanese forces. In 1944 the Viet Minh moved out of their bases along the Chinese border and expanded their influence in northern Vietnam, attracting peasant support while attacking the Japanese occupiers with guerrilla tactics. When a famine killed 2 million Vietnamese, the Viet Minh gained popular backing and recruits because the Japanese exported scarce food to Japan. The Viet Minh organized local village administrations led by peasants who sympathized with their movement.

Japanese fortunes waned as the United States gained the upper hand and bombed Japanese installations in Southeast Asia. Fearful, the Japanese encouraged Southeast Asians to resist Western attempts to reestablish colonial control. Japanese officials helped Indonesian nationalists prepare for Indonesian independence and Burmese nationalists to establish a government. Some nationalists began secretly working with the Western Allies. Changing sides, the Burmese nationalist army helped push Japanese forces out of Burma. Tired of economic deprivation and repression, few Southeast Asians regretted Japan's defeat, and some, especially in Malaya, British Borneo, and the Philippines, even welcomed the return of Western forces. The United States granted independence to the Philippines under pro-U.S. leaders in 1946. But often the returning Westerners faced volatility, setting the stage for dramatic political change in Vietnam, Indonesia, and Burma as nationalist forces successfully struggled for independence in the late 1940s and early 1950s.

Nationalism in Colonial Africa

Challenges to Nationalism

The roots of the African nationalist struggle were planted in the interwar years, although African nationalists lacked the mass base of the Vietnamese and Indians. African nationalists tried with limited success to overcome major barriers to widespread popular support. Few regimes prepared their colonies for political and economic independence by permitting African participation in government or producing a large educated class that could assume the responsibilities and burdens of nationhood. The artificial division of Africa was also a major hindrance to nationalist organizing. Colonial regimes, by using divide-and-rule strategies to govern the diverse ethnic groups living within artificial national boundaries, made creating viable national identities and uniting all people within a colony difficult. For example, Nigeria resulted from the British colonization of often-rival ethnic groups. While some Pan-Nigerian nationalists sought unity, most Nigerian nationalists found their greatest support only among particular regions or ethnic groups. In the 1940s a prominent Yoruba leader expressed the common fear that no Nigerian nation was really possible:

> *Nigeria is not a nation [but] a mere geographical expression. There are no "Nigerians" in the same sense as there are "English" or "French." The word "Nigerian" merely distinguish[es] those who live within the boundaries of Nigeria from those who do not.*[18]

Resistance to Colonialism

World War I and the unfulfilled expectations for better lives in its aftermath spurred nationalism. The British, French, and Germans had all drafted or recruited Africans to fight on European battlefields, where many thousands died. When the survivors returned home, the promises made to them about land or jobs proved empty, while taxes were raised. Returning Kenyan soldiers found that British settlers had seized their land. In response Harry Thuku (THOO-koo) (ca. 1895–1970), a Gikuyu, created an alliance of diverse Kenyans to confront the British. When the British arrested Thuku, rioting broke out led by Gikuyu women. The British fired on the rioters, killing many. Anticolonial protests were also common in the Belgian Congo, leading to rebellions by peasant farmers upset at Belgian demands for unpaid labor. Women often led resistance. Aline Sitoe Diatta (1920–1944), who led an uprising in Senegal when the French conscripted her village's rice supplies, was exiled and later executed. In Nigeria in 1929, tens of thousands of Igbo women, particularly the palm oil traders, rioted to protest taxes on them. After the British opened fire, killing thirty-two of them, the protests escalated and it took months to restore order.

Nationalist Organizations

In the 1920s urban-based nationalist organizations developed to press for African participation in local government. They were led by Western-educated Africans such as J. E. Casely Hayford (1866–1930), a lawyer and journalist in the British Gold Coast (today's Ghana) who was influenced by Gandhi. Some Africans, including Hayford, favored a Pan-African approach and sought support across colonial borders, which they did not view as the basis for nations. But both nationalists and Pan-Africanists were unable to overcome ethnic divisions and, unlike the Indian and Vietnamese nationalists, the gap between the cities and the villages. Furthermore, some African merchants, chiefs, and kings profited from their links to the colonizers and discouraged protests.

The nationalists, unable to capitalize on the brutal Italian invasion and occupation of Ethiopia in 1935–1936, had modest influence before World War II. West African nationalist currents were strongest in the multiethnic capital cities, which became the breeding grounds of new ideas. City life encouraged trade union movements, which sponsored occasional strikes to protest colonial policies or economic exploitation. Hence, market women in Lagos, Nigeria, protested taxation and demanded the right to vote. During World War II they refused to cooperate with price controls, forcing the British to back down. Rural people also asserted their rights. During the 1930s cocoa growers in the British-ruled Gold Coast held back their crops to protest low prices.

Cultural Nationalism

Colonial rule generated new cultural trends that allowed people to express their views, often critical, about colonial life. During the 1930s a musical style arose in the Gold Coast and soon spread into other British West African colonies, carried chiefly by guitar-playing Africans and West Indian sailors. **Highlife** was a mix of Christian hymns, West Indian calypso songs, and African dance rhythms. Later West African musicians added influences from Cuba, Brazil, and the United States, especially jazz, indicating the continuing cultural links between West Africa and the Americas. Although closely tied to dance bands and parties, some highlife musicians addressed social and political issues and the problems of everyday life. The very term *highlife* signified both an envy and disapproval of the Western colonizers and rich Africans, who lived in luxury in mansions staffed by servants. Many highlife songs were sung in **pidgin English**, the form of broken English that

highlife An urban-based West African musical style mixing Christian hymns, West Indian calypso songs, and African dance rhythms.

pidgin English The form of broken English that developed in Africa during the colonial era.

Courtesy, National Library of South Africa

African Jazz Band Jazz from the United States had a wide following in the world in the 1920s, 1930s, and 1940s. Jazz especially influenced the music of black South Africans, some of whom formed jazz groups such as the Harmony Kings.

developed during the colonial era. This mix of African and English words and grammar spread throughout British West Africa as a marketplace lingua franca among diverse urban populations.

South African Resistance

Racial inequality and white supremacy sparked nationalism and resistance to oppression in South Africa. The early South African nationalists, such as the founders of the African National Congress (usually known as the ANC, established in 1912), came from the urban middle class. The ANC encouraged education and preached African independence from white rule but did not directly confront the government until the 1950s. More militant African resistance flourished in the mining industry, where strikes were endemic despite severe government repression. Resistance was often subtle, involving noncooperation or affirmation of African cultural forms. Protest was often expressed in music, although usually veiled to avoid arrest. Knowing that few whites understood lyrics sung in African languages, African workers filled the mining camps with political music, offering messages such as "we demand freedom" and "workers unite." For decades, road gangs worked to songs such as "We Say: Oh, the White Man's Bad." Zulu and Swazi workers blended their own traditions with Western influences to create new dances. Virile, stamping dancers laced their performances with provocative songs: "Who has taken our land from us? Come out! Let us fight! The land was ours. Now it is taken. Fight! Fight!"[19]

Music and Protest

In South African cities jazz became a form of resistance. A potent vehicle for protest, this music, adapted from African Americans, reflected the African rejection of the racist Afrikaner culture. African American musicians such as the trumpeter Louis Armstrong (1901–1971) and the pianist Duke Ellington (1898–1974) were particularly popular in the 1930s, influencing South African jazz bands and new jazz-based musical styles. Educated urban Africans envisioned a modern African culture and sometimes rejected African traditions, as one Johannesburg resident proclaimed:

> *Tribal music! Chiefs! We don't care about chiefs! Give us jazz and film stars, man! We want Ellington, Satchmo [Louis Armstrong], and hot dames! Yes, brother, anything American. You can cut out this junk about [rural homesteads] and folk-tales—forget it! You're just trying to keep us backward!*[20]

The preferred music of the small black professional and business class, jazz ultimately became a symbol of black nationalism in South Africa.

SECTION SUMMARY

- Southeast Asian nationalism was strong in places such as Burma, which experienced harsh colonial rule, and even emerged as a rallying cry in Siam, which was never colonized but where a military coup overthrew the royal government.
- Vietnamese resistance to French rule was continued by the terrorist Vietnamese Nationalist Party, which the French harshly repressed, and the Viet Minh, a coalition led by the communist Ho Chi Minh.
- A variety of groups representing Muslims, women, and communists worked toward independence for the Dutch East Indies; the Indonesian Nationalist Party, which was led by Sukarno and incorporated both Islam and Marxism, was most influential.
- Southeast Asians suffered greatly under Japanese occupation, but Japanese control also showed that Westerners could be defeated and primed the colonized peoples to resist recolonization by Westerners after the war was over.
- Although African nationalist movements were hampered by the existence of rival ethnic groups within artificial colonies, anger over the poor treatment of Africans who had fought in World War I inspired many, especially in cities, to work for independence.
- In South Africa, nationalists opposed the repressive white supremacist government through education, strikes, and, most pervasively, music.

REMAKING THE MIDDLE EAST AND LATIN AMERICA

What factors promoted change in the Middle East and Latin America?

The peoples of both the Middle East and Latin America were also influenced by nationalism. While North Africans experienced Western colonial rule, Arabs in western Asian territories controlled by the Ottoman Turks stagnated economically. After World War I the Ottoman-ruled

Arab territories were transferred to Britain and France, sparking nationalist resentment, while Turkey remained independent. In Latin America, two world wars and the Great Depression caused turmoil, fostered dictatorships, and spurred feelings of nationalism.

CHRONOLOGY
The Middle East, 1914–1945

1916 Arab revolt against the Turks

1917 Balfour Declaration

1919–1922 Turkish Revolution by Ataturk

1921 Formation of Iranian republic by Reza Khan

1922 Formation of Turkish republic

1922 End of British protectorate in Egypt

1925 Formation of Pahlavi dynasty by Reza Khan

1928 Formation of Muslim Brotherhood in Egypt

1930 Independence for Iraq

1932 Formation of Saudi Arabia

1935 Discovery of oil in Saudi Arabia

1936 Britain-Egypt alliance

1936–1939 Civil war in Palestine

Reshaping the Ottoman Territories

World War I led to a dismantling of the Turkish-dominated Ottoman Empire and a reshaping of Arab politics. The Turks were allies of Germany, which shared their hatred of expansionist Russia. The Ottomans also dreamed of liberating Russian-controlled lands in the Caucasus and Central Asia, inhabited largely by peoples speaking languages related to Turkish. However, the Caucasus peoples, especially the Christian Armenians, desired independence. Suspecting them of aiding Russia, the Turks turned on the Armenians in eastern Anatolia (see Chapter 21). More than a million Armenians were deported, chiefly to Syria and Iraq, while perhaps another million died of thirst, starvation, or systematic slaughter by the Ottoman army. These sufferings created a permanent Turkish-Armenian hostility.

The hardships during World War I also spurred Arab nationalism against Ottoman rule. Hunger and disease affected millions of Arabs, with 200,000 dying in Syria alone during the war. Unrest in Syria brought on fierce repression, with dissidents sent into exile or hanged for treason. The most serious challenge came in Arabia, where Sharif Hussein ibn Ali (1856–1931), the Arab ruler of the Hejaz in western Arabia, which included Mecca and Medina, shifted his loyalties from the Ottomans to the British, who promised to support Arab independence. In 1916, at British urging, Sharif Hussein launched an Arab revolt (see Chronology: The Middle East, 1914–1945). British officers, including the flamboyant Lt. T. E. Lawrence (famous as "Lawrence of Arabia"), advised Sharif Hussein's tribal forces as they attacked Ottoman bases and communications. The British also invaded and occupied southern Iraq, an Ottoman province, which had a strategic position and was thought to have oil.

European Colonialism

The end of World War I brought crushed dreams and turmoil. The Arab nationalists such as Sharif Hussein did not know that Britain, France, and Russia had made secret agreements that ignored Arab interests. The czarist Russians had planned to incorporate Istanbul and nearby territories into their empire, while Britain and France agreed to partition the Ottoman provinces in western Asia between them. The Russian plans had to be modified after the communists took power and signed a peace treaty with Germany that allowed the Caucasus region, occupied by the Russians in the 1800s, to be returned to Germany's Ottoman ally. When the war ended with Ottoman defeat, British troops occupied much of Iraq and Palestine, French troops controlled the Syrian coast, and the Russians regained control of the Caucasus, including Armenia.

The Versailles treaty dismembered the Ottoman Empire (see Map 25.2). Turkey's neighbors—the Greeks, Italians, and Armenians—made claims on Anatolia and adjacent islands, and European Zionists asked for a Jewish national home in Palestine (see Chapter 21). The Allies promised eventual independence to the Kurds, a Sunni Muslim people, distinct from both Arabs and Turks, who inhabited a large, mountainous region of western Asia, including southeast Turkey. Both Syria and Iraq declared their independence. However, the League of Nations, dominated by Western countries, awarded France control over Syria and Lebanon, and Britain control over Iraq, Palestine, and Transjordan (today Jordan), under what the League called mandates, in theory less onerous than colonies because they were not considered permanent. Viewing mandates as a new form of colonialism, Arab nationalists in Syria proposed a democratic government, and some favored granting women the vote, which few Western nations had done. Ignoring Arab views, French forces quickly occupied Syria and, after facing armed resistance, exiled nationalist leaders. Despite promises, the Allies also ignored Kurdish desires for their own nation. The Kurds remained divided between Turkey, Persia (Iran), Iraq, and Syria, thus becoming the world's largest ethnic group without their own state.

Ataturk and Modern Turkey

The heart of the Ottoman Empire, Turkey, saw the most revolutionary changes. The disastrous defeat of the war and the humiliating agreements that followed left the Turks helpless, bitter, and facing a Greek invasion and Arab secession. But under the leadership of the daring war hero and ardent nationalist later known as Kemal Ataturk **(kuh-MAHL AT-uh-turk)** (1881–1938), the Turks enjoyed a spectacular resurgence. In 1919 Ataturk began mobilizing military forces in eastern Anatolia into a revolutionary organization to oppose the Ottoman sultan, discredited by defeats,

Map 25.2 Partition of the Ottoman Empire

Before 1914 the Ottoman Turks controlled much of western Asia, including western Arabia. After World War II the League of Nations awarded Iraq, Transjordan, and Palestine to Britain. Syria and Lebanon were given to France, and western Arabia was ruled by Arabs. Eventually the Saudi family, rulers of the Najd, expanded their rule into western Arabia and created Saudi Arabia.

e Interactive Map

and to restore Turkish dignity and preserve the Turkish majority areas and the Kurdish districts in eastern Anatolia. After establishing a rival Turkish government in the central Anatolia city of Ankara, Ataturk's forces fought both the sultan's government in Istanbul and the Greek forces that had moved deep into Anatolia. Ataturk finally pushed the Greeks back, and Turkey and Greece eventually agreed to a population transfer in which many Greeks living in Turkey moved to Greece and most Turks dwelling in Greece moved to Turkey. In 1922 Ataturk deposed the Ottoman sultan and set up a republic with himself as president.

Ataturk was a controversial figure among Turks. A religious agnostic, he violated Muslim customs by pursuing sexual promiscuity and drinking heavily in public. As a Turkish nationalist who glorified the pre-Islamic Turkish past, Ataturk dismissed Islamic culture as outdated. He favored modernization, announcing that "our eyes are turned westward. We shall transplant Western institutions to Asiatic soil. We wish to be a modern nation with our mind open, and yet to remain ourselves."[21] Ataturk claimed that secularization and the emancipation of women were the Turkish tradition. In the 1920s these ideas were put in action through reforms that challenged Muslim traditions. Ataturk revamped the legal system along Western lines, replaced Arabic-based script with a Western alphabet, prohibited polygamy, abolished Islamic schools and courts, removed reference to Islam as the state religion from the constitution, and granted women equal rights in divorce, child custody, and inheritance. While his government resembled a parliamentary democracy, he exercised near-dictatorial power and alienated the Kurds by suppressing their language and culture. Ataturk left a deeply changed nation. While many of his reforms never reached the villages, where Islam remained a strong influence, his secular approach remained popular with Turkish nationalists, including military officers, influencing Turkish politics today.

Hulton Archive/Getty Images

Ataturk Wedding Dance The Turkish leader Kemal Ataturk promoted and adopted Western fashions while defying Muslim customs. In this photo from around 1925, Ataturk dances with his daughter at her Western-style wedding.

Modern Iran, Egypt, and Iraq

Major changes also occurred in the other major Middle Eastern countries. The end of the war left Britain with the power to impose a protectorate over Persia, forcing the government to accept British loans, financial controls, advisers, and military forces. Growing Persian opposition prompted the British in 1921 to support General Reza Khan **(REE-za kahn)** (1877–1944), a soldier who wanted to end the corrupt, ineffective royal dynasty, establish a secular republic, and address economic underdevelopment. Reza Khan drew support from secular Shi'ites, who had long struggled for a more democratic society that could reduce the powerful Shi'ite clergy's domination. But in 1925, at the urging of Shi'ite clerics, Reza Khan abandoned the republican government and formed the Pahlavi **(PAH-lah-vee)** dynasty, with himself as king (known in Persia as a shah).

Reza Khan, like Ataturk, promoted modernization and, in 1935, renamed his nation Iran, a symbolic break with the past. The shah created a large national army through conscription, built railroads, established government factories to produce textiles, sugar, cement, and steel, and took control over the oil industry. The regime also made social changes that outraged Muslim conservatives, such as introducing a Western law code, encouraging men to wear Western hats and clothes, and outlawing the veiling of women in public. This had the unintended effect of forcing women who wanted to wear the veil to stay home. But while the modernists, merchants, and middle class supported Reza Khan's policies, poor Iranians saw little improvement, especially as Reza Khan expanded the landlord class at peasant expense. The shah lacked Ataturk's charisma and had less success in transforming Iran. When during World War II he favored Germany, Anglo-Russian forces occupied Iran. Humiliated, Reza Shah abdicated in favor of his son, Muhammad Reza Pahlavi **(REH-zah PAH-lah-vee)** (1919–1980), who ruled until 1979.

Egyptian Nationalism

British control of Egypt and Iraq also fostered nationalist feeling. In Egypt during World War I the British imposed martial law and drafted peasants to build roads and railroads and dig trenches in war zones, breeding resentment. A song of the period pleaded to be left alone and castigated British officials for carrying off the peasants' corn, camels, and cattle. After the war nationalists unsuccessfully sought an end to British domination. The leading nationalist party, the secular *Wafd*, led by Saad Zaghlul **(sod ZOG-lool)** (ca. 1857–1927), who had studied theology under Islamic modernists and then earned a French law degree, sought independence, representative government, civil liberties, and curtailed powers for the pro-British monarchy.

In 1919 the British arrested Wafd leaders. Enraged Egyptians—rich and poor, Muslims and Coptic Christians, men and women—responded with strikes, student demonstrations, sabotage of railroads, and the murder of British soldiers. The turmoil forced the British to release Zaghlul, who then went to the Paris Peace Conference to plead for national self-determination but, like Vietnam's Ho Chi Minh, was ignored. Upon returning, Zaghlul was arrested again, but the resulting unrest forced Britain to grant Egypt limited independence in 1922. Nationalists saw this agreement as a sham, since Britain still controlled Egypt's defense and foreign affairs. In 1936 Britain officially ended its occupation but still kept thousands of troops along the Suez Canal. It also shared with Egypt the administration of Sudan to the south. Resentment of the continuing British presence increased during World War II.

Britain and Iraq

The British also struggled to control Iraq, an artificial creation that united three Ottoman provinces, each dominated by a different group: Sunni Kurds, Sunni Arabs, and Shi'ite Arabs. Describing their occupation as a "liberation," the British promised the Iraqis an efficient administration, honest finance, impartial justice, and security. Planning to discourage self-government but wanting to give the appearance of popular support, they held a plebiscite but manipulated the results to suggest pro-British sympathies. Hating occupation, in 1920 Shi'ite clerics seeking an Islamic state proclaimed a holy war against the British, and various Shi'a and Sunni tribes rose in rebellion. The British, relying heavily on aerial bombing, suppressed the rebellion at a great cost, suffering 400 casualties themselves, killing some 10,000 Iraqis, and and flattening whole villages.

Shaken by the fierce resistance, the British changed direction and introducing limited self-government through an appointed Council of State. The skilled diplomacy of a pro-Arab British archaeologist, writer, and diplomat, Lady Gertrude Bell (1868–1926), defused tensions. Seeking a king for Iraq who would "reign but not govern, " in 1921 Britain installed a member of the Hashemite **(HASH-uh-mite)** royal family of Mecca, Sharif Hussein's son Faisal (1885–1935). In 1930 Faisal convinced Britain to grant Iraq independence after he agreed to accept continued British military bases and government advisers. By then the British had found oil, making them unwilling to cut their ties. Many Arabs considered Faisal and his successors to be British puppets, but a series of Sunni Arab military autocrats influenced government policies more than the kings.

Islam and Zionism

Debating Westernization

The stranglehold of European power and Western culture remained concerns of most Middle Eastern societies. Although various colonized peoples struggled to free themselves, nationalist success came slowly. Thinkers debated over how or whether to emulate the Western nations. While envying Western industrialization and consumer goods, they disagreed about how many Western patterns, such as freethinking, parliamentary democracy, and women's rights, should be adopted. Some sought wholesale transformation; some favored Islamic tradition; and still others sought a mixing of Western and Islamic traditions. Egypt, Iraq, Lebanon, Transjordan, and Syria adopted Western-style constitutions, providing for civil liberties and elected parliaments. But these parliaments were limited and unrepresentative. Real power remained with European officials or powerful kings who had little respect for civil liberties.

Inspired by Western modernity, Arabs made progress in education, public health, industrialization, and communications, but change came slowly. The Egyptian literacy rate rose from 9 percent in 1917 to only 15 percent in 1937. Some women asserted their rights, including Huda Shaarawi **(HOO-da sha-RAH-we)** (1879–1947). From a wealthy Cairo family, Huda had been married off at age thirteen to a much older cousin. Finding the marriage confining, she organized nonviolent anti-British demonstrations by women after World War I and then publicly removed her veil in 1923, shocking Egyptians. She also founded the Egyptian feminist movement, which succeeded in raising the minimum marriage age for girls to sixteen and increasing women's educational opportunities.

Islamic Thought

Muslim Brotherhood An Egyptian religious movement founded in 1928 that expressed popular Arab reaction to Westernization.

The debates over Westernization fostered new intellectual currents, some pro-Western, others anti-Western. A blind Egyptian, Taha Husayn (1889–1973), educated in traditional Islamic schools but also at the Sorbonne in Paris, became the key figure of Egyptian literature. He challenged orthodox Islam and, in 1938, proclaimed that Westernizing Arab culture would fit with Egypt's traditions, saying, "I want our new life to harmonize with our ancient glory." In contrast, the **Muslim Brotherhood**, founded in 1928 by schoolteacher Hasan al-Banna (1906–1949), reflected the popular reaction against Westernization. Al-Banna despised Western values, arguing that it "would be inexcusable for us to turn aside from the path of truth—Islam—and so follow the path of fleshly desires and vanities—the path of Europe."[22] The Brotherhood followed a strict interpretation of the Quran, though it also accepted modern technology and was open to a more active public role for women. Expressing a widespread resentment against Western films, bars, and figure-revealing women's fashions, the Brotherhood developed a following in Sudan and western Asia.

The Wahhabis and Saudi Arabia

The most extreme anti-Western reaction, the puritanical Wahhabi movement, which eventually dominated Arabia, sought a return to a supposedly pristine Islam uncorrupted by centuries of change. The Wahhabis opposed shaving beards, smoking tobacco, and drinking alcohol. Wahhabi influence grew when a tribal chief, Abdul Aziz Ibn Saud (sah-OOD) (1902–1969), expanded the power of the Saudi family in central and eastern Arabia (see Chapter 21). By 1932 his forces had taken western Arabia and the holy cities from the Hashemites and formed the country of Saudi Arabia. As king, Abdul Aziz strictly enforced Islamic law by establishing Committees for the Commendation of Virtue and the Condemnation of Vice to mentor personal behavior. Policemen used long canes to enforce attendance at the five daily prayers, punish alcohol use and listening to music, and harass unveiled women. Yet, the Saudis also welcomed material innovations from the West, such as automobiles, medicine, and telephones. In 1935 it was discovered that Saudi Arabia contained the world's richest oil reserves. The oil wealth chiefly benefited the royal family and the Wahhabi clergy.

Britain, Palestine, and the Jews

The roots of a long-term problem for Arab nationalists were planted in Palestine, part of Ottoman-ruled Syria that had a largely Arab population. The British took over Palestine after World War I. Meanwhile, the Zionist movement, which sought a homeland for the Jewish people, had been formed in the Jewish ghettoes of Europe (see Chapters 19 and 21). The Zionist slogan—"a land without a people for a people without a land"—offered a compelling vision: take the long-persecuted Jewish minorities and return them to Palestine, from where they had been expelled by the Romans two millennia earlier. Zionist leaders cultivated the British government, which in 1917 issued the **Balfour Declaration**, a letter from the British foreign minister to Zionist leaders giving British support for the establishment of Palestine as a national home for the Jewish people. But Palestine was not a land without a people. Arabs had lived there for many centuries, building cities, cultivating orchards, and herding livestock. In Arab eyes, Jewish immigrants were European colonizers planning to dispossess them.

Balfour Declaration A letter from the British foreign minister to Zionist leaders in 1917 giving British support for the establishment of Palestine as a national home for the Jewish people.

In the interwar years, thousands of European Jews migrated to Palestine with British support, some fleeing Nazi Germany, so that by 1939 the Palestine population of 1.5 million was one-third Jewish. Although Jewish settlers contributed by establishing businesses, industries, and productive farms, Arabs feared becoming a vulnerable minority in their own land. Land became a contentious issue. Zionist organizations began buying up the best land from absentee Arab landlords who disregarded the customary rights of villagers to use it, uprooting thousands of Arab peasants. As tensions increased, violence spread, bewildering the British. Sometimes hundreds of Arabs and Jews were killed in armed clashes, and in 1936 an Arab rebellion fostered a three-year civil war, with Arabs demanding an end to Jewish immigration, land sales to Jews, and plans for an independent Palestine. In response, Britain proposed a partition into two states and the removal of thousands of Arabs from the Jewish side, but both groups rejected the proposal. Then in 1939 Britain limited Jewish immigration and banned land transfers; however, the Holocaust against the Jews during World War II spurred a more militant Jewish desire for a homeland where they could govern themselves.

Politics and Modernization in Latin America

Latin America, with economies reliant on a few natural resource exports such as beef, copper, coffee, and sugar, became more vulnerable to global political and economic crises. Sometimes this weakness resulted in foreign interventions, as when military forces from the United States occupied Nicaragua from 1909 to 1933 and Haiti from 1915 to 1934. During the Great Depression, as foreign investment fell and foreign markets closed, the foreign trade of some countries was cut by 90 percent, and by 1932 Latin America as a whole exported 65 percent less than it had in 1929. These economic downturns led to political instability and the rule of military dictators, known as caudillos, all over the region (see Map 25.3).

Rising Dictatorships

In 1930–1931 armed forces overthrew governments in a dozen Latin American nations (see Chronology: Latin America and the Caribbean, 1909–1945). Some of the new governments, such as those in Argentina and Brazil, were influenced by European fascism. Dictators often increased their governments' role in the economy, beginning industries to provide products normally imported. They also amassed huge fortunes and repressed dissent. In El Salvador President Maximiliano Hernandez Martinez massacred 30,000 protesting Indian peasants while putting a "positive spin" on poverty by saying that people who went barefoot could better receive the "beneficial

Map 25.3 South and Central America in 1930

By 1930 Latin America had achieved its present political configuration, except that Britain, France, and Holland still had colonies in the Guianas region of South America, and Britain controlled British Honduras (today's Belize) in Central America.

Interactive Map

vibrations" of the earth than those with shoes. Some dictatorships continued for years. The repressive Cuban rightwinger Gerardo Machado (r. 1925–1933) was forced out of office when the collapse of sugar prices generated a massive strike, temporarily bringing leftwing nationalists and socialists to power. But the United States disliked the new government because it implemented reforms that hurt influential American business interests. In 1934 the United States encouraged a coup by Sgt. Fulgencio Batista **(fool-HEN-see-o bah-TEES-ta)** (1901–1973), who dominated Cuba for the next twenty-five years as a rightwing dictator.

CHRONOLOGY

Latin America and the Caribbean, 1909–1945

1909–1933 U.S. military force in Nicaragua

1930–1931 Military governments throughout Latin America

1930–1945 Estado Novo in Brazil

1934 Fulgencio Batista Cuban dictator

1934–1940 Presidency of Lazaro Cardenas in Mexico

The challenges also affected Chile, one of the most open Latin American nations. Although the military had occasionally seized power for short periods, Chile had generally enjoyed elected democratic governments and competitive elections involving several parties. The Great Depression helped reformist parties and social movements to gain support, and the squabbling leftist and centrist parties united in a Popular Front that came to power in the 1939 elections. Their reformist government, supported by labor unions, sponsored industrialization. In addition, a growing women's movement allied with Chile's political left brought once-forbidden ideas into the patriarchal, strongly Catholic country. Demanding respect for Chilean women and an end to "compulsory motherhood," women lobbied for prenatal health care, child-care subsidies, birth control, and the right to abortion, which was illegal but widely practiced. But while women won some basic legal rights, they still struggled for voting rights and could not get most of their social agenda approved.

Brazil experienced political change tinged with nationalism. In the 1920s middle-class reformers challenged a corrupt ruling class that did not listen to the common people or assert Brazil's national interests in the world. Their proposals for a more liberal society included official recognition of labor unions, a minimum wage, restraints on child labor, land reform, universal suffrage, and expansion of education to poor children. Worker unrest aided the growth of labor unions. But the Great Depression prompted a civilian-military coup by Getulio Vargas (jay-TOO-lee-oh VAR-gus) (1883–1954) in 1930. A former soldier, lawyer, and government minister, Vargas launched the **Estado Novo** ("New State"), a fascist-influenced, modernizing dictatorship that ruled until 1945. An anti-Vargas businessman described him as "intelligent, extremely perceptive, but also a demagogue who knew how to manipulate the masses."[23] While Vargas used torture and censorship to repress opponents, the Estado Novo also sponsored modernizing reforms that made Vargas popular with the lower classes. He nationalized the banks, financed industrialization, and introduced social security, an eight-hour workday, a minimum wage, the right to strike, and the vote for literate eighteen-year-olds and working women. Gradually the dictator became more populist and nationalist. After he was deposed by the army in 1945, tensions between rightwing and leftwing Brazilians remained.

Estado Novo ("New State") A fascist-influenced and modernizing dictatorship in Brazil led by Getulio Vargas between 1930 and 1945.

Politics in Mexico

Progressive and nationalist ideas also emerged in Mexico. After the decade-long Mexican Revolution (see Chapter 20), which ended only in 1920, Mexico badly needed reconstruction funds but faced sharply reduced export earnings and a deepening economic slump. A popular song noted the hardship on common Mexicans: "The scramble to be president is one of our oldest haunts. But to eat a peaceful tortilla is all the poor man wants."[24] President Plutarcho Elias Calles (KAH-yays) (r. 1924–1928) put the political system on a solid footing by creating a new party that brought together various factions. Yet many Mexicans saw little improvement in their lives, and women remained largely excluded from public life. In 1934 Mexicans elected Lazaro Cardenas (car-DAYN-es) (r. 1934–1940), an army officer with socialist leanings, as president. Peasants had grown cynical about the promises by political leaders to supply them with land, but Cardenas fulfilled this dream for some by assigning land ownership to the *ejidos* (eh-HEE-dos), the traditional agricultural cooperatives, who now apportioned land to their members. Cardenas hoped the ejidos would build schools and hospitals and supply credit to farmers, uplifting Mexico's poorest social class. But agricultural production fell, and promised government aid never materialized.

Cardenas also introduced reforms that made him popular. He encouraged the formation of a large labor confederation, allowing the working class to enjoy a higher standard of living and more dignity. He also followed a nationalist economic policy. After U.S.-owned oil companies ignored a Mexican Supreme Court order to improve worker pay, Cardenas nationalized the industry, spurring celebrations in Mexico and outraging U.S. leaders. The president also supported women's rights. In addition, Cardenas reorganized the ruling Party of Revolutionary Institutions around four functional groups: peasants, organized labor, the military, and the middle class. Cardenas gave the Mexican Revolution new life, while the wealthy Mexican landowners and merchants, as well as U.S. political and business leaders, hated him.

However, Cardenas was followed by more moderate leaders who reversed support for the ejidos, favoring instead individual farmers. They also ignored women's rights—Mexican women could not vote until 1953—and cooperated with the United States on immigration issues. While poor Mexicans had long moved to the United States, during World War II a Mexico-United States agreement sent more Mexican workers north to fill jobs in industry, agriculture, and the service sector left vacant by drafted American men. The flow northward of poor Mexicans became a floodtide after the war.

Primary Source: Speech to the Nation In this excerpt from a radio address given in 1938, President Lazaro Cardenas announces his decision to nationalize the Mexican oil industry.

Cultural Nationalism in Latin America and the Caribbean

Cultural nationalism greatly affected Latin American and Caribbean societies. A Brazilian literary trend, Modernism, explored the country's rich cultural heritage. Rather than emulating European literary trends, modernist writers reflected Brazil's uniqueness. For example, the poet, novelist, and critic Mario de Andrade (1893–1945) mixed words from regional dialects and Native American, African, and Portuguese folklore into his work. The more internationalist Oswald de Andrade (1890–1954) saw Brazil as a creative consumer of world culture, arguing that Brazilians should mix ideas from all over the world and turn them into something distinctively Brazilian. Meanwhile, nationalism shaped Brazilian music. The unconventional composer Heitor Villa-Lobos (1890–1959) was inspired by Afro-Brazilian and Indian religious rites and urban popular music, and the popular *samba* music and dance became not only a symbol of Brazilian society but also a way for the Afro-Brazilian lower classes to express themselves. Samba began as a street music associated with the annual pre-Lenten carnival in Rio de Janeiro. Professional samba groups competed for prizes awarded by a jury, making samba a major social activity of the city's shantytowns. Annual carnival processions grew increasingly extravagant, featuring elaborate floats, flamboyant costumes, and intricate group choreography.

Literature and Art

The progressive spirit spurred literary and artistic movements throughout Latin America. The work of Marxist-influenced Chilean writers such as the poet Pablo Neruda (ne-ROO-duh) (1904–1973) bristled with anger over economic inequalities. Sometimes governments retaliated against dissident artists, and Neruda wrote some of his greatest poetry while in hiding or exile. Mexican culture glorified the country's mixed-descent, or mestizo, heritage and addressed the poverty and powerlessness of the remaining Native American communities. In this tradition, several great artists painted, usually on walls of public buildings, magnificent murals showing the life of Mexico's people, most notably Diego Rivera (1885–1957), a Marxist who became one of the world's most famous artists. His huge, realistic murals depicted peasants and workers struggling for dignity or emphasized the conflicts between Indians and the Spanish colonizers. His wife, Frida Kahlo (1907–1954), the daughter of a German Jewish immigrant, specialized in vivid paintings expressing women's physical and psychological pain, reflecting her own health problems and stormy personal relationships.

Caribbean Thought

Caribbean intellectuals' search for an authentic West Indian identity involved overcoming the elite's reluctance to acknowledge influences from Africa. Adopting British and French stereotypes, West Indians had often associated Africa with the uncivilized. In contrast, some Afro-Caribbean intellectuals such as the Trinidadian Marxist C. L. R. James (1901–1989) sought to rebuild Afro-Caribbean pride by celebrating African roots and to use literature, art, and music to challenge Western colonialism. James was a well-traveled historian, prolific writer, political theorist, critic, skillful cricket player, and activist in Trinidad politics, equally at home in the Caribbean, Europe, Africa, and North America, who inspired intellectuals around the world.

Candido Portinari, *Coffee* Portinari, one of the finest Brazilian painters of the 1930s and 1940s, often portrayed urban and rural labor, reflecting his leftwing political views. He had grown up the son of Italian immigrants on a coffee plantation near Sao Paulo. This painting from 1935 shows plantation workers carrying heavy bags of coffee, much of which will be exported.

SECTION SUMMARY

- In the post–World War I breakup of the Ottoman Empire, lands such as Iraq, Syria, and Lebanon that sought freedom were instead colonized by Britain and France, but Turkey revived under the leadership of Ataturk, who modernized the country and minimized the role of Islam.
- Reza Khan, the British-supported shah of Persia, attempted to modernize his country as Ataturk had Turkey, though with less success, while Britain, in reaction to violent opposition, granted Egypt and Iraq increasing measures of autonomy and independence.
- Arab leaders debated how to balance modernization with Islam; the most puritanical form of Islam, Wahhabism, came to dominate Saudi Arabia; and the return of Jews to Palestine caused great tensions with the Arabs who had lived there for centuries.
- Vulnerable Latin American economies were greatly damaged during the Great Depression, which led to instability and the rise of military dictators in many countries, while in Chile, instability led to a progressive, prolabor government.
- Impoverished and frustrated after a long revolution, many Mexicans were pleased by the rule of Lazaro Cardenas, who gave land to agricultural cooperatives, nationalized industries, and supported women's rights, but who was followed by less-progressive leaders.
- Latin American and Caribbean artists, musicians, and writers worked to produce art that expressed their unique cultural perspectives.

Chapter Summary

During this era, nationalism became a strong force in the Western colonies and other dominated societies of Asia, Africa, and Latin America. Two world wars and the Great Depression destabilized local economies, capitalism reshaped rural life for millions of peasants, and many Asians and Africans resented the Western powers. Nationalism, often blended with Marxism, gained support as a strategy to oppose Western domination. Nationalists reunified China after two decades of warlord violence but could not improve rural life or halt Japanese expansion, providing an opening for the Chinese communists under Mao Zedong to gain support by offering a program to transform society. In India, nationalism opposing repressive British colonialism gained a mass following. Mohandas Gandhi mounted massive, nonviolent campaigns of civil disobedience, which undermined British rule. But Gandhi and other nationalist leaders, mostly Hindus, could not prevent the minority Muslims from seeking a separate nation.

Nationalism had an uneven history in Southeast Asia, sub-Saharan Africa, and the Middle East. In Vietnam, Ho Chi Minh organized an effective communist resistance to the French, while in Indonesia, Sukarno led opposition to Dutch rule. During World War II nationalists in Vietnam, Indonesia, and Burma organized to oppose a resumption of Western colonialism when the war ended. While political nationalist organizations developed in Africa and black South Africans resisted white domination, nationalism was often more influential as a cultural force, especially in music. World War I left the Middle East in turmoil, as Britain and France extended their power into Arab societies once ruled by the Ottoman Empire. But the Turks, led by Kemal Ataturk, and Iran developed modern states open to Western influences. Muslim intellectuals debated whether to adopt Western ideas or maintain Islamic traditions. Arab conservatives, including the Wahhabis, used Islam to oppose any social or cultural changes. The rise of Zionist immigration to Palestine posed another challenge to the Arabs. In many Latin American nations, while progressive social and literary movements proliferated, economic problems intensified and dictators gained power. Nationalism permeated literary, musical, and artistic expression in both Latin America and the Caribbean.

KEY TERMS

warlords
New Culture Movement
May Fourth Movement
Jiangxi Soviet
Long March
people's war
Maoism
nonviolent resistance
Viet Minh
lingua franca
highlife
pidgin English
Muslim Brotherhood
Balfour Declaration
Estado Novo

EBOOK AND WEBSITE RESOURCES

PRIMARY SOURCE
Speech to the Nation

INTERACTIVE MAPS
Map 25.1 Chinese Communist Movement and Chinese-Japanese War
Map 25.2 Partition of the Ottoman Empire
Map 25.3 South and Central America in 1930

LINKS

History of the Middle East Database (http://www.nmhschool.org/tthornton/mehistorydatabase/mideastindex.php). A useful site on history, politics, and culture.

Internet African History Sourcebook (http://www.fordham.edu/halsall/africa/africasbook.html). This site contains useful information and documentary material on Africa.

Internet East Asian History Sourcebook (http://www.fordham.edu/halsall/eastasia/eastasiasbook.html). An invaluable collection of sources and links on China, Japan, and Korea from ancient to modern times.

Internet Indian History Sourcebook (http://www.fordham.edu/halsall/india/indiasbook.html). An invaluable collection of sources and links on India from ancient to modern times.

Internet Islamic History Sourcebook (http://www.fordham.edu/halsall/islam/islamsbook.html). A comprehensive examination of Islamic societies and their long history, with many useful links and source materials.

Internet Modern History Sourcebook (http://www.fordham.edu/halsall/mod/modsbook.html). An extensive online collection of historical documents and secondary materials.

Latin American Resources (http://www.oberlin.edu/faculty/svolk/latinam.htm). An excellent collection of resources and links on history, politics, and culture.

WWW Southeast Asia Guide (http://www.library.Wisc.edu/guides/SEAsia/). An easy-to-use site.

Plus flashcards, practice quizzes, and more. Go to: www.cengage.com/history/lockard/globalsocnet2e.

SUGGESTED READING

Bogle, Emory C. *The Modern Middle East: From Imperialism to Freedom, 1800–1958.* Upper Saddle River, NJ: Prentice-Hall, 1996. An overview of the region during this era.

Brown, Judith M. *Gandhi: Prisoner of Hope.* New Haven: Yale University Press, 1991. One of the key studies of this seminal nationalist leader and thinker.

Brown, Judith M. *Modern India: The Origins of an Asian Democracy,* 2nd ed. New York: Oxford University Press, 1995. A strong introduction to modern Indian history.

Clayton, Lawrence A. and Michael L. Conniff, *A History of Modern Latin America,* 2nd ed. Boston: Wadsworth, 2005. Good coverage of this era.

Cleveland, William L. *A History of the Modern Middle East,* 4th ed. Boulder: Westview Press, 2008. One of the best surveys.

Erlmann, Veit. *African Stars: Studies in Black South African Performance.* Chicago: University of Chicago Press, 1991. Essays on South African music and nationalism in this era.

Findley, Carter Vaughn, and John A. M. Rothney. *Twentieth Century World,* 6th ed. Boston: Houghton Mifflin, 2006. A comprehensive survey of this era.

Freund, Bill. *The Making of Contemporary Africa: The Development of African Society Since 1800,* 2nd ed. Bloomington: Indiana University Press, 1999. An excellent discussion of the colonial era and the changes it brought.

Gonzalez, Michael J. *The Mexican Revolution, 1910–1940.* Albuquerque: University of New Mexico Press, 2002. Good scholarly study of this period.

Huynh Kim Khanh. *Vietnamese Communism, 1925–1945.* Ithaca: Cornell University Press, 1982. A valuable scholarly study of this topic.

Keen, Benjamin, and Keith Haynes. *A History of Latin America,* 8th ed. Boston: Houghton Mifflin, 2009. A comprehensive account with considerable coverage of these decades.

Lary, Diane, *China's Republic.* New York: Cambridge University Press, 2007. Well-written survey of China from 1912–1949.

Marlay, Ross, and Clark Neher. *Patriots and Tyrants: Ten Asian Leaders.* Lanham, MD: Rowman and Littlefield, 1999. Sketches of Asian nationalists such as Gandhi, Nehru, Ho, Mao, and Sukarno.

Martin, Cheryl E., and Mark Wasserman. *Latin America and Its People,* 2nd ed. New York: Longman, 2007. A readable introduction with much on this era.

Owen, Norman G., et al. *The Emergence of Modern Southeast Asia: A New History.* Honolulu: University of Hawai'i Press, 2005. The best survey of modern Southeast Asian history, comprehensive and readable.

Sheridan, James E. *China in Disintegration: The Republican Era in Chinese History, 1912–1949.* New York: Free Press, 1975. Dated but still a standard work on this period in China.

Spence, Jonathan D. *The Gate of Heavenly Peace: The Chinese and Their Revolution, 1895–1980.* New York: Penguin, 1982. A masterful account of China in this era through the eyes of artists, thinkers, and writers.

Stavrianos, Leften S. *Global Rift: The Third World Comes of Age.* New York: William Morrow, 1971. A provocative, innovative, and readable study that provides a global context.

Wolf, Eric R. *Peasant Wars of the Twentieth Century.* New York: Harper and Row, 1969. A pathbreaking study of the revolutions in China, Vietnam, Algeria, Cuba, and Mexico.

Modernization or World-System?

Historians and social scientists in the West have vigorously debated which theories best explain the modern world, especially how it became interconnected. One influential approach uses the concept of modernization and focuses on individual societies. The other approach, world-system analysis, emphasizes the links between societies. This second approach has often interested world historians.

THE PROBLEM

Historians and historically oriented social scientists have sought to understand societies and their changes over time. These efforts have spawned new intellectual approaches in the past several decades. Scholars have asked why some societies in the modern world, such as the United States, Britain, and Japan, became rich and powerful while others, such as Mozambique, Haiti, and Laos, remained poor and weak. Have societies developed as they did because of their own traditions or because of their connections to the larger world? Should we study societies as separate units, as the modernization approach advocates? Or should societies be examined as part of a larger system of exchange and power, or a world-system? Or are both of these approaches inadequate?

THE DEBATE

During the 1950s and 1960s modernization theory was developed in the United States by scholars such as C. E. Black and W. W. Rostow. In their classification, most societies were traditional, retaining centuries-old political and economic institutions and social and cultural values. These societies had despotic governments, extended family systems, and fatalistic attitudes. In contrast, a few dynamic societies became modern by adopting liberal democracy, secularism, flexible social systems, high-consumption lifestyles, and free market capitalism. This modernization began in Europe between 1500 and 1750 and reached its fullest development in the United States by the mid-twentieth century. All societies, these theorists asserted, were moving, rapidly or slowly, in the same direction toward U.S.-style modernization—some enthusiastically, others reluctantly—and this modernization was desirable.

Modernization theory was influential in the United States for several decades, but by the 1970s it began losing considerable support among historians. While the notion of modernity seemed helpful, critics found many flaws in the theory of modernization. They argued that it centered history on the West as the dynamic nursery of modernization and neglected other politically and economically successful societies, such as Qing China, Tokugawa Japan, Siam (today's Thailand), Ottoman Turkey, Morocco, and the Ashante kingdom in Africa. Although these societies had all either collapsed or struggled against Western imperialism during the nineteenth century, they had once flourished and fostered economic growth despite having few of the characteristics associated with modernity. Furthermore, by emphasizing the individual trees (societies) at the expense of the larger forest (the global context), the theory failed to explain the interconnections of societies through various international networks and processes that created global imbalances, such as the transfer of wealth and resources—Indonesian coffee, Iraqi oil, West African cocoa, Latin American silver, Caribbean sugar—from colonies to colonizers.

Modernization theory generally reflects the views of scholars who believe that U.S.-style individualism, democratic government, and free enterprise capitalism are the best strategies to promote personal freedom and economic growth, and who want to export these ideas to the world. Modernization theorists such as Rostow have considered challenges to U.S. influence and to capitalism, from Marxists and radical nationalists, to be diversions leading to despotic governments and an economic dead end. While agreeing that political and economic freedom were valuable ideas that generally benefited Western peoples, critics doubt these are the foundation of modernity or applicable everywhere. By characterizing traditional societies as "backward" and blaming them for being this way, modernization theory, critics contend, reflects Western prejudices about the world, such as the French "civilizing mission" and the U.S. notion of "Manifest Destiny, " and supports the expansion of Western political power and economic investment into Asia and Africa on the grounds that it fosters "progress." Furthermore, critics argue, most societies are a mix of "traditional" and "modern" traits. For example, the "modern" United States has been a highly religious society from its beginning, arguably less secular than "traditional" China. Nor have Asians and Africans always found Western social and cultural models, such as nuclear families and Christianity, to be more appealing or useful than their own traditions; some, often inspired by Western ideas, have hoped to reform Muslim, Hindu, Confucian, or Buddhist traditions, but most continued to find meaning in the beliefs and customs of their ancestors.

Challenging modernization theory's neglect of connections, scholars led by the American sociologist Immanuel Wallerstein developed the concept of the "world-system," a network of interlinked economic, political, and social relationships spanning the globe. To Wallerstein the world-system, originating in Europe in the 1400s and based on a capitalist world economy, rival European states, and imperialism, explains growing Western global dominance after 1500. By 1914 Western military expansion, colonialism, and industrialization had enriched Europe and brought other societies into the modern world-system. An Africa specialist, Wallerstein views the modern world-system as more widely spread than the more limited networks, such as those of the Mongols and Arabs, that linked Afro-Eurasian societies prior to the 1400s.

In this view, modernization involves not only changes within societies but also their changing relationship to the dominant political powers and the world economy. For example, the Ashante kingdom became a West African power in the 1700s by trading slaves to the West, but, in the late 1800s, it was conquered and absorbed into the British colony of the Gold

Coast (modern Ghana). Under British rule, the Ashante chiefly grew cocoa for export and thus were dependent on the fluctuations of the world price for cocoa. To understand modern Ghana, then, requires knowledge of the Ashante relations to both British colonialism and the world economy.

To describe the world political and economic structure, Wallerstein divided the world-system into three broad zones, or categories of countries: the *core, semiperiphery*, and *periphery*. In 1914 the core included the rich and powerful nations such as Britain, France, and the United States, which all benefited from industrialization, growing middle classes, democracy, a strong sense of nationhood, and political stability. They sometimes used their armies and financial clout to assert power over other societies, even independent ones such as China, where Western powers established spheres of interest patrolled by their gunboats. By 1914 Wallerstein's middle category, the semiperiphery, included countries such as Japan, Russia, and Italy, which were partially industrialized, politically independent nation-states but less prosperous and powerful than the core nations. Finally, the largest group in 1914, the periphery, comprised the colonized societies, such as French Vietnam, British Nigeria, and the U.S.-ruled Philippines, and the neocolonies such as Brazil, Thailand (Siam), and Iran (Persia). These societies were burdened with export economies based on natural resources, little or no industrialization, massive poverty, little democracy, and domination by more powerful core nations. Colonialism transferred wealth from the periphery to the core, which used the wealth for its own economic development. As Wallerstein acknowledges, the world-system is not rigid, and a few societies shifted categories over the centuries. For example, the United States was semiperipheral in 1800, but by 1900 industrialization and territorial expansion had propelled it into the core. By contrast, once-powerful China fell into peripheral status after 1800. But even with some movement up or down, Wallerstein argues, the core-semiperiphery-periphery structure still characterizes the world-system today.

If modernization theory predicts an increasing standardization around the world toward a Western-influenced pattern, world-system analysis suggests that the core and periphery, serving different functions in the world economy, have moved in opposite directions, toward wealth on the one hand and poverty on the other. Since the economic exchange between them was unequal, the periphery became dependent on the core for goods, services, investment, and resource markets, giving core societies, which exploited the resources of the periphery, great influence. For example, the Gold Coast's cocoa growers needed British markets, and British companies provided consumer goods to the shopkeepers, often Lebanese immigrants, who served these communities. The wealth and power of a country, then, reflect its political and economic position in the world-system.

Like modernization theory, world-system analysis has provoked controversy. Some scholars embrace a world-system approach but disagree with Wallerstein's version. Whereas Wallerstein believes a world-system began only around 1500, Christopher Chase-Dunn and Thomas Hall emphasize a longer history with diverse intersocietal networks that can be called world-systems beginning in ancient times. Andre Gunder Frank and Barry Gills identify one single world-system

Private Collection

A Japanese View of America This Japanese print records the impression of the United States and its wealth and power by a Japanese trade mission in 1860. It shows an American man and woman posing with symbols of modern technology, a pocket watch and a sewing machine.

existing for 5,000 years, since, they argue, some form of capitalism began with the earliest states, such as Sumeria, in Afro-Eurasia. Some critics accuse Wallerstein, like the modernization theorists, of overemphasizing the West and underestimating the key roles played by Asians in the Afro-Eurasian economy.

Other critics are harsher. Some charge that Wallerstein's stress on exchange between countries downplays inequitable economies and class structures within countries—such as rapacious landowners, privileged aristocrats, tyrannical chiefs, and greedy merchants—hence shifting the blame for poverty to the world economy. Others, such as Daniel Chirot, question whether exploitation of the periphery explains the economic growth of the core. Critics also wonder whether terms such as *core* and *periphery* constitute a more sophisticated version of "modernity" and "tradition, " marginalizing and perhaps demeaning poor societies. Finally, some think Wallerstein's focus on economic factors neglects politics and cultures, including religion, and places so much stress on the forest that it misses the trees.

EVALUATING THE DEBATE

The modernization and world-system theorists launched an ongoing debate about how world history can be understood, but neither approach fully explains modern history. World historians widely agree that the once-dominant modernization theory is inadequate for understanding the world as a whole. Some are attracted to one or another version of world-system analysis. While many details of Wallerstein's approach are open to challenge, the general concept of a global system, divided into several categories of countries each with common features, helps understand relations between societies and the exchanges within the world economy. Situating societies within an interlinked world helps explain the impact of colonialism, the background to military interventions by more powerful countries, and the political turbulence of the poorer states today. While each society has unique characteristics that shape its history, perceiving some sort of global system or systems that rise and fall over time helps us understand large-scale, long-term change and explains how thousands of small hunting and gathering bands 12,000 years ago became the contemporary global community of nation-states.

THINKING ABOUT THE CONTROVERSY

1. How do modernization and world-system approaches explain the modern world and its diverse societies differently?
2. What are the major advantages and problems of each of the two approaches?

EXPLORING THE CONTROVERSY

Among the major works of modernization theory are C. E. Black, *The Dynamics of Modernization: A Study in Comparative History* (New York: Harper and Row, 1966); and W. W. Rostow, *The Stages of Economic Growth: A Non-Communist Manifesto* (Cambridge: Cambridge University Press, 1960). Immanuel Wallerstein has summarized his ideas in *The Capitalist World-Economy* (New York: Cambridge University Press, 1979) and *World-Systems Analysis: An Introduction* (Durham, NC: Duke University Press, 2004). Alternative versions of the world-system concept include Christopher Chase-Dunn and Thomas D. Hall, *Rise and Demise: Comparing World-Systems* (Boulder, CO: Westview Press, 1997); and Andre Gunder Frank and Barry K. Gills, eds., *The World System: Five Hundred Years or Five Thousand?* (New York: Routledge, 1996). Daniel Chirot takes issue with much of world-system analysis in *Social Change in the Modern Era* (New York: Harcourt Brace Jovanovich, 1986). Excellent summaries and critiques of world-system analysis and competing ideas can be found in Thomas R. Shannon, *An Introduction to the World-System Perspective* (Boulder, CO: Westview Press, 1989); Alvin Y. So, *Social Change and Development: Modernization, Dependency, and World-System Theories* (Newbury Park, CA: Sage, 1990); Stephen K. Sanderson, ed., *Civilizations and World Systems: Studying World-Historical Change* (Walnut Creek, CA: Altamira Press, 1995); Pamela Kyle Crossley, *What Is Global History?* (Malden, MA.: Polity Press, 2008); and Thomas D. Hall, ed., *A World-Systems Reader: New Perspectives on Gender, Urbanism, Cultures, Indigenous Peoples, and Ecology* (Lanham, MD: Rowman and Littlfield, 2000). For a provocative critique of these debates and the rise of the world economy by an Indian scholar, see Amiya Kumar Bagchi, *Perilous Passage: Mankind and the Global Ascendancy*

Global Imbalances in the Modern World, 1750–1945

of Capital (Lanham, MD: Rowman and Littlefield, 2005).

A world traveler in the nineteenth century could not help but notice the imbalances in wealth and power between the world's societies, imbalances that became even wider in the early twentieth century. One of these travelers, the American writer Mark Twain, author of beloved novels about Tom Sawyer and Huckleberry Finn, became a critic of the imperialism that increased these imbalances. Returning to the United States after lengthy travels in the South Pacific, Asia, Africa, and Europe, Twain blasted U.S. policies in Asia, including the costly military occupation of the Philippines as part of the Spanish-American War, writing in 1900 that "I left these [American] shores a red-hot imperialist. I wanted the American eagle to go screaming into the Pacific. But I have thought more, since then. [Now] I am opposed to having the eagle put its talons on any other hand."[1] His travels had convinced him that, despite Western stereotypes, most peoples, including Filipinos, were capable of governing themselves and that efforts to impose U.S. models on others were doomed to failure.

The imbalances that Twain had observed in his travels or gleaned from news accounts were part of the modern world, which was shaped in part by revolutions and innovations in western Europe and North America. In these Western societies, capitalism and industrialization fostered wealth and inspired new technologies, such as the steamships and railroads that conveyed travelers like Twain, resources, and products over great distances. But the new technologies also included deadly new weapons, such as repeating rifles and machine guns, that enabled the Western conquest of Asian and African societies, reshaping the world's political and economic configuration. Just as Spain and Portugal controlled Latin America until the early 1800s, a half-dozen Western nations ruled, or influenced the governments of, most Asian, African, and Caribbean peoples by 1914. Western domination of the global economy fostered investment but also facilitated a transfer of vast wealth to the West.

While several Western societies exercised disproportionate power in this era, other societies were not passive actors, simply responding to the West. In whatever part of the world they lived, people were linked to a global system that, however imbalanced in terms of political and economic power, promoted often-useful exchanges between distant societies. Societies borrowed ideas, institutions, and technologies from each other, though redefining them to meet their own needs. Societies such as Siam (later Thailand), Persia (later Iran), Turkey, and, most spectacularly, Japan successfully resisted colonialism and, borrowing Western models, introduced some modernization. In fact, resistance to Western power was endemic in the global system. Even in colonized societies such as Vietnam, Indonesia, India, and South Africa, local peoples actively resisted domination and asserted their own interests. The movement of products, thought, and people, on a larger scale than ever before, transcended political boundaries, connecting distant societies. Europeans avidly imported Asian arts, Africans embraced Christianity, and peasants from India settled in the South Pacific and the West Indies. By the 1930s people around the world, often using borrowed Western ideas such as nationalism and Marxism, were challenging Western political and economic power.

Imperialism, States, and the Global System

The world's governments changed greatly during the Modern Era, fostering new types of empires and states. A more integrated international order, dominated by a few Western nations and, eventually, also by Japan, was built on the foundation of the varied Western and Asian empires that had been the main power centers during the Early Modern Era. Societies worldwide grappled with the global political trends that affected people's well-being and livelihoods.

Global Empires

Powerful societies had formed empires since ancient times, but over the centuries successive empires grew larger and more complex. In the mid-1700s over two-thirds of the world's people lived in one of several large, multiethnic empires whose economies were based largely on peasant agriculture. These empires stretched across the Eastern Hemisphere from Qing China and the Western colonies in Southeast Asia, such as Dutch Java and the Spanish Philippines, to the Ottoman, Russian, and Habsburg Empires. In the Americas the huge Spanish Empire, Portuguese Brazil, and British North America all resembled the Eurasian empires in their multiethnic populations and agrarian base, although much of the agriculture was done by unfree labor. In addition to empires but smaller, there were also strong states such as Tokugawa Japan, Siam, and the Ashante kingdom in West Africa. All empires and states depended on a command of military power, especially gunpowder weapons. Great Britain and the Netherlands differed from the other strong states mainly in their greater reliance on world trade.

Many of the empires of the mid-1700s had crumbled by the early twentieth century. The Spanish, Portuguese, and British lost most of their territories in the Americas, and the Habsburg and Ottoman Empires were dismantled after World War I. In their place, modern empires had emerged. Between 1870 and 1914, Britain and France established overseas empires on a grander scale than ever before in history, ruling colonies in Africa, Asia, and the Pacific, and Russia now controlled a vast expanse of Eurasia. On a smaller scale, Germany, Japan, and the United States also forged territorial empires. A huge portion of the globe, divided up into colonies or spheres of influence by the West, was incorporated into a Western-dominated world economic system. The influential British imperialist

Queen Victoria as Seen by a Nigerian Carver This wood effigy of the British monarch was made by a Yoruba artist in just-colonized Nigeria in the late nineteenth century.

Pitt Rivers Museum, Oxford University

and author Rudyard Kipling summarized the rationale for exercising imperial power: "That they should take who have the power, And they should keep who can."[2]

Like empires throughout history, modern imperial states, whatever their democratic forms at home, punished dissent in their colonies. Sometimes protests, such as those led by Mohandas Gandhi in India, forced Western colonizers to modify their policies; more commonly, protest leaders, such as Gandhi, Harry Thuku in Kenya, and Sukarno in Indonesia, were jailed or exiled. Some observers recognized the failure of democratic countries to encourage democracy in their own colonies. For example, British critics condemned the repressive colonial policies of their government, especially the harsh treatment designed to discourage rebellion in Ireland against Britain. A nineteenth-century English wit charged that "the moment the very name of Ireland is mentioned, the English seem to bid adieu to common feelings, common prudence and common sense, and to act with the barbarity of tyrants and the fatuity of idiots."[3]

Nations and Nationalisms

Whether parts of empires or not, all over the world societies struggled to become nations, enjoying self-government and a common identity. But Western peoples formed the most powerful nations. Many European nations were formidable forces because of their strong government structures and democratic practices that fostered debate; they also enjoyed economic dynamism, possessed advanced weapons, and engaged in fierce rivalries with each other. Across the Atlantic most Latin American nations struggled to achieve prosperity and internal unity, but the United States matched European capabilities and shared similar imperial ambitions by the later 1800s, much to the disgust of anti-imperialists such as Mark Twain. Americans believed in the tenets of Manifest Destiny, articulated by an influential U.S. politician: "God has marked the American people as his chosen nation to finally lead in the regeneration of the world."[4] By contrast, few people in the colonies shared any sense of common identity, let alone a national mission; colonial governments were unpopular and usually viewed by the colonized as illegitimate. By drawing up arbitrary colonial borders, often without regard to ethnic connections or economic networks, the British created Nigeria, the Dutch created Indonesia, the French created Laos, and the Belgians created the Congo, all colonies lacking any national cohesion. The ethnic diversity of most colonies—Indonesia and the Congo each contained several hundred ethnic groups—inhibited nationalist feeling and thus the formation of nationalist movements.

Still, despite the barriers, nationalism spread, often encouraged by travel, exile, or education. Giuseppi Garibaldi **(gee-you-SEP-ee gare-a-BALL-dee)** (1807–1882), for instance, who helped unify Italy, was born in France of Italian parents and nursed a love for his ancestral homeland during his years living in South America and then the United States before he returned to Italy. The Venezuelan Simon Bolivar, the Filipino Jose Rizal **(rih-ZALL)** (1861–1896), and the Vietnamese Ho Chi Minh (1890–1969), all disenchanted with colonial restrictions, embraced a nationalist agenda while living in Europe. Indian students discovered the writings of the English-born American revolutionary and exponent of liberty Tom Paine and wondered why their British rulers had ignored Paine's "rights of man" in India. Yan Fu, a Chinese student living in England in the 1870s, recalled spending "whole days and nights discussing differences and similarities in Chinese and Western thought and political institutions."[5] He perceived how Europeans became powerful by combining military aggression, well-defined national states, growing commerce, and a culture approving of political and religious debate. Back in China, Yan Fu translated the work of liberal British thinkers and used it to spread nationalism and other Western ideas in China. But nationalists seeking to confront Western power did not all look to the West for inspiration. By 1900 Japan was a role model of nationalism and modernization for many Asians, and the Vietnamese anticolonial leader Phan Boi Chau **(fan boy CHOW)** (1867–1940) advised his countrymen to look east to Japan.

But nationalism was not always an imported sentiment. Many Asians had a sense of identity similar to nationalism long before the nineteenth century. People in Korea, Japan, and Vietnam, for example, had long enjoyed some national feeling based on shared religion, a common language, bureaucratic government, and the perception of one or more common enemies. African kingdoms such as Ashante, Oyo, and Buganda enjoyed some attributes of nationhood. Reflecting such national feeling, in 1898, Hawaii's last monarch, Queen Liliuokalani **(luh-lee-uh-ohkuh-LAH-nee)**, pleaded with the United States not to colonize the islands, since her people's "form of government is as dear to them as yours is precious to you. Quite as warmly as you love your country, so they love theirs."[6] U.S. leaders ignored her pleas and annexed Hawaii. To protect their position, colonizers labored hard to crush these traditions and to counter anticolonial nationalism through the use of divide-and-rule strategies, such as the British encouragement of the Hindu-Muslim divide in India. Formerly well-defined states, such as Ashante and Buganda in Africa, lost their traditional cohesion as they now became parts of larger colonies. To resist colonial strategies, nationalists sought ways to regain the initiative and achieve sovereignty. The Indian nationalist Jawaharlal Nehru expressed the search for a successful anticolonial strategy: "What could we do? How could we pull India out of this quagmire of poverty and defeatism, which sucked her in?"[7]

Nationhood Through Revolutions

Some societies needed major rebellions and revolutions to transform old discredited orders and create new nations. The American and French Revolutions of the later 1700s began an Age of Revolution and inspired people elsewhere to take up arms against unjust or outdated governments. In the U.S. case, disgruntled colonists overthrew British rule, and key American revolutionaries, such as Thomas Jefferson and English-born Tom Paine, became known around the world as exponents of political freedom. During the mid-nineteenth century the Taiping **(TIE-ping)** Rebellion against China's Qing dynasty and the Indian Rebellion against the British East India Company, although they ultimately failed, provided fierce challenges to established governments in the world's two most populous societies. Like these upheavals, the rebellion by the southern states of the United States against the federal government, which resulted in some 600,000 deaths during the American Civil War, did not succeed. Nonetheless, the struggle reshaped American society by allowing President Abraham Lincoln to abolish slavery and forge a stronger national government. Early in the twentieth century, other revolutions overturned old governments and built nations in Mexico, Turkey, and China; the Chinese revolution ended 2,000 years of imperial control and established the foundation for a modern republic. The Russian Revolution of 1917 installed the world's first communist government, inspiring communist movements and revolutionary nationalists around the world.

The aftermath of World War I brought new revolutionary upheavals and ideologies. Old states collapsed in eastern Europe, fascism spread in Germany and Japan in the economic shambles caused by the Great Depression, and Spain erupted in civil war. In 1914 Marxism, the revolutionary socialist vision developed by Karl Marx (1818–1883), had relatively little influence outside of Germany and Russia, but by 1945 the ideology had mass support in many societies. Communist revolutionary movements percolated in China, Korea, Indonesia, and Vietnam. Karl Marx had supplied the critique of the old society, which he saw as shaped by class struggle and capitalism. Now the Russian leader, Vladimir Lenin (1870–1924), forged a revolutionary party and strategy to overthrow that society, and the Chinese communist leader Mao Zedong **(maow dzuh-dong)** (1893–1976) contributed a vision of a new, unselfish socialist society. Unlike Lenin, Mao believed that revolutionaries must work closely with the local people, writing that "the people are the sea, we [communists] are the fish, so long as we can swim in that sea, we will survive."[8] By combining communism with nationalism, the Vietnamese revolutionary Ho Chi Minh provided a workable model to overthrow colonialism. The ideas of Lenin, Mao, and Ho made Marxism a major vehicle for change after World War II.

Change in the Global System

During the Modern Era the global system expanded and changed as Western influence increased. Networks of trade and communication linking distant societies grew in number and extent. However, because some Western nations came to enjoy more political and military power than other societies, they benefited more from their exchanges with the rest of the world. Aided by this power, Western culture dominated local traditions, especially in Western colonies. For example, textbooks in French colonial schools, where the students were of African, Afro-Caribbean, Asian, or Pacific islander descent, celebrated the history of the French—"our ancestors the Gauls"—while children in the U.S.-ruled Philippines, a tropical and predominantly Catholic land, learned English from books showing American youngsters throwing snowballs, playing baseball, and attending Protestant church services. In some cases this deliberate Westernization reshaped beliefs and ways of life, as occurred among the Filipinos and the Igbos of southern Nigeria. However, Western cultural influence was weak in other colonized societies, especially Muslim ones such as Egypt, the Hausa of northern Nigeria, and the Achehnese of Indonesia.

Countries gained or lost power in the global system, depending on their wealth, type of government, and access to military power (see Historical Controversy: Modernization or World-System?). In 1750, Western overseas expansion, including military conquests, had already reshaped the Americas and some regions of Africa and southern Asia. Chinese, Indians, and western Europeans were the richest peoples at this time, the Chinese accounting for a third and India and western Europe each accounting for a fourth of the world's total economic production. Collectively they accounted for 70 percent of all the world's economic activity and 80 percent of its manufacturing. China remained the greatest engine of the world economy. Britain was the rising political and economic European power, but it faced challenges from France, Russia, Spain, and the Ottoman Empire. The more economically developed districts and the major cities within the two wealthiest countries, Britain and China, apparently enjoyed similar living standards, such as abundant food and long life spans, until at least 1800. As late as the 1830s British observers reported that residents of Britain's capital, London, and the key Chinese trading city of Guangzhou had a roughly comparable material life.

By 1914, however, after a century and a half of Western industrialization, imperial expansion, and colonization, the global system had become more divided than ever before into rich and poor societies. India was now among the poorer countries, and China had succumbed to Western military and economic influence, falling well behind the West. Meanwhile, a few Western nation-states—especially Great Britain, the United States, Germany, and France—had grown rich and powerful, enjoying substantial influence around the world and over the global economy. Because of their unparalleled military power, all four of these nations ruled colonial empires, from which they extracted valuable resources; played a leading role in world trade; and tried to spread, with some success, their cultures and ideas. Also among the richest nations, but having less international power, were a few other western European countries, including the Netherlands, Belgium, and Switzerland. A middle category of countries—Canada, Japan, and European nations such as Russia, Italy, Portugal, and Spain—had a weaker economic base and less military power than those of the richest nations, but they still enjoyed economic and political autonomy. A third category of countries were those that were economically poor and militarily weak, either ruled directly as Western colonies, such as India, Indonesia, Nigeria, or Jamaica, or under strong political and economic influence as neocolonies, such as China, Thailand, and Iran. Economically, Latin American countries, relative to the rich North American and western European nations, were also poor.

Living conditions and governments in the rich countries differed dramatically in 1914 from those in the poor societies. Capitalism fostered growth in Europe and North America, although it took many decades for the benefits to reach the common people. The rich countries, such as Britain and the United States, were highly industrialized and enjoyed well-diversified economies and large middle classes. Many of their people lived in cities and, owing to mass education systems, became literate. These countries also boasted efficient, well-financed, constitutional governments. Rich countries were typically democratic, with their governments being chosen by voters (though usually only men) through regular elections. These governments generally tolerated an independent mass media, including newspapers and magazines, and diverse political opinions, such as those represented by socialist and feminist movements. These patterns were also common in the less-powerful Western nations and in Japan.

By contrast, the poor societies, especially Western colonies in Asia and Africa, where many people worked the lands owned by foreign landlords or planters, were not industrialized and people earned meager wages. Economic growth was often determined by foreign investment and markets rather than by local needs. For example, rather than growing food for the local community, farmers in Honduras, in Central America, grew bananas for the U.S. market while farmers in French-ruled Senegal, in West Africa, raised peanuts for export. Politically, a small upper class—African chiefs, Indian princes, Javanese aristocrats—played a political role by cooperating with Western rulers. Only a small minority of people had access to formal education. A tiny middle class and low rates of literacy made democracy difficult, even if it had been allowed, but most Western colonies also prohibited or limited voting or officeholding by anyone who was not white and European.

Their general poverty and lack of economic and political options did not mean that people in poor societies were always miserable. For many generations, and through successive governments, they had learned how to make the best of poverty. Celebrating their survival skills in the early 1900s, the Indian writer and thinker Rabindranath Tagore **(rah-BIN-dra-NATH TUH-gore)** (1861–1941) found both triumphs and tragedies in Indian peasant life through the ages, which "with its everyday contentment and misery, has always been there in the peasants' fields and village festivals, manifesting their very simple and abiding humanity across all of history—sometimes under Mughal rule, sometimes under British rule."[9]

In the colonies, heavy Western cultural influence, such as the policies the French called their "civilizing mission" in Vietnam and West Africa, by which they tried to impose French ways on people they regarded as culturally inferior, was combined with psychological trauma as once-proud peoples succumbed to foreign rule and its racist restrictions. An anti-imperialist African organization complained in 1927 that colonialism had abruptly cut short "the development of the African people. These nations were later declared pagan and savage, an inferior race."[10] Although Western Christian missionaries often found eager converts, as in Vietnam, Nigeria, and Uganda, nationalists frequently criticized the well-funded Christian missions, accusing them of undermining traditional beliefs. Western domination, however, did not preclude cultural and scientific achievements by colonized people. For example, although their country was a British colony, various Indian mathematicians, biochemists, and astrophysicists won international renown. In Calcutta the experiments of Sir Chandrasekhara Raman **(CHAHN-dra-SEE-ker-ah RAH-man)** (1888–1970) led to significant advances in the theory of the diffusion of light, for which he won the Noble Prize for physics in 1930.

Between 1914 and 1945 the global system underwent further changes. Wars were now sometimes world wars, titanic struggles that reshaped world politics, fought on a greater scale than ever before and on battlefields thousands of miles apart. World Wars I and II were the deadliest conflicts in history. The United States became the world's richest, most powerful nation. Because of its military defeat in World War I, Germany temporarily lost wealth and power. Germany, Italy, and Japan—all middle-ranking nations by the 1930s—challenged the rich nations—Britain, France, and the United States—during World War II. Several Latin American nations and Turkey enjoyed enough economic growth and stability of government to move into the middle-ranking category by the 1940s. Yet most of the societies of Asia, Africa, Latin America, and the Caribbean remained poor colonies or neocolonies, exercising little diplomatic and economic influence in the global system.

The World Economy

Even before the Western overseas expansion that occurred between 1500 and 1914, trade had taken place over vast distances. Chinese, Indian, Arab, and Armenian merchants had long dominated the vigorous Asian trade, and for centuries Chinese silks and porcelains and Southeast Asian and Indian spices had reached Europe, the Middle East, and parts of sub-Saharan Africa. European explorers wished to locate the source of these riches, and after 1500 the Portuguese, Dutch, and British played key roles in this trade, beginning the rise of the world economy. European influence on the world economy increased in the 1700s and 1800s when Western traders, supported by their governments, sought new natural resources and markets in the tropical world, thereby creating a truly global economic exchange. By 1914 the entire world was enmeshed in a vast economic exchange that particularly benefited the more powerful nations. People often produced resources or manufactured goods—Middle Eastern oil, Indonesian coffee, British textiles—for markets thousands of miles away. Europe's Industrial Revolution, which provided manufactured goods to trade for resources, dramatically reshaped the Western economies in the 1800s but only slowly spread to other regions.

The Inequality of Global Economic Exchange

Economic exchange between societies within the world economy did not proceed on an even playing field. As had been the case for empires throughout history—Assyrian, Roman, Chinese, Inca, Spanish, Dutch—imperialism and colonialism remained the means for transferring wealth to the imperial nations, which used that wealth to finance their own development. The imperial powers, seeking to enhance the value of their colonial economies, also used their control of world trade to shift cash crops indigenous to one part of the world to another. For example, Europeans introduced South American peanuts and rubber to colonized Africa, and coffee from Arabia became a major cash crop in Brazil and Indonesia. This transfer benefited colonial treasuries and plantation owners but also sometimes earned income for the small farmers who started growing these crops.

Gearing economic growth chiefly to the needs of the imperial powers impeded economic development that might have benefited everyone. Many colonies developed economies that produced and exported only one or two primary resources, such as rice and rubber from French Vietnam, sugar from Spanish Cuba, and cocoa from the British Gold Coast. Most of these resource exports were transformed into consumer goods, such as rubber tires and chocolate candies, and sold in stores in Western nations, to the profit of their merchants. For instance, chocolate, whose use for over two millennia was confined to elites in Mexico, became popular among wealthy Europeans after 1500. During the nineteenth century European chemists figured out how to produce chocolate bars, and soon chocolate products gained an eager market among all classes throughout the Western world. Meanwhile, the Western manufactured goods exchanged for these resources, especially textiles, found markets in Africa, Asia, and Latin America. Although much of this exchange was largely at the expense of the colonized peoples, some of them, including a few women, managed to capitalize on it. For example, Omu Okwei **(OH-moo AWK-way)** (1872–1943), an Igbo, made a fortune trading palm oil for European imported goods, which she distributed widely in Nigeria through a vast network of women traders.

Societies specializing in producing one or two natural resources were especially vulnerable to a changing world economy. To take one case, British Malaya was a major rubber exporter, but most of its rubber plantations, worked chiefly by poorly paid Indian immigrants, were British-owned, and Malayans had little influence over the world price of rubber, which was determined largely by demand in the West. And the prices of agricultural and mineral exports fluctuated more than the prices for industrial goods, which were produced largely in the West. Furthermore, the rise and fall of rubber prices affected not only the rubber tappers and their families but also the shops, often owned by Chinese immigrants, who sold them goods or extended credit to them. Thus the livelihoods of people all over the world increasingly became subject to chronic fluctuations in the world prices of the resources they grew or mined. These prices rose or fell depending on the whims of Western consumers and decisions by the corporations who controlled the international trade.

The world economy widened the wealth gap between societies. In 1500 the differences in per capita income and living standards between people in the richer regions—China, Japan, Southeast Asia, India, Ottoman Turkey, and western Europe—had probably been minor. And these peoples were roughly only two to three times better off materially than the farmers and city folk of the world's poorest farming societies. By 1750, however, while China, western Europe, and British North America enjoyed similar levels of economic production, the wealth gap between them and others was increasing. By 1900 the wealth gap between the richest and poorest societies had grown to about 10 to 1. This trend accelerated throughout the twentieth century, in part because the wealth produced in Western colonies seldom contributed to local development. For example, by the 1950s, after seventy-five years of Belgian colonialism that produced vast wealth for Belgian corporations, mine owners, and rubber planters, the Belgian Congo still lacked all-weather roads linking the major cities and had only a few schools and health clinics for its millions of people.

Unequal economic exchange also fostered conflict. Wars erupted as one country threatened another's access to markets and resources. For example, British free trade policies caused the Opium War with China in the mid-1800s. The Qing government worked to end both the legal and illegal opium trade, but, as the leading opium supplier, Britain needed to protect the opium exports to China from British India, which earned 20 percent of its colonial revenues from charging duty on opium. Britain's defeat of China hastened Chinese decline. In the first half of the twentieth century, World War I was at least partly caused by the bitter competition between European nations for resources in Asia and Africa.

The Spread of Industrialization

The Industrial Revolution, which began in Britain in the late 1700s, was not just a Western development. China and India had once been the world's leading manufacturing countries, and knowledge of Chinese mechanical devices probably stimulated several British inventions. Between 1750 and 1850, however, Britain took the lead in industrialization, and by the mid-1800s it produced about half of the world's manufactured goods while China and India fell behind. Various other European nations, the United States, and Japan industrialized in the later 1800s. Only these few nations increased their resources and weapons as a result of industrialization, and hence only a few became world powers. Some of the profits from colonialism and other overseas activities stimulated or furthered European industrialization. For instance, the Dutch based some of their industrial and transportation growth on profits earned from selling coffee and sugar grown by peasants in their Indonesian colony. But even in Europe agriculture and other nonindustrial activities, such as trade, remained economically important. By 1881 only 44 percent of the British, 36 percent of the German, and 20 percent of the American labor force were employed in industrial or industry-related occupations.

Industrialization gradually spread beyond Europe and North America, but it was highly uneven in its impact and pace. Western policies commonly discouraged other societies, especially colonies, from maintaining or opening industries that might compete with Western manufacturers. For instance, India had been the world's greatest textile manufacturer for centuries, but British colonization gradually diminished the industry through tax and tariff policies, opening the way for British-made textiles to dominate the Indian market. The British saw India not only as a market for their goods but also as a source of cash crops, such as jute and opium. Hence, in 1840 a British official boasted that his nation had "succeeded in converting India from a manufacturing country into a country exporting raw materials."[11] The once-flourishing Indian textile center of Calcutta lost two-thirds of its population between 1750 and 1850 as its manufacturing declined.

Several nations sought to foster development by setting up manufacturing operations. China, Persia, Egypt, the Ottoman Empire, and Mexico introduced textile industries in the nineteenth century. However, the British, nominally proponents of free trade, used tariffs, or stiff duties on imports to Britain, to stifle many of these industries, thereby opening doors for the export of British fabrics and clothing to these countries. Between 1900 and 1945 there was resurgence of efforts at industrialization in various nations—China, Argentina, Brazil, and Australia—but agriculture remained the economic foundation for most of their population.

Before 1880 few industrial cities had emerged outside of northwestern Europe and North America, but, in a global economy, several cities far from factories had grown dependent on the Industrial Revolution for their livelihood, becoming hubs for the distribution of imported industrial products. For example, Shanghai thrived as the commercial gateway to central China's interior, Singapore served as the economic hub for much of Southeast Asia, and Alexandria was the import-export center for Egypt and the upper Nile basin.

Frontiers and Migrations

People have always been pushed to relocate by necessity or drawn to new lands by opportunity. But the rise of a modern world economy, and its constant quest for resources, markets, and labor, accelerated migration. Modern transportation networks, linked by larger and faster ships and later airplanes, facilitated the movement not only of commodities but also of people. Rapid population growth also spurred migration. Between 1800 and 1900 the world population grew from 900 million to 1,500 million, with two-thirds of these people living in Asia. While some people escaped poverty and overcrowding by moving into nearby frontier regions, many others, more than 100 million between 1830 and 1914, left for distant lands. Some, such as enslaved Africans transported to the Americas, were taken from their homes unwillingly. In contrast, millions of Europeans and Asians sought, and often found, a better life in other countries.

Settling Frontiers

From ancient times people left overcrowded lands to move into sparsely settled frontiers. Bantu-speaking Africans, for instance, took their ironworking and farming technologies from West Africa into the sparsely populated grasslands and forests of central, eastern, and southern Africa, and Chinese expanded from north China into central and south China. Similar movements continued in modern times. For example, millions of Russians migrated east into Siberia and Turkestan to settle what they wrongly considered virgin lands. White Americans and Canadians moved westward across the North American continent, subduing, marginalizing, and killing off the Native American peoples and seizing their land. In Australia, New Zealand, and South Africa, European colonists also settled the land at the expense of local peoples. In South America, Brazilians moved from the Atlantic coast westward into the rain forests and grasslands, setting up farms or ranches after pushing out or killing local Indians, and Argentines settled the vast interior grasslands they called the Pampas. Generally the frontier settlers thought they were bringing "progress" to a "wild" area. An influential leader in the United States, Benjamin Franklin, ignoring the native peoples who still inhabited America, wrote in 1784 about the "vast quantity of forest land we have yet to clear, and put in order for civilization."[12]

Remote from central government controls and traditional social structures, the frontier fostered innovations. Frontier social conditions were often freer and more fluid and flexible, promoting new ideas and offering new opportunities. Cultures met and mixed, and people of different groups intermarried, such as white backwoods hunters, trappers, and itinerant traders with Native Americans. Cultural blending produced hybrid social groups such as the Russian Cossacks, western American cowboys, and Argentine gauchos. The cowboys and gauchos, who chiefly herded cattle for ranchers, combined European and self-sufficient Native American customs, and many were themselves of mixed white and Native American ancestry. Eventually, however, as farmers, ranchers, towns, and states gradually replaced the frontier pioneers, the nearby states incorporated the frontier territories. In this way, for example, the settlers in frontier territories, such as Kentucky, Kansas, and Oregon, were gradually absorbed into the larger U.S. society, and the prairie provinces and British Columbia joined Canada.

African and European Population Movements

The largest population movements of the era involved the involuntary transport of African slaves across the Atlantic to the Americas and the chiefly voluntary migration of European emigrants to the Americas, southern Africa, Australia, and New Zealand. The Africans, shipped in chains and filth, were forced to work for whoever purchased them in the Americas. They typically faced lives shortened by harsh conditions. In contrast, most of the Europeans chose to leave their homelands to seek a better life, and often succeeded.

The major movement of Africans resulted from the trans-Atlantic slave trade, which reached its height between 1760 and 1800. During these years over 70,000 people a year were herded onto crowded slave ships and shipped from Africa. Between 1800 and 1850 the annual export of Africans to the Americas ranged between 36,000 and 66,000. The great majority of Africans were landed in Brazil and the Caribbean islands, where people of African ancestry today account for a large part of the population. But the gradual abolition of slavery in the Americas eroded the trade. Between 1851 and 1867 the flow of human cargo dropped dramatically. However, the longtime slave trade from East and Central Africa to the Middle East continued until the end of the nineteenth century. By the early 1900s slavery had declined significantly or been abolished in Africa, the Middle East, and Southeast Asia. Abolition resulted in part from the efforts of Western colonial governments, often prompted by humanitarian organizations and Christian missionaries, and both Western and local abolitionists. Some had themselves been slaves, such as Mary Prince, a slave from the British West Indies who was taken to London, freed, and became an active abolitionist, arguing eloquently in 1831: "All slaves want to be free. They work night and day, sick or well, till we are quite done up."[13] The end of plantation slavery in the Americas opened the doors to recruitment of impoverished workers from Asia, who chiefly came voluntarily but under restrictive contracts that limited their rights by requiring them to work for years under harsh conditions.

During the Modern Era the European migration across oceans to the Americas and the South Pacific dwarfed other population movements (see map). Unlike the African slaves, many European emigrants were escaping poverty or political repression and expected to improve their lives abroad. While the ships carrying the emigrants were often crowded and unhealthy and the emigrants sometimes struggled to find jobs that could support their families, Europeans did not arrive in chains, with no possibility of freedom. Some of them received free land upon arrival. The emigrants represented Europe's ethnic diversity but came largely from the British Isles, Germany, Italy, Spain, Poland, and Russia.

Between 1500 and 1940 some 68 million people left Europe, creating new societies in the Americas, Australia, New Zealand, and southern Africa. The largest movement came in the nineteenth and early twentieth centuries. For example, between 1820 and 1930 some 32 million Europeans moved to the United States, the major destination. In the same period another 20 million shipped off to Argentina, Canada, Brazil, and Australia. Not all movement was by ship, however; some 14 million Russians moved overland to the Asian regions of their empire. The result of this large population movement was a Europeanization of societies, as European cultures were implanted far from their ancestral homes. The tendency to look toward Europe for inspiration was especially strong in Argentina, Chile, Canada, Australia, and New Zealand. In these societies many immigrants and their descendants tended to maintain their native languages, churches, and social customs and to identify with their homeland. As a result, the numerous Italians in Argentina's capital, Buenos Aires, often spoke Italian, while Anglo-Argentines sent their children to private English-medium schools. Similarly, Canadians, Australians, and New Zealanders commonly revered the British crown. Immigrants contributed much to their new lands. For example, in the United States, the Scottish-born Andrew Carnegie (1835–1919) helped build the iron and steel industry and with his philanthropy sponsored libraries. Others found different ways to improve their new societies, such as working for social change. The controversial Lithuanian-born leftwing activist Emma Goldman (1869–1940) was one of these individuals. Goldman had moved with her family to Russia and then to Germany fleeing anti-Semitism. She finally reached the United States in 1885, where she was later arrested and deported for being an advocate for slum-dwellers and for opposing U.S. entry into World War I.

Asian Migrations

During this era, peoples from eastern and southern Asia also emigrated in large numbers, usually by ship to distant shores. They went in response to the demand among Western colonies and American nations for a labor force for the mines and plantations that supplied their wealth. As a result, Chinese mined tin in Southeast Asia and gold in California and Australia, while Indians worked on rubber plantations in British Malaya and sugar plantations in South Africa, Fiji in the South Pacific, and the Guianas in South America. Immigrants often died from overwork or ill health and, as happened with Chinese in California, sometimes suffered from violent attacks by local people who resented their presence. Yet, many Asians survived to raise families in their new homes. Today approximately 40 to 45 million Asians live outside, and often thousands of miles away from, their ancestral homelands. Chinese and Indians constituted the great majority of Asian migrants, settling in Southeast Asia while also establishing communities, often large, in the Americas, the Pacific islands, and parts of Africa. Their descendants became a vital presence in the world economy as merchants, miners, and plantation workers.

Although most moved as poor contract laborers, Asian emigrants often found success abroad, chiefly as merchants. Through hard work, organization, and cooperation many Chinese in Southeast Asia became part of a prosperous, urban middle class that controlled retail trade, operating everything from small general stores and coffee shops to large import-export firms and banks. Today the majority of Chinese in Southeast Asia, the South Pacific and Indian Ocean islands, the Caribbean, and Latin America are engaged in commerce. A Chinese man who settled in New Zealand in the 1920s recalled the hard work that brought him success: "My generation really worked for a living. We had to open the shop at 7 A.M. and we closed [at] 1 A.M. Then we had to clean the shop. It was seldom before 2 A.M. before we got to bed."[14] The descendants of Chinese immigrants have constituted the most dynamic economic sector in Southeast Asia, with their money and initiative spurring the dynamic economic growth since 1970. Indian merchants also prospered in the diaspora. Many were linked to Indian trade networks that moved capital and products around the Indian Ocean and Pacific Rim as well as into Central Asia and Russia. Lebanese and Syrians became merchants in the Americas and West Africa.

Pushed by poverty, overpopulation, or war, people also emigrated from Northeast and Southeast Asia, forming cohesive communities in new lands. Numerous Japanese and Koreans left their homelands between 1850 and 1940. Some settled in Hawaii to work on pineapple plantations or in the canning industry. Many Japanese migrated to the Pacific Coast of the United States and Canada, some taking up farming. In response to growing local prejudice against all Asian

Asian and European Migration, 1750–1940

During this era millions of Europeans emigrated to the Americas, South Africa, Australia, and New Zealand. Millions of Asians, especially Chinese and Indians, left their homes to work or settle in Southeast Asia, Africa, the Pacific islands, and the Americas.

e **Interactive Map**

immigrants, the United States and Canada restricted Japanese immigration in the early 1900s. As a result, the Japanese emigrant flow turned to Latin America, especially Peru and Brazil. Southeast Asians also departed from their homelands to live abroad. Between 1875 and 1940 Indonesians, mostly Javanese, were recruited to work on plantations in Malaya and British North Borneo but also in Dutch Guiana (today's Suriname), in South America, and on the French-ruled South Pacific island of New Caledonia. Some 50,000 Javanese today live in Suriname. After the United States colonized the Philippines, Filipinos began migrating to Hawaii and the U.S. Pacific coast as factory workers or farm laborers. Today one and a half million Filipinos live in the United States.

The Spread of Technology and Mass Culture

The modern global system owed much to innovations in technology. Improved methods of communication and transportation allowed people, ideas, and products to travel farther and faster than ever before, enhancing networks of power and

Courtesy, Singapore History Museum

Singapore's Chinatown By the early 1900s Singapore, a major Southeast Asian port and commercial crossroads, was predominantly Chinese in population. The bustling streets were lined by shops, workers' quarters, theaters, and brothels.

exchange. More effective military technologies enabled a few societies to gain control of other societies and to combat rival powers. Finally, the increasing connections around the world enabled cultural ideas and products to spread across national and regional borders.

Communication and Transportation

For much of history, communication over long distances had been slow, depending largely on beasts of burden carrying riders or pulling wagons, and later on sailing ships. In 500 B.C.E. a message carried by successive riders on horses could travel the 1,800-mile length of the Persian Empire in nine days. Two millennia later, in the 1600s, it took Dutch ships some nine months to sail from Amsterdam to Dutch-ruled Java to deliver news and orders. Then in the nineteenth century, thanks to the Industrial Revolution, communications changed dramatically. In 1844 the first telegraph messages were exchanged between Washington and Baltimore. By 1861 submarine telegraph cables linked Britain to North America, prompting a poet to write: "Two mighty lands have shaken hands, Across the deep blue sea; the world looks forward with new hope, Of better times to be."[15] By 1870 the cables had reached from Britain to India. The invention of the telephone in 1876 and radio in 1895 further increased the potential for communications. In 1906 a Canadian scientist, Reginald Fessenden, broadcast the first experimental entertainment program on radio, featuring Christmas carols and speeches. As the possibilities and advantages of broadcasting over great distances became apparent, the New Zealand premier proposed in 1911 that Britain build an empirewide radio network because of "the great importance of radio for social, commercial, and defensive purposes."[16] World War I postponed the scheme, but radio technology improved. By the 1920s radio transmissions had become commonplace in industrial nations and British broadcasts could reach Canada, South Africa, India, and Australia.

Some technologies conveyed people and commodities as well as messages, transforming peoples' lives around the world. Railroads were built all over the world to carry goods and passengers, and as trains reached stations, telegraph messages smoothed their journeys by passing on traffic and weather information. By 1869 railroads connected the Pacific and Atlantic coasts of North America, and by 1903 anyone determined to make the long journey could ride the 9,000 miles between Paris and Siberia's Pacific coast. While railroads extended land networks, shipping lines that employed steamships linked the world. The opening of the 105-mile-long Suez Canal in 1869 and the 51-mile Panama Canal in 1914, both of which cost the lives of thousands of workers during their construction, greatly reduced travel times for many sea journeys and also made it easier and cheaper to ship resources from Asia and Latin America to Europe and North America. Now it only took a few weeks to sail from China or Singapore to New York or London. Political and economic leaders took advantage of the new travel opportunities. For instance, seeking to forge diplomatic alliances and recruit laborers for his islands' plantations, in 1880–1881 Hawaii's king, David Kalakaua (KAH-la-COW-ah) (r. 1874–1891), sailed around the world by steamship and in the course of his journey met the Japanese emperor, the Siamese king, the pope, and Britain's Queen Victoria, among other dignitaries. In Japan, he signed an agreement to import thousands of Japanese laborers to his kingdom.

In the early 1900s motor cars and buses continued the revolution in land transportation begun by railroads, allowing people to more easily commute to city jobs and downtown stores or to travel between cities. After World War I thousands of middle-class Europeans and North Americans owned their own cars, and in the 1930s the first commercial air flights began, making long-distance journeys even faster. Transportation depended increasingly on fossil fuels, first coal and then oil. The use of vehicles fueled by oil increased the strategic importance of oil-rich regions such as the Middle East, Indonesia, Mexico, and the Gulf Coast of the United States.

Technologies of Warfare

New technologies included those devoted to warfare that made it easier to kill more people and at a greater distance. Most of these weapons remained largely a monopoly of Western nations and Japan during this era, and thus contributed to the imbalances in global power. White adventurers and settlers used the rifle invented by the American Philo Remington (1816–1889), which was effective at 1,500 yards, to defeat, and seize the lands of, the Native Americans and the Australian Aborigines. In 1878 an Argentinean observed that the Remington rifle has left "the land strewn with the bodies of those [local Indians] who dared to oppose it."[17] Effective rifles also proved devastating in Africa against warriors armed only with spears and arrows. The British-born American explorer Henry Morton Stanley boasted of his use of repeating rifles and terrorism to destroy a hostile Congo village that had greeted him with spears and arrows: "I skirmish in their streets, drive them pell-mell into the woods beyond; with frantic haste I fire the huts, and end the scene by towing their canoes into midstream and setting them adrift."[18]

Military weaponry quickly improved, including more powerful repeating guns. In 1861 an American doctor, Richard Gatling (1818–1903), invented what quickly came to be known as the Gatling gun, which could fire up to 3,000 rounds of ammunition a minute. The Gatling gun was quickly adopted by Western armies. The first totally automatic machine gun, spitting out 11 bullets a second, was invented in 1884 by Hiram Maxim (1840–1916), an American working in Britain, and gave the British an unparalleled military advantage. The Western powers used the Maxim gun and similar repeating weapons to subdue resistance to colonialism in Africa and Asia. During World War I, since most Western armies had an array of repeating weapons and field artillery, the two rival alliances in that war inflicted terrible casualties on each other. The Western nations had also by this time developed the first armored tanks and increasingly relied on battleships at sea. Air power was introduced to combat in World War I but did not become central to wars until the Spanish Civil War and World War II. The methods of warfare were now more indiscriminate in their targets and more lethal than ever before in history. In 1945 the United States used the most deadly weapon in history, the atomic bomb, to force Japanese surrender and end World War II.

The Spread of Mass Cultures

The revolution in communications and transportation technologies contributed to the creation and spread of mass cultures, popular entertainments appealing to a large audience that often crossed class divisions and national borders. People were increasingly exposed to cultural products, such as films and music, and pastimes, such as sports, that were common in other regions of their countries or imported from abroad. Mass cultures percolated into and spread outward from the major cities, where the emerging mass media, such as newspapers and radio, were centered. These media disseminated mass culture, reporting on film stars and sports events or playing popular music. The influence of Paris on the rest of France, Berlin on Germany, Tokyo on Japan, Istanbul on Turkey, Buenos Aires on Argentina, and New York City on the United States grew. As literacy rates rose, the print media gained particular influence. Between 1828 and 1900 the number of newspapers published around the world grew from 3,100 to 31,000, making available news and opinions in hundreds of languages. India alone supported 600 different newspapers in several dozen languages in 1900. Popular books, from Arab detective novels to romances written in South Africa's Xhosa (KHO-sa) language, competed with classic works of philosophy and religion for the hearts and minds of readers.

By spreading cultural influences into other societies, mass communications and increased travel sometimes fostered Westernization. Reflecting Westernization, orchestras playing Western classical music appeared in various Asian societies, including India, China, and Japan, by the early 1900s. Like Europeans, many educated Asians enjoyed the music of Beethoven, Bach, and Mozart. Films and popular music from the United States had an even larger international audience. American film stars such as Charlie Chaplin, born in Britain, became known throughout the world, and U.S.-born jazz musicians often made a living playing the nightclubs of Europe and Asia, where they inspired local musicians to take up jazz. Many societies adopted and excelled in Western sports. For example, Indians became skilled in British cricket; India's Prince Ranjitsinhji (RAHN-jeet-SING-jee) (1872–1933) became one of the world's best players. India's field hockey team remained unbeaten in the Olympics from 1932 through 1960. European football, also known as soccer, became an international sport that was played and watched all over the world.

But Westernization was only part of the story. Influences from non-Western cultures also spread, contributing to a creative cultural mixing. For example, in the eighteenth and nineteenth centuries the growing Western interest in Chinese painting, Japanese prints, Indonesian gamelan music, and African woodcarvings influenced Western arts. Later, in the 1930s, Indian films and Indian popular music became popular in Southeast Asia and the Middle East, and Cuban music, a mix of African and Western traditions, developed a large following in West and Central Africa, where it blended with local styles. Hawaiian music, which mixed Polynesian and Western influences, became popular in the continental United States in the 1920s and later developed a following in Southeast Asia. People found ways to combine imported ideas, whatever their source, with their own traditions. For instance, in his lyrical suite, *Bachianas Brasileiras*, of 1930, the Brazilian composer Heitor Villa-Lobos (1887–1959) adapted the Baroque influences of German composer Johann Sebastian Bach (1685–1750) to Brazilian folk and popular music.

The reach of organizations and social movements expanded, as did awareness of the world. Some organizations developed a global focus. For example, the Red Cross, a Christian organization formed in nineteenth-century Switzerland to alleviate human suffering by helping war victims, eventually became an international movement devoted to humanitarian aid around the globe. Its global reach encouraged it to adapt to non-Christian cultures; in the Islamic world it became the Red Crescent. Social movements also crossed borders. For instance, women in China, Japan, Indonesia, Egypt, and Chile, inspired in part by feminist movements in Europe and North America, sought to adapt the notions of women's rights and education to their own societies. The winning of women's suffrage resulted from the efforts of women worldwide. Thus, in the United States, Susan B. Anthony (1820–1906) began campaigning at age seventeen for equal pay for female teachers and later cofounded the key national and international organizations working for women's suffrage. Across the Pacific, Ichikawa Fusae (ITCH-ee-KAH-wa foo-SIGH) (1893–1918) fought for the rights of women to attend political meetings and, in 1924, formed the major women's suffrage group in Japan, which won the right to vote in 1945.

Global crises now became more widely known, and people followed world events in newspapers and radio newscasts. An avid news follower, the Trinidad calypso singer who humorously called himself Atilla the Hun, appraised the devastation in the world of the later 1930s:

> *All we can hear is of unrest, riots, revolutions; There is war in Spain and China. Man using all his skill and ingenuity making weapons to destroy humanity. In the [Italian invasion of Ethiopia] it is said, over six hundred thousand maimed and dead. The grim reaper has taken a gigantic toll. Why all the bloodshed and devastation, Decimating the earth's population? Why can't this warfare cease? All that the tortured world needs is peace.*[19]

Soon after Atilla's plea, World War II raised the level of violence even further, providing a fitting end to a turbulent, violent era during which the world's people had become more closely linked into a common global system.

Suggested Reading

Books

Abernathy, David B., *The Dynamics of Global Dominance: European Overseas Empires, 1415–1980*. New Haven: Yale University Press, 2002. One of the best studies of European imperialism.

Bayly, C. A. *The Birth of the Modern World, 1780–1914*. Malden, MA: Blackwell, 2004. A brilliant, detailed study.

Cohen, Robin. *Global Diasporas: An Introduction*. Seattle: University of Washington Press, 1997. A brief, valuable survey.

Cook, Scott B. *Colonial Encounters in the Age of High Imperialism*. New York: Longman, 1996. Examines Western imperialism.

Curtin, Philip D. *The World and the West: The European Challenge and the Overseas Response in the Age of Empire*. New York: Cambridge University Press, 2000. An interesting study of reactions to European imperialism.

Hobsbawm, Eric. *The Age of Extremes: A History of the World, 1914–1991*. New York: Pantheon, 1994. A masterful overview, especially strong on social and cultural history.

Hoerder, Dirk. *Cultures in Contact: World Migrations in the Second Millennium*. Durham, NC: Duke University Press, 2003. A comprehensive, detailed summary of migrations and diasporas.

Marks, Robert B. *The Origins of the Modern World: A Global and Ecological Narrative*, 2nd ed. Lanham, MD: Rowman and Littlefield, 2007. A concise, readable examination of some major themes.

Neiberg, Michael S. *Warfare in World History*. New York: Routledge, 2001. Good coverage of this era.

Ponting, Clive. *The Twentieth Century: A World History*. New York: Henry Holt and Company, 1998. A thematic study.

Stavrianos, Leften S. *Global Rift: The Third World Comes of Age*. New York: William Morrow, 1971. A provocative, innovative study.

Stearns, Peter N., *The Industrial Revolution in World History*, 3rd ed. Boulder: Westview Press, 2007. Useful comparative study with much on this era.

Wesseling, H. L. *The European Colonial Empires, 1815–1919*. Harlow, United Kingdom: Pearson, 2004. A useful overview of the entire colonial enterprise by a Dutch scholar.

Wolf, Eric R. *Europe and the People Without History*. Berkeley: University of California Press, 1982. A thought-provoking analysis of the Western impact on the wider world from 1400 to 1914.

WEBSITES

Modern History Sourcebook (***http://www.fordham.edu/halsall/***). An extensive online collection of historical documents and secondary materials.

Modern World History Links (***http://www.loeser.us/mhist.html***). A quirky site with links to various useful information sources.

Modern World History Resources (***http://www.historesearch.com/modworld.html***). Has links to sites on many topics and regions.

PART VI

Global System: Interdependence and Conflict in the Contemporary World, Since 1945

The key events of the first half of the twentieth century, including the rise of communism in Russia, the growth of anti-Western nationalism in Africa and Asia, the economic disaster of the Great Depression, and the traumas of World Wars I and II, laid a foundation for a new global system. Yet the world of today has also been shaped by the trends marking the decades since World War II, what historians often term the Contemporary Era. During this era, political and economic power in the world passed from huge Western colonial empires to Russia, Japan, China, and especially the United States. Meanwhile, the world's nations became more closely linked through trade, cooperation, and worldwide movements.

A key feature of world politics until the end of the 1980s was the conflict known as the Cold War. Marking this conflict was a competition for influence between the United States and its allies and the Soviet Union and its allies. Another major political trend was the ending of Western colonial control in Asia, Africa, and most of the Caribbean and Pacific islands by the 1970s. Nationalist movements in these colonized areas demanded and gained political independence but sometimes achieved their goals only through violent resistance, including revolutions in countries such as Indonesia, Algeria, and Mozambique. While the Soviet Union imposed communism on eastern Europe, communist-led movements came to power through revolution in countries such as China, Vietnam, and Cuba. Despite fierce competition between the major powers, new international organizations, among them the United Nations, fostered cooperation among nations on issues of common concern, such as women's rights, proliferating nuclear weapons, and threats to public health.

The world has also seen significant economic change since 1945. Western Europe and Japan recovered quickly from World War II, regaining prosperity. Economic links between nations became much stronger, greatly enlarging the world economy. A trend known as globalization spread, facilitating the flow of investment, jobs, resources, and products, not to mention information and ideas, around the world. New or improved technologies, from home appliances and automobiles to cell phones and computers, made life more convenient while fostering economic change. Capitalizing on globalization, several industrializing Asian nations, including India, South Korea, Malaysia, and especially China, grew economically, reshaping world trade. But Japan and the western nations, led by the United States, have controlled much of the world's wealth and have had the most productive economies. The gap between these industrialized countries and the world's poorest countries has grown even wider.

Furthermore, economic growth has come at a huge cost in environmental destruction, from the cutting down of forests to the polluting of the world's air, land, and water. Skyrocketing population growth has harmed the environment, diminished natural resources, and fostered poverty. While people in several

Corbis

dozen nations have enjoyed unprecedented affluence and longer, healthier lives, a fifth of the world's people live in desperate poverty, unable to meet their basic needs for food and shelter.

Social and cultural change has also characterized recent decades. Spurred by war or the quest for a better life, for example, people have left their homelands to settle in other lands. As a result, millions of Africans, Arabs, Turks, and South Asians live in Europe while Latin Americans and Asians have moved to North America. In many countries women have gained better job opportunities and political rights, and ethnic minorities have struggled for social equality. Popular culture products, such as Hollywood films, Caribbean reggae music, and Japanese video games, have spread around the world. Although secular thought has enjoyed increased influence, especially in western Europe and East Asia, Christianity and Islam have rapidly gained followers and influence in many lands. These social and cultural changes, however, are balanced by continuities. While people often enjoy the latest entertainment and gadgets, in many ways they remain like their ancestors, devoted to their families, faiths, and customs. Most societies are a mix of old and new, the traditional and the contemporary.

Since the collapse of European communist regimes and the Soviet Union at the end of the 1980s, which left the United States as the sole global superpower, the world's nations have faced other challenges. These include international terrorism, deadly diseases, food and energy shortages, weapons of mass destruction, global warming, unstable nations engulfed in conflict, and the growing inequality between rich and poor countries. How nations, working together, deal with these and other problems will determine the shape of the future.

EUROPE

Although western Europe recovered quickly from World War II, the imperial Western states were unable to maintain control of their colonies. The western European nations forged stable welfare states, providing a social safety net, and moved toward close cooperation and economic unity among themselves. The Soviet Union became a global superpower, controlling eastern Europe, but at the end of the 1980s it and its communist satellites collapsed. Germany, divided after World War II, was reunified, and Russia sought a new role in the world.

WESTERN ASIA

Nationalists gained control of the western Asian nations but faced new challenges. Israel, a new Jewish state in Palestine, won wars against Arab neighbors, and Arab-Israeli hostilities have remained a source of tension. Some nations, such as Turkey, pursued modernization. An Islamic revolution reshaped oil-rich Iran, which fought oil-rich Iraq in the 1980s. Saudi Arabia and several Persian Gulf states flourished from oil wealth. After 2001 U.S.-led forces invaded and occupied Afghanistan and Iraq but, while removing despotic governments, struggled to restore stability.

EASTERN ASIA

Coming to power through revolution in 1949, communists transformed China, creating a socialist society and fighting the United States during the Korean War. After 1978 new communist leaders mixed free markets with socialism and fostered modernization, turning China into an economic powerhouse. Japan recovered rapidly from World War II, embracing democracy and becoming an economic giant. Borrowing Japanese models, South Korea and Taiwan industrialized. North Korea remained a repressive communist state.

AFRICA

As Arab and African nationalism grew stronger, colonies became independent nations, sometimes, as in Algeria and Angola, through revolution. In North Africa, Egypt promoted Arab nationalism and became a regional power but faced economic problems. Most of the new sub-Saharan African nations, which were artificial creations of colonialism, struggled to maintain political stability and foster economic development, but South Africans finally achieved black majority rule.

SOUTHERN ASIA AND OCEANIA

Britain granted independence to predominantly Hindu India but also to largely Muslim Pakistan, which eventually split when Bangladesh seceded. India enjoyed democracy and economic progress, but Pakistan and Bangladesh often fell under military rule. In Southeast Asia, the U.S. and British colonies gained independence peacefully while Indonesians triumphed through revolution. Vietnamese communists first defeated the French and then the United States. Malaysia, Singapore, and Thailand developed economically. Australia and New Zealand established closer links to Asia, and most of the Pacific islands gained independence from Western colonialism.

CHAPTER

26

THE REMAKING OF THE GLOBAL SYSTEM, SINCE 1945

CHAPTER OUTLINE

- Decolonization, New States, and the Global System
- Cold War, Hot Wars, and World Politics
- Globalizing Economies, Underdevelopment, and Environmental Change
- New Global Networks and Their Consequences

PROFILE
Wangari Maathai, Kenyan Environmental Activist

WITNESS TO THE PAST
An Agenda for the New Millennium

AP/Wide World Photos

"Our World Is Not for Sale"
In 2004 tens of thousands of activists from all over the world, under the banner of "Our World Is Not for Sale," marched on the streets of Mumbai (formerly Bombay), India's largest city, to protest economic globalization, racial and caste oppression, and the U.S.-led war in Iraq. The march reflected the globalization of social movements and political protests in the contemporary world.

One heart, one destiny. Peace and love for all mankind. And Africa for Africans.

—Bob Marley, reggae superstar[1]

FOCUS QUESTIONS

1. How did decolonization change the global system?
2. What roles did the Cold War and superpower rivalry play in world politics?
3. What were some of the main consequences of a globalizing world economy?
4. How did growing networks linking societies influence social, political, and economic life?

In 1980, when the new African nation of Zimbabwe (formerly Southern Rhodesia) celebrated its independence from British rule, Bob Marley, a Jamaican reggae music star and a symbol of black empowerment, performed at Zimbabwe's national stadium. Marley's experience there reflected many late-twentieth-century politcal and cultural trends. He had been invited in part because his songs often dealt with issues such as poverty, racial prejudice, and asserting one's rights, realities for Zimbabweans, who had lived under an uncaring British colonial and then white supremacist government. But Marley's concert was disrupted by the local police, mostly whites fearing a riot and vandalism, who used tear gas to disperse thousands of black Zimbabweans, often poor, who gathered outside the overcrowded stadium. The next night Marley ignored threats of violence against him by local white racists and gave a free concert for 40,000 Zimbabweans. The violence of the previous night and the threats to his life showed Marley that the social ills and ethnic hatreds he knew in Jamaica also occurred elsewhere in the world. In Zimbabwe they would not be solved by a black majority government.

Marley's career reflected a world interconnected as never before. An eloquent advocate of political and cultural freedom whose music was enjoyed around the world, Marley came from the slums of a small island of barely 2 million people, yet his music touched hearts and minds across racial, political, religious, class, and cultural barriers. Reggae was a truly world music, an intoxicating mix of African, Caribbean, and North American traditions. To the world, Marley personified reggae's progressive politics and spiritual quest.

Some 2,500 years ago ancient thinkers such as the Buddha in India, Daoists in China, and the Greek philosopher Heraclitus had argued that nothing was permanent except change. Never was this more true than in the second half of the twentieth century and the early twenty-first. Since World War II the pace of change quickened and the global economy grew dramatically. Economic and cultural networks linked societies ever more closely while ideas, technologies, and products flowed across porous borders, affecting the lives of people everywhere. World politics were turbulent, reflecting the conflict between the United States and the Soviet Union (USSR) and the struggle of African, Asian, and Latin American countries for decolonization and development. Since 1989, when the Soviet bloc collapsed, the world has groped toward a new political configuration while dealing with mounting economic and environmental problems.

e Visit the website and eBook for additional study materials and interactive tools: www.cengage.com/history/lockard/globalsocnet2e

Decolonization, New States, and the Global System

How did decolonization change the global system?

The contemporary world derived both from Western imperialism and from the resistance waged against it. After World War II Asia, Africa, and Latin America became major battlegrounds between the United States and the Soviet Union, which had so much military, political, and economic might in comparison to other countries that they were known as superpowers. The struggle of Asian, African, and Latin American societies to end Western domination and to develop economically also shaped the postwar era. Nationalist movements proliferated, sometimes leading to interventions by Western powers or the USSR, which were anxious to preserve their political and economic influence. The former colonies now became part of a global system marked by continued imbalances in wealth and power.

Nationalism and Decolonization

Types of Nationalism

Nationalism became a powerful force in the colonized world by the mid-1900s (see Chapter 25). Three basic types of nationalist movements developed. In the first type, which occurred in most colonized societies, the goal was the end of colonial rule, but not necessarily major social and economic change. Colonial powers were often willing to grant independence where nationalist leaders, in countries such as Nigeria and the Philippines, accepted continued Western control of mines, plantations, and other resources. The second type of nationalist movement, mounted by social revolutionaries inspired by Marxism, wanted not only political independence but also a new social order free of Western economic domination. In China the communist movement led by Mao Zedong reorganized Chinese society while limiting contact with the world economy and the United States. Making up a third type were the nationalist movements by long-repressed nonwhite majorities in white settler colonies such as Algeria and Zimbabwe, which struggled against domination by the minority whites, who owned most of the land and resources.

Dismantling Empires

The dislocations caused by the Great Depression and World War II intensified anticolonial feelings. In the three decades after World War II, colonialism gradually crumbled, often after nationalist resistance led by charismatic figures such as Mohandas Gandhi in India and Sukarno in Indonesia. Most of the Western colonizers realized that the increased military force required to maintain their control was too expensive. In 1946 the United States began the decolonization trend, granting independence to the Philippines (see Chronology: Global Politics, 1945–1989). Weary of suppressing nationalist resistance, the British gave up their rule in India and Burma, and the Dutch left Indonesia. Between 1946 and 1975 most of the Western colonies in Asia, Africa, and the Caribbean achieved independence (see Map 26.1).

Some colonizers accepted decolonization only after failing to quell nationalist uprisings. The Dutch planned to regain Indonesia, a source of immense wealth, but the struggle against a nationalist army proved bloody and demoralizing. Similarly, the French had no plans to abandon their profitable colonies in Vietnam and Algeria, but uprisings by revolutionaries forced them to leave. In Vietnam, heavy U.S. aid could not prevent a humiliating French defeat by communist forces led by Ho Chi Minh in 1954. The ultimately successful anticolonial struggles by the Indonesian, Vietnamese, and Algerian nationalists had electrifying global effects, giving hope to colonized peoples elsewhere and warning the Western powers that they would pay a heavy cost for opposing decolonization.

Nationalism and the Superpowers

Both superpowers sought to capitalize on the nationalist surge. The Soviet Union generally supported nationalist movements, sometimes supplying arms to revolutionaries. The Soviets also offered economic aid and diplomatic support to Asian and African countries that achieved independence and had strategic value because of their size, location, or valuable resources, such as India, Egypt, and Indonesia. The United States followed a mixed policy on decolonization. Wanting access to trade and outlets for investment in Asia and Africa, the United States encouraged the Dutch to leave Indonesia and urged independence for some British colonies in Africa. But Americans also opposed communism and Soviet influence. Thus where nationalism had a leftist orientation, as in French-ruled Vietnam and Portuguese-ruled Mozambique, the United States supported continued colonial power, no matter how unpopular, and helped finance the French and Portuguese military efforts to suppress the revolutionaries. Portugal stubbornly resisted decolonization until festering African rebellions, growing demoralization at home, and the toppling of its fascist dictator forced it to abandon its African empire in 1975.

CHRONOLOGY

	International	Eurasia	The Americas
1940	**1945** Formation of the United Nations **1946–1975** Decolonization in Asia, Africa, and Caribbean **1946–1989** Cold War	**1950–1953** Korean War **1959–1975** U.S.-Vietnam War	
1960	**1968** Widespread political protests		**1962** Cuban Missile Crisis
1980		**1989–1991** Dismantling of Soviet bloc and Soviet Union	
2000			**2001** Al Qaeda attack on United States

Colonialism did not completely disappear. By the 1980s one major territorial empire, the USSR, remained, and it strained to repress the nationalist demands of the Baltic, Caucasus, and Central Asian peoples it ruled. The Soviet Empire was largely dismantled between 1989 and 1991, when the communist system collapsed, although Russians still controlled some unwilling subjects, such as the Muslim Chechens in southern Russia. Britain, France, and the United States still control small empires. Britain and France retain direct control of a few islands, mostly in the South Pacific, South Atlantic, and Caribbean, and some outposts such as French Guiana in South America. The territories, mostly self-governing, that are linked to the United States include Puerto Rico and the Virgin Islands in the Caribbean and a few Pacific islands such as American Samoa and Guam.

UPI/Bettmann/Corbis

African Independence In 1961 the British monarch, Queen Elizabeth II, made an official visit to newly independent Ghana, the former British colony of the Gold Coast. Here she walks under a ceremonial umbrella with the Ghanian president, Kwame Nkrumah.

Decolonization often resulted in neocolonialism, a continuing Western political and economic influence. In the Philippines, Americans maintained a major role in the economy, Philippine governments loyally supported U.S. foreign policies, and Filipinos avidly consumed American products and popular culture such as music, films, and fashions. Similarly, the French controlled much of the economy and advised the government in Cote d'Ivoire **(COAT dee-VWAHR)** (Ivory Coast), and many Ivoirians favored French cuisine, literature, and language. A West Indian–born writer offered a radical nationalist but oversimplified view of why most former colonies accepted neocolonialism: "The colonial power says, 'Since you want independence, take it and starve' [after economic aid ends]. Other countries refuse to undergo this ordeal and agree to [accept] the conditions of the former guardian power."[2] Some Asian and African intellectuals advocated "decolonizing the mind," to escape what Bob Marley called "mental slavery" that kept formerly colonized people in awe of Western power, wealth, and culture. This sometimes meant building a nationalist culture reflecting local traditions or abandoning the use of Western languages in literature. For example, the Kenyan novelist Ngugi wa Thiongo **(en-GOO-gey wah they-ON-go)** switched from writing in English to his native Gikuyu.

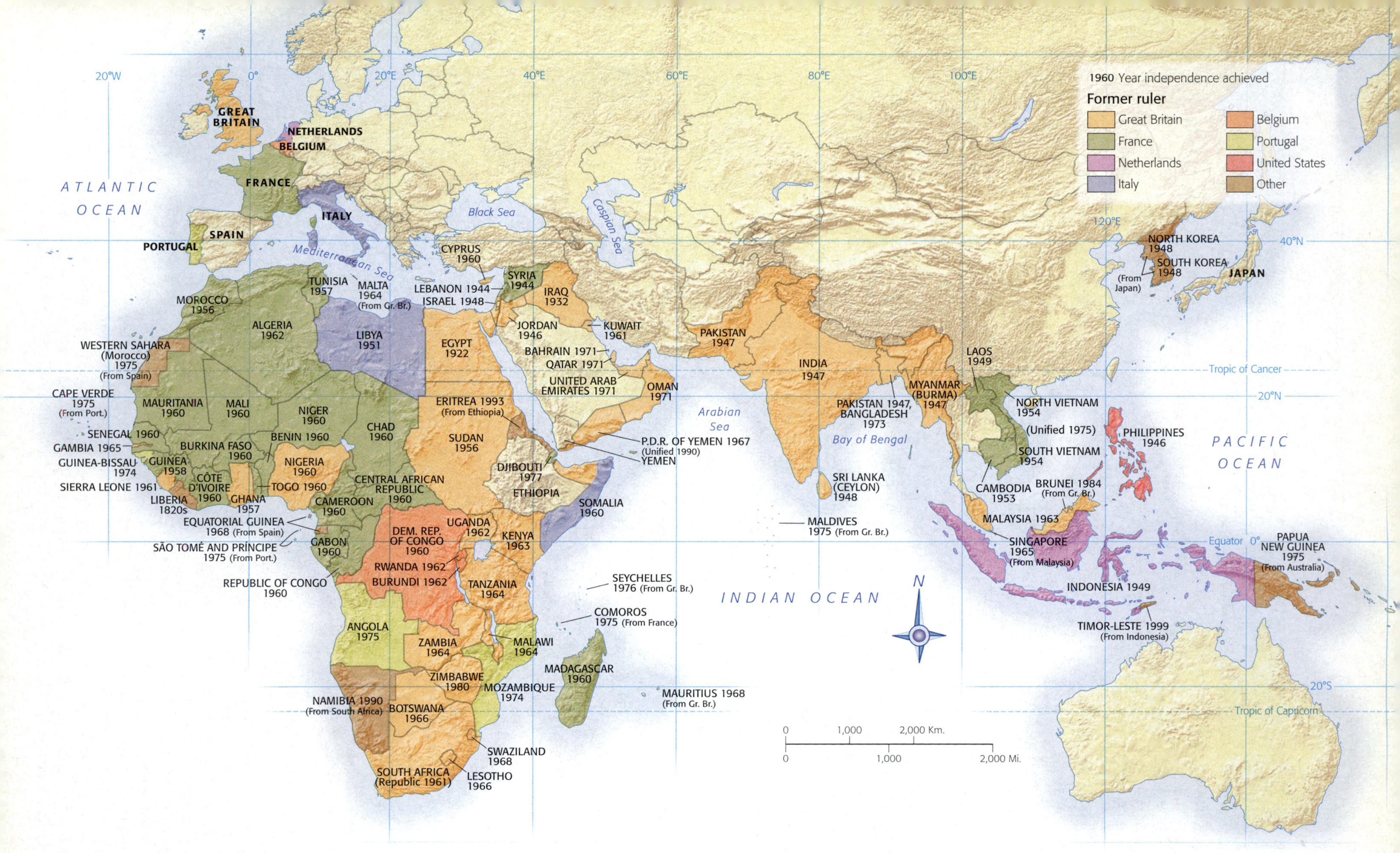

1960 Year independence achieved

Former ruler

- Great Britain
- France
- Netherlands
- Italy
- Belgium
- Portugal
- United States
- Other

Map 26.1 Decolonization

Between 1946 and 1975 most of the Western colonies in Asia, Africa, and the Caribbean won their independence, with the greatest number achieving independence in the 1960s. The decolonization reshaped the political map, particularly of Africa, South Asia, and Southeast Asia.

Interactive Map

Social Revolutionary States

During the twentieth century, revolutionary activity erupted in Asia, Africa, and Latin America, intensified by the drive to end Western domination. This revolutionary activity often engaged peasants impoverished by the loss of their lands or the declining prices for their crops. Revolutionary intellectuals spurred by a Marxist vision mobilized support. Amilcar Cabral **(AM-ill-car ka-BRAWL)** (1924–1973), the revolutionary leader in Portugal's colony of Guinea Bissau **(GIN-ee bi-SOW)**, advised his Marxist colleagues to "always bear in mind that the people are not fighting for ideas, for the things in anyone's head. They are fighting to live better, and in peace, to guarantee the future of their children."[3] Between 1949 and 1980 social revolutionary regimes came to power through force of arms in China, Vietnam, Algeria, Cuba, Nicaragua, Angola, and Mozambique. Opposed by the United States, they necessarily looked to the USSR for political, economic, and military support. Revolutionary movements were also active, although ultimately frustrated, in various other Latin American and Southeast Asian countries.

CHRONOLOGY
Global Politics, 1945–1989

1945 Formation of United Nations

1946–1975 Decolonization in Asia, Africa, Caribbean

1946–1989 Cold War

1949 Communist victory in China

1950–1953 Korean War

1954 Vietnamese defeat of French

1955 Bandung Conference

1959–1975 U.S.-Vietnam War

1959 Communist victory in Cuba

1962 Cuban Missile Crisis

1968 Widespread political protests

1975 End of Portuguese Empire

1979-1989 Soviet War in Afghanistan

Thinkers and activists around the world, such as the West Indian–born psychiatrist and writer Frantz Fanon (1925–1961), who joined the anti-French movement while working in colonial Algeria, often romanticized the revolutionaries' promise to create more just societies. Yet scholars of politics disagreed as to whether revolutions ultimately improved lives and righted injustice or instead generated tyranny and economic stagnation. While social revolutionary governments often raised the status and living standards of the poor, they also became bureaucratic, despotic, and intolerant of dissent, frequently compiling poor human rights records. Influenced by Stalinism, they had uneven relations with the capitalist nations. In order to rebuff outside interference, renounce foreign debts, and assume control of their economic direction, these states usually limited their involvement with the world economy, instead creating planned economies in which economic decisions, such as allocation of investment capital, were made by governments rather than through free markets. Nevertheless, many people welcomed the end of the uncaring, often repressive governments the revolutions replaced.

Social revolutionary approaches brought mixed results. Some countries saw their goals sidetracked by civil wars or rebellions. South Africa and the United States supported rebels in Angola who fought the Marxist-dominated government for over two decades, costing over 200,000 lives, ruining much of the country, and diverting resources to the military. In contrast to Angola's woes, between 1949 and 1978 communist-run China was able to increase its economic potential and address social problems, but at a heavy cost in limiting personal freedom. After 1978 China sparked even more rapid growth by modifying its socialist economy with foreign investment and free enterprise. The shift of China, followed by Vietnam, toward market economies and greater participation in the world economy suggested that revolution may have helped nations gain control of their resources but was insufficient to raise living standards to the levels of the richer nations. Yet, China and Vietnam also found that although free markets could create more wealth than socialism, they did not necessarily lead to an equitable distribution of wealth, breeding explosive social tensions.

A New Global System

A new global system emerged after 1945. The prewar world had been dominated by a few great Western powers, led by Britain and France, ruling over vast empires in Asia, Africa, and the Caribbean, but decolonization and the rise of the United States and Soviet Union to superpower status modified this pattern. Many observers now divided the world into three categories of countries, each one having a different level of economic development. The **First World** comprised the industrialized democracies of western Europe, North America, Australia–New Zealand, and Japan. The **Second World** referred to the communist nations, led by the USSR and China. The **Third World** was made up of most societies in Asia, Africa, Latin America, and the Caribbean that were marked by mass poverty and a legacy of Western colonization or neocolonialism. Some experts added a fourth category, the **Fourth World**, which included the poorest societies with very small economies and few exploitable resources, such as Laos, Afghanistan, Haiti, and Mali. However, critics argued that lumping the world's societies—with their very different histories,

First World The industrialized democracies of western Europe, North America, Australia–New Zealand, and Japan.

Second World The communist nations, led by the USSR and China.

Third World Societies in Asia, Africa, Latin America, and the Caribbean, which were shaped by mass poverty and a legacy of colonization or neocolonialism.

Fourth World The poorest societies, with very small economies and few exploitable resources.

cultures, and global connections—into a few categories was highly misleading. Furthermore, after the 1970s the global system changed. Countries such as Malaysia, South Korea, Dubai **(doo-BYE)**, and Chile, once grouped with the Third World, achieved rapid economic growth, and the communist systems that had defined the Second World often collapsed.

Rich and Poor Nations

At the developed end of the global system, most Western nations and Japan enjoyed new heights of prosperity from the 1960s through the 1980s. After World War II the dominant world power, the United States, offered generous aid and investment to its allies, restarting further economic growth in industrialized, diversified countries that already had literate, skilled, and mostly urban populations. Hence, western Europe and Japan recovered from the ashes of World War II and prospered. Japan's economy increased fivefold between 1953 and 1973, the fastest economic growth in world history. As Western and Japanese businesses invested heavily around the world, international trade soared. Japan and West Germany became the second and third largest capitalist economies. By the 1970s several Western nations, such as West Germany, Sweden, Canada, and Australia, had standards of living similar to those in the United States but far more income equality.

Although economic growth rates often slowed after 1990, Western prosperity relative to the rest of the world continued. Every year the United Nations issues a Human Development Report that rates the quality of life of the world's nations by examining per capita income, health, and literacy. Generally Norway, Sweden, Australia, Canada, and the Netherlands are rated as the most livable nations. A hundred years earlier Norway and Sweden were among the poorest European countries. Now Sweden has achieved the world's lowest poverty rate, largely because the Swedish state provides each citizen with free education, subsidized health care, and other welfare benefits, and the Swedish economy has grown steadily. The reports rank several dozen nations, mostly in sub-Saharan Africa, as having a low quality of life—massive poverty, inadequate health care, and low rates of literacy. Tanzanian president Julius Nyerere **(nye-RE-re)** put the gap between rich and poor nations in perspective: "While the United States is trying to reach the moon, Tanzania is trying to reach its villages."[4]

Some nations had more political stability and resources to secure their citizens' lives. Richer nations usually benefited from democracy and were nation-states where the large majority shared a common culture and language. Some of these nations did contain restless ethnic or religious minorities. For example, the Basques in northern Spain, whose language and identity differ completely from the Spanish majority, sought autonomy or independence. But democratic governments mostly diminished social tensions, while generous welfare systems prevented mass poverty. Many western European states, Canada, and New Zealand adopted ambitious welfare systems, including comprehensive national health insurance, which promoted social justice and equality. Poorer nations, often with highly diverse populations, small budgets, and limited resources, faced greater challenges in building stable nation-states. Violence, such as the repeated ethnic conflicts in Yugoslavia, occurred in nations that had abandoned communism and its safety net. The fighting between Yugoslavs sometimes resulted in brutal atrocities and the forced expulsion of minorities. Only a few non-European nations, such as Sri Lanka and oil-rich Brunei and Saudi Arabia, tried to mount welfare states with free education and health care, but they struggled to pay for them.

SECTION SUMMARY

- Between 1946 and 1975, most Western colonies achieved independence, in many cases as a result of violent opposition movements, though the United States continued to oppose leftist movements and the Soviet Union's vast colonial empire endured until 1989.
- Western nations maintained a great deal of influence over the economy and culture of many of their former colonies, which led some intellectuals to call for "decolonizing the mind."
- Revolutionary regimes, often inspired by Marxism, came to power in a number of Asian, African, and Latin American nations, though they met with mixed economic success and in some cases were embroiled in long-term civil war.
- The division of the world's nations into First, Second, and Third Worlds grew blurry as some Third World nations developed First-World-level economies and the Soviet Union collapsed, though democratic countries tended to be more stable and offer more support to their citizens.

COLD WAR, HOT WARS, AND WORLD POLITICS

What roles did the Cold War and superpower rivalry play in world politics?

Cold War A conflict lasting from 1946 to 1989 in which the United States and the USSR competed for allies and engaged in occasional warfare against their rival's allies rather than against each other directly.

A new global political configuration emerged after World War II. From 1946 to 1989 the two major superpowers, the United States and the USSR, engaged in the **Cold War**, a conflict in which they competed for allies and engaged in occasional warfare against their rival's allies rather than with each other directly. The United States enjoyed much greater influence and boasted more allies. While the Cold War did not lead to a military conflict in which U.S. and

Soviet military forces fought each other, it produced chronic tensions and led to covert and military interventions by each of the superpowers seeking to block gains by the other.

The Cold War: A Divided World

United States and Soviet Union

The world took on a bipolar political character. Nations practicing capitalism and often democracy, led by the United States, were on one side, while those marked by socialist authoritarianism, led by the USSR and known as the Soviet bloc, were on the other. For over four decades U.S.-USSR relations were a major factor in international affairs. The United States sought to contain communism, while the USSR worked to spread communism and undercut American influence. Leaders of nations such as Egypt, India, and Indonesia promoted nonalignment with either superpower. In 1955 leaders from twenty-nine nonaligned Asian and African countries held a conference in Bandung, Indonesia, to gain recognition for what they called a Third World bloc, but they had trouble maintaining unity in the decades to follow.

The United States became the world's most powerful nation, enjoying far greater wealth, military force, and cultural influence than any other nation, including the USSR. In 1945, the United States already had the atomic bomb, produced half of the world's industrial output, and held two-thirds of the gold. Americans seemed willing to bear a heavy financial and military burden to sustain their leading role in world affairs and to promote U.S. economic growth by obtaining raw materials and preserving profitable markets.

By 1948 the Soviets controlled all of eastern Europe and were allied with communist governments in Mongolia and North Korea. After World War II, therefore, U.S. concern shifted to countering the USSR, which Americans perceived as a rival for influence in the world. Americans tried to prevent communists from gaining control of China; then they became involved in the Korean War (1950–1953) to fight successfully the North Korean effort to forcibly reunify the Korean peninsula. Yet, in spite of U.S. efforts, communist regimes came to power in China in 1949, North Vietnam in 1954, and Cuba in 1959. Furthermore, waging the Cold War and using military force to contain communism, including a long war in Vietnam, cost the United States $4 trillion or $5 trillion and some 113,000 American lives, mostly soldiers, between 1946 and 1989.

Primary Source: The Long Telegram This critique of the Soviet Union's ideology, authored by an American diplomat in 1946, profoundly influenced the foreign policy of the United States.

Historians debate whether the USSR ever posed a serious military threat to the United States and how much both sides misinterpreted their rival's motives and actions. Remembering centuries of invasions from the west, the USSR occupied eastern Europe as a buffer zone and considered the United States and its western European allies a lethal danger whose combined military power greatly exceeded that of the USSR. For their part, Americans mistrusted Soviet leaders and despised communism. While Americans viewed themselves as protecting freedom, the Soviets claimed that they were helping the world's exploited masses and fighting imperialism.

Cold War Conflicts

Some historians believe the Cold War brought stability, while others point to some eighty wars between 1945 and 1989, resulting in 20 million deaths and perhaps 20 million refugees. The Cold War rivalries also dragged in emerging nations, already damaged by their long, humiliating subservience to Western power, and led to upheavals that bankrupted economies and devastated entire peoples. A series of small conflicts involved surrogates, governments, or movements allied to one superpower and fighting the troops from the other superpower. In Korea and Vietnam U.S. troops battled not Soviet armies but Soviet-supported communist forces. Similarly, the Soviets sent military supplies and advisers to help the Vietnamese communists fight first the French and then the United States, which had supported a pro-Western government in South Vietnam after the French defeat. The communists gained control of the entire country in 1975. Americans also used surrogates, such as when they supplied Islamic groups fighting the Soviets in Afghanistan in the 1980s. Insurgencies using unconventional warfare, such as sniping, sabotaging power plants, and planting roadside bombs, also became common. Insurgents often resorted to **guerrilla warfare**, an unconventional military strategy of avoiding full-scale direct confrontations in favor of small-scale skirmishes. For example, Vietnamese communist guerrillas staged hit-and-run attacks on American patrols and field bases and planted land mines on trails used by American troops.

guerrilla warfare An unconventional military strategy of avoiding full-scale direct confrontations in favor of small-scale skirmishes.

The Cold War fostered interventions—both covert and military—by both superpowers to protect their interests. The USSR sent military forces into Poland, Hungary, and Czechoslovakia to crush anti-Soviet movements and into Afghanistan to support a pro-Soviet government. Sometimes Soviet invasions proved disastrous; the heavy Soviet losses and humiliating withdrawal from Afghanistan in 1989 contributed to the collapse of the Soviet system. Communist parties established a strong presence in nations such as Indonesia, India, and Chile, where they participated openly in politics, but they also launched unsuccessful insurgencies against governments in countries such as Peru, Malaysia, and the Philippines. The United States actively sought to shape the political and economic direction of Asian, African, and Latin American societies, often giving generous aid and promoting human rights. Americans generously donated food, disaster and medical assistance, offered technical advice, and supported the growth of democratic organizations. But other efforts destabilized or helped overthrow governments deemed unfriendly to U.S. business and political interests, including left-leaning but democratically elected regimes in Brazil, Chile, and Guatemala.

U.S. Interventions

One of the earliest U.S. interventions came in 1953 in oil-rich Iran, which was governed by a nationalist but noncommunist regime that had angered the Americans and British by nationalizing British- and U.S.-owned oil companies that sent most of their huge profits abroad and paid their Iranian workers less than fifty cents a day. Britain and the United States imposed an economic boycott, making it hard for Iran to sell its oil abroad. American agents also recruited disaffected military officers and paid Iranians to spread rumors and spark riots that paralyzed the capital, forcing the nationalists from power and leading to a pro-U.S. but despotic government. For the first time ever the United States had overthrown a foreign government outside the Western Hemisphere. One result was the long-term hatred of the United States by many ordinary Iranians.

To critics, the U.S. interventions constituted a new form of imperialism. The interventions often proved costly as well. In Vietnam the communist-led forces achieved a military stalemate that cost the United States vast sums of money, killed some 58,000 Americans, and forced it to negotiate for peace and withdraw, harming U.S. prestige in the world. The war also created economic problems in the United States and reduced the U.S. willingness to exercise military power. But the Vietnam conflict also cost the lives of several million Vietnamese on all sides and required the USSR and China to spend scarce resources supplying their communist allies.

The Nuclear Arms Race and Global Militarization

nuclear weapons Explosive devices that owe their destructive power to the energy released by either splitting or fusing atoms.

The superpower arms race and increasing militarization around the world became major components of the Cold War. Both superpowers developed first atomic and then **nuclear weapons**, explosive devices that owe their destructive power to the energy released by either splitting or fusing atoms. These weapons were the most deadly result of the technological surge that can be traced back through Albert Einstein to Sir Isaac Newton and the scientific revolution. A nuclear explosion produces a powerful blast, intense heat, and deadly radiation over a wide area. The United States dropped the first atomic bombs on the Japanese cities of Hiroshima and Nagasaki to end World War II, and both the United States and the USSR eventually developed even more deadly nuclear warheads that could be placed on the tips of missiles. The growth of nuclear arsenals was only the most dangerous part of a larger trend toward the expansion of war-making ability by many nations.

Threats of Mass Destruction

Since 1945 the world has lived in the shadow of nuclear weapons; a small number of them could reduce whole countries to radioactive rubble and, many scientists believe, radically alter global weather patterns. Einstein fretted that the unleashed power of the atom would change everything except peoples' ways of thinking, and he worried that leaders would create a global catastrophe by rashly using the new technologies. Fortunately these weapons were never used after 1945, although the world was close to a nuclear confrontation on several occasions. For example, in 1962, after discovering that the USSR had secretly placed nuclear missiles in Cuba, just 90 miles from Florida, President John F. Kennedy (1917–1963) demanded they be removed but vetoed a U.S. invasion that might have sparked all-out nuclear war. Kennedy rejected attacking Cuba with nuclear weapons, but his firm stance created a tense crisis, ultimately forcing the Soviets to withdraw them. However, before that withdrawal, in response to a U.S. attack on his boat, a Soviet submarine commander armed but did not fire a nuclear missile aimed at Florida, averting catastophe.

The Cold War fostered a balance of terror, with both superpowers unwilling to use their weapons for fear the other would retaliate. Historians debate whether the nuclear arms race preserved the peace by discouraging an all-out U.S.-USSR military confrontation or unsettled international politics and wasted trillions of dollars. Britain, France, China, India, and Pakistan also constructed or acquired nuclear bombs, while countries like Israel, Iran, and North Korea began programs to do the same. Although in 1987 the two superpowers negotiated their first treaty to reduce their nuclear arms, concerns grew about nuclear proliferation, especially that North Korea or Pakistan could sell bombs to other countries or terrorist groups. But some outside the West argued that the monopoly on such weapons by a few powerful nations was unfair.

Costs of Militarization

The proportion of total world production and spending devoted to militaries grew dramatically during the Cold War. By 1985, the world was spending more on military forces and weapons

than the combined income of the poorest 50 percent of the world's countries. The two superpowers together, with 11 percent of the world population, accounted for 60 percent of military spending, 25 percent of the world's armed forces, and 97 percent of its nuclear weapons. They also sold conventional weapons to other countries with which they had friendly relations.

The varied wars since 1945 caused enormous casualties, with civilians accounting for some three-fourths of the casualties. Two million people died during the Chinese civil war (1945–1949), 800,000 during the violent partition of India (1948), 2 million during the American-Vietnamese War, 1 million during the Nigerian civil war (1967), and more than 2 million in the Cambodian violence from 1970 to 1978. Millions of these deaths resulted from genocide. For example, in the 1990s members of the Hutu majority slaughtered people belonging to the Tutsi minority in Rwanda **(roo-AHN-duh)**, while extremist Serbs killed Bosnian and Albanian Muslims in Yugoslavia, in a policy they called "ethnic cleansing." The Yugoslav killings were finally stopped when the United States and western European nations sent in troops to restore order and punish the worst human rights violators.

Global Organizations and Activism

The United Nations

During the Cold War, more than ever before in history, public and private organizations with a global reach and mission promoted political cooperation and addressed various social, political, economc, and environmental issues. The largest effort to cooperate for the common good, the United Nations, was founded in 1945 with fifty-one members, becoming a key forum for global debate and an agency for improving global conditions. The United Nations Charter enumerated the founding principles: "To develop friendly relations among nations based on respect for the principle of equal rights and self-determination of peoples and to take other appropriate measures to strengthen universal peace." The founding members aimed to "save succeeding generations from the scourge of war, reaffirm faith in fundamental rights, and respect international law."[5] As colonies gained independence and joined, the organization grew to nearly two hundred member states. The United Nations sponsored humanitarian agencies such as the World Health Organization, which monitored diseases, funded and fostered medical research, and promoted public health, and the United Nations Children Fund (UNICEF), which promoted children's welfare and education around the world. Such U.N.-sponsored programs helped increase average life expectancy from 45 in 1900 to 75 in 2000, as well as greatly reducing the risk of mothers dying in childbirth. Yet, critics believed that political differences often obstructed the United Nation's work.

The five major powers of 1945 (the United States, China, Britain, France, and the USSR) enjoyed permanent seats with veto power in the policy-making U.N. Security Council, and both superpowers vetoed decisions that challenged their national interests. Hence, the United States often vetoed resolutions aimed at penalizing Israel, and it also blocked the communist government from occupying China's seat in the United Nations. The Security Council also sometimes sent peacekeeping troops into troubled countries. However, the United Nations discouraged, but could not prevent, states from resorting to force. To gain support for a possible military action, nations often felt it necessary to make their case before the Security Council; sometimes they received support, as when a United States–led U.N. military force repulsed a North Korean invasion of South Korea. However, nations often ignored widespread disapproval by the organization's members, as the United States did when it invaded Iraq in 2003.

International Agreements

Nations also forged international agreements and treaties, such as an agreement in 1972 banning biological weapons. In 1997, 132 nations signed an international treaty to ban the production, use, and export of land mines, which kill and injure civilians years after the end of conflicts. In 1997 most nations also signed the Kyoto Protocol, pledging to reduce the harmful gases that contribute to global warming. In 2002 a treaty established an International Criminal Court to prosecute the perpetrators of genocide, war crimes, and crimes against humanity. But the United States and several other industrial nations refused to ratify these modest efforts to reduce weapons, promote environmental stability, and establish accountability for international crimes.

Private organizations and activists also worked for issues of peace, social justice, health, refugees, famine, conflict resolution, and environmental protection. For example, Doctors Without Borders offered medical personnel, and Amnesty International worked to free political prisoners. Some religious leaders promoted world peace, justice, and humanitarian issues. The Dalai Lama (b. 1935), the highest Tibetan Buddhist spiritual leader, won the Nobel Peace Prize in 1989 for his efforts to promote human rights, nonviolent conflict resolution, and understanding among different religions. In 1997 the Dalai Lama pleaded, "We all have a special responsibility to create

AP/World Wide Photos

U.N. Peacekeepers in Congo The United Nations has regularly sent peacekeepers into troubled countries such as the Congo. This photo, from 2003, shows U.N. troops from Uruguay guarding a U.N. office while a Congolese woman and her four children, displaced from her village by factional fighting, seek U.N. help.

a better world. No one loses, and everyone gains by a shared universal sense of responsibility to this planet and all living things on it."[6] Similarly, the Aga Khan IV (b. 1936), the spiritual leader of a largely Indian Shi'ite Muslim sect, funded schools and clinics all over the world. The World Council of Churches, supported by diverse Protestant and Eastern Orthodox churches, encouraged interfaith cooperation and understanding, and several Catholic popes favored interfaith dialogue and denounced war and capital punishment.

World Politics Since 1989

Between 1989 and 1991 the Soviet bloc disintegrated and the communist regimes in eastern Europe and the USSR collapsed, ending the Cold War and the bipolar world it had defined (see Chronology: Global Politics Since 1989). Longtime State Department official George Kennan (1904–2004), the architect of the U.S. policy to contain communism in the 1940s, concluded that no country or person "won" the Cold War because it was fueled by misconceptions and nearly bankrupted both sides. Other nations, especially Japan and West Germany, both protected by U.S. military bases, had gained the most economically from the conflict by investing heavily in economic growth. As both U.S. and Soviet leaders deescalated tensions in the later 1980s, the United States became the sole superpower. By 2008 it spent as much on defense as all other countries combined and was the world's major supplier of arms. Yet some observers perceived a tripolar system in which the United States had to share political and economic leadership with western Europe and several Asian nations, especially China, Japan, and India.

U.S. as Sole Superpower

The first major post–Cold War challenge for the United States came from Iraq's brutal dictator, Saddam Hussein (1937–2006), whose army invaded and occupied Iraq's small, oil-rich neighbor, Kuwait, in 1990. Since the United States opposed the Islamic government of Iran, it had supported Saddam's military with weapons in the 1980s, when Iraq was fighting Iran. Now the United States organized an international coalition and, in 1991, quickly defeated the Iraqis, pushing them out of Kuwait. In the aftermath, U.S. president George H. W. Bush proclaimed a "new world order" led by the United States and based on American values, envisioning the United States as a world policeman.

New World Disorder

The end of the long, costly Cold War did not result in universal peace or the triumph of American political values. Instead, the 1990s saw a new world disorder. Ethnic and nationalist conflicts exploded in violence in Yugoslavia, eastern Europe, Sri Lanka, west Africa, and Rwanda, and states with weak or dysfunctional governments, such as Haiti, Liberia, Sierra Leone, Congo, and Somalia, experienced chronic fighting and civil war. In addition, rising tides of religious militancy or conflict between rival faiths complicated politics in countries such a s India, Indonesia, Algeria, Egypt,and Nigeria. In particular, militant Islam demonstrated its potency in Iran, Sudan, and Afghanistan and led some extremists to form terrorist groups to fight moderate Islamic regimes, Israel, and Western nations. By the early 2000s Islamic radicals posed a greater challenge in Southeast Asia and the Middle East than the declining communist movements. The ambitions of aggressive dictators, such as Iraq's Saddam Hussein, and the communist regime in North Korea, which limited contact with the outside world, also fostered regional tensions. Then in 2008 a severe global recession added to the problems as businesses closed, world trade declined, and national economies floundered. The new world order promise of a peaceful world moving, with U.S. support, toward democracy foundered on the shoals of proliferating regional, nationalist, religious, and ethnic conflicts that, combined with economic collapse, produced a context for violence.

CHRONOLOGY
Global Politics, Since 1999

1989–1991 Dismantling of Soviet bloc and empire

1997 Kyoto Protocol on climate change

2001 Al Qaeda attack on United States

2003 U.S. invasion of Iraq

2008–2009 Global recession

SECTION SUMMARY

- During the Cold War, the United States and the USSR struggled for world control, with the United States generally favoring democracy and capitalism but also seeking access to resources and foreign markets, and the USSR supporting emerging communist regimes and movements.
- Though the United States and the USSR never fought directly, they were involved in wars in other countries, such as Vietnam, Korea, and Afghanistan, in which millions died, and they intervened in countries such as Guatemala, Iran, Poland, Hungary, and Czechoslovakia.
- The United States and the USSR participated in a massive arms race, spending trillions of dollars on nuclear weapons, which led to widespread fear of mass destruction, though some argue that this fear helped prevent all-out war.
- The United Nations was formed with the goal of promoting world peace and human rights, and various agreements have been signed to ban biological weapons and land mines, to prevent global warming, and to facilitate an international justice system, though they have encountered opposition by the United States and some other industrial nations.
- When the Soviet Union collapsed, the United States was the sole superpower, with a military budget dwarfing that of other countries and dreams of a peaceful democratic world, but religious extremism and ethnic and nationalist conflicts have ensured continuing conflict.

Globalizing Economies, Underdevelopment, and Environmental Change

What were some of the main consequences of a globalizing world economy?

The world economy was increasingly characterized by **globalization**, a pattern in which economic, political, and cultural processes reach beyond national boundaries. This trend reduced barriers between countries, allowing for more collaboration, and turned the world into a more closely integrated whole through worldwide commercial markets, finance, telecommunications, and the exchange of ideas. However, globalization also generated a widening inequality of nations and negative environmental consequences from industrialization and economic growth, including ever-increasing pollution and a warming climate. In response to population growth, people expanded agriculture into semidesert areas and cut down rain forests, causing environmental deterioration.

globalization A pattern in which economic, political, and cultural processes reach beyond nation-state boundaries.

The Transnational Economy

A world economy that links distant societies has been developing over the past 2,500 years, but after World War II globalization rapidly spread market capitalism as well as flows of capital, goods, services, and people. The world's production of goods and services was 120 times higher in 2000 than it had been in 1500, and average personal income grew fourfold between 1900 and

Economic Growth

2000. As the interconnectedness between societies has increased, events occurring or decisions taken in one part of the world affect societies far away. Rising or falling prices on the Tokyo or New York stock exchanges quickly reverberate around the world, influencing stock markets elsewhere. Similarly, the decision by Western governments to sell supplies of stockpiled rubber, hence depressing world prices, affects the livelihood of rubber growers, and the businesses that supply them, in Malaysia, Sri Lanka, Brazil, and the Congo. Not all the transnational economic activity has been legal, especially the flow of narcotics. Heroin and cocaine sold in North America and Europe, creating millions of addicts, originates largely in Asia and Latin America and is smuggled by transnational criminal syndicates.

Changing World Economy

Americans have been the major proponent of globalization, arguing that open markets, investment, and trade foster prosperity. By 2000 the United States produced nearly a third of the world's goods and services; Japan, with the next largest economy, accounted for around a sixth. International observers described U.S. leadership metaphorically: when the United States sneezes, the rest of the world catches cold. However, economic growth does not necessarily improve the living conditions for all people; well-functioning governments, legal and political rights, and health and education services are also required. Moreover, critics charge that globalization promises riches it does not always deliver, distributing the benefits unequally. By the 1990s the United States and China were gaining the most from removing trade barriers and fostering competitive markets worldwide. Both sucked in investment capital, aggressively acquired natural resources from around the globe, and supplied diverse products to foreign markets. China surpassed Germany to become the world's third largest economy as Chinese factories turned out clothing, housewares, and other consumer goods. The Chinese also began investing in Africa, Latin America, and the Middle East and buying U.S.-based companies. However, not all Chinese benefited. China's less-efficient state-owned enterprises often closed down, while peasants protested as their farmland was bulldozed to build foreign-owned factories, private housing developments, and golf courses for affluent Chinese.

A few other nations, such as India, Ireland, Singapore, and South Korea, also capitalized on globalization, fostering economic growth and becoming centers of high technology. But not all countries enjoyed such success. By the 1990s Japan and some European nations struggled to compete in the globalizing economy, while many Asian, African, and Caribbean nations fell deeper into poverty. Many people in developing nations—Mexican corn growers, West African wheat growers, Pakistani textile workers—faced trade barriers and well-funded, technologically superior Western competitors. As U.N. Secretary General Kofi Annan **(KO-fee AN-uhn)**, a Ghanaian, put it in 2002: "Our challenge today is to make globalization an engine that lifts people out of hardship and misery, not a force that holds them down."[7]

Although experiencing occasional setbacks, the Western industrial nations and Japan have generally maintained a favorable position in the global economy. They control most of the capital, markets, and institutions of international finance, such as banks, and their corporations also own assets in other nations. For example, U.S. citizens control businesses, mines, and plantations in Latin America, Japanese operate factories in Southeast Asia, and the French maintain a large economic stake in West Africa. The capitalist systems in the industrialized nations have ranged from limited government interference, common in the United States, to the mix of free markets and welfare states in western Europe, to the closely linked government-business relationship in Japan and South Korea. These contrast with the economies in many former colonies where power holders, often closely tied to foreign or domestic business interests, preside over largely poor populations. Hence, in the Congo, corrupt leaders protect Belgian-owned and local corporations who fund them.

Newly Industrializing Nations

Some once-poor countries have used the transnational economy to their advantage, achieving spectacular growth. If revenues are not stolen by corrupt leaders, as has happened in Iraq and Nigeria, possession of oil can enhance national wealth. A few oil-rich nations, such as Kuwait and the United Arab Emirates, use oil revenues to improve their citizens' lives. Various Asian countries, much like Japan in the late 1800s, have combined market economies, cheap labor, and powerful governments to promote industrialization. By repressing opposition, they have ensured political stability and attracted foreign investment. These countries have favored export-oriented growth, producing consumer goods—clothing, toys, housewares—for sale abroad, especially in Europe and North America, and fostering high growth rates and the import of industrial jobs from other, often Western, countries. Beginning in the 1980s China, South Korea, Taiwan, Malaysia, Thailand, Singapore, and eventually Vietnam created the world's fastest-growing economies and considerable prosperity, their major cities boasting well-stocked malls, freeways, diverse restaurants, and luxury condominiums.

Often the growing middle class and labor leaders have demanded a larger voice in government and political liberalization. By the 1990s Indonesians, South Koreans, Taiwanese, and Thais had

replaced dictatorships with democratic governments. The Asian systems became development models by mixing capitalism, which creates wealth, with socialism, which can distribute wealth equitably. With this combination, the Asian economic resurgence seemed to have the potential to restore the leading role some Asian societies had enjoyed in the world economy for many centuries before 1800. But in the late 1990s the economies of many Asian nations crashed and only slowly rebounded, only to be damaged again in 2008–2009 as the U.S. economic crisis affected Asia and the rest of the world. Factories closed and revenues declined, causing massive unemployment and hardship. By later 2009 some Asian nations, including China and India, re-established strong growth.

Various institutions shaped the transnational economy, especially the international lending agencies formed by the Allies in 1944 to aid postwar reconstruction. The World Bank funded development projects such as dams and agricultural schemes, and the International Monetary Fund (IMF) regulated currency dealings and addressed financial problems. Many Asian, African, Caribbean, and Latin American nations did not earn enough income from selling natural resources to buy food and medicine, import luxuries, or finance projects such as building dams and improving ports. Hence, they took out loans from the IMF or the World Bank, closely linked to the United States. Some Latin American and African countries fell deeply in debt. Moreover, the IMF, which had the right to dictate economic policies to borrowing countries, favored Western investment and free markets at the expense of social services.

CHRONOLOGY
The Global Economy and New Technologies

1947 Formation of GATT

1947 Invention of transistor

1958 Invention of silicon microchips

1995 Formation of World Trade Organization

1997 Asian economic collapse

2008–2009 Global recession

Trade Agreements and Blocs

Trade agreements and trading blocs have also reflected an economic connectedness unprecedented in world history. Formed in 1947, the General Agreements on Trade and Tariffs (GATT) set general guidelines for world trade and rules for establishing tariffs and trade regulations (see Chronology: The Global Economy and New Technologies). The World Trade Organization (WTO), founded by 124 nations in 1995, marked a new phase in the postwar economic system. The WTO had stronger dispute-resolution capabilities than GATT. Regional trading blocs also formed. The European Common Market (now the European Union) eventually included most European nations. The major industrial nations also cooperated to manage the global economy. By the 1990s leading economic officials in the seven richest industrial countries met regularly as the G7 (Group of 7) to discuss common concerns, later joined by Russia to form the G8. But China, India, and other newly industrialized nations sought more input. Thanks to the 2008–2009 economic crisis and the need for concerted action on a world scale, by late 2009 the G8 leaders agreed to permanently expand the discussion to include 12 other countries with large economies, such as China, India, Brazil, Indonesia, South Korea, and Argentina. This new G20 grouping confirmed the changing world economic leadership and especially the key role of China.

multinational corporations Giant business enterprises that operate all over the world, gaining a leading role in the global marketplace.

Another development is the growth of giant business enterprises, known as **multinational corporations** because they operate all over the world, which have gained a leading role in the

AP/World Wide Photos

The Global Economy Cambodian Buddhist monks, following ancient traditions, collect their food from the devout in the capital city, Phnom Penh, while advertising for American cigarettes entices Cambodians into the global economy, despite government concerns about the health danger posed by tobacco products.

global marketplace. Some 300 to 400 companies, two-thirds of them U.S.-owned, dominate world production and trade. These are now the world's third largest economic force, with great influence on governments. The multinationals set the world price for various commodities, such as coffee, copper, or oil; can play one country off against another to get the best deal; and can switch manufacturing jobs from one country to another. Multinationals have also created millions of jobs in poor countries. Increasingly women provide the majority of the labor force in the global assembly lines of factories producing for export. Supporters argue that outsourcing—moving jobs from high-wage to low-wage countries—creates a middle class of managers and technicians and offers work to people with few other job prospects. Critics reply that most of these jobs pay low wages, require long hours, and offer little future. For example, the U.S.-based Nike Corporation, praised for creating needed jobs in Vietnam, is also criticized because the Vietnamese employees, mainly women, work in unhealthy conditions, face sexual harassment, and are fired if they complain.

The Spread of Industrialization

Industrial Growth

During the later twentieth century, industrialization spread to other parts of the world, especially to Asia and Latin America. Entrepreneurs or state agencies in countries such as China, India, South Korea, Brazil, and Mexico built textile mills, steel mills, and automobile plants, and Chinese textiles, Indian steel, and South Korean cars found markets around the world. Meanwhile, the U.S. share of world industrial production fell from 50 percent in 1950 to 30 percent in the 1980s; whereas Americans built over 75 percent of all cars in 1950, by the early 1990s they built less than 20 percent. Malaysians could now drive Volvos made in Sweden, Hyundais made in South Korea, Toyotas made in Japan, and Proton Sagas manufactured locally.

Third Industrial Revolution The creation of unprecedented scientific knowledge and new technologies.

Technological innovations spurred economic growth. The so-called **Third Industrial Revolution** created unprecedented scientific knowledge and new technologies that made the creations of the first and second Industrial Revolutions seem obsolete. Traditional smokestack industries such as steel mills were displaced by nuclear power, computers, automation, and robotry. The technological surge also brought rocketry, genetic engineering, silicon chips, and lasers. Space technology produced the first manned trips to the moon and unmanned crafts exploring the solar system. In 2005 a probe from one of these crafts landed on Saturn's large, mysterious moon, Titan, sending back photographs of the surface. More powerful telescopes increased knowledge of the solar system and the universe, including the discovery of several hundred planets circling other stars. The British poet Archibald MacLeish observed that the astronauts on the space capsules circling the planet did not perceive national boundaries or international rivalries, but only oceans and lands containing people with a common planetary home: "To see the Earth as we now see it, small and blue and beautiful in that eternal silence [of space] where it floats, is to see ourselves as rulers on the Earth together."[8]

Green Revolution Increased agricultural output through the use of new high-yield seeds and mechanized farming.

The Third Industrial Revolution has had potentially dramatic consequences for people around the world. Part of it, the **Green Revolution**, has fostered increased agricultural output through the use of new high-yield seeds and mechanized farming. Farmers able to afford these innovations can shorten the growing season, thus raising more crops a year. Between 1965 and 1978, one village in India increased its food output by 300 percent. But not all farmers benefited. In countries such as India, the Philippines, and Mexico, the Green Revolution, which requires more capital for seeds and machines but fewer people to work the land, has often harmed poor peasants who could not afford the investment. And in many industries, such as automobile manufacturing, automation has taken over production, allowing companies to fire workers.

Globalizing Industry

Industry also became globalized. By the 1990s over two hundred industrial parks, occupied largely by foreign-owned factories paying low taxes and wages, existed around the world. For example, factories in northern Mexico, usually U.S.-owned, made goods largely for the U.S. market and employed nearly half a million workers, mainly women. The service and information exchange industries also grew. More people worked in service enterprises, such as fast-food restaurants, while others established transnational computer networks, such as AOL and Google, to help people use the Internet for communication and knowledge acquisition. Responding to these trends, India graduated each year thousands of people fluent in English and skilled in computer technology, becoming a world center for offshore information and technical services. Increasingly consumers calling North American companies for computer technical support, product information, or billing questions reached Indians working in cubicles in cities such as Bangalore and Bombay (Mumbai).

Yet, industrialization and its globalization have come with risks. Hoping to better compete, businesses have moved factories to countries with low wages and costs. Some Western and Japanese businesses have shifted operations to South Korea or Taiwan, where the average worker earns in a month what a U.S. or German worker earns in a week or ten days, yet produces as much. Others have estab-

lished operations in Asian, African, Latin American, or eastern European nations where workers earn even less. In 1990 the U.S. clothing maker Levi Strauss closed its plant in San Antonio, Texas; laid off 1,150 workers, most of them Mexican American women; and relocated the operation to Costa Rica. Viola Casares, one of the fired workers, expressed the despair: "As long as I live I'll never forget how the white man in the suit said they had to shut us down to stay competitive."[9] Levi Strauss closed fifty-eight U.S. plants with over 10,000 workers while shifting half of its production overseas.

Underdevelopment and Development

Growing Rich–Poor Gap

Uneven economic growth has contributed to a growing gap between rich nations and poor undeveloped nations. The gap was already wide in 1945, since colonialism seldom raised people's general living standards. As a Guyanese historian concluded, "the vast majority of Africans went into colonialism with a hoe and came out with a hoe."[10] But fluctuation in the world economy has also caused hardships. Many Asian, African, and Latin American economies grew rapidly in the 1950s and 1960s, when the world economy boomed. Then in the 1970s and 1980s, as the world economy soured and the world prices for many exports collapsed, the growth rates of these economies declined. Then the world economy revived for a few years, only to experience a dramatic downturn in the later 1990s and early 2000s. In 2008–2009 the world economy went into the worst crisis since the Great Depression, affecting many nations severely, but some Asian and European countries began to recover in later 2009.

Moreover, economic growth has not always fostered development that benefits the majority of the population. With globalization, rich countries encourage other nations to open their economies to foreign investment. Some Asian nations have prospered from this investment, building schools, hospitals, and highways, but elsewhere Western investment often has done little to foster locally owned businesses. In Nigeria, for example, British-owned enterprises have controlled banking, importing, and exporting, and foreign investment has gone mainly into cash crops and oil production, controlled largely by Western companies. Outraged that they gain little from the polluting oil wells around them, local people in Nigeria's main oil-producing region have sabotaged operations and kidnapped foreign oil workers. Some resorted to armed insurgency against government targets. Furthermore, foreign investment and aid has often been siphoned off to line the pockets of corrupt leaders, bureaucrats, and military officers.

Stephanie Maze/Woodfin Camp & Associates

Rich and Poor in Brazil The stark contrast between the wealthy and the poor in many nations can be seen in the Brazilian city of Rio de Janeiro. Seeking jobs in expanding industries, millions of migrants flock to the city, building shantytown slums and squatter settlements in view of luxury high-rise apartment and office buildings.

Scholars debate how poor countries can better profit from their connections to the world economy and spur local efforts at development. One of the most influential economists, the Indian Amartya Sen (b. 1933), had helped run evening schools for illiterate rural children as a youth. This experience laid a foundation for his studies of global poverty, for which he won the Nobel Prize in economics in 1998. Sen believes that the main challenges are how to use trade and technology to help the poorest people by addressing famine, poverty, and social and gender inequality. Influenced by his first wife, a prominent Indian writer and political activist, Sen focused on women in development. Sen argues that women's literacy and employment are the best predictors of both child survival and fertility rate reduction, prerequisites for development in poor villages. His views on poverty and gender inequality influenced the United Nations when, in 2000, they developed an agenda to address the world's pressing problems by 2020 (see Witness to the Past: An Agenda for the New Millennium). However, without outside financial support, few poor countries have sufficient resources to seriously combat widespread poverty or promote women's empowerment.

While some nations have become richer, others have become poorer. Most poor nations have suffered from some combination of rapid population growth, high unemployment, illiteracy, hunger, disease, corrupt or ineffective governments, and reliance on only a few exports. By the 1990s the richest fifth of the world's people received 80 percent of the total income

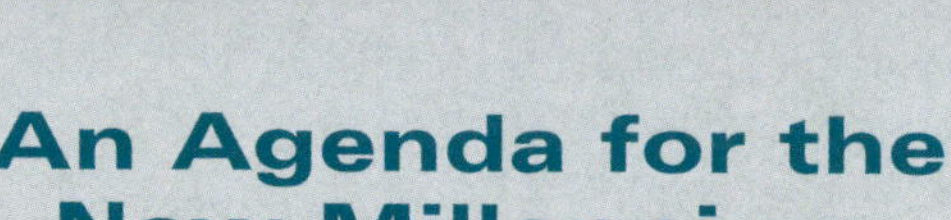

An Agenda for the New Millennium

In 2000 the United Nations called together the 188 member states for a summit at its headquarters in New York City to discuss the issues facing the world during the new millennium. In the following document, distributed before the summit, the United Nations secretary general, Kofi Annan of Ghana (GAH-nuh), laid out his vision for the organization and the challenges it faced in a world that had changed dramatically since the organization's formation over five decades earlier.

If one word encapsulates the changes we are living through, it is "globalization." We live in a world that is interconnected as never before—one in which groups and individuals interact more and more directly across State frontiers. . . . This has its dangers, of course. Crime, narcotics, terrorism, disease, weapons—all these move back and forth faster, and in greater numbers, than in the past. People feel threatened by events far away. But the benefits of globalization are obvious too: faster growth, higher living standards, and new opportunities—not only for individuals but also for better understanding between nations, and for common action.

One problem is that, at present, these opportunities are far from equally distributed. How can we say that the half of the human race which has yet to make or receive a phone call, let alone use a computer, is taking part in globalization? We cannot, without insulting their poverty. A second problem is that, even where the global market does reach, it is not yet underpinned by rules based on shared social objectives. In the absence of such rules, globalization makes many people feel they are at the mercy of unpredictable forces. So, . . . the overarching challenge of our times is to make globalization mean more than bigger markets. To make a success of this great upheaval we must learn how to govern better, and . . . how to govern together. . . . We need to get [our nations] working together on global issues—all pulling their weight and all having their say.

What are these global issues? . . . First, freedom from want. How can we call human beings free and equal in dignity when over a billion of them are struggling to survive on less than one dollar a day, without safe drinking water, and when half of all humanity lacks adequate sanitation? Some of us are worrying about whether the stock market will crash, or struggling to master our latest computer, while more than half our fellow men and women have much more basic worries, such as where their children's next meal is coming from. . . . I believe we can halve the population of people living in extreme poverty; ensure that all children—girls and boys alike, particularly the girls—receive a full primary education; and . . . transform the lives of one hundred million slum dwellers around the world.

The second main [issue] is freedom from fear. Wars between States are mercifully less frequent than they used to be. But in the last decade internal wars have claimed more than five million lives, and driven many times that number of people from their homes. . . . We must do more to prevent conflicts from happening. Most conflicts happen in poor countries, especially those which are badly governed or where power and wealth are very unfairly distributed between ethnic or religious groups. So the best way to prevent conflict is to promote [fair representation of all groups in government], human rights, and broad-based economic development.

The third [issue] is . . . the freedom of future generations to sustain their lives on this planet. Even now, many of us have not understood how seriously that freedom is threatened. We are plundering our children's heritage to pay for our present unsustainable practices. We must stop. We must reduce emissions of . . . "greenhouse gases," to put a stop to global warming. . . . We must face the implications of a steadily shrinking surface of cultivable land, at a time when every year brings many millions of new mouths to feed. . . . We must preserve our forests, fisheries, and the diversity of living species, all of which are close to collapsing under the pressure of human consumption and destruction. . . . We need a new ethic of stewardship to encourage environment-friendly practices. . . . Above all we need to remember the old African wisdom which I learned as a child—that the earth is not ours. It is a treasure we hold in trust for our descendants.

THINKING ABOUT THE READING

1. What does Annan see as the major global issues of the new millennium?
2. How are the problems he outlined connected to each other?

Source: United Nations, *The Millennium Report* (*http://www.un.org/millennium/sg/report/state.htm*). Reprinted with permission of the United Nations.

while the poorest fifth earned less than 2 percent. For example, in Guatemala, 90 percent of people lived below the official poverty line, and nearly half had no access to health care, indoor plumbing, piped water, or formal education. A fifth of the world's people earned less than $1 per day. By 2000 the world's three richest persons owned more assets than the forty-eight poorest nations together, and 358 billionaires had a combined net worth equal to that of the bottom 45 percent of the world's population combined. The United Nations estimated that one billion people suffered from hunger in 2009, a problem made worse by the global recession. Furthermore, despite preaching the benefits of free trade, rich nations have often blocked or restricted food and fiber exports from poor nations into their own markets while heavily subsidizing their own farmers. Hence, wheat farmers in Mali, however industrious, cannot compete with French or U.S. wheat farmers, who can sell their crops at much lower prices because of the financial support from their governments.

Yet, the nations outside of Europe and North America can boast of achievements. Between 1960 and 2000 they reduced infant mortality by half and doubled adult literacy rates. China, Sri Lanka, Malaysia, and Tanzania have been particularly successful in providing social services, such as schools and clinics, to rural areas. Various countries have developed their own locally based development strategies. In sub-Saharan Africa, for instance, some countries, such as Burkina Faso (buhr-KEE-nuh FAH-so) and Niger (nee-jer), have moved away from big, expensive prestige projects—such as building large dams to supply hydroelectric power—to small-scale labor-intensive projects that aid the environment, such as tree-planting campaigns, while local cooperative banks have provided credit to farmers. However, severe drought can still cause widespread starvation.

Improving Lives

Women and their children have faced the harshest problems. Economic change has not only undermined the handicrafts that once provided incomes for women, but it has also fragmented families: many men have to find work in other districts or countries, leaving their wives to support and raise the children. In Africa, men migrate each year from Burkina Faso to the Ivory Coast's cocoa plantations and logging camps, and from Mozambique to South African mines. Meanwhile, women leave India, Sri Lanka, and the Philippines to work as domestic servants in the Persian Gulf states and Saudi Arabia, some facing sexual harassment or cruel employers. Asian and Latin American women work in homes and sweatshops in North America and Europe.

Economic Change and Gender Relations

Development often leaves women behind because of their inferior social status and relative invisibility in national economic statistics. For example, women often face social customs that accord them little influence and, in case of divorce, award their children to the father. An Indian folk song expressed the bitterness of village women who, after marriage, have no claim on their birth family's property: "To my brother belong your green fields, O father, while I am banished afar."[11] While women do 60 percent of the world's work and produce 50 to 75 percent of the world's food, they own only 1 percent of the world's property and earn 10 percent of the world's income. Most of poor women's labor—food preparation, cleaning, child rearing—is unpaid, done at home, and often demanding. In Senegal a typical rural woman, married at a young age, gets up at 5 A.M. to pound millet, the staple food, for an hour. She then walks a few hundred yards or perhaps several miles to get water from a well, makes breakfast for the family, goes to the village shop, makes the family lunch, takes food to family members working in the fields, does laundry, makes supper, and then pounds millet again before bed. Some women combine all this with farm work.

Some nations help women and children through bottom-up policies relying on grassroots action. The Grameen (GRAH-mean) Bank in Bangladesh, which promotes a philosophy of self-help, provides an outstanding model. After meeting a woman matmaker who earned only four cents a day, the economist Muhammad Yunus (b. 1940) concluded that conventional economics ignored the poverty and struggles occurring in his nation's villages. Learning that few banks made loans to the poor, in 1983 Yunus opened the Grameen Bank, which makes loans under $100 on cheap terms to peasants, especially women, for buying the tools they needed to earn a living. A borrower might buy a cell phone that villagers could use to make business or personal calls, paying the owner for each call, or purchase bamboo to make chairs. Less than 2 percent of borrowers defaulted. The women earning an income now enjoyed higher social status and many began using contraceptives, helping lower the Bangladesh birthrate from 3 to 2 percent a year. For his vision and efforts, Muhammad Yunus won the Nobel Peace Prize in 2006.

Population, Urbanization, and Environmental Change

Rapid population growth and overcrowded cities have become manifestations of global imbalance. Since 1945 the world's population has grown faster than ever before in history (see Map 26.2). Two thousand years ago the earth had between 125 and 250 million people; it took roughly 10,000 generations for the world to reach 1 billion in 1830. At the end of World War II the population had risen to 2.5 billion, and by 2008 it had more than doubled to 6.7 billion. Some experts talked of a "population bomb" overwhelming the world's water, food sources, forests, and minerals and a population of perhaps 12 billion by 2100, which the earth's resources could not support. But fertility rates began dropping in much of the world, especially in industrialized nations, thanks to the widespread use of artificial birth control, such as contraceptive pills, better health care, and larger numbers of women entering the paid work force. By 1990 over half of the world's couples practiced some form of contraception to prevent births. As a result, demographers now envision a world population of some 9 billion by 2050, which will still impose a heavy burden on food supplies and services and intensify social, economic, and environmental problems. For example, overpopulation, and the ensuing competition for limited resources, probably contributed to violence in crowded countries such as Ethiopia,

Rising Population

Map 26.2 World Population Growth
This map shows dramatically which nations have the largest populations: China, India, the United States, Indonesia, and Brazil. It also shows which regions experience the most rapid population growth: Africa, South Asia, and Central America.

Interactive Map

Rwanda, and El Salvador. Several British studies in 2009 predicted a worldwide 50 percent rise in demand for food, 30 percent for water, and 50 percent for energy by 2030.

Population growth has been more rapid in some regions. Most of it has occurred in Asia, Africa, and Latin America. By 2000, China and India had the largest populations, with around a billion people each. While Asia has continued, as it has for millennia, to house at least 60 percent of humanity, Europe's share of population fell from a quarter in 1900 to an eighth. Because of their falling birthrates, various European nations, Russia, China, and Japan have declining and aging populations, which puts a growing burden on those of working age to produce more wealth to support elderly populations. Italy and Spain, both predominantly Roman Catholic nations that once had high birthrates, now have the world's lowest fertility rates. North American birthrates have also dropped, but the decline has been offset by immigration.

Nonetheless, the Western nations, Japan, and recently China, enjoying high rates of resource consumption, including fossil fuels, have done more harm to the environment than countries with large populations but low consumption rates. Owing to heavy use of energy and metals-dependent innovations—air conditioners, central heating systems, gasoline-powered vehicles, refrigerators—the average American or Canadian consumes some twenty times, and the average Australian, German, or Japanese ten to fifteen times, the resources of the average Pakistani or Peruvian.

Population Growth and Poverty

Population growth has diminished the possibility for economic development in overcrowded nations already struggling with a scarcity of food, health care, housing, and education. In countries such as the Philippines, Pakistan, and Uganda, the population of school-age children has expanded faster than the resources needed to build new schools and hire teachers. Many countries cannot afford compulsory education. By 2000, over 1 billion people around the world were desperately poor and unable to obtain basic essentials, such as adequate food. The Green Revolution, sparking dramatic increases in food production, averted mass famine, but by the 1990s harvests reached a plateau, producing only small food increases or sometimes even decreases in food supplies. Furthermore, fish catches have declined steeply, partly because of overfishing by Western and Japanese fleets using high-technology equipment. Feeding the new mouths has also required massive clearing of forests for new cropland.

For all these reasons, twentieth-century advances in health and welfare could be reversed unless nations find ways to slow population growth and reduce poverty. Predominantly Islamic and Roman Catholic nations often discourage birth control and outlaw abortion as contrary to their religious beliefs. But other nations have pursued vigorous population control programs, increasing their economic potential. Thailand cut its birthrate by a fifth between 1980 and 2000. Using harsher means, overcrowded China dramatically reduced fertility by mandating only one child per family; couples who flouted the laws faced stiff fines or, sometimes, forced abortions. The most successful campaigns have targeted women by giving them better education, health care, and a sense of dignity independent of their roles as mothers. In the past, many parents viewed having many children as insurance for their old age; for example, in Mali the average woman had seven children, of which four survived to adulthood. Economic development, including better health care to lower infant mortality, often changed these attitudes. Increasing affluence also reduces birthrates. Thus, as women in Bangladesh opened small businesses, they had fewer children.

Migration to Cities

Rural folk have often had to abandon the livelihoods that had sustained their ancestors, usually ending up in crowded cities—Jakarta in Indonesia, Calcutta in India, Cairo in Egypt, Mexico City—where they often live in shantytowns or on the sidewalks. Whereas cities held some 10 percent of the world population in 1900, they held 50 percent in 2000. Cairo grew from 900,000 in 1897 to 2.8 million in 1947 and 13 million in 1995. In 1950 Western cities, headed by New York, accounted for most of the world's ten largest metropolitan areas; fifty years later Asian and Latin American cities dominated the list. Tokyo, with 28 million people, was followed by Mexico City, Bombay (India), São Paulo (Brazil), and Shanghai (China). Huge traffic jams make driving in Bangkok, Tokyo, Mexico City, and Lagos a nightmare. Struggling to provide needed services, cities usually dump raw sewage into bays and rivers. Today cities are responsible for 75 percent of the world's resource consumption and produce 75 percent of its trash. City life has also reshaped traditional ways. In a pop song from Peru, a boy who migrated to Lima complained that his girlfriend had abandoned rural values: "You came as a country girl. Now you are in Lima you comb your hair in a city way. You even say, 'I'm going to dance the twist' [a popular dance from the United States]."[12]

Environmental Challenges

Industrialization, population growth, and urbanization have posed unprecedented environmental challenges and increased competition for limited resources such as oil, timber, and tin while contributing to a warmer, drier global climate. Over the twentieth century societies increased their industrial output twentyfold and their energy use fourteenfold. Industrialized nations as well as once-poor nations that became richer, such as China, South Korea, and Malaysia, paid the cost in noxious air, toxic waste, stripped forests, water pollution, and hotter climates. Some environmental disasters

WANGARI MAATHAI, KENYAN ENVIRONMENTAL ACTIVIST

Wangari Maathai (wahn-GAHR-ee muh-THIGH), who won the 2004 Nobel Peace Prize for her environmental activism, was born in 1940 and grew up in Nyeri, a small village in Kenya, East Africa. As a young girl, Wangari fetched water from a small stream. She grew fascinated by the creatures living in the stream and loved the lush trees and shrubs around her village. But over the years the stream dried up, silt choked nearby rivers, and the once green land grew barren. She lamented the assault on nature. Girls in rural Kenya in the 1940s and 1950s commonly spent their youth preparing for marriage and children. But a brother convinced Wangari's parents to send the inquisitive girl to the primary school he attended.

After graduating from a Roman Catholic high school, Wangari was awarded a scholarship to study in the United States, where she earned a B.A. in biology from a small Kansas college in 1964 and then completed an M.A. at the University of Pittsburgh in 1966. She credited her U.S. experience, including her observations of anti–Vietnam War protests, with encouraging her interest in democracy and free speech. Returning home, she earned a Ph.D. at Nairobi University in 1971, the first East African woman to achieve that degree, and then joined the faculty to teach biological sciences. She became a dean and joined a local organization that coordinated United Nations environmental programs.

Throughout her life Wangari has faced and overcome gender barriers, including in her marriage. Wangari married Mwangi Maathai and had three children, but their relationship soured and they divorced after he was elected to parliament in 1974. She attributed the breakup to gender prejudice:

AP/World Wide Photos

Wangari Maathai Wangari Maathai, winner of the 2004 Nobel Prize for peace, plants a tree outside the United Nations headquarters in New York in 2005. Earlier that day she challenged world leaders to dirty their hands by planting trees and working to stop the destruction of forests worldwide.

have affected large populations. In 1957 an explosion in a Russian nuclear waste dump killed some 10,000 people, contaminated 150 square miles of land, and forced the evacuation of 270,000 people. A massive die-off among varieties of frogs and some ocean species, a catastrophe perhaps due to pollution and ecological instability, suggested that diverse environments are increasingly dangerous to life. Sea turtle populations decreased drastically in regions as far apart as Southeast Asia, the Persian Gulf, and Central America.

Deforestation

Deforestation provides one sign of environmental destruction. In the twentieth century half of the world's rain forests were cut down, as commercial loggers obtained wood for housing, farmers converted forests into farms, and poor people collected firewood. This destruction continues at a furious pace today; an area larger than Hungary is cleared each year. Between 1975 and 2000 a quarter of the Central American rain forest was turned into grasslands, where beef cattle, raised chiefly to supply North American fast-food restaurants, now graze. Most of the world's tropical rain forest survives in only three nations: Brazil, Congo, and Indonesia. In tropical regions clearing the land exposes the thin topsoil to leaching of the nutrients by rains, so that often the cleared land can be farmed only for a few years before it becomes unusable desert. Deforestation has had enormous long-term consequences, ranging from decreasing rainfall to loss of valuable pharmaceuticals that might cure cancer or other illnesses. Millions of species of plants and animals have disappeared in recent decades, and by 2000 more than 11,000 species of plants and animals were threatened with extinction. A quarter to half of all current species could disappear by 2100. The destruction of forests, which absorb the carbon dioxide that heats up the atmosphere, has contributed, along with carbon dioxide–producing fossil fuels and industrial pollution, to the accelerating global warming. Scientists worry that this will raise ocean levels as glaciers and polar ice melts, flooding lowlands, river deltas, and small islands, ruin good farmland as drought increases, and make tropical regions unlivable as temperatures rise.

"I think my activism may have contributed to my being perceived as an [un]conventional [woman]. And that puts pressure on the man you live with, because he is then perceived as if he is not controlling you properly."

To stop the spread of desert in Kenya by planting trees, the dogged Wangari founded the Greenbelt Movement on Earth Day, 1977. She got the idea for the movement from talking to women when she served on the National Council of Women. Women told her they needed clean drinking water, nutritious food, and energy, and she realized trees could provide for all these needs: they stop soil erosion, help water conservation, bear fruit, provide fuel and building materials, offer shade, and also enhance the beauty of the landscape. Over 10,000 Kenyans, largely women, became involved, planting and nurturing more than 30 million trees. For each tree planted, the members earned a small income. The movement showed Kenyans that the health of their forests and rivers mattered for both their immediate well-being and their future.

Realizing that logging contracts enriched leaders of corrupt governments, including Kenya's repressive regime, Wangari began to see the link between environmental health and good governance. As a result, the Greenbelt Movement launched programs of civic education, linking human rights, ecology, and individual activism and helping thousands of women gain more control of their lives. Women took on local leadership roles, running tree nurseries and planning community-based projects. Thanks to the movement, she said, "women have become aware that planting trees or fighting to save forests from being chopped down is part of a larger mission to create a society that respects democracy, the rule of law, human rights, and the rights of women."

Wangari and her campaign to empower and educate rural women had many critics in Kenya, including the country's dictatorial president. She was threatened by violence, harassed, sometimes severely beaten, arrested over a dozen times, and had her public appearances broken up by police. When she led protests against the building of a 62-story tower that would destroy much of Nairobi's main public park in the mid-1970s, the police killed seven of her associates. Still, she continued to protest illegal forest clearing and the Kenya government's holding of political prisoners. Wangari's efforts inspired similar Greenbelt movements in the United States, Haiti, and over thirty other African countries, and she became an international environmental spokesperson. In 2002, during the first fair elections in years, Wangari ran for the Kenyan parliament as a Green Party member and gained election by a huge majority. In 2003 a reformist president appointed her to his cabinet as an Assistant Minister for Environment, Natural Resources, and Wildlife. In awarding her the Noble Peace Prize, the Nobel committee praised Wangari for taking a comprehensive "approach to sustainable development that embraces democracy, human relations, and women's rights," saying that she "thinks globally and acts locally." She celebrated winning the Noble Prize by planting a tree on the slopes of Mount Kenya, near her childhood home, and recommitting herself to the struggle for a better world.

THINKING ABOUT THE PROFILE

1. How did Wangari's activities help Kenyan women?
2. How did Wangari's efforts to protect the environment also foster change in the political and social realms?

Note: Quotations from Friends of the Greenbelt Movement North America website (*http://gbmna.org/a.php?id*).

desertification The transformation by which productive land is transformed into mostly useless desert.

Desertification, the transformation of once productive land into useless desert, has increased with government, market, and population pressure to expand agriculture onto marginal land. During the past half century in Africa, some 20,000 square miles of land became desert every year. To combat the resulting farming failures, Africans used more pesticides, fertilizers, and irrigation, but these often have negative consequences. Drier climates diminish water supplies. One of Africa's largest lakes, Lake Chad, has lost 90 percent of its water since 1975. Deforestation and desertification also undermine farming by causing soil erosion, since, with less vegetation to absorb water, rains wash away fertile topsoil and cause severe flooding. Drought has become a regular reality in Africa, forcing millions to become refugees in other lands. With less rain to feed it, the Niger River in West Africa, once the location of great trading cities, no longer supports farming on a level of five centuries ago. The problems are not confined to Africa. In Nepal, farmers have stripped the once-lush Himalayan mountainsides for wood. The rain has then washed unimpeded down the slopes into the rivers, causing, along with melting Himalayan glaciers, ever more destructive floods downstream in India and Bangladesh, while reducing fresh water supplies in the region.

Environmental Movements

Movements to counter environmental decay have emerged. Some, such as the Sierra Club in the United States and the Malaysian Nature Society, appeal chiefly to middle-class people. Others, such as the Chipko tree protection movement in India and the Greenbelt movement in Kenya, bring middle-class urbanites and rural peasants together in a common cause. In 2004 the Greenbelt leader and global environmental activist, Wangari Maathai, won the Noble Peace Prize (see Profile: Wangari Maathai, Kenyan Environmental Activist). The United Nations established an environmental program that issues regular reports warning that environmental destruction, combined with poverty and population growth, threatens the long-term health of the planet and its people.

SECTION SUMMARY

- Globalization has boosted world economies and has reaped great rewards for countries such as the United States and China, but it has not always benefited the lives of poor people and has also led to continued foreign domination of some groups and nations by others.
- The World Bank and the International Monetary Fund have lent money to developing nations but sometimes dictate economic policies to borrowers, while multinational corporations have become so large that they exert great influence over governments and set the world prices for some commodities.
- Industrialization has spread throughout Asia and Latin America, the Third Industrial Revolution has created powerful new technologies, the Green Revolution has allowed for increased agricultural production, and the service and information industries have grown rapidly; but some globalization practices, such as outsourcing jobs to countries with cheaper labor, have produced hardships.
- Despite worldwide economic growth, some countries remain underdeveloped and the gap between the wealthiest and poorest people is striking; however, the developing world has made great improvements in infant mortality and adult literacy.
- Women have faced great problems in the modern economy as they have been drastically underpaid for their contributions, but grassroots programs such as the Grameen Bank have offered some increased economic opportunity.
- Over the past fifty years, the world population has exploded, especially in Asia, Africa, and Latin America, prompting fears that it will eventually outstrip available resources; while in more developed countries, fertility rates have dropped and populations have grown older.
- Industrialization and population growth have led to increased pollution and deforestation, which have led to massive extinction of plant and animal species, global warming, and the rise of environmental groups.

NEW GLOBAL NETWORKS AND THEIR CONSEQUENCES

How did growing networks linking societies influence social, political, and economic life?

global village An interconnected world community in which all people, regardless of their nationality, share a common fate.

During the late twentieth century the world became connected in unprecedented ways, leading to talk of a "spaceship earth" or a **global village**, an interconnected world community in which all people, regardless of nationality, share a common fate. A study of the interconnectedness contended that "the boundaries of the 'global village' are fluid, the inhabitants are highly mobile. Each street has its own problems, but each problem impinges increasingly on the population as a whole. The 'tyranny of distance' has been overcome; isolation has been eliminated."[13] Globalization has reshaped politics and cultures, fostering the movement of people, diseases, cultures, and religions. Increasingly the world is marked by both unity and diversity, common influences mixing with local traditions.

The Global Spread of Migrants, Refugees, and Disease

Population Movement

Today, many people live in nations filled with immigrants and their descendants from the four corners of the globe. Forty percent of Australians are immigrants or the children of immigrants. Thirty million people moved to labor-short western Europe between 1945 and 1975, chiefly from North Africa, West Africa, Turkey, South Asia, and the Caribbean. Similarly, 4 million Mexicans legally entered the United States, many filling low-wage jobs. Immigrants rapidly transformed cities such as Vancouver, Los Angeles, Sydney, and Paris into internationalized hubs of world culture and commerce. The many educated people who have moved to Western nations constitute a "brain drain" from poor countries. For example, doctors from India and nurses from the Philippines have played key roles in North American health care. Cosmopolitanism—a blending of peoples and cultures—flavors cities closely linked to the world economy, such as Hong Kong, Singapore, São Paulo (POU-lo), London, Dubai, and New York.

Immigrants often trigger tensions and debates as local people feel threatened by the newcomers and resent their continuing attachment to their own languages and traditions. While the globalization of trade and jobs dissolves economic boundaries, governments increasingly impose tighter border controls to discourage illegal immigration. For example, the United States has devoted more resources to patrolling the long border with Mexico, even building a high fence hundreds of miles long, but has been unable to stop the flow of Latin Americans flocking north.

The world contains over 100 million voluntary migrants to foreign countries, the great majority moving for economic rather than political reasons. Many migrants—some from impoverished regions such as Central America and South Asia, others from more prosperous nations such as South Korea and Taiwan—have sought better economic opportunities in the industrialized West. Small Indian- and Pakistani-run sundry goods and grocery stores, known as corner shops, have become a fixture in British cities. Millions of Asians and Africans have moved to the Middle East seeking work. Filipinos are an especially mobile people, migrating for short periods to other Southeast Asian nations and the Middle East and more permanently to North America. Some 8 million Filipinos now live abroad. Moving to a faraway, alien society is often traumatic. A poem by a Moroccan woman whose husband worked in Europe and rarely returned home captured her distress: "Germany, Belgium, France and Netherlands, Where are you situated? I have never seen your countries, I do not speak your language. I am afraid my love forgets me in your paradise. I ask you, give him back to me."[14]

Political turbulence, wars, genocides, government repression, and famine have also created some 20 million refugees. Desperate people have fled nations engulfed in political violence, such as Sudan, Guatemala, Afghanistan, Somalia, and Cambodia, and drought-plagued states such as Ethiopia and Mali. Over 2 million African Muslims from the Darfur region of Sudan fled genocidal attacks by Arab militias for refuge in Chad, an equally impoverished nation. Cubans, Chinese, Laotians **(lao-OH-shuhnz)**, and Vietnamese have fled communist-run states that restricted their freedoms. Others, such as Haitians, Chileans, Iranians, and Congolese, have escaped brutal rightwing dictatorships or corrupt despotisms. Millions of refugees have remained for decades, even generations, in squalid refugee camps, often fed and housed by international aid organizations. Many Palestinians who fled conflict in Israel have lived in refugee camps in Egypt, Jordan, and Lebanon for over six decades. Many refugees have nurtured resentments against the governments whose policies they escaped from or who forced them out, and citizens in countries offering refuge have often resented the refugees. Moreover, by the 1990s many nations, especially in Europe, became more cautious in granting political asylum.

Spreading Diseases

Diseases traveling the routes of trade and migration have produced major pandemics, or massive disease outbreaks, throughout history. Today, although modern medicine has eliminated diseases that had long plagued humanity, such as smallpox, leprosy, and polio, other diseases, such as cholera and malaria, still bedevil people with little access to health care. Cholera, a bacterial disease that easily crosses borders, still kills several thousand people a year in poor countries, and malaria, spread by mosquitoes, debilitates millions of people in tropical regions. In the early twenty-first century, experts worried about a possible global spread of several viral diseases, perhaps killing millions of people, that passed from birds, poultry, and pigs to humans. Both United Nations agencies and private organizations have worked to reduce health threats and treat victims. But the travel of migrants, tourists, business people, armies, truck drivers, sailors, and others continues to spread diseases.

The most deadly contemporary scourge affecting nations rich and poor, autoimmune deficiency syndrome (AIDS), caused by a virus known as HIV, is partly spread through the increased trade and travel associated with globalization. The disease spreads through sexual contact, needle sharing by drug addicts, and selling or receiving blood. Long-distance truck drivers who visit prostitutes along their routes spread the infection, especially in Africa and India. By 2005 some 42 million people around the world were infected with either HIV or AIDS, and 3.1 million died annually, a fifth of them children and one-third of them adult women, infected by husbands or lovers, leaving millions of orphans. As much as 30 percent of the adult population of some African nations was HIV positive. The disease is less catastrophic in richer countries. Only 0.2 percent of Americans were infected, and the rate was even lower in Europe. Although the pandemic undermines economic development in Africa and parts of Asia, only a few African and Asian governments have mounted education campaigns to convince people to take precautions or to seek treatment. Treating AIDS patients stresses health care resources, and AIDS victims are often rejected by their families and communities, dying alone and neglected by society.

Cultures and Religions Across Borders

Popular Cultures

The spread of cultural products and religions across national borders and the creative mixing of these with local traditions have been hallmarks of the modern world. Popular culture, commonly produced for commercial purposes and spread by the mass media, such as radio, television, and films, has become a part of everyday life for billions of people. In recent decades, Western influences have been pervasive, although often superficial. Western videos, pop music recordings, jeans, and shopping malls have attracted some youth in Asia, Africa, and Latin America, but their influence on the broader society, especially in the rural areas, is often more limited. No common world culture has emerged, and Western technologies sometimes serve local needs. India developed the world's largest film industry, producing some 1,000 films a year by 2002, three times more films than the next largest producers, the United States and Japan. And cheap, often pirated, audio cassettes in the 1970s, videocassettes in the 1980s, and DVDs in the 1990s enabled even many more people to enjoy music and films while also enabling political or religious groups to spread their messages. Modern media have reshaped people's lives, especially in cities. One observer in the 1990s noted the global popularity of television:

> *Take a walk down any street, in any city or village, as the twilight fades and the darkness comes. Whether you are in London or Tokyo, Cairo or New York, Buenos Aires or Singapore, a small blue light will flicker at you from the unshuttered windows. These lights are the tiny knots in the seamless web of modern media.*[15]

Popular Musics

Popular musics reflect the mixing of cultures and the increasing role of the mass media. Some popular styles, such as American jazz and Brazilian samba, emerged well before World War II, but most appeared after 1945. Rock, jazz, and rap, all African American forms with African roots, have found audiences all over the world. Vaclav Havel **(VAH-slav HAH-vel)**, the leader of the movement that overthrew Czech communism, credited the songs of the U.S. rock musician Frank Zappa with inspiring him to become an activist. Havel had once written songs for a Czech rock group. Rebellious youth in Manila and São Paulo use rap to express their feelings. The sudden death in 2009 of American pop musician Michael Jackson, known equally for his spectacular musical talents and bizarre lifestyle, illustrated the global influence of U.S. popular culture. His passing and legacy dominated the mass media in many nations for weeks, a star-studded memorial tribute was televised around the world, and millions of fans bought his recordings and memorabilia. Through the global reputations they often enjoy, pop stars also mount concerts to address issues such as racism, political prisoners, famine, and African poverty. Bono, the lead singer for the Irish rock band U2, uses his fame to campaign among world leaders for causes such as debt relief for poor nations.

Many musicians have mixed indigenous and imported influences, often from outside the West. For example, Congolese popular music, which borrowed Latin American dance rhythms, gained audiences throughout Africa and Europe. Indian film music and Arab folk music have influenced the popular music of Southeast Asia and East Africa. Even pop music that does not cross many borders can reflect a creative blending. *Dangdut*, an Indonesian popular music, originated as a fusion of Western rock, Indian film music, and local folk music. The major dangdut star, Rhoma Irama **(ROW-muh ih-RAH-muh)**, sometimes faced arrest for offering political protests in songs that address poverty, human rights abuses, the struggle of the underdog, and the betrayal of the nationalist promise. Beginning in the 1970s he developed a huge following among poor rural folk and urban youth, who agree with the message of one of his more famous songs: "The rich get richer and the poor get poorer." Rhoma's music, which has a strong Islamic quality and promotes Muslim moral teachings, helped inspire the Islamic revival in Indonesia, but conservative Muslims have often condemned other dangdut singers for their erotic lyrics and suggestive performances.

Religions

Although secular thought has become more popular than ever before in history, over three-quarters of the world's people identify with one or another universal religion with roots deep in the past. The world contains over 2 billion Christians, 1.5 billion Muslims, 900 million Hindus, 375 million Buddhists, and 14 million Jews. Well over 1.5 billion practice a local faith, such as animism or Daoism, or profess no religion (see Map 26.3). Religion sometimes provides the basis for national identity, as in Roman Catholic Poland and Ireland and in Muslim Bangladesh and Pakistan. Religious leaders have debated how much, if at all, their faiths need to change to better engage the contemporary world. Pope John XXIII (pope 1958–1963) liberalized church practices, such as having the mass in a vernacular language rather than Latin, and encouraged a more active dialogue with other churches and religions. Meanwhile, a controversial movement arose among Catholic clergy and laypeople in Latin America, called liberation theology, that cooperated with socialist and communist groups to improve the lives of the poor. Muslim liberals and militants confronted each other over such issues as the role of women, relations with non-Muslims, and whether Muslim majority states should base their legal systems on Islamic law. In sub-Saharan Africa and Southeast Asia, where many Sunni Muslims are tolerant toward other beliefs, some people have become more devout, and more men have studied in the Middle East, often returning with more militant views.

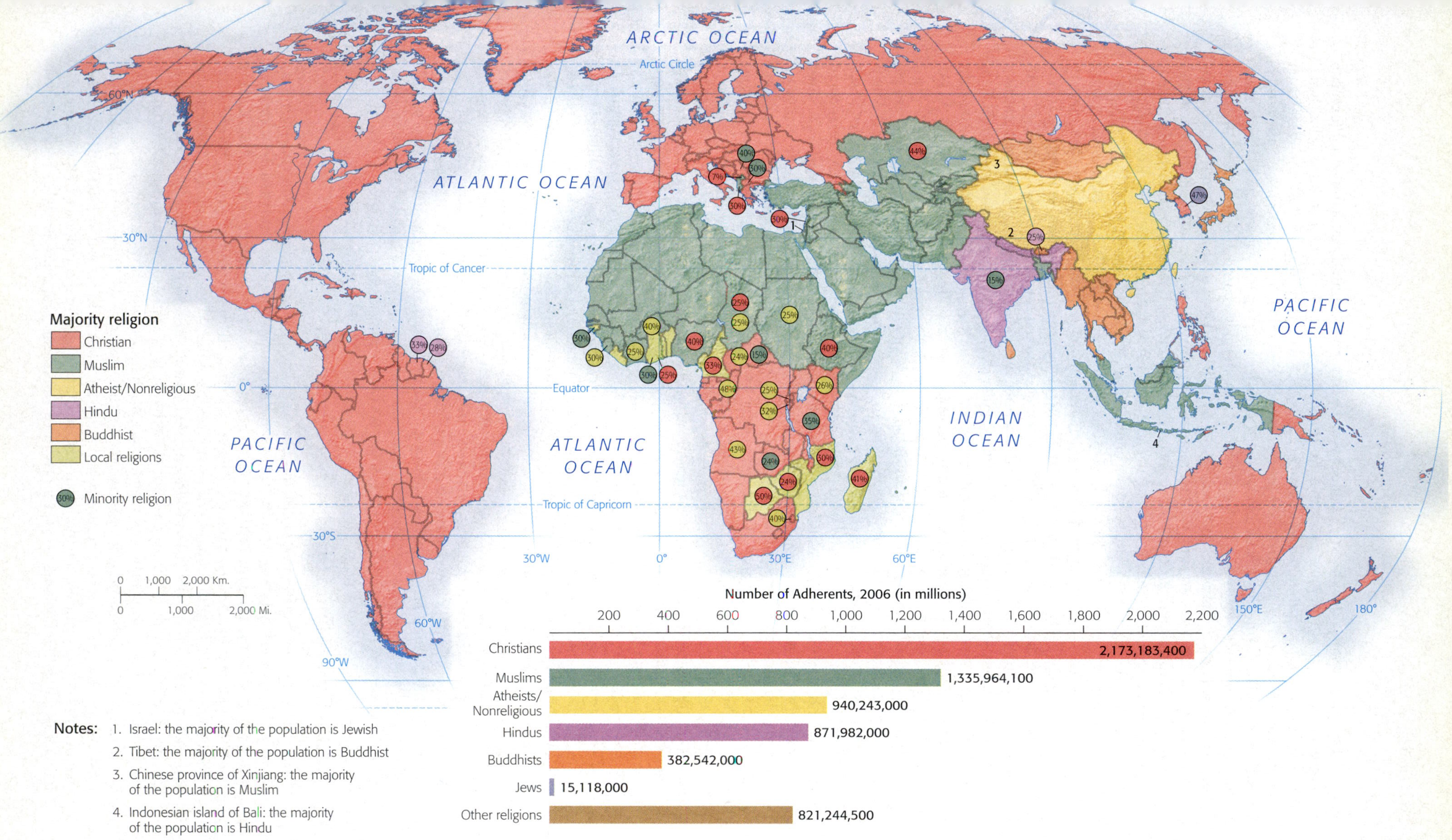

Map 26.3 World Religions
Christianity has the most believers and is the dominant faith in the Americas, Oceania, Europe, Russia, and central and southern Africa. Most people in the northern half of Africa, western Asia, and Central Asia embrace Islam. Hindus are concentrated in India, and Buddhists in East and Southeast Asia.

Interactive Map

The easy spread of ideas in the globalized world has worked to the advantage of portable creeds not dependent on one culture or setting. In Africa, polytheism and animism have faded while Christianity and Islam, promoted by missionary activity, have gained wider followings. Protestants have evangelized and gained ground in predominantly Catholic Latin America, and Pentacostalism, an American-born Christian tradition that promotes charismatic worship and faith healing, has developed a large following. Protestants and Catholics have competed with each other, and often with Muslims, for followers in Africa, Southeast Asia, and East Asia. Christianity has increasingly become a non-Western faith, with far more believers in Africa, Asia, and Latin America than in Europe and North America. Christian and Muslim missionaries have appealed to the downtrodden, suggesting that adopting their faith could lead not only to spiritual health but also to material wealth, and have recast their messages to recognize local cultural traditions.

Yet, organized religion has declined in East Asia and much of the West. Communist regimes discouraged religious observance, and many Japanese found neither their traditional faiths nor imported religions relevant to their lives. Church attendance and membership in Europe, Canada, and Australia fell dramatically after 1960. Traditional church attitudes have also competed with changing social attitudes. Even predominantly Catholic European nations have legalized abortion and moved toward equal rights for homosexuals, policies opposed by the Catholic Church. Both the Netherlands, once a center for puritanical Protestantism, and Spain, once one of the staunchest Catholic nations, have approved same-sex marriage, as have Belgium, Canada, South Africa, Mexico City, and several U.S. states.

Religious Tensions and Militancy

Tensions remain between different faiths. Sparked by political differences, some Christians and Muslims have violently attacked each other in Indonesia, the Philippines, Lebanon, Yugoslavia, and Nigeria, causing many casualities. Conflicts between Muslims and Hindus generated sporadic violence in India, Catholics and Protestants opposed each other in Northern Ireland and Uganda, and Sunni and Shi'ite Muslims occasionally fought in Pakistan and western Asia. Some Sunni Muslim regimes discriminated against or persecuted Shi'ites. In Iraq, where some 60 percent of the population is Shi'ite, the Sunni dictator, Saddam Hussein, restricted Shi'ite religious holidays and executed Shi'ites who opposed his regime. After his removal by the U.S. invasion, Shi'ite and Sunni conflict erupted, complicating U.S. efforts to restore stability.

Religious militancy has also grown. Some Muslim militants have turned the notion of *jihad*, or struggle within believers to strengthen their faith, into a campaign for holy war against unbelievers, secular Muslims, and countries or groups they consider anti-Muslim, and for turning secular states into Islamic ones. The militants, often known as Islamists or jihadis, appeal especially to the young and poor, often unemployed and embittered. Many Muslims oppose market capitalism and Western cultural influence, and the more puritanical Muslims despise the revealing clothing styles, open romantic behavior, independent women, and rebellious youth portrayed in Western television programs and movies. Similarly, some Christians, especially in the United States, Latin America, and Africa, have turned to literal, fundamentalist interpretations of the Bible and fund proselytizing efforts. Some Nigerian Protestant churches have even sent missionaries to the United States and Europe, while South Korean Protestants evangelize in China. Conservative churches have often opposed secular culture, rejected scientific findings they deem incompatible with biblical accounts, and condemned leftwing political and social movements, particularly those promoting socialism, feminism, legalized abortion, and homosexual rights. Christian and Islamic militancy has sparked similar movements in Buddhism, Hinduism, and Judaism, pitting the zealous believers against those with moderate, tolerant views.

Global Communications and Movements

Technological Breakthroughs

A worldwide communications network has been a chief engine of globalization. The introduction of radio in the early 1900s was followed by tape recording, television, and then the transistor, which allowed for the miniaturization of electronics. In 1953 portable transistor radios became available and soon reached even remote villages, opening them to world news and culture. Even villages without electricity could use transistor radios and cassette players. By the 1960s in central Borneo, a densely forested island divided between Indonesia and Malaysia, isolated villagers listened to radio broadcasts from the United States, Britain, and Australia and could often sing the songs of Western pop musicians such as the British rock group the Beatles.

Technological breakthroughs provided the foundation for more rapid and widespread communications. The first general-purpose computers were built in 1948, and in 1958 the first silicon microchips began a computer revolution that led to the first personal computers. By 2008 the world had nearly 800 million personal computers with 1.6 billion Internet users as well as countless web pages and blogs, all part of a vast network often termed the information superhighway. E-mail allows people in different countries, such as Canada and Malaysia, to communicate instantly with each other, and every minute millions of e-mails are dispatched via computer. An interested reader in Hong Kong, Ghana, or Finland can also access online versions of newspapers, such as the *New York Times*, *Al Ahram* in Cairo, or the *Deccan Herald* in India. Finally, the rise of 24-hour cable news networks able to reach worldwide audiences, such as U.S.-based CNN (Cable News Network) and the Arab-language Al Jazeera, based in the Persian Gulf state of Qatar, widened access to diverse views, enriching people's understanding of the wider world. Technologically literate people can send music, video, and photos around the world via computers and cell phones.

A Networked World

The rapid evolution of media and information technology has had many consequences. Through fax communications, orbiting communications satellites, portable phones, electronic mail, and the worldwide computer web, information can be transmitted outside the reach of governments, diminishing their power to shape their citizens' thinking. For this reason, repressive states seeking to limit information flow, such as Iran, Cuba, Burma, and China, have banned satellite dish receivers and tried to jam access to controversial and dissident websites, but these efforts have been only partly successful. In 2009, protesters in nations like China and Iran used cellphones, Twitter, and YouTube to coordinate their activities, spread their message, and circumvent government control of the mass media. The U.S.-based social media site Facebook claims 250 million members, seventy percent of them outside the U.S. Technologies, especially the World Wide Web, have enhanced the value of education and of English, which has gradually become a world language, like Latin in the Mediterranean zone 2,000 years ago and Arabic in the Islamic world 1,000 years ago. By 2005 some three-quarters of all websites were in English. Perhaps a quarter of the world's people know some English, and Asian countries with many educated people fluent in English, such as India and Singapore, have an advantage in competing for high-technology industries. But in the poorest nations, only a lucky few have access to satellite dishes, fax machines, and networked computers. Furthermore, many nations resent the strong U.S. influence over the Internet.

Social and Political Movements

The increasing links between far-flung peoples have allowed for social and political movements originating in different countries to transcend borders and link to similar movements elsewhere. A wide variety of transnational organizations promote issues such as the treatment of political prisoners, women's rights, and antiracism. Amnesty International, based in Britain, publicizes the plight of people imprisoned solely for their political views and activities, such as the Burmese opposition leader Aung San Suu Kyi (AWNG sahn soo CHEE) and, during the Cold War, the Soviet dissident scientist Andrei Sakharov (SAH-kuh-RAWF), organizing letter writing and pressure campaigns to seek their release. The World Social Forum, formed in 2001 and meeting annually in Brazil, brings together nongovernment organizations and activists who oppose globalizing free market capitalism and imperialism. They believe globalization undermines workers' rights and environmental protection.

Movements or upheavals in one nation or region sometimes spread widely. During the 1960s, students, workers, and political radicals in many nations organized protests against the U.S. war

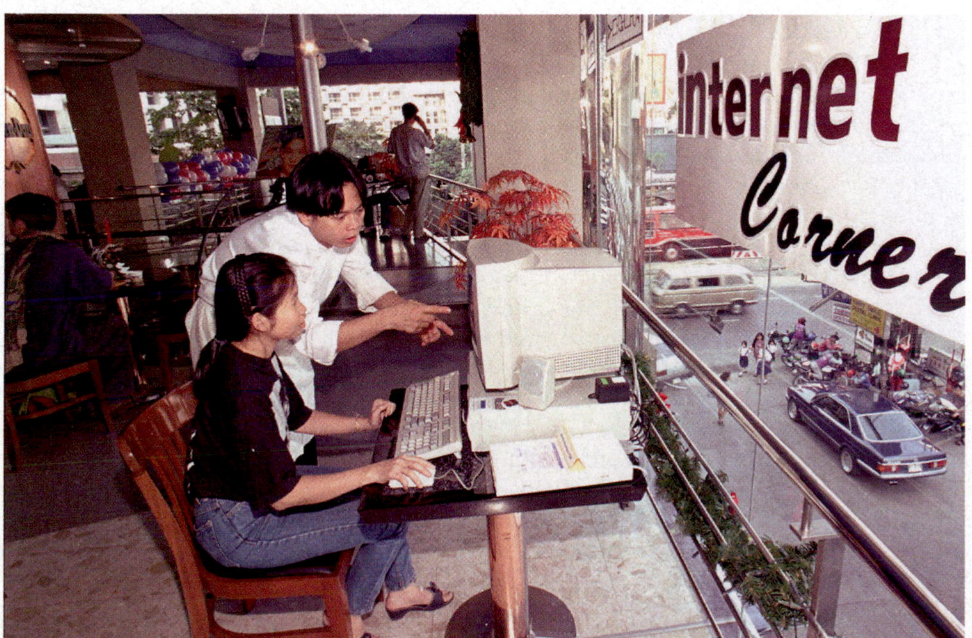

AP/Wide World Photos

Internet Cafe in Thailand In this photo, a waiter at a cyberspace café, operated by the Swiss multinational ice cream company, Häagen Dazs, in Bangkok, Thailand, helps a young Thai woman navigate one of the café's computers.

in Vietnam, racism, unresponsive governments, capitalism, and other concerns. In 1968 demonstrations, marches, and strikes intensified around the world. Although these movements were not coordinated, young protesters were often influenced by the same writers, music, and ideas. The more radical protesters wore t-shirts celebrating Che Guevara **(guh-VAHR-uh)** (1928–1967), an Argentinean-born revolutionary who helped Fidel Castro take power in Cuba and who became a communist martyr when he was killed in Bolivia. The 1968 turbulence affected over a dozen countries, from the United States and Mexico to France, Czechoslovakia, and Japan. However, other protesters have looked to noncommunists or even anticommunists, such as the dissidents—often devout Catholics—who opposed the communist regime in Poland. In the wake of the 1968 activism, environmental, peace, workers' rights, homosexual rights, and feminist movements grew, chiefly but not only in industrialized nations.

Women's Movements

Women have been particularly active in seeking to expand their rights, and some activists have placed women's issues on the international agenda. The United Nations periodically sponsors global conferences on women's issues such as gender equality. However, women who attend international conferences, divided by culture and nationality, do not always agree on goals and strategies. In the United Nation's fourth World Conference on Women, held in China in 1995, the 40,000 delegates disagreed sharply on priorities. Delegates from rich nations wanted to expand women's employment options, social freedom, and control over their bodies, while Asian, African, and Latin American delegates emphasized making their families more healthy and economically secure. One Indian delegate described the goals of U.S. delegates as irrelevant to Indian women: "They ask for abortion rights. We ask for safe drinking water and basic health care."[16] While abortion remained a controversial issue in most of the world, it became legal in most Western and many Asian nations.

Despite disagreements, women have worked across borders on issues such as preventing violence against women. For example, women activists and their male supporters from Muslim and Western nations have fought the tradition common in some conservative Muslim societies of jailing or killing women for adultery while exonerating the man responsible. In 2005 Mukhtaran Bibi **(MOOK-tahr-an BIH-bee)**, an illiterate woman from an impoverished Pakistani village without electricity, gained worldwide sympathy for her resistance to male brutality. The tribal council had ruled that she be gang-raped to punish her family, which had been involved in a village dispute. Instead of following custom by ending the "disgrace" through suicide, she bravely pursued the rapists in court. They were convicted, and she used the money awarded her by the court to start two village schools, one for boys and one for girls. When a higher court then overturned the men's convictions, her courageous refusal to accept the verdict caused an international outcry. While the Pakistani government tried to suppress the controversy, men and women around the world, alerted by news accounts and Internet appeals, donated money and made her a symbol of the need for women's rights. Mukhtaran Bibi inspired millions everywhere with her courage and faith in education and justice.

Global Terrorism

terrorism Small-scale but violent attacks aimed at undermining a government or demoralizing a population.

Terrorism, small-scale but violent attacks, often on civilian targets, aimed at undermining a government or demoralizing a population, intensified in the late twentieth and early twenty-first century, expanding to global dimensions and reshaping world politics. Terrorism has a long history, going back many centuries. After 1945 Palestinians under Israeli control, Basque nationalists in Spain, and Irish nationalists in Britain, among others, engaged in terrorism for their causes. Some states also carried out or sponsored terrorism against unfriendly governments or political movements. South Africa's white minority government financed insurgencies that opposed the Marxist governments of Angola and Mozambique, resulting in thousands of civilian deaths. Similarly, the United States sponsored terrorism against leftist-ruled Nicaragua in the 1980s, helping form a military force, known as the *Contras,* that often attacked civilian targets, such as rural schools, day-care centers, and clinics operated by the government. An increasingly interconnected world has spurred some terrorist organizations to operate on a global level, forming networks with branches in many countries. The most active of these networks, formed by militant Islamists, has capitalized on widespread Muslim anger at Israel, their own governments, and U.S. foreign policies. Muslim terrorist groups have become increasingly active in Egypt, Algeria, Lebanon, and Pakistan, attacking politicians, police, Western residents and tourists, and Israeli and U.S. targets.

Middle Eastern Terrorism

Terrorism became a growing threat to life in the Middle East. For example, the *Hezbollah* movement in Lebanon, formed by Shi'ite Arabs opposed to the U.S.-backed Lebanese government and to U.S. support for Israel, used suicide bombers driving explosive-filled trucks to destroy the U.S. Embassy and a Marine Corps base in Beirut in 1983, killing several hundred Americans. Later, to oppose Israeli occupation of Arab lands and demoralize Israelis, Palestinian militants strapped explosives to their bodies and detonated them in Israeli buses and businesses. Outraged by these murderous attacks, the Israelis responded with force, killing or arresting Palestinians and expelling families of suspected militants from their homes, often bulldozing the houses into rubble. Divided by politics, Israelis and Palestinians have shared the bitter experience of grieving for those lost in the chronic violence, among them innocent women and children.

The Soviet military intervention in 1979 to support a pro-Soviet government in Afghanistan provided the spark for forming a global network of Islamist terrorists. Militants from the Middle East and Pakistan flocked to Afghanistan to assist the Muslim Afghan insurgents resisting the Soviets. In 1988 the most extreme of the foreign fighters came together in a jihadi organization known as *Al Qaeda* ("The Base"). Al Qaeda's main leader, the Saudi Osama bin Laden (b. 1957), came from an extremely wealthy family and had been trained as an engineer. Bin Laden used his wealth to support the Afghan rebels, who were also funded and armed by the United States as part of its Cold War rivalry with the USSR. After the Soviets abandoned Afghanistan in 1989, bin Laden set up Al Qaeda cells in Saudi Arabia, whose government he viewed as corrupt, and aimed to target Egypt and Iraq, whose secular regimes suppressed Islamic militants. To recruit, support, and communicate with members, Al Qaeda used the information superhighway, setting up websites, using e-mail and satellite phones, and releasing videotapes to cable news networks of bin Laden's messages. Eventually Al Qaeda looked beyond the Middle East for targets. The Afghanistan-based bin Laden, a ruthless man willing to kill innocent people in pursuit of his goals, plotted terrorist efforts against his former ally in the Afghan resistance, the United States, whose military bases in Saudi Arabia, support for repressive Arab governments, and close alliance with Israel enraged many Arabs. Al Qaeda or related groups sponsored attacks on U.S. targets, such as the embassies in Kenya and Tanzania, causing hundreds of casualties.

Al Qaeda

On September 11, 2001, Al Qaeda members hijacked four U.S. commercial airliners and crashed two of them into New York's World Trade Center and another into the Pentagon near Washington, D.C., killing over 3,000 people, mostly civilians. A fourth airliner crashed into a Pennsylvania farm field before reaching Washington, D.C. The attacks shocked Americans and people everywhere who opposed indiscriminate killing and prompted U.S. president George W. Bush to declare a war on terrorism. U.S. forces attacked Al Qaeda bases in Afghanistan and then occupied the country, whose government, controlled by Islamists who had fought the Soviets, shielded bin Laden; but although they installed a new pro-U.S. government, the Americans failed to capture bin Laden and still faced resistance from Islamic militants.

United States and Iraq

In 2003 the United States, claiming that Saddam Hussein's Iraq was closely linked to Al Qaeda and possessed weapons of mass destruction, invaded Iraq, removed Saddam's brutal government, and imposed a U.S. military occupation supported chiefly by Britain. However, the U.S. troops found no evidence of any Saddam ties to Al Qaeda or any weapons of mass destruction, and the occupation sparked an insurgency, including suicide bombings, and unleashed sectarian divisions that hindered the U.S. efforts to stabilize and rebuild Iraq. While most of the insurgents were Sunni Iraqis fearing domination by the Shi'ite majority, Islamists from other countries also flocked to Iraq to attack Americans and destabilize the country. The U.S. invasion and occupation, and the resistance to it, killed over 100,000 Iraqis, resulted in 4,300 U.S. deaths and tens of thousands of wounded, and kept a large U.S. military force tied down in Iraq.

Eventually violence diminished. Whether the war in Iraq helped or harmed the U.S.-led war against terrorism remained subject to debate. The war alienated many U.S. allies and, like the earlier U.S. conflict in Vietnam, was unpopular around the world. Transferring U.S. troops and funds from Afghanistan to Iraq allowed the Islamic militants to regroup and fight the U.S.-backed Afghan government. Meanwhile, capitalizing on anti-U.S. sentiments among Muslims, Al Qaeda spawned loosely affiliated terrorist groups, often operating without direct Al Qaeda guidance, that launched terrorist attacks on several continents, from Spain and Britain to Indonesia, Kenya, and Morocco. Nations with despotic governments, such as China, Egypt, and Uzbekistan, also invoked terrorism as a reason to restrict civil liberties. In 1993 a German historian had perceptively predicted the challenges ahead in the post–Cold War world: "We are at the beginning of a new era, characterized by great insecurity, permanent crisis and the absence of any kind of *status quo*. We must realize that we find ourselves in one of those crises of world history."[17]

SECTION SUMMARY

- In the new global village, millions of people have immigrated to foreign countries seeking greater economic opportunity or an escape from insufferable conditions at home, including political repression, famine, and civil war.
- Modern medicine has eliminated many diseases, but cholera and malaria are still serious problems, and AIDS has seriously affected India, Southeast Asia, and especially Africa.
- Western consumer culture has spread around the world, while musical forms from different cultures have mingled and musicians and performers have expressed political and often controversial views.
- The world's major religious traditions have remained numerically strong, and some have worked to adapt to the modern world, while representatives of rival religions have fought for control of various areas and many Muslims and Christians have grown more fundamentalist.
- Worldwide communication was facilitated by technologies such as radio, television, and the Internet, making a vast array of information available, even in countries such as China, Iran, and Cuba, whose governments attempted to limit its availability.
- Increased global communication led to political movements that transcended conventional borders, such as Amnesty International, the 1968 youth protests, and women's rights movements.
- Terrorism, which had been used throughout the twentieth century by groups such as the Palestinians, the Basques, and the Irish, became more deadly, culminating in the radical Muslim group Al Qaeda's 2001 attack on the United States.

CHAPTER SUMMARY

The later twentieth century proved turbulent. Nationalism spread in Asia and Africa, leading to decolonization. During the 1950s and 1960s most of the Western colonies gained their independence through negotiations, the threat of violence, or armed struggle, and social revolutionaries gained power in some nations. However, the West maintained a strong economic presence in many former colonies. The rivalry between the United States and the USSR also shaped the global system, generating a Cold War in which the two superpowers faced each other indirectly or through surrogates. The powerful United States had a large group of allies and sometimes intervened in Asian and Latin American nations, while the USSR occupied eastern Europe. The collapse of the Communist bloc and then the USSR allowed the United States to become the world's lone superpower.

The world was also shaped by globalization, with its unprecedented flow of money, products, information, and ideas across national borders. The global economy grew rapidly but did not spread its benefits equally. As industrialization spread, most Western and some Asian and Latin American nations prospered, but many poor nations struggled to escape underdevelopment and raise living standards. A billion people remained mired in deep poverty. Meanwhile millions of people migrated, social and political movements addressed local and global problems, universal religions gained new converts, and the information superhighway and other technological innovations linked millions of people in new ways. New international terrorist networks also challenged governments and reshaped world politics.

KEY TERMS

First World
Second World
Third World
Fourth World
Cold War
guerrilla warfare
nuclear weapons
globalization
multinational corporations
Third Industrial Revolution
Green Revolution
desertification
global village
terrorism

EBOOK AND WEBSITE RESOURCES

PRIMARY SOURCE
The Long Telegram

INTERACTIVE MAPS
Map 26.1 Decolonization
Map 26.2 World Population Growth
Map 26.3 World Religions

LINKS

Global Problems and the Culture of Capitalism (http://faculty.plattsburgh.edu/richard.robbins/legacy/). An outstanding site, aimed at undergraduates, with a wealth of resources.

The Globalization Website (http://www.emory.edu/SOC/globalization/). A useful site with many resources and essays on globalization.

Human Rights Watch (http://www.hrw.org/wr2k3/introduction.html). The website of a major human rights organization that reports on the entire world.

Modern History Sourcebook (http://www.fordham.edu/halsall/mod/modsbook.html). A very extensive online collection of historical documents and secondary materials.

United Nations Environment Program (http://www.unep.org/geo2000/ov-e/index.htm). Provides access to United Nations reports on the world's environmental problems.

Plus flashcards, practice quizzes, and more. Go to: www.cengage.com/history/lockard/globalsocnet2e.

SUGGESTED READING

Ali, Tariq. *The Clash of Fundamentalisms: Crusades, Jihads and Modernity*. London: Verso, 2003. A controversial but powerful examination, by a London-based Indian writer, of Western policies and Islamic movements around the world.

Axford, Barrie. *The Global System: Economics, Politics and Culture*. New York: St. Martin's, 1995. A comprehensive, thoughtful review by a British scholar of approaches to understanding the global system.

Crossley, Pamela Kyle, et al. *Global Society: The World Since 1900*, 2nd ed. Boston: Houghton Mifflin, 2008. A comprehensive survey.

DeFronzo, James. *Revolutions and Revolutionary Movements*. Boulder, CO: Westview Press, 1991. Useful surveys of revolutions and the societies they made, with case studies of Russia, China, Vietnam, Cuba, Nicaragua, Iran, and South Africa.

Enloe, Cynthia. *Bananas, Beaches and Bases: Making Feminist Sense of International Relations*, 2nd ed. Berkeley: University of California Press, 2001. A provocative examination of women's experiences in global politics.

Ehrenreich, Barbara, and Arlie Russell Hochschild, eds. *Global Women: Nannies, Maids, and Sex Workers in the New Economy*. New York: Henry Holt, 2002. A provocative look at the feminization of the migrant work force.

Eriksen, Thomas Hylland. *Globalization: The Key Concepts*. New York: Berg, 2007. Useful introduction by a Norwegian scholar.

Frieden, Jeffrey A. *Global Capitalism: Its Fall and Rise in the Twentieth Century*. New York: W.W. Norton, 2006. Provocative examination of globalization and capitalism.

Hunt, Michael H. *The World Transformed, 1945 to the Present*. Boston: Bedford/St. Martin's, 2004. A readable and up-to-date survey.

Kechner, Frank J., and John Boli. *World Culture: Origins and Consequences*. Malden, MA: Blackwell, 2005. Examines the impact of globalization on world culture.

Khanna, Parag. *The Second World: Empires and Influence in the New Global Order*. New York: W.W. Norton, 2008. Exploration of world politics by India-born scholar.

LaFeber, Walter. *America, Russia and the Cold War, 1945–2006*, 10th ed. New York: McGraw-Hill, 2006. An excellent examination of the Cold War around the world.

Mazlish, Bruce, and Akira Iriye, eds. *The Global History Reader*. New York: Routledge, 2005. A provocative set of essays on global trends in the twentieth century, from the information revolution and environmental change to human rights and terrorism.

McNeill, J. R. *Something New Under the Sun: An Environmental History of the Twentieth-Century World*. New York: W.W. Norton, 2000. An outstanding examination of the interface between societies and environmental change.

Ponting, Clive. *The Twentieth Century: A World History*. New York: Henry Holt, 1999. A valuable thematic examination by a British scholar.

Reynolds, David. *One World Divisible: A Global History Since 1945*. New York: W.W. Norton, 2001. A comprehensive survey.

Sen, Amartya. *Identity and Violence: The Illusion of Destiny*. New York: Norton, 2006. An influential Indian economist's views on globalization, freedom, violence, and other global issues.

Stearns, Peter N. *The Industrial Revolution in World History*, 3rd ed. Boulder, CO: Westview Press, 2007. Useful comparative study.

Wang, Gungwu, ed. *Global History and Migrants*. Boulder, CO: Westview Press, 1997. Essays on recent population movements.

Weiss, Thomas G., et al. *The United Nations and Changing World Politics*, 5th ed. Boulder, CO: Westview Press, 2006. Examines the history and roles of the United Nations.

Westad, Odd Arne. *The Global Cold War*. New York: Cambridge University Press, 2005. A provocative study by a Norwegian scholar.

CHAPTER 27

East Asian Resurgence, Since 1945

CHAPTER OUTLINE

- Mao's Revolutionary China
- Chinese Modernization
- The Remaking of Japan
- The Little Dragons in the Asian Resurgence

PROFILE
Xue Xinran, a Chinese Voice for Women

WITNESS TO THE PAST
A Japanese Generation Gap

Wally McNamee/Corbis

The China Stock Exchange
The East Asian nations enjoyed an economic resurgence in this era. Since the 1980s, China has boasted the world's fastest-growing economy and a booming stock exchange.

> Once China's destiny is in the hands of the people, China, like the sun rising in the east, will illuminate every corner with a brilliant flame, and build a new, powerful and prosperous [society].
>
> —Mao Zedong, Chinese communist leader[1]

FOCUS QUESTIONS

1. How did Maoism transform Chinese society?
2. What factors explain the dramatic rise of Chinese economic power in the world since 1978?
3. How did Japan rise from the ashes of defeat in World War II to become a global economic powerhouse?
4. What policies led to the rise of the "Little Dragon" nations and their dynamic economies?

On October 1, 1949, Mao Zedong (1893–1976), the Chinese communist leader, was driven into Beijing accompanied by soldiers from the communist military force, the People's Liberation Army. Mao, fifty-five years old and a peasant's son, had never been out of China and had spent the previous twenty-two years living in remote rural areas while directing brutal warfare against the Japanese invaders and the Chinese government. Ahead of Mao's car rolled a Sherman tank, originally donated by the United States to the Republic of China government, headed by Jiang Jieshi (better known in the West as Chiang Kai-shek) (1887–1975), to help crush Mao's communist forces. But Chiang's army had lost, and the president had fled to the large offshore island of Taiwan. Wearing a new suit, Mao climbed to the top of the Gate of Heavenly Peace, the entrance to the Forbidden City of the Qing emperors overlooking spacious Tiananmen Square. He and his comrades had sacrificed much to reach this pinnacle of power. Chinese jammed the square to hear their new ruler announce the founding of a new communist government, the People's Republic of China. Referring to a century of corrupt governments and humiliation and domination by Western nations and Japan, Mao thanked all those who, starting with the Opium War, had "laid down their lives in the many struggles against domestic and foreign enemies," finally proclaiming: "The Chinese people have stood up. Nobody will insult us again."[2]

The formation of the People's Republic marked a watershed in the history of China and the world, bringing to an end a century of severe social and political instability, caused in part by China's inability to defend itself against foreign imperialism. Its communist leaders were committed to the revolutionary transformation of the society while making China respected abroad once again. Given China's size and a population of 1.3 billion by 2008, greater than that of North America, Europe, and Russia combined, any major transition there had global significance. By the early twenty-first century Mao was long gone and many of his policies discarded, but China, with a booming economy, had reclaimed some of the political and economic status it had lost two centuries earlier.

The Chinese were not the only East Asians to enjoy a resurgence. By the 1980s observers referred to the **Pacific Rim**, the economically dynamic Asian countries on the edge of the Pacific Basin: China, Japan, South Korea, Taiwan, and several Southeast Asian nations. Many predicted that the twenty-first century would be the **Pacific Century**, marked by a shift of global economic power from Europe and North America to the Pacific Rim, whose export-driven nations seemed poised to dominate a post–Cold War world where economic power might outweigh military might. The center of gravity of world economic life, for centuries located in the eastern half of Eurasia, had shifted to Europe and North America, and then in the 1990s had moved back toward a resurgent Asia. Although changing world

Pacific Rim The economically dynamic Asian countries on the edge of the Pacific Basin: China, Japan, South Korea, Taiwan, and several Southeast Asian nations.

Pacific Century The possible shift of global economic power from Europe and North America to the Pacific Rim in the twenty-first century.

e Visit the website and eBook for additional study materials and interactive tools: www.cengage.com/history/lockard/globalsocnet2e

politics and economic crises, especially an Asian financial collapse in 1997 and a severe global recession in 2008–2009, have challenged the Pacific Century concept, China, Japan, and their neighbors have remained major players in the global system.

MAO'S REVOLUTIONARY CHINA

How did Maoism transform Chinese society?

The Chinese Revolution that brought the Chinese communists to power was one of the three greatest upheavals in modern world history. The French Revolution (1789) destroyed the remnants of feudalism throughout western Europe, with its leaders extolling the rights of the common people, and the Russian Revolution (1917) charted a noncapitalist path to industrialization. Both events swept away old social classes and ruling elites. China's revolution remade a major world society while restoring its international status. The communists built a strong government that made China the most experimental nation on earth, veering from one innovative policy to another in an attempt to renovate Chinese life and overcome underdevelopment. In the process, the People's Republic created a new model of economic development different from both Western-dominated capitalism and highly centralized Soviet communism. But the path was littered with conflict and repression. Furthermore, the Chinese, like all societies, were products of their history. China remained partly an ancient empire and partly a modern nation, and its leaders often behaved much like the emperors of old in their autocratic exercise of power.

CHRONOLOGY
China Since 1945

1945–1949 Chinese civil war

1949 Chinese communist triumph

1949–1957 Stalinist model

1950 Occupation of Tibet

1950 New marriage law

1950–1953 Korean War

1957–1961 First use of Maoist model

1958–1961 Great Leap Forward

1960 Sino-Soviet split

1966–1976 Great Proletarian Cultural Revolution

1972 Nixon's trip to Beijing

1976 Death of Mao Zedong

1976 Arrest of Gang of Four

1978 Four Modernizations policy

1978 Normalization of U.S.-China diplomatic relations

1978–1989 Market socialism

1978–1997 Deng Xiaoping era

1989 Tiananmen Massacre

1989 Introduction of market Leninism

1997 Return of Hong Kong to China

The Communist Triumph and the New China

The U.S. defeat of Japan in 1945 sparked a fierce civil war between Mao's communists and Chiang Kai-shek's nationalist government for control of China. While Mao and Chiang despised each other, both men were patriotic, autocratic, and hungry for power. Chiang's 3.7-million-man army vastly outnumbered the 900,000 communist troops, and the United States lavished military aid on Chiang, providing planes and trucks to transport his soldiers so they could occupy as much territory as possible. The communists, aided by the Soviet Union (USSR), concentrated on north China and Manchuria. In trying to block Mao's forces, however, Chiang overstretched his supply lines. In addition, Chiang's Republic experienced corruption and a rapid decline in the value of Chinese currency that demoralized the population. Seeking change, many came to view the communist movement as a more honest alternative to Chiang's Nationalist Party.

Meanwhile, in the villages that they controlled, the communists promoted a social revolution, known as the "turning over," by encouraging villagers to denounce local landlords, transferring land from richer to poorer peasants, replacing government-appointed leaders with elected village councils, and protecting battered wives. Encouraged to air their grievances by "speaking pains to recall pains" in village meetings, women warned abusive men to mend their ways or face punishment or arrest. However, inevitably the release of pent-up rage against violent husbands or greedy landlords who mistreated tenants led to excesses, such as angry crowds beating them to death.

The military and political tide turned against the Republic, and in 1948 Chiang's troops in Manchuria surrendered to the communists. To revive Chiang's prospects, the United States pressured him unsuccessfully to broaden his political base with democratic reforms. Some American leaders demanded that the United States send troops to help Chiang, but others concluded that his regime had lost too much popular support to win the conflict. Through 1949 the communists took the major cities of north China and pushed Chiang's army south. Finally Chiang fled to the island of Taiwan, along with thousands of troops and 2 million supporters. On Taiwan, with massive U.S. aid and military protection, the leaders of the relocated Republic of China developed a successful capitalist strategy for economic growth. Meanwhile, mainland China's history now moved in a direction very different from that of Chiang's Republic of China.

CHRONOLOGY

	China	Japan	Korea and Taiwan
1940	**1945–1949** Chinese civil war **1949** Chinese communist triumph	**1946–1952** U.S. occupation of Japan	**1950–1953** Korean War
1960	**1960** Sino-Soviet split **1966–1976** Great Proletarian Cultural Revolution **1978** Four Modernizations policy	**1960s–1989** Rapid economic growth	
1980			**1997** Asian financial collapse

The key question confronting the Chinese communists after 1949 was how to achieve rapid economic development in an overpopulated, battered country. Two decades of war had ruined the economy, leaving little capital for industrialization. China had no overseas empire to exploit for economic resources, and the communists did not want loans and foreign investment that might reduce their independence. Furthermore, they faced a powerful enemy: propelled by alarm at Mao's policies and anticommunist Cold War concerns, the United States launched an economic boycott to shut China off from international trade, refused diplomatic recognition, and surrounded China with military bases. Isolated, China created its own models of economic and political development.

China's Challenges

Between 1949 and 1976 China followed two different models of economic development, each with its own priorities and consequences. The first, Stalinism, a system based on the Soviet model of central planning, heavy industry, a powerful bureaucracy, and a managerial system, dominated the early years (1949–1957) (see Chronology: China Since 1945). China received some Soviet aid but otherwise financed development before the late 1970s through self-reliance, limiting contact with the global system. As in Meiji Japan and the Soviet Union, the state took the lead, emphasizing austerity and making people work hard for low wages in hopes that future generations would live better. The communists also abolished private ownership of business and industry and transferred land to poor peasants. Soon they began collectivizing the rural economy into cooperatives, in which peasants helped each other and shared tools. As in the Soviet Union, new privileged elite emerged in the government and the ruling Communist Party, which cracked down on dissent.

Stalinism and Maoism

By the late 1950s Mao, disenchanted with Stalinism, reintroduced Maoism, a unique synthesis of Marxism and Chinese thought that emphasized the mass mobilization of the population. Under Maoism, China's guiding ideology from 1957 to 1961 and then again from 1966 to 1976, people were mobilized for development projects, such as building dams and pest elimination. Everyone was issued fly swatters and asked to kill as many flies as possible in hopes of reducing disease, and the party introduced tree-planting campaigns to reverse the ecological instability of recent centuries. Mao also reorganized the rural economy into **communes**, large agricultural units that combined many families and villages into a common administrative system for pooling resources and labor. A commune could build and operate a factory, secondary school, and hospital, tasks that would be impractical for a single village. The communes raised agricultural productivity, eliminated landlords, and promoted social and economic equality. Mao also located industry in rural areas, keeping the peasants at home rather than fostering movement to cities.

communes Large agricultural units introduced by Mao Zedong that combined many families and villages into a common system for pooling resources and labor.

The most radical Maoist policy was the **Great Leap Forward** (1958–1961), an ambitious attempt to industrialize China rapidly and end poverty through collective efforts. Farmers and workers built small iron furnaces in their backyards, courtyards, and gardens and spent their free time turning everything from cutlery to old bicycles into steel. But the poorly conceived campaign, pushing the people too hard, nearly wrecked the economy and, along with disastrous weather, caused 30 million people to starve. One of Mao's critics in the leadership charged: "Grains scattered on the ground, potato leaves withered; Strong young people have left to smelt iron, only children and old women reaped the crops; How can they pass the coming year?"[3] These failures diminished Mao's influence, bringing moderate policies in the early 1960s.

Great Leap Forward Mao Zedong's ambitious attempt to industrialize China rapidly and end poverty through collective efforts.

Chinese Politics and the World

Communist Rule

The Communist Party, led by Mao as chairman, dominated the political system; party members occupied all key positions in the government and military. Using the slogan "Politics Takes Command," the communists emphasized ideology, making political values pervasive and requiring all Chinese to become members of political discussion groups. Party activists monitored the discussions and reported dissenters, and political education was integrated into the schools, work units, and even leisure activities. The party also sought to eradicate inequalities and to alter thought patterns and attitudes, emphasizing the interests of the group over those of the individual. To eliminate class distinctions, officials and intellectuals had to perform physical labor, such as laying bricks for house construction or spreading manure to fertilize farm fields, so that they would understand the experience of the workers and peasants. The system required massive social control, enabled by a vast police apparatus; millions suspected of opposing the communists were harassed, jailed, exiled, or killed. Even communist sympathizers, such as the outspoken feminist writer Ding Ling (1902–1986), were purged after falling out of official favor. In exchange for accepting its policies, the state promised everyone the "five guarantees" of food, clothes, fuel, education, and a decent burial. But over the years thousands of people fled to British-ruled Hong Kong.

Despite these problems, the communists restored China's status as a major world power (see Map 27.1) and pursued a foreign policy that maximized stability at home. Mao reasserted Chinese sovereignty in outlying areas and in 1950 sent armies to occupy Tibet, once a Qing province, whose people were culturally and historically distinct from the Chinese and had broken away in 1912. Most Tibetans, however, opposed Chinese rule, sparking periodic unrest. The Chinese suppression of a Tibetan revolt led the highest Tibetan Buddhist leader, the Dalai Lama (b. 1935), to flee to India in 1959. Revered by devout Tibetans as both a spiritual and political leader, he became a defiant symbol of Tibetan resistance to Chinese rule, traveling the world to rally support for the Tibetan cause while promoting Buddhist ethics and world peace. China failed to reclaim another former Qing-ruled territory, Mongolia, which in 1924 had become a communist state allied to, and protected by, the USSR.

China and the World

China faced major challenges in foreign affairs. In 1950 China, which supported the communist North Korean government installed in 1948, was drawn into the Korean War between the USSR-backed North Korea and United Nations forces led by the United States, sent to defend pro-U.S. South Korea. When the U.N. forces pushed the North Korean army toward China's border and the U.S. commander, General Douglas MacArthur, talked recklessly of carrying the offensive across the Yalu River into China, the Chinese entered the conflict and pushed U.N. troops back south. The war produced huge casualties on both sides, including several hundred thousand Chinese, and reinforced the hostility and mutual fear between China and the United States. The Korean War

Honoring Chairman Mao Since the beginning of communist rule in China in 1949, this giant portrait of Mao Zedong, the chairman of the Chinese Communist Party, has hung on the Gate of Heavenly Peace, the entrance to the Forbidden City of the Qing dynasty emperors, in the heart of Beijing.

Map 27.1
China and Taiwan
China is a huge country, divided into many provinces, and occupies a large part of eastern Eurasia. In 1949 the government of the Republic of China, defeated by the Chinese communists, moved to the island of Taiwan, off China's Pacific coast.

Interactive Map

ended in a stalemate in 1953, and the United States signed a mutual defense treaty with Chiang Kai-shek's regime on Taiwan. The substantial U.S. forces stationed in Taiwan and South Korea joined the thousands of U.S. troops that had remained in Japan, Okinawa, and the Philippines after World War II, while the U.S. Navy patrolled the waters off China. But Mao used paranoia about this formidable U.S. military presence to mobilize the Chinese around his programs, and the ability to achieve a Korean stalemate with the powerful Americans improved China's international position. Many countries allied to the United States recognized the Republic of China, now based on Taiwan, as the official government of China, even while the United States continued to veto the Chinese communist effort to gain China's United Nations seat.

Relations with Russia and the United States

In the late 1950s tensions between China and the USSR grew. The Soviet policy of "peaceful coexistence" with the West enraged Mao, who labeled the United States "a paper tiger." Mao also opposed the 1956 decision of the Soviet leader, Nikita Khrushchev **(KROOSH-chef)**, to reveal the excesses of Stalinist police-state rule in Russia. By 1960 the Sino-Soviet split was official; the USSR withdrew advisers, technicians, and even the spare parts for the industries they had helped build. The Chinese built up their military strength, tested their first atomic bomb, and occasionally clashed with Soviet forces on their border. To counterbalance the power of the United States and the USSR, China sought allies and influence in Asia and Africa. Yet, despite fierce anti-U.S. and anti-Soviet rhetoric, Chinese leaders generally followed a cautious foreign policy.

During the 1970s Chinese foreign policy changed dramatically, symbolized by U.S. president Richard Nixon's trip to Beijing in 1972. The two nations shared a hostility toward the USSR; moreover, the bitter U.S. experience in Vietnam had opened the door to foreign policy rethinking in both the United States and China. Chinese leaders perceived the Americans as stepping back from Asian commitments, and hence a diminishing threat. The United States quit blocking Chinese membership in the United Nations and, in 1978, normalized diplomatic relations with China. Meanwhile, the Chinese developed better relations with noncommunist nations in Southeast Asia and Africa.

Cultural Revolution and Maoist Society

Mao was a complex figure, a self-proclaimed feminist who promoted women's rights but also a sexually promiscuous man who married several times and had many lovers, but who also seldom bathed or brushed his teeth. A poor public speaker, he could nevertheless inspire millions to follow his lead. A poet and philosopher but also power hungry and ruthless, he made many enemies, even within the leadership. Although many of his initiatives ultimately failed or resulted in misery for millions of people, he played a powerful role in modern world history, leading the communists to victory, reunifying China, focusing public attention on rural people, and placing his stamp on the world's most populous nation.

e **Primary Source: "One Hundred Items for Destroying the Old and Establishing the New"** Read this document of support for Mao's socialist ideology and commitment to destroy the old ways of Chinese thinking by a student group of Red Guards.

Great Proletarian Cultural Revolution A radical movement in China between 1966 and 1976 that represented Mao Zedong's attempt to implant his vision, destroy his enemies, crush the stifling bureaucracy, and renew the revolution's vigor.

Red Guards Young workers and students who were the major supporters of the Cultural Revolution in Mao's China.

Dissatisfied with China's development and his eclipse by the early 1960s, in the mid-1960s Mao regained his dominant status by resurrecting Maoism and its vision of a new society comprising unselfish, politically conscious citizens. In Mao's vision, individuals inspired by the slogan "Serve the People" subordinated their own needs to the broader social order. His allies emphasized the cult of Mao, and newspapers reported that, illuminated by Mao's revolutionary ideas, factory workers would discover better techniques for galvanizing, the manager of a food store would double his sales of watermelons, and farmers would learn to judge exactly the right amount of manure to fertilize their plots. Following these ideas, between 1966 and 1976 a radical movement generated by Mao convulsed and reshaped China like a whirlwind. The **Great Proletarian Cultural Revolution** represented Mao's attempt to implant his vision, destroy his enemies, crush the stifling bureaucracy, and renew the revolution's vigor. Workers and students known as **Red Guards** roamed around cities and the countryside in groups, attacking and arresting anti-Mao leaders and smashing temples, churches, and party and government headquarters. Mao's supporters also created revolutionary committees, led by students, workers, and soldiers, to run cities, factories, and schools. The Red Guards carried copies of a little red book containing short quotations from Mao's writings, such as his claim that Marxism cannot be understood through books alone but also requires contact with the workers and peasants. One observer noted that "giant portraits of [Mao] now hung in the streets, busts were in every chamber, his books and photographs were everywhere on display."[4]

The turmoil disrupted industrial and agricultural production, closed most schools for two years, and resulted in thousands killed, jailed, or removed from official positions. Millions of others were sent to remote rural areas to experience peasant life, and anti-Mao officials, intellectuals, and people with upper-class backgrounds faced public criticism and often punishment. A Chinese journalist whose grandparents were capitalists remembered the attacks on her family: "Red Guards swarming all over the house and a great fire in our courtyard onto which were thrown my father's books, my grandparent's precious traditional furniture and my toys."[5] Soon even Mao was dampening the radical fervor.

The communists reshaped Chinese society in many ways. Mao promoted a model of social equality, known as the **Iron Rice Bowl**, in which the people, especially in villages, shared resources—food, draft animals, farm equipment—and the peasants enjoyed dignity. As a result, Maoism generally improved life for the poorer Chinese. An emphasis on preventive medicine included the training of villagers as paramedics, known as barefoot doctors, who addressed everyday health care, such as distributing medication and setting broken bones. Where once famine and disease were common, most Chinese now enjoyed decent health care. In addition, mass education raised literacy rates to the levels of industrialized nations. Many peasants appreciated the changes. In 1971 an elderly peasant told visiting Western scholars what he had gained: "Now we are free to work full-time, have a secure home, eat enough food, have complete medical care, receive education—and take our future in our hands."[6]

Woodcut by Ku Yuan, from Mei-shu, 1944

Chinese Political Art This woodcut, carved during the Chinese civil war of the late 1940s, was typical of the political art made by the communists to rally popular support for their cause, a hallmark of Mao's era. Entitled "Support Our Common People's Own Army," the woodcut shows Chinese peasants working together with the communist military forces.

Iron Rice Bowl A model of social equality in Mao's China in which the people, especially in the villages, shared resources and the peasants enjoyed status and dignity.

The communists also tried to overturn Confucian-influenced patriarchy by raising the status of women. Mao praised women, who he said "held up half the sky," as a force in production. A new marriage law abolished arranged marriages, forbade men from taking concubines, and made divorce easier, while a land reform empowered women economically by expanding their property rights. Women now enjoyed legal equality with men and greater access to education, often worked for wages, and played a stronger public role, often leading local organizations. In conferences and periodicals, women debated the proper balance between housekeeping and paid work and whether they should devote their energies to the revolution as well as to their husbands and children. Women activists worked to build a democratic family, emphasizing love matches rather than arranged marriages, fostering closer emotional ties between husbands, wives, and children, and lessening male domination. But the rural areas remained more conservative than the cities. Moreover, few women held high national positions. Mao's last wife, Jiang Qing **(chang ching)** (1914–1991), a former film actress, wielded great power during the Cultural Revolution but was unpopular because of her radical policies. In 1976, after Mao's death, Jiang and her top party allies, the "Gang of Four," lost a power struggle and were imprisoned.

The communists often undermined traditional beliefs and culture. Calling religion a bond enslaving people, Mao moved to control religious behavior and marginalize Christian churches, Buddhist monasteries, and Islamic mosques, and by the 1970s only a small minority openly practiced religion. Only religious leaders who cooperated with the state maintained their positions. Mao also sought to use the arts as a weapon in the class struggle, fostering a "people's art" created by and for the common people. He wrote, "In the world today all culture, all literature and art belongs to definite political lines. Art for art's sake, art that stands above the class and party do not exist in reality."[7] During the Great Leap Forward, party activists collected literature written by common people and encouraged peasants and workers to compose poetry and songs. Peasants painted scenes of people at work, often in bright, cheerful colors conveying an optimistic tone, and part-time writers got a day off from the factory to work on literary projects. A 1958 poem proclaimed: "Labor is joy, how joyful it is, Bathed in sweat and two hands full of mud. Like sweet rain, my sweat waters the land."[8] However, critics argued that art serving revolutionary goals was reduced to political propaganda.

The politicization of the arts reached its peak levels during the Cultural Revolution, when elitism came under fierce attack. Red Guards sang new songs in praise of change and Chairman Mao, such as "The East is red, the sun has risen. China has produced a Mao Zedong; He is the great savior of the people."[9] Militant operas had a strong revolutionary message, such as the dignity of peasant life or Communist Party history. Rejecting Western-style ballet as decadent, dancers composed revolutionary ballets that integrated Chinese martial arts, such as kung fu, folk dances, and Russian ballet. For example, *The Red Detachment of Women* portrayed the experiences of a company of women soldiers during the civil war against Chiang's Republic.

Mao's Legacy

After Mao died in 1976, the Chinese took stock of Mao's legacy. The communists had restored China to great power status and renewed the people's confidence after a century of imperialistic exploitation and invasion. China was no longer a doormat; it even had nuclear weapons. Once again, the Chinese envisioned themselves as the Middle Kingdom exercising influence in the world. Whereas a generation earlier begging or prostitution had been common, now most Chinese, though enjoying little material surplus, could satisfy their basic food, housing, and clothing needs. The economy was also healthier and more broadly based than in 1949.

Mao's policies, however, had also resulted in failures and political repression. Although China may have gained control of its economic destiny, it was still poor by world standards. In addition, Mao had discouraged free enterprise and individual initiative, so that few private cars interfered with the bicycles that most Chinese used to get to work or go shopping. Chinese wanted better housing and more consumer goods now rather than in a distant future. With few luxuries or diversions available, life was dull. In addition, the fierce punishment of dissenters and the turmoil of the Great Leap Forward and Cultural Revolution had ruined numerous lives. People were disillusioned by government coercion, unfulfilled promises, and the chaos of the Cultural Revolution, and bitter disagreements had ripped the Communist Party leadership apart. Many blamed Mao and his radicalism for the problems, and reformers in the party charged that, in his later years, Mao had lost touch with common people's lives. The often erratic policies made people cynical, willing to give only passive cooperation and avoiding commitment to a particular line. Many Chinese were ready for change.

SECTION SUMMARY

- After Japan was defeated in World War II, Chinese communists and nationalists fought a civil war in which Mao Zedong's communists triumphed by appealing to people's frustration with the corruption of Chiang Kai-shek's nationalists.
- To develop its economy, China first employed Stalinism, which featured central planning dominated by a bureaucratic elite, and then shifted to Maoism, which emphasized mass mobilization of the people to industrialize and maximize output, but under Maoism millions starved to death and many suffered under political repression.
- China reasserted itself as a world power, reclaiming Tibet, becoming involved in the Korean War, ultimately splitting with the USSR, and only reestablishing formal relations with the United States in the 1970s.
- Frustrated with China's development, Mao led a decade-long cultural revolution, a period of radical upheaval in which young Red Guards attempted to destroy Mao's enemies and obstacles to progress, which caused great economic problems and brought misery to many.
- Mao reshaped Chinese society, improving literacy rates and health care, especially for rural people, expanding the rights of women, opposing traditional religious institutions and elitism, and encouraging the people to produce their own literature and art, but at the cost of many human rights abuses.
- While Mao restored China as a world power and brought many out of poverty, after his death in 1976 many Chinese wanted to join the modern world and gain increased access to material benefits.

CHINESE MODERNIZATION

What factors explain the dramatic rise of Chinese economic power in the world since 1978?

Deng Xiaoping **(dung shee-yao-ping)** (1904–1997), a longtime Communist Party leader who had often clashed with Mao, came to power in 1978 and changed China's direction. Deng and his allies rejected Mao's view of a self-sufficient, ideologically pure China outside the world economy, concluding that collectivized agriculture had failed to raise productivity enough to finance a jump into the high technology and industry needed to make China a major power. In 1978 Deng, portraying China as at a turning point in history, announced the policy of Four Modernizations: the development of agriculture, industry, military, and science and technology to turn China into a powerful nation by 2000. Deng's successors generally followed his pragmatic policies, which transformed China into an economic powerhouse and modified Maoist society.

Market Socialism and Repression

From 1978 to 1989 Chinese leaders pursued **market socialism**, a mix of free enterprise, economic liberalization, and state controls that produced economic dynamism. This pragmatic approach, unlike Mao's, was more concerned with economic results than socialist values. Twice purged for opposing Mao, Deng was fond of a Chinese proverb: "It doesn't matter whether a cat is black or white, only if it catches mice." Deng used the market to stimulate productivity, and China reentered the world economy to obtain capital investment to spur manufacturing. Like Meiji Japan, China now imported technology, foreign expertise, and capitalist ideas. Deng believed that China had reached a plateau; to move to the next levels required wider international participation. Hence, he improved ties with the United States, Japan, western Europe, and non-communist Southeast Asia. Dazzled by China's huge potential market of, as Western experts put it, 1 billion toothbrushes (for toothpaste) and 2 billion armpits (for deodorant), Western companies promoted increased trade.

market socialism A Chinese economic program used between 1978 and 1989 that mixed free enterprise, economic liberalization, and state controls and that produced economic dynamism in China.

Spurring Economic Growth

Introducing capitalist ideas, such as offering workers material incentives rather than ideological slogans, Deng's reforms sparked dramatic changes. The government first allowed small private enterprises, then larger ones; ultimately both private and state-owned enterprises competed with each other. In agriculture, Deng replaced Mao's communes with the contract system in which peasants could lease (but could not buy) land to work privately. In many districts this free market led to soaring productivity, with rural per capita incomes rising fourfold in the first decade. Tapping a skilled, industrious, but cheap labor force, hundreds of Western and Asian companies set up manufacturing operations, producing goods such as shirts, underwear, and toys chiefly for export. In the 1980s, China became a consumer society; even in small cities, shops stocked Japanese televisions and Western soft drinks. Over the next twenty-five years the economy quadrupled in size and foreign trade increased ten times over.

Cultural Life

Deng also loosened political and cultural controls. Intellectuals and artists enjoyed greater freedom; people long silenced or imprisoned were heard from again. The press was enlivened and the scope for public debate widened. Deng also increasingly tolerated organized religion. Western popular culture, especially films, rock music, and discos, won a huge audience; books and magazines from around the world became available; and foreign travelers backpacked in remote areas. The sentimental recordings of Taiwan's top female singer, Deng Lijun (deyn lee-choong), better known to her millions of fans in Hong Kong, Japan, and Southeast Asia as Teresa Teng, were so widely played in Chinese homes and restaurants that people said that "the day belongs to Deng Xiaoping but the night belongs to Deng Lijun."[10] At the same time, novels and short stories revealed the depth of suffering during the Cultural Revolution, and popular writers developed huge audiences for stories daring to use sexual themes. Chinese-made films won international acclaim, while creative directors associated with semi-independent film studios skirmished with wary government censors. Their films portrayed China as anything but a communist paradise. Rock musicians, especially Cui Jian (sway jen), a former trumpeter with the Beijing Symphony, became a major voice for alienated urban youth. Dressed in battered army fatigues and a coat style favored by Mao, Cui sang: "This guitar in my hands is like a knife. I want to cut at your hypocrisy till I see some truth." Cui's songs were indirect, focusing more on bureaucratic corruption, social problems, and young people's frustrations than on politics, but Chinese youth easily read between the lines for the hidden meanings. One fan commented that "Cui Jian says things we all feel, but cannot say."[11]

Tensions and Government Crackdown

Although many Chinese applauded the ideological loosening and the growing economic options, market socialism hid a dark underside. Many districts had seen few benefits from the reorganization of rural life. Chinese authorities imposed one policy for the vast nation rather than allowing districts and villages to find a policy that worked for them. Some villagers, because of their better land, political connections, or entrepreneurial skills, benefited more than others, opening a gap between newly rich and poor villagers. Prices rose rapidly, and corruption increased as bureaucrats and Communist Party officials lined their own pockets. Moreover, tension increased within the party, with Stalinists and Maoists viewing economic liberalization as undermining one-party rule and communism. The fall of communism in eastern Europe and the USSR in 1989 alarmed hardliners. But dissidents and some reformers, seeing strong controls as inhibiting initiative, pushed democracy as "the fifth modernization." In response, party hardliners called for cracking down, arresting dissidents.

In 1989 the tensions in Deng's China reached a boiling point, generating massive protests and government repression. Thousands of protesters, led by university students and workers, took over Tiananmen Square in downtown Beijing, demanding the resignation of the most unpopular leaders, an end to government corruption, and a transition to a fully open system. The party hardliners, in alliance with Deng, purged the moderate party leaders and ordered the army to clear out the demonstrators. In what became known as the Tiananmen Massacre, the army killed hundreds and arrested thousands, while millions around the world watched the violence on television. The courageous

Beijing protesters had overestimated their popular support. Since many Chinese outside the cities valued stability more than vague promises of a better world, the protesters had also miscalculated the prospects of democracy in a country with an authoritarian political tradition.

Economic Change and Politics Since 1989

market Leninism A policy followed after the Tiananmen Massacre in 1989 whereby the Chinese communist state asserted more power over society while also fostering an even stronger market orientation in the economy than had existed under market socialism.

After the Tiananmen Massacre the communists modified market socialism into **market Leninism**, a policy whereby the Chinese state, obsessed with stability, asserted more power over society while also fostering an even stronger market orientation in the economy. The communist leadership reestablished control in political, social, and cultural life, tolerating less dissent than in the 1980s, but the economy became further privatized. Remembering the chaos of the Cultural Revolution and the 1989 unrest, Chinese often valued political stability over individual rights, such as unfettered free speech and participation in government, especially at a time of overheated economic growth. For 2000 years Chinese governments have promoted social and political harmony to discourage conflict.

However, the control of the one-party state was not absolute. In some local elections communist officials permitted competition between candidates, and some dissenters still spoke out. Opponents of the environmentally damaging Three Gorges Dam project, constructed to control the Yangzi **(yahng-zeh)** River and provide electrical power, publicized their views but could not halt the expensive project, which forced several million people to move from their homes. However, the Chinese state, often arbitrary in its actions, used the military and police to intimidate dissidents. Assertive dissidents faced arrest, and public debate was dampened. China executed thousands of people a year, mostly criminals but including some accused of economic misbehavior or political opposition. Anxious to preserve national unity, China's leaders also suppressed dissent in Tibet and among Muslim Turkish groups in Xinjiang **(shinjee-yahng)**, in far western China, where people sought autonomy, greater religious freedom, and limits on large-scale Chinese immigration. In Tibet in 2008 and Xinjiang in 2009, the seething resentment against the government and Han Chinese newcomers led to riots and inter-ethnic violence, leaving hundreds of people dead or injured.

Social Unrest

Rapid Economic Growth

After 1980 China enjoyed the fastest economic growth in the world, often 10 percent a year, abetted by a "get-rich-quick" mentality among many Chinese. Deng claimed that to get rich is glorious. China's exports increased fifteenfold between 1980 and 2000, and the communist leadership sought popular support by offering consumer goods and wealth rather than political reform, providing shops with ample consumer goods and households with spending money. In the early days of reform people aspired to the "three bigs": bicycle, wristwatch, and sewing machine. Now they wanted televisions, washing machines, and video recorders. The urban middle class grew rapidly, and by 2009 China had moved ahead of Germany into third place in world economic strength. China also clearly benefited from the mobility of capital and products with globalization. If the economy maintains high annual growth rates, China may eventually have the world's largest economy.

Although the economic reforms have improved living standards for many Chinese, they have also produced numerous downsides. For example, economic dynamism is concentrated in a few coastal provinces and special economic zones, where living standards approach those of Taiwan and South Korea. Cities such as Shanghai and Shenzen boast towering skyscrapers and huge shopping malls with upscale shops. Elsewhere, conditions have often deteriorated. Unemployment grows dramatically as state enterprises close or become uncompetitive and inflation skyrockets. Although laws discourage migration to another district without government permission, millions of peasants seeking jobs or a less rustic life have nonetheless moved to cities, where they struggle. Their precarious position became clear in 2008, when the global economic crisis began to affect China as overseas markets collapsed. Thousands of factories closed, leaving millions of disillusioned workers without incomes. Many had little choice but to return to their home villages. Yet, unlike the Western nations and Japan, China's economy still grew, albeit at about half the rate of 2007. By later 2009, thanks to a huge government stimulus package and autocratic decision-making, China's economy began a recovery and many workers found jobs.

Resource and Energy Consumption

The Chinese have also become even greater users of world resources, such as oil and coal, and major polluters of the atmosphere. China has become the number two producer of greenhouse gases that cause global warming, although its output is only half that of the the United States. Mindful of the unhealthy air pollution of China's cities and fouled rivers and lakes fostered by industrialization, by 2009 Chinese leaders placed more emphasis than Americans do on developing cleaner, greener, and renewable energy sources such as wind and solar. Yet, China still relies heavily on coal-based power sources and now leads the world in carbon emissions. Water supplies have become badly overstretched, and, with private cars clogging the city streets where bicycles once dominated, smog blankets the cities. Land and energy grow more expensive.

Political and economic changes have influenced other areas of Chinese life. In the cities, the newly rich entrepreneurs enjoy luxury cars, access to golf courses, and vacations abroad. China has several hundred thousand millionaires and some billionaires. Even the middle class, numbering over 200 million and chiefly working in business, can enjoy a comfortable life. With money concentrated in the private sector, teachers, professors, and doctors leave their low-paying state jobs to open businesses or join foreign corporations, and some village leaders use their power to amass wealth and power. The wealthy flaunt their affluence, and the poor resent it. Street songs often mock the powerful: "I'm a big official, so I eat and drink, and I've got the potbelly to prove it. Beer, spirits, rice wine, love potions—I drink it all."[12] By 2005 peasant protests against seizure of village land to build polluting factories, luxury housing, and golf courses had become frequent, numbering in the thousands annually and resulting in the arrests of protest leaders. Meanwhile, the shift to market forces leaves millions unable to afford medical care and schooling for their children. Thanks to the decline in health care, especially in rural areas, between half a million and 1.5 million Chinese have HIV or AIDS. Some poorer Chinese long fondly for Mao and the dismantled Iron Rice Bowl. Yet, despite reduced job security and social services, people are now freer than before to travel, change jobs, enjoy leisure, and even complain.

Rich–Poor Divide

The Communist Party has faced problems Mao could never have anticipated. Once viewing itself as the protector of the working class and poor peasants, it now welcomes wealthy businessmen and professionals into its ranks. Many who have little faith in the communist vision still see party membership as helpful to their career prospects. And most young Chinese, preoccupied with seeking wealth, know little about the Tienanmen Massacre. Yet, powerful provincial leaders whose first priority is economic growth increasingly ignore Beijing. The rapid economic growth raises questions as to whether Chinese leaders can resolve the increasing inequalities and spread wealth more equitably to check the growth of social tensions. Some pessimists forecast more conflicts between rich and poor Chinese, or civil war between rich and poor regions.

Chinese Society and Culture Since 1989

The government struggles to maintain social stability. Mao's China had been one of the world's safest countries, but economic growth and the quest for wealth generated a rapid increase in crime. The close connection between government and business corruption, underworld activity, and financial success led to Chinese talking about the "Five Colors," or surest roads to riches: Communist Party connections, prostitution, smuggling, illegal drug dealing, and criminal gangs. Drug dealing became rampant once again, serving the growing number of people using narcotics for escape. Maintaining Confucian and Maoist attitudes, many Chinese view wealth as corrupting and mistrust rich business interests.

Although women's economic status has often improved, many still face restricted gender expectations. While the feminist journalist Xue Xinran **(shoe shin-rahn)** wrote that "Chinese women had always thought that their lives should be full of misery. Many had no idea what happiness was, other than having a son for the family"[13] (see Profile: Xue Xinran, a Chinese Voice for Women), many scholars consider the stereotype of the long-suffering, submissive Chinese woman misleading, noting that modern women are often strong-willed and resourceful. But many rural women may feel intimidated by men. Women now receive little support because government policies are aimed at economic growth, not gender equality. Millions of rural women migrate to the cities for industrial and service jobs, providing much of the labor force for the new factories that have helped turn China into an economic giant. Wherever they live, women commonly work long hours, and few women occupy high positions in the government, Communist Party, or top business enterprises.

Gender Relations

Since China already had 1 billion people, a fifth of humankind, Deng Xiaoping introduced a one-child-per-family policy to try to stabilize the population. Critics complained that children without siblings were pampered and self-centered. The policy also encouraged and sometimes mandated abortion and, since traditional attitudes favoring sons remained, resulted in widespread killing of female babies. With more boys than girls being born and raised, an imbalance in numbers between the sexes developed, with serious social consequences as men cannot find wives.

Global entertainment and consumer culture also affect China, with Western popular culture becoming a powerful force among youth. Cui Jian and other rock musicians, some of whom had participated in the Beijing student protest movement, now compete with heavy metal, punk, and rap musicians. Every city has clubs offering Western music, and Chinese imitators of Anglo-American boy bands and girl groups have found a vast teen audience. In 2005 more than 8 million Chinese voted for three finalists in a hugely popular Chinese television program, *Super Girl,* a local version of the popular U.S. television program, *American Idol.* Television offers U.S. series dubbed in Chinese, such as *The X-Files* and *Baywatch*, and in Shanghai a theme park very similar to Disney

Popular Culture

World features a Wild West Town. Chinese consumers are served by numerous McDonald's outlets (one near Mao's mausoleum), Hard Rock Cafes, Wal-Marts, and some 85,000 Avon agents selling American cosmetics and beauty products. Homosexuals, who faced condemnation and discrimination under Mao, have been slowly coming out, especially in the cities, where gay bars are common, and even have hundreds of their own websites. But South Korean popular culture and consumer products—music, clothing, television dramas, movies, cosmetics—also became very fashionable among young Chinese. Much of the conversion of millions of Chinese to evangelical Christianity is due to the thousands of South Korean Protestant missionaries in the country.

China and the Information Superhighway

Those Chinese able to afford satellite dishes, fax machines, and personal computers linked to the Internet have gained access to ideas from around the world. More than 300 million Chinese are Internet users, and 53 million own personal computers. E-commerce is becoming much more popular and China's biggest on-line auction site had some 145 million registered members in 2009. To restrict the free flow of information, officials crack down on cyberspace, sometimes closing down Internet cafes and preventing Internet providers—local and Western—from allowing access to banned websites. But websites and blogs proliferate rapidly, making complete monitoring difficult. By 2009 the government sought even stricter controls over the Internet and electronic tools such as Twitter, Facebook, and YouTube. The government also sometimes shuts down newspapers and magazines whose reporting is too daring, but brave journalists and officials have risked punishment by openly criticizing micromanagement of the media. Some liberal party members and intellectuals sign petitions and write articles calling for more attention to human rights abuses, actions that may cost them their jobs or invite police surveillance. Yet, several hundred thousand Chinese, including the children of high officials, have studied in Western universities.

Policies toward religion have been inconsistent. After 1978 the government tolerated millions of Chinese returning to their ancestral faith, but it has cracked down on movements deemed a threat or that refuse to accept official restrictions. Officials arrest and sometimes execute leaders and members of the assertive, missionary *Falun Gong* meditation sect, a mix of Daoist, Buddhist, and Christian influences, and have tried to close down rapidly proliferating independent Christian churches that do not seek government approval.

China in the Global System

Reclaiming Hong Kong and Macao

China's relations with the wider world have been colored by humiliation from the lost wars and foreign gunboats of the nineteenth century and by civil wars and Japanese invasions in the twentieth. Eventually the Chinese saw their nation once again stand tall, strong, and increasingly rich. In 1997 they celebrated the peaceful return of Hong Kong from British colonial control, rectifying the loss of that territory during the Opium War. Hong Kong, a prosperous enclave whose towering skyscrapers, dazzling neon-lit waterfront, bustling shopping malls, and dynamic film industry made it a symbol of East Asian capitalism, was incorporated under the policy of "one nation, two systems." At the same time, a vocal and popular pro-democracy movement in Hong Kong charges that China's occasional interference in Hong Kong politics threatens political freedoms. Another loss was rectified when in 1999 Portugal returned its small coastal colony of Macao to Chinese control. Macao's economy is based on gambling casinos, a lucrative enterprise the once-puritanical communists now seem happy to tolerate.

China and Global Power

Since 1976 China has pursued a pragmatic foreign policy designed to win friends and trading partners but to also avoid entangling alliances. China gradually improved relations with the United States and USSR, cultivated diplomatic ties with other nations, and became increasingly active in the world community, joining international institutions such as the World Trade Organization. To enhance China's competitive stance, some 200 million children study English. China now enjoys tremendous influence in the world economy, importing vast amounts of capital and natural resources, such as Zambian copper and Venezuelan oil, while exporting industrial products of every kind. Thousands of foreign investors have come from the West, Japan, Southeast Asia, South Korea, and even Taiwan, opening factories and negotiating joint ventures with Chinese firms. Meanwhile, China has supported the U.S. economy, becoming the major buyer of the treasury bonds that financed the growing U.S. national debt in the early 2000s. Chinese enterprises have also begun buying up companies in other nations. Hundreds of Chinese companies operate in Africa and Latin America. Many thousands of Chinese have followed them as workers or to open small enterprises. In addition, China provides investment and loans to governments but expects cooperation in return. Thus China has become the world's most successful newly industrializing economy, buttressed by a vast resource base, a huge domestic market, and a resourceful labor force.

Yet China has met roadblocks in enhancing its global power. The government continues to threaten forced unification if Taiwan, which enjoys a defense agreement with the United States,

XUE XINRAN, A CHINESE VOICE FOR WOMEN

In the 1980s Xue Xinran (shoe shin-rahn), known professionally as Xinran, began working for a radio network and went on to become one of China's most successful and innovative journalists. A radio call-in show that she launched in 1989 featured hundreds of poignant and haunting stories by women. The huge audience the show attracted and her sensitive handling of the callers made Xinran a role model and heroine for Chinese women. Her own life and career also revealed women's experiences in contemporary China.

Born in Beijing in 1958, Xinran had a difficult childhood that was complicated by the turmoil of the Cultural Revolution. Her mother came from a capitalist, property-owning family. But Xinran's grandfather, although he cooperated with the communists, lost his property and was imprisoned during the Cultural Revolution. Her mother joined the Communist Party and army at sixteen but was occasionally jailed or demoted in purges of those from capitalist class backgrounds. Xinran's father was a national expert in mechanics and computing but, like her mother, also from a once wealthy family. He too had been imprisoned. Xinran had been sent to live with a grandmother when she was one month old and seldom saw her parents during her childhood. Reflecting on her family, she wrote that, like many Chinese, her parents endured an unhappy marriage: "Did [my parents] love each other? I have never dared to ask." While working as an army administrator, Xinran married, had a son, PanPan, and later divorced.

Eventually Xinran became a radio journalist. But she had to persuade the station to let her begin a nightly call-in program, *Words on the Night Breeze*. Since 1949 the media had been the mouthpiece of the Communist Party, ensuring that it spoke with one identical voice. However, Xinran said, "I was trying to open a little window, a tiny hole, so that people would allow their spirits to cry out and breathe after the gunpowder-laden atmosphere of the previous forty years." In starting her call-in program, the question that obsessed her was, What is a woman's life really worth in a China where footbinding was a recent memory but women now lived and worked alongside men? Xinran's compassion and ability encouraged callers to talk freely about feelings. For eight groundbreaking years, women called in and discussed their lives, and Xinran was shocked by much of what they said. Broadcast all over China, the program offered an unflinching portrait of what it meant to be a woman in modern China, including the expectations of obedience to fathers, husbands, and sons. Women from every social status—daughters of wealthy families, wives of party officials, children of Cultural Revolution survivors, homeless street scavengers, isolated mountain villagers—called in stories, often heartbreaking tales of sexual abuse, gang rape, forced marriages, and enforced separation of families.

The stories Xinran heard did not fit the image promoted by the Communist Party of a happy, harmonious society. She told, for instance, of Jingyi and her boyfriend, Gu Da, university classmates who fell passionately in love but were sent by the government to work in different parts of the country. They had planned to eventually marry but lost touch during the chaos of the Cultural Revolution. For forty-five years Jingyi had first longed for and then searched for Gu Da. When they finally had a reunion in 1994, Jingyi was devastated to discover that Gu Da, despairing of ever seeing Jingyi again, had married another woman. Their saga provided a window on the disrupted personal and family lives common in China after 1949.

Courtesy, Asia Society, AustralAsia Centre

Xue Xinran The Chinese journalist, Xue Xinran, explored the lives of Chinese women on her radio program and in her writings.

In Xinran's view, "When China started to open up [to the outside world], it was like a starving child devouring everything without much discrimination. But China's brain had not yet grown the cells to absorb truth and freedom." In 1997 the conflict between what Xinran knew and what she was permitted to say caused her to give up her career and leave for Britain, where she hoped to find a freer life and reach a global audience. In Britain, after mastering English, she first taught at the University of London and then became a columnist for a national newspaper, *The Guardian*. She published several nonfiction books based on the stories she learned in China. In *The Good Women of China: Hidden Voices* (2002), she opened a window revealing the lives of Chinese women to the outside world. Her reports revealed strong, resourceful characters who offered insights into China's past and present. Another book, *The Sky Burial* (2004), told the extraordinary story of an intrepid Chinese woman who spent thirty years searching rugged Tibet, a thousand miles from her home city, for her beloved husband, an army doctor who was reported killed. In *China Witness* (2008), Xinran traced China's traumatic modern history through candid interviews with aging Chinese. In 2002 Xinran married an Englishman, the literary agent Toby Eady. Every year she returns to China for visits and reporting, and also sponsors a charity, The Mother's Bridge of Love, that helps disadvantaged children.

THINKING ABOUT THE PROFILE

1. Why did Xinran achieve such fame in China?
2. What does her journalism tell us about the experiences of Chinese women?

Note: Quotations from Xue Xinran, *The Good Women of China: Hidden Voices* (New York: Anchor, 2002), 3, 126, 227.

tries to declare a permanent break from China. Although economic and social links between China and Taiwan have increased, few in the island nation, which enjoys democracy and a much higher standard of living, want a merger with the mainland in the near future. Meanwhile, Chinese relations with Japan ebb and flow. The two nations have close economic ties—thousands of Japanese businessmen are based in China—but are also natural rivals, the Chinese remaining resentful of Japanese brutality during World War II and antagonistic to contemporary Japanese nationalism. However, China has improved political and economic relations with once-bitter enemies such as South Korea and anticommunist countries such as Malaysia, the Philippines, and Australia, which view China as the future regional power and hence seek friendly relations. In many Asian and some African and Latin American countries, large numbers of people are learning Chinese, and some 90,000 foreign students study in China. Nonetheless, historical resentment of Japan and the West stokes Chinese nationalism, sometimes resulting in anti-Japan or anti-U.S. protest demonstrations. In addition, although by the early 2000s China only ranked fifth among the world's nations in defense spending, its neighbors have feared Chinese military power.

China's Prospects

China's tremendous size, population, natural resources, military strength, national confidence, and sense of history have placed it in an unusual position of being a major global power while still having a much lower overall standard of living and far more poverty than North America, western Europe, Japan, and several industrializing Asian nations. Nonetheless, China, rather than the United States, led global recovery from the 2008–2009 recession, suggesting that the world's economic center of gravity may be shifting to East Asia. Perhaps China has been returning to its historical leadership as the Asian dragon and a major engine of the global economy. Experts debated whether either China or India might replace the United States as the major world power by 2050 or 2100. Some argued that India had advantages, such as democracy, a free press, and a sounder financial system, while others thought China had the better prospects, especially if the growing middle class fosters a more open political system. Still others doubted that a decline of U.S. power was imminent. As during the long period of Chinese power and prosperity between 600 and 1800, China is once again a major force in world affairs.

SECTION SUMMARY

- Under Deng Xiaoping, China opened up to Western economic ideas and investment, gradually introducing private ownership and competition, as well as to political, religious, and cultural currents that had been suppressed under Mao.
- Although many supported Deng's reforms, they led to increasing corruption and a growing gap between rich and poor, especially in rural areas, and, in 1989, a violent suppression of prodemocracy dissidents in the Tiananmen Massacre.
- Under market Leninism, the Chinese state increased political and social control while continuing to privatize the economy, which grew briskly, though there was stagnation in many rural areas and environmental damage in others.
- The growth of China's economy has improved access to consumer goods but has also led to increased crime and drug use, and an effort to limit population has led to many abortions and the killing of female babies.
- China has become more open to Western culture, though its government has attempted to restrict the free flow of information.
- China has enjoyed a great recovery and return to world prominence in recent decades, though it still has uncertain relations with Taiwan and Japan, and its living standard remains much lower than many of its rivals.

THE REMAKING OF JAPAN

How did Japan rise from the ashes of defeat in World War II to become a global economic powerhouse?

In August 1945, Japan lay in ruins, its major cities largely destroyed by U.S. bombing and its economy ruined (see Map 27.2). Having no concept of military defeat, the Japanese people were psychologically devastated. Yet, within a decade the country had recovered from the disaster of World War II. After several decades of the highest economic growth rates in world history, Japan became one of the world's major economic powers, and by the 1980s it was challenging the United States for world economic leadership. A system stressing cooperation rather than individualism provided the basis for economic and social stability in an overcrowded land. But beginning in the 1990s Japan experienced political and economic uncertainty.

Map 27.2
Japan and the Little Dragons
Japan fostered the strongest Asian economy through the second half of the twentieth century, but in recent decades the Little Dragons—South Korea, Taiwan, Hong Kong, and Singapore—also have had rapid economic growth.

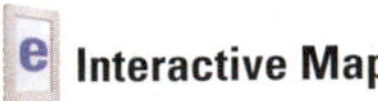
Interactive Map

Occupation, Recovery, and Politics

U.S. Occupation

The post–World War II occupation by the United States aided Japan's recovery. The emperor, Hirohito **(here-o-HEE-to)** (1901–1989), still a revered figure, asked them to cooperate with the Allied occupation forces, and by and large they did. Japan was placed under a U.S.-dominated military administration, the Supreme Command of Allied Powers (SCAP), that was tasked with rebuilding rather than punishing Japan. Japan also lost Korea, Taiwan, and Manchuria, while the United States took control of the Ryukyu Islands, which were returned to Japan in the 1970s,

CHRONOLOGY

Japan Since 1945

1946–1952 SCAP occupation of Japan

1946 First postwar Japanese elections

1951 U.S.-Japan peace treaty

1960s–1989 Era of rapid Japanese economic growth

1989 Beginning of Japanese economic downturn

1993 Fragmentation of Liberal Democratic Party

1997 Asian financial collapse

and Micronesia. SCAP hoped to demilitarize and democratize Japan, using the United States as the model, and to aid economic recovery. It dismantled the Japanese military, removed some civilian politicians, and tried and hanged seven wartime leaders as war criminals. Fearing that punishing the emperor, a member of an imperial family over 1,500 years old, would destabilize Japan, U.S. officials did not charge Hirohito with war crimes, but he was forced to renounce his godlike aura and become a more public figure.

SCAP fostered political and social changes. Sustaining democracy required a more egalitarian society in which once-disadvantaged people shared in the progress. A new constitution guaranteed civil liberties and forever renounced war as the nation's sovereign right. The first democratic elections, held in 1946, involved various competing political parties. All adult citizens, including women, could vote. Women gained legal equality in society and marriage but were only partly freed from the expectations of a patriarchal society. New universities opened, giving Japanese youth greater access than ever before to higher education. The economy also gradually recovered, using the same mix of government intervention and free markets that Japan had introduced in the Meiji era. Land reform subsidized the peasantry, making them strong government supporters and bringing prosperity to rural areas. Although SCAP attempted to break up entrenched economic power, large industrial-commercial-banking conglomerates still dominated manufacturing and foreign trade, making Japan more competitive in the world economy. But workers gained the right to unionize.

Japanese Politics

After the Chinese communist victory and the outbreak of the Korean War, the United States shifted its emphasis from restructuring Japanese society to integrating Japan into the anticommunist Western alliance, symbolized by the signing in 1951 of a formal U.S.-Japan peace treaty. U.S. military bases have remained in Japan ever since as part of a mutual defense pact. The policies implemented during the SCAP occupation, which officially ended in 1952, were most successful where U.S. and Japanese desires coincided or when the policies fit with the nation's traditions (see Chronology: Japan Since 1945). Democratic government fit both criteria. The Japanese had enjoyed several decades of democracy before the Great Depression, and borrowing from abroad also fit with Japanese tradition. They were again receptive to importing Western culture. With conditions stabilized, Japanese leaders embarked on a strategy of capitalizing on peace to strengthen the nation.

Despite stresses, Japan's democratic political system has endured. A variety of political parties—socialists, communists, liberals, Buddhists, and rightwing nationalists—have competed for parliamentary seats. But one major party, the center-right Liberal Democratic Party (LDP), has dominated politics, applying generally conservative, probusiness, and pro-U.S. policies. The SCAP-imposed electoral system gave greater weight to rural voters, the backbone of LDP support. But although prime ministers learned to negotiate with opposition parties as well as with the diverse LDP factions, critics believed that a political system dominated by one party and a few wealthy kingmakers, who faced little criticism from media largely owned by huge corporations, was at best a partial democracy.

Indeed, the need to finance political careers and raise money for elections from powerful corporations and criminal gangs has fostered political corruption. Bribery scandals have sometimes forced political leaders to resign, and a few have gone to prison. In 1993 the LDP fragmented in factional disputes, and various opposition parties gained support. But the LDP soon returned to power under a reform leader, though it faced challenges from opposition parties, and it has lost support for failing to resolve economic crises. Finally, in 2009, with Japan mired in severe recession and facing a huge national debt, the LDP experienced a huge defeat in national elections, losing power to the center-left Democratic Party, which promised reforms.

Japan and the United States

For self-protection, Japanese leaders forged a military alliance with the United States that allowed U.S. bases in Japan. As a result, Japan's military spending has long remained meager compared to that of the United States and the USSR, and Japan has been able to devote more resources to the civilian economy to help propel rapid economic growth. While the Cold War superpowers invested in weapons and armies, Japan devoted its economic surplus largely to industrial development. However, leftist parties, labor unions, and militant student groups long opposed the U.S. military presence as neocolonialism. Japanese also feared that the U.S. military interventions in places such as Vietnam and Iraq made Japan a potential target. Remembering the horrors of World War II, especially the atomic bombings that killed some 200,000 Japanese, many Japanese favored pacifism and believed that Japan's economic strength protected them from attack. Yet, with U.S. support, Japan began increasing military spending in the 1980s, and by 2009 it had the fourth largest military budget in the world, ahead of China but still much below that of the United States.

The Japanese decision to send soldiers to support, in noncombat activities, the U.S. war in Iraq was widely unpopular and, to critics, violated the constitutional ban against engaging in war.

The Japanese Economy and Growth

Adapting capitalism to its own traditions, Japan achieved phenomenal economic growth, its goods in demand on every continent only a century after it opened to the outside world. Wartime destruction required the rebuilding of basic industries using the latest innovations. Investing in new industries and high-tech fields, the Japanese became the world leaders in manufacturing products such as pianos, oil tankers, and automobiles, as well as electronics products such as watches, televisions, and cameras. As a result, from the 1960s through the 1980s Japan's annual growth rate was three times higher than that of other industrialized nations. Now an industrial giant possessing an advanced technology and distinctive economic and industrial structure, in 2000 Japan produced some 16 percent of the world's goods and services, half the U.S. percentage but twice that of third-place Germany. What observers often called an economic miracle was particularly impressive considering that the country has few mineral resources, limited productive farmland, and no major rivers to produce hydroelectric power. Consequently, the Japanese must import minerals needed for industry, such as iron ore, tin, and copper. Oil obtained from Alaska, Southeast Asia, and the Middle East powers Japan's transportation.

Getty Images

Japanese Protest Political demonstrations are common in Japanese cities. During this protest in 2001, liberals and leftists criticized new middle-school textbooks, approved by the Education Ministry, that, the critics claimed, distorted history by emphasizing nationalist viewpoints and downplaying Japanese atrocities in World War II.

Japan became known for innovative technologies and high-quality products. A magnificent mass transit system included the state-of-the-art bullet trains that whisked passengers around the country at 125 to 150 miles per hour and were always on time. Electronics manufacturers such as Sony, Atari, and Nintendo invented entertainment-oriented products, among them video and handheld game systems that became part of life on every continent, especially for youth. Millions of people, from Boston to Bogotá, Barcelona to Bombay, drove Toyotas, Hondas, and other Japanese-made cars. Enjoying living standards equal to those of most western Europeans, the Japanese themselves became Western-style consumers; everyone now sought to own cars, televisions, washing machines, and air conditioners. The Japanese also enjoyed the world's highest average life expectancy: seventy-nine or eighty years; in addition, a more varied diet, including more meat and dairy products, produced taller, healthier children. Western foods and beverages became popular, and Western fast-food outlets such as McDonald's proved a great success, serving the same items popular in the West as well as dishes adapted to local taste, such as teriyaki burgers and Chinese fried rice. The rural areas shared in the prosperity. However, most rural youth left their villages for the cities, and many workers had to make do with part-time jobs offering few benefits, and a small but growing underclass had no permanent jobs or homes.

Japan's capitalist economy has differed in fundamental ways from those of other industrial nations. The national government and big business work together in a cooperative relationship that became known as **Japan, Inc.** (Japan Incorporated). The government regulates business, setting overall guidelines, sponsoring research and development, and leasing the resulting products or technologies to private enterprise. Most Japanese businesses have accepted the guidelines because they take a longer-term view of profitability than was common among Western business leaders. But government-business cooperation has occurred chiefly in international trade, the country's lifeblood, and is made easier by the dominance of large Japanese conglomerates that own diverse enterprises such as factories, banks, and department stores. The government aids Japanese businesses by erecting protectionist barriers and bureaucratic hurdles that impede foreign businesses in the Japanese market.

Japan, Inc. The cooperative relationship between government and big business that has existed in Japan after 1945.

Environmental Problems

Economic growth has generated new problems. As in the West, industrialization has fostered wealth but also harmed the environment. Pollution of rivers and bays has wiped out coastal fishing, and smoggy air is so bad that city residents sometimes cover their noses and mouths with masks to avert respiratory difficulties. Thousands of people have died or been made ill by toxic waste dumped by factories. In addition, many younger people resent the long hours and sacrifices expected of both white-collar and blue-collar employees, especially since a high standard of living has already been achieved.

Industrial System

Japan's business and factory life has contributed to success. The system takes advantage of Japanese cultural values, such as conformity, hard work, cooperation, thrift, and foresight, while adding innovations. The 30 percent of workers employed in larger Japanese companies have often enjoyed lifetime job security and access to generous welfare benefits offered by their employer, such as health insurance, recreation, housing, and car loans. Some companies sponsor group tours abroad or own vacation retreats for their employees. When a corporation has faced financial trouble, top managers often accept responsibility for the problems, cutting their own pay rather than firing workers. Most workers remain with the same employer for life, though, by the 1980s, it became more common to change jobs. To encourage workers to feel a part of the corporate family, employers often gather the employees together to sing the company anthem each morning before they head for their workstations. Yet, many employees in smaller businesses, as well as temporary workers, do not enjoy generous benefits and are vulnerable to layoffs. Japanese companies also emphasize working in teams and "bottom-up" decision making through quality control circles and work groups, such as a factory team that installs a car engine; these groups decide how best to undertake their tasks. Business offices tend to be organized around large tables, where white-collar employees work collaboratively, rather than around the small cubicles common in North America. Businesses and factories have also expected their employees to put company over personal interests, including regularly working overtime.

Japanese Society, Culture, and Thought

City Life

Urbanization and affluence have contributed to social change. Sixty percent of Japanese now live in cities of over 100,000. With 35 million people, Tokyo is the world's largest metropolitan area by far. Some of Tokyo's legendary traffic jams take police several days to untangle. The city subways are convenient but overcrowded, and rush hour has evolved into "crush hour," with city employees equipped with padded poles pushing commuters into overflowing cars to enable subway train doors to close. Yet, despite Mafia-like organized crime syndicates, Japan's cities are the safest in the world; experts attribute low rates of violent crime in part to strict gun control.

salaryman An Japanese urban middle-class male business employee who commits his energies and soul to the company, accepts assignments without complaint, and takes few vacations.

The economy has changed men's lives. Most university-educated men want to become white-collar office workers for major corporations. Japanese observers describe the **salaryman**, an urban middle-class male business employee who commits his energies and soul to the company, accepts assignments without complaint, and takes few vacations. The cover of a local book on the salaryman pictures a harried middle-aged man eying the sundry items that define his work life: a computer, newspaper, lunch box, demanding boss, and subway strap. Many men working in white-collar jobs are also known as "7-11 husbands" because they leave for work at 7 A.M. and do not return until 11 P.M. After work they and their office mates socialize in restaurants, bars, and nightclubs while their wives take care of the home. In the 1980s one wife complained, "I don't know why Japanese men marry if they are never going to be home."[14]

Women's Roles

Meanwhile, while earning more money, gaining legal protections, and enjoying greater freedom, women still struggle for full social and economic equality in a hierarchical society obsessed with patriarchy and seniority. Most women are expected to marry and then retire from the work force to raise children, even though they often remain in paid work. According to one young woman, when she and other women graduated from a top Japanese university, "our bright appearance [for the graduation ceremonies] in vividly colored kimonos [traditional robes] was deceiving. Deep in our hearts we knew that our opportunities to use our professional education would be few."[15] As single women often discovered they could support themselves, the average age of marriage for women rose from twenty-two in the 1950s to twenty-seven in the 1990s. Indeed, in recent years, many women have avoided marriage altogether, preferring to concentrate on their careers or leisure interests. Accordingly, marriage rates have declined, alarming politicians.

Despite the popular image of the timid Japanese female, women have become more assertive. Feminist organizations and leaders have publicized women's issues, and working women have lobbied companies for equal treatment and pay. Some women have moved into middle management or prestige occupations, such as law, journalism, college teaching, and diplomacy. Yet, women also largely remain outside political and economic power, and only a few attain positions of political leadership. Women aspiring to gender equality admire activists such as Ichikawa Fusae (ee-CHEE-kah-wah foo-SIGH) (1893–1981), a former schoolteacher and journalist who organized the women's suffrage movement in the 1920s and served in the parliament as a political independent for twenty-five years after World War II, campaigning for women's equality and human rights. At the same time, family life has gradually changed. Although the traditional arranged marriage remains common, many men and women select their own spouse, and more Japanese get married late or opt to end unhappy marriages in divorce. The decline of marriage has made it easier for homosexuals to find social acceptance. Japanese society has always tolerated homosexual behavior, but now more have become open about their sexual orientation.

Social Problems

Urban housing remains cramped, and the elderly complain of neglect by their children, who have no room for them in their small homes. Birth control and abortion had been widely practiced in overcrowded Japan for centuries; the renewal of these practices after World War II, along with lower marriage rates, stabilized the population at 120 million for several decades. Yet, by 2000 Japan had a birthrate well below replacement standards and a rapidly aging population that placed a heavy burden on a shrinking work force to pay for retiree's benefits and a generous health care system. Despite this problem, the government has discouraged immigration to provide new workers. Thousands of Brazil-born Japanese who have returned to their ancestral homeland, mostly to work in factories, often face resentment, and those who became unemployed were encouraged to return to Brazil. In 2005, foreigners, mostly Chinese and Koreans, numbered less than 2 percent of the population; by contrast, the foreign-born accounted for 5 percent in Britain, 10 percent in Germany, 12 percent in the United States, and 22 percent in Australia. Despite laws banning discrimination, the Japanese have also largely failed to end prejudice against the *Burakumin,* a despised underclass for centuries, who number some 1 to 3 million people and traditionally did jobs considered unclean, such as leatherworking.

Japanese Youth

Youth face their own kinds of pressures. Young people take difficult exams to get into the better kindergartens, grade schools, and secondary schools, and the entrance exam for the top universities is so rigorous it is known as "exam hell." These varied pressures, and the expectations of conforming to the values of mainstream society, have encouraged youth rebellion. Indifferent students sometimes drop out and join motorcycle gangs that roar along the highways by day and neighborhood streets by night, annoying middle-class families trying to sleep. University students have often supported leftwing political organizations that protest issues such as U.S. military bases or the destruction of farmland to build new airports or business developments, but student activism has waned in recent years (see Witness to the Past: A Japanese Generation Gap). Eventually, however, most young people return to the mainstream upon graduation and take jobs in the corporate or industrial world. Some who cannot conform emigrate to North America, Europe, or Latin America in search of a more free-spirited life.

Arts and Film

The Japanese, while continuing to blend traditional and modern cultures and beliefs, East and West, debate this blending and its effect on cultural identity. Artists and writers ponder whether synthesizing foreign and local ideas has been the nation's salvation or its bane. Some worry that

Getty Images

Japanese Women Commuters A female passenger boards a train compartment reserved for women in a subway station in Tokyo. Tokyo's subways are usually jammed with passengers, and special cars allow women to travel without fear of possible sexual harassment.

A Japanese Generation Gap

The rapid pace of change since World War II has fostered growing generation gaps in many nations. In 1993 the Japanese essayist Yoshioka Shinobu (born in 1948) discussed the differences in perceptions between his "baby boomer" cohort born in the decade after 1945 and those Japanese of the next generation. Yoshioka's experiences reflected the exciting era of social experimentation during his teenage years in the 1960s. By contrast, young people in the 1970s faced a tighter economy and less official tolerance of radical ideas and organized political protests.

Whenever I hear someone mention Japan's baby boomers, . . . I think back to a conversation I had . . . [in] 1976 at a rock concert. . . . The band had the latest sound equipment, but its talent was no match for its technology. Bored, . . . I struck up a conversation with two young girls. . . . They had run away from home . . . because they were sick of school, and had come to Tokyo in search of adventure. . . . They had lied about their ages to get part-time jobs, were sharing a tiny apartment, and from time to time went out to concerts. . . . I told them I thought they must be having the time of their lives.

"Your generation had it good," one of the girls answered. "When you ran away from home, there was rock music, underground theater, demonstrations, all kinds of things—you could do whatever you wanted. Our generation has to walk a tightrope, . . . and there's nothing to catch us if we fall. We lose our balance, we die. You guys might have walked a tightrope too, but you had a safety net below. If you didn't like it up on the rope, you could always dive down and let yourself be caught in midair. You could do whatever you wanted to."

She had hit home. So that's how we look in the eyes of someone ten years younger, I thought. My generation . . . had an entirely different understanding of itself. [We] . . . had many names . . . : the baby boomers, the Beatles generation, the anti-Vietnam [War] generation. . . . [Our radical student movements] did much to discredit the established political system, but our generation was more than just a new political force. We began new trends in music, theater, art, and social customs . . . that defied the existing structure of authority and social conventions. In those days, nothing was worse than a willingness to capitulate to the "system" and adopt its narrow conventions.

Consequently, we tried our hands at everything. Singers of traditional [music], who had put in years of hard work climbing the rigid, hierarchical ladder before they were allowed to perform publicly, suddenly found themselves displaced by our barely rehearsed bands and spontaneous concerts. Some put on plays in . . . tents set up in vacant lots, ridiculing the empty and imitative formalism of Japan's commercial theater. Others . . . took off nearly penniless to wander about in foreign countries—their adventureousness helped make travel abroad commonplace.

The two girls were saying that these experiences . . . were only possible because we had a safety net underneath us. . . . The girls had a point. When [my] generation was growing up, the . . . confusion of the early postwar years had given way to spectacular economic growth. . . . This . . . engendered confidence in liberal politics and democratic government, and it also created a willingness to forgive the unruliness of the younger generation. . . . If we were arrested [in antiwar demonstrations] it did not worry us much. . . . The runaway girls told me that the age of such optimism was over. . . . Between my generation and the next, attitudes toward change took a 180-degree turn. For us, changes in society and the individual were exciting and intrinsically valuable. For the younger generation, however, change is frightening and the source of insecurity.

THINKING ABOUT THE READING

1. How did Yoshioka's generation contribute to change?
2. What does the essay tell us about Japan's connection to the wider world?

Source: Shinobu Yoshioka, "Talkin' 'bout My Generation," in Merry L. White and Sylvan Barnet, eds., *Comparing Cultures: Readings on Contemporary Japan for American Writers* (Boston: Bedford Books of St. Martin's Press, 1995), pp. 119–122. Reprinted with permission by Yoshioka Shinobu.

Japan's adoption of foreign culture has imperiled its own distinctive culture. Others contend that the Japanese needed to become more global-minded, even encouraging immigration that would make Japan a multicultural nation.

The questions about Japanese identity and problems facing society are often analyzed in films that have achieved worldwide recognition. While the Japanese film industry, the world's third largest, produces escapist films, such as those portraying samurai warriors and gigantic city-wrecking monsters, it also makes thought-provoking masterpieces, especially grand historical epics and introspective psychological or sociological studies. One of the most skillful directors, Kurosawa Akira **(kur-o-SAH-wa a-KEER-a)** (1910–1998), mixed a distinctive Japanese style and setting with a theme appealing to viewers in other cultures. *Rashomon* (1950), for example, deals with the relativity of truth by examining one event, the killing of a feudal lord and the violation of his wife by a bandit, through varied eyes. Another Kurosawa film, *Ikuru*, or "To Live" (1952), explores the meaning of life through the story of a Japanese bureaucrat dying of cancer who overcomes endless red tape to facilitate the building of a small neighborhood park.

The Japanese have the world's highest literacy rate (99.9 percent) and the largest numbers of newspaper readers, magazine subscribers, and bookstores per capita, which have fostered both popular and serious literature. Kawabata Yasunari (ka-wa-BAH-ta yah-suh-NAHR-ee) (1899–1972) became the first Japanese novelist, in 1968, to receive the Nobel Prize for literature. Directly addressing Japanese identity, the writings of Mishima Yukio (me-SHE-mah YOO-kee-oh) (1925–1970) portray an effete, decadent "nation of shopkeepers" that need a return to the martial values of the Tokugawa period. His best novel concerns a disturbed young man torn, like Mishima himself, between old samurai and modern Westernized values. For Mishima, a conflicted homosexual and avid body builder, life became art; in 1970 he publicly committed suicide in samurai style in front of his private army to sacrifice himself for what he called the "old beautiful tradition of Japan, which is disappearing day by day."[16] His action shocked the Japanese, but his message died with him; the Japanese continued to develop a consumer society.

Popular Culture

Continuity has long characterized Japanese popular culture. Every sport, art form, and religion that has appeared in the past 1,500 years in Japan still attracts practitioners or followers. Japanese remain passionate about sumo wrestling, a sport, going back centuries, in which two large, paunchy Japanese men attempt to push each other out of a small ring. Yet, while performances of kabuki or bunraku, theatrical forms that appeared in the 1600s, still attract devoted audiences, and young Japanese women preparing for marriage often master the even older tea ceremony, many more Japanese follow professional baseball teams; consume Japanese comics, or *manga* (mahn-gah), and animated films, or *anime*, that are popular worldwide; and flock to Japanese or Western films, discos, pinball palaces, and video-game arcades. Modern Japanese, especially young people, have avidly adopted cultural forms from around the world. Japanese also frequent nightclubs featuring many musical styles, including both local and imported versions of rock, jazz, reggae, country western, rap, and salsa.

Religion

Organized religion continues to decline, although some Japanese remain deeply religious. Militant Buddhist groups claim several million followers, and various new religions based on Buddhist or Shinto traditions, or a mix of the two, have flourished by addressing material prosperity and family problems. Nonetheless, the contemporary Japanese are a largely secular people. In census questionnaires, less than 15 percent reported any formal religious affiliation by 2000. Although Japan's Christian population is tiny, millions of non-Christians ardently celebrate Christmas as an opportunity to give and receive gifts, and Japanese department stores often feature elaborate Christmas displays, complete with Santa Claus and brightly decorated Christmas trees. However, the weak influence of religions has not resulted in social breakdown. Japanese remain among the world's most law-abiding, peaceful citizens, with a morality that mostly derives from the fear of bringing shame on the family or group rather than fear of retribution by gods or ancestors. The reluctance to disgrace the family suggests that Confucianism remains important. Yet the emphasis on conforming to the group and its rules has a downside. Criticizing the attitudes expressed by an old saying—"the nail that sticks up gets hammered down"—Japanese liberals have sought a less-conformist society that would nourish rather than inhibit individual genius.

Japan in the Global System

Economic Challenges

The Japanese have had to readjust their views of the economy and international relations over the past several decades. Like their North American and European counterparts, Japanese companies have sought cheaper labor by setting up factories in Southeast Asia, South Korea, and China, costing Japan jobs. In 1989 the Japanese economy went into a severe downturn, due in part to overvalued stocks that caused a crisis on the Tokyo Stock Exchange but also to global recession and competition from the newly industrializing nations of Southeast Asia. Only in the early 2000s did Japanese leaders introduce policies that fostered higher growth rates and renewed business confidence, but the recovery remained incomplete. The global economic crisis of 2008–2009 undermined export-oriented Japan, causing recession, bank failures, bankruptcies, and a huge drop in consumer spending abroad that even affected automobile manufacturers like Toyota. As in the United States, Japanese corporations have reacted to foreign competition and crises by slashing salaries, cutting benefits, and even firing employees, modifying the business system that brought Japan prosperity for a half century. Many newly unemployed men, especially office workers, ashamed to admit their humiliation to friends and families, spend each work day on park benches or in coffee houses. The economic problems caused disenchanted voters to turn the long-ruling Liberal Democratic Party out of office

Japanese Power in the World

While comfortable as an economic powerhouse, the Japanese remain reluctant to assert their political and military power in the world, remembering how the attempt to dominate eastern Asia brought them disaster during World War II. Japan's main concerns are the continued health of the world economy and continuing access to overseas resources and markets. To this end, the Japanese prefer that the country seek peaceful rather than military solutions to world problems. Japan has maintained a strategic alliance with its major trading partner, the United States, but the two nations have also remained keen economic rivals and have sometimes engaged in trade disputes. Japanese leaders have also worked to promote peaceful exchange with China and South Korea, two countries with long memories of Japanese imperialism during the first half of the twentieth century. Relations with China have often been strained, as the Chinese have demanded that Japan accept responsibility for World War II atrocities in China. Resurgent Japanese and Chinese nationalisms clash. As China and several other Asian nations rise economically, Japan faces more competition and the challenge of maintaining its position in the world economy.

SECTION SUMMARY

- After World War II, a U.S.-led occupation of Japan (SCAP) worked to rebuild Japan's economy while demilitarizing the country and encouraging the return of democracy, much of which was successful; however, it was difficult to break up large business conglomerates.
- The Liberal Democratic Party dominated Japanese politics for decades, with a brief break in the 1990s, and the presence of U.S. military bases within Japan was seen by some as neocolonialism but freed up resources to help fuel the economy.
- Relying on innovation and collaboration between government and big business, Japan's economy has grown at a phenomenal rate, though it has caused environmental problems and great personal sacrifices on the part of workers.
- Japan's cities have become increasingly congested, men are expected to devote all their energy to work, women struggle for equality and increasingly choose work over marriage, arranged marriages have become less common, and students face the pressure of an arduous education system.
- Japanese have managed to blend their traditions with modern and foreign influences and have maintained a high degree of social order in spite of low participation in organized religion, but some criticize Japanese society as too conformist.
- In the early 2000s, Japan's economy began to recover from a decade-long downturn, while in world politics, Japan has played an important role, though it has been hesitant to assert its power too forcefully.

THE LITTLE DRAGONS IN THE ASIAN RESURGENCE

What policies led to the rise of the "Little Dragon" nations and their dynamic economies?

Little Dragons South Korea, Taiwan, Singapore, and Hong Kong, which were strongly influenced by Chinese culture and built rapidly growing, industrializing economies.

While China and Japan were rising to regional and global power, a few of their East Asian neighbors also achieved economic development. Known as the **Little Dragons** because they were strongly influenced by Chinese culture, South Korea, Taiwan, Singapore, and Hong Kong built rapidly growing, industrializing economies. Except for Hong Kong, a British colony until 1997 and a bastion of free enterprise, these societies largely followed the Meiji Japan model of state-directed capitalism. They were also inspired by Japan's resurgence after World War II, which depended on participation in the world economy. All the Little Dragons shared a Confucian cultural heritage that emphasized hard work, discipline, cooperation, and tolerance for authoritarian governments. They all achieved an export-oriented industrialization that raised incomes, reduced poverty, and forged high standards in health and education. For South Korea, however, this development came only after a brutal war that left a hostile, rigidly communist North Korea on the border. Taiwan had to find its own path in the shadow of China, while Singapore (see Chapter 31) and Hong Kong (now part of China) are city-states with largely Chinese populations.

Korean Independence and War

Japanese Colonialism

The Korean War (1950–1953) was rooted in the Korean nationalism that, despite fierce repression, simmered during a half century of harsh Japanese colonial rule (see Chapters 23 and 24). While introducing some economic modernization, the Japanese arrested or executed Korean nationalists, conscripted Korean women to serve Japanese soldiers, relocated thousands of Korean workers to Japan, and manipulated the divisions within Korean society. Christians constituted one influential group, growing in numbers, and by the 1940s a fifth of Koreans had become Catholics or Protestants. Another group of Koreans had gravitated toward communism, some escaping to the USSR to form a revolutionary movement. In contrast, a majority of Koreans maintained their adherence to Buddhism and Confucianism as central to Korean identity. Although Christians, communists, and traditionalists all hated Japanese rule and worked underground to oppose it, they could not cooperate, and no unified nationalist movement emerged.

CHRONOLOGY

The Little Dragons Since 1945

1948–1994 Kim Il-Sung's leadership of North Korea

1950–1953 Korean War

1954 U.S.-Taiwan mutual defense treaty

1980s South Korean democratization movement

1989 First democratic elections in Taiwan

1989–1991 Collapse of Soviet bloc and Soviet Union

1997 Asian financial collapse

1998 Beginning of South Korean "sunshine policy"

Japan's crushing defeat by the United States in 1945 meant political liberation for Korea and a chance to reestablish the nation free of foreign interference. But the United States quickly occupied the southern half of the peninsula and the Soviet Union the north, bisecting Korea and making it a hostage to the Cold War. As the USSR and the United States imposed rival governments, unification quickly became impossible. With Soviet help, communists led by the ruthless Kim Il-Sung **(KIM ill-soon)** (1912–1994) formed a government in North Korea (see Chronology: The Little Dragons Since 1945). A clever strategist from a Christian family, Kim quickly built a brutal communist system, eliminated his opponents, and reorganized rural society. But the impatient Kim disastrously overestimated the revolutionary potential of the south and also misjudged the Americans, who were determined to stop the spread of Soviet influence. The United States helped create and then supported a South Korean state headed by Rhee Syngman **(REE SING-man)** (1865–1965). A politically conservative Christian from a powerful landlord family, Rhee had lived in exile in the United States for over two decades. Unpopular with the majority non-Christians, the autocratic Rhee imprisoned or eliminated his opponents and sparked a leftist rebellion supported by many factory workers and peasants, which United States troops helped crush. Although less repressive than Kim's North Korean regime, Rhee's South Korea held some 30,000 political prisoners.

Korean War

These developments set the stage for the Korean War (see Map 27.3), a result of mixing revolution and nationalism into a Cold War–driven stew. Both Korean states, threatening to reunify Korea with military force, had initiated border skirmishes. In this highly charged context, North Korea, with Soviet and Chinese approval, invaded the South in 1950. The Western-dominated United Nations agreed to let the United States lead a military intervention to support South Korea, thus turning a Korean crisis into a Cold War confrontation; the United States made the major commitment of troops, war materials, and funding. U.S. president Harry Truman secretly planned to strike North Korea with atomic weapons if the USSR entered the war. But while the Soviets gave military supplies and advice, they sent no combat troops.

U.N. troops, aided by U.S. air power, quickly pushed the North Koreans back across the north-south border. But the U.N. move into North Korea and push toward the Chinese border sparked a massive Chinese intervention that drove back U.N. troops and turned a likely victory into a bitter stalemate. U.S. leaders had misjudged the Chinese willingness to fight and had underestimated Chinese military capabilities. When the war ended in 1953 with peace talks, the boundary between the Koreas remained roughly in the same place it was before the war but was now a heavily fortified zone where North and South Korean troops glared at each other across the barbed wire. The war left 400,000 Korean troops and 1 or 2 million civilians dead, and some 400,000 Chinese and 43,000 U.N. forces, 90 percent of them American, were killed. The fighting also generated millions of Korean refugees who wandered the countryside, seeking food and shelter. Both Koreas were left in economic shambles.

The Two Koreas

Rise of South Korea

The postwar rise of South Korea was nearly as dramatic as that of Japan. Closely allied to the United States, the South Korean governments ranged from highly repressive military dictatorships from the 1950s through the mid-1980s, to moderate semidemocracies in the later 1980s, and then to liberal democracies with free elections since the early 1990s. All regimes aimed at economic development. The dictator Park Chung Hee (1917–1979) argued in 1970, "My chief concern was economic revolution. One must eat and breathe before concerning himself with politics, social affairs, and culture."[17] The United States protected the South Korean regimes by permanently stationing troops and supplying generous economic and military aid. A half-century after the war, some 40,000 U.S. troops remained in South Korea.

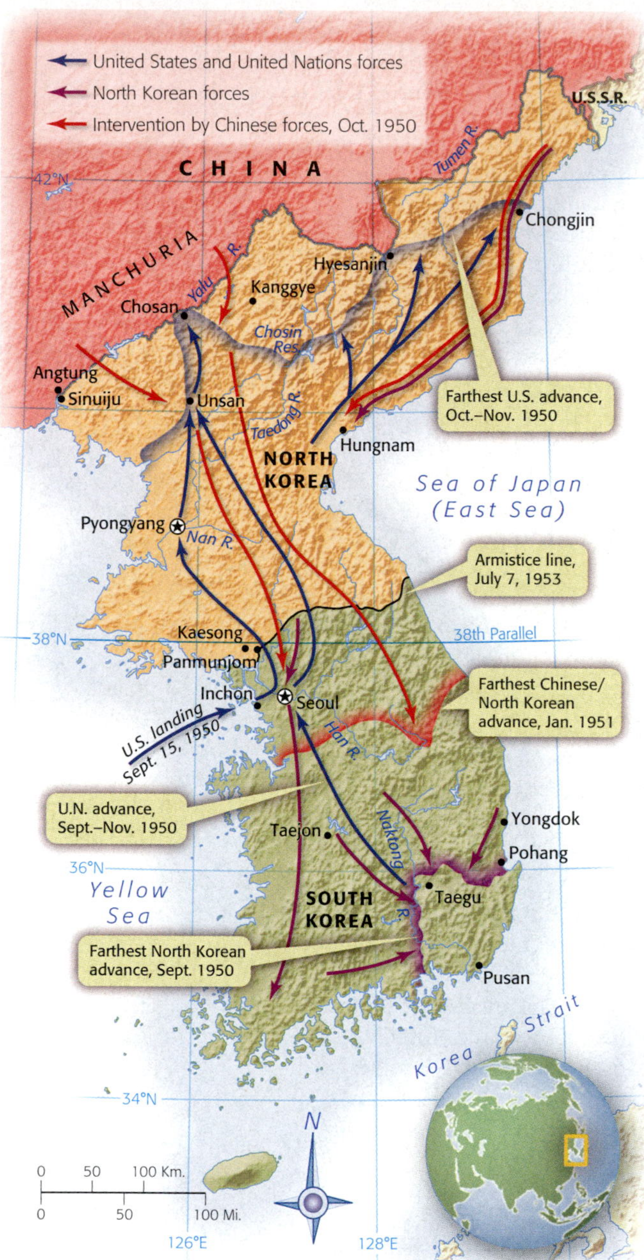

Map 27.3 The Korean War
In 1950, North Korean forces crossed the 38th parallel and invaded South Korea, but they were then pushed back north by United Nations forces led by the United States. The intervention of China in support of North Korea pushed the United Nations forces south and produced a military stalemate, preserving the border between North and South Korea at the 38th parallel.

Interactive Map

South Korea has enjoyed enormous economic growth, investing heavily in the Middle East, Southeast Asia, and Russia, while exporting automobiles and electronic products. By the 1990s South Korea had joined the ranks of advanced industrial nations, the first non-Western nation to make that transition since Japan in the late nineteenth century, and became a proud member of the G-20 grouping of major industrial nations. Having acquired a standard of living South Koreans could only dream of two decades earlier, with nearly full employment and universal literacy, South Koreans now enjoy the highest rate of high-speed Internet access in the world: some 75 percent of households are wired, far more than in North America and Europe, and 35 percent of the population play computer games online. The country became a high-technology model. Both boys and girls received free education through age twelve. South Korean women benefited from new job options in the professions and business. With more women in the work force and self-supporting, marriage rates declined and average births per woman fell dramatically from 6 in 1990 to 1.6 in 2005.

Economic growth has also fostered political change. Democracy movements had begun in the 1960s, but they often faced government repression. In 1980 the dictatorship brutally crushed an uprising in a southern province that began when some five hundred people demonstrated, demanding an end of martial law; paratroopers landed and slaughtered the protesters and local people. Hundreds of thousands of enraged people then drove the troops out of the city, only to face a much larger force, which shot their way into the city, killing over 2,000 people. Eventually, however, political tensions diminished. Governments fostered more liberalization, tolerated a freer press, and made overtures toward former enemies in the USSR and China. By the early 1990s, with the growth of the middle class and organized labor, democracy flowered, though it was sometimes sullied by political corruption. South Koreans took pride in their freedom, bustling cities, and the influence of their popular culture in both China and Japan.

But while the country clearly outshined repressive North Korea, problems arose. Many rural people and unskilled workers did not share in the prosperity, and factories expected long hours from poorly paid workers. Frustrated at their prospects, thousands of Koreans, many of them middle class, emigrated to the United States. Discontent also grew with the economic slowdown beginning in 1997, and then with the 2008–2009 global economic crisis, which cost many jobs. Furthermore, while many South Koreans welcomed U.S. bases, others viewed them as an affront to nationalism. Koreans yearned for reunification and an end to the peninsular cold war. After years of hostility, and owing partly to South Korean efforts to improve relations, North and South Korea finally achieved a wary peaceful coexistence. A dialogue known as the "sunshine policy," begun in 1998, resulted in limited cross-border trade and allowed a few South Koreans to visit family members in North Korea they had not seen since the early 1950s. Televised images of South Koreans tearfully embracing aging parents or siblings mesmerized the nation. Then in 2000 South Korean president Kim Dae-jung **(kim day-chung)** (1925–2009), a liberal reformer, visited North Korea, an event unthinkable a decade earlier. Yet national reconciliation still remains a dream, and South Koreans worry about North Korean military capabilities and its quest to build nuclear weapons. Tensions increased again in 2009 over these issues.

North Korea

North Korea's leaders chose a completely different path from that taken by South Korea. The Korean War devastated the country, though North Korea quickly recovered with aid from China

Tony Stone/Getty Images

South Korean Economic Growth One of South Korea's major, most diverse enterprises, the Hyundai Corporation, formed in 1976, engages in shipping, manufacturing, and trade, producing, among other products, chemicals, machinery, and information and telecommunications equipment. The ships in this company dry dock are being readied to carry Hyundai-made cars to distant markets around the world.

and the USSR. From 1948 until his death in 1994, Kim Il-Sung was the nation's president, creating a personality cult around himself as the "Great Leader." North Koreans were taught that they owed everything—jobs, goods, schooling, food, military security—to Kim. To ensure loyalty and deflect blame for failures, Kim purged many communist officials and jailed or executed thousands of dissidents. He also mixed Stalinism and Maoism to shape the economy and society, with Soviet-style economic planning and central direction emphasizing heavy industry and weapons at the expense of consumer goods. Hence, North Koreans did not enjoy the rising living standards of South Koreans. Kim invented a political philosophy of self-reliance that was heavily influenced by Mao Zedong's policies. Although North Korea contained most of Korea's factories and mines, built during Japanese colonial times, the huge military establishment drained resources as North Korea concentrated on deterring enemies and intimidating South Korea.

North Korea stressed group loyalty, ultranationalism, and independence from foreign influence, following the model of the Yi dynasty and Confucian bureaucracy in the nineteenth century. A small political and military elite, isolated from the bleak existence of the peasants and workers, enjoyed comfortable apartments and sufficient food, while controlling the people through regimentation and restricting information. To monitor activities and thoughts, the government required each citizen to register at a public security office and urged people to spy on their families and neighbors. To prevent people from hearing contrary views, radios were fixed to receive only the government station. Political prisoners and people caught trying to flee to China or South Korea faced long terms in harsh concentration camps or execution. As a result, the regime faced increasing international isolation. The economy declined rapidly, thanks to poor management, commodity shortages, and rigid policies. Satellite photos of the Korean peninsula at night revealed the stark differences in electrical power between a brilliantly lit South Korea and a completely dark North Korea. Even in the capital city nearly all lights are turned off each night by 9 P.M. U.S. diplomatic and economic pressure isolated the regime, making North Korea totally reliant economically on the Soviet bloc. Various efforts to strike back, such as assassination attempts on South Korean leaders, earned North Korea a reputation as an unpredictable terrorist state. When the Soviet bloc collapsed in 1989, Russia and China demanded that North Korea pay cash for oil and other imports.

North Korea's problems increased after Kim Jong-Il **(chong-ill)** (b. 1942), known as the "Dear Leader," succeeded his deceased father in 1995. When the nation soon faced mass starvation, South Korea, Japan, and the United States, anxious to discourage any desperate military action, sent food aid to North Korea. Even with the aid, many people died or were malnourished, and thousands of North Koreans fled to China to find food and work. Yet the regime avoided collapse. Thanks to isolation and tight information control, few North Koreans traveled abroad, studied foreign languages, met foreigners, or encountered foreign publications, films, and music. Meanwhile, a small dissident movement, risking harsh reprisals, smuggled in food from China and videotapes, books, and music from South Korea.

North Korea and the World

North Korea became a concern in both regional and world politics. Its military force was twice as large as South Korea's and was capable of building nuclear weapons. But with both Koreas possessing lethal military forces, and U.S. nuclear weapons in South Korea, war became less likely. This perception encouraged the search for common ground. The economic disasters, especially food shortages, softened the North Korean position, and after 1998 South Korea actively sought better relations to reduce the threat from its dangerous northern neighbor and its unpredictable leader. North Korea's neighbors and the United States also sought diplomatic ways to eliminate the possibility of a conventional war or a nuclear confrontation, but by 2008 tensions returned as North Korea continued to sporadically test nuclear weapons and missiles, unsettling the region.

Taiwan and China

The Chinese communist triumph on the mainland in 1949 led to the relocation of Chiang Kai-shek and his Nationalist government to the mountainous, subtropical Taiwan island, where he reestablished the Republic of China. Taiwan had only become a part of Chinese territory in the seventeenth and eighteenth centuries, and in 1910 it became a Japanese colony. Japan ruled Taiwan less harshly than it did Korea, financing industrialization that produced a higher standard of living than that known in mainland China. After World War II China reclaimed the island, but in 1947 local resentment of Chiang's heavy-handed regime led to an island-wide uprising. Chiang dispatched 100,000 troops from the mainland, who killed 30,000 to 40,000 Taiwanese, including many local leaders, in quelling the unrest.

Nationalist Government

As Chiang's Republic of China collapsed in 1948–1949, Chiang and 2 million mainlanders moved to Taiwan, taking with them their government, the Nationalist Party, the remaining military forces, the priceless art collections of the national museum, and China's national treasury. These mainlanders and their descendants eventually constituted some 15 to 20 percent of the total island population, which numbered 23 million by 2008. Because the minority mainlanders dominated politics, the economy, and the military, the majority Taiwanese, although Chinese in culture and language, often considered the mainlanders colonizers. Chiang viewed Taiwan as a temporary refuge, since he hoped to reconquer the mainland. But after his death in 1975, many mainlanders (and their children) realized that, with a return to the mainland unlikely, Taiwan might be their permanent home. They then cultivated better relations with the Taiwanese. However, two governments claiming to represent China created a long-term diplomatic problem for the world community. Both the governments of the People's Republic and of the Republic on Taiwan regarded the island as an integral part of China rather than a separate nation; this "one China policy" was endorsed by most of the world.

Economic Growth

Learning from their defeat in China, and using generous U.S. aid, the Republic's leaders promoted rapid industrial and agricultural growth, a more equitable distribution of wealth, and land reform. With land ownership and access to credit facilities, the peasantry prospered. As in South Korea and Meiji Japan, the economy mixed capitalism and foreign investment with government planning and investment. Light industry and manufacturing eventually accounted for half of Taiwan's economic production and the bulk of exports. Taiwan became the world's third largest producer, after the United States and Japan, of computer hardware. Between the early 1970s and the late 1990s it enjoyed more years of double-digit growth than any other nation. Taiwanese companies set up operations in Southeast Asia, China, Africa, and Latin America. The economic indicators far surpassed those on the mainland, including a per capita annual income of \$8,000, 99 percent of households owning a color television, 92 percent literacy, and a life expectancy of seventy-five. In the 1990s Taiwan businessmen built the world's tallest skyscraper, 1,667 feet high, in the capital city, Taipei. Rapid development, however, brought environmental destruction, traffic congestion, political corruption, and a severe economic slowdown in 1997 and 2008–2009. Concrete high-rise buildings increasingly displace the lush greenery of the mountains around Taipei.

Modernization has challenged Chinese values and traditions. The small roadside cafés selling noodle soup and meat dumplings often close, unable to compete with U.S. fast-food restaurants and convenience stores selling Coca-Cola, hamburgers, and ice cream. Rampant materialism concerns those who believe life should offer more than the quest for luxury goods and money. While Confucian values have fostered material success, some Taiwanese have worried that Confucian ethics, including respect for parents and concern for the community rather than the individual, are threatened. Despite the modernization, traditional Chinese culture remains stronger in Taiwan than the mainland. Over 90 percent of the people describe themselves as Buddhists, Daoists, Confucianists, or a mix of the three ancient traditions. Some 5 percent of Taiwan's people have adopted Christianity, while several million others infrequently attend temples or churches.

Like South Korea, Taiwan until the later 1980s followed the authoritarian Little Dragon political model, with Chiang Kai-shek and his family implementing a police state that held numerous political prisoners. Chiang made it illegal to advocate making Taiwan permanently independent of China, and the communists on the mainland also opposed those who advocated two separate Chinese nations. For four decades Chiang's Nationalist Party ruled, but in 1989, nudged by a growing middle class seeking liberalization, they permitted opposition candidates to run in elections. Gradually the regime recognized civil liberties, including the freedom of speech and press. The 2000 elections swept into office the Democratic Progressive Party (DPP), largely supported by the native Taiwanese; many party leaders advocated that Taiwan become a separate nation, a stance that angered both the Nationalist leaders on Taiwan and the communist leaders on the mainland. However, Taiwan's voters seemed less eager to confront China and in 2008 replaced the DPP government, beset by corruption, with the Nationalists, who sought friendlier ties with China.

Taiwan Politics

China has remained Taiwan's permanent challenge. Fearing an invasion to forcibly annex the island, Taiwan lavishly funded its military, kept a large standing army, and bought the latest fighter jets and gunboats, at the same time maintaining after 1954 a defense alliance with the United States and allowing U.S. bases. But in 1978 the United States recognized the People's Republic as China's only government and withdrew diplomatic recognition from the Republic of China. However, it has maintained a strong informal economic presence and repeatedly reaffirms a commitment to defend the island from attack. In the later 1980s Taiwan and China began informal talks about improving relations. As a result, informal trade between the two countries has grown substantially, and many people from Taiwan have visited the mainland to do business or look up relatives. However, doubts about whether China will move toward political liberalization and democracy, as well as alarm at occasional Chinese military exercises being conducted near Taiwan, have precluded any serious negotiations on reunification. China's leaders have threatened military action to prevent any move by Taiwan for permanent independence. Such action would alarm Japan, and might draw in the United States. Thus Taiwan's political future remains an open question, fiercely debated by Taiwanese and their several competing political parties.

Taiwan and China

The Little Dragons in the Global System

The rise of the Pacific Rim, including China, Japan, and the Little Dragons, in the late twentieth century reshaped the global system. The quarter of the world's population living along the western edge of the Pacific Basin outpaced the West and the rest of the world in economic growth while maintaining political stability. A global economy that had been based on the tripod of the United States, western Europe, and Japan now has to accommodate China and the Little Dragons. The Little Dragons industrialized and then diversified into high technology, making computers and other electronics products and thereby posing an economic challenge to Japan and the West. They successfully used the Meiji Japan model to develop and compete with Japan and the West.

Some trends suggested that the Pacific Rim nations were becoming an Asian counterpart to the European Community, the free-trade zone formed by western European nations, thus foreshadowing the possible Pacific Century in which Asian nations might dominate the world economy. Many East and Southeast Asian nations forged closer economic cooperation, with Japan and China forming the hubs. But in 1997 and again in 2008–2009 a severe economic meltdown hit South Korea, Taiwan, Japan, and the industrializing economies of Southeast Asia. As businesses closed, unemployment soared and economies went into deep recession. Thus both the Pacific Rim and the United States face uncertain futures, and China, Japan, and the United States will undoubtedly play major roles in the years to come. Yet in many respects, East Asia had returned to its historical role as a key engine of the world economy.

SECTION SUMMARY

- After World War II, communist North Korea, assisted by the USSR and China, fought a war with South Korea, assisted by a U.S.-dominated United Nations force, that caused thousands of deaths and economic devastation and ended with roughly the same border that existed at the start of the war.
- South Korean governments have grown more tolerant of internal dissent and more open to relations with former enemies such as communist North Korea and China, though their primary emphasis has been on economic growth.
- After the Korean War, North Korea recovered with support from the USSR and China and was ruled as a repressive communist dictatorship with a centrally planned economy whose shortcomings led to widespread food shortages in the 1990s.
- With the communists ruling mainland China, the nationalists took over Taiwan, which they ruled as a police state and turned into an economic powerhouse, but relations with mainland China have continued to be tense.
- China and the "Little Dragons" (Taiwan, South Korea, Singapore, and Hong Kong) grew rapidly in the late twentieth century, leading to predictions of a coming "Pacific Century," but several slowdowns dampened such expectations.

CHAPTER SUMMARY

In the decades after World War II, East Asia experienced revolutionary upheavals and dramatic economic development that led to a resurgence of the region's influence in the world. The communist triumph in China began the process of change. After experimenting with a Soviet-style Stalinist development model, China's leader, Mao Zedong, imposed his own version of communism. Emphasizing collective efforts, political values, and mass mobilization, Mao reorganized the rural economy into communes. He also sparked the Cultural Revolution, which attacked the bureaucracy and those who opposed his political and economic vision but also created turmoil. After Mao's death, Deng Xiaoping led China in a new direction; his market socialism energized the economy but led to tensions and then repression. During the 1990s market Leninism continued the economic reforms, providing a basis for rapid growth. China became a world economic power, but the growing inequalities of wealth have threatened to destabilize the nation.

The experiences of Japan and the Little Dragons differed from those of China. After the World War II defeat and U.S. occupation of Japan, the nation rapidly rose to become an economic powerhouse, based on a system mixing political democracy and a form of capitalism in which government and business worked together. The Japanese rebuilt their industries and fostered new forms of business and production. But social change came slowly, leaving Japan hierarchical. The Little Dragon nations of South Korea and Taiwan achieved industrial growth and prosperity by borrowing the Japanese model and mixing free markets with government intervention, eventually fostering democracy, while North Korea chose Stalinism and isolation from the world. The dynamism of most East Asian nations suggests that they have recovered from the disasters they experienced from the mid-1800s to the mid-1900s as a result of Western imperialism, Japanese expansion, and war, but their overall role remains unclear for the twenty-first century.

KEY TERMS

Pacific Rim
Pacific Century
communes
Great Leap Forward
Great Proletarian Cultural Revolution
Red Guards
Iron Rice Bowl
market socialism
market Leninism
Japan, Inc.
salaryman
Little Dragons

EBOOK AND WEBSITE RESOURCES

PRIMARY SOURCE

"One Hundred Items for Destroying the Old and Establishing the New"

INTERACTIVE MAPS

Map 27.1 China and Taiwan
Map 27.2 Japan and the Little Dragons
Map 27.3 The Korean War

LINKS

Asian Studies (http://coombs.anu.edu.au/WWWVL-AsianStudies.html). A vast metasite maintained at Australian National University, with links to hundreds of sites.

China-Profile: Facts, Figures, and Analyses (http://www.china-profile.com). Offers useful information on China today.

East and Southeast Asia: An Annotated Directory of Internet Resources (http://www.newton.uor.edu/Departments&Programs/AsianStudies-Dept/asianam.html). A superb set of links, maintained at the University of Redlands.

Internet East Asian History Sourcebook (http://www.fordham.edu/halsall/eastasia/eastasiasbook.html). An invaluable collection of sources and links on China, Japan, and Korea from ancient to modern times.

Internet Guide to Chinese Studies (http://www.sino.uni-heidelberg.de/igcs/). An excellent collection of links, maintained at a German university.

Plus flashcards, practice quizzes, and more. Go to: www.cengage.com/history/lockard/globalsocnet2e.

SUGGESTED READING

Benson, Linda. *China Since 1949.* New York: Longman, 2002. A brief overview.

Cheek, Timothy. *Living With Reform: China Since 1989.* New York: Zed Press, 2006. Lively and balanced review of post-Mao China.

Cumings, Bruce. *Korea's Place in the Sun: A Modern History*, 2nd ed. New York: W.W. Norton, 2005. A provocative and readable account emphasizing the years since World War II.

Dietrich, Craig. *People's China: A Brief History*, 3rd ed. New York: Oxford University Press, 1998. A fine study of China's Communist era.

Dower, John W. *Embracing Defeat: Japan in the Wake of World War II.* New York: W.W. Norton, 1999. Detailed look at the postwar U.S. occupation and its consequences.

Dreyer, June Teufel. *China's Political System: Modernization and Tradition*, 5th ed. New York: Longman, 2005. One of the best surveys of contemporary China.

Ebrey, Patricia Buckley, Anne Walthall, and James B. Palais. *East Asia: A Cultural, Social, and Political History*, 2nd ed. Boston: Houghton Mifflin, 2009. A readable, comprehensive survey.

Gamer, Robert E., ed. *Understanding Contemporary China*, 3rd ed. Boulder, CO: Lynne Rienner, 2008. An excellent collection of essays on all aspects of Chinese society.

Kingston, Jeffrey. *Japan in Transformation, 1952–2000.* New York: Longman, 2001. A useful study of Japan's recent history.

McCargo, Duncan. *Contemporary Japan*, 2nd ed. New York: Palgrave, 2004. A provocative survey by a British scholar.

Peerenboom, Randall. *China Modernizes: Threat to the West or Model for the Rest?* New York: Oxford University Press, 2007. Scholarly study of China's recent development.

Reischauer, Edwin O., and Marius B. Jansen. *The Japanese Today: Change and Continuity*, 2nd ed., enlarged. Cambridge: Harvard University Press, 2004. A classic examination of Japanese society.

Schirokauer, Conrad, and Donald N. Clark. *Modern East Asia: A Brief History*, 2nd ed. Belmont, CA: Wadsworth, 2007. Extensive coverage of China, Japan, and Korea in this era.

Schoppa, R. Keith. *Revolution and Its Past: Identities and Change in Modern Chinese History*, 2nd ed. Upper Saddle River, NJ: Prentice-Hall, 2006. A recent study offering a historical perspective.

Spence, Jonathan. *Mao Zedong.* New York: Viking, 1999. One of the best, most readable biographies of this major Chinese leader.

Stueck, William, ed. *The Korean War in World History.* Lexington: The University Press of Kentucky, 2004. A recent reassessment from multiple perspectives.

Tao Jie, et al., eds. *Holding Up Half the Sky: Chinese Women Past, Present, and Future.* New York: Feminist Press, 2004. Interesting essays on many aspects of women's lives in China today.

Terrill, Ross. *The New Chinese Empire.* New York: Basic Books, 2003. A readable recent study that places China's rise in historical context.

Yahuda, Michael. *The International Politics of the Asia-Pacific*, 2nd ed. New York: Routledge Curzon, 2005. A comprehensive study of the changing roles of China, Japan, Russia, and the United States in East Asia and the world.

CHAPTER

28

Rebuilding Europe and Russia, Since 1945

CHAPTER OUTLINE

- Western Europe: Revival and Unity
- Western European Societies and Cultures
- Communism in the Soviet Union and Eastern Europe
- Communist Collapse: A New Russia and Europe

PROFILE
Simone de Beauvoir, French Feminist and Philosopher

WITNESS TO THE PAST
Restructuring Soviet Society

AP/Wide World Photos

Fall of the Berlin Wall
In 1989, as communist governments collapsed in eastern Europe, peaceful protesters climbed on top of the Berlin Wall, which had already been decorated with graffiti. The wall, which divided communist East and democratic West Berlin, was soon torn down.

This [united] Europe must be born. And she will, when Spaniards say "our Chartres," Englishmen "our Cracow," Italians "our Copenhagen," and Germans "our Bruges." Then Europe will live.

—SPANISH WRITER SALVADOR DE MADARIAGA, 1948[1]

FOCUS QUESTIONS

1. What factors fostered the movement toward unity in western Europe?
2. How did the rise of welfare states transform western European societies?
3. What factors contributed to political crises in the Soviet Union and eastern Europe?
4. How did the demise of the communist system contribute to a new Europe?

Jacques Delors **(deh-LOW-er)** faced a challenge. This French banker's son turned socialist politician had lived through a tumultuous history, including the Great Depression, World War II, and the Cold War. Now, after holding high positions in the French government, he had dedicated himself to building a united Europe. In 1985 he became president of the European Commission, established to reconcile national loyalties with more political cooperation. In 1991, Delors convened the leaders of twelve closely linked European nations in the Dutch city of Maastricht, full of historic buildings, where, calling on all his diplomatic skills, he prodded them to conclude a historic agreement for increased cooperation. The Maastricht meeting affirmed a dream of European unity that had been percolating among European visionaries. Now Europeans, chastened by centuries of conflict, seemed ready to subordinate national interests to a common good. Delors asked the national leaders to transform the economic and political alliance begun in the late 1940s and expanded in the 1950s into a more comprehensive union.

This meeting took place in the same month that the Soviet Union (USSR) dissolved. With their biggest communist rival no longer a threat, European leaders hoped to link their countries to ensure a stable and peaceful future. In theory the European Union, as the grouping was called, would stretch from the Atlantic to the western frontier of Russia, allow goods and people to freely cross borders between member states, and use a single currency, the *euro.* Persuaded by Delors, conference leaders signed the Maastricht Treaty, and it was later ratified by voters in all member nations, though debates contin ued as new members joined. While facing bumps in the road, the European Union, given the centuries of European strife, was a huge achievement.

From 1945 until 1990 three themes dominated European history: (1) the Cold War shaped by the United States and the USSR, each with a political and military power vastly exceeding that of other nations; (2) the rebirth of western European wealth and power; and (3) the movement toward European unity represented by the Maastricht Treaty. After World War II, which had left most countries in shambles, Europe became divided into mutually hostile political and military blocs. While eastern Europe came under Soviet domination, enduring authoritarian communist governments, much of western Europe recovered its prosperity, ensuring freedom, peace, and the well-being of citizens. The trauma of two world wars had fostered a drive for unity involving consensus rather than military might. After 1989, when the communist governments collapsed, this movement accelerated, opening the way for a new, interconnected Europe.

Western Europe: Revival and Unity

What factors fostered the movement toward unity in western Europe?

Western Europe, emerging from the ashes of World War II economically bankrupt, made a rapid recovery with aid from the United States. Most western Europeans reestablished working multiparty democracies that accorded personal freedom to their citizens. Beginning in 1947, however, Europe was split into two mutually hostile camps with rival military forces—western and eastern Europe—each with a different model of postwar reconstruction. Gradually West Germany, France, and Britain served as the core of a rebuilt, increasingly unified western Europe and were able to regain influence in the world, while economic prosperity blunted the appeal of radicalism.

The Remaking of European Nations

World War II had cost some 50 million lives, reduced major cities to rubble, and destroyed bridges, tunnels, and roads. Transportation, food, housing, and fuel were in short supply. The chaos and the redrawing of political boundaries after the war had displaced people from their home countries, including 10 million Germans who were forced to leave eastern Europe and move to Germany. Emotionally traumatized by the war and the atrocities, Europeans also saw their prestige in tatters. War crimes trials held in Nuremberg, Germany, in 1946 condemned Nazi leaders to death and declared crimes against humanity, especially genocide, indefensible. A fresh start was needed.

Economic Recovery

Marshall Plan A recovery program created for western Europe by the United States that aimed to prevent communist expansion and to spread liberal economic principles.

Economic growth provided the foundation for a new Europe. In 1947 the U.S. secretary of state, World War II general George Marshall (1880–1959), proposed that, to achieve stability and guarantee peace, the United States assist in restoring Europe's economic health. This initiative, the **Marshall Plan**, created a recovery program aimed at preventing communist expansion and spreading liberal economic principles, such as free markets. Between 1948 and 1952 the United States offered $13 billion in aid, about half going to Britain, France, and West Germany. In exchange, American business enjoyed greater access to European markets. The Marshall Plan restored agricultural and industrial production while bolstering international trade. The rapid economic resurgence from 1948 to 1965, unmatched in world history except for Japan's recovery in the same years (see Chapter 27), also owed much to liberal democracy, modern production and managerial techniques, and advances in science, technology, transportation, and agriculture.

Promoting Unity

The British leader Winston Churchill (1874–1965), who served twice as prime minister (1940–1945, 1951–1955), prophesied the new trends for Europe. Churchill warned that the Soviet Union was expansionist and that "an iron curtain" had descended across Europe, dividing western Europe from eastern Europe and pro-Western, capitalist West Germany from communist East Germany. This Cold War division stimulated western European cooperation. When eight hundred delegates met at the Hague, in Holland, in 1948, where they called for a democratic European economic union, Churchill urged them to "design a United Europe, where men and women of every country will think of being European as of belonging to their native land, and wherever they go in this wide domain they will truly feel 'Here I am at home'"[2] (see Chronology: Western Europe, 1945–1989). The Hague Congress, which created a European assembly and a court of human rights, generated what soon became the "European Movement."

Western Europeans also committed to sustaining parliamentary democracy. This was true even for the surviving constitutional monarchies, including Belgium, Britain, the Netherlands, and the Scandinavian nations, where kings and queens remained symbols of their people but enjoyed little power. In the 1970s longtime dictators opposed to change were overthrown and replaced by democrats in Spain, Portugal, and Greece. Britain, France, Italy, and West Germany became the most influential European nations.

New political alignments also emerged. Political stability in western Europe depended on improved relations between France and Germany, as well as on German recovery from war. Although Charles De Gaulle (1890–1970), the crusty general and proud nationalist who dominated French politics between 1947 and 1969, imagined France "like the princess in the fairy stories, as dedicated to an exalted and exceptional destiny,"[3] he made French-German reconciliation the cornerstone

CHRONOLOGY

Western Europe, 1945–1989

1946–1949 Greek civil war

1947–1989 Cold War

1947–1969 De Gaulle era in France

1948 Hague Congress on European unity

1948–1949 Berlin crisis

1948–1952 Marshall Plan

1949 Formation of NATO

1951 Formation of European Coal and Steel Community

1957 Formation of European Common Market

1969 West German ostpolitik policy

CHRONOLOGY

	Western Europe	Russia	Eastern Europe
1940	**1946–1989** Cold War **1949** Formation of NATO **1957** European Common Market	**1955** Warsaw Pact	**1945–1948** Formation of communist governments
1960		**1979–1989** Soviet war in Afghanistan	
1980	**1991** Maastricht Treaty	**1991** Breakup of Soviet Union	**1989** End of communist governments

of French policy. Similarly, the West German leader, Konrad Adenauer **(ODD-en-HOUR)** (1876–1967), sought a cooperative relationship with France. Germany's reconciliation with its neighbors was furthered in the 1960s by West German chancellor Willy Brandt (1913–1992), a fervent anti-Nazi who had fled Adolph Hitler's government. Brandt accepted German responsibilities for the war and the new borders imposed after the war, which awarded a large chunk of German territory to Poland. Economic growth also improved French-German relations. Because of its sheer size and central location, West Germany's economy lay at the heart of western European recovery, and by 1960 West Germany, now firmly allied with France, accounted for a fifth of the world's trade in manufactured goods, surpassing Britain.

Political Parties

New political parties and movements took shape. On the right, Christian Democrats, who, aligned with the Catholic Church, emphasized Christian values and protecting the traditional family, either formed governments or led the opposition in a half dozen countries, including West Germany and Italy. But Christian Democratic corruption scandals erupted in West Germany and Italy, and by the 1990s the parties had lost considerable support. Parties on the left competed for support. The social democratic parties, which favored generous welfare programs to provide a safety net for all citizens, acquired more clout than they had enjoyed in the prewar years. Social democratic governments came to power in several countries, including Britain and France, and moved toward state ownership of large industries such as steel and railroads. Eventually most of the social democratic parties, such as the British Labor Party, abandoned state ownership and economic planning for free markets.

AP/Wide World Photos

Basque Terrorism The extremist Basque nationalist movement, the ETA, has waged a terrorist campaign against the Spanish government for decades, assassinating dozens of people and exploding bombs at government targets in cities and towns. The result is the sort of destruction shown here after one attack.

Eurocommunism A form of communism in western Europe that embraced political democracy and free elections and that rejected Soviet domination.

Greens A political movement in western Europe that rejected militarism and heavy industry and favored environmental protection over economic growth.

Meanwhile, the western European communist parties declined rapidly, maintaining a large following only in France, Italy, Portugal, and Spain. Seeking popular support, some adopted **Eurocommunism**, a form of communism that embraced political democracy and free elections and that rejected Soviet domination. Despite Eurocommunism, the communist parties lost most of their support in the 1990s, fragmenting into small feuding parties. By the 1980s a new political movement had an impact. The **Greens** rejected militarism and heavy industry and favored environmental protection over economic growth. Women such as Petra Kelly (1947–1992) were prominent in the West German Green Party leadership, helping it appeal to women voters and win seats in the West German parliament.

Ethnic and Religious Conflicts

However, western Europe was not immune to political unrest. Between 1946 and 1949 a civil war raged in Greece, where conservatives supporting the monarchy, aided by the United States, defeated revolutionaries who wanted to end the monarchy and establish a communist state. Elsewhere, the desire of ethnic minorities for their own nations spurred violence and sometimes terrorism. For example, a chronic ethnic conflict embroiled Spain, where the Basque people, who live mostly in the north and speak a language completely different from Spanish, have long sought either autonomy within, or independence from, Spain. An underground Basque independence movement, known as ETA (for "Basque Homeland and Freedom"), has carried out assassinations and bombings against people linked to the Spanish government. Similarly, for decades in Northern Ireland (Ulster), which remains part of Great Britain, the Catholic minority, often less affluent, have sought freedom from British rule and a merger with the largely Catholic Irish Republic, while the majority Protestants have wanted to remain a British province. For decades extremist Catholic and Protestant paramilitary groups attacked each other and the British army, causing thousands of civilian deaths, but violence ebbed as relations between Britain and Ireland improved.

Decolonization and the Cold War

Dismantling Empires

Both the end of colonial empires and the Cold War affected Europe. Most European colonizers gradually abandoned their efforts to quell nationalist movements in Asia and Africa and started to leave their colonial territories. The British, whose empire had occupied an area 125 times larger than Great Britain, realized that imperial glory was only memory. In 1947 they recognized the independence of India and in 1948 of Burma. The Dutch, facing a determined nationalist resistance, reluctantly abandoned their lucrative colony, Indonesia, in 1950. By the mid-1960s the British had also turned over most of their colonies in Africa, Asia, and the Caribbean to local leaders, retaining control of only a few tiny outposts, such as Gibraltar, a strategically valuable peninsula on the southern coast of Spain, and a few Caribbean, South Atlantic, and South Pacific islands. While postimperial Britain sought to balance a special relationship to the United States with closer links to Europe, it also continued economic ties to many former colonies. A more formal connection was maintained through the British **Commonwealth of Nations**, established in 1931 and comprising fifty-three states by 2009, which provided a forum for cooperating and discussing issues of mutual interest.

Commonwealth of Nations A forum, established by Britain in 1931, for discussing issues of mutual interest with its former colonies.

By contrast, the French and Portuguese only grudgingly recognized the inevitable. In the 1940s nationalist rebellions broke out in Algeria and Vietnam, which France attempted to quell at the cost of much bloodshed. In his criticism of torture used against rebels in Algeria, the French philosopher Jean-Paul Sartre, an outspoken opponent of colonialism, wrote: "We are sick, very sick. Feverish and prostrate, obsessed by old dreams of glory and the foreboding of its shame, France is struggling in the grip of a nightmare it is unable either to flee or to decipher."[4] In 1954, unable to defeat communist-led revolutionaries, the French withdrew from Vietnam. Then in 1962 they left Algeria, causing 800,000 European settlers, many embittered toward the French government, to flee to France. France retained a few small Caribbean, Pacific, and Indian Ocean islands and French Guiana, and eventually it established close relations with most of its former colonies, including an enduring economic connection that critics considered a form of neocolonialism, since French business interests and advisers remained prominent. Portugal wasted lives and wealth violently resisting African nationalist movements but, after democrats overthrew the long-standing fascist dictatorship, granted its African colonies independence in 1975.

Europe and the Cold War

Truman Doctrine A policy formed in 1947 that asserted that the United States, as the leader of the free world, was charged with protecting countries from communism.

Beginning in 1946, the Cold War shaped the European roles in the world. The USSR helped install communist governments in eastern Europe and East Germany, while the United States assumed the burden for protecting western Europe militarily. In 1947 the U.S. president, Harry Truman (president 1945–1953), introduced a policy, known as the **Truman Doctrine**, that asserted that the United States, as the leader of the free world, was charged with defending countries that were threatened by communist movements or Soviet pressure. Then in 1949 strong European and

U.S. fears of possible Soviet attack led to the formation of the North Atlantic Treaty Organization, **NATO**, a military alliance that linked nine western European countries with the United States and Canada. NATO allowed coordination of defense policies against the USSR and its communist allies, known as the **Soviet bloc**, with the aim of repulsing any potential Soviet military attack across the "iron curtain" frontier. Permanent U.S. military bases were set up in NATO countries, especially West Germany. The Soviets responded in 1955 by forming the **Warsaw Pact**, a defense alliance that linked the communist-ruled eastern European countries with the USSR (see Map 28.1). By the 1980s senior officers in NATO and the Warsaw Pact had spent their careers preparing for a war that, partly because both sides possessed nuclear weapons, never came. Western Europeans were alarmed by nuclear weapons, which could obliterate their cities in minutes, and worried that a nuclear conflict between the United States and the USSR would inevitably destroy Europe as well.

NATO A military alliance, formed in 1949, that linked nine western European countries with the United States and Canada.

Soviet bloc The Soviet Union and the communist states allied with it.

Warsaw Pact A defense alliance formed in 1955 that linked the communist-ruled eastern European countries with the USSR.

The Cold War and NATO were partly a response to the postwar division of Germany. Each of the four World War II allies—the United States, Britain, France, and the USSR—had an occupation zone in Germany and had also divided up the German capital, Berlin. In 1948 the three Western powers united their occupation zones. Angered, the USSR blockaded Berlin to prevent supplies from reaching the city's Western-administered zone by land through Soviet-controlled East Germany. For a year the allies supplied the city with food and fuel by airlift. In 1949 the USSR stopped the blockade and allowed the creation of the Federal Republic of Germany, or West Germany, while forming its own allied government, the German Democratic Republic, or East Germany. West Germany later joined NATO.

Reducing Tensions

Cold War fears gradually slackened as the danger of actual war faded, leading western Europeans to reappraise their policies toward both of the two superpowers. Some, especially in Britain, promoted the U.S. alliance, while many Europeans, resenting what they considered irresponsible U.S. foreign policies, wanted weaker ties. Most opposed the American war in Vietnam, as well as U.S. interventions to overthrow left-leaning governments in Latin America, such as Guatemala (1954) and Chile (1973). In 1969 the West German chancellor Willy Brandt, a Social Democrat and strong anticommunist, introduced his policy of **ostpolitik** ("eastern politics"), which sought a reconciliation between West and East Germany and an expanded western European dialogue with the USSR. This stance led to a thaw between West Germany and the Soviet bloc and gave hope to eastern Europeans who wanted more freedom. Gradually western Europeans, by building their own military forces, became less reliant on U.S. power. Despite the differences, however, the Western alliance and NATO remained strong because of mutual interests during the Cold War.

ostpolitik A West German policy, promoted by Chancellor Willy Brandt, that sought a reconciliation between West and East Germany and an expanded dialogue with the USSR.

From Cooperation to European Community

Western Europe's role in the global system changed. Between the two world wars Europeans owned enterprises all over the globe, including Indian tea plantations, Malayan rubber estates, African mines, and South American railroads. But during the 1940s Europeans lost influence to the United States. The Bretton Woods agreement on international monetary cooperation in 1944 made the U.S. dollar, pegged to the price of gold, the staple currency of the Western nations. Europeans concluded they had no choice but to cooperate with each other. In 1949 ten nations formed the Council of Europe, which operated on the basis of a shared cultural heritage and democratic principles. In 1950 the Council produced the European Convention on Human Rights, the root of a Europe-wide justice system and court. But some leaders wanted more. Jean Monnet (MOAN-ay) (1888–1979), a French economist, financier, and former League of Nations official who is often called the "Father of United Europe," and French prime minister Robert Schuman (1886–1963), a strong proponent of French-German reconciliation, wanted to make war not only unthinkable but impossible. To encourage better economic coordination, they proposed a European Coal and Steel Community (ECSC), which finally formed in 1951. They hoped that the ECSC, which brought together six nations, would be a first step for unity and peace. But some nations, including Britain, fearing loss of economic independence, declined to join.

Increasing Cooperation

The European Community

Building on the ECSC, the Common Market, later known as the European Community (EC), was formed in 1957 with six members: France, Italy, West Germany, the Netherlands, Belgium, and Luxembourg. By removing tariff barriers, it opened frontiers to the free movement of capital and labor. The members called upon other Europeans to join in their efforts and added Britain, Ireland, and Denmark in 1973. The EC created unprecedented economic unity in the world's largest free trade zone.

Monnet and Schuman dreamed of a Europe united politically: societies that depend on one another, they reasoned, won't go to war. But European nationalism occasionally flared up. The EC weathered many disagreements as the member nations squabbled to get the best deal for their own farmers or businesses, and the British, an island people proud of their distinctive traditions,

Map 28.1
Military Alliances and Multinational Economic Groupings, 1949–1989
Post–World War II Europe was divided by Cold War politics into communist and noncommunist blocs. Most western European nations joined the NATO defense alliance. Western Europeans also cooperated in economic matters. By 1989 the Common Market had expanded from six to eleven members. The Soviet bloc counterpart, COMECON, had eight members.

Interactive Map

Map 28.2
Europe's Gross Domestic Product
The gross domestic product, or the official measure of the output of goods and services in a national economy, provides a good summary of a nation's economic production. In the early twenty-first century, Norway, Ireland, and Switzerland were the most productive European countries on a per capita basis, while former Soviet bloc nations had the weakest performance.

Interactive Map

periodically threatened to quit the grouping. While every member economy had to adapt to the marketplace, dumping uncompetitive industries, some doubters, the "Euro-skeptics," believed cooperation had gone too far. Yet the EC greatly reduced old national tensions. The members eventually established an elected European Parliament, based in Brussels, Belgium, to discuss shared issues and to make policies that encouraged cooperation and standardization.

Growing Prosperity

The European Community spurred growth, creating a consumer society in western Europe (see Map 28.2). With higher wages, greater purchasing power, and more available consumer products, families bought automobiles, washing machines, refrigerators, and televisions. More people worked in the service sector and fewer in agriculture, and the middle classes grew rapidly, while blue-collar workers shared middle-class aspirations. Consumer markets reached from Europe's sprawling cities into remote villages. A journalist's description of an old French village in 1973 revealed the change: "The last horse trod its streets in 1968. The water mill closed down in 1952.

SECTION SUMMARY

- World War II devastated western Europe's population, infrastructure, and economy, but it enjoyed a remarkable period of growth, aided by extensive U.S. funding under the Marshall Plan.
- After World War II, Germany and France overcame centuries of mutual hatred, rightwing Christian Democrat parties competed with leftist social democrats, and the Greens agitated for environmental protection over economic growth.
- A wave of decolonization followed World War II, though the British Commonwealth maintained connections between Great Britain and its former colonies, and France, after struggling to maintain its colonies, maintained economic ties with its former holdings.
- The Cold War shaped European politics, with eastern Europe allied with the USSR and western Europe allied with the United States, but over time some European leaders distanced themselves from U.S. policies and advocated dialogue with the USSR.
- Having been surpassed economically by the United States, European countries joined together in the European Community, which became the world's largest free-trade zone and led to increased prosperity; however, the 1970s brought hard times, and European unity sometimes threatened to give way.

The washing machine replaced the wash house—and broke up the community of women—in the 1960s."[5] Europeans invested in high-speed railroads and turnpikes to link peoples together, as well as mass transit—subways and commuter trains—to make city life more convenient. Yet prosperity did not eliminate all poverty or regional disparities. For example, industrialized northern Italy remained much wealthier than largely agricultural southern Italy.

Despite the growing cooperation and successes, western Europe still faced economic problems. For one thing, Europeans were hurt by U.S. decisions that led to the dismantling of the Bretton Woods international monetary system. In 1971, with the U.S. economy undermined by the war in Vietnam, President Richard Nixon devalued the U.S. dollar, the staple currency of the Western nations, and ended its parity with gold. These moves destabilized world trade, triggering soaring prices and trade deficits. Then in 1973 European economies were brought to a standstill by a quadrupling of oil prices, followed by a short embargo on oil exports, by the major oil-producing nations, which were angered by Western support of Israel. The frustrated motorists waiting in long lines at gas stations showed how vulnerable prosperity could be in the global system. Western Europe also faced the environmental problems common to all industrial societies, such as noxious air, toxic waste, and lakes and forests dying from acid rain, the apparent price of industrialization.

The end of cheap energy and growing competition from industrializing Asian nations and Japan also hurt European industries and workers. Factories built a century or more earlier, often decaying and inefficient, scaled back operations or closed, causing high unemployment in industrial cities such as Birmingham and Manchester in England. Jobless young people, living in bleak row houses or apartments and surviving on welfare payments, hung out on street corners, some turning to drugs or crime. By 1983 unemployment rates in western Europe had risen to 10 percent, posing a special problem to women, immigrants, and those just out of school. As some blamed their problems on immigrant workers, especially the Arabs and Turks who competed with local people for jobs, these feelings gave a boost to rightwing, anti-immigrant parties. As a result, free market conservatives often regained political power, penalizing striking workers and weakening labor unions.

WESTERN EUROPEAN SOCIETIES AND CULTURES

How did the rise of welfare states transform western European societies?

In the ashes of World War II the wartime British prime minister, Winston Churchill, wrote, "What is Europe? A rubble heap, a charnel house, a breeding ground for pestilence and hate."[6] Seeing the need for change, western European nations embarked on reshaping their societies and improving the quality of life for all their citizens, often blending capitalism and socialism. The economic boom from the late 1940s to the 1970s allowed most western European states, influenced by socialism, to construct welfare programs that fostered political stability, ensured public health, and eliminated poverty for most citizens. Gender relations, family life, and sexual attitudes were also reshaped, while musicians, philosophers, and churches addressed the changes of the times.

Social Democracy and Welfare States

welfare states Government systems that offer their citizens a range of state-subsidized health, education, and social service benefits; adopted by western European nations after World War II.

The rise of western European **welfare states**, government systems that offer their citizens a range of state-subsidized health, education, and social service benefits, and the high quality of life they fostered, owed much to an influential political philosophy called social democracy. Social democracy derived from socialists in the early 1900s who favored evolutionary rather than revolutionary change, eventually promoting a mixing of liberal democracy, market economies, and a safety net for workers. Since 1945 social democratic parties have governed or been the dominant opposition in many Western countries. They have usually controlled the governments in the Scandinavian nations of Denmark, Finland, Norway, and Sweden and have often governed in several other nations, including Britain, France, Netherlands, West Germany, and Spain. They have also been influential in Australia, Canada, and New Zealand.

Social Democratic Policies

Social democracy has fostered welfare programs, a mix of free markets and government regulation, a commitment to parliamentary democracy and civil liberties, support for labor unions, and the goal of moderating the extremes of wealth and poverty. As a result, workers in northern and central Europe have gained more rights and protections than workers enjoy anywhere else in the world. In West Germany, for example, they received generous pensions and gained seats on the boards of directors of the enterprises that employed them. Often valuing leisure at the expense of work, Europeans boasted that they work to live while Americans, who on average earn more, live to work. By the 1990s both white-collar and blue-collar Europeans worked many fewer hours each year than their counterparts in the United States and Japan. The 35-hour workweek became the norm in France and West Germany, and by 2000 the average German spent around 400 fewer hours a year on the job than the average American. Moreover, the average paid vacation has been four to six weeks a year. During the most popular vacation month, August, the beach and mountain resorts are jammed, and, with many employees gone, stores often offer limited services.

Citizens in nations influenced by social democracy have received generous taxpayer-funded benefits from the state. Europeans tend to define welfare not just as assistance to the poor, as Americans do, but also as ensuring that everyone enjoys better living standards and opportunities. Free education through the university level (but with stiff university entrance exams) has helped people from working-class and farming backgrounds to move into the middle and upper classes, and generous unemployment insurance removes the pain of job loss. Governments also subsidize housing for the elderly, while inexpensive, widely available day care allows mothers to work outside the home for wages. Whether married or single, custodial parents receive child support payments from the welfare state. While extensive mass transit makes travel and commuting affordable for all, universal health coverage has removed the fear of serious illness, providing inexpensive prescription drugs and guaranteeing medical care to all citizens. These benefits have greatly improved public health. Most Western European nations spend less than Americans do on health care yet often see better outcomes. Using statistical methods the World Health Organization identified France as having the world's best health care system, with the lowest per capita number of avoidable deaths and a life expectancy three years longer than Americans. Where Europeans had once looked to the extended family for support in the early 1900s, now they expect the welfare state to care for the elderly and incapacitated. In addition, northern European nations have the most equitable distributions of income in the world and have nearly eliminated slums and deep poverty.

Scandinavian Welfare States

The Scandinavian nations, poor a century ago, have elected the strongest social democratic governments and become the world's most prosperous societies. Norway has achieved the highest standard of living in the Western world, thanks to North Sea oil and a generous welfare state.

B.O. Olsson, photographer

Swedish Father and Child Swedes have been the most innovative Europeans in social policy, including adopting in 1975 a law requiring employers to grant parental leave. While women mainly take advantage of the law, some men, including this man with his child, take off the full allotted time.

The annual Human Development Report, issued by the United Nations, usually ranks Norway and Sweden as having the highest quality of life in the world, along with several other countries in which social democracy has been influential, such as Australia, Canada, Iceland, and the Netherlands. The Scandinavian nations are also ranked, along with Ireland, the Netherlands, and Switzerland, as having the most press freedom in the world, with the least government interference in the free flow of information. In Sweden, which has been Europe's most creative country in experimenting with social change, women, youth, and even animals have more rights and protections than elsewhere. Swedish citizens enjoy housing subsidies, free hospitalization, and a pension that pays two-thirds of their salary upon retirement. By providing child care in kindergartens and preschools, the Swedes also attract women into the work force. Nor have the world's most level playing field and lowest poverty rate dampened economic growth. In recent decades, Sweden has often enjoyed the most dynamic economy in Europe. And, thanks to the social safety net and wise investment of oil revenues, Norway even thrived during the 2008–2009 global economic crisis that undermined most European economies.

Challenges to Welfare States

All welfare states have problems, however. Although they foster social stability, funding them has required high taxes, often half of a citizen's annual income. There are also some workplace consequences. Worker protections make it hard for companies to fire workers, prompting companies to hire fewer people. The shift in emphasis from work to leisure has given workers so much security that they may not need to strive harder, which has economic costs. Losing a job is less disastrous than for Americans, since the welfare state insulates people from many effects of economic slumps. Yet, many people with modest incomes, especially immigrants, live in drab apartment blocks or houses, often far from potential jobs and the best schools.

Beginning in the 1980s the welfare states experienced more problems related to sporadic downturns in the world economy. For decades governments had paid for social services by borrowing against future exports, a strategy known as deficit spending. Falling export profits, and hence revenues, placed the welfare systems under strain, forcing cutbacks in benefits, and also prompted nations to cut spending for military defense. Companies downsized, thus putting pressure on generous unemployment programs. As a result, in some countries conservative parties gained power and began to modify the welfare systems. For example, in Britain, the government led by Prime Minister Margaret Thatcher (governed 1979–1990), a free market enthusiast, reduced health services, with the result that people had to wait longer to receive medical attention. But the conservative regimes did not dismantle welfare state institutions such as national health insurance, which remained hugely popular.

Political and Economic Stability

Unlike in the 1930s, the economic problems did not bring serious violence or political instability. While occasionally a political party with an anti-immigrant or anti–European Union platform has gained a following, extremist rightwing and ultranationalist forces have remained weak in most countries. For example, the French National Front, led by the paratrooper turned lawyer Jean-Marie Le Pen (b. 1928), won 10 percent of the national vote in 1986 by calling for expulsion of Arab and African immigrants and secession from the European Community, but Le Pen's appeal faded. The welfare state, which allows even the unemployed to receive their basic necessities such as health care, provides stability because it diminishes workers' fear of job competition from immigrants. Hence, even most free market conservatives have accepted the broad framework of the welfare state, although they want to make it more efficient and cost-effective.

Social Activism, Reform, and Gender Relations

Social Protests and Problems

Although most people have seemed satisfied with their lives, occasional student and worker protests against capitalism and materialism have erupted. A serious challenge to mainstream society came in 1968, when youth protests broke out in France that were aimed at the aging, autocratic president Charles De Gaulle, an antiquated university education system, and the unpopular U.S. war in Vietnam, France's former colony. Protest posters urged students to "be realistic—ask for the impossible." University students went on strike, police beat hundreds of them, protesters blocked traffic, and activists fought pitched battles in the streets with police, who responded with teargas. As public sentiment shifted toward the protesters, industrial workers called a general strike, bringing some 10 million workers into the streets. Although De Gaulle outmaneuvered the protesters by rallying conservatives, raising workers' wages, and calling for a new national election, the protests begun in Paris soon spread to Italy and West Germany, where students resented conservative governments, staid bureaucracies, rigid university systems, and powerful business interests. Lacking strong public support, however, Europe's student protests soon fizzled; governments did not fall or need troops to restore order. However, De Gaulle resigned a year later after the public rejected, in a referendum, his proposals to reorganize the French government.

Europeans also dealt with social problems common to all industrialized nations, such as drug and alcohol abuse and high divorce rates. But European attitudes to the problems were often different from those in the United States. For example, while Americans harshly punished drug use and trafficking, by the 1980s many western Europeans generally treated drug use and minor drug sales as social and medical issues rather than criminal ones. Some European countries even decriminalized use of marijuana. Other laws in Europe also differed from those elsewhere. European nations generally abolished capital punishment, and most enacted strict gun control laws, often banning handguns. The scarcity of guns fostered low rates of violent crime.

Gender Relations

Attitudes toward marriage and gender relations also shifted. After World War II, governments tried to revitalize traditional marriage and family patterns, such as the view that women were chiefly homemakers and should have many children. But in the 1960s and 1970s the changing attitudes toward sexual activity, often known as the sexual revolution, facilitated by general access to birth control, undermined conventional practices. The contraceptive pill, which remained illegal in some Catholic countries until much later, gave women control over their reproduction and sexuality. The sexual revolution upset those with traditional values, such as the rural Spanish woman who ruefully observed the ease of pursuing sex outside of marriage: "If a boy wants to be alone with a girl there's no problem; they go off alone and whatever fires they have can burn."[7]

Changing social attitudes also eliminated or moderated the social shame of divorce, extramarital sex, and unmarried cohabitation. All these activities now became open, a challenge to cultural taboos. Although sex scandals involving politicians are not unknown, especially in Britain, most political leaders have little fear of public criticism for openly having extramarital relationships or children out of wedlock, and such practices are common in France and Italy. Pornography and obscenity laws were relaxed, allowing long banned work to be published, such as the racy 1920s novel *Lady Chatterly's Lover* by the British author D. H. Lawrence. British poet Philip Larkin satirized the changes: "Sexual intercourse began, in nineteen sixty-three (Which was rather late for me)—Between the end of the *Chatterly* ban, And the Beatles' first LP."[8]

Women's Movements

Inspired by feminist thinkers such as the French philosopher Simone de Beauvoir **(bo-VWAHR)** (see Profile: Simone de Beauvoir, French Feminist and Philosopher), women's movements grew in strength and, by the 1970s, pressed their agendas more effectively. An English women's group hoped that "a world freed from the economic, social and psychological bonds of patriarchy would be a world turned upside down, creating a human potential we can hardly dream of now,"[9] benefiting both men and women. Feminists wanted legal divorce, easier access to birth control, the right to abortion, and reform of family laws to give wives more influence. They had their most success in Protestant countries, which often adopted their agenda. In 1973 Denmark became the first nation to allow abortion on request. The feminist movements also made headway in Catholic nations. Although Pope John Paul II (pope 1978–2005) reiterated the long-standing church ban on contraception, abortion, and divorce, many Catholics ignored the conservative teachings of their church, and during the 1970s and 1980s most Catholic nations, including Italy and Spain, followed the earlier examples of France, Britain, and Germany and legalized both divorce and abortion.

The lives of both men and women were affected by changes in work, politics, and family life. Men and women now shared responsibility for financially supporting their families. By the 1980s women were half the work force in Sweden, a third in France and Italy, and a quarter in conservative Ireland. Women also moved into the professions, business, and even politics. Having won the right to vote, they constituted a majority of the electorate. In some nations, such as Belgium, France, and Italy, female suffrage came only in 1945, but as once-powerful male-dominated institutions such as the military and church declined in influence, more and more women voted for socialist and liberal parties supportive of the welfare state that guaranteed them and their children health care and education. At various times women headed governments in nations such as Britain, France, Germany, Iceland, and Norway. Even Ireland, where patriarchy remained strong, in 1991 elected its first woman president, social democrat Mary Robinson (b. 1944), an outspoken law professor, feminist, single parent, and supporter of homosexual rights.

Women political activists made their voices heard. In 1976 two Northern Ireland mothers, Mairead Corrigan (b. 1944) and Betty Williams (b. 1943), jointly shared the Nobel Peace Prize for their efforts to bridge the Catholic-Protestant divide and bring peace to their troubled land. Women wage earners became less dependent on men. Yet, some changes came slowly. So few women had been able to achieve high business and industry positions that, in 2006, Norway's social democratic government outraged corporate leaders by requiring that 40 percent of the board members of large private companies must be women.

Marriage Patterns

Less-rigid gender roles affected marriage patterns. In the 1970s the model of the married heterosexual couple remained the norm, and even rock stars known for their live-in girlfriends, such as Mick Jagger of the Rolling Stones, a popular British group, got married, surrounded by celebrities. Some celebrities, such as French rock star Johnny Halliday, changed spouses frequently. But by the 1980s more men and women remained single and lived on their own. In Scandinavia and Germany, the singles accounted for between a quarter and a third of the adult population. Increasing personal independence and mobility fostered small nuclear families instead of the large extended families of old. As unhappy couples no longer needed to stay married, divorce rates more than doubled between 1960 and 1990.

Homosexuality

Homosexuals also began to enjoy equal rights. Homosexual subcultures in European cities had been active for decades. Organizing to change discriminatory laws and attitudes, reform movements began in several countries. Yet, in the 1950s many governments still prosecuted homosexuals, some of them respected figures in the arts, for consensual sexual activity. In West Germany between 1953 and 1965 some 99,000 men were convicted, and frequently jailed, under still-existing Nazi-era laws prohibiting homosexual activity. Although governments began to eliminate laws opposing homosexual behavior by the 1960s, combating prejudice took longer. Hence, in 1974 a conservative Christian Democrat leader in Italy warned that "if divorce is allowed, it will be possible to have marriages between homosexuals, and perhaps your wife will run off with some pretty young girl."[10] However, most societies developed more tolerant attitudes. Denmark recognized domestic partnerships in 1989, and by 2001 most of northern Europe had such laws providing legal protection, while discrimination against homosexuals had ebbed. Several nations, including the Netherlands, Belgium, and Spain, legalized homosexual marriage in the early twenty-first century. At the same time, openly homosexual men and women served as high government officials or political leaders in nations as socially different as the liberal Netherlands and conservative Ireland. In 2009 Iceland, engulfed in economic collapse, chose the openly lesbian Johanna Sigurdarlottir, a leftwing former flight attendant and trade unionist, as prime minister.

Immigration: Questions of Identity

"Guest Workers"

In the later twentieth century several million immigrants settled in various European countries as "guest workers." In response to labor shortages in northern Europe and Britain in the 1950s and 1960s, poorer southern Europeans, especially Italians, Greeks, and Portuguese, migrated north in search of better jobs and pay. They were soon joined by Turks, Algerians, Moroccans, and people from West Africa and the Caribbean, fleeing even harsher poverty. At first many were single men who were brought for factory work and often housed in bleak shantytowns. Later entire families arrived. Many Indians, Pakistanis, and Bangladeshis sought a better life in their former imperial power, Britain, while people left the former Dutch colonies of Indonesia and Suriname for the Netherlands. By the early twenty-first century immigrants constituted 10 percent of the population in Germany, 6 percent in France, and 5 percent in Britain. Major European cities such as Berlin, London, and Paris took on an international flavor. By 2006 London's population was 40 percent nonwhite, and Islamic culture flourished in cities such as Hamburg (Germany) and Marseilles (France), where Arab- and Turkish-language radio stations had large audiences.

Immigrant Life

Immigrants contributed much to European societies. Paris became a center of Arab and African culture, including a large recording industry churning out music by Arab and African musicians, often for export to their homelands. Small Arab-run neighborhood grocery stores served vital functions in French urban life, and the Indian and Pakistani sundry goods and grocery shops and restaurants became features of English and Irish city life. Observers remarked that the favorite British food was now Indian curry, while in Ireland Chinese carry-out restaurants opened in nearly every town. In Britain many immigrants served as mayors, officials, doctors, professors, writers, and entertainers, and people of Asian, Middle Eastern, and African descent were elected to parliaments in countries such as Britain, France, and the Netherlands. In 2007 two Muslim women, of Algerian and Senegalese background respectively, were named to the French cabinet.

The immigration also posed problems of absorption into European society, fostering tensions between whites and the nonwhite immigrants. Over the years, as Turks, Arabs, Africans, and Pakistanis arrived to do the low-paying jobs nobody else wanted and then settled down, they and even their local-born children faced discrimination and sometimes violent attack by rightwing youth gangs. Neo-Nazis in Germany sometimes set fire to immigrant apartment buildings, and young toughs in England boasted of "Paki-bashing," or beating up people from the Indian subcontinent. In response, many immigrants retreated into their own cultures. While older immigrants often clung to the cultures and attitudes they brought from their Asian or Middle Eastern village, such as a husband's authority over his wife and the preference for arranged marriages, their children struggled to reconcile the contrasting expectations of their conservative parents and religious traditions with the materialistic, individualistic, secular societies of Europe.

SIMONE DE BEAUVOIR, FRENCH FEMINIST AND PHILOSOPHER

Few thinkers have had more influence on the study of women and on contemporary women's movements than Simone de Beauvoir (1908–1986), the first systematic feminist philosopher and a prolific writer of novels, essays, and autobiographical works. She was born in Paris to a middle-class family. Her father, a lawyer, and a devout mother with very traditional values sent her to fashionable Roman Catholic girls' schools that taught her, she remembered, "the habit of obedience." She believed that God expected her "to be dutiful." Her classmates aimed at marriage rather than careers. But when World War I impoverished de Beauvoir's family, Simone was pushed toward a career. During her teens she battled her parents for more freedom to leave the house on her own and alarmed her parents by becoming an atheist.

Simone loved the liberating intellectual atmosphere at the Sorbonne in Paris, the most prestigious French university, but found that, to succeed in her studies there, she had to overcome gender stereotypes: "My upbringing had convinced me of my sex's intellectual inferiority. I flattered myself that I had a woman's heart and a man's brain." Graduating at the top of her class, she then supported herself, first as a high school teacher and then as a writer. De Beauvoir began a romantic and intellectual partnership with Jean Paul Sartre, later to become Europe's most acclaimed philosopher, whom she had met at the Sorbonne, and became a vital contributor to Sartre's ideas and books. The two maintained an intense free union, and their lifelong connection provided a model of an adult relationship between a man and woman without wedlock or exclusive commitment. Both had lovers on the side.

De Beauvoir's life reflected the transformation of a privileged woman into a feminist icon. By the late 1940s she was the most famous female intellectual of the day. Throughout her life she enjoyed the new opportunities gained by women as French society liberalized, offering women legal equality, educational opportunities, the vote, and diverse economic roles, but she also saw the limits to these freedoms. Sartre suggested she write about what difference being a woman had made in her life. The result was the pioneering 1,200-page study *The Second Sex* (1949), which challenged conventional thinking on women's issues, becoming perhaps the most influential book on women ever written. The study ranged through biology, history, mythology, sociology, and Marxist and Freudian theory to conclude that all women were oppressed by the attitudes of society. It critically analyzed Western culture as dominated by males and argued that women are not born inferior but are made to view themselves as such. De Beauvoir showed how girls saw their future different from that of boys and had their choices, such as in careers, restricted. Men took themselves as the model: "There is an absolute human type, the masculine. He is the Absolute—she is the Other." In her view, marriage denied women's individuality, becoming a contract of subjugation rather than an equal partnership. Her writings greatly influenced the North American and European feminist movements. Later she addressed aging, including the way society dictated roles for the elderly.

Disillusioned by the slow pace of change in gender relations, in 1972 de Beauvoir became a feminist activist, acknowledging her solidarity with other women and arguing that they had to fight for an improvement in their social condition. She became president of the French League of Women's Rights and editor of journals that called attention to problems of violence, sexual assault, and lack of easily available contraception in Europe and the world. In 1976 she addressed the International Tribunal of Crimes against Women, noting, "You are gathered here to denounce the oppression to which women are subjected. Talk to the world, bring to light the shameful truths that half of humanity is trying to cover up." Admired by millions, de Beauvoir died in 1986 at age seventy-eight.

THINKING ABOUT THE PROFILE

1. How did de Beauvoir's personal life affect her ideas?
2. What were de Beauvoir's main arguments about how history and society shaped perceptions of gender?

Note: Quotations from Bonnie S. Anderson and Judith P. Zinsser, *A History of Their Own: Women in Europe from Prehistory to the Present,* vol. 2 (New York: Harper, 1988), 240, 169, 422; and Bonnie G. Smith, *Changing Lives: Women in European History Since 1700* (Lexington, MA: D.C. Heath, 1989), 519.

Time Life Pictures/Getty Images

Simone de Beauvoir and Jean Paul Sartre The French feminist thinker Simone de Beauvoir and her partner, the philosopher Jean Paul Sartre, were frequent visitors to the cafés of European cities and influential participants in the lively intellectual life of post–World War II Europe.

Rising Tensions

Tensions mounted further after 1989. Vanishing jobs put both the immigrants and the local people on the unemployment rolls or in competition for scarce work. Illegal immigration also increased as people fled extreme poverty or harsh repression. Boarding rickety boats, desperate Albanians headed to Italy and Africans tried to reach Spain. As a result, anti-immigrant (especially anti-Muslim) movements have emerged even in famously tolerant countries like Denmark and the Netherlands, especially after the terrorist attacks against the United States in 2001, which shocked Europeans. To express their alienation from European society, young people of Middle Eastern, South Asian, and African-Caribbean background have often turned to musical forms from their countries of origin, such as Algerian *rai* for Arabs and Jamaican dancehall and reggae for Afro-Caribbeans. Some immigrant youth have adapted African American rap to their needs, writing lyrics in their own languages. Hence, in France the Senegal-born M. C. Solaar achieved popularity for songs commenting on the lives of young people of African ancestry. Facing particular hostility since 2001, some young Muslims, rejecting Western culture as immoral and criticizing the Islam brought by their parents from North African, Turkish, or South Asian villages as corrupted by Sufi mysticism, have become more devout and rigidly orthodox than their parents. The most alienated have turned to militant Islamic groups for direction.

Reshaping Cultures, Thought, and Religion

Popular Culture

Enriched by imports from societies around the world, western Europeans enjoyed a resilient cultural and intellectual life. Mass culture from the United States became widespread. American cigarettes, Coca-Cola, and chewing gum symbolized postwar fashions, while American films and music reshaped cultural horizons. African American jazz musicians often settled in Europe, especially in France and Scandinavia, to escape racism at home. European governments tried to protect their languages and culture industries from the powerful American challenge by mandating how much foreign music could be played on government radio stations. Young people also enjoyed popular entertainments from outside of North America, such as Caribbean reggae music, Latin American dances, and Japanese animated films. Yet Europeans often treasured entertainers who reflected local culture, such as the waiflike French singer Edith Piaf (1915–1963), known for her sad, nostalgic songs of lost love and lost youth.

Rock, an exciting, edgy music that parents often disliked, helped define youth cultures. After rock emerged in the United States in the mid-1950s, it rapidly gained a huge following in Europe, with American rock stars such as Bill Haley, Buddy Holly, Elvis Presley, and Chuck Berry enjoying massive popularity. By the 1960s European musicians inspired by U.S. rock and blues, such as Francois Hardy in France and the Beatles and Rolling Stones in Britain, had reshaped the local music scenes. The Beatles, young working-class men from Liverpool, a gritty but cosmopolitan port city, matured as musicians while playing clubs in West Germany. Beatlemania, as their impact was called, reached around the world. Rock became known as "yeah yeah" music in nations as different as Brazil and Malaysia, after the Beatles lyric "she loves you yeah yeah yeah." The music and fashion, such as clothing and hair length, of the Beatles and other rockers represented an assertion of youth identity. But eventually rock music introduced more personal reflection and social commentary, as reflected in such top-selling Beatles albums as *Revolver* (1966), which lambasted the taxman, greedy for revenues, and introduced Eleanor Rigby, a fictive woman who died alone, ignored by society. The Beatles 1967 album, *Sgt. Pepper's Lonely Hearts Club Band*, became the prototype of the concept album, with a linking theme, cross-cultural musical explorations (including use of Indian instruments), and provocative lyrics, influencing popular musicians around the world for decades after.

By the mid-1970s a new style of rock, punk, appeared that expressed social protest. Although it gained a presence in North America and continental Europe, punk became especially influential in Britain, where working-class youth faced limited job options. The provocative songs of a leading British punk group, the Sex Pistols, deliberately insulted the monarchy and offended the deeper values of British society, much to the delight of their fans. As a leading punk magazine asserted: "[Punk] music is a perfect medium for shoving two fingers up at the establishment."[11] As punk's energy dissipated, it was largely replaced in the 1980s by escapist dance music. But punk provided a foundation for creative new forms of rock in the 1990s in Europe and North America.

bhangra A popular music that emerged in Britain from a blending of traditional folk songs brought by Indian immigrants with Caribbean reggae and Anglo-American styles, such as rock, hip hop, and disco.

Cultural forms from Asia and Africa also influenced European culture. For example, in Britain the popular **bhangra** music emerged from a blending of Indian folk songs with Caribbean reggae and Anglo-American styles, such as rock, hip hop, and disco. Using a mix of Indian and Western instruments, bhangra became a lively dance music, popular with both white and Indian youth in Britain. By the 1980s bhangra had spread to the Indian diaspora communities in North America, the Caribbean, and to India and Pakistan, sustaining Indian identity and encouraging Indian youth to have fun.

Cinema and Literature

Cultural life was influenced not only by the wave of cultural imports but also by local developments, especially political liberalism and a growing mass media such as television and cinema. The creative cinema of France, Italy, and Sweden developed a global audience by depicting the humblest lives and psychological and social dilemmas common to people in a rapidly changing world. Literature also reflected political change. Writers known as postcolonialists sought to escape the world-view shaped by Western dominance. The India-born British writer Salman Rushdie (b. 1947), a Cambridge University–educated former actor and advertising copywriter from a Muslim family, confronted Western ethnocentrism. Remembering the prejudice he faced in British schools, Rushdie criticized Western society but also challenged what he considered the antimodern sensibilities of Islamic culture. His books *Shame* (1983), a satire on Pakistan's history, and especially *The Satanic Verses* (1988), a critical look at Islamic history, created an uproar among conservative Muslims and earned him death threats.

Philosophy

As Europeans struggled to understand the horrors of World War II, which seemed to contradict the rational thought and tolerance that had been building in Europe since the Enlightenment, some turned to new philosophies. **Existentialism**, a philosophy whose speculation on the nature of reality reflects disillusionment with Europe's violent history and doubt that objectivity is possible, and Marxism, which envisions a noncapitalist future for societies, became the most influential schools of secular thought. At the same time organized religion declined as churches struggled to remain relevant in an increasingly secular society.

existentialism A philosophy, influential in post–World War II western Europe, whose speculation on the nature of reality reflects disillusionment with Europe's violent history and doubt that objectivity is possible.

The French philosopher Jean Paul Sartre (SAHRT) (1905–1980) and the French feminist thinker Simone de Beauvoir (1908–1986), his longtime partner, transformed existentialism from a little-known Scandinavian and German approach into a philosophy with wide appeal. Sartre argued that women and men are defined by a reality that they view as fate or imposed by others. He advised people not to let others determine their lives, but find their own meaning. They cannot banish uncertainty about the world and their place in it, but they can overcome it. People must accept responsibility for their actions, and this should lead to political engagement to create a better society. Sartre himself became active in leftwing movements promoting world peace and banning nuclear weapons, thus providing a philosophy that every individual could act upon and that reached across political boundaries. Sartre achieved fame unusual for a philosopher; when he died in 1980, thousands attended his funeral.

Other influential philosophies debated the nature of reality. Marxism emphasized social class and gender inequality, but as a political philosophy it lost many followers after the 1960s. In contrast to Marxism's certitude about truth, an approach called deconstruction, pursued by the Algeria-born Frenchman Jacques Derrida (DER-i-dah) (1930–2004), claimed that all rational thought could be taken apart and shown to be meaningless. Derrida questioned the entire Western philosophical tradition and the notion that Western civilization was superior to other cultures. Inspired by Derrida, by the 1990s literature and scholarship were influenced by **postmodernism**, which contends that truth is not absolute but constructed by people according to their society's beliefs. Hence, notions of different male and female aptitudes or of the superiority of one literary work over another are not objective but merely subjective attitudes acquired by people as they grow up in a society. Even scholars, postmodernists argue, cannot completely escape the prejudices of their gender, social class, ethnicity, and culture. Some thinkers, however, rejected the postmodernist notion that truth is relative and objectivity impossible.

postmodernism A European intellectual approach contending that truth is not absolute but constructed by people according to their society's beliefs.

Religion

Organized religious life went into decline, partly because the horrors of World War II and postwar materialism had destroyed many people's faith. Churchgoing ceased to be the social convention it once was, often leaving churches semideserted. Polls in the 1990s showed that, whereas some two-thirds of Americans had a moderate or strong religious faith, less than half of western Europeans did, and while 40 percent of Americans regularly attended church, only 10 percent of western Europeans did. Meanwhile, conflicts between rival Christian churches lost their intensity. Protestants and Catholics no longer lived in separate worlds, and ecumenical cooperation increased. Formed in 1948, the World Council of Churches, based in Switzerland, brought together the main Protestant and Eastern Orthodox churches. Appalled by the Holocaust, Christian thinkers began acknowledging their faiths' relationship to Judaism by referring, for the first time in history, to Europe's *Judeo-Christian* heritage. Although the Jewish population in Europe decreased sharply because of the Holocaust and post–World War II emigration to Israel and the Americas, Jews remained a key religious minority and active in public life. Christians also had to deal with another faith: by 2000 immigration and conversions had made Islam the second largest religion after Catholicism in France, Belgium, and Spain.

Protestant churches struggled to maintain their influence in increasingly secular societies, with churches often paying a price for their close ties to the state. Governments often subsidized state churches, as in Scandinavia and Britain, and church-operated schools, but many observers believed this only undermined religious devotion as people found traditional values irrelevant. Because churches funded partly by the state did not need to actively solicit support, they were unable to generate religious passion. This truth was expressed by a popular joke about a young British man joining the army, who wrote on his enlistment form "no religion" and was told, "We'll put you down as Church of England [Anglican] then."

The Roman Catholic Church also had to address the changes. Pope John XXIII (pope 1958–1963) began a comprehensive reform with the convocations of church leaders known as the Second Vatican Council (1962–1965), or Vatican II, which launched the most radical church changes since the Council of Trent in the 1500s. Vatican II officially ended the campaign against Protestantism sparked at Trent and reconciled the church with modernity, while giving the laity greater responsibility in worship; it no longer required Latin in the liturgy and removed blame from the Jews for the death of Jesus. Even after Vatican II, many Catholics ignored church teachings they disliked, such as the ban on artificial birth control, while some conservative Catholics turned to more traditionalist movements opposing Vatican II. Some Catholic women sought more influence and advocated allowing women to become priests, and every year fewer European and North American men and women entered Catholic religious vocations. Meanwhile, the church evangelized in Asia and Africa, and Asians, Africans, and Latin Americans made up a growing share of the priesthood and religious orders. As a result, Catholic churches in Europe and North America increasingly imported parish priests from countries such as Nigeria or Mexico, and some observers talked about a Third World rather than a Western church of the future.

e **Primary Source: Vatican II: The Catholic Church Engages the Modern World** Read how Pope John XXIII opened the Second Vatican Council, at which the Catholic Church reformed itself in significant ways.

SECTION SUMMARY

- Western European governments have generally instituted the welfare state, a mix of capitalism and socialism in which citizens pay high taxes in exchange for an extensive safety net, including national health coverage, generous pensions, and workers' rights.
- In 1968, a wave of radical protest swept Europe, and over the decades European society was changed by the sexual revolution; increasing divorce rates; acceptance of birth control, abortion, and homosexuals; and rising numbers of women in the work force.
- The large numbers of immigrants, legal and illegal, who have come to western Europe seeking work have given many of its cities an international flair but have also led to tensions and problems with assimilation.
- Rock music, originally imported from the United States, became extremely popular among European youth, as did punk, which expressed working-class frustrations, while other popular music showed Asian and African influences.
- Philosophies such as existentialism, which urged people to control their own lives, and postmodernism, which claimed that complete objectivity is impossible, became popular in postwar Europe.
- Organized religion became less influential in postwar Europe, while long-standing tensions among branches of Christianity faded, Roman Catholicism liberalized, and Muslims became a significant portion of the European population.

COMMUNISM IN THE SOVIET UNION AND EASTERN EUROPE

What factors contributed to political crises in the Soviet Union and eastern Europe?

Like western Europe, the Soviet Union changed after World War II. Western Europeans had struggled for centuries to understand Russia; Winston Churchill called Russia a riddle wrapped in a mystery inside an enigma. For several generations during the Cold War the USSR was the major political, military, and ideological rival to the North American and western European nations. The Soviets feared U.S. ambitions and NATO military power, viewing themselves as more threatened than threatening. The USSR was the last great territorial empire and enjoyed substantial natural resources while maintaining a powerful state and a planned economy. But while the communists had modernized society, by the 1980s the Soviet system was showing signs of decay.

Soviet Politics and Economy

The USSR emerged from World War II as the world's number two military and economic power, no mean achievement given the ravages of war: 20 million killed, millions left homeless, cities blasted into rubble, the countryside laid waste. The trauma of that war helps explain the hostility toward the West: Russians resented the sacrifices they had been forced to make because of Germany's conflict with Britain and France. These experiences reinforced traditional Russian paranoia, fostered by two centuries of invasions by Germany or France, and led Russians to maintain a huge defense establishment and their power in eastern Europe, keeping the region as a buffer zone between them and western Europe. While the Soviet political system was rigid, it was also subject to stresses that fostered some change over the decades.

The early postwar USSR reflected the policies of Josef Stalin **(STAH-lin)** (1879–1953), who believed that, because of their key role in the victory over Nazism and the Russian occupation of eastern Europe, the Soviets could deal as equals with the West. Soviet armies remained in eastern Europe and helped establish communist governments there, while Stalin also kept control of the Baltic states of Estonia, Latvia, and Lithuania, formerly independent nations that the Soviets occupied in World War II. Thus was created the Soviet bloc of nations, divided from the West by heavily fortified borders. In 1949 the USSR gained a key ally with the communist victory in China (see Chapter 27). By 1949 Soviet scientists, helped by information collected by spies in the United States, had built and tested an atomic bomb, enabling them to keep pace with the United States in the emerging arms race.

Stalin's years in power had been brutal. The paranoid dictator, imagining potential enemies everywhere, maintained an iron grip on power. Millions of Soviet citizens were exiled to Siberia, and hundreds of others, including top Communist Party officials and military officers Stalin suspected of disloyalty, were convicted of treason in show trials and then executed. The Communist Party also maintained a tight rein on the arts, education, and science. For instance, party officials banned the poetry of Anna Akhmatova **(uhk-MAH-tuh-vuh)** (1888–1966), who had courageously recorded the agonies of Stalin's purge victims, and detained her in a filthy hospital; they also imprisoned scientists whose research questioned theories favored by party-approved scientists in fields such as plant genetics, resulting in flawed studies. Stalin's government also stepped up the effort to spread Russian language and culture in the non-Russian parts of the empire, especially Muslim Central Asia.

CHRONOLOGY
The Soviet Union and Eastern Europe, 1945–1989

1945–1948 Formation of communist governments in eastern Europe

1948 Yugoslavia split from Soviet bloc

1953 Death of Stalin

1955 Formation of Warsaw Pact

1956 Khrushchev de-Stalinization policy

1956 Uprising in Hungary

1957 Launch of *Sputnik*

1960 Sino-Soviet split

1961 Building of Berlin Wall

1962 Cuban Missile Crisis

1968 Prague Spring in Czechoslovakia

1979–1989 Soviet war in Afghanistan

1980 Formation of Solidarity Trade Union in Poland

1985 Gorbachev new Soviet leader

De-Stalinization

The death of Stalin in 1953 sparked rethinking and modest political change (see Chronology: The Soviet Union and Eastern Europe, 1945–1989). The Russian poet Evgeni Evtushenko remembered that "all Russia wept tears of grief—and perhaps tears of fear for the future."[12] Stalin's successor, Nikita Khrushchev **(KROOSH-chef)** (1894–1971), courageously began de-Stalinization in 1956 with a secret speech to party leaders critical of Stalin's dictatorial ruling style and crimes. Khrushchev sought to cleanse communism of the brutal Stalinist stain in order to legitimize the system among the Soviet people and around the world. The speech circulated underground throughout the Soviet bloc, stirring up dissent in eastern Europe. In Poland workers went on strike, and hundreds died or were wounded when the government suppressed it with force. Twenty thousand Hungarians died in an abortive uprising against Soviet domination.

While it began a political thaw at home, de-Stalinization opened a split in the communist world, leading eventually to China breaking its alliance with the USSR in 1960, and perhaps planted the seed for the unraveling of the Soviet Empire and system three decades later. Khrushchev promised that the Soviet standard of living would eventually equal that of the United States. It never happened, but Khrushchev produced some achievements. In 1957 the USSR shocked the world by launching *Sputnik,* the first artificial satellite to orbit earth, and in 1961 cosmonaut Yuri Gagaran **(guh-GAHR-un)** (1934–1968) became the first man to fly aboard a rocket ship into earth orbit, returning to land a hero. In 1963, cosmonaut Valentina Tereshkova **(tare-esh-KO-va)** (b. 1937), the daughter of a tractor driver and textile mill worker, defied the conventional wisdom and became the first woman to fly in space. Along with these achievements came some old-style Soviet repressiveness: in 1957 Khrushchev prevented novelist Boris Pasternak **(PAS-ter-NAK)** (1890–1960) from publishing the novel *Dr. Zhivago,* a critical look at the Bolsheviks during the Russian Civil War that had won a Nobel Prize in 1959 after being smuggled to the West.

Repression

In 1964 Khrushchev was deposed, replaced by Leonid Brezhnev (1906–1982), a cautious bureaucrat who imposed a Stalinist system in which the state had a hand in everything. Russians still found subtle ways to express their discontent. As they had cautiously during Stalin's time, average Russians addressed their political powerlessness by passing jokes along to friends and relatives. In a popular joke, a man arrested for shouting "Brezhnev is an idiot" in Moscow's Red Square received fifteen days for hooliganism and fifteen years for revealing a state secret. Brezhnev led the country for the next two decades (1964–1982). Under Brezhnev and his successors the Soviet state, run mostly in secret by a group of elderly, bureaucratic men, was intolerant of dissent, although less brutal than in Stalin's time. The secret police (KGB) monitored thought and behavior; most citizens accepted Communist Party control as inevitable; and Russians learned how to cooperate just enough to avoid trouble. Active dissidence came from a few intellectuals and artists, who were often deprived of jobs and benefits, and some dissidents found themselves in the remote prison camps of Siberia, where poorly fed inmates spent their regimented days in hard labor. Many died there.

Some of the intellectuals persecuted had made notable achievements. In 1970 the writer Alexander Solzhenitsyn **(SOL-zhuh-NEET-sin)** (1918-2008), a Red Army veteran imprisoned by Stalin, was forbidden to receive the Nobel Prize for literature because his novel, *One Day in the Life of Ivan Denisovich*, had exposed the harsh life in the labor camps. He later went into exile in the United States. Another well-known dissident, Andrei Sakharov **(SAH-kuh-rawf)** (1921–1989), a physicist who had helped develop the first Soviet atomic bomb but became disillusioned, was exiled to a remote city after championing human rights, democracy, and an end to the nuclear arms race. Sakharov won the Nobel Peace Prize in 1975 but was not allowed to attend the ceremonies. Milovan Djilas **(JIL-ahs)** (1911–1995), a Yugoslav communist leader turned dissident, described the contrast between the two great political movements of modern Europe: "Fascism is a nightmare and madness; communism is force and taboo. Fascism is temporary, communism is an enduring way of life."[13]

Economic and Environmental Problems

While the Soviets achieved notable successes, they also experienced severe economic problems. Stalin's Five-Year Plans had rapidly transformed the USSR from a backward to a fairly modern society. To encourage more economic progress, Soviet leaders had three tools: the Communist Party, the bureaucracy, and the military. By the 1980s all three had proved inadequate in directing a modern economy and society. The authoritarian party tolerated little dissent and fostered rigidity; the overcentralized bureaucracy often bungled the planning and management; and officials planned the number of industrial products needed—from steel beams to dish pans—for five years ahead when they didn't know precisely how many they had produced five years earlier. Soviet bureaucrats were cautious, anxious to preserve their perks and power, while the military, large but inefficient, was held together by brutal discipline, promoted incompetent officers, and wasted resources. In 1987 a West German college student deliberately exposed the flaws by piloting his small, single-engine plane unnoticed right through Soviet air security to land in Red Square, where he was arrested by astonished police.

Increasingly the economy struggled. The Soviets spent vast sums to achieve nuclear and military parity with the United States, building a massive defense establishment and arms industry that sucked money from other scientific and technological projects. As a result, Soviet factories were unable to supply consumer goods to meet growing demand, and people often bought food and clothes through the black market from illegal vendors. Paying workers regardless of effort also caused absenteeism and indifference; bored shop clerks seemed annoyed to have their frequent tea breaks and gossip sessions interrupted by shoppers. The Soviets also failed to innovate high technology, completely missing the personal computer revolution sweeping the West. By the 1990s few citizens or schools had yet acquired computers. Thus, although better off than most Asians, Africans, or Latin Americans, most Soviet citizens lived well below North American and western European standards.

Industrial pollution also ravaged the environment, producing dying forests and lakes, toxic farmland, and poisoned air. Diverting rivers for farming and power caused the Aral Sea, once nearly as large as Lake Michigan, to practically dry up, and it also diminished the world's largest inland body of water, the Caspian Sea. Then in 1986 the nuclear power station at Chernobyl in the Ukraine exploded, causing numerous deaths and injuries, releasing radiation over a wide area of Europe, and revealing the Soviet Union's inadequate environmental protections.

Communist Decline

When living standards were rising under Krushchev in the 1950s, Soviet people turned optimistic about communism. Even U.S. intelligence analysts estimated in 1960 that the total Soviet production of goods and services would be three times higher than that of the United States by 2000. But Soviet leaders responded slowly to change and papered over problems, and by the 1970s fewer Soviet citizens believed in the communist future. People joked cynically: "Under capitalism man exploits man; under communism it's the other way around." In a supposedly classless society, the contrast between the wealth of the party, government, and military elite and that of everyone else was striking. Communism had fostered a favored elite that Djilas called a new class, enjoying special privileges denied to average citizens, such as weekend retreats in the countryside. Social decay was evident everywhere: drab working-class lives, rampant corruption and bribery, the shortage of goods, high rates of alcoholism, and demoralized youth seeking access to Western popular culture and consumer goods.

The Soviet Union in the Cold War

United States-Soviet Relations

United States–USSR tensions reached a height in the late 1940s through late 1950s. During the Korean War (1950–1953), the Soviets supplied communist North Koreans fighting the South Koreans and the United States. Then from the late 1950s through late 1970s, as Stalin's successors promoted a less aggressive policy, known as "peaceful coexistence," toward the West, the tensions eased somewhat, even though Soviet-backed forces took control of North Vietnam in 1954 and Cuba joined the communist camp in 1959. In 1961 the Soviet ally, East Germany, built a high, 27-mile-long wall around West Berlin to prevent disenchanted East Germans from fleeing to the West. However, the Berlin wall also symbolized the fears of exposing their people to Western culture and values. In 1962 a crisis caused by secretly placing Soviet nuclear missiles in Cuba, and by the U.S. demand that the missiles be removed, brought the two superpowers to the brink of nuclear war. The Soviets withdrew the missiles, easing tensions. The Soviets also helped arm the communist forces fighting U.S.-supported South Vietnam, Laos, and the Philippines in the 1950s and 1960s, conflicts that drew in U.S. advisers and troops.

Soviet Foreign Policies

The Soviets generally subordinated the global crusade for communism to the normal pursuit of allies, security, and political influence. While they supported nationalist and revolutionary movements in Asia, Africa, and Latin America, often supplying weapons and advice, on the whole, the Soviets followed pragmatic policies, usually sending military force into another country only when their direct interests were threatened. After China broke with the USSR in 1960 and became a rival for influence in international communism, Soviet and Chinese troops watched each other warily along their common border. In contrast, they tolerated no opposition to Soviet power in the east European satellites and intervened to protect their allied governments. Hence the Soviets moved quickly to use military force to suppress revolts in Poland and Hungary in the 1950s, liberalizing tendencies in Czechoslovakia in 1968, and dissident movements in Poland in the 1970s and 1980s. The **Brezhnev Doctrine** asserted Moscow's right to interfere in the satellites to protect communist governments and maintain the Soviet bloc.

Brezhnev Doctrine An assertion by Soviet leaders of Moscow's right to interfere in Soviet satellites to protect communist governments and the Soviet bloc.

Eventually, military interventions proved costly. In 1979 Soviet armies invaded neighboring Afghanistan to prop up a pro-Soviet government. But the United States, along with Arab nations and Pakistan, actively aided the Afghan rebels, mostly militant Muslims, who were fighting the secular Afghan regime and the Soviet occupation. Ultimately Afghanistan, where the mountain and desert terrain made fighting difficult, proved a disaster, costing 13,000 Russian lives and billions of dollars, and the Soviets withdrew their forces in 1989. Economic problems, restless subject peoples,

Gerd Ludwig/Corbis

Aral Sea As water from the rivers that supplied it was diverted for agriculture and industry, the Aral Sea in Soviet Central Asia lost over half its water between 1960 and 2000. This photo shows a stranded boat where rich lake fisheries once existed.

and the cost of supporting a huge military and its widespread commitments contributed to a major reassessment by Soviet leaders in the later 1980s.

Soviet Society and Culture

Soviet society changed over the decades. Population growth surged, from 180 million in 1950 to 275 million by the late 1980s. The Soviet people were far healthier, better paid, and more educated than their predecessors in 1917. Citizens enjoyed social services unimaginable fifty years earlier, such as free medical care, old-age pensions, maternity leaves, guaranteed jobs, paid vacations, and day-care centers. Most people were grateful to the state for providing such economic and physical security. In exchange for the security, however, people knew they had to accept state power and the subordination of individual rights. The benefits provided by the state, often termed "cradle to grave socialism," meant that individuals were not responsible for their own lives.

Gender Relations

The experiences of Soviet women reflected the provision of education and social services. While few women served in the Soviet hierarchy, most women were in the paid work force, and among the highly skilled, some three-quarters of doctors were women. Many young rural women migrated to the cities in search of a better life. While rural women often faced a hard life—no running water, indoor plumbing, central heating, or access to nearby shops—urban women also faced challenges. In addition to their paid jobs, women of modest means stood in long lines to buy food and necessities, took their kids to and from school, washed clothes and dishes in the bathroom sink, and sometimes prepared meals in communal kitchens. Meanwhile, because women increasingly divorced abusive husbands and the state legalized abortion, the average family became smaller. Except in Central Asia, both the birthrate and life expectancy fell dramatically. Schools perpetuated the Russian stereotype that women were weak and passionate while men were strong and rational, and sometimes feminist activists were harassed, arrested, or even deported.

Ethnic Tensions

Relations between ethnic Russians and the diverse ethnic minorities deteriorated. Restless ethnic minorities chafed at domination by ethnic Russians, who constituted only about half of the Soviet population by the 1980s. In Central Asian Soviet republics such as Kazakhstan and Uzbekistan, the newly built industrial cities attracted millions of ethnic Russian migrants, who monopolized most of the managerial and professional positions. Compared to neighboring regions of Asia, communism brought relatively high living standards to Soviet Central Asia. But many Muslim peoples resented the Russification of their cultures and the weakening of Islamic practice. Most Baltic peoples hated Russian domination and the replacement of local languages with Russian, and some Jews sought the freedom to openly practice their religion or to emigrate to Israel or North America.

Religion and Culture

The state marginalized organized religion but did not eliminate it. Soviet leaders promoted atheism and denounced Christianity as superstition, and the Russian Orthodox Church became an informal state agent, with a the clergy that carefully avoided contesting the Communist Party. Still, Russians often attended church and nurtured their faith, and in the 1980s, when the state became more tolerant, millions returned to the church. Yet, many Russians remained skeptical of or indifferent to organized religion.

Soviet state policies forced most cultural creativity underground. Intellectuals exchanged copies of forbidden books and magazines in secret, and writers sent their work abroad illegally to be published. Anti-Stalinist poets explored the breathing space between the official line and prison. Soviet and east European authorities were often baffled by youth movements. Considering Western rock degenerate, the authorities subjected innovative musicians to restrictions, although few faced arrest. Russian Vladimir Vysotski (VLAD-eh-meer vih-SOT-skee) (1938–1980), an irreverent singer-songwriter-actor-poet, expressed political disenchantment without incurring arrest, although he was harassed. Vysotski maintained a large cult following among the urban intelligentsia for songs that exposed the Russian soul, extolled sex and liquor, and mocked Soviet corruption, hypocrisy, labor camps, and even politics: "But wait—let's have a smoke, better yet, let's drink to a time, when there will be no jails in Russia."[14] Cassette tapes of his unofficial concerts in small theaters enjoyed wide underground distribution. After his death from cancer, hundreds of mourners left flowers at his Moscow grave every month for years.

Young people wanted a cultural liberalization. By the 1960s some young Russians were modeling themselves on the Anglo-American "hippie" counterculture, wearing jeans, bell-bottom pants, miniskirts, and peace medallions and listening to the Beatles or their Soviet clones. For youth, rock music, often spread by illicit cassettes, remained the chief escape from an oppressive society, and some 160,000 underground rock and jazz bands existed by the 1980s. While few musicians dared to

RIA-Novosti

Soviet Rock Band For Soviet youth, rock music became a way of escaping the restrictions of Soviet life. This long-haired rocker from the 1980s wears a shirt with the communist symbol, the hammer and sickle, but the lyrics of rock bands often addressed the problems of Soviet life.

challenge the system directly, like Vysotski, they explored the fringes, mocking the bureaucracy or the absurdity of Soviet life. Rather than seeking to change the Soviet government, rock musicians and their audience sought to live beyond the police and the bureaucracy.

Eastern Europe in the Soviet System

Communist Rule

During the late 1940s the Soviets installed communist governments in each eastern European nation, sealing the fate of eastern Europe for over forty years. Political parties were abolished, churches persecuted, and nationalistic leaders purged. In 1949 the communist nations formed COMECON (Council for Mutual Economic Assistance), which more closely integrated the Soviet and eastern European economies. Communism also fostered economic development in Romania and Bulgaria, which had little industrialization before World War II. But people in the more industrialized Czechoslovakia, Poland, and East Germany aspired to living standards closer to those in western Europe. To supply consumer goods and finance industrialization, the governments took out loans and built up huge debts. Increased industrial activity also had serious environmental side effects. Finally, while the Soviets treated the satellite countries as neocolonies, exploiting their resources, they also had to give them generous subsidies to maintain control.

Yugoslavia followed the most independent path, breaking with the USSR entirely in 1948. In 1945 the Yugoslav Communist Party, led by Marshal Josip Broz Tito (TEE-toe) (1892–1980), the popular leader of the anti-Nazi resistance, won national elections. Tito wanted to avoid Soviet domination, and his Yugoslavia cooperated with the nonaligned nations while also maintaining friendly relations with the West. Tito's unique form of communism, which experimented with worker rather than manager control of factories, created enough prosperity and popular support to neutralize his nation's powerful ethnic divisions.

Unrest and Revolt

The resentment of Soviet domination fostered unrest. After the Soviets crushed protest demonstrations in Poland in the early 1950s, a Polish poet daringly wrote: "They [the communists] ran to us shouting, 'Under socialism, a cut finger doesn't hurt.' But they [the people] felt pain [and] lost faith."[15] Poland, with its strong Catholic allegiances, was the most restless satellite, with its workers demanding more public input into the government. In 1956 Hungarian leaders tried to break with rigid communism by reinstating private property, inviting noncommunists into the government, and declaring the country neutral. In response, a Soviet bloc force occupied Hungary and executed the anti-Soviet leaders. But even under the new pro-Soviet leaders, Hungary remained open to the West and was more tolerant of dissent than other Soviet satellites. While the other satellites followed the Soviet pattern of highly centralized bureaucracies, Hungary's blend of state influence and free markets, known as market socialism, created the most prosperous Soviet bloc economy. Hungarians called it "goulash communism," after their favorite dish, a mix of pasta and meat.

Other disgruntled eastern Europeans later defied Soviet power. In Czechoslovakia in 1968 the reform-minded leader Alexander Dubček **(DOOB-check)** (1927–1993), during what was called the "Prague Spring," sought to shift to a more liberal "communism with a human face." Alarmed, the Soviets sent in Warsaw Pact troops and replaced Dubček and his supporters with repressive Soviet puppets. In Poland, the Soviets allowed Polish-born Pope John Paul II to make a triumphant visit in 1979 but were alarmed at the outpouring of religious and nationalist fervor. Then in 1980 shipyard workers led by Lech Walesa **(leck wa-LEN-za)** (b. 1943), an electrical engineer, went on strike. As food prices increased, thousands of women took to the streets, shouting, "We're hungry!" When the dissidents formed the Solidarity trade union, which aimed at economic liberalization, the government declared martial law and banned Solidarity. Even though illegal, Solidarity had 9.5 million members by 1981 and worked for political as well as economic goals. As one leader put it: "What we had in mind was not only bread, butter and sausage but also justice, democracy, truth, legality, human dignity, freedom of convicts, and the repair of the republic."[16]

Soviet Decline and Reform

Soviet Challenges

Soviet problems mounted, forcing a reappraisal of the political and economic system and the nation's place in the world. The USSR had steadily lost ground in world affairs to the United States and economic ground to Japan and West Germany. China became a bitter rival, and the Afghanistan war and the subsidizing of the east European satellites drained Soviet wealth. By the mid-1980s the USSR had few close remaining allies outside the Soviet bloc, which was restless, and few Asian, African, or Latin American revolutionaries looked toward Moscow for inspiration. Soviet power in the world had always been mostly military, whereas the United States and its Western allies also had cultural, economic, technological, and even linguistic influence. All over the world people studied English or French, not Russian, and some observers found more power in rock music, videos, fast food, youth fashions, and global news networks than in the Soviet Red Army. Young people from Bangkok to Buenos Aires avidly sought blue jeans and flocked to American adventure films; few of them knew or cared much about Soviet life. Thus the Beatles, McDonald's, and the Cable News Network (CNN) were at least as crucial, some scholars concluded, in the West winning the Cold War as was U.S. military power.

This declining international influence, combined with spiraling social and economic problems and a stifling bureaucracy, ultimately led to the rise of younger, reform-minded Soviet leaders who introduced dramatic change. Soviet leaders now had more contact with the outside world and an appreciation of their growing technological backwardness. The planned economy that had powered a largely peasant society into a superpower now seemed a severe drag. In 1985 Mikhail Gorbachev **(GORE-beh-CHOF)** (b. 1931) became Soviet leader. Because of the escalating costs of militarization, he realized the nation could not win an arms race, and while hoping to preserve the basics of the Soviet system, he understood the need to liberalize the economy, decentralize decision making, and relax ideological controls. However, Gorbachev inherited a Communist Party that allowed no political competition and managed a planned economy, run from the top with little room for individual initiative. With such a rigid system, he concluded, the USSR could never match the United States as a superpower.

Gorbachev introduced a dazzling series of reforms to reenergize the Soviet Union, developing closer relations with the West and abandoning the ideological struggle with the liberal democracies. In 1987 a United States–USSR treaty lessened

CHRONOLOGY
Europe, 1989–Present

1989 End of communist regimes in eastern Europe

1990 Reunification of Germany

1991 Breakup of Soviet Union

1991–2000 Yeltsin era in Russia

1991–2000 Crises in Yugoslavia

1991 Signing of Maastricht Treaty

2004 Expansion of European Union into eastern Europe

Restructuring Soviet Society

In 1987 Mikhail Gorbachev, the head of the Soviet Communist Party and government, published a book, *Perestroika*, outlining his policy of economic restructuring. His goal was to transform the inefficient, stagnant Soviet economy into one based on a decentralized market orientation similar to the market socialism of Hungary and China. The new policy gave greater autonomy to local government officials and factory managers and attempted to democratize the Communist Party itself. Causing a sensation, the book was ranked by some observers as the most important publication of the late twentieth century. By the early 1990s, with Gorbachev himself removed from office, the policy was eclipsed, but the book remained a testimony to the problems that led to the Soviet system's collapse. In this excerpt, Gorbachev defines perestroika.

Perestroika means overcoming the stagnation process, breaking down the braking mechanism, creating a dependable and effective mechanism for acceleration of social and economic progress and giving it dynamism.

Perestroika means initiative. It is the comprehensive development of democracy, socialist self-government, encouragement of initiative and creative endeavor, improved order and discipline, more glasnost (openness), criticism and self-criticism in all spheres of our society. It is utmost respect for the individual and consideration for personal dignity.

Perestroika is the all-round intensification of the Soviet economy, the revival and development of the principles of democratic centralism in running the national economy, the universal introduction of economic methods, the renunciation of management by injunction and by administration methods, and the overall encouragement of innovation and socialist enterprise.

Perestroika means a resolute shift to scientific methods, an ability to provide a solid scientific basis for every new initiative. It means the combination of the achievements of the scientific and technological revolution with a planned economy.

Perestroika means priority development of the social sphere aimed at ever better satisfaction of the Soviet people's requirements for good living and working conditions, for good rest and recreation, education and health care. It means unceasing concern for cultural and spiritual wealth, for the culture of every individual and society as a whole.

Perestroika means the elimination from society of the distortions of social ethics, the consistent implementation of the principles of social justice. It means the unity of words and deeds, rights and duties. It is the elevation of honest, highly-qualified labor, the overcoming of leveling tendencies in pay and consumerism.

This is how we see perestroika today. This is how we see our tasks, and the substance and content of our work for the forthcoming period. It is difficult now to say how long that period will take. Of course, it will be much more than two or three years. We are ready for serious, strenuous and tedious work to ensure that our country reaches new heights by the end of the twentieth century.

THINKING ABOUT THE READING

1. What did Gorbachev mean by perestroika?
2. What problems did the policy aim to solve?

Source: Mikhail Gorbachev, *Perestroika* (New York: HarperCollins, 1987), pp. 34–35.

the threat of nuclear war by having both countries destroy their short- and long-range missiles. With his **glasnost** ("openness") policy, Gorbachev democratized the political system, including free elections, a real parliament that included noncommunist parties, the release of most political prisoners, and a deemphasis on the role of the Communist Party. Gorbachev also loosened state control of the media and the arts and invited scholars to talk truthfully about the Soviet past. Furthermore, realizing the ruinous financial cost of maintaining the unpopular eastern European governments, Gorbachev made clear he would not intervene to preserve them. They collapsed or were toppled in 1989 (see Chronology: Europe, 1989–Present).

glasnost The policy introduced in the Soviet Union by Mikhail Gorbachev to democratize the political system.

Admitting the faults of Soviet communism, Gorbachev also liberalized the economy, using market mechanisms in a policy known as **perestroika** ("restructuring") (see Witness to the Past: Restructuring Soviet Society). But the economic changes failed to take off. While many in the intelligentsia wanted democratization, the working classes mostly preferred consumer goods, which did not come. Meanwhile, top bureaucrats, including the managers of state enterprises, resisted changes that might threaten their role. Conservatives in the Communist Party and the secret police also opposed reforms that might undermine their power. Soon the Soviet system collapsed.

perestroika ("restructuring") Mikhail Gorbachev's policy to liberalize the Soviet economy using market mechanisms.

SECTION SUMMARY

- Under Stalin, the USSR ruthlessly suppressed dissent, while under Khruschev, it moderated somewhat and focused on competing with the United States economically and technologically; under Brezhnev, it became somewhat more repressive again.
- Although the Soviet economy grew under communism, it suffered from lack of innovation, inept planning, and an overemphasis on the military, and it created a privileged class of Communist Party and military insiders who lived much better than the common people.
- U.S.-USSR relations were strained by the Cuban Missile Crisis, the Berlin Wall, and Soviet support for communist Cuba and North Vietnam, but the USSR's foreign interventions were usually motivated by its national interest rather than a desire to spread communism.
- In exchange for limited freedom, Soviet citizens were offered extensive social services, but many non-Russians in Central Asia and the Baltics resented Russian domination and the devaluing of their own cultures, while Soviet youth turned to rock music to express their rebellion.
- Much of eastern Europe was effectively colonized by the USSR, though Yugoslavia pursued an independent communist course, and citizens of Poland, Hungary, and Czechoslovakia mounted periodic challenges to Soviet rule.
- With the USSR losing ground economically and culturally, Soviet leader Mikhail Gorbachev introduced reforms designed to democratize the USSR, to liberalize its economy, and to allow eastern European countries greater self-determination.

COMMUNIST COLLAPSE: A NEW RUSSIA AND EUROPE

How did the demise of the communist system contribute to a new Europe?

For over four decades the Cold War and the iron curtain had provided the context for both western and eastern European politics. The breakup of the communist bloc of nations in 1989 and the USSR in 1991 reshaped the political and economic face of Russia, the former Soviet territories, eastern Europe, and western Europe, creating hope but also uncertainties. Russia struggled to rebuild and to revive its power. While Yugoslavia was torn apart by wars and Germany was reunited, western Europe pushed toward unification, seeking to include some of eastern Europe as well, but it still faced the conflicting forces of nationalism and cooperation. Most Europeans now chose governments through multiparty elections. By the beginning of the twenty-first century, Europe, though no longer the world leader it had once been, still influenced the age of globalization.

A New Russia and New Post-Soviet Nations

Soviet Collapse

The sudden collapse of the Soviet empire and communism in Europe was a major development of twentieth-century history. In 1985 there had been 5 million Soviet soldiers stationed from East Germany to eastern Siberia's Pacific coast, symbolizing the reach of imperial Soviet power. Six years later the Soviet Union and its satellite nations had unraveled, without a shot being fired. Though the collapse was not a complete surprise, its pace was astonishing. While outside factors, including east European unrest and escalating U.S. defense spending that was hard for the Soviets to match, played a role, Soviet economic decline was probably the decisive cause. The collapse showed the failure of the Soviet system, founded on Leninism and strongly shaped by Stalinism. Democratic governments and decentralized capitalism had adjusted better to global changes than the communist-planned economies, and nationalist yearnings among non-Russians had sapped the empire's foundations.

Gorbachev's greatest contribution was to face up to failure. By 1991 Gorbachev, unable to control the forces unleashed, had lost his credibility and resigned, replaced as leader by Boris Yeltsin (b. 1931), a communist bureaucrat turned reformer with strong U.S. support. Yeltsin ended seven decades of communist rule by outlawing the Communist Party. Russians who welcomed the party's demise toppled statues of Lenin and restored czarist names to cities that had been renamed during the Soviet era. Leningrad once again became St. Petersburg.

Dismantling the Soviet Union

Yeltsin acquiesced in the breakup of the USSR itself, while maintaining the unity of the largest Soviet republic, Russia, which stretched from the Baltic Sea through ten time zones to the eastern tip of Siberia, only a few miles from Alaska (see Map 28.3). But glasnost had opened a Pandora's box.

Ethnic hatreds, long suppressed by military force or alleviated by the government-provided safety net, soon exploded to the surface. In 1991 all of the fourteen Soviet republics outside of Russia, from Lithuania and the Ukraine in the west to Kyrgyzstan **(KER-giz-STAN)** in eastern Turkestan, declared their independence, often under former communist officials whose autocratic ruling style and intolerance of dissent resembled the old Soviet system.

Former Soviet Republics

Most of the new nations have struggled to achieve economic self-sufficiency and political stability. Some have been engulfed in conflict between rival ethnic or nationalist groups or have fought each other over territorial claims, as did Christian Armenia and Muslim Azerbaijan. In three of the former Soviet republics—Georgia, Ukraine, and Kyrgyzstan—what observers called "colored revolutions" because their proponents symbolized their cause with a color, such as orange in the Ukraine, pro-democracy activists, with U.S. and western European encouragement, forced out dictatorial regimes. But the results of revolutions are usually unpredictable, and the leaders soon disappointed their supporters by becoming less democratic or antagonizing the Russians. In Central Asia, inhabited largely by Muslims, some nominal and others devout, militant Muslims launched insurgencies against the secular post-Soviet governments, and Islam gained support among the disenchanted and marginalized, especially jobless young men. Islamic fervor also forced or prompted many women to don the headscarf or veil and to dress and behave modestly. Meanwhile, millions of ethnic Russians in the former Soviet republics faced resentment for their relative affluence and ties to the former colonizer. In Latvia, for example, the indigenous Lett people make up only half the population: Russians constitute a third. The Latvian government now requires everyone to learn the Latvian language, which was marginalized under Soviet rule.

Map 28.3
The Dissolution of the Soviet Union

In 1991 the leaders of Russia, who had abandoned communism, allowed the other fourteen republics to leave the Soviet Union, bringing an end to a vast federation that had endured for over seven decades. Even without the fourteen republics, Russia remained the world's largest nation in geographical size, stretching across ten time zones from the Pacific Ocean to the Baltic Sea.

Interactive Map

Shock Therapy

Yeltsin had difficulty solving Russia's problems. Taking the advice of Russian free market enthusiasts and of American advisers, who often knew little of Russian culture, he introduced a "shock therapy": rapid conversion of the stagnant planned economy to market capitalism, which produced more consumer goods and a growing middle class but created other problems. Party officials converted the enterprises they managed into their own private companies, becoming Russia's new capitalists, while organized crime groups and a few well-placed former communists, known as **oligarchs**, gained control of many economic assets. Yeltsin also faced secession movements within the Russian federation, especially in oil-rich Chechnya, a largely Muslim Caucasus region that declared independence in 1994. Yeltsin, fearing that Chechnya's independence would encourage other secession movements, tried to crush the separatists, sucking the Red Army into a quagmire with thousands of casualties.

oligarchs Well-placed former communists who amassed enough wealth to gain control of major segments of the post–Soviet Russian economy.

The economic pain in Russia was widespread. Millions of workers, the majority of them women, lost their jobs as inefficient, obsolete Soviet industries closed. Some leaders reemphasized the Soviet era ideal of men as soldiers and women as working mothers, and conservatives advocated that women stay at home and tend to family obligations. Moreover, with the end of free higher education, families preferred to devote their funds to their sons. Factory workers, miners, and state employees, such as teachers, were often not paid for years. As Yeltsin dismantled parts of the welfare state, health-care reductions, declining incomes, heavier drinking, and illegal drug use affected public health; men's life expectancy dropped from sixty-four in 1990 to fifty-nine in 2002. By 1992 inflation was 2,500 percent, devastating people who lived on pensions and fixed incomes. According to a popular local joke, "All the good things the communists said about communism were false, but all the bad things they said about capitalism were true."

Putin's Russia

In 2000, with the Russian economy near collapse and free markets discredited, Yeltsin resigned in disgrace and was replaced by Vladimir Putin (b. 1952), who ended shock therapy and brought back stability after fifteen years of turbulence. A former secret police colonel who kept a portrait of Peter the Great in his office, Putin espoused capitalism and democratic reforms, including multiparty elections, but also pursued more authoritarian and nationalist policies than Yeltsin. Political liberalism faded as Putin took control of much of the media, seizing or muffling opposition newspapers and television stations and prosecuting some oligarchs for alleged corruption The state also took over many large private companies, turning the economy into a form of state capitalism not unlike Meiji Japan. Eventually the economy made a substantial recovery because of improved tax collection and higher prices for two leading Russian exports, oil and natural gas, allowing Putin to assert Russian interests in the world. Through these measures Putin outmaneuvered the discredited pro-U.S. free market advocates, the rebuilt Communist Party, and extreme rightwing nationalists. However, the 2008–2009 global economic crisis brought a rapid decline in oil prices after Putin had committed oil to various trading partners, and drastic revenue declines brought cutbacks and recession, hurting Putin's prestige and fomenting dissent.

Putin's Russia mixed autocratic government with a more outward-looking attitude. The Russian Orthodox Church, for centuries closely connected to national identity and political power, regained influence, and even Putin claimed to be a believer. Within the church leadership, liberals promoted a tolerant and ecumenical view while conservatives denounced ecumenism, some even supporting anti-Semitic, anti-Muslim views and a return of the monarchy. Yet, in many places, Muslims—some 15 percent of the population—and Christians live in harmony. Putin also sought good relations with Germany, France, the United States, and China. In 2009 education officials announced that Alexander Solzhenitsyn"s long-banned book about Stalin-era Soviet labor camps, *The Gulag Archipelago*, would be taught in Russian secondary schools. However, while the middle class grew, the contrasts between rich and poor became stark. While elegantly dressed men and women in Moscow cavorted in fine restaurants and glitzy casinos, some remote towns went without heat and power. In addition, corruption, poverty, unaccountability, weak legal institutions, and the festering war in Chechnya stifled development. And while Russia still had a large military budget, it was only a fifth that of the United States. Some polls showed that a majority of Russians preferred the communist years to the new Russia, and many people expressed nostalgia for Stalin and Lenin. Future directions remained unclear.

The New Eastern Europe

Collapsing States

The changes in the USSR resonated throughout eastern Europe. In the late 1980s Mikhail Gorbachev, who admired Hungarian market socialism, promoted reform in eastern Europe. The USSR could no longer afford to subsidize these states, and when it became clear that the USSR was no longer willing to protect the largely unpopular eastern European governments, they began to fall like dominoes. Democratic movements once underground surfaced. Hungary adopted democracy, Solidarity came to power in Poland, and East Germans streamed across the border into West Germany. The world could watch on television as Berliners gleefully knocked down the Berlin Wall, the symbol of Cold War division, and carried off its bricks as souvenirs. Soon the East German regime and the other east European communist governments had collapsed or been overthrown. After massive demonstrations forced the communist leaders to resign in a largely peaceful "Velvet Revolution," Czechoslovaks elected as president the playwright and former rock group lyricist, Václav Havel **(vax-LAV hah-VEL)** (b. 1936), who had been frequently arrested for his prodemocracy activities. Havel announced, "Your government, my people, has been returned to you."[17]

New Governments and Economies

The new democratic or semidemocratic governments replaced planned economies with market forces, and east Europeans took up voting enthusiastically. Yet, reformers did not anticipate the results of their policies. The end of communism uncorked ethnic hatreds and rivalries going back centuries. Slovaks seceded from the Czechs, forming their own country, while Romanians repressed the large Hungarian minority. Several countries persecuted or avoided providing services, such as schools, to the Romany (Gypsies), and prejudice against Jews intensified.

The rapid move to capitalism, while providing abundant consumer goods, also proved destabilizing. Critics wrote of shock without therapy. While millions were thrown out of work as obsolete factories closed, western European or North American companies bought many of the remaining enterprises. Dazzled by the Western consumer goods just over the border, east Europeans may have underestimated the risks that came with Western-style capitalism. Shops were full of attractive goods, but few people had the money to buy them. Only Poland and the Czech Republic enjoyed robust economic growth. Protections of the communist welfare system, such as free education, health care, and subsidized housing, were removed. While some economies gradually improved, pockets of high unemployment remained and the rich-poor gap widened.

The political environment changed as diverse political parties competed for power. Capitalizing on popular support for the social safety net, former Communist Party members who now called themselves reform communists won some national elections, competing for power with free market advocates, pro-Western liberals, and rightwing nationalists. In a striking repudiation of the Soviet legacy, reform communists often supported joining the European Union and even NATO. Few anticommunists regretted the changes, however jarring they were. Adam Michnik, a leader of Polish Solidarity, concluded that "without the slightest hesitation it is much better to live in a country that is democratic, prosperous and thus boring."[18]

The greatest instability came to Yugoslavia, an artificial federation of states that self-destructed in bloody civil wars between ethnic groups (see Map 28.4). Created for political convenience after World War I, Yugoslavia contained antagonistic ethnic and religious groups. The nationalistic Orthodox Serbs tried to dominate the federation, while the Catholic Croats and Slovenians and the Bosnian and Albanian Muslims wanted independence for their regions. After Marshal Tito, the product of a mixed Croat-Serb marriage whose autocratic policies kept the lid on ethnic hatreds, died in 1980, Yugoslavia became a seething cauldron of ethnic conflict. In 1991 the Serb-dominated Yugoslav army tried to stop Slovenia and Croatia from breaking away, but the United Nations sent in peacekeeping troops to secure their independence. Then in 1992 the Muslim majority in multiethnic Bosnia declared independence, a move opposed by the minority Serbs and Croats in the state. Bosnian Serb militias, aided covertly by the largest Yugoslav state, Serbia, massacred thousands of Muslims, using a new term for genocide, "ethnic cleansing." The United Nations sent more peacemakers, and U.S. air strikes under NATO auspices forced the Serbs to accept a peace treaty in 1995. The Bosnia conflict killed 200,000 people and generated 4 million refugees. In 1999 violence returned when the Albanian majority in Kosovo, the southern region of Serbia, revolted and the Serbs responded with ferocity, prompting another NATO-imposed settlement in 2000. Thousands of NATO troops remained in Bosnia and Kosovo, a symbol of eastern Europe's unresolved challenges.

The Velvet Revolution Protesters took to the streets in Prague, Czechoslovakia, to protest communist government and demand democracy. These protests, known as the Velvet Revolution for their peaceful nature, were led by Václav Havel, pictured on the poster carried by a protester.

Peter Turnley/Corbis

Map 28.4
Ethnic Conflicts in Eastern Europe
Many of the nations in central and eastern Europe contain substantial ethnic minorities, and tensions between various groups have often led to conflict. In Yugoslavia, the conflicts between the major ethnic groups—Serbs, Croats, Bosnian Muslims, and Albanians—led to violence and civil war at the end of the twentieth century.

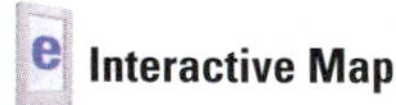

Toward European Unity

German Reunification

The reunification of Germany and the unity movement have dominated western Europe in the years after 1989. The East German state collapsed and Germany was quickly reunified in 1990, but the results have satisfied neither West nor East Germans. For many East Germans, merging with the prosperous West Germany promised access to a materially comfortable life they could only dream of before. But reunification cost billions and threw the German economy into a tailspin. Before reunification West Germany had enjoyed a long boom, but a decade later, the reunified nation's 80 million people were stuck in deep recession. Since Germany has western Europe's largest economy, the German slump dragged down the rest of Europe. Many East German workers lost jobs as obsolete factories were closed or sold to West Germans, who often downsized the work force. The unemployment rate in the east was twice as high as in the west and wages much lower. As a result, some angry youth turned to rightwing, often neo-Nazi, groups that favor heavy metal rock groups whose songs promote hatred of foreigners and immigrants.

Hastening Unity

Worried by Germany's problems, western European leaders believed that hastening unification would stabilize postcommunist Europe. The Maastricht Treaty, discussed in the chapter opening, set a goal of economic and monetary union that required budgetary and wage restraint as a prelude. Most signers of the treaty adopted the euro as their currency. Unity was aided by other factors as well. Millions of Europeans were multilingual, moving easily between cultures, and many studied in other countries. The cosmopolitanism also influenced the arts. For example, the popular Greek singer Nana Mouskeri **(NA-na mouse-KUR-ee)** gained a large international audience by recording in English, French, German, and Spanish. The Eurotunnel, which stretched ninety-four miles under the English Channel and made possible a three-hour train ride from London to Paris, symbolized the decline of both political and cultural borders.

Expanding the European Union

The European Union (EU) doubled its membership from twelve nations in 1993 to twenty-seven by 2009, including ten former Soviet bloc states and republics. The Czech Republic, Poland, Hungary, and Estonia had joined in 2004. The Danish prime minister told prospective new EU members: "In 1989 brave and visionary people brought about the collapse of the Berlin Wall. They could no longer tolerate the forced division of Europe. Today we are giving life to their hopes."[19] With the new members the EU became a bloc of nearly 500 million people encompassing most of Europe and enjoying a combined economic power larger than that of the United States. Some of the members, such as Sweden and Ireland, the latter once one of Europe's poorest countries but soon known as the Celtic Tiger because its rapid growth, resembled that of the "Little Tiger" nations of Southeast Asia (see Chapter 31), becoming models for the world. Many thousands of migrants from Europe and Asia moved to Ireland for jobs, fostering multiethnic neighborhoods in Dublin.

Conducting a quarter of the world's commerce and economic production, the EU became one of the world's three dominant economic forces, along with the U.S. and Japan. Some observers spoke of a tripolar world led by the United States, the EU, and East Asia (especially China and Japan). However, the European Union hit several major road bumps. Critics called the EU a faceless bureaucracy with innumerable rules that compromised national independence, and two of Europe's most prosperous nations, Norway and Switzerland, declined membership. The EU leaders have also been cautious in admitting former Soviet bloc states with weak economies and autocratic leaders. Turkey, a largely Muslim nation, has long sought membership, fostering an EU debate about how to define Europe. This debate spilled over into the effort to prepare an EU constitution. Amid much controversy, the proposed constitution rejected any mention of Europe's Christian heritage. But in 2005 voters in two of the most pro-unity countries, France and the Netherlands, fearing loss of control, shocked EU leaders by rejecting the constitution, raising questions about the EU's future. After the proposed constitution was modified into a treaty forming a stronger executive and European parliament while promising more democracy, transparency, and efficiency, it was approved by most member nations.

AP/Wide World Photos

European Economic Power Business and political leaders from India and the European Union met in a summit in 2005 to increase trade relations, reflecting the growing economic power of both India and western Europe. This photo shows British Prime Minister Tony Blair and India's Prime Minister Manmohan Singh in conversation.

Recent Developments

Increasing unity may have contributed to problems caused by the economic austerity policies of the 1990s, which unsettled welfare states. Social democrats, who had governed eleven of the sixteen western European nations in the early 1990s, now jockeyed with centrists, free market conservatives, Greens, anti-immigrant nationalists, and the fading communists for power. Attempts to roll back but not eliminate social benefits sometimes set off massive protests and long strikes. While many Europeans preferred to maintain what they termed the social market economy, even at the cost of slower economic growth, both the German and French governments replaced the 35-hour workweek with the 40-hour workweek to increase their competitiveness. Yet, some large companies continued to downsize or export jobs, and in 2006 thousands in France rioted against loosening job protections. Some observers compared Europe's sluggish social market economies unfavorably with the dynamic U.S. economy. Others disagreed, noting that many European nations have nearly as high a per capita income as the United States, less inequality, universal health insurance, a greater commitment to a high quality of life for all, and, collectively, a larger total production of goods and services. The 2008–2009 global economic crisis challenged both arguments. The crisis, the worst since the Great Depression, began in the United States with real estate, banking, and financial problems, discrediting the free-wheeling U.S. economic model. Yet, European economies also went into steep decline, greatly stressing welfare states and demonstrating government inadequacies in resolving the problems. Germany, saddled with an indecisive coalition government, reacted slowly as deficits mounted. The economy of Iceland collapsed from bank failures, while Ireland's economy plummeted so rapidly that many thousands of immigrants, losing jobs, returned home. Indeed, the grim job market prompted many Arabs, Africans, and East Europeans to leave western European countries. By later 2009 some economies, including France and Germany, were growing again but most East European economies remained deeply troubled

Europeans also faced other challenges. A century earlier overcrowded and the world's greatest exporter of people, Europe now has a declining population, due mainly to the world's lowest birthrate: 1.2 children per woman. Yet, Europeans became increasingly hostile to immigration from the Middle East. Tensions simmered, and in 2005 rioting and vandalism by young Arab and African residents in France, many of them unemployed and resenting discrimination and police harassment, caused much damage and raised the issue of what sort of integration into European societies was possible. The population decline also posed a long-term problem: with more people retiring from than entering the work force, younger workers had more responsibility for financing government services for the elderly. By the early twenty-first century, political disenchantment, an anti-incumbent mood, and stronger anti-U.S. sentiments often caused voters to reject the governing parties. Anti-immigrant parties became more influential, even in tolerant nations like Denmark and the Netherlands. Europeans still struggled to define their place in a changing world.

Europe and Russia in the Global System

Relations with the United States

With the end of the Cold War, Russia, western Europe, and the former Soviet bloc states searched for new roles in the world. Russia sought good relations with the EU, the United States, China, and the nearby Islamic nations, such as Iran, but also acted in its own self-interest, sometimes opposing U.S. or EU policies. NATO needed to redefine its mission as it added many of the former Warsaw Pact nations, discomforting Russia. After Russia warned NATO against admitting former Soviet republics such as Ukraine and Georgia, it reinforced its threat in 2008 by briefly invading Georgia, a small U.S. ally in the Caucasus, to protect pro-Russian enclaves. For their part, western Europeans seemed more reluctant than Americans to devote vast sums to the military or to send their armed forces into combat. The United States, not Europe, led the intervention to end the killing and restore order in Yugoslavia.

In the early twenty-first century, European relations with its military ally and main trading rival, the United States, became complicated. Various European nations, as part of NATO, sent troops to Afghanistan after the 2001 terrorist attacks on the United States and shared the goal of combating international terrorism. But most Europeans mistrusted the U.S. decision to invade oil-rich Iraq in 2003, believing it had little to do with fighting terrorism and fearing it would destabilize the Middle East. European nations such as France and Germany criticized the U.S. invasion and occupation. Although their people strongly opposed the war, some close U.S. allies, such as Italy, Poland, and Spain, sent small token forces, but only Britain had a sizable military presence in Iraq.

Relations with Islam

Europeans also disagreed on how best to respond to international terrorism and militant Islamic groups. The substantial Muslim immigrant populations complicated policies on the Islamic militancy that spread among some people of Arab or South Asian ancestry, especially unemployed youth. Some of the men who perpetrated the 2001 attacks on the United States had studied in Europe, where they were recruited by Islamic militants. Deadly terrorist attacks on commuter trains in Madrid in 2004 and the London subway in 2005, which killed several hundred people, showed the potential for terrorist violence but convinced many that military interventions in the Middle East might actually increase the terrorist threat. In 2006, shocked Europeans found how tense Muslim-Western relations had become when offensive cartoons insulting or satirizing the Islamic prophet Muhammad, published by a rightwing, anti-immigrant Danish newspaper, caused riots and demonstrations around the Muslim world and attacks on Danish embassies and business interests.

However, Europeans played key roles in resolving world problems. Before the 2008–2009 economic crisis, Europeans tended to identify global warming as the major world problem. Some nations strongly encouraged alternative energy strategies. Hence Denmark now imports no Middle Eastern oil. They also took the lead in developing international treaties on issues such as climate change, biological and chemical weapons, international criminal courts, and genocide. U.S. opposition to these treaties built resentment. Yet, by 2009, mired in recession, both European leaders and the new pro-environment Barack Obama administration in the U.S. struggled to develop joint policies to combat global warming. European workers also led movements against the economic globalization they saw as costing jobs and livelihoods. Saying the world is not for sale, French farmer José Bové drove a tractor into a McDonald's outlet and vandalized it to protest against the large global corporations that often displace local enterprises, becoming a hero to those Europeans opposed to globalization and the institutions that promote it.

With the move toward closer political and economic integration, Europe became much more than a geographical expression and a collection of separate countries sharing cultural traditions and history. A few European leaders have even envisioned a political federation, or united states of Europe, but many hurdles would have to be overcome first. While Europe is no longer the powerhouse it had been in the nineteenth century, its peoples are carving out a new place in the world.

SECTION SUMMARY

- The collapsing Soviet bloc and Soviet decay created problems for Mikhail Gorbachev, and he was replaced by Boris Yeltsin, who allowed independence for all the non-Russian Soviet republics, some of which ended up with authoritarian governments, and pursued a rapid shift to capitalism.
- However, as a result of this "shock therapy," a small group of former Communist Party officials became extremely wealthy while most Russians suffered economically, and Yeltsin was replaced by the more authoritarian Vladimir Putin, who brought back some stability and pursued good relations with Europe and the United States.
- With the fall of the USSR, formerly communist eastern Europe became more democratic, though many countries struggled economically and others suffered political upheaval, especially Yugoslavia, which experienced violent civil war and "ethnic cleansing."
- German reunification, celebrated at first, yielded mixed results, while the European Union grew to include many nations but faced questions over whether to admit non-Christian nations and over what form its constitution should take.
- European nations struggled to navigate the evolving world economy, to deal with Islamic terrorism, and to work out relations with each other and with the United States, whose 2003 invasion of Iraq was generally unpopular in most countries.

CHAPTER SUMMARY

Emerging shattered from World War II, western Europeans were determined to build a new Europe. Although the Cold War divided Europe, western Europeans rebuilt democracies and began a movement to foster unity. Sparked by French-German reconciliation, Europeans established institutions for economic cooperation. Eventually these became the European Union, which established a single currency and a European parliament. Stability also resulted from the rise of welfare states, which guaranteed all citizens fair access to housing, health care, and education. Social democratic parties took the lead in creating the safety net, but supporting it became more costly with growing economic problems and unemployment rates. Gradually family and gender relations changed, while millions of immigrants reshaped European societies.

After the war the Soviet Union maintained a communist-run government and economy, with a powerful state dominating life and work. The Soviets installed communist governments in eastern

Europe and brutally repressed opposition, but they failed to realize much economic dynamism and lost ground in the Cold War to a more powerful U.S.-western Europe alliance. By the 1980s the Soviet system and the Soviet bloc needed reform. Although communism generated modernization and improved living standards, ethnic minorities were restless, the bureaucracy was stifling, and the economy remained stagnant. Unsettling reforms resulted in the collapse of communism and the dismantling of the Soviet Empire in 1991. Since then the former communist nations have struggled to introduce capitalism and liberal democracy. Meanwhile, most of the European nations joined the European Union, the world's third largest economic power. Germany struggled to make reunification work, Russia debated a new role in the world, and the European Union sought the appropriate mix of cooperation and national sovereignty.

KEY TERMS

Marshall Plan
Eurocommunism
Greens
Commonwealth of Nations
Truman Doctrine
NATO
Soviet bloc
Warsaw Pact
ostpolitik
welfare states
bhangra
existentialism
postmodernism
Brezhnev Doctrine
glasnost
perestroika
oligarchs

EBOOK AND WEBSITE RESOURCES

PRIMARY SOURCE

Vatican II: The Catholic Church Engages the Modern World

INTERACTIVE MAPS

Map 28.1 Military Alliances and Multinational Economic Groupings, 1949–1989
Map 28.2 Europe's Gross Domestic Product
Map 28.3 The Dissolution of the Soviet Union
Map 28.4 Ethnic Conflicts in Eastern Europe

LINKS

EUROPA—Gateway to the European Union (http://europa.eu.int/index_en.htm). Provides information on many topics.

European Union in the US (http://www.eurunion.org/states/home.htm). Provides a wealth of data on the European Union.

Internet Resources on Russia and the CIS (http://www.ssees.ac.uk/russia.htm). A British site with a collection of links on many aspects of Russia and the Soviet Union.

Internet Modern History Sourcebook (http://www.fordham.edu/halsall/mod/modsbook.html). A very extensive online collection of historical documents and secondary materials.

Russian History Index: The World Wide Web Virtual Library (http://vlib.iue.it/hist-russia/Index.html). Contains useful essays and links on Russian history, society, and politics.

Plus flashcards, practice quizzes, and more. Go to: www.cengage.com/history/lockard/globalsocnet2e.

SUGGESTED READING

Bridenthal, Renate, et al., eds. *Becoming Visible: Women in European History*, 3rd ed. Boston: Houghton Mifflin, 1998. Offers readable essays.

Crockatt, Richard. *The Fifty Years War: The United States and the Soviet Union in World Politics, 1941–1991*. New York: Routledge, 1995. A detailed study of the Cold War and U.S.-Soviet relations.

Evtuhov, Catherine, et al. *A History of Russia: Peoples, Legends, Events, Forces*. Boston: Wadsworth, 2004. A readable survey.

Gleason, Gregory. *The Central Asian States: Discovering Independence*. Boulder, CO: Westview Press, 1997. A study of the peoples and modern history of Turkestan.

James, Harold. *Europe Reborn: A History, 1914–2000*. New York: Longman, 2003. A survey of the period.

McCormick, John. *Understanding the European Union: A Concise Introduction*, 4th ed. New York: Palgrave Macmillan, 2008. A broad-ranging introduction to European integration.

Meyer, Michael. *The Year That Changed the World: The Untold Story Behind the Fall of the Berlin Wall*. New York: Scribner, 2009. Account of the dramatic changes in 1989.

Pagden, Anthony, ed. *The Idea of Europe: From Antiquity to the European Union*. New York: Cambridge University Press, 2002. An interesting collection of essays on European unity through the ages, including the contemporary era.

Reid, T.R. *The United States of Europe: The New Superpower and the End of American Supremacy*. New York: Penguin, 2005. Interesting examination of a predicted "European Century."

Rifkin, Jeremy. *The European Dream: How Europe's Vision of the Future Is Quietly Eclipsing the American Dream*. New York: Tarcher/Penguin, 2004. A provocative, sympathetic examination by an American scholar.

Roskin, Michael G. *The Rebirth of Eastern Europe*, 4th ed. Englewood Cliffs, NJ: Prentice-Hall, 2001. A provocative survey emphasizing politics and economics.

Ryback, Timothy W. *Rock Around the Bloc: A History of Rock Music in Eastern Europe and the Soviet Union*. New York: Oxford University Press, 1990. A fascinating examination of the role of rock music in the communist bloc.

Smith, Bonnie G. *Changing Lives: Women in European History Since 1700*. Lexington, MA: D.C. Heath, 1989. A readable introduction with good coverage of the twentieth century.

Strayer, Robert. *The Communist Experiment: Revolution, Socialism, and Global Conflict in the Twentieth Century*. New York: McGraw-Hill, 2007. Useful comparative study with much on the Soviet Bloc and Cold War.

Suny, Ronald Grigor. *The Soviet Experiment: Russia, the USSR, and the Successor States*. New York: Oxford University Press, 1998. An excellent overview of Soviet history and the aftermath.

Tipton, Frank B., and Robert Aldrich. *An Economic and Social History of Europe: From 1939 to the Present*. Baltimore: Johns Hopkins University, 1987. An accessible and comprehensive introduction.

Vinen, Richard. *A History in Fragments: Europe in the Twentieth Century*. Cambridge: Da Capo Press, 2000. A provocative, wide-ranging narrative by a British historian.

Wilkenson, James, and H. Stuart Hughes. *Contemporary Europe: A History*, 10th ed. Upper Saddle River, NJ: Prentice-Hall, 2004. One of the best, most comprehensive general surveys.

CHAPTER 29

The Americas and the Pacific Basin: New Roles in the Contemporary World, Since 1945

CHAPTER OUTLINE

- The United States as a Superpower
- The Changing Societies of North America and the Pacific Basin
- Political Change in Latin America and the Caribbean
- Changing Latin American and Caribbean Societies

PROFILE
Violeta Parra, Chilean New Song Pioneer

WITNESS TO THE PAST
Justifying Preemptive Strikes

AP/Wide World Photos

A Naturalization Ceremony
Seeking political freedom or economic opportunities, immigrants flock to the United States, and many become citizens. At this ceremony, 800 residents, representing 88 countries, took the oath of citizenship in Columbus, Ohio, in April 2005.

It's curious. Our generals listen to the [U.S.] Pentagon. They learn the ideology of National Security and commit all these crimes [against the Argentine people]. Then the same [American] people who gave us this gift come and ask, "How did these terrible things happen?"

—President Raul Alfonsin of Argentina, 1984[1]

FOCUS QUESTIONS

1. How did the Cold War shape U.S. foreign policies?
2. How and why are the societies of the United States, Canada, and Australia similar to and different from each other?
3. Why have democracy and economic development proved to be difficult goals in Latin America?
4. How have Latin American and Caribbean cultures been dynamic?

The women appeared one day in 1977 in the historic Plaza de Mayo, adjacent to the presidential palace in downtown Buenos Aires, Argentina. For several years the military government had waged a bloody campaign to eliminate dissidents, killing or abducting some 30,000 people and arresting and torturing thousands more. Some of those targeted may have belonged to outlawed leftist groups, but many simply held progressive ideas or were friends with regime critics. Initially only the feared secret police paid attention to the dozen or so frightened women who came once a week, standing in silent protest. But soon the women's ranks swelled to over a hundred, and a year later the peaceful protesters numbered more than a thousand. Wearing kerchiefs on their heads and sensible flat shoes, the mothers and grandmothers pinned to their chests photographs of missing family members, victims of the state's terror. They all asked the same question: Where were their missing children, husbands, pregnant daughters, and grandchildren? The "Mothers and Grandmothers of the Plaza de Mayo" challenged one of Latin America's most brutal tyrannies. Whether rich, poor, or middle class, most were housewives fighting, as one put it, vicious armed forces, spineless politicians, complicit clergy, muzzled press, and co-opted labor unions. Their courageous protest inspired others in Argentina and around the world with hope and moral outrage at military repression. The gatherings continued weekly until 1983, when the regime fell and a civilian government could investigate the disappearances. Most of the women never learned the fates of their loved ones.

The Plaza de Mayo protest illustrates how some Latin Americans addressed the authoritarian governments under which they lived, sometimes for decades. Latin American countries often shifted back and forth between dictatorship and democracy, neither of which fostered widespread economic prosperity amid the stark contrasts between rich and poor. Many Latin Americans also resented the United States, which, as Raul Alfonsin (1927–2009), the democratically elected Argentine president who replaced the military dictatorship, noted, often supported the Latin American dictatorships that welcomed U.S. investment. The United States remained the hemisphere's dominant power while expanding its global influence. Wars in Korea and Vietnam were part of the U.S. effort to oppose the expansion of communism. U.S. president Harry Truman (president 1945–1953) argued in 1947 that American political and business practices could thrive at home only if foreign countries also embraced similar practices. Following this logic, the United States became the global workshop and banker, preacher and teacher, umpire and policeman. Between 1946 and 1989, it enjoyed unrivaled supremacy, a combination of military might, economic power, and political-ideological leadership, contested only by the Soviet Union. Meanwhile, U.S. society increasingly differed from its North American neighbor, Canada, and the Pacific Basin countries of Australia and New Zealand.

Visit the website and eBook for additional study materials and interactive tools: www.cengage.com/history/lockard/globalsocnet2e

The United States as a Superpower

How did the Cold War shape U.S. foreign policies?

By virtue of its size, power, and wealth, the United States has played a major world role. The Americans helped Europe and Japan to recover from World War II, espoused and often promoted human rights and freedom, lavished aid on allies, and provided leadership in a politically fragmented world. During the Cold War, competition with the Soviet bloc for allies and strategic advantage shaped U.S. policies, and these policies influenced the world's perceptions of the United States (see Chronology: North America and the Pacific Basin, 1945–Present). Soviet domination of eastern Europe, the communist victory in China, and the Korean War all convinced Americans that communism was on the march. But while people around the world admired America's democratic ideals, prosperity, and technological ingenuity, the drive to oppose communist expansion led to wars, interventions, support for often authoritarian allies, frequent neglect of human rights, and the globalization of capitalism that fostered widespread hostility. After the Cold War, the United States and its allies faced new challenges.

CHRONOLOGY
North America and the Pacific Basin, 1945–Present

1946–1989 Cold War

1947 Formation of CIA and National Security Council

1950–1953 Korean War

1954 U.S. Supreme Court invalidation of school segregation

1955 Sparking of Montgomery bus boycott by Rosa Parks

1960–1975 U.S. secret war in Laos

1962–1990 Decolonization of Pacific islands

1963 Assassination of U.S. president John F. Kennedy

1963–1975 U.S. war in Vietnam

1968 Assassination of Dr. Martin Luther King, Jr.

1969 Woodstock rock festival

1973 End of "white Australia" policy

1988 Canadian Multiculturalism Act

1991 Gulf War

1994 Formation of NAFTA

1999 Formation of Nunavut in northern Canada

2001 Al Qaeda terrorist attacks in United States

2003 U.S. invasion of Iraq

The American Century and the Cold War

World War II was a watershed that forged Americans' vision of world politics. As a result of the war, acceleration of U.S. political centralization and economic growth encouraged Americans to accept international involvements, thus promoting an activist foreign policy. Observers began referring to both the United States and the USSR as superpowers. As the United States became the global powerbroker and policeman, the two superpowers sought to block each other from gaining influence in other countries. The victory over Nazism and Japanese militarism reinforced American confidence and sense of mission. In 1941, Henry Luce, the publisher of one of the most influential news magazines in the United States, *Time*, declared that the twentieth century would be the American Century, and that Americans must accept their duty and opportunity to influence the world. Luce believed that America's idealistic Bill of Rights, magnificent industrial products, and technological skills would be shared with all peoples. His view, while arrogant, reflected Americans' longtime belief in the exportability of their country's values and institutions, that their nation was the world's model. But U.S.-style capitalism and democracy proved difficult to implant where they had no roots.

In 1941 a conference of influential Americans recommended strengthening U.S. economic influence around the globe. After the war, therefore, the U.S. government rebuilt defeated Germany and Japan, established global financial networks, lavished aid on western Europe to help stabilize it under democratic governments, and used military forces to protect U.S. allies in Asia. It also opposed radical nationalist and communist-led movements in Asia, Africa, and Latin America. For several decades, as the U.S. economy soared, the notion of an American Century seemed realistic. But the economic superiority of the United States in the 1940s and 1950s was founded on unusual conditions. Among the great powers, only the United States had not been bombed or financially drained, and therefore it was able to keep intact a modern industrial system. The United States alone could produce, on a large scale, the consumer goods needed by others. In 1950, it accounted for 27 percent of total world economic output. By supplying the world, Americans experienced an economic boom that lasted until the late 1960s and helped finance an activist U.S. foreign policy.

As the United States became the engine of the world economy, it forged close trade links with Canada, western Europe, and Japan while sponsoring large-scale foreign aid programs and investment, especially in Asia and Latin America. Such aid and investment sparked an economic renaissance and promoted political stability in western Europe and Japan after World War II. However, in developing nations the aid and investment often supported cash crop agriculture and mining and thus reinforced dependence on export of natural resources, promoting unbal-

CHRONOLOGY

	North America	Pacific Basin	Latin America and the Caribbean
1940	**1946–1989** Cold War **1950–1953** Korean War		**1959** Cuban Revolution
1960	**1963–1975** U.S. war in Vietnam	**1962–1990** Decolonization of Pacific islands **1973** End of "white Australia" policy	**1964–1985** Military government in Brazil **1973–1989** Military government in Chile
1980	**1994** Formation of NAFTA		
2000	**2001** Al Qaeda terrorist attacks in United States		

anced growth. Later, U.S. investment developed light industry, especially textile factories, that utilized cheap labor in countries such as Mexico and Thailand. Asian, African, and Latin America countries became key U.S. markets, acquiring over a third of American exports by the 1990s and enriching U.S. corporations. However, American consumption of ever more foreign imports, from Japanese cars to Middle Eastern oil, contributed to a chronic trade imbalance, as Americans spent more for foreign products than they earned from exports. By 2005 imports were 57 percent larger than exports as Americans lived beyond their means and globalization led to outsourcing of manufacturing and jobs.

Competing Ideologies

The Cold War produced long-term conflict between two competing ideologies: communism and capitalist democracy. For decades after World War II, U.S. foreign relations were shaped by the idea that the Soviet Union was pursuing global domination. Although they had good reason to worry about a Soviet state headed by dictators and possessing formidable military might, U.S. leaders and intelligence analysts often overestimated the Soviet threat. Two key U.S. institutions carrying out the anti-Soviet strategy, the Central Intelligence Agency (CIA) and the National Security Council, both established in 1947, operated in top secrecy, with little congressional oversight and ever larger budgets, reaching $40 billion per year for all intelligence agencies by the 1980s. In the early 1950s the **domino theory**, which envisioned countries falling one by one to communism, became a mainstay of U.S. policy.

domino theory A theory that envisioned countries falling one by one to communism and that became a mainstay of U.S. policy.

Anticommunism intensified after hard-drinking U.S. senator Joseph McCarthy (1909–1957) and his allies charged, without offering much proof, that communists had infiltrated the U.S. government and shaped foreign policy. During the early and mid-1950s a campaign, known as McCarthyism, to identify suspected communists in the government, the military, education, and the entertainment industry led to the firing or the blacklisting of thousands of Americans who held leftwing political views, which were condemned as "un-American." (Blacklisting prevented people from working.) For example, university experts on Asia lost their positions for criticizing U.S. Asian policies, forcing some to finish their careers overseas. McCarthy called hundreds of people, from movie actors to State Department officials, before his Senate committee, where he questioned them about their political activities or their friends' political views. In 1954 the U.S. Senate censured McCarthy for recklessly charging top military leaders with treason. To critics, McCarthy's investigation was a witch-hunt and a Cold-War-driven hysteria that violated the Bill of Rights.

For much of the Cold War era, as a broad consensus emerged around opposing the spread of communism and Soviet power, most American leaders favored an activist foreign policy and the use of military power. However, they disagreed on the approach. Some leaders pursued **multilateralism**, in which the United States sought a common front and a coordination of foreign policies with allies in western Europe, Japan, and Canada, avoiding activities that might enflame world opinion against the United States. In contrast, most policymakers, and the presidents they served, favored **unilateralism**, whereby the United States acted alone in its own perceived national interest even if key allies disapproved, as they did with the U.S. war in Vietnam. Unilateralism often led to support of repressive allies such as the Philippines and the Congo, while consensus stifled those who questioned the rationale, tactics, and cost of an activist policy. Ultimately the costly interventions abroad, especially the frustrating war in Vietnam, generated a debate about the

multilateralism A foreign policy in which the United States sought a common front and a coordination of foreign policies with allies in western Europe, Japan, and Canada, avoiding activities that might enflame world opinion against the United States.

unilateralism A foreign policy in which the United States acted alone in its own perceived national interest even if key allies disapproved.

goals, operation, and impact of U.S. foreign policy. By the later 1960s, this debate had undermined the consensus and provoked increasing dissent.

containment The main U.S. strategy aimed at preventing communists from gaining power, and the USSR from getting political influence, in other nations during the Cold War.

The main U.S. strategy, known as **containment**, was aimed at preventing communists from gaining power, and the USSR from getting political influence, in other nations. Containment resulted in wars, as in Korea and later Vietnam, and in briefer interventions in countries that were gaining independence from Western colonialism or seeking to weaken Western economic domination. An influential, top secret government report, known as NSC-68, prepared by the National Security Council in 1950, provided the rationale for activist policies by painting a bleak picture of the USSR's search for world supremacy: "The issues that face us are momentous, involving the fulfillment or destruction not only of this [U.S.] Republic but of civilization itself."[2] NSC-68, which sanctioned any tactics in the anticommunism struggle, remained a key basis for U.S. military and intelligence policies abroad until the mid-1970s.

Defense Spending

NSC-68 had called for a huge defense budget and expansion of the nuclear weapons arsenal as a deterrent, to be paid for by tax increases and major reductions in social welfare spending. Thus security was to take precedence at the expense of all other priorities. The Soviets matched the U.S. military buildup, creating a constant and costly escalation of military spending and ever more sophisticated weapons on both sides. Under the policy of **Mutually Assured Destruction**, or MAD, the United States and the USSR used the fear of nuclear weapons to deter each other. Historians debate whether MAD prevented a direct military confrontation that might have sparked World War III. Americans reacted to the threat of nuclear war in the 1950s by often building bomb shelters in their basements or backyards and having schools hold mock air raid drills, during which students learned to "duck and cover," jumping under their desks to protect themselves from a hypothetical nuclear attack.

Mutually Assured Destruction A policy, known as MAD, in which the United States and the USSR used the fear of nuclear weapons to deter each other.

Defense spending reshaped the U.S. economy. Despite the warning of U.S. president and World War II commander Dwight Eisenhower (g. 1953–1961) about the growing influence of what he termed the "military-industrial complex," an alliance of military leaders and weapons producers, defense became an enormous business. By the 1960s it employed a fifth of the U.S. industrial work force and a third of scientists and engineers, while costing U.S. taxpayers hundreds of billions of dollars a year. The United States also sold weapons to allied nations, among them dictatorships such as Argentina and Thailand. Unfortunately, these nations sometimes used the weapons against their own populations, while their military officers and police forces often used the tactics they learned from U.S. forces to eliminate dissidents.

United States Power and the World

Between 1945 and 1975 U.S. power was unmatched in the world, and the United States maintained military bases on every inhabited continent and in dozens of countries (see Map 29.1). Both the United States and the USSR intervened directly or indirectly in civil wars and revolutions to outflank the other. Americans employed military force, as in the long war in Vietnam and the invasion of the Dominican Republic in 1965, and covertly aided governments to suppress opposition or helped overthrow governments considered unfriendly to U.S. economic or political interests, even if, as in Chile in 1973, these governments were democratic and freely elected. Some foreign observers applauded American efforts to suppress leftwing governments and movements, while others criticized the U.S. for superpower imperialism. The U.S.-U.S.S.R. rivalry persisted until the collapse of many communist regimes in 1989.

U.S. power was less dominant between the mid-1970s and the early 1990s. Reasons included the resurgence of western Europe and Japan, Soviet military strength, the economic challenge from industrializing nations such as South Korea and China, the damage done to the U.S. economy and prestige by the widely unpopular war in Vietnam, and the economic price Americans paid for global power. The extension and cost of military commitments caused the nation's economic creativity to sag and industries to become obsolete as defense spending diverted U.S. wealth from the domestic economy. Over four decades the Cold War cost the United States around $4 trillion, money that did not go to improving education and health care or meeting other needs. The growing U.S. defense budgets helped undermine the Soviet Union, unable to match the lavish spending on expensive, often unproven, weapons, but they also transformed the United States into the world's largest debtor nation, leaving ballooning federal deficits. In the 1990s, President Bill Clinton (g. 1993–2001) eliminated the budget deficits, but the debts skyrocketed under his successor, George W. Bush (g. 2001–2009).

The United States, Wars, and the Developing Nations

Korean War

The 1949 communist victory in China, a country long allied with and armed by the United States (see Chapter 27), escalated U.S. concern about communist expansion, leading to the Korean War

Map 29.1 U.S. Military Presence in the World, 1945–Present
As the major superpower, the United States maintained several dozen military bases outside of North America while engaging in military operations in Latin America, Africa, Asia, the Middle East, and Europe. This map shows some of the major U.S. bases and military conflicts.

Interactive Map

(1950–1953) (see Chapter 27). The decision to send U.S. troops to Korea signaled the U.S. adoption of an interventionist foreign policy, with the U.S. president, Harry S. Truman, viewing the North Korean invasion as a second coming of Nazi aggression. The anticommunist mood in the United States made it politically unthinkable for Truman not to oppose the North Korean invasion of South Korea. Truman never consulted the Congress, which had the constitutional responsibility to declare war, and his approach thereafter made presidents supreme in decisions to go to war without congressional approval, enhancing the power of the executive branch. Furthermore, the Soviet support of North Korea and the intervention of the Chinese on the North Korean side deepened American fear of an expanding communism. However, despite the 38,000 Americans killed and over 100,000 wounded, the war ended not in victory but in stalemate. For the first time since the War of 1812, the United States had failed to decisively win a major military conflict. The U.S. intervention in Korea also reflected the idealistic American desire to spread democracy and free market capitalism around the world. An American official reported sarcastically the hope of his more idealistic American colleagues that South Korea "will institute a whole series of necessary reforms which will so appeal to the North Koreans that their army

On Patrol in Vietnam U.S. soldiers sought out National Liberation Front fighters and supporters in the villages, rice fields, and jungles of South Vietnam. They could not easily tell friend from foe and warily dealt with local people.

Corbis

will revolt, kill all the nasty communists, and create a lovely liberal democracy to the everlasting credit of the U.S.A.!"[3] North Korea, however, remained a rigid communist state, and South Korea did not become a democracy until the 1980s, over three decades after the war. By 2009 U.S. military bases and thousands of troops remained in South Korea.

War in Indochina

The domino theory, which predicted a communist sweep through Southeast Asia, as well as the desire to maintain military credibility and keep valuable Southeast Asian resources in friendly hands, also provided the rationale for financing the French effort to maintain colonial control (1946–1954) in Vietnam. When that effort failed, the U.S. military eventually fought Vietnamese communist forces armed by the USSR and China (see Chapter 31). But few U.S. leaders comprehended the historical and cultural factors that sparked, and generated much local support for, the Vietnamese communist movement. By the mid-1960s, as the unpopular U.S.-backed South Vietnamese regime lost support, the U.S. president, Lyndon B. Johnson (g. 1963–1969), committed military forces and launched an intensive air war against targets in North and South Vietnam and later in neighboring Cambodia and Laos. Using domino theory rhetoric that exaggerated the communist threat, Johnson asserted that "if we don't stop the [communists] in South Vietnam, tomorrow they will be in Hawaii and next week they will be in San Francisco,"[4] very unlikely scenarios. As a result, between 1963 and 1975, 2.5 million Americans served in Vietnam; 58,000 died and 300,000 were wounded there.

As support within the United States for the war ebbed with military stalemate and increasing casualties in what seemed a quagmire, Johnson's successor, President Richard Nixon (g. 1969–1973), placed more emphasis on South Vietnamese forces, negotiated a political settlement with North Vietnam, and gradually withdrew U.S. forces. But a wartime policy of spending lavishly on both "guns and butter"—military and domestic needs—generated huge deficits and other economic problems with which the United States struggled from the later 1960s into the 1990s. The war in Vietnam ultimately cost U.S. taxpayers around $1 trillion. Furthermore, the lack of a military victory made Americans temporarily wary of supporting other military interventions that might become quagmires.

United States and Decolonization

During the Cold War, decolonization, nationalism, the U.S.-Soviet struggle, and persistent poverty combined to make the Asian, African, and Latin American societies prone to crises. The United States often favored decolonization that presented opportunities to U.S. business; for example, it successfully pressured the Dutch to abandon Indonesia and the British to grant independence to most of their African colonies. However, it opposed independence for colonies, such as French-ruled Vietnam and Portuguese-ruled Mozambique, where communists or leftists dominated the nationalist movements. After decolonization, Americans offered generous aid to friendly nations and to victims of famine or natural catastrophes, and they also funded the Green Revolution in agriculture, which led to improved food production. However, Cold War challenges involved the United States in long-term confrontations with communist-led China, North Vietnam, and Cuba, as well as interventions, sometimes with military force, to help U.S. allies suppress leftist insurgencies and to oppose left-leaning governments. But some U.S.-supported governments lacked widespread popular support or lost their credibility, often surviving only by repressing and sometimes killing domestic opponents.

Interventions

While U.S. leaders used the threat of communism as the rationale, some interventions removed democratic governments, as in Guatemala and Chile, or suppressed democratic movements. For example, President Lyndon Johnson, fearing another Cuba, dispatched 20,000 U.S. Marines into the Dominican Republic in 1965 to support a military government under attack by the democratically elected leaders they had recently overthrown. However, Johnson consulted no other Latin American governments, and the antimilitary leaders, while left-leaning, were mostly noncommunist reformers with wide popular support. Former Dominican president Juan Bosch (1909–2001) declared that "this was a democratic revolution smashed by the leading democracy in the world."[5] Instead of troops, the United States also provided friendly governments or antileftist groups with weapons, military advisers, intelligence agents, and funding. For example, during the 1970s and 1980s it aided a pro-Western but often repressive government combating a leftist insurgency in El Salvador. In Laos from 1960 to 1975, during the CIA's "secret war," kept hidden from Congress and the U.S. public, Americans recruited an army from among hill peoples to fight communist Laotian and North Vietnamese forces (see Chapter 31).

A final type of intervention involved covert destabilization. American agents worked underground to help undermine or spark the overthrow of governments by spreading misinformation about government policies, subsidizing opposition political parties, providing weapons to the military, and arranging for assassinations of government leaders. U.S. clandestine activity undermined left-leaning democratic governments in Iran in the 1950s and Thailand and Chile in the 1970s, resulting in brutal dictatorships. Secretary of State Henry Kissinger defended the U.S.-supported military coup against the elected Chilean government, which respected civil liberties, by explaining, "I don't see why we [Americans] need to stand by and watch a country go communist due to the irresponsibility of its own people."[6] Only in the mid-1970s, with congressional hearings, did Americans learn of the U.S. role in Chile and other interventions, forcing debate on whether engaging in secret operations and foreign interventions unknown to the public is compatible with democracy and open, accountable government.

The United States in the Global System After 1989

Pax Americana

The demise of the Soviet bloc in 1989 and the dissolution of the USSR in 1991 left the United States the dominant world power, although the European Union, Japan, and rising China and India also enjoyed great influence in the global system. But the lack of a rival superpower under what some called the *Pax Americana* ("American Peace") did not mean the end of challengers. The United States now struggled to find a new role in a world characterized by small, deadly conflicts. During the early 1990s, for example, it sent a small number of U.S. troops, under United Nations auspices, to stabilize Somalia, a famine-racked northeast African state involved in a civil war. The intervention turned out badly when the forces of a local warlord paraded the mutilated bodies of dead U.S. soldiers through the streets, forcing a U.S. withdrawal. In the aftermath, the United States declined to intervene to stop bloody ethnic conflicts and genocides in the African states of Rwanda, Liberia, and Sierra Leone. However, working with European allies, President Clinton sent U.S. forces to help end the deadly civil wars in the former Yugoslavia. The Clinton administration also established diplomatic ties and lifted the trade embargo that had been imposed on Vietnam after 1975, which it viewed as counterproductive, forging better relations with Vietnam.

United States and Middle East

Cold War policies sometimes came back to haunt the United States. For example, Iranian resentment over the 1953 overthrow of their government still complicates U.S.-Iran relations. In the 1980s, when the United States gave military and financial aid to the Islamic rebels fighting Soviet troops and the pro-Soviet government in Afghanistan (see Chapter 30), some of this aid went to Arab volunteers fighting alongside the rebels, among them the Saudi militant Osama bin Laden (b. 1957). After the defeated Soviets left Afghanistan in 1989, Muslim extremists, the Taliban, ultimately took power, imposing a rigid Islamic state and offering a base for bin Laden to form the global terrorist network known as Al Qaeda ("the Base"). Al Qaeda now plotted terrorist attacks against the United States, sometimes using leftover U.S. weapons (see Chapters 26 and 30). Farther west, Iraq's ruthless dictator, Saddam Hussein, used weapons acquired from the United States, his ally against Iran in the 1980s, to threaten Iraq's neighbors and repress dissident groups. In 1991 the United States led a coalition of nations that pushed invading Iraqi forces out of Kuwait during the Gulf War and then later protected the Kurds in northern Iraq from Saddam's reprisals. The intervention in oil-rich Kuwait was part of a consistent U.S. policy over the decades to protect the flow of oil from the Middle East to the West.

International Terrorism

The terrorist attack carried out by Al Qaeda on the World Trade Center in New York and the Pentagon in Washington, D.C., in September 2001, which killed nearly 3,000 Americans, shocked the nation and led to a reshaping of both domestic and foreign policies. The new U.S. president, George W. Bush (g. 2001–2009), introduced policies, such as preventive detention, intercepting overseas phone calls, and monitoring of libraries, designed to prevent possible domestic terrorism but that critics believed infringed on civil liberties. The terrorists, young Muslim fanatics mostly from two close U.S. allies, Egypt and Saudi Arabia, attacked buildings that symbolized often-unpopular U.S. economic and military power to people around the world. However, people in most countries, even if they disliked U.S. power, deplored the bombings and the loss of innocent life.

As a result of September 2001, President Bush declared war on international terrorism. But unlike the USSR during the Cold War, whose leaders had to be cautious, terrorist networks had no clear command structure or military resources and could not be influenced by diplomacy. With international support, the United States invaded Afghanistan to destroy Al Qaeda terrorist bases and displace the Taliban government that tolerated their presence. Bush also announced a new doctrine of **preemptive war** that sanctioned unilateral military action against potential threats (see Witness to the Past: Justifying Preemptive Strikes), and he named Iraq, Iran, and North Korea as states at the core of an "axis of evil" that threatened their neighbors and world peace. The Bush doctrine advocated that the United States maintain overwhelming military superiority over all challengers. Critics perceived the Bush doctrine as a recipe for acquiring an American empire through military action, a violation, they charged, of international law and the United Nations charter.

preemptive war A U.S. doctrine, triggered by the 2001 terrorist attacks, that sanctioned unilateral military action against potential threats.

The U.S. and Iraq

The Bush administration's concern with international terrorism led to a resumption of unilateralist U.S. foreign policies. Rejecting opposition from the United Nations and key U.S. allies, among them Canada and Germany, in 2003 the Bush administration invaded and occupied Iraq, ending Saddam Hussein's brutal regime. On the basis of faulty or manipulated intelligence, Bush claimed that Iraq possessed weapons of mass destruction and aided Al Qaeda. But the U.S. forces found no such weapons or evidence of a Saddam–Al Qaeda link. Furthermore, the Bush administration had planned poorly for restoring stability in Iraq, a nation rich in oil but troubled by ethnic and religious divisions that threatened to explode into civil war and that frustrated U.S. attempts to foster democracy. A mounting insurgency by some Iraqi factions, as well as suicide bombings largely linked to foreign terrorists flocking to Iraq to fight Americans, caused many thousands of U.S. casualties and complicated political and economic reconstruction, making an early withdrawal of U.S. forces difficult. By 2007 oil production and basic services such as electricity had still not been restored to prewar levels, and the streets in many regions remained unsafe, demoralizing Iraqis. Only in 2008, after Bush dispatched more troops, did conditions stabilize, violence diminish, and political conditions improve, but over 130,000 U.S. troops remained in later 2009. The U.S.-led NATO force in Afghanistan also faced increased resistance from Islamist fighters led by a rejuvenated Taliban.

In both Afghanistan and Iraq, U.S. forces, although trained for conventional warfare relying heavily on air power, had to return to the counterinsurgency strategy they used in Vietnam. Moreover, the spiraling costs of the Iraq occupation and other expenses, combined with large tax cuts, ballooned U.S. budget deficits that damaged the U.S. economy. The ever-expanding appetite of Americans for oil also contributed to the Middle East interventions and support for dictatorial regimes; critics charged that the Iraq war was about oil. The Iraq war, unpopular in much of the world, the allegations that the U.S. tortured suspected terrorists, holding suspected enemies for years without trial, and the U.S. rejection of several international treaties, such as that on global warming, further alienated Western allies. Yet, the United States also earned praise for generous assistance to the victims of a catastrophic tidal wave in South and Southeast Asia in 2005.

The Price of World Power

Because of its unparalleled economic and military might, the United States had assumed heavy burdens, sending troops to Afghanistan, Iraq, and elsewhere while maintaining military bases around the world. By 2008 the U.S. accounted for some two thirds of arm sales to other nations, earning some $40 billion per year. While western Europeans and East Asians have generally concentrated on trade relations with other nations, Americans have attempted to balance trade with confronting the nations they perceive as dangerous. By 2008 the United States accounted for half of all military spending worldwide, devoting as much to its military and weapons as all other nations combined, and it also accounted for about half of all arms sales to the world's nations. While anti-U.S. sentiments grew steadily in the early twenty-first century, no coalition of nations has come together to oppose the U.S. role. However, the budget deficits that now pay for it, more than doubling the national debt between 2001 and 2008, are only possible because Asian investors, especially the Chinese, Japanese, and South Koreans, finance around half of the debt, giving these countries leverage with the United States.

The spiraling national debt, expensive global commitments, housing market crisis, and overly lax regulation of banks, corporations, and the stock market led to an economic meltdown in 2008–2009 that soon spread to the rest of the world. Millions of Americans lost their jobs and homes,

Justifying Preemptive Strikes

In the wake of the shocking terrorist attacks on the United States in September 2001, the administration of President George W. Bush produced a document, the National Security Strategy of the United States, that restated the U.S. desire to spread democracy and capitalism while announcing that the United States would act preemptively, striking first, unilaterally if necessary, against any hostile states that the Bush administration believed might be planning to attack U.S. targets. Depending on the observer, the document either reflected or exploited Americans' fear of terrorist attacks. In 2003 Bush used the preemptive strike rationale to order a military invasion and occupation of Iraq, which he claimed had weapons of mass destruction. After Saddam's fall, Bush offered a new mission: fostering democracy in Iraq as an example for the Middle East. To critics, however, the failure to find such weapons, the faulty intelligence about them, and the huge financial and human costs of the resulting occupation for both Americans and Iraqis all suggested the dangers of a preemptive strategy. Furthermore, they argued, many presidents before Bush had claimed to promote democracy abroad but had rarely done so, especially when they used military force to install a pro-U.S. government in another country.

The great struggles of the twentieth century between liberty and totalitarianism ended with a decisive victory for the forces of freedom—and a single sustainable model for national success: freedom, democracy, and free enterprise. . . . Only nations that share a commitment to protecting basic human rights and guaranteeing political and economic freedom will be able to unleash the potential of their people and assure their future prosperity. . . . Today the United States enjoys a position of unparalleled military strength and great economic and political influence. In keeping with our heritage and principles, we do not use our strength to press for unilateral advantage. We seek instead to create a balance of power that favors human freedom. . . . We will extend the peace by encouraging free and open societies on every continent.

Defending our Nation against its enemies is the first and fundamental commitment of the Federal Government. Today, that task has changed dramatically. Enemies in the past needed great armies and great industrial capabilities to endanger America. Now, shadowy networks of individuals can bring great chaos and suffering to our shores for less than it costs to purchase a single tank. Terrorists are organized to penetrate open societies and to turn the power of modern technologies against us. To defeat this threat we must make use of every tool in our arsenal. . . . The war against terrorists of global reach is a global enterprise of uncertain duration. . . . America will hold to account nations that are compromised by terror, including those who harbor terrorists—because the allies of terror are the enemies of civilization. . . . Our enemies have openly declared that they are seeking weapons of mass destruction. . . . The United States will not allow these efforts to succeed. . . . And, as a matter of common sense and self-defense, America will act against such emerging threats before they are fully formed. . . . We must be prepared to defeat our enemies' plans. History will judge harshly those who saw this coming danger but failed to act. In the new world we have entered, the only path to peace and security is the path of action. . . .

The struggle against global terrorism is different from any other war in our history. It will be fought on many fronts against a particularly elusive enemy over an extended period of time. . . . New deadly challenges have emerged from rogue states and terrorists. . . . Rogue regimes seek nuclear, biological, and chemical weapons. . . . We must be prepared to stop rogue states and their terrorist clients before they are able to threaten or use weapons of mass destruction against the United States and our allies. . . . The United States can no longer solely rely on a reactive posture as we have in the past. . . . We cannot let our enemies strike first. . . . We must adapt the concept of imminent threat to the capabilities and objectives of today's adversaries. . . . The greater the threat, the greater the risk of inaction—and the more compelling the case for taking anticipatory action to defend ourselves, even if uncertainty remains as to the time and place of the enemy's attack. To forestall or prevent such hostile acts by our adversaries, the United States will, if necessary, act preemptively.

THINKING ABOUT THE READING

1. How does the document reflect the tendency of U.S. leaders to claim a national goal of spreading U.S. political and economic models in the world?
2. What does the document offer as the rationale for preemptive actions?

Source: The National Security Strategy of the United States (http://www.whitehouse.gov/nsc/print/nssall.html).

consumer spending dropped dramatically, stock prices plummeted, pension funds dwindled, and state and local governments faced severe budget cuts. The government was forced to bail out major banks, the distressed automobile industry, and revenue-starved states, adding to budget deficits. While the severe recession was not as catastrophic as the Great Depression, it did force debate on the continuing relevance of the free-wheeling U.S. economic model and on the heavy cost of the nation's obligations in the world. Whether the United States will retain its dominance in the years ahead or whether the growing burdens will reduce U.S. power as other nations, perhaps China or India, surge ahead, remains unclear. Due to the economic crisis, some experts perceived a transition underway toward a multi-polar economy less dependent on U.S. leadership and consumption. Whatever the case, since the Romans two millennia ago, no other nation has been as dominant in military, economic, political, and social realms as the United States has been after 1990, forcing Americans to debate, as the Romans and the Athenians did, whether democracy and imperial power are consistent.

SECTION SUMMARY

- For several decades after World War II, the United States enjoyed a period of economic growth and lavished economic aid on western Europe and Japan, where it helped those countries to recover, and later on developing nations, where it was not used as effectively.
- During the Cold War, McCarthyism led to the persecution of many U.S. citizens for supposed communist sympathies, U.S. presidents aimed to contain the spread of communism through unilateral action, the two superpowers followed the Mutually Assured Destruction policy, and defense spending became a key factor in the U.S. economy.
- On the basis of the domino theory, which argued that if communism wasn't stopped it would take over the world, the United States adopted an interventionist foreign policy and fought communists in Korea and Vietnam, but neither war achieved U.S. goals, and the Vietnam War severely crippled the U.S. economy.
- During the Cold War, the United States opposed not only communist movements but also noncommunist leftist movements in several countries, in many cases helping to replace them with brutal military dictatorships.
- In response to the terrorist attacks of September 11, 2001, U.S. president George W. Bush proclaimed a policy of preemptive war and led the country to war in Afghanistan and then in Iraq, the second of which was fought despite United Nations disapproval and has been very controversial.

THE CHANGING SOCIETIES OF NORTH AMERICA AND THE PACIFIC BASIN

How and why are the societies of the United States, Canada, and Australia similar to and different from each other?

The United States, Canada, Australia, and New Zealand, all originally settled by people from the British Isles, shared a general prosperity, stable democracies, similar social patterns, and many cultural traditions. Millions of immigrants also helped to globalize their cultures and link them more closely to other nations. But the United States played a different role than the other countries and exercised more power in the world.

Prosperity, Technology, and Inequality in the United States

Economic Growth

Living in the world's richest nation, many Americans benefited from a growing economy and widespread affluence. During the 1960s, as many Americans worked in new automobile, aerospace, service, and information technology industries, the production of goods and services doubled and per capita income rose by half. By 2000 the United States accounted for a third of the world's total production of goods and services, over twice as much as second-place Japan, and enjoyed a median annual family income of over $40,000. Americans also owned the majority of the giant multinational corporations, such as General Motors and Wal-Mart, that played ever larger roles in the globalizing world. However, there were downsides to this growth. With 6 percent of the world population, Americans consumed around 40 percent of all the world's resources, such as oil and iron ore, and produced a large share of the chemicals, gases, and toxic wastes that pollute the atmosphere, alter the climate, and destroy the land. At the same time, the United States lagged in environmental protection; in 2005 it ranked twenty-eighth in meeting sustainable environmental goals, well behind most of western Europe, Japan, Taiwan, and several developing nations. Americans also worked longer hours than any industrialized people except the Japanese.

New Technologies

The rise of high technology and the decline of smokestack industries, such as steel production, reshaped the economy and workplace. Americans made innovations in medicine, space research, transportation, and electronics. Space satellites greatly improved weather forecasting, communications, and intelligence gathering, and computers revolutionized life with their convenience and versatility, since these machines could, as *Time* magazine concluded, "send letters at the speed of light, diagnose a sick poodle [and] test recipes for beer."[7] By 2008 many Americans carried with them pocket-sized devices, once the stuff of science fiction novels, that could make telephone calls, send text messages, take photos, play music and films, and access news and weather.

Economic Change and American Life

Beginning in the 1970s, a growing economy improved the lot of some people, especially those trained in the new technologies, but hurt millions of unskilled workers, younger workers, and children in single-parent households. While computers and robots increased efficiency, they also replaced workers, and in the 1980s a third of industrial jobs disappeared. Industrialists won corporate bonuses for relocating factories and exporting jobs to Latin America or Asia, devastating factory-dependent American communities. By the early 2000s, although life for the majority of Americans remained comfortable compared to that in most other nations, unemployment for men was the highest it had been in five decades, and millions of men and women had to work two jobs to support their families. Moreover, the United States generally ranked behind several European nations, Canada, and Australia in overall quality of life in the annual United Nations Human Development Report. Some economists referred to a "winner-take-all economy" that produced ever more millionaires—over 2 million of them by 2005—but also a struggling middle class and, at the bottom of the social ladder, more homeless people sleeping in city streets and parks. Except for the richest 1 percent of Americans, whose earnings skyrocketed, average incomes fell between 2001 and 2008. Yet, most Americans identified themselves with the middle class rather than, as Europeans often did, with the working class.

In contrast to most industrialized nations, the United States never developed a comprehensive welfare state. Hence, despite sporadic government efforts at abolishing poverty, a widening gap separated the richest third and the poorest third of Americans. The inequality of wealth grew dramatically after 1980, and by 2004, 12.5 percent of Americans lived below the poverty line, the highest poverty rate in the industrialized world. Today the gap between the richest 20 percent and the poorest 20 percent of Americans is three times wider than in Japan, the Netherlands, Sweden, or Germany, and millions of Americans today have no health insurance, a striking contrast to western Europe and Canada. A devastating hurricane that caused massive damage and flooding in the Gulf Coast in 2005, ruining New Orleans, rendering millions homeless, and killing several thousand people, starkly revealed the gap; most of the people who died or were only rescued days later were black and poor, unable to afford transportation out of the area.

Suburbs and Cities

Economic changes went hand in hand with the suburbanization of American life, deepening the inequalities. Following World War II families with young children wanted affordable housing and sought a better life in suburbia, the bedroom communities on the edges of major cities. Suburbs, occupied typically by white Americans, built shopping malls, offered well-funded schools, and seemed immune from city violence. Governments supported the suburban trend by subsidizing real estate developers. William Leavitt, who built vast suburban tracts, known as Leavittown, around New York City, argued that no person who owned his or her own house and yard could be a communist because he or she was too busy keeping up, and working to pay for, the property. The two-car, multitelevision family symbolized affluence. The increasingly affordable automobile, combined with government-funded highway construction, made long commutes from the suburbs to jobs in the central city possible. Later, as the jobs often moved to the suburbs, the city cores were increasingly dominated by the local-born poor, often nonwhite, or immigrants. Furthermore, increasing use of fossil fuels for gasoline, electricity, and heating caused pollution, while clearing land for housing and business development harmed the environment. Most suburbs lacked ethnic and cultural diversity and isolated residents from the stimulation, as well as the problems, of big city life. Suburban living also intensified the trend, begun before World War II, toward two-parent, single-breadwinner nuclear families that lived apart from other relatives. Finally, moving people farther away from city jobs encouraged mothers to stay at home. Until the mid-1960s the image of the fashionably dressed, stay-at-home suburban housewife, smiling proudly as she served breakfast to her husband and children, remained ingrained in the culture, even as women increasingly found it necessary to undertake paid work. Critics lambasted the conformity of life in the standardized suburban tract houses, which, according to a song from the 1950s, resembled "little boxes. There's a green one, a pink one, a blue one and a yellow one. And they're all made out of ticky-tacky, And they all look just the same."[8]

American Political Life: Conservatism and Liberalism

Americans tended to alternate between political conservatism and liberalism. For most of the postwar years, political conservatives, allied with big business groups favoring low taxes and religious groups who disliked social and cultural liberalization, dominated the presidency and often the Congress and the judiciary. Liberals played a key role in U.S. politics chiefly in the 1960s, the 1990s, and after 2006. They were generally supported by labor unions, environmentalists, and groups that sought social change and a stronger government safety net, such as women's and civil rights organizations.

1950s Conservatism

The widespread desire for stability after the Great Depression and a calamitous world war encouraged political and social conservatism throughout the 1950s. Prosperous, the middle and upper classes rarely questioned their government or the prevailing social patterns. Americans who criticized U.S. foreign policy or favored extensive social change faced harassment, expulsion from job or school, arrest, or grillings by congressional committees. More Americans than ever before married, producing a "baby boom" of children born in the years following the war. The mass media portrayed women as obsessed with bleaching their clothes a purer white and defined by kitchen, bedroom, babies, and home. Society expected homosexuals to remain deep in the closet, and those who did not faced taunting, beatings, or arrest. The growing consumer economy also emphasized pleasure and leisure activities, such as cocktail parties, backyard barbecues, and baseball games. Like their parents, teenagers became consumers, creating a market for youth-oriented clothes and music.

1960s Liberalism

During the 1960s, Americans became open to new ideas and lifestyles as liberalism became influential. The era saw the first people to walk on the moon and the Peace Corps, an agency that sent idealistic young Americans to help developing nations as teachers, health workers, and agricultural specialists. Presidents John F. Kennedy (g. 1961–1963) and Lyndon B. Johnson (g. 1963–1969) launched programs to address poverty and racism. But the 1960s was also a decade of doubts, anger, and violence. Three national leaders were assassinated, including Kennedy, shot in the head while riding in a motorcade in 1963. The war in Vietnam, the civil rights movement for African Americans, and issues of environmental protection and women's empowerment divided the nation. The country's social fabric fragmented as prowar "hawks" and antiwar "doves" competed for support, and riots and demonstrations punctuated the decade.

Much of the commotion came from a large segment of young people, chiefly middle class, who rebelled against the values of their parents and established society. The popular folksinger Bob Dylan (b. 1941) sang: "Come, mothers and fathers, throughout the land, And don't criticize what you can't understand. Your sons and your daughters are beyond your command, Your old world is rapidly aging. Please get out of the new one if you can't lend your hand, For the times, they are achanging."[9] Some youth, especially high school and university students, worked to change society and politics, registering voters, holding "teach-ins" to discuss national issues, and going door to door to spread their cause. Other youth forged a counterculture that often involved using illegal drugs, such as marijuana, and engaging in casual sex, with some emblazoning the slogan "Make love, not war" on bumper stickers, posters, and buttons. The Summer of Love in 1967, during which young people from North America and elsewhere gathered in San Francisco to hear rock music and share comradery, and the Woodstock rock music festival of 1969, which attracted over 300,000 young people to a New York farm to hear some of the most popular rock musicians, marked the zenith of both the youth counterculture and political activism.

Return to Conservatism

In the 1970s, with the winding down of the war, the nation returned to more conservative values and politics. With the exception of the 1990s, when the moderate Bill Clinton held the presidency, conservatives maintained their dominance of American politics and the social agenda until 2006, when Democrats reclaimed Congress, followed by the 2008 election of Democrat Barack Obama as president. President Ronald Reagan (g. 1981–1989), a former movie star and zealous anticommunist, symbolized conservative governance by weakening the labor movement and the welfare system while taking a hard line toward the Soviet Union. Religion has also remained a powerful force, with Americans more likely to attend churches and profess strong Christian beliefs than Canadians or most Europeans. While many Protestants, Catholics, and Jews supported liberal causes, by the 1980s conservative Catholics and evangelical Protestants became influential in public life, helping elect political conservatives to office. Some experts attributed Christian conservatism to a rejection of the Enlightenment emphasis on reason and tolerance as believers sought certainty and timeless rules. Others stressed the search for a personal spiritual experience. Many churches stressed membership in a supportive community or emphasized self-help. While Americans avidly consumed new technologies, such as cell phones and portable music players, polls showed that, because of religious conservatism, substantial numbers also mistrusted science, rejecting scientific explanations for the origins of the universe and human evolution in favor of biblical accounts.

Observers found much to deplore and much to praise in post-1960s U.S. politics. As money from big corporations and other special interests increasingly played a major role in politics, fostering corruption and political apathy, fewer Americans participated in the democratic process, with barely half of eligible voters bothering to vote in presidential elections—far lower numbers than in most other industrial democracies. However, a free media exposed government corruption,

XinHua/Xinhua Press/Corbis

President Obama Villagers in Kogelo, Kenya, celebrate the inauguration of Barack Obama as president of the United States in early 2009. While many around the world watched the ceremony on television, the interest was was especially strong in Kogelo, where Obama's father was born.

including abuse of power by presidents. President Richard Nixon, facing impeachment, resigned in 1973 for sanctioning and then covering up illegal activities by his subordinates, and the presidencies of both Reagan and Clinton were marred by congressional hearings examining their misdeeds. After the controversial, bitter 2000 and 2004 elections, Americans were sharply divided between the two major political parties and the divergent policies they supported.

The Obama Presidency

However, the apathy faded in 2008 during an exciting election campaign to replace a strongly conservative President George W. Bush, widely disliked for the unpopular Iraq war, an incompetent response to Hurricane Katrina, a spiraling national debt, controversial social and environmental policies, and the economic meltdown of 2008. Illinois Senator Barack Obama (b. 1961), the Hawaii-born son of a black Kenyan father and white mother from Kansas, won the Democratic nomination over New York Senator Hillary Rodham Clinton (b. 1947), a former First Lady. Obama had lived in Indonesia for a few years as a child. By mobilizing a coalition of racial minorities, women, youth, and labor unions, Obama went on to win the presidency over Arizona Senator and Vietnam War hero, Republican John McCain (b. 1936). Obama's victory as the first nonwhite president electrified the world, and suggested that U.S. society was changing. Obama urged global cooperation on pressing issues and many non-Americans hoped for a less unilateral and aggressive U.S. foreign policy than under Bush. Inheriting two wars and an economic crisis, and enjoying Democratic congressional majorities, Obama proposed New Deal–like policies to generate economic recovery, made plans to withdraw U.S. troops from Iraq, and promised to deliver universal health coverage and implement more environmentally friendly policies. However, while a government stimulus package averted a complete economic crash, reducing unemployment proved a challenge. Whether Obama had begun a new era of liberalism and economic resurgence remained to be seen.

American Society and Popular Culture

The changing American society affected ethnic minorities, families, women, and men. As they had since the end of slavery, African Americans, over 10 percent of the population, experienced much higher rates of poverty than whites and faced various forms of discrimination. Until the 1960s the southern states maintained strict racial segregation, forcing blacks to attend separate schools and to even use different public drinking fountains than whites, while in northern industrial cities racism and poverty often encouraged African Americans to concentrate in run-down inner-city neighborhoods, known as ghettos.

African Americans and Civil Rights

The civil rights movement, organized by African Americans in the 1950s, eventually forced courts, states, and the federal government to introduce reforms. In 1954 the Supreme Court outlawed segregated schools. A year later, in Montgomery, Alabama, Rosa Parks (1913–2005), a seamstress and community activist, bravely refused to follow the local custom to give up her front seat on a bus to a white man, sparking a mass movement for change. A black minister, Reverend Martin

Luther King, Jr. (1929–1968), led a bus boycott to protest her arrest and fine. Using the strategy of nonviolent resistance pioneered by Mohandas Gandhi, King led a protest movement all over the South. While leading the 1963 March on Washington to demand equal rights, he presented his vision: "I have a dream. When we let freedom ring, all of God's children will be able to join hands and sing in the words of that old spiritual, 'Thank God almighty, we are free at last!'"[10] King's assassination by a white racist in 1968 shocked the nation, but by then the African American struggle had inspired similar struggles elsewhere in the world, including black South Africans, Afro-Brazilians, and Australian Aborigines. Thanks to the efforts of King, Parks, and many others, African Americans gradually gained legal equality, and many moved into the middle and upper classes, although African Americans were still far more likely than whites to live in poverty, face unemployment, and be imprisoned. While they celebrated Obama's presidential victory as a sign of progress, they were also more likely to lose jobs and homes in the 2008–2009 recession.

Multiracial Society

Americans have often boasted that they live in a "melting pot" where ethnic groups merge and lose their separate identity, which has often been the case for people of European ancestry. However, because members of many nonwhite ethnic groups have often maintained their separate identities and cultures, Americans have increasingly faced a multiracial, multicultural society. By 2008 the U.S. population of 300 million, the third largest in the world, was more diverse than ever, and over 10 percent were foreign-born. As a result, American life took on a cosmopolitan flavor: Spanish became widely spoken, and Latin American grocery stores, Asian restaurants, and African art galleries opened in communities throughout the country. Alaska and Hawaii, both with large nonwhite populations, became states in 1959, adding to the nation's diversity.

Ethnic groups grew through both legal and illegal immigration. By 2006 the Hispanic/Latino population alone totaled around 45 million, two-thirds of Mexican origin, outnumbering the 41 million African Americans. Several million Asians arrived, mostly from China, South Korea, India, and Southeast Asia, and immigrants also came from Europe, the Middle East, the Caribbean, and South Pacific islands, especially Samoa and Tonga. Some immigrants labored for meager wages in crowded sweatshops in big cities, where bosses often allowed workers only one or two breaks during their shift and ignored city safety regulations. Chinese sewed clothing in New York City, and Mexicans did the same in Los Angeles. At the same time, immigration marginalized Native Americans. While many lived in cities, others remained isolated on reservations. Some joined movements to assert their rights, often seeking a return of lands seized by white settlers generations earlier. While a few tribes achieved prosperity by operating gambling casinos, most Native Americans remained poor.

Gender Relations

After the 1960s women's issues became more prominent. In the 1950s few women worked for high pay, colleges imposed strict quotas on female applicants, married women could not borrow money in their own names, there was no legal concept of sexual harassment, and men often joked of keeping women "barefoot and pregnant." By the early twenty-first century conditions had changed dramatically, but it took a long struggle for gender equality. Beginning in the 1960s many women joined feminist movements demanding equal legal rights with men and improved economic status. In 1963 Betty Friedan's (1921–2006) passionate book, *The Feminine Mystique*, identified women's core problem as a stunting of their growth by a patriarchal society and unfulfilling housework. With slogans such as "Sisterhood Is Powerful," women came together in groups, such as the National Organization for Women (NOW), founded by Friedan in 1966, to fight for expanded opportunities. Thanks in part to feminists' efforts, the median income of women workers climbed to 70 percent of that of men, and the number of women with paid work more than doubled between 1960 and 2000. Women now held governorships and federal cabinet posts, served in Congress, sat on the Supreme Court, and, as Hillary Clinton's campaign demonstrated, were serious candidates for president. Clinton became Obama's Secretary of State, the third woman to hold that influential post. By the twenty-first century more women than men finished secondary school and attended universities, some joining highly paid, traditionally male occupations such as law, university teaching, engineering, and medicine. Women pursuing satisfying, well-paid careers, running for political office, and enjoying personal freedoms unimaginable to their great grandmothers owed their gains largely to the feminist movement and its male supporters. However, most employed women struggled to juggle work with family and housekeeping responsibilities. One young mother of two complained in the 1990s that "it's like twenty-four hours a day you're working. My day never ends."[11] Moreover, sexual harassment in the workplace, stalking, and rape remained serious problems. Scholars wrote of a "feminization of poverty" as many women headed single-parent families.

Social and legal changes affected both women and men. As divorce became easier and more common, by the 1990s over half of all marriages ended in divorce. Single-parent households grew more frequent, and increasingly, as in Europe, many men and women never married, often living with partners out of wedlock. Americans remained deeply divided on some women's issues, especially abortion, which was long common but illegal in the United States before being declared legal by the Supreme Court in 1973. Americans also disagreed about homosexuality. By the 1960s gay men and lesbians actively struggled to end harassment and legal discrimination, gaining greater acceptance in society, yet the growing numbers who openly acknowledged their sexual identity still faced hostility. During the early twenty-first century Americans quarreled over allowing homosexuals to serve openly in the armed forces, marry, or establish legal partnerships, a pattern of acceptance common in Europe and Canada but opposed by many Christian churches. By 2009 several states had legalized homosexual marriages, while many other states passed laws forbidding it.

Popular Culture

Once importers of culture from Europe, Americans became the world's greatest exporters of popular culture products. U.S.-made films, television programs, books, magazines, and sports reached a global audience, and popular music had widespread influence. Various musical styles, including the Broadway musicals of songwriters such as Richard Rogers and Oscar Hammerstein, the blues of singer Billie Holiday and guitarist B. B. King, the jazz of saxophonist John Coltrane and trumpeter Miles Davis, and the country music of singer-songwriters Hank Williams and Dolly Parton, spread far and wide.

But no music style had the power of rock, which in the 1950s and 1960s helped spark a cultural revolution, especially among youth, in the United States and gained a huge following abroad. The first exhilarating blasts of rock and roll, notably from the white singer Elvis Presley (1935–1977), whose suggestive, hip-swinging performances earned him the nickname "Elvis the Pelvis," and the inventive black guitarist Chuck Berry (b. 1926), defied the Eisenhower era's puritanical emphasis on social and political conformity, often alarming adults. Rock music broke down social barriers by challenging sexual and racial taboos. The first American popular music that appealed across social class boundaries, rock was inspired by black rhythm and blues but also by the country and gospel music of white southerners, and early rock made a powerful statement that young Americans were less divided by race than their parents. Rock became the heart of the youth movement of the 1960s, when albums by key rock musicians, such as the poetic American singer-songwriter Bob Dylan and the British group the Beatles, seemed infused with political meaning. Rock later lost its political edge but, evolving into forms such as punk, grunge, and heavy metal, remained at the heart of U.S. popular music.

The music created by African Americans has also addressed the problems of American life. The soul music in the 1960s, from artists like James Brown and Aretha Franklin, promoted black self-respect and unity, paralleling the messages of black pride movements. In the 1980s rap music emerged out of urban black ghettos to become the cutting-edge, politicized form of Western pop music. An eclectic mix of rock, soul, rhythm and blues, and Caribbean music, rap expresses the tensions of urban black youth. The boastful, often angry tone highlights conflict between white and black, rich and poor, and male and female. Rap musicians have outraged segments of both white society and the black middle class. Musicians in nations around the world have adopted the rap style, often integrating it into their own traditions.

The Canadian Experience

English and French Canadians

Although they share cultural traditions and a democratic spirit with Americans, Canadians have remained proudly independent of their powerful southern neighbor while nurturing differences from Americans, such as by maintaining two official languages—English and French. Two main parties, one liberal and one conservative, have dominated national elections, but, in contrast to the United States, smaller leftwing and rightwing parties also play key roles, often governing Canadian provinces. The French Canadian nationalist Party Québécois **(KAY-be-KWAH)** has often governed French-speaking Quebec, which contains a quarter of Canada's population, and periodically holds provincial votes on independence from Canada (see Map 29.2). In 1985 the federal parliament, hoping to preserve a united Canada, recognized Quebec as a distinct society within largely English-speaking Canada and granted it more provincial autonomy. Canadians still debate how much power to allocate to the provinces and how much to the federal government.

Canada and the United States

Canadians, 34 million strong by 2009, cannot ignore their proximity to the United States, which has almost ten times Canada's population and vastly more global power. Former prime minister Pierre Trudeau **(troo-DOE)** (g. 1968–1984), a French Canadian, complained that sharing a border with the United States was "like sleeping with an elephant. No matter how friendly or even-tempered the beast, one is affected by every twitch and grunt."[12] Most Canadians live within a hundred miles of the U.S. border and thus have easy access to the U.S. mass media. Moreover, Americans own some 20 percent of the Canadian economy. While some Canadians welcome U.S. investment as a spur to economic growth, others resent U.S. domination. In 1994 the North American Free

Map 29.2 Canada
The Canadian federation includes eleven provinces stretching from Newfoundland in the east to British Columbia and the Yukon in the west. In 1999 a large part of northern Canada, inhabited chiefly by the Inuit, became the self-governing region of Nunavut.

e Interactive Map

Trade Agreement (NAFTA) further bound the Canadian, Mexican, and U.S. economies. Yet, despite usually friendly relations, Canadians have often opposed U.S. foreign policies, including the wars in Vietnam and Iraq.

Economy and Society

Canadians have generally enjoyed prosperity, which has fostered social stability. Agricultural, industrial, and natural resource exports have helped finance rising living standards, while vast oil reserves have enriched western provinces. As a result, Canada has consistently ranked among the top five nations in the annual United Nations Human Development Index of quality of life. Unlike the more individualistic Americans, Canada, influenced by social democratic ideals, built a strong social safety net, including national health insurance. Canadians have generally been more liberal on social and economic issues than Americans, approving same-sex marriage, banning the death penalty, and, in some provinces, decriminalizing marijuana use. Organized religion has had a declining influence in public life. The secularizing trend has been especially notable in Quebec, where the Catholic Church once enjoyed great influence. Even openly homosexual politicians have gained popular support, and Quebec's birth rate, one of the world's highest in the 1940s, has fallen by over half to become one of the world's lowest.

Canadian society has become increasingly diverse by welcoming several million immigrants from all over the world, many from Asia and the Caribbean. In 2005 one of those immigrants, Haitian-born Michaelle Jean, a television journalist in Quebec, became Canada's first female governor general, the official head of state as the representative of the British monarch. Rather than following the American "melting pot" ideal, Canadian laws, especially the Multiculturalism Act of 1988, allow ethnic minorities to maintain their cultures and languages. But some Canadians, resenting the recognition of Portuguese-Canadians or Chinese-Canadians, prefer unhyphenated Canadians. Canadians have also recognized the rights of the Native Americans, known as the "First Nations," who have pressed land claims. To address the desire for autonomy of the Inuit, or Eskimo, people of the Arctic region, in 1999 the federal government transformed much of northern Canada into the self-governing territory of Nunavut **(NOO-nuh-voot)**. Canadians are still debating how much to think of themselves as English or French or Inuit Canadians and how much to live comfortably with multiple identities.

The Pacific Basin Societies

Australian Society

The diverse societies scattered around the Pacific Basin experienced major changes as they adjusted to a new world. In the two largest, most populous countries, Australia and New Zealand, the majority population, descended from European, mainly British and Irish, settlers, had long identified with western European society, building economies that closely resembled those of the industrial West. Australia became one of the world's most affluent nations, known to its people as the "lucky country" because of its abundant resources and high living standards. Thanks in part to a comprehensive system of social welfare, health care, and education, Australians forged a quality of life that usually places the nation near the top in the annual United Nations Human Development Reports. However, the nation has also faced a chronic high unemployment rate and areas of persisting poverty. In addition, feminists complain that men dominate government, business, and churches and that women are less influential than in most Western nations. Nonetheless, women's organizations have won considerable gender equity.

Australia's 22 million people are increasingly diverse. In 1973 the federal government, seeking better relations with Asian nations, abandoned restrictions on nonwhite immigration—known as the "white Australia" policy—that had been in place since 1901. The shift to a policy based on skills stimulated immigration from Asia and the Middle East; as a result, predominantly Asian neighborhoods developed in major cities. Newcomers from Europe also continued to arrive. For example, one of the major cities, Melbourne, boasted the world's largest Greek emigrant population. Eventually nearly a quarter of Australia's people were born abroad. Race relations also improved as Aborigines, often poor and facing discrimination, gained some self-determination and land rights for their tribal territories. As a result, one group was able to block a dam project in the 1990s that threatened tribal land. Yet, those Aborigines living in run-down city neighborhoods have struggled in the largely white-owned urban economy. Moreover, occasional attacks on Arab and Indian immigrants by drunken white youth showed that racism had not been eliminated.

Changing global conditions forced new economic thinking. With an economy based primarily on the export of minerals, wheat, beef, and wool, Australia needed secure outside markets. But the formation of the European Community and NAFTA threatened traditional markets in Europe and North America, raising questions about the nation's link to Britain. In a 1995 referendum, 55 percent of Australians supported remaining a constitutional monarchy under the British queen. Yet, Britain was far away, while Asia was, as Australians put it, the "near north." Australians therefore

Glenn Hunt/AAP

Lion Dance In recent decades, many Asians have settled in Australia. This Chinese lion's dance, in Melbourne's large Chinatown, celebrates the Chinese New Year.

established closer trade and investment links to Southeast Asia, East Asia, and the Pacific islands, so that, by 2000, Asian nations accounted for some 60 percent of Australia's export market.

New Zealand

New Zealanders had long cultivated their British heritage and British patronage, but they now had to forge strategic and economic connections within the Asia-Pacific region. The economy relied heavily on tourism and the export of agricultural products, mostly to Britain. Suffering from a stumbling economy and jolted by Britain's membership in the European Community, New Zealand cultivated close relations with the United States. However, these relations cooled after New Zealand refused to allow nuclear-armed U.S. ships to make visits to its ports. New Zealand then fostered economic cooperation with nearby Asian and Pacific countries, and by 2000 these countries accounted for one-third of the nation's trade. While experiencing rising unemployment, New Zealanders were supported by an elaborate social welfare system. Owing in part to expanded educational opportunities, women gained new economic roles and served in politics. In 1999 Helen Clark (b. 1950), a former university professor, became the nation's first female prime minister. Closer ties to the Pacific region also resulted in increased immigration from Asia and the Pacific islands. The government also recognized the land rights of, and worked to end discrimination against, the native Maori minority, who sought to maintain their Polynesian culture while adding modern economic skills.

The Pacific Islands

While Australians and New Zealanders had long enjoyed independence, the decolonization of the Pacific islands, spurred by the United Nations, had to wait until the 1960s. Between 1962 and 1980 nine independent Pacific nations were formed in Polynesia and Melanesia, and in 1990 the United States gave up control of some of its Micronesian territories. The new states ranged from republics such as Fiji to kingdoms like Tonga to groupings such as the Federated States of Micronesia. Not all Pacific islanders, however, became independent. Some French-ruled islands, such as Tahiti and New Caledonia, became semiautonomous French territories with representation in the French parliament, but many islanders resented what they considered a disguised French colonialism. Most independent islands retained close ties to their former colonizer, as Micronesia did with the United States. Pacific islanders usually remained dependent on fishing, tourism, and the export of mineral and agricultural products to Japan, the United States, Australia, and New Zealand.

Islanders cooperated on common issues. For example, they formed regional organizations to promote everything from duty-free trade to art festivals, and they fought high-technology fishing fleets from industrialized nations that threatened their own low-technology fishing. To oppose nuclear weapons testing, they joined with Australia and New Zealand to declare the Pacific a nuclear-free zone. The international Law of the Sea Treaty gave the islands more control of adjacent sea beds, and hence their minerals. However, some problems have defied solution. Thanks to rising sea levels, which threaten low-lying atolls and coastal plains, many islanders will have to relocate over the next century. The Tuvalo islands in the central Pacific, home to 11,000 people and on average only three feet above sea level, will be inundated by 2050.

The Pacific islanders have held on to some indigenous traditions while also adapting to social and political change. While most islanders have become Christian, some pre-Christian customs have remained important. For example, although Western Samoa, first ruled by Germany and then by New Zealand, has an elected parliament, adopted from the West, clan chiefs still govern the villages, as they have for centuries. But poverty has fostered migration to island cities, such as Suva in Fiji and Pago Pago in American Samoa, and emigration to Australia, New Zealand, Hawaii, and the mainland United States. More Samoans and Cook Islanders live abroad than at home, and thousands of Tongans reside in California. The money sent back by migrants has become a valuable source of income. Some islands have also experienced ethnic or regional conflict over political power and scarce land. Occasional military coups have rocked Fiji, resulting from ten-

SECTION SUMMARY

- On average, U.S. residents are among the wealthiest in the world, yet in recent decades many industrial jobs have been moved overseas and the gap between rich and poor has grown wider, with the former often living in suburbs and the latter left behind in inner cities.
- In the 1950s, political conservatism dominated the United States and a large number of children were born; in the 1960s, liberalism was prominent, especially among the rebellious youth; since the 1970s, conservatism has been generally dominant, though the country is sharply divided politically; and the 2008 election of Barack Obama launched a new era.
- After 1945 African Americans gained legal rights through the civil rights movement, immigrants made America more diverse, women increasingly entered the work force, and gays and lesbians became more visible but still struggled for equal rights.
- American culture became popular around the world, particularly music such as rock, which energized youth in the 1950s and 1960s, and rap, which initially expressed the radical political sentiments of African Americans but became watered down in the twenty-first century.
- While Canada's culture and economy are strongly influenced by the United States, in many ways Canada resembles western Europe, with a strong social safety net and a more liberal attitude on social issues.
- Australia and New Zealand have maintained their traditional ties with Britain but have also traded increasingly with their Asian neighbors, while many Pacific islands have gained independence from former colonizers but still face challenges such as rising sea levels, poverty, and ethnic conflict.

sions between the descendants of Indian immigrants, nearly half of the population, and the native Fijians, who fear that Indians want to diminish the role of traditional Fijian chiefs and challenge tribal rights to land.

Political Change in Latin America and the Caribbean

Why have democracy and economic development proved to be difficult goals in Latin America?

The Latin American and Caribbean peoples (see Map 29.3) had a different experience than North Americans and Pacific Basin societies. Social inequality, economic underdevelopment, and the demands for change often created a pressure cooker, generating revolutionary and progressive political movements in impoverished villages and shantytowns. Sometimes leftists gained power, launching reforms, though only in Cuba did they remain in power for decades. A few Latin American countries and most small Caribbean islands enjoyed a consistent democratic tradition; elsewhere, however, military leaders or autocratic civilians often dominated governments. Most governments, whether democratic or dictatorial, proved unable to eliminate their nation's major problems.

Despotisms, Democracies, and the United States

Latin American governments struggled to raise living standards and expand political participation. Some paternalistic but authoritarian reformers mobilized workers and peasants for change, but they also failed to empower the people or significantly improve their lives. The charismatic Juan Peron **(puh-RONE)** (1895–1974), a former army officer, admirer of Benito Mussolini, and hypnotic public speaker, who was elected Argentina's president in 1946, was a major autocratic reformer who marginalized the legislature and crushed opposition (see Chronology: Latin America and the Caribbean, 1945–Present). With help from his hugely popular wife, Evita Peron (1919–1952), a radio and stage actress from a poor family and a proponent of social justice, the nationalistic Peron's regime won the support of workers and the middle class by emphasizing industrialization and buying up banks, insurance companies, railroads, and shipping companies often owned by unpopular foreign interests. Evita promoted women's issues, including voting rights. After Evita's death in 1952, corruption, growing unemployment, inflation, strikes, and human rights abuses led to Peron's overthrow in 1955. Peron returned to power briefly in 1973–1974, but otherwise the military mostly ruled Argentina from the 1950s through 1983, often killing opponents. Yet Peron's followers sustained a Peronist movement with a working-class base that often governed the nation after the restoration of democracy.

Argentina

Rightwing and leftwing forces have jockeyed for power in Latin America. In the majority of countries from the 1950s through the late 1980s, rightwing military governments and despots ruled, suppressing labor unions, student protesters, and democracy activists to maintain stability. Some rightwing governments, especially in Central American countries such as El Salvador and Guatemala, organized death squads to assassinate dissident peasants, liberal clergy, teachers, and journalists deemed threats to the regime. Despite the repression, leftwing movements increased their strength. By 1979 the Sandinistas, a revolutionary movement led by Marxists, defeated the long-standing dictatorship and gained control of Nicaragua. In 1970 an even more radical movement, the Shining Path, emerged in Peru; its leaders, half of them women, mixed Maoist ideas with a call to emancipate the impoverished Indians. Their rebellion terrorized Peruvians and brought the country to its knees before finally being crushed in the early 1990s.

Left-Right Conflicts

During the later 1980s, with rightwing rule largely discredited by being unable or unwilling to address mass poverty, many nations turned to democracy and free markets under centrist or moderate leftist leaders. But in most cases they were unable to resolve the severe problems or diminish social equalities. Some nations also faced racial and ethnic tensions. The large Indian communities in Bolivia, Peru, Colombia, Mexico, and Guatemala, often allied with the left, increasingly sought equal rights, a fairer share of the wealth, and recognition of their cultures and aspirations. In 2005, for example, chronic resentment by Bolivia's Indian majority led to the election, as president, of Evo Morales (b. 1959), a former small-town soccer player of humble origins who had led a movement of coca farmers fighting a white-dominated government and U.S. opposition to coca growing. At the

Democratization

Map 29.3 Modern Latin America and the Caribbean
Latin America includes the nations of Central and South America and those Caribbean societies that are Spanish-speaking, including Cuba and the Dominican Republic. Brazil, Argentina, and Mexico are the largest Latin American nations. The peoples, mostly English or French speaking, of the small Caribbean islands also formed independent states.

e Interactive Map

ruins of an ancient temple, Morales took part in a spiritual ceremony steeped in the pre-Inca traditions of his Aymara people. Walking barefoot up the pyramid steps, he donned a traditional tunic and cap and accepted a gold and silver baton from Aymara priests, then promised to "seek equality and justice" for the poor and do away with the vestiges of the Spanish colonial past. However, his efforts to redistribute wealth and power from the white minority, reshape the political system, and pursue nationalistic economic policies generated conflict within Bolivia and U.S. opposition.

Leftist Resurgence

By the later 1990s, as disillusionment with capitalism increased, the left regained the political initiative, working largely within a democratic context. Mobilizing workers and peasants, who had benefited little from the country's oil wealth, the former general Hugo Chavez (b. 1954) was elected president of oil-rich Venezuela and introduced socialist policies that alienated the wealthy and middle class, who organized mass protests against his regime. However, poor Venezuelans supported his marginalization of the congress and control of the courts. Chavez called his policies the Bolivaran Revolution, linking them to the nineteenth-century, Venezuelan-born liberator. But the United States moved to isolate the dictatorial, pro-Cuba Chavez regime and support the opposition. Chavez lambasted U.S. president George W. Bush, provided aid and oil to other Latin Americans, and tightened his grip on politics and the media, but declining oil prices in 2009 threatened his foreign policies and domestic support. Elsewhere, voters desperate for more equitable policies also elected pragmatic leftist leaders in countries such as Argentina, Brazil, Chile, Ecuador, Uruguay, and El Salvador. These leaders often began the process of prosecuting the human rights violations perpetrated under military rule. But whether imported economic ideas from the left or the right will work for Latin Americans remained unclear.

CHRONOLOGY

Latin America and the Caribbean, 1945–Present

1946–1955 Government of Juan Peron in Argentina

1954 CIA overthrow of Guatemalan government

1959 Triumph of Fidel Castro in Cuba

1962 Cuban missile crisis

1964–1985 Military government in Brazil

1973 Overthrow of Chilean government

1973–1989 Military government in Chile

1979–1989 Sandinista government in Nicaragua

1983 Restoration of Argentina's democracy

1990 U.S. invasion of Panama

1994 Formation of NAFTA

1998 Economic collapse in many nations

2000 Election of President Vicente Fox in Mexico

2002 Election of President Lula da Silva in Brazil

Latin Americans also had to deal with the United States, which has had a powerful presence in that area. Referring to longtime U.S. economic leverage, a leftist Nicaraguan leader lamented that his country's "function was to grow sugar, cocoa and coffee for the United States; we served the dessert at the imperialist dining table."[13] The United States served not only as the neighborhood bully at times but also as a leading trading partner, a major source of investment capital, a supplier of military and economic assistance, and an inspiration to the region's democrats and free market enthusiasts. Some Latin American leaders supported U.S. foreign policies, and U.S. popular culture, particularly films and music, reached a huge audience, influencing local cultures. Moreover, millions of people seeking a better life have moved to the United States legally or illegally. In 1999 the United States gained favor by transferring control over the Panama Canal to Panama, yet U.S. military bases remained along the canal, a symbol of U.S. regional power.

Under the banner of anticommunism, the United States often intervened in Latin American and Caribbean countries, arousing much local resentment. For example, in 1954 a force led by exiled Guatemalan military officers, covertly organized, armed, and trained by the U.S. Central Intelligence Agency (CIA), overthrew a democratically elected reformist government, led chiefly by liberals and socialists, that American leaders accused of being communist. The government angered U.S. business interests by implementing land reform and encouraging leftist labor unions. The powerful United Fruit Company controlled much of the Guatemalan economy, especially the banana plantations, and had close ties to officials in the Eisenhower administration. The removal of the democratic regime cheered wealthy Guatemalans and U.S. corporations, but the new Guatemalan leaders formed death squads that killed over 200,000 Guatemalans, especially poor Indian peasants and workers, over the next three decades. By 1990, when the repression diminished, 90 percent of Guatemalans still lived in poverty, and one-third of them lacked adequate food.

United States and Latin America

The successful ousting of the Guatemalan government encouraged U.S. leaders to use their power elsewhere, offering military assistance and advice to friendly governments against the challenge of revolutionary movements in El Salvador, Honduras, and Colombia. The United States also used covert operations to undermine or overthrow governments deemed too left-leaning in Brazil (1964), Chile (1973), and Nicaragua (1989). The American public was often unaware of the covert activities until years later. Sometimes the United States sent in military force, as in the Dominican Republic (1965) and Grenada (1982). Not all interventions were inspired by anticommunism. In 1990 U.S. troops invaded Panama to remove and arrest the dictator Manuel Noriega (b. 1940), a longtime U.S. ally and well-paid CIA informant who was also implicated in human rights abuses and smuggling narcotics into the United States. Then in 1994 U.S. troops were sent to Haiti to support a reform government that had replaced a brutal dictatorship. U.S. troops remained in Haiti promoting stability as leftwing and rightwing forces intermittently battled for control, leaving Haitians poorer and more desperate.

The Legacy of Revolution: Mexico and Cuba

Mexico

The Mexican Revolution in the early twentieth century inspired hopes of reducing social inequality, but the nation's leaders soon turned to emphasizing economic growth over uplifting the poor majority. Even today, in southern states where revolutionaries once promised to bring liberty and justice, peasant men, wearing traditional white cotton pants and shirt, still use a machete to cultivate their tiny plots of corn. Although Mexico's limited democracy offered regular elections, one party, the Party of Revolutionary Institutions (PRI), controlled the elections, often resorting to voter fraud. A coalition of factions ranging from left to right and led by businessmen and bureaucrats, the PRI fostered stability for decades while deflecting challenges to its power monopoly. Although it usually co-opted or arrested opponents, in 1968 it ordered police to open fire on a large demonstration, killing hundreds of university students and other protesters.

By the 1980s the PRI began to falter as leftist and rightwing parties, which struggled to overcome the PRI's vast power and wealth, made some national gains. In the early 1990s a peasant revolt in a poor southern state, Chiapas, revealed starkly the PRI's failure to redress rural poverty, and in 2000 the election of a non-PRI president, Vicente Fox, a pro-U.S. rancher and free market conservative, ended the seven-decades-long PRI monopoly on federal power. However, Fox proved unable to foster much economic or social change, while the PRI still held power in many states and enjoyed a national power base. Gradually a more open and pluralistic political system emerged, with stronger leftist and rightwing parties contending with the PRI for support. In 2008 elections another conservative edged out a leftist for the presidency, solidifying a multiparty system.

Mexico's economic system also gradually opened, but without diminishing poverty. For decades the PRI had mixed capitalism with a strong government role. However, the collapse of world oil prices in the 1980s damaged development prospects, since oil was the major foreign revenue source, and led to replacing protectionist policies with open markets. In 1994, after the North American Free Trade Agreement (NAFTA) helped integrate the U.S. and Mexican economies, many U.S.-owned factories opened on the Mexican side of the border. The majority of the new workers were poorly paid young women, usually housed in crowded dormitories or flimsy shacks, who often complained of harassment or assault by male workers or managers. Elsewhere Mexicans have lost jobs; peasant corn farmers were unable to compete with highly subsidized U.S. farmers. By 2000 half of the 100 million Mexicans lived on $4 a day or less, and the bottom 20 percent of Mexicans earned only 3.5 percent of the country's personal income. Even the urban middle class has felt the economic pain as wages stagnate. Whereas in 1980 Mexico's economy was nearly four times larger than South Korea's, by 2005 a dynamic South Korea had pushed ahead. At the same time, Mexico's population quadrupled between 1940 and 2000. Because of poverty and overpopulation, thousands of desperate Mexicans continue to cross the border to the United States each year, legally or illegally, in search of a better life. Others have taken up growing or smuggling illegal drugs, and bloody wars between rival drug cartels have made life dangerous in many districts.

Castro and Cuba

In contrast to Mexico, Cuba, led by Fidel Castro (b. 1927), built a society dominated by a powerful communist government. Castro, a onetime amateur baseball star who was nearly signed by a U.S. professional team but instead became a lawyer, came to power in 1959, the victor of a revolution against a corrupt U.S.-supported dictator. Although the son of a rich sugar planter, Castro allied with the Cuban Communist Party and promised to introduce radical change, prompting many thousands of affluent Cubans to flee to the nearby United States. In 1961 the United States moved to isolate and then overthrow his regime by organizing a military force of Cuban exiles that landed on a Cuban beach known as the Bay of Pigs. But the invasion, poorly planned and enjoying little popular support in Cuba, was routed—a humiliation for the United States. Castro became a firm Soviet ally, igniting even more U.S. opposition and soon precipitating the Cuban missile crisis. In 1962 U.S. air surveillance of Cuba discovered Soviet ballistic missiles with a 2,000-mile range and capable of carrying nuclear warheads. The United States demanded that the missiles be removed, imposed a naval blockade on Cuba, and considered invading the island. With the threat of nuclear confrontation looming, however, the Soviets backed down and removed the missiles, defusing the crisis. In the aftermath, the United States imposed an economic boycott, strongly supported by Cuban exiles, that endured into the twenty-first century, cutting off Cuba from sources of trade and investment.

e **Primary Source: Free Trade and the Decline of Democracy** Read a cogent critique by Ralph Nader, a consumer advocate and political activist, of international free trade agreements.

In the 1960s and 1970s Castro tried innovative socialist policies, often known as **Castroism**, to stimulate economic development while also tightly controlling its population. Castro called capitalism "repugnant, filthy, gross, alienating because it causes war, hypocrisy and competition"[14]; yet his own policies generated little surplus food and few consumer goods. Despite valiant efforts, Cubans also largely failed to diversify their sugar-based economy. Nonetheless, Castroism improved the life of the working classes by building schools and clinics, mounting literacy campaigns, and promoting equality for long-marginalized Afro-Cubans and women. By the mid-1980s Cuba had the lowest infant mortality and highest literacy rates and life expectancy in Latin America, with its citizens living as long as North Americans and ten years longer than Mexicans and Brazilians. Cuba also had nearly as many doctors per population as the United States. Moreover, in contrast to some Latin American dictatorships, the Cuban government did not form death squads

Castroism Innovative socialist policies introduced by Fidel Castro to stimulate economic development in Cuba while tightly controlling its population.

Corbis

Castro Addressing Crowd A spellbinding orator, the Cuban leader, Fidel Castro, often recruited support for his government and policies by speaking at large rallies.

or murder dissidents. However, government agencies monitored citizens and their opinions, and Castro placed limits on free expression, jailing or harassing those who defied the ban, including brave writers, homosexuals, and human rights and free speech advocates. Seeking political freedom, better-paying jobs, or higher living standards, several hundred thousand Cubans have fled over the years to the United States.

Castro exchanged dependence on the United States for dependence on the USSR, which poured billions of dollars of aid into the country. With the collapse of the USSR, however, Castro lost his patron, and since then Cuba has struggled. With the country having few markets or sources of capital, the social welfare system cracked, and the economy crumbled despite introducing some market forces. Yet, frustrating his opponents, Castro remained in power for fifty years. However, in 2008 an ailing Castro turned over leadership to his brother Raul Castro (b. 1931), who offered some cautious reforms, including leasing some state-owned land to private farmers, and hinted at more flexibility in domestic and foreign affairs. Critics of U.S. policy, including most U.S. allies, have opposed the embargo, arguing that it helps Castro by reinforcing anti-U.S. feelings and discrediting dissidents. In 2009 new U.S. President Barack Obama made it easier for U.S.-based Cubans to visit the island. Remembering American domination from 1898 to 1959, many Cubans, while desiring a freer system, remain wary of the United States.

Dictatorship and Democracy: Brazil and Chile

Brazilian Dictatorship

Few Latin American nations have had as much promise and experienced as many problems as Brazil and Chile. Occupying half of the South American continent and with a population of nearly 200 million, Brazil is Latin America's colossus, with its largest economy. From the mid-1940s to the mid-1960s the nation, despite economic crises, maintained a democratic government. In 1961 Joao Goulart **(jao joo-LART)** (1918–1976), a populist reformer supported by leftists, assumed the presidency, but the economy stumbled, and efforts to organize the impoverished peasants and rural workers antagonized powerful landlords. Seeking to impose order, the military overthrew Goulart in 1964 and ruled for the next two decades under a harsh dictatorship, which arrested some 40,000 opponents. Fearing a communist takeover, the United States had encouraged the military coup, while Brazilian industrialists, businessmen, planters, and affluent urbanites welcomed the change. Between 1964 and 1985 U.S.-supported authoritarian governments gave priority to economic growth and national security. Relying on brutal repression, they imposed censorship, outlawed political parties, and banned strikes and collective bargaining. Rightwing vigilante groups and death squads killed up to 100 dissidents a month and tortured countless others, among them labor leaders and slum dwellers.

The generals imposed a capitalist economic model recommended by American advisers. For a decade the economy boomed, eliciting American praise of the "Brazilian miracle" as annual growth rates averaged 10 percent between 1968 and 1974 and exports soared. The policies promoted a major shift in exports from natural resources, such as coffee, to manufactured goods, and the industrialization relied heavily on foreign investment, technology, and markets. The United States and international lending agencies also poured in $8 billion in aid. But the "miracle" depended on low wages and redistributing income upward to the rich and middle class, confirming the local saying that there is no justice for the poor. The top 10 percent of people enjoyed 75 percent of the income gain, while half of all households lived below the poverty line. While many people went barefoot and dressed in rags, Brazil made and exported shoes. Brazilian governments also encouraged land speculators and foreign corporations to open up the vast Amazon basin, the world's largest tropical rain forest and river system. The virgin forest was rapidly stripped for logging, farming, mining, and ranching, displacing many of the 200,000 Indians who lived off its resources and destabilizing the local environment.

Brazilian Democracy

By 1980 the "miracle" was fading as Brazil experienced an inflation rate of over 100 percent, a huge balance of payments deficit, a massive foreign debt, and sagging industrial production. Meanwhile, numerous Brazilians demanded democracy, and the Catholic Church criticized human rights violations and advocated for social justice. In 1985 democracy returned with the election of a civilian president. However, under the successive democratic governments led by moderate reformers, many problems remained unresolved, since leaders feared another military coup. Inflation soared to 2,500 percent by 1994. When landless peasants seized land, well-connected landowners hired gunmen to harass them. In addition, social inequities such as school dropout rates, malnutrition, bankrupt public health services, homelessness, and debt slavery grew. Brazil maintained one of the world's most unequal income distributions: the wealthiest 1 percent of people earned the same percentage of national income as the poorest 50 percent. As a result, many Brazilians became disillusioned with democracy.

Although the economy revived in the later 1990s, Brazilians, wanting further reform, turned to the political left. In 2002 they gave leftist candidates 80 percent of the vote and elected as president socialist labor leader Luis Ignacio da Silva (b. 1944), known as Lula, a former metalworker and longtime dissident. While Lula has fostered dramatic economic growth, and some observers compare Brazil to dynamic Southeast Asian nations such as Malaysia, Singapore, and Thailand, peasant and worker groups believe that Lula's moderate economic policies go too far in pleasing financial interests and international lenders, and that he has done too little for the poor and the environment. Yet, the booming economy, growing manufacturing, and discovery of offshore oil have given Brazil regional and international clout and restored national self-confidence. Brazil became a major player in the G-20 group of key industrial nations. Brazilians have often shared an optimistic outlook because of the nation's size and economic potential, reflected in the saying that "God is a Brazilian." But a perennial local joke reflects cynicism: "Brazil, Country of the Future, but the future never comes."[15]

Reform in Chile

Chileans, like Brazilians, tried a succession of strategies, from reform to dictatorship to democracy, to foster development. Chileans had enjoyed a long tradition, unusual in Latin America, of elected democratic governments sustained by a large middle class, high rates of literacy and urbanization, and multiple political parties. Nonetheless, a wealthy elite of businessmen, military officers, and landowners held political power and suppressed labor unrest. Chile depended on the export of minerals, especially copper. By the 1960s it was divided politically between the right, center, and left and had a stagnant economy, with two-thirds of Chileans earning under $200 a year. Chile shifted direction with the 1970 elections. Six liberal, socialist, and communist parties united in a coalition, the Popular Unity, supported by small businessmen, the urban working class, and peasants. Their winning presidential candidate, Salvador Allende **(ah-YEN-dee)** (1908–1973), promised a "Chilean road" to socialism, with red wine and meat pies, through constitutional means in a parliamentary democracy. His regime took over banks and a copper industry that had been dominated by powerful U.S. corporations, while land reform broke up underutilized ranches and divided the land among the peasant residents. Allende's government supported the labor unions and provided the urban shantytowns with health clinics and better schools. Both employment and economic production soared. The Popular Unity also fostered a Chilean cultural renaissance, arguing that American magazines, recordings, and films had overwhelmed Chilean-produced cultural products. A pro-Allende cultural organization protested that "Our folklore, our history, our customs, our way of living and thinking are being strangled [by] the uncontrolled invasion [of the U.S. media and popular culture]."[16]

Although democracy flourished and Allende enjoyed growing popularity, rapid reforms produced shortages of luxury goods, fostering middle-class resentment. Moreover, Allende's opponents controlled the mass media and judiciary and dominated the congress. The U.S. president, Richard Nixon, worried about Allende's friendship with Cuba's Fidel Castro and feared that Allende's socialism without revolution could spread, threatening U.S. power and economic interests. The United

States therefore mounted an international economic embargo on Chilean exports, while the CIA spread untrue rumors, helped assassinate pro-Allende military officers, and organized strikes to paralyze the economy.

Rise and Fall of Chilean Military Rule

In 1973 a U.S.-supported military coup overthrew Allende, who died while defending the presidential palace. The military imposed a brutal military dictatorship, led by General Agusto Pinochet **(ah-GOOS-toh pin-oh-CHET)** (b. 1915), that arrested some 150,000 Allende supporters and detained and tortured hundreds of political prisoners for years. The regime murdered thousands of dissidents, sometimes in front of other prisoners held in the national stadium. Thousands of Chileans fled the country. The junta forbade labor unions and strikes, prohibited free speech and political parties, restored nationalized U.S. property, and publicly burned books and records produced by leftist Chileans. Advised by U.S. economists, Pinochet shifted to a free enterprise economy, similar to military-ruled Brazil's, that generated growth and moderate middle-class prosperity purchased at the cost of a monumental foreign debt and environmental degradation. But little of this wealth trickled down to the poor, whose living standards deteriorated. By the later 1980s, unemployment had skyrocketed to 30 percent, and some 60 percent of people were poor. Two observers wrote that Pinochet's Chile "remained a dual society of winners and losers. The rich, roaring through traffic in their expensive sedans, seemed to mock those left behind, trapped in fuming buses."[17]

However, a severe economic crisis undermined the regime's legitimacy, and in 1989 escalating social tensions and political protests prompted the junta to hold an election. The resulting center-left governments, often headed by presidents from Allende's Socialist Party, retained free enterprise while boosting health, housing, education, and social spending. The poverty sector has been reduced by half, unemployment has plummeted, and tax increases and increased welfare have not stifled the annual economic growth of about 10 percent. Chile has become the most prosperous Latin American economy, enjoying a stable democratic system. While leaders have sought closer economic ties with the United States, many Chileans remain bitter toward the Americans for having helped perpetuate a brutal military regime.

SECTION SUMMARY

- In Latin America, rightwing and leftwing movements competed for power; rightwing movements were dominant from the 1950s through the 1980s, and moderates and leftists such as Venezuela's Hugo Chavez gained more power in the 1990s.
- Many Latin Americans resented U.S. interference in their economies and support for the overthrow of leftist governments, while others welcomed the U.S. example of democracy and free trade.
- The Mexican Revolution led to decades of single-party rule that failed to significantly help the poor, and a reformist president elected in 2000 also failed to improve their lot. Many Mexicans crossed the U.S. border in search of a better life.
- Under Castro, communist Cuba has attempted to control its people but has also provided excellent medical care and education; however, the withdrawal of aid from the USSR in 1991 and the U.S. embargo have left its economy struggling.
- Under a brutal U.S.-supported military dictatorship, Brazil enjoyed a period of impressive growth but then experienced extreme inflation and increasing gaps between rich and poor; democracy returned in the mid-1980s, and the economy recovered in the late 1990s.
- Alarmed by the popularity of a democratically elected leftist government in Chile, the United States supported a 1973 coup there as well as the brutal military dictatorship that resulted, which rewarded the wealthy and further impoverished the poor, and which was replaced by a democratic government in 1989.

Changing Latin American and Caribbean Societies

How have Latin American and Caribbean cultures been dynamic?

The societies of Latin America and the Caribbean, while facing daunting economic problems, have had social and cultural patterns different from those of North America and the Pacific Basin. Most have still emphasized export of traditional natural resources such as oil, sugar, coffee, bananas, wool, and copper. The Spanish-speaking nations, Portuguese-speaking Brazil, and the English-, Dutch-, and French-speaking Caribbean societies, being derived from varied mixes

U.S. Factory in Mexico Since the 1980s growing numbers of U.S. companies have relocated industrial operations to Mexico, building many factories along the Rio Grande River that separates Mexico from Texas. In this factory, in Matamoros, Mexico, the mostly female labor force makes toys for the U.S. market.

of peoples and traditions, often have little in common with each other but have fostered dynamic cultural forms that have gained international popularity.

Latin American Economies

Although often enjoying economic growth, no Latin American nations have achieved the affluence common in the industrialized West or eastern Asia. Latin Americans forged rising literacy rates and lowered infant mortality rates, and more people now own televisions, even in poor neighborhoods. Nonetheless, the world prices for most of their natural resource exports have declined over the years, leaving less money for development. As a result, most countries have experienced at best modest growth in per capita income and productivity. To pay the bills and import luxury items, governments have taken out loans, eventually owing billions to international lenders. Rapidly expanding populations, growing at 3 percent a year, add to the social burden and cause environmental problems. Governments have tried to satisfy land hunger, mineral prospecting, and timber exploitation by treating the rain forests as expendable resources.

Income Inequality

Latin America has also suffered severe income inequality. By 2000 the top 10 percent of the population earned half of all income, and 70 percent of the people lived in poverty. Often evading taxes, the small elite class drive Rolls Royces, while the poor lack bus service. In Brazil half of the people had no access to doctors in 2000, even while Rio de Janeiro became the world's plastic surgery capital, with hundreds of cosmetic surgeons catering to wealthy Brazilians and foreigners. In Caracas, Venezuela's capital, one shopping mall that serves the affluent boasts 450 stores, an amusement park, two movie theaters, and a McDonald's. But any customers coming from a slum of open sewers and tin shacks, perched a few miles away on unstable hillsides, would have to pay half a day's wage for a Big Mac. Such inequality fuels support for leftists like Hugo Chavez. To survive, poor peasants in some nations, especially after a decline of world coffee prices, have turned to growing coca and opium for making cocaine and heroin. But the drug trade, largely to the U.S. market, fosters political turbulence and government corruption and profits only a few drug kingpins. In recent years, violence between rival drug cartels has killed many people, and made life dangerous, in Colombia and Mexico.

Rural Economy

Agriculture has remained an economic mainstay, but landholding remains concentrated in a small group of aristocratic families and multinational corporations, such as the U.S.-based United Fruit Company. By the 1990s, 60 percent of all agricultural land was held in large estates and farmed inefficiently, contributing to food shortages. Although modern agriculture requires large investments for machinery, fertilizers, pesticides, and fuel, growing beans and corn to feed hungry peasants supplies inadequate revenue. Hence, vast tracts of rain forests and farms have been transformed into ranches that often raise beef cattle for fast-food outlets in North America and Europe. Latin America remains a food importer, mostly from North America, and malnutrition causes half of all child deaths. In Peru's major city, Lima, hundreds of poor children, known as "fruit birds," desperately compete with stray dogs for spoiled fruit. In Mexico, beef cattle consume more food than the poorest quarter of people.

Rural life has often been marked by hardship. A Brazilian novel captured the hopelessness in the drought-tortured northeast, where, in the 1980s, life expectancy was thirty years, and only two-thirds of children attended school. The herder Fabiano understands that everything prevents his escape from endless poverty: "If he could only put something aside for a few months, he would be able to get his head up. Oh, he had made plans, but that was all foolishness. Ground creepers were never meant to climb. Once the beans had been eaten and the ears of corn gnawed, there was no place to go but to the boss's cash drawer [for a loan]."[18] Unemployment and unprofitable farms generated migration to cities, so that by 2000 Latin America had become the world's most urbanized region, with 75 percent of people living in cities and towns. Living in festering shantytowns, migrants work as shoe-shine boys, cigarette vendors, car washers, or in other poorly paid work. Half the urban population lacks adequate water, housing, sanitation, and social services. But economic growth has also fostered growing middle classes, now a third of the population in Argentina, Chile, and Uruguay and a fifth in Brazil and Mexico.

Beginning in the 1980s many Latin American nations adopted **neoliberalism**, an economic model, encouraged by the United States, that promoted free markets, privatization, and Western investment. Neoliberalism generated growth for a decade, but more people than ever remained stuck in poverty because it failed to curb government corruption, install honest judicial systems, foster labor-intensive industries, or reduce the power of rich elites or the dependence on foreign loans and investment. Free markets have often meant that a few people enjoyed fabulous wealth while most people remained poor. The nation that most ardently adopted neoliberalism, Argentina, saw its economy collapse in 1998; unemployment soared, and by 2001 half of the people lived in poverty. The economy only revived after Argentineans elected pragmatic Peronist leftists into power in 2003. The economy grew by 9 percent a year, and in 2006 the nation paid back the money still owed to the International Monetary Fund, a symbol of recovery as well as of a turn to a more state-oriented economy. However, in 2008 Argentine economic growth dwindled and the Peronists lost some support. But although neoliberalism lost credibility, no other economic model, such as Cuban communism or Allende's socialism with democracy, had widespread support or a record of success in Latin America.

neoliberalism An economic model encouraged by the United States in the developing world that promoted free markets, privatization, and Western investment.

Latin American Societies and Religions

Gender Relations

Political and economic change has reshaped gender relations and family life. Although men dominate governments, militaries, businesses, and the Catholic Church, women's movements have reduced gender inequality. Once considered helpless and groomed as girls to be a wife and mother, many women now go out to paid work, some in male-dominated trades. Millions of women earn money selling clothing, handicrafts, and food in small markets or from street stalls. Factories relocating from North America prefer young women, who accept lower wages and have been raised to obey. Family life has also undergone strains. By the 1990s far fewer people married, especially among the poor. But divorce, banned by the Catholic Church, has remained difficult or impossible in some nations, and men still enjoy a double standard in sexual behavior: men's extramarital affairs are tolerated while women's are condemned. Although abortion is illegal everywhere in the region, Latin America has one of the world's highest abortion rates. Homosexuality remains illegal and often punished in many nations, including Castro's Cuba, although Brazil and Costa Rica have fostered more tolerant climates, and liberal Mexico City legalized homosexual marriage in 2009.

Women have become more active in politics. Between 1945 and 1961 women gained the right to vote, and in 1974 Isabel Peron (b. 1931) of Argentina, a former dancer who married Juan Peron after Evita's death, succeeded her late husband to become the region's first woman president; however, she was ousted in a military coup in 1976. In 1990 Violeta Chamorro (vee-oh-LET-ah cha-MORroe) (g. 1990-1996), a newspaper publisher, was elected president of Nicaragua, serving until 1996. Then in 2006 Chileans elected as president the pediatrician turned socialist politician Michelle Bachelet (BAH-she-let), a divorced mother of three and avowed agnostic whose father was murdered while she and her mother were jailed and tortured during the Pinochet years. Bachelet struck a blow for gender equity by filling half of her cabinet positions with women, including the key defense and economy ministries. Yet, men have often resented women's empowerment, and dictatorships have singled out women activists, such as Bachelet's mother, for torture. During military rule in Argentina, Brazil, and Chile, women political prisoners were kept naked and often raped. However, women have made gains in several areas. In Mexico, the feminist movement challenged inequitable laws and social practices, and in 1974 the Mexican legislature passed a law guaranteeing women equal rights for jobs, salaries, and legal standing. Meanwhile, in Argentina, Brazil, and Uruguay, liberal women's groups made loosening the antiabortion laws a top priority and gained more public support for their cause.

Religion

liberation theology A Latin American movement that developed in the 1960s to make Catholicism more relevant to contemporary society and to address the plight of the poor.

The religious landscape of Latin America has become increasingly diverse. In the 1960s progressive Latin American Roman Catholics developed **liberation theology**, a movement to make the church more relevant to contemporary society and address the plight of the poor. Until the Vatican prohibited the movement in the 1980s, priests favoring liberation theology, especially in Brazil, cooperated with Marxist and liberal groups in working for social justice. Meanwhile, the Roman Catholic hierarchy generally remained conservative. While fewer Catholics attended church, the popular Catholicism of fiestas, pilgrimages, and the family altar flourished. Protestantism, chiefly evangelical or pentecostal, grew rapidly with increased missionary efforts, attracting converts with its participatory, emotional services. By the 1990s Protestants numbered nearly 20 percent of the population in Guatemala and 8 percent in Brazil and Chile. But their active evangelization caused resentment among Catholic leaders.

Social Change and Popular Culture

Brazil has reflected both the region's social changes and its continuities. Between 1920 and 1980 Brazil's urban population grew from about a quarter to three-fifths of Brazilians. Migrants jammed into shantytowns, such as the notorious hillside shacks of Rio de Janeiro, and poverty remained pervasive. By the 1980s three-fourths of Brazilians were malnourished, a third of adults had tuberculosis, a quarter of the population suffered from parasitic diseases, and millions of abandoned or runaway children wandered city streets, living by their wits. Yet, the shantytowns were also well organized, led by community activists and filled with hard-working residents seeking a better future for their children.

Although Brazilians have increasingly tolerated racial and cultural diversity, race remains a central social category. Like the United States, Brazil has never become a true racial "melting pot." Afro-Brazilians often condemn what they view as a racist society steeped in prejudice. Race has often correlated with social status: whites dominate the top brackets, blacks the bottom, and mixed-descent Brazilians fall in between. The flexible Brazilian concept of race, however, differs from the biological concept that North Americans have. Dark-skinned people can aspire to social mobility by earning a good income, since, as a popular local saying claimed, "money lightens." Furthermore, Afro-Brazilian culture has increasingly influenced whites. Over a third of Brazilians, often devout Catholics, have adopted or been interested in one of the Afro-Brazilian faiths that link West African gods or other African traditions with Roman Catholic saints and ceremonies.

The mass media and professional sports have become popular entertainments and diversion from social problems. Immensely popular local television soap operas dominate prime time television viewing, with those from Brazil and Mexico enjoying the widest popularity and gaining a large market around the world. European football, or soccer, has been hugely popular, uniting people of all social backgrounds. From the late 1950s to late 1970s the storied career, fluid play, and magnetic personality of Brazilian superstar Pele (b. 1940), from a poor Afro-Brazilian family, did much to spread the popularity of soccer in the world. Brazilians are especially proud of the international success of their national team, which won the World Cup championships five times between 1958 and 2002 by employing a creative, teamwork-oriented strategy, known as "samba football." A playwright noted how Brazilians obsessively suspend their daily lives during the World Cup, held every four years: "The nation pauses, all of it. Robbers don't rob, ghosts don't haunt, no crimes, no embezzlements, no deaths, no adulteries."[19]

Latin American and Caribbean Cultures

Latin American Literature

Creative Latin American and Caribbean cultural forms have reached a global audience. Latin American literature flourished, with writers often describing social conditions and government failures. The popular Brazilian novelist Jorge Amado (HOR-hay ah-MAH-do) (1912–2001) blended fantasy, realism, and political commitment, providing insight into life in Brazil's impoverished northeast. Former journalist Gabriel García Márquez (MAHR-kez) (b. 1928), a Nobel Prize–winning Colombian novelist, developed an international audience for imaginative books full of "magic realism," the representation of possible events as if they were wonders and impossible events as commonplace. His most famous work, *One Hundred Years of Solitude* (1970), charts the history of a Colombian house, the family who live in it, and the town where it was located, through wars, changing politics, and economic crises. Some writers tested the tolerance of governments. In Chile, the greatest epic poem of the leftist writer and former diplomat Pablo

Neruda (neh-ROO-da) (1904–1973), *General Song,* published in 1950, portrays the history of the entire hemisphere, showing an innocent pre-Columbian America cruelly awakened by Spanish conquest. The poem romanticizes the Incas, extolls the liberators who ended Spanish rule, castigates foreign capitalists (often from the United States) as exploiters, and identifies an emerging mass struggle to establish government by and for the people rather than the rich. In 1971 Neruda won the Nobel Prize for literature, cheering his admirers and distressing those who considered his radical views a threat to society.

Latin American Cinema and Music

Other art forms also developed a social consciousness. The Brazilian New Cinema movement, launched in 1955, tried to replace Hollywood films with films reflecting Brazilian life. One of the movement's finest films, *Black Orpheus* (1959), which gained an international audience, employed a soundtrack of local popular music to examine the annual pre-Lenten Carnival in Rio de Janeiro's shantytowns and the extremes of wealth and poverty revealed in the different ways rich and poor celebrated Carnival. A musical style known as **New Song**, based chiefly on local folk music and closely tied to progressive politics and protest, gained popularity in a half-dozen countries in the 1960s and 1970s, becoming especially influential in Chile. Seeking an alternative to the Anglo-American popular culture favored by elite Chileans, Chilean musicians have used indigenous Andean instruments and tunes. For example, Chilean New Song pioneers such as Violeta Parra (1918–1967) and Victor Jara (HAR-a) (1932-1973) wrote or collected songs that addressed problems of Chilean society such as poverty and inequality (see Profile: Violeta Parra, Chilean New Song Pioneer). Jara put his goal of using music to promote his political goals in song: "I don't sing for the love of singing, Or to show off my voice, But for the statements, Made by my honest guitar."[20]

New Song A Latin American musical movement based chiefly on local folk music and closely tied to progressive politics and protest; became popular in the 1960s and 1970s, especially in Chile.

Because of its leftwing connections, New Song was vulnerable to changing political conditions. In 1970 Chilean New Song musicians had joined the electoral campaign of the leftist Popular Unity coalition. After Salvador Allende won the presidency, he encouraged the media to pay more attention to New Song and less to popular music from the United States. New Song musicians promoted the new government's programs, such as land reform, and some toured abroad to foster foreign support for Allende's government. In 1973, the Chilean military seized power and arrested, executed, or deported most of the New Song musicians while making it illegal to play or listen to New Song. Before thousands of other detainees held in the national stadium, soldiers publicly cut off Victor Jara's fingers, which he had used to play his guitar, and then executed him, symbolizing the death of free expression in Chile and the government's fear of the power of popular culture. New Song faded as a popular music in Latin America, replaced by local forms of rock and by distinctive dance-oriented hybrid musics such as *salsa* (originally from Cuba and Puerto Rico) and *meringue* from Colombia, both of which feature more of a big band sound.

Caribbean Culture

With diverse populations of blacks, whites, and Asians, the Caribbean islands also offered an environment for creative cultural development, especially in religion and music. Jamaica proved particularly fertile soil. **Rastafarianism**, a religion mixing Christian, African, and local influences, arose in Jamaica in 1930 and attracted the urban and rural poor by preaching a return of black people to Africa. The believers revered the emperor Ras Tafari of Ethiopia, the sole uncolonized African state in 1930. Its followers, known as Rastas, adopted distinctive practices, including smoking ganja, an illegal drug, and sporting dreadlocked hair, that outraged Jamaica's elite. The return to Africa became more a spiritual than a physical quest and was mixed with black nationalism. Rastafarianism became identified as a movement of the black poor, seeking to redistribute wealth.

Rastafarianism A religion from Jamaica that arose in 1930 and that mixed Christian, African, and local influences; Rastafarianism attracted urban slum dwellers and the rural poor by preaching a return of black people to Africa.

The most influential popular music to come out of the Caribbean had similar mixed origins. In the 1960s Jamaican musicians created **reggae**, a style blending North American rhythm and blues with Afro-Jamaican traditions and marked by a distinctive beat maintained by the bass guitar. The songs of reggae musicians, many of them Rastas, promoted social justice, economic equality, and the freedom of Rastas to live as they liked. The international popularity of reggae owed much to Bob Marley (1945–1981), a Rasta, and his group, the Wailers. Marley became the first international superstar from a developing nation (see Chapter 26). His perceptions were shaped by the status of blacks in Jamaica and the wider world and the degrading conditions of the nonwhite poor. His explosive performances and provocative lyrics offered clear messages: "Slave driver, the table is turned; Catch a fire, you gonna get burned."[21] Like New Song musicians in Chile, Marley and other reggae musicians became involved in politics. Many musicians supported socialist Michael Manley (1924–1997), whose antibusiness policies as prime minister (1972–1978) prompted crippling U.S. sanctions that caused the Jamaican people hardship. After Marley's death from cancer in 1981, many reggae musicians watered down their message. Raunchy party music soon dominated the Caribbean music scenes, but reggae was mixed with rock, rap, and Latin musics to create *reggaeton*, a hugely popular Spanish-language music around Latin America and among Hispanics in the United States.

reggae A popular music style that began in the 1960s and that blended North American rhythm and blues with Afro-Jamaican traditions; reggae is marked by a distinctive beat maintained by the bass guitar.

VIOLETA PARRA, CHILEAN NEW SONG PIONEER

Born in 1918 to a poor school-teaching family, Violeta Parra was the key figure in the early development of New Song, a Chilean music based chiefly on local folk music, and a multitalented artist in many mediums, including poetry, filmmaking, tapestry, and painting. Despite her lower-middle-class background, the unconventional Parra lived and dressed like a peasant, wearing her hair long and almost uncombed. Restless and unsuited for marriage, she struggled to find the best outlet for her talents while supporting herself and her two children, Isabel and Angel **(AHN-hell)**. After working as a commercial entertainer, she began collecting, writing, and singing folk music in the 1940s and eventually collected over 3,000 songs. She had clear musical goals: "Every artist must aspire to unite his/her work in a direct contact with the public. I am content to work with the people close to me, whom I can feel, touch, talk and incorporate into my soul." Yet, unlike her protégés, such as Victor Jara, who was deeply engaged in leftwing movements, she never became directly active in politics.

In the early 1950s Parra began Chile's first folk music radio program and recorded her debut album, with simple guitar-accompanied arrangements. She also taught briefly at a southern Chilean university. Parra and her children introduced Andean and African American folk music to Chile after a four-year sojourn in Paris, France, where they encountered musicians from various countries. Settling with her children in Chile's capital city, Santiago, she enjoyed cooking huge pots of beans for the young Chileans who gathered around her to drink wine, discuss Chilean affairs, and exchange songs and stories. A café the Parras opened in Santiago became a meeting place for performers and other Chileans interested in New Song and leftist politics. Parra greatly influenced younger urban musicians, who began learning from her how to play traditional Andean instruments while collecting or writing their own songs, and she provided a role model for other Latin American musicians. As Cuba's top New Song musician, Silvio Rodriguez, claimed: "Violeta is fundamental. Nothing would have been as it is had it not been for Violeta."

Parra's songs displayed two essential elements of later New Song: a base in folk music and concern with Chile's social, economic, and political problems. In "Look How They Tell Us About Freedom," she critiqued the Catholic Church establishment and her nation's ills: "look how the nation's religious and political leaders brag about freedom," she sang, "when they are actually keeping it from us; they boast about tranquility as their power tortures us." Her music attacked such issues as the brutality of the police, the inequalities of capitalism, the exploitation of Indians, and chronic conflict between Latin American governments. At the same time, her songs retained an intense, highly personal, and contemporary mood, which was both Chilean and universal.

Besides being held in contempt by the Chilean elite for her unconventional life and antiestablishment sympathies, Parra was plagued by poverty and increasing personal problems, including depression. Even her closest friends found her strong, often unpredictable personality difficult, and younger musicians began gravitating to Victor Jara and other New Song figures. Her later songs took on a more philosophical spirit. On her last album in 1966 she recorded her famous farewell, "Gracias a la Vida" (I Give Thanks to Life), a prayerlike expression of gratitude for the richness of life: "I am grateful for the life that has benefited me so much; It has given me both laughter and tears; because of this I can differentiate happiness from sadness; everybody's song is my own song." Not overtly political, the song reflected her identification with the common people and became the underground anthem of many Latin Americans living under dictatorships. As Parra's depression deepened, she committed suicide in 1967. But her career had built a bridge between an older, peasant-based folk tradition and the developing interest of younger musicians. She may have gone, but New Song flowered in Chile and around Latin America.

THINKING ABOUT THE PROFILE

1. Why did her peers consider Parra fundamental to the evolution of New Song in Latin America?
2. How did Parra's life reflect Chilean social and political conditions?

Notes: Quotations from *Studies in Latin American Popular Culture* 2 (1983): 177–178, and 5 (1986): 117; and Nancy E.Morris, *Canto Porque es Necesario Cantar: The New Song Movement in Chile, 1973–1983* (Albuquerque: Latin American Institute, University of New Mexico, Research Paper Series No. 16, July 1984), 6.

Archivo, La Fundacion Violeta Parra

Violeta Parra An influential Chilean musician, folklorist, and artist, Violeta Parra is credited with founding the folk-music-oriented New Song movement, influencing many musicians in Chile and throughout Latin America.

Latin America and the Caribbean in the Global System

Regional Cooperation

The peoples of Latin America and the Caribbean forged closer relations with one another and increased regional economic cooperation and trade, often through trade pacts. The Southern Cone Common Market, formed in 1996, included six South American nations with over 200 million people. Similarly, Caribbean countries cooperated in the Caribbean Community and Common Market, formed in 1973. Latin and North American leaders periodically met in summits to bolster hemispheric solidarity and enhance cooperation on immigration, tariff reduction, suppression of the illegal drug trade, and other issues. Some U.S.–Latin American issues remain contested. While people in the United States have blamed Latin American drug cartels for smuggling illegal drugs, Latin Americans have often resented the U.S. interventions and economic impositions they consider "Yankee imperialism." Latin American and Caribbean leaders have also feared being pushed aside in a world economy dominated by North American, European and, increasingly, Asian nations.

Globalization

Globalization has influenced Latin Americans and their economies. Asian nations, especially China, Japan, Taiwan, and South Korea, have captured a growing share of Latin America's traditional overseas markets while also investing in Latin America and the Caribbean. Energy-hungry China has been particularly active in seeking resources such as oil from countries like Brazil and Venezuela. In a globalized economy, a hiccup in Tokyo or New York causes a stomach ache in Ecuador or El Salvador. Since most Latin American and Caribbean economies have followed the track of the U.S. economy, they are particularly vulnerable to change in the United States. When the 2001 terrorist attacks diverted U.S. attention to the Middle East, the sudden U.S. disinterest in Latin America and its problems sparked a regional economic downturn that reduced demand for Latin American exports. The economic gains made in the mid-1990s slipped away, and the fifth of Latin America's 500 million people who lived in extreme poverty faced an even grimmer future, which leftists capitalized on to win elections and take power in many countries. Only a few nations, such as Brazil and Chile, had much hope of significantly improving their status in the global system. The 2008–2009 global economic crisis further damaged many Latin American and Caribbean economies as jobs disappeared, tourism declined, and many jobless migrants to North America returned home. Although U.S. exports to Latin America nearly matched those to Europe, by 2008, at the end of the George W. Bush presidency, U.S.–Latin American relations were at their lowest point since the Cold War.

Buffeted by political changes and economic crises, Latin Americans search for their identity and role in a world dominated by other societies. Calling on leaders to recognize the needs of all the people, regardless of class, ethnicity, and gender, and for both North and Latin Americans to find common ground with each other, the Panamanian salsa music star, lawyer, and part-time U.S. resident Ruben Blades **(blayds)** pondered the hemisphere's destiny in song: "I'm searching for America and I fear I won't find her. Those who fear truth have hidden her. While there is no justice there can be no peace. If the dream of one is the dream of all let's break the chains and begin to walk. I'm calling you, America, our future awaits us, help me to find her."[22]

SECTION SUMMARY

- Latin American economies have been marked by overdependence on natural resources, extreme inequality of income, agriculture that deemphasizes production of foodstuffs for domestic consumption, increasing urbanization, and failed experiments with free trade.
- Though men continue to dominate Latin American society, more women have entered the work force, and several have become national leaders, while liberation theology, a Catholic movement addressing the plight of the poor, became popular for a while but was outlawed by the Vatican; Protestantism also gained a following.
- Brazil, Latin America's largest nation, became increasingly urban and suffered widespread poverty, with a racial divide between lighter- and darker-skinned people, but Brazilians have found escape from their problems through popular sports such as soccer.
- Latin American culture has flourished, with writers employing magic realism to explore their region's experience, others airing political views through poetry and music, and many preferring to use local traditions and forms rather than foreign ones.
- In the Caribbean, the Jamaican religion of Rastafarianism promoted redistribution of wealth, while a closely related musical form, reggae, frequently included calls for social justice and freedom from police interference.
- Latin American and Caribbean nations forged closer relations, signed several trade pacts, and shared an uneasy economic relationship with the United States, while Asian nations also became important competitors with and investors in their economies.

CHAPTER SUMMARY

Having emerged from World War II as the dominant superpower, the United States soon engaged in a Cold War with the Soviet Union. The U.S. campaign to contain communism fostered the growth of a powerful military and a strong government. During the Cold War the United States lavished aid and investment on its allies and the developing nations and intervened in many nations, including some in Latin America and the Caribbean, to counter revolutionary movements or overthrow left-leaning governments. While the U.S. economy flourished for decades, American society and culture rapidly changed, as ethnic minorities and women struggled for equal rights. Although shaped, like the United States, by massive immigration from Europe, especially Britain, the societies of Canada, Australia, and New Zealand have more liberal attitudes on social issues and, unlike the United States, have extensive social welfare systems.

Latin American and Caribbean experiences differ from those in the United States and Canada and the Pacific Basin. Military dictatorships dominated many Latin American nations for decades. Most nations struggled to implement and sustain democracy, which became prevalent in the 1990s, and to find the right economic mix to foster economic development. Many people have remained in dire poverty. Women and nonwhites have worked to improve their status, with only modest success. The Latin American and Caribbean peoples have also fostered dynamic cultural forms, from innovative literatures to popular musical forms, that have often expressed protest and have gained worldwide audiences.

KEY TERMS

domino theory
multilateralism
unilateralism
containment
Mutually Assured Destruction
preemptive war
Castroism
neoliberalism
liberation theology
New Song
Rastafarianism
reggae

EBOOK AND WEBSITE RESOURCES

PRIMARY SOURCE

Free Trade and the Decline of Democracy

INTERACTIVE MAPS

Map 29.1 U.S.Military Presence in the World, 1945–Present
Map 29.2 Canada
Map 29.3 Modern Latin America and the Caribbean

LINKS

WWW-VL: History: United States (http://vlib.iue.it/history/USA/). A virtual library, maintained at the University of Kansas, that contains links to hundreds of sites.

Internet Modern History Sourcebook (http://www.fordham.edu/halsall/mod/modsbook.html). Extensive online collection of historical documents and secondary materials.

Internet Resources for Latin America (http://lib.nmsu.edu/subject/bord/laguia/). This outstanding site, from New Mexico State University, provides information and links.

Latin American Network Information Center (http://lanic.utexas.edu/). Very useful site on contemporary Latin America, maintained at the University of Texas.

Plus flashcards, practice quizzes, and more. Go to: www.cengage.com/history/lockard/globalsocnet2e.

SUGGESTED READING

Beezley, William, and Colin MacLachlan. *Latin America: The Peoples and Their History,* 2nd ed. Belmont, CA: Wadsworth, 2007. Comprehensive study.

Brown, D. Clayton. *Globalization and America Since 1945.* Wilmington, DE: Scholarly Resources, 2003. A brief but useful study of the U.S. role in a globalizing world.

Chafe, William H. *The Unfinished Journey: America Since World War II,* 5th ed. New York: Oxford University Press, 2003. An outstanding, readable survey of the era.

Clayton, Lawrence A., and Michael L. Conniff. *A History of Modern Latin America,* 2nd ed. Belmont, CA: Wadsworth, 2005. A readable general history, with much on the contemporary era.

DePalma, Anthony. *Here: A Biography of the New American Continent.* New York: Public Affairs, 2001. A U.S. jounalist's account of contemporary Canada, Mexico, and the United States.

Green, Duncan. *Faces of Latin America,* 3rd ed. New York: Monthly Review Press, 2006. An entertaining and provocative examination of Latin America's people and their vibrant cultures.

Guarneri, Carl. *America in the World: U.S. History in Global Context.* New York: McGraw-Hill, 2007. Places recent U.S. history in comparative perspective.

Hillman, Richard S., ed. *Understanding Contemporary Latin America,* 3rd ed. Boulder: Lynne Rienner, 2005. A valuable collection of essays.

Hillman, Richard S., ed. *Understanding the Contemporary Caribbean,* 2nd ed. Lynne Rienner, 2009. A valuable collection of essays.

Hobsbawm, Eric. *On Empire: America, War, and Global Supremacy.* New York: New Press, 2008. Provocative critique of U.S. role in the world by a British historian.

Hunt, Michael H. *The American Ascendancy: How the United States Gained and Wielded Global Dominance.* Chapel Hill: University of North Carolina Press, 2007. Tracks the factors behind the U.S. rise to global power.

Isserman, Maurice, and Michael Kazin. *America Divided: The Civil War of the 1960s.* New York: Oxford University Press, 2000. A comprehensive history of this important era.

Kinzer, Stephen. *Overthrow: America's Century of Regime Change from Hawaii to Iraq.* New York: Times Books, 2006. A critical examination of U.S. interventions and forced regime changes abroad over the past century.

Page, Joseph A. *The Brazilians.* Reading, MA: Addison-Wesley, 1995. A readable examination of Brazilian society and culture.

Paterson, Thomas, et al. *American Foreign Relations Since 1895,* 7th ed. Boston: Wadsworth, 2009. A readable survey with much on this era.

Rosen, Ruth. *The World Split Open: How the Modern Women's Movement Changed America.* New York: Viking, 2000. One of the best studies of the women's movement in the United States since World War II.

Schaller, Michael, et al. *Present Tense: The United States Since 1945,* 3rd ed. Boston: Houghton Mifflin, 2004. An informative survey.

Skidmore, Thomas E., and Peter H. Smith. *Modern Latin America,* 6th ed. New York: Oxford University Press, 2004. An excellent introduction to the recent history of the region and its nations.

Sullivan III, Michael J. *American Adventurism Abroad: Invasions, Interventions, and Regime Changes Since World War II,* revised and expanded ed. Malden, MA: Blackwell, 2008. Traces foreign policy from the 1940s to today.

Terrill, Ross. *The Australians.* New York: Touchstone, 1988. A readable introduction to Australian history and society.

Thompson, Roger C. *The Pacific Basin Since 1945,* 2nd ed. New York: Longman, 2001. An Australian scholar's broad examination of the East Asian, Pacific, Latin American, and North American societies and their relations.

Winn, Peter. *Americas: The Changing Face of Latin America and the Caribbean,* 3rd ed. Berkeley: University of California Press, 2006. A sweeping, highly readable examination of the region and its peoples.

CHAPTER 30

The Middle East, Sub-Saharan Africa, and New Conflicts in the Contemporary World, Since 1945

CHAPTER OUTLINE

- The Middle East: New Nations and Old Societies
- Change and Conflict in the Middle East
- Political Change in Sub-Saharan Africa
- African Economies, Societies, and Cultures

PROFILE
Nelson and Winnie Mandela, South African Freedom Fighters

WITNESS TO THE PAST
Assessing Arab Development

AP/Wide World Photos

Modern vs. Traditional
Wearing traditional clothing, including veils and head scarves, Egyptian women walk through downtown Cairo in 1998 in front of billboards promoting popular entertainers. The scene illustrates the encounter between Islamic customs and modern ideas in many Middle Eastern nations.

I saw the Berlin Wall fall, [Nelson] Mandela walk free. I saw a dream whose time has come change my history—so keep on dreaming. In the best of times and in the worst of times gotta keep looking at the skyline, not at the hole in the road.

—"Your Time Will Come" by South African pop group Savuka, 1993[1]

FOCUS QUESTIONS

1. How have Arab-Israeli tensions and oil shaped contemporary Middle Eastern politics?
2. What roles has Islam played in the contemporary Middle East?
3. What were the main political consequences of decolonization in sub-Saharan Africa?
4. What new economic, social, and cultural patterns have emerged in Africa?

In 1987 the Nigerian writer Chinua Achebe **(ah-CHAY-bay)** (b. 1930) dissected the underside of African politics in a controversial novel, *Anthills of the Savannah*, about a military dictatorship like the one he had experienced in his own country. *Anthills* portrays the problems faced by average people and throughout much of Africa, mercilessly depicting the immorality, vanity, and destructiveness of dictatorship. Achebe did not have to look far for examples: the Nigerian military leaders who overthrew a civilian government in 1983 had first arrested people well-known as corrupt, but then proceeded to jail anyone who questioned the regime's own economic mismanagement and human rights abuses. Achebe's satire on moral bankruptcy illustrated the dangers of unaccountable, repressive power. Just as the black and white musicians in the South African pop group, Savuka, could sing of dreams changing history and a new era beginning with the end of white minority rule, Achebe also offered a powerful message about the need for people to struggle to attain a better life. Achebe has argued that the artist and society cannot be separated, that no novel is ever politically neutral because even saying nothing about politics is a political statement that says everything is OK. *Anthills* argues eloquently that, in Achebe's view, everything is not OK. Like various other creative writers, musicians, and artists who used their art to spur political and social change, Achebe has had to live in exile from intolerant governments.

The problems Achebe vividly described—corruption, economic stagnation, combustible social tensions, and failed promises of democracy—have applied to most other nations in sub-Saharan Africa and the Middle East. Between 1945 and 1975 country after country became independent or escaped from Western political domination. In contrast to various Asian and Latin American nations, however, African and Middle Eastern nations have often struggled just to survive. While innovative in areas such as music, literature, and other forms of culture, few of the nations have successfully resolved their social and economic problems or substantially raised living standards. For some nations, Islam has become a rallying cry to assert political interests and preserve cultures. To serve their own ends, global superpowers have manipulated governments and intervened to shape the regions.

[1]Written by Johnny Clegg. Publisher: HRBV Music/Thythm Safari

Visit the website and eBook for additional study materials and interactive tools: www.cengage.com/history/lockard/globalsocnet2e

THE MIDDLE EAST: NEW NATIONS AND OLD SOCIETIES

How have Arab-Israeli tensions and oil shaped contemporary Middle Eastern politics?

Few world regions have witnessed more turbulence in the past half-century than the predominantly Muslim nations stretching from Morocco eastward across North Africa and western Asia to Turkey, Iran, and Afghanistan. The Arabs have dominated most of these nations, but Turks, Iranians, Kurds, and Israeli Jews also influence the region. After World War II the Middle Eastern societies ended Western colonization and asserted their own political interests, often under modernizing leaders. But they have also endured dictatorial governments, chronic political instability, and centuries-old hostilities between Sunni and Shi'a Muslims. Meanwhile, containing much of the world's oil reserves, the Middle East became crucial to the global system.

The Reshaping of the Middle East

In the decade after World War II nationalist governments replaced most of the remaining colonial regimes (see Chronology: The Middle East, 1945–Present). The French abandoned control of Morocco, Tunisia, Lebanon, and Syria, while the Italians left Libya. However, during the Algerian Revolution (1954–1962) nationalist guerrillas fought 500,000 French troops for eight years to bring independence to Algeria, which had a large European settler population. Some 250,000 Algerians died in the conflict. Seeing no clear end to the struggle, the French granted independence in 1962. Although some Middle Eastern nations, such as Egypt and Morocco, had a long history of national identity and unity, many states were fragile. For example, after World War I the British had formed the artificial states of Iraq, Jordan, and Palestine with arbitrary boundaries, while Afghanistan, Turkey, Lebanon, and Syria included diverse and often feuding ethnic and religious groups.

Iran and Turkey, which had never been colonized, sought influential roles in the region and built formidable military forces. Both also abused their citizens' human rights, arresting dissidents and restricting ethnic minorities. Turkey shifted from military-dominated to democratically elected governments by the 1980s, but the military remained powerful, and strict internal security laws resulted in the imprisonment of several thousand people for political offenses. Led largely by secular politicians, Turks looked increasingly westward, joining NATO (the North Atlantic Treaty Organization), hosting U.S. military bases, and applying for membership in the European Union. But Turkey's governments, while generally promoting a modern version of women's rights, have also suppressed the culture and language of the largest ethnic minority, the Kurds, who chiefly live in southeastern Turkey. Although the nation's 73 million people are largely Muslim, nationalist governments long limited political activity by groups favoring an Islamic state and discouraged conservative religious customs. However, the moderate Islamic Justice and Development Party, which came to power in 2002 and won successive elections, has loosened restrictions on Muslim practices, such as by allowing devout female students to wear head scarves, while pursuing a pro-Western policy and closer ties to Europe.

The hopes for development throughout the Middle East were soon dashed as vested interests, such as large landowners and most of the Muslim clergy, opposed significant changes. Many people also remained mired in illiteracy, poverty, and disease. But although freewheeling and enduring multiparty democracy has been hard to establish or maintain, some have made the effort. Lebanese could choose between many competing warlord or sectarian-based parties, and in recent years both men and women in the small Persian Gulf kingdoms of Bahrain **(BAH-rain)** and Kuwait have elected parliaments. In 2009 three Kuwaiti women won seats. Due to U.S. occupation, Iraq also now has an elected, although deeply factionalized, parliament with some women deputies. As another example, the Moroccan king,

CHRONOLOGY
The Middle East, 1945–Present

1948 Formation of Israel

1948–1949 First Arab-Israeli War

1951 Nationalist government in Iran

1954–1970 Nasser presidency in Egypt

1953 CIA overthrow of Iranian government

1954–1962 Algerian Revolution

1956 Suez crisis

1960 Formation of OPEC

1967 Arab-Israeli Six-Day War

1973 Arab-Israeli (Yom Kippur) War

1973 OPEC oil embargo

1978 Egypt-Israel peace treaty

1979 Islamic revolution in Iran

1979–1989 Soviet war in Afghanistan

1980–1988 Iran-Iraq War

1987 Beginning of Palestinian Intifada

1996–2001 Taliban government in Afghanistan

1993 Limited Palestinian self-government

2000 Renewed Israeli-Palestinian conflict

2001 U.S. invasion of Afghanistan

2003 U.S. invasion and occupation of Iraq

CHRONOLOGY

	The Middle East	Sub-Saharan Africa
1940	**1948** Formation of Israel **1954–1962** Algerian Revolution	**1948** Apartheid in South Africa **1957–1975** African decolonization
1960	**1967** Arab-Israeli Six-Day War **1973** OPEC oil embargo **1979** Islamic revolution in Iran	**1975** Independence for Portuguese colonies
1990	**2003** United States invasion of Iraq	**1994** Black majority rule in South Africa

Muhammad VI, who claims descent from the prophet Muhammad, has used a tolerant interpretation of Islam to try to modernize his nation, granting new rights to women and strengthening civil liberties and the role of an elected parliament. Yet, the king still controls vast power. In most countries elections are rigged, parliaments are weak, or governments make it hard for opposition candidates to run. Furthermore, the United States and the Soviet Union, attracted by the region's oil and strategic location along vital waterways, including the Persian Gulf and Suez Canal, soon filled the power vacuum created by decolonization. Pan-Arab nationalism, based more on Arabs' shared cultural and linguistic background than political interests, was never able to overcome political rivalries and superpower meddling. Divided by rival Muslim sects and differing outlooks toward the West, Arabs floundered in their quest for unity. As a result, the Middle East became a highly combustible region subject to many strains.

Arab Nationalism and Egypt

During the 1960s and 1970s confrontation between Arab nationalism and the world's superpowers was acute in Egypt, which, with 82 million people by 2008, is the most populous Arab country. In 1954 a charismatic Egyptian leader, General Gamal Abdul Nasser (NAS-uhr) (1918–1970), became Egypt's leader after a military coup in 1952 that ended the corrupt pro-British monarchy. From the lower middle class in cosmopolitan Alexandria, Nasser's frequent visits to his parents' impoverished farming village had sparked his sympathy for the poor and his resentment of rich landlords. He also despised the British and their Egyptian collaborators. As a radical student and then army officer with a commanding personality, he developed a vision of a new Egypt, free of Western domination and social inequality.

Rise of Nasser

President Nasser preached modernization, socialism, and unity, promising to improve the lives of the poor and to implement land reform, making him a hero in the Arab world. To generate electric power and improve flood control, Nasser used Soviet aid to build the massive Aswan High Dam along the Nile, completed in 1970. But his nonaligned foreign policy antagonized a Cold War–obsessed United States, and his support of pan-Arab nationalism also generated wars. In 1956 Nasser's government took over the British-operated Suez Canal, a key artery of world commerce. To Egyptians, foreign ownership of the canal had symbolized their subjugation to foreign powers, but to Europeans, the canal was the lifeline that moved oil and resources to the West from Asia. Britain, France, and Israel sent in military forces to reclaim the canal from Egyptian troops, but diplomatic opposition by the United States, which disliked Nasser but feared regional instability, and by the USSR, forced their withdrawal. By standing up to the West, Nasser became an even greater Arab hero and a leader of the movement among developing nations for nonalignment, or neutrality, between the two rival superpowers. However, the Israeli defeat of Egypt and its allies in a brief 1967 war humiliated Nasser. Furthermore, Nasser's social and economic reforms fostered little economic development or military strength.

Egypt after Nasser

Nasser's successors followed pragmatic, pro-U.S. policies. In 1978 Anwar Sadat (g. 1970–1981) signed a peace treaty with Israel brokered by the U.S. president, Jimmy Carter (g. 1977–1981). For his efforts Sadat was assassinated by hardline military officers. Sadat and his successor, Hosni Mubarak, dismantled the socialist economy, allowing a few well-connected capitalists to become fabulously rich while the poorest became even poorer. In Cairo, the contrast has grown more dramatic between the glittering rich neighborhoods, featuring luxury apartments and mansions surrounded by high walls, and the poor, overcrowded neighborhoods, where the most desperate families live in huts on top of ramshackle apartment buildings. As a result, millions of Egyptians have sought work in oil-rich Arab nations.

With little oil and few resources other than the fertile lands along the Nile, Egypt suffers from high malnutrition and unemployment, low rates of literacy and public health, and a huge national debt. In elections other candidates were able to run against the long-entrenched president Hosni Mubarak (r. 1981–present), but they were hampered in campaigning by limits on free speech, harassment, and the arrest of opposition leaders. While liberals seek more democracy, Islamic militants, feeding on these frustrations, challenge the secular but corrupt, repressive government.

Israel in Middle Eastern Politics

Birth of Israel

The conflict between Israel and the Arabs became the Middle East's most insurmountable problem, sustaining tensions for over half a century. Zionist Jews had been emigrating from Europe to Palestine since the late 1800s, building cities and forming productive socialist farming settlements. The growing Jewish presence triggered occasional conflicts with the Palestinian Arab majority. Then the Nazis' murder of 6 million Jews during World War II spurred a more militant Zionism and a Jewish desire for a homeland free of oppression, and in the later 1940s Jewish refugees poured into Palestine from Europe. Moderate Jewish leaders negotiated with the sympathetic British for a peaceful transfer of power to them in Palestine. However, Zionist extremists practiced "gun diplomacy," using bombings and assassinations against the British, Arabs, and moderate Jews, while Arabs, opposed to an Israeli state at their expense, attacked Jews. Unable to maintain order, Britain referred the Palestine question to the new Western-dominated United Nations. As the British withdrew in 1948, Jewish leaders proclaimed the establishment of Israel. By establishing a multiparty democracy and seeking to rebuild shattered Jewish lives, the Israelis gained the strong support of Western nations and especially the United States, which has pumped in generous aid ever since.

Arab-Israeli Conflicts

The establishment of a Jewish state led to full-scale war in 1948–1949 between Israel and its Arab neighbors, to whom Israel was a white settler state and a symbol of Western colonialism (see Map 30.1). As some 85 percent of Palestinian Arabs fled the fighting and attacks by Jewish extremists, or heeded the calls of opportunistic Arab leaders to leave, Israelis occupied their farms and houses. Through these means the Israelis won the war against the disorganized Arabs. Palestinian refugees settled in overcrowded, squalid refugee camps in Egypt, Lebanon, Jordan, and Syria. While some Palestinian exiles became a prosperous middle class throughout the Middle East, most remained in the camps, nursing their hatred of Israel. They supported the Palestine Liberation Organization (PLO), a coalition of Arab nationalist, Muslim, and Christian groups led by Yasser Arafat **(YA-sir AR-uh-fat)** (1929–2004), an engineer and journalist from a wealthy Jerusalem family. However, neither the Western nations nor Israel officially recognized or would negotiate with the PLO until the 1990s, prompting it to resort to terrorism, such as by attacking public buses and rural settlements.

Israel remained in a state of confrontation with its Arab neighbors and the PLO. The Palestinians still in Israel participated in democratic politics but were disproportionally poor and often saw themselves as second-class citizens. Meanwhile, thousands of Jewish immigrants arrived, many from Middle Eastern countries where they had faced discrimination or retribution. The immigration intensified the divisions in Israel between secular and devout Jews and between European and Middle Eastern Jews. Israeli, obsessed with military security, became well armed, especially by the United States, with half its total national budget going to the military. A cycle of violence followed as the PLO attacked and Israelis bombed a refugee camp in Lebanon in retaliation.

1967 War and Aftermath

An Arab-Israeli War in 1967 further complicated regional politics, heightening conflict and reshaping Israeli society. Responding to an ill-advised attack led by Egypt and Jordan, Israel gained control of the West Bank, that part of Jordan on the western side of the Jordan River; eastern Jerusalem, filled with both Jewish and Islamic holy places; the Gaza Strip, a small coastal enclave of Egypt; and the Golan Heights, a Syrian plateau overlooking northeast Israel. The Israeli victory greatly increased the amount of Israeli-controlled land but incorporated a large Arab population, a combustible situation. By 2005 Israel and the occupied territories contained some 5 million Jews and 4 million Arabs. Israel treated the occupied Palestinians as a colonized people, allowing them no political rights. In 1973 another Israeli war with Egypt and Syria proved costly to all sides.

Increasing Israeli control over the Palestinians exacerbated the conflict. Although many Israelis wanted to trade occupied land for a permanent peace settlement, others hoped to permanently annex the occupied lands as part of biblical Israel. Ultranationalist Israelis, with government support, began claiming and settling on Arab land, creating another problem: thousands of Jewish settlers, largely militant Zionists and religious conservatives, living amid hostile Arabs. Palestinians

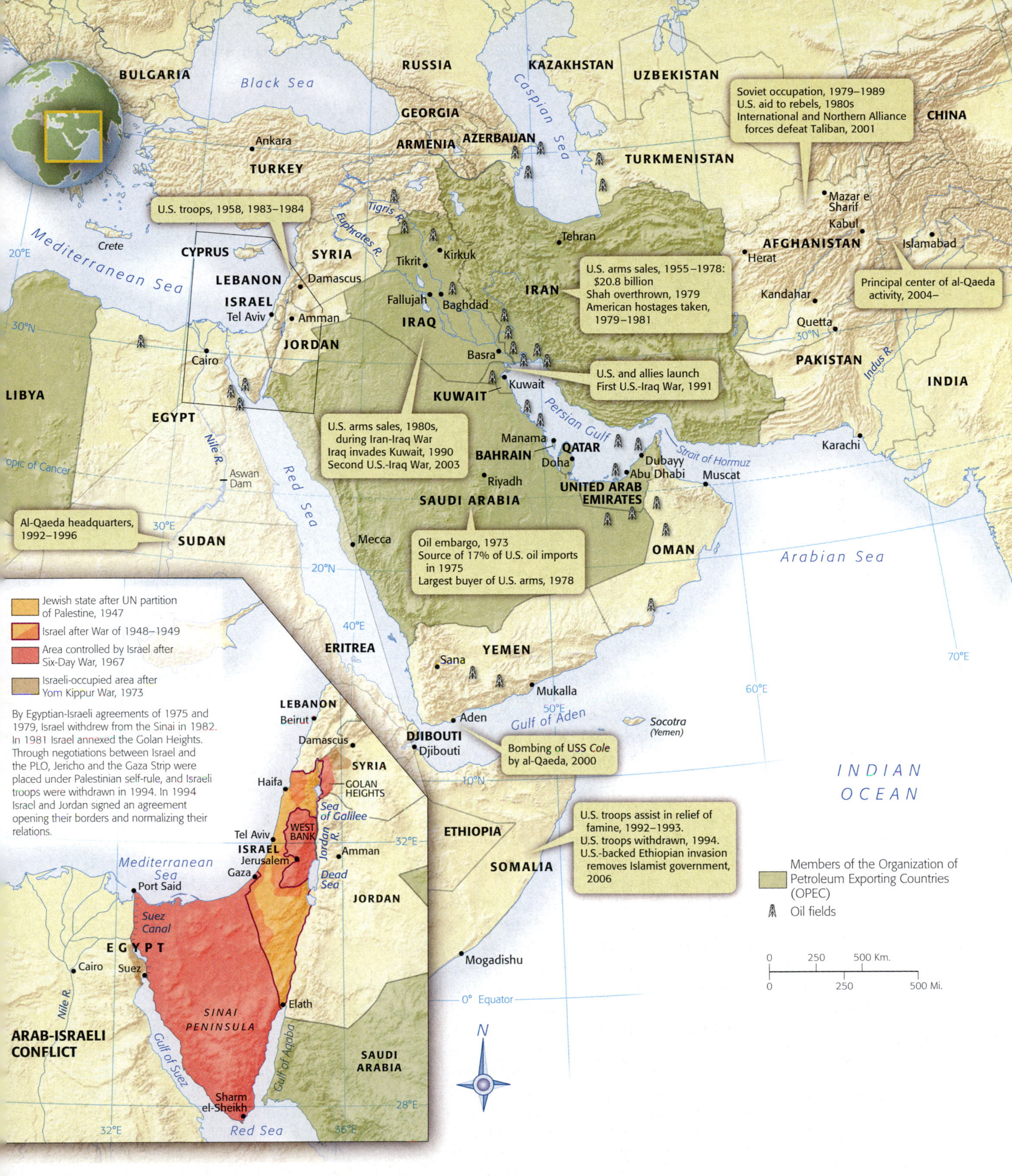

Map 30.1 Middle East Oil and the Arab-Israeli Conflict
Several Middle Eastern nations, including Saudi Arabia, Iran, Iraq, Libya, and the small Persian Gulf states, are rich in oil and active members of OPEC. Israel, founded in 1948, and the neighboring Arab countries of Egypt, Jordan, and Syria have been in chronic conflict that has resulted in four wars. Israel's victory in the 1967 war allowed it to take control of Gaza, the West Bank, and the Golan Heights.

e **Interactive Map**

Dismantling Israeli Settlements Palestinians have viewed the settlements built by ardent Zionists in the West Bank and Gaza as a provocation. Israeli troops have sometimes been ordered to dismantle settlements, which are expensive to protect, and remove the enraged settlers by force. In 2005 all the Israeli settlements were closed down in Gaza.

AP/Wide World Photos

resent the heavily fortified settlements, guarded by Israeli soldiers, that often overlook Palestinian cities and villages from nearby hilltops. Because Israel proper has remained a democracy with a vibrant free press, Israelis have heatedly debated these policies and the general treatment of Arabs. In 1987 desperate Palestinians began a resistance known as the **Intifada** ("Uprising") against the Israeli occupation. However, the turmoil spawned a rising Islamic militancy in the occupied territories that alarmed both the secular Fatah movement, the main party in the PLO, and the Israelis. Negotiations led in 1993 to limited self-government under the PLO in some parts of the occupied territories, the basis for a possible Palestinian state, and a peace agreement between Israel and Jordan. Optimists hoped a permanent peace agreement might be found to satisfy both sides. But the assassination in 1995 of Israeli president Yitzak Rabin by Jewish extremists proved a setback for peace talks.

Intifada ("Uprising") A resistance begun in 1987 by Palestinians against the Israeli occupation.

Recent Politics

In 2000 violence erupted again, returning the Israel-Palestine problem to center stage in Middle Eastern politics. Moderate Israelis and Palestinians lost hope as demoralizing Palestinian suicide bombings of civilian targets, such as restaurants and public buses, and Israeli reprisal attacks on Palestinian neighborhoods made life insecure for everyone. Israel also built a high security fence separating it from the West Bank that incorporated some occupied territory, enraging Palestinians. In a 2006 election promoted by the United States the Palestinians, tired of Fatah's ineffective and corrupt regime, unexpectedly gave the militant Islamic Hamas movement a majority of seats in the Palestinian parliament, alarming Israelis, since Hamas had sponsored terrorist attacks and refused to recognize Israel's right to exist. Soon Hamas seized Gaza, from where militants fired rockets into Israel, while Fatah controlled the West Bank. An inconclusive Israeli invasion of southern Lebanon in 2006 to stop terrorist attacks and a bloody military incursion in Gaza in 2008 that reduced some Gaza neighborhoods to rubble hardened Israeli and Palestinian attitudes and led to condemnation in the world community. As a hardline Israeli government took power in 2009, the future of Israeli-Palestinian relations remained uncertain. With only a third of the world's 14 million Jews living in Israel, the Zionist dream of a Greater Israel stretching from the Mediterranean coast through the West Bank to the Jordan River is fading. At the same time, with conflicting visions of how Israelis and Palestinians might coexist, no basis for ensuring long-term peace has yet emerged.

e **Primary Source: Arab and Israeli Soccer Players Discuss Ethnic Relations in Israel, 2000** Learn how Arabs and Jews get along in the world of professional soccer in Israel.

Islamic Revolution in Iran

Western Intervention

Rich in oil and strategically located along the Persian Gulf, Iran had been buffeted between rival European nations for a century. Outside interference continued after World War II, when internal politics revolved around a conflict between the young king, Shah Mohammed Pahlavi **(pah-LAH-vee)** (1919–1980), and nationalist reformers opposed to foreign domination. In 1951 nationalists came to power, reducing the shah to a ceremonial role. Because Iran had been receiving little of the oil revenue, the reformers also nationalized the British-dominated oil industry. Britain and its ally, the United States, which considered the nationalists sympathetic to the USSR, cut off aid and launched a boycott to close oil markets, bringing Iran to near bankruptcy and fostering unrest. Then in 1953, American CIA agents secretly organized opposition among military leaders and riots against the nationalist government. In the turmoil, royalists overthrew the government, imprisoned its leaders, and restored the unpopular shah to power, embittering many Iranians. Shah Pahlavi, a ruthless, pleasure-loving man who dreamed of restoring Persia as a great power, allied himself with the United States and allowed American companies to control the oil industry.

Iran under Shah Pahlavi

Along with the modernization, the shah's three and a half decades of rule also brought political repression and a huge military force built with oil revenues. What the shah termed his "white revolution," which promoted a market economy and women's rights while enlarging the middle class, was admired in the West but failed to improve living standards for most Iranians. While a corrupt elite siphoned off most of the development money, including generous U.S. aid, and the royal family lived extravagantly, 60 percent of peasants remained landless. As people flocked to the cities, choked in traffic and smog, the population of Tehran, the capital, increased fivefold between 1945 and 1977. To increase national pride and attract Western tourists, the shah spent billions to renovate the splendid palaces and tombs of Persepolis, a city built for Persian kings 2,400 years ago, but few Iranians had the money to visit the city. The absolute monarchy tolerated little dissent, and the shah's secret police eliminated opposition. Political prisoners numbered in the thousands. The poetess Faruq Farrukhzad **(fuh-ROOK fuh-ROOK-sad)** wrote of how the intellectuals, cowed into submission, retreated into "swamps of alcohol [while] the verminous mice gnawed through the pages of gilded books, stacked in ancient closets."[2] Conservative Shi'ite leaders opposed the modernization, such as the unveiled women and crowded bars, which they viewed as a threat to Muslim culture. Then in 1979, as the economy slumped, strikes and protests forced the shah into exile in the United States and turned the Americans and Iranians into bitter foes.

Islamic Revolution and the United States

An Islamic revolution began to reshape Iran. While some Shi'ite thinkers discouraged the clergy from political activism, others promoted a clergy-governed Islamic state. Militant Shi'ite clerics, led by the long exiled Ayatollah Ruhollah Khomeini **(roo-HOLE-ah KOH-may-nee)** (1902–1989), took power, eliminated leftists and moderate nationalists, and overturned the shah's modernization. Khomeini had long criticized the shah's secular policies, urging that they be replaced by the Islamic Shari'a law codes. As Iran became an Islamic state, thousands of Iranians fled abroad, many to the United States. Women were forced to wear veils and prohibited from socializing with men from outside their families. The regime restricted other personal freedoms as well, as reflected in a popular joke: "We used to drink in public and pray in private. Now we pray in public and drink in private." Like the shah, the clerics ruled by terror, suppressed ethnic minorities, such as the mostly Sunni Kurds in the northwest, and executed opponents.

The Iranian Revolution fostered opposition from outside. The United States became a bitter enemy after Islamic militants, led by women students and driven by hatred of the United States for its long support of the shah, seized the U.S. Embassy in 1979 and held it and the U.S. diplomats for one year. Iran's Arab neighbors, who had always feared Iran's territorial size, large population (70 million in 2006), military strength, and regional ambitions, were also alarmed. Now they had to worry about Islamic militancy aimed at their more secular governments. Animosity between the mostly Sunni Arabs and the mostly Shi'ite Iranians also fueled tensions and led to war with Iraq. Finally, an Iranian program to develop nuclear power and perhaps nuclear weapons gave worry to the international community.

Recent Iranian Politics

Eventually Iran mixed theocracy with the trappings of democracy. A more open electoral process allowed opposition parties to win seats in parliament. Beginning in 1997, reformers gained a share of power, fostering a power struggle between moderate reformers and the hardline clerics who controlled the judicial and electoral systems. With the economy floundering, the reformers sought closer ties to the outside world, democratization, and a loosening of harsh laws, but they found the United States unwilling to improve relations. Young people, resenting clerical leadership and Islamic laws, often supported reform and increasingly challenged restrictions on personal behavior. Young women, often unveiled or wearing fashionable head scarves, began socializing again with men. But the hardliners banned reformist newspapers and disqualified reformist candidates. Shirin Ebadi **(shih-RIN ee-BOD-ee)** (b. 1947), a feminist Iranian lawyer and human rights activist, won the Nobel Peace Prize in 2003 for bravely challenging the clerical leadership and favoring a reformist Islam, distressing the hardliners. But in 2005 Iranians lost faith in the ineffective reformist leaders and elected a hardline president, Mahmoud Ahmedinijad **(mah-MOOD ah-mah-DIH-nee-zhahd)** (b. 1956), who increased nuclear capabilities, restored conservative values, harassed dissidents, threatened Israel, and openly defied the United States. One of his first acts was to ban Western music from radio and television. However, as the economy declined, reformers and hardliners continued to struggle for influence. In 2009, a victory by Ahmedinijad and the hardliners—in a disputed election that many Iranians considered rigged and that generated massive street protests—intensified repression of dissidents, and divided the clerical leadership, leaving the nation's political future uncertain.

Iraq and Regional Conflicts

Iraqi Dictatorship

Ba'ath ("Renaissance") A political party in the Middle East that favored socialism and Arab nationalism and strongly opposed Israel.

Iraq proved a major source of regional instability. In 1958 the Iraqi army overthrew an unpopular monarchy and began over four decades of ruthless dictatorships that crushed all opposition. These governments also fostered secular policies and some economic development, making Iraq one of the most prosperous Arab societies by the 1980s. They were usually led by members of the **Ba'ath** ("Renaissance") Party, which favored socialism and Arab nationalism and strongly opposed Israel. Representing the Sunni Arab minority of 20 percent, the Ba'ath ruled a nation with a restless Arab Shi'ite majority, located mostly in the south, and a disaffected Sunni Kurdish minority in the north. In 1979 Saddam Hussein (1937–2006), a landless peasant's son, seized power and proved even more brutal than his predecessors.

Alarmed by the Iranian Revolution, and hated by Ayatollah Khomeini, who considered Saddam's secular regime godless, in 1980 Saddam launched an invasion of Iran, using poison gas against Iranian soldiers, but he was unable to achieve victory. The war drew in outsiders because it threatened Persian Gulf shipping lanes and hence the world supply of oil. The United States, with its vested interest in Iraq's oil—the world's second largest proven reserves—and hostility toward Iran, sided with Iraq, attacking Iranian shipping and arming Saddam's military. As the casualties mounted, both Iran and Iraq drafted teenagers to fight. The costs of war were staggering: over 260,000 Iranian and 100,000 Iraqi dead and grave damage to the Iraqi economy.

Iraq and the United States

When the war ended in 1988 with no victor, Saddam's actions fostered regional tension. U.S. president George H. W. Bush (r. 1989–1993) viewed Saddam as a useful strategic ally and continued providing him with weapons. But Iraqi leaders had long claimed that Kuwait, a British protectorate until 1961 that sits atop oil riches and blocks Iraq from enjoying greater access to the Persian Gulf, should be part of Iraq. In 1990 Iraq invaded prosperous Kuwait, ruled by an Arab royal family. Bush, worried that oil-rich Saudi Arabia might be next, formed a coalition and launched the Persian Gulf War (1991), which drove Iraqis from Kuwait and killed perhaps 30,000 Iraqi soldiers. The war restored Americans' faith in their military, which had been undermined by the bitter defeat in Vietnam, but the euphoria proved short-lived. Saddam remained in power, persecuting dissidents and slaughtering Shi'ites and Kurds, who rebelled with U.S. encouragement. At least 30,000 Shi'ites and many thousands of Kurds died from the fighting. Nevertheless, Saddam's war-making capabilities had been badly damaged, and the United States and United Nations eventually gave the Kurds some military and police protection, allowing them to set up a government with democratic trappings in their northern region. Meanwhile, U.N. sanctions imposed to restrict Iraq's foreign income and ability to buy weapons undermined Iraq's economy. The Iraqi people struggled to acquire food and medical supplies, and thousands died from the resulting shortages.

Saudi Arabia, Oil, and the World

Saudi Society

The Persian Gulf War pointed out the close connection between Saudi Arabia and the United States, which had military bases and a strong economic stake in the kingdom. Mostly bleak desert, Saudi Arabia possesses the world's largest known oil reserves. The Saudis used oil revenues to fund modernization projects, building highways, hospitals, and universities, and by the 1980s they had achieved high health and literacy rates for the Middle East. Glittering shopping malls offer the latest Western fashions and electronic gadgets serve affluent urbanites, who reach the malls in luxury cars often driven by chauffeurs. Yet, outside the cities, poor Saudis often still travel by camel and sleep in tents.

Despite the modernization, Saudi political and social life has remained conservative, with the royal family exercising absolute power and living extravagantly while tolerating corruption and quashing dissent. They have used their power to maintain traditional customs and social patterns. Indeed, the country became a laboratory for the clash between modern institutions (like television) and a highly puritanical, patriarchal Islamic culture. With the acquiescence of the Saudi royal family, the Wahhabis, followers of the most rigid form of Islam, maintain a stranglehold on religious thought, life, and education. Wahhabis are hostile to Western and often any modern ideas; they believe, for example, that women should stay at home and be controlled by men. Hence, although some educated women wish to enjoy freedom, thanks to Wahhabi-influenced laws they still cannot legally drive or work or study alongside men. Armed with canes, a special police force patrols the

Bill Strode/Woodfin Camp & Associates

Oil Wealth Saudi Arabia contains the world's largest oil operations, mostly located on or near the Persian Gulf. A Saudi worker overlooks one of the nation's many refineries, which produces the oil exports that have brought the nation wealth.

streets, markets, and city malls to punish women for violating the strict dress codes, which require them to be covered head to foot. In the 1990s the religious police prevented unveiled female students from fleeing a school dormitory fire, causing dozens of the girls to burn to death. The Shi'ite minority, despised by the Wahhabis, have also enjoyed few rights. These conflicts have fostered tensions. Saudi and Western critics believe that what they see as the narrow Islam taught in Saudi schools promotes extremism and anti-Western feeling, and some Saudi men and women have called for a liberalization and women's empowerment.

Oil Wealth

OPEC (Organization of Petroleum Exporting Countries) A cartel formed in 1960 to give producers more power over the price of oil and leverage with the consuming nations.

Saudi Arabia's policies have strongly influenced world oil prices and availability. The kingdom was the major player in the formation in 1960 of **OPEC** (Organization of Petroleum Exporting Countries), a cartel designed to give the producers more power over the price of oil and leverage over consuming nations. OPEC's members range from Middle Eastern nations such as Algeria, Iran, and the United Arab Emirates to more distant countries such as Mexico, Nigeria, and Indonesia. In 1973 OPEC members, angry at Western support of Israel, reduced the world oil supply to raise prices, badly discomforting industrialized nations by causing long lines at gasoline stations. After the embargo ended, the world price remained high, enriching OPEC members. High prices also forced the United States and western Europe to find ways to conserve fuel, such as by designing more fuel-efficient cars. But in the 1980s reduced oil consumption broke OPEC's power and prices plummeted, damaging the economies of most OPEC members.

Saudi Arabia remained the world's largest exporter of oil, ensuring political support and profits from industrialized nations but not guaranteeing Saudi prosperity. Indeed, by the 1990s the Saudi economy had soured. Between 1980 and 2000 income levels fell by two-thirds, resulting in the cutting of government welfare benefits and climbing unemployment. Meanwhile, members of the royal family spent money lavishly and often violated Wahhabi restrictions with their high living abroad, cavorting in the nightclubs of Beirut and the casinos of Europe. Resentment of the royal family and its U.S. allies increased. Many Saudis oppose the U.S. military bases on Saudi soil, which symbolize U.S. support for the royal family and materialistic interest in the kingdom's oil. Seeing little future, frustrated young people often drink alcohol and have mixed-gender parties behind closed doors. Others have embraced militant Islam, a few joining terrorist groups such as Al Qaeda. Most of the young men who hijacked four U.S. airliners and crashed them into the Pentagon and World Trade Center in 2001 were Saudis, often well educated. The Al Qaeda leader, Osama bin Laden (b. 1957), a militant Wahhabi from a large, wealthy Saudi family, had long raged against the presence of U.S. military bases in Saudi Arabia. Yet, Saudis also have been among the biggest investors in the U.S. and European economies, and many Saudis have studied in the West. Thanks to oil, Saudi Arabia and the industrialized nations have remained close allies despite vastly different social and political systems.

SECTION SUMMARY

- After World War II, nationalist governments replaced many colonial regimes in the Middle East, but the region has failed to develop many working multiparty democracies.
- Egyptian leader General Gamal Abdul Nasser became a hero when he threw off British influence, seized control of the Suez Canal, and pursued socialist policies, but neither Nasser nor his pro-American successors brought prosperity to Egypt.
- Traumatized by the Holocaust, many Jews moved to Palestine after World War II and established the state of Israel, which led to a war between Jews and Arabs, a mass exodus of Palestinians into refugee camps, and enduring tensions.
- After the 1967 Arab-Israeli War, Israel occupied lands with a large Arab population and severely limited Arabs' freedom, and, while Israelis debated how to achieve peace, Palestinians became increasingly militant in their opposition.
- After nationalists overthrew the Iranian shah, the United States helped organize a coup that returned him to power, and he ruled ruthlessly until 1979, when he was overthrown by Islamic fundamentalists.
- From 1958 on, Iraq was ruled by ruthless military dictatorships dominated by the Sunni minority, and in 1979 Saddam Hussein came to power, launched a costly war against Iran, and then was attacked by the United States after invading Kuwait.
- Saudi Arabia grew extremely wealthy from oil sales, but many citizens have remained poor, and Saudi society is dominated by extremely conservative religious leaders, some of whose followers resent the close relationship the Saudi royal family has forged with the United States.

CHANGE AND CONFLICT IN THE MIDDLE EAST

What roles has Islam played in the contemporary Middle East?

In 1979 the Islamic world celebrated thirteen centuries of Islamic history. For most of those centuries Muslims had made brilliant contributions to the world, fostering extensive trade networks, accommodating and introducing scientific knowledge, and founding powerful empires. By the mid-twentieth century the European powers dominated the political and economic life of these societies, though many older traditions remained relevant into the present. In recent decades new conflicts resulting from foreign interventions, Islamic militancy, and international terrorism unsettled the Middle East and world politics.

Social Change and Conflict

Divisions in Lebanon

In parts of the Middle East ethnic and religious hostilities have fostered long-term conflict. In Lebanon a series of political crises and a long civil war resulted from competition between a dozen rival factions, Christian, Sunni, and Sh'ia, for control of the small state. In this deeply fragmented land, a national government mostly existed only in name during the 1970s and 1980s. Beirut, once a prosperous, freewheeling mecca for trade, entertainment, and tourism, was devastated by factional fighting. Supporting various factions, Israel, Syria, and the United States were all sucked into the conflict. Syria stationed troops in the north and east, and Israel in the south. In the 1980s the United States intervened on behalf of a weak national government led by the largest, most pro-Western Christian faction. U.S. warships shelled areas around Beirut dominated by opposition, especially Shi'ite, factions while U.S. Marines secured the Beirut airport. The disastrous U.S. mission resulted in some five hundred U.S. deaths from suicide bombers and the holding of U.S. hostages. The intervention also made the United States a focus of Arab rage. In the 1990s the fighting ebbed, and Lebanon regained some stability but little national unity. However, the U.S. and Israeli interventions energized radical Shi'ites, who formed a militant Iran-backed organization, Hezbollah **(HEZ-bo-LAH)**, which shelled Israel. The Israelis responded by invading Lebanon in 2006 to weaken Hezbollah, but the incursion was costly in lives on all sides and failed to destroy Hezbollah, which remained a strong force in the deeply polarized Lebanon politics.

In the Sudan, a huge country, the Arab Muslim-dominated government, which imposed an Islamic state, used military force to control the rebellious black African Christians and animists in the south, a conflict that resulted in 2 million deaths. In 2005 the two sides agreed to end the conflict, but by then a rebellion in Darfur, an impoverished western region where African Muslim farmers competed for scarce land with Arab pastoralists, had erupted. The government launched, with the aid of local Arab militias, a genocide against the Africans, earning condemnation from around the world. Thousands of people died from military assaults on their villages or from disease and starvation after they fled, many into neighboring Chad. By 2009, violence also resurfaced in the south.

Ethnic Conflicts

Another longtime ethnic conflict concerned Kurds, a large ethnic group—over 20 million strong—inhabiting mountain districts in Iran, Iraq, Syria, and Turkey. Although deeply divided by clan and factional rivalries, Kurds had long sought either their own nation or self-government within their countries of residence, generating constant conflict with central governments. Kurdish rebel groups were especially active in eastern Turkey, where the Turkish government, hoping to build a national identity based on Turkish values and language, repressed Kurdish culture and language. Kurds were also restless in oil-rich northern Iraq, where the dictator, Saddam Hussein, made Kurds a special target of his repression, launching air raids and poison gas attacks against Kurdish villages.

Gender Relations

In almost all Arab countries, gender relations and family life have changed relatively little. Although women have been elected prime ministers in the predominantly Muslim nations of Bangladesh, Pakistan, Indonesia, and Turkey, no Arab or Iranian women have reached this goal. In Turkey, Iraq, Jordan, and Lebanon urban women have expanded their opportunities by running businesses and entering the professions. But many women have remained in the home, often secluded from the outside world, with their lives as daughters, wives, and mothers controlled by men. Liberals have advocated improving women's lives through education, and Turkey, Tunisia, and Iraq have adopted Western-influenced family laws allowing civil marriages that accord women rights in divorce and child custody. Blaming patriarchal cultural traditions for restrictions, some women activists have argued that the Quran supports women's rights, using such arguments to fight against controlling parents and spouses. But conservative Muslims have prevented the enactment of liberal laws in other Middle Eastern societies. Moreover, devout women have often opposed secular feminism, arguing that women are best protected by strict Islamic law. Zainab Al-Ghazali (1917–2005) in Egypt founded an organization that built mosques, trained female preachers, and promoted an active women's role in public life, but her staunch support of Islamic values upset not only liberal feminists but also Egypt's modernizing President Nasser, who had her jailed and tortured. The conflict between modernizers and traditionalists has often resulted in gender role confusion, as an Egyptian writer noted: "Our mothers understood their situation. We, however, are lost. We do not know whether or not we still belong to the harem, whether love is forbidden or permitted."[3]

Liberal and conservative Muslims disagree on women's dress. Liberals often see the veil as symbolizing female subjugation, and many women from the urban middle and upper classes have adopted Western dress. However, traditionalists have praised the veil as essential to female modesty. In secular nations such as Turkey and Egypt, women influenced by revivalist Islam have lobbied to wear the full veil or the head scarf as a symbol of piety. In Turkey the secular government, wary of Islamic militancy, long banned head scarves from schools, a policy that has been recently modified. A young Egyptian reflected the views of many religious women when she claimed that "being totally covered saves me from the approaches of men and hungry looks. I feel more free, purer, and more respectable."[4] Indeed, many independent-minded, well-educated Muslim women have not wanted to uncritically adopt Western ways. The liberal Moroccan sociologist and Quranic scholar Fatema Mernissi, a frequent visitor to the West, argued that Western women face their own version of the veil through their obsession with physical appearance, limiting their ability to compete with men for power: "I thank you, Allah, for sparing me the tyranny of the 'size six harem.' I am so happy that the conservative male elite [in the Middle East] does not know about it. Imagine the [Muslim] fundamentalists switching from the veil to forcing women to fit size 6."[5]

Attitudes toward homosexuality have often become more repressive. For centuries many Muslim societies tolerated, although did not approve, homosexual activity, and writings sympathetically exploring homosexual experiences circulated widely. By the late 1800s this changed, forcing homosexuals into the closet. In the 1990s the taboo began to slowly diminish, at least in some cities. The strict gender segregation in countries such as Saudi Arabia, where people spend most of their time, and enjoy emotional bonds, with other people of the same sex, and where hand holding between same-sex friends is common, makes it easier for homosexual couples to escape notice.

Yet, in many countries homosexual behavior, when discovered, frequently results in jail terms or even execution.

Religion and Culture

Islamic Divisions

Islamists Antimodern, usually puritanical Islamic militants who seek an Islamic state.

The clash between tradition and modernity has provided a fertile environment for creativity in religion, music, and literature. Islam has remained at the heart of Middle Eastern life, but, despite its message of peace, social justice, and community, it has often proved divisive (see Map 30.2). Age-old divisions between Sunni and Shi'a, liberal and conservative, secular and devout, Sufi and anti-Sufi, remain powerful. Antimodern, usually puritanical militants known as **Islamists**, who seek an Islamic state and are bitter rivals of secular Muslims, have become increasingly influential, especially in Egypt, Sudan, Algeria, Turkey, and Iran. After World War I the Islamist Muslim Brotherhood spread around the region. The Iranian Ali Shariati (SHAR-ee-AH-tee) (1933–1977), educated in France but a critic of the West who influenced Shi'ites, castigated Western democracy as subverted by the power of money but also social justice and blamed Islamic tradition for reducing women to, as he put it, the level of a washing machine. Egyptian writer Sayyid Qutb (SIGH-eed ka-TOOB) (1906–1966) sparked political Sunni Islam and redefined *jihad* ("struggle") as violent opposition to the West rather than personal struggle to maintain faith. Qutb lived in the United States for two years; he found Americans friendly but was appalled by the antiblack racism and by the hedonism, such as heavy drinking and casual romantic relations between men and women, that he witnessed. Returning to Egypt, Qutb promoted an Islamic state and joined the Muslim Brotherhood. Inspired by thinkers like Qutb, the most extreme Islamists, known as *jihadists,* plotted violence against secular Muslims, Sufis, and non-Muslims they considered obstacles to imposing their rigid version of Islam.

Disillusionment with repressive and corrupt governments, dissatisfaction with lack of material improvement, and resentment of Western world power have prompted a growing turn to Islam. When elections are allowed, Islamic groups with their large followings tend to triumph over secular parties, as happened in Iraq, Egypt, and Palestine in 2005, a reason why pro-Western modernists often fear democracy. In a troubled world the Islamic revival satisfies for millions a need for personal solace, a yearning for tradition, and a dream of a just political system as propounded by the earliest Muslims. Islamic dress and practice became more common in Egypt after war losses to Israel, as well as in Iraq after the U.S. invasion of 2003, which overthrew Saddam Hussein and the secular Ba'athist government. Devout Muslims dominate the U.S.-installed Iraqi government. While activists in Iraq have closed bars, harassed unveiled women, and terrorized Christians, Sunni militants in various lands have attacked followers of Sufi mysticism as heretics. Islamist movements in Algeria, Egypt, and Saudi Arabia have also challenged their governments, sometimes using terrorism; some, frustrated at home, join international terrorist groups.

Popular Culture

While Islamic militants have condemned music, dance, and other pleasures, many people—both the secular and the devout—have been fans of popular culture, especially popular music. Musicians often hope to encourage national unity or shape society, usually in a more liberal direction. The Egyptian singer Oum Kulthum (oom KAL-thoom) (1904–1975) symbolized Arab people's feelings. Attracting a region-wide following with her emotional songs of love and abandonment, Kulthum dominated Middle Eastern popular music from the 1940s through the 1960s. At her height she was one of the two most popular figures among Arabs, the other being her friend, Egypt's president Nasser. Her concerts attracted huge crowds, and her recordings were always on the radio and in films. Popular music also created a sense of community. The songs of peace and coexistence sung by hugely popular Lebanese singer Fairuz (fie-ROOZ) were sometimes credited with being the major symbol of hope in that turbulent, civil war–plagued land. Similarly, Israelis revered Yemen-born Shoshana Damari (1923–2006), whose optimistic songs encouraged Israeli unity by extolling the nation and its military forces.

In religiously dogmatic or ethnically divided states, popular music has sometimes stirred controversy. The Islamic government of Iran, opposed to women performing in public, tried to silence all female singers, especially the vocalist and film star Googoosh (GOO-goosh), whose melancholic Westernized pop music had a huge audience during the 1960s and 1970s. The clerics destroyed all her recordings, posters, and films, turning Googoosh into a popular symbol against clerical rule. The *arabesk* pop music of Turkey is rooted in the experiences of poor Arab and Kurdish migrants to Istanbul. One observer noted that "arabesk describes a decaying city in which poverty-stricken migrant workers are exploited and abused, and calls on its listeners to pour another glass of wine and curse fate and the world."[6] Some popular music styles blend Arab and

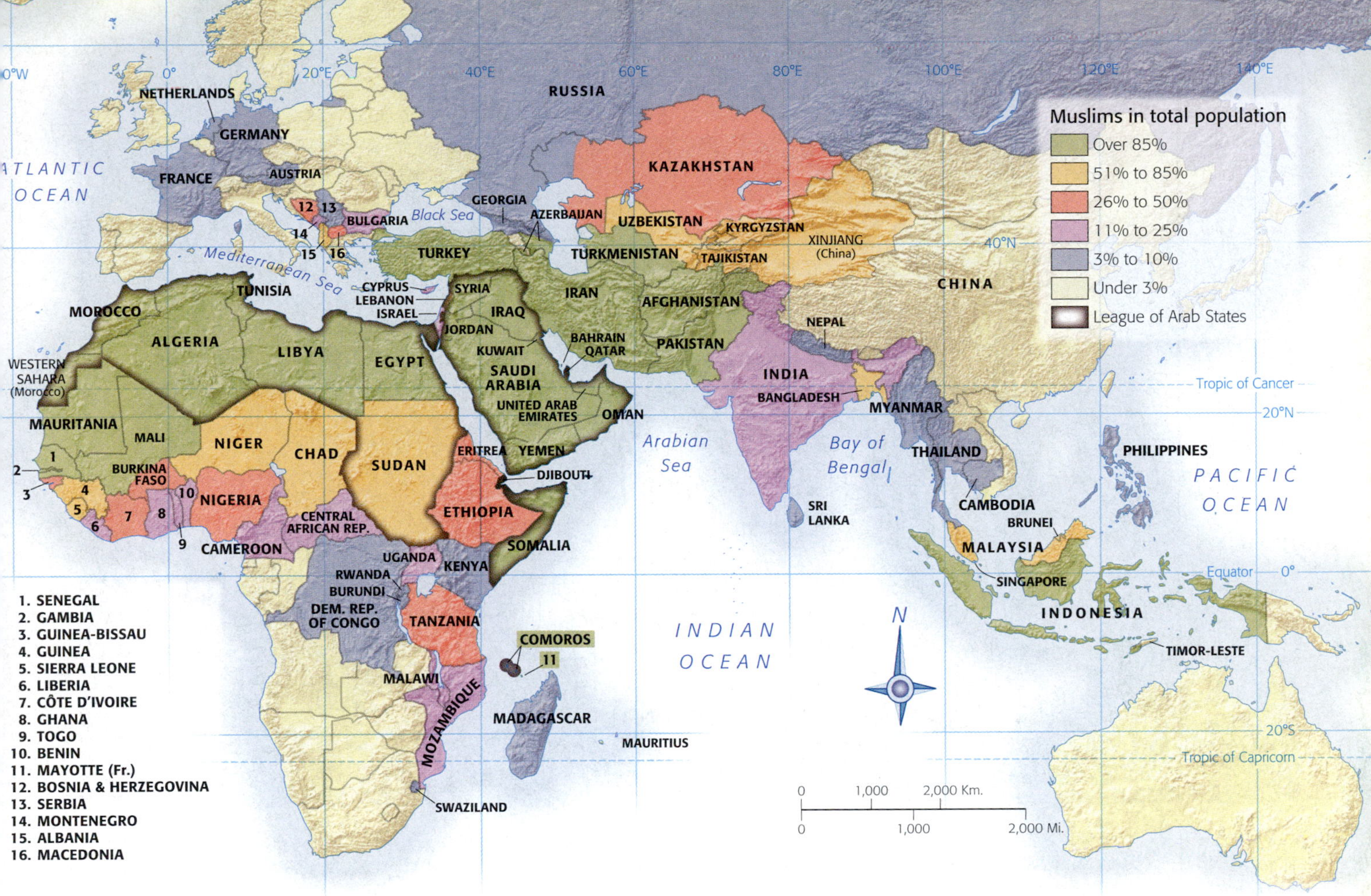

Map 30.2 The Islamic World

The Islamic world includes not only the Middle East—Western Asia and North Africa—but also countries with Muslim majorities in sub-Saharan Africa, Central Asia, and South and Southeast Asia. In addition, Muslims live in most other Eastern Hemisphere nations and in the Americas.

e Interactive Map

foreign forms while addressing social problems. The **rai** ("opinion") pop music of Algeria is based on local Bedouin chants, Spanish flamenco, French café songs, Egyptian pop, and other influences, and its improvised lyrics often deal with forbidden themes of sex and alcohol. By the 1970s synthesizers, drum machines, and electric guitars were added to the exciting mix. Rai holds great appeal to urban working-class youth in North Africa and to the offspring of Arab immigrants in France, but it is anathema to puritanical Islamic militants in Algeria, who have frequently forced singers into exile or even assassinated them. Rai musicians have often moved their base to Paris.

rai ("opinion") A pop music of Algeria based on local Bedouin chants, Spanish flamenco, French café songs, Egyptian pop, and other influences and featuring improvised lyrics that often deal with forbidden themes of sex and alcohol.

Literature

Middle Eastern writers have also expressed ideas forbidden in politics and religion. The novels of the Egyptian Naguib Mahfuz **(nah-GEEB mah-FOOZ)** (b. 1911–2006), a merchant's son turned government official and journalist, have addressed social problems, such as poverty, and questioned conservative religious values and blind faith, which he believes keep individuals from realizing their full potential. Many of his writings have been banned in Egypt and other nations. But in 1988 Mahfuz, strongly influenced by both Western and Arab writers, became the first Arab writer to win a Nobel Prize for literature. Iranian writers have often risked punishment attacking religious hypocrisy while satirizing the failings of governments and business. One famous Iranian novel recommended opportunism for career success: "Try to establish connections with the holders of high offices. Agree with everybody, no matter what his opinion is."[7]

Turmoil in Afghanistan and Iraq

Afghanistan and Russia

Afghanistan and Iraq have been two of the most troubled nations, and both were reshaped by foreign interventions. Violence and extreme militant Islamic movements generated instability in Afghanistan for three decades. Afghanistan's diverse Muslim ethnic groups, subdivided

Monument to Revolution, Liberation Square, Baghdad. Artist: Jawad Salim

Arab Art The large monument of Revolution, in Baghdad, sculpted by a major modern Iraqi artist, Jawad Salim (1920–1961), occupies a central place in the city. Commissioned in 1958 after the overthrow of the monarchy, it celebrates the Iraqi struggle for justice and freedom and often provided a motif for Iraqi poets.

into rival tribes, have little sense of national unity. From the early 1800s until 1978 kings from the largest ethnic group, the Pashtuns, loosely governed the territory. Some Afghan leaders advocated modernization, triggering revolts by conservative tribes. In 1978 procommunist generals seized power, forged close ties with the Soviet Union, and introduced radical social and economic reforms that challenged Islamic traditions. They implemented land reform, promoted women's education, and replaced Islamic law with a secular family law giving women more rights. When conservative Islamic rebels, known as **mujahidin** (moo-JAH-hi-deen) ("holy warriors"), rebelled against the pro-Soviet regime, the USSR invaded in 1979 to protect their allies, launching decades of turbulence. The mujahidin, while poorly armed and divided, won small victories against the 150,000 Soviet troops. Both sides were ruthless, attacking civilians suspected of aiding or supporting the enemy. Indiscriminate Soviet air attacks on the rebels created 5 million refugees and turned the population against the Soviet occupation. Meanwhile, the United States, Pakistan, and Arab nations sent military and financial aid to the rebels and to Islamic volunteers such as the wealthy Saudi Osama bin Laden (b. 1957). Afghanistan became an unwinnable quagmire for the Soviet forces, and they withdrew in 1989, a defeat that led to the ending of Soviet communism and the dismantling of the Soviet Empire. The pro-Soviet government collapsed, and rival mujahidin groups fought for control. With the USSR gone and the civil war over, the West offered little help to reconstruct the ruined country.

mujahidin ("holy warriors") Conservative Islamic rebels who rebelled against the pro-Soviet regime in Afghanistan in the 1970s and 1980s.

As conflict between rival militias continued, a group of Pashtun militants known as the **Taliban** ("Students"), many educated in Pakistani Islamic schools, organized a military force to impose order and stamp out what they considered immoral behavior among the tribal factions fighting each other. The Taliban conquered much of the Pashtun south, then seized the capital, Kabul, in 1996 and eventually extended their influence into the north. The puritanical Taliban introduced an especially harsh form of Islamic rule. Women in Kabul, who once wore jeans and T-shirts and attended universities, were now required to wear long black robes and stay at home. Education for women was banned and alcohol disappeared from stores. The Taliban also banned pleasures such as music and films as sinful and executed people for even minor infractions. Although the streets were safe, life offered no joy. Reflecting their disdain for Afghanistan's pre-Islamic past, the Taliban

Taliban ("Students") A group of Pashtun religious students who organized a military force in the 1980s to fight what they considered immorality and corruption and to impose order in Afghanistan.

also destroyed spectacular monumental Buddhas carved into a mountainside over a millennium ago, outraging the world.

Al Qaeda and the United States

Meanwhile, international terrorist groups with a jihadist agenda and hatred for the West and the Saudi royal family formed around radical Arab volunteers who had come to fight for the mujahidin and then remained. Osama bin Laden, who became the leader and chief financial backer of the largest group, Al Qaeda, called on Muslims to take up arms against the United States and other Western regimes, whom he called "crusaders" after those Christian knights who fought Muslims during the Intermediate Era: "Tell the Muslims everywhere that the vanguards of the warriors who are fighting the enemies of Islam belong to them."[8] These Islamic terrorist groups made Taliban-controlled Afghanistan their base, building camps to train more terrorists.

After the Al Qaeda attacks on the United States in September 2001, Americans, with widespread world support, sent military forces into Afghanistan, where, with local anti-Taliban allies, they soon displaced the Taliban from government and the main cities, destroyed the Al Qaeda bases, and installed a fragile pro-Western government. Many Afghans and most Muslims outside Afghanistan applauded the Taliban's demise, but instability ensued: the major Taliban and Al Qaeda leaders, including bin Laden, went into hiding, and the victors struggled to foster development and support a fledgling democracy, especially after the United States shifted much of its military force and development aid to Iraq. In 2005 the Taliban regrouped and mounted an insurgency against the pro-Western regime and the U.S.-European forces that supported it. By 2009, using Pakistan tribal areas as a refuge and recruiting base, the Taliban controlled large sections of the Pashtun south, forcing the new Obama administration in the United States to send in more troops, expand development efforts, and pressure Pakistan to better police the porous border.

U.S. Occupation of Iraq

The Afghan war was followed by a larger conflict in Iraq. Charging that Saddam Hussein had weapons of mass destruction and was linked to Al Qaeda, the U.S. president George W. Bush ordered an invasion and occupation of Iraq in 2003 by U.S. troops and small forces from a few other nations. But Bush got no support from the United Nations, many Western allies, and regional allies such as Turkey and Egypt. Massive looting followed the quick U.S. victory, as museums, ancient historical sites, power plants, armories, and communications networks were plundered. U.S. credibility suffered after American claims about the Iraqi threat proved wrong. Nor had the Americans adequately planned for the problems of the postwar reconstruction, forcing them to shift troops and resources from Afghanistan to Iraq. While the Bush administration changed its goal to fostering democracy, containing factional divisions and restoring basic services such as electricity and clean water proved a challenge.

Although Saddam was captured and executed, American forces, lacking enough troops, also struggled to maintain order against a persistent resistance movement, supported by many Sunnis and some Shi'ites, and to defend against terrifying suicide bombings by newly arrived foreign jihadis linked to Al Qaeda. Between 2003 and 2008 over 100,000 Iraqis died, 2 million became refugees in neighboring countries, and many were forced from their neighborhoods by "ethnic cleansing." Many Iraqis, especially Shi'ites and Kurds, had hated Saddam's bloody regime and welcomed its demise, but Iraqis, remembering British colonization after World War I, often resented yet another Western occupation and feared potential U.S. control of their oil industry. While some Arab liberals hoped democracy would flower in Iraq and throughout the region, the occupation of an oil-rich Arab country, at a high cost in U.S. and Iraqi casualties, tied down the U.S. military in a quagmire and intensified anti-U.S. feeling around the world, probably increasing support for Islamic militancy in the Muslim world generally. However, Iraqis now elected their own government, one whose Shi'ite leaders were closely tied to Iran, that had to handle ethnic and tribal rivalries while trying to hold the nation together. By 2009 violence had diminshed but had not ended, and a large U.S. military presence remained.

The Middle East in the Global System

Confronting Modernity

By the late twentieth century, many observers in the region argued that most Middle Eastern countries had adjusted poorly to a rapidly changing world, lagging behind much of Asia and Latin America in development. A Lebanese novelist wrote that the dictatorial Arab regimes succeeded in depriving people not only of dignity but also of air: the opportunity to discuss problems freely. In 2002 Arab thinkers issued an Arab Human Development Report that outlined economic and social failures, including the marginalization of women and the limited development in health and education (see Witness to the Past: Assessing Arab Development). Debate has been spurred by regional cable networks, such as Qatar-based Al Jazeera, that spread awareness of political and social developments while promoting a modern image, such as by using unveiled female news anchors. Some urban people have access to the Internet, often at cafés, and go online to access foreign news, shop, or arrange dates, and Arab and Turkish chat rooms and blogs abound. Religious and political groups also use the Web to recruit support, among them Al Qaeda and the Iraqi insurgents fighting the U.S. occupation.

Economic Problems

The region's economic record has been checkered. The Middle East has had the world's highest unemployment rate and, except for sub-Saharan Africa, the slowest economic growth and lowest productivity. Only Turkey has fostered much industrialization and high economic growth. Nations with oil, such as Algeria, Iran, and Libya, have remained dangerously dependent on oil revenues for survival. Some 10 million migrant workers from other Arab countries, South Asia, and Southeast Asia work in the Gulf states, though most are semiskilled or unskilled and often face abuse and discrimination. Oil wealth often leads to political corruption, spurs autocratic leaders to oppose democracy, and sometimes funds Islamist and terrorist groups. Yet several small Persian Gulf states have used their oil wealth to become centers of global commerce. For example, Dubai has become one of the world's most modern cities and the region's most globalized society, with luxury hotels, towering skyscrapers, futuristic architecture, the world's largest artificial port, local branches of Western universities, and thousands of businessmen and workers from all over the world. However, the 2008–2009 world economic crisis also hurt Dubai, and many foreigners left. Yet, the Western, Japanese, and new Chinese and Indian appetite for oil ensures that the profits will flow to oil-rich nations for years to come. Middle Eastern nations that are without oil and so must rely mostly on agriculture, such as Egypt and Lebanon, have struggled to build modern economies with limited resources.

Past and present, tradition and modernity, have been all jumbled in the contemporary Middle East, whose people have hoped to preserve revered traditional patterns while harmonizing them with the modern world. An Egyptian novelist wrote that a Cairo resident has a split personality: "Half of him believes, prays, fasts and makes the pilgrimage [to Mecca]. The other half renders his values void in banks and courts and in the streets, the cinemas, perhaps even at home among his family before the television set."[9] The recent history of the Middle East, like that of India and sub-Saharan Africa, challenges the notion that contact with the modern world automatically erodes all traditional cultures and steers people inevitably toward Western models. Older patterns of life and thought have persisted in much of the region. Observers disagree whether this constitutes a barrier to progress or gives the people an anchor to deal with the destabilizing effects of change.

Islamic Militancy

Islamic militancy has become a major force, tapping a strand of unease with Western ideas. Many Muslims reject what they see as the materialistic, hedonistic values of Western culture. The Iranian Revolution of 1979 was the first successful attempt by an Islamic country to become totally independent of Western political, economic, social, and cultural influence. Iranians and Arabs have often agreed with the Indian Muslim poet Muhammad Iqbal **(ik-BALL)** (1873–1938), who wrote in 1927: "Against Europe I protest, And the attraction of the West: Woe for Europe and her charm, Swift to capture and disarm! Earth awaits rebuilding; rise! Out of slumber deep, Arise!"[10] Militancy has emerged as a challenge to capitalism, secularism, failed governments, and Western-style democracy. Other Muslims have feared Islamic militancy, which has not delivered a better material life in the main countries it controls, Iran and Sudan. The hopes of modernist reformest Muslims for greater economic development, political freedom, and rights for women were expressed by Reza Aslan, an influential liberal Iranian based in the United States, who argued that a reformation has begun to cleanse Islam of the "false idols" of bigotry and fanaticism and return the faith to its roots as an egalitarian social reform movement.

The Middle East and the Superpowers

Interventions by outside powers, such as the USSR and the United States, reflected the global importance of the Middle East, especially its oil wealth and its strategic location among key waterways of world trade. Until cost-effective alternative power sources become common, all industrial economies need access to Middle Eastern oil, without which modern lifestyles would come to a screeching halt. The desires of some countries to control the oil flow have led to wars, since the world community will not tolerate anything that threatens the movement of oil tankers through the Persian Gulf. While U.S. leaders hope democracy will spread, many experts worry that instability in Iraq has unsettled the entire region, perhaps strengthening Iran and forcing the United States to maintain a large military presence. Furthermore, few conflicts or persistent problems, including the Arab-Israel conflict and Arab-Iranian tensions, seem resolvable anytime soon. These challenges make the Middle East a focus of world attention and, some fear, a potential tinderbox.

Assessing Arab Development

Under the auspices of the United Nations Development Programme, a group of Arab scholars and opinion makers from the twenty-two member states of the Arab League, a regional organization, met to consider the Arab condition. In 2002 they issued the first of four planned reports that offered both a description of the Arab condition and a prescription for change. Hailed by Arab and non-Arab observers as a pathbreaking effort by Arabs to foster a debate on the inadequacies of Arab development and local barriers to progress, the first document reported great strides in many areas but also unsolved problems. This excerpt is from the Executive Summary.

The Arab Human Development Report 2002 . . . places people squarely at the [center] of development in all its dimensions: economic, social, civil, political, and cultural. It provides a neutral forum to measure progress and deficits, propose strategies to policymakers, and draw attention to country problems that can benefit from regional solutions. It is guided by the conviction that solid analysis can contribute to the many efforts underway to mobilize the region's rich human potential. There has been considerable progress in laying the foundations for health, habitat, and education. Two notable achievements are the enormous quantitative expansion in educating the young and a conspicuous improvement in fighting death. For example, life expectancy has increased by 15 years over the last three decades, and infant mortality rates have dropped by two-thirds. Moreover, the region's growth has been "pro-poor": there is much less dire poverty (defined as an income of less than a dollar a day) than in any other developing region.

But there have been warning signs as well. Over the past twenty years, growth in per capita income was the lowest in the world except in sub-Saharan Africa. . . . If such trends continue [into] the future, it will take the average Arab citizen 140 years to double his or her income. . . . The decline in productivity has been accompanied by deterioration in real wages, which has accentuated poverty. It is evident that . . . Arab countries have not developed as quickly or as fully as other comparable regions. . . . The Arab region is richer than it is developed, . . . hobbled by a . . . poverty of capabilities and . . . opportunities. These have their roots in three deficits: freedom, women's empowerment, and knowledge. Growth alone will neither bridge these gaps nor set the region on the road to sustainable development.

The way forward involves tackling human capabilities and knowledge. It also involves promoting systems of good governance, those that promote, support and sustain human well-being, based on expanding human capabilities, choices, opportunities and freedoms, . . . especially for the poorest and most marginalized members of society. The empowerment of women must be addressed throughout. . . .

[The Report concludes that] People in most Arab countries live longer than the world average life expectancy of 67. However, disease and disability reduce life expectancy by between five and 11 years. Arab women have lower life expectancy than the world average. . . . Arab countries have made tangible progress in improving literacy: . . . female literacy rates tripled since 1970. Yet 65 million adults are illiterate, almost two-thirds of them women. . . . One out of every five Arabs lives on less than $2 per day . . . Arab countries had the lowest freedom score [in the world] in the late 1990s. . . . [Utilization] of Arab women's capabilities through political and economic participation remains the lowest in the world. . . . Serious knowledge deficits include weak systems of scientific research and development.

The Arab world is at a crossroads. The fundamental choice is whether its trajectory will remain marked by inertia, as reflected in much of the present institutional context, and by ineffective policies that have produced the substantial development challenges facing the region; or whether prospects for an Arab renaissance, anchored in human development will be actively pursued.

THINKING ABOUT THE READING

1. How have Arabs done in promoting freedom, women's empowerment, and knowledge?
2. What does the report consider the major improvements and the major failures and challenges of the Arab nations?

Source: Arab Human Development Report 2002: Creating Opportunities for Future Generations (UNDP, 2002), available online at http://www.rbas.undp.org/ahdr/press_kits2002/PRExecSummary.pdf. Reprinted with permission of the United Nations Development Program (UNDP).

SECTION SUMMARY

- For several decades, Lebanon was mired in civil war among a variety of factions supported by foreign governments, including the United States; in the Sudan, Arab Muslims fought with African Christians and launched a genocide against African Muslims; and the Kurds came into conflict with the governments of several Middle Eastern countries.
- Although some Middle Eastern women have attained greater freedom and adopted Western dress, many remain in the home and wear a veil, which some argue protects them from predatory men.
- Middle Eastern societies have been divided between Islamists and secular Muslims, and musicians and writers, popular among the people, have raised the ire of religious conservatives.
- In Afghanistan, U.S.-supported Islamic rebels and Soviet-assisted communists fought for a decade until the Soviets withdrew, after which the Taliban, led by extremely conservative, repressive Muslims, took over much of the country and allowed terrorist groups such as Al Qaeda to base themselves there.
- After Al Qaeda's September 2001 attack on the United States, a U.S.-led invasion overthrew the Taliban and set up a weak pro-Western government, and in 2003 the United States invaded Iraq, generating massive looting and persistent, violent opposition, even by Iraqis who hated life under Saddam Hussein.
- Middle Eastern societies have been torn between those who feel they have failed to adapt to the modern world and those who champion tradition and urge rejection of the modern, Western values, while the region has remained extremely important to outside powers, such as the United States, because of its oil reserves.

POLITICAL CHANGE IN SUB-SAHARAN AFRICA

What were the main political consequences of decolonization in sub-Saharan Africa?

As in the Middle East, the rise of nationalism and the consequent wave of decolonization in Africa between 1957 and 1975 reduced Western political influence, reshaping societies and politics (see Chronology: Sub-Saharan Africa, 1945–Present). Countries won political independence as the British, French, Belgians, Spanish, and eventually the Portuguese came to terms with rising nationalist activity. In the 1960s, as optimistic Africans celebrated their freedom and formed governments, some observers proclaimed that this was Africa's Age of Glamor. The times were electric with change, and hopes for a better future were high. The years since have been the most momentous and rapid time of change in all of Africa's history, though they have often been destabilizing. Africans still struggle to find the right mix of policies to resolve their problems.

Nationalism and Decolonization

Anti-Colonialism

Rising nationalism sparked decolonization. The European colonial powers did little to encourage national feeling among Africans and maintained control through divide and rule of the different ethnic groups. Nationalists also had to struggle to overcome the ethnic complexities within colonies whose boundaries were arbitrarily imposed by the colonialists. But the increasing nationalism often encouraged the Western colonizers to transfer power peacefully. World War II, during which Europeans slaughtered both one another and the Africans they drafted or recruited to fight in North Africa, Asia, and Europe, undermined Western credibility. Africans felt revulsion against the Western powers and their pretensions of superiority, represented by the British official in Nigeria who argued that Nigerian "barbarism" required maintaining the "civilizing mission" into the far future. While the British and French espoused freedom and democracy, Africans noticed that these values were seldom applied in the colonies. With Western vulnerability obvious, nationalist leaders negotiated for reforms in the 1940s. After the war the British encouraged African hopes by granting independence to India and Burma and by introducing local government in some African colonies. Yet most colonial governments did little to prepare their societies for true political and economic independence.

Independence Movements

The first change came in the British Gold Coast. In 1948 riots followed when small farmers boycotted European businesses they suspected of profiteering at their expense. A rising leader, Kwame

Nkrumah **(KWAH-mee nn-KROO-muh)** (1909–1972), who had graduated from both British and American universities, became convinced that only socialism could save Africa, and in 1949 he organized a political party. He was soon arrested by the British, who viewed Nkrumah as a dangerous leftist. However, because of the continued unrest the British allowed an election in 1951 for a legislative council, which was won by Nkrumah's party. After negotiations, in 1957 the Gold Coast became independent and was renamed Ghana, after the first great West African kingdom over a millennium earlier. Nkrumah became the nation's first prime minister and Africa's hero. His message was **pan-Africanism**, the dream that all Africans would cooperate to eventually form some sort of united states of the continent.

The anticolonial dam had now burst, and it was impossible to stem the tide. By 1963, after peaceful negotiations and workers' strikes, all the British colonies in West Africa had become independent. By contrast, the French had no plans to abandon their empire and fought brutal but unsuccessful wars in the 1950s to keep Vietnam and Algeria as colonies. Finally realizing that a peaceful transition might better maintain their economic influence, France gave its colonies the option of a complete break or autonomy within a French community of closely connected nations. Initially only Guinea opted to expel the French completely, prompting the French to withdraw all economic aid. Later all the French colonies became fully independent, though they usually maintained close political and economic ties to France.

Whereas peaceful power transfers succeeded in many colonies, widespread violence preceded or accompanied independence in others. Many British settlers had migrated to Kenya after both World War I and World War II, taking land from the Africans to establish farms. In 1952 many Gikuyu, Kenya's largest ethnic group, who had suffered the most land losses, began an eight-year uprising known as the **Mau Mau Rebellion**, during which they attacked British farmers and officials. The British sent thousands of troops and committed atrocities against pro-Mau Mau villages, ultimately killing 10,000 Gikuyu and detaining 90,000 others in harsh prison camps, where many died from disease or mistreatment. Finally realizing the futility of their cause, the British released from prison the leading nationalist leader, Jomo Kenyatta **(ken-YAH-tuh)** (ca. 1889–1978), a Gikuyu former herd boy who had studied anthropology in Britain. Negotiations resulted in Kenyan independence in 1963, and Kenyatta became the first freely elected prime minister. Britain also granted independence to its other East African colonies, Uganda and Tanzania. In Kenya white settlers who had strongly opposed political rights for the African majority often remained, sometimes serving in the Kenyan government.

CHRONOLOGY

Sub-Saharan Africa, 1945–Present

1948 Introduction of apartheid in South Africa

1949 First mass-based political party in Gold Coast

1952–1960 Mau Mau uprising in Kenya

1957 Independence for Ghana

1957–1975 African decolonization

1961 Assassination of Patrice Lumumba in Congo

1965–1980 White government in Southern Rhodesia

1967–1970 Nigerian civil war

1975 Independence for Portuguese colonies

1991–1994 Civil war in Somalia

1994 Genocide in Rwanda

1994 Nelson Mandela first black president of South Africa

1997 End of Mobuto era in Congo

pan-Africanism The dream that all Africans would cooperate to eventually form some sort of united states of the continent.

Mau Mau Rebellion An eight-year uprising in the 1950s by the Gikuyu people in Kenya against British rule.

Violence also engulfed the Belgian Congo, a vast, natural resource–rich territory containing some two hundred ethnic groups. The Belgians had failed to foster an educated leadership class, encourage national consciousness, or build adequate paved roads, bridges, and telephone systems. At independence the Congo had only a few university graduates. The only Congolese leader with any national following, the widely admired left-leaning visionary Patrice Lumumba **(loo-MOOM-buh)** (1925–1961), a former post office clerk and brewery director, opposed economic domination by Belgian business and mining interests. In 1959 riots broke out in Congolese cities, forcing the Belgians to announce the colony's first free elections, which were won by Lumumba's party. As Lumumba took power, some Congolese troops mutinied and attacked whites. Taking advantage of the chaos, Belgian-supported leaders in the mineral-rich Katanga region who opposed Lumumba announced their secession from the country. The United Nations sent in a peacekeeping force that restored order in the Congo. But Katanga leaders, with the complicity of Belgium and the United States, who feared that Lumumba favored the Soviet Union, abducted and murdered him in 1961. Both Belgium and the U.S. supported the Congo's new leader, General Joseph Mobuto **(mo-BOO-to)**, who became a dictator. In 1971 Mobuto, who had given his country a new name, Zaire, also changed his name to Mobuto Sese Seko, "Mobuto the All Powerful." He required his people to sing his praises every day at the workplace and in schools and to replace European names and values with African ones, including exchanging Western clothes, such as ties, for traditional garb. Wearing a tie then became an act of political resistance for men.

Dismantling Portuguese Rule

Portugal, ruled by a fascist dictator, had been reluctant to give up its empire. When revolts broke out in its three colonies—Angola, Guinea-Bissau, and Mozambique—in the 1960s, the Portuguese military struggled to crush them. Angola's liberation movement was divided into three rival

Hulton-Deutch Collection/Corbis

Mau Mau During the 1950s Africans in Kenya, especially the Gikuyu, rebelled against British colonial rule. The British responded by detaining some 90,000 suspected rebels and sympathizers in concentration camps such as this, where many died.

factions based on the country's major ethnic groupings, while Marxists led the major liberation movements in Mozambique and Guinea Bissau. The visionary Amilcar Cabral **(AH-mill-CAR kah-BRAHL)** (1924–1973), a university-educated agronomist who founded and led the Guinea-Bissau movement, emphasized educating the people to empower them, telling his followers: "Learn from life, people, books, the experiences of others, never stop learning."[11] Portuguese agents assassinated Cabral in 1973. In 1974, however, Portugal's war-weary army ended the dictatorship in Portugal, and the new democratic, socialist-led government granted the colonies their independence in 1975. In Angola, the nationalist factions fought each other for dominance for the next two decades, and Mozambique's revolutionary government faced a long insurgency supported by white-ruled South Africa.

The British colonies of the Rhodesias and Nyasaland in southern Africa, all containing white settlers who bitterly resisted efforts at political and social equality for Africans, were among the last colonies to gain independence under black majority rule. After African nationalists launched largely nonviolent resistance campaigns, the British granted independence to Zambia (Northern Rhodesia) and Malawi (formerly Nyasaland), both of which had only small white minorities in 1963. But the large white settler population in Southern Rhodesia declared independence from Britain in 1965 and installed a white racist government that imposed stricter racial segregation and prohibited nonwhite political activity. Africans took up arms in two rival Marxist-led liberation movements. By 1980 the African resistance was so strong that the United States and Britain pressured the white government to allow elections, which were won by Robert Mugabe **(moo-GAH-bee)** (b. 1924), a guerrilla leader and former political prisoner. The country became independent as Zimbabwe.

Political Change and Conflict

New Nations

A West African scholar called the term *nation* "a magical word meant to exorcise ethnic quarrels and antagonisms—and as such very precious"[12]; but, as he conceded, the magic usually failed to overcome disunity. New African nations typically experienced political and economic challenges that fostered instability: coups, prolonged civil wars, and recurring famines (see Map 30.3). Although most new nations started as parliamentary democracies, only a few sustained democratic systems. Rule by the military or by one dominant party has been more common. Militaries have often been the only groups that can govern effectively, since they have a sense of superiority over civilians, good internal communications, and a tradition of discipline. But military officers enjoying a privileged existence are also often out of touch with the population; used to giving orders, they have ruled with a heavy hand and often looted treasuries. Civilian leaders have often favored one-party states because such parties can minimize ethnic divisions. While some of these one-party states, such as in the Congo (Zaire), have been despotisms, others have been relatively open, even allowing some choice among candidates for office. Some nations, such as Nigeria and Ghana, have shifted back and forth between authoritarian military dictatorships and ineffective, corrupt civilian governments. Some of the despotic governments have brutally mistreated their own people. During the 1970s in Uganda, then ruled by Idi Amin **(EE-dee AH-meen)** (1925–2004), a poorly educated former amateur boxing champion who rose to become a general, some 300,000 people were killed, and thousands more were jailed or fled into exile.

Western-style democracy has had little chance to flower in these artificial countries with a tiny middle class and numerous poor people. Given the often deteriorating economic conditions, governments have had little money to spend on containing ethnic tensions or for building schools,

Map 30.3 Contemporary Africa and the Middle East
Sub-Saharan and North Africa contain over forty nations. Six sub-Saharan African nations and Algeria in North Africa experienced anticolonial revolutions, and a dozen sub-Saharan nations have been racked by civil wars since independence.

Interactive Map

hospitals, and roads. As a result, the nationalist leaders and parties that governed the new nations often lost their credibility and mass support after a few years. For instance, Ghana's Kwame Nkrumah was overthrown for economic mismanagement and an autocratic governing style and died in exile. Some African leaders have been highly respected, farsighted visionaries, such as Tanzania's Julius Nyerere **(NEE-ya-RARE-y)** (g. 1962–1985) and Mozambique's Samora Machel (g. 1975–1986), and pragmatic problem solvers, such as South Africa's first black president, Nelson Mandela. While not all their initiatives succeeded, these leaders have used political office largely to improve society rather than enrich themselves. However, many leaders, emulating the despotic kings of old Africa, have too often been reluctant to give up their power, rigging elections or having compliant parliaments declare them presidents for life. Others have disappointed or brutalized their people. Some, such as the Congo (Zaire) dictator Mobuto (g. 1965–1997) and the Nigerian military dictator Sani Abacha (g. 1993–1998), have been ruthless crooks, arresting or murdering opponents and plundering the public treasury to amass multibillion-dollar fortunes. When Abacha, hopped up on Viagra, died of a heart attack while he engaged in an orgy with prostitutes, few Nigerians lamented.

Social Conflict

Political instability, conflict, and social unrest have grown as people have struggled for their share of the wealth. The blatant corruption, conspicuous consumption, and smuggling in government and the business sector have increased inequalities and deepened public frustrations. Sub-Saharan Africa has the world's highest income inequality. In some countries, government officials were known as "Mr. 10 Percent," a reference to the share of public budgets they grab. East Africans chastise the **wabenzi**—"people who drive a Mercedes Benz"—a privileged urban class of politicians, bureaucrats, professionals, military officers, and businessmen who manipulate their connections to amass wealth. These elites have often squandered scarce resources on importing luxuries, such as fancy cars and hard liquor, signs of the continuing hold of Western taste and consumer goods.

wabenzi ("people who drive a Mercedes Benz") A privileged urban class in Africa of politicians, bureaucrats, professionals, military officers, and businessmen who manipulate their connections to amass wealth.

On the other hand, in some societies relations between governments and the governed have improved. New grassroots nongovernmental organizations have addressed issues such as human rights and the environment, and ordinary people have demanded greater responsibility for improving their lives. For example, by 2000 some 25,000 local women's groups in Kenya had pushed for improved rights and other issues, such as environmental protection. The Kenyan women's rights and environmental activist, Wangari Maathai (wan-GAHR-ee MAH-thai), won the Nobel Peace Prize in 2005 (see Chapter 26). Since few Africans can afford health insurance, in countries such as Senegal poor people have come together to form small mutual health organizations, negotiating with local clinics to get an affordable group rate for health care. In Liberia, strong support from women voters helped economist Ellen Johnson-Sirleaf (b. 1939), a Harvard-trained banker and former United Nations official, become Africa's first woman president in 2005, as her country sought to recover from a long civil war and then a corrupt dictatorship. But she faced a monumental challenge to bring progress to a maimed nation with no piped water or electric grid and few functioning schools and hospitals.

Nigeria and Its Challenges

Africa's hopes and frustrations are mirrored in Nigeria, home to some 140 million people, about a fifth of Africa's total population. Nigeria's ethnic and religious diversity and natural wealth have been both a blessing and a curse. Among the 250 ethnic groups, about two-thirds of the people belong to the Hausa-Fulani, Igbo (Ibo), or Yoruba groups. Nigeria's oil wealth has produced 80 percent of the nation's total revenues but has also corrupted politics and increased social inequality. Once a food exporter, Nigeria neglected agriculture and is now a food importer. Nearly two thirds of the people have insufficient food. Moreover, Nigeria's history has frequently been punctuated by coups, countercoups, riots, political assassinations, and civil war rooted in regional and ethnic rivalries. Between 1967 and 1970 Nigeria endured a bloody civil war to prevent the secession of the Igbo-dominated oil-rich southeast region. The religious divide between Christians, who dominate the south, and Muslims, who control the northern states, also complicates politics. Following a Muslim revival among the Hausa-Fulani, many northern states imposed strict Islamic law, antagonizing non-Muslims. Several Muslim women were sentenced to death by stoning for adultery while the men involved were not punished, causing an outcry in Nigeria and around the world. Sometimes severe Christian-Muslim fighting causes the death of hundreds of people. The chaos has often led to corrupt military rule, which has brought stability by suppressing opposition but pushed the people hard, alternated with periods of corrupt civilian democracy, which has increased political freedom but often governed ineffectively.

The Nigerian oil industry, while creating some prosperity, has also made Nigeria dependent on oil exports. A few politicians, bureaucrats, and businessmen have monopolized oil profits, fostering corruption, sometimes outright plunder of public wealth, and inequitable wealth distribution. By 2005 the top 20 percent of Nigerians received 56 percent of all the country's wealth, while the bottom 20 percent got only 4.4 percent. People in the southern oil-producing districts see few benefits and watch sullenly as pipelines through their villages move oil to the coastal ports, from where tankers carry the oil to European and North American consumers. Their sporadic protests, including sabotage of the oil pipelines, have been met with military force and sometimes execution of protest leaders. Meanwhile, local rebel groups harass the oil industry and fight the army. Disenchanted Nigerians refer to a "republic of the privileged and rich" and a "moneytocracy." After oil money created high expectations in the 1970s, world oil prices collapsed in the 1980s, forcing the nation to take on massive foreign debt.

Political Turmoil

The combination of artificial boundaries, weak national identity, and economic collapse has produced chronic turmoil in several African nations, resulting in what one discouraged African observer called the "dark night of bloodshed and death." Liberia and Sierra Leone, once among the more stable countries, disintegrated in the 1990s as ethnic-based rebel groups challenged governments for power. In both countries thousands fled the slaughter and the maiming of civilians, causing African nations like Nigeria to send in troops to bring stability. In drought-plagued Somalia, when longtime military rule collapsed in 1991, the country divided into regions ruled by feuding

Somali clans with their own armies. As the Somali economy disintegrated, causing thousands to starve to death, the United Nations dispatched a humanitarian mission. But some Americans with the mission were killed and the U.N. withdrew in 1994, unable to achieve a unified government. Somalia remained a country in name only, controlled by warlords and, more recently, engulfed in civil war involving various Islamist militias, a weak central government, and the Ethiopian army. In the chaos, desperate young men in coastal villages turned to piracy, disrupting shipping and prompting an international naval force to police the nearby seas.

Hatreds led to genocide in impoverished, densely populated Rwanda, divided between majority Hutus and minority Tutsis. The Belgians had ruled through Tutsi kings, and soon after independence, the Hutus rebelled, slaughtering thousands of Tutsis and forcing others into exile. The remaining Tutsis faced discrimination and repression. In 1994 the extremist Hutu government began a genocide against the Tutsis and moderate Hutus, murdering over 500,000 people. Tutsi exiles based in Uganda then invaded Rwanda, forcing the Hutu leaders and their followers—over 2 million–into the neighboring Congo. As a result, the new Tutsi-led government continued to face militant Congo-based Hutu resistance groups, leading to Rwandan military incursions into the Congo and support for Congolese rebel groups.

The New South Africa

White Supremacy

South Africa experienced a distinctive conflict and inequality for over three centuries. From World War II to the early 1990s, South Africa remained the last bastion of institutionalized white racism on a continent where white rule had once been widespread. The white population, in the 1990s some 15 percent of the total, and divided between an Afrikaner majority (descendants of Dutch settlers) and an English minority, ruled the black majority (74 percent) and the Indians (2 percent) and mixed-descent Coloreds (9 percent). Racial inequality became more systematic after 1948, when Afrikaner nationalists won the white-only elections and declared full independence from Britain. A top nationalist leader claimed: "We [whites] need [Africans] because they work for us but they can never claim political rights. Not now, nor in the future."[13] Their new policy, **apartheid** (uh-PAHRT-ate) ("separate development"), set up a ruthless police state to enforce racial separation; laws required all Africans to carry ID ("pass") cards specifying the locations where they could legally reside or visit. Interracial marriage and sexual relations were also outlawed. Apartheid created a nearly unparalleled cruelty, a chilling juxtaposition of comfort for whites and despair for blacks.

apartheid ("separate development") A South African policy to set up a police state to enforce racial separation.

Apartheid expanded segregation to include designated residential areas, schools, recreational facilities, and public accommodations. Urban black men were commonly housed in crowded dormitories near the mines or factories where they worked or, often with their families, in shantytown suburbs, from where they commuted to their jobs. While most white families lived comfortably in well-furnished apartments or houses with swimming pools, a typical house in Soweto, a dusty African suburb of Johannesburg, was bleak, with the residents using candles or gas lamps for lighting and most having no running water. Demoralized blacks, especially men, found escape in alcohol, frequenting the informal bars that dotted African urban neighborhoods.

Apartheid also created what white leaders called tribal homelands, known as **bantustans**, rural reservations where black Africans were required to live if they were not needed in the modern economy. The system allocated whites 87 percent of the nation's land and nonwhites the other 13 percent. Every year thousands of Africans were forcibly resettled to the impoverished bantustans, which contained too little fertile land and too few jobs, hospitals, and secondary schools. Infant mortality rates in the bantustans were among the world's highest. Under this system black families were fractured as men and women were recruited on annual contracts for jobs outside the bantustans. Even if a husband and wife were both recruited for jobs in the same city, they could not legally visit each other if their ID cards restricted each of them to a different neighborhood.

bantustans Rural reservations in South Africa where black Africans under apartheid were required to live if they were not needed in the modern economy.

Rich in strategic minerals such as gold, diamonds, uranium, platinum, and chrome, South Africa became the most industrialized African nation. But while whites enjoyed one of the world's highest standards of living, with access to well-funded schools and medical centers, Africans and the Colored and Indian minorities enjoyed few benefits. Whites controlled over two-thirds of the nation's wealth and personal disposable income, while a third of Africans were unemployed. By 1994 the ratio of average black to white incomes stood at 1:10, the world's most inequitable income distribution. The government enjoyed the open or tacit support of several industrialized countries, including the United States, Britain, and Japan, who feared that unrest or black majority rule might threaten their billions in investments and access to lucrative resources.

African Resistance

Africans resisted and often paid a price for their defiance. The police state featured brutal treatment of dissidents and the world's highest rate of execution. Stephen Biko (1946–1977), a former medical student who led an organization that encouraged black pride and self-reliance, was beaten to death in police custody. Hundreds of Africans were arrested each day for "pass law" violations and held for a few days or weeks. The police violently repressed protests and imprisoned thousands of dissidents, including numerous children, often without trial. Off-duty policemen sometimes assassinated black leaders, such as Victoria Mxenge **(ma-SEN-gee)**, a lawyer who defended anti-apartheid activists. Nevertheless, various forms of defiance, including strikes, work interruptions, and sabotage, became common. Resistance was often subtle, too; Nobel Prize–winning white South African novelist and apartheid critic Nadine Gordimer (b. 1923) described in her novel, *Something Out There*, how even domestic servants in white households could protest and assert their dignity in nonverbal ways:

> *Every household in the fine suburb had several black servants—a shifting population of pretty young housemaids whose long red nails and pertness not only asserted the indignity of being undiscovered fashion models but kept hoisted a cocky guerrilla pride against servitude to whites.*[14]

The African National Congress (ANC), the major opposition organization, remained multiracial, with some whites, Coloreds, and Indians serving in its leadership. In 1955, despairing of peaceful change, a more militant ANC leadership framed its inclusive vision in the Freedom Charter: "South Africa belongs to all who live in it, black and white."[15] But the government declared the ANC illegal and fierce repression forced it underground, where it adopted violent resistance. Several of its main leaders, including Nelson Mandela (b. 1918), spent almost thirty years in prison for their political activities (see Profile: Nelson and Winnie Mandela, South African Freedom Fighters). Women, among them Mandela's wife, Winnie Mandela, played an influential role in the ANC, often facing arrest and mistreatment.

Ultimately, international isolation, economic troubles, the need for more highly skilled black workers, and growing black unrest forced the government to relax apartheid and release Mandela from prison. The two parties agreed on a new constitution requiring "one man, one vote," and in 1994 an amazed world saw white supremacy come to an end in the first all-race elections in South African history, which installed Mandela as president and gave the ANC two-thirds of the seats in Parliament. The ANC government enjoyed massive goodwill but also faced daunting challenges in healing a deeply fragmented society while restoring the pride and spirits of Africans demoralized by apartheid. Mandela sought the right mix of racial reconciliation and major changes to benefit the disadvantaged black majority. In 1999 he voluntarily retired, a still-popular figure, and the ANC retained power in free elections. It improved services, such as electricity and water, in black communities, raised black living standards, and fostered a growing black upper and middle class.

Yet millions of other blacks have felt neglected, wanting better land and services and complaining about corruption and mismanagement. South Africa has one of the world's highest rates of HIV/AIDS, crime has rapidly increased, violent protests have broken out, and black unemployment has remained high. In 2009 the election of a more radical ANC leader, Jacob Zuma (b. 1942), prompted some blacks to leave the ANC and form or join opposition parties. Zuma has faced widespread discontent and strikes. But while some of the goodwill of the Mandela years has faded, given the long history of repression and fear, the rapid transition to multiparty democracy has been impressive. People all over the continent hope that the nation of 50 million succeeds in healing racial wounds while spreading the wealth to all its citizens.

SECTION SUMMARY

- European colonial rulers had played rival ethnic groups in Africa against each other, but after World War II, pressures for independence became stronger and Ghana, under the leadership of Kwame Nkrumah, became the first colony to achieve independence.
- Most British colonies attained independence through peaceful means, but Kenya's transition was long and violent, as was that of the Belgian Congo, Angola, Guinea-Bissau, Mozambique, and Zimbabwe.
- After independence, many African nations were ruled by military dictatorships or corrupt civilians, many nationalist leaders lost favor over time, the gap between rich and poor widened, and some nations experienced ongoing violence, disorder, and genocide.
- Nigeria, home to rival ethnic and religious groups, has experienced civil war, coups, and corrupt military rule, and while its oil reserves have brought wealth to the elite, they have hardly benefited the poor, and dependence on them led to economic problems in the 1980s.
- Under apartheid, a white minority in South Africa viciously suppressed the black majority with laws restricting their political, economic, and physical freedom, but the African National Congress, led by Nelson Mandela, resisted fiercely and ultimately won control of the government in 1994.

NELSON AND WINNIE MANDELA, SOUTH AFRICAN FREEDOM FIGHTERS

Courageous symbols of unbroken black determination, Nelson Mandela (b. 1918) and Winnie Mandela (b. 1934) made a mark on history in the struggle against apartheid, South Africa's policy of rigid racial separation, despite severe white supremacist repression. The inspirational Mandelas represented African ambitions for several generations.

Nelson Mandela was born in the Transkei reserve near South Africa's southeast coast, the son of a Xhosa (KHO-sa) chief. His middle name, Rolihlahla (ROH-lee-la-la), meant "troublemaker." Mandela was groomed to succeed his father as chief, but, after years of hearing stories about the valor of his ancestors in war, he wanted to help with the freedom struggle. After attending a Methodist school and then earning a B.A. from the only college for black South Africans, he qualified as a lawyer and opened the country's first black legal practice. He also joined the African National Congress (ANC), which had, for half a century, followed a policy of promoting education for blacks and cautiously criticizing rather than confronting the government. Mandela and his young colleagues transformed the ANC into an activist mass movement. In 1958 he married Winnie Madikizela (MAH-dee-kee-ZEH-la), a Xhosa nurse, but they had only a short life together before political repression separated them.

The white government tolerated little opposition. In 1960, after police opened fire on 20,000 peaceful black protesters, killing 69 of them (including women and children), the government banned the ANC and arrested black leaders. The ANC then became an underground movement committed to violence. In 1964, found guilty of sabotage and treason, Mandela was sentenced to life in prison. In his stirring statement to the court, Mandela articulated his goals: "During my lifetime I have dedicated myself to this struggle of the African people. I have fought against [both] white and black domination. I have cherished the ideal of a democratic and free society in which all persons live together in harmony and with equal opportunities. It is an ideal for which I am prepared to die."

Mandela spent most of the next three decades in the notorious Robben Island prison off Cape Town, where he was joined by dozens of other ANC leaders and members. He turned the prison experience into an ANC school, leading political discussions and studying other freedom fighters, such as Mohandas Gandhi and Jawaharlal Nehru in India. Over the years Mandela grew into an international hero. During his imprisonment, although jailed for a short time herself and then confined to a remote settlement, Winnie Mandela kept her husband's flame burning, gaining an international reputation as a freedom fighter. Returning to Johannesburg in 1985, Winnie campaigned ceaselessly for black rights and her husband's release, earning a reputation for courage and skill in negotiating a male-dominated society.

In 1990, after secret negotiations, a realistic new South African president, F. W. de Klerk, legalized the ANC and released Nelson Mandela from prison, and in 1993 Nelson Mandela and de Klerk shared a Nobel Peace Prize. In 1994 the first all-race elections made Nelson Mandela the first black president of South Africa. At his inauguration, he told the people: "Out of the experience of an extraordinary human disaster that lasted too long must be born a society of which all humanity will be proud. Let there be justice [and] peace for all. We must act together as a united people, for the birth of a new world. God bless Africa!"

Forgiving and pragmatic, Mandela remained popular with most South Africans, white and black. His moderate, accommodationist style reassured whites but also disappointed some impatient blacks. Meanwhile, his marriage to Winnie

Corbis

Nelson Mandela A symbol of black South African aspirations for nearly thirty years in prison, Mandela led the African National Congress after his release and, in 1994, was elected the nation's first black president.

became strained, in part because of her controversial activities, legal problems, and political ambitions. Her popularity declined after 1988 when bodyguards she hired to protect her from black and white foes were implicated in the kidnapping and murder of a black youth; Winnie herself was convicted of involvement in the kidnapping, but her sentence was commuted. In 1996 Nelson and Winnie Mandela divorced. Winnie remained active in the ANC, supporting a militant faction that mistrusted Nelson's conciliatory policy of bringing white and black South Africans together. Nelson later married Grace Machel, the widow of the respected Mozambique president Samora Machel, who had been killed in an airplane crash.

In 1999, at the age of eighty-one, Mandela voluntarily retired from politics and moved to his native village. In his autobiography, he wrote, "I have walked a long road to freedom. I have tried not to falter, I have made missteps along the way. After climbing a great hill, one only finds that there are many more hills to climb. With freedom come responsibilities. I dare not linger, for my long walk is not yet ended." The long walk taken by Nelson and Winnie Mandela changed history.

THINKING ABOUT THE PROFILE

1. Why did the Mandelas become international symbols of the freedom struggle?
2. How did the Mandelas change history?

Note: Quotations from Kevin Shillington, *History of Africa*, rev. ed. (New York: St. Martin's, 1995), 405; and Nelson Mandela, *Long Walk to Freedom: The Autobiography of Nelson Mandela* (Boston: Little, Brown, 1996), 620, 625.

AFRICAN ECONOMIES, SOCIETIES, AND CULTURES

What new economic, social, and cultural patterns have emerged in Africa?

Since the 1960s, for many sub-Saharan African nations, achieving economic development has seemed a desperate struggle rather than an exhilarating challenge. African nations have tried various strategies, including capitalism and socialism, to benefit the majority of people, but no strategy has proved effective over the long term. Economic problems have proliferated. But Africans have created new social and cultural forms to aid them in dealing with their problems.

Economic Change and Underdevelopment

Economic Problems

Africa has experienced severe economic problems. As during colonial times, Africans have mostly supplied agricultural and mineral resources, such as cocoa and copper, to the global economy, but this has not brought widespread wealth. For example, in Kenya, small farmers encouraged to abandon subsistence food growing and take up tobacco planting found that their new crops brought in little money, required cutting down adjacent forests, and leached nutrients from the soil. In 2004 one of the farmers, Jane Chacha, who still lived in the same two-room, mud-and-thatch house she and her husband built fifteen years earlier, complained that "this is a hopeless dream. Growing tobacco has been nothing but trouble."[16]

Only a few countries have enjoyed consistently robust economic growth, been able to escape reliance on producing one or two resources, or substantially raised living standards. As a result, sub-Saharan Africa contains most of the world's twenty poorest countries. With nearly 800 million people, this region accounts for only 1 percent of the world's production of goods and services, about the same as one of the smallest European nations, Belgium, with 10 million people. Most sub-Saharan African countries have annual per capita incomes of under $1,000 per year, and some are under $500. Half of the people earn less than $1 per day, the world's highest rate of desperate poverty. Sub-Saharan Africa has also had the world's highest infant mortality rates and lowest literacy rates and average life expectancies.

The economic doldrums are linked to other problems. The region's economies have generally grown by 1 to 2 percent a year, but its population increase is the world's highest, over 3 percent. Since 10 to 15 percent of babies die before their first birthday, parents have had an incentive to have many children to provide for old-age security. While the population may double by 2025, new jobs, classrooms, and food supplies will not keep pace. Only a few nations have enjoyed self-sufficiency in food production; most require food imports from Europe and North America. Women grow the bulk of the food, but the male farmers growing cash crops receive most of the government aid. Millions of people are chronically malnourished, and several million children die each year from hunger-related ailments. In addition, severe drought and the drying up of water sources results in numerous deaths from dehydration or starvation, or in migration in search of a better life. In Kenya some malnourished people are reduced to eating cactus. Some 25 million girls receive no elementary education, and less than half of school-age children attend school, while millions of others work in the labor force. Poverty means scraping by, physically and mentally exhausted by the struggle for survival.

Neocolonial Capitalism

As Africans have sought viable economic strategies to achieve economic development, neocolonial capitalism, involving close economic ties to the Western nations, foreign investment, and free markets, has became the most common model. Countries following this strategy have favored the cash crops and minerals that had dominated the colonial economy, and Westerners, especially British and French, have managed or owned a substantial portion of the economies. A few countries prospered with this strategy, but the political consequences were often negative. Ivory Coast (or Côte d'Ivoire) and Kenya were hospitable to a Western presence, and in the 1960s and 1970s they were rewarded with high growth and rising incomes. Ivory Coast remained a major exporter of coffee and cocoa, while Kenya, with world-famous game parks, lived from tourism and the export of coffee, tea, and minerals. By the 1980s both had per capita incomes about double the African average. That success came at some cost, however. The Ivory Coast rapidly logged the once-verdant forest, causing less rain, and more French lived there than during colonial times, owning, along with other non-Ivoireans, most of the economy. Both countries also eventually became one-party states that, while stable, grew despotic and corrupt. While the glittering major cities, Abidjan and Nairobi, had fancy restaurants, boutiques, and nightclubs, some rural people faced starvation. By the 1990s, as collapsing world prices for coffee and cocoa stressed their economies, protesters demanded more democracy, the delicate ecologies became dangerously unbalanced, and crime rates soared. Economic development became a fading memory. Ivory Coast became engulfed in civil war, while Kenyans forced out a dictator and elected a reformist government that, while spurring economic growth, failed to fulfill most of its promises. In 2008 a disputed Kenyan election led to riots, interethnic fighting, and hundreds of deaths.

The most disastrous neocolonial capitalist state was the Democratic Republic of the Congo (known as Zaire between 1971 and 1997). A huge country, with 66 million people, Congo enjoys a strategic location in the center of Africa and rich mineral resources, but it became Africa's biggest failure. The United States and Belgium poured in billions of investment and aid to support President Mobuto, who looted the treasury and foreign aid to amass a huge personal fortune—some 4 to 5 billion dollars—while repressing his opponents. Mobuto built palaces for himself all over the country and in Europe and hired top French chefs to prepare his food, spending little money on schools, roads, telephones, and hospitals. Hence, the Congo suffered one of the world's highest infant mortality rates, limited health care, and widespread malnutrition. In 1997 a long-festering rebellion gained strength, forcing Mobuto into exile, where he died. Rebels took over, but they have done little to foster democracy or development. The Congo soon fragmented in civil war and interethnic fighting that drew in armies from neighboring countries, and rebel groups controlled large sections of the sprawling country. Nearly 4 million Congolese died from the fighting and the collapse of medical care, causing a humanitarian crisis.

The most recent showcases for economic success have been Ghana and Botswana. Once a symbol of failure, Ghana has made steady progress. For several decades the country experienced a roller coaster of corrupt civilian governments interspersed with military regimes. But in the 1990s the leaders gradually strengthened democracy and adopted certain policies of the Asian Little Dragons, such as Taiwan and South Korea, by mixing capitalism and socialism. Ghana became increasingly prosperous: by 2009 it enjoyed one of the continent's highest annual per capital incomes, $2,700, a life expectancy of fifty-nine, democratic elections, and press freedom. In addition, investment in schools resulted in one of Africa's most educated populations. Botswana also made a turnaround. When it gained independence in 1966, it was one of the world's poorest countries, with an annual per capita income of $35. Gradually, however, using ethnic traditions as a foundation, Botswanans carved out a successful democracy; the economy, health care, education, and protection of resources all steadily improved, despite deadly droughts. By 2000 Botswanans had fostered living standards higher than those of most African and many Middle Eastern, Asian, and Latin American societies, boasting an annual per capita income of over $3,000, an economy growing by 11 percent a year, and a literacy rate of 70 percent. Unfortunately, the AIDs epidemic, which hit Botswana particularly hard, rapidly undermined economic and health gains and reduced life expectancy to thirty-four years.

Social Revolutionary States

Some African nationalists pursued revolutionary or reformist strategies. Since the political institutions, businesses, and plantations inherited from colonialism were geared to transfer wealth and resources to the West, the radicals argued that they could not spark economic development: after independence more wealth still flowed out of Africa than into it. To empower Africans, it was necessary to replace the colonial state with something entirely new. Thus various social revolutionary regimes emerged from the long wars of liberation against colonial or white minority governments. Looking toward China or the USSR for inspiration, Marxist revolutionary governments came to power in Angola and Mozambique after the Portuguese left. To counter these governments, white-ruled South Africa sponsored opposition guerrilla movements, aided by an anticommunist United States, that kept these countries in civil war for several decades. During Angola's conflict, over 1.5 million people died. While the war eventually ended, Angola, blessed with coffee, diamonds, and especially oil but plagued with corruption, still struggled to foster development despite considerable Western investment. The civil war in Mozambique resulted in 1 million deaths and 5 million refugees. Since its war ended in 1992, the pragmatic Marxist leaders introduced multiparty elections and liberalized the economy, raising the per capita income to $1,500.

One social revolutionary state, Zimbabwe, at first became Africa's biggest success story. The Marxist-influenced government, led by the liberation hero Robert Mugabe, proved pragmatic for over a decade, largely respecting democracy and human rights, encouraging the white minority to stay, and raising living standards and opportunities for black Zimbabweans. The country became one of Africa's few food-exporting nations. But Zimbabwe eventually faced severe problems, including tensions between rival African ethnic groups. Blacks resented continuing white ownership of the best farmland, and during the 1990s Mugabe became more dictatorial and used land disputes to divide the nation. As his support waned, he rigged elections, harassed or jailed his opponents, and ordered the seizure of white-owned farms. Meanwhile, uncontrolled inflation made local currency worthless. Commercial agriculture collapsed, the country was gripped by drought and a cholera outbreak, life expectancy dropped sharply, food disappeared from shops, refugees fled to neighboring countries, and Mugabe's police demolished the homes and shops of poor blacks who favored the opposition, driving them out of the cities. As the nation veered toward catastrophe, African nations forced Mugabe to form a coalition government with the opposition party in 2009, but he still held most of the power.

African Socialism and Reform

Tanzania experimented with an "African" socialism compatible with African traditions, especially cooperation and mutual sharing of resources. Under its visionary president, Julius Nyerere (1922–1999), Tanzania reorganized agriculture into cooperative villages with the goal of achieving national self-sufficiency. Nyerere encouraged some democracy in his one-party state by holding regular elections and allowing multiple candidates to run for each office or parliamentary seat. His emphasis on building schools and clinics improved literacy to 68 percent and health to well above African norms. But Nyerere's dreams were dashed as the government became overly bureaucratic, the planning proved inadequate, and many people lost enthusiasm for socialism. Because Tanzania imported few luxury goods, life was austere compared to that available to affluent residents in capitalist Kenya. Peasants often preferred their small family farms to the collective villages they were encouraged, or forced, to join. As the economy slumped, Tanzania had to take more foreign loans. Still admired by his people, Nyerere retired in 1985, one of the few founding African leaders to voluntarily give up power. His successors dismantled much of the socialist structure, promoted free enterprise, welcomed foreign investment and loans, and fostered a multiparty system. Yet life for most Tanzanians has improved little, malnutrition has become widespread, and Tanzania remains a poor nation.

Social Change

City Life

Modern Africa has seen rapid social change. More people live in cosmopolitan cities where traditional and modern attitudes meet, mix, and clash. City life offers more variety—jobs, department stores, movie theaters, nightclubs—than village life and hence attracts rural people. The cities that developed under colonial auspices, such as Nairobi (Kenya), Lagos (Nigeria), and Dakar (Senegal), which have grown nearly 5 percent a year since 1980, serve as economic centers and seats of government. Between 1965 and 2000 the percentage of Africans living in urban areas doubled to 30 percent. Abidjan in Ivory Coast and Luanda in Angola each contain a quarter of their country's population. Cities have grown so fast that services such as buses, water, power, police, schools, and health centers cannot meet peoples' needs. These problems are exemplified by Nigeria's largest city, Lagos, which grew from less than a million in 1965 to a megalopolis of some 12 million by 2008. A journalist described the urban chaos:

> *Lagos is a vast laboratory of helter-skelter expansion, a fount of confusion and frenzy. A tiny minority of people live extremely well, in villas or plush apartments, and they go to work in gleaming skyscrapers that sit awkwardly next to traditional marketplaces. A vastly larger number of people live in appalling slums, where open sewers may run under disintegrating floorboards. The traffic jam, or "go-slow," is a fact of life. Much of the everyday commerce occurs in this city through the windows of cars, trucks, and other vehicles.*[17]

Social changes have been numerous in cities. Interethnic mixing, even marriage, has become more common. Neighborhoods have developed their own slang, hairstyles, music, dance, art, and poetry. They forge their own institutions such as football (soccer) leagues, labor unions, and women's clubs, helping migrants adjust by creating a new community to replace the village left behind. Small traders set up shop along the sidewalks, hawking everything from food and drinks to cheap clothes, religious items, and music cassettes. Various African nations have enjoyed international football success, and Ethiopians and Kenyans have dominated long-distance running. Africans have also played in the U.S. National Basketball Association and the National Football League.

Families and Gender Relations

The family has also changed. The extended family of the villages is often replaced in cities by the smaller nuclear family. Individualism increasingly challenges the village tradition, where marriages were largely arranged by elders. In the cities, love has become a major criterion for selecting a spouse. Traditionally village men had an economic incentive to take more than one wife, since women did most of the routine farm work, especially food crops, which gave rural women economic status. With no farming option, urban women have lost economic status and men no longer need several wives. Men enjoy more educational opportunities and hence dominate wage labor in business and transportation.

Gender roles have changed as women have become more independent, and a growing number have served in governments and parliaments. Indeed, sub-Saharan Africa ranks ahead of the rest of the developing world in the percentage of women in legislative positions. Some women have achieved positions as politicians, professors, lawyers, and company heads. The Kenyan Grace Ogot (OH-got) (b. 1930) served in parliament while writing short stories in which her heroines confronted traditional values and change. In addition to organizations for work, savings, or worship, women have formed groups to work for society's improvement. The Nigerian Eka Esu-Williams (b. 1950), the daughter of a midwife, earned a Ph.D. in immunology and pursued an academic career before forming Women Against AIDS in Africa in 1988. Her goal was to educate and empower women, more likely than men to get HIV, through workshops, schools, and support groups. Some women have also become teachers, nurses, and secretaries, but these are poorly paid occupations. Most women are left with self-employment in low-wage activity, such as the small-scale trade of hawking goods and keeping stalls in city markets, a female near monopoly for centuries; domestic work as maids, cooks, or nannies; or hairdressing. Meanwhile, many men spend long hours commuting to and from work and socializing with their friends after work in bars or at club meetings. Although homosexuals face severe intolerance in many African countries, homosexuality has been more open in South Africa, where the courts legalized homosexual marriage in 2005.

African Culture and Religion

Popular Musics

In the area of culture, Africans have combined imported ideas with their own traditions, creating works that are loved around the world. As the Senegalese writer and president Leopold Senghor (sah-GAWR) (1906–2001) has asked, "Who else would teach rhythm to the world that has died of machines and cannons?"[18] Urbanization, the growth of mass media, and the mixing of ethnic groups and outside influences have all created a fertile ground for exciting new popular music styles that reflect social, economic, and political realities. Miriam Makeba (muh-KAY-ba) (1932–2008), the South African jazz and pop singer forced to spend decades in exile, described her mission as follows: "I live to sing about what I see and know. I don't sing politics, I sing truth."[19] Popular music styles that creatively blend local and imported influences have helped Africans adjust to change while affirming their spirit in the face of external influences and internal failures. For instance, the *juju* music of Nigeria reflects Yoruba traditions while adopting Western instruments, such as electric guitars.

African popular musicians also reach an international audience, performing and selling recordings around the world. Perhaps the greatest African superstar, the Senegalese Youssou N'Dour (YOO-soo en-DOOR) (b. 1959), often collaborates with leading Western and Arab musicians. Yet, he remains true to his roots, living in Dakar and following his tolerant Sufi Muslim faith. Some musicians are highly political. The Nigerian Fela Kuti (1938–1997), whose music mixed jazz, soul, rock, and Yoruba traditions, used his songs as a weapon to attack the Nigerian government and its Western sponsors, facing frequent arrests and beatings for his protests. Like Bob Marley, Bob Dylan, and Chile's Victor Jara, Fela gained worldwide fame for using music to attack injustice. Women have also expressed their views through music. For instance, Oumou Sangare of Mali had a massive hit with her account of a young woman torn between pleasing her parents and her loved one. In the Congo, a particularly influential (Zairean) pop music, known widely as **soukous** ("to shake"), was shaped by dance rhythms from Cuba and Brazil, created by the descendants of African slaves. Soukous depends heavily on the guitar as well as on traditional African songs and melodies. Congolese musicians, unable to make a living or speak freely in their troubled homeland, have often sought their fortunes elsewhere. Soukous became a major dance music throughout Africa and among African immigrants in Europe.

soukous ("to shake") A Congolese popular music that was shaped by dance rhythms from Cuba and Brazil.

Literature

As with popular musicians, writers combined old traditions with new influences to comment on modern society, assert African identity, and influence political change and economic development.

Many write in English or French to reach an international audience. The Nigerian Wole Soyinka **(WOE-lay shaw-YING-kuh)** (b. 1934), a Yoruba poet, playwright, novelist, and sometime filmmaker who won the 1986 Nobel Prize for literature, has mixed Yoruba mysticism with criticisms of Western capitalism, racism, and cultural imperialism and of African failures, including the brutalities of Nigerian political life. A former political prisoner, Soyinka denounced repressive African leaders, chastising "Nigeria's self-engorgement at the banquet of highway robberies, public executions, public floggings and other institutionalized sadisms, casual cruelties, wanton destruction."[20] The powerful criticism of governments offered by Soyinka and his Nigerian colleague Chinua Achebe has often forced both men to live in exile.

negritude A literary and philosophical movement to forge distinctively African views.

Writers and artists have also tried to find authentic African perspectives. **Negritude** is a literary and philosophical movement to forge distinctively African views that first developed in the 1930s. The Senegalese writer and later the first president of his country after independence, Leopold Senghor, attempted to balance the Western stress on rational thought with African approaches to knowledge, such as mysticism and animism, long disdained by Europeans as superstition. To Senghor, Africans needed to assert, rather than feel inferior about, their black skins and cultural traditions. Negritude influenced French artists and writers, and the philosopher Jean Paul Sartre praised it as a weapon against all forms of oppression.

One of the best-known writers in Francophone West Africa, Ousmane Sembene **(OOS-man sem-BEN-ee)** (b. 1923) of Senegal, was influenced more by Marxism than by negritude. Drafted into the French army during World War II, Sembene, the son of a poor fisherman, fought in Italy and Germany. After the war he worked in France as a dockworker and became a leader of the dockworkers' union, and his first novel portrayed the stevedore's hard life. After returning to Senegal, Sembene often wrote about the colonial period, showing African resistance to Western domination and social inequality while attacking Senegal's greedy businessmen and government officials. Sembene also achieved international acclaim for films satirizing corrupt bureaucrats and illustrating the exploitation of the poor by the rich.

English-language literature also flourished in South Africa and East Africa. Kenyan Ngugi Wa Thiongo **(en-GOO-gee wah thee-AHN-go)** (b. 1938), a journalist turned university professor, has written several novels that explore the relationship between colonialism and social fragmentation, showing Gikuyus struggling to retain their identity, culture, and traditions while adjusting to the modern world. Once a devout Christian, Ngugi later rejected Christianity, which he viewed as a legacy of colonialism. His 1979 novel, *Petals of Blood*, portrays a Kenya struggling to free itself from neocolonialism but also beset with corruption. His attacks on the privileged Kenyan elite allied with Western exploitation earned Ngugi several jail terms and later forced him into exile.

Religion has remained in constant flux. In general, Africans have maintained a triple religious heritage: animism/polytheism, Islam, and Christianity. All these faiths have many followers, although the believers in animism now account for only a tenth of Africans. With their links to wider worlds, Christianity and Islam are also globalizing influences, spreading Western or Middle Eastern political, social, and economic ideas. Africans often view religions in both theoretical and practical terms, adopting views that help them adjust to change while rejecting old ideas and adding new ones as needed.

Christianity has become Africa's largest religion, attracting some 46 percent of Africans by 2008, both the fervent and the nominal in faith. Some countries, such as Congo, South Africa, and Uganda, have become largely Christian. Christianity has proven a powerful force for social change, and mission schools have educated many African leaders, influencing their world-views. However, many Christian churches have prevented their followers from practicing traditional customs. Believers often favor the liberation of women, yet many criticize progressive social views common in the West such as tolerance for homosexuality. A growing number of independent churches, some blending African traditions into worship and theology, have no ties to the older Western-based denominations. By promising to help members acquire wealth and happiness, some African churches have enjoyed spectacular growth, which has enabled them to build big urban churches that attract thousands of congregants each Sunday. In a reversal of historical patterns, several evangelical Nigerian churches even send missionaries to revitalize Christianity in the West, establishing

African Cultural Expression Africans have developed diverse and vibrant popular music, often by mixing Western and local traditions. In Nigeria, juju music, played by bands such as Captain Jidi Oyo and his Yankee System in this 1982 photo, has been popular among the Yoruba people.

Courtesy, Christopher Waterman, UCLA

branches in Europe and North America. Yet many other Africans have viewed Christianity as connected to Western imperialism. According to a popular nationalist saying: "When the missionaries came the Africans had the land and the Christians had the Bible. They taught us to pray with our eyes closed. When we opened them they had the land and we had the Bible."[21]

Some 40 percent of black Africans follow Islam, and about a fourth of all sub-Saharan countries have Muslim majorities. Some revivalist and Wahhabi movements have gained influence, especially in northern Nigeria, where some states have imposed Islamic law, sparking deadly clashes with Christian minorities that have left hundreds dead. But most Muslims and Christians remain moderate and inclusive. While politicians use religion as a wedge issue, and Christian-Muslim clashes have occurred in countries such as Ivory Coast and Sudan, relations among Christians, Muslims, and animists have more often been marked by tolerance. Among the Yoruba, for example, members of each group mix easily and even intermarry. One sect in Lagos even mixes Islam and Christianity into a blend called "Chrislam." Ethnicity often divides people more than religion.

Africa in the Global System

Africa and the World Economy

The Cold War rivalry between the USSR and the United States gained some countries aid but also fostered manipulation by superpowers. Countries such as Congo and Angola often became pawns as superpowers helped to support or remove leaders. But with the Cold War over, the Western world has largely ignored Africa, providing it with little aid and investment. Furthermore, the wealth gap between African countries and the Western industrialized nations has grown even wider than during colonial times. Today the gap between the richest Western nations and the poorest African countries is around 400 to 1. Only when the world economy boomed in the 1950s and 1960s did African economies show steady growth. Between the 1970s and 2000, however, as world prices for many African exports collapsed, African economic growth rates steadily dropped.

Western experts have encouraged a policy of "structural adjustment," in which international lenders, such as the International Monetary Fund (IMF) and the World Bank, loan nations money on the condition that these nations open their economies to private investment and, to balance national budgets, reduce government spending for health, education, and farmers. The resulting hardship on average people—from eliminating money for poor children to attend the village primary school to closing the local office that aids small farmers—increases resentment both of governments and of the Western nations that control the IMF and World Bank. This private investment also promotes a shift away from traditional farming to more productive modern agriculture that relies on tractors, chemical fertilizers, and new seeds. However, this kind of farming has a large environmental and social cost: marginal land is often turned into desert, and small farmers lack the means to buy the modern supplies.

To obtain the cars, fashionable clothes, and electronic gadgets desired by the urban middle and upper classes, African nations have taken out loans. As a percentage of total output, African countries have had the largest foreign debts in the world. Yet, the world prices for most of Africa's exports, such as coffee, cotton, and tobacco from Tanzania and cocoa from Ghana, have steadily dropped since the 1960s. Some exports now bring in a third of what they once did, leaving ever larger revenue gaps. And small farmers, such as the cotton growers in Mali, cannot compete with highly subsidized Western farmers and the tariff barriers erected in Europe, North America, and Japan against food and fiber imports from Africa. Increasingly desperate, countries such as Guinea-Bissau and Somalia have agreed to allow dangerous toxic waste, such as deadly but unwanted chemicals produced in the West, to be buried on their land in exchange for cash. Although prices for exports, especially minerals and oil, rebounded by 2000, spurring faster economic growth, the 2008–2009 global economic crisis lowered growth rates from 6.1 percent in 2007 to 2.8 percent in 2009. Taking advantage of Western disinterest, in the past decade China has made huge investments in African oil, refining, mining, timber, agriculture, and banking as well as constructing railroads, dams, bridges and other infrastructure projects. Bilateral trade quintupled between 2000–2006, and perhaps 750,000 Chinese now live and work in Africa. The Chinese activity may foreshadow a change of direction for many Africans.

Colonial Legacies

Africa's economic problems have had diverse roots. Colonial economic policies caused severe environmental destruction, such as desertification and deforestation, while incorporating the people into the world economy as specialized producers of minerals or cash crops for export rather than food farmers. Hence, Zambia relies on exploiting copper (87 percent of exports), Uganda coffee (72 percent), Malawi tobacco (72 percent), and Nigeria oil (95 percent). In addition, the colonial regimes often failed to build roads, schools, and clinics. Bad policy decisions, poor leadership, corruption, unstable politics, and misguided advice from Western experts have also contributed to the economic challenges, while the rapid spread of HIV/AIDS has killed and affected millions (see Chapter 26). In some nations a third of the population has the HIV virus.

African Successes

But although falling behind much of Asia and Latin America, Africans have had successes. Using foreign aid and their own resources, they have made rapid strides in literacy, social and medical services, including active birth control campaigns, and road construction. Some nations, such as South Africa, Ghana, and Uganda, have a feisty free press. Nations have also worked together to resolve problems. The African Union, formed in 2000 with fifty-four members, has sent peacekeeping troops into violence-torn countries such as Sudan. By the 1990s Africans had grown skeptical about the usefulness of Western models of development, which often depend on expensive high technology, and were also disillusioned with socialist governments controlling economic activity. Many nations have moved toward more democratic systems and private enterprise. However, political leadership has often failed to root out corruption and poverty and foster food production. Africa also suffers a particularly acute "brain drain" as academics, students, and professionals, seeking a better life, move to Europe or North America. Thus Africans have not enjoyed complete control of their destiny. The Ghanaian historian Jacob Ajayi (a-JAH-yee) laid out the challenge: "The vision of a new [African] society will need to be developed out of the African historical experience. The African is not yet master of his own fate, but neither is he completely at the mercy of fate."[22]

SECTION SUMMARY

- African countries have struggled economically, with many being forced to import food and others, like the Congo, to enter into neocolonial relationships with Western powers, but Ghana and Botswana have managed to significantly improve their economies.
- Marxist revolutionary governments, which appealed to many Africans who wanted to erase the colonial legacy, came to power in Angola and Mozambique, both of which then entered into long civil wars, as well as in Zimbabwe.
- African cities have grown rapidly and often lack necessary services, individualism has grown more common, and women have lost some of the economic value they had in agricultural villages, though some have become successful professionals.
- African musicians, writers, and artists have drawn on local traditions as well as influences from the West to create original forms, such as soukous, as well as works that criticize both Western encroachment and homegrown corruption.
- While animism has grown less influential in Africa, Christianity is the most popular religion and has undermined traditions and been seen by some as connected to Western imperialism, while Islam is followed by 40 percent of Africans.
- The economic gap between Africa and the industrialized West continues to grow larger, and Western attempts to help Africa through the IMF and the World Bank often include requirements that harm the environment and the poor and inspire resentment, as do tariffs against African imports and the enduring colonial legacy.

CHAPTER SUMMARY

The Middle East and sub-Saharan Africa have shared certain experiences, including decolonization, mass poverty, reliance on exporting natural resources, political instability, and intervention by Western powers. The Middle East was reshaped by diverse developments since 1945. Arab nationalism, especially strong in Egypt, generated conflict with the West and with Israel, which became the major Arab enemy. The Arab-Israeli conflict greatly destabilized the region, while ethnic and religious divisions fostered violent struggles within nations. Islam proved most potent as a revolutionary political force in Iran, long a battleground for international rivalries over its oil supplies. The Middle East, especially the Persian Gulf region, provided much of the world's oil, fostering wealth but also global attention as world consumption increased. Oil-rich Saudi Arabia forged an alliance with the United States. Most Middle Eastern societies remained conservative but also fostered cultural creativity. The rivalry between militants and secular Muslims has provided a major cleavage in many countries.

By the 1970s the long-colonized African nations had achieved independence under nationalist leaders. But the hopes for a better life were soon dashed. Artificially created multiethnic nations have found it difficult to sustain democracy, and dictatorial governments have often gained power. Most nations have remained dependent on exporting one or two resources. Ambitious development plans have given way to economic stagnation and, as commodity prices fall, increasing poverty. Neither capitalism nor socialism has proved able to both stimulate growth and raise living standards for Africa's majority. But South Africa was finally transformed from a racist state to a multiracial democracy. Societies urbanized, redefined family life and gender roles, and created new music and literature. Africans still search for the right mix of imported ideas and local traditions to create better lives.

KEY TERMS

Intifida
Ba'ath
OPEC
Islamists
rai
mujahidin
Taliban
pan-Africanism
Mau Mau Rebellion
wabenzi
apartheid
bantustans
soukous
negritude

EBOOK AND WEBSITE RESOURCES

PRIMARY SOURCE

Arab and Israeli Soccer Players Discuss Ethnic Relations in Israel, 2000

INTERACTIVE MAPS

Map 30.1 Middle East Oil and the Arab-Israeli Conflict
Map 30.2 The Islamic World
Map 30.3 Contemporary Africa and the Middle East

LINKS

Africa South of the Sahara (http://www-sul.stanford.edu/depts/ssrg/africa/guide.html). A valuable gateway for links on many topics in African studies.

African Studies Internet Resources (http://www.columbia.edu/cu/lweb/indiv/). Provides valuable links to relevant websites on contemporary Africa.

Arab Human Development Reports (http://www.un.org/Pubs). The general United Nations site contains links to the reports, issued annually beginning in 2002 and available online, that assess the successes and challenges facing the Arab nations.

History of the Middle East Database (http://www.nmhschool.org/tthornton/mehistorydatabase/mideastindex.php). A useful site on history, politics, and culture.

Internet African History Sourcebook (http://www.fordham.edu/halsall/africa/africasbook.html). Contains useful information and documentary material on Africa.

Internet Islamic History Sourcebook (http://www.fordham.edu/halsall/islam/islamsbook.html). A comprehensive examination of Islamic societies and their long history, with useful links and source materials.

Plus flashcards, practice quizzes, and more. Go to: www.cengage.com/history/lockard/globalsocnet2e.

SUGGESTED READING

Anderson, Roy R., et al. *Politics and Change in the Middle East: Sources of Conflict and Accommodation*, 9th ed. Upper Saddle River, NJ: Prentice-Hall, 2008. An introductory survey of politics and economies.

Bates, Daniel G., and Amal Rassam. *Peoples and Cultures of the Middle East*, 2nd ed. Upper Saddle River, NJ: Prentice-Hall, 2001. A readable introduction to the social and cultural patterns of the region.

Clark, Nancy L., and William H. Worger. *South Africa: The Rise and Fall of Apartheid.* New York: Longman, 2004. A brief survey with documents.

Cleveland, William L. *A History of the Modern Middle East*, 4th ed. Boulder, CO: Westview, 2008. A political overview of the region during this era.

Cooper, Frederick. *Africa Since 1940: The Past of the Present.* New York: Cambridge University Press, 2002. A brief overview of contemporary history.

Danielson, Virginia. *The Voice of Egypt: Umm Kulthum, Arabic Song, and Egyptian Society in the Twentieth Century.* Chicago: University of Chicago Press, 1997. A fascinating view of modern Egypt through the life and work of the Arab world's most famous pop singer.

Davidson, Basil. *The Black Man's Burden: Africa and the Curse of the Nation State.* New York: Times Books, 1992. Reflections on modern Africa and its challenges by an influential historian.

Esposito, John L. *Islam: The Straight Path,* 3rd ed. revised. New York: Oxford University Press, 2005. A detailed examination of modern Islam.

Gerges, Fawaz A. *The Far Enemy: Why Jihad Went Global.* New York: Cambridge University Press, 2005. A gripping account of the rise of Islamism, Al Qaeda, and terrorism by a Lebanon-born, U.S.-based scholar.

Gerner, Deborah J., and Jillian Schwedler, eds. *Understanding the Contemporary Middle East,* 3rd ed. Boulder, CO: Lynne Rienner, 2008. A useful collection of essays on varied aspects of the Middle East today.

Gordon, April A., and Donald L. Gordon, eds. *Understanding Contemporary Africa,* 4th ed. Boulder, CO: Lynne Rienner, 2006. An excellent collection of essays on aspects of Africa.

Keddie, Nikki R. *Modern Iran: Roots and Results of Revolution,* updated ed. New Haven: Yale University Press, 2006. Updating and revision of a major study.

Martin, Phyllis M., and Patrick O'Meara, eds. *Africa,* 3rd ed. Bloomington: Indiana University Press, 1995. Essays on African history, politics, culture, and economies.

Nugent, Paul. *Africa Since Independence: A Comparative History.* New York: Palgrave Macmillan, 2004. A recent, detailed survey.

Smith, Charles D. *Palestine and the Arab-Israeli Conflict: A History with Documents,* 7th ed. Boston: Bedford/St. Martin's, 2009. A comprehensive, balanced survey.

Tenaille, Frank. *Music Is the Weapon of the Future: Fifty Years of African Popular Music.* Chicago: Lawrence Hill, 2000. A recent overview of varied African pop musicians and musical styles.

CHAPTER

31

South Asia, Southeast Asia, and Global Connections, Since 1945

CHAPTER OUTLINE

- The Reshaping of South Asia
- South Asian Politics and Societies
- Revolution, Decolonization, and New Nations in Southeast Asia
- Tigers, Politics, and Changing Southeast Asian Societies

PROFILE
Raj Kapoor, Bollywood Film Star

WITNESS TO THE PAST
A Thai Poet's Plea for the Environment

Mary Cross

Commuting to Work
Vietnam has largely recovered from its decades of war and has experienced increasing economic growth. These women in Hanoi are commuting to work by bicycle.

This music sings the struggle of [humanity]. This music is my life. This is the revolution we have begun. But the revolution is only a means to attain freedom, and freedom is only a means to enrich the happiness and nobility of human life.

—Hazil, the Indonesian revolutionary nationalist in Mochtar Lubis's Novel *A Road with No End* (1952)[1]

FOCUS QUESTIONS

1. What factors led to the political division of South Asia?
2. What have been the major achievements and disappointments of the South Asian nations?
3. What were the causes and consequences of the struggles in Southeast Asia?
4. What role do the Southeast Asian nations play in the global system?

In 1950 an idealistic group of Indonesian writers published a moving declaration promoting universal human dignity: "We [Indonesians] are the heirs to the culture of the whole world, a culture which is ours to extend and develop in our own way [by] the discarding of old and outmoded values and their replacement by new ones. Our fundamental quest is [helping] humanity."[2] These writers, hoping that Indonesia could combine the most humane ideas of East and West to become a beacon to the world, open to all cultures, had been shaped by Western Enlightenment traditions, including the ideals of democracy, free thought, and tolerance. Having witnessed the Indonesian Revolution against the Dutch, a nationalist struggle that raged between 1945 and 1950 and finally led to Indonesian independence, the writers also warned against a narrow nationalism. They had been inspired by the irreverent Sumatran poet Chairul Anwar **(CHAI-roll ON-war)** (1922–1949), who believed that the revolution had made possible a new, open society. A true bohemian, undisciplined in his personal life, Anwar had risen from poverty—his family was too poor to send him to secondary school—to master the Dutch, English, Spanish, and French languages. Influenced both by Western books and by an Indonesian sensibility, Anwar excited Indonesians with his pathbreaking poems that stretched the possibilities of the Indonesian language. But Anwar had died at twenty-seven, sapped by his appetite for the pleasures of the flesh. His death left it to others, among them the liberal Sumatran novelist and journalist Mochtar Lubis **(MOKE-tar LOO-bis)** (b. 1920), to carry on the campaign. Their goal, as expressed in the writers' declaration, was to blend widely admired ideas from abroad with Indonesian ideas, fostering change while also preserving continuity.

The declaration's noble aspirations and recognition of Indonesia's connection to the wider world reflected a new sense of possibility as colonial walls were being knocked down. But the writers' idealism was soon dashed by the realities of the early post–World War II years. While South and Southeast Asians longed for human dignity, other, more immediate goals took precedence: securing independence, building a new nation, and addressing poverty and underdevelopment. The cosmopolitan values of Anwar, Lubis, and their colleagues even came to seem quaint and contrary to the dominant nationalist agenda. But despite false starts and conflicts, over the following decades Indonesians and other nations of South and Southeast Asia sought, and sometimes found, answers to their challenges while increasing their links to global networks. As a result, these societies changed dramatically without destroying tradition. Except for East Asia, southern Asia is the most densely populated part of the world: well over 2 billion people live in the lands stretching eastward from Pakistan and India to Indonesia and the Philippines. It is also very diverse, containing a wide array of languages, ethnic groups, religions, world-views, governments, and levels of

e Visit the website and eBook for additional study materials and interactive tools: www.cengage.com/history/lockard/globalsocnet2e

economic development. Some nations have experienced destabilizing conflict; others have achieved widespread prosperity. This region of contrasts between wealth and poverty has played an important role in the world for over four millennia and continues to be one of the cornerstones of the world economy.

The Reshaping of South Asia

What factors led to the political division of South Asia?

World War II undermined British colonialism and led to independence for South Asians. The British, economically drained by the war and realizing that continued control would come only at a great cost in wealth and perhaps lives, handed power over to local leaders. The first prime minister of independent India, Jawaharlal Nehru **(JAH-wa HAR-lahl NAY-roo)** (1889–1964), told his people: "A moment comes, which comes rarely in history, when we step from the old to the new, when an age ends and when the soul of a nation, long suppressed, finds utterance."[3] Yet Nehru's idealism was tempered by the realities of the challenges ahead. India's long struggle for independence, marked by the nonviolent philosophy of Mohandas Gandhi (1868–1948), had ironically ended with Gandhi assassinated and British India divided into two separate, often hostile countries, predominantly Hindu India and largely Muslim Pakistan. Mostly Buddhist Sri Lanka and, in the 1970s, largely Muslim Bangladesh also gained independence. Each nation had its achievements and failures, but the largest and most populous, India, has been the regional colossus and a major player in world affairs.

Decolonization and Partition

South Asia's religious divisions undermined regional unity. During World War II relations between the British and the mainly Hindu leadership of the Indian National Congress ruptured (see Chapter 25). Taking advantage, and fearing domination by the Hindu majority, the Muslim League pressed its case with the British for a separate Muslim nation, to be called Pakistan. Negotiations to bring the Congress and the Muslim League together broke down in 1946. As the tension increased, rioting broke out, and Muslims and Hindus began murdering each other, pulling victims from buses, shops, and homes. In Calcutta alone 5,000 people died. The rioting undermined any pretence of Hindu-Muslim unity, and the Muslim League leader, Mohammed Ali Jinnah (1876–1948), announced that if India were not divided it would be destroyed. As the rioting spread, the Congress leaders and British officials now realized that some sort of partition was inevitable. In 1947 the British, Congress, and Muslim League agreed to create two independent nations, India and a Pakistan formed out of the Muslim majority areas of eastern Bengal and the northwestern provinces along the Indus River (see Chronology: South Asia, 1945–Present).

In a speech to his new nation, Prime Minister Nehru proclaimed: "Long years ago we made a tryst with destiny, and now the time comes when we shall redeem our pledge. At the stroke of the midnight hour, when the world sleeps, India will awake to life and freedom."[4] A similar mood of renewal struck people in Pakistan. But the euphoria in both new nations proved short-lived as a bloodbath ensued. Muslims and Hindus had often lived side by side, but partition sparked hatreds between local members of the majority faith, who felt empowered, and religious minorities, who feared discrimination. As violence flared, Hindus and Sikhs fled Pakistan for India, and Muslims fled India for Pakistan. Altogether some 10 to 12 million refugees crossed the India-Pakistan borders. Perhaps 1 million died and 75,000 women were raped. Religious extremists sometimes attacked whole villages or whole trainloads of refugees.

The sixty-eight-year-old Mohandas Gandhi labored to stop the killing. Moving into the Muslim quarter of Delhi, he toured refugee camps without escort, read aloud from the scriptures of all religions, including the Quran, and confronted Hindu mobs attacking mosques. Finally, in desperation, and hoping to send a message to everyone, Gandhi, who weighed only 113 pounds, began a fast until all the violence

CHRONOLOGY
South Asia, 1945–Present

1947 Independence for India and Pakistan

1948 Assassination of Mohandas Gandhi

1948 Sri Lankan independence

1950 Indian republic

1948–1964 Nehru era in India

1959 Sri Lanka's Sirimavo Bandaranaike first woman prime minister

1962 India-China border war

1971 Formation of Bangladesh

1975–1977 State of emergency under Indira Gandhi

1984 Assassination of Indira Gandhi

1988–1990 First Benazir Bhutto government in Pakistan

1993–1996 Second Benazir Bhutto government

1999–2006 Military government led by Pervez Musharraf

2006 Assassination of Benazir Bhutto

CHRONOLOGY		
	South Asia	Southeast Asia
1940	**1947** Independence for India and Pakistan **1948–1964** Nehru era in India	**1945–1950** Indonesian Revolution **1946–1954** First Indochina War **1948** Independence of Burma
1950		
1960	**1963–1975** U.S.-Vietnamese War	**1966–1998** New Order in Indonesia
1970	**1971** Formation of Bangladesh	**1975** Communist victories in Vietnam, Cambodia, Laos
1980	**1984** Assassination of Indira Gandhi	
1990		**1997** Asian economic crisis
2000		**2008–2009** World economic crisis

in the city had stopped or he died. He quickly fell ill, but Gandhi's effort worked, allowing him to break off his fast. After the violence subsided, a substantial Muslim and Sikh minority remained in India and a Hindu and Sikh minority in Pakistan. But partition had been shattering. A Muslim poet spoke for many disillusioned people: "This is not that long looked-for break of the day. Where did that fine breeze blow from—where has it fled?"[5] Gandhi's support for Muslim victims of Hindu violence outraged Hindu extremists, who regarded Gandhi as a traitor. In January 1948, one of them gunned down Gandhi as he walked to a meeting, shocking the whole country and the world.

Two New Nations

Despite its bloody start, India was built on a solid political foundation. Britain bequeathed the basis for democracy, a trained civil service, a good communications system, and an educated if Westernized elite committed to modernization. India became a republic with a constitution based on the British model, led by a prime minister chosen by the majority party in an elected parliament. However, given its huge ethnic, religious, and linguistic diversity (fourteen major languages and hundreds of minor languages), India has had difficulty building national unity. To accommodate the many religious minorities, regions, and cultures, India adopted a federal system, with elected state governments, and was officially secular with complete separation of religion and state. Kashmir, a mountainous Himalayan state on the India-Pakistan border, presented a long-term problem because it had a Muslim majority but a Hindu ruler who opted to join India. Kashmir has remained a source of constant tension and sometimes war between India and Pakistan.

The new Pakistan confronted numerous problems. It was an artificial country, with two wings separated by a thousand miles of India. The nation's founding leader, Jinnah, died soon after independence, and his successor was assassinated. Muslims had been overrepresented in the British Indian military, and the army now played a stronger role in Pakistan's politics than in India's. The loss of top civilian leaders, lack of a balanced economic base, massive poverty, and geographical division made Pakistan more vulnerable than India to political instability and military rule. Pakistan and India quarreled over issues from water use to trade to ownership of Kashmir.

Building a New India

Nehru's India

India's first prime minister, Nehru, a close associate of Gandhi, dominated Indian politics for a decade and a half (1948–1964). A gifted speaker and brilliant thinker, Nehru was supported by the small middle class, who wanted a modern India, and by the lower-class majority who lived in overcrowded, unhealthy urban slums or dusty villages that lacked electricity and running water. Nehru promised to raise living standards and address the nation's overwhelming poverty. He believed firmly in democracy. While India lagged behind China in economic development, it preserved personal freedom. Believing in peaceful coexistence with neighbors, renouncing military aggression, and hoping to prevent a nuclear conflict between the superpowers, Nehru became a major figure on the world stage. He helped found the Non-Aligned Movement of nations, such as Egypt and Indonesia, that were unwilling to commit to either the U.S. or Soviet camps in the Cold War. As India's stature grew, Nehru led the Congress Party to three smashing electoral victories.

Wide World Photos

Muslims Leaving India for Pakistan During Partition As India and Pakistan split into two new nations in 1947, millions of Muslims and Hindus fled their homes to escape violence. This photo shows displaced Muslims, carrying a few meager belongings, jamming a train headed from India to Pakistan.

Nehru's Policies

Nehru's policies derived from his complex ideals. Although the British-educated lawyer admired Western politics, literature, and dynamism, he also respected India's cultural heritage, speaking of its moral strength. Raised a Hindu brahman, Nehru was nevertheless a secularist who believed that Congress should represent and serve all religions and social groups. Perhaps his greatest contributions came in addressing social problems. Like Gandhi, he opposed the caste system and fought gender inequalities. Nehru convinced parliament to approve new laws on untouchability and women's rights that penalized discrimination. Untouchables, who have preferred the designation **Dalit** ("suppressed" or "ground down" people) since the 1970s, acquired special quotas in government services and universities, while Hindu women gained legal equality with men, including the right to divorce and inheritance. To discourage child marriage, Nehru set a minimum marriage age at eighteen for males and fifteen for females. But these laws challenging centuries of tradition were often ignored, especially in rural areas.

Dalit The designation commonly used for untouchables since the 1970s.

Nehru introduced a planning system to foster modern technology while mixing capitalism and socialism. He left established industries in private hands but set up public ventures to, for example, build power plants and dams, which doubled power production, and irrigation canals, which increased agricultural yields by 25 percent. In the 1960s the Green Revolution of new high-yield wheat and rice fostered a dramatic rise in food production. Thanks to Nehru's five-year plans, by the 1970s India produced many industrial products, including steel, and was nearly self-sufficient in food.

But some of Nehru's policies proved failures. Government control of the private sector through regulations gave bureaucrats great power, fostered corruption, and shackled private enterprise. Nehru also failed to cultivate good relations with Pakistan or with China, and in 1962 Chinese troops humiliated Indian forces during a border dispute. Moreover, Nehru did not recognize that a rapidly growing population, which rose from 389 million in 1941 to 434 million in 1961, would undermine most of India's economic gains; thus he only belatedly endorsed family planning. In addition, the government built schools and universities but failed to substantially raise literacy rates. Yet, when Nehru died in 1964, millions mourned the end of an idealistic era that had earned India respect in the world.

The Nehru Dynasty

Nehru also fostered a family political dynasty. With the sudden death of his respected successor in 1966, the Congress selected Nehru's daughter, Indira Gandhi (1917–1984), to be the nation's first woman prime minister. She had worked closely with her father while her husband (no relation to Mohandas Gandhi) served in parliament. Mrs. Gandhi enjoyed a decade and a half in power. When her support waned in the 1967 elections, she responded aggressively with policies to win back the poor. India's smashing military victory over archenemy Pakistan elevated her status. But

Jagadeesh/Reuters/Corbis

Global Communications A workroom in one of the hundreds of call centers in Indian cities such as Bangalore and Mumbai (Bombay). The workers, mostly well-educated and fluent in English, field customer service calls from around the world for Western companies, many of them in the financial services, computer, and electronic businesses.

mounting domestic problems precipitated increasingly harsh policies, which often made matters worse. Powerful vested interests ignored her reforms, the economy faltered, and many Indians turned against the Congress. As a result, Indian democracy faltered. In 1975 Gandhi declared a state of emergency, suspending civil rights, closing state governments, and jailing some 10,000 opposition leaders and dissidents. While her actions were condemned, some of her policies improved the economy. Meanwhile, her youngest son, Sanjay Gandhi (1946–1980), launched a controversial birth control campaign to forcibly sterilize any man with more than three children, and also implemented a slum-clearance program that forced thousands out of sidewalk shanties. Both programs became deeply unpopular. In 1977 Indira lifted the emergency. After thirty years in power, the Congress Party, and with it Indira Gandhi, was voted out of office and replaced by an uneasy coalition of parties, including Hindu nationalists opposed to secularism. But the coalition government, which solved few problems, collapsed.

Political Violence

Indira Gandhi returned to power in the 1980 elections, restoring the Nehru dynasty. But Mrs. Gandhi faced voter apathy, growing unemployment, and unrest. In 1980 Sanjay Gandhi died in a plane crash, and Indira Gandhi elevated her eldest son Rajiv (1944–1991), an apolitical airline pilot, as her heir apparent. Violence in the Punjab, India's richest state, which had a heavy Sikh population, provoked Mrs. Gandhi's final crisis. Many Sikhs, whose religion mixes Hindu and Muslim ideas, desired autonomy from India. In 1983 armed Sikh extremists occupied the Golden Temple at Amritsar (uhm-RIT-suhr), the holiest Sikh shrine, and turned it into a fortress, calling for an independent Sikh homeland and murdering those, including moderate Sikhs, who opposed them. In 1984 the Indian army stormed the Golden Temple. When the fighting ended, the temple was reduced to rubble and over a thousand militants and soldiers lay dead.

Violence had returned to Indian political life. The destruction of their holiest temple shocked the Sikhs and led to the shooting death of Indira Gandhi by two of her Sikh bodyguards. In response, Hindu mobs roamed Delhi, burning Sikh shops and killing Sikhs, often by pouring gasoline over them and setting them ablaze. The dead numbered in the thousands. Meanwhile, Rajiv Gandhi succeeded his mother but proved ineffective, and in 1991, while campaigning in the southern city of Madras, he was blown up by a young Sri Lankan woman handing him flowers. The suicide bomber opposed India's support of the Sri Lankan government in its war against the Tamil secessionist group to which she belonged. Yet despite this tumult, India remained a functioning democracy and a thriving nation.

The Making of Pakistan and Bangladesh

Awami League A Bengali nationalist party that began the move for independence from West Pakistan.

Pakistan faced greater challenges than did India. Jinnah had pledged to make the nation happy and prosperous, but the leaders who followed him had only limited success, in part because of tensions between ethnic groups who shared an Islamic faith but often little else. Hostilities flared between the nationalistic Bengalis, who dominated the east, and the Punjabis and Sindhis, who dominated the west. The two regions differed in language, culture, and outlook. The factionalized Pakistani parliament, whose members chiefly represented regions and ethnic groups rather than rival ideologies, proved unworkable, providing an excuse for military leaders to take over the government in 1958. But by 1969 dissatisfaction with military dictatorship led to riots, prompting martial law. The Bengalis felt they did not get a fair share of the nation's resources and political power, and eventually ethnic tensions came to a boil. After the **Awami League**, a Bengali nationalist party, won a majority of East Pakistan's seats in national elections, in early 1971 Pakistani troops arrested the party leader, Sheikh Mujiber Rahman **(shake MOO-jee-bur RAH-mun)** (1920–1975). Hoping to crush Awami League support, troops opened fire on university dormitories and Hindu homes, causing hundreds of casualties.

Inspired by Sheikh Mujiber, who asked his supporters to carry his message to every rice field and mango grove, the Awami League then declared independence. In response, West Pakistani troops poured into East Pakistan, terrorizing the Bengali population with massacres, arson, and the raping of thousands of women. At least half a million Bengalis died. The civil war caused 10 million desperate, starving refugees to flee to India. World opinion turned against Pakistan. India appealed for support of East Pakistan, armed the Bengali guerrillas, and, after an ill-advised Pakistani attack on Indian airfields, sent troops into both West and East Pakistan, rapidly gaining the upper hand. Meanwhile, Pakistan received military aid from China and the United States, both of which it had courted. But while the U.S. administration of President Richard Nixon ignored the slaughter of Bengalis and China threatened to intervene on behalf of Pakistan, Soviet backing of India discouraged such a move. By the end of 1971 Pakistani troops in Bengal had surrendered to Indian forces, and the Awami League, led by Sheikh Mujibur, established a new nation, Bangladesh (Bengali Nation) (see Map 31.1).

SECTION SUMMARY

- After World War II, when majority Muslim Pakistan broke off from majority Hindu India, widespread religious violence broke out and a dispute over the territory of Kashmir set the stage for continued tension between the two countries.
- Nehru attempted to expand the rights of women and, through a mix of capitalism and socialism, vastly increased India's industrial and agricultural output, but the population expanded at a dangerously rapid rate and not all policies were successful.
- Nehru's daughter, Indira Gandhi, was prime minister for over a decade, but she treated her opposition harshly and was assassinated in the midst of clashes between Hindus and Sikhs, and her son and successor, Rajiv Gandhi, was also assassinated.
- East and West Pakistan were divided along ethnic lines, and a military crackdown on a Bengali nationalist party led to a bloody civil war in which India intervened on behalf of East Pakistan, which then became a separate country, Bangladesh.

SOUTH ASIAN POLITICS AND SOCIETIES

What have been the major achievements and disappointments of the South Asian nations?

South Asian societies each forged their own political role in the region. With 1.2 billion people by 2009 and 65 percent of the land in the subcontinent, the Republic of India rose to regional dominance. Indian governments began to liberalize the economy, stimulating growth. But growing Hindu nationalism has challenged the domination of the Congress Party, threatening its secular vision. Meanwhile, India's neighbors have struggled to achieve stability and economic development. Both Pakistan and Sri Lanka have experienced persistent ethnic violence, while India and Pakistan remain wary, building up military forces and nuclear weapons to use against the other. In each South Asian nation ancient customs exist side by side with modern machines and ways of living.

Indian Politics and Economic Change

Indian Democracy

When India celebrated its fiftieth jubilee of independence in 1997, the nation's president reminded his people that India's challenge was to achieve economic growth with social justice. That goal remains elusive; India has been unable to mount the sort of concerted attack on mass poverty found in China. However, Indians can boast that they have maintained one of the few

Map 31.1 Modern South Asia

India, predominantly Hindu, is the largest South Asian nation and separates the two densely populated Islamic nations of Bangladesh and Pakistan. Buddhists are the majority in Sri Lanka, just off India's southeast coast. The small kingdoms of Bhutan and Nepal are located in the Himalayan mountain range.

e Interactive Map

working multiparty democracies outside the industrialized nation-states, one that fosters lively debate and forces candidates to appeal to voters. An Indian novelist described the campaign rhetoric leading up to elections: "The speeches were crammed with promises of every shape and size: promises of new schools, clean water, health care, land for landless peasants, powerful laws to punish any discrimination."[6] While such grandiose promises usually prove difficult to fulfill, millions of people vote in these elections, and changes in state and federal governments have regularly occurred.

To some observers, democracy fosters national unity by providing a flexible system for accommodating the diverse population. Others argue that democracy has intensified differences between groups. Certainly, tensions between Hindus and Muslims and between high-caste and low-caste Hindus, manipulated by opportunistic politicians, have complicated political life. While voting may give the poor an opportunity to put pressure on elites, elites can manipulate the system to preserve their privileges. Critics contend that democracy functions as a safety valve for popular frustration, creating the illusion of mass participation that prevents a frontal attack on caste and class inequalities. Yet, lower-caste voters sometimes force officials to meet their needs, such as by paving the pathways in their neighborhoods.

Political Parties

The Congress Party has remained nationally influential but has had to contend with rivals. On the left, several communist parties dominate politics in West Bengal and in Kerala in the southwest, repeatedly winning elections by promoting modernization and support for the poor. On the right are Hindu nationalist parties, which had limited success until the 1990s. In the southern states various parties representing regional interests have generally dominated state governments and joined federal coalitions. These regional parties, often led by stars of the local film industries, have protected local languages while preserving English, understood by educated people around the country, as a national language. All of India's parties have suffered from corruption.

Bharatha Janata The major Hindu nationalist party in India.

Since 1989 Indian politics has become more pluralistic. The major Hindu nationalist party, the **Bharatha Janata** (BJP), gained influence in north India by espousing hostility to Muslims and state support for Hindu issues, such as having schools teach Indian history in accordance with Hindu traditions and religious writings. The BJP slogan, "One Nation, One People, One Culture," confronts the Gandhi-Nehru vision of a tolerant multicultural state. By the late 1990s India, under a BJP-dominated government, suffered from rising political corruption, violent secessionist movements in border regions, caste conflict, religious hostilities, and fragmentation into several rival political factions. In 2002 major Hindu-Muslim violence broke out again, leaving over a thousand people dead and over 100,000 terrified Muslims, burned out of their cities, huddled in tent camps. In 2004 the Congress, led by Rajiv Gandhi's Italian-born, sari-wearing widow, Sonia Gandhi (b. 1946), a Roman Catholic who met Rajiv when both were students in England, capitalized on disenchantment among the poor and Muslims and, allied with leftist parties, unexpectedly defeated the ruling BJP-led coalition. A Pakistan-born Sikh economist, Manmohan Singh (b. 1932), became the first non-Hindu prime minister.

A free press monitors politics in India. In 2005 an investigation of corruption by a television station forced several members of parliament to resign, indicating the continued vibrancy of Indian democracy. Although India was rocked by a terrorist attack on Bombay by Pakistani militants and then by the global economic crisis, in 2009 the Congress and Singh won a big electoral victory with strong support from the poor, grateful for increased spending on rural health and education. While older politicians still dominated government, a quarter of the successful parliamentary candidates were younger than forty-five.

Economic Policies

India struggled to resolve economic backwardness, skyrocketing population growth, and crushing poverty for the majority. Nehru had sought to end ignorance, poverty, and inequality of opportunity. While his dream has not been fully realized, Indians can boast of many gains, especially after India changed directions economically in the 1970s. For example, in 1956 India had to import vital foodstuffs and manufactured goods. Twenty tears later it was a net exporter of grain and by 2000 was making and exporting its own cars, computers, and aircraft. To spur faster growth after 1991, Indian leaders began dismantling the socialist sector of the economy built by Nehru. Reform, deregulation, and liberalization contributed to an economic growth rate of 6 to 7 percent a year by the late 1990s, and several cities, especially Bangalore and Bombay, became high-tech centers closely linked to global communications. Hundreds of North American and European companies, taking advantage of a growing, educated Indian middle class, especially university graduates fluent in English, have moved information and technical service jobs, such as call-in customer service and computer programming, from North America and Europe to India. India's boom even prompted thousands of highly educated Indians living in North America and Europe to return and join its high-tech sector. These returnees often move into spacious, newly built California-style suburbs with names like Ozone and Lake Vista. Even greater progress has been made in agriculture. The nation now grows enough wheat and rice to feed the entire population.

However, persisting social, economic, and regional inequalities have prevented equitable food distribution. Hence, when inadequate monsoon rains caused a severe drought in 2009, millions of poor farmers lost income, perpetuating the cycle of rural poverty. Moreover, in spite of the economic revival and a growing middle class, many Indians have yet to enjoy its fruits. Compared to China, Malaysia, and South Korea, India's economy has been less able to deliver a better life to the majority. More than half of Indians still live below the poverty line, 25 percent lack an adequate diet, and nearly 80 percent earn less than $2.50 per day. While China nears universal literacy, only half of Indians can read and write. Meanwhile, population growth eats away at the national resources. Every year 30 million Indians are born, and by 2050 India will have 1.5 billion people, more than

China and four times more than the United States. Ironically, success in doubling life expectancy contributes to overpopulation, which causes overcrowded cities, a lack of pure drinking water and adequate sanitation, and insufficient primary health care. India has half as many physicians per population and over twice as much infant mortality as China; Chinese live twelve years longer than Indians. Millions of Indians sleep on city sidewalks for lack of money and housing. Many schools are inadequate, staffed by poorly-paid teachers. While affluent Indians increasingly buy fancy imported cars to drive along newly built highways, many commuters ride on the roofs of jammed buses and trains. India's greenhouse gas emissions are expected to triple in the next two decades.

Development and Underdevelopment

The stark contrasts between the modern and traditional sectors have produced development amid underdevelopment and raised questions as to who benefits from the changes. The "haves" can afford to pay for services that strapped governments cannot provide—good schools, clean water, decent health care, efficient transport—while ambitious birth control campaigns enjoy success in cities but less in the countryside. The Green Revolution has increased output but mostly benefits the big landowners, who can afford the large investments in tractors and fertilizers, and per capita calorie consumption remains well below world averages. Because successive Indian governments have been largely unable or unwilling to challenge vested interests such as the powerful landlords, half the rural population has become landless. Poverty fosters growing urban crime and rural banditry. Maoist guerrillas challenge local police in some impoverished districts. Economic growth and poverty also ravage the environment as cities encroach on farmland and people cut down trees for firewood. As in China, poor peasants protest, often violently, the taking of their land for building factories, often foreign-owned, and highways. The Chipko forest conservation movement, based on traditional and Gandhian principles and led mostly by women, is one of many groups working to protect the environment. A Chipko leader, the globetrotting Sunderlal Bahugana **(SUN-dur-LOLL ba-hoo-GAH-na)**, stresses the place of people in the larger web of nature.

Indian Societies and Cultures

Cities and Villages

In his will, India's first prime minister, Jawaharlal Nehru, asked that his ashes be scattered in the Ganges River, not because of the river's religious significance to Hindus but because it symbolized to him India's millennia-old culture, ever changing and yet ever the same. Ancient traditions have persisted but have also been modified, especially in the cities. The contrast between the villages, where 80 percent of Indians live, and the often-modern cities remains stark. The growing urban middle class enjoys recreations and technologies, from golf to video games, that are available to the affluent around the world. As young people move around the country, often on the new national highway system, they identify less with their home region and more with India, becoming cosmopolitan. Whether they live in the Punjab, Calcutta, or Bangalore, educated urban young people often like the same music and buy the same consumer goods, which conservatives see as a threat to local cultures. Conservatives fumed but many urbanites cheered when Indian courts struck down laws against homosexuality in 2009.

Moreover, practices that ensure strict divisions between castes, such as avoiding physical contact or sharing food, are harder to maintain in cities than in villages. While city people often still pay attention to caste, their approach to preserving it is different. For instance, high-caste families often place classified ads in national newspapers seeking marriage partners from similar backgrounds for their children, as in this example: "Suitable Brahman bride for handsome Brahman boy completing Ph.D. (Physics). Write with biodata, photograph, horoscope."[7] Meanwhile, caste remains much more firmly rooted in the villages. At the bottom of the caste system, the untouchables (Dalits), some 20 percent of India's population, still live difficult lives, especially in the villages, even though government policies to improve their status have enabled some low-caste people to succeed in high-status occupations or politics. The grooves of tradition run deep, particularly in the rural areas, and changes can bring demoralization and disorientation as well as satisfaction.

Families and Gender Relations

Modern life has also hastened the breakup of the traditional joint families, where parents lived in large compounds with their married and unmarried children and grandchildren; some Indians now live in smaller, nuclear families. New forms of employment, which can cause family members to move to other districts or countries, have undermined family cohesion. A traditional preference for male babies, however, has continued. Today the ability of technology to determine the sex of a fetus has led many Indians who want male children to terminate pregnancies. Experts worry that a gender-imbalanced population will experience increasing social problems.

Nehru had believed that India could progress only if women played a full part, and new laws banned once-widespread customs such as polygamy, child marriage, and sati. In addition, female literacy has risen, from 1 percent in 1901 to 27 percent in 2000, though it is still only half the male rate. But some changing customs have penalized women. The practice of requiring new brides to provide generous dowries to their in-laws, once restricted to higher castes, has become common in all castes. As a result, some families banish, injure, or kill young brides whose own families failed to supply the promised dowries. Moreover, notions of women's rights, common in cities, are less known in villages. In some towns the police harass unmarried couples in public parks for public displays of affection, and even in Bangalore, where many educated women work in high-tech jobs, conservatives sometimes harass young women who go with friends to bars and discos.

Nevertheless, many Indian women have benefited from education, even becoming forceful leaders in such fields as journalism, business, trade unions, and the arts. Women have been elected to parliament and serve as chief ministers of states, especially in south India. In 2009 the Congress Party challenged tradition by naming a Dalit woman, former diplomat Meira Kumar, as Speaker of the Parliament. An antipatriarchy women's movement, growing for a century, has also become more active. The Self-Employed Women's Association, founded by Ela Bhatt in 1972, has provided low-cost credit and literacy training to some of the poorest city women, the ragpickers and sidewalk vendors. Outside the big cities, however, women have remained largely bound by tradition, expected to demonstrate submission, obedience, and absolute dedication to their husband. Women's organizations affiliated with the Hindu nationalist BJP emphasize women as mothers who produce sons and portray Muslim men as a threat to them. But a more concrete threat has come from AIDS, which has rapidly become a health problem, a result largely of women being forced into prostitution to serve the sexual needs of increasingly mobile male workers such as long-haul truckers.

Religion

Religion still plays a key role in Indian life. Although Hindus form a large majority, India's population also includes 140 million Muslims, over 20 million Sikhs, and nearly 20 million Christians. However, religious differences have become politicized. Some upper-caste Hindus, particularly in the BJP, have used the notion of a Hindu nation to marginalize Muslims and low-caste Hindus. Violent attacks on Muslims by militant Hindu nationalists, often fundamentalists who interpret the ancient Hindu religious texts literally, have caused political crises. At other times Muslims have initiated the violence. In 2006 Muslims protesting Danish cartoons offensive to Muslims rioted and attacked Hindu and Western targets. Tensions are fueled by mass poverty among all the religious groups. Yet, Muslims occupy high positions in India's government, business, and the professions and play a key role in cultural expression, such as films and music. India's most famous modern artist, Tyeb Mehta (1925–2009), was a Shi'ite Muslim whose works, much of which address the Hindu-Muslim divide, sell all over the world. Yet, art can stir controversy. Many Indian galleries refuse to show the works of another acclaimed Muslim artist, Maqbool Fida Husain, because some of them depict Hindu goddesses in the nude.

Literature and Popular Culture

Bollywood The Mumbai film industry.

Indians have also eagerly embraced modern cultural forms. While Indian-born novelists such as Arundhati Roy (AH-roon-DAH-tee roy) and Salman Rushdie have achieved worldwide fame, a more popular cultural form has been film. India has built the world's largest film industry, making about a thousand movies a year. Many films also find a huge audience among both Indian emigrants and non-Indians in Southeast Asia, the Middle East, Africa, Europe, and the Caribbean. The Mumbai film industry, known as "**Bollywood**," (see Profile: Raj Kapoor, Bollywood Film Star), churns out films in the major north Indian language, Hindi. But other regions make films in local languages, such as Tamil in southeast India. Many films, especially musicals, have portrayed a fantasy world that enables viewers to forget the problem-filled real world. As one fan explained: "I love to sit in the dark and dream about what I can never possibly have. I can listen to the music, learn all the songs and forget about my troubles."[8] Religious divisions are muted in Bollywood, and many leading directors, writers, and stars come from Muslim backgrounds. Because of their superstar status, film stars are often able to move into state and federal politics. For example, voters in southern India have long favored stars of the local film industries as state leaders. By the 1980s that trend had even spread to parts of north India.

Islamic Societies and Sri Lanka

Politics in Pakistan

South Asia's two densely populated Muslim countries, Pakistan and Bangladesh, struggled to develop and maintain stability while alternating between military dictatorships and elected civilian governments. Containing 170 million people, over 95 percent of them Sunni Muslims, Pakistan has had difficulty transforming its diverse ethnic and tribal groups into a unified nation. The longest-serving civilian leader, Zulkifar Ali Bhutto (zool-KEE-far AH-lee BOO-toe) (r. 1971–1977), a lawyer from a wealthy landowning family and educated at top universities in Britain and California, pursued socialist policies to help the poor. Accusing him of corruption, the army took power and later executed Bhutto. The Soviet occupation of Afghanistan in 1979 and the Pakistan-supported Islamic resistance to the Soviets that followed (see Chapter 30) distracted Pakistanis

RAJ KAPOOR, BOLLYWOOD FILM STAR

Raj Kapoor (1924–1988) was a true pioneer: the first real superstar of Indian film, an accomplished actor, director, producer, and all-round showman. Kapoor skillfully combined music, melodrama, and spectacle to create a cinema with huge popular, even international, appeal, especially among the poor. He was born in Peshawar, the son of one of India's most distinguished stage and film actors, Prithviraj Kapoor, among whose hundreds of roles was that of Alexander the Great. The family settled in Bombay in 1929, when the Hindi-language film industry was in a formative stage (Hindi is the major language spoken in north India). At age twenty-two Kapoor entered an arranged marriage to Krishnaji. Although he had romances with actresses, the marriage endured and the couple had five children.

Handsome and vigorous, with a talent for comedy, music, and self-promotion, the young Kapoor formed his own film company in 1948 with hopes of appealing to the common person. Over the next three decades he starred in or oversaw dozens of films, many of them commercially successful. Kapoor's greatest success came during the Nehru years from the late 1940s to mid-1960s, when Indians were optimistic and looked outward. His films, often subtitled in local languages, brought him celebrity all over South Asia and in Southeast Asia, East Africa, the Middle East, the Caribbean, and the Soviet Union. He was largely responsible for the recognition of Indian cinema in the world. Songs from his films were sung or hummed on streets of cities and small towns thousands of miles from India, and he and his female costars became popular pin-ups in the bazaars of the Arab world and folk heroes in the Soviet lands. Kapoor, like Nehru, believed that an Indian could be international, enjoying foreign products and influences, while also remaining deeply Indian. A song from his film *The Gentleman Cheat* in 1955 reflected the hero's transnational identity: "The shoes I'm wearing are made in Japan, My trousers fashioned in England. The red cap on my head is Russian. In spite of it all my heart is Indian."

Dinodia Picture Agency

Raj Kapoor As the most influential male lead and director in Indian films, Kapoor could attract the top actresses to star in his films. He made many films with Nargis, the two of them shown here in a 1948 musical, *Barsaat.*

Kapoor believed that some of his films achieved international success because "the young people of those countries saw in the films their own sufferings, the strivings to achieve, and their own triumph over a world in chaos." Fans saw in his characters youth, optimism about life, and revolt against authority, the little man straddling the great divides of wealth and poverty, city and village, sophistication and innocence. For example, in *The Vagabond* (1951) he portrays a rebellious youth and petty thief growing up on the streets, both daring and vulnerable, charming and reckless, surviving by his wits.

The themes of Kapoor's films often touched on social problems or politics and were filled with humanism and sensitivity. They cried out against destitution and unequal wealth, offering underdog heroes who were poor but also happy. These themes permeated some of his most popular films, such as *The Vagabond,* which broke box-office records in the USSR and the Middle East, where it was dubbed into Arabic, Persian, and Turkish. An ardent fan of American comedians, especially Charlie Chaplin, Kapoor, like Chaplin, often portrayed a deglamorized tramp, the little man at odds with the world and hiding his pain behind a smiling face, a figure he thought "had a greater identity with the common man."

Kapoor's romanticism was evident in his sympathetic treatment of women. The heroine, often played by the actress Nargis **(NAR-ghis)** (1929–1981), a Muslim whose mother was a famed singer, was always a central player in his films. Sometimes Kapoor's films presented women as strong and without flaws, as was his character's love interest, Nargis, in *The Vagabond;* at other times women were victims, exploited and tormented by religion and tradition. Kapoor argued, "We eulogize womankind as the embodiment of motherhood but we always give our women the worst treatment. They are burnt alive [in sati], treated as slaves [by men]." Yet, in spite of his concern for the sexual exploitation of women, Kapoor's films presented sensuous actresses and opened the way to more sexually explicit scenes, shocking social conservatives.

Kapoor's career faded in the 1970s, when his style of romantic hero became old-fashioned. The newer films focused on the angry young man, often a gangster, and turned away from Kapoor's adoring treatment of women. At the time of his death in 1988 he was making a film exploring the taboo subject of love across the India-Pakistan border, between a Hindu and a Muslim. His sons, all actors, tried to keep his banner alive, but Bollywood moved in new directions, centering stories on men and their challenges rather than balancing strong male-female roles as Kapoor had done.

THINKING ABOUT THE PROFILE

1. Why is Kapoor often credited with spreading Indian film to other countries?
2. What social viewpoints were expressed in his films?

Note: Quotations from Sumita S. Chakravarty, *National Identity in Indian Popular Cinema, 1947–1987* (Austin: University of Texas Press, 1993), 138, 30; and Malti Sahai, "Raj Kapoor and the Indianization of Charlie Chaplin," *East-West Film Journal* 2, no. 1 (December 1987): 64.

from their unpopular military regime and brought more U.S. military aid to Pakistan. Bhutto's daughter, Benazir Bhutto **(BEN-ah-ZEER BOO-toe)** (1953-2006), a graduate of Oxford University, put together a movement to challenge the military regime. As unrest increased in 1988, Benazir Bhutto became prime minister and later the first head of a modern Asian government to give birth to a child while in office. She was respected abroad but, accused of abuse of power, was dismissed in 1990. Although Bhutto returned to power after the 1993 elections, she failed to resolve critical problems, including growing fighting between ethnic factions and attacks by militant Sunnis on the small Shi'a Muslim and Christian minorities. In 1996 she was once again removed.

In 1999 the military took over, installing as president General Pervez Musharraf **(per-VEZ moo-SHAR-uff)** (b. 1943), whose family had fled to Pakistan during the partition of India in 1947. He faced and largely failed to meet the same challenge as his predecessors: to halt factional violence, punish corruption, collect taxes from the wealthy, restore economic growth, solve high unemployment, and balance the demands of both militant and secular Muslims. Although Musharraf allied with the United States after the 2001 terrorist attacks on the United States and the resulting U.S. invasion of Afghanistan, many Pakistanis resented the United States and the West. While seeking Pakistani help in the war on international terrorism, the United States was reluctant to remove high tariff barriers against Pakistani textiles, a major export that accounts for nearly half of all manufacturing jobs—Pakistanis make everything from shirts to sheets for Western companies. After popular unrest forced Musharraf out in 2006, Benazir Bhutto won free elections, but she was soon assassinated by a Muslim zealot. Since then the government has been besieged by the rise of a Pakistani Taliban, Muslim extemists seeking to impose a rigid theocracy, leading to terrorist attacks and Taliban-army fighting that has displaced several million refugees.

Pakistani Society and Culture

Pakistani society and culture have remained conservative and deeply divided between Sufis and secular urbanites, generally moderate, and those who favor strict Islamic laws and conduct. Pakistan's founding leader, Jinnah, a cosmopolitan British-educated lawyer, had favored more rights for women, arguing that it was a crime that most Pakistani women were shut up within the four walls of the house as prisoners. But national leaders who shared this view were reluctant to challenge the strong opposition to women's rights, especially in rural areas. In 1979 an Islamizing military government pushed through discriminatory laws that made women who were raped guilty of adultery, a serious offense. Women enjoyed far fewer legal rights than men and were more commonly jailed or punished for adultery. Women's groups who courageously protested in the streets were attacked by military force, prompting the feminist poet Saeeda Gazdar **(SIGH-ee-da GAZ-dar)** to write: "The flags of mourning were flapping, the hand-maidens had rebelled. Those two hundred women who came out on the streets, were surrounded on all sides, besieged by armed force, [repressed by] the enemies of truth, the murderers of love."[9] By the 1990s things had changed little: only 10 percent of adult women were employed outside the home, and fewer than 20 percent were literate. In some districts Islamic militants succeeded in restricting women from voting or from attending school with males.

Repression exists in other areas as well. The attempts by Islamic leaders to prohibit the broadcasting of music by popular singers, especially women such as London-based Nazia Hassan, set off an ongoing debate about the role of Westernized popular culture and women entertainers. Finally, Pakistan remains a land of villages dominated by large, politically influential landowners. Although life expectancy improved from forty-three to sixty-three years between 1960 and 2005, 40 percent of children suffered from malnutrition. With far too few public schools, many Pakistani youngsters attend Islamic madrassahs with narrow religious curriculums.

Politics and Society in Bangladesh

Bangladesh, overcrowded with 155 million people, has also encountered barriers to development. Mostly flat plains, the land is prone to devastating hurricanes, floods, tornados, famine, and rising sea levels due to global warming. The nation's founder, Sheikh Mujiber Rahman, had hoped that the nation he envisioned—secular, democratic, and socialist—would rapidly progress, but, after tightening his power, he was assassinated by the military. None of the succession of governments after him, whether military or civilian, have had much success in resolving problems, and all have suffered from corruption. Several leaders have been assassinated. After 1991 democracy became the main pattern, and the two largest parties have been led by women. The conservative Islamic and pro-capitalist Khaleda Zia **(ZEE-uh)** (b. 1945), the widow of an assassinated leader, heads one party while the left-leaning Sheikh Hasina Wajed **(shake ha-SEE-nah WAH-jed)** (b. 1947), the daughter of the assassinated Sheikh Mujiber Rahman, the nation's first prime minister, leads the Awami League. Sheikh Hasina herself escaped an assassination attempt in 2004. The two women, bitter rivals, have alternated as the nation's prime minister.

Despite political turbulence, however, Bangladesh has been a pioneer in programs to eliminate poverty and now provides some formal education to 60 percent of its children. The Grameen Bank, which loans small amounts of money, particularly to poor women for starting a village business, has helped millions of people, earning world attention (see Chapter 26). A visionary activist, Fazle Hasan Abed, also launched a movement to improve rural life through forming cooperatives. But the nation's per capita income remains $120 per year (35 cents per day), only 43 percent of adults are literate, and nearly half the population live below the official poverty line. Conflict and instability continue to plague the country.

As in Pakistan, social and cultural issues have divided Bangladesh. Bangladesh is officially a secular state and has a large Hindu minority (16 percent). Although over the centuries the Bengalis incorporated Hindu and Buddhist influences as well as Sufi mysticism, creating a tolerant Islam, militant Muslim political movements seeking an Islamic state gained strength in the 1990s, heightening divisions. The militants, allied with Khaleda Zia's party, succeeded in restricting women's rights. Public universities implemented a regulation to require women students to return to their dormitories by sunset to, as they put it, protect the women's chastity. Zia's government also prosecuted feminist writers such as the medical doctor-turned-novelist Taslima Nasreen (b. 1962), who criticized religion and a conservative culture for holding Bengali women back, arguing that the basic division was not between religions but between those favoring modern, rational values and those steeped in irrational, blind faith. Muslim militants condemned Nasreen's writing as blasphemy against Islam, a capital offense. Nasreen fled Europe to escape death threats.

Sri Lankan Policies and Society

Sri Lanka shares problems of ethnic conflict and poverty with its neighbors but has generally maintained a democracy. In 1948 the leaders of the Sinhalese, some 75 percent of the population and mostly Theravada Buddhists, negotiated independence from Britain, inheriting a colonial economy based on rubber and tea plantations. The Sinhalese-dominated government has also discriminated against the language and culture of the major ethnic minority, the Tamils, who are mostly Hindus. In 1959 Sirimavo Bandaranaike **(sree-MAH-vo BAN-dar-an-EYE-kee)** (1916–2004), the widow of an assassinated leader, led her party to victory and became the world's first woman prime minister. Her enemies derided her as a "kitchen woman," someone who knew all about cooking but nothing about running a country, yet she proved to be a strong leader and dominated politics in the 1960s and 1970s. The successive governments promoted Sinhalese nationalism while sponsoring textile and electronics manufacturing to reduce dependence on cash crop exports. While socialist policies discouraged free enterprise, they fostered the highest literacy rates (85 percent) and, by providing rice and free medical care to the poor, South Asia's longest life span (seventy-three). In 1983 some of the Tamils seeking independence for their northern and eastern region began a rebellion that has kept the island in a constant state of tension, resulting in assassinations of top political leaders and communal fighting. In 1994 Chandrika Kumaratunga **(CHAN-dree-ka koo-MAHR-a-TOON-ga)** (b. 1945), the University of Paris–educated daughter of Sirimavo Bandaranaike, led her left-leaning party to victory and became Sri Lanka's second woman leader. She sought both military victory over the Tamils and political peace but achieved neither, narrowly escaping an assassination attempt in 2000. Nearly 60,000 people, many innocent civilians, have died in twenty years of violence between Tamils and Sinhalese. The violence has also split the Buddhist clergy between those advocating peace and tolerance and those demanding defeat of the Hindu Tamils, whom they view as a threat to Buddhism. In 2009 the Sri Lankan military finally defeated the main Tamil insurgent group, bringing hope for peace. But national reconciliation has long proved elusive, and the future for multiethnic democracy remains unclear.

South Asia in the Global System

Indian Economic Power

Since 1945 South Asian nations have grown in geopolitical and economic stature. Along with China and Brazil, India has become a major voice in the G-20 nations. Although Nehru strode the world stage as a major leader, seeking a middle ground between the United States and the USSR, his successors lacked his international influence. However, India has become a center of advanced technology, importing high-tech and service jobs from the West, and one of the most industrialized nations outside of Europe and North America, exporting heavy machinery, steel, and autos while producing abundant consumer goods for local consumption. Some Indian employees, such as those providing telephone technical support to users of U.S.-made computers, receive training in mastering an American or Australian accent to facilitate rapport. Even with the global recession of 2008–2009, outsourcing of jobs to India has continued. In addition, every year Indian universities, some of them world class, turn out thousands of talented engineers and computer scientists who have built up homegrown industries and also helped staff the high-tech "silicon valleys" of North America and Europe. As a result, experts have debated whether India or China might eventually compete for world economic leadership with the United States. Some point to India's large number of English-speakers, solid financial system, and vibrant democracy

SECTION SUMMARY

- India's multiparty democracy has endured despite religious and caste tensions, and the Congress Party has been consistently influential, though communist parties have often governed in the northeast and south and Hindu nationalists have gained strength since 1989.
- Despite great advances in agricultural and industrial production, India still suffers from extensive poverty, and its rapidly growing population is likely to perpetuate this problem.
- While caste distinctions have remained strong in villages, they have broken down somewhat in cities; women have advanced in education and opportunity, though they are still less educated than men; and religion continues to be a source of tension.
- Pakistan has alternated between civilian and military governments and has been slow to grant women equal rights, while Bangladesh has combated poverty in spite of great challenges and has generally accepted religious minorities, though militant Muslim groups have gained influence in recent years.
- Since it became independent, Sri Lanka has been a democracy; it elected the world's first woman prime minister, and it has nurtured a well-educated, long-lived population, but since 1983 the minority Tamils have fought for independence from majority Sinhalese.
- India has produced talented engineers and computer scientists and made advances in technology, although its nuclear weaponry has prompted Pakistan to also develop nuclear arms and thus raised the worry of nuclear weapons in the hands of Islamic terrorists.
- Though women's rights are not universal in South Asia, more South Asian women have achieved positions of great power than in other areas of the world.

as advantages. However, the nation's boom has added few jobs, and to become a world power, India, like China, needs to contain social tensions and find ways to better share the wealth and reduce rural poverty.

South Asian technology and ingenuity have led to scientific achievements. In 1975 the Indian government launched into orbit its first satellite, named after Aryabhata **(OUR-ya-BAH-ta)**, a major Indian scientist and mathematician who lived over fifteen hundred years ago. In 1998 India openly tested its first nuclear bomb. But these achievements have also triggered India-Pakistan rivalries. In response to the regional arms race with India, Pakistan also developed nuclear weapons. Since the late 1990s the weapons experts of many nations and international organizations have worried about Pakistan's nuclear abilities, since Islamic militants, some with possible links to global terrorist networks, have influence in Pakistan's military and play a key role in local and national politics. In 2004 a top Pakistani nuclear scientist admitted to selling nuclear secrets to other nations.

Global and regional politics have intensified Indian-Pakistani rivalries. After U.S. president George W. Bush, in the wake of the 2001 terrorist attacks on the United States, justified preemptive military attacks against potential threats and ordered U.S. forces into Afghanistan and Iraq, some Indians, adapting that justification to their own ends, wondered why India should not preemptively attack Pakistan: "If the United States can fly its bombs 10,000 miles to hit terrorist bases [in Afghanistan], why should India wait to knock out Pakistan's [military] bases?"[10] But while India-Pakistan relations have remained combustible, after 2000 Indian and Pakistani leaders promoted a thaw in relations, visiting each others' countries and giving hope that tensions might diminish. The thaw fostered cross-border visits and sports competitions. However, the Afghanistan conflict has spilled over into Pakistan. Islamist groups flourish among conservative Pashtuns in the tribal regions bordering Afghanistan, which have never been under firm government control. Over time the Islamists have extended their influence beyond the tribal areas, alarming moderate Muslims and the United States.

South Asians have made a distinctive contribution to world politics. Although maintaining traditional social patterns and cultural viewpoints, the four major South Asian nations, all democracies some or most of the time, have been led by women at various times, a striking difference from the preference for male leaders elsewhere in the world. Indeed, both Sri Lanka and Bangladesh elected two different women prime ministers. Hence, while women remain disadvantaged, they have enjoyed more high-level political power than in other nations. The political power of a few women is just part of the great complexity of this region.

Revolution, Decolonization, and New Nations in Southeast Asia

What were the causes and consequences of the struggles in Southeast Asia?

The nationalist thrust for independence from colonialism produced new nations in Southeast Asia after World War II (see Map 31.3). But the euphoria of independence proved short-lived, and the building of states capable of improving the lives of their people had only just begun. The peoples of Indochina experienced wrenching violence as two powerful Western nations—France and the United States—attempted to roll back revolutionary nationalism. During the First Indochina War (1946–1954), the French attempted to maintain their colonial control of Vietnam against communist-led opposition, a conflict that eventually ended in French defeat (see Chronology: Indochina, 1945–Present). The second and more destructive war, in which the United States and its Vietnamese allies waged an ultimately unsuccessful fight against communist-led Vietnamese forces, also dragged in Cambodia and Laos. Indonesia, the Philippines, Burma, and the other new nations, while often facing violent unrest, avoided the destructive warfare rocking Indochina but also had to overcome economic underdevelopment, promote national unity in ethnically divided societies, and deal with opposition to the new ruling groups. The years between 1945 and 1975 were marked by economic progress, but also by conflict and dictatorships. The leaders also had to forge new relationships with the former colonial powers and the new superpowers of a Cold War world—the United States and the Soviet Union—as well as with nearby China.

CHRONOLOGY
Indochina, 1945–Present

1945 Formation of Viet Minh government in Vietnam

1946–1954 First Indochina War

1953 Independence of Laos, Cambodia

1963 Assassination of South Vietnam president Ngo Dinh Diem

1963–1975 U.S.-Vietnamese War

1964 Gulf of Tonkin incident

1968 Tet Offensive

1970 Overthrow of Prince Sihanouk in Cambodia

1975 Communist victories in Vietnam, Cambodia, Laos

1978 Vietnamese invasion of Cambodia

The First Indochina War and Two Vietnams

For Vietnam, the first decade after World War II included an anticolonial revolution. In 1945 the Japanese army in southern Vietnam had surrendered to British forces, which moved into southern Vietnam to prepare the ground for a French return to power. Meanwhile the Viet Minh, the communist-led, U.S.-armed anti-Japanese guerrilla force that had occupied much of rural northern and central Vietnam during the Japanese occupation, captured the capital of colonial Vietnam, Hanoi, and declared the end of French colonialism. Controlling northern Vietnam and parts of the center and south, the Viet Minh–led government, headed by Ho Chi Minh, became the first non-French regime in over eighty years. In his address to a half-million jubilant Vietnamese who gathered in Hanoi's main square, Ho quoted the U.S. Declaration of Independence and added: "It means: All the peoples on earth are equal from birth, all the peoples have a right to live and to be happy and free."[11] Both French and American observers on the scene noted that the majority of Vietnamese supported the Viet Minh.

However, the French, desperate to retain their empire in Southeast Asia, quickly regrouped and reoccupied southern Vietnam. Meanwhile, the Republic of China sent its troops to disarm the remaining Japanese soldiers in northern Vietnam. This provocative move made the Vietnamese fear a permanent presence by their traditional enemy, China. Using earthy language, Ho told his followers he had to patiently negotiate with the French because it was better to sniff French manure for a while than to eat China's all their lives. The United States, influenced by Cold War thinking and an ally of both France and China, was alarmed at Ho Chi Minh's association with the USSR and communism. Hence, the Americans shifted from supporting the Viet Minh during World War II to opposing all left-wing nationalists, including Ho and the Viet Minh.

First Indochina War

Vietnam remained tense. The French, refusing to accept Ho's government, had allies among anticommunist Catholics and pro-Western nationalists. After Ho negotiated with the French for recognition of Vietnamese independence, the French arranged a Chinese troop withdrawal but refused to give up their claims. Ho also appealed to the U.S. president, Harry Truman, for political and economic support but received no answer. French leaders were determined to regain domination of all of Vietnam. In 1946 Ho warned a French diplomat that a war would be costly and unwinnable: "You will kill ten of my men while we will kill one of yours, but you will be the ones who will end up exhausted."[12] During the First Indochina War (1946–1954) the French attempted, with massive U.S. economic and military aid, to maintain their colonial grip. A large French military force pushed the Viet Minh out of the northern cities, but their brutal tactics alienated the population, while in the rural areas the Viet Minh won peasant support by transferring land to poor villagers. The French could not overcome an outgunned but determined foe with a nationalist message. As his forces became bogged down in what observers called a "quicksand war," a French general complained that fighting the Viet Minh was "like ridding a dog of its fleas. We can pick them, drown them, and poison them, but they will be back in a few days."[13] After a major military defeat in 1954, when Viet Minh forces overwhelmed a key French base in the mountains at Dien Bien Phu and took thousands of prisoners, the French abandoned their efforts and went home.

North and South Vietnam

The peace agreements negotiated at a conference in Geneva, Switzerland, in 1954 divided the country into two Vietnams. But while northern and southern Vietnamese spoke different dialects and had some cultural differences, few Vietnamese wanted separate nations. The agreements left the Viet Minh in control of North Vietnam and provided that elections be held in 1956 to determine whether the South Vietnamese wanted to join in a unified country. Ignoring the Geneva agreements, which it had not signed, the United States quickly filled the political vacuum and helped install Ngo Dinh Diem (no dinh dee-EM) (1901–1963), an anticommunist and longtime U.S. resident, as president of South Vietnam. Concerned that Ho would easily win a free election, with U.S. support Diem refused to hold reunification elections. Some Vietnamese opposed communist ideology and backed Diem and the United States.

North and South Vietnam differed dramatically. Ho's government built a disciplined state that addressed the inequalities of the colonial period, redistributing land from powerful landlords to poor peasants. However, the government's authoritarian style and socialist policies prompted nearly a million North Vietnamese, including many Catholics, to move to South Vietnam, where President Diem, an ardent Catholic from a wealthy family, established a government based in Saigon. The United States poured in economic and military aid and, to stabilize Diem's increasingly unpopular regime, sent military advisers to aid the South Vietnamese army.

However, the rigid Diem alienated peasants by opposing most land reform. In 1960 dissidents in South Vietnam, including former Viet Minh soldiers, formed a communist-led revolutionary movement, the **National Liberation Front (NLF)**, often known as the Viet Cong. Armed by North Vietnam, the insurgency in South Vietnam grew. Diem responded with repression, murdering or imprisoning thousands of suspected rebels and other opponents. Buddhists resented the Diem government's pro-Catholic policies, and nationalists generally viewed Diem as an American puppet. Meanwhile, the NLF spread their influence in rural areas, often assassinating government officials.

National Liberation Front (NLF) Often known as the Viet Cong, a communist-led revolutionary movement in South Vietnam that resisted American intervention in the American-Vietnamese War.

By the early 1960s the NLF, supplied by North Vietnam, controlled large sections of South Vietnam, and thousands more American troops, still called military advisers, became more involved in combat. In 1963 U.S. leaders, judging Diem ineffective, sanctioned his overthrow by his own military officers, who killed him. As the situation deteriorated and North Vietnamese troops moved south, U.S. concerns about a possible communist sweep through Southeast Asia provided the rationale for action. The stage was set for what Americans called the Vietnam War (1963–1975) and what many Vietnamese termed the American War.

The American-Vietnamese War

Escalating United States Intervention

The United States escalated the conflict into a full-scale military commitment (see Map 31.2). U.S. president Lyndon Johnson's (g. 1963–1969) excuse was an alleged North Vietnamese attack on a U.S. ship in the Gulf of Tonkin in 1964, which probably never occurred. When Johnson said in 1965, "I want to leave the footprints of America there [Indochina]. We can turn the Mekong into [an economically developed] Tennessee Valley,"[14] he was reflecting a longtime American sense of mission to change the world and spread democracy and capitalism. However, Johnson and other U.S. leaders, civilian and military, had little understanding of the nationalism and spirited opposition to foreign occupation that had shaped Vietnam, a country with many historical reasons for mistrusting foreign powers—whether Chinese, French, or American—on "civilizing" missions. Soon the war intensified, drawing in a larger U.S. presence. In 1965 Johnson ordered an air war against targets in both South and North Vietnam and a massive intervention of ground troops, peaki ng at 550,000 Americans by 1968. However, a series of military regimes never achieved credibility with the South Vietnamese majority. Meanwhile, military supplies and North Vietnamese troops regularly moved south through the mountains of eastern Laos and Cambodia, along what came to be known as the Ho Chi Minh Trail.

Despite their technological superiority, U.S. forces struggled to find effective strategies to overcome the communists, often ignoring South Vietnamese leaders and the consequences of U.S. military actions. Since the South Vietnamese army, largely conscripts, suffered from low morale and high desertion and casualty rates, Americans did much of the fighting. U.S. strategists viewed Vietnam chiefly in military terms: they measured success by counting the enemy dead and creating free fire zones, areas where civilians were ordered to evacuate so that U.S. forces could attack any people remaining as the enemy. Such policies made it hard for the Americans to win Vietnamese "hearts and minds," a key doctrine of counterinsurgency strategies, and diminishh local support for the NLF. Vietnam also became the most heavily bombed nation in history, with the United States dropping twice the total bomb tonnage used in World War II. The use of chemical defoliants to clear forests and wetlands, and the countless bomb craters, caused massive environmental damage. Thanks in part to the toxic chemicals, Vietnam today has the world's highest rate of birth defects and one of the highest rates of cancer.

South Vietnamese Divisions

South Vietnamese had to choose sides. For procommunist Vietnamese, the American-Vietnamese War was a continuation of the First Indochina War to expel the French and rebuild a damaged society. When the Viet Minh humbled the hated French colonizers, they gained a

Map 31.2 The U.S.-Vietnamese War

From the early 1960s until 1975 South Vietnam, aided by thousands of U.S. troops and air power, resisted a communist-led insurgency aided by North Vietnam, which sent troops and supplies down the Ho Chi Minh Trail through Laos and Cambodia.

Interactive Map

popularity with many Vietnamese that the United States could not overcome. The communists also gained peasant support by advocating reform to help landless peasants. Moreover, some U.S. policies, especially the air war, which killed thousands of innocent people, backfired. One of the thousands of women who fought for the NLF reported: "The first days I felt ill at ease—marching in step, lobbing grenades, taking aim with my rifle, hitting the ground. But as soon as I saw the American planes come back [to bomb], my timidity left me."[15] However, some South Vietnamese supported the pro-U.S. government or rejected both sides. Pham Duy **(fam do-ee)**, a folksinger in South Vietnam who, like many South Vietnamese, disliked both the corrupt Saigon government and the often ruthless communists, wrote a song describing the war's impact on average Vietnamese: "The rain of the leaves is the tears of joy, Of the girl whose boy returns from the war. The rain on the leaves is bitter tears, When a mother hears her son is no more."[16]

United States Withdrawal

Tet Offensive Communist attacks on major South Vietnamese cities in 1968, a turning point in the American-Vietnamese War.

By 1967 the U.S. military strategy had brought about a military stalemate, but a turning point came in 1968 with the **Tet Offensive**, when communist forces attacked the major South Vietnamese cities during the Vietnamese new year. Although the communists were pushed back and suffered high casualties, Tet proved a political and psychological setback for Americans, who watched on television as communist guerrillas attacked the U.S. embassy in Saigon and U.S. Marines fought their way, block by block, against fierce resistance into the old imperial capital of Hue.

The war bitterly divided Americans, and by the late 1960s a majority had turned against the commitment to a seemingly endless quagmire in which American soldiers were being killed or injured for uncertain goals. Even Ho Chi Minh's death in 1969 did not alter the situation. The United States began a gradual withdrawal of troops and negotiated peace agreements with North Vietnam. By 1973 U.S. ground forces had left Vietnam; the air war ended a year later; and in 1975 the NLF and North Vietnam defeated the South Vietnamese forces and reunified the country under communist leadership. As the victors marched into Saigon, many South Vietnamese fled the country, some 1.3 million eventually settling in the United States. General Maxwell Taylor, former U.S. ambassador to South Vietnam, later concluded that Americans lost because, never understanding the Vietnamese on either side, they overestimated the effectiveness of U.S. policies. The devastating war cost the United States 58,000 dead and 519,000 physically disabled. It cost the Vietnamese around 4 million killed or wounded—10 percent of the total population. After the fighting ended, Vietnam turned to reconstruction.

War in Laos and Cambodia

Laos and Cambodia became pawns in the larger conflict between the United States and the North Vietnamese. Anticolonial sentiment had grown during and after the Japanese occupation of World War II. In 1953 the French, wearying of their Indochinese experience, granted Laos independence under a conservative, pro-French government dominated by the ethnic Lao majority. Cambodia gained its independence under the young, charismatic, and widely popular Prince Norodom Sihanouk **(SEE-uh-nook)** (b. 1922), who won the first free election in 1955. However, both countries were eventually engulfed in the Vietnam conflict, in part because of U.S. military interventions.

Laos and the United States

Pathet Lao Revolutionary Laotian nationalists allied with North Vietnam during the American-Vietnamese War.

The U.S. intervention in Laos, which began in the late 1950s and continued until 1975, intensified conflict between U.S.-backed anticommunist rightwingers, people favoring neutrality between the superpowers, and the **Pathet Lao**, revolutionary Laotian nationalists allied with North Vietnam. In 1960 rightwing forces advised and equipped by the U.S. Central Intelligence Agency (CIA) seized the Laotian government. As fighting intensified, the Pathet Lao controlled the northern mountains while the government controlled the south and the Mekong Valley. Because the Laotian regime, bloated with corruption, had an ineffective U.S.-financed army, Americans turned to the hill peoples for recruits, among them a large faction of one group, the Hmong, that sought autonomy from the government. Promising them permanent U.S. support and protection, in 1960 the CIA recruited a secret army of some 45,000 soldiers, largely Hmong, that attacked North Vietnamese forces along the Ho Chi Minh Trail and fought the Pathet Lao. As a result, 10 percent of the Hmong population, some 30,000 people, died during a conflict that was largely unknown to the American public. U.S. bombing depopulated large areas, forcing many Laotians into refugee camps, and the war killed some 100,000 Laotians. After 1975, when the Pathet Lao took full control of a war-weary Laos, thousands of anticommunist Laotians fled into Thailand, many later moving to the United States and other Western nations.

Cambodia and the United States

Like Laos, Cambodia also became part of the Indochina conflict. Its first president, Prince Sihanouk, ruled as a benevolent autocrat while also writing sentimental popular songs, playing the saxophone, directing films, and publicizing his political views in foreign newspapers. Sihanouk diplomatically maintained Cambodian independence and peace. But both the Vietnamese communists, whose forces roamed the border area, and the United States, whose war planes bombed communist positions in Cambodian territory, violated Cambodian neutrality. Sihanouk faced other problems as well. The **Khmer Rouge** (kmahr roozh) ("Red Khmers"), a communist insurgent group seeking to overthrow the government and led by alienated intellectuals educated in French universities, built a small support base of impoverished peasants. Moreover, although Sihanouk remained popular among many peasants, military officers and big businessmen resented his dictatorial rule and desired to share in the U.S. money and arms flowing into neighboring South Vietnam, Laos, and Thailand.

Khmer Rouge ("Red Khmers") A communist insurgent group seeking to overthrow the government in Cambodia during the 1960s and 1970s.

In 1970 Sihanouk was overthrown by U.S.-backed generals and civilians. With Sihanouk in exile, U.S. and South Vietnamese forces soon invaded eastern Cambodia in search of Vietnamese communist bases, and the resulting instability created an opening for the Khmer Rouge to recruit mass support. The pro-U.S. government lacked legitimacy, becoming dependent on U.S. aid for virtually all supplies, and the ineffective Cambodian army suffered from corruption and low morale. Meanwhile, to attack the Khmer Rouge, U.S. planes launched an intensive, terrifying air assault through the heart of Cambodia's agricultural area, where most of the population lived, killing thousands of innocent civilians. Rice production declined by almost half, raising the possibility of massive starvation. Amid the destruction, the Khmer Rouge rapidly enlarged its forces, recruiting from among the displaced and shell-shocked peasantry. From 1970 through 1975, between 750,000 and 1 million Cambodians, mostly civilians, perished from the conflict between the Khmer Rouge, who were brutal toward their enemies, and the U.S.-backed government. In 1975 the Khmer Rouge seized the capital, Phnom Penh, and controlled the country until 1978 (discussed in next section).

CHRONOLOGY

Noncommunist Southeast Asia, 1945–Present

1945–1950 Indonesian Revolution

1948 Independence of Burma

1963 Formation of Malaysia

1965 Secession of Singapore from Malaysia

1965–1966 Turmoil in Indonesia

1966–1998 New Order in Indonesia

1997 Economic crisis in Southeast Asia

2008–2009 World economic crisis

Indonesia: The Quest for Freedom and Unity

Indonesian independence came through struggle. During the violent anti-Dutch resistance of the late 1940s, known as the Indonesian Revolution, the Dutch used massive force to suppress the nationalists, who fought back. In a short story about a brutal battle, a nationalist writer noted that, for the revolutionary soldiers, "everything blurred: the future and their heart-breaking struggle. They only knew that they had to murder to drive out the enemy and stop him trampling their liberated land. They killed [the Dutch soldiers] with great determination, spirit and hunger."[17] The United States, fearing regional instability, pressured the Dutch to grant independence in 1950 (see Chronology: Noncommunist Southeast Asia, 1945–Present).

Indonesia still faced the challenge of fostering a unified nation. Given the diversity of islands, peoples, and cultures, Indonesian leaders became obsessed with creating national unity and identity. Their national slogan, "unity in diversity," expressed more a goal than a solid reality. During the 1950s and early 1960s Indonesia was led by the charismatic but increasingly authoritarian president Sukarno (soo-KAHR-no) (1902–1970), an inspirational nationalist. A spell-binding orator able to rally popular support and bring different factions together, Sukarno worked to create national solidarity and unite a huge nation in which villagers on remote islands and cosmopolitan city dwellers on Java knew little about each other.

Political and Economic Turmoil

Despite his efforts, Sukarno proved unable to maintain stability. The multiparty parliamentary system became divisive. Regionalism also grew as outer islanders resented domination by the Javanese, who constituted over half of Indonesia's population and, many outer islanders believed, were favored by Sukarno. By the early 1960s Sukarno's nationalistic but poorly implemented economic policies had caused a severe economic crisis and deepened divisions between communist, Islamic, and military forces. A procommunist Javanese novelist described the economic failures: "Jakarta [the capital city] reveals a grandiose display with no relationship to reality. Great plans, enormous immorality. [There are] no screws, no nuts, no bolts, no valves, and no washers for the machinery we do have."[18]

By 1965 Indonesia had become a country of explosive social and political pressures and was experiencing its greatest crisis as an independent nation. After a failed attempt by a small military faction with communist sympathies to seize power, discontented generals arrested Sukarno, took power, and launched a brutal campaign to eliminate all leftists, especially members of the large Communist Party, influential among poor peasants in Java. The resulting bloodbath, led by the army and Muslim groups, killed perhaps half a million Indonesians, including members of the unpopular Chinese minority. Most communist leaders were killed or arrested, and thousands of leftists were held in remote prison camps for years. Sukarno died in disgrace in 1970.

Map 31.3 Modern Southeast Asia
Indonesia, covering thousands of islands, is the largest, most populous Southeast Asian nation. Southeast Asia also includes four other island nations (including the Philippines and Singapore), five nations on the mainland, and Malaysia, which sprawls from the Malay Peninsula to northern Borneo.

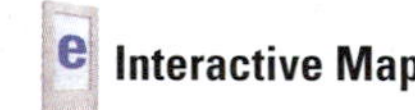

Making the Philippine and Malaysian Nations

Philippine Politics

The Philippines and Malaysia both became independent but troubled nations. The Philippines achieved independence from the United States on July 4, 1946, though the two countries remained bound by close political and economic links. The new nation soon faced problems sustaining democracy. A small group of landowners, industrialists, and businessmen who had prospered under U.S. rule manipulated elected governments to preserve their power and to protect U.S. economic interests. Free elections involved so much violence, bribery, and fraud that disillusioned Filipinos spoke of them as decided by "guns, goons, and gold." Furthermore, nationalists believed that continuing U.S. influence hindered a truly independent Filipino identity and culture. Several major U.S. military bases near Manila symbolized this influence, and the popular U.S. films, television programs, music, comics, and books helped to spread it. A prominent scholar wrote that her people "sing of White Christmases and of Manhattan. Their stereos reverberate with the American Top 40."[19] Outside influences—first Spanish and then American—on Filipino culture were often superficial, but Filipinos have struggled to create a clear national identity out of the diverse mosaic of local languages and regions.

Economic inequality and social divisions fueled conflict. A Filipino poet portrayed the gap between the rich and poor: "[For the affluent] there's pleasure and distraction, fiesta and dancing, night-long, day-long; who dares whisper that thousands have no roofs above their heads; that hunger stalks the town."[20] The communist-led Huk Rebellion from 1948 to 1954 capitalized on discontent among the rural poor and was suppressed only by heavy U.S. assistance. In the 1970s the communist New Peoples Army (NPA) controlled many rural districts. Like the Huks, the NPA's promise of radical social and economic change attracted support from rural tenant farmers and urban slum dwellers. Religious differences have also led to conflict. While most Filipinos became Christian in Spanish times, the southern islands have large Muslim populations, who have often resented domination by and favoritism toward Christians. Several Muslim groups have taken up arms to fight for autonomy. In 1972 President Ferdinand Marcos (1917–1989) used law and order as an excuse to suspend democracy, and from 1972 until 1986 he ruled as a dictator, resolving few problems.

Building Malaysia

Malayan governments proved more stable after independence. After World War II the British sought to dampen political unrest as communist-led insurgents kept the colony on edge for a decade. In 1957, with the insurgency crushed by the British, Malaya became independent as a federation of states under a government led by the main Malay party, **UMNO** (United Malays National Organization). However, the predominantly Chinese city-state of Singapore, a major trading center and military base, remained a British colony. In Malaya the majority ethnic group, the Malays, nearly all Muslim, dominated politics, but the Chinese, a third of the population, were granted liberal citizenship rights and maintained strong economic power. British leaders, seeing their colonial role in Singapore as well as in two northern Borneo states they controlled, Sabah and Sarawak, as burdensome, suggested joining them with Malaya in a larger federation, to be called Malaysia. This new, geographically divided Malaysia was formed in 1963.

UMNO The main Malay political party in Malaysia.

Malaysians struggled to create national unity out of deep regional and ethnic divisions. Singapore withdrew in 1965 and became independent. Given the need to reduce political tensions, sustain rapid economic growth, and preserve stability, the leaders of the key ethnic groups in Malaya—Malays, Chinese, and Indians—cooperated through political parties that allied in an UMNO-dominated ruling coalition, but below the surface ethnic tensions simmered. Street fighting between Chinese and Malays following the heated 1969 election led to a nationwide state of emergency. After 1970 Malay-dominated governments pursued policies designed to reshape Malaysia's society and economy.

Diversity and Dictatorship in Thailand and Burma

Thailand and Burma also struggled to create national unity and stability. Although historical rivals, the two countries have shared certain patterns. The majority Thais (Siamese) and the Burmans, both Theravada Buddhists, assert authority over diverse minorities, including various hill tribes, Malay Muslims, and Chinese. Both countries experienced insurgencies by disaffected ethnic, religious, or communist factions.

Thailand Policies and Society

In Thailand, leaders sought to build a national culture based on Thai cultural values, including reverence for Buddhism and the monarchy, which symbolized the nation, respect for those in authority, and social harmony. However, this conservatism fostered authoritarian governments and bureaucratic inertia. Various communist and Islamic insurgent groups operated during the 1960s and 1970s in ethnic minority regions. Partly because of this unrest, Thailand's political history after 1945 was characterized by long periods of military rule, often corrupt and oppressive, followed by short-lived democratically elected or semidemocratic governments. Not until the 1970s would opposition movements challenge the long-entrenched military regime. Many Thais resented the United States, which supported the military regime and had military bases and some 50,000 troops in the country. The presence of free-spending American soldiers created a false prosperity, while staunch Buddhists were outraged by the sleazy bars, gaudy nightclubs, and brothels that often exploited poor Thai women and served the Americans but also attracted eager Thai men.

In 1973 antigovernment feelings boiled over and the military regime was overthrown following massive student-led demonstrations. The military strongman fled the country, having lost public support after his troops arrested protest leaders and killed or wounded over a thousand demonstrators. The collapse of military rule opened a brief era of political liberalization as democracy and debate flourished. The civilian government tolerated these activities but proved fragile and unable to resolve major problems. Meanwhile, rightwing military officers and bureaucrats resisted challenges to their power and privileges, and Thai society became polarized between liberals and conservatives. Finally, in 1976, bloody clashes between leftist students and rightwing youth gangs led to a military coup and martial law, which resulted in the killing or wounding of hundreds and the arrest of thousands of students and their supporters. The return of military power reestablished order, but the massacres discredited the military.

Burma's Politics and Society

Burma emerged from the Japanese occupation devastated, whole cities blasted into rubble by Allied bombing. After the war the British returned to reestablish their colonial control. Facing a well-armed Burmese nationalist army and weary of conflict, they negotiated independence with the charismatic nationalist leader Aung San (1915–1947) and left in 1948. But newly elected Prime

Minister Aung San was assassinated by a political rival and replaced by his longtime colleague, U Nu (1907–1995), an idealistic Buddhist and democrat. Soon key ethnic minorities, fearful of domination by the majority Burmans, declared their secession and organized armies. For several decades the central government rarely controlled more than half the nation's territory as ethnic armies and communist insurgents, funded by opium revenues, battled the Burmese army. In 1962, however, the army deposed U Nu and seized control, suspended civil liberties, imposed censorship, and claimed most of the government budget. The military also took over industries, banks, and commerce and discouraged foreign investment. By the 1980s, economic stagnation and political repression had fostered dissent and the various secession movements continued, only to be largely suppressed in the 1990s.

SECTION SUMMARY

- After World War II, the communist Viet Minh, led by Ho Chi Minh, took partial control of Vietnam and declared independence, but the U.S.-supported French fought back in the First Indochina War, which ended in frustration for the French.
- Instead of allowing an election to determine the future of South Vietnam, the United States installed Diem as president, but he was opposed by the communist National Liberation Front, setting the stage for the Vietnam War.
- Using a questionable attack as a pretext, the United States went to war to rid Vietnam of communism, but despite vastly superior resources, the United States and its allies in South Vietnam could not triumph over the communists, who gained control of Vietnam two years after the United States pulled out its ground forces.
- In Laos the United States recruited Hmong hill people to fight the Pathet Lao revolutionaries, who took control of the country in 1975, while in Cambodia the United States bombed areas occupied by North Vietnamese and supported a weak, dependent government, which was overthrown in 1975 by the Khmer Rouge.
- After a difficult fight for independence from the Dutch, Indonesia's wildly diverse population struggled to attain unity under Sukarno, but different groups became more divided and a group of generals cracked down harshly on leftists and removed Sukarno from power.
- After attaining independence, the Philippines remained strongly influenced by the United States and struggled with economic inequality and a Muslim insurgency, while Malaysia experienced intermittent tensions between the politically dominant Malays and the economically strong Chinese.
- Thailand alternated between long periods of military rule and short periods of democratic or semidemocratic rule, while Burma endured decades of factional fighting and, since 1962, brutal military domination.

Tigers, Politics, and Changing Southeast Asian Societies

What role do the Southeast Asian nations play in the global system?

Southeast Asia changed dramatically after 1975, mixing influences from the past and from the wider world. The fast pace of change has reshaped life in both cities and villages. Indonesia, Malaysia, Singapore, and Thailand, with market economies geared to world commerce, have gained reputations as "tigers" because of their dynamism. At the same time, governments played a major role in stimulating economies and often became authoritarian to ensure social stability. When the fighting ended in Indochina, all the societies involved had to rebuild their societies and the lives shattered by the turmoil. Vietnam eventually developed a tiger economy.

The Resurgence of Southeast Asia

Economic Growth

A shift of economic direction allowed several Southeast Asian nations to develop and play a greater role in the world economy. In 1976, Indonesia, Burma, and Thailand were under military rule, the communist regimes in Indochina faced monumental reconstruction, a dictator governed in the Philippines, and only Malaysia and Singapore had semidemocracies. Few of the countries enjoyed impressive economic growth. But in the 1980s, the pace of change accelerated. Inspired by Japan's industrialization in the late nineteenth century and rapid recovery from World War II, leaders encouraged their people to "Look East" by mixing capitalism and activist government to spur economic expansion. Local entrepreneurs of Chinese ancestry provided much of the initiative and capital. Economic growth had drawbacks: for example, industrial activity and the expansion of agriculture, mining, and logging caused widespread environmental destruction. Yet, migrants crowding into cities rubbed elbows with other peoples, encouraging cultural mixing. Even though governments often squashed dissent and repressed personal liberties, an expanding education fostered larger middle classes, who sought more political influence. Experts identified a vibrant Pacific Rim that included the "tiger" nations as well as Japan, China, Taiwan, South Korea (see Chapter 27), and eventually Vietnam. Some forecast a Pacific Century in which these nations would lead the world economically and increase their political strength.

To promote growth and stability, Southeast Asian countries began cooperating as never before. Founded in 1967 by Malaysia, Indonesia, Thailand, Singapore, and the Philippines, **ASEAN** (Association of Southeast Asian Nations), a regional economic and political organization, promoted economic exchange among the noncommunist Southeast Asian nations and coordinated opposition to Vietnam. However, ASEAN's priorities shifted after the end of the Indochina wars. As Vietnam, Cambodia, Laos, Burma, and the tiny, oil-rich state of Brunei became members, ASEAN emerged as the world's fourth largest trading bloc. It also provided a forum for the members to work out their differences and deal with the wider world. Eventually ASEAN cultivated closer relations with China and Japan.

ASEAN A regional economic and political organization formed in 1967 to promote cooperation among the noncommunist Southeast Asian nations; eventually became a major trading bloc.

New Challenges

Many challenges remained. By 2008 there were some 580 million Southeast Asians. Population growth outstripped economic growth, placing a greater burden on limited resources such as food and water, especially in the Philippines, Indonesia, and Vietnam. These conditions sometimes generated riots or even full-blown insurgencies. But despite occasional violence and political upheavals, the destructive wars of the earlier years were not repeated. In some cases, dictatorships were eventually replaced by more open regimes. In 1997, however, most Southeast Asian countries faced a severe economic crisis, part of a broader collapse among Asian and world economies. The reasons for the troubles included poorly regulated banking systems, overconfident investments, and government favoritism toward well-placed business interests. The dislocations hit all social classes. The crisis eventually bottomed out, only to be rekindled in 2008–2009 by a larger world economic downturn that reduced demand for Southeast Asian products, caused massive job losses, and slowed foreign investment. The widespread dislocations called into question the prospect of a forthcoming Pacific Century. Southeast Asia is also one of the regions most threatened by global warming, which may foster erratic rains and will raise sea levels, flooding densely populated river deltas and lowlands.

New Orders in Indonesia and the Philippines

Indonesia under Suharto

Indonesia, with more than seven hundred ethnic groups and a rapidly growing population of 240 million, struggled to preserve political stability while developing economically. Between 1966 and 1998 the government, known as the **New Order**, headed by general-turned-president Suharto (1921–2008), a Javanese, mixed military and civilian leadership to maintain law and order. Suharto used force to repress independence movements in East Timor, a small, former Portuguese colony with a mostly Christian population, north Sumatra, dominated by the fiercely Islamic Achehnese, and West Irian (western New Guinea). However, although it limited political opposition, the New Order improved Indonesia's economic position and fostered an educated urban middle class. Per capita income, life expectancy, and adult literacy increased, aided by an annual economic growth rate of nearly 5 percent by the 1990s, though a third of the population remained desperately poor, earning less than a dollar a day. Creative musicians, writers, artists, and filmmakers shaped a vibrant popular culture.

New Order The Indonesian government headed by President Suharto from 1966 to 1998, which mixed military and civilian leadership.

Yet, the New Order also started some negative trends. Indonesia became dependent on exporting oil, which represented 80 percent of foreign earnings. As a result, whenever world oil prices decline and reduce the national budget, Indonesia adds to an enormous foreign debt. The rapid development of mining, forestry, and cash crop agriculture also has taken a toll on the environment. Rain forests were clear-cut so rapidly for timber and plantations that forest fires became common, polluting the air and creating a thick, unhealthy haze that spread into neighboring nations. Furthermore, income disparities between classes and regions widened while political and business corruption thrived. One Indonesian fiction writer criticized a society in which government officials and predatory businessmen solicited bribes and grabbed public funds for themselves: "Indonesia, Land of Robbers. My true homeland stiff with thieves. In the future, I shall plunder while my wife shall seize."[21] The wealthy frolicked in nightclubs, casinos, and golf courses built across the street from slums or on land appropriated from powerless villages. Suharto, the son of poor peasants, became one of the world's most corrupt leaders, and he and his family acquired over $15 billion in assets from their business enterprises and access to public coffers.

Indonesian Islam

Many Indonesians disliked the New Order, with Islam providing the chief vehicle for opposition. Some 87 percent of Indonesians are either devout or nominal Muslims, but few have supported militant Islamist movements. Suharto discouraged Islamic radicalism as a threat to national unity in a country that includes many Christians and Hindus. However, devout Muslims have often opposed secular policies and desired a more Islamic approach to social, cultural, and legal matters. Muslim conservatives denounce gambling casinos, racy magazines and films, and scantily clad female pop singers. At the same time, a progressive, democratic strand of Islamic thought has favored liberal social and political reform. Muslim liberals tap into the Javanese emphasis on harmony, consensus, and tolerance that was incorporated into Indonesian Islam, offering a stark contrast to the more dogmatic Islam common in Pakistan and Saudi Arabia. Nevertheless, Muslims blamed the New Order government for poor living standards and massive corruption.

By the 1990s Indonesian society suffered from increasing class and ethnic tensions, student protests, and labor unrest, setting the stage for dramatic changes. When the economy collapsed in 1997, throwing millions out of work and raising prices for essential goods, widespread rioting resulted in Suharto's resignation. The country fell into turmoil, and protests and ethnic clashes proliferated. Many among the urban middle class wanted to strengthen democracy, and in 1999 free elections were held. Later, Megawati Soekarnoputri (MEH-ga-WHA-tee soo-KAR-no-POO-tri), the daughter of Indonesia's first president, Sukarno, became Indonesia's first woman president. Like her father, Megawati followed secular, nationalist policies but also showed little faith in grassroots democracy and resolved few problems. By 2004 popular support for her regime had ebbed and she was defeated for reelection by a retired Javanese general, who was reelected in 2009.

Post-Suharto Politics

The disorderly democracy that replaced the New Order brought unprecedented freedom of the press and speech. But removing New Order restrictions allowed long-simmering ethnic hostilities to reemerge. East Timor, which had endured a long, unpopular occupation by Indonesia, finally achieved independence in 1999, but only after thousands of its people were killed by Indonesian troops and militias. Muslim-Christian conflicts also resulted in numerous deaths, with Islamic militants capitalizing on the instability to recruit support. Several terrorist bombings of popular tourist venues, most recently in 2009, added to the growing tensions. Then in 2005 over 100,000 Indonesians perished from earthquakes and a deadly tidal wave, or tsunami, that destroyed cities and washed away coastal villages on Sumatra. These setbacks raised questions about the long-term viability of Indonesian democracy. Yet, in 2009 voters decisively rejected anti-Western Islamist parties and reelected the centrist, secular government.

Marcos Dictatorship

Like Indonesia, the Philippines also experienced political turbulence and social instability, lagging well behind the most prosperous Southeast Asian nations in economic development. When Ferdinand Marcos ruled as a dictator, economic conditions worsened, rural poverty became more widespread, the population grew rapidly, and political opposition was limited by the murder or detention of dissidents, censorship, and rigged elections. The dictator, his family, and cronies looted the country, amassing billions. The regime built high walls along city freeways so that affluent motorists would not have to view slums along the route. A tiny minority lived in palatial homes surrounded by high walls topped with broken glass and barbed wire, and with gates manned by armed guards. Across the street from the glittering pavilions of Manila's Cultural Center, whose landscaped gardens were a gaudy monument to Marcos splendor, homeless families slept in bushes. The majority of rural families were landless, and child malnutrition increased. A Filipino novelist described rural society and its poverty, with villagers eking out a living on unproductive land: "Nothing in the countryside had changed, not the thatched houses, not the ragged vegetation, not the stolid people. Changeless land, burning sun."[22] To escape poverty, Filipinos often migrated, temporarily or permanently, to other Asian nations, the United States, or the Middle East. Some 10 million Filipinos lived abroad by 2009, with many women working as nurses, maids, or entertainers. About 2,500 Filipinos leave the country every day for overseas work.

The failures of the Marcos years led to massive public protests in 1986 that restored democracy. The opposition rallied around U.S.-educated Corazon Aquino (ah-KEE-no) (1933–2009), a descendant of a Chinese immigrant, whose popular politician husband had been assassinated by Marcos henchmen. In a spectacular nonviolent "people's power" revolution, street demonstrations involving students, workers, businessmen, housewives, and clergy demanded justice and freedom. Marcos and his family fled into exile in the United States, which had long supported his regime. As Marcos and his family escaped by helicopter, thousands of demonstrators who broke into the presidential palace found that the dictator's wife, Imelda Marcos, a former beauty queen, had acquired thousands of pairs of shoes and vast stores of undergarments, symbolizing the Marcoses' waste of public resources. Mrs. Aquino became president and reestablished democracy.

Recent Politics

Yet the hopes that the Philippines could resolve its problems proved illusory. The new government, while open to dissenting voices, was, as had been true since independence, dominated

Corbis

People's Power Demonstration in the Philippines In 1986 the simmering opposition to the dictatorial government of Ferdinand Marcos reached a boiling point, resulting in massive demonstrations in Manila. Under the banner of "people's power," businesspeople, professionals, housewives, soldiers, students, and cultural figures rallied to topple the regime.

by the wealthiest Filipinos, mostly members of the hundred or so landowning families who were favored during U.S. colonial rule. Mrs. Aquino, herself a member of one of these families, voluntarily declined reelection in 1992. Her successors had rocky presidencies; one of these men, a former film star with a reputation for heavy drinking, gambling, and womanizing, was impeached for corruption and vote-rigging. In 2001 another woman, Gloria Macapagal-Arroyo (b. 1947), a Ph.D. economist and the daughter of a former president, became president but also faced corruption allegations; however, she was reelected in 2005.

Two decades after the overthrow of Marcos the public seems disillusioned with the results. Many Filipinos also have resented the continuing close ties to, and influence from, the United States. A best-selling pop song reflected the opposition to what nationalists considered neocolonialism: "You just want my natural resources, And then you leave me poor and in misery. American Junk, Get it out of my bloodstream. Got to get back to who I am."[23] While democracy has returned, a free press flourishes, and the economy has improved, much of the economic growth has been eaten up by rapid population growth; the nation now has 85 million people. And none of the governments have successfully addressed poverty or seemed willing to curb the activities of influential companies exploiting marine, mineral, and timber resources, often harming the environment. A local Catholic priest noted how economic exploitation and environmental destruction have remained common: "A plunder economy, that's the post World War II Philippine history: plunder of seas, plunder of mines, plunder of forests."[24] At the same time, differences in access to health care, welfare, and related services have continued to reflect the great gaps in income between social classes and regions.

Politics and Society in Thailand and Burma

The striking contrasts between prosperous Thailand and stagnant Burma have increased. In the 1950s both nations had economies of similar size and growth rates, but the gap between them has become vast. While both nations have had a long history of military dictatorship, only the Thais, finding the repressive atmosphere chilling, made a transition to more open government. By the 1980s Thailand developed a semidemocratic system combining order and hierarchy, symbolized by the monarchy, with representative, accountable government. While most successful political candidates came from wealthy families, often of Chinese ancestry, the rapidly expanding urban middle class generally supported an expansion of democracy that would give them more influence. A new constitution adopted in 1997 guaranteed civil liberties and reformed the electoral system, and a lively free press emerged.

Thailand's Economy and Politics

Thailand generally has enjoyed high rates of economic growth. Despite a growing manufacturing sector, the export of rice, rubber, tin, and timber remains significant. Although the Chinese minority of some 10 percent controls much wealth, Thais enjoy high per capita incomes and standards of

A Thai Poet's Plea for Saving the Environment

Angkhan Kalayanaphong (AHN-kan KALL-a-YAWN-a-fong), born in 1926, the most popular poet in Thailand for decades, also gained fame as an accomplished graphic artist and painter. His poems often addressed social, Buddhist, and environmental themes. In his long poem, "Bangkok-Thailand," he examines Thailand and its problems in the 1970s and 1980s. The author pulls no punches in condemning Thai society for neglecting its heritage; he skewers politicians, government institutions, big business, and the entertainment industry. In this section, Angkhan pleads for Thais to save the forest environment being destroyed by commercial logging.

Oh, I do not imagine the forest like that
So deep, so beautiful, everything so special.
It pertains to dreams that are beyond truth. . . .
Dense woods in dense forests; slowly
The rays of half a day mix with the night.
Strange atmosphere causing admiration.
Loneliness up to the clouds, stillness and beauty.
Rays of gold play upon, penetrate the tree-tops
rays displayed in stripes, the brightness of the sun.
I stretch out my hand drawing down clouds mixing them with brandy.
This is supreme happiness. . . .
The lofty trees do not think of reward for the scent of their blossoms. . . .
Men kill the wood because they venerate money as in all the world. . . .
The lofty trees contribute much to morals.
They should be infinitely lauded for it.
The trace of the ax kills. Blood runs in streams. . . .
You, trees, give the flattering pollen attended by scents.
You make the sacrifice again and again.
Do you ever respond angrily? You have accepted your fate which is contemptuous of all that is beautiful.
But troublesome are the murderers, the doers of future sins.
Greedy after money, they are blind to divine work.
Their hearts are black to large extent, instead of being honest and upright.
They have no breeding, are lawless. . . .
Thailand in particular is in a very bad way.
Because of their [commercial] value parks are "purified," i.e., destroyed.
Man's blood is depraved, cursed and base.
His ancestors are swine and dogs. It is madness to say they are Thai.

THINKING ABOUT THE READING

1. What qualities does the poet attribute to the forest?
2. What motives does he attribute to the loggers and businessmen who exploit the forest environment?

Source: Klaus Wenk, *Thai Literature: An Introduction* (Bangkok: White Lotus, 1995), pp. 95–98.

public health by Asian standards. Indeed, thousands of people from North America and Europe come to Thailand each year for medical treatment. Yet perhaps a quarter of Thais are very poor, especially in rural areas. The economic "miracle" has, in many respects, been built on the backs of women and children, many from rural districts, who work in urban factories, the service sector, and the sex industry. Millions of Thai women have identified with the songs of popular singer Pompuang Duangjian (POM-poo-ahn DWONG-chen) (1961–1992), herself the product of a poor village, that often deal with the harshness of the lives of poor female migrants to the city: "So lousy poor, I just have to risk my luck. Dozing on the bus, this guy starts chatting me up. Say's he'll get me a good job."[25] Pompuang herself had only two years of primary school education and worked as a sugar-cane cutter before starting a music career. With much of her money stolen by lovers, managers, and promoters, she died at age thirty-one unable to afford treatment for a blood disorder.

The economic collapses of 1997 and 2008–2009 threw many Thais out of work. The overcrowded capital, Bangkok, is one of Asia's most polluted cities, drenched in toxic matter from factories and automobiles despite efforts by local environmental groups to clean up the air. The nation's once-abundant rain forests disappear at a rapid rate, a fact lamented by Thai musicians and poets (see Witness to the Past: A Thai Poet's Plea for Saving the Environment). The AIDs rate skyrockets. And, in recent years, massive street protests, political turmoil between rival factions, and a return of military influence have divided the country and weakened democracy. Yet, Thais possess a talent for political compromise, and Buddhism teaches moderation, tolerance, respect for nature, and a belief in individual worth. Thus Thais have the basis for a democratic spirit, a more equitable distribution of wealth, and an environmental ethic.

Burma's Economy and Politics

Whatever Thailand's problems, they seem dwarfed by a Burma ruled by a harsh, corrupt military regime. Few outside the ruling group have prospered, despite the country's natural riches of timber, oil, gems, and rice. As a result, Burma is now one of Asia's poorest nations. Sparked by economic decline and political repression, mass protests in 1988, led by students and Buddhist monks, demanded civil liberties, but the protests ended when soldiers killed hundreds and jailed thousands of demonstrators. In 1990 Burma (now renamed Myanmar **(my-ahn-MAH)**, under international pressure, allowed elections. Although most of its leaders were in jail, the opposition quickly organized and won a landslide victory. Aung San Suu Kyi **(AWNG sahn soo CHEE)** (b. 1945), daughter of the founding president and an eloquent orator, returned from a long exile in England to lead the democratic forces. But the military refused to hand over power, put Aung San Suu Kyi under house arrest, and jailed thousands of opposition supporters. Aung San Suu Kyi refused to compromise in exchange for the regime ending her house arrest. A courageous symbol of principled leadership, she won the Nobel Peace Prize in 1991.

Meanwhile, the military regime remains in power, detaining opposition leaders. Although many Burmese still dream of democracy, and illicit cassettes of protest music and opposition messages are exchanged from hand to hand, others have accommodated themselves to military rule, valuing stability and fearing civil war. To increase its own revenues, the government began welcoming some limited foreign investment. But investments by Western, Japanese, and Southeast Asian corporations in Burma, especially in the timber and oil industries, diminish the willingness of other countries to punish Burma for gross human rights violations. In recent years the brutal suppression of Buddhist-led protests, a refusal of foreign assistance for the victims of a devastasting hurricane, and increased military assaults on ethnic minority settlements, made clear that the generals would not relax their grip or modify their isolation from the world.

Diversity and Prosperity in Malaysia and Singapore

Malaysia and Singapore, both open to the world, have achieved the most political stability and economic progress. Both countries have successfully diversified their economies and stimulated development while raising living standards and spreading the wealth. The two nations, once joined in the same federation, have shared a similar mix of ethnic groups, though while Malays constitute slightly over half, Chinese a third, and Indians a tenth of the Malaysian population, around three-quarters of Singaporeans are Chinese. Malaysia and Singapore have maintained limited democracies, holding regular elections in which the ruling parties control the voting and most of the mass media. While opposition leaders sometimes face arrest or harassment, dissidents use the Internet to spread their views. By 2008 an opposition coalition overcame obstacles and made electoral gains against the ruling alliance in Malaysia, possibly foreshadowing a more open system.

Malaysian Society and Economy

In Malaysia religion has often divided the Muslim majority from the Christian, Hindu, Buddhist, and animist minority. Conflict also occurs within religious traditions. Islamic movements with dogmatic, sometimes militant views have gained support among some young Malays, especially rural migrants to the city alienated by a Westernized, materialistic society and looking for an anchor in an uncertain world. These movements, which encourage women to dress modestly and sometimes reject modern technology or products, often alarm secular Malays and non-Muslims who oppose taking Malaysia backward. In response, Malay women's rights groups use Islamic arguments to oppose restrictions favored by conservatives. Hence, Sisters in Islam, founded by the academic Zainab Anwar **(ZEYE-nab AN-war)**, espouses freedom, justice, and equality and fights strict interpretations of Muslim family law. Numerous women also hold high government positions. At the other extreme, aimless Malay youth mock the conventions of mainstream society, wearing long hair and listening to heavy metal and hip hop music.

Supported by abundant natural resources, such as oil and tin, economic diversification, and entrepreneurial talent, Malaysia has surpassed European nations like Portugal and Hungary in national wealth. High annual growth rates have enabled it to achieve a relatively high per capita income and to build export industries that employ cheap, often female, labor to make shoes, toys, and other consumer goods. The manufacturing sector has continued to grow rapidly—Malaysians even build their own automobiles—and timber and oil have become valuable export commodities. But economic growth comes at the price of toxic waste problems, severe deforestation, and air pollution. In 1969 violence between Chinese and Malays resulted in the New Economic Policy; aimed at redistributing more wealth to Malays, it has fostered a substantial Malay middle class. Televisions, stereos, cell phones, and videocassette recorders became nearly universal in the cities and increasingly common in the rural areas. Many Malaysians have personal computers or access to Internet cafés, and official poverty rates dropped from some 50 percent in 1970 to around 20 percent by 2000. Nevertheless, the gap between rich and poor remains and may have widened. In the bustling capital city, Kuala Lumpur, jammed freeways, glittering malls, and high-rise luxury condominiums contrast with shantytown squatter settlements and shabbily dressed street hawkers hoping to sell enough of their cheap wares to buy a meal.

Kuala Lumpur Dominated by new skyscrapers, including some of the world's tallest buildings, and a spectacular mosque, the Malaysian capital city, Kuala Lumpur, has become a prosperous center for Asian commerce and industry. Modern buildings gradually replace the older shophouses built decades ago. Yet, poor shantytowns have also grown apace to house the poor. Corbis

Singapore Politics and Society

Restricted to a tiny island, Singapore, despite few resources, has joined the world's most prosperous nations, with a standard of living second only to Japan in Asia. The numerical and political predominance of ethnic Chinese makes Singapore unique in Southeast Asia. The government has mixed freewheeling economic policies with an autocratic leadership that tightly controls the 5 million people and limits dissent. Singapore is run like a giant corporation, efficient and ruthless. People pay a stiff fine if caught spitting, littering, or even tossing used chewing gum on the street. Yet it is also one of the healthiest societies, enjoying the world's lowest rate of infant mortality. Singapore devotes more of its national budget to education than other nations, everyone studies English in school, and world-class universities attract international faculties. In the vanguard of the information revolution, the city has also become a hub of light industry, high technology, and computer networking. Businesspeople and professionals from around the world have flocked to this globalized city, just as they had flocked to the trading states of Srivijaya and Melaka centuries ago.

Conflict and Reconstruction in Indochina

After years of war and destruction, Vietnam, Laos, and Cambodia began to rebuild and deal with lingering tensions. In Vietnam, socialist policies failed to revitalize the economy, and the reunification of North and South Vietnam proved harsh. Because of mismanagement, natural disasters, a long U.S. economic embargo, and the devastation of the war, between 1978 and 1985 half a million refugees, known as "boat people," risked their lives to escape Vietnam in rickety boats, becoming easy targets for pirates. After spending months or years in crowded refugee camps in Southeast Asia, most of the refugees were resettled in North America, Australia, or France.

Vietnam's Politics and Economy

In the 1980s the government recognized its failures and introduced market-oriented reforms similar to those in China favoring private enterprise and foreign investment. These reforms increased productivity, fostered some prosperity in the cities, and ended the refugee flow. Emphasis on education also more than doubled the 1945 literacy rates to 85 percent of adults. But the shift from rigid socialism also widened economic inequalities, leaving most farmers living just above the poverty line. The Vietnamese have debated the appropriate balance between socialist and free market policies to resolve the rural problems. With the global recession of 2008, the Vietnamese experienced the full effects of globalization. Hundreds of villages which had shifted from farming to producing handicrafts for export saw their income collapse as foreign consumers cut spending.

Politically, Vietnam, like China, has remained an authoritarian one-party state, with little democracy, but restrictions on cultural expression have loosened. Several former soldiers became rock or disco stars, and many writers addressed contemporary problems and the war's legacy in fiction. For example, "The General Retires," a short story by a former North Vietnamese soldier, caused a sensation by depicting the despair of an old soldier contemplating the emptiness of the new society. However, the communists expanded ties to the West and the world economy, the United

States and Vietnam resumed diplomatic relations, and U.S. president Bill Clinton lifted the U.S. economic embargo. Urban streets are now jammed with motor scooters, and bustling Saigon, renamed Ho Chi Minh City, has enjoyed especially dynamic economic growth and prosperity. Consumers in the United States now buy shrimp and underwear imported from Vietnam, while many Americans, including former soldiers and Vietnamese refugees, visit Vietnam. Hundreds of American veterans operate businesses or social service agencies in Vietnam, sometimes in partnership with former communist soldiers. Still, the ruling communists have to satisfy the expectations of the 80 million Vietnamese struggling to overcome the devastation wrought by decades of war.

Laotians also needed to deal with the divisions and destruction caused by the war. Many Laotians fled into exile, among them over 300,000 Hmongs who settled in the United States. The Laotian government persecuted some remaining Hmong who they believed were supporting anti-communist guerillas. While Laotian leaders sought warmer relations with neighboring Thailand, China, and the United States, they failed to foster a more open society or energize the economy. Rigid communists still dominate the one-party state. While several places have attracted Western tourists, most Laotians remain poor. Looking across the Mekong at the busy freeways, neon lights, and high-rise buildings in Thailand, Laotians see a more successful development model.

Honoring Ho Chi Minh These schoolgirls, dressed in traditional clothing and parading before Ho Chi Minh's mausoleum in Hanoi, are part of an annual festival to honor the leading figure of Vietnamese communism.

Cambodia has faced a far more difficult challenge because war was followed by fierce repression and mass murder. Agriculture had been badly disrupted, raising the specter of widespread starvation. When the communist Khmer Rouge, hardened by years of brutal war, achieved power in 1975, they turned on the urban population with a fury, driving everyone into the rural areas to farm. The Khmer Rouge's radical vision of a propertyless, classless peasant society, combined with violence against suspected dissenters and resisters, led thousands to flee into neighboring countries. Even worse were the "killing fields": the Khmer Rouge executed thousands of victims in death camps and shot or starved many others, including both common people, such as peasants and taxi drivers, and Westernized and educated people. Ultimately the Khmer Rouge and their brutal leader, Pol Pot (1925–1998), in their attempt to create a new communist society, were responsible for 1.5 to 2 million deaths. Perhaps 500,000 were executed, and the rest died from illness, hunger, and overwork, sparking comparisons with Nazi Germany.

Cambodian Political Change

The situation changed in 1978, leading to a new government. The Vietnamese, alarmed at Khmer Rouge territorial claims and the murder of thousands of ethnic Vietnamese in Cambodia, allied with an exile army of disaffected former Khmer Rouge, invaded Cambodia, and rapidly pushed the Khmer Rouge to the Thailand border. The Vietnamese invasion liberated the Cambodian people from tyranny and installed a less brutal communist government. But military conflict continued for years as a Khmer Rouge–dominated resistance, subsidized chiefly by China and the United States, which both wanted to weaken Vietnam, controlled some sections of the country. Cambodia proved to be for Vietnam what Vietnam had been for the United States, an endless sinkhole of conflict that drained scarce wealth and complicated Vietnam's relations with the West.

In the early 1990s a coalition government was formed under United Nations sponsorship. The Khmer Rouge, which refused to take part, splintered and collapsed as a movement. While the resulting peace was welcomed by all, the government remained repressive and corrupt, tolerating some opposition but controlling the vote. Sihanouk returned from exile to become king but had little power and served largely as a symbol of Cambodia's link to its past. Life for many Cambodians remained grim as they faced everything from the high price of fuel to poor education, problems that have spurred some people to demand more democracy and attention to social problems. Nevertheless, the new government has transformed Cambodia, while still haunted by past horrors, from a traumatized to a functioning society, kept afloat largely by Western tourism and aid.

Southeast Asia in the Global System

Economic Models

Although Southeast Asians still export the natural resources they did in colonial times, some nations have seen major economic growth through industrialization and exploitation of other resources. The gold, pepper, and spice exports of earlier centuries have been largely replaced by oil, timber, rubber, rice, tin, sugar, and palm oil. The region's role in the world has also changed, fostering some of the fastest-growing economies. Malaysia, Thailand, Singapore, and, to some extent, Indonesia and Vietnam have become major recipients of foreign investment. Meanwhile, workers produce manufactured goods like shoes, clothing, computer chips, and sports equipment for European and North American markets. Several countries elsewhere in Asia, Africa, and Latin America now borrow economic models from the Southeast Asian "tigers." Recently Southeast Asians began shifting their focus from the United States to China, which they viewed as the rising world power with which they must cooperate.

Southeast Asia and Global Influences

Southeast Asians also influenced politics worldwide. The Indonesian Revolution, for instance, forced a major colonial power to abandon its control, giving hope to colonized Africans. Similarly, Vietnamese communists under Ho Chi Minh, in their ultimately successful fifty-year fight against French colonialism, Japanese occupation, and then U.S. intervention, stimulated a wave of revolutionary efforts, from Nicaragua to Mozambique, to overthrow Western domination. The Vietnamese struggle for independence also inspired student activists in Europe and North America; in the 1960s, while protesting against war and inequality, a few of the more radical shouted slogans in praise of the Vietnamese communist leader, Ho Chi Minh. Women have long played an influential role in Southeast Asia, and the political leaders Megawati Soekarnoputri in Indonesia, Corazon Aquino in the Philippines, and Aung San Suu Kyi in Burma have become inspirations to women worldwide.

Global influences and economic development have increasingly modified lives. For example, the resident of an upscale suburb of Kuala Lumpur, Bangkok, or Manila, connected through her home computer to the information superhighway and working in a high-rise, air-conditioned office reached by driving a late-model sports car along the crowded freeways, has a way of life vastly different from that of the peasant villager whose life revolves around traditional society. The modern cities boast malls, supermarkets, boutiques, Hard Rock Cafes, and Planet Hollywoods. Indonesian television now features many U.S.-style reality shows, which have replaced local soap operas in the ratings. Even rural areas have become more connected to wider networks by televisions, outboard motors, motor scooters, and telephones. Yet change has often been superficial. In poor-city neighborhoods restaurants may have compact disc players and cold beer, but they may also feature traditional music and dance and serve up fiery hot curries. For every youngster who joins the fan club for a Western or local pop star, another identifies with an Islamic, Buddhist, or Christian organization, sometimes a militant one. Many people find themselves perched uneasily between the cooperative village values of the past and the competitive, materialistic modern world.

SECTION SUMMARY

- Beginning in the late 1970s, Southeast Asia experienced rapid economic growth through a Japanese-style mix of capitalism and active government involvement, though a severe economic crisis hit the region in 1997.
- Under Suharto, the Indonesian New Order government repressed regional opposition and improved the economy, but Suharto was extravagantly corrupt and was forced to resign in 1997 amid widespread unrest and economic collapse.
- Under Marcos, the Philippines was divided between the very rich and the poor; Marcos was forced out after massive protests, and the democratically elected governments that followed were more open to dissent but still dominated by the wealthy.
- Since the 1980s, Thailand has developed a semidemocratic system and has grown economically, though it has endured widespread poverty and sexual exploitation, while Burma has been burdened with a corrupt regime that has failed to take advantage of ample natural resources and stifled its opposition.
- Malaysia has taken advantage of abundant natural resources to become highly successful, surpassing some European nations in wealth, while Singapore, with fewer resources, has been even more successful through a combination of economic freedom and political restriction.
- Vietnam struggled after the war, but in the 1980s it opened up its economy and by the 1990s had reestablished ties with the rest of the world, including the United States.
- Many Laotians fled into exile, while the communist-dominated government has opened somewhat to the world economy, and Cambodia endured vicious repression under the Khmer Rouge, who continued to wreak havoc even after a Vietnamese invasion pushed them out of power.
- With their rapidly growing economies, the Southeast Asian "tigers" have inspired developing nations around the world, and while most of the region has joined the modern world, tradition thrives in them as well.

CHAPTER SUMMARY

After decolonization, the societies of southern Asia struggled to shape their futures. Since Hindu and Muslim leaders could not agree on a formula for unity after independence, British India fragmented into two rival nations, predominantly Hindu India and mostly Muslim Pakistan. Under Nehru, India adopted democratic practices and modernizing policies. Indians generally sustained multiparty democracy, raised the legal status of untouchables and women, achieved a dramatic rise in food production, industrialized, and fostered high-technology enterprises. But they failed to transform rural society, distribute the fruits of economic growth equitably, and eradicate Hindu-Muslim conflict. Muslim-dominated Pakistan divided when Bangladesh broke away, and both Pakistan and Bangladesh have had difficulty maintaining democracy and generating economic development. India and Pakistan, both armed with nuclear weapons, have remained hostile neighbors.

Like South Asians, Southeast Asians also regained the independence they had lost under Western colonialism. Vietnamese communists led by Ho Chi Minh launched a revolutionary war that eventually forced the French to leave, giving the communists control of North Vietnam. The United States, influenced by Cold War thinking, supported anticommunist South Vietnam and, in response to a growing communist insurgency, sent American troops to South Vietnam. But the United States withdrew in 1975, unable to triumph over a determined foe. The conflict caused several million casualties and major environmental damage. With the war over, Vietnam, Cambodia, and Laos, all under communist control, struggled for reconstruction. Meanwhile Indonesia and Malaysia worked to build national unity in a complex mosaic of peoples and cultures. Burma, Thailand, and the Philippines experienced chronic unrest that often led to military or civilian dictatorships. But eventually Malaysia, Singapore, Thailand, Indonesia, and Vietnam achieved rapid economic growth, supplying natural resources and manufactured goods to the world.

KEY TERMS

Dalit	**Bollywood**	**Tet Offensive**	**UMNO**
Awami League	**National Liberation Front (NLF)**	**Pathet Lao**	**ASEAN**
Bharatha Janata		**Khmer Rouge**	**New Order**

EBOOK AND WEBSITE RESOURCES

INTERACTIVE MAPS

Map 31.1 Modern South Asia
Map 31.2 The U.S.-Vietnamese War
Map 31.3 Modern Southeast Asia

LINKS

Asian Studies: WWW Virtual Library (http://coombs.anu.edu.au/WWWVL-AsianStudies.html). A vast metasite maintained at Australian National University, with links to hundreds of sites.

East and Southeast Asia: An Annotated Directory of Internet Resources (http://newton.uor.edu/Departments&Programs/AsianStudies-Dept/). A superb set of links on Southeast Asia, maintained at the University of Redlands.

Internet Indian History Sourcebook (http://www.fordham.edu/halsall/india/indiasbook.html). An invaluable collection of sources and links on India from ancient to modern times.

Virtual Library: South Asia (http://www.columbia.edu/cu/libraries/indiv/area/sarai/). A major site maintained by Columbia University.

WWW Southeast Asia Guide (http://www.library.wisc.edu/guides/SEAsia/). An easy-to-use site.

Plus flashcards, practice quizzes, and more. Go to: www.cengage.com/history/lockard/globalsocnet2e.

SUGGESTED READING

Abinales, Patricio N., and Donna J. Amoroso. *State and Society in the Philippines.* Lanham, MD: Rowman and Littlefield, 2005. A readable study with much on recent politics.

Beeson, Mark, ed. *Contemporary Southeast Asia: Regional Dynamics, National Differences.* New York: Palgrave Macmillan, 2004. Essays on varied topics.

Brown, Judith M. *Nehru.* New York: Longman, 1999. A readable biography of an important Asian leader.

Chalmers, Ian. *Indonesia: An Introduction to Contemporary Traditions.* New York: Oxford University Press, 2006. Explores social and cultural life.

Chandler, David, 4th ed. *A History of Cambodia.* Boulder: Westview, 2008. Extensive coverage of contemporary era.

Ganguly, Sumit, ed. *South Asia.* New York: New York University Press, 2006. Recent essays on the South Asian countries.

Ganguly, Sumit, and Neal DeVotta, eds. *Understanding Contemporary India.* Boulder, CO: Lynne Rienner, 2003. An accessible collection covering most aspects of Indian society.

Guha, Ramachandra. *India After Gandhi: The History of the World's Largest Democracy.* New York: Harper, 2008. Explains factors behind India's recent rise.

Harrison, Selig S., et al., eds. *India and Pakistan: The First Fifty Years.* New York: Cambridge University Press, 1999. An excellent collection of essays covering many topics.

Karnow, Stanley. *Vietnam: A History,* 2nd ed. New York: Penguin, 1997. One of the better introductions to modern history and the American-Vietnamese War.

Kingsbury, Damien. *South-East Asia: A Political Profile,* 2nd ed. New York: Oxford University Press, 2005. A comprehensive, up-to-date survey by an Australian scholar.

Lockard, Craig A. *"Dance of Life": Popular Music and Politics in Southeast Asia.* Honolulu: University of Hawaii Press, 1998. An examination of politics and societies through popular culture.

Luce, Edward. *In Spite of the Gods: The Rise of Modern India.* New York: Anchor, 2008. Journalistic account of India today.

Marlay, Ross, and Clark Neher. *Patriots and Tyrants: Ten Asian Leaders.* Lanham, MD: Rowman and Littlefield, 1999. Sketches of Asian nationalists, such as Gandhi, Nehru, Ho, and Sukarno.

Neher, Clark D. *Southeast Asia: Crossroads of the World,* 2nd ed. DeKalb: Center for Southeast Asian Studies, Northern Illinois University, 2004. A general, readable introduction to cultures and politics.

Olson, James S., and Randy Roberts. *Where the Domino Fell: America and Vietnam, 1945–2006,* 5th ed. St. James, NY: Wiley-Blackwell, 2006. An outstanding survey with an emphasis on U.S. policies and actions.

Stein, Burton. *A History of India.* Malden, MA: Blackwell, 1998. A detailed history with good coverage of the contemporary era.

Varshney, Ashutosh. *Ethnic Conflict and Civic Life: Hindus and Muslims in India,* 2nd ed. New Haven, CT: Yale University Press, 2003. A key study of Hindu-Muslim relations in three cities, including peacemaking and violence.

Vickers, Adrian. *A History of Modern Indonesia.* New York: Cambridge University Press, 2005. A quirky but fascinating study.

Globalization: For and Against

The first pictures taken from the moon in 1969, which showed the earth as a blue oasis in the middle of nowhere, made clear that humans share a single home. The pictures also suggested that this home is shared by an interlinked future. Different kinds of networks have increasingly connected peoples across distance and borders, and globalization—the interconnections between societies, the rise in cross-border exchanges, and the creation of one world—has become a major subject of debate. Often used vaguely and inconsistently, the concept became a metaphor to explain capitalism spreading throughout the world. But to many observers, the concept has deeper meanings, describing a process that both unites and divides, creates winners and losers, and brings both new possibilities and new risks. The debates on globalization cut across political leanings and national divisions.

THE PROBLEM

Globalization inspires passionate support and bitter opposition, generating immense discussion and disagreement. The debate focuses on four questions: When did globalization begin? What are the arguments in favor of it? What are some of the major opposing views? Is the trend leading the world into a troubled era of increasing conflict or greater cooperation?

THE DEBATE

The first question, the roots of globalization, remains disputed. Some scholars argue that its origins lie deep in the past, going back to the interconnections that slowly enveloped people from the dawn of cities and states. The German historians Jurgen Osterhammel and Niels Petersson, for example, trace it back a millennium or two to the silk trade between China and the Mediterranean region, the sea trade between the Middle East and India, and the caravans crossing the deserts of Africa, all activities that moved people, ideas, artwork, natural resources, goods, and coins. By contrast, Robbie Robertson, an Australian, argues that history changed dramatically only five hundred years ago, when the gradual linking of the world by European voyages of discovery transformed societies and economic activities. Still other scholars trace it no further back than the mid-nineteenth century, pointing to the first permanent transoceanic telegraph cable in 1866, global social movements such as feminism, and global regulatory bodies such as the Universal Postal Union. Some other writers claim that globalization did not affect most of humanity until the 1960s or later. Whatever the roots, by 2000 a global system—defined by market capitalism, over two hundred nation-states, some four hundred international organizations, and 40,000 transnational corporations—existed with no central authority.

On the second and third questions, whether the effects are positive or negative, the debate has raged for years. Among the benefits attributed to globalization are higher living standards and the worldwide sharing of culture. British sociologist John Giddens identifies a worldwide trend toward democracy and intellectual freedom. Walter Anderson praises the opening of societies to one another, as reflected in communications satellites and the fiber-optic submarine cable system winding its way around the world. As a result, he notes, the Inuit people living in northern Alaska watch twenty-eight channels of satellite television, take courses through the Internet, and stay in touch with their families by cell phones. Free market enthusiasts, such as Indian-born, U.S.-based economist Jagdish Bhagwati, stress the fostering of economic freedom. Opposing antiglobalization movements as the misguided enemy of progress, all these thinkers complain that newspapers and television reports focus more on shuttered textile factories, as jobs move overseas, than on the African child at the computer. Bhagwati claims that when properly governed, globalization becomes a powerful force for social good, bringing prosperity to underdeveloped nations, reducing child labor, increasing literacy, and helping women by creating jobs that increase their income and status. Another enthusiast, Thomas Friedman, considers globalization the principal trend of the post–Cold War world, symbolized by the Lexus, a Japanese-made luxury car sold around the world. Yet, he argues, people often prefer to hold on to meaningful traditions, symbolized by the olive tree often found at the center of an Arab village, rather than embrace new ideas. The world, he argues, has gotten flat, and this level playing field has allowed over 2 billion Chinese, Indians, and Russians to contemplate eventually owning a car, house, refrigerator, and toaster, increasing competition and dramatically raising the demand for the world's resources.

The contrary views on globalization stress negative consequences. These consequences include a concentration of economic power, more poverty, and less cultural diversity. The challengers of economic globalization argue that powerful governments and multinational corporations bully the marketplace, control politics, and stack the deck in their favor. Walter LaFeber shows how U.S. basketball star Michael Jordan, whose games were broadcast all over the world, became an international phenomenon of great commercial appeal, benefiting the international corporations who used Jordan to create a demand for their expensive products, such as sneakers, often at the expense of local manufacturers making the same product. To LaFeber, the terrorist attacks on the United States, especially the World Trade Center in New York in 2001, must also be understood in the context of the growing opposition to globalization around the world as the rich become richer and the poor become poorer. Joseph Stiglitz, an ardent fan of capitalism and former World Bank official, believes that globalization can be positive but that misguided policies and the economic power of industrial nations have made free trade unfair for developing nations. Looking at other aspects of globalization, Cynthia Enloe explores the often-negative effects of tourism and U.S. military bases on women, who, enjoying fewer economic options than men, often need to sell their bodies to male tourists and soldiers to survive. James Mittelman argues that, experienced from below, globalization fosters the loss of local political control as power shifts upward and also a devaluation of a society's cultural achievements as foreign

Kuwaiti Stock Exchange Capitalism has spread widely in the world, and with it financial institutions such as investment banks and stock exchanges. The oil-rich, politically stable Persian Gulf sultanate of Kuwait has one of the most active stock exchanges.

Corbis

cultural products, such as music and films, become influential. All of these globalizing trends spur angry resistance, reflected in antiglobalization movements.

Experts also disagree about the fourth question, where globalization is taking the world. Some predict a growing divide both between and within societies. Benjamin Barber, for example, analyzes the conflict between consumerist capitalism (what he calls McWorld, after McDonald's) and tribalism or religious fundamentalism (what he terms jihad, after Islamic militants). Barber dislikes both trends: the dull homogeneity of McWorld, in which everyone, moved by capitalism and advertising, has the same tastes and ideas; and the balkanized world of jihad in which rival cultures, convinced of their own superior values and disdainful of others, struggle for dominance. Other scholars also predict tensions. John Giddens argues that the globalization of information, symbolized by the World Wide Web, that puts people in touch with others who think differently will promote a more cosmopolitan world-view respecting cultural differences but will also generate a backlash among narrow nationalists and religious fundamentalists who see only one path to truth. Preventing conflict between the factions and lessening the growing divide between rich and poor nations require cooperation between nations. Bhagwati, for example, supports managed rather than unfettered globalization, with world leaders discussing how to foster equality as well as growth. Taking a different approach, Mittelman doubts that globalization can be managed and calls for people around the world, rather than leaders and governments, to work together to decentralize political and economic power to build a future of greater equity.

EVALUATING THE DEBATE

The globalization discussion, much more than an academic debate, is a disagreement about profound transformations in the world and about what ethical and institutional principles should be applied to better organize human affairs for a brighter future. Some authors engaged in the debate have proposed catchy ideas, such as the Lexus and the olive tree, jihad and McWorld, but the reality of globalization is usually more complex. Both proponents and opponents make convincing points about the consequences of globalization; the truth may lie somewhere between. Globalization may indeed bring great benefits, at least to a section of the world's people. While the free flow of ideas inspires some people to demand more political rights or social inequality, many young women working long hours for low wages in foreign-owned factories may often prefer that life to the dead end of rural poverty. But improving the lives of those who do not benefit, as even globalization proponents Bhagwati and Friedman concede, will probably require action such as land reform to help poor peasants, more funding for schools, and stiffer environmental and worker protection laws to smooth the impacts on societies, cultures, and environments. Yet, the relations between business interests and their political supporters prompting globalization and the antiglobalization activists, often from worker or peasant backgrounds, remain tense. Local, national, regional, and global forces are intermingling in new and complex ways that may necessitate not just actions to remedy inequalities but also new ways of thinking.

THINKING ABOUT THE CONTROVERSY

1. When did globalization begin?
2. What are the positive arguments for globalization?
3. What main points do opponents make?

EXPLORING THE CONTROVERSY

Among the key historical studies are Robbie Robertson, *The Three Waves of Globalization: A History of a Developing Global Consciousness* (New York: Zed Books, 2003), and Jurgen Osterhammel and Niels P. Petersson, *Globalization: A Short History* (Princeton: Princeton University Press, 2005). Some of the major proponents are John Giddens, *Runaway World: How Globalization Is Reshaping Our Lives* (London: Routledge, 2000); Walter Truett Anderson, *All Connected Now: Life in the First Global Civilization* (Boulder, CO: Westview Press, 2001); Jagdish Bhagwati, *In Defense of Globalization* (New York: Oxford University Press, 2004); and Thomas L. Friedman, *The Lexus and the Olive Tree: Understanding Globalization* (New York: Anchor, 2000) and *The World Is Flat: A Brief History of the Twenty-First Century* (New York: Farrar, Straus, and Giroux, 2005). Writers questioning the benefits include Walter LaFeber, *Michael Jordan and the New Global Capitalism*, new and expanded ed. (New York: W.W. Norton, 2002); Joseph E. Stiglitz, *Globalization and Its Discontents* (New York: W.W. Norton, 1993); Cynthia Enloe, *Bananas, Beaches and Bases: Making Feminist Sense of International Politics*, updated ed. (Berkeley: University of California Press, 2001); and James H. Mittelman, *The Globalization Syndrome: Transformation and Resistance* (Princeton: Princeton University Press, 2000). For one view of future trends, see Benjamin R. Barber, *Jihad vs. McWorld* (New York: Times Books, 1995). On globalization generally, see Thomas Hyland Eriksen, *Globalization: The Key Concepts* (New York: Berg, 2007); David Held, ed., *A Globalizing World? Culture, Economics, Politics* (New York: Routledge, 2000); Mark Kesselman, ed., *The Politics of Globalization: A Reader* (Boston: Houghton Mifflin, 2007); George Ritzer, *Globalization: A Basic Text* (Hoboken, N.J.: John Wiley, 2009); Robert K. Schaeffer, *Understanding Globalization: The Social Consequences of Political, Economic, and Environmental Change* (Lanham, MD: Rowman and Littlefield, 1997); and Manfred B. Steger, *Globalization: A Very Short Introduction* (New York: Oxford University Press, 2003).

The Contemporary World, Since 1945

The world has changed dramatically since 1945. Some observers have described these years as the most revolutionary age in history, reshaping whole ways of life and world-views. All regions of the world, opening to ideas and products from everywhere, have become, as some experts put it, part of a global village or global system. The Indonesian thinker Soedjatmoko (so-jat-MOH-ko), summing up the era's trends, described a world of collapsing "national boundaries and horrifying destructive power, expanding technological capacity and instant communication [in which] we live in imperfect intimacy with all our fellow human beings."[1] This interconnected and rapidly changing global society, and the people who shape it, have produced both great good and indescribable horrors.

The contemporary world has become a global unity within a larger diversity. Globalization has fostered or intensified networks of exchange and communication: international trade pacts and electronic fund transfers, jet-speed travel and fax machines. These networks link distant societies. Yet, even as they have become more closely linked, nations have not been able to work together to meet the challenges facing humanity, such as poverty and environmental distress. No clear international consensus has emerged on maintaining strong local cultures in the face of global influences, correcting the widening gap between rich and poor nations, and achieving a better balance between environmental preservation and economic development. Solving these problems requires complex strategies and the joint efforts of many nations. Ensuring a brighter future also requires examining how the patterns of the past and the trends of the present may shape the years to come.

Globalization and Cultures

Over recent centuries the world's people have built a human web, or networked society—a global system that today encompasses most of the world's 6.8 billion people. All these terms imply transnational connections and the institutions that foster them, such as the World Bank, the Internet, and religious missionaries. Around the world people speak, with fear or enthusiasm, of globalization. Some observers see the trend as dangerous folly, others as a boon, and still others have mixed feelings. In recent decades, people have experienced global influences not only by, for some, frequent travel abroad but also because these influences have reshaped the cities, towns, and villages where they live. The interaction between global influences and local traditions, such as religion and music, has become a force in the world, helping to shape cultures.

Globalization and Its Impacts

The roots of globalization go deep into the past. During the first millennium of the Common Era trade networks such as the Silk Road, which linked China and Europe across Central Asia and the Middle East, and the spread of religions such as Buddhism, Christianity, and Islam, connected distant societies. A thousand years ago an Eastern Hemisphere–wide economy based in Asia and anchored by Chinese and Indian manufacturing and Islamic trade networks represented an early form of globalization. The links between the hemispheres forged after 1492, during which Europeans competed with each other and with Asians for a share of the growing trade in raw materials, expanded the reach of this economy. In the nineteenth century the Industrial Revolution, which produced desirable trade goods, and European imperialism, which led to the Western colonization of large parts of the world, extended the connections even further, aided by technological innovations such as steamships and transoceanic cables.

The integration of commerce and financial services today is more developed than ever before. As the global system has become increasingly linked, societies have become more dependent on each other for everything from consumer goods and entertainments to fuels and technological innovations. For example, all over the world people consume Chinese textiles, U.S. films, Persian Gulf oil, Indian yoga, and Japanese electronics. Videoconferencing allows business partners in Los Angeles, Berlin, and Hong Kong to confer instantaneously with one another. During the early twenty-first century the world's most powerful nation, the United States, has become increasingly reliant on Asian nations, especially China, to finance its skyrocketing national debt. The debt has grown in part because of a costly U.S. military engagement in Iraq and an increasing economic imbalance as Americans import more from abroad than they export. Such interdependence, as well as the reach of political, cultural, and social events across distances, has had an increasing impact in a shrinking world. This reality was demonstrated in 2005 when some faraway African societies were affected indirectly by Hurricane Katrina, which devastated the Gulf Coast of the United States, disrupting the export of corn from the U.S. Midwest through the port of New Orleans. Japan, a major consumer of that corn, then turned to South Africa for supplies, which deprived people in Malawi of South African corn, causing widespread starvation in Malawi. Yet, while globalization affects every country to some degree, the great bulk of world trade and financial flow and activity is concentrated in, and has the largest impact on, the peoples of three huge interlinked blocs: North America, Europe, and a group of Asian nations stretching from Japan to India.

Furthermore, many observers believe that globalization is unmanageable. U.S. journalist Thomas Friedman writes:

> *Globalization isn't a choice. It's a reality, and no one is in charge. You keep looking for someone to complain to, to take the heat off your markets. Well guess what, there's no one on the other end of the phone. The global market today is an electronic herd of anonymous stock, bond and currency traders sitting behind computer screens. Sure, this is unfair [but] there's nobody to call.*[2]

If governments are often somewhat powerless in the face of global economic trends, they need to adapt by educating their citizens, especially their young people, for a new, more competitive world. Various Asian nations, such as India, Taiwan, and

Singapore, have adapted to these changes more rapidly than North American and European nations, pouring money into education, science, and high technology. The Western nations that have successfully adjusted to globalization are mainly those, especially in Scandinavia, that have combined open markets with strong societal and environmental protections.

This impersonal globalization, operating independent of governments, has had major impacts on societies, politics, economies, cultures, and environments. Whether they are seen as positive or negative consequences depends on the observer. For example, some Western free market enthusiasts celebrate a new global order in which everybody on the planet is in the same economy, offering entrepreneurs unparalleled opportunities for profit. But graffiti by disillusioned Poles in the 1990s took a different view, complaining that when Poland abandoned communism it asked for democracy but ended up with the bond market and domination by transnational corporations. Scholars and others energetically debate the value and scope of globalization (see Historical Controversy: Globalization: For and Against).

Global forces, symbolized by advertising for foreign-made goods and satellites miles up in the sky relaying information around the world, interact with local cultures, raising questions about national and local identity. As a result, local traditions and products sometimes get replaced, and imported and local cultures blend. An example of blending comes from France, where, with its large Arab immigrant population, Arab entrepreneurs have prospered by selling fast-food hamburgers and pizza prepared according to Muslim requirements and adapted to Arab taste. People around the world consume global products, from fast food to fashionable footwear to action films, but still enjoy cultural traditions that are distinctly local and popular with earlier generations. Examples include the unique Thai style of boxing in which combatants can attack with both hands and feet, sumo wrestling in Japan, and the African-influenced martial arts of Brazil.

To adapt and flourish in an interconnected world, people have had to become aware of international conditions. In North America, activists seeking to fight inequality or preserve the environment have urged people to think globally but act locally. Thinking globally, for example, would include understanding how rapid deforestation in the tropics—especially in the Amazon and Congo Basins, where rain forests recycle vast amounts of water into the air—diminishes rainfall around the world. Acting locally, Brazilian environmental and citizens' groups work to save their rain forests, while environmentally conscious North Americans and Europeans support organizations, businesses, and political leaders committed to improving the global environment. Others wonder, however, if this is enough, arguing that, since the world is so interlinked, people must think and act both globally and locally—to embrace both a global citizenship and a local citizenship. But, despite greatly increased travel and migration, only a small minority of people have become true citizens of the world, comfortable everywhere. Few people have gone as far toward an ecumenical view as Australian Aboriginal writer Colin Johnson, who both embraced Hinduism, imported from India, and dedicated his first novel to the Jamaican reggae star Bob Marley and his Rastafarian faith. Moreover, world government remains a distant prospect at the beginning of the twenty-first century.

Cultural Imperialism: The Globalization of Culture

The inequitable relationship between the dominant West and the developing nations has compelled observers to examine global change. Arising from this effort has been the concept of cultural imperialism, in which the economic and political power of Western nations, especially the United States, enables their cultural products to spread widely. Some African writers have called this pattern a "cultural bomb" because, they believe, Western products and entertainments destroy local cultures. In this view, the developed countries export popular music, disco dancing, skimpy women's clothing, and sex-drenched films and publications reflecting these countries' own values and experiences. Other societies adopt these products, which modify or suffocate their own traditions. For instance, big budget Hollywood films attract large audiences while local films, made on small budgets, cannot compete, and the local film industries often die as a result. To survive, local filmmakers adopt the formulas used by successful Hollywood filmmakers: sex and violence. Critics of Western power argue that cultural exchange has been common throughout history but in the modern world has become largely a one-way street, leading to domination by Western, especially Anglo-American, culture.

Popular culture produced in the United States, entertaining but also challenging to traditional values, has emerged as the closest thing available to a global entertainment. The Monroe Doctrine—the early-nineteenth-century declaration by Congress that the United States would interfere in Latin American political developments—has now become, in the view of certain wags, the "Marilyn Monroe Doctrine," after the famous American actress who, for many non-Americans, symbolized U.S. culture in the 1950s. Other examples of American cultural influence were popular U.S. television programs, such as the drama series *Dallas*, the racy *Desperate Housewives,* and *The Muppet Show,* a variety show, which have been broadcast in dozens of nations.

Some American icons, from basketball star Michael Jordan to McDonald's, have become symbols of a new global modernity and capitalism. In 1989 two young East Germans crossed the Berlin Wall and discovered their first McDonald's restaurant. One of them remembered, "It was all so modern, the windows were so amazing. I felt like a lost convict who'd just spent twenty-five years in prison. I was in a state of shock."[3] Not even the Chinese, with one of the world's most admired cuisines, were immune to the appeal of modern U.S. marketing techniques and convenience for harried urbanites. In 1993 a famous roast duck restaurant in China's capital, Beijing, sent its management staff to study the McDonald's operation in British-ruled Hong Kong and then introduced its customers to "roast duck fast food." The restaurant also faced a challenge from the growing number of McDonald's franchises in Beijing. Yet, Chinese restaurants flourish around the world.

Still, popular American entertainments often face opposition. Governments, from the Islamic clerics running Iran to the more democratic leaders of India, have attempted to halt or control the influx of what they consider destabilizing, immoral pop culture. In 1995 an Islamic political party in Pakistan even demanded, unsuccessfully, that the United States turn over to them American pop stars Madonna and Michael Jackson so that they could be placed on trial as "cultural terrorists" destroying humanity. In 2005, representatives of many nations, meeting under the auspices of the United Nations cultural organization, agreed that all nations had the right to restrict cultural imports, outraging American political and entertainment leaders. To maintain their cultural traditions and boost local artists many nations have mandated, as Portugal did in 2006, that a set percentage of music on radio and television must be locally made.

Forming New World Cultures

Whatever the real scope of cultural imperialism, a new world culture appears to be on the rise. The world is becoming one vast network of relationships as ideas, people, and goods move between its different regions. Similar cultural forms, often Anglo-American in origin, develop across national boundaries, transcending any one territory, society, or tradition. Yet the rising world culture is not uniform. No total homogenization of expression and meaning has occurred.

Anglo-American cultural forms are not the only ones to reach a global audience. Mexican and Brazilian soap operas, Indian (Bollywood) films, Nigerian novels, Arab, African, and Caribbean pop music, and Japanese comics and electronic games have been popular all over the globe. For example, thanks in part to the popularity of Jamaican singer/songwriter Bob Marley, reggae music spread around the world, as one observer marveled in the 1980s:

> *In Papeete, Tahiti, the buses all have speakers the size of foot lockers, making them moving sound systems. Their routes are jumping with the rhythms of [reggae groups] Steel Pulse, Black Uhuru, and Bob Marley. Four thousand miles away in Tokyo, there is a reggae night spot called Club 69, where local youth wear dreadlocks and dance to the beats of the Wailers. Africa has its own reggae styles and hundreds of bands.*[4]

The cultural traffic flow is not one-way. In North America, western Europe, and Australia, people take up Indian yoga, Chinese *tai qi*, and other Asian spiritual disciplines; patronize Thai, Indian, Chinese, and Japanese restaurants; enjoy Brazilian and African pop music; learn Latin American dances; and master Asian martial arts, such as karate and judo. Even classical musicians in the West have embraced foreign influences. For instance, in 1998 the Chinese cellist Yo Yo Ma, born in Paris and later a U.S. resident, founded the Silk Road Ensemble, which brings together Western, East Asian, and Middle Eastern musicians to tour the world playing music that mixes the instruments and traditions of both East and West.

The meeting of global and local cultures fosters hybridization, the blending of two cultures, a process that can be either enriching or impoverishing. Record stores in Western cities set aside some of their display space to sell a hybrid form called "world music," popular music originating largely outside of the West that mixes Western influences with local and other traditions. Some experts contend that world music reflects Western cultural imperialism, since Western influence—rock beats and electric instruments, for example—are often strong, and Anglo-American rock stars such as Peter Gabriel, Paul Simon, and Sting have promoted and sometimes appropriated some of the music. Yet world music has introduced Western and global audiences to a rich variety of sounds, often rooted in Asian, African, Caribbean, and Latin American traditions. While reshaping music for a global market, world music has also given Asian, African, and Latin American musicians a larger audience. Just like Western pop stars, some world musicians such as the Brazilian singer-songwriter Caetano Veloso, the Indian film diva Asha Bhosle (the most recorded artist in history: 20,000 songs in over a dozen languages), and the Senegalese Youssou N'Dour, the descendant of griots, who mixes guitars with West African talking drums, perform around the world.

Inequality and Development

Globalization, resulting from interconnections transcending the boundaries of nations, benefits some people but not all equally. The gap between rich and poor nations, and rich and poor people within nations, has grown and remains one of the world's major problems. In 1960 the richest fifth of the world's population had a total income thirty times the poorest fifth; by 2000 the ratio had more than doubled. The former Soviet leader Mikhail Gorbachev, a keen student of world affairs, has asked: "Will the whole world turn into one big Brazil, into countries with complete inequality and [gated communities] for the rich elite?"[5] International and national leaders have addressed the challenges of development, considering a more equitable sharing of the world's diminishing resources.

The North-South Gap

With the changes in the global system since World War II, nations on every continent have improved their living standards, lowered poverty rates, and increased their stake in the global economy, which has more than quintupled in size since 1950. The average per capita income in the world grew 2.6 times in the same period, to some $5,000 per year. But the rising tide of the world economy has not lifted all ships, leaving some nations, especially in the southern lands near or below the equator, poor relative to the northern countries. The economies of these nations, known as underdeveloped nations, have stagnated or enjoyed only very modest growth, leaving the majority of their people in poverty. Over 1 billion people live in extreme poverty, with an income of less than $1 per day. Using a popular term for an underdeveloped nation, Jamaican reggae star Pato Banton reflected on the harshness of poverty in a 1989 song, "Third World Country":

> *In a Third World country, the plants are green, it's a beautiful scene. Seems like a nice place for human beings. But there's people on the streets, no shoes on their feet. They gotta hustle to get a little food to eat. Things shouldn't be this way.*[6]

The gap between the richest and poorest countries, often known as the North-South gap, has widened steadily (see map). For instance, the difference in average per capita incomes between industrialized and nonindustrialized nations grew from 2:1 in 1850 to 10:1 in 1950 to 30:1 by 2000. Today the industrialized North contains a quarter of the world's population but accounts for over three-quarters of its production of goods and services. Meanwhile, poor nations from Haiti to Sierra Leone have experienced civil war or insurgency as rival factions fight to control their limited resources and revenues.

The growing North-South gap has many aspects all documented in dry statistics that, however, represent real people. The disparity in consumption is striking. For example, while Americans, 5 percent of the world's population, consume 40 percent of the world's resources, people in a Bolivian valley consume few resources and experience an impoverished material life. According to a study of the valley: "In a man's lifetime, he will buy one suit, one white shirt, perhaps a hat and a pair of rubber boots. The only things which have to be purchased in the market are a small radio-record player, the batteries to run it, plaster religious figures, a bicycle, and some cutlery."[7] Food consumption also differs dramatically. On average, North Americans consume twice as many calories each day as Haitians and Bangladeshis. While overeating contributes to widespread obesity in industrialized nations, a sixth of the world's people are chronically malnourished, often suffering permanent brain damage because of it, and lack access to clean water. Fifteen million children die each year from hunger-related ailments.

There are also other indicators of difference in wealth. The 10 percent of people who live in the most industrialized nations consume two-thirds of the world's energy. Literacy rates range from a low of 14 percent in Niger, in West Africa, to a high of 99 percent in some twenty wealthy countries. Life expectancy ranges from a high of eighty in Japan to a low of thirty-seven in Sierra Leone, in West Africa. Over 60 percent of the world's poorest people are women, who often struggle to compete with men for resources or are often prevented by local custom from working outside the home.

Challenges of Development

Of course, the experiences of the Asian, African, and Latin American nations involve more than the bleak story of poverty and underdevelopment. Life expectancy worldwide has grown by nearly half, and infant mortality has dropped by two-thirds since 1955. Some Asian and Latin American nations have achieved literacy rates comparable to those of some European nations, and the number of countries the United Nations considers to have "high human development" grew from sixteen to fifty-five between 1960 and 2004. The rapidly industrializing nations of East and Southeast Asia have led the way: Singapore and South Korea achieved similar world economic rankings with such European nations as Italy, Greece, and Portugal. Several Latin American nations, Caribbean islands, and small oil-rich Persian Gulf states joined the top development category. Many rising nations—such as Malaysia, Thailand, India, and Brazil—formed a growing group of newly industrializing countries (NICs) which, since the 1960s, have enjoyed high economic growth rates. Malaysia, for example, has dramatically reduced poverty rates, while India and Singapore have become centers of high technology. Nor is technological innovation restricted to the well educated. In India, for example, creative farmers have made their work easier by inventing cotton-stripping machines and modifying motorcycles into tractors.

While some countries are on the rise, however, others struggle to spur economic growth that benefits all the population. Valiant efforts have failed to substantially raise living standards or create wealth for everyone. For instance, in much of Latin America the wealthiest 20 percent have enjoyed huge income increases while the poorest 40 percent have lost income. Capitalism supported by Western investment has helped a few countries, especially those that combine strong governments with social and economic reform, as in South Korea, Malaysia, and Thailand. But reliance on free markets and Western investment has often failed to sustain development. Little of the trickle down of wealth from the rich to the poor, predicted by Western economists who favor free enterprise, has occurred. Instead, the result has often been trickle out: the loss of a country's wealth to multinational corporations and international banks. Throughout the Contemporary Era, for example, more wealth has flowed out of Africa and Latin America in the form of resources and profits than has flowed in through aid and investment.

At the same time, alternatives to capitalism have not necessarily brought improvement. Communist and other social revolutionary countries have experienced severe problems. Some of these countries, such as Fidel Castro's Cuba and Mao Zedong's China, did a good job of delivering education and health care but were unable to create much wealth. Some communist countries, such as Angola and Vietnam, also sometimes faced civil wars and trade embargoes imposed by the West that drained their economies. Since in most cases neither capitalism nor socialism by itself proved the answer, most communist regimes eventually introduced economic liberalization, such as allowing private companies and Western investment while still maintaining strong, centralized governments. Since adopting this model after the end of the Maoist era, China, for example, has generated the world's most rapid economic growth; in recent years Vietnam has tried to follow the same path. However, economic liberalization that dismantles government services has deprived millions of Chinese and Vietnamese, especially peasants, of the free education and health care they enjoyed under socialism, fostering unrest. Meanwhile, the formula of mixing capitalism and socialism has worked well in much of East and Southeast Asia. In these regions, a dynamic, largely unfettered private sector has evolved along with government investment, planning, land reform, investment in education, and other public policies to benefit the common people.

Envisioning a New World Order

The challenge of development is only a part of a larger contemporary question: how societies, working together, can forge a new, more equitable world order. The old world order, built in the nineteenth century when powerful Western nations conquered much of Asia and Africa, was one in which a few rich nations politically and economically dominated most of the others. Even after World War II, decolonization, and the rise of revolutionary states such as China, a few nations, mostly in the West and East Asia, still held disproportionate power and influence. The United States has played the key role and borne the major costs in managing the global system through military alliances (such as NATO), trade pacts (such as GATT), and international organizations (such as the World Bank). However, since the 1960s experts and, often, leaders of underdeveloped nations have argued that fostering widespread economic development also requires addressing the inequalities within the global system, including adjusting power relations

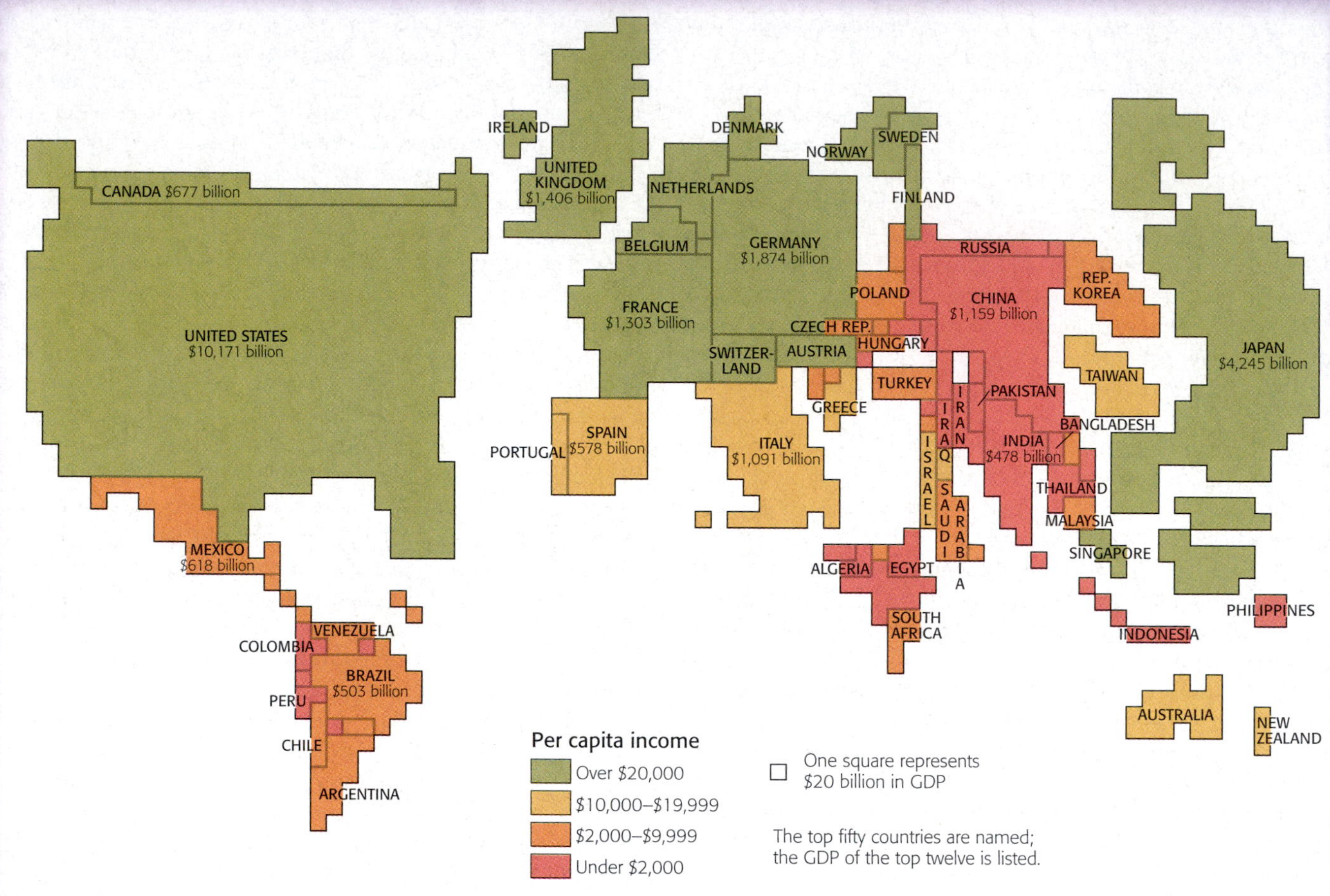

Global Distribution of Wealth

The countries of North America, northern Europe, and Japan have the most wealth and the world's highest per capita incomes, averaging over $20,000 per year. At the other extreme, many people in South America and most people in the poor countries of sub-Saharan Africa, South Asia, and the Middle East earn under $2,000 per year.

e **Interactive Map**

between the North and South, and spurring cooperation on international issues. The United Nations has been one major attempt at global cooperation but has had a mixed record.

The current world order contains many problems. The tensions resulting from governments unable significantly to raise living standards for the majority, to deal successfully with mounting social and economic problems, or to sustain hope for a better future have often led to political instability: coups, rebellions, and interventions by foreign powers. Conflicts in one nation then often spill over into neighboring nations, complicating international relations. Furthermore, people have experienced feelings of powerlessness in a world dominated by the governments, businesses, armies, and cultural influences of a few industrialized nations and the impersonal force of global markets. Leaders in the West have also expressed doubts about globalization. French president Jacques Chirac (g. 1995–present), for example, is suspicious of globalization, arguing that democracies "must tame it, accommodate it, humanize it, civilize it."[8]

The prospect of fostering a more equitable sharing of world resources raises questions about the availability of resources. Experts worry that the world's resources and environment could not support a Western standard of living for all the world. If every Chinese, Indian, Egyptian, and Peruvian, they argue, consumed the same products and calories as Americans, Swedes, or Japanese, world resources would quickly diminish. For all 6.8 billion people in today's world to live at a western European standard of living would require a 140-fold increase in the consumption of resources and energy. Present oil supplies would run out in one or two decades, assuming the oil could be pumped and refined into petroleum that fast. Furthermore, the world population is growing rapidly—4.4 people born every second—and most of the growth is occurring in the developing nations, putting even more pressure on diminishing resources.

China's recent economic success shows the challenges ahead. By the early twenty-first century a China rushing toward development had become a huge consumer of the world's industrial, agricultural, and natural resources, energizing global trade but causing shortages elsewhere. For example, world oil prices have soared since 2000 in part because of China's increasing energy appetite as Chinese switch from bicycles to cars. If the Chinese consumed as much oil per capita as Americans, their demand would exceed the present world production. By 2006 the Chinese consumed nearly twice as much meat and more than twice as much steel as Americans.

China's living standards remain far below those of Japan and South Korea. Should they rise to that level, however, in the next decade or two, China will import vastly more resources than it does today, further stressing supplies. Assuming China does not experience a revolution, civil war, or economic collapse, all of which are possible, experts expect it to surpass Japan in the next few years and to have the world's largest economy by 2035 or 2040, eclipsing the United States. As occurred in the industrializing West earlier, rapid Chinese development, including the growing use of polluting fossil fuels, has also led to environmental degradation, including dangerous air pollution. People in nations once poor but becoming developed, such as China, India, and Brazil, do not believe that the industrialized Western peoples have any more right to consume the world's resources than they do, and they want their fair share.

Resolving problems of underdevelopment, and the poverty it brings, requires change within individual countries, such as implementing land reform, curbing corruption, and reducing bureaucratic obstacles to enterprise. Many experts have advocated "bottom up" development that involves peasants, workers, and women, rather than bureaucratic elites, in decision making. Such decisions would include shaping policies that provide families with adequate economic security, hence reducing the desire among parents for many children to ensure their support in old age. The Grameen Bank in Bangladesh, which loans money to poor women, is an outstanding example of such a "bottom up" policy. The visionary Tanzanian leader Julius Nyerere argued that people cannot be developed by outsiders but must develop themselves, using their own efforts and visions to improve their lives. Self-development, however, requires more social and economic equality within societies so that the wealth can be shared more equitably.

International cooperation is hobbled because the leaders of rich and poor nations often disagree on how to address global inequality. For economic and strategic reasons, Western nations want to protect their access to and heavy consumption of resources such as oil and copper and also worry about trade competition from NICs. In democratic nations these leaders have had to answer to voters, who fear compromising their own prosperity. Beginning in the 1970s various conferences and movements have debated modifying the world economic order by, for example, stabilizing world prices for natural resource exports, which chiefly come from developing nations, so that governments could better anticipate annual revenues. Responding to a worldwide campaign to help poor nations, in 2005 the industrialized nations canceled the burdensome debts of the poorest nations. Yet critics wondered whether poor nations with corrupt, often dictatorial, governments would use increased revenues or aid wisely. Furthermore, several Western nations, including the United States, Britain, and France, have often opposed efforts to build a new economic order because such an order could threaten their powerful position in the world economy and transfer wealth to poor nations. Yet, the world demand for food, water, and energy may increase between 30 and 50 percent by 2030.

Sustainable Environments

The decades since the mid-twentieth century were unusual for the intensity of environmental deterioration and the centrality of human effort in sparking it. The industrialized nations especially had become used to rapid economic growth and were dependent on abundant cheap energy and fresh water, needs that led to environmental destruction on an unparalleled scale. By the dawn of the twenty-first century the challenge of a changing environment became obvious. On every continent, but especially in Eurasia and North America, gas-guzzling vehicles, smoky factories, coal-fired power plants, and large farming operations produce large amounts of carbon dioxide and other pollutants, contributing to rising average temperatures that scientists call global warming. This climate change, if it continues, may have a greater impact—possibly catastrophic—on human life than any conventional war or other destructive human activities. Problems such as global warming raise the question of whether in the long term the natural environment can maintain itself and support plant, animal, and human life—a pattern known as sustainability.

Societies and Environmental Change

Experts have wondered whether the world's resources—minerals, wild plants, food crops, fresh water—could sustain present living standards on a long-term basis. For the past several decades scientists have been alarmed at the human consumption of natural resources faster than nature can replenish them. A major scientific study in the 1990s concluded that a devastating environmental crash would occur during the twenty-first century as resources become exhausted, forests disappear, plant and animal species die off, a warming climate makes certain regions uninhabitable, and pollution increases.

Human activity has altered environments since prehistory, sometimes with catastrophic results. Environmental collapse triggered by agricultural practices or deforestation helped undermine the Mesopotamians, Romans, and Maya, among others. But modern industrial societies and rapidly growing populations encroach on their natural settings even more heavily than did earlier societies. In the twentieth century people used more energy than had been used in all previous history. Between the 1890s and the 1990s the world economy grew fourteen times larger, industrial output twenty times, energy use fourteen times, carbon dioxide emissions seventeen times, water use nine times, and marine fish catches thirty-five times. These increases contributed to, among other pressing problems, air and water pollution, disposal of hazardous waste, declining genetic diversity in crops, and a mass extinction of plant and animal species. With their heavy economic production and consumption, people today are borrowing from tomorrow.

The atmosphere faces particular dangers, including a measurable warming. Earth's climate changed little, with only minor fluctuations, between the last Ice Age, which ended 10,000 years ago, and the end of the eighteenth century, when the Industrial Revolution began in Europe, but it has been changing fast over the past two centuries. The global temperature rose by one degree during the twentieth century. Since 1985, the world has experienced the highest average annual temperatures on record and unprecedented droughts. Scientists now largely agree that global warming has been increasing, although they debate its causes and dangers. Without major efforts to curb warming, scientists forecast a rise of somewhere between an alarming 2.5 and a catastrophic 10.4 degrees by 2100, which, if it happens, will change human life

Protesting Global Warming People in societies around the world became alarmed at the increasing environmental damage brought by modern economic activity and exploitation of resources. This demonstration by environmental activists concerned with global warming, a potentially dangerous trend caused by burning fossil fuels such as coal that produces more carbon dioxide, took place in Turkey.

AP/Wide World Photos

dramatically. Referring to the enclosed buildings where warm-weather plants are raised in cold climates, scientists speak of a Greenhouse Effect, the overheating of earth from human-made pollutants. The main culprits are gases such as carbon dioxide, chlorofluorocarbons, and methane that accumulate in the atmosphere and trap heat. The amount of heat-trapping carbon dioxide in the atmosphere increased by a third between 1900 and 2000, mostly from burning coal and oil. The greenhouse gases come largely from factory smokestacks, coal-fired power plants, and gasoline-powered vehicle exhausts. The most industrialized nation, the United States, has become the major producer, accounting for some 25 percent of the carbon dioxide and up to 50 percent of the other polluting chemicals. Europe, Russia, Japan, and China produce much of the rest. Some pollutants also destroy the ozone layer, a gaseous region in the upper atmosphere that protects humans from the cancer-causing ultraviolet rays of the sun. Scientists discovered that the ozone depletion rate in the 1990s was twice as fast as was thought a decade earlier.

In the pessimistic scenarios, the consequences of rising temperatures for many of the world's peoples are devastating. Earth gets baked, rich farmland turns to desert, and forests wilt. Fresh water, already scarce, becomes even harder to find as lakes and streams dry up. Rising ocean temperatures damage fisheries and kill most protective coral reefs while also increasing the intensity of hurricanes, making them more often like the catastrophic storm that devastated New Orleans and the U.S. Gulf Coast in 2005. Tropical and subtropical nations find agriculture and life generally more difficult. In North America farming becomes tougher in the southern United States, though more productive in a warming Canada. As the ice on Greenland melts, pouring fresh water into the North Atlantic, the warming Gulf Stream may shift southward and bring harsher winters to Europe and eastern North America.

Some peoples might face even more daunting challenges. Global warming has reduced the ice covering the Arctic Ocean by half in recent years while thawing the adjacent land; these developments diminish the habitat for cold-adapted animals, such as polar bears, and threaten the livelihood and settlements of Arctic peoples. At the other end of the world, the West Antarctic ice shelf holds a vast amount of water and in some places has already begun to melt. If this trend accelerates, it will raise sea levels enough over the next two centuries to cover much low-lying coastal land. This will have disastrous consequences for regions such as the U.S. Gulf Coast and Florida, the Low Countries of northwest Europe, Bangladesh and eastern India, the Southeast Asian river deltas, and small island nations already now barely above sea level, including Tonga, Tuvalu, the Bahamas, and the Maldives.

Environmental Issues and Movements

The environmental challenges, such as diminishing resources, global warming, and deforestation, reinforce the scientific concept, first popularized in the 1970s, of global ecology—of the world, including human societies, as a complex web in which all living things interact with each other and their surroundings. From earliest times, societies have had complex relations with the environment, including interdependence with it. The Industrial Revolution, which has reshaped the world over the past two centuries, often for the better, came at great costs to the environment. Yet the world's leaders cannot agree on ways to better balance economic growth, which all nations desire, with environmental protection.

The exploitation of the earth's resources for human benefit, which has accelerated since 1945, has undermined sustainability. While soil, forests, and fisheries are renewable resources if properly managed, which they often were not in the past century, mineral resources such as oil and copper cannot be replaced once used up. Oil experts disagree as to when all known recoverable oil reserves will become exhausted. Optimists think oil supplies will be adequate through much of this century, and perhaps longer, before becoming scarce. Pessimists, noting the increased demand by countries such as China and India, believe all easily exploitable sources will be gone within two or three decades, causing conflict as nations scramble for oil supplies. Anticipating future resource and energy shortages, experts have for years recommended that industrial nations conserve oil by reducing dependence on it as the main fuel while developing renewable energy resources, such as solar, tidal, and wind power. Some nations have turned toward building more nuclear power plants, which are expensive and potentially dangerous but do less damage to the climate than burning fossil fuels. So far a few developing nations and some European countries have shown the most commitment to conservation and developing renewable energies.

Scientific conclusions about global warming and the need to reduce dependence on oil have often challenged powerful economic interests and upset governments that favor economic growth and worry about economic competition from rival nations. For example, since the 1970s U.S. presidents and Congress, fearing possible negative effects on U.S. business, have often opposed environmental agreements, such as the Kyoto Treaty of 1997, which was an effort, supported by most of the world's nations, to begin reducing greenhouse gases, as well as a European proposal seeking a 15 percent alternative energy use by 2010 (versus 1 percent today). Leaders of a few other powerful nations, including Japan, Russia, Britain, and China, have also been reluctant to cooperate with the world community on environmental issues. In 2005, 150 nations met in Montreal, Canada, and reaffirmed their commitment to the Kyoto treaty. Another international conference, scheduled for 2009 in Denmark, will determine whether heavy contributors to global warming will make binding commitments and cooperate on a common program. To sustain environmental health, a Canadian statesman has argued, requires a "revolution in [our] thinking as basic as the one introduced by Copernicus who [in the 1500s] first pointed out that the earth was not the center of the universe."[9]

An environmental movement began in the West in the late nineteenth century, eventually sparking similar movements around the world. Yet environmental awareness grew slowly. In the 1940s, the American environmentalist Aldo Leopold called for an ethic that treats the land with respect because all life belongs to a community of interdependent relationships: "Land is a fountain of energy flowing through a circuit of soils, plants, and animals, a sustained circuit, like a slowly augmented revolving fund of life."[10] Such ideas did not gain a large following. By the 1970s, however, views had changed; organizations such as Greenpeace, Earth First!, and the Rainforest Action Network pressed for a global commitment to stop environmental destruction. In 1992 a United Nations–sponsored global conference in Rio de Janeiro issued a proclamation urging sustainable development: "Human beings are entitled to a healthy and productive life in harmony with nature."[11] But the realities of modern politics, national rivalries, and fierce economic competition continue to make such a change difficult.

Global Pasts and Futures

The study of history helps us understand today's news and views as they are reported in daily newspapers, broadcast on radio and television, and disseminated on the World Wide Web. Historians often describe their work as involving a dialogue between past, present, and future. A few years ago French scientist René Dubos argued: "The past is not dead history. It is living material out of which makes the present and builds the future."[12] Current global problems have their roots in the patterns of world history: the rise of cities, states, and organized religions; the expansion of trade and capitalism to global dimensions; the unprecedented mastery and altering of nature represented by the scientific, industrial, and technological revolutions; the proliferation of competitive, unequal nations; and the myriad of social, economic, political, and cultural connections between peoples encompassed in the expanding global system. While seeking to understand how the past shaped the present, historians also speculate on how current trends may shape the future.

Understanding the Global Past

World historians offer several ways of understanding the world of yesterday, today, and tomorrow. One view is that contacts and collisions between different societies produce change. Whether through peaceful exchange or warfare or perhaps both, when societies encounter other societies they are exposed to different customs and ideas. For millennia after the transition to agriculture most of those contacts were with nearby peoples, but around two thousand years ago, thanks to advances in transportation and growing economies, increasingly mobile peoples began to encounter others much farther away, laying the roots for a global system to emerge after 1450. Historians also emphasize continuity, the persistence of social, cultural, political, and religious ideas and patterns, as well as change, the transformations in ways of life, work, and thought. Continuities are common. For example, many Christians, Muslims, Jews, Buddhists, and Hindus still look at the world through the prism of traditional religious values forged millennia ago and still meaningful today. Hence, in 2004 over 400,000 Christian missionaries—many from countries like Nigeria, the Philippines, and South Korea—were spreading the gospel around the world, at an annual cost of some $11 billion. Islam increased its following from 400 million people in 1960 to 1.3 billion by 2004. Yet changes, too, are everywhere. Thus most people, among them the devout followers of the old religions, also engage in activities, face challenges, and use forms of transportation and communication nonexistent a few generations ago. As a result, missionaries and clerics often use radio, television, and the Internet to spread their message. Another insight offered by global historians is that great transitions, such as the agricultural and industrial revolutions or, more recently, the rise of high technology, can turn history in new directions. Hence, thousands of years ago farming largely displaced hunting and gathering, two centuries ago industry transformed the world economy, and today instant communication and information bring distant peoples closer together. For instance, youngsters in Wisconsin can watch Australian-rules football matches from Melbourne on cable television while fans of Chinese rock and rap groups can hear their music on websites accessible from around the world.

As an example of the contacts and collisions that foster change, some scholars explain the changes of the past five hundred years in terms of the larger world's exposure and accommodation to the West, which led in turn to the political, economic, and military triumph of the West and often the adoption of its values and institutions. As a result of the spread of Western cultural influences, market economies, economic consumption practices, and individualistic values, they see a growing standardization of the world's societies. Many people welcome this standardization as a sign of progress, while others perceive it as a threat to local traditions. Still others consider the claim that societies and cultures are standardizing inaccurate, seeing instead a real increase in differences, especially the growing gap between rich and poor nations. In fact, living standards in the world have not been standardized. While people in the rich countries usually own several expensive electrical appliances, from washing machines to plasma televisions, millions of people in the poor nations do not even have electricity. Still, thanks to contacts between distant societies, the Western value of materialistic indulgence has become common, even if often out of reach for the poorest half of the world's people.

The experiences of most societies over the past half century reveal a mix of change and continuity. For example, Western ideas have gained even greater influence in the world since 1945 than they had before. People in different lands have adopted Western ideas of government, such as constitutions and elections, although not necessarily the substance of democracy, along with Western-rooted ideologies and faiths: capitalism, socialism, nationalism, and Christianity. Western pop culture, from rock music to soft drinks and blue jeans, has spread widely, leading to the "Coca-Colazation" of the world stemming from Western economic power, including advertising. Yet influences from the West are usually strongest in large cities and penetrate less deeply into the villages in Africa, Asia, and the Middle East, where traditional ways reflect continuity with the past. As a result, city youth in Malaysia or Tanzania may follow the latest recordings from Western pop stars, but these recordings may be unknown to their rural counterparts. Yet the urban youth may also share with rural youth traditional views about family and faith, and rural youth may, like their city counterparts, own motorcycles, boom boxes, and cell phones that make their lives different from those of their parents.

As a result of the transition to globalizing technology, culture, and commerce, the contacts between societies and their interdependence have vastly increased since 1945. In different ways nuclear weapons, multinational corporations, earth-circling satellites, World Cup soccer, and cable news networks draw people together, willingly or not. Imperialists once claimed proudly that "the sun never set on the British Empire." By the 1990s observers noted that "the sun never sets on McDonald's." Closer contact, of course, does not necessarily mean friendly relations and a less dangerous world; it can also bring collisions. Guided missiles and planes carrying bombs can reach 10,000 miles from their base. Over the past several decades over 60,000 Americans have died fighting in Vietnam, Afghanistan, and Iraq in support of U.S. efforts to reshape distant nations. On the other side, terrorist plots hatched in Afghanistan by Islamic militants who blame the United States for Middle Eastern problems killed Americans in New York City and Washington, D.C., in 2001. Some of the terrorists involved in planning or carrying out those and other attacks were once secular Muslims who went to Europe or the United States for college and, culturally disoriented and resentful of Western policies, became Islamic militants and then joined a terrorist organization with global reach and access to high technology such as satellite phones, computers, and the Internet. Experts also speak of cyberspace terrorism, in which political or religious extremists advertise their violent goals and deeds on websites. The same technologies that allow people to instantly access and share information around the world also allow governments to spy on citizens and criminals to use cyberspace for their own purposes. Meanwhile, hackers can live anywhere and disrupt computer operations all over the world. Technology also threatens governments. In 2005 the search engine company, Google, made available a program, Google Earth, that can be freely downloaded and allows a user anywhere to see aerial and satellite photos of any location in the world. Governments from Algeria to India to Russia protested unsuccessfully that this violated their laws and revealed data, such as the layout of military bases, that they did not want available to the general public.

The contacts, changes, and transitions since 1945 have created a global village, a single community of exchange and interaction. In some regions, such as Southeast Asia, even remote villages have become part of this global village. By the 1960s, for example, people living in the once-isolated interior of the island of Borneo, divided between Indonesia and Malaysia, could access the outside world through battery-powered transistor radios and cassette players, and also by means of visiting traders, Christian missionaries, and government officials. Borneo's interior people also often left their remote villages to find work at logging camps, oil wells, or plantations as their rain forest environment and small farms rapidly disappeared, destroyed by international timber and mining operations that cut forests and stripped land to procure resources to ship to distant countries. As once-remote peoples, like those in the Borneo interior, are brought into the global system, and ethnic minorities are incorporated into nations, they find it harder to maintain their cultures and languages. Half of all languages are in danger of dying out over the next several decades, and less than 1 percent of languages are used on the Internet.

Toward the Future

Women and men created the present world from the materials of the past and are now laying the foundation for the future. As a Belgian scholar wrote a few years ago, "We cannot predict the future, but we can prepare it."[13] But this raises the question of what kind of future. In 1974 the American economic historian Robert Heilbroner, asking what promise the future holds, doubted the permanence of modern industrial society and even democracy in the face of population explosion, environmental degradation, resource depletion, militarization, and the increasing economic desperation of people in the poorest countries. His question remains highly relevant in the early twenty-first century. For example, as industrialization spreads to other nations, the world requires more use of fossil fuels, which spurs more global warming. Heilbroner drew a gloomy picture of the future. He believed most people are not willing to sacrifice for the good of future generations. Like him, other experts often despair. The world's long history of war, inequality, and exploitation, even when seemingly offset by progress, does not foster optimism. Indeed, some respected experts predict human extinction if people do not adopt more sustainable ways, and scientific studies are more frequently pessimistic than optimistic about the future. Worried that we face environment collapse, one study concludes: "Our generation is the first to be faced with decisions that will determine whether the earth our children inherit will be habitable."[14]

Yet, since World War II humanity has produced many green shoots of hope. Western Europe moved rapidly to political and economic unity, defusing centuries of conflict. Eastern Europeans and Russians overturned dogmatic communist regimes, ending the long Cold War between the superpowers. The Scandinavian nations, a hundred years ago among the poorest European societies, have virtually eliminated poverty, achieving the world's highest quality of life. Several Asian nations rapidly developed, dramatically improving living standards and national wealth. A century ago desperately poor, China has become not only able to feed and clothe its huge population but also to export industrial products to the world. Thanks in part to global efforts, black majority rule came to South Africa. Over two dozen nations, including some in Asia, Latin America, and the Caribbean, have elected women presidents or prime ministers, and women, making their voices heard, have increasingly gained more power over their lives in many countries. Despite some notable conflicts, wars have become less common than before. Unlike the Cold War years between 1946 and 1992, when fighting between and within nations was frequent, between 1992 and 2005 the number of wars with over 1,000 battle deaths a year declined by 80 percent.

Hopeful developments have also resulted from international cooperation. A large majority of nations have signed agreements to ban weapons of mass destruction, punish genocide, and reduce gases contributing to global warming. Drastic reductions in the arms race have diminished the threat of nuclear war. United Nations agencies have improved lives for children and women in many countries and spurred cooperation on environmental issues. Local nongovernmental organizations, often with international connections, have also become active, working for the rights of women, children, workers, and peasants and for a healthier environment. Human rights groups with chapters around the world have worked courageously to promote civil liberties and the release of political prisoners. Encouraged by environmental activists abroad, brave tribal groups in tropical rain forests have resisted the logging and mining destroying their habitats. Not least in its effects, the growing information superhighway now instantly links millions of office or home computers with people, libraries, and other information sources around the world.

A history not only of cruelty and exploitation but also of compassion and sacrifice provides hope in navigating troubled times. Remembering when people behaved magnificently may foster inspiration to answer the challenges. The contemporary age offers ample examples of inspiring people: democracy activists such as Nelson Mandela, Vaclav Havel, Mohandas Gandhi, and Aung San Suu Kyi; social activists such as Wangari Maathai, Dr. Martin Luther King, Jr., Shirin Ebadi, and Mukhtaran Bibi; cultural figures such as Wole Soyinka, Violeta Parra, Simone de Beauvoir, and Cui Jian; and figures who have built links between societies such as Jean Monnet, Bono, and the Dalai Lama. Historians sometimes view the past as a stream with banks. The stream is filled with people killing, bullying, enslaving, and doing other things historians usually record, while on the banks, unnoticed, women and men build homes,

International Women's Day 2005 Women around the world became more willing to assert their rights. Activists from diverse Indian nongovernmental organizations interested in women's rights marched in New Delhi, India's capital, in 2005 to mark International Women's Day.

raise children, tend farms, settle disputes, sing songs, whittle statues, trade with their neighbors, and chat with travelers from other lands. Historians often ignore the banks for the stream, but what happens on the banks may be more reassuring.

Some observers, believing that cultural differences will increasingly drive international politics, forecast a clash of civilizations, such as between the Christian West and Islam, which are seen as irreconcilably opposed in world-views. But simplistic formulas miss the complexity of the global order. None of the great religions and the cultures that they shaped are monolithic, the divisions among Christians or Muslims, Westerners or Middle Easterners, being as great as their differences with other traditions. No cultures or religions have a monopoly on values such as peace, justice, charity, tolerance, public discussion, and goodwill. In any case, nations generally shape their foreign policies according to their national interests rather than ideology. Wars over resources, such as oil and water, some observers claim, are more likely to occur than wars over cultural differences. Other observers doubt that, whatever the tensions, any titanic military struggle like the two world wars of the twentieth century is inevitable; they expect that the world will cooperate on major issues and tolerate different concepts of economics, government, God, morality, and society for years to come. Furthermore, thanks to the many available information sources, people can become informed about why past societies, such as the Mesopotamians and Maya, destroyed their environments and collapsed, and how countries blundered into wars or failed to develop cooperative relations with their neighbors that maintained peace. These insights, if acquired, may help people today to avoid repeating the mistakes of the past and construct a better future.

Four centuries ago, the English playwright William Shakespeare wrote that the past is prologue to the present. The study of world history allows us to ask questions about the global future because we understand the changing patterns of the global past, including the building of societies, their interactions through networks, and the great transitions that reshaped humanity. These have led to an increasingly connected world in the past 1,500 years. The contemporary age has been marked by a complex mix of dividing and unifying forces, unique societies differing greatly in standards of living but linked into a global system of exchange. People today cannot yet know with certainty where the path will lead, but they can help build it. Nineteenth-century British novelist Lewis Carroll (1832–1898) suggested a way of looking at the problem in his novel *Through the Looking Glass*, about Alice in Wonderland. Lost and perplexed in Wonderland, Alice asked the Cheshire Cat: "Would you tell me, please, which way I ought to go from here?" The enigmatic cat pondered the query for a few moments and then replied: "That depends a great deal on where you want to get to."[15] Societies, working together, must chart that course into the future.

Suggested Reading

Books

Baylis, John, et al., eds. *The Globalization of World Politics: An Introduction to International Relations,* 4th ed. New York: Oxford University Press, 2008. Essays on world politics by British scholars.

Brown, Lester. *Plan B 2.0: Rescuing a Planet Under Stress and a Civilization in Trouble,* 3rd ed. New York: W.W. Norton, 2008. A survey of the world's environmental and resource challenges and some possible solutions.

Eriksen, Thomas Hylland. *Globalization: The Key Concepts.* New York: Berg, 2007. A Norwegian scholar's provocative introduction to the debates.

Hannerz, Ulf. *Transnational Connections: Culture, People, Places.* New York: Routledge, 1996. Interesting essays on cultures and networks in the age of globalization by a Swedish scholar.

Held, David, ed. *A Globalizing World? Culture, Economics, Politics,* 2nd ed. New York: Routledge, 2004. An excellent collection of essays and readings on various aspects of globalization, compiled by British scholars.

Hobsbawm, Eric. *On the Edge of the New Century.* New York: The New Press, 1999. Thoughts on the past, present, and future by a British historian.

Kennedy, Paul. *Preparing for the Twenty-First Century.* New York: Random House, 1994. A study of how population, technology, and the environment shaped the contemporary world and various regions.

Mayor, Federico, and Jerome Bindé. *The World Ahead: Our Future in the Making.* New York: Zed Books, 2001. A comprehensive study, prepared by European scholars for the United Nations, of political, economic, social, cultural, and environmental trends.

Mazrui, Ali. *Cultural Forces in World Politics.* London: Heinemann, 1990. A challenging examination of world-views and patterns by a distinguished African scholar.

Newland, Kathleen, and Kamala Chandrakirana Soedjatmoko, eds. *Transforming Humanity: The Visionary Writings of Soedjatmoko.* West Hartford, CT: Kumarian Press, 1994. Thoughtful essays on development, violence, religion, and other issues in the contemporary world by an influential Indonesian thinker.

Pieterse, Jan Nederveen, ed. *Global Futures: Shaping Globalization.* London: Zed Books, 2000. Provocative essays on world trends by scholars from around the world.

Pieterse, Jan Nederveen. *Globalization and Culture: Global Melange,* 2nd ed. Armonk, NY: Rowman and Littlefield, 2009. A study of cultural hybridization.

Sachs, Jeffrey. *The End of Poverty: Economic Possibilities for Our Time.* New York: Penguin, 2005. A controversial but stimulating discussion of global poverty issues.

Seager, Joni. *The Penguin Atlas of Women in the World,* 4th ed. New York: Penguin, 2008. A creative, indispensable examination of women around the world.

Sen, Amartya. *Identity and Violence: The Illusion of Destiny.* New York: W.W. Norton, 2006. A provocative critique by an India-born economist of the clash-of-civilizations idea.

Smith, Dan, and Ane Braein. *Penguin State of the World Atlas,* 8th ed. New York: Penguin, 2008. The latest edition of an invaluable map-based reference providing an overview of world conditions.

Worldwatch Institute. *State of the World.* New York: W.W. Norton. Informative annual surveys of the world's environmental health that are published annually by the Worldwatch Institute in Washington, D.C.

Taylor, Timothy D. *Global Pop: World Music, World Markets.* New York: Routledge, 1997. A fine study of the world music industry and major musicians.

WEBSITES

Global Problems and the Culture of Capitalism (***http://faculty.plattsburgh.edu/richard.robbins/legacy/***). An outstanding site, aimed at undergraduates, with a wealth of resources on many topics.

Globalization Guide (***http://www.globalisationguide.org***). A useful collection of essays and links.

The Globalization Website (***http://www.sociology.emory.edu/globalization/***). A very useful site with many resources and essays related to globalization.

United Nations (***http://www.un.org***). The pathway to the websites of the many United Nations agencies, operations, and ongoing projects.

The WWW Virtual Library (***http://vlib.org/***). The homepage of a vast and indispensable British-based network of links on many topics and issues.

Notes

Chapter 1 The Origins of Human Societies, to ca. 2000 B.C.E.

1. Brian Swimme and Thomas Berry, *The Universe Story* (San Francisco: Harper, 1992), 2.
2. From the *Rig Veda*, quoted in Carolyn Brown Heinz, *Asian Cultural Traditions* (Prospect Heights, IL: Waveland, 1999), 132.
3. Genesis 3:17–19, *The Holy Bible*, New King James Version (Chicago: Thomas Nelson, 1983), 3.
4. From Plato's *Critias*, quoted in L. S. Stavrianos, *Lifelines from Our Past: A New World History*, rev. ed. (Armonk, NY: M.E. Sharpe, 1997), 65.
5. Genesis 1:28, *Holy Bible*, 2.

Chapter 2 Ancient Societies in Mesopotamia, India, and Central Asia, 5000–600 B.C.E.

1. The quote is from the Oriental Institute, the University of Chicago.
2. The quote is from the Oriental Institute, the University of Chicago.
3. Quoted in Frederick Gentels and Melvin Steinfield, *Hangups from Way Back: Historical Myths and Canons*, vol. 1, 2nd ed. (San Francisco: Canfield, 1974), 64.
4. The quotes are from William H. Stiebing, Jr., *Ancient Near Eastern History and Culture* (New York: Longman, 2003), 48.
5. The quotes are from Brian Fagan, *The Long Summer: How Climate Changed Civilization* (New York: Basic Books, 2004), 138.
6. Quoted in Michael Wood, *Legacy: The Search for Ancient Cultures* (New York: Sterling, 1994), 34.
7. Quoted in G. R. Driver and John C. Miles, eds., *The Babylonian Laws*, vol. II (Oxford: Clarendon Press, 1952), 7.
8. Quoted in N. B. Jankowska, "Asshur, Mitanni, and Arrapkhe," in *Early Antiquity*, ed. I. M. Diakonoff (Chicago: University of Chicago Press, 1991), 256.
9. Samuel Noah Kramer, *The Cradle of Civilization* (New York: Time-Life Books, 1967), 75.
10. Quoted in Wood, *Legacy*, 32.
11. *The Epic of Gilgamesh*, trans. by N. K. Sandars (New York: Penguin Books, 1960), 108.
12. Quoted in John Keay, *India: A History* (New York: Atlantic Monthly Press, 2000), 35.
13. Quoted in Hermann Kulke and Dietmar Rothermund, *History of India*, 3rd ed. (New York: Routledge, 1998), 35.
14. William McNaughton, ed., *Light from the East* (New York: Laurel, 1978), 398.
15. Quoted in Burton Stein, *A History of India* (Malden, MA: Blackwell, 1998), 53.
16. Quoted in A. L. Basham, *The Wonder That Was India* (New York: Grove Press, 1959), 241.
17. Quoted in Romila Thapar, *Early India from the Origins to AD 1300* (Berkeley: University of California Press, 2002), 116.

Chapter 3 Ancient Societies in Africa and the Mediterranean, 5000–600 B.C.E.

1. Quoted in Lionel Casson, *Ancient Egypt* (New York: Time Incorporated, 1965), 120.
2. Quoted in David Phillipson, *African Archaeology*, 2nd ed. (Cambridge: Cambridge University Press, 1993), 152.
3. Quoted in *Egypt: Land of the Pharaohs* (Alexandria, Va.: Time-Life Books, 1992), p. 142.
4. Quoted in Casson, *Ancient Egypt*, p. 95.
5. Quoted in Carl Roebuck, *The World of Ancient Times* (New York: Charles Scribner's Sons, 1966), p. 72.
6. Quoted in Egypt: Land of Pharaohs, p. 89.
7. Quoted in Felipe Fernandez-Armesto, *Civilizations: Culture, Ambition, and the Transformation of Nature* (New York: Simon and Schuster, 2001), p. 195.
8. Quoted in Brian M. Fagan, *People of the Earth: An Introduction to World Prehistory*, 9th ed. (New York: Longmans, 1998), p. 407.
9. Quoted in Ezra Pound and Noel Stock, *Love Poems of Ancient Egypt* (Norfolk, Conn.: New Directions, 1962).
10. Quoted in Barbara Mertz, *Red Land, Black Land: Daily Life in Ancient Egypt*, rev. ed. (New York: Dodd, Mead and Company, 1978), p. 56.
11. Quoted in *Africa's Glorious Legacy* (Alexandria, Va.: Time-Life Books, 1996), p. 18.
12. Nahum 3:7, 19, *The Holy Bible*, New King James Version (Chicago: Thomas Nelson, 1983), p. 908.
13.. Psalm 137:1, *Holy Bible*, p. 639.
14. Isaiah 45:21–22, *Holy Bible*, p. 721.
15. Isaiah 42:6–7, *Holy Bible*, p. 717.
16. Ezekiel 27:3–4, 9, *Holy Bible*, p. 835.

Chapter 4 Around the Pacific Rim: Eastern Eurasia and the Americas, 5000–600 B.C.E.

1. From the ancient Chinese *Book of Songs*, quoted in Herlee Glessner Creel, *The Birth of China: A Survey of the Formative Period of Chinese Civilization* (New York: Frederick Unger, 1937), 64.
2. Quoted in Michael Wood, *Legacy: The Search for Ancient Cultures* (New York: Sterling, 1994), p. 96.
3. *The Book of Songs*, translated by Arthur Waley (London: George Unwin, 1954), p. 162.
4. Quoted in Felipe Fernandez-Armesto, *Civilizations: Culture, Ambition, and the Transformation of Nature* (New York: Simon and Schuster, 2001), p. 214.
5. The quotes are in John Minford and Joseph S. M. Lau, eds., *Classical Chinese Literature: An Anthology of Translations*, vol. 1 (New York: Columbia University Press, 2000), pp. 16–17, 20.
6. Quoted in Creel, *Birth of China*, pp. 228–229.
7. Quoted in Benjamin I. Schwartz, *The World of Thought in Ancient China* (Cambridge: Harvard University Press, 1985), p. 39.
8. In Minford and Lau, *Classical Chinese Literature*, p. 150.
9. The two songs come from Waley, *Book of Songs*, pp. 68, 203.
10. Waley, *Book of Songs*, p. 205.
11. Quoted in Nguyen Ngoc Bich, "The Power and Relevance of Vietnamese Myths," in David P. Elliott et al., eds., *Vietnam: Essays on History, Culture and Society* (New York: Asia Society, 1985), p. 62.
12. Quoted in Brian M. Fagan, *Kingdoms of Gold, Kingdoms of Jade: The Americas Before Columbus* (New York: Thames and Hudson, 1991), p. 55.

Societies, Networks, Transitions: Ancient Foundations of World History, 4000–600 B.C.E.

1. From Homer's *The Odyssey*, quoted in Rodney Castledon, *Minoans: Life in Bronze Age Crete* (New York: Routledge, 1993), 111.
2. Quoted in Lewis Mumford, *The City in History: Its Origins, Its Transformations, and Its Prospects* (New York: Harcourt, Brace and World, 1961), 68.
3. Quoted in Lionel Casson, *The Ancient Mariners: Seafarers and Sea Fighters of the Mediterranean in Ancient Times*, 2nd ed. (Princeton: Princeton University Press, 1991), 9.
4. From the *Brahmanas*, quoted in F. R. Allchin, *The Archaeology of Historic South Asia: The Emergence of Cities and States* (New York: Cambridge University Press, 1995), 86–87.
5. Quoted in John Keegan, *A History of Warfare* (New York: Alfred A. Knopf, 1993), 143.
6. Quoted in Barbara Mertz, *Red Land, Black Land: Daily Life in Ancient Egypt*, rev. ed. (New York: Dodd Mead, and Company, 1978), 135–136.
7. *The Book of Songs*, translated by Arthur Waley (London: George Allen and Unwin, 1954), 121.
8. Nahum 3:2–3, *Holy Bible*, 907.

9. Isaiah 2:4, *Holy Bible*, 683.
10. Quoted in Merry E.Wiesner-Hanks, *Gender in History* (Malden, MA: Blackwell, 2001), 61.
11. From Homer's *The Odyssey*, quoted in Castledon, *Minoans*, 9.
12. Quoted in Stephen L. Sass, *The Substance of Civilization: Material and Human History from the Stone Age to the Age of Silicon* (New York: Arcade, 1998), 13.
13. Quoted in Herlee Glessner Creel, *The Birth of China: A Survey of the Formative Period of Chinese Civilization* (New York: Frederick Unger, 1961), 256.

Chapter 5 Classical Societies in Southern and Central Asia, 600 B.C.E.–600 C.E.

1. Quoted in Jeannine Auboyer, *Daily Life in Ancient India: From 200 BC to 700 AD* (London: Phoenix, 2002), 62.
2. Quoted in Lionel Casson, *The Ancient Mariners: Seafarers and Sea Fighters of the Mediterranean in Ancient Times*, 2nd ed. (Princeton: Princeton University Press, 1991), 202.
3. Quoted in Stanley Wolpert, *A New History of India*, 5th ed. (New York: Oxford University Press, 1997), 48.
4. From Swami Prabhavananda and Frederick Manchester, eds., *The Upanishads: Breath of the Eternal* (New York: Mentor, 1957), 62.
5. C. E. Gover, *The Folk-Songs of Southern India* (London: Trubner and Co., 1872), 165.
6. Quoted in Wolpert, *New History*, 54.
7. Quoted in Roy C. Amore and Julia Ching, "The Buddhist Tradition," in *World Religions: Eastern Traditions*, ed. Willard G. Oxtoby (New York: Oxford University Press, 1996), 230.
8. Quoted in Rhoads Murphy, *A History of Asia*, 4th ed. (New York: HarperCollins, 2003), 74.
9. Quoted in Lucille Schulberg, *Historic India* (New York: Time-Life Books, 1968), 80.
10. From William McNaughton, ed., *Light from the East* (New York: Laurel, 1978), 377.

Chapter 6 Eurasian Connections and New Traditions in East Asia, 600 B.C.E.–600 C.E.

1. *Records of the Historian: Chapters from the Shih Chi of Ssu-ma Ch'ien*, translated by Burton Watson (New York: Columbia University Press, 1969), 274.
2. Quoted in Arthur Cotterell and David Morgan, *China's Civilization: A Survey of Its History, Arts, and Technology* (New York: Praeger, 1975), 58.
3. Quoted in H. G. Creel, *Chinese Thought from Confucius to Mao Tse-Tung* (New York: Mentor, 1953), 32.
4. Quoted in Ch'u Chai and Winberg Chai, *Confucianism* (Woodbury, NY: Barron's, 1973), 45.
5. Quoted in Dun J. Li, ed., *The Essence of Chinese Civilization* (Princeton: D. Van Nostrand, 1967), 6.
6. The quotes are from Patricia Buckley Ebrey, ed., *Chinese Civilization: A Sourcebook*, 2nd ed., revised and expanded (New York: Free Press, 1993), 43–44.
7. The quotes are from Lionel Giles, *The Sayings of Lao Tzu* (New York: E.P. Dutton, 1908), 19, 22, 25.
8. Quoted in Creel, *Chinese Thought*, 85.
9. Quoted in Arthur Waley, *The Way and Its Power: A Study of the Tao Te Ching and Its Place in Chinese Thought* (New York: Grove Press, 1958), 210.
10. Quoted in William McNaughton, ed., *Light from the East: An Anthology of Asian Literature* (New York: Laurel, 1978), 132.
11. Sima Qian, quoted in Arthur Cotterell, *The First Emperor of China* (New York: Penguin, 1988), 106.
12. Quoted in Frances Wood, *The Silk Road: Two Thousand Years in the Heart of Asia* (Berkeley: University of California Press, 2002), 55.
13. From John Minford and Joseph S. M. Lau, eds., *Classical Chinese Literature: An Anthology of Translations*, vol. 1 (New York: Columbia University Press, 2000), 387.
14. Ebrey, *Chinese Civilization*, 61–62.
15. Quoted in ibid., 73.
16. Quoted in Robin R. Wang, ed., *Images of Women in Chinese Thought and Culture: Writings from the Pre-Qin Period Through the Song Dynasty* (Indianapolis: Hackett, 2003), 254.
17. Ibid.
18. Quoted in David John Lu, ed., *Sources of Japanese History*, vol. 1 (New York: McGraw-Hill, 1974), 21–22.

Chapter 7 Western Asia, the Eastern Mediterranean, and Regional Systems, 600–200 B.C.E.

1. Quoted in Norman Davies, *Europe: A History* (New York: Harper, 1996), 117.
2. Quoted in Lindsay Allen, *The Persian Empire* (Chicago: University of Chicago Press, 2005), 27.
3. Quoted in A. T. Olmstead, *History of the Persian Empire* (Chicago: University of Chicago Press, 1959), 125.
4. Quoted in William H. Stiebing, *Ancient Near Eastern History and Culture* (New York: Longman, 2003), 303.
5. From George Rawlinson, trans., *The Histories of Herodotus*, vol. 1 (London: Dent, 1910), 131–140.
6. From Loren J. Samons III, ed., *Athenian Democracy and Imperialism* (Boston: Houghton Mifflin, 1998), 216–217.
7. Quoted in Robert Flaceliere, *Daily Life in Greece at the Time of Pericles* (London: Phoenix, 2002), 56.
8. Quoted in Rex Warner, *The Greek Philosophers* (New York: New American Library, 1958), 24.
9. The quote is from Martyn Oliver, *History of Philosophy: Great Thinkers from 600 B.C. to the Present Day* (New York: MetroBooks, 1997), 16–17.
10. Quoted in Mortimer Chambers et al., *The Western Experience*, vol. 1, 5th ed. (New York: McGraw-Hill, 1987), 96.
11. Quoted in C. Warren Hollister, *Roots of the Western Tradition: A Short History of the Ancient World*, 5th ed. (McGraw-Hill, 1991), 109.
12. From Barbara Hughes Fowler, *Archaic Greek Poetry: An Anthology* (Madison: University of Wisconsin Press, 1992), 131.
13. Quoted in Robert Flaceliere, "Women, Marriage, and the Family," in *Everyman in Europe: Essays in Social History*, ed. Allan Mitchell and Istvan Deak, vol. 1 (Englewood Cliffs, NJ: Prentice-Hall, 1974), 53.
14. From *Medea*, quoted in Frank J. Frost, *Greek Society*, 2nd ed. (Lexington, MA: D.C. Heath, 1980), 94.
15. From Aristophanes, *Lysistrata and Other Plays*, trans. Alan H. Sommerstein (New York: Penguin, 1973), 200–208.
16. Reported by Thucydides, quoted in L. S. Stavrianos, ed., *The Epic of Man to 1500* (Englewood Cliffs, NJ: Prentice-Hall, 1970), 120–122.
17. Quoted in Michael Chauveau, *Egypt in the Age of Cleopatra: History and Society Under the Ptolemies* (Ithaca: Cornell University Press, 2000), 188.
18. Quoted in Francis Chanoux, *Hellenistic Civilization* (Malden, MA: Blackwell, 2003), 319.
19. "Diogenes," in *Biographical Encyclopedia of Philosophy* (Garden City, NY: Doubleday, 1965), 76.

Chapter 8 Empires, Networks, and the Remaking of Europe, North Africa, and Western Asia, 500 B.C.E.–600 C.E.

1. Quoted in Tim Cornell and John Matthews, *The Roman World* (Alexandria, VA: Stonehenge, 1991), 51.
2. Livy, quoted in Frederick Gentles and Melvin Steinfield, eds., *Hangups from Way Back: Historical Myths and Canons*, vol. 1, 2nd ed. (San Francisco: Canfield, 1974), 173.
3. Diodorus, quoted in Barry Cunliffe, *The Extraordinary Voyage of Pytheas the Greek* (New York: Penguin, 2002), 52.
4. Gentles and Steinfield, *Hangups from Way Back*, 167.
5. From Plutarch, *Life of Antony*, in *Readings in Ancient History*, ed. William S. Davis, vol. 2 (Boston: Allyn and Bacon, 1913), 163–164.
6. Quoted in Jerome Carcopino, *Daily Life in Ancient Rome*, 2nd ed. (New Haven, CT: Yale University Press, 1968), 202.
7. Quoted in Norman Davies, *Europe: A History* (New York: Harper, 1998), 193.

8. Diodorus Siculus, in Jo Ann Shelton, *As the Romans Did: A Sourcebook in Roman Social History* (New York: Oxford University Press, 1988), 175.
9. The quotes are from Henry C. Boren, *Roman Society: A Social, Economic and Cultural History,* 2nd ed. (Lexington, MA: D.C. Heath, 1992), 279, 219.
10. Quoted in Susan Whitfield, *Life Along the Silk Road* (Berkeley: University of California Press, 1999), 21.
11. Tacitus, *Agricola,* quoted in Moses Hadas, ed., *A History of Rome from Its Origins to 529 A.D. as Told by the Roman Historians* (Garden City, NY: Doubleday Anchor, 1956), 126–127.
12. Matthew 22: 37–39, in *The Holy Bible,* New King James Version (Chicago: Thomas Nelson, 1982), 957.
13. Quoted in Michael McCormick, *Origins of the European Economy: Communication and Commerce, A.D. 300–900* (New York: Cambridge University Press, 2001), 27.
14. From A. Atwater, trans., *Procopius: The Secret History* (Ann Arbor: University of Michigan Press, 1963), 8.
15. Quoted in Daniel Del Castillo, "A Long-Ignored Plague Gets Its Due," *Chronicle of Higher Education,* February 15, 2002, A22.
16. Quoted in Philip Sharrard, *Byzantium* (New York: Time-Life, 1966), 36.
17. Quoted in Patricia Crone, "The Rise of Islam in the World," in *The Cambridge Illustrated History of the Islamic World,* ed. Francis Robinson (New York: Cambridge University Press, 1966), 4–5.

Chapter 9 Classical Societies and Regional Networks in Africa, the Americas, and Oceania, 600 B.C.E.–600 C.E.

1. From *The Horizon History of Africa* (New York: American Heritage, 1971), 207.
2. Ibn Battuta, quoted in Robert W. July, *Precolonial Africa: An Economic and Social History* (New York: Charles Scribner's, 1975), p. 183.
3. Quoted in Stanley Burstein, ed., *Ancient African Civilizations: Kush and Axum* (Princeton, N.J.: Markus Wiener, 1998), p. 41.
4. Quoted in Derek A. Welsby, *The Kingdom of Kush: The Napatan and Meroitic Empires* (Princeton: Markus Wiener, 1996), p. 40.
5. From *Horizon History,* p. 78.
6. Quoted in Basil Davidson, *African Kingdoms* (New York: Time-Life, 1966), p. 42.
7. Quoted in Graham Connah, *African Civilization. Precolonial Cities and States in Tropical Africa: An Archaeological Perspective* (Cambridge: Cambridge University Press, 1987), p. 78.
8. Quoted in Robert W. July, *A History of the African People,* 5th ed. (Prospect Heights, Ill.: Waveland, 1998), p. 45.
9. Rufinus, quoted in Burstein, *Ancient African Civilizations,* p. 95.
10. Quoted in Christopher Ehret, *An African Classical Age: Eastern and Southern Africa in World History, 1000 B.C. to A.D. 400* (Charlottesville: University of Virginia Press, 1998), p. 275.
11. From the Popul Vuh, quoted in Brian M. Fagan, *Kingdoms of Gold, Kingdoms of Jade: The Americas Before Columbus* (London and New York: Thames and Hudson, 1991), p. 94.
12. Father Bernardino de Sahagun, quoted in Richard E. W. Adams, *Prehistoric Mesoamerica* (Boston: Little, Brown, 1977), p. 110.
13. Frey Diego de Landa, quoted in T. Patrick Culbert, *Maya Civilization* (Washington, D.C.: Smithsonian, 1993), p. 23.
14. Quoted in Michael Wood, *Legacy: The Search for Ancient Cultures* (New York: Sterling, 1994), p. 166.
15. Frey Diego de Landa, quoted in Culbert, *Maya Civilization,* p. 22.
16. Fra Bernardino de Sahagun, quoted in Juan Schobinger, *The First Americans* (Grand Rapids, Mich.: William B. Eerdmans, 1994), p. 97.
17. Cieza de Leon, quoted in Fagan, *Kingdoms of Gold,* p. 192.
18. Quoted in Brian Fagan, *The Long Summer: How Climate Changed Civilization* (New York: Basic Books, 2004), p. 213.
19. Quoted in Judy Thompson and Allan Taylor, *Polynesian Canoes and Navigation* (Laie, Hawaii: Institute of Polynesian Studies, 1980), p. 32.
20. Quoted in Peter Bellwood, *The Polynesians: Prehistory of an Island People,* revised ed. (London: Thames and Hudson, 1997), p. 7.
21. Quoted in Peter Bellwood, *Man's Conquest of the Pacific: The Prehistory of Southeast Asia and Oceania* (New York: Oxford University Press, 1979), p. 300.

Societies, Networks, Transitions: Classical Blossomings in World History, 600 B.C.E.–600 C.E.

1. Quoted in Michael Wood, *Legacy: The Search for Ancient Cultures* (New York: Sterling, 1994), 192.
2. Quoted in Patricia Buckley Ebrey, *The Cambridge Illustrated History of China* (New York: Cambridge University Press, 1996), 46.
3. The quotes are from Felipe Fernandez-Armesto, *Ideas That Changed the World* (New York: DK, 2003), 117, 119.
4. Quoted in Lindsay Allen, *The Persian Empire* (Chicago: University of Chicago Press, 2005), 43.
5. From Patricia Buckley Ebrey, ed., *Chinese Civilization: A Sourcebook,* 2nd ed., revised and expanded (New York: Free Press, 1993), 57–58.
6. Quoted in Romila Thapar, *Asoka and the Decline of the Mauryas* (Delhi: Oxford University Press, 1997), 147.
7. Quoted in Robert P. Clark, *The Global Imperative: An Interpretive History of the Spread of Humankind* (Boulder: Westview, 1997), 3.
8. Quoted in Richard C. Foltz, *Religions of the Silk Road: Overland Trade and Cultural Exchange from Antiquity to the Fifteenth Century* (New York: St. Martin's, 1999), 62.
9. Tertullian, quoted in Erik Gilbert and Jonathan T. Reynolds, *Africa in World History: From Prehistory to the Present* (Upper Saddle River, NJ: Prentice-Hall, 2004), 74.
10. Quoted in Kenneth R. Hall, *Maritime Trade and State Development in Early Southeast Asia* (Honolulu: University of Hawaii Press, 1985), 29.
11. Hou Han Shu, quoted in *Monks and Merchants: Silk Road Treasures from Northwest China* (http://www.asiasociety.org/arts/monksandmerchants/index.html).
12. Quoted in Frances Wood, *The Silk Road: Two Thousand Years in the Heart of Asia* (Berkeley: University of California Press, 2001), 66.
13. Quoted in Lionel Casson, *The Ancient Mariners: Seafarers and Sea Fighters of the Mediterranean in Ancient Times,* 2nd ed. (Princeton: Princeton University Press, 1991), 166.
14. From Basil Davidson, *African Civilization Revisited: From Antiquity to Modern Times* (Trenton, NJ: Africa World Press, 1991), 64.
15. Quoted in Louis Crompton, *Homosexuality and Civilization* (Cambridge: Harvard University Press, 2003), 218.
16. Quoted in Peter N. Stearns, *Gender in World History* (New York: Routledge, 2000), 28.

Chapter 10 The Rise, Power, and Connections of the Islamic World, 600–1500

1. From *The Muqaddimah: An Introduction to History,* translated by Franz Rosenthal and edited by N. J. Dawood (Princeton: Princeton University Press, 1967), 25–27.
2. Quoted in Albert Hourani, *A History of the Arab Peoples* (Cambridge: Belknap Press, 1991), 3.
3. Quoted in Jonathan Bloom and Sheila Blair, *Islam: A Thousand Years of Faith and Power* (New Haven, CT: Yale University Press, 2002), 29.
4. Quoted in Wiebke Walther, *Women in Islam* (Princeton: Markus Wiener, 1993), 104.
5. Quoted in Karen Armstrong, *Muhammad: A Biography of the Prophet* (San Francisco: HarperSan Francisco, 1992), 160.
6. Quoted in Arthur Goldschmidt, Jr., *A Concise History of the Middle East,* 4th ed. revised (Boulder: Westview, 1991), p. 37.
7. Quoted in Francis Robinson, *The Cultural Atlas of the Islamic World Since 1500* (Oxford: Stonehenge, 1992), p. 180.
8. Quoted in Henry Bucher, *Middle East* (Guilford, Conn.: Dushkin, 1984), p. 19.
9. Quoted in Manuel Komroff, ed., *Contemporaries of Marco Polo* (New York: Horace Liveright, 1928), pp. 286–292.
10. Quoted in Alfred Guillaume, "Islamic Mysticism and the Sufi Sect," in Swisher, ed., *Spread,* p. 153.

11. "Baba Kuhi of Shiraz," translated by Reynold A. Nicholson. Quoted in Mary Ann Frese Witt et al., *The Humanities: Cultural Roots and Continuities*, vol. 1, 7th ed. (Boston: Houghton Mifflin, 2005), p. 270.
12. Quoted in Adam Goodheart, "Pilgrims from the Great Satan," *New York Times*, March 10, 2002, p. A12.
13. Quoted in Walther, *Women in Islam*, p. 40.
14. Quoted in Mervyn Hiskett, "Islamic Literature and Art," in Swisher, ed., *Spread*, p. 120.
15. Excerpted in John Yohannan, ed., *A Treasury of Asian Literature* (New York: New American Library, 1965), pp. 261–262.
16. Quoted in Jonathan P. Berkey, *The Formation of Islam: Religion and Society in the Near East, 600–1800* (New York: Cambridge University Press, 2003), p. 233.
17. Quoted in Hourani, *History of Arab Peoples*, p. 201.
18. Quoted in Bernard Lewis, *The Arabs in History* (New York: Harper and Row, 1960), p. 131.
19. Hariri, quoted in Fernand Braudel, *A History of Civilizations* (New York: Penguin, 1995), p. 71.
20. Ibn Al Athir, quoted in Mike Edwards, "Genghis Khan," *National Geographic* (December, 1996): p. 9.
21. Quoted in Francis Robinson, *The Cambridge Illustrated History of the Islamic World* (Cambridge: Cambridge University Press, 1996), p. 198.

Chapter 11 East Asian Traditions, Transformations, and Eurasian Encounters, 600–1500

1. Quoted in John Merson, *The Genius That Was China: East and West in the Making of the Modern World* (Woodstock, NY: Overlook Press, 1990), 14.
2. Quoted in John A. Harrison, *The Chinese Empire* (New York: Harcourt Brace Jovanovich, 1972), 239.
3. Quoted in C. P. Fitzgerald, *China: A Short Cultural History* (New York: Praeger, 1961), 336.
4. Quoted in Derk Bodde, *China's Cultural Tradition: What and Whither?* (New York: Holt, Rinehart and Winston, 1957), 31.
5. The Wang and Li poems are from Robert Payne, ed., *The White Pony: An Anthology of Chinese Poetry* (New York: Mentor, 1960), 154, 174.
6. Du's poems are from Cyril Birch, ed., *Anthology of Chinese Literature from Early Times to the Fourteenth Century* (New York: Grove Press, 1965), 240–241; and *Tu Fu: Selected Poems* (Peking: Foreign Languages Press, 1962), 100.
7. John Meskill, "History of China," in *An Introduction to Chinese Civilization*, ed. John Meskill (Lexington, MA: D.C. Heath, 1973), 127–128.
8. Yuan Tsai, from Patricia Buckley Ebrey, ed., *Chinese Civilization and Society: A Sourcebook* (New York: The Free Press, 1981), p. 96.
9. The quotes are from Dun J. Li, ed., *The Essence of Chinese Civilization* (Princeton, NJ: Van Nostrand, 1967), p. 88; and James Zee-Min Lee, *Chinese Potpourri* (Hong Kong: Oriental Publishers, 1950), p. 319.
10. Quoted in H. D. Martin, *The Rise of Chingis Khan and His Conquest of North China* (Baltimore: Johns Hopkins University Press, 1950), 5.
11. R. E. Latham, trans., *The Travels of Marco Polo* (Baltimore: Penguin Books, 1958), 184–187.
12. Zhang Tao, quoted in Timothy Brook, *The Confusions of Pleasure: Commerce and Culture in the Ming* (Berkeley: University of California Press, 1998), vii.
13. Quoted in Bruce Cumings, *Korea's Place in the Sun: A Modern History* (New York: W.W. Norton, 1997), 37.
14. Quoted in Yung Chung Kim, ed. and trans., *Women of Korea: A History from Ancient Times to 1945* (Seoul: Ehwa Women's University Press, 1977), 32.
15. Quoted in Donald Keene, "Literature," in *An Introduction to Japanese Civilization*, ed. Arthur E. Tiedemann (Lexington, MA: D.C. Heath, 1974), 395.
16. Quoted in Ivan Morris, *The World of the Shining Prince: Court Life in Ancient Japan* (New York: Kodansha, 1994), 229.
17. Quoted in ibid., 204.
18. Quoted in Mikiso Hane, *Japan: A Historical Survey* (New York: Charles Scribner's, 1972), 56.
19. From Ryusaku Tsunoda et al., eds., *Sources of Japanese Tradition*, vol. 2 (New York: Columbia University Press, 1958), 236.
20. Quoted in Noel F. Busch, *The Horizon Concise History of Japan* (New York: American Heritage, 1972), 58.

Chapter 12 Expanding Horizons in Africa and the Americas, 600–1500

1. Quoted in Patricia W. Romero, *Lamu: History, Society, and Family in an East African Port City* (Princeton: Markus Wiener, 1997), 14.
2. Quoted in Esmond Bradley Martin and Chryssee Perry Martin, *Cargoes of the East: The Ports, Trade and Culture of the Arabian Seas and Western Indian Ocean* (London: Elm Tree Books, 1978), 9.
3. Quoted in *Africa's Glorious Legacy* (Arlington, VA: Time-Life Books, 1994), 90.
4. Quoted in E. Jefferson Murphy, *History of African Civilization* (New York: Dell, 1972), 120.
5. The quotes are from E. W. Bovill, *The Golden Trade of the Moors*, 2nd ed. (London: Oxford University Press, 1970), 95.
6. Leo Africanus, quoted in Kevin Shillington, *History of Africa*, rev. ed. (New York: St. Martin's, 1995), 105.
7. Quoted in Constance B. Hilliard, ed., *Intellectual Traditions of Pre-Colonial Africa* (New York: McGraw-Hill, 1998), 311–312.
8. Quoted in John Middleton, *The World of the Swahili* (New Haven, CT: Yale University Press, 1992), 40.
9. Quoted in Bovill, *Golden Trade*, 96.
10. Djeli Mamoudou Kouyate, quoted in D. T. Niane, *Sundiata: An Epic of Old Mali* (London: Longman, 1965), 1.
11. John Smith, quoted in Charles Mann, "The Pristine Myth," *The Atlantic Online*, March 7, 2002 (http://www.theatlantic.com/unbound/interviews/int2002-03-07.htm)
12. Quoted in Richard F. Townsend, *The Aztecs*, rev. ed. (New York: Thames and Hudson, 2000), 59.
13. Quoted in Brian M. Fagan, *Kingdoms of Gold, Kingdoms of Jade: The Americas Before Columbus* (London: Thames and Hudson, 1991), 7.
14. Quoted in ibid., 224.
15. Quoted in Robert M. Carnack et al., *The Legacy of Mesoamerica: History and Culture of a Native American Civilization* (Upper Saddle River, NJ: Prentice-Hall, 1996), 415.
16. Quoted in Marysa Navarro, "Women in Pre-Columbian and Colonial Latin America," in *Restoring Women to History* (Bloomington, IN: Organization of American Historians, 1988), 6.
17. Pedro Cieza de Leon, quoted in Terence N. D'Altroy, *The Incas* (Malden, MA: Blackwell, 2002), 3.
18. The Chronicles of Michoacan, quoted in Melvin Lunenfeld, ed., *Discovery, Invasion, Encounter: Sources and Interpretations* (Lexington, MA: D.C. Heath, 1991), p. 262.

Chapter 13 South Asia, Central Asia, Southeast Asia, and Afro-Eurasian Connections, 600–1500

1. From L. S. Stavrianos, *The Epic of Man to 1500* (Englewood Cliffs, NJ: Prentice-Hall, 1970), 160, 162–163.
2. Quoted in Tansen Sen, *Buddhism, Diplomacy, and Trade: The Realignment of Sino-Indian Relations, 600–1400* (Honolulu: University of Hawaii Press, 2003), 11.
3. Al-Biruni, quoted in Romila Thapar, *Early India: From the Origins to AD 1300* (Berkeley: University of California Press, 2002), 437.
4. Quoted in Paul Thomas Welty, *The Asians: Their Evolving Heritage*, 6th ed. (New York: Harper and Row, 1984), 68.
5. Quoted in Lucille Schulberg, *Historic India* (New York: Time-Life Books, 1968), 11–12.
6. Quoted in Debiprasad Chattopadhyana, *History of Science and Technology in Ancient India*, vol. 3 (Calcutta: Firma KLM Private Ltd., 1996), 60.
7. Minhaju-s Siraj, quoted in John Keay, *A History of India* (New York: Atlantic Monthly Press, 2000), 245.
8. Quoted in Keay, *History of India*, 274.
9. Stanley Wolpert, *A New History of India*, 5th ed. (New York: Oxford University Press, 1997), 113.
10. Quoted in Richard Eaton, "Islamic History as Global History," in *Islamic and European Expansion: The Forging of a Global Order*, ed. Michael Adas (Philadelphia: Temple University Press, 1993), 21.

11. Quoted in Christopher Pym, *The Ancient Civilization of Angkor* (New York: New American Library, 1968), 118.
12. Quoted in David Chandler, *A History of Cambodia*, 2nd ed. updated (Boulder, CO: Westview Press, 1996), 74.
13. From ibid., 41.
14. Ibn Muhammad Ibrahim, from Michael Smithies, *Descriptions of Old Siam* (Kuala Lumpur: Oxford University Press, 1995), 91.
15. Quoted in Ralph Smith, *Viet-Nam and the West* (Ithaca, NY: Cornell University Press, 1971), 9.
16. Quoted in Anthony Reid, *Southeast Asia in the Age of Commerce, 1450–1680*, vol. 2 (New Haven: Yale University Press, 1993), 10.
17. Tome' Pires, quoted in Paul Wheatley, *The Golden Khersonese* (Kuala Lumpur: University of Malaya Press, 1961), 313.
18. Quoted in Kenneth R. Hall, *Maritime Trade and State Development in Early Southeast Asia* (Honolulu: University of Hawaii Press, 1985), 210.

Chapter 14 Christian Societies in Medieval Europe, Byzantium, and Russia, 600–1500

1. From a fourteenth-century legend, quoted in Amy G. Remensnyder, "Topographies of Memory: Center and Periphery in High Medieval France," in Gerd Althoff et al., eds., *Medieval Concepts of the Past: Ritual, Memory, Historiography* (New York: Cambridge University Press, 2002), p. 214.
2. Quoted in *What Life Was Like in the Age of Chivalry: Medieval Europe, AD 800–1500* (Alexandria, Va.: Time-Life Books, 1997), p. 17.
3. Quoted in James C. Russell, *The Germanization of Early Medieval Christianity* (Oxford: Oxford University Press, 1994), p. 186.
4. "Charlemagne's letter to Pope Leo III, 796," from C. Warren Hollister et al., *Medieval Europe: A Short Sourcebook*, 2nd ed. (New York: McGraw-Hill, 1992), p. 78.
5. Quoted in F. Donald Logan, *The Vikings in History*, 2nd ed. (New York: Routledge, 1991), p. 15.
6. Hugo of Santalla, quoted in Jerry Brotton, *The Renaissance Bazaar: From the Silk Road to Michelangelo* (Oxford: Oxford University Press, 2002), p. 195.
7. Quoted in John M. Hobson, *The Eastern Origins of Western Civilization* (New York: Cambridge University Press, 2004), p. 113.
8. Quoted in Jo Ann H. Moran Cruz and Richard Gerberding, *Medieval Worlds: An Introduction to European History, 300–1492* (Boston: Houghton Mifflin, 2004), p. 388.
9. Quoted in *Eileen Power, Medieval People*, new rev. ed. (New York: Barnes and Noble, 1963), p. 18.
10. Richard of Devizes, quoted in Jacques Le Goff, ed., *The Medieval World* (London: Postgate Books, 1997), p. 139.
11. The quotes are from Frederic Delouche, et al., *Illustrated History of Europe: A Unique Portrait of Europe's Common History* (New York: Barnes and Noble, 2001), p. 170; and Georges Duby, "Marriage in Early Medieval Society," in *Love and Marriage: The Middle Ages*, translated by Jane Dunnett (Chicago: University of Chicago Press, 1994), p. 11.
12. Quoted in Carolly Erickson, *The Medieval Vision: Essays in History and Perception* (New York: Oxford University Press, 1976), p. 73.
13. Quoted in Cruz and Gerberding, *Medieval Worlds*, p. 277.
14. Quoted in Clive Ponting, *A Green History of the World: The Environment and the Collapse of Great Civilizations* (New York: Penguin, 1991), p. 144.
15. Quoted in Thomas F. Madden, *A Concise History of the Crusades* (Lanham, Md.: Rowman and Littlefield, 1999), pp. 8–9.
16. Quoted in C. Warren Hollister, *Medieval Europe: A Short History*, 8th ed. (Boston: McGraw-Hill, 1998), p. 296.
17. Quoted in ibid., p. 273.
18. Quoted in Nicholas V. Riasanovsky, *A History of Russia*, 5th ed. (New York: Oxford University Press, 1993), p. 72.
19. Eustache Deschamps, quoted in J. Huizinga, *The Waning of the Middle Ages* (Garden City, N.Y.: Doubleday Anchor, 1954), p. 33.
20. Quoted in Delouche, *Illustrated History*, p. 168.
21. Quoted in Brotton, *Renaissance Bazaar*, p. 75.
22. Canon Pietro Casola, quoted in ibid., p. 38.
23. Quoted in Edith Simon, *The Reformation* (New York: Time-Life Books, 1966), p. 71.
24. Cadamosto, quoted in Peter Russell, *Prince Henry "the Navigator": A Life* (New Haven, Conn.: Yale University Press, 2000), p. 225.

Societies, Networks, Transitions: Expanding Horizons in the Intermediate Era, 600 B.C.E.–600 C.E.

1. Quoted in Jack Turner, *Spice: The History of a Temptation* (New York: Vintage, 2004), 103.
2. Quoted in Fernand Braudel, *The Wheels of Commerce* (New York: Harper and Row, 1979), 127.
3. Abdul Kassim ibn Khordadbeh, quoted in Elmer Bendiner, *The Rise and Fall of Paradise* (New York: Dorset Press, 1983), 101.
4. Quoted in John M. Hobson, *The Eastern Origins of Western Civilisation* (New York: Cambridge University Press, 2004), 40.
5. Quoted in M. N. Pearson, "Introduction," in *Spices in the Indian Ocean World*, ed. M. N. Pearson (Aldershot, UK: Valiorum, 1996), xv.
6. Quoted in Philip D. Curtin, *Cross-Cultural Trade in World History* (New York: Cambridge University Press, 1984), 125.
7. Quoted in John Kelley, *The Great Mortality* (New York: HarperCollins, 2005), 2.
8. Quoted in Peter N. Stearns, *Western Civilization in World History* (New York: Routledge, 2003), 52.
9. Al-Musabbihi, quoted in Heinz Halm, *The Fatimids and Their Traditions of Learning* (New York: I.B. Taurus, 1997), 73.
10. Leon Battista Alberti, quoted in Jeremy Brotton, *The Renaissance Bazaar: From the Silk Road to Michelangelo* (London: Oxford University Press, 2002), 73–74.
11. Quoted in Peter N. Stearns, *Gender in World History* (New York: Routledge, 2000), 52.
12. Quoted in Anthony Reid, *Southeast Asia in the Age of Commerce, 1450–1680*, vol. 1 (New Haven: Yale University Press, 1988), 1.
13. Quoted in Adriaan Verhulst, *The Carolingian Economy* (New York: Cambridge University Press, 2002), 48.
14. Ibn al-Athir, quoted in David R. Ringrose, *Expansion and Global Interaction, 1200–1700* (New York: Longman, 2001), 22.
15. Quoted in Rene Grousset, *The Empire of the Steppes: A History of Central Asia* (New Brunswick: Rutgers University Press, 1970), 249.
16. Quoted in L. S. Stavrianos, *Lifelines from Our Past: A New World History*, rev. ed. (Armonk, NY: M.E. Sharpe, 1997), 58.
17. Quoted in Frederick F. Cartwright, *Disease and History: The Influence of Disease in Shaping the Great Events of History* (New York: Thomas Y. Crowell, 1972), 37.
18. Quoted in Brian Fagan, *The Long Summer: How Climate Changed Civilization* (New York: Basic Books, 2004), 224.
19. Peter Martyr, quoted in Turner, *Spice*, xi.

Chapter 15 Global Connections and the Remaking of Europe, 1450–1750

1. From "The Tempest," *The Riverside Shakespeare*, 2nd ed. (Boston: Houghton Mifflin, 1997), 1684.
2. Franciscan friar Toribio de Montolinia, quoted in Marvin Lunenfeld, ed., *1492: Discovery, Invasion, Encounter: Sources and Interpretations* (Lexington, MA: D.C. Heath, 1991), 214.
3. Quoted in Carlo M. Cipolla, *Before the Industrial Revolution: European Society and Economy, 1000–1700*, 2nd ed. (New York: W. W. Norton, 1980), 270.
4. Quoted in Miriam Beard, *History of the Businessman* (New York: Macmillan, 1938), 239–240.
5. Quoted in H. O. Taylor, *Thought and Expression in the Sixteenth Century*, vol. 1 (New York: Macmillan, 1920), 175.
6. From "Hamlet," *The Riverside Shakespeare*, 2nd ed. (Boston: Houghton Mifflin, 1997), 1204.
7. Quoted in James Krokar et al., *Rhetoric and Civilization*, vol. 2 (Littleton, MA: Copley, 1988), 620.
8. Quoted in *What Life Was Like During the Age of Reason* (Alexandria, VA: Time-Life Books, 1999), 18.
9. Quoted in Blitzer, *Age of Kings*, 119.
10. From Hobbes, *The Leviathan*, Chapter 13 (oregonstate.edu/instruct/ph1302/texts/hobbes/leviathan-c.html)
11. Quoted in Norman Davies, *Europe: A History* (New York: Harper, 1996), 599.

12. Quoted in John M. Hobson, *The Eastern Origins of Western Civilisation* (Cambridge: Cambridge University Press, 2004), 194.
13. From Dena Goodman and Kathleen Wellman, eds., *The Enlightenment* (Boston: Houghton Mifflin, 2004), 167.
14. Quoted in Frederic Delouche et al., *Illustrated History of Europe* (New York: Barnes and Noble, 2001), 247.
15. Quoted in Diarmaid MacCulloch, *The Reformation: A History* (New York: Penguin, 2005), 609.
16. Quoted in Robert Wallace, *Rise of Russia* (New York: Time-Life Books, 1967), 140.

Chapter 16 New Challenges for Africa and the Islamic World, 1450–1750

1. Quoted in Ali Mazrui, *The Africans: A Triple Heritage* (Boston: Little, Brown, 1986), 11.
2. Quoted in Basil Davidson, ed., *African Civilization Revisited* (Trenton, NJ: African World Press, 1991), 118.
3. Quoted in Basil Davidson, *Africa in History* (New York: Touchstone, 1995), 176–177.
4. Quoted in Derek Nourse and Thomas Spear, *The Swahili: Reconstructing the History and Language of an African Society, 800–1500* (Philadelphia: University of Pennsylvania Press, 1985), 82.
5. Quoted in Michael Pearson, *The Indian Ocean* (New York: Routledge, 2003), 119.
6. From Roland Oliver and Caroline Oliver, eds., *Africa in the Days of Exploration* (Englewood Cliffs, NJ: Prentice-Hall, 1965), 111.
7. From Basil Davidson, ed., *The African Past: Chronicles from Antiquity to Modern Times* (New York: Grosset and Dunlap, 1964), 136.
8. Malcolm Cowley and Daniel Mannix, "The Middle Passage," in *The Atlantic Slave Trade,* ed. David Northrup (Lexington, MA: D.C. Heath, 1994), 99, 101.
9. Quoted in R. A. Houston, "Colonies, Enterprise, and Wealth: The Economies of Europe and the Wider World in the Seventeenth Century," in *Early Modern Europe: An Oxford History,* ed. Euan Cameron (New York: Oxford University Press, 1999), 165.
10. Quoted in Halil Inalcik, *The Ottoman Empire: The Classical Age, 1300–1600* (London: Phoenix Press, 2000), 41.
11. Quoted in Arthur Goldschmidt, Jr., *A Concise History of the Middle East,* 4th ed. revised and updated (Boulder, CO: Westview Press, 1991), 129.
12. Ibrahim Pecevi, quoted in Philip Mansel, *Constantinople: City of the World's Desire, 1453–1924* (New York: St. Martin's, 1995), 171.
13. Quoted in Inalcik, *Ottoman Empire,* 189.
14. From John J. Saunders, ed., *The Muslim World on the Eve of Europe's Expansion* (Englewood Cliffs, NJ: Prentice-Hall, 1966), 35.
15. Quoted in Francis Robinson, *The Cultural Atlas of the Islamic World Since 1500* (London: Stonehenge, 1987), 49.

Chapter 17 Americans, Europeans, Africans, and New Societies in the Americas, 1450–1750

1. Quoted in Michael C. Meyer and William L. Sherman, *The Course of Mexican History,* 2nd ed. (New York: Oxford University Press, 1983), 86.
2. From Lewis Hanke, ed., *History of Latin American Civilization: Sources and Interpretations,* vol. 1 (Boston: Little, Brown and Company, 1973), 64.
3. Quoted in Oliver Cox, "The Rise of Modern Race Relations," in *Racial Conflict, Discrimination, and Power,* ed. William Barclay et al. (New York: AMS Press, 1976), 91.
4. Quoted in Herman J. Viola, "Seeds of Change," in *Seeds of Change: A Quincentennial Commemoration,* ed. Herman J. Viola and Carolyn Margolis (Washington, DC: Smithsonian Institution Press, 1991), 13.
5. Quoted in L. S. Stavrianos, *Lifelines from Our Past: A New World History,* rev. ed. (Armonk, NY: M.E. Sharpe, 1997), 96.
6. Alonso de Zuazo, quoted in Kathleen Deagan and Jose Maria Cruxent, *Columbus's Outpost Among the Tainos: Spain and America at La Isabela, 1493–1498* (New Haven, CT: Yale University Press, 2002), 210.
7. Magá Lahen Hurao, quoted in Geoffrey C. Gunn, *First Globalization: The Eurasian Exchange* (Lanham, MD: Rowman and Littlefield, 2003), 194.
8. Quoted in Jane MacLaren Walsh and Yoko Sugiura, "The Demise of the Fifth Sun," in Viola and Margolis, *Seeds of Change,* 41.
9. Quoted in Noble David Cook, *Born to Die: Disease and New World Conquest, 1492–1650* (Cambridge: Cambridge University Press, 1998), vi.
10. From Hanke, *History of Latin American Civilization,* 388.
11. Quoted in Jonathan C. Brown, *Latin America: A Social History of the Colonial Period* (Belmont, CA: Wadsworth, 2000), 146.
12. Quoted in Marysa Navarro and Virginia Sanchez-Korrol, "Latin America and the Caribbean," in *Restoring Women to History* (Bloomington, IN: Organization of American Historians, 1988), 23.
13. Quoted in Felipe Fernandez-Armesto, *Millennium: A History of the Last Thousand Years* (New York: Scribner's, 1995), 300.
14. Gonzalo Fernandez de Oviedo, quoted in L. S. Stavrianos, *Global Rift: The Third World Comes of Age* (New York: William Morrow, 1981), 83.
15. Guzman Poma de Ayala, quoted in Brown, *Latin America,* 183.
16. Quoted in Robert Heilbroner and Aaron Singer, *The Economic Transformation of America, 1600 to the Present,* 3rd ed. (Fort Worth, TX: Harcourt Brace, 1994), 68.
17. Quoted in David Freeman Hawke, *Everyday Life in Early America* (New York: Harper and Row, 88), 120.
18. Quoted in Salvador de Madariaga, *The Rise of the Spanish American Empire* (New York: Macmillan, 1947), 90–91.
19. From Fray Toribio Motolinia, "The Ten Plagues of New Spain," in *Indian Labor in the Spanish Indies,* ed. John Francis Bannon (Boston: D.C. Heath, 1966), 45.
20. Quoted in Stuart B. Schwartz, "Brazil," in *A Historical Guide to World Slavery,* ed. Seymour Drescher and Stanley L. Engerman (New York: Oxford University Press, 1998), 101.
21. Gonzalez de Cellorigo, quoted in Jonathan Williams, *Money: A History* (New York: St. Martin's, 1997), 162.

Chapter 18 South Asia, Southeast Asia, and East Asia: Triumphs and Challenges, 1450–1750

1. Quoted in Anthony Reid, "Early Southeast Asian Categorizations of Europeans," in *Implicit Understandings,* ed. Stuart B. Schwartz (Cambridge: Cambridge University Press, 1994), 275.
2. Quoted in John E. Wills, Jr., *1688: A Global History* (New York: W.W. Norton, 2001), 276.
3. Quoted in Om Prakash, *European Commercial Enterprise in Pre-Colonial India* (New York: Cambridge University Press, 1998), 4.
4. Quoted in Francis Robinson, *The Cultural Atlas of the Islamic World Since 1500* (London: Stonehenge, 1992), 39.
5. The quotes are from Rhoads Murphey, *A History of Asia,* 4th ed. (New York: Longman, 2002), 185; and Michael Edwardes, *A History of India* (New York: Farrar, Straus and Cudahy, 1961), 191.
6. Quoted in Edwardes, *History of India,* 190.
7. Quoted in Klaus Wenk, *Thai Literature: An Introduction* (Bangkok: White Lotus, 1995), 14–16.
8. Joost Schouten, quoted in Michael Smithies, *Descriptions of Old Siam* (Kuala Lumpur: Oxford University Press, 1995), 19.
9. Quoted in Nicholas Tarling, "Mercantilism and Missionaries: Impact and Accommodation," in *Eastern Asia: An Introductory History,* ed. Colin Mackerras, 3rd ed. (Frenches Forest, NSW, Australia: Longmans, 2000), 115.
10. Pedro Chirino, quoted in Carolyn Brewer, "From Animist 'Priestess' to Catholic Priest: The Re/gendering of Religious Roles in the Philippines, 1521–1685," in *Other Pasts: Women, Gender and History in Early Modern Southeast Asia,* ed. Barbara Warson Andaya (Honolulu: Center for Southeast Asian Studies, University of Hawaii at Manoa, 2000), 69.
11. Quoted in Felip Fernandez-Armesto, *Millennium: A History of the Last Thousand Years* (New York: Scribner's, 1995), 324.

Societies, Networks, Transitions: Connecting the Early Modern World, 1450–1750

1. Francisco Lopez de Gomara, quoted in Roger Schlesinger, *In the Wake of Columbus: The Impact of the New World on Europe, 1492–1650* (Wheeling, IL: Harlan Davidson, 1996), 23.

2. Quoted in Peter J. Hugill, *World Trade Since 1431: Geography, Technology, and Capitalism* (Baltimore: Johns Hopkins University Press, 1993), vii.
3. Quoted in Roger Savory, *Iran Under the Safavids* (Cambridge: Cambridge University Press, 1980), 205.
4. Quoted in Gregory Blue, "China and Western Social Thought in the Modern Period," in *China and Historical Capitalism,* ed. Timothy Brook and Gregory Blue (New York: Cambridge University Press, 1999), 64.
5. Quoted in Kenneth Chase, *Firearms: A Global History to 1700* (New York: Cambridge University Press, 2003), 2.
6. Quoted in Patricia Risso, *Merchants and Faith: Muslim Commerce and Culture in the Indian Ocean* (Boulder, CO: Westview Press, 1995), 96.
7. Quoted in Robert B. Marks, *The Origins of the Modern World: A Global and Ecological Narrative* (Lanham, MD: Rowman and Littlefield, 2002), 81.
8. Quoted in Christine Dobbin, *Asian Entrepreneurial Minorities: Conjoint Communities in the Making of the World-Economy, 1750–1940* (Richmond, United Kingdom: Curzon, 1996), 23.
9. Quoted in J. Donald Hughes, "Biodiversity in World History," in *The Face of the Earth: Environment and World History,* ed. Hughes Armonk, NY: M.E. Sharpe, 2000), 31.
10. Quoted in G. William Skinner, *Chinese Society in Thailand: An Analytical History* (Ithaca, NY: Cornell University Press, 1957), 8.
11. Balthasar Barreira, quoted in George E. Brooks, *Landlords and Strangers: Ecology, Society, and Trade in Western Africa, 1000–1630* (Boulder, CO: Westview Press, 1983), 306.
12. Quoted in Annemarie Schimmel, *The Empire of the Great Mughals: History, Art, and Culture* (New Delhi: Oxford University Press, 2005), 113.
13. Quoted in Susan Mann, *Precious Records: Women in China's Long Eighteenth Century* (Stanford, CA: Stanford University Press, 1997), 108.
14. Quoted in Schimmel, *Empire of Great Mughals,* 130.
15. Juan Gimes de Sepulveda, in Marvin Lunenfeld, ed., *1492: Discovery, Invasion, Encounter: Sources and Interpretations* (Lexington, MA: D.C. Heath, 1991), 219–220.

Chapter 19 Modern Transitions: Revolutions, Industries, Ideologies, Empires, 1750–1914

1. Quoted in Eric Hobsbawm, *The Age of Revolution, 1789–1848* (New York: New American Library, 1962), 44.
2. From Charles Dickens, *A Tale of Two Cities* (New York: Bantam, 1989), 1.
3. From David A. Hollinger and Charles Capper, eds., *The American Intellectual Tradition: A Sourcebook,* vol. 1, 2nd ed. (New York: Oxford University Press, 1993), 131.
4. Quoted in William Appleman Williams, *America Confronts a Revolutionary World, 1775–1976* (New York: William Morrow, 1976), 15, 25.
5. Quoted in Peter N. Stearns, *Life and Society in the West: The Modern Centuries* (San Diego: Harcourt Brace Jovanovich, 1988), 164.
6. Quoted in Eric Hobsbawm, *Workers: World of Labor* (New York: Pantheon), 34.
7. Quoted in Michael Elliott-Bateman et al., *Revolt to Revolution: Studies in the 19th and 20th Century European Experience* (Manchester, England: Manchester University Press, 1974), 87.
8. Jose San Martin, quoted in Edwin Early, *The History Atlas of South America* (New York: Macmillan, 1998), 76.
9. Quoted in Carlos Fuentes, *The Buried Mirror: Reflections on Spain and the New World* (New York: Houghton Mifflin, 1992), 252.
10. Quoted in E. Bradford Burns and Julie A. Charlip, *Latin America: A Concise Interpretive History,* 7th ed. (Upper Saddle River, NJ: Prentice-Hall, 2002), 75.
11. Quoted in John R. Gillis, *A World of Their Own Making: Myth, Ritual, and the Quest for Family Values* (New York: Basic Books, 1996), 65.
12. Quoted in Fernand Braudel, *The Perspective of the World: Civilization and Capitalism, 15th–18th Century* (New York: Harper and Row, 1984), 553.
13. Quoted in Peter Gay, *Age of Enlightenment* (New York: Time, Inc., 1966), 105–106.
14. Quoted in Peter Hall, *Cities in Civilization* (New York: Fromm International, 1998), 310.
15. Quoted in Oliver Zimmer, *A Contested Nation: History, Memory and Nationalism in Switzerland, 1761–1891* (Cambridge: Cambridge University Press, 2003), 119.
16. Quoted in W. Raymond Duncan et al., *World Politics in the 21st Century,* 2nd ed. (New York: Longman, 2004), 311.
17. Quoted in Patrick Galvin, *Irish Songs of Resistance* (New York: Folklore Press, n.d.), 84.
18. Quoted in S. C. Burchell, *The Age of Progress* (New York: Time, Inc., 1966), 120.
19. Quoted in Reginald Nettel, *Sing a Song of England: A Social History of Traditional Song* (London: Phoenix House, 1969), 183.
20. Quoted in Robert A. Huttenback, *The British Imperial Experience* (New York: Harper and Row, 1966), 101.
21. Hillaire Beloc, quoted in Eric Hobsbawm, *The Age of Empire, 1875–1914* (New York: Vintage, 1987), 20.
22. Quoted in John Steele Gordon, *A Thread Across the Ocean: The Heroic Story of the Transatlantic Cable* (New York: Perennial, 2003), 215.
23. Quoted in Winnifred Baumgart, *Imperialism: The Idea and Reality of British and French Colonial Expansion, 1880–1914* (New York: Oxford University Press, 1986), 88.
24. Quoted in L. S. Stavrianos, *Global Reach: The Third World Comes of Age* (New York: William Morrow, 1981), 263.
25. Quoted in Baumgart, *Imperialism,* 52.

Chapter 20 Changing Societies in Europe, the Americas, and Oceania, 1750–1914

1. *Nostromo* (Garden City, NY: Doubleday, Page, and Company, 1924), 77.
2. The Kume quotes are from Donald Keene, *Modern Japanese Diaries: The Japanese at Home and Abroad as Revealed Through Their Diaries* (New York: Columbia University Press, 1998), 90–115.
3. Quoted in Frederic Delouche et al., *Illustrated History of Europe* (New York: Barnes and Noble, 2001), 312.
4. Quoted in Louise A. Tilly and Joan W. Scott, *Women, Work and Family* (New York: Holt, Rinehart and Winston, 1978), 64.
5. Quoted in T. W. C. Blanning, "The Commercialization and Sacralization of European Culture in the Nineteenth Century," in *The Oxford Illustrated History of Modern Europe,* ed. T. W. C. Blanning (Oxford: Oxford University Press, 1996), 147.
6. From Alexis De Tocqueville, *Democracy in America and Two Essays on America* (New York: Penguin, 2003), xxxiii.
7. Quoted in James Chase and Caleb Carr, *America Invulnerable: The Quest for Absolute Security from 1812 to Star Wars* (New York: Summit, 1988), 46.
8. From Peter Blood-Patterson, *Rise Up Singing* (Bethlehem, PA: Sing Out Publications, 1988), 246.
9. Quoted in Walter L. Williams, "American Imperialism and the Indians," in *Indians in American History: An Introduction,* ed. Frederick E. Hoxie (Arlington Heights, IL: Harlan Davidson, 1988), 233.
10. Quoted in Simon Serfaty, *The Elusive Enemy: American Foreign Policy Since World War II* (Boston: Little, Brown, 1972), 13.
11. Quoted in William Appleman Williams, *The Contours of American History* (Chicago: Quadrangle, 1966), 284.
12. Quoted in Robert Heilbroner and Aaron Singer, *The Economic Transformation of America, 1600 to the Present,* 3rd ed. (Fort Worth, TX: Harcourt Brace, 1994), 163.
13. Quoted in Juliet Haines Mofford, ed., *Talkin' Union: The American Labor Movement* (Carlisle, MA: Discovery Enterprises, 1997), 24.
14. From Mark Van Doren, ed., *The Portable Walt Whitman* (New York: Penguin, 1973), 210.
15. Quoted in Lloyd Gardner, *Safe for Democracy: The Anglo-American Response to Revolution, 1913–1923* (New York: Oxford University Press, 1984), 26.

16. From Mariano Azuela's novel *The Flies*, quoted in Lesley Byrd Simpson, *Many Mexicos*, 4th ed. rev. (Berkeley: University of California Press, 1967), 298.
17. Quoted in Stanley J. Stein and Barbara H. Stein, *The Colonial Heritage of Latin America: Essays on Economic Dependence in Perspective* (New York: Oxford University Press, 1970), 151.
18. Quoted in E. Bradford Burns, *Latin America: A Concise Interpretive History*, 5th ed. (Englewood Cliffs, NJ: Prentice-Hall, 1990), 213.
19. Quoted in Michael C. Meyer and William L. Sherman, *The Course of Mexican History*, 2nd ed. (New York: Oxford University Press, 1983), 416.
20. Quoted in Lloyd Braithwaite, "The Problem of Cultural Integration in Trinidad," in *Consequences of Class and Color: West Indian Perspectives*, ed. David Lowenthal and Lambors Comitas (Garden City, NY: Anchor, 1973), 248.
21. General Leonard Wood, quoted in Saul Landau, *The Dangerous Doctrine: National Security and U.S. Foreign Policy* (Boulder, CO: Westview Press, 1988), 80–81.
22. Quoted in Louis Hartz, *The Founding of New Societies* (New York: Harcourt, Brace and World, 1964), 248.

Chapter 21 Africa, the Middle East, and Imperialism, 1750–1914

1. Quoted in Edmund Burke III, *Prelude to Protectorate in Morocco: Precolonial Protest and Resistance, 1860–1912* (Chicago: University of Chicago Press, 1976), xi.
2. Quoted in Alan Palmer, *The Decline and Fall of the Ottoman Empire* (New York: Barnes and Noble, 1992), 58.
3. Quoted in John Iliffe, "Tanzania Under German and British Rule," in *Zamani: A Survey of East African History*, ed. B. A. Ogot, new ed. (Nairobi: Longman Kenya, 1974), 301.
4. Francois Coillard, quoted in John Iliffe, *Africans: The History of a Continent* (New York: Cambridge University Press, 1995), 208.
5. Quoted in ibid., 200–201.
6. H. H. Johnston, quoted in M. E. Chamberlain, *The Scramble for Africa* (Harlow, UK: Longman, 1974), 96.
7. Nnamdi Azikiwe, quoted in Minton F. Goldman, "Political Change in a Multi-National Setting," In David Schmitt, ed., *Dynamics of the Third World: Political and Social Change* (Cambridge: Winthrop, 1974), 172.
8. Rev. J. B. Murphy, quoted in Kevin Shillington, *History of Africa*, rev. ed. (New York: St. Martin's, 1995), 333–334.
9. Quoted in Dennis Austin, *Politics in Ghana* (London: Oxford University Press, 1964), 275.
10. Quoted in Tom Hopkinson, *South Africa* (New York: Time Inc., 1964), 93.
11. The lyrics are in David B. Coplan, *In Township Tonite: South Africa's Black City Music and Theater* (London: Longman, 1985), 44–45.
12. Quoted in Leroy Vail, "The Political Economy of East-Central Africa," in *History of Central Africa*, ed. David Birmingham and Phyllis M. Martin, vol. 2 (New York: Longman, 1983), 233.
13. Quoted in Andrew Wheatcroft, *The Ottomans* (New York: Viking, 1993), 146.
14. Quoted in Halil Inalcik, "Turkey," in *Political Modernization in Japan and Turkey*, ed. Robert E. Ward and Dankwart A. Rostow (Princeton: Princeton University Press, 1964), 57–58.
15. Quoted in Afaf Lufti al-Sayyid Marsot, *Egypt in the Reign of Muhammad Ali* (New York: Cambridge University Press, 1994), 28.
16. Quoted in Yahya Armajani and Thomas M. Ricks, *Middle East: Past and Present*, 2nd ed. (Englewood Cliffs, NJ: Prentice-Hall, 1986), 221.
17. Quoted in Charles Issawi, *The Middle East Economy: Decline and Recovery* (Princeton: Markus Wiener, 1995), 126.
18. Gertrude Bell, quoted in Emory C. Bogle, *The Modern Middle East: From Imperialism to Freedom, 1800–1958* (Upper Saddle River, NJ: Prentice-Hall, 1996), 103.
19. Quoted in Eric R. Wolf, *Peasant Wars of the Twentieth Century* (New York: Harper and Row, 1969), 209.
20. The quotes are from Akram Fouad Khater, ed., *Sources in the History of the Modern Middle East* (Boston: Houghton Mifflin, 2004), 75; Wiebke Walther, *Women in Islam* (Princeton: Markus Wiener, 1993), 221.
21. Quoted in Burke, *Prelude to Protectorate*, 38.
22. From Khater, *Sources*, 34.

Chapter 22 South Asia, Southeast Asia, and Colonization, 1750–1914

1. From Huynh Sanh Thong, *An Anthology of Vietnamese Poems from the Eleventh Through the Twentieth Centuries* (New Haven, CT: Yale University Press, 1996), 88.
2. The poem excerpts are in Helen B. Lamb, *Vietnam's Will to Live: Resistance to Foreign Aggression from Early Times Through the Nineteenth Century* (New York: Monthly Review Press, 1972), 134, 152.
3. Quoted in Sinharaja Tammita-Delgoda, *A Traveller's History of India*, 2nd ed. (New York: Interlink, 1999), 154.
4. The quotes are in Burton Stein, *A History of India* (Malden, Mass.: Blackwell, 1998), 265–266.
5. Charles Metcalfe, quoted in David Ludden, *An Agrarian History of South Asia* (New York: Cambridge University Press, 1999), 161.
6. Quoted in Tammita-Delgoda, *Traveller's History*, 167.
7. Quoted in ibid., 173.
8. Dadabhai Naoroji and R.C. Dutt, quoted in Ainslee T. Embree, *India's Search for National Identity* (New York: Alfred A. Knopf, 1972), 48–49.
9. Quoted in Clark D. Moore and David Eldridge, eds., *India Yesterday and Today* (New York: Bantam, 1970), 154–155.
10. The quotes are in Francis Robinson, *The Cultural Atlas of the Islamic World Since 1500* (Oxford: Stonehenge, 1992), 148–149.
11. From Rabindranath Tagore, *Gitanjali: A Collection of Indian Songs* (New York: Macmillan, 1973), 49–50.
12. Quoted in John McLane, ed., *The Political Awakening of India* (Englewood Cliffs, NJ: Prentice-Hall, 1970), 46.
13. Douwes Dekker, from Harry J. Benda and John A. Larkin, eds., *The World of Southeast Asia: Selected Historical Readings* (New York: Harper and Row, 1967), 127.
14. Quoted in Truong Buu Lam, *Resistance, Rebellion, Revolution: Popular Movements in Vietnamese History* (Singapore: Institute of Southeast Asian Studies, 1984), 11.
15. From Huynh, *Anthology of Vietnamese Poems*, 214.
16. The quotes are in Lamb, *Vietnam's Will to Live*, 229; and Truong Buu Lam, *Patterns of Vietnamese Response to Foreign Intervention, 1858–1900*, Monograph Series No. 11, Southeast Asia Studies (New Haven, CT: Yale University Press, 1967), 8.
17. Quoted in Teodoro A. Agoncillo, *A Short History of the Philippines* (New York: Mentor, 1969), 93.
18. Quoted in David Joel Steinberg et al., *In Search of Southeast Asia: A Modern History*, rev. ed. (Honolulu: University of Hawaii Press, 1987), 274.
19. Quoted in Daniel B. Schirmer, *Republic or Empire: American Resistance to the Philippine War* (Cambridge: Schenkman, 1972), 237.
20. The quotes are in David Howard Bain, *Sitting in Darkness: Americans in the Philippines* (Baltimore: Penguin, 1986), 2; and Gary R. Hess, *Vietnam and United States: Origins and Legacy of War* (Boston: Twayne, 1990), 25.
21. Quoted in Ngo Vinh Long, *Before the Revolution: The Vietnamese Peasants Under the French* (New York: Columbia University Press, 1991), v.
22. Tran Tu Binh, *The Red Earth: A Vietnamese Memoir of Life on a Colonial Rubber Plantation*, translated by John Spragens, Jr. (Athens, OH: Center for International Studies, Ohio University, 1985), 26.
23. Raden Ajoe Mangkoedimedjo, quoted in Norman Owen et al., *The Emergence of Modern Southeast Asia: A New History* (Honolulu: University of Hawaii Press, 2005), 197.

Chapter 23 East Asia and the Russian Empire Face New Challenges, 1750–1914

1. Quoted in Frederic Wakeman, Jr., *Strangers at the Gate: Social Disorder in South China, 1839–1861* (Berkeley: University of California Press, 1966), p. 126.
2. Quoted in Jonathan D. Spence, *The Search for Modern China*, 2nd ed. (New York: W.W. Norton, 1999), 148.
3. Quoted in Derk Bodde, *China's Cultural Tradition: What and Whither?* (New York: Holt, Rinehart and Winston, 1957), 62–63.

4. Chu Tsun, quoted in Hsin-Pao Chang, *Commissioner Lin and the Opium War* (New York: W.W. Norton, 1970), 89.
5. Quoted in Mark Borthwick, *Pacific Century: The Emergence of Modern East Asia* (Boulder, CO: Westview Press, 1992), 97.
6. Ssu-Yu Teng and John K. Fairbank, eds., *China's Response to the West: A Documentary Survey, 1839–1923* (New York: Atheneum, 1963), 26.
7. Quoted in Jean Chesneaux et al., *China: From the Opium Wars to the 1911 Revolution* (New York: Pantheon, 1976), 123.
8. S. Wells Williams, quoted in John A. Harrison, *China Since 1800* (New York: Harcourt, Brace and World, 1967), 42.
9. Hsu Tung, quoted in Joseph R. Levenson, *Confucian China and Its Modern Fate: A Trilogy* (Berkeley: University of California Press, 1968), 105.
10. Quoted in Earl Swisher, "Chinese Intellectuals and the Western Impact, 1838–1900," *Comparative Studies in Society and History* 1 (October 1958): 35.
11. Wang Pengyun, from Cyril Birch, ed., *Anthology of Chinese Literature* (New York: Grove Press, 1972), 294.
12. Quoted in Lloyd Gardner, *Safe for Democracy: The Anglo-American Response to Revolution, 1913–1923* (New York: Oxford University Press, 1984), 318.
13. Quoted in Jonathan D. Spence, *The Gate of Heavenly Peace: The Chinese and Their Revolution, 1895–1980* (New York: Viking, 1981), 52.
14. Quoted in Ono Kazuko, *Chinese Women in a Century of Revolution* (Stanford, CA: Stanford University Press, 1989), 30.
15. Otsuki Gentaku, quoted in Mikiso Hane, *Modern Japan: A Historical Survey*, 2nd ed. (Boulder, CO: Westview Press, 1992), 59.
16. Quoted in Patricia Fister, "Female *Bunjin*: The Life of Poet-Painter Ema Saiko," in *Recreating Japanese Women, 1600–1945,* ed. Gail Lee Bernstein (Berkeley: University of California Press, 1991), 109.
17. Quoted in Matthi Ferrer, *Hokusai* (New York: Barnes and Noble, 2002), 9.
18. Yanagawa Seigan, quoted in H. D. Hartoonian, *Toward Restoration: The Growth of Political Consciousness in Tokugawa Japan* (Berkeley: University of California Press, 1970), 1–2.
19. Quoted in Paul Varley, *Japanese Culture*, 4th ed. (Honolulu: University of Hawaii Press, 2000), 238.
20. Fukuzawa Yukichi, quoted in Mikiso Hane, *Peasants, Rebels, and Outcasts: The Underside of Modern Japan* (New York: Pantheon, 1982), 33.
21. Quoted in Conrad Totman, *A History of Japan* (Malden, MA: Blackwell, 2000), 341.
22. The quotes are from Varley, *Japanese Culture*, 272.
23. Quoted in L. S. Stavrianos, *Global Rift: The Third World Comes of Age* (New York: William Morrow, 1981), 344.

Chapter 24 World Wars, European Revolutions, and Global Depression, 1914–1945

1. Quoted in Anne Applebaum, *Gulag: A History* (New York: Doubleday, 2003), 3.
2. Quoted in S. L. Marshall, *World War I* (Boston: Houghton Mifflin, 1987), 53.
3. Quoted in Sir Michael Howard, "Europe 1914," in *The Great War: Perspectives on the First World War,* ed. Robert Cowley (New York: Random House, 2003), 3.
4. David Lloyd George, quoted in Holger H. Herwig, ed., *The Outbreak of World War I*, 6th ed. (Boston: Houghton Mifflin, 1997), 12.
5. The quotes are in Michael J. Lyons, *World War I: A Short History*, 2nd ed. (Upper Saddle River, NJ: Prentice-Hall, 2000), 195; and Ian Barnes and Robert Hudson, *The History Atlas of Europe: From Tribal Societies to a New European Unity* (New York: Macmillan, 1998), 131.
6. From L. S. Stavrianos, ed., *The Epic of Modern Man: A Collection of Readings* (Englewood Cliffs, NJ: Prentice-Hall, 1966), 354.
7. Quoted in A. J. Nicholls, *Weimar and the Rise of Hitler*, 2nd ed. (New York: St. Martin's, 1979), 11.
8. Quoted in Piers Brendon, *Dark Valley: A Panorama of the 1930s* (New York: Alfred A. Knopf, 2000), 6.
9. Quoted in L. S. Stavrianos, *Global Rift: The Third World Comes of Age* (New York: William Morrow, 1981), 499.
10. Quoted in Brendon, *Dark Valley*, 493.
11. Quoted in Kenneth B. Pyle, *The Making of Modern Japan*, 2nd ed. (Lexington, MA: D.C. Heath, 1996), 173.
12. Senator William Borah, quoted in William Appleman Williams, *American-Russian Relations, 1781–1947* (New York: Rinehart, 1952), 164.
13. *The Great Gatsby* (New York: Scribner's, 1925), 182.
14. Paul Reynaud, quoted in Brendon, *Dark Valley*, 153–154.
15. Quoted in Robert Heilbroner and Aaron Singer, *The Economic Transformation of America, 1600 to the Present* (Fort Worth: Harcourt Brace, 1994), 289.
16. From Harold Leventhal and Marjorie Guthrie, eds., *The Woody Guthrie Songbook* (New York: Grosset and Dunlap, 1976), 180–181.
17. Maurice Sachs, quoted in Brendon, *Dark Valley*, 168.
18. Quoted in Felix Gilbert with David Clay Large, *The End of the European Era, 1890 to the Present*, 4th ed. (New York: W.W. Norton, 1991), 263.
19. Quoted in Martin Kitchen, *A World in Flames: A Short History of the Second World War in Europe and Asia, 1939–1945* (London: Longman, 1990), vi.
20. Quoted in Stephen J. Lee, *European Dictatorships, 1918–1945*, 2nd ed. (London: Routledge, 2000), 207.
21. Quoted in George Donelson Moss, *America in the Twentieth Century*, 4th ed. (Upper Saddle River, NJ: Prentice-Hall, 2000), 257.
22. Quoted in James L. McClain, *Japan: A Modern History* (New York: W.W. Norton, 2002), 515.

Chapter 25 Imperialism and Nationalism in Asia, Africa, and Latin America, 1914–1945

1. Quoted in James C. Scott, *The Moral Economy of the Peasant: Rebellion and Subsistence in Southeast Asia* (New Haven: Yale University Press, 1976), 236.
2. Quoted in James W. Trullinger, *Village at War: An Account of Conflict in Vietnam* (Stanford, Calif.: Stanford University Press, 1994), 18.
3. Dick Spottswood, liner notes to the album *Calypsos from Trinidad: Politics, Intrigue and Violence in the 1930s* (Arhoolie 7004, 1991).
4. Quoted in Lester Langley, *Central America: The Real Stakes: Understanding Central America Before It's Too Late* (New York: Dorsey, 1985), 23.
5. Kenneth Wherry of Nebraska, quoted in John Brooks, *The Great Leap: The Past Twenty-five Years in America* (New York: Harper and Row, 1966), 327.
6. Quoted in *A Pictorial Biography of Luxun* (Beijing: Peoples Fine Arts Publishing House, n.d.), 157.
7. "Report on an Investigation of the Peasant Movement in Hunan," in *Selected Works of Mao Tse-Tung*, vol. 1 (Peking: Foreign Languages Press, 1965), 28.
8. Quoted in Stephen Uhalley, Jr., *Mao Tse-Tung: A Critical Biography* (New York: New Viewpoints, 1975), 55.
9. Quoted in John Meskill, "History of China," in *An Introduction to Chinese Civilization*, ed. John Meskill (Lexington, MA: D.C. Heath, 1973), 302.
10. Quoted in Sinharaja Tammita-Delgoda, *A Traveller's History of India*, 2nd ed. (New York: Interlink, 1999), 189.
11. From Clark D. Moore and David Eldridge, eds., *India Yesterday and Today* (New York: Bantam, 1970), 174.
12. Quoted in Martin Deming Lewis, ed., *Gandhi: Maker of Modern India?* (Lexington, MA: D.C. Heath, 1965), xii.
13. Quoted in Hermann Kulke and Dietmar Rothermund, *History of India*, 3rd ed. (New York: Routledge, 1998), 135–136.
14. Sir T.P. Sapru, quoted in Judith M. Brown, *Modern India: The Origins of an Asian Democracy*, 2nd ed. (New York: Oxford University Press, 1994), 280.
15. "Phan Boi Chau's Prison Reflections, 1914," in *Major Problems in the History of the Vietnam War: Documents and Essays*, ed. Robert J. McMahon (Lexington, MA: D.C. Heath, 1990), 32.
16. Hoai Thanh, quoted in David Marr, "Vietnamese Historical Reassessment, 1900–1944," in *Perceptions of the Past in Southeast Asia*, ed. Anthony Reid and David Marr (Singapore: Heinemann, 1979), 337–338.
17. Sitor Situmorang, quoted in Harry Aveling, ed., *From Surabaya to Armageddon: Indonesian Short Stories* (Singapore: Heinemann, 1976), vii.

18. Obafemi Awolowo, quoted in Chester L. Hunt and Lewis Walker, *Ethnic Dynamics: Patterns of Intergroup Relations in Various Societies*, 2nd ed. (Holmes Beach, FL: Learning Publications, 1979), 277.
19. Quoted in Veit Erlmann, *African Stars: Studies in Black South African Performance* (Chicago: University of Chicago Press, 1991), 95–96.
20. Quoted in Charles Hamm, "'The Constant Companion of Man': Separate Development, Radio Bantu and Music," *Popular Music* 10, no. (May 1991): 161.
21. Quoted in Hans Kohn, *A History of Nationalism in the East* (New York: Harcourt, 1929), 257.
22. The quotes are from Akram Fouad Khater, ed., *Sources in the History of the Modern Middle East* (Boston: Houghton Mifflin, 2004), 167, 176.
23. Severino Fama, quoted in Robert M. Levine, *The History of Brazil* (New York: Palgrave, 1999), 107.
24. From Frederick B. Pike, ed., *Latin American History: Select Problems. Identity, Integration, and Nationhood* (New York: Harcourt, Brace and World, 1969), 319.

Societies, Networks, Transitions: Global Imbalances in the Modern World, 1750–1945

1. From Jim Zwick, ed., *Mark Twain's Weapons of Satire: Anti-Imperialist Writings on the Philippine-American War* (Syracuse, NY: Syracuse University Press, 1992), 3–5.
2. Quoted in L. S. Stavrianos, *Lifelines from Our Past: A New World History*, rev. ed. (Armonk, NY: M.E. Sharpe, 1997), 114.
3. Rev. Sydney Smith, quoted in Frederic Delouche et al., *Illustrated History of Europe: A Unique Portrait of Europe's Common People* (New York: Barnes and Noble, 2001), 289.
4. Senator Albert Beveridge of Indiana, quoted in Henry Allen, *What It Felt Like Living in the American Century* (New York: Pantheon, 2000), 7.
5. Quoted in Benjamin Schwartz, *In Search of Wealth and Power: Yen Fu and the West* (New York: Harper Torchbooks, 1964), 29.
6. Quoted in Scott B. Cook, *Colonial Encounters in the Age of High Imperialism* (New York: Longman, 1996), 100.
7. From Clark D. Moore and David Eldridge, eds., *India Yesterday and Today* (New York: Bantam, 1970), 170.
8. Quoted in John A. Harrison, *China Since 1800* (New York: Harcourt, Brace and World, 1967), 161.
9. Quoted in Ranajit Guha, *History at the Limit of World-History* (New York: Columbia University Press, 2002), 91.
10. International Congress of the League Against Imperialism and Colonial Oppression, quoted in Clive Ponting, *The Twentieth Century: A World History* (New York: Henry Holt, 1998), 197.
11. Quoted in Richard H. Robbins, *Global Problems and the Culture of Capitalism* (Boston: Allyn and Bacon, 1999), 90.
12. Quoted in "Introduction," in *The Frontier in Perspective*, ed. Walter D. Wyman and Clifton B. Kroeber (Madison: University of Wisconsin Press, 1965), xviii.
13. Quoted in Pamela Scully, "Race and Ethnicity in Women's and Gender History in Global Perspective," in *Women's History in Global Perspective*, ed, Bonnie G. Smith, vol. 1 (Urbana: University of Illinois Press, 2004), 207.
14. Quoted in Ng Bickleen Fong, *The Chinese in New Zealand* (Hong Kong: Hong Kong University Press, 1959), 96.
15. Quoted in J. R. McNeill and William H. McNeill, *The Human Web: A Bird's-Eye View of World History* (New York: W. W. Norton, 2003), 217.
16. Quoted in Daniel R. Headrick, *The Tentacles of Progress: Technology Transfer in the Age of Imperialism, 1850–1940* (New York: Oxford University Press, 1988), 127.
17. Quoted in L. S. Stavrianos, "The Global Redistribution of Man," in *World Migration in Modern Times*, ed. Franklin D. Scott (Englewood Cliffs, NJ: Prentice-Hall, 1968), 170.
18. Quoted in Daniel R. Headrick, *The Tools of Empire: Technology and European Imperialism in the Nineteenth Century* (New York: Oxford University Press, 1981), 116.
19. Quoted in Gordon Rohlehr, *Calypso and Society in Pre-Independence Trinidad* (Port of Spain: Gordon Rohlehr, 1990), 80–81.

Chapter 26 The Remaking of the Global System, Since 1945

1. Quoted in Adrian Boot and Chris Salewicz with Rita Marley as Senior Editor, *Bob Marley: Songs of Freedom* (London: Bloomsbury, 1995), 278.
2. Frantz Fanon, *The Wretched of the Earth* (New York: Grove, 1968), 97–98.
3. Quoted in Goran Hyden, *Beyond Ujamaa in Tanzania: Underdevelopment and an Uncaptured Peasantry* (Berkeley: University of California Press, 1980), 202.
4. Quoted in Jennifer Seymour Whitaker, *How Can Africa Survive?* (New York: Harper and Row, 1988), 13.
5. The quotes are in Choi Chatterjee et al., *The 20th Century: A Retrospective* (Boulder, CO: Westview Press, 2002), 153, 306.
6. Dalai Lama, *My Land and My People* (New York: Warner Books, 1997), x.
7. Quoted in Peter Singer, "Navigating the Ethics of Globalization," *Chronicle of Higher Education*, October 11, 2002, B8.
8. Quoted in J. Donald Hughes, *An Environmental History of the World: Mankind's Changing Role in the Community of Life* (New York: Routledge, 2002), 206.
9. Quoted in Miriam Ching Louie, "Life on the Line," *The New Internationalist* (http://www.newint.org/issue302/sweat.html)
10. Walter Rodney, *How Europe Underdeveloped Africa* (London: Bogle-L'Ouverture, 1972), 162.
11. Quoted in Michael H. Hunt, *The World Transformed, 1945 to the Present* (Boston: Bedford/St. Martin's), 428.
12. Quoted in Eric Hobsbawm, *The Age of Extremes: A History of the World, 1914–1991* (New York: Pantheon, 1994), 365.
13. A. G. Hopkins, "Globalization: An Agenda for Historians," in *Globalization in World History*, ed. A. G. Hopkins (New York: W.W. Norton, 2002), 11.
14. From Hazel Johnson and Henry Bernstein, eds., *Third World Lives of Struggle* (London: Heinemann Educational, 1982), 173.
15. J. R. McLeod, "The Seamless Web: Media and Power in the Post-Modern Global Village," *Journal of Popular Culture* 15, no. 2 (Fall 1991): 69.
16. Quoted in David Reynolds, *One World Divisible: A Global History Since 1945* (New York: W.W. Norton, 2000), 491.
17. Michael Sturmer, quoted in Hobsbawm, *Age of Extremes*, 558.

Chapter 27 East Asian Resurgence, Since 1945

1. Quoted in Jerome Chen, *Mao and the Chinese Revolution* (New York: Oxford University Press, 1967), 6.
2. The quotes are from Ross Terrill, *Mao: A Biography* (New York: Harper, 1980), 198.
3. Peng Dehuai, quoted in Craig Dietrich, *People's China: A Brief History*, 3rd ed. (New York: Oxford University Press, 1998), 130.
4. Quoted in Maurice Meisner, *Mao's China and After: A History of the People's Republic*, 3rd ed. (New York: The Free Press, 1999), 281.
5. Xue Xinran, *The Good Women of China: Hidden Voices* (New York: Anchor, 2002), 175.
6. Quoted in the Committee of Concerned Asian Scholars, *China! Inside the Peoples Republic* (New York: Bantam, 1972), 34.
7. From Timothy Cheek, *Mao Zedong and China's Revolutions: A Brief History with Documents* (Boston: Bedford/St. Martin's, 2002), 116.
8. Quoted in Hu Kai-Yu, *The Chinese Literary Scene: A Writer's Visit to the People's Republic* (New York: Vintage, 1975), 227.
9. Quoted in Orville Schell, *Discos and Democracy: China in the Throes of Reform* (New York: Anchor, 1989), 101.
10. Quoted in June Teufel Dreyer, *China's Political System: Modernization and Tradition* (New York: Paragon House, 1993), 345.
11. The quotes are in Andrew F. Jones, *Like a Knife: Ideology and Genre in Contemporary Chinese Popular Music* (Ithaca, NY: East Asia Program, Cornell University, 1992), 97, 148.
12. Quoted in R. Keith Schoppa, *Revolution and Its Past: Identities and Change in Modern Chinese History* (Upper Saddle River, NJ: Prentice-Hall, 2002), 433.

13. Xue Xinran, author interview in *Random House: Reading Group for the Good Women of China* (http://www.randomhouse.co.uk/offthepage/guide.htm?command=Search&db=catalog/mai)
14. Quoted in James L. McClain, *Japan: A Modern History* (New York: W.W. Norton, 2002), 585.
15. Misuzu Hanikara, from Richard H. Minear, ed., *Through Japanese Eyes*, vol. 2 (New York: Praeger, 1974), 88.
16. Quoted in Mikiso Hane, *Modern Japan: A Historical Survey*, 2nd ed. (Boulder, CO: Westview Press, 1992), 371.
17. Quoted in Frank Gibney, *The Pacific Century: America and Asia in a Changing World* (New York: Charles Scribner's, 1992), 231.

Chapter 28 Rebuilding Europe and Russia, Since 1945

1. Quoted in Norman Davies, *Europe: A History* (New York: Harper, 1998), 1066.
2. Quoted in ibid.
3. Quoted in Felix Gilbert with David Clay Large, *The End of the European Era, 1890 to the Present*, 4th ed. (New York: W.W. Norton, 1991), 429.
4. Quoted in Harold James, *Europe Reborn: A History, 1914–2000* (New York: Longman, 2001), 248.
5. Quoted in Robert O. Paxton, *Europe in the Twentieth Century* (New York: Harcourt Brace Jovanovich, 1973), 576.
6. Quoted in Davies, *Europe*, 1065.
7. Quoted in Bonnie G. Smith, *Changing Lives: Women in European History Since 1700* (Lexington, MA: D.C. Heath, 1989), 509.
8. Quoted in Richard Vinen, *A History in Fragments: Europe in the Twentieth Century* (New York: Da Capo, 2000), 370.
9. Quoted in Bonnie S. Anderson and Judith P. Zinsser, *A History of Their Own: Women in Europe from Prehistory to the Present*, vol. 2 (New York: Harper Perennial, 1988), 334.
10. Amintore Fanfani, quoted in Vinen, *History in Fragments*, 493.
11. *Sniffin' Glue*, quoted in Peter Wicke, *Rock Music: Culture, Aesthetics and Sociology* (New York: Cambridge University Press, 1990), 148.
12. Quoted in Ronald Grigor Suny, *The Soviet Experiment: Russia, the USSR, and the Successor States* (New York: Oxford University Press, 1998), 387.
13. Quoted in James, *Europe Reborn*, 279.
14. Quoted in Timothy W. Ryback, *Rock Around the Bloc: A History of Rock Music in Eastern Europe and the Soviet Union* (New York: Oxford University Press, 1990), 35.
15. Quoted in Davies, *Europe*, 1102.
16. Quoted in James, *Europe Reborn*, 300.
17. Quoted in James Wilkenson and H. Stuart Hughes, *Contemporary Europe: A History*, 10th ed. (Upper Saddle River, NJ: Prentice-Hall, 2004), 559.
18. Quoted in Vinen, *History in Fragments*, 520.
19. Quoted in Wilkenson and Hughes, *Contemporary Europe*, 590.

Chapter 29 The Americas and the Pacific Basin: New Roles in the Contemporary World, SInce 1945

1. Quoted in James D. Cockcroft, *Latin America: History, Politics, and U.S. Policy*, 2nd ed. (Chicago: Nelson-Hall, 1996), 567.
2. Quoted in Marilyn B. Young, *The Vietnam Wars, 1945–1990* (New York: HarperCollins, 1991), 25.
3. Quoted in James Matray, *The Reluctant Crusade: American Foreign Policy in Korea, 1941–1950* (Honolulu: University of Hawaii Press, 1985), 3.
4. Quoted in L. S. Stavrianos, *Global Rift: The Third World Comes of Age* (New York: William Morrow, 1981), 712.
5. Quoted in Walter LaFeber, *America, Russia and the Cold War: 1945–1992*, 7th ed. (New York: McGraw-Hill, 1993), 248.
6. Quoted in Cockcroft, *Latin America*, 531.
7. Quoted in Walter LaFeber et al., *The American Century: A History of the United States Since 1941*, 5th ed. (Boston: McGraw-Hill, 1998), 519.
8. Folksinger Malvina Reynolds, quoted in Richard O. Davies, "The Ambivalent Heritage: The City in Modern America," in *Paths to the Present: Interpretive Essays on American Society Since 1930*, ed. James T. Patterson (Minneapolis: Burgess, 1975), 163.
9. From Peter Blood-Patterson, ed., *Rise Up Singing* (Bethlehem, PA: Sing Out Publications, 1988), 219.
10. Quoted in George Donelson Moss, *America in the Twentieth Century*, 4th ed. (Upper Saddle River, NJ: Prentice-Hall, 2000), 409.
11. Quoted in James T. Patterson, *America Since 1941: A History*, 2nd ed. (Fort Worth, TX: Harcourt, 2000), 254.
12. Quoted in Wayne C. Thompson, *Canada 1997* (Harpers Ferry, VA: Stryker-Post, 1997), 1.
13. Jaime Wheelock, quoted in Kyle Longley, *In the Eagle's Shadow: The United States and Latin America* (Wheeling, IL: Harlan Davidson, 2002), 291.
14. Quoted in Sebastian Balfour, *Castro*, 2nd ed. (New York: Longman, 1995), 167.
15. The quotes are in Thomas E. Skidmore and Peter H. Smith, *Modern Latin America*, 4th ed. (New York: Oxford University Press, 1997), 147; Joseph A. Page, *The Brazilians* (Reading, MA: Addison-Wesley, 1995), 5.
16. Quoted in David J. Morris, *We Must Make Haste—Slowly: The Process of Revolution in Chile* (New York: Vintage, 1973), 270–271.
17. Pamela Constable and Arturo Valenzuela, *A Nation of Enemies: Chile Under Pinochet* (New York: W.W. Norton, 1991), 38.
18. Graciliano Ramos, *Barren Lives*, quoted in E. Bradford Burns, *Latin America: A Concise Interpretive History*, 5th ed. (Englewood Cliffs, NJ: Prentice-Hall, 1990), 231.
19. Nelson Rodrigues, quoted in Warren Hoge, "A Whole Nation More Agitated than Spike Lee," *New York Times*, June 5, 1994, A1.
20. From Jara's song "Manifiesto." The song and the translation can be found on Jara's album *Manifiesto: Chile September 1973* (XTRA 1143, 1974).
21. See Marley's album *Catch a Fire* (Island ILPS 9241, 1973).
22. Quoted in Jan Fairley, "New Song: Music and Politics in Latin America," in *Rhythms of the World*, ed. Francis Hanly and Tim May (London: BBC Books, 1989), 90.

Chapter 30 The Middle East, Sub-Saharan Africa, and New Conflicts in the Contemporary World, Since 1945

1. See Savuka's album *Heat, Dust and Dreams* (EMI 9777-7-98795, 1993)
2. Quoted in James Alban Bill, *The Politics of Iran: Groups, Classes and Modernization* (Columbus, OH: Charles E. Merrill, 1972), 76–77.
3. Latifa az-Zayyat, quoted in Wiebke Walther, *Women in Islam from Medieval to Modern Times* (Princeton: Markus Wiener, 1993), 235.
4. Quoted in Daniel Bates and Amal Rassam, *Peoples and Cultures of the Middle East*, 2nd ed. (Upper Saddle River, NJ: Prentice-Hall, 2001), 235.
5. Fatema Mernissi, *Scheherazade Goes West: Different Cultures, Different Harems* (New York: Washington Square Press, 2001), 219.
6. Martin Stokes, *The Arabesk Debate: Music and Musicians in Modern Turkey* (Oxford: Clarendon Press, 1992), 1.
7. Sadiq Hidayat, in *Hajji Aqa*, quoted in Bill, *Politics of Iran*, 105.
8. From Akram Fouad Khater, ed., *Sources in the History of the Modern Middle East* (Boston: Houghton Mifflin, 2004), 362.
9. Naguib Mahfuz, quoted in Bates and Rassam, *Peoples and Cultures*, 199.
10. Quoted in Frances Robinson, *The Cultural Atlas of the Islamic World Since 1500* (Alexandria, VA: Stonehenge, 1982), 158.
11. Quoted in Basil Davidson, *The People's Cause: A History of Guerrillas in Africa* (Burnt Mill, UK: Longman, 1981), 165.
12. A. Toure, quoted in Bill Freund, *The Making of Contemporary Africa: The Development of African Society Since 1800* (Bloomington: Indiana University Press, 1984), 192.
13. Prime Minister John Vorster in 1968, quoted in L. S. Stavrianos, *Global Rift: The Third World Comes of Age* (New York: William Morrow, 1981), 759.
14. Quoted in Jean Comaroff, *Body of Power, Spirit of Resistance: The Culture and History of a South African People* (Chicago: University of Chicago Press, 1985), vi.
15. Quoted in Gwendolen Carter, "The Republic of South Africa: White Political Control Within the African Continent," in *Africa*, ed. Phyllis Martin and Patrick O'Meara, 2nd ed. (Bloomington: Indiana University Press, 1986), 353.

16. Quoted in Joe Asila, "No Cash in This Crop," in *Global Studies: Africa*, ed. Wayne Edge, 2nd ed. (Guilford, CT: Dushkin, 2006), 285.
17. Sanford Unger, *Africa: The People and Politics of an Emerging Continent* (New York: Simon and Schuster, 1985), 131–132.
18. Quoted in Richard A. Fredland, *Understanding Africa: A Political Economy Perspective* (Chicago: Burnham, 2001), 139.
19. Quoted in John Follain, "Only the First Step for 'Mama Africa,'" *New Straits Times*, February 23, 1990.
20. Quoted in Tejumola Olaniyan, "Narrativizing Postcoloniality: Responsibilities," *Public Culture* 5, no. 1 (Fall 1992): 47.
21. Quoted in Chinweizu, *The West and the Rest of Us: White Predators, Black Slavers, and the African Elite* (New York: Vintage, 1975), 1.
22. Quoted in Jennifer Seymour Whitaker, *How Can Africa Survive?* (New York: Harper and Row, 1988), 197.

Chapter 31 South Asia, Southeast Asia, and Global Connections, Since 1945

1. Mochtar Lubis, *Road with No End*, translated by Anthony Johns from 1952 Indonesian edition (Chicago: Henry Regnery, 1968), 9.
2. Quoted in Anthony Johns, "Introduction," in ibid., 4.
3. Quoted in John R. McLane, ed., *The Political Awakening of India* (Englewood Cliffs, NJ: Prentice-Hall, 1970), 178.
4. Quoted in B. N. Pandey, *The Break-up of British India* (New York: St. Martin's, 1969), 209.
5. Faiz Ahmed Faiz, quoted in Sugata Bose and Ayesha Jalal, *Modern South Asia: History, Culture, Political Economy* (New York: Routledge, 1998), 200.
6. Rohinton Mistry, *A Fine Balance* (London: Faber, 1996), 143.
7. Quoted in Susan Bayly, *Caste, Society and Politics in India from the Eighteenth Century to the Modern Age* (New York: Cambridge University Press, 1999), 315.
8. Quoted in Jeremy Marre and Hannah Charlton, *Beats of the Heart: Popular Music of the World* (New York: Pantheon, 1985), 150.
9. Quoted in Bose and Jalal, *Modern South Asia*, 232.
10. Quoted in Stanley Wolpert, *A New History of India*, 7th ed. (New York: Oxford University Press, 2004), 462.
11. Quoted in William J. Duiker, *Ho Chi Minh: A Life* (New York: Hyperion, 2000), 323.
12. Quoted in George Donelson Moss, *Vietnam: An American Ordeal*, 4th ed. (Upper Saddle River, NJ: Prentice-Hall, 2002), 40.
13. Jacques Philippe Leclerc, quoted in James S. Olson and Randy Roberts, *Where the Domino Fell: America and Vietnam, 1945–1995*, 3rd ed. (St. James, NY: Brandywine, 1999), 28.
14. Quoted in Thomas G. Paterson et al., *American Foreign Policy: A History Since 1900*, 3rd ed. rev. (Lexington, MA: D.C. Heath, 1991), 553.
15. Anh Vien, quoted in Arleen Eisen Bergman, *Women of Vietnam*, rev. ed. (San Francisco: Peoples Press, 1975), 123.
16. Quoted in Neil L. Jamieson, *Understanding Vietnam* (Berkeley: University of California Press, 1993), 290.
17. From Idrus, "Surabaya," in *From Surabaya to Armageddon: Indonesian Short Stories*, ed. Harry Aveling (Singapore: Heinemann, 1976), 13.
18. From Pramoedya Ananta Toer, "Letter to a Friend in the Country," in Aveling, *From Surabaya*, 72.
19. Doreen Fernandez, "Mass Culture and Cultural Policy: The Philippine Experience," *Philippine Studies* 37 (4th Quarter, 1980): 492.
20. "The Kingdom of Mammon," in Amado V. Hernandez, *Rice Grains: Selected Poems* (New York: International Publishers, 1966), 31.
21. From Taufiq Ismail's story "Stop Thief!" in *Black Clouds over the Isle of Gods and Other Modern Indonesian Short Stories*, ed. David M. E. Roskies (Armonk, NY: M.E. Sharpe, 1997), 97.
22. F. Sionel Jose, quoted in David G. Timberman, *A Changeless Land: Continuity and Change in Philippine Politics* (New York: M.E. Sharpe, 1991), xi.
23. "American Junk," by the Apo Hiking Society, quoted in Craig A. Lockard, *Dance of Life: Popular Music and Politics in Southeast Asia* (Honolulu: University of Hawai'i Press, 1998), 156.
24. Quoted in Robin Broad and John Cavanaugh, *Plundering Paradise: The Struggle for the Environment in the Philippines* (Berkeley: University of California Press, 1993), xvii.
25. Quoted in Pasuk Phongpaichit and Chris Baker, *Thailand: Economy and Politics* (Kuala Lumpur: Oxford University Press, 1995), 413–415.

Societies, Networks, Transitions: The Contemporary World, Since 1945

1. Kathleen Newland and Kamala Chandrakirana Soedjatmoko, eds., *Transforming Humanity: The Visionary Writings of Soedjatmoko* (West Hartford, CT: Kumarian Press, 1994), 186–187.
2. Quoted in Jan Pronk, "Globalization: A Developmental Approach," in *Global Futures: Shaping Globalization*, ed. Jan Nederveen Pieterse (London: Zed Books, 2000), 46.
3. Daphne Berdahl, quoted in James L. Watson, ed., *Golden Arches East: McDonald's in East Asia* (Stanford, CA: Stanford University Press, 1997), xvii.
4. Billy Bergman, *Hot Sauces: Latin and Caribbean Pop* (New York: Quill, 1985), 18.
5. Quoted in Hans-Peter Martin and Harald Schumann, *The Global Trap: Globalization and the Assault on Democracy and Prosperity* (New York: Zed Books, 1996), 163.
6. From Banton's album, *Visions of the World* (IRSD-82003, 1989).
7. Frank Cajka, quoted in Peter Worsley, *The Three Worlds: Culture and World Development* (Chicago: University of Chicago Press, 1984), xi.
8. Quoted in Robbie Robertson, *The Three Waves of Globalization: A History of a Developing Global Consciousness* (New York: Zed Books, 2003), 263.
9. Lester Pearson, quoted in Lester R. Brown, *World Without Borders* (New York: Vintage, 1972), ix.
10. Aldo Leopold, *A Sand County Almanac* (New York: Ballantine, 1966), 253.
11. Quoted in J. Donald Hughes, *An Environmental History of the World: Humankind's Changing Role in the Community of Life* (New York: Routledge, 2001), 230.
12. Rene Dubos, *So Human an Animal* (New York: Scribner's, 1968), 270.
13. Ilya Prigogine, quoted in Federico Mayor and Jerome Bindé, *The World Ahead: Our Future in the Making* (New York: Zed Books, 2001), 1.
14. Lester Brown et al., "A World at Risk," in *State of the World 1989* (New York: W.W. Norton, 1989), 20.
15. Lewis Carroll, "Alice's Adventures in Wonderland," in *The Complete Works of Lewis Carroll* (New York: Modern Library), 71–72.

Index